Merriam-Webster's Crossword Puzzle Dictionary

SECOND EDITION

Merriam-Webster, Incorporated
Springfield, Massachusetts

A GENUINE MERRIAM-WEBSTER

The name *Webster* alone is no guarantee of excellence. It is used by a number of publishers and may serve mainly to mislead an unwary buyer.

Merriam-Webster™ is the name you should look for when you consider the purchase of dictionaries or other fine reference books. It carries the reputation of a company that has been publishing since 1831 and is your assurance of quality and authority.

Library of Congress Cataloging in Publication Data

Main entry under title:

Merriam-Webster's crossword puzzle dictionary.—2nd ed.
        p.   cm.
    ISBN 0-87779-121-X (alk. paper)
    1. Crossword puzzles—Glossaries, vocabularies, etc.   I. Merriam-
Webster, Inc.
GV1507.C7M45 1996
793.73'2'03—dc20   96-24796
                                                        CIP

Made in the United States of America
  3456RRD99897

Preface

Merriam-Webster's Crossword Puzzle Dictionary, Second Edition, has been edited to meet the specific needs of crossword puzzles solvers. The extensive resources and editorial care that have placed Merriam-Webster general dictionaries among the most respected and sought-after reference books in this country have been utilized in preparing this specialized dictionary.

Based on actual crossword puzzle clues, entries have been selected from Webster's Third New International Dictionary and its venerable predecessor, Webster's New International Dictionary, Second Edition, as well as from Merriam-Webster's Collegiate Thesaurus, Webster's New Geographical Dictionary, Merriam-Webster's Biographical Dictionary, Merriam-Webster's Collegiate Dictionary, and Encyclopædia Britannica, making this book one of the most comprehensive of its kind. Because of the wide range of information contained in this book, it can also be used as a source of much general reference material.

Several members of the editorial department have contributed greatly to the development of this dictionary. Michael G. Belanger was chiefly responsible for revisions and updates going into this second edition. Editors who contributed to the first edition include JulieAnne Collier, Kathleen M. Doherty, Grace A. Kellogg, Daniel J. Hopkins, John M. Morse, Stephen J. Perrault, and Francine A. Roberts. Clerical work for the second edition was handled chiefly by Carol A. Fugiel. Production coordination was provided by Jennifer S. Goss. Proofreading was primarily done by Mary W. Cornog and Cynthia S. Ashby.

James G. Lowe
Editor

Introduction
Main Entries

The organization of Merriam-Webster's Crossword Puzzle Dictionary, Second Edition, is structured in accordance with the way in which crossword puzzles are constructed and solved. The main entries and their subcategories correspond to the numbered clues given in the puzzle, and the answer words that follow the main entries are possibilities for filling in the blanks provided.

Main entries appear in boldface type and are entered in alphabetical order letter by letter. Those beginning with *Mc-* are alphabetized as if spelled *Mac-*; thus **McTeague author** appears before **mad.** We have endeavored to make the range of entries as comprehensive as possible in a book of this size so as to enable the user to meet the challenges of even the most difficult puzzles.

These entries include names of persons (as biblical, famous, legendary, literary, and mythological), places (as countries, islands, mountains, rivers, states, and seas), and miscellaneous things (as chemical elements, coins, drinks, games, and wines). Also included are titles of famous books, operas, and works of art. The bulk of the main entries, however, consists of words that have synonyms or closely related words.

Entries may be a single word, a group of words, or a blank with a word or group of words (as **Damocles'** _____ or _____ **d'Azur**). Parts of speech are not indicated since they are not usually provided in puzzle clues.

Subcategories

When the main entry is a large category (as at **animal, composer,** and **river**), the list of answer words is broken down into alphabetically arranged subcategories for easy access. Each subcategory is introduced by an appropriate boldface italic word or words. If you want to find, for example, the name of a French composer, first look for the entry **composer** and then under it the subcategory *French.*

Subcategories may indicate various kinds of relationships to the main entry, for example, personal (father, mother, etc.), political (capital, kingdom, etc.), literary (author, character, etc.), or artistic (painter, sculptor, etc.). They may indicate a nationality, a language

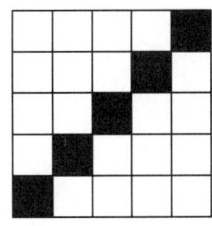

or dialect, or a particular example or type. Also included as subcategories are prefixes, suffixes, combining forms, and chemical symbols related to the main entry.

Answer Words

When more than one answer is possible to a clue represented by a main entry, the answer words are grouped together according to the number of letters they contain. The specific number appears in boldface before each numerical grouping, and within each grouping answer words are alphabetized. Even when only a single answer word is given, the boldface number of its letters precedes it. Answer words usually range from two to thirteen letters since longer answers are rarely asked for. However, some answers (as titles and nicknames) may consist of more than one words and may exceed thirteen letters. Some answers are not actual words; these include abbreviations, prefixes, suffixes, combining forms, and chemical symbols, which are commonly called for in crossword puzzles.

In a single list of answer words you may find grouped together words that seem unrelated to one another. This results when the answer words are of various parts of speech or are synonymous with only one meaning of a main entry that has more than one meaning. Thus, answer words, although related to the main entry, may not be synonymous with each other.

Guide Words

In order to facilitate finding a particular entry, the first main entry on each left-hand page is printed at the top of that page in large boldface type. Likewise, the last main entry on each right-hand page is printed at the top of that page. These two guide words indicate the alphabetical range of main entries on the two pages.

Cross-References

Occasionally a reduced boldface cross-reference to another main entry is given instead of answer words. For example, at **anywise** you are directed to see **anyhow** for answer words because these two main entries are synonymous, and at **Arthur** you are referred to **King Arthur** for the answer words. These cross-references save space and allow a greater number of main entries than would otherwise be possible.

Aaron

brother: **5** Moses
father: **5** Amram
sister: **6** Miriam
son: **5** Abiku, Nadab **7** Eleazer, Ithamar

aback

5 short **6** sudden **7** unaware **8** suddenly, unawares **10** unawaredly **12** unexpectedly

abacus

Chinese: **7** swanpan **8** shwanpan

abaft

3 aft **4** back **5** after **6** astern, back of, behind

abalienate

4 cede, deed **5** alien **6** assign, convey, remise **8** make over, sign over, transfer

abalone

5 ormer

abandon

3 fun **4** cede, drop, ease, junk, play, quit **5** chuck, leave, scrap, sport, waive, yield **6** desert, disuse, give up, laxity, maroon, reject, resign, turn up **7** cast off, discard, forsake, freedom, laxness, liberty, license, unguard **8** hand over, renounce, wildness **9** looseness, repudiate, surrender, throw over **10** exuberance, relinquish, unruliness, wantonness **11** naturalness, spontaneity, unrestraint **12** heedlessness, incontinence, unconstraint **13** impulsiveness

abandoned

4 lewd, lorn **6** wanton **7** corrupt, debased, riotous, uncouth **8** depraved, derelict, deserted, desolate, forsaken, solitary **9** debauched, dissolute, lecherous, perverted, reprobate **10** degenerate, lascivious, licentious, profligate **12** incorrigible, unprincipled

abase

4 fawn, sink **5** cower, lower, toady **6** bemean, cringe, debase, demean, demote, grovel, humble, reduce **7** degrade, truckle **8** cast down, diminish **9** downgrade, humiliate

abash

4 faze **5** abase **6** demean, humble, rattle **7** confuse **8** confound **9** discomfit, embarrass, humiliate **10** disconcert

abashment

6 unease **9** confusion **10** uneasiness **12** discomfiture, discomposure **13** disconcertion, embarrassment

abate

3 ebb **4** fall, lull, wane **5** annul, close, let up, quash, taper **6** lessen, negate, recede, reduce, relent, weaken **7** abolish, die away, die down, dwindle, ease off, nullify, slacken, subside, vitiate **8** abrogate, decrease, diminish, moderate, taper off **9** drain away, eradicate **10** annihilate, invalidate **11** exterminate

abatement

6 rebate **8** discount **9** deduction, reduction **11** subtraction

abbot

female: **6** abbess

abbreviate

3 cut **7** abridge, curtail, cut back, shorten

abbreviation

7 acronym **10** abridgment, shortening

abdicate

5 demit, leave **6** reject, resign **7** abandon **8** renounce, withdraw **9** surrender, throw away **10** relinquish

abdomen

3 gut, pot **5** belly, tummy **6** middle, paunch, venter **7** midriff, stomach **8** potbelly **9** bay window **10** midsection **11** breadbasket
combining form: **6** ventri, ventro
depression: **5** navel

abduct

5 seize **6** kidnap, snatch **10** spirit away

abecedarian

4 tyro **7** amateur, dabbler **9** smatterer **10** dilettante

Abel

brother: **4** Cain, Seth
father: **4** Adam
mother: **3** Eve
slayer: **4** Cain

Abelard

son: **9** Astrolabe
wife: **7** Heloise

abele

6 poplar

aberrant

3 odd **6** errant, erring **7** deviant, devious, strange, unusual **8** abnormal, atypical, peculiar **9** anomalous, deviative, different, disparate, divergent, eccentric, untypical **11** exceptional, heteroclite

aberration

4 slip **6** lunacy, oddity, rarity **7** madness, mistake, turning **8** insanity **9** curiosity, departure, deviation, diversion, unbalance **10** alienation, deflection, divergence, insaneness **11** abnormality, derangement, distraction, psychopathy

abet

3 aid, egg **4** goad, help, prod, spur, urge **6** assist, exhort, foment, incite, stir up **8** advocate **9** encourage, instigate **11** countenance

abettor
9 accessory 10 accomplice
11 confederate, conspirator
13 coconspirator

abeyance
5 break, pause 7 latency, respite
8 dormancy, interval 10 quiescence, quiescency, suspension
11 cold storage 12 intermission,
interruption

abeyant
6 latent 7 dormant, lurking 8 deferred 9 postponed, quiescent, repressed 10 suppressed
11 intermitted

abhor
4 hate 5 scorn 6 detest, loathe
7 contemn, despise, disdain 8 execrate 9 abominate

abhorrence
4 hate 6 dismay, hatred, horror
8 aversion, distaste, loathing
9 repulsion, revulsion 10 repellency, repugnance 11 abomination, detestation

abhorrent
6 horrid, odious 7 hatable, hateful
8 hateable 9 invidious, obnoxious,
repellent, repugnant, revulsive
10 abominable, detestable 11 uncongenial 12 antipathetic
13 unsympathetic

Abi
father: 9 Zechariah
husband: 4 Ahaz
mother: 8 Hezekiah

abide
4 bear, last, live, stay, take, wait
5 brook, cling, dwell, exist, stand,
stick, tarry 6 accede, accept, adhere, cleave, endure, linger, remain, reside, suffer 7 consent,
hang out, perdure, persist, receive,
stomach, subsist, swallow 8 continue, tolerate 11 stick around

abiding
4 firm, sure 6 steady 7 durable,
lasting 8 enduring 9 steadfast
10 perdurable, persistent 11 unfaltering, unqualified 12 never-failing,
wholehearted 13 unquestioning

Abiel
grandson: 4 Saul 5 Abner
son: 3 Ner 4 Kish

abigail
4 maid

Abigail's husband
5 David, Nabal

ability
5 knack, might, skill 6 talent 7 address, aptness, command, faculty,
know-how, mastery, prowess 8 adequacy, aptitude, capacity,
deftness, facility 9 dexterity, expertise, expertism, handiness, ingenuity
10 adroitness, capability, cleverness, competence, efficiency, expertness, mastership 11 proficiency
13 qualification, qualifiedness

Abital's husband
5 David

abject
9 underfoot 11 downtrodden

abjure
4 cede 5 unsay 6 desert, disown,
recall, recant 7 abandon, disavow,
forsake, retract 8 forswear, palinode, renounce, take back, withdraw 9 repudiate, surrender
10 relinquish

ablaze
5 afire, aglow, fiery 6 aflame,
alight 7 burning, flaming, flaring,
ignited 8 aflicker 11 conflagrant

able
4 good, keen 5 alert, sharp, smart
6 au fait, brainy, clever, expert,
proper, wicked 7 capable, goahead, skilled 8 skillful 9 brilliant,
competent, effective, effectual, efficient, qualified 10 proficient 11 intelligent 12 enterprising

abnegation
6 denial 10 self-denial 12 renouncement, renunciation

Abner
cousin: 4 Saul
father: 3 Ner
slayer: 4 Joab

abnormal
3 odd 5 undue, weird 6 off-key
7 deviant, offtype, unusual 8 aberrant, atypical 9 anomalous, deviative, divergent, irregular, paratypic,
unnatural, unregular, untypical
11 heteroclite, uncustomary 13 heteromorphic, preternatural
combining form: 3 mal 4 anom, poly
5 anomo, pseud 6 pseudo
prefix: 3 dys, par 4 para

abnormality
5 lusus

abode
4 home 5 house 8 domicile, dwelling 9 residence, residency
10 commoracy, habitation

abolish
4 undo 5 abate, annul, quash
6 cancel, negate, repeal, revoke,
vacate 7 blot out, nullify, rescind,
vitiate, wipe out 8 abrogate, disallow, disannul 9 eradicate, extirpate
10 annihilate, circumduct, extinguish, invalidate 11 exterminate

abolitionist
4 Mott (Lucretia), Weld (Theodore)
5 Lundy (Benjamin), Smith (Gerrit),
Stowe (Harriet Beecher) 6 Birney
(James), Lowell (James Russell), Parker (Theodore), Tappan (Arthur)
8 Douglass (Frederick), Garrison
(William Lloyd), Phillips (Wendell),
Whittier (John Greenlaef)

abominable
6 cursed, horrid, odious 7 hateful
8 accursed, hateable 9 abhorrent,
loathsome, offensive, repugnant, revolting 10 detestable

abominable snowman
4 yeti

abominate
4 damn, hate 5 abhor, curse 6 detest, loathe 8 execrate 9 objurgate

abomination
4 hate, pest 5 bogey, scorn, trial
6 hatred, horror, plague 7 bugaboo, bugbear, disdain, dislike, incubus 8 anathema, aversion, contempt, disfavor, distaste, loathing
9 annoyance, bête noire, disrelish,
repulsion, revulsion 10 abhorrence,
black beast, repugnance, repugnancy 11 detestation

aboriginal
6 native, savage 7 endemic 8 barbaric, primeval 9 barbarian, barbarous, primitive 10 indigenous,
primordial 13 autochthonous

aborigine
3 abo 6 native

abortive
4 vain 6 futile, unripe 7 useless
8 bootless, immature, unformed
9 fruitless 10 unavailing 11 ineffective, ineffectual, unavailable
12 unproductive

abound
4 flow, teem 5 crawl, swarm

abound in
suffix: 5 ulent

abounding
4 full, rife 5 alive 6 jammed,
packed 7 replete, stuffed, teeming
8 swarming, thronged 11 overflowing

abounding in
suffix: 3 ose, ous 4 ious

about
2 on, re 4 as to, back, in re, most, much, near, nigh, over, upon, with 5 again, anent, circa, round 6 all but, almost, anyhow, around, nearby, nearly 7 anywise, apropos, through 8 at random, backward, casually, randomly, to and fro 9 aimlessly, as regards, haphazard, in reverse 10 carelessly, concerning, near-at-hand, respecting, throughout 11 any which way, haphazardly, practically 12 circuitously 13 approximately, helter-skelter

about-face
4 turn 7 reverse 8 reversal 9 reversion, volte-face 11 reversement

above
3 o'er 4 over, past 5 aloft, supra 6 beyond 8 overhead
combining form: 6 supero
prefix: 3 sur 4 over 5 hyper, super, supra

above all
7 chiefly

aboveboard
4 open 7 artless 8 straight 9 ingenuous 10 forthright, scrupulous 12 plain dealing

abracadabra
4 cant 5 argot 6 jargon 7 mummery 9 gibberish 10 hocus-pocus, mumbo jumbo 13 mystification

abrade
3 bug, irk, rub 4 burn, fret, gall, rasp, wear 5 annoy, chafe, erode, grate, graze 6 bother, flurry, ruffle, scrape 7 corrade, corrode, eat away, perturb, provoke 8 exercise 9 excoriate

Abraham
birthplace: 2 Ur
brother: 5 Haran, Nahor
concubine: 5 Hagar
father: 5 Terah
grandfather: 5 Nahor
grandson: 4 Esau
nephew: 3 Lot
son: 5 Isaac, Medan, Shuah 6 Midian, Zimran 7 Ishmael
well: 9 Beer-Sheba
wife: 5 Sarah 7 Keturah

Abraham's bosom
4 Zion 5 bliss 6 Canaan, heaven 7 elysium, nirvana 8 empyrean, paradise 10 Civitas Dei 12 New Jerusalem

abrasive
5 emery

abreast
2 up 6 au fait, versed 7 versant 8 familiar, informed, up-to-date 9 au courant 10 acquainted, conversant 12 contemporary

abridge
3 cut 5 limit, slash 6 lessen, minify, narrow, reduce 7 curtail, cut back, shorten 8 condense, diminish, minimize, restrict, retrench 10 abbreviate

abridgment
3 sum 5 brief 6 apercu, digest, précis, sketch 7 capsule, epitome, outline, summary 8 abstract, boildown, breviary, breviate, syllabus, synopsis 9 summation, summing-up 10 compendium, conspectus 12 condensation

abroad
6 afield 7 oversea 8 overseas

abrogate
4 ruin, undo, void 5 abate, annul, quash, wreck 6 cancel, negate, vacate 7 abolish, blot out, nullify, vitiate 8 dissolve 9 discharge 10 annihilate, extinguish, invalidate, obliterate

abrupt
4 curt 5 bluff, blunt, brief, brisk, crisp, gruff, hasty, quick, ready, sharp, sheer, short, steep 6 casual, crusty, snippy, speedy, sudden 7 arduous, brusque, hurried, rushing 8 headlong, informal 9 impetuous 11 precipitant, precipitate, precipitous, short-spoken, subitaneous 13 unceremonious

abruptly
5 short 6 sudden 7 asudden 8 suddenly 9 forthwith

abruptness
10 brusquerie

Absalom
commander: 5 Amasa
father: 5 David
mother: 7 Maachah
sister: 5 Tamar
slayer: 4 Joab

abscess
4 boil, sore 5 botch, ulcer 6 lesion, pimple, trauma 7 pustule 8 furuncle 9 carbuncle

abscond
2 go 3 fly 4 flee, quit 5 break, leave, scape 6 decamp, escape 8 withdraw

absence
4 lack, need, void, want 6 dearth, defect, vacuum 7 default, drought, failure 9 privation 10 deficiency 13 insufficiency

absent
4 away, gone, lost 7 bemused, faraway, lacking, missing, omitted, wanting 8 distrait, heedless 9 forgetful 10 abstracted

absentminded
4 lost 7 bemused, faraway 8 distrait, heedless, unseeing 10 abstracted, unnoticing 11 inattentive, inconscient, preoccupied, unobserving 12 unperceiving

absent without leave
4 AWOL

absolute
4 hard, pure, real, true 5 ideal, sheer, utter 6 actual, simple 7 eternal, factual, genuine, perfect, unmixed 8 complete, despotic, flawless, infinite, outright, positive, ultimate, unflawed 9 arbitrary, autarchic, boundless, downright, fleckless, imperious, masterful, out-and-out, sovereign, tyrannous, unalloyed, undiluted, unlimited 10 autocratic, autonomous, consummate, impeccable, monocratic, tyrannical 11 categorical, dictatorial, domineering, independent, note-perfect, unmitigated, unqualified 12 indefectible, totalitarian, transcendent 13 authoritarian

absolutely
6 easily 9 doubtless 10 definitely, positively 11 doubtlessly 13 unequivocally

absolution
6 pardon 7 amnesty 11 condonation

absolutism
9 Caesarism 12 dictatorship

absolve
4 free 5 clear, spare 6 acquit, excuse, exempt, let off, shrive 7 release, relieve 8 dispense 9 discharge, exculpate, exonerate, vindicate 10 disculpate

absorb
5 imbue 6 embody, engage, imbibe, infuse, ingest, sponge 7 consume, engross, immerse, inhaust, in-

volve **8** permeate **9** preoccupy **10** assimilate, impregnate, monopolize **11** incorporate

absorbed
4 deep, rapt **6** intent **7** engaged, wrapped **8** immersed, involved **9** engrossed, wrapped up **11** preoccupied

absorbent cotton
7 pledget

absorbing
9 consuming **10** engrossing **12** monopolizing

abstain
4 curb, deny, keep **5** forgo, spurn **6** eschew, refuse, reject **7** decline, forbear, refrain **8** abnegate, hold back, teetotal, withhold **9** constrain

abstemious
5 sober **7** ascetic, austere, sparing **9** abstinent, continent, temperate **11** self-denying

abstentious
see **abstemious**

abstinence
8 sobriety **10** continence, temperance **12** renunciation

abstinent
see **abstemious**

abstract
4 lift **5** annex, brief, filch, ideal, pinch, steal, swipe, unfix **6** detach, divide, pilfer **7** epitome, neutral, purloin, utopian **8** academic, boil-down, breviary, breviate, detached, notional, separate, synopsis, uncouple **9** colorless, disengage, visionary **10** abridgment, conceptual, conspectus, disconnect, dissociate, impersonal, inconcrete **11** appropriate, impractical, speculative, theoretical, unpassioned **12** condensation, disassociate, hypothetical, transcendent **13** disinterested
being: **3** ens

abstracted
4 lost, rapt **6** absent, intent **7** bemused, faraway **8** distrait, heedless **9** engrossed, oblivious, unmindful, unminding **11** inattentive, inconscient, preoccupied **12** absentminded

abstruse
4 deep **5** heavy, ideal **6** knotty, occult, orphic, secret **7** complex **8** esoteric, hermetic, profound **9** intricate, recondite **10** acroamatic **11** complicated **12** hypothetical

absurd
5 balmy, comic, crazy, droll, funny, loony, potty, silly, wacky **6** insane **7** asinine, fatuous, foolish **8** farcical **10** irrational **11** harebrained **12** preposterous, unreasonable

absurdity
5 folly **7** inanity **8** insanity, nonsense **9** craziness, dottiness, silliness **11** foolishness, witlessness **13** senselessness

abundance
4 ease **6** enough, galore, plenty **7** lashins **8** adequacy, lashings, thriving **10** lavishness, prosperity **11** prodigality, sufficiency
Scottish: **5** routh, rowth

abundant
4 lush, rife **5** ample, thick **6** common, lavish, plenty **7** copious, crammed, crowded, liberal, profuse, replete **8** generous, prolific **9** bounteous, bountiful, luxuriant, plenteous, plentiful

abuse
3 mar, mud **4** harm, hurt **5** decry, spoil, wrong **6** damage, debase, impair, injure, mess up, misuse, rating, revile **7** calumny, corrupt, cursing, exploit, obloquy, oppress, outrage, pervert, profane, railing **8** belittle, berating, derogate, discount, ill-treat, maltreat, minimize, misapply, mistreat, reviling, swearing **9** contumely, desecrate, disparage, dispraise, invective, manhandle, misemploy, mishandle, persecute, profanity **10** defamation, depreciate, impose upon, malignment, scurrility **12** billingsgate, vilification, vituperation

abusive
5 dirty **6** odious **7** scurril **8** scurrile **9** aspersing, insulting, invective, maligning, offending, offensive, outraging, truculent, vilifying **10** affronting, scurrilous, vituperous **11** opprobrious **12** contumelious, vituperative, vituperatory

abut
4 join, line **5** flank, march, touch, verge **6** adjoin, border **8** neighbor **11** communicate

abutting
4 next **7** joining **8** adjacent, touching **9** adjoining, bordering, impinging **10** approximal, connecting, contiguous, juxtaposed **12** conterminous

abysm
4 gulf **5** chasm

abysmal
4 deep **8** infinite, profound **9** plumbless, soundless **10** bottomless, fathomless **11** illimitable, plummetless **12** unfathomable

abyss
3 pit **4** gulf, hell **5** chasm, depth, hades, Sheol **6** Tophet **7** Gehenna, inferno **8** deepness **9** perdition **10** profundity, underworld **11** netherworld **12** profoundness

academic
5 booky **6** closet **7** bookish, utopian **8** gownsman, pedantic **10** scholastic **11** book-learned, impractical, quodlibetic, speculative, theoretical

academic year part
4 term **7** quarter **8** semester **9** trimester

Academy Award Winner
picture:
1927-28: **5** Wings
1928-29: **14** Broadway Melody
1929-30: **25** All Quiet on the Western Front
1930-31: **8** Cimarron
1931-32: **10** Grand Hotel
1932-33: **9** Calvalcade
1934: **18** It Happened One Night
1935: **17** Mutiny on the Bounty
1936: **16** The Great Ziegfeld
1937: **15** Life of Emile Zola
1938: **20** You Can't Take It With You
1939: **15** Gone With the Wind
1940: **7** Rebecca
1941: **19** How Green Was My Valley
1942: **10** Mrs. Miniver
1943: **10** Casablanca
1944: **10** Going My Way
1945: **14** The Lost Weekend
1946: **22** The Best Years of Our Lives
1947: **19** Gentleman's Agreement
1948: **6** Hamlet
1949: **14** All the King's Men
1950: **11** All About Eve
1951: **17** An American in Paris
1952: **22** The Greatest Show on Earth
1953: **18** From Here to Eternity
1954: **15** On the Waterfront
1955: **5** Marty
1956: **26** Around the World in Eighty Days
1957: **23** The Bridge on the River Kwai

1958: 4 Gigi
1959: 6 Ben-Hur
1960: 12 The Apartment
1961: 13 West Side Story
1962: 16 Lawrence of Arabia
1963: 8 Tom Jones
1964: 10 My Fair Lady
1965: 15 The Sound of Music
1966: 17 A Man for All Seasons
1967: 19 In the Heat of the Night
1968: 6 Oliver
1969: 14 Midnight Cowboy
1970: 6 Patton
1971: 19 The French Connection
1972: 12 The Godfather
1973: 8 The Sting
1974: 12 The Godfather (Part Two)
1975: 25 One Flew Over the
   Cuckoo's Nest
1976: 5 Rocky
1977: 9 Annie Hall
1978: 13 The Deer Hunter
1979: 14 Kramer vs. Kramer
1980: 14 Ordinary People
1981: 14 Chariots of Fire
1982: 6 Gandhi
1983: 17 Terms of Endearment
1984: 7 Amadeus
1985: 11 Out of Africa
1986: 7 Platoon
1987: 14 The Last Emperor
1988: 7 Rain Man
1989: 16 Driving Miss Daisy
1990: 16 Dances With Wolves
1991: 20 The Silence of the Lambs
1992: 10 Unforgiven
1993: 14 Schindler's List
1994: 11 Forrest Gump
1995: 10 Braveheart

actor:
1927-28: 8 Jannings (Emil)
1928-29: 6 Baxter (Warner)
1929-30: 6 Arliss (George)
1930-31: 9 Barrymore (Lionel)
1931-32: 5 Beery (Wallace), March
   (Fredric)
1932-33: 8 Laughton (Charles)
1934: 5 Gable (Clark)
1935: 8 McLaglen (Victor)
1936: 4 Muni (Paul)
1937: 5 Tracy (Spencer)
1938: 5 Tracy (Spencer)
1939: 5 Donat (Robert)
1940: 7 Stewart (James)
1941: 6 Cooper (Gary)
1942: 6 Cagney (James)
1943: 5 Lukas (Paul)
1944: 6 Crosby (Bing)
1945: 7 Milland (Ray)
1946: 5 March (Fredric)
1947: 6 Colman (Ronald)
1948: 7 Olivier (Laurence)
1949: 8 Crawford (Broderick)

1950: 6 Ferrer (Jose)
1951: 6 Bogart (Humphrey)
1952: 6 Cooper (Gary)
1953: 6 Holden (William)
1954: 6 Brando (Marlon)
1955: 8 Borgnine (Ernest)
1956: 7 Brynner (Yul)
1957: 8 Guinness (Alec)
1958: 5 Niven (David)
1959: 6 Heston (Charlton)
1960: 9 Lancaster (Burt)
1961: 6 Schell (Maximilian)
1962: 4 Peck (Gregory)
1963: 7 Poitier (Sidney)
1964: 8 Harrison (Rex)
1965: 6 Marvin (Lee)
1966: 8 Scofield (Paul)
1967: 7 Steiger (Rod)
1968: 9 Robertson (Cliff)
1969: 5 Wayne (John)
1970: 5 Scott (George C.)
1971: 7 Hackman (Gene)
1972: 6 Brando (Marlon)
1973: 6 Lemmon (Jack)
1974: 6 Carney (Art)
1975: 9 Nicholson (Jack)
1976: 5 Finch (Peter)
1977: 8 Dreyfuss (Richard)
1978: 6 Voight (Jon)
1979: 7 Hoffman (Dustin)
1980: 6 DeNiro (Robert)
1981: 5 Fonda (Henry)
1982: 8 Kingsley (Ben)
1983: 6 Duvall (Robert)
1984: 7 Abraham (F. Murray)
1985: 4 Hurt (William)
1986: 6 Newman (Paul)
1987: 7 Douglas (Michael)
1988: 7 Hoffman (Dustin)
1989: 8 Day-Lewis (Daniel)
1990: 5 Irons (Jeremy)
1991: 7 Hopkins (Anthony)
1992: 6 Pacino (Al)
1993: 5 Hanks (Tom)
1994: 5 Hanks (Tom)
1995: 4 Cage (Nicholas)

actress:
1927-28: 6 Gaynor (Janet)
1928-29: 8 Pickford (Mary)
1929-30: 7 Shearer (Norma)
1930-31: 8 Dressler (Marie)
1931-32: 5 Hayes (Helen)
1932-33: 7 Hepburn (Katharine)
1934: 7 Colbert (Claudette)
1935: 5 Davis (Bette)
1936: 6 Rainer (Luise)
1937: 6 Rainer (Luise)
1938: 5 Davis (Bette)
1939: 5 Leigh (Vivien)
1940: 6 Rogers (Ginger)
1941: 8 Fontaine (Joan)
1942: 6 Garson (Greer)
1943: 5 Jones (Jennifer)

1944: 7 Bergman (Ingrid)
1945: 8 Crawford (Joan)
1946: 11 de Havilland (Olivia)
1947: 5 Young (Loretta)
1948: 5 Wyman (Jane)
1949: 11 de Havilland (Olivia)
1950: 8 Holliday (Judy)
1951: 5 Leigh (Vivien)
1952: 5 Booth (Shirley)
1953: 7 Hepburn (Audrey)
1954: 5 Kelly (Grace)
1955: 7 Magnani (Anna)
1956: 7 Bergman (Ingrid)
1957: 8 Woodward (Joanne)
1958: 7 Hayward (Susan)
1959: 8 Signoret (Simone)
1960: 6 Taylor (Elizabeth)
1961: 5 Loren (Sophia)
1962: 8 Bancroft (Anne)
1963: 4 Neal (Patricia)
1964: 7 Andrews (Julie)
1965: 8 Christie (Julie)
1966: 6 Taylor (Elizabeth)
1967: 7 Hepburn (Katharine)
1968: 7 Hepburn (Katharine)
   9 Striesand (Barbara)
1969: 5 Smith (Maggie)
1970: 7 Jackson (Glenda)
1971: 5 Fonda (Jane)
1972: 8 Minnelli (Liza)
1973: 7 Jackson (Glenda)
1974: 7 Burstyn (Ellen)
1975: 8 Fletcher (Louise)
1976: 7 Dunaway (Faye)
1977: 6 Keaton (Diane)
1978: 5 Fonda (Jane)
1979: 5 Field (Sally)
1980: 6 Spacek (Sissy)
1981: 7 Hepburn (Katharine)
1982: 6 Streep (Meryl)
1983: 8 MacLaine (Shirley)
1984: 5 Field (Sally)
1985: 4 Page (Geraldine)
1986: 6 Matlin (Marlee)
1987: 4 Cher
1988: 6 Foster (Jodie)
1989: 5 Tandy (Jessica)
1990: 5 Bates (Kathy)
1991: 6 Foster (Jodie)
1992: 8 Thompson (Emma)
1993: 6 Hunter (Holly)
1994: 6 Lange (Jessica)
1995: 8 Sarandon (Susan)

accede
3 let, yes 5 agree, allow 6 assent,
concur, permit 7 consent 9 acquiesce, cooperate, subscribe

accelerate
5 hurry, impel, speed 6 hasten,
step up 7 quicken, swiften

acceleration
7 speedup

accent
4 beat, tone 5 meter, pulse, throb
6 rhythm, stress 7 cadence 8 emphasis 9 pulsation 10 inflection,
intonation
Irish: 6 brogue
Scottish: 4 burr
Southern: 5 drawl

accent mark
5 acute, grave

accentuation
see **accent**

accept
3 bow, buy, see 4 bear, take
5 adopt, agree, catch, favor, go
for, grasp, yield 6 admire, endure,
esteem, follow, pocket, take in
7 agree to, approve, believe, compass, receive, respect, swallow
8 assent to, bear with, hold with,
tolerate, tough out 9 agree with,
apprehend, approbate 10 capitulate, comprehend, understand
11 countenance, subscribe to

acceptable
4 good 6 decent 7 average 8 adequate, all right, bearable, ordinary
9 endurable, tolerable 10 sufficient
11 commonplace, supportable
12 satisfactory 13 unexceptional,
unimpeachable

acceptably
4 well 5 amply, right 8 properly,
suitably 9 fittingly 10 adequately,
becomingly 13 appropriately

acceptant
8 suasible, swayable 9 receptive
10 responsive 11 persuadable,
persuasible 13 influenceable

acceptation
5 sense 6 import 7 meaning, message, purport 10 intendment
12 significance, significancy 13 signification, understanding

accepted
5 sound, usual 6 proper 7 chronic,
correct, routine 8 habitual, orthodox, received 9 customary
10 accustomed, recognized, sanctioned 11 established
12 conventional

access
3 fit, way 4 adit, door, gust, pang,
turn 5 burst, entry, onset, route,
sally, spell, throe 6 attack, entrée,
stitch, taking, twinge 7 flare-up, ingress, passage, seizure 8 entrance,
eruption, outburst 9 admission, explosion 10 admittance

accessible
4 open 6 public, usable 9 operative 10 employable 11 practicable
12 approachable, unrestricted

accession
4 rise 5 raise 8 addition, increase
9 accretion, increment
12 augmentation

accessory
7 abettor, adjunct, fitting 8 addition, adjuvant, appendix 9 accretion, ancillary, appendage, auxiliary, increment, secondary,
tributary 10 accomplice, coincident, collateral, concurrent, incidental, subsidiary 11 appurtenant, concomitant, confederate, conspirator,
subordinate, subservient 12 adventitious, appurtenance, contributory
13 accompaniment, coconspirator

accident
3 hap 4 fate, luck 5 fluke
6 chance, hazard, kismet, mishap
7 destiny, fortune 8 calamity, casualty, fortuity 9 mischance 10 misfortune 12 misadventure

accidental
3 odd 5 fluky 6 casual, chance,
random 7 unmeant 9 chromatic,
dependent, unplanned, unwitting
10 coincident, contingent, fortuitous, undesigned, unintended, unpurposed 11 conditional, inadvertent 13 unintentional

accidentally
5 haply

acclaim
4 hail 5 cheer, éclat, exalt, glory,
honor, roose 6 homage, kudize,
praise 7 applaud, commend, glorify, magnify, ovation, root for
8 applause, plaudits 9 recommend,
reverence 10 compliment

acclamation
8 applause, plaudits

acclimate
6 harden, season 7 toughen
9 climatize

acclimatize
see **acclimate**

accolade
4 bays 5 award, badge, honor, kudos 7 laurels 10 decoration
11 distinction

accommodate
3 fit 4 hold, suit, tune, vary
5 adapt, alter, defer, favor, house,
humor, lodge, put up, yield 6 adjust, attune, bestow, billet, change,
encase, harbor, modify, oblige,
square, submit, tailor 7 cater to,
conform, contain, enclose, indulge,
quarter 8 domicile 9 entertain, harmonize, integrate, reconcile 10 coordinate, proportion 11 convenience, domiciliate
12 reconciliate

accommodations
4 keep, room 7 housing, lodging,
shelter 8 lodgment 12 room and
board

accompaniment
4 mate 6 fellow 7 comrade, consort, partner 8 addition 9 accessory, associate, attendant, colleague, companion, corollary
10 assistance, complement, enrichment, equivalent, supplement
11 concomitant, enhancement
12 augmentation

accompany
4 join, lead 5 bring, guide, pilot,
steer 6 attend, convoy, escort
7 combine, conduct, consort, esquire 8 chaperon 9 associate
11 consort with

accompanying
8 incident 9 ancillary, attendant, attending, satellite 10 coincident, collateral 11 concomitant

accomplice
5 aider 6 flunky, helper, stooge
7 abettor 9 accessory, assistant
11 confederate, conspirator
13 coconspirator

accomplish
3 win 4 gain 5 reach, score 6 attain, fulfil, rack up 7 achieve, fulfill,
realize, succeed

accomplished
4 ripe 5 adept 6 expert 8 finished,
masterly 9 all-around, many-sided,
perfected, versatile, virtuosic
10 consummate, proficient

accomplishment
3 act, art 4 deed 5 craft, doing,
skill, thing 6 action, finish 8 fruition
9 adeptness, expertise 10 attainment, expertness 11 achievement,
acquirement, acquisition,
proficiency

accord
4 deal, fuse, give, jibe, tune
5 agree, award, blend, chime, fit
in, grant, merge, tally, union 6 chorus, concur, confer, square 7 concede, concert, conform, empathy,
harmony 8 affinity, coalesce, coincide, dovetail, sympathy 9 agree-

ment, harmonize, vouchsafe **10** attraction, consonance, correspond, solidarity **11** concordance **13** understanding

accordant
9 congruous **10** harmonious

accordingly
2 so **4** ergo, then, thus **5** hence **9** therefore, thereupon **12** consequently

accost
3 dog **4** dare, face, hail **5** annoy, front, greet, hound, worry **6** bother, call to, halloo, pester, salute **7** address, affront, apply to, bespeak, outface, outrage **8** approach, confront **9** challenge **10** buttonhole **11** memorialize

accouchement
7 lying in **8** childbed **11** confinement

account
3 tab, use **4** bill, deem, note, rate, view **5** avail, favor, score, story, value, worth **6** assess, esteem, reason, reckon, regard, report, repute **7** dignity, explain, expound, fitness, history, invoice, justify, recital, respect, service, utility, version **8** appraise, consider, estimate, evaluate **9** advantage, chronicle, elucidate, narrative, rationale, reckoning, relevance, statement, valuation **10** admiration, estimation, reputation, usefulness **11** consequence, distinction, explain away, explanation, rationalize **13** applicability, consideration, justification

accountable
6 liable **8** amenable **10** answerable **11** responsible

account book
6 ledger

accounting
branch of: **11** bookkeeping

accouter
3 arm, rig **4** deck, gear **5** adorn, dress, equip, fix up, ready **6** attire, fit out, outfit **7** appoint, furnish, prepare, turn out **8** decorate **9** embellish

accouterment
4 gear **6** outfit, tackle **7** bravery, regalia **8** matériel, tackling **9** apparatus, equipment, machinery, trappings **11** furnishings, habiliments **12** appointments **13** paraphernalia

accredit
2 OK **3** lay **4** okay **5** refer **6** assign, attest, charge, enable, impute **7** approve, ascribe, certify, commend, empower, endorse, license **8** sanction, vouch for **9** attribute, authorize, recommend **10** commission

accretion
4 rise **5** raise **7** adjunct **8** addition, increase **9** accession, appendage, increment **10** attachment **11** enlargement **12** augmentation

accumulate
4 heap, hive, mass, pile **5** amass, hoard, lay by, lay in, lay up, stock, uplay **6** garner, gather, roll up **7** backlog, collect, lay down, store up **8** assemble, treasure **9** stockpile

accumulation
4 bank, heap, mass, pile **5** hoard, stock, store, trove **7** buildup, cumulus, reserve **9** amassment **10** collection **11** aggregation **13** agglomeration

accumulative
5 chain **8** additive, additory **9** summative **11** aggregative **12** augmentative

accuracy
9 exactness, precision **10** definition, exactitude **11** correctness, preciseness **12** definiteness

accurate
4 nice **5** exact, right **6** proper **7** certain, correct, precise **8** reliable, rigorous **9** authentic **10** dependable

accursed
6 odious **7** hateful **8** damnable **9** abhorrent, execrable, offensive, repugnant, revolting **10** abominable, detestable

accusation
6 charge **8** delation **10** allegation, indictment
false: **7** calumny

accuse
3 tax **5** blame **6** charge, delate, indict **7** arraign, censure, impeach **8** denounce **9** criminate, criticize, inculpate, reprobate **11** incriminate

accustom
3 use **4** wont **5** adapt, inure **6** adjust, harden, season **9** habituate **11** acclimatize, familiarize

accustomed
5 usual **7** chronic, routine **8** accepted, everyday, habitual, stan-

dard **9** confirmed **10** habituated, regulation **11** commonplace **12** conventional

ace
3 bit, jot **4** atom, hair, iota, mite **5** crumb, minim, speck **7** whisker **8** molecule, particle **11** hairbreadth

ace and face card
7 natural **9** blackjack

acedia
5 sloth

acerb
3 dry **4** acid, sour, tart **7** acetose, caustic **9** acidulous, corrosive, sarcastic **12** archilochian

acerbate
7 envenom **8** embitter

acerbic
see *acerb*

acerbity
7 acidity, sarcasm **8** acrimony, asperity, dourness, mordancy, sourness, tartness **9** harshness, roughness, surliness **10** bitterness, causticity **11** crabbedness, saturninity

Achates' companion
6 Aeneas

ache
3 yen **4** hurt, long, lust, pain, pang, pine, pity, rack, sigh **5** crave, throe, yearn **6** hanker, hunger, injury, misery, stitch, suffer, thirst, twinge **7** feel for **8** yearning **10** sorrow over **11** commiserate **13** compassionate
Scottish: **5** stoun **6** stound

acheronian
5 black, bleak, drear **6** dismal, gloomy **7** joyless **8** desolate, funereal **9** cheerless

achieve
2 do **3** get, win **4** gain **5** reach, score **6** attain, finish, obtain, rack up, secure **7** acquire, execute, perform, realize **8** complete, conclude **9** actualize **10** accomplish

achievement
4 deed, feat **6** finish **7** exploit **10** attainment **11** acquirement, acquisition, tour de force

Achilles
adviser: **6** Nestor
companion: **9** Patroclus
father: **6** Peleus
horse: **7** Xanthus
lover: **7** Briseis
mother: **6** Thetis

slayer: **5** Paris
victim: **6** Hector
vulnerable part: **4** heel

Achilles' heel
8 soft spot

aching
4 sore **7** algetic, hurtful, hurting, painful **10** afflictive

Achsah
father: **5** Caleb
husband: **7** Othniel

achy
4 sore

acicular
5 acute, peaky, piked, sharp **6** peaked **7** pointed

acid
3 dry **4** sour, tart **5** acerb **7** acerbic, acetose
bleaching: **6** oxalic
combining form: **3** oxy **4** acet **5** aceto
fatty: **6** capric **7** caproic, stearic **8** caprylic
found in apples: **5** malic
found in cranberries: **7** benzoic
found in grapes: **8** tartaric
found in lemons: **6** citric
found in rhubarb: **6** oxalic
found in sour milk: **6** lactic
indicator: **6** litmus
kind: **5** amino, boric, iodic, malic, oleic **6** acetic, bromic, formic, nitric, oxalic, tannic **7** chloric, nitrous, silicic **8** carbolic, carbonic, chlorous, muriatic, sulfuric **9** aqua regia **12** hydrochloric
neutralizer: **4** base **6** alkali
tanning: **6** tannic **8** catechin
vinegar: **6** acetic

acid radical
combining form: **3** oyl

acidulous
3 dry **4** sour, tart **5** acerb, sharp **6** biting **7** acerbic, acetose, cutting, piquant, pungent

Acis
lover: **7** Galatea
slayer: **10** Polyphemus

acknowledge
3 own **4** avow, deem, tell, view **5** admit, agree, allow, grant, let on, own up **6** accept, fess up, reveal **7** concede, confess, declare, divulge **8** announce, consider, disclose, proclaim **9** recognize

acknowledgment
6 credit **11** recognition

acme
4 apex, peak **6** apogee, climax, summit, tiptop, vertex, zenith **8** capstone, meridian, pinnacle **11** culmination

acorn
combining form: **5** balan **6** balano
sprouter: **3** oak

acoustic
5 aural **6** audile **8** auditory

acquaint
4 clew, clue, post, tell, warn **6** advise, fill in, inform, notify, orient, wise up **7** apprise, present **8** accustom **9** habituate, introduce

acquaintance
4 mate **5** amigo, crony **6** friend **7** comrade **8** familiar, intimacy, intimate **9** associate, companion, confidant **10** experience **11** familiarity

acquainted
6 au fait, versed **7** abreast, versant **8** familiar, informed **9** au courant **10** conversant

acquiesce
3 bow, yes **5** agree **6** accede, assent, concur **7** consent **9** reconcile, subscribe

acquiescence
9 deference **10** compliance, conformity **11** resignation **12** complaisance

acquiescent
7 passive **8** resigned, yielding **10** submissive **11** unresistant, unresisting **12** nonresistant, nonresisting

acquire
3 add, get, win **4** earn, form, gain, land, make, reap **5** amass, annex, reach **6** garner, obtain, pick up, secure **7** bring in, collect, develop, rocure **8** cumulate **9** knock down **10** accumulate

acquirement
6 finish **7** advance **8** addition **9** accretion, erudition **10** attainment **11** achievement, acquisition, advancement

acquisition
see **acquirement**

acquisitive
5 itchy **6** grabby, greedy **8** covetous, desirous, grasping **10** prehensile

acquit
3 act **4** bear, free **5** carry, clear **6** behave, deport **7** absolve, comport, conduct, release **8** liberate **9** discharge, exculpate, exonerate, vindicate **10** disculpate

acres
4 land **5** manor **6** estate **7** demesne

acrid
4 sour **5** harsh, sharp **6** biting, bitter **7** austere, caustic, cutting **9** amaroidal **10** astringent

acrimonious
3 mad **5** angry, cross, irate, testy, wroth **6** cranky, ireful, wrathy, wrothy **8** wrathful, wrothful **9** indignant, irascible, splenetic **11** belligerent, contentious, quarrelsome

acrimony
5 spite **6** animus, malice, rancor **7** ill will **8** acerbity, asperity, mordancy **9** animosity, antipathy, malignity **10** bitterness **11** malevolence

Acrisius
daughter: **5** Danae
slayer: **7** Perseus

across
4 over **6** beyond **7** athwart **12** transversely
prefix: **2** di **3** dia **4** over **5** trans

act
2 do **3** run **4** bear, deed, fake, feat, play, sham, work **5** bluff, doing, feign, put on, serve **6** acquit, affect, assume, behave, demean, deport **7** comport, conduct, exploit, operate, perform, portray, pretend **8** function, simulate **9** discourse, officiate, personate **10** masquerade **11** counterfeit, impersonate
suffix: **2** cy, th **3** ade, ate, ice, ion, ism

acting
6 pro tem **7** interim **9** ad interim, temporary **10** pro tempore

actinium
symbol: **2** Ac

action
4 case, deed, fray, suit, work **5** cause, doing **6** affray, battle, combat **7** lawsuit, process, service **8** behavior, conflict, function **9** discharge, execution, operation, procedure **10** engagement, proceeding **11** performance
combining form: **3** cin, kin **4** cino, kine, kino **5** cinet, kinet **6** cineto, kineto, praxia, praxis
suffix: **2** al, cy **3** ade, ing, sis

4 ance, ence, esis, ment, osis
5 ation **7** isation, ization
unwise: **8** impolicy

action painting
7 tachism

activate
4 stir, wake **5** rally, rouse, waken
6 arouse, awaken **8** energize,
vitalize

activation
combining form: **7** kinesis

active
4 busy, live, spry, yare **5** agile,
alert, alive, brisk, zippy **6** brisky,
lively, nimble **7** driving, dynamic,
running, working **8** animated, spirited, vigorous **9** assiduous, energetic, operative, sprightly, vivacious
11 functioning, industrious
12 enterprising

activity
8 exercise, exertion **10** exercising

actor
4 mime **5** mimic, party **6** mummer,
player, sharer **7** trouper **8** histrion,
partaker, thespian **9** performer
11 participant **12** impersonator,
participator
name: **3** Cox (Wally), Dix (Richard),
Fox (James, Michael J.), Lee
(Bruce), Lom (Herbert), Mix (Tom),
Ray (Aldo) **4** Alda (Alan, Robert),
Bean (Orson), Blue (Ben), Bond
(Ward), Caan (James), Cage (Nich-
olas), Cobb (Lee J.), Coco (James),
Culp (Robert), Dean (James), Depp
(Johnny), Dern (Bruce), Duff (How-
ard), Egan (Richard), Falk (Peter),
Ford (Glenn, Harrison), Foxx
(Redd), Geer (Will), Gere (Richard),
Grey (Joel), Hale (Alan), Hill (Ar-
thur), Hope (Bob), Hurt (John Wil-
liam), Ives (Burl), Jory (Victor), Kaye
(Danny), Kean (Edmund), Keel
(Howard), Ladd (Alan), Lahr (Bert),
Lord (Jack), Lowe (Chad, Rob), Lunt
(Alfred), Marx (Chico, Groucho,
Harpo), Muni (Paul), Ngor (Haing
S.), Noth (Christopher), Peck (Greg-
ory), Penn (Sean), Pitt (Brad), Raft
(George), Roth (Tim), Ryan (Robert),
Shaw (Robert), Todd (Richard),
Tone (Franchot), Torn (Rip), Tune
(Tommy), Wahl (Ken), Webb (Clif-
ton, Jack), Wynn (Ed, Keenan),
York (Michael) **5** Adler (Luther), Al-
len (Tim, Woody), Arkin (Adam,
Alan), Asner (Ed), Autry (Gene),
Ayres (Lew), Bacon (Kevin), Barry
(Gene), Bates (Alan), Beery (Noah,
Wallace), Berle (Milton), Boone
(Richard), Brady (Scott), Brand (Ne-
ville), Burns (George), Caine (Mi-
chael), Candy (John), Chase
(Chevy), Clark (Dane), Clift (Mont-
gomery), Conte (Richard), Cooke
(Alistair), Corey (Wendell), Cosby
(Bill), Dafoe (Willem), Davis (Clif-
ton, Ossie, Sammy Jr.), Delon
(Alain), Donat (Robert), Evans (Mau-
rice), Ewell (Tom), Finch (Peter),
Firth (Colin, Peter), Flynn (Errol),
Fonda (Henry, Peter), Franz (Den-
nis), Gabin (Jean), Gable (Clark),
Gould (Elliot), Grant (Cary, Hugh),
Gwenn (Edmund), Hanks (Tom),
Hardy (Oliver), Hauer (Rutger),
Hawke (Ethan), Hayes (Gabby),
Irons (Jeremy), Jaffe (Sam), Jones
(Dean, James Earl, Tommy Lee), Ka-
zan (Elia), Keach (Stacy), Keith
(Brian, David), Kelly (Gene), Kiley
(Richard), Kline (Kevin), Kotto (Ya-
phet), Lamas (Fernando, Lorenzo),
Lanza (Mario), Lewis (Jerry, Rich-
ard), Lloyd (Harold), Lorre (Peter),
Lukas (Paul), Lynde (Paul), March
(Fredric), McCoy (Tim), Mills
(John), Mineo (Sal), Moore (Dudley,
Roger, Victor), Neill (Sam), Nimoy
(Leonard), Niven (David), Nolan
(Lloyd), Nolte (Nick), Oakie (Jack),
Oland (Warner), Olmos (Edward
James), O'Neal (Patrick, Ryan),
Payne (John), Perry (Luke, Mat-
thew), Pesci (Joe), Power (Tyrone),
Price (Vincent), Pryce (Jonathan),
Quaid (Dennis, Randy), Quale (An-
thony), Quinn (Aidan Anthony),
Rains (Claude), Reeve (Christo-
pher), Scott (Campbell, George C.,
Randolph), Segal (George), Sheen
(Charlie, Martin), Smits (Jimmy),
Stack (Robert), Stamp (Terence),
Tracy (Spencer), Tufts (Sonny),
Wayne (John), Wilde (Cornel),
Wills (Chill), Woods (James),
Young (Gig, Robert) **6** Abbott
(Bud), Albert (Eddie), Ameche
(Don), Arness (James), Backus (Jim),
Balsam (Martin), Barker (Lex), Bax-
ter (Warner), Beatty (Ned, War-
ren), Begley (Ed), Blades (Ruben),
Bogart (Humphrey), Bolger (Ray),
Bosley (Tom), Brando (Marlon),
Brooks (Albert, Mel), Burton (Rich-
ard), Caesar (Sid), Cagney (James),
Callan (Michael), Cantor (Eddie),
Cariou (Len), Carney (Art), Carrey
(Jim), Carvey (Dana), Chaney (Lon),
Coburn (Charles, James), Colman
(Ronald), Conrad (Robert, William),
Conway (Tim, Tom), Coogan
(Jackie), Cooper (Gary), Cotten
(Joseph), Crabbe (Buster), Crenna
(Richard), Cronyn (Hume), Crosby
(Bing), Cruise (Tom), Culkin (Ma-
caulay), Curtis (Tony), Dailey (Dan),
Dalton (Timothy), Danson (Ted),
Danton (Ray), Darren (James), De
Niro (Robert), De Vito (Danny), Dil-
lon (Matt), Downey (Robert), Dullea
(Keir), Duryea (Dan), Duvall (Rob-
ert), Ferrer (Jose, Mel), Fields
(W.C.), Finney (Albert), Garcia
(Andy), Garner (James), Gibson
(Hoot, Mel), Glover (Danny), Gor-
cey (Leo), Gordan (Gale), Graves
(Peter), Greene (Lorne, Richard),
Grodin (Charles), Hamlin (Harry),
Harris (Ed, Richard), Harvey (Lau-
rence), Hayden (Sterling), Heflin
(Van), Heston (Charlton), Hingle
(Pat), Holden (Bill), Hopper (Dennis,
William), Howard (Trevor), Hudson
(Rock), Hunter (Jeffrey, Tab), Huston
(John, Walter), Hutton (Jim, Timo-
thy), Jacobi (Lou), Jagger (Dean),
Keaton (Buster, Michael), Keitel
(Harvey), Kilmer (Val), Knotts (Don),
Kruger (Otto), Landau (Martin), Lan-
don (Michael), Laurel (Stan), Lem-
mon (Jack), Liotta (Ray), Lugosi
(Bela), MacRae (Gordon), Malden
(Karl), Martin (Dean, Steve), Marvin
(Lee), Massey (Raymond), Mature
(Victor), McCrea (Joel), Meeker
(Ralph), Menjou (Adolphe), Modine
(Matthew), Morgan (Harry), Morley
(Robert), Morris (Wayne), Morrow
(Vic), Mostel (Josh, Zero), Murphy
(Audie, Eddie), Murray (Bill, Don),
Neeson (Liam), Nelson (Ozzie),
Newley (Anthony), Newman (Paul),
O'Brian (Hugh), O'Brien (Edmund,
Pat), Oldman (Gary), O'Toole (Pe-
ter), Pacino (Al), Parker (Fess, Jame-
son), Poston (Tom), Powell (Dick),
Reeves (Keanu, Steve), Reiner (Carl,
Rob), Reiser (Paul), Rennie (Mi-
chael), Ritter (John, Tex), Rogers
(Roy, Wayne, Will), Romero
(Cesar), Rooney (Mickey), Rourke
(Mickey), Schell (Maximilian), Sea-
gal (Steven), Sharif (Omar), Slezak
(Walter), Snipes (Wesley), Spacey
(Kevin), Spader (James), Swayze
(Patrick), Talbot (Lyle), Taylor (Rob-
ert, Rod), Thomas (Danny, Richard),
Toomey (Regis), Tucker (Forrest), Tur-
pin (Ben), Vaughn (Robert), Voight
(Jon), Wagner (Jack, Robert),
Walker (Robert), Warden (Jack),
Wayans (Damon, Keenen Ivory),
Weaver (Dennis, Fritz), Welles (Or-
son), Werner (Oskar), Wilder
(Gene), Willis (Bruce) **7** Abraham

(F. Murray), Andrews (Dana), Assante (Armand), Astaire (Fred), Aykroyd (Dan), Baldwin (Alec, Daniel, Stephen, William), Bellamy (Ralph), Bogarde (Dirk), Branagh (Kenneth), Bridges (Beau, Jeff, Lloyd), Bronson (Charles), Brosnan (Pierce), Brynner (Yul), Bushman (Francis X.), Buttons (Red), Calhern (Louis), Calhoun (Rory), Cameron (Rod), Carlson (Richard), Carroll (Leo G.), Chaplin (Charlie), Clooney (George), Connery (Sean), Connors (Chuck, Mike), Conried (Hans), Costner (Kevin), Crystal (Billy), Daniels (Jeff, William), da Silva (Howard), DeLuise (Dom), Dennehy (Brian), Donahue (Troy), Donlevy (Brian), Douglas (Kirk, Melvyn, Michael, Paul), Dreyfuss (Richard), Edwards (Vince), Feldman (Marty), Fiennes (Ralph), Freeman (Morgan), Garrick (David), Gazzara (Ben), Gielgud (John), Gleason (Jackie), Goodman (John), Gossett (Louis), Grammer (Kelsey), Granger (Farley, Stewart), Guiness (Alec), Hackman (Gene), Henreid (Paul), Hoffman (Dustin), Homeier (Skip), Homolka (Oscar), Hopkins (Anthony), Hoskins (Bob), Ireland (John), Janssen (David), Johnson (Ben, Don, Van), Jourdan (Louis), Jurgens (Curt), Karloff (Boris), Kennedy (Arthur, George), Klugman (Jack), Lawford (Peter), Leonard (Robert Sean, Sheldon), Lithgow (John), Macchio (Ralph), MacLane (Barton), Maharis (George), Mathers (Jerry), Matthau (Walter), McCarey (Leo), McGavin (Darren), McQueen (Steve), Merrill (Gary), Milland (Ray), Mitchum (Robert), Montand (Yves), Navarro (Ramon), Newhart (Bob), O'Connor (Carroll, Donald), Olivier (Laurence), Palance (Jack), Paulsen (Pat), Peppard (George), Perkins (Anthony), Persoff (Nehemiah), Pickens (Slim), Pidgeon (Walter), Pinchot (Bronson), Poitier (Sidney), Preston (Robert), Randall (Tony), Redford (Robert), Rickman (Alan), Robards (Jason), Robbins (Tim), Robeson (Paul), Roberts (Pernell, Tony), Salvini (Tommaso), Sanders (George), Savalas (Telly), Scourby (Alexander), Selleck (Tom), Sellers (Peter), Shatner (William), Shepard (Sam), Silvers (Phil), Sinatra (Frank), Skelton (Red), Skinner (Otis), Steiger (Rod), Stewart (James, Patrick), Tamblyn (Russ), Ustinov (Pe-

ter), Vallone (Raf), Van Dyke (Dick, Jerry), Wallach (Eli), Widmark (Richard), Wilding (Michael), Winters (Jonathan), Woolley (Monty) **8** Banderas (Antonio), Basehart (Richard), Berenger (Tom), Bickford (Charles), Blackmer (Sidney), Borgnine (Ernest), Buchanan (Edgar), Buchholz (Horst), Carrillo (Leo), Chandler (Jeff), Costello (Lou), Crawford (Broderick, Michael), Cummings (Robert), Day-Lewis (Daniel), DiCaprio (Leonardo), Duchovny (David), Eastwood (Clint), Forsythe (John), Gardiner (Reginald), Garfield (John), Goldblum (Jeff), Harrison (Gregory, Noel, Rex), Hemmings (David), Holbrook (Hal), Holloway (Stanley), Jannings (Emil), Kilbride (Percy), Kingsley (Ben), Langella (Frank), Laughton (Charles), Lockhart (Gene), Marshall (E.G., Herbert), McDowall (Roddy), McDowell (Malcolm), McLaglen (Victor), Meredith (Burgess), Mitchell (Thomas), O'Connell (Arthur), O'Donnell (Chris), O'Herlihy (Dan), Rathbone (Basil), Redgrave (Michael), Reynolds (Burt), Ritchard (Cyril), Robinson (Edward G.), Sarrazin (Michael), Scofield (Paul), Stallone (Sylvester), Sullivan (Barry), Travolta (John), Turturro (John), Van Damme (Jean-Claude), Von Sydow (Max), Whitmore (James), Williams (Robin) **9** Amsterdam (Morey), Barrymore (John, Lionel), Brandauer (Klaus Maria), Broderick (Matthew), Carnovsky (Morris), Carradine (David, John, Keith, Robert), Courtenay (Tom), Depardieu (Gerard), Fairbanks (Douglas), Fishburne (Larry), Franciosa (Anthony), Hardwicke (Cedric), Harrelson (Woody), Hyde-White (Wilfrid), Lancaster (Burt), MacMurray (Fred), Malkovich (John), Montalban (Ricardo), Nicholson (Jack), Pleasance (Donald), Robertson (Cliff, Dale), Tarantino (Quentin), Zimbalist (Efrem) **10** Fitzgerald (Barry), Hasselhoff (David), Montgomery (Robert), Richardson (Ralph), Sutherland (Donald, Kiefer), Washington (Denzel) **11** Chamberlain (Richard), Greenstreet (Sydney), Larroquette (John), Mastroianni (Marcello) **13** Kristofferson (Kris) **14** Schwarzenegger (Arnold)

actor's
quest: **4** part, role
signal: **3** cue

actress
3 Bow (Clara), Cox (Courtney), Day (Doris), Dee (Sandra), Dru (Joanne), Gam (Rita), Loy (Myrna), May (Elaine), Rae (Charlotte) **4** Bara (Theda), Barr (Roseanne), Cass (Peggy), Cher, Coca (Imogene), Dahl (Arlene), Daly (Tyne), Dern (Laura), Duke (Patty), Eden (Barbara), Foch (Nina), Garr (Teri), Gish (Lillian), Hawn (Goldie), Holm (Celeste), Hunt (Helen, Linda, Marsha), Hyer (Martha), Kahn (Madeline), Kerr (Deborah), Lake (Veronica), Lisi (Virna), Main (Marjorie), Mayo (Virginia), Neal (Patricia), Olin (Lena), Raye (Martha), Rigg (Diana), Ross (Diana, Katharine), Rush (Barbara), Ryan (Meg, Peggy), Shue (Elisabeth), Weld (Tuesday), West (Mae), Wood (Natalie, Peggy), Wray (Fay), York (Susannah) **5** Adams (Maude), Aimee (Anouk), Allen (Joan, Karen, Nancy), Alley (Kirstie), Arden (Eve), Astor (Mary), Bates (Kathy), Berry (Halle), Bloom (Clair), Blyth (Ann), Booth (Shirley), Britt (May), Bruce (Virginia), Buzzi (Ruth), Caron (Leslie), Close (Glenn), Crain (Jeanne), Davis (Bette, Geena, Judy), Dunne (Irene), Eggar (Samantha), Field (Sally), Fonda (Bridget, Jane), Gabor (Eva, Zsa Zsa), Garbo (Greta), Gless (Sharon), Grant (Lee), Hagen (Uta), Hasso (Signe), Hayes (Helen), Henie (Sonja), Howes (Sally Ann), Jones (Jennifer, Shirley), Kelly (Patsy), Kurtz (Swoosie), Lahti (Christine), Lange (Hope, Jessica), Leigh (Janet, Jennifer Jason, Vivien), Lenya (Lotte), Lewis (Juliette), Loren (Sophia), Mason (Pamela), Meara (Anne), Miles (Sarah, Vera), Moore (Demi, Mary Tyler, Terry), North (Sheree), Novak (Kim), O'Hara (Maureen), Olson (Nancy), O'Neal (Tatum), Perez (Rosie), Picon (Molly), Pitts (Zasu), Roman (Ruth), Ruehl (Mercedes), Ryder (Winona), Saint (Eva Marie), Scott (Lizbeth, Martha), Smith (Alexis, Maggie), Storm (Gale), Tandy (Jessica), Tyson (Cicely), Welch (Raquel), Wiest (Dianne), Wyatt (Jane), Young (Sean Loretta) **6** Adjani (Isabelle), Angeli (Pier), Ashley (Elizabeth), Bacall (Lauren), Bardot (Brigitte), Barkin (Ellen), Barrie (Wendy), Baxter (Anne), Bening (Annette), Bergen (Candice, Polly), Bisset (Jacqueline), Blaine (Vivian), Bujold (Genevieve),

Butler (Brett), Cannon (Dyan), Carter (Dixie, Lynda, Nell), Curtin (Jane), Curtis (Jamie Lee), Davies (Marion), Delaney (Dana), Del Rio (Dolores), Dennis (Sandy), Diller (Phyllis), Duncan (Sandy), Durbin (Deanna), Fabray (Nanette), Farrow (Mia), Fisher (Carrie), Foster (Jodie), Garner (Peggy Ann), Garson (Greer), Gaynor (Mitzi), Gordon (Ruth), Grable (Betty), Grimes (Tammy), Hannah (Daryl), Harlow (Jean), Harper (Tess, Valerie), Harris (Julie, Rosemary), Hunter (Holly, Kim), Hussey (Ruth), Huston (Anjelica), Hutton (Betty), Keaton (Diane), Keeler (Ruby), Kidman (Nicole), Lamarr (Hedy), Lamour (Dorothy), Lasser (Louise), Laurie (Piper), Louise (Tina), Lupino (Ida), MacRae (Sheila), Malone (Dorothy), Martin (Mary), Matlin (Marlee), McGraw (Ali), Merkel (Una), Midler (Bette), Monroe (Marilyn), Moreau (Jeanne), Moreno (Rita), Oberon (Merle), O'Brien (Margaret), Palmer (Lili), Paquin (Anna), Parker (Eleanor, Mary-Louise, Sarah Jessica, Suzy), Powers (Stephanie), Prowse (Juliet), Rashad (Phylicia), Remick (Lee), Ritter (Thelma), Rogers (Ginger), Sidney (Sylvia), Spacek (Sissy), Streep (Meryl), Taylor (Elizabeth), Temple (Shirley), Thomas (Marlo), Tiffin (Pamela), Tomlin (Lily), Turner (Kathleen, Lana), Walker (Nancy), Weaver (Sigourney), Wilson (Marie), Winger (Debra), Wright (Teresa), Wynter (Dana) **7** Allyson (June), Andress (Ursula), Andrews (Julie), Bergman (Ingrid), Buckley (Betty), Bullock (Sandra), Burnett (Carol), Burstyn (Ellen), Collins (Joan, Pauline), Darnell (Linda), DeCarlo (Yvonne), Deneuve (Catherine), Dukakis (Olympia), Dunaway (Faye), Dunnock (Mildred), Fawcett (Farrah), Fleming (Rhonda), Fricker (Brenda), Gardner (Ava), Garland (Judy), Goddard (Paulette), Grayson (Kathryn), Hayward (Susan), Heckart (Eileen), Hershey (Barbara), Jackson (Ann, Glenda, Kate), Langtry (Lillie), Learned (Michael), Lombard (Carole), Madonna, Magnani (Anna), Mangano (Silvana), McGuire (Dorothy), McKenna (Siobhan), McQueen (Butterfly), Meadows (Audrey, Jayne), Mimieux (Yvette), Miranda (Carmen), Mulgrew (Kate), Natwick (Mildred), Perlman (Rhea), Perrine (Valerie), Podesta (Rosanna), Roberts (Julia), Russell (Jane, Rosalind, Theresa), Scacchi (Greta), Shearer (Norma), Simmons (Jean), Sorvino (Mira), Stevens (Connie, Stella), Swanson (Gloria), Thaxter (Phyllis), Tierney (Gene), Ullmann (Liv), Winfrey (Oprah), Winters (Shelley), Withers (Jane) **8** Anderson (Judith, Loni, Melissa Sue), Arquette (Patricia, Rosanna), Ashcroft (Peggy), Bancroft (Anne), Bankhead (Tallulah), Basinger (Kim), Blondell (Joan), Byington (Spring), Caldwell (Zoe), Channing (Carol, Stockard), Charisse (Cyd), Christie (Julie), Crawford (Joan), Dewhurst (Colleen), Dietrich (Marlene), Dressler (Marie), Fletcher (Louise), Fontaine (Joan), Fontanne (Lynn), Goldberg (Whoopi), Griffith (Melanie), Hayworth (Rita), Lansbury (Angela), Lawrence (Gertrude), Leachman (Cloris), Leighton (Margaret), Lindfors (Viveca), Lockhart (June), Lovelace (Linda), MacLaine (Shirley), Mercouri (Melina), Minnelli (Liza), Neuwirth (Bebe), O'Donnell (Rosie), Pfeiffer (Michelle), Pickford (Mary), Prentiss (Paula), Redgrave (Lynn, Vanessa), Roseanne, Rowlands (Gena), Sarandon (Susan), Shepherd (Cybill), Signoret (Simone), Stanwyck (Barbara), Sullavan (Margaret), Talmadge (Norma), Thompson (Emma, Sada), Williams (Esther), Woodward (Joanne) **9** Alexander (Jane), Barrymore (Drew, Ethel), Bernhardt (Sarah), Christian (Linda), Clayburgh (Jill), DeGeneres (Ellen), Dickinson (Angie), Kellerman (Sally), Mansfield (Jayne), McDonnell (Mary), Moorehead (Agnes), O'Sullivan (Maureen), Pleshette (Suzanne), Plowright (Joan), Schneider (Romy), Singleton (Penny), Stapleton (Jean, Maureen), Strasberg (Susan), Streisand (Barbra), Struthers (Sally), Thorndike (Sybil), Vera-Ellen **10** Lanchester (Elsa), Montgomery (Elizabeth), Richardson (Miranda, Natasha), Rutherford (Margaret), Tushingham (Rita) **11** Ann-Margaret, de Havilland (Olivia), McCambridge (Mercedes), Riefenstahl (Leni), Steenburgen (Mary) **12** Bonham-Carter (Helena), Lollabrigida (Gina), Mastrantonio (Mary Elizabeth)

actual

4 hard, real, true **6** extant **7** genuine **8** absolute, bona fide, concrete, existent, material, physical, positive, tangible, unfabled **9** authentic, objective, veridical **10** legitimate, phenomenal, undeniable **12** indisputable

actuality

4 fact **5** being **7** reality **9** existence, substance **10** embodiment **11** incarnation, materiality

actually

4 very **5** truly **6** really **7** de facto **9** genuinely, veritably

actuate

4 move, stir **5** drive, impel, rouse **6** arouse, propel, set off **7** provoke, trigger **8** mobilize, vitalize **9** circulate, galvanize

act up

9 misbehave

acumen

3 wit **8** astucity, keenness **9** acuteness, sharpness **10** astuteness, shrewdness **11** discernment, penetration, percipience **12** perspicacity

acute

4 dire, high, keen **5** peaky, piked, sharp **6** argute, peaked, piping, shrill, treble, urgent **7** crucial, cutting, exigent, pointed **8** acicular, critical, incisive, piercing, shooting, stabbing **9** aciculate, acuminate, acuminous, cuspidate, desperate, knifelike, observant, sensitive, trenchant **10** perceptive **11** climacteric, penetrating, penetrative, quick-witted, sharp-witted
combining form: 3 oxy

adage

3 saw **4** word **6** byword, saying, truism **7** proverb **8** aphorism, apothegm

Adah

husband: 4 Esau **6** Lamech
son: 5 Jabal, Jubal **7** Eliphaz

Adam

grandson: 4 Enos **5** Enoch
rib: 3 Eve
son: 4 Abel, Cain, Seth
teacher: 6 Raisel
wife: 3 Eve **6** Lilith

Adam___

4 Bede **5** Smith

adamant

5 rigid **8** immobile, obdurate **9** immovable, unbending, unswaying

10 inexorable, inflexible, relentless, unbendable, unyielding
12 unsubmitting

adapt
3 fit **4** suit **5** refit **6** adjust, square, tailor **7** conform **9** acclimate, reconcile **11** acclimatize, accommodate

adaptable
6 mobile, pliant, supple **7** ductile, plastic, pliable **8** moldable **9** all-around, malleable, many-sided, versatile

Ad astra per___
6 aspera

add
3 sum, tot **4** cast, foot, tote **5** affix, annex, tally, total **6** append, attach, figure, reckon, tack on, take on **7** augment, compute, enlarge, subjoin, summate **8** compound, increase, totalize **9** calculate

added
3 new **4** else, more **5** fresh, other **7** another, farther, further **10** additional

addendum
5 rider **7** allonge **8** addition **10** supplement

ad design
4 logo

addict
3 fan **4** bias, buff **5** hound, lover **6** adjust, junkie, votary, zealot **7** devotee, fanatic, habitué, hophead **9** habituate **10** aficionado, enthusiast, predispose

addition
4 plus, rise **5** extra, raise, rider **7** accrual, adjunct **8** addendum, appanage, increase **9** accession, accessory, accretion, extension, increment **10** accruement, supplement **12** appurtenance, augmentation
number: **6** addend **7** summand

additional
3 new **4** else, more **5** extra, fresh, other **7** another, farther, further **9** accessory **12** supplemental **13** supplementary

additionally
3 too, yea, yet **4** also, more, then **5** again **6** as well, withal **7** addedly, besides, further **8** likewise, moreover **11** furthermore

additive
5 chain **8** extender **9** summative **10** cumulative **12** accumulative

addle
5 mix up **6** ball up, fuddle **7** confuse, fluster, nonplus, perplex **8** befuddle, bewilder, confound, distract, throw off **9** dumbfound

address
3 aim, air, set, sue, woo **4** hail, mien, port, send, ship, tact, talk **5** apply, court, greet, level, point, poise, remit, route, skill, speak **6** accost, attend, call to, devote, direct, pursue, relate, salute, speech **7** bearing, bespeak, consign, forward, incline, know-how, lecture, prowess, tutoyer **8** appeal to, approach, converse, deftness, demeanor, dispatch, petition, presence, talk with, transmit **9** dexterity, diplomacy, expertise **10** adroitness, allocution, buckle down, competence, deportment, efficiency **11** comportment, memorialize, proficiency, savoir faire, superscribe, tactfulness **12** apostrophize

adduce
3 lay **4** cite **5** offer **6** allege, submit, tender **7** advance, present, proffer, propose, suggest **8** document **9** exemplify **10** illustrate

add up to
4 mean **5** spell **6** denote, import, intend **7** connote, express, signify

A Death in the Family author
4 Agee (James)

adept
4 deft, whiz **5** crack **6** adroit, expert, master, wizard **7** skilled **8** masterly, skillful, virtuoso **9** dexterous, masterful **10** proficient **11** crackerjack **12** professional

adequacy
5 might **6** enough **7** ability **8** capacity **10** capability, competence, sufficient **13** qualification

adequate
6 common, decent, enough **8** all right **9** competent, sufficing **10** acceptable, sufficient **11** comfortable **12** satisfactory **13** unexceptional, unimpeachable

adequately
4 well **5** amply, right **6** enough **8** properly, suitably **9** fittingly **10** becomingly **13** appropriately

adhere
5 cling, stick **6** adsorb, cleave, cohere

adherence
4 bond **5** cling **7** loyalty **8** adhesion, clinging, cohesion, fidelity, stickage, sticking **9** constancy **10** attachment, concretion **11** cementation **12** faithfulness **13** agglutination

adherent
6 cohort **7** sectary **8** disciple, follower, henchman, partisan, sectator, stalwart **9** satellite, supporter
suffix: **3** ite

adhering
8 osculant

adhesion
see **adherence**

adhesive
5 gluey, gooey, gummy, tacky **6** clingy, cloggy, sticky **7** stickum **8** mucilage

adieu
2 by **5** congé **6** bye-bye, so long **7** cheerio, good-bye, parting **8** farewell, toodle-oo **11** leave taking

ad interim
6 acting, pro tem, supply **9** temporary **10** pro tempore

adipose
3 fat **5** fatty

adiposity
7 fatness, obesity **10** corpulence, fleshiness

adit
3 way **4** door **5** entry **6** access, entrée **7** ingress **8** entrance **9** admission **10** admittance

adjacent
5 handy **6** nearby **7** close-by **8** abutting, touching **9** adjoining, bordering **10** approximal, contiguous, convenient, juxtaposed, near-at-hand **11** close-at-hand, neighboring **12** conterminous

adjoin
4 abut, line, meet **5** march, touch, verge **6** border, butt on **8** neighbor **11** communicate

adjoining
see **abutting**

adjourn
4 rise, stay **5** close, defer, delay **6** hold up, put off, recess, shelve **7** break up, disband, hold off, suspend **8** dissolve, hold over, postpone, prorogue **9** prorogate, terminate

adjudge
6 umpire **7** referee **9** arbitrate **10** adjudicate

adjudicate
see **adjudge**

adjunct
5 affix 8 addition, appanage, appendix 9 accessory, accretion, appendage 10 attachment 12 appurtenance

adjust
3 fit, fix, rig 4 suit, tune 5 adapt, order, right 6 accord, attune, orient, square, tailor, tune up 7 arrange, conform, correct, rectify 8 modulate, regulate 9 habituate, harmonize, reconcile 11 accommodate

adjuvant
9 accessory, ancillary, auxiliary 10 collateral, subsidiary 11 appurtenant, subservient 12 contributory

ad-lib
9 improvise 11 extemporize, improvisate

Admetus
father: 6 Pheres
wife: 8 Alcestis

administer
3 run 4 deal, give 5 issue 6 direct, govern, manage, render, strike 7 conduct, deal out, deliver, dole out, execute, give out, inflict, mete out 8 carry out, dispense, share out 9 apportion, supervise 10 distribute, portion out

administrate
6 govern, render 7 execute 8 carry out

administration
system of: 11 bureaucracy

administrator
4 exec 7 manager, officer 8 official 9 executive

admirable
6 august, worthy 8 laudable 9 deserving, estimable, meritable, praisable 11 commendable, meritorious, thankworthy 12 praiseworthy

admiral
American: 4 Byrd, Sims 5 Dewey, Stark 6 Halsey, Nimitz 7 Zumwalt 8 Farragut, Rickover, Spruance
Confederate: 6 Semmes
Dutch: 5 Tromp
English: 6 Nelson, Rodney, Vernon 7 Hawkins 8 Beaufort, Jellicoe, Villiers 11 Mountbatten
French: 10 Villeneuve
German: 4 Spee 6 Donitz, Raeder 7 Tirpitz

Japanese: 4 Togo 5 Yonai 8 Yamamoto
Spanish: 8 Menendez

admiration
5 amaze, favor 6 esteem, regard, wonder 7 account, respect 9 amazement, marveling 10 estimation, wonderment 12 appreciation

admire
5 adore, prize, value 6 esteem, regard, relish, revere 7 adulate, cherish, lionize, respect, worship 8 consider, treasure, venerate 9 delight in, reverence 10 appreciate

admirer
3 fan 6 votary 7 amateur, devotee, fancier

admission
3 way 4 adit, door 5 entry 6 access, entrée 7 ingress 8 entrance 10 admittance

admit
3 own 4 avow, take 5 agree, allow, enter, grant, let on, lodge, own up 6 fess up, harbor, permit, suffer, take in 7 concede, confess, receive, shelter 9 entertain, introduce, recognize 11 acknowledge

admittance
see **admission**

admix
5 merge 6 mingle 8 comingle, immingle 9 commingle 11 intermingle

admixture
4 dash 5 alloy, shade, smack, spice, taint, tinge 7 amalgam 8 compound 9 composite 10 adulterant, denaturant 12 amalgamation

admonish
4 warn 5 chide 6 lesson, monish, rebuke 7 caution, reprove, tick off 8 call down, reproach 9 reprimand

admonishing
7 warning 8 monitory 10 cautionary, cautioning, monitorial

admonition
3 rap, wig 6 caveat, rebuke 7 caution, chiding, reproof, warning 9 reprimand 11 forewarning

ado
4 fuss, stir 5 tizzy, whirl 6 bustle, flurry, furore, pother, uproar 7 turmoil 9 confusion

adolescence
5 youth 6 spring 7 puberty

9 greenness, youthhood 10 juvenility, pubescence, springtide, springtime 12 youthfulness

adolescent
4 teen 6 teener 8 preadult, teenager

Adonijah
brother: 5 Amnon 7 Absalom, Chileab
father: 5 David
mother: 7 Haggith
slayer: 7 Benaiah

Adonis
lover: 5 Venus 9 Aphrodite
mother: 5 Myrrh 6 Myrrha
slayer: 4 boar

adopt
4 take 6 affect, assume, take on, take up 7 embrace, espouse

adoption
8 espousal 9 embracing 11 embracement

adorable
4 lush 7 darling, lovable 8 heavenly, lovesome, luscious 9 ambrosial, delicious 10 delectable, delightful 11 scrumptious

adoration
4 love 7 passion, worship 8 devotion, idolatry 9 affection 11 idolization

adore
4 love 6 admire, dote on, esteem, revere 7 idolize, worship 8 dote upon, enshrine, venerate 9 affection, delight in, reverence

adorn
4 deck, trim 5 prank, primp, prink 6 bedeck, doll up, enrich, pretty, richen 7 bedizen, dress up, enhance, furbish, garnish, smarten 8 beautify, decorate, ornament, prettify, spruce up, titivate 9 embellish

adornment
5 decor 6 finery 7 garnish 8 ornament 9 caparison 10 decoration 11 centerpiece 13 embellishment

ad rem
7 apropos, germane 8 apposite, material, pointful, relevant 9 pertinent 10 applicable 11 applicative, applicatory

adroit
3 sly 4 deft 5 canny, handy, smart 6 astute, clever, nimble, shrewd 7 cunning 8 dextrous, skillful 9 dexterous, ingenious, workmanly 11 in-

telligent, quick-witted, workmanlike
13 perspicacious

adroitness
3 art 5 craft, skill 7 address, cunning, know-how, prowess, sleight
8 deftness 9 dexterity, expertise, readiness

adulation
7 acclaim, blarney 8 applause, flattery, soft soap 12 blandishment

adult
4 aged, ripe 5 grown 6 mature
7 grown-up, matured, ripened
9 full-blown, full-grown 11 full-fledged

adulterant
5 alloy 9 admixture 10 denaturant

adulterate
4 thin 5 taint 6 debase, defile, dilute, doctor, dope up, weight 7 pollute 8 denature, impurify
10 tamper with

adumbrate
3 dim, fog 4 bode, call, hint, mist, murk 5 augur, cloud, draft
6 darken, shadow, sketch 7 becloud, bespeak, betoken, obscure, outline, portend, predict, presage, suggest 8 block out, chalk out, forebode, forecast, foretell, indicate, prophesy, rough out, skeleton 9 obfuscate, prefigure 10 foreshadow, vaticinate 11 prefigurate, skeletonize 12 characterize

adumbration
4 hint, sign 5 shade, umbra
6 shadow 7 umbrage 8 penumbra
10 intimation, suggestion

advance
3 aid 4 cite, help, lend, loan, move 5 get on, march, raise, serve 6 adduce, allege, assist, course, foster, mature, prefer, uplift 7 develop, elevate, forward, further, headway, ongoing, present, proceed, promote, upgrade 8 anabasis, approach, encroach, get along, heighten, increase, overture, progress 9 encourage, evolution
11 development, furtherance, improvement, progression
12 breakthrough

advanced
7 forward, liberal, radical 8 tolerant 10 precocious 11 broad-minded, progressive

advancement
5 march 7 headway 8 progress
9 promotion 10 preference

advantage
3 use 4 boon, edge, good, lead, odds, sake 5 asset, avail, bulge, serve 6 better, profit 7 account, benefit, fitness, godsend, mastery, service, welfare 8 blessing, handicap, interest, leverage 9 allowance, head start, relevance, upper hand, well-being 10 ascendancy, domination, leadership, prosperity, usefulness 11 benediction, superiority 12 running start

advantageous
4 good 6 paying, toward, useful
7 benefic, gainful, helpful 8 favoring, remedial, salutary 9 conducive, desirable, expedient, favorable, lucrative 10 beneficial, profitable, propitious, well-paying, worthwhile 11 moneymaking
12 remunerative

advent
6 coming 7 arrival, hearing
8 approach

adventitious
6 casual 10 accidental, contingent, fortuitous, incidental
12 supervenient

adventure
4 feat, gest, risk 5 quest, wager
6 chance 7 emprise, exploit 8 escapade 10 enterprise

adventuresome
see **adventurous**

adventurous
4 bold, rash 5 brash 6 daring
7 doughty 8 intrepid, reckless
9 audacious, daredevil, foolhardy, impetuous, imprudent
11 temerarious

adversary
3 con 4 anti 5 match 7 opposer
8 opponent 9 oppugnant
10 antagonist

adverse
4 anti 7 counter, harmful, hurtful, opposed 8 contrary, negative, opposing 9 injurious, oppugnant
11 deleterious, detrimental, obstructive, unfavorable 12 antagonistic, antipathetic 13 counteractive

adversity
4 dole 6 misery, mishap 7 tragedy
8 distress 9 mischance, suffering
10 misfortune 11 contretemps

advert
4 note 5 refer 6 allude, notice, remark 7 bring up, observe 8 point out

advertent
6 arrect 7 heedful 9 attentive, intentive, observant, regardful

advertise
4 plug, puff, push 5 boost 6 blazon, report 7 build up, declare, promote, publish 8 announce, ballyhoo, proclaim 9 broadcast, publicize 10 annunciate, bruit about, promulgate

advertisement
2 ad 4 bill, plug, sign 5 blurb, flyer, promo 6 notice, poster 7 affiche 9 billboard, broadcast, promotion, publicity 10 commercial, propaganda 11 declaration, publication 12 announcement, proclamation, promulgation
13 pronouncement

advertising
7 buildup, puffery 9 publicity

advice
4 news, word 7 caution, counsel, tidings, warning 8 guidance, teaching 10 admonition 11 information, instruction 12 intelligence

advisable
4 wise 6 seemly 7 politic, prudent
8 sensible, suitable, tactical
9 expedient

advise
4 clew, clue, post, tell, warn 6 confab, confer, fill in, huddle, inform, notify, parley, powwow, wise up
7 apprise, caution, consult, counsel
8 acquaint, forewarn 9 recommend
11 confabulate

advised
7 studied 8 designed, intended, prepense, studious 10 considered, deliberate, thought-out 11 intentional 12 premeditated

advocacy
7 defense

advocate
4 back 5 favor 6 preach, uphold
7 promote, support 8 backstop, champion, exponent, side with
9 encourage, expounder, proponent, supporter 11 countenance
combining form: 4 crat
suffix: 5 arian

Aeacus
father: 4 Zeus
mother: 6 Aegina
son: 6 Peleus 7 Telamon

Aedon
brother: 7 Amphion
sister-in-law: 5 Niobe
son (victim): 6 Itylus

Aeetes
daughter: 5 Medea
father: 6 Helios

Aegaeon
see **Briareus**

Aegeon's wife
7 Aemilia

Aegeus's son
7 Theseus

aegis
4 ward 5 armor, guard 6 shield
7 backing, defense 8 armament,
auspices, security 9 patronage,
safeguard 10 protection
11 sponsorship

Aegisthus
father: 8 Thyestes
lover: 12 Clytemnestra
mother: 7 Pelopia
slayer: 7 Orestes
victim: 6 Atreus 9 Agamemnon

Aegyptus
brother: 6 Danaus
father: 5 Belus
mother: 8 Anchinoe
son: 7 Lynceus

Aeneas
companion: 7 Achates
father: 8 Anchises
mother: 5 Venus 9 Aphrodite
son: 5 Iulus 8 Ascanius
wife: 6 Creusa 7 Lavinia

Aeneid
author: 6 Vergil, Virgil
first words: 16 arma virumque cano
hero: 5 Aneas

Aeolus
brother: 5 Dorus 6 Xuthus
daughter: 6 Canace 7 Alcyone
8 Halcyone
father: 6 Hellen 8 Poseidon
mother: 9 Melanippe
son: 7 Athamas 9 Salmoneus

aeon
3 age 7 dog's age 8 blue moon,
coon's age, eternity

aerate
3 air 6 aerify 9 oxygenate,
ventilate

aerial
4 airy 5 lofty 6 towery, vapory
7 soaring, spiring, topless 8 ethe-

real, towering, vaporous 9 pneumatic 10 impalpable
11 atmospheric

aerie, aery, eyrie
4 nest 5 brood 9 penthouse

aeronaut
4 Fogg 5 pilot 7 aviator 8 Zeppelin 10 balloonist

Aerope
husband: 6 Atreus
lover: 8 Thyestes
son: 8 Menelaus 9 Agamemnon

aery
6 aerial 8 ethereal 9 visionary

Aesculapius
daughter: 6 Hygeia 7 Panacea
father: 6 Apollo
mother: 7 Coronis
slayer: 4 Zeus 7 Jupiter
son: 7 Machaon 9 Podalirus
teacher: 6 Chiron
wife: 6 Epione

Aeson
brother: 6 Pelias
son: 5 Jason

aesthete
10 dilettante 11 cognoscente,
connoisseur

Aether's father
6 Erebus

affable
6 genial, gentle, polite 7 amiable,
cordial 8 gracious, sociable 9 congenial, courteous

affair
4 love 5 amour, thing 6 matter
7 concern, liaison, palaver, romance 8 business, intrigue
10 proceeding

affect
3 act, get 4 fake, move, sham,
sway 5 bluff, carry, feign, haunt,
put on, touch 6 assume, resort,
strike 7 actuate, impress, inspire,
pretend 8 frequent, simulate 9 influence 11 counterfeit

affectation
4 airs, lugs, pose 9 mannerism,
prettyism

affected
5 put-on 6 chichi, la-di-da, too-too
7 assumed, feigned, genteel, mincing, stilted 8 involved, mannered,
overnice, précieux, precious, spurious 9 concerned, conscious 10 artificial, implicated, interested

11 alembicated, overrefined, pretentious 13 self-conscious

affected with/by
combining form: 6 pathic
suffix: 2 ic 4 ical

affecting
6 moving 8 poignant, touching
9 troubling 10 disturbing, impressive 11 distressful, distressing

affection
4 bias, love, mark 5 savor, trait
6 doting, malady, virtue, warmth
7 ailment, concern, disease, emotion, feature, feeling, leaning, passion, quality, worship 8 devotion,
disorder, fondness, interest, penchant, property, sickness, sympathy, syndrome 9 attention, attribute,
character, complaint, condition, infirmity, sentiment 10 attachment,
propensity, tenderness
12 predilection

affectionate
4 dear, fond, warm 6 doting, loving, tender 7 devoted 8 lovesome
11 sympathetic

affective
6 moving 7 emotive 9 emotional

affectivity
7 emotion, feeling, passion
9 sentiment

affianced
7 engaged 8 intended, plighted,
promised 9 betrothed
10 contracted

affiche
4 bill 6 poster 7 placard
8 handbill

affidavit certificate
5 jurat

affiliated
4 akin 6 agnate, allied 7 cognate,
connate, kindred, related 8 incident 10 connatural
11 consanguine

affiliation
5 tie-up 6 hookup 7 cahoots 8 alliance 10 connection 11 association, combination, conjunction,
partnership 12 conjointment

affinity
6 simile 7 analogy 8 likeness, sympathy 9 alikeness, semblance
10 attraction, comparison, similarity, similitude 11 resemblance
combining form: 5 phily, trope
6 philia 7 tropism

affirm
3 say, yes 4 aver, avow 5 state, vouch 6 assert, attest, avouch, depose 7 certify, declare, profess, protest, witness 9 guarantee

affirmative
2 ay 3 aye, yes 8 positive

affix
3 add 5 annex, rivet 6 append, attach, fasten 7 subjoin

afflict
3 try, vex 4 rack 5 annoy, harry, press, smite, worry, wound, wring 6 bother, harass, harrow, martyr, pester, plague, strike 7 agonize, crucify, torment, torture 9 martyrize 10 excruciate

afflicted
6 dolent, rueful, woeful 7 doleful, ruthful 8 dolorous, stricken, wretched 9 miserable, sorrowful

affliction
3 rue, woe 4 care, dole 5 cross, grief, trial 6 mishap, ordeal, regret, sorrow 7 anguish, illness 8 disorder, sickness, unhealth 9 heartache, infirmity, mischance 10 heartbreak 11 tribulation
suffix: 4 itis

afflictive
4 dire, sore 6 aching, bitter, woeful 7 algetic, galling, hurtful, hurting, painful 8 grievous 10 calamitous, deplorable, lamentable 11 distasteful, distressing, regrettable, unfortunate, unpalatable 13 heartbreaking

affluent
4 rich 7 moneyed, opulent, wealthy

affray
3 row 5 brawl, clash, fight, melee 6 fracas 7 ruction, scuffle 8 skirmish 9 scrimmage 10 donnybrook

affright
3 awe 5 alarm, scare, spook 7 startle, terrify 9 terrorize

affront
4 face, meet, slap 6 insult, offend, slight 7 despite, offense, outrage 8 dishonor 9 aspersion, contumely, criticize, encounter, indignity 10 defamation

aficionado
3 fan 4 buff 5 hound, lover 6 addict, votary 7 devotee, habitué

afield
4 away 5 amiss, badly, wrong 6 astray

afire
see **aflame**

aflame
5 afire, aglow, fiery 6 ablaze, alight 7 blazing, burning, flaming, flaring, ignited 8 aflicker 11 conflagrant

afraid
3 shy 4 wary 5 chary, jumpy, loath, scary, timid 6 aghast, averse, scared, trepid 7 afeared, anxious, ascared, fearful, uneager 8 cautious, hesitant, skittish, timorous 9 reluctant, terrified, unwilling 10 frightened 11 disinclined 12 apprehensive

afresh
3 new 4 anew, over 5 again, newly 6 de novo, lately, of late 8 once more, recently

Africa
country: 4 Chad, Mali, Togo 5 Benin, Congo, Egypt, Gabon, Ghana, Kenya, Libya, Niger, Sudan, Zaire 6 Angola, Gambia, Guinea, Malawi, Rwanda, Uganda, Zambia 7 Algeria, Burundi, Comoros, Lesotho, Liberia, Morocco, Namibia, Nigeria, Senegal, Somalia, Tunisia 8 Botswana, Cameroon, Djibouti, Ethiopia, Tanzania, Zimbabwe 9 Cape Verde, Mauritius, Swaziland 10 Ivory Coast, Madagascar, Mauritania, Mozambique, Seychelles 11 Burkina Faso, Sierra Leone, South Africa 12 Guinea Bissau 13 Comoro Islands
ethnic group: 3 Ibo 4 Akan, Arab, Boer, Copt, Fula, Issa, Moor, Zulu 5 Bantu, Fulah, Galla, Hausa, Kongo, Mande, Negro, Pygmy, Swazi, Wolof 6 Beduin, Berber, Fulani, Hamite, Herero, Kaffir, Kikuyu, Nubian, Somali, Tuareg, Ubangi, Yoruba 7 Ashanti, Bedouin, Bushman, Malinke, Swahili 8 Egyptian, Mandingo 9 Hottentot
language: 3 Ibo 4 Urdu 5 Bantu, Galla, Hausa 6 Arabic, Berber, Somali, Yoruba 7 Amharic, Bambara, Swahili 8 Malagasy 9 Afrikaans

aft
6 astern

after
3 for 4 back, hind, next, past, rear 5 below, later, since 6 behind, beyond, hinder, retral 7 by and by, ensuing 8 hindmost, latterly 9 following, posterior 10 subsequent 12 postliminary, subsequently

after all
3 yet 5 still 6 though 7 howbeit, however 11 nonetheless 12 nevertheless

aftereffect
5 issue 6 result, upshot 7 outcome 8 causatum 11 consequence, eventuality

afterlife
6 beyond 8 eternity 9 hereafter

aftermath
see **aftereffect**

afterward
4 next, to-be 5 later 6 behind, future, offing 7 by-and-by 8 latterly 9 hereafter 12 subsequently

afterword
8 epilogue

Agag
kingdom: 6 Amalek
slayer: 6 Samuel

again
4 also, anew, back, over 5 about 6 afresh, around, de novo 7 besides, further 8 once more 12 additionally
combining form: 2 an 3 ana 4 pali
prefix: 2 re

again and again
3 oft 4 much 5 often 8 ofttimes 10 frequently, oftentimes, repeatedly

against
4 agin 6 contra, facing, toward, versus 7 apropos, despite, vis-à-vis 8 fronting, touching 9 in spite of 10 concerning, respecting
prefix: 2 ob 3 ant 4 anti 6 contra 7 counter

Agamemnon
avenger: 7 Orestes
brother: 8 Menelaus
daughter: 7 Electra 9 Iphigenia
father: 6 Atreus
slayer: 9 Aegisthus
son: 7 Orestes
wife: 12 Clytemnestra

agape
6 aghast 7 shocked 8 dismayed 10 confounded 11 dumbfounded, overwhelmed 13 thunderstruck

agate
3 mib, taw 6 marble 7 shooter

Agave
father: 6 Cadmus
husband: 6 Echion
mother: 8 Harmonia

sister: 3 Ino 6 Semele 7 Autonoe
son: 8 Pentheus

age
3 eon, era 4 aeon, grow, ripe, time
5 epoch, ripen 6 grow up, mature,
mellow, period 7 develop 8 blue
moon, caducity, eternity, maturate

aged
3 old 4 ripe 5 hoary, olden 6 mellow, senior 7 ancient, antique, elderly, matured, ripened 8 Noachian, timeworn 9 senescent,
venerable 11 patriarchal
12 antediluvian

ageless
7 eternal 8 dateless, timeless
10 intemporal

agency
4 mean 5 cause, organ 6 medium
7 channel, vehicle 8 ministry
10 instrument

agenda
6 docket 7 program 8 calendar,
schedule 9 timetable
entry: 4 item

Agenor
brother: 5 Belus
daughter: 6 Europa
father: 7 Antenor, Neptune
8 Poseidon
mother: 5 Libya
son: 6 Cadmus

agent
3 fed, spy 4 doer, mean, tool 5 actor, organ, proxy, spook 6 deputy,
factor, medium 7 channel, proctor,
steward, vehicle 8 assignee, attorney, executor, institor, minister, ministry 9 activator, go-between, middleman 10 instrument, procurator
combining form: 4 stat
suffix: 3 ant

age-old
7 ancient, antique 8 timeworn
9 venerable 12 antediluvian

agglomerate
4 heap, mass, pile 9 aggregate
11 aggregation

agglomeration
5 hoard, trove 9 aggregate, amassment 10 collection, cumulation
11 aggregation

aggrandize
5 boost, exalt, honor 6 beef up, expand, extend 7 augment, build up,
dignify, enlarge, ennoble, glorify,
magnify, sublime 8 heighten, increase, multiply 11 distinguish

aggravate
4 gall 5 annoy, grate, mount,
peeve, pique, rouse, upset 6 burn
up, deepen, nettle, worsen 7 bedevil, disturb, enhance, magnify,
perturb, provoke 8 heighten, irritate 9 intensify 10 exasperate

aggravation
6 bother, pother 9 annoyance

aggregate
3 all, sum 4 body, bulk, floc 5 add
up, gross, total, whole 6 amount,
budget, number 7 quantum 8 entirety, quantity, totality 11 agglomerate 12 conglomerate
13 agglomeration
suffix: 3 ery

aggregation
4 ruck 5 crowd, group, hoard,
trove 6 muster 7 company 8 assembly 9 amassment, congeries,
gathering 10 assemblage, collection, cumulation 11 agglomerate
12 accumulation

aggression
4 raid 5 fight, onset 6 attack 7 assault, offense 8 invasion 9 incursion, offensive, onslaught, pugnacity 10 assailment 12 belligerence
13 combativeness

aggressive
5 pushy 6 fierce 7 scrappy, vicious
8 militant 9 assertive, combative,
imperious 11 belligerent, contentious, domineering, hard-hitting

aggressiveness
11 bellicosity 12 belligerence,
belligerency

aggrieve
4 hurt, pain 5 annoy, harry, worry,
wrong 6 harass, injure, plague
7 afflict, oppress, torment 8 distress
9 constrain, persecute

aghast
4 agog, awed 5 agape 6 afraid,
amazed, scared 7 anxious, fearful,
shocked 8 appalled, dismayed,
startled 9 horrified, terrified
10 astonished, confounded, frightened 11 awestricken, dumbfounded, overwhelmed 12 horror-
struck 13 flabbergasted,
thunderstruck

agile
4 deft, spry, yare 5 brisk, catty,
lithe, zippy 6 active, adroit, limber,
lively, nimble, supple, volant 7 lissome 8 dextrous 9 dexterous,
sprightly

agitate
4 rile, rock 5 argue, drive, impel,
peeve, shake, upset 6 bother, debate, flurry, joggle, ruffle 7 discuss,
dispute, disturb, fluster, perturb,
provoke, tempest, unhinge 8 convulse, irritate 9 thrash out 10 discompose, exasperate

agitation
4 flap, stew 6 bustle, dither, lather,
pother, tumult 7 tempest, turmoil
9 commotion, confusion
10 turbulence

agitator
7 inciter 8 fomenter 10 instigator

Aglaia
see **Graces**

Aglauros, Agraulos
father: 7 Cecrops
sister: 5 Herse 9 Pandrosos

aglow
5 afire 6 ablaze, aflame, alight, lucent 7 radiant, shining 8 aflicker,
gleaming, luminous

agnate
4 akin, like 5 alike 6 allied 7 cognate, connate, kindred, related,
similar 9 analogous 10 affiliated
11 consanguine 13 corresponding

agnostic
7 infidel, skeptic 11 disbeliever

"Agnus ___"
3 Dei

ago
2 by 4 gone, past, syne, yore
5 since

agog
4 avid 5 eager 6 ardent, roused
7 excited, popeyed 9 impatient

agonize
4 fret, gall, rack 5 chafe 6 harrow,
squirm, suffer, writhe 7 afflict, torment, torture, trouble 8 distress
10 excruciate

agonizing
7 intense, racking, tearing 9 harrowing, torturing, torturous 10 tormenting 12 excruciating

agony
4 pain 5 dolor 6 misery 7 passion
8 distress 9 suffering

agrarian
5 rural 6 rustic 8 agrestal, pastoral
10 campestral 12 agricultural

Agraulos
see **Aglauros**

agree

3 yes 4 jibe, suit 5 admit, check, equal, fit in, match, tally 6 accede, accord, assent, concur, square 7 comport, concede, concert, concord, conform, consent 8 check out, coincide, dovetail 9 acquiesce, harmonize, recognize, subscribe 10 correspond 11 acknowledge

agreeable

4 nice 7 affable, welcome 8 amenable, pleasant, pleasing 9 congenial, congruous, consonant, favorable 10 compatible, consistent, gratifying 11 pleasurable, pleasureful, sympathetic

agreed

2 OK 3 aye, yea, yep, yes 4 okay 8 all right, okeydoke

agreement

4 bond, deal, pact 6 accord, treaty, unison 7 bargain, compact, concord, entente, harmony 8 contract, covenant 9 concordat 10 consonance 11 concordance

agree with

3 fit 4 suit 5 befit 6 become 10 go together

agricultural

8 agrarian
combining form: 4 agro

agriculture

7 farming, tillage 8 agronomy 9 husbandry

Agrippina's son

4 Nero

aground

7 beached 8 stranded

Ahab

daughter: 8 Athaliah
father: 4 Omri
wife: 7 Jezebel

Ahasuerus

kingdom: 6 Persia
wife: 6 Esther, Vashti

Ahaz

kingdom: 5 Judah
son: 8 Hezekiah
wife: 3 Abi

Ahaziah

father: 4 Ahab 5 Joram 7 Jehoram
kingdom: 5 Judah 6 Israel
mother: 7 Jezebel 8 Athaliah
sister: 9 Jehosheba 11 Jehosobeath

ahead

4 alee, ante, fore 5 forth 6 before, onward 7 forward, onwards 8 forwards, previous 9 in advance 10 beforehand 11 precedently 12 antecedently

Ahinoam

father: 7 Ahimaaz
husband: 4 Saul 5 David
son: 5 Amnon

aid

4 abet, hand, help, lift 6 assist, helper, relief, succor 7 ancilla, backing, comfort, help out, succour, support 8 benefact, succorer 9 assistant, attendant, coadjutor 10 assistance, benefactor, coadjutant, lieutenant, ministrant, mitigation 11 alleviation, assuagement

Aida

composer: 5 Verdi
father: 8 Amonasro
lover: 7 Radames
rival: 7 Amneris

aide

6 deputy, second 7 orderly 9 assistant, coadjutor 10 coadjutant, lieutenant

ail

4 cark 5 upset, worry 7 afflict, trouble 8 distress

ailing

3 ill, low 4 mean, weak 6 donsie, droopy, offish, poorly, sickly, unwell 8 off-color 9 enfeebled 10 indisposed 11 debilitated

ailment

3 ill 6 malady, unrest 7 disease, ferment, turmoil 8 disorder, disquiet, sickness, syndrome 9 affection, complaint, condition, infirmity 10 inquietude 11 disquietude, restiveness 12 restlessness

aim

3 try 4 cast, goal, head, mark, mean, plan, want, wish 5 angle, essay, focus, level, point, slant, train 6 aspire, design, desire, direct, intend, strive, target, zero in 7 address, attempt, propose, purpose 8 ambition, endeavor 9 objective 11 contemplate

aimless

6 random 9 desultory, haphazard, hit-or-miss, irregular, unplanned 10 designless 11 purposeless

air

3 sky 4 aura, feel, mien, mood, port, song, tune, vent 5 state, style 6 aerate, aerify, manner, melody, reveal, strain 7 bearing, declare, divulge, express, feeling, melisma, publish, quality 8 demeanor, presence, proclaim 9 broadcast, character, semblance, ventilate 10 atmosphere, deportment 11 comportment
combining form: 3 aer, atm 4 aeri, aero, atmo 5 pneum 6 pneumo 7 pneumat 8 pneumato

aircraft

5 blimp, drone, plane 6 glider 7 airship, balloon, chopper 8 aerodyne, aerostat, airplane, jetliner, zeppelin 9 dirigible 10 helicopter
carrier: 7 flattop 8 birdfarm
designer: 6 Fokker, Martin 7 Junkers, Tupolev 8 Northrop, Sikorsky, Yakovlev 13 Messerschmitt

airless

5 close, stivy 6 stuffy, sultry 8 stifling 10 breathless 11 suffocating

airman

5 flier, pilot 6 fly-boy 7 aviator

air movement

5 draft 7 updraft 9 downdraft

air navigation system

5 loran, navar, radar

airplane

3 jet, SST 4 STOL, VTOL 5 avion, VSTOL 6 bomber 7 fighter 8 autogiro, autogyro 9 transport
A-bomb-dropper: 8 Enola Gay
battle: 8 dogfight
body: 8 fuselage
commercial: 5 liner
engine: 3 jet 6 fanjet 7 propjet 8 turbofan, turbojet 9 turboprop
engine casing: 7 nacelle
engineless: 6 glider
instrument: 5 radar, radio 7 compass 9 altimeter, gyroscope 10 tachometer 11 transponder
maneuver: 4 buzz, dive, loop, roll 8 nosedive 9 chandelle 10 barrel roll
movement: 3 yaw 4 bank, spin 5 pitch 8 tailspin
part: 3 fin 4 flap, nose, prop, tail, wing 5 cabin, wheel 6 engine, rudder 7 aileron 8 airscrew, elevator 9 empennage, propeller 10 stabilizer, stabilator, stabilizer
pilotless: 5 drone
shelter: 6 hangar
target: 6 drogue
vapor: 8 contrail

airport

5 drome, field 7 helipad 8 airdrome, airfield, heliport 9 aerodrome
building: 8 terminal

flag: 8 windsock
name:
  Amsterdam: 8 Schiphol
  Atlanta: 10 Hartsfield
  Boston: 5 Logan
  Chicago: 5 O'Hare
  Copenhagen: 7 Kastrup
  Dublin: 7 Shannon
  London: 7 Gatwick 8 Heathrow
  New York: 3 JFK 7 Kennedy 9 La
    Guardia
  Paris: 4 Orly 8 DeGaulle 9 Le
    Bourget
  Rome: 7 Da Vinci
  Washington: 6 Dulles
  part: 5 apron, tower 6 runway
    7 taxiway

airs
  4 lugs, pose, show 6 vanity 9 loftiness, mannerism, prettyism, vainglory 11 affectation, ostentation

airship
  8 zeppelin 9 dirigible

airtight
  8 hermetic, ironclad

airwaves nuisance
  6 static

airy
  4 rare, thin 5 blowy, gusty, light,
  lofty, windy 6 aerial, bouncy,
  breezy, dainty, towery, vapory
  7 buoyant, gaseous, soaring, spiring, tenuous 8 animated, delicate,
  ethereal, rarefied, spirited, supernal, towering, vaporous, volatile
  9 expansive, frivolous, pneumatic,
  resilient, windswept 10 diaphanous
  11 atmospheric, skyscraping 12 effervescent, high-spirited

Ajax's father
  6 Oileus 7 Telamon

akin
  4 like 5 alike 6 agnate, allied
  7 cognate, connate, kindred, related, similar, uniform 8 parallel
  9 analogous, consonant 10 affiliated, comparable, connatural
  11 consanguine 13 corresponding

Alabama
  capital: 10 Montgomery
  college, university: 5 Miles 6 Auburn,
    Mobile 8 Tuskegee 9 Talladega
    10 Huntingdon
  largest city: 10 Birmingham
  nickname: 11 Cotton State 12 Heart
    of Dixie
  state flower: 8 camellia

alacrity
  8 celerity, dispatch 9 briskness, eagerness, quickness, readiness

10 enthusiasm, expedition, prompt-
ness 11 promptitude

alamo
  6 poplar 10 cottonwood

a la mode
  4 chic, tony 6 modish, tonish,
  trendy 7 dashing, stylish 9 exclusive 11 fashionable

alarm
  3 SOS 4 fear 5 alert, dread,
  larum, panic, scare, siren, spook,
  upset 6 dismay, fright, horror, terror, tocsin 7 startle, terrify, warning
  8 affright, frighten 9 terrorize
  11 forewarning, trepidation
  13 consternation

alarmable
  4 edgy 8 agitable, skittery, skittish,
  volatile 9 excitable, startlish
  11 combustible

Alaska
  capital: 6 Juneau
  largest city: 9 Anchorage
  state flower: 11 forget-me-not

Albania
  capital: 6 Tirana, Tirane
  monetary unit: 3 lek

albatross
  5 goony 6 gooney, goonie

albeit
  5 while 6 much as, though
  7 whereas 8 although

Alberta
  capital: 8 Edmonton
  largest city: 7 Calgary
  university: 7 Calgary 10 Lethbridge

Albion
  7 England

album
  3 ana 6 record 7 garland, omnibus 8 register 9 anthology 10 miscellany 11 florilegium

Alcestis
  father: 6 Pelias
  husband: 7 Admetus
  rescuer: 8 Heracles, Hercules

alchemist
  10 Paracelsus

Alcina
  sister: 7 Morgana 10 Logistilla
  victim: 6 Rogero 8 Astolpho,
    Ruggiero

Alcinous
  daughter: 8 Nausicaa
  wife: 5 Arete

Alcmaeon
  father: 10 Amphiaraus
  mother: 8 Eriphyle
  wife: 10 Callirrhoe

Alcmene
  husband: 10 Amphitryon
  son: 8 Heracles, Hercules

alcohol
  4 grog 5 booze, drink, hooch,
  juice 6 liquor, tipple 7 spirits
  9 aqua vitae, firewater
  name: 4 amyl 5 butyl, cetyl, ethyl
    6 glycol, methyl, sterol 7 butanol,
    ethanol, mannite, menthol 8 glyc-
    erin, glycerol, inositol, mannitol,
    methanol 9 isopropyl
    11 cholesterol
  used in perfumes: 5 nerol 7 borneol,
    linalol 8 farnesol, geraniol, linalool

alcoholic
  4 hard 8 bibulous 9 spiritous
  10 spirituous 11 dipsomaniac
  12 intoxicating

alcoholic drink
  see under **beverage**

alcoholized
  5 drunk

alcove
  4 nook 5 niche 6 gazebo, pagoda, recess 9 belvedere
  Japanese: 8 tokonoma

Alcyone
  father: 5 Atlas 6 Aeolus
  husband: 4 Ceyx
  mother: 7 Pleione
  sisters: 8 Pleiades

ale
  3 nog 4 nogg

Alea
  6 Athena

alehouse
  3 pub 4 café 6 bistro 7 cabaret
  8 beer hall 9 bierstube, brasserie,
  honky-tonk, nightclub 10 beer garden 11 rathskellar

Alemanus
  father: 7 Histion
  grandfather: 6 Japhet

alert
  3 SOS 4 keen, warn 5 alarm,
  quick, ready, sharp, smart
  6 brainy, bright, clever, frisky,
  lively, tocsin 7 heedful, knowing,
  mindful, wakeful 8 animated, open-
  eyed, spirited, vigilant, watchful
  9 attentive, brilliant, mercurial,
  sprightly, vivacious, wide-awake

11 intelligent, quick-witted, ready-witted
Scottish: 4 gleg 8 wakerife

Alexander
birthplace: 5 Pella
conquest: 4 Tyre 5 Egypt, Issus 6 Arbela, Greece, Persia 7 Parthia 8 Granicus
father: 6 Philip
general: 9 Antipater
horse: 10 Bucephalus
kingdom: 9 Macedonia
mother: 8 Olympias
teacher: 9 Aristotle
wife: 6 Roxana

alfalfa
6 lucern 7 lucerne

Alfonso's queen
3 Ena

alfresco
7 open-air, outdoor, outside 9 out-of-door 10 hypaethral

alga
6 desmid, diatom 7 seaweed
blue-green: 6 nostoc
brown: 4 kelp 5 fucus 8 rockweed
combining form: 7 phyceae
green: 8 conferva 9 chlorella
red: 4 nori 7 amanori

algebra term
4 root 6 factor 8 binomial, equation, monomial, variable 9 quadratic 10 polynomial

Algeria
capital: 7 Algiers
ethnic group: 4 Arab 6 Berber
monetary unit: 5 dinar
port: 4 Oran

algetic
4 sore 6 aching 7 hurtful, hurting, painful 10 afflictive

Ali
son: 5 Hasan 6 Husayn
wife: 6 Fatima

alias
3 AKA 6 anonym 7 pen name 9 pseudonym 10 nom de plume 11 nom de guerre

alibi
4 plea 6 excuse 7 pretext

alien
6 exotic 7 foreign, inconnu, strange 8 estrange, outcomer, outsider, stranger, transfer 9 auslander, extrinsic, foreigner, outlander 10 extraneous, outlandish

alienate
4 part, wean 6 assign, convey, re-

mise 8 disunify, disunite, estrange, sign over, transfer 9 disaffect 10 relinquish

alienation
6 lunacy 7 madness 8 insanity 9 unbalance 10 aberration, insaneness 11 derangement, distraction, psychopathy 12 disaffection, estrangement

alight
4 land 5 afire, aglow, fiery, perch, roost 6 ablaze, aflame, bright, settle 7 blazing, burning, deplane, detrain, flaming, flaring, glowing, ignited, set down, sit down 8 aflicker, dismount 9 effulgent, refulgent, touch down 11 conflagrant

align
4 line, true 5 range 6 adjust, line up 8 regulate 9 allineate

alike
4 akin, same 7 similar, uniform 8 parallel 9 analogous, consonant 10 comparable 13 corresponding
combining form: 2 is 3 hom, iso 4 homo

alikeness
6 simile 7 analogy 8 affinity 9 semblance 10 comparison, similarity, similitude 11 resemblance

aliment
3 pap 4 food 7 pabulum 9 nutriment 10 sustenance 11 nourishment

alimentary
9 nutritive 11 nutritional

alimentary canal
7 enteron

alimentation
4 keep 5 bread 6 living 7 support 10 livelihood, sustenance 11 maintenance, subsistence

alimony
see **alimentation**

alive
4 rife 5 awake, aware, fresh, quick, vital 6 active, extant, living, zoetic 7 animate, dynamic, knowing, replete, running, teeming, working 8 animated, existent, existing, sensible, sentient, swarming, thronged 9 abounding, au courant, cognizant, conscious, operative, wide-awake 11 functioning, overflowing

alkali metal
6 cesium, sodium 7 lithium 8 francium, rubidium 9 potassium

alkaline substance
3 lye, reh 4 lime, soda, usar 5 borax 6 potash 7 ammonia, antacid 8 pearl ash, saltwort 11 caustic soda

alkali's opposite
4 acid

alkalize
6 basify

alkaloid
4 base
hallucinogenic: 7 harmine 9 harmaline
medicinal: 5 ergot 6 heroin 7 cocaine, codeine, emetine, eserine, harmine, quinine 8 atropine, caffeine, ecgonine, lobeline, morphine 9 ephedrine, harmaline, quinidine, reserpine 11 scopolamine
narcotic: 6 heroin 7 cocaine, codeine 8 morphine
poisonous: 6 conine 7 tropine 8 atropine, nicotine, solanine, thebaine 9 aconitine 11 scopolamine

all
3 sum 4 each 5 every, gross, quite, total, whole 6 apiece, entire, in toto, purely, wholly 7 exactly, totally, utterly 8 complete, entirety, everyone, outright, totality 9 aggregate, everybody 10 altogether, everything
combining form: 3 omn, pam, pan 4 omni, pano, pant 5 panta, panto

all-around
7 general, overall 8 complete, sweeping, synoptic 9 adaptable, many-sided, panoramic, versatile 10 consummate 11 wide-ranging 13 comprehensive

allay
4 balm, calm, ease, lull 5 quiet, still 6 settle, soothe, subdue 7 assuage, compose, lighten, mollify, quieten, relieve 8 mitigate 9 alleviate 11 tranquilize

all but
4 most, much, nigh 5 about 6 almost, nearly 8 as good as, as much as, well-nigh 11 essentially, practically 13 approximately

allegation
8 pleading 9 assertion

allege
3 lay 4 cite 5 offer, state 6 adduce, assert 7 advance, declare, present, profess

alleged
7 dubious, would-be 8 doubtful, so-

called, specious, supposed **9** pretended, professed, purported, soi-disant **10** ostensible, self-styled

allegiance
5 ardor, piety **6** fealty, homage **7** loyalty **8** devotion, fidelity **12** faithfulness

allegiant
4 true **5** liege, loyal **6** ardent **7** staunch **8** constant, faithful, resolute **9** steadfast

allegory
4 myth **5** fable **7** parable **8** apologue **9** symbolism **10** figuration **12** typification

allergy
5 atopy **8** aversion, dyspathy **9** antipathy, rejection, repulsion

alleviate
4 cure, ease **5** allay **6** remedy **7** assuage, lighten, mollify, relieve **8** mitigate

alleviation
4 ease **6** relief **8** easement **10** mitigation

all-fired
5 utter **6** blamed, dashed, deuced **7** blasted, blessed, doggone, goldarn **8** infernal

alliance
5 tie-up, union **6** hookup, league **7** cahoots **9** anschluss, coalition **10** connection, federation **11** affiliation, association, combination, confederacy, conjunction, partnership, unification **12** conjointment **13** confederation

allied
4 akin **6** agnate, linked, united **7** cognate, connate, kindred, related **8** incident **10** affiliated, connatural **11** consanguine

all in
5 spent **6** bleary, effete, used up **7** drained, far-gone, worn-out **8** depleted **9** exhausted, washed-out

all in all
5 quite **6** in toto, purely, wholly **7** en masse, totally, utterly **9** generally **10** altogether, by and large, on the whole

allineate
4 line **5** align, range **6** line up

allness
8 entirety, totality

allocate
4 give **5** allot, allow **6** assign

7 earmark, mete out **9** admeasure, apportion, designate

allocution
4 talk **6** speech **7** address, lecture

allot
4 give **5** grant **6** accord, assign **7** deal out, dole out, mete out **8** allocate, dispense **9** admeasure, apportion **10** distribute

allotment
3 cut **4** bite, meed, part **5** quota, share, slice **6** ration **7** measure, partage, portion, quantum **9** allowance

all-out
5 total **9** full-blown, full-scale, unlimited **12** totalitarian

all over
10 everyplace, everywhere, far and near, far and wide, high and low, throughout

allow
3 let, lot, own **4** give **5** admit, allot, brook, grant, leave, let on, stand **6** assign, endure, fess up, permit, suffer **7** concede, confess, mete out **8** allocate, tolerate **9** admeasure, apportion **11** acknowledge

allowance
3 aid, cut, lot **4** bite, edge, help, meed, odds, part, tret **5** grant, leave, quota, share, slice **6** corody, permit, ration **7** consent, corrody, measure, partage, portion, quantum, subsidy, vantage **8** handicap, pittance, sanction **9** advantage, allotment, head start **10** assistance, concession, permission, sufferance **13** accommodation, apportionment, authorization

alloy
5 blend **6** fusion **7** amalgam, mixture **8** compound **9** admixture, composite **10** adulterant, denaturant **11** interfusion **12** amalgamation, intermixture
brass-like: **6** latten, lattin
copper-sulfur: **6** niello
copper-tin: **6** bronze
copper-zinc: **5** brass **6** tambac, tombac, tombak **8** arsedine
gold-like: **6** oreide, ormolu, oroide
gold-silver: **8** electrum
iron-carbon: **5** steel
iron-nickel: **5** invar **7** elinvar
mercury: **7** amalgam
pewter-like: **5** bidri
tin-lead: **5** calin, terne **6** pewter, solder

tin-zinc: **6** oreide, oroide
used in jewelry: **6** oreide, oroide, tombac

all-powerful
8 almighty **10** omnipotent

all right
2 OK **3** aye, yea, yep, yes **4** good, jake, okay **6** agreed, decent **8** adequate, okeydoke **9** tolerable **10** acceptable **12** satisfactory

all round
7 overall **10** everyplace, everywhere, far and near, far and wide, high and low, throughout

all there
4 sane **5** lucid, right **6** normal **12** compos mentis

All the Way Home author
4 Agee (James)

allude
4 hint **5** imply, refer **6** advert **7** bring up, suggest **8** intimate

allure
4 bait, draw, take, tole, toll, wile **5** charm, decoy, tempt **6** appeal, entice, entrap, lead on, seduce **7** attract, bewitch, enchant, glamour **8** charisma, inveigle, witchery **9** captivate, fascinate, magnetism, magnetize **10** witchcraft **11** fascination

allurement
4 bait, call, draw, pull, trap **5** decoy, snare **6** appeal, come-on **9** seduction **10** attraction, enticement, seducement, temptation **12** drawing power, inveiglement

alluring
5 siren **8** charming **9** appealing, beguiling, glamorous, seductive **10** appetizing, attractive, bewitching, enchanting **11** captivating, fascinating

ally
4 join **5** unite **6** friend, helper **7** comrade, partner **8** federate **9** affiliate, associate, bedfellow, colleague, supporter **10** accomplice **11** confederate **12** collaborator

almighty
3 God **7** Creator **10** omnipotent **11** all-powerful

almost
4 nigh **5** about **6** all but, nearly **8** as good as, as much as, well-nigh **9** nearabout, virtually **11** essentially, practically **13** approximately
Scottish: **6** feckly

alms

7 charity 8 donation, offering
11 benefaction, beneficence
12 contribution

Aloeus

father: 7 Neptune 8 Poseidon
mother: 6 Canace
son: 4 Otus 9 Ephialtes
wife: 9 Iphimedia

aloft

4 high, over 5 above 6 upward
7 skyward 8 overhead
combining form: 4 hyps 5 hypsi,
hypso

Aloha State

6 Hawaii

alone

4 only, sole, solo 5 apart, solus
6 lonely, singly, solely, unique
7 isolate, removed 8 detached, entirely, isolated, lonesome, peerless,
singular, solitary 9 matchless, unequaled, unmatched, unrivaled
10 unexampled, unexcelled 11 exclusively, unsurpassed 12 unparalleled, unrepeatable 13 unaccompanied

aloneness

8 solitude 9 isolation

along

3 too, yet 4 also 5 forth 6 as well,
onward 7 besides, forward 8 likewise, moreover 11 furthermore
12 additionally

alongside

2 by 6 beside, next to 7 fornent
prefix: 3 par 4 para

along with

combining form: 3 sym, syn

aloof

4 cold, cool 5 proud 6 casual,
chilly, frigid, offish, remote 7 distant, haughty 8 arrogant, detached, reserved, reticent, solitary
9 unbending, uncurious, withdrawn
10 disdainful, restrained, unsociable 11 constrained, indifferent,
standoffish, unconcerned
12 uninterested

alp

4 peak 5 mount 8 mountain

alpaca's habitat

4 Peru 5 Andes 7 Bolivia

alpha

4 dawn 5 start 6 outset 7 dawning, genesis, opening 8 outstart
9 beginning 12 commence-
ment

alphabet

4 ABC's 7 grammar, letters 8 elements 9 rudiments 10 principles
12 fundamentals
Arabic: 2 ba, fa, ha, ra, ta, ya, za
3 ayn, dad, dal, gaf, jim, kaf, kha,
lam, mim, nun, sad, sin, tha, waw,
zay 4 alif, dhal, shin 5 ghayn
Greek: 2 mu, nu, pi, xi 3 chi, eta,
phi, psi, rho, tau 4 beta, iota, zeta
5 alpha, delta, gamma, kappa,
omega, sigma, theta 6 lambda
7 epsilon, omicron, upsilon
Hebrew: 2 he, pe 3 mem, nun, sin,
taf, tav, taw, tet, vav, waw, yod,
yud 4 alef, ayin, beth, caph, heth,
kaph, koph, qoph, resh, shin, teth
5 aleph, cheth, gimel, lamed, sa-
dhe, tsade, zayin 6 daleth, samekh
Old Irish: 4 ogam 5 ogham
runic: 7 futhark, futhorc, futhork

Alphenor's mother

5 Niobe

Alpheus

beloved: 8 Arethusa
father: 7 Oceanus
form: 5 river
mother: 6 Tethys

Alpine

animal: 4 ibex 7 chamois
climber: 10 alpestrian
dance: 5 gavot 7 gavotte
dress: 6 dirndl
goat: 4 ibex
herdsman: 4 senn
house: 6 chalet
lake: 4 Como, Iseo 5 Garda 6 Geneva 7 Lucerne 8 Maggiore
9 Constance, Neuchatel
pass: 3 col 5 Cenis 7 Brenner, Simplon 9 St. Bernard
peak: 5 Blanc, Eiger 7 Bernina
8 Jungfrau 10 Matterhorn
plant: 9 edelweiss
primrose: 8 auricula
resort: 5 Davos 7 Bolzano, Zermatt
8 Chamonix, Grenoble 9 Innsbruck
10 Interlaken 11 Saint Moritz
river: 5 Rhine, Rhone
snowfield: 4 firn, neve
staff: 10 alpenstock
state: 5 Tirol, Tyrol 7 Bavaria
tunnel: 5 Blanc, Cenis 7 Arlberg,
Simplon 10 St. Gotthard
wind: 4 bise, bora 5 foehn

already

4 even, once 6 before 7 earlier
8 formerly 9 erstwhile 10 heretofore, previously

also

3 too, yet 4 more 5 again, along,
still 6 as well, withal 7 besides, further 8 likewise, moreover 9 similarly 10 in addition 11 furthermore
12 additionally

also-ran

5 loser

altar

boy: 6 server 7 acolyte
cloth: 4 pall 5 palla 7 frontal
constellation: 3 Ara
hanging: 6 dorsal, dossal, dossel
platform: 8 predella
screen: 7 reredos
shelf: 6 gradin 7 gradine, retable
site: 4 apse, bema
table: 5 mensa
vessel: 5 cruet, paten 7 chalice 8 ciborium 10 monstrance

alter

4 geld, turn, vary 5 adapt 6 adjust,
change, jigger, modify, mutate,
neuter, temper 8 moderate, modulate 9 refashion

alteration

4 turn 5 shift 6 change 8 mutation
9 variation 10 adaptation, adjustment, changeover, conversion,
transition 12 modification
13 metamorphosis

altercate

4 spat, tiff 5 argue, scrap 6 bicker
7 brabble, quarrel, wran-
gle 8 squabble 9 caterwaul

altercation

3 row 4 tiff 6 combat, fracas
7 contest, dispute, quarrel, wrangle
8 argument, squabble 9 bickering
10 falling-out 11 controversy,
embroilment

alternate

3 sub 5 proxy 6 fill-in, rotate
7 stand-in 8 periodic 9 change off,
fluctuate, oscillate, recurrent, recurring, replacing, surrogate 10 equivalent, isochronal, periodical, substitute 11 isochronous, locum tenens,
pinch hitter, replacement 12 intermittent

alternately

6 in lieu, rather 7 instead

alternative

5 proxy 6 choice, option 8 druthers, election 9 selection, surrogate
10 preference, substitute 11 contingency, possibility

Althaea

father: 8 Thestius
husband: 6 Oeneus

son: 8 Meleager
victim: 8 Meleager

although
4 when 5 while 6 albeit, much as 7 howbeit, whereas

altitude
6 height 9 elevation

altitudinous
4 high, tall

altogether
4 well 5 quite 6 in toto, wholly 7 en masse, exactly, totally, utterly 8 all in all, entirely 9 generally, perfectly 10 by and large, completely, on the whole, thoroughly

altruistic
6 humane 7 liberal 8 generous 9 unselfish 10 benevolent, big-hearted, charitable, open-handed 11 magnanimous, noble-minded 12 eleemosynary, humanitarian 13 philanthropic

alum
4 grad 6 emetic 7 styptic 8 graduate 10 astringent

aluminum
symbol: 2 Al

always
4 ever 7 forever 8 evermore 9 eternally 10 constantly, invariably 11 forevermore, in perpetuum, perpetually 12 continuously

amalgam
see **amalgamation**

amalgamate
3 mix 4 fuse, meld 5 admix, merge, unify, unite 6 mingle 8 compound, intermix 9 interfuse 11 consolidate, intermingle

amalgamation
5 alloy, blend 6 fusion, merger 7 compost, mixture 8 compound 9 admixture, composite 10 commixture 13 consolidation

Amalthea
form: 4 goat
horn: 10 cornucopia
nursling: 4 Zeus

Amasa
father: 6 Hadlai, Jether
mother: 7 Abigail

amass
4 bulk, hive 5 hoard, lay up, uplay 6 garner, gather, roll up 7 store up 8 cumulate 9 stockpile 10 accumulate

amassment
5 hoard, trove 9 colluvies 10 collection, cumulation 11 aggregation 12 accumulation 13 agglomeration

Amata's husband
7 Latinus

amateur
4 tyro 6 novice, tinker, votary 7 admirer, dabbler, devotee 8 beginner, neophyte, putterer 9 greenhorn, smatterer 10 apprentice, enthusiast, uninitiate 11 abecedarian

amateurish
3 raw 5 crude, green 6 clumsy, flawed 7 jackleg 8 dabbling 9 deficient, unskilled, untutored 10 dilettante, unfinished 12 dilettantist

amative
6 erotic 7 amorous 11 aphrodisiac

amaze
6 wonder 7 astound 8 astonish, surprise 9 dumbfound, marveling 10 admiration, wonderment 11 flabbergast 12 confoundment

amazement
6 wonder 8 surprise 9 marveling 10 admiration, wonderment 12 confoundment

amazing
7 strange 8 wondrous 9 marvelous, wonderful 10 astounding, miraculous, prodigious, stupendous, surprising 11 astonishing

amazon
5 harpy, scold, shrew, vixen 6 ogress, virago 8 fishwife 9 termagant, Xanthippe

ambassador
5 agent, envoy 6 legate 8 diplomat, emissary 9 messenger
papal: 6 nuncio

ambience
6 medium, milieu 7 climate 10 atmosphere 11 environment, mise-en-scène 12 surroundings

ambiguity
7 evasion 9 equivoque, obscurity, vagueness 11 amphibology, uncertainty 12 equivocality, equivocation 13 double meaning

ambiguous
5 fishy, vague 6 opaque, unsure 7 dubious, obscure, suspect, unclear 8 doubtful 9 equivocal, tenebrous, uncertain, unsettled 10 inexplicit 11 problematic 12 questionable

ambit
5 limit, orbit, range, reach, scope, sweep 6 extent, radius 7 circuit, compass, purview 9 extension, perimeter, periphery 13 circumference

ambition
3 aim 4 goal, hope, mark, wish 5 dream, drive 6 desire, spirit, target 7 avidity, purpose 9 eagerness, intention, objective 10 aspiration, enterprise, get-up-and-go, initiative

ambitious
4 avid, bold, keen 5 eager 8 aspiring 9 energetic, grandiose, visionary 10 aggressive 11 hard-working 12 enterprising

ambivalent
see **equivocal**

amble
4 mope 5 dally, drift, mosey 6 bummel, dawdle, linger, stroll 7 saunter

ambrosial
4 lush 5 balmy, spicy, sweet, yummy 6 aromal, savory 7 darling 8 adorable, aromatic, fragrant, heavenly, luscious, perfumed, redolent 9 delicious 10 delectable, delightful 11 scrumptious

ambulant
6 roving 7 nomadic, vagrant, walking 8 vagabond 9 itinerant 11 peripatetic

ambulate
4 hoof, pace, step, walk 5 tread, troop 6 foot it 7 traipse

ambulatory
see **ambulant**

ambuscade
6 ambush 10 ambushment

ambush
4 trap 5 snare 6 assail, attack, entrap, lay for, waylay 7 assault, ensnare, scupper 8 surprise 9 ambuscade

ameliorate
4 help, mend 5 amend 6 better, perk up 7 improve, relieve 8 mitigate 10 convalesce, recuperate

amenable
4 tame 6 docile, liable, pliant 7 plastic, pliable, subdued, willing 8 biddable, obedient 9 adaptable, malleable, receptive, tractable

10 answerable, responsive 11 accountable, responsible

amend
4 help 5 right 6 better, repair 7 correct, improve, rectify 9 meliorate 10 ameliorate

amends
7 redress 8 reprisal 9 indemnity, quittance 10 recompense, reparation 11 restitution 12 compensation

amenities
5 mores 6 manner 8 decorums 9 etiquette 10 civilities 11 proprieties

amenity
5 charm, frill, luxus 6 luxury 7 comfort 8 civility, courtesy, facility 9 attention, gallantry, geniality, pleasance 10 affability, amiability, betterment, cordiality, enrichment, politeness 11 convenience, enhancement, improvement, sociability 12 agreeability, extravagance, graciousness, gratefulness, pleasantness 13 agreeableness, courteousness, enjoyableness

ament
4 fool, zany 5 idiot, moron 6 catkin, cretin 7 half-wit, natural 8 imbecile 9 simpleton

amerce
4 fine 5 mulct 6 punish 8 penalize

amercement
4 fine 5 mulct 7 forfeit, penalty

American
with Japanese-born parents: 5 nisei

American League
Baltimore: 7 Orioles
Boston: 6 Red Sox
California: 6 Angels
Chicago: 8 White Sox
Cleveland: 7 Indians
Detroit: 6 Tigers
Kansas City: 6 Royals
Milwaukee: 8 Brewers
Minnesota: 5 Twins
New York: 7 Yankees
Oakland: 9 Athletics
Seattle: 8 Mariners
Texas: 7 Rangers
Toronto: 8 Blue Jays

America, the Beautiful
music: 4 Ward (Samuel Augustus)
words: 5 Bates (Katherine Lee)

americium
symbol: 2 Am

Amfortas
father: 7 Titurel
opera: 8 Parsifal

amiability
7 amenity 9 geniality, pleasance 10 cordiality 12 gratefulness, pleasantness 13 agreeableness, enjoyableness

amiable
4 kind, mild, warm 6 benign, genial, gentle, kindly 7 affable, cordial, lenient 8 gracious, mannerly, obliging 9 courteous 10 responsive 11 complaisant, good-humored, good-natured, warmhearted 12 good-tempered

amicable
7 pacific 8 empathic, friendly, peaceful 9 congenial, peaceable 10 harmonious, like-minded, neighborly 11 sympathetic 13 understanding

amical
8 friendly 9 congenial 10 harmonious

amid
5 among, midst 6 during 10 throughout

amigo
4 mate 6 friend 8 familiar, intimate 9 confidant 12 acquaintance

amino acid
4 dopa 6 leucin, lysine, serine, toluid, valine 7 cystein, cystine, glycine, leucine, proline, toluide 8 cysteine, dopamine, histidin, thyroxin, toluidin, tyrosine

Amis novel
8 Lucky Jim

amiss
3 bad 4 awry, poor 5 badly, wrong 6 afield, astray, faulty, flawed, guilty, rotten, sinful, unholy 7 wrongly 8 blamable, blameful, culpable, faultily 9 defective, imperfect 10 censurable 11 blameworthy, incorrectly, unfavorably 12 inaccurately 13 demeritorious, reprehensible

amity
6 comity 7 concord, harmony 8 goodwill 10 friendship, kindliness 11 benevolence 12 friendliness

Ammonite god
6 Molech

Amneris's rival
4 Aida

amnesty
6 pardon 10 absolution

Amnon
father: 5 David
half sister: 5 Tamar
mother: 7 Ahinoam

Amon
father: 8 Manasseh
son: 6 Josiah

Amonasro's daughter
4 Aida

among
3 mid 4 amid 5 midst 7 between
prefix: 5 inter

amorist
5 lover, Romeo 7 Don Juan, gallant 8 Casanova, lothario, paramour

amorous
6 erotic 7 amative, amatory, lustful 8 enamored 10 infatuated 11 aphrodisiac

amorousness
4 love 5 amour 7 passion

amorphous
8 formless, inchoate, unformed, unshaped 9 shapeless

amount
4 body, bulk, core, dose 5 add up, equal, price, reach, run to, sense, total, touch 6 budget, burden, dosage, embody, matter, number, thrust, upshot 7 include, purport, quantum, run into, subsume 8 approach, comprise, quantity 9 aggregate, substance 12 correspond to
owed: 4 debt
Scottish: 4 haet 7 bittock
small: 3 bit, jot 4 atom, drop, iota, mite, whit 5 minim, spark, speck, trace 7 modicum, smidgen 8 molecule, particle 9 scintilla

amour
4 love 5 lover 6 affair 7 liaison, passion, romance 8 intimacy, intrigue 10 love affair 12 entanglement, relationship

amour propre
5 pride 6 vanity 7 conceit 8 self-love, vainness 9 vainglory 10 narcissism, self-esteem, self-regard 11 self-conceit, self-respect 13 conceitedness

amphetamines
5 speed 6 dexies, hearts, uppers 7 bennies, Dexoxyn 8 greenies, pep pills, Preludin 9 Dexedrine 10 Benzedrine, Methedrine

amphibian
burrowing: **9** caecilian
extinct: **7** eryopid
family: **7** Hylidae, Ranidae **9** Bufonidae, Proteidae, Sirenidae
genus: **4** Bufo, Hyla, Rana **5** Acris, Siren **7** Aneides, Eurycea **8** Ascaphus, Ensatina, Manculus, Necturus, Triturus **9** Ambystoma, Plethodon
legless: **9** caecilian
order: **5** Anura **7** Caudata **9** Salientia
tailed: **3** eft, olm **4** newt **7** caudate, proteus, uredele **10** salamander
tailless: **4** frog, hyla, toad **8** bullfrog, tree toad **10** batrachian, salientian
wormlike: **9** caecilian
young: **7** tadpole **8** polliwog

Amphion
brother: **6** Zethus
conquest: **6** Thebes
father: **4** Zeus
mother: **7** Antiope
sister: **5** Aedon
wife: **5** Niobe

Amphitrite
father: **6** Nereus
husband: **7** Neptune **8** Poseidon
mother: **5** Doris
son: **6** Triton

Amphitryon's wife
7 Alcmene

ample
5 great, large, roomy **6** lavish, plenty **7** copious, liberal, profuse **8** abundant, generous, handsome, prodigal, spacious **9** bounteous, bountiful, capacious, plenteous, plentiful **10** commodious

amplify
5 swell **6** dilate, expand **7** develop, distend, enlarge, inflate **8** increase **9** elaborate

amplitude
4 size **5** scope, space **6** spread **7** bigness, breadth, expanse, stretch **8** distance, fullness, wideness **9** expansion, greatness, largeness, magnitude, roominess **11** sizableness **12** sizeableness, spaciousness **13** capaciousness

Amram
father: **4** Bani **6** Dishon, Kohath
wife: **8** Jochebed

amulet
4 juju, luck, zemi **5** charm **6** fetish, grigri, mascot **7** periapt **8** greegree, gris-gris, talisman **10** lucky piece, phylactery, rabbit-foot

Amulius' brother
7 Numitor

amuse
4 wile **5** charm **6** divert **7** animate, beguile, delight, enchant, enliven **8** distract, recreate **9** entertain, fascinate

amusement
9 diversion **10** recreation **11** dissipation, distraction **13** entertainment

amusement park
7 funfair

amusement show
8 carnival

amusing
5 droll, funny **7** comical, risible **8** humorous **9** laughable, ludicrous

Amycus
father: **7** Neptune **8** Poseidon
friend: **8** Heracles, Hercules
mother: **5** Melia

Amymone
father: **6** Danaus
son: **8** Nauplius

ana
5 varia **9** anecdotes **10** collection, miscellany **11** memorabilia

anabasis
5 march **7** advance, headway, ongoing **8** progress **11** advancement, proficiency

anadem
5 crown **6** wreath **7** chaplet, coronal, coronet, garland

anagogic
6 mystic, occult **8** mystical, telestic **10** symbolical **11** allegorical

analects
4 posy **5** album **7** garland, omnibus **9** anthology **10** miscellany **11** florilegium

analgesic
7 anodyne **10** anesthetic, painkiller

analogous
4 akin, like **5** alike **7** kindred, similar, uniform **8** parallel **9** consonant **10** comparable

analogue
5 match **7** cognate **8** congener, parallel **9** correlate **11** counterpart, countertype **13** correspondent

analogy
6 simile **8** affinity, likeness, metaphor **9** alikeness, semblance **10** comparison, similarity, similitude **11** resemblance

analysis
4 scan, view **5** audit **6** review, survey **7** breakup, checkup **8** exegesis, scrutiny **9** breakdown **10** dissection, inspection, resolution **11** examination **13** perlustration

analytic
4 keen **5** acute, sharp **6** subtle **7** logical **8** piercing **11** penetrating **13** ratiocinative

analyze
7 dissect, examine, inspect, resolve **8** classify **9** anatomize, break down, decompose **10** decompound, scrutinize **11** investigate

analyze grammatically
5 parse

Ananias
4 liar **6** fibber **7** fibster **8** perjurer **9** falsifier **11** storyteller **12** prevaricator
coconspirator: **8** Sapphira
father: **9** Nedebaeus
wife: **8** Sapphira

anarch
see **anarchist**

anarchism
4 riot **7** misrule **8** disorder **9** distemper

anarchist
5 rebel **8** frondeur, mutineer, revolter **9** insurgent **10** malcontent

anarchy
4 riot **5** chaos **7** misrule **8** disorder **9** distemper, mobocracy **10** ochlocracy **11** lawlessness

anathema
5 curse **6** pariah **7** bugbear, censure, malison, outcast, reproof **9** bête noire **10** black beast **11** abomination, commination, detestation, imprecation, malediction **12** condemnation, denunciation

anathematize
4 damn **5** curse **8** execrate **9** objurgate

anatomical depression
5 fossa, fovea

anatomical tube
3 vas **4** duct **5** canal

anatomist
5 Wolff (Kaspar) **6** Harvey (William) **8** Vesalius (Andreas)

anatomize
7 analyze, dissect, resolve **9** break down, decompose **10** decompound

Anaxarete's lover
5 Iphis

Anaxo
brother: 10 Amphitryon
daughter: 7 Alcmene
father: 7 Alcaeus
husband: 9 Electryon

ancestor
8 forebear, foregoer 9 ascendant, precursor, prototype 10 antecedent, antecessor, forefather, forerunner, progenitor 11 predecessor 12 primogenitor

ancestral sequence
8 pedigree 9 bloodline, genealogy

ancestry
4 race 5 blood, breed, stock 6 family, origin, source 7 descent, kindred, lineage 8 pedigree 10 derivation, extraction

Anchises' son
6 Aeneas

anchor
3 fix 4 moor 5 catch 6 fasten, secure 7 grapnel, killick, killock
line: 7 catfall
part: 4 ring 5 crown, fluke, shank

anchorage
4 port 5 chuck, haven, roads 6 harbor, riding 7 mooring 9 harborage, roadstead

anchorite
5 loner 6 hermit 7 recluse

anchors ___
6 aweigh

ancient
3 old 4 aged 5 elder, hoary, olden 6 age-old, doting, primal, senior 7 antique, elderly, oldster 8 Noachian, old-timer, primeval, timeworn 9 doddering, venerable 10 primordial 12 antediluvian
combining form: 4 pale 5 palae, paleo 6 archae, archeo, palaeo 7 archaeo

ancient capital
4 Susa 5 Balkh, Calah, Isker, Kalhu, Ninus, Sibir 6 Bactra, Nimrud 7 Nineveh, Shushan 10 Persepolis

ancient city
Asia Minor: 4 Nice, Teos 5 Tyana 6 Edessa, Nicaea 7 Antioch 13 Halicarnassus
Babylonia: 4 Sura 5 Accad, Agade, Akkad, Eridu, Larsa 7 Ellasar
Bengal: 4 Gaur 9 Lakhnauti
Canaan: 5 Gezer

Cyprus: 7 Salamis
Egypt: 2 On 5 Tanis 6 Thebes 7 Memphis 10 Heliopolis
Etruria: 4 Veii
Euphrates River: 7 Babylon
Greece: 5 Crisa 6 Athens, Sparta 7 Calydon 10 Lacedaemon
Ionia: 4 Myus, Teos 5 Chios, Samos 6 Priene 7 Ephesus, Lebedos, Miletus, Phocaea 8 Colophon, Erythrae 10 Clazomenae
Italy: 5 Locri 7 Pompeii 11 Herculaneum
Latium: 5 Gabii 9 Alba Longa
Mayan: 4 Coba 5 Tikal
Nile River: 5 Meroe
North Africa: 5 Utica 8 Carthage
Palestine: 4 Gaza 5 Ekron, Endor, Sodom 6 Beroea, Bethel, Gilead, Hebron 7 Jericho, Samaria 8 Ashkelon 9 Capernaum, Jerusalem
Peloponnesus: 5 Tegea 6 Sparta 7 Corinth
Sumeria: 2 Ur 4 Kish, Uruk 5 Erech, Larsa 7 Lagash
Turkey: 5 Assos, Assus 9 Byzantium
Yucatan: 5 Uxmal

ancient country
Adriatic coast: 7 Illyria
Africa: 10 Mauretania
Arabian Peninsula: 5 Sheba
Asia: 4 Aram 5 Media, Minni, Syria 7 Armenia, Ash Sham, Bactria
Asia Minor: 5 Lydia, Mysia 6 Aeolis, Pontus 7 Cilicia, Phrygia 8 Bithynia
Balkan: 7 Macedon 9 Macedonia
Black Sea: 7 Colchis
Dead Sea: 4 Edom
Euphrates River: 9 Babylonia
Europe: 4 Gaul 5 Dacia 6 Gallia
gold-rich: 5 Ophir
Italy: 6 Latium 7 Etruria
Nile valley: 4 Cush
Peloponnesus: 4 Elis 7 Arcadia
Syria: 9 Phoenicia

ancient empire
6 Median 7 Hittite, Persian 8 Assyrian, Athenian, Chaldean, Egyptian, Seleucid 9 Ptolemaic 10 Babylonian

ancient kingdom
Anglo-Saxon: 6 Wessex
Asia: 4 Ghor, Ghur
Celtic: 7 Cumbria
China: 3 Shu
Euphrates valley: 4 Hira 7 Al-Hirah
Greece: 8 Pergamon, Pergamum
North Of Assyria: 3 Van 6 Ararat, Urartu
Palestine: 5 Judah 6 Israel
Persian Gulf: 4 Elam
Portugal: 7 Algarve

Spain: 4 Leon 6 Aragon 7 Castile, Galicia, Granada, Navarre
Syria: 4 Moab
Welsh: 5 Powys
West Sahara: 4 Gana 5 Ghana

ancient monument
6 sphinx 7 obelisk, pyramid

ancient royal forest
4 Dean 8 Sherwood

ancient town
Africa: 4 Zama
Armenia: 4 Dwin, Tvin
Asia Minor: 4 Soli 5 Derbe, Issus, Soloi
Attica: 6 Icaria
Black Sea: 5 Olbia 9 Apollonia
Greece: 4 Abae, Opus 8 Marathon
Italy: 4 Elea, Luna 5 Cumae, Velia
Latium: 5 Ardea, Cures
Macedonia: 5 Pydna, Stobi 9 Apollonia
Peloponnesus: 5 Asine
Persia: 6 Hormuz 8 Harmozia
Sicily: 5 Hybla
Spain: 5 Munda
Tatar: 5 Isker, Sibir
Wendish: 5 Julin

ancilla
3 aid 4 help 6 helper 7 striker 9 assistant, attendant

ancillary
8 adjuvant, incident 9 accessory, attendant, attending, auxiliary, satellite 10 coincident, collateral, subsidiary 11 appurtenant, concomitant, subservient 12 accompanying, contributory

Anderson, Maxwell
play: 7 High Tor 8 Key Largo 9 Winterset 11 Valley Forge 14 What Price Glory

Anderson, Sherwood
book 9 Poor White 10 Kit Brandon 12 Dark Laughter 13 Winesburg, Ohio

Andes native
4 Inca

andiron
7 firedog

androgynous
8 bisexual 13 hermaphrodite

android
5 robot 9 automaton

Andromache
husband: 6 Hector 7 Helenus, Pyrrhus 11 Neoptolemus
son: 8 Astyanax, Molossus

Andromeda
father: 7 Cepheus
husband: 7 Perseus
mother: 10 Cassiopeia
rescuer: 7 Perseus

___ and warp
4 woof

anecdote
4 tale, yarn 5 story 7 episode, recital 8 relation 9 narration, narrative

anemic
4 pale 6 pallid, watery 8 waterish 9 bloodless

anent
2 re 4 as to, in re 5 about, as for 7 apropos 8 touching 9 as regards 10 concerning 13 with respect to

anesthetic
4 dull, hard 5 rocky 7 anodyne 9 analgesic, bloodless, insensate 10 impassible, insensible, pain-killer 11 insensitive
combining form: 5 caine
medical: 5 ether 6 spinal 7 eucaine 8 morphine, procaine 9 halothane, novocaine 10 benzocaine, chloroform, tetracaine 11 scopolamine

anesthetized
4 dead, numb 6 asleep, numbed 8 benumbed, deadened 9 senseless, unfeeling 10 insensible 11 insensitive

anew
4 over 5 again 6 afresh, de novo, lately, of late 8 once more, recently
combining form: 2 an 3 ana 4 pali
prefix: 2 re

angel
6 backer, cherub, patron, surety 7 sponsor 8 backer-up 9 celestial, guarantor
biblical: 5 Uriel 7 Gabriel, Michael, Raphael
fallen: 7 Lucifer
hierarchy: 6 powers 7 thrones, virtues 8 cherubim, seraphim 9 dominions
Mormon: 6 Moroni
of death: 6 Azrael

Angel Clare's bride
4 Tess

angelic
4 holy 5 godly 7 saintly 8 cherubic

Angelica
father: 9 Galaphron
husband: 6 Medoro
lover: 7 Orlando

anger
3 ire, irk, vex 4 bile, boil, burn, fume, fury, huff, rage, rant, rave, rile 5 annoy, pique, storm, wrath 6 blow up, choler, dander, enrage, madden, nettle, offend, seethe 7 affront, bristle, dudgeon, flare up, incense, outrage, provoke, steam up, umbrage 8 boil over, irritate 9 aggravate, annoyance, infuriate 10 exasperate 11 indignation, infuriation 12 exasperation

angered easily
4 rily 5 riley 9 irascible

angle
3 aim, bow 4 axil, bend, bias, fish, hand, hint, skew, turn 5 facet, phase, slant 6 aspect, crotch 7 flexure, outlook, turning 8 flection 9 direction, viewpoint 10 standpoint
combining form: 3 gon 4 goni 5 gonio 6 anguli, angulo

Anglo-Saxon
army: 4 fyrd
assembly: 4 moot 5 gemot 6 gemote
coin: 3 ora 5 sceat 6 mancus
council: 9 heptarchy
county: 5 shire
court: 4 moot 5 gemot 6 gemote
crown tax: 4 geld
epic: 7 Beowulf
free servant: 5 thane, thegn
god: 3 Ing
goddess of fate: 4 Wyrd
historian: 4 Bede
king: 3 Ine, Ini 4 Edwy 5 Edgar, Edred 6 Alfred, Edmund, Edward, Egbert 8 Ethelred
kingdom: 4 Kent 5 Essex 6 Mercia, Sussex, Wessex 10 East Anglia 11 Northumbria
king's council: 5 witan
letter: 3 edh, eth, wen, wyn 4 wynn 5 thorn
nobleman: 4 earl
poet: 4 scop
prince: 8 atheling
sheriff: 5 reeve 6 gerefa
slave: 4 esne
tenant: 6 geneat
village: 3 ham
warrior: 5 thane, thegn

angry
3 mad 4 rily, sore, waxy 5 irate, riley, upset, vexed, wroth 6 heated, ireful, put out, shirty, wrathy, wrothy 7 enraged, furious, uptight 8 choleric, incensed, maddened, worked up, wrathful, wrothful 9 indignant, perturbed, wrought up

10 aggravated, infuriated 11 acrimonious, exasperated

anguish
3 rue, woe 4 ache, care, dole, pain, pang 5 grief, throe, worry 6 regret, sorrow, throes 7 anxiety, torment, torture 9 heartache 10 affliction, heartbreak

angular
4 bony, lank, lean 5 crude, gaunt, lanky, rough, spare 6 skinny 7 scraggy, scrawny 8 rawboned, unworked 9 roughhewn, undressed 10 unfinished, unpolished 11 unfashioned

anima
4 soul 6 pneuma, psyche, spirit 9 élan vital 10 vital force

animadversion
4 slam, slur 7 censure, obloquy 9 aspersion, criticism, stricture 10 accusation, imputation, reflection 11 insinuation 12 reprehension

animadvert
5 state, utter 6 remark 7 comment, declare, observe 10 commentate

animal
5 beast, brute, feral 6 brutal, carnal, ferine 7 beastly, bestial, brutish, critter, fleshly, sensual, swinish, wilding 8 creature, wildling
antlered: 3 elk 4 axis, deer 5 moose 7 caribou 8 reindeer
aquatic: 3 eel 4 fish, frog, seal 5 otter, whale 6 dugong, sea cow, walrus 7 dolphin, manatee, octopus 8 bryozoan, porpoise 9 alligator, crocodile
arboreal: 2 ai 4 bird, unau 5 chimp, coati, koala, lemur, sloth 6 gibbon, monkey 7 opossum, tarsier 8 kinkajou, marmoset, squirrel 9 orangutan
burrowing: 4 mole 5 brock, ratel 6 badger, gopher, marmot, rabbit 7 echidna 9 armadillo, groundhog, woodchuck
castrated: 2 ox 5 capon, spado, steer 6 barrow, wether 7 gelding
combining form: 2 zo 3 zoa (plural), zoo 4 zoon 6 theria (plural) 7 therium
draft: 2 ox 3 yak 4 mule, oxen (plural) 5 horse 6 donkey 8 elephant
exhibit: 3 zoo
extinct: 3 moa 4 dodo, urus 6 quagga 7 mammoth 8 dinosaur, eohippus, mastodon 9 solitaire, trilobite

female: **3** cow, dam, doe, ewe, hen, pen, roe, sow **4** mare, puss **5** bitch, goose, jenny, nanny, vixen **6** jennet **7** lioness

four-footed: **9** quadruped

four-limbed: **8** tetrapod

free-swimming: **6** nekton

hibernating: **4** bear, frog, toad **5** skunk, snake **7** polecat **8** chipmunk **9** groundhog, woodchuck

horned: **2** ox **3** ram, yak **4** bull, goat, ibex, kudu **5** addax, ariel, badak, bison, eland, rhino **6** cattle, koodoo **7** buffalo, gazelle, giraffe, unicorn **8** antelope

humped: **2** ox **3** elk, yak **4** zebu **5** bison, camel, moose

imaginary: **5** snark

insect-eating: **4** mole, newt **5** gecko, shrew **6** numbat **7** echidna **8** aardvark, anteater, hedgehog, pangolin, tamandua **10** salamander

lover: **8** zoophile

male: **3** cob, ram, tom **4** boar, buck, bull, cock, stag, stud **5** billy, steer **6** gander **7** gobbler, rooster **8** bachelor, stallion

many-celled: **8** metazoan

many-footed: **9** centipede, millipede

marsupial: **4** tait **5** koala **6** cuscus, numbat, wombat **7** dasyure, opossum, wallaby **8** kangaroo **9** bandicoot, phalanger

meat-eating: **9** carnivore

mythical: **4** yale **5** hodag, Hydra, kylin **6** bunyip, dragon, kraken, sphinx **7** centaur, griffin, mermaid, Pegasus, unicorn **8** basilisk, Cerberus, Minotaur

one-celled: **9** protozoan

Peruvian: **5** llama **6** alpaca, vicuna

plant-eating: **9** herbivore

skin disease: **6** mange

snouted: **5** coati, tapir **8** mongoose; (see also **animal,** *insect-eating*)

spotted: **4** axis, paca **6** calico, jaguar, ocelot **7** cheetah, leopard, piebald **8** skewbald **9** dalmatian

striped: **4** kudo **5** tiger, zebra **6** koodoo, quagga

suffix: **4** acea (plural) **5** acean

trail: **3** pug **4** foil, slot **5** spoor

tusked: **6** walrus **7** warthog **8** elephant

two-footed: **5** biped

web-footed: **4** duck, frog, toad **5** goose, otter **6** beaver **8** duckbill, platypus

young: **3** cub, kid, kit, pup **4** calf, colt, fawn, foal, joey, lamb **5** bunny, chick, kitty, poult, shoat, stirk, whelp **6** cygnet, farrow, heifer, kitten, piglet **7** bullock, gosling, lambkin **8** suckling, yeanling, yearling **9** fledgling

animal behavior
study of: **8** ethology

animal fat
    4 suet **6** tallow

animalism
    7 lechery **9** carnality **10** sensualism, sensuality, unchastity **11** fleshliness, lustfulness **13** lecherousness

animalize
    4 warp **6** debase **7** corrupt, deprave, pervert, vitiate **9** brutalize **10** bestialize, demoralize

animal life
    5 fauna

animals
suffix: **3** ata, ida, ini **4** idae, idea

animate
    4 fire **5** cheer, drive, exalt, impel, liven, nerve, steel **6** inform, vivify **7** actuate, chirk up, enliven, hearten, inspire, quicken, refresh **8** activate, embolden, inspirit, motivate, vitalize **9** encourage, enhearten **10** invigorate, vivificate

animated
    3 gay **4** cant, keen **5** alert, alive, canty, vital **6** lively, living, zoetic **7** zestful **8** spirited **9** exuberant, sprightly, vitalized, vivacious **12** high-spirited

animation
    3 vim **4** brio, dash, élan, life, zing **5** oomph, verve **6** esprit, spirit

animosity
    6 enmity, rancor **9** antipathy, hostility **10** antagonism

animus
    4 plan, soul **6** design, enmity, intent, pneuma, psyche, rancor, spirit **7** meaning, purpose **9** antipathy, élan vital, hostility, intention **10** antagonism, intendment, vital force

Anius
daughter: **4** Oeno **5** Elais **6** Spermo
father: **6** Apollo
mother: **5** Rhoeo

Anjou
    4 pear

ankle
    6 tarsus
combining form: **4** tars **5** tarso

annals
    7 history **9** chronicle

Anna's sister
    4 Dido

annex
    3 add, arm, cop, ell, nim, win **4** gain, hook, join, land, take, wing **5** affix, seize, steal, unite **6** append, attach, fasten, obtain, pick up, secure, take on **7** acquire, preempt, procure, purloin, subjoin **8** accroach, addition, arrogate, superadd **9** extension, sequester **10** commandeer, confiscate **11** appropriate, expropriate

Annie Oakley
    4 pass

annihilate
    4 raze, ruin, undo **5** abate, annul, crush, quash, quell, wrack, wreck **6** murder, negate, quench, squash, uproot **7** abolish, blot out, destroy, expunge, nullify, put down, root out, vitiate, wipe out **8** abrogate, decimate, demolish, massacre, suppress **9** eradicate, extirpate, slaughter **10** extinguish, invalidate, obliterate **11** exterminate

annihilative
    7 ruinous **8** wrackful, wreckful **10** shattering **11** destructive

anniversary
hundredth: **9** centenary **10** centennial
tenth: **9** decennial
thousandth: **10** millennial **11** millenniary

annotate
    5 gloss **7** comment, explain **9** elucidate **10** commentate

announce
    5 augur, sound **6** attest, blazon, herald **7** bespeak, betoken, declare, forerun, presage, present, publish, testify, witness **8** foreshow, foretell, indicate, proclaim **9** advertise, broadcast, harbinger **10** bruit about, promulgate **11** preindicate

announcement
    9 broadcast **11** declaration, publication **12** proclamation, promulgation **13** advertisement

annoy
    3 bug, irk, vex **4** bait, fret, gall, gnaw, miff **5** chafe, chivy, harry, peeve, tease, upset, worry **6** abrade, badger, bother, harass, heckle, hector, pester, plague, ruffle **7** agitate, bedevil, disturb, hagride,

perturb, provoke **8** distress, exercise, irritate **9** beleaguer
Scottish: **4** fash

annoyance
3 ire **4** pest **5** anger, trial **6** bother, irking, pester, plague, pother, vexing **7** teasing **8** distress, irritant, nuisance, vexation **9** besetment, bothering, pestering, provoking **10** affliction, botherment, harassment **11** aggravation, botheration, indignation, provocation **12** exasperation

annoying
5 pesky

annual
5 plant **6** flower, yearly **7** almanac **8** yearbook

annul
4 undo, void **5** abate, erase, quash **6** cancel, delete, efface, negate, revoke, vacate **7** abolish, blot out, expunge, nullify, redress, rescind, vitiate, wipe out **8** abrogate, dissolve **9** cancel out, discharge, frustrate **10** annihilate, counteract, extinguish, invalidate, neutralize, obliterate **11** countermand

annunciate
5 sound, state **7** declare, publish **8** proclaim **9** advertise, broadcast **10** bruit about, promulgate

anodyne
6 opiate **8** narcotic, nepenthe, sedative **9** analgesic, calmative, soporific **10** anesthetic, depressant, pain-killer **12** tranquilizer

anointing
7 unction

anomalous
6 off-key **7** deviant, foreign, strange **8** aberrant, abnormal, atypical, peculiar **9** deviative, divergent, irregular, unnatural, untypical **11** heteroclite **13** preternatural

anon
4 soon, then, when **5** again **7** by and by, shortly **8** directly **9** presently

anonym
5 alias **11** nom de guerre

anonymous
7 unknown, unnamed **8** nameless **9** incognito **10** innominate **11** unspecified **12** undesignated, unidentified, unrecognized

another
3 new **4** else, more **5** added, fresh **7** farther, further **10** additional

anschluss
5 union **6** league **8** alliance **9** coalition **10** federation **11** confederacy **13** confederation

anserine
5 silly **6** stupid **9** gooselike

answer
4 fill, meet **5** rebut, reply **6** come in, refute, rejoin, result, retort, return **7** fulfill, respond, satisfy **8** antiphon, rebuttal, response, solution **9** rejoinder **10** refutation **11** recriminate **13** countercharge

answerable
5 bound **6** liable **7** obliged **8** amenable **9** compelled, duty-bound, obligated **11** accountable, constrained, responsible

ant
5 emmet **9** carpenter
combining form: **6** myrmec **7** myrmeco
male: **4** aner
relating to: **6** formic
worker: **6** ergate

Antaean
4 huge **5** giant **6** heroic **7** titanic **8** colossal, gigantic **9** cyclopean, Herculean **10** gargantuan

Antaeus
father: **7** Neptune **8** Poseidon
mother: **2** Ge **4** Gaea
slayer: **8** Heracles, Hercules

antagonism
3 con **6** animus, enmity, rancor **7** discord **8** friction, opposure **9** animosity, antipathy, hostility **10** antithesis, opposition, oppugnancy, resistance **11** contrariety **12** disagreement

antagonist
3 con **4** anti **5** match **7** opposer **8** opponent **9** adversary, oppugnant

antagonistic
4 anti **6** averse, bitter **7** adverse, hostile, opposed **8** clashing, contrary, inimical, opposing **9** oppugnant, rancorous, vitriolic **10** antonymous, discordant **11** conflicting, contrariant, inconsonant **12** antipathetic, incompatible
combining form: **7** enantio

ante
3 bet, pot **5** stake, wager

anteater
see **animal**, *insect-eating*

antecede
7 forerun, precede, predate **8** foredate

antecedence
8 priority **12** previousness

antecedent
4 fore **5** cause, prior **6** former, reason **8** ancestor, anterior, forebear, foregoer, occasion, previous **9** condition, foregoing, precedent, preceding, precursor, prototype **10** forerunner **11** determinant, predecessor

antedate
see **antecede**

antediluvian
3 old **4** aged, fogy **5** hoary **6** age-old, fogram, fossil, square **7** ancient, antique **8** mossback, Noachian, timeworn **10** fuddy-duddy **12** old-fashioned **13** stick-in-the-mud

antelope
3 gnu, kob **4** guib, koba, kudu, oryx, poku, puku, suni, tora **5** addax, beira, beisa, bongo, eland, goral, nagor, nyala, oribi, saiga, serow, tiang **6** dik-dik, duiker, grimme, impala, lechwe, lelwel, nilgai **7** blesbok, bubalis, chamois, defassa, dibatag, gazelle, gemsbok, gerenuk, grysbok, rooibok, sassaby **8** agacella, bontebok, bushbuck, reedbuck, sing-sing, steinbok **9** duikerbok, kleeneboc, sitatunga, springbok, waterbuck **10** hartebeest **12** klipspringer
extinct: **7** blaubok **9** blaauwbok
family: **7** Bovidae
female: **3** doe
four-horned: **6** chouka **7** chikara **10** chousingha
male: **4** buck
mythical: **4** yale
young: **3** kid
(see also **gazelle**)

antenna
4 yagi **6** aerial, dipole **8** monopole

Antenor
father: **8** Aesyetes
son: **6** Agenor
wife: **6** Theano

anterior
4 past **5** prior **6** former **8** previous **9** foregoing, precedent, preceding **10** antecedent

Anteros
brother: **4** Eros
father: **4** Ares, Mars

mother: **5** Venus **9** Aphrodite
opposite: **4** Eros

anthology
3 ana **4** posy **5** album **7** garland, omnibus **8** analects, delectus, treasury **10** collection, miscellany **11** compilation, florilegium

anthropoid
3 ape **6** monkey **7** gorilla, manlike, primate **8** hominoid, humanoid **10** chimpanzee

anthropologist
4 Boas (Franz), Mead (Margaret) **5** Black (Davidson), Keith (Arthur), Sapir (Edward), Tylor (Edward Burnett) **6** Dubois (Eugène), Frazer (James George), Hooton (Earnest Albert), Leakey (Louis), Linton (Ralph), Morgan (Lewis Henry) **7** Kroeber (Alfred Louis), Wissler (Clark) **8** Benedict (Ruth), Washburn **10** Malinowski (Bronisław Kasper) **11** Weidenreich (Franz), Westermarck (Edward Alexander)

anti
3 con **7** adverse, opposed, opposer **8** opponent, opposing **9** adversary, oppugnant **10** antagonist **12** antagonistic, antipathetic

antiaircraft fire
4 flak

antibiotic
7 colicin **8** viomycin **9** polymyxin **10** bacitracin, novobiocin, penicillin **11** bacteriocin, tyrothricin **12** streptomycin, tetracycline

antic
4 dido, lark **5** caper, comic, prank, trick **6** frisky, frolic, lively, pranky, shines **7** bizarre, comical, foolish, playful, roguish **8** farcical, gamesome, prankful, prankish, spirited **9** fantastic, grotesque, laughable, ludicrous, sprightly **10** frolicsome, rollicking, shenanigan, tomfoolery **11** mischievous, monkeyshine

anticipate
3 see **5** await **6** divine, expect **7** foresee, preknow, presage, prevent, previse **8** forecast, forefeel, foreknow, foretell, outguess **9** apprehend, forestall, foretaste, prevision, visualize

anticipation
10 expectancy **11** expectation

anticipatory
7 atiptoe **9** expectant, expecting

Anticlea
father: **9** Autolycus

husband: **7** Laertes
son: **7** Ulysses **8** Odysseus

antidote
4 cure **6** remedy **7** negator **9** nullifier **10** corrective **11** counterstep, neutralizer **12** counteragent **13** counteractant, counteractive

Antigone
brother: **9** Polynices
father: **7** Oedipus
mother: **7** Jocasta
sister: **6** Ismene
uncle: **5** Creon

Antilochus
father: **6** Nestor
friend: **8** Achilles
slayer: **6** Memnon

antimony
7 stibium
combining form: **4** stib **5** stibi, stibo **6** stibio
symbol: **2** Sb

Antiope
father: **6** Asopus
husband: **5** Lycus **7** Theseus
queen of: **7** Amazons
son: **6** Zethus **7** Amphion **10** Hippolytus

antipasto
4 whet **7** zakuska **9** appetizer **11** hors d'oeuvre

antipathetic
7 adverse, opposed **8** aversive, clashing, contrary, opposing, opposite, ungenial **9** abhorrent, antipodal, loathsome, obnoxious, oppugnant, repellent, repugnant, repulsive **10** antonymous, discordant, disgusting **11** conflicting, contrariant, distasteful, uncongenial **12** antagonistic **13** contradictory, unsympathetic

antipathy
6 animus, enmity, rancor **7** allergy, dislike **8** aversion, distaste, dyspathy **9** animosity, hostility **10** abhorrence, antagonism, repellency

antiphon
5 reply **6** answer, retort, return **7** respond **8** response **9** rejoinder

antipodal
5 polar **7** counter, reverse **8** contrary, converse, opposite **9** diametric **11** diametrical **12** antithetical **13** contradictory

antipode
6 contra **7** counter, reverse **8** contrary, converse, opposite **10** antithe-

sis **11** counterpole **13** contradictory

antiquate
7 outdate, outmode **8** obsolete **9** obsolesce **12** superannuate

antiquated
5 dated, fusty, moldy, passé **7** antique, archaic **8** obsolete, old-timey, outmoded **10** oldfangled **12** old-fashioned

antique
3 old **4** aged **5** dated, hoary, passé **6** age-old **7** ancient, archaic **8** Noachian, old-timey, outdated, outmoded, timeworn **9** ancestral, out-of-date, venerable **10** antiquated, oldfangled **12** antediluvian, old-fashioned

antiquity
combining form: **6** archae, archeo **7** archaeo

antiseptic
6 iodine **7** alcohol **8** peroxide **9** boric acid, carvacrol, germicide, merbromin **10** gramicidin **12** carbolic acid, disinfectant
pioneer: **6** Lister (Joseph)

antisocial
7 ascetic, austere **8** eremitic, reserved, solitary **9** reclusive, withdrawn **11** introverted, standoffish **12** misanthropic

antithesis
3 con **6** contra **7** counter, reverse **8** antipode, antipole, contrary, converse, opposite, opposure **10** antagonism, opposition **11** contrariety, counterpole **13** contradictory

antithetical
5 polar **7** counter, reverse **8** contrary, converse, opposite **9** antipodal, diametric **10** antipodean **11** diametrical **13** contradictory

antitoxin
4 sera (plural) **5** serum

antlike
9 myrmecoid

Antony, Mark
defeat: **6** Actium
friend: **6** Caesar
lover: **9** Cleopatra
wife: **7** Octavia

Anubis' father
6 Osiris

anus
combining form: **3** ano **5** proct **6** procta, procti, procto

anvil
combining form: **5** incud **6** incudo

anxiety

4 care 5 doubt, dread, panic, worry 6 unease 7 concern 8 disquiet, distress, mistrust, suspense 9 suffering 10 solicitude, uneasiness 11 concernment, disquietude, uncertainty

anxious

4 agog, avid, keen 5 eager, scary, upset 6 afraid, aghast, ardent, scared, uneasy 7 alarmed, fearful, jittery, worried 8 agitated, appetent, troubled 9 impatient, perturbed, terrified 10 breathless, disquieted, frightened 12 apprehensive

any

4 some

anyhow

6 random 8 at random, randomly 9 haphazard 11 any which way, haphazardly 13 helter-skelter

anytime

4 ever 5 at all

anyway

4 ever, once 5 at all

anywise

see anyhow

A1

4 tops 5 prime 6 Grade A 8 five-star, superior 9 excellent, first rate, front-rank, number one, top-drawer 10 blue-ribbon, first-class

apace

4 fast 7 flat-out, hastily, quickly, rapidly, swiftly 8 speedily 9 posthaste 12 lickety-split 13 expeditiously

Apache chief

7 Cochise 8 Geronimo

apart

5 alone, aside 6 singly 7 asunder, isolate, removed, sky-high 8 detached, isolated, one by one 9 severally 10 separately 12 individually 13 independently, unaccompanied
combining form: 4 dich 5 chori, dicho
prefix: 3 dis

apart from

3 bar, but 4 save 6 except, saving 7 barring, besides 9 outside of 11 exclusive of

apartheid

10 separation, separatism 11 segregation 12 separateness

apartment

4 flat, room 5 rooms, suite 6 rental, walk-up 7 chamber, flatlet 8 lodgings, tenement

apathetic

3 dry 4 dull, limp 5 inert, stoic 6 stolid, torpid 7 callous, languid, unmoved 8 sluggish 9 impassive, untouched 10 anesthetic, insensible, phlegmatic, spiritless 11 indifferent, insensitive 12 matter-of-fact

apathy

6 acedia, phlegm, torpor 8 coldness, lethargy, obduracy, stoicism 9 disregard, inertness, lassitude, passivity, stolidity, torpidity, unconcern 10 detachment, dispassion 11 callousness, disinterest, impassivity, insouciance 12 heedlessness, indifference, listlessness 13 insensibility, insensitivity, unmindfulness

ape

4 copy, mime, mock 5 magot, mimic 6 baboon, gibbon, monkey, parody, pongid, simian 7 copycat, gorilla, imitate, take off 8 travesty 9 burlesque, orangutan 10 caricature, chimpanzee, orangoutan
combining form: 6 pithec 7 pitheco 8 pithecus

aperçu

6 digest, précis, sketch, survey 7 pandect, sylloge 8 syllabus 10 compendium

aperitif

4 whet 5 drink 8 cocktail 9 appetizer

aperitive

5 sapid, tasty 6 savory 8 saporous, tasteful 9 palatable, toothsome 10 appetizing, flavorsome 13 mouth-watering

aperture

3 gap 4 gash, hole, slit, vent 5 break, chasm, cleft, slash 6 breach, outlet 7 opening, orifice, pinhole 8 puncture 10 interstice 11 perforation 13 discontinuity

apery

7 mimicry

apex

3 cap, tip, top 4 acme, cusp, noon, peak, roof 5 crest, crown, limit, point 6 apogee, climax, comble, culmen, summit, vertex, zenith 8 capsheaf, capstone, meridian, noontide, pinnacle, ultimate 9 crescendo, fastigium, sublimity 11 cul-

mination, ne plus ultra 12 quintessence
combining form: 3 ace 4 apic 5 apici, apico

Aphareus' son

4 Idas 7 Lynceus

aphorism

4 rule 5 axiom, gnome, maxim, moral 6 dictum, truism 7 brocard 8 apothegm

aphrodisia

4 itch, lust 6 desire 7 passion 9 eroticism, prurience, pruriency 11 lustfulness 13 concupiscence, lickerishness

aphrodisiac

6 erotic 7 amative, amatory, amorous

Aphrodite

5 Venus
consort: 4 Ares 6 Vulcan 10 Hephaestus
father: 4 Zeus 7 Jupiter
goddess of: 4 love
mother: 5 Dione
son: 4 Eros 5 Cupid 6 Aeneas 7 Priapus

apiarist

6 beeman 9 beekeeper, beemaster

apical

3 top 7 highest, topmost 8 loftiest 9 uppermost

apiculture

10 beekeeping

apiece

3 all 4 each 5 aside 6 singly 8 one by one, per caput 9 per capita 12 individually, respectively

apish

7 slavish 9 emulative, imitative

aplomb

4 ease 5 poise 8 coolness, easiness 9 assurance, composure, sangfroid, self-trust 10 confidence, equanimity 11 nonchalance, savoir faire 13 self-assurance

apocalypse

6 oracle, vision 8 prophecy 10 revelation

apocalyptic

4 dire 5 vatic 6 mantic 7 baleful, baneful, direful, fateful, fatidic, ominous, unlucky 8 Delphian, oracular 9 ill-boding, prophetic, sibylline, vaticinal 11 prophetical, threatening 12 inauspicious

apocopate

5 elide

apocryphal
5 false, wrong **6** untrue **7** dubious **8** doubtful, spurious **9** incorrect, ungenuine **11** unauthentic

apogee
4 acme, apex, peak **6** climax, summit, zenith **8** capstone, meridian, pinnacle **11** culmination

Apollo
6 Helios **7** Phoebus
beloved: **6** Cyrene, Daphne **8** Calliope
birthplace: **5** Delos
father: **4** Zeus **7** Jupiter
mother: **4** Leto **6** Latona
oracle: **6** Delphi
sister: **5** Diana **7** Artemis
son: **3** Ion **7** Orpheus
temple: **6** Delphi

Apollyon
5 devil, fiend, Satan **6** diablo **7** Lucifer, Old Nick, serpent **9** Beelzebub **10** Old Scratch **13** Old Gooseberry

apologetic
5 sorry **7** defense **8** contrite, penitent **9** regretful, repentant **10** remorseful **11** attritional, penitential **12** compunctious **13** justification

apologia
7 defense **11** elucidation, explanation **13** clarification, justification

apologue
4 myth **5** fable **7** parable **8** allegory

apology
6 excuse **7** defense, redress, regrets, support **8** espousal, mea culpa **9** admission **10** advocating, advocation, concession, confession **11** championing **13** justification

aporetic
6 show-me **9** quizzical, skeptical **11** incredulous, questioning, unbelieving **12** disbelieving

apostasy
7 perfidy **9** defection, desertion, falseness, recreancy

apostate
8 defector, recreant, renegade, runagate, turncoat **9** turnabout **13** tergiversator

apostatize
4 turn **6** defect, desert **8** renounce **9** repudiate **10** tergiverse **12** tergiversate

a posteriori
9 inducible, inductive

apostle
4 John, Jude, Paul **5** James, Judas, Peter, Silas, Simon **6** Andrew, Philip, Thomas **7** Matthew **8** Barnabas, disciple, follower, Matthias, preacher **9** missioner **10** colporteur, evangelist, missionary **11** Bartholomew **12** propagandist
of Germany: **8** Boniface
of Ireland: **7** Patrick
of the English: **9** Augustine
of the French: **5** Denis
of the Gauls: **8** Irenaeus
of the Gentiles: **4** Paul
of the Goths: **7** Ulfilas
to the Indians: **9** John Eliot

apothecary
7 chemist **8** druggist **10** pharmacist

apothegm
4 rule **5** axiom, gnome, maxim, moral **6** dictum, truism **7** brocard **8** aphorism

apotheosis
6 height **7** epitome **8** last word, ultimate **9** elevation **10** exaltation **11** deification, ennoblement, idolization, lionization **12** enshrinement, quintessence **13** dignification, glorification

appall
3 awe **4** faze **5** daunt, shake **6** dismay **7** horrify, overawe **11** consternate

appalling
5 awful **7** fearful **8** daunting, dreadful, horrible, horrific, shocking, terrible, terrific **9** dismaying, frightful **10** formidable, horrifying

appanage
5 right **9** privilege **10** birthright, perquisite **11** prerogative

apparatus
4 gear, tool **6** outfit, tackle **7** utensil **8** materiel, tackling **9** equipment, implement, machinery **10** instrument **11** habiliments **13** accouterments, paraphernalia
combining form: **4** stat

apparel
4 clad, duds, garb, togs **5** array, dress **6** attire, clothe **7** clothes, garment, raiment **8** clothing, enclothe **10** attirement **11** habiliments

apparent
5 clear, plain **6** patent **7** evident, obvious, seeming **8** distinct, illu-

sive, illusory, manifest, palpable, semblant **9** prominent **10** Barmecidal, noticeable, observable, ostensible **11** discernible, perceivable, unambiguous, unequivocal

apparently
combining form: **5** quasi

apparition
5 bogey, ghost, shade, spook, umbra **6** shadow, spirit, wraith **7** eidolon, phantom, specter **8** illusion, phantasm, revenant, spectrum **13** hallucination

appeal
3 beg **4** call, lure, plea, pray, pull, suit **5** brace, charm, crave, plead **6** allure, excite, invoke, orison, prayer, sue for **7** attract, beseech, entreat, glamour, implore **8** charisma, entreaty, interest, intrigue, petition **9** fascinate, importune, magnetism, seduction **10** allurement, attraction, supplicate **11** application, fascination, imploration **12** drawing power, solicitation, supplication

appealing
5 siren **8** alluring, charming **9** seductive **10** attracting, attractive, bewitching, enchanting **11** captivating, fascinating

appear
4 look, loom, rise, seem, show **5** arise, issue, sound **6** arrive, emerge **7** emanate **11** materialize

appearance
3 air **4** face, look, mien, pose, show **5** front, guise **6** aspect, facade, facies, manner **7** bearing, seeming, showing **8** demeanor **9** semblance **10** simulacrum **11** countenance
combining form: **5** phane, phany

appease
4 calm **6** pacify, soothe **7** assuage, content, gratify, mollify, placate, relieve, satisfy, sweeten **10** conciliate, propitiate

appellation
4 name **5** nomen, style, title **7** moniker **8** cognomen **11** designation **12** denomination

append
3 add **5** annex **6** take on **7** subjoin **8** superadd

appendage
3 arm, fin, leg, tab, tag **4** barb, flap, horn, limb, seta, tail, wing

5 extra 6 cercus 7 adjunct, antenna, elytron, stipule 8 pedipalp, pendicle, tentacle 9 accessory, auxiliary 10 collateral, incidental, supplement 12 appurtenance, nonessential

appendix
5 rider 7 adjunct, codicil 8 addendum 9 accessory 10 supplement 12 appurtenance

apperception
5 grasp 11 recognition 12 apprehension, assimilation 13 comprehension, understanding

appertain
5 apply 6 bear on, belong, relate 8 bear upon

appetence
5 taste 7 stomach

appetent
4 agog, avid, keen 5 eager 6 ardent 7 anxious, athirst, craving, lusting, thirsty 8 desirous, yearning 9 impatient 10 breathless

appetite
4 bent, bias, itch, lust, urge 5 taste 6 desire, hunger, liking 7 craving, leaning, passion, stomach 8 cupidity, fondness, gluttony, penchant, soft spot, voracity, weakness 10 proclivity, propensity 11 inclination
combining form: 6 orexia
insatiable: 7 bulimia

appetizer
4 whet 6 canapé, savory, tidbit 7 zakuska 8 delicacy 9 antipasto 11 hors d'oeuvre

appetizing
5 sapid, tasty 6 savory 8 saporous 9 aperitive, palatable, relishing, toothsome 10 flavorsome 13 mouth-watering

applaud
4 clap, hail, laud, root 5 bravo, cheer, extol 6 kudize, praise, rise to 7 acclaim, commend 9 recommend 10 compliment

applause
4 hand 6 bravos, cheers 7 acclaim, ovation, rooting 8 cheering, clapping, plaudits 11 acclamation

apple
4 crab, pome 6 pippin, russet 7 Baldwin, costard, Duchess, Stayman, Wealthy, Winesap 8 Cortland, greening, Jonathan, McIntosh, pearmain 9 Delicious

10 Rome Beauty 11 Granny Smith, Gravenstein, Northern Spy, Transparent
combining form: 4 pomi
dessert: 5 crisp
genus: 5 Malus
juice: 5 cider
relating to: 5 malic

applejack
5 cider 6 brandy

apple knocker
4 hick, jake 5 yokel 6 rustic 7 bucolic, bumpkin, hayseed, hoosier, redneck 10 provincial

apple-polish
4 fawn 5 cower, toady 6 cringe, grovel, kowtow 7 honey up, truckle 8 bootlick 9 brownnose

apple-polisher
5 toady 8 bootlick, clawback, groveler, lickspit 9 brownnose, sycophant 10 bootlicker, brownnoser, footlicker 11 lickspittle

applesauce
5 fudge, hooey 6 bunkum 7 baloney, rubbish, twaddle 8 malarkey, nonsense 9 poppycock 12 blatherskite

appliance
3 use 4 play 6 usance 9 operation 10 employment 11 application
kitchen: 4 oven 5 mixer, range, stove 7 blender, toaster 9 can opener 10 dishwasher 12 refrigerator

applicability
3 use 5 avail 7 account, fitness, utility 9 advantage, relevance 10 usefulness

applicable
3 apt, fit 4 just, meet 5 ad rem 6 seemly 7 apropos, correct, fitting, germane 8 apposite, material, pointful, relevant, suitable 9 befitting, pertinent 10 felicitous 11 applicative, applicatory, appropriate

applicant
6 seeker 7 hopeful 8 aspirant 9 candidate

application
3 use 4 heed, plea, suit 5 study 6 appeal, debate, orison, prayer, usance 8 entreaty, exercise, exertion, petition 9 appliance, attention, operation 10 employment, exercising 11 imploration, imprecation 12 deliberation, supplication 13 concentration, consideration

applicatory
5 ad rem 7 apropos, germane 8 apposite, material, pointful, relevant 9 pertinent

applied
combining form: 6 techno

apply
3 dab, use 4 bend, give, turn, urge 5 press 6 accost, appeal, bear on, bestow, devote, direct, employ, handle, relate, resort, take on 7 address, beseech, entreat, implore, pertain, utilize 8 approach, bear upon, exercise, petition, set about 9 appertain, importune, undertake 10 buckle down

appoint
3 arm, rig, tap 4 gear, name 5 equip 6 assign, finger, fit out, outfit 7 dress up, furbish, furnish, turn out 8 accouter, accredit, delegate, nominate 9 authorize, designate, embellish 10 commission

appointment
3 job 4 date, post, spot 5 berth, place, tryst 6 billet, office 8 position 9 situation 10 connection, engagement, rendezvous 11 assignation

apportion
3 lot 4 give 5 allot, allow, divvy, quota, serve, share, split 6 assign, bestow, divide, parcel, ration 7 deal out, dish out, dole out, measure, mete out, prorate 8 allocate, dispense, separate, share out 9 admeasure, partition 10 administer, distribute

apportionment
4 meed, part 5 quota, share 6 ration 7 measure, quantum 9 allotment, allowance

apposite
5 ad rem 6 timely 7 apropos, germane 8 material, pointful, relevant 9 pertinent 10 applicable 11 applicative, applicatory

appositeness
5 order 9 propriety 10 expediency 11 suitability

appraisal
5 stock 8 estimate, judgment 9 valuation 10 assessment, estimation, evaluation

appraise
4 rate 5 assay, audit, judge, set at, value 6 assess, survey 7 adjudge, examine, inspect, valuate 8 estimate, evaluate 10 scrutinize

appreciable

5 clear, plain **7** evident, obvious **8** apparent, concrete, manifest, material, palpable, sensible, tangible **10** detectable, observable **11** discernible, perceptible, substantial

appreciate

4 know, like, love **5** enjoy, grasp, prize, savor, value **6** admire, esteem, fathom, regard, relish **7** apprize, cherish, cognize, respect **8** treasure **9** apprehend, delight in **10** comprehend, understand

appreciation

7 tribute **9** gratitude **11** recognition, testimonial **12** gratefulness

apprehend

3 dig, nab, see **4** bust, fear, know, take, twig **5** catch, grasp, pinch, run in, seize, sense **6** absorb, accept, arrest, detain, digest, divine, fathom, pick up, take in, wise up **7** catch on, cognize, compass, foresee, make out, preknow, previse, realize **8** conceive **9** penetrate, recognize, visualize **10** anticipate, appreciate, understand

apprehensible

5 lucid **8** knowable, luminous **10** fathomable

apprehension

4 care, fear, idea **5** alarm, angst, dread, pinch, worry **6** arrest, notion, pickup, unease **7** anxiety, capture, concern, thought **8** disquiet **9** agitation, detention, misgiving **10** conception, foreboding, perception, solicitude, uneasiness **11** disquietude, premonition

apprehensive

5 alive, awake, aware **6** afraid **7** anxious, fearful, knowing **8** sensible, sentient **9** cognizant, conscious

apprentice

4 colt, tyro **6** novice, rookie **7** learner, trainee **8** beginner, freshman, neophyte, newcomer **9** novitiate **10** tenderfoot

apprenticed

5 bound **8** articled **10** indentured

apprise

4 clue, post, tell, warn **6** advise, fill in, inform, notify, reveal, wise up **8** acquaint, announce **11** communicate

apprize

5 value **6** esteem **7** cherish **8** treasure **10** appreciate

approach

4 near, nigh **5** reach, rival, touch, verge **6** accost, advise, amount, border, trench **7** address, advance, apply to, attempt, bespeak, consult **8** endeavor, overture **11** approximate

approaching

6 coming **7** nearing **8** oncoming, upcoming **11** forthcoming

approbate

5 favor **6** accept **7** approve **11** countenance

approbation

2 OK **4** okay **5** favor **6** esteem **8** approval, blessing, goodwill, sanction **10** admiration **11** benediction

approbatory

9 favorable

appropinquity

9 immediacy, proximity **10** contiguity

appropriate

3 apt, cop, due, fit **4** grab, just, lift, meet, take, true **5** annex, claim, exact, filch, grasp, pinch, right, seize, steal, swipe, usurp **6** assume, pilfer, proper, snatch, snitch, timely, useful, worthy **7** condign, desired, fitting, germane, merited, preempt, purloin **8** accroach, apposite, arrogate, deserved, eligible, entitled, relevant, rightful, suitable **9** befitting, opportune, pertinent, requisite, sequester **10** acceptable, admissible, applicable, commandeer, confiscate, convenient, felicitous, seasonable

appropriately

4 well **5** amply, right **8** properly, suitably **9** fittingly **10** acceptably, adequately, becomingly

appropriateness

3 use **5** order **7** account, aptness, fitness, service, utility **8** meetness **9** advantage, propriety, relevance, rightness **10** expediency, usefulness

appropriation

5 grant **7** stipend, subsidy **9** allotment, allowance **10** subvention

approval

2 OK **4** okay **5** favor **8** applause, blessing, sanction, suffrage **10** acceptance, compliment **11** approba-

tion, benediction, endorsement **12** commendation

approve

2 OK **4** okay **5** clear, favor, go for **6** accept, back up, praise, ratify, uphold **7** applaud, certify, commend, condone, confirm, endorse, initial, stand by, support, sustain **8** accredit, hold with, sanction **9** approbate **10** compliment **11** countenance

approximal

8 abutting, adjacent, touching **9** adjoining, bordering **10** contiguous, juxtaposed **12** conterminous

approximate

4 near, nigh, rude **5** judge, place, rough **6** reckon **8** approach, estimate, relative **11** comparative

approximately

4 most, nigh **5** about **6** all but, almost, nearly **8** well-nigh **9** nearabout **11** practically

appurtenance

7 adjunct **8** appendix **9** accessory, appendage, equipment, furniture **11** furnishings

appurtenant

8 adjuvant **9** accessory, ancillary, auxiliary **10** collateral, subsidiary **11** subservient **12** contributory

a priori

8 dogmatic, reasoned **9** deducible, deductive, derivable

apriorism

5 posit **6** thesis **7** premise **9** postulate **10** assumption **11** postulation, presumption, supposition

apron

5 stage **8** pinafore

apropos

2 re **4** as to, in re, meet **5** about, ad rem, anent, as for **6** proper **7** germane **8** apposite, material, pointful, relevant, touching **9** as regards, pertinent, regarding **10** applicable, as respects, concerning, respecting **11** applicative, applicatory, in respect to **13** with respect to

Apsu

daughter: **6** Lahamu
son: **5** Lahmu
wife: **6** Tiamat

apt

3 fit **4** just, meet **5** alert, given, prone, quick, ready **6** bright, liable, likely, prompt, proper **7** apropos, fitting **8** apposite, disposed, inclined, relevant, suitable **9** befitting, pertinent **10** felicitous **11** appropriate

aptitude
4 bent, gift **5** flair, knack **6** genius, talent **7** ability, fitness **8** capacity, tendency **10** propensity **11** disposition

aptness
4 bent, gift **5** flair, knack, order **6** genius, talent **7** faculty, fitness **8** meetness **9** propriety, rightness **10** expediency **11** suitability

aquake
5 shaky **7** aquiver, shaking **9** quivering, shivering, trembling, tremorous, tremulant, tremulous

aqua vitae
4 grog **5** booze, drink, hooch **6** liquor, tipple **7** alcohol, spirits

aqueduct
5 canal **6** course **7** channel, conduit **11** watercourse

Aquila star
6 Altair

aquiver
see **aquake**

Arab chief
4 emir **5** sheik **6** sheikh, sultan

Arab country
4 Iraq, Oman **5** Egypt, Libya, Qatar, Sudan, Syria, Yemen **6** Jordan, Kuwait **7** Algeria, Bahrain, Lebanon, Morocco, Tunisia **11** Saudi Arabia

arable
7 fertile **8** fruitful, tillable **10** cultivable, productive

Arachne
father: **5** Idmon
form: **6** spider
mother: **6** Cyrene
rival: **6** Athena **7** Minerva

arachnid
4 mite, tick **6** acarus, spider **8** scorpion **9** phalangid, tarantula **10** harvestman

Aran
brother: **2** Uz
father: **6** Dishan

arbiter
5 judge **6** umpire **7** referee **9** moderator

arbitrary
4 rash **7** erratic, wayward **8** absolute, arrogant, despotic, freakish, heedless, oracular, whimsied **9** autarchic, impetuous, tyrannous, vagarious, whimsical **10** autocratic, capricious, monocratic, tyrannical **11** dictatorial, magisterial, precipitate **12** unreasonable **13** authoritarian

arbitrate
5 judge **6** umpire **7** adjudge, mediate, referee **9** intervene **10** adjudicate **12** intermediate

arbitrator
5 judge **6** umpire **7** referee **8** mediator **9** moderator

arbor
5 bower **6** casino, gazebo **7** pergola **9** belvedere **11** summerhouse

arc
3 bow, lob **4** arch, bend **5** curve, round **7** rainbow **9** curvation, curvature

arcadia
4 Eden, Zion **6** heaven, utopia **8** paradise **9** Cockaigne, fairyland, Shangri-la **10** lubberland, wonderland **12** promised land

arcane
6 mystic, secret **8** numinous **10** cabalistic, mysterious, unknowable **11** inscrutable **12** impenetrable **13** unaccountable

Arcas
father: **4** Zeus **7** Jupiter
mother: **8** Callisto

arch
3 bow, coy **4** bend, hump, pert **5** chief, cocky, curve, first, fresh, roach, round, saucy, vault **6** bantam, camber, cheeky, cocket, impish **7** leading, playful, premier, roguish **8** champion, flippant, foremost, malapert **9** curvation, curvature, principal **10** coquettish **11** mischievous
inner curve: **8** intrados
kind: **4** flat, ogee **5** ogive, round, Tudor **6** lancet **7** rampart, trefoil **9** horseshoe, primitive, segmental **10** shouldered **11** equilateral
outer curve: **8** extrados
part: **8** keystone, springer, voussoir
pointed: **4** ogee **5** ogive

archaeological site
Africa: **8** Zimbabwe
Crete: **7** Knossos
Egypt: **6** Naqada **9** Al-Bahnasa **11** Oxyrhynchus
England: **10** Stonehenge
Greece: **7** Mycenae, Olympia
Iraq: **2** Ur **4** Isin, Nuzi **5** Issin **7** Babylon, Nineveh
Israel: **7** Jericho
Italy: **7** Pompeii
Turkey: **4** Troy **9** Hissarlik

archaeologist
5 Evans (Arthur) **6** Carter (Howard) **7** Thomsen (Christian), Woolley (Leonard), Worsaae (Jens) **8** Breasted (James), Goodyear (William), Piranesi (Giambattista) **10** Schliemann (Heinrich) **11** Winckelmann (Johann)

archaic
3 old **5** dated, passé **6** bygone **7** antique **8** outdated **9** out-of-date, primitive, unevolved **10** antiquated **11** undeveloped **12** old-fashioned
combining form: **4** pale **5** palae, paleo **6** palaeo

arched
4 bent **5** bowed, round **6** curved **7** arrondi, rounded **8** arciform **11** curvilinear
combining form: **3** tox **4** toxi, toxo

archer
4 Tell (William) **5** Cupid **6** bowman **9** Robin Hood **11** Sagittarius, toxophilite

archery
9 toxophily
combining form: **3** tox **4** toxi, toxo

archetypal
5 ideal, model **7** classic, typical **9** classical, exemplary **12** paradigmatic, prototypical

archetype
5 ideal, model **6** mirror **7** example, pattern **8** exemplar, original, paradigm, standard **9** beau ideal, prototype **10** protoplast

archfiend
5 demon, devil, Satan **8** succubus

Archimedes' cry
6 eureka

archipelago
Asian: **5** Malay
Canada: **6** Arctic
Japan: **4** Goto **9** Gotoretto
Norway: **11** Spitsbergen
off Scotland: **7** Orcades, Orkneys **13** Orkney Islands
off South America: **14** Tierra del Fuego

architect
4 sire **5** maker **6** author, father **7** creator, founder **8** designer, inventor **9** generator, patriarch **10** originator
American: **3** Pei (Ieoh Ming) **5** McKim (Charles), Stone (Edward

Durell), Weese (Harry), White (Stanford) **6** Breuer (Marcel), Rogers (Isaiah), Soleri (Paole), Upjohn (Richard), Walter (Thomas), Warren (William), Wright (Frank Lloyd) **7** Johnson (Philip), Latrobe (Benjamin), Renwick (James), Sturgis (John Hubbard) **8** Bulfinch (Charles), Saarinen (Eero, Eliel), Sullivan (Louis), Thornton (William), Yamasaki (Minoru) **10** Richardson (Henry Hobson)

Brazilian: **8** Niemeyer (Oscar)

English: **4** Shaw (Richard), Wood (John), Wren (Christopher) **5** Jones (Inigo), Scott (George Gilbert), Wyatt (James) **6** Street (George Edmund), Voysey (Charles) **8** Vanbrugh (John)

Finnish: **5** Aalto (Alvar)

French: **6** Perret (Auguste) **11** Le Corbusier

German: **8** Schinkel (Karl)

German-American: **7** Gropius (Walter)

Italian: **6** Romano (Giulio) **7** da Vinci (Leonardo), Orcagna, Peruzzi (Baldassare), Raphael, Vignola (Giacomo da) **8** Palladio (Andrea), Sangallo (Giuliano da), Terragni (Giuseppe) **9** Sansovino (Jacopo) **12** Michelangelo

Japanese: **5** Tange (Kenzo)

Roman: **9** Vitruvius

architecture

6 design, makeup **9** formation **11** composition **12** constitution, construction

ornament: **4** boss, fret **5** gutta **6** finial, pampre, patera, volute **7** cabling, console, crocket, diglyph **8** encarpus, triglyph, vignette **9** arabesque, guilloche, modillion

style: **5** Doric, Greek, Ionic, Tudor **6** Gothic, Norman, Rococo **7** Baroque **8** Colonial, Georgian **9** Byzantine, Victorian **10** Corinthian, Romanesque **11** Renaissance **13** Mediterranean

archive

6 record **7** library **8** document, monument **9** athenaeum

arch-shaped

8 arciform

arctic

3 icy **4** cold, cool **5** chill, gelid, nippy **6** chilly, frosty, hiemal **7** glacial, numbing **8** freezing, hibernal **11** hyperborean

animal: **3** auk, fox **4** bear, hare, seal, vole **5** sable, whale **6** er-

mine, marten **7** caribou, lemming **8** reindeer **9** ptarmigan

base: **4** Etah (Greenland)

bird: **3** auk

cetacean: **7** narwhal

current: **8** Labrador

dog: **5** husky **7** Samoyed **8** malamute, malemute

explorer: **4** Byrd (Richard), Cook (Frederick) **5** Bylot (Robert), Davis (John), Peary (Robert) **6** Baffin (William), Bering (Vitus), Henson (Matthew), Hudson (Henry), Nansen (Fridtjof), Nobile (Umberto) **7** Barents (Willem), Bennet (Floyd), Wilkins (George), Wrangel (Ferdinand) **8** Amundsen (Roald) **9** Ellsworth (Lincoln), Mackenzie (Alexander), MacMillan (Donald) **10** Stefansson (Vilhjalmus)

forest: **5** taiga

jacket: **5** parka **6** anorak

people: **4** Lapp **5** Aleut, Yakut **6** Eskimo, Koryak, Tungus, Zyrian **7** Chukchi, Samoyed **9** Kamchadal

sea: **4** Kara **6** Laptev **7** Barents, Chukchi **8** Beaufort **9** Greenland

transport: **7** dogsled

treeless plains: **6** tundra

ardent

3 hot **4** agog, avid, keen, true **5** eager, fiery, loyal **6** fervid, heated, intent, red-hot, strong, torrid **7** anxious, athirst, blazing, burning, earnest, fervent, flaming, intense, staunch **8** appetent, constant, desirous, faithful, powerful, resolute, sizzling, vehement, whitehot **9** allegiant, impatient, impetuous, impulsive, scorching, steadfast **10** breathless, hot-blooded, passionate **11** impassioned **12** enthusiastic

ardor

4 fire, zeal, zest, zing **5** gusto, piety, verve **6** fealty, fervor, spirit, warmth **7** avidity, loyalty, passion **8** devotion, fidelity **9** calenture, eagerness **10** allegiance, enthusiasm **12** faithfulness

arduous

4 hard **5** rough, sheer, steep, tight **6** abrupt, trying, uphill **7** labored, operose, tricksy **8** sideling, toilsome **9** difficult, laborious, strenuous **11** precipitate, precipitous

area

4 belt, zone **5** field, place, range, realm, scene, space, tract **6** domain, locale, region, sector, sphere **7** expanse **8** district, locality, prov-

ince, vicinage, vicinity **9** bailiwick, territory **12** neighborhood

combining form: **3** gea **4** gaea

dark, shaded: **5** umbra

unit: **4** acre **7** hectare

arena

5 scene **7** stadium, theater **8** coliseum **10** hippodrome **12** amphitheater

Ares

4 Mars

consort: **5** Venus **9** Aphrodite

father: **4** Zeus **7** Jupiter

mother: **4** Enyo, Hera, Juno

sister: **4** Eris

son: **5** Remus **7** Romulus

arête

5 crest, merit **6** virtue **7** quality **10** excellence, excellency, perfection

Arethusa's pursuer

7 Alpheus

argent

6 silver **7** silvern, silvery

Argentina

capital: **11** Buenos Aires

monetary unit: **4** peso

Arges

7 Cyclops

brother: **7** Brontes **8** Steropes

father: **6** Uranus

mother: **4** Gaea

argon

symbol: **2** Ar

Argonauts' leader

5 Jason

argot

4 cant **5** lingo, slang **6** jargon, patois, patter **7** dialect **10** vernacular

arguable

4 moot **7** dubious **8** doubtful **9** debatable, uncertain **10** disputable **11** problematic **12** questionable

argue

4 moot **5** claim, clash **6** assert, attest, bicker, debate, differ, hassle, object **7** agitate, bespeak, canvass, contend, discept, discuss, dispute, dissent, justify, protest, quarrel, quibble, stickle, testify, witness, wrangle **8** announce, conflict, disagree, indicate, maintain, polemize, squabble **9** thrash out **10** polemicize **11** expostulate, remonstrate

argument

3 row **4** fuss **5** theme, topic **6** debate, dustup, hassle, motive, reason, rumpus **7** dispute, polemic, sorites, subject, wrangle **8** rebuttal **10** contention, dissension, squabbling **11** controversy, disputation, embroilment **12** disagreement

argumentation
6 debate **7** dispute, mooting, oratory **8** forensic, rhetoric **9** dialectic **11** controversy, disputation

argumentative
9 litigious, polemical **11** contentious **12** disputatious **13** controversial

Argus
father: **4** Zeus **7** Jupiter
mother: **5** Niobe
slayer: **6** Hermes **7** Mercury

argute
4 high **5** cagey, heady, savvy, sharp **6** piping, shrewd, shrill, treble **8** piercing **9** sagacious **13** perspicacious

aria
3 lay **4** hymn, lied, song **5** ditty **7** descant

Ariadne
father: **5** Minos
husband: **7** Theseus
mother: **8** Pasiphae

arid
3 dry **4** drab, dull, sere **5** dusty, tepid **6** barren, boring, dreary **7** bone-dry, insipid, sterile, tedious, thirsty **8** bromidic, droughty, weariful **9** dryasdust, infertile, unwatered, waterless, wearisome **10** unfruitful **12** moistureless **13** uninteresting

Ariel's master
8 Prospero

Aries
3 ram

aright
4 well **5** fitly **6** justly, nicely **8** decently, properly **9** correctly, fittingly **10** decorously

arise
4 lift, soar **5** begin, get up, issue, mount, start **6** ascend, aspire, spring, uprear **7** emanate, proceed **8** commence **9** originate

Aristaeus
father: **6** Apollo
mother: **6** Cyrene
son: **7** Actaeon
wife: **7** Autonoe

aristarch
5 momus **6** carper, critic, Zoilus **7** caviler, knocker **10** criticizer **11** faultfinder

Aristocles
5 Plato

aristocracy
5 elite **6** bon ton, gentry, jet set **7** who's who **8** nobility, noblesse, smart set **9** beau monde, blue blood, gentility, haut monde **10** patricians, patriciate, upper class, upper crust **13** carriage trade

aristocrat
9 blue blood, gentleman, patrician
ancient Greek: **8** eupatrid
Russian: **5** boyar **6** boyard

Aristophanes play
6 Plutus **8** The Birds, The Frogs **9** The Clouds

arithmetic
4 math **8** figuring **9** ciphering, reckoning **11** calculation, computation, mathematics

Arizona
capital: **7** Phoenix
college: **11** Grand Canyon
motto: **11** God Enriches
nickname: **16** Grand Canyon State
state bird: **10** cactus wren
state flower: **13** saguaro cactus

Arkansas
capital: **10** Little Rock
motto: **13** The People Rule
state bird: **11** mockingbird
state flower: **12** apple blossom

ark landfall
6 Ararat

arm
3 bay, ell, gun, rig **4** cove, gear, gulf, wing **5** annex, bayou, equip, firth, force, inlet, power **6** fit out, harbor, muscle, outfit, slough, weapon **7** appoint, furnish, turn out **8** accouter, strength **9** extension
bone: **4** ulna **6** radius **7** humerus
combining form: **6** brachi **7** brachio
muscle: **6** biceps **7** triceps

armada
4 navy **5** fleet

armadillo
genus: **7** Dasypus
giant: **4** tatu **5** tatou
nine-banded: **4** peba, peva
relative: **5** sloth **8** anteater
seven-banded: **6** mulita
six-banded: **5** poyou **6** peludo

small: **5** pichi **10** pichiciago **11** quirquincho
three-banded: **4** apar **5** apara
twelve-banded: **7** tatouay

armament
4 ward **5** aegis, armor, guard **6** shield **7** defense **8** security **9** safeguard **10** protection

armamentarium
4 fund **5** stock, store **6** supply **9** inventory

armchair
8 fauteuil

armed
combining form: **5** hoplo

armed attendant
9 bodyguard

armed forces
4 army, navy **6** troops **8** air force, military **10** servicemen

armistice
5 truce **9** cease-fire

armor
4 mail, ward **5** aegis, cover, guard **6** shield **7** buckler, defense, shelter **8** armament, security **9** safeguard **10** protection
arm: **8** brassart
body: **7** cuirass
armpit: **8** pallette
buttocks: **5** culet
coat: **7** hauberk **10** brigandine
combining form: **5** hoplo
elbow: **6** couter **9** cubitiere
face: **5** visor **6** beaver
flexible: **4** mail
foot: **7** sabaton, soleret **8** sabbaton, solleret
forearm: **8** vambrace
hand: **8** gauntlet
head: **6** helmet
horse: **4** bard **5** barde **6** crinet **7** peytral, peytrel, poitrel **8** chamfron, chanfron, criniere
knee: **11** genouillere
leg: **4** jamb **5** jambe **6** greave **7** jambeau
mail: **4** coif **7** hauberk **8** chausses
neck: **6** camail
shoulder: **7** ailette **8** pauldron, pouldron **9** epauliere
skirt: **6** tonlet
suit: **7** panoply
thigh: **4** tace **5** cuish, tasse **6** tasset, tuille **8** flancard **9** flanchard
throat: **6** gorget

armory
4 dump **5** depot **7** arsenal **8** magazine

armpit
6 axilla 8 underarm
Scottish: 5 oxter

arms
7 ensigns, warfare 8 weaponry

army
4 host, rout 5 crowd, flock, horde
6 legion, scores 7 militia
9 multitude
combat arm: 5 armor 8 infantry
9 artillery
commission: 6 brevet
Fort: 3 Dix, Lee, Ord 4 Hood, Knox,
Polk, Sill 5 Bliss, Bragg, Lewis,
Meade, Riley 6 Carson, Eustis, Gordon, Monroe, Rucker 7 Belvoir,
Benning, Jackson, Shafter 8 Campbell, Holabird, Huachuca, Monmouth 9 McClellan, McPherson
10 Sam Houston 11 Leavenworth
law enforcer: 2 MP
mascot: 4 mule
meal: 4 chow, mess
mine layer: 6 sapper
NCO: 8 corporal, sergeant
officer: 5 major 7 captain, colonel,
general, warrant 10 lieutenant
post: 4 base, camp, fort
postal abbreviation: 3 APO
relating to: 7 martial 8 military
school: 3 OCS, OTS 7 academy
9 West Point
store: 2 PX 10 commissary 12 post
exchange
unit: 5 corps, squad, troop 7 brigade, cavalry, company, platoon
8 division, regiment
vehicle: 4 jeep, tank 6 Humvee
9 half-track

Arnold's coconspirator
5 André

aroma
4 balm, odor 5 scent, smell, spice
7 bouquet, incense, perfume 9 fragrance, redolence

aromatic
5 balmy, spicy, sweet 6 savory
7 perfumy 8 fragrant, perfumed,
redolent 9 ambrosial

around
4 back, near, nigh, over 5 about,
again, circa 6 anyhow, extant,
nearby, random 7 anywise,
through 8 at random, existent, existing, randomly 9 haphazard
10 throughout 11 any which way,
haphazardly 13 helter-skelter
prefix: 4 ambi, amph, peri 5 amphi
6 circum

around-the-clock
8 constant 9 continual, incessant,
perpetual 10 continuous 11 unremitting 13 uninterrupted

arouse
4 fire, stir, wake, whet 5 alert,
pique, rally, waken 6 awaken, bestir, excite, incite, kindle, work up
7 inflame 9 challenge

arraign
3 tax, try 6 accuse, charge, indict
7 impeach 9 criminate, inculpate
11 incriminate

arrange
4 plan, sort 5 array, chart, order,
unify 6 assort, codify, design, devise, lay out, map out, scheme, set
out 7 dispose, marshal 8 organize,
sequence, tabulate 9 blueprint, harmonize, integrate, methodize
10 categorize, symphonize, synthesize 11 choreograph, orchestrate,
systematize

arrangement
5 order, setup 6 layout, lineup, series 8 ordering, sequence 9 structure 11 disposition 12 distribution
combining form: 4 taxy 5 taxis
6 tactic
of five objects: 8 quincunx
suffix: 4 osis

arrant
4 rank 5 gross, total, utter
6 brassy, brazen 7 blatant, flat-out
8 absolute, complete, impudent, infernal, overbold 9 barefaced,
downright, out-and-out, shameless,
unabashed 10 unblushing

arras
7 drapery 8 tapestry

array
3 lot 4 clad, garb, pomp, show
5 batch, bunch, clump, dress,
group, order 6 attire, bundle,
clothe, parade 7 apparel, arrange,
cluster, display, dispose, garment,
marshal, panoply, raiment 8 enclothe, organize, spectrum
11 systematize

arrears
3 due 4 debt 9 liability
12 indebtedness

arrect
6 raised 7 heedful, stand-up, upright 9 advertent, attentive, intentive, observant, regardful
10 straight-up, upstanding

arrest
3 nab 4 bust, halt, jail, stay, stem,
stop 5 catch, check, pinch, run in,
stall 6 collar, detain, lock up,
pickup, pull in, retard, stop up
7 capture, contain, seizure 8 imprison, obstruct, restrain 9 apprehend, detention, interrupt 11 incarcerate 12 apprehension

arresting
6 marked, signal 7 salient 9 affective, appealing, prominent
10 attractive, enchanting, impressive, noticeable, remarkable
11 conspicuous, outstanding

arride
6 divert, please 7 beguile, delight,
gladden, gratify 8 pleasure 9 delectate, entertain

arrival
6 advent, coming 7 success 8 entrance, incoming 9 emergence
10 appearance

arrive
4 come, show 5 get in, reach
6 show up, thrive, turn up 7 prosper, succeed 8 flourish

arriviste
7 parvenu, upstart 8 roturier
12 nouveau riche

arrogance
5 pride 6 hubris, hybris, morgue
7 disdain, hauteur 9 loftiness, superbity 11 haughtiness

arrogant
5 cocky, proud, puffy, wiggy
6 lordly, snooty, snotty, stuffy
7 bloated, haughty, pompous
8 cavalier, fastuous, insolent, superior 10 disdainful, peremptory,
pontifical 11 domineering, highfalutin, magisterial, overbearing
12 supercilious 13 high-and-mighty,
self-important
Scottish: 7 paughty

arrogate
4 grab, take 5 annex, seize, usurp
6 assume 7 preempt 8 accroach,
take over 9 sequester 10 commandeer, confiscate 11 appropriate,
expropriate

arrondi
4 bent 5 arced, bowed, round
6 arched, curved 7 rounded 8 arciform 11 curvilinear

arrow
combining form: 3 tox 4 toxi, toxo
7 hastato

poison: 4 upas 5 urare, urari 6 antiar, curara, curare, curari, oorali 7 woorali, woorari 8 antiarin

arrow-like
6 beloid 7 hastate 8 sagittal 9 sagittate

arrowroot
3 pia 5 araru, tuber 6 ararao 7 coontie, maranta

arroyo
3 gap 4 draw 5 brook, chasm, cleft, clove, creek, gorge, gulch, gully 6 clough, coulee, ravine, stream 7 channel

arsenal
4 dump 5 depot, store 6 armory 8 magazine 10 depository, repository, storehouse

arsenic
symbol: 2 As

arsonist
5 firer, torch 7 firebug 10 incendiary

art
5 craft, skill, trade 6 métier 7 cunning, finesse, know-how, slyness 8 artifice, foxiness, vocation, wiliness 9 cageyness, canniness, dexterity, expertise 10 adroitness, craftiness, handicraft, profession
combining form: 4 typy 6 techno
faddish: 6 kitsch
style: 2 op 3 pop 6 rococo 7 baroque, Bauhaus, Islamic, optical, surreal 8 abstract, cubistic, romantic 9 arabesque, Byzantine, Christian, classical, dadaistic, realistic 11 Renaissance 12 naturalistic, surrealistic
suffix: 3 ery 4 ship

Artegal's wife
11 Britomartis

Artemis
5 Diana
birthplace: 5 Delos
brother: 6 Apollo
father: 4 Zeus 7 Jupiter
mother: 4 Leto 6 Latona
priestess: 9 Iphigenia

artery
3 way 4 path, road 5 aorta, track 6 avenue, street, vessel 7 carotid, highway 8 coronary 9 boulevard 12 thoroughfare

artful
3 sly 4 foxy, oily, wily 5 suave 6 adroit, astute, crafty, smooth,

tricky 7 cunning 8 guileful 9 dexterous, insidious 10 diplomatic

arthropod
3 bee, fly 4 crab, moth 6 beetle, insect, shrimp 7 lobster 8 arachnid, barnacle, chilopod, diplopod, myriapod, myriopod 9 butterfly, centipede, cockroach, millipede 10 crustacean
body segment: 6 somite, telson 8 metamere
class: 7 Insecta 8 Symphyla 9 Arachnida, Chilopoda, Crustacea, Diplopoda, Pauropoda
limb segment: 6 podite 8 podomere

Arthur
see **King Arthur**

article
2 an 3 the 4 item 5 essay, paper, point, theme, thing 6 object 7 element 10 particular 11 composition, stipulation

articled
5 bound 10 indentured

articulate
3 say 4 join, oral 5 order, utter, vocal 6 fluent, prolix, relate, sonant, spoken, voiced 7 connect, phonate 8 eloquent 9 enunciate, garrulous, harmonize, integrate, pronounce, talkative 10 coordinate 11 concatenate 12 smooth-spoken

artifice
4 play, ploy, ruse, wile 5 craft, feint, guile, trick 6 deceit, device, gambit 7 cunning, knavery, slyness 8 foxiness, trickery, wiliness 9 adeptness, cageyness, canniness, chicanery, ingenuity, rascality, stratagem 10 adroitness, cleverness, craftiness 11 skulduggery

artificial
4 fake, faux, mock, sham 5 dummy, false, put-on 6 ersatz, forced, unreal 7 assumed, feigned, labored, man-made, pretend 8 affected, spurious 9 contrived, imitation, insincere, simulated, synthetic, unnatural 10 fabricated, factitious, fictitious, substitute

artillery
6 rocket 8 cannonry, howitzer, ordnance, weaponry

artillery plant
11 burning bush

artisan
7 builder, workman 9 carpenter, craftsman

artist
3 ace 4 whiz 5 adept 6 expert, master, wizard, wonder 8 virtuoso 10 first-rater, past master, topnotcher
garb: 5 smock
knife: 7 spatula
medium: 3 oil 5 chalk, paint 6 pastel 7 tempera 8 charcoal 10 watercolor
pigment board: 7 palette
stand: 5 easel
workshop: 6 studio 7 atelier
(see also **painter**)

artless
4 free 5 naive 6 simple 7 natural 8 trusting, unartful 9 childlike, ingenuous, unstudied 10 aboveboard, forthright, unaffected, unschooled 12 unartificial, unsuspicious

arty
8 imposing 9 overblown 11 pretentious 12 high-sounding

as
3 for 5 being, since, while 7 because 11 considering

Asa
father: 6 Abijam 7 Elkanah
grandfather: 8 Rehoboam
grandmother: 6 Maacah

____ as a pin
4 neat

as a rule
7 usually 8 commonly 9 generally 10 frequently, ordinarily

Ascanius
5 Iulus
father: 6 Aeneas

ascend
4 lift, rise, soar 5 arise, climb, crest, mount, scale 6 aspire, uprear 7 upclimb 8 escalade, escalate, surmount

ascendancy
8 dominion 9 dominance, masterdom, supremacy 10 domination, prepotency 11 preeminence, sovereignty 13 preponderance

ascendant
6 master 7 regnant 8 ancestor, dominant, forebear 9 paramount, precursor, prevalent, sovereign 10 forefather, forerunner, progenitor 11 overbearing, predecessor, predominant, predominate 12 preponderant, primogenitor

ascension
4 rise 6 rising

ascent
4 rise 5 climb 6 rising 7 raising
9 elevation, uplifting

ascertain
5 learn 7 catch on, find out, unearth 8 discover 9 determine

ascetic
3 nun 4 monk 5 stern, stoic 6 hermit, severe 7 austere, eremite, recluse 8 anchoret 9 abstinent, anchorite, mortified 10 abstemious, astringent, forbearing, restrained 11 disciplined, self-abasing, self-denying
ancient Hebrew: 6 Essene
Buddhist: 5 bonze 7 bhikshu
early Christian: 7 stylite
Hindu: 4 Yogi 5 fakir, Yogin

Asclepius
see **Aesculapius**

ascribe
3 lay 4 cite 5 refer 6 assign, charge, credit, impute 8 accredit 9 attribute

Asenath
husband: 6 Joseph
son: 7 Ephraim 8 Manasseh

aseptic
8 retiring 9 shrinking, unaffable, withdrawn 10 restrained 11 unexpansive

asexual
6 agamic 7 agamous
combining form: 4 agam 5 agamo

as for
2 re 4 in re 7 apropos 8 touching 9 regarding 10 concerning, respecting

as good as
4 nigh 5 about 6 all but, almost, nearly 8 well-nigh 9 just about, nearabout 11 essentially, practically 13 approximately

ash
4 soot 7 cinders, residue 8 clinkers

ashake
6 aquake 7 aquiver, ashiver, quaking 9 quivering, shivering, trembling, tremulous

ashamed
6 abased, abject 7 abashed, hangdog, humbled 8 contrite, penitent 9 chagrined, mortified, repentant 10 humiliated 11 discomfited, embarrassed

ashen
4 gray, pale 5 faded, livid, lurid, waxen 6 doughy, pallid 7 ghostly, macabre 8 blanched, bleached 9 cinereous, colorless 10 corpselike

Asher
daughter: 5 Serah
father: 5 Jacob
mother: 6 Zilpah
son: 4 Isui 6 Beriah, Ishuah, Jimnah

Ashhur
father: 6 Hezron
mother: 5 Abiah

ashiver
see **ashake**

Asia
country: 4 Iran, Iraq, Laos, Oman 5 Burma, China, India, Japan, Nepal, Qatar, Syria, Yemen 6 Bhutan, Cyprus, Israel, Jordan, Kuwait, Russia, Taiwan 7 Armenia, Bahrain, Georgia, Lebanon, Myanmar, Vietnam 8 Cambodia, Malaysia, Maldives, Mongolia, Pakistan, Sri Lanka, Thailand 9 Indonesia, Kampuchea, Singapore 10 Azerbaijan, Bangladesh, Kazakhstan, Kyrgyzstan, North Korea, South Korea, Tajikistan, Uzbekistan 11 Afghanistan, Philippines, Saudi Arabia 12 Turkmenistan
ethnic group: 3 Han, Jew, Lao, Tai 4 Arab, Kurd, Moor, Shan, Thai, Turk 5 Karen, Khmer, Malay, Tajik, Tamil, Uzbek 6 Burman, Indian, Korean, Lepcha, Manchu, Mongol, Sindhi 7 Baluchi, Bengali, Chinese, Iranian, Persian, Punjabi, Russian, Tibetan 8 Armenian, Assyrian, Japanese, Javanese, Nepalese 9 Dravidian, Indo-Aryan, Pakistani, Sinhalese 10 Circassian, Montagnard, Singhalese, Vietnamese 13 Khalkha Mongol
language: 3 Lao 4 Urdu 5 Hindi, Malay, Tamil, Uzbek 6 Arabic, Hebrew, Korean, Nepali 7 Bengali, Burmese, Khalkha, Kurdish, Persian, Tibetan, Turkish, Yiddish 8 Armenian, Japanese, Javanese, Mandarin 9 Cambodian 10 Vietnamese 15 Bahasa Indonesia

aside
4 awry 5 apart, askew 6 askant, aslant, aslope 7 askance, slantly 8 excursus, sideways 9 excursion, obliquely, slantways, slantwise 10 digression, discursion, divagation, slantingly 11 parenthesis

aside from
3 bar 4 save 6 bating, except 7 barring, besides 9 excluding, outside of 11 exclusive of

as if
combining form: 5 quasi

asinine
5 silly 6 absurd, simple 7 fatuous, foolish, puerile, witless 8 mindless 9 brainless 10 irrational, weakheaded

ask
3 beg, bid 4 quiz, seek 5 crave, exact, query 6 appeal, demand, desire, invite 7 beseech, call for, canvass, consult, enquire, entreat, examine, implore, inquire, request, require, solicit 8 question 9 catechize, importune 11 interrogate
Scottish: 5 speer, speir

askance
4 awry 5 askew 8 cockeyed 9 cock-a-hoop, crookedly, cynically 10 critically, doubtfully, doubtingly 11 skeptically 12 suspiciously 13 distrustfully, mistrustfully

asker
6 beggar, prayer, suitor 9 suppliant 10 petitioner, supplicant 11 supplicator

askew
4 awry 6 askant 7 askance 8 cockeyed 9 cock-a-hoop, crookedly

aslant
5 aside 6 aslope 8 sideways, sidewise 9 obliquely 11 slaunchways
combining form: 5 plagi 6 plagio

asleep
4 dead, idle, numb 5 inert 6 dozing, numbed 7 defunct, dormant, napping 8 benumbed, deadened, inactive 9 exanimate, senseless, unfeeling 10 insensible, unanimated 11 unconscious 12 anesthetized

as long as
3 for 5 cause, since 6 seeing 7 because, whereas 11 considering

as much as
6 all but, almost 8 well-nigh 11 essentially, practically

asomatous
8 bodiless 10 discarnate, immaterial, unphysical 11 disembodied, incorporeal 13 insubstantial

aspect
4 look, mien, side 5 angle, facet, phase 7 bearing, seeming 10 appearance

asperity
5 rigor **8** acerbity, acrimony, grimness, hardness, hardship, mordancy, tartness **9** harshness, roughness **10** bitterness, difficulty, inclemency, inequality, unevenness **11** vicissitude **12** irregularity, irritability

asperous
5 harsh, rough **6** craggy, jagged, rugged, uneven **7** scraggy, unlevel **8** scabrous, unsmooth

asperse
4 slur **5** libel **6** defame, insult, malign **7** baptize, immerse, slander, traduce **8** christen, sprinkle **9** denigrate **10** calumniate, scandalize

aspersion
4 muck, slam, slur **5** abuse **7** calumny, obloquy, slander **9** invective, stricture **10** detraction, reflection **12** vituperation **13** animadversion

asphalt
7 bitumen **8** blacktop

asphyxiate
5 choke **6** stifle **7** quackle, smother **9** suffocate

aspirant
6 seeker **7** hopeful **9** applicant, candidate

aspiration
3 aim **4** goal **6** desire **8** ambition **9** objective **10** pretension **13** ambitiousness

aspire
3 aim, try **4** long, pant, rise, soar **5** arise, mount **6** ascend, hunger, thirst, uprear

aspiring
7 emulous, wanting, wishful **8** vaulting, yearning **9** ambitious

as regards
2 re **4** in re **7** apropos **8** touching **10** concerning, respecting

ass
4 donk, fool, jerk, moke **5** burro, idiot **6** donkey **8** imbecile **10** nincompoop
female: **5** jenny
male: **4** jack
wild Asian: **5** kiang **6** onager **8** chigetai

assail
4 beat **5** beset, pound, storm **6** attack, buffet, fall on, oppugn, pummel, strike **7** aggress, assault **8** fall upon

assailment
5 onset **6** attack **7** assault, offense **9** offensive, onslaught **10** aggression

Assam silkworm
4 eria

assassin
3 gun **5** bravo **6** gunman, hit man **7** torpedo **8** murderer **9** cutthroat **10** gunslinger, hatchet man, triggerman
of Caesar: **6** Brutus **7** Cassius
of Garfield: **7** Guiteau (Charles Julius)
of J.F. Kennedy: **6** Oswald (Lee Harvey)
of Lincoln: **5** Booth (John Wilkes)
of Marat: **6** Corday (Charlotte)
of R.F. Kennedy: **6** Sirhan (Sirhan)

assassinate
4 cool, do in, kill **6** finish, murder, rub out **7** bump off, execute, put away **8** knock off **9** liquidate

assault
3 mug, war **4** raid **5** beset, fight, onset, set-to, storm **6** assail, attack, fall on, onfall, strike **7** aggress, mugging, offense **8** fall upon, invasion **9** offensive, onslaught **10** aggression, assailment

assay
3 try **4** rate, seek, test **5** offer, value **6** assess, strive, survey **7** attempt, valuate, venture **8** appraise, endeavor, estimate, evaluate, struggle **9** undertake

assemblage
4 ruck **5** crowd, group **6** muster **7** company, turnout **9** gathering **10** collection **11** aggregation **12** congregation

assemble
4 call, form, make, mass, mold **5** amass, build, clump, group, shape **6** gather, muster, summon **7** cluster, collect, convene, convoke, fashion, marshal, produce, round up **8** congress, contrive **9** aggregate, forgather **10** accumulate, congregate **11** manufacture, put together

assembly
4 band, bevy, crew, ruck **5** bunch, covey, crowd, group, party, rally **6** muster, troupe **7** cluster, company, meeting **8** conclave **9** congeries, gathering **10** collection **11** association **12** congregation
American Indian: **6** powwow
ancient Greek: **8** ecclesia
ancient Roman: **7** comitia
anglo-Saxon: **4** moot **5** gemot **6** gemote **8** folkmoot, folkmote
ecclesiastical: **5** synod **10** consistory
Hawaiian: **3** hui
Irish: **4** feis
legislative: **4** diet **6** senate **8** congress **10** parliament
medieval English: **7** husting
place: **4** hall, room **5** agora **10** auditorium
Russian: **4** duma
witches': **6** sabbat **7** sabbath

assent
3 yes **5** agree **6** accede **7** consent **9** acquiesce, subscribe

assert
4 aver, avow **5** argue, claim, state, utter, voice **6** adduce, affirm, allege, avouch, defend, depose, submit **7** advance, contend, declare, express, justify, profess, protest, publish, warrant **8** announce, constate, maintain, proclaim **9** broadcast, predicate, vindicate **10** promulgate **11** disseminate

assertive
4 sure **5** pushy **7** assured, certain, pushing **8** cocksure, emphatic, forceful, positive, sanguine **9** confident, insistent **10** aggressive, resounding **11** affirmative, self-assured **13** self-confident

assertory
5 pushy **7** pushing **8** militant **10** aggressive

assess
4 deem, levy, rate, scot **5** assay, exact, judge, put on, set at, value, weigh **6** impose, reckon, survey **7** account, valuate **8** appraise, consider, estimate, evaluate

assessment
3 tax **4** duty, levy **5** stock **6** impost, tariff **8** estimate, judgment **9** appraisal, valuation **10** estimation, evaluation **12** appraisement

asset
6 credit **8** resource **9** advantage **11** distinction
opposite: **9** liability

assets
5 means, money **6** wealth **7** capital **8** bankroll, property **9** resources, valuables

assiduous
4 busy **7** moiling, operose, zealous **8** diligent, sedulous, tireless **9** labo-

rious **11** hard-working, industrious **13** indefatigable

assiduously
4 hard **9** earnestly, intensely **10** thoroughly **11** intensively **12** exhaustively **13** painstakingly, unremittingly

assign
3 fix, set **4** cede, deed, give **5** allot, allow, refer **6** charge, convey, credit, define, impute, remise, settle **7** appoint, ascribe, lay down, mete out, station **8** accredit, allocate, make over, relegate, sign over, transfer **9** admeasure, apportion, attribute, establish, prescribe **10** pigeonhole

assignation
4 date **5** tryst **9** allotment **10** engagement, rendezvous **11** appointment, get-together

assignee
5 agent, proxy **6** deputy, factor **8** attorney

assignment
3 job **4** duty, task **5** chare, chore, stint **6** devoir **10** obligation

assimilate
5 adopt, liken, match **6** absorb, equate, imbibe, insorb **7** compare, inhaust, paragon **8** parallel **11** incorporate

assimilation
9 awareness **11** mindfulness, recognition **12** apperception **13** consciousness

assist
3 aid **4** abet, help, lift **5** do for, stead **6** relief, succor **7** comfort, help out, secours, support **8** benefact **9** cooperate

assistance
3 aid **4** help, lift **6** relief, succor **7** backing, comfort, secours, subsidy, support **9** upholding **10** subvention, supporting

assistant
3 aid **4** aide, help **5** aider **6** flunky, helper, lackey, minion, second, stooge **7** acolyte, ancilla, orderly, striker **8** adjutant, henchman **9** attendant, auxiliary, coadjutor **10** aide-de-camp, coadjutant, lieutenant **12** right-hand man

assistive
6 aidant, aiding **7** helpful **11** serviceable

assize
3 law **4** rule **5** canon, edict **6** decree **7** precept, statute **8** standard **9** ordinance, prescript **10** regulation

associate
3 pal **4** ally, chum, join, link, mate, yoke **5** buddy, crony, match, merge, unite **6** cohort, comate, couple, fellow, friend, hobnob, relate **7** bracket, combine, compeer, comrade, conjoin, connect, consort, partner **8** confrere, familiar, federate, intimate **9** affiliate, bedfellow, colleague, companion, copartner **10** accomplice, amalgamate, compatriot, complement, consociate **11** concomitant, confederate, correlative, counterpart, running mate **12** acquaintance **13** accompaniment, brother-in-arms, comrade-in-arms

associated
combining form: **3** sym, syn

associated with
suffix: **2** ic **4** ical

association
4 axis, bloc, club, hint **5** guild, order, tie-up, union **6** hookup, league **7** cahoots, circuit, concert, society **8** alliance, congress, overtone, relation, sodality, teamwork **9** coalition, undertone **10** conference, connection, federation, fellowship, fraternity, suggestion **11** affiliation, brotherhood, combination, conjunction, connotation, cooperation, implication, partnership **12** conjointment, organization, relationship, togetherness **13** collaboration

assort
5 class, group, order **7** arrange **8** classify, stratify **9** methodize **10** categorize, pigeonhole **11** systematize

assorted
5 mixed **6** fitted, motley, suited, varied **7** adapted, matched **8** chowchow **11** conformable, promiscuous **12** conglomerate, multifarious **13** heterogeneous, miscellaneous

assortment
4 olio **6** jumble, medley **7** mélange, variety **8** mishmash, pastiche **9** potpourri **10** hodgepodge, miscellany **11** gallimaufry

assuage
4 calm, ease **5** allay **6** pacify, soothe **7** appease, lighten, mollify, placate, relieve **8** mitigate **9** alleviate **10** conciliate, propitiate

as such
5 per se **13** intrinsically

assumably
6 likely **8** probably **9** doubtless

assume
3 act, don **4** fake, sham, take **5** bluff, feign, get on, posit, put on, seize, usurp **6** affect, draw on, expect, reckon, slip on, strike, take on **7** believe, imagine, preempt, premise, presume, pretend, suppose, suspect **8** accroach, arrogate, shoulder, simulate **9** postulate **10** commandeer, presuppose, understand **11** appropriate, counterfeit

assumed
5 put on **7** feigned **8** affected, delusory, putative, spurious **9** deceptive **10** artificial, factitious

assumption
5 posit **6** thesis **7** premise, surmise **9** apriorism, postulate **10** conjecture **11** supposition

assurance
5 nerve, troth **6** aplomb, parole, pledge, safety, surety **8** audacity, safeness, security, sureness, temerity **9** brashness, certainty, certitude, cockiness, composure, guarantee, hardiness, sangfroid, self-trust **10** brazenness, confidence, conviction, equanimity **11** presumption

assure
5 cinch **6** ensure, insure, secure **7** promise, satisfy **8** convince, persuade

assured
4 cool **6** secure **7** certain, decided **8** clear-cut, composed, definite, sanguine **9** collected, confident, unruffled **10** pronounced, undoubtful **11** unflappable **13** imperturbable, self-confident

assuredness
6 surety **9** certainty, certitude **10** confidence, conviction

Assyria
capital: **5** Calah **7** Nineveh
city: **4** Hara, Opis **5** Ashur, Assur, Kalhu **6** Asshur
god: **3** Sin **4** Asur, Nabu **5** Ashur, Assur, Nusku **6** Asshur, Tammuz **7** Ninurta
goddess: **6** Ishtar

king: 3 Pul 6 Sargon 11 Sennacherib, Shalmaneser 12 Ashurbanipal, Assurbanipal
language: 7 Aramaic
measure: 4 cane, foot 5 gasab, makuk 6 artaba, gariba 7 mansion
queen: 9 Semiramis
river: 6 Tigris
writing: 9 cuneiform

astatine
symbol: 2 At

astern
3 aft 4 rear 5 abaft

Asterope
father: 5 Atlas
mother: 7 Pleione
sisters: 8 Pleiades

as to
2 re 4 in re 7 apropos 8 touching 9 regarding 10 concerning, respecting

astonish
5 alarm, amaze 7 astound 8 affright, dumfound, surprise 9 dumbfound 11 flabbergast

astonishing
7 amazing 8 wondrous 9 marvelous, wonderful 10 astounding, miraculous, prodigious, stupendous, surprising 11 spectacular 12 breathtaking

astound
5 amaze 8 astonish, dumfound, surprise 9 dumbfound 11 flabbergast

astounding
see **astonishing**

Astraea
father: 4 Zeus 7 Jupiter
mother: 6 Themis

astral
6 dreamy, starry 7 exalted, highest, stellar 8 sidereal 9 daydreamy, stellular, top-drawer, unworldly, visionary 10 top-ranking 11 daydreaming 12 otherworldly

astray
4 awry 5 amiss, badly, wrong 6 afield

astricted
5 bound 7 costive 10 obstipated 11 constipated

astringent
4 keen 5 acrid, harsh, sharp, stern, tonic 6 biting, bitter, severe, strict 7 ascetic, austere, caustic, cutting,

styptic 8 incisive, roborant 11 contracting 12 constrictive

astrologer
11 Nostradamus

astrological aspect
5 trine 7 sextile 8 quartile 10 opposition 11 conjunction

astronaut
4 Ride (Sally) 5 Glenn (John), Young (John) 6 Aldrin (Edwin), Cooper (Gordon), Lovell (James), Worden (Alfred) 7 Bluford (Guion), Collins (Michael), Gagarin (Yuri), Grissom (Gus), Jemison (Mae), Schirra (Walter), Shepard (Alan), Yegorov (Boris) 8 Stafford (Thomas) 9 Armstrong (Neil), Carpenter (Scott), McAuliffe (Christa) 10 Tereshkova (Valentina)

astronomer
American: 3 See (Thomas Jefferson) 6 Lowell (Percival) 7 Langley (Samuel), Newcomb (Simon) 8 Tombaugh (Clyde) 9 Pickering (Edward) 11 Schlesinger (Frank)
Austrian: 13 Schwarzschild (Karl)
Dutch: 6 Sitter (Willem de) 7 Huygens (Christiaan)
English: 4 Ryle (Martin), Wren (Christopher) 6 Halley (Edmond), Lovell (Bernard) 7 Lockyer (Joseph), Parsons (William) 8 Herschel (Caroline, John, William)
French: 6 Picard (Jean) 7 Laplace (Pierre-Simon de), Messier (Charles)
German: 4 Wolf (Maximilian) 5 Vogel (Hermann) 6 Kepler (Johannes), Muller (Johann), Struve (Otto)
Greek: 12 Eratosthenes
Italian: 7 Galilei (Galileo) 12 Schiaparelli (Giovanni)
Persian: 11 Omar Khayyam
Polish: 10 Copernicus (Nicolaus)
Swedish: 7 Celsius (Anders)
Swiss: 6 Zwicky (Fritz)

astute
3 sly 4 deep, foxy, keen, wily 5 cagey, heady, savvy, sharp 6 argute, artful, crafty, shrewd, tricky 7 cunning, knowing 8 guileful 9 astucious, insidious, sagacious 13 perspicacious

astuteness
3 wit 6 acumen 8 keenness 10 shrewdness 11 discernment, penetration, percipience 12 perspicacity

Astyanax
father: 6 Hector
mother: 10 Andromache

asunder
5 apart

as usual
8 wontedly 10 habitually 11 customarily 12 consistently

asweat
5 puggy 8 perspiry 10 perspiring

as well
3 too, yet 4 also, even, just, more 7 besides, exactly 8 likewise, moreover 9 expressly, precisely 11 furthermore 12 additionally

as well as
6 beside, beyond 7 besides 12 over and above

as yet
5 so far 7 earlier, thus far 8 hitherto

asylum
4 home, port 5 cover, haven 6 covert, harbor, refuge 7 retreat, shelter 8 bughouse, loony bin, madhouse, nuthouse, security 9 harborage, sanctuary 10 booby hatch, crazy house, sanatorium 11 institution

asymmetric
6 uneven 7 unequal 8 lopsided 9 irregular 10 off-balance, unbalanced 12 overbalanced

Atalanta
husband: 8 Melanion
suitor: 10 Hippomenes

at all
4 ever, once 6 anyway, soever 7 anytime, anywise
Scottish: 3 ava

ataraxy
8 calmness, coolness 9 composure, sangfroid 10 equanimity

atavism
9 reversion, throwback

ataxia
5 chaos, snarl 6 huddle, muddle 7 clutter 8 disarray, disorder 9 confusion

at close hand
4 near, nigh 6 nearby

atelier
6 studio 7 bottega 8 workshop

Athamas
daughter: 5 Helle
father: 6 Aeolus
son: 7 Phrixos, Phrixus 8 Learchus
wife: 3 Ino 7 Nephele

Athena, Athene
7 Minerva
attribute: 3 owl 5 Aegis 7 serpent

father: 4 Zeus
names: 4 Alea, Nike 5 Areia 6 Ergane, Hippia, Hygeia, Itonia, Pallas, Polias 8 Apaturia 9 Parthenos, Promachos 10 Chalinitis
shield: 4 Egis 5 Aegis
statue: 9 Palladium
temple: 9 Parthenon

athenaeum
7 library 8 archives

Athens
citadel: 9 Acropolis
founder: 7 Cecrops
last king: 6 Codrus
marketplace: 5 agora
rival: 6 Sparta
senate: 5 boule
temple: 9 Parthenon

athirst
3 dry 4 avid, keen 5 eager 6 ardent 7 anxious, dried-up 8 appetent 9 impatient 10 dehydrated, desiccated

athlete
4 jock 6 player 7 acrobat, gymnast, tumbler

athlete's foot
8 ringworm

athletic
6 active, brawny, sinewy 8 muscular, vigorous 9 energetic, strenuous
contest: 4 agon, game 5 match
field: 4 oval, ring, rink 5 arena, court 7 diamond, stadium 8 gridiron
prize: 3 cup 5 medal 6 trophy

athletics
5 games 6 sports 8 exercise 10 gymnastics, recreation 12 calisthenics

athwart
4 over 5 cross 6 across, beyond 9 crossways, crosswise 12 transversely

atiptoe
9 expectant, expecting 10 anticipant 12 anticipative, anticipatory

Atlanta's civic center
4 Omni

Atlas
brother: 10 Prometheus
daughter: 5 Hyads 6 Hyades 8 Pleiades 10 Atlantides
father: 7 Iapetus
mother: 7 Clymene
race: 5 Titan
wife: 7 Pleione

at last
7 finally

Atli
slayer: 6 Gudrun
wife: 6 Gudrun

atmosphere
3 air 4 aura, mood 6 aether, medium, milieu 7 ambient, climate, feeling, quality 8 ambiance, ambience 9 semblance 11 environment, mise-en-scène 12 surroundings
stratum: 9 exosphere 10 ionosphere, mesosphere 11 chemosphere, ozonosphere, troposphere 12 stratosphere, thermosphere
sun's: 12 chromosphere

atmospheric
4 airy 6 aerial 9 pneumatic

atoll
6 island
equatorial area: 11 Baker Island
Indian Ocean: 4 Male
Kiribati: 4 Beru 7 Abaiang, Abemama, Apamama
Marshall Islands: 4 Ebon, Mili, Ujae 6 Bikini 8 Eniwetok 9 Kwajalein
Northern Cook Islands: 8 Manahiki
North of Samoa: 7 Fakaofo
Pacific: 5 Makin 8 Johnston 10 Butaritari, Palmerston
Tokelau: 5 Atafu 10 Duke of York
Tuamotu: 10 Anaa Island 11 Chain Island
Tuvalu: 8 Funafuti

atom
3 bit, jot 4 iota, mite 5 minim, touch, trace 6 tittle 7 modicum, smidgen 8 particle
charged: 3 ion 5 anion
group: 7 radical

atomic particle
3 ion 4 beta, muon, pion 5 alpha, boson, meson 6 baryon, hadron, lepton, proton 7 fermion, hyperon, neutron, nucleon 8 electron, mesotron, neutrino, positron, thermion
hypothetical: 5 quark 6 parton

atomize
4 ruin 5 smash, wreck 6 rub out 7 destroy, shatter 8 demolish, destruct, dynamite, nebulize 9 devastate, pulverize

at once
3 now 4 away 8 directly, first off, together 9 forthwith, instantly, right away 11 immediately, straightway 12 concurrently, straightaway

atone
3 pay 6 repent 7 expiate, satisfy 10 compensate, recompense

atoner
8 penitent

Atossa
father: 5 Cyrus
husband: 6 Darius 7 Smerdes 8 Cambyses
son: 6 Xerxes

atramentous
3 jet 4 ebon, inky 5 black, ebony, raven, sable 10 pitch-black

at random
5 about 6 anyhow 7 anywise 9 haphazard 11 any which way, haphazardly 13 helter-skelter

Atreus
brother: 8 Thyestes
father: 6 Pelops
mother: 10 Hippodamia
slayer: 9 Aegisthus
son: 8 Menelaus 9 Agamemnon 11 Pleisthenes
victim: 11 Pleisthenes
wife: 6 Aerope

atrocious
4 foul, vile 6 horrid, odious, savage 7 heinous, noisome, obscene 8 shocking 9 desperate, execrable, loathsome, monstrous, offensive, repulsive, sickening 10 abominable, despicable, disgusting, outrageous, scandalous 12 contemptible

atrocity
8 enormity, savagery 9 brutality 11 heinousness 13 monstrousness

atrophy
7 decline 8 downfall 9 decadence, downgrade 10 degeneracy, devolution 11 declination 12 degeneration 13 deterioration
combining form: 4 necr 5 necro

attach
3 add, fix, tie 4 bind 5 affix, annex, rivet 6 adhere, append, fasten

attached
7 sessile

attachment
4 love 6 fealty 7 loyalty 8 adhesion, devotion, fidelity, fondness 9 adherence, affection, constancy 10 allegiance 12 faithfulness

attack
3 fit 4 raid, rush 5 beset, blitz, drive, fight, foray, onset, sally, siege, spasm, spell, storm, throe 6 access, ambush, assail, banzai,

battle, charge, fall on, harass, have at, invade, irrupt, onfall, savage, sortie, strike, tackle, turn on **7** aggress, assault, besiege, bombard, offense, seizure **8** fall upon, outbreak, paroxysm **9** beleaguer, incursion, offensive, onslaught, pugnacity **10** aggression, assailment **11** bellicosity **12** belligerence **13** combativeness

combining form: 5 lepsy **6** lepsia, lepsis

attacker

combining form: 6 mastix

attain

3 get, win **4** gain **5** reach, score **6** rack up **7** achieve, realize **10** accomplish

attainment

11 achievement, acquirement, acquisition, realization

attempt

3 try **4** seek, stab **5** assay, essay, offer, trial **6** strive **7** venture **8** endeavor, striving, struggle **9** undertake **11** undertaking

attend

3 aid **4** hear, heed, help, mind **5** watch **6** assist, convoy, escort, listen **7** care for, conduct, hearken, oversee **8** chaperon **9** accompany, companion, supervise **11** consort with

attendant

3 aid **4** help **6** helper, lackey **7** ancilla, doorman, orderly, servant, striker **8** incident **9** ancillary, assistant, satellite **10** bridesmaid, coincident, collateral **11** chamberlain, concomitant **12** accompanying

ancient Roman: 6 lictor

in court: 7 bailiff **8** tipstaff

attendants

5 suite, train **7** cortege, retinue **9** entourage

attention

4 heed, mark, note **5** study **6** notice, regard, remark **7** amenity **8** courtesy, sedulity **9** assiduity, awareness, diligence, gallantry **10** absorption, cognizance, observance **11** application, engrossment, mindfulness, observation, sensibility **12** deliberation, sedulousness **13** concentration, consciousness, consideration

attention getter

4 ahem **5** gavel

attentive

5 alert, aware **6** arrect, intent

7 heedful, mindful **8** open-eyed **9** advertent, observant, open-eared, regardful **10** interested, thoughtful **11** considerate **13** concentrating

attenuate

3 sap **4** rare, slim, thin **5** blunt, reedy **6** lessen, rarefy, shrink, slight, stalky, subtle, twiggy, weaken **7** cripple, deflate, disable, slender, squinny, subtile, tenuous, unbrace **8** enfeeble, rarefied, wiredraw **9** dissipate, undermine **10** debilitate

attest

5 argue, swear, vouch **6** affirm, verify **7** bespeak, betoken, certify, point to, testify, witness **8** announce, indicate **10** asseverate

attestation

5 proof **7** witness **8** evidence **9** testament, testimony **11** testimonial **12** confirmation

attic

4 loft **6** garret **8** cockloft

at times

9 sometimes **10** now and then **11** ever and anon, now and again **12** here and there

attire

4 clad, duds, garb, togs **5** array, dress **6** clothe, outfit **7** apparel, clothes, garment, raiment **8** accouter, clothing, enclothe **11** habiliments

attirement

see **clothes**

attitude

4 pose **5** stand **6** stance **7** posture **8** carriage, demeanor, position, posture **11** point of view

attitudinize

4 pose **7** pass for, pass off, posture **10** masquerade

attorney

5 agent, proxy **6** deputy, factor, lawyer **7** counsel **8** assignee **9** barrister, counselor, solicitor **10** counsellor

attract

4 draw, lure, wile **5** charm, court, tempt **6** allure, appeal, draw in, entice, invite, seduce **7** beguile, bewitch, enchant, solicit **8** interest, intrigue, inveigle **9** captivate, fascinate, magnetize

attraction

4 bait, call, draw, lure, pull **5** charm, mecca **6** appeal, liking **8** affinity, cynosure, sympathy **9** se-

duction **10** allurement **12** drawing power

attractive

4 cute, fair, sexy **5** bonny, dishy, siren **6** comely, lovely, luring, pretty **7** Circean, likable **8** alluring, charming, engaging, enticing, fetching, handsome, inviting, magnetic, mesmeric, tempting **9** appealing, beauteous, beautiful, beckoning, glamorous, seductive **10** bewitching, enchanting **11** captivating, fascinating, good-looking, tantalizing **13** prepossessing

attractiveness

5 charm **6** appeal, beauty, glamor

attribute

4 mark **5** refer, trait **6** assign, charge, credit, emblem, impute, symbol, virtue **7** ascribe, earmark, feature, quality **8** accredit, property **9** character

attrition

3 rue **4** ruth, wear **7** penance, remorse **8** abrasion, friction **9** penitence, penitency **10** repentance **12** contriteness

attritional

5 sorry **8** contrite, penitent **9** regretful, repentant **10** apologetic, remorseful **11** penitential

attune

7 balance, conform **9** harmonize, integrate, reconcile **10** coordinate, proportion **11** accommodate

atypical

3 odd **5** queer **7** deviant, strange **8** aberrant, abnormal, peculiar **9** anomalous, deviative, different, irregular, unnatural **11** exceptional, heteroclite **13** preternatural

auberge

3 inn **5** hotel, lodge **6** hostel, tavern **7** hospice **8** hostelry **9** roadhouse **11** caravansary, public house

Auber opera

10 Fra Diavolo

au courant

5 awake, aware **6** au fait, versed **7** abreast, knowing, versant, witting **8** familiar, informed, sentient, up-to-date **9** cognizant, conscious **10** acquainted, conversant **12** contemporary **13** up-to-the-minute

auction

Scottish: 4 roup

audacious
4 bold, rash 5 brash, brave, saucy
6 brazen, daring 7 valiant 8 fearless, impudent, insolent, intrepid, reckless, unafraid, uncurbed, valorous 9 daredevil, dauntless, foolhardy, shameless, undaunted, venturous 10 courageous, ungoverned, unhampered 11 adventurous, impertinent, temerarious, uninhibited, untrammeled, venturesome 12 contumelious, unrestrained 13 adventuresome

audacity
4 gall 5 brass, nerve 6 mettle, spirit 7 courage 8 temerity 9 assurance, brashness, cockiness, hardihood, hardiness, impudence 10 brazenness

audible
5 aural 9 auricular

audibly
5 aloud

audience
6 public 7 hearing 8 audition 9 clientage, clientele, following 10 spectators

audile
5 aural 8 acoustic

audit
4 scan 5 check, probe 6 review, survey 7 checkup 8 analysis, scrutiny 10 inspection 11 examination 13 investigation, perlustration

audition
7 hearing 8 audience

auditory
4 otic 5 aural 8 acoustic

au fait
4 able 5 right 6 decent, proper, versed 7 abreast, capable, correct, versant 8 becoming, decorous, familiar, informed 9 au courant, befitting, competent, qualified 10 acquainted, conforming, conversant

au fond
8 at bottom 9 basically, in essence 11 essentially 13 fundamentally

Augean stable
3 sty 4 sink 5 Sodom 7 cesspit 8 cesspool

auger
combining form: 6 trypan 7 trypano

Auge's son
8 Telephus

aught
4 zero 5 zilch 6 cipher 7 nothing 8 goose egg

augment
3 wax 4 hike, rise 5 boost, build, exalt, mount, raise 6 beef up, expand, extend 7 enlarge, magnify, upsurge 8 compound, heighten, increase, manifold, multiply 10 aggrandize

augmentation
4 rise 5 annex, extra, raise 7 adjunct 8 addition, increase 9 accession, accretion, increment 10 complement, enrichment 11 enhancement 13 accompaniment

augur
4 bode, omen 7 betoken, portend, predict, presage, promise, prophet, suggest 8 forebode, forecast, foreshow, foretell, indicate, prophesy, soothsay 9 adumbrate, foretoken, predictor, prefigure 10 forecaster, foreshadow, foreteller, prophesier, vaticinate 11 Nostradamus 13 prognosticate

augury
4 omen 6 boding 7 portent, presage 8 bodement 9 foretoken 10 prognostic

august
5 grand, noble 6 lordly 7 stately 8 baronial, imposing, majestic, princely, splendid 9 grandiose 11 magnificent

auk genus
4 Alca

___ au lait
4 café

au naturel
3 raw 4 nude 5 naked 6 unclad 8 buff-bare, stripped 9 unclothed, undressed 10 stark-naked

aura
3 air 4 feel, glow, halo, mood 5 aroma 6 nimbus 7 aureole, feeling 8 mystique, radiance 9 emanation, semblance 10 atmosphere

aural
6 audile 7 audible 8 acoustic, auditory 9 auricular

aureate
7 flowery 8 sonorous 9 bombastic, overblown 10 euphuistic, rhetorical 11 declamatory 13 grandiloquent

auricular
5 aural 7 audible

Auriga star
7 Capella

aurora
4 dawn, morn 7 dawning, morning, sunrise 8 cockcrow, daybreak

Aurora
3 Eos
goddess of: 4 dawn
husband: 8 Tithonus
son: 6 Memnon

auslander
5 alien 7 inconnu 8 outcomer, outsider, stranger 9 foreigner

auspex
5 augur 7 prophet 8 foreseer 10 forecaster, foreteller, prophesier, soothsayer 11 Nostradamus

auspices
5 aegis 7 backing 9 patronage 11 sponsorship

auspicious
6 benign, bright, dexter, timely 7 hopeful, timeous 9 favorable, fortunate, opportune, well-timed 10 prosperous, seasonable

Austen novel
4 Emma 10 Persuasion 17 Pride and Prejudice

Auster
see **Notus**

austere
4 bare, dour, grim, hard 5 acrid, bleak, grave, harsh, sharp, stern 6 bitter, severe, simple, somber 7 ascetic, serious 9 stringent, unadorned 10 astringent

Australia
capital: 8 Canberra
largest city: 6 Sydney
monetary unit: 6 dollar

Austria
capital: 6 Vienna
dynasty: 8 Habsburg, Hapsburg
monetary unit: 9 schilling

autarchic
4 free 8 absolute, despotic, dogmatic, separate 9 arbitrary, imperious, sovereign, tyrannous 10 autocratic, autonomous, monocratic, tyrannical 11 independent, self-reliant

authentic
4 real, true 5 pukka, right, solid, sound, valid 6 trusty 7 certain, factual, genuine 8 accurate, bona

fide, credible, faithful, reliable **9** simon-pure, undoubted, veritable **10** convincing, dependable, sure-enough **11** indubitable, trustworthy **12** questionless

authenticate

6 verify **7** bear out, confirm, justify, voucher **8** validate **11** corroborate **12** substantiate

author

4 sire **5** maker **6** father, penman, proser, scribe, writer **7** creator, founder **8** inventor, novelist, prosaist **9** architect, generator, patriarch **10** originator

American: **3** Bly (Robert), Nin (Anaïs), Poe (Edgar Allan) **4** Agee (James), Buck (Pearl), Dana (Richard Henry), Grey (Zane), King (Stephen), Mann (Thomas), Rand (Ayn), Roth (Philip), Shaw (Irwin), Uris (Leon), West (Nathanael) **5** Aiken (Conrad), Alger (Horatio), Barth (John), Crane (Hart, Stephen), Harte (Bret), Oates (Joyce Carol), O'Hara (John), Paine (Thomas), Steel (Danielle), Stone (Irving), Stowe (Harriet Beecher), Turow (Scott), Twain (Mark), Tyler (Anne), White (Edmund, Elwyn Brooks, Theodore Harold), Wolfe (Thomas), Wylie (Elinor) **6** Alcott (Louisa May), Bellow (Saul), Cabell (James Branch), Cather (Willa), Clancy (Tom), Cooper (James Fenimore), Ferber (Edna), Harris (Frank, Joel Chandler), Hersey (John), Holmes (Oliver Wendell), Hughes (Langston), Irving (John, Washington), Jewett (Sarah Orne), Kidder (Tracy), London (Jack), Mailer (Norman), Miller (Arthur, Henry, Joaquin, May), Morley (Christopher), Norris (Frank), Parker (Dorothy), Porter (Katherine Anne, William Sydney), Runyon (Damon), Singer (Isaac Bashevis), Styron (William), Updike (John), Warren (Robert Penn), Wilder (Laura Ingalls, Thornton), Wilson (August, Edmund, Harriet, Lanford), Wister (Owen), Wright (James, Richard) **7** Baldwin (Faith, James), Beattie (Ann), Clemens (Samuel Langhorne), Cozzens (James Gould), Farrell (James Thomas), Gardner (Erle Stanley), Garland (Hamlin), Glasgow (Ellen), Heyward (DuBose), Howells (William Dean), Jarrell (Randall), Johnson (Diane, James), Kerouac (Jack), Lardner (Ring), Malamud (Bernard),

Masters (Edgar Lee), Mumford (Lewis), Nabokov (Vladimir), Rexroth (Kenneth), Richter (Conrad), Roberts (Elizabeth Madox, Kenneth), Saroyan (William), Sheehan (Neil), Thoreau (Henry David), Thurber (James), Wallace (Lew), Wharton (Edith) **8** Anderson (Maxwell, Poul, Regina, Sherwood), Caldwell (Erskine), Faulkner (William), Marquand (John Phillips), Melville (Herman), Michener (James), Mitchell (Donald Grant, Margaret, S. Weir), Remarque (Erich Maria), Rinehart (Mary Roberts), Salinger (Jerome David), Sandburg (Carl), Sinclair (Upton), Spillane (Mickey), Stockton (Frank R.) Vonnegut (Kurt) **9** Burroughs (Edgar Rice, John, William Seward), Dos Passos (John), Hawthorne (Nathaniel), Hemingway (Ernest), Isherwood (Christopher), McCullers (Carson), Steinbeck (John), Wodehouse (Pelham Grenville), Woollcott (Alexander) **10** Fitzgerald (F. Scott), Tarkington (Booth)

Australian: **4** West (Morris Langlo) **5** White (Patrick) **10** Richardson (Henry Handel)

Austrian: **5** Kafka (Franz) **7** Suttner (Bertha) **10** Schnitzler (Arthur)

Canadian: **3** Roy (Camille, Gabrielle) **5** Kirby (William) **6** Atwood (Margaret), Davies (Robertson) **7** Leacock (Stephen), Raddall (Thomas), Richler (Mordecai), Service (Robert) **8** Woodcock (George) **9** de la Roche (Mazo), MacLennan (Hugh)

Chinese: **5** Han Yu

Czech: **5** Capek (Karel)

Danish: **4** Rode (Helge), Wied (Gustav) **6** Jensen (Johannes Vilhelm) **7** Holberg (Ludwig)

Dutch: **6** Vondel (Joost van den)

English: **4** Amis (Kingsley, Martin), Ford (Ford Madox, John), Lyly (John), Saki, Snow (Charles Percy), Ward (Mrs. Humphry), West (Rebecca) **5** Defoe (Daniel), Doyle (Authur Conan), Eliot (Thomas Stearns), Hardy (Thomas), James (Henry, Phyllis Dorothy), Lewis (Clive Staples, Monk, Wyndham), Lowry (Malcolm), Milne (Alan Alexander), Powys (John Cowper, Llewelyn, Theodore Francis), Reade (Charles), Spark (Muriel), Waugh (Alec, Evelyn), Wells (Charles Jeremiah, Herbert George), White (Terence Hanbury), Woolf (Leonard, Virginia), Young (Arthur, Edward, Francis

Brett) **6** Archer (Jeffrey), Austen (Jane), Belloc (Hilaire), Brontë (Anne, Charlotte, Emily), Bunyan (John), Butler (Samuel), Conrad (Joseph), Graves (Robert), Greene (Graham, Robert), Hilton (James), Hudson (William Henry), Huxley (Aldous), Lytton (Robert Bulwer-), Malory (Thomas), Orwell (George), Potter (Beatrix), Powell (Anthony), Sayers (Dorothy), Sterne (Laurence), Storey (David), Walton (Izaak) **7** Ballard (James Graham), Burgess (Anthony), Dickens (Charles), Durrell (Lawrence), Fleming (Ian), Follett (Ken), Forster (Edward Morgan), Golding (Louis, William), Kipling (Rudyard), Maugham (Robin, William Somerset), Sassoon (Siegfried), Shelley (Mary, Wollstonecraft, Percy Bysshe), Sitwell (Edith, Osbert, Sacheverell), Southey (Robert), Surtees (Robert Smith), Tolkien (John Ronald Reuel), Walpole (Horace, Hugh), Wyndham (John) **8** Christie (Agatha), Forester (Cecil Scott), Koestler (Arthur), Lawrence (David Herbert, Thomas Edward), Macaulay (Rose, Thomas Babington), Meredith (George), Sillitoe (Alan), Smollett (Tobias), Strachey (Lytton), Trollope (Anthony), Zangwill (Israel) **9** De Quincey (Thomas), Du Maurier (Daphne, George), Goldsmith (Oliver), Mansfield (Katherine), Masefield (John), Priestley (John Boynton), Radcliffe (Ann), Thackeray (William Makepeace) **10** Chesterton (Gilbert Keith), Galsworthy (John), Richardson (Dorothy, Samuel) **12** Quiller-Couch (Arthur Thomas)

Finnish: **7** Waltari (Mika) **9** Sillanpaa (Frans Eemil)

French: **4** Gide (Andre), Hugo (Victor), Kock (Charles-Paul de), Sade (Marquis de), Sand (George), Zola (Emile) **5** Camus (Albert), Dumas (Alexandre), Sagan (Francoise), Stael (Germaine de), Verne (Jules), Vigny (Alfred-Victor) **6** Balzac (Honoré de), Daudet (Alphonse), France (Anatole), Proust (Marcel), Sartre (Jean-Paul) **7** Cocteau (Jean), Gautier (Leon, Theophile), Malraux (Andre), Mauriac (Claude, Francois), Maurois (Andre), Merimée (Prosper), Rolland (Romain), Romains (Jules), Simenan (Georges) **8** Beauvoir (Simone de), Flaubert (Gustave), Marivaux (Pierre), Rabelais (Francois), Stendhal, Voltaire

9 Giraudoux (Jean) 10 Maupassant (Guy de), Saint-Simon (Duke de) 12 Robbe-Grillet (Alain)
German: 4 Böll (Heinrich) 5 Grass (Gunter), Hesse (Hermann), Storm (Theodor Woldsen), Tieck (Ludwig), Zweig (Stefan) 6 Toller (Ernst) 7 Fontane (Theodor), Richter (Jean Paul), Wieland (Christoph Martin) 8 Hoffmann (Ernst Theodor Amedeus, Heinrich), Schlegel (August Wilhelm von, Friedrich von, Johann Elias) 9 Hauptmann (Gerhart), Sudermann (Hermann) 10 Wassermann (Jakob)
Greek: 6 Lucian 11 Kazantzakis (Nikos)
Hungarian: 5 Jokai (Mor)
Icelandic: 7 Laxness (Halldor)
Irish: 5 Joyce (James) 6 Stoker (Bram) 7 Beckett (Samuel), O'Connor (Frank), Russell (George William) 8 O'Faolain (Julia, Sean), Stephens (James) 9 O'Flaherty (Liam)
Italian: 5 Verga (Giovanni) 6 Silone (Ignazio) 7 Manzoni (Alessandro), Moravia (Alberto) 8 Boccacio (Giovanni) 9 Vittorini (Elio) 10 Pirandello (Luigi), Straparola (Gianfrancesco)
Japanese: 7 Mishima (Yukio) 8 Kawabata (Yasunari), Murasaki (Shikibu) 9 Yokomitsu (Riichi), Yoshikawa (Eiji)
Lebanese: 6 Gibran (Khalil)
Norwegian: 3 Lie (Jonas) 6 Hamsun (Knut), Undset (Sigrid) 8 Bjornson (Bjornstjerne Martinius), Kielland (Alexander Lange)
Norwegian-American: 7 Rolvaag (Ole Edvart)
Polish: 7 Reymont (Wladyslaw Stanislaw) 8 Zeromski (Stefan) 11 Sienkiewicz (Henryk)
Portuguese: 6 Pessoa (Fernando)
Roman: 5 Pliny, Varro (Marcus Terentius)
Russian: 5 Gorki (Maksim *or* Maxim) 7 Andreev (Leonid Nikoleyevich), Tolstoy (Leo) 8 Turgenev (Ivan), Zamyatin (Yevgeny Ivanovich) 9 Lermontov (Mikhail), Sholokhov (Mikhail) 10 Dostoevsky (Fyodor) 11 Dostoyevsky (Fydor), Yevtushanko (Yevgeny) 12 Solzhenitsyn (Aleksandr)
Scottish: 4 Lang (Andrew) 5 Scott (Alexander, Walter) 6 Barrie (James M.), Buchan (John) 8 Urquhart (Thomas) 9 Stevenson (Robert Louis)
Spanish: 6 Baroja (Pio) 7 Alarcon (Pedro Antonio de) 9 Cervantes (Miguel de)

Swedish: 7 Johnson (Eyvind), Rydberg (Viktor) 8 Lagerlof (Selma) 10 Lagerkvist (Par), Strindberg (August)
Swiss: 4 Wyss (Johann Rudolf) 6 Frisch (Max) 9 Spitteler (Carl)
Welsh: 4 Owen (Alun, Daniel, Goronwy, John) 5 Evans (David, Evan), Wynne (Ellis)
Yiddish: 4 Asch (Sholem)

authoritarian
6 strict 8 dogmatic 9 dictative, stringent 10 oppressive, totalistic 11 dictatorial, doctrinaire, magisterial 12 totalitarian

authoritative
4 sure, true 5 sound 8 accepted, attested, dogmatic, official, orthodox 9 canonical, dictative, ex officio, trustable 10 dependable, ex cathedra, sanctioned 11 cathedratic, dictatorial, doctrinaire, irrefutable, magisterial, trustworthy 12 indisputable

authority
4 rule, sway 6 credit, expert, master, weight 7 command, control, mastery 8 prestige, virtuoso 9 influence 10 domination, governance, government, past master 12 jurisdiction

authorization
5 leave 6 permit 7 consent, go-ahead, mandate 8 sanction 9 allowance, clearance 10 green light, permission, sufferance

authorize
3 let 4 vest 5 allow 6 enable, invest, permit 7 approve, empower, endorse, entitle, license, qualify, warrant 8 accredit, sanction 10 commission 11 countenance

auto
see **automobile**

autobiographer
9 memoirist

autobiography
4 life, vita 5 diary 6 memoir 7 journal 11 confessions

autochthonous
6 native 7 endemic 10 aboriginal, indigenous

autocracy
7 tyranny 9 despotism 12 dictatorship

autocratic
7 haughty 8 absolute, arrogant, despotic 9 arbitrary, tyrannous 10 tyrannical

autodidactic
10 self-taught 12 self-educated

autograph
3 ink 4 sign 9 signature, subscribe 11 John Hancock

autoist
6 driver 8 motorist, operator

Autolycus
daughter: 8 Anticlea
father: 6 Hermes 7 Mercury

automate
8 robotize

automatic
8 habitual 9 impulsive, reflexive 10 mechanical, self-acting, unprompted 11 instinctive, involuntary, perfunctory, spontaneous, unmeditated
combining form: 4 self

automaton
5 golem, robot 7 android, machine

automobile
3 bus, car 5 buggy, coupe, racer, sedan 6 jalopy, tourer 7 flivver, hardtop, machine 8 dragster, motorcar, roadster, runabout
British: 2 MG 6 Anglia, Austin, Jaguar 7 Bentley, Daimler, Hillman, Sunbeam, Triumph 8 Vauxhall 10 Rolls-Royce 11 Austin-Healy
French: 5 Simca 7 Citroen, Peugeot, Renault
German: 3 BMW 7 Porsche 10 Volkswagen 12 Mercedes-Benz
Italian: 4 Fiat 6 Lancia 7 Ferrari 8 Maserati 9 Alfa-Romeo
Japanese: 5 Honda, Mazda 6 Datsun, Subaru, Toyota
Korean: 6 Hundai
Swedish: 4 Saab 5 Volvo

automotive pioneer
4 Benz (Carl Friedrich), Ford (Henry), Olds (Ransom Eli) 5 Evans (Oliver), Roper (Sylvester) 6 Cugnot (Nicholas Joseph), Duryea (Charles E., J. Frank), Lenoir (Etienne), Winton (Alexander) 7 Daimler (Gottlieb), Stanley (Francis, Freelan) 8 Morrison (William)

Autonoe
father: 6 Cadmus
husband: 9 Aristaeus
mother: 8 Harmonia
sister: 5 Agave
son: 7 Actaeon

autonomous
4 free 8 separate 9 autarchic, sovereign 11 independent 12 self-governed, uncontrolled

autopsy
8 necropsy 10 postmortem

auto racer

8 Foyt (A. J.) **4** Hill (Graham)
5 Clark (Jim), Petty (Richard), Unser
(Al, Bobby) **6** Fangio (Juan)
7 Brabham (Jack), Stewart (Jackie)
8 Andretti (Mario)

autumn casualty

3 DST (Daylight Saving Time)
6 leaves

auxiliary

4 aide **6** helper **7** reserve **8** adjutant, adjuvant **9** accessory, ancillary, assistant, coadjutor **10** additional, collateral, subsidiary
11 appurtenant, subservient
12 contributory **13** complementary,
supplementary
verb: **2** am, do, is **3** are, can, did,
had, has, may, was **4** been, does,
have, must, were, will **5** could,
might, ought, shall, would **6** should

avail

3 use **5** serve **6** profit **7** account,
benefit, fitness, service **9** advantage, relevance **10** usefulness
13 applicability

available

8 gettable **9** securable **10** attainable, obtainable, procurable
11 purchasable

avalanche

5 flood, slide **8** mudslide, rockfall
9 landslide, rockslide, snowslide

avarice

5 greed **7** avidity **8** cupidity, rapacity **10** greediness **12** covetousness, graspingness

avenge

5 repay, right **7** pay back, redress,
requite **9** retaliate, retribute,
vindicate

avengement

7 revenge **8** reprisal, requital, revanche **9** vengeance **11** counterblow, retaliation, retribution

avenue

3 way **4** path, road **5** track **6** artery, street **7** highway **9** boulevard
12 thoroughfare

aver

4 avow **5** state **6** affirm, assert,
avouch, depose **7** declare, profess,
protest **8** constate, maintain
9 predicate

average

3 par **4** fair, mean, norm, so-so
6 common, median, medium **8** mediocre, middling, moderate, ordinary **11** indifferent **12** intermediate

averagely

4 so-so **6** enough, fairly, rather
8 passably **9** tolerably
10 moderately

avernal

7 hellish, stygian **8** infernal, plutonic **9** cimmerian, plutonian

averse

5 balky, loath **6** afraid **7** uneager
8 backward, hesitant **9** reluctant,
resistant, unwilling **10** indisposed
11 disinclined

aversion

4 fear, hate **5** dread **6** hatred, horror **7** allergy, disgust, dislike **8** disfavor, distaste, dyspathy, loathing
9 antipathy, disliking, disrelish, repulsion, revulsion **10** abhorrence,
antagonism, repugnance **11** abomination, detestation, displeasure
13 indisposition

aversive

8 ungenial **9** repellent, repugnant
11 uncongenial **12** antipathetic
13 unsympathetic

avert

4 foil, turn, veer, ward **5** check, deter **6** thwart **7** deflect, forfend, obviate, prevent, rule out **8** preclude,
stave off **9** forestall, frustrate

avian

8 ornithic

aviary

4 cage **6** volary **8** dovecote, ornithon **9** birdhouse, columbary,
dovehouse

aviator

3 ace **5** flier, pilot **6** airman, flyboy, Wright (Orville, Wilbur)
7 birdman, Earhart (Amelia) **9** Lindbergh (Charles) **10** Richthofen
(Manfred von) **12** Rickenbacker
(Eddie)

avid

4 agog, keen **5** eager **6** ardent,
greedy **7** anxious, athirst, craving,
thirsty, wanting **8** appetent, covetous, desirous **9** impatient
10 breathless

avidity

5 greed **7** avarice **8** cupidity,
rapacity

avoid

4 bilk, duck, shun, snub **5** avert,
elude, evade, shirk **6** bypass, divert, escape, eschew **7** obviate,
prevent **8** preclude

avoidance

6 escape **7** come-off, elusion, eva-
sion **8** escaping, escapism, eschewal, shunning **9** runaround
combining form: **4** phob **5** phobo

avouch

3 own **4** aver, avow **5** admit **6** affirm, assert, depose **7** confess, confirm, declare, profess, protest
8 constate **9** predicate **11** acknowledge, corroborate

avow

3 own **4** aver **5** admit, allow,
grant, let on, own up **6** affirm, assert, avouch, depose, fess up
7 concede, confess, declare, profess, protest **8** constate, maintain
9 predicate **11** acknowledge

await

4 hope **6** expect **7** count on

awake

4 stir **5** alive, aware, rouse
6 roused **7** aroused **8** sensible,
sentient **9** au courant, cognizant,
conscious, stirred up

awaken

4 stir, whet **5** alert, rally, rouse
6 arouse, bestir, kindle

awanting

4 sans **5** minus **7** lacking, without

award

4 give, kudo **5** badge, endow,
grant, honor, kudos, medal, prize
6 accord, bestow, confer **7** concede, laurels, tribute **8** accolade
9 vouchsafe **10** blue ribbon, decoration **11** distinction
motion picture: **5** Oscar
mystery novel: **5** Edgar
record: **6** Grammy
television: **4** Emmy
theater: **4** Tony

aware

5 alert, alive, awake **7** heedful,
knowing, mindful, witting **8** informed, sensible, sentient **9** au
courant, cognizant, conscious
10 conversant **12** apprehensive

awash

4 full **6** jammed, loaded, packed
7 brimful, crammed, crowded,
stuffed **8** brimming **9** chock-full

away

3 far, fro, now, off **4** afar, gone,
over **5** apart, aside, forth, hence
7 lacking, missing, omitted, wanting
8 directly, first off, right off **9** forthwith, instantly, therefrom
11 immediately

away from

prefix: **2** ap **3** aph, apo

awe
   4 fear **5** alarm, scare **6** fright, wonder **7** startle, terrify **8** affright, frighten **9** reverence, terrorize **10** veneration, wonderment

aweigh
   5 atrip

aweless
   4 bold **5** brave **7** valiant **8** fearless, intrepid, unafraid, valorous **9** dauntless, undaunted **10** courageous

awesome
   4 eery **5** eerie **6** august, dreary, solemn **7** sublime **8** dreadful, imposing, terrific

awful
   7 fearful **8** dreadful, horrible, horrific, shocking, terrible, terrific **9** appalling, frightful **10** formidable

awfully
   4 much, very **6** hugely **7** greatly **8** whacking, whopping **9** extremely

awhile
   Scottish: **4** awee

awkward
   5 gawky, inept, nerdy, splay

6 clumsy, gauche, wooden **7** gawkish, halting, lumpish, unhandy, unhappy **8** bumbling, bungling, ungainly **9** graceless, ham-handed, ill-chosen, lumbering, maladroit **10** blundering, bunglesome, unskillful **11** heavy-handed, splathering, unfortunate **12** discommoding, embarrassing, incommodious, inconvenient, infelicitous **13** discommodious

awning
   ancient Roman: **8** velarium

awry
   5 amiss, askew, badly, wrong **6** afield, askant, astray **7** askance **8** cockeyed **9** cock-a-hoop, crookedly **11** unfavorably
   Scottish: **5** aglee, agley

ax, axe
   3 adz, can **4** adze, fire, sack **5** hache **6** bounce **7** boot out, chopper, cleaver, dismiss, hatchet, kick out **8** tomahawk **9** discharge, terminate
   blade: **3** bit
   double-headed: **6** twibil **7** twibill
   handle: **5** helve
   ice: **6** piolet

axiom
   3 law **4** rule **5** gnome, maxim, moral **6** dictum, truism **7** brocard, theorem **8** aphorism, apothegm **9** principle **10** principium **11** fundamental

aye
   2 OK **3** yea, yep, yes **4** okay **8** all right

Azariah
   brother: **7** Ahimaaz
   father: **4** Obed **5** Zadok **6** Nathan **7** Ahimaaz, Hilkiah, Jeroham, Johanan **8** Hoshaiah, Maaseiah **11** Jehoshaphat
   son: **7** Seraiah

Azimov's forte
   5 sci-fi

Aztec
   capital: **12** Tenochtitlan
   conqueror: **6** Cortes, Cortez
   emperor: **9** Montezuma
   god: **4** Xipe **6** Eecatl, Meztli, Tlaloc **9** Xipetotec **11** Xiuhtecutli **12** Quetzalcoatl
   hero: **4** Nata
   language: **7** Nahuatl
   temple: **8** teocalli

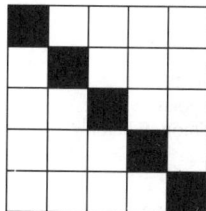

Bb

baa
5 bleat

Babbitt
4 boob 8 boeotian 10 middle-brow, philistine
author: 5 Lewis (Sinclair)

babblative
5 gabby, talky 6 chatty 9 garrulous, talkative 10 loquacious 11 loose-lipped 12 loose-tongued, multiloquent

babble
3 gab, jaw, yak, yap 4 blab, chat 5 clack, prate, run on 6 burble, drivel, gibber, jabber, patter, piffle, rattle, yammer 7 blabber, blather, chatter, maunder, palaver, prattle, twaddle 8 nonsense 9 gibberish 11 jabberwocky

babbler
Scottish: 7 blellum

babe
6 infant 7 neonate, newborn 8 bantling

babel
3 din 6 clamor, hubbub, jangle, racket, tumult, uproar 10 hullabaloo, tintamarre 11 pandemonium

baboon
6 chacma 8 mandrill 9 hamadryas

babushka
8 bandanna, kerchief

baby
3 tot 5 sissy, spoil 6 cocker, coddle, cosset, dote on, infant, pamper 7 bambino, cater to, indulge, neonate, newborn, papoose, toddler 8 bantling, dote upon, nursling, suckling, weakling, weanling 11 mollycoddle
ailment: 5 colic, croup
baptismal robe: 7 chrisom
bed: 4 crib 6 cradle 8 bassinet
bedroom: 7 nursery
breechcloth: 6 diaper
cap: 6 biggin, bonnet
carriage: 4 pram 5 buggy 8 stroller 12 perambulator
doctor: 12 pediatrician
food: 3 pap 4 milk 6 pablum
garment: 7 rompers
Italian: 7 bambino
napkin: 3 bib
nurse: 4 nana
outfit: 7 layette
powder: 4 talc
shoe: 6 bootee
Spanish: 4 bebé, nene
unborn: 5 fetus

baby grand
5 piano

babyhood
7 infancy

babyish
7 puerile 8 childish, immature 9 infantile, infantine

Babylonian
6 lavish 9 luxurious
abode of the dead: 5 Aralu
capital: 7 Babylon
chaos: 4 Apsu
city: 2 Ur 5 Accad, Akkad 6 Cunaxa, Cuthah
crown prince: 10 Belshazzar
division: 5 Accad, Akkad, Sumer
earth mother: 6 Ishtar
first ruler: 6 Nimrod
god: 2 Ea, Zu 3 Anu, Bel, Hea, Sin 4 Adad, Addu, Apsu, Enzu, Irra, Nabu, Nebo 5 Alala, Alalu, Dagan, Enlil, Kingu, Lahmu, Mummu, Ninib, Siris 6 Anshar, Marduk, Namtar, Nannar, Nergal, Ramman, Tammuz 7 Shamash 8 Ningirsu
goddess: 4 Gula, Nina 5 Aruru, Belit 6 Allatu, Belili, Beltis, Ishtar, Kishar, Lahamu, Ningal, Tiamat 7 Baalath, Damkina
hero: 5 Adapa, Etana 9 Gilgamesh
king: 6 Sargon 9 Hammurabi
priest: 2 en
priestess: 5 entum
river: 6 Tigris 9 Euphrates
ruler of the dead: 6 Nergal
storm god: 4 Adad, Adda, Addu
sun god: 3 Bel 7 Shamash
tower: 5 Babel 8 ziggurat
waters: 4 Apsu 6 Tiamat
winged dragon: 6 Tiamat

baccalaureate
6 degree 8 bachelor

bacchanal
4 orgy 5 party 7 debauch 10 saturnalia 11 bacchanalia

bacchanalian
7 drunken, reveler 9 orgiastic

bacchanal's cry
4 evoe 5 evohe

Bacchus
8 Dionysus
attendant: 6 maenad
father: 4 Zeus 7 Jupiter
lover: 5 Venus 9 Aphrodite
mother: 6 Semele
son: 7 Priapus
staff: 7 thyrsus

Bach
birthplace: 8 Eisenach
composition: 5 fugue, motet, suite 6 sonata 7 cantata, chorale, partita, prelude, toccata 8 concerto, fantasia, oratorio, sinfonia
deathplace: 7 Leipzig
musical style: 7 baroque
religion: 8 Lutheran

back
3 aid 4 abet, fund, help, hind, rear 5 about, again, dorsa (plural), round, spine, stake 6 around, assist, dorsum, hinder, rachis, recede, remote, retral, uphold 7 endorse, finance, promote, retract, retreat, reverse, sponsor, support 8 advocate, bankroll, champion, frontier,

hindmost, rearward, side with **9** in reverse, posterior, retrocede, vertebrae (plural) **10** outlandish, retrograde, round about
ailment: **7** lumbago **10** rheumatism
combining form: **2** an **3** ana, not **4** dors, noto **5** dorsi, dorso, notus **6** opisth **7** opistho
of a book: **5** spine
of an arthropod: **6** tergum
of an insect: **5** notum
of the neck: **4** nape **6** scruff
prefix: **2** re **4** post **5** retro
relating to: **6** dorsal

back answer
6 retort **7** riposte **8** comeback, repartee

backbiter
9 slanderer

backbiting
5 abuse **7** calumny, obloquy, scandal, slander **8** libelous **9** invective, maligning, traducing, vilifying **10** calumnious, defamation, defamatory, detracting, detraction, detractive, scandalous, slanderous **12** belittlement, depreciation, vituperation **13** disparagement

backbone
4 grit, guts **5** moxie, nerve, spine, spunk **6** pillar, rachis **8** mainstay **9** fortitude, vertebrae (plural) **12** spinal column

backcountry
4 bush **6** sticks **7** boonies **8** frontier **9** boondocks **10** hinterland

backcourtman
5 guard

back down
4 balk **5** demur, welsh **6** beg off, cry off, recall, recant, renege, resile **7** disavow, retract, stickle **8** withdraw **9** weasel out

backer
5 angel **6** patron, surety **7** sponsor **8** promoter **9** guarantor **10** bankroller, meal ticket

backfire
6 fizzle **8** kick back, miscarry **9** boomerang **11** fall through

background
7 scenery

backhanded
7 devious **8** indirect **9** sarcastic

backing
4 help **5** aegis **7** support **8** auspices **9** patronage **10** assistance **11** sponsorship

backland
see **backcountry**

backlash
5 slack **6** recoil **8** reaction

backlog
5 hoard, stock, store **7** nest egg, reserve **9** inventory, reservoir, stockpile

back of
5 abaft **6** behind

back off
see **back down**

backpack
8 knapsack, packsack, rucksack **9** haversack

backpedal
see **back down**

backset
5 check **7** reverse **8** reversal

backside
4 rear, rump, seat **5** fanny, hiney **6** behind, bottom, heinie **8** buttocks, derriere **9** posterior

backslide
5 lapse **6** return, revert **7** regress, relapse **9** retrovert **10** recidivate

backstabbing
7 calumny, scandal, slander **10** defamation, detraction **12** belittlement, depreciation **13** disparagement

backstairs
6 secret, sordid **7** furtive **10** scandalous

backstop
6 uphold **7** support **8** advocate, champion, side with

back talk
3 lip **4** guff, sass **5** mouth, sauce **9** impudence, insolence

backtrack
7 retrace, retreat, reverse

backward
3 shy **4** dull, slow **5** about, again, loath, round, timid **6** around, averse, demure, modest, retral, stupid **7** bashful, moronic, uneager **8** hesitant, ignorant, inverted, retarded, retiring, retrorse, reversed **9** benighted, diffident, dim-witted, in reverse, reluctant, unwilling **10** behindhand, half-witted, indisposed, retrograde, round about, slow-witted, uncultured **11** disinclined, thickheaded, undeveloped **12** feebleminded, self-effacing,

simpleminded, uncultivated **13** unprogressive

backwoods
see **backcountry**

backwoodsman
4 hick, jake **5** yokel **6** rustic **7** bumpkin, hillman **9** hillbilly **10** provincial

bacon
side: **6** flitch, gammon
slice: **6** rasher

Bacon, Francis
12 Baron Verulam
work: **12** Novum Organum

bacteria
5 cocci **7** bacilli, vibrios **8** spirilla
culture medium: **4** agar
destroyer: **10** antibiotic

bacterial disease
7 anthrax, leprosy, tetanus **8** syphilis **9** gonorrhea, pneumonia **10** diphtheria

bacteriologist
American: **6** Enders (John Franklin) **7** Noguchi (Hideyo), Theiler (Max)
British: **7** Fleming (Alexander)
French: **5** Widal (Fernand) **7** Nicolle (Charles-Jean-Henri), Pasteur (Louis)
German: **4** Cohn (Ferdinand Julius), Koch (Robert) **5** Klebs (Edwin) **7** Behring (Emil von), Loffler (Friedrick) **10** Wassermann (August von)
Japanese: **8** Kitasato (Shibasaburo)
Russian: **11** Metchnikoff (Elie)
Swiss: **6** Yersin (Alexandre-Emile-John)

bad
3 ill, low **4** down, evil, foul, null, poor, sour, void **5** amiss, lousy, rough, rowdy, tough, wrong **6** arrant, nocent, putrid, rancid, rotten, sinful, unruly, wicked **7** decayed, froward, harmful, hateful, hurtful, immoral, invalid, naughty, nocuous, noisome, noxious, peccant, spoiled, tainted, unhappy, unsound, vicious **8** damaging, dejected, downcast, inferior, perverse, wretched **9** abhorrent, defective, deficient, depressed, execrable, injurious, loathsome, miserable, obnoxious, offensive, putrefied, reprobate, repulsive, sickening, woebegone **10** decomposed, disgusting, disorderly, dispirited, ill-behaved, indecorous, iniquitous, unpleasant **11** deleterious, detrimental, displeasing, distasteful, distressing, downhearted, intolerable, misbehaving, mischievous, unfavorable

12 disagreeable, disconsolate, insufferable, unacceptable **13** objectionable
combining form: **3** cac, mal **4** caco
comparative: **5** worse
prefix: **3** dys, mis
superlative: **5** worst

Badebec
husband: **9** Gargantua
son: **10** Pantagruel

Baden, for one
3 spa

badge
3 pin **5** award, honor, kudos **6** button, emblem **7** laurels **8** accolade, insignia **10** decoration **11** distinction

badger
3 nag **4** bait, ride **5** brock, chivy, hound **6** heckle, hector **8** balisaur, bullyrag
group of: **4** cete

Badger State
9 Wisconsin

badinage
6 banter **7** joshing, kidding **8** backchat, repartee, snip-snap **9** cross talk **10** persiflage

badland
4 wild **5** waste **6** barren, desert **8** wildness **10** wilderness

badly
4 awry, illy **5** amiss, wrong **6** afield, astray **7** harshly, roughly **8** severely **9** painfully **10** rigorously **11** unfavorably
combining form: **3** mal

badman
4 hood, thug **6** bandit, outlaw **7** bandido, hoodlum, villain **8** criminal, hooligan **9** desperado

bad mark
3 gig **7** demerit

bad-tempered
6 cranky, crusty, touchy **8** choleric **9** dyspeptic **10** ill-humored, ill-natured, tempersome **12** cantankerous

Baedeker
5 guide **6** manual **8** handbook **9** guidebook, vade mecum **10** compendium **11** enchiridion

baffle
4 balk, bilk, foil, ruin **5** addle, mix up, stump **6** muddle, puzzle, thwart **7** confuse, flummox, mystify, nonplus **8** befuddle, confound **9** dumb-

found, frustrate **10** circumvent, disappoint

bafflement
9 confusion **10** perplexity

bag
3 cop, nab, net **4** grip, hook, land, nail, poke, sack **5** biddy, catch, crone, pouch, purse, seize, steal **6** beldam, collar, secure **7** capture, satchel **8** backpack, knapsack, reticule, suitcase **9** apprehend

bagatelle
6 trifle

baggage
4 gear **5** hussy, tramp, trull, wench **6** wanton **7** effects, luggage, trollop **8** slattern, strumpet

Baghdad
founder: **6** Mansur
river: **6** Tigris

bagnio
7 brothel **8** bordello, cathouse **10** bawdy house, whorehouse

Bagnold
4 Enid

bagpipe
part: **5** drone **7** bourdon, chanter
sound: **5** skirl

Bahamas' capital
6 Nassau

bail
3 dip **4** bond, lade **5** ladle, scoop **6** surety **8** guaranty, security, warranty **9** guarantee

bailiwick
5 field, realm **6** domain, sphere **7** demesne, terrain **8** district, dominion, province **9** champaign, territory **12** jurisdiction

bait
3 nag **4** lure, ride, toll, trap **5** chivy, decoy, harry, hound, leger, snare, tempt **6** allure, badger, come-on, entice, entrap, harass, heckle, hector, lead on, ledger, molest, pester, seduce **7** torment **8** bullyrag, inveigle **9** persecute **10** allurement, enticement, seducement, temptation **12** inveiglement

bake
4 burn, cook, fire, kiln **5** broil, roast **6** saggar, sagger, scorch **7** scallop, scollop, swelter

baked clay
7 ceramic

baker's dozen
8 thirteen

bakers' yeast
6 leaven

baking
3 hot **5** fiery **6** red-hot, torrid **7** burning **8** broiling, scalding, sizzling, white-hot **9** scorching
chamber: **4** kiln, oven

baksheesh
3 tip **4** alms **5** favor **6** reward **8** gratuity

Balaam
beast: **3** ass **6** donkey
father: **4** Beor

balance
4 rest **5** level, poise **6** adjust, attune, make up, offset, redeem, set off, stasis **7** harmony, remains, remanet, remnant, residue **8** atone for, coolness, leavings, outweigh, residual, residuum, symmetry **9** composure, congruity, equipoise, harmonize, remainder, stability **10** compensate, equanimity, proportion, steadiness **11** consistency, countervail, equilibrium, self-control **12** counterpoise
combining form: **5** stato

bald
4 bare, nude **5** naked, plain **6** shaven, smooth **8** glabrous, hairless **9** unadorned **11** undecorated, ungarnished **12** unornamented **13** unembellished

baldachin
4 silk **6** canopy, fabric

Balder, Baldur
father: **4** Odin
mother: **5** Frigg **6** Frigga
slayer: **4** Hoth, Loke, Loki **5** Hoder, Hothr
son: **7** Forsete, Forseti
wife: **5** Nanna

balderdash
3 rot **4** bosh **5** bilge **6** blague, bushwa **7** eyewash, rubbish **8** claptrap, malarkey, nonsense

baldness
8 alopecia

baldpate
7 widgeon **8** skinhead

balefire
6 beacon

baleful
4 dire, evil **6** malign **7** direful, fateful, malefic, ominous **8** sinister **9** illboding, ill-omened **10** maleficent, pernicious **11** apocalyptic, threatening **12** unpropitious

balk

3 gag, jib, shy **4** beam, dash, foil, ruin **5** demur **6** baffle, boggle, refuse, thwart, timber **7** scruple, stickle, stumble **8** hang back **9** frustrate **10** circumvent, disappoint

balky

5 loath **6** averse, ornery **7** froward, restive, wayward **8** contrary, hesitant, perverse **9** reluctant **11** wrongheaded **12** cross-grained

ball

3 orb, wad **5** dance, globe, round **6** sphere **7** rondure **8** conglobe, ensphere **10** conglobate
batted high: **3** fly
batted straight: **5** liner
combining form: **5** globo, spher **6** sphaer, sphero **7** sphaera, sphaero
of thread or yarn: **4** clew
ornamental: **6** pom-pom, pompon
tiny: **7** globule

ballad

3 lay **4** lied, poem, song **7** calypso
rhyme: **4** ABCB
singer: **8** minstrel **10** troubadour

ballast

5 poise **6** steady **9** stabilify, stabilize **11** stabilitate

ballerina

6 dancer **7** danseur **8** coryphee, danseuse **9** figurante **11** dancing girl

ballet

costume: **4** tutu **6** tights **7** leotard
dancer: **7** danseur **8** coryphee, danseuse, figurant **9** ballerina, figurante
for two: **9** pas de deux
handrail: **5** barre
jump: **4** jeté **8** ballonné **9** entrechat
knee bend: **4** plié
position: **6** pointe **8** attitude **9** arabesque
step: **3** pas **8** glissade
turn: **6** chaîné **9** pirouette

ball game

see at **game**

balloon sail

9 spinnaker

ball-shaped

7 globoid, globose **8** globular, spheroid **9** globulous, spherical

ball up

4 clew **5** addle **6** fuddle **7** confuse, fluster **8** befuddle, bewilder, distract, throw off

ballyhoo

4 tout **6** herald, hoopla **7** trumpet **9** publicity

balm

4 lull **5** allay, aroma, cream, quiet, salve, scent, spice, still **6** cerate, chrism, settle, soothe **7** bouquet, compose, incense, perfume, unction, unguent **8** ointment **9** fragrance, redolence **11** tranquilize

balmacaan

8 overcoat

balm of Gilead

6 poplar **9** balsam fir **12** balsam poplar

balmy

4 mild, soft **5** bland, faint, spicy, sweet **6** aromal, easing, gentle, insane, savory, smooth **7** foolish, lenient, perfumy **8** aromatic, fragrant, perfumed, pleasant, pleasing, redolent, soothing **9** agreeable, ambrosial

baloney

3 rot **4** bosh, bull, bunk **5** hokum **7** hogwash, rubbish **8** nonsense

balsam poplar

9 tacamahac **10** hackmatack **12** balm of Gilead

Balthazar's gift

5 myrrh

Baltic

native: **4** Lett **7** Latvian **8** Estonian **10** Lithuanian
state: **6** Latvia **7** Estonia **9** Lithuania

balustrade

4 rail **7** railing **8** banister

Balzac character

6 Goriot **7** Grandet **9** Birotteau

bamboozle

4 bilk, dupe, fool, gull, hoax **5** trick **6** befool **7** chicane, swindle **8** flimflam, hoodwink **11** hornswoggle

ban

4 tabu **5** taboo **6** enjoin, forbid, outlaw **8** prohibit **9** interdict **11** forbiddance, prohibition **12** interdiction, proscription

Ban

ally: **6** Arthur
son: **8** Lancelot

banal

4 flat **5** bland, corny, trite, vapid **6** watery **7** insipid, sapless **8** waterish **9** hackneyed **10** namby-pamby, pedestrian, wishy-washy **11** commonplace

banality

6 cliché, truism **7** bromide **8** prosaism **9** platitude **10** prosaicism, shibboleth **11** commonplace

banana oil

5 hokum

banausic

4 blah, dull, poky **6** dreary, earthy, stodgy **7** humdrum, mundane, sensual, worldly **8** temporal **10** monotonous, pedestrian **13** materialistic

band

4 belt, club, crew, gang, gird, tape **5** bunch, corps, covey, group, party, strap, strip, troop, unite **6** concur, fillet, girdle, league, outfit, ribbon, streak, team up, troupe **7** cluster, combine, company, conjoin **8** begirdle, cincture, coadjute, engirdle, symphony **9** cooperate, orchestra **10** encincture **12** philharmonic
combining form: **3** zon **4** taen, zono **5** taeni **6** taenio
Mexican: **8** mariachi
neck: **6** torque
of flowers: **7** wreathe
small: **5** combo

bandage

4 bind **5** dress **6** swathe **7** swaddle

bandanna

8 babushka, kerchief

bandeau

5 strip **6** fillet, ribbon, stripe **9** brassiere

banderilla

4 dart

banderole

4 flag, jack **6** banner, burgee, ensign, pennon **7** pennant **8** streamer

bandicoot

3 rat

bandit

6 badman, outlaw, raider, sacker **7** bandido, brigand, cateran, forager, ravager **8** marauder, pillager **9** cutthroat, desperado, holdup man, plunderer **10** freebooter, highwayman **11** bushwhacker
of India: **6** dacoit

bandleader

7 maestro **8** choragus **9** conductor

bandolier

4 belt

bandwagon

3 fad **4** chic, mode, rage **5** craze, style, vogue **7** fashion

bandy
4 flip, toss 6 banter 8 exchange
11 interchange

bane
4 ruin 5 venom, virus 6 poison
7 bugaboo, bugbear, undoing
8 downfall 9 contagion, destroyer,
ruination 11 destruction

baneful
4 dire 6 deadly 7 fateful, noxious,
ominous 9 ill-boding, ill-omened, injurious, pestilent, unhealthy 10 pernicious 11 apocalyptic, pestiferous,
threatening 12 pestilential,
unpropitious

bang
3 bat, hit, pep, pop, rap 4 bash,
beat, belt, blow, boom, clap, kick,
push, shot, slam, sock, wham,
whop 5 blast, burst, crash, noise,
punch, sharp, smack, smash,
sound, vigor, whack 6 thrill, wallop
7 surpass 8 smack-dab, squarely,
vitality 9 explosion

Bangladesh
capital: 5 Dacca, Dhaka
monetary unit: 4 taka

bang-up
5 dandy 7 capital 8 five-star, top-
notch, whiz-bang 9 excellent, first-
rate 10 first-class 11 first-string

banish
4 oust 5 debar, eject, evict, exile,
expel 6 deport, put out, run out
7 cast out, dismiss, exclude, expulse, shut out, turn out 8 displace,
drive out, relegate 9 discharge, ostracize, rusticate 10 expatriate
13 excommunicate

banishment
5 exile 9 expulsion, ostracism
10 relegation 11 deportation
12 displacement

Bani's son
3 Uel 5 Amram, Rehum

banister
4 rail 7 railing 10 balustrade

bank
4 heap, hill, mass, pile, save
5 beach, coast, levee, mound,
shore, stack, stash 6 invest, margin,
rely on, rivage, strand 7 build on,
count on, deposit, lay away, pyramid, trust in, trust to 8 depend on,
lay aside, reckon on, rely upon, salt
away, set aside, sock away 10 depend upon, streamside 11 calculate on 12 squirrel away

bank deal
4 loan

bankroll
4 back 5 stake 7 finance 9 grubstake 10 capitalize

bankrupt
4 bare, bust, do in, ruin 5 break,
drain, strip, use up, wreck 6 divest,
fold up, pauper 7 deplete, deprive,
exhaust 9 pauperize
10 impoverish

bankruptcy
4 ruin 7 failure 9 depletion, sterility
10 barrenness, exhaustion

banned
7 illegal, illicit, tabooed 8 en-
joined, verboten 9 forbidden
10 prohibited, proscribed

banner
4 flag, jack 6 bang-up, ensign,
pennon 7 pendant, pennant
8 champion, five-star, gonfalon,
gonfanon, standard, streamer, top-
notch 9 banderole, excellent, first-
rate, front-rank 10 blue-ribbon, first-
class 11 first-string
Roman: 7 labarum 8 vexillum

bannerol
4 flag, jack 6 ensign, pennon
7 pendant, pennant 8 streamer

banquet
4 feed 5 feast 6 dinner, junket, regale, repast, spread

banquette
4 seat 5 bench, shelf 8 platform

bantam
4 arch, fowl, grig, pert 5 saucy,
small 6 little, petite 8 malapert,
smallish

banter
3 fun, kid, rag, rib 4 fool, jest, jive,
joke, josh, razz 5 chaff, jolly, tease
7 teasing 8 backchat, badinage,
chitchat, exchange, repartee, snip-
snap 9 small talk 10 persiflage
11 give-and-take

bantling
4 babe, baby 6 infant 7 neonate,
newborn

baptize
3 dub 4 call, name 5 title 6 purify
7 asperse, cleanse, immerse
8 christen, sprinkle 9 designate
10 denominate

bar
3 ban, dam, pub, rod, tap 4 bate,
café, curb, dive, halt, save, slab,
snag, stop 5 block, brake, court,
estop, fence, ingot, limit, stick, strip
6 billet, bistro, except, hinder, impede, lounge, saloon, tavern 7 barrier, buvette, cabaret, cantina, confine, delimit, exclude, gin mill, rule
out, rummery, rumshop, suspend,
taproom 8 alehouse, blockade,
count out, drinkery, drunkery, grogshop, lawcourt, obstacle, obstruct,
pothouse, prelimit, restrict, traverse,
tribunal 9 aside from, barricade,
eliminate, excluding, honky-tonk,
nightclub, outside of, roadblock,
roadhouse 11 exclusive of, obstruction, rathskeller 12 circumscribe,
watering hole
fruit: 4 line 5 olive
iron: 6 rabble

barb
4 dart 5 shaft
combining form: 3 onc 4 onch, onci,
onco 5 oncho

Barbados
capital: 10 Bridgetown
monetary unit: 6 dollar

barbarian
3 Hun 4 Goth, rude, wild 5 brute
6 savage, Vandal 8 Visigoth 9 foreigner, Ostrogoth

barbarism
6 misuse 8 malaprop, slangism, solecism 9 neologism, vulgarism
10 corruption 11 impropriety, malapropism 13 vernacularism,
vernacularity

barbarity
7 cruelty 8 atrocity 10 inhumanity

barbarous
4 fell, grim, rude, wild 5 cruel
6 brutal, fierce, Gothic, savage, unholy, vulgar, wicked 7 Hunnish, inhuman, lowbrow, uncivil, ungodly,
wolfish 8 backward, fiendish, inhumane, sadistic 9 benighted, ferocious, graceless, heartless, primitive, tasteless, truculent
10 outlandish, outrageous, philistine, unmerciful 11 unchristian,
uncivilized 12 uncultivated

Barbary ape
5 magot

Barbary state
5 Tunis 7 Algiers, Morocco, Tripoli

barbate
7 bearded 9 whiskered
11 bewhiskered

barber
6 shaver 7 clipper, cropper, friseur

8 coiffeur 9 coiffeuse 10 haircutter
11 hairdresser, hair stylist

Barber of Seville
author: 12 Beaumarchais (Pierre-
Augustin)
character: 6 Figaro, Rosina, Rosine
7 Bartolo, Basilio 8 Almaviva,
Bartholo
composer: 7 Rossini (Gioacchino)
9 Paisiello (Giovanni)

barber's itch
8 ringworm

bard
4 muse, poet, scop 5 skald 8 jongleur, minstrel 10 Parnassian,
troubadour

bardlet
6 rhymer 8 poetling, verseman
9 poetaster, poeticule, rhymester,
versifier 10 versesmith 11 versemonger 12 versificator

Bard of Avon
11 Shakespeare (William)

bare
4 bald, mere, nude, open, show,
very, void 5 clear, empty, naked,
stark, strip 6 barren, denude, divest, expose, peeled, reveal, unclad, unveil, vacant 7 baldish, denuded, deprive, disrobe, emptied,
exhibit, exposed, uncover, unrobed, vacuous 8 bankrupt, denudate, disclose, stripped 9 dismantle, unattired, unclothed, uncovered,
undressed
combining form: 4 gymn, nudi, psil
5 gymno, psilo

barefaced
5 blunt 6 arrant, brassy, brazen
7 blatant 8 impudent, overbold
9 shameless, unabashed 10 unblushing 11 temerarious

barefoot
6 unshod 8 shoeless 9 discalced
10 unsandaled 11 discalceate

bareheaded
7 hatless

barely
4 just 6 hardly, scarce 8 scarcely

bargain
3 buy 4 bond, deal, pact, swap
5 steal, trade, truck 6 barter,
dicker, haggle, higgle, palter
7 chaffer, compact, traffic 8 closeout, contract, covenant, exchange,
giveaway, huckster 9 agreement,
negotiate 10 compromise, convention, loss leader, pennyworth
11 transaction

barge
4 scow 5 clump, stump 6 lumber
7 galumph, stumble

baritone
American: 5 Gorin (Igor) 6 Milnes
(Sherrill), Warren (Leonard) 7 Mac-
Neil (Cornell), Merrill (Robert),
Reardon (John), Tibbett (Lawrence)
8 Guarrera (Frank), Warfield
(William)
English: 6 Bailey (Norman)
German: 4 Prey (Hermann)
Italian: 5 Gobbi (Tito) 8 Raimondi
(Ruggero)

barium
symbol: 2 Ba

bark
3 arf, yap, yip 4 snap, woof, yelp
5 snarl
combining form: 6 phello 7 cortico
Scottish: 4 yaff

barkeeper
see **bartender**

barkentine
4 ship

bark remover
4 spud 7 spudder

Barlow epic
9 Columbiad

barman
see **bartender**

Barmecidal
8 apparent, illusive, illusory, semblant 10 ostensible

barn
6 stable 10 storehouse
area of: 4 loft 7 hayloft

barnacle
5 leech 7 sponger 8 hanger-on,
parasite 10 freeloader 11 bloodsucker 12 lounge lizard

barnstorm
4 tour 5 pilot 6 travel

Barnum
elephant: 5 Jumbo
midget: 8 Tom Thumb
partner: 6 Bailey

barnyard
4 foul 5 dirty, nasty 6 coarse,
filthy, smutty, vulgar 7 obscene,
raunchy 8 indecent

baron
4 czar, king 5 mogul 6 tycoon
7 magnate

baronial
5 grand, noble, royal 6 august,

lordly 7 stately 8 imposing, majestic 9 grandiose 11 magnificent

baroque
4 gilt, rich 6 florid, ornate, rococo
8 luscious 10 flamboyant,
ornamented

Baroque
architect: 7 Bernini (Gian Lorenzo)
8 Boromini (Francesco)
composer: 4 Bach (Johann Sebastian, Wilhelm Friedmann) 6 Handel
(George Frideric) 9 Scarlatti (Alessandro, Giuseppe) 10 Monteverdi
(Claudio)l
painter: 6 Rubens (Peter Paul) 7 El
Greco, Poussin (Nicolas) 8 Car-
racci (Agustino, Annibale, Lodov-
ico) 9 Velazquez (Diego)
10 Caravaggio
sculptor: 7 Bernini (Gian Lorenzo),
Coustou (Guillaume, Nicholas)
8 Coysevox (Antoine), Girardon
(Francois)

bar pin
9 brochette

barrack
6 billet, casern 7 caserne
8 quarters

barracuda
4 fish, spet 5 barry, senet 6 be-
cuna, becune, picuda, sennet
10 guaguanche, guaguancho

barrage
4 hail 5 burst, salvo, storm, surge
6 shower, stream, volley 8 drumfire
9 broadside, cannonade, fusillade
11 bombardment

barrel
3 keg, run, tun 4 butt, cask, much,
peck, pipe, rush, whiz 5 fleet,
hurry, speed 6 hasten 7 rundlet
8 hogshead 9 great deal
maker: 6 cooper
part: 4 hoop 5 stave
stopper: 4 bung
support: 6 gantry

barrelhouse
3 zip 4 dive, rush, whiz 5 hurry,
joint 6 hasten, hustle 7 hangout
9 honky-tonk

barren
3 dry 4 arid 5 bleak, stark, waste
6 desert, effete, fallow 7 badland,
parched, sterile 8 desertic, heirless,
impotent, infecund, wild land
9 childless, infertile, unbearing, unfertile, wasteland 10 unfruitful, untill-
able, wilderness 12 hardscrabble,
unproductive

barricade
3 bar 4 stop, wall 5 block, fence 7 barrier, railing 8 blockade 9 blank wall, roadblock
of trees: 6 abatis

Barrie character
4 John 5 Peter, Tommy, Wendy 7 Michael 8 Crichton 9 Tiger Lily 10 Tinker Bell 11 Captain Hook

barrier
see **barricade**

barring
3 but 4 save 6 bating, except, saving 9 aside from, excluding, outside of 11 exclusive of

barrister
6 lawyer 7 counsel 8 attorney

barroom
3 pub 6 lounge, saloon, tavern 7 taproom 8 dramshop, drinkery, groggery, grogshop

bar sinister
4 blot, blur, onus, slur, spot 5 brand, odium, stain 6 stigma 8 black eye

bartender
7 tapster 8 boniface 10 mixologist 12 saloonkeeper

barter
4 swap 5 trade, truck 7 bargain, traffic 8 exchange
Scottish: 6 niffer

Bartered Bride composer
7 Smetana (Bedrich)

Baruch
father: 6 Neriah, Zabbai
occupation: 6 scribe

basal
5 basic 6 bottom, lowest 7 primary, radical 8 simplest 10 bottommost, elementary, nethermost, pedimental, rudimental, underlying 11 fundamental, rudimentary 12 foundational

base
3 bad, bed, fix, low 4 evil, foot, mean, poor, prop, root, seat, ugly, vile 5 build, cheap, dirty, found, lousy, lowly, nadir, plant, set up, sorry, stand, tatty 6 bottom, common, filthy, ground, humble, paltry, scurvy, shoddy, sleazy, sordid, trashy, wicked 7 bedrock, caitiff, footing, ignoble, lowborn, lowdown, servile, squalid, support 8 beggarly, buttress, cowardly, pedestal, plebeian, recreant, un-

washed, unworthy, wretched 9 construct, dastardly, degrading, establish, framework, loathsome, low-minded, predicate 10 abominable, despicable, foundation, groundwork, substratum, unennobled 11 disgraceful, humiliating, ignominious 12 contemptible, meanspirited, substructure, underpinning

baseball
abbreviation: 2 AB, AL, BA, BB, BI, CF, DH, DP, ER, FA, HR, IP, LF, LP, NL, RF, SB, SO, SS, WP 3 ERA, HSP, LOB, MVP, PCT, RBI
reputed founder: 9 Doubleday (Abner)
glove: 4 mitt
official: 3 ump 6 umpire
pitch: 4 drop, heat 5 curve, smoke 6 change, heater, sinker, slider, slurve 7 spitter 8 change-up, fadeaway, fastball, fork ball, knuckler, palm ball, spitball 9 brushback, screwball 12 change of pace, knuckle curve
player: 6 batter 7 baseman, catcher, fielder, pitcher 9 infielder, shortstop 10 outfielder 11 left fielder 12 right fielder 13 center fielder
practice fly ball: 5 fungo
term: 3 bag, bat, box, fan, fly, out, run, tag, tap, tip 4 balk, ball, base, bean, bunt, cage, deck, foul, hook, line, mitt, pill, pole, save, walk 5 alley, apple, bench, bloop, clout, count, drive, error, flare, glove, homer, liner, mound, pop-up, slide, swing 6 assist, clutch, double, dugout, groove, ground, inning, inside, pop fly, pop-out, powder, putout, rubber, runner, single, strike, triple, windup 7 battery, blooper, bullpen, cleanup, diamond, floater, fly ball, home run, infield, manager, outside, pickoff, rhubarb, sidearm, squeeze, stretch 8 baseline, beanball, delivery, foul ball, grounder, keystone, outfield, pinch-hit, rosin bag, southpaw 9 full count, home plate, hot corner, line drive, sacrifice, strikeout, two-bagger 10 double play, frozen rope, ground ball, scratch hit, strike zone 11 knuckleball, pinch hitter, squeeze play, three-bagger 12 Texas leaguer

baseballer
3 Ott (Mel) 4 Bell (George), Cobb (Ty), Cone (David), Dean (Dizzy), Fisk (Carlton), Ford (Whitey), Foxx (Jimmy), Kaat (Jim), Mays (Willie), Rice (Jim), Rose (Pete), Ruth (Babe), Ryan (Nolan) 5 Aaron (Henry), An-

son (Cap), Banks (Ernie), Bench (Johnny), Berra (Yogi), Boggs (Wade), Bonds (Barry), Brett (George), Brock (Lou), Carew (Rod), Clark (Will), Davis (Mark), Grove (Lefty), Gwynn (Tony), Henke (Tom), Kiner (Ralph), Maris (Roger), Perez (Tony), Perry (Gaylord), Raines (Tim), Smith (Lee), Spahn (Warren), Staub (Rusty), Tiant (Louis), Viola (Frank), Young (Cy), Yount (Robin) 6 Dawson (Andre), Feller (Bob), Foster (George), Franco (John), Garvey (Steve), Gehrig (Lou), Gibson (Bob, Kirk), Gooden (Dwight), Herzog (Whitey), Hunter (Catfish), Koufax (Sandy), Maddox (Greg), Mantle (Mickey), Morgan (Joe), Murphy (Dale), Murray (Eddie), Musial (Stan), Palmer (Jim), Ripken (Cal), Seaver (Tom), Sutter (Bruce), Sutton (Don), Thomas (Frank), Wagner (Honus) 7 Bagwell (Jeff), Canseco (José), Carlton (Steve), Clemens (Roger), Coleman (Vince), Fingers (Rollie), Hornsby (Roger), Hubbell (Carl), Jackson (Reggie), Johnson (Walter), Justice (David), Puckett (Kirby), Reardon (Jeff), Schmidt (Mike), Speaker (Tris) 8 Anderson (Sparky), Blyleven (Bert), Clemente (Roberto), DiMaggio (Joe), Mitchell (Kevin), Righetti (Dave), Robinson (Brooks, Frank, Jackie), Williams (Ted), Winfield (Dave) 9 Alexander (Grover), Eckersley (Dennis), Henderson (Rickey), Hernandez (Willie), Hershiser (Orel), Killebrew (Harmon), Mattingly (Don) 10 Campanella (Roy), Conigliaro (Tony), Strawberry (Darryl), Valenzuela (Fernando) 11 Yastrzemski (Carl)

baseball team
see **American League; National League**

baseboard
7 molding 8 skirting

baseborn
3 low 4 mean 5 lowly 6 humble 7 bastard, ignoble, natural 8 plebeian, spurious, unwashed 11 misbegotten 12 illegitimate

baseless
4 idle, vain 5 empty, false, wrong 9 pointless, senseless, unfounded, untenable 10 gratuitous, groundless, ungrounded 11 uncalled-for, unnecessary, unsupported, unsustained, unwarranted 12 indefensible 13 unjustifiable

basement
6 bottom, ground 10 foundation, groundwork, substratum 12 substructure

base on balls
4 pass, walk

bash
3 bat 4 belt, blow, slam, whop 5 crack, party, smack, smash, whack 6 soiree, wallop 7 blowout, shindig

Bashan
last king: 2 Og
people: 7 Rephaim

Bashemath
father: 7 Ishmael
husband: 4 Esau
sister: 8 Nebaioth

bashful
3 coy, shy 5 mousy, timid 6 demure, modest 7 abashed 8 retiring, timorous 9 diffident, recoiling, shrinking, unassured 11 embarrassed, unassertive

basic
4 main 5 basal, chief 6 bottom 7 capital, element, primary, radical 8 rudiment 9 elemental, essential, primitive, principal 10 elementary, substratal, underlying 11 fundamental 12 foundational 13 part and parcel

basically
6 au fond 9 in essence 11 essentially 13 fundamentally

basic point
4 crux, gist 7 essence

basin
3 cwm, dip, sag 4 sink 6 cirque, hollow 7 sinkage 8 sinkhole, washbowl 9 concavity 10 depression
liturgical: 5 stoup 7 piscina

basis
4 root, seat 5 axiom, heart, right 6 bottom, ground, reason 7 bedrock, essence, footing, grounds, premise, theorem, warrant 9 postulate, principle 10 assumption, foundation, groundwork, substratum 11 fundamental, presumption 12 substructure, underpinning 13 justification

bask
3 sun 4 roll 5 revel 6 wallow, welter 7 indulge, rollick 9 luxuriate

basket
5 frail 6 dosser, gabion 7 pannier
angler's: 5 creel

basketball
inventor: 8 Naismith (James)
official: 6 umpire 7 referee
player: 5 cager, guard 6 center 7 forward 8 hoopster, swingman 10 point guard
team: 4 five 7 quintet
term: 3 gun, jam, key 4 cage, dunk, pass 5 board, lay-up, press, shoot, tip-in 6 freeze, tap-off, tip-off, travel 7 dribble, keyhole, rebound, throw-in, time-out 8 alley-oop, jump ball, slam dunk 9 backboard, backcourt, field goal, free throw 11 ball control

basketballer
3 Bol (Manute) 4 Bird (Larry), Reed (Willis), West (Jerry, Mark) 5 Barry (Rick), Cousy (Bob), Ewing (Patrick), Mikan (George), O'Neal (Shaquille), Price (Mark) 6 Baylor (Elgin), Cowens (Dave), Erving (Julius), Gervin (George), Jordan (Michael), Malone (Jeff, Karl, Moses), McAdoo (Bob), McHale (Kevin), Miller (Reggie), Parish (Robert), Pierce (Ricky), Pippin (Scottie), Skiles (Scott), Thorpe (Otis), Walton (Bill), Worthy (James) 7 Barkley (Charles), Dawkins (Darryl), Edwards (James), Frazier (Walt), Johnson (Magic), Russell (Bill), Rollins (Tree), Wilkins (Dominique) 8 Auerbach (Red), Havlicek (John), Olajuwon (Akeem), Robinson (David), Stockton (John), Williams (Buck) 9 Donaldson (James), Robertson (Oscar) 11 Abdul-Jabbar (Kareem), Chamberlain (Wilt)

Basmath's father
7 Solomon

Basque
cap: 5 beret
game: 6 pelota 7 jai alai
mountains: 8 Pyrenees
province: 5 Alava 7 Vizcaya 9 Guipuzcoa

bass
6 singer 7 crappie, jewfish, sunfish 8 cabrilla
American: 5 Hines (Jerome), Ramey (Samuel), Tozzi (Giorgio) 6 Morris (James) 7 Plishka (Paul), Robeson (Paul) 8 Flagello (Ezio)
Bulgarian: 8 Ghiaurov (Nicolai)
Italian: 5 Siepi (Cesare) 8 Raimondi (Ruggero)
Russian: 9 Chaliapin (Fyodor)
Swiss: 6 Corena (Fernando)

Bassanio's beloved
6 Portia

bassinet
4 pram 9 baby buggy 12 baby carriage, perambulator

bastard
5 cross 6 by-blow, hybrid 7 mongrel 8 baseborn, spurious, whoreson 10 fatherless, unfathered 11 chance child, misbegotten 12 filius populi, illegitimate, natural child 13 filius nullius
combining form: 4 noth 5 notho

bastardize
4 warp 6 debase 7 corrupt, debauch, deprave, pervert, vitiate 9 brutalize 10 bestialize, demoralize

bastardly
4 mean 12 contemptible

baste
3 wig 4 beat, drub, lash, mill, pelt, rail, whip 5 paste, scold 6 batter, berate, larrup, pummel, stitch, thrash, wallop 7 bawl out, belabor, chew out, clobber, tell off 8 bless out 10 tongue-lash

bastille
4 jail 6 prison

bastinado
3 bat 4 bash, beat, blow 5 crack, pound, smack, smash, stick, whack 6 cudgel, thwack, wallop 8 bludgeon

bastion
7 bulwark, parapet, rampart 10 breastwork

bat
3 bag, bop, bum, gad, hag, jag 4 belt, biff, blow, bust, club, mace, roam, rove, slam, sock, tear, trot, whop, wink 5 baton, biddy, binge, blink, booze, crack, crone, drunk, mooch, smack, spree, witch 6 beldam, bender, cudgel, ramble, rantan, thwack, wander 7 meander, nictate, traipse, twinkle 8 bludgeon 9 chiropter, flying fox, gallivant, nictitate, reremouse, truncheon 10 knobkerrie, shillelagh
combining form: 8 nycteris
European: 7 noctule 8 serotine 9 pipistrel 11 pipistrelle
Malaysian: 6 kalong

batch
3 lot, set 5 array, bunch, clump, group 6 bundle, clutch, parcel 7 cluster

bate
4 omit 6 deduct, except 7 exclude 8 moderate, restrain

bath
   3 spa, tub **4** wash **5** hydro, wells
6 shower **7** springs **13** watering
place
   combining form: **5** balne **6** balneo
   relating to: **7** balneal

bathe
   3 lap, lip, sop, tub **4** bask, lave,
soak, soap, wash **5** douse, flush,
souse **6** shower

bathetic
   5 mushy, soppy, stale, tired, trite
6 cliché **7** clichéd maudlin, mawkish **9** hackneyed **11** commonplace,
sentimental, stereotyped, tear-jerking **13** stereotypical

bathhouse
   5 sauna

bathing suit
   6 bikini, trunks **7** maillot

bathroom
   2 WC **6** toilet **8** lavatory

Bathsheba
   father: **5** Eliam
   husband: **5** David, Uriah
   son: **7** Solomon

bathtub gin
   5 hooch **7** bootleg **9** moonshine
11 mountain dew

bating
   3 bar, but **4** save **6** except, saving
7 barring **9** aside from, excluding,
outside of **11** exclusive of

baton
   4 club, mace, wand **5** billy
6 cudgel **7** war club **8** bludgeon
9 billy club, truncheon **10** nightstick

batrachian
   4 frog, toad **9** amphibian
10 salientian

batter
   4 beat, drub, lame, maim, maul
5 baste, pound, wreck **6** bruise,
buffet, bung up, mangle, pummel,
thrash, wallop **7** belabor, clobber,
contuse, cripple, disable, lambast,
shatter **8** lacerate, lambaste, mutilate **9** disfigure

battery
   3 lot **4** body **5** array, batch,
bunch, clump, group **6** bundle
7 cluster

battery terminal
   5 anode **7** cathode

battle
   3 tug, war **5** brush, clash, fight

6 action, assail, attack, combat, oppugn, sortie **7** assault, bombard,
contend, contest **8** conflict, skirmish
9 encounter, onslaught, scrimmage
10 engagement **11** hostilities
   combining form: **5** machy

battle-ax
   6 twibil **7** twibill

Battle Born State
   6 Nevada

battle cry
   5 motto **9** catchword
   Japanese: **6** banzai

battlement
   7 parapet

battlesome
   6 brawly **7** scrappy **8** brawling
9 brawlsome **11** quarrelsome

batty
   4 nuts **5** crazy, wacky **6** crazed,
insane, maniac, screwy **7** cracked
8 deranged **9** bedlamite

bauble
   5 curio **6** gewgaw, trifle **7** bibelot,
novelty, trinket, whatnot **8** gimcrack
9 objet d'art **10** knickknack

Baucis' husband
   8 Philemon

bavardage
   6 by-talk **8** chitchat, trifling **9** small
talk

Bavaria
   6 Bayern
   capital: **6** Munich
   city: **8** Augsburg, Bayreuth, Wurzburg **9** Nuremburg
   king: **6** Ludwig
   patron saint: **6** Rupert

bawd
   4 drab, moll **5** poule, whore **6** harlot, hooker **8** meretrix **10** prostitute
11 nightwalker **12** streetwalker

bawdy house
   4 stew **6** bagnio **7** brothel **8** bordello, cathouse, joyhouse
10 whorehouse **11** parlor house
13 sporting house

bawl
   3 cry, sob **4** howl, roar, rout, wail,
weep, yell, yowl **5** shout **6** bellow,
boohoo, clamor, holler, scream,
shriek, squall, yammer **7** blubber,
bluster, screech

bawl out
   3 wig **4** lash **5** scold **6** berate
7 chew out, condemn, tell off, up-

braid **8** bless out, denounce
10 tongue-lash

bay
   3 arm **4** cove, gulf, howl, wail
5 award, badge, bayou, bight,
creek, firth, honor, inlet, kudos,
quest **6** harbor, slough **7** laurels,
ululate **8** accolade **10** decoration
11 distinction
   Aegean Sea: **5** Anzac
   Africa: **6** Walvis
   Alaska: **7** Glacier
   Angola: **5** Bengo, Tiger **6** Tigres
   Antarctica: **3** Ice **8** Amundsen
   Arabian Sea: **4** Qamr **5** Kamar
   Argentina: **6** Blanca
   Australia: **5** Anson, Shark **6** Botany,
Sharks **9** Discovery
   Baltic: **4** Hano, Kiel **6** Danzig, Kieler
9 Pomerania **10** Pomeranian,
Pommersche
   Barents Sea: **4** Kola **7** Pechora
   Beaufort Sea: **7** Prudhoe
9 Mackenzie
   Bismarck Sea: **5** Kimbe
   Brazil: **9** Guanabara
   Bristol Channel: **10** Carmarthen
   California: **5** Morro **8** Monterey, San
Diego **12** San Francisco
   Canada: **5** Fundy
   Cape Breton Island: **4** Mira
   Capetown: **5** Table
   Caribbean Sea: **5** Limon **8** Chetumal
   Central America: **7** Fonseca
   China: **4** Mirs
   Crete: **4** Suda **5** Canea
   Cuba: **4** Broa, Mora, Nipe
10 Guantanamo
   Dominican Republic: **4** Ocoa
   East River: **8** Flushing
   Ecuador: **5** Manta
   Egypt: **6** Abukir **7** Aboukir
   Eire: **4** Clew **7** Brandon
   English Channel: **3** Tor **4** Lyme
5 Seine
   Estonia: **5** Parnu **6** Pyarnu
   Europe: **6** Biscay **11** Aquitanicus
   Florida: **8** Biscayne
   Greenland: **5** Disko **6** Baffin
8 Melville
   Gulf of Alaska: **3** Icy **5** Woman
12 Resurrection
   Gulf of Boothia: **5** Pelly
   Gulf of California: **5** Adair
   Gulf of Guinea: **5** Benin, Bonny
6 Biafra
   Gulf of Mexico: **5** Tampa **6** Mobile
7 Aransas **8** Campeche, Sarasota
9 Matagorda, Pensacola **10** San
Antonio, Terrebonne **11** Atchafa-
laya, Ponce de Leon **12** Apalachi-
cola **13** Corpus Christi

Gulf of St. Lawrence: **5** Bonne, Gaspé
Hawaii: **5** Koloa, Lawai
Hong Kong: **4** Deep
Honshu: **3** Ise **5** Mutsu, Osaka, Owari, Tokyo **6** Atsuta, Sagami
Hudson River: **7** New York
Iceland: **4** Faxa, Huna **8** Faxafloi
Indian Ocean: **6** Bengal **15** Great Australian
Indonesia: **4** Bima, Kayo **5** Saleh **8** Humboldt
Irish Sea: **4** Luce **7** Dundalk
Jamaica: **4** Long
Japan: **4** Tosa
Java: **4** Lada **5** Peper
Java Sea: **7** Batavia **8** Djakarta
Kara Sea: **6** Enisei **7** Yenisei
Lake Erie: **8** Sandusky
Lake Huron: **7** Saginaw, Thunder
Lake Michigan: **5** Green **13** Grand Traverse
Lake Ontario: **11** Irondequoit
Lake Superior: **5** Huron **8** Keweenaw **9** Whitefish
landlocked: **5** Lamon
Long Island Sound: **6** Oyster
Madagascar: **8** Antongil
Maine: **5** Casco **7** Machias **9** Penobscot
Marquesas Islands: **5** Anaho
Maryland-Virginia: **10** Chesapeake **12** Chincoteague
Massachusetts: **6** Boston **7** Cape Cod **8** Buzzards, Plymouth
Mediterranean: **9** Famagusta
Mozambique: **5** Memba, Pemba
Nantucket Sound: **5** Lewis
New Brunswick: **13** Passamaquoddy
Newfoundland: **4** Hare **5** White **7** Fortune
New Guinea: **3** Oro **5** Berau, Hansa, Milne
New Jersey: **5** Great **6** Newark **7** Raritan **8** Barnegat
New York: **7** Jamaica
New Zealand: **5** Hawke **6** Tasman **11** Hauraki Gulf
North Carolina: **6** Onslow
North Sea: **4** Jade **9** Jadebusen
Northwest Territories: **5** Wager **7** Repulse **8** Franklin **9** Frobisher
Nova Scotia: **8** Cobequid
Oregon: **4** Coos
Philippines: **5** Baler, Pilar, Sogod **6** Butuan
Puerto Rico: **5** Sucia
Quebec: **6** Ungava
Red Sea: **4** Foul
Rhode Island: **12** Narragansett
Russia: **4** Amur **5** Aniva, Chaun **6** Ussuri **7** Amurski
Scotland: **5** Enard
Sea of Japan: **13** Peter the Great

Solomon Islands: **4** Deep
South Africa: **5** Algoa, False
South Carolina: **4** Bull, Long
South China Sea: **4** Bias, Datu, Taya **5** Dasol, Subic, Subig **6** Brunei, Paluan **7** Camranh
Spain: **5** Cadiz **9** Gibraltar
Spitsbergen: **5** Cross, Kings
Sri Lanka: **4** Palk
Strait of Gibraltar: **7** Tangier
Sumatra: **5** Bajur **10** Koninginne
Sydney: **6** Botany
Tasmania: **5** Storm
Texas: **7** Trinity
Tyrrhenian Sea: **6** Naples **7** Paestum
Wales: **9** Carnarvon **10** Caernarvon
Washington: **5** Dabob **6** Skagit
Western Sahara: **8** Rio de Oro
West Indies: **5** Coral
White Sea: **5** Onega
Yellow Sea: **5** Korea

baygall
3 bog, fen **4** mire, moss, quag, sump **5** marsh, swamp **6** morass **9** swampland

bayou
3 arm, bay **4** cove, gulf **5** bight, creek, firth, inlet **6** harbor, slough
Louisiana: **5** Macon **9** Lafourche **10** Terrebonne
Mississippi: **9** Chickasaw

Bay State
13 Massachusetts

bay window
3 pod, pot **6** paunch **8** potbelly **11** corporation

bazoo
3 boo **4** bird, hiss, hoot, pooh, razz **7** catcall **8** pooh-pooh **9** raspberry **10** Bronx cheer

bazooka's target
4 tank

be
4 go on, hold, live, move **5** abide, exist, stand **6** endure, obtain, remain **7** breathe, persist, prevail, subsist **8** continue

beach
4 bank **5** coast, shore, wreck **6** pile up, strand **8** cast away, lakeside **9** lakeshore, shipwreck **10** oceanfront
Hawaii: **7** Waikiki
Massachusetts: **9** Nantasket
New York: **10** Fire Island

___ Beach
5 Dover

beached
7 aground **8** grounded, stranded

beachhead
8 foothold

beachwear
see **bathing suit**

beacon
5 flare **6** pharos **7** bonfire **8** balefire **9** watchfire **10** lighthouse

beak
3 neb, nib **4** bill, cape, naze, nose, peck, pick **5** point, snoot, snout **6** beezer, pecker **7** sneezer **8** foreland, headland **9** proboscis, schnozzle **10** promontory
combining form: **5** rostr **6** rhamph, rostri, rostro **7** rhampho **8** rhynchus

beaklike part
7 rostrum

be-all and end-all
3 sum **4** pith, root, soul, tote **5** stuff, total, whole **6** bottom, marrow **7** essence **8** entirety, sum total, totality **9** aggregate, substance **10** rock bottom **12** quintessence

beam
3 can, ray **4** balk, burn, grin, rear, seat **5** fanny, gleam, shaft, shine, shoot, smile **6** behind, bottom, lintel, rafter, timber **7** radiate **8** backside, buttocks, crosstie, derriere **9** posterior

beaming
6 bright, lucent **7** fulgent, lambent, radiant **8** luminous **9** brilliant, effulgent, refulgent **12** incandescent

bean
3 dry, wax **4** bush, coco, conk, dome, head, lima, mung, navy, pole, poll, snap, soya **5** baked, brain, broad, horse, jelly, pinto **6** belfry, coffee, frijol, kidney, noddle, noggin, noodle, string **7** frijole, jumping **9** headpiece **10** stringless
of india: **3** urd

beano
5 bingo

Bean Town
6 Boston

beany
5 fiery **6** spunky **7** gingery, peppery **8** spirited **10** mettlesome **11** high-hearted **12** high-spirited

bear
2 go **3** act, bow, jag, jam, lug, try **4** born, buck, form, go on, have, head, hump, lump, make, pack, push, quit, show, take, tote **5** abide, allow, apply, beget, birth, breed, bring, brook, bruin, carry, crowd, crush, defer, ferry, fruit,

press, refer, shape, squab, stand, stick, touch, yield 6 accept, acquit, affect, attend, behave, convey, convoy, create, demean, deport, digest, endure, escort, invent, permit, pocket, relate, seller, set out, squash, squish, squush, submit, suffer 7 afflict, comport, concern, condone, conduct, deliver, display, exhibit, fashion, involve, pertain, possess, produce, squeeze, stomach, support, sustain, swallow, take off, torment, torture, turn out 8 chaperon, engender, fructify, generate, light out, multiply, parallel, shoulder, stick out, sweat out, tolerate, tough out 9 accompany, acquiesce, appertain, companion, fabricate, procreate, propagate, reproduce, strike out, transport 10 bring forth, correspond 11 consort with, countenance
Alaskan: 5 polar 6 kodiak
Australian: 5 koala
combining form: 4 arct 5 arcto
family: 7 Ursidae
genus: 5 Ursus
kind: 3 sun 5 black, brown, honey, koala, polar, sloth 6 kodiak 7 grizzly 10 spectacled
relating to: 6 ursine
young: 3 cub

bearable
7 livable 9 allowable, endurable, tolerable 10 acceptable, admissible, sufferable 11 supportable, sustainable 12 satisfactory

bear cat
5 panda 9 binturong

beard
4 barb, dare, defy, face, fuzz 5 brave, front 6 beaver, goatee 7 galways, outdare, outface, stubble, Vandyke, venture 8 imperial, whiskers 9 burnsides, challenge 11 muttonchops 12 side-whiskers
combining form: 5 pogon 6 pogono
on grain: 3 awn
pointed: 6 goatee 7 Vandyke

bearded
5 hairy 7 barbate, goateed, stubbed, stubbly 8 unshaven 9 whiskered 11 bewhiskered

bear down
5 crush 6 defeat, reduce, subdue 7 conquer 8 vanquish 9 overpower, subjugate

bearer
5 envoy 6 coolie, porter, redcap, skycap 7 bellboy, bellhop, bellman, carrier, courier, drogher 8 cargador, emissary 9 messenger 11 internuncio
combining form: 3 fer 4 pher, phor 5 phora, phore 6 phorae (plural), phorum

bearing
3 air, set 4 brow, look, mien, port, pose 5 birth, front, poise, stand 6 aspect, stance 7 address, conduct, display, posture 8 attitude, behavior, birthing, carriage, delivery, demeanor, presence 10 childbirth, deportment 11 comportment, parturition
combining form: 6 ferous, gerous, parous 7 igerous, phorous

bearish
5 waspy 6 cranky, ornery 7 dubious, waspish 8 cankered, vinegary 9 crotchety, declining 10 vinegarish 11 pessimistic 12 cantankerous

bearlike
6 ursine, ursoid 8 ursiform

bear out
6 verify 7 confirm, justify 8 validate 11 corroborate 12 authenticate, substantiate

bear up
4 prop 5 brace, carry 6 uphold 7 bolster, shore up, support, sustain 8 buttress

beast
5 brute 6 animal 7 beastie, critter, varmint 8 behemoth, creature 9 quadruped
combining form: 4 ther 5 thero 6 theria (plural), therio 7 therium

beastly
5 brute, feral 6 animal, brutal, ferine 7 bestial, brutish, swinish

beat
2 do 3 get, gyp, lam, tan, top, wag, win 4 balk, best, bilk, cane, comb, dash, drub, drum, dump, flog, foil, grub, lace, lash, lick, maul, pelt, rake, ruin, trim, wale, wave, welt, whip, whop 5 baste, baton, cheat, cozen, curry, excel, lay on, meter, outdo, paste, pound, pulse, rhyme, scoop, scour, smear, stick, stump, swing, throb, tromp, whisk 6 baffle, batter, better, buffet, chouse, cudgel, diddle, exceed, forage, hammer, larrup, muss up, pummel, rhythm, search, switch, thrash, thwart, waggle, wallop, woggle 7 belabor, buffalo, cadence, cadency, clobber, conquer, defraud, lambast, measure, nonplus, prevail, pulsate, ransack, rough up, rummage, shellac, smother, surpass, triumph, trounce 8 bludgeon, finecomb, flimflam, lambaste, malleate, outshine, outstrip, overcome, rhythmus 9 bastinado, exclusive, frustrate, fustigate, overreach, palpitate, transcend 10 circumvent, disappoint, pistolwhip

beat down
5 crush 6 defeat, reduce, subdue 7 conquer 8 vanquish 9 overpower, subjugate

beating
4 rout 5 lumps 6 defeat, hiding 7 debacle, licking 8 drubbing 9 overthrow, pulsating, thrashing 10 defeasance 11 shellacking 12 vanquishment

beatitude
5 bliss 7 ecstasy, rapture 9 happiness, transport 11 blessedness 12 blissfulness

Beatles
4 John, Paul 5 Ringo 6 George

beau
5 flame, lover, swain 6 steady 7 beloved 8 truelove, young man 9 boyfriend, inamorato 10 sweetheart

Beau Brummel
3 fop 5 dandy 7 coxcomb 8 macaroni 9 exquisite 11 petit-maître 12 lounge lizard

beau ideal
5 model 6 mirror 7 example, pattern 8 ensample, exemplar, paradigm, standard 9 archetype

Beaumarchais' hero
6 Figaro

beauteous
4 fair 5 bonny 6 comely, lovely, pretty 8 handsome 10 attractive 11 good-looking

beautiful
4 fair 5 bonny 6 choice, comely, lovely, pretty, proper, superb 7 elegant, sublime 8 glorious, gorgeous, handsome, pleasing, splendid, stunning 9 exquisite 10 attractive, eye-filling, personable 11 good-looking, resplendent, well-favored 12 eye-appealing
combining form: 4 cali, calo 5 calli, callo

beautiful people
6 jet set 8 smart set

beautify
4 deck, trim 5 adorn, grace, prank 6 bedeck 7 dress up, garnish 8 dec-

orate, ornament, prettify **9** embellish, glamorize

beauty
5 belle, dream, peach, toast **6** eyeful, looker, lovely **7** charmer, dazzler, stunner **8** knockout **9** eye-opener **10** good-looker
combining form: **4** cali, calo **5** calli, callo

beaver
5 beard **6** rodent **8** whiskers
family: **10** Castoridae
genus: **6** Castor
home: **5** lodge
young: **3** kit, pup

Beaver State
6 Oregon

becalm
4 lull **5** allay, quiet, still **6** settle, soothe **7** compose, quieten **11** tranquilize

because
2 as **3** for, now **5** being, since **6** seeing **7** whereas **8** as long as **10** inasmuch as **11** considering

because of
4 over **5** due to **7** owing to, through

Becher's father
7 Ephraim **8** Benjamin

Beckett work
4 Play, Watt **6** Molloy, Murphy **7** Endgame **9** Happy Days **14** Krapp's Last Tape **15** Waiting for Godot

becloud
3 dim, fog **4** blur **5** bedim, befog, muddy **6** darken, puzzle **7** confuse, eclipse, obscure, perplex **8** befuddle **9** obfuscate

become
2 go **3** fit, get, run, wax **4** come, grow, rise, soar, suit, turn **5** arise, befit, mount **6** go with **7** enhance, flatter **9** agree with **10** go together
suffix: **3** ize

becoming
4 nice **5** right **6** decent, proper, seemly **7** correct, fitting **8** decorous, suitable, tasteful **9** befitting **10** attractive, conforming, flattering **11** appropriate, comme il faut
suffix: **6** escent **7** escence

bed
3 cot **4** base, bunk, flop, rest, seat, twin **5** basis **6** bottom, cradle, double, ground, Murphy, pallet, pile in, retire, roll in, tuck in, turn in **7** bed-

rock, trundle **8** rollaway **10** foundation, substratum
combining form: **4** clin **5** clino
of India: **7** charpai, charpoy

Bedad's son
5 Hadad

bedamn
4 cuss **5** curse, swear **8** execrate **9** imprecate

bedaub
3 dab **5** smarm, smear **6** smudge **7** besmear, plaster

bedaze
4 stun **6** bemuse, benumb **7** petrify, stupefy **8** paralyze

bedazzle
4 daze **5** blind

bedbug
5 cimex **6** chinch **7** cimices (plural)

bedcover
5 quilt **6** afghan, spread **8** coverlet, coverlid **11** counterpane

bedeck
4 trim **5** adorn, prank **6** bedaub **7** bedizen, dress up, garnish **8** beautify, decorate, ornament **9** embellish

Bedeiah's father
4 Bani

bedevil
5 annoy, harry, tease, worry **6** harass, pester, plague **7** hagride, wherret **9** tantalize

bedevilment
7 trouble **8** disorder, vexation **9** confusion

bedfellow
4 ally **9** associate

bedim
3 fog **5** befog, cloud, gloom **6** darken **7** becloud, eclipse, obscure **9** obfuscate

bedlamite
3 mad, nut **4** loon, nuts **5** batty, crazy, loony **6** dement, insane, madman, maniac **7** cracked, lunatic, madling **8** demented, deranged **9** non compos

bedog
3 tag **4** tail **5** trail **6** shadow

bedouin
4 Arab **5** nomad

bedraggled
5 faded, seedy **6** shabby, tagrag **7** rundown **8** decrepit, tattered

10 down-at-heel, threadbare **11** dilapidated

bedridden
4 weak **6** feeble, infirm, laid up, sickly **7** bedfast **8** confined **13** incapacitated

bedrock
4 base, root **5** basis **6** ground **7** footing **10** foundation, groundwork, substratum **12** substructure, underpinning

bedroom
7 boudoir

bedspread
8 coverlet, coverlid **11** counterpane

bed-wetting
8 enuresis

bee
combining form: **3** api
family: **6** Apidae **8** Bombidae
food: **6** nectar
genus: **4** Apis **5** Osmia **6** Bombus **8** Ceratina **9** Megachile
glue: **8** propolis
group: **5** swarm **6** colony
house: **6** apiary
kind: **5** drone, mason, queen **6** cuckoo, mining, sewing, worker **8** honeybee, quilting, spelling **9** bumblebee, carpenter **10** leafcutter
nest: **4** hive, skep
product: **3** wax **5** honey
relating to: **5** apian **8** apiarian
study of: **8** apiology
wax cells: **9** honeycomb

beechnuts
4 mast

beef
3 arm **4** crab, fuss, miff, thew, tiff, yaup, yawp **5** bitch, bleat, boost, brawl, brawn, force, gripe, might, power, sinew, steam, vigor **6** energy, expand, extend, muscle, squawk, yammer **7** augment, blow off, dispute, enlarge, magnify, quarrel, rhubarb **8** heighten, increase, multiply, squabble, strength **9** bellyache, bickering, strong arm **10** aggrandize, falling-out **11** altercation
cut: **3** rib **4** loin, rump, side **5** chuck, flank, plate, round, shank **7** brisket, sirloin **10** tenderloin
grade: **4** good **5** prime **6** choice **7** utility **8** standard **10** commercial
order: **4** rare **6** medium **8** well-done

beefeater
6 warder, yeoman

beefheaded
4 dull 5 dense 6 stupid
10 numskulled

beefy
5 burly, hefty, husky

Beehive State
4 Utah

beekeeper
8 apiarian, apiarist 12 apiculturist

beekeeping
10 apiculture

Beeliada's father
5 David

beeline
3 nip, zip 4 whiz 5 hurry, speed
6 bullet, hustle, rocket 7 hotfoot
8 highball

Beelzebub
5 devil, fiend, Satan 6 diablo 7 Lucifer, Old Nick, serpent 8 Apollyon
10 Old Scratch 13 Old Gooseberry

beer
3 ale 4 bock, brew 5 draft, lager,
stout, weiss 6 porter 7 pilsner
8 pilsener
cup: 3 mug 4 toby 5 stein 6 flagon,
seidel 7 tankard 8 schooner
9 blackjack
drinking place: 3 inn, pub 6 saloon,
tavern
ingredient: 4 hops, malt 5 yeast
6 barley
maker: 6 brewer
mythical inventor: 9 Gambrinus
plant: 7 brewery
Russian: 5 kvass
Scottish: 10 barley-bree, barley-broo
slang: 4 suds
Tibetan: 5 chang

beer hall
5 stube 8 alehouse, mughouse

Beeri
daughter: 6 Judith
son: 5 Hosea

beet
5 chard 6 mangel, wurzel
7 mangold
family: 9 goosefoot

Beethoven, Ludwig van
birthplace: 4 Bonn
opera: 7 Fidelio
overture: 6 Egmont 7 Leonore
10 Coriolanus, Prometheus
sonata: 8 Kreutzer, Pastoral 9 Moon-
light 10 Pathetique
symphony: 6 Choral, Eroica 8 Pastoral

beetle
3 jut 4 hang, poke, pout 5 bulge,
pouch 7 project 8 bend over, lean
over, overhang, protrude, stand
out, stick out
click: 6 cucuyo, elater 7 firefly
8 cucubano, skipjack
dung: 6 scarab 9 tumblebug
front wing: 6 elytra (plural) 7 elytron
fruit-eating: 8 curculio
insect-eating: 7 ladybug 8 ladybird
kind: 3 dor 4 bean, dorr, dung, fire,
June, stag 5 click, flour, grain, tiger, water 6 carpet, chafer, dor
bug, ground, May bug, meloid, museum 7 blister, cadelle, carabid,
firefly, goldbug, goliath, June bug,
vedalia 8 ambrosia, figeater, Japanese, lampyrid, passalid, pinch
bug 9 bombadier, longicorn, potato bug 10 cockchafer, rhinoceros
order: 10 Coleoptera
ornamental: 6 scarab
sacred: 6 scarab
snouted: 6 weevil 7 billbug 8 curculio 9 wood borer
young: 4 grub 5 larva 8 wireworm

beetlehead
4 dolt, dope 5 dunce 8 dumbbell

beetleheaded
4 dull 5 dense 6 stupid
10 numskulled

beet soup
6 borsch, borsht 7 borscht

befall
2 go 3 hap 5 break, occur 6 betide, chance, happen 7 come off,
develop, fall out

befit
4 suit 6 become, go with 9 agree
with 10 go together

befitting
3 apt 4 just, meet, nice 5 happy,
right 6 decent, proper, seemly
7 correct 8 becoming, decorous,
suitable 10 conforming, felicitous
11 appropriate, comme il faut
suffix: 2 ly

befog
3 dim 4 blur 5 bedim, cloud,
muddy 6 darken, puzzle 7 becloud, confuse, eclipse, obscure,
perplex, stumble 8 bewilder, confound 9 obfuscate, overcloud
13 metagrobolize

befool
4 dupe, gull, hoax 5 trick 7 chicane 8 hoodwink 9 bamboozle,
victimize 11 hornswoggle

before
2 to 3 ere 4 ante, once, then, till,
up to 5 ahead, until 6 facing,
sooner, up till 7 ahead of, already,
earlier, forward, prior to 8 formerly, previous 9 erstwhile, in advance, preceding 10 heretofore,
previously 11 confronting, in advance of, precedently
12 antecedent
combining form: 4 fore 6 proter
7 protero
prefix: 2 ob 3 pre, pro 4 ante

befoul
4 slur 5 dirty, smear 6 defame, malign 7 blacken, pollute, slander,
spatter, traduce 9 bespatter, denigrate 11 contaminate

befuddle
4 daze 5 addle, mix up 6 ball up
7 confuse, fluster 8 bewilder, distract, throw off 9 bumfuzzle

befuddlement
3 fog 4 daze, haze, maze 5 mix-
up 9 confusion 10 muddlement
11 muddledness

beg
3 ask, nag, sue 4 pray 5 brace,
cadge, crave, plead, press, worry
6 appeal, call on, demand, invoke,
obtest 7 beseech, besiege, conjure,
entreat, implore, request, solicit
8 petition 9 importune
10 supplicate

begem
5 beset, jewel 7 bejewel, enjewel

beget
4 bear, sire 5 breed 6 father 7 produce 8 generate, multiply 9 procreate, propagate, reproduce
11 progenerate

begetting
combining form: 4 gony

beggar
4 hobo 5 asker, tramp 6 bummer,
cadger, pauper, prayer, sponge,
suitor 7 moocher, sponger 8 deadbeat 9 schnorrer, suppliant
10 down-and-out, freeloader, panhandler, petitioner, supplicant
11 bindle stiff, supplicator

beggared
4 flat, poor 5 broke, needy 8 dirt
poor, indigent 9 destitute
11 fortuneless, impecunious
12 impoverished

beggarly
4 mean 5 cheap, sorry 6 cheesy,
measly, paltry, scurvy, shabby,

trashy **7** pitiful **8** pitiable, wretched **10** despicable, despisable **12** contemptible

Beggar's Opera
music: **7** Pepusch (John)
painting: **7** Hogarth (William)
text: **3** Gay (John)

beggarweed
6 dodder, spurry **9** knotgrass

beggary
4 need, want **6** penury **7** bumming, cadging, poverty **8** mooching **9** indigence, mendicity, neediness, pauperism **10** mendicancy **11** destitution, panhandling

begin
4 open **5** arise, dig in, enter, found, set to, start **6** attack, broach, get off, launch, spring, tackle, take up, tee off **7** break in, jump off, kick off, lead off, prepare, usher in **8** commence, embark on, initiate **9** establish, institute, introduce, originate **10** embark upon, inaugurate

beginner
4 colt, tiro, tyro **6** novice, rookie **8** freshman, neophyte, newcomer **9** novitiate **10** apprentice, tenderfoot

beginning
4 dawn, rise, root **5** alpha, basal, birth, onset, start **6** anlage, origin, outset, primal, setout, source, spring, sprout **7** dawning, genesis, infancy, initial, nascent, opening **8** creation, exordium, outstart, prologue, rudiment, simplest **9** dayspring, elemental, emergence, inception, inceptive, incipient **10** appearance, elementary, incipiency, initiative, initiatory, opening gun, rudimental **11** origination, rudimentary **12** commencement, introductory
combining form: **3** acr, akr **4** acro, akro, arch
suffix: **6** escent

begird
3 hem **4** band, belt, ring **5** beset, round **6** circle, girdle **8** cincture, encircle, engirdle, surround **9** encompass **10** encincture

begirdle
4 band, belt **6** engird **8** cincture **10** encincture

begone
4 kite **5** scram **6** decamp, get out **7** buzz off, skiddoo, take off, va-

moose **8** clear out, hightail **9** skedaddle

begrime
4 foul, soil **5** dirty **6** besoil, smirch, smooch, smudge, smutch **7** tarnish

begrudge
4 envy

beguile
4 lure, play, wile **5** bluff, fleet, while **6** betray, delude, entice, humbug, illude, jockey, juggle, seduce, take in **7** deceive, exploit, finesse, mislead **8** maneuver **10** manipulate **11** double-cross

beguiling
5 false **8** deluding, delusive, delusory **9** deceiving, deceptive **10** fallacious, misleading

Behan's autobiography
10 Borstal Boy

behave
2 do **3** act **4** bear, go on, move, quit, take, work **5** carry, react **6** acquit, demean, deport, direct, manage **7** comport, conduct, control, disport, operate, perform **8** function

behavior
6 manner **7** bearing, conduct **8** demeanor **10** deportment **11** comportment

behead
4 neck **9** decollate **10** decapitate, guillotine

beheaded noblewoman
4 Grey (Lady Jane) **6** Boleyn (Anne), Howard (Catherine) **10** Antoinette (Marie)

behemoth
5 giant, whale **7** mammoth, monster **9** leviathan

behemothic
4 huge **7** mammoth, titanic **8** colossal, gigantic **9** Herculean, monstrous **10** gargantuan, mastodonic **11** elephantine

behest
4 word **5** order **6** charge, demand **7** bidding, command, dictate, mandate, request **9** prompting **10** injunction **12** solicitation

behind
3 can **4** next, rump **5** abaft, after, below, fanny, hiney, infra, later, since **6** back of, bottom, heinie **7** by and by **8** backside, buttocks, derriere, latterly **9** afterward, fol-

lowing, posterior **10** afterwhile **12** subsequently, subsequent to
combining form: **7** postero
prefix: **3** met **4** meta, post **5** retro

behindhand
3 lax **4** late **5** lated, slack, tardy **6** in debt, remiss **7** belated, overdue **8** backward, careless, derelict **9** in arrears, negligent **10** delinquent, neglectful, regardless, unpunctual **11** undeveloped **12** disregardful **13** unprogressive

behold
3 see **4** espy, mark, note, view **6** descry, notice **7** discern, observe **11** distinguish
French: **5** voilà
Latin: **4** ecce

beholden
7 obliged **8** indebted **9** obligated

beholder
6 viewer **7** watcher, witness **8** bysitter, looker-on, observer, onlooker **9** bystander, spectator **10** eyewitness

being
2 as **3** for, man **4** body, esse, soul **5** human, since, stuff, thing, wight **6** entity, matter, mortal, nature, object, person, seeing **7** because, essence, texture, whereas **8** as long as, creature, essentia, existent, material **9** actuality, character, existence, personage, something, substance **10** inasmuch as, individual **11** considering, personality **12** essentiality **13** individuality
suffix: **2** ic **3** ant, ent **4** ical

bejewel
3 gem **5** begem, beset **7** diamond, encrust, spangle **9** bespangle

Bel
father: **2** Ea
wife: **5** Belit **6** Beltis

bel ___
5 canto **6** esprit

Bel ___
5 Paese

Bela
father: **4** Beor **8** Benjamin
son: **3** Ard

belabor
4 beat, drub **5** baste, pound **6** batter, buffet, pummel, thrash, wallop **7** lambast **8** lambaste

Belait
6 Europe

belated

   5 dated, passé, tardy 7 antique, archaic, overdue 8 outdated, outmoded 9 out-of-date 10 antiquated, behindhand, oldfangled, unpunctual 12 old-fashioned

belch

   4 burp, spew 5 eject, erupt, expel 6 irrupt 8 disgorge, eructate

beldam

   3 hag 5 crone 6 virago

beleaguer

   4 gnaw 5 annoy, beset, harry, siege, storm, tease, worry 6 harass, invest, pester, plague 7 bedevil, besiege, hagride 8 blockade

belfry

   7 clocher 8 carillon 9 bell tower, campanile
   dweller: 3 bat

Belgium

   capital: 8 Brussels
   commercial center: 4 Gent 5 Ghent
   horse breed: 9 Brabançon
   language: 6 French 7 Flemish
   monetary unit: 5 franc
   people: 7 Fleming, Flemish, Walloon
   province: 5 Liège, Namur 7 Antwerp, Brabant, Hainaut, Limburg 8 Flanders 10 Luxembourg
   violinist: 5 Ysaye (Eugene-Auguste)

belie

   4 hide, warp 5 color, twist 6 garble 7 conceal, distort, falsify, pervert 8 disguise, disprove, miscolor, misstate, negative 10 contradict, contravene, controvert 12 misrepresent

belief

   3 ism 4 idea, mind, view 5 credo, creed, dogma, faith, tenet, trust 6 assent, credit 7 concept, feeling, opinion, precept 8 credence, doctrine, religion, sureness 9 assurance, certainty, certitude, principle, sentiment 10 conviction, persuasion

believable

   5 solid 6 likely 7 tenable 8 credible, possible, probable, rational 9 colorable, plausible 10 convincing, creditable, impressive, meaningful, persuasive, presumable, reasonable, satisfying, supposable 11 conceivable, substantial

believe

   3 buy 4 deem, feel, hold, take 5 admit, sense, think, trust 6 accept, assume, credit, expect,

gather, reckon, repute 7 imagine, suppose, suspect, swallow 8 accredit, consider 10 understand

belittle

   5 decry 8 derogate, diminish, discount, minimize, write off 9 criticize, discredit, disparage, dispraise, underrate 10 depreciate, undervalue 11 detract from 13 underestimate

belittlement

   4 tale 7 calumny, scandal, slander 10 backbiting, defamation, detraction 12 backstabbing, depreciation 13 disparagement

bell

   4 bong, peal, ring, toll 5 chime, knell

bell-bottoms

   5 pants 8 trousers

bell cow

   4 dean, lead 5 doyen, guide, pilot 6 leader

Bellerophon

   father: 7 Glaucus 8 Poseidon
   grandfather: 8 Sisyphus
   horse: 7 Pegasus
   victim: 7 Chimera

belles lettres

   10 literature

belletrist

   4 poet 6 author, writer

bellflower

   9 campanula

___ belli

   5 casus

bellicose

   7 scrappy, warlike 8 factious, fighting, militant 9 assertive, combative, truculent 10 aggressive, pugnacious, rebellious 11 belligerent, contentious, quarrelsome 12 gladiatorial

belligerence

   5 fight 6 attack 9 pugnacity 10 aggression, truculence 13 combativeness

belligerent

   3 hot 6 ardent, fierce 7 hostile, scrappy, warlike, warring 8 battling, fighting, invading, militant, ructious 9 attacking, bellicose, combative, truculent 10 aggressive, pugnacious 11 contentious, hot-tempered, quarrelsome 12 antagonistic, gladiatorial

Bellini

   opera: 5 Norma 8 Il Pirata 9 I Puritani 12 La Sonnambula
   sleepwalker: 5 Amina

bell metal

   6 bronze

bellow

   3 bay, cry, low, moo 4 bark, bawl, roar, rout, wail, yelp 6 clamor 7 bluster

Bellow character

   6 Herzog 7 Sammler 9 Henderson 10 Augie March

bell ringer

   3 hit, wow 4 bang 5 smash 6 toller 7 success 12 carillonneur

bell ringing

   11 campanology

bell-shaped

   11 campanulate

bell sound

   4 ding, dong, peal, ring, ting, toll 5 clang, knell 6 tinkle

bell tower

   6 belfry 7 clocher 8 carillon 9 campanile

___ bellum

   4 ante, post

bellwether

   4 dean, lead 5 doyen, guide, pilot 6 leader

belly

   3 gut 5 tummy 6 paunch, venter 7 abdomen, stomach
   combining form: 5 gastr 6 gaster, gastro, ventri, ventro 7 gastero, gastria
   Scottish: 4 wame

bellyache

   4 beef, crab, fuss, yaup, yawp 5 bitch, bleat, colic, gripe 6 gripes, squawk, yammer 7 blow off 12 collywobbles

bellyacher

   4 crab 5 crank 6 griper, grouch, kicker 7 grouser 8 grumbler 10 complainer, malcontent 11 faultfinder

belly button

   5 navel

belong

   2 go 3 fit, set 4 suit, vest 5 agree, befit, chime, match, tally 6 accord, become, inhere 7 indwell, pertain 9 appertain, harmonize 10 correspond

belonging
suffix: **2** an, ar **3** ary, ean, ian, ine

belongings
5 goods **6** estate, things **7** effects
8 chattels, movables **10** possession

beloved
3 pet **4** baby, beau, dear, love
5 flame, honey, lover, sweet
6 steady **7** darling, sweetie **8** blue-
eyed, favorite, ladylove, loveling,
precious, truelove **9** boyfriend, inamorata, inamorato, sweetling
10 fair-haired, girl friend, heartthrob, sweetheart

below
4 next **5** after, infra, since, under
6 behind, nether **7** beneath **9** following **10** underneath **12** subsequent to
combining form: **6** infero
prefix: **3** sub **5** infra

belt
3 bat, bop **4** area, band, bash,
biff, blow, gird, loop, ring, sash,
slam, slug, sock, whop, zone
5 blast, smack, smash, strap, strip,
tie up, tract **6** begird, cestus, circle,
engird, girdle, region, wallop
7 baldric, caestus, clobber, stretch
8 begirdle, ceinture, cincture, encircle, engirdle **9** bandoleer, bando-
lier, territory, waistband **10** cummer-
bund, encincture
celestial: **6** zodiac
combining form: **3** zon **4** zono

belt highway
8 ring road

Belus
brother: **6** Agenor
daughter: **4** Dido
father: **7** Neptune **8** Poseidon
mother: **5** Libya
son: **6** Danaus **7** Cepheus, Phineus
8 Aegyptus

belvedere
6 alcove, gazebo, pagoda **11** garden house, summerhouse

bemean
4 sink **5** abase, lower **6** debase,
humble **7** degrade **8** cast down
9 humiliate

bemedaled
9 decorated **10** beribboned

bemired
4 miry, oozy **5** muddy **6** claggy,
clarty

bemoan
3 rue **4** weep **6** bewail, grieve, lament, regret **7** deplore **8** complain

bemuse
4 daze, stun **5** addle **6** bedaze,
benumb, puzzle **7** fluster, perplex,
petrify, stupefy **8** paralyze

bemused
4 lost **6** absent **7** faraway **8** distrait **10** abstracted **11** inconscient,
preoccupied **12** absentminded

bench
6 settee
church: **3** pew
outdoor: **6** exedra
upholstered: **9** banquette

benchmark
5 gauge **7** measure **8** standard
9 criterion, yardstick **10** touchstone

bend
2 go **3** arc, bow, jut, nod, yaw
4 arch, bias, cave, curl, flex, give,
hang, hook, lean, tack, turn **5** angle, apply, break, crook, curve,
round, shift, stoop, throw, yield
6 beetle, buckle, devote, direct, double, fold up, inflex **7** address, crumple, dispose, flexure, incline, turning **8** collapse, flection, lean over,
overhang **9** curvation, curvature,
deviation **10** buckle down, deflection, predispose

bendable
6 pliant, supple **7** elastic, pliable
8 flexible

bender
see **binge**

bending
combining form: **7** sphingo

___ bene
4 nota

beneath
5 below, under
prefix: **3** hyp, sub **4** hypo **5** infra

___ Benedict
4 eggs

benediction
2 OK **4** boon, good, okay **5** favor,
grace **7** thanks **7** benefit, benison,
godsend **8** approval, blessing
9 advantage **11** approbation
12 thanksgiving

benefact
3 aid **4** abet, help **5** do for, stead
6 assist **7** help out

benefaction
4 alms **7** charity **8** donation, offering **11** beneficence **12** contribution

beneficence
see **benefaction**

beneficial
4 good **5** brave **6** toward, useful
7 helpful **8** favoring, salutary
9 favorable, wholesome **10** propitious **12** advantageous

beneficiary
4 heir **5** donee **6** vassal **7** legatee
9 feudatory
suffix: **2** ee

beneficiate
5 treat **6** reduce **7** prepare,
process

benefit
3 aid **4** boon, gain, good, help,
sake **5** avail, build, favor, serve
6 assist, behalf, behoof, better,
profit, succor **7** account, advance,
further, godsend, improve, promote, relieve, welfare, work for
8 blessing, interest **9** advantage,
well-being **10** ameliorate, prosperity **11** benediction **12** contribute to

benevolence
4 boon, gift **5** amity, favor **6** comity **7** largess, present **8** goodwill
10 compliment, friendship, kindliness **12** friendliness

benevolent
3 big **4** good, kind **5** lofty **6** do-
good, humane, kindly **7** liberal
8 generous **10** altruistic, beneficent,
bighearted, charitable, chivalrous,
openhanded **11** considerate, freehearted, magnanimous **12** eleemosynary, greathearted, humanitarian,
largehearted **13** compassionate,
philanthropic, tenderhearted

benighted
8 backward, ignorant, untaught
9 untutored **10** illiterate, uneducated, uninformed, unlettered, unschooled **11** empty-headed, know-
nothing **12** uninstructed
13 unenlightened, unprogressive

benign
4 kind, mild **6** bright, dexter, gentle, humane, kindly **7** clement
8 gracious, merciful **9** favorable,
fortunate **10** auspicious, benevolent, charitable, forbearing, propitious **11** good-hearted

Benin
capital: **9** Porto Novo
largest city: **7** Cotonou
monetary unit: **5** franc

benison
8 blessing **11** benediction

Benjamin
brother: **6** Joseph

father: 5 Jacob
mother: 6 Rachel

bent
  3 set 4 bias, gift, head, nose, turn
  5 arced, bowed, flair, knack, round
  6 arched, curved, genius, intent, talent 7 arrondi, decided, faculty,
  leaning, rounded, settled, uncinal
  8 arciform, decisive, inflexed, penchant, resolute, resolved, tendency,
  uncinate 9 inclining 10 determined, proclivity, propensity
  11 curvilinear, disposition, inclination 12 predilection
  combining form: 4 cyrt 5 ancyl, ankyl, curvi, cyrto 6 anchyl, ancylo,
  ankylo, campto 7 anchylo

benumb
  4 daze, dull, mull, stun 5 blunt
  6 bedaze, bemuse, deaden 7 petrify, stupefy 8 paralyze
  11 desensitize

benumbed
  6 asleep 9 senseless, unfeeling
  10 insensible 11 insensitive
  12 anesthetized

benzene
  combining form: 4 phen 5 pheno

Beor's son
  4 Bela 6 Balaam

bequeath
  4 will 5 leave 6 devise, hand on,
  legate, pass on 8 hand down,
  transmit

bequest
  6 devise, legacy 11 inheritance

berate
  3 jaw 4 rail, rate 5 scold 6 revile
  7 bawl out, chew out, upbraid
  10 tongue-lash, vituperate

berceuse
  7 lullaby 10 cradlesong

bereave
  3 rob 4 lose, oust 6 divest 7 deprive 10 disinherit, dispossess

bereaved
  6 bereft 9 sorrowing 10 distressed

Berechiah's son
  9 Zechariah

Bergen's dummy
  5 Snerd (Mortimer) 8 McCarthy
  (Charlie)

Beriah's father
  5 Asher 6 Shimei, Shimhi
  7 Ephraim

berkelium
  symbol: 2 Bk

Bermuda grass
  4 doob

Bernice
  brother: 7 Agrippa
  father: 5 Herod
  husband: 6 Polemo
  lover: 5 Titus 9 Vespasian

berry
  4 wort 5 bacca, fruit, grape, whort
  6 banana, tomato 7 bramble, currant, madrona, madrone, madrono,
  whortle 8 allspice
  combining form: 4 cocc 5 cocci,
  cocco
  Latin: 6 acinus
  medicinal: 5 cubeb

berry-bearing
  7 baccate 11 bacciferous

berrylike
  7 baccate, coccoid

berth
  3 job 4 dock, pier, post, quay, slip,
  spot 5 jetty, levee, place, wharf
  6 billet, office 8 position 9 situation
  10 connection 11 appointment

Bertha's son
  7 Orlando

beryllium
  symbol: 2 Be

beseech
  see **beg**

beset
  3 gem, hem 4 gird, ring 5 begem,
  jewel, storm 6 assail, attack, circle,
  fall on, girdle, infest, invest, strike
  7 aggress, assault, bejewel, besiege, encircle, environ,
  overrun 8 blockade, encircle, fall
  upon, surround 9 beleaguer,
  encompass, overswarm
  10 overspread

besetment
  4 pest 6 bother, pester, plague
  8 irritant, nuisance 9 annoyance
  10 botherment 11 botheration
  12 exasperation

besetting
  8 dominant, haunting 9 obsessive,
  principal 10 persistent

beside
  2 by 3 bar, but 4 near, nigh, save
  5 round 6 beyond, except, nearby,
  next to 7 barring 8 as well as, opposite 9 alongside, aside from, excluding, outside of 11 exclusive of
  12 over and above
  prefix: 2 ep 3 eph, epi, par 4 para

besides
  3 bar, but, new, too, yet 4 also,
  else, more, save, then 5 added,
  again, along, other 6 as well, beyond, except 7 barring, farther, further 8 as well as, likewise, moreover 9 aside from, excluding,
  otherwise, outside of 10 additional,
  in addition 11 exclusive of, furthermore 12 additionally, over and
  above

besiege
  4 trap 5 beset, hem in 6 assail, attack, invest 7 assault 8 blockade,
  encircle, surround 9 beleaguer,
  encompass

besmear
  3 dab, tar 4 daub, soil 5 smarm,
  stain, sully, taint 6 bedaub, defile,
  smudge 7 plaster, tarnish 8 besmirch, discolor

besmirch
  see **besmear**

besoil
  4 foul 5 dirty, grime 6 smirch,
  smooch, smudge, smutch 7 begrime, tarnish

besom material
  5 twigs

besotted
  5 dotty, drunk 8 enamored 9 infatuate 10 infatuated

bespatter
  4 slur, spot 5 smear 6 befoul, bespot, defame, malign 7 asperse,
  blacken, slander, traduce
  9 denigrate

bespeak
  3 ask 4 book, hire 6 accost, attest,
  desire 7 address, apply to, betoken, request, reserve, solicit, testify,
  witness 8 announce, approach, indicate 9 preengage

bespeckle
  3 dot 6 pepper 7 freckle, stipple
  8 sprinkle

best
  3 gem, pip, top 4 beat, down,
  most, pick 5 cream, elite, excel,
  model, outdo, pride, prime, prize,
  worst 6 better, choice, defeat, exceed, flower, master 7 conquer,
  greater, largest, paragon, pattern,
  prevail, surpass, triumph 8 exemplar, nonesuch, outshine, outstrip,
  overcome, primrose 9 nonpareil,
  transcend 10 bettermost
  combining form: 6 aristo

bestial
5 brute, feral **6** animal, brutal, ferine **7** beastly, brutish, swinish

bestialize
4 warp **6** debase **7** corrupt, debauch, deprave, pervert, vitiate **9** brutalize **10** bastardize, demoralize

bestir
4 wake, whet **5** rally, rouse, waken **6** arouse, awaken, kindle **9** challenge

bestow
3 use **4** bunk, give, pack **5** apply, board, grant, house, lodge, put up, store **6** billet, confer, devote, donate, employ, handle, harbor, lavish **7** exploit, hand out, present, quarter, utilize **8** domicile, exercise, give away **9** entertain, warehouse
Scottish: **7** propine

bestower
5 donor, giver **7** donator **9** conferrer, presenter

bestrew
3 sow **5** straw **7** disject, scatter **9** broadcast **11** disseminate

bestride
4 back **5** mount **8** straddle, striddle

bet
3 lay, pot, set **4** ante, game, play, risk **5** banco, put on, stake, wager **6** gamble, parlay
racing: **6** exacta **8** perfecta, quinella, quiniela
taker: **6** bookie

Betelgeuse
4 star
constellation: **5** Orion

betel palm
5 areca

bête noire
4 hate **7** bugbear **8** anathema **10** black beast **11** abomination, detestation

bethink
4 cite, mind **6** recall, remind, retain, revive **8** remember **9** recollect, reminisce **10** retrospect

Bethuel
daughter: **7** Rebekah
father: **5** Nahor
mother: **6** Milcah
son: **5** Laban
uncle: **7** Abraham

betide
2 go **3** hap **5** break, occur **6** befall, chance, happen **7** come off, develop, fall out

betimes
4 soon **5** early **6** timely **8** oversoon **10** seasonably **11** prematurely

betoken
4 bode, omen **5** argue, augur **6** attest **7** bespeak, portend, presage, promise, testify, witness **8** announce, forebode, foreshow, indicate **9** foretoken **10** foreshadow

betray
4 sell, show, tell, trap **5** bluff, cross, snare, spill, split **6** delude, desert, entrap, evince, humbug, illude, inform, juggle, reveal, take in, turn in, unveil **7** beguile, betoken, blab out, deceive, divulge, ensnare, mislead, sell out, uncover **8** disclose, discover, evidence, give away, indicate, manifest, renegade **10** apostatize **11** collaborate, demonstrate, double-cross

betrayal
7 treason

betrayer
3 rat **4** fink, nark **6** snitch **7** stoolie, tattler, traitor **8** informer, squealer, turncoat **10** talebearer, tattletale **11** stool pigeon

betroth
6 pledge **8** affiance

betrothal
8 espousal **10** engagement

betrothed
6 fiancé **7** engaged, fiancée, pledged **8** intended, plighted, promised, wife-to-be **9** affianced, bride-to-be **10** contracted **11** husband-to-be

better
3 top, win **4** beat, best, good, help, more, most **5** amend, elder, excel, outdo **6** choice, exceed, senior **7** greater, improve, largest, success, surpass, triumph, victory **8** brass hat, higher-up, outshine, outstrip, superior, whip hand **9** advantage, desirable, exceeding, excellent, meliorate, transcend, upper hand **10** ameliorate, preferable, surpassing **11** exceptional, superiority

bettor
7 wagerer

between
5 among, twixt **6** atwixt **7** betwixt
prefix: **5** inter, intra

betweentimes
11 at intervals

bevel
4 bias **6** biased **7** slanted **8** diagonal, slanting

beverage
3 ade, nog, pop, tea **4** mate, milk, soda **5** cider, cocoa, drink, juice, shake **6** coffee, eggnog, frappe, malted, nectar **7** potable **8** lemonade, libation, potation **9** drinkable, milk shake
alcoholic: **3** ale, gin, rum **4** beer, grog, mead, wine **5** cider, julep, negus, punch, stout, toddy, vodka **6** bishop, brandy, caudle, cooler, liquor, rickey, shandy, sherry, whisky **7** liqueur, martini, sangria, tequila, whiskey **8** cocktail, highball, sillabub, sillibub, syllabub, vermouth
Australasian: **4** kava
British: **5** perry, stout **6** stingo
carbonated: **4** cola, soda **6** rickey **8** root beer **9** ginger ale
central Asian: **5** kumys **6** koumis, koumys, kumiss, kumyss **7** koumiss, koumyss
Dutch: **7** schnaps **8** schnapps
from camel's milk: **5** kumys **6** koumis, koumys, kumiss, kumyss **7** koumiss, koumyss
from cow's milk: **5** kefir
Greek: **4** ouzo **7** oenomel, oinomel, retsina, retzina
Irish: **5** usque **6** poteen **7** potheen, potteen **8** usquabae, usquebae **10** usquebaugh
medicinal: **6** elixir
Mexican: **6** pulque **7** tequila
of the gods: **6** nectar
Oriental: **4** sake, saki **6** arrack, samshu
Russian: **5** kefir, kvass, quass, vodka
Scottish: **4** yill **6** scotch
South American: **4** maté **5** yerba
Swedish: **5** glogg
Turkish: **4** raki
West Indies: **3** rum **5** tafia

bevy
4 band, crew **5** bunch, covey, group, party **7** cluster **8** assembly

bewail
4 moan, weep **6** bemoan, grieve **7** deplore

beware
4 heed, mind **5** watch **6** attend, notice **7** look out **8** watch out

bewhiskered
7 barbate, bearded

bewilder

3 fog 4 stun 5 addle, befog, mix up 6 baffle, ball up, fuddle, muddle, puzzle 7 confuse, fluster, perplex, stumble 8 befuddle, confound, distract 9 bumfuzzle 13 metagrobolize

bewitch

3 hex 4 draw, snow, take, wile 5 charm, spell, trick 6 allure, dazzle, voodoo 7 attract, bedevil, enchant, possess 8 demonize, ensorcel, overlook 9 beglamour, captivate, ensorcell, fascinate, magnetize, sorcerize

bewitching

8 alluring, charming, magnetic, mesmeric 9 seductive 10 attractive

bewitchment

5 magic 7 sorcery 8 witchery, wizardry 9 conjuring, magicking 10 necromancy, witchcraft 11 incantation

beyond

3 new, yon 4 else, more, over, past 5 above, added, after, other 6 across, beside, yonder 7 athwart, besides, farther, further, outside, without 8 as well as 9 afterlife, hereafter, otherwise 10 additional, afterworld, otherworld 12 over and above, transversely

combining form: 6 preter 7 praeter

prefix: 3 met, par 4 meta, over, para 5 extra, hyper, super, trans, ultra

bias

4 bend, bent, skew 5 angle, bevel, slant 7 beveled, dispose, incline, leaning, slanted 8 diagonal, penchant, slanting 9 inclining, influence, prejudice, viewpoint 10 partiality, predispose, prepossess, proclivity, standpoint 11 disposition, inclination 12 one-sidedness, predilection

biased

6 swayed, warped 7 bigoted, colored, partial, slanted 8 disposed, inclined, one-sided, partisan, slanting 9 jaundiced, unneutral 10 influenced, interested, prejudiced 11 opinionated, predisposed, tendentious 12 prepossessed 13 unindifferent

bibelot

5 curio 6 bauble, gewgaw, trifle 7 novelty, trinket, whatnot 8 gimcrack 9 objet d'art 10 knickknack

Bible

abbreviation: 2 Ex, Is, Jn, Lk, Mk, Mt, Ps 3 Col, Cor, Dan, Eph, Gal, Gen, Hab, Heb, Hos, Jas, Jer, Jon, Lam, Lev, Mal, Mic, Neh, Num, Pet, Rev, Rom, Sam, Tim, Tit 4 Deut, Ezek, Josh, Judg, Obad, Phil, Prov, Zech, Zeph 5 Chron, Thess 6 Eccles, Philem

Apocrypha book: 5 Tobit 6 Baruch, Esdras, Esther, Judith 7 Susanna 8 Manasseh, Manasses 9 Maccabees

New Testament book: 4 Acts, John, Jude, Luke, Mark 5 James, Peter, Titus 6 Romans 7 Hebrews, Matthew, Timothy 8 Philemon 9 Ephesians, Galatians 10 Colossians, Revelation 11 Corinthians, Philippians 13 Thessalonians

Old Testament book: 3 Job 4 Amos, Ezra, Joel, Ruth 5 Hosea, Jonah, Kings, Micah, Nahum 6 Daniel, Esther, Exodus, Haggai, Isaiah, Joshua, Judges, Psalms, Samuel 7 Ezekiel, Genesis, Malachi, Numbers, Obadiah 8 Habakkuk, Jeremiah, Nehemiah, Proverbs 9 Leviticus, Zechariah, Zephaniah 10 Chronicles 11 Deuteronomy 12 Ecclesiastes, Lamentations 13 Song of Solomon

part: 4 book 5 verse 7 chapter 9 testament

translator: 4 Knox (Ronald Arbuthnott) 5 Eliot (John) 6 Jerome, Luther (Martin) 7 Erasmus, Tyndale (William), Zwingli (Huldrych) 8 Wycliffe (John) 9 Coverdale (Miles)

version: 4 Geez 5 Douay, Itala 6 Coptic, Gothic, Syriac, Targum 7 Vulgate 8 Peshitta 9 Jerusalem, King James, Masoretic, Serampore 10 New English, Septuagint

Biblical

animal: 4 reem 5 daman 8 behemoth

ascetic order: 6 Essene

battle: 7 Jericho

battle site: 10 Armageddon

charioteer: 4 Jehu

city, town: 2 Ai, Ur 3 Ain, Dan, Lod, Luz, Nob 4 Bela, Cana, Gath, Gaza, Nain, Nebo, Tyre, Zoar 5 Bezer, Calno, Derbe, Ekron, Endor, Gerar, Golan, Haifa, Haran, Joppa, Lydda, Ramah, Sidon, Sodom, Tekoa, Zorah 6 Ashdod, Asshur, Beroea, Bethel, Calneh, Dothan, Emmaus, Gadara, Gibeah, Gibeon, Gilgal, Hebron, Kadesh, Lystra, Mizpah, Ophrah, Rimmon,

Shiloh, Shunem, Siloan, Smyrna, Tarsus 7 Antioch, Askelon, Baalbec, Bethany, Corinth, Ephesus, Ephraim, Iconium, Jericho, Jezreel, Magdala, Nineveh, Samaria, Shechem 8 Caesarea, Chorazin, Damascus, Gomorrah, Michmash, Nazareth, Philippi, Tiberias 9 Beersheba, Beth-horon, Bethlehem, Bethsaida, Capernaum, Jerusalem

coin: (see at **Hebrew**)

coney: 5 daman

desert: 5 Sinai

garden: 4 Eden 8 Paradise

giant: 4 Anak, Emim 7 Goliath

giant slayer: 5 David

hill: 4 Zion

hunter: 6 Nimrod

judge: 3 Eli 4 Ehud, Elon, Jair, Tola 5 Abdon, Ibzan 6 Gideon, Samson, Samuel 7 Deborah, Othniel, Shamgar 8 Jephthah

king: 2 Og 3 Asa 4 Agag, Ahab, Ahaz, Amon, Bera, Elah, Jehu, Omri, Reba, Saul 5 David, Herod, Hiram, Joash, Joram, Nadab, Pekah, Rezin, Zimri 6 Abijam, Baasha, Birsha, Hoshea, Japhia, Josiah, Jotham, Uzziah 7 Ahaziah, Amaziah, Azariah, Jehoash, Jehoram, Menahem, Shallum, Solomon 8 Hezekiah, Jehoahaz, Jeroboam, Manasseh, Rehoboam, Zedekiah 9 Jehoiakim, Zechariah 10 Jehoiachin 11 Jehoshaphat

land: 3 Nod, Pul 4 Aram, Elam, Moab, Seba, Seir 5 Judah, Judea, Perea 6 Bashan, Canaan, Goshen, Israel 7 Chaldea, Galilee, Samaria 9 Palestine

land of plenty: 6 Goshen

measure: (see at **Hebrew**)

mountain: 3 Hor 4 Ebal, Nebo, Peor, Seir 5 Horeb, Sinai, Tabor 6 Abarim, Ararat, Carmel, Gilboa, Gilead, Hermon, Moriah, Olivet, Pisgah 7 Gerizim, Lebanon

name: 2 Er, Ir, Ur 3 Abi, Asa, Bel, Dan, Eli, Eri, Eve, Gad, Ham, Hen, Hod, Hul, Hur, Ira, Iri, Iru, Job, Lot, Ner, Nun, Ram, Reu, Toi, Uel, Uri, Zur 4 Abel, Adah, Adam, Agag, Ahab, Ahaz, Amon, Aran, Bela, Beor, Boaz, Buzi, Cain, Cush, Dodo, Ebal, Ebed, Eber, Eder, Ehud, Elah, Elam, Elon, Enan, Enos, Eram, Esau, Ezer, Gaal, Gadi, Gera, Guni, Hazo, Heli, Hori, Ibri, Iddo, Igal, Irad, Iram, Ishi, Izri, Jada, Jael, Jair, Jehu, Joab, Joah, Joel, John, Kish, Kore, Lael, Leah, Levi, Lois, Maon, Mark, Mary, Mica, Moab, Moza, Naam, Nebo,

Neri, Noah, Obal, Obed, Oded, Ohad, Ohel, Omar, Omri, Onam, Onan, Oreb, Oren, Ozem, Ozni, Paul, Puah, Reba, Rosh, Ruth, Salu, Saph, Sara, Saul, Seth, Shem, Shua, Sodi, Suah, Susi, Tema, Tola, Ucal, Ulam, Uzai, Uzal, Uzzi, Zeeb, Zeri, Ziza, Zuar 5 Aaron, Abiel, Abner, Amasa, Amnon, Amram, Asher, Bedad, Bedan, Beeri, Caleb, Carmi, Chuza, Cozbi, David, Debir, Deuel, Dinah, Eliab, Eliam, Elias, Eliel, Eliud, Emmor, Enoch, Ephah, Ephai, Ephod, Esrom, Ethan, Ezbon, Gaham, Galal, Gazez, Gomer, Hadad, Hagar, Haggi, Haman, Hamul, Hanan, Hanun, Haran, Harum, Heber, Helah, Heleb, Helek, Helon, Hemam, Heman, Herod, Hirah, Hobab, Horam, Hosea, Ibhar, Imlah, Imnah, Isaac, Iscah, Ishui, Ithra, Ittai, Izhar, Jaasu, Jabal, Jacob, Jahdo, Jakeh, Jalam, Jalon, James, Jamin, Janna, Jared, Jarib, Jeiel, Jerah, Jered, Jesse, Jeush, Jezer, Joash, Jobab, Jogli, Jonah, Jonas, Joram, Jubal, Judah, Judas, Korah, Laban, Lahad, Lahmi, Laish, Libni, Lotan, Mahli, Mahol, Mamre, Maoch, Massa, Merab, Mered, Mesha, Micah, Moses, Mushi, Nabal, Nadab, Nahor, Naomi, Nehum, Nogah, Nohah, Ocram, Onias, Ophir, Orpah, Othni, Palal, Pallu, Palti, Pekah, Peleg, Pelet, Perez, Peter, Puvah, Rahab, Raham, Raphu, Regem, Rekem, Reuel, Rezon, Rizia, Rufus, Sacar, Sallu, Sarah, Segub, Seled, Serah, Sered, Serug, Shama, Shaul, Sheal, Sheba, Shema, Shiza, Shobi, Shuah, Shual, Shuni, Simon, Tahan, Tamar, Tarah, Tebah, Terah, Tibni, Tilon, Timna, Tubal, Uriah, Uriel, Uthai, Uzzah, Zabad, Zabdi, Zabud, Zadok, Zaham, Zebah, Zephi, Zepho, Zerah, Zibia, Zimri, Zohar 6 Abital, Achsah, Ashhur, Balaam, Baruch, Becher, Beriah, Bilhah, Binnui, Canaan, Cheran, Chesed, Daniel, Dathan, Dishan, Dishon, Elasah, Eliada, Elijah, Elisha, Elpaal, Eshban, Eshcol, Esther, Eunice, Gesham, Gideon, Gilead, Ginath, Hanani, Hannah, Hanoch, Hareph, Hebron, Hemdam, Hepher, Hezion, Hezron, Hodesh, Hoglah, Hophni, Hoshea, Hotham, Hothir, Huldah, Hupham, Hushim, Isaiah, Ishbak, Ishpah, Ishpan, Ishuah, Israel, Ithiel, Ithran, Izliah, Izziah, Jaalam, Jabesh, Jachin, Jahath, Japhia, Jashub, Jehiel, Jehush, Jemuel, Jesher, Jeshua, Jether, Jethro, Jeziel, Jezoar, Joahaz, Joakim, Joanna, Joelah, Joiada, Joktan, Joseph, Joshah, Joshua, Josiah, Jotham, Judith, Kareah, Kemuel, Keziah, Kohath, Laadah, Lamech, Maacah, Maadai, Machir, Mahali, Mahlah, Mahlon, Malcam, Manoah, Martha, Matred, Mattan, Melech, Merari, Midian, Milcah, Miriam, Mirmah, Misham, Naamah, Naaman, Naarah, Nahash, Nahath, Nathan, Nemuel, Nepheg, Neriah, Nimrod, Ochran, Ophrah, Pagiel, Paruah, Pasach, Paseah, Peleth, Penuel, Peresh, Philip, Pilate, Pispah, Pithon, Prisca, Putiel, Raamah, Rachel, Raddai, Ramiah, Ramoth, Raphah, Reaiah, Rechab, Reuben, Rimmon, Rinnah, Rizpah, Rohgah, Salmon, Salome, Samson, Samuel, Shaaph, Shamir, Sharai, Sheber, Shelah, Shemer, Shephi, Shepho, Shilem, Shilhi, Shimea, Shimei, Shimri, Shiphi, Shobab, Shobal, Shoham, Shomer, Shuham, Simeon, Tahash, Tahath, Talmai, Thomas, Tikvah, Tirzah, Tobias, Urijah, Uzziah, Uzziel, Vaniah, Vashni, Vashti, Vophsi, Zaavan, Zabbai, Zaccur, Zalaph, Zebiah, Zephon, Zeresh, Zereth, Zeruah, Zetham, Zibiah, Zichri, Zillah, Zilpah, Zimmah, Zimran, Zippor, Zoheth, Zophah, Zuriel
patriarch: (see at **Hebrew**)
people: 6 Kenite, Levite 7 Amorite, Edomite, Elamite, Moabite 9 Israelite
plains: 4 Maab 5 Mamre 6 Sharon 7 Jericho
plotter: 5 Haman
poem: 5 psalm
pool: 5 Gihon 6 Shelah, Siloam 8 Bethesda
priest: 3 Eli 4 Levi 5 Aaron, Annas 8 Caiaphas
Promised Land: 6 Canaan
pronoun: 2 ye 3 thy 4 thee, thou 5 thine
prophet: (see **prophet** entry)
Psalmist: 5 David
punishment: 7 stoning
queen: 5 Sheba 6 Esther, Vashti 7 Candace, Jezebel 8 Athaliah
reproach: 4 raca
river: 3 Zab 4 Nile 5 Abana, Arnon 6 Abanah, Jabbok, Jordan, Kishon
sacred object: 4 urim 7 thummin
scribe: 6 Baruch
sea: 3 Red 4 Dead 7 Galilee
sea monster: 9 Leviathan

spice: 5 aloes, myrrh 6 cassia, onycha, stacte 7 calamus 8 cinnamon, galbanum 12 frankincense
spy: 5 Caleb
temptress: 3 Eve 7 Delilah
thief: 8 Barabbas
tree: 5 cedar
valley: 4 Baca, Elah 6 Hinnon, Kidron, Shaveh, Siddim
verb ending: 3 eth
weed: 4 tare
well: 3 Ain 4 Esek 6 Jacob's
witch's home: 5 Endor

bibliography
4 list 7 catalog, history

bibliopole
7 bookman 10 bookdealer, bookseller

bicker
3 row, war 4 spat, tiff 5 argue, clack, fight, scrap 6 argufy, battle, hassle, rattle, ruttle 7 brabble, clatter, clitter, contend, dispute, fall out, quarrel, quibble, shatter, wrangle 8 squabble 9 altercate, caterwaul

bickering
3 row 4 spat 5 run-in 6 hassle 7 dispute, quarrel, wrangle 8 squabble 11 altercation, embroilment

bicycle
4 bike 9 high-riser 11 high-wheeler
brake: 7 caliper, coaster
for two: 6 tandem
rider: 6 cycler 7 cyclist
ten-speed: 10 derailleur

bid
3 ask 4 tell, warn 5 order 6 charge, direct, enjoin, invite, summon 7 command, request 8 instruct

biddable
6 docile 7 amiable, docious 8 amenable, obedient, obliging 9 tractable 11 good-natured

bidding
4 call, word 5 order 6 behest, charge 7 command, dictate, mandate 9 summoning 10 injunction

biddy
3 bag, bat, hag 4 drab, girl, maid, trot 5 crone, witch 6 beldam

bide
4 live, stay, wait 5 dwell, tarry 6 linger, remain, reside 7 hang out 8 continue 11 stick around

bier
10 catafalque

biff

3 bop, hit 4 belt, blow, ding, nail, sock, whop 5 catch, clout, devel, pound, slosh, smack, whack 6 strike, thwack, wallop

bifold

see **binary**

bifurcate

4 fork 5 split 6 branch, divide 8 separate 11 dichotomize, dichotomous

bifurcation

4 fork 6 branch 8 division 9 dichotomy 10 separation

big

3 fat 4 arty, bull, full, gone, lion, much, very 5 ample, awash, awful, great, heavy, hefty, husky, large, lofty, major, roomy, sated 6 biggie, bigwig, bumper, clumsy, gravid, hugely, packed, parous 7 awfully, brimful, copious, crammed, crowded, glutted, greatly, hulking, notable, replete, sizable, stuffed, swollen, weighty 8 enceinte, generous, imposing, inflated, material, oversize, pregnant, spacious 9 capacious, chock-full, distended, expectant, expecting, extensive, extremely, important, momentous, overblown, satisfied 10 benevolent, chivalrous, commodious, large-scale, meaningful, voluminous 11 considerate, heavyweight, magnanimous, overflowing, pretentious, significant, substantial 12 considerable, greathearted, high-sounding 13 comprehensive, consequential

Big Bertha's birthplace

5 Essen

Big Dipper

constellation: 9 Ursa Major

star: 5 Alcor, Dubhe, Merak, Mizar

bigfoot

4 Omah 9 Sasquatch

biggety

4 bold, wise 5 fresh, nervy, sassy 6 cheeky 7 forward 8 impudent 10 procacious 11 smart-alecky

bighearted

7 liberal 10 openhanded

big house

3 can, jug, pen 4 jail 5 clink 6 lockup, prison 7 slammer 8 hoosegow 11 reformatory 12 penitentiary

bight

3 arm, bay 4 cove, gulf 5 bayou, creek, firth, inlet 6 harbor, slough

bigmouthed

4 loud 10 boisterous

bigness

4 size 9 amplitude, greatness, largeness, magnitude 11 sizableness

bigot

6 maniac, racist, zealot 7 fanatic

bigoted

6 biased, narrow 9 hidebound, illiberal, lily-white 10 brassbound, intolerant, prejudiced, unenlarged 11 small-minded 12 conservative, narrow-minded

big shot

3 VIP 5 celeb, nabob 6 bigwig, fat cat 7 notable 8 big wheel 9 big cheese, celebrity, dignitary 13 high-muck-a-muck

bijouterie

6 jewels 7 jewelry 8 trinkets

bile

combining form: 4 bili, chol 5 chole, cholo

bilge

4 bunk 5 hooey, trash 6 bushwa 7 hogwash, malarky, rubbish 8 nonsense 10 balderdash

Bilhah's son

3 Dan 8 Naphtali

Bilhan's father

7 Jediael

bilk

3 gyp, shy 4 balk, beat, dash, duck, foil, kite, ruin, shun 5 avoid, cheat, cozen, dodge, elude, evade, shake 6 baffle, chouse, diddle, double, escape, eschew, thwart 7 defraud 8 flimflam 9 frustrate, overreach 10 circumvent, disappoint

bill

3 neb, nib, tab 4 beak, bone, buck, cape, fish, head, naze, oner, peak, skin 5 check, point, score, visor 6 damage, dollar, pecker, poster 7 account, affiche, charges, invoice, ironman, placard, smacker 8 foreland, frogskin, handbill, headland 9 reckoning, smackeroo, statement 10 promontory

five-dollar: 3 fin

of a bird: 3 neb, nib 4 beak

one-dollar: 4 buck

ten-dollar: 7 sawbuck

billet

3 bar, bed, hut, job, rod 4 post, slab, spot 5 berth, board, house,

ingot, lodge, place, put up, stick, strip 6 bestow, canton, harbor, office 7 quarter 8 domicile, position 9 entertain, situation 10 connection 11 appointment

billet-doux

8 mash note 10 love letter

billfold

6 wallet

billiards term

3 cue 4 foot, head, pool, rack, spot 5 break, carom, chalk, masse 6 bridge, cannon, corner, inning, miscue, pocket, string 7 bricole, cue ball, cushion, scratch 8 balkline, cue stick, rotation 9 eight ball 10 object ball

billingsgate

5 abuse 7 obloquy 9 contumely, invective 10 scurrility 12 vituperation

billion

British: 8 milliard

combining form: 4 giga

billionth

combining form: 4 nano

bill of fare

4 menu 7 program 11 carte du jour

bill of lading

7 receipt

Billy Budd's captain

4 Vere

billy club

5 baton 6 cudgel 8 bludgeon 9 truncheon 10 knobkerrie, nightstick

bin

3 box 4 crib, vina 5 frame, pungi, stall 6 hamper, trough 9 container 10 receptacle

for coal: 6 bunker

for fish: 5 kench

binary

4 dual 5 duple 6 bifold, double, duplex 7 twofold 9 dualistic

bind

3 tie 4 frap, gird, tape 5 chain, dress, tie up 6 cement, enserf, fetter, ligate 7 bandage, confine, enchain, spancel 8 astringe, enfetter, ligature 9 constrict

bird's wings: 6 pinion

to secrecy: 4 tile, tyle

with twigs: 5 withe

binding

combining form: 5 desis

binge
3 bat, bum, bun, jag **4** bust, orgy, soak, tear, time, toot **5** blast, booze, drunk, fling, souse, spree **6** bender, ran-tan **7** blowoff, blow-out, carouse, debauch, rampage, splurge, wassail **8** carousal, rowdy-dow **9** bacchanal, brannigan **11** bacchanalia, compotation

bingo
5 beano

Binnui
father: 7 Henadad
son: 7 Noadiah

biographer
9 memoirist
American: 5 Weems (Parson) **6** Parton (James) **7** Freeman (Douglas) **8** Bradford (Gamaliel), Sandburg (Carl)
English: 6 Aubrey (John), Morley (John), Walton (Izaak) **7** Boswell (James) **8** Strachey (Lytton)
French: 7 Maurois (Andre)
German: 6 Ludwig (Emil)
Greek: 8 Plutarch
Italian: 6 Vasari (Giorgio)
Roman: 9 Suetonius

biography
3 bio **4** life, obit **5** diary, story **6** memoir **7** history, journal, letters, profile **8** obituary **11** confessions

biological category
5 class, genus, order **6** family, phylum **7** species, variety **10** subspecies

bionomics
7 ecology

birchbark
5 canoe

bird
African: 4 coly, fink, taha, tock **5** paauw **6** barbet, bulbul, jabiru, quelea, whidah **7** courser, finfoot, marabou, ostrich, touraco **8** hornbill, oxpecker, parakeet, umbrette **9** beefeater, broadbill, francolin, napecrest, trochilus **10** hammerhead, tambourine
antarctic: 4 skua **7** penguin **10** sheathbill
aquatic: 3 auk, cob, ern, mew **4** cobb, coot, duck, erne, gony, gull, loon, skua, swan, teal, tern **5** booby, cahow, goose, grebe, murre, rotch, solan **6** fulmar, gannet, hagdon, petrel, puffin, rotche, scoter, wigeon **7** anhinga, dovekey, dovekie, finfoot, mallard, moorhen, pelican, penguin, skim-mer, widgeon **8** alcatras, baldpate, dabchick, murrelet **9** albatross, cormorant, gallinule, guillemot, kittiwake **10** shearwater, sheathbill
arctic: 3 auk **4** knot, skua, xema **5** murre, rotch **6** fulmar, jaeger, rotche **7** dovekey, dovekie **9** guillemot
Asian: 4 kora, myna, ruff, smew **5** mynah, pewit, pitta **6** chukar, drongo, dunlin, hoopoe **7** courser, hill tit, lapwing, peacock, sirgang **8** accentor, dotterel, hornbill, parakeet, tragopan, wheatear **9** brambling, francolin
Australian: 3 emu **4** kahu, koel, koil, lory **5** arara, galah, pitta **6** drongo, leipoa **7** boobook, bustard, figbird, waybung **8** bellbird, bushlark, cockatoo, lorikeet, lyrebird, manucode, megapode, morepork, parakeet **9** cassowary, coachwhip, frogmouth, pardalote
blackbird: 3 ani, daw, pie **4** crow, merl, rook **5** amsel, merle, ousel, ouzel, raven **6** chough, magpie, thrush **7** grackle, jackdaw, redwing
carrion-eating: 4 aura **5** urubu **6** condor **7** buzzard, vulture
Central American: 4 guan, ibis **5** booby, macaw **6** barbet, jabiru, toucan **7** bittern, cotinga, jacamar, quetzal, tinamou **8** curassow, troupial
chimney-nesting: 5 swift
class: 4 Aves
colony: 5 roost **7** rookery
combining form: 5 ornis **6** ornith **7** ornitho **8** ornithes (plural)
corvine: (see **crow family** below)
crocodile: 9 trochilus
crow family: 3 daw, jay, kae **4** rook **5** raven **6** chough, corbie, magpie **7** jackdaw
diving: 3 auk **4** smew **5** grebe, murre **6** dipper, petrel **8** murrelet **9** guillemot, merganser
European: 3 mag, mew, nun **4** clee, darr, gled, mall, merl, pope, rook, ruff, shag, smew, wren **5** amsel, crake, egret, finch, glede, merle, ousel, ouzel, pewit, pipit, terek, whaup **6** cuckoo, dunlin, hoopoe, linnet, martin, merlin, missel, redleg, roller, thrush **7** bustard, jackdaw, kestrel, lapwing, martlet, ortolan, redwing, ruddock, sparrow, wagtail, wryneck **8** accentor, blackcap, brantail, dabchick, dotterel, garganey, nightjar, nuthatch, peesweep, redstart, reedling, starling, throstle, wheatear, whimbrel, whinchat, woodcock **9** brambling, chaffinch, crossbill, fieldfare, stonechat **10** chiffchaff, goatsucker, kingfisher **11** lammergeier
extinct: 3 moa **4** dodo, mamo **8** Diatryma **9** aepyornis, solitaire
fabulous: 3 roc **5** hansa **6** simurg **7** phoenix, simurgh
fish-eating: 4 erne
flightless: 3 emu, moa **4** dodo, kagu, kiwi, rhea, weka **6** kakapo, ratite, takahe **7** apteryx, ostrich, penguin, roatelo **8** Diatryma, notornis **9** cassowary
fruit-eating: 4 coly **6** parrot, toucan
game: 4 duck, guan, rail, sora, teal **5** brant, goose, quail, snipe **6** chukar, grouse, turkey **7** bustard, mallard, pintail, widgeon **8** baldpate, bobwhite, moorfowl, pheasant, shoveler, tragopan, wildfowl, woodcock **9** merganser, partridge, ptarmigan
ground-dwelling: 5 colin, quail **6** grouse, peahen, turkey **7** chicken, peacock, peafowl **8** bobwhite, moorfowl, pheasant **9** partridge, ptarmigan
Hawaiian: 2 io **3** ava, ioa, iwa **4** koae, mamo, moho, omao
Indian: 4 baya, kala, koel, koil **5** sarus, shama **6** argala, bulbul, homrai, luggar **7** peacock **8** adjutant, amadavat, tragopan
Jamaican: 7 vervain
large: 3 emu, moa **4** guan **5** eagle **6** curlew, jabiru, willet **7** bustard, megapod, ostrich, pelican, seriema **8** curassow, megapode, shoebill
largest: 7 ostrich
Madagascar: 6 drongo **7** anhinga, kirombo, roatelo
marsh: 4 coot, rail, sora **5** crane, snipe, stilt **8** reedling **9** gallinule
Mexican: 6 jacana
mythical: 3 roc **7** phoenix **9** fenghuang, feng-hwang
New Zealand: 3 ihi, kea, poe, tui **4** huia, kaka, kaki, kiwi, koko, ruru, titi, weka **6** kakapo **7** apteryx **8** morepork, notornis
nocturnal: 3 owl **5** cahow, owlet **7** bullbat, dorhawk **8** guacharo, nightjar **9** nighthawk **10** goatsucker
North American: 3 ani, tit **4** coot, pape, sora, stib, wamp, wren **5** booby, colin, crane, egret, junco, murre, robin, swift, veery, vireo **6** chebec, darter, dunlin, fulmar, grouse, hagdon, phoebe, towhee, turkey, verdin, willet **7** anhinga, blue jay, catbird, flicker, grackle, tanager **8** bobolink, bobwhite, car-

dinal, killdeer, nuthatch, thrasher, titmouse, wheatear **9** chickadee, crossbill, nighthawk, partridge, snakebird **10** bufflehead **12** whippoorwill

of Arabian Nights: **3** roc

of brilliant plumage: **4** lory, toco, tody **5** macaw, pitta **6** oriole, parrot, toucan, trogon **7** jacamar, kirombo, minivet **8** lorikeet, parakeet, pheasant, tragopan

of omen: **7** waybird

of peace: **4** dove

of prey: **3** owl **4** gled, hawk, kite **5** buteo, eagle, glead, glede, harpy **6** condor, elenet, falcon, osprey, raptor **7** buzzard, goshawk, harrier, kestrel, vulture **8** caracara **9** accipiter **11** lammergeier

passerine: (see **songbird** below)

razorbilled: **3** auk

relating to: **5** avian, avine **8** ornithic

shore: **3** auk **4** gull, ruff, tern **5** reeve, snipe, stilt **6** avocet, avoset, curlew, dunlin, plover, puffin, willet **7** lapwing, skimmer **8** dotterel, killdeer, redshank, whimbrel, woodcock **9** phalarope, sandpiper, turnstone

small: **3** tit **4** tody, wren **5** finch, pewee, pipit, serin, sylph, vireo **6** canary, sappho, tomtit, verdin **7** manakin, sparrow **8** titmouse **9** chickadee

songbird: **3** jay, tit **4** chat, crow, lark, wren **5** finch, mavie, mavis, pipit, robin, shama, veery, vireo **6** bulbul, canary, dipper, linnet, oriole, shrike, thrush **7** catbird, creeper, hill tit, kinglet, redwing, skylark, sparrow, swallow, tanager, titlark, wagtail, warbler, waxwing **8** accentor, amadavat, bobolink, brantail, cardinal, nuthatch, philomel, redstart, starling, thrasher, whinchat, woodlark **9** chickadee, stonechat **10** chiffchaff, flycatcher **11** nightingale

South American: **3** ara, hia **4** anna, guan, jacu, loro, mitu, rhea, soco, toco, yeni **5** chaja, egret, macaw, potoo, sylph **6** chunga, cracid, jabiru, motmot, sappho, toucan **7** cariama, cotinga, hoatzin, jacamar, limpkin, manakin, seriema, tinamou **8** boatbill, caracara, curassow, guacharo, hoactzin, screamer, tapacolo, tapaculo, terutero, troupial **9** campanero, trumpeter

talking: **4** myna **5** mynah **6** parrot

tropical: **3** ani **6** barbet, drongo, motmot, quezal, toucan, trogon **7** cacique, hoatzin, jacamar, mana-

kin, quetzal, sawbill, waxbill **8** guacharo, hoactzin, troupial

turkey-like: **8** curassow

unfledged: **4** eyas **5** chick **6** gorlin **8** nestling

wading: **4** ibis, rail **5** crane, egret, heron, stork **6** godwit, jabiru, jacana **7** bittern, courlan, limpkin, tattler **8** boatbill, flamingo, shoebill, umbrette **9** spoonbill **10** hammerhead

web-footed: **3** auk **4** duck, loon, swan **5** goose, murre **6** avocet, avoset, darter, fulmar, gannet, petrel, puffin **7** anhinga, pelican, penguin **8** shoveler **9** albatross, cormorant, guillemot, merganser, razorbill, snakebird **10** shearwater

West Indian: **3** ani **4** tody

birdbrain
5 dummy, dunce, idiot, moron **7** dullard **8** dullhead, dumbbell **9** ignoramus, simpleton **10** rattlehead **11** featherhead

birdcage
large: **6** aviary, volary, volery

birdlife
5 ornis **8** avifauna

bird pepper
8 capsicum

birds' eggs
study of: **6** oology

bird's head
top: **5** pilea (plural) **6** pileum

birr
3 pep **4** tuck **5** moxie, vigor **6** energy **7** potency **9** hardihood

birth
4 dawn, flow, rise, slip, stem **5** arise, issue, onset, start **6** outset, spring **7** bearing, emanate, genesis, opening, proceed **8** geniture, nascence, nascency, nativity, outstart **9** beginning, originate **10** derive from **12** commencement

combining form: **4** toky

birth-control leader
6 Sanger (Margaret)

birth flower
April: **5** daisy
August: **9** gladiolus
December: **10** poinsettia
February: **8** primrose
January: **9** carnation
July: **8** sweet pea
June: **4** rose
March: **6** violet
May: **15** lily of the valley

November: **13** chrysanthemum
October: **6** dahlia
September: **5** aster

birthmark
4 mole **5** nevus, point, trait **7** feature **9** character

birthright
6 legacy **8** appanage, heritage **9** heritance, patrimony, privilege **10** perquisite **11** inheritance, prerogative

birthroot
8 trillium

birthstone
April: **7** diamond **8** sapphire
August: **7** peridot **8** sardonyx
December: **6** zircon **9** turquoise
February: **8** amethyst
January: **6** garnet
July: **4** ruby
June: **5** agate, pearl **11** alexandrite
March: **6** jasper **10** aquamarine, bloodstone
May: **7** emerald
November: **5** topaz
October: **4** opal **10** tourmaline
September: **8** sapphire **10** chrysolite

biscuit
3 bun **4** roll, rusk, snap **6** bisque, cookie **7** cracker **8** cracknel, hardtack

Scottish: **4** bake

bishop
district: **7** diocese
headdress: **5** miter, mitre
seat of office: **3** see
skullcap: **9** zucchetto
staff: **7** crosier, crozier
throne: **8** cathedra

bishopric
3 see **7** diocese

bismuth
symbol: **2** Bi

bison
European: **6** wisent **7** aurochs
family: **7** Bovidae
North American: **7** buffalo

bistered
4 dark **5** brown, dusky, swart **6** brunet, swarth **7** swarthy **11** dark-skinned

bistro
4 café **6** nitery **7** cabaret, hot spot **8** nightery **9** nightclub, night spot **11** discotheque **13** watering place

bit
3 end, jot **4** atom, bite, curb, drop, iota, mite, time, whet **5** check, minim, scrap, space, speck, spell,

while **6** bridle, hold in, morsel **7** inhibit, smidgen, stretch **8** fragment, hold back, hold down, molecule, mouthful, particle, restrain, withhold **9** constrain

bit by bit
9 gradually, piecemeal

bitch goddess
7 success

bite
3 cut, eat, lot **4** burn, chaw, chew, gnaw, part, tapa **5** bever, chack, champ, chomp, erode, mug-up, munch, piece, quota, scour, share, slice, smart, snack, stang, sting, tooth **6** crunch, morsel, nibble **7** corrode, eat away, partage, portion, scrunch **8** mouthful **9** allotment, allowance, masticate

Bithiah's husband
5 Mered

biting
5 crisp, nippy **7** cutting, ingoing, mordant **8** clear-cut, incisive **9** sarcastic, trenchant **11** penetrating

bitter
3 bad **4** acid, hard, tart **5** acerb, acrid, harsh, sharp **6** brutal, picric, rugged, severe, woeful **7** austere, divided, galling, hostile, painful **8** grievous, rigorous, virulent **9** alienated, amaroidal, rancorous, vexatious, vitriolic **10** afflictive, disturbing, unpleasant **11** distasteful, distressing, intemperate, unpalatable **12** antagonistic, disagreeable
combining form: **4** picr **5** picro

bitterness
8 acrimony, asperity

bitterroot
7 dogbane

bitumen
3 tar **5** pitch **7** asphalt, naphtha **8** blacktop

bivalve
4 clam, spat **6** cockle, mussel, oyster, pholas **7** geoduck, goeduck, mollusk, pandora, piddock, scallop **10** brachiopod

bivouac
4 camp **6** encamp, laager, maroon **10** encampment

bizarre
3 odd **5** antic, queer, weird **7** curious, oddball, strange, unusual **8** peculiar, singular **9** fantastic, grotesque **10** outlandish

Bizet opera
6 Carmen

blab
3 gab, yak **4** chat, talk, tell **5** rumor **6** babble, betray, gabble, gossip, jabber, reveal, tattle **7** chatter, divulge, palaver **8** disclose, give away

blabber
3 gab **4** chat **5** clack, drool, prate **6** babble, drivel, gabber, gabble, jabber, magpie, prater **7** blather, chatter, palaver, prattle, twaddle **8** jabberer, prattler **9** chatterer **10** chatterbox

blabbermouth
6 gabber, magpie, prater **7** windbag **8** jabberer, prattler **9** bandarlog **10** chatterbox

black
3 jet **4** ebon, foul, inky, noir, onyx **5** bleak, dirty, ebony, nasty, raven, sable, slate, soily, utter **6** bruise, dismal, dreary, filthy, gloomy, grubby, impure, pitchy, somber **7** contuse, piceous, squalid, unclean **8** absolute, charcoal, complete, funereal, outright **9** downright, out-and-out, pitch-dark **10** depressing, depressive, oppressive **11** dispiriting
combining form: **3** mel **4** atro, mela, melo **5** melam, melan **6** melano

blackball
4 veto **7** boycott, exclude **9** ostracize

black bass
7 sunfish **10** priestfish

black beast
4 hate **7** bugbear **8** anathema **9** bête noire **11** abomination, detestation

blackbird
see at **bird**

black cohosh
7 bugbane

black crappie
7 sunfish **10** calico bass

black death
6 plague

black diamond
4 coal **8** hematite **9** carbonado

blacken
4 slur, soot **5** libel, smear **6** defame, malign, vilify **7** asperse, slander, traduce **10** calumniate

black eye
4 blot, onus, slur **5** mouse, odium, stain **6** shiner, stigma **11** bar sinister

blackfish
5 whale **6** bowfin, salmon, tautog **7** galjoen **8** luderick

Black Forest
city: **10** Baden-Baden
peak: **8** Feldberg
river: **5** Rhine **6** Danube

black gold
3 oil **9** maldonite, petroleum

blackguard
4 heel **5** knave, rogue **6** rascal **7** lowlife, villain **9** miscreant, scoundrel

blackhead
4 clam **5** sebum **6** comedo, mussel **9** scaup duck

blackheart
9 sandpiper **12** whortleberry

blackjack
3 oak **6** coerce **7** tankard **9** scaup duck **10** sphalerite

black lead
8 graphite

black letter
6 Gothic **10** Old English

black magic
10 witchcraft

blackmail
6 extort **8** chantage **9** extortion

Black Muslim founder
4 Fard (Wallace) **6** Farrad (Walli)

black out
5 annul, erase, faint, swoon **6** cancel, delete, efface **7** expunge **10** obliterate

blackpoll
7 warbler

Black Prince
6 Edward

Blackshirt
7 fascist

blacksmith
4 fish **6** forger, plover **7** farrier, striker **10** horseshoer

blacktail
6 dassie **11** salmon trout

blackthorn
4 cane, plum **7** pear haw **8** cocktail

black vomit
11 hematemesis, yellow fever

blackwash
5 libel **6** malign, vilify **7** asperse,

slander, traduce **9** denigrate
10 calumniate, scandalize, villainize

black widow
6 spider

bladder
3 sac **4** cyst **5** pouch **6** vesica
7 blister, vacuole **7** vesicae (plural),
vesicle **8** vesicula **9** vesiculae
(plural)
combining form: **3** asc **4** asci, asco,
cyst, phys **5** cysto, physo

blah
4 bosh, dull **5** hooey **6** bunkum,
dreary, humbug, stodgy **7** humdrum **8** banausic, nonsense, pishposh, plodding **10** balderdash, monotonous, pedestrian

blamable
see **blameworthy**

blame
3 rap **4** onus **5** fault, guilt, knock
6 accuse **7** censure, condemn
8 denounce, reproach **9** criticize,
reprehend, reprobate **10** accusation, denunciate, imputation
12 condemnation, denunciation,
reprehension
Scottish: **4** wite, wyte **6** dirdum

blameless
4 good, pure **5** clean **8** innocent,
unguilty **9** crimeless, exemplary,
faultless, guiltless, lily-white, righteous **10** inculpable

blameworthy
5 amiss **6** guilty, sinful, unholy
8 culpable, faultful **10** censurable,
delinquent, illaudable, punishable
13 reprehensible, uncommendable

blanch
4 pale **5** quail, start, white, wince
6 bleach, flinch, recoil, shrink,
whiten **7** decolor, squinch

blanched
3 wan **4** ashy, pale **5** ashen, livid,
waxen **6** doughy, pallid
9 colorless

Blancheflor's beloved
6 Flores, Floris

bland
4 flat, mild, soft **5** balmy, banal,
suave, vapid **6** gentle, smooth, urbane, watery **7** insipid, lenient,
sapless **8** waterish **10** nambypamby, wishy-washy

blandish
3 con **4** coax **6** cajole **7** blarney,
flatter, wheedle **8** soft-soap
9 sweet-talk

blandishment
3 oil **7** blarney, incense **8** flattery,
soft soap **9** adulation

blank
4 skip **5** chasm, empty, utter **6** vacant **7** deadpan **8** absolute, omission **9** downright, out-and-out,
oversight **11** preterition **12** inexpressive, unexpressive

blanket
3 cap **5** cover, crown **6** afghan,
stroud **7** overlay **8** overcast
10 overspread
Spanish: **6** sarape, serape

blankness
7 vacancy, vacuity **9** emptiness
11 vacuousness

blare
5 shout **6** scream, shriek

blaring
4 loud **7** roaring **8** piercing
10 stentorian **11** full-mouthed, stentorious **12** earsplitting

blarney
3 con, oil **4** coax **6** cajole **7** incense, wheedle **8** blandish, flattery,
soft soap **9** adulation, sweet-talk
12 blandishment

blasé
5 jaded **7** knowing, worldly **8** mondaine **9** apathetic **11** indifferent,
worldly-wise **12** disenchanted,
disentranced, sophisticate **13** disillusioned, sophisticated

blaspheme
5 abuse, curse, swear **6** revile
7 profane

blasphemous
7 profane **12** sacrilegious

blasphemy
5 abuse **7** cursing, cussing, shaming **8** swearing **9** befouling, profanity, sacrilege, violation **10** execration **11** desecration,
imprecation, profanation

blast
4 bang, beat, belt, boom, clap,
dash, drub, ruin, slam, slug, toot,
wham, whip **5** burst, crack, crash,
smash, wreck **6** blight, wallop
7 destroy, lambast **8** lambaste
9 overwhelm

blat
6 cry out **7** exclaim **8** blurt out
9 ejaculate

blatant
4 loud **5** gaudy, overt **6** arrant,
brassy, brazen, flashy, garish, patent, tawdry **7** glaring **8** impudent,
overbold, strident **9** barefaced,
clamorous, shameless, unabashed
10 boisterous, unblushing, vociferant, vociferous **11** loudmouthed
12 obstreperous

blather
4 bosh, rave **5** drool, hokum, prate
6 babble, bunkum, drivel, gabble
7 blabber, prattle, twaddle **8** nonsense **10** balderdash, double-talk,
flapdoodle

blaze
4 glow **5** blare, flame, flare, glare,
shine **7** declare **8** announce, proclaim **10** incandesce **11** scintillate
Scottish: **3** low **4** lowe

blazes
4 hell **5** abyss, hades, Sheol **6** Tophet **7** Gehenna, inferno **9** perdition

blazing
5 afire, fiery **6** aflame, alight, ardent, fervid, red-hot **7** burning, fervent, flaming, flaring, ignited **9** perfervid **10** passionate
11 conflagrant, impassioned

blazing star
8 tritonia **9** colicroot

blazon
5 sound **7** declare, publish **8** announce, proclaim **9** advertise,
broadcast **10** annunciate, bruit
about, promulgate

bleach
5 white **6** blanch, blench, whiten
7 decolor **8** peroxide

bleak
4 dour, grim, hard **5** harsh **6** dismal, dreary, gloomy, severe, somber **7** austere **8** funereal **9** stringent **10** depressing, oppressive
13 disheartening

blear
3 dim **4** blur, dull **5** faint, vague
7 obscure, shadowy, unclear **10** illdefined, indistinct

bleary
3 dim **5** all in, faint, spent, vague
6 effete, used up **7** drained, fargone, obscure, shadowy, unclear,

worn-out **8** depleted **9** exhausted, washed-out **10** ill-defined, indistinct

bleat
3 baa **4** crab, fuss, yawp **5** gripe **6** squawk, yammer **7** blow off

bleed
4 ooze, seep, weep **5** exude, mulct, stick, sweat **6** extort, fleece, strain **8** transude

bleeding heart
8 dicentra **11** sympathizer

blemish
3 mar **4** flaw, harm, hurt, scar, vice, wart **5** fault, spoil **6** blotch, damage, defect, impair, injure **7** blister, tarnish, vitiate **8** pockmark **13** disfigurement

blench
5 quail, start, white, wince **6** bleach, flinch, recoil, shrink, whiten **7** decolor, squinch

blend
3 mix **4** fuse, meld **5** alloy, immix, unify, unite **6** commix, fusion **7** amalgam, arrange, combine, mixture **8** coalesce, compound, conflate, immingle, intermix **9** commingle, composite, harmonize, integrate, interfuse **10** amalgamate, commixture, symphonize, synthesize **11** interfusion, orchestrate **12** amalgamation, intermixture

blender setting
4 whip **5** puree

bless
4 laud **5** extol **6** hallow, praise **7** glorify **8** eulogize, sanctify **9** celebrate **10** consecrate, panegyrize

blessed
4 holy **6** sacred **7** saintly **8** hallowed **9** unprofane **10** sanctified **11** consecrated

blessedness
5 bliss **9** beatitude, happiness **12** blissfulness

blessing
2 OK **4** boon, good, okay **5** favor, grace **6** thanks **7** benefit, benison, godsend **8** approval **9** advantage **11** approbation, benediction **12** thanksgiving

blight
3 nip **4** dash, ruin **5** blast **7** disease

blimp
5 fatso, fatty **7** airship **8** zeppelin **9** dirigible

blind
4 daze, dull **5** decoy, drunk, front, shill **6** capper, dazzle **7** eyeless, muddled, shutter **8** bedazzle, unseeing **9** pixilated, shillaber, sightless **10** inebriated, lackluster, lusterless, visionless **11** intoxicated
combining form: **5** typhl **6** typhlo

blind alley
6 pocket **7** dead end, impasse **8** cul-de-sac

blind god
4 Hoth **5** Cupid, Hoder, Hodur, Hothr

blindworm
6 lizard

blink
3 bat **4** wink **5** flash **7** flicker, nictate, twinkle **9** nictitate

blink at
4 omit **6** forget, ignore, slight **7** connive, neglect **8** discount, overlook **9** disregard

blip
3 box **4** cuff, slap **5** smack, spank **6** buffet, censor, screen **9** expurgate **10** bowdlerize

bliss
4 Zion **6** Canaan, heaven **7** elysium, nirvana **8** empyrean, paradise **9** beatitude, happiness **11** blessedness

blissful
5 happy **6** elated **8** beatific, ecstatic, euphoric **9** contented

blissfulness
7 ecstasy **8** euphoria **9** beatitude, happiness **10** exaltation **11** blessedness

blister
4 bleb, flay **5** blain, bulla, slash **6** canker, scathe, scorch **7** lambast, scarify, scourge, vesicle **8** lambaste, vesicate **9** castigate, excoriate
combining form: **7** vesicul **8** vesiculo

blithe
3 gay **4** boon **5** jolly, merry, sunny **6** cheery, chirpy, jocund, jovial **7** gleeful **8** cheerful, chirrupy, mirthful, sunbeamy **9** lightsome **12** lighthearted

blithering
4 rank **5** gross, utter **7** blasted **8** absolute, outright, positive **9** downright, out-and-out

blithesome
see **blithe**

blitz
4 raid **7** bombard **10** mass attack **11** bombardment

bloated
5 puffy **6** stuffy **7** pompous **8** arrogant **10** pontifical **11** magisterial **13** self-important

bloc
4 ring **5** party **7** combine, faction **8** alliance **9** coalition **11** combination

block
3 bar, dam, ell **4** clog, fill, plug, stop, wall, wing **5** annex, brake, choke, close **6** cut off, hinder, impede **7** barrier, congest, occlude, stopper **8** obstruct **9** barricade, extension, intercept
iron: **5** anvil

blockade
3 bar **4** stop, wall **5** beset, siege **6** invest **7** barrier, besiege **9** barricade, beleaguer, blank wall, roadblock

blockbuster
4 bomb

blockhead
4 dolt, dope **5** dunce, idiot, ninny **8** clodpate, dumbbell, numskull **9** simpleton **10** thickskull

blockheaded
4 dumb **5** dense, thick **6** stupid **7** doltish **10** numskulled

block out
5 close, draft **6** screen, shroud, sketch **7** outline, shut off **8** obstruct, skeleton **9** adumbrate **12** characterize

block up
4 clog, plug, stop

bloke
3 guy, man **4** chap, gent **6** fellow **9** gentleman

blond
4 fair **5** light, straw **6** flaxen, golden **7** towhead **8** platinum **9** towheaded

blood
4 gore **6** murder, origin **7** descent, lineage **8** ancestry **10** extraction
cancer of: **8** leukemia
cell: **3** red **4** poly **5** white **8** hemocyte, monocyte, platelet **9** corpuscle, leukocyte **10** lymphocyte **11** erythrocyte, granulocyte
clot: **8** thrombus

clotted: **4** gore
coloring matter: **10** hemoglobin
combining form: **3** hem **4** emia,
  haem, hema, hemi, hemo **5** aemia,
  haema, haemo, hemat, hemia
  6 haemat, haemia, hemato, sangui
  7 haemato **8** sanguini, sanguino
disease: **6** anemia **8** leukemia
  10 hemophilia
factor: **2** RH
feud: **8** vendetta
fluid part: **5** serum **6** plasma
of the gods: **5** ichor
particle in: **7** embolus
poisoning: **6** pyemia **7** toxemia
  8 copremia, sapremia
  10 septicemia
pressure: **8** systolic **9** diastolic
relating to: **5** hemal, hemic
  7 hematal
serum: **6** plasma
study of: **10** hematology
sugar: **7** glucose

bloodbath
  7 carnage **8** butchery, massacre
  9 slaughter

bloodless
  4 dull, hard, pale **6** anemic, pallid,
  watery **8** waterish **9** insensate
  10 anesthetic, insensible
  11 insensitive

bloodletting
  10 phlebotomy **11** venesection

bloodlike
  8 hematoid

bloodline
  6 family, strain

bloodroot
  7 puccoon **8** turmeric **10** tetterwort
  11 Indian paint

bloodshed
  place of: **8** aceldama

bloodstained
  4 gory **7** imbrued **8** sanguine
  10 sanguinary **11** ensanguined,
  sanguineous

bloodstone
  10 chalcedony

bloodsucker
  4 tick **5** lamia, leech **6** lizard,
  sponge **7** sponger, vampire
  8 barnacle, hanger on, parasite
  10 freeloader **12** lounge lizard

bloodthirsty
  8 sanguine **9** homicidal, murdering, murderous **10** sanguinary
  11 sanguineous

blood vessel
  4 vein **5** aorta **6** artery **7** jugular
  9 capillary
combining form: **3** vas **4** angi, vasi,
  vaso **5** angio
rupture: **6** rhexis

bloodwort
  6 yarrow **8** centaury **10** herb robert **11** salad burnet

bloody
  4 gory, grim **7** imbrued **8** sanguine
  9 cutthroat, homicidal, murdering,
  murderous **10** sanguinary **11** ensanguined, sanguineous
  12 slaughterous

bloom
  4 blow, glow, posy **5** blush
  6 flower **7** blossom, burgeon
  10 effloresce

blooper
  4 slip, trip **5** boner, break, error,
  fluff, gaffe, lapse **6** boo-boo, bungle **7** blunder, faux pas, mistake
  8 solecism **9** indecorum
  11 impropriety

blossom
  3 bud **4** blow, glow, open, posy
  5 bloom, blush, flush **6** flower, unfold **7** burgeon **10** effloresce

blot
  4 blur, onus, slur, smut, spot
  5 brand, odium, stain **6** stigma
  7 bestain, blemish **8** black eye, discolor **11** bar sinister

blotch
  6 macula, macule, mottle
  7 splodge, splotch
combining form: **5** macul **6** maculi,
  maculo

blot out
  5 abate, annul, erase **6** cancel, delete, efface **7** abolish, expunge
  9 eradicate, extirpate **10** annihilate, extinguish, obliterate
  11 exterminate

blotto
  see **drunk**

blouse
  5 middy, shirt, smock, tunic
  6 basque, guimpe

bloviate
  4 rant, rave **5** mouth, orate **7** declaim, soapbox **8** harangue,
  perorate

blow
  3 bop, fan, hit, jar **4** bang, bash,
  belt, biff, brag, bump, cuff, gasp,
  gust, huff, jolt, pant, puff, slam,

slug, swat, whop, wind **5** bloom,
boast, break, crack, pound, prate,
punch, shock, slosh, smack, smash,
vaunt, waste, whack **6** flower, impact, ruffle, thwack, wallop, winnow **7** blossom, burgeon, consume,
fritter, respite **8** breather, knockout,
outbloom, squander **9** bastinado,
collision, dissipate, gasconade,
throw away **10** concussion, effloresce, frivol away, percussion, trifle
away **11** rodomontade

blow-by-blow
  6 minute **8** detailed, itemized, thorough **9** clocklike **10** particular

blowhard
  see **boaster**

blow in
  4 come **6** arrive, show up, turn up

blowout
  4 bash **6** shindy **7** shindig

blowsy
  5 dowdy **6** frowsy, sordid **8** slattern **10** slatternly **13** draggletailed

blow up
  4 boil, burn, fume, rage **5** anger,
  burst, go off **6** seethe **7** bristle, explode **8** boil over, detonate, disprove, dynamite **9** discredit

blowy
  4 airy **5** gusty, windy **6** breezy

blubber
  3 cry, sob **4** pipe, wail, weep
  6 boohoo

bludgeon
  3 bat **4** club **5** baton, billy, bully
  6 cudgel, hector **7** bluster, war club
  8 browbeat, bulldoze, bullyrag
  9 bastinado, billy club, strong-arm,
  truncheon **10** intimidate, nightstick
British: **4** cosh

blue
  3 low, sea **4** down, racy **5** ocean,
  salty, shady, spicy **6** purple, risqué,
  wicked **7** profane **8** dejected,
  downcast, off-color **9** depressed,
  woebegone **10** dispirited, suggestive **11** downhearted
  12 disconsolate
combining form: **3** ind **4** cyan, indi,
  indo **5** cyano
dark: **5** perse **6** indigo
grayish: **5** merle, slate **7** celeste
greenish: **4** aqua, bice, cyan, teal
  5 beryl **6** cobalt **7** azurite **8** calamine **9** turquoise
moderate: **5** copen
reddish: **5** smalt **6** marine, purple, vi-

olet **7** cyanine, gentian, lobelia
8 mazarine
sky: **5** azure **8** cerulean

___ Blue
3 Ben

blue blood
5 elite **6** aristo, gentry **7** aristoi
9 gentility, gentleman, patrician
10 aristocrat, upper class
11 aristocracy

bluebonnet
4 Scot **6** parrot **10** cornflower

Blue Boy painter
12 Gainsborough (Thomas)

bluecoat
3 cop **5** bobby **6** copper **8** Dogberry **9** constable, policeman

blue-eyed
8 favorite, precious **10** fair-haired

Bluegrass State
8 Kentucky

Blue Grotto site
5 Capri

bluejacket
6 sailor

blue jeans
6 denims

blue moon
3 age, eon **4** aeon **7** dog's age
8 coon's age, eternity **12** donkey's
years

bluenose
4 prig **5** prude **7** puritan **8** comstock **9** Mrs. Grundy, nice Nelly
10 goody-goody

bluenosed
4 prig, prim **6** prissy, stuffy **7** prudish **8** priggish **9** Victorian **10** tightlaced **11** puritanical, straitlaced

blue-pencil
4 edit **6** delete, revise

bluepoint
6 oyster

blueprint
4 cast, plan **5** chart **6** design, devise, scheme, sketch **7** arrange,
outline, project **8** game plan,
strategy

blue-ribbon
3 top **5** prime **6** Grade A **7** capital
8 five-star, top-notch **9** excellent,
first-rate, top-drawer **10** first-class
11 first-string

blues
5 dumps, gloom **7** dismals, sadness

9 dejection **10** depression, melancholy **11** unhappiness
12 mournfulness

bluff
3 act **4** curt, fake, fool, sham
5 blunt, feign, frank, gruff, rough,
sharp, trick **6** abrupt, affect, assume, betray, candid, crusty, delude, direct, humbug, illude, snippy
7 beguile, brusque, deceive, mislead, pretend **8** snippety **9** outspoken **10** forthright, no-nonsense
11 counterfeit, double-cross, plainspoken, short-spoken

blunder
4 bull, goof, mess, slip, trip
5 boner, botch, error, fluff, gaffe,
gum up, lapse **6** bobble, bollix,
bumble, bungle, goof up
7 blooper, louse up, mistake, stumble **8** flounder

blunderbuss
3 gun **7** bungler, firearm

blunt
4 bald, curt, dull, mull, numb
5 bluff, brief, gruff, short **6** abrupt,
benumb, crusty, deaden, obtund,
obtuse, snippy, snubby, weaken
7 brusque, cripple, disable, disedge, stupefy **8** enfeeble, hebetate,
snippety **9** attenuate, undermine
10 debilitate **11** desensitize
12 unstrengthen

blur
3 dim, fog **4** blot, dull, mist, onus,
slur, spot **5** befog, blear, brand,
cloud, muddy, odium, smear, stain,
taint **6** smudge, stigma **7** becloud,
besmear, confuse, tarnish **8** besmirch, black eye, discolor **11** bar
sinister
in printing: **6** mackle

blurb
2 ad **4** plug, puff **6** notice **7** puffing, write-up **12** commendation

blurt
4 blat, bolt **6** cry out **7** exclaim
9 ejaculate

blush
4 glow, rose **5** bloom, color, flush,
rouge **6** mantle, pinken, redden
7 blossom, crimson, roseate

bluster
4 bawl, huff, rage, roar, rout
5 blast, bully, storm **6** bellow,
clamor, hector **7** dragoon **8** bludgeon, browbeat, bulldoze, bullyrag
10 intimidate

blustery
4 wild **5** rough **6** raging, stormy
7 furious **8** stormful **9** turbulent
11 tempestuous

boa
5 scarf, snake

board
4 slab **5** get on, house, lodge, put
up, table **6** bestow, billet, embark,
harbor **7** emplane, entrain, quarter
artist's: **7** palette

board game
see at **game**

boarding house
7 pension **8** pensione

boardwalk
9 promenade

boast
4 blow, brag, crow, puff **5** exalt,
mouth, prate, preen, vaunt **7** bluster, show off, swagger **9** gasconade **11** rodomontade

boaster
6 blower, gascon **7** bragger,
vaunter **8** blowhard, braggart,
puckfist, rodomont **11** braggadocio, rodomontade

boastful
6 braggy **8** arrogant, braggart,
vaunting **9** big-headed, conceited
11 pretentious, rodomontade
12 braggadocian, vainglorious
13 swelled-headed
Scottish: **6** vaunty

boat
3 ark **4** ship **6** vessel **7** steamer
above-water: **9** hydrofoil
Arab: **4** dhow
bottom projection: **4** keel
British: **5** coble **6** wherry **7** coracle
Canadian: **6** bateau
canoe-like: **7** pirogue
captain: **7** skipper
cargo: **3** hoy **4** scow **5** barge
6 wherry **7** drogher, gabbard, gabbart, lighter **8** canaller
Chinese: **4** junk **6** sampan
dock, basin: **6** marina
Dutch: **6** dogger, hooker, schuit,
schuyt **8** bilander
Egyptian: **6** sandal **8** dahabeah
Eskimo: **5** kayak, umiak **6** oomiak
7 bidarka **8** bidarkee
fishing: **4** dory **5** coble, smack
6 dogger, lugger **7** caravel, coracle, tartana, trawler
flat-bottomed: **4** dory, keel, punt,

scow **5** barge, coble **6** bateau, bugeye **7** lighter, pontoon
French: **7** caravel
front end of: **3** bow **4** fore, prow
hide-covered: **7** coracle
Indian: **4** doni **5** dhoni **7** masoola
Indonesian: **4** prao, prau, proa **5** prahu
Irish: **7** currach, curragh
Italian: **7** gondola
landing: **3** LST
Levantine: **4** saic **6** caique
mail: **6** packet
Mediterranean: **6** settee
motor: **7** cruiser, inboard **8** outboard, runabout
narrow: **4** punt **5** canoe, scull, shell **7** gondola **8** canaller
Nile river: **6** sandal **8** dahabeah
on a ship: **3** gig **5** jolly **6** launch **7** pinnace
Philippine: **5** banca, casco
pole-propelled: **4** punt **7** gondola
Polynesian: **4** pahi
race: **7** regatta
racing: **3** gig **5** scull, shell, yacht **6** torpid
rear end of: **3** aft **5** stern
river: **4** scow **5** barge, canoe, ferry **6** packet, sampan, wherry
round: **4** gufa **5** goofa, guffa **6** goofah
rowing: **4** dory **5** coble, scull, shell, skiff **6** caique, dinghy, randan
sailing: **4** yawl **5** ketch, skiff, sloop, smack, yacht **6** cutter, lateen, lugger, settee **7** pinnace **8** lateener, schooner
Scandinavian: **4** pram **5** praam
Scottish: **5** coble **7** currach, curragh, gabbard, gabbart
scouting: **7** vedette, vidette
small: **3** cog **4** dory **5** coble, skiff **6** bugeye, cockle, dinghy **7** coracle, shallop
song: **9** barcarole **10** barcarolle
three-hulled: **8** trimaran
three-oared: **6** randan
towing: **3** tug
twin-hulled: **9** catamaran
two-masted: **4** yawl **5** ketch **8** schooner

boatman
5 poler **6** Charon **7** oarsman, paddler **8** deckhand **9** gondolier

boat-shaped
8 scaphoid **9** cymbiform, navicular
combining form: **5** scaph **6** scapho
ornament: **3** nef

boatswain
4 bos'n **5** bosun **6** jaeger **10** tropic bird

Boaz's wife
4 Ruth

bob
3 jig, nod, rap, tap **4** buff, crop, dock **5** bunch, float, gigue **6** weight **7** cluster, nosegay

bobbery
3 row **4** fray **5** brawl, fight, melee **6** affray, fracas, hubbub **7** ruction **10** donnybrook **11** disturbance

bobbin
4 pirn **5** quill, spool **7** spindle

bobble
4 mess **5** botch, gum up **6** bollix, bungle, goof up **7** louse up

bobby
6 copper, peeler **7** officer **9** constable, policeman

bobwhite
5 quail **9** partridge

Boccaccio
beloved: **9** Fiammetta
tales: **9** Decameron

bode
4 omen **5** augur **7** betoken, portend, presage, promise **8** foreshow **9** foretoken **10** foreshadow

bodement
4 omen **6** augury **7** portent, presage **9** foretoken **10** prognostic

bodiless
9 asomatous, unfleshly **10** discarnate, immaterial, unphysical **11** disembodied, incorporeal **13** insubstantial

bodily
6 carnal **7** fleshly, sensual, somatic **8** corporal, physical **9** corporeal

body
4 bulk, core, mass, mort, pith, soma **5** array, batch, bunch, clump, group, stiff, stock, torso **6** amount, budget, bundle, burden, corpse, corpus, object, parcel, staple, upshot, volume **7** cadaver, carcass, cluster, corpora (plural), purport, quantum, remains **8** physique, quantity **9** aggregate, substance
combining form: **4** dema, soma, some, somi (plural) **5** somat, somia, somus **6** somata (plural), somato
suffix: **2** cy

body cavity
5 cecum, sinus **6** coelom **7** abdomen **8** hemocoel

body check
5 block

bodyguard
9 attendant, protector

body of water
3 bay, sea **4** gulf, lake, pond, pool **5** bight, brook, creek, fiord, firth, fjord, inlet, ocean, river **6** lagoon **7** channel, estuary **9** reservoir

body passage
4 duct, iter, vein **5** canal **6** artery, meatus, vessel **7** trachea

body politic
5 state **6** nation

boeotian
4 boob **7** Babbitt **10** middlebrow, philistine

bog
3 fen **4** mire, quag **5** marsh, swamp **6** morass **8** quagmire **9** swampland
combining form: **4** helo

Bogart film
6 Sahara **7** Dead End, Sabrina **8** Key Largo **10** Casablanca, High Sierra **11** The Big Sleep **15** The African Queen

bog down
5 delay **6** detain, hang up, retard, slow up **7** set back, slacken **10** decelerate

bogey
5 ghost, shade, spook **6** scarer, spirit, wraith **7** phantom, specter **8** revenant **10** apparition

boggle
3 gag, jib, shy **4** balk, mess **5** botch, demur, gum up, stick **6** bollix, bungle, cobble, goof up, strain **7** louse up, nonplus, scruple, stagger, stickle, stumble **9** dumbfound

bogus
4 fake, sham **5** false, phony, snide **6** forged, pseudo **8** spurious **9** brummagem, imitation, pinchbeck **11** counterfeit

Boheme, La
character: **4** Mimi **7** Rodolfo
composer: **7** Puccini (Giacomo)
setting: **5** Paris

Bohemian
7 beatnik, dropout **8** maverick **9** eccentric **10** iconoclast **13** nonconformist

bohunk
3 oaf **4** gawk, lout, lump **5** klutz **6** lubber, lummox **7** palooka

boil
4 bolt, burn, dash, fume, race, rage, rush, stew 5 anger, churn, fling, poach, shoot 6 blow up, bubble, charge, coddle, pimple, seethe, simmer 7 abscess, bristle, ferment, flare up, pustule, smolder 8 furuncle 9 carbuncle

boil down
8 simplify 10 streamline

boiled
combining form: 5 cocto

boiler suit
8 coverall

boiling
3 hot 5 fiery 6 baking, red-hot 7 burning 8 scalding, sizzling 9 scorching 10 blistering

boil over
4 burn, fume, rage 5 anger 6 blow up, seethe 7 bristle, flare up

boisterous
5 noisy, rowdy 6 unruly 7 blatant, raucous, riotous 8 rowdyish, strident 9 clamorous, termagant, turbulent 10 disorderly, rollicking, rowdydowdy, tumultuous, vociferant, vociferous 11 loudmouthed, openmouthed 12 obstreperous, rambunctious

Boito opera
11 Mefistofele

bold
4 pert, wise 5 bluff, brave, fresh, nervy, sassy, saucy 6 brazen, cheeky 7 doughty, forward, valiant 8 fearless, impudent, insolent, intrepid, unafraid 9 audacious, dauntless, undaunted 10 courageous, procacious 11 impertinent, smart-alecky 12 contumelious

boldhearted
5 brave 7 doughty, valiant 8 fearless, intrepid, unafraid 9 audacious, dauntless, undaunted 10 courageous

boldness
4 gall 5 nerve 7 chutzpa 8 audacity, chutzpah, temerity 9 hardihood, impudence, insolence, insolency 10 brazenness, disrespect 12 impertinence

Bolero composer
5 Ravel (Maurice)

Bolivia
capital: 5 La Paz, Sucre
monetary unit: 9 boliviano

bollix
4 flub, mess 5 botch, gum up 6 bobble, bungle, fumble, goof up 7 louse up

Bolshevik
3 Red 6 commie 7 comrade 9 communist

bolshevism
9 communism

bolster
4 prop 5 brace, carry 6 bear up, buoy up, upbear, uphold 7 shore up, support, sustain 8 backstop, buttress 9 reinforce, underprop 10 strengthen

bolt
3 fly, run 4 cram, dash, flee, gulp, jump, lash, race, rush, tear 5 chase, rivet, scoot, shoot, skirr, slosh, start 6 charge, cry out, englut, gobble, guzzle, spring 7 exclaim, kingpin, make off, scamper, startle 8 blurt out 9 ejaculate, skedaddle 11 ingurgitate 13 thunderstroke

bomb
3 dud 4 bust, flop 5 blitz, lemon, loser, shell 7 failure 9 cannonade

bombard
4 pelt 5 blitz, shell 6 strike 7 assault 9 cannonade

bombardment
4 hail 5 burst, salvo 6 shower, volley 7 barrage 8 drumfire 9 broadside, cannonade, fusillade

bombardon
4 bass 7 helicon 8 bass tuba

bombast
4 rant 7 fustian 8 rhapsody, rhetoric, tumidity 9 turgidity 11 highfalutin, rodomontade

bombastic
7 aureate, flowery, swollen 8 sonorous 9 overblown 10 euphuistic, rhetorical 11 declamatory 12 magniloquent 13 grandiloquent

bombed
5 drunk 11 intoxicated

bombinate
3 hum 4 buzz 5 drone, strum, thrum 6 bumble

bombshell
8 surprise

bomb shelter
4 abri

bona fide
4 real, true 7 genuine 9 authentic, undoubted, veritable 10 sure-enough 11 indubitable

bona fides
9 good faith, sincerity 11 sincereness

bonanza
4 mine 8 eldorado, Golconda, gold mine, treasury 13 treasure trove

bonbon
5 candy 7 fondant 8 confetti (plural), confetto

bond
3 tie 4 bail, knot, link, pact, yoke 5 nexus 6 surety 7 bargain, compact 8 adhesion, clinging, cohesion, contract, covenant, guaranty, ligament, ligature, security, stickage, sticking, vinculum, warranty 9 adherence, agreement, coherence, guarantee 10 connection, connective, convention 11 transaction
combining form: 4 desm 5 desmo

bondage
4 yoke 6 thrall 7 helotry, peonage, serfage, serfdom, slavery 9 servility, servitude, thralldom, villenage 11 enslavement, subjugation

bondsman
5 slave 7 chattel 9 mancipium

bone
ankle: 5 talus 6 tarsus
arm: 4 ulna 6 radius 7 humerus
back: 5 spine 8 vertebra 9 vertebrae (plural)
breast: 7 sternum
calf: 6 fibula
cavity: 5 fossa
change into: 6 ossify
cheek: 5 malar 6 zygoma
chest: 3 rib
collar: 8 clavicle
combining form: 3 ost 4 osse, ossi, oste 5 osseo, osteo 6 osteon, osteus
face: 5 malar, nasal 7 frontal 8 temporal
finger: 7 phalanx 8 phalange
foot: 6 tarsus 9 calcaneum, calcaneus 10 astragalus, metatarsus
hand: 10 metacarpus
head: 5 skull, vomer 7 cranium 8 parietal, sphenoid 9 occipital
heel: 9 calcaneum, calcaneus
hip: 5 ilium, pubis 6 pelvis 7 ischium
jaw: 7 maxilla 8 mandible
kneecap: 7 patella
Latin: 2 os 5 ossa (plural)

leg: 5 femur, tibia 6 fibula 7 patella
lower back: 6 coccyx, sacrum
middle ear: 5 anvil, incus 6 hammer, stapes 7 malleus, stirrup
relating to: 6 osteal
shin: 5 tibia
shoulder blade: 7 scapula
small: 7 ossicle
substance: 6 ossein
thigh: 5 femur
toe: 7 phalanx 8 phalange
U-shaped: 5 hyoid
wrist: 6 carpus

bonehead
5 dunce 8 clodpate, numskull 10 thick-skull

bone-like
7 osseous, osteoid

boner
see **blooper**

bone up
4 cram 5 study 6 review

bong
4 bell, peal, ring, toll 5 chime, knell

boniface
8 publican, taverner 9 barkeeper, innholder, innkeeper, saloonist 12 saloonkeeper

bonkers
5 crazy 6 insane

bonny
4 fair 6 comely, lovely, pretty 9 beauteous, beautiful 10 attractive 11 good-looking

bon vivant
7 epicure, gourmet 8 gourmand 10 gastronome 11 gastronomer 12 gastronomist, man-about-town

bon voyage
8 farewell, good trip

bony
4 lank, lean 5 gaunt, lanky, spare 6 skinny 7 angular, scraggy, scrawny 8 rawboned

boo
4 hiss, hoot, razz 5 bazoo 7 catcall 8 cannabis 9 marijuana, raspberry

boob
3 oaf 4 dolt, goof, goon 5 chump, dunce 7 Babbitt, fathead 8 boeotian, dolthead, lunkhead 10 middlebrow, philistine

boo-boo
see **blooper**

booby hatch
6 asylum 8 loony bin, madhouse, nuthouse 9 funny farm

booby trap
7 pitfall, springe 8 deadfall, trapfall

boodle
4 bilk, loot, mint 5 booty, cheat, cozen, prize, spoil 6 bundle, chisel, chouse, diddle, packet 7 defraud, fortune, plunder 8 flimflam 10 plunderage

boohoo
3 cry, sob 4 blub, wail, weep 7 blubber

book
4 list, tome 5 album, codex, novel, tract 6 enroll, folder, manual, scroll, volume 7 catalog, edition, leaflet, reserve, writing 8 brochure, hardback, inscribe, pamphlet, schedule, softback, treatise 9 monograph, preengage 10 compendium 11 publication
combining form: 6 biblio
of hours: 5 Horae
of psalms: 7 psalter
of public records: 5 liber

bookdealer
10 bibliopole 11 bouquiniste

bookie
see **bookmaker**

bookish
7 learned 8 academic, literary, pedantic 9 scholarly

bookkeeping term
4 loss 5 asset, audit, check, debit, entry 6 budget, credit, income, ledger, profit 7 account, balance, expense, invoice, voucher 8 discount, interest 9 liability 12 depreciation

bookmaker
6 binder, bookie, editor 7 printer 9 publisher

book of account
6 ledger, record 7 journal 8 register

bookplate
5 label 8 ex libris

bookstall
5 kiosk 9 newsstand

boom
4 bang, clap, slam, wham 5 blast, burst, crack, crash, smash 7 thunder 10 prosperity

boomerang
8 backfire, backlash, kick back 10 bounce back

booming
6 robust 7 roaring, thrifty 8 thriving 10 prospering, prosperous 11 flourishing

boon
4 gift, good 5 favor, jolly, merry 6 blithe, jocund, jovial 7 benefit, festive, gleeful, godsend, largess, present 8 blessing, mirthful 9 advantage 10 blithesome 11 benediction, benevolence

boondocks
6 sticks 8 backland, backwash, frontier 9 backwater, backwoods 10 hinterland 11 backcountry

boor
3 oaf 4 lout 5 chuff, churl, clown, yahoo, yokel 6 lummox, mucker, rustic 7 buffoon, bumpkin, grobian, peasant 10 clodhopper

boorish
4 rude 6 coarse, rugged, vulgar 7 ill-bred, loutish, lowbred, lumpish, uncivil 8 churlish, cloddish, clownish, impolite, lubberly, swainish 9 graceless, tasteless, unrefined 10 robustious, uncultured, ungracious, unpolished 11 clodhopping, ill-mannered, uncivilized

boost
2 up 3 wax 4 hike, jump, plug, push, rise 5 put up, raise 6 beef up, expand, extend, jack up 7 augment, enlarge, magnify, promote, upgrade 8 heighten, increase, multiply 9 advertise 10 aggrandize 12 breakthrough

boot
2 ax 4 bang, fire, kick, sack, tyro 5 chase, chuck, eject, evict 6 bounce, novice, rookie, thrill 7 dismiss, extrude, kick out 8 beginner, freshman, neophyte, throw out 9 discharge, terminate 10 apprentice, tenderfoot
kind: 5 kamik, wader 6 arctic, chukka, crakow, gaiter, galosh, golosh, mucluc, mukluk 7 bottine, cothurn, gambado, jodhpur, shoepac 8 balmoral, cothurni (plural), muckluck, overshoe, shoepack 9 cothurnus 10 Wellington
Scottish: 8 gamashes (plural)

Boötes star
8 Arcturus

booth
5 kiosk, stall, stand

boot hill
8 cemetery 9 graveyard 12 burial ground

bootleg
3 run 5 hooch 7 smuggle 9 moon-

shine **10** bathtub gin, contraband
11 mountain dew

bootless
4 vain **6** futile **7** useless **8** abortive
9 fruitless **10** profitless, unavailing
11 ineffective, ineffectual **12** unproductive, unprofitable

bootlick
4 fawn **5** cower, toady **6** cringe,
grovel, kowtow **7** truckle **9** brownnose **11** apple-polish

bootlicker
4 toad **5** toady **7** spaniel **8** lickspit
9 sycophant, toadeater
11 lickspittle

booty
4 loot, swag **5** prize, spoil **6** boodle **7** plunder **10** plunderage

booze
3 jag **4** grog, swig **5** binge, drink,
hooch, sauce, souse, swill
6 bender, guzzle, imbibe, liquor,
tipple **7** carouse, spirits, swizzle
8 liquor up **9** aqua vitae, brannigan, firewater

boozehound
4 lush, wino **5** drunk **6** sponge
7 guzzler **8** drunkard **9** inebriate

boozer
see **boozehound**

bop
3 bat **4** bash, belt, biff, blow, sock,
whop **5** pound, smack

borax
6 tincal

Bordeaux wine
district: **5** Medoc **6** Graves
grape: **6** Malbec, Merlot **8** Cabernet
name: **5** Arsac, Ludon, Macau
6 Moulis **7** Labarde, Margaux,
Pomerol **8** Cantenac, Pauillac **9** St.
Julien, St. Emilion, St. Estephe, St.
Laurent
red: **6** claret

bordello
see **brothel**

border
3 hem, lip, rim **4** abut, brim, edge,
join, line **5** bound, brink, flank,
frame, march, marge, skirt, touch,
verge **6** adjoin, butt on, define,
fringe, limbus, margin, trench
7 outline, selvage **8** approach, be-
fringe, boundary, frontier, neighbor, sideline, surround **9** marchland, perimeter, periphery **11** butt
against, communicate
embroidered: **6** orfray **7** orphrey

inlaid: **8** purfling
raised: **7** coaming

bordereau
4 note **10** memorandum

bordering
8 abutting, adjacent, touching
9 adjoining **10** approximal, contiguous, juxtaposed **12** conterminous

borderland
5 march **8** frontier **9** marchland

borderline
7 unclear **8** doubtful **9** ambiguous,
dubitable, equivocal, uncertain,
undecided, unsettled
11 problematic

border line
8 boundary **11** demarcation

border state
8 Delaware, Kentucky, Maryland,
Missouri, Virginia

bore
4 gape, gawk, gaze, pall, peer,
ream, tire **5** auger, drill, ennui,
glare, gloat, prick, punch, stare,
weary **6** goggle, wimble **7** fatigue
8 puncture **9** perforate

boreal
3 icy **4** cold, cool **5** chill, gelid
6 arctic, chilly, frosty **7** glacial
8 freezing

Boreas
beloved: **8** Orithyia
brother: **5** Notus **8** Hesperus,
Zephyrus
father: **8** Astraeus
mother: **3** Eos
son: **5** Zetes **6** Calais

boredom
4 yawn **5** ennui **6** tedium **7** fatigue
8 doldrums **9** weariness

borer
combining form: **6** trypan **7** trypano

Borgia
6 Alonso, Cesare **7** Rodrigo
8 Lucrezia

boring
4 dull **6** dreary, stodgy, tiring
7 humdrum, irksome, tedious
8 drudging, tiresome
10 monotonous

boring tool
6 trepan

born
3 née **6** inbred **7** built-in **8** inherent
9 intrinsic **10** congenital, deep-
seated, ingenerate
combining form: **3** gen **4** gene
6 genous **7** genetic

borne by the wind
5 eolic **6** aeolic, eolian **7** aeolian

Borodin opera
10 Prince Igor

borough
4 burg, town **5** burgh **7** village
8 township
Scottish: **5** brugh

bosh
see **bunkum**

bosom
4 soul **5** heart **6** breast

bosomy
5 busty, buxom **6** chesty

boss
4 head **5** chief **6** honcho, leader,
master, survey **7** headman, oversee
8 chaperon, hierarch, overlook, superior **9** chieftain, dominator, supervise **11** quarterback,
superintend
African: **5** bwana

bossy
8 imperial **9** imperious, masterful
10 high-handed, imperative, peremptory **11** domineering, magisterial, overbearing

botanist
American: **4** Gray (Asa) **5** Sears
(Paul B.) **6** Bailey (Liberty), Bessey
(Charles), Carver (George Wash-
ington) **7** Bartram (John), Burbank
(Luther) **9** Fairchild (David)
Austrian: **6** Mendel (Gregor)
British: **6** Sloane (Sir Hans)
Danish: **7** Warming (Johannes)
Dutch: **7** De Vries (Hugo)
French: **7** Lamarck (Chevalier de)
German: **4** Cohn (Ferdinand), Mohl
(Hugo Von) **5** Sachs (Julius von)
Irish: **6** Harvey (William)
Scottish: **5** Brown (Robert)
Swedish: **8** Linnaeus (Carolus)
Swiss: **6** Nageli (Karl) **8** Candolle
(Augustin)

botany branch
8 algology, bryology, mycology
9 phycology **10** palynology **11** hydroponics, pteridology
12 bacteriology

botch
3 dub **4** blow, flub, mess, muck,
muff, mull, muss **5** fluff, gum up,
mix-up, spoil **6** bobble, boggle,
bollix, bumble, bungle, cobble, foozle, fumble, goof up, mess up,
mucker, muddle **7** blunder, louse
up **8** bugger up, shambles **9** mishandle, mismanage **10** misconduct

botchy
5 messy 6 sloppy, untidy 8 careless, slapdash, slipshod, slovenly 10 unthorough

both
combining form: 3 bis
prefix: 4 ambi, amph 5 amphi

bother
3 bug, irk, vex 4 fret, pest 5 annoy, chafe, upset 6 abrade, flurry, harass, pester, plague, ruffle 7 agitate, disturb, fluster, perturb, provoke, unhinge 8 disquiet, irritant, nuisance 9 annoyance, besetment 10 discompose 11 aggravation 12 exasperation 13 inconvenience

botheration
4 pest 6 pester, plague 8 irritant, nuisance 9 annoyance, besetment 11 aggravation 12 exasperation

Botswana
capital: 8 Gaborone
monetary unit: 4 pula

bottle
4 vial 5 ampul, cruet, cruse, flask, phial 6 ampule, carafe, fiasco, flacon, magnum, vessel 8 decanter, jeroboam 9 container
baby's: 6 nurser

bottle gourd
8 calabash

bottleneck
7 impasse 8 obstruct, paralyze, slowdown, throttle

bottom
3 bed 4 base, foot, seat, sole 5 basal, basic, fanny, found, hiney, nadir 6 behind, breech, heinie, lowest 7 bedrock, essence, footing, primary, rear end 8 backside, buttocks, derriere 9 establish, lowermost, posterior, predicate, underbody, undermost, underside 10 foundation, nethermost, underlying, underneath 11 fundamental 12 foundational, quintessence, substructure, undersurface

bottom dog
4 prey 6 victim 8 casualty

bottomless
4 deep 7 abysmal 8 baseless 9 plumbless, soundless, unfounded 10 fathomless, gratuitous, groundless, ungrounded 11 plummetless, uncalled-for, unwarranted 12 unfathomable

bottommost
6 lowest 9 lowermost, undermost 10 nethermost

bough
4 limb 6 branch

boulevard
3 way 4 path, road 5 track 6 artery, avenue, street 7 highway 12 thoroughfare

boulevardier
7 flaneur, trifler 9 bon vivant 12 man-about-town

bounce
2 ox 3 hop 4 fire, jump, leap, sack 5 bound, vault 6 hurdle, spring 7 boot out, dismiss, kick out, saltate 9 discharge, terminate

bounce back
7 rebound, recover 8 backfire, backlash 9 boomerang

bounce off
5 carom

bouncer
4 goon 7 chucker 8 houseman 9 muscleman, strong arm

bouncy
4 airy 7 buoyant, elastic 8 volatile 9 expansive, resilient 12 effervescent

bound
3 end, hem, hop, rim 4 edge, jump, leap, term 5 limit, skirt, vault, verge 6 border, bounce, define, demark, finite, fringe, hurdle, margin, spring 7 delimit, limited, mark out, measure, saltate 8 articled, confines, surround 9 demarcate, determine 10 delimitate, indentured, limitation 11 apprenticed

boundary
5 ambit 6 limits 7 compass 8 confines, environs, purlieus 9 precincts

bounder
3 cad, cur 6 rotter

boundless
7 endless 8 infinite 9 limitless, unlimited 10 indefinite, unmeasured 11 measureless 12 immeasurable

bounteous
4 free 5 ample 6 plenty 7 copious, liberal 8 abundant, generous, handsome 9 plenteous, plentiful, unsparing 10 freehanded, munificent, openhanded

bountiful
see **bounteous**

Bounty captain
5 Bligh (William)

bouquet
4 balm, kudo, posy 5 aroma,

scent, spice 7 corsage, garland, incense, nosegay, orchids, perfume 9 fragrance, redolence 10 compliment 11 arrangement, boutonniere

bourgeois
10 philistine 11 middle-class 12 capitalistic

bourgeoisie
11 middle class

bout
4 tour, turn 5 shift, siege, spell, stint, trick

bovine
2 ox 3 cow, yak 4 anoa, bull, calf, gaur, neat, zebu 5 bison, gayal, steer, stirk 6 catalo, cattle, wisent 7 aurochs, banteng, buffalo, bullock, cattalo 8 longhorn
genus: 3 Bos
sound: 3 low, moo

bow
3 arc 4 arch, bend, lout, turn 5 angle, crook, curve, defer, round, yield 6 congee, curtsy, salaam, submit 7 flexure, succumb, turning 8 flection 9 curvation, curvature 10 capitulate 11 buckle under 12 knuckle under

bowdlerize
4 blip 6 censor, screen 9 expurgate

bowed
4 bent 5 arced, bandy, round 6 arched, curved 7 arrondi, rounded 8 arciform 9 bowlegged 11 bandy-legged, curvilinear
combining form: 3 tox 4 toxi, toxo

bowel
3 gut 4 draw 6 paunch 10 eviscerate, exenterate

bower
5 arbor 7 pergola

bowery
7 skid row 8 skid road

bowfin
7 mudfish

bowl
5 arena, basin, jorum, mazer, stade 6 tureen, vessel 7 stadium 8 coliseum
ornamental: 5 tazza

bowlegged
5 bandy

bowler
3 hat 5 derby 6 kegler 7 kegeler

Bowl game
3 Sun (El Paso) 4 Rose (Pasadena) 5 Aloha (Honolulu), Gator (Jackson-

ville), Peach (Atlanta), Pecan (Abilene), Sugar (New Orleans), Super **6** Copper (Tucson), Cotton (Dallas), Fiesta (Tempe), Orange (Miami), Senior (Mobile) **7** Freedom (Anaheim), Holiday (San Diego), Liberty (Memphis) **8** Carquest (Miami), Las Vegas (Las Vegas) **10** Bluebonnet (Houston), California (Fresno) Hall of Fame (Tampa) **12** Independence (Shreveport) **13** Florida Citrus (Orlando)

bowling
7 kegling **8** kegeling
British: **8** skittles
Italian: **5** bocce, bocci **6** boccia, boccie
term: **3** pin **4** hook, lane, spot **5** curve, frame, spare, split **6** gutter, strike, string, turkey **7** duckpin **9** candlepin

bowl over
3 wow **4** stun **5** floor **6** dismay **8** surprise **9** overwhelm **10** disconcert

box
3 bin **4** case, cell, chop, cuff, kist, loge, slap, sock **5** booth, chest, clout, crate, fight, punch, smack, spank, stall, trunk **6** buffet, carton, casket, coffin, encase, hopper, packet, square **7** confine, enclose, package **8** canister **9** container, enclosure, rectangle **10** pigeonhole, receptacle **11** compartment
ancient: **4** arca
for a document: **7** hanaper
for ammunition: **7** caisson
for an official seal: **7** skippet

boxer
7 fighter, palooka, puncher, slugger **8** pugilist **9** flyweight **11** heavyweight, lightweight **12** bantamweight, middleweight, welterweight **13** featherweight
champ: **3** Ali (Muhammad) **4** Bowe (Riddick) **5** Bruno (Frank), Lewis (Lennox), Louis (Joe), Moore (Archie), Tyson (Mike) **6** Hearns (Thomas), Holmes (Larry), McCall (Oliver), Moorer (Michael), Seldon (Bruce), Spinks (Leon, Michael), Tunney (Gene), Walker (Mickey) **7** Charles (Ezzard), Corbett (James), Dempsey (Jack), Douglas (Buster), Foreman (George), Frazier (Joe), Johnson (Jack), Leonard (Sugar Ray), Sharkey (Jack), Walcott (Joe) **8** Marciano (Rocky), Robinson (Sugar Ray), Sullivan (John L.)

9 Armstrong (Henry), Holyfield (Evander), Patterson (Floyd), Schmeling (Max)

boxing
8 pugilism **10** fisticuffs **13** prizefighting
term: **2** KO **3** jab, TKO **4** bell, blow, bout, duck, foul, hook, ring, rope, spar **5** break, count, feint, glove, judge, match, parry, punch, round, swing, towel **6** bucket, canvas, corner, sponge **7** low blow, referee **8** heavy bag, knockout, pugilism, speed bag, uppercut **9** knockdown **11** punching bag

boy
3 lad, son **5** gamin, sonny **6** laddie, nipper, shaver **7** gossoon **9** shaveling, stripling, youngster
combining form: **3** ped **4** paed, paid, pedo **5** paedo, paido
country: **5** swain
errand: **5** gofer **8** lobbygow
French: **6** garçon
Latin: **4** puer
mischievous: **6** urchin
small: **3** tad
Spanish: **4** niño

boyfriend
4 beau **5** beaux (plural), flame, lover, swain **6** fiancé, steady **7** beloved **8** paramour, truelove **9** inamorato **10** heartthrob, sweetheart

Boy Scout
founder: **11** Baden-Powell (Robert)
gathering: **8** jamboree
motto: **10** be prepared
rank: **9** Life Scout, Star Scout **10** Eagle Scout, Tenderfoot
unit: **5** troop **6** patrol

Boys Town
founder: **8** Flanagan (Edward)
state: **8** Nebraska

B.P.O.E. member
3 Elk

Brabantio's daughter
9 Desdemona

brabble
3 gab, row **4** chat, spat, tiff **5** clack, scrap **6** bicker, cackle, hassle, jabber **7** chatter, dispute, fall out, palaver, prattle, quarrel, wrangle **8** squabble **9** bickering, brannigan, caterwaul **10** falling-out **11** altercation **12** tittle-tattle

brace
3 beg, duo **4** dyad, gird, pair, pray, prop, stay **5** plead, ready, shore, steel **6** appeal, bear up, col-

umn, couple, splent, splint, upbear, uphold **7** beseech, bolster, doublet, entreat, fortify, implore, prepare, refresh, shore up, support, sustain, twosome **8** buttress **9** importune **10** strengthen, supplicate **11** underpinner **12** underpinning **13** underpropping

bracelet
6 bangle **8** wristlet

bracing
5 tonic **9** animating **10** quickening, vitalizing **11** stimulating, stimulative **12** exhilarating, exhilarative, invigorating

bracket
3 wed **4** join, link **5** unite **6** couple, relate **7** collate, combine, compare, conjoin, connect **8** contrast **9** associate

bract
4 leaf **5** glume, palea, palet **6** paleae (plural), spathe **8** phyllary

brad
4 nail

Bradamant
brother: **7** Rinaldo
husband: **6** Rogero **8** Ruggiero

Bradbury's forte
5 sci-fi

brag
4 blow, crow, puff **5** boast, mouth, prate, vaunt **9** gasconade **11** rodomontade

braggadocian
8 boastful, braggart, vaunting **11** rodomontade

braggadocio
7 boaster **8** boasting, braggart, bragging **9** cockiness **10** cockalorum

braggart
6 blower **7** boaster, vaunter, windbag **8** blowhard, boastful, fanfaron, puckfist, rodomont, vaunting **11** braggadocio, rodomontade **12** braggadocian

Brahmin
7 egghead **8** highbrow **10** doubledome **12** intellectual

braid
4 plat **5** plait, queue **7** galloon, pigtail **8** soutache **10** intertwine, interweave
gold or silver: **5** orris
hemp: **5** tagal

brain
3 wit 4 bean, conk, head, mind
7 concuss 9 intellect 10 gray matter 12 intelligence
bone: 5 skull 7 cranium
clot: 10 thrombosis
combining form: 6 cerebr, enceph
7 cerebri, cerebro 8 cerebell
9 cerebelli, cerebello, encephalo,
encephaly 10 encephalia,
encephalus
gland: 6 pineal 9 pituitary
layer: 4 obex 6 cortex
lobe: 6 limbic, vermis 7 frontal
8 parietal, temporal 9 occipital
membrane: 3 pia 4 dura, tela 6 meninx 8 pia mater 9 arachnoid,
dura mater
part: 4 aula, lobe 7 medulla 8 cere-
brum, thalamus 9 sensorium, ventricle 10 cerebellum, hemisphere
12 diencephalon
relating to: 8 cerebral 10 encephalic
ridge: 4 gyri (plural) 5 gyrus
vertebrate: 10 encephalon
wave record: 3 EEG
white matter: 4 alba

brainchild
7 coinage 9 invention
11 contrivance

brainless
6 simple 7 asinine, foolish, unwitty,
witless 8 mindless 9 nitwitted,
senseless 10 weak-minded

brainless one
5 ament

brainpower
3 wit 5 sense 9 mentality, mother
wit 12 intelligence

brainsick
4 daft 5 batty, crazy 6 crazed, insane 7 cracked, lunatic 8 demented, deranged 9 bedlamite

brainstorm
4 idea 11 inspiration

brainteaser
6 puzzle

brainwashing
10 persuasion

brainwork
7 thought 10 cogitation, reflection
11 cerebration, speculation
12 deliberation

brainy
5 alert, sharp, smart 6 bright,
clever 7 knowing 9 brilliant 11 intelligent, quick-witted, ready-witted

brake
3 bar, dam 4 slow, stop 5 block
6 hinder, impede 8 obstruct
10 overslaugh

branch
4 gill, limb, rami (plural) 5 bough,
brook, creek, ramus 6 ramify, runnel, stream 7 rivulet
relating to: 5 ramal 7 ramular

branched
6 ramate, ramose, ramous 8 ramu-
lose, ramulous
combining form: 7 cladous

brand
4 blot, blur, logo, mark, onus, slur,
spot 5 odium, stain 6 stigma
8 black eye, logotype 9 trademark
11 bar sinister

brandish
4 show 5 flash 6 expose, flaunt,
parade 7 display, disport, exhibit,
show off, trot out

brand-new
4 mint 5 clean, fresh 6 unused
8 pristine 9 untouched 12 spick-
and-span

brandy
4 marc 5 pisco, rakia 6 cognac,
grappa, kirsch, rakija 7 quetsch
8 armagnac, calvados, slivovic
9 applejack, framboise, mirabelle,
slivovitz 11 aquardiente

brannigan
3 row 4 bust 5 binge, fight, spree
6 bender, hassle, ruckus 7 brabble,
carouse, dispute, quarrel, wassail,
wrangle 10 falling out
11 altercation

brash
4 bold 5 hasty 6 brazen, madcap,
uppish, uppity 7 forward, pushful,
pushing 8 reckless, tactless 9 ebullient, exuberant, hot-headed, impetuous, impolitic, maladroit, presuming, unpolitic, untactful, vivacious
10 ill-advised, incautious 11 overweening, thoughtless 12 effervescent, high-spirited, presumptuous,
undiplomatic 13 inconsiderate, self-
asserting, self-assertive

brashness
4 gall 5 brass, cheek, crust, nerve
8 audacity, temerity 9 assurance,
hardihood, hardiness 10 confidence, effrontery 11 presumption

brass
4 gall 5 cheek, crust, nerve 9 brashness 10 confidence, effrontery
11 presumption
combining form: 5 chalc, chalk
6 chalco, chalko

brassbound
5 brash, rigid 6 narrow, uppish,
uppity 7 adamant, bigoted, forward, pushful 8 obdurate 9 illiberal, presuming, unbending 10 inexorable, inflexible, intolerant,
relentless, unyielding 11 overweening, small-minded 12 narrow-
minded, presumptuous, single-
minded 13 self-asserting,
self-assertive

brass hat
5 elder 6 better, senior 8 higher-
up, superior

brass tacks
7 details

brass worker
7 brasier, brazier

brassy
see **brazen**

brat
3 imp

brave
4 bold, dare, defy, face, game,
good 5 gutsy, hardy, manly, noble,
stout, vivid 6 daring, gritty, heroic,
manful, plucky, spunky, useful
7 aweless, benefic, defiant,
doughty, gallant, helpful, outdare,
outface, valiant, venture 8 colorful,
fearless, intrepid, resolute, spirited,
stalwart, unafraid, valorous 9 audacious, challenge, dauntless, favorable, soldierly, steadfast, undaunted, unfearful, unfearing
10 beneficial, courageous, propitious, unblenched 11 boldhearted,
lionhearted, unblenching, undauntable, unflinching, venturesome
12 advantageous, greathearted,
stouthearted, unfrightened

Brave New World author
6 Huxley (Aldous)

bravery
4 grit 5 pluck 6 daring, spirit
7 courage, heroism 8 audacity,
boldness 9 fortitude, gallantry
11 intrepidity 12 intrepidness
false: 7 bravado

brawl
3 row 4 feud, fray, maul, riot, spat,
tiff 5 broil, fight, melee, scrap, set-
to 6 affray, bicker, dustup, fracas,
hassle, mellay, rumble, tussle

7 bobbery, brabble, dispute, quarrel, ruction, scuffle, wrangle **8** dogfight, eruption, rowdydow, slugfest, squabble, struggle, upheaval **9** bickering, caterwaul, commotion, fistfight, imbroglio, scrimmage **10** donnybrook, fisticuffs, free-for-all **11** altercation, disturbance

brawn
4 beef, thew **5** might **6** muscle

brawny
5 beefy, lusty, tough **6** sinewy **8** athletic, muscular, vigorous

bray
4 buck **5** crush **6** powder **9** comminute, pulverize, triturate **12** contriturate

brazen
4 bold, loud **5** gaudy, saucy **6** arrant, brassy, flashy, garish, tawdry, tinsel **7** aeneous, blatant, chintzy, glaring **8** impudent, insolent, overbold **9** audacious, barefaced, shameless, unabashed **10** procacious, unblushing **11** impertinent **12** contumelious, meretricious

Brazil
explorer: **6** Cabral (Pedro)
largest city: **8** Sao Paulo
monetary unit: **8** cruzeiro

breach
3 gap **4** hole, open, rent, rift **5** break, split **6** hiatus, lacuna, offend, schism **7** discord, disrupt, fissure, infract, interim, opening, rupture, violate **8** disunity, division, fracture, infringe, interval, trespass **9** severance, violation **10** alienation, contravene, infraction, separation, transgress **12** estrangement, infringement, interruption **13** contravention, discontinuity, transgression

bread
3 bun **4** feed, food, grub **5** money **6** cocket, living, simnel, viands **7** biscuit, edibles, nurture, support **8** victuals **9** provender **10** livelihood, provisions, sustenance **11** comestibles, maintenance, subsistence
blessed: **7** eulogia **9** antidoron
boiled: **4** cush **6** panada
browned: **5** toast **6** sippet **7** crouton **8** zwieback
combining form: **4** arto
communion: **4** azym, host **5** azyme, wafer **9** eucharist
consecrated: **9** eucharist
cube: **7** crouton

from heaven: **5** manna
hard and crisp: **4** rusk **8** zwieback
ingredient: **4** meal **5** flour, yeast **6** leaven
Jewish: **5** matzo **6** hallah, matzoh **7** challah
maker: **5** baker
relating to: **6** panary
roll: **5** bagel
Scottish: **7** bannock
small piece: **6** sippet
soup: **6** panada
spread: **3** jam **4** oleo **5** jelly **6** butter
unleavened: **4** azym **5** azyme, matzo **6** matzoh
with fruit and nuts: **7** stollen

bread and butter
4 keep **6** living **7** support **10** livelihood, sustenance **11** maintenance, subsistence **12** alimentation

breadbasket
7 stomach

breadth
5 range, reach, scope, space, sweep **6** spread **7** compass, expanse, stretch **8** distance, fullness, wideness **9** amplitude, expansion

break
3 gap **4** bust, cave, fail, flee, fold, hole, leak, plow, rent, rift, ruin **5** boner, burst, crack, crash, gaffe, rebut, scape, solve, spell, split, yield **6** befall, betide, breach, chance, convey, decode, demote, escape, fold up, get out, happen, hiatus, lacuna, offend, plow up, reduce, refute, schism, sunder **7** abscond, blooper, come off, come out, confute, crumble, crumple, declass, degrade, demerit, fall out, faux pas, fissure, infract, interim, opening, respite, rupture, shatter, time-out, violate **8** bankrupt, breather, collapse, confound, decipher, disprove, dissolve, fracture, fragment, interval **9** downgrade, interlude, pauperize **10** contravene, controvert, impoverish, transgress **11** communicate, impropriety, interregnum, opportunity, parenthesis **12** intermission, interruption **13** discontinuity

breakable
5 frail **7** fragile **8** delicate, shattery **9** frangible **11** fracturable, shatterable

breakaway
4 prop **10** escarpment, scrummager

breakdown
5 crash, smash, wreck **7** crack-up, debacle, smashup **8** analysis, collapse **10** dissection, resolution

break down
3 rot **4** wilt **5** decay, spoil, taint **6** cave in, digest, molder **7** analyze, crumble, dissect, give out, putrefy, resolve, succumb **9** anatomize, decompose **10** decompound **12** disintegrate

breaker
combining form: **5** clast **7** clastic

Breakfast at Tiffany's author
6 Capote (Truman)

breakfront
7 cabinet **8** bookcase

break in
5 train **8** initiate **9** interrupt

breaking up
combining form: **7** schises (plural), schisis
suffix: **4** lyse, lyze

breakneck
4 fast **5** fleet, hasty, quick, rapid, swift **6** speedy **10** expeditive, harefooted **11** expeditious

break out
5 erupt **6** escape **7** explode **10** burst forth

breakthrough
4 hike, rise **5** boost **7** advance, upgrade **8** increase

break through
5 burst **6** breach **7** rupture

breakup
8 analysis **10** dissection

break up
4 part **6** divide, sunder **7** disband, disjoin, disrupt, rupture **8** disjoint, disperse, dissever, dissolve, disunite, separate

breast
5 bosom, chest, heart
animal: **7** brisket
combining form: **3** maz **4** mast, mazo **5** masto, stern, steth **6** mastia (plural), sterno, stetho

breastbone
7 sternum

breast-feed
5 nurse **6** suckle **7** nourish

breast-shaped
9 mammiform

breastwork
7 bastion, bulwark, parapet, rampart

breath
4 blow, dash, hint 5 break, spell, trace, whiff 6 streak 7 respite, soupçon 9 suspicion 10 suggestion
combining form: 4 pnea 5 pneum, pnoea 6 pneumo 7 pneumat 8 pneumato

breathe
2 be 4 live, rest, sigh 5 exist 6 exhale, expire, inhale 7 confide, inspire, respire, subsist, whisper

breather
4 rest 5 break, spell 7 respite

breathing
labored: 7 dyspnea 8 dyspnoea
normal: 6 eupnea 7 eupnoea
rapid: 8 polypnea 9 polypnoea

breathing apparatus
10 respirator
underwater: 5 scuba

breathing orifice
8 blowhole, spiracle

breathless
4 agog, avid, keen 5 close, eager, stivy 6 ardent, stuffy, sultry 7 airless, anxious, athirst, thirsty 8 appetent, stifling 9 impatient 11 suffocating

breathtaking
8 exciting 9 thrilling 11 astonishing

Brecht play
4 Baal 7 Galileo 13 Mother Courage

breech
4 rear, rump 5 fanny 6 behind, bottom 8 backside, buttocks, derriere 9 fundament, posterior

breechclout
9 loincloth

breed
3 ilk 4 bear, grow, kind, sire, type 5 beget, cause, class, hatch, raise 6 father, induce, nature 7 produce, species, variety 8 engender, generate, multiply, muster up 9 character, cultivate, procreate, propagate, reproduce 11 progenerate

breeding
5 grace 6 polish 7 culture 9 gentility 10 refinement 11 cultivation

breeding ground
6 hotbed 8 hothouse 10 forcing bed 12 forcing house

breeze
3 zip 4 snap 5 cinch, waltz 6 zephyr 8 duck soup, kid stuff, pushover 10 child's play

breezy
4 airy 5 blowy, gusty, windy 6 casual, dégagé 7 relaxed, unfussy 8 informal 9 easygoing 11 low-pressure 13 unconstrained

breviary
5 brief 7 epitome 8 abstract, boildown, synopsis 10 conspectus 11 abridgement 12 condensation

breviloquent
4 curt 5 bluff, blunt, brief, gruff, rough, short, terse 6 abrupt, crusty 7 brusque, concise, laconic, summary 8 succinct 11 compendious 13 short and sweet

brevity
8 laconism 9 briefness, shortness, terseness 11 conciseness 12 succinctness

brew
4 loom 6 foment, gather, impend 9 forthcome, potpourri 10 miscellany

Briareus
7 Aegaeon
father: 6 Uranus
mother: 2 Ge 4 Gaea

bribe
3 buy, fix, sop 6 buy off, square, suborn 7 corrupt 10 tamper with

bric-a-brac
6 curios

brick
5 block
handler: 6 hacker
layer: 5 mason
laying: 7 masonry
material: 4 clay, marl
oven: 4 kiln
pile: 4 hack
row: 6 course
sun-dried: 3 bat 5 adobe
trough for carrying: 3 hod
wooden: 3 nog

bridal
7 spousal, wedding 8 marriage, nuptials 9 espousals

bridal wreath
6 spirea

bridewell
4 jail 5 prison

bridge
4 span
kind: 4 arch, draw, rope 5 swing, truss 7 bascule, covered, natural, pontoon, trestle, viaduct 10 cantilever, suspension
term: 3 bid 4 book, east, pass, ruff, slam, suit, void, west 5 bonus,

dummy, north, raise, south, trick, trump 6 double, renege, rubber 7 auction, finesse, no-trump, overbid 8 contract, jump call, redouble 9 grand slam, overtrick, singleton 10 little slam, undertrick, vulnerable

bridge-like game
5 whist 6 hearts

bridle
3 bit 4 curb, rein 5 check 6 hold in, manage 7 control, inhibit, repress 8 hold back, hold down, restrain, suppress, withhold 9 constrain

brief
4 curt 5 bluff, blunt, gruff, short, terse 6 abrupt, crusty, snippy 7 brusque, concise, epitome, laconic, passing 8 abstract, boildown, breviary, breviate, fleeting, snippety, succinct, synopsis 9 momentary, transient 10 conspectus 11 abridgement, compendary, compendious 12 breviloquent, condensation 13 short and sweet
combining form: 5 brevi

brig
4 jail 6 cooler, lockup, prison 7 slammer 8 stockade 9 guardroom

brigand
6 bandit, bummer, looter 7 cateran, forager 8 marauder, pillager 9 plunderer 10 depredator, freebooter

brigandage
7 pillage 11 depredation

bright
4 glad, keen 5 alert, brave, clear, light, lucid, nitid, sharp, shiny, smart, vivid 6 benign, brainy, cheery, clever, colory, dexter, lively, lucent 7 animate, beaming, blazing, flaming, fulgent, glowing, knowing, lambent, lighted, radiant 8 animated, cheerful, colorful, gleaming, luminous, lustrous, spirited, sunshiny 9 brilliant, effulgent, favorable, fortunate, refulgent, sparkling, sprightly, vivacious 10 auspicious, glistening, glittering, precocious, propitious, shimmering 11 illuminated, intelligent, quick-witted, ready-witted 12 incandescent 13 scintillating
combining form: 6 lampro

brighten
5 cheer, shine 6 polish 7 burnish, enliven, furbish, gladden 8 illumine 10 illuminate

brightness
5 éclat 6 luster, reflet 8 radiance, radiancy, splendor 9 luminance 10 brilliance, luminosity
measure of: 3 lux 4 phot 5 lumen 6 candle 7 candela 10 footcandle

brilliance
see **brightness**

brilliant
4 sage, wise 5 sharp, smart 6 brainy, bright, clever, lucent 7 beaming, fulgent, knowing, lambent, radiant 8 luminous 9 effulgent, refulgent 11 intelligent, quick-witted, ready-witted 12 incandescent 13 knowledgeable

brilliantine
6 pomade

brim
3 hem 4 edge 5 brink, skirt, verge, visor 6 border, fringe, margin 9 perimeter, periphery

brimful
see **brimming**

brimming
3 big 4 full 5 awash 6 filled, jammed, loaded, packed 7 crammed, crowded, replete, stuffed, teeming, welling 8 swelling 9 chock-full

brimstone
6 sulfur
combining form: 3 thi 4 thio

brine
3 sea 4 deep, main 5 ocean

bring
4 lead, sell 5 fetch 7 convert 8 persuade

bring about
4 make 5 cause 6 draw on, effect, secure 7 produce

bring around
6 induce, prompt 7 win over 8 convince, persuade, talk into 9 argue into 11 prevail upon

bring back
6 recall, return, revive 7 restore 8 retrieve, revivify

bring down
4 drop, fell 5 floor, level 6 ground, tumble 9 prostrate

bring forth
4 bear 7 deliver

bring forward
6 adduce 7 present, produce 9 introduce

bring in
3 get, pay, win 4 earn, gain, make, sell 5 fetch, yield 6 return 7 acquire

bringing
suffix: 3 fic

bring off
6 effect 8 carry out 10 effectuate 12 carry through

bring out
3 say 4 tell 5 educe, state, utter 7 chime in, declare, deliver

bring together
4 join 5 batch, blend, merge, unify, unite 7 collect, compact, compile 9 integrate 10 synthesize 11 consolidate

bring up
4 halt, moot, rear, stop 5 breed, raise, refer, train 6 advert, allude, broach, draw up, foster, haul up, pull up 7 educate, mention, nourish, nurture 8 point out 9 cultivate, introduce 10 provide for

brink
3 hem 4 brim, edge 5 point, skirt, verge 6 border, fringe, margin 9 perimeter, periphery, threshold

briny
5 salty

brio
3 vim 4 dash, élan, zing 5 oomph, verve 6 esprit, spirit 9 animation

brioche
4 roll

briolette
7 diamond

Briseis' lover
8 Achilles

brisk
4 spry, yare 5 agile, quick, zippy 6 active, adroit, lively, nimble, volant 9 sprightly

bristle
4 boil, burn, fume, rage, seta 5 anger, setae (plural) 6 blow up, chaeta, seethe 7 chaetae (plural), flare up 8 boil over
combining form: 4 seti 5 chaet 6 chaeta, chaeto 7 chaetae (plural), chaetes, chaetus
Scottish: 5 birse

British
air force: 3 RAF
airplane: 8 Spitfire

bailiff: 5 reeve
bar: 3 pub 5 local
bard: 4 scop
barge: 6 wherry
bed: 4 doss
beer: 6 swipes
boat, ancient: 7 coracle
boat, fishing: 5 coble 6 hooker
boy: 6 nipper
cathedral city: 3 Ely 4 York 5 Truro 6 Durham, Exeter 7 Lincoln 8 Coventry, Hereford, St. David's 9 Salisbury, Worcester 10 Canterbury, Gloucester
Channel Island: 4 Sark 6 Jersey 8 Alderney, Guernsey
china: 5 Spode
coal carrier: 4 corf
coin, current: 5 pence (plural), penny 9 halfpenny
coin, old: 3 bob, ora 5 ackey, angel, crown, groat, noble 6 bawbee, florin, George, guinea, seskin, sovran, tanner, teston 7 angelot, carolus 8 farthing, shilling 9 dandiprat, halfcrown, sovereign 10 threepence
colony, former: 4 Aden, Cape 5 Adana, Kenya, Malta, Natal 6 Ceylon, Cyprus, Gambia 7 Jamaica, Sarawak 9 Gold Coast, Singapore, Transvaal 10 Basutoland, New Zealand 11 Orange River, Sierra Leone 12 Bechuanaland
conservative party: 4 Tory
country gentleman: 6 squire
county: 4 Kent, York 5 Derby, Devon, Essex, Hants, Salop 6 Dorset, Durham, Oxford, Surrey, Sussex 7 Bedford, Rutland, Suffolk, Warwick 8 Cheshire, Cornwall, Hereford, Hertford, Somerset, Stafford 9 Berkshire, Hampshire, Lancaster, Leicester, Wiltshire, Worcester 10 Cumberland, Gloucester, Shropshire 11 Westmorland
court, local: 8 hustings
court, medieval: 4 eyre
cow barn: 4 byre
dance, ancient: 6 morris
dandy: 4 toff
elevator: 4 lift
farm, small: 5 croft
field: 5 croft
flashlight: 5 torch
football: 5 rugby
forest: 5 Arden, weald 8 Sherwood
freeman: 5 ceorl, churl, thane
game: 5 darts, rugby 6 soccer 7 cricket
gasoline: 6 petrol

gun: **4** Bren, Sten
hat: **6** bowler
hat, military: **5** busby
headmaster: **4** beak
horse: **5** screw **6** garron
horse dealer: **5** coper
hunt: **5** chevy, chivy
hut: **6** Nissen
idler: **4** spiv
innkeeper: **8** publican
jail: **4** gaol
king, legendary: **3** Lud **4** Beli, Bran **6** Arthur **7** Artegal, Belinus, Elidure **8** Brannius
laborer: **5** navvy, prole
landowner: **6** squire
language, ancient: **6** Celtic, Cymric **9** Brythonic
lawyer: **9** barrister, solicitor
legislature: **10** parliament
letter, old: **3** wen **5** thorn
liberal party: **4** Whig
magistrate: **4** beak
malt liquor: **6** porter
measure: **3** ell, pin **4** boll, comb, coom, cran, goad, hand, hide, last, pool, rood, trug, yoke **5** bodge, coomb, digit, float, floor, hutch, jugum, stack, truss **6** bovate, cranne, firkin, oxgang, pottle, runlet, strike, sulung, tierce **7** rundlet, tertian, virgate **8** carucate, chaldron, puncheon **9** kilderkin, shaftment, shathmont **10** barleycorn
molasses: **7** treacle
news agency: **7** Reuters
nobleman: **4** duke, earl, lord, peer **5** baron **6** prince **8** marquess, viscount
nurse: **6** sister
order: **6** Garter
ore carrier: **4** corf
peasant: **5** churl
peddler: **7** chapman
people, early: **4** Celt, Jute, Pict **5** Angle, Iceni, Saxon
poet: **4** scop
policeman: **5** bobby **6** copper, peeler
political party: **4** Tory, Whig **6** Labour
pope: **8** Adrian IV
pottery: **5** Spode
prince: **5** Harry **6** Andrew, Edward **7** Charles, William
princess: **4** Anne **5** Diana **8** Margaret
printer: **6** Caxton
prison: **7** Newgate **8** Dartmoor **13** Tower of London
queen, ancient: **8** Boadicea
racetrack: **5** Ascot **10** Epsom Downs

resort: **4** Bath **7** Margate **8** Brighton **9** Blackpool
rifle: **7** Enfield
royal house: **4** York **5** Tudor **6** Stuart **7** Hanover, Windsor **9** Lancaster **11** Plantagenet
royal residence: **7** Windsor **8** Balmoral **10** Buckingham
school: **4** Eton **5** Rugby **6** Harrow
school, military: **9** Sandhurst
seaman: **6** rating
serf: **4** esne **6** thrall
solitaire: **8** patience
spa: **4** Bath **5** Epsom **6** Buxton **7** Matlock **8** Brighton **10** Cheltenham
stables: **4** mews
stool pigeon: **4** nark
streetcar: **4** tram
tavern: **3** pub
tax: **3** VAT **4** geld **6** excise
thicket: **7** spinney
tinworks: **8** stannary
tobacco packet: **5** screw
tourist: **7** tripper
truck: **5** lorry
tutor: **3** don
valley: **4** dene
wage earner: **5** prole
weight: **4** keel **5** stone
woman in the navy: **4** Wren
wrench: **7** spanner

British Columbia
capital: **8** Victoria
largest city: **9** Vancouver

Britomartis
7 Artemis **8** Dictynna

brittle
5 crisp, short **7** crackly, crumbly, crunchy, friable

broach
3 pin **4** clip, moot **7** bring up, mention **9** introduce, ventilate **10** speak about

broad
4 wide **6** risqué, scopic **7** liberal, radical **8** advanced, extended, off-color, scopious, tolerant **9** expansive, extensive **10** suggestive **11** broad-minded, progressive
combining form: **4** eury, lati, plat **5** platy

broadcast
3 sow **5** straw, strew **6** blazon **7** bestrew, declare, disject, publish, scatter **8** announce, proclaim, televise, transmit **9** advertise **10** annunciate, bruit about, promulgate **11** blaze abroad, declaration, disseminate, publication **12** announce-

ment, proclamation, promulgation **13** advertisement, pronouncement

broaden
4 open **5** widen **6** expand **9** breadthen, spread out

broadloom
6 carpet

broad-minded
4 wide **7** liberal, radical **8** advanced, tolerant **11** progressive

broadside
4 hail **5** burst, salvo, storm **6** shower, volley **7** barrage **9** cannonade, fusillade **11** bombardment

broadtail
5 sheep **6** parrot **7** karakul, rosella **8** lambskin

Brobdingnagian
4 huge **5** giant **7** Antaean, mammoth, titanic **8** colossal, gigantic **9** cyclopean, monstrous **10** gargantuan

brocade
medieval: **4** acca

brocaded
6 broché

brocard
4 rule **5** axiom, gnome, maxim, moral **6** dictum, truism **8** aphorism, apothegm

brochette
4 spit **6** skewer

broil
4 bake, burn, cook, fray **5** brawl, fight, grill, roast **6** affray, fracas, scorch **7** bobbery, ruction, swelter **10** donnybrook, free-for-all

broiling
3 hot **5** fiery **6** baking, red-hot, torrid **7** burning **8** scalding, sizzling **9** scorching **10** sweltering

broke
4 flat, poor **5** needy, stony **8** beggared, dirt poor, indigent, strapped **9** destitute

broken-down
5 dingy, seedy, tacky **6** shabby, tagrag **8** decrepit, tattered **10** threadbare **11** dilapidated

brokenhearted
7 crushed **8** dejected **9** depressed

broker
8 mediator **9** go-between, middleman **10** interagent, interceder **11** intercessor **12** entrepreneur, in-

termediary, intermediate
13 intermediator

bromide
6 cliché, truism **8** banality, prosa-ism **9** platitude **10** prosaicism, shibboleth **11** commonplace, rub-ber stamp

bromidic
3 dry **4** arid, dull **5** dusty **7** in-sipid, tedious **8** weariful **9** dryas-dust, wearisome **13** uninteresting

bromine
symbol: **2** Br

bronco
5 horse **6** cayuse **7** mustang
Australian: **6** brumby

broncobuster
6 cowboy

Brontë
character: **9** Catherine, Rochester
10 Heathcliff
novel: **8** Jane Eyre **16** Wuthering Heights
sisters: **4** Anne **5** Emily **9** Charlotte

Bronx cheer
3 boo **4** hiss, razz **5** bazoo **7** cat-call **9** raspberry

brooch
3 pin **4** clip

brood
3 set, sit **4** mope, seed **5** cover **6** scions **7** despond, progeny **8** children **9** offspring **11** descen-dants, progeniture
member: **7** sibling

brook
4 bear, gill, race, rill, take **5** abide, creek, stand **6** arroyo, endure, rillet, runnel, stream, suffer **7** rivu-let, stomach, swallow **8** tolerate
Scottish: **6** burnie

broom
5 besom, brush, shrub, sweep, whisk **7** heather
combining form: **5** scopi

broth
5 stock **6** brewis **8** bouillon, consomme
Scottish: **4** bree, broo

brothel
6 bagnio **7** lupanar **8** bordello, cat-house, seraglio **9** call house **10** bawdy house, fancy house **11** parlor house **13** sporting house

brother
3 bub, kin **4** monk **5** friar **7** comrade
French: **5** frère

Italian: **3** fra **5** frate **8** fratello
Latin: **6** frater
relating to: **9** fraternal
Spanish: **7** hermano

brotherhood
4 club **5** guild, order, union **6** league **7** society **8** sodality **10** fellowship, fraternity **11** association

brotherly
4 kind **10** cherishing **12** affectionate

Brothers Karamazov
4 Ivan **6** Alexei, Dmitri **10** Smerdyakov

brouhaha
3 din **4** coil, fuss **5** babel **6** clamor, furore, hubbub, hurrah, jangle, racket, ruckus, rumpus, shindy, tumult, uproar **8** foofaraw **9** commotion **10** hullabaloo **11** pandemonium

brow
5 frons, front **8** forehead

browbeat
3 cow **5** bully **6** harass, hector **7** bluster, dragoon **8** bludgeon, bulldoze, bullyrag **10** intimidate

brown
4 dark, sear **5** dusky, toast **6** gloomy, scorch, tanned **7** swarthy
dark: **5** sepia, umber **9** chocolate
grayish: **3** dun **6** bister, bistre
light: **3** tan **4** ecru, fawn **5** beige, hazel, khaki, tawny
moderate: **4** teak **6** sahara, sienna
reddish: **3** bay **4** roan **5** henna **6** auburn, russet, sorrel, titian **8** chestnut
yellowish: **6** bronze, havana **8** bismarck **12** butterscotch

Brown Bomber
5 Louis (Joe)

brown coal
7 lignite

brownie
3 elf, fay **5** fairy, nisse, pixie **6** sprite

Browning poem
8 Prospice **11** Pippa Passes **12** Rabbi Ben Ezra **13** Fra Lippo Lippi, My Last Duchess

brown recluse
6 spider

brownshirt
4 Nazi **12** storm trooper

browse
4 scan, shop **6** go over, peruse **7** dip into, run over **8** glance at, look over **10** glance over, run through **11** flip through, leaf through, riff through, skim through **12** thumb through **13** riffle through

bruise
4 mash, pulp **5** black, crush **6** bat-ter, squash **7** becrush, contuse **8** abrasion, black eye **9** contusion

bruit about
6 blazon **7** declare, publish **8** an-nounce, proclaim **9** advertise, broadcast **10** annunciate, promul-gate **11** blaze abroad

bruja
3 hag, hex **5** lamia, witch **9** sorcer-ess **10** witchwoman **11** enchantress

brume
4 film, haze, mist **5** smaze

brummagem
4 fake, sham **5** bogus, false, phony, snide **6** pseudo, tinsel **8** spu-rious **9** pinchbeck **11** counterfeit

brunet
4 dark **5** dusky, swart **6** swarth **7** swarthy **8** bistered

Brunhild's husband
6 Gunnar **7** Gunther

brush
4 clip, fray, kiss, skim **5** clash, graze, melee, run-in, set-to, shave, sweep **6** affray, glance, mellay, scrape **7** contact **8** skirmish **9** en-counter, scrimmage, sideswipe **10** velitation
combining form: **5** scopi

brusque
4 curt **5** bluff, blunt, brief, gruff, short **6** abrupt, crusty, snippy **8** snippety

brutal
4 hard **5** feral, harsh **6** animal, bit-ter, ferine, rugged, severe **7** beastly, bestial, swinish **8** rigor-ous **9** inclement **11** intemperate

brutalize
4 warp **6** debase **7** corrupt, de-bauch, deprave, pervert, vitiate **10** bastardize, bestialize, demoralize

brute
5 beast, feral **6** animal, ferine **7** beastly, bestial, swinish **8** crea-ture

brutish
3 low 4 base, mean, vile 5 crude, feral 6 animal, coarse, ferine, scurvy 7 beastly, bestial, swinish 11 animalistic

bryophyte
4 moss 9 liverwort

Brythonic
see **Cymric**

bubble
3 lap 4 boil, stir, wash 5 churn, dream, slosh, swash 6 burble, gurgle, seethe, simmer 7 chimera, fantasy, ferment, smolder 8 illusion 9 pipe dream

bubbly
8 effusive 9 champagne, exuberant, sparkling

buccaneer
5 rover 6 pirate, sea dog 7 corsair, sea wolf 8 picaroon, sea rover 9 sea robber 10 freebooter

buck
3 fop, guy, lug, man 4 bear, bill, bray, chap, dude, duel, gent, pack, tote 5 carry, crush, dandy, ferry, fight, horse, pitch, repel, throw 6 combat, convey, dollar, fellow, oppose, powder, resist, unseat 7 contest, coxcomb, dispute, sawbuck, trestle, unhorse 8 sawhorse, traverse 9 comminute, exquisite, gentleman, pulverize, transport, triturate, withstand, workhorse 11 Beau Brummel 12 contriturate

bucket
3 fly, run 4 pail, rush, whiz 5 hurry, speed 6 barrel, hasten, hustle 7 grapple 9 clamshell

Buckeye State
4 Ohio

buckle down
5 apply, set to 6 devote, direct, fall to, jump in, wade in 7 address, pitch in 8 jump into, wade into

buckle under
3 bow 4 cave, give 5 defer, yield 6 submit 7 knuckle, succumb 10 capitulate

Buck novel
12 The Good Earth

buckram
5 stiff 6 wooden 7 stilted 9 cardboard 11 muscle-bound

buck up
5 cheer 6 solace 7 comfort, console, upraise

buckwheat tree
4 titi

bucolic
4 hick, jake 5 rural, yokel 6 rustic 7 bumpkin, country, hayseed, hillman, hoosier, outland 8 agrestic, pastoral 9 chawbacon 10 campestral, out-country, provincial 11 countrified

bud
4 germ, seed 5 chick, child, spark 6 embryo 8 juvenile, young one 9 youngling, youngster
combining form: 5 blast 6 blasto

Buddha
7 Gautama 10 Siddhartha
Chinese: 2 Fo
dialogues: 5 sutra
disciple: 6 Ananda
Japanese: 5 Amida, Amita
mother: 4 Maya
son: 6 Rahula
teachings: 6 dharma
wife: 9 Yasodhara

Buddhism
5 Daijo, Foism, Kegon 7 Lamaism 8 Hinayana, Mahayana

Buddhist
bronze image: 8 Daibutsu
chant: 6 mantra
column: 3 lat
dialogues: 5 sutra
doctrine: 7 trikaya
enlightenment: 6 satori
evil spirit: 4 Mara
fate: 5 karma
fertility spirit: 6 yaksha, yakshi
gateway: 5 toran 6 torana
god: 4 deva
hatred: 4 dosa
hell: 6 Naraka
language: 4 Pali
mendicant: 7 bhikshu
monastery: 4 tera
monk: 2 bo 4 lama 5 arhat, bonze, yahan 7 bhikshu, poongee 8 poonghee, poonghie, talapoin
monument, mound: 5 stupa
novice: 5 goyin
paradise: 4 Jodo
religious community: 6 sangha
sacred city: 5 Lhasa
saint: 5 arhat
school: 5 ritsu
scripture: 9 Tripitika
sect: 3 Zen 6 tendai
shrine: 4 tope 5 stupa 6 dagaba, dagoba 7 chorten
spell: 6 mantra
spiritual leader: 4 guru 9 Dalai Lama
state of happiness: 7 nirvana

temple: 6 pagoda, vihara
throne: 5 asana
title: 7 mahatma
tree of enlightenment: 2 bo 5 bodhi, pipal
tutelary spirit: 6 yaksha, yakshi
will to live: 5 tanha

buddy
3 pal 4 chum 5 crony 6 comate, friend 7 comrade 9 associate, companion 11 running mate

buddy-buddy
4 cozy 5 pally 6 chummy 8 intimate

budgerigar
6 parrot 8 lovebird, parakeet 9 parrakeet

budget
4 body, bulk 5 total 6 amount 7 quantum 8 quantity 9 aggregate

budtime
6 spring 10 springtide

Buenos ____
5 Aires

buff
3 fan, rub 5 glaze, gloss, shine 6 addict, glance, polish, votary 7 burnish, devotee, furbish, habitué 10 aficionado

buffalo
4 anoa, balk, beat, bilk, dash, foil, ruin 5 bison, stump 6 baffle 7 carabao, nonplus 9 frustrate 10 circumvent, disappoint
Philippines: 7 tamarao, tamarau, timarou

buffalo grass
5 grama 6 gramma

buffet
3 box 4 beat, blip, chop, cuff, drub, poke, slap, sock 5 clout, pound, punch, smack, spank 6 batter, pummel, thrash, wallop 7 belabor, lambast 8 lambaste

buffoon
4 zany 5 clown 9 harlequin 11 merry-andrew

bug
3 irk, nut, vex 4 fret, gall 5 annoy 6 bother, insect, zealot 7 fanatic, provoke, wiretap 10 enthusiast

bugaboo
see **bugbear**

bugbear
4 bogy, fear, ogre 5 bogey 6 goblin 7 problem, specter, spectre 8 anathema, bogeyman 9 bête noire, boogeyman, hobgoblin

10 black beast 11 abomination, detestation

bugle
blare: 7 tantara
call: 4 mess, taps 6 sennet, tattoo 7 retreat 8 assembly, reveille

Bugs ___
4 Baer 5 Bunny

build
3 wax 4 form, make, mold, rise 5 boost, erect, forge, frame, mount, put up, raise, run up, shape 6 expand, uprear 7 augment, enlarge, fashion, habitus, magnify, produce, throw up, upsurge 8 assemble, compound, heighten, increase, multiply, physique 9 construct, fabricate 10 aggrandize 11 manufacture 12 constitution

builder
10 contractor

builder's knot
10 clove hitch

building
3 hut 6 fabric 7 edifice 9 structure
addition: 3 ell 4 wing 5 annex
compartment: 3 bay 4 room 6 office
connector: 9 breezeway
farm: 4 barn, crib, shed, silo
for apartments: 8 tenement
for arms: 7 arsenal
for fodder: 4 silo
for gambling: 6 casino
for grain: 4 silo 7 granary 8 elevator
for horses: 6 stable
for manufacture: 4 shop 5 plant 7 factory
for music: 4 hall 10 auditorium, opera house
for sports: 3 gym 4 bowl 5 arena 7 stadium 8 coliseum 9 gymnasium 10 hippodrome
material: 4 iron, wood 5 adobe, brick, glass, steel, stone 6 cement 8 concrete
medieval: 6 castle
projection: 3 bay, ell 4 wing 5 annex 6 dormer 7 cornice
round: 7 rotunda

build up
4 puff 5 erect 9 advertise, construct, establish, publicize 10 press-agent

built-in
6 inborn, inbred, innate 8 inherent 9 essential, ingrained 10 congenital, deep-seated, indwelling

bulb
3 bud 4 leek, lily, sego 5 onion, tu-

lip 6 garlic, squill 8 daffodil, hyacinth 9 amaryllis, narcissus
segment: 5 clove

bulb-like bud
4 corm 5 tuber 7 rhizome

Bulgaria
capital: 5 Sofia
monetary unit: 3 lev

bulge
3 jut 4 bump, edge, lump, poke, pout 5 pouch, swell 6 beetle, dilate, expand 7 distend, project 8 handicap, overhang, protrude, stand out, stick out, swelling 9 advantage, allowance, head start, outthrust 10 projection, protrusion 11 protuberate 12 protuberance

bulk
4 body, core, loom, mass 5 total 6 amount, budget, corpus, object, staple, volume 7 bigness, quantum 8 quantity, stand out 9 aggregate, greatness, largeness, magnitude, substance
combining form: 4 onco 5 oncho

bull
3 big, fat 4 slip, toro, trip 5 boner, buyer, error, fluff, husky, lapse, large 6 bungle 7 blooper, blunder, mistake 8 oversize
combining form: 4 taur 5 tauri, tauro

bulldoze
3 cow 4 push 5 bully, press, shove 6 hector, hustle, jostle 7 bluster, dragoon 8 bludgeon, browbeat, bullyrag, shoulder 10 intimidate

bullet
3 fly, zip 4 whiz 5 hurry 6 barrel, dumdum, tracer
size: 7 caliber, calibre

bull fiddle
10 contrabass, double bass

bullfighter
6 torero 7 matador, picador 8 toreador 9 cuadrilla 11 cuadrillero 12 banderillero
famous: 6 Arruza 8 Belmonte, Joselito, Manolete 10 El Cordobes

bullfighting
arena: 5 plaza
cheer: 3 olé
hero: 6 torero 7 matador 8 toreador
lancer: 7 picador
red cloth: 6 muleta
Spanish: 7 corrida
team: 9 cuadrilla

bullheaded
6 mulish 8 perverse 9 obstinate, pigheaded 10 headstrong, refrac-

tory, self-willed 11 intractable, stiff-necked 12 pertinacious

bullwork
4 moil, toil 5 grind, labor, sweat 6 drudge 7 travail 8 drudgery

bully
3 cow 4 fine, punk 5 meany 6 hector, meanie, menace, pander 7 bluster, dragoon, harrier, torment 8 ballyrag, bludgeon, browbeat, bulldoze, bullyrag, harasser, threaten 9 bulldozer, excellent, first-rate, front-rank, tormenter 10 browbeater, intimidate, macquereau, persecutor 11 antagonizer, intimidator

bullyrag
see **bulldoze**

bulwark
4 fend 5 cover, guard 6 defend, screen, secure, shield 7 bastion, parapet, protect, rampart 8 fortress 9 safeguard 10 breastwork, stronghold

bum
3 beg, jag, vag 4 bust, hobo, idle, laze, lazy, loaf, loll, slug 5 binge, cadge, drunk, idler, mooch, tramp 6 bender, dawdle, loafer, loiter, lounge, slouch 7 carouse, drifter, floater, goof off, vagrant, wassail 8 derelict, dolittle, faineant, slugabed, sluggard, vagabond 9 brannigan, do-nothing, goldbrick, lazybones, panhandle 10 street arab

bumbershoot
8 umbrella

bumble
3 hum 4 buzz, muff 5 botch, drone, lurch, strum, thrum 6 bobble, bollix, bungle, fumble, mucker 7 blunder, stumble 9 bombinate

bumbling
5 inept 6 gauche, wooden 7 awkward, halting, unhandy, unhappy 9 ham-handed, maladroit 11 heavy-handed

bummer
6 bandit, beggar, cadger, looter 7 brigand, cateran, forager, moocher 8 marauder, pillager 9 plunderer 10 depredator, freebooter, panhandler

bump
3 hit, jar 4 bang, bust, jolt, knot, knur, lump, slam 5 break, bunch, carom, clash, crash, gnarl, knock, shock 6 demote, impact, jostle, reduce, strike, wallop 7 collide, declass, degrade, demerit, disrate,

mudhole, pothole **8** disgrade, pumpknot, swelling **9** chuckhole, collision, downgrade **10** concussion, percussion **12** protuberance

bumpkin
4 hick, jake, rube **6** joskin, rustic **7** bucolic, hayseed, hoosier **9** chawbacon **10** clodhopper, provincial

bump off
4 do in, kill **6** finish, murder **7** execute, put away **9** liquidate **11** assassinate

Bumppo, Natty
alias: **7** Hawkeye **10** Deerslayer, Pathfinder
creator: **6** Cooper (James Fenimore)

bumptious
8 arrogant **9** conceited, obtrusive

bumpy
5 jerky, nubby, ridgy, rough **6** bouncy, jouncy **7** jolting

bunch
3 lot, set **4** band, bevy, body, bump, crew, knot, lump, push **5** batch, clump, covey, crowd, group, party **6** bundle, circle, clutch, parcel **7** cluster **8** assembly

bunco steerer
3 gyp **6** con man **7** diddler, sharper **8** swindler **9** defrauder, trickster **12** double-dealer **13** confidence man

bundle
3 lot, pot, set, wad **4** bale, body, mint, pile **5** array, batch, bunch, clump, group, sheaf **6** bindle, boodle, fardel, packet, parcel **7** cluster, fortune
of grain: **5** sheaf, shock, stook
of hay: **4** bale, wase
of sticks: **5** fagot **6** faggot **7** fascine
small: **8** fascicle

bungle
4 bull, flub, muff, slip, trip **5** boner, botch, error, fluff, gum up, lapse **6** bollix, foozle, goof up **7** blooper, blunder, louse up, mistake

bungler
5 klutz **8** shlemiel **9** blunderer, schlemiel **10** stumblebum **11** blunderbuss

bunglesome
6 clumsy **7** awkward

bunk
3 hut **5** board, hokum, house, lodge, put up **6** bestow, billet, harbor, humbug **7** eyewash, baloney, quarter **8** domicile, nonsense **9** poppycock

bunkum
4 jazz **5** hokum **7** baloney **8** flimflam, nonsense **9** poppycock **10** balderdash

Bunyanesque
4 huge **7** mammoth, titanic **8** colossal, gigantic **9** Herculean, monstrous **10** behemothic, gargantuan, prodigious

Bunyan's ox
4 Babe

buoy
4 prop **6** uphold **7** bolster, support, sustain **9** underprop

buoyancy
10 ebullience, exuberance, exuberancy **13** effervescence

buoyant
4 airy **6** bouncy **7** elastic **8** volatile **9** expansive, resilient **12** effervescent

burble
3 yak **4** chat, wash **5** clack, run on, slosh, swash **6** babble, bubble, gabble, gurgle, rattle, yammer **7** chatter, prattle

burden
3 tax **4** clog, duty, gist, haul, lade, load, onus, task **5** cargo, weigh **6** amount, charge, cumber, lading, lumber, saddle, upshot, weight **7** afflict, freight, oppress, payload, purport **8** encumber, handicap, overload **9** millstone, substance **10** deadweight

burdensome
5 tough **6** taxing **7** exigent, onerous, weighty **8** exacting, grievous **9** demanding **10** oppressive

bureau
5 chest **7** dresser **10** chiffonier

bureaucrat
8 mandarin, official **11** functionary **12** civil servant

burg
6 hamlet, Podunk **7** cowtown, mudhole, village **8** hick town, tank town **11** whistle-stop **12** one-horse town **13** jerkwater town

burgee
4 flag, jack **6** banner, ensign, pennon **7** pendant, pennant **8** standard, streamer

burgeon
4 blow **5** bloom, build, mount, run up **6** expand, flower, sprout **7** augment, blossom, enlarge **8** heighten, increase, multiply, outbloom, snowball **10** effloresce

burghal
4 city **5** urban **9** municipal

burgher
3 cit **5** towny **6** towner **7** citizen, townman **8** townsman

burglar
4 yegg **5** thief **6** robber **7** yeggman
loot: **4** swag

burglarize
3 rob **6** burgle **7** ransack **10** housebreak

burgomaster
5 mayor **10** magistrate

Burgundy wine
grape: **5** Gamay **9** Pinot Noir **10** Chardonnay
red: **8** Mercurey **10** Beaujolais
white: **5** Rully **6** Chagny **7** Chablis **10** Montrachet **13** Pouilly-Fuissé

burial
4 tomb **5** grave **7** funeral **8** exequies **9** interment, obsequies, sepulcher, sepulture **10** entombment, inhumation
box: **6** casket, coffin
ceremony: **7** funeral
coffin stand: **4** bier
mound: **3** low **6** barrow **7** tumulus
tomb: **9** mausoleum, sepulcher, sepulchre

burial ground
8 boot hill, cemetery **8** God's acre **9** graveyard **10** necropolis **11** polyandrium **12** memorial park, potter's field
early Christian: **8** catacomb

burlap
5 gunny **6** fabric **7** bagging, sacking **10** wrappering
fiber: **4** hemp, jute

burlesque
3 ape **4** mock, sham **5** farce, mimic **6** parody **7** imitate, mockery, takeoff **8** travesty **10** caricature

burly
5 beefy, hefty, husky

Burma
7 Myanmar
capital: **6** Yangon **7** Rangoon

burn
4 bake, beam, bite, boil, char, cook, fire, fume, kiln, melt, rage, sear **5** anger, blaze, broil, chark, creek, flame, flare, gleam, light, parch, roast, scald, shine, singe, smart, smoke, sting, toast **6** blow up, ignite, kindle, scorch, seethe, stream **7** bristle, combust, consume,

cremate, flare up, inflame, radiate, smolder, sputter, swelter 8 boil over, smoulder 9 carbonize, cauterize 10 incinerate
Scottish: 7 scowder 8 scouther

burnable
9 flammable, ignitable 11 combustible, inflammable

burned-out
7 worn-out 8 fatigued 9 destroyed, exhausted 10 broken-down 11 debilitated

burning
3 hot 4 dire 5 afire, aglow, fiery 6 ablaze, aflame, alight, ardent, fervid, heated, hectic, red-hot, torrid, urgent 7 blazing, clamant, exigent, fervent, fevered, flaming, flaring, glowing, ignited, instant, lighted 8 broiling, feverish, pressing, sizzling, white-hot 9 clamorous, scorching 10 imperative, passionate 11 conflagrant, impassioned, importunate 12 incandescent
combining form: 4 igni
malicious: 5 arson
relating to: 5 pyric

burnish
3 rub 4 buff 5 glaze, gloss, shine 6 glance, polish 7 furbish

burnished
5 shiny 6 glossy, sheeny 7 shining 8 gleaming, lustrous, polished 10 glistening

burnsides
5 beard 8 whiskers 10 sideboards 11 dundrearies, muttonchops 12 side-whiskers

burp
5 belch, eruct 8 eructate

burro
3 ass 4 donk 6 donkey 7 jackass

Burroughs' hero
6 Tarzan

burrow
3 den 4 hole, lair, snug 5 couch, hovel, lodge 6 cuddle, nestle, nuzzle 7 snuggle

burst
4 bang, boom, clap, gust, rive, slam, wham 5 blast, crack, crash, erupt, flare, go off, lunge, sally, salvo, smash, storm 6 access, blow up, plunge, shiver, shower, volley 7 barrage, explode, flare-up, rupture, shatter 8 break out, detonate, drumfire, eruption, fragment, mushroom, outbreak, splinter, splitter

9 broadside, cannonade, explosion, fusillade 11 bombardment

bursting
8 erumpent
combining form: 7 rrhexis, rrhexes (plural)

bury
4 hide, tomb 5 cache, cover, inter, plant, stash 6 coffin, entomb, inhume, screen 7 conceal, lay away, put away, secrete 8 ensconce 9 sepulcher, sepulture

bush
4 rose 5 lilac, shrub, wahoo 6 azalea, cassis, privet 7 currant, weigela 8 backland, backwash, barberry, frontier, hazelnut 9 backwater, backwoods, forsythia, manzanita, up-country 10 gooseberry, hinterland 11 pussy willow 12 rhododendron
combining form: 5 thamn 6 thamno

bush-league
5 minor 8 mediocre 10 inadequate, second-rate

bushranger
8 woodsman 12 frontiersman

bushwa
4 bosh 5 hooey 6 bunkum 7 baloney, eyewash 8 malarkey, nonsense 9 poppycock 10 balderdash, flapdoodle

bushwhacker
6 bandit, outlaw, raider, sniper 8 woodsman 9 guerrilla

bushy
5 bosky

business
3 job 4 duty, firm, line, role, work 5 trade 6 affair, custom, matter, office, outfit, racket 7 calling, company, concern, lookout, palaver, pursuit, traffic 8 commerce, function, industry, province 9 patronage 10 employment, enterprise, occupation 13 establishment
expense: 8 overhead
syndicate: 6 cartel

businesslike
7 serious 9 efficient, practical 10 purposeful, systematic

businessman
6 dealer, trader, tycoon 7 magnate 8 merchant 9 tradesman 10 trafficker 12 merchandiser

buss
4 kiss, peck 5 smack 6 smooch 8 osculate

bust
3 dud, jag, nab 4 bomb, bump, fail, flop, fold, raid, ruin 5 binge, break, crash, lemon, loser, spree 6 arrest, bender, demote, fold up, pauper, reduce 7 carouse, declass, degrade, demerit, disrate, failure 8 bankrupt, disgrade 9 downgrade, pauperize 10 impoverish

bustard
African: 7 korhaan 8 knorhaan
genus: 4 Otis
relating to: 7 otidine

bustle
3 ado, fly, run 4 flit, fuss, rush, stir, to-do 5 hurry, whirl, whisk 6 clamor, flurry, furore, hassle, hasten, hubbub, hustle, pother, tumult, uproar 7 turmoil 9 commotion, whirlpool, whirlwind 10 hurlyburly

bustling
4 busy 5 brisk, fussy 6 active, lively 7 hopping, humming, popping 9 energetic

busty
5 buxom 6 bosomy, chesty 11 full-bosomed

busy
5 fussy 6 engage, lively, occupy 7 engaged, engross, hopping, humming, immerse, popping, working 8 bustling, employed, hustling, occupied 9 assiduous, intrusive, obtrusive, officious 10 meddlesome 11 impertinent

busybody
5 prier, pryer, snook, snoop 6 butt-in, gossip, rubber 7 meddler, Paul Pry 8 informer, kibitzer, quidnunc 9 pragmatic 10 newsmonger, pragmatist, rubberneck 11 nosey Parker, rumormonger 12 gossipmonger, intermeddler

but
3 bar, yet 4 just, only, save 5 alone 6 bating, except, merely, saving, simply, solely, unless 7 barring, besides, however 8 entirely 9 aside from, excluding, outside of 11 exclusively

butcher
4 slay 9 slaughter

butcher-bird
6 shrike

butcherly
6 bloody, clumsy, savage 10 unskillful

butchery
7 carnage 8 massacre 9 bloodbath, bloodshed, slaughter

Butler, Samuel
novel: **7** Erewhon **16** The Way of All Flesh
poem: **8** Hudibras

butt
3 keg, tun **4** abut, cask, dupe, fool, gull, jest, join, joke, line, mark, mock, pipe **5** chump, touch, verge **6** adjoin, barrel, border, jestee, pigeon, sucker, target, victim **7** fall guy, gudgeon, mockery **8** derision, hogshead, neighbor **9** cigarette, pilgarlic **11** communicate, sitting duck **13** laughingstock

butter
artificial: **4** oleo **9** margarine **13** oleomargarine
Indian: **3** ghi **4** ghee
piece: **3** pat
semifluid: **3** ghi **4** ghee
tree: **4** shea
tub: **6** firkin

butterball
5 blimp, fatty **8** dumpling

butterfish
5 coney **6** gunnel

butterfly
5 diana, satyr, zebra **6** copper, morpho **7** admiral, buckeye, kallima, monarch, satyrid, skipper, sulphur, troilus, vanessa, viceroy **8** crescent, grayling, milkweed, victoria **9** aphrodite, metalmark, nymphalid, wood nymph **10** fritillary, hairstreak, parnassius **11** checkerspot, swallowtail
bush: **8** buddleia
fish: **6** blenny, chiton **7** gurnard
larva: **11** caterpillar
lily: **8** mariposa
order: **11** Lepidoptera
plant: **8** oncidium
pupa: **9** chrysalis
scientist: **13** lepidopterist

butterlike
8 butyrous **11** butyraceous

butt-in
7 meddler **8** busybody, kibitzer, quidnunc

butt in
6 horn in, meddle **7** intrude, obtrude **8** busybody, chisel in **9** interfere, interlope **10** intertrude, monkey with, tamper with **11** intermeddle

buttinsky
see **butt-in**

buttocks
4 prat, rear, rump, seat, tail **5** fanny, hiney, nates, podex **6** behind, bottom, breech, heinie **7** hind

end, hunkers, keester, keister, rear end, tail end **8** backside, derriere, haunches **9** fundament, posterior
combining form: **3** pyg **4** pyga, pygo **5** pygia **6** procta

button
Japanese: **7** netsuke

buttonball
8 sycamore

button-down
6 square **8** orthodox, straight **12** conventional

buttonwood
8 sycamore **13** white mangrove

buttress
4 prop, stay **5** brace, shore **6** bear up, column, upbear, uphold **7** bolster, shore up, support, sustain **11** underpinner **12** underpinning **13** underpropping

buxom
5 busty **6** bosomy, chesty **7** shapely, stacked **10** curvaceous **11** full-bosomed, full-figured

buy
3 get **5** bribe **6** obtain, ransom, redeem **7** acquire, bargain, believe **8** closeout, purchase **10** pennyworth, tamper with
Scottish: **4** coff

buy back
6 redeem

buyer
6 emptor, vendee **8** customer **9** purchaser

buy off
3 fix, sop **5** bribe **10** tamper with

Buzi's son
7 Ezekiel

buzz
3 hum **4** fizz, hiss, whir, whiz **5** drone, rumor, strum, thrum, whirr, whish **6** bumble, fizzle, gossip, report, rumble, sizzle, wheeze, whoosh **7** whisper **8** sibilate **9** bombinate **11** scuttlebutt

by
3 per, via **4** as to, near, nigh, over, with **5** adieu, round **6** beside, nearby, next to, so long **7** goodbye, through **8** farewell **9** alongside **11** according to

by and by
4 anon, next, soon **5** after, infra, later **7** shortly **8** directly, latterly **9** afterward, presently **10** afterwhile **12** subsequently

by and large
7 en masse **8** all in all **9** generally **10** altogether, on the whole

by dint of
see **by means of**

bye-bye
5 adieu **6** so long **7** cheerio **8** farewell, toodle-oo

bygone
3 old **4** dead, late, lost, once, past **5** dated, olden **6** former, whilom **7** antique, archaic, belated, defunct, extinct, old-time, onetime, quondam **8** departed, sometime, vanished **9** erstwhile, out-of-date **10** antiquated, oldfangled **12** old-fashioned

by means of
3 per, via **4** with **7** through

byname
7 moniker **8** nickname **9** sobriquet **10** hypocorism

bypass
5 burke, skirt **6** detour **8** sidestep **10** circumvent

byplace
4 nook **5** niche **6** cranny

by-product
7 spin-off **8** offshoot **9** outgrowth **10** derivative, descendant

Byron work
4 Cain, Lara **5** Beppo **6** Werner **7** Don Juan, Manfred **9** The Giaour **10** The Corsair **12** Childe Harold

bystander
6 viewer **7** watcher, witness **8** beholder, looker-on, observer, onlooker **9** spectator **10** eyewitness

by stealth
7 sub rosa **8** covertly, secretly **9** furtively, privately **13** clandestinely

by virtue of
see **by means of**

by way of
see **by means of**

byword
3 saw **5** adage **6** phrase, saying, slogan **7** proverb **8** nickname **9** sobriquet **10** hypocorism, shibboleth **11** catchphrase

Byzantine
6 daedal, knotty **7** complex, gordian **8** involved **9** elaborate, intricate **11** complicated **12** labyrinthine **13** sophisticated
emperor: **3** Leo **4** Zeno **5** Basil **6** Bardas, Justin, Phocas **7** Michael, Romanus **9** Heraclius, Justinian **10** Nicephorus, Theodosius
empress: **3** Zoe **5** Irene **8** Theodora

Cc

cab
4 hack, taxi

cabal
3 mob 4 camp, clan, plot, ring
5 covin 6 circle, clique, scheme
7 coterie, ingroup 8 intrigue, practice 9 camarilla 10 conspiracy
11 machination

cabaletta
4 aria, song

cabalistic
6 arcane, mystic 8 numinous
9 mysterial, unguessed 10 mysterious, unknowable 11 inscrutable
12 impenetrable 13 unaccountable

caballero
6 knight 8 cavalier, horseman
9 chevalier

cabaret
4 café 6 nitery 7 hot spot 8 nightery 9 nightclub, night spot 10 supper club 11 discotheque 12 watering hole

cabbage
3 nab, nip 4 hook, lift 5 kraut,
money, pinch, steal 6 collar 7 purloin 10 greenbacks, sauerkraut
11 appropriate
disease of: 6 mildew, mosaic 7 root
rot, yellows 8 blackleg, club root
family: 4 cole, kail, kale, rape
5 colza, savoy 6 turnip 7 collard,
mustard 8 broccoli, coleseed, colewort, kohlrabi, rutabaga
11 cauliflower

cabbagehead
see **dunce**

cabdriver
4 hack 5 cabby 6 cabbie

cabin
3 cot, hut 4 camp 5 lodge, shack
6 cabana, shanty 7 cottage
9 stateroom

cabin cruiser
4 boat 9 motorboat

cabinet
7 armoire, commode 8 cupboard

cabinetmaker
American: 5 Eames (Charles), Phyfe
(Duncan) 6 Belter (John Henry),
Wright (Frank Lloyd) 7 Goddard
(John, Stephen, Thomas) 8 McIntire
(Samuel), Townsend (Christopher,
Edmund, James, Job, John,)
English: 4 Adam (James, Robert),
Hope (Thomas), Kent (William)
6 Morris (William) 8 Sheraton
(Thomas) 11 Chippendale
(Thomas), Hepplewhite (George)
French: 6 Boulle (Andre-Charles)
8 Caffieri (Jacques, Jean-Jacques,
Philippe), Cressent (Charles)
German: 10 Weisweiler (Adam)

cable
4 rope, wire 6 stitch

cabriolet
8 carriage

cache
4 bury, hide 5 cover, plant, stash,
store 7 conceal, secrete
8 ensconce

cachet
4 rank 5 state 6 status 7 dignity,
stature 8 position, prestige, standing 11 consequence

cachinnate
5 laugh

cackle
3 gab, jaw 4 blab, chat 5 clack,
run on 6 babble, burble, gabble,
gaggle 7 blabber, blatter, chatter,
prattle

cacoëthes
5 mania

cacophonic
9 dissonant, immusical, unmusical
10 discordant, inharmonic 11 dis-
harmonic 12 inharmonious, unharmonious 13 disharmonious

cacophonous
see **cacophonic**

cacophony
10 dissonance

cactus
5 dildo, nopal 6 cereus, cholla,
mescal, peyote 7 airampo, bisnaga, biznaga, opuntia, saguaro,
sahuaro 8 chichipe 11 prickly pear
fruit: 6 cochal

cad
3 cur 4 heel, lout 5 creep, louse
6 rotter 7 bounder 9 yellow dog

cadaver
4 body, mort 5 stiff 6 corpse 7 carcass, remains

cadaverous
5 gaunt 6 wasted 7 ghastly,
ghostly, shadowy 8 skeletal, spectral 9 deathlike, emaciated, ghostlike 10 corpselike

cadence
4 beat 5 meter, pulse, rhyme,
swing, throb 6 rhythm 7 measure
8 rhythmus 9 pulsation

cadency
see **cadence**

cadet
4 pimp 5 bully, plebe 6 pander
8 fancy man 10 macquereau

cadge
3 beg, bum 5 mooch 6 sponge
9 panhandle

cadmium
symbol: 2 Cd

Cadmus
daughter: 3 Ino 5 Agave 6 Semele
7 Autonoe
father: 6 Agenor
sister: 6 Europa
victim: 6 dragon
wife: 8 Harmonia

caducity
3 age 6 old age 7 dotardy 10 dotingness, senescence 11 elderliness, senectitude

Caesar
assassin: 6 Brutus (Marcus Junius) 7 Cassius (Gaius)
battle: 4 Zela 9 Pharsalus
conquest: 4 Gaul
eulogist: 6 Antony (Marc)
message: 12 veni, vidi, vici
river: 7 Rubicon
utterance: 9 et tu Brute
wife: 7 Pompeia 8 Cornelia 9 Calpurnia

Caesarism
10 absolutism 12 dictatorship

café
5 diner 6 nitery 7 beanery, cabaret, hot spot 8 cookshop, nightery 9 lunchroom, nightclub, night spot 10 coffee shop, supper club 11 discotheque, eating house 12 luncheonette, watering hole 13 watering place

café ___
6 au lait, filtre

cage
3 hem, mew, pen 4 coop, jail 6 immure, shut in 7 close in, enclose, envelop 8 imprison 11 incarcerate

cagey
3 sly 5 heady 6 argute, astute, shrewd 9 astucious, sagacious 13 perspicacious

cageyness
3 art 5 craft 7 cunning, slyness 8 artifice, foxiness, wiliness 9 canniness 10 artfulness, craftiness

cahoots
5 tie-up 6 hookup 8 alliance 10 connection 11 affiliation, association, combination, conjunction, partnership 12 togetherness

caiman
6 jacare 9 crocodile

Cain
brother: 4 Abel, Seth
father: 4 Adam
land: 3 Nod
mother: 3 Eve
nephew: 4 Enos
son: 5 Enoch
victim: 4 Abel

Caine Mutiny author
4 Wouk (Herman)

cajole
3 con 4 coax 7 beguile, blarney, wheedle 8 blandish, soft-soap 9 sweet-talk

cake
3 dry, set 4 coat, rime 5 cover, crust 6 harden 7 congeal, encrust, incrust 8 indurate, solidify 10 incrustate
almond: 8 macaroon
chocolate: 7 brownie
coffee: 5 babka 6 kuchen
cornmeal: 4 pone 8 tortilla
crisp, thin: 5 wafer
flat: 5 cooky 6 cookie
oatmeal: 4 farl 5 farle, scone 7 bannock
of food: 5 patty 6 pattie
ring-shaped: 5 donut 6 jumbal, jumble 8 doughnut
rum-soaked: 4 baba
Scottish: 4 farl 5 farle, scone
shell-shaped: 9 madeleine
toasted: 7 crumpet
topping: 5 icing 8 frosting, streusel
twisted: 7 cruller
unleavened: 8 tortilla
wheat: 4 puri
without flour: 5 torte
without shortening: 6 sponge

Cakes and Ale author
7 Maugham (W. Somserset)

cakewalk
4 romp, rout 5 dance, strut 6 prance 7 runaway

calaboose
4 jail 5 clink, pokey 6 cooler, lockup, prison 8 hoosegow

Calais
brother: 5 Zetes
father: 6 Boreas
mother: 8 Orithyia

calamitous
4 dire 5 fatal 6 woeful 7 fateful, ruinous 8 grievous 10 afflictive, deplorable, disastrous, lamentable 11 cataclysmic, distressing, regrettable, unfortunate 12 catastrophic 13 heartbreaking

calamity
4 ruin, woes 5 wreck 7 tragedy 8 disaster 9 cataclysm 10 affliction 11 catastrophe, tribulation 12 misadventure

Calamity ___
4 Jane

calamity howler
9 Cassandra, pessimist, worrywart

calcar
4 oven

calcium
symbol: 2 Ca

calculate
5 count, value 6 assess, cipher, figure, reckon 7 compute 8 appraise, estimate, evaluate 9 ascertain, determine

calculated
7 planned

calculating
3 sly 4 wary, wily 5 chary 6 artful, crafty 7 careful, cunning, guarded 8 cautious, discreet, gingerly, guileful 11 circumspect, considerate

calculating device
6 abacus
ancient Peruvian: 5 quipo, quipu

calculation
8 figuring 9 ciphering, reckoning 10 arithmetic, estimation 11 computation

calculus
combining form: 4 lith 5 litho

Caleb
daughter: 6 Achsah
father: 6 Hezron 9 Jephunneh
son: 3 Hur, Iru

Caledonia
8 Scotland

calembour
3 pun 11 paronomasia

calendar
4 card, sked 6 agenda, docket 7 program 8 schedule 9 programma, timetable
abbreviation: 3 Apr, Aug, Dec, Feb, Fri, Jan, Mar, Mon, Nov, Oct, Sat, Sep, Sun, Tue, Wed 4 Sept 5 Thurs
ecclesiastical: 4 ordo 8 menology

calenture
4 fire, zeal 5 ardor 6 fervor, hurrah 7 passion 10 enthusiasm

calf
hide: 3 kip
leather: 3 elk
meat: 4 veal
relating to: 8 vituline
stray: 4 dogy 5 dogie
unbranded: 8 maverick

Caliban
5 slave
master: 8 Prospero
witch-mother: 7 Sycorax

caliber
5 class, grade, merit, value, worth
6 virtue 7 quality, stature

calibrate
7 measure 9 systemize
11 standardize

California
capital: 10 Sacramento
college, university: 3 USC 4 UCLA
5 Biola 8 Stanford 10 Pepperdine
12 San Francisco
colonizer: 6 Sutter (John Augustus)
fault zone: 10 San Andreas
largest city: 10 Los Angeles
motto: 6 Eureka
nickname: 11 Golden State
state flower: 11 golden poppy

californium
symbol: 2 Cf

caliginous
3 dim 4 dark, dusk 5 dusky, murky
6 gloomy 7 obscure 9 lightless, tenebrous 13 unilluminated

Caligula's mother
9 Agrippina

caliology topic
4 nest

caliph's name
3 Ali 7 Abu Bakr

Calista's seducer
8 Lothario

calisthenics
9 exercises

call
3 bid, cry, dub 4 bawl, draw, hail,
hoot, howl, lure, name, note, page,
pull, roar, song, term, yell, yowl
5 augur, cause, claim, exact, greet,
hallo, hollo, phone, pop in, shout,
title, visit 6 accost, appeal, bellow,
come by, drop by, drop in, holler,
invite, look in, look up, reckon, salute, stop by, stop in, summon
7 address, baptize, convene, convoke, entitle, portend, predict, presage, round up, solicit, summons
8 assemble, christen, estimate, forecast, foretell, occasion, prophesy
9 adumbrate, challenge, designate,
necessity, postulate, seduction, telephone 10 allurement, attraction,
denominate, vaticinate, visitation,
vociferate 11 approximate, requisition 12 drawing power
13 prognosticate

calla
4 lily

call down
5 chide 6 lesson, monish, rebuke
7 reprove, tick off 8 admonish, reproach 9 reprimand

called
6 yclept 7 ycleped

caller
5 guest 7 visitor 8 visitant

call for
3 ask 5 crave 6 demand 7 require
11 necessitate

call forth
5 evoke 6 elicit 7 conjure

calligrapher
6 penman 7 copyist 9 engrosser

calligraphist
see **calligrapher**

calligraphy
4 hand 6 ductus, script 10 penmanship 11 handwriting

call in
6 summon 7 convene

calling
3 art, job 4 work 5 craft, trade
6 métier 7 mission, pursuit 8 business, lifework, vocation 10 employment, handicraft, occupation,
profession

Calliope
4 Muse
father: 4 Zeus 7 Jupiter
mother: 9 Mnemosyne
son: 7 Orpheus

Callisto
lover: 4 Zeus 7 Jupiter
son: 5 Arcas

call off
5 scrub 6 cancel

Call of the Wild
author: 6 London (Jack)
dog: 4 Buck

call on
5 visit 7 require

callosity
8 hardness 9 thickness

callous
5 stony 8 obdurate 9 heartless, indurated, unfeeling 11 coldhearted,
hardhearted, unemotional 12 casehardened, stonyhearted
13 unsympathetic

callow
3 raw 5 fresh, green, young 6 infant, unripe 7 untried 8 immature,
juvenile, unversed, youthful 9 unfledged 10 unseasoned 11 unpracticed 13 inexperienced,
unexperienced

call's partner
4 beck

call up
5 draft, evoke 6 summon
8 mobilize

calm
4 cool, easy, hush, lull 5 allay,
peace, quiet, relax, salve, still
6 hushed, pacify, placid, poised,
sedate, serene, settle, smooth,
soothe, stable, steady, stilly 7 appease, assuage, compose, halcyon,
mollify, pacific, placate, resting,
staunch 8 composed, inactive,
peaceful, reposing, tranquil 9 collected, easygoing, impassive, possessed, quiescent, unruffled
10 nonchalant, phlegmatic, untroubled 11 tranquilize, unflappable
12 even-tempered, self-composed
13 imperturbable, self-possessed

calmant
8 quietive, sedative

calmative
see **calmant**

calmness
6 phlegm 7 ataraxy 8 coolness
9 composure, sangfroid
10 equanimity

calumniate
5 libel 6 defame, malign, vilify
7 asperse, slander, traduce 9 denigrate 10 scandalize, villainize

calumnious
8 libelous 9 maligning, traducing,
vilifying 10 backbiting, defamatory, detracting, detractive, scandalous, slanderous

calumny
7 scandal, slander 10 backbiting,
defamation, detraction, reflection
12 backstabbing, belittlement, depreciation 13 disparagement

Calvados
6 brandy

calvary
5 cross, trial 6 ordeal 10 affliction,
visitation 11 tribulation

Calypso
beloved: 7 Ulysses 8 Odysseus
island: 6 Ogygia

calyx part
5 sepal

camaraderie
5 cheer 7 jollity 10 affability

11 sociability 12 conviviality, friendliness

camarilla
3 mob 4 camp, clan, ring 5 cabal 6 circle, clique 7 coterie, ingroup

Cambodia
9 Kampuchea
capital: 9 Phnom penh
monetary unit: 4 riel

camel
driver: 6 sarwan
one-humped: 9 dromedary
two-humped: 8 Bactrian

camel hair fabric
3 aba

camelopard
7 giraffe

Camelot
6 palace
lord: 6 Arthur

Camembert
6 cheese

cameraman
6 photog 7 lensman 8 photoist 12 photographer

Cameroon
capital: 7 Yaounde
largest city: 6 Douala
monetary unit: 5 franc

Camilla
father: 7 Metabus
slayer: 5 Aruns

Camille's creator
5 Dumas (Alexandre)

camouflage
4 mask 5 cloak 8 disguise 9 dissemble 11 dissimulate

camp
3 cot, hut, mob 4 clan, ring, tent 5 cabal, cabin, lodge, shack 6 circle, clique, shanty 7 bivouac, caboose, coterie, cottage, ingroup 9 camarilla

campaigner
9 candidate

campanile
6 belfry 8 carillon 9 bell tower

campestral
5 rural 6 rustic 7 bucolic, country, outland 8 agrestic, pastoral 10 outcountry, provincial 11 countrified

campus
see **college**

Camus work
5 Rebel 6 Plague 8 Caligula, Stranger

can
4 fire 7 dismiss 9 container, discharge 10 receptacle
combining form: 5 scyph 6 scyphi, scypho

Canaan
4 Zion 5 bliss 6 heaven 7 elysium, nirvana 8 empyrean, paradise
father: 3 Ham
grandfather: 4 Noah

Canaanite god
3 Mot 4 Baal 6 Molech, Moloch

Canace
brother: 8 Macareus
father: 6 Aeolus

Canada
capital: 6 Ottawa
college, university: 6 McGill 8 McMaster 9 Concordia
largest city: 8 Montreal
monetary unit: 6 dollar
province: 6 Quebec 7 Alberta, Ontario 8 Manitoba 10 Nova Scotia 12 New Brunswick, Newfoundland, Saskatchewan
provincial park: 5 Gaspé 7 Rondeau 9 Garibaldi

Canadian insurgent
4 Riel (Louis)

canaille
3 mob 6 masses, rabble 8 riffraff, unwashed 11 proletariat

canal
4 duct 6 course 7 channel, conduit 8 aqueduct 11 watercourse
Africa: 4 Suez 8 Ismailia
Belgium: 6 Albert
Canada: 7 Welland
Central America: 6 Panama
China: 5 Grand 7 Da Yunhe
combining form: 4 meat 5 meato
Florida: 10 Saint Lucie
Germany: 4 Kiel
Greece: 7 Corinth
Massachusetts: 7 Cape Cod
Michigan: 3 Soo
Netherlands: 8 Noord Zee, North Sea 13 Amsterdam Ship
New York: 4 Erie 6 Oswego 9 Champlain
Ontario: 6 Rideau
Thailand: 6 khlong
Venice: 5 Grand

canapé spread
4 paté

canard
3 fib, lie 4 tale 5 spoof 7 falsity, untruth 8 untruism 9 falsehood 13 prevarication

canary
4 fink 6 snitch 7 stoolie 8 informer, squealer

Canary Islands
5 Ferro, Lobos, Palma 6 Gomera, Hierro 7 Inferno 8 Graciosa, Tenerife 9 Alegranza, Lanzarote

canary yellow
6 meline

cancel
3 end 4 drop, x out 5 annul, erase, scrub 6 delete, efface, negate, revoke 7 blot out, call off, expunge, redress, rescind, sublate, wipe out 8 black out 9 frustrate, terminate 10 counteract, invalidate, neutralize, obliterate 12 countercheck

cancer
5 tumor 9 carcinoma
combining form: 6 carcin 7 carcino
treatment: 5 X rays 7 surgery 9 radiation 12 chemotherapy

cancer-causing
12 carcinogenic
substance: 10 carcinogen

cancer-like
8 cancroid

candescent
7 glowing 8 dazzling

Candia
5 Crete

candid
4 fair, just, open 5 frank, plain 6 honest 8 unbiased 9 equitable, impartial, objective, uncolored 10 aboveboard, forthright, scrupulous, unreserved 11 openhearted, unconcealed, undisguised 12 undissembled, unprejudiced 13 dispassionate, undissembling

candidate
6 seeker 7 hopeful, nominee, stumper 8 aspirant 9 applicant, dark horse 10 campaigner

Candide
author: 8 Voltaire
lover: 9 Cunegonde
tutor: 8 Pangloss
valet: 7 Cacambo

candle
6 bougie 8 bayberry
holder: 6 lampad, sconce 7 menorah, pricket 9 girandole 10 candelabra 11 candelabrum
material: 3 wax 4 wick 6 tallow 7 stearin 8 paraffin
religious: 6 votive 7 paschal
slender: 5 taper

candlefish
8 eulachon
relative: 5 smelt

candlelit service
5 vigil

candlepins
7 bowling

candy
5 honey 7 sweeten 9 sugarcoat, sugar over
kind: 4 rock 5 fudge, gundy, lolly, sweet, taffy, toffy 6 bonbon, comfit, dragée, jujube, nougat, toffee 7 brittle, caramel, fondant, gumdrop, penuche, praline 8 licorice, lollipop, lollypop, marzipan, sourball, taiglach, teiglach 9 chocolate, jelly bean, nonpareil, sweetmeat 10 confection 12 butterscotch
medicated: 7 lozenge 9 cough drop

Canea's land
5 Crete

canine
3 dog 4 tyke 5 hound, pooch

Canis Major star
6 Sirius

Canis Minor star
7 Procyon

canker
5 stain 6 debase 7 corrupt, debauch, deprave, pervert, vitiate 9 animalize 10 bestialize, demoralize

cankered
5 waspy 6 cranky, ornery 7 bearish, waspish 8 vinegary 9 crotchety 10 vinegarish 12 cantankerous, cross-grained

canker sore
5 ulcer 6 lesion 10 ulceration

cannabis
3 pot 4 hemp 5 bhang, ganja, grass 7 hashish 9 marijuana

canned
6 pocket, potted 7 capsule 9 condensed 10 epitomized

Cannery Row author
9 Steinbeck (John)

cannibalic
4 grim 5 cruel 6 fierce, savage 7 inhuman, wolfish 8 inhumane 9 barbarous, ferocious, truculent

canniness
3 art 5 craft 7 caution, cunning, slyness 8 artifice, foxiness, pru-

dence, wiliness 9 cageyness, foresight 10 artfulness, craftiness, discretion, precaution, providence 11 forethought 12 discreetness

cannon
6 pom-pom 8 howitzer, ordnance 9 artillery
part: 5 chase 6 breech 8 cascabel, trunnion
slang: 6 pistol 10 pickpocket

cannonade
4 bomb, hail 5 blitz, burst, salvo, shell 6 shower, volley 7 barrage, bombard 8 drumfire 9 broadside, fusillade 11 bombardment

cannonball
4 dive 5 speed 7 missile

cannoneer
6 gunner

cannon fodder
8 infantry, soldiers

canny
3 sly 4 wise 5 chary, quick, sharp, slick, smart 6 adroit, clever, frugal, saving 7 cunning, knowing, sparing, thrifty 9 dexterous, ingenious, provident, stewardly 10 economical, unwasteful 11 quick-witted, sharp-witted 12 nimble-witted

canoe
6 dugout 7 pirogue, piroque
ancient: 7 coracle
Central American: 6 pitpan
Eskimo: 5 kayak, umiak 6 oomiak 7 bidarka
Guianan: 6 corial
Latin American: 5 bungo
Malabar Coast: 6 ballam
Maori: 4 waka
Philippine: 5 banca 6 baroto
Polynesian: 4 pahi

canon
3 law 4 rule 5 dogma, edict, tenet 6 assize, decree 7 precept, statute 8 decretum, doctrine 9 ordinance 10 regulation

canonical
5 sound 8 accepted, orthodox, received 10 sanctioned 13 authoritative

canonical hour
4 none, sext 5 lauds, prime, terce 6 matins, tierce 7 vespers 8 compline

canonicals
9 vestments

can opener
9 church key

canopy
3 sky 5 cover 6 awning 7 marquee, shelter 8 covering 9 baldachin 10 baldachino 11 baldacchino
canvas: 4 tilt

cant
3 tip 4 heel, lean, list, tilt 5 argot, idiom, lingo, slang, slant, slope 6 jargon, patois, patter, speech 7 dialect, diction, incline, lexicon, palaver, recline 8 language 9 hypocrisy 10 dictionary, pharisaism, sanctimony, Tartuffery, Tartuffism, vernacular, vocabulary 11 phraseology, terminology 12 pecksniffery

cantaloupe
5 melon 9 muskmelon

cantankerous
4 dour, sour 5 cross, huffy, waspy 6 cranky, crusty, morose, ornery 7 bearish, crabbed, prickly, waspish 8 cankered, liverish, petulant, snappish, vinegary 9 crotchety, dyspeptic, irascible, irritable 10 ill-natured, vinegarish 12 cross-grained

canter
3 bum, vag 4 gait, hobo 5 tramp 7 drifter, vagrant 8 derelict, vagabond 10 street arab 11 bindle stiff

Canterbury
archbishop: 3 Oda 6 Anselm, Becket (Thomas), Parker (Matthew) 7 Cranmer (Thomas), Dunstan 9 Augustine

Canterbury Tales
author: 7 Chaucer (Geoffrey)
inn: 6 Tabard

canticle
3 ode 4 hymn, song 10 Benedicite, Benedictus, Magnificat 12 Nunc Dimittis

canticles
11 Song of Songs 13 Song of Solomon

cantilever
6 bridge 7 support

cantillate
4 sing 5 chant 6 recite

cantina
3 bar, pub 6 saloon, tavern 7 barroom, gin mill, rum hole 8 drinkery, groggery, pothouse

canton
6 billet 7 quarter 8 district, division

cantor
5 hazan 6 chazan, hazzan 7 chazzan 9 precentor

canvas
4 duck, sail, tarp, tent 6 awning
8 painting 9 tarpaulin

canvasback
4 duck

canvass
3 con, vet 4 case, drum, moot 5 argue, study 6 debate, drum up, survey 7 agitate, check up, discept, discuss, dispute, examine, inspect, solicit 9 check over, thrash out
10 scrutinize

canyon
5 cajon, chasm, gorge, gulch 6 ravine, valley 10 depression
Colorado River: 5 Grand
mouth: 4 abra
Snake river: 5 Hells

cap
3 cob, top 4 best, pass 5 beret, cover, crest, crown, trump 6 barret, beanie, climax, exceed, top off 7 blanket, overlay, surpass 8 outshine, outstrip, overcast, round off, surmount 9 culminate, finish off, transcend 10 overspread
academic: 11 mortarboard
brimless: 3 tam 5 beret, calot
7 calotte
clergyman's: 5 miter, mitre 7 biretta
9 zucchetto
combining form: 8 calyptri, calyptro
cone-shaped: 3 taj
hoodlike: 4 coif
hunter's: 7 montero
jester's: 7 coxcomb 9 cockscomb
Jewish: 8 yarmulke
knitted: 5 toque, tuque
military: 4 kepi
mushroom: 6 pileus
Muslim: 3 taj
part: 4 bill, brim, flap, peak 5 visor
7 earflap
Roman: 6 pileus
Scottish: 3 tam 5 mutch 6 bonnet
8 balmoral 9 glengarry 11 tam-o'-shanter
sheepskin: 6 calpac, kalpak
7 calpack
Turkish: 6 calpac, kalpak 7 calpack

capability
3 art 5 craft, might, skill 7 ability, cunning, potency 8 adequacy, capacity, efficacy 10 competence, efficiency 13 effectiveness, qualification, qualifiedness

capable
4 able, good 6 au fait, proper, wicked 9 competent, qualified
suffix: 3 ile 4 able, ible

capacious
4 wide 5 ample, roomy 7 copious
8 abundant, spacious
10 commodious

capacitance
unit of: 5 farad

capacity
4 bent, gift, rank 5 knack, might, place, state 6 status, talent 7 ability, caliber, faculty, footing, station, stature 8 adequacy, position, standing 9 character, situation
10 capability, competence 13 qualification, qualifiedness
unit of: 4 gill, peck, pint 5 liter, minim, quart 6 bushel, gallon 8 fluidram 10 fluidounce, milliliter

Capaneus
slayer: 4 Zeus
wife: 6 Evadne

caparison
8 clothing 9 adornment

cape
4 beak, bill, head, naze, ness
5 point 8 foreland, headland, pelerine 10 promontory
clergyman's: 7 mozetta 8 mozzetta
papal: 5 fanon, orale

Cape
Africa: 4 Juby, Yubi 5 Blanc
6 Blanco 7 Agulhas
Alaska: 3 Icy 4 Nome 5 Ocean
11 Krusenstern
Algeria: 3 Fer
Antarctica: 3 Ann 4 Dart 5 Adare
Arctic: 5 North 8 Nordkaap
Asia: 5 Aniva
Australia: 5 Byron, Otway, Sandy, Smoky 6 Arnhem 9 Van Diemen
Baffin Island: 4 Dyer
Black Sea: 5 Yasun
Borneo: 4 Datu 6 Datoek
Brazil: 4 Frio, Raso 5 Norte
California: 9 Mendocino
Canada: 5 North
Caribbean: 8 Honduras
Colombia: 5 Aguja
Costa Rica: 5 Velas
Crete: 5 Plaka
Croatia: 5 Ploca 6 Planka
Cuba: 4 Cruz 5 Maisi
Denmark: 4 Skaw 6 Skagen
Desolación island: 5 Pilar 6 Pillar
Djibouti: 3 Bir
Egypt: 5 Banas
England: 8 Bolerium, Lands End
Florida: 5 Sable 7 Kennedy
9 Canaveral
Greece: 4 Busa 5 Gallo, Malea, Papas, Vouxa 6 Araxos, Maleas
7 Akritas

Guadalcanal: 4 West
Guinea: 5 Verga
Gulf of California: 5 Lobos
Gulf of Guinea: 5 Lopez
Gulf of Mexico: 4 Rojo
Hawaii: 5 Ka Lae, South 10 South Point 11 Diamond Head
Hispaniola: 5 Beata
Honshu: 3 Iro, Oma 5 Inubo, Kyoga, Nyudo
Iceland: 4 Horn 5 North
Indonesia: 4 Vals 5 False
Japan: 4 Esan, Nomo, Sata, Soya
5 Erimo, Kamui
Liberia: 5 Mount
Libya: 3 Tin 4 Milh
Long Island Sound: 10 Throgs Neck
Malay Peninsula: 5 Bulat 7 Romania
Malaysia: 4 Piai 5 Sirik
Massachusetts: 3 Ann, Cod
Mediterranean: 5 Ajdir
Mexico: 4 Buey
Morocco: 3 Sim 4 Guir, Rhir
Namibia: 4 Fria 5 Cross
Newfoundland: 4 Pine 5 Bauld
New Jersey: 3 May
New Zealand: 4 East 5 Brett, North, South, Table
North Carolina: 4 Fear 7 Lookout
8 Hatteras
Northwest Territories: 8 Bathurst
Nova Scotia: 5 Canso 6 Breton
Oman: 3 Nus 4 Hadd
Ontario: 4 Hurd, Rich
Pakistan: 5 Monze, Muari
Portugal: 4 Roca
Puerto Rico: 4 Rojo
Quebec: 5 Gaspé
Red Sea: 5 Kasar
Sicily: 4 Boeo, Faro 7 Lilibeo, Passero, Pelorus
Solomon Islands: 5 Zelee
Somalia: 4 Asir 5 Assir, Hafun
South Africa: 4 Seal 8 Good Hope
South America: 4 Horn
Spain: 3 Nao 4 Gata 5 Creus, Penas 9 Trafalgar
Syria: 5 Basit
Taiwan: 5 O-luan 7 Garam Bi
Tasmania: 5 Table
Tierra del Fuego: 5 Penas
Tunisia: 5 Blanc
Turkey: 3 Boz 4 Baba, Ince, Kara, Krio 6 Lectum 8 Bozburun 9 Inceburun, Karaburun
Vancouver Island: 5 Scott
Virginia: 5 Henry
Washington: 5 Alava

Čapek
coinage: 5 robot
play: 3 R.U.R.

caper
4 dido, lark, romp 5 antic, frisk, prank, shine, trick 6 cavort, frolic, gambol 7 roguery, rollick 8 escapade, mischief 9 capriccio, devilment 10 impishness, shenanigan, tomfoolery 11 monkeyshine, waggishness

Capetown's famous son
5 Smuts (Jan)

capillary
4 tube 6 vessel 8 hairlike 11 blood vessel

capital
3 top 4 cock, fine, main, rank 5 basic, chief, dandy, gross, major, prime, vital 6 assets, famous, wealth 7 glaring 8 cardinal, dominant, five-star, flagrant, top-notch 9 egregious, essential, excellent, first-rate, number one, principal, resources 10 first-class, preeminent, underlying 11 fundamental, outstanding, predominant
Afghanistan: 5 Kabul
Alberta: 8 Edmonton
Angola: 6 Luanda
Antigua: 7 St. Johns
Armenia: 7 Yerevan
Assam: 6 Dispur
Azerbaijan: 4 Baku
Belize: 8 Belmopan
Belarus: 5 Minsk
Bhutan: 6 Thimbu
Botswana: 8 Gaborone
Dominica: 6 Roseau
Equatorial Guinea: 6 Malabo
Estonia: 7 Tallinn
Ethiopia: 10 Addis Ababa
Faeroe Islands: 9 Thorshavn
Falkland Islands: 7 Stanley
French Guiana: 7 Cayenne
Galapagos Islands: 12 San Cristobal
Georgia, Republic of: 7 Tbilisi
Ghana: 5 Accra
Greenland: 8 Godthaab
Guam: 5 Agana
Guinea: 7 Conakry
Kazakhstan: 7 Alma-Ata
Kiribata: 6 Tarawa
Kyrgyzstan: 7 Bishkek
Latvia: 4 Riga
Lithuania: 7 Vilnius
Malaysia: 11 Kuala Lumpur
Manitoba: 8 Winnipeg
Mauritania: 10 Nouakchott
Moldova: 8 Chişinău
Mongolia: 9 Ulan Bator
Montserrat: 8 Plymouth
Mozambique: 6 Maputo
Myanmar: 6 Yangon

Namibia: 8 Windhoek
Newfoundland: 10 Saint Johns
Northern Ireland: 7 Belfast
Northern Territory: 6 Darwin
North-West Frontier Province: 8 Peshawar
Northwest Territories: 11 Yellowknife
Nova Scotia: 7 Halifax
Orange Free State: 12 Bloemfontein
Pakistan: 9 Islamabad
Papua New Guinea: 11 Port Moresby
Prince Edward Island: 13 Charlottetown
Puerto Rico: 7 San Juan
Queensland: 8 Brisbane
Réunion: 10 Saint Denis
Saint Helena: 9 Jamestown
Saint Lucia: 8 Castries
Saskatchewan: 6 Regina
Scotland: 9 Edinburgh
Seychelles: 8 Victoria
Shetland: 7 Lerwick
Sicily: 7 Palermo
Sierra Leone: 8 Freetown
Sikkim: 7 Gangtok
Sind: 7 Karachi
Slovenia: 9 Ljubljana
Solomon Islands: 7 Honiara
South Australia: 8 Adelaide
South-West Africa: 8 Windhoek
Suriname: 10 Paramaribo
Swaziland: 7 Mbabane
Tahiti: 7 Papeete
Tajikistan: 8 Dushanbe
Tasmania: 6 Hobart
Tibet: 5 Lhasa
Tirol: 9 Innsbruck
Tonga: 9 Nukualofa
Turkmenistan: 9 Ashkhabad
Ukraine: 4 Kiev
Uruguay: 10 Montevideo
Uttar Pradesh: 7 Lucknow
Uzbekistan: 8 Tashkent
Victoria: 9 Melbourne
Vietnam: 5 Hanoi
Wales: 7 Cardiff
Western Australia: 5 Perth
Yukon: 10 Whitehorse
(see also names of individual countries and states)

capitalist
8 investor 9 bourgeois, financier, plutocrat

capitalistic
9 bourgeois

capitalize
3 aid 4 back, fund, help 5 stake 6 assist 7 finance, promote, sponsor, support 8 bankroll 9 grubstake, subsidize

capital sin
see **deadly sin**

Capitol Hill sound
3 aye, nay

capitulate
3 bow 4 cave 5 defer, yield 6 submit 7 knuckle, succumb 11 buckle under 12 knuckle under

capitulation
8 dedition 9 surrender 10 submission

capper
5 blind, decoy, shill, stick 9 shillaber

capriccio
5 caper, fancy, prank 6 whimsy

caprice
3 bee 4 mood, vein, whim 5 crank, fancy, freak, habit, humor, trait, trick 6 foible, maggot, megrim, notion, temper, vagary, whimsy 7 boutade, conceit 8 crotchet 9 mannerism 11 peculiarity 12 whigmaleerie 13 inconsistency

capricious
4 iffy 5 moody 6 chancy, fickle 7 erratic, wayward 8 freakish, ticklish, unstable, variable, volatile, whimsied 9 arbitrary, fluctuant, humorsome, mercurial, uncertain, vagarious, whimsical 10 changeable, inconstant, lubricious 12 effervescent, incalculable 13 temperamental, unpredictable

caprid
4 goat

capsheaf
see **capstone**

capsize
4 keel 5 upset 8 collapse, overturn

capstone
4 acme, apex, peak 6 apogee, climax, summit 8 capsheaf, meridian, pinnacle 11 culmination

capsule
6 canned, pocket, potted 9 condensed 10 epitomized
combining form: 4 thec 5 theci, theco

capsulize
7 enclose 8 condense

captain
7 skipper 11 four-striper
fictional: 4 Ahab, Nemo 5 Queeg
historical: 5 Bligh (William)
pirate: 4 Kidd (William)

Captains Courageous author
7 Kipling (Rudyard)

caption
6 legend 7 cutline 8 overline
9 underline

captious
5 testy 6 critic, snappy 7 carping,
finicky, peevish 8 caviling, contrary, critical, exacting, perverse,
petulant, snappish 9 cavillous, demanding, irritable 10 censorious
12 faultfinding, overcritical
13 hypercritical

captivate
4 draw, grip, hold, take, wile
5 charm 6 allure, please 7 attract,
bewitch, delight, enchant, gratify
8 enthrall 9 fascinate, magnetize,
mesmerize, spellbind

captivating
8 magnetic 9 appealing, glamorous, seductive

captive
7 hostage 8 prisoner

captivity
11 confinement 12 imprisonment

capture
3 bag, get, nab 4 nail, take
5 catch, cotch 6 collar, secure
7 prehend

Capuan
4 lush 5 plush 6 deluxe 7 opulent
8 luscious, palatial 9 luxuriant,
luxurious, sumptuous
11 upholstered

car
4 auto, heap 5 buggy, coach,
coupe, crate, motor, sedan, wreck
6 hotrod, jalopy, junker 7 clunker,
flivver, hardtop, machine, phaeton
8 dragster, motorcar, roadster, runabout 9 limousine 10 automobile,
touring car 11 convertible 12 station wagon
(see **automobile**)

caramel-like
5 chewy

caravansary
3 inn 5 hotel, lodge 6 hostel, tavern 7 auberge, hospice 8 hostelry
9 roadhouse 11 public house

carbohydrate
5 sugar 6 starch 7 glucose, lactose, sucrose 8 fructose, glycogen
9 cellulose, galactose
suffix: 3 ose

carbon
4 coal, coke, soot 8 graphite, plumbago 9 lampblack
combining form: 7 anthrac
8 anthraco

carbonate
6 aerate

carbon compound
suffix: 2 an 3 ane, ene, yne 5 ylene

carbon copy
5 ditto 7 replica 9 duplicate, facsimile 11 replication 12 reproduction 13 reduplication

carbonize
4 burn, char

carboxyl
suffix: 3 oic 4 onic

carbuncle
4 boil 6 pimple 7 abscess, pustule
combining form: 7 anthrac
8 anthraco

carcass
4 body, mort 5 stiff 6 corpse,
deader 7 cadaver, remains

carcinoid
5 tumor

carcinoma
5 tumor 6 cancer

card
3 wag, wit 4 menu, sked, zany
5 joker, trump 6 agenda, docket
7 program 8 calendar, comedian,
humorist, schedule 9 programma,
timetable 11 carte du jour
fortune-telling: 5 tarot
performer's: 3 cue 5 idiot
spot: 3 pip

cardboard
5 stiff 6 unreal, wooden 7 bristol,
buckram, stilted 10 unlifelike
11 muscle-bound, stereotyped,
unrealistic

card-carrying
7 genuine 11 full-fledged

card game
see at **game**

cardiac stimulant
7 ouabain 9 digitalis

cardialgia
9 heartburn

cardinal
5 vital 6 ruling 7 central, pivotal
9 essential 10 overriding, overruling 11 fundamental 12 constitutive

cardinal point
4 east, west 5 north, south

cardinal suffix
2 ty 4 teen

Cardinal Virtue
7 justice 8 prudence 9 fortitude
10 temperance

care
3 rue, woe 4 dole, fear, heed,
mind, reck, tend, ward 5 alarm,
grief, nurse, pains, serve, trial, trust,
watch, worry 6 attend, charge, dismay, effort, mother, regard, regret,
sorrow, strain, stress, unease, wait
on 7 anguish, anxiety, concern,
conduct, custody, keeping, running,
tension, trouble 8 disquiet, exertion, handling, interest, suspense,
tendance 9 agitation, alertness, attention, curiosity, heartache, misgiving, oversight, vigilance 10 affliction, enthusiasm, foreboding,
heartbreak, intendance, management, minister to, solicitude, uneasiness 11 concernment, disquietude,
disturbance, heedfulness, safekeeping, supervision 12 apprehension, guardianship, perturbation,
watchfulness 13 consciousness,
consideration, consternation

careen
4 sway 5 lurch, swing, weave
6 wobble 7 stagger

career
4 race, rush, tear 5 chase, speed
6 course 7 calling 8 vocation

care for
4 like, mind, tend 5 nurse 6 foster

carefree
4 wild 6 breezy 8 feckless, reckless
9 lightsome 10 free-minded, incautious, insouciant 12 happy-go-
lucky, lighthearted 13 irresponsible

careful
4 safe, wary 5 chary, exact, fussy
6 intent 7 duteous, dutiful, finical,
finicky, guarded, heedful, precise,
prudent, studied 8 accurate, cautious, critical, discreet, gingerly,
punctual 9 attentive, observant,
provident, religious 10 deliberate,
meticulous, particular, scrupulous
11 calculating, circumspect, considerate, foresighted, painstaking,
punctilious 12 conscionable
13 conscientious

carefully
8 gingerly

careless
3 lax 4 rash, wild 5 messy, slack, unfit 6 botchy, remiss, sloppy, unneat, untidy 7 raunchy, unkempt 8 derelict, feckless, heedless, reckless, slapdash, slipshod, slovenly, uncaring 9 forgetful, incapable, negligent, oblivious, unheeding, unmindful, unrecking 10 behindhand, delinquent, disheveled, inadequate, incautious, neglectful, regardless, unthinking, unthorough 11 inadvertent, inattentive, thoughtless, unconcerned, unqualified 12 disregardful, irreflective, unfastidious, uninterested, unreflective 13 irresponsible

caress
3 pat, pet, toy 4 love, neck 5 dally, flirt 6 cocker, coddle, coquet, cosset, cuddle, dandle, fondle, nuzzle, pamper, stroke, trifle 7 indulge

caressive
7 calming 8 soothing

caretaker
9 custodian

careworn
5 drawn, jaded 6 fagged 7 haggard, pinched 8 troubled, tuckered 9 exhausted 10 distressed

cargo
4 haul, load 6 burden, lading 7 freight, payload

caricature
4 fake, mock, sham 5 farce, phony 6 parody 7 cartoon, lampoon, mockery, takeoff 8 travesty 9 burlesque, clinquant, imitation 10 pasquinade 13 laughingstock

carillon
6 belfry 9 bell tower, campanile

caritas
5 grace, mercy 6 lenity 7 charity 8 clemency

cark
3 ail 4 fret, fuss, stew 5 upset, worry 6 pother 7 trouble 8 distress

Carlsbad feature
6 cavern

Carmen
author: 7 Mérimée (Prosper)
composer: 5 Bizet (Georges)
lover: 7 Don José
toreador: 9 Escamillo

Carmi
father: 6 Reuben
son: 5 Achan

carnage
8 butchery, massacre 9 bloodbath, bloodshed, slaughter

carnal
4 lewd 5 gross 6 animal, bodily, coarse, earthy, vulgar, wanton 7 earthly, fleshly, lustful, mundane, obscene, sensual, somatic, worldly 8 corporal, material, physical, sensuous 9 corporeal 10 lascivious

carnation
4 pink 5 color 6 flower

carnival
attraction: 4 ride 6 midway 8 sideshow 10 concession
character: 5 shill 6 barker, hawker 7 grifter, spieler
New Orleans: 9 Mardi Gras
performer: 4 geek

carol
4 song 6 ballad
Christmas: 4 noel

carom
3 dap 4 skim, skip 5 graze 6 glance 8 ricochet

Caron role
4 Gigi, Lili

carotid's relative
5 aorta

carousal
3 bat, jag 4 tear 5 binge, booze, drunk, spree 6 bender 7 blowoff 9 brannigan
Scottish: 6 splore

carouse
4 hell, riot 5 revel 6 frolic 7 roister, wassail
Scottish: 4 birl 5 birle

carp
3 nag 4 fuss 5 cavil 6 peck at 7 henpeck

carpe ___
4 diem

carpenter
3 ant, bee 6 joiner, wright 7 artisan, builder, workman 9 craftsman

carpentry
7 joinery

carper
5 momus 6 critic, Zoilus 7 caviler, knocker 9 aristarch 10 criticizer 11 faultfinder, smellfungus

carpet
3 mat, rug 5 tapis 6 velvet, Wilton 8 Brussels, moquette, Venetian 9 Axminster, broadloom
Afghan: 5 Herat 6 Herati
Indian: 4 Agra
Persian: 4 kali 6 Kerman, Keshan, Kirman, Sarouk
Turkish: 5 Koula, Ladik 8 Ghiordes

carpet beetle
10 buffalo bug

carpet knight
8 hedonist, sybarite

carping
6 critic, jawing 7 blaming, railing 8 blameful, captious, caviling, critical 9 cavillous, damnatory 10 censorious, upbraiding 11 criticizing, objurgatory, reproachful, reprobating, reprobatory 12 condemnatory, faultfinding, overcritical, reprehending 13 hypercritical

carrageen
7 seaweed 9 Irish moss

carrefour
5 plaza 6 square 10 crossroads

carriage
3 rig 4 pose 6 stance 7 posture, transit, voiture 8 attitude, carrying, posture 9 transport 10 conveyance 12 transporting
American: 5 buggy 8 dearborn, rockaway 9 buckboard
attendant: 6 flunky 7 flunkey, footman
baby: 4 pram 5 buggy 8 stroller 12 perambulator
driver: 4 hack 5 cabby 8 coachman
folding top: 6 calash
four-wheeled: 4 sado, trap 5 buggy, coupe 6 berlin, calash, fiacre, landau, surrey 7 britska, cariole, dos-a-dos, hackney, phaeton 8 barouche, britzska, brougham, carriole, carryall, clarence, dearborn, rockaway, sociable, stanhope, tarantas, victoria 9 buckboard
Indian: 6 gharri, gharry
Javanese: 4 sado
man-drawn: 6 riksha 7 rikisha, rikshaw 10 jinrikisha
Philippine: 6 calesa 7 calesin 9 carromata
Russian: 6 drosky, troika 7 droshky 8 tarantas 9 tarantass
stately: 7 caroche
three-horse: 6 troika
two-wheeled: 3 gig 4 shay, trap 5 buggy, sulky 6 calesa, chaise, dennet, hansom, herdic, whisky 7 caleche, calesin, dogcart, tilbury, whiskey 8 curricle 9 cabriolet, carromata
with attendants: 8 equipage

carriage trade
5 elite 6 flower, gentry 7 quality
9 blue blood, gentility 10 upper
class, upper crust 11 aristocracy

carrick bend
4 knot

carrier
5 envoy 6 bearer, porter, vector
7 airline, courier, drogher, vehicle
8 emissary 9 messenger
11 internuncio
combining form: 4 pher, phor
5 phora, phore 6 phorae (plural),
phorum

Carroll character
5 Alice, snark 6 boojum, Hatter
8 Dormouse 9 March Hare
10 Mock Turtle 11 White Rabbit
12 Humpty Dumpty

carrot
4 meed, plum 5 prize 6 reward
7 guerdon, premium 8 dividend

carry
3 act, get, jag, lug 4 bear, buck,
have, hump, keep, move, pack,
pipe, prop, quit, send, sway, take,
tote, waft 5 brace, bring, ferry,
fetch, shift, stock, touch 6 acquit,
affect, bear up, behave, convey,
demean, deport, funnel, remove, siphon, strike, upbear, uphold 7 bolster, channel, comport, conduct,
disport, impress, inspire, possess,
shore up, support, sustain, traject
8 buttress, transfer, transmit 9 influence, transport

carrying
combining form: 7 phorous

carrying case
7 holdall

carry off
4 down, kill, slay 6 cut off, finish,
lay low, spirit 7 destroy, put away,
take off 8 dispatch

carry on
3 run 4 go on, keep, rant, rave
5 act up, cut up, horse 6 direct,
hang on, manage, ordain 7 conduct, operate, persist 9 horseplay,
persevere

carry out
6 effect, govern, render 7 execute,
fulfill 8 bring off, complete, finalize, transact 9 discharge, prosecute 10 administer, effectuate
12 administrate

carry over
8 postpone, transfer

carrytale
5 clack, tabby 6 gossip 8 gossiper,
quidnunc 10 newsmonger 12 gossipmonger 13 scandalmonger

carry through
4 last 5 abide 6 effect, endure
7 perdure, persist 8 bring off, continue 10 effectuate

cart
4 dray, haul 5 carry 6 barrow, convey 7 tumbrel, tumbril 8 carriage
9 transport
Indian: 5 tonga
racing: 5 sulky

___ carte
3 a la

___ Carte
5 D'Oyly

carte blanche
3 say 5 power, right, say-so 7 license 8 free hand 9 authority
10 blank check 11 prerogative

carte d'entrée
6 ticket

carte du jour
4 menu

cartel
4 bloc, dare, defy, pool 5 chain,
group, stump, trust 7 combine
8 defiance 9 challenge, syndicate
10 consortium

Carthaginian
goddess of the moon: 5 Tanit
6 Tanith
queen: 4 Dido 6 Elissa

cartilage
6 tissue 7 gristle
combining form: 6 chondr 7 chondri,
chondro

cartogram
3 map

cartographer
English: 5 Smith (Willian)
Flemish: 6 Kremer (Gerhard) 8 Mer-
cator (Gerardus), Ortelius
German: 13 Waldseemuller (Martin)
Greek: 7 Ptolemy

cartography
9 mapmaking

cartoonist
4 Capp (Al), Nast (Thomas), Szep
5 Davis (Jim), Gould (Chester), Kelly
(Walt), Young (Chic) 6 Addams
(Charles), Disney (Walt), Larson
(Gary), Schulz (Charles) 7 Mauldin
(Bill), Trudeau (Garry) 8 Goldberg
(Rube), Groening (Matt), Herblock

cartouche
5 brown, frame 6 shield

cartridge
4 case, tube 5 shell 8 cylinder

cartwheel
4 coin 6 tumble 10 handspring

carve
3 cut 5 sculp, sever, slice, split
6 chisel, cleave, sculpt, sunder
7 dissect 8 dissever 9 sculpture

Casanova
4 wolf 5 Romeo 6 chaser, masher
7 amorist, Don Juan, gallant 8 lothario, paramour 9 ladies' man,
philander, womanizer 10 lady-
killer 11 philanderer

cascade
5 chute, falls, sault, spout 8 cataract 9 waterfall

case
3 con, pod, vet 4 etui, hull, husk,
skin, suit, view 5 cause, event, order, shape, shell, shuck, spook,
state, study 6 action, estate, oddity,
repair, sample 7 canvass, check
up, episode, examine, example, inspect, lawsuit, oddball 8 incident,
instance, original, sampling, specimen 9 character, check over, condition, eccentric, situation 10 occurrence, scrutinize 11 eventuality
12 circumstance, illustration
combining form: 4 thec 5 theca,
theci, theco 6 thecae (plural), the-
cia (plural) 7 thecium
grammatical: 6 dative 8 ablative,
genitive, vocative 9 objective
10 accusative, nominative,
possessive

casebearer
5 larva 11 caterpillar

case-hardened
7 callous 10 insensible

case history
6 sample 7 example 8 instance,
sampling, specimen 12 illustration

casement
6 window

Casey at the Bat poet
6 Thayer (Ernest Lawrence)

cash
4 coin, jack 5 bread, dough,
money 6 mazuma, wampum
7 scratch, shekels 11 legal tender

cashier
2 ax 3 bar, can 4 cast, fire, oust,
sack, shed 5 eject, expel, scrap
6 bounce, reject, shelve, slough

7 boot out, discard, dismiss, exclude, kick out **8** abdicate, jettison, pass over, throw out **9** discharge, eliminate, terminate, throw away

cash in
3 die **4** conk, drop **5** croak **6** pop off **7** kick off, succumb **8** check out, pass away

casino attendant
8 croupier

cask
3 keg, tun **4** butt, pipe **6** barrel **8** hogshead

casket
3 box **5** chest **6** coffin

Cassandra
7 seeress **9** doomsayer, pessimist, worrywart **10** prophetess **11** crepehanger
brother: **7** Helenus
father: **5** Priam
lover: **9** Agamemnon
mother: **6** Hecuba
slayer: **12** Clytemnestra

casserole
4 dish

Cassiopeia
daughter: **9** Andromeda
husband: **7** Cepheus
kingdom: **8** Ethiopia

Cassio's mistress
6 Bianca

cassock
7 soutane

cast
3 add, aim, hue, lay, sum, tot, way **4** dash, drop, face, fire, foot, form, hint, hurl, junk, kind, look, mold, plan, shed, sort, tint, tone, toss, tote, turn, type **5** chart, class, color, fling, heave, leave, level, pitch, point, scrap, shade, shape, sling, smack, throw, tinge, total, touch, trace, train, weird, yield **6** design, devise, direct, figure, launch, nature, reject, slough, stripe, visage, zero in **7** address, arrange, cashier, discard, dope out, incline, moulage, project, scatter, soupçon, summate, variety **8** abdicate, disperse, forecast, jettison, prophecy, totalize **9** blueprint, broadcast, character, prevision, prognosis, suspicion, throw away **10** distribute, expression, intimation, prediction, suggestion **11** countenance, description, foretelling **12** conformation **13** configuration

cast about
4 hunt, seek **5** quest **9** ferret out, search for, search out

cast a spell
3 hex

cast away
4 blow **5** beach, waste, wreck **6** pile up, strand **7** consume, fritter **8** squander **9** dissipate, shipwreck

castaway
5 leper **6** pariah **7** Ishmael, outcast **8** derelict **10** Ishmaelite **11** offscouring, untouchable

cast down
3 bad, low **4** down, sink **5** abase, lower **6** bemean, debase, demean, humble **7** degrade **8** dejected, downcast **9** depressed, humiliate, woebegone **10** dispirited **11** crestfallen **12** disconsolate

castigate
3 wig **4** beat, drub, flay, rail, rate **5** baste, slash **6** berate, pummel, punish, scathe, scorch, thrash **7** belabor, blister, chasten, correct, lambast, scarify, scourge, upbraid **8** chastise, lambaste, lash into, penalize **9** excoriate **10** discipline, tongue-lash

castigation
3 rod **8** punition **10** correction, discipline, punishment **12** chastisement

cast iron
7 spiegel

castle
5 manor, villa **7** chateau, mansion
adjunct: **4** moat
gate: **10** portcullis
ledge: **7** rampart
structure: **6** turret
tower: **4** keep **6** donjon
wall: **6** bailey **10** battlement

castle-builder
7 dreamer, utopian **8** idealist **9** ideologue, visionary

cast off
5 fling, let go, loose, untie **6** slough, unmoor **7** unhitch **8** unfasten

Castor
brother: **6** Pollux **10** Polydeuces
constellation: **6** Gemini
father: **4** Zeus **9** Tyndareus
mother: **4** Leda
sister: **5** Helen
slayer: **4** Idas

castor oil
9 cathartic, lubricant

cast out
4 oust **5** exile, expel **6** banish, deport **7** expulse **8** displace **9** ostracize, transport **10** expatriate

cast overboard
8 jettison

castrate
3 fix **4** geld **5** alter, unman, unsex **6** neuter **7** unnerve **8** enervate, mutilate, unstring **9** sterilize **10** emasculate **11** desexualize

castrato singer
9 Farinelli

casual
5 aloof, fluky, light, minor, petty **6** breezy, chance, degage, little, remote **7** offhand, relaxed, trivial, unfussy **8** detached, informal **9** easygoing, extempore, impromptu, impulsive, incurious, small-beer, uncurious, unplanned, withdrawn **10** accidental, contingent, fortuitous, improvised, incidental, shoestring **11** indifferent, low-pressure, spontaneous, unconcerned, unimportant **12** uninterested **13** disinterested, insignificant, unconstrained

casualty
4 prey **5** death, fatal **6** mishap, victim **8** accident, fatality, underdog **9** bottom dog, mischance **12** misadventure

casuistry
7 fallacy, sophism **8** delusion **9** deception, sophistry **12** equivocation, speciousness, spuriousness **13** deceptiveness

casus ____
5 belli

cat
4 eyra, lion, lynx, puma, puss **5** felid, kitty, ounce, pussy **6** bobcat, cougar, feline, kaffir **7** caracal **12** mountain lion
Alice's: **5** Dinah
catlike animal: **5** civet, genet, zibet **6** zibeth **7** linsang
combining form: **5** aelur, ailur **6** aeluro, ailuro
disease: **9** distemper
domestic: **3** Rex **4** Manx **5** tabby **6** calico **7** Burmese, Persian, Siamese **8** longhair **9** Himalayan, shorthair **10** Abyssinian
extinct: **10** saber-tooth
fastest: **7** cheetah

female: 5 queen 7 lioness, tigress
9 grimalkin
genus: 5 Felis
grinning: 8 Cheshire
group: 7 clowder
male: 3 gib, tom
relating to: 6 feline
ring-tailed: 6 serval
Scottish: 8 baudrons
sound: 3 mew 4 hiss, meow, purr,
roar 5 miaou, miaow, miaul
9 caterwaul
spotted: 4 pard 6 jaguar, margay,
ocelot, serval 7 cheetah, leopard,
panther
striped: 5 tiger
tailless: 4 Manx
young: 6 kitten

cataclysm
4 pour, woes 5 flood, spate 6 deluge 7 niagara, torrent, tragedy
8 calamity, cataract, disaster, flooding, overflow 10 inundation 11 catastrophe 12 misadventure

cataclysmic
5 fatal 7 fateful, ruinous 10 calamitous, disastrous 12 catastrophic

catacomb
5 crypt, vault 10 undercroft

catafalque
4 bier

catalog
4 book, list, roll 5 admit, count, enter, tally 6 enroll, number, roster
7 itemize, program 8 inscribe, register, roll call, schedule, syllabus
9 enumerate, introduce, inventory
10 prospectus
of books: 11 bibliotheca
of goods: 9 inventory
of saints: 9 hagiology

catalyst
4 goad, spur 7 impetus, impulse
8 stimulus 9 incentive, stimulant
10 incitation, incitement, motivation

catamaran
4 boat, raft

catamount
4 lynx 6 cougar

cataract
5 chute, falls, flood, sault, spate,
spout 6 deluge 7 cascade, niagara, torrent 8 flooding, overflow
9 cataclysm, waterfall
10 inundation

catastrophe
3 woe 7 tragedy 8 calamity, disaster 9 cataclysm 12 misadventure

catastrophic
5 fatal 7 fateful, ruinous 10 calamitous, disastrous 11 cataclysmic

Catawba
4 wine 5 river

catcall
3 boo 4 bird, hiss, hoot, pooh,
razz 5 bazoo 8 pooh-pooh
9 raspberry 10 Bronx cheer

catch
3 bag, con, fix, get, hit, nab, net,
see, wed 4 ding, dupe, espy, find,
fool, grab, grip, gull, hoax, hook,
moor, nail, snag, sock, spot, take,
trap 5 abash, benet, block, clasp,
clout, grasp, hit on, marry, reach,
seize, smite, snare, stick, stump,
trick, whack 6 accept, anchor, arrest, baffle, clutch, collar, cut off,
descry, detect, entrap, fasten,
flurry, follow, put out, rattle, secure,
snatch, strike, take in, tangle, turn
up 7 capture, chicane, confuse,
disturb, ensnare, espouse, fluster,
grapple, hit upon, nonplus, perplex, prehend 8 confound, contract, entangle, flimflam, hoodwink,
meet with, overhaul, overtake 9 apprehend, bamboozle, embarrass,
encounter, intercept 10 comprehend, understand 12 come down
with

catchall term
3 etc.

Catcher in the Rye
author: 8 Salinger (Jerome David)
character: 9 Caulfield (Holden)

catcher's glove
4 mitt

catching
6 taking 10 contagious, infectious
12 communicable

catch on
3 see 4 hear 5 learn 6 tumble
7 find out, unearth 8 discover 9 ascertain, determine

catchphrase
see **catchword**

Catch-22 author
6 Heller (Joseph)

catch up
4 hold 8 enthrall 9 fascinate, mesmerize, spellbind

catchword
5 maxim, motto 6 byword, phrase,
slogan 9 battle cry, watchword
10 shibboleth

catchy
6 fitful, spotty, tricky 8 sporadic
9 appealing, desultory, irregular,
spasmodic

catechist
7 teacher

catechize
3 ask 4 quiz 5 query 7 examine,
inquire 8 question 11 interrogate

catechumen
7 convert, student

categorical
4 sure 6 direct 7 certain, decided,
express 8 absolute, clean-cut, clear-
cut, definite, explicit, positive, specific, ultimate 9 downright 10 definitive, forthright 11 unambiguous,
unequivocal

categorize
3 peg 4 sort 5 class, group 6 assort 7 put down 8 classify, identify,
nail down 10 pigeonhole

category
4 tier 5 class, genre, grade, group
6 league 8 grouping
10 pigeonhole

catenation
6 series 10 connection

catercorner
9 slantways, slantwise 10 cornerwise, diagonally 12 slantingways

caterpillar
5 larva 7 cutworm, webworm 8 ar-
myworm, silkworm 10 casebearer
combining form: 5 campa, eruci

cater to
4 baby 5 humor, spoil 6 cocker,
coddle, cosset, cotton, pamper
7 gratify, indulge 11 mollycoddle

caterwaul
3 row 4 howl, meow, spat, tiff
5 miaou, miaow, miaul, scrap
6 bicker 7 brabble, fall out, quarrel, wrangle 8 squabble

catfish
see **fish**

catharsis
9 cleansing, purgation 10 lustration
11 expurgation 12 purification

cathartic
9 castor oil, purgative

Cathay
5 China

cathedral
5 duomo 6 church
passage: 5 slype

Cather novel
9 A Lost Lady, My Antonia, One of Ours, O Pioneers **12** Lucy Gayheart **13** My Mortal Enemy, Song of the Lark **16** Alexander's Bridge

catholic
6 cosmic, global **7** general, generic **8** eclectic **9** extensive, inclusive, planetary, universal, worldwide **10** ecumenical, large-scale **12** cosmopolitan **13** comprehensive

catholicity
10 liberality **12** universality

catholicon
6 elixir **7** cure-all, nostrum, panacea

catkin
5 ament

catlike
5 catty **6** feline **7** furtive **8** stealthy

catnap
6 siesta, snooze **10** forty winks

Cato
title: **5** edile **6** aedile, censor, consul **7** praetor, tribune **8** quaestor

Cat on a Hot ____
7 Tin Roof

cat's-paw
4 pawn, tool **6** puppet, stooge

cattail
4 rush

cattle
4 kine, neat, oxen **5** bovid **6** bovine
breed: **5** Angus, Devon, Kerry **6** Durham, Jersey, Sussex **7** Brahman, Hariana, Red Poll, Sahiwal **8** Ayrshire, Charbray, Galloway, Guernsey, Hereford, Highland, Holstein, Limousin, Longhorn **9** Charolais, Red Polled, Shorthorn, Simmental **10** Brown Swiss, Charollais **11** Dutch Belted
call: **4** sook **6** sookie
castrated: **5** steer
catching rope: **5** lasso **6** lariat
combining form: **4** bovi
cry: **3** low, moo
dehorn: **4** poll
disease: **4** loco **5** bloat **6** garget, nagana **7** anthrax, locoism, measles, murrain **8** blackleg, lumpy jaw, mastitis, staggers **10** rinderpest, Texas fever **11** brucellosis
extinct breed: **9** Teeswater
family: **7** Bovidae
feed: **6** fodder **7** farrago
female: **3** cow

foot: **4** hoof
genus: **3** Bos
goddess: **6** Bubona
grazing land: **5** range **7** pasture
group: **4** herd **5** drove
herdsman: **6** cowboy, drover, gaucho **7** vaquero **8** wrangler **10** cowpuncher
hornless: **5** muley **6** mulley
hybrid: **7** cattalo
identification: **5** brand
Indian: **4** dhan
jowl: **6** dewlap
male: **4** bull
pen: **6** corral
round up: **7** wrangle
stable: **4** barn, byre
steal: **6** rustle
unbranded: **8** maverick
wild flight: **8** stampede
young: **4** calf
young, motherless: **5** dogie

catty
4 evil, spry, yare **5** agile, brisk, zippy **6** active, bitchy, feline, lively, nimble, volant, wicked **7** catlike, furtive, hateful, vicious **8** spiteful, stealthy **9** malicious, rancorous, sprightly **10** despiteful, malevolent

Caucasian
capital: **4** Baku **7** Tbilisi, Yerevan
republic: **7** Armenia, Georgia **10** Azerbaijan

Caucasus
peak: **6** Elbrus
people: **5** Osset

caucho
3 ule **4** hule **6** rubber

caudal
appendage: **4** tail
combining form: **2** ur **3** uro

cause
4 call, case, goad, make, root, suit **5** breed, evoke, get up, hatch **6** action, author, draw on, effect, elicit, induce, motive, origin, reason, secure, source, spring, work up **7** creator, impulse, lawsuit, produce, provoke **8** engender, generate, muster up, occasion **9** generator, incentive, necessity **10** antecedent, bring about, inducement, obligation, originator, prime mover **11** determinant **13** consideration
combining form: **4** etio **5** aetio, aitio

cause ____
7 célèbre

caused by
suffix: **2** ic **4** ical

causerie
3 rap **4** chat, chin, talk, yarn **5** prose

causing
combining form: **7** facient, factive
suffix: **3** fic **4** able, ible

caustic
4 keen, tart **5** acerb, acrid, acute, crisp, harsh, rough, salty, sharp, terse **6** biting, bitter, ironic, severe **7** acerbic, cutting, mordant, pungent, satiric **8** incisive, scathing, stinging, succinct **9** corrosive, sarcastic, stringent, trenchant **10** mordacious **12** archilochian
solution: **3** lye

cauterize
4 burn, sear

caution
4 warn **6** caveat **7** warning **8** forewarn, monition, prudence **9** canniness, chariness, foresight **10** admonition, discretion, precaution, providence **11** commonition, forethought, forewarning **12** discreetness

cautionary
4 wary **6** surety **8** cautious, monitive, monitory, security **10** admonitory

cautious
4 cozy, safe, wary **5** alert, cagey, canny, chary **6** shrewd **7** careful, guarded, politic, prudent **8** discreet, gingerly, scheming, vigilant, watchful **9** judicious, provident **11** calculating, circumspect, considerate, foresighted **13** prethoughtful

cavalcade
6 parade, series **8** sequence **10** procession

cavalier
5 lofty, proud **6** knight **7** haughty **8** arrogant, horseman, insolent, superior **9** caballero **10** disdainful **11** overbearing **12** supercilious **13** high-and-mighty

cavalryman
6 lancer **7** dragoon, trooper
Algerian: **5** spahi **6** spahee
horse: **5** waler
Prussian: **4** ulan **5** uhlan
Russian: **7** cossack
Turkish: **5** spahi **6** spahee
weapon: **5** lance, saber **7** carbine

cave
3 bow, den **4** bend, drop, give, grot, lair **5** antre, break, defer,

yield **6** fold up, grotto, hollow, submit **7** crumple, knuckle, succumb **8** collapse **9** break down **10** capitulate, subterrane **11** buckle under **12** knuckle under, subterranean
combining form: **6** speleo
dweller: **3** bat **4** bear, lion **6** hermit **9** Cro-Magnon **10** troglodite **11** Neanderthal
explorer: **9** spelunker
formation: **10** stalactite, stalagmite
France: **7** Lascaux **10** Rouffignac **13** Gouffre Berger
Iceland: **7** Singing
Indiana: **9** Wyandotte
Iraq: **8** Shanidar
Kentucky: **7** Mammoth
New Zealand: **7** Waitomo
rock: **8** dolomite **9** limestone
South Africa: **5** Cango
Spain: **8** Altamira
study of: **10** speleology

caveat
6 notice **7** caution, warning **8** monition **10** admonition **11** commonition, forewarning

caveat ____
6 emptor

cave-dwelling
combining form: **6** troglo

cavern
6 grotto **10** subterrane **12** subterranean
Capri: **10** Blue Grotto
combining form: **4** antr **5** antro
Montana: **13** Lewis and Clark
New Mexico: **8** Carlsbad
Tennessee: **10** Cumberland
Virginia: **5** Luray

cavernous
4 vast **6** gaping, hollow **7** chasmal, yawning **10** commodious, sepulchral **11** reverberant

caviar
3 roe **4** eggs **6** relish
source: **6** beluga **7** sterlet **8** sturgeon

cavil
4 carp, momi (plural) **7** chicane, quibble

caviler
5 momus **6** carper, critic, Zoilus **7** knocker **9** aristarch **10** criticizer **11** faultfinder, smellfungus

caviling
4 mean **5** fussy, petty, small **6** critic, pickly **7** carping, finicky **8** captious, contrary, critical, exacting, niggling **9** demanding **10** censorious, nitpicking **12** faultfinding,

overcritical **13** hairsplitting, hypercritical

cavity
3 pit **4** bore, hole, void **6** boring, hollow **7** vacuity
body: **5** antra (plural), sinus **6** antrum **8** follicle, hemocoei
combining form: **3** cel **4** antr, caec, ceci, ceco, cele, celo, coel **5** antro, caeci, caeco, coele, coelo
in a glacier: **6** moulin

cavort
4 romp **5** caper, cut up, frisk **6** frolic, gambol **7** carry on, rollick **9** horseplay **10** roughhouse **11** horse around

caw
4 yaup, yawp **6** squall, squark, squawk

cay
3 key **4** isle, reef

cayenne
6 pepper
genus: **8** Capsicum

cayman
see **caiman**

Cayuga chief
5 Logan (James)

cease
3 erd **4** halt, quit, stop **5** close **6** desist, ending, finish, period **8** conclude, give over, intermit, knock off, leave off, surcease **9** cessation, terminate **10** conclusion, desistance **11** discontinue, termination

cease-fire
5 truce **9** armistice

ceaseless
7 endless, eternal **8** constant, immortal, unending **9** continual, perpetual, unceasing **10** continuous **11** amaranthine, everlasting, neverending, unremitting **12** interminable **13** uninterrupted

Cecrops' daughter
5 Herse **8** Aglauros **9** Pandrosos

cecum
combining form: **5** typhl **6** typhlo

cede
4 deed **5** alien, grant, leave, waive, yield **6** accord, assign, convey, give up, remise, resign **7** abandon, concede **8** alienate, hand over, make over, sign over, transfer **9** surrender, vouchsafe **10** abalienate, relinquish

ceiling
elaborate: **7** plafond

ceinture
4 belt, sash **6** girdle **8** cincture **9** waistband

Celaeno
father: **5** Atlas
mother: **7** Pleione
sisters: **8** Pleiades

celebrate
4 fete, hymn, keep, laud **5** bless, cry up, extol **6** praise **7** glorify, maffick, magnify, observe **8** eulogize **9** solemnize **10** panegyrize **11** commemorate

celebrated
5 famed, great, noted **6** famous **7** eminent, notable **8** renowned **9** prominent **11** illustrious **13** distinguished

celebration
4 fete, gala **6** fiesta **7** jubilee **8** festival, jamboree

célèbre
5 cause

celebrity
3 VIP **4** fame, hero, lion, name, star **5** éclat **6** renown, repute, worthy **7** big name, mahatma, notable **8** cynosure, immortal, luminary, somebody **9** notoriety, personage, superstar **10** notability, reputation

celerity
4 gait, pace **5** haste, hurry, speed **6** hustle, rustle **8** alacrity, dispatch, legerity, rapidity, velocity **9** briskness, quickness, swiftness **10** expedition, speediness

celery
genus: **5** Apium
green: **6** pascal
relative: **6** carrot **7** parsley, parsnip
white: **8** blanched
wild: **8** smallage

celestial
7 blessed, elysian **8** beatific, empyreal, empyrean, ethereal, heavenly, Olympian, supernal **9** unearthly **12** otherworldly, transmundane

celestial body
3 sun **4** moon, star **5** comet **6** meteor, nebula, planet **8** asteroid **9** satellite
hypothetical: **9** black hole

Celestial Empire
5 China

cell
4 room, zoid 5 cubby, zooid 7 cubicle 11 compartment
blood: 8 hemocyte
combining form: 3 cyt 4 cyte, cyto, phag 5 blast, gamet, phage 6 gameto, gonidi 7 gonidio
disease: 6 cancer
division: 7 meiosis, mitosis
fertilized egg: 6 zygote
material: 3 DNA, RNA 7 protein 9 chromatin, cytoplasm 10 protoplasm
nerve: 6 neuron
part: 4 gene 7 nucleus, vacuole 8 ribosome 10 chromosome
reproductive: 3 egg 4 germ, ovum 5 sperm 6 gamete 8 gonidium

cellist
American: 4 Rose (Leonard) 6 Lesser (Laurence), Parnas (Leslie) 7 Nelsova (Zara), Parisot (Aldo), Starker (Janos) 8 Schuster (Joseph)
English: 5 du Pré (Jacqueline)
Russian: 11 Piatigorsky (Gregor) 12 Rostropovich (Mstislav)
Spanish: 6 Casals (Pablo)

cellophane
4 wrap 7 wrapper 8 wrapping 9 packaging

celluloid
4 film 7 plastic

cement
4 bind, join 5 unify, unite 6 mortar 8 concrete
combining form: 4 lith
ingredient: 4 lime 6 silica 7 alumina 8 magnesia, pozzolan 9 iron oxide, pozzolana

cemetery
8 boneyard, boot hill, catacomb 8 God's acre 9 graveyard 10 churchyard, necropolis 11 polyandrium 12 burial ground, memorial park, potter's field
underground: 8 catacomb

cense
7 thurify

censer
8 thurible
carrier: 8 thurifer

censor
4 blip, edit 5 purge 6 cut out, delete, excise, narrow, purify, screen 7 clean up, exscind 8 restrain, restrict 9 expurgate, red-pencil 10 blue-pencil, bowdlerize

censorious
6 critic 7 carping, chiding 8 captious, caviling, critical 9 cavillous, culpatory 10 accusatory, condemning, denouncing 11 reproachful 12 condemnatory, denunciatory, faultfinding, overcritical, reprehending 13 hypercritical

censurable
5 amiss, wrong 6 guilty, sinful, unholy 8 blamable, blameful, culpable, doubtful, improper, wrongful 9 incorrect 11 blameworthy 12 inadmissible, questionable, unacceptable 13 demeritorious, discreditable, objectionable, reprehensible

censure
3 rap 4 skin 5 blame, knock, scorn, scout 6 oppose, rebuke, reject, strafe 7 condemn, contemn, disdain, reprove 8 denounce, disallow, reproach 9 criticize, reprehend, reprimand, reprobate 10 denunciate, disapprove, stigmatize

centaur
6 Chiron, Nessus

Centaurus star
4 Beta 5 Alpha

Centennial State
8 Colorado

center
3 hub, mid 4 core, mean, pith, root, seat 5 focus, heart, midst, quick 6 dynamo, inside, medial, median, middle 7 central, essence, halfway, midmost 8 interior, midpoint, omphalos, polestar 9 activator, energizer, stimulant 10 focal point, middlemost 11 equidistant 12 intermediary, intermediate

centerboard
4 keel

centerfold
7 foldout 8 gatefold

centipede
9 arthropod
class: 9 Chilopoda

central
3 key, mid 4 main, mean 5 basic, chief, focal 6 master, medial, median, middle, ruling, signal 7 leading, pivotal, primary, radical, salient 8 cardinal, dominant, foremost 9 essential, important, paramount 10 overriding, overruling 11 controlling, fundamental, outstanding, predominant, significant 12 all-absorbing, intermediary, intermediate, preponderant

Central African Republic
capital: 6 Bangui
monetary unit: 5 franc

Central America
country: 6 Panama 8 Honduras 9 Costa Rica, Guatemala, Nicaragua 10 El Salvador
ethnic group: 6 Indian 7 Mestizo, Spanish
language: 7 Nahuatl, Spanish

centripetal
8 unifying 10 compacting 11 integrative 12 centralizing 13 concentrating, consolidating

centurion
7 officer, soldier 9 commander

century plant
genus: 5 Agave

cephalalgia
8 headache

cephalopod
5 squid 7 mollusk, octopus 10 cuttlefish

Cepheus
daughter: 9 Andromeda
kingdom: 8 Ethiopia
wife: 10 Cassiopeia

cerate
4 balm 5 cream, salve 6 chrism 7 unction, unguent 8 ointment

cerberus
6 custos, keeper, warden 8 claviger, guardian, watchdog 9 custodian

Cerberus
father: 6 Typhon
form: 3 dog
mother: 7 Echidna

cereal
4 meal, mush 5 gruel 6 farina 7 oatmeal 8 cornmeal, porridge
grass: 3 rye 4 corn, oats, ragi, rice 5 emmer, maize, spelt, wheat 6 barley, millet 7 sorghum 9 buckwheat
North African: 8 couscous
Russian: 5 kasha

cerebral
6 mental 7 psychic 8 highbrow 9 psychical 10 highbrowed 12 intellective, intellectual 13 psychological
combining form: 5 psych 6 psycho

cerebrate
5 think 6 reason 7 reflect 8 cogitate 9 speculate 10 deliberate

cerebration

7 thought **9** brainwork **10** cogitation, reflection **11** speculation
12 deliberation

ceremonial

3 set **5** fixed, lofty, rigid, stiff **6** august, formal, ritual, solemn
7 courtly, starchy, stately, studied
8 mannered, stylized **10** liturgical
11 ritualistic

ceremonious

6 formal, moving, proper, seemly, solemn **7** stately **8** decorous, imposing, majestic, striking **9** grandiose **10** impressive **12** conventional

ceremony

4 form, rite **6** ritual **7** liturgy, service **9** formality **10** observance
Jewish: **5** berit, brith **6** berith **8** habdalah, havdalah **10** bar mitzvah, bas mitzvah **11** bath mitzvah
university: **8** encaenia

Ceres

7 Demeter
daughter: **10** Persephone, Proserpina, Proserpine
father: **6** Cronus, Saturn
mother: **3** Ops **4** Rhea

cerium

symbol: **2** Ce

certain

3 one, set **4** firm, many, some, sure, true **5** fated, fixed **6** divers, stated, sundry **7** assured, ensured, insured, settled, several, various
8 accurate, cocksure, credible, definite, numerous, positive, provable, reliable, sanguine, surefire, unerring **9** authentic, certified, confident, doubtless, necessary, plausible, unfailing, warranted **10** dependable, guaranteed, inarguable, ineludible, inevasible, inevitable, infallible, returnless, stipulated, undeniable, unevadable, verifiable **11** confirmable, indubitable, ineluctable, inescapable, irrevocable, trustworthy, unalterable, unavoidable, undoubtable, unescapable **12** demonstrable, indefeasible, indisputable, wellgrounded **13** establishable, incontestable, predestinated, predetermined, uncontestable

certainty

6 surety **8** firmness, sureness **9** assurance, certitude, dogmatism
10 confidence, conviction, positivism, steadiness **11** assuredness, staunchness **12** absoluteness, definiteness, positiveness

certificate

3 IOU **4** bond, note **6** coupon, notice, ticket **7** diploma, license, receipt, voucher **8** contract, document **9** testimony **10** credential

certifier

6 notary

certify

2 OK **4** aver, avow, okay **5** vouch
6 assert, attest, avouch **7** approve, endorse, license, profess, warrant, witness **8** accredit, guaranty, notarize, sanction **9** authorize, guarantee **10** commission

Cervantes' hero

10 Don Quixote

cesium

symbol: **2** Cs

cessation

3 end **4** stop **5** cease, close **6** ending, finish, period **10** conclusion, desistance **11** termination

cesspool

3 den, sty **4** sink **5** Sodom **11** pandemonium **12** Augean stable

Cetus star

4 Mira

cgs unit

3 erg **4** dyne, gram, phot **5** gauss, poise, stilb **6** second, stokes **7** lambert, maxwell, oersted
10 centimeter

Chablis

4 wine **8** Burgundy

Chad

capital: **8** N'Djamena
monetary unit: **5** franc

chafe

3 irk, rub, vex **4** flay, fret, gall, hurt, peel, skin, wear **5** annoy, erode, graze **6** abrade, bother, damage, impair, injure, ruffle, scrape **7** corrode, inflame, provoke, scratch **8** exercise, irritate
9 excoriate

chaff

3 fun, kid, rag, rib **4** jest, joke, josh, razz **5** jolly **6** banter

chaffer

3 beg **4** coax **5** plead **6** dicker, haggle, higgle, palter **7** bargain
8 huckster

chafing

7 fretful **9** impatient, unpatient

chagrined

5 upset **6** shamed **7** ashamed,

crushed **9** mortified, perturbed
11 discomposed **12** disconcerted

chain

3 row **4** bond, gyve, iron **5** group, train, trust **6** cartel, catena, fetter, hobble, series, string, tether **7** combine, manacle, shackle **8** additive, additory, handcuff, sequence
9 summative, syndicate **10** cumulative, succession **11** alternation, concatenate, consecution, progression, stereotyped **12** accumulative, conglomerate **13** concatenation, stereotypical
adjunct: **8** sprocket
collar: **6** torque
combining form: **6** strept **7** strepto
gang: **6** coffle
ornamental: **10** chatelaine
ship's: **3** tye
sound: **5** clank

chain ___

3 saw **4** gang, mail **5** smoke, store
6 letter **8** reaction

Chained Lady

9 Andromeda

chainlike

8 catenate

chain-shaped

10 catenulate

chair

4 seat **5** stool **6** rocker **7** preside
back: **5** splat
bishop's: **8** cathedra
designer: **5** Eames
portable: **5** sedan
reclining: **12** chaise longue, chaise lounge
royal: **6** throne
type: **4** club, easy **6** morris **7** rocking **8** captain's, cogswell **9** reclining **10** ladder-back

chalcedony

4 onyx, sard **5** agate **6** jasper, quartz **9** carnelian **10** bloodstone
11 chrysoprase

chalice

3 ama, cup **5** amula, grail

chalk

combining form: **4** calc **5** calci, calco
8 calcareo

chalk out

5 draft **6** sketch **7** outline **8** block out, rough out, skeleton **9** adumbrate **11** skeletonize
12 characterize

chalk up

3 get, win **4** gain, have **5** annex

6 obtain, pick up, secure **7** acquire, procure

challenge
3 try **4** call, dare, defi, defy, face, stir, wake, whet **5** beard, brave, claim, demur, doubt, exact, front, rally, rouse, stump, waken **6** arouse, awaken, banter, bestir, cartel, demand, kindle, strive **7** calling, dispute, outdare, protest, require, solicit, venture **8** claiming, defiance, demurral, demurrer, exacting, mistrust, question, struggle **9** demanding, objection, postulate **10** difficulty, insistence **11** importuning, requisition **12** remonstrance **13** remonstration

challenger
5 rival **8** opponent **9** adversary, contender **10** competitor, contestant

chamber
4 cell, room **5** haven, house **6** harbor, shield **7** cubicle, shelter **9** apartment
combining form: **6** thalam **7** thalamo
in Egyptian tomb: **6** serdab
underground: **8** hypogeum

chambered
10 cancellate, cancellous

chamberlain
6 priest **7** officer, servant **9** attendant, treasurer

chameleon
6 lizard

chameleonic
6 fickle **10** changeable, inconstant

chamois
4 gems **5** gemse **6** shammy **7** leather **8** antelope, ruminant
habitat: **4** Alps
Old Testament: **6** aoudad

chamois-like animal
4 ibex **5** goral **6** gooral **7** klipbok **12** klipspringer

champ
3 gum, nip **4** bite, chew, mash, peck, pick **5** chomp, crush, mouth, munch **6** crunch, mumble, nibble **7** chumble, scrunch **8** macerate, ruminate **9** masticate

champagne
4 wine **5** color **6** bubbly
bucket: **4** icer
center: **5** Reims

Champagne
capital: **6** Troyes

champaign
5 field **6** domain, sphere **7** demesne, terrain **8** dominion, province **9** bailiwick, territory

champignon
6 fungus **8** mushroom

champion
4 arch, back, boss, head **5** chief, dandy, first, prime **6** uphold **7** capital, contend, leading, premier, support, titlist **8** advocate, backstop, exponent, fight for, foremost, side with, splendid, superior, top-notch, whiz-bang **9** excellent, expounder, principal, proponent, supporter **10** blue-ribbon **11** illustrious, outstanding, titleholder **13** distinguished
medieval: **7** paladin

championing
prefix: **3** pro

championship
5 crown, title **7** defense, pennant **8** advocacy

chance
2 go **3** hap, hit, lot, odd **4** bump, fate, luck, meet, risk, shot, show, time **5** break, fluke, fluky, light, occur, wager **6** befall, betide, casual, gamble, happen, hazard **7** come off, fall out, fortune, offhand, opening, outlook, stumble, venture **8** accident, careless, fortuity, heedless, occasion, prospect **9** advantage, adventure, transpire **10** accidental, fortuitous, incidental, likelihood **11** opportunity, possibility, probability
even: **6** toss-up

chancellor
5 judge **6** priest **7** adviser, officer **8** minister **9** secretary
German: **6** Brandt (Willy), Erhard (Ludwig), Hitler (Adolf) **7** Schmidt (Helmut) **8** Adenauer (Konrad), Bismarck (Otto)

chancy
4 iffy **5** dicey, fluky, hairy, risky **6** touchy, tricky **7** erratic, unsound **8** perilous, ticklish **9** dangerous, fluctuant, hazardous, uncertain, whimsical **10** capricious, jeopardous, precarious **11** speculative, treacherous **12** incalculable **13** unpredictable

change
3 fix **4** geld, swap, turn, vary **5** alter, shift, sport, trade, unsex **6** avatar, invert, modify, mutate, neuter, reform, revamp, revert, revise, switch **7** commute, convert, inverse, novelty, replace, reverse **8** castrate, exchange, mutation, mutilate, revision, transfer **9** deviation, diversify, permutate, refashion, sterilize, transform, transmute, transpose, variation, variegate **10** aberration, alteration, conversion, divergence, innovation, substitute, transplace **11** desexualize, interchange, permutation, transfigure, vicissitude **12** metamorphose, modification, transmogrify **13** metamorphosis, transmutation
sudden: **8** peripety **10** peripeteia

changeable
5 fluid **6** fickle, labile, mobile, pliant, shifty **7** movable, mutable, plastic, protean, unfixed **8** moveable, restless, slippery, ticklish, unstable, unsteady, variable, volatile, weathery **9** adaptable, mercurial, uncertain, unsettled **10** capricious, inconstant, lubricious **13** kaleidoscopic, temperamental

change decor
4 redo

changeless
5 fixed **6** steady **7** regular, uniform **8** constant, resolute **9** steadfast **10** invariable

change off
9 alternate

change of heart
8 reversal

change of life
9 menopause **11** climacteric

change of pace
5 pitch, shift

changeover
5 shift **10** alteration, conversion

channel
3 way **4** duct, mean, pass, pipe **5** agent, canal, carry, organ **6** agency, convey, course, funnel, groove, medium, siphon, strait **7** conduct, conduit, passage, vehicle **8** aqueduct, ministry, pipeline, transmit **10** instrument **11** watercourse
Africa-Madagascar: **10** Mozambique
Atlantic-Nantucket Sound: **8** Muskeget
Atlantic-North Sea: **7** English
California: **12** Santa Barbara
Caribbean-Gulf of Mexico: **7** Yucatan
combining form: **3** vas **4** vasi, vaso **5** solen **6** soleno
Ellesmere-Greenland: **7** Robeson **10** Smith Sound

Ganges: 5 Hugli 7 Hooghly
Hawaii: 5 Kaiwi, Kauai
Japan: 5 Bungo
Long Island: 13 Rockaway Inlet
Mediterranean: 5 Malta
Northwest Territories: 9 M'Clintock
Pakistan: 4 Nara
Scotland: 5 Minch
Tierra del Fuego: 6 Beagle
Tigris-Euphrates: 11 Shatt al Arab
Virginia: 12 Hampton Roads
West Indies: 9 Old Bahama 10 Saint Lucia

channel bass
4 drum 7 redfish

"Chanson ___"
6 Triste

chanson de
5 geste

chant
4 sing, tune 8 vocalize
10 cantillate
Gregorian: 9 plainsong 12 cantus firmus
Jewish: 6 Hallel

chanteuse
6 singer 10 cantatrice

chanticleer
4 cock 7 rooster

chaos
4 void 5 snarl 6 ataxia, huddle, muddle 7 anarchy, clutter, misrule 8 disarray, disorder 9 confusion, mobocracy 10 ochlocracy, unruliness 11 lawlessness

Chaos
daughter: 3 Nox, Nyx 4 Gaea
son: 6 Erebus

chap
3 guy, man 4 gent 6 fellow
9 gentleman
British: 5 bloke

chaparral
7 thicket

chaparral bird
10 roadrunner

chaperon
4 boss 5 guide 6 attend, convoy, escort, survey 7 conduct, oversee 9 accompany, companion, supervise 11 consort with, quarterback, superintend

chapfallen
see **crestfallen**

chaplain
5 padre 8 sky pilot

chaplet
5 crown 6 anadem, rosary, wreath 7 coronal, coronet, garland

char
4 burn 9 carbonize

character
3 ilk, rep, VIP 4 case, fame, kind, mark, mind, name, quiz, rank, role, sign, sort, soul, type 5 chief, humor, nabob, place, point, savor, state, trait 6 bigwig, cipher, device, kidney, letter, makeup, mettle, nature, oddity, report, repute, spirit, status, stripe, symbol, temper, virtue, zombie 7 big shot, courage, feature, footing, notable, oddball, persona, quality, station, variety 8 big-timer, capacity, eminence, identity, monogram, original, position, property, standing, uniquity 9 affection, attribute, birthmark, dignitary, eccentric, intellect, reference, situation 10 complexion, notability, reputation, resolution, uniqueness 11 credentials, description, disposition, distinction, personality, temperament, testimonial 13 individualism, individuality
chief: 4 hero 11 protagonist
defect: 8 hamartia
suffix: 3 ery

character assassination
7 calumny, scandal, slander 10 backbiting, defamation, detraction 12 backstabbing, belittlement, depreciation 13 disparagement

characteristic
4 mark, odor, sign, tang 5 badge, point, savor, smack, token, trait 6 flavor, normal, proper, virtue 7 feature, natural, quality, regular, special, typical 8 especial, peculiar, property, specific 9 affection, attribute, birthmark, character, diacritic 10 diagnostic, individual, particular 11 differentia, distinctive, singularity 13 idiosyncratic

characteristic of
suffix: 2 ic, ly 3 ish, ist 4 ical 5 istic 7 istical

characterize
4 mark 5 draft 6 define, sketch 7 outline, qualify 8 block out, chalk out, describe, identify, rough out, skeleton 9 adumbrate, signalize 11 distinguish, individuate, peculiarize, personalize, singularize, skeletonize 13 differentiate, individualize

characterized by
suffix: 2 al, ic 3 ful, ial, ous 4 ical

characterless
4 weak 5 sissy 6 futile 7 unmanly 8 childish, impotent 9 infantile, powerless, sissified 10 namby-pamby, panty-waist, wishy-washy

charade
7 pageant 8 disguise, pretense 10 pretension 11 make-believe

chare
3 job 4 duty, task 5 chore, stint 6 devoir 10 assignment

charge
3 ask, bid, fee, lay, tab, tax 4 bill, boil, bolt, care, clog, cost, dash, duty, fill, heap, lade, lash, load, must, need, onus, pack, pile, race, rate, rush, task, tear, tell, toll, warn, word 5 chase, choke, fling, order, ought, place, price, refer, right, shoot, trust, weigh 6 accuse, adjure, assign, behest, burden, credit, cumber, devoir, direct, enjoin, impugn, impute, indict, saddle, tariff, weight 7 arraign, ascribe, bidding, command, conduct, dictate, entrust, expense, impeach, mandate, pervade, request, running, solicit 8 accredit, business, encumber, handling, instruct, permeate, price tag, reproach, saturate 9 attribute, committal, criminate, inculpate, millstone, oversight, penetrate, percolate, reprehend, transfuse 10 commitment, deadweight, impregnate, injunction, intendance, management, obligation 11 impenetrate, incriminate, supervision

chargeable
6 liable 11 responsible

chargeless
4 free 6 gratis 8 costless 10 gratuitous 13 complimentary

charger
5 horse, mount, steed 7 courser 8 war-horse

chariness
7 caution 8 prudence

chariot
5 essed 6 esseda, essede
four-horse: 8 quadriga
two-horse: 4 biga

charioteer
5 drive, pilot 6 Auriga, driver

charisma
5 charm 6 allure, appeal, duende, glamor 7 glamour 8 witchery 9 magnetism 10 witchcraft 11 fascination

charitable

4 easy, good **6** benign, humane, kindly **7** clement, helpful, lenient **8** merciful, obliging, tolerant **9** indulgent **10** altruistic, benevolent, forbearing, thoughtful **11** considerate, kindhearted, sympathetic **12** eleemosynary, humanitarian **13** accommodating, philanthropic

charity

4 alms, love **5** amity, grace, mercy **6** lenity **7** caritas **8** altruism, clemency, donation, goodwill, offering **9** affection **10** attachment, humaneness, kindliness **11** benefaction, beneficence, benevolence **12** contribution, friendliness

charivari

5 babel **6** medley **8** serenade, shivaree **10** hodgepodge **11** celebration

charlatan

4 sham **5** bluff, quack **8** imposter **9** quackster **10** mountebank **11** fourflusher, quacksalver **12** saltimbanque

Charlemagne

brother: **8** Carloman
father: **5** Pepin
knight: **4** Ivon, Oton **5** Gerin, Ivory **6** Anseis, Gerard, Gerier, Oliver, Roland, Samson **7** Olivier, paladin **8** douzeper, Engelier **9** Berengier
nephew: **6** Roland **7** Orlando
sword: **7** Joyeuse
traitor: **4** Gano **7** Ganelon

Charles's Wain

9 Big Dipper

charleston

5 dance

Charley's Aunt author

6 Thomas (Brandon)

Charlie Brown creator

6 Schulz (Charles)

Charlie McCarthy

5 dummy **6** stooge
friend: **5** Snerd (Mortimer)
voice: **6** Bergen (Edgar)

charm

3 hex **4** draw, juju, luck, lure, rune, take, wile, zemi **5** spell, witch **6** allure, amulet, appeal, enamor, fetish, glamor, mascot, voodoo **7** attract, bewitch, enchant **8** enthrall, entrance, talisman, witchery **9** captivate, ensorcell, fascinate, magnetism, magnetize **10** allurement, attraction, phylactery, witchcraft **11** conjuration, fascination, incanta-

tion **12** gratefulness **13** agreeableness

charmed

8 enamored **9** bewitched, enchanted, entranced **10** captivated, fascinated

charmer

4 mage **5** magus **6** magian, wizard **7** warlock **8** conjurer, magician, sorcerer **9** enchanter **11** necromancer

charming

5 siren **7** drawing, winsome **8** adorable, alluring, magnetic **9** glamorous, seductive **10** attracting, attractive, enchanting **11** captivating

Charon

7 boatman **8** ferryman
father: **6** Erebus
mother: **3** Nox
river: **4** Styx

Charpentier opera

6 Louise

charpoy

3 bed, cot

chart

3 map **4** cast, plan, plat, plot **5** graph, table **6** design, devise, scheme **7** arrange, dope out, project **9** blueprint **10** tabulation

charter

3 let **4** deed, hire, rent **5** lease **10** conveyance

Chartreuse

7 liqueur

chary

4 safe, wary **5** canny, loath **6** frugal, saving **7** careful, guarded, sparing, thrifty **8** cautious, discreet, gingerly, hesitant **9** inhibited, provident, reluctant, stewardly **10** economical, restrained, unwasteful **11** calculating, circumspect, considerate, constrained, disinclined

Charybdis

9 whirlpool
rock associated with: **6** Scylla

chase

3 out, run **4** boil, bolt, dash, game, hunt, lash, prey, race, rush, tear **5** chivy, chuck, eject, evict, fling, shoot, speed, trail **6** career, charge, course, follow, pursue, quarry, venery **7** boot out, dismiss, extrude, hunting, kick out, pursuit **8** throw out

chase away

4 shoo

chaser

4 wolf **6** masher **7** Don Juan **8** Casanova **9** ladies' man, philander, womanizer **10** lady-killer **11** philanderer

chasm

3 gap **4** gulf, skip **5** abysm, abyss, blank, cleft, clove, gorge, gulch, split **6** arroyo, clough, ravine, schism **8** cleavage, omission, overlook **9** oversight **11** preterition **13** pretermission

chasmal

7 yawning **9** cavernous

chassepot

5 rifle

chaste

4 pure **5** clean, moral **6** decent, modest, proper, seemly, vestal, virgin **7** ethical **8** becoming, decorous, maidenly, spotless, virginal, virtuous **9** abstinent, continent, righteous, stainless, undefiled, unsullied **10** immaculate **11** unblemished

chasten

3 try **5** abase **6** humble, punish **7** afflict, correct **8** chastise **9** castigate, humiliate **10** discipline

chastise

4 beat **5** baste **6** pummel, punish, thrash **7** belabor, chasten, correct **9** castigate **10** discipline

chastisement

3 rod **8** punition **10** correction, discipline, punishment **11** castigation

chat

3 gab, jaw, rap, yak, yap **4** blab, chin, gush, talk, yarn **5** clack, prate, prose, run on, visit **6** babble, burble, cackle, confab, dither, gabble, gossip, jabber, parley, patter, rattle, yak-yak, yammer, yatter **7** chatter, clatter, palaver, prattle, smatter, twaddle, twitter **8** causerie, chin-chin, colloque, colloquy, converse, dialogue, lallygag **9** tête-à-tête, yakety-yak **11** confabulate **12** bibble-babble, conversation, tittle-tattle **13** confabulation

chateau

5 manor, villa **6** castle **7** mansion

chateaubriand

5 steak **10** tenderloin

Chateaubriand novel

4 René **5** Atala **10** Les Natchez

chatelain
6 warden 8 governor 9 castellan

chatelaine
4 hook, wife 5 clasp 8 mistress

chattel
5 slave 7 bondman 8 bondsman
9 bondslave, mancipium

chatter
3 gab, jaw, yak 4 blab, bull, chat
5 clack, prate 6 babble, burble,
cackle, gabble, gibber, gossip, jabber, natter, patter, yak-yak, yammer, yatter 7 blabber, blather, blatter, blither, brabble, palaver,
prattle 8 chin-chin, chitchat 9 small
talk, yakety-yak 12 bibble-babble,
gibble-gabble, talkee-talkee, tittle
tattle

chatterbox
5 tabby 6 chewet, gabber, gossip,
magpie, prater 7 blabber 8 busybody, jabberer, prattler, quidnunc
9 bandar-log, blabmouth, chatterer
10 newsmonger, tattletale 12 blabbermouth 13 scandalmonger

chatty
5 gabby, talky, wordy 9 garrulous,
talkative 10 babblative, loquacious
11 loose-lipped 12 loose-tongued,
multiloquent 13 multiloquious

chauffeur
5 drive 6 driver 9 transport

chauvinism
8 jingoism 10 partiality, patriotism
11 nationalism

cheap
3 bad, low 4 base, fake, mean,
poor, sham, vile 5 petty, phony,
sorry, tatty, wrong 6 cheesy, common, flashy, garish, measly, paltry,
rotten, scurvy, shabby, shoddy,
sleazy, tawdry, trashy, undear
7 chintzy, cut-rate, low-cost, pitiful,
popular, reduced 8 beggarly, inferior, pitiable, rubbishy, terrible, trifling, trumpery, uncostly 9 brummagem, low-priced, rubbishly,
valueless, worthless 10 despicable,
despisable, reasonable, rubbishing
11 inexpensive 12 contemptible,
meretricious

cheapen
5 decry, lower 7 devalue 8 mark
down, write off 9 devaluate, downgrade, write down 10 depreciate,
undervalue

cheap-jack
6 hawker, monger, vendor 7 hig-

gler, packman, peddler 8 huckster,
inferior, outcrier 9 worthless

cheapskate
4 skin 5 chuff, miser, stiff 7 niggard 8 muckworm, tightwad 9 skinflint 11 cheeseparer

cheat
3 con, gyp 4 beat, bilk, burn,
dupe, fool, gull, hoax, ream, sell,
take 5 bunco, cozen, crook, fraud,
fudge, hocus, put-on, screw, short,
slick 6 befool, boodle, chisel,
chouse, con man, deceit, delude,
diddle, extort, fleece, humbug,
sucker 7 beguile, chicane, deceive,
defraud, diddler, hoaxing, mislead,
sharper, swindle 8 cozening, flimflam, swindler, trickery 9 chicanery, deception, defrauder, fourberie, imposture, overreach,
trickster 10 dishonesty, hanky-
panky 11 double-cross, highbinding 12 double-dealer 13 bamboozlement, confidence man,
double-dealing
on a check: 4 kite

check
2 go 3 bit, tab, try 4 balk, bill,
curb, foil, halt, jibe, rein, stay,
stem, stop, test, tick 5 agree,
cease, prove, score, stall, tally
6 accord, arrest, baffle, bridle,
damage, desist, hold in, square,
thwart 7 backset, conform, examine, inhibit, obviate, prevent, repress, reverse, setback 8 dovetail,
hold back, hold down, preclude, restrain, reversal, suppress, withhold
9 constrain, frustrate, interrupt
10 circumvent, correspond
11 discontinue

checklist
7 catalog 9 catalogue, inventory

checkmate
6 arrest, corner, defeat, thwart
7 counter

check over
3 con, vet 4 view 5 study 6 survey
7 canvass, check up, examine, inspect 10 scrutinize

checkup
7 medical 8 physical 10 inspection
11 examination

cheek
4 face, gall 5 brass, crust, nerve
9 brashness 10 confidence, effrontery 11 presumption
combining form: 3 mel 4 melo
5 bucco

cheekbone
5 malar

cheeky
4 bold, pert, wise 5 fresh, nervy,
sassy, smart 7 forward 8 impudent
11 smart-alecky

cheep
4 chip, peep 5 chirp, tweet 7 chipper, chirrup, chitter, tweedle, twitter

cheer
3 rah 4 root 5 bravo, huzza,
nerve, steel 6 buck up, hoorah,
hooray, hurrah, hurray, huzzah,
solace 7 animate, applaud, comfort, console, hearten, upraise
8 embolden, inspirit 9 encourage,
enhearten 10 strengthen
corrida: 3 olé

cheerful
3 gay 4 airy, glad, rosy 5 chirk,
corky, jolly, merry, riant, sunny
6 blithe, bright, chirpy, jaunty, joc-
und, lively 7 beamish, buoyant, radiant 8 animated, carefree, chirrupy, debonair, sunbeamy
9 lightsome, vivacious
12 lighthearted
Scottish: 5 cadgy

cheerio
2 by 5 adieu 6 bye-bye, so long
7 good-bye 8 farewell, toodle-oo

cheerless
4 drab 5 bleak 6 dismal, dreary,
gloomy, somber 8 funereal 9 de-
jecting 10 depressing, oppressive,
tenebrific 11 dispiriting

cheese
3 pot 4 blue, jack 5 brick, cream,
store 6 farmer 7 cottage, process
9 pineapple, smearcase
American: 8 Longhorn 11 Lieder-
kranz 12 Monterey Jack
Belgian: 9 Limburger
brown: 6 mysost 7 gjetost
Canadian: 3 Oka
combining form: 3 tyr 4 case, tyro
5 caseo
curdling agent: 6 rennet, rennin
Danish: 4 Tybo 5 Esrom 6 Samsoe
7 Havarti
dish: 6 fondue 7 rarebit, soufflé
Dutch: 4 Edam 5 Gouda 6 Leyden
English: 7 cheddar, Stilton 8 Cheshire 10 Lancashire
French: 4 Brie 7 fromage, Livarot
9 Camembert, reblochon, Roquefort
10 Neufchâtel 11 Pont l'Évêque,
Port du Salut
German: 4 kase 6 Tilsit 7 Munster
8 Muenster, Tilsiter

Greek: **4** feta **7** kasseri

green: **7** sapsago

Italian: **6** Romano **7** fontina, ricotta **8** Bel Paese, Parmesan, pecorino **9** provolone **10** Gorgonzola, mozzarella **12** caciocavallo

lover: **9** turophile

main ingredient: **6** casein

Norwegian: **6** mysost **7** gjetost, primost **9** gammelost, Jarlsberg, taffelost **10** Noekkelost

Oriental: **4** tofu

protein: **6** casein

Scottish: **6** Dunlop, Orkney **7** kebbock, kebbuck

Swedish: **8** graddost

Swiss: **6** Saanen **7** Gruyère, sapsago **8** Vacherin **10** Emmentaler **11** Emmenthaler

uncured: **7** cottage

Welsh: **10** Caerphilly

whey: **5** ziger **6** zieger

cheesecloth
5 gauze

cheeselike
6 caseic **7** caseous

cheeseparer
4 skin **5** chuff, miser, stiff **7** niggard **8** muckworm, tightwad **9** skinflint **10** cheapskate

cheeseparing
4 mean **5** cheap, close, tight **6** shabby, stingy **7** miserly **8** grudging **9** illiberal, niggardly, penurious **11** closefisted, tightfisted **12** parsimonious **13** penny-pinching

cheesy
4 mean, poor **5** cheap, tatty **6** common, shoddy, sleazy, trashy **7** caseous **8** rubbishy

chef d'oeuvre
7 classic **9** showpiece **10** magnum opus, masterwork **11** masterpiece, tour de force

Chekhov, Anton
play: **6** Ivanov **7** Seagull **10** Uncle Vanya **12** Three Sisters **13** Cherry Orchard

chelonian
6 turtle **8** tortoise

chemical
agent: **8** catalyst

combining form: **2** is, ol, ox, yl **3** aci, hex, iod, iso, mer, ole, oxa, oxo, oyl, pyr, thi, tri, ure **4** acet, amid, amin, hept, hexa, hydr, iodo, orth, poly, pyro, quin, tetr, thio **5** aceto, amido, amino, hepta, hydro, ortho, quino, tetra, xanth **6** ammino, xantho

combining power: **7** valence

compound: **4** acid, base, diol, enol, imid, oxim, salt, tepa, urea **5** amide, amine, diene, ester, imide, imine, indol, orcin, oxime, purin, pyran, salol, tolan, triol **6** alkali, benzin, benzol, diamin, emodin, guanin, halide, hydrid, indole, inulin, ionone, isatin, isolog, isomer, ketone, lactam, maltol, metepa, natron, nitril, pterin, purine, pyrone, pyrrol, quinol, retene, silane, skatol, tannin, tetryl, thiram, thymol, tolane, triene, trimer, uracil, ureide, yttria, zeatin **7** barilla, benzene, benzole, cumarin, diamide, diamine, diazine, diazole, diester, flavone, guanine, heptose, hydride, indamin, indican, indoxyl, isatine, levulin, metamer, monomer, naphtol, nitrile, orcinol, oxazine, phytane, picolin, polyene, polymer, pyrrole, quinoid, quinone, salicin, skatole, steroid, taurine, terpene, thiazin, thiazol, thymine, tolidin, triazin, urethan, uridine, vitamer, xylidin **8** cephalin, cyanamid, disulfid, elaterin, fluorene, furfural, guaiacol, hematein, hexamine, indamine, isologue, kephalin, lichenin, limonene, melamine, naloxone, naphthol, palmitin, phenazin, phosphid, phthalin, picoline, piperine, pristane, quinolin, resorcin, salicine, santonin, siloxane, sodamide, sorbitol, spermine, squalene, stilbene, strontia, tautomer, thiazine, thiazole, thiophen, thiotepa, thiourea, tolidine, triazine, triazole, triptane, tyramine, urethane, vanillin, warfarin, xanthene, xanthine, xanthone, xylidine, ytterbia, zaratite, zirconia

element: (see at **element**)

prefix: **2** di **3** dia, met **4** meta

quantity: **4** mole

radical: **4** acyl, amyl, cyan **5** allyl, butyl, ethyl, tolyl **6** acetyl, formyl, methyl, oxalic, phenyl, propyl, toluyl **7** benzoyl

reaction: **5** redox

salt: **5** niter, nitre, urate, ziram **6** haloid, humate, malate, oleate, phytin **7** ferrate, formate, gallate, maleate, pectate, persalt, picrate, tannate, toluate, zincate **8** fumarate, pyruvate, racemate, selenate, silicate, stearate, tartrate, thionate, titanate, valerate, vanadate, xanthate

suffix: **2** id, il, in, ol, on **3** ane, ase, ate, ein, ene, ide, ile, ine, ite, ium, oic, oin, one, ose, ous, yne **4** eine, idin, itol, oate, olic, onic **5** idine, onium, oside, ylene

warfare agent: **7** tear gas **8** vesicant **10** mustard gas

chemist
7 analyst **8** druggist **10** apothecary, pharmacist

American: **4** Urey (Harold) **6** Remsen (Ira), Sumner (James) **7** Onsager (Lars), Pauling (Linus), Seaborg (Glenn) **8** Hoffmann (Roald), Langmuir (Irving), Mulliken (Robert), Richards (Theodore), Woodward (Robert)

Austrian: **4** Kuhn (Richard) **5** Pregl (Fritz)

British: **6** Ramsay (William) **8** Smithson (James)

Dutch: **8** van't Hoff (Jacobus)

English: **4** Abel (Frederick), Davy (Humphry) **5** Soddy (Frederick) **6** Dalton (John) **7** Faraday (Michael) **9** Priestley (Joseph), Wollaston (William) **10** Williamson (Alexander)

French: **5** Curie (Irene, Marie, Pierre) **7** Moissan (Henri), Pasteur (Louis) **8** Sabatier (Paul) **9** Lavoisier (Antoine-Laurent)

German: **5** Haber (Fritz) **6** Bunsen (Robert), Liebig (Justus von), Nernst (Walther), Wittig (Georg), Wohler (Friedrich) **7** Fischer (Emil, Ernst, Hans), Hofmann (August), Ostwald (Friedrich), Wallach (Otto), Wieland (Heinrich), Windaus (Adolf), Ziegler (Karl) **9** Zsigmondy (Richard) **10** Erlenmeyer (Richard), Staudinger (Hermann) **11** Willstatter (Richard)

Italian: **5** Natta (Giulio) **8** Avogadro (Amedeo)

Russian: **7** Semenov (Nikolay) **8** Zelinsky (Nikolay) **9** Mendeleev (Dmitry)

Scottish: **4** Todd (Alexander)

Swedish: **8** Svedberg (The, Theodor)

Swiss: **6** Karrer (Paul), Werner (Alfred)

(see also under **Nobel Prize Winner**)

chemist's vessel
4 vial **5** ampul, flask, phial **6** aludel, ampule, beaker, mortar, retort **7** ampoule, matrass **8** bolt head, crucible, cylinder, test tube

chemoreceptor
8 taste bud

cheongsam
5 dress

Cheops
5 Khufu **7** pyramid

Cheran's father
6 Dishon

cherish

4 keep, save **5** guard, nurse, prize, value **6** admire, defend, esteem, foster, harbor, nursle, relish, revere, shield **7** apprize, nourish, nurture, shelter **8** conserve, preserve, treasure, venerate **9** cultivate, delight in, entertain, reverence, safeguard **10** appreciate

Cherokee

chief: **4** Ross (John)
historian: **7** Sequoya

cherry

dark: **4** Bing
family: **4** rose **8** Rosaceae
genus: **6** Prunus
hybrid: **4** Duke
sour: **7** morello **8** amarelle
sweet: **4** Bing, gean **7** mazzard, oxheart **9** Bigarreau
wild: **7** marasca, mazzard **10** maraschino

cherry bomb

11 firecracker

Cherry Orchard author

7 Chekhov (Anton)

cherrystone

4 clam **6** quahog

chersonese

9 peninsula

Chesed

father: **5** Nahor
wife: **6** Milcah

chess

champion: **3** Tal (Mikhail) **4** Euwe (Max) **6** Karpov (Anatoly), Lasker (Emanuel) **7** Fischer (Bobby), Smyslov (Vassily), Spassky (Boris) **8** Alekhine (Alexander), Kasparov (Gary), Steinitz (Wilhelm) **9** Botvinnik (Mikhail), Petrosian (Tigran) **10** Capablanca (Jose)
draw game: **9** stalemate
goal: **4** mate **9** checkmate
move: **6** castle, gambit **10** fianchetto
opening: **6** gambit
piece: **4** king, pawn, rook **5** queen **6** bishop, knight
risk: **6** gambit
term: **3** net, pin **4** biff, draw, file, fork, mate, rank **5** check **6** attack, castle, gambit, skewer **7** capture, develop, end game **9** checkmate, en passant **10** fianchetto, middle game **11** combination

chest

4 kist **6** breast, bureau, coffer, lowboy, thorax, wangan, wangun **7** dresser, highboy, wanigan

8 treasury, wannigan **9** exchequer **10** chiffonier
combining form: **5** stern **6** sterno, stetho, thorac **7** thoraci, thoraco

chesterfield

4 sofa **8** overcoat **9** davenport

chestnut

4 tree **5** color, horse **6** cliché, marron **10** brownstone, chinquapin
extract: **6** tannin
Polynesian: **4** rata
water: **4** ling

cheval glass

6 mirror

chevalier

5 noble **6** knight **8** horseman **9** caballero, gentleman

chevron

6 stripe

chew

3 eat, gum **4** bite, chaw, gnaw **5** champ, chomp, chump, crump, munch **6** crunch, devour, mumble, nibble **7** chumble, consume, scrunch **8** ruminate **9** masticate

chewing gum

6 chicle

chew out

3 jaw, wig **5** scold **6** revile **7** bawl out, tell off **10** tongue-lash, vituperate

Chiang ___

7 Kai-shek

chic

3 cry, fad **4** mode, rage **5** craze, smart, style, swank, swish, vogue **6** furore, modish, trendy, with-it **7** dashing, fashion, stylish **9** exclusive **10** dernier cri **11** fashionable

chicane

4 dupe, fool, gull, hoax, ploy, ruse, wile **5** cavil, feint, fraud, trick **6** befool, gambit **7** quibble **8** artifice, flimflam, hoodwink, maneuver, trickery **9** bamboozle, deception, stratagem, victimize **10** dishonesty, hanky-panky **11** furtiveness, highbinding **13** double-dealing

chicanery

4 plot **5** fraud **8** intrigue, trickery **11** machination

chichi

5 showy, swank **6** dressy, la-di-da **7** splashy **8** affected, overnice, peacocky, précieux, precious **10** flamboyant, peacockish **11** alembicated, overrefined, pretentious **12** orchidaceous, ostentatious

chick

3 kid **5** child **6** moppet, nipper **8** juvenile, young one **9** youngling, youngster

chickadee

8 titmouse
family: **7** Paridae

chicken

4 fowl, funk **5** sissy **6** coward, craven, funker **7** dastard, gutless, quitter, unmanly **8** cowardly, poltroon **9** spunkless **11** lily-livered, poltroonish, yellowbelly **12** poor-spirited **13** pusillanimous
breed: **4** Java **6** Ancona, Brahma, Cochin, Lamona, Redcap, Sussex **7** Buckeye, Cornish, Dorking, Holland, Leghorn, Minorca **8** Delaware, Dominick, Langshan **9** Buttercup, Dominique, Orpington, Wyandotte **10** Australorp **11** Jersey Giant, Rock Cornish
castrated: **5** capon
cooking: **5** fryer **7** broiler, roaster
disease: **5** gapes **8** pullorum **11** coccidiosis
female: **3** hen **6** pullet
genus: **6** Gallus
male: **4** cock **7** rooster **8** cockerel
pen: **4** coop
small: **6** bantam
sound: **6** cackle

chicken feed

7 peanuts **8** pittance

chicken pox

9 varicella

chickpea

8 garbanzo

chickweed

4 pink **7** potherb

chicle

3 gum **10** chewing gum

chicory

7 witloof

chide

4 rate **5** scold, sneap **6** berate, lesson, monish, rebuke **7** reprove, tick off, upbraid **8** admonish, call down, reproach **9** reprimand

chiding

3 rap, wig **6** rebuke **7** reproof **8** reproach **9** reprimand **10** admonition **12** admonishment

chief

4 arch, boss, cock, duce, head, jefe, lion, main, star **5** first, major, prime **6** bigwig, führer, honcho, leader, master, potent, primal, ruling, sachem **7** capital, headman, leading, notable, premier, primary,

stellar, telling, weighty **8** bigtimer, big wheel, champion, dictator, dominant, eminence, foremost, hierarch, luminary **9** dignitary, dominator, effective, important, momentous, number one, principal, prominent **10** notability, preeminent **11** controlling, outstanding, predominant, significant **13** consequential
combining form: 4 prot **5** proto
commander: 4 CINC
prefix: 4 arch **5** archi
Spanish: 4 jefe

Chief Justice
3 Jay (John) **4** Taft (William Howard) **5** Chase (Salmon P.), Stone (Harlan), Taney (Roger B.), Waite (Morrison), White (Edward Douglass) **6** Burger (Warren), Fuller (Melville W.), Holmes (Oliver Wendell), Hughes (Charles Evans), Vinson (Frederick M.), Warren (Earl) **8** Marshall (John) **9** Ellsworth (Oliver)

chiefly
6 mainly, mostly **7** largely, overall **9** generally, primarily **11** principally **13** predominantly

chiffchaff
4 bird **7** warbler

chiffonier
5 chest **6** bureau **7** dresser

chigger
4 mite **6** chigoe, red bug

chignon
3 bun **4** knot

chilblain
4 sore **8** swelling **12** inflammation

child
3 kid **5** minor, youth **6** cherub, moppet, nipper, teener **7** dickens **8** innocent, juvenile, runabout, teenager, young one **9** sweetling, youngling, youngster **10** adolescent **11** teenybopper
combining form: 3 ped **4** paed, paid, pedo **5** paedo, paido, tecno
gifted: 7 prodigy
homeless: 4 waif
parentless: 6 orphan
Scottish: 5 bairn
spoiled: 4 brat
young: 3 tot **4** baby, tike, tyke **6** infant, kiddie **8** bantling, weanling

childish
4 slow **5** naive, silly **6** simple **7** asinine, babyish, fatuous, foolish, kid-

dish, moronic, puerile **8** arrested, backward, immature, retarded **9** infantile, infantine
Scottish: 7 bairnly **8** bairnish

childless
6 barren **7** sterile

childlike
6 docile, filial **7** natural **8** innocent, trustful, trusting **9** ingenuous

child's play
4 snap **5** cinch, setup **6** breeze, picnic **8** duck soup, kid stuff, pushover

Chile
capital: 8 Santiago
chief export: 6 copper
conqueror: 8 Valdivia (Pedro de)
monetary unit: 4 peso

Chileab
father: 5 David
mother: 7 Abigail

chili con _____
5 carne

Chilion
father: 9 Elimelech
mother: 5 Naomi

chill
3 icy **4** ague, cold, cool **5** gelid, nippy **6** arctic, chilly, deject, formal, frigid, frosty **7** distant, glacial **8** dispirit, freezing, reserved, solitary **9** disparage, withdrawn **10** abstracted, demoralize, discourage, dishearten **11** emotionless, indifferent, standoffish, unemotional **12** uninterested **13** disinterested

chiller
7 shocker **8** thriller

chilly
3 raw **4** cold **5** algid **7** coldish

chilopod
9 centipede

chime
4 bell, bong, peal, ring, toll, tune **5** knell **6** accord **7** concord, harmony **9** agreement **10** consonance **11** concordance

chime in
3 say **4** tell **5** state, utter **6** chip in **7** break in, declare, deliver **8** bring out, throw out **9** interrupt

chimera
5 dream **6** bubble **7** fantasy, rainbow **8** illusion, phantasy **9** pipe dream

Chimera
father: 6 Typhon

mother: 7 Echidna
slayer: 11 Bellerophon

chimerical
6 absurd, unreal **7** fictive, utopian **8** delusive, delusory, fabulous, fanciful, illusory, mythical **9** ambitious, deceptive, fantastic, fictional, imaginary **10** fictitious **11** pretentious **12** preposterous, suppositious

chiming
7 musical **8** blending, harmonic **9** consonant, symphonic **10** harmonious **11** symphonious

chimney
3 lum **4** flue, tube **5** stack **10** smokestack
corner: 8 fireside **9** inglenook
output: 3 gas **4** fume, soot **5** smoke

chimpanzee
3 ape **6** monkey **7** primate **10** anthropoid
kin: 7 gorilla

chin
3 rap **4** chat, talk, yarn **5** prose, visit **6** mentum **8** causerie, colloque, converse
combining form: 5 genio, mento

china
6 dishes **7** ceramic **8** crockery **9** porcelain **11** earthenware
maker: 3 Bow **5** Hizen, Imari, Spode **6** Doccia, Sèvres **7** Bristol, Chelsea, Dresden, Limoges, Meissen **8** Caughley, Haviland, Wedgwood

China
capital: 6 Peking **7** Beijing
largest city: 8 Shanghai
monetary unit: 4 yuan
old name: 6 Cathay
province: 5 Anhui, Gansu, Hebei, Henan, Hubei, Hunan, Jilin **6** Fujian, Shanxi, Yunnan **7** Guizhou, Jiangsu, Jiangxi, Qinghai, Shaanxi, Sichuan **8** Liaoning, Shandong, Szechwan, Zhejiang **9** Guangdong **12** Heilongjiang
region: 5 Tibet **6** Xizang **10** Nei Monggol **12** Ningxia Huizu **13** Inner Mongolia, Xinjiang Uygur

china clay
6 kaolin

chinchilla
3 fur **6** rodent

chine
5 crest, ridge **7** hogback

Chinese
administrative unit: 2 fu **5** hsien
archway: 6 pai-lou

aromatic root: 7 ginseng
artichoke: 6 crosne 7 chorogi, crosnes 8 knotroot
assembly: 3 hui
bamboo: 7 whangee
boat: 4 junk 6 sampan
boat-dweller: 3 Tan 5 Tanka
bow: 6 kowtow
Buddha: 2 Fo
Buddhism: 5 Foism
cabbage: 6 pechay 7 pakchoi
card game: 6 fan tan
cauterizing agent: 4 moxa
civet: 5 rasse
combining form: 4 Sino 5 Chino 6 Sinico
conveyance: 7 pedicab, ricksha 10 jinrikisha
date: 6 jujube
deer: 8 elaphure
dialect: 2 Wu 4 Amoy 5 Hakka 6 Swatow 7 Foochow 8 Mandarin 9 Cantonese, Pekingese
dictator: 10 Mao Tse-tung
distance unit: 2 li
dog: 4 chow, Peke 9 Pekingese
dulcimer: 7 yang-kin 8 yang ch'in
dynasty: 2 Wu 3 Ch'i, Han, Sui, Wei, Yin 4 Ch'en, Ch'in, Chou, Hsia (first), Ming, Sung, T'ang, Tsin, Yuan 5 Ch'ing, Liang, Shang 6 Manchu, Mongol, Shu Han
fabric: 5 pekin 6 pongee, tussah 7 tsatlee 8 shantung
feminine principle: 3 yin
festival: 8 Ch'in Ming
feudal state: 3 Wei
figurine: 5 magot
food: 6 subgum, won ton 7 foo yong
fruit: 6 lichee, litchi, loquat 7 kumquat 8 mandarin
gambling game: 6 fan tan
gazelle: 6 dzeren, dzeron
god: 4 joss, Shen 7 Shang-ti, Tien Chu
gong: 6 tam-tam
grass: 3 bon
gruel: 6 congee
herb: 4 ramee, ramie 7 ginseng
idol: 4 joss
jute: 7 chingma
laborer: 6 coolie
legendary emperor: 7 Huang Ti
liquid measure: 5 cheng, sheng
liquor: 6 samshu
magnolia: 5 yulan
mandarin's residence: 5 yamen
masculine principle: 4 yang
military leader: 7 warlord
money, silver: 5 sycee
moon guitar: 6 yue-kin 8 yueh-ch'in
musical instrument: 3 kin 4 ch'in, pi-

pa 5 cheng, hsiao 6 yue-kin 8 yang ch'in, yueh ch'in
nurse: 4 amah
official: 4 kuan 8 mandarin
official seal: 4 chop
oil: 4 tung
omelet: 7 foo yong
ox: 4 zebu
pagoda: 2 ta 3 taa
peony: 6 moutan
permit: 4 chop
porcelain: 4 chin, Ming 7 celadon, Nankeen 8 mandarin
pottery: 4 Kuan, Ming 5 Chien 7 boccaro, tz'u-chou
prefecture: 2 fu
puzzle: 7 tangram
race: 9 Mongoloid
religion: 5 Foism 6 Taoism 8 Buddhism 12 Confucianism
rice song: 6 yang ko
sauce: 3 soy
secret society: 4 tong
sheep: 3 sha 5 urial 6 oorial
silkworm: 6 tussah 7 tussore 9 ailanthus
string money: 4 tiao
tea: 5 bohea, congo, hyson 6 congou, oolong 8 souchong
temple: 2 ta 3 taa 6 pagoda
tree: 4 tung 6 gingko, ginkgo, loquat, wampee 7 kumquat 8 mandarin
unicorn: 3 lin
vine: 5 kudzu 7 yangtao
weight: 3 fan, fen, tan 4 mace, tael 5 catty, liang, picol, picul

chink

4 rift, rima, rime 5 cleft, clink, crack, split 6 jingle, tingle, tinkle 7 fissure 8 rimation

chinquapin

3 nut 8 chestnut

chintzy

4 loud 5 cheap, gaudy 6 brazen, flashy, garish, tawdry, tinsel 7 blatant, glaring 12 meretricious

chip in

6 kick in 7 break in, chime in, pitch in 9 interrupt, subscribe 10 contribute 11 come through

chipmunk

6 hackee, rodent
family: 8 squirrel 9 Sciuridae

chipper

3 gay 4 keen, neat, peep, snug, tidy, trig, trim 5 alert, cheep, chirm, chirp, tweet 6 bright, lively 7 animate, chirrup, chitter, orderly, tweedle, twitter 8 animated, spirited 9 shipshape, sprightly, vivacious

11 uncluttered, well-groomed 12 spick-and-span

chirk

3 gay 5 cheer 6 blithe, bright, cheery, chirpy, lively 7 animate, chipper, hearten 8 animated, cheerful, chirrupy, embolden, inspirit, sunbeamy 9 encourage, enhearten, lightsome, sprightly, vivacious 10 strengthen

chirography

4 fist, hand 6 ductus, script 10 penmanship 11 calligraphy, handwriting

chiromancy

9 palmistry

Chiron

7 centaur
father: 6 Cronus
mother: 7 Philyra
pupil: 5 Jason 8 Achilles, Heracles, Hercules 9 Asclepius 11 Aesculapius

chiropody

8 podiatry

chiropractic

founder: 6 Palmer

chiropter

3 bat

chirp

4 chip, peep 5 cheep, chirm, tweet 7 chipper, chirrup, clutter, tweedle, twitter

chirpy

5 chirk, sunny 6 blithe, cheery 8 cheerful, chirrupy, sunbeamy 9 lightsome

chirrup

4 chip, peep 5 cheep, chirm, chirp, tweet 7 chipper, chitter, tweedle, twitter

chisel

3 gyp 4 beat, bilk 5 carve, cheat, cozen, cut in, sculp 6 butt in, diddle, horn in, sculpt 7 defraud, intrude, obtrude 9 sculpture 10 intertrude

chiselly

3 bad 4 sour 6 rotten 7 unhappy 10 unpleasant 11 displeasing 12 disagreeable

chit

3 kid 4 memo, note 5 chick, child 6 moppet 8 juvenile, notandum, notation, young one 9 youngster 10 memorandum

chitchat
5 clack 6 babble, by-talk, cackle, gabble 7 chatter, prattle 8 trifling 9 bavardage, small talk 12 talkee-talkee, tittle-tattle

chitter
4 chip, peep 5 cheep, chirp, tweet 7 chipper, chirrup, tweedle, twitter

chivalric
see **chivalrous**

chivalrous
3 big 5 lofty, manly, noble 8 generous, knightly 10 benevolent 11 considerate, magnanimous 12 greathearted

chivy, chivvy
3 try 4 bait, ride 5 chase, hound, trail 6 badger, follow, heckle, hector, pursue 7 afflict, torment 8 bullyrag

Chloe
11 shepherdess
beloved: 7 Daphnis

chlordane
11 insecticide

chloride
4 salt 5 ester 7 muriate

chlorine
symbol: 2 Cl

Chloris
father: 7 Amphion
husband: 6 Neleus 8 Zephyrus
mother: 5 Niobe
son: 6 Nestor

chloroform
7 anodyne, solvent 10 anesthetic

choate
4 full 5 whole 6 entire 7 perfect 8 complete, integral

chockablock
4 full 6 jammed, packed 7 brimful, crammed, crowded, jam-full, stuffed 8 bung-full 9 jam-packed

chocolate
3 bar 5 candy, cocoa, color, drink 8 beverage

Chocolate Soldier composer
6 Straus (Oscar)

chocolate tree
5 cacao

choice
3 fat, top 4 best, pick, rare 5 cream, elite, pride, prime, prize 6 chosen, culled, dainty, flower, option, picked, rating, select 7 elegant, finding, supreme, verdict 8 decision, delicate, druthers, election, judgment, peerless, selected, superior, volition 9 appraisal, exquisite 8 recherché 9 selection 10 evaluation, preeminent, preference, surpassing 11 alternative, superlative, unsurpassed 12 incomparable, transcendent 13 determination
even: 6 toss-up

choicy
4 nice 5 fussy, picky 6 choosy 7 finical, finicky 9 finicking 10 fastidious, particular 11 persnickety

choir
6 chorus
area: 4 loft 7 chancel, gallery
assistant: 9 succentor
leader: 6 cantor 8 choragus 9 precentor
member: 9 chorister
section: 4 alto, bass 5 tenor 7 soprano
vestment: 4 gown, robe 5 cotta 8 surplice

choke
4 clog, fill, heap, hush, load, pack, pile, plug, stop 5 block, close, quiet, shush, still 6 charge, shut up, stifle 7 congest, occlude, quieten, silence, smother, stopper 8 obstruct, strangle, throttle 9 suffocate 10 asphyxiate

choking
8 quashing, stifling 9 quenching, squashing 10 repression, smothering, squelching, strangling 11 suppression

choleric
3 mad 4 waxy 5 angry, fiery, irate, ratty, testy, wroth 6 cranky, heated, ireful, spunky, tetchy, touchy, wrathy 7 carping 8 captious, wrathful 9 indignant, irascible, temperish 11 acrimonious, hot-tempered 12 fault-finding 13 quick-tempered

cholla
6 cactus

chomp
4 bite, chew 5 champ, chump, munch 6 crunch 7 scrunch 8 ruminate 9 masticate

choose
3 opt 4 cull, like, love, mark, pick, take, want, will, wish 5 adopt, elect, favor, optate, opt for, please, prefer, select 7 embrace, espouse, pick out 8 handpick 9 single out

choosy
4 nice 5 fussy 7 finical, finicky 8 delicate 9 finicking 10 fastidious, particular, pernickety 11 persnickety

chop
3 box, cut, hew 4 cuff, dice, fell, hack, hash, poke, slap 5 clout, cut up, mince, smack, spank 6 buffet, hackle 8 fragment

chop-chop
4 fast 7 flat-out, hastily, quickly, rapidly 8 full tilt, promptly, speedily 9 posthaste 12 lickety-split

chophouse
10 restaurant

Chopin
birthplace: 6 Poland
instrument: 5 piano
lover: 4 Sand (George)

chord
4 line 5 triad 6 tetrad 9 harmonize
sequence: 7 cadence

chore
3 job 4 duty, task 5 stint, trial 6 devoir, effort 8 taskwork 10 assignment 11 tribulation

choreograph
6 direct 7 arrange, compose

choreographer
American: 4 Feld (Elliot), Lang (Pearl) 5 Ailey (Alvin), Fosse (Bob), Shawn (Ted), Tharp (Twyla) 6 Fokine (Michel), Graham (Martha), Taylor (Paul), Tetley (Glen) 7 de Mille (Agnes), Massine (Leonide), Robbins (Jerome), Tamiris (Helen), Weidman (Charles) 8 Humphrey (Doris) 10 Balanchine (George), Cunningham (Merce)
English: 5 Tudor (Antony) 6 Ashton (Frederick), Weaver (John) 9 MacMillan (Kenneth)
French: 6 Béjart (Maurice), Perrot (Jules-Joseph), Petipa (Marius) 7 Noverre (Jean-Georges)
German: 5 Jooss (Kurt)
Mexican: 5 Limon (José)
Russian: 8 Nijinska (Bronislawa)

chorography
3 map 9 mapmaking

chortle
5 laugh, tehee 6 giggle, guffaw, hee-haw, titter 7 chuckle, snicker, sniggle

chorus
4 tune 6 accord 7 concert, concord, harmony 10 consonance

chorus girl
7 chorine

chosen
4 pick 5 elect 6 picked, select 8 selected 9 exclusive

Chou ___
5 En-Lai

chouse
3 gyp, jig 4 beat, bilk, play, ploy, ruse 5 cheat, cozen, feint, trick 6 diddle, gambit 7 defraud, gimmick, whizzer 8 artifice, flimflam

chow
4 feed, food, grub, meal 6 repast, viands 7 edibles, nurture 8 victuals 9 provender, refection 10 provisions 11 comestibles

chowchow
4 brew, hash, stew 5 mixed 6 jumble, medley, motley, relish, varied 7 mélange 8 assorted, mishmash, preserve 9 potpourri 10 hodgepodge, miscellany 11 promiscuous 12 conglomerate, multifarious 13 heterogeneous, miscellaneous

chowderhead
4 dope 5 dunce, noddy 6 noodle 7 schnook 9 lame-brain

chowhound
7 glutton 8 gourmand

chrism
3 oil 4 balm 5 cream, salve 6 cerate 7 unction, unguent 8 ointment

christen
3 dub 4 call, name, term 5 style, title 7 asperse, baptize, entitle, immerse 8 sprinkle 9 designate 10 denominate

christening
7 baptism

Christian
5 right 6 decent, proper, seemly 8 becoming, decorous 9 befitting, civilized
denomination: 6 Mormon, Quaker 7 Baptist 8 Anglican, Catholic, Lutheran 9 Calvinist, Methodist 12 Episcopalian
Eastern rite: 5 Uniat 6 Uniate
Egyptian: 4 Copt
love feast: 5 agape
martyr, first: 7 Stephen
symbol: 3 IHS 4 rood 5 cross 7 ichthus, ichthys

Christian Science founder
4 Eddy (Mary Baker)

___ Christie
6 Agatha

Christina's World painter
5 Wyeth (Andrew)

Christmas
4 Noel, Xmas, yule 8 Nativity, yuletide
symbol: 7 Yule log

Christmas Carol, A
author: 7 Dickens (Charles)
character: 7 Scrooge, Tiny Tim 8 Cratchit

Christogram
6 Chi-Rho

Christopher Robin creator
5 Milne (Alan Alexander)

chromatic
8 colorful 10 accidental

chromatin thread
7 spireme

chromium
symbol: 2 Cr

chromosome component
3 DNA 4 gene 8 telomere 10 centromere, chromomere

chronic
5 usual 6 wonted 7 routine 8 accepted, habitual 9 confirmed, customary 10 accustomed, habituated

chronicle
4 list 5 story 6 annals, record, relate, report 7 account, history, recital, version 8 describe 9 narration, narrative, recount

chronograph
5 watch 9 timepiece

chronometer
5 clock, watch 9 timepiece

chrysalis
4 pupa 8 covering

Chryseis
captor: 9 Agamemnon
father: 7 Chryses

Chrysippus
father: 6 Pelops
slayer: 6 Atreus 8 Thyestes

chthonian
6 Hadean 8 infernal, plutonic 9 plutonian, Tartarean 10 sulphurous

chubby
5 plump, podgy, pudgy, round, tubby 6 plumpy, rotund 8 plumpish, roly-poly 10 roundabout

chuck
4 cast, junk, quit, shed 5 chase, ditch, eject, evict, scrap 6 desert, reject, slough 7 abandon, boot out, discard, dismiss, extrude, forsake, kick out 8 jettison, renounce, throw out 9 throw away, throw over

chucker
7 bouncer 8 houseman

chuckle
5 laugh, tehee 6 giggle, guffaw, hee-haw, titter 7 chortle, snicker, sniggle

chucklehead
4 dope 5 dunce, noddy 6 noodle 7 schnook 9 lame-brain

chuff
4 boor, glum, ugly 5 churl, clown, hunks, miser, nabal, stiff, sulky, surly 6 gloomy, morose, mucker, sullen 7 crabbed, grobian, niggard, scrooge 8 muckworm 9 skinflint 10 clodhopper 12 moneygrubber

chum
3 pal 5 buddy, crony, cully 6 comate, friend 7 comrade 9 associate, companion 11 running mate

chumble
4 chew 5 champ, chomp, munch 6 crunch 7 scrunch 8 ruminate 9 masticate

chummy
4 cozy 5 close, pally, thick 8 familiar, intimate 10 buddy-buddy, palsy-walsy 12 confidential

chump
3 oaf, sap 4 boob, butt, chaw, chew, dolt, dupe, fool, goof, goon, gull, mark 5 booby, dunce, munch 6 crunch, pigeon, sucker 7 fall guy, fathead, gudgeon, scrunch 8 dolthead, lunkhead, ruminate 9 masticate

chunk
3 gob, wad 4 clod, hunk, lump 5 clump, hunch 6 nugget

chunky
5 dumpy, squat 6 chubby, rotund, stocky, stubby, stumpy 8 heavyset, thickset 11 thick-bodied

church
4 cult, fane, kirk, sect 5 creed, faith 6 temple 7 minster 8 basilica, reli-

gion **9** cathedral, communion, spiritual **10** connection, house of God, persuasion, tabernacle **12** denomination **13** house of prayer

adjunct: **6** belfry **7** steeple **9** bell tower

basin: **4** font **5** stoup

bench: **3** pew

bishop's: **9** cathedral

Buddhist: **2** ta **3** taa **6** pagoda

calendar: **4** ordo

caretaker: **6** sexton

chapel: **7** oratory

combining form: **7** ecclesi **8** ecclesio

council: **5** synod

court: **4** Rota **10** consistory

creed: **6** Nicene **8** Apostles'

district: **6** parish **7** diocese

father: **5** Basil **6** Jerome, Justin, Origen **7** Clement **8** Ignatius **9** Augustine **10** Chrysostom, Tertullian, theologian

fund-raiser: **6** bazaar

governing body: **5** curia **7** classis **10** consistory

head: **4** pope **7** pontiff

land: **5** grebe

law: **5** canon

member: **11** communicant

Muslim: **6** mosque

of a monastery: **7** minster

officer: **5** elder, vicar **6** beadle, deacon, sexton, verger, warden **9** presbyter, sacristan

part: **4** apse, bema, loft, nave **5** aisle, altar, choir **6** vestry **7** chancel, gallery, narthex, steeple **8** sacristy, transept **9** baptistry, sanctuary **10** baptistery, clerestory

porch: **6** parvis **7** galilee

pulpit: **4** ambo

reader: **6** lector

recess: **4** apse

revenue: **5** tithe

room: **6** vestry **8** sacristy

Scottish: **4** kirk

seat for clergy: **7** sedilia

service: **4** mass **6** matins **7** vespers **8** evensong **9** communion

small: **6** chapel

tribunal: **4** Rota

vault: **5** crypt

Churchill, Winston

daughter: **4** Mary **5** Diana, Sarah

father: **8** Randolph

mother: **6** Jennie

Order: **6** Garter

phrase: **11** Iron Curtain

son: **8** Randolph

trademark: **5** cigar

wife: **10** Clementine

church key

9 can opener

churchman

6 cleric, divine, parson, priest **8** clerical, minister, preacher, reverend **9** clergyman **12** ecclesiastic

churl

4 boor, clod **5** chuff, clown **6** mucker **7** grobian **10** clodhopper

churlish

4 curt, dour **5** blunt, crude, gruff, naive, surly **6** coarse, crusty **7** boorish, brusque, loutish, lowbred **8** cloddish, clownish **10** uncultured, unpolished, unschooled **11** clodhopping, uncivilized **12** discourteous

churn

4 boil, stir **6** bubble, seethe, simmer **7** ferment, smolder

Scottish: **4** kirn

chute

5 falls, sault, spout **7** cascade **8** cataract **9** waterfall

Chuza's wife

6 Joanna

CIA

predecessor: **3** OSS

cicatrix

4 scar **13** scarification

Cicero

forte: **7** oratory

target: **8** Catiline **10** Mark Antony

Cid

4 epic, hero, play, poem **5** opera

composer: **8** Massenet (Jules)

meaning: **4** lord

name: **4** Díaz (Rodrigo, Ruy) **5** Bivar

playwright: **9** Corneille (Pierre)

sword: **6** Colada, Tizona

wife: **6** Jimena, Ximena

cigar

4 toby **5** breva, stogy **6** concha, corona, Havana, Manila, stogie **7** bouquet, cheroot, culebra, Londres, regalia, trabuco **8** panatela, perfecto, pickwick, puritano **9** belvedere

case: **7** humidor

color: **5** claro **6** maduro **8** colorado

cigarette

3 cig, fag **4** butt **5** smoke **6** gasper **10** coffin nail

cigarfish

4 scad

cilium

4 hair, lash **7** eyelash **8** barbicel

combining form:

7 blephar **8** blepharo

cimmerian

7 avernal, hellish, stygian **8** infernal, plutonic **9** plutonian **11** pandemoniac

cinch

4 snap **5** setup **6** assure, breeze, ensure, insure, picnic, secure **8** duck soup, kid stuff, pushover **10** child's play

cinchona bark extract

7 quinine

cincture

4 band, belt, gird, sash **6** begird, engird, girdle **8** begirdle, engirdle **9** waistband

cinders

3 ash **5** ashes **8** clinkers

cinema

4 film, show **5** flick, movie **7** picture **9** photoplay **11** picture show **13** motion picture, moving picture

cinereous

4 gray **5** ashen

cinnabar

3 ore **7** mineral **9** vermilion

color: **3** red

cinnamon bark

6 cassia

cinnamon stone

6 garnet **8** essonite

cipher

3 zip **4** zero **5** aught, digit, ought, zilch **6** figure, naught, nobody, nought, number, reckon **7** chiffer, compute, integer, nothing, nullity, numeral, whiffet, whipster **8** estimate, goose egg, monogram, whipster **9** calculate, nonentity **11** whole number

ciphering

10 arithmetic **11** calculation, computation

circa

4 near, nigh **5** about **6** around, nearby **7** close on

circadian

5 daily **7** diurnal **9** quotidian

Circe

5 siren **9** sorceress

brother: **6** Aeetes

father: **3** Sol **6** Helios

home: **5** Aeaea

lover: **7** Ulysses **8** Odysseus

niece: **5** Medea

son: **5** Comus **9** Telegonus

Circean
6 luring 8 enticing, fetching, tempting

circinate
6 coiled

circle
3 hem, lot, mob, set 4 camp, clan, gird, gyre, halo, loop, push, ring, roll, turn 5 bunch, cabal, crowd, cycle, group, orbit, range, round, scope, wheel, whorl 6 begird, clique, corona, extent, girdle, gyrate, length, radius, rotary, rotate 7 compass, coterie, cronies, environ, friends, ingroup, revolve, rondure 8 comrades, encircle, surround 9 camarilla, dimension, encompass, extension, extensity, intimates 10 associates, circumduct, companions 12 acquaintance
bisector: 8 diameter
colored: 6 areola, areole
combining form: 3 gyr 4 cycl, gyro 5 cyclo
graph: 8 pie chart
luminous: 4 aura, halo 6 corona, nimbus 7 aureola, aureole
part: 3 arc 6 sector 8 quadrant
small: 4 disk 7 annulet 8 roundlet

circlet
4 band, ring 8 bracelet, headband
for head or helmet: 7 coronal, coronel

circuit
3 way 4 gyre, loop, tour, trip, turn 5 ambit, round, route, wheel, whirl 6 course, league 7 compass, journey, travels 8 gyration, rotation 9 perimeter, periphery, round trip 10 conference, revolution, roundabout 11 association, circulation 13 circumference

circuitous
7 oblique 8 circular, indirect 10 collateral, roundabout

circuit rider
9 clergyman

circular
4 bill 5 flier, flyer, gyral, round 7 annular, cycloid, discoid 8 handbill 10 circuitous
file: 11 wastebasket
motion: 4 eddy, gyre, spin 5 whirl 8 gyration, rotation 10 revolution
plate: 4 disc, dish, disk

circularize
4 poll 9 publicize

circulate
4 flow 5 strew 6 rotate, set off,

spread 7 actuate, diffuse, radiate, revolve 8 disperse, exchange, mobilize 9 propagate 10 distribute 11 disseminate, interchange

circulation
4 gyre, turn 5 round, wheel, whirl 7 circuit 8 gyration, rotation 10 revolution

circulator
6 gossip 8 gossiper, quidnunc 9 carrytale 10 newsmonger 11 rumormonger 12 gossipmonger

circumambulate
4 roam, rove 5 drift, mooch, range, stray 6 ramble, wander 7 meander 8 straggle

circumciser
5 mohel

circumcision
Jewish: 5 Berit, Brith 10 Brith Milah

circumference
3 rim 5 ambit 6 border, bounds, limits, margin 7 circuit, compass 8 boundary, confines 9 perimeter, periphery

circumflex
9 diacritic

circumfuse
7 envelop 8 surround

circumjacent
11 surrounding

circumlocution
8 pleonasm, verbiage 9 tautology, verbality 10 periphrase, redundancy, roundabout 11 periphrasis 13 circumambages

circumnavigate
5 skirt 6 bypass, detour 10 circumvert

circumnavigator
4 Cook (James) 5 Drake (Francis) 8 Magellan (Ferdinand), van Noort (Oivier) 9 Cavendish (Thomas)

circumscribe
3 bar 5 limit 6 fetter, hamper 7 confine, delimit, trammel 8 prelimit, restrict 10 delimitate

circumscribed
5 bound, fixed 6 finite, narrow, strait 7 bounded, cramped, precise 8 definite 11 determinate

circumscription
5 cramp, stint 9 restraint, stricture 10 constraint, limitation 11 confinement, restriction 12 ball and chain 13 constrainment

circumspect
4 safe, wary 5 chary 7 careful, guarded 8 cautious, discreet, gingerly 10 meticulous, scrupulous 11 calculating, considerate, punctilious

circumstance
4 fate, item 5 event, moira, thing 6 detail, factor, kismet 7 destiny, element, episode, portion 8 incident, occasion 9 component, happening 10 occurrence, particular 11 constituent

circumstantial
4 full, nice 5 close, exact 6 minute, strict 7 precise, replete 8 accurate, complete, detailed, itemized, thorough 9 clocklike 10 blow-by-blow, particular

circumvent
4 balk, beat, bilk, dash, dupe, foil, ruin 5 avoid, burke, elude, evade, skirt, trick 6 baffle, befool, bypass, detour, escape, thwart 8 hoodwink, outflank, sidestep 9 frustrate 10 disappoint

circumvolution
4 gyre, turn 5 round, wheel, whirl 7 circuit 8 gyration, rotation 10 revolution 11 circulation

circus
4 ring 5 arena 6 big top, cirque 9 spectacle 12 amphitheater
animal: 4 bear, flea, lion, seal 5 horse, tiger 8 elephant
attraction: 5 freak 8 sideshow
owner: 6 Bailey, Barnum 8 Ringling
performer: 5 clown, tamer 7 acrobat, athlete, juggler, tumbler 9 aerialist, fire eater
worker: 7 rouster 10 roustabout

citadel
4 fort 7 redoubt 8 fastness, fortress 10 stronghold
of Carthage: 5 Bursa, Byrsa
Russian: 7 kremlin

citation
5 award 6 eulogy, reward 7 guerdon, tribute 8 encomium 9 panegyric 10 salutation

cite
4 name, tell 5 count, offer, quote 6 adduce, allege, number, recall, remind, retain, revive 7 advance, bethink, mention, present, specify 8 instance, remember 9 enumerate, recollect, reminisce 10 retrospect

citizen
5 towny 6 towner 7 burgess,

burgher, subject, townman **8** national, townsman

Citizen Kane director
6 Welles (Orson)

citron
4 tree **5** melon **6** yellow

citrus
family: **3** rue **8** Rutaceae
fruit: **4** lime **5** lemon **6** citron, orange **7** kumquat, tangelo **8** bergamot, mandarin, shaddock **9** tangerine **10** grapefruit

city
4 burg **5** urban **7** burghal **9** municipal
Alamo: **10** San Antonio
combining form: **5** polis
Eternal: **4** Rome
French: **5** ville
heavenly: **4** Sion, Zion
Latin: **4** urbs
Motor: **7** Detroit
of Bells: **10** Strasbourg
of Bridges: **6** Bruges
of Brotherly Love: **12** Philadelphia
of David: **9** Jerusalem
official: **5** mayor **7** manager **8** alderman **10** councilman
of God: **6** heaven **8** paradise
of Gold: **8** Eldorado
of Kings: **4** Lima
of Lights: **5** Paris
of Lilies: **8** Florence
of Masts: **6** London
of Rams: **6** Canton
of Refuge: **6** Medina
of Saints: **8** Montreal
of Seven Hills: **4** Rome
of the dead: **10** Necropolis
of Victory: **5** Cairo
planner: **8** urbanist
section: **4** slum, ward **5** block, plaza **6** barrio, ghetto, square, uptown **8** business, downtown, red-light **11** residential
slicker: **4** dude
windy: **7** Chicago

city-state
Greek: **5** polis **6** poleis (plural)

city, town, village
(see also **capital**) *Afghanistan:* **5** Balkh, Farah, Herat, Kushk
Alabama: **3** Opp **4** Arab, Boaz, Elba **5** Eutaw, Selma **6** Dothan, Mobile **7** Decatur, Florala **8** Prichard **10** Birmingham, Huntsville, Tuscaloosa
Alaska: **5** Kenai, Sitka **6** Bethel, Kodiak, Valdez **9** Anchorage, Fairbanks, Ketchikan

Albania: **4** Fier **5** Berat, Korce, Kukes, Vlore
Alberta: **4** Olds **5** Hanna, Leduc, Taber **7** Calgary **10** Lethbridge
Algeria: **4** Oran **5** Batna, Blida, Medea, Saida, Setif **6** Annaba, Bechar
Argentina: **4** Azul, Goya **5** Junin, Lanus, Lujan, Merlo, Salta, Tigre **6** Parana **7** Cordoba, La Plata, Mendoza, Rosario, San Juan, Santa Fe **11** Bahia Blanca
Arizona: **3** Ajo **4** Eloy, Mesa,Yuma **5** Globe, Tempe **6** Tucson **7** Sun City, Winslow **8** Glendale, Prescott **9** Flagstaff **10** Casa Grande, Scottsdale
Arkansas: **4** Mena **5** Beebe, Cabot, Earle, Ozark, Wynne **9** Fort Smith, Pine Bluff, Texarkana
Australia: **3** Ayr **5** Dalby, Dubbo, Unley **8** Randwick **9** Bankstown, Blacktown, Newcastle **10** Kalgoorlie, Parramatta, Sutherland, Wollongong **12** Alice Springs
Austria: **4** Enns, Graz, Linz, Wels **5** Lienz, Steyr, Traun **8** Salzburg **9** Innsbruck **10** Klagenfurt
Azerbaijan: **8** Gyandzha
Bangladesh: **5** Bogra, Pabna **6** Khulna **10** Chittagong
Belarus: **5** Brest, Gomel, Mazyr, Pinsk **6** Grodno **7** Mogilev, Vitebsk
Belgium: **3** Ath, Hal, Huy, Mol **4** Amay, Dour, Geel, Genk, Gent, Hoei, Luik, Mons, Vise **5** Aalst, Arlon, Diest, Dison, Eupen, Evere, Ghent, Gilly, Halle, Hamme, Hornu, Ieper, Jette, Jumet, Leuze, Liege, Menen, Namen, Namur, Ronse, Theux, Thuin, Uccle, Ukkel, Wavre, Ypres **6** Bruges **7** Antwerp
Bolivia: **5** Oruro, Uyuni **9** Santa Cruz **10** Cochabamba
Bosnia and Herzegovina: **5** Bihac, Brcko, Jajce, Tuzla **8** Sarajevo
Botswana: **4** Maun **5** Kanye
Brazil: **4** Codo, Para **5** Bahia, Bauru, Belem, Ceara, Natal **6** Campos, Canoas, Caxias, Ilheus, Maceio, Manaus, Olinda, Recife, Santos **7** Aracaju, Caruaru, Goiania, Jundiai, Marilia, Niteroi, Pelotas, Sao Luis, Uberaba, Vitoria **8** Campinas, Colatina, Curitiba, Londrina, Salvador, Santarem, Sao Paulo, Sorocaba, Teresina **9** Caratinga, Fortaleza, Guarulhos, Rio Grande **10** Guarapuava, Joao Pessoa, Juiz de Fora, Nova Iguacu, Pernambuco, Petropolis, Piraci-

caba, Santa Maria, Santo Andre, Uberlandia **11** Campo Grande, Caxias do Sul, Ponta Grossa, Porto Alegre **12** Montes Claros, Rio de Janeiro, Teofilo Otoni, Volta Redonda **13** Belo Horizonte, Campina Grande, Duque de Caxias, Florianopolis, Mogi das Cruzes, Riberiao Preto
British Columbia: **5** Comox **9** Vancouver
Bulgaria: **3** Lom **4** Ruse **5** Varna, Vidin **6** Burgas **7** Plovdiv **11** Stara Zagora
Burkina Faso: **13** Bobo Dioulasso
California: **4** Brea, Galt, Lodi, Ojai **5** Arvin, Azusa, Ceres, Chico, Chino, Dixon, Hemet, Indio, Norco, Ripon, Ukiah, Wasco, Yreka **6** Downey, Encino, Fresno, Oxnard, Pomona, Sonoma **7** Anaheim, Burbank, Compton, Fremont, Hayward, Modesto, Oakland, San Jose, Seaside, Soledad, Van Nuys **8** Berkeley, Glendale, Palo Alto, Pasadena, San Diego, Santa Ana, Stockton, Torrance, Yuba City **9** El Segundo, Hollywood, Long Beach, Menlo Park, Riverside, Sausalito **10** Carmichael, Chowchilla, Chula Vista, Culver City, Los Angeles, Pismo Beach, San Leandro, Santa Clara **11** Bakersfield, Laguna Beach, Pebble Beach, Redwood City, San Clemente, Santa Monica **12** Beverly Hills, Mission Viejo, Redondo Beach, San Francisco, Santa Barbara **13** San Bernardino, San Luis Obispo
Cameroon: **4** Buea, Edea **5** Kribi, Lomie **6** Douala
Canada: **5** Banff, Edson, Hanna, Leduc, Rouyn **6** Regina **7** Calgary, Halifax, Toronto, Windsor **8** Hamilton, Montreal, Moose Jaw, Victoria, Winnipeg **9** Saint John, Saskatoon, Vancouver **10** Lethbridge, Saint Johns, Sherbrooke, Thunder Bay, Whitehorse **11** Fredericton, Yellowknife **12** Peterborough **13** Charlottetown, Trois Rivieres
Central African Republic: **5** Bouar
Chad: **4** Sarh
Chile: **4** Lebu, Lota, Tome **5** Ancud, Angol, Arica, Maipu, Penco, Rengo, Talca **10** Concepcion, Talcahuano, Valparaiso **11** Antofagasta
China: **4** Amoy, Jian, Luan, Yaan **5** Hefei, Jilin, Jinan, Lhasa, Qinan, Ssuan, Wuhan, Yenan, Yibin, Yumen **6** Andong, Anqing, Anshan,

Anshun, Anyang, Beihai, Canton, Datong, Foshan, Fushun, Guilin, Haikou, Handan, Harbin, Hoihao, Jilong, Luzhou, Mukden, Ningbo, Pengbu, Suzhou, Urumqi, Xiamen, Xuzhou, Yanggu, Yichun, Yining, Zhangi, Zhaoan **7** Baoding, Changan, Chengdu, Dandong, Guiyang, Huainan, Jiamusi, Jiaxing, Kaifeng, Kunming, Luoshan, Luoyang, Nanking, Nanning, Shantou, Taiyuan, Wanxian, Weifang, Yizhang **8** Changchi, Changsha, Dangshan, Hangzhou, Hanzhong, Hengyang, Huangshi, Jiangmen, Jiujiang, Kueiyang, Liaoyang, Nanchang, Shanghai, Shangrao, Shaoyang, Tianshui, Zhenjiang **9** Changchun, Chenjiang, Chongqing, Chungking, Huangshih, Zhenjiang **10** Jingdezhen, Laojunmiao **11** Qinhuangdao, Zhangjiakou
Colombia: 4 Buga, Cali **5** Bello, Mocoa, Neiva, Ocana, Pasto, Tulua, Tunja **6** Cucuta, Ibague **7** Cienaga, Palmira, Pereira **8** Medellin, Monteria **9** Cartagena, Manizales **10** Santa Marta **11** Bucaramanga **12** Barranquilla
Colorado: 5 Craig **6** Arvada, Salida **7** Alamosa, Durango, Greeley, La Junta **8** Brighton, Gunnison, Lakewood, Longmont, Loveland, Montrose, Thornton **9** Englewood, Estes Park, Leadville, Littleton, Rocky Ford **10** Broomfield, Castle Rock, Fort Lupton, Fort Morgan, Monte Vista, Northglenn, Walsenburg, Wheat Ridge **11** Fort Collins **13** Grand Junction
Connecticut: 5 Byram **6** Bethel, Bolton, Darien, Easton, Granby, Groton, Haddam, Hamden, Moosup, Somers, Weston **7** Ansonia, Bethany, Danbury, Enfield, Ledyard, Meriden, Milford, Newtown, Niantic, Norwalk, Norwich, Old Lyme, Pomfret, Seymour, Tolland, Windham, Winsted, Wolcott **8** Branford, Cromwell, East Lyme, Guilford, New Haven, Simsbury, Stamford, Suffield, Westport **9** Danielson, Deep River, East Haven, Ellington, Greenwich, Harwinton, Killingly, Montville, New Canaan, Newington, New London, Pawcatuck, Rocky Hill, Southbury, Thomaston, Waterbury, Waterford, West Haven **10** Bridgeport, Brookfield, East Granby, East Haddam, Farmington, Gales Ferry, Kensington, Litchfield, New Britain, New Mil-

ford, North Haven, Plainville, Ridgefield, Stonington, Terryville, Torrington **11** Beacon Falls, East Norwalk, East Windsor, Forestville, Glastonbury, Marlborough, Middlefield, Old Saybrook, Southington, Wallingford, Willimantic **12** Collinsville, East Hartford, New Fairfield, South Norwalk, South Windsor, West Hartford, Wethersfield, Windsor Locks **13** North Branford, Thompsonville
Croatia: 4 Pula **5** Sisak, Zadar **6** Rijeka, Zagreb **9** Dubrovnic
Cuba: 5 Banes, Bauta **7** Holguin **8** Camaguey, Marianao, Matanzas **10** Cienfuegos
Cyprus: 7 Kyrenia, Larnaca **8** Limassol **9** Famagusta
Czech Republic: 4 Brno, Cheb **5** Decin, Opava, Pisek, Plzen, Tabor **7** Ostrava
Delaware: 5 Lewes **7** Seaford **10** Harrington, Wilmington
Denmark: 5 Arhus, Skive, Vejle **6** Alborg, Odense, Viborg **13** Frederiksberg
Dominican Republic: 4 Azua, Bani, Moca **5** Cotui, Nagua, Neiba
Ecuador: 4 Loja **5** Canar, Daule, Manta, Pinas **9** Guayaquil
Egypt: 4 Giza, Idfu, Isna, Qena **5** Asyut, Benha, Disuq, Girga, Luxor, Minuf, Tahta, Tanta **6** Helwan **7** El Arish, Zagazig **8** Damanhur, Damietta, El Faiyum, Ismailia, Port Said
Eire: 4 Athy, Birr, Cobh, Naas, Tuam **5** Ennis, Sligo **6** Carlow, Galway, Tralee **7** Dundalk, Kildare, Wexford, Wicklow **8** Kilkenny, Monaghan **9** Castlebar, Killarney, Tipperary, Waterford **10** Balbriggan
England: 4 Bath, Eton, Hove, Ryde, York **5** Bacup, Brent, Brigg, Colne, Corby, Cowes, Egham, Eling, Esher, Eston, Goole, Leeds, Leigh, Lewes, Luton, Oadby, Poole, Ryton, Wigan **6** Bexley, Bolton, Dudley, Merton, Oldham, Torbay, Warley, Welwyn **7** Bristol, Bromley, Croydon, Hackney, Ipswich, Malvern, Norwich, Salford, Seaford, Walsall **8** Abingdon, Basildon, Brighton, Coventry, Hastings, Hatfield, Havering, Hertford, Lewisham, Plymouth, Wallsend **9** Aylesbury, Blackpool, Islington, Leicester, Liverpool, Sheffield **10** Birkenhead, Canterbury, Colchester, Manchester, Nottingham, Portsmouth, Sunderland

11 Bournemouth, Northampton, Southampton **12** Peterborough, Stoke-on-Trent, West Bromwich **13** Melton Mowbray, Middlesbrough, Southend-on-Sea, Wolverhampton
Estonia: 5 Parnu, Tartu
Ethiopia: 5 Aksum, Harar **6** Asmara **8** Dire Dawa
Finland: 4 Kemi, Oulu, Pori **5** Espoo, Hango, Kotka, Lahti, Rauma, Turku, Vaasa **7** Tampere
Florida: 4 Leto, Mims, Ojus, Tice **5** Dania, Davie, Largo, Miami, Ocala, Ocoee, Oneco, Tampa **6** DeLand **7** Hialeah, Key West, Orlando **8** Gulfport, Key Largo, Lakeland, Sarasota **9** Boca Raton, Bradenton, Fort Myers, Hollywood, Kissimmee, Palm Beach, Pensacola, Vero Beach **10** Clearwater, Cocoa Beach, Fort Pierce, Miami Beach, Titusville **11** Coral Gables, Gainesville, Key Biscayne, St. Augustine, Winter Haven **12** Apalachicola, Daytona Beach, Ft. Lauderdale, Jacksonville, Pompano Beach, St. Petersburg **13** Chattahoochee
France: 3 Dax, Pau **4** Agde, Agen, Albi, Ales, Auch, Caen, Gien, Laon, Lyon, Metz, Orly, Reze, Sens, Sete, Vire **5** Arles, Arras, Auray, Auton, Avion, Berck, Blois, Bondy, Brest, Creil, Digne, Dijon, Douai, Dreux, Flers, Gagny, Laval, LePuy, Lille, Lunel, Meaux, Melun, Muret, Nimes, Niort, Noyon, Reims, Revin, Rodez, Rouen, Royan, Tours, Tulle, Vichy, Vitre **6** Amiens, Angers, Calais, Cannes, Evreux, LeMans, Nantes, Nevers, Rennes, Thiers, Toulon **7** Ajaccio, Avignon, Bethune, Bourges, LeHavre, Limoges, Lorient, Lourdes, Orleans, Roubaix **8** Bordeaux, Gentilly, Grenoble, Toulouse **9** Cherbourg, Le Creusot, Marseille, Montreuil **10** Draguignan, Strasbourg, Versailles **11** Montpellier **12** Saint Etienne **13** Aix en Provence
Georgia: 4 Adel, Alma, Arco **5** Jesup, Macon, McRae **7** Calhoun **8** Americus, Marietta, Savannah, Valdosta **9** Brunswick
Georgia, Republic of: 6 Batumi **7** Kutaisi, Sukhumi, Tbilisi
Germany: 3 Aue, Hof, Ulm **4** Gera, Goch, Hamm, Jena, Kehl, Kiel, Koln, Marl, Suhl **5** Aalen, Ahlen, Borna, Bruhl, Calbe, Celle, Duren, Emden, Essen, Forst, Fulda, Furth, Gotha, Greiz, Hagen, Halle, Ha-

nau, Herne, Hurth, Kleve, Lemgo, Lobau, Mainz, Neuss, Peine, Pirna, Riesa, Stade, Thale, Trier, Wesel, Zeitz **6** Aachen, Bremen, Coburg, Dachau, Dessau, Erfurt, Kassel, Lubeck, Munich, Rheydt **7** Cologne, Dresden, Koblenz, Krefeld, Leipzig, Munchen, Munster, Potsdam, Rostock, Zwickau **8** Augsburg, Bayreuth, Chemnitz, Cuxhaven, Dortmund, Duisburg, Hannover, Mannheim, Nurnburg, Wurzburg **9** Bielefeld, Brunswick, Darmstadt, Karlsruhe, Magdeburg, Nuremburg, Oldenburg, Osnabruck, Remscheid, Stuttgart, Wiesbaden, Wuppertal **10** Baden Baden, Dusseldorf, Heidelberg, Oberhausen, Regensburg, Salz·gitter **11** Brandenburg, Bremerhaven, Saarbrucken **12** Braunschweig **13** Gelsenkirchen
Ghana: 2 Wa **4** Axim, Keta, Tema **5** Lawra, Yendi **6** Kumasi
Greece: 3 Kos **4** Arta **5** Argos, Lamia, Nemea, Volos **6** Sparta **7** Corinth **12** Thessaloniki
Guatemala: 5 Coban
Guinea: 4 Labe
Hawaii: 4 Aiea, Hilo, Laie **5** Kapaa, Lihue, Maili **6** Kailua **7** Kaneohe, Wailuku
Honduras: 5 Danli
Hong Kong: 7 Kowloon
Hungary: 3 Ozd **4** Eger, Gyor, Pecs **5** Abony, Bekes **6** Szeged **7** Miskolc **8** Debrecen
Idaho: 4 Buhl **5** Nampa **6** Driggs, Dubois, Weiser **7** Gooding, Orofino, Payette, Rexburg **8** Caldwell **9** Blackfoot, Pocatello, Sandpoint, Twin Falls **11** Coeur d' Alene, Grangeville, Saint Maries, Soda Springs **12** Bonners Ferry, Mountain Home, Saint Anthony **13** American Falls
Illinois: 4 Dupo, Pana **5** Aledo, Alsip, Alton, Carmi, Elgin, Galva, Lacon, Niles, Olney, Pekin, Plano, Posen **6** Albion, Cicero, DeKalb, Galena, Hardin, Joliet, Macomb, Moline, Paxton, Peoria, Skokie, Toulon, Urbana **7** Chicago, Decatur, Glencoe, Oak Lawn, Oquawka, Tuscola, Watseka, Wheaton **8** Carthage, Evanston, Golconda, Hennepin, Kankakee, La Grange, Monmouth, Rockford, Vandalia, Waukegan **9** Belvidere, Effingham, Galesburg, Park Ridge, Rushville, Yorkville **10** Belleville, Carbondale, Carrollton, Des Plaines, Metropolis, Northbrook,

Rock Island **11** Carlinville, Jerseyville, Lindenhurst, McLeansboro, Murphysboro, Shawneetown, Taylorville **12** Edwardsville, Highland Park, Mount Carroll **13** Lawrenceville, Mount Sterling, Pinckneyville
India: 3 Mau **4** Agra, Ahwa, Bhuj, Durg, Gaya, Kota, Mhow, Puri, Rewa, Tonk, Ziro **5** Adoni, Aimer, Akola, Alwar, Arcot, Arrah, Banda, Barsi, Bidar, Bihar, Churu, Damoh, Delhi, Dewas, Eluru, Gonda, Jalna, Jammu, Karur, Miraj, Morvi, Nasik, Patan, Patna, Poona, Sagar, Satna, Sikar, Simla, Surat, Thana **6** Baroda, Bhopal, Bombay, Guntur, Howrah, Jaipur, Jhansi, Kanpur, Meerut, Mysore, Nagpur, Raipur, Rajkot, Ranchi, Ujjain **7** Aligarh, Asansol, Belgaum, Bikaner, Burdwan, Cuttack, Gauhati, Gwalior, Jodhpur, Kurnool, Lucknow, Madurai, Mathura, Nellore, Patiala, Vellore **8** Alleppey, Amravati, Amritsar, Bareilly, Bhatpara, Calcutta, Dehra Dun, Jabalpur, Jamnagar, Kakinada, Kolhapur, Ludhiana, Malegaon, Sholapur, Srinagar, Varanasi **9** Ahmadabad, Allahabad, Bangalore, Bhagalpur, Bhavnagar, Darbhanga, Gorakhpur, Hyderabad, Jullundur, Kamarhati, Mangalore, Moradabad, Nagercoil, Thanjavur, Tuticorin **10** Ahmadnagar, Chandigarh, Coimbatore, Jamshedpur, Saharanpur, Trivandrum, Ulhashagar, Vijayawada **11** Garden Reach, Muzaffarpur, Rajahmundry **12** Hubli Dharwar, Secunderabad, Shahjahanpur **13** Machilipatnam
Indiana: 5 Berne, Paoli, Vevay **6** Delphi, Kokomo, Marlon, Muncie, Tipton **7** Bedford, Corydon, Elkhart, La Porte, Winamac **8** Bluffton, Kentland **9** Boonville, Cannelton, Fort Wayne, New Albany, Rushville, South Bend, Vincennes **10** Brookville, Brownstown, Crown Point, Evansville, Logansport, Scottsburg, Terre Haute, Valparaiso **11** Greencastle, Noblesville, Shelbyville **12** Connersville, Lawrenceburg, Martinsville
Indonesia: 4 Pati **5** Bogor, Garut, Kudus, Medan, Tegal, Turen **6** Batang, Kediri, Madiun, Malang, Manado, Padang **7** Bandung **8** Semarang, Surabaja, Tjirebon **9** Palembang, Pontianak, Surakarta **10** Pekalongan **11** Tasikmalaja **12** Bandjarmasin
Iowa: 4 Adel, Tama **5** Albia, Clive, Onawa, Pella **6** Algona, Cresco,

Eldora, Harlan, Keokuk, Le Mars, Red Oak, Sibley, Waukon **7** Allison, Anamosa, Carroll, Clinton, Corydon, Creston, Decorah, Denison, Dubuque, Elkader, Marengo, Osceola, Ottumwa, Wapello, Waverly **8** Camanche, Chariton, Clarinda, Ida Grove, Mount Ayr, Primghar **9** Davenport, Fort Dodge, Indianola, Keosauqua, Maquoketa, Muscatine, Oskaloosa, Storm Lake, West Union, Winterset **10** Emmetsburg, New Hampton, Rock Rapids, Spirit Lake **11** Cedar Rapids, Estherville, Fort Madison **12** Grundy Center **13** Council Bluffs, Guthrie Center
Iran: 3 Qum **4** Amul, Arak, Khoi, Sari, Yazd, Yezd **5** Ahwaz, Babol, Rasht **6** Abadan, Meshed, Shiraz, Tabriz **7** Esfahan, Hamadan, Isfahan, Mashhad
Iraq: 3 Ana, Kut **5** Amara, Basra, Erbil, Hilla, Mosul, Rutba **6** Kirkuk **7** An Najaf
Ireland: (see Eire, above)
Israel: 5 Afula, Haifa, Holon **8** Nazareth, Ramat Gan **9** Beersheba
Italy: 4 Acri, Alba, Asti, Atri, Bari, Enna, Este, Fano, Gela, Iesi, Lodi, Lugo, Pisa **5** Adria, Agira, Anzio, Aosta, Arola, Cantu, Capua, Carpi, Crema, Cuneo, Eboli, Fermo, Fondi, Forli, Gaeta, Imola, Ivrea, Lecce, Lecco, Lucca, Massa, Melfi, Menfi, Monza, Padua, Parma, Prato, Siena, Turin **6** Assisi, Foggia, Modena, Naples, Rimini, Venice, Verona **7** Bergamo, Bolzano, Brescia, Catania, Leghorn, Palermo, Pescara, Salerno, Taranto, Trieste **8** Cagliari, La Spezia, Piacenza
Ivory Coast: 6 Bouake
Jamaica: 6 May Pen **10** Montego Bay
Japan: 3 Ina, Ise, Ito, Ota, Tsu, Ube, Uji, Yao **4** Ageo, Anan, Gifu, Hagi, Himi, Hofu, Iida, Joyo, Kaga, Kobe, Kofu, Kure, Miki, Mito, Naha, Nara, Noda, Oita, Otsu, Saga, Saku, Soka, Tosu, Ueda, Yono **5** Akita, Atami, Beppu, Chiba, Chofu, Daito, Fukui, Hanno, Hyuga, Imari, Itami, Iwaki, Iwata, Izumi, Izumo, Kiryu, Kochi, Kyoto, Minoo, Odate, Ogaki, Okawa, Okaya, Omiya, Omuta, Osaka, Otaru, Oyama, Sabae, Saiki, Sanjo, Suita, Tenri, Urawa, Yaizu, Zushi **6** Akashi, Aomori, Himeji, Kadoma, Kurume, Matsue, Mitaka, Nagano, Nagoya, Numazu, Sa-

sebo, Suzuka, Toyama, Yonago **7** Fukuoka, Hitachi, Ibaraki, Imabari, Iwakuni, Kawagoe, Kodaira, Kushiro, Machida, Matsudo, Morioka, Muroran, Niigata, Niihama, Nobeoka, Obihiro, Odawara, Okayama, Okazaki, Sapporo, Shimizu, Takaoka, Tottori **8** Ashikaga, Fujisawa, Fukuyama, Hachioji, Hakodate, Hirakata, Hirosaki, Ichihara, Ichikawa, Kakogawa, Kamakura, Kanazawa, Kawasaki, Koriyama, Kumagaya, Kumamoto, Maebashi, Miyazaki, Nagasaki, Neyagawa, Onomichi, Shizuoka, Takasaki, Toyonaka, Wakayama, Yamagata, Yokohama, Yokosuka **9** Amagasaki, Asahikawa, Chigasaki, Fukushima, Funabashi, Hachinohe, Hamamatsu, Hiratsuka, Hiroshima, Kagoshima, Kawaguchi, Kishiwada, Koshigaya, Kurashiki, Matsubara, Matsumoto, Matsusaka, Matsuyama, Moriguchi, Musashino, Tachikawa, Takamatsu, Takatsuki, Tokushima, Tomakomai, Toyohashi, Yamaguchi, Yokkaichi **10** Ichinomiya, Ishinomaki, Kitakyushu, Miyakonojo, Takarazuka, Utsunomiya, Yatsushiro **11** Nishinomiya, Shimonoseki
12 Higashiosaka
13 Aizuwakamatsu
Jordan: **5** Irbid **6** Nablus
Kansas: **4** Gove, Iola **5** Colby, Hoxie, Lakin, Leoti, Paola, Pratt **6** Atwood, Beloit, Girard, Holton, Larned, Olathe, Salina **7** Abilene, Dighton, Emporia, Garnett, Hugoton, Jetmore, Kinsley, Mankato, Oberlin, Osborne, Wichita **8** Cimarron, Goodland, La Crosse, Sublette, Wakeeney **9** Coldwater, Fort Scott, Great Bend, Oskaloosa **10** Clay Center, Hutchinson **11** Leavenworth, Smith Center, Yates Center **12** Council Grove, Overland Park **13** Medicine Lodge, Sharon Springs
Kazakhstan: **6** Guryev, Uralsk **8** Balkhash, Chimkent, Dzhambul, Kyzl Orda, Pavlodar **9** Karaganda **10** Aktyubinsk **11** Tselinograd **13** Petropavlovsk, Semipalatinsk
Kentucky: **4** Inez **5** Cadiz, Hyden, McKee **6** Elkton, Harlan **7** Ashland, Campton, Greenup, Hickman, Hindman, Owenton, Paducah, Stanton **8** Bardwell, Carlisle, Fort Knox, La Grange, Mayfield **9** Bardstown, Covington, Cynthiana, Eddyville, Lexington, Maysville, Owensboro, Pikeville, Pineville, Smithland, Southgate,

Vanceburg, Wickliffe **10** Booneville, Frenchburg, Hawesville, Louisville, Whitesburg **11** Beattyville, Brooksville, Burkesville, Hardinsburg, Harrodsburg, Hodgenville, Leitchfield, Morganfield, Mount Olivet, Owingsville, Paintsville, Scottsville, West Liberty **12** Barbourville, Bowling Green, Catlettsburg, Flemingsburg, Hopkinsville, Madisonville, Munfordville, Prestonsburg, Russellville, Salyersville, Taylorsville **13** Elizabethtown, Mount Sterling, Nicholasville, Tompkinsville
Kenya: **4** Embu **5** Nyeri **6** Kisumu, Nakuru **7** Mombasa
Kyrgyzstan: **3** Osh **5** Naryn
Laos: **5** Pakse **11** Savannakhet **12** Luang Prabang
Latvia: **9** Ventspils **10** Daugavpils
Lebanon: **5** Sidon, Zahle
Libya: **4** Homs **5** Derna, Zawia **6** Tobruk **8** Benghazi
Lithuania: **6** Kaunas **8** Klaipeda
Louisiana: **4** Jena **5** Amite, Arabi, Houma, Mamou, Norco, Rayne **6** Colfax, Edgard, Gretna, Minden, Ruston **7** Arcadia, Bastrop, Marrero, Oberlin **8** Bogalusa, De Ridder, Metairie, New Roads, Oak Grove, Westwego **9** Abbeville, Chalmette, Coushatta, Hahnville, Leesville, New Iberia, Opelousas, Port Allen, Thibodaux, Winnfield, Winnsboro **10** Marksville, New Orleans, Plaquemine, Shreveport **11** Farmerville, Franklinton, Lake Charles, Ponchatoula, Ville Platte **12** Natchitoches **13** Napoleonville
Macedonia: **4** Stip **5** Debar, Ohrid **6** Skopje
Madagascar: **8** Tamatave **9** Antsirane, Mahajanga **11** Antsiranana **12** Fianarantsoa
Maine: **4** Milo, Saco **5** Eliot, Orono **6** Auburn, Bangor, Gorham **7** Berwick, Houlton, Kittery, Machias, Rumford **8** Lewiston, Portland, Rockland **9** Bar Harbor, Biddeford, Brunswick, Ellsworth, Kennebunk, Skowhegan, Wiscasset **10** South Paris **11** Millinocket, Presque Isle **13** South Portland
Malawi: **5** Zomba **8** Blantyre
Malaysia: **4** Ipoh **5** Gemas, Klang **6** Kelang, Penang, Pinang **11** Johore Bahru
Mali: **5** Kayes, Mopti, Segou **7** Sikasso
Maryland: **5** Bowie **6** Denton, Elkton, Towson **8** Bethesda, Landover, Snow Hill **9** Baltimore, Rockville

10 Beltsville, Hagerstown **11** Chestertown, College Park, Leonardtown **12** Havre de Grace, Silver Spring **13** Upper Marlboro
Massachusetts: **4** Ayer **5** Acton, Athol, Lenox, Salem **6** Agawam, Boston, Dedham, Hadley, Ludlow, Malden, Monson, Natick, Saugus, Woburn **7** Danvers, Duxbury, Holyoke, Hyannis, Medford, Methuen, Needham, Raynham, Seekonk, Swansea, Taunton, Walpole, Waltham, Wareham **8** Brockton, Chicopee, Falmouth, Plymouth, Rockport, Scituate, Somerset, Uxbridge, Yarmouth **9** Attleboro, Braintree, Brookline, Deerfield, Edgartown, Fall River, Fitchburg, Haverhill, Lexington, Southwick, Tewksbury, Westfield, Wilbraham, Worcester **10** Barnstable, Framingham, Gloucester, Greenfield, Leominster, Longmeadow, New Bedford, North Adams, Swampscott, Winchendon **11** Belchertown, Easthampton, Northampton, South Hadley, Springfield **12** Mattapoisett, Provincetown, Turners Falls, West Yarmouth, Williamstown
Mauritania: **4** Atar **5** Kaedi **6** Dakhla
Mexico: **4** Leon **5** Ameca, Choix, Tepic **6** Celaya, Colima, Merida, Oaxaca, Puebla, Toluca **7** Durango, Guasave, Morelia, Reynosa, Tampico, Tijuana, Tlalpan, Torreon, Uruapan **8** Chetumal, Coyoacan, Culiacan, Ensenada, Mazatlan, Saltillo, Tuxtepec **9** Fresnillo, Ixtacalco, Monterrey, Queretaro, Salamanca, Tapachula **10** Cuernavaca, Hermosillo, Ixtapalapa, Xochimilco **11** Guadalajara, Nueva Laredo **12** Azcapotzalco **13** Ciudad Obregon, Coatzacoalcos, San Luis Potosi, Veracruz Llave
Michigan: **3** Mio **4** Alma, Caro, Holt, Novi **5** Ionia, L'Anse, Niles **6** Adrian, Alpena, Bad Axe, Lapeer, Otsego, Paw Paw **7** Allegan, Corunna, Detroit, Gladwin, Livonia, Midland, Saginaw **8** Ann Arbor, Bessemer, Dearborn, Escabana, Grayling, Hastings, Houghton, Kalkaska, Manistee, Munising, Muskegon, Newberry, Petoskey, Sandusky **9** Big Rapids, Cheboygan, Coldwater, Hillsdale, Kalamazoo, Ludington, Menominee, Ontonagon, Port Huron, Roscommon, Ypsilanti **10** Cassopolis, Charlevoix, Eagle River, Grand Haven, Manistique, West Branch, White Cloud

11 Battle Creek, East Lansing, Grand Rapids, Harrisville, Saint Ignace 12 Crystal Falls, Highland Park, Iron Mountain, Mount Clemens 13 Mount Pleasant

Minnesota: 3 Ely 4 Mora 5 Anoka, Edina, Osseo 6 Aitkin, Bagley, Benson, Chaska, Duluth, Milaca, New Ulm, Wadena, Waseca, Windom, Winona 7 Bemidji, Glencoe, Hallock, Hibbing, Luverne, Mankato, Red Wing, Slayton, Wabasha, Wheaton 8 Baudette, Brainerd, Elk River, Le Center, Mahnomen, Moorhead, Owatonna, Shakopee 9 Albert Lea, Blue Earth, Caledonia, Crookston, Elbow Lake, Fairbault, Pipestone, Saint Paul, Silver Bay 10 Ortonville, Park Rapids, Saint Cloud, Saint James, Saint Peter, Stillwater, Two Harbors 11 Bloomington, Fergus Falls, Grand Marais, Little Falls, Long Prairie, Mantorville, Minneapolis, Worthington 12 Breckenridge, Detroit Lakes, Granite Falls, Red Lake Falls, Redwood Falls

Mississippi: 4 Iuka 5 Amory 6 Biloxi, Leland, McComb, Purvis, Sardis, Sumner, Tunica, Tupelo, Vaiden, Winona 7 Belzoni, Brandon, Fayette, Okolona, Quitman, Wiggins 8 Ackerman, Gulfport, Hernando, Lucedale, Meridian, Paulding, Pontotoc, Rosedale, Walthall 9 Greenwood, Indianola, Meadville, New Albany, Pittsboro, Senatobia, Vicksburg, Woodville 10 Batesville, Bay Springs, Booneville, Brookhaven, Clarksdale, Ellisville, Hazlehurst, New Auguste, Pascagoula, Port Gibson, Starkville, Waynesboro 11 Coffeeville, Hattiesburg, Leakesville, Mayersville, Poplarville, Rolling Fork, Water Valley 12 Holly Springs 13 Bay Saint Louis

Missouri: 3 Ava 4 Linn 5 Eldon, Hayti, Ladue, Rolla 6 Galena, Kahoka, Neosho, Potosi 7 Hermann, Ironton, Kennett, Linneus, Osceola, Palmyra, Sedalia 8 Doniphan, Gallatin, Hannibal 9 Boonville, Camdenton, Cassville, Hartville, Hillsboro, Maryville, Maysville, New Madrid, Pineville, Tuscumbia, Warrenton 10 Kirksville, Marble Hill, Marshfield, Perryville, Saint Louis, Steelville, Unionville, West Plains 11 Keytesville, Poplar Bluff, Saint Joseph, Warrensburg 12 Saint Charles 13 Harrisonville

Mongolia: 5 Kobdo 6 Darhan 10 Choybalsan

Montana: 5 Havre, Libby 6 Hardin, Hysham, Polson, Scobey, Wibaux 7 Bozeman, Broadus, Choteau, Cut Bank, Ekalaka, Ryegate, Winnett 8 Billings, Glendive, Missoula, Red Lodge 9 Big Timber, Deer Lodge, Harlowton, Kalispell, Wolf Point 10 Fort Benton, Great Falls, Plentywood 13 Thompson Falls

Montenegro: 9 Podgorica 10 Podgoritsa

Morocco: 4 Safi, Taza 5 Nador, Oujda 6 Agadir, Meknes 7 Kenitra 9 Marrakesh 10 Casablanca

Mozambique: 5 Beira 7 Nampula 9 Quelimane, Quilimane

Myanmar: 3 Pyu 4 Paan 5 Akyab, Bhamo, Chauk, Katha, Magwe, Minbu, Mogok, Tavoy 7 Bassein 8 Mandalay

Namibia: 5 Outjo 6 Tsumeb 12 Keetmanshoop

Nebraska: 3 Ord 5 Cozad, Omaha, Ponca, Tryon, Wahoo 6 Elwood, Gering, McCook, Minden, Muilen, Neligh, Pender, Sidney, Wilber 7 Burwell, Chadron, Fremont, Kearney, Kimball, Osceola, Tekamah 8 Beatrice, Chappell, Fairbury, Hastings, Holdrege, Ogallala, Red Cloud, Schuyler, Tecumseh, Thedford 9 Ainsworth, Benkelman, Broken Bow, Fullerton, Papillion 10 Clay Center, Hartington, Springview, Stockville 11 Grand Island, Hayes Center, North Platte, Plattsmouth

Netherlands: 3 Ede, Epe, Oss 4 Echt, Tiel, Uden 5 Aalst, Assen, Delft, Emmen, Soest, Vaals, Venlo, Vught, Weert, Weesp, Zeist 6 Arnhem 7 Haarlem, Tilburg, Utrecht 8 Enschede, Nijmegen 9 Apeldoorn, Eindhoven, Groningen, Rotterdam, Zandvoort

Nevada: 3 Ely 4 Elko, Reno 6 Fallon, Minden, Pioche 7 Tonopah 8 Las Vegas, Lovelock 9 Goldfield, Yerington 10 Winnemucca

New Brunswick: 5 Minto 9 Dalhousie 10 Edmundston, Richibucto 12 Hopewell Cape, Perth Andover, Saint Andrews

Newfoundland: 5 Burin 6 Wabana

New Hampshire: 5 Derry, Keene 6 Exeter, Gorham, Nashua 7 Hanover, Laconia, Ossipee 8 Hinsdale, Seabrook 9 Littleton, Merrimack 10 Portsmouth

New Jersey: 4 Atco, Lodi 6 Camden, Newark, Nutley, Rahway 7 Bayonne, Clifton, Hoboken, Hohokus, Paramus, Passaic, Raritan, Teaneck 8 Freehold, Metuchen, Paterson, Vauxhall, Woodbury 9 Belvidere, Bridgeton, Glassboro, Lakehurst, Maplewood, Menlo Park, Montclair, Riverside, Toms River 10 Asbury Park, Bloomfield, Cherry Hill, East Orange, Flemington, Hackensack, Mount Holly, Perth Amboy, Piscataway, Plainfield, Somerville, West Orange 11 Mays Landing, South Orange 13 Palisades Park

New Mexico: 4 Mora, Taos 5 Belen, Hobbs, Raton 6 Clovis, Deming, Grants 7 Roswell, Socorro 8 Estancia, Los Lunas, Mosquero, Portales 9 Carrizozo, Las Cruces, Lordsburg, Los Alamos, Lovington, Santa Rosa, Tucumcari 10 Alamogordo, Bernalillo, Fort Sumner 11 Albuquerque

New York: 4 Elma, Ovid 5 Depew, Ilion, Islip, Le Roy, Nyack, Olean, Owego, Utica 6 Attica, Cohoes, Delmar, Elmira, Ithaca, Oneida 7 Batavia, Corning, Geneseo, Katonah, Mineola, Penn Yan, Suffern, Yonkers 8 Bay Shore, Cortland, Herkimer, Hyde Park, Lockport, Mayville, Ossining, Syracuse, Valhalla 9 Greenport, Hempstead, Patchogue, Riverhead, Rochester, Scarsdale, Schoharie 10 Binghamton, Glens Falls, Haverstraw, Huntington, Lackawanna, Lake George, Lake Placid, Mamaroneck, Massapequa, Mount Kisco, Rensselaer, Wampsville, Watervliet 11 Ballston Spa, Canajoharie, Canandaigua, Cheektowaga, Cooperstown, Farmingdale, Hudson Falls, Irondequoit, Plattsburgh, Port Chester, Saint George, Schenectady, Southampton, Watkins Glen, White Plains 12 Lake Pleasant, Little Valley, Poughkeepsie 13 Mechanicville, Port Jefferson

New Zealand: 4 Hutt, Tawa 5 Levin, Taupo, Waihi 7 Dunedin 8 Auckland 12 Christchurch

Nicaragua: 4 Leon 5 Boaco, Rivas

Nigeria: 3 Aba, Ado, Ede, Ife, Iwo, Jos, Owo, Oyo 4 Kano, Ondo 5 Akure, Enugu, Gusau, Okene, Zaria 6 Ibadan, Ilesha, Ilorin, Kaduna, Mushin, Sokoto 7 Onitsha, Oshogbo 8 Abeokuta 9 Maiduguri, Ogbomosho 12 Port Harcourt

North Carolina: 4 Dunn 5 Ayden, Elkin, Erwin, Oteen, Sylva 6 Burgaw, Dobson, Durham, Lenoir, Manteo, Marion, Shelby, Sparta, Winton 7 Bayboro, Brevard, Edenton, Kinston, New Bern, Newland,

Raeford, Roxboro, Sanford, Tarboro **8** Asheboro, Beaufort, Gastonia, Snow Hill **9** Albemarle, Asheville, Charlotte, Currituck, High Point, Louisburg, Lumberton, Morganton, Pittsboro, Southport, Wadesboro, Warrenton, Wentworth **10** Burnsville, Chapel Hill, Gatesville, Greensboro, Hayseville, Laurinburg, Lillington, Lincolnton, Mocksville, Reidsville, Rockingham, Smithfield, Whiteville, Wilkesboro **11** Bakersville, Kenansville, Statesville, Swanquarter, Waynesville, Williamston, Yadkinville, Yanceyville **12** Fayetteville, Hillsborough, Murfreesboro, Robbinsville, Taylorsville, Winston Salem **13** Rutherfordton

North Dakota: 4 Mott **5** Cando, Fargo, Minot, Rolla **6** Amidon, Ashley, Bowman, Formon, Lakota, Linton, Medora, Mohall **7** La Moure, Langdon **8** Bowbells, McClusky, Wahpeton, Washburn **9** Bottineau, Dickinson, Ellendale, Fessenden, Fort Yates, Hettinger, Williston **10** Carrington, Devils Lake, Grand Forks **11** Minnewaukan, New Rockford

Northern Ireland: 5 Derry, Larne, Newry, Omagh **6** Antrim, Armagh **8** Limavady **9** Ballymena, Banbridge, Coleraine, Craigavon, Dungannon, Newcastle **10** Bally money **11** Ballycastle, Downpatrick, Enniskillen, Londonderry, Magherafelt **13** Carrickfergus

North Korea: 5 Haeju, Nampo **6** Wonsan **7** Hamhung, Kaesong, Sinuiju **8** Ch'ongjin, Kimchaek **9** P'yongyang

Norway: 4 Bodo **5** Hamar, Skien **6** Tromso **9** Stavanger, Trondheim

Nova Scotia: 5 Digby **6** Pictou **7** Arichat, Baddeck **8** Port Hood **9** Kentville, Lunenburg, Shelburne, Westville **10** Antigonish **11** Guysborough

Ohio: 4 Kent **5** Akron, Berea, Bryan, Cadiz, Carey, Eaton, Heath, Logan, Niles, Parma, Piqua, Solon, Xenia **6** Canton, Celina, Dayton, Elyria, Euclid, Kenton, Lorain, Marion, Medina, Sidney, Tiffin, Toledo **7** Ashland, Batavia, Bucyrus, Chardon, Findlay, Ironton, Oakwood, Pomeroy, Ravenna, Van Wert, Wauseon, Waverly, Wooster **8** Caldwell, Conneaut, Marietta, Paulding, Sandusky **9** Ashtabula, Cleveland, Coshocton, Mansfield, West Union **10** Cincinnati, Galli-

polis, Wapakoneta, Woodsfield, Zanesville **11** Chillicothe, Circleville, Millersburg, Mount Gilead, Painesville, Port Clinton **12** New Lexington, Steubenville **13** Bellefontaine, Cuyahoga Falls, Upper Sandusky

Oklahoma: 3 Ada **4** Alva, Enid **5** Altus, Atoka, Sayre, Tulsa **6** Arnett, Durant, El Reno, Guymon, Hollis, Idabel, Lawton, Madill, Mangum, Nowata, Okemah, Poteau, Taloga, Vinita, Wewoka **7** Antlers, Ardmore, Cordell, Eufaula, Newkirk, Purcell, Sapulpa, Stigler, Watonga, Waurika **8** Anadarko, Coalgate, Okmulgee, Pawhuska, Sallisaw, Stilwell **9** Chickasha, Claremore, Frederick, McAlester, Tahlequah, Wilburton **10** New Cordell, Stillwater, Tishomingo **11** Holdenville, Pauls Valley **12** Bartlesville

Oman: 3 Sur **6** Matrah **7** Salalah

Ontario: 4 Ajax, Wawa, York **6** Barrie, Guelph, Kenora, Minden, Picton, Sarnia, Simcoe **7** Cobourg, Gore Bay, Napanee, Sudbury, Windsor **8** Brampton, Cochrane, Goderich, North Bay, Pembroke, Prescott **9** Brantford, Kitchener, L'Original, Newmarket, Owen Sound, Walkerton **10** Belleville, Brockville, Haileybury, Parry Sound, Thunder Bay **11** Bracebridge, Fort Frances, Mississauga, Orangeville **12** Peterborough, St. Catharines

Oregon: 4 Moro **5** Canby, Nyssa **6** Condon, Eugene **7** Heppner **8** Coquille, La Grande, Lakeview, Portland, Roseburg **9** Clackamas, Corvallis, Gold Beach, Hood River, Pendleton, The Dalles, Tillamook **10** Grants Pass, Prineville **11** McMinnville **12** Klamath Falls

Pakistan: 5 Bannu, Bhera, Kasur, Kohat **6** Gujrat, Lahore, Mardan, Multan, Quetta, Sukkur **7** Karachi, Sialkot **8** Lyallpur, Peshawar, Sargodha **9** Hyderabad **10** Bahawalpur, Gujranwala, Rawalpindi

Paraguay: 3 Ita **4** Yuty **5** Belen, Luque, Pilar

Pennsylvania: 4 York **5** Avoca, Darby, Muncy, Paoli **6** Easton **7** Altoona, Bedford, Clarion, Hanover, Hershey, Laporte, Latrobe, Reading, Ridgway, Sunbury **8** Carlisle, Edinboro, Hazleton, Montrose, Scranton, Somerset, Tionesta **9** Allentown, Ebensburg, Honesdale, Jim Thorpe, Lancaster, Lewis-

burg, Lock Haven, Meadville, New Castle, Smethport, Wellsboro **10** Bellefonte, Bloomsburg, Brookville, Carbondale, Clearfield, Gettysburg, Greensburg, Huntingdon, Kittanning, McKeesport, Middleburg, Pittsburgh, Pottsville, Waynesburg **11** Coudersport, Stroudsburg, Tunkhannock, Valley Forge, West Chester, Wilkes Barre **12** Chambersburg, Conshohocken, Philadelphia, State College, Williamsport **13** Hollidaysburg, Kennett Square, New Bloomfield

Peru: 3 Ica, Ilo **5** Ancon, Cuzco, Jauja, Junin, Lamas, Pisco, Piura, Tacna **6** Callao **8** Arequipa, Chiclayo, Trujillo

Philippines: 3 Iba **4** Bago, Bais, Boac, Bogo, Cebu, Daet, Jolo, Lipa, Mati **5** Basco, Bulan, Cadiz, Danao, Davao, Digos, Gapan, Gubat, Iriga, Laoag, Ormoc, Silay, Tagum, Vigan **6** Butuan, Iloilo **7** Angeles, Bacolod, Basilan **8** Batangas, Calbayog **9** Zamboanga **13** General Santos

Poland: 4 Lodz, Nysa, Pila, Zary **5** Brzeg, Bytom, Bytow, Chelm, Gubin, Ilawa, Jaslo, Konin, Kutno, Lomza, Luban, Lubin, Mlawa, Olawa, Opole, Plock, Radom, Rumia, Sanok, Sopot, Tczew, Torun, Tychy, Ursus, Zagan **6** Gdansk, Gdynia, Kielce, Lublin, Poznan, Zabrze **7** Chorzow, Gliwice, Wroclaw **8** Katowice, Szczecin **9** Bialystok, Bydgoszcz, Sosnowiec, Walbrzych **10** Ruda Slaska **11** Czestochowa **12** Bielsko Biala

Portugal: 4 Faro **5** Braga, Evora **6** Oporto

Prince Edward Island: 10 Summerside

Puerto Rico: 5 Ponce **7** Bayamon

Quebec: 4 Alma **5** Amqui, Anjou, Granb, Laval, Levis, Magog, Percé, Rouyn **6** Ham Sud, Matane, Val d'Or **7** Bedford, Lachute **8** Cap Santé, Joliette, LacBrome, Maniwaki, Montreal, Rimouski, Roberval, Sept Iles, Waterloo **9** Becancour, Cookshire, Iberville, Inverness, La Malbaie, La Prairie, Longueuil, Montmagny, Saint Jean, Tadoussac, Vaudreuil, Vercheres **10** Ayers Cliff, Baie Comeau, Chicoutimi, Huntingdon, Marieville, St. Henedine, St. Julienne, Ville Marie, Yamachiche **11** Beauharnois, Lac Megantic, L'Assomption, Louiseville, Mont Laurier, Napierville, New Carlisle, Sainte Croix, Saint Pascal **12** Loretteville, Saint Liboire, Saint

Raphael **13** Baie Saint Paul, Berthierville, Chateau Richer, Coteau Landing, Drummondville, Papineauville, Riviere du Loup, Sainte Martine, Thetford Mines, Trois Rivieres

Rhode Island: **7** Newport, Rumford, Warwick **8** Apponaug, Coventry, Cranston, Tiverton, Westerly **9** Hopkinton, Pawtucket **10** Woonsocket **11** West Warwick **12** Narragansett, West Kingston **13** East Greenwich

Romania: **3** Dej **4** Aiud, Arad, Cluj, Deva, Husi, Iasi **5** Anina, Bacau, Buzau, Carei, Lugoj, Sibiu, Turda **6** Braila, Brasov, Galati, Oradea **7** Craiova **8** Ploiesti **9** Constanta, Timisoara

Russia: **3** Kem, Ufa **4** Inta, Luga, Okha, Omsk, Orel, Orsk, Perm, Tula, Tura, Zima **5** Aldan, Artem, Chita, Ishim, Kansk, Lysva, Onega, Penza, Pskov, Rzhev, Salsk, Serov, Sochi, Sokol, Tomsk, Tulun, Volsk, Yurga **6** Bratsk, Kaluga, Kovrov, Kurgan, Rostov, Ryazan, Samara, Syzran, Tambov, Tyumen, Vyborg, Yelets **7** Angarsk, Armavir, Barnaul, Bryansk, Irkutsk, Ivanovo, Izhevsk, Kalinin, Kolomna, Lipetsk, Magadan, Nalchik, Norilsk, Rybinsk, Saransk, Saratov, Shakhty, Ulan Ude, Vologda, Yakutsk, Zhdanov **8** Belgorod, Kemerovo, Kostroma, Murmansk, Nakhodka **7** Novorod **8** Orenburg, Smolensk, Taganrog, Vladimir, Voronezh **9** Archangel, Astrakhan, Berezniki, Kiselevsk, Krasnodar, Rubtsovsk, Serpukhov, Stavropol, Syktyvkar, Ulyanovsk, Volgograd, Yaroslavl **10** Cheboksary, Dzerzhinsk, Khabarovsk, Yoshkar Ola **11** Chelyabinsk, Cheremkhovo, Cherepovets, Krasnoyarsk, Makhachkala, Novosibirsk, Prokopyevsk, Sterlitamak, Verkhoyansk, Vladikavkaz, Vladivostok **12** Magnitogorsk, Novokuznetsk, Novomoskovsk, Severodvinsk **13** Yekaterinburg

Saskatchewan: **8** Moose Jaw **10** Assiniboia

Saudi Arabia: **4** Jauf, Taif **5** Jidda **6** Medina

Scotland: **3** Ayr **4** Alva, Caol, Dyce, Oban **5** Alloa, Annan, Beith, Cowie, Cupar, Dalry, Ellon, Kelso, Kelty, Largs, Leven, Nairn, Patna, Troon **6** Dundee **7** Glasgow **8** Aberdeen **9** Inverness

Senegal: **5** Thies **6** Kaolak **7** Kaolack

Serbia: **3** Bor, Nis, Pec **4** Ruma

5 Becej, Cacak, Pirot, Sabac, Senta, Vrbas, Vrsac **7** Novi Sad **8** Subotica

Slovakia: **5** Nitra **6** Kosice **10** Bratislava

Slovenia: **4** Bled **5** Celje, Koper, Kranj **9** Ljubljana

Somalia: **3** Eil **5** Afgoi, Alula, Brava, Burao, Obbia **7** Berbera, Kismayu

South Africa: **5** Brits, Ceres, De Aar, Nigel, Paarl **6** Benoni, Durban **7** Springs **8** Boksburg, Mafeking **9** Germiston, Kimberley, Uitenhage **10** East London **11** Krugersdorp, Vereeniging **12** Johannesburg **13** Port Elizabeth

South Carolina: **5** Aiken, Cayce, Saxon **6** Saluda, Sumter **7** Bamberg, Gaffney, Laurens, Manning, Pickens **8** Barnwell, Beaufort, Newberry, Rock Hill, Walhalla **9** Abbeville, Allendale, Edgefield, Greenwood, Kingstree, McCormick, Ridgeland, Winnsboro **10** Charleston, Darlington, Greenville, Orangeburg, Walterboro **11** Bishopville, Myrtle Beach, Spartanburg **12** Moncks Corner **13** Bennettsville, Saint Matthews

South Dakota: **5** Burke, Hayti, Leola, Murdo, Onida, Selby **6** Armour, De Smet, Dupree, Kadoka, Olivet **7** Milbank, Sturgis, Tyndall, Yankton **8** Deadwood, Elk Point, Faulkton, Highmore, Kennebec, Redfield **9** Brookings, Clear Lake, Flandreau, Lake Andes **10** Fort Pierre, Gannvalley, Plankinton, Sioux Falls, Timber Lake **12** Belle Fourche

South Korea: **3** Iri **4** Yosu **5** Cheju, Masan, Mokpo, Pusan, Suwon, Taegu, Ulson, Wonju **6** Chinju, Chonju, Inchon, Kunsan, Taejon **7** Kwangju

Spain: **4** Adra, Baza, Elda, Jaca, Jaen, Leon, Loja, Lugo, Olot, Reus, Vich, Vigo **5** Albox, Alcoy, Alora, Baena, Cadiz, Ceuta, Cieza, Ecija, Eibar, Elche, Gijon, Ibiza, Jodar, Lorca, Mahon, Oliva, Osuna, Palma, Ronda, Soria, Ubeda **6** Bilboa, Burgos, Cuenca, Malaga, Murcia, Oviedo **7** Almaden, Almeria, Cordoba, Durango, Granada, Seville, Tarrasa, Vitoria **8** Alicante, La Coruna, Pamplona, Sabadell, Valencia **9** Barcelona, Salamanca, Santander, Saragossa **10** Hospitalet, Valladolid **12** San Sebastion

Sri Lanka: **5** Galle, Kandy **6** Jaffna **10** Batticaloa

Sudan: **4** Juba **5** Kodok, Kosti **8** Omdurman

Sweden: **4** Lund, Umea **5** Boden, Boras, Falun, Gavle, Lulea, Malmo, Nacka, Pitea, Solno, Vaxjo, Visby, Ystad **7** Uppsala **8** Goteborg **9** Jonkoping

Switzerland: **3** Zug **4** Biel, Chur, Thun **5** Aarau, Arbon, Baden, Basel, Koniz **6** Lugano, Zurich **7** Lucerne **8** Lausanne

Syria: **4** Hama, Homs **5** Idlib **6** Aleppo **7** Latakia

Tanzania: **5** Lindi, Mbeya, Tanga **6** Dodoma **8** Zanzibar

Tennessee: **5** Alcoa, Erwin, Rives **6** Celina, Dunlap, Loudon, Ripley, Selmer **7** Memphis, Waverly **8** Gallatin, Oak Ridge, Rutledge, Tazewell, Wartburg **9** Dandridge, Dyersburg, Hohenwald, Jacksboro, Jonesboro, Knoxville, Lewisburg, Maryville, Pikeville **10** Cookeville, Crossville, Gainesboro, Hartsville, Smithville, Sneedville, Somerville, Waynesboro **11** Blountville, Chattanooga, Clarksville, Greeneville, McMinnville, Rogersville, Sevierville, Shelbyville, Tiptonville **12** Decaturville, Elizabethton, Lawrenceburg, Madisonville, Maynardville, Murfreesboro

Texas: **4** Azle, Roby, Vega, Waco **5** Alvin, Anson, Baird, Bowie, Bryan, Clute, Cuero, Emory, Ennis, Freer, Hondo, Marfa, Mexia, Olney, Ozona, Pampa, Pecos, Pharr, Plano, Sealy, Tulia, Vidor, Wylie **6** Belton, Boerne, Bonham, Burnet, Conroe, Dallas, Del Rio, Denton, El Paso, Gilmer, Goliad, Jayton, Lamesa, Laredo, Linden, Lufkin, Menard, Morton, Odessa, Quanah, Sarita, Seguin, Sinton, Tahoka, Tilden, Uvalde **7** Abilene, Anahuac, Bandera, Bastrop, Big Lake, Brenham, Cotulla, Crowell, Dalhart, Denison, Dimmitt, Farwell, Houston, Kaufman, Kountze, Lubbock, Mentone, Mertzon, Midland, Refugio, San Saba, Stanton, Van Horn, Wharton **8** Amarillo, Angleton, Beaumont, Beeville, Cleburne, Eastland, Eldorado, Floydada, Giddings, Glen Rose, Gonzales, Granbury, Groveton, Hemphill, La Grange, Lampasas, Lipscomb, Longview, McKinney, Monahans, Montague, Muleshoe, Pearsall, Perryton, Rockwall, Spearman, Stinnett **9** Arlington, Aspermont, Ballinger, Bellville, Big Spring, Brownwood, Childress, Clarendon, Corsicana, Crosbyton, Eagle Pass, Fort Davis, Fort Worth, Galveston, Groesbeck, Henrietta, Hillsboro, Jacksboro,

Kerrville, Levelland, Paint Rock, Palo Pinto, Plainview, San Angelo, Sanderson, San Marcos, Silverton, Woodville **10** Brownfield, Coldspring, Falfurrias, Gatesville, George West, Jourdanton, Kingsville, Port Arthur, Port Lavaca, San Antonio, Sweetwater, Waxahachie **11** Brownsville, Floresville, Goldthwaite, Littlefield, Nacogdoches, Rocksprings, Weatherford **12** Breckenridge, Daingerfield, Fort Stockton, Hebbronville, New Braunfels, Raymondville, San Augustine, Sierra Blanca, Stephenville, Throckmorton, Wichita Falls **13** Brackettville, Corpus Christi, Hallettsville

Thailand: 3 Nan, Tak **5** Phrae, Roi Et, Surin **8** Songkhla

Tunisia: 4 Beja, Sfax **5** Gabes, Gafsa **7** Bizerte

Turkey: 5 Adana, Bursa, Izmir, Konya, Sivas **6** Erzurm, Samsun **7** Kayseri, Malatya **8** Istanbul **9** Eskisehir, Gaziantep **10** Diyarbakir

Turkmenistan: 8 Nebit Dag

Uganda: 5 Jinja, Mbale **7** Entebbe

Ukraine: 4 Lvov, Sumy **5** Lutsk, Rovno **6** Odessa **7** Donetsk, Kharkov, Kherson, Poltava **8** Vinnitsa, Zhitomir **9** Chernigov, Krivoy Rog, Nikolayev **10** Chernovtsy, Kirovograd, Kremenchug, Sevastopol, Simferopol, Zaporozhye

United Arab Emirates: 5 Ajman, Dubai **7** Sharjah **8** Fujairah **12** Ras al Khaimah

Uruguay: 4 Melo **5** Minas, Pando, Rocha, Salto

Utah: 3 Loa **4** Lehi, Moab, Orem **5** Konab, Manti, Nephi, Ogden, Provo **6** Tooele **7** Parowan **8** Duchesne **9** Coalville, Panguitch **10** Castle Dale **11** Saint George

Uzbekistan: 5 Nukus **6** Kokand **7** Bukhara, Fergana **8** Andizhan, Chirchik, Namangan **9** Samarkand

Venezuela: 4 Coro **5** Anaco, Cagua **6** Merida **7** Cabimas, Maracay **8** Valencia **9** Maracaibo **12** Barquisimeto, San Cristobal

Vermont: 5 Barre **7** Chelsea, Newfane, Rutland **8** Winooski **9** Guildhall, North Hero **10** Bennington, Burlington, Middlebury **11** Brattleboro, Saint Albans, St. Johnsbury **12** Bellows Falls

Vietnam: 3 Hue **4** Vinh **5** Da Lat, Hoi An, My Tho **6** Da Nang **7** Nam Dinh, Qui Nhon **8** Haiphong, Nha Trang

Virginia: 4 Tabb **5** Luray, Surry **6** Grundy, Saluda **7** Accomac, Boydton, Mathews, New Kent, Nor-

folk **8** Abingdon, Culpeper, Leesburg, Manassas, Montross, Nottoway, Poquoson, Powhatan, Rustburg, Tazewell **9** Arlington, Clintwood, Courtland, Dinwiddie, Eastville, Farmville, Fincastle, Goochland, Lunenburg, Lynchburg **10** Appomattox, Berryville, Front Royal, Hillsville, Jonesville, King George, Lovingston, Pearisburg, Portsmouth, Rocky Mount, Wytheville **11** Heathsville, King William, Newport News, Warm Springs **12** Prince George, Spotsylvania, Tappahannock **13** Stanardsville

Wales: 4 Rhyl **5** Neath, Risca, Tenby, Tywyn **7** Cardiff, Cwmbran, Denbigh, Swansea **8** Aberdare, Bridgend **10** Llangollen

Washington: 4 Omak **5** Brier, Camas, Kelso, Lacey, Pasco, Selah **6** Asotin, Colfax, Tacoma, Yakima **7** Ephrata, Everett, Pomeroy, Prosser, Seattle, Spokane **8** Bellevue, Chehalis, Colville, Okanogan **9** Cathlamet, Montesano, Ritzville, Snohomish, Wenatchee **10** Bellingham, Coupeville, Ellensburg, Goldendale, Walla Walla, Waterville **11** Port Angeles, Port Orchard **12** Friday Harbor, Port Townsend

West Virginia: 5 Nitro, Welch **6** Elkins, Hamlin, Hinton, Keyser, Ripley **7** Beckley, Parsons, Weirton **8** Kingwood, Philippi, Wheeling **9** Glenville, Marlinton, Pineville, Wellsburg **10** Buckhannon, Clarksburg, Huntington, Moorefield, Morgantown, Petersburg, Saint Marys, Williamson **11** Grantsville, Harrisville, Martinsburg, Moundsville, Parkersburg **12** Middlebourne, Summersville **13** New Cumberland, Point Pleasant

Wisconsin: 4 Kiel **5** Ripon, Tomah **6** Antigo, Barron, Durand, Hurley, Oconto, Racine, Wausau **7** Baraboo, Chilton, Crandon, Elkhorn, Hayward, Kenosha, Keshena, Mauston, Merrill, Oshkosh, Shawano, Viraqua, Waupaca, Wautoma **8** Appleton, Green Bay, Kewaunee, La Crosse, Montello, Phillips, Washburn, Waukesha, West Bend **9** Eau Claire, Ellsworth, Fond du Lac, Green Lake, Ladysmith, Manitowoc, Marinette, Menomonie, Milwaukee, Sheboygan, Shell Lake, Wauwatosa, West Allis, Whitehall **10** Balsam Lake, Darlington, Dodgeville, Eagle River, Grantsburg, Janesville **11** Neillsville, Sturgeon Bay **12** Stevens Point, Whitefish Bay **13** Chippewa Falls

Wyoming: 4 Lusk **6** Casper, Lander **7** Laramie, Rawlins, Worland **8** Gillette, Kemmerer, Pinedale, Sheridan, Sundance **9** Wheatland **10** Green River **11** Rock Springs, Thermopolis

Yemen: 5 Taizz **7** Hodeida, Mukalla

Zaire: 4 Boma **6** Bukavu, Likasi **7** Kananga **9** Kisangani, Mbuji Mayi **10** Lubumbashi

Zambia: 5 Kabwe, Kitwe, Mansa, Mbala, Mongu, Ndola

Zimbabwe: 5 Gwelo **6** Umtali

civet

3 cat

African: 7 nandine

Asian: 5 zibet **6** zibeth

Chinese: 5 rasse

East Indian: 6 musang **9** tangalung

Indian: 6 bondar

Madagascar: 5 fossa **8** fanaloka

Malaysian: 8 mampalon

relative: 5 genet

civic

6 public **8** national

civil

5 bland, suave **6** polite, public, urbane **7** affable, cordial, courtly, genteel, politic, refined **8** gracious, mannerly, national, obliging, wellbred **9** courteous **10** cultivated, diplomatic **12** well-mannered **13** accommodating

civil court

9 nisi prius

civility

6 comity **7** amenity, decorum **9** etiquette, propriety **10** politeness

civilization

7 culture

civilized

5 bland, suave **6** decent, polite, proper, smooth, urbane **7** refined **8** decorous **9** befitting, Christian **10** conforming **11** comme il faut **13** sophisticated

civil rights

leader: 4 King (Martin Luther)

organization: 4 ACLU, CORE **5** NAACP

Civil War

admiral: 8 Buchanan (Franklin), Farragut (David)

battle: 6 Shiloh **7** Bull Run **8** Antietam, Manassas **9** Mobile Bay, Nashville, Vicksburg **10** Cold Harbor, Gettysburg **11** Chattanooga, Chickamauga

general: 3 Lee (Robert E.) **4** Hood (John Bell), Pope (John) **5** Bragg

(Braxton), Buell (Don Carlos), Ewell (Richard Stoddart), Grant (Ulysses S.), Meade (George), Sykes (George) **6** Hooker (Joseph) **7** Forrest (Nathan Bedford), Jackson (Thomas "Stonewall"), Sherman (Thomas West, William Tecumseh) **8** Burnside (Ambrose), Johnston (Albert Sidney, Joseph Eggleston), Sheridan (Philip) **9** McClellan (George Brinton), Rosecrans (William), Schofield (John) **10** Beauregard (Pierre)
ship: **7** Monitor **9** Merrimack

civil wrong
4 tort

Civitas Dei
4 Zion **5** bliss **6** Canaan, heaven **7** elysium, nirvana **8** empyrean, paradise **12** New Jerusalem **13** Abraham's bosom

clabber
5 curds

clack
3 gab, jaw, yak **4** blab, chat **5** prate, sieve, tabby **6** babble, bicker, gabble, gossip, jabber, rattle **7** blabber, chatter, clatter, clitter, palaver, prattle, shatter **8** quidnunc, telltale **9** carrytale, yakety-yak **10** talebearer **11** rumormonger **13** scandalmonger

clad
4 face, garb, side, skin **5** array, dress **6** attire, clothe **7** apparel, garment, raiment, sheathe **8** enclothe

claim
4 call, dibs **5** argue, exact, right, share, stake, title **6** adduce, allege, assert, defend, demand **7** advance, contend, justify, purport, require, solicit, warrant **8** interest, maintain, pretense **9** assertion, challenge, postulate, privilege, vindicate **10** birthright, pretension **11** affirmation, declaration, prerogative, requisition **12** protestation

clairvoyance
3 ESP

clairvoyant
4 seer

clam
5 razor **6** gweduc, quahog **7** bivalve, coquina, geoduck, goeduck, gweduck, mollusk, quahaug, steamer **11** cherrystone
genus: **3** Mya

clamant
4 dire **6** crying, urgent **7** burning, exigent, instant **8** pressing **9** clamorous **10** imperative **11** importunate

clamber
5 climb, crawl, scale **8** scrabble, scramble, struggle

clamor
3 din **4** bawl, roar, rout, to-do **5** babel, claim, noise, whirl **6** bellow, bustle, debate, demand, hassle, hubbub, jangle, outcry, racket, tumult, uproar, upturn **7** agitate, bluster, dispute, ferment, turmoil **8** upheaval **9** commotion **10** convulsion, hullabaloo, hurly-burly, tintamarre **11** pandemonium

clamorous
4 dire **5** noisy, vocal **6** crying, urgent **7** begging, blatant, burning, clamant, exigent, instant, voluble **8** adjuring, eloquent, pressing, strident **9** imploring **10** articulate, boisterous, imperative, multivocal, vociferant, vociferous **11** importunate, loudmouthed, openmouthed **12** obstreperous

clamp
4 grip, hold, vise **5** clasp, grasp, gripe **6** clench, clinch, clutch, tenure **7** grapple

clamshell
6 bucket **7** grapple

clan
3 mob **4** camp, folk, race, ring, sept **5** cabal, house, stock, tribe **6** circle, clique, family **7** coterie, ingroup, kindred, lineage **9** camarilla
emblem: **5** totem

clandestine
3 sly **4** foxy **6** artful, covert, secret **7** furtive, illicit **8** hush-hush, stealthy **10** undercover **12** hugger-mugger, illegitimate **13** surreptitious, under-the-table

clang
3 din **4** ding, peal **5** noise **6** jangle

clangorous
5 noisy **7** rackety **8** clattery, noiseful, sonorous **10** uproarious

clap
4 bang, boom, slam, wham **5** blast, burst, crack, crash, smash **7** applaud

claptrap
4 bull **5** hokum **6** bunkum, drivel,

humbug **7** baloney, twaddle **8** malarkey, nonsense **10** flapdoodle

Clare Boothe ___
4 Luce

claret
3 red **4** wine **8** Bordeaux

clarify
5 clean, clear **6** define, purify, settle **7** analyze, cleanse, clear up, explain **8** depurate, simplify **9** break down, delineate, elucidate, formulate **10** illuminate, illustrate **13** straighten out

clarion
4 fair, fine **5** clear, sunny **8** pleasant, rainless, sunshiny **9** cloudless, unclouded **10** undarkened

clarity
4 care **6** nicety **8** accuracy, lucidity **9** clearness, fussiness, limpidity, plainness, precision, propriety **10** exactitude **11** perspicuity **12** articulation, correctitude

clash
3 jar, row, try **4** bump, fray, fret, gall, jolt, riot **5** brawl, broil, brush, crash, grate, melee, scrap, set to, shock, smash **6** action, affray, battle, fracas, impact, jangle, mellay, rumpus, wallop **7** collide, discord **8** conflict, mismatch, skirmish **9** collision, disaccord, encounter, scrimmage **10** concussion, engagement **11** embroilment **12** disharmonize

clasp
3 hug **4** clip, coil, grip, hold, take **5** clamp, grasp, gripe, press, tache **6** clench, clinch, clutch, enfold, tenure **7** embrace, grapple, squeeze **10** chatelaine

class
3 ilk **4** head, hold, kind, mark, part, rank, rate, sort, tier, type **5** allot, brand, caste, color, gauge, genre, genus, grade, grain, group, judge, order, score, stamp, style **6** assess, assign, assort, branch, divide, kidney, league, nature, reckon, regard, stripe **7** account, bracket, caliber, feather, quality, section, species, variety **8** appraise, category, consider, division, evaluate, grouping, separate **10** categorize, pigeonhole **11** description **12** denomination
Hindu: **5** caste, varna
middle: **11** bourgeoisie
school: **6** junior, senior **8** freshman **9** sophomore

scientific: 5 genus 6 genera (plural)
suffix: 2 cy
working: 11 proletariat

classic
3 top 4 fine 5 ideal, model, prime 6 famous 7 capital, typical, vintage 8 champion, superior, top-notch 9 classical, excellent, exemplary 10 magnum opus, masterwork, prototypal 11 chef d'oeuvre, masterpiece, tour de force 12 paradigmatic, prototypical

classification
4 sort, type 5 genre, genus, grade, order 6 family, genera (plural), phylum, rating 7 species 8 category, division, grouping, taxonomy, typology 11 arrangement

classified
6 secret 9 top secret 12 confidential

classify
4 rank, rate, sort 5 grade, group 6 assort 8 evaluate 10 categorize, pigeonhole

classy
2 in 4 tony 5 sharp, swank, swish 6 modish, tonish 7 dashing, stylish 11 fashionable

clatter
3 gab, jaw 4 chat, to-do 5 clack, run on 6 babble, bicker, clamor, dither, hassle, hubbub, pother, rattle, tumult, uproar 7 chatter, clitter, shatter, turmoil 9 commotion 10 hurly-burly
Scottish: 7 brattle

clattery
5 noisy 7 rackety 8 noiseful, sonorous 10 clangorous, uproarious

Claudia's husband
6 Pilate

Claudio's beloved
4 Hero

Claudius
nephew: 6 Hamlet
slayer: 6 Hamlet 9 Agrippina
successor: 4 Nero

claviger
6 custos, keeper, warden 8 cerberus, guardian, watchdog 9 custodian

claw
3 dig 4 nail, tear 5 chela, grasp, grope, seize, talon, uncus 6 clutch, scrape, ungual, unguis, ungula 7 scratch

combining form: 4 chel 5 cheli, on-ych, ungui 6 onycho 8 onychium

clay
3 cob, pug 4 galt, leck, loam, lute, marl 5 argil, brick, earth, gault, loess, ocher, ochre, rabat 6 clunch 8 camstone
baked: 4 bole, tile 5 adobe, brick
box: 6 saggar, sagger
brick: 3 bat
building: 5 adobe
ceramic: 10 terra-cotta
combining form: 3 pel 4 pelo 6 argill 7 argilli, argillo 10 argillaceo
constituent: 6 silica 7 dickite, nacrite 8 feldspar, silicate 9 kaolinite
friable: 4 bole
in glass: 4 tear
made of: 7 fictile
mold: 3 dod
porcelain: 6 kaolin 7 kaoline
red: 4 bole 8 laterite, sinopite
rock: 5 shale
slab: 3 bat
sticky: 8 gumbotil
tobacco pipe: 6 dudeen
watery mixture: 4 slip
white: 6 kaolin 7 kaoline

clay pigeon
6 target

clean
3 gut 4 dust, fair, pure, swab, tidy, trim, wash, wipe 5 dress, fresh, groom, order, purge, renew, scour, scrub, sweep 6 bright, chaste, decent, modest, neaten, police, purify, spruce, vacuum 7 clarify, freshen, furbish, shining, sinless 8 brighten, depurate, innocent, renovate, spotless, unguilty, unsoiled 9 blameless, crimeless, faultless, guiltless, sparkling, stainless, taintless, undefiled, unsullied, untainted, wholesome 10 immaculate, inculpable 11 recondition, sportsmanly, unblemished 12 spick-and-span, straighten up 13 sportsmanlike
ship's bottom: 5 bream

clean-cut
7 express 8 definite, explicit, specific 10 definitive 11 categorical, unambiguous

cleaner
see **cleanser**

cleanhanded
8 innocent

clean-limbed
4 trim 7 shapely 8 shapeful 10 statuesque, well-turned

cleanse
5 purge, rinse 6 purify, refine 7 clarify, deterge 8 depurate, lustrate, sanitize 9 disinfect, expurgate, sterilize

cleanser
3 lye 4 soap 6 bleach 9 detergent

cleansing
9 catharsis, purgation 10 lustration 11 expurgation 12 purification

Cleante
father: 8 Harpagon
lover: 9 Angelique

clear
3 net, pay, rid, win 4 bare, earn, fade, fair, fine, gain, leap, lose, make, over, pure, quit, sink, void, well 5 à fond, close, empty, exact, fully, glean, lucid, milky, overt, pay up, plain, quite, repay, solve, stark, sunny, untie, vault 6 acquit, better, gather, hurdle, limpid, lucent, obtain, patent, pay off, pick up, public, secure, settle, simple, square, vacant, vacate, vanish 7 absolve, acquire, clarify, clarion, cleanse, clean up, crystal, defined, evanish, evident, explain, improve, obvious, precise, rule out, satisfy, untwine, utterly, vacuous 8 apparent, definite, distinct, entirely, evanesce, explicit, knowable, luculent, luminous, manifest, overleap, palpable, pellucid, pleasant, rainless, scot-free, sensible, shake off, sunshiny, surmount, tangible, throw-off, unburden, unhidden, univocal, untangle 9 cloudless, disappear, discharge, eliminate, elucidate, evaporate, exculpate, exonerate, extricate, graspable, liquidate, meliorate, negotiate, perfectly, published, stabilize, tralucent, unblurred, unclouded, vindicate 10 accumulate, altogether, ameliorate, completely, disculpate, disentwine, illuminate, illustrate, opalescent, openhanded, see-through, translucid, undarkened, unentangle, unobscured, unscramble 11 appreciable, conspicuous, disencumber, disentangle, open-and-shut, perceptible, perspicuous, translucent, transparent, unambiguous, unequivocal, unperplexed 12 recognizable, transpicuous, unmistakable 13 apprehensible, uncomplicated

clearance
7 go-ahead 10 green light 13 authorization

clear away
6 remove 7 take out 9 discumber
10 disembroil 12 disembarrass

clear-cut
4 nice 5 crisp, exact, lucid, plain
6 biting, lucent 7 assured, crystal,
cutting, decided, express, ingoing,
precise 8 definite, distinct, explicit,
incisive, luminous, manifest, pellucid, specific 9 trenchant, unblurred,
undoubted 10 definitive, pronounced, undisputed 11 categorical, indubitable, penetrating, translucent, transparent, unambiguous
12 transpicuous, unquestioned

clear-eyed
10 discerning

clearheaded
10 perceptive

clear out
4 kite 5 scram 6 begone, decamp,
get out 7 skiddoo, take off, vamoose 8 hightail 9 skedaddle

clear-sightedness
3 wit 6 acumen 8 astucity, keenness 10 astuteness, shrewdness
11 discernment, penetration,
percipience

clear up
5 solve 6 cipher, unfold 7 clarify,
dope out, explain, resolve, unravel
8 decipher, dissolve 9 elucidate,
figure out, puzzle out 10 illuminate,
illustrate

clearwing
4 moth

cleat
4 bitt 5 cavel, chock, kevel 6 batten 7 bollard, coxcomb, dolphin

cleavage
5 chasm, cleft, split 6 schism

cleave
3 cut, hew, rip 4 chop, join, link,
rend, rive, tear 5 carve, cling, sever, slice, split, stick, unite 6 adhere, cohere, divide, sunder 7 combine, conjoin, dissect, divorce
8 dissever, separate 9 associate

cleft
3 gap 4 rift, rima, rime, slit
5 chasm, chink, clove, crack,
gorge, gulch, split 6 arroyo,
clough, ravine, schism 7 crevice,
fissure 8 cleavage, rimation
combining form: 5 fissi, schiz
6 schizo 7 schisto

clemency
5 grace, mercy 6 lenity 7 caritas,

charity 8 fairness, justness, lenience, leniency, mildness 9 endurance, tolerance 10 gentleness, indulgence, sufferance, toleration
11 forbearance 12 mercifulness
13 equitableness

clement
4 easy, kind, mild 6 benign, humane, kindly, tender 7 lenient
8 merciful, tolerant 9 benignant, indulgent 10 benevolent, charitable,
forbearing 11 sympathetic
13 compassionate

clench
4 grip, grit, hold 5 clamp, clasp,
grasp, gripe 6 clinch, clutch, tenure
7 grapple

Cleopatra
attendant: 4 Iras 8 Charmian
brother: 7 Ptolemy
husband: 7 Ptolemy
killer: 3 asp
lover: 6 Antony, Caesar
river: 4 Nile

Cleopatra's Needle
7 obelisk

clepsydra
9 timepiece 10 water clock

clerestory
7 gallery

clergyman
5 clerk, padre, vicar 6 bishop,
cleric, curate, divine, father, parson, pastor, priest, rector 7 domi-
nie, pontiff, prelate 8 chaplain,
clerical, minister, ordinary,
preacher, pulpiter, reverend, shepherd, sky pilot 9 churchman, predi-
cant, pulpiteer 10 ecclesiast, evangelist, missionary, sermonizer
11 pulpitarian 12 ecclesiastic
American: 4 Hale (Edward Everett),
King (Martin Luther, Thomas Starr)
5 Eliot (John), Stone (Barton Warren), Weems (Parson) 6 Dwight
(Timothy), Holmes (John Haynes),
Hooker (Thomas), Mather (Cotton,
Increase, Richard), Merton
(Thomas), Parker (Samuel, Theodore), Powell (Adam Clayton), Tay-
lor (Edward, Graham, Nathaniel
William) 7 Beecher (Henry Ward,
Lyman), Harvard (John), Russell
(Charles Taze) 10 Muhlenberg
(Frederick Augustus, Henry Mel-
chior, John Peter Gabriel)
English: 4 Ward (Nathaniel, Seth,
William George) 5 Donne (John),
Paley (William), Smith (Henry "Sil-
ver-Tonqued," John "The Sebap-

tist," Sidney) 6 Cotton (John), Fuller
(Andrew, Thomas), Taylor (Jeremy,
Rowland) 7 Cranmer (Thomas),
Parsons (Robert) 8 Kingsley
(Charles)
French: 8 Teilhard (Pierre)
10 Schweitzer (Albert)
home: 5 manse 6 priory 7 rectory
8 vicarage 9 monastery, parsonage
traveling: 12 circuit rider

cleric
see **clergyman**

clerisy
8 literati 10 illuminati
13 intellectuals

clerk
3 nun 4 monk 5 steno 6 cleric,
scribe 7 scholar 8 minister 9 clergyman, secretary 11 salesperson
12 stenographer

clerkish
4 nice 5 fussy, picky 6 choosy
7 finical, finicky 9 finicking, squeamish 10 fastidious, particular

clever
3 apt, sly 4 able, deft, good, racy,
slim 5 adept, alert, canny, funny,
handy, quick, ready, salty, sharp,
slick, smart, witty 6 adroit, brainy,
bright, crafty, expert, nimble,
pretty, prompt, tricky, wicked
7 amusing, capable, cunning,
knowing, piquant, risible, skilled
8 dazzling, fanciful, humorous,
masterly, pleasing, skillful 9 all-
around, brilliant, competent, deceitful, dexterous, facetious, ingenious,
laughable, many-sided, qualified,
sparkling, sprightly, versatile, whimsical, workmanly 10 neat-handed,
proficient 11 coruscating, intelligent, quick-witted, ready-witted,
workmanlike 12 entertaining
13 scintillating

cliché
5 stale, trite 6 truism 7 bromide
8 banality, bathetic, prosaism, timeworn 9 hackneyed, platitude
10 prosaicism 11 commonplace,
stereotyped 13 stereotypical

click
2 go 4 tick 6 go over, pan out
7 come off, succeed 8 prove out

click beetle
6 elater 8 elaterid

client
6 patron 8 customer

cliff

4 crag 5 bluff, cleve, scarp 7 clog-wyn 8 headland, palisade 9 precipice

Scottish: 5 heuch, heugh

climacteric

4 dire 5 acute 7 crucial 8 critical 9 desperate, menopause 12 change of life

climate

6 medium, milieu 7 ambient 8 ambience 10 atmosphere 11 environment, mise-en-scène 12 surroundings

combining form: 6 meteor 7 meteoro

climatize

6 harden, season 7 toughen 9 acclimate

climax

3 cap, end 4 acme, apex, peak 5 crown 6 apogee, finish, summit, top off 8 capsheaf, capstone, conclude, meridian, pinnacle, round off 9 culminate, finish off, terminate 11 culmination

in drama: 10 catastasis

climb

4 shin, upgo 5 mount, scale, speel 6 ascend 7 clamber 8 escalade, escalate

climbing

8 scandent

climbing iron

7 crampon

clinch

3 hug 4 grip, hold 5 clamp, clasp, grasp, gripe, press 6 clutch, enfold, tenure 7 embrace, grapple, squeeze

cling

4 bond 5 stick 6 adhere, cleave, cohere 8 adhesion, cohesion, stickage, sticking 9 adherence, coherence

clingfish

6 remora

clingstone

5 peach

clink

3 can, jug 4 jail, stir 5 pokey 6 cooler, jingle, lockup, tingle, tinkle 7 chinkle, slammer 8 hoosegow 9 calaboose

clinkers

3 ash 5 ashes 7 cinders

clinquant

6 tinsel 10 glittering

Clio

see **Muse**

clip

3 cut, mow, pin 4 crop, pare, skin, soak, trim 5 lower, prune, shave, shear, skive, slash, stick 6 broach, brooch, fleece, reduce 7 cut back, cut down 8 mark down 10 overcharge

clique

3 mob, set 4 camp, clan, ring 5 cabal 6 circle 7 coterie, faction, in-group 9 camarilla

cloak

4 cape, face, mask, robe, show, veil, wrap 5 cover, guise 6 facade, joseph, mantle, poncho, screen, shroud, veneer 7 blanket, curtain, dress up, manteau 8 disguise 9 dissemble, semblance 10 camouflage 11 dissimulate

ancient Greek: 7 chlamys

ancient Roman: 5 palla, sagum 6 abolla 7 paenula, pallium

Arab: 3 aba

combining form: 6 pallio

fur: 7 pelisse

hooded: 5 capot 6 capote 7 burnous 8 burnoose, cardinal

Indian: 5 choga

Jewish: 6 kittel

liturgical: 4 cope

monk's: 8 analabos

Moroccan: 5 jelab 7 jellaba 8 djellaba

over armor: 6 tabard 7 surcoat

Spanish: 4 capa 5 manta

Turkish: 6 dolman

waterproof: 6 poncho

clobber

4 belt, slam, slug 5 blast, brain, clout, smash 6 wallop

clochard

3 vag 4 hobo 5 tramp 6 canter 7 drifter, floater, vagrant 8 roadster, vagabond 11 bindle stiff

clock

4 time 9 timepiece 11 chronometer

ship-shaped: 3 nef

water: 9 clepsydra

clocklike

4 full 6 minute 7 precise, regular 8 detailed, itemized, thorough 10 blow-by-blow, particular

clockmaker

10 horologist

clockwise

6 deasil, dextro 8 positive 11 right-handed

clod

3 gob, wad 4 boob, dolt, dope, hunk, lump 5 chump, chunk, clump, dummy, dunce, hunch 6 dimwit, nugget 8 dumbbell 9 blockhead, lamebrain

cloddish

7 boorish, ill-bred, loutish 8 churlish, clownish 9 unrefined 10 uncultured, unpolished 11 uncivilized

clodhopper

4 boor, hick, lout, shoe 5 chuff, churl, clown, yokel 6 mucker, rustic 7 bumpkin, grobian, hayseed, hoosier, redneck 9 chawbacon

clog

3 gum, tax, tie 4 curb, fill, lade, load, plug, stop 5 block, choke, close, leash, weigh 6 burden, charge, cumber, fetter, hamper, hobble, hog-tie, lumber, saddle 7 congest, occlude, shackle, stopper, trammel 8 encumber, obstruct 9 cumbrance, entrammel, hindrance, impedance 10 impediment 11 encumbrance

cloister

7 seclude 9 sequester

Cloister and the Hearth author

5 Reade (Charles)

cloistered

7 recluse, secluse 8 hermetic, secluded 9 seclusive 11 sequestered

cloistered one

3 nun 4 monk

Clorinda

beloved: 7 Tancred

father: 6 Senapo

guardian: 6 Arsete

slayer: 7 Tancred

close

3 end 4 bang, clap, clog, face, fill, firm, halt, hard, meet, near, next, nigh, plug, quit, seal, shut, slam, stop, taut 5 abate, block, cease, choke, debar, dense, front, handy, humid, muggy, solid, stivy, taper, tense, thick, tight 6 almost, chummy, desist, ending, finale, finish, lessen, narrow, nearby, nearly, period, reduce, screen, shroud, silent, sticky, stingy, stuffy, sultry, windup, wrap up 7 airless, compact, congest, crowded, dwindle, exclude, miserly, nearest, occlude, shut off, stopper 8 abutting, adjacent, block out, complete, conclude, decrease, diminish, familiar, finalize, intimate, nearmost, ob-

struct, obturate, reserved, reticent, stifling, taciturn, taper off, ultimate, write off **9** adjoining, cessation, compacted, condensed, determine, drain away, encounter, immediate, nearabout, niggardly, penurious, proximate, terminate **10** breathless, compressed, conclusion, consummate, contiguous, contracted, convenient, desistance, near-at-hand **11** constricted, impermeable, neighboring, substantial, suffocating, termination, tight-lipped **12** cheeseparing, confidential, consolidated, impenetrable, parsimonious, tightmouthed **13** pennypinching
combining form: **4** pync, sten **5** plesi, pynco, steno **6** plesio

closed
combining form: **5** clist **6** cleist, clisto, occlus **7** cleisto, occluso

closed-minded
4 deaf **8** unpliant **9** obstinate, pigheaded, unpliable **10** bullheaded, hardheaded, self-willed, unyielding **11** intractable

closefisted
6 stingy **7** miserly **8** clinging, grasping **9** clutching, niggardly, tenacious **13** penny-pinching

close in
3 hem, mew **4** cage, coop **5** fence, hedge **6** corral, immure **7** enclose, envelop

close-knit
8 intimate

close-lipped
6 silent **8** reserved, reticent, taciturn **12** tight-mouthed

closely
4 hard **7** sharply **8** intently, minutely **9** carefully, heedfully, mindfully **11** searchingly **12** meticulously, scrupulously, thoughtfully **13** punctiliously

close match
6 tossup

closemouthed
see **close-lipped**

closeness
8 intimacy

close off
6 cut off, enisle, island **7** isolate **8** insulate, separate **9** segregate, sequester

closet
6 hushed, inside, office **7** private **8** academic **11** speculative, theoretical **12** confidential

closing
3 end, lag **4** last, stop **5** final **6** ending, finish, latest, latter, period **8** eventual, hindmost, terminal, ultimate **9** cessation **10** concluding, desistance **11** termination

closure
3 cap, lid **8** fastener **9** cessation
combining form: **6** clisis **7** cleisis

clot
3 gel, set **4** body, jell **5** array, batch, bunch, clump, group, jelly **6** bundle, gelate **7** battery, cluster, congeal, jellify **8** coagulum, thrombus **9** coagulate **10** gelatinize
combining form: **6** thromb **7** thrombo

cloth
see **fabric**

clothe
3 tog **4** clad, deck, do up, garb, robe **5** array, cloak, drape, dress, endue, equip, tog up **6** attire, bedeck, invest, mantle, outfit, rig out, swathe, tog out **7** apparel, bedrape, costume, dress up, garment, raiment, vesture **8** accouter, enclothe

clothes
3 rig **4** duds, garb, rags, togs **5** array, dress, getup **6** attire, outfit, things **7** apparel, costume, raiment, rigging, toggery, vesture **8** clothing **9** vestments **10** attirement **11** habiliments
basket: **6** hamper
civilian: **5** mufti
relating to: **8** vestiary

clothes moth genus
5 Tinea

clothespress
3 kas **7** armoire **8** wardrobe

clothes tree
8 costumer

cloud
3 dim, fog, tar **4** army, blur, host, rout **5** addle, befog, crowd, flock, gloom, muddy, smear, sully, taint **6** legion, muddle, puzzle, scores, shadow, smudge **7** becloud, besmear, confuse, obscure, perplex, tarnish **8** befuddle, besmirch, discolor, distract, overcast **9** adumbrate, multitude
combining form: **4** cirr **5** cirrh, cirri, cirro, nepho, nimbo **6** cirrhi, cirrho, nephel **7** nephelo
type: **7** cirrus, nimbus **7** cumulus, stratus **11** altocumulus, altostratus **12** cirrocumulus, cirrostratus, cumulonimbus, nimbostratus **13** stratocumulus

cloudburst
6 deluge, shower **8** downpour, rainfall

clouded
4 open **5** shady **7** dubious, unclear **8** doubtful **9** ambiguous, equivocal, uncertain, unsettled **11** problematic

cloudless
4 fair, fine **5** clear, sunny **7** clarion **8** pleasant, rainless, sunshiny **10** undarkened

cloud-like mass
6 nebula

cloudy
4 dull, hazy **5** foggy, heavy, misty, mucky, murky, mushy, vague **6** vapory **7** louring **8** lowering, nubilous, overcast, vaporous

clough
3 gap **5** chasm, cleft, clove, gorge, gulch **6** arroyo, ravine

clout
2 in **3** box, hit **4** biff, chop, cuff, ding, drag, nail, poke, pull, slam, slap, slog, slug, sock **5** paste, punch, smack, smite, whack **6** buffet, strike **9** influence

clove
3 gap **5** chasm, cleft, gorge, gulch **6** arroyo, clough, ravine

clove hitch
4 knot

cloven-footed
8 fissiped

clover
5 lotus **6** alsike, ladino, lucern **7** alfalfa, berseem, lucerne, melilot, trefoil **8** four-leaf, shamrock **9** lespedeza
family: **3** pea
genus: **9** Trifolium

clown
3 wag **4** boor, fool, hick, jake, mime, rube, zany **5** chuff, churl, cutup, joker **7** jester, mucker, mummer, rustic **7** bucolic, buffoon, bumpkin, farceur, grobian, hayseed, hoosier **8** comedian, jokester **9** harlequin **10** mountebank **11** merry-andrew
French: **7** pierrot
operatic: **5** buffo
Spanish: **8** gracioso

clownish
3 row **4** rude, zany **6** clumsy, gauche **7** awkward, boorish, ill-

bred, loutish, lumpish, uncouth
8 churlish, cloddish **9** unrefined
10 uncultured, unpolished
11 uncivilized

cloy
4 fill, glut, jade, pall, sate **5** gorge
6 stodge **7** satiate, surfeit

club
3 bat **4** mace **5** baton, billy, guild,
order, union **6** bistro, cudgel,
league **7** society **8** bludgeon, sodality, sorority **9** truncheon **10** fellowship, fraternity, knobkerrie,
nightstick **11** association,
brotherhood
Australian: **5** waddy
college: **8** sorority **10** fraternity
combining form: **5** clavi **6** rhopal
7 rhopalo
Irish: **8** shillala **10** shillelagh
women's: **7** sorosis

clubfoot
7 talipes

cluck
4 fowl, simp **5** dunce **6** dimwit, nitwit **7** lackwit, pinhead, wantwit
9 dumb bunny **13** featherweight

clue
3 cue **4** hint, post, tell, warn, wind
6 advise, fill in, inform, notify, notion, wise up **7** apprise, inkling
8 acquaint, telltale **10** indication,
intimation, suggestion

clump
3 gob, lot, set, wad **4** body, clod,
hunk, lump **5** array, barge, batch,
bunch, chunk, group, hunch, stump
6 bundle, jumble, lumber, nugget,
parcel **7** cluster, clutter, galumph,
stumble **10** hodgepodge

clump of grass
4 tuft **6** tuffet

clumsy
5 bulky, gawky, inept, splay
6 gauche, klutzy, wooden **7** awkward, hulking, lumpish, uncouth,
unhandy, unhappy **8** bumbling, ungainly, unwieldy **9** graceless, ham-
handed, inelegant, lumbering, maladroit **10** bunglesome
11 heavy-handed

clumsy one
3 oaf **4** lout **5** klutz **6** lummox
7 bungler

clunk
4 thud **5** clonk, thump

clunker
4 heap **5** crate, wreck **6** jalopy,
junker

cluster
3 lot, set **4** band, bevy, body, crew
5 array, batch, bunch, clump,
covey, group, party **6** bundle,
clutch, gather, parcel **7** collect,
package, round up **8** assemble, assembly, cumulate **9** aggregate,
associate **10** accumulate
combining form: **3** cym, kym **4** cymo,
kymo

cluster bean
4 guar

clutch
3 nab, set **4** body, grab, grip,
hold, keep, take **5** array, batch,
bunch, catch, clamp, clasp, clump,
grasp, gripe, group, seize **6** bundle, clench, clinch, harbor, parcel,
snatch, tenure **7** cherish, cluster,
grapple
Scottish: **5** cleek **7** claucht, claught

clutter
4 hash, mash, mess, muss, ruck
5 chaos, snarl **6** ataxia, huddle,
jumble, jungle, litter, medley, muddle, tumble **7** mélange, rummage,
shuffle **8** disarray, disorder, mishmash, scramble **9** confusion, macedoine **10** hodgepodge
12 huggermugger

Clydesdale
5 horse

Clymene
father: **7** Oceanus
husband: **7** Iapetus
mother: **6** Tethys
son: **5** Atlas **10** Epimetheus,
Prometheus

Clytemnestra
brother: **6** Castor, Pollux
10 Polydeuces
daughter: **7** Electra **9** Iphigenia
father: **9** Tyndareus
husband: **9** Agamemnon
lover: **9** Aegisthus
mother: **4** Leda
slayer: **7** Orestes
son: **7** Orestes
victim: **9** Agamemnon, Cassandra

Clytie
beloved: **6** Apollo
form: **9** sunflower **10** heliotrope

coach
5 stage, train, tutor **6** mentor **8** carriage **10** instructor

coadjutant
3 aid **4** aide **9** assistant **10** aide-
de-camp, lieutenant

coadjute
4 band **5** unite **6** concur, league
7 combine, conjoin **9** cooperate

coadjutor
see **coadjutant**

coadunation
5 union **6** merger **7** melding, merging **8** mergence **9** coalition
11 combination, unification

coagulate
3 dry, gel, set **4** clot, jell **5** jelly
6 curdle, freeze, gelate, harden
7 compact, congeal, jellify, thicken
8 coalesce, concrete, condense, solidify **9** dehydrate **10** gelatinize,
inspissate **11** concentrate,
consolidate

coal
combining form: **7** anthrac, carboni
8 anthraco
distillate: **3** tar
dust: **4** coom, smut, soot **5** coomb,
slack
element: **6** carbon
fused leavings: **4** slag **7** clinker
glowing: **5** ember, gleed
hard: **10** anthracite
lump: **3** cob
miner: **7** collier
region: **4** Saar
residue: **4** coke
shaly: **9** tasmanite
soft: **6** cannel **10** bituminous

coalesce
3 mix, wed **4** fuse, join, link
5 blend, cling, merge, stick, unite
6 adhere, cleave, mingle, relate
7 bracket, combine, conjoin, connect **9** associate

coalition
4 bloc, ring **5** party, union
6 league, merger **7** combine, faction, melding, merging **8** alliance,
mergence **9** anschluss **10** federation **11** coadunation, combination,
confederacy, unification **13** confederation, consolidation

coarse
3 low, raw **4** foul, rude **5** caked,
cakey, crass, crude, dirty, gross,
lumpy, nasty, rough, rowdy, tacky
6 common, filthy, grainy, incult,
smutty, vulgar **7** boorish, obscene,
raffish, raunchy, uncouth **8** granular, indecent, inexpert, prentice
9 inelegant, roughneck, unrefined,
vulgarian **10** uncultured **11** particu-
late **12** scatological, uncultivated
food: **6** fodder

coast
4 bank 5 beach, drift, shore, slide
6 strand 8 littoral
of Antarctica: 4 Knox
of west Africa: 5 Ivory
swampy: 7 maremma

coastal
8 littoral

coaster
4 sled

coat
5 layer, plate, tunic 6 blazer,
duster, jacket, patina, raglan,
reefer, ulster, veneer 7 cutaway,
paletot 8 covering, mackinaw, tegument 9 newmarket, redingote
10 integument
animal: 3 fur 4 hide, pelt, wool
6 pelage
arctic: 5 parka
fur-lined: 7 pelisse
glossy: 5 glacé
kind: 3 car, pea, top 5 frock
6 trench
Levantine: 6 caftan
medieval: 8 gambeson
of arms: 5 crest 6 blazon, emblem,
shield, tabard 7 surcoat 8 bla-
zonry 9 escucheon 10 escutcheon
of egg white: 5 glair 6 glaire
of gold: 4 gild, gilt
of mail: 6 byrnie 7 hauberk
Scottish: 4 jupe
seaman's: 5 grego
soldier's: 5 frock, tunic 6 capote
waterproof: 7 slicker 10 mackintosh

coating
4 film 5 layer 6 finish, patina, veneer 7 lacquer 8 covering

coax
3 con, get 4 lure, urge 5 press,
tease, tempt 6 cajole, entice,
fleech, induce, pester, plague
7 blarney, prevail, wheedle 8 blandish, butter up, inveigle, persuade,
soft-soap 9 importune, sweet talk
Scottish: 7 cuittle

cob
3 cap 4 ding, swan 5 excel, horse,
outdo 6 exceed 7 surpass 8 outmatch, outshine, outstrip

cobalt
symbol: 2 Co

cobble
4 make, mend, mess 5 botch,
patch, snafu, stone 6 bollix, bungle, foul up, goof up, mucker, repair 7 confuse, louse up, screw up,
snarl up

cobbler
3 pie 4 fish 5 drink 7 catfish, pompano 9 shoemaker 10 threadfish

cobbler's form
4 last

cobelligerent
4 ally

cobweb
3 net 4 mesh, toil, trap 8 gossamer
12 entanglement

coccyx
8 tailbone

cochineal
3 dye 6 insect

cochleate
6 spiral 11 shell-shaped

cock
3 tap 4 bank, boss, gate, head,
heap, hill, lord, mass, pile, rick
5 chief, drift, mound, stack, swank,
swell, valve 6 faucet, honcho,
leader, master, spigot 7 headman,
hydrant, pyramid, rooster, swagger
8 hierarch, mountain 9 chieftain,
dominator, number one, principal
10 preeminent 11 chanticleer,
pontificate

cock-a-doodle-doo
4 blow, brag, crow, puff 5 boast,
mouth, prate, vaunt 9 gasconade
11 rodomontade

cock-a-hoop
4 awry 5 askew 6 askant
7 askance 8 exultant, exulting, jubilant 9 crookedly, triumphal
10 triumphant

Cockaigne
4 Zion 6 heaven, utopia 7 arcadia
8 paradise 9 fairyland, Shangri-la
10 lubberland, wonderland
12 promised land

cockalorum
8 leapfrog 11 braggadocio

cockamamy
10 incredible, ridiculous

cock-and-bull story
3 fib, lie 6 canard 7 falsity, untruth
9 falsehood 13 prevarication

cockatoo bush
9 blueberry

cockcrow
4 dawn, morn 5 light, sunup 6 aurora 7 dawning, morning, sunrise
8 daybreak, daylight

cocker
4 baby 5 humor, spoil 6 coddle,

cosset, pamper 7 cater to, indulge
11 mollycoddle

cockeyed
4 awry 5 askew, boozy, drunk
6 askant 7 askance, muddled
9 crookedly, disguised, pixilated,
plastered 10 inebriated
11 intoxicated

cockle
4 fret 6 dimple, riffle, ripple

cockleshell
4 boat

cockscomb
see **coxcomb**

cocksure
7 certain 8 positive 9 confident

cocktail
5 Bronx, drink, zombi 6 zombie
7 martini, Sazerac, sidecar 8 aperitif, daiquiri, pink lady, salty dog,
sangrita, sombrero 9 aperitive, appetizer, Manhattan 10 Bloody
Mary, Margharita
fruit: 9 macedoine
gasoline: 7 Molotov

cocktail lounge
3 bar, pub 6 saloon, tavern 7 barroom, gin mill, taproom 8 groggery, pothouse

Cocktail Party author
5 Eliot (Thomas Stearns)

coconspirator
7 abettor 9 accessory 10 accomplice 11 confederate

coconut
husk fiber: 4 coir
meat: 5 copra

coddle
4 baby 5 humor, spoil 6 cosset,
cotton, pamper 7 cater to, indulge
11 mollycoddle

code
6 cipher 7 encrypt 8 encipher
kind: 3 zip 4 area 5 Morse, penal
message in: 10 cryptogram

code word
see **communications code word**

codicil
5 rider 8 addendum, appendix
10 supplement

codswallop
8 nonsense

coefficient
8 coacting, coactive, conjoint, synergic 10 synergetic 11 cooperative

coelenterate
5 coral 7 hydroid 9 jellyfish
10 sea anemone

coerce
3 cow 4 make, push, urge 5 beset,
bully, force 6 compel, menace,
oblige 8 browbeat, bulldoze,
threaten 9 blackjack, constrain, terrorize 10 intimidate

coercion
5 force 6 duress, menace, threat
8 menacing 10 compulsion, constraint 11 threatening

coeval
see **contemporary**

coexistent
see **contemporary**

coffee
alkaloid: 7 caffein 8 caffeine
bean: 3 nib
cake: 6 kuchen
cup: 9 demitasse
cup holder: 4 zarf
French: 4 café
grinder: 4 mill
kind: 4 drip, java 5 latte, mocha
  7 arabica, instant 8 espresso
  10 cappuccino
maker: 6 biggin 10 percolator
pot: 3 urn

coffee shop
4 café 5 diner 8 snack bar 9 hash
house, lunchroom 11 eating house,
greasy spoon 12 luncheonette

coffer
5 chest 8 treasury, war chest
9 exchequer

coffin
3 box 4 kist 6 casket
carrier: 6 hearse 10 pallbearer
nail: 9 cigarette
stand: 4 bier 10 catafalque

cogency
5 force, point, punch 7 bearing,
concern 8 validity 9 relevance, validness 10 connection, pertinence
13 effectiveness

cogent
5 solid, sound, valid 6 potent 7 telling, weighty 8 forceful, forcible,
powerful, puissant 9 justified
10 compelling, convincing, meaningful, persuasive, satisfying 11 influential, significant, well-founded
12 constraining, satisfactory, well-
grounded 13 consequential

cogitate
4 plot 5 think 6 devise, reason
7 collude, connive, imagine, reflect

8 conceive, conspire, contrive, envisage, envision, intrigue 9 cerebrate, machinate, scheme out, speculate 10 deliberate

cogitation
7 thought 9 brainwork 10 reflection 11 cerebration, speculation
12 deliberation

cogitative
7 pensive 8 thinking 9 pondering
10 meditative, reflecting, reflective,
ruminative, thoughtful 11 speculative 13 contemplative

cognate
4 akin 6 agnate, allied, common
7 connate, general, generic, kindred, related 8 incident 9 universal
10 affiliated, connatural
11 consanguine

cognition
9 knowledge 10 perception
combining form: 5 gnosy 6 gnosia,
gnosis

cognizance
4 heed, mark, note 6 notice, regard, remark 9 attention 10 observance 11 observation

cognizant
5 alive, awake, aware 7 knowing, witting 8 sensible, sentient
9 au courant, conscious
12 apprehensive

cognize
4 know 5 grasp 6 fathom 9 apprehend 10 appreciate, comprehend,
understand

cognomen
4 name 5 style, title 7 epithet, moniker 11 appellation, appellative,
designation 12 compellation,
denomination

cognoscente
5 judge 6 critic, expert 8 aesthete
9 authority 10 dilettante, proficient,
specialist 11 connoisseur

cognoscible
8 knowable

cohere
2 go 4 fuse, join 5 agree, blend,
check, cling, fit in, merge, stick,
unite 6 accord, cleave 7 combine,
comport, conform, connect 8 check
out, coalesce, dovetail 9 associate
10 correspond

coherence
4 bond 5 cling, union, unity 8 adhesion, clinging, cohesion, stickage, sticking 9 congruity, integrity

10 conformity, solidarity
11 consistency

coherent
7 unified 9 connected
10 consistent

cohesion
see **coherence**

cohort
4 mate 6 fellow 7 partner, sectary
8 adherent, confrere, disciple, follower, henchman, partisan, sectator
9 associate, copartner, satellite,
supporter 10 consociate

coif
3 cap 4 hood 6 hairdo 8 skullcap

coiffure
6 hairdo 9 headdress
aid: 3 net, rat 5 snood

coil
4 curl, fuss, loop, ring, turn, wind
5 helix, twine, twist 6 furore, rotate,
ruckus, rumpus, shindy, spiral, tumult, uproar 7 entwine, revolve,
shindig, turmoil, wreathe 8 brouhaha, foofaraw 9 commotion,
corkscrew
combining form: 4 spir 5 spiri, spiro

coiled
7 tortile 9 circinate

coin
4 mint
Afghanistan: 3 pul
Albania: 3 lek
Algeria: 5 dinar 7 centime
ancient Greek: 4 obol
ancient Muslim: 5 dinar
ancient Roman: 6 follis 8 denarius
Argentina: 4 peso 7 centavo
Australia: 4 cent 6 dollar
Austria: 8 groschen 9 schilling
Bahamas: 4 cent 6 dollar
Bahrain: 4 fils 5 dinar
Barbados: 4 cent 6 dollar
Belgium: 5 franc 7 centime
Benin: 5 franc
Bhutan: 7 chetrum 8 ngultrum
Bolivia: 7 centavo
Botswana: 4 pula 5 thebe
Brazil: 7 centavo 8 cruzeiro
Bulgaria: 3 lev 8 stotinka
Burundi: 5 franc
Cameroon: 5 franc
Canada: 4 cent 6 dollar
Cape Verde Islands: 6 escudo
Chile: 4 peso 7 centavo
China: 3 fen 4 jiao, yuan 5 chiao
Columbia: 4 peso 7 centavo
Costa Rica: 5 colon
Cuba: 4 peso 7 centavo
Cyprus: 4 cent 5 pound

Czech Republic: 5 haler 6 koruna
defective: 4 fido
Denmark: 3 ore 5 krone
Dominican Republic: 4 peso
   7 centavo
Ecuador: 5 sucre 7 centavo
edge: 7 milling
Egypt: 7 piastre 8 millieme
Ethiopia: 4 cent
European gold: 5 ducat
Fiji: 4 cent 6 dollar
Finland: 5 penni 6 markka
former: 3 ecu, lek, mil, pie, sol
   4 anna, besa, cash, doit, duit, kran,
   para, pice, real, reis (plural)
   5 crown, fanam, litas, mohur,
   paisa, rupia, shahi, soldo, toman
   6 centas, denier, heller, kopeck,
   macuta, pagoda, tangka 7 san-
   tims, sapeque 8 farthing, mara-
   vedi, sixpence, skilling 9 half
   penny, rigsdaler 10 Indian head,
   reichsmark, threepence 13 reich-
   spfennig
France: 5 franc 7 centime
Gambia: 5 butut 6 dalasi
Germany: 4 mark 7 pfennig
Ghana: 4 cedi 6 pesewa
Great Britain: 6 guinea 8 new penny
   9 sovereign
Greece: 6 lepton 7 drachma
Guatemala: 7 centavo, quetzal
Guinea-Bissau: 4 peso
Guyana: 4 cent 6 dollar
Haiti: 6 gourde 7 centime
Honduras: 7 centavo, lempira
Hungary: 6 forint
Iceland: 5 eyrir, krona
India: 5 paisa, rupee
Indonesia: 3 sen 6 rupiah
Iran: 4 rial
Iraq: 4 fils 5 dinar
Ireland: 5 penny 8 farthing
Israel: 5 agora 6 shekel
Italy: 4 lira
Jamaica: 4 cent 6 dollar
Japan: 3 rin, sen, yen
Jordan: 3 fil 5 dinar
Kenya: 8 shilling
Korea, North: 3 won 4 chon
Korea, South: 3 won
Kuwait: 4 fils
large: 9 cartwheel
Lebanon: 5 livre 7 piaster, piastre
Lesotho: 4 loti
Liberia: 4 cent 6 dollar
Libya: 6 dirham
Luxembourg: 5 franc
Madagascar: 5 franc
Malawi: 6 kwacha 7 tambala
Malta: 4 cent 5 pound
Mauritania: 7 ouguiya

Mauritius: 4 cent 5 rupee
Mexico: 4 peso 7 centavo
Monaco: 5 franc
Morocco: 6 dirham
Mozambique: 7 metical
Nepal: 5 paisa, rupee
Netherlands: 4 cent 6 florin, gulden
New Zealand: 4 cent 6 dollar
Nicaragua: 7 centavo, cordoba
Nigeria: 4 kobo
Norway: 3 ore 5 krone
old Hungarian: 5 pengo
old Italian: 5 scudo
old Swedish: 8 skilling
Oman: 4 rial
Pakistan: 4 pice 5 paisa
Panama: 6 balboa 9 centesimo
Papua-New Guinea: 4 kina, toea
Paraguay: 7 centimo, guarani
Peru: 3 sol 7 centimo
Philippines: 4 piso 7 sentimo
Poland: 5 grosz, zloty
Portugal: 6 escudo 7 centavo
Qatar: 6 dirham
Roman: 6 aureus, bezant 7 solidus
Romania: 3 leu
Russia: 5 ruble 6 kopeck
Rwanda: 5 franc
San Marino: 4 lira
Saudi Arabia: 6 halala
Seychelles: 4 cent 5 rupee
side of a: 7 obverse
Sierra Leone: 4 cent
Singapore: 4 cent 6 dollar
Slovakia: 5 haler 6 koruna
South Africa: 4 cent, rand
   10 krugerrand
Spain: 6 peseta 7 centimo
Sri Lanka: 4 cent 5 rupee
stamping metal: 8 planchet
Suriname: 4 cent 6 gulden
Swaziland: 4 cent 9 lilangeni
Sweden: 3 ore 5 krona
Switzerland: 5 franc 6 rappen
Syria: 5 pound
Tanzania: 8 shilling
Thailand: 4 baht 6 satang
thick: 7 piefort 8 piedfort
Tonga: 6 pa'anga, seniti
Trinidad and Tobago: 4 cent 6 dollar
Tunisia: 5 dinar
Turkey: 4 lira 5 kurus
Uganda: 8 shilling
United Arab Emirates: 6 dirham
United States: 4 dime 5 penny 6 dol-
   lar, nickel 7 quarter 10 half dollar
Uruguay: 4 peso 9 centesimo
Vatican City: 4 lira
Venezuela: 9 bolivar
Western Samoa: 4 sene, tala
Zambia: 5 ngwee 6 kwacha
Zimbabwe: 4 cent 6 dollar

coinage
   9 invention, neologism 10 brainchild 11 contrivance

coincide
   4 jibe 5 agree, equal, match, tally
   6 accord, concur 7 concert, concord 9 harmonize 10 correspond

coincident
   9 ancillary, attendant, attending,
   satellite 10 collateral 11 concomitant 12 accompanying

coincidentally
   6 at once 8 together
   12 concurrently

coin-shaped
   8 nummular

___ **colade**
   4 piña

colander's cousin
   5 sieve 6 sifter 8 strainer

cold
   3 icy, raw 4 cool, dead, iced 5 algid, aloof, bleak, brisk, chill, crisp,
   drear, frore, gelid, nippy, polar
   6 arctic, biting, chilly, dismal,
   frigid, frosty, frozen, gloomy, somber, wintry 7 bracing, cutting, defunct, extinct, glacial, joyless, nipping, shivery 8 chilling, comatose,
   deceased, departed, freezing, heat-
   less, lifeless 9 cheerless, chillsome,
   exanimate, inanimate, inhibited,
   senseless 10 impersonal, insensible, oppressive, undersexed 11 dispiriting, emotionless, inconscious,
   indifferent, passionless, unconscious, unemotional 12 matter-of-
   fact, unresponsive 13 unimpassioned, unsympathetic
combining form: 3 cry, kry 4 cryo,
   kryo 5 frigo 7 psychro
common: 6 coryza
symptom: 5 cough, fever 6 sneeze
   7 catarrh

cold ___
   3 war 4 cash, cuts, feet, fish, pack,
   room, sore, wave 5 cream, frame,
   front, patch, steel, sweat, water
   6 turkey 7 storage 8 shoulder

cold-blooded
   7 callous 8 hardened, obdurate
   9 heartless, unfeeling 10 hard-
   boiled, impersonal 11 emotionless,
   hardhearted 12 matter-of-fact,
   stonyhearted 13 unimpassioned

cold box
   4 icer

cold feet

4 fear 5 alarm, dread, panic 6 dismay, fright, horror, terror
11 trepidation 13 consternation

coldhearted

see **cold-blooded**

cold-shoulder

3 cut 4 snob, snub 9 ostracize

cold storage

7 latency 8 abeyance, abeyancy, doldrums, dormancy 10 quiescence, quiescency, suspension
12 intermission, interruption

cole

4 rape 7 cabbage 8 broccoli, kohlrabi 11 cauliflower

Coleridge poem

9 Kubla Khan 10 Christabel

Colette character

4 Gigi 5 Cheri 8 Claudine

colewort

4 kale 7 cabbage

colic

5 gripe 9 bellyache 11 stomachache 12 collywobbles

coliseum

4 bowl 5 stade 7 stadium

collapse

2 go 4 bend, cave, drop, fail, flag, give, tire, wilt 5 break, crash, droop, smash, weary, wreck, yield 6 cave in, fold up, peg out, weaken 7 breakup, crack-up, crumple, debacle, deflate, exhaust, failure, founder, give out, play out, ruining, shatter, smashup, succumb, undoing 8 flake out, languish 9 breakdown, cataclysm, ruination 10 disruption 11 catastrophe, destruction 12 disintegrate

collar

3 bag, cop, get, nab, nip 4 hook, lift, nail, take 5 catch, steal 6 corner, secure 7 capture, prehend 8 bottle up 11 appropriate
armor: 6 gorget
boy's: 4 Eton
chain: 4 torc 6 torque
horse: 7 bargham
jeweled: 6 carcan 8 carcanet
lace-edged: 6 rabato, rebato
medieval: 10 chevesaile
metal: 4 torc 6 torque
Philippine: 7 panuelo
pleated: 4 ruff
wooden: 4 cang 6 cangue

collarbone

8 clavicle

collate

5 order 7 arrange, bracket, compare 8 assemble, contrast
9 integrate

collateral

3 sub 5 under 6 allied 7 cognate, kindred, oblique, related, subject 8 adjuvant, circular, incident, indirect 9 accessory, ancillary, attendant, attending, auxiliary, dependent, satellite, secondary, tributary 10 circuitous, coincident, reciprocal, roundabout, subsidiary 11 adminicular, appurtenant, concomitant, subordinate, subservient 12 accompanying, confirmative, confirmatory, contributory, verificatory 13 complementary, corresponding, corroborative, corroboratory

colleague

3 pal 4 aide, chum 5 buddy, crony 6 fellow, helper 7 compeer, partner 8 confrere, co-worker 9 assistant, associate, companion, copartner 10 compatriot, consociate, workfellow

collect

4 draw, make, rank, rein 5 array, group, infer, judge, order, raise 6 deduce, deduct, derive, gather, muster 7 cluster, compile, compose, control, dispose, make out, marshal, round up 8 assemble, conclude, congress, restrain 10 congregate, rendezvous, simmer down

collected

4 calm, cool, easy, smug, sure 5 quiet, still 6 placid, poised, serene 7 assured 8 composed, peaceful, sanguine, tranquil 9 confident, easygoing, possessed, unruffled 10 complacent, nonchalant 11 unflappable 13 imperturbable, self-possessed, self-satisfied

collection

3 ana, kit, lot 4 band, bevy, clan, crew, olio, ruck 5 bunch, clump, crowd, group, hoard, party, trove 6 medley, muster, outfit 7 cluster, company, variety 8 assembly, caboodle 9 aggregate, amassment, colluvies, congeries, gathering 10 assemblage, assortment, cumulation, miscellany 11 aggregation 12 accumulation, congregation 13 agglomeration, armamentarium

miscellaneous: 4 hash, olio 6 jumble, medley 7 mélange, mixture 8 mishmash, pastiche 9 bric-a-brac, potpourri 10 hodgepodge, salmagundi 11 olla podrida
of anecdotes: 3 ana
of animals: 3 zoo 9 menagerie
of artistic works: 6 museum 7 gallery
of clothes: 8 wardrobe
of dried plants: 9 herbarium
of facts: 4 data
of literary pieces: 5 sylva 8 analecta, analects 9 anthology
of proper names: 11 onomasticon
of reports: 4 file 7 dossier
of trinkets: 10 bijouterie
suffix: 3 ery

collective

association, Russian: 5 artel
farm, Israeli: 7 kibbutz
farm, Russian: 7 kolkhoz

collector

of bird's eggs: 8 oologist
of books: 11 bibliophile
of coins: 11 numismatist
of fares: 9 conductor
of phonograph records: 10 discophile
of postcards: 12 deltiologist
of stamps: 11 philatelist

colleen

4 girl, lass
country: 4 Eire, Erin 7 Ireland

college

building: 3 gym, lab 4 dorm, hall
campus area: 4 quad 10 quadrangle
class meeting: 3 lab 7 lecture, seminar 8 tutorial, workshop
degree: 2 AA, AB, BA, BD, BS, CE, DD, MA, MD, MM, MS 3 BLS, DST, LLB, LLD, MBA, MEd, MFA, MLS, PhD 5 LittD
graduate: 6 alumna, alumni (plural) 7 alumnae (plural), alumnus
official: 4 dean 5 prexy 6 bursar, regent 7 proctor, provost, trustee 8 chairman, chaplain, director 9 counselor, librarian, president, registrar
oldest in U.S.: 7 Harvard
oldest women's in U.S.: 12 Mount Holyoke
permit for absence: 5 exeat
relating to: 8 academic 10 collegiate
social group: 4 frat 8 sorority 10 fraternity
song: 9 alma mater
student class: 4 soph 5 frosh 6 junior, senior 8 freshman 9 sophomore

Carnegie Mellon = Tartans

teacher: **3** don **4** prof **5** tutor **8** academic **9** professor **10** instructor
term: **7** quarter, session **8** semester **9** trimester
VIP: **4** BMOC
woman: **4** coed

college athletic team

Air Force: **7** Falcons
Alabama: **11** Crimson Tide
Arizona: **8** Wildcats
Arizona State: **9** Sun Devils
Arkansas: **10** Razorbacks
Arkansas State: **7** Indians
Army: **6** Cadets
Auburn: **6** Tigers
Baylor: **5** Bears
Boston College: **6** Eagles
Boston University: **8** Terriers
Brigham Young: **7** Cougars
Brown: **5** Bears
California: **11** Golden Bears
Central Michigan: **9** Chippewas
Cincinnati: **8** Bearcats
Citadel: **8** Bulldogs
Clemson: **6** Tigers
Colgate: **10** Red Raiders
Colorado: **9** Buffaloes
Colorado State: **4** Rams
Columbia: **5** Lions
Connecticut: **7** Huskies
Cornell: **6** Big Red
Dartmouth: **8** Big Green
Davidson: **8** Wildcats
Delaware State: **7** Hornets
Drake: **8** Bulldogs
Duke: **10** Blue Devils
Eastern Kentucky: **8** Colonels
Eastern Michigan: **6** Eagles
Florida: **6** Gators
Florida State: **9** Seminoles
Fresno State: **8** Bulldogs
Furman: **8** Palidans
Georgia: **8** Bulldogs
Georgia Tech: **13** Yellow Jackets
Harvard: **7** Crimson
Hawaii: **15** Rainbow Warriors
Holy Cross: **9** Crusaders
Houston: **7** Cougars
Howard: **6** Bisons
Idaho: **7** Vandals
Idaho State: **7** Bengals
Illinois: **6** Illini
Illinois State: **8** Redbirds
Indiana: **8** Hoosiers
Indiana State: **9** Sycamores
Iowa: **8** Hawkeyes
Iowa State: **8** Cyclones
Kansas: **8** Jayhawks
Kansas State: **8** Wildcats
Kent State: **13** Golden Flashes
Kentucky: **8** Wildcats
Lehigh: **9** Engineers

Louisiana State: **6** Tigers
Louisiana Tech: **8** Bulldogs
Maine: **10** Black Bears
Maryland: **5** Terps **9** Terrapins
Massachusetts: **9** Minutemen
Miami (Florida): **10** Hurricanes
Miami (Ohio): **8** Redskins
Michigan: **10** Wolverines
Michigan State: **8** Spartans
Minnesota: **7** Gophers
Mississippi: **6** Rebels
Mississippi State: **8** Bulldogs
Missouri: **6** Tigers
Montana: **9** Grizzlies
Montana State: **7** Bobcats
Navy: **10** Midshipmen
Nebraska: **11** Cornhuskers
Nevada: **6** Rebels **8** Wolfpack
New Hampshire: **8** Wildcats
New Mexico: **5** Lobos
New Mexico State: **6** Aggies
North Carolina: **8** Tar Heels
North Carolina State: **8** Wolfpack
Northeastern: **7** Huskies
Northwestern: **8** Wildcats
Notre Dame: **13** Fighting Irish
Ohio State: **8** Buckeyes
Ohio University: **7** Bobcats
Oklahoma: **7** Sooners
Oklahoma State: **7** Cowboys
Oregon: **5** Ducks
Oregon State: **7** Beavers
Pennsylvania: **7** Quakers
Pennsylvania State: **12** Nittany Lions
Pittsburgh: **8** Panthers
Princeton: **6** Tigers
Purdue: **12** Boilermakers
Rhode Island: **4** Rams
Rice: **4** Owls
Rutgers: **14** Scarlet Knights
San Diego State: **6** Aztecs
San Jose State: **8** Spartans
South Carolina: **9** Gamecocks
South Carolina State: **8** Bulldogs
Southern California: **7** Trojans
Southern Illinois: **7** Salukis
Southern Methodist: **8** Mustangs
Stanford: **9** Cardinals
Syracuse: **9** Orangemen
Temple: **4** Owls
Tennessee: **10** Volunteers
Tennessee State: **6** Tigers
Tennessee Tech: **12** Golden Eagles
Texas: **9** Longhorns
Texas A&M: **6** Aggies
Texas Christian: **11** Horned Frogs
Texas Southern: **6** Tigers
Texas Tech: **10** Red Raiders
Toledo: **7** Rockets
Tulane: **9** Green Wave
UCLA: **6** Bruins
UNLV: **12** Runnin' Rebels
Utah: **4** Utes

Utah State: **6** Aggies
Vanderbilt: **10** Commodores
Villanova: **8** Wildcats
Virginia: **9** Cavaliers
VMI: **7** Keydets
VPI: **8** Gobblers
Wake Forest: **12** Demon Deacons
Washington: **7** Huskies
Washington State: **7** Cougars
West Virginia: **12** Mountaineers
William & Mary: **5** Tribe
Wisconsin: **7** Badgers
Wyoming: **7** Cowboys
Yale: **4** Elis **8** Bulldogs

collide
3 hit, ram **4** bump **5** carom, clash, crash, smash **6** strike **7** impinge **8** conflict

collision
4 bump, jolt **5** clash, crash, shock, smash, wreck **6** impact, pileup **7** crack-up, smashup **10** concussion, percussion **11** destruction **12** demolishment

collocate
3 set **5** place **7** arrange **8** position

collogue
5 treat **6** advise, confab, confer, huddle, parley, powwow **7** consult **11** confabulate

colloid
3 gel, sol **4** agar **8** hydrogel, hydrosol

colloque
4 chat, chin, talk, yarn **5** visit **8** converse

colloquial
6 patois, vulgar **7** vulgate **8** familiar, informal **10** vernacular

colloquium
7 palaver, seminar **10** conference, rap session

colloquy
4 chat, talk **6** parley **7** palaver, seminar **8** converse, dialogue **10** conference, rap session **12** conversation **13** confabulation

collude
4 plot **6** devise **7** connive **8** cogitate, conspire, contrive, intrigue **9** machinate, scheme out

collusion
10 complicity, connivance

colluvies
4 hash **5** hoard, trove **6** jumble, medley **7** mélange **8** mishmash, pastiche **9** amassment, potpourri **10** assortment, collection, cumulation, hodgepodge, miscellany

11 aggregation 12 accumulation
13 agglomeration

collywobbles
5 colic, gripe 9 bellyache
11 stomachache

Colombia
capital: 6 Bogota
highest peak: 9 Cristobal
monetary unit: 4 peso

Colonel Blimp
10 fuddy-duddy 12 stuffed shirt

colonnade
4 stoa

color
3 dye, hue 4 cast, flag, glow, jack,
pink, rose, show, tint, tone 5 belie,
blush, flush, paint, rouge, shade,
stain, tinct, tinge, twist 6 banner,
ensign, mantle, pennon, pinken,
redden, stance 7 crimson, distort,
falsify, pennant, pigment 8 attitude,
disguise, dyestuff, gonfalon, misstate, overdraw, position, standard,
streamer, tincture 9 embellish, embroider, oriflamme, overpaint, overstate, semblance 10 exaggerate
12 chromaticity, misrepresent
band: 5 facia, vitta 6 fascia
combining form: 5 chrom 6 chromo
7 chromat 8 chromato 9 chromasia
primary: 3 red 4 blue 6 yellow
relating to: 9 chromatic
secondary: 5 green 6 orange, purple
soft: 6 pastel

Colorado
academy, college: 5 Regis 10 U.S.
Air Force
capital: 6 Denver
nickname: 15 Centennial State
park: 5 Estes
state bird: 11 lark bunting
state flower: 9 columbine

colorant
3 dye 5 stain 7 pigment 8 dyestuff,
tincture

coloration
combining form: 6 chroia, chromy
7 chromia

colored
6 biased, warped 7 bigoted, partial 8 one-sided, partisan 9 jaundiced 10 prejudiced 11 tendentious 12 prepossessed
combining form: 6 chroic, chrome
7 chromat, chroous 8 chromato

colorful
3 gay 5 gaudy, showy, vivid
6 bright, flashy, florid, garish
7 splashy

coloring
4 face, mask, show 5 front, guise,
put-on 6 facade 8 disguise 9 hyperbole, semblance 12 embroidering,
exaggeration 13 embellishment,
overstatement

coloring matter
combining form: 5 phyll

colorist
6 tinter

colorless
3 wan 4 ashy, drab, dull, flat, pale
5 ashen, livid, lurid, prosy, waxen,
white 6 albino, doughy, pallid
7 insipid, neutral, prosaic 8 abstract, blanched, detached, lifeless,
tintless 10 achromatic, impersonal,
lackluster, lusterless, poker-faced
11 unpassioned 13 disinterested,
dispassionate, unimaginative
combining form: 4 leuc, leuk 5 leuco,
leuko

colossal
4 huge, vast 7 mammoth, titanic
8 gigantic 9 cyclopean, monstrous
10 behemothic, gargantuan
11 elephantine

Colossus of
6 Rhodes

colporteur
7 apostle 9 missioner 10 evangelist, missionary 12 propagandist

colt
4 tyro 6 novice, rookie 8 beginner,
freshman, neophyte, newcomer
9 fledgling, novitiate

coltish
6 elvish, frisky, impish 7 larkish,
playful, puckish, waggish 10 frolicsome 11 mischievous

columbary
8 dovecote, pigeonry 9 dovehouse
11 culverhouse, pigeon house

Columbine
beloved: 9 Harlequin
father: 9 Pantaloon

columbium
symbol: 2 Cb

Columbus
birthplace: 5 Genoa
patron: 8 Isabella 9 Ferdinand
ship: 4 Nina 5 Pinta 10 Santa
Maria
son: 5 Diego
starting point: 5 Palos

column
3 row 4 pier, prop 5 brace, shore
6 pillar 7 support 8 buttress, pilas-

ter 11 underpinner 12 underpinning 13 underpropping
base: 4 ordo 5 socle 6 plinth
9 stylobate
bulge: 7 entasis
female figure: 8 caryatid
male figure: 5 atlas 7 telamon 8 at-
lantes (plural)
style: 5 Doric, Ionic 10 Corinthian
top: 7 capital 8 chapiter

coma
5 faint, sleep, swoon 6 stupor, torpor 7 languor, slumber, syncope
8 blackout, dullness, hebetude, lethargy 9 lassitude, torpidity

comate
3 pal 4 chum 5 buddy, crony
7 comrade 9 associate, companion
11 running mate

comatose
5 dopey, heavy 6 stupid, torpid
8 sluggish 9 lethargic, senseless
10 insensible, slumberous 11 inconscious, unconscious
12 hebetudinous

comb
4 grub, rake, sift, sort 5 probe,
scour 6 forage, search, winnow
7 ransack, rummage 8 finecomb,
separate 11 investigate
combining form: 4 loph 5 lopho
6 pectin 7 pectini

combat
3 war 4 buck, duel 5 fight, repel
6 action, battle, oppose, resist,
strife 7 contend, contest, dispute,
service 8 traverse 9 withstand

combating
prefix: 4 anti

combative
7 warlike 8 militant, vigorous 9 ag-
onistic, bellicose, truculent
10 pugnacious 11 belligerent, contentious, quarrelsome
12 gladiatorial

combativeness
5 fight 6 attack 9 pugnacity 10 aggression 11 bellicosity
12 belligerence

combe
4 dale, glen, vale 6 valley

combination
4 bloc, pool, ring 5 party, tie-up,
union 6 hookup, merger 7 cahoots, faction, melding, merging
8 alliance, mergence 9 aggregate,
coalition 10 connection 11 affiliation, association, coadunation, con-

junction, partnership, unification
13 consolidation
combining form: **4** hapt **5** hapto

combine
3 add, mix, wed **4** band, bloc, fuse, join, link, pool, ring **5** blend, chain, group, merge, party, trust, unify, union, unite **6** cartel, concur, embody, league, mingle, relate **7** bracket, conjoin, connect, faction **8** coadjute, coalesce **9** associate, coalition, commingle, cooperate, integrate, syndicate **10** amalgamate **11** consolidate, incorporate **12** conglomerate
Japanese: **8** zaibatsu

combined action
7 synergy **8** synergia

combust
4 burn **10** incinerate

combustible
4 edgy, fuel **8** agitable, burnable, skittery, skittish, volatile **9** alarmable, excitable, flammable, ignitable, startlish **11** inflammable
material: **3** gas, oil **4** coal, peat, wood **6** tinder

come
4 flow, grow, near, show, stem **5** add up, arise, get in, issue, occur, reach, run to, sum to, total **6** amount, arrive, befall, betide, happen, number, show up, spring, turn up **7** advance, develop, emanate, proceed **8** approach, hail from **9** aggregate, originate, transpire **10** derive from
a cropper: **4** fail, fall
across: **4** find, meet **8** discover **9** encounter
apart: **12** disintegrate
at: **6** attack, attain
away: **5** leave **6** depart
before: **7** precede
between: **9** interfere, interpose
clean: **7** confess
down from: **6** alight
forth: **5** issue **6** appear, emerge
forward: **9** volunteer
from: **6** derive, result
into: **5** enter **7** acquire
near: **5** verge **8** approach
round: **5** rally **7** get well, recover
to pass: **5** occur **6** happen
up: **5** arise
upon: **4** find, meet **6** affect, attack **7** afflict **8** discover **9** encounter

comeback
6 retort **7** riposte **8** repartee

come by
3 see **4** call, gain **5** pop in, run in,

visit **6** attain, drop in, look in, look up, step in **7** acquire, inherit

comedian
3 wag, wit **4** card, zany **5** comic, droll, joker **6** jester **8** funnyman, humorist, jokester, quipster

comedo
9 blackhead

comedown
4 fall, ruin **5** crash **7** descent, setback **8** collapse

come down with
3 get **5** catch **8** contract

comedy
5 humor **8** drollery **9** drollness, funniness, wittiness **10** comicality **12** humorousness

come in
5 enter, reply **6** answer, rejoin, retort, return **7** ingress, respond **9** penetrate

comely
4 fair, nice **5** bonny, sonsy **6** lovely, pretty, proper, seemly, sonsie **7** correct **8** becoming, decorous, handsome **9** beauteous, beautiful, befitting, civilized **10** attractive **11** good-looking

come off
3 hap **5** break, click, occur **6** befall, betide, go over, happen, pan out **7** develop, succeed **8** prove out

come-off
6 escape **7** elusion, evasion **8** escaping, eschewal, shunning **9** avoidance, runaround

come-on
4 bait, lure, trap **5** cheat, decoy, rogue, snare **6** con man, gypper **8** swindler **9** trickster **10** allurement, enticement, seducement, temptation **11** flimflammer **12** bunco steerer, double-dealer, inveiglement **13** confidence man

come out
4 leak **5** break, debut **6** emerge **9** transpire

come out with
3 say **4** tell **5** state, utter **7** declare, deliver

comestible
6 edible **7** eatable **8** esculent

comestibles
4 feed, food, grub **6** viands **7** edibles **8** victuals **9** provender **10** provisions

come through
6 chip in, kick in **7** pitch in, ride out, survive **9** subscribe **10** contribute

come together
4 meet **7** synapse **8** converge

comeuppance
3 due **5** lumps, merit **6** rights **7** deserts **9** deserving

comfort
3 aid **4** help, lift **5** cheer **6** assist, buck up, relief, solace, succor **7** amenity, condole, console, relieve, secours, support, upraise **8** facility, reassure **10** assistance, sympathize **11** commiserate, convenience

comfortable
4 cozy, easy, homy, snug, soft **5** comfy, cushy, homey **6** loungy **7** content, easeful, pleased, restful, welcome, well-off **8** adequate, homelike, pleasant, pleasing, well-to-do **9** agreeable, competent, satisfied, sufficing, well-fixed **10** gratifying, prosperous, sufficient, well-heeled **11** substantial **12** satisfactory

comforter
4 pouf, puff **5** quilt **9** eiderdown

comfortless
5 harsh **7** uncomfy **12** inconsolable **13** discomforting

comfy
4 cozy, easy, homy, snug, soft **5** cushy, homey **7** easeful **8** homelike **11** comfortable

comic
3 wag, wit **5** antic, droll, funny, joker **6** jester **7** risible **8** comedian, farcical, funnyman, gelastic, humorist, jokester, quipster **9** laughable, ludicrous **10** ridiculing, ridiculous
strip: **7** funnies

comical
4 zany **5** droll, funny, silly **6** absurd, impish **7** foolish, risible, roguish, waggish **8** farcical, gelastic, sportive **9** laughable, ludicrous **10** ridiculous

coming
4 next **6** advent **7** arrival, ensuing, nearing **9** following **11** approaching
forth: **7** issuant

comity
5 amity **7** concord, harmony **8** goodwill **10** friendship, kindliness

11 benevolence, camaraderie, comradeship **12** friendliness

comma
4 lull **5** pause **8** interval **9** pausation

command
3 bid, law **4** rule, sway, tell, warn, word **5** canon, might, order, power, skill **6** adjure, behest, charge, compel, direct, enjoin, manage **7** ability, bidding, captain, conduct, control, dictate, know-how, mandate, mastery, precept, statute **9** authority, constrain, direction, directive, expertise, expertism, ordinance **10** domination, expertness, injunction, mastership **11** instruction **12** jurisdiction
to go: **4** mush **6** avaunt, begone, giddap
to stop: **4** whoa **5** avast

commandeer
4 take **5** annex, seize, usurp **6** assume **7** preempt **8** accroach, arrogate **9** sequester **10** confiscate **11** appropriate, expropriate

commander
4 boss, head **6** honcho, leader, master **7** captain, general, headman, officer **8** decurion, hierarch **9** dominator

commandment
3 law **4** rule **5** edict, order **6** decree **7** mitsvah, mitzvah, precept, statute

Commedia dell' ___
4 Arte

comme il faut
4 nice **5** right **6** decent, proper, seemly **7** correct **8** becoming, decorous **9** befitting **10** conforming

commemorate
4 keep **7** observe **8** monument **9** celebrate, solemnize **11** memorialize **13** monumentalize

commemorative
8 memorial

commence
4 open **5** arise, begin, enter, start **6** launch, take up **7** kick off, lead off **8** embark on **9** originate **10** embark upon, inaugurate

commencement
4 dawn **5** alpha, birth, onset, start **6** outset **7** dawning, genesis, opening **8** outstart **9** beginning

commend
4 hail, laud **5** extol **6** commit, kudize, praise, tender **7** acclaim, applaud, approve, confide, consign,

entrust, proffer **8** hand over, relegate, turn over **10** compliment

commendable
6 worthy **8** laudable **9** admirable, deserving, estimable, meritable, praisable **11** meritorious, thankworthy **12** praiseworthy

commensurable
see **commensurate**

commensurate
4 even **5** equal **11** symmetrical **12** proportional

comment
4 note **6** notice, remark, review **7** observe **8** critique, reviewal **9** criticism **10** animadvert **11** observation **12** obiter dictum

commerce
5 trade, truck **7** contact, traffic **8** business, congress, dealings, exchange, industry **9** communion **11** interchange, intercourse **13** communication

commercial
2 ad **8** business **10** mercantile **13** advertisement

commie
3 Red **9** Bolshevik, communist

commination
5 curse **7** malison **8** anathema **11** imprecation, malediction

commingle
3 mix **5** immix, merge, unify **8** compound, intermix **9** integrate **10** amalgamate

comminute
4 bray, buck **5** crush **6** powder **9** pulverize, triturate **12** contriturate

commiserable
4 poor **6** rueful **7** piteous, pitiful **8** pathetic, pitiable

commiserate
4 ache, pity **7** feel for **10** sympathize **13** compassionate

commiseration
3 rue **4** pity, ruth **8** sympathy **10** compassion

commission
3 bid **4** name **5** board, order **6** charge, depute, enable, enjoin **7** appoint, command, council, empower, license **8** accredit, delegate, deputize, instruct, nominate **9** authorize, designate

commit
2 do **5** allot **6** assign, invest, ordain **7** commend, confide, consign, entrust, execute, perform, pull off,

trustee **8** hand over, relegate, turn over **10** perpetuate

commitment
4 duty, must, need **5** ought **6** charge, devoir **10** obligation

committal
see **commitment**

commixture
6 fusion **7** compost **9** composite **11** interfusion

commodious
4 wide **5** ample, roomy **8** spacious **9** capacious

commodities
5 goods, items, wares **6** things **8** articles **9** vendibles **11** merchandise

common
4 flat, park, poor **5** cheap, joint, plaza, prosy, stale, tatty, trite, typic, usual **6** decent, garden, impure, mutual, normal, paltry, shared, shoddy, sleazy, square, trashy **7** defiled, general, generic, natural, prosaic, regular, routine, typical **8** adequate, all right, communal, conjoint, conjunct, déclassé, everyday, familiar, frequent, inferior, low-grade, ordinary **9** customary, pleasance, prevalent, tolerable, universal **10** desecrated, second-rate, sufficient, uneventful, unexciting **11** intermutual, second-class **12** matter-of-fact, satisfactory, second-drawer, unnoteworthy **13** unexceptional, unimpeachable, uninteresting
combining form: **3** cen **4** caen, ceno, coen **5** caeno, coeno

commonalty
3 mob **5** plebs **6** masses, people, plebes, public, rabble **7** commune **8** populace **9** hoi polloi, multitude, plebeians **11** proletariat, rank and file, third estate

commoners
see **commonalty**

commonition
6 caveat **7** caution, warning **11** forewarning

commonplace
5 lowly, tired, trite, usual **6** cliché, normal, truism **7** bromide, clichéd, general, inanity, mundane, natural, prosaic, regular, typical, workday **8** banality, bromidic, chestnut, everyday, ordinary, prosaism, shopworn, timeworn, well-worn, workaday **9** platitude, prevalent, triteness **10** prosaicism, shibboleth, stereo-

type, threadbare, uneventful **11** stereotyped **12** unnoteworthy **13** stereotypical, unexceptional

common sense
6 wisdom **8** gumption, judgment

Common Sense author
5 Paine (Thomas)

commorancy
4 home **5** abode, house **8** domicile, dwelling **9** residence, residency **10** habitation

commotion
3 din, row **4** coil, flap, fuss, moil, riot, stew, stir, to-do **5** hurly, storm, upset, whirl **6** bustle, clamor, dither, flurry, fracas, furore, hassle, hoopla, hubbub, hurrah, lather, outcry, pother, racket, ruckus, rumpus, shindy, tow-row, tumult, uproar, upturn **7** clatter, ferment, fluster, ruction, shindig, turmoil, whoopla **8** brouhaha, disquiet, foofaraw, rowdydow, upheaval, uprising **9** agitation, confusion **10** convulsion, hullabaloo, hurly-burly, turbulence **11** pandemonium **12** perturbation

commove
5 elate **6** excite **7** inspire **9** stimulate **10** exhilarate

communal
5 joint **6** common, mutual, public, shared **8** conjoint, conjunct **11** intermutual

commune
6 confer **8** commerce, converse, district **10** collective **12** conversation
Israeli: **7** kibbutz
Russian: **3** mir **7** kolkhoz

communicable
8 catching **9** expansive, garrulous, talkative **10** contagious, infectious

communicate
4 abut, join, tell **5** touch, verge **6** adjoin, border, butt on, convey, impart, pass on, reveal, signal **7** contact, divulge **8** disclose, neighbor, transmit

communication
4 talk, word **7** contact, message, missive, talking **8** commerce, converse, exchange **9** directive **10** conversing, discussing, discussion **11** interchange, intercourse **12** conversation
means: **2** TV **4** drum, note **5** media, phone, radio **6** letter, medium, pi-

geon, speech **9** telegraph, telephone **10** television
system: **8** language

communications code word
4 Alfa, Echo, Golf, Kilo, Lima, Mike, Papa, Xray, Zulu **5** Bravo, Delta, Hotel, India, Oscar, Romeo, Tango **6** Quebec, Sierra, Victor, Yankee **7** Charlie, Foxtrot, Juliett, Uniform, Whiskey **8** November

communicative
7 voluble **9** expansive, garrulous, talkative **10** loquacious

communion
4 cult, sect **5** creed, faith, truck **6** church **7** contact, traffic **8** commerce, converse, dealings, religion **10** connection, persuasion **11** intercourse **12** denomination
cloth: **8** corporal
cup: **3** ama **7** chalice
plate: **5** paten

communism
8 Leninism **10** bolshevism

Communist
3 red **5** pinko **6** commie **7** comrade, Marxist **8** Leninist **9** Bolshevik, Stalinist **10** Trotskyist

Communist leader
Chinese: **10** Mao Tse-tung
Russian: **5** Lenin (Vladimir) **6** Stalin (Joseph) **7** Trotsky (Leon) **10** Khrushchev (Nikita)

community
4 city, town **6** people, public **7** enclave, society **12** neighborhood
ecological: **10** biocenosis

commute
5 alter **6** change, travel **7** convert **8** exchange, transfer **9** transform, translate, transmute, transpose **10** compensate, substitute **11** interchange, transfigure **12** metamorphose, transmogrify

compact
4 bond, firm, hard **5** close, dense, pithy, thick, tight, unify **6** packed **7** bargain, bunched, crowded **8** compress, condense, contract, covenant **9** agreement, integrate **10** convention **11** concentrate, consolidate, transaction **12** epigrammatic
combining form: **4** pycn **5** pycno

companion
3 pal **4** chum, fere, mate, twin **5** buddy, crony, match **6** attend, cohort, comate, double, escort, fellow **7** comrade, conduct, consort,

partner **8** chaperon, helpmate, helpmeet **9** accompany, associate, colleague, duplicate **10** coordinate, reciprocal **11** concomitant, consort with, running mate **13** accompaniment

companionable
6 social **7** amiable **8** sociable **9** convivial **11** good-natured

companionship
7 company, society **10** fellowship

company
3 mob **4** band, club, crew, firm, gang, pack, ruck, team **5** corps, group, house, party, troop **6** attend, clique, convoy, guests, muster, outfit, troupe **7** concern, conduct, coterie, society, visitor **8** assembly, business, chaperon, visitors **9** companion, gathering **10** assemblage, collection, enterprise, fellowship **11** aggregation, association, camaraderie, comradeship **12** congregation, consocation **13** companionship, establishment

comparable
4 akin, like **5** alike **6** agnate **7** similar, uniform **8** parallel **9** consonant **13** corresponding, undifferenced

comparative
4 near **8** relative **11** approximate
suffix: **2** er

compare
5 liken, match **6** equate **7** bracket, collate, paragon **8** contrast, parallel **9** correlate **10** assimilate

comparison
6 simile **7** analogy **8** affinity, likeness **9** alikeness, semblance **10** similarity, similitude **11** resemblance

compass
3 get, hem, see, win **4** gain, gird, ring **5** ambit, annex, catch, field, grasp, orbit, range, reach, round, scope, sweep **6** bounds, circle, domain, extent, girdle, limits, obtain, radius, secure, sphere, take in **7** acquire, circuit, environ, procure, purview **8** boundary, confines, encircle, environs, purlieus, surround **9** apprehend, enclosure, extension, perimeter, periphery, precincts **10** comprehend, understand **13** circumference
kind: **4** gyro **5** solar **8** lensatic, magnetic
stand: **8** binnacle

compassion

3 rue 4 pity, ruth 5 mercy 7 charity, empathy 8 clemency, humanity, sympathy 10 humaneness 11 benevolence 13 commiseration, fellow feeling

compassionate

4 pity, warm 6 humane, tender 7 clement, feel for 10 responsive 11 commiserate, kindhearted, softhearted, sympathetic, warmhearted

compassionless

5 stony 7 callous 8 obdurate 9 heartless, unfeeling 11 coldblooded, hardhearted, ironhearted 12 stony-hearted

compass point

2 NE, NW, SE, SW 3 ENE, ESE, NNE, NNW, SSE, SSW, WNW, WSW 4 east, west 5 north, rhumb, south
Scottish: 4 airt

compatible

6 proper 8 suitable 9 agreeable, congenial, congruous, consonant 10 consistent 11 sympathetic

compatriot

7 compeer 8 confrere 9 associate, colleague

compeer

see **compatriot**

compel

4 hale, make, urge 5 drive, force 6 coerce, impose, oblige 7 concuss, enforce 9 constrain
Scottish: 3 gar

compellation

4 name 5 nomen, style, title 7 moniker 8 cognomen 11 appellative, designation 12 denomination

compendious

4 curt 5 brief, short 7 compact, concise, laconic, summary 8 succinct 12 breviloquent 13 short and sweet

compendium

5 brief, guide 6 aperçu, digest, manual, précis, sketch, survey 7 pandect, sylloge 8 Baedeker, handbook, overview, syllabus 9 guidebook, vade mecum 10 abridgment, conspectus 11 enchiridion

compensate

3 pay 5 atone, repay 6 make up, offset, redeem, set off 7 balance, guerdon, requite 8 atone for, outweigh 9 indemnify, reimburse 10 counteract, neutralize, recompense, remunerate 11 countervail 12 counterpoise

compensation

6 amends, reward, salary 7 payment, redress 8 reprisal, requital, solatium 9 indemnity, quittance 10 recompense, reparation 11 restitution

compete

3 vie 5 fight, match, rival 6 battle, strive 7 contend, contest, dispute, emulate, tourney 8 rivalize, struggle

competence

5 might 6 enough 7 ability 8 adequacy, capacity 10 capability 11 sufficiency 13 qualification, qualifiedness

competent

4 able 5 adept 6 au fait, decent, enough, proper 7 capable, skilled 8 adequate, masterly 9 qualified, sufficing 10 sufficient 11 comfortable 12 satisfactory

competition

4 game, meet 5 match, rival 6 strife 7 contest, rivalry, warfare 8 concours, conflict, corrival, striving, struggle, tug-of-war 9 emulation, rencontre

competitor

5 rival 8 corrival, opponent 9 adversary 10 antagonist, contestant

compile

4 edit 6 gather, muster, select 7 collect 8 assemble

complacence

see **complacency**

complacency

5 pride 6 egoism 7 conceit, egotism 9 vainglory 10 narcissism 11 amour propre, consequence 13 conceitedness

complacent

4 smug 7 assured 8 egoistic, priggish 9 conceited, confident, egotistic 11 self-assured, self-pleased 13 self-confident, self-contented, self-possessed, self-satisfied

complain

3 nag 4 beef, crab, fuss, kick, wail 5 gripe, grump, whine 6 grouch, grouse, murmur, pester, repine, yammer 7 grizzle, grumble, protest 9 bellyache

complainer

4 crab 5 crank 6 griper, grouch, kicker 7 grouser 8 grumbler, sourpuss 10 malcontent 11 faultfinder

complaint

3 ill 5 gripe 6 malady 7 ailment, disease, protest 8 disorder, sickness, syndrome 9 affection, condition, infirmity

complaisant

4 easy, mild 7 amiable, lenient 8 generous, obliging 9 agreeable, indulgent 11 good-humored, goodnatured 12 good-tempered

complement

4 crew 7 pendant 9 correlate 10 enrichment, supplement 11 counterpart, enhancement 12 augmentation 13 accompaniment

complementary

prefix: 7 counter

complete

3 end 4 done, full, halt 5 close, ended, gross, total, uncut, utter, whole 6 choate, entire, finish, wind up, wrap up 7 achieve, fulfill, perfect, perform, plenary, through 8 absolute, conclude, finished, integral, outright, realized, thorough, totalize, ultimate, undocked, wholehog 9 concluded, determine, discharge, downright, full-dress, implement, out-and-out, terminate 10 accomplish, consummate, exhaustive, terminated, unabridged 11 uncondensed, unmitigated 13 thoroughgoing, unabbreviated
combining form: 3 hol, tel 4 holo, tele, telo 5 teleo

completed

4 done, over 5 ended 7 through 8 finished 9 concluded 10 terminated

completion

3 end 6 finish
combining form: 6 teleut 7 teleuto

complex

5 vague 6 daedal, knotty, system, varied 7 gordian, mixed-up, network, obscure 8 baffling, compound, confused, involved, puzzling 9 Byzantine, composite, confusing, elaborate, intricate 10 mysterious, mystifying, perplexing 11 bewildering, complicated, confounding 12 labyrinthine 13 heterogeneous, sophisticated

complexion

3 hue 4 tint 5 color, humor, tinge 6 makeup, nature, temper 8 tincture 9 character 11 disposition, personality, temperament 13 individualism, individuality

complexionless
4 ashy, pale 5 ashen, livid, lurid, waxen 6 doughy, pallid 8 blanched 9 colorless

compliance
8 docility 9 obedience 10 conformity 11 amenability, resignation 12 acquiescence, tractability

complicate
5 mix up, ravel, snarl, upset 6 jumble, muddle, tangle 7 perplex 8 disorder, entangle 10 disarrange

complicated
4 hard 5 fancy 6 daedal, knotty 7 complex, gordian 8 abstruse, involved 9 Byzantine, elaborate, intricate, recondite 12 labyrinthine 13 sophisticated

complicity
9 collusion 10 connivance 11 involvement

compliment
4 hail, kudo, laud 6 kudize, praise 7 acclaim, applaud, bouquet, commend, orchids, tribute 8 accolade, encomium 9 laudation, recommend 12 commendation

complimentary
4 free 6 gratis 8 costless 10 chargeless, gratuitous

comply
4 keep, mind, obey 6 follow, submit 7 conform, observe 9 acquiesce

component
4 part 6 factor 7 element 10 ingredient 11 constituent

comport
3 act 4 bear, go on, quit 5 agree, carry, check, fit in, tally 6 accord, acquit, behave, demean, square 7 conduct 8 dovetail 9 harmonize 10 correspond

comportment
3 air, set 4 mien 5 tenue 7 address, bearing, conduct 8 behavior, demeanor, presence

compose
4 balm, calm, cool, form, lull, make, rein 5 allay, quiet, relax, still, verse, write 6 becalm, create, devise, indite, invent, make up, settle, solace, soothe 7 collect, comfort, console, contain, control, dream up, repress, versify 8 comprise, melodize, mitigate, moderate, modulate, restrain, suppress,

tune down 9 originate, re-collect 10 constitute, simmer down 11 tranquilize
type: 3 set

composed
4 calm, cool, easy 5 quiet, staid, still 6 placid, poised, sedate, serene 8 tranquil 9 collected, easygoing, possessed, repressed, unruffled 10 nonchalant, suppressed 11 unflappable 13 imperturbable, self-possessed

composer
4 bard, poet 5 odist 6 author, lyrist, penman, scorer, writer 7 elegist, hymnist 8 compiler, essayist, lyricist, melodist, monodist, novelist 9 balladist, dramatist, harmonist, scenarist, songsmith, tunesmith, wordsmith 10 compositor, typesetter
American: 3 Kay (Hershy, Ulysses) 4 Cage (John), Hill (Edward Burlingame, Jackson), Ives (Charles), Kern (Jerome), Work (Henry Clay) 5 Arlen (Harold), Bland (James), Bloch (Ernest), Cohan (George M.), Dylan (Bob), Friml (Rudolf), Glass (Philip), Gould (Morton), Grofé (Ferde), Handy (William Christopher), Loewe (Frederick), Mason (Daniel Gregory, Lowell), Moore (Douglas), Sousa (John Philip), Still (William Grant) 6 Barber (Samuel), Berlin (Irving), Cowell (Henry), Emmett (Daniel), Foster (Stephen), Hanson (Howard), Harris (Roy), Joplin (Scott), McKuen (Rod), Morton (Ferdinand Joseph "Jelly Roll"), Oliver (Joe "King"), Parker (Charlie "Bird," Horatio), Piston (Walter), Porter (Cole), Seeger (Charles, Pete), Taylor (Deems, James), Varese (Edgar) 7 Babbitt (Milton), Brubeck (Dave), Copland (Aaron), Gilbert (Henry F.), Gilmore (Patrick), Goldman (Edwin), Guthrie (Arlo, Woody), Herbert (Victor), Loesser (Frank), Maxwell (Elsa), Menotti (Gian-Carlo), Rodgers (Richard), Romberg (Sigmund), Schuman (William), Thomson (Virgil), Tiomkin (Dimitri) 8 Billings (William), Burleigh (Henry Thacker), Damrosch (Leopold, Walter), Gershwin (George, Ira), Kreisler (Fritz), Sessions (Roger), Sondheim (Stephen), Spalding (Albert), Williams (Clarence, Bert, Hank, John) 9 Bacharach (Burt), Bernstein (Elmer, Leonard), Ellington (Duke), Ledbetter (Huddie "Leadbelly"), MacDowell

(Edward) 10 Blitzstein (Marc), Gottschalk (Louis Moreau)
Argentinian: 9 Ginastera (Alberto)
Australian: 8 Grainger (Percy)
Austrian: 4 Berg (Alban), Wolf (Hugo) 5 Haydn (Joseph) 6 Czerny (Karl), Mahler (Gustav), Mozart (Leopold, Wolfgang Amadeus), Straus (Oscar), Sulzer (Salomon), Webern (Anton von) 7 Strauss (Eduard, Johann, Josef, Richard) 8 Bruckner (Anton), Schubert (Franz) 9 Schönberg (Arnold)
Belgian: 5 Ysaye (Eugene-Auguste)
Brazilian: 10 Villa-Lobos (Heitor)
Czech: 3 Suk (Josef) 6 Dvořák (Antonín) 7 Janáček (Leoš), Kubelik (Jan, Rafael), Smetana (Bedřich)
Danish: 7 Nielsen (Carl)
Dutch: 9 Sweelinck (Jan)
English: 4 Arne (Thomas), Byrd (William) 5 Elgar (Edward William) 6 Delius (Frederick), Morley (Thomas), Tallis (Thomas), Walton (William), Wesley (Charles, Samuel) 7 Britten (Benjamin), Dowland (John), Gibbons (Orlando), Purcell (Henry), Weelkes (Thomas) 8 Sullivan (Arthur) 11 Lloyd Webber (Andrew)
Finnish: 8 Palmgren (Selim), Sibelius (Jean)
Flemish: 5 Dufay (Guillaume), Lasso (Orlando di) 6 Lassus (Orlande de) 8 Willaert (Adriaan)
French: 4 Indy (Vincent d'), Lalo (Edouard) 5 Auber (Esprit), Bizet (Georges), Dukas (Paul-Abraham), Fauré (Gabriel-Urbain), Ibert (Jacques), Jarre (Maurice), Lully (Jean-Baptiste), Ravel (Maurice), Satie (Erik), Widor (Charles-Marie) 6 Boulez (Pierre), Campra (Andre), Franck (Cesar), Gounod (Charles-François), Rameau (Jean-Philippe), Thomas (Ambroise) 7 Berlioz (Hector), Debussy (Claude), Delibes (Leo), Milhaud (Darius), Poulenc (Francis) 8 Chabrier (Emmanuel), Couperin (Francois, Louis), Honegger (Arthur), Massenet (Jules), Messiaen (Olivier) 9 Offenbach (Jacques)
German: 4 Bach (Carl Philipp, Johann Christian, Johann Christoph, Johann Sebastian, Wilhelm Friedmann, Wilhelm Friedrich), Orff (Carl) 5 Bruch (Max), Gluck (Christoph), Reger (Max), Spohr (Louis), Weber (Carl Maria von), Weill (Kurt) 6 Brahms (Johannes), Handel (George Frideric), Schutz (Heinrich), Vogler (Abt), Wagner (Rich-

ard, Siegfried) **7** Hassler (Hans Leo), Richter (Ernst, Franz), Silcher (Friedrich), Strauss (Richard) **8** Schumann (Georg, Robert), Telemann (Georg Philipp) **9** Beethoven (Ludwig van), Buxtehude (Dietrich), Hindemith (Paul), Meyerbeer (Giacomo) **10** Praetorius (Michael) **11** Humperdinck (Engelbert), Mendelssohn (Felix), Stockhausen (Karlheinz)

Hungarian: **5** Lehar (Franz), Liszt (Franz) **6** Bartok (Bela), Kodaly (Zoltan), Ligeti (Gyorgy) **8** Dohnanyi (Erno)

Italian: **4** Peri (Jacopo) **5** Boito (Arrigo), Verdi (Giuseppe), Vinci (Leonardo) **6** Busoni (Ferruccio), Viotti (Giovanni), Vitali (Giovanni) **7** Bellini (Vincenzo), Corelli (Arcangelo), Martini (Padre), Puccini (Giacomo), Rossini (Gioacchino), Tartini (Giuseppe), Vivaldi (Antonio) **8** Clementi (Muzio), Gabrieli (Andrea, Giovanni), Mascagni (Pietro), Paganini (Niccolo), Respighi (Ottorino) **9** Cherubini (Luigi), Donizetti (Gaetano), Pergolesi (Giovanni), Scarlatti (Alessandro, Giuseppe), Tommasini (Vincenzo) **10** Boccherini (Luigi), Monteverdi (Claudio), Palestrina (Giovanni da), Ponchielli (Amilcare), Zingarelli (Niccolo) **11** Frescobaldi (Girolamo), Leoncavallo (Ruggero) **12** Dallapiccola (Luigi)

Mexican: **6** Chavez (Carlos)

Norwegian: **5** Grieg (Edvard), Olsen (Sparre)

Polish: **6** Chopin (Frederic) **10** Paderewski (Ignacy), Penderecki (Krzysztof), Wieniawski (Henryk)

Romanian: **7** Xenakis (Iannis)

Russian: **6** Glinka (Mikhail) **7** Borodin (Aleksandr) **8** Glazunov (Aleksandr), Scriabin (Aleksandr) **9** Prokofiev (Sergey) **10** Mussorgsky (Modest), Rubinstein (Anton), Stravinsky (Igor), Tcherepnin (Nikolay) **11** Tchaikovsky (Pyotr Ilich) **12** Rachmaninoff (Sergey), Shostakovich (Dmitry)

Spanish: **5** Falla (Manuel de), Vives (Amadeo) **6** Garcia (Manuel) **7** Albéniz (Isaac) **8** Granados (Enrique), Victoria (Tomas Luis de)

composite
3 mix **6** hybrid **7** amalgam, complex, compost, mixture, montage **8** compound **9** immixture **10** commixture **11** combination **12** amalgamation, intermixture

composition
5 essay, paper, theme **6** design, makeup **7** article, morceau, writing **8** fantasia **9** formation **10** compromise **12** architecture, constitution, construction

choral: **5** motet

for eight: **5** octet

for five: **7** quintet

for four: **7** quartet

for nine: **5** nonet

for one: **4** solo **5** scena

for seven: **6** septet

for six: **6** sextet

for three: **4** trio

for two: **4** duet **6** duetto

instrumental: **3** jig **4** reel **5** étude, fugue, gigue, march, rondo, suite **6** sonata **7** caprice, partita, prelude, scherzo **8** allemand, concerto, fantasia, overture, rhapsody, saraband, sinfonia, symphony, tone poem **9** capriccio, sarabande **10** intermezzo

vocal: **4** aria, lied, mass, song **5** canon, carol, chant, motet, opera, round **6** arioso, ballad, chorus **7** cantata, chanson, chantey, chorale, lullaby, requiem **8** berceuse, madrigal, oratorio **9** barcarole, plainsong, spiritual **12** cantus firmus

compos mentis
4 sane **5** lucid **6** normal

composure
6 phlegm **7** ataraxy **8** calmness, coolness **9** sangfroid **10** equanimity

compound
3 mix **4** join, link **5** admix, alloy, blend, boost, immix, unite **6** commix, couple, expand, extend, fusion, make up, mingle **7** amalgam, augment, bracket, complex, compost, connect, enlarge, magnify, mixture **8** coagment, coalesce, comingle, heighten, increase, intermix, multiply **9** admixture, associate, coadunate, commingle, composite **10** aggrandize, commixture **11** intermingle **12** amalgamation

aromatic: **7** depside

chemical: (see at **chemical**)

combining form: **5** genin

medicinal: **7** quassin **8** magnesia

protein: **7** peptone

sulfur: **5** thiol **6** sulfid **7** sulfide, sulfone **8** sulfonal, sulfuryl, sulphide, sulphone

volatile: **8** cymogene

comprehend
3 dig, get, see **4** know **5** catch, grasp **6** accept, embody, fathom, take in **7** cognize, compass, contain, embrace, include, involve, subsume **8** perceive **9** encompass **10** appreciate, understand

comprehendible
5 lucid **8** knowable, luminous **9** graspable **10** fathomable **12** intelligible **13** apprehensible

comprehensible
see **comprehendible**

comprehensive
4 full, wide **5** broad **6** global **7** general, overall **8** sweeping **9** all-around, inclusive **12** encyclopedic

comprehensiveness
5 scope **7** breadth **8** fullness, wideness **9** amplitude

compress
3 jam **4** bear, cram, push **5** crowd, crush, press, stupe **6** shrink, squash, squish **7** bandage, compact, pledget, squeeze **8** condense, contract, laminate **9** constrict **11** concentrate

comprise
4 form, make **6** make up **7** compose, contain, include **10** constitute

compromise
4 mean, pact, risk **5** peril **6** hazard, menace **7** bargain, compact, imperil, jeopard **8** contract, endanger, jeopardy **9** agreement, middle way **10** golden mean, jeopardize **11** composition **12** middle ground

compulsion
4 itch, need, urge **5** drive, force **6** duress **8** coercion, exigency, violence **9** necessity **10** constraint

compulsory
8 required **9** imperious, mandatory **10** imperative, obligatory

compunction
3 rue **4** ruth **5** demur, qualm **6** squeam **7** penance, remorse, scruple **9** attrition, hesitancy, penitence, penitency **10** conscience, contrition, hesitation, repentance **12** contriteness

compunctious
5 sorry **8** contrite, penitent **9** regretful, repentant **10** apologetic, remorseful **11** attritional, penitential

computation
8 figuring **9** ciphering, reckoning

10 arithmetic, estimation
11 calculation

compute
5 total 6 cipher, figure, reckon
8 estimate 9 calculate

computer
6 abacus 7 machine 10 calculator
13 adding machine
data: 7 readout 8 printout, software
information: 4 data
instruction: 5 macro
inventor: 7 Babbage (Charles)
language: 5 ALGOL, BASIC, COBOL
7 FORTRAN
operator: 9 programer 10 programmer
printer: 5 laser 9 dot matrix
type: 6 analog 7 digital

comrade
3 pal 4 ally, chum, mate 5 buddy,
crony 6 comate, fellow, frater
7 brother, consort 8 tovarich, tovarish 9 associate, communist,
companion

comstock
4 prig 5 prude 6 Grundy 7 puritan
8 bluenose 9 Mrs. Grundy, nice
Nelly 10 goody-goody

con
4 anti, bilk, coax, dupe, fool, hoax,
scam, view 5 learn, study, trick
6 befool, cajole, gammon, inmate,
survey 7 blarney, canvass, chicane, convict, deceive, examine, inspect, opposer, swindle, wheedle
8 blandish, flimflam, hoodwink, jailbird, memorize, opponent, opposure, prisoner, soft soap 9 adversary, bamboozle, check over,
oppugnant, sweet-talk 10 antagonism, antagonist, antithesis, opposition, scrutinize 11 contrariety,
hornswoggle

concatenate
4 join, link 5 unite 7 connect 9 integrate 10 articulate

concave
6 arched 7 vaulted 8 bowllike
9 depressed
combining form: 7 coelous

concavity
3 dip, sag 4 bowl, dent, sink 5 basin 6 hollow 7 sinkage 8 sinkhole
10 depression

conceal
4 bury, hide, veil 5 cache, cloak,
cover, stash 6 occult, screen 7 secrete 8 ensconce, enshroud, palliate 10 camouflage

concealed
5 privy 6 buried, covert, hidden,
secret 7 guarded 8 obscured,
shrouded, ulterior 11 clandestine
combining form: 4 adel 5 adelo

concede
3 own 4 avow 5 admit, allow,
award, grant, let on, own up 6 accord, fess up 7 confess 9 vouchsafe 11 acknowledge

conceit
4 idea, whim 5 fancy, freak, humor, image, pride 6 egoism, megrim, notion, vagary, vanity 7 boutade, caprice, concept, egotism,
thought 8 crotchet, self-love, smugness, snobbery, vainness 9 selfglory, self-pride, vainglory 10 conception, impression, narcissism,
perception, self-esteem 11 amour
propre, complacence, complacency, consequence, self-opinion,
swelled head 12 apprehension, intellection 13 outrecuidance

conceited
4 vain 6 snobby, snooty 7 pompous, stuck-up 8 snobbish 12 narcissistic, vainglorious

conceitedness
6 vanity 8 self-love, vainness
9 vainglory 10 narcissism, self-esteem 11 amour propre

conceivable
6 likely, mortal 7 earthly 8 possible, probable 9 thinkable
10 imaginable, supposable

conceive
4 form, make 5 beget, fancy,
grasp, think 6 accept, assume, expect, follow, gather, ponder, vision
7 believe, compass, feature, imagine, realize, suppose, suspect
8 cogitate, envisage, envision, meditate, ruminate 9 apprehend, speculate, visualize 10 comprehend, excogitate, understand

concentrate
3 fix 4 heap, mass, meet, pile 5 focus, rivet, unify 6 fasten, fixate,
gather, shrink 7 collect, compact
8 assemble, compress, condense,
contract, converge 9 constrict, integrate 11 consolidate

concentrated
5 fixed, lusty, whole 6 fierce, potent, robust, strong 7 furious, intense 8 vehement 9 exclusive, exquisite, undivided 10 full-bodied
unswerving 12 undistracted

concentrating
8 unifying 10 compacting 11 centripetal, integrative 12 centralizing
13 consolidating

concentration
4 heed 5 study 6 debate 9 attention 11 application 12 deliberation
13 consideration

concept
4 idea 5 image 6 notion 7 conceit,
thought 10 impression, perception
12 apprehension, intellection

conception
4 idea 5 image, start 6 notion
7 conceit, thought 9 beginning
10 impression, perception 12 apprehension, intellection

conceptual
5 ideal 8 abstract, notional
9 imaginary, visionary 10 ideational 12 transcendent

concern
4 care, firm, heed 5 doubt, worry
6 affair, gadget, matter, outfit, regard, unease, wonder 7 anxiety,
company, dubiety, lookout, palaver
8 business, disquiet, interest, mistrust 9 attention, curiosity, dubiosity, misgiving, occasions, suspicion
10 enterprise, inquietude, skepticism, solicitude, uneasiness
11 carefulness, disquietude, heedfulness, incertitude, uncertainty, uncertitude 12 apprehension 13 consciousness, consideration,
establishment

concerned
8 affected, involved 10 implicated,
interested

concerning
2 re 4 as to, in re 5 about, anent,
as for 7 against, apropos 9 as regards, regarding 10 respecting

concert
4 tune 5 agree 6 accord, chorus,
concur, settle 7 arrange, benefit,
concord, harmony, recital 8 coincide 9 cooperate, harmonize, negotiate 10 consonance
11 performance

concert hall
5 odeon, odeum 10 auditorium

concession
5 favor 6 gambit 9 allowance,
privilege 10 compromise
12 acquiescence

conch
5 shell 6 mussel 7 mollusk

concierge
6 porter, warden 7 doorman, janitor 9 custodian 10 doorkeeper

conciliate
4 calm, ease 5 quiet 6 pacify, soothe 7 appease, assuage, mollify, placate, sweeten 10 propitiate 11 tranquilize

concise
4 curt 5 brief, pithy, short, terse 7 compact, laconic, summary 8 abridged, succinct 9 condensed 10 compressed, contracted 11 compendiary, compendious 12 breviloquent 13 short and sweet

conclude
3 end 4 draw, halt, rule, stop 5 close, infer, judge 6 decide, deduce, deduct, derive, figure, finish, gather, reason, settle, wind up, wrap up 7 collect, resolve 8 complete, ultimate 9 determine, terminate

concluding
4 last 5 final 6 latest, latter 7 closing 8 eventual, hindmost, terminal, ultimate

conclusion
3 end 4 stop 5 cease, close, finis 6 ending, epilog, finale, finish, period, windup 7 closing, closure 8 decision, epilogue, illation, judgment, sequitur 9 cessation, deduction, inference 10 desistance, resolution, settlement 11 termination 13 determination, ratiocination

conclusive
4 last 5 final 6 cogent 7 telling 8 deciding, decisive 10 compelling, convincing, definitive 11 determinant, determinate, irrefutable 12 irrefragable, unanswerable

concoct
3 mix 4 brew, cook 5 frame, hatch 6 cook up, create, devise, invent, make up, vamp up 7 dream up, hatch up 8 conceive, contrive 9 formulate, originate

concomitant
4 mate 6 fellow 7 consort 8 adjuvant, incident 9 accessory, ancillary, associate, attendant, attending, companion, satellite 10 coincident, collateral 12 accompanying 13 accompaniment, supplementary

concord
4 pact, tune 5 agree, chime, unity 6 accord, chorus, concur, treaty 7 concert, harmony, rapport 8 coincide 9 agreement, harmonize 10 consonance, convention

concordance
4 tune 5 chime 6 accord 7 harmony 9 agreement 10 consonance

concordant
8 agreeing 9 congruous 10 harmonious

concourse
6 throng 7 joining, meeting 8 junction 9 gathering 10 concursion, confluence

concrete
3 set 4 join, link 5 beton, solid, unite 6 couple, harden 7 bracket, combine, congeal, connect 8 coalesce, compound, indurate, solidify 9 associate
component: 4 sand 5 water 6 gravel

concubine
7 hetaera, hetaira, odalisk 8 mistress 9 odalisque

concupiscence
4 lust 6 desire 7 passion 9 eroticism, prurience, pruriency 10 aphrodisia 11 lustfulness 13 lickerishness

concupiscent
3 hot 7 goatish, lustful, satyric 8 prurient 9 lickerish 10 lascivious, libidinous, passionate

concur
4 band, jibe 5 agree, unite 6 accord, league 7 combine, concert, concord, conjoin, go along 8 coadjute, coincide 9 cooperate, harmonize

concurrent
6 coeval 10 coetaneous, coexistent, coexisting, synchronal, synchronic 11 synchronous 12 contemporary, simultaneous

concurrently
6 at once 8 together 12 coincidently

concuss
3 jar 4 rock 5 force, shake, shock 6 coerce, compel, oblige 7 agitate, shotgun 8 convulse 9 constrain

concussion
3 jar 4 bump, jolt 5 clash, clout, crash, shock, smack 6 impact 7 beating, jarring, jolting, shaking 8 pounding 9 buffeting, collision

condemn
3 rap 4 damn, doom 5 blame, decry, knock 7 censure, convict 8 de-nounce, sentence 9 criticize, proscribe, reprehend, reprobate 10 denunciate

condensation
3 dew 5 brief 7 epitome, summary 8 abstract, boildown, breviary, breviate, synopsis 10 abridgment, conspectus

condense
3 sum 5 sum up 6 digest, reduce, shrink 7 abridge, capsule, compact, shorten, summate 8 boil down, compress, contract 9 capsulize, constrict, epitomize, inventory, summarize, synopsize 10 abbreviate 11 concentrate, consolidate

condescend
5 deign, stoop 6 unbend

condign
3 due, fit 4 fair, just 5 right 7 merited 8 deserved, rightful, suitable 9 requisite 11 appropriate 13 rhadamanthine

condiment
3 soy 4 salt 5 caper, curry, sauce, spice 6 catsup, pepper, relish 7 chutney, ketchup, mustard, paprika, vinegar 8 dressing, turmeric 9 seasoning 10 mayonnaise

condition
2 if 3 ill 4 case, mode 5 order, shape, state, terms 6 estate, fettle, kilter, malady, repair, status 7 ailment, disease, fitness, posture, proviso, strings 8 disorder, sickness, syndrome 9 affection, complaint, essential, exception, infirmity, necessity, provision, requisite, situation 10 limitation, sine qua non 11 requirement, reservation, stipulation 12 prerequisite 13 qualification
suffix: 2 or, th, ty 3 dom, ery, ice, ile, ion, ism 4 ance, ancy, ence, ency, ment, ness, oses (plural), osis, ship 5 ation

conditional
4 iffy 7 reliant 8 relative 9 dependent, provisory, qualified, tentative, uncertain 10 contingent, restricted 11 provisional 12 provisionary

condolence
3 rue 4 pity, ruth 8 sympathy 10 compassion 13 commiseration

condonable
7 tenable 9 excusable, tolerable 10 acceptable, defensible, vindicable 11 justifiable, warrantable

condone
5 remit 6 excuse, pardon 7 forgive
8 overlook

conduce
4 lead, tend 7 redound
10 contribute

conduct
3 act, run 4 bear, care, head,
lead, quit, show 5 guide, pilot,
route, steer, tenue, usher 6 acquit,
attend, behave, charge, convey,
convoy, demean, deport, direct, escort, funnel, handle, keep up, manage, ordain 7 arrange, carry on,
channel, company, comport, control, operate, oversee, running, traject 8 behavior, chaperon, handling, shepherd, transmit
9 accompany, companion, oversight, supervise 10 administer, deportment, intendance, management
11 comportment, supervision

conductor
5 guide 6 copper, escort, leader
7 maestro 8 conveyor, director, mo-
torman 10 bandleader impresario
American: 4 Shaw (Robert) 5 Grofé
(Ferde), Stock (Frederick August),
Szell (George) 6 Levine (James),
Maazel (Lorin), Previn (Andre), Reiner (Fritz), Thomas (Theodore, Mi-
chael Tilson), Walter (Bruno)
7 Fiedler (Arthur), Monteux (Pierre),
Ormandy (Eugene) 8 Damrosch (Le-
opold, Walter), Williams (John)
9 Bernstein (Elmer, Leonard), Leins-
dorf (Erich), Rodzinski (Artur), Stein-
berg (William), Stokowski (Leopold)
11 Kostelanetz (Andre), Mitropoulos
(Dimitri)
Australian: 7 Bonynge (Richard)
Austrian: 4 Bohm (Karl) 6 Mahler
(Gustav) 10 von Karajan (Herbert)
Belgian: 5 Ysaye (Eugene-Auguste)
British: 5 Solti (Georg)
Canadian: 9 MacMillan (Ernest)
Czech: 7 Kubelik (Jan, Rafael)
English: 4 Wood (Henry) 5 Boult
(Adrian) 7 Beecham (Thomas), Mal-
colm (George), Sargent (Malcolm)
8 Goossens (Eugene) 10 Barbirolli
(John)
French: 5 Munch (Charles) 6 Boulez
(Pierre), Pretre (Georges)
German: 4 Muck (Carl) 5 Spohr
(Louis), Weber (Carl Maria von)
9 Klemperer (Otto), Scherchen (Her-
man) 11 Furtwangler (Wilhelm),
Mendelssohn (Felix)
Hungarian: 5 Seidl (Anton) 7 Ni-
kisch (Arthur), Richter (Hans)

Indian: 5 Mehta (Zubin)
Italian: 6 Abbado (Claudio) 9 Tos-
canini (Arturo)
Japanese: 5 Ozawa (Seiji)
Mexican: 6 Chavez (Carlos)
Russian: 12 Koussevitzky (Serge)
Spanish: 6 Iturbi (Jose)
Swiss: 8 Ansermet (Ernest)
stick: 5 baton
suffix: 3 eer

conduit
4 duct, main, pipe 5 canal
6 course 7 channel 8 aqueduct,
penstock, pipeline 11 watercourse

coney
4 pika 5 hyrax 6 rabbit
10 butterfish

confab
4 chat 5 treat 6 advise, confer,
huddle, parley, powwow 7 consult
8 collogue

confabulate
see **confab**

confabulation
3 rap 4 chat, talk 6 parley 8 colloquy, converse, dialogue 10 conference, discussion 12 conversation, deliberation

confection
see **candy**

confederacy
5 union 6 league 8 alliance 9 anschluss, coalition 10 federation

confederate
3 reb 4 ally 5 rebel, unite 6 fellow
7 abettor, partner 8 conspire 9 accessory, associate, colleague
10 accomplice 11 conspirator
12 collaborator 13 coconspirator
admiral: 6 Semmes
capital: 8 Richmond
color: 4 gray
general: 3 Lee (Robert E.) 4 Hill (Ambrose), Hood (John Bell) 5 Bragg
(Braxton), Ewell (Richard Stoddart),
Price (Sterling), Smith (Edmund
Kirby) 6 Morgan (John Hunt), Stuart
(James Ewell Brown) 7 Forrest (Nathan Bedford), Hampton (Wade),
Jackson (Thomas Jonathan "Stonewall"), Pickett (George) 8 Johnston
(Albert Sidney, Joseph Eggleston)
9 Pemberton (John Clifford)
10 Beauregard (Pierre G. T.), Longstreet (James)
president: 5 Davis (Jefferson)
soldier: 9 butternut
spy: 4 Boyd (Belle)
vice-president: 8 Stephens (Alexander
Hamilton)

confederation
see **confederacy**

confer
4 give, meet, talk 5 allot, award,
grant, speak, treat 6 accord, advise, bestow, confab, huddle, parley, powwow 7 consult, discuss,
present 8 collogue, colloque, converse 10 deliberate 11 confabulate

conference
3 rap 4 loop, talk 5 synod, wheel
6 league, parley, powwow 7 circuit, meeting, palaver, seminar
8 colloquy 9 symposium 10 colloquium, discussion, rap session,
round robin, round table 11 association 12 deliberation
13 confabulation

confess
3 own 4 avow, sing 5 admit, allow, grant, let on, own up 6 reveal
7 concede, divulge 8 disclose
11 acknowledge

confession
5 creed 6 avowal 7 peccavi 9 admission, statement 10 disclosure

confidant
4 mate 5 amigo 6 friend 8 familiar, intimate 11 cater-cousin
12 acquaintance

confide
4 tell 6 bestow, commit 7 breathe,
commend, consign, entrust, present,
whisper 8 hand over, relegate, turn
over

confidence
4 gall, hope 5 brass, cheek, faith,
nerve, stock, trust 6 aplomb, surety
7 courage 8 reliance, sureness
9 assurance, brashness, certainty,
certitude, self-trust 10 conviction,
dependence, effrontery, equanimity
11 assuredness
game: 4 scam 5 bunco, bunko, grift,
sting 7 swindle

confidence man
3 gyp 7 diddler, grifter, sharper,
sharpie 8 swindler 9 defrauder,
trickster 11 bunco artist 12 bunco
steerer

confident
4 bold, sure 5 brash, brave, cocky,
perky, pushy 6 secure, uppity 7 assured, certain, pushful 8 cocksure,
fearless, intrepid, positive, sanguine, trustful, unafraid 9 dauntless, presuming, undaunted
10 brassbound, courageous, un-

doubtful **11** overweening, self-assured, self-reliant **12** presumptuous **13** self-assertive, self-possessed

confidential
5 close, privy, thick **6** chummy, closet, hushed, inside, secret **7** private **8** familiar, intimate **9** auricular

configuration
4 cast, form **5** shape **6** figure **7** contour, outline, pattern **12** conformation

confine
3 bar, box, end, mew, pen **4** cage, coop, crib, jail, term **5** bound, cramp, limit, orbit, range, reach, scope, sweep **6** embank, encage, extent, immure, intern, radius **7** delimit, enclose, pinfold, purview **8** bastille, boundary, imprison, localize, prelimit, restrict **9** constrain, periphery **10** delimitate, limitation **11** incarcerate **12** circumscribe **13** circumference

confinement
5 cramp **7** lying-in **8** childbed **9** captivity, restraint **10** constraint **11** restriction **12** accouchement, imprisonment **13** constrainment

confines
6 bounds, limits **7** compass **8** boundary, environs, purlieus **9** precincts

confirm
3 fix, set **4** back **5** check, prove, vouch **6** attest, ratify, uphold, verify **7** bear out, certify, justify, support **8** check out, validate **11** corroborate **12** authenticate, substantiate

confirmation
5 proof **7** witness **8** evidence **9** testament, testimony **11** attestation, testimonial

confirmed
3 set **5** fixed, sworn **7** chronic, settled **8** deep-dyed, definite, habitual, ratified **9** hard-shell **10** accustomed, deep-rooted, deep-seated, entrenched, habituated, inveterate **13** bred-in-the-bone, dyed-in-the-wool

confiscate
4 take **5** annex, seize, usurp **7** escheat, preempt **8** accroach, arrogate **9** sequester **10** commandeer **11** appropriate, expropriate

confiture
3 jam **8** conserve, preserve

conflagrant
5 afire, fiery **6** ablaze, aflame, alight **7** blazing, burning, flaming, flaring, ignited

conflagration
4 fire **5** blaze **7** inferno **9** holocaust

conflict
3 jar, war **4** bout, duel, meet, rift, vary **5** clash, fight **6** battle, combat, differ, jangle, oppose, strife **7** contest, discord, dispute, dissent, meeting, rivalry, warfare **8** argument, concours, disagree, disunity, mismatch, striving, struggle, tug-of-war, variance **9** disaccord, emulation, encounter, rencontre **10** contention, difference, dissension, dissidence **11** competition, controversy **12** disharmonize

conflicting
7 warring **8** clashing, contrary **9** dissonant **10** contending, discordant, discrepant **11** contrariant, incongruent, incongruous, inconsonant **12** antagonistic, antipathetic, disconsonant, incompatible, inconsistent, inharmonious

confluence
7 meeting **8** junction **9** concourse, gathering **10** concursion

conform
3 fit **4** jibe, mind, obey, suit, tune **5** adapt, agree, fit in, yield **6** accord, adjust, attune, comply, follow, square, submit, tailor **7** observe **8** dovetail, quadrate **9** acquiesce, harmonize, integrate, reconcile **10** coordinate, correspond, proportion, tailor-make **11** accommodate **12** reconciliate

conformable
6 fitted, suited **7** adapted, matched **8** assorted, suitable

conformation
4 cast, form **5** shape **6** figure **13** configuration

conforming
4 nice, typy **5** typey **6** decent, proper, seemly **7** uniform **8** becoming, decorous **9** befitting, civilized **11** comme il faut

conformity
7 decorum, harmony **8** affinity, legalism, normalcy **9** coherence, congruity, obedience **10** compliance, submission **11** consistency, resignation **12** acquiescence

confound
3 mix **4** faze, pose, stun **5** abash, befog, evert, mix up, rebut **6** baffle, puzzle, rattle, refute **7** confuse, confute, misdeem, mistake, perplex, stumble, stupefy **8** bewilder, disprove **9** discomfit, dumbfound, embarrass **10** controvert, disconcert, disconfirm **11** misidentify **13** metagrobolize

confounded
4 rank **5** agape, gross, utter **6** aghast, blamed, cursed, cussed, damned **7** blasted, blessed, shocked **8** absolute, dismayed, infernal, outright **9** consarned, dadburned, execrable, out-and-out **11** dumbfounded, overwhelmed, straight-out, unmitigated **13** thunderstruck

confrere
see **colleague**

confront
4 defy, face, meet **5** brave **6** accost, breast, oppose **9** challenge, encounter

Confucian way of life:
3 tao

confuse
3 fog, mix **4** blur, faze, mull, pose, warp **5** abash, addle, befog, cloud, dizzy, mix up, muddy, twist, upset, wrest **6** baffle, ball up, bemuse, flurry, foul up, fuddle, garble, jumble, mess up, muddle, puzzle, rattle, wrench **7** agitate, becloud, derange, disrupt, distort, flummox, fluster, misdeem, mislead, mistake, nonplus, perplex, perturb, pervert, snarl up **8** bedazzle, befuddle, bewilder, confound, disorder, disquiet, distract, throw off, unsettle **9** discomfit, embarrass **10** disarrange, discompose, disconcert **11** disorganize, misidentify **12** misrepresent **13** metagrobolize

confused
4 lost **5** muddy, muzzy, vague **7** at a loss, mixed up **9** perplexed **10** bewildered, topsy-turvy **12** disconcerted

confusion
3 din **4** flap, loss, mess, muck, ruin, stew **5** babel, chaos, havoc, mix-up, snafu, snarl **6** ataxia, bedlam, dither, foul-up, hubbub, huddle, jumble, lather, muddle, pother, tumult, unease **7** clutter, turmoil **8** disarray, disorder, misorder, pellmell **9** abashment, agitation, com-

motion, ruination **10** hullabaloo, turbulence, uneasiness **11** bedevilment, derangement, destruction, devastation, disturbance, pandemonium **12** discomfiture, discomposure, razzle-dazzle **13** disconcertion, embarrassment

confute
4 deny **5** break, evert, rebut **8** confound, disprove **10** controvert, disconfirm

congé
3 bow **5** adieu **7** good-bye, parting **8** farewell **9** dismissal **11** leave-taking

congeal
3 dry, gel, set **4** cake, clot, curd, jell **5** jelly **6** curdle, gelate, harden **7** jellify, stiffen, thicken **8** concrete, indurate, solidify **9** coagulate **10** gelatinize

congener
3 ilk **4** kind, sort, type **5** class, genus

congenial
4 good, nice **6** amical, social **7** affable, cordial, kindred, welcome **8** amicable, friendly, gracious, pleasant, pleasing, sociable **9** agreeable, congruous, consonant, favorable **10** compatible, consistent, gratifying, harmonious **11** cooperative, pleasurable, sympathetic **13** companionable

congenital
6 inborn, inbred, innate, native **7** connate, natural **8** inherent **9** essential, ingrained, inherited, intrinsic **10** connatural, deep-seated, indigenous, indwelling, unacquired

conger
3 eel **4** pike

congeries
4 ruck **5** group **6** muster **7** company **8** assembly **9** gathering **10** assemblage, collection **11** aggregation **12** congregation

congest
3 jam **4** clog, fill, plug, stop **5** block, choke, close, crowd **7** occlude **8** obstruct

conglobate
4 ball **5** round **6** sphere **8** ensphere

conglomerate
4 heap, mass, pool **5** chain, group, mixed, trust **6** cartel, motley, varied **7** combine **8** assorted, chowchow **9** aggregate, syndicate **11** aggregation, promiscuous **12** multifarious **13** agglomeration, heterogeneous, miscellaneous

conglomeration
5 hoard, trove **9** aggregate, amassment, colluvies **10** collection, cumulation **11** agglomerate, aggregation **12** accumulation

Congo
capital: **11** Brazzaville
monetary unit: **5** franc

congratulate
4 laud **6** salute **10** compliment, felicitate

congregate
4 meet, teem **5** raise, swarm **6** gather, muster **7** collect, convene **8** assemble, congress **9** forgather **10** rendezvous

congregation
4 host, mass, ruck **5** crowd, group **6** muster **7** company, meeting **8** assembly, audience **9** gathering **10** assemblage, collection

congress
4 club, diet **5** guild, synod, union **6** gather, league, muster **7** collect, society **8** assemble, assembly **9** forgather **10** congregate, fellowship, fraternity, parliament, rendezvous **11** association, brotherhood, Capitol Hill, legislature

congressman
7 senator **8** delegate **10** legislator **14** representative

congruity
9 agreement, coherence **10** conformity **11** consistency

congruous
3 apt, fit **7** fitting **9** accordant, agreeable, congenial, consonant **10** compatible, concordant, consistent, harmonious **11** appropriate, sympathetic

conjectural
7 reputed **8** putative, supposed **11** suppositive, suppository **12** hypothetical, supposititious **13** suppositional

conjecture
5 fancy, guess, infer **6** assume, theory **7** presume, pretend, suppose, surmise, suspect **9** inference, speculate **11** speculation, supposition

conjoin
3 wed **4** band, knit, link, yoke **5** unite **6** concur, couple, league, relate **7** combine, connect **8** coadjute **9** associate, cooperate

conjoint
6 common, mutual, public, shared **8** coacting, coactive, communal, conjunct, synergic **10** synergetic **11** coefficient, cooperative, intermutual

conjointly
8 mutually, together

conjointment
5 tie-up, union **6** hookup **7** cahoots, wedding **8** alliance **9** coalition **10** connection **11** affiliation, association, combination, conjunction, partnership

conjugal
6 wedded **7** marital, married, nuptial, spousal **8** hymeneal **9** connubial **11** matrimonial

conjugality
7 wedlock **8** marriage **9** matrimony **12** connubiality

conjugate
4 join, link, yoke **5** yoked **6** couple, joined, linked **7** bracket, combine, conjoin, connect, coupled **8** coalesce **9** associate, connected

conjunct
5 joint **6** common, mutual, public, shared **8** communal **11** intermutual

conjunction
2 as, if, or, so **3** and, but, for, nor, tho, yet **4** as if, lest, than, then, when **5** since, tie-up, union, until, while **6** either, hookup, though, unless, whenas, whilst **7** because, neither, wedding, whereas, whether **8** alliance, although, moreover **9** coalition, therefore **10** connection **11** affiliation, association, combination, partnership **12** conjointment

conjuration
4 rune **5** charm, spell, trick **11** incantation, legerdemain

conjure
3 beg **4** pray **5** brace, crave **6** appeal, invoke **7** beseech, entreat, implore **9** importune **10** supplicate

conjurer
4 mage, seer **5** magus **6** magian, shaman, wizard **7** warlock **8** magician, sorcerer **9** enchanter, trickster, voodooist **11** illusionist, necromancer

conjuring
5 magic **7** sorcery **8** witchery, wizardry **10** necromancy, witchcraft

11 bewitchment, enchantment, legerdemain, thaumaturgy

conk
3 die, hit, rap 4 swat 5 knock
7 decease 8 pass away

con man
see **confidence man**

connate
4 akin 6 allied, inborn, native
7 kindred, natural, related 8 incident, inherent 9 elemental, essential, inherited, intrinsic 10 affiliated, congenital, deep-seated, indigenous, indwelling, unacquired
11 consanguine

connatural
see **connate**

connect
3 tie, wed 4 bind, join, link, yoke
5 marry, unite 6 attach, bridge, couple, fasten, relate 7 combine, conjoin 9 affiliate, associate, interlock

connected with
suffix: 3 ast 4 aria 5 arium, orial

Connecticut
academy, college, university: 4 Yale 7 Trinity 8 Hartford, New Haven, Wesleyan 9 Fairfield 10 Bridgeport, Quinnipiac 11 Sacred Heart, Saint Joseph 12 U.S. Coast Guard
capital: 8 Hartford
nickname: 11 Nutmeg State 12 Blue Law State, Constitution State
state bird: 13 American robin
state flower: 14 mountain laurel

connection
3 job 4 cult, post, seam, sect, spot
5 creed, joint, nexus, tie-in, tie-up, union 6 billet, hookup 7 joining
8 alliance, coupling, junction, juncture, position, religion 9 communion, situation 10 catenation 11 affiliation, appointment, association, combination, conjunction, partnership 12 conjointment, denomination, togetherness

connective
2 or 3 and, nor 6 either 7 neither
8 syndetic 11 conjunction, conjunctive

connivance
9 collusion 10 complicity

connive
4 plot, wink 5 blink 6 devise, wink at 7 blink at, collude 8 cogitate, conspire, contrive, intrigue 9 machinate, scheme out

connoisseur
6 expert 7 epicure, gourmet
8 aesthete, gourmand, highbrow
9 bon vivant 10 dilettante
11 cognoscente

connotation
4 hint 7 meaning 8 overtone 9 undertone 10 suggestion 11 association, implication

connote
4 hint, mean 5 imply, spell 6 import, intend 7 add up to, express, signify, suggest 8 intimate
9 insinuate

connubial
6 wedded 7 marital, married, nuptial, spousal 8 conjugal, hymeneal
11 matrimonial

connubiality
7 wedlock 8 marriage 9 matrimony 11 conjugality

conquer
3 win 4 beat, best, foil, lick, tame, whip 5 crush 6 defeat, hurdle, master, outwit, reduce, subdue, thwart 7 prevail, triumph 8 bear down, beat down, overcome, override, surmount, vanquish 9 checkmate, overpower, overthrow, overwhelm, subjugate 10 overmaster

conquest
3 win 4 rout 7 routing, subdual, triumph, victory 9 overthrow

Conrad
character: 3 Jim 4 Axel, Lena
5 Flora, Kurtz 6 Marlow 7 Almayer
8 MacWhirr, Nostromo
work: 5 Youth 6 Chance 7 Lord Jim, Typhoon, Victory 8 Nostromo
11 Secret Agent 14 Almayer's Folly

consanguine
4 akin 6 agnate, allied 7 cognate, connate, kindred, related 8 incident 10 affiliated, connatural

conscience
5 demur, qualm, sense 6 psyche, squeam 7 scruple 11 compunction

conscienceless
6 amoral, shifty, tricky, unfair 7 devious 12 unprincipled

conscientious
4 fair, just, true 5 exact, fussy, right
6 honest 7 careful, dutiful, heedful, upright 8 punctual, studious 9 honorable 10 meticulous, scrupulous
11 painstaking, punctilious 12 conscionable

conscionable
see **conscientious**

conscious
5 alive, awake, aware 7 knowing, mindful, witting 8 affected, mannered, sensible, sentient, vigilant, watchful 9 attentive, au courant, cognizant 10 conversant, perceptive

consciousness
4 care, heed 6 regard 7 concern
9 awareness 11 carefulness, needfulness

conscribe, conscript
5 draft 6 enlist, enroll, muster

consecrate
5 bless 6 anoint, devote, hallow
8 dedicate, sanctify

consecrated
4 holy 6 sacred 7 blessed 8 hallowed 9 unprofane 10 sanctified
oil: 6 chrism
thing: 6 sacrum

consecution
3 row 5 chain, order, train 6 sequel, series 8 sequence 10 procession, succession 11 progression

consecutive
4 next 5 after, later 6 serial 7 ensuing, sequent 9 enlarging, following, succedent 10 increasing, sequential, subsequent, succeeding, successive 11 progressive 12 successional 13 subsequential

consent
3 let, yes 5 agree, allow, leave, yield 6 accede, accord, assent, comply, concur, permit 7 approve
8 sanction 9 acquiesce, agreement, allowance, subscribe 10 permission, sufferance 13 authorization, understanding

consentaneous
5 solid 9 unanimous 11 consentient

consequence
3 end 4 fame, pith, rank 5 event, honor, issue, pride, state 6 cachet, effect, egoism, import, moment, renown, repute, result, sequel, status, upshot, weight 7 conceit, dignity, egotism, outcome, stature 8 position, prestige, sequence, standing
9 aftermath, magnitude, vainglory
10 importance, narcissism, reputation 11 aftereffect, amour propre, complacence, complacency, weightiness 12 significance
13 conceitedness, momentousness

consequent
5 sound 7 logical 8 rational, sensible 9 following, resulting
10 reasonable 11 intelligent

consequential
3 big 7 weighty 8 material 9 important, momentous 10 meaningful
11 significant, substantial
12 considerable

consequently
2 so 4 ergo, then, thus 5 hence
9 therefore, thereupon
11 accordingly

conservation
4 care 6 saving 7 control, keeping
8 managing 9 attention, directing, governing, preserval, salvation
10 cherishing, husbanding, management, protection 11 safekeeping 12 preservation, sustentation

conservative
4 tory, wary 5 chary, right
6 proper 7 diehard, puritan 8 cautious, discreet, moderate, old liner, orthodox, rightist, standpat 9 temperate, unextreme 10 controlled, reasonable, restrained 11 bitterender, circumspect, reactionary, right-winger, standpatter, unexcessive

conserve
3 can, jam 4 save 6 keep up
7 support, sustain 8 maintain, preserve 9 confiture

consider
3 eye, see 4 deem, feel, hold, mind, muse, rate, rule, scan, view
5 fancy, infer, judge, sense, study, think, weigh 6 admire, credit, esteem, gather, look at, ponder, reason, reckon, regard 7 account, believe, bethink, examine, imagine, inspect, perpend, reflect, respect
8 cogitate, conceive, conclude, gaze upon, look upon, meditate, prescind, ruminate, think out
9 speculate, think over 10 excogitate, scrutinize 11 contemplate

considerable
3 big 4 good, tidy 5 hefty, large, major 6 active, goodly, pretty
7 notable, sizable, weighty 8 material, sensible 9 effective, extensive, important, momentous 10 largescale, meaningful 11 efficacious, respectable, significant, substantial
13 consequential

considerably
3 far 4 well 5 quite 6 rather
8 somewhat 13 significantly

considerate
3 big 4 kind, safe, wary 5 chary, lofty 6 kindly, polite, tender 7 amiable, careful, guarded 8 cautious, discreet, generous, gingerly, obliging 9 attentive 10 benevolent, chivalrous, thoughtful 11 calculating, circumspect, complaisant, magnanimous, sympathetic, warm-hearted
12 greathearted 13 compassionate

consideration
4 heed 5 cause, favor, mercy, study 6 debate, esteem, motive, reason, regard, spring 7 account, concern, respect 9 attention, awareness 10 admiration, estimation, solicitude 11 application, forbearance, heedfulness, mindfulness
12 deliberation 13 concentration

considered
7 advised, studied, willful 8 designed, prepense, studious 9 voluntary 10 deliberate, thought-out
11 intentional 12 aforethought, premeditated

consign
4 give, send, ship 5 allot, award, remit, route, yield 6 commit, devote
7 address, commend, confide, entrust, forward 8 dispatch, hand over, relegate, transmit, turn over
9 surrender

consist
2 be, go 3 lie 4 rest 5 abide, agree, dwell, exist, fit in 6 accord, inhere, repose, reside 7 comport, conform, consort, subsist 8 dovetail
10 correspond

consistency
7 aptness, concord, fitness, harmony 8 evenness, felicity, firmness, likeness 9 agreement, coherence, congruity 10 apposition, conformity, consonance, similarity
11 suitability

consistent
4 same, true 8 constant 9 agreeable, congenial, congruous, consonant, unfailing, unvarying 10 compatible, invariable, unchanging
11 sympathetic

consistently
7 as usual, usually 8 wontedly
10 habitually 11 customarily

console
4 calm 5 cheer, table 6 buck up, solace 7 animate, cabinet, comfort, hearten, relieve, upraise 8 inspirit
11 tranquilize

consolidate
3 mix, set 4 fuse 5 blend, merge, unify, unite 7 compact 8 compress, condense, solidify 9 integrate
10 amalgamate, strengthen
11 concentrate

consolidation
5 union 6 merger 7 melding, merging 8 mergence 9 coalition 11 coadunation, combination, unification
12 amalgamation

consonance
4 tune 5 chime 6 accord, chorus
7 concert, concord, harmony
9 agreement 11 concordance

consonant
4 akin, like 5 alike, round 6 agnate, fortis, rotund 7 chiming, musical, orotund, ringing, similar, uniform, vibrant 8 blending, harmonic, parallel, plangent, resonant, sonorant 9 accordant, agreeable, analogous, congenial, congruous 10 coincident, comparable, compatible, consistent, harmonious, resounding
11 conformable, sympathetic, symphonious 13 corresponding
kind: 4 stop, surd 5 nasal, velar
6 atonic, voiced 7 lateral, palatal, spirant 8 alveolar, bilabial, unvoiced 9 fricative, voiceless

consort
4 bear, mate, wife 5 agree, group, tally 6 accord, attend, convoy, fellow, spouse, square 7 company, comport, conduct, conform, husband 8 assembly, chaperon, dovetail 9 accompany, associate, companion, harmonize 10 correspond
11 concomitant 13 accompaniment

consortium
4 club 5 guild, order, union
6 league 7 society 8 congress
10 fellowship, fraternity
11 association

conspectus
5 brief 7 epitome 8 abstract, boildown, breviary, breviate, synopsis
10 abridgment 12 condensation

conspicuous
5 clear, plain, showy 6 marked, patent, signal 7 blatant, eminent, evident, obvious, pointed, salient
8 apparent, distinct, flagrant, manifest, striking 9 arresting, arrestive, egregious, prominent 10 celebrated, noticeable, openhanded, remarkable 11 illustrious, outstanding

conspiracy
4 plan, plot 5 cabal, covin
6 scheme 8 intrigue, sedition
9 treachery 11 machination

conspirator
7 abettor 9 accessory 10 accomplice 11 confederate

conspire
4 plot 5 cabal 6 devise 7 collude, complot, connive 8 cogitate, contrive, intrigue 9 machinate, scheme out

constancy
6 fealty 7 loyalty 8 adhesion, fidelity 9 adherence, diligence
10 attachment 12 faithfulness

constant
4 even, fast, same, true 5 fixed, liege, loyal 6 ardent, dogged, stable, steady 7 abiding, chronic, endless, equable, lasting, stabile, staunch, uniform 8 clinging, enduring, faithful, unending 9 allegiant, ceaseless, confirmed, continual, immovable, immutable, obstinate, perpetual, steadfast, unceasing, unfailing, unmovable, unvarying
10 changeless, consistent, continuous, inflexible, invariable, inveterate, persistent, persisting, unchanging, unwavering 11 everlasting, inalterable, persevering, unalterable, unremitting 12 interminable, pertinacious, unchangeable, unmodifiable 13 unfluctuating

Constantine
birthplace: 4 Nish
mother: 6 Helena
son: 7 Crispus
victim: 6 Fausta 7 Crispus
wife: 6 Fausta

constantly
4 ever 6 always 10 invariably
11 perpetually 12 continuously

constellation
5 group 7 pattern 10 assemblage, collection 11 arrangement
Altar: 3 Ara
Archer: 11 Sagittarius
Arrow: 7 Sagitta
Balance: 5 Libra
Big Dipper: 9 Ursa Major
Bird of Paradise: 4 Apus
Bull: 6 Taurus
Centaur: 9 Centaurus
Chained Lady: 9 Andromeda
Chameleon: 10 Chamaeleon
Champion: 7 Perseus
Charioteer: 6 Auriga
Clock: 10 Horologium
Colt: 8 Equuleus

Crab: 6 Cancer
Crane: 4 Grus
Cross: 4 Crux
Crow: 6 Corvus
Crown: 6 Corona
Cup: 6 Crater
Dolphin: 9 Delphinus
Dove: 7 Columba
Dragon: 5 Draco
Eagle: 6 Aquila
Fishes: 6 Pisces
Fly: 5 Musca
Flying Fish: 6 Volans
Furnace: 6 Fornax
Graving Tool: 6 Caelum
Greater Dog: 10 Canis Major
Hare: 5 Lepus
Herdsman: 6 Boötes
Horned Goat: 11 Capricornus
Hunter: 5 Orion
Indian: 5 Indus
Keel: 6 Carina
Lady in the Chair: 10 Cassiopeia
Larger Bear: 9 Ursa Major
Larger Dog: 10 Canis Major
Lesser Dog: 10 Canis Minor
Lion: 3 Leo
Little Dipper: 9 Ursa Minor
Little Fox: 9 Vulpecula
Lizard: 7 Lacerta
Lyre: 4 Lyra
Mariner's Compass: 5 Pyxis
Monarch: 7 Cepheus
Net: 9 Reticulum
Painter's Easel: 6 Pictor
Pair of Compasses: 8 Circinus
Peacock: 4 Pavo
Pump: 6 Antlia
Ram: 5 Aries
Rescuer: 7 Perseus
River Po: 8 Eridanus
Sails: 4 Vela
Scorpion: 8 Scorpius
Serpent: 7 Serpens
Serpent Holder: 9 Ophiuchus
Sextant: 7 Sextans
Shield: 6 Scutum
Smaller Bear: 9 Ursa Minor
Square: 5 Norma
Stern: 6 Puppis
Swan: 6 Cygnus
Table: 5 Mensa
Toucan: 6 Tucana
Triangle: 10 Triangulum
Twins: 6 Gemini
Unicorn: 9 Monoceros
Virgin: 5 Virgo
Water Carrier: 8 Aquarius
Water Monster: 5 Hydra
Water Snake: 6 Hydrus
Whale: 5 Cetus
Winged Horse: 7 Pegasus
Wolf: 5 Lupus

consternate
5 daunt, shake 6 appall, dismay
7 horrify

consternation
4 fear 5 alarm, dread, panic 6 dismay, fright, horror, muddle, terror 9 confusion, trepidity 10 muddlement, perplexity 11 distraction, trepidation 12 bewilderment

constipate
6 stifle 7 trammel 8 stagnate, stultify

constituent
4 part 5 piece, voter 6 factor, member 7 element, portion 8 division, fraction 9 component, principal 10 ingredient

constitute
4 form, make 5 enact, found, set up, start 6 create, embody, make up 7 compose 8 complete, comprise, organize 9 establish, institute

constitution
3 law 4 code 5 build, canon, habit 6 design, makeup, nature 7 habitus 8 physique 9 formation, ordinance, structure 11 composition 12 architecture, construction

Constitution
12 Old Ironsides

constitutional
4 turn, walk 6 inborn, inbred, innate, ramble, stroll 7 built-in, saunter 8 inherent 9 essential, ingrained, intrinsic 10 congenital, deep-seated

Constitution State
11 Connecticut

constitutive
5 vital 8 cardinal 9 essential
11 fundamental

constrain
3 ban, bar, jam, jug 4 bear, curb, deny, hurt, jail, make, pain, push 5 check, crowd, crush, force, press 6 bridle, coerce, compel, enjoin, grieve, hold in, immure, injure, intern, oblige, squash, squish 7 abstain, concuss, confine, deprive, inhibit, refrain, shotgun, squeeze 8 aggrieve, bastille, disallow, distress, hold back, hold down, imprison, restrain, restrict, withhold 11 incarcerate

constraint
4 bond 5 check, cramp, force 6 duress 8 coercion, violence 9 restraint 10 compulsion, repression

11 confinement, restriction, suppression

constrict
4 curb, stop 5 choke, limit, strap 6 hamper, narrow, pucker, shrink 7 confine, inhibit, squeeze, tighten 8 astringe, compress, condense, contract, restrain, strangle, stultify 9 constrain 10 constipate, constringe 11 concentrate 12 circumscribe

constrictor
3 boa 5 snake 6 muscle 8 anaconda 9 sphincter, strangler

construct
4 form, make, rear 5 build, erect, forge, frame, put up, raise, set up 6 devise, uprear 7 build up, fashion, produce 8 assemble 9 establish, fabricate, hammer out 11 put together

construction
6 design, expose, makeup 8 building, exegesis 9 construal, formation 10 exposition 11 composition, explanation, explication 12 architecture, constitution

constructive
7 helpful, virtual 8 implicit 9 practical

construe
7 analyze, explain, expound 8 spell out 9 explicate, interpret, translate

consuetude
3 use 4 wont 5 habit, trick, usage 6 custom, manner, praxis 8 habitude, practice

consult
3 ask 5 refer, treat 6 advise, confab, confer, huddle, parley, powwow 7 counsel, examine 8 collogue, consider 11 confabulate

consume
2 go 3 eat, use 4 down, gulp, meal, raze, ruin, take, wolf 5 crush, drink, eat up, gorge, sew up, shift, spend, swill, use up, waste, wreck 6 absorb, devour, expend, feed on, finish, guzzle, ingest 7 destroy, engross, exhaust, fritter, put away, put down, swallow 8 gobble up, squander 9 dissipate, overwhelm, partake of, polish off, throw away 10 annihilate, extinguish, frivol away, monopolize, run through, trifle away

consumer advocate
5 Nader (Ralph)

consuming
9 absorbing 10 engrossing 12 monopolizing

consummate
3 end 4 able, halt, ripe 5 close, utter 6 finish, gifted, superb, wind up, wrap up 7 perfect, skilled, supreme, trained 8 absolute, complete, conclude, finished, flawless, outright, peerless, positive, talented, ultimate 9 downright, faultless, out-and-out, perfected, practiced, terminate, virtuosic 10 impeccable, inimitable 11 superlative, unmitigated 12 accomplished 13 thoroughgoing, unsurpassable

consumption
2 TB 3 use 5 decay, waste 8 phthisis 11 white plague 12 tuberculosis

contact
3 get 4 abut, meet 5 reach, touch, union 6 accord 7 harmony, oneness, rapport, taction 8 commerce, nearness, relation, tangency, touching 9 closeness, communion, proximity 10 connection, contiguity, fellowship 11 association, contingence, impingement, intercourse, propinquity 13 communication, companionship
combining form: 4 hapt 5 hapto

contagion
3 pox 4 bane 5 taint, venom, virus 6 miasma, poison 7 disease 9 pollution 10 corruption 13 contamination

contagious
6 catchy, taking 8 catching 10 infectious 12 communicable

contain
4 have, hold, keep, take 5 admit, house, lodge 6 embody, take in 7 collect, compose, control, embrace, include, involve, receive, repress, smother, subsume 8 comprise, restrain 9 encompass 10 comprehend, simmer down 11 accommodate

container
3 bag, bin, box, can, cup, jar, keg, mug, pod, pot, tin, tub, urn, vat 4 cage, case, cask, drum, etui, ewer, pail, sack, silo, tank, vase, vial, well 5 chest, crate, cruet, flask, glass, gourd, phial, pouch 6 basket, bottle, carafe, carton, casket, coffin, cooler, goblet, hamper, hatbox, holder, inkpot, shaker 7 bandbox, capsule, chalice, ink-

well, package, pitcher, thermos 8 canister, catchall, decanter, envelope, hogshead, jerrican, puncheon 10 receptacle
liturgical: 3 pix, pyx 7 chalice 8 ciborium

containing
suffix: 2 ic 4 ical

contaminate
4 foul, harm, soil 5 dirty, spoil, stain, taint 6 befoul, debase, defile, infect, injure, poison 7 corrupt, deprave, pervert, pollute, tarnish, vitiate 9 desecrate 10 adulterate

conte
4 tale 5 story 9 narrative

contemn
4 hate 5 abhor, scorn, scout, spurn 7 despise, disdain 8 look down

contemplate
3 aim, eye 4 mean, mull, muse, plan, scan, view 5 study, think, weigh 6 design, intend, look at, ponder 7 examine, inspect, perpend, propose, purpose, reflect 8 consider, gaze upon, look upon, meditate, think out 9 think over 10 excogitate, scrutinize

contemplation
5 study 6 musing 7 thought 8 thinking 9 brainwork, pondering 10 cogitation, meditation, reflection, rumination 11 cerebration, speculation 12 deliberation

contemplative
6 musing 7 pensive 8 thinking, weighing 9 pondering, reasoning 10 cogitative, meditative, reflecting, reflective, ruminative, thoughtful 11 speculative

contemporary
2 up 6 coeval, extant 7 abreast, current, instant, present 8 existent, existing, todayish, up-to-date 9 au courant 10 coetaneous, coexistent, coexisting, coincident, concurrent, present-day, synchronal, synchronic 11 concomitant, synchronous 12 simultaneous 13 up-to-the-minute

contempt
5 scorn, shame 6 hatred, infamy 7 despite, disdain, mockery, sarcasm 8 aversion, defiance, despisal, disfavor, disgrace, dishonor, distaste, ignominy 9 antipathy, contumacy, discredit, disesteem, disrepute 10 opprobrium, repugnance 11 despisement 12 stubbornness 13 disparagement, recalcitrance

contemptible
3 bad, low 4 base, evil, mean, poor, vile 5 cheap, sorry 6 abject, odious, scummy, scurvy, shabby, sordid 7 hateful, ignoble, pitiful 8 beggarly, infamous, inferior, pitiable, shameful 9 abhorrent 10 abominable, despicable, despisable, detestable, disgusting 11 ignominious

contemptible one
suffix: 3 een, eer

contemptuous
7 haughty 8 arrogant, scornful 10 disdainful 12 supercilious

contend
3 say, tug, vie, war 4 cope, face, meet, tell, urge 5 argue, brawl, claim, fight, rival 6 assert, battle, charge, combat, defend, enjoin, oppose, oppugn, report, resist 7 compete, contest, justify, warrant 8 confront, cope with, maintain 9 encounter, vindicate, withstand

___ contendere
4 nolo

content
4 cozy, gist 5 happy 6 at ease 7 appease, gratify, satisfy 9 satisfied, substance 12 significance

contention
3 war 4 feud 6 hurrah, rumpus, strife, thesis 7 discord, dispute, dissent, quarrel, rivalry, wrangle 8 argument, conflict, disunity, squabble, variance 9 disaccord 10 difference, dissension, dissidence 11 altercation, competition, controversy 12 contestation
Scottish: 5 sturt

contentious
5 fiery 7 carping, froward, peppery, scrappy, warlike 8 captious, caviling, contrary, militant, perverse 9 bellicose, combative, hotheaded, impetuous, litigious, polemical, truculent 10 pugnacious 11 belligerent, quarrelsome 12 disputatious, faultfinding, gladiatorial 13 argumentative, controversial

conterminous
8 abutting, adjacent, touching 9 adjoining, bordering 10 approximal, contiguous, juxtaposed

contest
3 sue, vie 4 bout, buck, duel, feud, fray, game, meet, race, tilt 5 clash, fight, match, repel, rival, trial 6 battle, combat, debate, oppose, resist, strife, strive, trying 7 compete, contend, dispute, rivalry, testing, warfare 8 argument, concours, conflict, endeavor, skirmish, striving, struggle, tug-of-war 9 emulation, encounter, rencontre, withstand 10 engagement, tournament 11 competition
combining form: 5 machy

contiguity
9 adjacency, confinity, immediacy, proximity 11 propinquity 13 appropinquity

contiguous
4 near, next, nigh 5 close 6 nearby 7 close-by 8 abutting, adjacent, touching 9 adjoining, bordering 10 approximal, juxtaposed, near-at-hand 11 close-at-hand, neighboring 12 conterminous

continence
6 purity, virtue 8 chastity, sobriety 10 abstinence, chasteness, moderation, temperance 13 self-restraint, temperateness

continent
4 Asia, mass, pure 5 sober 6 Africa, chaste, curbed, Europe 7 America, bridled 8 mainland 9 abstinent, Australia, inhibited, temperate 10 abstemious, Antarctica, restrained 11 abstentious 12 North America, South America
lost: 8 Atlantis

continental pool
3 EEC 12 Common Market

contingence
5 touch 7 contact

contingency
4 pass 5 break, event, pinch 6 chance, crisis, strait 8 exigency, juncture, occasion, zero hour 9 emergency 10 crossroads 11 opportunity, possibility 12 turning point

contingent
3 odd 5 fluky 6 casual, chance, likely 7 reliant 8 possible, probable, relative 9 dependent 10 accidental, fortuitous, incidental, unforeseen 11 conditional 13 unanticipated, unforeseeable

continual
6 steady 7 abiding, endless, running, staying 8 constant, enduring, minutely, timeless, unending, unwaning 9 ceaseless, incessant, perpetual, unceasing, unfailing, unvarying 10 continuous, persistent, persisting, relentless, unchanging, unflagging 11 everlasting, unremitting 12 interminable 13 unintermitted, uninterrupted

continually
4 ever 6 always 7 forever, running 8 together 10 constantly 11 incessantly, night and day 12 successively 13 consecutively

continuance
3 run 4 stay 5 delay 6 sequel 8 duration, survival 9 constancy, longevity 10 permanence 11 persistence 12 postponement, prolongation

continuation
3 run 8 duration 9 endurance, extension 11 persistence, protraction 12 prolongation

continue
4 go on, last, ride, stay 5 abide, renew, run on 6 endure, pick up, remain, reopen, resume, retain, take up 7 carry on, outlast, outlive, perdure, persist, prolong, restart, survive 8 maintain, postpone 9 carry over, persevere 10 recommence 12 carry through

continuing
3 old 7 ongoing 8 constant, enduring, lifelong 9 long-lived, perennial 10 inveterate 11 long-lasting

continuity
6 script 8 duration, scenario 9 endurance 11 persistence

continuous
see **continual**

continuously
see **continually**

contort
3 wry 4 bend, warp, wind 5 curve, gnarl, twist, wring 6 deform, writhe 7 distort, grimace, torture 8 misshape

contortionist
7 acrobat

contour
4 form, line 5 curve, shape 7 outline, profile 9 lineament, lineation 10 figuration, silhouette 11 delineation

contra
5 again 6 facing, toward 7 against, counter, reverse, vis-à-vis 8 antipode, antipole, converse, fronting, opposite 9 vice versa 10 antithesis, conversely, oppositely

contraband
3 hot 5 taboo 6 banned 7 bootleg, illegal, illicit, shut out, smuggle 8 excluded 9 forbidden 10 prohibited, proscribed 11 disapproved

contract
3 get 4 bond, fail, knit, pact, sink, take 5 catch, cause, incur, lease, limit, upset 6 engage, induce, lessen, obtain, reduce, shrink, treaty, weaken 7 abridge, acquire, afflict, bargain, betroth, bring on, compact, decline, derange, dwindle, wrinkle 8 affiance, compress, condense, covenant, decrease, diminish, disorder, restrict, sicken of 9 agreement, betrothal, constrict, indispose, succumb to 10 convention, sicken with 11 concentrate, transaction 12 come down with
maritime: 8 bottomry
part: 6 clause 7 article, proviso

contraction
3 it's, tic 4 ain't, can't, don't, flex, isn't, won't 5 aren't, cramp, didn't, spasm 7 elision 9 reduction, shrinkage 10 abridgment 12 abbreviation
heart's: 7 systole
poetic: 3 e'en, e'er, o'er, 'tis 4 ne'er, 'twas 5 'twere, 'twill

contradict
4 deny 5 belie, cross, rebut 6 impugn, negate 7 dispute, gainsay 8 negative, traverse 9 disaffirm 10 contravene

contradiction
6 denial 7 paradox 8 antinomy, negation 10 gainsaying

contradictory
7 counter, reverse 8 antipode, antipole, contrary, converse, negating, opposite 9 antipodal 10 antipodean, antithesis, nullifying 11 counterpole 12 antagonistic, antithetical 13 counteractive

contraption
3 rig 6 device, gadget 7 machine 11 contrivance

contrariety
3 con 8 opposure 10 antagonism, antithesis, opposition

contrariwise
5 again 9 vice versa 10 conversely, oppositely

contrary
5 balky, polar 6 averse, ornery, unruly 7 counter, froward, restive, reverse, wayward 8 antipode, anti-pole, clashing, converse, opposite, perverse, recusant, stubborn 9 antipodal, diametric, dissident, obstinate, vice versa 10 antipodean, antithesis, conversely, discordant, headstrong, oppositely, rebellious, refractory 11 conflicting, counterpole, dissentient, intractable, wrongheaded 12 antagonistic, antipathetic, antithetical, contumacious, cross-grained, recalcitrant 13 contradictory, insubordinate, nonconforming, nonconformist
prefix: 3 dis 5 retro 6 contra 7 counter

contrast
7 compare 9 diversity 10 comparison, difference, divergence

contravene
4 defy, deny 5 break, cross, fight, spurn 6 abjure, breach, combat, disown, impugn, negate, offend, oppose, reject, resist 7 exclude, gainsay, infract, violate 8 disclaim, infringe, negative, traverse 9 disaffirm, repudiate 10 contradict, transgress

contravention
3 sin 4 vice 5 crime 6 breach 7 offense 8 trespass 9 violation 10 infraction 12 infringement 13 transgression

contretemps
4 slip 6 mishap 7 tragedy 9 adversity, mischance 10 misfortune

contribute
3 aid 4 give, help, tend 5 add to 6 assist, chip in, donate, kick in, submit, supply 7 augment, conduce, fortify, pitch in, recruit, redound 9 reinforce, subscribe 10 strengthen, supplement 11 come through

contribution
4 alms, gift 5 share 7 charity, present 8 donation, offering 11 benefaction, beneficence

contributory
8 adjuvant 9 accessory, ancillary, auxiliary 10 collateral, subsidiary 11 appurtenant, subservient

contrite
5 sorry 8 penitent 9 regretful, repentant 10 apologetic, remorseful 11 attritional, penitential 12 compunctious

contriteness
see **contrition**

contrition
3 rue 4 ruth 7 penance, remorse 9 attrition, penitence, penitency 10 repentance 11 compunction

contrivance
3 art 6 device 7 coinage, machine 8 artifice 9 apparatus, invention 10 brainchild 11 contraption

contrive
3 rig 4 fake, make, move, plan, plot 5 fix up, frame 6 cook up, devise, handle, invent, make up, scheme, vamp up, wangle 7 collude, concoct, connive, develop, dream up, fashion, hatch up, project, work out 8 cogitate, conspire, intrigue 9 elaborate, fabricate, formulate, machinate, scheme out

contrived
5 hokey 6 forced 7 labored 10 artificial

control
4 curb, rein, rule, sway 5 might, power, quell 6 adjust, bridle, corner, direct, govern, handle, manage, master, subdue 7 command, compose, contain, mastery, repress, smother, strings 8 dominate, monopoly, regulate, restrain 9 authority, supervise 10 discipline, domination 12 jurisdiction

controlled
4 tame 8 discreet, moderate 9 temperate, unextreme 10 reasonable, restrained 11 unexcessive 12 conservative

controversial
7 eristic 9 litigious, polemical 11 contentious 12 disputatious 13 argumentative

controversy
3 row 4 miff, tiff 6 debate, rumpus, strife 7 dispute, quarrel, wrangle 8 argument, squabble 9 bickering 10 contention, falling-out 11 altercation, embroilment

controvert
4 deny 5 break, rebut 6 oppugn, refute 7 confute 8 confound, disprove, question 9 challenge 10 disconfirm

contumacious
6 unruly 7 froward 8 contrary, factious, insolent, mutinous, perverse 9 insurgent, seditious 10 rebellious 13 insubordinate

contumacy
7 despite 8 contempt, defiance 12 stubbornness 13 recalcitrance

contumelious
4 bold 5 saucy 6 brazen 7 abusive, scurril 8 impudent, insolent, scurrile 9 audacious, invective, truculent 10 scurrilous, vituperous 11 impertinent, opprobrious 12 vituperative, vituperatory

contumely
4 slap 5 abuse 6 insult 7 affront, despite, obloquy 9 aspersion, indignity, invective, stricture 10 scurrility 12 billingsgate, vituperation 13 animadversion

contuse
5 black 6 bruise, injure

conundrum
3 why 6 enigma, puzzle, riddle 7 mystery, problem 10 puzzlement 13 Chinese puzzle, mystification

convalesce
4 mend 7 improve, recover 10 recuperate

convene
3 sit 4 call, meet, open 6 call in, gather, muster, summon 7 convoke, summons 8 assemble 10 congregate

convenience
4 ease 6 toilet 7 amenity, benefit, comfort

convenient
3 fit 4 good, meet, near, next, nigh 5 close, handy 6 nearby, proper, useful 7 close-by 8 adjacent, suitable 9 immediate 10 accessible, near-at-hand 11 appropriate, close-at-hand

convent
5 abbey 6 friary, priory 7 nunnery 9 monastery, sanctuary

convention
3 law 4 bond, form, pact, rule 5 canon, usage 6 accord, custom, treaty 7 bargain, compact, concord, meeting, precept 8 assembly, contract, covenant, practice 9 agreement, gathering, tradition 10 convenance 11 transaction 13 understanding

conventional
5 trite, usual 6 decent, formal, normal, proper, seemly, solemn, square 7 correct, stately 8 decorous, moderate, ordinary, orthodox, priggish, reliable, straight 9 temperate 10 button-down, ceremonial, dependable, fastidious, restrained, scrupulous 11 ceremonious, commonplace, constrained, responsible, traditional 12 conservative 13 conscientious

conventionalize
5 adapt 7 conform, stylize

converge
4 join, meet 5 focus 8 approach 9 concenter 11 concentrate

conversant
5 awake, aware 6 au fait, versed 7 abreast, knowing, witting 8 familiar, informed, sensible, sentient, up-to-date 9 au courant, cognizant, conscious 10 acquainted, perceptive, percipient 12 apprehending, apprehensive 13 comprehending

conversation
4 chat, talk 6 confab, debate, parley, speech 7 comment, talking 8 causerie, colloquy, dialogue, duologue, repartee, shoptalk 9 cross talk, discourse, tête-à-tête 10 discussion 13 confabulation

conversation piece
6 oddity 9 curiosity

converse
4 chat, chin, talk, yarn 5 polar, speak, visit 6 contra, parley 7 commune, counter, reverse 8 antipode, antipole, colloque, colloquy, contrary, dialogue, opposite 9 antipodal, communion, diametric, discourse 10 antipodean, antithesis 11 counterpole 12 antithetical 13 communication, confabulation, contradictory

conversely
6 contra 8 contrary 9 vice versa 10 contrawise, oppositely 12 contrariwise

conversion
5 shift 6 change 7 novelty, rebirth, turning 8 metanoia, mutation, reversal 9 about-face 10 alteration, changeover, innovation 11 permutation, reclamation 12 modification, regeneration 13 metamorphosis, qualification, transmutation

convert
4 lead, make, move, save, sway 5 alter, bring, forge 6 change, redeem, reform 7 commute, incline 8 persuade 9 proselyte, transform, translate, transmute, transpose 11 proselytize, transfigure 12 metamorphose, transmogrify
Christian: 10 catechumen

convex
5 bowed, toric 6 arched, curved 7 bulging, gibbous, rounded

convey
3 lug 4 bear, buck, cart, cede, deed, pack, pipe, send, tote 5 bring, carry, ferry 6 assign, funnel, impart, pass on, remise, siphon 7 channel, conduct, consign, project, traject 8 make over, sign over, transfer, transmit 9 put across, transport 11 communicate

conveyance
3 car 4 auto, cart, deed, sled 5 coach, coupe, sedan, stage, wagon 7 charter, trailer, transit, vehicle 8 carriage, carrying 9 transport 10 automobile 12 transporting
public: 2 el 3 bus, cab 4 taxi, tram 5 plane, train 7 ricksha, trolley 8 airplane, monorail, railroad, rickshaw 9 streetcar 10 jinricksha, jinrikisha

convict
4 find 5 felon, lifer 6 inmate, trusty 7 captive 8 criminal, jailbird, prisoner, sentence 10 malefactor

conviction
4 mind, view 5 creed, faith 6 belief, surety 7 feeling, opinion 8 doctrine, sureness 9 assurance, certainty, certitude, sentiment 10 confidence, persuasion 11 assuredness

convince
3 get 4 draw 6 assure, induce, prompt 7 satisfy, win over 8 persuade, talk into 9 argue into, prevail on 11 bring around, prevail upon

convincing
5 solid, sound, valid 6 cogent, trusty 7 telling 8 credible, faithful 9 authentic 10 persuasive, satisfying 11 trustworthy 12 satisfactory

convivial
3 gay 5 jolly, merry 6 jocund, jovial, lively, social 7 festive 8 sociable 9 vivacious 13 companionable

convocation
5 synod 7 council, meeting 8 assembly 9 gathering 10 assemblage 12 congregation

convoke
3 ask, bid, sit 4 call, meet 6 gather, invite, summon 7 collect, convene, request 8 assemble 10 congregate

convoluted
5 snaky 6 coiled 7 complex, sinuous, winding 8 flexuous, tortuous

9 meandrous 10 meandering, serpentine 11 anfractuous

convoy
4 bear 5 guard, guide, train 6 attend, defend, escort, shield 7 company, conduct, protect 9 accompany, companion, safeguard 11 consort with

convulse
4 rock 5 shake 7 agitate, concuss 8 tetanize

convulsion
3 fit 5 spasm 6 attack, clamor, outcry, tumult, uproar, upturn 7 ferment, quaking, rocking, shaking 8 disaster, laughter, upheaval 9 commotion, trembling

cook
3 fix, fry 4 bake, boil, burn, chef, melt, stew 5 broil, frame, grill, poach, roast, sauté, steam 6 braise, devise, invent, make up, scorch, simmer 7 concoct, dream up, griddle, hatch up, parboil, prepare, swelter 8 barbecue, cocinero, contrive 9 formulate

cooked
4 done
combining form: 5 cocto
with tomatoes: 10 cacciatore

cookery
7 cuisine 8 magirics
expert: 3 Yan (Martin) 4 Chen (Joyce), Kerr (Graham), Puck (Wolfgang), Root (Waverley) 5 Beard (James), Child (Julia), Hines (Duncan), Smith (Jeff) 6 Bocuse (Paul), Carême (Marie Antonin), Farmer (Fannie), Fisher (Mary Frances Kennedy), Franey (Pierre), Waters (Alice) 7 Crocker (Betty), Stewart (Martha) 8 Rombauer (Irma) 9 Claiborne (Craig), Escoffier (Auguste), Prudhomme (Paul) 14 Brillat-Savarin (Anthelme)

cookie
4 cake, snap 7 biscuit, brownie 8 macaroon 10 gingersnap

cooking
appliance: 4 oven 5 mixer, range, stove 7 blender, toaster 10 rotisserie
implement: 3 cup, pan, pot, wok 4 olla 5 ladle, sieve, spoon, whisk 6 frypan, grater, masher, sifter, tureen 7 griddle, skillet, spatula 8 colander 9 eggbeater 10 rolling pin 12 measuring cup
room: 6 galley 7 kitchen

cool
3 fan, ice 4 calm, cold 5 allay, aloof, chill, frore, gelid, nippy, sober 6 arctic, chilly, frigid, frosty, offish, placid, serene, stolid 7 assured, collect, compose, control, distant, repress 8 composed, detached, freezing, reserved, restrain, solitary, suppress, tranquil 9 collected, confident, impassive, unruffled, withdrawn 10 nonchalant, phlegmatic, simmer down, unsociable 11 indifferent, standoffish, unflappable 12 happy-go-lucky 13 imperturbable, self-possessed

cooler
3 fan 4 coop, icer, jail 6 lockup, prison 11 refrigerant 12 refrigerator

cooling device
3 fan 4 icer 6 icebox 7 freezer 12 refrigerator

coolness
6 aplomb, phlegm 7 ataraxy 8 calmness 9 composure, sangfroid 10 equanimity

coop
3 hem, mew, pen 4 cage, jail 5 cramp, fence 6 corral, shut in 7 close in, confine, enclose, envelop 9 enclosure

cooperate
5 agree, unite 6 concur, league 7 combine, conjoin, connive 8 coadjute, coincide 11 collaborate

cooperation
8 teamwork

cooperative
8 coacting, coactive, conjoint, synergic 9 concerted 10 synergetic 11 coefficient 13 collaborative, uncompetitive

Cooper hero
11 Natty Bumppo

coordinate
4 mate, tune 5 adapt, atune, match 6 fellow 7 conform, vis-à-vis 9 companion, harmonize, integrate, reconcile 10 proportion, reciprocal 11 accommodate 12 reconciliate

cop
3 nab 4 lift, take 5 filch, pinch, steal, swipe 7 gumshoe, officer, purloin 8 bluecoat 9 patrolman, policeman 11 appropriate

copacetic
4 fine, okay 5 dandy 12 satisfactory

cope
4 arch, bend, face 5 cover, dress, get by, match, notch, vault 6 canopy, handle, make do, manage, mantel, muzzle 8 deal with 9 encounter

copestone
5 crown

copious
4 full, lush, rich 5 ample 6 lavish, plenty 7 liberal, profuse, replete 8 abundant, generous 9 abounding, bounteous, bountiful, exuberant, luxuriant, plenteous, plentiful

Copland work
5 Rodeo

cop-out
6 excuse 7 pretext, retreat

copper
4 cent, coin 5 metal, penny, token 6 cuprum 9 butterfly, policeman
combining form: 4 cupr 5 chalc, chalk, cupri, cupro 6 chalko
item: 4 cent 5 penny 6 kettle
sulfate: 7 vitriol 9 bluestone 11 blue vitriol
symbol: 2 Cu

copperhead
5 snake, viper 8 squirrel

coppice
4 bosk, wood 5 copse, grove 6 bosque, forest, growth 7 thicket 9 brushwood, underwood

copse
see **coppice**

Copt
8 Egyptian

copula
4 link 5 union 7 coupler

copy
3 ape 4 echo, fake, mock, sham 5 ditto, mimic 6 carbon, ectype, effigy, ersatz, parody, repeat 7 emulate, imitate, replica, takeoff 8 knockoff, likeness, simulate, travesty 9 burlesque, duplicate, facsimile, imitation, replicate, reproduce 10 carbon copy, impression, simulacrum, transcribe 11 counterfeit, counterpart, reduplicate, replication 12 reproduction 13 reduplication

copyist
6 scribe 9 engrosser 10 plagiarist 12 calligrapher 13 calligraphist

copyread
4 edit

coquet
　3 toy 4 fool 5 dally, flirt 6 lead on, trifle 11 string along

coquette
　4 vamp 5 flirt 11 hummingbird

coquettish
　3 coy 4 arch 7 roguish

coral
　3 red 4 pink 5 palus, polyp 6 palule 8 skeleton 9 limestone

coral reef
　5 atoll
　off Australia: 5 Wreck
　world's largest: 12 Great Barrier

cord
　3 tie 4 band, lace, pile, rope, whip, wire, yarn 5 cable, nerve, stack 6 strand, string, tendon, thread 7 amentum
　twisted: 7 torsade

cordage
　4 rope 5 ropes 7 rigging
　fiber: 4 bast, eruc, hemp, imbe, jute, pita 5 sisal

Corday's victim
　5 Marat (Jean-Paul)

Cordelia
　father: 4 Lear
　sister: 5 Regan 7 Goneril

cordial
　4 warm 5 drink, sonsy 6 genial, hearty, tender 7 affable, liqueur, sincere 8 friendly, gracious, sociable 9 congenial, courteous, heartfelt 10 hospitable, responsive 11 sympathetic, warmhearted 12 wholehearted

cordiality
　5 ardor, favor 6 warmth 7 amenity 8 approval, sympathy 9 geniality, mutuality, pleasance 10 amiability 12 agreeability, friendliness, pleasantness 13 agreeableness, enjoyableness

cordon
　4 lace 5 braid 6 circle, ribbon 7 barrier
　blue: 4 chef, cook 6 ribbon 10 decoration

core
　3 hub, nub 4 base, body, bulk, gist, mass, meat, pith, root 5 basis, cadre, focus, heart, midst, quick 6 amount, burden, center, corpus, middle, origin, staple, thrust, upshot 7 purport 8 midpoint 9 substance 10 foundation

corf
　3 tub 4 cage 5 truck 6 basket

corium
　4 skin 5 cutis, layer 6 dermis

cork
　4 bark, plug, seal, stop 5 float 6 bobber 7 stopper, stopple
　combining form: 6 phello

corker
　4 lulu 5 dandy, dilly 8 jim-dandy, knockout 9 humdinger 11 crackerjack, lalapalooza

corkscrew
　4 coil, curl, wind 5 twine, twist 6 spiral 7 entwine, wreathe

cormorant
　4 bird, shag 7 glutton 8 Scottish
　norie: 5 scart

corn
　3 zea 4 meal, salt, samp 5 grain, maize 6 clavus, hominy 9 granulate
　bread: 4 pone 7 bannock
　Indian: 3 zea 5 maize 6 mealie
　kind: 3 pop 4 dent 5 flint, flour, sweet 6 Indian
　pest: 5 borer
　piece: 3 cob, ear 5 spike 6 kernel, nubbin

Corncracker State
　8 Kentucky

corner
　3 box, fix, jam, nab 4 hole, nook, trap, tree 5 angle, catch, coign, niche, seize 6 collar, cranny, dogleg, pickle, plight, recess, scrape 7 capture, dilemma, impasse, trouble 8 bottle up, monopoly 10 bring to bay 11 predicament
　combining form: 4 goni 5 gonio 6 anguli, angulo
　of eye: 7 canthus

cornerstone
　4 base 5 basis 7 support 10 foundation, groundwork

cornet
　4 cone, horn 5 zinke 8 woodwind 9 cornopean 10 instrument

cornflower
　5 bluet 10 bluebonnet, bluebottle

Cornhusker State
　8 Nebraska

cornice
　3 cap 4 band, eave 5 crown 6 geison 7 molding 8 swanneck
　combining form: 6 geisso

cornmeal
　4 masa, samp 5 atole 7 hoecake
　mush: 7 polenta

cornucopia
　4 cone, horn 9 abundance 12 horn of plenty

Cornwallis
　adversary: 6 Greene (Nathanael)
　surrender site: 8 Yorktown

corny
　5 banal, stale, tired, trite 6 old hat 7 clichéd 8 shopworn 9 hackneyed 10 warmed over 11 commonplace, sentimental, stereotyped

corollary
　6 effect, result, sequel, upshot 8 sequence 9 resulting 10 associated, end product, equivalent 11 aftereffect, consequence, precipitate

corona
　4 halo 5 cigar, crown, glory 6 circle, rosary, wreath 7 aureola, aureole, circlet, fermata, garland

coronal
　see **coronet**

coroner
　7 crowner, officer 8 examiner

coronet
　4 band 5 crown 6 anadem, circle, wreath 7 chaplet, circlet, garland

Coronis
　form: 4 crow
　son: 9 Asclepius 11 Aesculapius

corporal
　3 NCO 5 fanon 6 bodily, carnal 7 fleshly, somatic 8 physical

corporate
　6 united 7 unified 8 combined 9 aggregate

corporeal
　5 hylic, somal 6 bodily, carnal 7 fleshly, somatic 8 material, physical, sensible, tangible 9 objective 10 phenomenal 11 substantial

corps
　4 band 5 party, troop 6 outfit, troupe 7 company

corpse
　4 body, mort 5 bones, stiff 7 cadaver, carcass, carrion, remains
　combining form: 4 necr 5 necro

corpselike
　4 dead 6 deadly 7 deathly, ghastly, ghostly, shadowy 8 deadened, deathful, spectral 10 cadaverous

corpulence
7 fatness, obesity 9 adiposity
10 fleshiness

corpulent
3 fat 5 bulky, gross, heavy, obese, plump, stout 6 fleshy, portly
7 weighty 9 overblown
10 overweight

corpus
4 body, bulk, core, mass 6 oeuvre, staple 9 substance

corpuscle
4 cell 7 hematid 8 hemocyte, monocyte 9 leukocyte 10 lymphocyte 11 erythrocyte, granulocyte

corral
3 hem, mew, pen 4 cage, coop
5 fence, hedge 6 shut in 7 close in, confine, enclose 8 surround
9 enclosure

correct
3 fit, fix 4 done, edit, mend, true
5 amend, emend, exact, right 6 adjust, better, decent, proper, punish, reform, remedy, revise, seemly
7 chasten, improve, perfect, precise, rectify, redress 8 accurate, becoming, chastise, decorous, emendate, flawless, make over, regulate 9 castigate, faultless, veracious, veridical 10 conforming, discipline, impeccable, meticulous, scrupulous 11 comme il faut, punctilious, undistorted 12 conventional
combining form: 4 orth 5 ortho

correction
3 rod 8 punition 10 discipline, punishment 11 castigation
12 chastisement

corrective
4 cure 6 remedy 8 antidote, remedial 11 counterstep 12 counteragent 13 counteractant, counteractive

correctness
5 order 7 decorum 8 accuracy
9 coherence, congruity, exactness, precision, propriety 10 definitude, exactitude, properness, seemliness
11 orderliness, preciseness 12 decorousness, definiteness

correlate
5 match 6 analog 7 pendant 8 analogue, parallel 10 complement
11 counterpart, countertype
13 correspondent

correlative
2 if, or 3 nor 4 then 6 either 7 nei-

ther, related 10 reciprocal
13 corresponding

correspond
4 jibe, suit 5 agree, equal, match, write 6 accord, concur 7 conform, consort 8 dovetail 9 harmonize
11 communicate

correspondence
4 mail 7 letters 8 homogeny, symmetry 9 agreement, congruity
10 conformity 11 consistency
mathematical: 7 mapping 8 function

correspondent
5 match 6 analog, pen pal, writer
7 fitting 8 analogue, parallel, suitable 9 correlate 11 counterpart, countertype

corresponding
4 akin, like 5 alike 6 agnate 7 similar 8 parallel 9 analogous, consonant 10 comparable
prefix: 7 counter

correspondingly
2 so 4 also 8 likewise 9 similarly

corrida
9 bullfight
shout: 3 olé

corridor
4 hall 7 couloir, hallway, passage
10 passageway

corroborate
6 verify 7 bear out, confirm, justify
8 validate 12 authenticate, substantiate

corroborative
7 helping 9 ancillary, assisting, auxiliary 10 collateral, supportive
11 adminicular 12 confirmative, confirmatory, verificatory

corroboratory
see **corroborative**

corrode
3 eat 4 bite, gnaw, rust 5 erode, scour 7 eat away 8 wear away

corrosive
5 acerb 7 acerbic, caustic 9 sarcastic 12 archilochian

corrosiveness
7 sarcasm 8 acerbity 10 causticity

corrugation
4 fold, ruck 5 plica, ridge, rivel
6 crease, furrow, rimple 7 crinkle, wrinkle

corrupt
3 low, rot 4 foul, ruin, turn, warp
5 abase, decay, snide, spoil, stain, taint, venal, wreck 6 abased, be-

foul, debase, defile, molder, rotten, smirch 7 baneful, crooked, crumble, debauch, degrade, deprave, devious, knavish, noxious, oblique, pervert, putrefy, tarnish, vicious, vitiate 8 bribable, degraded, depraved, infamous, perverse, two-faced 9 animalize, break down, decompose, dishonest, faithless, mercenary, miscreant, nefarious, reprobate, unethical 10 bastardize, degenerate, demoralize, flagitious, inconstant, perfidious, pernicious, unfaithful, unreliable, villainous
11 deleterious, detrimental, treacherous 12 blackguardly, disintegrate, undependable, unprincipled, unscrupulous 13 double-dealing, untrustworthy

corruptible
5 venal 7 buyable 8 bribable
11 purchasable

corruption
4 vice 7 jobbery 8 slangism, solecism 9 barbarism, depravity, vulgarism 10 immorality, wickedness
11 impropriety 13 vernacularism, vernacularity

corsair
5 rover 6 pirate, sea dog 7 sea wolf 8 picaroon, sea rover 9 buccaneer, sea robber 10 freebooter

corset
6 bodice, girdle 7 support

cortex
4 bark, peel, rind 8 peridium
combining form: 7 cortico

Cortland
5 apple

corundum
4 ruby 5 emery, topaz 7 emerald
8 abrasive, amethyst, sapphire

coruscate
5 flash, gleam, glint 7 glisten, glitter, sparkle 11 scintillate

Corvino's wife
5 Celia

corybantic
3 mad 4 wild 5 rabid 7 frantic, furious 8 frenetic, frenzied
9 delirious

coryphée
6 dancer, hoofer 7 danseur 8 danseuse, figurant 9 ballerina, figurante 10 ballet girl 11 dancing girl

Cosi fan tutte composer
6 Mozart (Wolfgang Amadeus)

cosmetic
4 kohl 5 henna, rouge 6 ceruse, makeup, powder 7 blusher, bronzer, mascara 8 lipgloss, lipstick 9 eye shadow 10 nail polish 11 beautifying, superficial

cosmetologist
10 beautician

cosmic
6 global 8 catholic 9 planetary, universal, worldwide 10 ecumenical 12 cosmopolitan

cosmopolitan
6 cosmic, global, smooth, urbane 8 catholic, cultured, polished 9 civilized, planetary, universal, worldwide 10 cultivated, ecumenical 11 worldly-wise 12 metropolitan 13 sophisticated

cosmos
5 world 6 nature 8 creation, universe

Cossack
army: 3 Don 4 Ural 5 Kuban 6 voisko
district: 6 okrugi
land: 7 Ukraine
leader: 5 Razin (Stenka) 6 ataman, hetman, Mazepa (Ivan) 7 Bulavin (Kondraty) 8 Pugachev
novel: 10 Taras Bulba
village: 8 stanitsa, stanitza

cosset
3 pet 4 baby, love 5 humor, spoil 6 caress, cocker, coddle, cuddle, dandle, fondle, pamper 7 cater to, indulge 11 mollycoddle

cost
3 tab 4 rate, toll 5 price 6 charge, outlay, tariff 7 expense 8 price tag 11 expenditure 12 disbursement
business: 8 overhead

Costa Rica
capital: 7 San José
monetary unit: 5 colon

costermonger
6 hawker 7 peddler 9 barrow boy, barrowman

costive
4 mean 5 bound, close, tight 6 stingy 7 miserly 9 astricted, penurious 10 hardfisted, obstipated 12 cheeseparing, parsimonious

costless
4 free 6 gratis 10 chargeless, gratuitous 13 complimentary

costly
4 dear, high 5 fancy, pricy, steep, stiff 6 pricey 7 premium 8 precious, valuable 9 excessive, expensive, priceless 10 exorbitant, inordinate, invaluable 11 extravagant, inestimable

costume
3 rig 4 garb, mode 5 dress, getup, guise, style 6 outfit, setout 7 fashion, turnout

cot
3 hut 4 camp 5 cabin, lodge, shack 6 shanty 7 cottage
hanging: 7 hammock
wheeled: 6 gurney

coterie
3 mob 4 camp, clan, ring 5 cabal 6 circle, clique 7 ingroup 9 camarilla

cottage
3 hut 4 camp 5 cabin, lodge, shack 6 shanty 8 bungalow
Russian: 5 dacha
Swiss: 6 chalet

cotton
4 take 5 agree, grasp, toady 6 accept, coddle, kowtow 7 cater to, honey up 8 bootlick, perceive 9 apprehend, harmonize 10 comprehend, fraternize, understand
cleaner: 3 gin 5 willy 6 linter, willow
cloth: 4 jean, pima 5 khaki 6 canvas 7 galatea, jaconet, percale, silesia
cloth, Indian: 5 Surat 6 humhum 7 dhurrie
comb: 4 card
Egyptian: 4 maco
fabric: 3 rep 4 duck, lawn, leno, mull, repp 5 chino, crash, denim, doria, drill, manta, scrim, terry, wigan 6 calico, chintz, dimity, madras, muslin, nankin, sateen, satine 7 batiste, etamine, fustian, nankeen, nanking, organdy 8 drilling, nainsook 9 grenadine 10 seersucker
fabric, lustrous: 6 sateen, satine
fabric, sheer: 5 voile
fiber, short: 4 noil
fuzz remover: 6 linter
knot: 3 nep 4 slub
measure: 3 lea 4 hank, pick, yard 5 count, skein
pad: 7 pledget
pod: 4 boll
refuse: 5 flock 8 grabbots
seed separator: 3 gin
sheet: 3 bat 4 batt
thread: 5 lisle

Cotton State
7 Alabama

cottonwood
5 alamo 6 poplar

cottony
4 soft 5 silky 6 satiny, silken 7 velvety

Coty or Descartes
4 René

couch
3 den, put 4 lair, sink, sofa, word 5 divan, droop, lodge, lower 6 burrow, daybed, phrase 7 depress, express, let down 9 davenport, formulate 12 chesterfield

cougar
3 cat 4 puma 7 panther 9 catamount

cough
6 tussis
drop: 6 troche 7 lozenge

couloir
4 hall 5 gorge 7 hallway, passage 8 corridor 10 passageway

council
4 diet 5 junta 6 senate 7 cabinet, meeting 8 assembly, conclave, congress, ministry 10 conference, federation 12 consultation
ancient Greek: 5 boule
church: 5 synod 10 consistory
medieval English: 4 moot 5 gemot 6 gemote 7 husting 8 hustings
Muslim: 5 divan, diwan
Russian: 4 duma, douma 6 soviet
secret: 5 cabal, junto
Spanish: 7 cabildo

counsel
4 urge, warn 5 order 6 advice, advise, charge, direct, enjoin, lawyer, prompt 7 suggest 8 admonish, advocate, attorney 9 prescribe, recommend, reprehend 10 advisement
British: 9 barrister, solicitor

count
3 add, sum, tot 4 hope, look, mean 5 tally, total, weigh 6 bank on, census, expect, figure, import, matter, number, reckon, rely on 7 build on, compute, signify, trust in, trust to 8 bank upon, depend on, estimate, militate, numerate, quantify, reckon on, rely upon 9 calculate, enumerate 10 depend upon 11 calculate on

countenance
3 mug 4 back, cast, face, look, phiz 5 favor, go for 6 accept, visage 7 approve, commend, support

8 advocate, features, hold with
9 approbate, encourage
10 expression
combining form: 6 prosop 7 prosopo

counter
3 pit, vie 4 anti 5 match, polar
6 oppose 7 adverse, hostile, reverse 8 antipode, antipole, contrary, converse, impeding, opposite
9 antipodal, diametric, hindering, oppugnant 10 antipodean, antithesis 11 obstructive 12 antagonistic, antithetical 13 contradictory

counteract
3 fix 5 annul 6 negate 7 correct, rectify, redress 8 negative 9 cancel out, frustrate 10 neutralize

counteractant
4 cure 6 remedy 8 antidote
10 corrective

counteragent
see **counteractant**

counterbalance
6 make up, offset, redeem, set off
7 correct, rectify 8 atone for, outweigh 10 compensate

counterblow
7 revenge 8 avenging, reprisal, requital, revanche 9 vengeance
10 avengement 11 retaliation, retribution

countercheck
5 annul 6 negate 7 redress 8 negative 9 cancel out, frustrate
10 neutralize

counterclockwise
4 levo

counterfeit
3 act, ape, gyp 4 copy, fake, hoax, sham 5 bluff, bogus, dummy, false, feign, fraud, mimic, phony
6 affect, assume, deceit, pseudo
7 feigned, imitate, pretend 8 delusive, delusory, simulate, spurious
9 brummagem, deception, deceptive, imposture, pinchbeck, pretended, simulated 10 fraudulent, misleading, simulacrum
combining form: 5 pseud 6 pseudo

counterpane
6 spread 8 bedcover, coverlet
9 bedspread

counterpart
4 like 5 equal, match 6 analog
7 vis-à-vis 8 analogue, parallel
9 correlate 10 complement, coordinate, equivalent 13 correspondent

counterpoise
4 trim 6 make up, offset, redeem, set off, stasis, steady 7 balance, ballast 8 atone for, outweigh 9 stabilize 10 compensate
11 equilibrium

counterpole
see **opposite**

countersign
4 word 8 password 9 watchword

countertype
5 match 6 analog 8 analogue, parallel 9 correlate 13 correspondent

countervail
4 foil 6 offset, redeem, set off, thwart 7 balance, correct, rectify
8 atone for, outweigh, overcome, surmount 9 frustrate
10 compensate

countless
6 untold 10 innumerous, numberless, unnumbered 11 innumerable 12 unnumberable
combining form: 4 myri 5 myria, myrio

Count of Monte Cristo
6 Dantes
author: 5 Dumas (Alexandre)

count out
3 bar 4 bate 5 debar 6 except
7 exclude, rule out, suspend
9 eliminate

countrified
5 rural 6 rustic 7 bucolic 8 agrestic, pastoral 10 campestral, provincial

country
4 home, land, soil 5 rural 6 nation, rustic 7 bucolic, outland 8 agrestic, homeland, pastoral 10 campestral, fatherland, motherland, provincial
dance: 4 reel
home: 5 manor, ranch, villa
8 hacienda
music: 9 bluegrass
road: 4 lane, path 5 byway

country jake
4 hick, rube 5 clown 6 rustic
7 bumpkin, hayseed 9 hillbilly
10 clodhopper 12 backwoodsman

coup
4 blow, plan 5 d'etat, upset
6 putsch, stroke 8 takeover
9 stratagem

couple
3 duo 4 dyad, join, link, mate, pair, span, team, yoke 5 brace,

hitch, marry, unite 6 hook up
7 bracket, combine, conjoin, connect, doublet, harness, twosome
8 coalesce

coupler
4 link, ring 7 shackle
in an organ: 7 tirasse
railroad: 7 drawbar

couplet
4 pair 5 twins 7 distich

coupling
4 seam 5 joint, union 7 joining
8 junction, juncture 10 connection

courage
4 grit, guts 5 heart, moxie, pluck, spunk, valor 6 mettle, spirit 7 bravery, heroism 8 audacity, backbone, boldness, firmness, tenacity, valiance, valiancy 9 assurance, fortitude, gallantry 10 resolution
11 doughtiness, intrepidity, persistence 12 fearlessness 13 dauntlessness, determination

courageous
4 bold 5 brave, fiery, stout 6 manful, plucky, spunky, strong
7 doughty, valiant 8 fearless, intrepid, unafraid, valorous 9 audacious, dauntless, tenacious, undaunted 12 high-spirited

courier
5 envoy 6 bearer, legate, nuncio
7 carrier 8 emissary 9 go-between, messenger 11 internuncio

course
3 row, run, way 4 dart, dash, duct, line, path, plan, race, road, rush, tear 5 canal, chain, chase, hurry, orbit, order, range, route, scoot, scope, speed, trend 6 career, design, hasten, hustle, manner, policy, polity, scheme, scurry, sequel, series, sprint, string, system 7 advance, channel, circuit, conduit, passage, pattern, program, regimen, routine, scamper 8 aqueduct, progress, sequence 9 procedure
10 succession 11 progression
combining form: 4 drom 5 dromo
dinner: 5 salad 6 entrée 7 dessert
9 blue plate
of study: 8 syllabus 10 curriculum

courser
4 bird 7 charger 8 huntsman, warhorse

court
3 bar, woo 4 quad, yard 5 charm, judge, spark 6 allure, pursue 7 address, justice, romance 8 tribunal

9 captivate, curtilage, enclosure
10 magistrate, quadrangle, sweetheart
action: 4 suit 5 trial 6 appeal, assize 7 hearing, inquest, lawsuit 10 proceeding
calendar: 6 docket
call to: 7 summons 8 subpoena 11 arraignment
circuit: 4 eyre
crier's call: 4 oyes, oyez
decision: 6 assize 7 finding, verdict 8 judgment
ecclesiastical: 4 Rota 5 Curia 10 consistory
former English: 4 leet
Indian: 6 durbar
kind: 4 moot 5 civil 6 county, family 7 circuit, customs, federal, supreme 8 chancery, criminal, district, juvenile, kangaroo, superior 9 appellate, municipal 11 territorial
medieval English: 4 eyre, moot 5 gemot 6 gemote 7 husting 8 hustings
minutes: 4 acta
of equity: 8 chancery
officer: 2 DA 5 clerk, crier, judge 6 puisne 7 bailiff, justice, marshal, sheriff 10 prosecutor
order: 4 writ 5 arret, edict 6 decree 7 summons 8 mandamus, subpoena
panel: 4 jury
relating to: 5 aulic 8 judicial
session: 6 assize 7 sitting 8 sederunt

courteous
5 civil 6 polite 7 genteel 8 mannerly 9 attentive 10 thoughtful 11 considerate 12 well-mannered

courter
5 wooer 6 suitor

courtesy
5 favor 6 comity 7 amenity, service 8 chivalry, civility, kindness 9 attention, gallantry, geniality 10 affability, cordiality, indulgence 11 courtliness 12 complaisance, dispensation, graciousness 13 attentiveness, consideration

court game
see under **game**

courtly
4 prim 5 civil, lofty, preux, stiff 6 august, formal 7 gallant, starchy, stately, stilted, studied 8 gracious, imposing 9 civilized, dignified 11 ceremonious 12 conventional

courtship
4 suit 6 wooing 7 romance
former custom of: 8 bundling

courtyard
4 quad 5 garth, patio 6 atrium 7 cortile 9 curtilage 10 quadrangle

Cousteau, Jacques
ship: 7 Calypso
vehicle: 11 bathysphere

cove
3 arm, bay 4 gulf 5 bayou, bight, creek, firth, inlet 6 harbor, slough

covenant
3 vow 4 bond, pact 5 agree, swear 6 concur, pledge, plight 7 bargain, compact 8 contract 9 agreement 10 convention 11 transaction

cover
3 cap, lid 4 bury, fend, hide, hood, mask, wrap 5 brood, cache, cloak, crown, guard, guise, haven, put-on, stash, track 6 asylum, bush up, canopy, defend, enfold, enwrap, facade, harbor, hiding, refuge, safety, screen, secure, shield, shroud, travel 7 blanket, bulwark, conceal, enclose, envelop, overlay, protect, retreat, secrete, shelter 8 disguise, ensconce, overcast, pass over, security, traverse 9 harborage, safeguard, sanctuary, semblance, superpose 10 false front, masquerade, overspread 11 concealment, superimpose
combining form: 8 operculi
rooflike: 6 awning, canopy
the eyes: 9 blindfold
the face: 4 mask, veil
the mouth: 6 muzzle
with asphalt: 4 pave
with cloth: 5 drape
with dirt: 6 bemire, besoil 8 besmirch
with jewels: 5 begem
with straw: 6 thatch

coverall
10 boiler suit

covered
combining form: 5 crypt, krypt 6 crypto, krypto

covered wagon
9 Conestoga

covering
anatomical: 5 theca, velum 6 tegmen 7 velamen 8 tegument 10 integument
close-fitting: 6 sheath 9 sheathing
cloth: 5 sheet
combining form: 4 cole, derm, steg 5 coleo, derma, stego
flap: 9 operculum

for a book: 6 jacket
for a cigar: 7 wrapper
for a coffin: 4 pall
for a corpse: 6 shroud 8 cerement
for a package: 7 wrapper
for concealment: 10 camouflage
for food: 4 cosy, cozy
for soil: 5 mulch
metal: 4 mail 5 armor
of a diatom: 6 lorica
of a plant ovary: 8 pericarp
of a seed: 4 aril, case 5 testa
of fruits: 4 peel, rind
of gloom: 4 pall
of grain: 4 hull, husk 5 chaff
shell-like: 8 carapace
thin: 4 film 6 patina, veneer
waterproof: 4 tarp 9 tarpaulin

coverlet
6 spread 8 bedcover 9 bedspread 11 counterpane

covert
5 haven, privy 6 asylum, buried, harbor, hidden, masked, refuge, secret 7 cloaked, furtive, guarded, retreat, shelter, sub-rosa 8 hush-hush, obscured, shrouded, stealthy, ulterior 9 concealed, disguised, harborage, sanctuary 10 dissembled, undercover 11 camouflaged, clandestine 12 hugger-mugger 13 surreptitious, under-the-table

covertly
7 sub rosa 8 in camera, secretly 9 by stealth, furtively, privately 10 stealthily 12 hugger-mugger 13 clandestinely

covet
4 want, wish 5 crave 6 desire 10 desiderate

covetous
4 avid, keen 5 eager, itchy 6 grabby, greedy 7 envious, hoggish, jealous, piggish, selfish, swinish 8 desirous, esurient, grasping, grudging, ravenous 9 rapacious, voracious 10 gluttonous 11 acquisitive

covey
4 band, bevy, crew 5 bunch, group, party 7 cluster 8 assembly

covin
4 plot 5 cabal 6 scheme 8 intrigue 10 conspiracy 11 machination

cow
(see also **cattle**) 4 faze, kine (plural), neat 5 abash, bossy, bully, daunt 6 appall, bovine, dismay,

hector, rattle **7** bluster, dragoon **8** bludgeon, browbeat, bulldoze, bullyrag **9** discomfit, embarrass, strong-arm **10** disconcert, intimidate

cud: **5** rumen

French: **5** vache

hornless: **5** doddy, muley **6** doddie, mulley **7** pollard

mammary gland: **5** udder

pasture: **7** vaccary

pen: **6** corral

shed: **4** barn, byre **7** shippen, shippon

Spanish: **4** vaca

young: **4** calf **5** stirk **6** heifer

coward
4 baby **6** craven **7** caitiff, chicken, dastard, gutless, milksop, quitter, unmanly **8** poltroon, recreant, weakling **9** fraidy-cat, jellyfish, spunkless **10** scaredy-cat **11** lily-livered, poltroonish, yellowbelly **12** invertebrate, poor-spirited **13** pusillanimous

___ Coward
4 Noel

cowardly
4 vile **6** afraid, craven, yellow **7** caitiff, chicken, fearful, gutless, panicky, unmanly **8** cravenly, poltroon, recreant, timorous **9** dastardly, spunkless, worthless **11** lily-livered, milk-livered, poltroonish **12** fainthearted, poor-spirited, white-livered **13** pusillanimous

cowboy
5 waddy **6** drover, herder, waddie **7** puncher, rancher **8** buckaroo, buckeroo, herdsman, wrangler **9** cattleman **10** cowpuncher **12** broncobuster

contest: **5** rodeo

legendary: **9** Pecos Bill

leggings: **5** chaps

movie: **3** Mix (Tom) **5** Autry (Gene) **6** Rogers (Roy) **8** Cisco Kid **15** Hopalong Cassidy

rope: **5** lasso, reata, riata **6** lariat

Spanish-American: **6** charro, gaucho **7** llanero, vaquero

cower
4 fawn **5** quail, toady, wince **6** blench, cringe, flinch, grovel, kowtow, recoil, shrink **7** honey up, truckle **8** bootlick **9** brownnose **11** apple-polish

cowfish
6 dugong, sea cow **7** grampus, manatee **8** sirenian

cowl
3 cop **4** hood, monk **5** amice **6** almuce **7** capuche

cowpox
8 vaccinia

cowpuncher
see **cowboy**

coxcomb
3 fop **4** buck, dude **5** blood, dandy **8** macaroni **9** exquisite **11** Beau Brummel **12** lounge lizard

coy
3 shy **4** arch **5** timid **6** decent, demure, proper, seemly **7** bashful, playful **8** decorous, retiring, skittish **9** diffident, kittenish, unassured **10** capricious, coquettish **11** mischievous, unassertive **12** self-effacing

Coyote State
11 South Dakota

coypu
6 rodent

fur: **6** nutria

Cozbi's father
3 Zur

cozen
3 gyp **4** beat, bilk **5** cheat **6** betray, delude, diddle, humbug, illude, take in **7** beguile, deceive, defraud, mislead, sell out, swindle **8** flimflam **11** double-cross

cozy
4 easy, safe, snug, soft **5** comfy, cushy, pally **6** chummy, secure **7** easeful **8** covering, intimate **10** buddy-buddy, palsy-walsy

crab
4 beef, fuss, yaup, yawp **5** bleat, gripe **6** griper, grouch, kicker, squawk, yammer **7** decapod, grouser, growler **8** arthopod, grumbler **9** bellyache, shellfish **10** bellyacher, complainer, crosspatch, crustacean **11** faultfinder

claw: **5** chela **6** nipper

combining form: **6** carcin **7** carcino

constellation: **6** Cancer

genus: **3** Uca **6** Birgus **7** Limulus, Pagurus

hermit: **8** pagurian

kind: **3** pea **4** blue, king, pine, rock **5** ghost, purse **6** hermit, partan, spider **7** fiddler **9** Dungeness, horseshoe

king, horseshoe: **7** limulus **8** limuloid

relating to: **7** cancrid

resembiing: **8** cancroid

crabbed
4 dour, glum **5** blunt, gruff, huffy, sulky, surly, testy **6** cranky, crusty, gloomy, morose, sullen **7** brusque **8** choleric, snappish **9** irascible, irritable, saturnine, splenetic

crabby
see **crabbed**

crab-like
8 cancroid

crabwise
8 sidelong, sideward, sideways **9** laterally

crack
2 go **3** gag, try **4** bang, bash, belt, blow, boom, chap, clap, jape, jest, joke, quip, rent, rift, rima, rime, shot, slam, slap, slit, snap, stab, wham, whop **5** adept, blast, break, burst, chink, cleft, crash, flash, fling, jiffy, smack, smash, split, whack, whirl **6** cranny, decode, expert, master, moment **7** crevice, decrypt, fissure, instant, skilled **8** crevasse, decipher, drollery, interval, masterly, rimation, skillful, superior **9** bastinado, excellent, masterful, witticism **10** interstice, percussion, proficient **11** split second **12** cryptanalyze **13** discontinuity

crackbrain
3 nut **4** kook **5** crank **6** cuckoo **7** lunatic **8** crackpot **9** ding-a-ling, screwball

crackdown
8 quashing **10** repression **11** suppression

cracked
3 mad **4** daft, nuts **5** batty, crazy, daffy **6** crazed, cuckoo, insane, maniac, rimose, rimous, screwy **7** lunatic **8** demented

cracker
5 wafer **7** biscuit, saltine **8** Georgian **9** Floridian

crackerjack
4 lulu **5** adept, dandy, dilly, nifty **6** corker, expert, master **7** skilled **8** jim-dandy, knockout, masterly, skillful **9** humdinger, masterful **10** proficient **11** lalapalooza

crackle
4 snap **7** sparkle **9** crepitate

crackpot
3 nut **4** case, kook, loon **5** crank, loony **6** cuckoo, madman, maniac, oddity **7** dingbat, lunatic, oddball

9 character, ding-a-ling, eccentric, harebrain, screwball

crack-up
5 crash, smash, wreck **6** pileup **7** debacle, decline, smashup **8** collapse **9** breakdown **13** deterioration

cradlesong
7 lullaby **8** berceuse

craft
3 art, job **5** skill, trade **6** métier **7** calling, cunning, know-how, slyness **8** artifice, foxiness, vocation, wiliness **9** cageyness, canniness, dexterity, expertise **10** adroitness, artfulness, profession
combining form: **6** techno, techny

craftiness
3 art **7** cunning, slyness **8** artifice, foxiness, wiliness **9** cageyness, canniness **10** artfulness

craftsman
5 smith **6** carver, potter, weaver, wright **7** artisan, builder, jeweler **9** carpenter

crafty
3 sly **4** foxy, keen, wily **5** acute, sharp **6** adroit, artful, astute, clever, tricky **7** cunning, fawning **8** guileful **9** deceitful, insidious
Scottish: **6** sleeky **7** sleekit

cragged
5 harsh, rough **6** jagged, rugged, uneven **7** scraggy **8** asperous, scabrous, unsmooth

craggy
see **cragged**

cram
3 jam, ram **4** bolt, fill, gulp, heap, load, pack, tamp, wolf **5** chock, crowd, crush, drive, force, press, shove, study, stuff, wedge **6** bone up, englut, gobble, guzzle, review, squash, thrust **7** jam-pack, overeat, squeeze **11** ingurgitate

crammed
4 full **5** awash **6** jammed, loaded, packed **7** brimful, crowded, stuffed **8** brimming **9** chock-full

cramp
5 stint **7** shackle **8** confined **9** restraint, stricture **10** constraint, limitation **11** confinement, restriction **12** incommodious **13** constrainment

cramped
4 tiny **5** close, small, tight **6** little, minute, narrow **8** confined **9** two-by-four **12** incommodious

cranberry
9 vaccinium
tree: **7** pembina

crane
4 bird, boom **7** derrick **9** cormorant **10** demoiselle
arm: **3** jib
genus: **4** Grus
Indian: **5** sarus
resembling: **6** gruine
ship's: **5** davit
traveling: **5** jenny, titan **7** goliath

Crane's hero
12 Henry Fleming

cranium
5 skull

crank
3 bee, nut **4** crab, kook **5** fancy **6** cuckoo, griper, grouch, notion, vagary **7** boutade, caprice, conceit, grouser, growler, lunatic **8** crackpot, crotchet, grumbler, sourpuss **9** ding-a-ling, harebrain, screwball **10** bellyacher, crackbrain, crosspatch **11** faultfinder

cranky
4 daft **5** crazy, cross, daffy, ratty, testy, waspy **6** crazed, cuckoo, insane, ornery, tetchy, touchy **7** bearish, cracked, froward, waspish **8** cankered, choleric, contrary, vinegary **9** crotchety, irascible, temperish **10** bad-humored, ill-humored, vinegarish **11** hot-tempered **12** cantankerous, crackbrained, cross-grained, disagreeable **13** quick-tempered

cranny
4 nook **5** niche **7** byplace

crash
3 din, jar, ram **4** bang, boom, bump, bust, clap, fail, fold, jolt, slam, wham **5** blast, break, burst, crack, shock, smash, wreck **6** impact, pileup **7** collide, crack-up, debacle, smashup **8** accident, collapse **9** breakdown, collision **10** concussion, percussion

crashing
5 gross, utter **7** blasted **8** absolute, infernal, positive **9** downright **10** confounded, consummate

crass
3 raw **4** rude **5** crude, gross, rough **6** coarse, vulgar **7** loutish, uncouth **8** churlish **9** inelegant, unrefined

crate
4 heap **5** wreck **6** jalopy, junker **7** clunker

crater
3 pit **4** hole, pock **6** cavity **7** caldera **10** depression
Hawaiian: **7** Kilauea

cravat
3 tie **4** band **5** scarf **7** bandage, necktie

crave
3 ask, beg **4** ache, long, lust, pine, pray, sigh, want, wish **5** brace, covet, plead **6** appeal, demand, desire, hanker, hunger, thirst **7** beseech, call for, entreat, implore, require, suspire **9** importune **10** desiderate, supplicate **11** necessitate

craven
4 funk **6** coward, funker **7** chicken, dastard, gutless, quitter, unmanly **8** cowardly, poltroon **9** spunkless **11** lily-livered, plotroonish, yellowbelly **12** poor-spirited **13** pusillanimous

craving
4 itch, lust, urge **6** desire **7** passion **8** appetite **10** appetition

crawl
4 flow, inch, teem **5** creep, slide, snail, snake, swarm **6** abound, grovel **9** pullulate

crawling
6 repent **7** reptant

craze
3 fad **4** chic, rage **5** crack, fever, furor, mania, style, vogue **6** frenzy, furore, madden **7** derange, fashion, unhinge **8** distract **9** unbalance **10** dernier cri, enthusiasm

craziness
5 folly **7** inanity **8** insanity **9** absurdity, dottiness, silliness **11** foolishness, witlessness **13** senselessness

crazy
3 fey, mad **4** daft, gaga, loco, luny, nuts, wack **5** balmy, batty, daffy, dotty, goofy, loony, nutty, silly, wacky, whack **6** absurd, cuckoo, insane, looney, madman, maniac, screwy, teched, whacky **7** bonkers, cracked, foolish, lunatic, tetched, touched, unsound **8** crackpot, demented, deranged **9** bedlamite, possessed, senseless **10** crackbrain, moonstruck, unbalanced **11** harebrained **12** preposterous
British: **5** potty **6** scatty
Scottish: **3** wud

crazy house

6 asylum 8 loony bin 9 funny farm
10 booby hatch

cream

3 top 4 balm, beat, best, pick,
whip 5 blast, elite, pride, prime,
prize, salve 6 cerate, choice,
chrism 7 clobber, unction, unguent
8 lambaste, ointment

crease

4 fold, ruck 5 plica, ridge, rivel
6 furrow, rimple 7 crinkle, wrinkle
11 corrugation

create

4 make, sire 5 found, hatch, set up,
spawn, start 6 father, parent
7 compose, produce 8 conceive,
engender, generate 9 establish,
formulate, institute, originate, procreate 10 constitute

creation

5 world 6 cosmos, kosmos, nature
8 megacosm, universe 9 macrocosm 11 macrocosmos

creative

8 original 9 demiurgic, deviceful,
ingenious, inventive 10 innovative,
innovatory 11 originative
12 innovational

creator

4 sire 5 maker 6 author, father
7 founder 8 inventor 9 architect,
generator, patriarch 10 originator

creature

3 man 5 beast, being, brute, human, toady 6 animal, minion, mortal, person 7 critter 8 truckler
9 personage, sycophant
fabled: 3 elf, imp 4 ogre, puck
5 dwarf, fairy, giant, gnome, troll
6 dragon, goblin, merman, sprite
7 brownie, gremlin, mermaid, monster, unicorn 9 hobgoblin 10 leprechaun; (see also **monster**)
winged: 4 bird, fowl 8 volatile

credence

5 faith, trust 6 belief, credit 8 reliance 10 confidence

credentials

6 papers 9 character, documents,
reference 11 testimonial
13 documentation

credible

5 solid, sound, valid 6 trusty
8 faithful, rational 9 authentic, colorable, plausible 10 believable,
convincing, reasonable, satisfying
11 trustworthy 12 satisfactory

credit

3 lay 4 deem, feel 5 asset, faith,
honor, refer, sense, think, trust 6 assign, belief, charge, impute, notice,
weight 7 ascribe, believe 8 consider, credence, prestige, reliance
9 attribute, authority, influence
10 confidence 11 recognition

creditable

7 reputed 9 colorable, estimable,
plausible, reputable 10 believable
11 respectable 13 well-thought-of

credo

5 creed 6 belief 8 ideology

credulous

5 naive 6 unwary 7 dupable 8 gullible, trustful, trusting 9 accepting,
believing 12 unsuspecting, unsuspicious 13 unquestioning

creed

4 cult, sect 5 credo, faith 6 belief,
church 8 ideology, religion 9 communion 10 connection, persuasion
12 denomination

creek

3 ria 4 gill, race, rill 5 brook 6 arroyo, rillet, runlet, runnel, stream
7 freshet, rivulet 8 brooklet
9 streamlet

creep

4 edge, inch, lurk, slip 5 crawl,
glide, shirk, skulk, slide, slink,
snake, sneak, steal 6 tiptoe 7 gumshoe, slither, sniggle, wriggle
9 pussyfoot

creeping

6 repent 7 reptant
combining form: 6 herpet 7 herpeto

crème de la crème

4 best 5 elite 6 gentry 7 aristoi
8 optimacy 9 blue blood, haut
monde 10 upper crust
11 aristocracy

Cremona family

6 Amatis

Creon

daughter: 6 Creusa, Glauce, Glauke
sister: 7 Jocasta
son: 6 Haemon
victim: 8 Antigone

crepehanger

9 Cassandra, pessimist, worrywart

crescendo

4 acme, apex, peak 5 crest 6 apogee, climax, culmen 8 capstone,
meridian 11 culmination

crescent-shaped

6 lunate 7 lunated

body or surface: 8 meniscus
combining form: 5 selen 6 seleni,
seleno

crest

3 cap, top 4 acme, apex, noon,
peak,
roof 5 arête, chine, crown, ridge
6 apogee, climax, summit, vertex
7 hogback 8 pinnacle, surmount
9 crescendo, fastigium
11 culmination
combining form: 4 loph 5 lophi, lopho 6 lophio
of a wave: 8 whitecap

crestfallen

3 low 4 blue, down 8 cast down,
dejected, downcast 9 depressed
10 dispirited 11 downhearted
12 disconsolate

Crete

ancient city: 7 Cnossus, Knossos
8 Phaistos
ancient name: 6 Candia
capital: 5 Canea
goddess: 8 Dictynna 11 Britomartis
guard: 5 Talos
king: 5 Minos 9 Idomeneus
maze: 9 labyrinth
monster: 8 Minotaur
mountain: 3 Ida
princess: 7 Ariadne

cretin

4 fool, zany 5 ament, idiot, moron
6 zombie 7 half-wit 8 imbecile
9 simpleton

Creusa

father: 5 Priam
husband: 6 Aeneas
mother: 6 Hecuba
son: 3 Ion 8 Ascanius

crevice

4 seam, slit 5 chink, cleft, crack,
grike 6 cranny 7 fissure 8 cleavage, crevasse 10 interstice

crew

4 band, bevy, gang, team
5 bunch, covey, group, party
7 cluster, retinue 8 assembly

crib

3 bed, bin, box, hut, key 4 pony,
trot, weir 5 cheat, crate, hovel,
stall, steal 6 cradle, crèche, manger, pilfer 7 barrier, brothel, purloin 8 bassinet, bedstead, bordello
9 enclosure 10 plagiarism,
plagiarize

cricket

period of play: 7 innings

team: 6 eleven
term: 2 on 3 leg, off, rot 4 bowl
5 pitch 6 bowler, wicket, yorker
7 batsman, striker 9 fieldsman
turn at bat: 4 over

crime
3 sin 4 evil, tort 6 breach, delict, felony 7 misdeed, offense 8 delictum, iniquity 9 diablerie, violation 10 illegality, wrongdoing 11 misdemeanor 13 transgression
instructor: 5 Fagin

Crimea
capital: 10 Simferopol
city: 5 Kerch, Yalta 10 Sevastopol
river: 4 Alma
sea: 4 Azov
strait: 5 Kerch

criminal
4 hood, thug 5 crook, felon 6 outlaw 7 convict, illegal, illicit, lawless, mobster 8 fugitive, gangster, jailbird, offender, unlawful, wrongful 9 racketeer, wrongdoer 10 lawbreaker, malefactor, trespasser 12 illegitimate, transgressor
habitual: 8 repeater 10 recidivist

criminate
3 tax 6 accuse, charge, indict 7 arraign, impeach 9 inculpate

crimp
3 bar, bit, rub 4 friz, snag 5 check, frizz, screw 6 bridle, hamper, hold in, hurdle, rimple, ruck up, rumple 7 crinkle, crumple, inhibit, scrunch, wrinkle 8 hold back, hold down, mountain, obstacle, restrain, withhold 9 constrain 10 impediment 11 Chinese wall, obstruction

crimple
5 screw 6 ruck up, rumble 7 crinkle, crumple, scrunch, wrinkle

crimson
3 red 4 glow, pink, rose 5 blush, color, flush, rouge 6 mantle, pinken, redden

cringe
4 fawn 5 cower, quail, toady, wince 6 blench, flinch, grovel, kowtow, recoil, shrink, slaver 7 truckle 8 bootlick 11 apple-polish

crinkle
4 fold, ruck 5 crimp, plica, ridge, rivel, screw 6 crease, furrow, rimple, ruck up, rumple 7 crimple, crumple, scrunch 11 corrugation

crinkly
5 crepy 6 crepey

cripple
3 sap 4 lame, maim 5 blunt, palsy 6 disarm, mayhem, weaken 7 disable, dislimb, unbrace 8 enfeeble, mutilate, paralyze 9 attenuate, dismember, prostrate, undermine 10 debilitate, immobilize 12 incapacitate, unstrengthen

cripples' patron saint
5 Giles

crisis
4 pass 5 pinch 6 strait 8 exigency, juncture, zero hour 9 emergency 10 crossroads 11 contingency 12 turning point

crisp
5 short 6 biting 7 brittle, crumbly, crunchy, cutting, friable, ingoing 8 clear-cut, incisive 9 trenchant 11 penetrating

crisscross
9 decussate, intersect

criterion
5 gauge 7 measure 8 standard 9 benchmark, yardstick 10 touchstone

critic
5 momus 6 carper, Zoilus 7 carping, caviler, knocker 8 captious, caviling, censurer, quibbler 9 aristarch, belittler, cavillous, muckraker, nitpicker 10 censorious, disparager, mudslinger 11 faultfinder, smellfungus

critical
4 dire 5 acute, fussy 7 carping, crucial, finicky, pivotal, weighty 8 captious, caviling, decisive 9 cavillous, demeaning, desperate, important, momentous 10 belittling, censorious, conclusive, particular 11 climacteric, disparaging, significant 12 faultfinding 13 consequential, determinative
study: 6 examen 8 exegesis

criticism
5 blame 6 notice, rebuke, review 7 censure, comment, opinion, reproof 8 analysis, critique, diatribe, judgment, reproval, reviewal 9 appraisal 10 assessment, commentary 11 examination, observation

criticize
3 pan, rap 4 carp 5 blame, blast, cavil, cut up, fault, knock, roast, scold 6 rebuke, scathe 7 censure, condemn, reprove 8 badmouth, denounce, lambaste 9 castigate, fusti-

gate, reprehend, reprobate 10 denunciate

criticizer
5 momus 6 carper, Zoilus 7 caviler, knocker 9 aristarch 11 faultfinder

critique
see **criticism**

critter
5 beast, brute 6 animal 8 creature

Crius
father: 6 Uranus
mother: 4 Gaea
son: 8 Astraeus

croak
3 die 5 scold 6 grouch, grouse, murmur, mutter 7 grumble, quarrel 8 complain

croaking
5 gruff, husky 6 hoarse

croaky
see **croaking**

Croatia
capital: 6 Zagreb
city: 5 Split 6 Osijek, Rijeka

crock
3 jar, pot 4 smut, soot 7 disable 8 potsherd 11 earthenware

crocodile
7 reptile
bird: 6 plover 9 trochilus
Indian: 6 gavial
relative: 9 alligator
South American: 6 caiman, cayman, jacare
Southeast Asian: 6 muggar, mugger, muggur

Croesus' kingdom
5 Lydia

Cromwell, Oliver
regiment: 9 Ironsides
son: 7 Richard
victory site: 6 Naseby

crone
3 hag 4 drab, trot 5 biddy, witch 6 beldam

Cronus
5 Titan 6 Saturn
daughter: 4 Hera 6 Hestia 7 Demeter
father: 6 Uranus
mother: 4 Gaea
sister: 4 Rhea 6 Cybele, Tethys
son: 4 Zeus 5 Hades 7 Jupiter, Neptune 8 Poseidon
wife: 4 Rhea 6 Cybele

crony
3 pal 4 chum 5 buddy 6 comate
7 comrade 9 associate, companion
11 running mate

crook
3 bow 4 bend 5 curve, round, thief
6 bandit, robber

crooked
5 lying, snaky, snide, venal
6 curved, errant, shifty, zigzag
7 bending, corrupt, curving, devious, winding 8 rambling, ruthless,
tortuous, twisting 9 deceitful, dishonest, underhand 10 fraudulent,
meandering, serpentine, untruthful
12 unscrupulous 13 double-dealing
combining form: 5 ancyl, ankyl 6 anchyl, ancylo, ankylo 7 anchylo

crookedly
4 awry 5 askew 6 askant
7 askance 8 cockeyed 9 cock-a-
hoop

croon
3 hum, low 4 lull, moan, sing, wail
6 lament, murmur

crooner
4 Cole (Nat "King"), Como (Perry),
6 Crosby (Bing), Martin (Dean), Val-
lee (Rudy) 7 Sinatra (Frank) 8 Williams (Andy)

crop
3 cut, hew, mow, top 4 chop, clip,
pare, snip, trim 5 prune, shave,
shear, skive 7 harvest, pollard
8 fruitage, truncate 10 detruncate

cropping
7 harvest, reaping 9 gathering
10 harvesting 11 ingathering

croquet
5 roque

crosier
5 staff

cross
4 deny, mule, over, rood 5 ratty,
testy, trial 6 betray, cranky, hybrid,
impugn, negate, ordeal, tetchy,
touchy 7 athwart, calvary, carping,
gainsay, mongrel, sell out 8 captious, choleric, traverse 9 decussate, disaffirm, half blood, half-
breed, hybridize, intersect,
irascible, temperish 10 affliction,
contradict, contravene, interbreed,
transverse, visitation 11 tribulation
13 quick-tempered
a river: 4 ford
bearer: 8 crucifer
combining form: 6 stauro
decoration: 4 Iron 8 Victoria

Egyptian: 4 ankh
kind: 3 tau 5 Greek, Latin, papal
6 Celtic, fleury, formée, moline,
pommée, potent 7 avellan, boto-
née, Calvary, Maltese 8 crucifix,
fourchée, Lorraine, quadrate
11 patriarchal 12 Saint Andrew's
13 Saint Anthony's
section: 5 slice
stroke of a letter: 5 serif

crossbow
8 arbalest, arbalist

crossbreed
4 mule 6 hybrid 7 bastard, mongrel 9 half blood, half-breed, hybridize 10 interbreed

crosscut
9 decussate, intersect

cross-examination
5 grill 8 grilling 11 questioning,
third degree 13 interrogation

cross-eye
6 squint 9 esotropia 10 strabismus

crossing
6 thwart 8 traverse 10 transverse
11 transversal

cross out
6 cancel, delete

crosspatch
4 crab 5 crank 6 griper, grouch
7 grouser, growler 8 grumbler,
sorehead, sourpuss 10 complainer

crossroads
4 pass 5 pinch 6 crisis, strait 8 exigency, juncture, zero hour 9 carrefour, emergency 11 contingency
12 intersection, turning point
goddess: 6 Hecate, Hekate, Trivia

cross-shaped
8 cruciate 9 cruciform

crossways
6 across 7 athwart 10 diagonally
12 transversely

crosswise
see **crossways**

crotchet
4 whim 5 fancy, freak, quirk 6 megrim, vagary 7 boutade, caprice,
conceit 12 eccentricity

crotchety
5 waspy 6 cranky, ornery 7 bearish, waspish 8 cankered, contrary,
vinegary 10 vinegarish 12 cantankerous, cross-grained

crouch
4 bend, duck 5 cower, hunch,

squat, stoop 6 huddle 10 hunker
down 11 scrooch down

crow
4 blow, brag, puff 5 boast, exult,
gloat, mouth, prate, vaunt 9 gasconade 11 rodomontade
colony: 7 rookery
combining form: 5 corax
cry: 3 caw
family: 3 daw, jay 4 rook 5 raven
6 chough, corvid, hoodie, magpie
7 jackdaw 8 Corvidae
genus: 6 Corvus
Hawaiian: 5 alala
relating to: 7 corvine

crowbar
3 pry 5 jimmy, lever 7 gablock
8 gavelock

crowd
3 jam, lot, mob, set 4 army, bear,
cram, herd, host, push, rout, ruck
5 bunch, cloud, crush, drove, flock,
group, horde, press, serry, shove,
swarm, troop 6 circle, gaggle, huddle, legion, rabble, scores, squash,
squish, squush, throng 7 cluster,
company, squeeze 8 assembly
9 congeries, gathering, multitude
10 assemblage, collection 11 aggregation 12 congregation

crowded
4 full 5 awash, close, dense, thick,
tight 6 jammed, loaded, packed
7 brimful, compact, crammed,
stuffed 8 brimming, populous
9 chock-full

crow-like
7 corvoid

crown
3 cap, top 4 acme, apex, peak,
roof 5 cover, crest, tiara 6 anadem, climax, diadem, laurel, summit, top off, vertex, wreath, zenith
7 chaplet, coronal, coronet, garland, overlay 8 meridian, overcast,
pinnacle, round off, surmount 9 culminate, fastigium, finish off
10 overspread 11 culmination
combining form: 6 corono 7 stephan
8 stephano
Egyptian: 7 pschent

crucial
4 dire 5 acute, vital 8 critical, decisive 9 desperate, important, necessary 10 imperative 11 climacteric

crucible
4 test 5 trial 6 ordeal 10 affliction
11 tribulation

crucifix
4 rood 5 cross

crucifixion site
7 Calvary 8 Golgotha

crucify
4 kill 5 smite 6 harrow, martyr
7 afflict, agonize, mortify, torment,
torture 10 excruciate

crud
3 goo 4 gook, gunk, junk, muck
5 filth, slime, trash 6 debris, sludge
7 rubbish

crude
3 raw 4 foul, poor 5 crass, dirty,
gross, rough 6 coarse, filthy,
gauche, impure, native, ribald, risqué, smutty, unhewn, vulgar
7 boorish, ill-bred, loutish, lowbred,
obscene, raunchy, uncouth 8 backward, barnyard, cloddish, ignorant, immature, indecent, inexpert,
inferior, prentice, unformed, ungraded, unsorted, unworked
9 graceless, inelegant, roughhewn,
run-of-mine, unrefined, unskilled, untrained 10 amateurish, unfinished,
unpolished 11 clodhopping, ineffective 12 unproficient
13 unenlightened

cruel
4 fell, grim, mean 6 brutal, fierce,
savage 7 bestial, brutish, heinous,
inhuman, wolfish 8 inhumane, ruthless 9 atrocious, barbarous, ferocious, heartless, monstrous, truculent, unpitying 10 relentless
12 bloodthirsty

cruise
4 sail 6 voyage

cruiser
4 boat 7 warship 9 patrol car,
powerboat

crumb
3 bit, jot 4 iota 5 ounce, scrap,
shred 7 smidgen 8 particle

crumble
3 rot 5 decay, spoil, taint 6 molder
7 putrefy 8 collapse 9 break down,
decompose 12 disintegrate

crumbly
5 crisp, short 7 brittle, crunchy,
friable

crumple
3 wad 4 bend, cave, give 5 break,
crimp, screw, yield 6 fold up, rimple, ruck up 7 crinkle, scrunch,
wrinkle 8 collapse

crunch
4 chew 5 champ, chomp, chump,
munch 7 chumble 8 ruminate
9 masticate

Crusader
English: 7 Richard
French: 6 Philip, Robert 7 Godfrey,
Raymond 8 Montfort
German: 9 Frederick
Norman: 7 Tancred 8 Bohemund
Preacher: 7 Bernard 14 Peter the
Hermit

crusading
11 evangelical 12 evangelistic

crush
3 jam 4 bear, beat, bray, buck,
cram, dash, mash, pulp, push, ruin
5 crowd, drove, horde, press,
quash, quell, smash, wreck 6 béguin, bruise, defeat, pestle, powder, quench, reduce, squash,
squish, squush, subdue, throng
7 abolish, blot out, conquer, contuse, destroy, passion, put down,
repress, scrunch, squeeze, squelch
8 bear down, beat down, demolish,
suppress, vanquish 9 comminute,
multitude, overpower, pulverize,
puppy love, subjugate, triturate
10 annihilate, extinguish, obliterate
11 infatuation 12 contriturate

crust
4 cake, rime

crustacean
4 crab, flea, scud 5 louse, prawn
6 isopod, shrimp, slater, sow bug
7 copepod, daphnia, decapod, lobster, pill bug 8 amphipod, anomu-
ran, barnacle, crawfish, crayfish,
macruran, ostracod, sand flea 9 arthropod, beach flea, schizopod,
shellfish, water flea, wood louse
10 brachyuran, stomatopod, whale
louse 11 branchiopod
aggregate of: 5 krill
appendage: 5 exite 6 endite
7 pleopod
body segment: 6 somite, telson
8 metamere
claw: 5 chela 6 pincer
covering substance: 6 chitin
larva: 5 alima 8 nauplius
limb segment: 6 podite 8 podomere

crusty
4 curt, foul, rank 5 bluff, blunt,
brief, dirty, gross, gruff, short, testy
6 abrupt, coarse, cranky, filthy,
snippy 7 brusque, crabbed, obscene, raunchy, waspish 8 choleric, snippety 9 irascible, irritable,
saturnine, splenetic 10 fescennine

crux
3 nub 4 core, gist, meat, pith 6 kernel, thrust 7 purport 9 substance

cry
(see also **exclamation**) 3 sob
4 bawl, blub, call, howl, moan,
pule, rage, song, wail, weep,
yaup, yawp, yell, yowl 5 bleat,
craze, groan, hallo, hollo, motto,
mourn, on-dit, rumor, shout, sniff,
trend, vogue, whine, whoop
6 boohoo, furore, gossip, holler,
lament, report, rumble, scream,
snivel, squawk, squeak, squeal
7 blubber, fashion, hearsay,
screech, groan, ululate, whimper 9 advertise, publicize 10 vociferate
11 scuttlebutt
bacchanals': 4 evoe
calf: 5 bleat
cat: 3 mew 4 meow 5 miaou
cattle: 3 low, moo
chick: 4 peep 5 cheep
court: 4 oyes, oyez
crane: 5 clang
crow: 3 caw
dog: 3 arf 4 bark, woof
donkey: 4 bray 6 hee-haw
duck: 5 quack
frog: 5 croak
goat: 5 bleat
goose: 4 honk 5 clang, cronk
hen: 6 cackle
horse: 5 neigh 6 nicker, whinny
7 whicker
lion: 4 roar
owl: 4 hoot
pig: 4 oink 5 grunt
raven: 5 croak, cronk
sheep: 5 bleat
songbird: 5 chirp, tweet
turkey: 6 gobble

cry down
5 decry 8 belittle, derogate, diminish 9 disparage 10 depreciate
11 detract from, opprobriate

crying
4 dire 6 urgent 7 burning, clamant,
exigent, heinous 8 pressing, shocking 9 atrocious, clamorous, desperate, monstrous 10 imperative, outrageous, scandalous
11 importunate

cry off
5 welsh 6 renege, resile 7 back out
8 back down 9 backpedal,
backwater

cry out
4 blat, bolt 7 exclaim 9 ejaculate

crypt
4 cave, cell 5 vault 7 chamber
8 catacomb 10 undercroft 11 compartment

cryptanalyze
5 break, crack 6 decode 7 decrypt
8 decipher

cryptic
4 dark 5 murky, vague 6 opaque
7 obscure, unclear 8 abstruse, Delphian 9 enigmatic, tenebrous
10 mysterious, mystifying
12 unfathomable

crystal
5 clear, lucid 6 lucent 8 clear-cut,
luminous, pellucid 9 unblurred
11 translucent, transparent
12 transpicuous
combining form: 5 blast 6 hedron
gazer: 4 seer

**Cry, the Beloved Country
author**
5 Paton (Alan)

cry up
4 laud 5 bless, extol 6 praise
7 glorify, magnify 8 eulogize 9 celebrate 10 panegyrize

Cuba
capital: 6 Havana
chief export: 5 sugar
monetary unit: 4 peso
premier: 6 Castro (Fidel)

cubbyhole
5 niche 6 recess 7 cubicle

cube
3 die 4 dice (plural)

cubic meter
5 stere

Cub Scout
rank: 4 Bear, Wolf 6 Bobcat
7 Webelos
unit: 3 den 4 pack

Cuchulainn
father: 3 Lug 4 Lugh
foe: 4 Medb 5 Maeve
kingdom: 6 Ulster
mother: 8 Dechtire
son: 8 Conlaoch
victim: 8 Conlaoch
wife: 4 Emer

cuckoo
3 nut 4 daft, kook 5 crank, crazy,
daffy, nutty 6 crazed, insane
7 cracked, lunatic 8 crackpot
9 ding-a-ling, harebrain, screwball
12 crackbrained
bird: 3 ani

cucumber
4 pepo 6 gerkin 7 gherkin

cuddle
3 pet 4 snug 6 burrow, caress, cosset, dandle, fondle, nestle, nuzzle
7 embrace, snuggle

cuddlesome
8 huggable

cudgel
3 bat 4 cane, club, mace 5 baton,
billy 6 paddle 7 war club 8 bludgeon, spontoon 9 billy club, blackjack, truncheon 10 knobkerrie,
nightstick

cue
4 clue, hint 6 notion 7 inkling 8 telltale 10 indication, intimation,
suggestion

cuff
3 box, hit 4 blip, chop, clip, poke,
slap, sock 5 clout, punch, smack,
spank 6 buffet, wallop 8 haymaker

cul-de-sac
6 pocket 7 dead end, impasse
10 blind alley

cull
4 pick 5 elect, glean 6 choose,
garner, gather, optate, opt for, pick
up, prefer, select 7 extract 9 single
out

culminate
3 cap 5 crown 6 climax, top off
8 round off 9 finish off

culmination
4 acme, apex, noon, peak 6 apogee, climax, summit 8 meridian, pinnacle 11 ne plus ultra

culpability
4 onus 5 blame, fault, guilt

culpable
5 amiss 6 guilty, sinful, unholy
8 blamable, blameful 10 censurable 11 blameworthy, impeachable
13 demeritorious, reprehensible

cult
4 sect 5 creed, faith 6 church 8 religion 9 communion 10 connection,
persuasion 12 denomination
suffix: 3 ism

cultivable
6 arable 8 tillable

cultivatable
see **cultivable**

cultivate
4 farm, grow, tend, till, work
5 breed, dress, nurse, raise 6 foster, nursle, refine 7 cherish, nourish, nurture, produce 9 propagate

cultivated
6 urbane 7 genteel, refined 8 cultured, polished, well-bred 9 courteous, distingué

cultivation
6 polish 7 culture 8 breeding
10 refinement

culture
5 class 6 polish 8 breeding, elegance, learning, urbanity 9 education, erudition, gentility 10 refinement 11 cultivation, savoir faire
12 civilization 13 enlightenment

cultured
6 urbane 7 erudite, genteel,
learned, refined 8 educated, liter-
ate, polished, well-bred 9 civilized,
distingué 10 cultivated
11 enlightened

culture medium
4 agar

culverhouse
8 dovecote, pigeonry 9 columbary

cumber
3 tax 4 clog, lade, load, task
6 burden, charge, saddle

cumbersome
7 awkward, unhandy 8 cumbrous,
unwieldy 9 ponderous

cumbrance
4 clog 6 burden 7 trouble 9 hindrance, impedance 10 impediment

cumbrous
see **cumbersome**

cum ___ salis
5 grano

cumshaw
3 tip 7 largess 8 gratuity 9 lagniappe, pourboire 10 perquisite

cumulate
4 hive 5 amass, lay up, uplay
6 garner, roll up 7 store up
9 stockpile

cumulation
5 hoard, trove 9 amassment, colluvies, stockpile 10 collection
11 aggregation 13 agglomeration

cumulative
5 chain 8 additive, additory 9 summative 10 increasing
11 multiplying

cunning
3 art, sly 4 deep, foxy, keen, wary,
wily 5 acute, canny, craft, guile,
savvy, sharp, skill, smart 6 adroit,
artful, astute, clever, crafty, deceit,
tricky 7 finesse, know-how, knowing, slyness 8 artifice, deftness, facility, foxiness, guileful, subtlety, wiliness 9 adeptness, cageyness,
canniness, dexterity, dexterous, duplicity, expertise, ingenious, ingenuity, insidious, masterful, sharpness,

slickness **10** adroitness, artfulness, cleverness, craftiness, shiftiness, shrewdness, trickiness **12** dissemblance **13** dexterousness, dissimulation, ingeniousness

cup
3 mug **4** toby **5** grail, jorum, stein **6** beaker, seidel **7** chalice, tankard **8** schooner
assayer's: **5** cupel
combining form: **5** cotyl, cyath, scyph **6** cotyli, cotylo, cyatho, scyphi, scypho
diamond cutter's: **3** dop
handle: **3** ear, lug
holder: **4** zarf
liturgical: **3** ama **5** amula, calix **7** chalice
Scottish: **4** tass
small: **6** noggin **7** canakin, canikin **8** cannikin **9** demitasse
sports: **5** Davis, Ryder **6** Curtis **7** Stanley **8** America's, Wightman
two-handled: **3** tyg

cupbearer of the gods
4 Hebe **8** Ganymede

cupboard
3 kas **5** ambry, cubby, cuddy **6** buffet, closet, larder, pantry **7** armoire, cabinet **8** credence, credenza **9** sideboard

Cupid
4 Amor, Eros **6** cherub **7** amorino **8** amoretto
beloved: **6** Psyche
brother: **7** Anteros
father: **6** Hermes **7** Mercury
mother: **5** Venus **9** Aphrodite
title: **3** Dan

cupidity
4 lust **5** greed **6** desire **7** avarice, avidity, craving, passion **8** rapacity, voracity **9** eagerness **10** greediness **11** infatuation **13** rapaciousness

cupola
4 dome **5** vault **6** turret **7** furnace, lantern, lookout

cup-shaped
8 scyphate

cur
3 cad, dog **4** scum, toad **5** skunk, snake **6** rotter **7** bounder, stinker **8** riffraff, stinkard **9** yellow dog

curative
5 tonic **7** healing **8** remedial, salutary, sanative, sanatory **9** medicinal, remedying, vulnerary, wholesome **10** beneficial, corrective, medicative **11** restorative, therapeutic **12** invigorating

curb
3 bit, tie **4** clog, deny **5** check, leash, tie up **6** bridle, fetter, hamper, hobble, hog-tie, hold in **7** abstain, inhibit, refrain, repress, shackle **8** hold back, hold down, restrain, suppress, withhold **9** constrain, entrammel
British: **4** kerb

curd
see **curdle**

curdle
4 clot, sour **5** spoil **7** clabber, thicken **9** coagulate
Scottish: **6** lapper, lopper

cure
3 age **4** heal **6** physic, remedy **7** restore **8** antidote, medicant, medicine **9** pharmacon **10** corrective, medicament, medication **11** counterstep **12** counteragent **13** counteractant, counteractive
fish: **6** kipper

cure-all
6 elixir **7** nostrum, panacea **10** catholicon

cureless
8 hopeless **9** incurable, insanable, uncurable **10** impossible **11** immedicable, irreparable **12** irremediable **13** uncorrectable

curio
3 toy **6** bauble, gewgaw, trifle **7** bibelot, trinket, whatnot **9** bric-a-brac, objet d'art, **10** knickknack

curiosity
6 marvel, oddity, rarity, regard, wonder **7** anomaly, concern **8** interest, nonesuch

curious
3 odd **4** nosy **5** nosey, peery, queer, weird **6** prying, quaint, snoopy **7** bizarre, oddball, strange, unusual **8** peculiar, singular **9** inquiring **11** inquisitive, inquisitory, questioning **12** disquisitive **13** inquisitorial, investigative

curium
symbol: **2** Cm

curl
4 coil, friz, kink, wind **5** frizz, twine, twist **6** spiral **7** entwine, frizzle, ringlet, wreathe **9** corkscrew

curling
match: **8** bonspiel
period of play: **3** end
team: **4** four
term: **3** tee **4** hack, rink **5** house, stone

curly
5 kinky **6** frizzy

currency
4 cash **5** dough, lucre, money, scrip **11** legal tender
premium: **4** agio
unit: (see individual country)

current
3 run **4** eddy, flow, flux, rife, rush, tide **5** drift, flood, spate, tenor, trend **6** extant, modern, stream **7** instant, popular, present, rampant, regnant, topical **8** existent, tendency, up-to-date **9** prevalent **10** present-day, prevailing, widespread **11** fashionable **12** contemporary
air: **4** gale, gust, wind **5** blast, draft **6** breeze, squall, vortex, zephyr **7** cyclone, indraft, tornado, twister, typhoon, updraft **8** outdraft **9** downdraft, hurricane, whirlwind **10** slipstream
combining form: **4** rheo
ocean: **7** riptide **8** undertow **9** maelstrom, whirlpool
unit: **3** amp **6** ampere **8** abampere **10** statampere

Currier's partner
4 Ives (James)

curry
4 drug, whip **6** thrash **9** overwhelm

curse
4 cuss, damn, oath **5** swear **6** bedamn, plague **7** damning, malison, scourge **8** anathema, cussword, execrate **9** blaspheme, blasphemy, expletive, imprecate, objurgate, profanity, sacrilege, swearword **10** execration, pestilence **11** commination, imprecation, malediction, objurgation, profanation **12** anathematize, denunciation

cursed
6 damned, odious **7** blasted, blessed, doggone, dratted **8** damnable, infernal **9** execrable **10** confounded **13** blankety-blank

cursive
4 easy **6** fluent, smooth **7** flowing, running **10** effortless

cursory
5 brief, hasty, quick, rapid, short **7** hurried, shallow, sketchy **9** depthless **10** uncritical **11** superficial

curt
5 bluff, blunt, brief, gruff, short **6** abrupt, crusty, snippy **7** brusque, concise, laconic, summary **8** snippety, succinct **11** compendiary,

compendious **12** breviloquent
13 short and sweet

curtail

3 cut **5** slash **6** lessen, minify
7 abridge, cut back, shorten **8** diminish, retrench **10** abbreviate

curtain

4 drop, veil **5** drape **6** screen
7 barrier
doorway: **8** portiere
holder: **3** rod
Indian: **6** pardah, purdah
rod concealer: **7** valance
sash: **7** tieback
stage: **4** drop **8** backdrop

curtains

3 end **5** death **6** demise **7** decease, drapery

curtilage

4 quad, yard **5** court **9** enclosure
10 courthouse, quadrangle

curvaceous

5 buxom **7** rounded, shapely,
stacked **9** Junoesque **13** well-
developed

curvation

3 arc, bow **4** arch, bend **5** round

curvature

(see **curvation**)
of the spine: **8** kyphosis, lordosis
9 scoliosis

curve

3 arc, bow **4** arch, bend, coil, curl,
turn, veer, wind **5** crook, round,
twist **6** convex, spiral, swerve
7 concave, flexure, rondure, sinuate
of an arch: **8** extrados, intrados
pitcher's: **4** hook
plane: **7** cissoid, cycloid, limaçon
8 parabola, sinusoid, trochoid
9 hyperbola
S-shaped: **3** ess **4** ogee **7** sigmoid

curved

4 bent **5** arced, bowed, round
6 arched **7** arcuate, arrondi, bending, crooked, embowed, falcate,
rounded, twisted **8** arciform, twisting **9** declinate
combining form: **4** cyrt **5** ancyl, ankyl, curvi, cyrto **6** anchyl, ancylo,
ankylo, campto **7** anchylo, clastic
implement: **6** sickle
molding: **4** ogee
sword:
8 scimitar

curvilinear

see **curved**

curvy

see **curvaceous; curved**

Cush

father: **3** Ham
son: **6** Nimrod

cushion

3 mat, pad **5** squab **6** absorb,
buffer, pillow **7** bolster, hassock,
pillion **8** palliate
Indian: **4** gadi **5** gaddi

cushy

4 cozy, easy, snug, soft **5** comfy
7 easeful **11** comfortable

cusp

3 tip **4** apex, peak **5** point

cuspid

6 canine **8** eyetooth

cuspidate

5 acute, piked, sharp **6** peaked
7 pointed **8** acicular **9** aciculate,
acuminate, acuminous

cuss

3 guy, man **4** chap, damn, oath
5 curse, swear **6** bedamn, fellow
8 execrate **9** expletive, imprecate,
swearword

cussword

4 oath **5** curse, swear **9** expletive,
swearword

custard

4 flan **5** apple, papaw **8** sweetsop

custodian

6 keeper, warden **7** curator, steward **8** cerberus, claviger, guardian,
overseer, watchdog **9** caretaker
10 supervisor

custody

4 care, ward **5** trust **6** charge
7 keeping **10** caretaking, management, protection **11** safekeeping,
supervision **12** guardianship

custom

3 use **4** want **5** habit, mores (plural), trade, trick, usage **6** manner,
praxis, ritual **7** folkway, precept,
traffic **8** business, habitude, practice **9** patronage **10** consuetude,
tailor-made **11** made-to-order
Latin: **3** mos

customary

5 usual **6** common, wonted
7 chronic, general, routine **8** accepted, everyday, familiar, frequent, habitual, orthodox, standard
10 accustomed **11** traditional
12 conventional

custom-built

10 tailor-made **11** made-to-order

customer

5 buyer **6** client, patron **7** shopper
8 consumer **9** purchaser

aggregate of: **9** clientele
frequent: **7** habitué

customized

see **custom-built**

custom-made

see **custom-built**

cut

3 hew, ilk, lop, mow, saw **4** bite,
chop, clip, crop, dice, dock, fell,
gash, hack, kind, nick, pare, part,
reap, slit, snip, snob, snub, sort,
tear, thin, trim, type **5** bevel, carve,
ditch, drunk, filet, knife, lathe,
lower, mince, notch, piece, prune,
quota, sever, share, shave, shear,
skive, slash, slice, split, stamp,
wound **6** cleave, dilute, divide, fillet, hackle, incise, member, moiety,
open up, parcel, pierce, reduce,
scythe, sickle, sunder, trench,
weaken **7** abridge, curtail, dissect,
operate, partage, portion, scissor,
section, segment, shorten **8** amputate, dissever, division, lacerate,
mark down, retrench, separate
9 allotment, allowance, ostracize
10 abbreviate **11** description, intoxicated **12** cold-shoulder
combining form: **4** sect, tomy
6 tomous
of beef: **3** rib **4** loin,
rump **5** baron, chine, chuck, flank,
plate, roast, round, shank, steak
6 cutlet,
saddle **7** brisket, sirloin **8** shoulder
9 aitchbone

cut across

8 transect **9** transcend

cut-and-dried

7 routine

cutaneous

6 dermal

cutaway

4 coat, dive

cut back

4 clip, pare **5** lower, shave, slash
6 reduce **7** abridge, curtail, shorten
8 mark down, retrench
10 abbreviate

cut down

4 clip, pare **5** lower, shave, slash
6 reduce

cute

3 sly **5** sharp **6** clever, dainty,
pretty, quaint, shrewd **7** cunning
8 affected **9** ingenious
10 attractive

cut in

6 horn in **7** intrude, obtrude
8 chisel in **10** intertrude

cutlass
5 sword 7 machete

cut off
2 ax 3 axe, lop 4 kill, slay
5 block, catch, scrag 6 enisle, finish, lay low 7 destroy, isolate
8 amputate, dispatch, insulate, separate 9 intercept, segregate, sequester 10 disinherit

cut out
5 usurp 6 delete, excise, exsect, resect 7 exscind 8 displace, supplant 9 eliminate, extirpate

cutpurse
5 thief 10 pickpocket

cut short
3 bob 4 clip, crop, dock, poll
5 abort, check, shear 7 curtail

cuttable
7 sectile 8 scissile

cutter
4 boat, sled 6 editor, sleigh 7 incisor 9 cutthroat

cutthroat
3 gun 5 bravo 6 gunman, hit man
7 torpedo 8 assassin 10 gunslinger, hatchet man, triggerman

cutting
5 crisp 6 biting 7 ingoing 8 clearcut, incisive, piercing 9 trenchant
11 penetrating
combining form: 5 cidal
edge: 5 blade
remark: 3 dig
tool: 2 ax 3 adz, axe, hob, saw
4 adze 5 knife, lathe, mower, plane, razor 6 reaper, scythe, shears, sickle 7 hatchet 8 scissors, tomahawk

cutting out
combining form: 6 ectomy

cuttlefish
7 mollusk 10 cephalopod
ink: 5 sepia
relative: 5 squid 7 octopus

cut up
3 pan, rap 4 dice, hash, romp
5 caper, clown, horse, knock, mince 6 cavort, sliver 7 carry on, censure, condemn, show off 8 denounce 9 criticize, horse-play, misbehave, reprehend, reprobate
10 roughhouse

cutup
3 wag 4 zany 5 clown, joker 7 farceur 8 jokester

Cybele
4 Rhea
beloved: 5 Attis
brother: 6 Cronus
father: 6 Uranus
husband: 6 Cronus
mother: 2 Ge 4 Gaea
son: 4 Zeus 7 Jupiter, Neptune
8 Poseidon

cybernetics founder
6 Wiener (Norbert)

cycle
4 bike, loop, ring 5 chain, round, wheel 6 circle, course, series 7 circuit 8 sequence 10 succession, two-wheeler, velocipede

cyclone
7 tornado, twister

cyclopean
4 huge 7 Antaean, mammoth, titanic 8 colossal, gigantic 9 Herculean, monstrous 10 gargantuan
11 elephantine

Cyclops
5 Arges 7 Brontes 8 Steropes
10 Polyphemus

Cycnus
father: 4 Ares, Mars
slayer: 8 Hercules

cygnet
4 swan
dam: 3 pen
sire: 3 cob

Cygnus
form: 4 swan
friend: 7 Phaeton
star: 5 Deneb

cylinder
4 drum, lock, pipe, tube 5 spool
6 barrel, bobbin, platen, roller

cylindrical
5 tubal 6 terete, tubate 7 tubular
8 tubelike, tuberoid, tubiform, tubulose, tubulous

cyma recta
4 ogee

cymbals
dancer's: 3 tal 7 crotala

Cymbeline
daughter: 6 Imogen
son: 9 Arviragus, Guiderius

Cymric
5 Welsh 6 Celtic 9 Brythonic
bard: 8 Taliesin
Elysium: 6 Annwfn
god: 5 Lludd
of Elysium: 5 Arawn
of the dead: 5 Pwyll
of the seas: 3 Ler 4 Llyr 5 Dylan
of the sky: 7 Gwydion
of the sun: 4 Lleu, Llew
of the underworld: 4 Gwyn
goddess: 3 Don 9 Arianrhod
magician: 6 Merlin

Cymry land
5 Wales

cynical
3 wry 6 ironic 8 sardonic

Cynthia
4 Luna, moon 5 Diana 7 Artemis

cyprian
4 jade, slut 5 hussy, tramp 6 wanton 7 jezebel, trollop 8 slattern, strumpet

Cyprus
capital: 7 Nicosia
language: 5 Greek 7 Turkish

Cyrano
4 poet 7 duelist
author: 7 Rostand (Edmond)
feature: 4 nose

Cyrus
conquest: 5 Lydia, Media 7 Babylon
daughter: 6 Atossa
empire: 7 Persian
father: 8 Cambyses
son: 8 Cambyses

Cytherea
5 Venus 9 Aphrodite

czar
4 king 5 baron, mogul 6 prince, tycoon 7 magnate
Russian: 4 Ivan 5 Basil, Peter
6 Alexis, Feodor, Fyodor 7 Michael, Romanov 8 Nicholas, Romanoff, Theodore 9 Alexander
12 Boris Godunov

czar's wife
7 czarina 8 czaritza

Czech Republic
capital: 6 Prague
monetary unit: 6 koruna

Dd

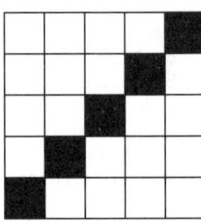

D.A., e.g.
4 atty

dab
3 hit, pat 4 blow, chit, lump, peck, spot 5 clout, smear 6 bedaub, blotch, smudge 7 besmear, plaster, portion, splotch

dabbler
4 tyro 7 amateur 9 smatterer 10 dilettante, uninitiate 11 abecedarian

dabbling
7 jackleg, shallow 8 ungifted 9 unskilled 10 amateurish, dilettante, unfinished 11 superficial 12 dilettantish, dilettantist

dabchick
5 grebe 9 hell-diver

Dadaist
3 Arp (Jean), Ray (Man) 4 Ball (Hugo) 5 Grosz (George), Tzara (Tristan) 7 Duchamp (Marcel), Picabia (Francis) 10 Schwitters (Kurt)

daedal
6 knotty 7 complex, gordian 8 involved 9 Byzantine, elaborate, intricate 11 complicated 12 labyrinthine 13 sophisticated

Daedalus
9 architect, artificer
construction: 9 Labyrinth
father: 6 Metion
son: 6 Icarus
victim: 5 Talos 6 Perdix

daffy
see **daft**

daft
3 mad 4 loco, luny, wild 5 balmy, crazy, giddy, potty, silly 6 crazed, cuckoo, insane, maniac 7 cracked, foolish, idiotic, lunatic, unsound 8 demented, deranged, imbecile 9 bedlamite 10 unbalanced

Dag
father: 7 Delling
horse: 9 Skinfaksi
mother: 4 Nott

Dagda
chief god of the: 5 Gaels, Irish
daughter: 6 Brigit
instrument: 4 harp
son: 6 Aengus
wife: 5 Boann

dagger
4 dirk 5 skean, skeen, skene 6 bodkin 8 stiletto
handle: 4 hilt
Malay: 4 kris
medieval: 6 anlace

daily
7 diurnal 9 circadian, quotidian

dainty
4 airy, nice, rare 5 fussy, goody, light, treat 6 choice, morsel, select, tidbit, titbit 7 elegant, finical, finicky 8 delicacy, delicate, ethereal, kickshaw, superior 9 exquisite, finicking, recherché 10 delightful, diaphanous, fastidious, particular, pernickety 11 persnickety

dairy
8 creamery

dais
7 rostrum, terrace 8 platform

daisy
5 oxeye
British: 10 moonflower
Scottish: 5 gowan

Daisy Miller author
5 James (Henry)

Daksha's father
6 Brahma

dale
4 glen 6 valley

dally
3 lag, toy 4 drag, fool, idle, play, poke 5 delay, flirt, tarry, trail 6 coquet, dawdle, frolic, lead on, linger, loiter, put off, trifle, wanton 11 string along 13 procrastinate

Dalphon's father
5 Haman

dam
3 bar 4 stay, stem, stop, weir 5 block, brake, check, choke 6 hinder, impede 7 barrier, repress 8 blockade, obstacle, obstruct, suppress 10 overslaugh

damage
3 mar 4 blot, harm, hurt, loss, ruin 5 abuse, burst, cloud, spoil, wound 6 deface, impair, injure, injury, scathe 7 blemish, destroy, marring, tarnish, vitiate 8 destruct, ill-treat, maltreat, mischief, mistreat, mutilate, sabotage 9 prejudice, vandalism 10 dilapidate, impairment
relating to: 5 noxal

damaging
3 bad 4 evil 6 nocent 7 harmful, hurtful, nocuous 9 injurious 11 deleterious, detrimental, mischievous

dame
4 lady 5 woman 6 beldam, gammer, matron 7 dowager, grandam 9 matriarch

Damien's island
7 Molokai

Damkina
husband: 2 Ea
son: 6 Marduk

damn
4 cuss, doom, drat, durn 5 curse, swear, whoop 7 condemn, doggone 8 execrate, sentence 9 abominate, imprecate, objurgate, proscribe 10 vituperate 12 anathematize

damnable
4 dang, darn 5 gross, utter 6 blamed, cursed, cussed, odious

7 blasted, dratted, hateful **8** accursed, infernal, outright **9** abhorrent, dad-burned, downright, execrable, out-and-out **11** unmitigated

damned

4 dang, darn, durn, lost, rank, very **5** gross, utter **6** blamed, cursed, cussed, dashed, doomed **7** awfully, blasted, doggone, dratted, goldarn **8** absolute, accursed, blighted, blinding, complete, infernal, outright, whopping **9** dad-blamed, downright, execrable, extremely, out-and-out, perishing, reprobate **10** confounded, dad-blasted **11** straight-out, unmitigated **13** anathematized, blankety-blank

Damocles' ____

5 sword

Damon's friend

7 Pythias

damp

3 wet **4** dank, dewy, mist **5** humid, juicy, moist, muggy, musty, rainy, soggy **6** clammy, moisty **7** bedewed, moisten, wettish **8** humidify, humidity, moisture

dampen

4 mute **6** deaden, muffle, sponge, stifle

damsel

3 gal **4** girl, lass, maid, miss **5** missy, wench **6** lassie, maiden, moppet **8** donzella, princess **10** demoiselle

Dan

father: **5** Jacob
mother: **6** Bilhah
son: **6** Hushim

Danaë

father: **8** Acrisius
lover: **4** Zeus
son: **7** Perseus

Danaus

brother: **8** Aegyptus
daughters: **8** Danaides
father: **5** Belus
founder of: **5** Argos
grandfather: **7** Neptune **8** Poseidon

dance

3 hop, jig, tap **4** ball, duet, flit, foot, giga, heel, hoof, juba, leap, lope, move, reel, skit, step **5** bamba, brawl, cooch, galop, gigue, hover, lindy, mambo, mixer, polka, rumba, sally, stomp, swing, tread, valse **6** adagio, ballet, bolero, boogie, Boston, cancan, chassé, chi-chi, foot it, formal, frolic, german, hoof it, redowa, rhumba, shimmy **7** beguine, coranto, courant, flicker, flitter, flutter, hoedown, onestep, shuffle **8** Alley Cat, cakewalk, chaconne, cotillon, courante, couranto, fandango, flamenco, galliard, galopade, glissade, hula-hula, rigadoon, rigaudon **9** allemande, jitterbug

art of: **11** terpsichore
12 choreography
Austrian: **7** ländler
ballroom: **5** congo, rumba, tango **6** chacha **7** fox-trot, mazurka, two-step **8** merengue **9** cotillion **10** Charleston
Bohemian: **5** polka
Brazilian: **5** samba **6** maxixe **9** bossa nova
chorus: **5** strut
combining form: **5** chore **6** choreo, chorio
country: **3** hay **8** anglaise, hornpipe
couple: **5** polka
court: **6** pavane **8** saraband **9** allemande, sarabande
Cuban: **5** conga **8** habanera
designer: **13** choreographer
East Indian: **5** mudra
English: **6** morris
folk: **4** hora, kolo **8** hornpipe **10** tarantella, tarantelle
formal: **4** prom
French: **5** gavot **7** bourrée, gavotte **8** lanciers **10** carmagnole
garment: **4** tutu **7** leotard
graceful: **6** minuet
Haitian: **4** juba
Hungarian: **7** Csardas, Czardas
Indian: **6** nautch
instrument: **8** castanet
Irish: **6** fading
Israeli: **4** hora **5** horah
Italian: **9** rigoletto **10** tarantella, tarentelle
lively: **4** reel, trot **6** rhumba **7** bourrée **9** shakedown
modern: **3** toe
movement: **4** step **6** minuet **8** glissade **9** allemande, pirouette
1920's: **10** Charleston
old-time: **7** hoedown **8** chaconne
Polish: **5** polka **7** mazurka **8** mazourka
Polynesian: **4** hula
round: **5** carol, waltz **6** carole
shoes: **5** pumps **8** slippers
slipper: **7** toeshoe
slow: **5** pavan, pavin **6** adagio, pavane
South American: **7** carioca
Spanish: **4** jota **6** bolero **7** zapateo **8** cachucha, saraband

springy: **3** jig
square: **7** lancers **9** quadrille
stately: **5** pavan **8** saraband **9** sarabande
step: **3** pas **4** riff, shag **6** pickup
voluptuous: **5** belly
woman's: **6** cancan

dancer

6 hoofer, hopper **7** chorine, clogger, danseur, prancer, stepper **8** coryphée, danseuse, figurant **9** ballerina, chorus boy, chorus man, figurante **10** ballet girl, cakewalker, chorus girl
American: **4** Feld (Elliot), Lang (Pearl), Tune (Tommy) **5** Kelly (Gene) **6** Duncan (Isadora), Graham (Martha), Taylor (Paul) **7** Astaire (Fred), Bujones (Fernando), de Mille (Agnes), Gregory (Cynthia), Martins (Peter), Massine (Leonide), McBride (Patricia), St. Denis (Ruth), Tamiris (Helen) **8** Kirkland (Gelsey), Villella (Edward) **9** Tallchief (Maria)
ballet: **6** étoile **7** soliste
Danish: **8** Tomasson (Helgi)
English: **5** Somes (Michael), Tudor (Antony) **7** Markova (Alicia) **8** Fonteyne (Margot)
female: **8** devadasi
French: **6** Bejart (Maurice), Perrot (Jules-Joseph), Petipa (Marius)
German: **5** Jooss (Kurt)
Italian: **5** Grisi (Carlotta)
Javanese: **7** serimpi
Mexican: **5** Limon (Jose)
Russian: **5** Lifar (Serge) **7** Nureyev (Rudolf), Pavlova (Anna), Ulanova (Galina) **8** Danilova (Aleksandra), Makarova (Natalia), Nijinsky (Vaslav), Vaganova (Agrippina) **9** Karsavina (Tamara), Semyonova (Marina) **11** Baryshnikov (Mikhail)
Scottish: **7** Shearer (Moira)
sword: **7** bouffon **8** matachin
Zuni: **7** shalako

dancing

6 ballet **7** saltant **11** choreography, terpsichore **12** choreography
mania: **9** tarantism

dandle

3 pet **4** love **6** caress, cosset, cuddle, pamper

dandruff

5 scurf **6** furfur

dandy

3 fop **4** beau, buck, dude, fine, lulu, toff **5** dilly, nifty, peach, swell **6** peachy **7** coxcomb **8** popinjay, terrific **9** excellent, first-rate, hum-

dinger, hunky-dory, marvelous
11 Beau Brummel, crackerjack
12 lounge lizard

dang
4 darn, durn **5** utter **6** cursed, cussed, damned **7** blasted, blessed, dratted, goldarn, regular **8** absolute, outright **9** downright **10** confounded, consummate **11** unmitigated

danger
4 risk **5** peril **6** hazard, menace, plight, threat **7** pitfall **8** distress, jeopardy
signal: **4** bell **5** alarm, siren **6** redeye, tocsin

dangerous
4 fell **5** dicey, grave, hairy, nasty, risky **6** chancy, scathy, unsafe, unsure, wicked **7** parlous, serious, unsound, vicious **8** grievous, insecure, menacing, perilous **9** hazardous, unhealthy **10** jeopardous, precarious **11** threatening

dangle
4 hang **5** droop, sling, swing **6** depend **7** suspend

Daniel
American pioneer: **5** Boone
father: **5** David
mother: **7** Abigail
statesman: **7** Webster

Danish
hero: **5** Ogier
king: **9** Christian, Frederick
queen: **9** Margrethe

dank
3 wet **4** damp **5** humid, moist **6** clammy, dampen, moisty **7** dampish, wetness, wettish **8** moisture

Dante
beloved: **8** Beatrice
birthplace: **8** Florence
daughter: **7** Antonia
deathplace: **7** Ravenna
party: **6** Guelph **7** Bianchi
patron: **5** Scala
teacher: **6** Latini
wife: **5** Gemma
work: **7** Inferno **8** Commedia, Convivio **9** Vita Nuova

Dantean division
5 canto

Danton's colleague
5 Marat (Jean-Paul)

Danzig
6 Gdańsk

dap
4 skim, skip **5** carom, graze **6** glance **8** ricochet

Daphne
father: **5** Ladon **6** Peneus
form: **10** laurel tree
pursuer: **6** Apollo **9** Leucippus

Daphnis' lover
5 Chloe

dapper
4 neat, trim **5** natty, sassy **6** jaunty, rakish, spiffy, spruce, sprucy **7** bandbox, doggish, foppish, stylish **8** sparkish **11** well-groomed

dapple
4 spot **5** fleck, patch

dappled
6 dotted, motley **7** flecked, mottled, spotted **8** freckled **9** multihued **10** discolored, multicolor, variegated, versicolor **11** varicolored **12** multicolored, particolored, versicolored

Dardanelles
10 Hellespont

Dardanus
descendants: **7** Trojans
father: **4** Zeus **7** Jupiter
mother: **7** Electra

dare
4 defi, defy, face, risk **5** beard, brave, front, stump **6** brazen, cartel, hazard **7** attempt, outface, venture **8** confront, defiance **9** challenge

daredevil
see **daring**

darer
4 hero **6** risker

daring
4 bold, pert, rash, wild **5** brave, nerve **6** heroic **7** courage, heroism **8** boldness, devilish, fearless, reckless, temerity **9** audacious, daredevil, foolhardy, venturous **10** courageous, jeopardous **11** adventurous, temerarious, venturesome **13** adventuresome

Darius
father: **9** Hystaspes
son: **6** Xerxes
wife: **6** Atossa

Darjeeling
3 tea

dark
3 dim, dun, sad, wan **4** dusk, murk **5** black, blind, brown, cloud, dingy, dusky, mirky, murky, night,

shady, sooty, swart, umber, unlit, vague **6** brunet, cloudy, dismal, gloomy, opaque, somber, sombre, swarth, swarty, wicked **7** aphotic, cryptic, duskish, obscure, rayless, shadowy, stygian, subfusc, sunless, swarthy, unclear **8** abstruse, bistered, Delphian, gloomful, ignorant, mystical, sinister **9** ambiguous, enigmatic, lightless, secretive, tenebrous, unlighted **10** caliginous, indistinct, mysterious, mystifying, pitch-black **11** black-a-vised **13** unilluminated
combining form: **3** mel **4** mela, melo **5** melam, melan **6** melano
poetic: **4** ebon

darken
3 dim, fog **4** dull, dusk, haze, murk **5** bedim, blind, cloud, gloom, lower, shade, sully, umber **6** shadow **7** becloud, benight, blacken, eclipse, embrown, obscure, opacate, tarnish **8** melanize, overcast **9** obfuscate, overcloud **10** overshadow
Scottish: **5** gloam

dark-haired
female: **8** brunette
male: **6** brunet

darkness
4 dusk, mirk, murk **5** black, gloom, night, shade, umbra **6** shadow **7** privacy, secrecy **8** midnight, twilight

dark-skinned
5 dusky, swart **6** brunet, swarth **7** swarthy **8** bistered, melanous **11** black-a-vised

darling
3 pet **4** chou, dear, duck, love, lush **5** deary, ducky, flame, honey, loved, sweet **7** beloved, pigsney, sweetie **8** adorable, favorite, heavenly, precious **9** ambrosial **10** delectable, delightful, fair-haired, honeybunch, sweetheart

darn
4 mend **5** patch, utter **6** blamed, cursed, cussed, damned, repair **7** blasted, doggone **8** infernal, outright **9** downright **10** confounded **11** straight-out **13** blankety-blank

darn it
French: **3** zut

Darrow client
4 Debs (Eugene), Loeb (Richard) **6** Scopes (John) **7** Leopold (Nathan)

dart
3 fly, jet, run, shy 4 barb, bolt, buzz, flit, leap, sail, scud, skim 5 arrow, bound, fling, hurry, lance, scamp, scoot, shaft, shoot, skirr, spear, speed, spurt 6 glance, hasten, scurry, spring, sprint, squirt 7 javelin, missile, scamper 8 jaculate
barbed: 10 banderilla

D'Artagnan's friends
5 Athos 6 Aramis 7 Porthos

Dartmouth location
7 Hanover

darts terms
3 leg 4 bust 5 split 6 dosser, double, flight, hockey, treble 8 bull's-eye 10 clock board

Darwin
7 Charles
ship: 6 Beagle
theory: 9 evolution

dash
3 nip, pep, run, vim, zip 4 balk, bang, beat, bilk, boil, bolt, brio, élan, foil, hint, hurl, life, pelt, race, ruin, rush, slam, tear, tick, zing 5 ardor, blast, break, chase, crush, drive, fling, oomph, scoot, shoot, smack, speed, spice, style, throw, trace, verve 6 baffle, blight, charge, energy, esprit, hurtle, hyphen, scurry, spirit, sprint, streak, thrust, thwart, trifle 7 bravura, collide, scamper, shatter, soupçon, spatter, splotch 8 confound, tincture 9 animation, bespatter, frustrate 10 circumvent, disappoint, sprinkling, suggestion

dashboard reading
4 fuel 5 speed 7 mileage

dashing
3 gay 4 bold, chic, keen 5 alert, showy, smart, swank, swish 6 bright, dapper, jaunty, lively, modish, swanky, with-it 7 animate, rousing, stylish 8 animated, spirited 9 vivacious 11 fashionable

Das Kapital author
4 Marx (Karl)

dassie
9 blacktail

dastard
4 funk 6 coward, craven, funker 7 chicken, quitter 8 poltroon 11 yellowbelly

dastardly
4 base, mean

data
5 facts, input 8 material 11 information

date
3 age, era, woo 5 court, epoch, tryst 6 cutoff, escort 7 take out 8 deadline 9 accompany 10 engagement, rendezvous 11 anniversary, appointment, assignation
abbreviation: 4 appt

dated
3 old 5 passé 6 démodé, old hat 7 archaic 8 obsolete, outmoded 10 antiquated 12 old-fashioned 13 unfashionable

Dathan's father
5 Eliab

datum
4 fact

daub
4 blob, blot, spot 5 fleck, paint, smear 6 dapple, smudge, splash 7 besmear, dribble, plaster, spatter, speckle, splotch 9 variegate

daughter
Carter's: 3 Amy
Cher's: 8 Chastity
Clinton's: 7 Chelsea
Cole's: 7 Natalie
Elizabeth II's: 4 Anne
Fonda's: 4 Jane
Ford's (Gerald): 5 Susan
Garland's: 12 Liza Minnelli
Johnson's (Lyndon): 4 Lucy 5 Linda
Kennedy's (John F.): 8 Caroline
Nixon's: 5 Julie 6 Tricia
Sinatra's: 5 Nancy

Daughter of the Moon
7 Nokomis

daunt
3 cow 6 dismay, subdue 7 conquer, horrify, terrify 8 frighten 10 disconcert, discourage, dishearten, intimidate

dauntless
4 bold, game 5 brave 8 fearless, unafraid 9 unfearful, unfearing 10 courageous, invincible 11 indomitable, lionhearted

dauntlessness
4 guts 5 heart, pluck, spunk 6 mettle, spirit 7 cojones, courage 10 resolution

davenport
4 desk, sofa 12 chesterfield

David
commander: 4 Joab 5 Amasa
companion: 8 Jonathan

daughter: 5 Tamar
father: 5 Jesse
rebuker: 6 Nathan
scribe: 7 Seraiah
singer: 5 Heman
son: 5 Amnon 7 Absalom, Solomon
wife: 7 Abigail, Ahinoam 9 Bathsheba

David, for one
4 camp

David Copperfield
author: 7 Dickens (Charles)
character: 4 Dora, Heep 5 Agnes, Uriah 6 Barkis, Betsey 7 Creakle 8 Micawber 9 Murdstone, Wickfield 10 Steerforth
nurse: 8 Peggotty (Clara)

dawdle
3 lag 4 drag, idle, jauk, laze, lazy, loaf, loll, poke 5 dally, delay, tarry, trail 6 linger, loiter, lounge, put off, putter, trifle 7 fritter 8 lallygag, lollygag 13 procrastinate

dawn
4 morn 5 alpha, light, onset, start, sunup 6 aurora, outset 7 genesis, morning, opening, sunrise 8 cockcrow, daybreak, daylight, outstart 9 beginning 11 cockcrowing 12 commencement
goddess: 3 Eos 6 Aurora
relating to: 4 eoan

day
3 era, sun 4 time 8 lifetime
abbreviation: 3 Fri, Mon, Sat, Sun, Thu, Tue, Wed 4 Thur, Tues 5 Thurs
before: 3 eve
church calendar: 5 feria
French: 4 jour
German: 3 Tag
holy: 5 feast
hot: 8 scorcher
hour: 4 noon
Latin: 4 dies
Spanish: 3 dia

day blindness
11 hemeralopia

daybreak
4 dawn, morn 5 sunup 6 aurora 7 dawning, morning, sunrise 8 cockcrow 11 cockcrowing

daydream
4 muse 5 fancy 6 revery, vision 7 fantasy, reverie 8 phantasm, phantasy

days
fourteen: 9 fortnight
of yore: 3 eld

daystar
3 Sol, sun 7 phoebus

daze
3 fog 4 haze, stun 5 blind, dizzy
6 bemuse, benumb, dazzle, fuddle,
muddle, trance 7 confuse, mystify,
petrify, stupefy 8 astonish, bedazzle, befuddle, bewilder, confound,
disorder, distract, paralyze
9 dumbfound, overwhelm 10 muddlement 11 muddledness
12 befuddlement

dazed
5 woozy 6 doiled, groggy, punchy
7 witless 8 dithered

___ d'Azur
4 Cote

dazzle
5 blind, shine 8 bewilder, outshine

dazzling
6 flashy, garish 7 fulgent, glowing,
radiant 9 brilliant 10 candescent

deacon
4 calf 6 cleric, doctor, layman 7 officer 10 adulterate

dead
3 dim 4 cold, dull, flat, gone, late,
lost, numb 5 bleak, blind, inert,
muted, passé, quiet, slain, utter
6 asleep, buried, bygone, dismal,
fallen, lapsed, numbed 7 defunct,
disused, exactly, expired, extinct,
outworn, tedious 8 benumbed, deceased, departed, inactive, lifeless,
obsolete, outmoded 9 apathetic,
deathlike, exanimate, inanimate,
senseless, unfeeling 10 breathless,
corpselike, insensible, insentient,
lackluster, lusterless, monotonous,
motionless, spiritless, unanimated,
unexciting 11 inoperative, insensitive, unconscious 12 anesthetized,
extinguished, unresponsive
Australian: 4 bung
British: 5 napoo 6 napooh
combining form: 4 necr 5 necro

dead duck
5 goner

deaden
4 dull, kill, mull, mute, numb, stun
5 blunt 6 benumb, dampen, muffle,
obtund, opiate, stifle 7 mortify, petrify, smother, stupefy 8 paralyze
10 devitalize 11 anesthetize,
desensitize

dead end
4 halt 6 pocket 7 impasse 8 cul-de-
sac 10 blind alley, bottleneck,
standstill

deadened
4 numb 6 asleep, corpsy, numbed
7 deathly 8 benumbed, deathful
9 deathlike, senseless, unfeeling
10 corpselike, insensible 11 insensitive 12 anesthetized

deadfall
4 trap 7 springe 9 booby trap,
mousetrap

deadliness
8 fatality 9 lethality, mortality

deadlock
3 tie 4 draw 6 logjam 7 dogfall,
impasse 8 standoff, stoppage
9 stalemate 10 standstill

deadly
4 dire 5 fatal, toxic 6 corpsy, lethal, mortal 7 baneful, capital, killing, noxious, ruinous, slaying
8 deathful, lethally, venomous, virulent 9 deathlike, pestilent, poisonous 10 corpselike, pernicious
11 destructive, mortiferous, pestiferous 12 pestilential

deadpan
5 blank, empty 6 vacant 12 inexpressive, unexpressive

dead shot
8 marksman

Dead Souls author
5 Gogol (Nikolay)

dead to rights
9 red-handed

deadweight
3 tax 4 duty, load, onus, task
6 burden, charge 9 millstone

deafen
3 din

deal
4 dole, give, sale 5 allot, serve,
shake, share, trade, treat 6 accord,
bestow, divide, impart, lot out, parcel, strike 7 bargain, deliver, dish
out, dole out, inflict, mete out, portion, scatter, wrestle 8 disburse, dispense, disperse, separate, share
out 9 agreement, apportion, negotiate, partition 10 administer, distribute, measure out, portion out
11 transaction 13 understanding
great: 4 lots 5 loads
out: 8 dispense 9 apportion 10 administer, distribute
secretly: 7 trinket
with: 4 play 5 serve, treat 6 handle

dealer
4 bank 5 agent 6 banker, broker,
seller, trader 8 chandler, merchant,

operator 9 tradesman 10 negotiator, trafficker 11 businessman, dis-
tributer, distributor
12 merchandiser
British: 6 draper, jobber, mercer
7 chapman
card: 6 farmer
horse: 5 coper
women's clothing: 7 modiste

dealings
5 truck 7 affairs, matters, traffic
8 business, commerce, concerns
11 intercourse

dealing with
suffix: 2 ic 4 ical

dean
4 head 5 doyen, guide, pilot
6 leader, priest, senior 7 officer
10 bellwether

dear
3 hon, pet 4 fond, high, lamb, love
5 honey, loved, sweet 6 costly, doting, loving, scarce 7 beloved, darling, devoted, lovable, machree,
querida, special, tootsie 8 especial, favorite, loveling, lovesome,
precious, valuable 9 cherished, expensive, heartfelt, sweetling 10 fair-
haired, heartthrob, honeybunch,
sweetheart 12 affectionate
French: 4 cher 5 chère
Irish: 4 agra
Scottish: 2 jo

dear one
suffix: 3 een

dearth
4 lack, want 6 defect, famine 7 absence, default, paucity, poverty
8 scarcity 9 privation, scantness
10 deficiency, meagerness,
scantiness
combining form: 5 penia

death
3 end 4 bane, exit 5 decay, night,
sleep 6 demise, ending, expiry
7 decease, parting, passage, passing, quietus, silence 8 biolysis, casualty, curtains, fatality, necrosis,
thanatos 9 bloodshed, departure
10 defunction, expiration, extinction, grim reaper 11 dissolution,
termination 12 annihilation
after: 10 posthumous
combining form: 6 thanat 7 thanato
easy: 10 euthanasia
music: 5 dirge, elegy 8 threnody
notice: 4 obit 8 obituary
9 necrology
of tissue: 8 gangrene
personification: 10 grim reaper

portending: 6 funest
put to: 3 gas 4 hang, kill, slay
5 choke, lynch 6 murder, stifle
8 strangle, throttle 9 suffocate
11 assassinate, electrocute
rate: 9 mortality
rites: 7 funeral

deathless
7 abiding, eternal, lasting, undying
8 immortal 10 persisting
12 imperishable

deathlike
see **deathly**

deathly
5 fatal 6 grisly, lethal, mortal
7 ghastly, haggard, macabre, stygian 8 deadened, gruesome, mortally 9 pestilent 10 cadaverous,
corpselike 11 mortiferous
12 pestilential

debacle
4 rout 5 crash, smash, wreck 6 defeat 7 beating, crack-up, failure,
licking, smashup 8 collapse, drubbing 9 breakdown, cataclysm,
overthrow, trouncing 10 defeasance 11 shellacking
12 vanquishment

debar
4 bate 6 except, forbid, refuse
7 deprive, exclude, prevent, rule
out, suspend 8 count out, preclude,
prohibit 9 eliminate

debark
4 land

debase
3 mar, rot 4 harm, sink, warp 5 alloy, lower, spoil, stain, stoop, taint
6 bemean, canker, damage, defile,
demean, dilute, dope up, humble,
impair, injure, poison, reduce, vilify, weaken, worsen 7 corrupt, degrade, deprave, devalue, pervert,
pollute, traduce, vitiate 8 cast
down, dishonor 9 animalize, brutalize, humiliate, undermine
10 adulterate, bastardize, bestialize, degenerate, demoralize
11 contaminate

debatable
4 moot 7 dubious 8 arguable,
doubtful, mootable 9 uncertain
11 problematic 12 questionable

debate
4 fray, heed, moot 5 argue, fight,
plead, rebut, study 6 hassle 7 agitate, canvass, contend, contest, discept, discuss, dispute, mooting,
quarrel, wrangle 8 argument, consider, forensic, question 9 alter-

cate, attention, dialectic, thrash out
10 toss around 11 application, controversy, disputation 12 deliberation 13 argumentation, concentration, consideration
art of: 9 forensics
expert: 7 eristic
place for: 5 forum

debauch
4 orgy, undo, warp 5 party 6 seduce 7 corrupt, deprave, pervert,
vitiate 8 bacchanal, brutalize
10 bastardize, bestialize, demoralize, saturnalia 11 bacchanalia

debauched
4 lewd 6 wanton 7 vitiate 8 depraved, vitiated 9 corrupted, dissolute, lecherous, libertine, perverted
10 lascivious, libidinous, licentious

debilitate
3 sap 5 blunt 6 weaken 7 cripple,
disable, unbrace 8 enfeeble
9 attenuate, extenuate, undermine
10 devitalize 12 unstrengthen

debilitated
4 weak 6 feeble, infirm, sapped
8 burnt-out, decrepit 9 burned-out

debility
7 astheny, disease, malaise 8 asthenia, weakness 9 infirmity
10 feebleness, infirmness, sickliness
11 decrepitude 13 unhealthiness
combining form: 6 asthen 7 astheno

Debir
kingdom: 5 Eglon
slayer: 6 Joshua

debonair
5 suave 6 urbane 8 carefree,
charming, graceful 10 nonchalant
12 lighthearted

Deborah's husband
9 Lappidoth

debris
4 junk, slag 5 offal, trash, waste
6 litter, refuse, rubble, spilth 7 garbage, rubbish 8 detritus, riffraff
rock: 5 talus 7 eluvium 8 colluvia

debt
3 due, sin 4 evil 5 wrong 6 arrear
7 arrears, default, deficit 9 arrearage, demurrage, liability 10 obligation, wickedness 11 delinquency
acknowledgment: 3 IOU 4 bill
5 check

debtless
7 solvent

debunk
6 expose, show up, unmask 7 un-

cloak, undress 8 discover,
unshroud

Debussy's La ___
3 Mer

debut
7 come out, opening 8 entrance,
premiere 9 beginning
12 introduction

decadence
7 decline 8 downfall 9 downgrade
10 declension, degeneracy, devolution 11 declination, degradation
12 degeneration, dégringolade
13 deterioration

decadent
6 effete 8 overripe 10 degenerate

decalogue verb
5 shalt

Decameron, The
author: 9 Boccaccio (Giovanni)
heroine: 8 Griselda

decamp
2 go 3 fly 4 exit, flee 5 break,
leave, scape, scram 6 begone, escape, get out, retire 7 abscond, run
away, skiddoo, slip off, take off
8 clear out, hightail, withdraw
9 skedaddle

decanter
6 bottle, carafe

decapitate
4 head, raze, ruin, undo 5 wrack,
wreck 6 behead, unmake 7 destroy, unbuild 8 decimate, demolish
9 decollate 10 guillotine

decapod
6 shrimp 7 mollusk 10 crustacean

decathlon champ
6 Jenner (Bruce), Schenk (Christian),
Toomey (Bill), Zmelik (Robert)
7 Johnson (Rafer), Mathias (Bob)
8 Campbell (Milton), Thompson
(Daley)

decay
3 ebb, rot 4 fade, sour, turn, wane
5 spoil, taint, waste 6 blight, curdle, fading, molder, wither 7 corrupt, crumble, failure, ferment,
moulder, putrefy 8 putresce
9 break down, decompose 11 deteriorate 12 dilapidation, disintegrate, putrefaction 13 deterioration

decayed
3 bad 6 effete, putrid, rotten 7 carious, spoiled 8 decadent, overripe
10 degenerate

decease
3 die 4 fail, pass 5 death, sleep
6 cash in, demise, depart, expire,
perish 7 passing, quietus, succumb
8 pass away 9 departure 10 defunction 11 dissolution

deceit
3 gyp 4 hoax, sham 5 fraud, guile
6 humbug 7 chicane, cunning,
swindle 8 artifice, flimflam, spoofery, trickery 9 chicanery, duplicity,
imposture 12 dissemblance 13 dissimulation, double-dealing

deceitful
3 sly 4 foxy, wily 5 false, lying
6 artful, crafty, fickle, hollow, shifty,
sneaky, tricky 7 cunning, knavish,
roguish 8 delusive, delusory, guileful, unhonest 9 dishonest, insidious,
insincere, underhand 10 fallacious,
mendacious, misleading, untruthful
11 treacherous, underhanded

deceivable
7 dupable 8 gullible

deceive
3 con, fob, fop, fub, lie 4 bilk,
dupe, flam, fool, gaff, gull, hoax,
jilt, mock, wyle 5 blind, bluff,
cheat, cozen, dodge, hocus, spoof,
trick 6 baffle, befool, betray, delude, humbug, illude, juggle, palter,
take in 7 beguile, defraud, mislead, sell out, two-time 8 flimflam,
hoodwink 9 bamboozle, four-flush
11 double-cross 12 misrepresent

deceiving
5 false 8 deluding, delusive, delusory 9 beguiling 10 fallacious,
misleading

decelerate
5 delay 6 retard, slow up
7 slacken 8 slow down

decency
7 decorum, dignity, fitness 9 etiquette, propriety 10 seemliness

decent
4 fair, good, just, nice, pure
5 clean, right 6 chaste, common,
enough, honest, modest, proper,
seemly 7 average, correct, fitting
8 adequate, all right, becoming,
decorous, spotless 9 befitting,
competent, stainless, sufficing, tolerable, undefiled, unsullied 10 acceptable, conforming, immaculate,
sufficient 11 comfortable, comme il
faut, presentable, respectable, unblemished 12 satisfactory
13 unexceptional, unimpeachable

deception
3 gyp 4 flam, gaff, gull, hoax,

hype, ruse, sham, wile 5 cheat,
craft, fraud, guile, magic, put-on,
spoof, trick 6 dupery, humbug, mirage 7 chicane, cunning, fallacy,
fantasm, knavery, sophism 8 cheating, cozening, flimflam, illusion, intrigue, phantasm, subtlety, trickery,
trumpery, wiliness 9 casuistry, chicanery, duplicity, fourberie, imposture, sophistry, treachery 10 artfulness, camouflage, defrauding,
dishonesty, hanky-panky, subterfuge 11 dipsy-doodle, highbinding,
indirection 12 speciousness, spuriousness 13 double-dealing
Scottish: 7 blaflum

deceptive
5 false 6 artful, crafty, tricky
7 seeming, trickie 8 deluding, delusory, illusory, specious, trickish
9 beguiling 10 fallacious,
misleading

deceptiveness
7 fallacy, sophism 8 delusion 9 casuistry, sophistry 12 equivocation,
speciousness, spuriousness

decide
3 opt 4 rule, will 5 judge 6 figure,
settle 7 adjudge, resolve 8 conclude 9 determine 10 adjudicate

decided
3 set 4 firm, flat, sure 5 fixed 6 intent 7 assured, certain, obvious, settled 8 clear-cut, cocksure, definite,
explicit, positive, resolute, resolved
10 determined, pronounced 11 categorical, established, unequivocal
12 unmistakable

decimate
4 raze, ruin, undo 5 wrack, wreck
6 unmake 7 destroy, unbuild, unframe, wipe out 8 demolish, massacre 9 slaughter 10 annihilate
11 exterminate

decipher
5 break, crack, solve 6 decode, reveal, unfold 7 analyze, decrypt, resolve, unravel 8 unriddle 9 figure
out, puzzle out, translate
12 cryptanalyze

decision
4 fiat 6 choice, ruling 7 resolve,
verdict 8 firmness, judgment, sentence, umpirage 9 selection
10 conclusion, resolution, settlement
12 resoluteness 13 determination,
purposiveness
rabbinical: 9 responsum

decisive
3 set 4 bent 6 intent 7 assured,
crucial, settled 8 critical, resolute,

resolved 9 imperious, masterful
10 determined, imperative, peremptory 11 self-assured 13 self-
confident

deck
4 trim 5 adorn, array, dress, equip,
floor, prank 6 attire, blazon, clothe
7 apparel, appoint, furnish, garland, garnish 8 accouter, accoutre,
beautify, decorate, emblazon, ornament, platform 9 embellish
chief: 4 bos'n 9 boatswain
high: 4 poop
lowest: 5 orlop
out: 5 fix up, primp, slick, spiff, tog
up 6 doll up 7 dress up, gussy up
8 spruce up
part: 7 scupper

deckhand
3 gob 6 sailor 7 rouster, swabbie

declaim
4 rant, rave 5 mouth, orate, speak,
utter 6 recite 7 elocute, inveigh,
soapbox 8 bloviate, harangue,
perorate

declamatory
7 aureate, flowery 8 sonorous
9 bombastic, high-flown 10 euphuistic, oratorical, rhetorical 12 magniloquent 13 grandiloquent

declaration
4 word 6 avowal, oracle, report
9 broadcast, statement 10 disclosure 12 announcement 13 advertisement, pronouncement

declare
3 say, vow 4 aver, avow, deny,
tell, toot, vend, vent 5 sound, state,
utter, voice 6 affirm, allege, assert,
assure, avouch, blazon, depone,
depose, herald, report, reveal
7 chime in, deliver, divulge, express, profess, protest, publish, signify, testify 8 announce, bring out,
constate, disclose, indicate, proclaim, throw out 9 advertise,
broadcast, predicate, pronounce
10 annunciate, bruit about, promulgate 11 blaze abroad, come out
with, disseminate
a saint: 8 canonize
in cards: 3 bid 4 meld
invalid: 5 annul

declare off
5 welsh 6 renege, resile 7 back out
8 back down 9 backpedal,
backwater

declass
4 bump, bust 5 break 6 demote,
reduce 7 degrade, demerit, disrate
8 disgrade 9 downgrade

déclassé

4 hack, mean, poor **6** common
8 inferior, low-grade **10** second-
rate **11** second-class **12** second-
drawer

declension

8 downfall **9** decadence, downgrade **10** degeneracy
12 dégringolade

declination

6 ebbing, waning **7** failure
8 downfall **9** decadence, downgrade **10** degeneracy
12 dégringolade

decline

3 dip, ebb, jib, rot, sag, set **4** balk,
dive, drop, fade, fail, fall, flag,
loss, sink, slip, wane **5** abate, demur, droop, lapse, lower, slide,
slope, slump, spurn **6** ebbing, go
down, recede, refuse, reject, renege, waning, weaken, worsen
7 abstain, atrophy, descend, descent, dismiss, drop-off, dwindle,
failure, falloff, forbear, refrain, relapse, sell-off, sinkage, subside
8 comedown, decrease, downfall,
downturn, languish, lowering, toboggan, turn down **9** backslide,
decadence, downgrade, downslide, downswing, downtrend, reprobate, repudiate, weakening
10 degeneracy, degenerate, depression, devolution, disapprove,
disimprove, falling off, retrograde
11 backsliding, deteriorate **12** degeneration, dégringolade, disintegrate **13** deterioration
combining form: **4** clin **5** clino

declivitous

6 sloped, tilted, tipped **7** leaning,
oblique, pitched, sloping **8** inclined
9 inclining

declivity

3 dip **4** drop, fall **5** slope **7** descent **8** gradient **11** inclination

decode

see **decipher**

decollate

4 head **6** behead **10** guillotine

decolor

5 white **6** blanch, bleach, blench,
whiten **7** wash out **11** achromatize

decompose

3 rot **4** turn **5** decay, spoil, taint
6 molder **7** analyze, break up,
crumble, dissect, putrefy, resolve
8 dissolve **9** anatomize, break
down **12** disintegrate

decomposition

combining form: **4** lyses (plural)
5 lysis

decorate

4 pink, trim **5** adorn, dress, frill,
prank **6** bedeck, emboss **7** cornice, dress up, festoon, furnish, garnish, miniate, appliqué **8** beautify,
emblazon, ornament **9** embellish
a border: **6** purfle

decorated

6 ornate **7** adorned, wrought **9** bemedaled **10** beribboned

decoration

2 PH **3** DSC, DSM **4** bays
5 award, badge, honor, kudos,
medal **6** boulle, doodad, plaque
7 laurels **8** accolade, fretting, fret-
work, ornament, vignette
cutout: **8** appliqué
furniture: **4** buhl **8** buhlwork

decorous

3 fit **4** done, good, nice, prim
5 right **6** au fait, comely, decent,
proper, seemly **7** correct, elegant,
fitting **8** becoming, suitable **9** befitting, civilized, de rigueur **10** conforming **11** appropriate, respectable, well-behaved

decorously

4 well **5** fitly **6** justly, nicely
7 rightly **8** properly **9** correctly, fittingly **11** befittingly

decorousness

5 order **9** propriety **11** orderliness
12 correctitude

decorticate

4 flay, hull, peel, skin **5** scale,
scalp, strip **6** denude

decorum

5 order **7** decency, dignity, modesty **9** etiquette, propriety **10** properness, seemliness **11** correctness,
orderliness **12** correctitude,
decorousness

decoy

4 bait, lure, toll, trap **5** blind, plant,
shill, snare, stick, tempt **6** allure,
capper, delude, entice, entrap,
lead on, pigeon, seduce **7** deceive,
mislead **8** inveigle, trickery **9** deception, shillaber **10** allurement,
enticement, seducement, temptation
12 inveiglement

decrease

3 cut, ebb **4** bate, clip, drop, ease,
fall, loss, sink, trim, wane **5** abate,
allay, close, lower, taper, waste
6 deduct, lessen, rebate, recede, reduce, shrink **7** abridge, atrophy,
curtail, cut back, cut down, dwindle, letdown, lighten, peak out,
shorten, slacken, subside **8** contract, diminish, downturn, moderate, peter out, retrench, rollback,
subtract, taper off **9** alleviate, drain
away **10** abbreviate, diminution

decree

3 act, law, set **4** fiat, rule **5** canon,
edict, enact, judge, order, tenet,
ukase **6** assize, behest, charge,
dictum, firman, impose, ordain, ruling **7** adjudge, appoint, bidding,
command, dictate, lay down, mandate, precept, statute **8** judgment,
sentence **9** directive, enactment,
judgement, ordinance, prescribe,
prescript **10** adjudicate, injunction,
plebiscite, regulation **11** declaration **12** adjudication, announcement, proclamation, promulgation
13 pronouncement
Muslim: **5** irade

decrepit

3 old **4** aged, lame, weak, worn
5 frail, seedy, tacky, tired **6** creaky,
feeble, flimsy, infirm, senile,
shabby, sloppy, tagrag, wasted,
weakly **7** cast-off, failing, fragile,
haggard, run-down, unkempt, unsound **8** slipshod **10** bedraggled,
broken-down, down-at-heel, threadbare **13** insubstantial, unsubstantial

decrepitude

7 disease, malaise **8** debility **9** infirmity **10** infirmness, sickliness
13 unhealthiness

decretum

3 law **4** rule **5** canon, edict **6** assize **7** precept, statute **9** ordinance
10 regulation

decry

3 boo **4** slur **5** abuse, lower
6 lessen **7** asperse, censure, condemn, degrade, detract, devalue,
run down **8** belittle, denounce, derogate, diminish, discount, mark
down, minimize, take away, take
from, write off **9** criticize, deprecate, devaluate, disparage, dispraise, downgrade, reprehend,
reprobate, underrate, write down
10 depreciate, disapprove, undervalue **11** detract from, opprobriate

decrypt

see **decipher**

decumbent

4 flat **5** prone **9** prostrate, reclining

decussate

5 cross **8** crosscut **9** intersect
10 criss-cross, intercross

dedicate
3 vow 6 devote, hallow
10 consecrate

deduce
4 draw, lead 5 infer, judge, trace
6 derive, evolve, gather 7 collect,
explain, extract, make out 8 cogitate, conclude

deduct
4 bate, dock, draw, take 5 abate,
allow, infer, judge 6 derive,
gather, remove 7 collect, make out,
take off, take out 8 abstract, conclude, discount, knock off, roll
back, subtract, take away

deduction
3 cut 6 rebate 7 dockage 8 decrease, discount, illation, judgment,
sequitur, write-off 9 abatement,
decrement, inference 10 conclusion
13 ratiocination

deductive
7 a priori 8 dogmatic, illative, reasoned 9 derivable 11 inferential
13 ratiocinative

deed
3 act 4 cede, fact, fait, feat, pact
5 doing, quest, thing, title 6 action,
assign, convey, escrow, remise
7 charter, compact, exploit 8 alienate, contract, covenant, make over,
practice, sign over, transfer
9 adventure 10 abalienate, conveyance, enterprise 11 achievement,
performance, tour de force
brutal: 8 atrocity
evil: 3 sin 11 malefaction

deem
3 say 4 feel, hold, hope, know, tell,
view 5 judge, opine, sense, think
6 credit, divine, reckon, regard
7 account, adjudge, believe 8 consider, proclaim 10 conjecture

de-emphasize
8 downplay, play down 9 soft-
pedal

deep
3 low, sly 4 foxy, hard, late, rapt,
wily, wise 5 abyss, acute, grave,
heavy, ocean 6 artful, astute,
crafty, growly, intent, middle, occult, orphic, remote, secret, shrewd,
tricky 7 abysmal, complex, cunning, devious, engaged, extreme,
intense, obscure, serious, unmixed
8 absorbed, abstruse, esoteric,
grievous, guileful, hermetic, immersed, involved, profound 9 developed, engrossed, firmament,
insidious, intensive, recondite, sagacious, unalloyed, wrapped up
10 acroamatic, bottomless, mysterious, profoundly 11 complicated,
preoccupied
combining form: 5 bathy
pink: 5 coral

deep-dyed
5 sworn 7 settled 9 confirmed,
hard-shell 10 entrenched, inveterate 13 bred-in-the-bone

deepen
4 rise 5 mount, rouse 6 darken
7 enhance, magnify, thicken
8 heighten, redouble 9 aggravate,
intensate, intensify 10 strengthen

deepness
4 drop 5 abyss, depth
10 profundity

deep-rooted
see **deep-dyed**

deep-sea
combining form: 5 bathy

deep-seated
5 sworn 6 inborn, inbred, innate
7 connate, settled 8 inherent, profound 9 confirmed, hard-shell, ingrained, intrinsic 10 congenital, entrenched, indwelling, inveterate
13 bred-in-the-bone, dyed-in-the-
wool

deep water
6 plight 7 dilemma
11 predicament

deer
3 elk, roe 4 buck, musk, stag
5 brown, moose 6 wapiti 7 caribou, venison 8 bobolink 10 camel's hair
Asian: 4 axis 5 maral 6 chital, sambar, sambur 7 muntjac, sambhar,
sambhur 8 muntijak
British: 4 hart
combining form: 5 cervi
female: 3 doe
female red: 4 hind
Japanese: 4 sika
male: 4 hart 7 roebuck
male red: 4 stag 8 staggard,
   staggart
meat: 5 jerky 7 venison
path: 3 run 5 trail
red: 7 brocket
relating to: 6 damine 7 cervine
track: 4 slot 5 spoor
young: 3 kid 4 fawn

Deerslayer
author: 6 Cooper (James Fenimore)
character: 11 Natty Bumppo
12 Chingachgook

deface
3 mar 4 foul, harm, ruin, scar
5 spoil 6 batter, damage, deform,
injure, mangle 7 blemish, distort
8 misshape, mutilate 9 disfigure,
vandalize 10 disfashion, disfeature

de facto
6 really 8 actually 9 genuinely,
veritably

defalcation
4 lack 7 deficit, failing, failure
8 shortage, underage 10 deficiency, inadequacy, negligence,
scantiness 13 insufficience,
insufficiency

defamation
4 tale 7 calumny, scandal, slander
10 backbiting 12 backstabbing,
belittlement 13 disparagement

defamatory
8 libelous 9 maligning, traducing,
vilifying 10 backbiting, calumnious,
detracting, detractive, scandalous,
slanderous

defame
4 foul 5 abase, cloud, libel, smear
6 injure, malign, vilify 7 asperse,
blemish, scandal, slander, traduce
8 dishonor, vilipend 9 blackwash,
denigrate 10 calumniate, scandalize, villainize

default
4 fail, lack, omit, want 6 dearth,
defect 7 absence, failure, neglect
9 oversight, privation 10 negligence 11 delinquency, dereliction
12 imperfection

defeasance
4 rout 7 beating, debacle, licking
8 drubbing 9 overthrow 11 shellacking 12 discomfiture,
vanquishment

defeat
4 best, down, drub, foil, lick, loss,
rout, ruin, sink, stop, undo, whip
5 check, crush, outdo, skunk,
swamp, waste, whomp, worst
6 outgun, reduce, subdue 7 beating, conquer, debacle, destroy, failure, licking, nose out, outplay, out-
vote, repress, setback, shellac,
trounce 8 outfight, outtrump, overcome, overvote, vanquish, waterloo
9 downthrow, frustrate, insuccess,
overpower, overthrow, subjugate,
thrashing, trouncing, unsuccess
10 nonsuccess 11 shellacking
12 discomfiture, vanquishment

defecate
5 purge, stool 6 purify, refine
7 clarify 9 discharge

defect
3 bug 4 flaw, lack, vice, want
5 botch, error, fault 6 damage,
dearth, desert, foible, injury, malady 7 absence, blemish, default,
failing, frailty 8 drawback, renounce, weakness 9 infirmity, privation, repudiate 10 apostatize,
deficiency, tergiverse 11 shortcoming 12 imperfection, tergiversate
timber: 4 knot
visual: 6 myopia, squint 9 ambly-
opia, hyperopia 10 presbyopia,
strabismus 11 hemeralopia

defection
8 apostasy 9 falseness, forsaking,
recreancy 10 disloyalty
11 abandonment

defective
3 bad, ill 4 poor, sick 5 amiss,
flawy 6 broken, faulty, flawed
7 damaged, lacking, unsound,
wanting 8 deranged, impaired
9 corrupted, deficient, imperfect,
unhealthy 10 disordered, inaccurate, inadequate, incomplete, uncomplete 12 insufficient
combining form: 4 atel 5 atelo

defector
3 rat 7 traitor 8 apostate, recreant,
renegade, runagate, turncoat
9 turnabout 13 tergiversator

defend
4 back, hold, save 5 argue, claim,
cover, fight, guard 6 assert, screen,
secure, shield, uphold 7 bulwark,
contend, justify, protect, support,
warrant 8 advocate, champion,
conserve, garrison, maintain, preserve 9 safeguard, vindicate
11 rationalize

defendable
see **defensible**

defendant
7 accused, libelee 8 libellee

defender
8 advocate, champion, guardian
9 protector
of people's rights: 7 tribune

defense
4 egis, fort, ward 5 aegis, alibi, armor, guard 6 answer, excuse,
sconce, shield 7 apology, bulwark,
rampart, shelter 8 apologia, armament, fastness, fortress, muniment,
security 9 safeguard 10 apologetic, protection, stronghold
11 exculpation, explanation
13 justification
organization: 4 NATO 5 NORAD,
SEATO
outer: 6 tenail 8 tenaille

defenseless
8 helpless 11 unprotected

defensible
7 tenable 9 excusable
10 condonable

defer
3 bow 4 cave, stay, wait 5 adapt,
delay, remit, stall, waive, yield
6 accede, adjust, hold up, put off,
shelve, submit 7 adjourn, conform,
hold off, knuckle, lay over, put
over, succumb, suspend 8 hold
over, intermit, postpone, prorogue
9 acquiesce 10 capitulate 11 accommodate, buckle under
12 knuckle under 13 procrastinate

deference
5 honor 6 homage 9 obeisance
10 compliance, submission

deferential
5 silky 6 silken 7 duteous, dutiful
9 disarming, regardful 10 respectful, saccharine 11 insinuating, insinuative 12 ingratiating,
ingratiatory

defiance
4 dare 5 stump 6 cartel 7 bravado, despite 8 audacity, boldness, contempt, temerity 9 challenge, contumacy, enjoinder,
hardihood, impudence, insolence
10 brazenness, effrontery, insur-
gency, unruliness 12 contrariness,
factiousness, stubbornness

deficiency
3 sin 4 lack, want 5 fault, minus
6 dearth 7 absence, blemish, demerit, failing, failure 8 scarcity,
shortage, underage 9 privation
10 inadequacy, scantiness 11 defalcation, shortcoming
12 imperfection
combining form: 5 penia
mental: 6 idiocy 7 amentia
oxygen: 8 asphyxia

deficient
3 shy 5 minus, scant, short 6 faulty,
flawed, meager, meagre, measly,
scanty, scarce 7 bobtail, failing,
lacking, unsound, wanting 8 impaired 9 defective, imperfect 10 inadequate, incomplete, uncomplete
combining form: 6 privic

deficit
4 lack 7 failure 8 shortage, underage 10 inadequacy, scantiness
11 defalcation 13 insufficience,
insufficiency

defile
3 tar 4 foul, pass, rape, soil
5 dirty, shame, smear, spoil, stain,
sully, taint 6 befoul, debase, ravish
7 besmear, corrupt, outrage, pollute, profane, tarnish, violate 8 besmirch, deflower, discolor, dishonor
9 deflorate, desecrate
11 contaminate

defiled
6 impure 7 unclean 8 profaned
10 desecrated

define
3 fix, hem, rim, set 4 edge, etch,
term 5 bound, limit, skirt, verge
6 assign, border 7 clarify, delimit,
lay down, mark off, mark out, outline 8 surround 9 delineate, demarcate, prescribe 12 characterize

definite
3 set 4 sure 5 clear, final, fixed,
sharp, solid 6 narrow 7 assured,
certain, decided, express, limited,
precise, settled 8 clean-cut, clear-
cut, distinct, explicit, limiting, positive, specific 10 conclusive, determined, forthright, pronounced,
restricted 11 categorical, determinate, established, unambiguous, unequivocal 12 unmistakable
13 circumscribed

definiteness
8 accuracy 9 exactness
10 exactitude

definitive
4 last 5 final 7 express 8 absolute,
clean-cut, clear-cut, explicit, settling,
specific, terminal, ultimate 10 concluding, conclusive 11 categorical,
determining, unambiguous

definitiveness
see **definiteness**

definitude
see **definiteness**

deflect
4 bend, warp 5 avert, parry, pivot,
sheer, wheel, whirl 6 detour, divert, swerve 7 deviate, diverge,
hold off, keep off, refract 9 volte-
face

deflection
3 yaw 4 bend, tack, turn, veer
5 curve, shift 6 double, swerve
7 bending, turning, veering

8 swerving 9 departure, diversion
10 divergence
combining form: 7 sphingo

deflorate
see **deflower**

deflower
4 rape 5 force, harry, havoc, spoil
6 defile, devast, devour, ravage,
ravish 7 despoil, outrage, violate
8 desolate 9 depredate, desecrate,
devastate

Defoe
character: 6 Crusoe, Friday, Roxana
12 Moll Flanders
heroine: 4 Moll

deform
3 mar 4 flaw, maim, warp, wind
5 spoil 6 batter, damage, deface,
impair, injure, mangle 7 blemish,
contort, cripple, distort, torture
8 misshape, mutilate 9 disfigure
10 disarrange

deformity
4 flaw 7 blemish, harelip 8 misshape, ugliness 10 aberration, corruption, impairment 11 abnormality, impropriety 12 irregularity,
malformation

___ de France
3 Île

defraud
3 gyp 4 beat, bilk, hoax, take
5 cheat, cozen, mulct, rogue, trick
6 chouse, fleece 7 swindle 8 flimflam 9 bamboozle

deft
4 neat 5 adept, agile, handy, quick
6 adroit, clever, expert, nimble
8 dextrous, skillful 9 dexterous, ingenious 10 neat-handed

deftness
7 address, prowess, sleight 9 dexterity, readiness

defunct
4 cold, dead, gone, late, lost 5 inert 6 asleep, bygone 7 extinct
8 deceased, departed, finished, inactive, lifeless, vanished 9 exanimate, inanimate

defy
4 dare, face, gibe, mock 5 beard,
brave, flout, front, scorn, spurn,
stump 6 cartel, ignore 7 affront,
outdare, outface, venture
9 challenge

dégagé
6 breezy, casual 7 relaxed, unfussy
8 informal 9 easygoing 10 unre-

served 11 low-pressure
13 unconstrained

degeneracy
see **degeneration**

degenerate
3 rot 4 sink 5 lapse 6 effete, rotten, worsen 7 corrupt, decayed,
decline, descend, vicious, vitiate
8 decadent, depraved, infamous,
overripe 9 backslide, miscreant,
nefarious, unhealthy 10 disimprove, flagitious, villainous

degeneration
7 atrophy, decline 8 downfall, lowering 9 decadence, depravity,
downgrade 10 perversion, regression 12 dégringolade,
depravedness

degradation
4 fall 7 decline, descent
11 downgrading

degrade
4 bump, bust, sink 5 abase, break,
decry, lower 6 bemean, damage,
debase, demean, demote, depose,
expose, humble, lessen, reduce
7 corrupt, declass, demerit, deprive, detract, disrate, pervert, put
down 8 belittle, cast down, derogate, diminish 9 decompose, disparage, humiliate, reduction
12 depolymerize

degree
3 peg 4 heat, rank, rate, rung,
step, term, tier 5 grade, honor,
notch, order, pitch, point, ratio,
scale, shade, stage, stair 6 extent
7 measure, station 8 standing 9 dimension, magnitude 10 proportion
academic: 2 BA, BS, MA, MD, MS
3 DDS, LLB, LLD, MBA, MFA, PhD
highest: 8 cum laude 13 magna cum
laude, summa cum laude
of combining power: 7 valence
of height: 5 grade
of importance: 7 caliber, calibre
of outward slope: 5 splay
seeker: 9 candidate
slight: 4 hair
suffix: 2 ty 3 ity 4 ance, ness
utmost: 4 acme

dégringolade
see **degeneration**

___ de guerre
3 nom

dehydrate
3 dry 4 sear 5 parch 9 desiccate,
exsiccate

Deianira
brother: 8 Meleager
father: 6 Oeneus
husband: 8 Heracles, Hercules
mother: 7 Althaea
victim: 8 Heracles, Hercules

Deidamia
father: 9 Lycomedes
husband: 9 Pirithous
son: 11 Neoptolemus

deific
5 godly 6 divine 7 godlike

deification
10 apotheosis

deign
5 stoop 10 condescend

Deiphobus
brother: 5 Paris 6 Hector
father: 5 Priam
mother: 6 Hecuba
wife: 5 Helen

Deirdre
beloved: 5 Noisi
father: 5 Felim

deity
3 god 4 deva 5 numen 6 numina
(plural) 7 goddess, godhead, god-
hood, godling, godship 8 Almighty, divinity 12 supreme being
(see also at **Greek; Hindu; Norse;
Roman**)

deject
5 chill 8 dispirit 9 disparage
10 demoralize, discourage,
dishearten

dejected
3 low, sad 4 blue, down,
glum, sunk 6 gloomy, somber, sombre 7 hangdog, humbled, unhappy
8 downcast, wretched 9 cheerless,
depressed, woebegone 10 despondent, spiritless 11 crestfallen, downhearted 12 disconsolate

dejection
5 dumps 7 despair 10 melancholy
12 mournfulness

Delaware
capital: 5 Dover
largest city: 10 Wilmington
nickname: 10 First State 12 Blue Hen
State, Diamond State
state flower: 12 peach blossom

delay
3 lag 4 drag, hold, mire, mull,
poke, slow 5 check, defer, deter,
embog, stall, tarry, trail 6 dawdle,
detain, hang up, hinder, hold up,

impede, linger, loiter, put off, retard, shelve, slow up **7** adjourn, bog down, hold off, prolong, respite, set back, slacken, suspend **8** hangfire, hesitate, hold over, intermit, obstruct, postpone, prorogue, reprieve, slow down **9** detention, hindrance, lingering **10** decelerate, dillydally, moratorium, suspension **13** procrastinate

delaying
8 dilatory, moratory

delectable
4 lush **5** sapid, tasty, yummy **6** choice, savory **7** darling **8** heavenly, luscious, pleasing **9** ambrosial, delicious, exquisite, toothsome **10** delightful **11** scrumptious

delectation
3 joy **6** relish **7** delight, joyance **8** fruition, pleasure **9** diversion, enjoyment

delegate
4 name, send **5** agent, envoy, proxy **6** assign, charge, commit, depute, deputy **7** appoint, ascribe, consign, empower, entrust **8** deputize, emissary, transfer **9** authorize, catchpole, spokesman **10** commission, mouthpiece **12** representant

delete
4 omit, x out **5** annul, blank, erase, purge **6** cancel, censor, efface, remove **7** blot out, destroy, expunge, wipe out **8** black out, cross out **9** eliminate, eradicate **10** blue-pencil, obliterate

deleterious
3 bad **6** nocent **7** harmful, hurtful, nocuous, ruinous **8** damaging **11** destructive, detrimental, mischievous, prejudicial

deletion
7 erasure **8** omission **10** deficiency

deliberate
4 cool, muse, pore, slow **5** chary, meant, study, think, weigh **6** ponder, reason, regard **7** advised, careful, heedful, laggard, planned, reflect, schemed, studied, unhasty, willful, willing, witting **8** cautious, cogitate, consider, designed, dilatory, intended, measured, meditate, mull over, prepense, ruminate, studious, talk over, turn over, unforced **9** leisurely, meditated, projected, speculate, unhurried, voluntary **10** calculated, considered, purposeful, thought-out **11** circum-

spect, intentional **12** aforethought, premeditated, unprescribed

deliberately
9 on purpose, purposely **10** purposedly **11** purposively

deliberation
3 rap **4** heed **5** study **6** debate **7** thought **9** brainwork **10** conference, discussion

Delibes
ballet: **6** Sylvia **8** Coppelia, La Source
opera: **5** Lakmé

delicacy
4 cate **5** goody, treat **6** caviar, dainty, luxury, morsel, nicety, tidbit, titbit **7** caviare **8** kickshaw **10** daintiness **11** bonne bouche

delicate
4 airy, fine, lacy, mild, nice, rare, soft, weak **5** balmy, frail, fussy, light **6** aerial, choice, dainty, flimsy, gentle, pastel, petite, queasy, select, slight, subtle, tender, touchy, tricky **7** elegant, finical, finicky, fragile, lenient, politic, refined, tactful, tenuous **8** ethereal, feathery, finespun, gossamer, graceful, hairline, shattery, superior, tactical, ticklish **9** breakable, exquisite, finicking, frangible, recherché, sensitive, squeamish **10** diplomatic, fastidious, particular, precarious **11** fracturable, persnickety, shatterable **13** hair-splitting

delicatesse
4 tact **5** poise **7** address **9** diplomacy **11** savoir faire, tactfulness

delicatessen
11 charcuterie

delicious
4 lush **5** sapid, yummy **6** choice, savory **7** darling **8** adorable, heavenly **9** ambrosial, exquisite, palatable, toothsome **10** appetizing, delectable

delight
3 joy **4** glee **5** amuse, bliss, charm, enjoy, exult, glory, mirth, revel **6** arride, divert, please, regale, relish **7** enchant, gladden, gratify, happify, jollity, joyance, rapture, rejoice, triumph **8** enravish, entrance, fruition, hilarity, jubilate, pleasure, savoring **9** delectate, enjoyment, enrapture, entertain **11** contentment, delectation **12** satisfaction
in: **4** like, love **5** adore, enjoy, savor **6** admire **7** cherish **10** appreciate

delightful
4 lush **5** yummy **6** dreamy, savory **7** darling, elysian **8** adorable, alluring, charming, heavenly, luscious, pleasant, pleasing **9** agreeable, ambrosial **10** attractive, delectable, enchanting, gratifying **11** fascinating, scrumptious

Delilah's victim
6 Samson

delimit
3 bar **5** bound **6** demark **7** confine, mark out, measure **8** restrict **9** demarcate, determine **12** circumscribe

delineate
3 map **4** etch, limn **5** chart, image, trace **6** define, depict, render, survey **7** outline, picture, portray **8** describe **9** interpret, represent

delineation
5 story **7** account, contour, drawing, outline, picture, profile **10** silhouette **11** portraiture, presentment

delinquency
5 lapse **7** default, failure, misdeed, neglect **8** omission **9** oversight **10** misconduct **11** dereliction

delinquent
3 lax **5** slack **6** remiss **8** careless **9** negligent **10** behindhand, regardless **12** disregardful, transgressor

deliquesce
3 run **4** flux, fuse, melt, thaw **5** decay **7** liquefy **8** dissolve **9** decompose, disappear **12** disintegrate

delirious
3 mad **4** wild **5** crazy, manic, rabid **6** crazed, insane, maniac, raving **7** frantic, lunatic **8** confused, demented, deranged, ecstatic, frenetic, frenzied, rambling **9** rapturous, wandering **10** bewildered, corybantic, distracted, irrational **11** overexcited, overwrought **12** unreasonable
Scottish: **8** brainish

delirium
5 furor **6** fervor, frenzy, ravery **7** ecstasy, jimjams, rapture

delirium ____
7 tremens

deliver
3 say **4** bail, bear, deal, feed, find, give, hand, save, take, tell, yean **5** bring, pitch, serve, speak, state, throw, utter, whelp **6** convey, re-

deem, rescue, strike, supply, unbind
7 chime in, consign, declare, inflict,
present, provide, release **8** bring
out, dispatch, dispense, hand over,
liberate, transfer, transmit, turn over
9 surrender **10** administer, bring
forth, emancipate **11** come out with

deliverance
6 rescue **7** opinion, release **8** decision **10** liberation **12** disburdening

delivery
5 birth **6** rescue **7** address, bearing **8** shipment **9** rendition
10 childbirth **11** parturition
12 childbearing
combining form: **4** toky

dell
4 dale **6** dingle, hollow, valley

Delphian
4 dark **5** vatic **6** mantic **7** cryptic,
fatidic **8** oracular **9** enigmatic, prophetic, sibylline, vaticinal **10** mystifying **11** apocalyptic, prophetical

delude
5 bluff, trick **6** betray, humbug, juggle, take in **7** beguile, deceive, mislead **8** impose on **11** double-cross

deluge
3 sea, sop, wet **4** gush, pour, soak
5 douse, drown, flood, souse,
spate, swamp, whelm **6** drench,
engulf **7** niagara, torrent **8** cataract, downpour, flooding, inundate,
overcome, overflow, submerge
9 cataclysm, overwhelm **10** cloudburst, inundation

delusion
5 dream, fancy **6** mirage **7** eidolon, fallacy, fantasy, figment, phantom, sophism **8** daydream, phantasm **9** casuistry, deception,
sophistry **10** apparition, misleading
11 ignis fatuus **12** equivocation,
speciousness, spuriousness
13 deceptiveness, hallucination

delusive
5 false **8** fanciful, illusory, quixotic
9 beguiling, deceiving, deceptive,
fantastic, imaginary, visionary
10 chimerical, fallacious,
misleading

delusory
see **delusive**

deluxe
4 lush **5** plush **6** Capuan, choice
7 elegant, opulent **8** luscious, palatial **9** exquisite, luxuriant, luxurious,
recherché, sumptuous **11** upholstered

delve
3 dig, dip **4** hole, mine, void **6** cavity, fathom, hollow, pocket, quarry,
vacuum **7** vacancy, vacuity
into: **4** sift **5** probe **7** explore
8 prospect **11** investigate

delving
5 probe, quest **7** inquest, inquiry,
probing **8** research **11** inquisition
13 investigation

demagnetize
6 deperm **7** degauss

demagogue
6 leader **7** inciter **8** agitator, fomenter **9** firebrand **10** instigator
12 rabble-rouser

demand
3 ask, use **4** call, need, take, want
5 claim, crave, exact, force, order
6 compel, direct, elicit, enjoin, expect, insist, oblige **7** call for, request, require, solicit **8** occasion
9 challenge, constrain, postulate
11 requirement, requisition

demanding
5 rigid, stern, tough **6** severe, strict,
taxing, trying **7** exigent, onerous,
weighty **8** grievous, rigorous
9 stringent **10** burdensome,
oppressive

demarcate
5 bound, limit **6** define, set off
7 delimit, mark out, measure **8** separate, set apart **9** determine, segregate **10** delimitate **11** distinguish
12 circumscribe, discriminate
13 differentiate

demarcation
10 border line, separation
11 distinction

demean
3 act **4** bear, go on, mien, quit,
sink **5** abase, carry, decry, lower
6 acquit, behave, debase, deport,
humble **7** comport, conduct, degrade, detract **8** behavior, belittle,
cast down, derogate **9** disparage,
humiliate

demeanor
3 air, set **4** mien, port **7** address,
bearing, conduct **8** behavior, carriage, portance, presence
10 deportment **11** comportment

demented
3 mad **4** luny **5** crazy, nutty
6 crazed, insane, maniac **7** lunatic,
unsound **8** deranged, frenzied
9 delirious **10** hysterical, unbalanced

___ **de mer**
3 mal

demerit
3 sin **4** bump, bust, mark **5** break,
fault **6** demote, reduce **7** declass,
degrade, disrate **8** disgrade
9 downgrade **10** deficiency
11 shortcoming **12** imperfection

demesne
5 field **6** domain, estate, sphere
7 terrain **8** dominion, province
9 bailiwick, champaign, territory
house: **5** manor

Demeter
see **Ceres**

demigod
8 superman **10** superhuman

demise
3 die **4** drop, pass **5** death, sleep
6 cash in, depart, ending, expire
7 decease, passing, quietus, silence, succumb **8** curtains, pass
away **10** defunction, expiration,
extinction **11** dissolution
12 annihilation

demit
4 sink **5** couch, droop, lower **6** resign **7** depress, let down **8** abdicate, renounce, withdraw

demiurgic
8 creative, original **9** deviceful, formative, ingenious, inventive
10 innovative, innovatory **11** originative **12** innovational

demobilize
6 dispel **7** break up, disband, scatter **8** disperse, separate **9** discharge, muster out

democratic
7 popular **10** self-ruling **13** self-
governing

Democratic party symbol
6 donkey

démodé
5 dated, passé **7** antique, archaic,
belated **8** old-timey, outdated
9 out-of-date **12** old-fashioned

demoiselle
5 crane **6** damsel **9** damselfly
10 damselfish **11** earth pillar

demolish
4 raze, ruin, undo **5** crush, level,
smash, total, wrack, wreck **6** unmake **7** destroy, unbuild, unframe
8 decimate

demolition bomb
11 blockbuster

demon

3 hag, imp 4 ogre 5 devil, fiend, genie, ghoul, Satan, witch 7 incubus, villain, warlock 9 archfiend
Arabic: 5 afrit 6 afreet
female: 5 lamia 7 succuba, succubi (plural) 8 succubae (plural), succubus
Samoan: 4 aitu
small: 8 devilkin

demoniac

see **demonic**

demonian

see **demonic**

demonic

7 satanic 8 devilish, diabolic, fiendish 10 serpentine, unhallowed 11 diabolonian

demonstrate

3 try 4 mark, show, test 5 prove 6 evince, expose, ostend 7 display, exhibit, make out 8 evidence, manifest, proclaim 9 determine, establish

demonstration

4 show 5 proof 7 display 9 spectacle

demonstrative

4 here, open, that, this 7 profuse 8 effusive, outgoing 9 expansive, exuberant, outspoken 10 epideictic, outpouring, unreserved 12 unrestrained 13 unconstrained

demoralize

4 warp 5 chill, unman 6 debase, deject, weaken 7 corrupt, debauch, deprave, pervert, unnerve, vitiate 8 dispirit 9 disparage, undermine 10 bastardize, debilitate, discourage, dishearten

Demosthenes

for one: 6 orator
oration: 9 Olynthiac, Philippic

demote

4 bump, bust 5 break, lower 6 reduce 7 declass, degrade, demerit, disrate 8 disgrade 9 downgrade

demulcent

8 soothing 9 softening

demur

3 gag, jib, shy 4 balk 5 qualm, stick, waver 6 boggle, falter, object, oppose, squeam, strain 7 protest, scruple, stickle, stumble 8 aversion, hesitate, question
9 challenge, hesitancy, objection, vacillate 10 conscience, difficulty, hesitation, indecision, reluctance
11 compunction, deprecation, dis-

approval, remonstrate, uncertainty 12 protestation, remonstrance 13 remonstration, unwillingness

demure

3 coy, mim, shy 4 prim 5 timid 6 modest, silent 7 bashful 8 backward, reserved, reticent, retiring 9 diffident, unassured 11 unassertive

demurral

7 protest 8 question 9 challenge, objection 10 difficulty 12 remonstrance 13 remonstration

demurrer

see **demurral**

den

3 sty 4 base, cave, goal, home, lair, room, sink 5 couch, lodge, Sodom, study 6 burrow, cavern, hollow 7 cesspit, dayroom, hideout 8 cesspool, hideaway, playroom, workroom 11 pandemonium 12 Augean stable
rabbit: 6 warren

denial

2 no 3 nay 7 refusal, refutal 8 disproof, negation, rebuttal 9 rejection 10 abnegation, gainsaying, refutation 11 declination, repudiation 12 disallowance, renouncement, renunciation 13 contradiction, controversion

denigrate

5 libel, sully 6 darken, defame, malign, vilify 7 asperse, slander, traduce 8 belittle, tear down 10 calumniate, scandalize

denims

9 blue jeans

denizen

5 liver 6 native 7 dweller, habitué, haunter, resider 8 habitant, occupant, resident 9 indweller 10 frequenter, inhabitant

Denmark

capital: 10 Copenhagen
monetary unit: 5 krone

denominate

3 dub 4 call, name, term 5 style, title 7 baptize, entitle 8 christen

denomination

4 cult, name, sect 5 creed, faith, nomen, style, title 6 church 8 category, cognomen, religion 9 communion 10 persuasion 11 appellative
religious: 6 Jewish, Muslim 7 Baptist 8 Lutheran 9 Adventist, Episcopal,

Mennonite, Methodist 12 Presbyterian 13 Roman Catholic

denotation

4 name, sign 7 meaning 10 signifying

denote

4 mark, name, show 5 spell 6 import, intend 7 add up to, express 8 indicate 9 designate, insinuate, represent

denouement

6 result 7 outcome

denounce

3 rap 4 skin 5 blame, blast, decry, knock 6 accuse, scathe 7 arraign, censure, condemn, redbait, upbraid 9 criticize, reprehend, reprobate 10 denunciate, vituperate 11 incriminate 12 anathematize

de novo

4 anew, over 5 again 6 afresh 8 once more 9 over again

dense

4 dull, dumb 5 close, heavy, massy, solid, thick, tight 6 obtuse, opaque, stupid 7 compact, crammed, crowded, doltish, serried 8 blockish, imporous 9 fatheaded, jam-packed 10 numskulled 11 block-headed, thickheaded 12 impenetrable
combining form: 4 pycn, pykn 5 pachy, pycno, pykno

dent

4 bash, nick 5 dinge, notch, tooth 6 dimple

dental structures

5 brace 6 bridge 10 bridgework

denticulate

7 serrate, serried 8 saw-edged, saw-tooth, serrated 10 saw-toothed

dentin

6 enamel

denude

4 bare 5 strip 6 divest 7 deprive, disrobe 8 bankrupt, unclothe 9 dismantle

denunciate

see **denounce**

deny

4 curb 5 cross, forgo, rebut 6 disown, eschew, forbid, impugn, negate, refuse, refute, reject, renege 7 abstain, confute, deprive, disavow, forbear, forsake, gainsay, refrain 8 abnegate, disallow, disclaim, forswear, hold back, keep back, negative, renounce, traverse,

withhold **9** constrain, disaffirm **10** contradict, contravene, controvert

depart

2 go **3** die **4** exit, flee, pass, quit **5** leave, stray **6** begone, decamp, demise, desert, differ, expire, get off, perish, ramble, recede, retire, set out, skidoo, swerve, wander **7** abandon, abscond, decease, deviate, digress, diverge, excurse, forsake, get away, pull out, skiddoo, succumb **8** divagate, pass away, withdraw

departing

7 good-bye **8** farewell **11** valedictory

department

6 branch, sphere **8** division, province **11** subdivision

departure

4 exit **5** break, death, going **6** egress, exodus, flight **7** exiting, leaving, retreat, turning **8** farewell, offgoing, outgoing, quitting **9** deviation, diversion, egression **10** aberration, decampment, deflection, divergence, setting-out, withdrawal **11** leave-taking
of a ship: **6** sortie
point: **7** outport

depend

4 bank, hang, lean, rely, rest, turn **5** count, hinge, sling **6** bank on, dangle, hang on, rely on, turn on **7** build on, count on, hinge on, stand on **8** reckon on **11** calculate on

dependable

4 sure, true **5** loyal, solid, tried **6** secure, steady, trusty **7** certain, staunch **8** accurate, constant, faithful, reliable, surefire **9** authentic, steadfast **11** responsible, trustworthy **12** tried and true **13** authoritative
Scottish: **6** sicker

dependence

4 hope **5** faith, stock, trust **8** reliance

dependent

3 sub **4** iffy **5** child, under **6** minion, sponge, vassal **7** limited, reliant, relying, sponger **8** clinging, relative **9** accessory, ancillary, provisory, secondary, tributary, uncertain **10** collateral, contingent, restricted **11** appurtenant, conditional, provisional, subordinate

depict

4 draw, limn **5** image, paint **6** recite, relate, render, report, sketch **7** depaint, express, impaint, narrate, outline, picture, portray, recount **8** describe, emblazon **9** delineate, interpret, represent **12** characterize

depiction

7 picture **9** portrayal **11** portraiture, presentment

deplete

3 sap **4** draw **5** bleed, drain, empty, use up **6** expend, lessen, reduce, weaken **7** consume, disable, draw off, exhaust **8** bankrupt, decrease, diminish, draw down, enfeeble **9** undermine **10** impoverish

depleted

5 all in, spent **6** bleary, effete, used up **7** far-gone, worn-out **8** bankrupt **9** washed-out

deplorable

4 dire **5** awful **6** woeful **8** dolorous, dreadful, grievous, mournful, terrible, wretched **9** sickening **10** afflictive, calamitous, disastrous, horrifying **11** distressing, unfortunate **12** heartrending **13** heartbreaking

deplore

3 rue **4** moan, weep **5** mourn **6** bemoan, bewail, grieve, lament, regret, repent, sorrow **9** deprecate **10** disapprove, sorrow over

____ de plume

3 nom

depone

5 swear **6** assert **7** testify

____ -de-pont

4 tête

deport

3 act **4** bear, go on, oust, quit **5** carry, exile, expel **6** acquit, banish, behave, demean **7** conduct, expulse **8** displace, relegate **10** expatriate

deportee

2 DP **5** exile **8** expellee

deportment

3 air, set **4** mien, port **5** tenue **7** address, bearing, conduct **8** behavior, carriage, demeanor, presence

depose

4 aver, avow, oust **5** swear **6** affirm, assert, avouch, devest, divest, remove, unmake **7** declare, de-

crown, profess, protest, testify, uncrown **8** constate, dethrone, discrown, displace, throw out, unthrone **9** disthrone, overthrow, predicate **11** disenthrone

deposit

3 lay, set **4** bank, drop, dump, fund, lees, pawn, stow **5** chest, dregs, lodge, place, put by, store **6** entomb, settle **7** consign, grounds **8** sediment **9** settlings **11** precipitate **13** precipitation
alluvial: **5** delta
black: **4** soot
calcium carbonate: **10** stalactite, stalagmite
containing gold: **6** placer
eggs: **5** spawn
geologic: **7** horizon
glacial: **4** till **5** drift, esker **7** moraine
loam: **5** loess
mineral: **4** lode **10** concretion
muddy: **6** sludge
sand: **4** bank **5** beach
sedimentary: **4** silt
skeletal: **5** coral
stolen goods: **5** fence
stream: **8** alluvium, sediment
tooth: **6** tartar

deposition

6 burial **7** placing **8** sediment **9** testimony **10** testifying

depository

4 bank, safe **5** attic, store, vault **7** arsenal **8** magazine **10** storehouse
for bones: **7** ossuary

depot

4 bank, base, dump **5** store **6** armory **7** arsenal, station **8** magazine, terminal, terminus **9** warehouse **10** repository, storehouse **12** station house

deprave

4 warp **6** debase, malign **7** corrupt, debauch, pervert, vitiate **9** brutalize **10** bastardize, bestialize, demoralize

depraved

3 bad **4** evil, ugly, vile **6** putrid, rotten, warped, wicked **7** bestial, corrupt, debased, immoral, twisted, vicious, vitiate **8** degraded, perverse, vitiated **9** corrupted, debauched, miscreant, nefarious, perverted, unhealthy **10** degenerate, flagitious, villainous

depravity

4 vice **8** villainy **10** corruption, immorality, wickedness

deprecate

5 frown **6** object **7** detract **8** derogate, disfavor **9** disesteem **10** disapprove, discommend **12** disapprove of

depreciate

5 abate, abuse, decry, erode, lower **6** lessen, reduce, soften **7** cheapen, devalue, dwindle **8** belittle, decrease, derogate, diminish, discount, mark down, minimize, write off **9** devaluate, disparage, dispraise, downgrade, underrate, write down **10** devalorize, undervalue **11** detract from

depreciation

7 calumny, scandal, slander **8** discount **10** backbiting **12** backstabbing, belittlement **13** disparagement

depreciative

9 slighting **10** derogatory, detracting **11** disparaging, dyslogistic, underrating **12** undervaluing

depreciatory

see **depreciative**

depredate

4 sack **5** waste **6** devour, ravage **7** despoil, pillage, plunder **8** desolate, lay waste, prey upon, spoliate **9** desecrate, devastate

depredator

6 looter, raider **7** forager, spoiler **8** marauder **10** freebooter

depress

4 damp, dash, dent, fall, sink **5** chill, couch, demit, droop, lower, slump **6** dampen, deject, dismay, indent, sadden **7** decline, let down, oppress, trouble **8** contrist, dispirit, enfeeble **9** disparage, weigh down **10** discourage, dishearten

depressant

5 black, bleak **6** dismal, dreary, gloomy **9** cheerless **10** oppressive **11** dispiriting

depressed

3 bad, low, sad **4** blue, down, glum, sunk **6** broody, gloomy, glumpy, hollow, lonely, somber **7** hippish, letdown **8** dejected, downcast **9** woebegone **10** dispirited, lugubrious, melancholy, spiritless **11** downhearted, melancholic **12** disconsolate **13** disadvantaged

depressing

3 sad **4** blue **5** black, bleak, chill **6** dismal, dreary, gloomy, somber, triste **7** joyless **8** funereal, mournful

9 saddening **10** melancholy, oppressive **11** melancholic **13** disheartening

depression

3 dip, low, pit, sag **4** drop, hole, sink, vale **5** basin, blues, crash, dumps, gloom, notch, scoop, slump **6** cavity, crater, hollow, pocket, valley **7** cyclone, decline, sadness, sinkage, sinking **8** sinkhole **9** concavity **10** melancholy, stagnation **11** unhappiness **12** mournfulness
anatomical: **5** fossa, fovea **6** foveae (plural) **7** foveola, foveole **8** foveolae (plural), foveolet
between breasts: **8** cleavage
geographic: **7** Qattara
in ridge: **3** col
in snow: **8** sitzmark
small: **4** dent **6** dimple

depressive

see **depressant**

deprivation

4 loss **11** bereavement, deprivement, divestiture **13** dispossession

deprive

3 rob **4** bare, lose, oust **5** strip **6** denude, divest **7** bereave, disrobe **8** bankrupt, denudate, disseize **9** dismantle **10** disinherit, dispossess
of brilliancy: **4** dull **6** deaden
of courage: **7** unnerve
of sensation: **6** benumb
of sense and judgment: **9** inebriate
of virginity: **8** deflower

deprive of

prefix: **2** de **3** dis

depth

4 drop **5** abyss **7** lowness **8** deepness **9** acuteness **10** profundity **11** penetration **12** profoundness
combining form: **4** bath **5** batho, bathy
measure: **6** fathom
measuring instrument: **4** gage **5** gauge
of water: **5** draft **7** draught

depthless

7 cursory, shallow, sketchy **10** uncritical **11** superficial

dept. of ___

2 ed **3** agr, com, def, int **4** comm **5** labor, state, trans **7** justice

depurate

5 clean **6** purify **7** clarify, cleanse

deputize

8 delegate **10** commission

deputy

5 agent, proxy **6** factor **8** assignee, attorney, delegate **9** catchpole **12** representant
prefix: **2** co

derange

5 craze, upset **6** frenzy, madden, mess up, sicken **7** disturb, perturb, rummage, unhinge **8** disarray, disorder, distract, unsettle **9** interrupt, unbalance **10** discompose **11** disorganize

deranged

3 mad **5** crazy **6** crazed, insane, maniac **7** cracked, lunatic, unsound **8** demented **9** disturbed **10** disordered, unbalanced

derangement

6 lunacy **7** madness **8** disorder, insanity **9** confusion, unbalance **10** aberration, alienation, insaneness **11** distraction, disturbance, psychopathy, unsoundness

derby

3 hat **4** race, shoe **6** cheese **7** contest **9** horse race **10** field trial

derelict

3 bum, lax, vag **4** hobo, lorn **5** dingy, faded, leper, seedy, slack, tramp **6** pariah, remiss, shabby, unused **7** drifter, floater, Ishmael, outcast, run-down, uncouth, vagrant **8** careless, castaway, deserted, desolate, forsaken, solitary, vagabond **9** abandoned, forgotten, negligent **10** behindhand, delinquent, Ishmaelite, neglectful, regardless, street arab, threadbare, unreliable **11** dilapidated, offscouring, untouchable **12** disregardful, undependable **13** irresponsible, untrustworthy

dereliction

5 fault **7** default, failure, neglect **9** deviation, oversight **11** abandonment, delinquency, shortcoming

deride

4 lout, mock, quiz, razz, twit **5** fleer, rally, scoff, scout, taunt **7** catcall **8** ridicule

de rigueur

4 nice **5** right **6** au fait, decent, proper **7** correct **8** becoming, decorous **11** comme il faut

derision

4 butt, jest, joke, mock **5** sport **6** jestee **7** mockery **9** pilgarlic **13** laughingstock

derisive sound
3 boo 4 hiss

derivable
7 a priori 8 dogmatic, reasoned
9 deducible, deductive

derivation
4 root, well 6 origin, source,
whence 7 descent 8 fountain
9 etymology 10 provenance, wellspring 11 provenience

derivative
7 spin-off 8 offshoot 9 by-product,
outgrowth, secondary
10 descendant

derive
3 get 4 draw, stem, take 5 adapt,
educe, infer, judge 6 deduce, deduct, evolve, gather 7 acquire, collect, emanate, make out, work out
8 arrive at, conclude 9 formulate,
originate 10 excogitate

derive from
4 flow, head, rise, stem 5 arise, issue 6 spring 7 emanate, proceed
9 originate

dernier cri
3 cry, fad 4 chic, mode, rage
5 craze, style, vogue 6 furore
7 fashion 8 last word

derogate
5 decry 8 belittle, diminish, minimize, write off 9 disparage, dispraise 10 depreciate 11 detract
from, opprobriate

derogatory
5 snide 8 decrying, scornful, spiteful 9 degrading, demeaning, malicious, maligning, slighting, vilifying
10 belittling, calumnious, detracting, disdainful, malevolent, pejorative 11 disparaging, dyslogistic
12 contumelious, depreciative

derout
8 stampede

derrick
5 hoist

derriere
4 beam, rear, seat 5 fanny 6 behind, bottom 7 rear end 8 backside, buttocks 9 posterior

derring-do
5 nerve 7 bravado, bravery,
courage

dervish
4 monk 9 mendicant
cap: 3 taj
in Arabian Nights: 4 Agib

practice: 7 dancing, howling
8 whirling
wandering: 8 calender

descant
3 air, lay 4 aria, hymn, lied, sing,
song, tune 5 ditty 6 melody, remark, strain, warble 7 discuss, dissert, measure, melisma, melodia
8 diapason, dilate on 9 discourse,
expatiate, sermonize 10 dilate
upon, dissertate 11 observation
12 counterpoint

Descartes' axiom
13 cogito ergo sum

descend
3 rot 4 drop, fall, pass, sink
5 lower, stoop, swoop 6 alight, derive, go down, worsen 7 decline
8 come down 9 originate 10 degenerate, disimprove, retrograde,
spring from 11 deteriorate
12 disintegrate
by rope: 6 rappel

descendant
3 son 5 scion 7 progeny, spin-off
8 offshoot, relative 9 by-product,
outgrowth 10 derivative
suffix: 3 ite

descendants
4 seed 5 brood, issue 7 progeny
8 children 9 offspring, posterity
11 progeniture

descent
3 dip 4 drop, fall 5 birth, blood,
slope 6 origin 7 decline, drop-off,
incline, lineage, sinking 8 ancestry,
comedown, gradient, pedigree,
plunging, stooping 9 declivity,
downgrade 10 derivation, extraction, plummeting 11 origination
12 discomfiture
airplane: 8 approach
parachute: 4 jump 7 bailout

describe
4 limn 5 image, label, state 6 denote, depict, recite, relate, render,
report 7 explain, express, mark
out, narrate, outline, picture, portray, recount, signify 8 rehearse, vignette 9 chronicle, delineate, interpret, represent 10 illustrate
11 distinguish 12 characterize
grammatically: 5 parse

description
3 ilk 4 kind, sort, tale, type, yarn
5 story 6 nature 7 account, picture,
recital, variety, version 8 anecdote
9 character, chronicle, narrative,
portrayal, recountal 10 recounting
11 portraiture, presentment

descry
3 see 4 espy, find, mark, note,
spot, view 5 catch, hit on 6 behold, detect, spy out, turn up 7 discern, hit upon, observe 8 discover,
meet with, perceive 9 encounter
11 distinguish

Desdemona
father: 9 Brabantio
husband: 7 Othello
slanderer: 4 Iago
slayer: 7 Othello

desecrate
4 sack 5 waste 6 defile, devour,
ravage 7 despoil, pillage, profane
8 spoliate 9 depredate, devastate

desecration
9 blasphemy, sacrilege

desensitize
4 dull, mull, numb 5 blunt 6 benumb, deaden

desert
2 go 3 fly, rat 4 flee, quit, turn,
wild 5 chuck, leave, waste 6 barren, betray, decamp, defect, depart, escape, maroon, strand, Tan-
ami 7 abandon, abscond,
badland, forsake 8 Karakumy, renounce, wild land, wildness 9 repudiate, throw over, wasteland
10 apostatize, tergiverse, wilderness 12 tergiversate
African: 6 Libyan, Sahara 7 Arabian
8 Kalahari
Arizona: 7 Painted
Asian: 4 Gobi, Thar 6 Syrian
7 Kara Kum, Qara Qum 8 Kyzyl
Kum 10 Great Sandy
basin bottom: 5 playa
beast: 5 camel 9 dromedary
California: 6 Mohave, Mojave
clay: 5 adobe
combining form: 4 erem 5 eremo
dweller: 4 Arab 5 nomad 6 Berber,
Libyan, Malian, Nubian 8 Algerian, Egyptian, Maghrebi, Magh-
ribi, Sudanese 11 Mauritanian
fertile area: 5 oases (plural), oasis
garb: 3 aba
hallucination: 6 mirage
region: 3 erg
Saudi Arabia: 7 An Nafud
Sudan: 6 Nubian
travel group: 7 caravan
valley: 6 bolson
wind: 7 sirocco

deserted
4 bare, lorn 5 empty 6 barren, vacant 7 uncouth 8 derelict, desolate, forsaken, solitary 9 aban-

doned **10** unoccupied
11 uninhabited

deserter
3 rat **4** AWOL **6** bolter **7** runaway
8 apostate, fugitive, renegade, runagate, turncoat

desertion
7 perfidy **8** apostasy **9** falseness,
recreancy, treachery
11 abandonment

deserts
3 due **11** comeuppance

deserve
3 get, win **4** earn, gain, rate
5 merit **6** demand

deserved
3 due **4** just **5** right **7** condign,
merited **8** rightful, suitable **9** requisite **11** appropriate
13 rhadamanthine

deserving
3 due **5** lumps, merit **6** rights, worthy **8** laudable **9** admirable, estimable, meritable, praisable
11 comeuppance, commendable,
meritorious, thankworthy
12 praiseworthy

desexualize
3 fix **4** geld **5** alter, unsex
6 change, neuter **8** castrate,
mutilate

desiccate
3 dry **4** fade, sear **5** decay, drain,
dry up, parch, wizen **6** divest,
wither **7** deplete, exhaust, shrivel
9 dehydrate **10** devitalize

desiderate
4 want, wish **5** covet, crave
6 choose, desire

design
3 aim **4** cast, draw, form, mean,
mind, plan, plot, will **5** chart, de-
cal, draft, frame, model, motif
6 animus, create, device, devise,
devote, figure, intend, intent, invent, lay out, makeup, map out,
motive, scheme, set out, sketch
7 arrange, diagram, dope out,
drawing, execute, fashion, meaning, outline, pattern, prepare, produce, project, propose, purpose,
thought, tracing **8** conation, contrive, creation, game plan, intrigue,
strategy, thinking, volition **9** blueprint, construct, delineate, direction,
formation, intention, invention
10 decoration, figuration, intendment, reflection **11** arrangement,
composition, contemplate, delinea-

tion, disposition, machination
12 architecture, constitution, construction, deliberation
book: **6** fillet **8** vignette
carpet: **3** gul **9** medallion
incised: **8** intaglio
Indonesian: **5** batik
inlaid: **6** mosaic
of squares: **5** check
openwork: **8** filigree
perforated: **7** stencil
raised: **8** repoussé
skin: **6** tattoo
textile: **8** polka dot
velvety: **8** flocking

designate
3 dub, opt, tap **4** call, make,
name, pick, term **5** allot, elect, label, style, title **6** assign, choose, denote, depute, finger, induct, select,
single **7** appoint, baptize, declare,
dictate, earmark, entitle, mete out,
reserve, signify, specify **8** allocate,
christen, identify, stand for **9** apportion, stipulate **10** decide upon
11 appropriate **12** characterize

designation
4 name **5** nomen, style, title **6** naming **8** cognomen, monicker **9** allotment **10** indicating, pigeonhole
11 appellative, identifying
12 pigeonholing

designed
7 advised, decided, studied **8** prepense, resolved, studious **10** considered, deliberate, determined,
thought-out **12** aforethought,
premeditated

designedly
9 on purpose, purposely **10** prepensely **11** purposively **12** deliberately **13** intentionally

designless
4 spot **6** random **9** desultory, haphazard, hit-or-miss, unplanned
12 unconsidered

desirable
6 suited **7** optimal **9** excellent,
expedient

desire
3 aim, ask, yen **4** envy, eros, hope,
itch, like, long, lust, pant, pine,
urge, want, wish **5** covet, crave,
enjoy, fancy, greed, yearn **6** asking, aspire, choice, choose, hanker, hunger, pining, thirst **7** avarice, bespeak, craving, entreat,
impulse, longing, passion, request,
solicit **8** appetite, cupidity, petition,
rapacity, striving, yearning **9** appe-

tency, eroticism, hankering, hunger-
ing, prurience, pruriency, thirsting
10 aphrodisia, appetition, attraction, preference **11** inclination, lustfulness **13** concupiscence,
lickerishness
combining form: **6** orexia
for liquids: **6** thirst
restless: **4** itch

desired
4 true **5** right **6** proper **7** fitting
11 appropriate

desirous
5 itchy **6** grabby, greedy **7** athirst,
envious, wishful **8** appetent, covetous, grasping **10** prehensile, solicitous **11** acquisitive

desist
4 halt, quit, stop **5** cease, deval,
yield **6** resign **7** abandon, abstain,
forbear, hold off **8** give over, knock
off, leave off, surcease **10** relinquish **11** discontinue, refrain from

desistance
3 end **4** stop **5** cease, close **6** ending, finish, period **9** cessation
10 conclusion **11** termination

desk
5 booth, stand, table **7** counter, lectern, roll top **8** lapboard **9** secretary **10** escritoire, secretaire
adjunct: **8** inkstand, standish
item: **3** pad **7** blotter, inkwell
library: **6** carrel **7** carrell
Scottish: **3** pew

desman
3 fur **4** pelt **6** mammal

_____ de soie, French silk
4 peau

desolate
4 bare, dark, lorn, poor, sack
5 black, bleak, drear, empty,
murky, stark, waste **6** barren, devoid, devour, dismal, gloomy, ravage, ruined, somber, vacant **7** despoil, joyless, pillage, uncouth
8 bereaved, derelict, deserted, forsaken, funereal, lay waste, lifeless,
solitary, spoliate **9** abandoned,
cheerless, depredate, desecrate,
destitute, devastate, sorrowful
10 acheronian, unoccupied **11** dilapidated, uninhabited **12** inconsolable, unconsolable
13 disheartening

desolation
6 sorrow **7** sadness **9** wasteland
11 abandonment

despair
4 drop **5** yield **6** give up, resign **7** abandon **8** renounce **9** surrender **10** relinquish

despairing
7 cynical, forlorn **8** hopeless **9** depressed, oppressed **10** melancholy **11** atrabilious, melancholic, pessimistic, weighed down **12** misanthropic **13** brokenhearted

desperado
6 badman, bandit, outlaw **7** bandido, convict **8** criminal **10** lawbreaker

desperate
4 dire, rash **5** acute **6** balked, crying, fierce, foiled **7** baffled, crucial, forlorn, furious, heinous, intense, vicious, violent **8** critical, headlong, hopeless, reckless, shocking, terrible, thwarted, vehement **9** atrocious, exquisite, foolhardy, monstrous, outwitted **10** frustrated, outrageous, scandalous **11** climacteric, precipitate, venturesome **12** circumvented, concentrated, overpowering **13** irretrievable, overmastering, uncollectable

despicable
3 low **4** base, mean, ugly, vile **5** cheap, sorry **6** abject, scummy, scurvy, shabby, sordid **7** ignoble **8** beggarly, infamous, wretched **9** loathsome **11** disgraceful, ignominious **12** contemptible

despisable
see **despicable**

despise
4 hate, shun, snub **5** abhor, avoid, scorn, scout, spurn **6** detest, eschew, ignore, loathe, reject, slight **7** contemn, disdain **8** execrate, look down, misprize, overlook, renounce **9** abominate, disregard, repudiate

despised one
6 pariah

despisement
4 hate **5** scorn **6** hatred, malice **7** disdain, ill will **8** aversion, contempt, loathing **10** abhorrence **11** detestation, malevolence

despite
3 cut **4** harm, hate, hurt, slap, snub **5** altho, scorn **6** grudge, hatred, injury, insult, malice, rebuff, slight, spleen **7** affront, against, disdain, disgust, dislike, ill will **8** although, aversion, contempt, defiance, disfa-

vor, distaste, loathing, spurning **9** contumacy, contumely, indignity, insolence, in spite of, malignity, rejection **10** abhorrence, incivility, malignancy **11** abomination, detestation, discourtesy, indignation, in the face of, malevolence, repudiation **12** cold shoulder, regardless of, spitefulness, stubbornness **13** disparagement, maliciousness, recalcitrance

despiteful
4 evil **5** catty **6** bitchy, wicked **7** vicious **9** malicious, rancorous **10** malevolent

despoil
4 sack **5** blast, strip, waste, wreck **6** denude, devour, ravage **7** pillage, plunder **8** desolate, spoliate **9** depredate, desecrate, devastate, strip away, wrest away

despoiler
6 looter, ruiner, sacker, vandal **7** defacer, forager, wrecker **8** marauder, pillager, ruinator **9** destroyer, plunderer, spoliator **10** depredator, freebooter

Despoina
8 mistress **10** Persephone
husband: **5** Hades
realm: **10** underworld

despond
3 sag **4** mope **5** brood, droop **6** give up **8** languish

despondency
5 blues, dumps, gloom **6** misery, sorrow **7** despair **9** dejection **10** blue devils, depression, melancholy

despondent
3 sad **7** forlorn **8** dejected, downcast, grieving, hopeless, mourning **9** depressed, sorrowful, woebegone **10** dispirited, melancholy **11** discouraged **12** disconsolate, disheartened

despot
4 duce **5** ruler **6** tyrant **7** autarch, emperor **8** autocrat, dictator **9** oppressor, strong man

despotic
8 absolute, tyrannic **9** arbitrary, autarchic, tyrannous **10** autocratic, monocratic, tyrannical

despotism
7 tsarism, tyranny, tzarism **8** autarchy **9** autocracy **10** domination **12** dictatorship

despotize
7 dictate, oppress **8** dominate, domineer, overlord **9** tyrannize

desquamate
4 peel **5** scale **7** peel off **8** flake off, scale off **9** exfoliate

dessert
3 ice, pie **4** cake, flan, fool, tart **5** Betty, bombe, coupe, fruit, grunt, halva, melba, slump, torte **6** afters, cheese, Danish, éclair, frappe, gateau, halvah, hermit, junket, kuchen, mousse, pastry, sorbet, sundae, trifle **7** cassata, cobbler, custard, gelatin, mazarin, parfait, pudding, sabayon, sherbet, spumone, spumoni, strudel **8** Bismarck, flummery, ice cream, marquise, napoleon, pandowdy, streusel, taiglach, teiglach, turnover **9** charlotte, cream puff, petit four, shortcake **10** blancmange, brown Betty, cheesecake, frangipane, marguerite, zabaglione **11** baked Alaska, banana split, gingerbread **12** hasty pudding, zuppa inglese
chilled: **6** mousse
custard: **8** zabaione, zabaione
French: **5** bombe **6** éclair, frappe, gateau, mousse **7** mazarin, parfait, sabayon **8** marquise **9** petit four **10** blancmange, frangipane
frozen: **5** bombe **7** parfait, sherbet **8** sherbert
German: **6** kuchen **7** strudel
Italian: **7** cannoli, cassata, spumone, spumoni **10** zabaglione **12** zuppe inglese
Jewish: **8** taiglach, teiglach
pastry: **6** quiche
soft: **3** pud **7** pudding
Turkish: **5** halva **6** halvah

destination
3 end, use **6** object **7** purpose **10** appointing

destine
3 fix **4** fate **6** assign, decree, devise, direct, doom to, intend **7** preform **8** dedicate, set aside **9** determine, preordain **10** foreordain **12** predetermine

destiny
3 lot **4** doom, fate, goal **5** moira, weird **6** design, future, intent, kismat, kismet **7** fortune, portion **9** intention, objective **12** circumstance

destitute
4 bare, poor, void **5** empty, needy **6** bereft, devoid **7** drained **8** bankrupt, depleted, dirt poor, divested, indigent, innocent, stripped **9** defi-

cient, exhausted, penurious
10 bankrupted, stone-broke 11 impecunious, necessitous
12 impoverished
of water: 9 anhydrous

destitute of
prefix: 2 an
suffix: 4 less

destitution
4 lack, need, want 6 dearth, penury 7 absence, poverty 9 adversity, indigence, neediness
10 misfortune

destroy
3 zap 4 doom, down, kill, raze, ruin, sack, slay, undo, wipe
5 fordo, havoc, shoot, smash, total, waste, wrack, wreck 6 cut off, finish, foredo, injure, lay low, mangle, quench, ravage, rubble, rub out, unmake 7 abolish, atomize, nullify, pillage, put away, ruinate, shatter, subvert, take off, unbuild, unframe, wipe out 8 carry off, decimate, demolish, dispatch, dissolve, dynamite, fumigate, mutilate, pull down, sabotage, tear down 9 devastate, discreate, dismantle, eradicate, extirpate, pulverize 10 annihilate, counteract, decapitate, extinguish, neutralize 11 exterminate
suffix: 4 lyse, lyze

destroyer
4 bane, ruin 6 ruiner, tin can, vandal 7 defacer, undoing, warship, wrecker 8 downfall, ruinator 9 despoiler, ruination
combining form: 4 cide 5 clast
7 clastic, phthora

destroying
combining form: 5 cidal 7 clastic
prefix: 3 ant 4 anth, anti

destruction
4 bane, loss, ruin 5 havoc 7 killing, undoing 8 downfall 9 confusion 10 impairment
combining form: 4 lyses (plural) 5 lysis 6 clasia, clasis

destructive
5 fatal 6 deadly, lethal, mortal
7 baneful, ruinous 8 wrackful, wreckful 9 injurious 10 calamitous, disastrous, shattering 11 deleterious, detrimental

desuetude
3 end 5 cease, close 6 disuse, ending 7 closing, closure, neglect 8 disusage 9 cessation 10 conclusion, suspension 11 abandonment

desultory
6 casual, catchy, fickle, fitful, random, spotty 7 aimless, erratic, vagrant 8 shifting, sporadic, wavering 9 haphazard, hit-or-miss, mercurial, spasmodic, unplanned
10 capricious, designless, digressive, disorderly, inconstant 11 purposeless 12 unconsidered, unmethodical, unsystematic

detach
4 part, wean 5 sever, unfix 6 cut off, sunder, unhang 7 disjoin, divorce 8 abstract, dismount, disunite, separate, uncouple, withdraw 9 disengage, dismantle, dismember 10 disconnect, dissociate 11 disassemble 12 disaffiliate, disassociate

detached
5 alone, aloof, apart 6 casual, remote 7 distant, isolate, neutral, removed 8 abstract, isolated, separate, unbiased 9 colorless, incurious, uncurious, withdrawn
10 impersonal, poker-faced
11 indifferent, unconcerned, unconnected, unpassioned 12 uninterested 13 disinterested, dispassionate, unaccompanied
combining form: 2 ap 3 aph, apo

detachment
7 divorce, rupture, split up 8 disunion, division 9 partition 10 neutrality, separation 11 dissolution, divorcement 12 unworldliness
combining form: 5 lyses (plural), lysis

detail
4 item, list, part 5 point, thing 6 assign, relate, report 7 article, element, listing, minutia, program, specify 8 elements, minutiae (plural) 9 enumerate, stipulate
10 brass tacks (plural), particular
11 specificate, specificize
12 circumstance 13 particularize

detailed
4 full 6 minute 7 copious 8 abundant, itemized, thorough 9 clocklike 10 blow-by-blow, exhausting, exhaustive, particular
13 thoroughgoing

detain
3 nab 4 bust, curb, hold, keep, mire 5 check, delay, embog, pinch, run in 6 arrest, hang up, pick up, pull in, retard, slow up 7 bog down, inhibit, keep out, reserve, set back, slacken 8 hold back, keep back, restrain, slow down, withhold 9 apprehend
10 buttonhole, decelerate
in conversation: 10 buttonhole

detect
4 espy, find, spot 5 catch, hit on 6 descry, turn up 7 discern, hit upon, rectify 8 discover, meet with 9 ascertain, encounter
10 demodulate

detectable
8 sensible, tangible 11 perceptible

detecting device
5 radar, sonar 6 solion 7 antenna, sferics 8 spherics 13 Geiger counter

detection
4 find 6 espial, strike 9 discovery
10 laying open, unearthing
system: 5 radar, sofar

detective
3 tec 4 dick, G-man 5 roper 6 shamus, sleuth 7 gumshoe, shoofly 8 hawkshaw, informer, Sherlock 9 inspector 12 investigator 13 police officer
fictional: 4 Chan (Charlie), Moto (Mr.) 5 Dupin (Auguste), Lecoq, Lupin (Arsene), Spade (Sam), Trent (Philip) 6 Carter (Nick), Holmes (Sherlock), Poirot (Hercule), Wimsey (Peter) 7 Charles (Nick, Nora)
11 Father Brown

detective story writer
3 Poe (Edgar Allan) 5 Doyle (Arthur Conan), James (Phyllis Dorothy), Queen (Ellery), Stout (Rex) 6 Parker (Robert), Sayers (Dorothy) 7 Bentley (Edmund Clerihew), Biggers (Earl), Collins (Wilkie), Fleming (Ian), Gardner (Erle Stanley), Hammett (Dashiell) 8 Chandler (Raymond), Christie (Agatha), Gaboriau (Emile), Marquand (John) 10 Chesterton (Gilbert Keith)

detent
3 dog 4 pawl 5 catch, click

detention
3 nab 5 delay, pinch 6 arrest, pickup 10 arrestment, internment
12 apprehension, imprisonment

deter
5 avert, block, debar, scare 6 divert, hinder, impede 7 forfend, inhibit, obviate, prevent, rule out, shut out, ward off 8 dissuade, frighten, obstruct, preclude, restrain, stave off 9 disadvise, forestall, turn aside
10 discourage

deterge
7 cleanse, wash off

detergent
4 soap 6 alkali 8 cleanser
9 cleansing

deteriorate

3 mar, rot 4 fade, fail, flag, sink
5 decay, dwine, spoil 6 impair,
lessen, weaken, worsen 7 crumble,
decline, descend 8 languish 9 decompose, undermine 10 debilitate,
depreciate, disimprove, retrograde

deterioration

4 ruin 5 decay 6 dry rot, ebbing,
waning 7 atrophy, decline, ero-
sion, failure, rotting 8 decaying,
downfall, spoiling 9 crumbling,
decadence, downgrade, lessening
10 debasement, declension,
degeneracy, impairment
12 dégringolade

determinant

4 gene, mark 5 agent, cause, trait
6 factor, reason, weight 7 radical
8 occasion 9 attribute, authority,
influence 10 antecedent
11 differentia

determinate

4 spot 5 fixed, place 6 cymose, finger, narrow 7 limited, precise, settled 8 constant, definite, diagnose,
identify, pinpoint 9 arbitrary, ascertain, immovable, immutable, recognize 10 definitive, inflexible, invariable, restricted 11 distinguish,
established, inalterable, unalterable
12 unchangeable, unmodifiable
13 circumscribed, diagnosticate

determination

6 fixing 7 purpose, resolve 8 decision, firmness 9 resolving 10 conclusion, settlement 11 decidedness
12 resoluteness 13 purposiveness

determine

3 end, fix, see, set 4 bias, fate,
halt, hear, move, rule, show
5 bound, close, drive, impel, learn,
limit, prove 6 decide, direct, doom
to, figure, finish, induce, ordain,
settle, tumble, wind up, wrap up
7 actuate, catch on, control, delimit,
destine, dispose, find out, incline,
make out, mark out, measure, preform, purpose, resolve, unearth
8 complete, conclude, discover,
persuade, regulate, ultimate 9 ascertain, demarcate, establish, preordain, resolve on, terminate
10 delimitate, foreordain, predestine, predispose 11 demonstrate

determined

3 set 4 bent 6 intent 7 decided,
earnest, serious, settled 8 decisive,
hellbent, resolute, resolved 10 purposeful, unwavering 11 unfaltering
12 unhesitating

detest

4 hate 5 abhor, spurn 6 loathe, reject 7 despise, dislike 8 execrate
9 abominate, repudiate

detestable

4 foul, vile 5 sorry 6 damned, horrid, odious 7 hateful, heinous
9 abhorrent, execrable, loathsome
10 abominable, despicable
12 contemptible

detestation

4 hate 6 hatred, horror 7 bugbear,
disgust, dislike 8 anathema,
aversion, loathing 9 antipathy,
bête noire, repulsion, revulsion
10 abhorrence, black beast,
repugnance

dethrone

6 depose, divest, unmake 7 uncrown 8 discrown, displace

detonate

5 burst, go off 6 blow up 7 explode 8 mushroom

detonator

3 cap 4 fuse, fuze 9 explosive
11 blasting cap

detour

5 avoid, skirt 6 bypass 7 deflect
9 deviation, runaround 10 circumvent, roundabout

detract

4 draw 5 decry, libel 6 divert,
lessen, reduce 7 slander 8 belittle,
decrease, derogate, diminish, discount, minimize, write off 9 disparage, dispraise 10 depreciate

detracting

8 libelous 9 maligning, traducing,
vilifying 10 calumnious, defamatory, derogatory, pejorative, scandalous, slanderous 11 disparaging,
dyslogistic 12 depreciative,
depreciatory

detraction

4 harm, hurt, tale 5 libel, wrong
6 damage, injury 7 calumny, scandal, slander 8 libeling 9 aspersion,
injustice, maligning, traducing
10 backbiting, slandering, sycophancy 12 backstabbing, belittlement 13 disparagement

detriment

4 harm, hurt 6 damage, injury
7 marring 8 drawback, handicap,
mischief, spoiling 10 disability
12 disadvantage

detrimental

3 bad, ill 4 evil 7 adverse, harmful, hurtful, nocuous 8 damaging,

negative 9 injurious 11 deleterious,
mischievous, unfavorable

detritus

4 tufa, tuff 5 scree, talus 6 debris

Detroit

county: 5 Wayne
founder: 8 Cadillac (Sieur de)
lake: 4 Erie 10 Saint Clair
sobriquet: 6 Motown 9 Motor City

de trop

5 extra, spare 6 excess 7 surplus
11 superfluent, superfluous
13 supernumerary

detruncate

3 top 4 crop 7 pollard

Deucalion

father: 10 Prometheus
kingdom: 6 Phthia
mother: 7 Clymene
son: 6 Hellen
wife: 6 Pyrrha

Deuel's son

8 Eliasaph

Deutschland über ___

4 alles

dev, deva

3 god

Devaki's son

7 Krishna

deval

4 halt, quit, stop 5 cease 6 desist
8 give over, knock off, leave off,
surcease 11 discontinue

De Valera

5 Eamon

devaluate

5 decry, lower 8 mark down, write
off 9 underrate, write down
10 depreciate, undervalue

devaluation

7 atrophy, decline 8 downfall
9 decadence 10 declension,
degeneracy

devalue

see **depreciate**

devastate

4 sack 6 devour, ravage 7 despoil,
pillage 8 desolate, lay waste, overcome, spoliate 9 depredate, desecrate, overpower, overwhelm

devastation

4 loss, ruin 5 havoc 9 confusion

devel

3 hit 4 biff, ding, nail, sock 5 clout,
slosh, smite, whack 6 strike

develop

2 go 3 age, get 4 form, gain,

grow, ripe **5** break, occur, phase, reach, ripen **6** attain, befall, betide, chance, dilate, enroot, evolve, expand, grow up, happen, lay out, mature, mellow, obtain, open up, thrive, unfold, unfurl **7** achieve, acquire, advance, amplify, burgeon, come off, convert, enlarge, expound, fall out, prepare, promote, prosper, realize **8** flourish, maturate **9** actualize, elaborate, establish, transpire **11** come to light, materialize **13** differentiate
rapidly: **7** burgeon **8** bourgeon

development
5 phase **6** growth, phasis **7** advance, ongoing **8** ontogeny, progress, upgrowth **9** evolution, expansion, flowering, phylogeny, unfolding **11** elaboration, progression
combining form: **5** plasy **6** plasia, plasto
of life: **10** biogenesis

Devi
7 goddess
consort: **4** Siva
father: **7** Himavat
name: **3** Uma **4** Kali **5** Durga, Gauri **6** Chandi **7** Parvati

deviant
6 off-key **8** aberrant, abnormal, atypical **9** anomalous, divergent, irregular, unnatural, unregular, untypical **11** heteroclite **13** preternatural

deviate
3 err, yaw **4** veer **5** sheer, stray **6** depart, swerve, wander **7** digress, diverge, pervert **9** turn aside **13** sexual pervert

deviation
3 yaw **4** bend, tack, turn **5** error, fault, lapse, shift **6** breach, change, double **7** anomaly, blunder, failing, turning, veering **9** departure, diversion **10** divergence **13** transgression

device
4 play, ploy, tool, type, wile, will **5** feint, motif, motto, shift, trick **6** design, desire, dingus, emblem, figure, gadget, gambit, hickey, motive, resort, scheme, symbol **7** gimmick, machine, pattern, project, utensil **8** artifice, creation, insignia, maneuver, resource **9** apparatus, appliance, attribute, doohickey, expedient, implement, invention, makeshift, mechanism, stratagem

10 instrument, thingumbob **11** contraption, contrivance, inclination
automatic: **5** servo
baseball: **11** batting cage
binding: **5** clamp
combining form: **4** stat
cooking: **7** hibachi
electrical: **8** inverter
electronic: **7** vocoder
energy changing: **9** converter, convertor
fastening: **6** zipper
grasping: **4** tong
heating: **8** radiator
hoisting: **5** lewis **8** lewisson
holding: **4** vise **5** clamp
in an airplane: **7** gosport
irrigation: **6** shaduf **7** shadoof
light-generating: **7** lampion
literary: **5** irony
mechanical: **6** gadget
oil lamp: **8** pickwick
remote-control: **6** selsyn **7** synchro
respiratory: **8** pulmotor
restraining: **8** holdback
seed-sewing: **11** broadcaster
ship's: **7** euphroe
speed of rotation: **4** tach
stabilizing: **8** gyrostat
temperature measurement: **7** thermal
warning: **5** siren
weighing: **5** scale, trone
wiretapping: **3** bug

devil
4 deil, haze, limb **5** annoy, beast, brute, demon, error, fiend, knave, rogue, Satan, scamp, tease **6** Belial, Cloots, diablo, dybbuk, pester, rascal, spirit **7** caitiff, Clootie, dickens, Lucifer, Old Nick, serpent, tempter, torment, villain **8** Apollyon, Mephisto, mischief, scalawag, Succubus **9** Archfiend, Beelzebub, cacodemon, scoundrel, skeezicks **10** blackguard, Old Scratch **11** firecracker, rapscallion **13** Old Gooseberry
combining form: **6** diabol **7** diabolo

devil-devil
4 rune **5** charm, spell **11** conjuration, incantation

devilfish
3 ray **5** manta **7** octopus **10** cephalopod

devilish
3 bad **4** evil **6** cursed, wicked **7** demonic, extreme, satanic **8** accursed, damnable, demoniac, demonian, diabolic, fiendish **9** excessive, execrable, nefarious **10** diabolical, iniquitous, serpen-

tine, unhallowed, villainous **11** diabolonian, excessively

devilkin
3 imp

devil-may-care
3 gay **4** fast, rash, wild **6** rakish, sporty **7** raffish **8** rakehell, reckless

devilment
see **deviltry**

devilry
see **deviltry**

devil's-bones
4 dice, tats **5** cubes, ivory

deviltry
7 roguery, waggery **8** mischief **9** diablerie **11** roguishness, waggishness **12** sportiveness

devious
3 sly **4** foxy **5** stray **6** artful, astray, crafty, errant, erring, remote, roving, secret, shifty, sneaky, tricky, unfair **7** bending, crooked, cunning, curving, erratic, obscure, removed, retired, winding **8** aberrant, guileful, indirect, lonesome, sneaking, twisting **9** diverting, underhand, wandering **10** digressing, roundabout

devise
4 cast, form, plan, plot, will **5** chart, forge, frame, leave, shape **6** cook up, create, design, invent, legacy, legate, make up, scheme, vamp up **7** arrange, bequest, collude, concoct, connive, dope out, dream up, hatch up, project **8** bequeath, cogitate, collogue, conspire, contrive, discover, intrigue, property **9** blueprint, determine, formulate, machinate, scheme for, scheme out **11** inheritance

devitalize
5 dry up **6** weaken **7** deprive, destroy **9** desiccate **10** eviscerate

devoid
4 bare **5** empty **6** barren **7** lacking, wanting **8** free from, innocent **9** deficient, destitute

devoir
3 job **4** duty, must, need, task **5** chare, chore, ought, right, stint **6** charge **9** committal **10** assignment, commitment, obligation

devolution
7 atrophy, decline, passing **8** downfall, receding, transfer **9** conferral, decadence, recession **10** declension, degeneracy, regres-

sion **12** dégringolade, retrograding, transference **13** retrogression

devolve
4 pass **8** hand down, transfer

devote
3 try, use, vow **4** bend, damn, doom, give, turn **5** apply, throw **6** addict, adjust, attach, bestow, commit, direct, donate, employ, give up, hallow, strive, take to, wrap up **7** address, attempt, confide, consign, entrust, hand out, present, provide, utilize **8** dedicate, endeavor, give away, sanctify, struggle **9** confirm in, habituate **10** buckle down, consecrate

devoted
4 dear, fond, true **5** loyal **6** ardent, doting, fervid, loving **7** zealous **8** constant, faithful, lovesome **10** thoughtful **12** affectionate
religiously: **6** oblate

devotee
3 fan **4** buff **5** hound, lover **6** addict, votary **7** admirer, amateur, fancier, habitué **8** follower **9** supporter **10** aficionado, enthusiast
suffix: **3** ite

devotion
4 love, zeal **5** ardor, piety **6** fealty, fervor, prayer **7** loyalty, passion **8** fidelity, fondness **9** reverence **10** allegiance, attachment, enthusiasm **12** faithfulness
combining form: **5** latry
religious: **6** novena

devour
3 eat **4** meal, ruin, sack, take, wolf **5** eat up, enjoy, use up, waste, wreck **6** absorb, engulf, feed on, ingest, ravage, relish **7** consume, despoil, destroy, exhaust, feast on, gloat on, pillage, revel in **8** demolish, desolate, dispatch, prey upon, spoliate, squander **9** delight in, depredate, desecrate, devastate, dissipate, feast upon, gloat over, partake of, polish off, rejoice in, swallow up **10** annihilate

devouring
4 avid **6** greedy **9** voracious
combining form: **6** vorous

devout
4 holy **5** godly, pious **6** ardent, fervid, hearty **7** adoring, fervent, sincere, zealous **8** reverent, revering **9** pietistic, prayerful, religious **10** venerating, worshiping

devoutness
5 piety

dew
3 wet **5** sweat, tears **8** moisture **12** perspiration

dexter
5 right, white **6** benign, bright **9** favorable, fortunate **10** auspicious, propitious

dexterity
3 art **5** craft, skill **7** address, cunning, know-how, prowess, sleight **8** deftness **9** adeptness, expertise, readiness **10** adroitness, smoothness **12** skillfulness

dexterous
3 sly **4** deft, easy, slim **5** adept, agile, canny, coony, handy **6** adroit, artful, clever, expert, facile, nimble, smooth **7** cunning, skilled **8** masterly, skillful, sleighty **9** ingenious **10** effortless, neat-handed, proficient

diablerie
3 sin **4** evil, tort **5** crime, wrong **7** devilry, roguery, sorcery, waggery **8** deviltry, iniquity, mischief, satanism **9** devilment **10** black magic, wickedness, witchcraft, wrongdoing **11** roguishness, waggishness **12** sportiveness

diablo
5 devil, fiend, Satan **7** Lucifer, Old Nick, serpent **8** Apollyon **9** Beelzebub **10** Old Scratch **13** Old Gooseberry

diabolic
4 evil **6** wicked **7** demonic, satanic **8** demoniac, demonian, devilish, fiendish **10** serpentine, unhallowed **11** diabolonian

diabolism
see **diablerie**

diacritic
5 breve, haček, tilde **6** macron, proper **7** cedilla **8** dieresis, peculiar **9** diaeresis **10** circumflex, individual **11** distinctive **13** idiosyncratic
Arabic: **5** hamza **6** hamzah

diadem
5 crown **6** empire **8** headband **11** sovereignty

diagnose
4 spot **5** place **6** finger **8** identify, pinpoint **9** recognize **11** determinate, distinguish

diagnostic
6 proper **8** peculiar **9** diacritic

10 indicating, indicative, individual **11** distinctive **13** idiosyncratic

diagonal
4 bias **5** bevel **6** biased **7** beveled, slanted **8** inclined, slanting **9** slantways

diagonally
8 bendwise **9** slantwise **10** cornerwise **11** catercorner, catty-corner, kitty-corner, slaunchways **12** slantingways

diagram
5 chart, graph **7** isotype **9** represent

dial
3 map, mug, pan **4** face, phiz, puss, tune **6** kisser, visage **7** control **8** features **10** manipulate **11** countenance

dialect
4 cant **5** argot, idiom, koine, lingo, slang **6** jargon, patois, patter, speech, tongue **8** language, localism **10** vernacular **11** regionalism, terminology **13** provincialism
Georgia: **6** Gullah
London: **7** cockney

dialectic
5 logic **6** debate **7** mooting **8** forensic **11** disputation **13** argumentation

dialogue
4 chat, talk **6** parley **8** colloquy, converse **12** conversation **13** confabulation

diameter
5 chord **8** bisector **9** thickness

diametric
5 polar **7** counter, opposed, reverse **8** contrary, converse, opposite **9** antipodal **10** antipodean **12** antithetical **13** contradictory

diamond
3 gem **5** stone **6** bright **9** brilliant, sparkling
baseball: **7** infield
element: **6** carbon
famous: **4** Hope, Pitt **5** Sancy **6** Orloff, Regent **8** Braganza, Cullinan, Kohinoor **9** Excelsior **10** Great Mogul
holder: **3** dop **4** dopp
inferior: **4** bort **5** boart, bortz
oval: **9** briolette
playing card: **7** lozenge
state: **8** Delaware
surface: **5** facet

Diana
see **Artemis**

Diana monkey
7 roloway

diapason
3 air, lay 4 tune 5 range, scope 6 melody, strain, warble 7 compass, descant, measure, melisma, melodia 10 tuning fork

diaper
4 didy 5 didie, nappy 6 nappie

diaphanous
5 filmy, gauzy, sheer, vague 6 flimsy 7 tiffany 8 ethereal, gossamer 11 transparent 13 insubstantial

diaphragm
4 stop 9 partition
combining form: 5 phren 6 phreni, phreno

diarist
1 Gide (André) 5 Frank (Anne), Pepys (Samuel), Scott (Walter) 6 Burney (Fanny) 7 Boswell (James) 8 Robinson (Henry) 10 chronicler, journalist

diary
6 record 7 daybook, diurnal, journal, logbook 8 register 9 chronicle

diaskeuast
6 editor

diastase
6 enzyme

diatribe
6 tirade 7 polemic 8 harangue, jeremiad 9 criticism, philippic

dibs
4 gelt 5 blunt, brass, bread, chips, claim, dough, money, syrup, title 6 dinero, do-re-mi, rights 7 cabbage 8 pretense 10 pretension 11 reservation

dice
4 cast, shed, tats 5 bones, cubes, ivory, scrap 6 reject, slough 7 cashier, checker, discard 8 jettison, throw out 9 throw away 11 devil's-bones
combining form: 8 astragal 9 astragalo
game: 5 craps
losing throw: 7 missout
singular: 3 die
throw: 7 boxcars 9 snake eyes

dicer
7 gambler

dichotomize
4 part 5 sever 6 divide, sunder 7 break up, disjoin, dissect 8 disjoint, disunite, separate

dichotomous
9 bifurcate

dichotomy
7 forking 9 bisection, branching, splitting 11 bifurcation

Dickens
birthplace: 10 Portsmouth
captain: 6 Cuttle
character: 3 Pip, Tim 4 Dora, Gamp, Nell 5 Fagin 6 Bumble, Carton, Cuttle, Darnay, Dombey, Oliver 7 Barnaby, Defarge, Manette, Scrooge, Tiny Tim 8 Micawber, Pickwick 9 Bill Sikes, Pecksniff, Uriah Heep 10 Chuzzlewit
hero: 6 Carton (Sidney)
nationality: 7 English
pen name: 3 Boz
villain: 5 Fagin
work: 9 Hard Times 10 Bleak House 11 Oliver Twist 12 Barnaby Rudge 15 Tale of Two Cities 16 David Copperfield 17 Great Expectations

dicker
4 deal, swap 6 barter, haggle, higgle, palter 7 bargain, chaffer 8 huckster 11 negotiation

dickey
4 weak 5 gilet, shaky 6 unsure, wobbly 8 insecure, rootless, unstable, wavering 9 fluctuant 10 shirtfront 11 vacillating

dictate
3 bid, say, set 4 lead, rule, tell, word 5 guide, order, speak, utter 6 behest, charge, decree, diktat, direct, enjoin, govern, impose, manage, ordain, recite 7 bidding, command, control, lay down, mandate, read off 8 instruct 9 directive, prescribe 10 injunction 12 prescription

dictative
8 dogmatic 11 doctrinaire, magisterial 13 authoritarian

dictator
4 duce 6 despot, tyrant 7 arbiter 8 martinet 9 oppressor, strong man 10 magistrate
German: 6 Hitler (Adolf)
Italian: 9 Mussolini (Benito)
military: 8 caudillo
Spanish: 6 Franco (Francisco)

dictatorial
4 firm 5 bossy, proud, stern 7 haughty 8 absolute, arrogant, despotic, dogmatic 9 arbitrary, imperious, masterful 10 autocratic, imperative, peremptory, tyrannical 11 doctrinaire, domineering,

overbearing 12 totalitarian 13 authoritarian, authoritative

dictatorship
7 tyranny 9 autocracy, Caesarism, despotism 10 absolutism

diction
6 phrase 7 wordage, wording 8 parlance, phrasing, verbiage 9 verbalism 11 phraseology
suffix: 3 ese

dictionary
4 cant 6 jargon 7 lexicon, palaver 8 language, wordbook 10 repository, vocabulary 11 terminology 13 reference book
compiler: 7 Johnson (Samuel), Webster (Noah) 13 lexicographer
geographical: 9 gazetteer
of prosody: 6 gradus
of synonyms: 8 thesauri (plural) 9 thesaurus

dictum
4 rule 5 axiom, gnome, maxim, moral 6 saying, truism 7 brocard, opinion 8 aphorism, apothegm 9 statement 13 pronouncement

didactic
3 dry 5 moral 6 teachy 7 preachy 8 advisory, sermonic 9 hortative 10 moralizing, preceptive 11 exhortative, sermonizing

diddle
3 gyp 4 beat, bilk, hoax, idle, laze, loaf, loll, take 5 cheat, cozen, drone 6 chouse, dawdle, delude, loiter, lounge 7 defraud 8 lallygag 9 overreach, waste time

diddler
3 gyp 5 cheat 6 con man 7 grifter, sharper 9 defrauder, trickster 12 double-dealer 13 confidence man

dido
3 toy 5 curio, frill 6 bauble, gewgaw, trifle 7 bibelot, trinket, whatnot 8 furbelow, gimcrack 10 knickknack

Dido
6 Elissa
brother: 9 Pygmalion
city founded by: 8 Carthage
father: 5 Belus 6 Mutton
husband: 7 Acerbas 8 Sichaeus
lover: 6 Aeneas

Dido and Aeneas composer
7 Purcell (Henry)

die
3 ebb, pip 4 bate, conk, dado, drop, fall, fate, long, mold, pass,

stop, wane **5** abate, block, cease, croak, let up, swelt **6** cash in, chance, cop out, demise, depart, expire, kick in, matrix, peg out, perish, pop off, recede **7** decease, ease off, fortune, kick off, pass out, slacken, subside, succumb **8** check out, languish, moderate, pass away, snuff out **9** disappear, grow faint
from hunger: **6** starve
loaded: **6** fulham, fullam

___ die
4 sine **3** bis in (twice a day), ter in (thrice a day) **6** quater in (four times a day)

die-away
4 limp **7** languid **8** listless **9** enervated **10** languorous, spiritless **11** languishing **13** lackadaisical

diehard
4 tory **5** blimp, fixed, right, white **7** Bourbon, old fogy **8** mossback, old liner, pullback, rightist, royalist, standpat, true blue **9** right wing **10** praetorian **11** bitter-ender, reactionary, reactionist, right-center, right-winger, standpatter **12** conservative, intransigent **13** reactionarist, stick-in-the-mud

___ diem
5 carpe

Dies ___
4 Irae **7** faustus

diet
4 fast, feed **8** assembly **10** parliament

Diet of ___
5 Worms **6** Speyer, Spires **8** Augsburg

___ -dieu
4 prie

Dieu ___ , British motto
10 et mon droit

differ
3 jar **4** vary **5** argue, clash **6** bicker, debate, depart, divide, oppose **7** deviate, discord, dispute, dissent, diverge, quarrel **8** conflict, disagree, squabble **9** disaccord

difference
4 know **5** clash, sever **6** change, effect, strife **7** discern, discord, dissent **8** alterity, conflict, disunity, separate, variance **9** disaccord, extricate, otherness, variation **10** contention, discrepate, dissension, divergency, severalize, unlikeness

11 controversy, discrepancy, distinction, distinguish **12** disagreement, discriminate, dissemblance, modification **13** dissimilarity, dissimilitude
slight: **5** shade **8** hairline

different
5 other **6** divers, single, sundry, unlike **7** another, distant, diverse, several, special, unalike, unequal, unusual, various **8** discrete, distinct, opposite, peculiar, separate **9** disparate, divergent, otherwise, unsimilar **10** dissimilar, individual, particular **11** distinctive
combining form: **3** all **4** allo **5** heter **6** hetero **7** diversi

differentiate
4 know **5** sever **7** discern **8** separate **9** extricate **10** comprehend, discrepate, severalize, understand **11** distinguish **12** discriminate

difficult
4 hard **6** uphill **7** arduous, awkward, labored, obscure, operose, problem **8** perverse, puzzling, stubborn, toilsome **9** effortful, hampering, laborious, strenuous **11** problematic
combining form: **4** mogi
prefix: **3** dys

difficulty
3 fix, jam **4** beef, nodi (plural) **4** pass, snag **5** cavil, demur, fight, nodus, pinch, rigor **6** bother, hassle, pickle, plight, scrape, strait **7** dilemma, dispute, pitfall, problem, protest, quarrel, trouble **8** asperity, demurral, demurrer, exigency, hardness, hardship, obstacle, quandary, question, squabble **9** bickering, challenge, emergency, objection **10** falling-out, impediment **11** altercation, arduousness, controversy, obstruction, predicament, vicissitude **12** disagreement, remonstrance **13** embarrassment, inconvenience, remonstration

diffidence
7 modesty, reserve **8** distrust **11** bashfulness

diffident
3 coy, shy **5** timid **6** demure, modest **7** bashful **8** hesitant, retiring **9** blenching, flinching, reluctant, shrinking, unassured **11** distrustful, unassertive **12** self-effacing

difform
6 uneven **7** unequal **8** lopsided **10** asymmetric **13** unsymmetrical

diffuse
3 lax **4** full, long **5** loose, slack, strew, windy, wordy **6** casual, expand, extend, lavish, prolix, random, spread **7** copious, lengthy, osmolar, osmotic, perfuse, radiate, scatter, send out, verbose **8** disperse, intersow, permeate **9** broadcast, circulate, desultory, exuberant, interlard, propagate, redundant, scattered, spreading, spread out **10** distribute, longwinded, palaverous, widespread **11** disseminate, intersperse **13** intersprinkle

diffusion
7 osmoses (plural), osmosis **9** broadcast, prolixity, spreading **10** scattering

dig
3 jab, jog, ram, run **4** grub, hole, holk, howk, like, mind, mine, poke, prod, root, sift, sink, site, spud, stab **5** delve, ditch, drive, enjoy, enter, grind, nudge, probe, punch, scoop, spade, stick **6** burrow, drudge, go into, pierce, plunge, quarry, relish, rootle, shovel, thrust, trench, tunnel **7** explore, root out, unearth **8** excavate, look into, prospect **9** delve into, hollow out, penetrate **10** excavation **11** inquire into, investigate
out: **6** exhume
up: **7** unearth

digest
2 go **3** sum **4** bear, cook, take **5** abide, brook, stand, sum up **6** aperçu, codify, endure, précis, sketch, survey **7** pandect, stomach, summate, swallow, sylloge **8** compress, condense, nutshell, syllabus, synopsis, tolerate **9** epitomize, inventory, summarize, synopsize **10** abridgment, compendium, comprehend, periodical **11** compilation

digestion
combining form: **6** pepsia, peptic
good: **7** eupepsy **8** eupepsia
poor: **9** dyspepsia

digger
4 plow **5** miner

digit
3 toe **5** thumb **6** cipher, figure, finger, number, pinkie **7** chiffer, integer, numeral **11** whole number
abbreviation: **2** no.
combining form: **6** dactyl, digiti **7** dactylo, dactyly **8** dactylia **9** dactylism, dactylous

dignified
4 prim 6 proper 7 stately
8 decorous

dignify
5 erect, exalt, honor 6 uprear 7 ennoble, glorify, sublime 10 aggrandize 11 distinguish

dignitary
3 VIP 4 lion 5 chief, nabob
6 leader 7 notable 8 eminence, luminary 10 notability 13 high-muck-a-muck

dignity
4 rank 5 grace, honor, merit, poise, state, worth 6 cachet, ethics, status, virtue 7 address, decency, decorum, majesty, stature 8 elegance, grandeur, morality, nobility, position, prestige, standing 9 etiquette, grandness, nobleness, propriety 10 augustness, excellence, perfection, seemliness 11 consequence, ethicalness
12 magnificence
suffix: 3 dom 4 ship

digress
4 roam 5 drift, stray 6 depart, ramble, swerve, wander 7 deviate, diverge, excurse 8 divagate

digression
5 aside 7 episode, excurse 8 drifting, excursus, incident, rambling, straying 9 departure, deviation, wandering 10 deflection, divagation, divergence 11 parenthesis, underaction

dike
4 bank, pond, pool 5 drain, fix up, levee, slick, spiff 6 doll up, dude up 7 barrier, deck out, doll out, dress up, gussy up 8 aboideau, causeway, spruce up
11 watercourse

dilapidate
4 do in, ruin 5 decay, wreck 6 forget, ignore, slight 7 crumble, neglect 8 bankrupt, overlook 9 decompose, disregard, shipwreck
12 disintegrate

dilapidated
5 dingy, faded, seedy, tacky
6 beat-up, marred, shabby, tagrag
7 damaged, decayed, injured, rundown 8 crumbled, impaired
10 broken-down, down-at-heel, threadbare

dilapidation
5 decay, waste 6 debris

dilate
5 swell, widen 6 expand, extend, recite 7 amplify, augment, broaden, descant, discuss, dissert, distend, enlarge, narrate, prolong, recount 8 describe, expanded, increase, lengthen, protract, rehearse
9 discourse, expatiate, sermonize
10 dissertate

dilatory
3 lax 4 slow 5 slack, tardy 6 remiss 7 laggard, unhasty 9 leisurely, negligent, unhurried 10 deliberate, neglectful

dilemma
3 box, fix, jam 4 hole, spot
6 choice, corner, pickle, plight, scrape 7 problem 8 argument, quandary 10 perplexity 11 predicament 12 bewilderment
13 mystification

dilettante
4 tyro 7 amateur, dabbler, jackleg
8 aesthete, dabbling, ungifted
9 smatterer, unskilled 10 amateurish, unfinished, uninitiate 11 abecedarian, cognoscente, connoisseur

dilettantish
see **amateurish**

diligence
8 industry 9 assiduity 11 persistence 12 perseverance

diligent
7 operose 8 sedulous 9 assiduous
10 persistent, persisting, unflagging
11 industrious, persevering

dill plant
4 anet

dilly
3 pip 4 lulu 5 dandy, nifty, peach
6 corker, dinger, doozer, pippin, ripper, rouser 8 jim-dandy, knockout 9 humdinger 10 ripsnorter
11 crackerjack, lalapalooza

dillydally
see **delay**

dilute
3 cut 4 thin, weak 5 alter, washy
6 debase, modify, temper, watery, weaken 7 liquefy, qualify, reduced
8 deprived, diminish, impaired, moderate, waterish, weakened
9 enfeebled, water down 10 deliquesce 11 adulterated, watered-down 12 impoverished
13 sophisticated

dim
3 fog, mat 4 blur, dark, dead, dull, dusk, fade, flat, haze, hazy, pale
5 befog, blear, blind, cloud, dusky, faint, muddy, murky, muted, vague
6 bleary, darken, gloomy 7 becloud, dislimn, eclipse, low beam, obscure, shadowy, subdued, tarnish, unclear 9 lightless, obfuscate, tenebrous 10 caliginous, ill-defined, indistinct, lackluster, lusterless
12 parking light, undetermined
13 unilluminated

dime novel
4 pulp 7 chiller, shocker 8 dreadful, thriller 10 yellowback 12 bloodcurdler, killer-diller 13 penny dreadful

dimension
4 size 5 scope, trait, width 6 aspect, extent 7 measure, quality
8 lifelike 9 magnitude 10 yard lumber 11 proportions

diminish
3 ebb 4 bate, wane 5 abate, abuse, close, decry, peter, taper
6 lessen, minify, reduce, temper
7 abridge, curtail, dwindle, subside
8 belittle, decrease, derogate, minimize, moderate, taper off, write off
9 attenuate, disparage, dispraise, drain away, extenuate 10 depreciate 11 detract from

diminishing
7 calando

diminutive
3 wee 4 tiny 5 small, teeny, weeny
6 minute, teensy 9 miniature
10 teeny-weeny 11 lilliputian
12 teensy-weensy

diminutive one
suffix: 2 el, et, ey, ia (plural), ie
3 cle, ium, kin, ock, ula, ule, uli (plural) 4 ella, ette, illa, ling, ulae (plural), ulum, ulus 5 ellae (plural), illae (plural)

" ___ dimittis"
4 nunc

dimmet
4 dusk 7 evening 8 eventide, gloaming, owl-light, twilight
9 nightfall

dimple
4 fret 5 mound 6 cockle, hollow, riffle, ripple 10 depression

dim-sighted
8 purblind 9 half-blind

dimwit
4 simp 5 cluck, dunce 7 pinhead
9 dumb bunny, dumb cluck
13 feather-weight

dim-witted
4 dull, slow 7 moronic 8 backward, imbecile, retarded 12 feebleminded, simpleminded

din
3 row 5 babel, chirm, clash, music, noise, sound 6 bedlam, clamor, deafen, hubbub, jangle, racket, rattle, tumult, uproar 7 clangor, clatter, resound 8 blatancy, brouhaha, racketry 9 commotion, stridency 10 hullabaloo, percussion, tintamarre 11 pandemonium 13 clamorousness

Dinah
5 Shore
brother: 4 Levi 6 Simeon
father: 5 Jacob
mother: 4 Leah

dine
3 eat, sup 4 feed

diner
3 bar 4 café 6 eatery 7 counter, hashery 8 snack bar 9 hash house 10 coffee shop, quick-lunch, restaurant 11 eating house, greasy spoon 12 lunch counter, sandwich shop

dinette
ancient Roman: 5 oecus

ding
3 hit 4 beat, best, damn, sock 5 catch, clang, clout, outdo, outgo, whack 6 better, exceed, strike 7 surpass 8 outmatch, outshine

ding-a-ling
3 nut 4 kook 5 crank 6 cuckoo 7 lunatic 8 crackpot 9 harebrain, screwball 10 crackbrain

dinge
4 dent 5 blues, dumps, gloom 6 batter 7 sadness 9 dejection 10 depression, melancholy 11 unhappiness 12 mournfulness

dinghy
5 yacht 7 rowboat 8 life raft, sailboat

dingle
4 dale, dell 6 ravine, valley 9 storm door 10 passageway

dingus
5 gizmo 6 doodad, gadget, jigger 7 do-funny, thingum 9 doohickey 10 thingumbob 11 thingumajig

dingy
4 dark, drab, dull, mean 5 dirty, dusky, faded, murky, seedy, tacky, tired 6 gloomy, grimed, shabby, smutty, soiled 7 run-down, squalid, sullied 8 smirched 9 tarnished 10 broken-down, discolored, down-at-heel, threadbare 11 dilapidated

dinky
5 minor, small 6 lesser 8 small-fry 9 secondary, small-time 11 minor league 13 insignificant

dinner
4 fete, meal 5 feast 6 entrée, junket, regale, spread 7 banquet 8 festival, luncheon 9 breakfast, collation 10 table d'hôte
coat: 3 tux 6 tuxedo
course: 4 meat, soup 6 entrée 7 dessert 9 appetizer
Jewish: 5 seder 7 sedarim (plural)

"Dinner ___"
7 at Eight

dinosaur
8 theropod 10 allosaurus 11 stegosaurus, triceratops 12 brontosaurus 13 tyrannosaurus

dinosauric
4 huge 7 mammoth 8 colossal, enormous 9 cyclopean, leviathan 10 behemothic, gargantuan, mastodonic 11 elephantine

dint
5 force, might, notch, power, sinew, vigor 6 energy, hollow, virtue 7 drive in, impress, imprint, potency 8 strength 9 puissance 10 impression 11 indentation

diocese
3 see 9 bishopric
Eastern Orthodox: 7 eparchy
subdivision: 6 parish

diode
9 rectifier 12 electron tube
type of: 8 kenotron

Diomedes
city founded by: 4 Arpi
father: 4 Ares, Mars 6 Tydeus
foe: 6 Aeneas, Hector
slayer: 8 Hercules
victim: 6 Rhesus

Dione
5 Titan
cult partner: 4 Zeus
daughter: 5 Venus 9 Aphrodite
father: 7 Oceanus
lover: 4 Zeus
mother: 6 Tethys

Dionysus
see **Bacchus**

Dionyza's husband
5 Cleon

Dioscuri
5 twins 6 Anaces, Anakes, Castor, Gemini, Pollux

father: 4 Zeus 9 Tyndareus
mother: 4 Leda
sister: 5 Helen

dip
3 sag, set 4 bail, dish, draw, drop, duck, dunk, fall, lade, sink, skew, skid, slip, slue, tilt, veer 5 basin, depth, douse, ladle, lower, pitch, reach, sauce, scoop, sheer, slope, slump, souse, spoon, stoop 6 candle, go down, hollow, plunge, swerve, thrust, tumble 7 decline, delving, descend, descent, explore, falloff, immerse, plummet, sinkage 8 bucket up, decrease, downturn, lowering, nose-dive, sinkhole, submerge, submerse, train off 9 concavity, declivity, downslide, downswing, downtrend, immersion 10 depression, divergence, plunge into 11 inclination
kind: 4 clam 5 onion 10 blue cheese

diphthong
2 ae, ai, ea, ei, oe, oi, ou, oy 7 digraph 8 ligature

diploma
6 letter 7 charter, writing 8 document

diplomacy
4 tact 5 poise 7 address 10 adroitness, artfulness, settlement 11 delicatesse, savoir faire, tactfulness

diplomatic
4 wily 5 bland 6 artful, astute, crafty, polite, shrewd, smooth 7 politic, tactful 8 delicate, guileful, tactical 9 courteous 12 paleographic

diplomat's office
7 embassy

diplopod
9 millipede

dipper
3 cup 4 bird, grab 5 ladle, scoop 6 bucket, holder 10 bufflehead, water ouzel

dippy
5 crazy, silly, wacky 6 absurd, insane 7 foolish 9 fantastic 11 harebrained 12 preposterous

dipsomania
10 alcoholism

dire
5 acute, awful 6 crying, dismal, urgent, woeful 7 baleful, baneful, burning, clamant, crucial, exigent, extreme, fateful, fearful, instant, ominous, painful 8 critical, dreadful, grievous, horrible, pressing, shock-

ing, sinister, terrible, terrific **9** appalling, cheerless, clamorous, desperate, frightful, ill-boding **10** afflictive, calamitous, deplorable, depressing, imperative, lamentable, oppressing, oppressive **11** apocalyptic, climacteric, distressing, importunate, regrettable, threatening, unfortunate **12** inauspicious, unpropitious **13** heartbreaking

direct
3 aim, bid, due, fix, lay, run, see, set **4** beam, bend, cast, dead, give, head, keep, lead, mark, next, open, show, tell, turn, warn **5** allot, apply, focus, frank, guide, issue, label, level, order, pilot, plain, point, refer, right, route, steer, throw, train **6** assign, candid, charge, custos, define, devote, divert, enjoin, escort, extend, fasten, govern, handle, lineal, linear, manage, ordain, settle, zero in **7** address, carry on, command, conduct, control, genuine, incline, nonstop, operate, oversee, present, preside, primary, project, request, through **8** dispatch, dominate, instruct, man-to-man, point out, regulate, shepherd, straight, unbroken, verbatim **9** determine, effective, firsthand, immediate, literally, literatim, out-and-out, prescribe, proximate **10** administer, buckle down, channelize, contiguous, continuous, explicitly, inevitable, proceeding, straightly, unhampered, unreserved, unswerving **11** categorical, substantive, superscribe, unconcealed, undeviating, undisguised, unequivocal, word for word **12** undissembled **13** undeviatingly, uninterrupted
a helmsman: **4** conn
proceedings: **7** preside

direction
3 way **4** east, line, path, role, side, west **5** angle, north, order, point, slant, south, tenor **6** charge, course, design, sphere **7** bearing, channel, command, guiding, outlook, respect **8** guidance, pointing **9** clockwise, viewpoint **10** standpoint
blowing: **7** leeward **8** windward
combining form: **5** phoro
court: **5** order
for Muslims praying: **5** kibla **6** keblah, kildah
horizontal: **7** azimuth
main line of: **4** axis
musical: (see **musical direction**)
of a linear arrangement: **5** grain

square dance: **4** call
without fixed: **7** astatic
(see also **compass point**)

directive
4 memo, word **5** edict, ukase **6** decree, notice, ruling **7** bidding, message **8** exemplar **10** assignment, injunction, memorandum **11** instruction **13** communication, pronouncement

directly
3 due **4** anon, away, dead, soon **5** right, spang **6** at once **7** by and by, shortly **8** first off, in person, squarely, straight, verbatim **9** forthwith, instanter, instantly, literally, literatim, presently, right away **10** face-to-face, straightly **11** immediately, straight off, straightway, word for word **12** contiguously **13** undeviatingly, unqualifiedly

director
4 head **5** chief **6** leader **7** manager **9** conductor **10** supervisor

directory
4 list, ordo **5** guide, index **8** treatise **11** compilation

direful
see **fearful; ominous**

dirge
4 hymn, song **6** lament **7** epicede, requiem **8** threnody **9** epicedium **11** lamentation
Gaelic: **8** coronach

dirigible
7 airship **8** zeppelin **9** steerable

dirk
4 stab **5** sword **6** dagger

dirt
4 land, sand, soil, spot **5** earth, filth, fraud, grime, stain **6** gossip, gravel, ground **7** chicane, dry land, squalor **9** chicanery, deception, excrement, fourberie **10** corruption, dishonesty, hanky-panky, terra firma **11** highbinding, uncleanness **13** double-dealing, sharp practice

dirt poor
4 flat **5** broke **8** beggared, indigent **9** destitute, penurious **10** stone-broke **12** impoverished

dirty
3 low, tar **4** foul, smut, soil, wild **5** bawdy, black, dungy, grime, grimy, messy, mucky, muddy, murky, nasty, rough, smear, soily, sooty, stain, sully, taint **6** basely, befoul, begrim, besoil, coarse, dreggy, filthy, grubby, impure, rag-

ing, smirch, smooch, smudge, smudgy, smutch, smutty, soiled, sordid, stormy, vulgar **7** abusive, begrime, besmear, clouded, defiled, draggly, dullish, furious, hateful, immoral, obscene, piggish, raunchy, smoochy, smutchy, squalid, sullied, tainted, tarnish, unclean **8** begrimed, besmirch, blustery, discolor, draggled, grievous, indecent, polluted, scroungy, stormful, unchaste **9** uncleanly **10** blustering, scurrilous **11** distressing, regrettable, tempestuous **12** contaminated, contemptible, scatological **13** draggletailed

Dis
see **Pluto**

disability
8 drawback, handicap **9** detriment

disable
3 mar, sap **4** harm, hurt, maim, ruin **5** blunt, spoil, wreck **6** batter, disarm, mangle, weaken **7** cripple, deprive, invalid, unbrace **8** enfeeble, mutilate, paralyze **9** attenuate, prostrate, undermine **10** debilitate, disqualify, immobilize **12** incapacitate, unstrengthen
a racehorse: **6** nobble

disabuse
4 free **5** amend, emend, purge **7** correct, rectify, redress, release, unblind **8** liberate, undelude **9** disillude, enlighten, undeceive **10** illuminate **11** disillusion

disaccharide
7 lactose, maltose, sucrose

disaccord
3 jar **4** vary **5** clash **6** differ, divide, jangle, strife **7** dissent **8** conflict, disunity, mismatch, variance **10** contention, difference, dissension, dissidence **12** disharmonize

disadvantage
3 bar **4** harm, loss **6** hamper **8** blocking, drawback, handicap, obstacle **9** detriment, hindrance, prejudice **10** impediment, imposition **11** obstruction

disadvantaged
7 lacking **8** deprived **9** depressed

disadvise
5 deter **6** divert **8** dissuade **10** discourage

disaffect
4 wean **5** alien, upset **7** agitate, disturb **8** alienate, diminish, disquiet, disunify, disunite, estrange **10** discompose

disaffection
9 hostility 12 estrangement

disaffirm
4 deny 5 annul, cross 6 impugn, negate 7 gainsay, reverse 8 negative, traverse 9 repudiate 10 contradict, contravene

disagree
4 vary 5 clash 6 differ, divide 7 discord, dissent

disagreeable
3 bad 4 sour 5 waspy, whiny 6 rotten, snappy, twitty, woeful 7 helluva, peevish, pettish, unhappy, waspish 8 annoying, petulant 9 offensive, querulous 10 disturbing, unpleasant 11 displeasing, distressing

disagreement
3 row 4 spat 5 clash 7 discord, dispute, quarrel 8 variance 10 contention, difference, dissension, divergence, unlikeness 11 controversy, discrepancy, incongruity

disallow
4 deny, veto 5 debar 6 disown, refuse, reject 7 disavow, exclude, shut out 8 disclaim, keep back, withhold 9 repudiate

disallowance
6 denial 7 refusal 9 rejection

____ -disant
3 soi

disappear
2 go 4 fade 5 clear, leave 6 vanish 7 evanish 8 evanesce 9 evaporate

disappoint
4 balk, beat, bilk, dash, foil, ruin 6 baffle, defeat, thwart 7 let down 9 frustrate 10 circumvent

disappointment
7 failure 9 bringdown 11 frustration

disapproval
4 veto 7 censure, dislike 9 rejection
expression of: 3 boo 4 hiss, hoot, jeer 7 catcall 9 raspberry 10 Bronx cheer

disapprove
5 blame, decry, frown, pshaw, spurn 6 object, refuse, reject 7 censure, condemn, decline, detract, dislike, dismiss 8 denounce, disfavor, turn down 9 criticize, deprecate, disesteem, disparage, dispraise, reprehend, reprobate,

repudiate 10 depreciate, discommend 11 expostulate, remonstrate

disarm
5 charm 6 allure 7 attract, bewitch, cripple, enchant, unsteel, win over 8 paralyze 9 captivate, deprive of, fascinate, prostrate 10 immobilize 12 incapacitate

disarming
5 silky 6 silken 10 saccharine 11 deferential, insinuating, insinuative 12 ingratiating, ingratiatory

disarrange
4 mess 6 jumble, mess up, mislay 7 disturb, replace, rummage 8 disorder, displace, misplace, overturn, unsettle 10 discompose 11 disorganize

disarray
5 chaos, snarl 6 ataxia, huddle, jumble, mess up, muddle, unrobe 7 clutter, derange, disturb, rummage 8 disorder, unsettle 9 confusion 10 discompose 11 disorganize

disassemble
8 dismount, separate, take down, tear down 9 dismantle, dismember, take apart

disassociate
5 unfix 6 detach 8 abstract, uncouple 9 disengage 10 disconnect

disaster
3 woe 4 rock, ruin 6 fiasco, injure, mishap 7 failure, tragedy 8 accident, calamity, casualty, distress, fatality 9 adversity, cataclysm, mischance 10 misfortune 11 catastrophe 12 misadventure

disastrous
4 dire 5 fatal 7 fateful, hapless, ruinous 8 luckless 10 calamitous 11 cataclysmic, destructive, unfortunate 12 catastrophic

disavow
4 deny 6 disown, impugn, negate, recant 8 disclaim, negative 9 repudiate

disband
4 part 5 sever 6 dispel, divide, sunder 7 break up, disjoin, dissect, divorce, scatter 8 disjoint, disperse, dissever, dissolve, disunite, separate 9 dissipate 11 dichotomize

disbelieve
5 doubt, scorn, scout 6 eschew, reject 7 suspect 8 distrust, mistrust, question 9 discredit

disbeliever
5 cynic 7 doubter, sceptic, skeptic

disbelieving
6 show-me 8 aporetic 9 quizzical, skeptical 11 incredulous, questioning

disburden
6 unlade, unload, unship, unstow 7 discard, off-load 8 get rid of, jettison 9 discharge

disburse
3 pay 4 deal, give 5 divvy, spend 6 defray, divide, expend, lay out, lot out, outlay, pay out 7 dole out, fork out 8 dispense, disperse, shell out 9 partition 10 distribute, measure out

disbursement
4 cost 6 outlay 7 expense 11 expenditure

discard
4 cast, drop, dump, junk, oust, shed, waif 5 chuck, ditch, eject, let go, scrap, sluff, spurn 6 desert, reject, slough 7 abandon, cashier, cast off, deep-six, dismiss, forsake, wash out 8 abdicate, get rid of, jettison, lay aside, shuck off, throw out 9 repudiate, throw away

discarnate
8 bodiless 9 asomatous, unfleshly 10 immaterial, unembodied, unphysical 11 disembodied, incorporeal, nonphysical 13 insubstantial

discept
4 moot 5 argue 6 debate 7 agitate, canvass, dispute 9 thrash out 10 toss around

discern
3 see 4 know, note, view 5 sever 6 behold, descry, detect, divine, notice, remark 7 foresee, observe 8 perceive, separate 9 apprehend, ascertain, extricate 10 anticipate, difference, severalize 11 distinguish 13 differentiate

discernible
8 palpable 10 detectable, observable 11 appreciable

discerning
4 sage, wise 5 acute 7 gnostic, knowing 9 clear-eyed, insighted, sagacious 10 insightful, perceptive 11 wisehearted 13 knowledgeable

discernment
3 wit 6 acumen, reason 8 keenness, sagacity 9 intuition 10 astuteness, shrewdness 11 penetration, percipience 12 perspicacity 13 sagaciousness

discharge
2 ax 3 can, pay, run 4 drop, emit, fire, flow, free, oust, pour, quit, sack, vent, void 5 annul, clear, eject, empty, expel, exude, let go, loose, pay up, quash, rheum, shoot, spare, utter 6 bounce, excuse, exempt, let fly, let off, loosen, outlet, remove, settle, square, unbind, unlade, unload, unship, unstow, vacate 7 absolve, boot out, cashier, deliver, dismiss, exclude, execute, fulfill, give off, kick out, manumit, off-load, release, relieve, removal, replace, satisfy, unchain 8 abrogate, clear off, clear out, dispense, displace, dissolve, emission, get rid of, liberate, separate, set aside, supplant, throw off 9 acquittal, bleach out, disburden, disenroll, eliminate, explosion, expulsion, liquidate, muster out, pour forth, pronounce, send forth, supersede, terminate, unloading, unshackle 10 deactivate, demobilize, disembogue, emancipate, give vent to, inactivate, liberation, separation 11 acquittance, exoneration, fulfillment 13 privilege from
combining form: 5 rrhea 6 rrhoea 7 rrhagia
concentrated: 7 barrage
electrical: 5 spark 6 leader 8 streamer 9 lightning 12 leader stroke
from the body: 5 egest 7 excrete
simultaneous: 5 salvo

discinct
3 lax 5 slack 6 remiss 8 careless, derelict 9 negligent 10 behindhand, delinquent, neglectful 12 disregardful

disciple
6 cohort, zealot 7 apostle, fanatic, sectary 8 adherent, follower, henchman, partisan, sectator 9 satellite, supporter 10 enthusiast

disciplinarian
6 ramrod 8 martinet

disciplinary
7 ordered 8 punitive, punitory 9 punishing 11 castigatory

discipline
3 rod 4 curb, lead, whip, will 5 check, drill, guide, spank, teach, train 6 bridle, direct, manage, method, punish, reduce, school, subdue 7 chasten, conduct, control, correct, educate, inhibit, scourge 8 approach, chastise, instruct, overcome, penalize, punition, restrain, training 9 castigate, obedience, subjugate, will-power 10 correction, experience, punishment 11 castigation, self-command, self-control, self-mastery 12 chastisement 13 self-restraint

disclaim
4 deny 5 spurn 6 abjure, disown, recant, refuse, reject 7 disavow, gainsay, retract 8 belittle, disallow, forswear, minimize, renounce, traverse 9 challenge, criticize, deprecate, disparage, repudiate 10 contradict, contravene

disclose
3 own 4 avow, open, tell 5 admit, mouth, spill 6 betray, expose, reveal, unveil 7 blab out, confess, display, divulge, unclose, uncover 8 discover, give away, unclothe 9 make known 11 acknowledge

disclosure
6 exposé 10 confession, revelation 11 divulgation

discolor
3 tar 4 blot, dull, fade, smut, soil 5 smear, stain, sully, taint, tinge 6 defile, motley, streak 7 besmear, bestain, dappled, tarnish 8 besmirch 9 multihued 10 variegated

discoloration
5 stain
combining form: 6 chroia

discomfit
3 irk, vex 4 faze, foil, rout 5 abash, annoy, upset 6 bother, defeat, rattle, thwart 7 confuse, disturb, perturb 8 confound 9 embarrass

discomfiture
4 rout 5 upset 6 damage, defeat, injury, unease 7 beating, debacle, descent, licking 8 comedown, disquiet, drubbing, prickles 9 abashment, agitation, commotion, confusion, overthrow 10 defeasance, uneasiness 11 frustration, shellacking 12 perturbation, vanquishment 13 embarrassment, inconvenience

discomfort
6 unease 7 malaise, misease 9 annoyance 10 uneasiness 13 embarrassment

discomforting
see **uncomfortable**

discommend
5 frown 6 object 7 censure 8 admonish, disfavor 9 criticize, deprecate, disesteem, reprehend 10 disapprove

discommode
3 irk, vex 5 upset 6 bother, flurry, put out 7 fluster, perturb, trouble 8 put about 9 disoblige 13 inconvenience

discompose
3 irk, vex 5 annoy, harry, upset, worry 6 bother, dismay, flurry, harass, mess up, pester, plague, untune 7 agitate, derange, disturb, fluster, perturb, rummage, unhinge 8 disagree, disarray, disorder, disquiet, unsettle 9 embarrass 10 disarrange 11 disorganize

discomposure
6 unease 9 abashment, agitation, confusion 10 uneasiness 12 perturbation 13 embarrassment

disconcert
4 faze 5 abash, upset 6 puzzle, rattle, ruffle 7 break up, confuse, nonplus, perplex 8 bewilder, confound 9 embarrass, frustrate

disconfirm
5 break, evert, rebut 6 refute 7 confute 8 confound, disprove 10 controvert

disconnect
5 sever, unfix 6 detach 8 abstract, separate, uncouple

disconnected
7 muddled 8 inchoate 10 incoherent, incohesive 11 unorganized 12 uncontinuous

disconsolate
3 bad, low, sad 4 cold, down 5 bleak, drear 6 gloomy, somber, woeful 7 doleful, joyless, unhappy 8 dejected, downcast 9 cheerless, depressed, saddening, sorrowful, woebegone 10 depressing, melancholy 11 comfortless, crestfallen, downhearted

discontent
9 dysphoria 10 inquietude, uneasiness

discontented
5 upset 6 uneasy 7 unhappy 8 restless 9 perturbed 11 ungratified, unsatisfied

discontented one
see **complainer**

discontinuance
see **discontinuation**

discontinuation
3 end 5 cease, close 6 ending, finish 7 closing 9 desuetude 10 conclusion, desistance

discontinue
3 end 4 halt, quit, stop 5 cease, sever 6 desist, give up 8 break off,
give over, knock off, leave off, surcease 9 terminate

discontinuity
3 gap 4 hole 5 break 6 breach,
lacuna 7 opening

discontinuous
7 muddled 8 inchoate, separate
10 incoherent, incohesive 11 unconnected, unorganized

discord
3 jar 4 vary 5 clash 6 differ, divide, enmity, jangle, rancor, strife
7 unpeace 8 conflict, contrast, division, mischief, mismatch, variance
9 animosity, antipathy, collision,
hostility, inharmony 10 antagonism, contention, difference, opposition 11 incongruity 12 inconso-
nance, polarization
13 inconsistency
goddess: 3 Ate 4 Eris

discordant
5 harsh 7 jarring 8 clashing, contrary 9 immusical, unmixable,
unmusical 10 cacophonic, inharmonic 11 cacophonous, conflicting, contrarient, incongruent, incongruous, inconsonant, quarrelsome,
uncongenial 12 antagonistic, antipathetic, incompatible, inconsistent,
inharmonious, unharmonious

discotheque
4 café, go-go 6 nitery 7 cabaret,
hot spot 8 nightery 9 nightclub,
night spot 10 supper club 12 watering hole 13 watering place

discount
4 fail, omit, take 5 abuse, decry
6 deduct, forget, ignore, lessen, rebate, slight 7 neglect, take off, take
out 8 belittle, derogate, diminish,
draw back, knock off, minimize,
overlook, overpass, subtract, take
away 9 abatement, deduction, reduction, substract, underrate 10 anticipate, depreciate 11 detract
from, subtraction

discountenance
4 faze 5 abash, frown 6 object,
rattle 7 confuse, reprove 8 confound, reproach 9 deprecate, embarrass 10 put to shame

discourage
3 irk, try, vex 4 damp 5 check,
chill, deter, droop, scare, weigh
6 bother, dampen, deject, divert,
hinder, lessen 7 afflict, depress, inhibit, prevent, trouble 8 frighten, restrain 10 demoralize

discouraging
5 black, bleak 6 dreary, gloomy
9 deterring, hindering 10 depressing, depressive, oppressive

discourse
3 act 4 play, talk 5 argue, enact,
essay, orate, paper, speak, voice
6 expand, memoir, remark, sermon,
speech, thesis 7 amplify, article,
comment, descant, develop, enlarge, explain, expound, lecture,
perform, playact 8 converse, harangue, perorate, rhetoric, speaking, tractate, treatise 9 elaborate,
expatiate, monograph, personate,
sermonize, utterance 10 commentate, expression, monography
11 impersonate, interchange
12 conversation 13 verbalization
art of: 8 rhetoric
combining form: 3 log 4 logo, logy
5 logia, logue
religious: 6 homily, sermon

discourteous
4 rude 7 ill-bred, incivil, uncivil
8 impolite 10 ungracious, unmannerly 11 ill-mannered, impertinent

discover
3 see 4 espy, find, hear, note, spot,
tell 5 learn, mouth, spill 6 betray,
debunk, descry, detect, expose, reveal, show up, tumble, unmask
7 catch on, divulge, find out, observe, publish, uncloak, unclose, undress, unearth 8 give away, perceive, proclaim, unshroud
9 advertise, ascertain, determine,
encounter, make known

discovery
4 find 5 trove 6 espial, strike
7 finding 8 exposure 9 detection
10 exposition, revelation, unearthing 11 recognition

discredit
4 ruin 5 doubt, odium, shame,
shoot 6 blow up, expose, infamy,
show up 7 asperse, destroy, explode, obloquy 8 ignominy, puncture, reproach 9 unbelieve
10 opprobrium

discreditable
5 shady 6 shabby, shoddy
8 shameful 10 inglorious
11 ignominious

discreet
4 safe, wary 5 chary, muted, plain
6 modest, simple 7 careful,
guarded, prudent, tactful 8 cautious, gingerly, moderate 9 temperate, unadorned, unextreme 10 controlled, reasonable, restrained
11 calculating, circumspect, considerate, inelaborate, unelaborate,
unexcessive, unobtrusive 12 conservative, unbeautified
13 unpretentious

discrepancy
8 alterity 9 otherness, variation
10 difference, divergence, divergency, unlikeness

discrepant
7 diverse, varying 8 contrary 9 different, divergent, unmixable
11 conflicting, incongruent, incongruous, inconsonant 12 incompatible, inconsistent

discrete
8 detached, separate 9 countable
13 noncontinuous

discretion
4 tact 5 sense 6 wisdom 7 caution,
secrecy 8 delicacy, judgment, prudence, wariness 9 canniness, foresight, restraint 10 providence
11 forethought

discriminate
4 know, note 5 sever 6 remark
7 analyze, compare, make out
8 contrast, perceive, separate 9 extricate 10 difference, severalize
13 differentiate

discriminating
4 wise 6 select 7 careful, prudent
8 eclectic 9 judicious, selective
10 analytical

discrimination
3 wit 5 sense 6 acumen 8 astucity,
judgment, keenness 10 astuteness,
shrewdness 11 percipience
12 perspicacity

discriminatory
6 biased, unfair, unjust 7 partial
8 partisan 10 prejudiced 11 inequitable 12 prepossessed

disculpate
5 clear 6 acquit 7 absolve 9 exonerate, vindicate

discursion
5 aside 8 excursus 10 divagation
11 parenthesis

discursive
6 chatty, roving 7 roaming 8 rambling 9 desultory
group discussion: 11 bull session

discuss
4 moot 5 argue, parle, weigh
6 caucus, debate, parley 7 agitate,
canvass, descant, expound 8 con-

sider, converse, hash over, talk over **9** elucidate, expatiate, explicate, interpret, talk about, thrash out **10** deliberate, toss around **11** investigate
business: **8** talk shop
lightly: **5** bandy
thoroughly: **7** exhaust

discussion
3 rap **6** confab **8** argument **10** conference **11** ventilation **12** deliberation **13** confabulation

discus thrower
6 Oerter (Al) **10** discobolus **11** Rashchupkin (Viktor)

disdain
5 abhor, pride, scorn, scout **6** morgue **7** contemn, despise, despite, hauteur **8** aversion, contempt, despisal, disprize, look down **9** antipathy, arrogance, insolence, loftiness, superbity **11** despisement, haughtiness

disdainful
5 proud **6** averse, lordly **7** haughty **8** arrogant, cavalier, insolent, scorning, scouting, spurning, superior **9** despising, rejecting **10** contemning **11** overbearing, repudiating **12** antipathetic, contemptuous, supercilious **13** high and mighty, unsympathetic

disease
3 bug, ill **4** AIDS **5** virus **6** blight, malady, scurvy **7** ailment, anthrax, cholera, derange, endemic, illness, malaise, mycosis, purpura, rickets **8** debility, epidemic, leukemia, myxedema, paludism, pandemic, pellagra, rachitis, sickness, syndrome, zoonoses (plural), zoonosis **9** affection, black lung, complaint, condition, infirmity, sclerosis **10** alteration, blackwater, bronchitis, feebleness, impairment, infirmness, rachitides (plural), sickliness **11** decrepitude, derangement **13** unhealthiness
animal: **5** mange, surra **8** enzootic, epizooty
blood: **8** leucemia, leukemia, leukoses (plural), leukosis
cabbage: **8** clubroot
cattle: **6** cowpox **7** murrain, vaccina **8** blackleg, vaccinia
caused by bacteria: **11** brucellosis
cereal grass: **4** smut
children's: **7** rubella **10** chicken pox
citrus tree: **8** tristeza
classification: **8** nosology
combining form: **3** nos **4** noso, path **5** patho

communicable: **12** tuberculosis
disseminator: **7** carrier
eye: **8** glaucoma, trachoma
fish: **3** ich
foretelling of: **9** prognosis
hair follicle: **7** sycoses (plural), sycosis
heart: **11** cardiopathy
horse: **4** clap **5** faroy **6** nagana, spavie, spavin **7** dourine, sarcoid **8** glanders
identification of: **9** diagnosis
industrial: **10** byssinosis
infectious: **4** mono **6** typhus **7** malaria, tetanus, typhoid
liver: **9** cirrhosis, hepatitis
livestock: **7** locoism
lung: **8** phthisic, phthisis **9** pneumonia
lymph glands: **6** struma **8** scrofula
metabolic: **4** gout
nervous system: **4** kuru
of beets: **8** heartrot
of mammals: **10** babesiasis
parasitic: **3** rot
plant: **4** wilt **5** edema, scurf **6** blotch **7** frogeye **8** gummosis
poultry: **7** fowlpox
respiratory: **6** asthma
sheep: **3** gid **7** scrapie **10** bluetongue
skin: **4** acne **5** favus, hives, lupus, mange, pinta, tinea **6** eczema, tetter **7** leprosy, pemphix, prurigo, scabies **8** impetigo, keratoma, miliaria, pyoderma, ringworm, vitiligo, xanthoma **9** keratomas (plural), psoriasis, xanthomas (plural) **10** keratomata (plural), xanthomata (plural)
suffix: **3** ses (plural), sis **4** itis, oses (plural), osis **5** iases (plural), iasis
swine: **8** bullnose
syphilitic: **5** tabes
throat: **5** croup
tropical: **4** pian **5** sprue **6** carate, dengue **8** psiloses (plural), psilosis
venereal: **8** syphilis **9** chancroid, gonorrhea
viral: **3** flu **4** noma **5** mumps, polio **6** grippe, rabies, zoster **7** ecthyma, measles, rubella, rubeola, variola **8** morbilli, psorosis, smallpox **13** poliomyelitis

diseased
6 sickly **7** fevered
combining form: **3** cac **4** cace, caco
prefix: **3** dys

disembark
4 land **6** alight **8** go ashore

disembarrass
3 rid **5** clear, untie **7** relieve, un-

twine **8** unburden, untangle **9** extricate **10** unentangle

disembodied
9 asomatous, unfleshly **10** immaterial, unphysical **11** incorporeal, nonphysical **13** insubstantial

disembogue
4 emit, flow, pour, void **6** emerge **7** give off, pour out **9** discharge

disembowel
3 gut **6** paunch, remove **7** exhaust **10** eviscerate, exenterate

disembroil
7 untwine **8** untangle **9** extricate **10** unentangle, unscramble

disemploy
2 ax **3** can **4** drop, fire, sack **5** let go **6** bounce, let out **7** boot out **9** terminate

disenchanted
5 blasé **7** knowing, worldly **8** mondaine **9** world-wise **11** worldlywise **12** sophisticate **13** sophisticated

disencumber
5 untie **7** lighten, relieve, untwine **8** free from, untangle **9** alleviate, extricate **10** unentangle, unscramble

disengage
4 free, undo **5** loose, unfix **6** detach, unbind **7** release, unloose **8** abstract, liberate, uncouple, unfasten, unloosen **9** extricate

disentangle
4 part **5** sever, untie **6** detach, sunder **7** unravel, untwine **8** separate **9** extricate **10** unscramble **13** straighten out

disenthrall
4 free **5** loose **6** loosen, unbind **7** manumit, release, unchain **8** liberate **10** emancipate

disenthrone
6 depose, unmake **7** uncrown

disentranced
see **disenchanted**

disentwine
5 untie **8** untangle **9** extricate **10** unentangle, unscramble

disesteem
see **disfavor**

disfavor
5 frown, odium **6** infamy, object **7** obloquy **8** aversion, bad books, disgrace, ignominy, mistrust **9** deprecate, detriment **10** opprobrium **13** indisposition

disfigure
3 mar 4 foul 5 spoil 6 deface, deform, injure, mangle 8 mutilate

disfranchise
7 deprive 8 take away

disgorge
4 barf, spew 5 belch, eject, empty, eruct, erupt, expel, vomit 6 irrupt, spit up 7 bring up, throw up, upchuck

disgrace
4 blot, spot 5 brand, odium, shame, shend, stain 6 infamy, stigma 7 attaint, ill luck, obloquy, stigmas (plural) 8 black eye, contempt, debasing, humbling, ignominy, stigmata (plural) 9 abasement 10 debasement, misfortune, opprobrium 11 degradation, humiliation

disgraceful
5 shady 6 indign, shabby, shoddy 10 inglorious, unbecoming 11 ignominious 13 unrespectable

disgruntled
4 sore 9 uncontent 10 malcontent 11 uncontented, ungratified 12 malcontented

disguise
4 face, hide, mask, sham, show 5 belie, cloak, color, feign, front, put on 6 affect, assume, facade, garble, veneer 7 charade, conceal, dress up, falsify, obscure, pageant, pretend 8 artifice, coloring, delusion, pretense, simulate 9 deception, obfuscate 10 camouflage, false front, pretension 11 counterfeit, insincerity, make-believe 12 misrepresent, speciousness

disguisement
4 face, mask 5 cloak, color, cover, front 6 facade 8 coloring 10 false front

disgust
5 repel, shock 6 nausea, offend, reluct, revolt, sicken 7 outrage, repulse 8 aversion, nauseate 10 repugnance 13 squeamishness

disgusted
4 sick 5 fed up, tired, weary

disgusting
4 foul, vile 5 nasty 7 noisome 9 loathsome, offensive, repellent, repugnant, repulsive, revolting, sickening
behavior: 11 beastliness

dish
4 food, stew, tray 5 salmi 6 shelve, tureen 7 platter 8 cup of tea, get rid of, scrapple, set aside
baked: 7 soufflé
baking: 7 scallop 12 scallop shell
cheese: 6 fondue 7 ramekin, rarebit 8 raclette, ramequin
Chinese: 6 won ton
deep: 9 casserole
Hungarian: 7 goulash
Italian: 7 lasagna, lasagne, ravioli
Japanese: 7 sashimi, tempura 8 sukiyaki
Mexican: 5 tamal 6 tamale 7 burrito 11 chimichanga
Middle Eastern: 8 moussaka
ornamental: 7 epergne
principal: 6 entrée
rice: 7 risotto
rice and meat: 5 pilaf, pilau, pilaw 6 pilaff
Scottish: 6 haggis
shallow: 6 saucer

Dishan's son
2 Uz 4 Aran

disharmonic
see **discordant**

disharmonious
see **discordant**

disharmonize
3 jar 5 clash 6 jangle 8 conflict, mismatch

disharmony
6 strife 7 discord, unpeace 8 conflict, variance 10 contention, difference, dissension, dissention

dishearten
5 chill 6 deject 7 depress 10 demoralize

disheartening
5 black, bleak 6 dreary, gloomy, somber 8 funereal 10 depressing, depressive, despondent, oppressive 11 pessimistic

dishes
4 ware
clay: 7 pottery
porcelain: 5 china

dishevel
5 touse, towse 6 tousel, tousle, touzle

disheveled
5 messy 6 sloppy, untidy 7 raunchy, ruffled, unkempt 8 ill-kempt, slipshod, slovenly, straggly, uncombed 12 unfastidious

dishonest
5 false, lying, snide 6 shifty, tricky 7 corrupt, crooked, devious, furtive, knavish, oblique, roguish 8 cheating, cozening, two-faced 9 deceitful, faithless, insidious, swindling 10 defrauding, fraudulent, mendacious, perfidious, untruthful 13 double-dealing, untrustworthy

dishonesty
5 fraud 7 chicane, roguery 8 trickery 9 chicanery, deception, fourberie 10 hanky-panky 11 highbinding 13 double-dealing, faithlessness

dishonor
see **disgrace**

dishonorable
see **disgraceful**

Dishon's father
4 Anah

dish out
4 dole, give, hand 6 supply 7 deliver, furnish, provide 8 dispense, hand over, transfer, turn over

disillusioned
see **disenchanted**

disimprison
4 free 5 loose 6 unbind 7 manumit, release, unchain 8 liberate 9 unshackle 10 emancipate

disinclination
7 dislike 8 aversion 13 indisposition, unwillingness

disinclined
3 shy 5 loath 6 afraid, averse, shying 7 balking, dubious, uneager 8 backward, boggling, doubtful, hesitant, opposing, sticking 9 objecting, reluctant, resisting, stickling, unwilling, unwishful 10 indisposed, protesting 12 antipathetic 13 unsympathetic

disinfect
7 cleanse 9 sterilize

disingenuous
3 sly 4 foxy, wily 5 false 6 artful, crafty, tricky 7 cunning, devious, feigned, oblique, unfrank 8 guileful, indirect, uncandid 9 insidious, insincere

disinherit
3 rob 4 lose, oust 6 cut off 7 bereave, deprive 9 deprive of, repudiate

disintegrate
3 rot 4 sink, turn 5 break, decay, spoil, taint 6 molder, worsen 7 crumble, decline, descend, putrefy, scatter, shatter 8 separate 9 break down, decompose 10 deliquesce, retrograde
suffix: 4 lyse, lyze

disintegrating
combining form: 7 clastic

disintegration
combining form: 5 lyses (plural), lysis

disinter
5 dig up 6 exhume, unbury 7 unearth 8 exhumate 9 uncharnel

disinterest
6 apathy 8 lethargy 9 lassitude, unconcern 11 insouciance 12 heedlessness, indifference, listlessness 13 unmindfulness

disinterested
4 fair, just 5 aloof 6 casual, remote 7 neutral 8 abstract, detached, negative, unbiased 9 apathetic, colorless, impartial, incurious, withdrawn 10 impersonal, poker-faced 11 indifferent, unconcerned, unpassioned

disjoin
4 part 5 sever 6 divide, sunder, unglue, unlink 7 break up, divorce, unstick 8 separate

disjoint
4 part 5 sever, upset 6 divide, luxate, mess up, muddle, sunder 7 break up, rummage 8 disorder, separate 9 uncombine

disjointed
7 muddled 8 inchoate 10 incoherent, incohesive 11 unconnected, unorganized 12 uncontinuous

disk
4 chip, puck 5 wafer 6 record
metal: 4 slug
ornamental: 6 bangle, sequin

dislike
4 hate 6 detest, hatred, resent 8 aversion, distaste 9 prejudice 10 repugnance 11 deprecation, detestation 13 indisposition
object of: 8 anathema

disliking
8 aversion 13 indisposition

dislimb
4 maim 6 mayhem 7 cripple 8 mutilate

dislimn
3 dim 5 bedim, cloud, gloom 6 darken 7 becloud, obscure 8 overcast 9 adumbrate, obfuscate

dislocate
4 move, ship 5 mix up, shift 6 jumble, remove 7 rummage 8 disorder, transfer

dislodge
5 expel 6 remove 8 drive out

disloyal
5 false 6 untrue 8 recreant 9 alienated, estranged, faithless 10 perfidious, traitorous, unfaithful 11 treacherous

disloyalty
7 falsity, perfidy, treason 9 falseness, treachery 10 infidelity 13 faithlessness

dismal
5 black, bleak 6 dreary, gloomy, somber 8 funereal 10 depressing, depressive, oppressive 13 disheartening

dismantle
4 bare, lift, raze, ruin, undo 5 annul, strip, wrack, wreck 6 denude, divest, recall, repeal, revoke 7 deprive, destroy, rescind, reverse, strip of, unbuild, uncloak 8 bankrupt, decimate, demolish, denudate, dismount, take down, wear down 10 annihilate, do away with

dismay
4 faze, fear 5 abash, alarm, appal, daunt, dread, panic, scare, shake, upset 6 appall, bother, flurry, fright, horror, puzzle, rattle, subdue, terror 7 agitate, fluster, horrify, mystify, nonplus, perplex, perturb, terrify, unhinge 8 affright, bewilder, confound, frighten 9 dumbfound, embarrass 10 discompose 11 consternate, trepidation 12 perturbation 13 consternation

dismayed
5 agape, fazed 6 aghast 7 rattled, shocked 10 confounded 11 dumbfounded, overwhelmed 13 thunderstruck

dismember
4 maim, part 5 sever 6 mangle, mayhem, sunder 7 cripple 8 dismount, mutilate, separate, take down

dismiss
2 ax 3 can, out 4 cast, drop, fire, sack, shed 5 chase, chuck, eject, evict, let go, scoff, scorn, spurn 6 bounce, depose, lay off, let out, refuse, reject, remove, retire, slough, unseat 7 boot out, cashier, contemn, decline, divorce, extrude, kick out, kiss off, put away, suspend, turn off 8 furlough, poohpooh, ridicule, throw out, turn

away, turn down 9 reprobate, repudiate, terminate

dismissal
5 congé 6 layoff, ouster 7 removal 8 brushoff

dismount
6 alight, detach, get off 7 unhorse 8 separate, take down 10 alight from

Disney
4 Walt 10 cartoonist
character: 4 Huey 5 Daisy, Dewey, Dumbo, Goofy, Louie, Pluto 6 Donald, Mickey, Minnie
classic: 8 Fantasia

disobedient
6 unruly 7 naughty, willful 8 contrary 10 headstrong, rebellious 12 contumacious, obstreperous, recalcitrant 13 insubordinate

disoblige
6 offend, put out 7 affront, trouble 8 put about 9 incommode 13 inconvenience

disorder
3 ill 4 riot, turn 5 chaos, mix up, snarl, upset 6 anomie, ataxia, huddle, jumble, malady, mess up, muddle, muss up, rumple, sicken, tumble, tumult 7 ailment, anarchy, clutter, confuse, derange, disease, embroil, illness, misdeed, misrule, rummage, shuffle, turmoil, unhinge 8 disjoint, sickness, syndrome, unhealth, unsettle, upheaval 9 affection, agitation, anarchism, commotion, complaint, condition, confusion, infirmity 10 affliction, convulsion, misconduct, turbulence 11 bedevilment, misdemeanor 13 indisposition
mental: 8 paranoia

disordered
4 daft 5 crazy 6 crazed, insane 7 cracked, lunatic, muddled 8 demented, deranged, inchoate 9 bedlamite 10 incoherent, incohesive 11 unconnected, unorganized 12 uncontinuous

disorderly
5 rowdy 6 unruly 7 raucous 8 rowdyish 9 termagant, turbulent 10 boisterous, rowdydowdy, tumultuous 11 rumbustious

disorderly house
6 bagnio 7 brothel 8 bordello

disorganize
5 upset 6 jumble, mess up 7 derange 8 unsettle

disoriented
4 lost

disown
4 deny 8 disclaim, renounce
9 repudiate

disparage
5 abuse, chill, decry 6 deject, slight
7 downcry, run down 8 bad mouth,
belittle, derogate, minimize, write
off 10 demoralize, depreciate
11 detract from

disparagement
4 tale 5 scorn 7 calumny, despite,
scandal, slander 8 contempt, despisal 9 aspersion, indignity, stricture 10 backbiting, defamation, detraction, diminution, reflection
11 despisement 12 backstabbing,
belittlement, depreciation
13 animadversion

disparate
6 unlike 7 diverse, unalike, unequal, various 9 different, divergent, unsimilar 11 inconsonant
12 incompatible, inconsistent

disparity
8 alterity 9 otherness 10 difference, divergence, divergency, inequality, unevenness, unlikeness

dispassionate
4 calm, cool, fair, just, open
5 aloof, equal, frank 7 neutral
8 abstract, composed, detached, judicial, unbiased 9 colorless, equitable, impartial, uncolored, unruffled
10 aboveboard, impersonal, poker-
faced 11 indifferent, unflappable
12 uninfluenced, unprejudiced
13 imperturbable

dispatch
4 kill, send, ship, slay 5 eat up,
haste, hurry, remit, route, scrag,
speed 6 cut off, devour, finish, hasten, hustle, lay low, rustle 7 address, consign, destroy, forward,
killing, message, put away,
quicken, take off 8 alacrity, carry
off, celerity, get rid of, goodwill,
riddance, shipment, transmit 9 diligence, polish off, readiness, swiftness 10 expedition, put to death,
speediness 11 promptitude

dispatch boat
5 aviso 6 packet

dispel
4 oust 5 eject 7 crumble, scatter
9 clear away, drive away

dispensable
5 minor 7 trivial 8 needless, unneeded 9 redundant 10 unre-

quired 11 superfluous, unessential,
unimportant, unnecessary
12 nonessential

dispensary
6 clinic

dispensation
5 favor 7 service 8 courtesy, kindness, ordering 9 remission 10 indulgence, management

dispense
3 ply 4 deal, give, hand 5 spare,
swing, wield 6 divide, excuse, exempt, handle, let off, let out, supply
7 absolve, deal out, deliver, dish
out, dole out, furnish, mete out, portion, prorate, provide, release, relieve 8 deal with, hand over, maneuver, share out, transfer, turn
over 9 apportion, discharge, partition 10 administer, distribute, manipulate, measure out, portion out

disperse
3 sow 4 deal 5 spray, strew 6 divide, lot out, spread 7 break up,
diffuse, disband, disject, dole out,
radiate, scatter 9 circulate, partition, propagate 10 distribute, measure out

dispersion
7 colloid 9 spreading 10 scattering
combining form: 3 lyo

dispirit
5 chill 6 deject 7 depress 10 demoralize, discourage

dispirited
3 low, sad 4 blue, flat 8 cast
down, dejected, downcast, lifeless
9 depressed, woebegone 10 melancholy 11 downhearted

dispiriting
5 black, bleak 6 dreary, gloomy
8 funereal 9 cheerless 10 depressing, depressive, oppressing

displace
4 oust 5 exile, expel, shift, usurp
6 banish, cut out, deport, depose,
unmake, winkle 7 expulse, uncrown 8 crowd out, dethrone, redi-
rect, relegate, supplant 9 transport
10 expatriate, substitute

displaced person
2 DP 6 émigré 7 evacuee, refugee
8 fugitive

display
4 open, pomp, show 5 array, flash,
offer, shine 6 evince, expose,
flaunt, lay out, parade, reveal,
setout, spread, unfold, unveil 7 exhibit, fanfare, panoply, showing,
show off, trot out, uncover 8 bla-

zonry, brandish, describe, evidence, manifest, unclothe 9 showiness, spectacle 10 exhibiting,
exhibition, pretension 11 demonstrate, ostentation 13 demonstration, manifestation

displeasing
3 bad 4 sour 6 rotten, vexing
7 irksome, unhappy 8 annoying
10 bothersome, unpleasant

displeasure
4 pain 5 anger 6 sorrow 8 aversion, vexation 10 uneasiness 11 indignation, unhappiness
13 indisposition

disport
3 act, fun 4 bear, game, go on,
play, show 5 amuse, carry, flash
6 acquit, behave, demean, divert,
expose, flaunt, parade 7 conduct,
exhibit, jollity, pastime, show off,
trot out 8 brandish, recreate 9 diversion, entertain, merriment
10 recreation

disposal
5 order 7 dumping, junking 8 bestowal, chucking, jettison, ordering,
riddance, sequence 9 clearance,
scrapping 10 demolition, destroying, relegation 11 arrangement,
demolishing, destruction 12 throwing away, transference

dispose
4 bend, bias 5 array, order 7 arrange, incline, marshal, prepare
8 organize 9 make ready, methodize 11 systematize
of: 4 sell 5 scrap 6 finish, handle
7 destroy, discard

disposed
4 fain 5 prone, ready 6 minded
7 willing 8 inclined

disposition
4 bent, cast, mood, tone, type, vein
5 being, humor, order, stamp, tenor
6 makeup, nature, temper 7 control, dumping, junking, leaning
8 jettison, ordering, penchant, riddance, sequence, tendency 9 character, direction, inclining, scrapping 10 complexion, management,
proclivity, propensity 11 arrangement, controlling, inclination, personality, temperament 12 predilection, throwing away
13 individualism, individuality
favorable: 8 optimism
unfavorable: 9 pessimism

dispossess
3 rob 4 lose, oust 5 eject 6 banish,
divest 7 bereave, deprive

dispossession
4 loss 6 ouster 9 privation 11 deprivation, deprivement, divestiture

dispraise
5 decry 8 belittle, derogate, diminish, minimize 10 depreciate 11 detract from, opprobriate 12 depreciation

disproportion
8 imparity, mismatch 10 inequality, unevenness

disproportionate
6 uneven 7 unequal 8 lopsided 9 irregular 10 asymmetric, off-balance, unbalanced 12 overbalanced 13 unsymmetrical

disprove
5 break, evert, rebut, shoot 6 blow up, impugn, refute 7 confute, explode 8 confound, negative, overturn, puncture, traverse 9 discredit, overthrow 10 contravene, controvert

disputable
4 moot 7 dubious 8 doubtful 9 uncertain 11 problematic

disputation
6 debate 7 mooting 8 forensic 9 dialectic 11 controversy

dispute
4 buck, duel, miff, moot, tiff 5 argue, doubt, fight, rebut, repel 6 argufy, bicker, combat, debate, hassle, oppose, refute, resist, rumpus, strife 7 agitate, canvass, confute, contend, contest, discuss, quarrel, quibble, wrangle 8 argument, conflict, mistrust, question, squabble, traverse 9 bickering, challenge, thrash out, withstand 10 contention, controvert, falling-out, toss around 11 altercation, controversy, embroilment
Scottish: 6 threap, threep

disqualified
5 unfit 8 unfitted 9 incapable 10 ineligible, unequipped 11 incompetent

disqualify
3 bar 5 debar 6 except 7 exclude, rule out, suspend 9 deprive of, eliminate, make unfit 12 incapacitate
as judge: 6 recuse

disquiet
4 care 5 upset, worry 6 bother, flurry, unease, unrest, untune 7 agitate, ailment, anxiety, concern, ferment, fluster, perturb, trouble, turmoil, unhinge 10 discompose,

solicitude, uneasiness 11 concernment, restiveness 12 restlessness 13 Sturm und Drang

disquietude
4 care 5 worry 6 unease, unrest 7 ailment, anxiety, concern, ferment, turmoil 9 agitation 10 uneasiness 11 concernment, restiveness 12 restlessness 13 Sturm und Drang

Disraeli, Benjamin
novel: 7 Tancred

disregard
4 fail, omit 5 belay 6 apathy, forget, ignore, slight 7 blink at, neglect 8 ignoring, lethargy, omission, omitting, overlook, overpass 9 blink away, lassitude, slighting, unconcern 10 forgetting, neglecting 11 insouciance, overlooking 12 heedlessness, indifference, listlessness 13 unmindfulness

disregardful
3 lax 5 slack 6 remiss 8 careless, derelict, heedless 9 negligent 10 behindhand, delinquent, neglectful, regardless

disremember
6 forget

disreputable
4 mean 5 cheap, dingy, faded, seedy, shady, sorry 6 abject, scurvy, shabby, shoddy, sordid 7 run-down 8 beggarly, decrepit, pitiable, shameful 10 bedraggled, down-at-heel, inglorious, threadbare 11 dilapidated, ignominious 12 contemptible

disrepute
5 odium, shame 6 infamy 7 obloquy 8 disgrace, ignominy 10 opprobrium

disrespect
8 boldness 9 hardihood, impudence, insolence, insolency 10 incivility 12 impertinence, insolentness

disrespectful
4 rude 7 ill-bred, incivil, uncivil 8 impolite, impudent 10 ungracious 11 ill-mannered, impertinent

disrobe
4 bare 5 strip 6 denude, divest 7 deprive, strip of, undress 8 bankrupt, denudate, unclothe

disrupt
4 hole, open 5 upset 6 breach, mess up, muddle 7 rummage, rupture 8 disorder, unsettle 10 break apart

dissatisfaction
7 dislike 8 aversion 10 uneasiness

dissatisfactory
3 bad 4 poor 5 amiss, wrong 6 rotten

dissatisfied
5 irked, vexed 7 annoyed 8 bothered 9 uncontent 10 malcontent 11 uncontented 12 discontented, malcontented

dissect
3 cut 4 part 5 carve, probe, sever, slice, split 6 cleave, divide, pierce, sunder 7 analyze, break up, resolve 8 separate 9 anatomize, break down, decompose, penetrate 10 decompound 11 dichotomize

dissection
of animals: 7 zootomy

dissemblance
5 guile 6 deceit 7 cunning 8 alterity 9 duplicity, otherness 10 difference, divergence, divergency, unlikeness

dissemble
4 mask 5 cloak, feign 7 conceal, dress up 8 disguise 10 camouflage

dissembler
8 pharisee, Tartuffe 9 hypocrite, lip server

disseminate
3 sow 5 straw, strew 6 blazon, spread 7 bestrew, declare, diffuse, publish, radiate, scatter, send out 8 announce, permeate, proclaim 9 advertise, broadcast, circulate, propagate, publicize, spread out 10 annunciate, promulgate 11 blaze abroad

dissension
6 strife 7 discord, quarrel, wrangle 8 argument, conflict, variance 9 bickering 10 contention, difference, quarreling 11 altercation, controversy

dissent
3 shy 4 balk, vary 5 demur 6 boggle, differ, divide, heresy, object, schism, strife 7 stickle 8 conflict, variance 9 misbelief 10 contention, difference, heterodoxy 11 unorthodoxy 12 nonagreement 13 nonconformism, nonconformity

dissenter
7 heretic, sectary 10 schismatic, separatist 11 misbeliever, schismatist 13 nonconformist

dissertation
6 memoir, thesis 8 tractate, treatise

9 discourse, monograph, treatment
10 monography

disservice
6 injury 8 mischief

dissever
3 cut 4 part 5 carve, slice, split
6 cleave, divide, sunder 7 divorce
8 separate 11 dichotomize

dissidence
6 heresy, schism, strife 7 discord
8 conflict 9 misbelief 10 contention, heterodoxy 11 unorthodoxy
13 nonconformism, nonconformity

dissident
7 heretic, sectary 9 differing, heretical, heterodox, sectarian 10 schismatic, separatist, unorthodox
11 contentious, misbeliever, quarrelsome, schismatist 12 unharmonious
13 nonconformist

dissimilar
6 unlike 7 diverse, unalike, unequal, various 8 contrary, opposite
9 different, divergent 10 antonymous 12 antithetical
13 contradictory

dissimilarity
8 variance 9 diversity, otherness,
severance 10 difference, divergence, divergency, unlikeness
11 incongruity 12 divarication, in-
consonance 13 heterogeneity,
inconsistency

dissimulate
see **dissemble**

dissimulation
5 guile 6 deceit, hiding 7 cunning,
masking 8 cloaking, feigning, pretense, shamming 9 duplicity, hypocrisy, secreting 10 catabolism,
concealing, pharisaism, pretend-
ing, sanctimony 12 camouflaging

dissimulator
see **dissembler**

dissipate
4 blow 5 waste 6 vanish 7 consume, crumble, fritter, scatter 8 evanesce, fool away, squander
9 evaporate, throw away 10 frivol
away, trifle away 11 blunder away

dissociate
5 unfix 6 cut off, detach 8 abstract,
alienate, estrange, uncouple

dissolute
3 lax 4 fast, wild 5 light, loose,
slack 6 rakish, wanton 7 lawless,
raffish, wayward 9 abandoned,
reprobate 10 licentious, profligate

12 unprincipled, unrestrained
13 self-abandoned

dissolution
5 death, decay, sleep 6 demise
7 decease, divorce, passing, quietus, rupture, silence, split-up 8 curtains, division 10 detachment, prof-
ligacy 11 divorcement
combining form: 3 lys 4 lysi, lyso
5 lyses (plural), lysis

dissolvable
7 soluble

dissolve
3 end 4 flux, fuse, melt, ruin, thaw,
undo, void 5 annul, quash, wrack,
wreck 6 recess, unfold, vacate,
vanish 7 adjourn, break up, clear
up, destroy, disband, immerse, liquefy, resolve, shatter, unravel 8 abrogate, decimate, decipher, demolish, destruct, fade away, get rid of,
liquesce, prorogue, separate 9 decompose, figure out, lose power,
prorogate, puzzle out, terminate,
waste away 10 annihilate, deliquesce, do away with
13 superimposing
suffix: 4 lyse, lyze

dissonance
6 strife 7 discord 8 conflict 9 cacophony 10 contention, difference
11 incongruity

dissonant
4 rude 5 harsh 6 hoarse, rugged
7 grating, jarring, raucous 8 strident 9 immusical, unmixable, unmusical 10 cacophonic, inharmonic
11 cacophonous, conflicting, incongruent, incongruous 12 incompatible, inconsistent, inharmonious

dissuade
5 deter 6 dehort, divert 10 discourage, disincline

distaff
6 female

distance
3 way 4 area, size, ways 5 ambit,
orbit, piece, range, reach, route,
scope, space, spell, sweep
6 course, degree, extent, length,
milage, outrun, radius, spread
7 breadth, compass, expanse, mileage, outpace, purview, reserve,
spacing, stretch 8 alterity, coldness, interval, outspeed, outstrip
9 amplitude, expansion, extension,
otherness 10 difference, divergence, divergency, remoteness,
separation, unlikeness 11 dis-

tinction, perspective 12 dissemblance 13 dissimilarity,
dissimilitude
angular: 8 latitude 9 longitude
between levels: 4 drop
between rails: 4 gage
between supports: 4 span
from bottom to top: 6 height
geometric: 8 altitude
greatest perpendicular: 6 camber
measuring instrument: 8 odograph,
odometer 9 pedometer, telemeter
11 range finder
minute: 4 hair
perpendicular: 5 depth
shortest: 7 beeline 12 straight line
the wind blows: 5 fetch

distant
3 far, shy 4 afar, cold, cool
5 aloof, apart 6 far-off, remote
7 diverse, faraway, haughty, obscure, removed, spacial, spatial,
unalike, unequal, various 8 far-
flung, isolated, off-lying, outlying,
reserved, retiring, secluded, solitary
9 different, divergent, separated,
unsimilar, withdrawn 10 unsociable
11 out-of-the-way, sequestered,
standoffish
combining form: 3 tel 4 tele, telo

distaste
7 dislike 8 aversion 9 antipathy,
hostility, revulsion 10 abhorrence,
repugnance 13 indisposition

distasteful
4 flat 6 bitter, odious 7 galling, insipid, painful 8 grievous, unsavory
9 loathsome, obnoxious, repellent,
repugnant, repulsive, savorless,
tasteless 10 abominable, afflictive,
detestable, flavorless 11 ill-flavored, unpalatable
12 unappetizing

distemper
4 riot 5 mix up, paint 6 choler,
muddle 7 anarchy, derange, disease, misrule, rummage 8 disorder
9 anarchism, strangles 10 affliction
11 derangement 13 panleucopenia

distend
5 bloat, swell 6 dilate, expand, extend 7 amplify, augment, enlarge,
inflate 8 increase, lengthen
10 stretch out

distill
4 drib, drip, drop, weep 6 infuse,
purify 7 dribble, trickle
11 concentrate

distillation apparatus
5 still 7 alembic, limbeck

distinct

4 sole 5 clear, lucid, plain 6 patent, single 7 defined, diverse, evident, express, notable, obvious, special, unusual, various 8 apparent, clear-cut, definite, especial, explicit, manifest, palpable, peculiar, separate, specific 9 different, divergent 10 individual, particular, prescribed 11 categorical, perspicuous, unambiguous, unequivocal
combining form: 4 idio 5 chori 7 chorist 8 choristo

distinction

4 bays, rank 5 award, badge, class, grade, honor, kudos 6 nicety, renown 7 laurels 8 accolade, alterity, eminence, prestige 9 otherness 10 difference, divergence, divergency, prominence, prominency, unlikeness 11 differentia, preeminence 12 significance 13 dissimilarity

distinctive

6 proper, single, unique 8 peculiar, separate 9 diacritic 10 diagnostic, individual 11 outstanding 13 idiosyncratic

distingué

6 urbane 7 genteel, refined 8 cultured, polished, well-bred 10 cultivated

distinguish

3 see 4 know, mark, note, part, spot, view 5 erect, exalt, honor, place 6 descry, finger, notice, remark, set off 7 dignify, ennoble, glorify, magnify, mark off, observe, pick out, qualify, sublime 8 diagnose, identify, perceive, pinpoint, separate 9 demarcate, extricate, recognize, signalize, single out 10 aggrandize, difference 11 determinate, individuate, singularize 12 characterize 13 diagnosticate, differentiate, individualize

distinguished

5 famed, grand, great 6 famous 7 courtly, eminent, notable, stately 8 imposing, renowned 9 dignified, prominent 10 celebrated, celebrious 11 illustrious

distort

4 bend, warp, wind 5 alter, belie, color, curve, twist, wrest 6 change, deform, garble 7 falsify, pervert, torture 8 miscolor, misshape, misstate 11 misconstrue 12 misinterpret, misrepresent

distortion

8 misshape 9 deformity

distract

5 addle, craze, mix up 6 ball up, frenzy, fuddle, harass, madden 7 confuse, derange, fluster, unhinge 8 befuddle, bewilder, confound, throw off 9 unbalance

distraction

6 lunacy 7 madness 8 insanity 9 amusement, diversion, unbalance 10 insaneness, perplexity 11 derangement, psychopathy 13 entertainment

distrait

4 lost 5 upset 6 absent 7 bemused, faraway, worried 8 harassed, troubled 9 tormented 10 abstracted 11 inattentive, inconscient, preoccupied 12 absentminded

distraught

3 mad 4 daft, nuts 5 crazy, upset 6 addled, crazed, insane 7 cracked, frantic, muddled, worried 8 agitated, confused, demented, deranged, harassed, troubled 9 flustered, perturbed, tormented 10 bewildered, nonplussed

distress

3 ail, irk, try, woe 4 ache, cark, hurt, need, pain, pang, pass, rack 5 agony, annoy, cross, dolor, grief, harry, pinch, rigor, throe, trial, upset, weigh, worry 6 bother, grieve, harass, injure, misery, pester, plague, sorrow, strain, strait, stress, twinge 7 afflict, anguish, exhaust, passion, torment, torture, trouble 8 aggrieve, calamity, exigency, hardship 9 adversity, constrain, suffering 10 affliction, difficulty, heartbreak, misfortune, visitation 11 tribulation, vicissitude
call: 6 Mayday
signal: 3 SOS 5 alarm

distressing

4 dire 6 woeful 8 grievous, poignant 10 afflictive, calamitous, deplorable, lamentable 11 regrettable, unfortunate 13 heartbreaking

distribute

3 lot 4 deal, give, mete 5 allot, place, strew 6 assign, assort, bestow, divide, donate, lot out, parcel, ration, spread 7 deal out, deliver, diffuse, dole out, dribble, give out, mete out, portion, present, prorate, radiate, scatter 8 allocate,

classify, dispense, position, separate 9 apportion, circulate, partition, propagate, spread out 10 administer, measure out
in a tournament: 4 seed

distribution

5 order 7 density 8 ordering, sequence 9 allotment, placement 10 scattering 11 arrangement, probability 12 spreading out 13 apportionment

distributor

6 jobber 7 carrier 10 wholesaler

district

4 area 5 tract 6 barrio, parcel, region, sector 7 quarter, section 8 division, locality, precinct, vicinage, vicinity 11 subdivision 12 neighborhood
ecclesiastical: 5 synod 6 parish 7 diocese
Greek: 4 deme
Indian: 6 tahsil
judicial: 7 circuit
London: 4 Soho
theater: 6 rialto
Turkish administrative: 6 sanjak

distrust

5 doubt 7 suspect 8 wariness 9 suspicion 10 disbelieve

distrustful

4 wary 7 jealous 10 suspicious

distrusting

7 cynical 9 sceptical, skeptical 10 suspicious

disturb

4 faze, move, ship 5 alarm, fease, feaze, feeze, rouse, scare, shift, unset, upset 6 bother, damage, flurry, jumble, meddle, mess up, puzzle, remove, stir up, tamper 7 agitate, break up, derange, destroy, fluster, inquiet, perplex, replace, terrify, trouble, unhinge 8 bewilder, disorder, frighten, transfer, unsettle 9 incommode, interfere 11 intermeddle 13 inconvenience, interfere with

disturbance

6 rumpus, unrest 7 bobbery, cyclone, tornado, unquiet 9 agitating, agitation, commotion, variation 10 alteration 11 derangement 12 diastrophism, interruption
atmospheric: 5 storm
emotional: 8 neuroses (plural), neurosis
mental: 6 frenzy 7 phrensy 8 delirium
oceanic: 7 tsunami

disunify
see **disunite**

disunion
6 strife 7 divorce, rupture, split-up
8 conflict, division, variance 9 partition 10 contention, detachment, difference, separation
11 divorcement

disunite
4 part, wean 5 alien 6 divide, sunder 7 break up, divorce, split up
8 alienate, estrange, separate
9 fall apart, uncombine
11 dichotomize

disunity
6 strife 7 discord 8 conflict, variance 10 alienation, contention, difference

ditch
3 cut, dig, pit 4 cast, foss, junk
5 chuck, fosse, scrap 6 reject, sheuch, sheugh, trench, trough
7 abandon, cashier, discard, dismiss, foxhole 8 jettison, throw out
9 throw away 10 excavation

dither
3 gab, jaw, yak 4 chat, flap, halt, stew 5 clack, jumps, quake, run on, shake, waver 6 babble, cackle, falter, quaver, shakes, shiver, tremor, tumult 7 jitters, shivers, shudder, stagger, tremble, turmoil, twitter, whiffle, willies 8 hesitate 9 agitation, commotion, confusion, vacillate, whim-whams 10 turbulence
12 shilly-shally, wiggle-waggle
13 heebie-jeebies

dithyramb
4 hymn, poem 5 chant

dithyrambic
4 wild 5 fiery 6 ardent, fervid, torrid 7 burning, fervent, flaming
9 perfervid, rhapsodic 10 boisterous, passionate 11 impassioned

ditto
4 copy 6 carbon, repeat 7 replica
9 duplicate, facsimile 10 carbon copy 11 replication 12 reproduction 13 reduplication

ditty
3 lay 4 aria, hymn, lied, song
7 descant

diurnal
5 daily 9 circadian, ephemeral, quotidian

divagate
5 stray 6 depart, ramble, wander
7 digress, diverge, excurse

divan
4 sofa 5 couch 7 council 9 davenport 11 smoking room

diva's solo
4 aria

dive
3 bar, pub 4 dash, dump, hole, jump, leap 5 joint, lunge, pitch, sound 6 gainer, lounge, plunge, saloon, tavern 7 barroom, decline, descend, descent, hangout, taproom 8 submerge 9 belly-flop, honky-tonk, jackknife, roadhouse
10 cannonball, submerging
position: 4 pike, tuck 8 straight

diver
4 loon
combining form: 4 dyta 5 dytes

diverge
4 part, vary 5 stray 6 depart, differ, ramble, swerve, wander 7 deflect, deviate, digress, excurse
8 disagree, separate 9 draw apart

divergence
7 parting, turning, variety, varying
8 alterity 9 departure, deviation, differing, otherness 10 aberration, deflection, difference, digression, separation, unlikeness 11 disagreeing, discrepancy, distinction 12 disagreement, dissemblance 13 dissimilarity, dissimilitude

divergent
6 off-key, radial, unlike 7 deviant, distant, unalike, unequal, various
8 aberrant, abnormal, atypical, contrary, opposite 9 anomalous, different, differing, disparate, irregular, radiating, spreading, unnatural, unregular, unsimilar 10 dissimilar 12 antithetical 13 contradictory

divers
4 many, some 6 sundry 7 several, various
combining form: 4 poly, vari 5 parti, party, vario

diver's disease
5 bends 12 aeroembolism

diverse
6 unlike 7 distant, several, unalike, unequal, various 8 contrary, discrete, distinct, manifold, opposite, separate 9 different, differing, disparate, multifold, multiform, multiplex, unsimilar 10 contrasted, dissimilar 11 contrasting, contrastive 12 multifarious
13 contradictory
meanings: 8 polysemy

diversion
3 fun 4 play 5 sport 6 levity, relish 7 disport, turning 8 pleasure, sideshow 9 amusement, departure, deviation, enjoyment, frivolity 10 aberration, deflection, recreation
11 delectation, distraction
13 entertainment

diversity
7 variety 8 multeity 10 difference, unlikeness 11 distinction, variousness 12 multiformity, multiplicity
13 dissimilarity

divert
4 turn, veer 5 alter, amuse, deter
6 swerve 7 deflect, deviate, digress
8 dissuade, distract 9 disadvise, disengage, entertain, turn aside
10 discourage
water: 5 flume

divest
3 rob 4 bare, lose, oust 5 spoil, strip 6 denude 7 bereave, deprive, disrobe, undress 8 bankrupt, denudate, take away 9 dismantle
10 disinherit, dispossess

divide
3 cut 4 chop, deal, fork, part, vary
5 allot, carve, halve, quota, sever, share 6 assign, cleave, differ, lot out, parcel, ration, sector, sunder
7 break up, comport, discord, disjoin, dissect, dissent, divorce, dole out, furcate, portion, prorate, quarter, section, segment, share in, split up 8 allocate, classify, disagree, disburse, disjoint, dispense, disperse, disunite, fraction, graduate, separate 9 apportion, branch out, disaccord, partition, watershed
10 distribute, measure out 11 dichotomize, distinguish
into four parts: 7 quarter
into three parts: 7 trisect
into two parts: 5 halve 6 bisect
9 bifurcate

divided
6 cloven 7 asunder, partite 8 multifid 9 disunited, separated
combining form: 3 fid 4 sect 5 fissi, schiz 6 fidate, schizo, tomous
7 chorist 8 choristo

dividend
4 meed, plum 5 bonus, prize
6 carrot, return, reward 7 guerdon, premium

divider
6 bunton 7 compass 9 partition

divination
6 augury 7 insight 8 prophecy

by communication with the dead:
10 necromancy
by dreams: 11 oneiromancy
by figures: 8 geomancy
by lots: 9 sortilege
by numbers: 10 numerology
by rods: 7 dowsing
11 rhabdomancy
by stars: 9 astrology
combining form: 5 mancy

divine
4 holy 5 clerk, godly, infer 6 cleric,
deific, parson, priest, sacred
7 foresee, godlike, preknow, previse, suppose 8 clerical, discover,
forefeel, foreknow, minister,
preacher, prophesy, reverend
9 apprehend, chthonian, churchman, clergyman, marvelous, prevision, religious, visualize 10 anticipate, conjecture, superhuman,
theologian 12 ecclesiastic, extra-
mundane, transmundane
13 superphysical

Divine Comedy author
5 Dante

divining ability, for short
3 ESP

divinity
3 god 5 deity 7 godhead
8 theology
female: 5 nymph 7 goddess

division
3 cut 4 part, unit 5 class, piece
6 member, moiety, parcel, schism
7 discord, dissent, divorce, parting,
portion, rupture, section, segment,
split-up 8 category, conflict, district,
disunion, disunity, variance 9 disaccord, partition 10 detachment,
difference, disharmony, dissidence,
dissonance, separation 11 dissolution, divorcement 12 disagreement
13 apportionment
Bible: 5 verse
book: 7 chapter
British territorial: 5 shire
building: 4 wing
cell: 7 meiosis, mitosis
city: 4 ward 7 borough 8 precinct
combining form: 7 kineses (plural),
kinesis
contest: 4 heat 6 inning, period
corolla: 5 petal
country: 5 state 6 canton 8 province
10 department, prefecture
family: 4 side 6 branch
geologic time: 5 epoch 6 period
hospital: 4 ward, wing
into two: 9 bisection 11 bifurcation,
bipartition

mankind: 4 race
meal: 6 course
music: 3 bar 4 line 7 measure
8 movement
opera, play: 3 act 5 scene
poem: 5 canto, verse 6 stanza
population: 7 segment, stratum
race: 3 lap 4 heat
social: 5 caste, class, tribe
state: 6 county, parish
term: 8 quotient
time: 3 day, eon 4 week, year
5 month 6 decade, minute, moment, second 7 weekend
9 fortnight
tribal: 4 clan
word: 8 syllable
zodiac: 4 sign

divisive
8 factious

divorce
4 part 5 annul, sever, split 6 cancel, sunder 7 break up, disjoin, dismiss, put away, rupture, split-up, unmarry 8 disjoint, dissever, disunion,
disunite, separate 9 disaffect, partition 10 detachment, separation
11 dissolution

divot
4 turf

divulge
4 tell 5 mouth, spill 6 betray, gossip, reveal, tattle 7 blab out 8 disclose, discover, give away, proclaim 13 spill the beans

"Dixie" composer
6 Emmett (Daniel)

___ dixit
4 ipse

dizziness
7 vertigo

dizzy
4 daze 5 addle, dazed, giddy, inane, light, mix up, silly, undue
6 addled, ball up, fuddle, muddle,
swimmy 7 asinine, confuse, daz-
zled, extreme, fatuous, flighty, fluster, foolish, fuddled, muddled, puz-
zled, reeling, stupefy 8 befuddle,
bewilder, confused, heedless, skittish, swimming, throw off, towering,
whirling 9 befuddled, confusing,
excessive, frivolous 10 bewildered,
bird-witted, confounded, distracted,
exorbitant, immoderate, inordinate
11 empty-headed, extravagant,
harebrained, light-headed, vertiginous 12 unmeasurable

DNA
component: 7 adenine, guanine, thy-

mine 8 cytosine 10 nucleotide
11 deoxyribose
segment: 7 cistron

do
3 act, end, gyp, pay, put, set
4 bear, beat, bilk, cook, fare, feel,
go on, halt, play, quit, show, suit,
tire, tour, wash, work 5 break,
cheat, clean, close, cover, cozen,
enact, exert, get by, get on, occur,
serve, shift, tonic, track 6 acquit,
befall, behave, betide, chance,
chouse, commit, demean, deport,
diddle, effect, finish, happen, manage, render, travel, wind up, work
at, wrap up 7 achieve, approve,
arrange, come off, comport, conduct, defraud, develop, execute, exhaust, fall out, furbish, perform,
playact, suffice, undergo, wear out
8 carry out, complete, conclude,
decorate, flimflam, get along, pass
over, traverse 9 determine, discourse, overreach, personate, stagger on, terminate, transpire 11 impersonate 12 stagger along
13 muddle through
away with: 5 abate 6 banish
7 abolish 8 demolish, dissolve
without: 5 forgo 6 forego
wrong: 3 err

doable
8 feasible, possible

docent
7 teacher 8 lecturer, teaching
10 instructor 11 instructive

docile
4 tame 5 tawie 6 pliant 7 pliable
8 amenable, biddable, obedient
9 adaptable, teachable, tractable
10 submissive

dock
4 pier, quay, rump, slip 5 berth,
jetty, levee, wharf 6 hangar,
lessen, marina, reduce 7 abridge
8 platform
worker: 6 lumper 9 stevedore
12 longshoreman

docket
4 card, sked 6 agenda 7 program
8 calendar, schedule 9 timetable

doctor
2 MD 3 fix, vet 4 load, mend
5 medic, patch, treat 6 breeze, debase, dope up, medico, repair, revamp 7 dentist, medical, rebuild,
scholar, surgeon 8 overhaul 9 clini-
cian, internist, mediciner, physician
10 adulterate, specialist 11 medicine man, recondition, reconstruct
animal: 3 vet 12 veterinarian

children's: 12 pediatrician

famous baby care: 5 Spock (Benjamin)

foot: 10 podiatrist 11 chiropodist

heart: 12 cardiologist

slang: 8 sawbones

teeth: 7 dentist

women's: 12 gynecologist

Doctor of the Church
5 Basil 6 Jerome 7 Ambrose, Gregory 9 Augustine 10 Athanasius

doctrinaire
6 dogged, mulish 8 dogmatic, stubborn 9 dictative, obstinate, pigheaded 10 bullheaded 11 dictatorial, magisterial, stiff-necked 12 pertinacious 13 authoritarian, authoritative

doctrine
3 ism 4 doxy 5 axiom, basic, canon, dogma, doxie, tenet 7 plenism 8 teaching 9 principle 11 fundamental, instruction

combining form: 4 logy 5 logia

legal: 6 cypres

occult: 6 cabala, kabala 7 cabbala, kabbala 8 cabbalah, kabbalah

philosophical: 8 monadism, vitalism

religious: 8 chiliasm

suffix: 3 ism

document
5 paper 6 record 8 evidence, monument 9 testimony 11 certificate

travel: 8 passport

Dodavah's son
7 Eliezer

dodder
8 love vine

doddering
6 doting, senile

dodge
4 duck, jink, jouk, slip 5 avoid, elude, evade, fence, parry, shirk, skirt, slide 6 escape, scheme, weasel 7 evasion, shuffle 8 malinger, sidestep 9 avoidance, expedient, pussyfoot 10 equivocate, tergiverse 12 short circuit, tergiversate

dodger
7 haggler 8 circular, handbill 9 throwaway

Dodger
5 Davis (Tommy) 6 Garvey (Steve), Karros (Eric), Koufax (Sandy), Piazza (Michael), Snider (Duke), Sutton (Don) 8 Newcombe (Don), Robinson (Jackie) 9 Hershiser (Orel) 10 Campanella (Roy)

field: 7 Ebbetts

manager: 6 Alston (Walter) 7 Lasorda (Tommy)

dodo
4 boob, dolt 5 dummy, dunce, idiot, moron 6 dimwit, nitwit 8 numskull 9 simpleton

Dodo's son
7 Eleazar, Elhanan

doe
4 deer 6 almond

young: 3 teg

doer
suffix: 2 er, or 3 ast, eer, ier, ist 4 ater, ster

doff
5 douse, uncap, unhat 6 remove, unhelm 7 take off

dog
3 cur, pug, pup, tag 4 bird, chap, chow, fice, mutt, peke, puli, stop, tail, tyke 5 boxer, click, feist, frank, hound, lemon, pooch, puppy, spitz, trail 6 Afghan, bawtie, bowwow, briard, canine, collie, detent, poodle, rascal, saluki, shadow, wiener, wretch 7 andiron, Maltese, mastiff, mongrel, pointer, Samoyed, spaniel, terrier, whippet 8 Airedale, inferior, keeshond, papillon, Pekinese, pinscher, spurious, wirehair 9 Chihuahua, dachshund, Dalmation, Great Dane, greyhound, Pekingese, retriever, schnauzer 10 bloodhound, Pomeranian, Weimaraner 11 frankfurter, wienerwurst 12 Newfoundland, Saint Bernard 13 cocker spaniel

Alaskan: 8 malamute, malemiut, malemute

Australian: 5 dingo 8 warragal, warrigal

barkless: 7 basenji

bird: 6 setter 7 pointer, spaniel 9 retriever

Buster Brown's: 4 Tige

Charlie Brown's: 6 Snoopy

combining form: 3 cyn 4 cyno

Dorothy's: 4 Toto

Eskimo: 5 husky

family: 7 Canidae

FDR's: 4 Fala

fictional: 4 Lady 5 Astro, Pluto 6 Big Red 8 McBarker

"Garfield": 4 Odie

genus: 5 Canis

Hungarian: 6 vizsla

hunting: 4 alan 5 alant, hound 6 alaunt, beagle, borzoi, saluki, setter, Talbot 7 harrier, pointer, redbone 8 elkhound, foxhound 9 wolfhound 10 bloodhound 11 basset hound

Indian: 5 dhole

L.B.J.'s: 3 Her

long-bodied: 9 dachshund

movie: 4 Asta, Toto 5 Benji 9 Beethoven, Old Yeller, Rin Tin Tin

name: 4 Fido, Spot 5 Rover 6 Bowser

Nixon's: 8 Checkers

Odysseus's: 5 Argos

of Hades: 8 Cerberus

Orphan Annie's: 5 Sandy

powerful: 11 bull mastiff

Roy Rogers's: 6 Bullet

Russian: 6 borzoi 7 Samoyed

shaggy-coated: 8 komondor

short-legged: 5 corgi

small: 3 pom, pug, pup 4 alco, peke 7 whiffet 8 Pekinese 9 Chihuahua, Pekingese 10 Pomeranian

space traveler: 5 Laika

Steinbeck's: 7 Charley

television: 4 King 5 Eddie, Tramp 6 Lassie, Murray 8 Wishbone 9 Rin Tin Tin

terrier: 7 scottie

three-headed: 8 Cerberus

Tibetan: 9 Lhasa apso

tiny: 9 Chihuahua

tooth: 4 fang

tracking: 10 bloodhound

two-headed: 6 Orthos

Welsh: 5 corgi

Wendy's: 4 Nana

young: 3 pup 5 puppy, whelp

dogbane
10 bitterroot

dog days
8 canicule

dogfall
3 tie 4 draw 8 deadlock, standoff 9 stalemate

dogfight
3 row 4 fray 5 brawl, broil, melee, set-to 6 fracas 7 ruction 10 donnybrook, free-for-all

dogfish
6 bowfin, burbot 8 mud puppy

genus: 7 Squalus

dogged
5 rigid 7 adamant 8 obdurate 9 insistent, steadfast, unbending 10 brassbound, inexorable, inflexible, persistent, persisting, persistive, relentless, unshakable 11 perseverant, persevering, unremitting 12 single-minded 13 perseverative

doggone
4 damn, darn, rank 5 utter 6 damned 7 blasted, blessed, dratted 8 absolute, infernal, outright

9 dad-burned, out-and-out 10 confounded 11 unmitigated 13 blankety-blank

dogma
5 canon, credo, creed, tenet 6 belief 8 doctrine 10 conviction, persuasion

dogmatic
7 a priori 8 reasoned 9 deducible, deductive, derivable, dictative, doctrinal 11 dictatorial, doctrinaire, magisterial 13 authoritarian, authoritative

dog-paddle
4 swim

dog's age
3 eon 4 aeon, long 8 blue moon, eternity 12 donkey's years

Dog Star
6 Sirius

dogwood
5 sumac 6 cornel 8 red osier 9 boobyalla 11 native broom

do in
4 ruin, slay 5 wreck 6 finish, murder 7 execute, exhaust, frazzle, outtire, outwear, put away, wear out 8 bankrupt, knock off, knock out 9 liquidate, prostrate, shipwreck 10 dilapidate 11 assassinate

doing
3 act 6 action
combining form: 6 praxes (plural), praxia, praxis
good: 10 beneficent
suffix: 3 ant, ent

doit
3 bit, jot 4 damn, dram, drop, hoot, iota, whit 5 whoop 6 trifle 8 particle

doldrums
4 yawn 5 blues, dumps, ennui, gloom, slump 6 apathy, tedium 7 boredom, latency 8 abeyance, abeyancy, dormancy 9 dejection 10 depression, inactivity, quiescence, quiescency, stagnation 12 indifference, listlessness

doleful
4 down 7 piteous, pitiful, ruthful 8 cast down, dejected, downcast, grieving, mournful, mourning, wretched 9 afflicted, cheerless, depressed, miserable, plaintive, sorrowful, sorrowing, woebegone 10 dispirited, lamentable, lugubrious, melancholy 11 crestfallen, downhearted 12 disconsolate

dole out
4 deal, mete 6 divide, parcel, ration 7 mete out 8 disburse, dispense, disperse, share out 9 apportion, partition 10 administer, distribute

doll
3 Ken 6 Barbie, figure, Kewpie, puppet 10 Betsy Wetsy, Raggedy Ann 11 Raggedy Andy
grotesque: 8 golliwog

dollar
4 bill, buck, oner 8 simoleon

dollop
3 nip, tot 4 dram, drop, jolt, shot, slug 5 snort 7 snifter 8 toothful

Doll's House, A
author: 5 Ibsen (Henrik)
heroine: 4 Nora

dolly
4 cart 5 truck 7 stirrer

dolomite
6 marble 9 limestone 10 bitter spar

dolor
5 agony 6 misery, sorrow 7 anguish, passion 8 distress 9 suffering

dolorous
4 dire 6 rueful, woeful 7 ruthful 8 grievous, mournful, wretched 9 afflicted, miserable, plaintive, sorrowful 10 afflictive, calamitous, deplorable, lamentable, lugubrious, melancholy 11 distressing, regrettable 13 heartbreaking

dolphin
5 whale 7 bollard 8 porpoise 9 butterfly
combining form: 7 delphis

dolt
3 ass, oaf 4 boob, clod, goof 5 booby, chump, dunce 7 dullard, fathead, jughead, saphead, schnook 8 dumnkopf, lunkhead, meathead, numskull 9 blockhead
Scottish: 4 coof

doltish
4 dull, dumb 5 dense, thick 6 stupid 8 blockish, duncical 9 fatheaded 11 blockheaded 12 beetleheaded

domain
4 walk 5 field, realm 6 sphere 7 demesne, terrain 8 dominion, province 9 bailiwick, champaign, territory
nether: 4 hell
transcendent: 6 heaven
Turkish: 6 beylic, beylik

dome
4 roof 7 ceiling 12 snap fastener

domed hut
5 igloo

Domesday Book money
4 oras

domestic
4 home, tame 6 family, native 7 subdued 8 internal, national 9 household, municipal 10 indigenous, submissive

domesticate
4 tame 5 adopt, train 6 master, subdue 10 housebreak, naturalize 11 familiarize

domicile
3 hut 4 home 5 abode, board, house, lodge, put up 6 bestow, billet, harbor 7 quarter 8 dwelling 9 entertain, residence, residency 10 commorancy, habitation

domiciliate
3 hut 4 bunk, tame 5 board, house, lodge, put up 6 billet, harbor, master, reside 7 quarter

dominance
9 masterdom, supremacy 10 ascendancy, prepotence, prepotency 11 preeminence, sovereignty

dominant
4 main 5 chief, first, major 6 master, ruling 7 capital, leading, regnant, stellar, supreme 8 foremost 9 ascendant, governing, number one, paramount, prevalent, principal, sovereign 10 preeminent, prevailing, surpassing 11 outweighing, overbearing 12 overweighing, preponderant, transcendent 13 overbalancing

dominate
4 rule 5 reign 6 direct, govern, handle, manage, obsess 7 control, overtop, prevail, repress 8 domineer, look down, overarch, overlook, override 9 tower over 10 tower above
at home: 12 wear the pants

domination
4 sway 5 might, power 7 command, control, mastery, strings 9 authority, masterdom, supremacy 10 ascendancy, prepotence, prepotency, suzerainty 11 preeminence, sovereignty 13 preponderancy

dominator
4 boss, cock, head 5 chief, ruler 6 honcho, leader, master 7 headman 8 hierarch 9 chieftain

domineer

4 rule 5 reign 7 prevail 11 predominate 12 preponderate

domineering

5 bossy 6 lordly 8 arrogant, imperial, insolent 9 imperious, masterful 10 highhanded, imperative, peremptory, tyrannical 11 magisterial

Dominican Republic

capital: 12 Santo Domingo
island: 10 Hispaniola
monetary unit: 4 peso
product: 5 cocoa, sugar 6 coffee 7 bauxite, tobacco

dominion

3 raj 4 rule, sway 5 field, realm, regna (plural) 6 domain, empery, regnum, sphere 7 demesne, terrain 8 property, province 9 ascendant, bailiwick, champaign, masterdom, ownership, supremacy, territory 10 ascendancy, possession, prepotence, prepotency 11 preeminence, proprietary, sovereignty 13 possessorship

domino

4 mask 5 amice, visor 6 vizard 9 doughface, false face
spot: 3 pip

don

3 sir 4 lord, pull 5 get on, put on 6 assume, draw on, slip on, strike, take on 7 throw on 8 huddle on

Donalbain

brother: 7 Malcolm
father: 6 Duncan

Donar

see **Thor**

donate

4 emit, give, loan 6 bestow, devote, hansel, supply 7 hand out, handsel, present 8 give away, transfer 10 contribute

donation

3 aid 4 alms, gift, help 5 grant 7 bequest, charity, handsel, subsidy 8 offering 9 endowment 10 assistance 11 beneficence 12 contribution

donator

see **donor**

Don Camillo

6 priest

Don Carlos

author: 8 Schiller (Friedrich von)
composer: 5 Verdi (Giuseppe)
father: 6 Philip

done

5 all in, ended, right, spent 6 decent, doomed, effete, gone by, proper, used up 7 correct, drained, dressed, far-gone, through, worn-out 8 becoming, complete, decorous, depleted, finished, washed-up 9 befitting, completed, concluded, exhausted, fitted out 10 conforming, terminated
for: 4 gone, sunk 5 kaput 8 finished
poetic: 3 o'er

donee

7 grantee 8 receiver 9 appointor, recipient

done in

5 spent 6 effete, used up 7 fargone, worn-out 8 depleted 9 exhausted, washed-out

Don Giovanni composer

6 Mozart (Wolfgang Amadeus)

Donizetti

hero: 7 Roberto
opera: 5 Lucia 10 Anna Bolena, La Favorita 11 Don Pasquale 12 Maria Stuarda

Don Juan

4 rake, wolf 5 Romeo 6 chaser, masher 7 amorist, gallant 8 Casanova, lothario, paramour 9 ladies' man, libertine, philander, womanizer 10 lady-killer, profligate 11 philanderer
drama: 13 The Stone Guest
home: 7 Seville
mother: 4 Inez
poet: 5 Byron (Lord)

donkey

3 ass 4 fool, jerk 5 burro, idiot 7 jackass 8 imbecile 10 nincompoop
female: 5 jenny

donkey's years

3 age 4 aeon 7 dog's age 8 blue moon, coon's age, eternity

donkeywork

4 moil, toil 5 grind, labor 6 drudge 7 slavery 8 drudgery, plugging

Donner

see **Thor**

donnybrook

4 fray 5 brawl, fight, melee, set-to 6 affray, fracas 7 bobbery, ruction 10 free-for-all

donor

5 giver 7 donator, granter, grantor 8 bestower 9 conferrer, presenter 11 contributor

do-nothing

3 bum 4 slug 5 idler 6 loafer, slouch 8 dolittle, fainéant, slugabed, sluggard 9 lazybones

Don Quixote

author: 9 Cervantes (Miguel de)
beloved: 8 Dulcinea
companion: 11 Sancho Panza
giant: 8 windmill
home: 8 La Mancha
horse: 9 Rocinante, Rosinante, Rozinante
squire: 11 Sancho Panza

doodad

5 gizmo 6 dingus, gadget, jigger 7 do-funny, thingum, trinket 9 doohickey, rigamajig, thingummy 10 thingumbob 11 thingumajig

doodle

3 ass, toy 4 fool, jerk, mess 5 cheat, idiot, ninny 6 donkey, fiddle, potter, puddle, putter, tinker, trifle 7 jackass 8 imbecile, scribble 10 mess around, nincompoop

doohickey

see **doodad**

doom

3 lot 4 damn, fate 5 moira, weird 6 decree, kismet 7 condemn, destine, destiny, portion, preform, tragedy 8 calamity, disaster, sentence 9 cataclysm, determine, ordinance, preordain, proscribe 10 foreordain, predestine 11 catastrophe 12 circumstance, last judgment, predetermine

doomful

4 dire 7 baleful, baneful, direful, ominous, unlucky 9 ill-boding 10 portentous 11 apocalyptic 12 inauspicious, unpropitious

doomsayer

7 killjoy 9 Cassandra, pessimist 11 crepehanger

____ Doone

5 Lorna

door

3 way 4 adit 5 entry 6 access, entrée, portal 7 gateway, ingress, opening 8 entrance, entryway 9 admission 10 admittance 11 entranceway
rear: 7 postern

doorkeeper

6 porter 7 gateman, ostiary

doormat

7 milksop 8 sufferer, weakling 9 jellyfish 10 namby-pamby, pantywaist 11 Milquetoast, mollycoddle

doorway

5 entry 6 portal 8 entrance, entryway 11 entranceway
column: 7 trumeau 8 trumeaux
(plural)

dope

4 drug 5 dunce, noddy 6 doctor,
heroin, nitwit, noddle, opiate, sedate 7 cocaine 8 narcotic 9 lamebrain, marijuana 10 dunderhead
11 chowderhead, chucklehead,
preparation 12 spinning bath

doped

4 high 6 stoned, zonked
7 drugged 8 hopped-up, turned on
9 spaced-out 10 tripped out

dope up

4 load 6 debase, doctor, weight
10 adulterate 12 sophisticate

dopey

5 heavy 6 stupid, torpid 7 bemused, fuddled 8 comatose, sluggish 9 lethargic 10 slumberous
12 hebetudinous

dor

6 beetle

Doric Zeus

3 Zan

Doris

brother: 6 Nereus
daughters: 7 Nereids
father: 7 Oceanus
husband: 6 Nereus

dormancy

7 latency 8 abeyance, diapause,
doldrums 10 quiescence, quiescency, suspension 11 cold storage
12 intermission, interruption

dormant

6 drowsy, latent 7 abeyant, lurking,
relaxed 8 immobile, inactive, sluggish 9 lethargic, potential, prepatent, quiescent 10 slow-moving
13 unprogressive

dormer

6 window

dorry

4 boat

dorsal

6 aboral 7 abaxial
combining form: 6 opisth 7 opistho

___ d'Orsay

4 Quai

dorsum

4 back

Dorus

brother: 6 Aeolus
father: 6 Hellen

dose

7 measure, portion 8 quantity
10 proportion

Dos Passos trilogy

3 U.S.A.

dot

4 mark, mote, stud 5 dower,
dowry, point, speck 6 bestud, pepper, period, pimple 7 freckle,
speckle, stipple 8 fly-speck, sprinkle
9 bespeckle 11 intersperse 12 dec-
imal point

dotage

8 senility 11 elderliness, senectitude

dote on

4 like 5 adore, enjoy, fancy 7 idolize, worship

doting

4 dear, fond 5 silly 6 loving, senile
7 asinine, devoted, doddery, fatuous, foolish 8 imbecile, lovesome,
overfond 9 doddering 12 affectionate 13 over-indulgent

dotted

6 spotty 8 cribbled, punctate,
stippled
with stars: 4 semé

dotty

5 crazy, loony, wacky 6 absurd, insane 7 foolish 8 besotted, enamored 9 eccentric, fantastic, infatuate 10 infatuated, ridiculous
12 feebleminded, preposterous

double

3 dub, shy, yaw 4 bend, bilk,
copy, dual, duck, dupe, fold, mate,
shun, tack, turn, twin 5 avoid, duple, elude, evade, image, match,
shift 6 bifold, binary, clench, duplex, escape, eschew, paired,
ringer, wraith 7 dualize, enlarge,
magnify, two-fold 8 increase
9 companion, deceitful, deviation,
dualistic, duplicate, insincere, replicate 10 coordinate, deflection, reciprocal, simulacrum, understudy
12 ambidextrous, hypocritical
13 spitting image
combining form: 2 di 3 bin 4 dipl,
diss 5 diphy, diplo, disso
prefix: 2 bi 3 dis

double agent

3 spy

double-barreled

4 dual 5 duple 6 bifold, binary,
duplex 7 twofold 9 dualistic

double bass

10 bull fiddle

double-cross

4 sell 5 bluff 6 betray, humbug, illude, juggle, take in 7 beguile, deceive, mislead, sell out 8 betrayal
9 four-flush

doubled

combining form: 3 bis

double dagger

6 diesis

double-dealer

3 gyp 5 cheat 6 con man 7 diddler, sharper 8 swindler 9 defrauder 10 mountebank
11 flimflammer 13 confidence man

double-dealing

5 fraud 7 chicane 8 mala fide,
trickery 9 chicanery, deception, duplicity, fourberie, insincere
10 hanky-panky, left-handed
11 highbinding 12 ambidextrous,
hypocritical 13 sharp practice

double-dome

7 Brahmin, egghead 8 highbrow
12 intellectual

double-edged

5 vague 7 obscure, unclear 9 ambiguous, ancipital, equivocal, tenebrous, uncertain

double entendre

9 ambiguity, equivoque 11 amphibology 12 equivocality,
equivocation

double-faced

5 vague 7 obscure, unclear 8 mala
fide 9 ambiguous, equivocal, insincere, tenebrous, uncertain 10 left-
handed 12 ambidextrous,
hypocritical

double fold

5 pleat

double meaning

see **double entendre**

double-minded

7 halting 8 hesitant, wavering
10 hesitating, indecisive, irresolute,
undecisive 11 vacillating
12 ambidextrous, hypocritical

doublet

3 duo 4 dyad, pair 5 brace 6 couple, jacket 7 twosome

double-talk

4 jazz 5 hokum 6 bunkum, drivel
7 twaddle 8 flimflam, newspeak,
nonsense 9 gibberish 10 balderdash 12 gobbledygook

double vision

8 diplopia

doubly
prefix: **2** bi

doubt
5 qualm **6** wonder **7** concern, dispute, dubiety, misgive, perhaps, suspect, swither **8** distrust, mistrust, question, unbelief **9** challenge, disbelief, dubiosity, suspicion **10** skepticism **11** dubiousness, incertitude, incredulity, uncertainty, uncertitude

doubtable
4 open **7** dubious, suspect **9** ambiguous, equivocal, undecided **10** borderline **11** problematic

doubter
7 skeptic, zetetic **10** headshaker, Pyrrhonian, Pyrrhonist, unbeliever

doubtful
4 hazy, iffy, moot, open **5** fishy, shady, shaky **6** chancy, queasy, uneasy, unsure **7** clouded, dubious, obscure, suspect, unclear **8** arguable, insecure, mootable, unlikely, unstable, wavering **9** ambiguous, debatable, dubitable, equivocal, uncertain, undecided, unsettled **10** borderline, contingent, disputable, hesitating, improbable, impugnable, indecisive, precarious, suspicious, touch-and-go **11** problematic, speculative **12** questionable

doubtfulness
7 concern, dubiety **8** mistrust **9** dubiosity, dubitancy, suspicion **10** skepticism **11** uncertainty, uncertitude

doubting Thomas
see **doubter**

doubtless
4 sure **6** easily, likely **7** certain **8** probably **9** assumably **10** absolutely, definitely, positively, presumably **13** presumptively, unequivocally

doubtlessly
4 well **5** truly **6** easily, indeed, really **8** provenly **10** absolutely, definitely, positively **11** undoubtedly **13** unequivocally

douceur
4 gift **7** present **8** gratuity

dough
4 cash **5** bread, money **8** currency **11** legal tender
cooked in honey: **8** taiglach, teiglach
inflator: **5** yeast

doughboy
11 infantryman

doughty
4 able, bold **5** brave, manly **6** plucky, spunky, strong **7** valiant **8** fearless, unafraid **9** dauntless, undaunted

doughy
4 ashy, pale **5** ashen, livid, lurid, waxen **6** pallid **8** blanched **9** colorless

do up
3 fix **4** mend, wrap **5** patch **6** doctor, repair, revamp **7** rebuild **8** overhaul **11** recondition, reconstruct

dour
4 glum, grim, hard, ugly **5** bleak, harsh, rigid, sulky, surly **6** dogged, gloomy, morose, severe, strict, sullen **7** austere, crabbed **8** rigorous **9** saturnine, stringent **10** forbidding, implacable, unyielding

douse
3 bat, bop, dip, out, sop, wet **4** doff, duck, dunk, slop, soak **5** bathe, drown, lower, plash, slosh, swash, throw **6** deluge, drench, put off, put out, quench, remove, splash, splosh **7** immerse, slacken, spatter, splurge, spurtle, take off **8** downpour, splatter, submerge, submerse **9** drenching **10** extinguish

douzeper
4 Ivon, Oton **5** Gerin, Ivory, peers **6** Anseis, Gerard, Gerier, Oliver, Roland, Samson **7** Olivier, paladin **8** Engelier **9** Berengier

dove
6 culver, pigeon **8** pacifist **10** pacificist
call: **3** coo
genus: **7** Columba

dovecote
6 aviary **8** pigeonry **9** birdhouse, columbary **11** culver house, pigeon house

dovehouse
see **dovecote**

dovelike
4 mild, pure **6** gentle **7** lovable **9** columbine

dovetail
4 jibe **5** agree, fit in, tally **6** accord, square **8** check out **9** harmonize **10** correspond **13** interlock with

dovish
7 antiwar **8** pacifist **10** pacifistic

dowager
4 dame **6** matron **9** matriarch **10** grande dame

dowdy
4 drab, slut **5** dated, passé, tacky **6** blowsy, bygone, démodé, frowsy, frumpy, old hat, sordid, stodgy **7** archaic, traipse, vintage **8** frumpish, outdated, outmoded, slattern, slovenly **9** out-of-date, unstylish **10** antiquated, slatternly **11** draggle-tail **12** old-fashioned **13** draggletailed
woman: **5** frump

dowel
3 pin, rod **5** stick

dower
3 dot **5** endow, endue **6** talent **9** crown with, endowment

dowitcher
5 snipe **8** grayback **9** brownback

down
3 bad, fur, ill, low, off, out **4** best, blue, done, drop, fell, flue, fuzz, kill, lick, lint, pile, sick, slow **5** below, ended, floor, floss, fluff, fully, level, lower, outdo, scrag, slack, throw, under, worst **6** cut off, defeat, fallen, finish, hipped, hurdle, lay low, master, nether **7** conquer, descent, destroy, flatten, for real, handout, swallow, through **8** actively, at hazard, bowl over, carry off, complete, consumed, defeated, dejected, dispatch, feathers, finished, inferior, lay aside, overcome, sluggish, suppress, surmount **9** completed, concluded, depressed, earnestly, earthward, liquidate, processed, seriously, subjacent **10** completely, dispirited, groundward, terminated, vigorously **11** netherwards **12** discomfiture
combining form: **4** ptil **5** ptilo
prefix: **2** de **3** cat, hyp, kat **4** cata, cath, cato, hypo, kata

down-and-outer
6 beggar, pauper, wretch

down-at-heel
5 seedy, tacky **6** shabby, tagrag **7** rundown **8** tattered **10** bedraggled, broken down, threadbare **11** dilapidated

downcast
3 bad, low, sad **4** blue, dull, glum, rout, sunk **5** moody, mopey, shaft **6** defeat, droopy, gloomy, hipped, morose **7** beating, debacle, doleful, forlorn, licking **8** dejected,

drubbing, listless, soul-sick, troubled **9** depressed, heartsick, heartsore, oppressed, overthrow, woebegone **10** chapfallen, defeasance, despondent, dispirited, distressed, spiritless **11** crestfallen, discouraged, low-spirited **12** disconsolate, disheartened

downcry
5 abuse **8** belittle, derogate, diminish, discount **9** disparage, dispraise **10** depreciate **11** detract from

downfall
4 bane, ruin **7** atrophy, decline, descent, undoing **9** decadence, destroyer, ruination **10** declension, degeneracy, devolution **11** declination, destruction **12** degeneration, dégringolade **13** deterioration

downgrade
4 bump, bust **5** break, decry, lower **6** demote, reduce **7** atrophy, declass, decline, demerit, devalue, disrate **8** mark down, write off **9** decadence, devaluate, write down **10** declension, degeneracy, depreciate, devalorize, devolution, undervalue **12** degeneration, dégringolade **13** deterioration

downhearted
see **downcast**

down-in-the-mouth
see **downcast**

down payment
7 deposit, earnest

downpour
4 rain **6** deluge **8** rainfall **9** drenching **10** cloudburst

down quilt
5 duvet

downright
4 flat, very **5** gross, plain, utter **8** absolute, complete, positive **9** out-and-out, up-and-down **10** sure-enough **11** indubitable, unmitigated **13** thoroughgoing

downslide
3 dip, sag **4** drop, slip **5** slump **7** decline, falloff

downstage area
5 apron

downstairs
5 below **8** servants

downswing
see **downslide**

down-to-earth
4 hard **5** sober **9** practical, pragmatic, realistic **10** hard-boiled, hardheaded **11** unfantastic **12** matter-of-fact, unidealistic

downtown sign
6 Main St.

downtrend
see **downslide**

downtrodden
6 abject, abused **9** oppressed, underfoot **10** maltreated, mistreated, persecuted

downturn
see **downslide**

downward
8 debasing **9** declining **10** descending, netherward
combining form: **4** bath **5** batho

downwardly, downwards
see **downward**

downy
4 soft **6** fluffy **8** feathery, soothing
combining form: **4** hebe
filler: **5** eider

doxy
3 ism **4** tart **5** creed, wench **6** harlot **7** opinion, trollop **8** doctrine

doyen
4 dean, lead **5** guide, maven, pilot **6** artist, expert, leader, master **8** virtuoso **9** authority **10** bellwether, master-hand, past master, proficient **12** passed master

Doyle's detective
6 Holmes

D'Oyly Carte offering
8 operetta

doze
3 nap **5** sleep **6** catnap, drowse **7** drop off, slumber **9** drowse off

dozy
see **drowsy**

DP
6 émigré **7** evacuee, refugee **8** fugitive

drab
3 hag **4** bawd, dowd, dull, flat, slut, trot **5** biddy, bleak, crone, dingy, dowdy, faded, mousy, muddy, murky, prosy, wench, whore, witch **6** beldam, dismal, dreary, harlot, mousey **7** hustler, prosaic, subfusc, traipse **8** desolate, dullness, lifeless, slattern **9** cheerless, colorless **10** lackluster, lusterless, prostitute **11** dispiriting,

draggle-tail, fille de joie, nightwalker **12** streetwalker

draconian
5 harsh, rigid **6** strict **8** rigorist, rigorous **9** stringent **10** ironhanded **12** unpermissive

Dracula author
6 Stoker (Bram)

draffy
6 drossy, no-good **7** inutile, nothing **8** unworthy **9** valueless, worthless

draft
3 tap **4** dose, plan, plot, pull, pump, swig **5** check, claim, drink, frame, press, swill, taper **6** call up, demand, design, devise, drench, enroll, induct, potion, scheme, siphon, sketch **7** compose, concoct, current, draught, harness, impress, outline, portion, prepare, project **8** block out, chalk out, contrive, muster in, rough out, skeleton, traction **9** adumbrate, allowance, conscribe, conscript, fabricate, formulate, muster out **11** delineation, skeletonize **12** characterize
avoider: **6** dodger
of a law: **4** bill

drag
3 lug, peg, tow, tug **4** hang, haul, poke, puff, pull, swig **5** dally, delay, draft, drain, drink, float, swill, tarry, trail **6** burden, daggle, dawdle, drench, harrow, loiter, put off, schlep, search, strain **7** ransack, sagging, schlepp, skidpan, traipse **8** drooping, friction **9** lag behind, sea anchor **10** conveyance **11** inclination **13** procrastinate
off: **4** cart

dragging
4 long **7** lengthy, tedious **8** drawn-out, longsome, overlong **9** prolonged **10** protracted **12** long-drawn-out

draggle
5 trail **7** shuffle, traipse **8** besmirch

draggle-tail
4 dowd, drab, slut **5** dowdy **7** traipse **8** slattern

draggletailed
5 dowdy **6** blowsy, frowsy, sordid, untidy **8** slattern, sluttish **10** slatternly

dragnet
5 trawl

dragon
5 beast, Satan **6** wivern **8** basilisk **9** water arum **10** cockatrice

Babylonian: 6 Tiamat
biblical: 5 Rahab
Canaanite: 3 Yam 4 Yamm 5 Lotan
Chinese: 4 lung
French: 8 Tarasque
genus: 5 Draco
Greek: 5 Ladon 9 Eurythion
horse: 6 Fafner, Fafnir
slayer: 4 Baal, Enki, Zeus 5 Indra
6 Cadmus, Marduk, Sigurd, Yahweh 7 Beowulf, Jupiter, Ninurta,
Perseus 8 St. George 9 St. Michael
10 St. Margaret
Sumerian: 3 Kur
two-legged: 5 wiver 6 wivern,
wyvern
Vadic: 3 Ahi 6 Vritra

dragoon
3 cow 5 bully 6 harass, hector
8 browbeat, bulldoze, bullyrag
9 persecute, strong-arm, terrorize
10 cavalryman, intimidate

drag race entry
6 hot rod

drain
3 tap 4 jade, pump, sink, sump,
swig, tire, vent, wear 5 bleed,
draft, drink, empty, leech, sewer,
swill, use up, weary 6 burden,
drench, gutter, siphon, trench
7 conduit, deplete, draw off, exhaust, fatigue 8 bankrupt, draw
down, wear down 9 discharge
10 impoverish 11 watercourse
transverse: 7 culvert

drain away
5 abate, close, taper 6 lessen, reduce 7 dwindle 8 decrease, diminish, taper off

drained
5 all-in, spent 6 bleary, effete, used
up 7 far-gone, worn-out 8 depleted
9 exhausted, washed-out

drainpipe
5 spout 9 downspout

drain pit
4 sump

dram
3 bit, nip, tot 4 dash, drop, hoot,
iota, jolt, mite, shot, slug, spot, swig
5 crumb, draft, drink, ounce, shred,
snort, swill 6 dollop 7 modicum,
smidgen, snifter, snorter 8 particle,
potation, toothful

drama
4 play 6 boards 7 theater, theatre
8 the stage 10 footlights
award: 4 Tony
former English: 6 masque

Japanese: 3 Noh
main part: 8 epitasis
musical: 5 opera 8 operetta
suspenseful: 11 cliff-hanger

dramatic
8 striking, theatral, theatric, thespian 10 histrionic, theatrical
conflict: 4 agon
scene: 4 skit

dramatis personae
4 cast

dramatist
10 playwright
American: 4 Hart (Moss), Inge (Wil-
liam), Rice (Elmer), Uhry (Alfred)
5 Albee (Edward), Mamet (David),
Odets (Clifford), Payne (John How-
ard), Simon (Neil) 6 Miller (Arthur),
O'Neill (Eugene), Thomas (Augus-
tus), Wilson (August, Lanford, Rob-
ert) 7 Hellman (Lillian), Kaufman
(George S.) 8 Anderson (Maxwell,
Robert), Sherwood (Robert), Wil-
liams (Tennessee) 11 Hammerstein
(Oscar), Wasserstein (Wendy)
Austrian: 10 Schnitzler (Arthur)
Belgian: 11 Maeterlinck (Maurice)
English: 3 Fry (Christopher), Gay
(John) 4 Rowe (Nicholas), Tate
(Nahum) 5 Milne (Alan Alexander),
Peele (George), Wilde (Oscar)
6 Coward (Noel), Jonson (Ben), Pi-
nero (Arthur), Pinter (Harold), Steele
(Richard), Storey (David) 7 Mar-
lowe (Christopher), Marston (John),
Osborne (John), Shaffer (Peter),
Webster (John) 8 Congreve (Wil-
liam), Shadwell (Thomas), Stoppard
(Tom), Tourneur (Cyril), Vanbrugh
(John), Zangwill (Israel) 9 Middle-
ton (Thomas), Wycherley (William)
11 Shakespeare (William)
French: 5 Camus (Albert), Genet
(Jean) 6 Musset (Alfred de), Racine
(Jean), Sardou (Victorien), Sartre
(Jean-Paul), Scribe (Eugene)
7 Anouilh (Jean), Ionesco (Eugene),
Labiche (Eugene-Marin), Moliere,
Rostand (Edmond) (8 Marivaux
(Pierre) 9 Corneille (Pierre), Girau-
doux (Jean) 12 Beaumarchais
(Pierre-Augustin Caron de)
German: 5 Weiss (Peter) 6 Brecht
(Bertolt), Goethe (Johann Wolfgang
von), Kleist (Heinrich von) 8 Schiller
(Friedrich von) 9 Hauptmann (Ger-
hart), Zuckmayer (Carl)
Greek: 8 Menander 9 Aeschylus, Eu-
ripides, Sophocles 12 Aristophanes
Hindu: 8 Kalidasa
Irish: 4 Shaw (George Bernard)
5 Behan (Brendan), Yeats (William

Butler) 6 O'Casey (Sean) 8 Sheri-
dan (Richard Brinsley)
Italian: 7 Alfieri (Vittorio), Giacosa
(Giuseppe), Goldoni (Carlo) 8 Tris-
sino (Gian Giorgio)
Japanese: 5 Zeami
Norwegian: 5 Ibsen (Henrik) 8 Bjorn-
son (Bjornstjerne Martinius)
Roman: 7 Plautus, Terence
Russian: 7 Chekhov (Anton) 8 Zam-
yatin (Yevgeny)
Spanish: 4 Vega (Lope de) 8 Quin-
tero (Serafin, Joaquin) 11 Garcia
Lorca (Federico)
Swedish: 5 Sachs (Nelly) 10 Strind-
berg (August)
Swiss: 6 Frisch (Max)

dramaturge
see **dramatist**

dramaturgic
see **dramatic**

drape
4 roll 5 adorn, cover 6 enfold, enwrap, sprawl, swathe, wrap up
7 curtain, swaddle 8 enswathe, envelope, spraddle, swathe in
11 spread-eagle

drapery
7 curtain 8 hangings

drastic
6 severe 7 extreme, radical 8 rigorous, vigorous 9 purgative

Dravidian language
5 Gondi, Khond, Malto, Tamil
6 Brahui, Kurukh, Telugu 8 Kanar-
ese 9 Malayalam

draw
3 gut, lug, pen, tap, tie, tow, tug,
win 4 call, edge, gain, haul, limn,
lure, make, move, odds, puff, pull,
pump, rise, sink, take, wile 5 alter,
angle, bowel, bulge, charm, draft,
drain, educe, evoke, infer, judge,
paint, start, steep, taper, use up
6 allure, appeal, coulee, crayon,
deduce, derive, elicit, entice, extend, gather, indite, induce, infuse,
inhale, paunch, pencil, prompt,
pucker, seduce, siphon, sketch
7 attract, bewitch, collect, deplete,
dogfall, enchant, exhaust, extract,
make out, prolong, spin out, stencil,
stipple, stretch, vantage, win over
8 bankrupt, conclude, contract, convince, dead heat, deadlock, elongate, handicap, lengthen, persuade, protract, standoff
9 advantage, allowance, argue
into, captivate, delineate, drain
away, fascinate, formulate, head
start, magnetize, represent, seduc-

tion, stalemate **10** allurement, attraction, disembowel, eviscerate, exenterate, impoverish, prolongate **11** bring around

forth: **5** educe **6** elicit **7** extract
from: **4** milk, pump **5** bleed
the main features of: **4** etch **6** sketch **7** outline
together: **3** tie **4** join, lace

draw back
5 wince **6** deduct, recede, recoil, retire **7** retreat, take off, take out **8** discount, knock off, subtract, take away **9** substract

drawback
6 defect, refund **7** trouble **8** handicap **9** detriment, hindrance **10** disability **12** disadvantage **13** inconvenience

draw down
3 get, win **4** earn, gain, make **5** drain, use up **7** acquire, bring in, deplete, exhaust **8** bankrupt **10** impoverish

drawer
9 draftsman
for money: **4** till

draw in
3 get **6** induce, prompt **7** win over **8** convince, persuade, talk into **9** argue into, prevail on **11** bring around, prevail upon

drawing
4 plan **6** sketch **8** alluring, charming, magnetic **9** appealing **10** attracting, attractive, bewitching, enchanting **11** captivating, fascinating
combining form: **4** gram
humorous: **7** cartoon

drawing power
4 call, lure, pull **6** appeal **9** seduction **10** allurement, attraction

drawing room
5 salon **6** saloon **9** reception

drawn
4 worn **7** haggard, pinched **8** careworn

drawn-out
4 long **7** lengthy **8** dragging, extended, longsome, overlong **9** prolonged **10** protracted

draw off
3 tap **4** pump **5** bleed, draft, drain **6** remove, siphon, syphon **8** withdraw

draw on
3 don **5** cause **6** assume, effect, induce, prompt, secure **7** produce,

win over **8** convince, persuade, talk into **9** argue into **10** bring about **11** bring around, prevail upon

draw out
6 extend, remove **7** extract, prolong, stretch **8** elongate, lengthen, protract **10** prolongate

draw up
4 halt, make, stop **5** draft, frame **7** prepare **9** formulate

dray
4 cart **7** travois **9** stoneboat

dray horse
4 peon **5** slave **6** drudge, slavey, toiler **11** galley slave

dread
4 fear **5** alarm, panic **6** dismay, fright, horror, terror **7** anxiety **9** trepidity **11** frightening, trepidation **13** consternation
combining form: **5** phobe **6** phobia, phobic **7** phobous

dreadful
5 awful **6** tragic **7** direful, extreme, fearful, shocker **8** horrible, horrific, shocking, terrible, terrific **9** appalling, dime novel, frightful, revolting, unrefined **10** formidable, unpleasant, yellowback **11** frightening

dreadfully
4 very **6** damned **8** horribly **9** extremely **10** strikingly **11** exceedingly **12** surpassingly **13** frighteningly

dreadnought
10 battleship

dream
4 ache, long, lust, moon, pine, sigh **5** crave, fancy, ideal **6** bubble, hanker, hunger, thirst, vision **7** chimera, fantasy, imagine, rainbow, reverie, suspire **8** illusion, phantasm, phantasy **9** nightmare **10** conceive of
combining form: **4** onir **5** oneir, oniro **6** oneiro
god: **8** Morpheus
interpreter: **12** oneirocritic

dreamer
6 mystic **7** utopian **8** idealist, theorist **9** ideologue, visionary **10** Don Quixote, lotus-eater **11** illusionist **13** castle-builder

dreamlike
5 vague **7** shadowy, surreal **8** nebulous

Dream of Gerontius composer
5 Elgar (Edward)

dream up
5 frame, hatch **6** devise, invent **7** concoct **8** contrive **9** formulate

dreamy
4 hazy, idle **5** ideal, nifty, super, vague **6** astral, divine, groovy, peachy **8** fanciful, glorious, pleasing, romantic **9** marvelous, unworldly, visionary, whimsical **10** delightful, idealistic, indistinct **12** otherworldly

dreary
4 blah, dull, poky **5** black, bleak **6** dismal, gloomy, somber, stodgy **7** forlorn, humdrum **8** banausic, funereal, monotone **10** depressing, depressive, enervating, monotonous, oppressive, pedestrian **11** dispiriting **12** discouraging
Scottish: **5** dowie

dreck
4 junk **5** offal, swill **6** litter, refuse **7** garbage, rubbish **12** outsweepings

dredge
3 dig **5** scoop **6** deepen, search **8** excavate

dregs
3 mob **4** lees, scum **5** trash **6** masses, rabble **7** deposit, grounds **8** canaille, riffraff, sediment, unwashed **9** settlings **11** precipitate, proletariat **13** precipitation

Dreiser
character: **5** Clyde **6** Carrie, Sondra **7** Roberta **10** Cowperwood
novel: **8** The Stoic, The Titan **9** The Genius **12** The Financier **17** An American Tragedy

drench
3 sop, wet **4** drag, dunk, lash, pour, soak, swig, teem, wash **5** douse, draft, drain, drink, drouk, drown, souse, steep, swill **6** deluge, seethe, sodden **7** immerse, overwet, pervade **8** oversoak, saturate, submerge, waterlog **10** impregnate

dress
3 gut, rig, tan **4** bind, clad, deck, doll, duds, garb, gown, sack, tend, till, togs, trim, work **5** adorn, align, array, clean, frock, getup, guise, habit, prank, smock **6** attire, bedeck, clothe, dirndl, enrobe, outfit, sacque, setout, tailor **7** apparel, bandage, bedizen, chemise, clothes, costume, garment, garnish, raiment, turnout **8** beautify, beclothe, clothing, covering, deco-

rate, enclothe, ornament **9** cultivate, embellish, make ready
10 attirement **11** habiliments
a wound: **7** bandage
designer: **4** Dior (Christian) **12** Saint-
Laurent (Yves)
extravagantly: **8** overdeck
finically: **5** primp
hair: **6** barber
Hawaiian: **6** muumuu
leather: **3** taw
line: **3** hem
mode of: **5** habit
of the clergy: **5** cloth
oriental: **9** cheongsam
South Seas: **6** sarong
with the beak: **5** preen
with vulgarity: **7** bedizen

dress down
4 lash, rail **5** scold **6** berate
7 bawl out, tell off **10** tongue-lash

dresser
5 chest **6** bureau **10** chiffonier
11 flour bolter
gaudy: **9** butterfly

dressing
5 sauce **6** catsup **7** bandage,
catchup, ketchup **8** stuffing
salad: **6** French **7** Italian, Russian
10 blue cheese

dressing room
8 vestiary
church: **6** vestry

dressmaker
6 tailor **7** modiste **9** couturier
10 seamstress

dress up
3 tog **4** clad, mask, smug, tart **5** array, cloak, prank, preen, primp,
slick, spiff **6** attire, clothe, tog out
7 apparel, deck out, doll out,
smarten **8** disguise, enclothe, prettify, trick off, trick out **9** dissemble
10 camouflage **11** dissimulate

dressy
4 chic **6** formal, frilly, ornate **7** elegant, stylish **9** elaborate

Dreyfus' defender
4 Zola (Emile)

drib
4 drop, weep **5** trill **6** gobbet
7 distill, droplet, globule, trickle

dribble
4 blow, drip, drop, weep **5** drool,
trill, waste **6** drivel, slaver **7** consume, distill, fritter, slabber, slobber, trickle **8** pittance, salivate,

squander **9** throw away **10** frivol
away, trifle away **11** blunder away

driblet
4 drop **6** gobbet **7** globule
8 pittance

dried acorns
6 camata **8** camatina

dried brick
5 adobe

dried coconut meat
5 copra

dried grape
6 raisin

dried grass
3 hay

dried meat
5 jerky **7** charqui **8** pemmican

dried orchid tubers
5 salep

dried plum
5 prune

drift
3 bat, gad, run **4** bank, bent, cock,
flow, flux, heap, hill, mass, mope,
pile, ride, roam, rush, sail, skid,
skim, tide, wash **5** amble, coast,
creep, dance, float, flood, mosey,
mound, range, shock, shoot, slant,
slide, spate, stack, stray, tenor,
trend **6** bummel, linger, motion,
ramble, stream, stroll, upwaft, wander **7** current, leaning, maunder,
meander, meaning, purport, pyramid, saunter **8** mountain, movement, penchant, sideslip, tendency
9 deviation, gallivant, inclining,
substance **10** partiality, propensity
11 disposition, inclination, progression **12** predilection
languidly: **5** swoon
of a ship: **6** leeway
unstratified: **4** till

drifter
3 bum, vag **4** hobo **5** rover, tramp
6 roamer **7** floater, rambler, vagrant **8** derelict, vagabond, wanderer **9** meanderer **10** street arab,
temporizer **12** rolling stone

driftwood
6 jetsam **7** flotsam **8** wreckage

drill
4 bore, skid **5** prick, punch, snail
6 pierce **7** wildcat **8** exercise,
practice, practise, puncture, rehearse, sideslip **9** penetrate, perforate **10** discipline
command: **6** at ease **8** left face
9 about face, attention, right face

drink
3 ade, nip, sea, sip, tea **4** brew,
deep, drag, grog, gulp, soak, swig,
tope, toss **5** booze, draft, drain, julep, ocean, quaff, slosh, slurp, sup
up, swill **6** absorb, drench,
guzzle, imbibe, jigger, liquid, liquor, pledge, potion, sup off, tank
up, tipple **7** potable, spirits, swallow, swizzle **8** aperitif, beverage,
libation, liquor up **9** aqua vitae
after-dinner: **6** frappe
British: **5** spree
drugged: **6** mickey
honey: **4** mead
hot: **5** toddy **6** saloop
liquor: **5** booze
mixed: **3** nog **5** zombi **6** zombie
mixer: **7** swirler
noisily: **5** slurp
of liquor: **4** dram, shot **5** snort
8 highball
of the gods: **6** nectar
Scottish: **6** waught
soft: **7** soda pop
stimulating: **6** bracer
tall: **4** fizz
(see also **beverage**)

drinkable
6 liquor **7** potable **8** beverage

drinkery
3 bar, pub **4** café **6** lounge, saloon, tavern **7** barroom, taproom

drinking
8 potation
fountain: **7** bubbler
horn: **6** rhyton
spree: **5** binge **6** bender **8** carousal

drip
4 weep **5** trill **7** distill, dribble,
spatter, spurtle, trickle **8** sprinkle

dripping
3 wet **5** runny, soppy **6** soaked,
sodden, soused **7** soaking
8 drenched **9** saturated **11** wringing-wet

drippy
5 mushy, rainy, sappy, sobby,
soupy **6** slushy, sobful **7** drizzly,
maudlin, mawkish **11** sentimental

drive
2 go **3** dig, pep, ram, run, sic, tug
4 auto, bang, dash, élan, goad,
herd, moil, move, prod, push, ride,
road, roll, sink, snap, spin, spur,
stab, taxi, toil, tool, trip, turn, urge
5 burst, chase, defer, force, getup,
grave, guide, impel, labor, lunge,
motor, pilot, pitch, pound, punch,
shove, stamp, steer, stick, surge,
tract, vigor, wheel, whirl **6** attack,

coerce, compel, convey, exhort, hammer, plunge, propel, strain, strike, strive, thrust **7** actuate, impetus, impress, joyride, operate, produce **8** ambition, mobilize, momentum, navigate, protract, shepherd, vitality **9** chauffeur, excursion, impelling, urge along **10** charioteer, enterprise, get-up-and-go, initiative
air: **4** blow
away: **4** shoo **5** exile, stave **6** aroint
back: **5** repel **6** defend **7** repulse
close: **8** tailgate
off: **6** dispel
out: **8** exorcise

drivel
4 blow, bosh **5** drool, Greek, hooey, prate, waste **6** babble, gabble, jabber, slaver **7** blabber, blather, consume, dribble, fritter, prattle, rubbish, slabber, slobber, twaddle **8** cast away, claptrap, nonsense, pishposh, salivate, squander **9** gibberish, throw away **10** double-talk, flapdoodle, frivol away, trifle away **11** blunder away, jabberwocky **12** blatherskite

driveling
4 flat **5** inane, vapid **6** jejune **7** insipid, sapless **9** innocuous **10** namby-pamby, wishy-washy **12** milk-and-water

driver
5 cabby **6** cabbie, cabman, hackie, jarvey, mallet, vanman **7** autoist, hackman, spanker **8** motorist, muleteer, operator **9** chauffeur, dowitcher **10** taskmaster **11** tamping iron **12** automobilist
fast: **4** jehu
of an elephant: **6** mahout
Roman: **10** charioteer
truck: **8** teamster

driver's light
8 headlamp

driving
6 active, lively **7** dynamic **9** energetic **12** enterprising

drizzle
8 sprinkle

Dr. Jekyll and Mr. ___
4 Hyde

drogher
6 bearer, porter **7** carrier

drôlerie
see **drollery**

droll
3 odd, wag, wit **5** comic, funny, joker **6** jester **7** comical, risible

8 comedian, farcical, funnyman, gelastic, humorist, humorous, jokester, quipster **9** burlesque, laughable, ludicrous, whimsical **10** puppet show, ridiculous

drollery
3 gag, yak **4** jape, jest, joke, quip **5** crack, humor **6** comedy **7** waggery **9** funniness, wisecrack, witticism, wittiness **10** comicality **11** comicalness **12** humorousness

drollness
see **drollery**

dromedary
5 camel

drone
3 hum **4** buzz, idle, laze, loaf, loll **5** idler, strum, thrum **6** bumble, dawdle, loiter, lounge **7** bagpipe, male bee **8** parasite **9** bombinate **10** pedal point **12** diddle-daddle

dronish
see **drony**

drony
4 lazy **7** work-shy **8** fainéant, indolent, slothful **9** easygoing, slowgoing

drool
4 guff, rave **5** prate, water **6** babble, bushwa, drivel, gabble, hot air, saliva, slaver **7** blabber, blather, dribble, enthuse, prattle, slabber, slobber, twaddle **8** claptrap, nonsense, rhapsody, salivate **10** balderdash, rhapsodize

droop
3 sag **4** fall, flag, hang, loll, sink, swag, wilt **5** couch, demit, lower, slump **6** dangle, go down, slouch, weaken **7** decline, depress, let down, subside, trollop **8** languish, pine away **11** deteriorate

droopy
3 bad **4** blue, down **6** gloomy **7** doleful **8** cast down, dejected, downcast **9** depressed **10** dispirited **11** downhearted

drop
3 die, dip, nip, sag, tot **4** down, dram, drib, dump, fall, fell, fire, iota, jolt, lose, pass, plop, quit, shot, skid, slip, slot, slug, thud, weep, wilt **5** cease, crumb, depth, floor, gutta, lapse, leave, lower, ounce, pitch, plonk, plump, plunk, scrub, shred, slide, snort, speck, spend, trill **6** bounce, cancel, cave in, crouch, curtsy, demise, depart, expire, fumble, give up, gobbet, go

down, goutte, ground, lay low, peg out, plunge, pop off, reduce, resign, smitch, topple, tumble, unload, vanish **7** abandon, boot out, call off, decease, decline, deposit, descend, descent, dismiss, distill, dribble, driblet, fall off, forfeit, give out, globule, lose out, pendant, plummet, relapse, smidgen, snifter, spatter, succumb, trickle **8** bowl down, bowl over, break off, collapse, comedown, deepness, defecate, downturn, fall away, keel over, molecule, nose-dive, particle, pass away, toothful **9** backslide, break down, bring down, declivity, disappear, discharge, downslide, downswing, downtrend, knock down, prostrate, reduction, sacrifice, terminate, throw down **10** depository
of liquid: **5** gutta
saline: **4** tear

drop in
3 see **4** call **5** visit **6** come by, look up, stop by **8** come over

droplet
4 drib **6** gobbet **7** globule

drop off
3 sag **4** fall, slip **5** slide, slump **8** fall away

dropout's loss
7 diploma

dropsical
5 puffy, tumid, windy **6** turgid **7** swollen **8** inflated **9** flatulent, overblown, tumescent

dropsied
see **dropsical**

dropsy
5 edema **7** hydrops **8** anasarca

dross
4 scum, slag **7** schlock **8** impurity

drossy
6 draffy, no-good **7** inutile, nothing **8** unworthy **9** worthless

drought
4 lack **6** dearth **8** scarcity, shortage

droughty
3 dry **4** arid, sere **7** bone-dry, thirsty **9** unwatered, waterless **12** moistureless

drove
4 herd, push **5** crowd, crush, flock, horde, press **6** chisel, squash, throng **9** multitude

drown

3 sop, wet **4** sink, soak, stun
5 douse, flood, souse, swamp,
whelm **6** dazzle, deluge, drench,
engulf **7** immerse, repress **8** inundate, overcome, overflow, submerge **9** knock over, overpower,
overwhelm, prostrate, suffocate,
tower over **10** extinguish

drowse

3 nod **4** doze **7** doze off, drop off,
slumber

drowsy

4 dozy **6** sleepy, snoozy **7** languid, nodding **8** indolent, slumbery
9 lethargic, somnolent, soporific
10 languorous, slumberous
13 lackadaisical

drub

3 tap **4** beat, flay, lick, trim, whip
5 baste, paste, pound, score, slash,
smear, stamp **6** batter, berate, buffet, pummel, scorch, thrash, wallop
7 belabor, blister, censure, scourge,
shellac **8** lambaste, lash into **9** castigate, excoriate, overwhelm

drubbing

4 rout **6** defeat **7** beating, debacle,
licking **9** overthrow, trouncing
10 defeasance **11** shellacking
12 vanquishment

drudge

4 grub, hack, moil, peon, plod,
slog, toil, work **5** grind, labor,
slave **6** slavey, toiler **7** grubber,
slavery **8** bullwork, hireling, plugging **9** dray horse, mercenary,
workhorse **10** donkeywork **11** galley slave

drudgery

4 moil, toil, work **5** grind, labor,
sweat **7** travail **8** bullwork, plugging, taskwork **10** donkeywork

drudging

6 boring, tiring **7** irksome, tedious
8 boresome, tiresome
10 monotonous

drug

4 dope, lull **5** sulfa **6** downer, opiate, physic, poison, sulpha **7** generic, stupefy, tetanic **8** biologic,
medicine, narcotic, nepenthe, pem-
oline, relaxant, roborant, sedative,
thiazide **9** medicinal **10** medicament, medication **12** pharmaceutic
addict: **6** junkie
agent: **4** narc
antibiotic: **8** neomycin
calming: **8** sedative
combining form: **8** pharmaco
experience: **4** trip
seller: **10** pharmacist
sleep-inducing: **8** hypnotic **9** soporific

drugged

4 high **5** doped **6** stoned, zonked
8 hopped-up, turned on **9** spaced-
out **10** tripped out

druggist

7 chemist **10** apothecary,
pharmacist

drugstore

8 pharmacy **10** apothecary

druid

4 bard **6** priest **7** prophet
8 sorcerer
sacred object: **3** oak **9** mistletoe

drum

4 cask **5** taber, tabla, tabor **6** atabal, barrel, enlist, gather, summon,
tabour, tom-tom, tymbal, tympan
7 canvass, solicit, taboret, taborin,
tympani **8** cylinder, taborine, ta-
bourer, tabouret, tympanum
Arab: **6** atabal
Indian: **8** mridanga
large: **4** bass **6** timbal
small: **5** bongo, tabor **6** tabret **7** taborin, timbrel
string: **5** snare

drumbeat

3 dub **4** flam, roll, tuck **6** ruffle, tattoo **8** berloque, rataplan

drumfire

4 hail **5** salvo, storm **6** shower, volley **7** barrage **9** broadside, cannonade, fusillade **11** bombardment

drumhead

4 skin **7** summary

drummer

4 Rich (Buddy) **5** Krupa (Gene)
7 swagman **8** weakfish

drum up

6 invent **7** canvass, solicit
9 originate
interest: **8** ballyhoo

drunk

3 fou, jag, lit, sot **4** bust, lush,
soak, tear, wino **5** binge, booze,
souse, spree, tight, tipsy **6** bender,
blotto, boozer, soused, stewed,
stinko, tiddly, zonked **7** crocked,
guzzler, pie-eyed, squiffy, stewbum,
tippler **8** squiffed **9** brannigan, inebriate **10** boozehound, inebriated
11 intoxicated

drunkard

3 sot **4** lush, soak, wino **5** rummy,
stiff, toper **6** bibber, boozer, rumdum, soaker, sponge **7** drammer,
fuddler, guzzler, swiller, tippler,
tosspot **9** alcoholic, inebriate, juice-
head, swillbowl **10** boozehound
11 dipsomaniac

drunken

5 boozy, tight, tipsy **6** wobbly
7 pie-eyed **8** lurching, unsteady
10 inebriated **11** intoxicated

drupaceous fruit

4 plum **5** peach **6** almond, cherry

Drusilla

brother: **8** Caligula
father: **5** Herod **10** Germanicus
husband: **5** Felix
mother: **9** Agrippina
sister: **8** Berenice **9** Agrippina

dry

3 set **4** acid, arid, bare, blot, brut,
cake, dull, sear, sere, sour, tart
5 acerb, baked, dusty, empty,
harsh, parch, plain, rough, slack,
stoic, wizen **6** barren, harden,
hoarse, modest, stingy, stolid, thirst,
wither **7** acerbic, acetose, athirst,
congeal, grating, insipid, jarring,
parched, rasping, sapless, shrivel,
sterile, tedious, thirsty **8** bromidic,
discreet, droughty, indurate, rainless, scariose, scarious, solidify, strident, tearless, teetotal, weariful,
withered **9** acidulous, anhydrate,
anhydrous, apathetic, dehydrate,
desiccate, exsiccate, impassive,
juiceless, sugarless, thirsting, unadorned, unwatered, waterless,
wearisome **10** dehydrated, desiccated, phlegmatic, stridulous
11 inelaborate, unemotional, ungarnished **12** matter-of-fact, moistureless, unproductive **13** unembellished, unembroidered, uninteresting,
unpretentious
biscuit: **7** cracker **8** hardtack
combining form: **3** xer **4** xero **5** scler
6 dehydr, sclero **7** dehydro
goods: **4** wear **6** linens, napery
8 clothing, textiles
out: **5** sober **8** soberize
period: **4** sere **6** drouth **7** drought
wine: **3** sec **4** brut

dryasdust

4 arid, dull **5** dusty **6** pedant **7** insipid, prosaic, tedious **8** bromidic,
pedantic, weariful **9** wearisome
10 uninspired **13** uninteresting

dry measure

4 peck, pint **5** quart **6** bushel

Dryope

form: **5** lotus

husband: 9 Andraemon
sister: 4 Iole

dry up
4 wilt 5 mummy, wizen 6 welter, wither 7 mummify, shrivel 8 pipe down 9 desiccate, disappear 10 devitalize

dual
4 twin 5 duple 6 bifold, binary, double, duplex, paired 7 twofold

dualistic
5 duple 6 bifold, binary, double, duplex 7 twofold

dualize
4 dupe 6 double 9 duplicate

dub
4 call, flub, muff, name, term, trim 5 botch, fluff, style, title 6 bobble, boggle, bollix, double, duffer, goof up, thrust 7 baptize, blunder, entitle 8 christen, nickname, rerecord 9 designate 10 denominate

dubiety
see **dubiosity**

dubiosity
5 doubt 6 wonder 7 concern 8 mistrust 9 addlement, confusion, suspicion 10 muddlement, skepticism 11 incertitude, uncertainty, uncertitude

dubious
4 moot, open 5 fishy 6 unsure 7 suspect, unclear 8 arguable, doubtful, hesitant, mootable, unlikely, untrusty 9 debatable, dubitable, equivocal, skeptical, trustless, uncertain, undecided 10 disputable, fly-by-night, improbable, unreliable 11 mistrustful, problematic, questioning, unpromising 12 questionable, undependable, undetermined 13 untrustworthy

dubitable
4 open 5 fishy 7 suspect 8 doubtful 9 ambiguous, uncertain, unsettled 10 borderline

duce
6 despot, tyrant 8 dictator 9 Mussolini, oppressor

duck
3 bob, bow, dip, shy 4 bend, bilk, dive, dunk, shun 5 avoid, dodge, douse, elude, evade, fence, parry, shirk, souse, stoop 6 double, escape, eschew, plunge 7 back out, immerse 8 sidestep, submerge, submerse 10 canvasback
Asian: 5 Pekin 8 mandarin
dabbling: 7 gadwall, mallard

diving: 4 smew 7 pochard 9 merganser 10 bufflehead
eggs: 5 pidan
Eurasian: 4 smew
European: 8 garganey, shelduck
genus: 4 Anas
group: 4 sord, team 5 brace, flock, skein 6 flight
Hawaiian: 5 koloa
hunter's screen: 5 blind
male: 5 drake
red-wattled: 7 Muscovy
relating to: 7 anatine
river: 4 teal 6 wigeon 7 pintail, widgeon
scaup: 8 bluebill
sea: 5 eider, scaup 6 scoter

duckbill
8 platypus 9 monotreme 10 mallangong

duck soup
3 pie 4 snap 5 cinch, setup 6 breeze, picnic 8 kid stuff, pushover 10 child's play

duckweed
6 lemnad

ducky
4 cute, fine 7 darling 8 pleasant, splendid 9 excellent

duct
4 pipe, tube 5 canal 6 course 7 channel, conduit 11 ink fountain, watercourse
anatomical: 3 vas 4 vasa (plural)
combining form: 3 vas 4 vasi, vaso

ductile
6 pliant, supple 7 plastic, pliable 8 flexible, moldable 9 adaptable, compliant, malleable, tractable
metal: 4 wire

ductless gland
see **endocrine gland**

ductus
4 fist, hand 6 script 10 penmanship 11 calligraphy, chirography, handwriting

dud
3 bad 4 bomb, bust, fake, flop 5 lemon, loser 7 failure 11 ineffective

dude
3 fop 4 buck 5 blood, dandy 7 coxcomb 8 macaroni 9 exquisite 10 tenderfoot 11 Beau Brummel, petit-maître 12 lounge lizard

dudgeon
4 fury, huff, miff, rage 5 pique, wrath 7 offense, umbrage 10 resentment

duds
4 togs 5 dress 6 attire, things 7 apparel, clothes, raiment 8 clothing 10 attirement 11 habiliments

due
4 debt, fair, good, just, owed 5 lumps, merit, owing, right 6 direct, earned, lawful, mature, reward, rights, unpaid 7 arrears, condign, deserts, exactly, merited, payable, payment, regular 8 adequate, deserved, directly, rightful, straight, suitable 9 arrearage, deserving, equitable, liability, requisite, scheduled, unsettled 10 recompense, satisfying, straightly, sufficient 11 appropriate, comeuppance, outstanding 12 compensation, indebtedness, satisfaction 13 rhadamanthine, undeviatingly

duel
4 buck 5 fight, repel 6 combat, oppose, resist 7 contest, dispute 8 conflict, traverse 9 withstand

duenna
8 chaperon 9 chaperone, governess

duet
dancer's: 9 pas de deux

due to
4 over 7 through 9 because of

duff
5 slack 7 pudding 8 coal dust, fine coal

duffer
4 dolt, dope 5 dunce, idiot 6 dimwit 8 dumbbell, numskull 9 blockhead, ignoramus

dugout
4 abri 5 banca, canoe 7 piragua, pirogue

dukedom
5 duchy

dulcet
5 sweet 7 melodic, tuneful, winning, winsome 8 engaging, euphonic, luscious, pleasant, soothing 9 melodious 10 euphonious 11 mellisonant

dulcimer
Chinese: 7 yang-kin
Hungarian: 8 cimbalom
Persian: 6 santir 7 santour

dull
3 bad, dim, dry, dun, mat 4 arid, blah, blue, blur, dead, down, drab, dumb, fade, flat, hard, hazy, numb, pale, poky, slow 5 befog, blear,

blind, blunt, cloud, dense, dingy, dusty, heavy, inert, matte, muddy, murky, muted, prosy, thick **6** benumb, blurry, boring, cloudy, deaden, dreary, gloomy, leaden, obtund, obtuse, retard, simple, somber, stodgy, stupid, tiring, weaken **7** becloud, blunted, disedge, doltish, humdrum, insipid, irksome, louring, moronic, muffled, prosaic, stupefy, subfusc, tarnish, tedious, wash out **8** backward, banausic, bromidic, cast down, deadened, dejected, deluster, discolor, downcast, duncical, enfeeble, hebetate, hopeless, imbecile, lifeless, listless, lowering, monotone, nubilous, overcast, plodding, retarded, sluggish, weariful **9** bloodless, brainless, colorless, depressed, dim-witted, dryasdust, insensate, ponderous, unfeeling, wearisome **10** anesthetic, beef-witted, devitalize, dispirited, half-witted, impassible, indistinct, insensible, lackluster, lusterless, monotonous, numskulled, pedestrian, spiritless **11** blear-witted, desensitize, downhearted, insensitive, overclouded, thickheaded, thick-witted, unsharpened **12** disheartened, feebleminded, simpleminded **13** uninteresting
combining form: **5** brady

dullard
5 dummy, dunce, idiot, moron **6** stupid **8** dumbbell **9** ignoramus, simpleton

dulled
combining form: **5** ambly **6** amblyo

dullness
4 coma **5** sleep **6** apathy, stupor, torpor **7** languor, slumber **8** hebetude, lethargy, monotony **9** bluntness, denseness, lassitude, stupidity, torpidity **10** drowsiness

duly
8 properly **9** regularly **12** sufficiently

Dumas character
5 Athos **6** Aramis, Dantes **7** Camille, Porthos **9** D'Artagnan

dumb
3 mum **4** dull, mute **5** dense, quiet, thick **6** deaden, silent, stupid **7** doltish, foolish **8** duncical, reticent, taciturn, wordless **9** fatheaded, voiceless **10** numskulled, speechless, tongue-tied **11** blockheaded, thick-witted, tight-lipped **12** close-mouthed, close-tongued,

inarticulate, inexpressive, tightmouthed, unarticulate, unresponsive

dumbbell
see **dullard**

dumbfound
5 amaze **6** boggle **7** astound, nonplus, stagger **8** astonish, surprise **11** flabbergast

dumbfounded
5 agape **6** aghast, amazed **7** shocked **8** confused, dismayed **10** bewildered **11** overwhelmed **13** thunderstruck

dummy
4 dolt, mock, sham **5** dunce, false, idiot, moron **6** effigy, ersatz, layout, stooge, stupid, yes-man **7** dullard **8** dullhead, dumbbell, spurious **9** ignoramus, imitation, simpleton, simulated **10** artificial, fictitious, substitute

dump
3 sty **4** cast, drop, junk **5** chuck, depot, ditch, scrap **6** armory, pigpen, pigsty, plunge **7** arsenal, discard, eyesore **8** jettison, magazine, throw out **9** throw away

dumpling
5 blimp, fatty **8** quenelle **10** butterball

dumps
5 blues, gloom **7** sadness **9** dejection **10** depression, melancholy, the dismals **11** unhappiness **12** mournfulness

dumpy
5 squat, thick **6** chunky, slummy, squdgy, stocky, stubby **8** heavyset, thickset **9** shapeless **11** thickbodied

dun
3 dim **4** dark, dusk, gnaw **5** annoy, brown, dusky, murky, worry **6** darken, gloomy, harass, needle, pester, plague, somber **7** bedevil, hagride, obscure **9** beleaguer, caddis fly, lightless **10** caliginous **12** grayish brown

Duncan's slayer
7 Macbeth

dunce
3 mug, oaf **4** boob, clod, dodo, dolt, dope, fool, goof, jerk, lunk, mutt, poke, simp **5** booby, chump, dummy, idiot, moron, ninny, noddy, prune **6** dimwit, donkey, duffer, nitwit, noodle, stupid, turnip, zombie **7** dullard, fathead, jackass, lackwit, muggins, pinhead, wantwit **8** bone-

head, clodpate, clodpoll, dolthead, dullhead, dumbbell, imbecile, ironhead, knothead, lunkhead, numskull **9** birdbrain, blockhead, ignoramus, lamebrain, simpleton, thickhead **10** beetlehead, dunderhead, dunderpate, hammerhead, muddlehead, muttonhead, nincompoop, squarehead, thickskull, woodenhead **11** cabbagehead, chowderhead, chucklehead, knucklehead, pumpkin head **12** featherbrain, scatterbrain **13** featherweight

Dunciad author
4 Pope (Alexander)

duncical
4 dull, dumb **5** dense **6** stupid **7** doltish **8** blockish **9** pinheaded **10** numskulled **11** blockheaded, thickheaded

dunderhead
see **dunce**

dunderpate
see **dunce**

dundrearies
9 burnsides, sideburns **10** sideboards **11** muttonchops **12** sidewhiskers

dune
5 twine **8** sandbank
area: **3** erg

dung
4 muck **6** manure, ordure **9** excrement
beetle: **3** dor **6** scarab **9** tumblebug
combining form: **4** copr, scat **5** copro, scato

dungaree fabric
5 denim

dungeon
4 cell, jail **5** vault **6** donjon, prison **9** black hole, oubliette

dunghill
6 midden

dungy
4 foul **5** black, dirty, nasty, soily **6** filthy, grubby, sordid **7** squalid, unclean

dunk
3 dip, sop **4** soak **5** douse, souse **7** immerse **8** saturate, submerge, submerse

dunlin
4 stib **9** sandpiper

duo
4 dyad, pair **5** brace **6** couple **7** doublet, twosome

dupe
3 con, job, kid, sap 4 butt, dust, fool, gull, hoax, mark, tool 5 catch, cheat, chump, cozen, patsy, slave, spoof, trick 6 befool, delude, double, outwit, pigeon, puppet, sucker 7 chicane, deceive, defraud, dualize, fall guy, gudgeon, mislead 8 flimflam, hoodwink 9 bamboozle, duplicate, victimize 11 double-cross, hornswoggle

dupery
5 cheat, fraud 7 chicane 9 chicanery, deception 10 dishonesty, hanky-panky 13 double-dealing, sharp practice

duple
4 dual 6 bifold, binary, double, duplex 7 twofold 9 dualistic

duplex
see **duple**

duplicate
4 copy, mate, same, twin 5 ditto, equal, match 6 carbon, double, fellow 7 dualize, identic, imitate, replica 9 companion, facsimile, identical, reproduce 10 carbon copy, coordinate, equivalent, reciprocal, tantamount 11 counterpart, replication 12 reproduction
prefix: 7 counter

duplicitous
6 shifty, sneaky 7 devious 8 guileful, indirect, sneaking 9 underhand 11 underhanded

duplicity
5 guile 6 deceit 7 cunning, perfidy 9 treachery 10 doubleness 12 dissemblance 13 dissimulation, double-dealing, faithlessness

durability
4 wear 11 lastingness

durable
5 stout 6 strong, sturdy 7 lasting 8 enduring 9 diuturnal, perduring, permanent, tenacious

duramen
9 heartwood

durance
9 restraint 11 confinement 12 imprisonment

duration
3 run 4 span, term, time 6 period 9 endurance 10 continuity 11 continuance, lastingness, persistence

duress
5 force 8 coercion, violence 10 compulsion, constraint

Durga
see **Devi**

during
3 mid 4 amid, over 5 midst 10 throughout
prefix: 2 di 3 dia 5 intra

durra
7 sorghum 10 guinea corn 12 Indian millet

durum
5 wheat

dusk
3 dim 4 dark 5 murky 6 darken, gloomy 7 evening, obscure 8 darkness, eventide, glooming, owl-light, twilight 9 lightless, nightfall, tenebrous 10 caliginous 12 semidarkness 13 unilluminated

dusky
3 dim 4 dark 5 black, bleak, drear, murky, swart 6 brunet, dismal, gloomy, opaque, swarth 7 joyless, obscure, swarthy 8 bistered, blackish, desolate, funereal, nubilous 9 ambiguous, cheerless, equivocal, lightless, sibylline, tenebrous 10 acheronion, caliginous, depressing 11 black-a-vised, dark-skinned, double-edged, double-faced 13 unilluminated
combining form: 4 pheo 5 phaeo

dust
3 row 4 beat, drub, dupe, fool, gull, hoax, lick, sift, whip 5 run-in, trick 6 fracas, hassle, powder, thrash 7 chicane, confuse, dispute, quarrel, shellac 8 flimflam, hoodwink, lambaste, levigate, sprinkle 9 bamboozle, bickering, confusion, overwhelm, powdering 10 besprinkle, falling-out, sprinkling 11 altercation, disturbance, hornswoggle
combining form: 4 coni 5 conio
Scottish: 5 stour

dustbowl victim
4 Okie

dustup
3 row 5 run-in 6 fracas, hassle 7 dispute, quarrel 8 argument 9 bickering 10 falling-out 11 altercation

dusty
3 dim, dry 4 arid, dull 5 blowy, stale 6 barren, sordid, stormy 7 clouded, insipid, powdery, tedious 8 bromidic, weariful 9 dryasdust, miserable, wearisome, worth-

less 12 contemptible, unproductive, unsatisfying 13 uninteresting
Scottish: 6 stoury

Dutch
7 trouble 8 hot water 9 Afrikaans
commune: 3 Ede
housewife: 4 frow
scholar: 7 Erasmus
uncle: 3 oom

dutiful
7 duteous 9 regardful 10 respectful 11 deferential

duty
3 job, tax, use 4 goal, levy, load, mark, must, need, onus, role, task 5 chare, chore, ought, stint 6 burden, charge, devoir, impost, object, office, target, tariff, weight 7 purpose, respect, service 8 business, function, province 9 committal, millstone, objective 10 assessment, assignment, commitment, deadweight, obligation

Duvalier's land
5 Haiti

dwarf
3 wee 4 runt, tiny 5 gnome, midge, pygmy, stunt, troll 6 midget, minify, peewee, teensy 7 manikin, minikin 8 suppress, Tom Thumb 9 miniature 10 diminutive, homunculus 11 hop-o'-my-thumb, lilliputian
combining form: 3 nan 4 nann, nano 5 nanno
in Snow White: 3 Doc 5 Dopey, Happy 6 Grumpy, Sleepy, Sneezy 7 Bashful
Scottish: 7 blastie

dwarf elder
8 danewort, goutweed

dwarfish
4 tiny 6 midget 7 minikin 9 itsy-bitsy, itty-bitty, miniature 10 diminutive 11 lilliputian

dwell
3 lie, won 4 bide, live 5 abide, exist 6 inhere, reside 7 consist, hang out

dweller
5 liver 7 denizen, resider 8 habitant, occupant, resident 10 inhabitant
monastic: 4 monk 5 friar 6 oblate
suffix: 3 ite

dwelling
4 casa, home 5 abode, house 8 domicile 9 residence, residency 10 brownstone, commoracy, habitation

American Indian: 4 tipi 5 hogan, tepee 6 pueblo, teepee, wigwam
clergyman's: 5 manse 7 rectory
9 parsonage
crude: 5 shack 6 shanty
Eskimo: 4 iglu 5 igloo
Hindu: 6 ashram, asrama
7 ashrama
Navaho: 5 hogan

dwindle
3 ebb 4 fail, wane 5 abate, close,
taper 6 lessen, reduce, shrink,
weaken 7 decline, subside 8 decrease, diminish, taper off 9 attenuate, drain away, extenuate, fall
short, waste away

dyad
3 duo 4 pair 5 brace 6 couple
7 doublet, twosome

dye
5 color, stain 6 reddle, ruddle
7 pigment 8 colorant, nigrosin, py-
ronine, tincture
blue: 4 woad 5 cyanin, indigo 7 cyanine, indulin 8 indigoid, induline
for hair: 5 henna
green: 7 gallein
plant: 4 chay, woad 5 chaya, sumac 6 madder
purple: 6 orchil
red: 5 eosin 6 eosine, kermes 7 cro-
cein, cudbear, fuchsin, kermess,
magenta 8 alizarin, anchusin, cro-
ceine, fuchsine, rhodamin, safranin
9 cochineal
reddish: 5 henna 8 purpurin

reddish brown: 6 orcein
violet: 7 thionin 8 thionine
yellow: 8 orpiment
yellowish red: 7 achiote, annatto

dyed-in-the-wool
5 sworn 7 devoted, settled 9 confirmed, hard-shell 10 deep-rooted,
deep-seated, entrenched, inveterate
13 bred-in-the-bone

dyeing process
5 batik

dyeleaves
8 inkberry 9 sweetleaf

dye red
6 ruddle

dyer's grape
8 pokeweed

dyer's mulberry
6 fustic

dyestuff
see **dye**

dyewood
6 brasil, brazil, fustet, fustic

dying
8 expiring, moribund

dynamic
4 live 5 alive, lusty, vital 6 active
7 intense, running, working 8 forceful, forcible, vigorous 9 energetic,
operative, strenuous 10 functional,
red-blooded 11 functioning

dynamite
4 raze, ruin 7 destroy, shatter

8 decimate, demolish, destruct, dissolve 9 dismantle, explosive
10 annihilate
inventor: 5 Nobel (Alfred)

dynamo
6 peeler 7 hustler, rustler 8 go-getter, live wire 9 generator 11 self-
starter

dysentery
4 flux 6 scours 8 diarrhea

dyslogistic
9 slighting 10 derogatory, detracting, pejorative 11 disparaging
12 depreciative, depreciatory

dyspathy
7 allergy 8 aversion

dyspepsia
7 pyrosis 9 gastritis, heartburn
11 indigestion

dyspeptic
6 morose 10 ill-humored, ill-natured, tempersome 11 bad-tempered, hot-tempered, ill-tempered

dysphoria
5 gloom, mopes 7 sadness 9 dejection 10 depression, melancholy
11 unhappiness 12 mournfulness,
wretchedness

dysprosium
symbol: 2 Dy

Dzhugashvili
6 Stalin (Joseph)

Ee

each
3 all, per 5 every 6 apiece 8 every-one, per caput 9 per capita

eager
3 hot 4 agog, avid, keen 5 itchy, ready 6 ardent, gung ho, heated, hungry, intent, pining, raring 7 anxious, athirst, craving, longing, restive, thirsty, wishful 8 appetent, covetous, desirous, on tiptoe, restless, yearning 9 ambitious, hankering, impatient 10 breathless, solicitous 11 acquisitive 12 enthusiastic

eagerness
4 zeal, zest, zing 5 ardor, gusto 6 fervor 7 avidity 8 alacrity, ambition, fervency, keenness 9 quickness 10 enthusiasm

eagle
4 hawk 9 accipiter
combining form: 4 aeto 5 aetus
nest: 4 aery 5 aerie, eyrie
North American: 4 bald 6 golden 10 bald-headed
sea: 3 ern 4 erne 6 osprey

eagle-eyed
7 lyncean 12 sharp-sighted

eagre
4 bore, flow, wave 5 flood

ear
4 heed, mark, note 6 notice, regard, remark 7 auricle 8 auricula 9 attention 10 observance 11 observation
bone: 5 anvil, incus 6 hammer, stapes 7 malleus, stirrup
canal: 5 scala
combining form: 2 ot 3 aur, oto 4 auri, otic
doctor: 9 otologist
inner: 9 labyrinth
middle: 8 tympanum
outer: 5 pinna
part: 4 drum, lobe 5 canal 6 tragus 7 cochlea

relating to: 4 otic 5 aural 9 auricular
science: 7 otology

earache
7 otalgia

eardrum
8 tympanum
combining form: 6 tympan 7 tympano

___ Earhart
6 Amelia

earl
4 lord, peer 5 noble 8 nobleman 10 aristocrat

earlier
3 ere, yet 4 once 5 as yet, so far 6 before, sooner 7 already, thus far 8 formerly, hitherto, previous 9 erstwhile, preceding 10 beforehand, heretofore, previously
combining form: 4 fore 6 proter 7 protero

earlier than
prefix: 3 pre, pro

earliest
5 first, prime 6 maiden 7 initial, pioneer, primary 8 original, primeval, pristine
combining form: 2 eo

earlike projection
3 lug

Earl of Avon
4 Eden (Anthony)

early
3 old 5 first, prior 6 primal, timely 7 ancient, betimes 8 germinal, original, oversoon, previous, primeval, pristine, untimely 9 preceding, premature, primitive 10 antecedent, antiquated, beforehand, precocious, prevenient, primordial, seasonably 11 precipitant, prematurely

combining form: 4 pale 5 palae, paleo 6 palaeo, palaio

earn
3 bag, get, net, win 4 gain, make, rate, reap 5 gross, merit, score 6 attain, come by, effect, obtain, secure 7 acquire, bring in, deserve, harvest, procure, realize, receive 8 draw down 9 knock down

earnest
4 busy, pawn, warm, zeal 5 grave, sober, staid, token 6 ardent, pledge, sedate, solemn, somber, warmth 7 serious, sincere, warrant, weighty, zealous 8 diligent, interest, pressing, security, sedulous 9 assiduous, attention, heartfelt 10 enthusiasm, intentness, no-nonsense, passionate, sobersided 11 industrious, perseverant, seriousness 12 enthusiastic, wholehearted

earnestly
4 down, hard 7 for real, soberly 8 actively, dingdong, solemnly 9 intensely, seriously, zealously 10 thoroughly 11 assiduously, intensively 12 exhaustively, thoughtfully 13 painstakingly

earnestness
7 gravity, resolve 8 decision, firmness, sobriety 10 absorption, intentness 11 engrossment, persistence, seriousness 12 deliberation, perseverance 13 concentration, determination

earnings
4 gain 5 lucre 6 income, living, profit, return 8 proceeds

ear shell
7 abalone

earshot
5 sound 7 hearing

earsplitting
4 loud 6 shrill 7 blaring, roaring

8 piercing 10 stentorian 11 full-mouthed, stentorious

earth

3 mud, orb 4 clay, clod, dirt, fill, land, loom, sand, soil, turf, vale 5 glebe, globe, humus, terra, world 6 cosmos, gravel, ground, planet, sphere 7 dry land, subsoil, terrain 8 creation, universe 9 macrocosm 10 terra firma
combining form: 2 ge 3 geo 6 tellur 7 telluri, telluro
core: 12 centrosphere
god: 3 Geb, Keb, Seb 5 Dagan
goddess: 2 Ge, Ki 4 Erda, Gaea 5 Ceres, Nintu 6 Kishar 7 Demeter, Nerthus
relating to: 8 telluric 9 planetary, tellurian 11 terrestrial
satellite: 4 moon
science: 7 geology 9 geography
Scottish: 4 yird 5 yirth

earthenware

4 delf 5 delft 7 biscuit, faience, pottery 8 crockery, majolica 9 stoneware 10 terra-cotta

earthlike

7 terrene 11 terrestrial

earthly

6 carnal, likely, mortal 7 mundane, terrene, worldly 8 material, physical, possible, probable, telluric, temporal 9 corporeal, potential, sublunary, tellurian 10 imaginable 11 conceivable, terrestrial, uncelestial, unspiritual

earthquake

5 seism, shake, shock 6 tremor 7 temblor 8 trembler, tremblor
combining form: 5 seism 6 seismo
measuring device: 11 seismograph, seismometer
relating to: 7 seismic
science: 10 seismology 11 seismometry

earthwork

4 bank, wall 7 bulwark, rampart 10 embankment 13 fortification

earthworm

7 annelid 9 brandling

earthy

3 low 5 dusty, gross, muddy, sandy 6 clayey 7 mundane, sensual, terrene, worldly 8 banausic, telluric, temporal 9 practical, pragmatic, realistic, sublunary, tellurian 10 hard-boiled, hardheaded 11 terrestrial, uncelestial, unfantastic 12 matter-of-fact 13 materialistic, unsentimental

earwax

7 cerumen

ease

3 aid, lax 4 bate, calm, dull, free, help, rest 5 allay, knock, loose, poise, relax, slack, speed 6 assist, better, deaden, loosen, relief, repose 7 abandon, assuage, calming, fluency, forward, further, improve, inertia, leisure, lighten, mollify, promote, relieve, slacken 8 calmness, deftness, diminish, dispatch, facility, idleness, mitigate, moderate, security, soothing, supinity, thriving 9 abundance, alleviate, disengage, expertise, inertness, passivity, readiness, reduction, untighten, well-being 10 adroitness, ameliorate, artfulness, cleverness, efficiency, expertness, facilitate, inactivity, mitigation, moderation, prosperity, relaxation, smoothness 11 alleviation, naturalness, spontaneity, tranquility 12 skillfulness, tranquillity

easel

5 frame, stand 7 support

easement

6 relief 9 allayment 10 mitigation 11 alleviation 13 mollification

ease off

3 ebb, lax 4 fall, wane 5 abate, let up, loose, relax, slack, unlax 6 loosen, relent, unbend, unwind 7 die away, die down, slacken, subside 8 loosen up, moderate 9 untighten

easily

4 well 6 freely, indeed, simply 7 handily, lightly, readily 8 facilely, smoothly 9 assuredly, certainly, decidedly, doubtless 10 absolutely, definitely, positively 11 competently, dexterously, doubtlessly, efficiently, undoubtedly 12 effortlessly 13 unequivocally
combining form: 2 eu

east

4 Asia 6 Levant, Orient
German: 3 ost

Easter

5 Pasch
relating to: 7 paschal
symbol: 3 egg 4 lamb 5 bunny 6 rabbit

eastern

8 oriental 9 Levantine
countries: 6 Orient
name: 3 Ali 4 Abou
title: 3 sri

East Indies

9 Indonesia
animal: 7 tarsier
bark: 5 niepa
bird: 4 baya 5 argus
boatman: 6 serang
civet: 6 musang
fish: 5 dorab
fruit: 6 durian, durion
grass: 4 kans 5 glaga 6 raggee
herb: 3 pia 4 chay, sola 6 sesame 7 roselle
monkey: 7 hanuman 8 entelles
musical instrument: 4 bina, vina
plant: 2 da 4 bene, jute, sola, sunn 5 benne, kenaf 6 ambary, sesame 9 patchouli
ship: 7 patamar 8 pattamar
tree: 3 nim 4 dhak, neem, poon, toon 5 mahua, niepa, salai, simal, siris 6 banyan, deodar, illupi, sissoo 7 champac, hollong 8 mastwood 10 hursinghar
warrior: 5 singh
wood: 3 eng

easy

3 lax 4 calm, cozy, fast, glib, mild, soft, well 5 clear, comfy, cushy, light, loose, naive, plain, royal, suave 6 benign, facile, fluent, kindly, placid, poised, polite, secure, serene, simple, smooth, urbane, wanton 7 amiable, clement, courtly, cursive, evident, flowing, lenient, obvious, relaxed, well-off, whorish 8 apparent, clear-cut, composed, distinct, familiar, graceful, gullible, informal, manifest, merciful, obliging, pleasant, sociable, tolerant, tranquil, trusting, unchaste, well-to-do 9 collected, credulous, forgiving, indulgent, lethargic, possessed, well-fixed 10 charitable, diplomatic, effortless, fleeceable, forbearing, prosperous, successful, uninvolved, well-heeled 11 comfortable, complaisant, good-humored, good-natured, susceptible, sympathetic, unambitious 12 good-tempered 13 compassionate, mollycoddling, self-possessed, uncomplicated, untroublesome

easygoing

3 lax 4 calm, lazy 5 drony 6 breezy, casual, dégagé, folksy, placid, poised, serene 7 affable, offhand, relaxed, unfussy, work-shy 8 carefree, careless, composed, fainéant, flexible, indolent, informal, moderate, slothful, tranquil 9 apathetic, collected, off-handed 10 unaffected, unreserved 11 indifferent,

low-pressure, unambitious, uncon-cerned, uninhibited **12** devil-may-care, happy-go-lucky, self-com-posed **13** self-possessed, unconstrained

easy mark
3 sap **4** butt, dupe, fool, gull **5** chump **6** pigeon, sucker **7** fall guy **9** soft touch

easy street
8 thriving **9** abundance, well-being **10** prosperity

eat
3 sup **4** bite, chow, dine, gnaw, meal, pick, take, wolf **5** erode, feast, gorge, lunch, mouth, scoff, scour, snack, use up **6** devour, feed on, gobble, ingest, nibble **7** banquet, consume, corrode, ex-haust, gorge on, swallow **8** dis-solve, wear away **9** breakfast, de-compose, partake of, polish off **10** gormandize, nibble away

eatable
6 edible **8** esculent **10** comestible

eater
8 consumer
combining form: **4** phag, vora, vore **5** estes, phaga, phage **6** phagus

eating
combining form: **4** phag **5** phago, phagy **6** phagia, vorous **7** phagous

eating place
4 café, mess **5** diner, grill **7** automat, beanery, dinette, tea-room **8** cookshop, messroom, snack bar **9** cafeteria, chophouse, lunchroom **10** coffee shop, restau-rant **12** luncheonette

Ebal's father
6 Shobal

ebb
4 fade, fall, tide, wane **5** abate, let up **6** recede, relent **7** decline, die away, die down, ease off, retreat, slacken, subside **8** decrease, dimin-ish, moderate **10** retrograde

Ebed's son
4 Gaal

Eber
father: **6** Elpaal **7** Shashak
son: **6** Joktan

Eblis
5 Satan
son: **3** Tir **4** Awar **5** Dasim **8** Za-lambur

ebon, ebony
3 jet **4** inky **5** black, jetty, raven, sable **9** pitch-dark **10** pitch-black **11** atramentous

éboulement
9 avalanche, landslide

ebullience
6 gaiety **7** ferment **8** buoyancy, vi-tality **9** agitation, animation **10** en-thusiasm, excitement, exuberance, exuberancy, liveliness **12** exhilara-tion **13** effervescence

ebullient
5 brash **7** boiling **8** agitated **9** ex-uberant, vivacious **12** effervescent, high-spirited

eccentric
3 odd **4** case, coot, kook, quiz **5** crank, freak, kooky, queer, wacky, weird **6** oddity, quirky, zombie **7** bizarre, caution, curious, erratic, heretic, oddball, strange **8** bohemian, crackpot, maverick, original, peculiar, singular **9** anom-alous, beheaded, character, dis-senter, fantastic, grotesque, irregu-lar, off-center, quizzical, screwball, unnatural **10** off-balance, unbal-anced, uncentered **11** exceptional **12** unconformist **13** exceptionable, idiosyncratic, nonconformist

eccentricity
5 quirk **6** oddity **10** aberration **11** peculiarity, strangeness **12** idiosyncrasy

ecclesiastic
5 clerk **6** cleric, divine, parson **8** clerical, minister, preacher, rever-end **9** churchman, clergyman

ecclesiastical
5 papal **6** church **8** churchly, cleri-cal, pastoral, priestly **9** apostolic, canonical, episcopal, prelatial, spir-itual, synagogal **10** churchlike, pan-theonic, pontifical, rabbinical, sac-erdotal, templelike
11 churchmanly, ministerial, patriar-chal, synagogical, theological **12** episcopalian, evangelistic, tabernacular

ecdysiast
6 peeler, teaser **8** stripper **10** strip-tease **11** stripteaser

echelon
3 row **4** file, line, rank, tier **5** queue **6** string **9** formation

echidna
5 bitis, snake, viper **8** anteater

Echidna
father: **7** Phorcys **8** Chrysaor
mother: **4** Ceto **10** Callirrhoe
offspring: **5** Hydra **6** dragon, Or-thus, Sphinx **7** Chimera **8** Cer-berus, Chimaera

echinoderm
6 urchin **8** starfish

echo
4 ring **5** oread **6** repeat, reverb, second **7** imitate, iterate, reflect, re-sound, revoice **8** resonate, re-sponse **9** reiterate **10** reflection, repetition **11** reverberate **12** reper-cussion **13** reverberation

echoic
9 imitative **12** onomatopoeic **13** onomatopoetic

Echo's beloved
9 Narcissus

éclat
4 bang, dash, fame, pomp **5** kudos **6** luster, renown, repute **7** acclaim, display **8** applause, standing **9** ce-lebrity, notoriety **10** brilliance, bril-liancy, prominence, reputation **11** distinction, ostentation

eclectic
5 broad, fussy, mixed, picky **6** choosy, select, varied **7** derived, diverse, finicky, mingled **8** as-sorted, catholic, elective **9** inclu-sive, multiform, selective **10** dis-cerning, fastidious, particular **11** diversified **12** multifarious **13** comprehensive, heterogeneous

eclipse
3 dim **4** murk **5** bedim, cloud, cover, excel, shade **6** darken, ex-ceed, shadow **7** becloud, decline, obscure, surpass **8** downfall **9** ad-umbrate, overcloud **10** overshadow

eclogue
4 idyl, poem **5** idyll **7** bucolic

ecological
8 bionomic
community: **5** biome
succession: **7** subsere

ecology
7 bionomy **9** bionomics
group: **3** EPA

economic
8 material **10** profitable
doctrine: **12** laissez-faire
system: **7** fascism **9** communism, so-cialism **10** capitalism **11** syndical-ism **12** mercantilism

economical
4 mean **5** canny, chary, close, spare **6** frugal, saving, stingy **7** careful, miserly, prudent, sparing, thrifty **8** skimping **9** niggardly, penny-wise, penurious, provident, scrimping, stewardly **10** forehanded, unwasteful **12** cheeseparing **13** penny-pinching

economist
American: 6 George (Henry), Veblen (Thorstein), Walker (Amasa), Weaver (Robert) **8** Friedman (Milton) **9** Galbraith (John Kenneth), Samuelson (Paul)
Canadian: 7 Leacock (Stephen)
Dutch: 9 Tinbergen (Jan)
English: 4 Mill (John Stuart) **5** Pigou (Arthur) **6** Keynes (John Maynard) **7** Malthus (Thomas Robert), Ricardo (David)
French: 6 Turgot (Anne-Robert-Jacques), Walras (Leon) **7** Quesnay (Francois)
German: 5 Weber (Max)
Scottish: 5 Smith (Adam)
Swedish: 6 Myrdal (Gunnar)
Swiss: 8 Sismondi (Simonde de)

economize
4 save **5** skimp **6** scrimp **7** husband **8** conserve

economy
6 thrift **7** parcity **8** meanness, prudence, skimping **9** frugality, husbandry, parsimony, scrimping **10** discretion, providence, stinginess **11** carefulness, miserliness, thriftiness **13** niggardliness

ecru
5 beige

ecstasy
3 joy **5** bliss **6** frenzy, heaven **7** delight, elation, madness, rapture **8** euphoria, felicity, gladness, paradise, pleasure, rhapsody **9** beatitude, happiness, transport **10** exaltation, joyfulness **11** blessedness, delectation, enchantment, inspiration **12** blissfulness, exhilaration, intoxication **13** seventh heaven

Ecuador
capital: 5 Quito
monetary unit: 5 sucre

ecumenical
6 cosmic, global **7** general **8** catholic **9** inclusive, planetary, universal, worldwide **10** heaven-wide **11** all-covering **12** all-including, all-pervading, cosmopolitan **13** comprehensive

ecumenical council
4 Lyon **5** Trent **6** Nicene, Vienne **7** Ephesus, Lateran, Vatican **9** Chalcedon, Constance

eczema
6 tetter **9** malanders **10** mallenders

edacious
8 ravening, ravenous **9** voracious **10** gluttonous

eddo
4 root, taro

eddy
4 purl **5** gurge, surge, swirl, twirl, whirl, whorl **6** swoosh, vortex **8** backwash **9** backwater, maelstrom, whirlpool **10** back stream **11** back current, counterflow, counterflux
combining form: 4 dino

edema
5 tumor **6** dropsy **8** anasarca, swelling

Eden
6 heaven, utopia **7** arcadia, elysium **8** paradise
river: 5 Gihon **6** Pishon **8** Hiddekel **9** Euphrates

edentate
5 sloth **8** anteater **9** armadillo, toothless

Ederyn's father
4 Nudd

Edessa's king
5 Abgar

edge
3 cut, end, hem, lip, rim **4** bank, bite, brim, draw, hone, side, whet **5** bound, brink, bulge, ledge, picot, point, ridge, sidle, skirt, start, sting, verge **6** border, fringe, margin, nosing **7** acidity, outline, serrate, sharpen, vantage **8** acerbity, acridity, boundary, emborder, handicap, keenness, surround, thinness **9** acuteness, advantage, allowance, extremity, head start, knife-edge, perimeter, periphery, sharpness, threshold **10** causticity, shrillness, stringency **11** astringency, penetration **12** incisiveness

edged
5 sharp **7** crenate, cutting, vallate

edge in
4 worm **5** foist **9** insinuate **10** infiltrate

edging
3 hem **4** lace **5** braid **6** border, fringe, lacing

edgy
5 nervy, tense **6** touchy, uneasy **7** excited, restive, uptight **8** agitable, restless, skittery, skittish, volatile **9** alarmable, excitable, impatient, irritable, startlish **10** high-strung

edible
7 eatable **8** esculent **9** palatable **10** comestible
root: 3 oca, yam **4** beet, taro **6** carrot, radish, turnip **7** parsnip **8** rutabaga **11** sweet potato
seed: 3 nut, pea **4** bean **6** peanut

edibles
4 food, grub **6** viands **7** nurture **8** victuals **9** provender **10** provisions **11** comestibles

edict
3 law **4** bull, fiat, rule **5** canon, order, ukase **6** decree, dictum, ruling **7** command, precept, statute **8** decretum **9** directive, manifesto, ordinance, prescript **10** instrument, regulation **12** proclamation **13** pronouncement
papal: 4 bull **8** decretal

Edict of ___
5 Milan **6** Nantes

edifice
4 pile **6** church **8** building, erection **9** structure

edify
5 teach **6** better, illume, uplift **7** educate, elevate, enhance, improve **8** illumine, instruct **9** elucidate, enlighten, irradiate **10** illuminate

edit
3 cut **4** omit **5** adapt, alter, amend, emend **6** delete, redact, refine, review, revise, reword, select **7** compile, correct, rewrite **8** assemble, copyread **9** rearrange

edition
4 copy **5** issue, print **7** reissue, version **8** printing, variorum **10** impression, reprinting **12** reproduction

editor
8 redactor **10** copyreader **11** proofreader

Edomite's ancestor
4 Esau

educate
4 rear **5** brief, teach, train **6** inform, school **7** explain, nurture **8** instruct **9** enlighten **10** discipline **12** indoctrinate

education

7 culture, science, tuition **8** breeding, coaching, guidance, learning, literacy, pedagogy, teaching, training, tutelage, tutorage, tutoring **9** erudition, knowledge, schooling, tutorship **11** instruction, learnedness, scholarship **13** enlightenment

educational

11 informative, informatory, instructive **13** informational, instructional
institution: **6** school **7** academy, college **9** institute **10** university **12** conservatory

educator

5 tutor **7** teacher **9** professor **10** instructor
American: **4** Mann (Horace) **6** Conant (James Bryant) **8** McGuffey (William) **10** Washington (Booker T.)
Italian: **10** Montessori (Maria)
Swiss: **10** Pestalozzi (Johann Heinrich)

educe

4 drag, draw, gain, milk, pull **5** evoke, wrest, wring **6** derive, elicit, evince, evolve, extort, obtain, secure **7** distill, draw out, extract, procure **10** excogitate

eel

4 worm **5** moray, siren, snake **6** conger, murena **7** hagfish, lamprey, muraena, sniggle **8** wriggler **9** muraenoid
young: **5** elver

eelboat

5 shuyt

eelpout

6 blenny, burbot **10** muttonfish

eely

6 slippy, wiggly **7** elusive, wriggly **8** slippery, slithery **9** wriggling

eerie

5 scary, weird **6** arcane, crawly, creepy, spooky **7** bizarre, strange, uncanny **9** fantastic, grotesque, unearthly **10** mysterious **11** frightening

efface

4 dele, x out **5** annul, erase **6** cancel, delete **7** blot out, destroy, exclude, expunge, rule out, wipe out **8** black out **9** eliminate, eradicate, extirpate **10** obliterate

effect

3 end **4** make **5** cause, enact, event, fruit, issue, yield **6** create, draw on, induce, invoke, render, result, secure, sequel, upshot **7** achieve, bring on, enforce, fulfill, outcome, perform, procure, produce, realize, turn out **8** bring off, carry out, causatum, conceive, generate, sequence **9** actualize, aftermath, corollary, implement, outgrowth, pursuance **10** accomplish, bring about, conclusion, denouement, end product **11** consequence, development, eventuality, precipitate **12** carry through, ramification, repercussion

effective

4 able **5** sound, valid **6** causal, cogent, direct, potent, useful **7** capable, dynamic, telling, virtual **8** adequate, virtuous **9** competent, efficient, operative **10** compelling, convincing **11** efficacious

effectiveness

5 force, point, power, punch, verve, vigor **7** cogency, potency **8** efficacy, strength, validity **9** validness **10** capability, efficiency **11** performance

effects

5 goods **6** things **8** chattels, movables **10** belongings **11** possessions

effectual

5 sound, valid **6** potent, strong, toothy, useful **8** decisive, powerful, virtuous, workable **9** achieving, efficient **10** conclusive, fulfilling **11** efficacious, influential, practicable **13** accomplishing, authoritative, determinative

effectuate

7 execute, fulfill **8** bring off, carry out **10** accomplish **12** carry through

effeminate

5 sappy, sissy **6** chichi, female, prissy, silken **7** epicene, foppish, unmanly **8** overnice, precious, womanish **9** pansified, sissified **10** old-maidish **12** Miss-Nancyish

effervescence

7 fizzing, foaming **8** bubbling, buoyancy **10** ebullience, ebullition, exuberance, exuberancy

effervescent

3 gay **4** airy **5** brash, jolly **6** bouncy, bubbly, lively **7** boiling, buoyant, elastic, excited, gleeful **8** animated, mirthful, volatile **9** ebullient, expansive, exuberant, hilarious, resilient, sparkling, sprightly, vivacious **12** high-spirited

effete

4 done, sere, soft, weak **5** all in, spent **6** barren, bleary, done in, used up **7** decayed, drained, far-gone, immoral, sterile, worn-out **8** consumed, decadent, decaying, depleted, fatigued, impotent, infecund, overripe **9** declining, dissolute, enfeebled, exhausted, infertile, washed-out **10** degenerate, unfruitful **11** debilitated

efficacious

6 active, potent, strong **8** forceful, forcible, powerful, puissant, virtuous **9** effective, effectual, efficient, operative **10** productive **11** influential

efficacy

see **effectiveness**

efficiency

see **effectiveness**

efficient

4 able **5** adept **6** expert, fitted **7** capable, skilled **8** masterly, skillful, virtuous **9** competent, effective, effectual, qualified **11** efficacious **12** businesslike

effigy

5 dummy, image **7** waxwork **8** likeness, portrait

effloresce

4 blow **5** bloom **6** flower **7** blossom, burgeon **8** outbloom

effluvium

4 odor **5** smell **6** efflux **7** exhaust **9** emanation **10** exhalation

efflux

4 flow **7** outflow **8** effusion **9** emanation

effort

3 job, try **4** task, toil, work **5** chore, essay, force, labor, might, nisus, pains, power, while **6** energy, strain **7** attempt, travail, trouble **8** endeavor, exertion, struggle, taskwork **9** puissance **11** application, elbow grease

effortful

4 hard **5** rough **6** uphill **7** arduous, labored, operose **8** toilsome **9** difficult, laborious, strenuous

effortless

4 easy **5** adept, light, ready, royal **6** expert, facile, fluent, simple, smooth **7** cursive, flowing, running, skilled **8** masterly, skillful **10** proficient **13** untroublesome

effrontery

4 face, gall **5** brass, cheek, nerve
8 audacity, boldness, temerity **9** assurance, brashness, hardihood, impudence, insolence **10** brazenness, confidence **11** presumption
12 impertinence **13** self-assurance

effulgence

4 glow **5** blaze **8** radiance, splendor **10** brightness, brilliance, luminosity

effulgent

5 vivid **6** bright, lucent **7** beaming, lambent, radiant **8** glorious, luminous, splendid **9** brilliant **11** resplendent **12** incandescent

effuse

4 flow, gush, pour, shed **7** emanate, radiate

effusive

5 gushy **6** sloppy, slushy, smarmy
7 cloying, fulsome, gushing, profuse
8 expansive, exuberant
10 outpouring, slobbering, unreserved **12** unrestrained **13** demonstrative, unconstrained

eft

4 newt **6** triton **10** salamander

egest

4 void **7** excrete **9** discharge

egg

3 ova (plural), sic **4** goad, ovum, prod, seed, spur, urge **5** drive, ovule, pique, prick, rally **6** arouse, excite, exhort, prompt, stir up **7** agitate **9** instigate, stimulate
before maturation: **6** oocyte
case: **5** shell **6** ovisac **7** ootheca
combining form: **2** oo, ov **3** ovi, ovo
dish: **6** omelet **8** omelette
fertilized: **6** zygote **7** oosperm, oospore
fish: **3** roe **6** caviar
French: **4** oeuf
part: **4** yelk, yolk **5** glair, shell, white **7** albumen, latebra
10 blastodisc
product: **3** zoa (plural) **4** zoon
white: **5** glair **7** albumen
yolk: **6** yellow **8** vitellus

egghead

7 Brahmin **8** highbrow **10** doubledome **12** intellectual

eggplant

7 brinjal **8** brinjaul **9** aubergine

egg-shaped

4 ooid, oval **5** ovate, ovoid **6** ooidal **7** oviform

eggshell

8 cascaron

Egil's brother

6 Volund

Eglah

husband: **5** David
son: **7** Ithream

eglantine

7 dog rose **10** sweetbrier

Eglantine

father: **5** Pepin
husband: **9** Valentine

Eglon

king: **5** Debir
slayer: **4** Ehud

ego

4 self **6** vanity **7** conceit **10** self-esteem

egocentric

7 pompous, selfish, stuck-up **9** conceited **10** self-loving **11** self-seeking, self-serving **12** megalomaniac, narcissistic, self-absorbed, self-affected, self-centered, self-involved, vainglorious **13** individualist, self-conceited, self-concerned, self-indulgent

egoism

5 pride **6** vanity **7** conceit **9** self-glory, self-pride, vainglory **11** self-opinion **13** self-assurance

egomaniacal

7 selfish **11** self-serving **12** self-absorbed, self-centered, self-exalting, self-involved, vainglorious **13** self-concerned

egotism

5 pride **6** vanity **7** conceit **8** boasting, bragging, self-love, vainness, vaunting **9** arrogance, gasconade, gasconism, self-glory, self-pride, vainglory **10** narcissism, self-esteem **11** megalomania, self-opinion, superiority **12** boastfulness **13** conceitedness

egotistic

5 cocky, proud **7** selfish, stuck-up **8** boastful, inflated, puffed up **9** conceited **11** pretentious, self-serving **12** self-absorbed, self-centered, self-involved **13** self-concerned, self-satisfied

egregious

4 rank **5** gross, stark **6** arrant
7 blatant, capital, glaring, heinous
8 flagrant, infamous, outright, shocking **9** atrocious **10** deplorable, outrageous

egress

4 door, exit **5** issue **6** escape, exodus, outlet **7** doorway, exiting, opening, passage **8** emerging, offgoing **9** departure, emergence **10** setting-out, withdrawal

egression

4 exit **6** exodus **7** exiting **8** offgoing **9** departure **10** setting-out, withdrawal

Egypt

capital: **5** Cairo
monetary unit: **5** pound

Egyptian

4 Arab, Copt **6** Coptic **7** African, Arabian
burial jar: **7** canopic
Christian: **4** Copt
cross: **4** ankh
dam: **4** sudd **5** Aswan
dancing girl: **4** alme **7** ghawazi (plural) **8** ghawazee (plural)
dynasty: **5** Saite, Xoite **6** Hyksos, Tanite, Theban **7** Persian, Thinite **8** Memphite **9** Bubastite, Ethiopian **10** Diospolite
god:
  chief: **6** Amen-Ra
  crocodile-headed: **5** Sebek
  falcon-headed: **4** Ment **5** Horus, Mentu **6** Sokari **7** Sokaris
  ibis-headed: **5** Thoth **6** Dhouti
  jackal-headed: **6** Anubis
  of chaos: **2** Nu
  of creation: **4** Ptah **5** Phtha
  of day: **5** Horus
  of earth: **3** Geb, Keb, Seb
  of evil: **3** Set **4** Seth **5** Sebek
  of life: **4** Amen, Amon **5** Ammon
  of magic: **5** Thoth **6** Dhouti
  of Memphis: **4** Ptah **5** Phtha **6** Sokari **7** Sokaris
  of pleasure: **3** Bes
  of procreation: **3** Min
  of the air: **3** Shu
  of the heavens: **5** Horus
  of the morning sun: **5** Horus **7** Khepera
  of the primeval flood: **2** Nu
  of the setting sun: **3** Tem, Tum **4** Atmu
  of the sun: **2** Ra, Re **6** Amen-Ra
  of Thebes: **4** Amen **6** Khensu, Khonsu
  of the underworld: **6** Osiris
  of war: **4** Ment **5** Mentu
  of wisdom: **5** Thoth **6** Dhouti
  ram-headed: **4** Amen, Amon **5** Ammon, Khnum **6** Khnemu
  snake: **4** Apep **5** Apepi
goddess:
  cat-headed: **4** Bast **5** Pakht

cow-headed: 5 Athor 6 Hathor
lioness-headed: 4 Bast 5 Pakht
6 Sekhet
of arms: 4 Anta
of fertility: 4 Isis
of love and mirth: 5 Athor 6 Hathor
of moisture: 6 Tefnut
of motherhood: 4 Apet, Isis
of Thebes: 3 Mut
of the dead: 8 Nephthys
of the heavens: 3 Nut
of truth and justice: 4 Maat
queen of the gods: 4 Sati
vulture-headed: 3 Mut 7 Nekhebt
8 Nekhebet
king: (see king entry)
language: 6 Arabic, Coptic
measure: 3 apt, dra, hen, pik, rob
4 draa, roub 5 ardab, ardeb, cubit, farde, keleh, kilah, sahme 6 artaba, aurure, feddan, keddah, rob-
bah 7 choryos, daribah, malouah,
roubouh, toumnah 8 kassabah,
kharouba 10 dira baladi
month: 4 Apap, Tybi 5 Payni, Thoth
6 Choiak, Hathor, Mechir, Mesore,
Paophi 7 Pachons 9 Phamenoth,
Pharmuthi
native: 4 Arab, Copt 5 Nilot
president: 5 Sadat 6 Nasser
7 Mubarak
queen: 9 Cleopatra, Nefertiti
sacred bird: 4 ibis
season: 4 Ahet, Pert 5 Shemu
skink: 4 adda
snake symbol: 6 uraeus
solar disk: 4 Aten
soul: 2 ba, ka 3 akh
sultan: 7 Saladin
talisman: 6 scarab
underworld: 4 Aaru, Duat 6 Amenti
weight: 3 kat, oka, oke 4 heml,
okia, rotl 5 artal, artel, deben,
kerat, okieh, uckia 6 hamlah, kantar 7 quintal
wind: 7 chamsin, khamsin, sirocco
8 khamseen

Ehud's victim
5 Eglon

eider
4 down, duck 8 shoreyer

eidetic
5 vivid 8 lifelike

eidolon
4 icon 5 ghost, ideal, image
7 phantom, specter 8 exemplar,
phantasm

eight
combining form: 3 oct 4 octa, octo
group of: 5 octad, octet 6 octave,
ogdoad 7 octette 8 octuplet

eight bells
4 noon

eighth note
6 quaver

Einstein
6 genius
birthplace: 3 Ulm

einsteinium
symbol: 2 Es

Eire
see **Ireland**

ejaculate
4 blat, bolt, yell 5 eject, shout 6 cry
out 7 exclaim 8 blurt out
10 vociferate

ejaculation
see **exclamation**

eject
3 out 4 boot, bump, fire, oust, rout,
sack, shed, spew 5 belch, chase,
chuck, debar, eruct, erupt, evict, expel, spout, spurn 6 banish, disbar,
irrupt, run off, squirt 7 boot out, discard, dismiss, exclude, extrude,
kick out, rule out, shut out, sputter
8 disgorge, displace, drive off,
throw out 9 discharge, ejaculate,
eliminate, repudiate 10 dispossess

eke
4 fill 7 squeeze, stretch
10 supplement

elaborate
4 busy 5 fancy 6 daedal, dressy,
evolve, expand, knotty, ornate, unfold 7 amplify, clarify, comment,
complex, develop, discuss, elegant,
enlarge, explain, expound, gordian
8 detailed, involved, overdone
9 Byzantine, decorated, interpret,
intricate 10 overworked 11 complicated, embellished, overwrought,
painstaking 12 labyrinthine

Elah
father: 4 Uzzi 5 Caleb 6 Baasha
slayer: 5 Zimri
son: 6 Hoshea

Elaine
father: 6 Pelles
lover: 7 Lancelot 9 Launcelot
son: 7 Galahad

Elam
capital: 4 Susa 7 Shushan
father: 4 Shem
king: 12 Chedorlaomer

élan
3 vim 4 brio, dash, life, zeal, zest,
zing 5 ardor, gusto, oomph, verve,
vigor 6 esprit, spirit 7 impetus, potency 9 animation, eagerness
10 enthusiasm

élan vital
4 soul 5 anima 6 animus, pneuma,
psyche, spirit

elapse
2 go 4 flow, pass, slip 5 glide,
slide 6 expire, run out 8 pass
away

Elasah's father
6 Pashur 7 Shaphan

elastic
4 airy 5 lithe 6 bouncy, garter, limber, lively, pliant, rubber, supple,
whippy 7 buoyant, ductile, pliable,
rubbery, soaring, springy, stretch
8 animated, flexible, moldable,
spirited, stretchy, volatile 9 adaptable, ebullient, expansive, malleable, resilient, sprightly, vivacious
10 mettlesome, rubberlike
11 stretchable

elate
4 buoy 5 cheer, exalt, flush, set up
6 excite, uplift 7 cheer up, commove, delight, gladden, gratify, inspire, overjoy 8 brighten, inspirit,
spirit up 9 encourage

elated
4 glad 5 happy 6 jovial 7 excited,
exulted 8 ecstatic, euphoric, exultant, gladsome, jubilant, turned-on
9 overjoyed 10 enraptured 11 exhilarated, intoxicated

elater
6 beetle 8 skipjack 11 click beetle

Elatha's son
4 Bres

elation
3 joy 4 glee 7 rapture 8 buoyancy, euphoria 9 happiness, transport 10 exaltation, excitement
12 exhilaration, intoxication

Elbe tributary
4 Eger, Iser

elbow
4 push 5 ancon, joint, nudge,
press, shove 6 hustle, jostle
8 bulldoze
relating to: 7 anconal

El Camino ____
4 Real

elder
5 prior 6 senior 7 ancient, oldster
8 brass hat, higher-up, old-timer, superior 9 presbyter 10 golden-ager
13 senior citizen
French: 4 aîné 5 aînée

elderliness

3 age **5** years **6** old age **8** caducity **10** senescence **11** senectitude

elderly

3 old **4** aged, gray **5** aging, olden **6** senile **7** ancient **9** declining

eldorado

4 mine **7** bonanza **8** Golconda, gold mine, treasury **13** treasure-house, treasure trove

eldritch

5 eerie, weird **7** uncanny

Eleanor's husband

7 Henry II

Eleazar

brother: **5** Abihu, Nadab
father: **4** Dodo **5** Aaron **6** Parosh **8** Abinadab, Phinehas
son: **8** Phinehas

elect

3 opt **4** cull, like, mark, name, pick, rare, take, vote, will, wish **5** admit, co-opt, judge, saved **6** accept, ballot, choice, choose, chosen, decide, optate, opt for, picked, please, prefer, settle, single, vote in **7** appoint, receive, resolve **8** conclude, destined, nominate, ordained, redeemed **9** delivered, designate, determine, exclusive, single out **10** designated, handpicked, singled out

election

6 choice **7** primary **9** balloting **10** preference **11** alternative

electioneer

5 stump **8** campaign, politick

elective

6 chosen **8** optional **9** voluntary **13** discretionary, nonobligatory

Electra

brother: **7** Orestes
father: **5** Atlas **7** Oceanus **9** Agamemnon
husband: **7** Pylades, Thaumas
mother: **6** Tethys **7** Pleione **12** Clytemnestra
sister: **4** Styx **9** Iphigenia
son: **6** Iasion **8** Dardanus

electric

appliance: **3** fan **4** iron, oven **5** clock, drier, mixer, range, stove **6** washer **7** blender, freezer, toaster **12** refrigerator
coil: **5** tesla **8** solenoid
device: **4** coil, fuse, plug **6** dynamo, magnet, switch **7** battery **8** resistor, rheostat, varistor **9** amplifier, capacitor, condenser, generator, rheotrope **11** transformer
generator: **6** dynamo
particle: **3** ion **8** thermion
resistance: **6** ohmage
unit: **3** amp, ohm, rel **4** volt, watt **5** farad, henry, joule **6** abvolt, ampere **7** coulomb, faraday **8** kilovolt, kilowatt

electric current

2 AC, DC
combining form: **5** potam **6** potamo
kind: **6** direct **11** alternating
power: **7** wattage
strength: **8** amperage

electricity

5 juice, spark **7** current **8** voltaism **9** galvanism, lightning **10** enthusiasm, excitement
kind: **6** static **7** current

electrify

3 jar **4** send, stun **6** excite, thrill **7** enthuse, provoke, stagger, startle

electrode

6 dynode
negative: **7** cathode
positive: **5** anode

electron

3 ion **7** polaron **8** negatron
stream: **10** cathode ray
tube: **6** triode **7** tetrode **8** dynatron, klystron

Electryon

brother: **6** Mestor
daughter: **7** Alcmene
father: **7** Perseus
mother: **9** Andromeda
wife: **5** Anaxo

eleemosynary

6 humane **7** liberal **8** generous **10** altruistic, beneficent, benevolent, charitable, munificent, openhanded **12** humanitarian **13** philanthropic

elegance

4 chic, pomp, tone **5** charm, grace, style, taste **6** beauty, luxury, polish **7** culture, dignity **8** chicness, lushness, poshness, richness, splendor **10** ornateness, refinement **11** cultivation **12** magnificence, tastefulness **13** sumptuousness

elegant

4 chic, fine, posh, rare **5** grand, noble, swank **6** august, choice, classy, dainty, lovely, select, swanky, urbane **7** courtly, genteel, opulent, refined, stately **8** cultured, delicate, finished, graceful, handsome, majestic, polished, superior, tasteful **9** beautiful, exquisite, luxurious, recherché, sumptuous **10** cultivated

elegy

4 poem, song **5** dirge **6** lament, monody **7** epicede **9** epicedium
Hebrew: **5** kinah

Elektra composer

7 Strauss (Richard)

element

4 item, part **5** basic, facet, metal, piece, point, thing **6** aspect, detail, factor, member, sector **7** article, feature, portion, section **8** division, particle, rudiment **9** component, essential, principle **10** ingredient, particular **11** constituent, fundamental **13** part and parcel
chemical: **3** tin **4** gold, iron, lead, neon, zinc **5** argon, boron, radon, xenon **6** barium, carbon, cerium, cesium, cobalt, copper, curium, erbium, helium, indium, iodine, nickel, osmium, oxygen, radium, silver, sodium **7** arsenic, bismuth, bromine, cadmium, calcium, fermium, gallium, hafnium, holmium, iridium, krypton, lithium, mercury, niobium, rhenium, rhodium, silicon, sulphur, terbium, thorium, thulium, uranium, yttrium **8** actinium, aluminum, antimony, astatine, chlorine, chromium, europium, fluorine, hydrogen, illinium, lutecium, masurium, nitrogen, nobelium, platinum, polonium, rubidium, samarium, scandium, selenium, tantalum, thallium, titanium, tungsten, vanadium **9** americium, berkelium, beryllium, columbium, germanium, lanthanum, magnesium, manganese, neodymium, neptunium, palladium, plutonium, potassium, ruthenium, strontium, tellurium, virginium, ytterbium, zirconium **10** dysprosium, gadolinium, lawrencium, molybdenum **11** californium, einsteinium, mendelevium, phosphorous **12** praseodymium **13** protoactinium
hypothetical: **8** coronium

elemental

4 pure **5** basal, basic, crude, prime **6** inborn, innate, primal, simple **7** connate, primary, radical **8** inherent, intimate, simplest **9** beginning, essential, ingrained, intrinsic, primitive **10** deep-seated, primordial, substratal, underlying **14** constitutional

elementary

4 easy **5** basal, basic **6** simple **8** simplest, unsubtle **9** beginning,

essential, prefatory, primitive 10 rudimental, substratal, underlying 11 fundamental, preliminary 12 introductory

elemi
5 animé, resin 9 oleoresin

elephant
5 hathi 6 muckna, tusker 9 pachyderm
boy: 4 Sabu
driver: 6 mahout
enclosure: 5 kraal 6 keddah
extinct: 7 mammoth 8 mastodon
female: 3 cow
goad: 5 ankus 7 ankusha
group: 4 herd
keeper: 6 mahout
male: 4 bull
maverick: 5 rogue
nose: 5 trunk 9 proboscis
seat: 6 howdah
sound: 4 barr 6 bellow 7 trumpet
tooth: 4 tusk
tusk: 5 ivory
young: 4 calf

elephant-headed god
6 Ganesa 7 Ganesha

elephantine
4 huge 6 clumsy 7 awkward, mammoth 8 colossal, enormous, gigantic 9 graceless, maladroit, monstrous, ponderous 10 behemothic, gargantuan, mastodonic, prodigious, ungraceful, uninspired 11 heavy-footed, heavy-handed

elevate
4 lift, rear, rise 5 boost, elate, ensky, erect, exalt, hoist, raise 6 pick up, prefer, take up, uphold, uplift, uprear 7 advance, enhance, glorify, promote, upgrade, upraise 8 heighten 10 exhilarate

elevated
4 high 5 grand, great, lofty, moral, noble 6 aerial, formal, lifted, raised, superb 7 ethical, exalted, stately, sublime, upright, uprisen 8 eloquent, majestic, towering, upheaved, uplifted, upraised, virtuous 9 dignified, grandiose, high-flown, honorable, righteous 10 high-minded, upstanding 13 grandiloquent

elevation
4 hill, rise 5 boost, mount, raise 6 ascent, height 7 advance, raising 8 altitude, highness, mountain 9 acclivity, promotion, upgrading 10 apotheosis, preference, preferment 11 advancement, ennoblement

indication: 9 bench mark

elevator
4 cage, lift, silo 5 hoist 6 lifter, raiser 7 hoister
maker: 4 Otis

eleven
combining form: 5 undec 6 hendec 7 hendeca

elf
3 fay 4 ouph, peri, pixy 5 fairy, nisse, ouphe, pixie 6 goblin, sprite 7 brownie, gremlin 10 leprechaun

elfin
5 child 6 urchin

elfish
see elvish

Elgin ___
7 marbles

Eli
4 Yale
son: 6 Hophni 8 Phinehas
successor: 6 Ahitub

Eli ___
7 Whitney

Eliab
brother: 5 David
daughter: 7 Abihail
father: 5 Helon, Pallu
son: 6 Abiram, Dathan

Eliada
father: 5 David
son: 5 Rezon

Eliakim's father
6 Josiah 7 Hilkiah

Eliam's daughter
9 Bathsheba

Eliasaph's father
4 Lael

Eliashib's father
4 Bani 5 Zattu 8 Elioenai

Eliathah's father
5 Heman

elicit
4 draw, milk 5 bring, cause, educe, evoke, fetch 6 derive, evince, extort 7 extract, provoke 8 bring out 9 call forth

elide
4 fail, omit, pass, skip 6 forget, ignore, slight 7 neglect 8 discount, overlook, suppress 9 disregard

Eliel's father
6 Hebron, Shimhi 7 Shashak

Eliezer's father
5 Harim, Moses 6 Zichri 7 Dodovah

eligible
3 fit 6 fitted, likely, nubile, seemly, suited, worthy 7 capable 8 suitable 9 desirable, qualified, visitable 10 acceptable, preferable 12 marriageable

Elihu ___
4 Root, Yale

Elijah
5 Elias 7 prophet 8 Tishbite
father: 5 Harim 7 Jeroham

Elimelech's wife
5 Naomi

eliminate
3 bar 4 bate, oust 5 debar, eject, erase, evict, expel, purge 6 delete, except, remove 7 dismiss, exclude, expunge, obviate, rule out, shut out, suspend, take out 8 count out 9 clear away, freeze out, liquidate

Eliot, George
novel: 6 Romola 8 Adam Bede 11 Middlemarch, Silas Marner 14 Mill on the Floss

Eliot, T.S.
poem: 9 Gerontion 12 Ash Wednesday, The Hollow Men, The Waste Land

Eliphal's father
2 Ur

Eliphaz
father: 4 Esau
mother: 4 Adah
son: 5 Teman

Eliphelet's father
5 David 6 Hashum 7 Ahasbai 8 Adonikam

eliquate
4 melt 5 smelt

Elisabeth
husband: 9 Zacharias
son: 4 John (the Baptist)

Elisha
father: 7 Shaphat
servant: 6 Gehazi

Elishah's father
5 Javan

Elishama's father
5 David 7 Ammihud

Elisheba
brother: 7 Nahshon
father: 9 Amminadab
husband: 5 Aaron
son: 5 Abihu, Nadab 7 Eleazar, Ithamar

Elishua's father
5 David

Elissa
see **Dido**

elite
3 top 4 best, pick 5 cream, elect, pride, prime, prize 6 choice, flower, gentry, jet set, select 7 aristoi, quality, society 8 optimacy, smart set 9 gentility 10 upper class, upper crust 11 aristocracy

Eliud
father: 5 Achim
son: 7 Eleazar

elixir
4 balm, cure 6 potion 7 arcanum, cure-all, nostrum, panacea, therapy 10 catholicon 11 therapeutic

Elizabeth I, name for
6 Oriana

Elizaphan
see **Elzaphan**

elk
4 deer, losh 5 moose 6 sambar, sambur, wapiti

Elkanah
brother: 5 Assir 8 Abiasaph
father: 4 Joel 5 Korah 6 Mahath 7 Jeroham
son: 6 Samuel
wife: 6 Hannah 8 Peninnah

ell
3 arm 4 wing 5 annex, block 8 addition 9 extension

ellipse
4 oval 5 curve

elliptical
5 brief, ovate, short 7 concise, cryptic, summary 9 condensed, enigmatic

elm
5 wahoo

Elmire's husband
5 Orgon

elocution
7 oratory 8 rhetoric 11 speechcraft

elongate
4 draw 6 extend, string 7 draw out, lengthy, spin out, stretch 8 extended, lengthen, protract, wiredraw 10 lengthened

elongation
9 extension 10 production 11 lengthening, protraction

Elon's father
7 Zebulun

elope
4 flee 6 escape 7 run away

eloquence
5 force, power, vigor 6 fervor, spirit 7 passion 9 facundity 10 expression 12 expressivity, forcefulness

eloquent
4 glib, high, rich 5 lofty, vocal 6 ardent, facund, fervid, fluent, moving, potent 7 fervent, graphic, telling, voluble 8 elevated, forceful, poignant, powerful, pregnant, touching 9 affecting, revealing 10 articulate, expressive, impressive, indicative, meaningful, passionate, persuasive, suggestive 11 impassioned, sententious, significant 12 smooth-spoken 13 silvertongued

Elpaal's father
9 Shaharaim

Elpalet's father
5 David

else
2 or 3 new 4 more 5 added, fresh, other 7 another, besides, farther, further 9 otherwise 10 additional

elucidate
5 clear, prove 7 clarify, clear up, explain 8 annotate, spell out 9 enlighten, exemplify, interpret 10 illuminate, illustrate

elude
3 fly, shy 4 bilk, duck, flee, foil, shun 5 avoid, dodge, evade 6 baffle, double, escape, eschew, outwit, thwart 9 frustrate 10 circumvate

elusion
6 escape 8 escaping, eschewal, shunning 9 avoidance, runaround

elusive
6 subtle, tricky 7 evasive, phantom 8 baffling, fleeting, fugitive, slippery 10 evanescent, intangible, mysterious 12 imponderable 13 insubstantial

elusory
5 vague 7 evasive 8 nebulous 10 intangible

elvish
5 antic 6 frisky, impish 7 coltish, larkish, playful, puckish, roguish 8 prankish, spiteful 9 kittenish 11 mischievous

elysium
4 Eden, Zion 5 bliss 6 Canaan, heaven 7 nirvana 8 empyrean, paradise 10 Civitas Dei 12 New Jerusalem

elytron
4 wing 5 scale, shard

Elzaphan's father
6 Uzziel 7 Parnach

emaciated
4 bony, lean 5 gaunt 6 skinny, wasted 7 scrawny, starved, wizened 8 skeletal, underfed 10 cadaverous

emaciation
5 tabes 7 atrophy 8 marasmus 10 starvation 11 attenuation

emanate
4 emit, flow, rise, stem 5 arise, birth, exude, issue 6 spring 7 proceed 9 originate 10 derive from

emanation
4 aura, flow 6 efflux 7 outcome 9 effluence 11 consequence

emancipate
4 free 5 loose 6 loosen, unbind 7 manumit, release, unchain 8 liberate, unfetter 9 discharge, unshackle 11 enfranchise

emancipation
7 freedom, release 10 liberation 11 deliverance

emancipator
5 Moses 7 Lincoln (Abraham) 9 deliverer

emasculate
3 wan 4 geld, weak 5 unman 6 soften, weaken 7 unnerve 8 boneless, castrate, enervate, impotent, unstring 9 forceless, spineless 10 devitalize, inadequate 11 ineffective, ineffectual

embalm
5 mummy 7 mummify, perfume 8 preserve

embankment
4 bund, dike, quay 5 levee, mound 7 parados 9 banquette

embargo
5 edict, order 8 blockade, stoppage 10 impediment 11 prohibition

embark
4 open 5 begin, board, enter, set to, start 6 engage, enlist, get off, set out, take up, tee off 7 jump off 8 commence

embarrass
3 vex 4 faze 5 abash, queer, upset 6 bother, flurry, hamper, impede,

rattle 7 agitate, chagrin, confuse, flummox, fluster, nonplus, perturb **8** confound, distress **9** discomfit **10** discompose, disconcert

embarrassing
7 awkward **12** discommoding, incommodious, inconvenient **13** discommodious

embarrassment
5 shame **6** strain, unease **7** chagrin **8** distress, vexation **9** abashment, agitation, confusion **10** constraint, difficulty, discomfort, uneasiness **11** humiliation **12** discomfiture, discomposure, perturbation **13** disconcertion, mortification

embassy
5 envoy **8** legation **10** ambassador

embattle
7 fortify, prepare **9** crenelate **10** crenellate

embay
6 shut in **7** shelter **8** encircle, surround

embed
3 fix, set **4** root **5** infix, lodge **7** ingrain **8** entrench

embellish
3 pad **4** deck, gild, trim **5** adorn, array, color, dress, fudge, prank **6** bedeck, blazon, emboss, enrich **7** apparel, dress up, garnish, magnify **8** beautify, decorate, ornament **9** embroider **10** exaggerate

embellishment
7 garnish, melisma, mordent **8** coloring, ornament **9** fioritura, floridity, hyperbole **11** ostentation **12** embroidering, exaggeration **13** ornamentation

ember
3 ash **4** coal **6** cinder

embezzle
4 loot **5** steal **6** pilfer, thieve **8** peculate

embitter
4 sour **7** envenom **8** acerbate **9** acidulate **10** exacerbate

emblaze
5 adorn **6** kindle **9** embellish **10** illuminate

emblazon
4 deck, laud **5** adorn, extol **7** display, glorify **8** inscribe **9** celebrate

emblem
3 bar **4** mace, sign **5** badge, crest, image, token **6** device, symbol

8 insignia, monogram **9** attribute **10** coat of arms **11** adumbration
of mercy: **8** red cross

embodiment
6 avatar **7** epitome **9** archetype **11** incarnation **13** manifestation

embody
4 fuse, have **5** blend, merge, reify, unify, unite **6** absorb, evince, mirror, take in, typify **7** combine, compose, contain, embrace, exhibit, include, involve, realize, subsume **8** manifest **9** actualize, encompass, epitomize, exemplify, incarnate, integrate, objectify, personify, personize, represent, symbolize **10** amalgamate, assimilate, comprehend, constitute, illustrate **11** consolidate, demonstrate, emblematize, exteriorize, externalize, hypostatize, incorporate, materialize, personalize **12** substantiate

embog
4 mine **5** delay **6** detain, hang up, retard, slow up **7** set back, slacken **8** slow down **10** decelerate

embolden
5 cheer, impel, nerve, steel **6** chance, hazard **7** animate, chirk up, hearten, inspire, venture **8** inspirit **9** encourage, enhearten **10** strengthen

embolus
4 clog, clot

embosom
7 enclose **8** surround

emboss
5 adorn, raise **8** ornament **9** embellish, embroider

embouchure
5 mouth **10** mouthpiece

embowel
3 gut **4** draw **6** paunch **10** eviscerate, exenterate

embrace
3 hug **4** clip, fold, grip, have, hold, lock, wrap **5** admit, adopt, bosom, clasp, cling, cover, press, twine **6** accept, cradle, cuddle, embody, enfold, enwind, fondle, nuzzle, take in, take on, take up **7** cherish, compose, contain, embosom, enclose, entwine, envelop, espouse, include, involve, receive, snuggle, squeeze, subsume, welcome **8** comprise, encircle **9** encompass **10** comprehend **11** accommodate, incorporate

embrangle
7 confuse

embrocation
8 liniment

embroider
3 pad, sew, tat **5** color, couch, fudge **6** emboss, expand, overdo, stitch **7** amplify, build up, distend, enhance, magnify, stretch, tambour **8** decorate, ornament **9** dramatize, elaborate, embellish, overstate **10** aggrandize, exaggerate **11** hyperbolize

embroidery
4 lace **6** edging **7** cutwork, orphery, pinwork **8** couching, smocking, tapestry **10** needlework

embroil
4 mire **6** tangle **7** confuse, involve **8** disorder, distract, entangle **9** implicate

embroilment
4 tiff **6** fracas **7** dispute, quarrel, wrangle **8** squabble **9** bickering **10** falling-out **11** altercation, controversy, involvement **12** entanglement

embryo
3 bud **4** germ, seed **5** fetus, spark **7** nucleus **8** blastula, gastrula
combining form: **5** blast **6** blasto

emend
4 edit **5** alter, right **6** polish, revise **7** correct, improve, rectify, retouch

emerald
3 gem **5** beryl, green, stone

Emerald Isle
4 Eire, Erin **7** Ireland

emerge
4 flow, loom, rise, show, stem **5** arise, issue **6** appear, derive, spring **7** come out, proceed **9** originate **11** materialize

emergency
3 fix **4** hole, pass, push **5** pinch **6** climax, clutch, crisis, strait **7** squeeze **8** juncture
money: **5** scrip

Emerson
forte: **5** essay
friend: **7** Thoreau (Henry David)

emery
5 board **6** powder **8** abrasive, corundum

Emesh
brother: **5** Enten
father: **5** Enlil

émeute
4 riot 6 tumult 8 outbreak, uprising

emigrant
7 pioneer, settler 8 colonist

emigré
2 DP 5 alien, exile 7 evacuee, refugee 8 expellee, fugitive 9 immigrant 10 expatriate

Emilia
husband: 4 Iago 7 Palamon
slayer: 4 Iago

eminence
3 VIP 4 fame, note, peak, rise 5 chief, glory, honor, kudos, power, raise 6 bigwig, credit, height, leader, renown, repute, uprise, weight 7 dignity, notable 8 altitude, big-timer, highness, luminary, prestige 9 authority, dignitary, elevation, greatness, influence, loftiness 10 famousness, importance, notability, prepotency, projection, prominency, reputation 11 distinction, superiority

eminent
3 big 4 high 5 famed, great, large, lofty, noble, noted 6 august, famous 7 big-name, big-time, exalted, notable 8 dominant, renowned, towering 9 big league, important, well-known 10 celebrated, celebrious 11 conspicuous, illustrious, outstanding 13 distinguished

eminently
4 very 6 highly 7 notably 9 extremely 10 remarkably, strikingly 11 exceedingly 12 surpassingly 13 exceptionally

emir
5 chief, noble, ruler, title 8 nobleman 9 chieftain

emissary
see **envoy**

emission
4 flow 9 discharge, effluvium, emanation

emit
4 beam, drip, flow, glow, ooze, pour, reek, vent, void 5 expel, exude, issue, loose, utter 6 exhale, expire, let out 7 emanate, excrete, extrude, give off, give out, radiate, release, secrete 8 evacuate, throw off 9 discharge 10 disembogue

emmer
5 grain, spelt, wheat 6 speltz

emmet
3 ant 7 pismire

Emmor's son
7 Shechem

emolliate
6 soften, weaken

emollient
7 lenient 8 lenitive, sedative, soothing

emolument
3 fee, pay 4 hire, wage 6 salary 7 guerdon, stipend 11 pay envelope 12 compensation

emote
3 act 4 gush, rage, rant 5 storm 6 take on 7 carry on, overact

emotion
3 ire, joy 4 fear, glee, hate, love 5 agony, ardor, grief, shame 6 relief, sorrow 7 ardency, despair, disgust, ecstasy, feeling, passion, sadness 8 jealousy, movement, surprise 9 affection, agitation, happiness, sentiment 11 affectivity, sensibility, sensitivity 12 excitability 13 sensitiveness
combining form: 4 thym 5 thymo 6 thymia

emotional
6 ardent, moving 7 feeling, fervent, soulful 8 sentient, stirring, touching 9 affecting, affective, rhapsodic, sensitive 10 hysterical, passionate, responsive, susceptive 11 rhapsodical, softhearted, susceptible, sympathetic

emotionless
3 icy 4 cold, cool 5 chill, staid 6 frigid, torpid 7 deadpan, distant, glacial 8 reserved 9 apathetic, immovable, impassive, unfeeling 10 impersonal 11 cold-blooded, indifferent 12 matter-of-fact 13 dispassionate, unimpassioned

empathy
4 pity 6 accord, warmth 7 concord, rapport 8 affinity, sympathy 9 communion 10 compassion 12 appreciation, congeniality 13 compatibility, comprehension, fellow feeling, understanding

emperor
4 czar, king, shah, tsar, tzar 5 ruler 6 caesar, kaiser, sultan 7 monarch 8 autocrat, dictator, imperial, padishah 9 sovereign
Japanese: 6 mikado 7 Akihito 8 Hirohito

emphasis
5 focus, force 6 accent, stress, weight 9 attention 10 insistence 12 accentuation

emphasize
4 mark 5 press 6 accent, assert, charge, play up, stress 7 feature 8 pinpoint 9 highlight, italicize, punctuate, spotlight, underline 10 accentuate, underscore

emphatic
6 marked 7 decided, earnest, pointed 8 accented, forceful, positive, stressed, vigorous 9 assertive, energetic, insistent, insistive 10 aggressive, emphasized, resounding, underlined 11 accentuated, assertative

empire
4 rule, sway 5 power, realm, state 6 domain 7 demesne, kingdom, tsardom, tzardom 8 dominion, province 9 territory
ancient: (see **ancient empire**)

Empire State
7 New York

empirical
7 factual 9 experient 12 experiential, experimental 13 observational

emplacement
7 battery, gallery 8 position

employ
3 add, use 4 busy, hire, work 5 apply, avail, exert, put on 6 bestow, devote, engage, handle, obtain, occupy, retain, secure, take on 7 engross, exploit, procure, utilize 8 exercise, practice

employee
4 hand, help 6 worker 7 servant 8 factotum 9 underling
bank: 5 clerk, guard 6 teller
hotel: 4 maid 5 clerk 7 bellboy, bellhop, doorman 9 concierge

employer
4 boss, user

employment
3 job, use 4 line, play, post, task, toil, work 5 trade, usage 6 hiring, office, usance 7 calling, mission, purpose, pursuit 8 business, engaging, exercise, exertion, function, handling, position, vocation 9 appliance, operation, situation 10 engagement, exercising, occupation 11 application, disposition, recruitment, utilization 12 exploitation

emporium
4 mall, mart, shop 5 store 6 bazaar, market 11 marketplace

empower
4 vest 5 endow 6 charge, enable, invest 7 entitle, entrust, license 8 accredit, deputize, sanction 9 authorize, privilege 10 commission

empress
5 queen
French: 7 Eugenie 9 Josephine
Japanese: 5 Suiko
of India: 8 Victoria
Russian: 4 Anna 7 czarina, tsarina, tzarina 9 Catherine, Elizabeth

empressement
6 fervor, warmth 10 cordiality

emprise
4 feat, gest 7 exploit, venture 9 adventure 11 undertaking

emptiness
4 void 6 hunger, vacuum 7 inanity, vacancy, vacuity

emptor
5 buyer 6 vendee 9 purchaser

___ **emptor**
6 caveat

empty
3 rid 4 bare, dumb, dump, flat, idle, pour, vain, void 5 banal, blank, clear, drain, inane, petty, silly, stark, vapid 6 barren, devoid, hollow, jejune, otiose, paltry, unload, vacant, vacate 7 deadpan, deplete, drained, exhaust, fatuous, foolish, insipid, trivial, vacated, vacuous 8 depleted, deserted, evacuate, forsaken, ignorant, innocent, nugatory, trifling, unfilled 9 abandoned, destitute, exhausted 10 unoccupied, untenanted 11 godforsaken, ineffectual 12 inexpressive, unexpressive 14 expressionless
combining form: 3 ken 4 keno
Scottish: 4 toom

empty-headed
4 rude 5 dizzy, giddy, silly 6 simple, vacant 7 flighty, vacuous 8 ignorant, skittish, untaught 9 benighted, brainless, frivolous 10 illiterate, uneducated, unlettered, unschooled 11 harebrained, knownothing 12 uninstructed 13 rattlebrained

empyreal
4 airy, holy 6 aerial, divine 7 sublime 8 heavenly 9 celestial, spiritual

empyrean
3 sky 4 Zion 5 bliss, ether 6 heaven, welkin 7 elysium, heavens, nirvana 8 heavenly, paradise 9 celestial, firmament 10 civitas Dei 12 New Jerusalem

emu
4 bird, rhea 6 ratite 9 cassowary

emulate
3 ape 4 copy 5 equal, rival 6 outvie 7 compete, imitate 8 rivalize 9 challenge

emulation
6 strife 7 contest, rivalry, warfare 8 conflict, striving, tug-of-war 9 imitation 10 contention 11 competition

emulous
5 vying 6 aiming 7 athirst 8 aspiring, striving, vaulting 9 ambitious 11 competitive

emulsifier
4 soap

enable
3 fit, let 5 allow, ready 6 permit 7 empower, entitle, license, prepare, qualify 8 accredit, sanction 9 authorize, condition 10 commission

enact
2 do 4 make, pass, play 6 decree, depict, effect, ordain, ratify 7 execute, perform, portray 8 proclaim 9 authorize, discourse, establish, institute, legislate, personate, represent 10 accomplish, bring about, constitute, effectuate 11 impersonate

enactment
3 law 6 action, assize, decree 7 statute 9 ordinance

enamel
5 email, glaze, gloss, paint

enamored
4 fond 5 dotty 6 loving, mashed, soft on 7 charmed, devoted, smitten 8 besotted, spoony on 9 bewitched, enchanted, entranced, infatuate 10 captivated, fascinated, infatuated, spoony over

Enan's son
5 Ahira

encamp
4 tent 6 settle 7 bivouac

encampment
6 laager 7 bivouac, hutment

encase
7 enclose, envelop, sheathe

enceinte
8 pregnant 9 expectant, expecting 10 parturient

enchain
4 bind 6 fetter

enchant
3 hex 4 draw, send, take, wile 5 charm, spell, witch 6 allure, delude, please, thrill, voodoo 7 attract, bewitch, delight 9 captivate, ensorcell, fascinate, magnetize, mesmerize, spellbind

enchanter
4 mage 5 magus 6 wizard 7 charmer, warlock 8 conjurer, magician, sorcerer 9 voodooist 11 necromancer

enchanting
5 siren 7 sirenic 8 alluring, charming 9 appealing, glamorous, seductive 10 attractive, bewitching, delectable, delightful, intriguing 11 captivating, fascinating

enchantment
3 hex 5 charm, magic, spell 7 sorcery 8 gramarye, witchery, wizardry 9 conjuring, magicking 10 necromancy, witchcraft 11 incantation

enchantress
3 hag, hex 5 bruja, Circe, lamia, Medea, witch 9 sorceress 10 witchwoman

enchiridion
4 book, text 5 guide 6 manual 8 Baedeker, handbook 9 guidebook, vade mecum 10 compendium

encincture
4 band, belt, gird 6 begird, engird, girdle 8 begirdle, engirdle

encipher
4 code

encircle
3 hem 4 band, belt, gird, halo, hoop, ring 5 girth 6 begird, engird, enlace, girdle 7 compass, embrace, enclose, environ, wreathe 8 cincture, surround 9 encompass 12 circumscribe

enclose
3 box, hem, mew, pen, rim 4 cage, coop, mure, veil, wall, wrap 5 bound, fence, hedge, limit 6 circle, closet, corral, encase, enfold, enlock, enwrap, immure, invest, shroud, shut in 7 compass, confine,

contain, embosom, envelop, environ, harness **8** encircle, enshroud, ensphere, imprison, insheath, restrict, surround **9** capsulize, encompass **12** circumscribe

enclosed
   6 obtect

enclosure
   3 box, haw, mew, pen, sty
   4 bawn, cage, cell, coop, cote, fold, quad, tank, trap, wall, weir, yard **5** booly, booth, court, crawl, fence, kench, pound, stall **6** aviary, cancha, corral, cowpen, garden, kennel, paling, prison **7** barrier, cockpit, paddock **8** cincture, cloister, sepiment, stockade **9** cofferdam, courtyard, curtilage **10** quadrangle, sheephouse
   African: **4** boma **5** kraal
   elephant: **6** keddah

encomiast
   7 praiser **8** eulogist **10** panegyrist

encomiastic
   9 laudative, laudatory, praiseful **11** panegyrical

encomium
   4 laud **5** kudos **6** eulogy, praise **7** acclaim, tribute **8** accolade, applause, approval, citation, plaudits **9** laudation, panegyric **10** compliment, salutation **11** acclamation **12** commendation

encompass
   3 hem **4** belt, gird, have, ring **5** beset, bound **6** begird, circle, embody, engird, girdle, take in **7** contain, delimit, embrace, enclose, environ, include, involve, subsume **8** encircle, surround **10** comprehend

encore
   6 recall, repeat **8** call back **10** repetition

encounter
   4 espy, face, find, fray, meet, spot **5** brush, catch, clash, close, fight, front, hit on, run-in, scrap, set-to **6** battle, descry, detect, engage, take on, turn up **7** affront, collide, contest, hit upon, meeting, quarrel **8** argument, conflict, confront, meet with, skirmish **10** contention, velitation

encourage
   4 abet, back, push, stir **5** boost, cheer, favor, nerve, pique, rally, serve, steel **6** assist, assure, buck up, excite, foster, incite, induce **7** advance, animate, approve, chirk

up, develop, endorse, fortify, forward, further, hearten, improve, prevail, promote, provoke, quicken, support, sustain **8** advocate, embolden, energize, inspirit, reassure, sanction **9** enhearten, galvanize, instigate, patronize, reinforce, stimulate, subsidize **10** invigorate, strengthen **11** countenance

encouragement
   4 lift, push **5** boost **7** backing, support

encouraging
   4 rosy **6** likely **7** hopeful, roseate **9** promising **10** promiseful **11** rose-colored

encroach
   5 poach **6** invade, meddle, trench **7** impinge, intrude **8** entrench, infringe, overstep, trespass **9** interfere, interpose, intervene

encumber
   3 tax **4** clog, lade, load **5** beset, block, weigh **6** burden, charge, fetter, hamper, hinder, impede, retard, saddle, weight **7** freight, oppress **8** handicap, obstruct, overload **9** incommode **10** discommode, overburden **13** inconvenience

encumbrance
   4 clog, load **6** burden **8** handicap, hardship, mortgage **9** albatross **10** difficulty, impediment **12** disadvantage **13** inconvenience

encyclical
   6 letter **7** general **8** circular

encyclopedic
   5 broad **7** general **8** complete **9** extensive, inclusive **10** discursive **12** all-embracing, all-inclusive **13** comprehensive

encyclopedist
   7 Diderot (Denis)

end
   3 aim, bit, tip **4** coda, goal, halt, part, quit, stop, tail, term **5** bound, cease, close, death, finis, limit, piece, scrap **5** teloi (plural), telos **6** expire, finale, finish, object, period, scotch, windup, wrap up **7** abolish, closing, closure, extreme, leaving, lineman, purpose, remnant, residue **8** boundary, complete, conclude, confines, curtains, finality, fragment, particle, surcease, terminal, terminus, ultimate **9** cessation, desuetude, determine, extremity, objective, remainder, terminate **10** borderline, completion,

conclusion, desistance, expiration, limitation **11** culmination, discontinue, termination **12** consummation
   combining form: **3** acr, akr, tel **4** acro, akro, tele, telo

endanger
   4 risk **5** peril **6** chance, expose, hazard, menace **7** imperil, jeopard, venture **8** jeopardy **10** compromise, jeopardize

endeavor
   3 aim, try **4** push, seek, toil, work **5** apply, assay, essay, labor, offer, trial **6** hassle, intend, strain, strive **7** address, attempt, purpose, travail **8** exertion, striving, struggle **9** determine, undertake **11** undertaking

ended
   4 done, down, over, past **7** through **8** complete, finished **9** completed **10** terminated

endemic
   5 local **6** native **8** home-bred **10** aboriginal, indigenous, native-born

ending
   4 stop **5** close **6** finale, finish, period, windup **7** closing **9** cessation **10** conclusion, desistance **11** termination

endive
   4 herb **7** witloof **8** escarole

endless
   7 eternal, forever, undying **8** constant, immortal, infinite, overlong, unending **9** ceaseless, continual, limitless, perpetual, unbounded, unceasing, unlimited **10** continuous, indefinite, unmeasured **11** amaranthine, everlasting, measureless **12** immeasurable, interminable

endmost
   8 farthest, furthest

endocrine gland
   5 gonad, ovary **6** pineal, testis, thymus **7** adrenal, thyroid **8** pancreas **9** pituitary **11** parathyroid **12** hypothalamus

endomorphic
   6 pyknic

endorse
   2 OK **4** okay, sign, visa, visé **5** vouch **6** attest, ratify, second, uphold **7** approve, certify, command, stand by, support, witness **8** accredit, advocate, champion, sanction **9** recommend **12** authenticate

endorsement

2 OK 4 fiat, visa 7 support 8 approval, sanction 9 signature

endow

4 back, fund 5 award, dower, found, grant 6 accord, bestow, confer, donate, enable, enrich, supply 7 empower, enhance, finance, promote, provide, sponsor, support 8 bequeath, heighten, organize 9 crown with, subscribe, subsidize 10 contribute

endowment

4 fund, gift 5 dower, dowry, grant, power, skill 6 talent 7 ability, chantry 8 appanage, dotation

end product

5 issue 6 effect, result, sequel, upshot 7 outcome 8 sequence 9 aftermath 11 aftereffect, consequence

endue

4 vest 5 dower, equip 6 clothe, invest, outfit 7 furnish 8 accouter 9 crown with

endurance

4 wind 5 pluck 7 stamina 8 duration, patience, strength 9 tolerance 10 continuity, toleration 11 persistence 12 continuation, perseverance

endure

2 go 4 bear, bide, last, take, wear 5 abide, allow, brook, stand 6 accept, linger, pocket, suffer 7 outlast, outlive, persist, stomach, sustain, swallow, undergo 8 bear with, continue, tolerate, tough out 9 withstand 12 carry through

enduring

3 old 4 fast, firm, sure 5 solid, sound 6 stable, steady, sturdy 7 abiding, durable, eternal, lasting, staunch 8 lifelong, resolute 9 diuturnal, long-lived, perennial, permanent, steadfast 10 continuing, inveterate, perdurable 11 long-lasting, substantial, unfaltering, unqualified 12 never-failing

Endymion

father: 8 Aethlius
lover: 5 Diana 6 Selene

enemy

3 foe 5 rival 7 hostile, invader 8 attacker, emulator, opponent 9 adversary, assailant, combatant, contender 10 antagonist, competitor

energetic

4 spry 5 brisk, fresh, lusty, peppy, vital, zippy 6 active, breezy, lively 7 driving, dynamic, vibrant 8 animated, spirited, tireless, vigorous 9 sprightly, strenuous, vivacious 10 aggressive, red-blooded 12 enterprising 13 indefatigable

energize

3 arm, pep 4 fuel 5 liven 6 actify, enable 7 empower, fortify, sustain 8 activate, activize, vitalize 9 reinforce 10 invigorate, strengthen

energy

2 go 3 pep, vim, zip 4 beef, birr, life, tuck 5 force, might, power, sinew, steam, vigor 6 effort, muscle, spirit 7 potency 8 activity, efficacy, strength 9 hardihood, puissance, toughness 10 mightiness 11 application 12 forcefulness, powerfulness 13 effectiveness, operativeness
excessive: 7 sthenia
unit: 3 erg 4 dyne, volt 5 joule 7 quantum 10 horsepower

enervate

3 sap 4 jade, tire 5 unman, weary 6 soften, weaken 7 disable, exhaust, fatigue, unnerve 8 enfeeble, unstring 10 devitalize

enfant terrible

4 limb 5 devil, rogue, scamp 6 rascal 7 villain 8 mischief, scalawag 9 skeezicks 11 rapscallion

enfeeble

3 sap 5 blunt 6 soften, weaken 7 cripple, disable, exhaust, unbrace 8 enervate 9 attenuate, undermine 10 debilitate, devitalize 12 unstrengthen

enfold

3 hug 4 gird, veil, wrap 5 clasp, cover, drape, press 6 encase, enwrap, girdle, invest, shroud, swathe 7 embrace, enclose, envelop, environ, squeeze 8 encircle, enshroud, surround 9 encompass, ensheathe

enforce

5 exact 6 compel, effect, invoke, oblige 7 execute, fulfill 9 discharge, implement, prosecute 10 accomplish, administer

enfranchise

4 free 6 rescue 7 deliver, manumit, release 8 liberate 9 extricate 10 emancipate

engage

3 tie 4 bind, busy, face, grip, hire,
meet, mesh, pass, soak 5 fight, imbue, put on, troth 6 absorb, arrest, attack, battle, commit, employ, enlist, occupy, pledge, strike, take on 7 assault, betroth, engross, immerse, involve, promise 8 affiance, enthrall, interact 9 captivate, encounter, fascinate, interlace, interlock, intermesh, interplay, preoccupy, undertake
passage: 4 book

engaged

4 busy, deep, rapt 6 intent 7 working, wrapped 8 absorbed, employed, immersed, intended, occupied, plighted 9 affianced, betrothed, committed, engrossed, wrapped up 10 contracted 11 preoccupied
person: 6 fiancé 7 fiancée

engage in

4 wage 5 enter
suffix: 3 ize

engagement

4 date, word 5 troth, tryst, visit 6 action, battle, hiring, pledge, plight 7 booking, meeting, promise 8 espousal 9 betrothal, interview 10 betrothing, employment, invitation, rendezvous 11 assignation

engaging

5 siren, sweet 6 dulcet 7 winning, winsome 8 magnetic, mesmeric 9 glamorous 10 attractive, bewitching, employment, intriguing 11 fascinating 13 prepossessing

engender

4 stir 5 beget, breed, cause, hatch, rouse 6 arouse, excite, induce, work up 7 develop, produce, provoke, quicken 8 generate, muster up, occasion 9 stimulate

engine

5 motor, turbo 7 turbine 10 locomotive
kind: 3 gas, jet 5 steam 6 diesel 7 turbine 8 gasoline 9 hydraulic
jet: 8 turbofan, turbojet
part: 3 cam, rod 4 gear, plug, pump 5 choke 6 filter, piston, tappet 8 cylinder, manifold, throttle 9 condenser, crankcase 10 carburetor 12 transmission
siege: 3 ram 12 battering ram
sound: 4 chug

engineer

4 plan, plot 5 set up, swing 6 devise, driver, manage, scheme, wangle 7 arrange, finagle 8 contrive, intrigue, maneuver 9 machinate,

negotiate **10** manipulate, mastermind

kind: 5 civil **6** mining **8** chemical, sanitary **10** electrical, mechanical **12** aeronautical

military: 6 sapper

engineers' group
abbreviation: 4 IEEE

England
6 Albion **7** Britain **9** Britannia **12** Great Britain

capital: 6 London

monetary unit: 5 pound

English
7 British

cathedral city: 3 Ely **4** York **5** Wells **6** Durham, Exeter **7** Lincoln, Norwich **8** Coventry, Hereford **9** Salisbury, Worcester **10** Canterbury, Winchester

coin: 5 angel, crown, groat, pence **6** florin, guinea, seskin **7** angelet **8** farthing, shilling, sixpence, twopence **9** fourpence, half crown, halfpenny, sovereign **10** threepence

combining form: 5 Anglo

farm: 5 croft

forest: 5 Arden **8** Sherwood

letter: 3 zed

measure: 3 ell, pin, rod, tun **4** comb, coom, gill, hand, hide, line, peck, pint, pipe, pole, pool, span, yard, yoke **5** chain, coomb, crane, digit, hutch, jugum, perch, point, truss **6** barrel, bovate, bushel, fathom, firkin, runlet, strike, sulung **7** furlong, quarter, rundlet, virgate **8** carucate, chaldron, hogshead, puncheon, quartern, standard **9** kilderkin **10** barleycorn

military college: 9 Sandhurst

patron saint: 6 George

person: 4 chap **5** bloke **6** Briton

pirate: 4 Kidd

prince: 5 Harry **6** Andrew, Edward, Philip **7** Charles, William

princess: 4 Anne **5** Diana **8** Margaret

professor: 3 don

royal family: 7 Windsor

saint: 7 Dunstan **8** Cuthbert

spa: 4 Bath

sport: 5 rugby **7** cricket

tavern: 3 pub

university: 5 Leeds **6** Oxford **9** Cambridge

weight: 3 kip, tod **4** keel **5** barge, fagot, stand, stone, tross **6** firkin, fother, fotmal, pocket **7** quintal **8** quartern

English Channel swimmer
6 Ederle (Gertrude)

englut
4 bolt, cram, gulp, slop, wolf **5** slosh **6** gobble, guzzle **11** ingurgitate

engrave
3 cut, fix **4** etch, root **5** carve, chase, embed, infix, print **6** incise, scrive **7** enchase, impress, imprint, ingrain, insculp, instill **8** entrench, inscribe

engraver
6 chaser, etcher

German: 5 Dürer (Albrecht) **10** Schongauer (Martin)

Italian: 8 Raimondi (Marcantonio)

engraving
7 etching, woodcut **8** drypoint, intaglio **9** xylograph

combining form: 5 glypt **6** glypto

engross
4 bury, busy, fill, grip, hold, soak **5** apply, sew up, write **6** absorb, arrest, engage, indite, occupy, scribe, scroll, take up **7** attract, consume, immerse, involve **8** enscroll, enthrall, inscribe **9** captivate, preoccupy **10** assimilate, monopolize **11** superscribe

engrosser
7 copyist **12** calligrapher **13** calligraphist

engulf
5 drown, flood, swamp, whelm **6** deluge, devour **7** swallow **8** inundate, overflow, submerge **9** overwhelm

enhance
4 lift, rise, suit **5** adorn, exalt, mount, raise, rouse **6** become, deepen **7** augment, elevate, flatter, magnify **8** beautify, heighten, increase, redouble **9** aggravate, embellish, embroider, intensate, intensify **10** exaggerate, strengthen

enhearten
5 cheer, nerve, steel **7** animate, chirk up **8** embolden, inspirit **9** encourage

enigma
3 why **4** crux, knot **5** rebus **6** puzzle, riddle **7** mystery, problem, puzzler, sticker **8** question **9** conundrum **10** closed book, perplexity, puzzlement **12** bewilderment, question mark **13** Chinese puzzle, mystification

enigmatic
4 dark **6** mystic **7** cryptic, obscure **8** Delphian, puzzling **10** mystifying

enisle
6 cut off **7** isolate **8** close off, insulate, separate **9** segregate, sequester

enjoin
3 ban, bid **4** deny, rule, tell, warn **5** order, taboo **6** adjure, advise, charge, decree, direct, forbid, impose, outlaw **7** caution, command, counsel, dictate, inhibit **8** admonish, disallow, forewarn, instruct, prohibit **9** interdict, prescribe

enjoy
3 own **4** fill, have, hold, like, love **5** boast, eat up, fancy, savor **6** occupy, relish, retain **7** command, possess **8** maintain **10** appreciate

a break: 8 take five

enjoyableness
7 amenity **8** pleasure **9** geniality, pleasance **10** amiability, cordiality **12** agreeability

enjoyment
4 ease, zest **5** gusto, savor **6** relish **7** delight **8** felicity, fruition, pleasure **9** diversion **10** indulgence, recreation, relaxation **11** delectation **12** satisfaction **13** gratification

Enki
consort: 5 Nintu

son: 6 Ninsar

enkindle
4 fire **5** light **6** ignite **7** inflame

enlarge
3 wax **4** grow, rise **5** add to, boost, build, mount, widen **6** beef up, expand, extend **7** amplify, augment, develop, greaten, magnify, stretch, upsurge **8** heighten, increase, multiply **9** elaborate, embroider **10** aggrandize, exaggerate

enlargement
4 node **5** tumor **6** growth, nodule **8** addition, increase, swelling **9** accretion, expansion, extension

combining form: 4 auxe **5** auxae (plural) **6** megaly **7** megalia

enlarging
combining form: 4 micr **5** micro

enlighten
5 edify, guide, teach, train **6** advise, direct, illume, inform, school, uplift **7** apprise, educate, improve

8 acquaint, illumine, instruct 9 irradiate 10 illuminate

Enlil

father: 2 An
mother: 2 Ki
son: 5 Nanna 6 Nergal, Ninazu
wife: 6 Ninlil

enlist

4 join 5 enter 6 enroll, join up, muster, sign on, sign up 8 register 9 volunteer

enlistment

5 hitch

enliven

3 pep 4 fire, warm 5 amuse, cheer, pep up, renew, rouse 6 excite, jazz up, vivify 7 animate, inspire, quicken, refresh, restore 8 enspirit, recreate 9 entertain, galvanize, stimulate 10 exhilarate, invigorate, rejuvenate, vivificate

enmesh

4 hook, trap 5 catch 6 draw in, tangle 7 ensnarl, trammel 8 drag into, entangle 9 embrangle, implicate

enmity

4 feud, gall, hate 5 spite 6 animus, hatred, malice, rancor, spleen 7 dislike, ill will 8 aversion, bad blood, loathing 9 animosity, antipathy, hostility, malignity 10 abhorrence, alienation, antagonism, bitterness, malignancy 11 detestation, malevolence 12 disaffection, estrangement, uncordiality

ennoble

5 exalt, honor, raise 6 uplift, uprear 7 dignify, glorify, magnify, sublime 10 aggrandize 11 distinguish

ennui

4 bore, pall, tire, yawn 5 blues, dumps, weary 6 apathy, tedium 7 boredom, fatigue, languor, sadness, satiety, surfeit 8 doldrums 9 dejection, tiredness, weariness 10 depression, melancholy 11 languidness 12 listlessness

Enoch

father: 4 Cain
son: 10 Methuselah

Enoch Arden author

8 Tennyson (Alfred)

enormity

7 bigness, outrage 8 atrocity, hugeness, rankness, vastness 9 depravity, flagrancy, graveness, great-

ness, grossness, immensity, magnitude 11 heinousness, massiveness, seriousness, weightiness 13 atrociousness, monstrousness

enormous

3 big 4 huge, vast 5 great, large 7 immense, mammoth, titanic 8 colossal, gigantic 9 monstrous 10 gargantuan, prodigious, stupendous, tremendous

Enos

father: 4 Seth
grandfather: 4 Adam
grandmother: 3 Eve
uncle: 4 Abel, Cain

enough

6 fairly, plenty 8 adequacy, adequate, decently, passably 9 abundance, ampleness, averagely, competent, sufficing, tolerably 10 abundantly, acceptably, adequately, admissibly, competence, moderately, sufficient 11 comfortable, sufficiency 12 satisfactory, sufficiently
poetic: 4 enow

enounce

3 say 5 state, utter 8 proclaim

enrage

3 ire, mad 5 anger 6 madden 7 incense, inflame, steam up, umbrage 9 infuriate

enrapture

5 charm, elate 6 allure, please, ravish, trance 7 attract, enchant, gladden, gratify, rejoice 8 enravish, enthrall, entrance 9 captivate, fascinate, transport

enrich

5 adorn, endow 6 fatten, richen 9 embellish

enroll

4 book, join, list 5 enter 6 enlist, induct, insert, join up, line up, muster, record, sign on, sign up 7 catalog, recruit 8 inscribe, register 11 matriculate

ensconce

4 bury, hide 5 cache, cover, place, plant, stash 6 locate, settle 7 conceal, install, secrete, situate 9 establish

ensemble

5 decor, group, suite, whole 6 outfit 7 costume 9 aggregate

enshroud

4 hide, veil, wrap 5 cloak 6 en-

fold, enwrap, invest 7 conceal, curtain, enclose, envelop

ensign

4 flag, jack 5 color 6 banner, pennon 7 pennant 8 gonfalon, standard, streamer 9 oriflamme

enslave

4 yoke 5 chain 6 thrall 7 oppress, shackle, subject 8 enthrall 9 subjugate 12 disfranchise

enslavement

4 yoke 6 thrall 7 bondage, helotry, peonage, serfdom, slavery 9 servitude, thralldom, villenage

ensnare

3 bag, net 4 hook, lure, mesh, snag, trap 5 benet, catch, decoy 6 enmesh, entice, entrap, tangle 7 capture, catch up 8 entangle, inveigle

ensnarl

6 enmesh, tangle 7 perplex, trammel 8 entangle 9 embrangle 11 intertangle

ensorcell

3 hex 5 charm, spell, witch 6 voodoo 7 bewitch, enchant

ensorcellment

5 magic 7 sorcery 8 witchery, wizardry 9 conjuring 10 necromancy, witchcraft 11 bewitchment, enchantment, incantation

ensphere

4 ball 5 round 8 conglobe 10 conglobate

ensue

4 stem 5 issue 6 attend, derive, follow, result 7 emanate, proceed, succeed 9 supervene

ensuing

4 next 5 after, later 6 coming 9 following, posterior 10 subsequent 12 postliminary 13 subsequential

ensure

5 cinch 6 secure 7 certify, warrant 9 establish, guarantee

enswathe

4 roll 5 drape 6 enwrap, wrap up 7 envelop, swaddle

entail

6 assign, confer, impose 7 require 8 transmit 11 necessitate

entangle

3 bag 4 clog, mesh, mire, trap 5 benet, catch, ravel, snare, snarl,

tie up, twist **6** ball up, burden, enmesh, entrap, fetter, hamper, impede, muddle **7** capture, catch up, embroil, ensnare, ensnarl, involve, perplex, trammel **10** complicate, intertwine, interweave

entanglement

3 web **4** knot, mesh, toil **6** affair, cobweb **7** contact, liaison **8** intrigue **10** enmeshment **11** association, embroilment, ensnarement, involvement

Enten

brother: **5** Emesh
father: **5** Enlil

entente

6 treaty **8** alliance **9** agreement, coalition

enter

4 go in, join, list, open, post **5** admit, begin, probe, put in, set to, start **6** come in, docket, enlist, enroll, go into, inject, insert, join up, muster, pierce, record, sign on, sign up, take up **7** ingress, lead off **8** come into, commence, embark on, inscribe, register **9** introduce, penetrate **10** embark upon, inaugurate

enterprise

4 deed, feat, firm, gest, push, task **5** cause, drive, house, vigor **6** action, daring, effort, energy, hustle, outfit **7** attempt, company, concern, courage, exploit, project, pursuit, venture **8** ambition, boldness, business, campaign, endeavor, industry, interest, striving, struggle **9** adventure, eagerness **10** enthusiasm, get-up-and-go, initiative **11** corporation, speculation, undertaking **12** organization, self-reliance **13** ambitiousness, establishment, inventiveness

enterprising

4 bold, busy **5** eager **6** active, daring, hungry, lively **7** craving, dashing, driving, go-ahead, itching, lusting, pushing, zealous **8** aspiring, diligent, hustling, yearning **9** ambitious, audacious, energetic, gumptious **10** aggressive **11** adventurous, hard-working, industrious, up-and-coming, venturesome

entertain

4 host **5** amuse, board, house, lodge, put up **6** bestow, billet, divert, foster, harbor, invite, please, regale **7** cherish, delight, enliven,

gladden, gratify, nourish, receive, rejoice **8** domicile, recreate

entertainer

4 host, mime **5** actor, comic **6** amuser, busker, dancer, singer **7** actress, trouper **8** comedian, minstrel
female: **7** actress, diseuse, hostess **10** comedienne

entertainment

4 fete, play, show, skit **5** cheer, revue, sport **6** circus, gaiety, relief **7** banquet, concert, disport, ridotto **8** pleasure **9** amusement, diversion, enjoyment **10** recreation, relaxation **11** dissipation, distraction

enthrall

4 grip, hold **5** charm **6** absorb, engage, master, subdue **7** catch up, enchant, engross, enslave **8** intrigue **9** fascinate, mesmerize, preoccupy, spellbind, subjugate

enthuse

4 rave, send **5** drool **6** thrill **8** rhapsody **9** electrify **10** rhapsodize

enthusiasm

4 élan, fire, zeal, zest, zing **5** ardor, craze, mania, verve **6** fervor, hurrah, spirit **7** ardency, earnest, passion **8** interest **9** eagerness **10** ebullience

enthusiast

3 bug, fan, nut **4** bear, buff **5** fiend, freak, lover **6** addict, maniac, votary, zealot **7** devotee, fanatic, habitué **8** partisan **9** extremist, supporter **10** aficionado

enthusiastic

4 gaga, keen **5** eager, nutty, rabid **6** ardent, gung ho, hearty, hipped, raring **7** devoted, fervent, zealous **8** hopped-up, obsessed, spirited, vascular **10** passionate

entice

4 bait, coax, lure, toll, wile **5** charm, decoy, tempt **6** allure, cajole, entrap, lead on, seduce **8** inveigle, persuade

enticement

4 bait, lure, trap **5** decoy, snare **6** come-on **10** allurement, seducement, temptation **12** inveiglement

enticer

4 bait, vamp **5** Circe, decoy, siren **7** Lorelei, seducer, taunter, tempter **9** attractor, enchanter, temptress

10 attraction, seductress **11** enchantress, femme fatale

enticing

5 siren **6** luring **7** circean, likable **8** fetching, inviting, pleasant, pleasing, tempting, witching **9** beguiling **10** attractive, bewitching, enchanting, intriguing **11** captivating, fascinating

entire

3 all **4** full **5** gross, sound, total, whole **6** choate, intact, unhurt **7** perfect, plenary, unified **8** complete, integral, outright, unbroken, unmarred **9** compacted, undamaged, uninjured **10** integrated, unimpaired **12** concatenated, consolidated
combining form: **3** hol **4** holo **7** integri

entirely

3 but **4** only, well **5** alone, fully, quite **6** solely, wholly **7** utterly **9** perfectly **10** altogether, completely, thoroughly **11** exclusively
combining form: **3** pam, pan **4** pano

entirety

3 all, sum **5** gross, total, unity, whole **7** allness, complex, omneity, oneness **8** sum total, totality **9** aggregate, integrity, plenitude, wholeness **10** everything **12** collectivity, completeness, universality

entitle

3 dub, let **4** call, name, term **5** allow, style **6** enable, permit **7** baptize, empower, license, qualify **8** christen, headline, nominate **9** authorize, designate **10** denominate

entity

3 ens, sum **4** body, unit **5** being, stuff, thing, whole **6** matter, object, system **8** existent, integral, material, totality **9** existence, integrate, something, substance **10** individual

entomb

4 bury **5** inter, inurn **6** inhume, shrine **8** enshrine **9** sepulcher, sepulture **11** ensepulcher

entombment

6 burial **9** interment, sepulture **10** inhumation

entourage

5 suite, train **7** retinue, toadies **9** courtiers, followers, following, hangers-on, retainers **10** associates, attendants, sycophants

entr'acte
8 interval 9 interlude
12 intermission

entrails
4 guts 5 pluck 6 bowels, tripes, vitals 7 giblets, innards, insides, inwards, viscera 8 stuffing 9 internals 10 intestines
combining form: 9 splanchno

entrammel
3 tie 4 clog, curb 5 leash 6 fetter, hamper, hobble, hog-tie 7 shackle

entrance
3 way 4 adit, door, gate 5 charm, entry, foyer, mouth 6 access, coming, entrée, please, portal, ravish 7 arrival, attract, bewitch, doorway, enchant, gladden, ingoing, ingress, opening, rejoice 8 aperture, enravish, enthrall, entryway, incoming, open door 9 admission, captivate, enrapture, fascinate, hypnotize, spellbind, threshold, transport 10 admittance, ingression 11 penetration

entrant
7 starter 10 competitor, contestant 11 participant

entrap
3 bag, net 4 bait, lure, toll 5 benet, catch, decoy, snare, tempt 6 allure, entice, entoil, lead on, seduce, tangle 7 catch up, ensnare 8 entangle, inveigle

entreat
3 ask, beg, bid 4 coax, pray, urge 5 crave, plead, press 6 appeal, invoke, pester, plague 7 beseech, implore, wheedle 8 blandish 9 importune 10 supplicate

entreaty
4 plea, suit 6 appeal, orison, prayer 8 petition 11 application, imploration, imprecation 12 supplication

entre ___
4 nous

entrechat
4 leap

entrée
3 way 4 adit, door 6 access 7 ingress 8 entrance, main dish 9 admission 10 admittance, main course

entrench
3 fix 4 root 5 embed, found, infix, lodge 6 define, ground, invade, settle 7 confirm, implant, ingrain 8 encroach, infringe, trespass 9 establish, interfere, intervene 10 strengthen

entrenched
5 sworn 7 settled 8 deep-dyed 9 confirmed, hard-shell 10 deep-rooted, deep-seated, inveterate 13 bred-in-the-bone, dyed-in-the-wool

entrepôt
9 warehouse 10 storehouse

entrepreneur
6 backer, broker 7 manager 8 mediator, producer, promoter 9 go-between, middleman, organizer 10 contractor, impresario, interagent, interceder, undertaker 11 intercessor 12 intermediary, intermediate 13 administrator, intermediator

entresol
9 mezzanine

entrust
4 bank, give, rely 5 allot, count, leave 6 assign, charge, commit, confer, depend, impose, reckon 7 commend, confide, consign, deliver, deposit 8 allocate, delegate, hand over, relegate, turn over

entry
3 way 4 adit, door 5 debit 6 access, credit, portal 7 doorway, ingress, opening 9 admission, threshold 10 admittance, enlistment, enrollment, ingression

entwine
4 coil, curl, lace, wind 5 braid, twist 6 enmesh, spiral 7 entwist, wreathe 8 entangle 9 corkscrew, interlace 10 interplait, intertwine, interweave

enumerate
4 list, tell 5 count, tally 6 detail, number, recite, relate 7 itemize, mention, recount, specify, tick off 8 identify 9 inventory 10 specialize 13 particularize

enunciate
3 say 4 show 5 state, utter, voice 6 affirm, intone, submit 7 advance, declare, develop, enounce, express, lay down, outline, phonate 8 announce, modulate, proclaim, vocalize 9 formulate, postulate, pronounce 10 articulate

envelop
3 hem, pen 4 cage, coop, hide, mask, roll, veil, wrap 5 cloak, drape, fence, guard, hedge 6 cocoon, corral, enfold, enwrap, immure, invest, sheath, shield, shroud, shut in, swathe, wrap up 7 enclose, protect, swaddle 8 enshroud, enswathe, surround 10 circumfuse

envenom
6 poison 7 corrupt 8 acerbate, embitter 10 exacerbate

envious
6 greedy 7 jealous, longing 8 appetent, coveting, covetous, desirous, grasping, grudging, yearning 9 green-eyed, invidious, resentful 10 begrudging, umbrageous

environ
3 hem 4 gird, ring 5 beset, fence, limit, round 6 circle, suburb 7 compass, enclose, envelop 8 encircle, go around, surround 9 encompass

environment
6 medium, milieu 7 ambient, climate, context, element, habitat, setting 8 ambience, backdrop 9 situation 10 atmosphere, background, mise-en-scène 12 surroundings
combining form: 2 ec 3 eco, oec 4 oeco, oiko
science: 7 ecology

environmentalist
6 Carson (Rachel) 9 ecologist

environs
6 bounds, limits 7 compass, fringes, suburbs 8 boundary, confines, locality, purlieus, vicinity 9 outskirts, precincts 12 neighborhood, surroundings

envisage
4 view 5 fancy, grasp, image, think 6 behold, regard, survey, vision 7 feature, foresee, imagine, picture, realize 8 conceive, envision, look upon 9 objectify, visualize

envision
4 view 5 dream, fancy, image, think 7 feature, foresee, imagine, picture, realize 8 conceive, summon up 9 conjure up, visualize

envoy
6 bearer, consul, deputy, legate, nuncio 7 attaché, carrier, courier 8 diplomat, emissary, minister 9 messenger 10 ambassador, councillor 11 internuncio

envy
4 long, want 5 covet, crave, yearn 6 desire, grudge, hanker 8 begrudge, grudging, jealousy 10 re-

sentment **12** covetousness
13 invidiousness

enwrap
4 roll, veil **5** clasp, drape **6** enfold, invest, shroud, swathe **7** enclose, envelop, sheathe, swaddle **8** enshroud, enswathe

enzyme
5 ficin, lyase, renin, urase **6** kinase, ligase, lipase, mutase, papain, pepsin, rennin, urease, zymase **7** amidase, amylase, cyclase, enolase, guanase, hydrase, inulase, isozyme, lactase, maltase, oxidase, pectase, pepsine, plasmin, ptyalin, rennase, sucrase, trypsin, zymogen **8** aldolase, diastase, elastase, esterase, fumarase, lyzozyme, nuclease, protease, steapsin, thrombin, zymogene **9** biogenase, cellulase, invertase **10** amygdalase
combining form: 3 zym **4** zyme, zymo
suffix: 2 in **3** ase

eon
see **aeon**

Eos
see **Aurora**

épée
5 sword

epergne
5 stand **11** centerpiece

Ephah
father: 6 Jahdai
lover: 5 Caleb

ephelis
7 freckle

ephemeral
5 brief, short **7** passing **8** episodic, fleeting, fugitive, volatile **9** fugacious, momentary, temporary, transient **10** evanescent, short-lived, transitory, unenduring **11** impermanent

Ephialtes
5 giant
brother: 4 Otus
father: 6 Aloeus **8** Poseidon
mother: 9 Iphimedia
slayer: 6 Apollo

Ephod's son
7 Hanniel

Ephraim
brother: 8 Manasseh
father: 6 Joseph
grandfather: 5 Jacob
mother: 7 Asenath

Ephratah
husband: 5 Caleb
son: 3 Hur

epic
4 epos, poem, saga **5** grand, Iliad **6** Aeneid, heroic **7** Beowulf, Odyssey **8** imposing **9** narrative
suffix: 2 ad

epicene
5 sissy **6** prissy **7** unmanly **9** pansified, sissified **10** effeminate

epicure
7 glutton, gourmet, ravener **8** gourmand, sybarite **9** bon vivant, high liver **10** gastronome **11** connoisseur, gastronomer **12** gastronomist

epicurean
4 lush **7** sensual **8** luscious, sensuous **9** luxurious **10** voluptuous **12** sensualistic

epidemic
3 flu **4** rash **6** plague **8** outbreak **10** pestilence

epidermis
4 skin **7** cuticle

epigram
4 poem **6** saying

epigrammatic
5 meaty, pithy **7** compact, concise, marrowy, piquant

epigraph
5 motto **11** inscription

epilogue
6 ending, sequel **8** follow-up, postlude **9** afterword **10** conclusion, postscript

Epimetheus
brother: 10 Prometheus
father: 7 Iapetus
wife: 7 Pandora

epinard
7 spinach

episode
5 event **8** incident, occasion **9** happening **10** occurrence **12** circumstance

epistaxis
9 nosebleed

epistle
4 note **6** letter **7** missive **13** communication

epitaph
3 R.I.P. **8** hic jacet **11** inscription

epithet
4 name, term **5** title **7** agnomen, moniker **8** cognomen, monicker,

nickname **9** sobriquet
11 appellation

epitome
3 sum **5** brief **6** resumé **7** summary **8** abstract, boildown, breviary, breviate, last word, synopsis, ultimate **9** summation, summing-up **10** abridgment, apotheosis, conspectus **12** condensation, quintessence

epitomize
5 sum up **6** digest, embody, mirror, typify **7** outline, summate **8** boil down, condense, nutshell, tabulate **9** capsulize, exemplify, incarnate, inventory, personify, represent, summarize, symbolize, synopsize **10** illustrate **11** emblematize, incorporate

epoch
3 age, day, era **4** date, term, time **6** period **8** interval

equable
4 even, just, same **6** stable, steady **7** orderly, regular, stabile, uniform **8** constant **9** immutable, unvarying **10** equivalent, invariable, methodical, systematic, unchanging **12** unchangeable **13** unfluctuating

equal
3 tie **4** even, fair, just, like, mate, meet, peer, same, twin **5** agree, alike, match, reach, rival **6** accord, amount, equate, even-up **7** emulate, identic, similar, uniform **8** alter ego, parallel **9** duplicate, identical, impartial, measure up, objective **10** competitor, fifty-fifty, tantamount **11** counterpart, symmetrical **12** commensurate, correspond to, proportional, unprejudiced **13** commensurable, corresponding, dispassionate, proportionate
combining form: 2 is **3** iso **4** equi, pari **5** aequi
French: 4 égal

equality
3 par **6** equity, parity **7** balance, égalité **8** sameness **10** adequation

Equality State
7 Wyoming

equalize
4 even **5** level **6** square **7** balance

equalizer
6 pistol **8** handicap **10** tying score

equally
6 evenly **8** squarely **10** fifty-fifty **11** impartially

equanimity
5 poise 6 aplomb, phlegm 7 ataraxy, balance 8 calmness, coolness, evenness, serenity 9 assurance, composure, equipoise, placidity, sangfroid 10 confidence, detachment 11 equilibrium, tranquility 12 tranquillity 13 self-assurance

equate
4 even 5 liken, match, treat 6 regard, relate 7 compare, paragon 8 consider, equalize, parallel, similize 9 associate, represent 10 assimilate

equestrian
5 rider 8 horseman

equidistant
3 mid 6 center, medial, median, middle 7 central, halfway, midmost 10 centermost, middlemost

equilibrium
5 poise 6 stasis 7 balance 9 equipoise, steadying 10 steadiness 12 counterpoise 13 stabilization
combining form: 5 stato

equine
4 colt, mare 5 horse, steed

equip
3 arm, rig 4 gear 5 dress, endow, rig up 6 attire, fit out, outfit, rig out, supply 7 appoint, furnish, prepare, provide, qualify, turn out 8 accouter, accoutre

equipment
3 rig 4 gear 5 traps 6 attire, outfit, tackle, things 7 baggage, fitment 8 fittings, material, materiel, tackling 9 apparatus, machinery, trappings 10 provisions 11 accessories, attachments, habiliments, impedimenta 12 accouterment, accoutrement, provisioning 13 appurtenances, paraphernalia

equitable
4 even, fair, just, same 5 level 6 stable 8 unbiased 9 identical, impartial, objective, uncolored 10 impersonal 12 unprejudiced 13 dispassionate

equity
3 law 7 justice 8 equality, justness

equivalence
3 par 6 parity 8 equality, likeness, sameness 10 adequation 11 correlation

equivalent
4 akin, like, same 5 alike, match 6 agnate 7 identic, obverse, similar

8 parallel 9 analogous, duplicate, identical 10 comparable, reciprocal, substitute, tantamount 11 convertible, correlative, counterpart 12 commensurate 13 corresponding, proportionate

equivocal
4 hazy 5 fishy, vague 7 clouded, dubious, obscure, suspect, unclear 8 doubtful 9 ambiguous, tenebrous, uncertain, undecided 10 ambivalent, borderline, indecisive, indistinct, multivocal, unexplicit 11 problematic 12 disreputable, questionable 13 indeterminate

equivocate
3 fib, lie 5 avoid, cavil, dodge, elude, evade, fence, hedge, parry, skirt 6 escape, eschew, palter, weasel 7 falsify, quibble, shuffle 8 sidestep 9 pussyfoot 10 tergiverse 11 prevaricate 12 tergiversate

equivocation
3 fib, lie 5 lying 6 deceit 7 fallacy, fibbing, hedging, sophism 8 coloring, delusion, haggling 9 ambiguity, casuistry, deception, duplicity, quibbling, sophistry 10 distortion 11 amphibology 12 speciousness, spuriousness 13 deceptiveness, dissimulation, double meaning

equivoque
3 pun 4 quip

era
3 age, day 4 date, term, time 5 epoch, stage 6 period

eradicate
4 dele, raze 5 abate, erase, purge 6 delete, uproot 7 abolish, blot out, destroy, root out, wipe out 8 demolish 9 extirpate, liquidate 10 annihilate, extinguish 11 exterminate

Eran
father: 9 Shuthelah
grandfather: 7 Ephraim

erase
4 dele, x out 5 annul, blank 6 cancel, cut out, delete, efface, excise, negate, remove, rub out, scrape 7 abolish, blot out, expunge, nullify, scratch, take out, wipe out 8 black out, blank out, cross off, cross out, disannul, withdraw 9 eliminate, extirpate, sponge out, strike out 10 neutralize, obliterate

Erato
see **Muse**

Erbin
father: 9 Custennin
nephew: 6 Arthur
son: 7 Geraint

erbium
symbol: 2 Er

ere
6 before

Erebus
daughter: 3 Day 6 Hemera
father: 5 Chaos
home: 5 Hades
sister, wife: 3 Nox, Nyx
son: 6 Aether, Charon

Erec et ___
5 Enide

Erechteus
daughter: 8 Chthonia
father: 6 Vulcan 10 Hephaestus
mother: 2 Ge 4 Gaea
slayer: 4 Zeus 7 Jupiter

erect
4 form, lift, make, rear 5 build, exalt, forge, frame, hoist, honor, put up, raise, run up, set up, shape, upend 6 create, effect, lifted, make up, raised, uprear 7 build up, compose, dignify, elevate, ennoble, fashion, glorify, magnify, produce, stand-up, sublime, upraise, upright 8 elevated, heighten, standing, upraised, vertical 9 construct, establish, fabricate, hammer out 10 aggrandize, bring about, straight-up, upstanding 11 distinguish, manufacture 13 perpendicular

erection
4 pile 7 edifice 8 building 9 structure

eremite
6 hermit 7 ascetic, recluse

Erewhon
6 utopia
author: 6 Butler (Samuel)

ergo
2 so 4 then, thus 5 hence 9 therefore, thereupon 11 accordingly 12 consequently

Erichthonius
father: 8 Dardanus
son: 4 Tros

Eridanus star
8 Achernar

Erigone
dog: 5 Maera
father: 7 Icarius
festival: 5 Aeora

Erin
see **Eire**

Erinyes
6 Alecto, Furies 7 Megaera 9 Eumenides, Tisiphone

Eriphyle
brother: 8 Adrastus
husband: 10 Amphiaraus
slayer, son: 8 Alcmaeon

Eris
brother: 4 Ares, Mars
daughter: 3 Ate
fruit: 5 apple
mother: 3 Nox, Nyx

Eri's father
3 Gad

ermine
3 fur 5 stoat 6 weasel

erode
3 eat, rub 4 bite, gall, gnaw, rust, wear 5 chafe, decay, grate, graze, scour 6 abrade, rub off, ruffle 7 consume, corrade, corrode, crumble, eat away, rub away 8 wear away 9 scrape off 10 scrape away 11 deteriorate 12 disintegrate

Eroica composer
9 Beethoven (Ludwig van)

Eros
see **Cupid**

erotic
4 lewd, sexy 5 bawdy, spicy 6 ardent, carnal, earthy, fervid 7 amative, amatory, amorous, fervent, fleshly, sensual 8 lovesome, prurient, sensuous 9 epicurean, lecherous, lickerish, salacious 10 lascivious, passionate, voluptuous 11 aphrodisiac, impassioned 12 concupiscent

err
3 sin 4 slip, trip 5 lapse, misdo, stray 6 bungle, offend, slip up, wander 7 blunder, deviate, misplay, stumble 8 trespass 10 transgress 12 miscalculate

errand
3 job 4 task 5 chore 7 mission

errand boy
4 page 5 gofer 7 bellboy, bellhop, courier

errant
5 stray 6 roving 7 devious, erratic, naughty, ranging, roaming 8 drifting, fallible, rambling, shifting,

straying 9 deviating, itinerant, wandering 10 meandering, unreliable 11 misbehaving, mischievous

erratic
4 iffy, wild 5 queer, stray, wacky, weird 6 chancy 7 bizarre, curving, devious, dubious, oddball, strange, unusual, wayward, winding 8 doubtful, freakish, peculiar, shifting, singular, unstable, variable, volatile, whimsied 9 anomalous, arbitrary, eccentric, fluctuant, irregular, mercurial, uncertain, unnatural, vagarious, wandering, whimsical 10 capricious, changeable, inconstant, meandering, roundabout, undirected 12 incalculable, inconsistent 13 idiosyncratic, unpredictable

erring
see **errant**

erroneous
3 off 4 awry 5 amiss, askew, false, wrong 6 untrue 7 unsound 8 mistaken, specious 9 defective, incorrect, misguided 10 inaccurate

error
3 sin 4 bull, flub, muff, slip, trip 5 boner, botch, fault, fluff, lapse 6 boo-boo, bungle, fumble, howler, miscue, slipup 7 blooper, blunder, fallacy, falsity, faux pas, misplay, misstep, mistake, stumble, untruth 8 delusion, illusion, misdoing, screamer 9 falsehood, falseness, indecorum, oversight 10 inaccuracy, misreading 11 impropriety, misjudgment
printing: 4 typo 6 errata (plural) 7 erratum

ersatz
4 copy, fake, mock, sham 5 dummy, false 8 spurious 9 imitation, simulated, synthetic 10 artificial, factitious, simulacrum, substitute

Erse
5 Irish 6 Celtic, Gaelic 8 Scottish

Er's father
5 Judah

erstwhile
3 old 4 late, once, past 6 before, bygone, former, whilom 7 already, earlier, onetime, quondam 8 formerly, sometime 10 heretofore, previously

eruct
4 burp, emit, spew 5 belch, eject, expel 6 irrupt 8 disgorge

erudite
7 learned 8 lettered, studious, well-read 9 scholarly 10 scholastic

erudition
4 lore 7 culture, letters, science 8 learning, literacy, pedantry 9 education, knowledge 11 bookishness, cultivation, learnedness, scholarship 12 studiousness 13 scholarliness

erupt
3 jet 4 boil, emit, hurl, spew 5 belch, burst, eject, expel, go off, spout, spurt 6 cast up, irrupt 7 cast out, explode 8 break out, detonate, disgorge, throw off, touch off 9 discharge 10 burst forth 11 extravasate

eruption
4 gust, rush 5 burst, flare, sally 6 access 7 flare-up 8 outbreak, outburst 9 commotion, explosion
skin: 3 zit 4 rash 6 pimple 7 serpigo 8 exanthem

Esau
brother: 5 Jacob
country: 4 Edom
descendant: 7 Edomite
father: 5 Isaac
father-in-law: 4 Elon
grandson: 6 Amalek
mother: 7 Rebekah
new name: 4 Edom
son: 5 Korha, Reuel 7 Eliphaz
wife: 4 Adah 10 Aholibamah

escalade
5 climb, mount, scale 6 ascend

escalate
4 grow, upgo 5 climb, mount, scale, widen 6 ascend, expand, spread 7 broaden, enlarge, upclimb 8 heighten, increase 9 intensify

escapade
4 lark 5 antic, caper, fling, prank, spree 6 frolic, vagary 7 roguery, rollick 8 mischief

escape
3 fly, lam, shy 4 bilk, duck, flee, flit, jump, miss, shun, skip, skit, slip 5 avoid, break, burke, dodge, elude, evade, shake, skirt 6 bypass, decamp, depart, eschew, flight, outlet, vanish 7 abscond, bail out, come-off, dodging, ducking, duck out, elusion, evasion, get away, make off, release, run away 8 breakout, eschewal, shunning 9 avoidance, bypassing, departure, disappear, runaround 10 circum-

vent, liberation **11** deliverance, elusiveness, evasiveness **12** sidestepping **13** circumvention
artist: **7** Houdini (Harry)
narrow: **9** close call **10** close shave

escargot
5 snail

escarole
6 endive

escarpment
5 cliff, slope

eschar
4 scab **5** crust **6** lesion

eschew
3 shy **4** bilk, duck, shun **5** avoid, elude, evade, forgo **6** double, escape, forego **7** abstain, forbear, refrain **8** forebear **9** sacrifice

eschewal
6 escape, shying **7** come-off, elusion, evasion **8** escaping, shirking, shunning **9** avoidance, runaround

escort
3 see **4** bear, beau, date, lead, show **5** bring, guard, guide, pilot, route, steer **6** attend, convoy, direct, fellow, squire **7** company, conduct, gallant, vis-à-vis **8** cavalier, chaperon, shepherd **9** accompany, attendant, boyfriend, companion **11** consort with

escritoire
4 desk **9** secretary **10** secretaire **11** writing desk

escrow
4 bond, deed, fund **7** deposit

esculent
6 edible **7** eatable **10** comestible

escutcheon
6 shield

Eshban's father
6 Dishon

Eshcol
ally: **7** Abraham
brother: **4** Aner **5** Mamre

esker
2 os **3** ose **4** kame **5** mound, ridge

Eskimo
3 Ita **4** Yuit **5** Aleut, Inuit
boat: **5** bidar, kayak, umiak **7** bidarka
boot: **5** kamik **6** mukluk
dog: **5** husky **8** malamute
dwelling: **5** igloo **9** barrabora
outer garment: **5** parka
sledge: **7** komatik

esophagus
4 tube **6** gullet, throat **7** pharynx

esoteric
5 inner **6** mystic, occult, orphic, secret **7** private **8** abstruse, hermetic, profound **9** recondite **10** acroamatic **12** confidential

ESP
9 intuition **12** clairvoyance

espadrille
4 shoe **6** sandal

espalier
7 lattice, railing, trellis

esparto
4 alfa **5** grass

especial
4 main **5** chief **7** express, notable, supreme, unusual **8** dominant, singular, specific, uncommon **9** paramount **10** individual, particular, preeminent, surpassing **11** exceptional, predominant **12** preponderant

especially
7 notably **8** in specie, markedly, uniquely **9** eminently, expressly, supremely, unusually **10** peculiarly, remarkably, singularly **12** particularly, preeminently, specifically **13** distinctively, exceptionally

espial
4 find **6** notice, strike **9** detection, discovery **10** unearthing

espionage
6 spying **8** watching **9** sleuthing **11** observation **12** surveillance

espousal
3 aid **5** troth, union **6** mating **7** support **8** adoption, advocacy, approval, ceremony, marriage **9** betrothal, embracing, promotion **10** acceptance, betrothing, engagement **11** betrothment

espouse
3 wed **4** back, mate **5** adopt, catch, marry **6** accept, take on, take up, uphold **7** approve, embrace, support **8** advocate, champion, maintain

esprit
3 vim, wit **4** brio, dash, élan, life, mind, zing **5** humor, oomph, verve **6** acumen, brains, fervor, mettle, morale, spirit **7** courage, loyalty, passion **8** devotion, tenacity **9** acuteness, animation, sharpness **10** brightness, cleverness, enthusiasm, fellowship **11** camaraderie

esprit de corps
see **morale**

espy
3 see **4** find, mark, note, spot, view **5** catch, hit on, sight, watch **6** behold, descry, detect, notice, remark, take in, turn up **7** discern, hit upon, make out, observe, witness **8** meet with **9** encounter, recognize **11** distinguish

___ es Salaam
3 Dar

essay
3 try **4** seek, toil, work **5** assay, labor, offer, paper, piece, study, theme, tract, trial **6** hassle, strive, thesis **7** article, attempt, travail, venture **8** endeavor, exertion, striving, struggle, treatise **9** discourse, undertake **10** discussion, exposition **11** composition, explication, undertaking **12** dissertation

essayist
American: **4** Agee (James), Will (George) **5** Baker (Russell), Cooke (Alistair), Gould (Stephen Jay), White (Elwyn Brooks) **6** Brooks, (Cleanth), Fisher (Mary Frances Kennedy), Holmes (Oliver Wendell), Sontag (Susan) **7** Buckley (William Frank), Cousins (Norman), Emerson (Ralph Waldo), Mencken (Henry Louis) **8** Benchley (Robert), Repplier (Agnes) **10** Crevecoeur (Jean de)
English: **4** Lamb (Charles) **5** Bacon (Francis), Pater (Walter), Smith (Sydney) **6** Morris (Jan), Ruskin (John), Steele (Richard) **7** Addison (Joseph), Hazlitt (William)
French: **9** Montaigne (Michel Eyquem de)
Greek: **8** Xenophon
Scottish: **7** Carlyle (Thomas)

esse
5 being **9** existence

essence
3 ens, nub **4** body, crux, form, gist, pith, root, soul **5** being, fiber, fibre, stuff **6** aspect, bottom, center, entity, kernel, marrow, nature, nubbin, spirit, timber **7** element, quality, texture **8** property **9** attribute, substance **10** distillate, inwardness, rock bottom, virtuality **12** distillation, significance

essential
4 main, must **5** basal, basic, chief, prime, vital **6** inborn, inbred, in-

nate, needed, primal, wanted
7 capital, connate, element, leading, needful, primary **8** cardinal, foremost, inherent, required, rudiment **9** condition, elemental, intrinsic, necessary, necessity, primitive, principal, requisite, right hand, substance **10** congenital, deep-seated, elementary, imperative, sine qua non, substratal, underlying **11** fundamental, necessitous, requirement **12** constitutive, precondition, prerequisite **13** indispensable, part and parcel

essentially
6 almost, au fond, really **8** actually, as good as, as much as, well-nigh **9** basically, virtually **11** practically **13** fundamentally, substantially

essonite
6 garnet **13** cinnamon stone

establish
3 fix, lay, put, set **4** base, make, moor, rest, root, show, stay **5** build, enact, endow, erect, found, infix, place, prove, rivet, set up, start, stick **6** attest, bottom, create, decree, enroot, ground, impose, secure, settle, verify **7** build up, clarify, confirm, implant, instill, make out, provide, set down **8** document, entrench, organize **9** authorize, construct, determine, formulate, hammer out, inculcate, institute, legislate, originate, predicate, prescribe **10** constitute **11** corroborate, demonstrate **12** authenticate, substantiate

establishment
4 firm **5** house **6** outfit **7** company, concern, diehard **8** business, Old Guard **9** institute, workplace **10** enterprise, foundation **11** institution **12** conservative

estate
4 case, farm, form, land, rank **5** acres, caste, class, grade, level, manor, order, place, ranch, shape, state, villa **6** quinta, repair **7** station **8** category, hacienda, mesnalty, position, property, standing **9** condition **10** plantation
feudal: **4** fief **7** fiefdom
first: **6** clergy
fourth: **5** press
Indian: **5** taluk **6** taluka
manager: **7** steward **8** executor, guardian
second: **6** nobles **8** nobility
third: **7** commons

esteem
5 favor, honor, prize, value **6** admire, credit, liking, regard, revere **7** account, apprize, cherish, idolize, respect, worship **8** approval, consider, treasure, venerate **9** valuation **10** admiration, appreciate, estimation **12** appreciation **13** consideration

ester
6 oleate **7** acetate **8** compound **9** phosphate
suffix: **4** oate

Esther
cousin: **8** Mordecai
father: **7** Abihail
festival: **5** Purim
Hebrew name: **8** Hadassah
husband: **9** Ahasuerus

estimable
4 good **5** noble **6** worthy **7** admired, reputed **8** esteemed, laudable, sterling **9** admirable, deserving, honorable, meritable, praisable, reputable, respected **10** creditable **11** commendable, meritorious, respectable, thankworthy **12** praiseworthy

estimate
3 put, set, sum **4** call, cast, rank, rate **5** assay, count, fancy, guess, infer, judge, place, price, prize, round, set at, stock, value **6** assess, cipher, decide, deduce, figure, rating, reckon, settle, survey **7** adjudge, compute, imagine, suppose, surmise, valuate **8** appraise, discover, evaluate, forecast, judgment, round off, sizing up **9** appraisal, ascertain, calculate, determine, enumerate, reckoning, valuation **10** adjudicate, assessment, conjecture, evaluation, projection **11** approximate, calculation, measurement **12** appraisement

estimation
4 fame **5** favor, honor, stock **6** esteem, regard **7** account, opinion, respect **8** figuring, judgment **9** appraisal, ciphering, reckoning, valuation **10** admiration, arithmetic, assessment, evaluation, impression **11** calculation, computation **12** appraisement **13** consideration

estop
3 bar **7** prevent **8** preclude, prohibit

estrange
4 part, wean **5** alien, sever, split **6** divide, sunder **7** break up, divorce **8** alienate, disunify, disunite, separate **9** disaffect

estrangement
6 schism **7** divorce **8** division **10** alienation, withdrawal **12** disaffection

estreat
4 copy **5** exact **6** record **7** extract **9** duplicate

estuary
5 firth, frith, inlet, mouth **6** estero **10** tidal river

esurient
6 greedy, hungry **9** voracious

étagère
7 cabinet, whatnot

Etats ____
4 Unis

etch
5 grave **6** define, depict, incise **7** engrave, impress, imprint, outline, picture, portray **8** describe, inscribe, set forth **9** delineate, represent

etcher
American: **7** Pennell (Joseph) **8** Whistler (James Abbott McNeil)
Dutch: **9** Rembrandt
French: **5** Redon (Odilon) **6** Villon (Jacques)
Italian: **8** Piranesi (Giambattista)
Spanish: **6** Ribera (Jose)
Swiss: **4** Zorn (Anders)

Eteocles
brother: **9** Polynices
father: **7** Oedipus
mother: **7** Jocasta
slayer: **9** Polynices

eternal
7 ageless, endless, lasting, undying **8** constant, dateless, immortal, infinite, timeless, unending **9** ceaseless, continual, deathless, immutable, permanent, perpetual, unceasing **10** immemorial, intemporal, perdurable, unchanging **11** amaranthine, everlasting, illimitable, inalterable, never-ending, sempiternal, unalterable, unremitting **12** interminable

Eternal City
4 Rome

eternally
4 ever **6** always **7** forever **8** evermore **11** forevermore, in perpetuum

eternity
3 age, eon **4** aeon, long **7** dog's age **8** blue moon, coon's age, in-

finity **9** afterlife **10** eviternity, infinitude, perpetuity **11** endlessness, immortality **12** infiniteness, sempiternity, timelessness

etesian
4 wind **6** annual

Ethan ___
5 Allen, Brand, Frome

Ethan's father
5 Kishi

Ethbaal's daughter
7 Jezebel

ether
3 air, gas, sky **6** heaven **8** empyrean **10** anesthetic, atmosphere

ethereal
4 aery, airy **5** filmy, light **6** aerial, vapory **7** fragile **8** delicate, empyreal, empyrean, gossamer, heavenly, vaporish, vaporous **9** celestial, vaporlike **13** unsubstantial

ethic
5 ideal, mores, value **6** belief, morals **8** criteria, morality, standard **9** standards **10** moralities, principles

ethical
5 moral, noble **7** upright **8** elevated, virtuous **9** righteous **10** moralistic, principled, upstanding **11** right-minded

Ethiopia
9 Abyssinia
battle site: **5** Adowa
capital: **10** Addis Ababa
emperor: **7** Menalik **8** Selassie **9** Ras Tafari **13** Haile Selassie
language: **7** Amharic
measure: **3** tat **4** cubi, kuba **5** derah, messe **6** cabaho, sinjer, sinzer, tanica **7** farsakh, farsang
monetary unit: **4** birr
region: **4** Bale, Kefa, Welo **5** Arusi, Gojam, Harer, Shewa, Tigre **6** Gonder, Sidamo, Welega **7** Eritrea **4** Gemu, Gefa **8** Ilubabor

ethnic
5 pagan **6** racial, tribal **7** gentile, heathen, infidel, profane **8** national **9** infidelic **11** unchristian **12** non-Christian

etiolate
4 pale **6** bleach, weaken **9** colorless

etiquette
4 form **5** mores **7** conduct, decency, decorum, dignity, manners **8** behavior, protocol **9** amenities, propriety **10** civilities, convention, deportment, seemliness **11** formalities, proprieties

etna
4 lamp **7** volcano

Etruscan
city, town: **4** Roma, Veii **5** Caere, Vulci **6** Arezzo **7** Clusium, Felsina, Perugia **8** Volsinii **9** Florentia, Tarquinia, Vetulonia
deity: **3** Tiv, Uni **4** Turm, Usil **5** Tinia **6** Menfra, Nethun, Trithn **7** Velchan **8** Voltumna
king: **7** Porsena, Tarquin
kingdom: **7** Etruria

etui
4 case

etymology
6 origin **7** history, origins

etymon
4 root **5** radix

eucalypt
4 yate

eucalyptus eater
5 koala

Eucharist
container: **3** pyx
plate: **5** paten
service: **4** Mass **9** Communion **11** Lord's Supper
vessel: **8** ciborium
wafer: **4** host **8** viaticum

___ **Eulenspiegel**
4 Till, Tyll

eulogistic
9 approving, laudative, laudatory, praiseful **11** approbatory, encomiastic, panegyrical **12** commendatory **13** complimentary

eulogize
4 hymn, laud **5** bless, cry up, extol **6** belaud, praise **7** applaud, glorify, magnify **8** bepraise **9** celebrate **10** panegyrize

eulogy
5 eloge **6** praise **7** oration, tribute **8** citation, encomium **9** adulation, panegyric **10** salutation **13** glorification

Eumenides
see **Erinyes**

Eunice's son
7 Timothy

eunuch
7 gelding **8** castrate, castrato

euphonic
5 sweet **6** dulcet **7** melodic, tuneful **9** melodious **11** mellisonant

euphony
7 harmony

euphoria
4 glee **6** frenzy **7** ecstasy, elation, madness **10** exaltation **12** exhilaration, intoxication

Euphrosyne
see **Graces**

euphuistic
7 aureate, flowery, swollen, verbose **8** colorful, elevated, sonorous **9** bombastic, elaborate, overblown **10** rhetorical **11** declamatory **12** magniloquent **13** grandiloquent

eureka
3 aha

Euridice's husband
7 Orpheus

Euripides play
3 Ion **5** Helen, Medea **6** Hecuba **7** Electra, Orestes **8** Alcestis **10** Andromache, Hippolytus **11** Trojan Women

Europa
brother: **6** Cadmus
father: **6** Agenor **7** Phoenix
husband: **8** Asterius
son: **5** Minos **8** Sarpedon

Europe
9 continent
country: **4** Eire **5** Italy, Malta, Spain **6** France, Greece, Latvia, Monaco, Norway, Poland, Russia, Sweden, Turkey **7** Albania, Andorra, Armenia, Austria, Belarus, Belgium, Croatia, Denmark, Estonia, Finland, Georgia, Germany, Hungary, Iceland, Ireland, Moldova, Romania, Rumania, Ukraine **8** Bulgaria, Portugal, Slovakia, Slovenia **9** Lithuania, Macedonia, San Marino **10** Azerbaijan, Luxembourg, Yugoslavia **11** Netherlands, Switzerland, Vatican City **13** Czech Republic, Liechtenstein, United Kingdom **17** Bosnia-Herzegovina
ethnic group: **4** Finn, Lapp, Pole, Serb, Turk, Wend **5** Croat, Czech, Dutch, Greek, Gypsy, Irish, Latin, Swede, Swiss, Welsh **6** Basque, French, German, Magyar, Polish, Scotch, Slovak **7** Bosnian, Catalan, English, Finnish, Fleming, Italian, Russian, Slovene, Spanish, Swedish, Walloon **8** Albanian, Andorran, Armenian, Croatian, Romanian **9** Bulgarian, Hungarian, Ukrainian **10** Macedonian, Monegasque, Phoenician **12** Byelorussian, Scandinavian

language: 4 Lapp 5 Czech, Dutch, Greek, Irish, Latin, Welsh 6 Basque, Breton, Danish, French, Gaelic, German, Polish, Slovak 7 Catalan, English, Finnish, Flemish, Italian, Maltese, Romansh, Russian, Slovene, Spanish, Swedish, Turkish 8 Albanian, Romanian, Rumanian 9 Bulgarian, Hungarian, Icelandic, Norwegian 10 Macedonian, Portuguese 13 Serbo Croatian

mountain: 3 Alp 8 Dolomite

europium
symbol: 2 Eu

Euryale
see **Gorgon**

Eurytus
daughter: 4 Iole
slayer: 8 Hercules

Euterpe
see **Muse**

evacuant
6 emetic 8 diuretic, emptying 9 cathartic, purgative

evacuate
4 void 5 clear, empty, expel 6 remove 7 excrete, exhaust 8 withdraw

evacuee
2 DP 6 émigré 7 refugee 8 fugitive

evade
3 fly, shy 4 bilk, duck, flee, foil, shun 5 avoid, dodge, elude, hedge, parry, shirk 6 bypass, double, escape, eschew, outwit, thwart, weasel 7 shuffle 8 sideslip, sidestep, slip away 9 pussyfoot, turn aside 10 circumvent, equivocate, tergiverse 12 tergiversate

Evadne
father: 5 Iphis
husband: 8 Capaneus

evaluate
4 rank, rate 5 assay, class, gauge, grade, set at, value 6 assess, ponder, survey 8 appraise, classify, estimate 9 criticize

evaluation
5 stock 6 rating 7 judging 8 decision, estimate, judgment 9 appraisal 10 assessment, estimation 12 appraisement, appreciation, interpreting

Evander
father: 6 Hermes 7 Mercury
mother: 8 Carmenta 9 Carmentis
son: 6 Pallas

evanesce
4 fade 5 clear, empty 6 dispel, vanish 7 scatter 8 disperse, dissolve 9 disappear, dissipate, evaporate 12 disintegrate

evanescent
6 fading, flying 7 cursory, melting, passing 8 fleeting, fugitive, volatile 9 ephemeral, fugacious, momentary, temporary, transient, vanishing 10 dissolving, short-lived, transitory 12 disappearing

evangelical
6 ardent, fervid 7 zealous 8 militant 9 crusading 10 missionary 11 impassioned 13 proselytizing

Evangeline
author: 10 Longfellow (Henry Wadsworth)
beloved: 7 Gabriel
home: 6 Acadia

evangelist
4 John, Luke, Mark 5 Baker (Jim), Moody (Dwight) 6 Graham (Billy), Sunday (Billy), Wesley (John) 7 apostle, Edwards (Jonathan), Falwell (Jerry), Matthew, Roberts (Oral) 9 McPherson (Aimee Semple), missioner, Robertson (Pat) 10 colporteur, missionary, revivalist

evangelistic
9 crusading, reforming 10 missionary

evangelize
6 preach 8 homilize 9 sermonize

evaporate
4 fade 5 clear 6 vanish 7 evanish 8 evanesce, vaporize 9 disappear

evasion
5 dodge 6 escape, excuse 7 comeoff, dodgery, dodging, elusion 8 escaping, escapism, eschewal, haggling, shunning 9 avoidance, quibbling, runaround

evasive
3 sly 4 eely 5 dodgy, vague 6 shifty 7 elusive, elusory, sliding, unclear 8 slippery 9 ambiguous, equivocal, shuffling 10 intangible 12 equivocating

eve
4 dusk 5 night 7 sundown

Eve
husband: 4 Adam
son: 4 Abel, Cain, Seth

even
3 tie, yet 4 fair, flat, just, same, tied 5 align, equal, exact, flush, grade, level, plane, quite, still, truly 6 as well, equate, honest, indeed, really, smooth, square, stable, steady, verily 7 already, balance, equable, exactly, flatten, pancake, planate, stabile, uniform 8 balanced, constant, equalize, smoothen, so much as, straight, unvaried 9 continual, equitable, expressly, identical, precisely, unvarying 10 absolutely, comparable, consistent, continuous, fifty-fifty, positively, symmetrize, unchanging 11 undeviating 12 unprejudiced 13 fair and square, proportionate, unfluctuating

combining form: 5 homal 6 homalo

evening
4 dusk 6 soiree, sunset 7 sundown 8 duskness, eventide, gloaming, twilight 9 afternoon, duskiness, nightfall
French: 4 soir
Italian: 4 sera
service: 7 vespers
star: 5 Venus 6 Hesper, Vesper 8 Hesperus

evenness
7 balance 8 equality, fairness, flatness 10 equanimity, uniformity 11 consistency

event
3 act, hap 4 case, deed, fact, feat, meet 5 issue, match, treat 6 action, affair, chance, effect, result, sequel, upshot 7 contest, delight, episode, exploit, fortune, outcome, product, sequent 8 accident, causatum, fortuity, incident, landmark, milepost, occasion, offshoot 9 aftermath, happening, milestone, outgrowth, resultant 10 occurrence, phenomenon 11 achievement, aftereffect, competition, consequence, eventuality 12 circumstance, happenstance

eventful
4 busy 9 important, momentous

eventual
3 lag 4 last 5 final 6 ending, latest, latter 7 closing, endmost, ensuing 8 hindmost, terminal, ultimate 10 concluding, consequent, inevitable, succeeding

eventuality
4 case 5 issue 6 effect, result, sequel, upshot 7 outcome 9 aftermath 11 aftereffect, consequence, contingency, possibility

eventually
3 yet 7 finally, someday 8 sometime 10 ultimately 13 sooner or later

eventuate
5 occur 6 happen, result

ever
3 too 4 once, over 5 at all, super 6 always, anyway, overly, unduly 7 anytime, anywise, forever, plaguey, usually 8 mortally, overfull, overmuch 9 eternally, extremely, immensely, regularly 10 annoyingly, constantly, consumedly, grievously, invariably 11 excessively, in perpetuum, perpetually 12 consistently, continuously

evergreen
3 fir, ivy, yew 4 ilex, pine, tree 5 cedar, holly, savin 6 laurel, myrtle, spruce 7 conifer, cypress, hemlock, juniper, redwood, sequoia 8 magnolia 9 mistletoe 12 rhododendron

Evergreen State
10 Washington

everlasting
7 endless, eternal, forever, lasting 8 constant, immortal, infinite, termless, unending 9 boundless, ceaseless, continual, limitless, permanent, perpetual, unceasing 10 continuous, perdurable 11 amaranthine, never-ending, unremitting 13 uninterrupted

evermore
6 always 9 eternally 11 in perpetuum

evert
5 upset 9 overthrow

every
3 all 4 each
combining form: 3 pam, pan 4 pano
suffix: 2 ly

everybody
3 all 4 each 8 everyone

everyday
5 banal, lowly, plain, usual 6 common 7 mundane, prosaic, routine, workday 8 familiar, frequent, ordinary, workaday 9 customary, plain Jane, quotidian 11 commonplace 12 unremarkable

everyplace
see **everywhere**

everything
3 all
French: 4 tout
German: 5 alles

everywhere
7 all over, overall 8 all round, wherever 9 all around 10 far and near, far and wide, high and low, throughout

evict
3 out 4 oust 5 chase, chuck, eject, expel 6 put out 7 boot out, dismiss, extrude, kick out, shut out, turn out 8 dislodge, force out, throw out 10 dispossess

evidence
4 clue, mark, show, sign 5 index, proof, prove, token, trace 6 attest, evince, expose, ostend 7 bespeak, betoken, confirm, display, exhibit, indicia, symptom, testify, witness 8 indicate, manifest, proclaim 9 testament, testimony 10 illustrate, indication 11 attestation, demonstrate, significant, testimonial 12 confirmation

evident
5 clear, overt, plain 6 patent 7 glaring, obvious, visible 8 apparent, distinct, manifest, palpable 9 prominent 10 noticeable, pronounced 11 unambiguous

evidently
9 outwardly, seemingly 10 apparently, officially, ostensibly 11 professedly

evil
3 bad, ill, low, sin 4 base, debt, foul, hard, tort, ugly, vice, vile 5 angry, black, catty, crime, fetid, wrong 6 malice, nocent, putrid, sinful, trying, wicked 7 badness, baleful, baneful, corrupt, devilry, harmful, hateful, hideous, hurtful, immoral, malefic, misdeed, nocuous, obscene, offense, ominous, satanic, unlucky, vicious 8 damaging, damnable, iniquity, satanism, satanity, spiteful, stinking, wrathful 9 atrocious, diablerie, diabolism, difficult, evildoing, execrable, ill-boding, ill-omened, injurious, loathsome, malicious, nefarious, offensive, rancorous, repellent, reprobate, repugnant, repulsive, revolting 10 calamitous, despiteful, disastrous, flagitious, iniquitous, malevolent, misconduct, pernicious, sinfulness, unpleasant, wickedness, wrongdoing 11 deleterious, destructive, detrimental, distasteful, maleficence, mischievous, unfavorable, unfortunate 12 disagreeable, inauspicious
combining form: 3 mal

evildoer
3 cur 5 crook, felon 6 bad lot, sinner 7 culprit, villain 8 criminal 9 miscreant

evil spirit
3 imp 5 demon, devil, fiend 6 daemon

evince
4 mark, milk, show 5 argue, cause, educe, evoke, prove 6 attest, elicit, expose, extort, ostend 7 bespeak, betoken, confirm, display, exhibit, extract, provoke, signify 8 evidence, indicate, manifest, proclaim 9 stimulate 10 bring about, illustrate 11 demonstrate

evirate
4 geld 8 castrate 10 emasculate

eviscerate
3 gut 4 draw 5 bowel 6 paunch 7 embowel 10 disembowel, exenterate

evocative
6 moving 7 causing, weighty 8 arousing, inducing, pregnant, stirring 9 effecting, producing 10 meaningful, suggestive 11 stimulating

evoke
4 milk, stir 5 educe, raise, rally, rouse, waken 6 arouse, awaken, call up, elicit, evince, excite, extort 7 extract 8 summon up 9 call forth, conjure up, stimulate 11 summon forth

evolution
6 change, growth 8 progress, upgrowth 9 flowering, unfolding 10 biogenesis 11 development, progression

evolve
4 grow 5 educe, get at, ripen 6 change, derive, mature, obtain, open up, unfold 7 advance, develop 8 progress 9 elaborate 10 excogitate

evulse
4 pull, tear, yank 7 extract

ewe
5 sheep
young: 6 theave

ewer
3 jug 4 vase 5 basin 7 pitcher

ex
6 former 7 without

exacerbate
5 annoy 6 worsen 7 envenom, inflame, provoke 8 embitter, heighten, irritate 9 aggravate, intensify 10 exasperate

exact

4 call, even, levy, nice, same, true, very **5** claim, force, fussy, gouge, pinch, put on, right, screw, wrest, wring **6** assess, coerce, compel, demand, extort, impose, oblige, proper, square, wrench **7** careful, correct, extract, precise, require, solicit, squeeze **8** accurate, punctual, rigorous, selfsame **9** challenge, constrain, identical, postulate, shake down **10** meticulous, scrupulous **11** painstaking, punctilious, requisition **12** consciable **13** conscientious

combining form: **4** orth **5** ortho

exacting

5 fussy, rigid, stern, tough **6** severe, strict, taxing, trying **7** exigent, finicky, onerous, weighty **8** critical, grievous, rigorous **9** demanding, stringent **10** burdensome, oppressive, particular

exactitude

8 accuracy **9** precision **10** definitude **11** correctness, preciseness **12** definiteness

exactly

3 all **4** bang, even, just **5** quite, right, sharp, spang, stick **6** as well, in toto, square, to a tee, wholly **7** totally, utterly **8** all in all, smack-dab, squarely **9** expressly, on the nose, precisely **10** absolutely, accurately, altogether, completely, positively **12** specifically

exaggerate

3 pad **5** color, fudge **6** overdo **7** amplify, magnify, overact, romance **8** overdraw, overrate **9** embellish, embroider, overstate **10** overcharge **11** hyperbolize, romanticize

exaggeration

7 romance **8** coloring **9** hyperbole **10** caricature, stretching **11** enlargement, overdrawing **12** embroidering, overcoloring **13** amplification, embellishment, overstatement

exalt

4 fire, laud, lift **5** boost, elate, erect, extol, honor, pique, raise **6** deepen, enhalo, inform, praise, uplift, uprear **7** acclaim, animate, build up, dignify, elevate, enhance, ennoble, glorify, inspire, magnify, promote, quicken, sublime, upgrade **8** heighten, inspirit, pedestal, spirit up, stellify **9** encourage, intensify, stimulate **10** aggrandize **11** apotheosize, distinguish

exaltation

3 joy **5** bliss **6** praise **7** delight, ecstasy, elation, rapture **8** euphoria, rhapsody **9** extolment, laudation, upgrading, uplifting **10** apotheosis **11** deification, delectation **12** exhilaration, intoxication **13** dignification, glorification

exalted

4 high **5** first, grand, lofty, noble **6** astral, august, superb **7** eminent, highest, leading, sublime **8** elevated, foremost **9** number one, prominent, top-drawer **10** top-ranking **11** high-ranking, illustrious, outstanding

examination

4 oral, quiz, scan, test, view **5** assay, audit, trial **6** review, survey **7** autopsy, canvass, checkup, hearing, inquest, inquiry, sifting, testing **8** analysis, quizzing, scanning, scrutiny **9** breakdown, check-over, diagnosis, winnowing **10** dissection, inspection **11** questioning **13** catechization, investigation, perlustration

kind: **4** oral **5** final **7** medical, midterm **8** physical

of accounts: **5** audit

of a corpse: **7** autopsy

examine

3 ask, con, try, vet **4** pump, quiz, scan, sift, test, view **5** audit, check, grill, probe, prove, query, study **6** go over, look at, peruse, survey **7** canvass, check up, inquire, inspect, observe **8** check out, look into, look over, overhaul, question **9** catechize, check over **10** scrutinize **11** contemplate, interrogate, investigate

eggs: **6** candle

examiner

6 censor, critic, tester **7** auditor, coroner **9** inspector

examining tool

combining form: **5** scope

example

4 case **5** ideal, model **6** mirror, sample **7** pattern, problem **8** ensample, exemplar, instance, paradigm, sampling, specimen, standard **9** archetype **11** case history **12** illustration

exanimate

4 dead **8** lifeless **10** spiritless

exasperate

3 get, irk **4** gall, huff, rile, roil

5 peeve, pique **6** nettle, work up **7** agitate **8** irritate **9** aggravate

exasperation

4 pest **6** bother, pester, plague, pother **8** irritant, nuisance, vexation **9** annoyance, besetment **10** botherment, irritation, resentment **11** aggravation, botheration, displeasure

ex cathedra

8 official **9** ex officio **13** authoritative

excavate

3 dig **4** grub **5** scoop, spade **6** dig out, shovel **7** unearth **8** gouge out, scoop out **9** hollow out, quarry out, scrape out

excavation

3 dig, pit **4** hole, mine **5** stope **6** trench

exceed

3 top **4** beat, best, dare, pass **5** break, excel, outdo **6** better, overdo **7** outstep, overrun, presume, surpass, venture **8** outreach, outshine, outstrip, outweigh, overstep **9** overreach, transcend

exceedingly

4 very **6** hugely **7** notably, parlous, vitally **9** extremely **10** remarkably, strikingly **12** surpassingly **13** exceptionally

prefix: **3** pre **5** ultra

excel

3 top **4** beat, best **5** outdo, shine **6** better, exceed **7** surpass **8** outclass, outshine, outstrip **9** transcend

excellence

5 arête, class, merit, value, worth **6** virtue **7** quality **8** fineness, goodness, niceness **10** perfection, superbness **11** distinction, superiority

excellent

3 top **4** brag, fine, good **5** bully, dandy, nobby, noble, prime, royal, smart **6** bang-up, banner, famous, Grade A, proper, superb, tip-top **7** capital, classic, premium, quality, supreme **8** champion, five-star, splendid, stunning, superior, terrific, top-notch, whiz-bang **9** classical, first-rate, front-rank, high-class, high-grade, marvelous, number one, sovereign **10** blue-ribbon, first-class **11** exceptional, first-string, magnificent, sensational, superlative, unsurpassed **12** incomparable

except

3 bar, but, yet **4** bate, kick, omit,

only, save 5 debar 6 bating, beside, exempt, object, reject, saving, unless 7 barring, besides, exclude, however, outside, protest, rule out, suspend 8 count out, pass over 9 apart from, aside from, eliminate, excluding, outside of 11 exclusive of, expostulate, remonstrate

exception
5 demur 7 dissent 9 exclusion, objection

exceptionable
8 unwanted 9 unwelcome 10 ill-favored 11 undesirable 12 inadmissible, unacceptable 13 objectionable

exceptional
4 rare 6 scarce, unique 7 notable, premium, special, strange, unusual 8 distinct, singular, superior, uncommon, unwonted 9 excellent, marvelous, wonderful 10 infrequent, noteworthy, phenomenal, remarkable, unordinary 11 outstanding, uncustomary, unthinkable 12 unimaginable 13 extraordinary

exceptionally
4 very 6 hugely 7 notably, parlous, vitally 9 extremely, unusually 10 especially, remarkably, strikingly 11 exceedingly, marvelously, wonderfully 12 particularly, phenomenally, stupendously, surpassingly

excerpt
4 cite, cull, pick 5 glean, quote 6 choose, select, single 7 extract, pick out

excess
3 fat 4 plus 5 extra, flood, spare 6 de trop 7 overage, surfeit, surplus 8 overflow, overkill, overmuch, overplus, plethora 9 boundless, indulgent, limitless, overboard, overdoing, overspill, overstock, profusion, redundant, unbounded 10 immoderacy, indulgence, oversupply, Saturnalia, surplusage 11 dissipation, overbalance, overmeasure, prodigality, superfluent, superfluity, superfluous, unessential 12 extravagance, immoderation, intemperance 13 overabundance, supernumerary

excessive
4 over 5 dizzy, steep, stiff, super, undue 6 too-too 7 extreme, sky-high 8 overmuch, prodigal, towering 10 dissipated, exorbitant, immoderate, inordinate, untempered 11 extravagant, intemperate, overweening 12 supernatural, unmea-

surable, unrestrained 13 overindulgent
combining form: 4 poly
prefix: 3 sur

excessively
3 too 4 ever, over 6 overly, unduly 7 parlous 8 overfull, overmuch 9 extremely, immensely 12 inordinately
prefix: 5 hyper

exchange
4 swap 5 bandy, trade, truck 6 barter, change, market, switch 7 bargain, commute, pay back, replace, traffic 8 displace 10 substitute 11 reciprocate
premium: 4 agio

exchequer
5 chest 6 coffer 8 treasury, war chest

excise
3 tax 4 toll 5 elide, slash 6 cut off, cut out, delete, exsect, remove, resect 7 exscind, root out 8 amputate 9 eradicate, expurgate, extirpate, strike out

excision
3 cut 7 erasure, removal, surgery 9 resection 11 destruction, extirpation

excitable
4 edgy 6 touchy 8 agitable, skittery, skittish, unstable, volatile 9 alarmable, mercurial, startlish 10 high-strung 11 combustible 13 temperamental

excite
4 fire, move, spur, stir 5 elate, pique, prime, rouse, set up, waken 6 appeal, arouse, stir up, thrill, turn on 7 agitate, attract, commove, disturb, innerve, inspire, perturb, provoke, quicken 8 charge up, disquiet, energize, interest, intrigue, motivate, spirit up, touch off 9 fascinate, galvanize, impassion, innervate, stimulate 10 discompose, exhilarate

excited
3 hot 4 avid 5 eager 6 hectic 7 fevered, frantic 8 aflutter

excitement
3 ado 4 stir 6 furore, warmth 8 delirium, hysteria 9 commotion 11 disturbance, pandemonium

exclaim
4 blat, bolt, roar 5 snort 6 cry out 8 blurt out, burst out 9 ejaculate

exclamation
2 ah, ai, ay, ha, hi, ho, lo, oh, ow, so 3 aah, aha, bah, boo, cry, eek, feh, fie, gee, hah, hey, hic, huh, och, oho, ooh, pah, tsk, tut, ugh, wow, yeh 4 ahem, alas, damn, dang, darn, drat, egad, gosh, heck, hell, oops, ouch, phew, pish, posh, rats, whew, yell, yipe 5 alack, bravo, faugh, golly, humph, pshaw, shout 6 clamor, hurrah, indeed, phooey, shucks 7 doggone, gee whiz, hosanna, jeepers, whoopee 9 expletive 12 interjection
of disgust: 3 bah, feh, ugh 5 yecch 6 phooey
of dismay: 4 oh no
of pain: 2 ow 4 ouch
of relief: 4 phew
of sorrow: 4 alas 5 alack
of surprise: 2 ah, oh 3 aha, oho, wow
of triumph: 3 hah
(see also **interjection**)

exclude
3 ban, bar 4 bate 5 block, debar, estop 6 banish, disbar, except, put out 7 keep out, lock out, obviate, prevent, rule out, shut out, suspend, ward off 8 close out, count out, preclude, prohibit 9 blackball, blacklist, eliminate, ostracize
prefix: 3 dis

excluding
3 bar, but 4 less, save 6 bating, except, saving 7 barring, besides 9 outside of 11 exclusive of

exclusive
4 chic, lone, only, pick, sole, tony 5 aloof, elect, elite, scoop, smart, swank, swish, whole 6 chosen, cliquy, picked, select, single, with-it 7 barring, dashing, high-hat, stylish 8 clannish, cliquish, limiting, selected, snobbish, unshared 9 debarring, excluding, preferred, undivided 10 individual, limitative, privileged, unswerving 11 fashionable, prohibitive, restrictive, standoffish 12 aristocratic, concentrated, undistracted

exclusively
3 but 4 only 5 alone 6 solely, wholly 8 entirely 10 completely 12 particularly

excogitate
4 mind 5 educe, study, weigh 6 derive, evolve, invent, ponder 7 develop, perpend, think up

8 consider, contrive, think out
9 think over 11 contemplate

excommunicate
8 unchurch

excoriate
3 rub 4 flay, fret, gall 5 chafe,
slash 6 abrade, scathe, scorch
7 blister, scarify, scourge 8 lambaste, lash into 9 castigate

excorticate
4 peel, skin 5 scale, strip

excrement
4 dirt 5 feces 6 ordure, refuse
combining form: 4 copr, scat 5
copro, scato
of animals: 4 dung, muck 6 manure
of sea birds: 5 guano

excrescence
4 wart 6 pimple 7 process 9 outgrowth, processus

excruciate
3 try 4 hurt, pain, rack 5 wound,
wring 6 harrow, martyr 7 afflict,
agonize, crucify, inflame, torment,
torture 8 convulse, irritate

excruciating
5 acute, sharp 7 extreme, racking,
rending, tearing 8 piercing, shooting, stabbing 9 agonizing, consuming, harrowing, torturing, torturous
10 tormenting

exculpate
4 free 5 clear, remit 6 acquit, excuse, let off, pardon 7 absolve, amnesty, condone, explain, forgive,
justify 9 exonerate, vindicate
11 rationalize

excurse
5 stray 6 depart, ramble, wander
7 digress, diverge 8 divagate

excursion
4 ride, tour, trek, trip, walk
5 aside, jaunt, paseo, sally, tramp
6 cruise, junket, outing, safari 7 circuit, journey 9 round trip 10 digression, divagation, expedition,
one-way trip, roundabout
11 parenthesis 12 pleasure trip

excusable
6 venial 7 tenable 10 condonable,
defensible, forgivable, pardonable,
remittable, vindicable 11 justifiable

excuse
4 plea 5 alibi, clear, remit, shift,
spare 6 acquit, cop-out, exempt, let
off, pardon, reason, wink at 7 absolve, apology, condone, defense,
explain, forgive, justify, pretext, regrets, relieve, stopgap 8 dispense,

overlook, palliate, pass over, shrug
off 9 discharge, exculpate, exonerate, extenuate, gloss over, makeshift, vindicate, whitewash 10 substitute 11 explanation, rationalize
13 justification

execrable
3 bad, low 4 base, foul, vile
6 cursed, cussed, damned
7 blasted, heinous 8 accursed,
damnable, horrific, infernal 9 atrocious, loathsome, monstrous, repulsive, revolting 10 confounded,
despicable, detestable, horrifying,
nauseating

execrate
3 ban 4 cuss, damn, hate 5 abhor,
curse, swear 6 bedamn, detest,
loathe, revile 7 accurse, censure,
condemn, reprove 8 denounce
9 abominate, imprecate, objurgate,
reprehend, reprobate
12 anathematize

execute
2 do 3 act 4 do in, hang, kill, slay
5 cause, lynch, purge 6 finish, gibbet, govern, handle, murder, render
7 achieve, bump off, conduct, fulfill,
perform, put away 8 carry out,
complete, dispatch, knock off, transact 9 discharge, eliminate, implement, liquidate 10 administer,
bring about, put through 11 assassinate 12 administrate

execution
6 murder 7 facture, garrote, hanging 8 garrotte 9 beheading
11 performance

executioner
6 hanger 7 hangman, headman
8 headsman

executive
4 dean 6 leader 7 manager, officer 8 director, governor, higher-up,
official 9 president 10 supervisor
11 businessman 12 entrepreneur
13 administrator, businesswoman

executor
4 doer 5 agent 9 performer

exegesis
6 exposé 9 construal 10 exposition
11 explanation, explication
12 construction

exemplar
4 soul 5 ideal, model 6 mirror
7 example, pattern 8 ensample, exponent, paradigm, standard 9 archetype, prototype 12 illustration

exemplary
4 good, pure 5 ideal, model

6 worthy 7 classic, typical 8 innocent, laudable, virtuous 9 admirable, blameless, classical, guiltless,
righteous 10 inculpable, prototypal, unblamable 11 commendable 12 paradigmatic, praiseworthy,
prototypical

exemplify
4 cite 5 quote 6 embody, mirror,
typify 7 clarify, clear up 8 spell out
9 enlighten, epitomize, personify,
represent, symbolize 10 illuminate,
illustrate 11 demonstrate,
emblematize

exempt
4 free 5 spare 6 except, excuse, let
off 7 absolve, relieve 8 dispense
9 discharge
combining form: 6 immuno

exemption
7 freedom, release 8 immunity, impunity 9 discharge, exception

exenterate
3 gut 4 draw 5 bowel 6 paunch
7 embowel 10 disembowel,
eviscerate

exercise
3 irk, ply, use, vex 4 fret, gall 5 annoy, apply, chafe, drill, exert, situp, sport, study, throw, train, wield
6 abrade, action, bestow, bother,
employ, foster, handle, lesson,
pushup, put out 7 develop, exploit,
improve, prepare, problem, provoke, utilize, workout 8 activity,
drilling, exertion, movement, practice, rehearse 9 athletics, condition,
cultivate, operation 10 employment
11 application 12 calisthenics

exert
3 ply, use 5 apply, throw, wield
6 employ, put out, strain 8 exercise

exertion
3 use 4 toil, work 5 labor, pains,
trial, while 6 effort, strain 7 trouble
8 activity, exercise, striving, struggle 9 operation 10 employment,
exercising 11 application, elbow
grease

exfoliate
4 peel 5 scale 8 flake off
10 desquamate

exhalation
6 breath 7 halitus 9 breathing, effluvium, emanation 10 expiration

exhale
4 blow, emit 6 expire, let out
7 breathe 10 breathe out, outbreathe

exhaust
3 fag, sap 4 do in, draw, tire
5 drain, eat up, spend, use up
6 devour, dispel, expend, finish,
overdo, run out, tucker, wash up,
weaken 7 consume, deplete, frazzle, outtire, outwear, overply, scatter, wear out 8 bankrupt, disperse,
draw down, enfeeble, knock out,
overwork 9 dissipate, overdrive,
overexert, prostrate 10 debilitate,
impoverish, overextend, run
through

exhausted
4 beat, dead, done, limp, weak
5 all in, spent, tired 6 bleary, effete, used up 7 drained, far-gone,
run-down, worn-out 8 consumed,
depleted, dog-tired 9 washed-out

exhaustion
7 fatigue 8 collapse 9 lassitude,
tiredness, weariness 11 prostration

exhaustive
5 total 6 all-out 7 radical 8 complete, profound, sweeping, thorough, whole-hog 9 full-blown, full-
dress, full-scale, intensive,
out-and-out 13 comprehensive,
thoroughgoing

exhibit
3 air 4 fair, look, mark, show
5 flash, sight 6 evince, expose,
flaunt, ostend, parade 7 display,
disport, show off, trot out 8 brandish, evidence, manifest, proclaim,
showcase 10 exposition, illustrate
11 demonstrate

exhibition
4 fair, show 5 sight 7 display, pageant, showing 8 offering 9 spectacle 10 exposition 12 presentation
13 demonstration, manifestation

exhilarate
4 buoy, lift 5 boost, cheer, elate,
exalt, pep up, set up 6 excite, thrill,
uplift 7 animate, commove, delight,
enliven, gladden, inspire 8 inspirit,
spirit up, vitalize 9 stimulate
10 invigorate

exhilaration
6 firing, gaiety, uplift 7 ecstasy,
elation 8 euphoria, gladness 9 animation, elevation 10 exaltation,
excitation, excitement, quickening
11 enlivenment, inspiration, stimula-
tion 12 invigoration, vitalization,
vivification 13 galvanization

exhort
3 sic 4 goad, prod, spur, urge
5 egg on, plead, prick 6 insist,

prompt, propel 8 admonish, call
upon 9 stimulate

exhume
3 dig 5 dig up 6 unbury 7 unearth
8 disinter 9 disembalm, disentomb,
disinhume, uncharnel

exigency
3 fix, jam 4 need, pass, want
5 pinch, rigor 6 crisis, demand, duress, pickle, scrape, strait 7 dilemma 8 coercion, hardship, juncture, pressure, zero hour
9 necessity 10 compulsion, constraint, crossroads, difficulty, insistence 11 requirement, vicissitude
12 turning point

exigent
5 acute, tough, vital 6 crying, taxing 7 burning, clamant, instant, onerous, weighty 8 exacting, grievous, menacing, pressing
9 clamorous, demanding, insistent,
necessary 10 burdensome, imperative, oppressive 11 importunate,
threatening

exiguous
4 poor, thin, tiny 5 scant, skimp,
small, spare 6 little, meager, narrow, scanty, scrimp, skimpy, slight,
sparse 7 limited, scrimpy, slender,
tenuous 8 confined 10 diminutive,
restricted, straitened

exile
4 oust 5 expel 6 banish, deport,
emigré 7 cast out, expulse, outcast,
refugee 8 diaspora, displace, drive
out, evacuate, expellee, unperson
9 exclusion, expulsion, extradite,
migration, nonperson, ostracism,
ostracize, transport 10 banishment,
dispersion, dispossess, expatriate,
relegation, scattering 11 deportation, extradition 12 displacement,
expatriation
place of: 7 Siberia

exist
2 am, be, is 3 are, lie 4 live, move
5 dwell 6 inhere, reside 7 breathe,
consist, subsist

existence
3 ens 4 esse, life 5 being, thing
6 entity 7 reality 8 perseity
9 actuality, something
13 individuality
combining form: 3 ont 4 onto

existent
4 real 5 alive, being, thing 6 actual, around, entity, living 7 instant,
present 8 todayish 10 present-day
12 contemporary

existentialist writer
5 Buber (Martin), Camus (Albert)
6 Marcel (Gabriel-Honore), Sartre
(Jean-Paul) 7 Jaspers (Karl) 9 Heidegger (Martin) 11 Kierkegaard
(Soren)

existing
5 alive, being, ontic 6 around, extant, living
from birth: 6 innate 10 congenital
Latin: 6 in esse

exit
2 go 4 door, gate, move, quit
5 going, leave 6 depart, egress,
exodus, get off, outlet, portal, retire
7 doorway, get away 8 offgoing,
withdraw 9 departure, egression
10 setting-out, withdrawal

exode
5 farce 8 travesty

exodus
4 exit 6 egress, flight 7 exiting
8 offgoing 9 departure, egression,
migration 10 emigration, setting-
out, withdrawal

Exodus author
4 Uris (Leon)

exonerate
4 free 5 clear 6 acquit, excuse
7 absolve 9 disburden, exculpate,
vindicate 10 disculpate

exorbitant
5 dizzy, undue 7 extreme 8 exacting, overmuch, towering 9 excessive, overboard 10 immoderate,
inordinate, outrageous
11 extravagant, unwarranted
12 preposterous, unmeasurable

exordium
5 proem 7 preface, prelude 8 foreword, overture, preamble, prologue
9 prelusion 11 preliminary 12 introduction, prolegomenon

exotic
5 alien 7 foreign, strange, unusual
8 alluring, enticing, imported, romantic 9 different, glamorous
10 introduced, mysterious, romanesque 11 fascinating

expand
3 wax 4 grow, open, rise 5 boost,
built, mount, swell, widen 6 beef
up, detail, dilate, fan out, spread,
unfold 7 amplify, augment, bolster,
develop, distend, enlarge, inflate,
magnify, prolong, stretch, upsurge
8 escalate, heighten, increase, multiply, mushroom, protract 9 discourse, elaborate, expatiate, expli-

cate, outspread **10** aggrandize, outstretch

expanse
   4 area, room **5** field, ocean, orbit, range, reach, scope, space, sweep, tract **6** domain, extent, sphere, spread **7** breadth, compass, stretch **8** distance **9** amplitude, immensity, magnitude, territory

expansion
   5 space **6** growth, spread **7** breadth, stretch **8** distance, increase **9** amplitude **11** enlargement

expansive
   3 big **4** airy, free, wide **5** ample, broad, great, gushy, large **6** bouncy, lavish, scopic **7** buoyant, elastic, liberal **8** effusive, extended, generous, outgoing, scopious, volatile **9** resilient **10** gregarious, openhanded, unreserved **11** extroverted **12** communicable, effervescent, unrestrained **13** communicative, demonstrative, unconstrained

expatiate
   6 ramble, recite, relate, wander **7** descant, discuss, dissert, recount **8** dilate on, rehearse **9** discourse, sermonize **10** dilate upon, dissertate

expatriate
   4 oust **6** banish, deport, emigré **8** displace, expellee, relegate **9** transport

expect
   4 feel, hope, look, take **5** await, sense, think **6** assume, divine, gather **7** believe, count on, foresee, imagine, presume, suppose **8** foreknow **9** apprehend, count upon **10** anticipate, presuppose

expectant
   3 big **5** alert, eager, heavy **6** gravid, parous **7** atiptoe, hopeful **8** childing, enceinte, open-eyed, pregnant, watchful **10** parturient **11** openmouthed **12** anticipative, anticipatory

expectation
   4 hope **6** design, motive **8** prospect

expectorate
   4 spit

expediency
   4 step **5** order, shift **6** design, resort, tactic **7** aptness, fitness, measure, stopgap **8** meetness, recourse, resource, strategy

9 makeshift, propriety, rightness, surrogate **10** substitute **11** suitability **12** appositeness, suitableness

expedient
   3 fit **4** wise **5** dodge, means, shift **6** agency, medium, refuge, resort, timely, useful **7** fitting, politic, prudent, stopgap **8** feasible, possible, recourse, resource, suitable, tactical **9** advisable, judicious, makeshift, opportune, practical, well-timed **10** beneficial, convenient, instrument, profitable, seasonable, substitute **11** appropriate, practicable, utilitarian **12** advantageous

expedite
   3 hie **4** send **5** hurry, issue, speed **6** hasten **7** quicken **8** dispatch **10** accelerate, facilitate

expedition
   4 trek, trip **5** haste, hurry, speed **6** hustle, rustle **7** entrada, journey, travels **8** alacrity, campaign, celerity, dispatch, goodwill **9** excursion, readiness, swiftness **10** speediness **11** promptitude, punctuality

expeditious
   4 fast **5** fleet, hasty, quick, rapid, ready, swift **6** prompt, speedy **9** breakneck, effective, effectual, efficient **10** harefooted **11** efficacious

expeditiousness
   5 haste, hurry, speed **6** hustle, rustle **8** celerity, dispatch **9** swiftness

expel
   4 oust, spew **5** belch, eject, eruct, erupt, evict, exile **6** banish, deport, disbar, irrupt **7** blow off, blow out, cast out, drum out, exhaust, expulse, kick out, read out, turn out **8** disgorge, displace **9** ejaculate, eliminate, transport **10** expatriate
   prefix: **3** dis

expellee
   6 emigré

expend
   2 go **3** pay **4** blow, give **5** spend, use up, waste **6** finish, lay out, outlay, wash up **7** consume, exhaust, fork out **8** disburse, dispense, shell out **10** distribute, run through

expenditure
   4 cost **6** outlay **12** disbursement

expense
   4 cost, loss, toll **5** price **6** charge, outlay **7** forfeit **8** overhead **9** dec-

rement, sacrifice **10** forfeiture **11** deprivation **12** disbursement

expensive
   4 dear, high **6** costly **9** big-ticket **10** high-priced, immoderate **12** uneconomical

experience
   3 see **4** feel, have, know, live, meet, view **5** savor, skill, taste, trial **6** accept, behold, ordeal, suffer, survey, wisdom **7** know-how, receive, sustain, undergo **8** intimacy, practice **9** encounter, go through **10** background, inwardness **11** familiarity, observation, savoir faire **12** acquaintance
   anew: **6** relive
   combining form: **7** empirio **8** empirico

experienced
   3 old, vet **4** wise **6** versed **7** oldline, old-time, skilled, veteran, worldly **8** broken in, seasoned, skillful **9** practical, practiced, qualified, underwent **10** proficient **12** accomplished

experiential
   see **empirical**

experiment
   3 try **4** test **5** probe, study, trial, try on, weigh **6** search, try out **7** analyze, test out **8** analysis, research, trial run **10** scrutinize **11** examination, investigate **13** investigation, trial and error
   combining form: **7** empirio **8** empirico

experimental
   4 test **5** trial **9** empirical, temporary, tentative **11** preliminary, preparatory, provisional **13** developmental

experimentation
   4 test **5** trial **8** trial run **13** trial and error

expert
   3 ace, pro, wiz **4** deft, whiz **5** adept, crack, doyen, maven, mavin, swell **6** adroit, artist, master, mayvin, wizard **7** artiste, skilled, trained **8** masterly, schooled, skillful, virtuoso **9** authority, dexterous, masterful **10** master-hand, past master, proficient, specialist **11** crackerjack **12** passed master, professional
   suffix: **5** ician

expertise
   3 art **5** craft, knack, savvy, skill **7** ability, command, cunning, fi-

nesse, know-how, mastery **9** dexterity, quickness, readiness **10** adroitness, cleverness, competence, mastership **12** skillfulness **13** ingeniousness

expertness
5 knack, skill **7** ability, command, know-how, mastery **8** facility **10** mastership

expiate
3 pay **5** amend, atone, avert **6** remedy **7** correct, rectify, redress

expiation
9 atonement

expiatory
7 atoning, lustral **9** purgative **10** lustratory **11** purgatorial **12** propitiatory **13** expurgatorial

expiration
3 end **5** death **10** exhalation **11** termination

expire
2 go **3** die **4** conk, pass **5** lapse **6** demise, depart, elapse, exhale, perish, run out **7** decease **8** pass away **10** breathe out, outbreathe

explain
4 undo **5** clear, gloss, gloze, solve **6** acquit, define **7** absolve, account, analyze, clarify, clear up, condone, justify, resolve, unravel **8** annotate, construe, decipher, footnote, spell out, unriddle, untangle **9** break down, elucidate, exculpate, exonerate, interpret, vindicate **10** illuminate, illustrate, unscramble **11** disentangle, rationalize

explain away
7 account, justify **11** rationalize

explanation
3 key **6** excuse, motive, reason **7** account, example, grounds, meaning **8** exegesis **9** construal, rationale **12** unscrambling **13** enlightenment

explanatory
8 exegetic **10** discursive **12** enlightening, illuminating, illustrative, interpretive **13** demonstrative

expletive
4 cuss, oath **5** curse, swear **8** cussword **9** swearword (see also **exclamation**)

explicate
6 unfold **7** amplify, develop, explain, expound **8** construe, spell out **9** interpret

explication
8 exegesis **9** construal **11** development, enlargement

explicative
8 exegetic **10** scholastic **12** interpretive

explicit
4 open, sure **5** clear, exact, lucid, overt, plain **7** certain, correct, obvious, precise **8** accurate, clean-cut, clear-cut, definite, distinct, specific **10** definitive **11** categorical, perspicuous, unambiguous, unequivocal

explode
3 pop **4** fire **5** blast, burst, erupt, go off, shoot **6** blow up **7** deflate **8** break out, detonate, disprove, dynamite, mushroom, puncture **9** discharge, discredit **10** burst forth

exploit
3 act, job, use **4** blow, coup, deed, feat, gest, play, skin, soak, work **5** abuse, apply, bleed, stick, stunt **6** bestow, effort, employ, fleece, handle, jockey, parlay, stroke **7** beguile, emprise, finesse, utilize, venture **8** exercise, impose on, maneuver **9** adventure, cultivate **10** enterprise, impose upon, manipulate **11** achievement, performance, tour de force

explore
3 try **4** feel, sift, test **5** probe **6** burrow, go into, quarry, search **7** dig into, examine **8** look into, prospect, question **9** delve into, inquisite **11** inquire into, investigate

explorer
African: 3 Cam, Cao (Diogo) **4** Park (Mungo) **5** Grant (James), Laird (Macgregor), Speke (John Hanning) **6** Akeley (Carl, Mary), Burton (Richard), Lander (John, Richard) **7** Covilha (Pero da), Stanley (Henry) **8** Covilhao (Pero da) **10** Clapperton (Hugh) **11** Livingstone (David)
American: 4 Byrd (Richard), Hall (Charles Francis), Kane (Elisha Kent), Pike (Zebulon) **5** Clark (William), Lewis (Meriwether), Peary (Robert) **6** Henson (Matthew), Powell (John Wesley), Wilkes (Charles) **7** Fremont (John Charles)
Antarctic: 4 Byrd (Richard), Cook (Frederick), Ross (James Clark) **5** Fuchs (Vivian), Ronne (Finn), Scott (Robert Falcon) **6** Palmer (Nathaniel), Rymill (John Riddoch), Wilkes (Charles) **7** Weddell (James), Wilkins (George) **8** Amundsen (Roald),

d'Urville (Dumont) **9** Ellsworth (Lincoln) **10** Shackleton (Ernest)
Arctic: 3 Rae (John) **4** Byrd (Richard), Cook (Frederick) **5** Davis (John), Peary (Robert) **6** Baffin (William), Bering (Vitus), Henson (Matthew), Hudson (Henry), Nansen (Fridtjof), Nobile (Umberto) **7** Barents (Willem), Bennett (Floyd), Wilkins (George), Wrangel (Ferdinand von) **8** Amundsen (Roald) **9** Mackenzie (Alexander), MacMillan (Donald) **10** Stefansson (Vilhjalmur)
Australian: 7 Wilkins (George)
Austrian: 9 Weyprecht (Carl)
British: 12 Younghusband (Francis)
Canadian: 9 Mackenzie (Alexander) **10** Stefansson (Vilhjalmur)
Danish: 9 Rasmussen (Knud)
Dutch: 6 Tasman (Abel Janszoon)
English: 4 Cook (James) **5** Drake (Francis), Scott (Robert Falcon), Smith (John) **6** Baffin (William), Burton (Richard), Hudson (Henry) **7** Raleigh (Walter), Stanley (Henry) **9** Vancouver (George) **10** Shackleton (Ernest)
French: 7 Cartier (Jacques), La Salle (Sieur de), Nicolet (Jean) **8** Cousteau (Jacques) **9** Champlain (Samuel de), La Perouse (Comte de), Marquette (Jacques)
French Canadian: 6 Joliet (Louis) **7** Jolliet (Louis) **9** Iberville (Sieur d')
German: 6 Peters (Carl) **7** Humboldt (Alexander von)
Italian: 5 Cabot (John) **6** Nobile (Umberto)
New Zealand: 7 Hillary (Edmund)
Norwegian: 6 Nansen (Fridtjof) **8** Amundsen (Roald), Sverdrup (Otto) **9** Heyerdahl (Thor)
Portuguese: 6 Cabral (Pedro) **8** Magellan (Ferdinand)
Scottish: 3 Rae (John) **4** Park (Mungo), Ross (James Clark) **7** Thomson (Joseph) **11** Livingstone (David)
Spanish: 6 Balboa (Vasco Nunez de), Cortes (Hernando), de Soto (Hernando), Pinzon (Martin Alonso) **7** Mendoza (Pedro de), Pizarro (Francisco) **8** Bastidas (Rodrigo de), Coronado (Francisco de) **11** Ponce de Leon (Juan)

explosion
3 pop, pow **4** bang, gust **5** blast, burst, sally **6** access **7** flare-up **8** outburst **10** detonation

explosive
3 TNT **4** bomb, mine **5** nitro, troty **6** amatol, petard, powder **7** am-

monal, cordite, dunnite, grenade, lyddite **8** cheddite, dynamite, fulminic, melinite **9** fulminate **10** detonative **13** nitroglycerin
device: **3** cap **4** bomb, mine **5** shell **6** petard **7** grenade **8** firework
display: **9** fireworks
expert: **5** Maxim (Hudson)
sound: **3** pop, pow **4** bang, boom

exponent
6 backer **7** booster **8** advocate, champion, defender, partisan, promoter, upholder **9** supporter

expose
3 air **4** bare, open, risk, show **5** flash, peril, strip **6** debunk, flaunt, hazard, parade, reveal, show up, unfold, unmask, unveil **7** display, disport, exhibit, imperil, jeopard, lay open, publish, show off, subject, trot out, uncloak, uncover, undress **8** brandish, disclose, discover, endanger, jeopardy, muckrake, unclothe, unshroud **9** advertise, broadcast

exposé
10 revelation

exposed
4 bare, open **5** naked, prone **6** liable, likely, peeled **7** denuded, evident, menaced, subject, visible **8** apparent, manifest, revealed, stripped, unhidden **9** obnoxious, sensitive, uncovered **10** threatened **11** susceptible, unconcealed

exposition
4 fair, show **7** display, exhibit **8** analysis, exegesis **9** construal, discourse, statement **10** discussion, exhibition **11** delineation

expository
8 critical, exegetic **11** explanative, explanatory **12** interpretive

expostulate
4 kick **5** argue, fight **6** combat, debate, except, object, oppose, resist **7** discuss, dispute, protest **11** remonstrate

exposure
4 risk **5** peril **6** danger **8** jeopardy, openness **9** liability **12** helplessness, susceptivity **13** vulnerability

expound
5 state, teach **7** clarify, comment, explain, express, lecture, present **8** construe, describe, spell out **9** delineate, discourse, exemplify, explicate, interpret **10** illustrate

expounder
7 teacher **8** advocate, champion **9** proponent, supporter

express
3 air, put, say, set **4** give, mean, tell, vent, word **5** couch, crush, frame, spell, state **6** broach, convey, denote, impart, import, intend, phrase, voiced **7** add up to, connote, declare, signify, special, uttered **8** announce, clean-cut, clearcut, definite, disclose, especial, explicit, intended, proclaim, put about, specific **9** circulate, enunciate, formulate, out-and-out, pronounce, ventilate **10** definitive, individual, particular **11** categorical, communicate, intentional, unambiguous, unqualified
gratitude: **5** thank
regret: **9** apologize

expression
4 cast, face, form, look, mien, show, sign, vent, word **5** idiom, issue, motto, token, voice **6** clause, phrase, symbol, visage **7** gesture **8** locution, reminder **9** eloquence, facundity, statement, utterance, verbalism, vividness **10** embodiment, indication, reflection **11** countenance, graphicness, observation **13** demonstration, manifestation
combining form: **4** logy **5** logia
facial: **4** grin, phiz **5** frown, scowl, smile, wince **7** grimace
of assent: **3** aye, nod, yea, yes **4** okay **6** placet **9** exequator
of sorrow: **4** alas, tear
trite: **6** cliché **7** bromide **8** banality
witty: **4** quip **8** atticism

expressionless
4 dead, dull **5** blank, empty, stony **6** stolid, vacant, wooden **7** deadpan, vacuous **9** impassive **10** lackluster **11** inscrutable

expressive
4 rich **5** vivid **6** facund, lively, poetic **7** graphic **8** eloquent, emphatic, pregnant, senseful, spirited **9** pictorial, revealing **10** meaningful, revelatory **11** sententious, significant

expressly
4 even, just **6** as well, namely **8** in specie

expressway
4 road **7** freeway, highway, parkway **8** turnpike

expropriate
4 take **5** annex, seize **7** preempt

8 accroach **9** sequester **10** commandeer, confiscate, dispossess

expulse
4 oust **5** eject **6** banish, deport **7** cast out **8** displace, relegate **9** transport

expulsion
5 exile **7** ousting, removal **8** ejection **9** ostracism **10** banishment, driving out, forcing out, relegation **11** deportation **12** displacement

expunge
4 dele, drop, omit, x out **5** annul, erase **6** cancel, delete, efface **7** blot out, destroy, discard, exclude, wipe out **8** black out **9** eradicate **10** annihilate, obliterate

expurgate
4 blip **5** purge **6** censor, purify, screen **7** cleanse **10** bowdlerize

expurgation
9 catharsis, cleansing

exquisite
3 top **4** buck, dude, nice, rare **5** acute, blood, dandy **6** choice, dainty, fierce, select, superb **7** coxcomb, elegant, extreme, furious, intense, vicious, violent **8** delicate, finished, flawless, macaroni, superior, terrible, vehement **9** desperate, errorless, faultless, recherché **10** consummate, immaculate, impeccable

exsanguine
6 anemic **9** bloodless

exsect
6 cut out, excise

exsiccate
3 dry **4** sear **5** parch

exsuccuous
3 dry **4** sere **7** sapless **8** withered

extant
5 alive, being **6** actual, around, living **7** current, present **8** todayish **9** immediate **10** present-day **12** contemporary

extemporaneous
4 snap **6** casual **7** offhand **8** informal **9** impromptu, impulsive, unstudied **10** improvised, unprepared **11** unrehearsed **12** unthought-out

extempore
see **extemporaneous**

extemporize
3 act **5** ad-lib **7** dash off, toss off **8** knock off **9** improvise **11** improvisate

extend
2 go 3 eke, run 4 draw, give, grow, make, open, pose, span, vary 5 allot, award, boost, grant, offer, range, reach 6 accord, attain, beef up, bestow, confer, donate, fan out, spread, tender, unfold 7 advance, amplify, augment, draw out, enlarge, hold out, magnify, present, proceed, proffer, project, prolong, spin out, stretch 8 allocate, continue, elongate, heighten, increase, lengthen, multiply, protract 9 outspread 10 aggrandize, outstretch, prolongate

extended
combining form: 3 meg 4 mego 5 megal 6 megalo

extension
3 arm, ell 4 area, size, wing 5 ambit, annex, block, orbit, range, reach, scope, sweep 6 radius, spread 7 compass, purview, stretch 8 increase 9 magnitude 10 continuing, drawing out, elongation, production, stretch-out 11 enlargement, lengthening, prolongment, protraction 12 augmentation, continuation, prolongation, spreading out

extensity
5 ambit, orbit, range, reach, scope, sweep 6 radius 7 compass, purview

extensive
3 big 4 vast, wide 5 broad, hefty, large, major 6 scopic 7 blanket, general, immense, sizable 8 scopious, spacious 9 boundless, wholesale 10 large-scale 11 far-reaching, wide-ranging 12 considerable, far-spreading

extent
4 size, tune, writ 5 ambit, field, orbit, order, range, reach, scope, sweep, width 6 amount, degree, domain, matter, radius, sphere 7 breadth, compass, measure, purview 8 province, vicinity 9 magnitude 10 dimensions, proportion

extenuate
4 thin 5 white 6 temper, veneer, whiten 7 explain, justify, qualify, varnish 8 palliate, wiredraw 9 apologize, gloss over, gloze over, sugarcoat, whitewash 10 blanch over 11 rationalize

exterior
4 over 5 ectal, outer 6 facade 7 outmost, outside, outward, surface 8 external 9 outermost

exterminate
4 kill 5 abate 6 uproot 7 abolish, blot out, root out, wipe out 8 massacre 9 finish off, slaughter 10 annihilate, extinguish

external
3 out 4 over 5 ectal, outer 7 outmost, outside, outward 9 outermost 10 peripheral 11 superficial
combining form: 3 ect 4 ecto

externalize
6 embody 8 manifest 9 incarnate, objectify, personify 12 substantiate

extinct
4 cold, dead, gone, late, lost 5 passé 6 asleep, bygone, fallen 7 archaic, defunct, disused, outworn 8 deceased, departed, lifeless, obsolete, outmoded, perished, vanished 9 collapsed 10 antiquated, overthrown, superseded, unanimated 11 disappeared, nonexistent 12 old-fashioned
combining form: 4 necr 5 necro

extinction
5 death 11 destruction 12 annihilation, obliteration

extinguish
3 out 5 abate, check, crush, douse, erase, quash, quell 6 put out, quench, squash, stifle, uproot 7 abolish, blot out, blow out, destroy, expunge, put down, root out, smother, wipe out 8 suppress 9 eradicate 10 annihilate, obliterate

extirpate
4 raze 5 erase 6 cut out, efface, excise, resect, uproot 7 abolish, blot out, destroy, expunge, kill off, root out, wipe out 8 demolish 10 annihilate

extol
4 hymn, laud 5 bless, cry up, exalt 6 praise 7 applaud, commend, elevate, glorify, magnify 8 eulogize 9 celebrate 10 panegyrize

extort
3 get 4 milk, skin 5 bleed, cheat, educe, evoke, exact, force, gouge, pinch, screw, wrest, wring 6 coerce, compel, demand, elicit, evince, fleece, obtain, secure, wrench 7 squeeze 9 blackmail, shake down

extortion
8 chantage, exaction 9 blackmail

extra
3 odd 4 more, over 5 added,

spare 6 de trop, rarely 7 surplus 8 markedly 9 lagniappe, unusually 10 additional, especially, noticeably, uncommonly 11 superfluent, superfluous 12 considerably, particularly, supplemental 13 supernumerary, supplementary
prefix: 5 hyper, super

extract
3 dig, pry 4 cull, draw, milk, pull, tear, yank 5 educe, evoke, glean, wring 6 avulse, eke out, elicit, evince, evulse, garner, gather, pick up 7 abridge, distill, excerpt, scratch, shorten, squeeze 8 condense

extraction
5 birth, blood 6 origin 7 descent, essence, lineage 8 ancestry, pedigree 9 parentage

extraneous
5 alien, outer 6 exotic 7 foreign 9 pointless, unrelated 10 accidental, immaterial, inapposite, incidental, irrelative, irrelevant 11 impertinent, unessential 12 adventitious, inapplicable 13 inappropriate

extraordinary
3 odd 4 rare 6 unique 7 amazing, notable, unusual 8 singular, terrific, uncommon, unwonted 9 wonderful 10 noteworthy, remarkable, stupendous, tremendous 11 exceptional, unthinkable

extravagance
5 frill, luxus, waste 6 luxury 7 amenity 8 squander, unthrift 9 overdoing 10 lavishness 11 prodigality, superfluity 12 wastefulness

extravagant
4 wild 5 crazy, dizzy, outré, silly, undue 6 absurd, lavish 7 bizarre, foolish, profuse 8 prodigal, towering, wasteful 9 fantastic, ludicrous 10 immoderate, inordinate, profligate, ridiculous, unbalanced 11 exaggerated, implausible, nonsensical 12 preposterous, unmeasurable, unrestrained

extreme
3 top 4 deep, dire, last, peak, wild 5 crest, crown, dizzy, final, limit, rabid, ultra, undue 6 ardent, climax, excess, height, moving, summit, utmost 7 ceiling, drastic, fanatic, intense, maximum, outmost, radical, violent 8 farthest, furthest, pinnacle, remotest, towering, ultraist 9 desperate, excessive, outer-

most, uttermost **10** immoderate, inordinate, outlandish **11** culmination, furthermost, inordinancy, intolerable, unwarranted **12** consummation, revolutional, unmeasurable, unreasonable **13** revolutionary
degree: **3** nth

extremely
3 too **4** ever, over, very **6** mighty **7** parlous **8** overfull, overmuch **11** exceedingly

extremist
5 rabid, ultra **7** fanatic, radical **12** revolutional **13** revolutionary

extremity
3 arm, end, leg, tip **4** acme, apex, foot, hand, tail **5** limit, verge **6** apogee, vertex, zenith **8** terminal, terminus
combining form: **3** acr, akr **4** acro, akro

extricate
4 free **5** clear, loose, sever, untie **6** detach, rescue **7** deliver, discern, release, resolve, unravel, untwine **8** abstract, untangle **9** clear away, disburden, discumber, disengage **10** discrepate, disembroil, disentwine, disinvolve, severalize, unentangle, unscramble **11** disemburden, disencumber, disentangle, distinguish **12** disembarrass

extrinsic
5 alien, outer **6** gained **7** foreign, outside, outward **8** acquired, external **10** accidental, extraneous

extrude
3 out **4** spew **5** chase, chuck, eject, evict **7** boot out, dismiss, kick out, project **8** throw out

exuberance
4 life, zest **5** ardor **6** spirit **7** abandon, gayness **8** buoyancy **10** friskiness, liveliness **11** zestfulness **13** sprightliness

exuberant
3 gay **4** glad, lush, rank **5** brash, happy **6** ardent, fecund, lavish, lively **7** diffuse, fertile, opulent, profuse, riotous, zestful **8** fruitful, prodigal, prolific, spirited **9** ebullient, profusive, sprightly, vivacious **10** frolicsome, passionate **12** effervescent, high-spirited

exude
4 emit, ooze, seep, weep **5** bleed, sweat **6** strain **7** emanate, secrete, trickle **8** perspire **9** discharge, percolate

exult
4 brag, crow **5** boast, gloat, glory **7** delight, rejoice, show off, triumph **8** jubilate **9** celebrate

exultant
4 glad **5** happy **6** elated, joyous **7** flushed **8** jubilant **9** cock-a-hoop, overjoyed, rejoicing, triumphal **10** cock-a-whoop, delighting

exultation
3 joy **7** delight, rapture, triumph **8** gloating **9** jubilance, rejoicing **10** jubilation

exuviate
4 molt, shed, slip **5** moult **6** slough

eye
3 orb, tab **4** gape, gaze, lamp, look, loop, mind, ring, tail, view **5** grasp, optic, sight, stare, watch **6** behold, belief, goggle, look at, ocular, oculus, peeper, regard, seeing, size up, staple, vision, winker **7** blinker, feeling, opinion **8** attitude, consider, gaze upon, judgment, look upon, position, scrutiny, thinking **9** sentiment, viewpoint **10** conception, conclusion, conviction, persuasion, rubberneck, scrutinize **11** contemplate **12** surveillance
combining form: **3** ope, opy **4** ocul, opia, opto **5** oculo **8** ophthalm **9** ophthalma, ophthalmo **10** ophthalmia, ophthalmus
defect: **6** myopia **9** hyperopia **10** emmetropia, presbyopia **11** astigmatism
disease: **8** cataract, glaucoma, trachoma
doctor: **7** oculist **11** optometrist
opening: **5** pupil
part: **4** iris, lens, uvea **5** pupil **6** cornea, retina, sclera
relating to: **5** optic **7** optical
socket: **5** orbit
Spanish: **3** ojo

eyeball
3 see **4** ogle **6** look at **7** examine, observe

eye-catching
6 marked, signal **7** pointed, salient **9** prominent **10** noticeable, remarkable **11** conspicuous

eyedropper
7 pipette

eyeful
6 beauty, looker, lovely **7** stunner **8** knockout

eyeglass
4 lens **5** lense **7** monocle

eyeglasses
5 specs **6** lenses **7** lorgnon **8** pince-nez **9** lorgnette

eyelash
6 cilium

eyelid
8 palpebra **9** palpebrae (plural)
combining form: **7** blephar **8** blepharo

eyepiece
4 lens **6** ocular

eye-popping
8 exciting, stirring **9** thrilling **10** exhilarant **11** astonishing **12** exhilarative

eyesore
4 mess **5** sight **6** defect, fright **7** blemish, desight **11** monstrosity

eyespot
7 disease, ocellus

eyetooth
6 canine

eyewash
3 rot **5** bilge, hooey **6** bunkum **7** twaddle **8** malarkey, nonsense

eyewitness
6 viewer **7** watcher **8** beholder, bysitter, looker-on, observer, onlooker **9** bystander, spectator

eye worm
3 loa

eyrie
see aerie

Ezbon's father
3 Gad

Ezekiel's father
4 Buzi

Ezer's father
6 Jeshua **7** Ephraim

Ff

Fabian
4 Shaw (George Bernard) 8 cautious 9 socialist

fable
4 myth, tale 5 story 6 legend 7 fiction, figment 8 allegory, apologue
animal: 8 bestiary

fabric
3 rep, web 4 repp 5 cloth, fiber, grain 7 texture 8 building, material, shirting 9 structure
coarse: 5 crash, gunny 6 burlap, linsey, ratiné 7 cheviot, hopsack 8 homespun, osnaburg
corded: 3 rep 4 repp 5 piqué 6 calico, moreen, poplin 7 pinwale 8 corduroy, paduasoy 9 bengaline
cotton: 4 jean, leno 5 baize, chino, drill, scrim, swiss, wigan 6 chintz, dimity, faille, madras, muslin 7 etamine, galatea, gingham, nankeen, percale, silesia, ticking 8 chambray, dungaree, nainsook, osnaburg, tarlatan
cotton and linen: 4 huck 7 fustian 9 huckaback
crepe: 8 marocain
dealer: 6 draper, mercer
durable: 4 huck, jean 5 chino, denim, drill 6 frieze, moreen 7 lasting, ticking 8 cretonne, dungaree, osnaburg
embroidered: 9 baldachin, baldaquin 10 baldachino 11 baldacchino
finishing process: 8 lustring 9 mercerize 10 causterize
flag material: 7 bunting
glazed: 6 chintz 7 cambric, holland
knitted: 6 tricot 10 balbriggan
linen: 7 cambric, lockram
looped: 6 bouclé
lustrous: 4 silk 5 moiré, satin, surah 7 silesia, taffeta 12 brilliantine
metallic: 4 lamé
net: 5 tulle 8 bobbinet, illusion
openwork: 4 lace 8 filigree

ornamental: 4 lace 5 braid 6 ribbon 7 bunting
pebbly-surface: 6 armure 8 barathea
pile-surface: 5 panne, plush, terry 6 velour, velvet 7 bolivia, duvetyn, velours 8 chenille, moleskin, velveret 9 velveteen
plaid: 6 tartan
printed: 5 batik, toile 6 calico, chintz, damask 7 allover, challis, dornick, pintado 8 cretonne, jacquard 11 toile de jouy
raised pattern: 7 brocade 10 brocatelle
satin weave: 5 panne
sheer: 4 lawn 5 gauze, ninon, swiss, voile 6 barege, dimity, tissue 7 batiste, chiffon, cypress, organdy, organza, tiffany 8 tarlatan
silk: 4 acca, fuji 5 pekin 6 cendal, chappe, pongee, samite, sendal 7 alamode, foulard, grogram, schappe 8 paduasoy, sarcenet, sarsenet, shantung 9 bombazine
striped: 3 aba 4 abba 5 abaya, pekin 7 galatea, ticking 8 algerine 10 algerienne
synthetic: 5 ninon, nylon, Orlon, rayon 6 Dacron
twill: 4 jean 5 chino, drill, serge 7 foulard, galatea, nankeen, silesia, ticking 8 dungaree, shalloon 9 bombazine 10 broadcloth
unfinished: 6 greige
waterproof: 7 oilskin
wool: 5 baize, loden, tweed 6 caddis, camlet, duffel, duffle, melton, merino, wadmad, wadmel, wadmol, witney, woolen 7 caddice, delaine, whitney, woollen 8 algerine, mackinaw, prunella 9 cassimera 10 algerienne
wool, poor quality: 5 mungo 6 shoddy
wool mixture: 5 tammy 6 saxony, wincey, winsey 7 drugget, ratteen 8 moquette, shalloon, zibeline
woven: 4 weft 7 textile

fabricate
4 form, make 5 build, frame, shape 6 devise, invent, make up 7 concoct, fashion, produce, turn out 8 assemble, contrive 9 construct 11 manufacture

fabrication
3 fib, lie 4 opus, work 6 deceit 7 fiction, figment, product, untruth 9 falsehood

fabulist
French: 10 La Fontaine (Jean de)
Greek: 4 Esop 5 Aesop
Indian: 6 Bidpai, Pilpai, Pilpay
Roman: 8 Phaedrus
Russian: 6 Krylov (Ivan)

fabulous
7 amazing 8 mythical 9 legendary, wonderful 10 astounding, exorbitant, fictitious, incredible, inordinate, outrageous, prodigious, stupendous 11 astonishing, extravagant 12 mythological
animal: 6 dragon 7 centaur, unicorn
bird: 3 roc 6 simurg 7 simurgh
serpent: 8 basilisk 10 cockatrice

facade
4 face, mask, show 5 color, front, guise, put-on 6 veneer 8 disguise, pretense

face
3 mow, mug, top 4 cast, clad, dare, defy, gall, gaze, look, mask, meet, moue, phiz, pout, show, side, skin, veil 5 await, beard, brass, brave, cheek, cloak, close, cover, fight, front, frown, glare, guise, lower, mouth, nerve, paint, scowl, stare, watch 6 accost, border, brazen, breast, engage, expect, glower, makeup, mazard, muzzle, oppose, resist, take on, visage 7 affront, contend, grimace, outdare, seeming, sheathe, showing, venture 8 confront, disguise, features, mouthing, war paint 9 brashness,

challenge, encounter, semblance, withstand **10** appearance, confidence, effrontery, expression, false front, lineaments, maquillage, masquerade, simulacrum **11** countenance, physiognomy

facet
4 hand, side **5** angle, bezel, front, phase **6** aspect

facetious
5 comic, droll, funny, jolly, merry, witty **6** blithe, jocose, jocund, joking, jovial **7** comical, jesting, jocular **8** humorous **9** laughable, ludicrous **12** wisecracking

face-to-face
7 vis-à-vis

facile
4 able, deft, easy, glib **5** light, quick, royal **6** adroit, expert, fluent, simple, smooth **7** cursory, shallow, voluble **9** dexterous **10** effortless, uncritical

facilitate
3 aid **4** ease, help **6** assist **8** expedite

facility
3 aid, wit **4** bent, ease, tact, turn **5** poise, skill **7** abandon, address, amenity, comfort, fitting, leaning **8** aptitude **9** advantage, dexterity, lightness, readiness **10** smoothness **11** convenience, spontaneity **13** accommodation

facing
5 front, panel **6** before, contra, toward, veneer **7** against, vis-à-vis **8** covering, opposite, paneling **11** over against
down: **5** prone
up: **6** supine

facsimile
4 copy **5** ditto **6** carbon **7** replica **9** duplicate, imitation **10** carbon copy **11** replication **12** reproduction

fact
5 datum, event, truth **6** detail **7** episode, reality **8** incident **9** actuality, happening **10** observable, occurrence, particular, phenomenon **11** genuineness **12** authenticity, circumstance

faction
4 bloc, camp, part, ring, sect, side, wing **5** junto, party **7** combine **8** offshoot **11** combination

factious
7 warring **8** fighting **9** alienated, estranged, insurgent, seditious **10** contending **11** belligerent, contentious, disaffected, quarrelsome **13** insubordinate

factitious
4 sham **5** false **6** forced **7** assumed, feigned, man-made, shammed **8** affected **9** pretended, simulated, synthetic **10** artificial **13** counterfeited

___facto
4 ipso

factor
3 aid **4** doer, gene **5** agent, cause, maker, means, proxy **6** agency, deputy, helper **7** bailiff, element, steward **8** adjutant, assignee, attorney **9** assistant, coadjutor, component, consignee, majordomo, seneschal **10** antecedent, ingredient, instrument **11** determinant

factory
4 mill, shop **5** plant, works

factual
4 hard, true **5** valid **7** certain, genuine **8** absolute, positive **9** authentic, undoubted, veritable

faculty
4 bent, bump, gift, nose, turn **5** flair, knack, power **6** genius, talent **7** aptness, leaning **8** aptitude, capacity, function, instinct, penchant, property **12** predilection

facund
4 rich **8** eloquent, pregnant **10** expressive, meaningful **11** sententious, significant

fad
3 cry **4** chic, mode, rage, whim **5** craze, fancy, style, trend, vogue **6** furore, vagary, whimsy **7** caprice, conceit, fashion **10** dernier cri

fade
3 die, dim, ebb **4** dull, flag, melt, pale, thin **5** abate, clear, muddy **6** lessen, rarefy, vanish, weaken, wither **7** decline, dwindle, evanish, tarnish **8** diminish, dissolve, evanesce, languish, moderate **9** attenuate, disappear, evaporate **10** deliquesce **11** deteriorate

Faerie Queen, The
author: **7** Spenser (Edmund)
character: **3** Ate, Una **4** Alma **5** Guyon, Talus **6** Abessa, Amavia, Amoret, Arthur, Cambel, Duessa, Palmer **7** Artegal, Corceca, Fidessa, Maleger, Sansloy **8** Calidore, Florimel, Fradubio, Gloriana, Lucifera, Orgoglio, Satyrane **9** Archimago, Britomart **11** Britomartis

Fafner, Fafnir
brother: **5** Regin **6** Fasolt, Reginn
father: **8** Hreidmar
form: **6** dragon
slayer: **6** Sigurd **9** Siegfried
victim: **6** Fasolt **8** Hreidmar

fag
4 flag, tire **5** smoke, weary **6** drudge, tucker **7** exhaust, frazzle, outtire, outwear, servant, wear out **8** knock out **9** cigarette, prostrate

fag end
4 butt **7** remnant **8** last part

fail
3 ebb, end **4** bomb, bust, flag, fold, jade, lose, miss, omit, sink, slip, wane **5** break, close, crash, drain, flunk, short **6** falter, finish, forget, ignore, lessen, run out, shrink, slight, weaken, worsen **7** blink at, bust out, decline, default, deplete, dwindle, exhaust, flummox, founder, gazette, give out, neglect, wash out **8** bankrupt, decrease, diminish, discount, languish, miscarry, overlook, overpass **9** blink away, disregard, terminate **10** impoverish **11** deteriorate

failing
3 shy **4** vice **5** fault, scant, short **6** foible, scanty, scarce **7** frailty **8** weakness **9** deficient **10** deficiency, inadequate **12** imperfection, insufficient, unsufficient

failure
3 dud **4** bomb, bust, flop, hash, lack, miss **5** botch, fault, lemon, loser **6** dearth, defeat, ebbing, fiasco, fizzle, laxity, muddle, outage, waning **7** absence, debacle, decline, default, deficit, neglect, paucity, washout **8** collapse, flagging, poorness, scarcity, shortage, underage, weakness **9** insuccess, oversight, slackness, unconcern, unsuccess **10** bankruptcy, deficiency, exhaustion, inadequacy, meagerness, negligence, nonsuccess, remissness, scantiness, skimpiness **11** declination, defalcation, delinquency, dereliction, inferiority, miscarriage, shortcoming **12** debili-

tation, enfeeblement, imperfection, indifference **13** deterioration, insufficience, insufficiency, might-have-been

fain
4 glad **5** eager, prone, ready **6** minded **7** willing **8** desirous, disposed, inclined **11** predisposed

faint
3 dim, low, wan **4** coma, mild, pale, soft, swim, thin, weak **5** balmy, bland, blear, dusty, fuzzy, small, swoon, vague **6** bleary, feeble, gentle, hushed, smooth **7** blurred, grayout, languid, lenient, muffled, obscure, pass out, shadowy, stifled, syncope, unclear, vertigo **8** black out, listless **9** dizziness, inaudible, undefined **10** ill-defined, indistinct, undistinct

fair
4 calm, even, fine, just, mean, mild, pure, sane, show, so-so **5** balmy, blond, clean, clear, equal, light, right, ruddy, sunny, tawny **6** bazaar, blonde, candid, chaste, comely, common, dainty, decent, honest, lawful, lovely, medium, placid, pretty, square **7** average, clarion, clement, exhibit **8** balanced, carnival, charming, delicate, detached, festival, handsome, mediocre, middling, moderate, ordinary, pleasant, rainless, rational, straight, sunshine, sunshiny, tranquil, unbiased **9** beauteous, beautiful, cloudless, equitable, exquisite, impartial, objective, unclouded, uncolored **10** attractive, enchanting, exhibition, exposition, impersonal, open-minded, reasonable, sunshining, undarkened **11** good-looking, indifferent, nonpartisan, sportsmanly **12** intermediate, unprejudiced **13** disinterested, dispassionate, sportsmanlike, undistinctive, unthreatening

fair-haired
3 pet **4** dear **5** blond, loved **6** blonde **7** beloved, darling **8** blue-eyed, favorite, precious

fairness
6 equity **12** impartiality

fairy
3 elf, imp **4** pixy, puck **5** dwarf, elfin, gnome, nisse, pixie **6** goblin, kobold, sprite **7** banshee, brownie, gremlin **10** leprechaun
king: **6** Oberon
palace: **4** shee **5** sidhe

queen: **3** Mab **7** Titania
shoemaker: **10** leprechaun

fairy tale
author: **5** Grimm (Jacob, Wilhelm), Wilde (Oscar) **8** Andersen (Hans Christian), Perrault (Charles)
character: **6** Gretel, Hansel **8** Rapunzel **9** Snow White **10** Cinderella, Goldilocks

faith
4 cult, hope, sect **5** creed, stock, troth, trust **6** belief, church, credit, dogmas, tenets **8** credence, reliance, religion **9** communion, doctrines **10** confidence, connection, dependence, persuasion **12** denomination
article of: **5** tenet **9** credendum

faithful
4 fast, firm, just, true **5** exact, liege, loyal, pious, right, tried **6** ardent, loving, steady, strict, trusty **7** binding, devoted, staunch **8** constant, credible, reliable, resolute, trueblue **9** allegiant, authentic, steadfast, veracious, veridical **10** convincing, dependable **11** trustworthy, undistorted **12** affectionate **13** conscientious, dyed-in-the-wool

faithfulness
5 ardor, piety **6** fealty **7** loyalty **8** adhesion, devotion, fidelity **9** adherence, constancy **10** allegiance, attachment

faithless
5 false **6** fickle, untrue **7** erratic, unloyal **8** disloyal, recreant, unstable, wavering **9** changeful **10** capricious, changeable, inconstant, perfidious, traitorous **11** fluctuating, treacherous

faithlessness
7 falsity, perfidy, treason **8** betrayal **9** treachery **10** disloyalty, infidelity

fake
3 act, gyp **4** hoax, mock, sell, sham **5** bluff, bogus, false, feign, fraud, phony, put on, snide, spoof **6** affect, assume, doctor, forged, framed, humbug, pseudo **7** falsify, pretend **8** impostor, invented, simulate, spurious **9** brummagem, charlatan, concocted, fabricate, imitation, imposture, pinchbeck, pretended, pretender, simulated **10** fabricated, fictitious, fraudulent, simulation **11** counterfeit
combining form: **5** pseud **6** pseudo

fakir
7 ascetic **9** mendicant

falcon
4 hawk **5** hobby, saker **6** lanner, luggar, merlin **7** kestrel **9** peregrine
male: **4** jack **6** musket, tassel, tercel **7** sakeret, tiercel **8** lanneret
mature: **7** haggard, passage
young: **4** eyas **5** eyess **8** brancher

falcon-headed god
see at **Egyptian**

falconry
7 hawking
equipment: **4** bell, hood, jess, lure **5** bewet, bewit **7** creance
procedure: **3** imp **4** cope, seel

fall
3 dip, ebb, sag **4** drag, drip, drop, flop, plop, sink, skid, slip, trip, wane **5** abate, beset, crash, droop, lapse, let up, lower, pitch, plonk, plunk, slide, slump, storm, trail, yield **6** assail, attack, dangle, give up, go down, lessen, plunge, relent, sprawl, strike, submit, topple, tumble **7** aggress, assault, cascade, decline, descend, descent, die away, die down, drop off, ease off, go under, plummet, relapse, slacken, stumble, subside, succumb, wipeout **8** decrease, diminish, downcome, downfall, keel over, moderate, nose-dive **9** declivity, surrender

fallacious
3 mad **6** untrue **7** invalid **8** deluding, delusive, delusory **9** beguiling, deceiving, deceptive, illogical, sophistic **10** irrational, misleading, reasonless, unreasoned **11** nonrational **12** unreasonable

fallacy
4 idol **5** error, idola (plural) **6** idolum **7** elusion, evasion, falsity, quibble, sophism, untruth **8** delusion **9** casuistry, deception, falsehood, falseness, quibbling, sophistry **12** equivocation, misconstrual, speciousness, spuriousness **13** deceptiveness, erroneousness, misconception

fall back
6 recede, retire **7** relapse, retract, retreat **8** withdraw **9** retrocede **10** retrograde

fall behind
3 lag

fall flat
4 fail 5 flunk 7 bust out, flummox, wash out

fall guy
3 sap 4 butt, dupe, fish, fool, goat, gull 5 chump, patsy 6 pigeon, sucker 7 gudgeon 9 scapegoat 11 whipping boy

falling-out
3 row 4 beef, feud 5 run-in 6 hassle 7 dispute, quarrel 9 bickering 11 altercation, controversy

falloff
3 dip, sag 4 drop, slip 5 slump 7 decline 8 downturn 9 downslide, downswing, downtrend

fall out
2 go 3 row 4 spat, tiff 5 break, occur, scrap 6 betide, bicker, chance, happen, result 7 brabble, come off, develop, quarrel, wrangle 8 disagree, squabble

false
4 fake, mock, sham 5 bogus, dummy, hokey, lying, phony, snide, wrong 6 ersatz, hollow, pseudo, untrue 7 crooked, devious, seeming, unloyal, unsound 8 apostate, apparent, deluding, delusive, delusory, disloyal, recreant, renegade, specious, spurious 9 beguiling, brummagem, deceitful, deceiving, deceptive, dishonest, distorted, erroneous, faithless, illogical, imitation, incorrect, pinchbeck, simulated 10 artificial, fictitious, fraudulent, inaccurate, mendacious, misleading, ostensible, perfidious, substitute, traitorous, unfaithful, untruthful 11 backsliding, counterfeit, treacherous
combining form: 5 pseud 6 pseudo

false face
4 mask 5 visor 6 domino, vizard

false front
4 face, mask, show, veil 5 cloak, cover 6 facade 8 disguise 10 masquerade

falsehood
3 fib, lie 4 sham, tale 5 error, fraud, story 6 canard, deceit, fakery 7 fallacy, falsity, fibbery, untruth 8 feigning, pretense, untruism 9 mendacity 10 unveracity 11 fabrication 13 dissimulation, erroneousness, prevarication, truthlessness

falseness
5 error 7 fallacy, perfidy, untruth

8 apostasy 9 defection, desertion, recreancy 10 disloyalty, infidelity

false teeth
7 denture 8 dentures

falsify
3 fib, lie 4 cook, deny, fake, warp 5 alter, belie, color, fudge, twist 6 change, doctor, garble, palter 7 contort, distort, pervert 8 miscolor, misstate, traverse 10 contradict, contravene, equivocate 11 prevaricate 12 misrepresent

falsity
3 fib, lie 4 sham, tale 5 bluff, error, story 6 canard 7 perfidy, untruth 8 untruism 9 falsehood, hypocrisy 10 disloyalty, infidelity 11 fabrication, insincerity 12 uncandidness 13 erroneousness, faithlessness, prevarication

Falstaff
companion: 3 Nym 4 Peto 6 Pistol 8 Bardolph
composer: 5 Verdi
creator: 11 Shakespeare (William)
play: 7 Henry IV
prince: 3 Hal
tavern: 9 Boar's Head

Falstaffian
3 fat 6 coarse, jovial 8 boastful, humorous 9 dissolute

falter
4 halt, limp 5 lurch, quail, quake, shake, waver 6 blench, dither, flinch, quaver, recoil, shrink, topple, wobble 7 shudder, stagger, stumble, tremble, whiffle 8 hesitate, tick over 9 vacillate 12 shilly-shally

fame
4 note 5 éclat, glory, honor 6 renown, report, repute 7 acclaim 8 applause, eminence 9 celebrity, character, greatness, notoriety 10 prominence, reputation 11 acclamation, distinction, preeminence, recognition

famed
5 great, noted 7 eminent, notable 8 renowned 9 prominent 10 celebrated, celebrious 11 illustrious 13 distinguished

familiar
2 up 4 boon, cozy, easy, mate, snug 5 amigo, aware, close, fresh, thick 6 au fait, chummy, common, friend, genial, versed, wonted 7 abreast, affable, cordial, forward, mindful, prosaic, versant 8 amicable, everyday, frequent,

friendly, gracious, habitual, informed, intimate, sociable 9 au courant, cognizant, confidant, conscious, customary, intrusive, obtrusive, officious 10 accustomed, acquainted, conversant, neighborly 11 cater-cousin, comfortable, commonplace, impertinent

familiarity
8 intimacy 9 awareness, cognition, knowledge 10 experience, inwardness 12 acquaintance 13 comprehension, understanding

familiarize
3 use 4 wont 5 adapt, inure 6 adjust, season 8 accustom, acquaint 9 condition, habituate

family
3 kin 4 clan, folk, home, line, race 5 brood, folks, house, issue, stirp, stock, tribe 6 ménage, strain 7 dynasty, kindred, lineage, progeny 8 domestic 9 bloodline, household, offspring
branch: 6 stirps
lineage: 4 tree 6 stemma 8 pedigree 9 genealogy

famished
6 hungry 7 starved 8 ravenous, starving

famous
3 top 5 great, noted 7 capital, eminent, leading, notable, popular 8 five-star, renowned, superior, topnotch 9 estimable, excellent, first-rate, honorable, notorious, prominent, reputable, well-known 10 celebrated, celebrious, first-class 11 first-string, illustrious, prestigious, redoubtable, respectable 13 distinguished, well-thought-of

fan
4 blow, buff, open, wind 5 hound, lover 6 addict, expand, extend, rooter, ruffle, spread, unfold, votary, winnow 7 admirer, amateur, devotee, habitué 8 follower 9 outspread 10 aficionado, enthusiast, outstretch
combining form: 5 rhipi 6 rhipid 7 rhipido 8 flabelli
horseracing: 7 turfman
India: 5 punka 6 punkah
movie: 7 cineast

fanatic
3 bug, nut 5 bigot, fiend, freak, rabid, ultra 6 maniac, zealot 7 extreme, radical 8 ultraist 9 extremist 10 monomaniac 12 revolutional 13 revolutionary, revolutionist

fancier
6 votary 7 admirer, amateur, devotee

fanciful
5 false, wrong 6 absurd, unreal 7 bizarre, fictive, shadowy, strange 8 fabulous, illusory, imagined, mythical, notional, romantic 9 fantastic, fictional, grotesque, imaginary, legendary 10 apocryphal, chimerical, fictitious 11 unrealistic 12 preposterous

fancy
3 bee, fad 4 idea, like, mind, whim, will 5 dream, fable, freak, humor, image, think 6 liking, megrim, mirage, notion, vagary, vision, whimsy 7 approve, boutade, caprice, chimera, conceit, concept, endorse, feature, fiction, figment, imagine, realize, whimsey 8 conceive, crotchet, daydream, delusion, envisage, envision, illusion, phantasm, phantasy, pleasure, sanction, velleity 9 capriccio, elaborate, intricate, invention, nightmare, visualize 10 conception 11 complicated, envisioning, fabrication, fata morgana, imagination, inclination 12 contrariness, envisagement, perverseness 13 hallucination, irrationality

fan dancer
4 Rand (Sally)

fandango
4 ball 5 dance

fanfare
4 pomp, show 5 array, shine 6 parade 7 display, panoply 8 flourish
trumpet: 6 tucket

fanlike
7 plaited, plicate

fanny
4 seat 5 hiney 6 behind, bottom, heinie 7 hind end 8 backside, buttocks, derriere 9 posterior

fanon
5 cloth, orale 7 maniple 8 corporal

fan palm
7 talipot 8 palmetto

fantasize
7 imagine 8 daydream

fantastic
3 odd 4 wild 5 crazy, loony, queer, silly, wacky 6 absurd, adroit, clever, insane, mortal, unreal 7 bizarre, fictive, foolish, massive, strange 8 cracking, delusive, delusory, fanciful, illusory, romantic, singular, towering 9 deceptive, eccentric, fictional, grotesque, imaginary, ingenious, monstrous, unearthly, whimsical 10 capricious, chimerical, fictitious, incredible, irrational, misleading, monumental, prodigious, ridiculous, stupendous, tremendous 11 extravagant, implausible, nonsensical 12 preposterous, suppositious, unbelievable, unreasonable

fantasy
4 whim 5 dream, freak 6 bubble, vagary, vision, whimsy 7 caprice, chimera, rainbow, whimsey 8 daydream, illusion, phantasm 9 imagining, nightmare, pipe dream 10 bizarrerie, conceiving 11 envisioning, imagination 12 grotesquerie

Fantine's daughter
7 Cosette

far
4 deep, long, well 5 quite 6 rather, remote 7 distant, removed 8 off-lying, outlying, somewhat 12 considerably
combining form: 3 tel 4 tele, telo

far and away
4 just, very 5 quite 6 by odds 9 by all odds, decidedly, doubtless 10 absolutely, by long odds, definitely, positively 11 by a long shot, undoubtedly

far and near
7 all over, overall 8 all round 9 all around 10 everyplace, everywhere, throughout

far and wide
see **far and near**

faraway
4 lost 6 absent, dreamy, remote 7 bemused, distant, removed 8 distrait, heedless, off-lying, outlying 9 oblivious, unheeding, unmindful 10 abstracted, stargazing 11 inconscient, preoccupied 12 absentminded, disregardful

farce
4 mock, sham 7 mockery 8 travesty 9 burlesque 10 caricature

farceur
3 wag 4 zany 5 clown, cutup, joker 8 jokester

farcical
5 comic, droll, funny 6 absurd 7 risible 8 gelastic 9 laughable, ludicrous 10 outrageous, ridiculous 11 extravagant 12 preposterous

fare
2 do, go 3 hie, way 4 diet, food, pass, path, rate, wend 5 get by, get on, shift, track 6 manage, push on, repair, travel 7 advance, journey, proceed 8 get along, progress 12 stagger along

farewell
2 by 3 ave, bye 5 adieu, adios, aloha, congé 6 bye-bye, so long 7 good-bye, parting 9 bon voyage, departing 11 leave-taking, valedictory

farfetched
5 queer 6 forced 7 bizarre, erratic, labored, strange 8 strained 9 eccentric, fantastic, grotesque, recherché

far-flung
6 remote 7 distant, removed 8 off-lying, outlying

farinaceous
5 mealy 7 starchy
food: 4 meal 5 flour, salep 6 cereal 7 pudding, tapioca

farm
4 till 5 croft, ranch 6 grange, rancho 7 hennery 8 estancia, hacienda, hatchery, steading 9 cultivate, farmstead
building: 4 barn, shed, silo
Dutch: 6 bowery
Israeli collective: 7 kibbutz
Russian: 7 kolkhoz, sovkhoz

farmer
6 grower, tiller, yeoman 7 granger, planter, rancher 8 ranchero, ranchman 13 agriculturist
Israeli: 6 halutz
Russian: 5 kulak
South African: 4 Boer
tenant: 6 cotter 7 cottier, crofter 12 sharecropper

farming
7 tillage 8 agronomy 9 geoponics, husbandry 11 agriculture, cultivation, hydroponics

faro
5 monte
bet: 7 sleeper
card: 4 case, hock, soda

Faroes whirlwind
2 oe

far-off
6 remote 7 distant, removed 8 outlying

farrier
5 smith 10 blacksmith

farsighted
9 hyperopic, sagacious
10 presbyopic

farther
3 now 4 else, more 5 added, fresh
6 beyond, longer, yonder
10 additional

farthest
6 utmost 7 endmost, extreme, outmost 9 outermost, uttermost

fascinate
4 draw, grip, hold, sway, take, wile
5 charm, touch 6 absorb, affect, allure, appeal, engage, excite, occupy, please, strike 7 attract, bewitch, catch up, delight, enchant, engross, gladden, impress, rejoice
8 enthrall, entrance, interest, intrigue 9 captivate, enrapture, influence, magnetize, mesmerize, preoccupy, spellbind

fascination
5 charm 6 allure, appeal, glamor
7 glamour 8 charisma, witchery
9 magnetism 10 witchcraft
11 enchantment

Fascist
4 Nazi 6 Hitler (Adolph) 9 Mussolini (Benito)

fashion
3 cry, fad, ton, way 4 chic, form, make, mode, mold, plan, plot, rage, tone, vein, wise, wont
5 build, craft, craze, drift, erect, forge, frame, habit, modus, sculp, shape, style, thing, trend, usage, vogue 6 create, custom, design, devise, furore, manner, method, sculpt, system 7 produce, turn out
8 contrive, practice, tendency
9 bandwagon, construct, fabricate, technique 10 convention, dernier cri

fashionable
4 chic, tony 5 smart, swank, swish
6 modish, with-it 7 a la mode, current, dashing, popular, stylish 9 exclusive, prevalent 13 up-to-the-minute

fashion designer
American: 4 Head (Edith) 5 Beene (Geoffrey), Blass (Bill), Dache (Lilly), Ellis (Perry), Karan (Donna), Klein (Anne, Calvin) 6 Lauren (Ralph), Mackie (Bob) 7 Galanos (James), Halston, Mizrahi (Isaac) 8 Hilfiger

(Tommy) 9 Claiborne (Liz), de la Renta (Oscar), Gernreich (Rudi)
Anglo-French: 5 Worth (Charles)
French: 4 Dior (Christian) 6 Chanel (Coco) 6 Ungaro (Emanuel)
7 Montana (Claude) 8 Givenchy (Hubert) 9 Lagerfeld (Karl)
12 Saint-Laurent (Yves)
Italian: 5 Pucci (Emilio) 6 Armani (Giorgio) 7 Cassini (Oleg), Versace (Gianni)

fast
3 gay, lax, set 4 diet, easy, firm, hard, held, keen, lewd, soon, sure, true, wild 5 alert, apace, bawdy, brisk, fixed, fleet, hasty, liege, light, loose, loyal, quick, rapid, slack, stuck, swift, tight, wingy 6 active, ardent, firmly, lively, presto, pronto, raking, rakish, secure, snappy, speedy, sporty, stable, starve, strong, wanton, wedged 7 fixedly, flat-out, fleetly, hastily, lustful, quickly, raffish, rapidly, riotous, satyric, solidly, staunch, swiftly, tightly, whorish 8 careless, chopchop, constant, faithful, full tilt, heedless, indecent, promptly, rakehell, resolute, speedily, unchaste
9 breakneck, immovable, lecherous, libertine, lickerish, posthaste, salacious, tenacious 10 expeditive, harefooted, lascivious, libidinous, licentious, stationary 11 expeditious, incontinent 12 devil-may-care, inextricable, lickety-split 13 expeditiously

fasten
3 bar, bed, fix, gib, peg, pin, put, set, tie 4 bind, hank, hasp, hook, join, lash, link, lock, moor, seal, turn, weld 5 affix, apply, catch, clamp, clasp, cling, embed, focus, hitch, infix, latch, lodge, reeve, rivet, screw, stake, stick, strap, train, unite, wedge 6 adhere, anchor, attach, bundle, button, cleave, cohere, devote, direct, fixate, secure, settle, staple, zipper
7 address, connect, implant, mortise 9 concenter, establish
11 concentrate

fastener
3 pin 4 frog, snap, tack 5 catch, rivet 6 button, needle, staple, toggle 10 clothespin

fastidious
4 nice 5 fussy 6 choosy, dainty
7 choosey, finical, finicky 8 critical, exacting 9 demanding, finicking,

squeamish 10 particular, pernickety 11 persnickety 13 hypercritical

fastness
4 fort 5 guard 6 adytum, castle
7 citadel, defense, redoubt, retreat, sanctum, shelter 10 protection, stronghold

fast-talking
4 glib

fat
3 big, oil, top 4 best, bull, deep, flab, lard, pick, rich, suet, wide
5 beefy, broad, bulky, burly, cream, dumpy, elite, great, gross, heavy, husky, large, lipid, obese, pride, prime, pudgy, pursy, round, squat, stout, thick, tubby 6 brawny, choice, chunky, excess, fleshy, flower, grease, portly, rotund, stocky, stubby, tallow 7 adipose, blubber, fertile, orotund, paunchy, pinguid, porcine, ringing, surfeit, surplus, vibrant, wealthy, weighty
8 blubbery, heavyset, overflow, overkill, overmuch, overplus, oversize, plethora, resonant, sonorant, sonorous, thickset 9 consonant, corpulent, overblown 10 full-bodied, overweight, potbellied, productive, prosperous, resounding 11 superfluity, upholstered 13 overabundance
combining form: 3 lip 4 adip, lipo, sebi, sebo 5 adipo, lipar, steat
6 liparo, steato

fatal
5 death 6 deadly, doomed, lethal, malign, mortal 7 baleful, baneful, deathly, malefic, ruinous, unlucky
8 casualty, sinister 9 pestilent
10 calamitous, disastrous, ill-starred, maleficent, pernicious
11 cataclysmic, mortiferous
12 catastrophic, pestilential

fatality
5 death 9 virulence 10 deadliness, malignancy 11 noxiousness

fata morgana
6 mirage

fate
3 end, lot 4 doom 5 issue, karma, moira, weird 6 chance, doom to, effect, ending, kismet, result, upshot
7 destine, destiny, fortune, outcome, portion, preform 9 determine, preordain 10 foreordain, predestine 12 circumstance, predetermine 13 inevitability

fateful

5 acute 7 crucial, ominous, ruinous 8 critical, decisive 9 ill-boding, important, momentous 10 calamitous, conclusive, disastrous 11 apocalyptic, cataclysmic, significant, threatening 12 catastrophic, inauspicious, unpropitious 13 determinative

Fates

see at **Greek; Norse; Roman**

fathead

3 oaf 4 boob, dolt, goof 5 booby, chump, dunce

fatheaded

5 dense, thick 6 stupid 10 numskulled

father

2 pa 3 dad, get, pop 4 dada, make, papa, père, sire 5 beget, breed, daddy, hatch, maker, motor, mover, padre, pappy, pater, poppa, spawn 6 author, create, parent, priest 7 builder, creator, founder, produce 8 engender, generate, inventor, producer, promoter 9 architect, generator, initiator, organizer, originate, patriarch, procreate, supporter 10 encourager, ingenerate, introducer, originator, prime mover 11 inaugurator, progenerate, promulgator
combining form: 4 patr 5 patri, patro
of his country: 6 Cicero 10 Washington (George)
of history: 9 Herodotus
of medicine: 11 Hippocrates
of modern surgery: 4 Paré (Ambroise)
of the symphony: 5 Haydn (Joseph)
of waters: 11 Mississippi

Father Brown creator

10 Chesterton (Gilbert Keith)

fatherland

4 home, soil 7 country

fatherless

7 bastard, natural 8 baseborn, spurious 11 misbegotten 12 illegitimate

Father Time's implement

6 scythe

fathom

4 have, know 5 grasp, plumb, probe, savvy, sound 6 pierce 7 cognize 8 perceive 9 apprehend, penetrate, plumb-line, recognize 10 appreciate, comprehend, understand

fathomless

7 abysmal

fatidic

8 Delphian, oracular 9 prophetic, sibylline, vaticinal 11 prophetical

fatigue

3 irk, vex 4 jade, tire, wear 5 annoy, drain, ennui, spend, weary 6 bother, tucker, weaken 7 deplete, disable, exhaust, languor, wear out 8 weakness, wear down 9 faintness, lassitude, tiredness, weariness 10 debilitate, enervation, exhaustion, feebleness 12 debilitation, listlessness

Fatima

father: 8 Mohammed, Muhammad
husband: 9 Bluebeard
step-brother: 3 Ali

fatness

7 obesity 9 adiposity 10 corpulence

fatten

5 plump 6 batten, enrich 7 plumpen, stouten, thicken

fatty

4 oily 5 blimp, lardy, pudge, suety 6 greasy 7 adipose 8 blubbery, dumpling, potbelly, roly-poly, strapper, unctuous 10 butterball, oleaginous, overweight
combining form: 3 lip 4 adip, lipo 5 adipo, lipar 6 liparo

fatuous

4 dumb, fond 5 inane, silly 6 absurd, simple, stupid 7 asinine, foolish, idiotic, moronic, unwitty, witless 8 besotted, imbecile 9 brainless, insensate 10 infatuated, weak-headed, weak-minded 11 sheepheaded

faucet

3 tap 4 bung, cock, gate 5 spile, valve 6 spigot 7 bibcock, hydrant, petcock 8 stopcock

Faulkner

character: 5 Caddy, Jason 7 Candace, Quentin 8 Benjamin
family: 7 Compson
novel: 8 Sartoris 9 Sanctuary, The Hamlet 11 As I Lay Dying 13 Light in August

fault

3 nag, sin 4 carp, flaw, flub, lack, onus, slip, vice 5 blame, crime, error 6 defect, foible 7 blemish, blunder, demerit, failing, frailty, mistake, offense 8 weakness

9 infirmity, liability 10 deficiency 11 culpability, shortcoming 12 imperfection 13 answerability, transgression

faultfinder

4 crab 5 grump, momus 6 critic, grouch, Zoilus

faultfinding

6 critic 8 captious, critical 9 cavillous 10 censorious, particular, pernickety 12 overcritical 13 hypercritical

faultless

4 pure 5 clean, whole 6 entire, intact 7 correct, perfect 8 flawless, innocent, unguilty 9 blameless, exquisite 10 immaculate, impeccable, inculpable 13 unimpeachable

faulty

4 sick 5 amiss, wrong 6 flawed, marred 7 damaged, defaced, inexact 8 fallible, specious 9 blemished, defective, deficient, erroneous, imperfect, imprecise, incorrect, uncorrect 10 disfigured, fallacious, inaccurate, inadequate, incomplete
prefix: 3 dys

Faunus

grandfather: 6 Saturn
son: 4 Acis 7 Latinus

Faust

author: 6 Goethe (Johann von) 7 Marlowe (Christopher)
beloved: 8 Gretchen
composer: 6 Gounod (Charles)

faux pas

4 slip 5 boner, break, error, gaffe 6 boo-boo, bungle, howler 7 blooper, blunder, misstep, mistake, stumble 8 pratfall, screamer, solecism 9 indecorum, oversight 11 impropriety, misjudgment 12 indiscretion

favor

2 OK 3 aid, for, pro 4 back, boon, gift, help, okay 5 prize, value 6 accept, esteem, oblige, pamper, regard 7 account, approve, backing, endorse, forward, indulge, largess, present, respect, service, support 8 advocate, approval, blessing, courtesy, goodwill, hold with, kindness, resemble, sanction, simulate 9 approbate, encourage, patronage 10 admiration, appreciate, assistance, estimation, indulgence 11 accommodate, approbation, benediction, benevolence, convenience, cooperation, counte-

nance **12** dispensation **13** consideration, encouragement

favorable
4 good, kind, nice **5** brave, happy, lucky, white **6** benign, bright, dexter, kindly, timely, toward, useful **7** benefic, helpful, timeous, welcome **8** cheering, grateful, pleasant, pleasing, salutary **9** approving, benignant, fortunate, healthful, laudatory, opportune, praiseful, promising, well-timed, wholesome **10** auspicious, beneficial, gratifying, propitious, prosperous, reassuring **11** approbative, approbatory, encouraging, pleasureful **12** advantageous, commendatory, providential, well-disposed **13** complimentary

favoring
4 good **5** brave **6** toward, useful **7** benefic, helpful **10** beneficial, propitious **12** advantageous
prefix: **3** pro

favorite
3 pet **4** dear **5** loved **6** adored, prized **7** admired, beloved, darling, popular, revered **8** blue-eyed, esteemed, laudable, pleasant, precious **9** cherished, preferred, treasured, well-liked **10** fair-haired

favoritism
4 bias **8** cronyism, nepotism **9** prejudice

fawn
3 bow, woo **4** cave, coax, deer **5** abase, court, cower, crawl, defer, toady, yield **6** cajole, cotton, cringe, debase, demean, grovel, invite, kowtow, slaver, submit **7** flatter, honey up, truckle, wheedle **8** blandish, bootlick **10** ingratiate **11** apple-polish

fawning
4 mean **6** abject, humble, smarmy **7** ignoble, servile, slavish **8** toadyish, toadyism **9** adulatory, compliant, flunkyish, groveling, kowtowing, parasitic, spineless, sycophant, truckling **10** flattering, obsequious, submissive **11** bootlicking, deferential, subservient, sycophantic **12** mealy-mouthed, sycophantish

fay
3 elf **5** fairy, nisse, pixie **6** sprite **7** brownie

faze
3 vex **5** abash, annoy, daunt, worry **6** appall, bother, dismay, muddle, puzzle, rattle **7** confuse,

horrify, mystify, nonplus, perplex **8** confound, irritate **9** discomfit, dumbfound, embarrass **10** disconcert

FBI director
5 Freeh (Louis) **6** Hoover (John Edgar)

fealty
5 ardor, faith, truth **7** loyalty, support **8** devotion, fidelity, trueness **10** allegiance **11** devotedness **12** faithfulness

fear
3 awe **4** funk **5** alarm, angst, dread, panic, scare, worry **6** dismay, esteem, fright, horror, phobia, terror **7** anxiety, concern, respect **8** cold feet, disquiet, timidity **9** agitation, cowardice, misgiving, reverence, trepidity **10** foreboding **11** disquietude, trepidation **12** apprehension, cowardliness, discomposure, perturbation, presentiment, timorousness
combining form: **4** phob **5** phobe, phobo **6** phobia, phobic **7** phobous
of animals: **9** zoophobia
of being buried alive: **11** taphephobia
of cats: **12** aelurophobia, ailurophobia
of crowds: **11** ochlophobia
of darkness: **11** nyctophobia
of dirt: **10** mysophobia
of fire: **10** pyrophobia
of heights: **10** acrophobia
of men: **11** androphobia
of new things: **9** neophobia
of open areas: **11** agoraphobia
of pain: **10** algophobia
of strangers: **10** xenophobia
of thunder: **12** brontophobia
of water: **11** hydrophobia
of women: **10** gynophobia

fearful
4 dire, grim **5** awful, lurid, scary, timid **6** afraid, aghast, grisly, malign, scared, uneasy **7** alarmed, anxious, ghastly, jittery, macabre, nervous, panicky, sublime, worried **8** aflutter, agitated, alarming, dreadful, gruesome, horrible, horrific, shocking, sinister, terrible, terrific, timorous **9** appalling, concerned, disturbed, frightful, perturbed, terrified **10** disquieted, formidable, frightened, horrendous, solicitous, terrifying, tremendous **11** discomposed, frightening, redoubtable **12** apprehensive

fearless
4 bold, game, sure **5** brave **6** daring **7** assured **8** intrepid, sanguine, unafraid **9** audacious, confident, dauntless **10** courageous **11** lionhearted

feasible
6 doable, likely, viable **8** possible, workable **9** practical **11** practicable

feast
3 eat **4** dine, meal **6** dinner, regale, repast, spread **7** banquet **8** potlatch
Hawaiian: **4** luau
Scottish: **3** foy

Feast of Lights
8 Hanukkah

Feast of Lots
5 Purim

Feast of Tabernacles
7 Sukkoth

Feast of Weeks
8 Shabuoth

feat
3 act **4** deed, gest **5** geste, stunt, trick **6** action **7** emprise, exploit, venture **9** adventure **10** enterprise **11** achievement, tour de force

feather
3 ilk **4** down, kind, sort, type **5** breed, order, pinna, plume, quill **6** fledge, fletch, pinion **7** species, variety
combining form: **4** pinn, pter, ptil **5** penni, penno, pinni, ptero, ptile, ptilo
kind: **4** down **5** penna, remex **6** covert **7** contour, plumule, rectrix, tectrix, tertial **8** scapular, tertiary
part: **3** web **4** barb, vane **5** shaft **7** barbule **8** barbicel

featherbrained
5 dizzy, giddy, silly **7** flighty **8** skittish **9** frivolous **11** empty-headed, hare-brained **13** rattlebrained

feathered
7 pennate, plumose **8** pennated

feather-like
7 pinnate, plumate **8** pinnated

feathers
7 plumage

featherweight
4 simp **5** dunce, light **6** dimwit, nitwit **7** lackwit, pinhead, unheavy, wantwit

feature

4 item, mark 5 fancy, image, point, savor, think, trait 6 aspect, detail, factor, play up, stress, virtue, vision 7 article, element, imagine, quality, realize 8 conceive, envisage, envision, property 9 affection, attribute, birthmark, character, component, emphasize, italicize, underline, visualize 10 ingredient, particular, underscore 11 constituent

febrile

5 fiery 7 fevered, pyretic 8 feverish

feces

4 dung 5 waste 7 excreta 9 excrement
combining form: 4 copr, scat 5 copro, scato

feckless

4 wild 6 remiss 7 fustian, useless 8 careless, heedless, uncaring 9 shiftless, uncareful, unheeding, unrecking, worthless 10 incautious, unpurposed, unreliable, unthinking 11 inadvertent, meaningless, purposeless, thoughtless 12 irreflective, undependable, unreflective 13 irresponsible, lackadaisical, untrustworthy

fecund

4 rich 7 fertile 8 childing, fruitful, prolific, spawning 10 productive 11 proliferant

fecundity

9 eloquence, fertility 10 expression 11 prodigality, profuseness, prolificacy 12 expressivity, fruitfulness, productivity

Federalist writer

3 Jay (John) 7 Madison (James) 8 Hamilton (Alexander)

federation

5 union 6 league 8 alliance 9 coalition 11 association, confederacy

fedora

3 hat

fed up

4 sick 5 bored, tired, weary 9 disgusted

fee

3 pay, tax 4 cost, dues, hire, wage 5 price 6 charge, salary 7 expense, payment, stipend, tuition 8 retainer 9 emolument 10 recompense
minting: 8 brassage 10 seignorage 11 seigniorage
wharf: 7 quayage

feeble

4 puny, weak 5 frail 6 ailing, flimsy, infirm, senile, sickly, weakly 7 doddery, fragile, sapless, tenuous 8 decrepit 9 doddering 13 insubstantial

feebleminded

4 dull, slow 7 moronic 8 backward, imbecile, retarded 9 dim-witted 10 half-witted, slow-witted 12 simpleminded

feebleness

7 disease, malaise 8 debility 9 infirmity 10 infirmness, sickliness 11 decrepitude

feed

3 eat 4 find, food, give, grub, hand, meal 5 feast, graze 6 devour, fatten, fodder, ingest, repast, supply, viands 7 banquet, consume, deliver, dish out, edibles, furnish, nourish, nurture, provide, sustain 8 dispense, hand over, victuals 9 partake of, provender, refection 10 provisions
combining form: 4 phag 5 phago

feed the kitty

4 ante

feel

3 air, paw 4 aura, deem, hold, know, mood 5 grope, guess, savor, sense, sound, taste, think, touch 6 assume, credit, endure, finger, fumble, handle, notice, suffer 7 believe, explore, grabble, observe, palpate, presume, suppose, surmise, suspect, undergo 8 consider, perceive 9 semblance, tactility

feeler

4 palp, test 5 probe, query 6 palpus 7 antenna, inquiry 10 intimation, prospectus 12 trial balloon

feeling

3 air 4 aura, mind, mood, vein, view 5 humor, sense, touch 6 belief, morale, notion, temper 7 emotion, opinion, outlook, passion, sensate 8 attitude, passible, reaction, sentient 9 affection, emotional, semblance, sensation, sensitive, sentiment 10 atmosphere, conviction, persuasion 11 affectivity, emotionable, palpability, sensibility, sensitivity, tangibility
combining form: 5 pathy 6 pathic

feign

3 act 4 fake, sham 5 bluff, put on 6 affect, assume 7 connive, pretend 8 simulate 11 counterfeit

feint

3 jig 4 fake, hoax, play, ploy, ruse, sham, wile 5 trick 6 gambit 7 whizzer 8 maneuver 9 stratagem
fencing: 5 appel
hockey: 4 deke

feldspar

6 albite 8 andesine, sanidine 9 anorthite, moonstone 10 microcline, orthoclase 11 labradorite, plagioclase
clay: 6 kaolin

felicitate

6 salute 7 commend 10 compliment 12 congratulate

felicitous

3 apt, fit 4 just, meet 5 happy 6 proper, timely 7 apropos, fitting 8 apposite, suitable 9 well-timed 10 applicable, seasonable 11 appropriate

feline

3 cat, tom 4 lion, lynx, pard, puma, puss 5 catty, felid, pussy, tiger 6 bobcat, cougar, jaguar, margay, ocelot, tomcat 7 catlike, cheetah, furtive, leonine, leopard, lioness, panther, tigress, wildcat 8 pussycat, stealthy
hybrid: 5 liger, tigon 6 tiglon

fell

3 cut, fur, hew 4 chop, down, drop, grim, hide, kill, pelt, raze, skin, ugly 5 cruel, floor, grave, level, major 6 deadly, fierce, ground, jacket, lay low, savage, tumble 7 fearful, flatten, inhuman, mow down, serious, wolfish 8 bowl down, bowl over, grievous, horrible, horrific, inhumane 9 barbarous, bring down, dangerous, ferocious, knock down, knock over, prostrate, shoot down, throw down, truculent

Fellini film

8 Amarcord, Casanova, La Strada 9 Satyricon 11 La Dolce Vita

fellow

2 he 3 boy, bub, guy, joe, lad, man 4 bozo, buck, chap, gent, mate, peer, twin 5 bloke, match 6 codger, cohort, double, hombre, person 7 consort, partner 8 confrere 9 associate, companion, copartner, duplicate, gentleman 10 consociate, coordinate, reciprocal 11 concomitant 12 contemporary
prefix: 2 co

fellowship

4 club 5 guild, order, union
6 league 7 company, society 8 alliance, sodality 10 fraternity 11 association, brotherhood, camaraderie 13 companionship

felon

8 criminal, offender 10 lawbreaker, malefactor

felt hat

6 fedora

female

4 girl 5 woman 7 womanly 8 feminine, womanish
combining form: 3 gyn 4 gyne, gyno, gyny 5 gynec, gyneo, thely 6 gynaec, gynaeo, gyneco, gynous 7 gynaeco
suffix: 3 ess, ine 4 ette, trix

femme fatale

5 siren 7 Lorelei 9 temptress
10 seductress

fen

3 bog 4 mire, quag 5 marsh, swamp 6 morass, slough 7 baygall 8 quagmire

fence

3 bar, hem, mew, pen 4 cage, duck, mure, stop, wall, weir
5 block, dodge, hedge, parry, shirk 6 corral, immure, paling 7 barrier, enclose, railing 8 blockade, palisade, sidestep, stockade 9 barricade, roadblock 12 circumscribe

fencer

7 duelist, épéeist 8 foilsman
9 swordsman

fencing

9 swordplay
attack: 5 lunge 6 thrust 7 reprise, riposte
defense: 5 parry
movement: 4 volt
ploy: 5 appel
position: 5 prime, sixte, terce 6 octave, quarte, quinte, tierce 7 seconde, septime
term: 4 jury 5 forte, lunge, piste 6 flèche, foible, pointe, touché 7 sabreur, stop cut, stop-hit 11 corps-à-corps
touch: 3 cut, hit 5 punto
weapon: 4 épée, foil 5 blade, guard, saber, sabre 6 pommel

fend

4 ward 5 avert, avoid, cover, guard, parry, rebut, repel 6 defend, rebuff, resist, screen, secure, shield 7 bulwark, deflect, hold off, keep off, protect, repulse, ward off 8 stave off 9 safeguard

fender

5 guard 6 buffer, shield
8 mudguard

Fenrir

chain: 8 Gleipnir
father: 4 Loki
form: 4 wolf
mother: 9 Angerboda
10 Angerbotha
slayer: 5 Vidar 6 Vithar
victim: 4 Odin

feral

4 wild 5 brute 6 animal, brutal, ferine, fierce, savage 7 beastly, bestial, brutish, inhuman, swinish, untamed, vicious 8 barbaric 9 barbarous, ferocious

Ferber novel

5 Giant, So Big 8 Cimarron, Show Boat, The Girls 9 Ice Palace

Ferber or Millay

4 Edna

Ferdinand

beloved: 7 Miranda
father: 6 Alonso

Ferdinand, King

conquest: 7 Granada
daughter: 6 Joanna
wife: 8 Germaine, Isabella

ferment

4 boil, stir 5 churn 6 bubble, clamor, foment, leaven, outcry, seethe, simmer, tumult, unrest, upturn 7 agitate, ailment, smolder, turmoil 8 disquiet, upheaval 9 commotion 10 convulsion, inquietude 11 disquietude, restiveness 12 restlessness

fermentation

7 zymosis

fern

4 tree 5 brake, holly, royal 6 Boston 7 bracken, woodsia 8 polypody 10 maidenhair, spleenwort
combining form: 6 pterid, pteris 7 pterido
leaf: 5 frond

ferocious

4 fell, grim 5 brute, cruel, feral 6 brutal, fierce, savage 7 bestial, inhuman, vicious, violent, wolfish 8 inhumane, ravening, ravenous 9 barbarous, rapacious, truculent 10 implacable, relentless 12 bloodthirsty

ferret out

4 hunt, seek 5 learn, probe, quest 6 elicit 7 extract 8 discover 9 ascertain, cast about, determine, search for, search out

Ferrex's brother

6 Porrex

ferrule

3 cap, tip 4 band, knob

ferry

3 lug 4 bear, buck, pack, tote
5 carry 6 convey 9 transport

ferryman of Hades

6 Charon

fertile

4 lush, rich 6 fecund 7 bearing, copious 8 abundant, childing, creative, fruitful, pregnant, prolific, spawning, yielding 9 bountiful, ingenious, inventive, luxuriant, plenteous, producing 10 productive 11 proliferant

fertilize

6 enrich 9 pollenate, pollinate
10 impregnate, inseminate

fertilizer

4 dung, marl 5 guano 6 manure
7 compost

ferule

3 rod 5 ruler, stick 6 switch

fervent

3 hot 4 keen 5 eager, fiery 6 ardent, devout, hearty 7 blazing, burning, earnest, glowing, intense, sincere 8 vehement 9 heartfelt, perfervid 10 hot-blooded, passionate 11 impassioned 12 enthusiastic, wholehearted

fervor

4 fire, zeal 5 ardor 6 hurrah, warmth 7 passion 9 calenture, sincerity, vehemence 10 devoutness, enthusiasm, heartiness 11 earnestness

fess up

3 own 4 avow 5 admit, allow, grant, let on, own up 7 concede, confess 11 acknowledge

fester

3 rot 5 ulcer 6 rankle 7 influme, putrefy 8 ulcerate 9 suppurate

festina _____

5 lente

festival

4 fair, fete, gala 5 feast, gaudy
6 fiesta 8 carnival 9 festivity
11 celebration

festive
3 gay 4 gala 5 jolly, merry
6 blithe, jocund, jovial, joyous
7 gleeful 8 mirthful 10 blithesome
12 lighthearted

festivity
5 revel 6 gaiety 7 jollity, revelry,
whoopee 8 reveling 9 merriment,
revelment 11 celebration,
merrymaking

fetch
4 sell 5 bring 7 bring in

fetching
6 luring 7 Circean 8 alluring, enticing, tempting

fete
4 fair 5 party 6 bazaar 8 festival
9 entertain 11 celebration

fetid
4 foul, rank 6 putrid, rancid, smelly
7 rankish, reeking 8 mephitic, stinking 10 malodorous

fetish
4 idol, juju, luck, zemi 5 charm,
mania, thing 6 amulet, mascot
7 periapt 8 fixation, gris-gris, penchant, talisman 9 obsession
10 phylactery

fetter
3 tie 4 clog, curb 5 leash 6 hamper, hobble, hog-tie 7 manacle,
shackle, trammel 8 handcuff, restrain 9 entrammel

fettle
4 trim 5 order, shape 6 kilter, repair 7 fitness 9 condition

feud
3 row 5 run-in 6 combat, fracas
7 contest, dispute, quarrel 8 argument, squabble, vendetta 9 bickering 10 falling-out 11 altercation,
controversy

feudal
estate: 4 feod, feud, fief
jurisdiction: 3 soc 4 soke
laborer: 4 serf
lord: 5 liege 8 suzerain
service: 5 avera
status: 9 vassalage
tax: 5 tallage
tenant: 6 vassal 7 homager, socager, sokeman, vavasor
8 vavasour
tenure of land: 6 socage
tribute: 6 heriot

fever
4 ague, fire 6 dengue 7 ferment,
pyrexia 9 calenture

combining form: 5 febri, pyret
6 pyreto
recurrent: 6 sextan 7 malaria, quar-
tan, quintan, tertian

feverish
3 hot 5 fiery 6 fervid, heated, hectic 7 burning, excited, febrile,
flushed, furious, pyretic 8 febrific,
frenzied, inflamed 10 passionate
11 overwrought

fever tree
7 blue gum

few
4 rare 6 scarce, seldom, smatch
7 handful, smatter, spatter 8 sporadic, uncommon 10 infrequent,
occasional, scattering, smattering,
spattering, sprinkling, unfrequent
combining form: 4 olig 5 oligo,
pauci

———-fi
2 hi 3 sci

fiat
5 edict, order 6 decree 7 command 8 sanction 11 endorsement
12 proclamation

fib
3 lie 4 tale 5 story 6 canard, palter 7 falsify, falsity, untruth 9 falsehood, mendacity 10 equivocate
11 evasiveness, prevaricate
13 prevarication

fiber
3 web 4 noil, pita 5 grain, istle
6 fabric, strand, thread 7 texture
basketry: 5 istle
brain: 4 pons
coarse: 4 adad, jute 8 piassava
coconut husk: 4 coir, kyar
combining form: 2 in 3 ino 4 fibr
5 fibro
knot: 3 nep
rope: 5 sisal 8 henequen
silky: 5 kapok
small: 6 fibril
substructure: 7 micelle, spongin
synthetic: 5 nylon, rayon, saran,
vinal
woody: 4 bast
woollike: 7 lanital

fibrous
4 ropy, wiry 6 sinewy 7 stringy
8 muscular

fibula
5 clasp 7 leg bone

fickle
7 flighty, moonish 8 ticklish, unstable, variable, volatile 9 mercurial

10 capricious, changeable, inconstant, lubricious, unfaithful, unreliable 12 undependable
13 temperamental

fiction
4 tale, yarn 5 fable, story 6 deceit
7 fantasy, figment 9 fish story, invention, narrative 10 concoction
11 fabrication

fictional
5 false, phony 6 unreal 7 fictive
8 fanciful, illusory 9 fantastic, imaginary 10 chimerical, fictitious
12 suppositious

fictitious
4 fake, mock, sham 5 false 6 ersatz, made-up, unreal, untrue 7 assumed, created, fictive 8 cooked-
up, fanciful, illusory, invented
9 concocted, fantastic, fashioned,
fictional, imaginary, simulated,
trumped-up 10 artificial, chimerical,
fabricated 12 suppositious
combining form: 5 pseud 6 pseudo

fiddle
4 fool, mess, play 6 dabble, doodle, fidget, handle, monkey, potter,
puddle, putter, tinker, trifle, violin
10 mess around

fiddle-faddle
4 bosh 5 fudge, hooey 6 bunkum,
piffle 8 nonsense, pishposh
10 flapdoodle

Fidelio
composer: 9 Beethoven (Ludwig van)
hero: 9 Florestan
heroine: 7 Leonora

——— fidelis
6 semper

fidelity
5 ardor, piety 6 fealty 7 loyalty
8 adhesion, devotion 9 adherence,
constancy 10 allegiance, attachment 11 reliability, staunchness
12 faithfulness 13 dependability,
steadfastness

fidget
4 play 6 fiddle, jitter, trifle
7 twiddle

fidgety
5 fussy, jumpy, nervy 6 goosey,
spooky 7 jittery, nervous, restive,
twitchy 8 restless, twittery 9 unrestful 10 high-strung

field
4 area, walk 5 milpa 6 domain,
meadow, region, sphere 7 demesne, terrain 8 dominion, pre-

cinct, province **9** bailiwick, champaign, territory **10** department
combining form: 4 agro

fieldbird
6 plover

field crop
3 hay **5** grain **6** cotton

field deity
3 Pan **4** Faun **5** Fauna

field glasses
10 binoculars

field hand
4 hoer **5** sower **6** picker **7** laborer, planter

Fielding novel
6 Amelia **8** Tom Jones **13** Joseph Andrews

field marshal
Austrian: **8** Radetzky (Joseph)
British: **6** Napier (Robert), Raglan (Baron), Wavell (Archibald), Wilson (Henry) **7** Roberts (Frederick) **8** Wolseley (Garnet) **9** Kitchener (Horatio) **10** Montgomery (Bernard)
French: **4** Foch (Ferdinand) **6** Joffre (Joseph-Jacques-Cesaire), Pétain (Philippe)
German: **6** Keitel (Wilhelm), Paulus (Friedrich), Rommel (Erwin), Rupert (Prince) **9** Mackensen (August von), Rundstedt (Karl von), Waldersee (Alfred von) **10** Kesselring (Albert)
Japanese: **8** Sugiyama (Gen)
Prussian: **6** Moltke (Helmuth von)
Russian: **7** Kutuzov (Mikhail), Suvorov (Aleksandr) **8** Potemkin (Grigory)

field mouse
4 vole

Field of Blood
8 Aceldama

field officer
5 major **7** colonel

field rat
5 metad

fiend
3 bug, nut **5** bigot, demon, devil, freak, Satan **6** diablo, maniac, zealot **7** fanatic, Lucifer, Old Nick, serpent **8** Apollyon, succubus **9** Beelzebub **10** enthusiast, Old Scratch **13** Old Gooseberry

fiendish
5 cruel **6** malign, savage, wicked **7** baleful, demonic, hellish, inhuman, malefic, satanic, vicious **8** demoniac, demonian, devilish, diabolic, infernal, sinister **9** barbarous, ferocious, malicious, malignant

fierce
4 fell, grim, wild **5** cruel **6** brutal, savage **7** brutish, enraged, furious, inhuman, intense, vicious, violent, wolfish **8** inhumane, maddened, pitiless, ruthless, terrible, tigerish, vehement **9** barbarous, bellicose, desperate, ferocious, merciless, truculent **10** aggressive, cannibalic, infuriated, pugnacious **11** belligerent

fiery
3 hot **5** afire **6** ablaze, aflame, ardent, fervid, fierce, heated, red-hot, spunky, torrid **7** blaring, blazing, burning, febrile, fervent, fevered, flaming, flaring, gingery, igneous, ignited, intense, peppery **8** broiling, feverish, inflamed, scalding, sizzling, spirited, vehement, white-hot **9** hot-headed, perfervid, scorching **10** mettlesome, passionate **11** conflagrant, impassioned **12** high-spirited

fifteen
combining form: 8 pentadec **9** pentadeca

fifth
combining form: 5 quint **6** quinti

fig
genus: **5** Ficus
sacred: **5** pipal
variety: **5** eleme, elemi **6** Smyrna

fight
3 row, tug, war **4** beef, bout, buck, duel, feud, fray, spat, tiff **5** brawl, broil, clash, joust, melee, repel, scrap, words **6** affray, attack, battle, bicker, combat, debate, fracas, hassle, oppose, oppugn, resist, strive, tussle **7** contend, contest, crusade, dispute, quarrel, scuffle, wrangle, wrestle **8** skirmish, slugfest, squabble, struggle, traverse **9** bickering, pugnacity, withstand **10** aggression, donnybrook **11** altercation **12** belligerence, disagreement **13** combativeness
combining form: 5 machy

fighter
2 GI **4** swad **5** boxer **7** soldier, warrior **8** pugilist, scrapper **9** man-at-arms

fighter plane
3 MiG, Roc **4** Zero **5** Sabre **6** Fokker, Hawker, Mirage, Voodoo **7** Corsair, Harrier, Stealth **8** Spitfire

fighting fish
5 betta

figment
5 dream, fable, fancy **6** bubble **7** chimera, fiction **8** daydream, illusion **9** invention **11** fabrication

figurant
6 dancer, hoofer **7** danseur **8** coryphée

figuration
4 line **5** shape **7** contour, outline, profile **8** allegory **9** lineament, lineation, symbolism **10** silhouette

figure
3 add, sum, tot **4** cast, foot, form, rule, tote **5** build, count, digit, frame, motif, shape, total **6** cipher, decide, design, device, motive, number, reckon, settle, symbol **7** chiffer, compute, integer, numeral, outline, pattern, resolve, summate **8** conclude, estimate, physique, totalize **9** calculate, character, determine, enumerate **11** whole number **12** conformation **13** configuration
geometric: **4** cone, cube **5** rhomb **6** circle, isogon, square **7** decagon, ellipse, hexagon, nonagon, octagon, polygon, rhombus **8** pentacle, pentagon, rhomboid, tetragon, triangle **9** rectangle **10** hexahedron, octahedron **11** icosahedron **12** dodecahedron, rhombohedron **13** quadrilateral
human: **4** nude **5** atlas **7** telamon **8** caryatid
ornamental: **6** statue **8** gargoyle

figure of speech
5 trope **6** aporia, simile **7** imagery, litotes **8** metaphor, metonymy **10** synecdoche

figure out
4 dope **5** crack, solve **6** decode, unfold **7** clear up, resolve, unravel **8** decipher, unriddle, untangle **9** puzzle out **10** unscramble **11** disentangle

figure skating
jump: **4** axel, loop, lutz **5** split **6** rocker **7** bracket, counter, salchow **11** spreadeagle
spin: **3** sit **5** camel

Fiji
capital: **4** Suva
monetary unit: **6** dollar

filch
3 nim, nip, rob **4** lift **5** pinch, steal, swipe **6** pilfer, snitch **7** purloin

file
3 row 4 line, rank, rasp, tier
5 queue 6 string 7 dossier, echelon

fill
3 gob, jam, jug 4 brim, clog, cloy, cram, glut, heap, jade, load, meet, pack, pall, pile, plug, sate, stop
5 block, choke, close, gorge 6 answer, bumper, charge, stodge
7 congest, engorge, occlude, satiate, satisfy, stopper, surfeit
interstices: 3 pug 4 calk 5 chink, putty

filled
4 full 5 sated 7 replete 9 saturated

fillet
4 band, orle, tape 5 snood, strip
6 ribbon, stripe 7 bandeau, banding 8 headband
anatomical: 9 lemniscus
architectural: 6 cimbia, listel, reglet, taenia
combining form: 4 taen 5 taeni 6 taenio
meat: 10 tenderloin

fill-in
3 sub 7 stand-in 9 alternate, surrogate 10 substitute 11 locum tenens, pinch hitter, replacement, succedaneum

fill in
4 clew, clue, post, tell, warn 6 advise, inform, insert, notify, wise up
7 apprise, throw in 8 acquaint
9 insinuate, interject, interpose, introduce 11 intercalate, interpolate

film
4 cine, haze, mist, show, skin, veil
5 brume, flick, layer, movie, smaze
6 patina 7 picture 8 pellicle 9 celluloid, photoplay 10 cinematize
11 picture show 13 motion picture, moving picture

filmy
4 fine, hazy 5 gauzy, misty, sheer, wispy 6 cloudy, dainty, flimsy
7 tiffany 8 delicate, gossamer
10 diaphanous 11 transparent

filter
4 sift 5 leach, sieve 6 purify, refine, screen, strain 8 filtrate
9 percolate

filth
4 dirt, dung, gore 6 ordure
7 squalor 9 obscenity
combining form: 4 copr 5 copro

filthy
4 foul, vile 5 black, dirty, dungy, gross, mucky, nasty, soily 6 coarse,
grubby, impure, ribald, sloppy, smutty, sordid, vulgar 7 obscene, raunchy, squalid, unclean 8 indecent 9 loathsome, offensive, repulsive, revolting, uncleanly, verminous 12 scatological

filthy lucre
4 cash, loot, pelf 5 dough, money
8 currency 11 legal tender

fin
4 anal 5 pinna 6 caudal, dorsal, pelvic 7 acantha, flipper, ventral
8 pectoral

finagle
5 cheat, trick 6 wangle 7 deceive, snaffle, swindle 8 engineer, maneuver 9 machinate

final
3 lag 4 last 6 ending, latest, latter
7 closing 8 crowning, decisive, eventual, hindmost, terminal, ultimate 9 finishing 10 concluding, conclusive, definitive 11 terminating

finale
3 end 5 close, finis 6 climax, ending, finish, payoff, windup 7 closing 9 cessation 10 conclusion, denouement 11 culmination, termination

finalize
3 end 5 close 6 finish, wind up
8 conclude, solidify 9 terminate
10 consummate

finance
4 back, bank, fund 5 endow, stake
7 promote, revenue, sponsor, support 8 bankroll 9 grubstake, patronize, subsidize 10 capitalize, underwrite

financial
6 fiscal, pocket 8 business, economic, monetary 9 pecuniary
10 commercial
plan: 6 budget
statement: 12 balance sheet

financier
American: 4 Hill (James Jerome), Ryan (Thomas Fortune), Sage (Russell) 5 Baker (George Fisher), Eaton (Cyrus), Field (Cyrus West), Gould (Jay), Grace (William Russell), Green (Hetty) 6 Boesky (Ivan), Girard (Stephen), Mellon (Andrew), Morgan (John Pierpont, Junius Spencer), Morris (Robert), Rogers (Henry Huttleston), Yerkes (Charles Tyson) 7 Peabody (George)
10 Vanderbilt (Cornelius, William)

British: 6 Rhodes (Cecil) 7 Gresham (Thomas)
French: 6 Necker (Jacques)
German: 7 Schacht (Hjalmar)
10 Rothschild (Amschel, Jakob, Karl, Mayer, Nathan, Salomon)

finch
4 pape 5 junco, serin, zebra 6 linnet, siskin, towhee 7 bunting, chewink, redpoll 8 grosbeak, longspur

find
4 espy, give, hand, note, spot
5 catch, dig up, hit on, sight, solve
6 descry, detect, espial, locate, strike, supply, turn up 7 discern, dish out, furnish, hit upon, provide, scare up 8 discover, dispense, hand over, meet with, transfer, treasure, turn over 9 detection, discovery, encounter 10 unearthing
13 treasure trove

find out
3 see 4 hear 5 learn 6 tumble
7 catch on, unearth 8 discover
9 ascertain, determine

fine
3 tax, top 4 fair, levy, nice
5 bonny, clear, dandy, mulct, sheer, sunny 6 amerce, choice, minute, sconce, subtle 7 capital, clarion, damages, elegant, forfeit, penalty, powdery, refined 8 delicate, five-star, hairline, penalize, pleasant, rainless, splendid, sunshiny, superior, top-notch 9 beautiful, cloudless, enjoyable, excellent, first-rate, unclouded 10 amercement, assessment, first-class, impalpable, pulverized, reparation, undarkened 11 first-string
13 hairsplitting

finery
5 frill 6 gewgaw, tawdry 7 apparel, bravery, clothes, gaudery, regalia 8 foofaraw, frippery, ornament, trimming, war paint 9 full dress 10 Sunday best

finesse
3 art 4 play 5 skill 6 jockey, outwit
7 beguile, cunning, exploit 8 maneuver, subtlety 9 dexterity
10 manipulate

Fingal's Cave island
6 Staffa

finger
3 paw, tap, toy 4 feel, make, name, spot 5 digit, index, pinky, place, strum, touch 6 handle, medius, pilfer, pinkie 7 appoint, palpate 8 diagnose, identify, nomi-

nate, pinpoint **9** designate, determine, recognize **11** distinguish **13** diagnosticate
bone: 7 phalanx **9** phalanges (plural)
combining form: 6 dactyl, digiti **7** dactylo, dactyly **8** dactylia **9** dactylism, dactylous
cymbal: 8 castanet

fingernail
combining form: 4 onyx **7** onychia **8** onychium
crescent: 6 lunule

fingerprint
4 arch, loop **5** whorl

finicky
4 nice **5** fussy **6** choosy, dainty, prissy **7** choosey **9** squeamish **10** fastidious, particular, pernickety **11** persnickety

finish
3 die, end **4** cool, do in, down, halt, kill, slay, stop **5** cease, close, glaze, scrag, spend, use up **6** cut off, ending, expend, finale, murder, polish, wash up, windup, wrap up **7** closing, consume, destroy, execute, exhaust, put away, surface, take off **8** carry off, complete, conclude, dispatch, finalize, knock off, terminus, ultimate **9** cessation, determine, liquidate, terminate **10** attainment, conclusion, desistance, run through **11** achievement, acquirement, acquisition, assassinate, termination
dull: 3 mat **4** matt **5** matte
second: 5 place
third: 4 show

finished
4 done, down, over, ripe **5** ended, suave **6** closed, smooth, urbane **7** done for, refined, through **8** complete, washed-up **9** completed, concluded, perfected, virtuosic **10** consummate, terminated **12** accomplished

finish off
3 cap **5** crown **6** climax, top off **8** round off **9** culminate

finite
5 bound **7** bounded, defined, limited **9** definable **10** restricted

Finland
capital: 8 Helsinki
monetary unit: 6 markka

Finlandia composer
8 Sibelius (Jean)

Finnish
bath: 5 sauna
combining form: 5 Fenno
epic: 8 Kalevala
god: 6 Jumala

fin's double
7 tenspot

fir
7 conifer **9** evergreen
genus: 5 Abies

fire
2 ax **3** can, pep, vim, zip **4** bake, burn, cast, dash, drop, hurl, kiln, sack, stir, toss, zeal, zest, zing **5** ardor, blaze, drive, exalt, flame, flare, fling, glare, gusto, heave, ingle, light, loose, pitch, rouse, salvo, shoot, sling, spark, throw, torch, verve, vigor **6** arouse, bounce, energy, excite, fervor, hurrah, ignite, inform, kindle, launch, spirit, thrill **7** animate, boot out, burnout, dismiss, enliven, enthuse, inferno, inflame, inspire, kick out, passion, provoke **8** enkindle, heighten **9** calenture, discharge, holocaust, intensify, terminate **10** enthusiasm, heartiness, liveliness **13** conflagration
combining form: 3 pyr **4** igni, pyro
god: 4 Agni, Loki **6** Vulcan **10** Hephaestus

firearm
see **gun**

firebrand
7 hothead, hotspur **8** agitator

firebug
5 torch **8** arsonist **10** incendiary, pyromaniac

firecracker
5 squib **9** explosive **10** cherry bomb, noisemaker

firedog
7 andiron

firedrake
6 dragon

firefly
7 glowfly **12** lightning bug

fire opal
7 girasol

fireplace
5 ingle
equipment: 6 fender, screen **7** andiron, fireset
part: 3 hob **6** hearth, mantel

fireplug
7 hydrant

fire up
5 rouse **6** excite, ignite, incite, kindle **7** enflame, enliven, inflame, inspire, provoke **8** enkindle **9** intensify

firework
4 gerb **5** gerbe **6** fizgig, petard, rocket **8** sparkler **10** tourbillon **11** pyrotechnic, tourbillion
cluster: 9 girandole

firm
3 set **4** fast, hard, sure **5** exact, fixed, house, rigid, solid, sound, stiff, tight, tough **6** outfit, secure, stable, stated, steady, stolid, strong, sturdy **7** abiding, adamant, certain, company, concern, confirm, fixedly, settled, solidly, staunch, tightly, unmoved **8** business, constant, definite, enduring, faithful, resolute, specific **9** inelastic, steadfast, tenacious **10** determined, enterprise, inflexible, stipulated, unwavering, unyielding **11** established, steadfastly, substantial, unfaltering, unqualified **12** never-failing **13** establishment

firmament
3 sky **6** welkin **7** heavens **8** empyrean

firmness
7 resolve **8** decision, security, solidity, strength, tenacity **9** constancy, soundness, stability **10** resolution, stableness, steadiness **11** decidedness **12** resoluteness **13** determination, purposiveness

first
4 arch, head **5** alpha, chief, least, prime **6** maiden, primal **7** eminent, highest, initial, leading, pioneer, premier, primary, supreme **8** champion, dominant, earliest, foremost, headmost, original, smallest **9** inaugural, initially, paramount, principal, slightest, sovereign **10** aboriginal, preeminent, primordial
combining form: 4 prot **5** proto

firstborn
4 heir **5** eigne **6** eldest

first-class
3 top **4** A-one, fine **5** prime **6** tiptop **7** capital **8** five-star, superior, top-notch **9** excellent, top-drawer

first fruits
7 annates

firsthand
6 direct **7** primary **9** immediate

first man in space
7 Gagarin (Yury)

first-rate
see **first-class**

first showing
8 premiere

First State
8 Delaware

first-string
see **first-class**

firth
3 arm, bay 4 cove, gulf 5 inlet
6 harbor, slough 7 estuary

fiscal
6 pocket 8 monetary 9 financial

fish
3 net, sap 4 butt, cast, dupe, fool,
gill, hint 5 angle, chump, seine,
trawl, troll 6 sucker 7 fall guy, gill-
net, gudgeon, sniggle
angler: 7 lophiid 9 goosefish
aquarium: 4 barb 5 betta, danio,
guppy, limia, platy, tetra 6 mollie
7 cichlid, gourami, rasbora 8 goldfish 9 angelfish
basket: 5 creel
catfish: 4 wels 5 dorad 6 madtom
7 candiru 8 bullhead, bullpout,
hornpout, stonecat
cod: 4 cusk, hake, ling 5 torsk
6 burbot, tomcod 7 pollack,
pollock
combining form: 6 ichthy 7 ichthyo,
ichthys
croaker: 4 drum 7 corbina 8 kingfish, seatrout, weakfish 10 sque-
teague, squiteague
eellike: 5 moray 6 conger 7 hagfish, lamprey
eggs: 3 roe 5 spawn
electric: 4 raad 7 torpedo
9 stargazer
extinct: 10 coelacanth
flatfish: 3 dab 4 butt, dace, sole
5 bream, brill, fluke 6 plaice, turbot
7 halibut 8 flounder
food: 3 cod, eel, ide 4 bass, carp,
cero, hake, ling, scup, shad, sole,
tuna 5 jurel, perch, scrod, skate,
smelt, trout 6 bonito, caviar, kipper, mullet, plaice, pompon,
salmon, tautog, weever, wrasse
7 alewife, catfish, cavalla, escolar,
grouper, haddock, halibut, herring,
morwong, pollack, pollock, pompano, pompoon, sardine, sea carp,
snapper, tautaug 8 brisling, cre-
valle, flounder, mackerel 9 barracuda
game: 4 bass, pike, tuna 5 perch,

trout 6 grilse, marlin, salmon, tarpon 8 pickerel 9 swordfish
grunt: 5 sargo 7 pigfish, tomtate
8 porkfish 10 bluestripe
herring: 4 shad, sild 5 sprat 7 alewife, sardine 8 brisling, pilchard
kind: 3 ray 4 bass, cero, chub,
dory, goby, jack, opah, pike, rudd,
scup, tuna 5 balao, bream, cisco,
loach, perch, porgy, sargo, shark,
skate, smelt, snook, tench, tunny,
wahoo 6 anabas, blenny, bonito,
dorado, marlin, minnow, mullet,
permit, puffer, remora, sauger,
splake, sucker, tarpon, tautog, warsaw, wrasse 7 anchovy, boxfish,
buffalo, cabezon, capelin, cavalla,
chimera, cowfish, crappie, dolphin,
grunion, haddock, hogfish, jewfish,
mojarra, muddler, mudfish, oarfish,
opaleye, piranha, pupfish, sardine,
sawfish, sculpin, snapper, sunfish,
tilapia, vendace, whiting 8 albacore, blowfish, bluefish, bluegill,
bonefish, burrfish, chimaera, file-
fish, gambusia, grayling, halfbeak,
ladyfish, lookdown, lumpfish, lung-
fish, mackerel, menhaden, moon-
fish, pickerel, pipefish, rockfish,
sailfish, seahorse, skipjack, sting-
ray, sturgeon, tilefish, topsmelt,
warmouth, wolffish 9 amberjack,
barracuda, greenling, jacksmelt, kil-
lifish, mummichog, pilotfish, spade-
fish, swordfish, topminnow, trunk-
fish, whitebait, whitefish
10 butterfish, flying fish, lizardfish,
needlefish, parrotfish, silverside, tripletail, yellowtail 11 harvestfish,
muskellunge, pumpkinseed, stickle-
back, triggerfish 12 schoolmaster
luminescent: 9 viperfish 10 midshipman 11 hatchetfish, lanternfish
minnow: 4 carp, chub, dace
6 shiner
pan: 5 bream, perch, trout 7 crappie, sunfish 8 bluegill, rock bass
11 pumpkinseed
porgy: 4 scup 7 pinfish 8 jolthead
10 sheepshead
relating to: 7 piscine 8 ichthyic
rockfish: 8 bocaccio, lionfish, rose-
fish 11 chilipepper
salmon: 3 dog 4 chum, coho 6 sebago 7 chinook, sockeye
spear: 3 gig 7 harpoon, trident
stew: 8 cioppino, matelote
13 bouillabaisse
trap: 3 dam 4 weir 6 eelpot
9 fishgarth
trout: 5 charr 7 oquassa, rainbow
9 cutthroat 11 Dolly Varden
voracious: 6 caribe 7 piranha

young: 3 fry 4 parr 5 larva, smolt
6 alevin, grilse

fisherman
6 angler 8 piscator

fish hawk
6 osprey

fishhook
5 drail
adjunct: 5 snell
part: 4 barb 5 shank

fishing area
7 piscary

fishing line
4 trot 7 boulter, setline 8 longline,
trotline
float: 3 bob 5 quill 6 dobber
leader: 5 snell

fishing lure
3 fly 4 herl

fishing net
5 seine, trawl

fishlike mammal
3 orc 5 whale 7 dolphin
8 porpoise

fish owl
6 ketupa

fishwife
5 harpy, scold, shrew, vixen
6 amazon, ogress, virago 9 termagant, Xanthippe

fishy
4 cold, dull 7 dubious, suspect
8 doubtful 9 ambiguous, doubtable, dubitable, equivocal, uncertain 10 suspicious

fission element
7 uranium 9 plutonium

fissure
3 gap 4 gash, hole, rent, rift, rima,
rime 5 break, chasm, chink, cleft,
crack, split 6 breach, schism
7 crevice, opening, rupture 8 crevasse, fracture, rimation

fist
3 job 4 grip, hand 5 grasp, index
6 clench, clutch, ductus, effort, handle, script 7 attempt 10 penmanship 11 calligraphy, chirography,
handwriting

fisticuffs
4 ring 6 boxing 8 pugilism
13 prizefighting

fit
2 go 3 apt, set 4 good, hale, jibe,
just, meet, sane, suit, turn, well
5 adapt, agree, frame, happy,
joint, ready, right, sound, spasm,

spell, tally, throe **6** access, accord, adjust, attack, become, belong, decent, go with, make up, proper, seemly, square, tailor, useful **7** capable, conform, healthy, prepare, qualify, seizure, tantrum **8** apoplexy, assemble, decorous, dovetail, eligible, paroxysm, quadrate, rightful, suitable **9** agree with, befitting, congruous, consonant, harmonize, reconcile, wholesome **10** applicable, convenient, correspond, felicitous, go together, tailor-make, well-liking **11** accommodate, appropriate
suffix: **4** able, ible

fitful
6 catchy, random, spotty **8** periodic, sporadic, unstable, variable **9** desultory, haphazard, hit-or-miss, irregular, recurrent, spasmodic **10** capricious, changeable, inconstant **11** interrupted

fitness
3 use **4** trim **5** order, shape **6** fettle, kilter, repair **7** account, aptness, service, utility **8** capacity, justness, meetness **9** advantage, condition, propriety, relevance, rightness, soundness **10** expediency, usefulness **11** eligibility, suitability **12** appositeness, suitableness **13** applicability

fit out
3 arm, rig **4** gear **5** equip **6** outfit **7** appoint, furnish, turn out **8** accouter, accoutre

fitting
3 apt **4** just, meet, true **5** happy **6** proper, seemly **7** adjunct, apropos, desired, germane **8** apposite, relevant, suitable **9** accessory, accordant, befitting, pertinent **10** applicable, attachment, concordant, felicitous, harmonious **11** appropriate

fit together
4 join, mesh **5** unite **6** hook up **7** connect **8** dovetail

Fitzgerald novel
13 The Last Tycoon **14** The Great Gatsby

five
combining form: **3** pen **4** pent **5** penta **6** quinqu **7** quinque
group of: **6** pentad **7** quintet
of trumps: **5** pedro

five-dollar bill
3 fin

fivefold
7 quinary **9** quintuple

Five Nations
8 Iroquois
member: **7** Cayugas, Mohawks, Oneidas, Senecas **9** Onondagas

five-sided figure
8 pentagon

five-year period
6 luster, lustre **7** lustrum

fix
3 buy, jam, lay, put, set, sop **4** do up, geld, make, mend, moor, root, spot, work **5** alter, bribe, catch, embed, focus, lodge, patch, place, ready, rivet, solve, stick, unsex **6** adjust, anchor, attach, buy off, change, corner, doctor, fasten, make up, neuter, pickle, plight, repair, revamp, scrape, secure, settle, square, steady, tune up **7** appoint, arrange, dilemma, ingrain, instill, prepare, rebuild, resolve, specify, work out **8** castrate, entrench, mutilate, overhaul, regulate, renovate **9** concenter, establish, stabilize, sterilize **10** tamper with **11** concentrate, desexualize, predicament, recondition, reconstruct

fixation
5 craze, mania, thing **9** obsession **11** fascination, infatuation

___ fixe
4 idée

fixed
3 pat, set **4** fast, firm, sure **5** tight, whole **6** frozen, narrow, secure, stable, stated, steady **7** abiding, certain, limited, precise, settled **8** constant, definite, enduring, immobile, immotile, immotive, resolute **9** exclusive, immovable, immutable, permanent, steadfast, tenacious, undivided, unmovable **10** inflexible, invariable, restricted, stationary, stipulated, unswerving, unwavering **11** determinate, inalterable, irremovable, unalterable, unfaltering, unqualified **12** concentrated, never-failing, unchangeable, undistracted, unmodifiable **13** circumscribed
combining form: **6** aplano

fix up
5 equip, primp, slick, spiff **6** devise, doll up, supply **7** deck out, doll out, dress up, furnish, gussy up **8** contrive, spruce up **9** smarten up **11** accommodate

fizzle
4 fail, hiss **6** fiasco **7** failure, sputter

fjord
Baffin Island: **9** Admiralty
Denmark: **3** Ise, Lim **5** Lamme
Iceland: **4** Axar, Eyja **5** Horna, Skaga, Vopna
Norway: **3** Tys **4** Bokn, Nord, Salt, Stor, Tana, Vest **5** Lakse, Ranen, Sogne **9** Stavanger, Trondheim
Spitsbergen: **3** Ice
Svalbard: **4** Stor

flabbergast
5 amaze, shock **7** astound **8** astonish, surprise **9** dumbfound, overwhelm

flabby
see **flaccid**

flaccid
4 limp, soft, weak **6** feeble, flabby, flimsy, floppy, sleazy **8** weakened, yielding

flag
3 ebb, sag **4** fade, fail, jack, sign, swag, tire, wane, wilt **5** abate, color, droop **6** banner, burgee, colors, ensign, fanion, guidon, motion, pencel, pennon, signal, weaken **7** decline, gesture, pendant, pennant **8** bannerol, gonfalon, gonfanon, languish, penoncel, standard, streamer, tricolor **9** banderole, oriflamme, pennoncel, signalize **10** Jolly Roger **11** deteriorate

flagellate
4 flog, hide, lash, whip **5** whale **6** stripe, switch, thrash **7** scourge

flagellum
4 whip **5** shoot **6** runner, stolon **7** scourge

flagitious
6 rotten, sinful, wicked **7** corrupt, vicious **8** criminal, depraved, infamous, perverse, shameful **9** miscreant, nefarious **10** degenerate, scandalous, villainous **11** disgraceful

flagon
3 cup, mug **5** stoup **7** tankard

flagpole
4 mast **5** staff
rope: **7** halyard

flagrant
3 bad **4** bold, rank **5** gross **6** wanton **7** capital, glaring, heinous, obvious **8** striking **9** atrocious, egregious, monstrous **10** outrageous **11** conspicuous

flagstone
5 shale, slate

flag-waver
7 patriot 10 patrioteer
12 superpatriot

flail
4 beat, flog, skin, whip 6 strike,
thrash, thresh 7 scourge

flair
4 bent, bump, gift, head, turn
5 knack 6 genius, talent 7 aptness,
faculty 8 aptitude

flake
3 bit 4 chip, peel, rack, snow, tray
5 fleck, scale 6 lamina 8 fragment

flake off
4 peel 5 scale 9 exfoliate
10 desquamate

flamboyant
4 rich 5 showy, swank 6 chichi,
florid, ornate, rococo 7 baroque,
splashy 8 luscious, peacocky
10 peacockish 11 pretentious
12 orchidaceous, ostentatious

flame
4 beau, dear, fire, glow, love 5 ardor, blare, blaze, flare, flash,
glare, honey, light, lover 7 beloved, darling, sweetie 8 ladylove,
loveling, truelove 9 boyfriend,
inamorata, inamorato 10 girlfriend

flamen
6 priest

flamenco
5 dance, gypsy, music

flaming
5 afire, fiery, flamy 6 ablaze,
aflame, alight, ardent, flambé, red-
hot 7 blazing, burning, fervent,
flaring, ignited 8 white-hot 10 hot-
blooded, passionate 11 conflagrant, impassioned

flammable
8 burnable 9 ignitable
11 combustible

flammable liquid
3 oil 6 acetyl 7 acetone, alcohol
8 gasoline, kerosene 10 turpentine

Flanders
capital: 5 Lille
language: 7 Flemish

flannelflower
7 mullein

flap
3 tab 4 clap, fold, leaf, stew 6 crisis, dither, lather, pother, tongue,

tumult 7 aileron, flutter, turmoil
9 agitation, commotion, confusion

flapdoodle
4 bosh 5 fudge 6 bunkum 7 rubbish 8 malarkey, nonsense
9 poppycock 12 blatherskite, fiddle-faddle

flapjack
7 hotcake, pancake 11 griddle
cake

flare
4 glow 5 blaze, burst, flame, flash,
torch 6 signal 7 flicker 8 eruption,
outbreak, outburst

flare-up
4 gust 5 burst, sally 6 access
8 eruption, outburst 9 explosion

flaring
5 afire, fiery 6 ablaze, aflame,
alight 7 blazing, burning, flaming,
ignited 11 conflagrant

flash
3 ray 4 beam, burn, glow, show
5 blare, blaze, blink, crack, flame,
flare, glare, gleam, glint, jiffy,
shake, shine, spark 6 dazzle, expose, flaunt, glance, minute, moment, parade, quiver, second 7 display, disport, exhibit, flicker,
glimmer, glisten, glitter, instant, radiate, shimmer, show off, spangle,
sparkle, trot out, twinkle 8 brandish
9 breathing, coruscate 10 incandesce 11 coruscation, scintillate,
split second 13 scintillation

flashy
4 loud 5 gaudy, showy 6 brazen,
florid, garish, ornate, tawdry, tinsel
7 blatant, chintzy, glaring 9 sparkling 10 flamboyant, glittering
12 meretricious

flask
5 frame 6 bottle, fiasco, flacon
7 ampulla, canteen, costrel

flat
3 dim, mat 4 dead, drab, dull,
even, poor 5 banal, bland, blind,
broke, flush, inane, level, muted,
needy, plane, prone, prosy, rooms,
stale, stony, suite, vapid 6 jejune,
planar, rental, smooth 7 insipid,
planate, prosaic, sapless 8 dirt
poor, lifeless, lodgings, strapped,
tenement, unsavory 9 apartment,
colorless, decumbent, destitute,
downright, innocuous, penurious,
prostrate, reclining, recumbent,
savorless, tasteless 10 flavorless,
lackluster, lusterless, monotonous,

namby-pamby, procumbent, stone-
broke

flatfish
see at **fish**

flatland
4 mesa, moor 5 plain 6 steppe,
tundra 7 plateau 9 tableland

flat-out
4 fast, rank 5 apace, utter
6 damned 7 blasted, goldarn, hastily, quickly, rapidly, swiftly 8 absolute, outright, speedily 9 out-and-
out, posthaste 11 straight-out,
unmitigated 12 lickety-split
13 expeditiously

flatten
3 lay 4 down, even, fell, flat
5 floor, flush, level, plane 6 deject,
ground, lay low, smooth 7 depress,
mow down 8 smoothen 9 bring
down, knock down, prostrate

flattened at the poles
6 oblate

flatter
4 coax, suit 5 toady 6 become, cajole, praise 7 blarney, enhance,
gratify, wheedle 8 blandish, bootlick, inveigle

flattery
3 oil 4 laud 6 praise 7 blarney,
fawning, incense 8 cajolery, soft
soap, toadying 9 adulation, laudation, truckling 10 sycophancy
11 bootlicking, compliments
12 blandishment, ingratiation

flatulent
4 vain 5 empty, gassy, tumid,
windy 6 hollow, turgid 8 dropsied,
inflated 9 dropsical, overblown,
tumescent

Flaubert
heroine: 4 Emma
novel: 8 Salammbo 12 Madame
Bovary

flaunt
4 show, wave 5 flash, flout, vaunt
6 expose, parade 7 display, disport, exhibit, flutter, show off, trot
out 8 brandish, flourish

flavor
4 tang, zest 5 sapor, savor, smack,
taste, tinge 6 relish, season
8 sapidity

flavorless
4 drab, flat 5 stale 7 insipid 8 unsavory 9 tasteless 11 distasteful
unpalatable

flavorsome
5 sapid, tasty 6 savory 9 aperitive, flavorful, palatable, relishing, toothsome 10 appetizing 11 goodtasting

flaw
3 gap, rip 4 rent, tear, vice 5 crack, fault 6 breach, defect 7 blemish, fissure 12 imperfection

flawed
4 sick 5 amiss 6 faulty, marred 7 damaged, spoiled 8 impaired 9 defective, imperfect

flawless
4 pure 5 ideal, model, sound, whole 6 entire, intact 7 perfect 8 absolute, unbroken, unmarred 9 errorless, exquisite, faultless, fleckless, undamaged 10 immaculate, impeccable, unimpaired 11 note-perfect, unblemished 12 indefectible

flax
5 linen
fiber: 3 tow 4 harl 5 harle 6 strick
prepare: 3 ret 4 card 5 dress 6 hackle, scutch
refuse: 5 hards, hurds

flaxen
5 blond, straw 6 blonde, golden

flay
4 skin 5 slash 6 assail, attack, berate, scathe, scorch 7 blister, censure, scarify, scourge 8 lambaste, lash into 9 castigate, excoriate 10 tongue-lash

flea
5 pulex 6 chigoe, jigger 7 chigger
water: .7 daphnid

Fleance's father
6 Banquo

fleckless
7 perfect 8 absolute, flawless, unflawed 10 impeccable 11 noteperfect

flection
3 bow 4 bend, turn 5 angle 7 flexure, turning

Fledermaus, Die
3 bat
character: 5 Adele, Falke, Frank 6 Alfred 9 Rosalinde 10 Eisenstein
composer: 7 Strauss (Johann)

fledgling
4 boot, colt, tyro 6 novice, rookie 8 beginner, freshman, neophyte, newcomer 10 apprentice

flee
3 fly, lam, run 4 bolt, scat, shun, skip 5 break, elude, scape, scoot, scram, skirr 6 decamp, escape 7 abscond, make off, scamper, scarper 9 skedaddle

fleece
3 web 4 bilk, clip, milk, rook, skin, soak, wool 5 bleed, cheat, cozen, mulct, shear, stick, sweat 6 extort, hustle 7 defraud, despoil, plunder, swindle 10 overcharge

fleeceable
4 easy 5 naive 8 gullible 11 susceptible

fleecy
5 hairy 6 pilose, woolly 7 hirsute, pileous 9 whiskered

fleer
4 gibe, gird, jeer, jest, mock 5 flout, laugh, scoff, sneer, taunt 6 quip at 7 scout at 8 fugitive

fleet
3 fly, run 4 fast, flit, navy, sail, spry, wile, wing 5 agile, brisk, hasty, hurry, quick, rapid, speed, sweep, swift, while 6 armada, hasten, hustle, nimble, rocket, speedy 7 beguile 8 flotilla 9 breakneck 10 evanescent, expeditive, harefooted 11 expeditious

fleeting
5 brief 7 passing 8 fugitive, volatile 9 ephemeral, fugacious, momentary, transient 10 evanescent, short-lived, transitory

Fleming, Ian
hero: 9 James Bond
novel: 4 Dr. No 10 Goldfinger 11 Thunderball 12 Casino Royale

fleshly
3 lay 6 animal, bodily, carnal 7 profane, secular, sensual, somatic 8 corporal, physical, sensuous, temporal 9 corporeal, epicurean, luxurious, sybaritic 10 voluptuous

fleshy
3 fat 5 beefy, gross, heavy, obese, plump, stout 6 portly 7 porcine, sarcous, weighty 9 corpulent 10 overweight
fruit: 4 pome 5 bacca, berry, drupe

Fletcher's partner
8 Beaumont (Francis)

fleur-de-____
3 lis, lys

flex
4 bend 5 tense 7 pliancy, tension

flexible
5 withy 6 docile, floppy, limber, pliant, supple, whippy 7 elastic, pliable, springy, stretch, willowy 8 amenable, stretchy, yielding 9 resilient, tractable 10 manageable

flexuous
5 snaky 7 sinuous, winding 8 tortuous 9 meandrous 10 circuitous, convoluted, meandering, serpentine 11 anfractuous

flick
3 hit 4 blow, cine, film, show 5 movie 6 strike 7 picture 9 photoplay 11 picture show 13 motion picture, moving picture

flicker
4 flit 5 blink, dance, flash, gleam, glint, hover, waver 7 flitter, flutter, glitter, sparkle, twinkle

flickering
7 lambent 8 unsteady

flier
3 ace 5 pilot 6 airman, fly-boy 7 aviator, birdman 8 aviatrix

flight
3 lam 4 rout, slip 5 floor, story 6 escape 7 getaway 8 breakout, escaping 10 escapement

flighty
5 dizzy, giddy, silly, swift 7 foolish 8 freakish, skittish, unstable, volatile 9 frivolous, mercurial, transient 10 capricious, changeable, inconstant 11 empty-headed, harebrained 13 irresponsible, rattlebrained

flimflam
3 gyp 4 beat, bilk, dupe, fake, fool, gull, hoax, jazz, sell, sham 5 cheat, cozen, fraud, freak, hokum, trick 6 befool, chouse, deceit, diddle, drivel, hot air, humbug, pigeon, trifle 7 chicane, deceive, defraud, eyewash, swindle 8 hoodwink, nonsense 9 bamboozle, deception, imposture, moonshine, overreach 10 balderdash, doubletalk 11 hornswoggle

flimflammer
3 gyp 4 skin 5 cheat 6 con man 7 diddler, sharper 8 swindler 9 defrauder 12 double-dealer

flimsy
4 limp, thin, weak 5 filmy, frail, gauzy, sheer 6 feeble, flabby, floppy, infirm, sleazy, slight, slimsy, weakly 7 flaccid, fragile, rickety,

slimpsy, tiffany, unsound **8** decrepit, delicate, gossamer **10** diaphanous, improbable, incredible **11** implausible, transparent **12** unbelievable, unconvincing

flinch
5 quail, start, wince **6** blanch, blench, recede, recoil, shrink **7** retreat, squinch **8** withdraw

fling
2 go **3** pop, try **4** boil, bolt, cast, dash, emit, fire, gibe, hurl, lash, orgy, race, rush, shot, slap, stab, tear, toss **5** binge, chase, crack, dance, heave, pitch, shoot, sling, spree, throw, whack, whirl **6** charge, launch **7** discard, rampage, sarcasm, splurge **9** disregard, overthrow

flip
3 tap **4** blow, flap, glib, pert, riff **5** drink, flick **6** riffle **8** flippant **10** somersault **11** smart-alecky

flippancy
6 levity **8** archness, pertness **9** cockiness, freshness, frivolity, lightness, sauciness **10** cheekiness, impishness, volatility **11** flightiness, playfulness, roguishness

flippant
4 flip, glib, pert

flip through
4 scan **6** browse **7** dip into, run over **8** glance at **10** glance over

flirt
3 toy **4** dart, flip, flit, fool, minx, ogle, play, toss, vamp **5** dally, flick **6** coquet, lead on, trifle, wanton **8** coquette

flit
3 fly, run, zip **4** dart, pass, rush, sail, scud, whiz, wing **5** dance, fleet, flick, float, hover, hurry, scoot, speed, sweep **6** dartle, hasten **7** flicker, flutter

flitter
3 bit **5** dance, flake, hover **7** flicker, flutter, skitter

float
3 bob, fly **4** buoy, cork, dart, hang, raft, ride, sail, scud, skim, waft, wash **5** drift, drink, flood, hover, poise, shoot, skirr **8** levitate **9** negotiate

floater
3 bum, vag **4** hobo, raft **5** tramp **6** boomer **7** drifter, vagrant **8** derelict, vagabond

floating
5 loose **6** adrift, afloat, natant **7** buoyant, movable **8** moveable, shifting

flocculent
6 woolly

flock
3 mob **4** army, bevy, herd, host, pack, rout **5** bunch, cloud, covey, crowd, drove, group **6** flight, legion, scores, volary **9** multitude **11** aggregation
of mallards: **4** sute

flog
3 tan **4** beat, cane, hide, lash, whip **5** birch, flail, knout, tawse, whale **6** larrup, stripe, switch, thrash **7** exhaust, scourge **10** flagellate

flood
4 bore, flow, flux, pour, rush, tide **5** drift, drown, eager, eagre, spate, swamp, whelm **6** deluge, engulf, stream, current, freshet, niagara, torrent **8** cataract, flooding, inundate, overflow, submerge **9** cataclysm, overwhelm **10** inundation, outgushing, outpouring

floor
4 down, drop, fell **5** level, story **6** defeat, ground, lay low **7** flatten, silence **8** audience, bowl down, bowl over **9** bring down, knock down

flop
3 dud **4** bomb, bust, fail, fall, flap **5** lemon, loser **6** fizzle **7** failure

floppy
4 limp **5** loose **6** flabby, flimsy, sleazy **7** flaccid **8** flexible

flora
6 plants **10** vegetation

flora and fauna
5 biota

Florence
bridge: **12** Ponte Vecchio
cathedral: **5** Duomo
family: **6** Medici
gallery: **6** Uffizi
museum: **8** Bargello
palace: **5** Pitti
river: **4** Arno

florid
4 rich **5** flush, gaudy, ruddy, showy **6** ornate, rococo **7** aureate, baroque, flowery, flushed, glowing **8** figurate, luscious, rubicund, sanguine, sonorous **9** bombastic, over-

blown **10** euphuistic, flamboyant, rhetorical **11** declamatory, full-blooded **12** magniloquent **13** grandiloquent

Florida
capital: **11** Tallahassee
college, university: **4** Nova **5** Barry **6** Eckerd **7** Stetson
discoverer: **11** Ponce de Leon (Juan)
Key: **4** Long, Vaca, West **5** Largo **7** Big Pine **9** Sugarloaf
largest city: **12** Jacksonville
motto: **12** In God We Trust
nickname: **13** Sunshine State
state bird: **11** mockingbird
state flower: **13** orange blossom

florilegium
3 ana **4** posy **5** album **7** garland, omnibus **8** analects **9** anthology **10** miscellany

Florimel's husband
7 Marinel

florist's milieu
10 greenhouse

floss
3 fur **4** down, flue, fuzz, lint, pile **5** fluff

flotilla
5 fleet

Flotow opera
5 Indra **6** L'Ombre, Martha

flotsam
6 jetsam **8** wreckage **9** driftwood

flounce
5 fling, frill, mince, strut **6** prance, ruffle, sashay **8** flounder, struggle

flounder
5 fling, labor, lurch **6** muddle, wallow **7** blunder, stumble **8** flatfish, struggle

flour
4 atta, bolt, meal, mill **5** grind **6** pinole, powder **9** pulverize
beetle: **6** weevil

flourish
3 wax **4** brag, grow, wave **5** adorn, bloom, boast, score, swing **6** arrive, flower, stroke, thrive **7** blossom, develop, fanfare, make out, prosper, succeed **8** brandish, curlicue, decorate, ornament **9** grace note

flout
4 gibe, gird, jeer, jest, mock **5** fleer, scoff, scorn, sneer, taunt **6** deride, insult, quip at **7** jeering, mockery **9** disregard

flow

3 run **4** emit, flux, gush, hang, head, pour, rill, rise, roll, rush, stem, teem, tide, void, well **5** arise, crawl, drift, flood, issue, spate, surge, swarm **6** abound, course, gurgle, onrush, ripple, series, sluice, spring, stream **7** cascade, current, emanate, give off, indraft, outflow, proceed **8** fountain, inundate, sequence **9** discharge, originate, pullulate **10** continuity, derive from, disembogue, inundation, menstruate, succession **11** continuance, progression **12** continuation, menstruation

combining form: 4 rheo **5** rrhea **6** rrhoea **7** rrhagia

flower

3 top **4** best, blow, pick, posy **5** bloom, cream, elite, pride, prime, prize **6** choice, gentry **7** aristoi, blossom, burgeon, develop, fleuron, quality, society **8** optimacy, outbloom **9** gentility **10** effloresce, upper class, upper crust **11** aristocracy **13** inflorescence

buttonhole: 11 boutonniere

cluster: 4 cyme **5** spike, umbel **6** corymb, floret, raceme, spadix, thyrse **7** panicle **8** spikelet **9** capitulum, dichasium, glomerule **11** monochasium, polychasium **13** inflorescence

combining form: 4 anth **5** antho, anthy, flori **6** anthes, anthus **7** anthous, florous

cup: 5 calyx

garden: 4 iris, lily, pink, rose **5** aster, canna, daisy, pansy, peony, phlox, poppy, tulip **6** azalia, cosmos, crocus, dahlia, orchid, violet **7** jonquil, petunia **8** camellia, daffodil, gardenia, geranium, gloxinia, hyacinth, larkspur, marigold, primrose **9** carnation, gladiolus, narcissus **10** delphinium, heliotrope **13** chrysanthemum

opening: 8 anthesis

part: 5 bract, calyx, ovary, ovule, petal, sepal, style **6** anther, pistil, spathe, stamen, stigma **7** corolla, nectary, pedicel, petiole **8** calyptra, filament, gynecium, peduncle, perianth

spike: 5 ament **6** catkin, spadix

stalk: 7 pedicel **8** peduncle

type: 3 ray **4** disk **6** annual, simple **9** composite, perennial

wild: 4 flag **5** bluet, daisy, gilia, vetch **6** lupine **7** anemone, arbutus, cowslip, gentian, vervain

8 bluebell, hepatica, trillium **9** buttercup, columbine, dandelion, saxifrage **10** cinquefoil **11** lady slipper **12** lady's slipper

flower arranging

7 ikebana

flowering

6 growth **8** progress, upgrowth **9** evolution, unfolding **10** evolvement **11** development, florescence, progression

flowerless plant

4 fern, moss **6** fungus, lichen **9** liverwort

flower-shaped ornament

7 fleuron

flowery

5 wordy **6** florid, ornate **7** aureate, swollen, verbose **8** sonorous **9** bombastic, overblown **10** euphuistic, rhetorical **11** declamatory **12** magniloquent **13** grandiloquent

Flowery Kingdom

5 China

flowing

4 easy **5** fluid **6** afflux, fluent, smooth **7** copious, cursive, running, streamy **8** freeform **10** effortless

back: 6 reflux **8** refluent

in: 6 influx **8** influent

together: 7 conflux **9** confluent

flow regulator

5 valve

flub

4 mess, muff **5** boner, botch, error, fluff **6** bollix, bungle, goof up **7** blunder, louse up

fluctuate

4 sway, wave **5** swing, waver **8** undulate **9** oscillate, vacillate **10** irresolute

flue

3 fur **4** down, fuzz, lint, pile **5** floss, fluff **7** channel, dragnet, feather, fishnet, passage

fluent

4 easy, free, glib **5** fluid, vocal **6** facile, liquid, smooth **7** cursive, flowing, running, voluble **8** eloquent **9** talkative **10** articulate, effortless, loquacious **12** smoothspoken

fluff

3 fur **4** bull, down, flub, flue, fuzz, lint, mess, muff, pile, slip, trip **5** boner, botch, error, floss, lapse

6 bollix, bungle, goof up **7** blooper, blunder, louse up, mistake

fluid

4 free **5** lymph, water **6** liquid, mobile **7** mutable, protean **8** unstable, unsteady, variable, weathery **9** changeful, unsettled **10** changeable

combining form: 4 sero

excessive: 5 edema

fluid pressure record

8 kymogram

fluky

3 odd **6** casual, chance **8** unsteady **9** uncertain **10** accidental, capricious, contingent, fortuitous, incidental

flume

5 chute **6** sluice, stream **7** channel

flummox

4 fail **7** confuse, perplex **8** confound **9** embarrass **10** disconcert

flunky

5 toady **7** footman, servant, steward

flurry

3 ado **4** fuss, gust, stir **5** haste, upset, whirl **6** bother, bustle, furore, pother, scurry **7** agitate, confuse, disturb, fluster, perturb, turmoil, unhinge **8** disquiet **9** agitation, confusion, whirlpool, whirlwind **10** discompose, excitement, turbulence

flush

3 lay **4** even, flat, glow, pink, rich, rose **5** bloom, blush, color, level, plane, rouge, ruddy **6** florid, mantle, pinken, redden, smooth **7** blossom, crimson, flatten, flushed, glowing, moneyed, opulent, planate, wealthy **8** abundant, affluent, rubicund, sanguine, smoothen **11** fullblooded

fluster

5 addle, dizzy, shake, upset **6** ball up, bother, flurry, fuddle, muddle, puzzle, rattle, ruffle **7** agitate, confuse, disturb, mystify, nonplus, perplex, perturb, unhinge **8** befuddle, bewilder, confound, disquiet, distract **10** discompose

flute

4 fife, roll **5** pleat **6** goffer, groove **7** chamfer, channel, flutist, piccolo, shuttle **8** recorder **9** wineglass

combining form: 3 aul **4** aulo

player: 5 piper **7** flutist **8** flautist

flutist

American: **5** Baker (Julius), Baron (Samuel) **7** Robison (Paula) **8** Zukerman (Eugenia)

British: **6** Galway (James)

French: **6** Rampal (Jean-Pierre)

flutter

4 beat, flap, flit **5** dance, hover, quake, shake, throb **6** flurry, quaver, quiver, wobble **7** flicker, flitter, pulsate, tremble, vibrate **8** disorder **9** agitation, confusion, palpitate, vibration **11** fluctuation, oscillation

flux

3 run **4** flow, fuse, melt, rush, thaw, tide **5** drift, flood, spate **6** scours, stream **7** current, flowing, liquefy, outflow **8** diarrhea, dissolve, liquesce **9** dysentery **10** deliquesce

fly

3 run, zip **4** bolt, dart, dash, flee, flit, lure, rush, sail, scud, skip, soar, whiz, wing **5** break, fleet, float, glide, hover, hurry, pilot, scape, scoot, shoot, skirr, speed, sweep, whish, whisk **6** aviate, decamp, escape, flight, hasten, hustle **7** abscond, airlift, flutter, hotfoot, make off, scamper **8** highball **9** skedaddle

combining form: **3** myi **4** myia, myio **5** musci

insect: **4** gnat, zimb **5** fruit, midge **6** botfly, gadfly, mayfly, tsetse **7** deerfly, sandfly, tachina **8** blackfly, dipteron, horsefly, housefly, mosquito, tachinid **10** bluebottle

larva: **3** bot **4** bott **6** maggot

fly-by-night

6 unsure **7** dubious **8** untrusty **9** trustless **10** unreliable **12** questionable, undependable **13** untrustworthy

flycatcher

4 tody

flying

5 aloft, brief **6** volant **7** soaring **8** airborne, volitant

Flying Dutchman

composer: **6** Wagner (Richard)

heroine: **5** Senta

flying fish

7 gurnard

flying fox

3 bat **6** kalong **8** fruit bat

flying horse

7 Pegasus **10** hippogriff

flying island

6 Laputa

flying lemur

6 colugo

flying mammal

3 bat

flying saucer

3 UFO

fly in the ointment

5 catch

foam

4 head, scud, scum, suds **5** froth, spume, yeast **6** lather

fob

4 seal **5** chain **6** pocket, ribbon **8** ornament

fob off

5 foist **6** palm on, put off **7** palm off

focus

3 fix, hub, put **4** meet, seat **5** heart, rivet **6** center, fasten, fixate **8** converge, polestar **9** concenter **11** concentrate, nerve center

fodder

4 feed, food **6** forage, silage **9** provender

crop: **3** hay, oat, rye **4** corn **5** maize, vetch, wheat **6** barley, clover, millet **7** alfalfa, sorghum **9** broad bean

storage structure: **4** silo

store: **6** ensile

foe

5 enemy, rival **8** opponent **9** adversary **10** antagonist

fog

3 dim **4** blur, daze, haze, mist, murk **5** addle, bedim, brume, cloud, muddy, vapor **6** darken, muddle, puzzle **7** becloud, confuse, eclipse, mystify, obscure, perplex, pogonip **8** bewilder, distract **9** obfuscate, overcloud **10** muddlement **11** muddledness **12** befuddlement, bewilderment

foggy

4 hazy **5** misty, murky, soupy, vague **7** brumous, muddled, obscure, tenuous **8** confused, vaporous

foghorn

8 diaphone

fogy

6 square **7** diehard **8** mossback, standpat **10** back number, fuddy-duddy **12** antediluvian, conservative, mid-Victorian **13** stick-in-the-mud

fogyish

4 tory **5** right **7** die-hard, old-line **8** orthodox **9** out-of-date **10** antiquated **11** reactionary **12** conservative, old-fashioned

foible

5 fault **7** failing, frailty **8** weakness **11** shortcoming **12** imperfection

foil

4 balk, beat, bilk, curb, dash, faze **5** sword **6** baffle, defeat, rattle, thwart, tissue **7** buffalo, repulse **8** restrain **9** discomfit, embarrass, frustrate **10** circumvent, disappoint, disconcert

foist

3 fob **4** dupe, gull, hoax, wish, worm **5** cheat, trick **6** delude, edge in, fob off, impose, palm on, work in **7** beguile, deceive, defraud, inflict, mislead, palm off, pass off, swindle, work off **8** hoodwink **9** bamboozle, insinuate, overreach **10** infiltrate

fold

3 lap, pen, ply **4** bend, bust, coat, fail, leaf, ruck, tuck **5** break, crash, drape, flock, layer, plait, pleat, plica, purse, ridge, rivel **6** crease, cuttle, double, furrow, pucker, rimple **7** confine, crinkle, crumple, embrace, entwine, envelop, flexure, overlap, plicate, wrinkle **8** surround **9** plication **11** corrugation

combining form: **5** ptych **6** ptycho, valvul **7** valvulo

skin: **4** ruga **5** plica, rugae (plural) **6** dewlap, plicae (plural)

folder

4 file **5** cover **6** binder **8** circular

foliage

6 growth, leaves **7** leafage, verdure **9** greenness **10** vegetation

folk

4 clan, race **5** house, laity, stock, tribe **6** family, people **7** kindred, lineage **9** relatives

folklore

4 myth **6** belief, custom, legend, mythos **9** mythology, tradition **12** superstition

folksinger

4 Baez (Joan), Ives (Burl) **5** Dylan (Bob), Niles (John Jacob), White (Josh) **6** Seeger (Pete) **7** Chapman (Tracy), Guthrie (Arlo, Woody) **9** Ledbetter (Huddie)

folktale

7 märchen

follow

3 ape, dog, see, spy, tag 4 copy, hunt, keep, mind, obey, seek, tail, take 5 after, catch, chase, chivy, ensue, grasp, hound, trace, track, trail 6 accept, attend, comply, convoy, pursue, search, shadow, take in 7 conform, imitate, observe, replace, succeed 8 displace, exercise, postdate, practice, supplant 9 accompany, apprehend, supersede, supervene 10 comprehend, understand

follower

3 fan 5 freak, toady 6 addict, cohort, patron, sequel, votary 7 devotee, groupie, habitué, sectary, sequent, trailer 8 adherent, advocate, disciple, faithful, hanger-on, henchman, myrmidon, parasite, partisan, sectator, tagalong 9 dependent, satellite, supporter, sycophant 10 aficionado 11 lickspittle
of Theodore Roosevelt: 9 Bull Moose
suffix: 3 ite

following

4 next 5 after, below, since, suite, train 6 behind, public 7 ensuing, retinue, sequent 8 audience 9 clientage, clientele, entourage 10 sequential, subsequent, succeeding, successive 12 subsequent to

follow-up

6 sequel

folly

4 whim 6 lunacy, vanity 7 fatuity, foolery, inanity, madness 8 insanity, nonsense 9 absurdity, craziness, dottiness, silliness, stupidity 10 imprudence, indulgence 11 foolishness, witlessness

foment

3 set 4 abet, brew, goad, spur 5 nurse, raise, rouse, set on 6 arouse, excite, foster, incite, stir up, whip up 7 agitate, ferment, nurture, provoke 9 cultivate, encourage, instigate

Fomorian one-eyed giant

5 Balor

fond

4 dear, warm 5 basis, silly 6 doting, loving, tender, upbeat 7 devoted, foolish 8 enamored, lonesome, romantic, sanguine 9 indulgent 10 groundwork, infatuated, optimistic, responsive 11 sentimental, sympathetic 12 affectionate

fondle

3 hug, pet 4 love 5 clasp 6 caress, cosset, dandle 7 embrace

fondness

4 love 5 taste 6 liking, relish 8 appetite, devotion, soft spot 9 affection 10 attachment, partiality, propensity 11 inclination 12 predilection

fondness for

combining form: 5 phily 6 philia
suffix: 4 itis

fond of

combining form: 4 phil 5 phile, philo 6 philic 7 philous

food

3 pap 4 bite, chow, diet, fare, grub, meal, meat 5 bread, manna, scoff 6 fodder, viands, vivres 7 aliment, edibles, nurture, pabulum 8 delicacy, victuals 9 nutriment, provender 10 provisions, sustenance 11 comestibles, nourishment
combining form: 4 sito 6 phagia
craving for: 7 bulimia
divine: 8 ambrosia
element: 5 sugar 6 starch 7 mineral, protein, vitamin 12 carbohydrate
from heaven: 5 manna
lover: 7 epicure, gourmet 8 gourmand
provision: 4 mess 6 ration 7 serving
scarcity: 6 famine
waste: 4 orts 7 garbage

foofaraw

4 coil, fuss 6 furore, hurrah, ruckus, rumpus, shindy 8 brouhaha 9 commotion

fool

3 ass, fun, kid, rag, rib, sap, toy 4 blow, butt, dolt, dope, dupe, fish, gull, hoax, jerk, jest, joke, josh, mark, poop, razz, simp, wolf, zany 5 amble, ament, chump, clown, comic, dally, dummy, dunce, flirt, goose, idiot, jolly, loser, moron, ninny, noddy, patsy, schmo, silly, trick, waste 6 banter, befool, butt in, coquet, cretin, cuckoo, dimwit, donkey, doodle, horn in, jester, lead on, loiter, madman, meddle, monkey, motley, nincom, nitwit, pigeon, schmoe, simple, stooge, stupid, sucker, trifle, victim, wanton 7 asshead, buffoon, chicane, consume, deceive, fall guy, foolish, fritter, gudgeon, half-wit, jackass, natural, pinhead, saphead, schmuck, tomfool 8 busybody, comedian, dumbbell, easy mark, flimflam, hoodwink, imbecile, lunkhead, mooncalf, numskull, pushover, softhead, squander, underwit, womanize 9 bamboozle, birdbrain, blockhead, dissipate, interfere, interlope, philander, simpleton, throw away 10 frivol away, instrument, mess around, monkey with, nincompoop, play around, tamper with, trifle away 11 featherhead, hornswoggle, merry-andrew, ninnyhammer, rattlebrain, string along 12 featherbrain, scatterbrain 13 laughingstock

foolhardy

4 rash 6 daring 8 headlong, reckless 9 audacious, daredevil, impetuous, venturous 11 adventurous, precipitate, temerarious, venturesome 13 adventuresome

foolish

3 mad 4 daft, fond, rash, zany 5 batty, crazy, dippy, dizzy, dotty, goofy, inane, jerky, loony, loopy, sappy, silly, wacky 6 absurd, insane, simple, stupid, unwise 7 asinine, doltish, fatuous, idiotic, lunatic, moronic, offbeat, unwitty, witless 8 headless, reckless 9 brainless, fantastic, half-baked, imbecilic, laughable, ludicrous, senseless, unearthly 10 halfcocked, half-witted, idleheaded, irrational, ridiculous, unorthodox, weak-headed, weak-minded 11 harebrained, nonsensical

foolishness

4 bull, bunk 5 folly 6 lunacy 7 fatuity, inanity, waggery 8 drollery, insanity, nonsense, unwisdom 9 absurdity 10 imprudence 12 indiscretion 13 senselessness

fool's gold

6 pyrite

foot

3 add, sum, tot 4 base, cast, pace, step, tote, walk 5 dance, nadir, total, tread, troop 6 bottom, figure, hoof it, prance, tootsy 7 summate, tootsie, traipse 8 ambulate, totalize
ailment: 4 corn 6 bunion, callus
animal: 3 pad, paw 4 hoof 7 fetlock, flipper, pastern, trotter
bones of: 5 talus, tarsi (plural) 6 cuboid, tarsal, tarsus 7 phalanx 9 calcaneus, cuneiform, navicular, phalanges (plural) 10 metatarsal

combining form: **3** ped, pod, pus **4** pede, pedi, pedo, poda, pode, podo **5** podia **6** podium
doctor: **10** podiatrist **11** chiropodist
metric: **4** iamb **5** arsis **6** dactyl, thesis **7** anapest, pyrrhic, spondee, trochee
part: **3** toe **4** arch, ball, claw, nail **5** ankle, digit, talon **6** hallux, instep

football

5 rugby **6** rugger, soccer **7** pigskin
field: **8** gridiron
foul: **7** holding, offside **8** clipping **12** interference
official: **6** umpire **7** referee **8** linesman **9** back judge, line judge **10** field judge
play: **4** dive, trap **5** sneak, sweep **6** option, screen **7** audible, counter, handoff, rollout, runback **8** dropback **9** crossbuck, off-tackle **10** buttonhook
player position: **3** end **4** back **5** guard **6** center, safety, tackle **7** flanker, lineman, wideout **8** fullback, halfback, slotback, split end, tailback, tight end, wingback **9** noseguard **10** cornerback, linebacker, nose tackle **11** quarterback **12** defensive end, wide receiver
scoring: **6** safety **9** field goal, touchdown **10** conversion
starting play: **7** kickoff
team: **6** eleven
term: **4** down, kick, pass, punt, rush, snap **5** blitz, block, squad **6** fumble, huddle, onside, option, safety, spiral **7** end zone, handoff, kickoff, offside, pigskin, quarter, spinner, yardage **8** clipping, crossbar, goal line, goalpost, gridiron, halftime **9** backfield, defensive, field goal, intercept, offensive, placekick, scrimmage, touchback, touchdown **11** broken field **12** interception

footballer

4 Kemp (Jack), Moon (Warren), Rice (Jerry) **5** Allen (Marcus), Baugh (Sammy), Berry (Raymond), Brown (Jim), Ditka (Mike), Elway (John), Jones (Bert, Deacon), Kelly (Jim), Kosar (Bernie), Shula (Don), Simms (Phil), Smith (Emmitt), Starr (Bart), Swann (Lynn), Young (Steve) **6** Aikman (Troy), Blanda (George), Butkus (Dick), Carter (Ki-Jana), Csonka (Larry), Dawson (Len), Graham (Otto), Grange (Red), Greene (Joe), Jaeger (Jeff), Marino (Dan), Namath (Joe), Payton (Walter), Rypien (Mark), Sayers (Gale), Thorpe

(Jim), Tittle (Y. A.), Unitas (Johnny), Walker (Herschel) **7** Bledsoe (Drew), Dorsett (Tony), Esiason (Boomer), Gifford (Frank), Hornung (Paul), Luckman (Sid), Montana (Joe), Riggins (John), Sanders (Barry, Deion), Simpson (O. J.), Stabler (Ken), Thurman (Thomas) **8** Anderson (Ottis), Bradshaw (Terry), Nagurski (Bronko), Plunkett (Jim), Staubach (Roger) **9** Dickerson (Eric), Jurgensen (Sonny), Hostetler (Jeff), Tarkenton (Fran)

footed

combining form: **3** ped, pod **6** podous

footfall

4 step **5** tread

footing

4 base, rank, seat, term **5** basis, place, state **6** bottom, ground, status **7** bedrock, seating, station, warrant **8** basement, capacity, position **9** character, situation **10** foundation, groundwork, substratum

footless

6 apodal

foot lever

5 pedal **7** treadle

footlike

6 pedate **8** pediform

footpad

6 robber **10** highwayman

footprint

3 pug **4** sign, step **5** spoor, trace, track, tract **7** pugmark, vestige
fossil: **7** ichnite **9** ichnolite

footslog

4 plod, slop, toil **6** stodge, trudge **8** plunther

footstep

5 spoor, track, tract **7** vestige

footstone

6 ledger **8** monument **11** grave marker

footstool

7 hassock, ottoman

fop

4 buck, dude **5** blade, blood, dandy, spark, sport, swell **6** masher **7** coxcomb, gallant **8** cavalier, macaroni, popinjay **9** exquisite **10** ladies' man, ladykiller **11** Beau Brummel, petit-maître **12** fashion plate, lounge lizard, man-about-town

for

prefix: **3** pro

forage

4 beat, comb, grub, raid, rake **5** scour **6** browse, fodder, ravage, search **7** ransack, rummage **8** finecomb, scrounge **9** pasturage; (see also **fodder**)

forager

6 raider, sacker **8** marauder, ravisher

foray

4 raid **5** harry **6** attack, harass, inroad, invade, maraud, sortie **7** overrun, pillage **8** invasion **9** incursion, irruption

forbear

4 curb, keep, shun **5** avoid, cease, evade, forgo, spare **6** bridle, desist, endure, escape, eschew, forego, suffer **7** abstain, decline, inhibit, refrain **8** restrain, tolerate, withhold **9** sacrifice

forbearance

5 grace, mercy **6** lenity **7** charity **8** clemency, lenience, leniency, mildness, patience **9** restraint, tolerance **10** abstinence, toleration

forbearing

4 easy, mild **6** gentle **7** clement, lenient, patient **8** merciful, tolerant **9** indulgent **10** charitable, thoughtful **11** considerate

Forbes hero

8 Tremaine (Johnny)

forbid

3 ban, bar **4** curb, deny, halt, stop, veto **5** block, check, debar, estop, taboo **6** enjoin, hinder, impede, outlaw, refuse **7** exclude, inhibit, obviate, prevent, rule out, shut out **8** obstruct, preclude, prohibit, restrain **9** interdict, proscribe

forbidden

5 taboo **6** banned **8** verboten **10** prohibited

Forbidden City

5 Lhasa

force

2 od **3** arm, jam, vim, vis **4** beef, cram, make, move, odyl, push, rape **5** cause, drive, exact, foist, impel, karma, might, odyle, order, pains, point, power, press, punch, sinew, speed, spoil, vigor, visit, wreak, wreck, wrest **6** coerce, compel, defile, demand, duress, effort, energy, enjoin, extort, impose, in-

ject, legion, muscle, oblige, ravish, strain, stress **7** cogency, command, concuss, headway, impetus, inflict, outrage, potency, require, sandbag, shotgun, tension, trouble, violate **8** coercion, deflower, manpower, momentum, obligate, occasion, pressure, shoehorn, strength, validity, velocity, violence **9** constrain, deflorate, exertions, intensity, puissance, strong arm, validness, vehemence **10** compulsion, constraint
apart: **5** wedge
unit: **4** dyne

forced
5 rigid, stiff **6** wooden **7** labored **9** contrived, fatiguing, unnatural **10** artificial, compulsory, exhausting, factitious, farfetched, inflexible **11** involuntary

forceful
6 cogent, mighty, potent, virile **7** dynamic, telling **8** emphatic, forcible, powerful, puissant, vigorous **9** assertive, effective, energetic, insistent **10** compelling, resounding **12** constraining

forceless
4 weak **5** wimpy **6** feeble **8** impotent **10** emasculate, inadequate **11** ineffective, ineffectual, slackspined **12** invertebrate

force out
see **expel**

forcible
6 mighty, potent **7** intense, violent **8** coercive, emphatic, militant, powerful, puissant, vehement **9** assertive **10** aggressive

Ford's folly
5 Edsel

for each
3 per

forearm bone
4 ulna **6** radius

forebear
8 ancestor **9** ascendant **10** progenitor **11** antecedents **12** primogenitor

forebode
4 omen **5** augur **7** betoken, portend, predict, presage, promise **8** foretell

foreboding
4 omen **5** dread **6** augury **7** anxiety, portent, presage, warning **9** prenotion **10** prediction, prognos-

tic **11** premonition, presagement **12** presentiment

forecast
5 augur, guess, infer, weird **6** gather **7** foresee, portend, predict, presage, surmise **8** conclude, foreshow, foretell, prophecy, soothsay **9** adumbrate, prevision, prognosis **10** conjecture, prediction, vaticinate **13** prognosticate

forecaster
4 seer **5** augur **6** auspex, oracle **7** prophet **8** haruspex **9** predictor **10** prophesier **11** Nostradamus **13** meteorologist

foreclose
3 bar **5** debar **6** cut off, hinder **7** prevent **8** preclude

forefather
see **forebear**

forefeel
6 divine **7** preknow, previse **9** apprehend, prevision, visualize

forefinger
5 index

forefront
8 vanguard

foregoer
7 example **8** ancestor **9** precursor, prototype **10** antecedent, antecessor **11** predecessor

foregoing
4 past **5** prior **8** anterior, previous **9** precedent, preceding **10** antecedent

forehanded
7 prudent, thrifty

forehead
4 brow **5** frons, front **8** sinciput **9** sincipita (plural)
combining form: **6** fronto
ornamental spot: **5** tilak

foreign
5 alien **6** exotic **7** strange **9** extrinsic, obnoxious, repellent, repugnant **10** accidental, extraneous, immaterial, inapposite, irrelative, irrelevant **11** distasteful, impertinent, incongruous, inconsonant **12** adventitious, inapplicable, incompatible, inconsistent **13** inappropriate
combining form: **3** xen **4** xeno

foreigner
5 alien **7** inconnu **8** outsider, stranger

foreknow
6 divine **7** previse **8** conclude

9 apprehend, prevision, visualize **10** anticipate

foreland
4 beak, bill, cape, head, naze **5** point **8** headland **10** promontory

forelock
5 bangs, quiff **8** linchpin, split pin **9** cotter pin

foreman
4 boss **5** chief **6** gaffer, ganger, honcho, leader **7** captain, headman, manager, overman, steward **8** overseer **10** supervisor

foremost
4 arch, head, main **5** chief, first, front **7** initial, leading, premier, supreme **8** champion, headmost **9** inaugural, principal **10** preeminent

forenoon
4 morn **7** morning

forensics
6 debate **7** mooting **11** disputation **13** argumentation

foreordain
4 fate **6** doom to **7** destine, preform **9** determine **10** predestine **12** predestinate, predetermine

forerun
4 pace **6** herald **7** precede, predate, presage **8** announce, antecede, antedate **9** harbinger **10** anticipate, foreshadow

forerunner
4 mark, omen, sign **5** model, token **6** augury, author, herald **7** example, pattern, pioneer, portent, presage, symptom, warning **8** ancestor, exemplar **9** announcer, harbinger, initiator, messenger, precursor, prototype **10** antecedent, antecessor, originator, prognostic **11** anticipator, predecessor **12** announcement

foresee
4 espy **6** descry, divine **7** discern, predict, preknow, presage, previse **8** perceive, prophesy **9** apprehend, prevision, visualize **10** anticipate **13** prognosticate

foreseer
5 augur **6** auspex, oracle **7** diviner, prophet **8** haruspex **9** predictor **10** prophesier, soothsayer **11** Nostradamus

foreshadow
4 bode, hint, omen **5** augur **7** betoken, portend, presage, promise **9** adumbrate, prefigure **11** prefigurate

foresight

6 vision 7 caution 8 prudence, sagacity 9 canniness 10 discretion, perception, precaution, prescience, providence 11 discernment 12 clairvoyance

forest

4 bosk, wood 5 copse, grove, weald, woods 6 timber 7 coppice, thicket, woodlot 8 wildwood, woodland 10 timberland, wilderness
combining form: 3 hyl 4 hylo
deity: 5 dryad 6 sylvan 8 Sylvanus
English: 5 Arden 8 Sherwood
opening: 5 glade
relating to: 6 sylvan
subarctic: 5 taiga
tropical: 5 selva 6 jungle

forestall

4 ward 5 avert, deter 7 obviate, prevent, rule out 8 preclude, stave off 10 anticipate

Forester

hero: 10 Hornblower (Horatio)
novel: 12 African Queen

foretell

4 bode, call, warn 5 augur 6 divine, reveal 7 declare, divulge, portend, predict, presage, promise 8 announce, disclose, proclaim, prophesy, soothsay 9 adumbrate, apprehend, prefigure 10 anticipate, vaticinate 13 prognosticate

foreteller

see **foreseer**

forethought

5 sense 7 caution 8 gumption, judgment, prudence 9 canniness, foresight 10 discretion, precaution, providence 12 deliberation, discreetness 13 premeditation

foretime

4 past, yore 9 yesterday 10 yesteryear

foretoken

4 bode, hint, mark, note, omen, sign 5 augur, badge 6 augury, boding, herald, ostent, shadow 7 inkling, portend, portent, presage, promise, symptom, warning 8 bodement, forecast 9 harbinger, precursor 10 indication, intimation

forever

3 aye 4 ever 6 always 7 endless, eternal 8 eternity, evermore 9 endlessly, eternally 11 ceaselessly, continually, everlasting, incessantly, in perpetuum, perpetually, unceasingly 13 everlastingly

forewarning

6 caveat 7 caution 8 monition 10 admonition 11 commonition

foreword

5 proem 7 preface, prelude 8 exordium, overture, preamble, prologue 9 prelusion 12 introduction, prolegomenon

for example

2 as, e.g. 6 such as

for fear that

4 lest

forfeit

4 drop, fine, lose 5 mulct 7 penalty 9 sacrifice 10 amercement

forfend

4 ward 5 avert, deter 6 secure 7 obviate, prevent, protect, rule out, ward off 8 preclude, preserve, stave off

forge

4 beat, copy, make, mold 5 build, pound, shape 6 smithy 7 advance, fashion, imitate, produce, turn out 8 bloomery, progress 9 construct, fabricate 11 counterfeit, manufacture, put together

forget

4 fail, omit 5 fluff 6 blow up, ignore, slight, unknow 7 blink at, neglect, unlearn 8 discount, overlook 9 blink away, disregard 11 disremember 12 misrecollect

forgetful

3 lax 5 slack 6 absent, remiss 7 bemused 8 careless, heedless 9 negligent, oblivious, unwitting 10 abstracted, neglectful 11 inattentive, thoughtless 12 absentminded

forgetfulness

5 lethe 7 amnesia 8 oblivion

forgivable

6 venial 10 pardonable

forgive

5 remit 6 excuse, pardon, slight 7 absolve, condone, neglect 8 overlook

forgo

5 leave, waive 6 eschew, give up, resign 7 abandon, forbear 8 abdicate, abnegate, renounce 9 sacrifice, surrender 10 relinquish

fork

6 bisect, branch, crotch 7 utensil
prong: 4 tine

fork out

3 pay 5 spend

forlorn

4 vain 5 alone 6 bereft, futile, lonely 7 cynical 8 deserted, desolate, forsaken, helpless, homeless, hopeless, lonesome, solitary, wretched 9 abandoned, depressed, desperate, destitute, fruitless, miserable, oppressed 10 bedraggled, despairing, despondent, desponding, disordered, friendless 11 defenseless, pessimistic 12 disconsolate

form

3 law, way 4 body, cast, make, mode, mold, plan, plot, rite, rule 5 build, canon, forge, found, frame, habit, image, model, shape, style, usage 6 create, custom, design, devise, figure, invent, make up, manner, method, ritual, scheme, system 7 acquire, anatomy, compose, contour, decorum, develop, economy, fashion, liturgy, outline, precept, process, produce, profile, project, turn out 8 ceremony, comprise, organism, organize, practice, skeleton 9 construct, establish, etiquette, fabricate, formality, framework, procedure, propriety, structure 10 ceremonial, constitute, convenance, convention, proceeding, regulation, silhouette 11 manufacture 13 configuration
combining form: 3 gen 4 gene 5 morph, plasm, plast 6 morpha, morphi (plural) 6 morpho, plasma 7 morphae (plural), morphic 8 morphism 9 morphosis
suffix: 2 fy 3 ify

formal

3 set 4 prim 5 exact, rigid, stiff 6 dressy, proper, seemly, solemn 7 distant, nominal, orderly, precise, regular, stately, titular 8 decorous, reserved, so-called 9 essential, unbending 10 ceremonial, methodical, systematic 11 ceremonious, syntactical 12 constitutive, conventional

formality

4 form, rite 6 ritual 7 liturgy, service 8 ceremony, insignia 10 ceremonial, convenance, convention, observance

format

4 plan, size 5 shape, style 6 makeup

formation

4 form, rank 6 design, makeup

9 structure 10 production 11 arrangement, composition, development 12 architecture, construction

formative material
combining form: 5 plasm 6 plasma

former
3 old 4 late, once, past 5 maker, prior 6 bygone, shaper, whilom 7 creator, earlier, onetime, quondam 8 anterior, previous, sometime 9 erstwhile, precedent, preceding 10 antecedent
combining form: 6 proter 7 protero

formerly
4 erst, once 6 before, whilom 7 already, earlier 9 erstwhile 10 heretofore, previously

formidable
4 hard 5 awful, tough 6 uphill 7 arduous, fearful, labored 8 alarming, dreadful, horrific, shocking, terrible, terrific, toilsome 9 appalling, difficult, effortful, frightful, laborious, strenuous

formless
3 raw 4 rude 5 crude, rough, vague 7 chaotic, obscure, unclear 8 inchoate, unshaped 9 amorphous, shapeless, undefined, unordered 10 immaterial, indefinite, indistinct 11 unorganized

Formosa
6 Taiwan
capital: 6 Taipei

formulate
3 put 4 make, word 5 couch, draft, frame, hatch 6 cook up, devise, draw up, invent, make up, phrase, vamp up 7 concoct, dream up, express, hatch up, prepare 8 contrive

forsake
4 quit 5 avoid, chuck, leave, spurn 6 defect, depart, desert, reject, resign 7 abandon 8 abdicate, renounce 9 throw over

forsaken
4 lorn 7 uncouth 8 derelict, deserted, desolate, solitary 9 abandoned

forsaker
8 apostate

Forseti
father: 6 Balder
palace: 7 Glitnir

forswear
4 deny 5 unsay 6 abjure, recall, recant, reject 7 perjure, retract

8 palinode, renounce, take back, withdraw

fort
6 castle 7 bastion, bulwark, citadel, redoubt 8 fastness, fortress, martello 10 stronghold
Baltimore: 7 McHenry
California: 3 Ord
New Jersey: 3 Dix
New York: 7 Niagara, Stanwix 8 Schuyler 11 Ticonderoga
Ontario: 9 Frontenac
San Antonio: 8 The Alamo
South Carolina: 6 Sumter
Spanish: 7 alcazar 8 presidio

forte
3 bag 5 thing 6 medium, métier, oyster 7 ability 8 ableness, eminency, long suit, strength 10 competence, efficiency, strong suit 11 strong point

forth
2 on 3 out 4 alee 5 ahead, along 6 onward 7 forward

forthcoming
6 future 7 affable, awaited 8 approach, expected, imminent, sociable 11 anticipated, approaching 12 approachable

for the most part
9 generally 10 on the whole

for the time being
6 pro tem 10 pro tempore

forthright
4 open 5 frank, plain 6 candid, direct, single 7 frankly 10 aboveboard 11 openhearted, undisguised, unvarnished

forthwith
3 now 4 away 5 short 6 at once, sudden 7 asudden 8 abruptly, directly, suddenly 9 instanter, instantly, right away, thereupon 11 immediately, straightway 12 straightaway

fortification
4 boma, moat, wall 5 agger, redan 6 abatis, glacis, sangar, sungar 7 barrier, parapet, rampart, ravelin, redoubt 8 barbican, enceinte, palisade 9 barricade, earthwork 10 breastwork
part: 7 salient

fortify
3 arm 4 gird, stir 5 brace, rally, ready, renew, rouse, steel 6 arouse 7 bulwark, prepare, protect, rampart, refresh, restore 8 energize,

palisade 9 encourage 10 invigorate, strengthen

fortitude
4 grit, guts, pith, sand 5 nerve, pluck, spunk, valor 6 bottom, mettle, spirit 7 bravery, courage, stamina 8 backbone, boldness, strength, tenacity, valiancy 9 constancy, endurance 10 resolution 11 intrepidity 12 fearlessness, perseverance, resoluteness, valorousness 13 dauntlessness, determination

fortress
see **fort**

fortuitous
3 odd 5 fluky 6 casual, chance 10 accidental, contingent, incidental

fortuity
3 hap 4 luck 6 chance 8 accident

Fortuna
5 Tyche
symbol: 5 wheel 6 rudder

fortunate
4 good, well 5 happy, lucky, white 6 benign, bright, dexter 9 favorable 10 auspicious, propitious 12 providential

Fortunate Islands
8 Canaries

fortune
3 lot, pot, wad 4 doom, fate, luck, mint, pile 5 worth 6 boodle, bundle, chance, hazard, packet, riches, wealth 7 destiny, portion, success 8 property 9 luckiness, resources, substance

fortune-teller
4 seer 7 palmist; (see also **foreteller**)

fortune-telling
see **divination**

forty winks
3 nap 6 catnap, dog nap, siesta, snooze

forward
2 on, to 3 aid 4 abet, alee, ante, back, bold, help, pert, send, ship, wise 5 ahead, along, brash, eager, fresh, nervy, ready, relay, remit, route, sassy, saucy, serve, smart, ultra 6 cheeky, foster, hasten, onward, uphold, uppish, uppity 7 address, advance, anxious, consign, extreme, further, promote, pushful, pushing, radical, support 8 advanced, champion, dispatch, impudent, previous, transmit 9 en-

courage, in advance, presuming **11** overweening, precedently, smart-alecky **12** antecedently, presumptuous **13** self-asserting, self-assertive
prefix: **4** ante

For Whom the Bell Tolls
author: **9** Hemingway (Ernest)
character: **5** Maria, Pablo, Pilar **6** Jordan

foss, fosse
4 moat **5** canal, ditch **6** trench

fossa
3 pit **6** cavity **10** depression

fossil
4 fogy **5** amber **6** square **7** antique **8** calamite, conodont, moss-back **10** antiquated, fuddy-duddy **12** antediluvian, mid-Victorian **13** stick-in-the-mud
combining form: **4** lite, lith, lyte, necr **5** necro, oryct **6** orycto
fuel: **3** oil **4** coal, peat **9** petroleum

foster
4 back, help, rear, warm **5** favor, house, lodge, nurse, serve **6** assist, harbor, nursle, oblige, uphold **7** advance, cherish, forward, further, nourish, nurture, promote, shelter, support, sustain **8** champion **9** cultivate, encourage, entertain

foul
4 base, soil, vile **5** black, block, dirty, fetid, grime, muddy, nasty, soily **6** besoil, coarse, defile, filthy, grubby, horrid, impure, odious, putrid, rotten, smirch, smooch, smudge, smutch, smutty, vulgar, wicked **7** abusive, begrime, noisome, obscene, pollute, profane, raunchy, squalid, tarnish, unclean **8** dishonor, feculent, indecent, obstruct, polluted, stinking **9** dangerous, desecrate, entangled, loathsome, obnoxious, offensive, repellent, repugnant, repulsive, revolting, uncleanly **10** detestable, disgusting, malodorous **11** contaminate **12** scatological

foul play
5 blood **6** murder **7** killing **8** homicide, violence **12** manslaughter

found
4 base, cast, rear, rest, stay **5** begin, erect, raise, set up, start **6** bottom, create **7** fashion, support, sustain **8** commence, initiate, organize **9** establish, institute, originate, predicate

foundation
3 bed **4** base, rest, sill **5** basis **6** bottom **7** bedrock, footing, roadbed, support, warrant **9** endowment **10** substratum **11** institution **12** organization, substructure, underpinning

foundational
5 basic **6** bottom **7** primary **10** underlying **11** fundamental

founder
4 fail, sink, sire **5** wreck **6** author, damage, go down **7** creator **8** collapse, inventor, submerge, submerse **9** architect, generator, patriarch **10** originator

fountain
3 jet **4** head, root **6** origin, source, spring, whence **8** wellhead **9** inception, reservoir **10** wellspring
nymph: **6** Egeria

four
6 tetrad **7** quartet **10** quaternion
bagger: **5** homer **7** homerun
combining form: **4** tetr **5** quadr, tetra **6** quadri, quadru, quater, tessar **7** tessara, tessera
gills: **4** pint
hundred: **5** elite **10** upper crust
inches: **4** hand
pecks: **6** bushel
quarts: **6** gallon

fourberie
5 fraud **7** chicane **8** trickery **9** chicanery, deception **10** dishonesty, hanky-panky

four-flush
5 bluff **6** betray, delude, humbug, juggle, take in **7** beguile, deceive **11** double cross

four-footed animal
8 tetrapod **9** quadruped

Four Horsemen
3 War **5** Death **6** Famine **10** Pestilence

four-in-hand
3 tie **7** necktie

fourpence
5 groat

four-poster
3 bed

fourscore
6 eighty

four-sided figure
6 square **7** rhombus **9** rectangle

foursquare
7 solidly **8** quadrate **9** quadratic

10 forthright **11** quadratical **12** forthrightly

fourteen pounds
5 stone

fourth
7 quarter **8** quadrant, quartern
combining form: **5** quadr, quart **6** quadri, quadru **7** tetarto

fowl
3 hen **4** bird, cock **5** chick, poult **6** Bantam, pullet **7** chicken, rooster; (see also **chicken; poultry**)

fox
4 fool **5** trick **6** baffle, outwit **7** confuse, Reynard **8** bewilder **9** dissemble
female: **5** vixen
kind: **6** corsac, corsak, fennec
Scottish: **3** tod
young: **3** cub

foxglove
7 mullein **8** pokeweed **9** fairy bell **10** fingerroot

fox grape
9 muscadine

foxiness
3 art **5** craft **7** cunning **8** artifice **10** cleverness

foxlike
7 vulpine

foxy
3 sly **4** deep, wily **6** artful, astute, clever, crafty, shrewd, tricky **7** cunning **8** guileful **9** deceitful, dishonest, insidious

foyer
5 lobby **8** anteroom, entrance **9** vestibule

fracas
3 row **4** feud **5** brawl, broil, fight, melee, run-in, set-to **6** affray, hassle **7** dispute, quarrel, ruction **8** squabble **9** bickering **10** donnybrook **11** altercation

fraction
3 bit, cut **4** part **5** piece, scrap **6** divide, little **7** portion, section **8** fragment

fractious
4 wild **5** cross, huffy, waspy **6** unruly **7** fretful, peevish, pettish, waspish **8** contrary, indocile, petulant, snappish **9** irritable **10** refractory **11** indomitable, intractable, quarrelsome **12** recalcitrant, ungovernable, unmanageable

fracturable
7 fragile 8 delicate, shattery
9 breakable

fracture
4 rent, rift, tear 5 break, cleft, crack, split 6 breach, schism 7 rupture, violate
combining form: 7 rrhexis

Fra Diavolo composer
5 Auber (Esprit)

fragile
4 fine, thin, weak 5 crisp, frail, short 6 feeble, flimsy, infirm, slight, weakly 7 brittle, crumbly, crunchy, friable, slender, tenuous, unsound 8 decrepit, delicate, shattery

fragment
3 ace, bit, end, jot 4 atom, chip, iota, part, rive 5 burst, crumb, flake, grain, minim, piece, scrap, shard, sherd, shive, shred, smash, spall 6 morsel, shiver, sliver 7 flinder, shatter 8 particle, splinter, splitter 11 splinterize

fragmentary
4 part 6 broken 7 partial 10 fractional, incomplete 12 disorganized

fragrance
4 balm, odor 5 aroma, scent, smell, spice 7 bouquet, incense, perfume 9 redolence

fragrant
5 balmy, spicy, sweet 6 aromal, savory 7 perfumy 8 aromatic, perfumed, redolent 9 ambrosial, delicious

frail
4 puny, slim, thin, weak 5 petty 6 feeble, flimsy, infirm, sickly, slight, weakly 7 fragile, slender, tenuous, unsound 8 decrepit, delicate, shattery 9 breakable, frangible 11 fracturable, shatterable

frailty
3 sin 4 vice 5 fault 6 foible 7 failing 8 weakness 9 infirmity 11 tenuousness 12 imperfection

frame
4 body, form, make, mold, plan, sash 5 build, cause, draft, easel, erect, forge, shape, state, utter 6 cook up, deckle, devise, draw up, figure, invent, make up, system, vamp up 7 arrange, chassis, concoct, dream up, fashion, hatch up, imagine, prepare, produce 8 casement, conceive, contrive, regulate 9 cartouche, construct, fabricate, formulate

part: 4 sill, stud 5 joist, plate

framework
4 rack 7 trestle 8 cribbing, cribwork, scaffold, skeleton, studding, studwork, trussing 9 structure
of crossed strips: 7 lattice, trellis

France
ancient name: 4 Gaul 6 Gallia
capital: 5 Paris
combining form: 5 Gallo
historic province: 4 Foix 5 Anjou, Aunis, Bearn, Berry, Maine 6 Alsace, Artois, Marche, Poitou 7 Gascony, Guyenne, Picardy 8 Auvergne, Brittany, Burgundy, Dauphine, Flanders, Limousin, Lorraine, Lyonnais, Normandy, Provence, Touraine 9 Angoumois, Champagne, Languedoc, Nivernais, Orleanais, Saintonge, Venaissin 10 Roussillon 11 Bourbonnais, Ile de France 12 Franche Comte
monetary unit: 5 franc

Francesca's lover
5 Paolo

franchise
4 vote 6 ballot 8 suffrage 9 exemption

frangible
7 brittle, fragile 8 delicate, shattery 9 breakable

frank
3 dog 4 fair, free, just, open 5 bluff, blunt, naive, plain 6 brazen, candid, direct, honest, hot dog, simple, single, wiener 7 natural, sincere, upright 8 man-to-man, unbiased 9 barefaced, impartial, ingenuous, outspoken 10 forthright, scrupulous, single-eyed, unmannered, unreserved 11 openhearted, plainspoken, unconcealed, undisguised, uninhibited, unvarnished, wienerwurst

Frankenstein author
7 Shelley (Mary)

frankfurter
3 dog 6 hot dog, wiener 11 wienerwurst

Frankie's lover
6 Johnny

Frankish hero
6 Roland

Franklin
birthplace: 6 Boston
invention: 5 stove 8 bifocals
pen name: 11 Poor Richard

frankness
6 candor 8 openness

frantic
3 mad 4 wild 5 rabid 6 insane 7 extreme, furious, violent 8 deranged, feverish, frenetic, frenzied 9 delirious, desperate 10 distraught

fraternal society
4 Elks 5 Moose 6 Eagles, Masons 10 Hibernians, Odd Fellows

fraternity
4 club 5 guild, order, union 6 league 7 company 10 fellowship 11 association, brotherhood 13 brotherliness

fraud
4 fake, hoax, sell, sham 5 cheat, faker, phony, trick 6 deceit, dupery, duping, humbug 7 chicane, defraud, swindle 8 impostor, trickery 9 chicanery, deception, fourberie, imposture, pretender, trickster 10 hanky-panky 11 bamboozling, highbinding, hoodwinking 13 bamboozlement, double-dealing, sharp practice

fraudulence
6 deceit 8 quackery, trickery 9 chicanery, deception, fourberie, phoniness 10 dishonesty

fraudulent
4 fake 5 false 7 crooked 8 cheating, guileful, quackish 9 deceitful, deceiving, deceptive, dishonest 10 fallacious

fray
3 row 4 fret 5 brawl, broil, brush, clash, fight, melee 6 combat, debate, strife, tumult 7 discord, dispute, quarrel, ruction, scuffle 8 skirmish 9 commotion, scrimmage 10 contention, dissension, donnybrook

frayed
4 worn 6 ragged 7 shreddy 10 threadbare

frazzle
4 fray, wear 5 upset 6 tucker 7 exhaust, outtire, outwear, wear out 8 knock out 9 prostrate

freak
3 bug, nut 4 whim 5 fancy, fiend, lusus 6 maniac, megrim, oddity, rarity, vagary, whimsy, zealot 7 anomaly, boutade, caprice, chimera, conceit, fanatic, monster, whimsey 8 crotchet, misshape, mutation, rara avis 9 androgyne, curiosity 10 aberration, enthusiast

11 abnormality, miscreation, monstrosity 12 malformation, whimsicality

freckle
3 dot 4 spot 7 ephelis, lentigo, speckle, stipple

free
3 lax, rid 4 open 5 clear, loose, round, unmew, unpen, untie, vocal 6 acquit, detach, exempt, gratis, loosen, ransom, redeem, rescue, unbind, uncurb, unpaid, untied, vagile 7 absolve, deliver, liberal, manumit, release, unbound, unchain, unclasp, unleash, unloose 8 autarkic, costless, detached, generous, handsome, liberate, released, separate, sui juris, unburden, unfasten, unloosen, untether 9 autarchic, bounteous, bountiful, delivered, discharge, disengage, exculpate, exonerate, extricate, liberated, outspoken, sovereign, unchained, unchecked, unshackle, unsparing 10 autonomous, chargeless, democratic, emancipate, gratuitous, heart-whole, munificent, openhanded, self-ruling, unconfined, unenslaved, unfettered, unshackled 11 affranchise, disencumber, disentangle, disenthrall, disimprison, emancipated, enfranchise, independent, untrammeled 12 enfranchised, unregimented, unrestrained, unrestricted 13 complimentary, self-directing, self-governing, unconstrained, unrecompensed, unremunerated

freebie
4 gift, pass 7 present 8 giveaway

freebooter
5 rover 6 bandit, bummer, pirate, raider, sea dog 7 brigand, cateran, corsair, forager, sea wolf 8 marauder, picaroon, pillager

freedom
4 ease 5 right, scope, sweep 7 compass, liberty, license, release 8 facility, immunity, latitude, vagility 9 exemption, privilege 10 generosity 11 magnanimity, prerogative 12 emancipation, independence

free-for-all
4 fray 5 brawl, broil, fight, melee, spree 6 affray, fracas 7 ruction 10 donnybrook

freehanded
7 liberal 8 generous 9 bounteous, bountiful, unsparing 10 munificent, openhanded

freeloader
5 leech 6 sponge 8 barnacle, hanger-on, parasite 12 lounge lizard

freeman
4 carl 5 carle, churl, thane, thegn 6 yeoman 7 burgess, burgher, citizen

Free State
8 Maryland

free ticket
4 pass 11 Annie Oakley

freezing
3 icy 4 cold 5 chill, gelid, nippy 6 arctic, chilly, frigid, frosty 7 glacial, shivery
combining form: 3 cry 4 cryo, kryo

freight
4 haul, load 5 cargo 6 burden, charge, lading 7 payload 9 transport

French
article: 2 la, le, un 3 les, une
attendant: 9 concierge
back: 3 dos
bed: 3 lit 6 couche
boy: 6 garçon
brother: 5 frère
cap: 5 beret
cardinal: 7 Mazarin (Jules) 9 Richelieu (Duc de)
castle: 7 château
cathedral city: 4 Albi 5 Paris, Reims, Rouen 6 Amiens, Nantes, Rheims 8 Chartres
clergyman: 4 abbé, curé, père
combining form: 5 Gallo 6 Franco
conjunction: 2 et, ou 4 mais
couturier: 4 Dior (Christian) 5 Patou (Jean) 6 Chanel (Coco) 7 Balmain (Pierre) 8 Givenchy (Hubert) 9 Courrèges (Andre), St. Laurent (Yves)
daughter: 5 fille
day: 5 jeudi, lundi, mardi 6 samedi 8 dimanche, mercredi, vendredi
dear: 4 cher
department head: 7 prefect
direction: 3 est, sud 4 nord 5 ouest
down with: 4 a bas
dream: 4 rêve
drink: 5 boire
dynasty: 5 Capet 6 Valois 7 Bourbon
egg: 4 oeuf
emblem: 10 fleur-de-lis
empress: 7 Eugénie 9 Joséphine
evening: 4 soir
exclamation: 3 zut 4 eheu, hein 9 sacrebleu

farewell: 5 adieu 8 au revoir
father: 4 père
forest: 7 Argonne, Belleau
friend: 3 ami 4 amie
game: 3 jeu 4 jeux (plural)
God: 4 dieu
good: 3 bon
hat: 7 chapeau
here: 3 ici
income: 5 rente
king: 3 roi
language: 9 Provençal
month: 3 mai 4 août, juin, mars, mois 5 avril 7 février, janvier, juillet
mother: 4 mère
national anthem: 12 Marseillaise
opera: 5 Faust, Lakmé, Manon, Thaïs 6 Carmen, Mignon 7 Werther
pancake: 5 crêpe
pastry: 6 éclair 8 napoleon
patron saint: 5 Denis
policeman: 4 flic 8 gendarme
porcelain: 6 Sèvres 7 Limoges
preposition: 2 de 3 par, sur 4 avec, dans, pour, sans, sous
pretty: 4 joli 5 jolie
prison: 8 Bastille
pronoun: 2 il, je, te, tu, un 3 eux, ils, mes, moi, toi, une 4 elle, nous, vous
Protestant: 6 Calvin 8 Huguenot
pupil: 5 élève
queen: 5 reine
rabbit: 5 lapin
railroad station: 4 gare
resort: 3 Pau 4 Nice 5 Vichy 6 Cannes, Menton 7 Antibes 8 Biarritz
resort area: 7 Riviera
restaurant: 6 bistro
revolutionist: 5 Marat (Jean-Paul) 6 Danton (Georges-Jacques)
Revolution party: 7 Gironde, Jacobin 8 Mountain
Revolution song: 5 Caira
saint: 4 Joan 6 Martin
school: 5 école, lycée
sea: 3 mer
season: 3 été 5 hiver 7 automne 9 printemps
servant: 5 valet
shop: 8 boutique
shrine: 7 Lourdes
singer: 4 Piaf (Edith) 8 chanteur 9 chanteuse
sister: 5 soeur
small: 5 petit 6 petite
soldier: 5 poilu 6 soldat, Zouave 8 chasseur
son: 4 fils
star: 6 étoile

state: 4 état
stock exchange: 6 bourse
street: 3 rue
subway: 5 metro
there!: 5 voilà
too much: 4 trop
very: 4 très
waiter: 6 garçon
wartime capital: 5 Vichy
water: 3 eau
well: 4 bien
wineshop: 6 bistro
wood: 4 bois
yesterday: 4 hier

frenetic
3 mad 4 wild 5 crazy, rabid
6 hectic 7 frantic, furious, violent
8 frenzied 9 delirious

frenzied
see **frenetic**

frenzy
3 mad 4 amok, fury, rage
5 amuck, craze, furor, mania
6 madden 7 derange, madness,
unhinge 8 delirium, distract, insanity 9 unbalance
of a bull elephant: 4 must 5 musth

frequency unit
5 hertz 7 fresnel

frequent
5 haunt, often, usual, visit 6 affect,
attend, common, infest, resort
7 hang out, overrun 8 everyday, familiar, habitual 9 customary
10 hang around

frequenter
7 denizen, habitué, haunter

fresh
3 new, raw 4 anew, bold, else,
more, pert, pure, rude, wise
5 added, alive, brisk, crude, green,
naive, nervy, novel, other, renew,
sassy, saucy, smart, sweet, vital,
vivid, young 6 bright, callow,
cheeky, lively, modern, recent, unused 7 another, artless, farther, forward, further, natural, uncouth,
untried 8 gleaming, impudent, neoteric, original, striking, unversed,
virginal, youthful 9 new-sprung,
sparkling, unspoiled 10 additional,
glistening, newfangled, unseasoned
11 impertinent, modernistic, smart-
alecky, unpracticed 12 invigorating, new-fashioned 13 inexperienced

freshet
5 flood, spate

freshman
4 colt, tyro 5 frosh, plebe 6 novice,
rookie 8 beginner, neophyte, newcomer 9 novitiate 10 apprentice,
tenderfoot

fret
3 irk, nag, rub, vex 4 cark, fray,
fume, fuss, gall, gnaw, mope, stew,
wear 5 annoy, brood, chafe,
grate, ravel, worry 6 abrade,
bother, cockle, dimple, dither, harass, nettle, plague, pother, rankle,
riffle, ruffle 7 agitate, corrode, disturb, provoke, roughen, torment
8 exercise, irritate 9 excoriate
10 irritation

fretful
5 angry, cross, huffy, waspy 7 carping, chafing, peevish, pettish, waspish 8 captious, caviling, contrary,
critical, perverse, petulant, restless,
snappish 9 fractious, impatient,
irascible, irritable, querulous, unpatient 12 faultfinding

Frey
father: 5 Njord 6 Njorth
sister: 5 Freya
wife: 4 Gerd 5 Gerda, Gerth

Freya
brother: 4 Frey
father: 5 Njord 6 Njorth
husband: 4 Odin

friable
5 crisp, mealy, short 7 crumbly,
crunchy

fribble
5 dizzy, giddy, light 7 flighty, trifler
8 trifling 9 frivolous 11 harebrained, light-headed

friction
7 discord, rubbing 8 abrasion 9 attrition 10 disharmony, dissension,
resistance 12 disagreement

friction match
5 vesta 7 lucifer 8 locofoco

Friday's rescuer
6 Crusoe (Robinson)

friend
3 aid, pal 4 ally, chum, mate
5 buddy, crony, matey, serve
7 comrade, partner 8 alter ego,
compadre, familiar, intimate, play-
mate, sidekick 9 associate, colleague, companion, confidant
10 confidante 11 cater-cousin
12 acquaintance
French: 3 ami 4 amie
Scottish: 3 eme

Spanish: 5 amiga, amigo

Friend
6 Quaker
founder: 3 Fox (George)

friendly
5 close, pally 6 amical, chummy,
loving 7 affable, amiable, cordial,
devoted 8 amicable, amicably, familiar, intimate, sociable 9 congenial, favorable, receptive 10 harmonious, hospitable 11 sympathetic 12 affectionate, well-disposed

Friendly Islands
5 Tonga

friends
4 kith

friendship
5 amity 6 accord, comity, fusion,
league 7 concord, empathy, harmony 8 affinity, alliance, goodwill
9 coalition 10 attraction, consonance, federation, kindliness
11 benevolence

frigate bird
3 ioa, iwa 8 alcatras
genus: 7 Fregata

Frigga, Frigg
husband: 4 Odin
son: 6 Balder

fright
3 awe 4 fear, mess 5 alarm,
dread, panic, scare, shock 6 dismay, horror, terror 7 eyesore, startle, terrify 9 terrorize, trepidity
11 trepidation

frighten
3 awe, cow 4 faze 5 alarm, daunt,
scare, shock, unman, upset 6 affray, appall, dismay 7 agitate,
astound, horrify, perturb, startle, terrify, unnerve 8 affright, browbeat,
bulldoze, disquiet 9 terrorize
10 demoralize, discompose, disconcert, intimidate

frightful
4 grim 5 awful, scary 6 horrid
7 fearful, ghastly, hideous
8 alarming, dreadful, fearsome,
horrible, horrific, shocking, terrible,
terrific 9 appalling 10 formidable,
horrendous

frigid
3 icy 4 cold, cool, dull 5 bleak,
chill 6 arctic, chilly, frosty 7 glacial, hostile, insipid 8 freezing
9 inhibited 10 undersexed 11 emo-

tionless, indifferent, passionless, un-emotional **12** unresponsive

frill

3 air **5** jabot, luxus, ruche **6** luxury, ruffle **7** amenity, flounce, ruching **8** furbelow **11** affectation, superfluity **12** extravagance

fringe

3 hem, rim **4** brim **5** bound, brink, skirt, verge **6** border, define, edging, margin **7** fimbria **8** surround, trimming **9** perimeter, periphery

frippery

6 finery **7** bravery, regalia **8** trumpery **9** full dress **10** Sunday best **11** ostentation

frisk

4 leap, romp, skip **5** caper, dance **6** cavort, curvet, frolic, gambol, search **7** disport, rollick **9** shake down

frisky

3 gay **5** antic **6** feisty, lively **7** larkish, playful, waggish **8** gamesome, prankish, sportive **9** kittenish **10** frolicsome

fritter

4 blow **5** shred, spend, waste **7** consume **8** cast away, diminish, disperse, fool away, fragment, squander **9** dissipate, throw away **10** trifle away

frivolity

3 fun **4** game, jest, play **5** sport **6** levity, toying **8** dallying, flirting, nonsense, trifling **9** flippancy, lightness **10** coquetting **11** flightiness

frivolous

3 gay **5** dizzy, giddy, light, silly **6** toyish **7** flighty, playful, shallow, trivial **8** carefree, careless, heedless **10** bird-witted, unprofound **11** empty-headed, harebrained, superficial **13** rattlebrained

frog

4 toad **5** ranid **6** anuran **9** amphibian **10** batrachian
combining form: **4** rani **7** batrach **8** batracho **9** batrachus
family: **7** Ranidae
genus: **4** Rana
kind: **4** hyla **6** peeper **8** bullfrog, tree toad
larva: **7** tadpole
relating to: **6** ranine

frogmouth

8 morepork

frolic

3 fun, gay **4** hell, lark, riot, romp **5** caper, dance, frisk, merry, party, prank, revel, sport, spree, trick **6** cavort, didoes, gaiety, gambol, prance, shines **7** carouse, disport, roister, rollick, wassail **9** merriment **10** shenanigan, tomfoolery

frolicsome

3 gay **5** antic **6** frisky, impish **7** coltish, playful, roguish, waggish **8** sportive **9** sprightly **10** rollicking **11** mischievous

from

French, Portuguese, Spanish: **2** de
German: **3** von
Italian: **2** da
Scottish: **4** frae

frondeur

5 rebel **6** anarch **8** mutineer, revolter **9** anarchist, dissident, insurgent **10** malcontent

front

3 bow, van **4** brow, dare, defy, face, fore, look, mask, meet, prow, show, veil **5** beard, blind, brave, close, color, put-on **6** accost, before, facade, facing **7** forward, outdare, outface, venture **8** anterior, coloring, disguise, forehead **9** challenge, encounter **10** appearance, figurehead **11** countenance
combining form: **6** antero
prefix: **3** pro

frontier

4 back, bush **5** march **6** border, remote, sticks **8** backland, backwash, boundary **9** backwater, backwoods, bordering, marchland, unsettled, up-country **10** borderland, hinterland, outlandish **11** backcountry, exploratory **12** conterminous

frontiersman

5 Boone (Daniel), Clark (George Rogers, William) **6** Carson (Kit) **7** pioneer, settler **8** Crockett (Davy) **10** bushranger

fronton game

7 jai alai

front-rank

5 prime **6** Grade A **8** five-star, superior, top-notch **9** excellent, first-rate, top-drawer **10** blue-ribbon, first-class **11** first-string

frontward

8 anterior

frost

4 hoar **6** freeze
combining form: **4** crym **5** crymo

frostfish

5 smelt **6** tomcod

frost heave

5 pingo

frosting

5 icing **7** topping

frosty

3 icy **4** cold, cool, rimy **5** chill, gelid, hoary, nippy, rimed **6** chilly, frigid **7** glacial, shivery **8** freezing, reserved **10** unfriendly

froth

4 barm, foam, scum, suds, vent **5** spume, yeast **6** lather, levity **9** flippancy, frivolity, lightness

froward

5 balky, cross **6** ornery **7** peevish, restive **8** contrary, perverse, petulant **10** refractory **11** disobedient

frown

4 pout, sulk **5** glare, gloom, lower, scowl **6** glower, object **7** grimace **8** disfavor **9** deprecate, disesteem **10** disapprove

frowsy

3 lax **4** mean, rank **5** dowdy, funky, fusty, musty, slack, stale **6** blowsy, remiss, shabby, smelly, sordid **7** noisome, reeking, squalid, unkempt **8** slattern, slovenly, stinking **9** negligent **10** disheveled, disordered, malodorous, neglectful, slatternly **13** draggletailed

frozen

4 hard **5** fixed, frore, gelid, rigid, stiff **6** chilly, frigid **7** chilled **8** benumbed, immobile **9** congealed, impassive, petrified **10** mechanical, unyielding **12** refrigerated

frugal

4 mean, wary **5** canny, chary, spare **6** saving, scanty, Scotch **7** careful, prudent, sparing, thrifty **8** discreet, stinting **9** scrimping, stewardly **10** conserving, economical, meticulous, preserving, unwasteful **12** cheeseparing, parsimonious **13** penny-pinching

frugality

6 thrift **7** economy **8** prudence **9** husbandry **10** providence **11** thriftiness

fruit
5 issue, young 6 result 7 progeny
9 offspring

citrus: 4 lime 5 lemon 6 citron, orange, pomelo 7 kumquat, tangelo
8 bergamot, mandarin, shaddock
9 tangerine 10 calamondin,
grapefruit

combining form: 4 carp 5 carpo
6 carpia (plural), carpic, carpus,
fructi 7 carpium, carpous

decay: 4 blet

dried: 5 prune 6 raisin

drink: 3 ade 5 juice, punch

fleshy: 7 syconia (plural) 8 syconium

hard-shelled: 3 nut 4 seed 5 gourd
7 coconut

residue: 4 marc 6 pomace

seed: 3 pip

study of: 8 pomology 9 carpology

subtropical: 3 fig 4 date, lime
5 lemon, olive 6 citron, orange
7 avocado, kumquat 9 tangerine
10 grapefruit

sugar: 7 glucose 8 fructose, levulose

temperate zone: 4 pear, plum, sloe
5 apple, grape, melon, peach,
prune 6 casaba, cherry, loquat,
quince 7 apricot, azarole, currant
8 dewberry 9 blueberry, cranberry,
muskmelon, nectarine, raspberry
10 blackberry, gooseberry, logan-
berry, strawberry 11 boysenberry,
huckleberry, pomegranate

tropical: 5 guava, mango 6 ajowan,
banana, papaya 7 acerola
8 breadnut, rambutan, tamarind
9 cherimoya, persimmon, pineapple 10 calamondin, mangosteen

type: 3 nut 4 pepo, pome 5 berry,
drupe 6 achene, legume, loment,
samara 7 capsule, cypsela, silicle,
silique, utricle 11 hesperidium

undeveloped: 6 nubbin

woody: 8 xylocarp

fruit basket
8 calathos, calathus

fruitful
4 rich 6 fecund 7 fertile 8 abundant, breeding, childing, prolific,
spawning 9 abounding, plenteous,
plentiful 10 productive 11 proliferant, propagating, reproducing

fruition
3 joy 7 delight, joyance 8 pleasure
9 enjoyment 10 attainment, conclusion 11 achievement, delectation,
fulfillment, realization

fruitless
4 vain 6 barren, foiled, futile
7 sterile, useless 8 abortive,

thwarted 9 infertile 10 unavailing
11 ineffective, ineffectual, infruc-
tuous, unavailable 12 unproductive, unprofitable

frumpy
4 drab, dull 5 dowdy, tacky
6 stodgy 8 outmoded 9 out-of-date,
unstylish

frustrate
3 bar 4 balk, beat, bilk, dash, foil,
halt, lick, null, ruin, vain 5 annul,
block, check, cross, elude 6 arrest,
baffle, blight, cancel, defeat, forbid, hinder, impede, outwit, thwart
7 buffalo, conquer, inhibit, nullify,
prevent, redress 8 confound, negative, obstruct, overcome, preclude,
prohibit 9 cancel out, checkmate,
forestall, interrupt 10 circumvent,
counteract, disappoint, neutralize

fry
5 sauté 6 sizzle

frying pan
6 spider 7 griddle, skillet

fuddle
5 mix up 6 ball up, jumble, muddle, tipple 7 confuse, fluster, stupefy 8 bewilder, distract, throw off
10 intoxicate

fuddy-duddy
4 fogy 5 Blimp, fussy 6 fogram,
fossil, square 7 fusspot 8 mossback, outdated 10 fuss-budget
12 antediluvian, Colonel Blimp,
mid-Victorian, stuffed shirt 13 stick-
in-the-mud

fudge
3 pad 4 blur, bosh, fake 5 cheat,
color, dodge, hedge, hooey, welsh
6 bunkum 7 distort, hogwash, magnify, traddle 8 contrive, nonsense,
overdraw 9 embellish, embroider,
overpaint, overstate, poppycock
10 exaggerate, overcharge

fuel
3 gas, oil 4 coal, coke, food, peat,
wood 5 stoke 6 petrol 7 support
8 charcoal, gasoline, hypergol, kerosene 9 petroleum, stimulate
13 reinforcement

fugacious
6 flying 7 passing 8 fleeting, volatile 9 ephemeral, momentary, transient 10 evanescent, short-lived,
transitory

fugitive
2 DP 5 exile 6 emigré, outlaw
7 evacuee, lamster, passing, refugee, runaway 8 deserter, fleeting,

vagabond, volatile 9 ephemeral,
momentary, transient 10 evanescent, perishable, short-lived,
transitory

fugue master
4 Bach (Johann Sebastian)

Führer, der
6 Hitler (Adolf)

fulfill
4 fill, meet 6 answer, effect, finish
7 achieve, execute, perform, satisfy
8 complete 9 discharge, implement
10 accomplish, effectuate

fulgent
6 bright 7 beaming, radiant, shining 8 luminous 9 brilliant

full
3 big 5 awash, jaded, plumb,
round, sated, total, whole
6 choate, entire, gorged, jammed,
loaded, minute, packed 7 brimful,
copious, crammed, crowded, glutted, orotund, perfect, replete, satiate, stuffed, teeming 8 brimming,
complete, detailed, integral, itemized, satiated, thorough 9 abounding, clocklike, jam-packed, plentiful,
surfeited

full-blooded
4 rich 5 flush, ruddy 6 ardent,
florid 7 flushed, genuine, glowing
8 forceful, pedigree, purebred, rubicund, sanguine 9 impelling, pedigreed, pureblood 12 thoroughbred

full bloom
8 anthesis

full-blown
4 lush, ripe 5 adult, total 6 all-out,
mature 7 grown-up, matured, ripened 9 unlimited 12 totalitarian

full-bodied
5 lusty, stout 6 potent, robust,
strong 9 corpulent 11 substantial

full-bosomed
5 busty, buxom 6 chesty

full dress
6 finery 7 bravery, regalia 8 frippery 10 Sunday best

full-figured
6 zaftig, zoftig

full-fledged
4 ripe 5 adult, grown 6 mature
7 genuine, grown-up, matured, ripened 12 card-carrying

full-grown
4 ripe 5 adult 6 mature 7 matured,
ripened

fullness
5 scope **6** plenty **7** breadth, satiety **9** abundance, amplitude, repletion **10** perfection **12** completeness

full of
suffix: **3** ose, ous **4** ious

full-scale
5 total **6** all-out **8** complete **9** unlimited **12** totalitarian

full tilt
4 fast **7** flat-out, hastily, quickly, rapidly, swiftly **8** speedily **9** posthaste **12** lickety-split **13** expeditiously

fulsome
3 fat **4** full, glib, oily **5** bland, plump, slick, soapy, suave **6** lavish, sating, smarmy, smooth **7** buttery, canting, cloying, copious, profuse **8** abundant, unctious, unctuous **9** bombastic, excessive, exuberant, repulsive, satiating, sickening, wheedling **10** disgusting, flattering, nauseating, oleaginous **11** extravagant, oily-tongued, pharisaical **12** honey-mouthed, honey-tongued, hypocritical, ingratiating, magniloquent, mealy-mouthed, pecksniffian

Fulton's steamboat
8 Clermont

fumble
3 paw **4** feel, flub, mess, muff **5** botch, error, grope **6** bobble, bollix, bungle, goof up, muddle, mumble, murmur, mutter **7** blunder, louse up, misplay, swallow **8** flounder

fume
4 boil, burn, odor, rage, reek, snit, stew **5** anger, smoke, sweat, tizzy, vapor **6** blow up, seethe, swivet **7** bristle, flare up **8** boil over **10** exhalation

fun
3 gag, kid, rag, rib **4** fool, game, glee, jest, joke, josh, play, razz **5** jolly, mirth, sport **6** banter, gaiety **7** disport, jollity, teasing, whoopee **8** hilarity, mischief, ridicule **9** amusement, diversion, high jinks, horseplay, jocundity, joviality, merriment **10** blitheness, pleasantry, recreation **13** entertainment

function
2 do, go **3** act, job, run, use **4** duty, goal, mark, role, take, task, work **5** power, react, serve **6** affair, behave, object, office, target **7** concern, faculty, operate, perform, purpose, service **8** activity, behavior, business, ceremony, occasion, province **9** objective, officiate, operation
suffix: **2** cy **3** ure
trigonometric: **4** sine **6** cosine, secant **7** tangent **8** cosecant **9** cotangent

functional
5 handy, utile **6** useful **7** working **9** practical **11** practicable, serviceable, utilitarian **12** occupational

functioning
4 live **5** alive **6** active **7** dynamic **9** operative

fund
4 pool **5** endow, stock, store **6** supply **7** capital, finance, reserve **9** inventory, subsidize **10** accumulate

fundament
4 beam, rear, rump, seat **6** behind, bottom **8** backside, buttocks, derriere **9** posterior **10** foundation

fundamental
3 law **4** pure **5** axiom, basal, basic, prime, vital **6** bottom, factor, primal **7** needful, primary, radical, theorem **8** cardinal, dominant **9** component, essential, formative, important, necessary, paramount, primitive, principal, principle, requisite **10** elementary, primordial, principium, substratal, underlying **11** constituent, irreducible **12** constitutive, foundational

fundamentalist
4 tory **5** right **7** diehard **8** old liner, standpat **11** bitter-ender, right-winger, standpatter **12** conservative

fundamental nature
7 essence

fund-raiser
6 dinner **8** telethon

funeral
6 burial
car: **6** hearse
director: **9** mortician **10** undertaker
oration: **6** eulogy **8** encomium **9** panegyric
procession: **6** exequy **7** cortege
service: **7** requiem **9** obsequies
song: **5** dirge, elegy **7** epicede **8** threnody **9** epicedium

funereal
4 back **5** bleak, grave **6** dismal, dreary, gloomy, solemn, somber **8** mournful **10** depressing, depressive, lugubrious, oppressive **13** disheartening

fungus
4 cepe, mold, rust, smut **5** ergot, morel, yeast **6** agaric, bolete, mildew **7** amanita, truffle **8** mushroom, polypore, puffball **9** earthstar, stinkhorn, toadstool **10** champignon **11** chanterelle
combining form: **3** myc **4** myco **5** myces, mycet **6** mycete, myceto **7** mycetes
part: **3** cap **4** gill, umbo **5** ascus, gleba, hypha, stipe, volva **7** annulus, cortina **8** basidium, conidium, mycelium

fungus disease
3 rot **4** mold, rust, scab, smut **5** ergot, tinea **6** blight, mildew, thrush **7** mycosis **8** lumpy jaw, ringworm **12** athlete's foot
suffix: **4** oses (plural), osis

funk
4 odor, rage, reek **5** dread, panic, smell, stink **6** coward, craven, flinch, stench **7** chicken, dastard, quitter, shirker **8** poltroon **11** yellowbelly

funky
4 foul, rank **5** musty, stale **6** frowsy, smelly **7** noisome, panicky, reeking **8** stinking **10** malodorous

funnel
4 pipe **5** carry, widen **6** convey, narrow, siphon **7** conduct, traject **8** transmit

funny
3 odd **4** zany **5** antic, comic, droll, fishy, queer **6** sneaky **7** amusing, bizarre, comical, jocular, risible, strange **8** farcical, gelastic, humorous **9** facetious, fantastic, grotesque, laughable, ludicrous **10** ridiculous **11** underhanded

funnyman
3 wag, wit **5** comic, droll, joker **6** jester **8** comedian, humorist, jokester, quipster

fur
4 down, fell, flue, hide, lint, pelt, pile, skin **5** floss, fluff, stole **6** jacket, pelage, peltry
kind: **3** fox **4** mink, seal **5** fitch, otter, sable **6** ermine, fisher, marten, nutria, tanuki **7** raccoon **10** chinchilla
lamb: **6** galyak, mouton **7** caracul, karakul, krimmer **9** broadtail
medieval: **4** vair **7** miniver

furbish
3 rub 4 buff 5 glaze, gloss, shine
6 glance, polish, revive 7 burnish
8 renovate

Furies
6 Alecto 7 Erinyes, Megaera
9 Eumenides, Tisiphone

furious
3 mad 4 wild 5 angry, dirty, hasty, irate, rabid, rough, upset 6 crazed, fierce, insane, maniac, raging, stormy 7 enraged, excited, extreme, fanatic, frantic, intense, violent 8 blustery, demented, feverish, frenetic, frenzied, furibund, incensed, maddened, provoked, terrible, vehement, vigorous, wrathful 9 desperate, energetic, excessive, exquisite, fanatical, impetuous, turbulent 10 bewildered, blustering, boisterous, corybantic, distracted, hysterical, infuriated, inordinate, irrational

furl
4 curl, fold, roll, wrap 5 cover
6 enfold 7 wrinkle

furnace
4 kiln, oven 5 forge, stove 6 heater
7 smelter 8 bloomery, tryworks
11 incinerator
part: 4 port, vent 5 bocca 6 trompe, tuyere
tender: 6 stoker

furnish
3 arm, rig 4 feed, gear, give, hand, lend 5 array, dower, endow, endue, equip, mount, yield 6 afford, clothe, fit out, outfit, supply 7 apparel, appoint, deliver, provide, turn out 8 accouter, dispense, hand over, transfer, turn over 10 contribute

furnishings
4 gear 5 decor 9 equipment, trappings

furniture
8 equipage, hardware 9 equipment 10 furnishing
shoddy: 5 borax
style: 4 Adam 6 Empire 8 Colonial, Sheraton 9 Queen Anne 11 chinoiserie, Chippendale, Hepplewhite

furniture designer
American: 5 Phyfe (Duncan) 7 Goddard (John, Stephen, Thomas), Haldane (William)
British: 6 Morris (William) 7 Gibbons (Grinling), Shearer (Thomas) 8 Sheraton (Thomas) 11 Chippendale (Thomas), Hepplewhite (George)
French: 5 Marot (Daniel) 6 Boulle (André-Charles)
Scottish: 4 Adam (James, Robert)

furor
3 ado, cry, fad 4 chic, coil, fury, mode, rage, stir, to-do 5 craze, mania, style, vogue, whirl 6 bustle, flurry, frenzy, pother, ruckus, rumpus, uproar 7 fashion, madness, shindig 8 foofaraw 9 commotion, whirlpool, whirlwind 10 dernier cri

furore
4 stir 5 craze 6 uproar
11 controversy

furrow
3 rut 4 fold, plow, ruck 5 plica, ridge, rivel, stria, sulci (plural) 6 cleave, course, crease, groove, rimple, striae (plural), sulcus, trench 7 channel, crinkle, wrinkle 11 corrugation

furrowed
6 rugose 7 sulcate 8 sulcated, wrinkled 10 corrugated

further
3 new 4 abet, also, else, help, more, then 5 added, again, fresh, serve 6 beyond 7 advance, besides, forward, promote 8 engender, generate, moreover 9 encourage, propagate 10 additional, in addition 12 additionally

furthermore
3 and, too, yea, yet 4 also 5 along 6 as well, withal 7 besides 8 likewise, moreover

furthermost
7 extreme 8 farthest, remotest

furthest
6 utmost 7 extreme, outmost 9 outermost, uttermost

furtive
3 sly 4 foxy, wary, wily 5 catty 6 artful, covert, crafty, feline, masked, secret, shifty, sneaky, stolen, tricky 7 catlike, cloaked, cunning, sub-rosa 8 cautious, guileful, hush-hush, scheming, stealthy 9 disguised, insidious 11 calculating, circumspect, clandestine 12 hugger-mugger 13 surreptitious, under-the-table
look: 4 peek, peep

furuncle
4 boil 7 abscess

fury
3 ire, mad 4 rage 5 anger, wrath 6 frenzy 7 madness, passion 8 acerbity, acrimony, afflatus, asperity, violence 9 vehemence 11 indignation

furze
4 whin 5 gorse
genus: 4 Ulex 7 Genista

fuse
3 mix, run 4 flux, frit, meld, melt, thaw, weld 5 blend, merge, smelt, unify, unite 6 anneal, mingle, solder 7 compact, liquefy 8 dissolve, intermix, liquesce 9 integrate 10 amalgamate, deliquesce, interblend 11 consolidate, incorporate

fusillade
4 hail 5 burst, salvo 6 shower, volley 7 barrage 8 drumfire 9 broadside 11 bombardment

fusion
5 alloy, blend, union 6 merger 7 amalgam, mixture 8 compound 9 admixture, coalition, immixture, synthesis
combining form: 3 zyg 4 zygo

fuss
3 ado, nag, row 4 cark, coil, crab, flap, fret, kick, miff, stew, stir, to-do, wail, yaup 5 annoy, bleat, fight, gripe, haste, hurry, speed, upset, whine, whirl, worry 6 bother, bustle, carp at, flurry, hassle, hurrah, murmur, peck at, pother, putter, racket, repine, ruckus, rumpus, shindy, squawk, yammer 7 agitate, dispute, fluster, henpeck, protest, quarrel, shindig 8 complain 9 bickering, commotion, complaint, objection, whirlpool, whirlwind 11 controversy 12 perturbation

fussbudget
5 crank 8 stickler 10 fuddy-duddy 12 precisionist 13 perfectionist

fussy
4 nice 5 exact, picky 6 dainty, lively, ornate 7 careful, fidgety, finical, finicky, fretful, heedful 8 bustling, hustling 9 finicking, irritable, querulous, squeamish 10 fastidious, meticulous, particular, pernickety, scrupulous 11 painstaking, persnickety, punctilious 13 conscientious

fustian
4 rant 7 bombast, pompous, use-

less **8** feckless, rhapsody, rhetoric **9** worthless **10** unpurposed **11** exaggerated, highfalutin, meaningless, purposeless

fusty
4 rank **5** close, dated, fetid, moldy, musty, passé, stale **6** bygone, filthy, old hat, putrid, rancid, sloppy, smelly **7** archaic, noisome, squalid, unkempt **8** outdated **10** antiquated, disheveled, malodorous **12** old-fashioned

futile
4 idle, vain **5** empty **6** hollow, otiose **7** useless **8** abortive, bootless, hopeless, nugatory **9** frivolous, fruitless, worthless **10** inadequate, unavailing **11** ineffective, ineffectual, inefficient **12** insufficient, unprevailing, unproductive, unsuccessful

future
4 to-be **5** later **6** offing **7** by-and-by **9** afterward, hereafter **10** subsequent

Futurism
founder: **9** Marinetti (Filippo Tommaso)
painter: **5** Balla (Giacomo), Carra (Carlo) **7** Russolo (Luigi) **8** Boccioni (Umberto), Severini (Gino)
sculptor: **8** Boccioni (Umberto)

fuzz
3 nap **4** blur, down, flue, lint, pile **5** floss, fluff

fuzzy
3 dim **5** faint, vague **6** bleary, blurry, frizzy **7** blurred, muddled, obscure, shadowy, unclear **8** confused **9** undefined **10** ill-defined, incoherent, indefinite, indistinct **12** inconclusive

fylfot
8 swastika

Gg

Gaal's father
4 Ebed

gab
see **gabble**

gabbard
4 scow, ship 5 barge 7 lighter

gabber
6 magpie, prater 7 blabber 8 jabberer, prattler 9 bandar-log, blabmouth, chatterer 10 chatterbox

gabble
3 gab, jaw, yak 4 chat, talk
5 clack, drool, prate 6 drivel, gibber, gossip, jabber 7 blabber,
blather, chatter, palaver, prattle,
twaddle 9 yakety-yak

gabby
5 talky 6 chatty 9 garrulous, talkative 10 babblative, loquacious
11 loose-lipped 12 loose-tongued

gaberdine
4 coat, suit 5 cloth, cover, smock
7 garment

gable
4 wall 8 pediment
ornament: 6 finial

Gabon
capital: 10 Libreville
monetary unit: 5 franc

gad
3 bat 4 band, roam, rope, rove
5 mooch, range, stray 6 ramble,
wander 7 maunder, traipse
9 gallivant

Gad
brother: 5 Asher
father: 5 Jacob
mother: 6 Zilpah
son: 3 Eri 5 Ezbon, Haggi

gadfly
4 pest 6 bother, critic

gadget
4 tool 5 gizmo 6 device, dingus,
doodad, hickey, jigger, widget
7 concern, dofunny, gimmick, utensil 9 apparatus, appliance, doohickey, rigamajig 11 contraption,
thingamajig, thingumajig

Gadi's son
7 Menahem

gadwall
4 duck

Gaea
2 Ge
husband: 6 Uranus
offspring: 6 Giants, Titans, Typhon,
Uranus 7 Erinyes 8 Cyclopes
parent: 5 Chaos

Gaelic
4 Erse 5 Irish 6 Celtic 8 Scottish
god: 3 Ler 5 Dagda
hero: 5 Oisin 6 Ossian 11 Finn
MacCool
king: 9 Conchobar, Conchobor
language: 4 Manx
poem: 7 aisling
poet: 4 bard, fili 6 Ossian
queen: 4 Medb
soldier: 4 kern 6 Fenian
spirit: 7 banshee
tale: 4 tain

gaff
3 fix 4 hoax, hook, spar, spur
5 abuse, fraud, trick 6 clamor,
fleece, outcry, uproar 7 gimmick

gaffe
5 boner, break 7 blooper, faux pas
8 solecism 9 indecorum
11 impropriety

gag
3 jib, shy 4 balk, hoax, jape, jest,
joke, keck, quip, ruse, wile
5 choke, crack, demur, heave,
retch, sally, stick, trick 6 boggle,
muzzle, strain 9 wisecrack, witticism

gage
6 pledge 8 security; (see also
gauge)

Gaham
father: 5 Nahor
mother: 6 Reumah

Gaheris
brother: 6 Gareth, Gawain
father: 3 Lot
mother: 8 Margawse, Morgause
uncle: 6 Arthur
victim: 8 Margawse, Morgause

gaiety
3 joy 4 glee 5 mirth, revel 7 jollity,
revelry, whoopee 8 gladness, hilarity, radiance, reveling, vivacity
9 animation, festivity, geniality,
happiness, merriment, revelment
10 liveliness 11 merrymaking

gain
3 get, net, win 4 earn, have, land,
make, mend, reap 5 annex, clear,
lucre, reach, score 6 attain, look
up, obtain, perk up, pick up, profit,
rack up, return, secure 7 achieve,
acquire, bring in, clean up, improve, procure, realize 8 draw
down, earnings, proceeds, windfall
9 knock down 10 accomplish

gainful
4 good, rich 6 paying 8 fruitful
9 lucrative 10 productive, profitable, satisfying, well-paying,
worthwhile

gainly
8 graceful, pleasing

gainsay
4 deny 5 cross, fight 6 combat, impugn, negate, oppose, resist 7 dispute, subvert 8 disprove, negative,
traverse 9 disaffirm, withstand
10 contradict, contravene, controvert

Gainsborough painting
7 Blue Boy

gait
3 run 4 lope, pace, rate, step, trot, walk 5 speed, strut 6 canter, gallop

gaiter
4 boot, shoe 8 overshoe

gala
3 gay 4 fair, fete 5 merry, party 6 festal, lively 7 festive 8 festival 9 festivity 11 celebration

Galahad
father: 8 Lancelot 9 Launcelot
mother: 6 Elaine
quest: 9 Holy Grail

Galatea
father: 6 Nereus
husband: 9 Pygmalion
lover: 4 Acis
mother: 5 Doris

galaxy
6 nebula 8 Milky Way

Galba
predecessor: 4 Nero
successor: 4 Otho

gale
4 blow, gust, wind 5 blast, storm 6 squall 7 tempest 8 outburst 9 hurricane

Galen's forte
8 medicine

galilee
5 porch 6 chapel 7 portico

Galilee
town: 4 Cana 7 Gergesa 8 Nazareth, Tiberias 9 Bethsaida, Capernaum

Galileo's birthplace
4 Pisa

gall
3 get, irk, rub, vex 4 face, fray, fret, rile, roil, wear 5 annoy, brass, chafe, cheek, chide, erode, grate, graze, harry, nerve, scurr, worry 6 abrade, blurt, burn up, harass, ruffle, scrape 7 conceit, corrade, disturb, frazzle, inflame, provoke, scratch, torment 8 exercise, irritate 9 aggravate, arrogance, brashness, excoriate 10 confidence, effrontery
combining form: 4 chol 5 chole, cholo

gallant
3 fop 4 beau, bold, buck, dude, game 5 blade, blood, brave, dandy, lover, manly, preux, Romeo, suave, swain, wooer 6 he-roic, manful, suitor, urbane 7 amorist, courtly, coxcomb, Don Juan, stately 8 Casanova, gracious, lothario, paramour 9 dauntless, exquisite

gallantry
5 poise, valor 6 mettle, spirit 7 amenity, bravery, courage, heroism, prowess, suavity 8 courtesy, urbanity, valiance, valiancy 9 attention 10 resolution

gallery
5 porch 6 arcade, loggia, museum, piazza 7 balcony, passage, portico, veranda 8 audience, corridor 9 colonnade, promenade
ancient Greek: 4 stoa

galley
4 boat, ship, tray 5 cuddy, proof 6 bireme 7 dromond, galliot, kitchen, trireme, unireme 9 cookhouse

Gallic
6 French

gallimaufry
4 hash, olio 6 jumble, medley 7 mélange, mixture 8 pastiche 9 potpourri 10 assortment, hodgepodge, miscellany, salmagundi

gallinaceous bird
3 hen 5 quail 6 grouse, turkey 7 chicken, hoatzin 8 curassow, megapode, pheasant 9 partridge

gallivant
3 bat, gad 4 roam, rove 5 mooch, range, stray 6 ramble, travel, wander 7 meander, traipse

gallows
5 frame 6 gibbet 7 hanging, potence
bird: 7 villain 8 criminal

galore
7 aplenty, profuse 8 abundant 9 plentiful

galosh
4 boot, shoe 6 arctic 8 overshoe

Galsworthy work
7 Justice 14 The Forsyte Saga

galvanize
4 coat, move 5 pique, prime 6 arouse, excite 7 innerve, provoke, quicken 8 activate, energize, motivate, vitalize 9 innervate, stimulate

gam
3 leg, pod 5 visit

Gambia
capital: 6 Banjul
monetary unit: 6 dalasi

gambit
3 jig 4 move, play, ploy, ruse 5 trick 6 device 7 gimmick, whizzer 8 artifice, maneuver 9 stratagem

gamble
3 bet, lay, set 4 game, play, risk 5 put on, stake, wager 6 chance, hazard 7 venture 9 speculate

gambler
5 dicer, shark, sharp 6 bettor, player 7 sharper 8 gamester 10 speculator

gambling place
4 Reno 5 Vegas 6 casino 8 Las Vegas 10 Monte Carlo 12 Atlantic City

gambol
3 hop 4 lark, leap, romp 5 bound, caper, frisk, revel 6 cavort, frolic, spring 7 roister, rollick

Gambrinus' invention
4 beer

game
3 bet, fun, lay, set 4 bold, jest, joke, lark, play, prey 5 brave, chase, put on, sport, stake, trick, wager 6 gamble, quarry, spunky 7 contest, pastime, valiant, willing 8 fearless, intrepid, resolute, unafraid, valorous 9 amusement, dauntless, diversion, undaunted 10 courageous
ball: 3 tut 4 golf, polo, pool 5 fives, rogue, rugby 6 hockey, pelota, soccer, squash, tennis 7 cricket, croquet, jai alai 8 baseball, football, handball, hardball, lacrosse, racquets, rounders, softball 9 billiards 10 basketball, volleyball 11 racquetball
Basque: 6 pelota 7 jai alai
bird: 5 quail 6 chukar, turkey 7 bustard 8 bobwhite, pheasant 9 partridge
board: 5 chess, darts, salta 7 pachisi, reversi, squails 8 checkers 9 crokinole 10 backgammon
card: 3 gin, loo, nap, pam, war 4 brag, faro, fish, skat, solo 5 monte, omber, ombre, pitch, poker, rummy, stuss, whist 6 Boston, bridge, casino, écarté, euchre, fan-tan, hearts, piquet 7 auction, bezique, canasta, cassino, coon-can, muggins, old maid, primero, reversi, setback 8 baccarat, Can-

field, conquian, cribbage, Michigan, napoleon, pinochle **9** blackjack, matrimony, Newmarket, solitaire, twenty-one, vingt-et-un **11** chemin de fer
child's: **3** tag **5** potsy **8** leapfrog, peekaboo **9** hopscotch
confidence: **4** scam **5** bunco, bunko, sting
court: **5** roque **6** pelota, squash, tennis **7** jai alai **8** handball, racquets **9** badminton **10** basketball, volleyball
electric: **7** pinball
English: **5** kails, rugby **7** cricket, loggats, loggets **8** draughts
Irish: **6** hurley **7** hurling
of chance: **4** faro, keno **5** beano, bingo, boule, craps, lotto, rondo **6** fan-tan, hazard, policy, raffle **7** lottery, rondeau **8** crack-loo, roulette **9** crackaloo
parlor: **5** jacks **8** charades
racket: **5** bandy **6** squash, tennis **8** lacrosse, racquets **9** badminton **11** racquetball, table tennis
roulette-like: **5** boule
rule maker: **5** Hoyle
string: **10** cat's cradle
table: **4** pool **5** craps **7** mah-jong, snooker **8** dominoes, mah-jongg, roulette **9** bagatelle, billiards **11** table tennis
word: **5** rebus **6** crambo, ghosts **7** anagram, hangman **8** acrostic, charades **9** crossword, logograph

game plan
6 design, scheme **7** project **8** strategy **9** blueprint

gamete
3 egg **4** ovum **5** sperm **8** oosphere

gamin
3 imp, tad **6** monkey, urchin

gamine
6 hoyden, tomboy

gaming cubes
4 dice

gammadion
8 swastika

gammon
3 ham **4** dupe, fool **5** bacon, feign **6** delude, humbug **7** deceive, pretend

gamut
4 note **5** range, scale **6** extent, series

gamy
4 olid, rank **5** fetid, funky **6** plucky, smelly, sordid, stinky, strong **7** noisome, reeking **10** malodorous

gander
4 fool, look **5** goose **6** glance **9** simpleton

Gandhi
5 Rajiv **6** Indira **7** Mahatma

ganef
5 thief **6** rascal

Ganesa, Ganesh
father: **4** Siva **5** Shiva
head: **8** elephant
mother: **7** Parvati

gang
3 mob, set **4** band, crew, pack, team **5** group, horde **6** clique, outfit

gangling
4 bony **5** gaunt, lanky, rangy **6** skinny **7** spindly **9** spindling

ganglion
5 tumor **7** nucleus

gangly
see **gangling**

gangrene
3 rot **5** decay **7** mortify **8** necrosis

gangster
4 goon, hood, thug **5** rough, thief, tough **6** bandit, gunman **7** mafioso, mobster **8** criminal **9** cutthroat
girl friend: **4** moll

gangway
4 hall **5** aisle **7** passage **8** corridor

gannet
4 bird, ibis **5** solan

ganoid fish
3 gar **6** beluga, bowfin **8** sturgeon

Ganymede
abductor: **4** Zeus **7** Jupiter
brother: **4** Ilus
father: **4** Tros
function: **9** cupbearer

gaol
4 jail **6** prison

gap
3 col **4** hole, lull, pass, slit, slot **5** break, chasm, chink, cleft, clove, crack, gorge, gulch, pause **6** arroyo, breach, clough, cranny, hiatus, lacuna, ravine **7** caesura, crevice, fissure, interim, opening, orifice, rupture **8** aperture, cleavage, division, fracture, interval **10** separation **12** intermission, interruption **13** discontinuity

gape
3 eye, yaw **4** bore, gawk, gaze, look, ogle, peer, yawn **5** glare, gloat, stare **6** goggle **10** rubberneck

gaping
4 open **7** chasmal, yawning **9** cavernous

gar
4 fish, pike **8** billfish **10** needlefish

Garand
5 rifle

garb
4 clad **5** array, dress, getup, style **6** attire, clothe, outfit **7** apparel, garment, raiment **8** enclothe

garbage
4 junk, orts, slop **5** dregs, filth, offal, trash, waste **6** debris, kelter, litter, refuse, rubble, sewage **7** rubbish **8** riffraff
heap: **6** midden

garble
4 sift, warp **5** belie, color, twist **6** jumble, mangle **7** becloud, distort, falsify, obscure, pervert **8** miscolor, misstate, mutilate **9** obfuscate **12** misrepresent

garçon
3 boy **6** waiter **7** servant

garden
3 hoe **4** Eden, farm, hall, park, plot, till, yard **5** grove, tract **8** rosarium **9** cultivate **11** commonplace
shelter: **5** arbor **6** arbour

Garden City
7 Chicago

gardener
7 yardman **9** topiarist

garden house
6 alcove, gazebo, pagoda **9** belvedere

Garden State
9 New Jersey

garden tool
3 hoe **4** claw, fork, rake **5** mower, spade **6** pruner, scythe, sickle, trowel, weeder **8** clippers

Gareth
brother: **6** Gawain **7** Gaheris
father: **3** Lot
mother: **8** Margawse, Morgause
slayer: **8** Lancelot **9** Launcelot
uncle: **6** Arthur
wife: **6** Liones

Gargamelle's son
9 Gargantua

Gargantua
abbey: 7 Theleme
author: 8 Rabelais (François)
father: 12 Grandgousier
first word: 5 drink
mother: 10 Gargamelle
son: 10 Pantagruel

gargantuan
see gigantic

Garibaldi follower
8 redshirt

garish
4 loud 5 gaudy, showy 6 brazen,
flashy, tawdry, tinsel 7 blatant,
chintzy, glaring 12 meretricious

garland
3 ana, lei 4 band, posy 5 album,
crown 6 anadem, wreath 7 chaplet, coronal, coronet, omnibus 8 analects 9 anthology 10 miscellany
11 florilegium

garlic
4 moly, ramp 5 clove 6 ramson

garment
4 cape, clad, coat, garb, gear,
gown, robe, vest 5 array, cloak,
dress, frock, habit, shirt, skirt, talar,
tunic 6 attire, blouse, clothe 7 apparel, chemise, raiment 8 clothing,
enclothe, vestment, wearable
10 habiliment
Afghan: 6 postin 7 posteen
8 poshteen
African: 6 kaross 7 dashiki
Arab: 3 aba 4 haik
British: 4 brat 10 mackintosh
Burmese: 6 tamein
clergy's: 3 alb 4 cope 7 cassock,
soutane 8 vestment
close-fitting: 6 girdle, tights 7 leotard
for sleeping: 6 pajama 7 nightie
9 nightgown
Greek: 5 tunic 6 chiton, peplos, tri-
bon 7 chlamys 8 himation
Hindu: 4 sari 5 saree
hooded: 7 jellaba 8 djellaba
Japanese: 6 kimono
lace: 10 chemisette
Malay: 6 sarong
men's: 3 tie 4 vest 5 pants, shirt,
socks 6 jacket, slacks 7 drawers
8 trousers
Muslim: 4 izar
outer: 4 cape, coat, robe, wrap
5 cloak, parka, shawl, smock, stole,
wamus 6 capote, jacket, kimono,
poncho, sarong, ulster, wammus

7 overall, paletot, pelisse, surtout,
sweater, topcoat, zamarra 8 overcoat, pinafore, pullover, scapular
9 coveralls, gaberdine, polonaise
patchwork: 5 cento 7 khirkah
Polynesian: 5 pareu 8 lavelava
rain: 6 poncho 7 oilskin, slicker
Roman: 4 toga 5 stola, tunic
Scottish: 4 jupe, kilt 7 sporran
sleeveless: 3 aba 4 cape 6 mantle,
tabard
trim: 7 falbala
Turkish: 6 dolman
women's: 4 gown 5 dress, skirt
6 blouse, vestee 7 blouson, nightie,
partlet 8 negligee, peignoir,
pelerine

garner
4 cull, hive, reap 5 amass, glean,
hoard, lay up, store, uplay
6 gather, pick up, roll up 7 extract,
granary, harvest, store up 8 cumulate, ingather 9 stockpile
10 accumulate

garnet
5 jewel, stone 6 pyrope 8 essonite
black: 8 melanite
red: 9 almandite

garnish
4 deck, trim 5 adorn, prank 6 bedeck 7 dress up 8 beautify, decorate, ornament 9 embellish

garret
4 loft, room 5 attic, solar 6 sollar,
soller 7 mansard 8 cockloft

garrison
4 fort, post 6 occupy 7 station
10 stronghold

garrote
4 kill 5 choke 7 execute 8 strangle, throttle 9 execution

garrulous
see gabby

garter
4 band, belt 5 snake 7 elastic
9 supporter

garth
3 dam 4 weir, yard 5 close

gas
4 fuel, fume 5 steam, vapor 6 petrol 8 gasoline 9 petroleum
atmospheric: 4 neon 5 argon, oxide,
ozone, xenon 6 helium, oxygen
7 krypton, methane 8 hydrogen,
nitrogen
combining form: 3 aer 4 mano
5 pneum 6 pneumo 7 pneumat
8 pneumato

flammable: 6 butane, ethane, ethyne
7 methane, propane, propene
8 ethylene
inert: 4 neon 5 argon, radon, xenon
6 helium 7 krypton
intestinal: 7 flatus
mine: 8 firedamp 9 blackdamp,
chokedamp
oxygen: 5 ozone
toxic: 5 sarin 6 arsine, ketene
7 mustard, stibine, yperite
8 phosphin

gasconade
4 brag 7 bravado 8 boasting

gash
3 cut 4 slit 5 carve, slash, slice,
split, wound 6 incise, pierce

gasket
4 band, line, ring, seal 6 sealer

gasoline
4 fuel 6 petrol
rating: 6 octane

gasp
4 blow, huff, pant, puff 5 heave

Gaspar
companion: 8 Melchior 9 Balthazar
gift: 12 frankincense

gassy
5 windy 8 inflated, vaporous

gastronome
7 epicure, gourmet 8 aesthete,
gourmand 9 bon vivant

gastronomer, gastronomist
see gastronome

gastropod
4 slug 5 cowry, murex, snail, whelk
6 cowrie, limpet, volute 7 abalone,
mollusk 8 pteropod

gat
3 gun 6 pistol 7 channel, passage

gate
3 tap, way 4 cock, door, exit
5 hatch, valve 6 faucet, portal,
spigot, wicket 7 hydrant, opening,
petcock 8 stopcock 9 turnstile

gatefold
6 insert 7 foldout

Gates of Hercules
9 Gibraltar

gateway
4 arch, door 5 pylon, toran 6 portal, torana 8 entrance

gather
4 brew, cull, draw, heap, herd,
loom, mass, meet, pick, pile, reap,
take 5 amass, bunch, flock, glean,

group, horde, infer, judge, pluck, raise, shirr, stack, think, troop **6** assume, deduce, deduct, derive, expect, garner, impend, muster, pick up, take in **7** believe, cluster, collect, extract, harvest, imagine, make out, round up, suppose, suspect **8** assemble, conclude, congress **9** aggregate, forthcome **10** accumulate, congregate, rendezvous, understand

gathering
4 bevy, crew, gang, mass, ruck **5** bunch, crowd, crush, flock, group, horde, party, press, swarm **6** klatch, muster **7** company, harvest, klatsch, meeting, reaping, reunion, turnout **8** assembly, cropping, junction **9** concourse, congeries **10** assemblage, collection, concursion, confluence, harvesting **11** aggregation **12** congregation
combining form: **4** fest

Gath's giant
7 Goliath

gauche
5 crude, inept **6** clumsy, wooden **7** awkward, halting, unhappy **8** bumbling **9** ham-handed, maladroit

gaucho
6 cowboy **8** herdsman
weapon: **4** bola **7** machete

Gaudeamus ___
6 igitur

gaudy
4 loud **5** crude, feast, gross, showy **6** brazen, coarse, flashy, garish, tawdry, tinsel, vulgar **7** blatant, chintzy, glaring **8** festival **9** tasteless **12** meretricious, ostentatious

gauge
5 judge, meter, scale **7** measure **8** estimate, standard **9** benchmark, criterion, yardstick **10** touchstone

Gauguin's island home
6 Tahiti

Gaul
4 Celt **6** France **9** Frenchman

Gaulish
6 French
combining form: **5** Gallo
god: **4** Esus **7** Taranis
goddess: **8** Belisama
priest: **5** druid

gaunt
4 bony, lank, lean **5** lanky, spare

6 skinny, wasted **7** angular, scraggy, scrawny **8** rawboned, skeletal **9** emaciated **10** cadaverous

gauntlet
4 dare, test **5** glove **6** cestus, ordeal **9** challenge

Gautama
6 Buddha **10** Siddhartha
mother: **4** Maya
son: **6** Rahula
wife: **9** Yasodhara

gauze
4 film, haze, leno, mist **5** cloth, crepe, lisse, tulle **6** fabric, tissue **7** bandage, chiffon **11** cheesecloth

gauzy
5 filmy, sheer **6** flimsy **7** tiffany **8** gossamer **10** diaphanous **11** transparent

gavel
6 hammer, mallet

gavial
7 reptile **9** crocodile

gavotte
5 dance

Gawain
brother: **6** Gareth **7** Gaheris
father: **3** Lot
mother: **8** Margawse, Morgause
slayer: **8** Lancelot **9** Launcelot
uncle: **6** Arthur
victim: **6** Uwayne **7** Lamerok **9** Pellinore

gawk
3 oaf **4** bore, gape, gaze, lout, lump, peer **5** glare, gloat, klutz, looby, stare

gawky
5 splay **6** clumsy, gauche **7** awkward, lumpish **8** ungainly **9** lumbering

gay
4 glad, keen, wild **5** alert, bonny, brash, brave, happy, jolly, merry, queer, riant, vivid **6** blithe, bright, colory, festal, frisky, jocund, jovial, lively, rakish, sporty **7** animate, festive, forward, gleeful, playful, pushful, raffish, rakehell, spirited, sportive **9** confident, homophile, presuming, sprightly, vivacious **10** blithesome, brassbound, frolicsome, homoerotic, homosexual

___ Gay
4 John **5** Enola

Gaza victor
7 Allenby (Edmund)

gaze
3 eye, see **4** bore, gape, gawk, leer, look, ogle, peer, pore, scan, view **5** glare, gloat, stare, watch **6** goggle, look at **7** observe **8** consider, look upon

gazebo
6 alcove, pagoda **8** pavilion **9** belvedere **11** garden house, summerhouse

gazelle
3 ahu, goa **4** admi, cora, dama, kudu, mohr, oryx **5** ariel, mhorr **6** dorcus **7** chikara, corinne **8** antelope

gazette
5 paper **6** record **7** courant, journal **9** newspaper

gazetteer
5 atlas, guide

Gazez's father
5 Caleb

Ge
see **Gaea**

gear
3 arm, cam, cog, rig **5** dress, equip, goods, stuff **6** fit out, outfit, tackle, things **7** apparel, appoint, furnish, rigging, turn out **8** accouter, accoutre, cogwheel, materiel, property, tackling **9** apparatus, equipment, machinery **10** belongings **11** accessories, habiliments, possessions **13** accouterments, accoutrements, paraphernalia

Geats
king: **7** Hygelac
prince: **7** Beowulf

Geb
daughter: **4** Isis **8** Nephthys
father: **3** Shu
mother: **6** Tefnut
sister: **3** Nut
son: **3** Set **6** Osiris
wife: **3** Nut

gecko
6 lizard

Gedaliah
father: **6** Ahikam **7** Pashhur **8** Jeduthun
slayer: **7** Ishmael

Gehenna
3 pit **4** hell **5** abyss, hades, Sheol **6** Tophet **7** inferno **9** perdition **10** underworld **11** netherworld

geisha wear
6 kimono

gel
3 dry, set 4 clot, jell 5 jelly 6 gelate 7 congeal, jellify 9 coagulate

gelatin
4 agar 5 jelly 7 sericin

geld
3 fix 4 spay 5 alter, unsex 6 change, neuter 8 castrate, mutilate 9 sterilize 10 emasculate 11 desexualize

gelid
3 icy 4 cold, cool 5 chill, nippy 6 arctic, chilly, frosty 7 glacial 8 freezing

gem
3 jet 4 jade, onyx, opal, ruby, sard 5 agate, amber, beryl, coral, jewel, pearl, stone, topaz 6 amulet, garnet, jasper, scarab, sphene, spinel, zircon 7 bejewel, cat's-eye, citrine, diamond, emerald, enjewel, peridot 8 amethyst, diopside, fluorite, intaglio, obsidian, sapphire, sardonyx, tigereye 9 carnelian, danburite, moonstone, phenakite, scapolite, spodumene, turquoise 10 aquamarine, cordierite, tourmaline 11 alexandrite, chrysoberyl, chrysoprase, lapis lazuli, masterpiece
blue: 6 zircon 8 sapphire 9 turquoise 10 aquamarine 11 lapis lazuli
carved: 8 intaglio
changeable: 9 chatoyant
cut: 7 navette 8 baguette, cabochon, marquise 9 brilliant
face: 5 facet
green: 4 jade 7 emerald, peridot, smaragd 10 chrysolite 11 chrysoprase
red: 4 ruby, sard 6 garnet, pyrope, spinel 9 carnelian
support: 7 setting
weight: 5 carat
yellow: 5 amber, topaz 6 sphene 7 citrine

Gemariah
brother: 6 Ahikam
father: 7 Hilkiah, Shaphan

Gemini star
6 Castor, Pollux

gemmule
3 bud 8 antelope

gemsbok
4 oryx

Gem State
5 Idaho

gemütlich
see **genial**

gendarme
7 soldier 9 policeman

gender
3 sex 4 kind, male, sort, type 5 class 6 female, neuter

genealogy
6 stemma 7 descent, history, lineage 8 pedigree 10 family tree

general
4 wide 5 broad, typic, usual 6 common, global, normal, public, vulgar 7 generic, natural, overall, regular, routine, typical 8 everyday, sweeping 9 all-around, inclusive, prevalent, universal 11 commonplace 12 run-of-the-mill 13 comprehensive
American: 3 Lee (Robert E.) 4 Pike (Zebulon), Wood (Leonard) 5 Clark (Mark, William), Grant (Ulysses S.), Meade (George), Scott (Charles, Hugh, Winfield), Smith (Andrew Jackson, Giles, Holland, Morgan, Samuel, Walter, Bedell), Stark (John), Worth (William) 6 Abrams (Creighton), Custer (George Armstrong), Kearny (Philip, Stephen), Patton (George S.), Porter (Fitz-John), Powell (Colin), Slocum (Henry), Spaatz (Carl), Taylor (Maxwell, Richard, Zachary) 7 Bradley (Omar), Fremont (John Charles), Houston (Samuel), Jackson (Andrew, Thomas "Stonewall"), Lejeune (John), Ridgway (Matthew B.), Sherman (William Tecumseh), Twining (Nathaniel), Wallace (Lewis), Wheeler (Joseph) 8 Burnside (Ambrose), Goethals (George Washington), Marshall (George), Mitchell (Billy), Pershing (John J.), Sheridan (Philip), Stilwell (Joseph) 9 MacArthur (Arthur, Douglas), McClellan (George), Rosecrans (William), Schofield (John), Wilkinson (James) 10 Eisenhower (Dwight David), Vandegrift (Alexander), Wainwright (Jonathan) 11 Schwarzkopf (Norman)
American Revolutionary: 4 Knox (Henry), Ward (Artemas) 5 Gates (Horatio), Wayne ("Mad Anthony") 6 de Kalb (Baron), Greene (Nathanael), Morgan (Daniel), Putnam (Israel, Rufus) 8 Moultrie (William), Sullivan (John) 10 Washington (George)

Austrian: 11 Wallenstein (Albrecht von)
British: 4 Gage (Thomas), Howe (William) 5 Clive (Robert), Monck (George), Wolfe (James) 6 Rupert (Prince) 7 Amherst (Jeffrey), Wingate (Orde Charles, Reginald) 8 Burgoyne (John), Cromwell (Oliver) 10 Abercromby (Ralph, Robert), Cornwallis (Charles), Wellington (Duke of)
Carthaginian: 8 Hamilcar, Hannibal 9 Hasdrubal
Chinese: 3 Yen (Hsishan) 4 Feng (Kuo-chang, Yü-hsiang) 5 Chang (Tso-lin)
combining form: 3 cen, pan 4 caen, ceno, coen, pano 5 caeno, coeno
Confederate: 3 Lee (Robert E.) 4 Hill (Ambrose), Hood (John Bell) 5 Bragg (Braxton), Ewell (Richard Stoddart), Price (Sterling), Smith (Edmund Kirby) 6 Morgan (John Hunt), Stuart (Jeb) 7 Forrest (Nathan Bedford), Hampton (Wade), Jackson (Thomas "Stonewall"), Pickett (George) 8 Johnston (Albert Sidney, Joseph Eggleston) 9 Pemberton (John) 10 Beauregard (Pierre G. T.), Longstreet (James)
French: 4 Foch (Ferdinand) 6 Moreau (Victor), Petain (Philippe) 7 Lefebre (Pierre), Weygand (Maxime) 8 de Gaulle (Charles), Montcalm (Marquis de), Saint-Cyr (Laurent de Gouvion-) 9 Frontenac (Comte de) 10 Rochambeau (Comte de)
German: 4 Jodl (Alfred) 6 Kleist (Paul Ludwig von) 10 Ludendorff (Erich)
Greek: 6 Nicias 9 Miltiades 10 Alcibiades 12 Themistocles
Japanese: 4 Tojo (Hideki) 5 Koiso (Kuniaki), Yasuda (Yoshisada) 8 Yamagata (Aritomo) 9 Yamashita (Tomoyuki)
Mexican: 9 Santa Anna (Antonio Lopez de)
Prussian: 11 Scharnhorst (Gerhard von)
Roman: 5 Sulla (Lucius Cornelius) 6 Caesar (Julius), Fabius (Quintus), Marius (Gaius), Pompey (the Great), Scipio (Gnaeus Cornelius, Publius Cornelius) 7 Regulus (Marcus Atilius), Ricimer (Flavius) 8 Agricola (Gnaeus Julius), Lucullus (Lucius Licinius), Stilicho (Flavius) 9 Marcellus (Marcus Claudius), Sertorius (Quintus) 10 Theodosius (the Great) 11 Cincinnatus (Lucius Quinctius)

Russian: 7 Wrangel (Pyotr), Zhdanov (Andrey) 9 Yeremenko (Andrey)
Spanish: 4 Alba (Duke of), Alva (Duke of) 6 Franco (Francisco)
Swedish: 7 Wrangel (Karl Gustav)

general assembly
6 plenum

generalize
5 infer, widen 6 extend, induce, spread

generally
6 mainly, mostly 7 as a rule, chiefly, en masse, largely, overall, usually 8 all in all, commonly 9 primarily 10 altogether, by and large, by ordinary, frequently, on the whole, ordinarily 11 principally 13 predominantly

generate
4 bear, make, sire 5 beget, breed, cause, get up, hatch, spawn 6 create, father, induce, parent, whip up, work up 7 develop, produce, provoke 8 engender, multiply, muster up 9 originate, procreate, propagate, reproduce 10 bring about

generic
6 common 7 general 9 universal

___ generis
3 sui

generosity
7 charity, largess 8 largesse 10 liberality

generous
3 big 4 free, kind 5 ample, lofty, noble 6 kindly, lavish, plenty 7 copious, helpful, liberal, profuse 8 abundant, handsome 9 bounteous, bountiful, plenteous, plentiful, unselfish, unsparing 10 altruistic, benevolent, bighearted, charitable, chivalrous, freehanded, munificent, openhanded, thoughtful, ungrudging 11 considerate, kindhearted, magnanimous

genesis
4 dawn 5 alpha, birth, start 6 origin, outset, setout 7 dawning, opening 8 outstart 9 beginning 12 commencement

genetic
10 hereditary
material: 3 DNA, RNA 7 cistron 9 chromatid 10 chromosome
term: 8 synapsis 9 backcross

genial
4 warm 5 jolly, merry 6 benign, blithe, gentle, jocund, jovial, kindly 7 affable, amiable, cordial 8 ami-

cable, cheerful, friendly, gracious, sociable 9 congenial 10 neighborly

genie
4 jinn 5 afrit, jinni 6 afreet, spirit, yaksha

genitor
6 father, parent 7 creator

geniture
5 birth 8 nativity

genius
4 bent, bump, gift, head, turn 5 flair, knack 6 brains, talent, wizard 7 aptness, faculty 9 ingenuity, intellect 10 creativity 12 intelligence 13 inventiveness

Genoa's liberator
5 Doria (Andrea)

genre
3 ilk 4 kind, sort, type 5 class, style 7 species 8 category

gens
4 clan 5 group 6 family, people

Genseric's subjects
7 Vandals

genteel
4 nice, prig, prim 5 civil, noble 6 la-di-da, polite, prissy, stuffy, tootoo, urbane 7 elegant, mincing, prudish, refined, stilted, stylish 8 affected, cultured, graceful, knightly, ladylike, mannerly, polished, precious, priggish, well-bred 9 courteous, distingué, Victorian 10 chivalrous, cultivated, tight-laced 11 fashionable, gentlemanly, pretentious, well-behaved 12 aristocratic, well-mannered 13 straightlaced

gentile
3 goy 4 Arya 5 Aryan

gentility
5 elite 6 flower, gentry 7 aristoi, quality, society 8 breeding, optimacy 10 upper class, upper crust 11 aristocracy

gentle
4 calm, easy, kind, meek, mild, soft, tame 5 balmy, bland, faint, quiet, tamed 6 benign, genial, kindly, mellow, placid, serene, smooth, tender 7 affable, amiable, lenient 8 delicate, peaceful, pleasant, pleasing, soothing, tranquil 9 agreeable 11 softhearted, sympathetic, warmhearted 13 compassionate
creature: 4 lamb

gentleman
6 aristo, fellow, mister 8 cavalier 9 blue blood, chevalier, patrician 10 aristocrat
English: 6 milord
French: 8 monsieur
Hindu: 4 babu
Spanish: 3 don 5 senor

gentleman friend
4 beau 5 swain

gentry
4 rank 5 elite 6 flower 7 aristoi, quality, society 8 optimacy 9 gentility 10 upper class, upper crust 11 aristocracy

genu
4 knee 5 joint

Genubath's father
5 Hadad

genuflect
5 kneel 6 kowtow

genuine
4 hard, real, true, very 5 plain, pucka, pukka 6 actual, dinkum, honest 7 factual, natural, sincere 8 absolute, bona fide, positive, trueborn 9 authentic, undoubted, unfeigned, veritable 10 heart-whole, sure-enough, unaffected

genus
4 kind, mode, sort, type 5 class, group, order 8 category

geode
6 cavity, nodule

geographer
American: 10 Huntington (Ellsworth)
Flemish: 8 Mercator (Gerardus)
German: 6 Ratzel (Friedrich)
Greek: 6 Strabo 7 Ptolemy

geologic
period: 5 azoic 6 Eocene 7 Miocene, Permian 8 Cambrian, Cenozoic, Devonian, Jurassic, Mesozoic, Pliocene, Silurian, Triassic 9 Oligocene, Paleocene, Paleozoic 10 Cretaceous, Ordovician 13 Mississippian, Pennsylvanian
study: 4 rock 5 earth 6 fossil

geometer
6 Euclid

geometric
coordinate: 8 abscissa
curve: 3 arc 6 spiral 7 cissoid, ellipse, evolute 8 parabola
solid: 4 cone, cube 5 prism 7 pyramid 8 spheroid, spherule
surface: 5 nappe, torus 6 toroid

geometric figure
4 cone, cube 5 prism, rhomb 6 circle, oblong, sphere, square 7 ellipse, hexagon, octagon, polygon, pyramid, rhombus 8 cylinder, heptagon, pentagon, rhomboid, spheroid, triangle 9 rectangle
combining form: 5 hedra (plural) 6 hedron

geometry letters
3 Q.E.D.

geophagy
4 pica

Georgia
capital: 7 Atlanta
college, university: 4 Tift 5 Clark, Emory, Paine
founder: 10 Oglethorpe (James)
nickname: 10 Peach State

Gera
father: 4 Bela
grandfather: 8 Benjamin
son: 4 Ehud 6 Shimei

Geraint's wife
4 Enid

Gerda's husband
4 Frey

germ
3 bud, bug 4 seed 5 spark, spore, virus 6 embryo 7 microbe, nucleus 9 bacterium
cell: 3 egg 4 ovum 5 sperm

German
4 Goth 6 Teuton
article: 3 das, der, des, die
bomber: 5 Gotha, Stuka
child: 4 kind
coin: 4 mark 5 taler 6 thaler 7 pfennig
empire: 5 reich
head: 4 kopf
highway: 8 autobahn
leader: 6 führer, kaiser
measles: 7 rubella
mister: 4 herr
no: 4 nein
nobleman: 6 Junker
pronoun: 2 du, er, es 3 ich, sie, wir
rifle: 6 Mauser
weight: 3 lot 5 pfund, stein 8 vierling
woman: 4 frau 8 fräulein

germane
5 ad rem 7 apropos, related 8 apposite, material, pointful, relevant 9 pertinent 10 applicable

Germany
11 Deutschland

capital: 6 Berlin
monetary unit: 4 mark

germinate
3 bud 6 evolve, sprout

Gerontion poet
5 Eliot (Thomas Stearns)

Gershom, Gershon
father: 4 Levi
son: 5 Libni 6 Shimei

Gershwin
3 Ira 6 George
opera: 12 Porgy and Bess

Gertrude
husband: 8 Claudius
son: 6 Hamlet

Gervaise's daughter
4 Nana

Geryon
dog: 6 Orthus
father: 8 Chrysaor
mother: 10 Callirrhoe
slayer: 8 Hercules

Gesham's father
6 Jahdai

gest, geste
4 deed, feat 7 emprise, exploit, venture 9 adventure 10 enterprise

Gestapo chief
7 Himmler (Heinrich)

gesticulate
6 motion 7 gesture

gesture
3 act, nod 4 flag, sign 5 token 6 motion, salute, signal 8 reminder 9 signalize 10 expression, indication
graceful: 9 beau geste

get
3 bag, fix, win 4 beat, come, draw, earn, gain, gall, grow, have, land, move, rile, sire, sway, turn 5 annex, breed, catch, educe, evoke, learn, peeve, reach, ready, touch, upset 6 accept, affect, arrive, attain, become, bother, burn up, collar, elicit, extort, father, induce, make up, master, obtain, pick up, secure, show up, turn up 7 acquire, bring in, capture, chalk up, compass, disturb, extract, impress, nonplus, perturb, prehend, prepare, procure, realize, receive, win over 8 contract, convince, distress, draw down, irritate, memorize, persuade, sicken of, talk into 9 aggravate, argue into, influence, knock down, prevail on, procreate 10 exasperate, sicken with

11 bring around, prevail upon, progenerate 12 come down with

get around
5 evade

get away
see **get out**

getaway
3 lam 4 slip 6 escape, flight 8 breakout, escaping 10 escapement

get back
6 recoup, regain 7 recover, recruit 8 retrieve 9 repossess

get by
4 fare 5 shift 6 manage

get off
2 go 4 exit, open, quit 5 begin, leave, start 6 depart, launch, retire 7 jump off, kick off, pull out 8 commence
prefix: 2 de

get out
2 go 4 exit, kite, leak 5 break, issue, leave, scram, split 6 begone, decamp, depart, egress, escape 7 publish, skiddoo, take off 8 clear out, hightail 9 skedaddle

Gettysburg general
3 Lee (Robert E.) 5 Meade (George)

get up
4 rise 5 arise, breed, cause, hatch, mount, stand 6 induce, uprise 7 pile out, produce, roll out, turn out 8 engender, generate, muster up, occasion, upspring 12 rise and shine

getup
2 go 3 pep, rig 4 bang, push, snap, togs 5 dress, drive, guise, punch, vigor 6 outfit, setout 7 costume 8 vitality

get-up-and-go
3 pep 4 bang, push, snap 5 drive, punch, vigor 8 ambition, vitality 10 enterprise, initiative

gewgaw
3 toy 5 curio 6 bauble, trifle 7 bibelot, novelty, trinket, whatnot 8 gimcrack 9 objet d'art 10 knickknack

geyser
5 spurt 6 spring 11 Old Faithful

Ghana
capital: 5 Accra
monetary unit: 4 cedi

ghastly
3 wan 4 grim, pale 5 awful
6 grisly, horrid, shadow 7 hideous,
macabre 8 dreadful, gruesome,
horrible, nauseant, shocking, spectral, terrible 9 appalling, deathlike,
frightful, ghostlike, sickening 10 cadaverous, corpselike, disgustful, disgusting, horrifying, nauseating, terrifying 11 frightening

ghee
3 fat 6 butter

gherkin
6 pickle 8 cucumber

ghetto
4 slum

ghost
5 shade, spook 6 shadow, spirit,
wraith 7 phantom, specter 8 phantasm 10 apparition 11 poltergeist

ghostlike
see **ghostly**

ghostly
5 eerie, scary 6 spooky 7 shadowy
8 spectral 9 deathlike 10 cadaverous, corpselike

ghoul
4 ogre 5 fiend 7 monster

GI
7 fighter, soldier, warrior 9 man-at-
arms 10 serviceman

giant
4 huge, ogre, Otus 5 gross, Gyges,
Hymir, jumbo, titan, troll, whale
6 Cottus, Typhon 7 Aloadae (plural), Antaeus, Cyclops, mammoth,
monster, titanic 8 behemoth, Briareus, colossal, colossus, gigantic,
Orgoglio 9 cyclopean, Enceladus,
Ephialtes, Gargantua, Herculean,
leviathan, monstrous, polypheme
10 behemothic, gargantuan
armadillo: 4 tatu 5 tatou
biblical: 4 Anak 7 Goliath
cactus: 7 saguaro
clam: 8 tridacna
grass: 5 otate
killer: 4 Jack 5 David
one-eyed: 5 Arges 7 Cyclops
10 Polyphemus
100-armed: 9 Enceladus
100-eyed: 5 Argus
perch: 5 begti, bekti 6 cockup
rime-cold: 4 Ymer, Ymir
sea god: 5 Aegir

Giant author
5 Ferber (Edna)

gibber
5 prate 6 babble, drivel, gabble,
jabber, yammer 7 blather, chatter,
prattle

gibberish
5 Greek 6 babble, bunkum, drivel,
gabble, jabber 7 blabber, blather,
mummery, palaver, prattle, twaddle
8 claptrap, nonsense 10 double-
talk, hocus-pocus, mumbo jumbo
11 abracadabra, jabberwocky
12 gobbledygook

gibbet
4 hang 5 noose, scrag 7 gallows,
turn off 8 string up

gibbon
3 ape, lar 6 monkey 7 primate,
siamang 10 anthropoid

gibbous
6 convex, humped 7 rounded,
swollen 10 humpbacked

gibe
4 gird, jeer, jest, mock, quip
5 fleer, flout, gleek, scoff, sneer
6 quip at 7 scout at 8 ridicule

Gibraltar
colony of: 12 Great Britain
conqueror: 5 Tarik, Tariq
country: 5 Spain
opposite: 5 Ceuta

Giddalti
father: 5 Heman
occupation: 6 singer

giddy
5 dizzy, light, silly 6 swimmy, volage, yeasty 7 flighty, fribble 8 skittish, swimming 9 fribbling, frivolous
10 bird-witted, hoity-toity 11 empty-
headed, harebrained, light-headed,
vertiginous 13 rattlebrained

___ Gide
5 André

Gideon
father: 5 Joash
servant: 5 Purah
son: 9 Abimelech

Gideoni's son
6 Abidan

gift
3 set, tip 4 alms, bent, boon,
bump, head, turn 5 award, favor,
flair, grant, knack 6 genius, legacy, reward, talent 7 aptness, cumshaw, faculty, handout, largess,
present, subsidy 8 bestowal, donation, gratuity, offering 9 lagniappe
11 benefaction, benevolence
12 contribution, presentation

gig
3 jab, job 4 boat, fool, goad, prod
5 annoy, rotor, spear 6 chaise, harass 7 demerit, provoke

gigantic
3 big 4 huge, vast 5 giant, large
7 hulking, immense, mammoth
8 colossal, enormous 9 cyclopean,
monstrous 10 gargantuan, prodigious, stupendous 11 elephantine

giggle
5 laugh, tehee 6 guffaw, hee-haw,
teehee, titter 7 chortle, chuckle,
snicker, snigger

Gilbert and Sullivan opera
8 Iolanthe, Patience 9 Ruddigore,
The Mikado 11 H.M.S. Pinafore,
Princess Ida, The Sorcerer, Trial by
Jury 12 The Grand Duke 13 The
Gondoliers

Gil Blas author
6 Lesage (Alain-René)

gild
5 adorn, cover, tinge 7 overlay
8 brighten 9 embellish

Gilda's father
9 Rigoletto

Gilead
father: 6 Machir
grandfather: 8 Manasseh
son: 8 Jephthah

Gilgamesh
4 epic
companion: 6 Eabani, Engidu,
Enkidu
home: 5 Erech
mother: 6 Ninsun
victim: 7 Humbaba

gill
4 race 5 brook, creek 6 runnel,
stream, wattle 7 rivulet
relating to: 9 branchial

gilly flower
4 pink 9 clove pink

gilt
3 hog, pig, sow 4 gold 5 swine
6 gilded, golden

gimlet
4 tool 5 drink 6 pierce 7 gum tree
8 eucalypt 10 eucalyptus
ingredient: 3 gin 9 lime juice

gimmick
4 ploy, ruse, wile 5 feint, gizmo,
trick 6 gadget, gambit, jigger,
widget 7 concern, whizzer 8 artifice, maneuver 9 stratagem

gimpy
4 lame 7 limping 8 crippled

gin
3 net 4 sloe, trap 5 catch, rummy,

snare **6** liquor **7** springe
8 Hollands

Ginath's son
5 Tibni

ginger
3 fig, pep, vim **4** herb, stir **5** liven,
spice, vigor **6** mettle, revive, spirit
cookie: **4** snap

gingerly
4 safe, wary **5** chary **7** careful,
guarded **8** cautious, discreet
11 calculating, circumspect,
considerate

gingery
5 beany, fiery **6** spunky **7** peppery
8 spirited **10** mettlesome **11** high-
hearted **12** high-spirited

gingham
5 cloth **6** fabric

gingiva
3 gum

ginseng
4 herb, root

Gioconda, La
8 Mona Lisa
composer: **10** Ponchielli (Amilcare)
painter: **7** da Vinci (Leonardo)

giraffe
3 car **5** piano **8** ruminant
10 camelopard

girandole
6 mirror **7** earring, pendant
11 candelabrum

girasol
4 opal **8** fire opal **9** artichoke

gird
3 hem **4** band, belt, gibe, jeer, jest,
ring, wrap **5** beset, brace, fleer,
flout, ready, round, scoff, sneer,
steel **6** circle, quip at **7** bolster,
forearm, fortify, prepare, scout at,
shore up, wreathe **8** begirdle, buttress, cincture, encircle, engirdle,
surround **9** encompass, reinforce
10 encincture, strengthen

girdle
3 hem **4** band, bark, belt, ring,
sash **5** beset, round **6** begird, cestus, circle, engird **8** ceinture, cincture, encircle, surround **9** encompass, waistband **10** encincture
combining form: **3** zon **4** zono
6 pleura
of Aphrodite: **6** cestus **7** caestus

girl Friday
9 secretary

girth
4 band, belt, bind, size **5** brace,
cinch, strap **6** girdle **7** measure

8 cincture, encircle **10** dimensions
13 circumference

gist
3 nub **3** core, meat, pith **5** sense,
short **6** burden, matter, thrust, upshot **7** bearing **9** substance

gitano
5 gypsy

give
3 air, lot, pay **4** bend, cave, deal,
fail, feed, find, hand, pose, sell,
vend, vent **5** allot, allow, apply,
award, break, grant, issue, offer,
spend, throw, yield **6** accord, afford, assign, befall, bestow, betide,
chance, confer, devote, direct, donate, expend, extend, fold up, happen, lay out, lot out, market, outlay,
relent, render, strike, supply, tender, weaken **7** address, crumple,
deliver, dish out, dole out, express,
fall out, fork out, furnish, hand out,
hold out, inflict, mete out, present,
produce, proffer, provide, slacken
8 allocate, collapse, disburse, dispense, disperse, give away, hand
over, shell out, transfer, turn over
9 admeasure, apportion, ventilate
10 buckle down, contribute, distribute

give away
4 tell **5** grant, mouth, spill **6** bestow, betray, devote, donate, re-
veal **7** blab out, divulge, hand out,
present, unclose **8** disclose,
discover

give back
4 echo **6** refund, retire, return **7** replace, restore, retreat **8** withdraw
9 reinstate

give in
5 yield **6** relent **7** indulge, succumb
9 surrender

give off
4 emit, flow, pour, vent, void **5** issue **7** release **8** throw off
9 discharge

give out
4 deal, dole, drop, emit, fail, mete,
vent, wilt **5** issue **6** cave in, peg
out, run out **7** release, succumb
8 collapse, throw off **9** break down

giver
5 donor **7** donator **8** bestower
9 conferrer, presenter

give up
4 cede, quit, sell **5** forgo, leave,
waive, yield **6** forego, resign, vacate **7** abandon, despair, despond

8 abdicate, hand over **9** surrender
10 relinquish

gizmo
see **gadget**

glabrous
4 bald **6** shaven, smooth **8** hairless
9 beardless **12** smooth-shaven

glacial
3 icy **4** cold **5** chill, gelid, nippy
6 arctic, chilly, frigid, frosty
8 freezing

glacier
3 ice **6** ice cap **8** ice sheet
Alaska: **4** Muir, Taku **6** Bering
Antarctica: **9** Beardmore
deposit: **4** kame **5** esker **6** placer
7 moraine **8** diluvium
fissure: **8** crevasse
fragment: **4** berg **7** iceberg
hill: **7** drumlin
Karakoram: **5** Biafo **7** Baltoro
New Zealand: **6** Tasman
pinnacle: **5** serac

glad
4 fain **5** happy, jolly, merry
6 blithe, bright, cheery, genial, jocund, jovial, joyful, joyous **7** beaming, gleeful, pleased, radiant, tick-
led **8** cheerful, mirthful, pleasant,
rejoiced **9** delighted, gratified
11 exhilarated **12** lighthearted

gladden
5 cheer, elate **6** arride, please
7 delight, gratify, happify, rejoice
8 pleasure

glade
5 grove, marsh **8** clearing

gladiator
7 battler, fighter **9** combatant
Roman: **9** retiarius

gladly
4 fain, lief

gladness
3 joy **4** glee **5** bliss, cheer, mirth
7 jollity, joyance **9** happiness
10 joyfulness

gladstone
3 bag

glamorous
5 siren **8** alluring, charming, magnetic **9** seductive **10** attractive, bewitching, enchanting **11** captivating, fascinating

glamour
5 charm, magic **6** allure, appeal
8 charisma, witchery **9** magnetism
10 witchcraft **11** fascination

glance
3 rub 4 buff, kiss, peek, peep,
skim, skip 5 brush, carom, flash,
glaze, gleam, glime, glint, gloss,
graze, shave, shine, touch
6 bounce, careen, polish, scrape
7 burnish, contact, furbish, glimmer,
glimpse, glisten, glitter, shimmer,
sparkle, twinkle 8 ricochet
9 coruscate
sinister: 4 leer

gland
5 gonad, liver, organ 6 thymus
7 adrenal, mammary, thyroid
8 exocrine, pancreas, prostate
9 endocrine, pituitary 11 parathyroid
secretion: 7 hormone
sex: 5 gonad
swelling: 4 bubo

glare
4 bore, gape, gawk, gaze, glow,
peer 5 blaze, flame, flash, frown,
gleam, gloat, lower, scowl, stare
6 dazzle, glower, goggle 7 glisten,
glitter

glaring
4 loud, rank 5 gaudy, plain, vivid
6 brazen, flashy, garish, tawdry,
tinsel 7 blatant, capital, chintzy
8 flagrant 9 egregious, obtrusive
10 noticeable 11 conspicuous,
outstanding

Glasgow's patron saint
5 Mingo 9 Kentigern

glass
4 lens, pane 5 image, lense, prism
6 mirror 7 reflect 9 barometer,
telescope
combining form: 4 hyal, vitr 5 hyalo,
vitro
container: 3 jar 6 beaker, bottle
decorative: 7 schmelz 8 schmelze
drinking: 3 mug 4 pony 5 stein
6 goblet, jigger, rummer, seidel
7 snifter, tumbler 8 schooner
gem: 5 paste 6 strass
magnifying: 5 loupe
milky: 7 opaline
volcanic: 7 perlite 8 obsidian

glasses
5 specs 6 shades 7 goggles
10 spectacles

glass-like
6 vitric 8 vitreous

glassmaker
6 blower 7 glazier, Tiffany (Louis
Comfort)

glassmaking
oven: 4 lehr
tool: 5 ponty 6 pontil 8 blowpipe

Glaucus
father: 5 Minos 8 Sisyphus
mother: 6 Merope 8 Pasiphae
son: 11 Bellerophon

glaze
3 rub 4 buff, coat 5 glint, gloss,
sheen, shine 6 enamel, glance, luster, polish 7 burnish, furbish

gleam
3 ray 4 beam, glow 5 flash, glint,
sheen, shine 6 glance 7 glimmer,
glisten, glitter, radiate, shimmer,
sparkle, twinkle 8 radiance 11 coruscation, scintillate 13 scintillation

gleaming
5 shiny 6 glossy, sheeny 7 shining
8 lustrous, polished 9 burnished
10 glistening

glean
4 cull, reap 6 garner, gather, pick
up 7 extract

glede
4 kite 6 osprey

glee
3 joy 5 mirth 6 gaiety, levity
7 delight, jollity 8 hilarity, pleasure
9 enjoyment, jocundity, joviality,
merriment

gleeful
3 gay 4 boon 5 jolly, merry
6 blithe, jocund, jovial 8 mirthful
10 blithesome

glen
4 dale, vale 6 dingle, valley
deep: 5 gorge 6 ravine
Scottish: 5 heuch, heugh

glib
4 easy 5 slick 6 facile, fluent,
smooth 7 voluble 8 eloquent, flippant, vocative, well-hung 9 talkative 10 articulate

glide
3 fly 4 flow, sail, skim, slip, soar
5 creep, float, mouse, skate, skulk,
slick, slide, slink, sneak, steal
7 gumshoe, slither 8 glissade, vol-
plane 9 pussyfoot

glimmer
4 glow 5 flash, gleam, glint
6 glance 7 glisten, glitter, shimmer,
sparkle, twinkle 9 coruscate
11 coruscation 13 scintillation

glimpse
4 look, peek, peep 5 stime
6 glance

glint
5 flash, glaze, gleam, gloss, sheen,
shine 6 glance, luster, polish

7 glimmer, glisten, glitter, shimmer,
sparkle, twinkle 9 coruscate
11 coruscation 13 scintillation

glissade
4 skim, slip 5 glide, slick, slide
7 slither

glisten
5 flash, gleam, glint, shine
6 glance 7 glimmer, glitter, shimmer, sparkle, twinkle 9 coruscate
11 coruscation

glitter
5 flash, gleam, glint, shine
6 glance 7 glimmer, glisten, shimmer, spangle, sparkle, twinkle
9 bespangle, coruscate 11 coruscation 13 scintillation

glittering
5 gaudy, showy 7 shining 9 brilliant, clinquant, sparkling

gloaming
3 eve 4 dusk 7 evening 8 eventide, owl-light, twilight 9 nightfall

gloat
4 bore, gape, gawk, gaze, peer
5 exult, glare, stare 6 goggle

global
5 grand 6 cosmic 7 general, overall 8 all-round, catholic 9 inclusive,
planetary, universal, worldwide

globe
3 orb 4 ball 5 earth, round, world
6 planet, sphere 7 rondure
half: 10 hemisphere

globule
4 bead, drib, drip, drop 6 gobbet
7 driblet, droplet 8 spherule

gloom
3 dim 4 dusk, murk 5 bedim,
blues, cloud, dumps, frown, lower,
scowl 6 darken, glower 7 becloud,
obscure, sadness 8 darkness, overcast 9 adumbrate, dejection 10 depression, melancholy, overshadow,
the dismals 11 unhappiness
12 mournfulness

gloomy
3 dim, dun, sad 4 cold, dark, dour,
drab, dull, glum, ugly 5 black,
bleak, drear, dusky, morne, murky,
muzzy, sulky, surly 6 dismal,
dreary, morose, solemn, somber,
sullen 7 crabbed, joyless, obscure,
stygian, unhappy 8 dejected, desolate, downcast, funereal, mournful
9 cheerless, depressed, lightless,
mirthless, oppressed, saturnine, tenebrous, woebegone 10 acheronian, acherontic, caliginous, depres-

sant, depressing, depressive, despondent, lugubrious, melancholy, oppressive, tenebrific **11** dispiriting, pessimistic **12** disconsolate, discouraging

glorify

4 hymn, laud **5** bless, cry up, erect, exalt, extol, honor **6** praise, uprear **7** dignify, ennoble, magnify, sublime **8** eulogize **9** celebrate **10** aggrandize, panegyrize

glorious

5 grand, great, noble, proud **6** divine, groovy, superb **7** radiant, sublime **8** gorgeous, lustrous, majestic, splendid, stunning **9** beautiful, brilliant, effulgent, hunky-dory, marvelous, ravishing **11** magnificent, resplendent, splendorous

glory

4 fame, halo **5** exult, honor **6** praise, renown **7** acclaim, aureole, delight, triumph **8** eminence, jubilate, splendor **9** greatness **11** distinction **12** magnificence

gloss

4 buff **5** glaze, glint, sheen, shine **6** enamel, glance, luster, polish **7** burnish, furbish, varnish **8** annotate **9** sleekness, slickness

glossary

6 clavis **7** lexicon

gloss over

5 white **6** veneer, whiten **7** falsify, varnish **8** palliate **9** extenuate, sugarcoat, whitewash **12** misrepresent

glossy

5 shiny, sleek **6** sheeny, sleeky, smarmy **7** shining **8** gleaming, lustrous, polished **9** burnished **10** glistening
fabric: **4** silk **5** satin
paint: **6** enamel

glove

4 mitt **5** cover **6** mitten, sheath **8** gauntlet

glow

4 pink, rose **5** blare, blaze, bloom, blush, color, flame, flare, flush, glare, rouge, shine **6** mantle, pinken, redden **7** blossom, crimson, foxfire

glower

4 gaze **5** frown, gloom, scowl, stare

glowing

3 hot **5** fiery, flush, ruddy, shiny **6** ardent, fervid, florid, heated **7** blazing, burning, candent, fer-

vent, flaming, flushed, radiant **8** dazzling, rubicund, sanguine **10** candescent, hot-blooded, passionate **11** full-blooded, impassioned **12** enthusiastic

gloze over

see **gloss over**

Gluck opera

5 Orfeo **6** Armide **7** Alceste

glucose

5 sugar

glue

3 fix **4** join **5** epoxy, paste, stick **6** adhere, attach, cement **8** adhesive, mucilage

gluey

5 gooey, gummy **6** cloggy, sticky, stodgy **8** adhesive

glum

4 dour **5** moody, sulky, surly **6** gloomy, morose, silent, sullen **7** crabbed **8** taciturn **9** depressed, oppressed, saturnine

glut

4 clog, cloy, cram, fill, jade, pall, sate **5** feast, gorge, stuff **6** stodge **7** satiate, surfeit

glutinous

4 ropy **5** gluey, gummy **6** sticky **7** viscous

glutton

3 hog, pig **5** gulch **8** gourmand **9** chowhound

gluttonous

7 hoggish, piggish **8** edacious, ravening, ravenous **9** indulgent, rapacious, voracious **11** intemperate

gluttony

7 edacity **8** gulosity

G-man

3 fed

gnarl

4 bend, knot **5** snarl, twist **6** deform **7** contort, distort

gnash

4 bite **5** grind

gnat

3 fly **4** pest **6** insect

gnaw

3 eat **4** bite, chew **5** annoy, erode, harry, scour, tease, worry **6** harass, nibble, pester, plague **7** bedevil, consume, corrode, eat away, hagride **8** wear away

gnome

3 elf, saw **4** rule **5** axiom, dwarf, maxim, moral, troll **6** dictum, gob-

lin, sprite, truism **7** brocard **8** aphorism, apothegm

gnostic

4 sage, wise **6** sophic **7** knowing **9** insighted, sagacious **10** discerning, insightful, perceptive **13** knowledgeable

go

3 act, die, fit, fly, hie, pep, run, set, try **4** bear, bout, exit, fare, flee, give, jibe, like, move, pass, quit, shot, wend, work **5** abide, agree, apply, brook, drive, enjoy, event, fit in, fling, leave, occur, range, recur, refer, siege, spell, stint, vigor, whirl **6** accord, become, belong, decamp, demise, depart, elapse, endure, energy, escape, expire, extend, get off, happen, pan out, pop off, push on, repair, resort, retire, thrive, travel **7** abscond, advance, come off, conform, crumble, decease, episode, get away, journey, potency, proceed, prosper, pull out, push off, succeed, success, succumb, take off **8** collapse, flourish, function, incident, occasion, pass away, run along, shove off, tolerate, vitality, withdraw **9** happening, hardihood **10** correspond, get-up-and-go, occurrence
against: **5** fight **6** oppose
ahead: **4** lead **7** precede, proceed **8** continue, progress
along: **5** agree **6** concur
around: **5** avoid **7** compass **10** circumvent
at: **6** attack **8** approach
away: **3** off **4** exit, quit, scat, shoo **5** leave, scram **6** depart, retire
back: **6** recede, return, revert **7** regress, retreat
back on: **6** betray, renege **7** abandon
back over: **6** review **7** retrace
before: **4** lead **7** precede **8** antedate
beyond: **6** exceed **7** surpass
forward: **7** advance, proceed **8** continue, progress
in: **5** enter **7** ingress **9** penetrate
out: **4** date, exit **5** leave **6** egress
Scottish: **3** gae
through: **3** cut **6** endure **7** undergo **9** penetrate **10** experience
together: **3** fit **4** suit **5** agree, befit **6** become **9** agree with, harmonize
with: **4** date, suit **5** befit **6** escort **9** accompany

goad

3 egg, sic **4** prod, spur **5** drive, egg on, impel, prick **6** exhort, needle, prompt, propel **7** impetus, impulse **8** catalyst, stimulus **9** impulsion, incentive, stimulant

go-ahead
4 okay **9** clearance, gumptious **10** green light **11** up-and-coming **12** enterprising **13** authorization

goal
3 aim, end, use **4** duty, mark **6** object, target **7** purpose **8** ambition, function **9** objective, quaesitum

goat
3 kid, ram **5** billy, nanny, patsy **6** alpaca, angora, caprid, nubian **7** fall guy **8** cashmere **9** scapegoat
combining form: **5** capri
female: **3** doe **5** nanny
flesh: **6** chevon
genus: **5** Capra
Himalayan: **4** tahr, thar
male: **4** buck **5** billy
wild: **4** ibex **7** markhor

goat antelope
5 goral, serow **7** chamois

goatee
5 beard **7** Vandyke

goatfish
6 mullet

goatish
3 hot **4** lewd **7** caprine, hircine, lustful, satyric **8** prurient **9** lickerish **10** lascivious, libidinous, passionate **12** concupiscent

goat-man deity
3 Pan

goat nut
6 jojoba

goatsfoot
8 goutweed

goatskin
9 chevrette

gob
3 wad **4** clod, hunk, lump, mass **5** chunk, mouth **6** nugget

gobbet
4 drip, drop **7** driblet, droplet, globule

gobble
4 bolt, cram, gulp, slop, wolf **5** slosh **6** englut, guzzle **11** ingurgitate

gobbledygook
see **gibberish**

go-between
5 agent, envoy **6** broker **8** attorney, emissary, mediator **9** middleman **10** arbitrator, interagent, interceder, matchmaker, negotiator

11 intercessor **12** entrepreneur, intermediary, intermediate **13** intermediator

goblet
5 glass **6** vessel

goblin
3 elf, fay **4** bhut, bogy **5** bogie, bogle, fairy, gnome, pooka **6** booger, sprite **7** brownie **8** barghest, bogeyman

gobs
4 heap, wads **5** loads, reams, scads **6** oodles **8** slathers **10** quantities

god
4 idol **5** deity **7** creator **8** Almighty, divinity, immortal
combining form: **3** the **4** theo
false: **4** baal
French: **4** dieu
Latin: **4** deus
Spanish: **4** dios; (see specific entries (as **Greek; Roman**) for names of specific gods and goddesses)

God Bless America composer
6 Berlin (Irving)

goddess
4 idol **5** deity **8** divinity, immortal
Latin: **3** dea; (see note at **god**)

godfather
3 don **4** capo **7** sponsor

God-fearing
5 pious **6** devout **8** reverent **9** religious

godforsaken
6 dismal **7** pitiful **8** desolate, pitiable, wretched **9** miserable, neglected **11** unfortunate

Godiva's husband
7 Leofric

godless
6 wicked **7** impious, infidel **8** agnostic **9** atheistic **11** irreligious, unreligious

godlike
6 deific, divine **8** deifical, immortal

godly
4 holy **5** pious **6** deific, devout, divine **7** angelic, saintly **9** pietistic, prayerful, religious

go down
3 dip, sag, set **4** drop, fall, fold, sink **5** droop, pitch, slump **6** cave in, plunge, submit, topple, tumble **7** crumple, decline, descend, founder, go under, succumb **8** collapse, keel over, submerge, submerse **9** surrender

God's acre
8 cemetery **9** graveyard **10** churchyard, necropolis **11** polyandrium **12** burial ground, memorial park, potter's field **13** burying ground

godsend
4 boon, good **7** benefit **8** blessing **9** advantage **11** benediction

Goethe work
5 Faust **6** Egmont, Stella **7** Clavigo **10** Prometheus

goffer
5 crimp, flute, plait

go-getter
6 dynamo, peeler **7** hustler, rustler **8** live wire **11** self-starter

goggle
3 eye **4** bore, gape, gawk, gaze, look, ogle, peer **5** glare, gloat, stare

goggles
5 specs **7** glasses **8** blinkers **10** spectacles

Gogol novel
9 Dead Souls **10** Taras Bulba

Gog's land
5 Magog

goiter
6 struma **8** swelling

gola
4 cyma **7** granary **9** storeroom, warehouse

Golconda
see **gold mine**

gold
4 gilt **5** aurum, metal, money **6** riches, wealth, yellow **7** bullion, element **8** treasure
bar: **5** ingot
combining form: **4** auri, auro **5** chrys **6** chryso
fool's: **6** pyrite
heraldic: **2** or
imitation: **6** ormolu
measure: **5** carat, karat
Spanish: **3** oro
symbol: **2** Au

goldbrick
3 bum **4** idle, laze, lazy, loaf, loll **6** dawdle, loiter, lounge **7** shirker, slacker, slinker

Gold Bug author
3 Poe (Edgar Allan)

gold cloth
4 lamé

gold-covered
4 gilt

golden
4 gilt, rich 5 blond, straw
6 blonde, flaxen, gilded, liquid,
mellow, yellow 7 aureate, aureous,
honeyed 8 Hyblaean

golden-ager
5 elder 6 senior 7 ancient, oldster
8 old-timer 13 senior citizen

golden apple
3 bel 6 tomato 7 hog plum

golden-apples guardian
5 Ithun 6 Ithunn

golden bough
9 mistletoe

Golden Boy playwright
5 Odets (Clifford)

golden-crowned accentor
8 ovenbird

goldeneye
4 duck 8 lacewing 9 merrywing

Golden Fleece seeker
5 Jason 8 Argonaut

Golden Hind captain
5 Drake (Francis)

Golden Horde
6 Tatars 7 Mongols

golden horse
8 palomino

golden shiner
4 dace

Golden State
10 California

golden wolf
6 chanco

goldfinch
8 graypate 12 yellowhammer

gold mine
7 bonanza 8 El Dorado, Golconda, treasury 13 treasure-house,
treasure trove

golem
4 dolt 5 robot 7 machine 9 automaton, blockhead

golf
assistant: 5 caddy 6 caddie
award: 8 Ryder Cup 9 Curtis Cup,
Walker Cup
club: 4 iron, wood 5 baffy, cleek,
spoon, wedge 6 driver, mashie,
putter 7 brassie, niblick, pitcher
9 metal wood, sand wedge
club part: 3 toe 4 face, grip, head,
heel, neck, sole 5 hosel, shaft
6 socket
course: 5 links
hazard: 4 trap 6 bunker 8 sand trap

mound: 3 tee
score: 3 ace, par 5 bogey, bogie,
eagle 7 birdie 9 albatross
stroke: 4 baff, chip, draw, fade,
hook, putt 5 drive, pitch, shank,
slice 6 sclaff
target: 3 cup, par, pin 4 flag
5 green 7 fairway
term: 3 lie 4 ball, club, fore, hole,
loft 5 divot, rough, round, swing
6 course, hazard, marker, stance,
stroke 8 approach, foursome,
handicap 9 backswing, downswing, flagstick 10 Vardon grip

golfer
8 linksman
man: 3 Els (Ernie) 4 Daly (John),
Ford (Doug), Kite (Tom), Lyle
(Sandy), Mize (Larry), Tway (Bob)
5 Boros (Julius), Faldo (Nick), Floyd
(Ray), Grady (Wayne), Green (Hu-
bert), Hagen (Walter), Hogan
(Ben), Jones (Bobby), Irwin (Hale),
North (Andy), Pavin (Corey), Price
(Nick), Shute (Denny), Snead (Sam)
6 Casper (Billy), Graham (David),
Janzen (Lee), Langer (Bernhard),
Miller (Johnny), Nelson (Byron,
Larry), Norman (Greg), Ouimet
(Francis), Palmer (Arnold), Player
(Gary), Sluman (Jeff), Sutton (Hal),
Vardon (Harry), Watson (Tom)
7 Azinger (Paul), Couples (Fred),
Guldahl (Ralph), Mayfair (Billy),
Sarazen (Gene), Simpson (Scott),
Stewart (Payne), Strange (Curtis),
Trevino (Lee), Woosnam (Ian),
Zoeller (Fuzzy) 8 Crenshaw (Ben),
Nicklaus (Jack), Olazabal (Jose),
Weiskopf (Tom), Rodriguez (Chi
Chi) 9 Elkington (Steve) 10 Middle-
coff (Cary) 11 Ballesteros (Seve)
woman: 4 Berg (Patty), King (Betsy)
5 Baker (Kathy), Lopez (Nancy),
Rawls (Betsy), Stacy (Hollis), Suggs
(Louise) 6 Alcott (Amy), Carner
(Joanne), Daniel (Beth), Davies
(Laura), Geddes (Jane), Mallon
(Meg), Merten (Lauri), Wright
(Mickey) 7 Bradley (Pat), Mochrie
(Dottie), Sheehan (Patty) 8 Zaharias
(Babe) 9 Sorenstam (Annika), Whit-
worth (Kathy) 10 Stephenson (Jan)

Goliath
5 giant 10 Philistine
deathplace: 4 Elah
home: 4 Gath
slayer: 5 David

Gomer
father: 7 Diblaim
husband: 5 Hosea

gonad
5 gland, ovary 6 testis

gondola
3 car 4 boat 5 chair

gone
4 away, dead, left, lost 6 absent,
gravid, parous 7 defunct, extinct,
lacking, missing, omitted, wanting
8 childing, departed, enceinte,
pregnant, vanished

gonef
see **ganef**

Goneril
father: 4 Lear
husband: 6 Albany
sister: 5 Regan 8 Cordelia
victim: 5 Regan

Gone with the Wind
author: 8 Mitchell (Margaret)
character: 6 Ashley 7 Melanie
11 Rhett Butler 13 Scarlett O'Hara
plantation: 4 Tara

gonfalon
4 flag 6 banner, ensign 7 pendant,
pennant 8 standard 9 banderole

goo
4 crud, gook, goop, guck, gunk,
muck

goober
3 nut 6 peanut

good
3 apt, fit 4 able, boon, just, meet,
nice, pure 5 brave, right, sound,
whole 6 adroit, au fait, clever, cogent, common, decent, humane, intact, kindly, proper, seemly, toward, useful 7 benefic, benefit,
capable, fitting, gainful, godsend,
healthy, helpful, welcome, welfare
8 adequate, all right, blessing, decorous, flawless, hygienic, innocent,
interest, pleasant, pleasing, salutary, sensible, skillful, straight, unmarred, virtuous 9 advantage,
agreeable, blameless, competent,
congenial, exemplary, favorable,
guiltless, healthful, incorrupt, justified, lily-white, lucrative, qualified,
righteous, tolerable, undamaged,
untainted, well-being, wholesome,
workmanly 10 acceptable, altruistic, beneficial, benevolent, charitable, gratifying, inculpable, profitable, propitious, prosperity,
salubrious, sufficient, unblamable,
unimpaired, worthwhile 11 appropriate, benediction, considerate,
pleasurable, pleasureful, respectable, unblemished, uncorrupted,

well-behaved, well-founded, work-manlike **12** advantageous, considerable, eleemosynary, humanitarian, remunerative, salutiferous, satisfactory, well-grounded **13** philanthropic
combining form: **2** eu **5** agath **6** agatho
French: **3** bon
German: **3** gut
Spanish: **5** bueno

good-bye
4 ta-ta **5** adieu, congé **6** so long **7** cheerio, parting **8** farewell, toodle-oo **9** departing **11** leave-taking, valedictory
French: **5** adieu
German: **8** lebe wohl
Japanese: **8** sayonara
Spanish: **5** adios

Good Earth author
4 Buck (Pearl)

good-for-nothing
6 drafty, drossy, no-good, waster **7** fustian, inutile, nothing, rounder, useless, wastrel **8** feckless, unworthy **9** valueless, worthless **10** ne'er-do-well, profligate, scapegrace, unpurposed **11** meaningless, purposeless

good-humored
see **good-natured**

good-looking
4 fair **6** comely, lovely, pretty **8** handsome **9** beauteous, beautiful **10** attractive

goodly
5 ample, large **6** comely, pretty **8** handsome **9** excellent **12** considerable

good-natured
4 easy, mild **6** genial, jovial **7** amiable, lenient **8** cheerful, obliging **9** gemütlich **10** altruistic, benevolent, charitable **11** complaisant

goodness
5 honor, merit **6** purity, virtue **7** honesty, probity **8** chastity, morality **9** integrity, rectitude, rightness **11** benevolence, uprightness **13** righteousness

goods
4 gear, line **5** stock, wares **7** effects **8** chattels, movables **9** vendibles **10** belongings **11** commodities, merchandise, possessions
smuggled: **10** contraband
stolen: **4** loot **5** booty **6** spoils

thrown overboard: **5** lagan, ligan **6** jetsam

good-tasting
5 sapid, tasty **6** savory **8** tasteful **9** palatable, relishing, toothsome **10** appetizing, flavorsome

goodwill
5 amity, favor **6** comity **7** charity, rapport **8** alacrity, altruism, dispatch, kindness, sympathy **9** readiness, tolerance **10** expedition, friendship, generosity, kindliness **11** benevolence, helpfulness, promptitude **12** friendliness

goody
5 candy, treat **6** bonbon, dainty, morsel, tidbit, titbit **8** delicacy, kickshaw

goody-goody
4 prig **5** prude **6** Grundy **7** puritan **8** bluenose, comstock **9** Mrs. Grundy, nice Nelly

gooey
5 gluey, gummy, mushy, sappy, sobby, soupy **6** cloggy, drippy, slushy, sticky, stodgy **7** maudlin **8** adhesive **11** sentimental

goof
3 err **4** boob, dolt, mess **5** booby, botch, chump, dunce, gum up **6** bobble, bollix, bungle **7** blunder, fathead, louse up **8** dolthead, lunkhead

go off
4 blow **5** burst **7** explode **8** detonate

goofy
5 crazy, silly **6** stupid **7** foolish

gook
3 rot **4** crud, goop, gunk, muck **5** bilge, gumbo, hooey, trash **6** drivel

go on
3 act **4** bear, quit **5** carry **6** acquit, behave, demean, deport, hang on **7** carry on, comport, conduct, persist **8** continue **9** persevere

goon
3 sap **4** boob, dolt, dope, thug **7** hoodlum

gooney
9 albatross

goop
4 gook, gunk, muck **5** gumbo

goose
4 bird, dolt, poke **5** solan **9** simpleton

cry: **4** honk, yang
genus: **5** Anser
Hawaiian: **4** nene
male: **6** gander
relating to: **8** anserine
snow: **4** chen, wavy **5** wavey
wild: **5** brant **7** graylag, greylag **8** barnacle, bernicle
young: **7** gosling

goose egg
4 zero **5** aught, ought, zilch **6** cipher, naught, nought **7** nothing

gooseflesh
5 bumps **7** pimples

gopher
6 marmot, rodent **8** squirrel, tortoise

Gopher State
9 Minnesota

Gordian knot cutter
9 Alexander

Gordius' son
5 Midas

gore
4 stab, tush, tusk **5** blood, slime, wound **6** pierce

gorge
3 gap **4** cloy, fill, glut, jade, pall, sate **5** chasm, cleft, clove, flume, gulch, stuff **6** arroyo, clough, devour, gobble, guzzle, ravine, stodge **7** couloir, overeat, satiate, surfeit **11** overindulge
Arizona: **11** Grand Canyon
China: **7** Yangtze
Colorado: **5** Royal

gorgeous
5 grand, plush, proud **6** lavish, lovely, pretty, superb **7** opulent, sublime **8** glorious, splendid **9** beautiful, luxurious, sumptuous **10** impressive **11** magnificent, resplendent, splendorous

Gorgon
6 Medusa, Stheno **7** Euryale
father: **7** Phorcus, Phorcys
mother: **4** Ceto
sentinel: **4** Enyo **5** Deino **6** Graeae, Graiae **8** Pephredo

gorilla
3 ape **6** monkey **7** primate **10** anthropoid

Gorki drama
14 The Lower Depths

gorse
5 furze **7** juniper

gory
6 bloody 7 imbrued 8 sanguine 10 sanguinary 11 ensanguined, sanguineous 12 bloodstained

gospel
5 truth 6 truism 8 doctrine, teaching

gossamer
3 web 5 filmy, gauzy, sheer 6 flimsy 7 tiffany 10 diaphanous 11 transparent

gossip
3 cry 4 blab, buzz, chat, dirt, talk 5 clack, on-dit, prate, rumor, sieve, tabby 6 babble, claver, report, rumble, tattle 7 chatter, hearsay, prattle, rumorer 8 bigmouth, busybody, informer, quidnunc, telltale 9 carrytale, grapevine 10 circulator, mumblenews, newsmonger, talebearer 11 rumormonger, scandalizer, scuttlebutt

Gotham
7 New York

Gothic
4 rude, wild 5 crude 6 brutal, coarse, Hunnic, savage 7 Hunnish 8 barbaric 9 barbarian, barbarous 11 uncivilized

Gouda
6 cheese

gouge
3 con, dig 4 tool 5 cheat, exact, pinch, screw, wrest, wring 6 extort, wrench 7 squeeze, swindle 9 shake down 10 overcharge

goulash
4 stew 6 jumble, medley 8 mishmash

go under
4 fall, sink 6 go down, submit 7 founder, succumb 8 submerge, submerse 9 surrender

Gounod work
5 Faust 8 Ave Maria

gourd
4 pepo 5 fruit, melon 6 bottle, vessel 7 pumpkin 8 calabash, cucurbit
instrument: 6 maraca

gourmand
see **glutton; gourmet**

gourmet
7 epicure 9 bon vivant 10 gastronome 11 gastronomer 12 gastronomist

gout
4 blob, clot 5 spurt 6 splash 7 podagra 8 swelling

govern
3 run 4 head, lead, rule, sway 5 guide, reign, steer 6 direct, handle, manage, master, render 7 command, conduct, control, execute, oversee 8 carry out, dominate, overrule, regulate, shepherd 9 supervise 10 administer

governess
4 nana 5 nanny, nurse 6 duenna, nannie 8 mistress 9 nursemaid

government
4 rule 5 power 6 polity, regime 7 conduct, control, regency, regimen, tyranny 8 guidance, monarchy, republic 9 authority, autocracy, democracy, direction, hierarchy, oligarchy 10 management 11 aristocracy 12 dictatorship, organization
autocratic: 7 czarism 9 despotism 10 absolutism 12 dictatorship
by a few: 9 oligarchy
by eight: 8 octarchy
by one: 8 monarchy
by three: 8 triarchy 11 triumvirate
by women: 8 gynarchy
combining form: 5 archy, cracy 6 ocracy
official: 6 consul, syndic 8 diplomat 10 bureaucrat
relating to: 9 political
science: 8 politics
without: 7 anarchy

government agency
2 VA 3 CIA, FAA, FBI, FCC, FDA, FHA, GAO, GPO, HUD, ICC, NBS, NRC, TVA 4 FEPC, NASA

governor
3 bey 4 head, lord 5 chief, nabob, pilot, ruler 6 leader, rector, regent 7 captain, manager, viceroy 8 director, official 9 executive, regulator 10 commandant, controller, magistrate
Chinese: 6 tuchun
of a fort: 7 alcaide 9 castellan, chatelain
Persian: 6 satrap
Turkish: 8 hospador

gown
4 robe, toga 5 dress, frock, habit, tunic 6 banian, banyan, camise, clothe, kimono, mantua 7 cassock, chemise, garment 8 peignoir
hospital: 6 johnny

goy
7 gentile

grab
3 hog, nab 4 nail, take 5 catch, clasp, grasp, seize 6 clutch, snatch, tackle 7 grapple

grabby
5 itchy 6 greedy 8 covetous, desirous, grasping 10 prehensile 11 acquisitive

grace
4 ease 5 adorn, charm, favor, mercy 6 lenity, polish, prayer, thanks, virtue 7 caritas, charity, dignify, dignity 8 blessing, clemency, easiness, elegance, goodness, kindness, leniency, petition 9 embellish 10 indulgence, invocation, suppleness 11 benediction, forbearance 12 thanksgiving

graceful
4 airy, deft, easy 6 featly, gainly, smooth, urbane 7 elegant, flowing, genteel, refined 8 debonair, polished

graceless
4 wild 5 inept 6 vulgar 7 awkward, unhappy 8 barbaric 9 barbarian, barbarous, ill-chosen, tasteless 10 outlandish 11 unfortunate 12 infelicitous

Graces
6 Aglaia (brilliance), Charis, Thalia (bloom) 8 Charites (plural) 10 Euphrosyne (joy)
mother: 5 Aegle

gracious
4 easy, kind, mild 5 preux 6 benign, clubby, genial, kindly 7 affable, amiable, cordial, courtly, gallant, starchy, stately 8 mannered, obliging, outgoing, sociable 9 benignant, bonhomous, congenial, courteous

grackle
3 jaw 7 jackdaw 9 blackbird

gradation
4 step 5 range, shade 6 ablaut, change, degree, nuance, series 8 position 9 variation 10 difference, divergence

grade
3 peg 4 lean, rank, rate, rung, sort, step, tier, tilt 5 class, group, notch, order, slant, slope, stage 6 assort, degree, estate, league 7 arrange, caliber, incline, leaning, quality

8 appraise, category, classify, evaluate, grouping

Grade A
3 top 4 fine 5 prime 7 capital 8 five-star, superior, top-notch 9 excellent, first-rate, top-drawer 10 first-class

gradient
4 lean, ramp, tilt 5 slant, slope 7 incline, leaning 11 inclination
combining form: 5 cline 6 clinal

gradine
4 seat, step 5 shelf 6 chisel

gradually
8 bit by bit 9 piecemeal 10 step by step

graduate
female: 6 alumna 7 alumnae (plural)
male: 6 alumni (plural) 7 alumnus

Graeae, Graiae
4 Enyo 5 Deino 8 Pephredo
father: 7 Phorcus, Phorcys
mother: 4 Ceto
sisters: 7 Gorgons

graft
4 join, mend 5 crime, scion, unite 6 attach, boodle, fasten, inarch 7 implant, topwork

grail
3 cup 7 chalice, platter

grain
3 bit, jot, rye 4 corn, iota, meal, mite, oats, rice 5 crumb, fiber, maize, speck, trace, wheat 6 barley, cereal, tittle 7 granule, smidgen, sorghum, texture 8 molecule, particle
bundle: 4 bale 5 sheaf
chute: 6 hopper
ear: 5 spica, spike
elevator: 4 silo
mixture: 6 fodder
row: 5 swath 7 windrow

grainy
6 coarse 8 granular

grammarian
Roman: 7 Donatus (Aelius)

grammatical case
6 dative 8 ablative, genitive, locative, vocative 9 objective 10 accusative, nominative, possessive, subjective

grampus
5 whale 8 cetacean, scorpion 9 blackfish

Granada
building: 8 Alhambra

citadel: 8 Alcazaba
last Moorish king: 7 Boabdil

granary
3 bin 4 gola, silo 10 repository, storehouse

grand
4 epic, huge 5 gaudy, lofty, noble, royal, showy 6 august, flashy, garish, lavish, lordly, ornate, superb 7 exalted, stately, sublime 8 baronial, elevated, gorgeous, imposing, magnific, majestic, princely, splendid, towering 9 luxurious, sumptuous 10 impressive, monumental, prodigious, stupendous, tremendous 11 magnificent 12 ostentatious

Grand Canyon
explorer: 6 Powell (John Wesley)
state: 7 Arizona

grande dame
6 matron 7 dowager 9 matriarch

grandee
5 pasha 6 bashaw 8 nobleman

grandeur
4 pomp 7 dignity, majesty 8 nobility, splendor, vastness 9 greatness, largeness, loftiness, nobleness, sublimity 10 augustness 11 stateliness 12 magnificence

grand inquisitor
Spanish: 10 Torquemada (Tomas de)

grandiose
4 epic, vast 5 lofty, noble, royal, showy 6 august, cosmic, lordly 7 stately, utopian 8 imposing, majestic, princely 9 ambitious, visionary 11 magnificent, pretentious 12 ostentatious

grandmother
Russian: 8 babushka
Scottish: 6 gudame

grange
4 farm 5 lodge 9 farmhouse

granite
4 rock 6 aplite

Granite State
12 New Hampshire

grant
3 aid, own 4 alms, avow, cede, dole, gift, give 5 admit, allow, award, let on, own up, yield 6 accord, bestow, confer, donate, fess up, permit 7 charity, concede, confess, entitle, handout, present, subsidy 8 bequeath, donation 9 vouchsafe 10 assistance, relin-

quish, subvention 11 acknowledge, benefaction 12 contribution 13 appropriation

granular
5 rough, sandy 6 coarse, grainy

granule
4 pill, spot 5 grain 6 pellet 8 particle

grape
3 fox, uva 4 Bual 5 Gamay, Pinot 6 Arinto, Burger, Gentil, Merlot, muscat 7 Albillo, Aligote, Barbera, Catawba, Concord, Furmint, Niagara, sultana 8 Aleatico, Cabernet, Charbono, Delaware, Friularo, Grenache, Isabella, labrusca, malvasia, muscadel, Nebbiolo, Riesling, Semillon, Sylvaner, Thompson, Traminer, vinifera, Viognier 9 Chasselas, Lambrusco, Malvoisie, muscadine, Pinot Gris, Pinot Noir, Sauvignon, Trebbiano, zinfandel 10 Grignolino, muscadelle, Pinot Blanc, Verdicchio 11 Chenin Blanc, Mavrodaphne, Petite Sirah, scuppernong
disease: 4 esca
dried: 6 raisin
drink: 4 wine
pulp: 4 rape 6 pomace
residue: 4 marc

grapefruit
6 pomelo

Grapes of Wrath
author: 9 Steinbeck (John)
family: 4 Joad
people: 5 Okies

grapevine
4 buzz, talk 5 on-dit, rumor 6 gossip, report, rumble 7 hearsay

graph
3 map 5 chart 6 sketch 7 diagram, outline 8 nomogram

graphic
5 clear, lucid, vivid 6 cogent, visual 7 precise, telling 8 clear-cut, definite, explicit, incisive, pictoric, striking 9 pictorial, realistic 10 compelling

graphite
4 lead 6 carbon 8 plumbago

grapnel
4 hook 6 anchor

grapple
3 nab 4 grab, grip, hold, take 5 catch, clamp, clasp, grasp, gripe, seize 6 bucket, clench, clinch,

clutch, snatch, tenure, tussle **7** scuffle, wrestle

grasp
3 dig, see **4** grip, have, hent, hold, know, take **5** catch, clamp, clasp, gripe **6** accept, clench, clinch, clutch, fathom, follow, take in, tenure **7** cognize, compass, grapple **8** envisage, perceive **9** apprehend **10** appreciate, comprehend, understand

graspable
5 lucid **8** knowable **10** fathomable **12** intelligible **13** apprehensible

grasping
4 avid **5** itchy **6** grabby, greedy **8** covetous, desirous **9** extorting **10** prehensile **11** acquisitive

grass
3 pot, sod, tea **4** lawn, reed, turf, weed **6** moocah, redtop **7** herbage, panicum, pasture **8** cannabis, Mary Jane **9** cocksfoot, marijuana
African: **6** imphee
annual: **6** darnel **8** teosinte
Asian: **7** vetiver, whangee
Australian: **8** spinifex
beach: **6** marram
cereal: **3** oat, rye **4** milo, teff **5** kafir, maize, proso, wheat **6** kaffir, millet, sorgho **7** sorghum **8** feterita, triticum
clump: **4** tuft **7** tussock
combining form: **6** gramin **7** gramini
dried: **3** hay
European: **7** Bermuda, timothy
fiber: **4** flax
forage: **7** setaria
fragrant: **10** citronella
giant: **5** otate
Mexican: **7** zacaton
pasture: **5** Bahia, grama
perennial: **5** muhly **6** fescue, quitch, zoysia **7** esparto, galleta
prairie: **8** bluestem
second growth: **5** rowen
tropical: **5** cogon **6** bamboo

grasshopper
4 grig **6** locust **7** katydid

grassland
3 lea **5** field **6** meadow **7** pasture, prairie
African: **4** veld **5** veldt
flat: **7** savanna **8** savannah
South American: **5** pampa

grate
3 get, jar **4** bark, fray, gall, rasp, rile, skin **5** chafe, peeve, pique, scuff **6** abrade, burn up, nettle,

scrape **7** provoke, scratch **8** irritate **9** aggravate

grateful
4 good **7** obliged, pleased, welcome **8** beholden, pleasant, renewing, solacing, thankful **9** agreeable, congenial, consoling, delicious, favorable, gratified

Gratiano
brother: **9** Brabantio
friend: **7** Antonio **8** Bassanio
niece: **9** Desdemona
wife: **7** Nerissa

gratify
4 baby, feed, sate **5** favor, feast, humor **6** arride, coddle, oblige, pamper, pander, please **7** appease, cater to, content, delight, gladden, happify, indulge, satisfy

grating
3 dry **4** grid, rasp **5** grill, harsh, rough **6** grille, hoarse **7** jarring, rasping, raucous **8** gridiron, strident **10** stridulent

gratis
4 free **8** costless **10** chargeless, gratuitous **13** complimentary

gratuitous
4 free **6** gratis, wanton **7** unasked, willing **8** baseless, costless **9** unfounded, voluntary **10** bottomless, chargeless, groundless, reasonless, ungrounded **11** uncalled-for, unwarranted **12** indefensible, supererogant **13** complimentary

gratuity
3 fee, tip **4** alms, gift, perk **5** bonus **6** reward **7** cumshaw, douceur, largess **8** donation, offering **9** baksheesh, lagniappe, pourboire **10** perquisite **11** benefaction **12** contribution

grave
3 pit, sad **4** dire, etch, fell, grim, tomb, ugly **5** awful, crypt, drive, fatal, heavy, major, pound, sober, staid, stamp, vault **6** burial, deadly, hammer, incise, sedate, severe, solemn, somber **7** austere, earnest, ghastly, impress, killing, ossuary, serious, weighty **8** catacomb, dreadful, grievous, horrible, terrible **9** dangerous, mausoleum, murderous, ponderous, saturnine, sepulcher, sepulture
marker: **5** stela, stele **6** ledger **8** memorial, monument **9** footstone, headstone, tombstone **11** sarcophagus

mound: **6** barrow **7** tumulus
robber: **5** ghoul

gravel
4 dirt, grit, sand
ridge: **5** esker

graven image
4 idol

graver
5 burin **8** sculptor

graveyard
8 boot hill, cemetery, God's acre **10** necropolis **11** polyandrium **12** burial ground, memorial park, potter's field **13** burying ground

gravid
6 parous **8** childing, enceinte, pregnant **9** expectant, expecting **10** parturient

gravity
6 weight **7** dignity **8** sobriety **9** heaviness, solemnity **10** importance, somberness **11** seriousness

gravy
5 juice, sauce **8** dressing, windfall
French: **3** jus

gray
3 ash, old **4** aged, ashy, blah, drab, dull **5** ashen, bleak, color, hoary, slate, slaty, taupe **6** dismal, gloomy, leaden **7** elderly, grizzly, neutral **8** cinerous, gunmetal, overcast **9** colorless
brownish: **7** fuscous
combining form: **4** poli **5** glauc, polio **6** glauco

gray dawn
4 zinc

gray duck
7 gadwall, mallard, pintail

grayfish
7 pollack

gray matter
3 wit **4** head, mind, obex **5** brain **9** intellect

graze
3 dop, rub **4** feed, gall, harm, hurt, kiss, skim, skip, wear **5** brush, carom, chafe, erode, shave, wound **6** abrade, bruise, glance, injure, ruffle **7** contuse, corrade, pasture **8** ricochet

grease
3 fat, oil **4** lard, soil **5** smear **6** smooth **7** lanolin **9** lubricant, lubricate
combining form: **4** sebi, sebo

greasy
4 oily 5 fatty, slick 6 slippy 7 pinguid 8 slippery, slithery, unctuous 10 lubricious, oleaginous

greasy spoon
4 café 5 diner 7 beanery, hashery 9 hash house, lunchroom 10 coffee shop

great
3 big, fat 4 bull, huge, vast 5 famed, grand, husky, large 6 famous, heroic 7 eminent, extreme, immense, notable, supreme, titanic 8 enormous, oversize, renowned 9 excellent, fantastic, important, prominent, wonderful 10 celebrated, celebrious, surpassing 11 illustrious, magnificent, superlative 13 distinguished
combining form: 3 meg 4 mega 5 megal 6 megalo

Great Bear
9 Big Dipper, Ursa Major

Great Britain
see **England**

Great Commoner, the
4 Pitt (William)

Great Emancipator, the
7 Lincoln (Abraham)

greater
4 more, over 6 better, higher, larger 8 superior 9 overlying 11 superjacent

greatest
4 best, most 6 utmost 7 largest, noblest, supreme
amount: 7 maximum

Great Expectations
author: 7 Dickens (Charles)
character: 3 Pip 5 Biddy 7 Estella, Jaggers 8 Havisham, Magwitch

greathearted
3 big 5 brave, lofty, manly 6 heroic 7 gallant 8 fearless, generous 10 benevolent, chivalrous, courageous 11 considerate, magnanimous

Great Lake
4 Erie 5 Huron 7 Ontario 8 Michigan, Superior
acronym: 5 HOMES

Great Lake State
8 Michigan

grebe
4 bird, fowl 8 dabchick, didapper

Greece
capital: 6 Athens
monetary unit: 7 drachma

greed
7 avarice, avidity 8 cupidity, gluttony, rapacity, voracity 12 ravenousness

greedy
5 itchy 6 grabby 7 miserly, selfish 8 covetous, desirous, esurient, grasping 10 avaricious, gluttonous 11 acquisitive

Greek
6 babble, drivel, jabber 7 Achaean 8 Hellenic, nonsense 9 gibberish
alien resident: 5 metic
assembly: 5 agora, boule
coin: 4 obol 5 hecte 6 lepton, stater
column: 5 Doric, Ionic 10 Corinthian
contest: 4 agon
counselor: 6 Nestor
cup: 5 kylix
dictator: 7 Metaxas (Ioannis)
dragon: 9 Eurythion
drink: 4 ouzo
epic: 5 Iliad 7 Odyssey
Fates: 6 Clotho, Moirae 7 Atropos 8 Lachesis
god:
  chief: 4 Zeus
  messenger: 6 Hermes
  of agriculture: 6 Cronus
  of death: 8 Thanatos
  of fire: 10 Hephaestus
  of healing: 9 Asclepius
  of love: 4 Eros
  of marriage: 5 Hymen
  of physicians: 6 Hermes
  of the sea: 6 Triton 7 Oceanus 8 Poseidon
  of the sun: 6 Helios
  of the underworld: 5 Pluto
  of the wind: 5 Eurus, Notus 6 Aeolus, Boreas 8 Zephyrus
  of war: 4 Ares
  of wine: 8 Dionysus
  of woods: 3 Pan
goddess:
  of agriculture: 7 Demeter
  of beauty: 9 Aphrodite
  of dawn: 3 Eos
  of discord: 4 Eris
  of flowers: 7 Chloris
  of harvests: 4 Rhea
  of hunting: 7 Artemis
  of justice: 7 Astraea
  of love: 9 Aphrodite
  of marriage: 4 Hera
  of night: 3 Nyx
  of peace: 5 Irene
  of retribution: 7 Nemesis
  of ruin: 3 Ate
  of the earth: 2 Ge 4 Gaea, Gaia
  of the moon: 6 Hecate, Hekate, Selena, Selene 7 Artemis, Astarte
  of the seasons: 5 Horae
  of the underworld: 6 Hecate, Hekate
  of vengeance: 7 Nemesis
  of victory: 4 Nike
  of wisdom: 6 Athena
  of witchcraft: 6 Hecate, Hekate
  of womanhood: 4 Hera
  of youth: 4 Hebe
hero: 4 Aias, Ajax 5 Jason 7 Theseus 8 Achilles, Argonaut, Heracles, Hercules, Odysseus 9 Achilleus
historian: 8 Xenophon 9 Herodotus 10 Thucydides
lawgiver: 5 Draco, Solon
leader: 9 Agamemnon
letter: 2 mu, nu, pi, xi 3 chi, eta, phi, psi, rho, tau 4 beta, iota, zeta 5 alpha, delta, gamma, kappa, omega, sigma, theta 6 lambda 7 epsilon, omicron, upsilon
magistrate: 6 archon
marketplace: 5 agora
measure: 3 ona, pik 4 bema 5 cados, chous, digit, maris, pygon, xylon 6 acaena, bachel, barile, cotula, dichas, gramme, hemina, koilon, pechys, pelame, schene 7 amphora, cyathos, diaulos, hekteus, stadion, stadium, stremma 8 condylos, daktylos, dekapode, dolichos, medimnos, metretes, palaiste, plethron, spithame, stathmos 9 oxybaphon
porch: 4 stoa
sandwich: 4 gyro
shield: 5 pelta
soldier: 7 hoplite
theater: 5 odeon, odeum
underworld: 5 Hades
war cry: 5 alala
warrior: 4 Ajax 7 Ulysses 8 Achilles, Diomedes, Odysseus 9 Agamemnon, Palamedes
weight: 3 mna, oka 4 mina 5 litra, livre 6 diobol, kantar, obolus, stater 7 chalcon, chalque, drachma 8 diobolon, talanton
wine: 7 retsina, retzina

green
3 raw 5 alive, fresh, plaza, virid, young 6 callow, common, infant, square, unripe 7 celadon, emerald, untried, verdant 8 immature, juvenile, pistache, unversed, youthful

9 unfledged 10 unseasoned 11 unpracticed 13 inexperienced
bluish: 8 glaucous
combining form: 4 verd 5 chlor,
verdo 6 chloro
grayish: 5 olive
yellowish: 7 luteous 10 chartreuse

greenbacks
4 cash, jack 5 bread, dough,
money 6 wampum 7 scratch 8 currency 11 legal tender

green-eyed
7 envious, envying, jealous
9 invidious
monster: 8 jealousy

greenfish
7 opaleye, pollack

greenfly
5 aphid

greengage
4 plum

greenhead
3 fly 5 scaup 7 mallard

greenheart
4 tree 7 bebeeru

greenhorn
4 hick, jake, rube, tyro 5 clown
6 novice, rustic 7 bumpkin, hayseed 9 hillbilly 10 clodhopper, provincial 12 backwoodsman

greenhouse
12 conservatory

Greenland
capital: 7 Godthab 8 Godthaab
discoverer: 10 Eric the Red
native: 3 Ita
settlement: 4 Etah

green light
2 OK 7 go-ahead 9 clearance
13 authorization

Green Mansions
author: 6 Hudson (William Henry)
character: 4 Rima

green monkey
6 guenon

Green Mountain State
7 Vermont

greenness
5 youth 6 spring 7 puberty, rawness 8 verdancy, viridity 9 freshness, youthhood 10 callowness, juvenility, pubescence, springtide,
springtime 11 adolescence 12 inexperience, youthfulness

green osier
7 dogwood

green plover
7 lapwing

green poppy
8 foxglove

greenroom
6 lounge

greenstone
7 diabase, diorite 8 nephrite

greet
3 cry 4 hail 6 accost, call to, salute
7 address, receive, welcome

greeting
3 ave, bow 4 hail 5 aloha, hello
6 salute 7 address, welcome 9 reception 10 salutation

gregarious
6 social 8 friendly, outgoing,
sociable

gremlin
3 elf, imp 5 gnome 6 sprite

grenade
4 bomb 5 shell 7 missile
9 explosive

grenadier
4 fish 7 rattail, soldier

grenadine
4 pink, yarn 5 syrup 9 carnation

Grendel's slayer
7 Beowulf

Gretchen's lover
5 Faust

Grey's forte
7 Western

grid
5 grate 7 grating, network

griddle
3 pan 5 grill

griddle cake
7 pancake 8 flapjack

gridiron
5 field, grill 7 grating, network

grief
3 rue, woe 4 care 5 dolor, tears
6 regret, sorrow 7 anguish, chagrin, emotion, sadness, trouble
8 distress, hardship 9 bemoaning,
bewailing, deploring, heartache,
lamenting, suffering 10 affliction,
heartbreak 11 lamentation

Grieg work
8 Peer Gynt

grievance
5 cross, rigor, trial, wrong 6 burden, injury 8 hardship 9 complaint, injustice 10 affliction
11 tribulation

grieve
3 cry, rue 4 bear, hurt, keen,
moan, pain, wail, weep 5 mourn
6 bemoan, bewail, endure, injure,
lament, sorrow, suffer 7 deplore
8 distress 9 constrain

grievous
3 sad 4 dire, fell, sore, ugly
5 grave, major, tough 6 bitter, taxing, woeful 7 exigent, galling, onerous, painful, serious, weighty
8 exacting 9 dangerous, demanding 10 afflictive, burdensome, calamitous, deplorable, lamentable,
oppressive 11 distasteful, distressing, regrettable, unfortunate, unpalatable

grill
3 vex 4 cook, grid 5 broil, grate
7 afflict, griddle, torment 8 gridiron, question 11 third degree
12 cross-examine 13 interrogation

grilse
4 fish 6 salmon

grim
3 set 4 cold, dour, fell, firm, hard
5 angry, bleak, cruel, fixed, harsh,
lurid, rigid, stern 6 dogged, fierce,
grisly, mortal, savage, severe 7 adamant, austere, certain, ghastly,
hideous, inhuman, macabre, ominous, wolfish 8 gruesome, horrible,
inhumane, obdurate, resolute, ruthless, stubborn, terrible 9 barbarous, ferocious, loathsome, merci-
less, offensive, repugnant, revolting, stringent, truculent 10 determined, forbidding,
foreboding, horrifying, implacable,
inevitable, inexorable, inflexible,
ironfisted, off-putting, relentless, terrifying, unyielding, vindictive
11 unflinching, unforgiving

grimace
3 mop, mow, mug 4 face, moue
5 mouth, smirk, sneer 6 deform
7 contort, distort

grimalkin
3 cat, hag 6 feline

grime
4 dirt, foul, soil 5 dirty, sully 6 besoil, smirch, smooch, smudge,
smutch 7 tarnish

grim reaper
5 death

grin
4 beam 5 fleer, risus, smile, smirk

grind
3 rut, vex 4 chew, grub, mill, moil,
pace, plod, rote, slog, toil, work
5 crush, gnash, grate, labor, slave,
sweat 6 crunch, drudge, groove,
kibble 7 routine, travail 8 bullwork,
drudgery, plugging 9 treadmill
10 donkeywork

grinder
4 hero 5 molar, stone, tooth
8 sandwich 9 submarine

grinding
5 harsh 6 severe 7 grating,
wearing
stone: 4 mano 6 muller, pestle

grip
4 hold, take, vice 5 clamp, clasp,
grasp, seize 6 clench, clinch,
clutch, duress, handle, tenure, valise 7 catch up, grapple 8 coercion, enthrall, handfast, handhold
9 fascinate, mesmerize, restraint,
spellbind 10 constraint

gripe
4 beef, crab, fuss, hold, kick, yaup,
yawp 5 bitch, bleat, brawl, clamp,
clasp, croak, grasp 6 clench,
clinch, clutch, grouch, grouse, murmur, mutter, squawk, take on, tenure, yammer 7 blow off, grapple,
grumble 8 complain 9 bellyache

griper
see **grumbler**

grippe
3 flu 7 disease 9 influenza

gripper
4 clip, hand, vice 5 clamp, clasp,
tongs 6 pliers

gris-gris
5 charm, spell 6 amulet 8 talisman
11 incantation

grisly
4 grim 5 eerie, lurid, weird 6 horrid 7 ghastly, hideous, macabre,
uncanny 8 gruesome, horrible, terrible 10 horrifying, terrifying

grist
3 lot 5 grain, stint 6 output
8 quantity

gristle
9 cartilage

grit
4 dirt, guts, sand, soil 5 earth,

moxie, nerve, spunk 6 gravel
7 courage 8 backbone 9 fortitude

gritty
4 game 5 brave, dirty, sandy
6 plucky, soiled 8 resolute

groan
4 moan, rasp 5 creak, grate

grocery
5 store 11 supermarket
Spanish: 6 bodega

grog
3 rum 5 booze, drink, hooch, juice
6 liquor, tipple 7 alcohol, spirits

groggy
4 logy, weak 5 dazed, foggy, tired
6 sleepy 7 muddled 8 sluggish

groin
4 fold 6 crotch, inguen
combining form: 6 inguin 7 inguino

groom
4 comb, tidy 5 brush, clean, curry,
ready, shave 6 neaten, polish, refine, toilet 7 prepare, servant
8 benedict 9 attendant
11 horsekeeper
Chinese: 5 mafoo
Indian: 4 syce

groove
3 rut 4 nurl, pace, rote, slot 5 canal, flute, glyph, grind, stria
6 fuller, furrow, gutter, hollow
7 chamfer, channel, routine

grope
3 pry 4 feel, poke, root, test
5 probe 6 fumble, handle, search
7 examine, explore, grabble
8 scrabble

grosbeak
4 bird 5 finch 8 haw finch

gross
3 all, big, fat, raw, sum 4 foul,
mass, rank, rude 5 brute, crass,
crude, heavy, obese, rough, stout,
total, utter, whole 6 animal, carnal,
coarse, damned, entire, fleshy,
portly, smutty, vulgar 7 capital, extreme, glaring, obscene, perfect,
porcine, sensual, uncouth, weighty
8 absolute, barnyard, complete, entirety, flagrant, improper, material,
outright, physical, sensible, sum total, tangible, totality 9 aggregate,
corporeal, corpulent, downright,
egregious, excessive, inelegant,
loathsome, objective, offensive, out-
and-out, repulsive, revolting, unrefined 10 exorbitant, immoderate

grotesque
5 antic, comic, droll, eerie, weird
6 rococo 7 baroque, bizarre, comical, extreme, uncanny 9 fantastic,
ludicrous

grotto
4 cave, hole 5 crypt, vault
6 cavern
Capri: 4 Blue

grouch
4 crab, sulk 5 crank, croak, grump,
scold 6 griper, grouse, kicker, murmur, mutter 7 crabber, grouser,
growler, grumble 8 grumbler, sorehead, sourpuss 10 bellyacher, complainer, crosspatch, malcontent
11 faultfinder

ground
3 bed, why 4 base, dirt, down,
drop, fell, land, rest, root, seat, soil,
stay, test 5 basis, cause, earth,
floor, level, proof, trial 6 bottom,
reason, whyfor 7 bedrock, dry
land, flatten, footing, mow down,
support, sustain 8 argument, basement, buttress, evidence 9 bring
down, establish, knock down, predicate, testimony, throw down,
wherefore 10 antecedent, foundation,
substratum, terra firma
combining form: 2 ge 3 geo, ped
4 pedo 5 chame 6 chamae

grounded
7 beached 8 stranded

groundhog
6 marmot 9 woodchuck

groundless
4 idle 5 false 8 baseless 9 unfounded 10 bottomless, gratuitous,
ungrounded 11 uncalled-for,
unwarranted

groundwork
3 bed 4 base, root 5 basis 6 bottom 7 bedrock, footing, support
8 basement 10 foundation, substratum 12 substruction, substructure,
underpinning

group
3 lot, set 4 band, bevy, body, clot,
club, crew, gang, mess, pool, push,
ruck, sect, sort, team, tier 5 array,
batch, bunch, chain, class, clump,
covey, crowd, grade, horde, party,
place, squad, suite, trust 6 adjust,
assort, bundle, cartel, circle, clique,
clutch, gather, huddle, league, muster, parcel, passel 7 arrange, battery, brigade, cluster, collect, combine, company, coterie, council,

dispose, echelon, platoon, round up **8** assemble, assembly, category, classify, ensemble, organize **9** congeries, gathering, harmonize, syndicate **10** assemblage, categorize, collection
of angels: **4** host
of ants: **6** colony
of badgers: **4** cete
of bears: **6** sleuth
of bees: **4** hive **5** grist, swarm
of birds: **6** flight, volery
of boars: **7** sounder
of cats: **7** clowder, clutter
of cattle: **5** drove
of chicks: **5** brood **6** clutch
of clams: **3** bed
of cranes: **5** sedge, siege
of crows: **6** murder
of ducks: **5** brace
of eight: **5** octet
of elephants: **4** herd
of elks: **4** gang
of fish: **5** shoal **6** school
of five: **5** quint **6** pentad **7** quinary, quintet
of four: **6** tetrad **7** quartet
of foxes: **5** leash, skulk
of geese: **5** flock, skein **6** gaggle
of gnats: **5** cloud, horde
of goats: **4** trip **5** tribe
of goldfinches: **5** charm
of gorillas: **4** band
of greyhounds: **5** leash
of grouse: **5** covey
of hares: **4** down, husk
of hawks: **4** cast
of hounds: **3** cry **4** mute, pack
of kangaroos: **3** mob **5** troop
of kittens: **6** kendle, kindle
of larks: **10** exaltation
of leopards: **4** leap
of lions: **5** pride
of locusts: **6** plague
of monkeys: **5** troop
of mules: **4** span
of nightingales: **5** watch
of nine: **5** nonet
of oysters: **3** bed
of partridges: **5** covey
of peacocks: **6** muster
of pheasants: **3** nye **4** nest, nide
of plovers: **4** wing **12** congregation
of quail: **4** bevy **5** covey
of seals: **3** pod **5** patch
of seven: **6** pleiad, septet
of sheep: **5** drove, flock
of six: **5** hexad **6** hexade, sextet
of swans: **4** bevy
of swine: **7** sounder
of teals: **6** spring
of three: **4** trio **5** triad **7** ternary, trinity, triplet

of toads: **4** knot
of vipers: **4** nest
of whales: **3** gam, pod
of wolves: **4** pack
suffix: **2** ad, et **3** ome **4** some

grouper
4 fish **8** rockfish **10** tripletail

grouse
5 croak, gripe, quail, scold **6** gorhen, grouch, murmur, mutter **7** gorcock, greyhen, grumble **8** complain, pheasant **9** blackcock, ptarmigan **10** whitebelly **12** capercaillie
extinct: **8** heath hen
red: **8** moorfowl
strut: **3** lak

grouser
see **grumbler**

grout
4 lees **5** dregs **6** cement, mortar **7** grounds, plaster **8** concrete

grove
3 bed **4** holt, wood **5** copse, hurst **7** boscage, coppice, orchard, thicket
suffix: **3** eta (plural) **4** etum

grovel
4 fawn **5** cower, toady **6** cringe, kowtow, wallow **7** honey up, truckle **8** bootlick **9** brownnose **11** apple-polish

grow
3 age, get, run, wax **4** come, rear, rise, tend, turn **5** breed, nurse, raise, ripen, swell **6** become, expand, foster, mature, mellow, sprout, thrive **7** care for, develop, enlarge, gestate, nurture, produce **8** escalate, increase, maturate, mushroom **9** cultivate, propagate

growing
8 crescive, vegetive **10** vegetative

growl
3 grr **4** roll **5** snarl **6** mutter, rumble **7** grumble **8** complain **9** complaint

growler
3 can **4** crab, floe **5** crank, grump **6** griper, grouch **7** grouser, iceberg, pitcher **8** grumbler, sorehead, sourpuss **9** container **10** bellyacher

grow old
3 age **5** ripen **6** mature

growth
4 rise **5** swell, tumor **7** merisis **8** increase, progress, swelling **9** accre-

tion, evolution, expansion, flowering, unfolding **10** evolvement **11** development, enlargement, progression
malignant: **6** cancer
skin: **3** wen **4** corn, mole, wart **6** bunion, keloid

grub
3 dig **4** beat, chow, comb, feed, food, hack, plod, poke, rake, root, slog, toil **5** grind, larva, scour, slave, spade, stump **6** burrow, drudge, forage, search, shovel, slavey, uproot, viands **7** edibles, grubber, nurture, ransack, rummage **8** excavate, finecomb, hireling, victuals **9** mercenary, provender

grubby
4 foul **5** black, dirty, grimy, nasty, soily **6** filthy, impure **7** squalid, unclean

grubstake
4 back **7** finance **8** bankroll

grudge
4 deny, envy **5** spite **6** injury, malice, refuse, spleen **7** despite, ill will **9** grievance, injustice, malignity **10** malignancy **11** malevolence **12** spitefulness

gruel
5 atole **8** porridge
Scottish: **6** crowdy

gruesome
see **grisly**

gruff
4 curt, dour, sour **5** bluff, blunt, husky, short, surly **6** abrupt, croaky, crusty, fierce, hoarse, morose, snippy, sullen **7** bearish, boorish, brusque, crabbed **8** churlish, croaking, snippety **9** saturnine

grumble
4 beef, crab, fuss, kick, moan, roll **5** bitch, brawl, croak, gripe, groan, growl, scold, snarl, whine **6** grouch, grouse, holler, murmur, mutter, repine, rumble, squawk **8** complain **9** bellyache

grumbler
4 crab **6** grouch **7** grouser, growler **8** sorehead **10** bellyacher, complainer, crosspatch, malcontent **11** faultfinder

grump
3 pet **4** crab, pout, sulk **5** crank **6** griper, grouch, kicker **7** growler **8** grumbler, sorehead, sourpuss **10** bellyacher

grumpy
5 moody, surly 6 crabby, cranky

guacharo
7 oilbird

Guam
capital: 5 Agana
native: 8 Chamorro

guanaco
5 llama 6 alpaca
kin: 5 camel

guarantee, guaranty
3 vow 4 bail, bond, oath, seal,
word 5 token, vouch 6 assure, ensure, insure, pledge, surety 7 certify, earnest, promise, warrant
8 security, warranty 9 assurance
11 undertaking

guarantor
5 angel 6 backer, patron, surety
7 sponsor 8 backer-up
11 underwriter

guard
4 fend, keep, mind, tend, ward
5 aegis, armor, cover, watch 6 attend, convoy, defend, escort, jailer,
keeper, patrol, picket, screen, secure, sentry, shield, warden, warder 7 bulwark, conduct, defense,
lookout, protect, turnkey 8 armament, chaperon, security, sentinel,
shepherd, watchdog, watchman
9 accompany, patrolman, protector
10 protection

guarded
4 safe, wary 5 chary, privy 6 buried, covert, hidden 7 careful 8 cautious, discreet, gingerly, obscured,
shrouded, ulterior 9 concealed
11 calculating, circumspect, considerate

guardhouse
4 brig 6 prison

guardian
6 custos, keeper, parent, patron,
warden 7 sponsor 8 cerberus, claviger, watchdog 9 custodian,
protector

guardianship
4 care, ward 5 trust 7 custody,
keeping, tuition 11 safekeeping

guava
4 inga, tree 5 fruit

gudgeon
3 pin 4 fish 5 pivot 6 socket

Gudrun
brother: 6 Gunnar 7 Gunther
father: 5 Hetel

husband: 4 Atli 5 Etzel 6 Sigurd
9 Siegfried

guerrilla
7 fighter, patriot, soldier 8 partisan
9 irregular 11 bushwhacker
Greek: 6 klepht

guess
4 call, shot, stab 5 fancy, infer,
think 6 deduce, reason, reckon
7 predict, presume, pretend, suppose, surmise 8 estimate 9 speculate 10 conjecture

guest
6 caller, lodger, patron, roomer
7 visitor

guff
3 jaw, lip 4 sass 5 hokum, hooey,
mouth, sauce, trash 6 bunkum
7 hogwash 8 back talk, claptrap,
malarkey, nonsense 9 poppycock
10 balderdash

guffaw
5 laugh, tehee 6 giggle, hee-haw,
titter 7 chortle, chuckle, snicker,
sniggle

guidance
7 auspice, conduct, control 9 direction 10 leadership, management

guide
3 see 4 airt, clue, dean, lead, show
5 airth, doyen, pilot, route, steer,
teach 6 beacon, convoy, direct, escort, leader, manage, manual, vector 7 conduct, control, marshal 8 Baedeker, chaperon,
contrive, director, engineer, handbook, maneuver, navigate, shepherd 9 accompany, conductor,
lead pilot, vade mecum 10 bellwether, compendium 11 enchiridion

guidebook
6 manual 8 Baedeker, handbook
9 itinerary, vade mecum
10 compendium 11 enchiridion

guided missile
3 ABM 4 Hawk, ICBM, IRBM,
Nike, Thor, Zuni 5 Atlas, drone,
Snark, Titan 6 Bomarc, Falcon
7 Bullpup, Polaris, Terrier 8 Red-
stone 9 Minuteman 10 Sidewinder

Guiderius
brother: 9 Arviragus
father: 9 Cymbeline

Guido's scale
2 fa, la, mi, re, ut 3 Ela, sol

guild
4 club 5 order, union 6 cartel,
league 7 society 8 sodality 10 fel-

lowship, fraternity 11 association,
brotherhood
medieval: 5 Hansa, Hanse

guile
4 wile 5 craft, fraud 6 deceit 7 cunning 9 duplicity 12 dissemblance

guileful
3 sly 4 deep, foxy, wily 6 artful,
astute, crafty, shifty, sneaky, tricky
7 cunning, devious 8 indirect,
sneaking 9 insidious, underhand
11 duplicitous, underhanded

guileless
5 naive 6 honest 7 artless, natural
8 unartful 9 ingenuous, unstudied,
untutored

guillemot
3 auk 5 murre

guillotine
6 behead 9 decollate
10 decapitate

guilt
3 sin 4 onus 5 blame, crime, fault,
shame 7 offense, remorse
11 culpability

guiltless
4 good, pure 5 clean 8 innocent,
unguilty, virtuous 9 blameless, crimeless, exemplary, faultless, righteous 10 inculpable, unblamable

guilty
5 amiss 6 nocent, sinful, unholy,
wicked 7 ashamed 8 blamable,
blameful, culpable, indicted 9 im-
peached 10 answerable, censurable 11 accountable, blameworthy,
responsible 12 incriminated

guinea fowl
genus: 6 Numida
young: 4 keet

guinea pig
4 cavy 6 rodent
genus: 5 Cavia

Guinevere
husband: 6 Arthur
lover: 8 Lancelot 9 Launcelot

guise
3 hue, rig 4 face, mask, show
5 cloak, color, cover, dress, getup
6 facade, outfit, setout 7 costume
8 coloring 9 semblance
10 appearance

guitar
part: 3 nut, peg 4 fret, neck 5 brace
6 bridge, string 7 peghead
player: 7 plucker 8 strummer
small: 3 uke 7 ukulele

soprano: 5 tiple
tool: 4 pick 8 plectrum

guitarist
American: 9 Parkening (Christopher)
Australian: 8 Williams (John)
British: 5 Bream (Julian)
Italian: 7 Ghiglia (Oscar)
Spanish: 5 Yepes (Narciso) 6 Romero (Celedonio) 7 Segovia (Andrés)

guitarlike instrument
3 uke 4 lute, vina 5 banjo, sitar 6 sancho 7 bandore, pandora, samisen, ukulele

gulch
3 gap 5 chasm, cleft, clove, gorge, gully 6 arroyo, canyon, clough, ravine

gulf
3 arm, bay, pit 4 cave, cove, eddy, well 5 abysm, abyss, bayou, bight, chasm, firth, gulch, inlet, shaft 6 cavity, harbor, hollow, ravine, slough 8 crevasse
Adriatic Sea: 6 Venice
Aegean Sea: 7 Saronic 8 Salonika
Africa: 6 Guinea
Arabian Sea: 4 Oman 7 Persian
Arctic Ocean: 2 Ob
Australia: 9 Van Diemen 11 Carpentaria
Baltic Sea: 4 Riga 6 Danzig, Gdansk 7 Bothnia, Finland
Bering Sea: 6 Anadyr
Canada: 13 Saint Lawrence
Caribbean Sea: 8 Honduras 9 Venezuela
Central America: 6 Panama 7 Fonseca
Djibouti: 6 Tajura 8 Tadjoura
Europe: 7 Bothnia, Gascony 8 Gascogne
Greece: 7 Corinth, Lepanto
Indian Ocean: 5 Aden
Ionian Sea: 4 Arta 7 Taranto
Iran: 7 Arabian
Italy: 5 Genoa
Mediterranean Sea: 5 Sidra, Tunis 8 Valencia 10 Khalij Surt 11 Syrtis Major
Mexico: 10 California
New Guinea: 5 Papua 7 McCluer
New Zealand: 7 Hauraki
North America: 6 Alaska, Mexico
Northwest Territories: 7 Boothia 8 Amundsen 9 Queen Maud
Philippines: 4 Asid 5 Davao, Leyte, Panay, Ragay
Red Sea: 4 Suez 5 Aqaba 11 Aelaniticus
Russia: 8 Sakhalin
Solomon Sea: 4 Huon, Kula 5 Vella

South China Sea: 4 Siam 6 Tonkin 8 Lingayen, Thailand
Tyrrhenion Sea: 7 Paestum
Yellow Sea: 2 Bo, Po 6 Chihli

Gulf State
5 Texas 7 Alabama, Florida 9 Louisiana 11 Mississippi

gull
3 mew, sap 4 bird, dupe, fish, fool, hoax 5 chump 6 befool, fleece, pigeon, sucker 7 chicane, fall guy, gudgeon, saphead 8 flimflam, hoodwink 9 bamboozle 11 hornswoggle
relating to: 6 larine, laroid

gullet
3 maw 4 tube 6 dewlap, ravine, throat 7 channel 9 esophagus

gullible
4 easy 5 naive 9 credulous 10 fleeceable 11 susceptible

Gulliver's Travels
author: 5 Swift (Jonathan)
land: 6 Laputa 8 Lilliput 11 Brobdingnag
people: 6 Yahoos

gully
5 gorge, gulch 6 arroyo, hollow, ravine, valley 7 couloir

gulp
4 bolt, cram, glut, slop, swig, wolf 5 slosh, stuff, swill 6 devour, englut, gobble, guzzle 7 swallow 11 ingurgitate

gum
4 chew, kino 5 botch, cheat, nyssa, stick, tuart 6 bobble, bollix, bungle, chicle, gluten, goof up, mucker, tupelo 7 bilsted, exudate, gingiva, louse up 8 adhesive, mucilage 9 sapodilla 10 eucalyptus
kind: 6 acacia, Arabic, balata, bubble 7 chewing, dextrin
resin: 5 myrrh 7 gamboge 8 ammoniac, galbanum, scammony 9 asafetida 12 frankincense

gummy
5 gooey 6 cloggy, sticky, stodgy 7 viscous 8 adhesive

gumption
5 sense 6 wisdom 8 judgment, sagacity 9 good sense 10 astuteness, enterprise, horse sense, shrewdness 11 common sense

gums
3 ula 8 gingivae

gumshoe
3 cop, tec 4 dick, fuzz, heat, lurk, slip 5 creep, shirk, skulk, slink,

sneak, snoop, steal 6 peeler, sleuth 7 officer 8 flatfoot, hawkshaw, Sherlock 9 detective, policeman, pussyfoot 12 investigator

gun
3 gat, rod 5 rifle 6 cannon, heater, mortar, musket, pistol, weapon 7 bazooka, carbine, firearm 8 howitzer, revolver 9 derringer
antiaircraft: 6 ack-ack, Bofors
big-game: 4 roer
British: 4 sten
French: 8 arquebus
German: 5 Luger
mount: 6 turret
part: 3 pin 4 bolt, bore, butt, lock 5 sight, stock 6 barrel, breech, hammer, muzzle, safety 7 chamber, trigger 8 cylinder, magazine 9 buttstock

gunfire
4 shot 5 salvo 6 ack-ack, strafe, volley 7 barrage 9 fusillade

gung ho
4 keen 7 zealous 12 enthusiastic

Guni's father
8 Naphtali

gunk
3 goo 4 crud, gook, goop, muck

gunman
5 bravo 6 hit man 7 torpedo 8 assassin 9 cutthroat

Gunnar
brother-in-law: 6 Sigurd
father: 5 Hetel
sister: 6 Gudrun
wife: 8 Brynhild

gunnel
6 blenny 10 butterfish

gunner
7 shooter 8 marksman, rifleman 9 cannoneer 12 artilleryman

Gunther
sister: 7 Gutrune 9 Kriemhild
slayer: 5 Hagen
uncle: 5 Hagen
wife: 8 Brunhild 9 Brynhilde 11 Brunnehilde

guppy
4 fish 6 minnow

gurgle
3 lap 4 wash 5 slosh, swash 6 bubble, burble

Gurkha knife
5 kukri

gurney
3 cot 9 stretcher

guru
5 guide 6 mentor 7 teacher

gush
4 flow, pour, roll, teem 5 flood, flush, issue, spout, spurt, surge 6 sluice, spring, stream 7 emanate

gusset
4 fold 5 armor, pleat 6 insert

gust
4 gale, puff, waft, wind 5 blast, burst, draft, sally, whiff 6 access, breeze, squall 7 bluster, flare-up 8 eruption, outburst

gusto
4 élan, zeal, zest 5 ardor, heart, taste 6 fervor, palate, relish, spirit 7 delight, passion 8 pleasure 9 enjoyment 10 enthusiasm 11 delectation

gut
4 draw 5 belly, bowel, clean, dress, inner 6 paunch 7 embowel, passage, stomach 8 interior, internal, intimate, visceral 9 viscerous 10 disembowel, eviscerate, exenterate

Gutenberg
city: 5 Mainz
invention: 11 movable type
partner: 4 Fust (Johann)

gutless
6 coward, craven 7 chicken, unmanly 8 cowardly 9 spunkless 11 lily-livered, poltroonish 13 pusillanimous

guts
4 grit 5 moxie, nerve, pluck, spunk 6 mettle, spirit, tripes 7 courage, innards, insides, viscera 8 backbone, entrails, stuffing 9 fortitude, internals 10 resolution

gutsy
4 bold 5 brave, manly 6 manful, plucky, spunky 7 valiant 8 intrepid 9 unfearful 10 courageous

gutter
5 ditch, gully 6 furrow, groove, trench, trough 7 channel

guttural
4 deep 5 harsh, rough, velar 7 palatal, rasping, throaty

Guyana
capital: 10 Georgetown
monetary unit: 6 dollar

guzzle
4 bolt, cram, gulp, slop, soak, swig, wolf 5 booze, drink, slosh, swill 6 englut, gobble, imbibe, tank up, tipple 7 swizzle

Gwendolen's husband
7 Locrine

gymnast
7 acrobat, athlete, tumbler
American: 5 Rigby (Cathy) 6 Conner (Bart), Retton (Mary Lou), Thomas (Kurt)
Romanian: 8 Comaneci (Nadia)
Russian: 3 Kim (Nelly) 6 Korbut (Olga)

gymnastics
5 sport 8 exercise, tumbling 9 athletics 10 acrobatics 12 calisthenics
apparatus: 3 bar 4 beam, buck, ring, rope 5 horse

feat: 3 kip 4 flip 5 vault 6 tumble 9 handstand, headstand 10 handspring, headspring, somersault

gyp
4 beat, bilk, fake, hoax, sell 5 cheat, cozen, fraud, phony, spoof 6 chisel, chouse, con man, diddle, humbug, rip off 7 defraud, diddler, sharper, swindle 8 swindler 9 defrauder, imposture, overreach, trickster 10 mountebank 11 flimflammer 12 double-dealer

gypsum
4 yeso 8 selenite 9 alabaster

gypsy
4 caló 5 caird, nomad 6 roamer, Romany 7 tzigane, zingana, zingano 8 Bohemian, wanderer
Spanish: 6 gitano

gyrate
4 roll, spin, turn 5 twirl, whirl 6 circle, rotate 7 revolve 9 pirouette, whirligig

gyration
4 turn 5 round, wheel, whirl 7 circuit 8 rotation 10 revolution 11 circulation

gyre
4 ring, spin 5 twirl, whirl 6 rotate, spiral, vortex 7 revolve 10 revolution

gyro
8 sandwich 9 gyroscope

gyve
4 bond, iron 5 chain 6 fetter 7 shackle

H
    4 high 5 aitch 7 hundred

habeus corpus
    4 writ

habilimented
    4 clad 7 clothed

habilitate
    5 dress 6 clothe

habit
    3 rut, set, use, way 4 bent, form, mode, rote, turn, wont 5 build, dress, style, trick, usage 6 clothe, custom, groove, manner, praxis 7 carcass, contour, fashion, habitus, outline, pattern, routine 8 behavior, physique, practice, tendency 9 addiction, framework 10 consuetude, convention, proclivity 11 disposition, inclination
    riding: 6 joseph 8 jodhpurs
    wearer: 3 nun 5 rider

habitant
    5 liver 7 denizen, dweller, resider 8 occupant, resident 9 indweller

habitat
    4 home, site 5 abode, haunt, range 6 locale 7 station 8 locality 9 territory 11 environment 12 surroundings
    combining form: 2 ec 3 eco, oec 4 oeco

habitation
    3 pad 4 digs, flat, home, nest, nook, roof, seat 5 abode, astre, haunt, haven, house, place, roost 6 colony, hearth 7 housing, lodging 8 domicile, dwelling, fireside, lodgment, peopling, quarters, rooftree, tenement 9 apartment, homeplace, homestead, occupancy, residence, residency

habitual
    6 addict, inborn, native, steady, wonted 7 chronic, regular, routine 8 accepted, addicted, constant, frequent 9 automatic, confirmed, continual, customary, ingrained 10 accustomed, inveterate, persistent 11 established, instinctive, involuntary

habituate
    3 use 4 bear, wont 5 enure, inure 6 addict, adjust, devote, endure, season, take to 7 support 8 accustom, devote to, tolerate 9 condition, confirm in 11 familiarize

habitué
    3 fan 4 buff, user 5 hound, lover 6 addict, patron, votary 7 denizen, devotee, haunter 8 customer 10 frequenter

Hacaliah, Hachaliah
    son: 8 Nehemiah

hacienda
    4 farm 5 ranch 6 estate 10 plantation

hack
    3 cab, cut, hew, old, try 4 chip, chop, dull, fell, gash, grub, jade, mean, nick, poor, taxi, trim, turn 5 cabby, cough, frame, grind, horse, notch, petty, shape, slash, slave, stale, tired, trite, usual 6 cabbie, cliché, common, drudge, haggle, lackey, mangle, slavey 7 clichéd, grating, grubber, machine, outworn, plodder, potboil, servant, taxicab, trivial 8 déclassé, hireling, inferior, low grade, mediocre, ordinary, outmoded, timeworn, wellworn 9 cabdriver, mercenary, potboiler 10 second-rate, uninspired 11 commonplace

hackneyed
    4 worn 5 stale, stock, tired, trite 6 cliché 7 archaic, clichéd, wornout 8 bathetic, everyday, obsolete, outmoded, timeworn, well-worn 9 moth-eaten, out-of-date, quotidian 10 antiquated 11 commonplace

Hadad
    father: 5 Bedad 7 Ishmael
    victim: 6 Midian

Hadadezer
    father: 5 Rehob
    kingdom: 5 Zobah

hades
    3 pit 4 hell 5 Sheol 6 Tophet 7 Abaddon, Avernus, Gehenna, inferno 8 Tartarus 9 barathrum, perdition 10 underworld 11 netherworld, Pandemonium
    Babylonian: 5 Aralu
    god: 3 Dis 5 Orcus, Pluto
    guard: 8 Cerberus
    lake: 7 Avernus
    river: 4 Styx 5 Lethe 7 Acheron, Cocytus 10 Phlegethon

hafnium
    symbol: 2 Hf

hag
    3 hex 4 drab, trot 5 biddy, bruja, crone, harpy, lamia, shrew, vixen, witch 6 beldam, gorgon, virago 7 grandam 8 battle-ax, fishwife, harridan, slattern 9 sorceress 10 witchwoman 11 enchantress

Hagar's son
    7 Ishmael

Hagen
    father: 8 Alberich
    nephew: 7 Gunther
    slayer: 9 Kriemhild
    victim: 9 Siegfried

haggard
    3 wan 4 lank, lean, pale, worn 5 ashen, drawn, faded, gaunt, spare, tired 6 fagged, pallid, skinny 7 angular, pinched, scraggy, scrawny, wearied 8 careworn, fatigued, harrowed, worndown 9 exhausted

Haggard novel
    3 She

Haggi's father
3 Gad

Haggith
husband: 5 David
son: 8 Adonijah

haggle
4 deal, hack 5 cavil, slash, trade
6 barter, bicker, dicker, hackle, palter 7 bargain, chaffer, dispute,
quibble, stickle, wrangle 8 huckster, squabble 10 horse-trade

hagiography subject
5 saint

hail
4 ahoy 5 greet, hallo, salvo, shout,
storm 6 accost, call to, hallow, holler, kudize, praise, salute, shower,
volley 7 acclaim, address, applaud, barrage, call out, commend
8 come from, drumfire 9 broadside, cannonade, fusillade, originate, recommend 10 salutation
11 bombardment

Haile Selassie
nation ruled: 8 Ethiopia

hair
3 ace, bit, jot 4 hint, mite, wool
5 pilus, trace 6 nicety, trifle
7 whisker 8 fraction, particle
animal: 3 fur 4 mane, pelt 8 vibrissa 9 vibrissae (plural)
braid of: 5 queue 7 pigtail
clip: 8 barrette
coarse: 7 bristle
combining form: 3 pil 4 coma, pili,
pilo 5 chaet, crini, thrix, trich
6 chaeta, chaeto, tricha, trichi, tricho, trichy 7 chaetae (plural), chaetes, chaetus, trichia 8 trichous
covering of: 3 wig
facial: 5 beard 6 goatee 8 mustache, whiskers 9 moustache, sideburns 11 muttonchops
fine: 6 lanugo
front: 4 bang
head of: 9 chevelure
instrument: 4 comb
knot of: 3 bun 6 tangle
lock of: 4 curl 5 tress 7 cowlick
loose roll: 4 pouf 5 pouff 6 pouffe
matted: 4 shag
ornament: 7 topknot
preparation: 6 pomade
12 brilliantine
relating to: 8 hirsutal
root: 6 fibril
set: 4 perm
stiff: 4 seta 5 setae (plural)
style: 9 pompadour

tangled: 7 elflock
tuft of: 7 fetlock
unruly: 3 mop 7 cowlick
without: 4 bald

haircutter
6 barber 7 friseur

hairdo
4 perm 7 chignon 8 bouffant

hairdresser
6 barber 7 friseur 10 beautician
13 cosmetologist

hair-raising
4 eery 5 eerie 9 thrilling
10 terrifying

hairsplitter
8 quibbler

hairstyle
2 DA 4 Afro 5 bangs 7 beehive,
crew cut, pageboy 8 bouffant, coiffure, ducktail, ponytail

hairy
5 bushy, crude, downy, furry,
fuzzy, harsh, nappy, risky, rough
6 chancy, craggy, fleecy, fluffy, jagged, lanate, pilose, rugged,
shaggy, tufted, uneven, wicked,
woolly 7 bristly, hirsute, pileous,
scraggy, unshorn, unsound, villous
8 asperous, perilous, scabrous, strigose, unsmooth 9 dangerous, hazardous, pubescent, tomentose, unhealthy, whiskered 10 jeopardous,
unpleasant 11 frightening,
treacherous
combining form: 4 dasy, hebe

Haiti
capital: 12 Port au Prince
export: 6 coffee 7 bauxite
island: 10 Hispaniola
location: 10 West Indies
monetary unit: 6 gourde
ruler: 8 Duvalier

Hajji Baba creator
6 Morier (James Justinian)

hake
5 gadid 7 codling, whiting
relative: 3 cod

halcyon
4 calm 5 happy, quiet, still
6 golden, hushed, placid, serene,
stilly 8 affluent 10 kingfisher, prosperous, untroubled

Halcyone
father: 6 Aeolus
husband: 4 Ceyx

hale
3 fit, tug 4 draw, pull, sane, well

5 husky, right, sound, stout 6 robust
7 healthy, summons 9 strapping,
wholesome

Hale character
5 Nolan (Philip)

haleness
6 health

Haley (Alex) epic
5 Roots

half
prefix: 3 sam 4 demi, hemi, semi

half-assed
7 lacking, wanting 9 defective, deficient 10 inadequate, incomplete,
uncomplete

half-breed
4 mule 5 cross 6 hybrid 7 bastard,
mestizo, mongrel, mulatto
8 mixblood

halfhearted
5 tepid 8 lukewarm

half-moon
7 scalare 8 demilune 9 blue perch

halfway
3 mid 6 almost, center, medial, median, middle 7 midmost, partial
8 amenably 9 partially 10 centermost, middlemost, more or less
11 equidistant

half-wit
4 dolt, fool, zany 5 ament, idiot,
moron 6 cretin 7 natural 8 imbecile 9 blockhead, simpleton

half-witted
4 dull, slow 5 silly 7 foolish, moronic 8 backward, imbecile, retarded 9 senseless 12 feebleminded, simpleminded

hall
4 dorm 5 foyer, lobby, lycea (plural) 6 lyceum 7 couloir, passage
8 building, corridor 9 dormitory
10 auditorium, corridor, living room, passageway 12 entrance room
ancient Roman: 5 oecus
exhibition: 5 salon
Salvation Army: 7 citadel

Halley's ___
5 comet

Hallohesh's son
7 Shallum

hallow
5 bless 6 devote, revere 8 dedicate, sanctify, venerate 10 consecrate

hallucination
6 mirage, wraith 7 fantasy, phantom 8 delusion, illusion, phantasm 11 fata morgana, ignis fatuus

hallucinogen
3 LSD 9 mescaline 10 psilocybin 11 scopolamine

halo
4 aura 5 nimbi (plural) 6 corona, gloria, nimbus 7 aureole 8 encircle, gloriole
combining form: 7 stephan 8 stephano

halogen
6 iodine 7 bromine 8 astatine, chlorine, fluorine

halt
3 end 4 lame, limp, quit, stay, stop 5 cease, check, close, hitch, lapse, stall, waver 6 arrest, desist, dither, draw up, falter, finish, haul up, hobble, pull up, wind up, wrap up 7 bring up, fetch up, stagger, suspend, whiffle 8 complete, conclude, give over, hesitate, knock off, leave off, surcease, ultimate 9 determine, interrupt, terminate, vacillate 11 discontinue

ham
4 hock 5 emote, thigh 7 buttock, overact 8 overplay, strutter 13 exhibitionist

Ham
brother: 4 Shem 7 Japheth
father: 4 Noah
son: 4 Cush, Phut 6 Canaan 7 Mizraim

Haman's father
10 Hammedatha

hamartiology subject
3 sin

Hamilcar
conquest: 5 Spain
home: 8 Carthage
son: 8 Hannibal
surname: 5 Barca

hamlet
5 moray 7 grouper, village
Irish, Scottish: 7 clachan

Hamlet
author: 11 Shakespeare (William)
beloved: 7 Ophelia
castle: 8 Elsinore
country: 7 Denmark
friend: 7 Horatio
mother: 8 Gertrude
slayer: 7 Laertes
uncle: 8 Claudius

victim: 7 Laertes 8 Claudius, Polonius

Hamlet, The
author: 8 Faulkner (William)
family: 6 Snopes

Hammedatha's son
5 Haman

hammer
4 beat, cock, drub, form, maul, peen, pein, pelt, toil 5 drive, erect, gavel, labor, pound, set up, shape, stamp, swage, thump 6 batter, mallet, pummel, sledge, thrash, wallop 7 belabor, build up, fashion, foliate, impress, malleus, planish, trippet 8 lambaste, malleate
type: 3 air 4 claw 6 sledge 8 ball peen 9 pneumatic

hammerhead
3 bat 5 dunce, shark, stork 8 clodpate, numskull 9 hog sucker 10 thickskull

Hammoleketh's brother
6 Gilead

hamper
3 bar, bin, rub, tie 4 balk, clog, curb, foil, snag 5 block, check, crimp, leash, limit, tie up 6 baffle, basket, cumber, fetter, hinder, hobble, hog-tie, hurdle, impede, lumber, retard, thwart 7 disrupt, inhibit, shackle, trammel 8 encumber, handicap, obstacle, obstruct, restrain, restrict 9 discomfit, embarrass, entrammel, frustrate

hamstring
6 hinder, impair, tendon 7 cripple, disable

Hamul's father
5 Perez 6 Pharez

Hamutal
father: 8 Jeremiah
husband: 6 Josiah
son: 8 Jehoahaz, Zedekiah

Hanameel
cousin: 8 Jeremiah
father: 7 Shallum

Hanani
brother: 8 Nehemiah
father: 5 Heman, Immer
son: 4 Jehu

Hananiah
father: 4 Azur 5 Azzur, Bebai, Heman 7 Shashak 10 Zerubbabel
son: 8 Jeshaiah, Pelatiah, Zedekiah

Hanan's father
4 Azel 6 Zaccur 7 Maachah, Shashak 8 Igdaliah

hand
3 aid 4 buck, feed, find, fist, furl, give, help, lift, pass, side 5 angle, facet, index, manus, phase, reach, skill, touch 6 aspect, assist, ductus, inning, pledge, relief, script, succor, supply, worker 7 ability, comfort, concern, conduct, deliver, dish out, laborer, provide, secours, support, workman 8 dispense, employee, interest, transfer, turn over 9 direction, operative, signature 10 assistance, penmanship, roustabout, workingman 11 calligraphy, chirography
clenched: 4 fist
combining form: 4 chir 5 cheir, chiro, palmi 6 cheiro, palmat 7 palmati
counting zero: 8 baccarat
covering: 5 glove 6 mitten
declarer's: 7 laydown
down: 8 bequeath
gestures: 5 mudra
make: 5 craft
on hip: 6 akimbo
part: 4 palm 5 thumb 6 finger
poker: 5 flush 8 straight 9 full house
protector: 5 glove 8 gauntlet

handbag
5 purse 8 reticule

handbill
5 flier, flyer 6 dodger, poster 7 affiche, leaflet, placard 8 circular

handbook
5 guide 6 manual 8 Baedeker 9 vade mecum 10 compendium 11 enchiridion
religious: 9 catechism

handcuff
7 manacle 8 restrain
British: 7 darbies (plural)

hand down
6 pass on 8 bequeath, transmit

Handel
aria: 5 Largo
birthplace: 5 Halle (Germany)
opera: 4 Nero 5 Serse 6 Almira, Xerxes 7 Rodrigo 8 Berenice 9 Agrippina
oratorio: 4 Saul 6 Esther, Joshua, Samson 7 Messiah 8 Jephthah

handicap
4 edge, load, odds 5 bulge, start 6 burden 8 drawback 9 advantage, allowance, detriment, head start 10 disability 11 encumbrance 12 disadvantage

handicraft
3 art 5 trade 6 métier 7 calling
8 vocation 10 profession

handkerchief
5 hanky 6 hankie 7 bandana
8 bandanna, mouchoir

handle
3 aim, ear, lay, paw, ply, run, try,
use 4 ansa, bail, feel, grip, haft,
knob, knop, name, play, take, test,
wave, work 5 apply, guide, level,
nomen, point, serve, shake, style,
swing, title, touch, treat, wield
6 bestow, byname, byword, direct,
employ, finger, govern, manage
7 act upon, conduct, control, exploit, moniker, operate, palpate,
trade in, utilize 8 brandish, cognomen, deal with, dispense, dominate, doorknob, exercise, flourish,
maneuver, nickname
scythe: 5 snath 6 snathe

handle-shaped
6 ansate

handling
4 care 6 charge 7 conduct, running 9 oversight 10 intendance,
management 11 supervision

hand out
4 give 6 bestow, devote, donate
7 present 8 give away
10 administer

hand over
4 cede, feed, find, give 5 leave,
waive, yield 6 commit, give up, resign, supply 7 abandon, commend,
confide, consign, deliver, entrust,
provide 8 dispense, relegate, transfer 9 deliver up, surrender 10 relinquish

handrail
8 banister

handsome
3 apt 4 chic, fair, free 5 ample, noble, smart, sonsy 6 adroit, august,
comely, lovely, modish, pretty, sonsie 7 dashing, liberal, sizable,
stately, stylish 8 generous, majestic
9 beauteous, beautiful, bounteous,
bountiful, unsparing 10 attractive,
munificent, openhanded 11 fashionable, good-looking

handspring
6 tumble
lateral: 9 cartwheel

handwriting
6 ductus, script 8 longhand
10 manuscript, penmanship 11 calligraphy, chirography

bad: 10 cacography
study of: 10 graphology

handy
4 deft 5 adept, utile 6 adroit,
clever, nearby, nimble, useful,
wieldy 7 close-by 8 adjacent, skillful 9 adaptable, dexterous, practical 10 beneficial, convenient, functional 11 practicable

handyman
6 jumper 8 factotum

hang
3 art, fix, jut, lop, pin, sag 4 hook,
idle, lean, loll, pend, rest 5 await,
cling, craft, drape, droop, float,
hover, knack, lynch, noose, pause,
poise, scrag, skill, sling, slope,
stick, swing, trail, trick 6 adhere,
attach, dangle, depend, gibbet, impend, loiter, tack up, turn on
7 execute
back: 3 lag
loosely: 3 sag 6 dangle

hangbird
6 oriole

hangdog
5 cowed 6 guilty 7 ashamed, pitiful 8 dejected

hanger-on
5 leech 6 sponge, sucker
7 sponger 8 barnacle, follower,
parasite 9 bystander, spectator,
sycophant 10 freeloader 11 bloodsucker 12 lounge lizard

hanging
7 pendent, pensile 9 declivity, pendulant, pendulous, suspended

Hanging Gardens
7 Babylon

hangings
5 arras 6 drapes 7 drapery 8 curtains, tapestry

hangout
4 dive 5 haunt, joint 6 resort 7 purlieu 9 honky-tonk 10 rendezvous
11 barrelhouse 12 watering hole

hang up
4 mire 5 delay, embog 6 detain,
retard 7 achieve, bog down, set
back, slacken 8 slow down
10 decelerate

hank
4 coil, loop, ring

hanker
3 yen 4 ache, long, lust, pine, sigh,
wish 5 covet, crave, yearn 6 desire, hunger, thirst

hanky-panky
5 fraud 7 chicane 8 trickery 9 chicanery, deception, fourberie
11 highbinding 13 double-dealing,
sharp practice

Hannah
husband: 7 Elkanah
son: 6 Samuel

Hannibal
defeat: 4 Zama
father: 8 Hamilcar
home: 8 Carthage
surname: 5 Barca
vanquisher: 6 Scipio
victory: 6 Cannae

Hanniel's father
4 Ulla 5 Ephod

Hanoch's father
6 Midian, Reuben

hansa, hanse
5 guild 6 league 11 association

Hans Brinker author
5 Dodge (Mary Mapes)

Hanseatic League City
6 Bremen, Lubeck, Wismar 7 Cologne, Hamburg, Rostock

Hansen's disease
7 leprosy

Hanun's father
6 Nahash

haphazard
5 about 6 anyhow, around,
chance, random 7 aimless, anywise, unaimed 8 accident, at random, careless, casually, randomly,
slipshod 9 aimlessly, desultory, hit-
or-miss, irregular, unplanned 10 accidental, carelessly, designless
11 any which way, unorganized
12 accidentally, unconsidered, unsystematic 13 helter-skelter

hapless
4 poor 6 woeful 7 unhappy, unlucky 8 ill-fated, untoward,
wretched 9 miserable 10 ill-starred
11 star-crossed, unfortunate 12 infelicitous, misfortunate

happen
2 do, go 3 hit 4 bump, come, fall,
give, luck, meet, pass, rise
5 break, light, occur 6 befall, betide, chance, drop in, tumble, turn
up 7 come off, develop, fall out,
stumble, turn out 8 bechance
9 transpire
again: 5 recur
together: 6 concur

happening
5 event, thing 7 episode 8 incident, occasion 10 occurrence
12 circumstance

happiness
3 joy 4 glee 5 bliss, cheer, mirth
6 gaiety 7 content, delight, jollity
8 felicity, gladness, pleasure 9 beatitude, enjoyment 11 delectation
12 satisfaction

happy
3 apt, fit, pat 4 glad, just, meet, nice, well 5 lucky, right 6 casual, cogent, joyful, joyous, proper, timely, upbeat 7 content, correct, fitting, pleased, telling 8 friendly, pleasant, suitable 9 befitting, congenial, contented, effective, effectual, efficient, favorable, fortunate, opportune, satisfied, well-timed
10 accidental, convincing, felicitous, fortuitous, harmonious, incidental, propitious, prosperous, seasonable 11 appropriate, efficacious 12 lighthearted

happy-go-lucky
4 cool, easy 6 blithe, casual
8 carefree, careless, cheerful, debonair, feckless, heedless, reckless
9 easygoing, lightsome 10 freeminded, insouciant, nonchalant
11 unconcerned 12 devil-may-care, light-hearted 13 lackadaisical

hara-kiri
7 seppuku, suicide 8 felo-de-se
10 self-murder 12 self-violence
13 self-slaughter

Haran
brother: 7 Abraham
daughter: 5 Iscah 6 Milcah
father: 5 Terah 6 Shimei
son: 3 Lot

harangue
4 rant, rave 5 mouth, orate 6 tirade 7 declaim, lecture, oration, soapbox 8 bloviate, diatribe, jeremiad, perorate 9 philippic
11 declamation

harass
3 irk, try, vex 4 bait, gnaw, pain, raid, ride 5 annoy, chivy, devil, foray, harry, hound, tease, worry
6 badger, hassle, heckle, hector, maraud, pester, plague, ratten, strain, stress 7 bedevil, dragoon, exhaust, fatigue, hagride, torment, trouble 8 bullyrag, distress 9 beleaguer

harasser
5 bully 6 hector 7 harrier, hassler

9 bulldozer 10 browbeater
11 intimidator

harassment
6 irking, vexing 8 vexation 9 annoyance, bothering, provoking
10 irritation 11 aggravation, disturbance, provocation 12 exasperation, perturbation

harbinger
4 omen, sign 6 herald, symbol
7 apostle, forerun, portent, presage
8 announce, foreshow, outrider
9 precursor 10 forerunner, indication 11 preindicate

harbor
3 arm, bay, hut 4 bunk, camp, cove, gulf, hide, live, port, roof, room 5 bight, board, cabin, cover, firth, guard, haven, house, inlet, lodge, nurse, put up, roost 6 asylum, bestow, billet, covert, encamp, foster, refuge, screen, shield, take in 7 chamber, cherish, conceal, contain, nurture, protect, quarter, retreat, seaport, secrete, shelter
8 domicile 9 anchorage, entertain, safeguard, sanctuary 11 accommodate
fee: 7 keelage
Greece: 5 Aulis
Guam: 4 Apra
Hawaii: 5 Pearl
Ireland: 4 Cork
Long Island Sound: 8 New Haven
Massachusetts: 4 Lynn 9 Annisquam
New Jersey: 9 Little Egg
Solomon: 4 Viru
Washington: 5 Grays

hard
3 bad, set 4 dark, deep, dour, dull, fast, firm, grim, iron, near, nigh
5 amiss, badly, bleak, close, crisp, cruel, fixed, harsh, heavy, horny, madly, rocky, rough, sharp, sober, solid, stark, tight, tough, vivid 6 actual, ardent, bitter, brazen, brutal, coarse, firmly, flinty, keenly, knotty, meanly, nearby, packed, rugged, severe, sorely, sticky, strict, strong, thorny, tiring, trying, unjust, uphill, wildly 7 angrily, arduous, austere, binding, briskly, callous, closely, compact, complex, cruelly, durable, factual, fixedly, genuine, glaring, harshly, hostile, intense, irksome, labored, largely, obscure, onerous, operous, petrous, precise, roughly, rowdily, serious, sharply, slavish, solidly, tightly, tiredly, toilful, violent, wearing 8 absolute, actively, bitterly, brutally, concrete, definite,

dingdong, exacting, fiercely, forcibly, frugally, granitic, grievous, grinding, indurate, intently, involved, mightily, petrosal, pitiless, positive, profound, reliable, rigorous, savagely, scabrous, severely, shabbily, snappily, stormily, strident, strongly, tempered, terrible, toilsome, unfairly, urgently, wearying 9 alcoholic, arduously, austerely, awkwardly, bloodless, compacted, demanding, difficile, difficult, earnestly, effortful, fatiguing, furiously, inclement, indurated, insensate, intensely, intensive, intricate, laborious, massively, merciless, offensive, onerously, painfully, pointedly, practical, pragmatic, punishing, realistic, resentful, resistant, searching, seriously, shameless, sprightly, straining, strenuous, stringent, unfeeling, unhandily, unsparing, viciously, violently, wearisome 10 adamantine, anesthetic, animatedly, bothersome, burdensome, compressed, cumbrously, exhausting, forbidding, forcefully, formidable, frenziedly, gruelingly, impassible, insensible, oppressive, perplexing, powerfully, rigorously, spiritedly, spirituous, sure-enough, thoroughly, toilsomely, unpleasant, unwieldily, unyielding, vigorously
11 assiduously, at close hand, complicated, difficultly, distressing, down-to-earth, exuberantly, ferociously, frantically, inequitable, insensitive, intemperate, intensively, intractable, laboriously, ponderously, rancorously, resentfully, searchingly, steadfastly, strenuously, troublesome, turbulently, unfantastic, unfavorable, unpalatable, unrelenting, unremitting, vivaciously
12 backbreaking, blood-and-guts, boisterously, burdensomely, concentrated, consolidated, cumbersomely, exhaustingly, exhaustively, incorrigible, intoxicating, matter-of-fact, meticulously, might and main, relentlessly, tumultuously
combining form: 5 scler, stere
6 sclero, stereo
to please: 7 finicky

hard-boiled
5 crude, rough, sober, stiff, tough
6 coarse 7 callous 8 obdurate, seasoned 9 heartless, practical, pragmatic, realistic, unfeeling 11 coldhearted, down-to-earth, unemotional, unfantastic, worldlywise 12 matter-of-fact, stony-

hearted, unidealistic **13** sophisticated, unsympathetic

harden
3 dry, set **4** cake, firm **5** adapt, enure, inure, steel **6** adjust, anneal, callus, freeze, ossify, season, temper **7** calcify, callous, compact, conform, congeal, densify, lithify, petrify, stiffen, toughen **8** accustom, concrete, indurate, sclerose, solidify **9** acclimate, climatize, fossilize, habituate **10** strengthen

hardfisted
4 mean **5** close, tight, tough **6** stingy, strong **7** save-all **9** niggardly **11** tough-minded **13** penny-pinching

hardheaded
5 sober **6** mulish **7** willful **8** perverse, stubborn **9** obstinate, practical, pragmatic, realistic **10** self-willed **11** down-to-earth, intractable, unfantastic **12** matter-of-fact, pertinacious, unidealistic

hardhearted
see **hard-boiled**

hardihood
3 pep **4** birr, grit, guts, sand, tuck **5** moxie, nerve, pluck, vigor **6** energy **7** potency **8** audacity, boldness, temerity **9** assurance, brashness, cockiness, fortitude, impudence, insolence, insolency **10** brazenness, disrespect, robustness

hardly ever
6 little, rarely, seldom **7** unoften **12** infrequently, unfrequently

hardness
5 rigor **8** adamancy, asperity, obduracy, severity **9** callosity **10** difficulty, inclemency

hardscrabble
6 barren **8** marginal **9** infertile, unbearing, unfertile **12** impoverished, unproductive

hardship
4 toil **5** peril, rigor, trial **6** danger, hazard **7** travail **8** asperity, distress, drudgery **9** adversity, mischance, privation, suffering **10** affliction, difficulty, discomfort, misfortune **11** tribulation

Hard Times author
7 Dickens (Charles)

hardy
4 bold **5** brave, tough **6** brazen, daring, robust, rugged, strong **8** resolute **9** audacious

Hardy
character: **3** Sue **4** Alec, Clym, Jude, Tess **5** Angel **8** Arabella, Eustacia, Henchard
setting: **6** Wessex

hare
3 wat **4** fool **6** rabbit **7** leporid **8** leporine
Belgian: **8** leporide
combining form: **3** lag **4** lago
female: **3** doe
genus: **5** Lepus
male: **4** buck
relating to: **7** leporid **8** leporine
young: **7** leveret

harebrained
5 balmy, crazy, dizzy, giddy, loony, silly, wacky **6** absurd, insane **7** flighty, foolish **8** skittish **9** frivolous **11** empty-headed **12** preposterous

harefooted
4 fast **5** fleet, hasty, quick, rapid, swift **6** speedy **9** breakneck **10** expeditive **11** expeditious

harem
6 serail, zenana **8** seraglio
concubine: **3** oda **4** odah **7** odalisk **9** odalisque
room: **3** oda **4** odah

Hareph's father
5 Caleb

Harhaiah's son
6 Uzziel

hark
4 hear, heed, mind, note **6** attend, listen, notice

harlequin
4 zany **5** clown **6** mottle **7** buffoon

Harlequin
beloved: **9** Columbine
rival: **7** Pierrot

harm
3 mar, sap **4** hurt, ruin **5** abuse, spoil **6** damage, ill-use, impair, injure, injury, misuse, molest **7** blemish, marring, outrage, tarnish, vitiate **8** maltreat, mischief, mistreat, sabotage **9** incommode, mischance, prejudice, undermine **10** dilapidate, discommode, disservice, impairment, misfortune **11** banefulness, noxiousness

harmful
3 bad, ill **4** evil **5** risky, toxic **6** malign, nocent, unsafe **7** baleful, baneful, hurtful, malefic, nocuous, noisome, noxious **8** damaging **9** dangerous, hazardous, injurious,

malignant, unhealthy **10** pernicious **11** deleterious, detrimental, mischievous, prejudicial, troublesome, unhealthful, unwholesome **12** insalubrious

harmless
4 safe **6** unhurt **8** innocent, nontoxic **9** innocuous, innoxious **11** inobnoxious, inoffensive, unoffending, unoffensive

Harmonia
daughter: **3** Ino **5** Agave **6** Semele **7** Autonoe
father: **4** Ares, Mars
husband: **6** Cadmus
mother: **5** Venus **9** Aphrodite
son: **9** Polydorus

harmonious
4 calm **5** sweet **6** amical, dulcet, irenic **7** chiming, chordal, musical, pacific, silvery, tuneful **8** amicable, blending, canorous, coactive, empathic, friendly, peaceful, pleasing, sonorous **9** accordant, agreeable, congenial, congruous, consonant, simpatico, symphonic **10** compatible, concinnate, concordant, empathetic, polyphonic, satisfying **11** cooperative, mellifluous, mellisonant, symmetrical, sympathetic **12** contrapuntal

harmonize
2 go **3** fit **4** jibe, tune **5** adapt, agree, blend, coapt, fit in, match, tally, unify, unite **6** accord, adjust, attune, concur, relate, square **7** arrange, concert, concord, conform **8** coincide, dovetail **9** cooperate, correlate, integrate, reconcile **10** coordinate, correspond, proportion, synthesize **11** accommodate, orchestrate **12** reconciliate

harmony
4 tune **5** chime, grace, peace, unity **6** accord, chorus, melody, unison **7** balance, concert, concord, dignity, empathy, kinship, oneness, rapport **8** affinity, diapason, elegance, sonority, symmetry **9** agreement, congruity, integrity, polyphony **10** accordance, coaptation, concinnity, conformity, consonance, musicality, proportion **11** concordance, concurrence, conformance, consistency, integration, tunefulness **12** articulation, togetherness
lack of: **7** discord
of movement: **8** eurythmy

Harnepher's father
6 Zophah

harness
4 gear, leaf, yoke **5** armor, hitch
6 couple, tackle **7** utilize **8** clothing
9 equipment
part: **3** bit **4** rein **5** girth, trace
6 collar **7** blinder, crupper **9** belly-
band, breeching, checkrein
12 breast collar
ring: **6** terret, territ

harp
4 lyre **9** harmonica
Irish: **8** clarsach

harpsichord
7 cembalo **8** clavecin

harpsichordist
American: **6** Fuller (Albert, David),
Kipnis (Igor), Newman (Anthony)
7 Marlowe (Sylvia), Pinkham (Dan-
iel), Valenti (Fernando) **11** Kirkpa-
trick (Ralph)
English: **7** Malcolm (George)
German: **7** Richter (Karl) **9** Leonhardt
(Gustav)
Italian: **7** Sgrizzi (Luciano)
Polish: **9** Landowska (Wanda)

harpy
5 leech, scold, shrew, vixen **6** amazon, ogress, virago **8** fishwife,
swindler **9** termagant, Xanthippe

Harpy
5 Aello **7** Celaeno, Ocypete
father: **7** Thaumas
mother: **7** Electra
sister: **4** Iris

harrier
3 dog **4** hawk **5** bully **6** hector,
runner **8** harasser **9** bulldozer
10 browbeater **11** intimidator

harrow
3 try **4** bait, fret, rack **5** devil,
tease, wring **6** badger, heckle, hector, martyr, needle, pester **7** afflict,
agonize, bedevil, crucify, torment,
torture **8** irritate **9** tantalize
10 excruciate

harry
3 irk **4** gnaw, raid, sack **5** annoy,
foray, havoc, tease, upset, worry
6 attack, badger, harass, maraud,
pester, plague, ravage, worrit **7** assault, bedevil, despoil, disturb, hagride, perturb, pillage, torment
8 desolate, irritate, spoliate, vexation **9** beleaguer, depredate

harsh
3 dry, raw **4** dour, grim, sour, tart
5 acerb, acrid, bleak, crude, cruel,
gruff, loose, rough, rusty, sharp,
stark, stern, tangy **6** biting, bitter,
brassy, brutal, coarse, craggy,
gruffy, hoarse, jagged, rugged, severe, shaggy, shrill, uneven **7** acerbic, austere, blaring, bristly, burning, grating, jarring, mordant,
pungent, rasping, raucous,
scraggy, squawky, squeaky, stubbly, uncomfy, unlevel **8** asperous,
exacting, granular, grinding, jangling, piercing, rigorous, scabrous,
scraggly, scraping, scratchy, strident, unsmooth **9** amaroidal, dissonant, inclement, stringent, unmusical **10** astringent, discordant,
irritating, stridulent, stridulous

hart
4 stag **7** red deer
mate: **4** hind

Hart, Moss
autobiography: **6** Act One
collaborator: **7** Kaufman (George S.)

hartebeest
4 tora **5** bubal **6** lelwel **7** bubalis
8 antelope
family: **7** Bovidae

Hartford
college: **7** Trinity
economic activity: **9** insurance

Harumaph's son
7 Jedaiah

Harum's son
7 Aharhel

haruspex
5 augur **7** prophet **8** foreseer
9 predictor **10** forecaster, foreteller,
prophesier, soothsayer **11** Nostradamus

harvest
2 in **3** bin **4** crop, hide, reap
5 amass, cache, hoard, stash, yield
6 garner, gather **7** bearing, collect,
reaping, store up, storing, vintage
8 assemble, cropping, fruitage, ingather, squirrel, stow away **9** gar-
nering, gathering **10** accumulate
bug: **4** mite **7** chigger
fly: **6** cicada
former festival: **6** Lammas
goddess: **3** Ops

harvester
grain: **6** header
of grapes: **8** vintager

Harvey
5 pooka **6** rabbit
author: **5** Chase (Mary)

Hasadiah's father
10 Zerubbabel

hash
4 chop, mess, mull, muss, stew
5 botch, mince, mix-up **6** jumble,
jungle, litter, medley, mess-up, muddle, review, tumble **7** clutter, mélange, mixture, rummage **8** botchery, consider, scramble, shambles
9 patchwork, talk about **10** assortment, hodgepodge, miscellany
11 gallimaufry

Hashabiah's father
6 Kemuel **8** Jeduthun

Hashabniah's son
7 Hattush

hashish
5 bhang, ganja **6** charas **8** cannabis, narcotic
plant: **4** hemp

Hashubah's father
10 Zerubbabel

hasp
6 fasten **8** fastener

Hassenuah's son
8 Hodaviah

hassle
3 row, try **4** beef, miff, spar, to-do
5 argue, brawl, cavil, essay, fight,
run-in, trial, whirl **6** argufy, bicker,
clamor, hubbub, pother, tumult, uproar **7** attempt, dispute, quarrel,
quibble, rhubarb, turmoil, wrangle
8 endeavor, squabble, striving,
struggle **9** bickering, commotion
10 hurly-burly **11** altercation,
controversy

hassock
4 gadi, pouf **5** gaddi **7** cushion,
ottoman **9** footstool

haste
3 run **4** dash, pace, rush **5** drive,
hurry, speed **6** barrel, bucket, bustle, flurry, hustle, rocket, rustle
7 beeline, hotfoot **8** celerity, dispatch, fastness, highball, rapidity,
velocity **9** fleetness, quickness, swiftness **10** expedition, nimbleness,
speediness **11** hurriedness, impetuosity **12** precipitance, precipitancy
13 impetuousness, impulsiveness,
precipitation

hasten
3 fly, run **4** flit, rush **5** fleet, hurry,
speed **6** barrel, hustle, step up,
urge on **7** hotfoot, quicken, shake
up, speed up, swiften
10 accelerate

hasty
4 fast, rash **5** agile, brash, brisk,
eager, fleet, quick, rapid, swift
6 abrupt, brashy, madcap, nimble,
speedy, sudden **7** cursory, hurried,
rushing **8** headlong, reckless, slam-

bang, slapdash **9** breakneck, hot-headed, impatient, impetuous, irritable, quickened **10** expeditive, harefooted, ill-advised, incautious, mad-brained **11** expeditious, precipitant, precipitate, precipitous, subitaneous, thoughtless

hat

5 derby, tuque **6** cloche, fedora, panama, topper **7** bicorne, chapeau, haircap, homburg, porkpie, stetson, tricorn **8** sombrero, tricorne **9** headpiece **11** chapeau bras
ancient Greek: **7** petasus
brimless: **7** pillbox
close-fitting: **5** toque, tuque **6** toquet, turban
cone-shaped: **3** fez
felt: **5** derby **6** bowler, trilby
fur: **5** busby
helmetlike: **4** topi **5** topee
lightweight: **6** panama
maker: **8** milliner
military: **5** shako **6** shacko
Muslim: **6** turban **7** tarbush **8** tarboosh
Near East: **3** fez
sheepskin: **6** calpac, kalpak **7** calpack
soft: **5** toque
straw: **6** boater, panama, sailor **7** bangkok **8** sombrero
sun: **5** terai
tall: **9** stovepipe
wide-brimmed: **9** sou'wester **11** southwester
woman's: **4** coif **5** beret

hatch

4 door, line, make, sire **5** breed, brood, cause, cover, frame, get up, spawn **6** cook up, create, devise, father, induce, invent, make up, parent, stroke, vamp up, work up **7** concoct, dream up, produce, provoke **8** contrive, engender, generate, incubate, occasion **9** floodgate, formulate, originate, procreate **11** compartment

hatchet

8 dispatch, tomahawk

hatchet man

3 gun **6** critic, killer **7** torpedo **8** assassin **9** cutthroat **10** highbinder

hate

5 abhor, gripe, scorn, spite **6** animus, bother, detest, horror, loathe, rancor, resent **7** bugbear, contemn, despise, disdain, disgust, dislike, ill will, trouble **8** anathema, aversion, distaste, execrate, irritant, loathing,

nuisance **9** animosity, antipathy, bête noire, deprecate, grievance, hostility, repulsion, revulsion **10** abhorrence, black beast, disapprove, repugnance **11** abomination, detestation

hateful

4 evil, foul, mean, vile **5** catty, nasty **6** bitchy, bitter, horrid, malign, odious, scurvy **7** vicious **8** accursed, annoying, damnable, infamous **9** abhorrent, execrable, malicious, obnoxious, repellent, repulsive, resentful **10** abominable, despicable, despiteful, detestable, ill-natured, malevolent **11** acrimonious, blasphemous, distasteful, distressing, opprobrious, uncongenial, unspeakable **12** contemptible **13** reprehensible

Hatfield vs. ___

5 McCoy

Hathath's father

7 Othniel

hatred

5 odium, spite **6** animus, enmity, rancor **7** dislike **8** aversion, loathing **9** animosity, antipathy, hostility, repulsion, revulsion **10** abhorrence, repugnance **11** abomination, detestation, malevolence
combining form: **3** mis **4** miso
of mankind: **11** misanthropy
of marriage: **8** misogamy
of women: **8** misogyny

hats

9 millinery

Hattush's father

8 Shemaiah **10** Hashabniah

hauberk

5 armor **9** chain mail, habergeon

haughtiness

5 pride **6** morgue **7** disdain, hauteur **9** arrogance, insolence, superbity

haughty

5 aloof, lofty, proud **6** lordly, sniffy **7** distant **8** arrogant, cavalier, detached, insolent, parvenue, reserved, scornful, sniffish, superior, toplofty **9** egotistic **10** disdainful **11** indifferent, overbearing **12** contemptuous, supercilious

haul

2 go **3** lug, tow, tug **4** cart, come, drag, draw, lift, load, move, pull, take **5** boost, cargo, hoist, raise, shift **6** burden, lading, remove **7** elevate, freight, payload
with a tackle: **5** bouse, bowse

haul up

4 stop **5** hoise, hoist
with a rope: **5** trice

haunches

4 beam, rump, tail **7** hind end, hunkers, rear end **8** backside, buttocks **9** fundament, posterior

haunt

4 home, howf, site **5** ghost, howff, range, shade **6** affect, linger, molest, resort, shadow, spirit, wraith **7** habitat, hang out, phantom, purlieu, specter, trouble **8** frequent, locality, phantasm **10** apparition, hang around, rendezvous **12** watering hole

haunter

7 denizen, habitué **10** frequenter

hautbois

4 oboe

hauteur

see **haughtiness**

haut monde

5 elite **6** gentry **7** quality, society, who's who **8** optimacy **9** blue blood **10** patriciate **11** aristocracy **13** carriage trade

have

3 buy, eat, fix, get, let, own, see, sop, use, win **4** bear, fool, gain, hire, hold, keep, know, land, lead, must, need, pass, show, take, undo, wear **5** admit, allow, annex, beget, bribe, carry, cheat, drink, enjoy, grasp, leave, smoke, trick **6** accept, buy off, convey, defeat, embody, fathom, obtain, outfox, outwit, permit, pick up, retain, square, suborn, suffer, take in **7** achieve, acquire, carry on, chalk up, cherish, cognize, compass, compose, contain, control, embrace, execute, exhibit, include, involve, outplay, perform, possess, procure, receive, subsume, support, sustain, undergo **8** comprise, dominate, engage in, exercise, manifest, outreach, outslick, outsmart **9** apprehend, bamboozle, encompass, outjockey, overreach, partake of **10** appreciate, categorize, comprehend, experience

haven

4 port, roof **5** cover, house, roads **6** asylum, covert, harbor, refuge, riding, shield **7** chamber, retreat, shelter **9** anchorage, harborage, roadstead, sanctuary

haversack

3 bag **4** case **8** backpack

havoc

4 loss, ruin, sack **5** waste **6** ravage **7** despoil, destroy, pillage **8** calamity, desolate, lay waste, ravaging, spoliate **9** cataclysm, confusion, depredate, desecrate, devastate, pillaging, ruination, vandalism **10** despoiling **11** catastrophe, destruction, devastation

haw

4 tree, yard **5** berry, fruit, shrub

Hawaii

author: **8** Michener (James A.)
capital: **8** Honolulu
discoverer: **4** Cook (Captain James)
highest point: **8** Mauna Kea
island: **4** Maui, Oahu **5** Kauai, Lanai **6** Niihau **7** Molokai **9** Kahoolawe
nickname: **10** Aloha State
state bird: **4** nene
state flower: **11** red hibiscus

Hawaiian

dance: **4** hula
duck: **5** koloa
feast: **4** luau
food: **3** poi
god: **2** Ku **4** Kane, Lono **5** Wakea **7** Kanaloa
goddess: **4** Pele
goose: **4** nene
instrument: **3** uke **7** ukulele
lava: **2** aa
neckwear: **3** lei
nonnative: **8** malihini
resident: **8** kamaaina
thrush: **4** omao

hawk

4 vend **5** buteo **6** monger, osprey, peddle **7** goshawk, haggard **8** caracara, huckster, roughleg **9** accipiter
Hawaiian: **2** io
young: **4** eyas

hawker

6 coster, monger, pedlar, pedler, vendor **7** packman, peddler **8** falconer, pitchman

hawk-eyed

7 lyncean **12** sharp-sighted

Hawkeye State

4 Iowa

Hawthorne

birthplace: **5** Salem
novel: **13** The Marble Faun **16** The Scarlet Letter

hay-building machine

5 baler

Haydn oratorio

10 The Seasons **11** The Creation

hay fever

10 pollenosis, pollinosis
cause: **6** pollen **7** ragweed

haymaker

3 box **4** chop, cuff, poke, sock **5** clout, punch, smack **6** buffet

hayseed

see **hick**

haywire

4 amok **5** amuck, crazy **8** confused **10** broken-down, out of order

hazard

3 bet **4** luck, risk **5** peril, wager **6** chance, danger, gamble, menace **7** fortune, imperil, venture **8** accident, endanger, jeopardy

hazardous

5 hairy, risky **6** chancy, wicked **7** unsound **8** aleatory **9** dangerous, unhealthy

haze

3 dim, fog **4** film, mist, murk, smog **5** befog, bloom, brume, cloud, dream, fog up, smoke, vapor **6** stupor, trance **7** becloud, obscure, reverie **8** overcast **9** mistiness, murkiness, overcloud, smokiness **10** bemusement, cloudiness, muddlement **11** muddledness **12** befuddlement

hazel

3 nut **6** muffin **7** filbert **8** noisette

Hazo

father: **5** Nahor
mother: **6** Milcah

hazy

3 dim **5** filmy, foggy, misty, murky, mushy, smoky, vague **6** cloudy, dreamy, vapory **7** bemused, blurred, clouded, nebular, obscure, tranced, unclear **8** nebulous, vaporous **9** stuporous, uncertain **10** indefinite, indistinct

head

2 go **3** aim, top, wit **4** arch, bent, bill, boss, bump, cape, cast, cock, flow, gift, john, make, mind, naze, neck, pate, poll, rise, stem, text, turn **5** arise, brain, caput, chief, crown, first, flair, front, issue, knack, level, motif, point, poise, privy, scalp, skull, start, theme, topic, train **6** climax, crisis, direct, genius, honcho, johnny, leader, master, matter, mazard, motive, noddle, noggin, noodle, scolex,

sconce, set out, talent, toilet, zero in **7** address, aptness, cranium, emanate, faculty, incline, latrine, leading, premier, proceed, subject, surpass, take off **8** argument, brainpan, champion, coiffure, director, foreland, foremost, hierarch, lavatory, light out **9** capitulum, chieftain, decollate, dominator, originate, principal, strike out **10** decapitate, derive from, gray matter, guillotine, individual, promontory **11** convenience, water closet
area: **5** crown **6** temple
back part: **7** occiput
bone: **5** skull **7** cranium **8** parietal
combining form: **5** crani **6** cephal, cranio **7** cephalo **8** cephalic **9** cephalous
covering: **3** cap, hat **8** kerchief
flower: **6** arnica, button
monastery: **4** dean **5** abbot **8** superior
nunnery: **4** dame **6** abbess **8** superior
of hair: **6** fleece
relating to: **8** cephalic
shaving of: **7** tonsure
skin: **5** scalp
tapeworm's: **6** scolex
top: **4** pate **5** crown

headache

6 megrim **7** problem **8** migraine **11** cephalalgia

headband

7 bandeau
ancient Greek: **6** taenia **7** taeniae (plural)

headdress

bishop's: **5** miter, mitre
medieval: **5** barbe
military: **5** busby, shako **6** helmet
nobleman's: **7** coronet
prelate's: **9** zucchetto
priest's: **7** biretta
royal: **5** crown, tiara **6** diadem
Spanish women's: **8** mantilla
women's: **6** bonnet; (see also **hat**)

headland

4 beak, bill, cape, naze, ness **5** point **10** promontory

headline

6 banner **7** feature **8** screamer

headlong

4 rash **5** hasty **6** abrupt, daring, rashly, sudden **7** hurried, rushing **8** gadarene, reckless **9** daredevil, foolhardy, impetuous **10** heedlessly, recklessly **11** precipitant, precipitate, precipitous, subitaneous

headmaster
9 principal

headshaker
7 skeptic, zetetic 9 pessimist
10 Pyrrhonian, Pyrrhonist

head-shaped
7 globose 8 capitate

head start
4 draw, edge, odds 5 bulge 7 vantage 8 handicap 9 advantage, allowance

headstone
6 ledger 8 monument 11 grave marker

headstrong
6 mulish 7 willful 8 stubborn 9 obstinate 10 refractory, self-willed 11 stiff-necked

heady
4 rash 5 cagey, giddy, smart 6 argute, astute, clever, shrewd 7 violent, willful 9 astucious, impetuous, sagacious 11 exhilarated, intoxicated 12 intoxicating

heal
4 cure, mend, scab 6 cement, remedy

healer
combining form: 7 iatrist

healing
8 curative, remedial, sanative, sanatory 9 vulnerary, wholesome 11 restorative
combining form: 5 iatro, iatry 7 iatrics
goddess of: 3 Eir

health
7 stamina 8 euphoria, haleness, tonicity, vitality 9 soundness, well-being, wholeness
club: 3 spa

healthful
4 good 6 aiding 8 curative, hygienic, remedial, salutary, sanative 9 wholesome 10 beneficial, corrective, mitigative, profitable, salubrious 11 alleviative, restorative

healthy
3 fit 4 good, hale, iron, rosy, safe, sane, spry, well 5 agile, lusty, right, ruddy, sound, tough, whole 6 robust, rugged, strong, sturdy, vegete, viable 7 chipper, massive 8 blooming, hygienic, positive, rubicund, salutary, stalwart, thriving, vigorous 9 desirable, wholesome

10 beneficial, prosperous, salubrious, well-liking 11 flourishing, uninjurious
Scottish: 5 gawsy 6 gawsie

heap
3 lot 4 bank, cock, cord, dump, fill, gobs, hill, load, lump, mass, much, pack, pile, rick, scad 5 amass, bunch, choke, clump, crate, drift, group, loads, mound, shock, stack, wreck 6 barrel, charge, gather, jalopy, junker, lumber, oodles 7 clunker, collect, deposit, jillion, million 8 assemble, cumulate, mountain, slathers, thousand, trillion 9 congeries, gathering, great deal, stockpile 10 accumulate, cumulation, quantities
combining form: 5 cumul 6 cumuli, cumulo
combustible: 4 pyre
of dead bodies: 7 carnage

hearing
4 test 5 sound, trial 6 parley, tryout 7 earshot, meeting 8 audience, audition 9 interview 10 conference, discussion
combining form: 4 acou 5 acouo, audio 6 acusia 7 acousia
distance: 7 earshot

hearken
6 attend, listen

hearsay
3 cry 4 buzz, talk 5 on-dit, rumor 6 gossip, report, rumble 7 account 9 grapevine 11 scuttlebutt

heart
3 hub 4 core, guts, love, mood, pith, root, seat, soul, zest 5 ardor, bosom, focus, gusto, pluck, quick, spunk, taste 6 breast, center, mettle, palate, relish, spirit 7 courage 8 feelings, polestar 9 character 10 affections, compassion, conscience, enthusiasm, focal point
combining form: 5 cardi 6 cardia, cardio 7 cardium
contraction: 7 systole
dilation: 8 diastole
part: 6 atrium, septum 9 ventricle

heartache
3 rue, woe 4 care, pang 5 grief 6 regret, sorrow 7 anguish 10 affliction, cardialgia

heartbeat
5 pulse, throb 9 pulsation
irregular: 8 arythmia

heartbreak
3 rue, woe 4 bale, care 5 agony,

grief 6 regret, sorrow 7 anguish, torment 10 affliction

heartbreaking
4 dire 8 grievous 10 afflictive, calamitous, deplorable, lamentable 11 regrettable, unfortunate

heartburn
7 pyrosis 10 cardialgia

hearten
4 stir 5 cheer, nerve, rally, rouse, steel 6 arouse 7 animate, chirk up, enliven 8 energize, inspirit 9 encourage

heartfelt
4 deep, true 6 honest 7 earnest, genuine, sincere 8 bona fide, profound 9 unfeigned 11 wholesouled

heartleaf
6 ginger

heartless
5 cruel 7 callous 8 obdurate 9 unfeeling 10 hard-boiled 11 unemotional 13 unsympathetic

Heart of Dixie
7 Alabama

heartrending
see **heartbreaking**

heartsease
5 pansy, viola 6 violet 9 smartweed

heart-shaped
7 cordate

heartsick
4 blue, down 8 cast down, dejected, downcast 9 depressed 10 dispirited 12 disconsolate

heartthrob
4 love 5 flame, honey, sweet 7 beloved, darling, passion 10 sweetheart

heartwood
7 duramen

hearty
4 deep, warm 5 ample 6 jovial, sailor 7 profuse, sincere 8 abundant, profound, vehement 9 approving, exuberant, flavorful, unfeigned 10 full-bodied, responsive 11 whole-souled 12 enthusiastic

heat
3 hot 4 cook, move, warm 6 excite, simmer, warmth 7 caloric, convect, furnace, hotness, inflame 8 pyrolyze
combining form: 3 pyr 4 pyro 5 therm 6 calori, thermo, thermy 7 thermia

measuring device: 11 colorimeter, thermometer
quantity: 3 BTU

heated
3 hot, mad 4 warm, waxy 5 angry, fiery, irate, wroth 6 ardent, baking, fervid, fierce, hectic, ireful, steamy, wrathy 7 boiling, burning, fevered 8 broiling, feverish, scalding, sizzling, wrathful 9 indignant, scorching 11 acrimonious

heater
5 stove 7 furnace 8 radiator

heathbird
7 gray hen 9 blackcock 11 black grouse

heathen
5 pagan 6 ethnic 7 foreign, gentile, infidel, profane, strange 8 paganish, paganist 9 infidelic 10 unfamiliar

heat-producing
9 calorific

heave
3 gag 4 blow, cast, fire, gasp, huff, hurl, keck, pant, puff, rock, roll, toss 5 fling, labor, pitch, retch, sling, throw, vomit

heaven
3 God 4 Zion 5 bliss, glory 6 Canaan, utopia 7 arcadia, ecstasy, elysium, nirvana, rapture 8 empyrean, eternity, paradise, rhapsody 9 Cockaigne, hereafter, Shangri-la 10 afterworld, Civitas Dei, lubberland, wonderland 11 immortality, kingdom come 12 New Jerusalem, promised land 13 Abraham's bosom

heavenly
4 lush 5 yummy 6 divine, sacred 7 blessed, darling 8 adorable, empyreal, empyrean, luscious 9 ambrosial, celestial, delicious 10 delectable, delightful, enchanting 11 exceedingly, scrumptious

heavenly body
see **celestial body**

heavy
3 big, fat 4 deep, drab, dull, gone, hard, loud, rich 5 acute, bulky, dopey, grave, gross, hefty, inert, obese, steep, stout, tough 6 clayey, cloggy, cloudy, clumsy, coarse, drowsy, fleshy, gravid, leaden, occult, orphic, parous, portly, secret, severe, sleepy, stupid, torpid 7 arduous, awkward, doleful, intense, labored, louring, massive, porcine,

serious, unhandy, villain, weighty 8 abstruse, burdened, childing, comatose, cumbrous, enceinte, esoteric, grievous, hermetic, inactive, lowering, nubilous, overcast, pregnant, profound, sluggish, toilsome, unwieldy 9 corpulent, difficult, effortful, expectant, expecting, laborious, lethargic, lumbering, ponderous, recondite, strenuous 10 acroamatic, afflictive, burdensome, cumbersome, encumbered, formidable, lumbersome, oppressive, overweight, parturient, slumberous

combining form: 4 bary, hadr 5 gravi, hadro

heavy-handed
5 inept 6 gauche, wooden 7 awkward, halting, unhappy 8 bumbling 9 maladroit, ponderous 10 uninspired

heavyhearted
3 sad 5 sorry 7 unhappy 8 mournful, saddened 10 dispirited, melancholy

heavyset
5 dumpy, thick 6 chunky, squdgy, stocky, stubby, stumpy 11 thickbodied

heavyweight
3 VIP 4 lion 5 chief 6 big boy, leader 7 notable 8 big-timer

Hebe
father: 4 Zeus 7 Jupiter
husband: 8 Hercules
mother: 4 Hera, Juno
successor: 8 Ganymede

Heber
father: 6 Beriah
grandfather: 5 Asher
mother: 4 Jael

hebetude
4 coma 5 sleep 6 stupor, torpor 7 languor, slumber 8 dullness, lethargy 9 torpidity

hebetudinous
5 dopey, heavy 6 stupid, torpid 8 comatose, sluggish 9 lethargic

Hebrew
bushel: 4 epha 5 ephah
coin: 4 beka, gera, mina, mite 5 bekah, gerah, maneh 6 lepton, shekel
festival: 5 Pesah, Purim, Seder 6 Pesach, Succos, Sukkos 7 Hanukah, Sukkoth 8 Chanukah, Hanukhah, Hanukkah, Lag b'Omer, Passover, Shabuoth 9 Chanukhah, Chanukkah, Tishah-b'Ab, Yom Kippur

11 Rosh Hashana 12 Simhath Torah
God: 2 El 5 Eloah, Yahwe 6 Adonai, Elohim, Yahweh 7 Jehovah
instrument: 4 Asor 5 nabla, nebel
judge: 6 Gideon
lawgiver: 5 Moses
letter: (see at **alphabet**)
measure: 3 cor, hin, kab, log 4 bath, omer, seah, span 5 cubit, ephah, homer 6 finger 11 handbreadth
month: 2 Ab 4 Adar, Elul, Iyar 5 Nisan, Sivan, Tebet 6 Kislev, Shebat, Tammuz, Tishri 6 Veadar (in leap year) 7 Heshvan
patriarch: 3 Dan, Gad 4 Cain, Levi, Seth 5 Asher, David, Isaac, Jacob, Judah 6 Joseph, Reuben, Simeon 7 Abraham, Zebulun 8 Benjamin, Issachar, Naphtali
sacred city: 5 Safad, Safed 6 Hebron 8 Tiberias 9 Jerusalem; (see also **Jewish**)

Hebron's father
6 Kohath

Hecate
father: 6 Perses
mother: 7 Asteria

heckle
3 nag 4 bait, faze, gibe, ride 5 chivy, hound, tease, worry 6 badger, harass, hector, molest, needle, plague, rattle 7 torment 8 bullyrag

hectic
3 red 6 fervid 7 burning, fevered, flushed 8 feverish, habitual, restless 10 persistent

hector
3 cow 4 bait, ride 5 bully, chivy, hound 6 badger 7 dragoon, harrier, swagger 8 bludgeon, braggart, browbeat, bulldoze, bullyrag, harasser

Hector
brother: 5 Paris 7 Helenus, Troilus 9 Deiphobus, Polydorus
father: 5 Priam
mother: 6 Hecuba
sister: 6 Creusa 8 Polyxena 9 Cassandra
slayer: 8 Achilles
victim: 9 Patroclus
wife: 10 Andromache

Hecuba
daughter: 6 Creusa 8 Polyxena 9 Cassandra
father: 5 Dymas
husband: 5 Priam

son: 5 Paris 6 Hector 7 Helenus, Troilus 9 Deiphobus, Polydorus
victim: 11 Polymnestor

hedge

3 mew, pen 4 cage, coop, mure, trim 5 evade, fence, guard 6 corral, hinder, immure, weasel 7 enclose, protect, shuffle 8 encircle, restrict, roadside, sidestep

hedonist

4 rake 7 epicure, gourmet 8 gourmand, sybarite 9 bon vivant, debauchee, epicurean, libertine 10 voluptuary

heebie-jeebies

5 jumps 6 dither, shakes 7 jitters, shivers

heed

3 see 4 care, hark, mark, mind, note, obey 5 study, watch 6 attend, beware, debate, listen, notice, regard, remark 7 concern, hearing, hearken, observe, respect 8 audience, consider, interest 9 attention, awareness 10 cognizance, observance 11 application, carefulness, mindfulness

heedful

5 alert, exact, fussy 6 arrect 7 careful 8 punctual 9 advertent, attentive, intentive, observant, observing 10 meticulous, scrupulous, thoughtful 11 observative, painstaking, punctilious 12 conscionable 13 conscientious

heedless

8 uncaring 9 oblivious, unmindful, unrecking 10 unthinking 11 inadvertent, inattentive, unobservant 12 unreflective

heedlessness

6 apathy 8 lethargy 9 disregard, lassitude, unconcern 11 disinterest, insouciance 12 indifference

hee-haw

4 bray 5 laugh 6 giggle, guffaw, titter 7 chortle, chuckle, snicker

heel

3 run, tip 4 cant, hock, lean, list, rest, tilt 5 knave, rogue, slant, slope 6 rascal 7 balance, incline, lowlife, recline, remains, remanet, remnant, residue, villain 8 leavings, residual, residuum 9 miscreant, remainder, scoundrel 10 blackguard
bones: 8 calcanea, calcanei

heft

4 lift 5 hoist, raise, weigh 6 weight 9 heaviness

hefty

3 big 5 beefy, burly, husky, large, major 6 mighty, rugged 7 massive, sizable 8 abundant, imposing, powerful 9 extensive, good-sized, plentiful, ponderous

Heidi

author: 5 Spyri (Johanna)
setting: 4 Alps

height

4 apex, rise 6 climax, summit, zenith 7 stature 8 altitude, highness, pinnacle, tallness 9 elevation, loftiness
combining form: 3 acr, akr 4 acro, akro, hyps 5 hypsi, hypso

heighten

3 wax 4 lift, rise 5 boost, build, mount, raise, rouse 6 better, deepen, expand, extend 7 amplify, augment, elevate, enhance, enlarge, improve, magnify, sharpen, upsurge 8 compound, increase, multiply, redouble 9 aggravate, highlight, intensate, intensify 10 aggrandize

heinous

6 crying 8 shocking 9 desperate, execrable 10 abominable, outrageous

heinousness

8 atrocity, enormity

heir

3 son 5 heres 6 haeres 7 heredes (plural), heritor 8 haeredes (plural) 9 inheritor, successor
joint: 8 parcener

Hel, Hela

father: 4 Loki
hall: 7 Niflhel 8 Niflheim
mother: 9 Angerboda

Helah's husband

5 Ashur 6 Ashhur

Heleb's father

6 Baanah

Helek's father

6 Gilead

Helenus

brother: 5 Paris 6 Hector 7 Troilus 9 Deiphobus, Polydorus
father: 5 Priam
mother: 6 Hecuba
sister: 6 Creusa 8 Polyxena 9 Cassandra
wife: 10 Andromache

helical

6 spiral

helicopter

7 chopper 10 whirlybird
armed: 7 gunship

Helios

6 Apollo
daughter: 5 Circe 8 Pasiphae
father: 8 Hyperion
mother: 5 Theia
sister: 3 Eos 6 Aurora, Selene
son: 8 Phaethon

heliotrope

10 bloodstone

Heli's daughter

4 Mary

helium

symbol: 2 He

hell

see **hades**

Hellen

father: 9 Deucalion
mother: 6 Pyrrha
son: 5 Dorus 6 Aeolus, Xuthus

hellhole

8 dystopia

hellish

7 avernal, stygian 8 infernal, plutonic 9 cimmerian, plutonian 11 pandemoniac

helm

5 steer

helmet

3 cap 5 salet 6 barbut, casque, morion, salade, sallet 7 morrion 8 burgonet, headgear
medieval: 5 armet 6 heaume, sallet 7 basinet
part: 7 ventail 8 aventail
sun: 4 topi 5 topee

helmet-shaped

7 galeate

Heloise

husband: 7 Abelard
son: 9 Astrolabe

Helon's son

5 Eliab

helotry

4 yoke 6 thrall 7 bondage, peonage, serfdom 9 servitude, thralldom, villenage 11 enslavement

help

3 aid, use 4 abet, ally, back, cure, hand, lift, mend 5 amend, avail, avoid, boost, do for, serve, stead 6 assist, better, fail in, profit, relief, remedy, second, succor, uphold

7 advance, ancilla, benefit, bestead, bolster, comfort, forward, further, improve, prevent, promote, relieve, secours, service, striker, support 8 befriend, benefact, champion, minister, mitigate, palliate 9 alleviate, assistant, attendant, extricate, meliorate 10 ameliorate, assistance, facilitate 11 cooperation
forward: 7 further
hired: 5 labor

helper
3 aid 4 aide 6 deputy, server 7 ancilla, servant 8 employee 9 assistant, associate, attendant, auxiliary 10 apprentice, benefactor 11 subordinate

helpful
4 good 5 brave 6 aidant, aidful, aiding, toward, usable 7 benefic 8 favoring, salutary 9 assistive, effective, favorable, practical 10 beneficial, profitable, propitious 11 encouraging, serviceable 12 advantageous, constructive

helping
7 portion 8 friendly 9 auxiliary

helpless
4 weak 6 feeble, futile 7 forlorn 8 desolate, forsaken, impotent 9 abandoned 10 bewildered 11 unprotected

helter-skelter
6 anyhow, around, random 7 anywise, flighty, hotfoot, turmoil 8 at random, pellmell, randomly 9 haphazard, hit-or-miss 11 any which way, haphazardly, hurry-scurry, impetuously, precipitate

helve
4 haft 6 handle

Helvetian
5 Swiss

hem
3 pen, rim 4 brim, cage, edge, gird, ring, seam, shut 5 beset, bound, brink, fence, hedge, round, skirt, verge 6 begird, border, circle, corral, define, edging, fringe, girdle, immure, margin, stitch 7 close in, enclose, envelop, selvage, shorten 8 encircle, surround 9 encompass, perimeter, periphery
turned-back: 4 cuff

Hemam's father
5 Lotan

Heman
father: 4 Joel
grandfather: 6 Samuel

hematite
3 ore 10 bloodstone 12 black diamond

Hemdam's father
6 Dishon

Hemingway work
9 In Our Time 14 A Moveable Feast 15 A Farewell to Arms, The Sun Also Rises 16 To Have and Have Not 18 Islands in the Stream, The Old Man and the Sea 19 For Whom the Bell Tolls 21 The Snows of Kilimanjaro

hemlock
4 herb, tree 6 conium

hemophiliac
7 bleeder

hemp
3 kef, kif 4 kaif, keef, kief 8 cannabis
fiber: 5 oakum
kind: 4 aloe

hemplike
4 towy

hen
broody: 6 sitter
coop: 5 cavie
spayed: 7 poulard 8 poularde
young: 6 pullet

hence
2 so 4 away, ergo, thus 5 since 9 therefore, thereupon 11 accordingly 12 consequently

henceforth
9 from now on, hereafter

henceforward
see **henceforth**

henchman
6 cohort, lackey, minion, stooge 7 sectary 8 adherent, disciple, follower, partisan, retainer, sectator 9 attendant, supporter

Hengist
brother: 5 Horsa
kingdom: 4 Kent
people: 5 Jutes

Henley poem
8 Invictus

henpeck
3 nag 4 fuss 6 carp at

henpecked
8 uxorious

Henry II
adversary: 6 Becket (Thomas à)
son: 7 Richard

surname: 5 Anjou 11 Plantagenet
wife: 7 Eleanor

Henry IV
surname: 9 Lancaster
victim: 7 Richard

Henry VIII
daughter: 9 Elizabeth
son: 6 Edward
surname: 5 Tudor
victim: 4 Anne 9 Catherine 10 Thomas More
wife: 4 Anne, Jane 9 Catherine

Hen's father
9 Zephaniah

hepatic, hepatica
9 liverwort

Hephaestus
6 Vulcan
father: 4 Zeus 7 Jupiter
mother: 4 Hera, Juno
wife: 6 Charis

Hepher's father
5 Ashur 6 Ashhur, Gilead

Hephzibah
husband: 8 Hezekiah
son: 8 Manasseh

Hera
4 Juno
father: 6 Cronus, Saturn
husband: 4 Zeus 7 Jupiter
messenger: 4 Iris
mother: 4 Rhea

Heracles, Hercules
beloved: 4 Iole
brother: 8 Iphicles
charioteer: 6 Iolaus
father: 4 Zeus 7 Jupiter
mother: 7 Alcmene
son: 6 Hyllus
victim: 5 Hydra, Ladon 6 Geryon, Megara, Orthus 10 Nemean lion
wife: 4 Hebe 6 Megara 8 Deianira

herald
4 hail, tout 5 crier, greet 6 signal 7 courier, forerun, precede, presage, trumpet 8 announce, ballyhoo, foreshow, outrider 9 announcer, harbinger, messenger, precursor, publicize, spokesman 10 forerunner, foreshadow 11 preindicate

heraldic
animal: 7 gardant
border: 4 orle
cross: 6 fitchy, fleury, formée 7 fitchée 8 fourchée
design: 5 giron, gyron 6 manche

7 saltier, saltire, sautoir **8** sautoire, tressour, tressure
term: **4** ente, paty, pily **6** pattée **7** passant

heraldry

6 armory **9** pageantry
term: **4** vert **6** moline, pommée, sejant **7** nombril, purpure, sejeant, statant

herb

4 forb, leek, mint, sage, wort
5 chive **6** allium, endive, garlic, pusley, pussly **7** campion, caraway, comfrey, gerbera, puccoon, pussley, spinach, spinage, tobacco **8** angelica, brassica, cilantro, costmary, deerweed, erigeron, gerardia, gromwell, hawkweed, marjoram, plantain, polygony, purslane, tithonia **9** buckwheat, clintonia, nemophila
African: **7** freesia, tritoma
annual: **4** dill, flax, okra **5** blite **6** crambe **7** bugseed, clarkia, clivers, sandbur, tampala, waxweed **8** euphrasy, sandburr, tidytips **9** bush basil **10** calliopsis
aquatic: **6** elodea **7** nelumbo **8** hornwort
aromatic: **4** nard **5** basil, clary, thyme **6** catnip **7** catmint, chervil, monarda, oregano **8** origanum, woodruff **9** spikenard
Asian: **7** perilla, skirret **8** chickpea
biennial: **11** blazing star
bitter: **9** chamomile
bulb: **5** onion
composite: **8** knapweed **9** centaurea **10** bitterweed **11** bur marigold
cultivated: **7** parsley
East Indian: **8** pachouli, turmeric **9** patchouli, patchouly
Eurasian: **6** mullen, squill **7** mullein
European: **5** paris **6** axseed, betony **7** parsnip, salsify **8** earthnut, fleawort, lungwort, mandrake, oxtongue, rapeseed, samphire, snowdrop, wormwood **9** birthwort **13** Christmas rose
evergreen: **5** galax
fragrant: **6** cicely **7** pinesap **10** basil thyme **12** balm of Gilead
garlic: **6** ramson
genus: **7** solanum
Japanese: **3** udo
leafless: **9** broomrape
marjoram: **6** origan
medicinal: **6** borage, eringo, eryngo, hyssop **7** allheal, sanicle **8** blueball, camomile, centaury **9** chamomile
Mexican: **4** chia **8** tuberose

mythical: **4** moly
ornamental: **8** dianthus
perennial: **4** geum, sego **5** avens, camas, orpin, tansy **6** arnica, asarum, bennet, burnet, camass, fennel, henbit, lovage, madder, orpine, pyrola, yarrow **7** bistort, boneset, bugbane, chicory, cicoree, cudweed, dittany, dogbane, genseng, ginseng, jonquil, milfoil, pinweed, primula, quamash, redroot, rhubarb, shortia, succory, witloof **8** agrimony, boltonia, calamint, chiccory, dicentra, dropwort, eggplant, eremurus, feverfew, finochio, fireweed, gaywings, harebell, hepatica, honewort, licorice, mayapple, nutgrass, nutsedge, pokeroot, pokeweed, primrose, roseroot, sainfoin, selfheal, shinleaf, soapwort, stokesia, tarragon, toadflax, valerian **9** bloodwort, finocchio, squawroot
poisonous: **6** conium **7** aconite, hemlock, henbane **8** veratrum
prickly: **8** acanthus
purple: **12** checkerbloom
Rocky mountain: **10** bitterroot
salad: **7** lettuce
seaside: **8** saltwort
small-flowered: **11** baby's breath
South African: **12** Cape marigold
South American: **3** oca
summer-blooming: **11** bunchflower
tall: **4** hemp
tropical: **6** crinum **7** begonia, episcia, petunia **8** abelmosk, capsicum, cardamom, cardamon, cardamum
twining: **8** lovevine
weedy: **7** ragweed
wild garlic: **4** moly
woody: **8** bedstraw
yellow: **9** celandine
yellow-rayed: **9** calendula

herbicide

6 diquat, diuron **7** dalapon, monuron **8** picloram, simazine

Herculean

4 huge, vast **5** giant **7** immense, mammoth, titanic **8** colossal, enormous, gigantic **10** superhuman

Hercules

see **Heracles**

herd

3 mob, run **4** lead **5** drive, drove, flock **6** gather **9** associate
sheep: **6** hirsel

here and there

6 passim **7** at times **9** sometimes **11** irregularly

hereditary

9 ancestral

heredity unit

4 gene

heresy

5 error **6** schism **7** dissent, fallacy, impiety **9** defection, misbelief **10** dissidence, heterodoxy, infidelity, radicalism **11** revisionism, unorthodoxy **13** nonconformism, nonconformity

heretic

7 infidel, sectary **8** apostate, defector, recreant, recusant, renegade **9** dissenter, dissident, innovator **10** iconoclast, schismatic, separatist, unbeliever **11** misbeliever, revisionist, schismatist **12** deviationist **13** nonconformist

heretical

7 infidel **8** apostate **9** differing, dissident, heterodox, miscreant, sectarian **10** dissenting, dissentive, schismatic, unorthodox **11** disagreeing, dissentient, revisionist, unbelieving **12** misbelieving **13** nonconformist

heritage

6 legacy **9** patrimony, tradition **10** birthright

Hermes

7 Mercury
attribute: **7** petasos, petasus, talaria **8** caduceus
father: **4** Zeus **7** Jupiter
mother: **4** Maia
winged cap: **7** petasos, petasus
winged shoes: **7** talaria

hermetic

4 deep **5** heavy **6** occult, secret **7** recluse, secluse **8** abstruse, airtight, profound, secluded **9** alchemist, recondite, seclusive **10** cloistered **11** sequestered

Hermia

beloved: **8** Lysander
father: **5** Egeus

Hermione

father: **8** Menelaus
husband: **7** Orestes, Pyrrhus **11** Neoptolemus
mother: **5** Helen

hermit

5 loner **7** eremite, recluse **8** solitary **9** anchorite

hermitage

8 hideaway **9** monastery

hernia

6 breach **7** rupture **10** protrusion
combining form: **4** cele

of the bladder: **9** cystocele
support: **5** truss
type: **6** cystic, hiatal **7** femoral **9** umbilical **10** incisional

hero
6 knight **7** demigod, paladin **8** champion **11** protagonist
American: **6** Bunyan (Paul) **8** Superman
Babylonian: **9** Gilgamesh
Celtic-French: **7** Tristam, Tristan **8** Tristram
Crusades: **7** Tancred **8** Tancredi
English: **6** Arthur **7** Beowulf **9** Robin Hood
French: **6** Roland **11** Charlemagne
German: **5** Etzel **9** Siegfried
Greek: **4** Ajax **5** Jason **7** Perseus, Ulysses **8** Achilles, Heracles, Hercules, Odysseus
Hebrew: **5** David **6** Samson
Irish: **9** Cuchullin **10** Cuchullain
Italian: **7** Orlando
Roman: **7** Romulus **8** Horatius
Scandinavian: **6** Sigurd
Scottish: **5** Bruce (Robert) **6** Rob Roy
Spanish: **5** El Cid
Spartan: **8** Leonidas
Trojan: **6** Aeneas, Hector

Herod
daughter: **6** Salome
father: **7** Antipas **9** Antipater
kingdom: **5** Judea **6** Judaea
mother: **6** Cyprus
son: **5** Herod (Antipas) **6** Joseph **7** Pheroas **9** Phasaelus

Herodias
daughter: **6** Salome
father: **11** Aristobulus
husband: **5** Herod (Antipas)

heroic
4 bold, huge **5** brave **6** mighty **7** extreme, radical, valiant **8** colossal, enormous, fearless, gigantic, intrepid, unafraid, valorous **9** cyclopean, dauntless, Herculean, undaunted **10** courageous

heroin
4 skag **5** horse, smack **8** narcotic **11** diamorphine

heroism
5 valor **6** spirit **7** bravery, courage, prowess **8** boldness, chivalry, nobility, valiance, valiancy **9** gallantry **11** intrepidity **12** fearlessness, valorousness

Hero's love
7 Leander

herring
8 brisling

smoked: **7** bloater
young: **4** brit **5** britt

Herse
father: **7** Cecrops
sister: **8** Aglauros
son: **8** Cephalus

Hersey
novel: **7** The Wall **13** A Bell for Adano
town: **5** Adano

Hesione
brother: **5** Priam
father: **8** Laomedon
husband: **7** Telamon
rescuer: **8** Heracles, Hercules
son: **6** Teucer

hesitant
3 shy **5** chary, loath **6** afraid, averse, wobbly **7** halting, uneager **8** backward **9** faltering, tentative, uncertain, unwilling **10** indisposed, irresolute **11** disinclined, vacillating, vacillatory **12** wiggle-waggle

hesitate
4 balk, halt **5** delay, demur, pause, stall, stick, swing, waver **6** boggle, dawdle, dither, falter, mammer **7** scruple, stagger, stammer, stickle, stutter, whiffle **8** hang back **9** temporize **10** dillydally **12** shilly-shally, wiggle-waggle **13** procrastinate

Hesperia
5 Italy, Spain **9** butterfly

Hesperides
5 Aegle **8** Erytheia, Hesperis

Hesperus
5 Venus **11** evening star
father: **8** Astraeus
mother: **3** Eos

Hesse novel
6 Demian **11** Steppenwolf **12** Magister Ludi

Hestia
5 Vesta
father: **6** Cronus, Saturn
mother: **4** Rhea

heterodox
9 dissident, heretical, sectarian **10** schismatic **13** nonconformist

heterodoxy
6 heresy, schism **7** dissent **9** misbelief **10** dissidence **13** nonconformism, nonconformity

heterogeneous
5 mixed **6** motley, varied **8** assorted, chowchow **9** disparate **12** conglomerate

hew
3 cut **4** chop, fell **5** stick **6** adhere **7** conform, cut down

hex
3 hag **4** jinx **5** bruja, charm, lamia, queer, spell, witch **6** hoodoo, voodoo, whammy **7** bewitch, enchant **9** ensorcell, sorceress **10** Indian sign, witchwoman **11** enchantment, enchantress

heyday
4 acme **5** prime **6** spring

Hezekiah
father: **4** Ahaz **7** Neariah
mother: **3** Abi
son: **8** Manasseh
wife: **9** Hephzibah

Hezion
grandson: **8** Benhadad
son: **8** Tabrimon **9** Tabrimmon

Hezron's father
5 Perez **6** Pharez, Reuben

hiatus
3 gap **5** break **6** breech, lacuna **7** interim **8** aperture, interval **12** interruption

Hiawatha
author: **10** Longfellow (Henry Wadsworth)
grandmother: **7** Nokomis
mother: **7** Wenonah
tribe: **6** Ojibwa **7** Ojibway
wife: **9** Minnehaha

Hibernia
4 Eire, Erin **7** Ireland

hick
4 jake, rube **5** yokel **6** rustic **7** bucolic, bumpkin, country, hayseed **8** cornball, ruralist, ruralite **10** clodhopper, provincial

hick town
4 burg **6** Podunk **7** mudhole **11** whistlestop

hidden
5 privy **6** buried, covert, secret **7** guarded, obscure **8** obscured, shrouded, ulterior **9** concealed **11** undisclosed
combining form: **5** crypt, krypt **6** crypto, krypto

hide
3 fur **4** bury, coat, fell, flog, lash, life, lurk, mask, pelt, skin, veil, whip **5** cache, cloak, cover, inter, lodge, plant, shade, stash **6** entomb, harbor, jacket, lather, mantle, occult, screen, shield, shroud, stripe, thrash **7** conceal, cover up, curtain,

leather, obscure, retreat, scourge, seclude, secrete, shelter, veiling 8 ensconce 10 flagellate

combining form: 4 derm 5 derma 6 dermia, dermis 9 dermatous

hideaway
3 den 4 lair 6 refuge 7 retreat 8 secluded 9 concealed

hideous
4 ugly 5 lurid, nasty 6 grisly, horrid 7 ghastly, hateful, macabre 8 gruesome, horrible, shocking, terrible, uncomely 9 dismaying, frightful, loathsome, ludicrous, monstrous, offensive, repellent, repugnant, repulsive, revolting, unsightly 10 disgusting, horrifying, ill-favored, ill-looking, terrifying

hideout
3 den 4 lair 5 haven 6 covert, refuge 7 retreat, shelter 9 hermitage, sanctuary

hiding place
5 cache, cover 6 covert, refuge 7 retreat

hie
2 go 4 fare, pass, wend 6 hasten, push on, repair, travel 7 journey, proceed

hiemal
6 wintry

hierarch
4 boss, cock, head 5 chief 6 honcho, leader, master 7 headman 9 chieftain

hieratic
8 priestal, priestly 9 priestish 10 priestlike, sacerdotal 12 sacerdotical

high
3 big, gay 4 acme, dear, loud, olid, rank, rick, tall, thin 5 acute, doped, drunk, fetid, grand, grave, knoll, large, lofty, noble, sharp 6 aerial, argute, bright, costly, elated, florid, height, piping, putrid, raised, rancid, remote, richly, shrill, smelly, stoned, strong, treble, whiffy, zonked 7 ancient, drugged, eminent, extreme, intense, keyed up, reeking, serious, soaring, supreme, violent 8 abstruse, arrogant, cheerful, critical, edifying, elevated, eloquent, exciting, gigantic, hopped-up, long past, nidorous, piercing, powerful, stinking, towering, turned on, vehement, wrathful 9 ambitious, climactic, excellent, expensive, imperious, important, intensive, luxurious, prominent,

spaced-out 10 boisterous, malodorous, pronounced, tripped out 11 anti-cyclone, extravagant, intoxicated

combining form: 4 alti

high-and-mighty
5 proud 6 lordly 8 arrogant, cavalier, insolent, superior 9 imperious 10 disdainful 11 overbearing 12 supercilious

highball
3 fly, run 4 rush, whiz 5 hurry, speed 6 barrel, hustle 7 hotfoot

highbinding
5 fraud 7 chicane 8 trickery 9 chicanery, deception, fourberie 10 dishonesty, hanky-panky 11 skulduggery

highboy
5 chest 6 bureau

highbrow
4 snob 7 Brahmin, egghead 8 cerebral 10 doubledome 12 intellectual

highest
3 top 5 chief 6 apical, astral, upmost 7 exalted, supreme, topmost 9 top-drawer, uppermost 10 top-ranking

point: 4 acme, apex 5 crest 6 summit, zenith 8 pinnacle

highfalutin
4 rant 6 florid 7 aureate, bombast, flowery, fustian, pompous 8 rhapsody, rhetoric 9 bombastic 10 oratorical, rhetorical 11 declamatory, pretentious

high-handed
5 bossy 8 imperial 9 arbitrary, imperious, masterful 10 imperative, peremptory 11 domineering, magisterial, overbearing

high-hat
4 snub 5 potty 6 snobby, snooty 8 snobbish 12 aristocratic

high jinks
5 revel 7 fooling, revelry, wassail, whoopee, whoopla, whoop-up 9 horseplay, revelment, rowdiness, whoop-de-do 10 roughhouse, skylarking 12 roughhousing

highlight
6 stress 7 feature 9 emphasize

high-minded
5 moral, noble 8 elevated

high-muck-a-muck
3 VIP 5 nabob 6 big boy, bigwig 7 big shot, mugwump, notable

high-pitched
6 shrill 7 shrieky 8 agitated

high-principled
5 noble 6 worthy 8 sterling 9 estimable, honorable

high roller
7 gambler, spender, wastrel 8 prodigal, unthrift 10 profligate 11 scattergood, spendthrift, wastethrift

high sign
3 nod, tip 4 wink 5 alarm 6 signal, tipoff 7 warning

high-sounding
3 big 4 arty 7 pompous 9 overblown 10 arty-crafty 11 pretentious

high-spirited
5 beany, brash, fiery, jolly, merry 6 joyful, lively, spunky 7 gingery, gleeful, peppery 8 mirthful 9 ebullient, exuberant, vivacious 10 mettlesome 12 effervescent, light-hearted

high-strung
4 taut 5 jumpy, tense, tight 6 goosey, spooky 7 fidgety, jittery, nervous, uptight 8 twittery 9 excitable, unrelaxed

hightail
3 run 4 kite 5 scram 6 begone, decamp, get out 7 skiddoo, take off 8 clear out 9 skedaddle

highway
4 path, pike, road 5 track 6 artery, avenue, street 8 turnpike 9 boulevard 12 thoroughfare

German: 8 autobahn

Italian: 10 autostrada

Highwayman author
5 Noyes (Alfred)

hike
2 up 3 wax 4 jump, rise, rove, trek, walk 5 boost, march, put up, raise, tramp, tromp 6 jack up, ramble, stroll, trapes, travel, wander 7 explore, journey, traipse, upgrade 8 backpack, footslog, increase 9 walkabout 12 breakthrough

hilarious
5 funny, merry 8 humorous, mirthful

hilarity
4 glee 5 cheer, mirth 6 gaiety 8 jocosity, laughter 9 merriment 12 cheerfulness

Hilkiah
father: 4 Amzi 5 Hosah

son: 7 Eliakim 8 Gemariah, Jeremiah

hill
3 kop 4 bank, bump, cock, heap, knob, pile, rick 5 butte, drift, mound, ridge, shock, slope, stack 6 cuesta, height 7 hummock, incline 8 mountain 9 elevation, monadnock
African veld: 5 kopje
Charlestown: 6 Bunker
craggy: 3 tor
Cuba: 7 San Juan
D.C.: 7 Capitol
elongate: 7 drumlin
high: 5 mount
level-topped: 4 mesa 5 butte
of stratified drift: 4 kame
rounded: 5 swell
sand: 4 dune
small: 5 knoll, kopje, mound 6 koppie
surrounded by ice: 7 nunatak

hillbilly
4 rube 5 yokel 6 rustic 7 bucolic, bumpkin, hayseed 10 clodhopper 12 backwoodsman

hillock
5 knoll, mound
British: 4 toft

hillside
5 slope
Scottish: 4 brae

Himavat's daughter
4 Devi

hind
3 doe 4 back, deer, rear 5 after 6 retral, rustic 7 bailiff, grouper 9 posterior
mate: 4 hart

hind end
4 beam, rear, rump, tail 7 hunkers 8 backside, buttocks, haunches 9 fundament, posterior

hinder
3 bar, dam, let 4 back, balk, clog, curb, mire, rear 5 after, block, brake, check, deter, embog 6 arrest, baffle, burden, cumber, fetter, hamper, hog-tie, impede, lumber, retard, retral, thwart, tramel 7 inhibit, manacle, shackle, tramell, trammel 8 blockade, handicap, obstruct, restrain 9 entrammel, frustrate, hamstring, interrupt 10 overslaugh

hindmost
3 lag 4 back, last, rear 5 after, final 6 latter, retral 7 closing

8 eventual, terminal, ultimate 9 posterior 10 concluding

hindquarters
8 haunches

hindrance
4 clog 5 block 8 drawback, obstacle 10 impediment

Hindu
age: 4 yuga
ascetic: 4 yogi
caste (varna): 5 Sudra 6 Vaisya 7 Brahman 9 Kshatriya
class: 5 caste, varna
dancing girl: 8 devadesi
demon: 4 Rahu 6 Ravana
essence: 5 atman
force: 5 karma
garment: 4 sari 5 saree
god: 3 dev 4 deva
goddess: 4 devi
goddess of beauty: 7 Lakshmi
goddess of destruction: 4 Kali
god of fire: 4 Agni
god of love: 4 Kama
god of the heavens: 7 Krishna
god of war: 6 Skanda 10 Karttikeya
god of wisdom: 6 Ganesa, Ganesh
hell: 6 Naraka
holy man: 5 sadhu 6 saddhu
leader: 6 Gandhi (Mahatma)
lowest caste: 5 Sudra
lute: 5 sitar
marriage: 9 gandharva
nobleman: 4 raja 5 rajah
precept: 5 sutra, sutta
prince: 4 raja 5 rajah 8 maharaja 9 maharajah
queen: 4 rani 5 ranee 8 maharani 9 maharanee
sacred thread: 7 upavita
salvation: 7 nirvana
scripture: 12 Bhagavad Gita
social group: 5 caste, varna
teacher: 4 guru
term of respect: 5 sahib
treatise: 9 Upanishad
twice-born: 6 Vaisya 7 Brahman 9 Kshatriya

hinge
4 pawl 5 joint, mount 12 turning point
kind: 4 butt 5 piano 10 hook-and-eye

hint
3 beg, cue, key, tip 4 cast, clue, coax, dash, fish, hair, lick, seek, sign, vein 5 angle, imply, plead, point, press, shade, smack, smell, spice, taint, taste, tinge, touch, trace, twang, whiff 6 advice, aiming, breath, notion, shadow,

smatch, strain, streak, tipoff, trifle 7 connote, inkling, pointer, presage, solicit, soupçon, suggest, vestige, whisper 8 indicate, innuendo, intimate, overtone, particle, pointing, telltale, tincture 9 adumbrate, direction, importune, insinuate, prefigure, prompting, scintilla, suspicion, undertone 10 assistance, foreshadow, indication, intimation, sprinkling, suggestion 11 adumbration, association, connotation, forewarning, implication, insinuation

hinterland
4 bush 6 sticks 8 backwash, frontier, interior 9 backwater, backwoods, up-country 10 background, wilderness 11 back-country

hip
4 coxa 6 haunch, huckle
bone: 5 ilium, pubis 6 pelvis 7 ischium
cattle: 5 thurl
combining form: 5 ischi 6 ischio
disorder: 8 sciatica

hippie
8 bohemian, longhair

Hippocratic ___
4 oath

Hippodamia
father: 8 Oenomaus
husband: 6 Pelops 9 Pirithous 10 Peirithous
son: 6 Atreus 8 Thyestes

Hippolytus
father: 7 Theseus
mother: 7 Antiope 9 Hippolyte
stepmother: 7 Phaedra

Hippomenes' wife
8 Atalanta

Hirah's friend
5 Judah

hire
3 fee, let, pay 4 book, rent, wage 5 lease, put on, wages 6 employ, engage, salary, sublet, take on 7 charter, recruit

hireling
4 grub, hack 6 drudge, slavey 7 grubber 9 mercenary

hirsute
5 hairy 6 fleecy, pilose, shaggy, woolly 7 pileous 9 whiskered

Hispania
5 Spain 6 Iberia

hiss
3 boo 4 bird, buzz, fizz, hoot, pooh, sizz, whiz 5 bazoo, swish,

whish, woosh **6** fizzle, sizzle, wheeze, whoosh **7** catcall, whisper, whistle **8** pooh-pooh, sibilate **9** raspberry

historian
8 annalist **10** chronicler
American: **4** Webb (Charles Richard) **5** Adams (Brooks, Charles Kendall, Hannah, Henry, Herbert Baxter), Beard (Charles, Mary), Foote (Shelby) **6** Durant (Ariel, Will), Malone (Dumas), Miller (Perry), Muzzey (David), Nevins (Allen), Sarton (George Alfred), Sparks (Jared), Turner (Frederick Jackson) **7** Morison (Samuel Eliot), Parkman (Francis), Ridpath (John Clark), Tuchman (Barbara), Woodson (Carter G.) **8** Channing (Edward), Commager (Henry Steele), Prescott (William H.), Robinson (James Harvey) **11** Schlesinger (Arthur Meier)
English: **4** Bede (Venerable), Stow (John), Ward (Adolphus) **5** Acton (Lord), Grote (George), Wells (Herbert George) **6** Camden (William), Gibbon (Edward), Namier (Lewis Bernstein), Stubbs (William) **7** Hakluyt (Richard), Raleigh (Walter), Toynbee (Arnold), Whewell (William) **8** Geoffrey (of Monmouth), Macaulay (Thomas Babington) **9** Holinshed (Raphael), Trevelyan (George)
French: **5** Renan (Joseph-Ernest), Taine (Hippolyte-Adolphe) **6** Guizot (Francois-Pierre-Guillaume), Thiers (Louis-Adolphe), Volney (Comte de) **8** Hanotaux (Gabriel), Michelet (Jules)
German: **5** Ranke (Leopold von) **7** Mommsen (Theodor), Niebuhr (Barthold Georg) **8** Spengler (Oswald)
Greek: **8** Polybius, Xenophon **9** Dionysius, Herodotus **10** Thucydides
Italian: **5** Croce (Benedetto) **9** Salvemini (Gaetano)
Jewish: **8** Josephus (Flavius)
Roman: **4** Livy **7** Sallust, Tacitus (Cornelius) **9** Suetonius
Scottish: **7** Carlyle (Thomas) **9** Robertson (William)
Swiss: **6** Müller (Johannes von)
Welsh: **7** Nennius

historical period
3 age, era **5** epoch **7** ancient **8** medieval

history
4 epic, saga, tale **5** diary, story **6** annals, memoir, report **7** ac-

count, journal, recital, version **8** relation **9** chronicle, narrative

histrionic
5 actor **6** staged **8** dramatic, theatral, thespian **10** theatrical **11** dramaturgic

hit
3 bop, rap, wow **4** bang, bash, bean, biff, blow, bump, bunt, butt, conk, cuff, ding, fill, fist, lick, luck, meet, slap, slog, slug, sock, swat, swot, wipe **5** clout, knock, light, occur, pound, skelp, smash, smite, swipe, whack **6** affect, attack, buffet, chance, happen, stress, strike, stroke, thwack, tumble **7** censure, stumble **8** bludgeon **9** collision, emphasize
baseball: **5** homer, liner **6** double, single, triple **7** home run **9** line drive
golf ball: **5** shank

hitch
4 jerk, lift, limp, yoke **5** thumb **6** couple, hobble **7** harness **8** stoppage **10** impediment **11** obstruction **12** entanglement

Hitchcock forte
8 suspense

hitchhike
5 thumb

hither
4 here **6** nearer **11** to this place

hitherto
3 yet **4** here, once **5** as yet, prior, so far **6** before **7** earlier, thus far **8** formerly, previous **10** heretofore, previously

Hitler
follower: **4** Nazi
title: **6** Führer **7** Fuehrer
wife: **5** Braun (Eva)

hit man
3 gun **5** bravo **7** torpedo **8** assassin, gangster **9** cutthroat **10** gunslinger

hit-or-miss
6 chance, random **7** aimless, unaimed **9** desultory, haphazard, irregular, unplanned **10** designless **12** unconsidered

hive
5 amass, lay up, uplay **6** apiary, garner, roll up **7** store up **8** cumulate **9** stockpile **10** accumulate

hoar
4 rime **5** frost

hoard
4 save **5** lay by, lay up, stash, stock, store, trove **6** garner **7** backlog, nest egg, reserve **8** squirrel, treasure **9** amassment, colluvies, inventory, reservoir, stockpile **10** accumulate, collection, cumulation **11** aggregation **12** accumulation

hoarder
5 miser

hoarfrost
4 rime

hoarse
3 dry **5** gruff, harsh, husky, rough, thick **6** croaky, rasped **7** grating, jarring, rasping, raucous, throaty **8** croaking, guttural, strident **10** discordant, stridulent, stridulous
Scottish: **5** roupy **6** roupet

hoary
3 old **4** aged **5** stale, trite **6** ageold, remote **7** ancient, antique **8** Noachian, timeworn **9** canescent, hackneyed, venerable **12** antideluvian

hoax
3 gyp **4** dupe, fake, fool, gull, sell **5** fraud, phony, put-on, spoof, trick **6** befool, delude, humbug, take in **7** chicane, mislead **8** flimflam, hoodwink **9** bamboozle, imposture, mare's nest, victimize **11** hornswoggle

hob
4 nail **6** ferret, leader

Hobab
brother-in-law: **5** Moses
father: **5** Reuel

Hobbit creator
7 Tolkien (John Ronald Reuel)

hobble
3 tie **4** clog, curb, halt, limp **5** hitch, leash **6** fetter, hamper, hog-tie, impede **7** cripple, trammel **8** obstruct **9** entrammel

hobby
7 pastime **9** avocation, diversion

hobgoblin
5 bogey **7** bugaboo

hobnail
4 stud

hobo
3 bum, vag **5** tramp **7** drifter, floater, swagman, vagrant **8** derelict, vagabond **10** street arab

hock
4 knee, pawn **6** pledge **8** mortgage **9** hamstring **11** impignorate

hockey
6 shinny **7** shinney
arena: **4** rink
cup: **7** Stanley
implement: **4** puck **5** stick
official: **7** referee **8** linesman
player: **3** Orr (Bobby), Roy (Patrick)
4 Bure (Pavel), Fuhr (Grant), Howe
(Gordie), Hull (Bobby, Brett), Jagr
(Jaromir), wing **5** Bossy (Mike), Bu-
cyk (John), Hasek (Dominik), Kurri
(Jari), Maruk (Dennis), Shore
(Eddie), Shutt (Steve) **6** center,
Clarke (Bobby), Coffey (Paul),
Dionne (Marcel), Dryden (Ken),
goalie, Harvey (Doug), Juneau
(Joe), Leetch (Brian), Mikita (Stan),
Morenz (Howie), Parent (Bernie),
Potvin (Denis), Recchi (Mark), Sa-
vard (Denis), Sundin (Mats) **7** Bel-
four (Ed), Bourque (Ray), Brodeur
(Martin), Chelios (Chris), Fedorov
(Sergei), forward, Francis (Ron),
Gretzky (Wayne), Lafleur (Guy),
Lemieux (Claude, Mario), Lindros
(Eric), Messier (Mark), Mogilny
(Alexander), Richard (Maurice), Se-
lanne (Teemu), Stastny (Peter), Yzer-
man (Steve) **8** Beliveau (Jean), Es-
posito (Phil, Tony), Nicholls
(Bernie), pointman, Trottier (Bryan),
Ysebaert (Paul) **9** Hawerchuk (Dale)
10 Carbonneau (Guy), defense-
man, goalkeeper
stick: **5** caman (Scottish, Irish),
camog (Irish) **7** cammock (Scottish)
team: **4** Jets **5** Blues, Kings, Stars
6 Bruins, Devils, Flames, Flyers, Oilers, Sabres, Sharks **7** Canucks,
Rangers, Whalers **8** Capitals, Panthers, Penguins, Red Wings, Senators **9** Canadiens, Islanders, Lightning, Nordiques **10** Black Hawks,
Maple Leafs, North Stars
11 Mighty Ducks
term: **3** box **4** cage, goal, puck, rink
5 bandy, bench, check, icing, stick
6 charge, crease, shinny **7** face-off,
off-side **8** blue line **9** back-check,
body-check **10** center line, penalty
box
variation of: **9** broomball

hod
4 tray **6** trough **7** scuttle **11** coal
scuttle

Hodaviah's father
8 Elioenai **9** Hassenuah

Hoder, Hoth
brother: **6** Balder
slayer: **4** Vali
victim: **6** Balder

Hodesh's husband
9 Shaharaim

hodgepodge
4 hash **6** jumble, medley **7** mélange, mixture **8** eclectic, mishmash
9 patchwork, potpourri **10** hotchpotch, miscellany **11** gallimaufry

Hod's father
6 Zophah

hoe
4 till **9** cultivate

hog
3 pig, sow **4** boar **5** roach, swine
8 boshvark
family: **6** Suidae
female: **3** sow **4** gilt
genus: **3** Sus
red: **5** duroc
young: **5** shoat, shote

hogback
5 chine, crest, ridge

Hoglah's father
10 Zelophehad

Hogni's victim
6 Sigurd

hogshead
3 keg, tun **4** butt, cask, pipe
6 barrel

hog-tie
4 clog, curb **5** leash **6** fetter, hamper, hobble **7** shackle, trammel
9 entrammel

hogwash
4 slop **5** bilge, hokum, hooey, swill
8 nonsense **9** poppycock

hoi polloi
3 mob **4** scum **5** dregs, trash
6 masses, rabble **8** populace, riffraff **9** multitude **11** proletariat

hoist
4 lift, rear, rise **5** boost, raise,
winch **6** pick up, take up, uphold,
uplift, uprear **7** derrick, elevate, upraise **8** windlass

hoity-toity
5 dizzy, giddy, silly **7** flighty,
pompous **8** skittish **9** frivolous
11 harebrained, thoughtless
13 rattlebrained

hokum
4 bosh, jazz **5** hooey **8** flimflam,
malarkey, nonsense **9** poppycock
11 foolishness

hold
3 fix, own **4** bear, deem, feel,
grab, grip, halt, have, keep, last,
stay, stop **5** apply, carry, clamp,

clasp, cling, delay, enjoy, grasp,
gripe, judge, limit, pause, poise,
sense, think, value **6** accept, arrest,
clench, clinch, clutch, credit, detain,
esteem, harbor, prison, regard, retain, steady, tenure **7** believe,
catch up, comport, contain, convene, convoke, custody, fermata,
grapple, keep out, possess, reserve,
support, sustain **8** conceive, consider, enthrall, keep back, maintain, preserve, purchase, restrict
9 fascinate, handclasp, mesmerize,
spellbind
as precious: **8** treasure
close: **6** cuddle
dear: **7** cherish
from proceeding: **4** stay
in check: **7** repress
in common: **5** share
out: **4** last **6** endure
together: **4** bond **5** clamp **6** fasten
wrestling: **8** headlock, scissors

hold back
3 bit **4** curb, deny, keep **5** check
6 bridle, detain, retain **7** abstain,
inhibit, keep out, refrain, reserve
8 restrain **9** constrain

hold in
3 bit **4** curb **5** check **6** bridle **7** inhibit **8** restrain **9** constrain
10 keep silent

hold off
4 stay **5** defer, delay, rebut, remit,
repel **6** rebuff, shelve **7** abstain,
adjourn, repulse, suspend **8** hesitate, postpone, prorogue
9 withstand

hold up
4 halt, lift, stay **5** check, defer, delay, raise, remit, waive **6** put off
7 prevail, support, suspend, sustain
8 postpone, prorogue

hole
3 box, den, fix, gap, jam, pit
4 cave, cove, flaw, open, rent, rift,
spot, vent, void **5** break, fault,
niche **6** breach, burrow, cavity,
corner, cranny, eyelet, hiatus, lacuna, outlet, pickle, pierce, plight,
scrape, vacuum **7** dilemma, disrupt, fissure, opening, orifice, rupture, vacancy, vacuity **8** aperture
9 perforate **10** excavation, interstice **11** perforation

hole in one
3 ace

holiday
5 leave **6** May Day **7** festive, Flag
Day **8** Arbor Day, carefree, vaca-

tion **9** Halloween **10** Father's Day, Mother's Day **12** All Saints' Day, Groundhog Day **13** St. Patrick's Day, Valentine's Day
Alaska: **10** Seward's Day
British: **9** Boxing Day
Canadian: **11** Dominion Day, Victoria Day
Federal: **8** Labor Day, New Year's **9** Christmas **11** Veterans Day **12** Armistice Day, Thanksgiving
Hawaii: **8** Kuhio Day **13** Kamehameha Day
Jewish: **8** Passover
Maryland: **12** Defender's Day
Newfoundland: **12** Discovery Day, St. George's Day **13** Orangemen's Day
Rhode Island: **10** Victory Day
Texas: **13** San Jacinto Day
Utah: **10** Pioneer Day

holiness
5 piety **8** devotion, divinity, sanctity **12** consecration, spirituality

Holland
see **Netherlands**

holler
3 cry **4** call, yell **5** gripe, shout **6** outcry **7** grumble **8** complain **9** complaint **10** vociferate

hollow
3 dip, sag **4** idle, sink, vain, void **5** basin, empty, false, notch, womby **6** cavity, dingle, otiose, ravine, sunken **7** channel, concave, echoing, sinkage, vacuity **8** complete, nugatory, resonant, sinkhole, sounding, thorough **9** cavernous, concavity, deceitful **10** depression, resounding, sepulchral
out: **3** dig, gut **4** mine **5** gouge **8** excavate

holly
4 tree **5** shrub
genus: **4** Ilex

holocaust
4 fire **7** inferno **9** sacrifice **11** destruction **13** conflagration

Holofernes' slayer
6 Judith

holy
3 god **5** pious **6** adored, devout, divine, sacred **7** angelic, awesome, blessed, revered, saintly **8** hallowed, priestly **9** glorified, pietistic, prayerful, religious, sanctuary, spiritual, unprofane, venerated, worshiped **10** reverenced, sanctified **11** consecrated, frightening
bread: **7** eulogia **9** antidoron
combining form: **4** hagi, hier **5** hagio, hiero
communion: **9** eucharist
oil: **6** chrism
person: **5** saint **6** zaddik **8** zaddikim (plural)
Spirit: **9** Paraclete
vessel: **7** chalice **8** ciborium

holy place
6 shrine **7** sanctum **9** sanctuary **10** sanctorium

Holy Roman Emperor
4 Karl, Otho, Otto **5** Adolf, Franz, Henry, Louis **6** Albert, Arnulf, Conrad, Joseph, Lothar, Ludwig, Philip, Rudolf, Rupert, Wenzel **7** Charles, Francis, Leopold, Lothair **8** Heinrich **9** Ferdinand, Frederick, Friedrich, Sigismund **10** Maximilian

Holy Writ
4 Book **5** Bible **9** Scripture

homage
5 honor **7** respect, tribute **9** deference, obeisance, reverence

home
4 land, site, soil **5** abode, haunt, house, local, range **6** family, native **7** country, habitat, housing **8** domestic, domicile, dwelling, internal, locality, location, national **9** household, intestine, municipal, residence, residency **10** commoracy, fatherland, focal point, habitation, motherland **12** headquarters **13** mother country
country: **7** cottage **8** bungalow

homely
3 dry **4** ugly **5** plain **6** direct, kindly, modest, simple **8** familiar, intimate, unpretty **10** unalluring, unhandsome **11** commonplace, inelaborate, unbeauteous, unbeautiful, unelaborate, ungarnished **12** unattractive, unornamented **13** plainfeatured, unpretentious

Homer epic
5 Iliad **7** Odyssey

homesickness
9 nostalgia

homespun
6 folksy **9** practical **13** unpretentious

Home, Sweet Home
music: **6** Bishop (Henry)
words: **5** Payne (John Howard)

homicidal
6 bloody **8** sanguine **9** murdering, murderous **10** sanguinary **11** sanguineous **12** bloodthirsty

homicide
5 blood **6** killer, murder, slayer **7** killing **8** foul play, murderer **9** manslayer **12** manslaughter

homilize
6 preach

homily
6 sermon **7** lecture **9** discourse **10** admonition

homogeneous
4 like, same **7** similar, uniform **10** comparable, compatible, consistent, equivalent
combining form: **2** is **3** hol, iso **4** holo

Homo sapiens
3 man **5** flesh **7** mankind **8** humanity **9** humankind, mortality

homunculus
4 runt **5** dwarf, midge, pygmy **6** midget, peewee **7** manikin **8** Tom Thumb **11** hop-o'-my-thumb, lilliputian

honcho
4 boss, cock, head **5** chief **6** leader, master **7** headman **8** hierarch **9** chieftain

Honduras
capital: **11** Tegucigalpa
monetary unit: **7** lempira
neighbor: **9** Guatemala, Nicaragua **10** El Salvador
product: **6** coffee **7** bananas

hone
4 edge, whet **7** sharpen

honest
4 open, real, true **5** frank, plain, right **6** candid, humble, simple **7** genuine, sincere, upright **8** innocent, reliable, truthful **9** objective, reputable, unfeigned, veracious **10** forthright, heart-whole, legitimate, scrupulous, unaffected **11** undesigning **12** praiseworthy, undissembled **13** conscientious, dispassionate, unimpeachable

honesty
6 virtue **7** probity **8** goodness, justness **9** integrity, rectitude, sincerity **11** uprightness **12** incorruption, truthfulness

honey
combining form: **4** meli, mell **5** melli
drink: **4** mead

honey badger
5 ratel

honey bear
8 kinkajou

honeybee genus
4 Apis

honeyberry
5 genip

honey bread
5 carob

honey buzzard
4 hawk, kite, pern

honeydew
5 melon

honeyed
6 golden, liquid, mellow 8 Hyblaean 9 sweetened 11 mellifluent, mellifluous

honeysuckle
8 rewa-rewa 9 columbine 11 swamp azalea 13 pinxter flower

Hong Kong's capital
8 Victoria

honky-tonk
4 dive 5 joint 7 hangout 11 barrelhouse

honor
4 bays, fete, kudo 5 adorn, asset, award, badge, erect, exalt, glory, kudos, medal, mense 6 esteem, homage, praise, regard, trophy, uprear 7 dignify, ennoble, glorify, laurels, magnify, respect, sublime, worship 8 accolade, approval, carry out, devotion 9 adoration, adulation, deference, integrity, obeisance, privilege, recognize, reverence 10 admiration, aggrandize, blue ribbon, compliment, decoration, reputation, veneration 11 distinction, distinguish, recognition 12 incorruption

honorable
4 just, true 5 right 6 august, worthy 7 ethical, upright 8 reverend, sterling 9 dignified 10 scrupulous, worshipful 11 illustrious 13 conscientious

hood
4 cowl, hide 5 cover 6 bonnet, helmet 7 bashlyk, blinder, capouch, capuche 8 covering
clergyman's: 6 almuce

hoodlum
4 thug 7 mobster, ruffian 8 plug-ugly 9 strong arm

hoodwink
4 dupe, fool, gull, hoax 5 blind, trick 6 befool 7 chicane 8 flimflam 9 bamboozle 10 impose upon 11 hornswoggle

hooey
4 bosh, bunk 5 bilge 6 bunkum 7 baloney 8 claptrap, malarkey, nonsense

hoof
4 boot, foot, kick, pace, walk 5 eject, troop 6 unguis, ungula 7 traipse, trample, ungulae (plural) 8 ambulate, throw out
cloven: 5 cloot

hoofer
6 dancer 7 danseur 8 coryphée, danseuse, figurant 9 ballerina, figurante

hooflike
6 ungual

hook
3 ear, nab, nim, nip 4 flag, gore, lift 5 catch, curve, hitch, pinch, steal 6 anchor, fasten, pilfer, scythe, secure, sickle 7 cabbage, hamulus 8 crotchet
a fish: 4 gaff, snag
combining form: 3 onc 4 onch, onci, onco 5 oncho
for a watch: 10 chatelaine

hooklike
7 falcate 8 unciform
part: 5 uncus 7 hamulus

hookup
7 cahoots, circuit 8 alliance 10 connection 11 affiliation, association, combination, conjunction, partnership

hooky
7 truancy 8 truantry

hooligan
see **hoodlum**

hoop
4 band, ring 5 clasp 6 circle 7 circlet, enclose 8 surround 10 finger ring

Hoosier State
7 Indiana

hoot
3 boo, jot 4 bird, damn, hiss, iota, jeer, whit 5 bazoo, ounce, scrap, shout, whoop 7 catcall, modicum 8 particle, pooh-pooh 9 raspberry

hooter
3 owl 5 owlet

hop
3 run 4 ball, jump, leap, skip, tend, trip 5 bound, dance, serve, vault 6 bounce, hurdle, spring, wait on 7 rebound, saltate, skitter 8 jump over

hope
4 look 5 await, faith, stock, trust 6 aspire, desire, expect 7 count on, promise 8 reliance 9 count upon 10 confidence
loss of: 7 despair

hopeful
4 easy, fond, rosy 5 happy, sunny 6 bright, cheery, golden, hoping, likely, secure, seeker, upbeat 7 assured, budding, content, halcyon, roseate 8 aspirant, cheerful, cheering, sanguine 9 applicant, candidate, confident, expectant, promising, satisfied 10 auspicious, optimistic, propitious 11 encouraging, rose-colored, undisturbed, up-and-coming 12 advantageous, anticipative, Pollyannaish

hopeless
4 glum, vain 6 futile, gloomy, morose 7 forlorn 8 downcast 9 desperate, incurable, insanable, insoluble, uncurable 10 despairing, despondent, desponding, impossible 11 immedicable, ineffectual, irreparable 12 incorrigible, irredeemable, irremediable 13 uncorrectable

hoper
8 optimist 9 Pollyanna

Hophni
brother: 8 Phinehas
son: 3 Eli

hopped-up
4 high 6 stoned, zonked 7 drugged

hopper
3 box 4 frog, hare, toad 5 bunny, chute 6 rabbit 7 cricket

—— Hopper
5 Hedda

hopping
4 busy 5 fussy 6 lively

Horae
4 Dike 6 Eirene 7 Eunomia

Horam
kingdom: 5 Gezer
slayer: 6 Joshua

horde
4 army, push 5 crowd, crush, drove, press, swarm 6 squash, throng 9 multitude

hordeolum
3 sty

Hori's son
7 Shaphat

horizon
3 ken 4 goal, zone 5 limit, range, reach 7 purview, skyline 8 prospect

horizontal
4 flat 7 general, overall

hormone
5 kinin 6 estrin 7 estriol, estrone, gastrin, insulin, relaxin 8 autacoid, estrogen, glucagon, kallidin, secretin
female: 8 estrogen
insect: 7 ecdyson 8 ecdysone
pituitary: 8 oxytocin
sex: 6 prolan

horn
4 gore, toot 5 cornu, drink, glory, power, pride 6 antler, claxon, klaxon, shofar, tootle 7 cuckold 10 cornucopia, projection
ancient Greek: 5 rhyta (plural) 6 rhyton
animal: 6 antler
combining form: 4 cera 5 ceras, cerus, corne 6 corneo
signal: 6 typhon

___ Hornblower
7 Horatio

horn in
4 fool 6 meddle 7 intrude, obtrude 8 busybody 9 interfere, interlope 10 intertrude, monkey with, tamper with

hornlike
8 ceratoid, corneous 10 keratinous

horn-shaped
7 cornute 8 cornuted

hornswoggle
4 dupe, fool, gull, hoax 6 befool, pigeon 7 chicane 8 flimflam, hoodwink 9 bamboozle

horny
4 hard 7 callous 8 keratoid

horrible
4 grim 5 awful, lurid, nasty 6 grisly 7 fearful, ghastly, hateful, hellish, hideous 8 dreadful, gruesome, shocking, terrible 9 abhorrent, appalling, frightful, loathsome, obnox-ious, offensive, repellent, repugnant, repulsive, revolting 10 disgusting, terrifying

horrid
see **horrible**

horrific
5 awful 7 fearful 8 dreadful, shocking, terrible 9 appalling, frightful 10 formidable

horrify
5 daunt, shake, shock 6 appall, dismay

horrifying
4 grim 5 lurid 6 grisly 7 ghastly, hideous 8 gruesome, terrible

horror
4 fear, hate, pain 5 alarm, dread, panic, shock, throe 6 dismay, fright, hatred, wrench 8 aversion, distress, loathing 9 repulsion, revulsion, trepidity 10 abhorrence, repugnance 11 abomination, detestation, trepidation

Horsa's brother
7 Hengist

hors d'oeuvre
4 whet 7 zakuska 9 antipasto, appetizer

horse
3 kid 4 buck, roam 5 act up, bronc, cut up, pacer, steed 6 bayard, bronco, brumby, equine, padnag 7 broncho, carry on, cavalry, palfrey, sawbuck, trestle, trotter 8 footrope, jackstay, palomino, skewbald, stallion, traveler
Asian: 6 tarpan
Australian-bred: 5 waler
battle: 7 charger
breed: 6 Morgan 7 Arabian, Belgian, Iceland 8 Shetland 9 Percheron 10 Lippizaner 12 Thoroughbred
collar: 7 brecham, brechan
collar part: 4 hame
combining form: 4 hipp 5 hippo 6 hippus
covering: 8 trapping
draft: 10 clydesdale
extinct: 8 eohippus
farm: 6 dobbin
female: 4 mare 5 filly
foot part: 7 pastern
gait: 4 trot 6 canter, gallop
gear: 3 bit 4 rein 6 saddle 7 harness 9 checkrein
leg joint: 7 fetlock
leg part: 6 gaskin 7 gambrel
male: 4 colt 8 stallion
mark: 5 blaze
naturalized: 7 mustang
nervous: 5 shier, shyer
of the movies: 6 Flicka, Silver 7 Trigger 8 Champion 11 Black Beauty
race: 5 derby 6 mudder 8 Affirmed, Citation 9 Preakness 11 Seattle Slew, Secretariat 13 Belmont Stakes, Kentucky Derby
rump: 7 crupper
saddle: 9 Appaloosa
small: 6 garron, jennet
spotted: 5 Pinto 7 piebald
tan: 8 palomino
thoroughbred: 8 hotblood
war: 8 destrier
wild: 7 mustang

horseman
6 cowboy, knight 7 vaquero 8 cavalier 9 caballero, chevalier 10 equestrian

horsemanship
6 manege 10 equitation

horse opera
5 oater 7 western

horseplay
5 act up, cut up 7 carry on, fooling 8 clowning 9 high jinks, rowdiness 10 buffoonery, roughhouse, skylarking 12 roughhousing

horseshoer
6 smithy 10 blacksmith

horticulturist
7 Burbank (Luther)

Horus
brother: 6 Anubis
father: 6 Osiris
mother: 4 Isis
victim: 4 Seth

hose
4 tube 5 water 8 stocking

Hosea's father
5 Beeri

Hoshaiah's son
7 Azariah 8 Jezaniah

Hoshea
father: 3 Nun 4 Elah 7 Azaziah
victim: 5 Pekah

hospice
see **hostel**

hospitable
6 social 7 cordial 8 friendly 9 convivial 10 gregarious 11 cooperative

hospital
6 clinic 7 lazaret 9 infirmary

attendant: **7** orderly
ship's: **7** sickbay

Hospitallers' island
5 Malta **6** Rhodes

host
4 army **5** cloud, crowd, emcee, flock **6** angels, legion, myriad, scores **7** compere **8** assemble **9** innkeeper, multitude

hostage
4 pawn **5** token **6** pledge, surety **7** earnest **8** guaranty, security **9** guarantee

hostel
3 inn **5** lodge **6** tavern, travel **7** auberge **9** roadhouse **11** caravansary, public house

hostile
3 dim, ill **4** dour, sour **5** enemy **6** bitter, fierce **7** adverse, opposed, warlike **8** contrary, inimical, militant, opposite, virulent **9** bellicose, rancorous, vitriolic **10** inimicable, pugnacious, unfriendly **11** belligerent, competitive, contentious, disaffected, unfavorable **12** antagonistic, disapproving **13** argumentative

hostility
6 animus, enmity, rancor **9** antipathy **10** antagonism

hot
5 eager, fiery, fresh, nifty, super **6** ardent, baking, banned, biting, groovy, heated, hectic, raging, stolen, sultry, torrid, tropic, unsafe, urgent **7** boiling, burning, febrile, fevered, goatish, lustful, peppery, pungent, satyric, summery, sweltry, violent, zealous **8** broiling, feverish, feverous, glorious, prurient, scalding, sizzling, tropical, vehement **9** lecherous, lickerish, marvelous, scorching **10** blistering, contraband, lascivious, libidinous, passionate, sweltering **11** radioactive **12** concupiscent

hot air
4 bosh **6** bunkum **7** blather, twaddle **8** flimflam, malarkey, nonsense **9** poppycock **10** double-talk

hot-blooded
5 fiery **6** ardent **7** blazing, burning, fervent, flaming **9** excitable **10** passionate **11** impassioned **12** high-spirited

hotchpotch
see **hodgepodge**

hot dog
5 frank **6** weenie, weiner, wiener,

wienie **7** show-off **11** frankfurter, wienerwurst

hotel
3 inn, spa **5** lodge **6** boatel, tavern **7** auberge, hospice, pension **8** motor inn **9** roadhouse **11** caravansary, public house **12** lodging house, rooming house **13** boardinghouse
chain: **5** Hyatt **6** Hilton, Westin **8** Marriott, Radisson, Sheraton, Stouffer **9** Ramada Inn **10** Holiday Inn **11** Four Seasons
inferior: **7** fleabag

Hoth
see **Hoder**

Hotham's father
5 Heber

hotheaded
4 rash **5** brash, fiery, hasty **6** madcap **8** reckless **9** impetuous

Hothir's father
5 Heman

hot spot
4 café **6** nitery **7** cabaret **8** nightery **9** nightclub **10** supper club **11** discotheque **12** watering hole **13** watering place

hot springs
7 thermae

hot-tempered
5 ratty, testy **6** cranky, tetchy, touchy **7** peppery **8** choleric **9** dyspeptic, irascible **10** passionate

hot water
3 box, fix, jam **4** hole **5** Dutch **6** corner, pickle **7** dilemma, trouble **8** quagmire **10** difficulty **11** predicament

____ Houdini
5 Harry

hound
3 dog, fan **4** bait, buff, ride, tyke **5** chivy, lover **6** addict, badger, bowwow, canine, heckle, hector, votary **7** devotee, dogfish, habitué **8** bullyrag **10** aficionado
Russian: **6** borzoi

house
3 hut, ken **4** casa, clan, firm, folk, home, race, roof, shed **5** abode, board, dwell, folks, haven, hotel, lodge, put up, stock, tribe **6** bestow, biggin, billet, casino, encase, family, harbor, ménage, outfit, shield **7** château, company, concern, contain, cottage, enclose, kindred, lineage, mansion, quarter,

saltbox, shelter, theater **8** audience, business, domicile, dwelling, messuage **9** caparison, entertain, residence, residency
clergyman's: **5** manse **7** rectory **9** parsonage
country: **5** manor **7** cottage **8** bungalow
dog: **6** kennel
earth: **5** adobe
Eskimo: **5** igloo
lower: **8** assembly
mean: **5** hovel
of prostitution: **4** crib **6** bagnio **7** brothel **8** bordello
religious: **5** abbey **6** priory **7** convent, nunnery **9** monastery
room in a: **7** chamber
rooming: **5** lodge
Russian: **5** dacha
small: **5** shack
Spanish: **4** casa
women's (Muslim): **5** harem

housebreak
3 rob **4** tame **5** rifle **6** subdue **7** ransack **9** knock over **10** burglarize

household
4 home **5** folks **6** common, family, ménage **8** domestic, familiar
combining form: **2** ec **3** eco, oec **4** oeco, oiko
gods (Roman): **5** lares **7** penates

house of God
see **house of worship**

house of prayer
see **house of worship**

house of worship
5 abbey, stupa **6** bethel, chapel, church, pagoda, shrine, temple **7** chantry, minster, oratory **8** basilica **9** cathedral, sanctuary **10** tabernacle **11** conventicle
Aztec: **6** teopan **8** teocalli
Jewish: **7** synagog **9** synagogue
Muslim: **6** masjid, mosque, musjid

housewife
5 hussy **8** hausfrau

housing
4 case **7** shelter **9** enclosure
run-down: **4** slum

hovel
3 hut, sty **5** hutch, shack **6** burrow, pigpen, pigsty, shanty **10** tabernacle

hover
4 flit, hang **5** cower, dance, float, poise **7** flicker, flitter, flutter **9** hang about

howbeit

3 yet **4** when **5** still, while **6** much as, though, withal **7** whereas **8** after all, although **11** nonetheless, still and all **12** nevertheless

however

3 but, yet **4** only, save **5** still **6** except, though, withal **8** after all, although **9** per contra **11** nonetheless, still and all

howl

3 bay, cry, yip **4** bark, keen, riot, wail, weep, yell, yelp **5** quest **6** scream, squall, squawl, squeal **7** blubber, protest, ululate, whimper **9** caterwaul, complaint **11** oscillation **12** sidesplitter

hoyden

6 gamine, tomboy

Hreidmar's son

5 Regin **6** Fafnir, Reginn

Hrimfaxi's rider

4 Nott

H-shaped

5 zygal

hub

4 band, bell, nave, seat **5** focus, heart **6** barrel, center **8** polestar **9** master tap **10** focal point **11** nerve center
opposite: 3 rim

hubbub

3 din **4** stir, to-do **5** babel, whirl **6** clamor, hassle, jangle, pother, racket, rumpus, tumult, uproar **7** turmoil **8** brouhaha **9** commotion **10** hullabaloo, hurly-burly, tintamarre **11** disturbance, pandemonium

hubristic

4 vain **5** proud **7** haughty **8** arrogant, cavalier, insolent, superior **10** disdainful **11** overbearing **12** supercilious **13** high-and-mighty

Huckleberry Finn

author: 5 Twain (Mark)
character: 3 Jim, Tom
river: 11 Mississippi

huckster

4 hawk, vend **5** adman **6** dicker, haggle, hawker, higgle, monger, palter, peddle, vendor **7** bargain, chaffer, higgler, packman, peddler **8** outcrier

huddle

3 don **4** lump **5** bunch, chaos, crowd, get on, hunch, put on, snarl, throw, treat **6** advise, assume, ataxia, confab, confer, crouch,

draw on, jumble, parley, powwow, slip on **7** clutter, consult, cover up, meeting **8** assemble, colloque, disarray, disorder **9** confusion **10** conference, discussion **11** confabulate, scrooch down

Hudson's ship

8 Half Moon

hue

4 cast, tint, tone **5** color, shade, shape, tinge **6** aspect, outcry **10** complexion

huff

4 blow, gasp, pant, rant, rile, roil, snap **5** annoy, grate, heave, peeve, pique, storm **6** nettle, put out **7** bluster, dudgeon, flounce, inflame, inflate, offense, provoke, umbrage **8** irritate **10** resentment

huffy

5 proud, waspy **6** touchy **7** fretful, haughty, peevish, pettish, waspish **8** arrogant, cavalier, insolent, petulant, snappish, superior **9** fractious, irritable, querulous **10** disdainful **11** overbearing **12** supercilious **13** high-and-mighty

hug

5 clasp, crowd, press **6** clutch, cuddle, enfold **7** cherish, embosom, embrace, squeeze **10** felicitate **12** congratulate

huge

4 vast **5** bulky, giant, grand, great, jumbo, large, lusty, massy, Titan **6** heroic, mighty, untold **7** Antaean, immense, mammoth, massive, monster, outsize, titanic, whaling **8** colossal, enormous, gigantic, oversize, pythonic, towering, whacking, whopping **9** cyclopean, extensive, gigantean, Herculean, leviathan, monstrous, planetary, unbounded, walloping **10** behemothic, dinosauric, gargantuan, mastodonic, monumental, prodigious, tremendous, unfathomed **11** Bunyanesque, elephantine, gigantesque, magnificent, mountainous

hugeness

8 enormity **9** immensity, magnitude

hugger-mugger

4 hash, hush, mash **6** covert, jumble, jungle, litter, muddle, secret, tumble **7** clutter, furtive, jumbled, rummage, secrecy, silence, subrosa **8** covertly, hush-hush, in camera, scramble, secretly **9** by stealth, confusion, furtively, privately **10** mumbo jumbo, secretness,

stealthily, undercover **11** clandestine **13** clandestinely

Hugo, Victor

character: 6 Javert **7** Cosette, Fantine, Valjean **9** Esmeralda, Quasimodo

Huguenot leader

5 Condé (Prince de) **6** Adrets (Baron des), Mornay (Philippe)

Huguenots composer

9 Meyerbeer (Giacomo)

Huldah's husband

7 Shallum

hulk

4 loom, ship

hull

3 pod **4** bark, case, peel, rind, skin **5** chaff, shell, shuck **6** casing **8** covering **9** cartridge **11** decorticate

hullabaloo

3 din **5** babel **6** clamor, hubbub, jangle, racket, tumult, uproar **8** ballyhoo **10** tintamarre **11** pandemonium

Hul's father

4 Aram

hum

4 buzz, moan, purr, sing, zing **5** drone **6** bumble, melody, murmur **7** vibrate

human

4 body, life, soul **5** being, party, wight **6** mortal, person **7** hominid, mankind **8** creature, hominine, hominoid **9** enigmatic, personage **10** anthropoid, ethnologic, individual **12** ethnological
being: 6 mortal, person **7** primate
combining form: 7 anthrop **8** anthropo
race: 7 mankind

humane

4 good, kind, mild **6** gentle, kindly **8** merciful **10** altruistic, benevolent, charitable **11** kindhearted, softhearted **12** eleemosynary **13** compassionate, philanthropic

humanitarian

4 good **10** altruistic, benevolent, charitable **12** eleemosynary **13** philanthropic

humanity

3 man, men **5** flesh **6** people **7** mankind **9** mortality **10** compassion **11** benevolence, Homo sapiens

Humbaba's slayer
9 Gilgamesh

humble
3 low **4** base, mean, meek, sink
5 abase, abash, lower, lowly, quiet
6 bemean, debase, demean, modest, simple **7** chagrin, degrade, ignoble, lowborn, lowbred, mortify, subdued **8** baseborn, cast down, plebeian, resigned, unwashed
9 compliant, discomfit, embarrass, humiliate **10** submissive, unassuming, unennobled **11** acquiescent, unobtrusive **13** insignificant, unpretentious

humbug
3 gyp, rot **4** bosh, fake, hoax, sell, sham **5** bluff, faker, fraud, hokum, phony, spoof **6** betray, bunkum, cajole, delude, drivel, illude, juggle, piffle, take in **7** beguile, deceive, mislead **8** flimflam, impostor, malarkey, nonsense, quackery
9 hypocrite, imposture, pretender
10 balderdash

humdinger
5 dandy, doozy, nifty, peach **8** jimdandy **11** crackerjack

humdrum
4 blah, dull **6** dreary, stodgy **7** prosaic **8** banausic, monotone, monotony, plodding, workaday **10** monotonous, pedestrian

humid
4 damp, dank **5** close, moist, mucky, muggy, soggy **6** clammy, sodden, sticky, stuffy, sultry **8** stifling, vaporous **10** oppressive, sweltering

humiliate
4 sink **5** abase, lower, shame **6** bemean, debase, demean, humble
7 chagrin, degrade, mortify **8** belittle, cast down, disgrace

humming
4 busy **5** brisk, fussy **6** lively
7 hopping, popping **8** bustling, hustling

hummingbird
5 sylph **6** sappho **7** vervain
9 thorntail, trochilus
genus: **6** Sappho

humor
3 bee, wit **4** baby, mind, mood, tone, vein, whim **5** fancy, freak, spoil **6** banter, cocker, coddle, comedy, cosset, cotton, esprit, joking, levity, makeup, megrim, nature, pamper, strain, temper, vagary **7** boutade, caprice, cater to,

conceit, gratify, gruntle, indulge, jesting, kidding **8** chaffing, chitchat, crotchet, drollery, jocosity, repartee **9** character, drollness, flippancy, funniness, jocundity, lightness, wittiness **10** comicality, complexion, jocularity, jocundness, pleasantry

humorist
3 Ade, wag, wit **4** card, Nash (Ogden), Shaw (Henry Wheeler), Ward (Artemus, Edward), zany
5 Adams (Franklin Pierce), Allen (Fred), clown, comic, cutup, droll, Dunne (Finley Peter), joker, Twain (Mark), White (Elwyn Brooks)
6 Browne (Charles Farrar), gagman, jester, kidder, Rogers (Will), Runyon (Damon), Thorpe (Thomas Bangs) **7** buffoon, Burgess (Gelett), Clemens (Samuel Langhorne), gagster, Hubbard (Kin), Marquis (Don), punster, Thurber (James) **8** Aleichem (Shalom), banterer, Benchley (Robert), comedian, funnyman, jokester, Perelman (Sidney Joseph), quipster **9** jokesmith, prankster
11 merry-andrew
Canadian: **7** Leacock (Stephen)

humorous
5 funny, witty **6** jocose **7** jocular, waggish, wagsome **9** facetious

humpback
5 whale **8** kyphosis

humpbacked
7 gibbous

Humperdinck opera
15 Hansel und Gretel

humus
3 mor **4** mull, soil

hunch
3 gob, wad **4** arch, clod, lump, push, rear **5** chunk, clump, crook, fudge, shove, squat **6** crouch, curl up, huddle, jostle, nugget
11 scrooch down

Hunchback of Notre Dame
9 Quasimodo
author: **4** Hugo (Victor)

hundred
combining form: **4** hect **5** centi, hecto **6** hecato **7** hecaton

hundredth
combining form: **5** centi

Hungary
capital: **8** Budapest
dog: **4** puli
ethnic group: **6** Magyar
monetary unit: **6** forint

national hero: **5** Arpad
wine: **5** tokay

hunger
3 yen **4** ache, long, lust, pine, sigh
5 crave, yearn **6** famine, famish, hanker, thirst **7** craving

hungry
4 avid, poor **6** barren **7** starved
8 famished, ravenous, starving, underfed

hunk
3 gob, wad **4** clod, lump **5** chunk, clump, piece **6** nugget

hunker down
5 squat

Hunnish
4 rude, wild **6** Gothic, savage
7 uncivil **9** barbarian, barbarous
11 uncivilized **12** uncultivated

hunt
3 dog, gun, run **4** hawk, kill, prey, rout, seek **5** chase, drive, hound, quest, shoot, snare, stalk, start, track **6** battue, course, dig out, ferret, pursue, rabbit, safari, shikar
7 capture, explore, rummage
9 cast about, ferret out, search for, search out
birds: **4** fowl
illegally: **5** poach

hunter
5 jager, yager **6** chaser, jaeger, nimrod **7** stalker **8** chasseur, predator
biblical: **6** Nimrod
cap: **5** terai **7** montero
constellation: **5** Orion
cry: **6** yoicks **7** tallyho
horn: **5** bugle
mythological: **5** Orion **7** Actaeon

hunting
5 chase **6** venery **7** angling, fishing, gunning, hawking **8** coursing, falconry **9** predatory **10** predacious
bird: **6** falcon
call: **7** recheat
cry: **4** toho **7** tallyho, tantivy
dog: **4** alan **5** alant, hound
6 alaunt, basset, beagle, borzoi, setter **7** pointer, spaniel
expedition: **6** safari

huntress
5 Diana **7** Artemis **8** Atalanta

Hupham's father
8 Benjamin

Hur
grandson: **8** Bezaleel
son: **8** Rephaiah

hurdle

3 bar, hop, lop, rub 4 down, jump, leap, lick, over, snag 5 bound, clear, throw, vault 6 bounce, hamper, master, spring 7 barrier, conquer, saltate 8 mountain, obstacle, overcome, overleap, surmount, traverse 9 negotiate 10 impediment 11 obstruction

hurl

4 cast, fire, rush, toss 5 drive, fling, heave, pitch, sling, throw, whirl 6 launch, thrust 8 catapult
stones: 8 lapidate

hurly-burly

4 to-do 5 melee, whirl 6 clamor, hassle, hubbub, pother, tumult, uproar 7 turmoil 8 confused 9 commotion, confusion

hurrah

4 coil, fire, fuss, romp, to-do, zeal ardor, cheer, scold, spree, tease 6 fervor, furore, harass, ruckus, rumpus, shindy, uproar 7 dispute, fanfare, passion 8 argument, raillery 9 calenture, commotion 10 contention, enthusiasm 11 controversy

hurricane

5 storm 7 tornado, typhoon 8 williwaw 9 whirlwind 13 tropical storm
tropical: 7 typhoon

hurried

4 fast 5 hasty 6 abrupt, sudden 7 rushing 8 headlong 9 impetuous 10 tumultuous 11 precipitant, precipitate, precipitous, subitaneous

hurry

3 fly, hie, jog, peg, run, zip 4 flit, pelt, post, rock, rush, skin, trot, whiz 5 dig in, fleet, haste, scoot, scour, skelp, skirr, skite, smoke, speed, stave, whirl, whish, whisk, whizz 6 barrel, breeze, bucket, bullet, bustle, hasten, hustle, rocket, rustle, step up, tumult, whirry 7 beeline, hotfoot, quicken, scutter, scuttle, shake up, skelter, swiften 8 celerity, dispatch, expedite, highball 9 bowl along, commotion, swiftness 10 accelerate, expedition, speediness

hurt

3 mar 4 ache, harm, pain, ruin 5 abuse, check, smart, spoil, wound, wrong 6 damage, grieve, hamper, impair, injure, injury, misuse, offend, suffer, weaken 7 afflict, blemish, damaged, outrage, tarnish, vitiate, wounded 8 aggrieve, distress, mischief, mistreat 9 constrain, detriment, prejudice, resentful, suffering 10 resentment

hurtful

4 evil, sore 6 aching 7 algetic, harmful, nocuous, painful 8 damaging 9 injurious 10 afflictive 11 deleterious, detrimental, mischievous, prejudicial 12 prejudicious

hurtle

4 rush 5 crash, fling, shoot, throw 6 clater 8 catapult 9 collision

husband

3 man 4 lord, mate, save 6 manage, mister, spouse 7 consort, hoarder 8 benedict, conserve, helpmate, helpmeet 9 other half 10 bridegroom

husbandry

6 thrift 7 economy, farming 8 prudence 9 frugality 10 management, providence 11 agriculture, thriftiness 12 conservation

hush

4 calm, lull 5 burke, quell, quiet, shush, still, whist 6 shut up, silent, stifle, stilly, whisht 7 mollify, secrecy, silence 8 choke off, suppress 9 cessation, noiseless, soundless, stillness 10 secretness 12 huggermugger 13 hugger-muggery, secretiveness

hush-hush

6 covert, secret 7 secrecy, silence, sub rosa 10 censorship, secretness, undercover 11 clandestine, suppression 12 confidential, hugger-mugger 13 hole-and-corner, huggermuggery, surreptitious, under-the-table

Hushim

father: 3 Dan
husband: 9 Shaharaim

husk

3 pod 4 case, peel, skin 5 bract, carob, hoose, shell, shuck, strip
combining form: 4 lepo 7 siliqui

husky

3 big, fat 4 bull 5 beefy, burly, empty, great, gruff, hefty, large, stout 6 brawny, croaky, hoarse, mighty, robust, strong, sturdy 8 croaking, gigantic, muscular, oversize, powerful, rattling, stalwart 9 Herculean, strapping, well-built 10 membranous 11 Bunyanesque

hustle

3 fly, rob, run 4 earn, move, push, rush, work 5 cheat, elbow, haste, hurry, press, shove, speed 6 gather, hasten 7 hotfoot, swindle 8 bulldoze, celerity, dispatch, shoulder 9 swiftness

hustler

4 bawd, doer, drab, moll 5 whore 6 dynamo, harlot, hooker, hummer, peeler, vendor 8 call girl, go-getter, live wire, new broom 9 humdinger 10 powerhouse, prostitute 11 self-starter 12 streetwalker

hustling

4 busy 5 fussy 6 lively 7 hopping, humming, popping 9 energetic

hut

3 cot 4 camp, crib, room, shed 5 cabin, dacha, house, hovel, hutch, jacal, lodge, roost, shack 6 bestow, billet, cabana, chalet, harbor, lean-to, shanty 7 cottage, edifice, quarter 8 building, domicile
American Indian: 6 wikiup 7 wickiup, wickyup
Russian: 4 isba, izba
shepherd's: 5 sheal, shiel 8 shealing, shieling

hutch

3 bin 4 cage 5 shack 6 locker, shanty

Huxley novel

11 Crome Yellow 13 Brave New World, Eyeless in Gaza

Hyacinthus

father: 7 Amyclas
slayer: 6 Apollo

hybrid

4 mule 5 cross 7 bastard, incross, mixture, mongrel 8 outcross 9 composite, crossbred, half blood, half-breed, loan-blend 10 crossbreed 11 combination

hybridize

5 cross 9 cross-mate 10 crossbreed, interbreed, intercross

Hydra

father: 6 Typhon
mother: 7 Echidna
slayer: 8 Heracles, Hercules

hydrant

3 tap 4 cock, gate 5 valve 6 faucet, spigot 7 petcock 8 fireplug, stopcock

hydraulic device

3 ram 4 jack, lift, pump 5 brake, press 8 elevator

hydrocarbon

5 xylol 6 ethane, indene, xylene
liquid: 6 octane 7 retinol, styrene 8 menthene
suffix: 5 ylene

hydroid
5 polyp 6 medusa, obelia 9 jelly-fish, millepore

hydrometer scale
4 Brix 5 Baumé

hydrophobia
5 lyssa 6 rabies

hydroponics
11 aquiculture, tank farming

Hygeia
5 Salus
father: 9 Asclepius 11 Aesculapius
goddess of: 6 health

hygienic
4 good 7 healthy 8 salutary, sanitary 9 healthful, wholesome
10 salubrious

Hyllus' father
8 Heracles, Hercules

hymeneal
6 wedded 7 marital, married, nuptial, spousal 8 conjugal 9 connubial 11 matrimonial

hymn
3 lay 4 aria, laud, lied, sing, song
5 bless, carol, chant, cry up, ditty, extol, paean, trill, troll 6 choral, intone, praise, warble 7 chorale, descant, glorify, gradual, magnify
8 antiphon, canticle, doxology, eulogize 9 celebrate 10 panegyrize

hyperbole
8 coloring 12 embroidering, exag-geration 13 embellishment, overstatement

hyperbolic function
4 cosh, coth, csch, sech, sinh, tanh

hypercritical
7 carping 8 captious, caviling
9 cavillous 10 censorious
12 faultfinding

Hyperion
daughter: 3 Eos 6 Aurora, Selene
father: 6 Uranus
mother: 2 Ge 4 Gaea
son: 6 Helios
wife: 5 Theia

hypnotic
6 opiate, sleepy 8 mesmeric, somnific 9 somnolent, soporific 10 somnorific 11 somniferous

hypnotize
5 charm 6 trance 8 entrance
9 mesmerize, spellbind

hypocorism
6 byname, byword 8 nickname
9 sobriquet

hypocrisy
4 cant, sham 6 humbug 7 pietism
8 glibness, quackery 9 casuistry
10 pharisaism, sanctimony, Tartuffery, Tartuffism 11 charlatanry, insincerity, religiosity 12 pecksniffery, unctuousness

hypocrite
4 sham 5 actor, faker, fraud, phony, poser, quack 6 humbug, phoney, poseur 7 bluffer, pietist, Tartufe 8 deceiver, impostor, pharisee, Tartuffe 9 charlatan, lip server, pretender 10 dissembler 11 fourflusher, masquerader 12 dissimulator

hypocritical
4 glib, oily 5 bland, false 6 smooth
7 canting 8 affected, janiform, malafide, specious, unctuous 9 casuistic, insincere, pharisaic, pietistic, religiose 10 goody-goody, left-handed, moralistic 11 dissembling, double-faced 12 ambidextrous, double-minded, mealymouthed, pecksniffian, smooth-spoken
13 double-dealing, doublehearted, double-tongued, sanctimonious, self-righteous, smooth-tongued

hypothesis
6 theory 8 supposal 11 supposition

hypothetical
5 ideal 7 assumed, reputed 8 abstract, doubtful, putative, supposed
11 conditional, conjectural, implication, problematic, suppositive, suppository 12 supposititious, transcendent 13 suppositional

Hypsipyle's father
5 Thoas

hyrax
4 cony 5 coney

hysterical fear
5 panic

Ii

Iago
general: 7 Othello
victim: 6 Cassio, Emilia 7 Othello
9 Desdemona
wife: 6 Emilia

Iapetus
father: 6 Uranus
mother: 2 Ge 4 Gaea
son: 5 Atlas 9 Menoetius 10 Epimetheus, Prometheus
wife: 7 Clymene

Iasion
brother: 8 Dardanus
father: 4 Zeus 7 Jupiter
lover: 5 Ceres 7 Demeter
mother: 7 Electra
son: 6 Plutus

ibex
3 tur 4 tahr 8 wild goat
family: 7 Bovidae
genus: 5 Capra

Ibhar's father
5 David

ibis-headed god
5 Thoth

Ibneiah's father
7 Jeroham

Ibnijah's son
5 Reuel

Ibri's father
7 Jaaziah

Ibsen
character: 3 Ase 4 Nora 5 Brand,
Hedda 7 Solness 8 Peer Gynt
country: 6 Norway
play: 6 Ghosts 8 Peer Gynt 11 A
Doll's House, Hedda Gabler, Little
Eyolf, Rosmersholm, The Wild Duck

Icarius
brother: 9 Tyndareus
daughter: 7 Erigone 8 Penelope
mother: 10 Gorgophone

Icarus' father
8 Daedalus

ice
4 rime, sish 5 chill, frost, glace
6 freeze
area: 4 rink
combining form: 6 glacio 8 crystall
9 crystallo
floating: 4 berg, floe
glacial: 5 serac
hanging: 6 icicle
on rock: 7 verglas
pinnacle: 5 serac

ice cream
7 spumone, spumoni, tortoni
dish: 4 soda 6 frappe, sundae

iced
5 glacé 6 glazed

ice field
7 glacier

ice game
6 hockey 7 curling

ice house
4 iglu 5 igloo

Iceland
capital: 9 Reykjavik
monetary unit: 5 krona

Icelandic
epic: 4 Edda
hero: 7 Grettir

Ichabod
father: 8 Phinehas
grandfather: 3 Eli

Ichabod Crane's beloved
8 Caterina

icing
7 topping 8 frosting

icky
4 vile 5 nasty 6 sticky 7 noisome
8 horrible 9 loathsome, offensive,
repellent, revolting, sickening
10 disgusting

icon
5 image

icy
4 cold 5 chill, gelid 6 arctic, chilly,
frigid, frosty 7 glacial 8 chilling,
freezing 11 emotionless, indifferent, unemotional

Idaho
capital: 5 Boise
nickname: 8 Gem State
state flower: 7 syringa

Idas
brother: 7 Lynceus
father: 8 Aphareus
slayer: 4 Zeus
victim: 6 Castor
wife: 8 Marpessa

Iddo
father: 9 Zechariah
grandson: 9 Zechariah
son: 8 Ahinadab

idea
4 view, whim 5 fancy, guess,
image 6 belief, notion, theory, vagary, whimsy 7 caprice, conceit,
concept, fantasy, feeling, figment,
inkling, opinion, subject, surmise,
thought 8 judgment, reaction
9 sentiment, suspicion 10 assumption, brainstorm, conception, conclusion, conjecture, conviction, estimation, hypothesis, impression,
perception, persuasion, reflection
11 inspiration

ideal
4 goal, very 5 jewel, model 6 mirror 7 classic, example, paragon,
pattern, perfect, phoenix, typical,
utopian 8 abstract, ensample, exemplar, flawless, nonesuch, notional, paradigm, standard 9 archetype, classical, exemplary,
imaginary, nonpareil, visionary
10 archetypal, conceptual, ideational, prototypal 11 theoretical

idealist
7 dreamer, quixote, utopian 9 ideologue, visionary 13 castle-builder

idealistic
6 starry 7 utopian 8 poetical, quixotic, romantic 9 visionary 10 starry-eyed 11 impractical, unrealistic

idée ___
4 fixe

identical
3 one 4 like, same, self, very 5 alike, equal, exact 8 selfsame

identification
abbreviation: 2 ID
mark: 5 brand, label

identify
3 tag 4 find, mark, name, spot 5 brand, place 6 finger, select 7 make out, pick out 8 diagnose, pinpoint 9 determine, establish, recognize

ideology
3 ism 4 view 5 credo, creed 7 outlook 10 philosophy

idiocy
5 folly 7 amentia, fatuity 9 stupidity

idiosyncratic
3 odd 5 queer, weird 6 proper 7 curious, erratic, oddball, strange 8 peculiar, singular 9 diacritic, eccentric 10 diagnostic, individual 11 distinctive

idiot
3 ass 4 fool, jerk, simp, zany 5 ament, dummy, dunce, moron, ninny, schmo 6 cretin, donkey, jester, motley, schmoe, stupid 7 dullard, half-wit, jackass, natural, tomfool 8 dullhead, dumbbell, imbecile, numskull 9 ignoramus, simpleton 10 nincompoop

idiotic
4 daft 6 stupid 7 foolish, moronic 9 senseless

idle
3 bum 4 laze, lazy, loaf, loll, rest, vain 5 amble, dally, drone, empty, inert, mooch, mosey, quiet, relax, sit by, tarry 6 asleep, dawdle, diddle, futile, hollow, linger, loiter, lounge, otiose, potter, repose, sleepy, stroll, unused, vacant 7 aimless, passive, saunter, sit back, useless 8 inactive, indolent, nugatory, slothful

idleness
4 laze 5 sloth 6 acedia, slouch 8 flânerie, laziness 9 indolence 12 slothfulness

idler
3 bum 4 slug 5 drone 6 loafer, slouch 8 dolittle, fainéant, slugabed, sluggard 9 do-nothing, lazybones

Idmon
daughter: 7 Arachne
father: 6 Apollo
mother: 6 Cyrene

idol
3 god 4 hero, icon 5 image
Chinese: 4 joss

idolatry
7 baalism, worship 9 adoration 11 idolization

idolize
5 adore 6 admire, dote on, revere 7 worship 8 dote upon, venerate

Idylls of the King
author: 8 Tennyson (Alfred)
character: 4 Enid 6 Arthur, Elaine, Gareth, Merlin, Vivien 7 Geraint, Lynette 8 Lancelot

iffy
5 dicey 6 chancy 7 erratic 8 doubtful 9 fluctuant, uncertain, whimsical 10 capricious 12 incalculable 13 unpredictable

Igal's father
6 Nathan 8 Shemaiah

Igdaliah's son
5 Hanan

igneous rock
4 lava 5 magma 6 basalt, gabbro, pumice, scoria 7 diabase, granite 8 obsidian, porphyry

ignis fatuus
6 mirage 8 delusion, illusion, phantasm 12 will-o'-the-wisp 13 hallucination

ignitable
8 burnable 9 flammable 11 combustible, inflammable

ignite
4 fire 5 light 6 excite, kindle 7 inflame 8 enkindle

ignited
3 lit 5 afire, fiery 6 ablaze, aflame, alight 7 blazing, burning, flaming, flaring, lighted

ignoble
3 low 4 base, mean, poor, vile 5 lowly, plain 6 abject, coarse, common, homely, humble, modest, scurvy, simple, sordid, vulgar 7 lowborn, peasant, popular, ser-vile 8 baseborn, inferior, ordinary, plebeian, shameful, unwashed, wretched 10 despicable, inglorious, unennobled 11 disgraceful 12 dishonorable

ignominious
5 shady 6 shabby, shoddy 8 shameful 10 inglorious 11 disgraceful 12 dishonorable, disreputable 13 discreditable, unrespectable

ignominy
5 odium, scorn, shame 6 infamy 7 chagrin, despite, disdain, obloquy 8 contempt, disgrace, dishonor 9 discredit, disesteem, disrepute 10 opprobrium 13 mortification

ignoramus
4 dolt, fool 5 dummy, dunce, idiot, moron 6 nitwit, stupid 7 dullard 8 dullhead, dumbbell 9 simpleton

ignorance
7 naiveté, rawness 8 darkness 9 greenness, innocence, inscience, nescience 10 callowness, illiteracy, simpleness, simplicity 11 unawareness, uncouthness, witlessness

ignorant
3 raw 4 rude 5 crude, green, gross, naive 6 callow, simple, stupid 7 lowbrow, unaware, uncouth 8 backward, nescient, untaught 9 benighted, ingenuous, oblivious, unknowing, untutored, unwitting 10 illiterate, uncultured, uneducated, unfamiliar, uninformed, unlettered, unschooled 11 emptyheaded, incognizant, know-nothing 12 inconversant, unacquainted, uninstructed

ignore
3 cut 4 fail, omit, snub 5 avoid, evade 6 forget, slight 7 blink at, neglect 8 discount, overlook, overpass 9 blink away, disregard

Igraine, Ygerne
husband: 5 Uther 7 Gorlois
son: 6 Arthur

iguana
6 lizard 7 tuatara

ilex
5 holly 7 holm oak

Iliad
4 epic
author: 5 Homer
character: 4 Ajax 5 Helen, Paris, Priam 6 Aeneas, Hector 8 Achilles, Diomedes, Odysseus 9 Agamemnon, Patroclus
city: 4 Troy

Ilion, Ilium
4 Troy

ilk
4 kind, sort, type 5 breed, class
6 family, kidney, nature, stripe
7 variety

ill
3 bad 4 down, evil, rude, sick
5 amiss 6 malady, nocent 7 ailment, disease, harmful, hostile, hurtful, ill-bred, nocuous, noxious, uncivil 8 damaging, disorder, feverish, feverous, impolite, inimical, nauseous, sickness, syndrome 9 affection, complaint, condition, infirmity, injurious

ill-adapted
5 inapt, unfit 6 unmeet 8 unfitted, unsuited 9 ill-suited 10 unsuitable 13 inappropriate

ill-advised
4 rash 5 brash, hasty 6 madcap, unwise 8 reckless 9 hotheaded, ill-judged, impolitic, imprudent 10 incautious, indiscreet, mad-brained 11 inadvisable, inexpedient, injudicious, thoughtless, unadvisable, unexpedient 13 inconsiderate

ill-boding
4 dire 7 baleful, baneful, fateful, ominous, unlucky 9 ill-omened 11 apocalyptic 12 inauspicious, unpropitious

ill-bred
4 rude 6 rugged 7 boorish, incivil, loutish, lowbred, uncivil 8 churlish, cloddish, impolite 9 unrefined 10 uncultured, ungracious, unpolished 11 disgracious, ill-mannered, impertinent, uncivilized 12 discourteous 13 disrespectful

ill-defined
3 dim 5 blear, faint, fuzzy, vague 6 bleary 7 shadowy, unclear 9 undefined 10 indistinct

illegal
3 hot 6 banned 7 illicit, lawless 8 criminal, nonlegal, outlawed, unlawful, wrongful 9 felonious, forbidden, irregular 10 actionable, contraband, prohibited, proscribed, unlicensed 11 interdicted, unwarranted 12 illegitimate, unauthorized
act: 5 crime 6 felony
scheme: 4 scam

illegible
5 faint 7 obscure, unclear 10 indistinct, unreadable

illegitimacy
8 bastardy 10 illegality 11 bar sinister, illicitness 12 unlawfulness

illegitimate
6 by-blow 7 bastard, bootleg, illegal, illicit, lawless, natural 8 baseborn, criminal, spurious, unlawful, wrongful

ill-fated
7 hapless, unhappy, unlucky 8 luckless, untoward 11 star-crossed, unfortunate 12 misfortunate

ill health
7 cachexy 8 cachexia

ill-humored
5 cross 6 cranky 7 peevish 8 choleric 9 dyspeptic 10 tempersome 11 bad-tempered, hot-tempered

illiberal
4 mean 5 petty, rigid, small 6 biased, little, narrow, paltry, stingy 7 bigoted, insular, partial 8 grudging, one-sided, partisan, rigorous 9 hidebound, jaundiced, parochial, stringent 10 brassbound, intolerant, prejudiced, provincial, unenlarged, ungenerous 11 opinionated, small-minded 12 narrow-minded, uncharitable

illicit
7 bootleg, illegal, lawless 8 criminal, unlawful, wrongful 12 illegitimate

illimitable
7 endless, eternal 8 infinite 9 boundless 10 perdurable 11 measureless, sempiternal 12 immeasurable, interminable

Illinois
capital: 11 Springfield
college, university: 5 Barat 6 De Paul 7 Wheaton 12 Northwestern
largest city: 7 Chicago
nickname: 11 Sucker State 12 Prairie State
state bird: 8 cardinal
state flower: 6 violet

illiterate
4 rude 8 ignorant, untaught 9 benighted, unlearned, untutored 10 analphabet, uncultured, uneducated, unlettered

ill-kempt
5 messy 6 sloppy, unneat, untidy 8 careless, slipshod, slovenly, uncombed 10 disheveled

ill-mannered
4 rude 7 incivil, uncivil 8 impolite 10 ungracious 11 disgracious, impertinent 12 discourteous 13 disrespectful

ill-natured
5 cross, nasty, surly 6 crabby 8 choleric 9 dyspeptic 10 tempersome 11 bad-tempered, hot-tempered

illness
6 malady 7 ailment, disease 8 cachexia, disorder, sickness, unhealth 9 infirmity 10 affliction 13 indisposition
mental: 8 dementia

illogical
3 mad 5 false 6 absurd 7 invalid, unsound 8 specious 9 plausible, senseless, sophistic 10 fallacious, irrational, reasonless, unreasoned 11 meaningless, nonrational 12 unreasonable, unscientific

ill-starred
6 malign 7 baleful, bodeful, fateful, hapless, malefic, ominous, unhappy, unlucky 8 luckless, sinister, untoward 10 foreboding, portentous 11 star-crossed, unfavorable, unfortunate, unpromising 12 misfortunate, unpropitious

ill-suited
5 inapt, unfit 6 unmeet 8 unfitted 10 unsuitable 13 inappropriate

ill-tempered
4 sour 5 cross, huffy, surly 6 crabby, grumpy 7 crabbed, grouchy, peevish, waspish 8 choleric, petulant, shrewish, snappish, vixenish 9 dyspeptic, fractious, irritable, querulous

ill-timed
5 inept 8 improper, mistimed, unseemly, untimely 10 malapropos, unbecoming, unsuitable 11 inopportune, unbefitting 12 unseasonable 13 inappropriate

ill-treat
5 abuse, harry 6 harass, misuse, molest 7 outrage 8 aggrieve, maltreat, mistreat

illude
4 bilk 5 bluff, cheat, elude 6 betray, delude, humbug, juggle, take in 7 beguile, deceive, mislead 11 double-cross

illume
5 edify, light 6 uplift 7 improve, lighten 8 illumine 9 enlighten, irradiate

illuminate
4 fire 5 clear, edify, exalt, gloss, light 6 better, define, finish, ignite,

kindle, mature, polish, refine, uplift **7** clarify, clear up, ennoble, explain, expound, express, improve, lighten, perfect **8** brighten, construe **9** dramatize, elucidate, enlighten, highlight, interpret, irradiate, spotlight

illuminati

7 clerisy **8** literati **13** intellectuals

illumination

8 lighting

unit of: **3** lux **4** phot **5** lumen **6** candle **7** candela **10** footcandle

illumine

see **illuminate**

illusion

5 dream **6** bubble, mirage **7** chimera, fantasy, rainbow, seeming **8** delusion, phantasm, phantasy **9** invention, pipe dream, semblance **10** appearance **11** ignis fatuus **12** will-o'-the-wisp **13** hallucination

illusionist

8 conjurer, magician **9** trickster

illusive

5 false **6** unreal **7** seeming **8** apparent

illusory

6 unreal **7** fictive, seeming **8** apparent, delusive, delusory, fanciful, illusive, semblant **9** deceptive, fantastic, fictional, imaginary, visionary **10** Barmecidal, chimerical, fictitious, misleading, ostensible

illustrate

4 mark, show **5** clear **6** embody, evince, expose, mirror, ostend, reveal, typify, vivify **7** clarify, clear up, display, enliven, exhibit, explain, expound, picture **8** disclose, discover, evidence, instance, manifest, proclaim **9** elucidate, epitomize, exemplify

illustration

4 case **6** sample **7** example, problem **8** ensample, instance, sampling, specimen

illustrative

7 graphic **8** pictoric **9** pictorial **12** iconographic

illustrator

American: **5** Flagg (James Montgomery), Wyeth (Newell Convers) **7** Burgess (Gelett) **8** Rockwell (Norman) **9** Remington (Frederic)
English: **6** Potter (Beatrix) **7** Tenniel (John) **9** Beardsley (Aubrey), du Maurier (George)
French: **4** Doré (Gustave)
German: **5** Dürer (Albrecht)

illustrious

5 famed, great, lofty, noted **6** famous, signal **7** eminent, exalted, notable, sublime **8** glorious, renowned, splendid, striking **9** prominent **10** celebrated, celebrious **11** conspicuous, outstanding, resplendent **13** distinguished

illustriousness

6 renown **8** eminence, prestige **10** prominence, prominency **11** distinction, preeminence

ill will

5 spite, venom **6** animus, grudge, malice, rancor, spleen **7** despite **9** hostility, malignity **10** malignancy **11** malevolence **12** spitefulness **13** maliciousness

Ilus

father: **4** Tros
grandson: **5** Priam
mother: **10** Callirrhoe
son: **8** Laomedon

image

4 copy, form, icon, idea, idol, limn **5** equal, fancy, glass, match, split, think **6** depict, double, effigy, mirror, notion, recept, render, ringer, vision **7** conceit, concept, fantasm, feature, imagine, picture, portray, realize, reflect, thought **8** conceive, describe, envisage, envision, likeness, phantasm, portrait **9** delineate, interpret, represent, semblance, visualize **10** conception, equivalent, impression, perception, simulacrum

Polynesian: **4** tiki
Semitic: **6** teraph **8** teraphim (plural)

imaginary

5 ideal **6** unreal **7** fancied, fictive, shadowy **8** abstract, chimeric, fanciful, illusory, imagined, notional, quixotic, spectral, visional **9** fantastic, fictional, figmental, visionary **10** chimerical, fictitious, phantasmal, phantasmic **11** imaginative **12** apparitional, hypothetical, suppositious **13** hallucinatory, unsubstantial

imagination

5 fancy **7** fantasy **8** phantasy **9** invention **10** creativity **11** inspiration **13** inventiveness, visualization

imagine

4 take **5** dream, fancy, guess, image, think **6** assume, expect, gather, vision **7** believe, feature, picture, realize, suppose, suspect **8** conceive, envisage, envision

9 fabricate, visualize **10** conjecture, understand

imbecile

3 ass **4** dolt, dull, fool, jerk, slow, zany **5** ament, idiot, moron, ninny **6** cretin, donkey **7** half-wit, jackass, moronic, natural, tomfool **8** backward, retarded **9** dim-witted, simpleton **10** half-witted, nincompoop, slow-witted **12** feebleminded, simpleminded

imbibe

3 sip **4** soak, swig, toss **5** booze, drink, quaff, sup up, swill **6** absorb, guzzle, insorb, sup off, tank up, tipple **7** inhaust, swallow, swizzle **8** liquor up **10** assimilate

imbricate

3 lap **4** ride **7** overlap, overlie, shingle **8** override

imbroglio

3 row **4** miff, spat **7** dispute, quarrel **8** squabble **9** bickering **10** falling-out **11** altercation, embroilment **12** disagreement

imbue

3 dye **4** soak **5** steep, tinge **6** infuse, invest, leaven **7** ingrain, suffuse **8** permeate, saturate **9** inoculate **10** impregnate

imitate

3 ape **4** copy, echo, mime, mock **5** mimic **6** parody **7** emulate, take off **8** travesty **9** burlesque, duplicate, replicate, reproduce **11** reduplicate

combining form: **3** mim **4** mimo

imitation

4 copy, fake, mock, sham **5** dummy, false, phony **6** ersatz **7** forgery, replica **8** likeness, spurious **9** duplicate, semblance, simulated **10** artificial, simulacrum, simulation, substitute **11** counterfeit, counterpart **12** reproduction

suffix: **3** een **4** ette

imitative

5 apish **6** echoic **7** parodic, slavish **9** emulative **12** onomatopoeic **13** onomatopoetic

Imlah's son

7 Micaiah

immaculate

4 pure **5** clean **6** chaste, decent, modest **7** cleanly, perfect **8** flawless, innocent, spotless, unsoiled **9** errorless, exquisite, faultless, stainless, taintless, undefiled, unsullied **10** impeccable **11** unblemished

immaterial

4 airy **6** aerial **7** foreign, ghostly, psychic, shadowy **8** bodiless, ethereal, heavenly, unbodied **9** asomatous, celestial, disbodied, spiritual, unearthly, unfleshly, unworldly **10** discarnate, extraneous, impalpable, inapposite, insensible, intangible, irrelative, irrelevant, subjective, unembodied, unmaterial, unphysical **11** disembodied, impertinent, incorporeal, nonmaterial, nonphysical **12** apparitional, imponderable, inapplicable, metaphysical, supernatural **13** insubstantial, unsubstantial

immature

3 raw **5** green, vealy, young **6** callow, infant, unripe **7** babyish, puerile **8** childish, juvenile, youthful **9** infantile, infantine, premature, unfledged **10** precocious **11** undeveloped

immaturity

6 nonage

immeasurable

7 endless **8** infinite **9** boundless, limitless, unbounded, unlimited **10** indefinite, unmeasured **11** illimitable, inestimable, measureless, uncountable **12** incalculable, unmeasurable, unreckonable

immediate

4 near, next, nigh **5** close **6** direct, nearby, urgent **7** instant, primary **9** first-hand, proximate **10** near-at-hand **11** hair-trigger **12** straightaway **13** instantaneous

immediately

3 now, PDQ **4** anon, away, soon, stat **6** at once, presto, pronto **7** shortly **8** directly, hereupon **9** forthwith, instanter, instantly, right away **11** straightway

immense

4 huge, vast **5** great, large **6** mighty **7** titanic **8** colossal, enormous, gigantic **9** monstrous **10** prodigious, tremendous

immensely

3 too **4** ever, over, very **6** overly, unduly **8** overfull, overmuch **9** extremely **11** exceedingly, excessively **12** inordinately

immensity

8 enormity, hugeness, vastness **9** magnitude **12** enormousness

immerse

3 dip **4** bury, busy, duck, dunk, sink, soak **5** bathe, douse, embed, souse **6** absorb, engage, occupy, plunge **7** asperse, baptize, engross, include **8** christen, saturate, sprinkle, submerge, submerse

immigrant

6 emigré
Israeli: **6** halutz **7** chalutz **8** halutzim (plural) **9** chalutzim (plural)
Japanese: **5** issei

imminent

5 loury **6** coming, likely, lowery **7** brewing, louring, nearing, ominous, pending **8** alarming, lowering, menacing, minatory, possible, probable, sinister, upcoming **9** gathering, impending, proximate **10** inevasible, inevitable **11** approaching, ineluctable, inescapable, overhanging, threatening, unavoidable, unescapable

immobile

3 set **5** fixed, inert, still **6** frozen, stable, static **8** immotile, immotive, stagnant, unmoving **9** immovable, steadfast, unmovable **10** motionless, stationary **11** irremovable

immobilize

6 disarm **7** cripple, disable **8** paralyze **9** prostrate **12** incapacitate

immoderate

5 dizzy, undue **7** extreme **8** towering **9** boundless, excessive, voracious **10** exorbitant, inordinate, untempered **11** extravagant, intemperate **12** unmeasurable, unreasonable, unrestrained **13** overindulgent

immoderation

6 excess **12** intemperance

immodest

4 bold, lewd **5** brash, gross **6** brazen **8** boastful, indecent, unchaste

immolate

4 kill **7** destroy **8** abnegate **9** sacrifice, victimize

immoral

3 bad **4** evil **5** dirty, loose, wrong **6** impure, sinful, wanton, wicked **7** corrupt, unclean, vicious **8** depraved, indecent, unchaste **9** dissolute, reprobate, uncleanly **10** iniquitous, licentious

immorality

4 vice **9** depravity **10** corruption, unchastity, wickedness

immortal

6 divine **7** abiding, endless, eternal, undying **8** enduring, timeless, unending **9** ceaseless, deathless, perpetual **11** amaranthine, everlasting, never-ending, sempiternal **12** imperishable

immotile

5 fixed **8** immobile, immotive **9** immovable, steadfast, unmovable **11** irremovable

immovable

3 pat, set **4** fast, firm **5** fixed, rigid, stuck **6** rooted, stable **7** adamant **8** constant, immobile, immotile, immotive, obdurate, unmoving **9** immutable, impassive, steadfast, unmovable **10** inflexible, invariable, stationary, unyielding

immunity

7 freedom **8** impunity **9** exemption

immunizer

7 vaccine **8** antibody

immure

3 hem, jug, pen **4** cage, coop, jail, mure, wall **5** fence, hedge **6** corral, intern **7** confine, enclose **8** bastille, cloister, imprison **9** constrain **11** incarcerate

immutable

4 firm **5** fixed **7** eternal **8** constant **9** immovable, unmovable **10** inflexible, invariable, unchanging **11** inalterable, unalterable **12** unchangeable, unmodifiable

Imnah

father: **5** Asher
son: **4** Kore

Imogen

father: **9** Cymbeline
husband: **9** Posthumus

imp

3 elf **4** brat, ouph, puck **5** cutup, demon, devil, gamin, gnome, pixie, scamp, troll **6** goblin, kobold, monkey, sprite, urchin **7** gremlin **9** hobgoblin

impact

3 hit, jar, rap **4** blow, bump, jolt, rock, slam, slap **5** brunt, clash, crash, crowd, pound, punch, quake, shake, shock, smash **6** bounce, buffet, jounce, quiver, strike, stroke, tremor, wallop **7** appulse, congest, impulse, meeting, smiting, tremble **9** collision, encounter **10** concussion, percussion

impair

3 mar, sap **4** harm, hurt **5** spoil **6** damage, debase, injure, lessen, weaken **7** blemish, cripple, tarnish, vitiate **8** enfeeble **9** prejudice, undermine

impaired
6 flawed, marred **7** damaged, spoiled **9** afflicted
prefix: **3** dys

impala
7 rooibok **8** antelope

impale
4 spit, stab **5** lance, prick, punch, spear, spike **6** pierce, skewer, skiver **8** puncture, transfix **9** perforate **11** transpierce

impart
4 give, lend, tell **5** break, grant, share, yield **6** bestow, convey, pass on **8** disclose, transmit **11** communicate
knowledge: **5** teach **6** inform **7** educate **8** instruct

impartial
4 even, fair, just **5** equal **7** neutral **8** unbiased **9** equitable, objective, uncolored **12** unprejudiced **13** disinterested, dispassionate

impasse
3 box, fix, jam **4** hole **6** corner, pickle, plight, pocket, scrape **7** dead end, dilemma **8** cul-de-sac, deadlock **9** stalemate **10** blind alley **11** predicament

impassioned
4 deep, warm **5** fiery, gushy, mushy **6** ardent, fervid, fierce, red-hot, torrid **7** blazing, burning, fervent, flaming, furious, glowing, gushing, intense, maudlin, violent, zealous **8** eloquent, feverish, profound, romantic, vehement, white-hot **9** perfervid **10** hot-blooded, overheated, passionate **11** dithyrambic, sentimental **12** melodramatic **13** overemotional

impassive
3 dry **4** calm, cold, cool **5** stoic **6** bovine, placid, stolid, wooden **7** callous **8** composed, hardened, reserved, reticent, taciturn **9** apathetic, collected, heartless, inanimate, indurated **10** insensible, insentient, motionless, phlegmatic, spiritless **11** cold-blooded, cold-hearted, emotionless, inexcitable, insensitive, passionless, unconcerned, unemotional, unexcitable, unflappable **12** inexpressive, matter-of-fact, unexpressive, unresponsive **13** dispassionate, imperturbable, unimpressible, unsusceptible

impassivity
6 apathy, phlegm **8** stoicism **9** stolidity **13** insensibility

impatient
3 hot **4** agog, avid, edgy, keen **5** eager, harsh, hasty, itchy **6** abrupt, ardent **7** anxious, athirst, chafing, fidgety, fretful, nervous, thirsty **8** appetent, headlong, restless **9** demanding, impetuous, irascible, irritable

impeach
3 tax **6** accuse, charge, indict **7** arraign, censure **9** criminate, inculpate **11** incriminate

impeccable
4 nice **5** clean, exact, right **7** correct, perfect, precise **8** absolute, accurate, flawless, unerring, unflawed **9** errorless, exquisite, faultless, fleckless **10** immaculate, infallible **12** indefectible

impecunious
4 poor **5** needy **8** dirt poor, indigent **9** destitute, penniless, penurious **11** necessitous **12** impoverished, unprosperous

impecuniousness
4 need, want **6** penury **7** poverty **8** poorness **9** indigence, neediness, privation **11** destitution

impedance
4 clog **9** cumbrance, hindrance **10** impediment **11** encumbrance

impede
3 bar, bog, dam **4** clog, faze **5** block, brake, check, debar **6** hinder, hold up, rattle **8** obstruct **9** discomfit, embarrass

impediment
3 bar, rub **4** clog, snag **5** block, hitch **6** hamper, hurdle **8** obstacle **9** cumbrance, hindrance **10** difficulty **11** encumbrance, obstruction

impel
4 good, move, spur, urge **5** drive, force **6** compel, foment, incite, propel **7** actuate, inspire **8** mobilize, motivate **9** constrain, instigate, stimulate

impend
4 brew, hang, loom **6** gather, menace **8** approach, overhang **9** forthcome

impenetrable
4 firm, hard **5** dense, solid **6** arcane, mystic **8** numinous **9** mysterial, unguessed **10** cabalistic, impassable, impervious, mysterious,

unknowable **11** impermeable, imperviable, inscrutable, substantial, ungraspable **12** incognizable, unfathomable

imperative
4 need, rule **5** acute, basic, bossy, guide, harsh, order, stern **6** crying, urgent **7** bidding, burning, claimed, clamant, command, crucial, exacted, exigent, instant **8** critical, demanded, imperial, ordering, pressing, required **9** clamorous, essential, imperious, insistent, mandatory, masterful, necessary, necessity **10** commanding, compulsory, high-handed, obligatory, peremptory **11** domineering, fundamental, importunate, magisterial, necessitous, overbearing **12** compulsatory, prerequisite

imperceptible
5 faint, vague **6** slight **7** obscure, trivial **8** fugitive **9** ephemeral, invisible, momentary **10** evanescent, impalpable, indistinct, insensible, intangible, unapparent **12** imponderable, unnoticeable, unobservable **13** inappreciable, inconspicuous, indiscernible, insignificant, unappreciable, undiscernible, unperceivable

imperceptive
7 cursory, shallow **8** slapdash **11** superficial, unobservant **12** impercipient, undiscerning, unperceiving, unperceptive

imperfect
4 sick **5** amiss **6** faulty, flawed, second **9** defective **10** defeasible, inadequate, incomplete, unfinished

imperfection
3 sin **4** flaw **5** fault **6** defect, foible **7** blemish, demerit, failing, frailty **8** weakness **10** deficiency **11** shortcoming

imperial
5 bossy, regal, royal **6** kingly **7** haughty **8** majestic **9** grandiose, imperious, masterful, sovereign **10** high-handed, imperative, peremptory **11** domineering, magisterial, overbearing

imperil
4 risk **6** hazard, menace **7** jeopard, venture **8** endanger, jeopardy, threaten **10** compromise, jeopardize

imperious
5 bossy **6** lordly, strict, urgent **7** haughty **8** absolute, arrogant,

despotic, dominant, imperial, required **9** arbitrary, mandatory, masterful, stringent **10** commanding, compulsory, high-handed, imperative, obligatory, oppressive, peremptory, tyrannical **11** dictatorial, domineering, heavy-handed, magisterial, overbearing

impermanent
7 passing **8** fleeting, fugitive, unstable **9** ephemeral, fugacious, momentary, temporary, tentative, transient **10** evanescent, short-lived, transitory

impersonal
4 cold, fair **5** equal **7** neutral **8** abstract, detached, unbiased **9** colorless, equitable, impartial, objective, uncolored **10** poker-faced **11** cold-blooded, emotionless, unpassioned **12** matter-of-fact, unprejudiced **13** disinterested, dispassionate, unimpassioned

impersonator
4 mime **5** actor, mimic **6** mummer, player **7** actress, trouper **8** thespian **9** performer, playactor **13** impressionist

impertinence
4 sass **8** audacity, boldness **9** hardihood, impudence, insolence, insolency, unfitness **10** disrespect, incivility **11** irrelevance **12** insolentness

impertinent
4 bold, busy, nosy, pert, rude **5** brash, fresh, sassy, saucy **6** brazen, prying **7** foreign, ill-bred, uncivil **8** arrogant, impolite, impudent, insolent, meddling **9** audacious, intrusive, obtrusive, offensive, officious **10** extraneous, immaterial, inapposite, irrelative, irrelevant, meddlesome, procacious, ungracious **11** ill-mannered, inquisitive, interfering, uncalled-for **12** contumelious, discourteous, inapplicable, presumptuous **13** disrespectful

imperturbability
6 phlegm **7** ataraxy **8** calmness, coolness **9** composure, sangfroid **10** equanimity

imperturbable
4 calm, cool, smug **6** placid, serene **7** unmoved **8** composed, tranquil **9** collected, impassive, unruffled, untouched **10** complacent, nonchalant, phlegmatic, unaffected **11** unflappable **13** self-satisfied

impervious
5 tight **8** hardened **10** impassable **11** impermeable, imperviable **12** impenetrable, unpierceable

impetuous
3 hot **4** rash **5** eager, fiery, hasty **6** abrupt, ardent, fervid, sudden **7** furious, hurried, restive, rushing, violent **8** headlong, vehement **9** hotheaded, impulsive **10** passionate **11** impassioned, precipitant, precipitate, precipitous, spontaneous

impetus
4 good, spur **5** force **7** impulse **8** catalyst, momentum, stimulus **9** incentive, stimulant **10** incitation, incitement, motivation

impious
6 sinful, unholy, wicked **7** froward, godless, profane, ungodly, wayward **8** contrary, indevout, perverse, undevout **9** atheistic, unduteous, undutiful **10** irreverent, scandalous, unfaithful, unhallowed **11** disobedient, irreligious, wrongheaded **12** iconoclastic, sacrilegious

impish
4 arch, pert **5** elfin, fresh, giddy, saucy **6** casual, elfish, elvish **7** coltish, offhand, playful, puckish, roguish, waggish **8** flippant, pixieish, sportive **10** frolicsome **11** free and easy, mischievous

impishness
7 devilry, roguery, waggery **8** deviltry, mischief **9** devilment **11** roguishness, waggishness **12** sportiveness

implacable
4 grim **6** mortal **8** ruthless **9** merciless **10** inexorable, ironfisted, relentless, unyielding **11** unflinching, unrelenting **12** unappeasable

implant
4 root **5** embed, imbue, infix, inset **6** enroot, infuse, leaven **7** impress, ingrain, inspire, instill, pervade **8** permeate, saturate **9** inculcate, inoculate, insinuate, introduce, penetrate **10** impregnate, inseminate **11** impenetrate

implausible
4 thin, weak **5** fishy, thick **6** flimsy **7** dubious, suspect, tenuous **8** doubtful, puzzling **10** improbable, incredible **11** problematic **12** unconvincing

implement
4 tool **6** device, effect, gadget, invoke **7** enforce, execute, fulfill, perform, realize, utensil **8** complete **9** actualize, apparatus, appliance **10** accomplish, instrument, supplement **11** contraption, contrivance
cleaning: **3** mop **5** broom, brush **6** vacuum **7** sweeper **10** whiskbroom
cutting: **5** knife, mower, razor **6** scythe, shears, sickle **8** scissors
digging: **5** spade **6** shovel
drawing: **3** pen **6** eraser, pencil **7** compass **8** charcoal, template
eating: **4** fork **5** knife, spoon
engraving: **5** burin **6** graver
farm: **4** disc, dish, plow **6** dibber, harrow, seeder, tiller **8** gangplow, reaphook
fireplace: **5** tongs **7** andiron
fishing: **3** rod **4** hook **7** harpoon, trident
garden: **3** hoe **4** rake **6** trowel
grooming: **4** comb **5** brush **8** tweezers **10** toothbrush
kind: **3** die, saw **4** file **5** brace, clamp, drill, punch, tongs **6** chisel, hammer, pliers, reamer, sander, wrench **7** hacksaw, scraper **9** blowtorch **11** screwdriver
kitchen: **3** pan, pot **4** mold **5** mixer **6** kettle, mortar, pestle **7** blender, skillet, spatula
logging: **4** pevy **5** peavy, peevy **6** peavey **8** cant hook
measuring: **4** gage, rule **5** gauge, ruler, scale **7** caliper, divider, trammel, T-square **10** micrometer, protractor
stone: **5** burin **6** colith **7** neolith **9** paleolith

implicate
4 mire **5** imply **6** affect, tangle **7** concern, embroil, implied, include, involve **8** implicit **11** incriminate

implication
4 hint **8** overtone **9** inference, undertone **10** suggestion **11** association, connotation

implicit
4 real **5** tacit **6** unsaid **7** genuine, implied, virtual **8** absolute, complete, inferred, unspoken **9** potential, practical, unuttered **10** undeclared, understood **11** unexpressed, unqualified

implied
5 tacit **6** unsaid **8** implicit, inferred,

unspoken, wordless **9** unuttered **10** undeclared, understood

imploration
4 plea, suit **6** appeal, orison, prayer **8** entreaty, petition **11** application, imprecation **12** supplication

implore
3 ask, beg **4** coax, pray **5** crave, plead **6** appeal **7** beseech, conjure, entreat **9** importune **10** supplicate

imply
4 hint **5** point **7** connote, include, suggest **8** indicate, intimate **9** insinuate

impolite
4 rude **5** crude, rough **7** ill-bred, incivil, uncivil **10** ungracious, unmannerly, unpolished **11** disgracious, ill-mannered, uncourteous **12** discourteous **13** disrespectful

impolitic
5 brash **6** unwise **8** tactless **9** ill-judged, imprudent, maladroit, unpolitic, untactful **10** ill-advised, indiscreet **11** inadvisable, inexpedient, injudicious, unadvisable, unexpedient **12** undiplomatic

import
4 mean, pith **5** count, sense, spell, value, weigh, worth **6** convey, denote, design, intend, intent, matter, moment, object, stress, weight **7** add up to, concern, connote, express, meaning, message, purport, purpose, signify **8** emphasis, indicate **9** magnitude, objective, substance **10** importance, intendment **11** acceptation, consequence, weightiness **12** significance, significancy

importance
4 mark, note, pith **5** value, worth **6** import, moment, weight **7** account, gravity **8** eminence, priority, salience, standing **9** magnitude, substance **10** notability, prominence, reputation, worthiness **11** consequence, distinction, seriousness, weightiness **12** significance

important
3 big **5** grave, great, noted, puffy, wiggy **6** famous, marked, potent, stuffy, urgent, worthy **7** big-time, bloated, crucial, eminent, fateful, notable, pompous, salient, serious, telling, unusual, weighty **8** arrogant, eventful, material, powerful,

top-notch, valuable **9** effective, essential, first-rate, front-page, memorable, momentous, ponderous, prominent **10** first-class, impressive, meaningful, noteworthy, noticeable, pontifical, remarkable, worthwhile **11** conspicuous, distinctive, exceptional, magisterial, outstanding, significant, substantial **12** considerable **13** consequential, distinguished

importune
3 beg **4** pray, urge **5** annoy, crave, plead, worry **6** appeal, invoke **7** beseech, entreat, implore, solicit, trouble **10** supplicate

impose
3 fob, set, use **4** lade, levy, wish **5** abuse, exact, foist, order, put on, visit, wreak, wreck **6** assess, burden, charge, compel, create, decree, demand, enjoin, fob off, oblige, ordain, saddle **7** command, dictate, exploit, force on, inflict, intrude, lay down, obtrude, palm off, presume, put upon, require **8** encroach, generate, infringe, trespass **9** constrain, force upon

imposing
3 big **4** arty **5** grand, noble, regal, royal **6** august, moving **7** stately **8** baronial, imperial, majestic, princely **9** grandiose, overblown **10** arty-crafty, commanding, impressive **11** magnificent, pretentious **12** high-sounding

imposition
3 tax **4** duty, fine, levy **6** burden **7** penalty **9** deception

impossible
6 absurd **8** cureless, hopeless **9** incurable, insanable, uncurable **10** infeasible, unfeasible, unworkable **11** immedicable, impractical, irreparable, unthinkable **12** inexecutable, irrealizable, irremediable, unacceptable, unattainable, unobtainable, unrealizable, unreasonable

impost
3 tax **4** duty, levy **6** tariff, weight **7** tribute **10** assessment

imposter
4 fake **5** cheat, faker, fraud, mimic, phony, quack **6** humbug **7** bluffer, shammer, shyster **8** beguiler, deceiver, imitator **9** charlatan, hypocrite, misleader, pretender, trickster **10** dissembler, mountebank **11** four-flusher, pettifogger

imposture
3 gyp **4** copy, fake, flam, hoax, ploy, ruse, sell, sham, wile **5** cheat, feint, fraud, phony, put-on, spoof, trick **6** deceit, gambit, humbug **7** forgery, sleight, swindle **8** artifice, flimflam, maneuver, pretense **9** deception, falsehood, imitation, mare's nest, stratagem **10** pretension **11** counterfeit, fabrication, make-believe

impotent
4 weak **5** frail **6** barren, effete, feeble **7** sterile **8** boneless, crippled, disabled, helpless, infecund **9** enfeebled, forceless, infertile, powerless, spineless **10** emasculate, inadequate, unfruitful **11** ineffective, ineffectual, slack-spined **12** invertebrate

impoverish
4 bust, draw, ruin **5** break, drain, use up **6** beggar, fold up, pauper **7** deplete, exhaust **8** bankrupt, draw down **9** pauperize

impoverished
4 poor **5** needy **6** scanty **8** bankrupt, beggared, indigent **9** destitute, penurious **10** stone-broke **11** impecunious

impoverishment
4 need, want **6** penury **7** poverty **8** poorness **9** indigence, neediness, privation **11** destitution

impracticable
6 unwise **7** awkward, useless **8** unusable **9** imprudent **10** impossible, infeasible, unfeasible, unworkable

impractical
5 viewy **7** useless **8** quixotic, romantic, unusable **9** visionary **10** idealistic, impossible, infeasible, ivory-tower, starry-eyed, unfeasible, unworkable **11** theoretical, unrealistic

imprecation
4 oath, plea, suit **5** curse **6** appeal, orison, prayer **7** cursing, cussing, malison **8** anathema, entreaty, petition, swearing **9** blasphemy, profanity

impregnable
4 safe **6** secure **7** guarded **8** defended, shielded **9** protected **10** invincible, unbeatable **11** indomitable

impregnate
3 sop **4** soak **5** imbue, souse, steep **6** charge, drench, infuse, leaven,

seethe, sodden **7** pervade **8** permeate, saturate, waterlog **9** fertilize, inoculate, penetrate, percolate, transfuse **10** inseminate

impresario
5 agent, Carte, Hurok (Sol) **7** manager **9** Diaghilev (Sergei) **10** D'Oyly Carte (Richard)

impress
3 fix, get, set **4** etch, mark, move, seal, sway **5** brand, carry, drive, exert, force, grave, infix, pique, pound, print, stamp, touch **6** affect, effect, excite, hammer, strike, thrill **7** engrave, enthuse, implant, imprint, ingrain, inspire, provoke **8** inscribe **9** electrify, establish, galvanize, inculcate, influence, stimulate

impression
4 dent, dint, idea, mark, sign **5** image, print, shock, stamp, trace, track **6** hollow, impact, notion **7** conceit, concept, edition, impress, imprint, reissue, thought, vestige **8** printing, reaction

impressionable
7 plastic, sensile **8** sensible, sentient **9** sensitive **10** affectable, responsive, susceptive **11** impressible, susceptible **13** influenceable

impressionist
composer: **5** Ravel (Maurice) **7** Debussy (Claude)
mimic: **6** Little (Rich)
painter: **5** Degas (Edgar), Manet (Edouard), Monet (Claude) **6** Renoir (Pierre-Auguste), Sisley (Alfred) **7** Cassatt (Mary) **8** Pissarro (Camilla); (see also **postimpressionist**)

impressive
5 grand, noble **6** august, lavish, moving, superb **7** notable **8** gorgeous, imposing, majestic, poignant, splendid, striking, touching **9** affecting, arresting, grandiose, luxurious, sumptuous

imprimatur
7 license **8** approval, sanction

imprint
4 etch, mark **5** press, stamp **7** engrave, impress **8** inscribe **10** impression

imprison
3 jug **4** cage, curb, jail **5** check, limit **6** detain, immure, intern **7** confine, enclose **8** bastille, restrain, restrict **9** constrain **11** incarcerate **12** circumscribe

impromptu
7 offhand **9** extempore, makeshift, unstudied **10** improvised **11** extemporary, unrehearsed **13** autoschediasm, improvisation

improper
5 amiss, crude, fresh, inapt, inept, outré, rough, sassy, unapt, undue, unfit, wrong **6** gauche, unmeet **7** illicit, ungodly, unhappy **8** ill-timed, indecent, informal, tactless, uncomely, unseemly, untimely, untoward **9** incorrect, unfitting **10** inaccurate, inapposite, indecorous, indelicate, malapropos, malodorous, unbecoming, undecorous, unsuitable **11** impertinent, unbefitting **12** illegitimate, inadmissible, inapplicable, infelicitous, intempestive, unseasonable **13** inappropriate, unceremonious
prefix: **3** mis

impropriety
5 boner, break, error, gaffe **7** blooper, faux pas **8** slangism, solecism **9** barbarism, indecorum, vulgarism **10** corruption, inelegance, unmeetness **12** unseemliness, untowardness **13** incorrectness

improve
4 edit, gain, help, mend **5** amend, edify, emend, rally, rub up **6** better, enrich, illume, look up, perk up, refine, reform, remedy, revise, revive, uplift **7** advance, augment, benefit, correct, develop, enhance, enlarge, perfect, recover, rectify, upgrade **8** illumine, increase, progress **9** cultivate, enlighten, intensify, irradiate, meliorate **10** ameliorate, convalesce, illuminate, recuperate, strengthen

improvident
6 lavish **7** profuse **8** careless, heedless, prodigal, reckless, unthrift, wasteful **9** imprudent, negligent, unthrifty **10** profligate, thriftless **11** extravagant, spendthrift **12** uneconomical

improvise
5 ad-lib **6** devise, invent **7** concoct **8** contrive **11** extemporize

improvised
7 offhand **9** extempore, impromptu, unstudied **11** extemporary, unrehearsed

imprudent
4 rash **6** unwary, unwise **7** foolish **8** reckless **10** ill-advised, incautious, indiscreet **11** inadvisable,

inexpedient, injudicious, unadvisable, unexpedient **12** shortsighted

impudence
4 gall **8** audacity, boldness **9** arrogance, hardihood, insolence, insolency **10** disrespect, effrontery **11** presumption **12** impertinence, insolentness

impudent
4 bold, flip, pert, wise **5** brash, fresh, lippy, nervy, sassy, saucy, smart **6** arrant, brassy, brazen, cheeky **7** blatant, forward **8** flippant, insolent, overbold **9** audacious, barefaced, shameless, unabashed **10** procacious, unblushing **11** brazenfaced, impertinent, smart-alecky **12** contumelious **13** disrespectful

impugn
4 deny **5** cross, fight **6** assail, attack, negate, oppose, resist **7** gainsay **8** negative, traverse **9** disaffirm **10** contradict, contravene

impugnable
5 fishy, shady **7** suspect **8** doubtful **9** doubtable, equivocal, uncertain **10** borderline, suspicious **11** problematic

impulse
3 ate **4** goad, lust, push, spur, urge, whim **5** drive, force **6** impact, motive, thrust, whimsy **7** impetus, passion, whimsey **8** catalyst, excitant, stimulus **9** actuation, impulsion, incentive, stimulant **10** incitation, incitement, motivation **11** instigation

impulsive
5 hasty **6** abrupt, sudden **8** headlong, will-less **9** automatic, impetuous **10** unprompted **11** instinctive, involuntary, precipitate, spontaneous, unmeditated

impure
3 raw **4** foul, lewd, vile **5** black, crude, dirty, gross, mixed, nasty, soily **6** carnal, common, filthy, grubby, native, unholy **7** bastard, defiled, immoral, lustful, obscene, scarlet, sensual, squalid, unclean **8** immodest, indecent, polluted, profaned, prurient, unchaste, ungraded, unsorted **9** run-of-mine, uncleanly, unrefined **10** desecrated, indecorous, lascivious, unhallowed **11** adulterated

impute
3 lay **4** give, hint **5** refer **6** accuse,

adduce, assign, charge, credit, impart, indict **7** ascribe **8** accredit, intimate **9** attribute

inability
9 inaptness, ineptness **10** inadequacy, inaptitude, incapacity, inefficacy, ineptitude **11** inadeptness **12** incapability, incompetence, inefficiency

inaccessible
3 far **6** closed, far-off, remote **7** distant, faraway **8** abstruse, esoteric **11** out-of-the-way, ungetatable, unreachable **12** unattainable, unobtainable

in accordance with
5 as per **10** pursuant to

inaccurate
5 false, wrong **6** faulty, untrue **7** inexact, unsound **8** specious **9** defective, erroneous, incorrect

inaction
5 drift **8** idleness, lethargy **9** indolence, inertness, slackness, torpidity **10** inactivity, quiescence **12** inactiveness, slothfulness

inactive
4 dead, idle, slow **5** inert, quiet, slack, still **6** asleep, latent, sleepy, static, supine, torpid **7** abeyant, dormant, jobless, passive **8** indolent, ossified, slothful, sluggish **9** do-nothing, lethargic, lymphatic, quiescent, sedentary, unworking **10** disengaged, motionless, unemployed, unoccupied

in addition
4 also, then **5** again **7** besides, further **8** moreover **12** additionally

inadequacy
4 lack **7** deficit, failure **8** shortage, underage **9** inability **10** deficiency, incapacity, inefficacy, scantiness **11** defalcation **12** incapability, incompetence **13** insufficience, insufficiency

inadequate
3 shy **4** weak **5** scant, short **6** meager, scanty, scarce, skimpy **7** failing, lacking, scrimpy, wanting **8** boneless, impotent **9** defective, deficient, forceless, spineless **10** emasculate, incomplete, uncomplete **11** ineffective, ineffectual, slack-spined **12** insufficient

inadmissible
5 inapt, inept, unapt **8** ill-timed, improper, unseemly, unwanted **9** un-

welcome **10** ill-favored, malapropos, unbecoming **11** undesirable **12** unacceptable

inadvertent
8 careless, feckless, heedless, uncaring **9** negligent, undevised, unheeding, unplanned, unrecking, unthought **10** undesigned, unintended **13** unintentional

inadvisable
4 rash **6** unwise **7** foolish **8** careless **9** foolhardy, impolitic, imprudent, pointless **10** ill-advised, incautious, indiscreet, unsensible **11** harebrained, inexpedient, undesirable, unexpedient **13** inappropriate

inalterable
5 fixed **8** constant **9** immovable, immutable, steadfast, unmovable **10** inflexible, invariable **12** unchangeable, unmodifiable

inamorata
5 flame, honey, lover, woman **6** steady **7** beloved, sweetie **8** ladylove, mistress, paramour, truelove **10** girl friend, sweetheart

inamorato
4 beau **5** flame, lover **6** steady **7** beloved **8** truelove **9** boyfriend **10** sweetheart

inane
4 flat, idle, vain **5** blank, empty, silly, vapid **6** hollow, jejune, vacant **7** asinine, fatuous, foolish, idiotic, insipid, sapless, shallow, vacuous **8** mindless, trifling **9** driveling, frivolous, innocuous, pointless, senseless

inanimate
4 cold, dead, dull, late **5** inert **6** asleep **7** defunct, extinct **8** deceased, departed, lifeless **9** exanimate, insensate, senseless, unfeeling **10** insensible, insentient

inanity
5 folly **7** vacuity **8** insanity, unwisdom, vapidity **9** absurdity, craziness, dottiness, emptiness, frivolity, silliness **10** hollowness, triviality **11** foolishness, shallowness, wittlessness **13** senselessness

inappreciable
6 meager, scanty, skimpy **7** scrimpy **10** impalpable, inadequate, insensible, intangible, unapparent **12** imponderable, insufficient, unobservable

inappropriate
5 inapt, inept, undue, unfit **6** clumsy, unmeet **8** ill-timed, improper, unfitted, unseemly, unsuited, untimely **9** ill-suited **10** ill-adapted, indecorous, malapropos, unbecoming, unsuitable **11** inconsonant, unbefitting **12** unseasonable

inapt
4 flat **5** banal, undue, unfit **6** clumsy, gauche, jejune, unmeet **7** awkward, inadept, insipid, unhandy **8** ill-timed, improper, inexpert, unfacile, unfitted, unsuited, untimely **9** ill-suited, maladroit, unfitting **10** amateurish, ill-adapted, inadequate, malapropos, unskillful, unsuitable

in arrears
6 behind **10** behindhand

inarticulate
4 dumb, mute **5** tacit **6** silent, unsaid **7** blurred, halting, implied, unvocal **8** implicit, inferred, mumbling, unspoken, wordless **9** faltering, stammered, unuttered, voiceless **10** hesitating, incoherent, indistinct, maundering, speechless, stammering, tongue-tied, undeclared **11** unexpressed

inasmuch as
2 as **3** for, now **5** since **7** because, whereas **8** as long as **11** considering

inattentive
3 lax **5** bored **6** ennuyé, remiss **8** careless, distrait, heedless **9** forgetful, negligent, unheeding, unmindful **10** abstracted, distracted, distraught, unnoticing, unthinking, unwatchful **11** inobservant, thoughtless, unobservant, unobserving

inaugural
5 first **7** initial, leading **8** foremost, headmost **9** induction **10** initiation **11** investiture **12** installation

inaugurate
4 open **5** begin, enter, set up, start **6** get off, induct, invest, launch **7** install, instate, jump off, kick off, usher in **8** commence, dedicate, initiate **9** institute, introduce, originate **10** consecrate

inauspicious
3 bad **4** dire, evil **7** adverse, baleful, baneful, fateful, ominous, unlucky **8** sinister **9** ill-boding, ill-omened **11** threatening **12** unpropitious

inborn
6 inbred, innate, native 7 connate, natural 8 inherent 9 essential, ingrained, inherited, intrinsic 10 congenital, connatural, deep-seated, hereditary, indigenous, indwelling, unacquired

inbred
6 inborn, innate 7 connate 8 inherent 9 ingrained, intrinsic 10 congenital, deep-seated, indwelling

Inca
beverage: 5 chica
capital: 5 Cusco, Cuzco
conqueror: 7 Pizarro (Francisco)
god: 4 Inti 9 Viracocha
10 Pachacamac
half-breed: 5 Cholo
language: 8 Quechuan
priest: 3 umu
record: 5 quipu
ruler: 9 Atahualpa, Pachacuti
sacred object: 5 huaca 8 apacheta
socioeconomic unit: 5 ayllu

incalculable
4 iffy, vast 6 chancy, untold 7 erratic 8 enormous, infinite 9 boundless, countless, fluctuant, limitless, uncertain, whimsical 10 capricious, unmeasured, unnumbered 11 illimitable, inestimable, innumerable, measureless, uncountable 12 immeasurable, unmeasurable

in camera
7 sub rosa 8 covertly, secretly 9 by stealth, furtively, privately 10 stealthily 12 hugger-mugger 13 clandestinely

incandescent
3 hot 5 lucid 6 ardent, bright, lucent 7 beaming, fulgent, glowing, lambent, radiant 8 luminous 9 brilliant, effulgent, refulgent

incantation
4 rune 5 chant, charm, magic, spell 7 sorcery 8 witchery, wizardry 9 conjuring, magicking 10 necromancy, witchcraft 11 bewitchment, conjuration, enchantment
Buddhist, Hindu: 6 mantra

incapable
5 inept, unfit 6 unable 8 inexpert, unexpert, unfitted 9 unskilled 10 ineligible, unequipped, unskillful 11 incompetent

incapacitate
6 disarm 7 cripple, disable 8 paralyze 9 disenable, prostrate 10 disqualify, immobilize

incapacity
9 inability 10 inadequacy, inefficacy 12 incapability, incompetence

incarcerate
3 jug 4 jail 6 immure, intern 7 confine, enclose 8 bastille, imprison 9 constrain

incarnadine
3 red 4 ruby 5 ruddy 6 redden, rubify, rubric, ruddle

incarnate
5 utter 6 embody 8 embodied, manifest 9 actualize, objectify, personify, personize 11 exteriorize, externalize, materialize, personalize, unspeakable 12 substantiate

incarnation
6 avatar 7 avatara 10 embodiment
Of Christ: 7 kenosis

incautious
4 bold, rash, wild 5 brash, hasty 6 madcap, unwary 7 unalert 8 carefree, careless, feckless, heedless, reckless 9 hotheaded, impetuous, impolitic, imprudent, negligent, uncareful, unguarded, unmindful 10 ill-advised, indiscreet, madbrained, neglectful, regardless, unvigilant, unwatchful 11 injudicious, thoughtless 13 inconsiderate, irresponsible

incendiary
5 torch 7 exciter, firebug 8 agitator, arsonist 10 pyromaniac 12 inflammatory

incense
3 ire, mad, oil 4 balm, burn 5 anger, aroma, scent, spice 6 arouse, enrage, homage, incite, madden
vessel: 6 censer 8 thurible

incentive
4 goad, spur 5 spark 6 motive 7 impetus, impulse 8 catalyst, stimulus 9 stimulant 10 incitation, incitement, inducement, motivation 11 provocation, stimulative 13 encouragement

inception
4 root, well 5 start 6 origin, source, whence 8 fountain 9 beginning 10 derivation, initiation, provenance, wellspring 11 provenience 12 commencement

inceptive
7 initial, nascent 9 beginning, incipient 10 initiative, initiatory 12 introductory

incertitude
5 doubt 6 wonder 7 concern, dubiety 8 mistrust 9 dubiosity, suspicion 10 indecision, skepticism 11 uncertainty

incessant
6 steady 7 endless, eternal 8 constant, timeless 9 ceaseless, continual, perpetual, unceasing 10 continuous 11 everlasting, unremitting 12 interminable

inchoate
7 muddled 8 formless, unformed, unshaped 9 amorphous, expectant, incipient, potential, shapeless 10 contingent, disjointed, disordered, incoherent, incohesive, incomplete 11 imperfected, unconnected, unorganized 12 disconnected, uncontinuous 13 discontinuous

incident
4 akin 5 event 6 agnate, allied 7 cognate, connate, episode, kindred, related 8 accident, external, occasion 9 ancillary, attendant, attending, happening, satellite 10 affiliated, collateral, connatural, occurrence 11 concomitant, consanguine 12 accompanying, circumstance

incidental
3 odd 5 fluky 6 casual, chance 8 episodic 9 accessory 10 accidental, contingent, digressive, fortuitous 11 subordinate 12 nonessential

incidentally
6 obiter 8 by the bye, by the way, casually 9 in passing 12 accidentally, fortuitously

incipient
7 initial, nascent 8 inchoate 9 beginning, inceptive 10 commencing, initiative, initiatory 12 introductory

incise
3 cut 4 etch, gash, kerf, slit 5 grave, slash, slice 6 pierce 7 engrave

incisive
4 keen, tart 5 acerb, acute, crisp, sharp, terse 6 biting 7 acerbic, caustic, concise, cutting, ingoing, laconic, mordant 8 clear-cut, drilling, piercing, scathing, slashing, succinct 9 sarcastic, trenchant 11 penetrating

incite
3 egg, set 4 abet, goad, prod,

spur, urge **5** raise, rouse, set on **6** arouse, compel, excite, exhort, foment, motive, set off, stir up, whip up **7** actuate, agitate, forward, further, inflame, promote, provoke, solicit, trigger **8** motivate **9** encourage, instigate, stimulate

incitement
see **incentive**

inclement
3 raw **4** hard **5** harsh, rough **6** bitter, brutal, rugged, severe, stormy **8** rigorous **10** unmerciful **11** intemperate

inclination
3 bow, nod **4** bent, bias, lean, love, mind, tilt, will **5** fancy, grade, slant, slope, taste **6** ascent, desire, liking **7** descent, incline, leaning **8** affinity, appetite, fondness, gradient, penchant, pleasure, soft spot, tendency, velleity, weakness **9** affection **10** attachment, proclivity, propensity **11** disposition **12** predilection
rate of: **8** gradient

incline
3 aim, lay, tip **4** bend, bias, cant, cast, hade, heel, lean, list, look, move, sway, tend, tilt, turn **5** drive, grade, impel, level, point, slant, slide, slope, train **6** affect, direct, induce, prompt, zero in **7** address, deflect, dispose, leaning **8** gradient, persuade **9** influence, prejudice
combining form: **4** clin **5** clino

inclined
3 apt **4** fain, wont **5** given, prone, raked, ready **6** biased, graded, liable, likely, minded, sloped, tilted, tipped **7** dipping, leaning, oblique, pitched, sloping, tilting, willing **8** diagonal, disposed, pitching **9** declivate **11** declivitous, predisposed
way: **4** ramp

include
4 have, hold **5** admit, bound, cover **6** embody, enfold, number, take in **7** confine, contain, embrace, enclose, involve, receive, subsume **8** comprise, encircle **9** encompass **10** comprehend

inclusive
6 global **7** general, overall **8** sweeping **9** all-around, enclosing **12** encompassing, encyclopedic **13** comprehensive

incognizant
7 unaware **8** ignorant **9** oblivious, unknowing, unwitting **10** unfamiliar, uninformed **12** inconversant, unacquainted, uninstructed

incoherent
5 loose **6** broken, raving **7** muddled **8** inchoate **9** illogical **10** discordant, disjointed, disordered, incohesive, maundering, tongue-tied **11** incongruous, inconsonant, nonadhesive, unconnected, unorganized **12** disconnected, inarticulate, incompatible, inconsequent, inconsistent, inharmonious, uncontinuous **13** discontinuous

incombustible
7 apyrous **12** nonflammable

income
4 gain, take **6** profit, return **7** annuity, comings, produce, revenue **8** interest, proceeds, receipts **9** emolument

incommode
3 irk, vex **5** annoy, block **6** bother, hinder, impede, molest, plague, put out **7** disturb, trouble **8** disquiet, obstruct, put about **9** disoblige **13** inconvenience

incommodious
5 cramp **7** awkward, cramped, squeezy **8** confined **12** discommoding, embarrassing, inconvenient

incommunicable
8 reserved, taciturn **9** ineffable, withdrawn **10** restrained, untellable **11** constrained, indefinable, inenarrable, unspeakable, unutterable **12** noncommittal **13** indescribable, inexpressible, undescribable, unexpressible

incomparable
7 supreme **8** peerless, towering, ultimate **9** matchless **10** preeminent, surpassing **11** unequalable, unmatchable **12** transcendent **13** unsurpassable

incompatible
7 adverse, counter **8** contrary, opposite **9** antipodal, dissonant, unmixable **10** antipodean, discordant, discrepant **11** conflicting, disagreeing, incongruent, incongruous, inconsonant, unadaptable **12** antagonistic, antipathetic, antithetical, disconsonant, inconsistent, inharmonious **13** contradictory, inconformable, unconformable, unsympathetic

incompetence
9 inability, unfitness **10** disability, inadequacy, incapacity, inefficacy **12** incapability **13** insufficiency

incompetent
5 inept, unfit **8** helpless, inexpert, unexpert, unfitted **9** incapable, unskilled **10** ineligible, unequipped, unskillful **11** inefficient, unqualified **12** disqualified, insufficient
legally: **12** inadmissible

incomplete
4 part **5** bitty, short **6** broken **7** lacking, partial, scrappy, sketchy, wanting **8** immature **9** composite, defective, deficient **10** fractional, inadequate, incoherent, uncomplete, unfinished **11** fragmentary, imperfected **12** insufficient

incompliant
5 rigid, stiff **6** mulish **8** perverse, stubborn **9** impliable, obstinate, pig-headed, resistant, unbending **10** bull-headed, headstrong, inflexible, self-willed, unflexible, unyielding **11** immalleable, intractable **12** pertinacious

incomprehensible
7 cryptic, obscure, unclear **8** abstruse **9** enigmatic **10** fathomless, mysterious, mystifying, unknowable, unreadable **11** inscrutable, ungraspable **12** impenetrable, incognizable, unfathomable, unimaginable, unsearchable **13** imperceptible, inconceivable

inconceivable
4 thin, weak **6** flimsy **10** improbable, incredible, unknowable **11** implausible, incogitable, unthinkable **12** insupposable, unbelievable, unconvincing, unimaginable

in conclusion
6 lastly **7** finally

inconclusive
4 open **9** uncertain, undecided, unsettled **10** incomplete, indecisive, indefinite, unfinished **11** ineffective

incongruous
5 alien **6** absurd **7** bizarre, foreign **9** dissonant, fantastic, grotesque, unmixable **10** discordant, discrepant, extraneous **11** conflicting, inconsonant **12** disconsonant, incompatible, inconsistent, inharmonious

inconscient
4 lost **6** absent **7** bemused, faraway **8** distrait, mindless **10** ab-

stracted **11** preoccupied
12 absentminded

inconsequential
5 petty, small **6** measly, paltry
7 trivial **8** picayune, trifling
10 irrelevant, picayunish

inconsiderable
4 puny **5** light, minor, petty, small
6 casual, little, meager, paltry, peanut, scanty, skimpy **7** scrimpy, trivial **8** picayune, trifling **9** small-beer
10 inadequate, negligible, shoestring **11** unimportant **12** inconsequent, insufficient, unconsidered
13 inappreciable, insignificant

inconsiderate
4 rash **5** brash, hasty, sharp, short
6 madcap, unkind **8** careless,
heedless, reckless **9** hotheaded
10 ill-advised, incautious, ungracious **11** precipitate, thoughtless

inconsistent
6 fickle **8** ticklish, unstable **9** dissonant, mercurial, uncertain, unmixa-
ble **10** capricious, changeable, discordant, discrepant, inconstant,
lubricious **11** conflicting, incongruent, incongruous, inconsonant
12 disconsonant, incompatible,
inharmonious **13** contradictory,
inconformable

inconsolable
7 forlorn **8** dejected, desolate
9 heartsick **11** comfortless, heartbro-
ken **12** disconsolate

inconspicuous
5 vague **7** obscure **10** indistinct,
unemphatic **11** unobtrusive
12 unnoticeable

inconstant
5 false, light **6** fickle, shifty, untrue
7 elusive, erratic, mutable, protean,
vagrant, variant, wayward **8** disloyal, slippery, ticklish, unstable,
unsteady, variable, volatile, wavering **9** changeful, faithless, frivolous,
mercurial, uncertain, unsettled
10 capricious, changeable, irresolute, lubricious, perfidious, traitorous, unreliable **11** chameleonic,
light-minded, treacherous,
vacillating **12** inconsistent, shilly-
shally, undependable **13** temperamental

incontestable
4 sure **7** certain **8** positive **9** undoubted **10** undeniable **11** indubitable, irrefutable, unequivocal
12 indisputable

incontinent
4 fast, lewd **7** lustful, satyric **9** lecherous, libertine, salacious **10** lascivious, libidinous, licentious
12 unrestrained

incontrovertible
4 sure **7** certain **8** positive **10** inarguable, undeniable **11** indubitable,
unequivocal **12** indisputable,
undisputable **13** incontestable,
uncontestable

inconvenience
3 try **4** fuss, stew **5** annoy, trial
6 bother, meddle, pother, put out
7 disturb, trouble **8** handicap, put
about **9** aggravate, annoyance,
disoblige, incommode, interfere
10 discomfort, discommode, discompose, exasperate **11** aggravation, awkwardness, intermeddle
12 disadvantage, discomfiture,
exasperation **13** embarrassment

inconvenient
7 awkward, unhandy **8** annoying
10 bothersome, unsuitable **11** detrimental, inexpedient, inopportune,
pestiferous, prejudicial, troublesome
12 discommoding, embarrassing,
incommodious, unreasonable
13 discommodious

incorporate
3 mix **4** fuse, join **5** blend, merge,
unite **6** absorb, embody, imbibe,
insorb, mingle **7** combine, inhaust
9 integrate **10** assimilate

incorporeal
4 airy **8** bodiless **9** asomatous,
spiritual **10** discarnate, immaterial,
unembodied, unphysical **11** disembodied, nonmaterial, nonphysical
12 metaphysical **13** unsubstantial

incorrect
5 false, wrong **6** faulty, untrue
7 unsound **8** improper, specious
9 erroneous, imprecise **10** inaccurate, unbecoming
combining form: **3** cac **4** caco
prefix: **3** mis

increase
2 up **3** add, rev, wax **4** gain,
grow, hike, jump, plus, push, rise,
soup, teem **5** boost, build, mount,
put up, raise, run up, swarm, swell
6 accrue, amount, beef up, dilate,
expand, extend, gather, growth,
jack up, markup **7** advance, amplify, augment, burgeon, distend,
enhance, enlarge, inflate, magnify,
prolong, pyramid, upgrade, upsurge **8** addition, compound, elon-

gate, escalate, flourish, heighten,
lengthen, manifold, multiply, protract, snowball **9** accession, accretion, aggravate, expansion, extension, increment, intensify, pullulate,
reinforce **10** accelerate, accumulate, aggrandize, appreciate,
strengthen **11** enlargement
12 augmentation, breakthrough
13 amplification
Scottish: **3** eke
suddenly: **4** zoom

increasing
8 crescent, crescive

incredible
4 thin, weak **5** thick **6** absurd,
flimsy **8** unlikely **9** cockamamy, untenable **10** cockamamie, impossible, improbable, outlandish, ridiculous **11** implausible, incogitable,
unthinkable **12** insupposable, preposterous, unbelievable, unconvincing, unimaginable
13 inconceivable

incredulity
7 unfaith **8** unbelief **9** disbelief

incredulous
4 wary **6** show-me **7** dubious
8 aporetic, doubting, hesitant
9 faithless, quizzical, skeptical, uncertain **10** suspicious **11** distrustful,
distrusting, mistrustful, questioning,
unbelieving, unconvinced, unsatisfied **12** disbelieving

increment
4 gain, rise **5** raise **6** growth **8** addition, increase **9** accession, accretion **11** enlargement
12 augmentation

incriminate
6 accuse, charge, indict **7** arraign,
impeach, involve **9** implicate,
inculpate

incrustation
4 rime, scab **5** scale **6** plaque,
tartar

incubus
4 onus **5** demon **6** burden **9** nightmare **10** evil spirit

inculcate
5 infix, teach **6** impart, infuse
7 educate, implant, impress, instill
8 instruct **10** inseminate
11 communicate

inculpable
4 good, pure **5** clean **8** innocent,
unguilty, virtuous **9** blameless,
crimeless, exemplary, faultless,
guiltless, righteous

incumbent
7 binding, leaning 8 occupant
9 overlying 12 superimposed

incur
3 get 6 induce 7 acquire, bring on
8 contract 9 encounter

incurable
8 cureless, hopeless 9 insanable
10 impossible 11 immedicable,
irreparable 12 irremediable
13 irretrievable, uncorrectable,
unrecoverable

incursion
4 raid 5 foray 6 attack, inroad
7 assault 8 invasion 9 irruption

incus
4 bone 5 anvil

indebted
7 obliged 8 beholden 9 duty-
bound, obligated 10 honor-bound

indebtedness
3 due 4 debt 7 arrears, failure
8 beholden 9 arrearage, liability
10 bankruptcy, insolvency, nonpay-
ment, obligation 11 delinquency

indecent
4 foul, racy 5 dirty, gross, nasty
6 coarse, filthy, impure, risqué,
smutty, vulgar 7 immoral, obscene,
raunchy, ungodly 8 immodest, improper, off-color, unseemly, untoward 10 indecorous, indelicate,
malodorous, ridiculous, scurrilous,
unbecoming, undecorous
12 scatological

indecision
5 doubt 8 to-and-fro, wavering
9 hesitancy 10 hesitation 11 uncertainty, vacillation 12 irresolution,
shilly-shally

indecisive
4 open 5 shaky, vague 7 dubious,
halting, unclear, unfixed 8 doubtful, hesitant, wavering 9 equivocal,
faltering, tentative, uncertain, undecided, unsettled 10 borderline, hesitating, indistinct, irresolute
11 problematic, vacillating

indecorous
4 rude 5 gross, loose, rough, unfit
6 coarse, vulgar 7 uncivil, ungodly
8 immodest, impolite, improper, indecent, shameful, unlawful, unseemly, untoward 9 incorrect, inelegant, irregular, offensive, tasteless,
unfitting 10 indelicate, malodorous,
ridiculous, unbecoming 11 ill-mannered, unbefitting, undignified
12 discourteous 13 inappropriate

indecorum
5 boner, break, gaffe 7 blooper,
faux pas 8 solecism 10 inelegance, unmeetness 11 impropriety

indeed
3 nay, yea 4 even, well 5 truly
6 easily, really, verily 7 in truth
8 forsooth, honestly 9 assuredly,
certainly 10 admittedly, positively,
undeniably 11 doubtlessly, undoubtedly

indefatigable
6 dogged 7 patient 8 diligent, sedulous, stubborn, tireless, untiring,
vigorous 9 assiduous, energetic,
steadfast, strenuous, tenacious,
weariless 10 determined, persistent, relentless, unflagging, unwavering, unwearying 11 painstaking,
persevering, unfaltering, unflinching, unrelenting, unweariable
13 inexhaustible

indefensible
9 untenable 10 inexpiable 11 inexcusable 12 unforgivable, unpardonable 13 unjustifiable

indefinable
5 vague 9 ineffable, uncertain
10 untellable 11 inenarrable,
unspeakable, unutterable 13 indescribable, indeterminate, inexpressible, undescribable, unexpressible

indefinite
4 wide 5 broad, loose, vague
7 endless, general, inexact, obscure, unclear, unfixed 8 infinite
9 ambiguous, boundless, imprecise,
limitless, unbounded, uncertain, undefined, unlimited 10 indistinct, inexplicit, unmeasured, unspecific
11 measureless 12 immeasurable,
inconclusive 13 indeterminate
article: 2 an
pronoun: 3 all, any, few 4 each,
many, most, none, some 6 anyone,
nobody 7 anybody, several, someone 8 everyone, somebody
9 everybody

indehiscent fruit
3 nut 4 pepo 5 akene, berry,
grain, grape, melon 6 achene, loment, samara, squash 7 pumpkin
8 cucumber 9 caryopsis
10 schizocarp

indelible
4 fast 5 fixed 7 lasting 8 enduring
9 permanent 10 inerasable,
unerasable 12 ineffaceable, ineradicable, inexpungible, inextirpa-

ble, uneradicable 13 undestroyable

indelicate
3 raw 4 lewd, rude 5 crude, gross,
rough 6 callow, coarse, wanton
7 uncouth, ungodly 8 impolite, improper, indecent, tactless, unseemly, untoward 9 unrefined
10 indecorous, malodorous, unbecoming

indemnify
3 pay 5 repay 7 requite 9 reimburse 10 compensate, recompense,
remunerate

indemnity
6 amends 7 amnesty, redress 8 reprisal, security 9 exemption, quittance 10 protection, recompense,
reparation 11 restitution 12 compensation

indentation
3 bay 4 dent, nick 5 notch, print,
stamp 6 recess 7 impress, imprint

indenture
4 nick 5 notch 11 indentation

indentured
5 bound 8 articled 11 apprenticed

independent
4 free 6 closed 8 autarkic, separate 9 autarchic, sovereign
10 autonomous 11 self-reliant
12 self-centered 13 self-contained,
self-sufficing, self-supported, self-
sustained
combining form: 4 self

indescribable
9 ineffable 10 untellable 11 indefinable, inenarrable, unspeakable,
unutterable 13 inexpressible,
unexpressible

indestructible
7 durable, lasting, undying 8 enduring, immortal 9 deathless, immutable, indelible, permanent, perpetual 10 changeless, inviolable,
quenchless 11 unalterable 12 imperishable, ineradicable, inextirpable, irrefragable, unchangeable,
unperishable, unquenchable
13 incorruptible, irrefrangible,
undestroyable

indeterminate
5 vague 7 inexact, unfixed 9 uncertain, unlimited 10 indefinite,
indistinct

index
4 list, mark, sign 5 table, token
7 catalog, indices (plural), indicia,
symptom 8 evidence 9 catalogue

India

bread: 7 chapati 8 chapatti
butter: 3 ghi 4 ghee
capital: 8 New Delhi
caste: 5 Sudra 6 Vaisya 7 Brahman
9 Kshatriya
female dancer: 8 bayadere
groom: 4 syce
harem: 6 zenana
lady: 4 bibi 5 begum 8 mem-sahib
language: 4 Urdu 5 Hindu, Tamil
6 Telugu 7 Bengali, Kannada, Ma-
rathi, Punjabi 8 Assamese, Guja-
rati, Kashmiri 9 Malayalam
10 Hindustani, Rajasthani
largest city: 6 Bombay
monetary unit: 5 rupee
nurse: 4 amah, ayah
official: 5 dewan, diwan
outcast: 6 pariah
prime minister: 5 Nehru (Jawaharlal)
6 Gandhi (Indira, Rajiv)
prince: 4 raja, rana 5 rajah 8 maharaja 9 maharajah
princess: 4 rani 5 begum, ranee
scholar: 6 pandit, pundit
servant: 4 maty
screen: 6 purdah
seal, stamp: 4 chop
soldier: 4 peon 5 sepoy
teacher: 4 guru
viceroy: 5 nabob, nawab
weight unit: 3 ser 4 cash, dhan,
pank, pice, powe, rati, tank, tola
5 adpao, fanam, hubba, masha,
maund, pally, pouah, ratti
6 dhurra, pagoda, pollam 7 chin-
nam, chittak

Indian, American

baby: 7 papoose
ball game: 8 lacrosse
carrier: 7 travois
Central and South American: 2 Ge
3 Ona 4 Cuna, Inca, Maya 5 Arara, Aztec, Carib, Huave, Olmec,
Yagua 6 Arawak, Aymara, Jivaro,
Omagua, Toltec, Yahgan 7 Chib-
cha, Quechua, Zapotec 8 Taras-
can 10 Araucanian 11 Tupi-
Guarani
colonists' greeting to Indian friend:
5 netop
drink: 6 chicha
food: 4 samp 5 maize 8 pemmican
game: 6 chunky 7 chunkey
home: 5 hogan, lodge, tepee
6 pueblo, teepee, wigwam
7 wickiup
leader: 4 Popé 6 Wovoka 7 Cochise, Osceola, Pontiac, Sequoya
8 Geronimo, Hiawatha, Powhatan,
Tecumseh 9 Massasoit 10 Crazy
Horse 11 Cornplanter, Sitting Bull
money: 5 sewan 6 wampum
North American: 3 Oto, Sac, Ute
4 Cree, Crow, Hopi, Hupa, Iowa,
Otoe, Pima, Pomo, Sauk, Taos,
Yuma 5 Aleut, Caddo, Creek,
Haida, Huron, Kansa, Kiowa,
Maidu, Miami, Modoc, Omaha,
Osage, Sioux 6 Apache, Cayuga,
Dakota, Lenape, Mandan, Micmac,
Mohawk, Munsee, Navaho, Nav-
ajo, Nootka, Ojibwa, Oneida, Pai-
ute, Pawnee, Pueblo, Quapaw,
Seneca, Siwash 7 Arapaho, Ari-
kara, Bannock, Chilkat, Chinook,
Choctaw, Dakotah, Esselen, Klam-
ath, Kutenai, Mohican, Naskapi,
Natchez, Ojibway, Pontiac, Shaw-
nee, Tlingit 8 Cherokee, Cheyenne,
Chippewa, Comanche, Delaware,
Illinois, Iroquois, Kickapoo, Kwak-
iutl, Nez Percé, Onondaga, Powhatan, Seminole, Shoshoni 9 Blackfoot, Chickasaw, Menominee,
Tsimshian, Tuscarora, Wampa-
noag, Winnebago 10 Assiniboin,
Chiricahua, Gros Ventre, Potawat-
omi 11 Massachuset, Narraganset
pipe: 7 calumet
spirit: 5 totem 7 kachina

Indiana

college, university: 6 De Pauw, Marion, Purdue 9 Ball State, Notre
Dame
nickname: 12 Hoosier State
state bird: 8 cardinal
state flower: 5 peony

indicate

3 say 4 bode, hint, mark, mean,
read, show 5 argue, augur, imply,
point, prove 6 attest, denote,
evince, import, record, reveal 7 bespeak, betoken, connote, display,
exhibit, express, presage, signify,
suggest, testify, witness 8 announce, disclose, evidence, intimate, manifest, register 9 designate 10 illustrate 11 demonstrate

indication

3 cue 4 clue, hint, mark, omen,
sign, type, wind 5 index, proof, token, trace 6 notion, signal, symbol
7 gesture, indicia, inkling, reading,
symptom 8 evidence, reminder, telltale 9 testimony 10 expression, intimation, suggestion 11 significant
13 manifestation, prefiguration

indicative

8 denotive, evincive, indicial, sym-
bolic 9 testatory 10 denotative,
evidential, exhibitive, expressive,
suggestive 11 designative, symp-
tomatic 13 demonstrative

indicia

4 fact, mark, sign 5 index, token
7 symptom 8 evidence 9 criterion

indict

6 accuse, charge 7 arraign, impeach 9 criminate, inculpate
11 incriminate

indifference

6 apathy 8 lethargy 9 aloofness,
disregard, lassitude, unconcern
10 negligence 11 disinterest, insouciance 12 carelessness, heedlessness 13 unmindfulness

indifferent

3 icy 4 cold, cool, fair, mean,
numb, so-so 5 aloof, blasé, chill,
equal, stoic 6 casual, frigid, medium, remote 7 average, fairish,
glacial, neutral, off-hand, unmoved
8 by-the-way, careless, detached,
heedless, inferior, listless, mediocre,
middling, moderate, passable, unbiased, uncaring 9 apathetic, equitable, impartial, impassive, incurious, negligent, objective, uncurious,
unmindful, withdrawn 10 impersonal, insensible, nonchalant, regardless, unaffected, unsociable
11 unconcerned, unemotional,
unobserving 12 unimpressive, uninterested, unprejudiced 13 disinterested, dispassionate

indigence

4 lack, need, want 6 penury 7 poverty 9 neediness, privation
11 destitution

indigenous

6 inborn, innate, native 7 connote,
endemic, natural 8 inherent 9 inherited 10 aboriginal, congenital, connatural, unacquired 13 autochthonous

indigent

4 poor 5 needy 6 beggar, pauper
8 dirt poor 9 destitute, penniless,
penurious 11 impecunious, necessitous 12 impoverished

indigestion

9 dyspepsia

indignant

3 mad 5 angry, irate, wroth
6 heated, wrathy, wrothy 7 annoyed 8 incensed, wrathful, wrothful 9 irritated, resentful

indignation

3 ire, mad 4 fury, rage 5 anger, wrath 10 resentment

indignity

3 cut 4 slap 5 wrong 6 injury, insult, slight 7 affront, despite, outrage 9 contumely, grievance, injustice 13 disparagement

indigo

4 anil, blue

indigo bird

5 finch 7 bunting

indigo plant

4 anil

Indira Gandhi's father

5 Nehru

indirect

6 errant, shifty, sneaky 7 crooked, devious, oblique, sinuous, vagrant, winding 8 circular, guileful, sneaking, tortuous, twisting 9 deceitful, dishonest, underhand, wandering 10 circuitous, collateral, meandering, roundabout, serpentine 11 duplicitous, underhanded

indiscreet

6 unwary, unwise 9 ill-judged, impolitic, imprudent, untactful 10 ill-advised, incautious 11 injudicious 13 inconsiderate

indiscretion

4 slip 5 folly 9 incaution 10 imprudence, unwariness

indiscriminate

4 spot, wide 5 broad, mixed 6 motley, random, varied 7 aimless, jumbled, mingled, shallow 8 assorted, chowchow, confused, sweeping 9 desultory, extensive, haphazard, hit-or-miss, unplanned, wholesale 10 designless, uncritical 11 promiscuous, purposeless, superficial 12 conglomerate, multifarious, unconsidered

indispensable

5 basic, vital 6 needed 7 exigent, needful 8 cardinal 9 essential, necessary, requisite 10 imperative 11 fundamental

indisposed

3 ill, low 4 mean, sick 5 loath 6 afraid, ailing, averse, offish, poorly, sickly, unwell 7 hostile, underly, uneager 8 backward, hesitant, inimical, off-color 9 reluctant, unwilling, unwishful 11 disinclined

indisposition

6 malady 7 ailment, dislike, illness, malaise 8 aversion, bad books, disfavor, disorder, distaste, sickness, unhealth 9 disliking, disrelish, infirmity 10 affliction, reluctance 11 displeasure

indisputable

4 real, sure, true 6 actual 7 certain, evident 8 positive, unfabled 9 veridical 10 undeniable 11 indubitable, irrefutable, unequivocal 12 irrefragable 13 incontestable, uncontestable

indistinct

3 dim 4 hazy 5 faint, misty, vague 6 bleary, cloudy 7 blurred, inexact, obscure, shadowy, unclear 8 confused 9 uncertain, undefined 10 ill-defined, indefinite 12 undetermined 13 indeterminate

indistinguishable

4 same 5 equal 7 identic 9 duplicate, identical 10 equivalent, tantamount

indite

3 pen 5 write 6 scribe 7 compose, engross 8 inscribe

individual

3 one 4 body, lone, self, sole, soul, unit 5 being, human, party, stuff, thing 6 entity, matter, mortal, object, person, proper, single 7 several, special 8 creature, especial, existent, material, peculiar, personal, separate, singular, solitary, specific 9 diacritic, existence, personage, something, substance 10 diagnostic, individual, particular, respective 11 distinctive 13 idiosyncratic

combining form: 4 idio

individualist

10 egocentric

individuality

4 self 5 seity, unity 6 makeup, nature, temper 7 ipseity, oneness, selfdom 8 identity, selfhood, selfness 9 character 10 complexion, difference, singleness, uniqueness, unlikeness 11 disposition, personality, singularity, temperament 12 independence, separateness, singularness

individualize

4 mark 7 qualify, specify 9 signalize 11 distinguish, singularize 12 characterize 13 particularize

Indochina country

4 Laos 5 Burma 7 Vietnam 8 Cambodia, Thailand

indoctrinate

5 teach, tutor 7 educate 8 instruct

indolence

4 laze 5 sloth 6 slouch 7 inertia, languor 8 idleness, laziness 10 inactivity 12 slothfulness, sluggishness

indolent

4 idle, lazy 5 drony 7 work-shy 8 fainéant, inactive, slothful, sluggish 9 easygoing, slowgoing

indomitable

4 wild 6 dogged, unruly 7 staunch 8 indocile, resolute, stubborn 9 fractious, steadfast 10 impassable, invincible, unbeatable 11 impregnable, insuperable, intractable 12 inexpugnable, invulnerable, pertinacious, recalcitrant, unassailable, undefeatable, ungovernable, unmanageable 13 unconquerable, undisciplined

Indonesia

capital: 7 Jakarta 8 Djakarta
monetary unit: 6 rupiah
president: 7 Suharto

indubitable

4 flat, real, sure, true 7 assured, certain, evident, genuine 8 bona fide, positive 9 authentic, downright, undoubted, up-and-down, veritable 10 inarguable, sure-enough, undeniable 11 irrefutable 12 indisputable, irrefragable 13 incontestable, uncontestable

induce

3 get 4 abet, draw, lead, move, sway, urge 5 breed, cause, get up, hatch, impel, infer, tempt 6 arouse, draw in, draw on, effect, elicit, incite, prompt, work up 7 actuate, inspire, procure, produce, win over 8 activate, conclude, convince, engender, generate, motivate, muster up, occasion, oversway, persuade, talk into 9 argue into, encourage, influence, prevail on

inducement

4 bait, lure 6 motive 9 incentive 10 enticement 13 consideration

induct

4 lead 6 enroll, invest 7 conduct, install, instate 8 initiate 9 introduce

inductance unit

5 henry 6 henrys (plural) 7 henries (plural)

induction

8 entrance 9 accession, inaugural, inference 10 initiation 11 investi-

ture **12** inauguration, installation, introduction

inductive
8 Baconian, epagogic **9** inducible, prefatial, prefatory, preludial, prelusive **11** a posteriori, prefatorial, preliminary, preparative, preparatory **12** introductory

indulge
3 pet **4** baby, bask, roll **5** favor, humor, revel, spoil **6** cocker, coddle, cosset, oblige, pamper, please, regale, wallow, welter **7** cater to, delight, gratify, rollick, satisfy **9** luxuriate **11** mollycoddle

indulgence
5 favor **6** liking, luxury **7** service **8** clemency, courtesy, fondness, kindness, lenience, leniency, mildness **9** benignity, tolerance **10** benignancy, benignness, gentleness, kindliness, toleration **11** forbearance **12** dispensation, mercifulness **13** gratification

indulgence seller
5 Tezel (Johann) **6** Tetzel (Johann)

indulgent
4 easy, kind, mild **6** benign, kindly **7** clement, lenient **8** excusing, merciful, tolerant **9** benignant, compliant, condoning, cosseting, forgiving, pampering, pardoning **10** charitable, forbearing, permissive

indurate
3 dry, set **4** cake **5** inure **6** harden **7** confirm, congeal **8** concrete, hardened, solidify, stubborn **9** unfeeling

industrialist
6 tycoon **7** magnate

industrious
4 busy, live **6** active **7** dynamic, operose, zealous **8** diligent, sedulous **9** assiduous

industry
4 work **5** labor, trade **7** traffic **8** business, commerce **9** diligence

inebriant
5 booze, drink **6** liquor **7** alcohol, spirits **9** aqua vitae **10** intoxicant

inebriate
3 sot **4** lush, soak **5** drunk, toper **6** bibber, boozer **7** tippler, tosspot **8** drunkard

inebriated
5 drunk, tight, tipsy **7** muddled **9** disguised, pixilated **11** intoxicated

inedible
7 baneful, insipid, noxious **9** poisonous, uneatable **10** inesculent **11** unwholesome **12** indigestible, unappetizing

ineffable
4 holy **5** ideal, taboo **6** divine, sacred **8** abstract, empyreal, empyrean, ethereal, heavenly **9** celestial, spiritual **10** untellable **11** indefinable, inenarrable, unspeakable, unutterable **12** transcendent **13** indescribable, inexpressible, undescribable, unexpressible

ineffaceable
9 indelible **10** inerasable, unerasable **12** ineradicable, inexpungible, inextirpable, uneradicable

ineffective
4 vain, weak **6** futile **7** useless **8** abortive, boneless, bootless, impotent, inferior **9** forceless, fruitless, incapable, spineless, worthless **10** emasculate, inadequate, unavailing **11** incompetent, ineffectual, inefficient, slack-spined, unavailable **12** invertebrate, unproductive **13** inefficacious

ineffectiveness
9 inability **10** inadequacy, incapacity, inefficacy **12** incapability, incompetence

ineffectual
see **ineffective**

ineffectualness
see **ineffectiveness**

inefficacious
see **ineffective**

inefficacy
see **ineffectiveness**

inefficient
5 inept **8** careless, inexpert, slipshod, slovenly, unexpert, unfitted **9** incapable, unskilled, untrained **10** unprepared, unskillful **11** incompetent, ineffective, ineffectual, unqualified **12** insufficient **13** inefficacious, unworkmanlike

inelaborate
5 plain **6** modest, simple **11** undecorated, ungarnished **12** unbeautified **13** unembellished, unembroidered, unpretentious

inelastic
5 rigid, stiff **9** impliable, unbending **10** inflexible, unflexible, unyielding **11** immalleable, incompliant

inelegant
3 raw **4** rude **5** crass, crude, gross, rough **6** coarse, vulgar **7** awkward, uncouth **9** graceless, unrefined

ineligible
5 unfit **8** unfitted, unworthy **9** incapable **10** unequipped **11** incompetent, unqualified **12** disqualified

ineluctable
4 sure **5** fated **6** doomed **7** certain **9** necessary **10** ineludible, inevasible, inevitable, returnless, unevadable **11** ineluctable, inescapable, unavoidable, unescapable

ineludible
7 certain **9** necessary **10** inevasible, inevitable, returnless, unevadable **11** ineluctable, unavoidable, unescapable

inept
4 dull **5** inapt, unapt, undue, unfit **6** clumsy, gauche, wooden **7** awkward, foolish, halting, inadept, unhandy, unhappy **8** bumbling, bungling, ill-timed, improper, inexpert, unexpert, unfacile, unseemly **9** graceless, ham-handed, ill-chosen, incapable, lumbering, maladroit, unskilled **10** inadequate, malapropos, unskillful, unsuitable **11** incompetent, inefficient, undexterous, unfortunate

inequality
8 asperity, imparity, rugosity **9** disparity, roughness **10** cragginess, jaggedness, ruggedness, unevenness **12** irregularity, variableness **13** disproportion

inequitable
3 bad **5** undue, wrong **6** unfair, unjust **8** wrongful **9** arbitrary, inequable, unmerited **10** highhanded, oppressive, undeserved **11** unequitable, unrighteous

inequity
5 wrong **9** injustice **10** unfairness, unjustness

inerasable
9 indelible **12** ineffaceable, ineradicable, inexpungible, inextirpable, uneradicable

inert
4 dead, idle **5** quiet, still **6** asleep, sleepy, stolid **7** neutral, passive **8** immobile, impotent, inactive, indolent, lifeless, sluggish **9** apathetic, impassive, inanimate, lethar-

gic, powerless **10** motionless, phlegmatic

inert gas
4 neon **5** argon, radon, xenon **6** helium **7** krypton **8** nitrogen, noble gas **13** carbon dioxide
suffix: **2** on

inescapable
see **inevitable**

inescapably
see **inevitably**

inesculent
8 inedible **9** uneatable

in essence
6 au fond **7** morally **9** basically, virtually **11** essentially, practically **13** fundamentally

inessential
see **unessential**

inestimable
6 costly **8** precious, valuable **9** priceless **10** invaluable, unmeasured **11** measureless, uncountable **12** immeasurable, incalculable, unmeasurable, unreckonable

inevitable
4 sure **5** fated **7** certain, decided, settled **8** destined **9** necessary **10** ineludible, inevasible, inexorable, inflexible, returnless, unevadable **11** ineluctable, inescapable, unavoidable, unescapable **12** foreordained, ineliminable **13** unpreventable

inevitably
8 perforce **10** helplessly, willy-nilly **11** inescapably, unavoidably, whether or no

inexcusable
8 blamable **9** untenable **10** censurable, inexpiable **11** blameworthy, intolerable, unallowable **12** criticizable, indefensible, unforgivable, unpardonable **13** impermissible, reprehensible, unjustifiable

inexhaustible
8 tireless, untiring **9** unfailing, weariless **10** unflagging, unwearying **11** unweariable **13** indefatigable

in existence
6 extant

inexorable
5 rigid **6** dogged, strict **7** adamant **8** immobile, obdurate, resolute **9** immovable, unbending **10** inflexible, relentless, unyielding **11** unrelenting **12** single-minded

inexpensive
3 low **5** cheap **6** frugal, undear **7** low-cost, popular **8** uncostly **9** low-priced **10** reasonable

inexperience
7 naiveté, rawness **8** verdancy **9** freshness, greenness, ignorance **10** callowness **13** unfamiliarity

inexperienced
3 row **5** fresh, green, inept, naive, young **6** callow **7** untried **8** ignorant, immature, inexpert, prentice, unversed **9** incapable, unskilled, untrained **10** amateurish, unfamiliar, unseasoned **11** unpracticed **12** unacquainted, unconversant

inexpert
see **inexperienced**

inexplicable
3 odd **7** strange, uncanny **8** peculiar **9** ambiguous, enigmatic **10** mysterious, unsolvable **11** inscrutable, undefinable **12** unfathomable **13** indescribable, inexplainable, unaccountable, unexplainable

inexpressible
8 nameless **9** ineffable **10** untellable **11** indefinable, inenarrable, unspeakable, unutterable **13** indescribable

inexpressive
4 dull **5** blank, empty **6** vacant, wooden **7** deadpan

inexpugnable
5 fixed **6** stable **10** invincible, unbeatable **11** impregnable, indomitable, unopposable **12** invulnerable, irresistible, unassailable, undefeatable **13** unconquerable

inextricable
8 involved **9** insoluble, intricate, unsoluble **10** insolvable, unsolvable

infallible
4 sure **5** exact **7** certain, correct, perfect **9** flawless, inerrant, surefire, unerring **9** faultless, inerrable, unfailing **10** impeccable **11** indubitable **12** undeceivable

infamous
4 base, evil, vile **5** sorry **6** odious, rotten, scurvy **7** corrupt, hateful, heinous, vicious **8** ill-famed, perverse, shameful **9** abhorrent, atrocious, miscreant, nefarious, notorious, unhealthy **10** abominable, degenerate, despicable, detestable, flagitious, iniquitous, scandalous, villainous **11** disgraceful, ignomini-

ous, opprobrious **12** contemptible, disreputable

infamy
5 odium, shame **7** obloquy **8** disgrace, dishonor, ignominy **9** discredit, disesteem, disrepute, notoriety **10** opprobrium **13** notoriousness

infancy
6 nonage **8** babyhood, minority **9** childhood, juniority **10** immaturity, infanthood, juvenility

infant
4 babe, baby **5** child, green, minor, young **6** callow, unripe **7** neonate, newborn, toddler **8** bantling, immature, juvenile, nursling, youthful **9** unfledged
bed: **4** crib **6** cradle **8** bassinet
food: **3** pap **4** milk
room: **7** nursery

infantile
7 babyish, puerile **8** childish, immature

infantryman
7 dogface **8** doughboy **11** foot soldier
Algerian: **6** Zouave

infatuated
3 mad **5** dotty, silly **7** foolish **8** besotted, enamored, obsessed **9** bewitched **10** captivated, enraptured

infatuation
4 rage **5** ardor, craze, crush, folly **6** beguin **7** passion **8** devotion **9** obsession **11** fascination

in favor of
3 for, pro **4** with **10** impossible, unworkable **11** impractical **12** irrealizable, unattainable, unrealizable **13** impracticable

infect
5 taint **6** defile, infest, poison **7** pollute **11** contaminate

infection
6 plague, sepses (plural), sepsis **7** disease, illness
fungous: **8** mycetoma
skin: **6** herpes

infectious
5 toxic **6** taking **7** miasmic, noxious **8** catching, mephitic, virulent **9** pestilent, poisonous, vitiating **10** contagious, corrupting **11** sympathetic **12** communicable, pestilential **13** contaminating

infecund
6 barren, effete **7** sterile **8** impotent **9** infertile **10** unfruitful

infelicitous
5 inapt, inept, unapt 6 gauche
7 awkward, unhappy 9 defective,
graceless, ill-chosen, imperfect, ina-
propos 10 deplorable, malapropos
11 regrettable, unfortunate
13 inappropriate

infer
4 draw, hint, make 5 glean, guess,
judge, think 6 bestow, confer, deduce, deduct, derive, gather, induce, reason, reckon 7 collect, inflict, make out, surmise 8 conclude,
construe

inference
5 guess 7 surmise 8 guessing, illation, judgment, sequitur 9 deduction, reckoning 10 assumption, conclusion, conjecture, derivation
11 presumption, supposition

inferior
3 bad, low 4 base, cull, fair, hack,
mean, poor, punk, puny 5 cheap,
lousy, lower, minor, petty, scrub,
sorry, under 6 common, deputy,
feeble, heeler, impure, junior,
lesser, minion, nether, no-good, paltry, puisne, satrap, shoddy, sleazy,
tawdry, tinpot, vassal 7 average,
subject, unequal 8 adherent, declassé, disciple, follower, hanger-
on, henchman, hireling, low-grade,
mediocre, middling, ordinary, retainer, unworthy, wretched 9 attendant, auxiliary, no-account, satellite, secondary, subaltern,
subjacent, sycophant, underling,
valueless, worthless 10 inadequate,
second-rate
prefix: 3 sub 4 demi 5 infra

inferior one
suffix: 3 een 4 ling 5 aster

infernal
6 Hadean 7 avernal, hellish, satanic, stygian 8 chthonic, damnable, demoniac, devilish, diabolic,
fiendish, plutonic 9 chthonian, plutonian, Tartarean 10 diabolical,
sulphurous

inferno
3 pit 4 fire, hell 5 abyss, hades,
Sheol 6 blazes, Tophet 7 Gehenna
9 holocaust, perdition
11 netherworld

Inferno
division: 5 canto
poet: 5 Dante
verse form: 9 terza rima

infertile
6 barren, effete 7 drained, sterile
8 depleted, impotent, infecund
9 exhausted, unbearing, unfertile
10 unfruitful 12 hardscrabble,
impoverished, unproductive

infest
4 teem 5 annoy, beset, crawl,
harry, haunt, swarm, worry
6 abound, harass, pester, plague
7 overrun 8 parasite 9 overswarm
10 overspread, parasitize

infidel
5 pagan 6 ethnic 7 gentile, heathen, profane, skeptic 9 infidelic
10 unbeliever

infidelity
7 falsity, perfidy, treason 9 falseness, treachery 10 disloyalty, fickle-
ness 11 inconstancy
13 faithlessness

infiltrate
4 leak, seep, worm 5 foist 6 edge
in, work in 9 insinuate

infinite
4 vast 7 endless, eternal, immense
9 boundless, countless, limitless,
perpetual, unbounded, unlimited
10 indefinite, perdurable, unmeasured 11 everlasting, illimitable,
measureless, sempiternal
12 immeasurable

infirm
4 lame, weak 5 anile, frail 6 ailing, feeble, flimsy, senile, weakly
7 fragile, unsound 8 decrepit 10 irresolute 11 debilitated, vacillating
13 unsubstantial

infirmity
3 ill 5 decay 6 foible, malady
7 ailment, disease, failing, frailty,
illness, malaise 8 debility, disorder,
sickness, syndrome, unhealth,
weakness 9 affection, complaint,
condition, weakening 10 affliction,
feebleness, infirmness, sickliness,
unwellness 11 decrepitude 12 debilitation, diseasedness, enfeeblement 13 indisposition, unhealthiness

infix
4 root 5 embed, lodge 6 insert
7 implant, impress, ingrain, instill
8 entrench 9 inculcate
10 inseminate

inflame
3 get 4 fire, gall, good, heat, rile,
roil, stir 5 grate, light, rouse
6 arouse, burn up, enrage, excite,
ignite, kindle, madden, put out, red-

den 7 incense, provoke 8 enkindle, irritate 9 aggravate, intensify
10 exasperate

inflammable
5 fiery 6 ardent 8 burnable 9 excitable, ignitable, irascible, irritable
11 combustible

inflammation
4 gout, sore 5 felon 6 quinsy 7 catarrh, coxitis, gonitis, rickets 8 ade-
nitis, cystitis, neuritis, pleurisy, rachitis, swelling 9 arthritis, chilblain,
gastritis, phlebitis 10 combustion
12 encephalitis 13 conflagration,
poliomyelitis
ear: 6 otitis
eye: 6 iritis 7 pinkeye 9 keratitis
horse: 6 thrush 7 fistula, quittor
8 poll evil
intestines: 7 ileitis 9 enteritis
suffix: 4 itis

inflammatory
8 exciting, incitive 9 seditious
10 incendiary 11 instigative,
provocative, seditionary 13 revolutionary

inflate
4 fill 5 bloat, elate, swell 6 dilate,
expand, tumefy 7 amplify, distend

inflated
5 showy, tumid, windy, wordy
6 elated, prolix, turgid 7 aureate,
bloated, diffuse, flowery, fustian,
pompous, ranting, swollen, verbose
8 bladdery, dropsied 9 bombastic,
distended, dropsical, flatulent, overblown, tumescent 10 rhetorical
11 exaggerated, pretentious,
rhapsodical

inflection
4 bend, tone 5 curve 6 accent,
timbre 8 tonality 9 accidence
10 intonation 11 enunciation
12 articulation 13 pronunciation

inflexible
3 set 4 grim, hard, iron 5 fixed,
rigid, stiff, tough 6 dogged, strict
7 adamant, settled 8 constant, granitic, hard-line, immobile, ironclad,
obdurate, rigorous, stubborn 9 immovable, immutable, impliable, inelastic, obstinate, rockbound, steadfast, unbending, unmovable
10 adamantine, brassbound,
changeless, implacable, inexorable, invariable, invincible, relentless, rock-ribbed, unbendable, unchanging, unswayable, unyielding
11 unalterable, uncompliant, unrelenting 12 single-minded,

unchangeable, unmodifiable 13 dyed-in-the-wool

inflict
4 deal, give 5 visit, wreak, wreck 6 expose, impose, strike 7 force on, subject

inflow
6 influx, inpour, inrush 9 influxion

influence
4 move, pull, sway 5 alter, bribe, carry, clout, force, impel, lobby, touch 6 affect, compel, credit, induce, modify, moment, strike, weight 7 command, control, impress, inspire, mastery 8 dominion, eminence, militate, persuade, prestige 9 authority, dominance

influenceable
8 suasible, swayable 9 acceptant, acceptive, receptive 10 responsive 11 persuadable, persuasible

influential
6 potent 8 powerful 9 effective, important

influx
6 inflow, inpour, inrush 7 illapse 8 increase 9 accession, inpouring 11 debouchment 12 augmentation

inform
3 rat 4 blab, clew, clue, fire, post, talk, tell, warn 5 endow, endue, exalt, imbue, peach, teach, train 6 advise, betray, fill in, infuse, leaven, notify, preach, snitch, squeak, squeal, tattle, turn in, wise up 7 animate, apprise, arrange, caution, educate, inspire 8 acquaint, forewarn, give away, instruct, permeate 9 advertise, enlighten 10 illuminate 11 familiarize

informal
6 breezy, casual, dégagé, simple 7 natural, private, relaxed, special, unfussy 8 familiar 9 easygoing, irregular 10 colloquial, unofficial

information
4 data (plural), fact, lore, news, word 5 datum 6 advice, notice, wisdom 7 science, tidings 9 complaint, knowledge, speerings 11 instruction 12 intelligence
second hand: 7 hearsay
suffix: 3 ana 4 iana

information bureau
abbreviation: 4 USIA, USIS

informative
8 edifying 9 educative 11 educational, elucidative, explanatory, informatory, instructive 12 enlighten-

ing, illuminating 13 informational, instructional

informed
2 up 3 hip 4 wise 5 aware 6 au fait, posted, versed 7 abreast, knowing, versant 8 apprised, educated, familiar 9 au courant 10 acquainted, conversant, cultivated 11 enlightened, intelligent

informer
3 rat, spy 4 fink 5 stool 6 canary, gossip, snitch 7 stoolie, tattler, tipster 8 betrayer, busybody, squawker, squealer, telltale 10 talebearer, tattletale 11 stool pigeon

infra
4 next 5 after, below, later, under 6 behind, within 7 beneath

infract
5 break 6 breach, offend 7 violate 8 infringe 10 contravene, transgress

infraction
3 sin 4 slip 5 crime, error, lapse 6 breach 7 faux pas, offense 8 trespass 9 intrusion, violation 12 encroachment, infringement 13 contravention, transgression

infrastructure
4 base, root 5 basis 6 bottom, ground 7 bedrock, footing 10 foundation, groundwork, substratum 12 substructure, underpinning

infrequent
3 few, odd 4 rare 5 scant, stray 6 meager, scanty, scarce, seldom, sparse 7 limited, unusual 8 isolated, sporadic, uncommon, unwonted 9 scattered, spasmodic 10 occasional 11 exceptional

infringe
5 break 6 breach, defeat, impose, invade, offend, refute 7 confute, infract, intrude, obtrude, presume, violate 8 encroach, entrench, trespass 10 contravene, transgress

infuriate
3 ire, mad 5 anger 6 enrage, madden 7 incense, steam up, umbrage

infuse
4 fill, fire 5 imbue, steep 6 inform, invest, leaven 7 animate, diffuse, implant, ingrain, inspire, instill, pervade, suffuse, suggest 8 intersow, permeate, saturate 9 inculcate, inoculate, insinuate, interfuse, interlard, introduce 10 impregnate 11 intersperse 12 indoctrinate 13 intersprinkle

ingenious
3 sly 4 slim 5 acute, canny, sharp, smart 6 adroit, clever, crafty 7 cunning 8 creative, original 9 demiurgic, deviceful, inventive 11 intelligent, originative, resourceful 12 innovational

ingenuous
4 open 5 naive 6 simple, unwary 7 artless, natural, unaware 8 innocent, unartful 9 childlike, guileless, unstudied 10 unaffected, unschooled 12 unartificial

Inge play
6 Picnic 7 Bus Stop

ingest
3 eat 4 meal, take 6 absorb, devour, feed on, take in 7 consume, swallow

inglorious
5 shady 6 shabby, shoddy 8 shameful 11 disgraceful, ignominious 12 dishonorable, disreputable 13 discreditable, unrespectable

ingot
3 bar, rod 4 slap 5 stick, strip 6 billet

ingrained
7 built-in, chronic 8 inherent 10 congenital, deep-rooted, deep-seated, indwelling, inveterate

ingratiating
5 silky 6 silken 8 pleasing 9 adulatory 10 flattering, saccharine 11 deferential, sycophantic

ingredient
6 factor 7 element 9 component 11 constituent

ingress
3 way 4 adit, door, go in 5 enter, entry 6 access, come in, entrée 8 entrance 9 admission, penetrate 10 admittance

ingurgitate
4 bolt, cram, gulp, slop, wolf 5 slosh, stuff, swill 6 devour, englut, gobble, guzzle 7 swallow

inhabit
4 live 5 abide, dwell 6 occupy, people, settle, tenant 8 populate

inhabitant
5 liver 6 inmate, native 7 citizen, denizen, dweller, resider 8 indigene, resident 9 aborigine 10 autochthon
foreign: 5 alien
indigenous: 6 native 9 aborigine
suffix: 3 ese, ite, ote

inhale
7 breathe, consume, respire
9 breathe in

inharmonious
6 atonal 7 jarring 9 cat-and-dog, differing, dissonant, immusical, unmusical 10 cacophonic, discordant 11 conflicting, conflictive, disagreeing, quarrelsome, uncongenial 12 antagonistic

inhere
3 lie 5 dwell, exist 6 belong, reside 7 consist

inherent
4 born 5 basic 6 inborn, innate, normal 7 built-in, connate, infixed, natural, regular, typical 8 immanent, peculiar 9 elemental, essential, ingrained, intrinsic 10 congenital, deep-seated, elementary, individual, indwelling, ingenerate

inherit
7 possess, receive, succeed

inheritance
6 devise, legacy 7 bequest 8 heritage 9 patrimony 10 birthright, entailment 13 primogeniture

inherited
6 innate, native 7 connate, natural 10 congenital, connatural, indigenous

inheritor
4 heir 7 heretor, heritor, legatee
female: 7 heiress 8 heretrix, heritrix 10 heretrices (plural), heritrices (plural)

inhibit
3 ban 4 curb, ward 5 avert, check, taboo 6 bridle, enjoin, forbid, hinder, hold in, outlaw, reduce, retard 7 prevent, repress 8 diminish, hold back, hold down, prohibit, restrain, suppress, withhold 9 constrain

inhibited
4 cold 6 frigid 9 repressed 11 passionless 12 unresponsive

inhibition
3 ban, bar 6 hangup 9 restraint 10 impediment

inhuman
4 cold, fell 5 cruel 6 brutal, fierce, malign, savage 7 beastly, bestial, brutish, wolfish 8 devilish, fiendish, nonhuman 9 barbarous, ferocious, malicious, malignant, truculent 10 cannibalic, diabolical, impersonal, implacable, mechanical

inhumane
4 fell, grim 5 cruel 6 brutal, fierce, savage 7 wolfish 9 barbarous, ferocious, truculent

inhumation
6 burial 9 interment, sepulture 10 entombment

inhume
4 bury, tomb 5 inter, plant 6 entomb 7 lay away, put away 9 sepulcher, sepulture

inimical
3 ill 7 adverse, harmful, hostile 10 unfriendly 11 unfavorable

iniquitous
3 bad 4 evil 5 wrong 6 sinful, unjust, wicked 7 immoral, vicious 9 nefarious, reprobate

iniquity
3 sin 4 evil, tort 5 crime, wrong 9 diablerie, injustice 10 wickedness, wrongdoing

initial
5 basic, early, first, prime 6 letter, maiden 7 leading, nascent, opening, pioneer, primary 8 earliest, foremost, germinal, headmost, monogram, original 9 beginning, embryonic, incipient

initiate
4 open 5 admit, begin, enter, set up, start 6 enroll, get off, induct, invest, launch, take in, take up 7 install, kick off, usher in 8 commence 9 originate 10 inaugurate

initiation
7 baptism 9 admission, beginning, induction 10 admittance 11 origination 12 commencement, introduction

initiative
4 push 6 energy 8 ambition, aptitude, gumption 9 beginning 10 enterprise, get-up-and-go

injudicious
6 unwise 9 ill-judged, impolitic, imprudent 10 ill-advised, indiscreet 11 inexpedient

injunction
4 word 5 order 6 behest, charge 7 bidding, command, dictate, mandate 9 direction 11 prohibition

injure
3 mar 4 foul, harm, hurt, maim, pain 5 spoil, wound, wrong 6 batter, blight, bruise, damage, deface, deform, foul up, grieve, impair, mangle, offend, weaken 7 afflict,

blemish, contort, cripple, disable, distort, louse up, tarnish, torment, torture, vitiate 8 aggrieve, disserve, distress, maltreat, mutilate 9 bespatter, constrain, disfigure, prejudice 12 incapacitate

injurious
3 bad 4 evil 6 nocent 7 abusive, harmful, hurtful 8 damaging 9 offensive 10 defamatory 11 detrimental

injury
3 bad, ill 4 evil, harm, hurt, loss, pain, pang, ruin 5 agony, wound, wrong 6 damage, trauma 7 outrage 8 distress, mischief 9 detriment, grievance, injustice

injustice
4 harm, hurt, ruin, tort 5 crime, wrong 6 breach, damage, injury 7 outrage 8 inequity, mischief, trespass, villainy 9 grievance, violation 10 favoritism, partiality, unfairness, wrongdoing

ink
4 sign 9 autograph, signature, subscribe

inkling
3 cue 4 clue, hint, idea, wind 6 notion 8 telltale 10 intimation, suggestion

ink or rubber
5 India

inky
3 jet 4 ebon 5 black, ebony, jetty, raven, sable 9 cimmerian, pitch-dark 10 pitch-black 11 atramentous

inlaid
5 piqué

Inland Empire
8 Illinois

inlet
3 arm, bay, cay, ria, voe 4 cove, gulf 5 bayou, bight, creek, fiord, firth, fjord, sound 6 harbor, slough, strait 9 estuary
Admiralties: 4 Kali
Adriatic Sea: 5 Vlorë
Aegean Sea: 7 Saronic 12 Gulf of Aegina
Africa: 6 Walvis 12 Gulf of Guinea
Alaska: 4 Cook 5 Cross, Taiya 7 Glacier 8 Chilkoot
Aleutians: 5 Holtz, Nazan
Angola: 5 Bengo, Tiger 6 Tigres
Antarctica: 3 Ice 7 McMurdo 8 Amundsen 10 Shackleton
Arabian Sea: 4 Qamr 5 Kamar

Arctic Ocean: 8 Gulf of Ob
Australia: 4 King 6 Botany 9 Discovery 10 Broad Sound 13 Van Diemen Gulf
Baffin Bay: 8 Melville
Baffin Island: 9 Admiralty
Baltic Sea: 4 Hano 6 Danzig, Gdansk 9 Pomerania 10 Gulf of Riga, Pomeranian
Barents Sea: 4 Kola 7 Pechora
Beaufort Sea: 7 Prudhoe 9 Mackenzie
Bering Sea: 12 Gulf of Anadyr
Bismarck Sea: 5 Kimbe
Brazil: 9 Guanabara
Bristol Channel: 10 Carmarthen
California: 5 Morro 8 Monterey, San Diego 12 San Francisco
Canada: 5 Fundy 9 Howe Sound
Cape Breton Island: 4 Mira
Caribbean Sea: 5 Limon 8 Chetumal, Honduras 9 Venezuela
Central America: 7 Fonseca
Chile: 5 Otway
China-Korea: 8 Huang Hai, Hwang Hai 9 Yellow Sea
Crete: 4 Suda 5 Canea
Denmark: 3 Ise
Djibouti: 6 Tajura 8 Tadjoura
East River: 8 Flushing
Ecuador: 5 Manta
Eire: 4 Clew 7 Brandon
English Channel: 3 Tor 5 Seine 8 Plymouth
Florida: 8 Biscayne 10 Saint Lucie 11 Indian River
France-Spain: 6 Biscay 13 Gulf of Gascony
Georgia: 8 Altamaha
Greece: 13 Gulf of Corinth, Gulf of Lepanto
Greenland: 6 Baffin
Gulf of Alaska: 3 Icy 5 Woman 12 Resurrection
Gulf of Mexico: 5 Tampa 6 Mobile 7 Aransas 8 Sarasota, Suwannee 9 Matagorda, Pensacola 10 San Antonio, Terrebonne 11 Atchafalaya, Mississippi, Ponce de Leon 12 Apalachicola 13 Corpus Christi
Gulf of St. Lawrence: 5 Bonne, Gaspé
Hawaii: 11 Pearl Harbor
Honshu: 3 Ise 5 Osaka, Owari, Tokyo 6 Atsuta
Hudson Bay: 7 Repulse
Hudson River: 7 New York
Iceland: 4 Axar, Eyja, Huna 5 Horna, Skaga, Vopna 8 Hunafloi
Indonesia: 4 Bima 5 Saleh
Ionian Sea: 7 Taranto
Irish Sea: 4 Luce 7 Dundalk

Italy: 11 Gulf of Genoa 14 Lagoon of Venice
Japan: 4 Tosa
Java: 4 Lada 5 Peper
Java Sea: 7 Batavia 8 Djakarta
Kara Sea: 6 Enisei 7 Yenisei
Labrador: 8 Hamilton
Lake Erie: 8 Put-in-Bay, Sandusky
Lake Huron: 7 Saginaw, Thunder
Lake Michigan: 5 Green 13 Grand Traverse
Lake Ontario: 11 Irondequoit
Lake Superior: 5 Huron 8 Keweenaw 9 Whitefish
Long Island: 8 Rockaway
Long Island Sound: 6 Oyster 8 New Haven
Madagascar: 8 Antongil
Maine: 5 Casco 7 Machias 9 Penobscot 12 Damariscotta
Maryland-Virginia: 10 Chesapeake
Massachusetts: 8 Buzzards, Plymouth 9 Annisquam
Massachusetts Bay: 10 Lynn Harbor
Mediterranean Sea: 8 Valencia 9 Famagusta 10 Khalij Surt 11 Gulf of Sidra, Gulf of Tunis, Syrtis Major
Mozambique: 5 Memba, Pemba
Nantucket Sound: 5 Lewis
New Brunswick: 13 Passamaquoddy
Newfoundland: 4 Hare 5 White 7 Fortune
New Guinea: 3 Oro 5 Berau, Hansa 11 McCluer Gulf
New Jersey: 5 Great 7 Raritan 8 Barnegat 9 Little Egg
New York: 7 Jamaica
New Zealand: 5 Hawke 6 Tasman
North Carolina: 7 Roanoke 9 Albemarle
Northern Ireland: 12 Belfast Lough
North Sea: 4 Lyse 9 Hardanger
Northwest Territories: 5 Wager 8 Bathurst, Franklin 9 Frobisher 12 Prince Albert
Norway: 3 Tys 4 Bokn, Tana 5 Lakse, Sogne
Norwegian Sea: 4 Nord, Salt, Stor, Vest 8 Ranen 8 Scoresby 9 Trondheim
Ontario: 4 Owen
Oregon: 4 Coos
Philippines: 5 Baler, Pilar, Sogod 6 Butuan 9 Davao Gulf, Leyte Gulf, Panay Gulf
Puget Sound: 4 Carr, Case
Quebec: 6 Ungava
Red Sea: 4 Foul
Rhode Island: 12 Narragansett 13 Sakonnet River
Russia: 5 Chaun 8 Sakhalin, White Sea 12 Sea of Okhotsk
Santo Cruz Islands: 8 Basilisk

Sea of Japan: 13 Peter the Great
Solomon Islands: 4 Deep 8 Huon Gulf
South Africa: 5 Table
South Carolina: 4 Bull
South China Sea: 4 Bias, Datu, Siam, Taya 5 Dasol, Subic, Subig 6 Brunei, Paluan 7 Camranh 8 Lingayen, Thailand
Spain: 5 Cadiz
Spitsbergen: 3 Ice 4 Bell 5 Kings
Strait of Gibraltar: 7 Tangier
Sumatra: 5 Bajur 10 Koninginne
Tasmania: 5 Storm
Tyrrhenian Sea: 6 Naples 7 Paestum 13 Gulf of Salerno
Wales: 5 Burry
Washington: 5 Dabob 6 Skagit 11 Grays Harbor

inmate
7 convict 8 occupant, prisoner 10 inhabitant

inmost part
4 core, pith 5 heart 6 center, depths, kernel, marrow 7 nucleus

inn
5 fonda, hotel, house, lodge, motel 6 hostel, posada, tavern 7 auberge, hospice 8 hostelry, wayhouse 9 roadhouse 11 caravansary, public house 13 boardinghouse
German: 8 gasthaus
Turkish: 6 imaret

innards
4 guts 6 tripes 7 viscera 8 entrails, stuffing

innate
see **inherent**

inner
3 gut 5 close, focal 6 hidden, inside, inward, middle, secret 7 central, nuclear, private 8 familiar, interior, internal, personal, visceral 9 concealed, essential
combining form: 3 ent 4 ento

innervate
4 move 5 pique, rouse 7 provoke, quicken 9 galvanize

Innisfail
4 Eire, Erin 7 Ireland

innkeeper
4 host 8 boniface, hosteler, publican

innocence
6 purity 7 naiveté 8 chastity 9 ignorance, silliness 10 simplicity 11 artlessness, sinlessness, unawareness

innocent

4 free, good, pure, void **5** clean, empty, legal, licit, naive, white **6** candid, chaste, devoid, lawful, simple **7** artless, natural, unaware **8** harmless, ignorant, unguilty, virtuous **9** blameless, childlike, crimeless, destitute, exemplary, faultless, guileless, guiltless, ingenuous, innocuous, permitted, righteous, stainless, unstained, unstudied, unsullied, untainted **10** inculpable, legitimate, tenderfoot, unaffected, unblamable, unschooled **11** inobnoxious, inoffensive, unoffending, unoffensive, white-handed **12** simpleminded, unartificial, unsuspecting

innocuous

4 flat **5** banal, bland **6** jejune, pallid **7** insipid, sapless **8** harmless **9** driveling **10** namby-pamby **11** inoffensive, unoffending, unoffensive **13** insignificant

innovation

6 change **7** novelty, wrinkle **11** vicissitude

innovative

3 new **5** novel **8** creative, original **9** demiurgic, deviceful, inventive

innovator

5 maker **7** builder **8** original, producer **9** architect, developer **10** originator

innuendo

4 clue, hint, slur **8** allusion **10** intimation **11** implication, insinuation

innumerable

4 many **6** legion, myriad, untold **9** countless, uncounted **10** numberless

Ino

brother: **9** Polydorus
father: **6** Cadmus
grandfather: **6** Agenor
husband: **7** Athamas
mother: **8** Harmonia
sister: **5** Agave **6** Semele **7** Autonoe
son: **8** Learchus, Palaemon **10** Melicertes

inobtrusive

5 quiet, tasty **7** subdued **8** tasteful **10** restrained

inoculate

5 admit, enter, imbue, steep **6** infuse, leaven **7** implant, suffuse

inoffensive

8 harmless **9** innocuous, peaceable

inopportune

8 ill-timed, mistimed, untimely

inordinate

5 dizzy, extra, undue **6** wanton **7** extreme, surplus **8** towering **9** excessive **10** disorderly, exorbitant, gratuitous, immoderate, irrational, untempered **11** extravagant, intemperate, superfluous, uncalled-for **12** unmeasurable, unreasonable, unrestrained **13** extraordinary

in passing

6 obiter **8** by the bye, by the way **12** incidentally

in perpetuum

4 ever **6** always **7** forever **8** evermore **9** eternally **11** forevermore

inquest

5 probe **6** search **7** delving, inquiry, probing **8** research **11** examination **13** investigation

inquietude

6 unrest **7** ailment, anxiety, ferment, turmoil **10** uneasiness **11** restiveness **12** restlessness **13** Sturm und Drang

inquire

3 ask **4** seek **5** query, study **6** search **7** examine **8** question **9** catechize **10** scrutinize **11** interrogate, investigate

inquiry

5 audit, check, probe, query, quest **7** delving, hearing, probing **8** question, research, scrutiny **11** catechizing, examination, questioning **13** investigation

inquisition

4 hunt **5** probe, quest **6** search **7** delving, inquiry, probing **8** grilling, research **11** examination **13** investigation

inquisitive

4 nosy **5** peery **6** prying, snoopy **7** curious **11** questioning

inquisitor

Spanish: **10** Torquemada (Tomas de)

in re

4 as to **5** about, as for **7** apropos **9** as regards, regarding **10** as respects, concerning, respecting

in respect to

see **in re**

inroad

4 raid **5** foray **6** invade **7** overrun **8** invasion **9** incursion, irruption, overswarm **12** encroachment

ins and outs

5 ropes **6** quirks **7** details **8** minutiae, oddities **11** incidentals, particulars **13** peculiarities, ramifications

insane

3 mad, off **4** daft, nuts **5** crazy, daffy, dotty, loony, manic, nutsy, nutty, rocky, silly, wacky, wrong **6** absurd, crazed, cuckoo, maniac, screwy, teched **7** cracked, foolish, lunatic, strange, tetched, touched, unsound, witless **8** demented, deranged, fanciful, mindless **9** bedlamite, brainsick, eccentric, fantastic, imaginary, visionary **10** bewildered, disordered, distracted, distraught, irrational, reasonless, ridiculous, unbalanced **11** harebrained, impractical, unrealistic **12** crackbrained, preposterous, unreasonable

insane asylum

6 bedlam **8** loony bin, madhouse, nuthouse **9** funny farm **10** booby hatch, sanatorium, sanitarium

insanity

5 folly, mania **6** dotage, frenzy, lunacy **7** madness **8** delirium, delusion, dementia, hysteria, illusion **9** acromania, craziness, dottiness, silliness, unbalance **10** aberration, alienation **11** derangement, distraction, fatuousness, foolishness, psychopathy, witlessness **13** hallucination, senselessness

insatiable

6 crying, greedy, urgent **7** exigent **8** pressing, yearning **9** clamorous, demanding, voracious **10** quenchless **11** importunate **12** unappeasable, unquenchable

inscribe

4 book, etch, list **5** enter, print, write **6** enroll **7** catalog, engrave, engross, impress, imprint **8** enscroll

inscription

5 title **6** legend **7** epigram, epitaph, heading **8** epigraph **10** enrollment

inscrutable

6 arcane, mystic, secret **8** numinous **9** mysterial, unguessed **10** cabalistic, mysterious, unknowable **12** impenetrable, unfathomable

insect

3 bee, bug, fly **6** beetle
adult: **5** imago
antenna: **4** palp **6** feeler

butterfly: (see **butterfly** entry)

combining form: **5** entom **6** entomo

covering: **6** chitin

immature: **4** grub, pupa **5** larva, nymph **6** larvae (plural), maggot **8** wriggler **9** chrysalis **11** caterpillar

kind: **3** ant **4** flea, moth, wasp **5** aphid, scale **6** bedbug, beefly, beetle, cicada, earwig, hornet, mantid, mantis, mayfly **7** ant lion, cricket, firefly, June bug, katydid, ladybug, termite **8** honeybee, horsefly, housefly, lacewing, mosquito, stinkbug **9** bumblebee, butterfly, damselfly, dragonfly **10** silverfish, springtail **11** grasshopper **12** walkingstick

luminous: **7** firefly **8** glowworm

molt: **7** ecdysis

moth: **4** luna **6** sphinx **8** Cecropia **10** Polyphemus

multi-legged: **8** diplopod **9** centipede, millepede, millipede

part: **4** palp **5** cerci (plural) **6** cercus, labium, labrum, ocelli (plural), thorax **7** antenna, maxilla, ocellus **8** antennae (plural), mandible, maxillae (plural) **9** proboscis, spiracles **10** ovipositor **11** exoskeleton

pest: **4** flea, lice (plural), mite **5** louse, midge, scale **7** blowfly, termite **8** horsefly, housefly, mealybug **9** cockroach, gypsy moth **10** boll weevil, Hessian fly, silverfish

science: **10** entomology

winged: **5** alate

wingless: **4** flea, lice (plural) **5** louse **8** firebrat **10** silverfish **11** bristletail

insecticide

3 DDT **5** mirex, naled **6** endrin, ronnel **7** lindane, phorate **8** carbaryl, dieldrin, rotenone **9** chlordane

insecure

4 weak **5** shaky **6** dickey, infirm, unsafe, unsure, wobbly **8** hesitant, rootless, unstable, wavering **9** fluctuant, unassured, uncertain **11** questioning, unconfident

inseminate

7 implant, instill **9** fertilize **10** impregnate

insensate

4 dull, hard **5** rocky, silly **6** simple **7** fatuous, foolish, witless **8** mindless **9** bloodless, brainless, nitwitted, unfeeling **10** anesthetic, unanimated **11** sheepheaded

insensibility

4 coma **6** apathy, phlegm, torpor **8** lethargy, stoicism **12** indifference

insensible

4 cold, dead, dull, hard, numb, rapt **5** blunt, rocky, stoic **6** asleep, intent, numbed, obtuse, stolid **7** brutish, callous **8** absorbed, benumbed, comatose, deadened, hardened, obdurate **9** apathetic, bloodless, engrossed, impassive, unfeeling **10** anesthetic, phlegmatic, unapparent **11** unconscious **12** anesthetized

insensitive

4 dead, dull, hard, numb **5** aloof, rocky **6** asleep, numbed **8** benumbed, deadened **9** bloodless, unfeeling **10** anesthetic, impossible **11** indifferent, unconcerned **12** anesthetized, unresponsive **13** insusceptible, unimpressible, unsusceptible

insert

5 admit, enter, infix, inlay, inlet, inset **6** fill in **7** implant, obtrude, throw in **9** interpose **11** intercalate, interpolate

in short

7 briefly, tersely **9** concisely **10** succinctly **11** laconically

inside

5 inner **6** closet, hushed, inward, within **7** private **8** interior **11** withindoors **12** confidential

combining form: **3** end **4** endo

insidious

3 sly **4** deep, foxy, wily **6** artful, astute, crafty, subtle, tricky **7** cunning, gradual **8** guileful **9** deceitful **10** fraudulent **11** treacherous

insight

6 wisdom **8** sagacity, sageness, sapience **9** intuition **10** anschauung **11** discernment, penetration **13** intuitiveness, sagaciousness, understanding

insightful

4 sage, wise **6** sophic **7** gnostic, knowing **9** sagacious **10** discerning, perceptive **11** penetrating **13** knowledgeable

insignia

4 mark, sign **5** badge **6** emblem **8** brassard **10** decoration

insignificant

4 puny **5** dinky, light, minor, petty, small **6** casual, lesser, little, paltry **7** trivial **8** inferior, small-fry, trifling **9** pointless, secondary, senseless, small-beer, small-time, unmeaning **10** shoestring **11** meaningless, minor-league, unimportant

insincere

5 false, lying **6** double, shifty, tricky **7** feigned **8** mala fide, slippery **9** deceitful, deceptive, dishonest **10** left-handed, mendacious, untruthful **11** double-faced **12** hypocritical

insinuate

4 hint, worm **5** foist, imply **6** allude, edge in, fill in, impugn, impute, insert, work in **7** ascribe, connote, implant, instill, suggest, throw in **9** introduce

insipid

3 dry **4** arid, dull, flat, mild, pale, soft, tame, thin, weak **5** banal, bland, dusty, plain, vapid **6** feeble, jejune, slight, swashy, watery **7** mundane, prosaic, sapless, subdued, tedious, tenuous **8** bromidic, lifeless, ordinary, unsavory, waterish, weariful **9** driveling, dryasdust, innocuous, pointless, savorless, tasteless, wearisome **10** flavorless, monotonous, namby-pamby, spiritless, wishy-washy **11** commonplace

insistent

4 dire **6** crying, dogged, urgent **7** burning, clamant **8** emphatic, forceful, pressing **9** assertive, clamorous, obtrusive **10** imperative, resounding **11** persevering

insolence

5 nerve **6** insult **8** audacity, boldness, contempt, rudeness **9** arrogance, hardihood, impudence **10** brazenness, disrespect, effrontery **11** haughtiness, presumption **12** impertinence

insolent

4 bold, pert, rude **5** lofty, proud, saucy **6** brazen **7** defiant, haughty, uncivil **8** arrogant, cavalier, impolite, impudent, superior **9** audacious **10** disdainful, imperative, peremptory, procacious, ungracious **11** dictatorial, impertinent, magisterial, overbearing **12** contumelious, discourteous, supercilious **13** high-and-mighty

insouciance

6 apathy **8** lethargy **9** disregard, lassitude, unconcern **11** disinterest **12** heedlessness, indifference, listlessness

insouciant

8 carefree, heedless **9** lightsome **10** free-minded **11** indifferent, unconcerned **12** happy-go-lucky, lighthearted

inspect
3 con, vet **4** view **5** check, study **6** notice, review, survey **7** canvass, check up, examine, observe **8** question **9** catechize, check over **10** scrutinize

inspiration
4 muse **6** animus, genius, vision **8** afflatus **9** brainwave, influence **10** brainstorm **13** enlightenment

inspire
3 get **4** fire, move, stir, sway **5** carry, elate, endow, endue, exalt, imbue, set up, touch **6** affect, excite, foment, incite, inhale, strike **7** animate, commove, enliven, impress, quicken **8** motivate, spirit up **9** breathe in, encourage, influence, stimulate **10** exhilarate

instability
9 shakiness **10** insecurity **11** inconstancy, unfixedness **12** unsteadiness **13** changeability, unsettledness

install
4 seat, vest **5** chair **6** induct, invest, settle **8** ensconce, enthrone, initiate **9** establish

instance
4 case, cite, item, name **5** proof **6** detail, ground, reason, sample **7** example, mention, request, specify **8** exponent, sampling, specimen **9** exemplify **10** illustrate, particular, suggestion **11** case history, instigation **12** illustration

instant
4 dire, time, wink **5** crack, flash, jiffy, point, shake, trice, while **6** minute, moment, second, urgent **7** current, exigent, present, twinkle **8** existent, juncture, occasion, pressing, todayish **9** immediate, insistent, twinkling **10** imperative, present-day

instantaneous
4 fast **5** quick, rapid **9** immediate, momentary **10** transitory **11** hair-trigger

instanter
3 now **4** away **5** right **6** at once **8** directly, first off **9** forthwith, right away **11** immediately

instantly
3 now **4** away **5** right **6** at once **8** directly, first off **9** forthwith, right away **10** pressingly

instead
4 else **6** in lieu, rather **11** alternately **13** alternatively

instigate
3 set **4** abet, fire, goad, hint, move, plan, plot, prod, spur, urge **5** impel, raise, set on **6** excite, foment, incite, scheme, stir up, whip up **7** provoke, suggest **8** motivate **9** stimulate

instill
5 imbue, infix **6** impart, infuse **7** implant **9** inculcate, introduce

instinctive
6 innate, normal **7** natural, regular, typical **8** inherent, visceral, will-less **9** automatic, intuitive, unlearned **10** congenital, unprompted, unreasoned **11** involuntary, spontaneous, unmeditated

institute
3 law **4** rule **5** begin, edict, found, set up, start **6** decree, launch, ordain **7** precept, usher in **8** decretum, initiate, organize **9** establish, introduce, ordinance, originate **10** inaugurate **12** organization

institution
4 rite **5** habit **6** custom **7** fixture **9** enactment **10** foundation **13** establishment
kind: **6** school **7** academy, college **8** hospital **10** university

instruct
3 bid **4** lead, show, tell, warn **5** coach, drill, guide, order, pilot, steer, teach, train, tutor **6** assign, charge, define, direct, enjoin, inform, school **7** apprise, command, counsel, educate **8** acquaint, engineer **9** prescribe **10** discipline

instruction
6 advice, lesson **7** precept **8** teaching, training, tutelage **9** catechism, education, schooling **10** directions
place of: **6** school **7** academe

instructive
8 didactic **10** moralistic, moralizing **11** educational

instrument
4 deed, gear, mean, tool **5** agent, means, organ **6** agency, device, medium, tackle **7** channel, utensil, vehicle **8** ministry **9** appliance, machinery **13** paraphernalia
aircraft: **3** aba **5** radar, radio **7** compass **8** yawmeter **9** altimeter, gyroscope **10** altazimuth, tachometer **11** transponder

calculating: **6** abacus **8** computer **9** slide rule
combining form: **4** labe, stat **5** meter
graphic: **6** camera **8** otoscope **9** telescope **10** binoculars, microscope **11** fluoroscope, stethoscope, stroboscope **12** bronchoscope, oscilloscope, spectrograph, spectroscope
measuring: **5** clock, gauge, radar, scale, sonar **7** alidade, ammeter, balance, caliper, sextant, transit **8** quadrant **9** altimeter, astrolabe, barometer, bolometer, manometer, pedometer, sonometer, voltmeter **10** anemometer, fathometer, hydrometer, hygrometer, micrometer, radiometer, radiosonde, spirometer, tachometer, theodolite **11** chronometer, lie detector, range finder, seismograph, speedometer, thermometer **12** electroscope, galvanometer, oscillograph, oscilloscope **13** Geiger counter, potentiometer
medical: **5** curet **6** lancet, plexor, trocar **7** curette, forceps, probang, specula (plural), tenacula (plural) **9** tenaculum
radiation-producing: **5** laser, maser; (see also **implement; musical instrument; tool**)

instrumental
6 useful **7** helpful **9** conducive **11** serviceable

instrumentality
5 agent, force, means, might, organ, power **6** agency, energy, medium **7** channel, vehicle **8** ministry

insubordinate
5 rebel **6** unruly **7** riotous **8** factious, mutinous **9** seditious **10** headstrong, rebellious, refractory **11** disaffected, disobedient, dissentious, intractable, uncompliant, uncomplying **12** contumacious, recalcitrant, ungovernable

insubstantial
4 airy, puny, weak **5** frail **6** feeble, flimsy **7** fragile, tenuous, unsound **8** bodiless, decrepit **9** imaginary, unfleshly **10** intangible, unembodied **11** disembodied **12** apparitional

insufferable
7 painful **10** unbearable **11** distressing, intolerable

insufficiency
4 lack **7** failure, paucity, poverty **8** scarcity, shortage, underage **9** inability **10** inadequacy, scantiness, scarceness **11** defalcation

insufficient
3 shy 5 scant, short, unfit 6 scanty, scarce 7 failing, lacking, unequal, wanting 9 defective 10 inadequate, incomplete

insular
5 local 6 narrow 7 limited 8 confined, detached, islander, isolated, regional, secluded 9 illiberal, insulated, parochial, sectarian, sectional, small-town 10 prejudiced, provincial, restricted

insulate
6 cut off, enisle, island 7 isolate 8 close off 9 segregate, sequester

insult
4 gibe, gird, jeer, mock, rump, slap, slur 5 abase, abuse, fleer, flout, scoff, scorn, shame, sneer, taunt 6 debase, deride, humble, offend, revile 7 affront, degrade, despite, disdain, obloquy, offense, outrage 8 contempt, disgrace, ignominy, ridicule 9 contumely, humiliate, insolence 10 opprobrium 12 unpleasantry, vituperation

insurance
8 guaranty, warranty 10 protection
agency: 7 actuary 8 adjuster 11 underwriter
term: 6 policy 7 annuity 8 coverage 9 bordereau 11 beneficiary

insure
5 cinch, guard 6 assure, shield 7 protect 9 safeguard 10 underwrite

insurgent
5 rebel 6 anarch 8 factious, frondeur, mutineer, mutinous, revolter 9 anarchist, seditious 10 rebellious 12 contumacious 13 insubordinate

insurrection
6 mutiny, revolt 8 uprising 9 rebellion

insurrectionist
5 rebel 6 anarch 8 frondeur, mutineer, revolter 10 malcontent

insusceptible
6 immune 9 impassive, unfeeling 10 insentient 12 unresponsive

intact
5 sound, whole 6 entire, maiden, unhurt, virgin 7 perfect 8 complete, flawless, unbroken, unmarred, virginal 9 undamaged, uninjured, untouched 10 unimpaired

intangible
4 airy, rare, thin 5 vague 6 aerial, slight 8 aeriform, ethereal 10 immaterial, impalpable, unapparent 11 incorporeal

integer
5 digit 6 figure, number 7 chiffer, numeral 11 whole number

integral
3 sum 4 full 5 whole 6 choate, entire, entity, system 7 inbuilt, perfect 8 complete, inherent, totality 9 component, composite 11 constituent

integrate
3 mix, sum 4 fuse, join, link, tune 5 blend, merge, unify, unite, whole 6 attune, embody, entity, system 7 arrange, combine, compact, conform, conjoin 8 coalesce, organize, totality 9 harmonize, reconcile 10 articulate, coordinate, proportion, symphonize, synthesize 11 desegregate

integrity
5 honor 7 honesty, probity 9 constancy, soundness, wholeness 10 entireness, honestness, perfection 12 absoluteness, completeness, incorruption 13 honorableness

integument
4 coat 5 testa 7 coating, cuticle 8 covering, envelope 10 investment
combining form: 4 derm, scyt 5 derma, scyto 6 dermia, dermis 9 dermatous

intellect
3 wit 4 mind, nous 5 brain 6 genius, pundit, reason 7 egghead, thinker 9 intuition, mentality 12 intelligence 13 comprehension, understanding

intellectual
5 brain 6 brainy, mental 7 Brahmin, egghead, psychic 8 highbrow, longhair 9 reasoning 10 double-dome, highbrowed, reflective

intelligence
3 wit 4 mind, news, word 5 brain, sense 6 acumen, advice, brains, notice, reason, wisdom 7 tidings 8 judgment, learning, sagacity 9 knowledge, mentality, mother wit, speerings 10 brainpower, shrewdness

intelligent
4 keen, wise 5 acute, alert, aware, sharp, smart, sound 6 adroit, astute, brainy, bright, clever, shrewd 7 cunning, knowing, logical 8 rational, sensible 9 brilliant, ingenious, sagacious 10 reasonable 11 quick-witted, ready-witted 13 knowledgeable, perspicacious

intelligentsia
7 clerisy 8 literati, vanguard 10 avant-garde, illuminati

intelligible
5 clear, lucid, plain 8 luminous 10 conceptual 13 supersensible, suprasensuous

intemperance
6 excess 10 debauchery 11 drunkenness 12 immoderation

intemperate
4 hard 5 harsh 6 bitter, brutal, rugged, severe 7 drunken, extreme, violent 8 bibulous, rigorous 9 bibacious, crapulous, excessive, inclement 10 gluttonous, immoderate, inordinate 12 unrestrained 13 overindulgent

intend
3 aim, try 4 mean, plan, plot 5 essay, spell 6 assign, denote, design, import, scheme, strive 7 add up to, attempt, connote, destine, express, propose, purpose, signify 8 endeavor 9 designate

intended
6 fiancé 7 engaged, fiancée 8 proposed 9 affianced, betrothed

intense
3 hot 4 deep, hard, keen 5 acute, great, vivid 6 ardent, fervid, fierce, severe, strong 7 extreme, fervent, furious, serious, vicious, violent, zealous 8 enhanced, powerful, profound, stressed, terrible, vehement 9 assiduous, desperate, excessive, exquisite 10 aggravated, emphasized, heightened 11 accentuated 12 concentrated

intensify
4 rise 5 exalt, mount, rouse 6 accent, deepen, stress 7 enhance, sharpen 8 heighten, increase, redouble 9 aggravate, emphasize 10 accentuate, aggrandize 11 concentrate

intensity
5 depth 6 energy, fervor 7 passion 8 fervency, loudness

intensive
5 eager 7 zealous 10 exhaustive 12 concentrated
pronoun: 6 itself, myself 7 herself, himself 8 yourself 9 ourselves 10 themselves, yourselves

intent

3 aim, set 4 deep, plan, rapt, will 5 eager, fixed, sense 6 animus, design, import 7 decided, earnest, engaged, meaning, minding, purport, purpose, riveted, settled, wrapped 8 absorbed, conation, decisive, diligent, immersed, resolute, resolved, sedulous, volition, watching 9 engrossed, wrapped up 10 determined

intention

3 aim, end 4 goal, hope, plan, wish 6 animus, design, desire, object, scheme 7 meaning, purpose

intentional

5 meant 7 advised, studied, willful, willing, witting 8 designed, proposed, purposed, unforced 9 designful, voluntary 10 considered, deliberate 12 premeditated, unprescribed

intentionally

9 on purpose, purposely

inter

4 bury, tomb 5 plant 6 entomb, inhume 7 lay away, put away 9 sepulcher, sepulture

interact

4 join 5 merge, unite 7 combine 9 cooperate 11 collaborate

interbreed

5 cross 9 cross-mate, hybridize

intercede

6 step in 7 mediate 9 arbitrate, interpose, intervene

intercept

4 curb, grab, stop, take 5 block, catch, check, seize 6 cut off, hinder 9 forestall, interrupt

intercessor

6 broker 8 advocate, mediator 9 go-between, middleman 12 entrepreneur

interconnect

4 join 5 blend, unite 10 anastomose, inosculate

intercourse

5 truck 7 contact, dealing, traffic 8 business, commerce, converse 9 communion 10 connection 12 conversation 13 communication

intercross

9 decussate, hybridize

interdict

3 ban 4 veto 5 taboo 6 enjoin, forbid, outlaw 8 prohibit 9 proscribe

interest

4 care, good, lure, pull 5 claim, pique, share, snare, stake, tempt 6 appeal, arouse, behalf, excite, regard 7 attract, benefit, concern, passion, welfare 9 advantage, attention, curiosity, fascinate, tantalize, titillate, well-being 10 absorption, enthusiasm, excitement, prosperity

interested

4 rapt 6 caring 7 partial 8 partisan

interfere

3 bar 4 balk, foil, fool 5 block 6 baffle, butt in, hamper, hinder, horn in, impede, meddle, step in, tamper, thwart 7 intrude, mediate, trouble 8 busybody, obstruct 9 frustrate, incommode, intervene 10 discommode, monkey with, tamper with

interim

3 gap 5 break 6 acting, breach, hiatus, lacuna, pro tem, supply 8 meantime 9 temporary 10 pro tempore

interior

3 gut 5 belly, bosom, heart, inner 6 center, inland, inside, inward, within 8 visceral 9 viscerous

interject

6 fill in 7 throw in 9 introduce

interjection

agreement: 6 righto 7 right on
attention-getter: 3 hey 4 ahem, psst 5 heigh
calling pigs: 5 sooey
cheer: 3 rah 6 hooray, hurrah, hurray
contempt: 3 poh 4 pooh 5 pshaw
disappointment: 4 rats 6 shucks
disapproval: 3 fie
disbelief: 2 aw 3 huh
disgust: 3 bah, pah, ugh 4 pugh, rats 5 faugh, nerts, yecch 6 phooey
dismay: 2 oy 4 oh no
dismissal: 3 git
farewell: 4 by-by, ciao 6 bye-bye, so long
gratitude: 8 gramercy
greeting: 2 hi 4 ciao 5 aloha, hello
hesitation: 2 er, um
in golf: 4 fore
in hunting: 6 yoicks
in marching: 3 hup
joy: 4 whee 6 hooray, hurrah, hurray, yippee 7 whoopee

mild apology: 4 oops 5 woops 6 whoops
mild oath: 3 gad, gor 4 darn, drat, egad, geez, gosh, heck, jeez 5 egads, golly, zooks 6 cracky, jiminy, zounds 7 begorra, begorry, gee whiz, jeepers, jimminy 8 gadzooks, gee whizz 13 gee whillikers, gee whillikins
of warning: 8 gardyloo
O.K.: 5 wilco
pain: 2 ow 4 ouch, yipe 5 yipes
peace: 6 shalom, sholom
regret: 4 alas 5 alack 8 lackaday
relief: 4 phew
request: 7 prithee
silence: 2 sh 3 shh
sneeze: 5 achoo 6 atchoo 7 kerchoo
sorrow: 4 alas 5 alack 8 lackaday
stop: 4 whoa
surprise: 2 ah, ho, lo, oh 3 aha, huh, oho, wow 4 gosh, oops, yipe 5 blimy, yipes, zowie 6 blimey
to a horse: 4 whoa 6 giddap
toast: 5 salud, skoal 6 cheers, prosit 7 l'chayim
triumph: 3 aha, hah 6 eureka; (see also **exclamation**)

interlace

3 mix 5 braid, twine, weave 9 alternate, interlock 10 intertwine, interweave 11 intersperse

interlard

3 mix 6 mingle 7 diffuse

interlope

4 fool 6 butt in, horn in, meddle 7 intrude 8 busybody 9 interfere 10 monkey with, tamper with 11 intermeddle

interlude

4 lull, rest 5 break, idyll, pause, spell 7 episode, respite 8 breather, entr'acte, interval, meantime 9 meanwhile

intermediary

3 mid 4 mean 5 agent, organ 6 agency, broker, center, medium, middle 7 central, channel, vehicle 8 mediator, ministry 9 go-between, middleman 10 interagent

intermediate

3 mid 4 fair, mean, so-so 6 broker, center, medium, middle, step in 7 average, between, central, fairish 8 middling 9 go-between, middleman 11 intervening 12 entrepreneur
combining form: 3 mes 4 medi, meso 5 medio

intermediator
6 broker 9 go-between, middleman 12 entrepreneur

interment
6 burial 9 sepulture 10 inhumation

interminable
7 endless, eternal, lasting 8 constant, infinite, unending 9 boundless, ceaseless, continual, limitless, permanent, perpetual, unceasing, unlimited 10 continuous 11 everlasting

intermission
4 rest, stop 5 break, pause 6 recess 7 latency, respite 8 abeyance, abeyancy, doldrums, dormancy, interval 10 quiescence, quiescency, suspension 11 cold storage, parenthesis 12 interruption

intermit
4 stay 5 check, defer, delay 6 arrest, hold up, put off 7 hold off, suspend 8 hold over, postpone, prorogue 9 interrupt

intermittent
6 broken, cyclic, fitful, serial 7 checked, iterant 8 arrested, cyclical, metrical, periodic, rhythmic, seasonal, sporadic 9 alternate, iterative, recurrent, recurring, spasmodic 10 alternated, isochronal, occasional, periodical, rhythmical 11 interrupted, isochronous

intermix
6 mingle 8 comingle, immingle 9 commingle 11 intermingle

intermixture
5 blend 7 amalgam 12 amalgamation 13 miscegenation

intern
3 jug 4 jail 6 immure 7 confine, impound, trainee 8 bastille, imprison 9 constrain

internal
3 gut 4 home 5 inner 6 inward, native 7 private 8 domestic, inherent, interior, visceral 9 intrinsic, viscerous 10 subjective
prefix: 5 intra

internal organs
4 guts 6 vitals 7 viscera 8 entrails

international organization
2 UN 3 FAO, IAM, ICJ, IFC, ILO, ITO, ITU, OAS, WHO, WMO 4 IAAF, IABA, IAEA, IARU, IATA, ICAO, IFIP, IMCO, NATO 5 ICFTU, SEATO 6 UNESCO, UNICEF

internuncio
5 envoy 6 bearer 7 carrier, courier 8 emissary 9 messenger

interpolate
3 add 5 admit, annex, enter 6 append, fill in, insert 7 throw in 8 superadd 9 introduce 11 intercalate

interpose
4 cast, push, toss 5 shove, throw 6 butt in, fill in, insert, meddle, step in, thrust 7 intrude, mediate, obtrude, throw in 8 moderate 9 arbitrate, insinuate, intercede, interfere, intervene, introduce, negotiate

interpret
4 limn 5 gloss, image 6 decode, depict, render 7 comment, explain, expound, picture, portray 8 annotate, construe, describe, spell out 9 delineate, exemplify, explicate, represent 10 commentate

interpretation
7 meaning, reading, version 8 exegesis 9 construal, rendering 11 explanation, translation

interpretive
8 exegetic 10 expository 11 explanatory, explicatory 12 expositional

interregnum
5 break 8 interval

interrogate
3 ask 4 quiz 5 grill, query 7 examine, inquire 8 question 9 catechize

interrupt
4 halt, stay, stop 5 break, check, cut in, defer, put in, stall 6 arrest, chip in 7 break in, chime in, disturb, suspend 8 postpone 9 intercept

interruption
3 gap 4 rent, rift 5 break, pause, split 6 breach, hiatus, lacuna 7 caesura, latency

intersect
4 meet 5 cross 8 crosscut, traverse 9 decussate 10 crisscross

intersection
8 crossing, junction 10 crossroads

intersperse
7 diffuse, scatter

interval
3 gap 4 lull 5 break, comma, pause, space 6 breach, hiatus, lacuna 7 caesura, interim, respite 9 pausation 11 parenthesis
music: 4 rest

intervene
4 part 5 sever 6 divide, step in 7 mediate 8 separate 9 intercede, interpose

interweave
3 mix 4 fuse, join, link 5 blend 9 associate

intestinal fortitude
4 grit, guts, sand 5 nerve, pluck, spunk 6 mettle, spirit 7 courage 8 backbone 10 resolution

intestine
3 gut 4 tube 5 bowel, canal 6 inward, viscus 7 viscera (plural)
combining form: 3 col 4 coli, colo 5 enter 6 entero
part: 5 cecum, colon, ileum 6 rectum 7 jejunum 8 duodenum

in the same place
6 ibidem

intimacy
7 liberty 9 closeness 10 experience 11 familiarity 12 acquaintance

intimate
3 gut 4 cozy, fond, hint, next 5 amigo, close, crony, imply, inner, pally, privy, thick 6 attest, chummy, friend, impart, loving, notify, secret, sexual 7 bespeak, betoken, comrade, connote, devoted, nearest, suggest 8 announce, familiar, inherent, visceral 9 close-knit, companion, confidant, elemental, essential, ingrained, insinuate, intrinsic, viscerous 10 deep-seated, indwelling 11 cater-cousin 12 acquaintance, confidential

intimation
3 cue 4 clue, hint, wind 5 shade, tinge, trace 6 breath, shadow, strain, streak 7 inkling 8 telltale 10 suggestion

intimidate
3 awe, cow 4 bait, ride 5 abash, alarm, bully, chivy, daunt, deter, force, hound, scare 6 badger, coerce, compel, hector, oblige 7 bluster, buffalo, dragoon, overawe, terrify 8 bludgeon, browbeat, bulldoze, bullyrag, dispirit, disquiet, frighten 9 constrain, strongarm, terrorize

intolerant
5 irate, upset 6 averse, narrow, stuffy 7 bigoted, waspish 8 dogmatic, obdurate, outraged, snappish, worked up 9 fractious, hidebound, illiberal, impatient, irritable

10 brassbound, disdainful, inflexible, prejudiced, unenlarged **11** small-minded, unindulgent **12** antipathetic, contemptuous, narrow-minded, unforbearing **13** unsympathetic

intonation
4 tone **5** chant **6** accent **10** recitation

in toto
3 all **4** just **5** quite, stick **6** wholly **7** exactly, utterly **10** altogether

intoxicant
5 booze, drink **6** liquor **7** alcohol, spirits **9** aqua vitae

intoxicated
3 cut, wet **4** high **5** blind, dopey, drunk, fried, loopy, soppy, stiff, tight, tipsy **6** elated, looped, rumdum, sloppy, sodden, soshed, stewed, stoned, tanked, zonked **7** drunken, excited, maudlin, muddled, slopped, sozzled, unsober **8** cockeyed, polluted, squiffed, turned-on **9** inebrious **11** alcoholized, exhilarated

intoxication
7 elation **8** euphoria **11** drunkenness, inebriation

intractable
4 wild **6** mulish, unruly **7** willful **8** indocile, mutinous, obdurate, perverse, stubborn **9** fractious, obstinate **10** bullheaded, headstrong, refractory, self-willed, unyielding **11** unteachable **12** pertinacious, recalcitrant, ungovernable **13** undisciplined

intransigent
5 tough **7** willful **8** stubborn **9** obstinate, unpliable **10** self-willed, unyielding **12** pertinacious

intrepid
4 bold **5** brave, hardy **6** daring, heroic **7** gallant, valiant **8** fearless, resolute, unafraid, valorous **9** audacious, dauntless, undaunted **10** courageous

intricate
4 hard **5** fancy **6** daedal, knotty **7** arduous, complex, gordian **8** involved **9** Byzantine, difficult, elaborate **11** complicated **12** labyrinthine **13** sophisticated

intrigue
4 plot **5** amour, cabal, covin **6** affair, appeal, devise, excite, scheme **7** attract, beguile, collude, connive,

liaison **8** cogitate, conspire, contrive, interest, practice **9** fascinate, machinate, scheme out **10** conspiracy **11** machination

intrinsic
see **inherent**

intrinsically
5 per se **6** as such

introduce
4 lead, moot **5** admit, begin, enter, found, set up, usher **6** broach, fill in, insert, launch, unveil, work in **7** bring up, implant, install, instill, pioneer, precede, preface, present, throw in, usher in **8** acquaint, initiate, innovate, organize **9** establish, insinuate, institute, interject, interpose, originate

introduction
5 debut, proem **7** introit, preface, prelude **8** entrance, exordium, foreword, overture, preamble, prologue, protases (plural), protasis **9** prelusion **12** prolegomenon

introductory
7 initial, nascent **8** proemial **9** beginning, prefatial, prefatory, preludial, prelusive **11** prefatorial, preliminary, preparative

intrude
5 cut in **6** bother, butt in, horn in, impose, invade, meddle, muscle, pester **7** disturb, presume **8** chisel in, encroach, entrench, infringe, trespass **9** interfere, interlope, interpose

intrusive
4 busy **7** curious **9** butting in, officious **10** meddlesome **11** impertinent **13** polypragmatic

in truth
6 indeed, really, verily **8** actually

intuition
7 insight **8** instinct **10** anschauung, sixth sense **11** second sight

inundate
5 drown, flood, swamp, whelm **6** deluge, engulf **8** overflow, submerge **9** overwhelm

inundation
4 pour **5** flood, spate **6** deluge **7** niagara, torrent **8** cataract, flooding, overflow **9** cataclysm

inure
3 use **4** wont **5** steel, train **6** harden, season **7** toughen **8** accustom **9** habituate **10** discipline **11** familiarize

inutile
6 draffy, drossy, no-good **7** nothing **8** unworthy **9** valueless, worthless

invade
4 loot, raid **5** foray **6** ravage **7** assault, overrun, pillage, plunder **8** encroach, entrench, infringe, permeate, trespass **9** overswarm **11** impenetrate

invalid
3 bad, mad **4** null, void **6** infirm, sickly **9** illogical, sophistic **10** fallacious, irrational, reasonless, unreasoned **11** nonrational, null and void **12** unreasonable

invalidate
4 undo **5** abate, annul, quash **6** offset **7** abolish, nullify **8** negative **9** discredit **10** circumduct, counteract, neutralize

invaluable
6 costly **8** precious **9** priceless **11** inestimable

invariable
4 same **5** fixed **6** steady **7** uniform **8** constant **9** continual, immovable, immutable, unfailing, unmovable, unvarying **10** consistent, inflexible, unchanging **11** inalterable, unalterable **12** unchangeable, unmodifiable

invariably
4 ever **6** always **7** forever **10** constantly **11** continually, perpetually

invasion
4 raid **5** foray **6** attack, inroad **9** incursion, intrusion, irruption, offensive **12** encroachment, entrenchment

invective
5 abuse **6** tirade **7** abusive, obloquy **8** diatribe, jeremiad, scurrile **9** contumely, damnatory, philippic, truculent **10** censorious, scurrility, scurrilous, vituperous **11** opprobrious, reproachful **12** billingsgate, condemnatory, contumelious, denunciatory, vituperation, vituperative, vituperatory

inveigh
4 kick, rail **6** except, object **7** protest **9** fulminate **11** expostulate, remonstrate

inveigle
4 bait, coax, lure, toll **5** decoy, snare, tempt **6** allure, cajole, entice, entrap, lead on, seduce **8** persuade

invent

4 coin, mint **5** frame **6** cook up, create, design, devise, make up, patent, vamp up **7** concoct, dream up, fashion, hatch up, pioneer **8** conceive, contrive, discover, engineer, envision **9** fabricate, formulate, originate

invention

7 coinage, fiction **8** creation **10** brainchild, concoction, innovation **11** contrivance, origination

inventive

7 fertile, teeming **8** creative, fruitful, original **9** demiurgic, deviceful, ingenious **10** innovative, innovatory, productive

inventor

4 sire **5** maker **6** author, father **7** creator, founder **8** engineer, original **9** architect, generator, innovator, patriarch **10** discoverer, introducer, originator

air brake: **12** Westinghouse (George)
air conditioning: **7** Carrier (Willis)
automobile: **7** Daimler (Gottlieb)
ballpoint pen: **4** Loud (John)
barbed wire: **7** Glidden (Joseph Farwell)
barometer: **10** Torricelli (Evangelista)
bifocal lens: **8** Franklin (Benjamin)
camera: **7** Eastman (George)
cash register: **5** Ritty (James)
cotton gin: **7** Whitney (Eli)
cylinder lock: **4** Yale (Linus)
dirigible: **8** Zeppelin (Ferdinand von)
dynamite: **5** Nobel (Alfred)
electric battery: **5** Volta (Alessandro)
electric fan: **7** Wheeler (George)
electric organ: **7** Hammond (Laurens)
electric razor: **6** Schick (Jacob)
electric stove: **7** Hadaway
elevator: **4** Otis (Elisha)
fountain pen: **8** Waterman (Lewis)
friction match: **6** Walker (John)
gyrocompass: **6** Sperry (Elmer)
helicopter: **8** Sikorsky (Igor)
hot-air balloon: **11** Montgolfier (Jacques, Joseph)
incandescent lamp: **6** Edison (Thomas Alva)
induction motor: **5** Tesla (Nikola)
lawn mower: **5** Hills
Linotype: **12** Mergenthaler (Ottmar)
logarithm: **6** Napier (John)
machine gun: **7** Gatling (Richard)
microphone: **8** Berliner (Emile)
movable type: **9** Gutenberg (Johannes)
parachute: **9** Blanchard (Jean-Pierre)
pendulum clock: **7** Huygens (Christiaan)
phonograph: **6** Edison (Thomas Alva)
photography: **6** Niepce (Joseph), Talbot (William Henry) **8** Daguerre (Louis)
piano: **10** Cristofori (Bartolomeo)
radio: **7** Marconi (Guglielmo)
reaper: **9** McCormick (Cyrus)
revolver: **4** Colt (Samuel)
rocket engine: **7** Goddard (Robert)
safety pin: **4** Hunt (Walter)
safety razor: **8** Gillette (King Camp)
sewing machine: **4** Howe (Elias)
sleeping car: **7** Pullman (George)
spinning jenny: **10** Hargreaves (James)
steamboat: **5** Fitch (John) **6** Fulton (Robert), Miller (Patrick), Rumsey (James) **8** Jouffroy (Claude de)
steam engine: **4** Watt (James)
steam locomotive: **10** Stephenson (George)
stethoscope: **7** Laennec (Rene)
submarine: **7** Holland (John Philip)
tank: **7** Swinton (Ernest)
telegraph: **5** Morse (Samuel F. B.)
telephone: **4** Bell (Alexander Graham)
telescope: **10** Lippershey (Hans)
television: **5** Baird (John) **6** Nipkow (Paul) **8** Zworykin (Vladimir) **10** Farnsworth (Philo)
torpedo: **9** Whitehead (Robert)
vulcanized rubber: **8** Goodyear (Charles)
writing for the blind: **7** Braille (Louis)
zipper: **6** Judson (Whitcomb)

inventory

3 sum **4** fund, list **5** hoard, stock, store, sum up, tally **6** digest, record, supply, survey **7** account, backlog, catalog, itemize, nest egg, reserve, specify, summary, summate **8** condense, nutshell, register, tabulate **9** checklist, enumerate, epitomize, reservoir, stockpile, summarize, synopsize

inverse

4 turn **6** change, revert **7** reverse **8** contrary, opposite **9** transpose **10** transplace
prefix: **2** ob

inversion

4 turn **7** reverse, turning **8** reversal **9** about-face, turnabout, volte-face **11** changeabout, reversement

invert

4 flip, turn **6** change **7** reverse, uranian, uranist **8** turn over **9** transpose **10** homosexual, transplace

invertebrate

4 weak **5** sissy **7** doormat, milksop **8** boneless, impotent, weakling **9** forceless, jellyfish, spineless **10** emasculate, inadequate, namby-pamby, pantywaist **11** ineffective, ineffectual, Milquetoast, mollycoddle, slack-spined
kind: **4** worm **6** insect, sponge **7** mollusk **8** arachnid **12** coelenterate

invest

4 gird, veil, wrap **5** adorn, array, beset, dress, endow, endue, imbue, steep **6** clothe, confer, enfold, enwrap, induct, infuse, leaven, ordain, shroud **7** besiege, empower, enclose, envelop, ingrain, install, instate, suffuse

investigate

3 pry **4** poke, sift **5** probe, study **6** go into, search **7** dig into, examine, explore, inquire **8** look into, muckrake, prospect, research **9** delve into **10** scrutinize **11** inquire into

investigation

5 probe, quest **6** survey **7** delving, inquest, inquiry, probing **8** research, sounding **9** surveying **11** inquisition

investigator

4 dick **6** sleuth **7** gumshoe **8** hawkshaw, sherlock **9** detective

investiture

5 siege **8** blockage **9** inaugural, induction **10** initiation **12** inauguration, installation

inveterate

3 old, set **5** fixed, sworn **6** rooted **7** abiding, chronic, settled **8** deep-dyed, enduring, habitual, hardened, lifelong **9** confirmed, hardshell, ingrained, long-lived, perennial **10** continuing, deep-rooted, deep-seated, entrenched, persistent, persisting **11** established

Invictus author

6 Henley (William Ernest)

invidious

6 bitter, odious **7** envious, envying, hateful, jealous **8** libelous **9** abhorrent, green-eyed, injurious, malignant, maligning, obnoxious, repellent, repugnant, revulsive, vilifying **10** abominable, calumnious, defamatory, detestable, detracting, detractive, detractory, scandalous, slanderous

invigorate

4 stir, zest **5** brace, cheer, rally,

renew, rouse **7** animate, enliven, fortify, refresh, restore **8** energize, vitalize **9** reinforce, stimulate **10** exhilarate, rejuvenate, strengthen

in vino ____
7 veritas

inviolable
4 holy, pure **6** chaste, divine, sacred **7** blessed **8** hallowed **9** undefiled **10** sacrosanct **11** consecrated **13** incorruptible

Invisible Man, The
author: **5** Wells (Herbert George)

Invisible Man author
7 Ellison (Ralph)

invitation
4 call, lure **7** bidding, proffer, request **8** entreaty, proposal, stimulus **9** incentive **10** attraction, suggestion **11** proposition

invite
3 ask, bid **4** call, lure **5** tempt **6** allure, call in, entice, summon **7** request, solicit

invoice
3 tab **4** bill **5** score **7** account **9** reckoning, statement

invoke
3 beg **4** pray **5** crave, plead **6** appeal, effect **7** beseech, enforce, entreat, implore **9** implement, importune **10** supplicate

involuntary
6 forced, reflex **8** will-less **9** automatic, impulsive, unwitting **10** compulsory, unintended, unprompted **11** instinctive, spontaneous, unmeditated **13** unintentional

involve
4 mire **6** embody, engage, entail, take in, tangle **7** concern, contain, embrace, embroil, include, subsume **8** comprise, entangle **9** encompass, implicate **10** complicate, comprehend

involved
6 daedal, knotty **7** complex, gordian, muddled **8** affected, confused, enmeshed **9** Byzantine, concerned, elaborate, entangled, intricate **10** implicated, interested **11** complicated **12** labyrinthine

invulnerable
10 invincible, unbeatable **11** impregnable, indomitable

inward
5 entad, inner **6** inside, mental **8** interior, internal **9** innermore, intestine, spiritual

inwards
4 guts **6** inside, tripes, within **7** innards, insides, viscera **8** entrails, interior **9** internals

Io
father: **7** Inachus
guard: **5** Argus
son: **7** Epaphus

iodine source
4 kelp

Iolcus king
5 Aeson **6** Pelias

Iole
captor: **8** Heracles, Hercules
father: **7** Eurytus
husband: **6** Hyllus

ion
6 ligand
kind: **5** anion **6** cation **8** thermion
suffix: **3** ium **5** onium

Ion
father: **6** Apollo
mother: **6** Creusa
stepfather: **6** Xuthus

Ionesco play
5 Chairs (The) **10** Rhinoceros (The) **11** Bald Soprano (The)

iota
3 bit, jot, ray **4** atom, mite, whit **5** crumb, grain, ounce, speck **6** tittle **7** smidgen **8** molecule, particle

IOU
4 debt
part: **3** owe, you

Iowa
capital: **9** Des Moines
college, university: **3** Coe **5** Dordt, Drake, Loras
nickname: **12** Hawkeye State
state bird: **9** goldfinch
state flower: **8** wild rose

Iphicles
brother: **8** Heracles, Hercules
mother: **7** Alcmene
son: **6** Iolaus

Iphigenia
brother: **7** Orestes
father: **9** Agamemnon
mother: **12** Clytemnestra
sister: **7** Electra

Iphis' daughter
6 Evadne

Iran
capital: **6** Tehran **7** Teheran
monetary unit: **4** rial
oil center: **6** Abadan

Iranian
7 Persian
language: **5** Farsi **7** Kurdish, Persian
non-Persian people: **5** Kurds
parliament: **6** Majlis
sect: **4** Shia **5** Sunni
sect member: **6** Shiite **7** Sunnite
title: **4** shah

Iraq
capital: **7** Baghdad
monetary unit: **5** dinar

irascible
5 cross, huffy, irate, ratty, surly, testy **6** cranky, ireful, snappy, tetchy, touchy **7** bristly, peevish, peppery **8** choleric, petulant, snappish **9** fractious, impatient, irritable, querulous, temperish **10** passionate **11** belligerent, hot-tempered **12** cantankerous **13** quick-tempered

Ira's father
6 Ikkesh

irate
3 mad **4** waxy **5** angry, wroth **6** ireful, wrathy, wrothy **7** enraged, furious **8** choleric, incensed, provoked, wrathful

ire
3 mad **4** fury, rage **5** anger, wrath **6** enrage, madden, temper **7** incense, steam up, umbrage **9** infuriate **10** exasperate **11** indignation **12** exasperation

Ireland
4 Eire, Erin **5** Ierne **8** Hibernia **9** Innisfail
capital: **6** Dublin
monetary unit: **5** pound

Irene
3 Pax
father: **4** Zeus **7** Jupiter
mother: **6** Themis

irenic
4 calm **7** pacific **8** pacifist, peaceful **9** peaceable **10** nonviolent **12** conciliatory, pacificatory

Iris
father: **7** Thaumas
mother: **7** Electra

Irish
4 Erse **6** Celtic, Gaelic
accent: **6** brogue
battle cry: **3** abu **4** aboo
cattle: **5** Kerry

clan: 4 sept
combining form: 7 Hiberno
coronation stone: 7 Lia Fail
cudgel: 9 shillalah 10 shillelagh
death spirit: 7 banshee
dirge: 8 ullagone
dog: 6 setter 7 terrier
elf: 10 leprechaun
exclamation: 3 aru 5 arrah
festival: 4 feis
flag color: 5 green, white 6 orange
flower: 8 shamrock
girl: 4 lass 6 lassie 7 colleen
goblin: 5 pooka
god: 3 Ler 5 Dagda 6 Aengus
goddess: 4 Badb, Bodb 6 Brigit
   8 Morrigan
harp: 8 clarsach
hero: 9 Cuchulain, Cuchullin
   11 Chuchulainn
heroine: 7 Deirdre
king: 9 Brian Boru
lake: 5 lough
language: 6 Gaelic
legislature: 4 Dail
militant force: 3 IRA
nationalist: 7 Parnell (Charles)
   8 O'Connell (Daniel)
nationalist society: 8 Sinn Fein
noble: 6 flaith
patron saint: 7 Patrick
theater: 5 Abbey
writing system: 4 ogam 5 ogham;
   (see also **Gaelic; Celtic**)

Irish moss
   7 seaweed 9 carrageen

irk
   3 try, vex 4 fret, gall, pain 5 anger, annoy, peeve, pique, upset
   6 abrade, bother, harass, nettle,
   ruffle, strain, stress 7 provoke, trouble 8 distress, exercise, irritate
   10 exasperate

Irma ___
   7 La Douce

iron
   4 hard 5 gyves, press 6 ferrum, fetter, strong 7 adamant, manacle,
   shackle 8 handcuff, obdurate 9 unbending 10 adamantine, brassbound, inexorable, inflexible, relentless, unyielding
combining form: 5 ferri, ferro, sider
   6 sidero
German: 5 eisen
relating to: 6 ferric 7 ferrous
symbol: 2 Fe
wrought: 5 mitis

ironbound
   5 harsh, rough 6 craggy, jagged,

rugged, uneven 7 scraggy 8 asperous, scabrous, unsmooth

Iron City
   10 Pittsburgh

ironclad
   5 fixed 8 constant 9 immovable,
   immutable 10 inflexible, invariable
   11 inalterable, unalterable 12 unchangeable

ironhanded
   5 rigid 6 strict 8 rigorist, rigorous
   9 draconian, stringent 12 unpermissive

ironhearted
   5 stony 7 callous 8 hardened, obdurate 9 heartless, unfeeling
   10 hard-boiled 11 cold-blooded
   13 unsympathetic

ironic
   3 wry 6 biting 7 caustic, cutting,
   cynical, mordant, satiric 8 sardonic
   9 sarcastic, trenchant

iron ore
   8 goethite, hematite, limonite, siderite, taconite 9 magnetite

Iron Pants
   6 Patton (George)

irons
   5 bonds, gyves 6 chains 7 fetters
   8 manacles, shackles

Iroquois tribe
   6 Cayuga, Mohawk, Oneida, Seneca 8 Onondaga

irradiate
   5 edify 6 illume, uplift 7 improve
   8 illumine 9 enlighten 10 illuminate

irrational
   3 mad 5 crazy 6 absurd, insane
   7 invalid 8 demented 9 illogical,
   senseless, sophistic 10 fallacious,
   reasonless, ridiculous, unreasoned
   11 nonrational 12 unreasonable

irrefutable
   4 sure 7 certain 8 positive 10 conclusive, inarguable 11 indubitable
   12 indisputable 13 incontestable,
   uncontestable

irregular
   3 odd 5 queer 6 fitful, off-key,
   patchy, random, spotty, uneven,
   unique 7 aimless, deviant, devious,
   erratic, strange, unaimed, unequal
   8 aberrant, abnormal, atypical, informal, lopsided, partisan, peculiar,
   singular, sporadic, unstable, unsteady, variable 9 anomalous, desultory, divergent, eccentric, guerrilla, haphazard, hit-or-miss,

spasmodic, unnatural, unregular,
unsettled 10 asymmetric, changeable, designless, inconstant, off-
balance, unbalanced, unofficial
11 exceptional, purposeless
12 overbalanced, unconsidered,
unsystematic
combining form: 4 anom 5 anomo
   6 anomal 7 anomali, anomalo

irregularity
   7 anomaly 8 asperity, disorder
   9 roughness 10 inequality,
   unevenness

irrelevant
   7 foreign 9 unrelated 10 extraneous, immaterial, inapposite, irrelative 11 impertinent, inessential,
   unessential, unimportant 12 inapplicable 13 insignificant

irreligious
   5 pagan 6 amoral, unholy 7 godless, impious, profane, ungodly,
   unmoral 8 indevout, undevout
   11 blasphemous 12 sacrilegious

irreparable
   8 cureless, hopeless 9 incurable, insanable, uncurable 10 impossible
   11 immedicable 12 irredeemable,
   irremediable 13 irreclaimable, irre-
   coverable, irretrievable, uncorrectable, unrecoverable

irreproachable
   4 good, pure 8 flawless, innocent,
   spotless, virtuous 9 blameless, errorless, exemplary, exquisite, faultless, guiltless, righteous 10 immaculate, impeccable, inculpable,
   unblamable

irresolute
   6 fickle, unsure, wobbly 7 halting
   8 doubtful, hesitant, unstable, wavering 9 faltering, tentative, uncertain,
   undecided 10 changeable, inconstant 11 fluctuating, vacillating,
   vacillatory 12 wiggle-waggle

irresponsible
   4 wild 8 carefree, careless, feckless, reckless 9 uncareful 10 incautious, unreliable 12 unanswerable,
   undependable 13 unaccountable,
   untrustworthy

irreverent
   6 unholy 7 impious, profane, ungodly 10 unhallowed

irrevocable
   4 firm 5 final 9 immutable 11 unalterable 12 irreversible, unchangeable, unmodifiable, unrepealable
   13 nonreversible

irrigation ditch
5 flume 6 sluice 7 acequia

irritability
6 choler 9 petulance 11 fretfulness
abnormal: 8 erethism

irritable
4 edgy 5 cross, huffy, raspy, techy,
testy, waspy, whiny 6 cranky, ornery, snappy, tetchy, touchy, twitty
7 fretful, peevish, pettish, prickly,
raspish, waspish 8 choleric, petulant, prickish, snappish 9 fractious,
impatient, irascible, querulent, querulous, splenetic 12 cantankerous,
disagreeable, querulential

irritant
4 pest 6 bother, pester, plague
8 nuisance 9 annoyance, besetment 10 botherment 11 botheration 12 exasperation

irritate
3 get, irk, rub, try, vex 4 fret, gall,
goad, huff, rile, roil 5 anger, annoy, chafe, grate, peeve, pique,
spite 6 abrade, badger, bother,
burn up, harass, hector, madden,
needle, nettle, offend, put out, ruffle
7 affront, inflame, provoke 8 acerbate 9 aggravate, stimulate 10 exacerbate, exasperate

irritated
5 irate, testy 7 fretful, peevish
8 choleric 9 impatient, irascible
11 hot-tempered

irritation
4 itch, rash, sore 5 uredo 9 annoyance 10 excitation

irrupt
4 spew 5 belch, eject, eruct, expel
7 intrude 8 disgorge

irruption
4 raid 5 foray 6 inroad 8 invasion
9 incursion

I.R.S. employee
4 acct 10 accountant

Iru's father
5 Caleb

Isaac
father: 7 Abraham
mother: 5 Sarah
son: 4 Esau 5 Jacob
wife: 7 Rebekah

Isabella
brother: 7 Claudio
husband: 9 Vincentio

Isabella I
country: 5 Spain

home: 7 Castile
husband: 9 Ferdinand

Isaiah's father
4 Amoz

Iscah
brother: 3 Lot
father: 5 Haran
sister: 6 Milcah

Iseult, Isolde
beloved: 7 Tristan
husband: 4 Mark

Ishbak
father: 7 Abraham
mother: 7 Keturah

Ishbosheth's father
4 Saul

Ishi
father: 6 Appaim
son: 6 Zoheth

Ishmael
6 pariah 7 outcast 8 castaway,
derelict, outsider 11 offscouring,
untouchable
father: 4 Azel 7 Abraham, Pashhur
9 Jehonanan, Nethaniah
mother: 5 Hagar
son: 5 Massa 8 Zebadiah

Ishmaiah's father
7 Obadiah

Ishpah's father
6 Beriah

Ishpan's father
7 Shashak

Ishtar
brother: 7 Shamash
father: 3 Anu, Sin
lover: 6 Tammuz

Ishuah's father
5 Asher

Ishui's father
4 Saul 5 Asher

Isis
brother: 6 Osiris
father: 3 Geb
husband: 6 Osiris
mother: 3 Nut
son: 4 Sept 5 Horus

Islam
adherent: 6 Moslem, Muslim
founder: 8 Mohammed, Muhammad
god: 5 Allah
priest: 4 imam
scriptures: 5 Koran; (see also **Muslim**)

island
3 ait, cay, key 4 holm, isle 5 atoll,
islet 6 cut off, enisle, skerry 7 cran-
nog, isolate 8 close off, insulate,
separate 9 segregate, sequester

Admiralty group: 5 Manus
Adriatic Sea: 3 Vis 4 Brac, Cres,
Hvar 5 Brach, Ciovo, Mljet, Solta
6 Lesina, Pharus
Aegean Sea: 4 Scio 5 Chios, Khios,
Samos, Thira 6 Ikaria, Lemnos, Les-
bos, Limnos 7 Nikaria 8 Mitilini,
Mytilene, Santorin 10 Sakis-Adasi,
Susam-Adasi
Alaska: 4 Adak, Atka, Attu, Kuiu
8 Wrangell
Aleutian group: 3 Rat 4 Adak, Akun,
Attu 5 Amlia, Kiska, Umnak 6 Kan-
aga, Tanaga, Unimak 8 Amchitka,
Unalaska
American Samoa: 3 Ofu, Tau 4 Rose
6 Swains
Andaman Sea: 4 Mali 5 Tavoy
Antarctica: 5 Scott, Young
Apostle group: 3 Oak 4 Long, Sand
5 Outer 8 Madeline, Michigan,
Stockton
Arafura Sea: 5 Dolak
Arctic Archipelago: 6 Baffin
8 Victoria
Arctic Ocean: 5 Senja
Australian: 5 Cocos 8 Tasmania
Azores: 4 Pico 5 Corvo, Faial
Bahamas: 3 Cat, Rum 4 Long
5 Abaco, Exuma 6 Andros, Inagua
7 Acklins, Crooked 8 Watlings
9 Eleuthera, Mayaguana 11 San
Salvador
Bahrain: 5 Sitra 8 Muharraq
Balearic group: 5 Ibiza 7 Majorca,
Menorca, Minorca 8 Mallorca
Baltic Sea: 4 Moon, Muhu 5 Faron,
Mukhu, Rugen, Worms 6 Vormsi
7 Gotland 8 Bornholm, Gothland,
Gottland
Barents Sea: 4 Bear
Bay of Biscay: 2 Re
Bay of Naples: 5 Capri
Bay of Panama: 4 Naos
Bering Sea: 5 Medny 7 Nunivak
10 Big Diomede 13 Little Diomede
Bismarck Archipelago: 5 Lihir
10 New Britain
Bristol Channel: 5 Lundy
Buzzards Bay: 9 Cuttyhunk
Canadian: 5 Banks, Devon 6 Baffin
8 Bathurst, Melville, Somerset, Vic-
toria 9 Anticosti, Ellesmere
10 Cape Breton 11 Axel Heiberg,
Southampton 12 Newfoundland,
Prince Edward
Canaries: 6 Gomera 7 La Palma
8 Tenerife 9 Lanzarote
Cape Verde: 4 Fogo, Maio, Mayo
5 Brava, Rombo
Caribbean Sea: 4 Cuba 5 Aruba,
Utila, Vache 6 Tobago 7 Antigua,
Cura%cao, Jamaica 8 Barbados,

Dominica, Trinidad **10** Guadeloupe, Martinique, Puerto Rico; (see also **Virgin group**)
Carolines: 5 Sorol **6** Ponape **9** Ascension
Chagos Archipelago: 11 Diego Garcia
Channel group: 4 Herm, Sark **5** Lihou, Sercq **6** Jersey **8** Guernsey
Chesapeake Bay: 4 Deal, Kent **5** Smith, Watts
Chukchi Sea: 6 Herald
Comoro group: 7 Mayotte
Congo River: 4 Bamu
Cook group: 4 Atiu **5** Mauke
Croatia: 3 Krk, Pag, Rab **5** Susak, Unije
Cyclades: 3 Ios, Kea, Nio **4** Ceos, Keos, Milo **5** Delos, Melos, Milos, Naxos, Paros, Siros, Syros **6** Andros, Dhilos **7** Amorgos, Cythnos, Kithnos, Kythnos, Mykonos
Denmark: 3 Als, Fyn, Mon **4** Aero, Fano, Moen, Mors **5** Alsen, Funen, Moers, Samso **8** Bornholm **13** Fanum Fortunae
D'Entrecasteaux group: 8 Kaluwawa **9** Fergusson
Dodecanese group: 3 Coo, Cos, Kos **4** Caso, Lero, Simi, Syme **5** Kasos, Leros, Lipso, Lisso, Patmo, Telos **6** Calino, Lipsos, Nisiro, Patmos **7** Calimno, Nisiros, Nisyros **8** Kalymnos
East River: 5 Ward's **7** Welfare **9** Roosevelt
England's: 7 Britian **9** Britannia **12** Great Britain
English Channel: 5 Wight
Faeroes: 4 Vago **5** Bordo, Sando
Fiji: 4 Koro **5** Mango, Vatoa
Florida Keys: 4 Long, Vaca, West **5** Largo **7** Big Pine **9** Matecumbe, Sugarloaf
Fox group: 5 Umnak **6** Akutan, Unimak **8** Unalaska
French: 7 Corsica **12** New Caledonia
French Polynesia: 4 Rapa, Reao, Ua Pu **9** Ua Pau
Frisian group: 3 Rom **4** Föhr, Sylt **5** Amrum, Juist, Mando, Texel **6** Borkum **7** Ameland **8** Langeoog, Pellworm, Vlieland **9** Helgoland, Norderney
Futunas: 5 Alofi
Galápagos: 5 Pinta **7** Chatham, Isabela **8** Abingdon **10** Albermarle
Georgia: 5 Tybee
Germany: 4 Fohr **7** Fehmarn **9** Helgoland **10** Heligoland
Greater Antilles: 4 Cuba **7** Jamaica **10** Hispaniola, Puerto Rico

Greece: 4 Milo, Rodi **5** Creta, Crete, Hydra, Idhra, Kriti, Rodos, Tenos, Tinos **6** Euboea, Evvoia, Hydrea, Rhodes, Rhodus **9** Negropont **10** Negroponte
Grenadines: 5 Union
Gulf of Alaska: 6 Kodiak
Gulf of Bothnia: 5 Karlö
Gulf of Carpentaria: 5 Maria **6** Groote **7** Eylandt
Gulf of Guinea: 7 Sao Tomé **8** Principe, Sao Thomé **11** Saint Thomas
Gulf of Mexico: 3 Cat **5** Lobos
Gulf of Panama: 3 Rey
Gulf of St. Lawrence: 5 Brion
Gulf of Thailand: 3 Kut **5** Samui
Haiti: 6 Gonave
Hawaii: 4 Maui, Oahu **5** Kauai, Lanai **6** Niihau **7** Molokai **9** Kahoolawe
Hudson Bay: 5 Coats
Indian Ocean: 4 Mahé, Nias **5** Heard, Pemba **7** La Dique, Praslin, Réunion **8** Sri Lanka, Zanzibar **9** Mauritius **10** Madagascar
Indonesia: 4 Bali, Biak, Java, Maja, Muna, Nias, Rhio, Riau, Roma, Roti, Savu, Sawu **5** Batam, Boano, Buton, Djawa, Japen, Lakor, Moena, Riouw, Rotti, Rupat, Sawoe, Solor, Sumba, Wetar, Wokam **6** Butung, Flores, Jappen, Lombok, Madura, Padang, Roepat, Romang, Soemba **7** Celebes, Madoera, Sumatra, Sumbawa **8** Boetoeng, Soembawa, Sulawesi **10** Bandanaira, Banda Neira, Sandalwood
Inner Hebrides: 4 Coll, Eigg, Iona, Jura, Muck, Mull, Skye **5** Canna, Gigha, Islay, Tiree, Tyree
Ionian group: 5 Corfu, Paxos, Zante **6** Cerigo, Ithaca, Leukas, Levkas **10** Santa Maura
Iran: 5 Shahi
Ireland: 4 Aran
Irish Sea: 4 Man
Italy: 4 Elba **6** Sicily **8** Sardinia
Japan: 3 Iki, Uku **4** Naru, Yezo **5** Awaji, Fukae, Fukue, Hondo, Shodo **6** Honshu, Kyushu **7** Shikoku **8** Hokkaido **10** Shodoshima
Java Sea: 4 Laut
Kiribati: 6 Tarawa
Kuril group: 4 Urup **5** Ketoi, Matua **6** Iturup **7** Etorofu, Matsuwa **8** Kunashir **9** Kunashiri
Lake Champlain: 5 Grand
Lake Erie: 9 North Bass, South Bass **10** Middle Bass
Lake Huron: 8 Drummond **10** Manitoulin

Lake Michigan: 3 Hog **4** High **6** Beaver
Lake Ontario: 5 Wolfe
Lake Superior: 4 Sand **6** Royale **7** Manitou
Lake Winnipeg: 5 Hecla
largest: 9 Greenland
Leeward group: 5 Nevis **7** Antigua, Barbuda, Redonda **8** Anguilla, Sombrero **10** Montserrat, Saint Kitts **13** St. Christopher
legendary: 7 Cipango
Lesser Sundas: 4 Alor **5** Ombai
Leti group: 3 Moa **5** Lakor
Line group: 5 Flint **6** Malden, Vostok **7** Fanning, Palmyra **8** Starbuck **9** Christmas
Long Island Sound: 4 City, Hart **5** Goose, Harts
Loyalty group: 3 Uea **4** Lifu, Maré, Uvea **5** Lifou
Malay Archipelago: 5 Kisar, Larat, Timor **6** Borneo **9** New Guinea
Malaysia: 6 Penang, Pinang **13** Prince of Wales
Malta: 4 Gozo
Marianas: 4 Maug, Rota **5** Pagan **6** Saipan
Marquesas group: 4 Eiào, Ua Pu **6** Hatutu, Hiva Oa, Ua Huka **7** Tahuata **8** Fatu Hiva, Nuku Hiva
Marshall group: 5 Wotho, Wotje **8** Eniwetok **9** Kwajalein
Massachusetts: 9 Nantucket
Mediterranean Sea: 4 Elba **5** Corfu, Crete, Malta **6** Cyprus, Euboea, Rhodes, Sicily **7** Corsica **8** Sardinia
Midway group: 4 Sand **7** Eastern
Moluccas: 4 Buru **5** Ambon, Ceram, Seram **6** Boeroe
Mozambique channel: 10 Juan de Nova
Myanmar: 5 Daung, Kadan, Lanbi
Narragansett Bay: 5 Rhode **8** Prudence **9** Aquidneck, Conanicut
Netherlands: 5 Texel **7** Ameland **8** Vlieland
Netherlands Antilles: 7 Curaçao
New York: 4 Fire, Long **9** Gardiners, Roosevelt
New York Bay: 5 Ellis **6** Staten **7** Liberty **9** Governors, Manhattan
New Zealand: 5 South, White **7** Chatham, Stewart **8** D'Urville
Niagara River: 4 Goat
Nile River: 4 Argo, Roda, Ruda **5** Rhoda **6** Rawdah **11** Elephantine
North Channel: 3 Mew
Northern Cook group: 7 Penrhyn **8** Manihiki **9** Tongareva
North Pacific: 4 Wake
Northwest Territories: 5 Banks, Bylot,

Devon **8** Bathurst, Melville **9** Ellesmere **10** Cornwallis, Resolution **13** Prince of Wales
Norwegian: 8 Jan Mayen
Norwegian Sea: 5 Donna, Smola, Vikna
Nova Scotia: 5 Sable **10** Cape Breton
off Alaska: 4 Dall **5** Kayak
off Albania: 5 Sazan **6** Saseno
off Australia: 4 Dunk
off Belize: 9 Ambergris
off Brazil: 4 Apeu **5** Rocas
off British Columbia: 4 King, Pitt **9** Vancouver
off Cape Cod: 8 Muskeget **9** Nantucket
off Chile: 5 Guafo, Mocha
off China: 4 Amoy **5** Ma-tsu **6** Hainan, Quemoy, Taiwan
off Crete: 3 Dia
off Ecuador: 4 Puna
off England: 3 Man **5** Wight **6** Walney
off Florida: 3 Dog **4** Pine **6** Amelia **7** Pelican, Sanibel **9** Anastasia
off France: 2 If
off French Guiana: 6 Devil's
off Georgia: 10 Cumberland **11** Saint Simons
off Germany: 4 Sylt
off Greenland: 5 Disko
off Guinea: 5 Tombo
off Hispaniola: 5 Beata
off Honduras: 5 Tigre
off Iceland: 7 Surtsey
off India: 5 Sagar
off Ireland: 4 Tory **5** Clare, Clear
off Kenya: 4 Lamu
off Long Island: 7 Fishers
off Louisiana: 5 Marsh
off Maine: 4 Deer, Orrs **5** Swans **8** Monhegan **11** Mount Desert
off Malay Peninsula: 6 Phuket **9** Singapore
off Maryland: 10 Assateague
off Massachusetts: 4 Plum **7** Naushon
off Mexico: 7 Cozumel
off Mississippi: 4 Horn, Ship
off Mozambique: 3 Ibo
off New Brunswick: 10 Campobello
off Newfoundland: 4 Bell
off Nigeria: 5 Lagos
off North Carolina: 5 Bodie
off Norway: 5 Bomlo, Froya, Hitra, Sotra, Stord, Vardo **8** Hitteren
off Panama: 5 Coiba **6** Parida
off Poland: 5 Wolin **6** Wollin
off Puerto Rico: 4 Crab **7** Culebra, Vieques
off Rhode Island: 5 Block
off Scotland: 4 Bute **5** Arran

off South Carolina: 5 North **6** Parris **10** Hilton Head
off Sri Lanka: 5 Delft
off Staten Island: 7 Hoffman
off Sumatra: 2 We **3** Weh
off Sweden: 5 Graso, Oland, Vaddo
off Syria: 5 Arvad, Arwad, Rouad **6** Aradus
off Tanzania: 5 Mafia, Pemba
off Tasmania: 5 Bruni, Bruny
off Tunisia: 5 Jerba **6** Djerba, Meninx
off Venezuela: 5 Aruba **7** Bonaire **8** Buen Aire
off Virginia: 5 Wreck
off Wales: 5 Caldy **6** Caldey
Okinawa group: 4 Kume
Orkneys: 3 Hoy
Outer Hebrides: 5 Barra, Scarp
Palmer Archipelago: 6 Anvers **7** Antwerp, Brabant
Pearl Harbor: 4 Ford
Persian Gulf: 4 Qeys **5** Kharg, Khark
Philippines: 4 Buad, Cebu, Fuga, Ilin, Poro, Sulu **5** Balut, Batan, Bohol, Coron, Daram, Leyte, Luzon, Panay, Samal, Samar, Sugbu, Talim, Ticao, Verde **6** Negros **7** Masbate, Mindoro, Palawan, Paragua **8** Limasawa, Mindanao **10** Corregidor
Phoenix group: 4 Hull, Mary **6** Birnie, Canton **9** Enderbury
Puerto Rico: 4 Mona
Quebec: 4 Alma
Queen Charlotte group: 7 Moresby
Red Sea: 5 Tiran, Zugur, Zuqar
Russia: 7 Wrangel
Ryukyu group: 7 Okinawa
St. Lawrence River: 4 Hare **5** Jesus **8** Montreal
San Francisco Bay: 5 Angel
Santa Cruz: 5 Anuda, Ndeni **6** Cherry
Sea of Japan: 4 Sado **5** Rebun
Sea of Marmara: 4 Avsa
second largest: 9 New Guinea
Senegal: 5 Gorée
Seychelles: 4 Mahé **7** La Digue, Praslin
Shetland archipelago: 4 Unst, Yell **5** Foula
Shumagin group: 4 Unga
Sierra Leone: 5 Tasso
Society group: 5 Eimeo, Tahaa, Tahao, Taiti **6** Moorea, Tahiti **8** Otaheite
Solomon group: 4 Buka, Gizo, Savo **7** Malaita **11** Guadalcanal **12** Bougainville
South Atlantic: 5 Gough **6** Gough's **11** Saint Helena

South Korea: 5 Cheju
South of Tokyo: 3 Iwo **7** Iwo Jima, Naka Iwo
South Orkneys: 10 Coronation
South Pacific: 3 Hiu **4** Niue **5** Raoul **6** Savage, Sunday **7** Norfolk **8** Pitcairn
Spitsbergen archipelago: 4 Edge
Strait of Hormuz: 5 Qeshm, Qishm
Sulu Archipelago: 4 Jolo **5** Lapac
Svalbard: 4 Hope
Sverdrup: 11 Axel Heiberg **12** Amund Ringnes
Swedish: 3 Ven **4** Hven **5** Hveen, Orust
Tanzania: 8 Zanzibar
Texas: 5 Padre
Thames River: 7 Sheppey
third largest: 6 Borneo
Tierra del Fuego: 5 Hoste
Tonga: 3 Eua, Foa **4** Uiha **5** Haano
Treasury group: 4 Mono
Truk group: 3 Tol **4** Haru, Moen, Udot, Uman **5** Fefan
Tuamotu Archipelago: 4 Anaa **5** Chain
Turkish: 5 Imroz **6** Imbros
Tuvalu: 7 Nanumea **9** Nukufetau
Tyrrhenian Sea: 6 Ischia **11** Montecristo
Vanuatu: 3 Api, Epi, Oba **4** Aoba, Gaua, Tana, Vate **5** Efate, Maewo, Tanna
Venezuelan: 5 Patos **9** La Tortuga
Virgin group, American: 9 Saint John **10** Saint Croix **11** Saint Thomas
Virgin group, British: 5 Peter **6** Norman **7** Anegada, Tortola **11** Jost Van Dyke
volcanic: 5 Tofua **7** Iwo Jima
Wales: 8 Anglesea, Anglesey, Holyhead
Weddell Sea: 4 Ross **6** Hearst
Western Samoa: 5 Upolu **6** Savaii
West Indies: 4 Mona, Saba, Salt **5** Nevis, Peter, Saona **6** Tobago, Tortue **7** Grenada, Tortuga **8** Trinidad **9** Santa Cruz **10** Concepción, Hispaniola, Montserrat, Saint Croix; (see also **Bahamas; Greater Antilles; Leeward group; Virgin group; Windward group**)-
West of England: 7 Ireland
West Pacific: 5 Dyaul, Fauro, Ocean **6** Banaba, Marcus **7** Iwo Jima, Kita Iwo **9** Minami Iwo
Windward group: 10 Martinique
with former penitentiary: 8 Alcatraz

island group

Alaska: 3 Rat **8** Aleutian, Pribilof **9** Andreanof, Catherine

Aleutians: 4 Near
American Samoa: 5 Manua
Arabian Sea: 9 Laccadive
Arctic Archipelago: 8 Sverdrup
Arctic Ocean: 8 Svalbard 12 Novaya Zemlya
Bahamas: 5 Berry, Exuma 6 Bimini
Banda Sea: 5 Damar
Bangladesh: 5 Hatia, Hatya
Bay of Bengal: 7 Andaman, Nicobar
between England and France: 7 Channel
Bismarck Archipelago: 4 Feni 5 Tabar, Tanga
Bismarck Sea: 4 Vitu
British: 7 Bermuda
Caribbean Sea: 4 Swan 5 Pearl 6 Cayman, Perlas, Pigeon 8 Pichones 10 Grenadines, West Indies
Carolines: 3 Uap, Yap 4 Truk 5 Nomoi 7 Hogoleu
Central Pacific Ocean: 4 Line 5 Samoa, Union 6 Danger, Midway 7 Phoenix, Tokelau 8 Manihiki 9 Polynesia 12 Northern Cook
Coral Sea: 4 Huon
Cuba: 8 Camaguey
East of Philippines: 10 Micronesia
East Siberian Sea: 4 Bear 8 Medvezhi
Ecuador: 5 Colon 9 Galápagos
England: 5 Farne
Fiji: 3 Lau 7 Eastern
Formosa Strait: 4 Hoko 6 Peng hu 10 Pescadores
French: 5 Salut 6 Safety 9 Kerguelen
French Polynesia: 3 Low 6 Tubuai 7 Austral, Paumotu, Société, Society, Tuamotu 9 Marquesas, Touamotou
Germany: 8 Halligen
Greece: 6 Aegean, Ionian 8 Cyclades 10 Dodecanese 11 Dodecanesus
Hudson Bay: 7 Belcher
Indian Ocean: 7 Aldabra
Indonesia: 4 Asia, Batu, Pagi, Sula 5 Babar, Batoe, Pagai, Pageh, Penju, Spice, Wakde 6 Maluku
Ireland: 4 Aran
Japan: 5 Osumi
largest: 5 Malay 8 Malaysia
Lesser Antilles: 8 Windward
Malay Archipelago: 5 Sunda 6 Soenda
Mediterranean Sea: 8 Baleares, Balearic
Moluccas: 3 Kai, Kei, Obi 4 Leti 5 Banda, Letti 8 Tanimbar 9 Timorlaut
New Caledonia: 7 Loyalty 9 Loyalties

North of Australia: 9 Melanesia
North of British Isles: 5 Faroe 7 Faeroes
North off Fiji: 5 Hoorn 6 Futuna
North of Madagascar: 7 Aldabra 8 Farquhar
North of New Caledonia: 5 Belep
North of New Guinea: 8 Bismarck 9 Admiralty 11 Admiralties
Northwest Territories: 5 Parry
off Alaska: 3 Fox
off Alaska Peninsula: 8 Shumagin
off Cape Cod: 9 Elizabeth
off eastern Asia: 5 Kuril 6 Kurile
off England: 6 Scilly
off Florida: 11 Dry Tortugas
off Guinea: 3 Los 4 Loos
off Honduras: 5 Bahia
off Morocco: 7 Madeira
off New Guinea: 3 Aru 4 Aroe
off Nicaragua: 4 Corn
off northern Africa: 6 Canary 8 Canaries
off northern Australia: 6 Wessel 7 Dampier
off Sicily: 5 Egadi 8 Aegadian
Outer Hebrides: 4 Uist
Pago Pago's: 13 American Samoa
Papua New Guinea: 5 Green
Persian Gulf: 4 Tunb
Philippines: 4 Cuyo 5 Tapul 6 Lubang 7 Basilan, Bisayas, Visayan
Portuguese: 5 Azores
Quebec: 8 Magdalen 9 Madeleine
Ryukyus: 5 Amami
St. Lawrence River: 8 Thousand
Sea of Japan: 3 Oki
Sea of Marmara: 5 Kizil 7 Princes 11 Kizil Adalar
South Atlantic Ocean: 8 Falkland, Malvinas
South China Sea: 6 Hirata 7 Paracel, Spratly
South of New Zealand: 8 Auckland
South Pacific: 11 Austronesia
Sulu Sea: 7 Cagayan 9 Cagayanes
Tonga: 5 Vavau
Tyrrhenian Sea: 5 Ponza
Venezuelan: 4 Aves, Bird 9 Los Roques
West Europe: 12 British Isles
West Indies: 6 Virgin 10 Guadeloupe
West of French Polynesia: 4 Cook
West of Scotland: 7 Western 8 Hebrides
West Pacific Ocean: 4 Duff 5 Bonin, Mapia, Palau, Pelew 7 Ladrone, Mariana, Solomon, Vanuatu 8 Marshall, Treasury 9 Ogasawara 10 Saint David

island nation
  Atlantic Ocean: 9 Cape Verde
  Indian Ocean: 8 Malagasy, Malgache, Sri Lanka 10 Madagascar, Seychelles
  Mediterranean Sea: 6 Cyprus
  Mozambique Channel: 6 Comoro 7 Comores
  off southern China: 6 Taiwan
  south of Greenland: 7 Iceland
  West Indies: 4 Cuba 7 Jamaica 8 Barbados 10 Saint Lucia
  West Pacific Ocean: 5 Nauru
  Windward group: 8 Dominica

island province
  12 Prince Edward

island state
  6 Hawaii

isle
  see **island**

Ismene
  brother: 9 Polynices
  father: 7 Oedipus
  mother: 7 Jocasta
  sister: 8 Antigone
  uncle: 5 Creon

isochronous
  8 periodic 9 alternate, recurrent, recurring 10 periodical 12 intermittent

isolate
  5 alone, apart 6 cut off, detach, enisle, island, remove 7 removed, seclude 8 block off, close off, detached, insulate, pinpoint, separate 9 segregate, sequester 13 unaccompanied

Isolde
  see **Iseult**

Israel
  4 Zion 5 Jacob 6 Canaan 9 Palestine
  capital: 9 Jerusalem
  district: 5 Haifa 7 Central, Tel Aviv 8 Northern, Southern 9 Jerusalem
  legislature: 7 Knesset
  monetary unit: 6 shekel

Israelite
  see **Hebrew; Jewish**

Issachar
  father: 5 Jacob
  mother: 4 Leah

issue
  4 emit, flow, gush, pour, rise, seed, stem, vent 5 arise, birth, brood, child, topic 6 effect, emerge, get out, put out, result, scions, sequel,

source, spring **7** descent, edition, emanate, give off, give out, outcome, problem, proceed, progeny, publish, release, subject **8** bulletin, causatum, children, question, throw off **9** offspring, originate, posterity **10** derive from, distribute, end product **11** consequence, descendants, eventuality, progeniture

Istanbul
ancient name: **9** Byzantium
business section: **6** Galata
country: **6** Turkey
foreign quarter: **4** Pera **7** Beyoglu
park: **8** Seraglio
residentiai section: **7** Uskudar

isthmus
Africa-Asia: **4** Suez
Greece: **7** Corinth
North America-South America: **6** Panama

Italian
article: **2** il, la **3** gli
automobile: **4** Fiat
cathedral: **5** duomo
condiment: **6** tamara
dialect: **6** Tuscan **8** Sicilian
dictator: **9** Mussolini (Benito)
family: **4** Este **5** Cenci, Savoy **6** Borgia, Medici, Orsini, Pepoli, Sforza **7** Colonna, Gonzaga, Spinola **8** Visconti
fascist: **10** Blackshirt
game: **4** mora **5** bocce, bocci, morra **6** boccie
gentleman: **3** ser **6** signor **7** signore
highway: **10** autostrada
lady: **5** donna **7** signora **9** signorina
magistrate: **7** podesta
opera house: **7** La Scala
patriot: **6** Cavour (Conte di), Rienzo (Cola di) **7** Mazzini (Giuseppe) **9** Garibaldi (Giuseppe)
reformer: **10** Savonarola (Girolamo)
resort: **4** Lido **5** Abano, Capri **7** Locarno **8** Sorrento
road: **6** strada
sausage: **6** salami

soup: **10** minestrone
square: **6** piazza
street: **3** via **5** corso
weight: **5** libra, oncia

Italy
capital: **4** Rome
monetary unit: **4** lira

itch
4 ache, long, lust, pine, sigh, stew, urge **5** crave, yearn **6** desire, hanker, hunger, seethe, thirst **7** craving, longing, passion **8** appetite, pruritus **9** eroticism, hankering, prurience, pruriency **10** aphrodisia, appetition **11** lustfulness **13** concupiscence, lickerishness
combining form: **4** psor **5** psoro

itching
8 pruritus **10** avaricious

itchy
5 jumpy **6** grabby, greedy **7** restive **8** covetous, desirous, grasping, prurient **10** prehensile **11** acquisitive

item
3 bit, too **4** also, more, well **5** along, entry, point, scrap, thing, topic **6** detail, matter **7** account, article, besides, element, feature, product **8** clipping, likewise, moreover **9** commodity **10** particular

itemize
4 list **5** count, tally **6** number **7** catalog, specify **8** document, spell out **9** catalogue, enumerate, inventory **10** specialize **13** particularize

iterate
5 renew, resay **6** repeat **7** reprise **10** ingeminate

Ithaca king
8 Odysseus

Ithamar's father
5 Aaron

Ithiel's father
7 Jesaiah

Ithra
son: **5** Amasa
wife: **7** Abigail

Ithran's father
6 Dishon, Zophah

Ithream
father: **5** David
mother: **5** Eglah

Ithunn's husband
5 Brage, Bragi

itinerant
6 moving, roving **7** migrant, nomadic, ranging, roaming, vagrant **8** ambulant, rambling, shifting, traveler, vagabond, wanderer **9** transient, unsettled, wandering, wayfaring **10** ambulatory **11** perambulant, peripatetic

Ittai's father
5 Ribai

Ivanhoe
author: **5** Scott (Walter)
character: **5** Isaac **6** Cedric, Rowena, Ulrica **7** Rebecca, Wilfred **9** Robin Hood

Ivory Coast
11 Cote d'Ivoire
capital: **7** Abidjan
monetary unit: **5** franc

ivory-tower
6 dreamy **8** escapist **11** impractical, unpractical, unrealistic **12** nonrealistic

Ixion
descendant: **7** Centaur
father: **8** Phlegyas

Izhar's father
6 Ashhur, Kohath

Izliah's father
6 Elpaal

Izrahiah's father
4 Uzzi

Izri's father
8 Jeduthun

Izziah's father
6 Parosh

Jj

jaal goat
4 ibex

Jaazaniah's father
4 Azur 5 Azzur 7 Shaphan
8 Jeremiah

jab
3 dig, hit, jog 4 poke, prod, stab
5 nudge, prick, punch 8 puncture

Jabal
brother: 5 Jubal
father: 6 Lamech
mother: 4 Adah

jabber
3 gab, jaw, yak 4 chat 5 clack,
Greek 6 babble, drivel, gabble,
gibber 7 blabber, chatter, palaver,
prattle 8 nonsense 9 gibberish
11 jabberwocky

jabberer
6 gabber, gossip, magpie, prater
7 blabber 8 prattler 9 bandar-log,
blabmouth, chatterer 10 chatterbox
12 blabbermouth

Jabberwocky author
7 Carroll (Lewis)

Jabesh's son
7 Shallum

jabot
4 fall 5 frill 6 ruffle

jacamar
4 bird

jacare
6 caiman 9 crocodile

____ jacet
3 hic

Jachin's father
6 Simeon

jack
2 up 3 tar 4 card, flag, hike, jump,
lift, salt 5 boost, color, knave, put
up, raise 6 banner, ensign, pennon, sailor, seaman 7 mariner,
pendant, pennant 8 bannerol, increase, standard, streamer 9 sailorman, tarpaulin

jackal god
5 Apuat 6 Anubis

jackanapes
3 ape 6 monkey 7 coxcomb

jackass
4 dolt, donk, fool, jerk 5 burro, idiot 6 donkey 8 imbecile
10 nincompoop

jackass deer
3 kob 8 antelope

jackdaw
4 bird 7 grackle 9 blackbird

jacket
3 fur 4 coat, Eton, fell, hide, pelt,
skin 5 grego, parka, wamus 6 anorak, blazer, bolero, dolman, jerkin, reefer, wammus, wampus
7 cassock, doublet, peacoat, spencer 8 camisole 10 roundabout
armored: 5 acton 7 hauberk
9 habergeon
cowboy's: 8 chaqueta
Scottish: 4 jupe
sleeveless: 4 vest 6 bolero, jerkin
9 waistcoat

jackhammer
5 drill 9 rock drill

jackknife
4 dive 6 barlow
game: 11 mumblety-peg

jackleg lawyer
7 shyster 11 pettifogger

jack-of-all-trades
6 tinker 8 handyman

Jack of clubs
3 pam

jack-o'-lantern
7 pumpkin

jackpot
4 pool 5 award, kitty 7 bonanza
8 windfall 9 pot of gold

jackrabbit
4 hare

Jack's companion
4 Jill

jackstay
3 bar, rod 4 rope 5 horse 7 rigging, support

Jacob
brother: 4 Esau
daughter: 5 Dinah
father: 5 Isaac
father-in-law: 5 Laban
mother: 7 Rebekah
new name: 6 Israel
son: 3 Dan, Gad 4 Levi 5 Asher, Judah 6 Joseph, Reuben, Simeon
7 Zebulun 8 Benjamin, Issachar,
Naphtali
variant: 5 James
wife: 4 Leah 6 Rachel

Jacob's rod
8 asphodel

jade
3 fag, gem 4 cloy, fill, glut, minx,
pall, sate, slut, snip, tire, wear
5 drain, gorge, hussy, jewel, stone,
tramp, weary, wench 6 stodge,
wanton 7 fatigue, jezebel, satiate,
surfeit, trollop 8 malapert, saucebox, slattern, strumpet, wear down

jaded
4 full, worn 5 sated, tired, weary
6 gorged 7 glutted, satiate, wearied, worn-out 8 fatigued, satiated,
worn down 9 surfeited

jaeger
4 bird, skua 6 hunter 8 huntsman,
rifleman 9 boatswain

Jael
husband: 5 Heber
victim: 6 Sisera

jag
3 bum, dag, tab 4 barb, bolt, bust,
soak, tear 5 binge, booze, drunk,

notch, prick, souse, spell, spree
6 bender, thrill **7** portion **8** quantity

jagged
5 erose, harsh, rough, sharp
6 craggy, hackly, rugged, uneven
7 scraggy, unlevel **8** asperous,
scabrous, unsmooth

____ Jagger
4 Mick

Jaggers' ward
3 Pip

Jahaziah, Jahzeiah
father: **6** Tikvah

Jahaziel's father
9 Zechariah

Jahzeel, Jahziel
father: **8** Naphtali

jai alai
6 pelota
basket: **5** cesta
court: **6** cancha **7** fronton

jail
3 can, jug, pen **4** coop, gaol,
keep, poky, stir **6** cooler, immure,
intern, lockup, prison **7** confine,
freezer, slammer **8** bastille, hoosegow, imprison, rock pile, stockade
9 bridewell, constrain, guardroom
11 incarcerate, reformatory
12 penitentiary

jailbird
3 con **5** loser **7** convict **8** prisoner

jailer
5 guard, screw **6** keeper, warden
7 turnkey

Jair
father: **5** Segub
grandfather: **6** Hezron
son: **7** Elhanan **8** Mordecai

Jakeh's son
4 Agur

jakes
5 privy **8** outhouse **9** backhouse

Jalam
father: **4** Esau
mother: **9** Oholibama

jalopy
3 car, dog **4** auto, heap **5** crate,
wreck **6** junker **7** clunker
10 automobile

jalousie
5 blind **6** window **7** shutter

jam
3 fix, ram **4** bear, bind, cram,
push, tamp **5** crowd, crush, jelly,
press, stuff **6** plight, scrape,
squash, squish, squush **7** dilemma,

squeeze **8** bar-le-duc, conserve,
preserve **9** confiture, marmalade
11 predicament

Jamaica
capital: **8** Kingston
monetary unit: **6** dollar

Jamaican
export: **3** rum
hair style: **10** dreadlocks
music: **3** ska **6** reggae
nationalist: **6** Garvey (Marcus)

James
brother: **4** John **5** Jesus, Joses
cousin: **5** Jesus
father: **7** Zebedee **8** Alphaeus
mother: **4** Mary **6** Salome

James novel
10 Confidence **11** Daisy Miller, The
American **12** The Europeans
13 The Bostonians, The Golden
Bowl, The Tragic Muse

Jamin's father
6 Simeon

Jammy and ____
7 Kashmir

Jane Eyre
author: **6** Brontë (Charlotte)
lover: **9** Rochester

jangle
3 din, jar **4** ring **5** babel, clash
6 clamor, hubbub, racket, tumult,
uproar **7** discord, conflict, mismatch **9** disaccord **10** hullabaloo,
tintamarre **11** pandemonium
12 disharmonize

jangling
5 harsh **7** grating **9** dissonant
10 discordant

janitor
6 porter **7** charman **9** caretaker,
custodian **10** doorkeeper

japan
7 varnish

Japan
5 Nihon **6** Nippon
capital: **5** Tokyo
monetary unit: **3** yen

Japanese
aborigine: **4** Ainu
apricot: **3** ume
baron: **6** daimio, daimyo
battle cry: **6** banzai
Buddha: **5** Amida, Amita
coin: **2** bu **3** rin, sen, yen **4** oban
5 koban, obang **6** kobang
court: **5** dairi
dancing girl: **6** geisha

dish: **5** kombu **7** tempura **8** sukiyaki, teriyaki
drink: **4** sake, saki
emperor: **6** Mikado **7** Akihito
8 Hirohito
festival: **3** Bon
fish: **3** ayu, tai **4** fugu
garment: **5** haori **6** kimono
god: **4** kami **5** Ebisu, Hotei **7** Dai-
koku, Jurojin **8** Bishamon
goddess: **6** Benten **9** Amaterasu
governor: **6** shogun
grill: **7** hibachi
instrument: **4** koto **7** samisen
martial art: **4** judo **6** karate **7** jujitsu,
jujutsu
measure: **2** bu, go, jo, mo, ri, se, to
3 boo, cho, ken, rin, sho, sun, tan
4 hiro, koku **5** shaku, tsubo
monastery: **4** tera
money: **3** sen, yen
persimmon: **4** kaki
plum: **6** loquat
poem: **5** haiku, hokku, tanka
6 haikai
pottery: **7** Satsuma
radish: **6** daikon
religion: **6** Shinto **8** Buddhism
9 Shintoism
rice wine: **4** sake, saki
robe: **6** kimono
samurai clan: **5** Taira **8** Minamoto
servant: **6** geisha
ship: **4** maru
song: **3** uta
suicide: **7** seppuku **8** hara-kiri, hari-
kari, kamikaze
sword: **5** catan **6** cattan, katana
theater: **2** No **6** Kabuki
tidal wave: **7** tsunami
tree: **4** kiri, kozo, sugi **5** akeki, kiaki
6 hinoki, keyaki
vehicle: **7** ricksha **8** rickshaw
warrior: **7** samurai
weight: **2** mo **3** fun, kin, rin, shi
4 kwan, niyo **5** momme **8** hiyak-
kin, hiyaku-me
wrestling: **4** sumo
writing: **4** kana **8** hiragana,
katakana
zither: **4** koto

Japanese-American
5 Issei, Kibei, Nisei
second generation: **6** Sansei

jape
3 gag **4** fool, jeer, jest, joke, mock,
quip **5** crack, taunt **7** waggery
8 drollery **9** wisecrack, witticism

Japheth
brother: **3** Ham **4** Shem
father: **4** Noah

son: 5 Gomer, Javan, Madai, Magog, Tiras, Tubal 7 Meshech

Japhia's father
5 David

jar
4 bump, ewer, jolt, olla, vase 5 clash, crash, cruse, quake, shake, shock, smash, upset 6 impact, jangle, jounce, tinaja, tremor 7 discord, terrine, tremble, vibrate 8 conflict, gallipot, mismatch 9 collision, container, disaccord, vibration 10 concussion 12 disharmonize
ancient: 6 hydria, krater 7 amphora 8 lecythus, lekythos, lekythus
Egyptian: 7 canopic
long-necked: 6 goglet
Mexican: 6 pinata
Philippine: 5 banga

jardiniere
3 pot, urn 4 vase 5 stand 7 garnish 9 flowerpot

Jared
father: 10 Mahalaleel
son: 5 Enoch

jargon
4 cant 5 argot, idiom, lingo, slang 6 patois, patter, pidgin 7 chatter, dialect, lexicon, palaver, twitter 8 language 9 gibberish 10 dictionary, vernacular, vocabulary 11 terminology
lawyer's: 8 legalese

jarl
4 earl 5 chief, noble 8 nobleman

jarring
3 dry 5 harsh, rough 6 hoarse 7 grating, rasping, raucous 8 strident 9 dissonant 10 discordant, stridulous

Jashub's father
4 Bani 8 Issachar

jasmine
4 vine 5 shrub 6 flower 7 perfume

Jason
father: 5 Aeson
helper: 5 Medea
lover: 6 Creusa, Glauce, Glauke
quest: 12 Golden Fleece
ship: 4 Argo
shipmate: 8 Argonaut
teacher: 6 Chiron 7 Cheiron
uncle: 6 Pelias
wife: 5 Medea

jasper
6 morlop, quartz 10 chalcedony

jaundice
4 bias 7 disease, icterus 9 prejudice
combining form: 5 icter 6 ictero
Scottish: 7 gulsach

jaunt
4 perk, ride, trip 5 sally 6 junket, outing, ramble 7 journey, joyride 9 excursion

jaunty
4 airy 5 light, perky 7 perkish 8 debonair 9 sprightly 10 nonchalant

java
6 coffee

Java almond
7 talisay

Java cotton
5 kapok

Java jute
5 kenaf

Javanese
carriage: 4 sado
civet: 5 rasse
instrument: 5 saron 6 bonang, gender 7 gamelan
measure: 4 paal
skunk: 6 teledu
tree: 4 upas 7 gondang
village: 4 desa 5 dessa

Javan squirrel
8 jelerang

Java plum
5 jaman 6 jambul 7 jambool

javelin
5 lance, shaft, spear 6 weapon 7 assagai, assegai, harpoon

Javert's prey
7 Valjean

jaw
3 gab, wig, yak 4 chat, rail, rate, talk 5 baste, clack, prate, scold 6 babble, berate, gabble 7 chatter, prattle, upbraid 9 yakety-yak 10 tongue-lash
kind: 5 glass
relating to: 7 gnathal, gnathic

jawbone
7 maxilla 8 mandible

jawbreaker
5 candy

jay
4 bird, hick, jake, rube 5 clown, dandy 6 rustic 7 bumpkin, hayseed 9 greenhorn

Jayhawker
6 Kansan, outlaw 9 guerrilla
State: 6 Kansas

jazz
4 guff, jive 5 bebop, swing 6 boogie 7 ragtime 8 malarkey, nonsense
up: 7 enliven 10 popularize

jealous
5 green 7 envious, envying 8 doubting 9 demanding, green-eyed, invidious 10 possessive, possessory, suspicious 11 distrustful, mistrustful

Jecoliah's Son
6 Uzziah

Jediael's father
8 Benjamin

Jedidah
husband: 4 Amon
son: 6 Josiah

jeer
4 gibe, gird, jest, jibe, mock 5 fleer, flout, scoff, sneer, taunt 6 deride, quip at 7 scout at 8 ridicule

Jeeves
creator: 9 Wodehouse (Pelham Grenville)
employer: 7 Wooster (Bertie)
position: 5 valet 6 butler

Jefferson
home: 10 Monticello
state: 8 Virginia

Jehiel
father: 4 Elam 8 Hachmoni 11 Jehoshaphat
son: 7 Obadiah 10 Shechaniah

Jehizkiah's father
7 Shallum

Jehoaddan's Son
7 Amaziah

Jehoahaz
brother: 9 Jehoiakim
father: 4 Jehu 6 Josiah 7 Jehoram
mother: 7 Hamutal
son: 5 Joash 7 Jehoash

Jehohanan
father: 5 Bebai 6 Tobiah 8 Eliashib
son: 7 Ishmael

Jehoiada
father: 6 Paseah 7 Benaiah
son: 7 Benaiah
wife: 9 Jehosheba

Jehoiakim
father: 6 Josiah
mother: 7 Zebidah
son: 10 Jehoiachin

Jehoram
brother: 7 Ahaziah
father: 4 Ahab 11 Jehoshaphat
kingdom: 5 Judah
slayer: 4 Jehu
wife: 8 Athaliah

Jehoshaphat
father: 3 Asa 6 Ahilud, Nimshi, Paruah
father-in-law: 4 Ahab
son: 4 Jehu 7 Jehoram
wife: 8 Athaliah

Jehosheba
father: 7 Jehoram
husband: 8 Jehoiada
sister: 7 Ahaziah
son: 5 Joash

Jehovah
3 God 5 Yahwe 6 Adonai, Elohim, Yahweh

Jehozabad's father
8 Obededom

Jehozadak
see **Jozadak**

Jehu
6 driver
father: 6 Hanani 11 Jehoshaphat
grandfather: 6 Nimshi
son: 8 Jehoahaz
victim: 5 Joram 7 Jehoram

Jehudijah's husband
5 Mered

Jehush
father: 4 Esau 5 Eshek 6 Bilhan, Shimei 8 Rehoboam
mother: 10 Oholibamah

jejune
4 dull, flat 5 banal, bland, inane, trite, vapid 7 insipid, sapless, tenuous 9 innocuous 10 namby-pamby 12 milk-and-water

Jekyll's alter ego
4 Hyde

jell
3 set 4 clot 6 gelate 7 congeal, pectize, thicken 9 coagulate 10 gelatinize

jelly
3 gel, set 4 clot, pulp 5 aspic 6 gelate, pectin, spread 7 congeal, gelatin, pectize, thicken 9 coagulate 10 gelatinize

jellyfish
3 sop 4 baby 5 sissy 6 medusa 7 acaleph, doormat, medusan, milksop 8 medusoid, weakling

10 pantywaist 11 Milquetoast, mollycoddle 12 invertebrate

Jemimah's father
3 Job

Jemuel's father
6 Simeon

jennet
3 ass 5 hinny, horse 6 donkey

jeopardize
4 risk 5 peril 6 expose, hazard, menace 7 imperil 8 endanger 10 compromise

jeopardy
4 risk 5 peril 6 danger, hazard, menace 7 imperil 8 endanger, exposure 9 liability 10 compromise

Jephthah's father
6 Gilead

Jephunneh's son
5 Caleb

jeremiad
6 lament, tirade 8 diatribe, harangue 9 complaint, philippic

Jeremiah
daughter: 7 Hamutal
father: 8 Hilkiath 10 Habaziniah
scribe: 6 Baruch
son: 8 Jaazniah

Jericho's conqueror
6 Joshua

Jerimoth
daughter: 8 Mahalath
father: 5 David

Jerioth's husband
5 Caleb

jerk
3 ass, lug, tic 4 fool, nerd, snap, yank 5 idiot, lurch, ninny, throw, wrest, wring 6 twitch, wrench 7 flounce, jackass, tomfool 9 vellicate 10 nincompoop

jerked beef
7 charqui

jerkin
4 coat 6 jacket 9 gyrfalcon

jerky
4 meat 5 inane, wagon 7 charqui, foolish, jolting 8 saccadic

Jeroboam
father: 5 Joash, Nebat
foe: 6 Abijam 8 Rehoboam
mother: 6 Zeruah
son: 5 Nadab 9 Zechariah

Jerome's Bible
7 Vulgate

jersey
3 cow 5 shirt 6 tricot 7 sweater 8 pullover 10 undershirt

Jerusalem
4 Sion, Zion 5 Salem 8 Holy City
hill: 4 Sion, Zion 6 Moriah
market: 4 souk
mosque: 4 Omar
pool: 6 Siloam 8 Bethesda

Jerusalem artichoke
5 tuber 7 girasol 8 girasole 9 sunflower

Jerusalem thorn
5 shrub 6 retama 7 catechu 9 horsebean

Jerusha
father: 5 Zadok
husband: 6 Uzziah
son: 6 Jotham

Jeshaiah
father: 7 Athalia 8 Hananiah, Jeduthun, Rehabiah
son: 6 Ithiel

Jeshua
father: 7 Jozadek
son: 4 Ezer

jess
5 strap

Jesse
daughter: 7 Abigail, Zeruiah
father: 4 Obed
grandfather: 4 Boaz
son: 4 Ozem 5 David, Eliab, Elihu 6 Raddai 7 Shammah 8 Abinadab, Nethanel
youngest son: 5 David

Jessica
father: 7 Shylock
husband: 7 Lorenzo

jest
3 fun, gag, kid, rag, rib 4 butt, game, gibe, gird, jape, jeer, joke, josh, mock, play, quip, razz 5 chaff, crack, fleer, flout, scoff, sneer, sport 6 banter, quip at 7 mockery, scout at, waggery 8 derision, drollery, ridicule 9 pilgarlic, wisecrack, witticism 13 laughing stock

jester
3 wag, wit 4 fool 5 clown, comic, droll, idiot, joker 6 motley 8 comedian, funnyman, humorist, jokester, quipster

Jesuit's founder
6 Loyola, Ignatius

jet
4 ebon, inky 5 black, ebony, plane, raven, sable, sprit, spurt 6 engine, splurt, squirt 8 airplane, fountain 9 pitch-dark

Jether
father: 4 Ezra 6 Gideon, Zophah
son: 5 Amasa

Jethro
daughter: 8 Zipporah
son-in-law: 5 Moses

jetsam
7 flotsam 8 wreckage 9 driftwood

jettison
4 cast, dump, junk, shed 5 scrap 6 reject, slough 7 cashier, discard, dumping, junking 8 abdicate, disposal, riddance 9 scrapping, throw away 10 discarding

jetty
4 dock, ebon, inky, pier, quay, slip 5 berth, black, ebony, groin, levee, raven, sable, wharf 9 pitch-dark 10 pitch-block

Jew
6 Essene, Semite 8 Judahite 9 Israelite

jewel
3 gem 5 adorn, begem, beset, bijou, ideal, stone 7 paragon, phoenix 8 nonesuch, ornament 9 nonpareil; (see also **gem**)

jeweler
8 lapidary, lapidist
famous: 7 Tiffany (Charles Lewis)

jewelry
10 bijouterie
artificial: 5 glass, paste 6 strass 7 costume
piece: 3 pin 4 ring 6 brooch 7 earring 8 bracelet, lavalier, necklace, tieclasp 9 lavaliere
set: 6 parure

Jewish
bread: 5 matzo 6 matzoh, matzos 8 afikomen
ceremony: 5 berit, brith 6 berith 10 bar mitzvah
combining form: 5 Judeo 6 Judaeo
doctrine: 6 Mishna 7 Mishnah
liturgy: 6 maarib, maariv, minhah 7 minchah 9 shaharith
New Year: 11 Rosh Hashana
organization: 8 Hadassah 9 B'nai B'rith
pioneer: 6 halutz 7 chalutz
prayer book: 6 mahzor, siddur 7 machzor

sabbath: 8 Saturday
scripture: 6 Talmud
synagogue: 4 shul 5 schul
teacher: 5 rabbi 6 Hillel; (see also Hebrew)

jezebel
4 jade, slut 5 hussy, tramp, trull, wench 6 wanton 7 trollop 8 slattern, strumpet

Jezebel
father: 7 Ethbaal
home: 5 Sidon
husband: 4 Ahab
slayer: 4 Jehu
victim: 6 Naboth

Jezer's father
8 Naphtali

Jezreel's father
5 Hosea

jib
3 gag, shy 4 balk, sail 5 demur, stick

jibe
2 go 5 agree, fit in, tally 6 accord, square 7 conform 8 dovetail 9 harmonize 10 correspond

jiffy
5 crack, flash, hurry, shake, trice 6 minute, moment, second 7 instant 9 breathing 11 split second

jig
4 hook, play, ploy, ruse, wile 5 dance, feint, trick 6 device, gambit 7 gimmick

jigger
3 cup 4 boat, mast 5 gizmo, glass 6 dingus, doodad, gadget, widget 7 concern, dofunny, gimmick, thingum 9 doohickey, shot glass

jiggle
5 shake 9 oscillate

jigsaw
4 tool 6 puzzle

jihad
3 war 6 strife 7 crusade, holy war 8 campaign

jilt
6 reject 7 abandon, cast off, discard

jim-dandy
5 nifty 8 knockout 9 humdinger

jimmy
3 bar, pry 4 open 5 lever 7 crowbar

jingle
4 ring, song 5 chime, chink, clink, verse 6 tinkle 7 chinkle

jinn
5 afrit, genie 6 afreet, spirit, yaksha

jinx
3 hex 5 charm, curse, spell 6 hoodoo, voodoo, whammy 7 evil eye

jitters
5 jumps, panic 6 dither, nerves, shakes 7 shivers, willies 9 whimwhams 13 heebie-jeebies

jittery
5 jumpy, nervy 6 goosey, spooky 7 fidgety, nervous 9 unrestful 10 high-strung

jive
3 kid 4 jazz, talk 5 dance, music, swing 6 jargon

Joab
brother: 6 Asahel 7 Abishai
father: 7 Seraiah, Zeruiah
slayer: 7 Benaiah
uncle: 5 David
victim: 5 Abner, Amasa

Joah
father: 5 Asaph 6 Joahaz, Zimmah 8 Obededon
son: 4 Eden

Joanna's husband
5 Chuza

Joan of Arc
birthplace: 7 Domremy
epithet: 7 Pucelle 13 Maid of Orleans
victory: 7 Orleans

Joan's husband
5 Darby

Joash
father: 4 Ahab 7 Ahaziah 8 Jehoahaz
son: 6 Gideon 7 Amaziah 8 Jeroboam
victim: 9 Zechariah

job
4 dupe, duty, fool, gull, hoax, line, post, spot, task, work 5 berth, chare, chore, place, stint, trade 6 befool, billet, devoir, effort, office, pigeon 7 calling, chicane, posting, pursuit 8 business, flimflam, position, sinecure, taskwork, vocation 9 bamboozle, situation, victimize 10 assignment, connection, employment, engagement, occupation, profession 11 appointment

Job
daughter: 6 Keziah 7 Jemimah
father: 8 Issachar
friend: 6 Bildad, Zophar 7 Eliphaz
home: 2 Uz

Jobab's father
5 Zerah 6 Joktan 9 Shaharaim

jobber
6 trader 10 contractor, wholesaler

job-training program
4 CETA

Jocasta
daughter: 6 Ismene 8 Antigone
husband: 5 Laius 7 Oedipus
son: 7 Oedipus 8 Eteocles
9 Polynices

Jochebed
brother: 6 Kohath
father: 4 Levi
husband: 5 Amram

jock
7 athlete

jockey
4 play 5 rider, trick 7 beguile, exploit, finesse 8 maneuver
10 manipulate
famous: 5 Baeza (Braulio) 6 Arcaro
(Eddie), Murphy (Isaac), Pincay
(Laffit) 7 Cauthen (Steve), Cordero
(Angel), Hartack (Bill), Longden
(Johnny) 8 McHargue (Darrel), Turcotte (Ron) 9 Shoemaker (Willie)

jocular
3 gay 5 comic, jolly, merry, silly,
witty 6 blithe, jocose, jovial 7 comical, playful 8 cheerful, humorous,
sportive 9 facetious

jocularity
4 glee 5 mirth 7 jollity 8 hilarity
9 jocundity, joviality, merriment

jocund
3 gay 5 jolly, merry 6 blithe, jovial
7 festive, gleeful, playful 8 mirthful,
sportive 10 blithesome
12 lighthearted

Joel
brother: 6 Nathan
father: 4 Nebo 5 Ladan 6 Samuel,
Zichri 7 Azariah, Pedaiah, Pethuel
son: 5 Heman

jog
3 dig, jab, run 4 lope, poke, prod,
trot 5 nudge, punch, shake
6 remind

jogger
6 layboy, runner

joggle
5 dowel, joint, notch, shake 6 jostle

Johanan
father: 6 Josiah, Kareah, Tobiah
8 Eliashib, Elioenai, Hakkatan
son: 7 Azariah

john
2 WC 4 head 5 privy 6 toilet 7 latrine 8 lavatory 11 convenience,
water closet

John
father: 5 Accos, Simon
10 Mattathias
son: 5 Peter 9 Eupolemus 10 Mattathias; (see also **John the Baptist;
John the Evangelist**)

John
Irish: 4 Sean

John Hancock
9 autograph, signature

Johnson's biographer
7 Boswell (James)

John the Baptist
father: 9 Zacharias
mother: 9 Elisabeth

John the Evangelist
brother: 5 James
father: 7 Zebedee
mother: 6 Salome

join
3 fay, mix, tie, wed 4 abut, ally,
bind, bond, fuse, knot, line, link,
mate, weld, yoke 5 affix, blend,
march, marry, merge, piece, touch,
unify, unite, verge 6 attach, border,
butt on, couple, enlist, enroll, fasten, relate, sign up, splice
7 bracket, combine, connect
8 coagment, coalesce, compound,
concrete, neighbor 9 associate, coadunate, conjugate, integrate

joint
3 ell, hip, tie 4 butt, crux, dive,
knee, link, seam 5 ankle, elbow,
hinge, scarf, union, wrist 6 common, mutual, public, shared, suture
7 hangout, knuckle, shiplap 8 abutment, communal, conjunct, coupling, junction, juncture, shoulder
9 honky-tonk 10 connection
combining form: 5 arthr 6 arthro,
condyl 7 condylo
disease: 9 arthritis 10 rheumatism
prefix: 2 co

join up
5 enter 6 enlist, enroll, muster, sign
up

joist
4 beam, stud 6 timber 7 sleeper,
support

joke
3 fun, gag, kid, pun, rag, rib, wit,
yak 4 butt, dido, fool, game, jape,
jest, josh, mock, play, quip, razz
5 antic, caper, crack, humor, jolly,
prank, sally, sport 6 banter, jestee,
parody 7 mockery, sarcasm, waggery 8 badinage, derision, drôlerie, drollery, one-liner, repartee
9 burlesque, pilgarlic, wisecrack,
witticism 10 caricature 11 monkeyshine 13 laughing stock
stale: 8 chestnut

joker
3 wag, wit 4 card, zany 5 clown,
comic, cutup, droll 6 gagman,
jester 7 farceur 8 comedian, funnyman, humorist, quipster

Jokshan
father: 7 Abraham
mother: 7 Keturah
son: 5 Dedan, Sheba

Joktan
brother: 5 Peleg
father: 4 Eber
son: 4 Obal 5 Ophir

jollity
3 fun 4 glee, play, romp 5 cheer,
mirth, revel, sport 6 frolic, gaiety,
gambol 7 disport, revelry, rollick,
whoopee 8 hilarity, reveling 9 festivity, jocundity, joviality, merriment, revelment 10 blitheness,
jocularity 11 merrymaking

jolly
3 fun, gay, kid, rag, rib 4 glad,
jest, josh, razz 5 chaff, merry
6 banter, blithe, jocund, jovial
7 festive, gleeful, jocular, playful, roguish, waggish 8 mirthful,
sportive 10 blithesome, frolicsome

Jolly Roger
4 flag 6 ensign
user: 6 pirate

jolt
3 jar, nip, tot 4 blow, bump, dram,
drop, shot, slug 5 clash, crash,
knock, shake, shock, snort 6 impact, jounce 7 snifter, startle
8 toothful 9 collision

Jonadab
cousin: 5 Amnon
father: 6 Rechab 7 Shimeah
uncle: 5 David

Jonah
4 jinx 7 prophet
father: 7 Amittai
son: 5 Peter, Simon
swallower: 5 whale

Jonathan
brother: 7 Johanan
father: 4 Jada, Saul 6 Joiada, Kareah, Uzziah 7 Absolom, Shimeah 8 Abiathar 10 Mattathias
friend: 5 David

Jones, John Paul
ship: 15 Bonhomme Richard
victim: 7 Serapis

jongleur
4 bard 6 singer 8 minstrel 10 troubadour

jonquil
8 daffodil 9 narcissus

Jonson play
6 The Fox 7 Epicene, Volpone

Joplin creation
3 rag

Joram
brother: 7 Ahaziah
father: 3 Toi 4 Ahab 11 Jehoshaphat
slayer: 4 Jehu
son: 7 Ahaziah

Jordan
capital: 5 Amman
king: 7 Hussein
monetary unit: 5 dinar

jorum
3 cup, jug 4 bowl

Joseph
brother: (see **Jacob**, son)
buyer: 8 Potiphar
father: 5 Asaph, Jacob 9 Zacharias 10 Mattathias
mother: 6 Rachel
son: 5 Jesus 7 Ephraim 8 Manasseh
wife: 4 Mary 7 Asenath

Joseph's coat
6 coleus 7 tampala

josh
3 fun, guy, kid, rag, rib 4 jest, joke, razz 5 chaff, jolly, tease 6 banter

Joshua's father
3 Nun

Joshua tree
5 yucca

Josiah
father: 4 Amon 9 Zephaniah
mother: 7 Jedidah

son: 8 Jehoahaz 9 Jehoiakim

joss
4 idol 5 image

Jo's sister
3 Amy, Meg 4 Beth

jostle
3 jar, jog 4 push 5 elbow, press, shove 6 hustle 8 bulldoze, shoulder

jot
3 bit 4 atom, iota, whit 5 grain, minim, speck 6 tittle 7 modicum, smidgen, smidgin 8 particle, smidgeon

jot down
4 note 5 write

Jotham
father: 6 Gideon, Jahdai, Uzziah
mother: 8 Jerushah

joule component
3 erg

jounce
3 jar, jog 4 bump, jolt 5 shock 6 impact, wallop 9 collision 10 concussion

journal
3 log 5 diary, organ, paper 6 record, review 7 gazette 8 magazine 9 newspaper 10 periodical

journalist
3 Bly (Nellie) 4 Drew (Elizabeth), Pyle (Ernie), Reed (John), Will (George F.) 5 Baker (Russell), Cooke (Alistair), Evans (Rowland), Hersh (Seymour), Novak (Robert), Rowan (Carl), Royko (Mike), Smith (Hedrick), Stone (I. F.), Szulc (Tad), Wolfe (Tom) 6 Bierce (Ambrose), Broder (David), Ephron (Nora), Greene (Bob), Kennan (George), Koppel (Ted), Lehrer (Jim), Moyers (Bill), Murrow (Edward R.), Reston (James), Runyon (Damon), Safire (William), Shirer (William L.), Thomas (Helen, Lowell), Zenger (John Peter) 7 Breslin (Jimmy), Cousins (Norman), Greeley (Horace), Gunther (John), McGrory (Mary), Mencken (H. L.), Pearson (Drew), St. Johns (Adela Rogers), Tarbell (Ida), Trillin (Calvin), Wallace (Mike), Walters (Barbara) 8 Amanpour (Christiane), Anderson (Jack, Terry), Atkinson (Brooks), Brinkley (David), Garrison (William Lloyd), Lippmann (Walter), Pulitzer (Joseph), Salinger (Pierre), Steffens (Lincoln), Thompson (Dorothy, Hun-

ter), Winchell (Walter), Woodward (Bob) 9 Bernstein (Carl), Donaldson (Sam), Frederick (Pauline), Hohenberg (John), Salisbury (Harrison), Watterson (Henry)

journey
2 go 3 hie 4 eyre, fare, pass, tour, trek, trip, wend 5 jaunt, sally 6 cruise, junket, push on, repair, safari, travel, voyage 7 odyssey, proceed, travels 8 progress 9 excursion 10 expedition, pilgrimage
route: 9 itinerary
stage: 3 leg

joust
4 tilt 5 fight 6 combat 10 tournament
arena: 8 tiltyard

Jove
see **Jupiter**

jovial
see **jocular**

jowl
3 jaw 5 cheek 6 dewlap, wattle 8 mandible

joy
4 glee 5 bliss, mirth 6 gaiety 7 delight, ecstasy, elation, rapture 8 fruition, gladness, pleasure 9 enjoyment 11 delectation

Joyce, James
birthplace: 6 Dublin
character: 5 Bloom (Leopold), Bloom (Molly) 7 Dedalus (Stephen)
work: 6 Exiles 7 Ulysses 9 Dubliners 13 Finnegans Wake

joyful
see **joyous**

joyous
3 gay 4 glad 5 happy, merry 7 buoyant, festive, gleeful 8 ecstatic, mirthful 9 delighted, rapturous 12 lighthearted

Jozabad's father
6 Jeshua 7 Pashhur

Jozacar
mother: 8 Shimeath
victim: 5 Joash

Jozadak's son
6 Jeshua

Jubal
father: 6 Lamech
mother: 4 Adah

jubilant
6 elated 8 exultant, exulting 9 cock-a-hoop, triumphal 10 cock-a-whoop, triumphant

jubilate
5 exult, glory 7 delight, triumph

Judah
brother: (see **Jacob**, son)
father: 5 Jacob
king: 3 Asa 4 Ahaz, Amon 5 Joash
6 Abijam, Josiah, Jotham, Uzziah
7 Ahaziah, Amaziah, Jehoram
8 Hezekiah, Jehoahaz, Manasseh,
Rehoboam, Zedekiah 9 Jehoiakim
10 Jehoiachin 11 Jehoshaphat
mother: 4 Leah
son: 2 Er 4 Onan 6 Shelah

Judas
7 traitor
father: 5 Simon 7 Chalphi
10 Mattathias
replacement: 8 Matthias
suicide place: 8 Aceldama,
Akeldama

judge
3 put, ref, try, ump 4 call, draw,
make, rule, test 5 check, court, infer 6 critic, decide, deduce, derive,
gather, jurist, reckon, settle, umpire
7 arbiter, collect, justice, make out,
referee 8 conclude, critique,
doomster, estimate, mediator, sentence 9 arbitrate, criticize, determine 10 adjudicate, arbitrator,
chancellor, magistrate, negotiator,
reconciler 11 approximate, concili-
ator 12 intermediary
Athenian: 6 dicast 7 heliast
bench: 4 banc
chamber: 6 camera
gown: 4 robe, toga
in Hades: 5 Minos 6 Aeacus
12 Rhadamanthys
mallet: 5 gavel
Muslim: 4 cadi 5 mufti

judgment
4 doom 5 award, sense, stock,
taste 6 acumen, ruling, wisdom
7 insight, opinion, verdict 8 decision, estimate, gumption, illation,
sagacity, sequitur 9 appraisal, criticism, deduction, good sense, inference 10 assessment, astuteness,
conclusion, discretion, estimation,
evaluation, horse sense, shrewdness 11 common sense, discernment 12 appraisement, perspicacity 13 determination, ratiocination

Judgment Day
8 doomsday

___judicata
3 res

judicial
8 critical 10 judgmental

assembly: 5 court
document: 4 writ

judicious
4 fair, sage, sane, wise 7 prudent,
sapient 8 rational, sensible
9 equitable, judgmatic, objective,
sagacious 10 reasonable 13 dispassionate

Judith
father: 5 Beeri
home: 8 Bethulia
husband: 4 Esau
victim: 10 Holofernes

Judy's husband
5 Punch

jug
3 jar, pen 4 coop, ewer, jail,
toby 5 gotch 6 cooler, immure, intern, lockup, prison, urceus 7 confine, pitcher 8 bastille, demijohn,
imprison 9 constrain 11 incarcerate

jug band instrument
5 kazoo 6 bottle 7 washtub
9 stovepipe, washboard

Juggernaut's temple
4 Puri

juggle
5 bluff 6 betray, delude, humbug,
illude, take in 7 beguile, deceive,
mislead, shuffle

juice
3 sap 4 fuel, must, stum 5 cider,
fluid 7 essence, vinegar 8 vitality
10 succulence 11 electricity
combining form: 3 opo 4 chyl
5 chyli, chylo
fermented: 4 wine 5 cider
Scottish: 4 broo

juicy
4 racy 7 piquant 9 succulent

juju
4 luck, zemi 5 charm 6 amulet, fetish, mascot 7 periapt 8 talisman
10 phylactery

jujube
3 ber 7 gumdrop, lozenge

julep
5 drink

Julian's epithet
8 Apostate

Juliet
betrothed: 5 Paris
father: 7 Capulet
lover: 5 Romeo

July 14
11 Bastille Day

jumble
3 mix, pie 4 hash, mess, olio 5 mix
up, shake, snafu 6 foul up, litter,
medley, mess up, muddle, muss up
7 clutter, confuse, derange, disturb,
rummage, shuffle, snarl up 8 disorder, mishmash, pastiche, scramble
9 patchwork, potpourri 10 assortment, disarrange, miscellany, salmagundi 11 disorganize, gallimaufry

jumbo
4 huge 5 giant 6 mighty 7 mammoth 8 colossal, enormous, gigantic 9 cyclopean 10 prodigious
11 elephantine

jump
3 hop, lop 4 bolt, hike, jink, leap,
loup 5 boost, bound, lunge, put up,
raise, vault 6 bounce, hurdle, jack
up, pounce, spring 7 saltate, startle
8 increase

jumper
5 dress, shirt, smock 6 blouse,
jacket

jumping
7 saltant

jumping frog county
9 Calaveras

jump over
8 leapfrog

jumps
6 dither, shakes 7 jitters, shivers,
willies 9 whim-whams 13 heebie-
jeebies

jumpy
see **jittery**

junction
4 seam 5 joint, union 6 suture
7 joining, meeting 8 coupling
9 concourse, gathering 10 concursion, confluence, connection

juncture
4 pass, seam 5 joint, pinch, point,
union 6 crisis, moment, strait 7 instant, joining 8 coupling, exigency,
zero hour 9 emergency 10 connection, crossroads 11 contingency
12 turning point

june bug
6 beetle

jungle
3 web 4 hash, knot, mash, maze,
mesh 5 skein, snarl 6 jumble, litter,
morass, muddle, tangle 7 clutter,

mizmaze, rummage **8** mishmash, scramble **9** labyrinth

Jungle, The
author: **8** Sinclair (Upton)
locale: **7** Chicago

Jungle Books, The
author: **7** Kipling (Rudyard)
character: **6** Mowgli
python: **3** Kaa

juniper
4 cade, tree **5** cedar, larch, retem, savin

junk
4 boat, cast, dope, drug **5** offal, scrap, trash, waste **6** debris, kelter, litter, refuse, reject, slough **7** cashier, discard, garbage, rubbish, wash out **8** jettison, throw out **9** narcotics, throw away

junker
4 heap **5** crate, noble, wreck **6** jalopy **10** aristocrat

junket
4 trip **5** jaunt, sally **6** outing, picnic **9** excursion **10** roundabout

junkyard
4 dump

Juno
bird: **7** peacock
epithet: **6** Moneta; (see also **Hera**)

Junoesque
5 curvy **7** rounded **9** curvesome **10** curvaceous **11** curvilinear **13** well-developed

junta
5 group **7** council **9** committee **10** government

junto
5 cabal, group **7** coterie, faction

Jupiter
4 Jove, Zeus
angel: **7** Zadkiel
cupbearer: **8** Ganymede
daughter: **5** Venus **7** Minerva
epithet: **6** Fidius, Fulgur, Stator, Tonans **7** Pluvius

father: **6** Saturn
lover: **2** Io **6** Europa **8** Callisto
mother: **3** Ops
satellite: **2** Io **6** Europa **8** Callisto, Ganymede
son: **5** Arcas **6** Castor, Pollux
temple: **7** Capitol
wife: **4** Juno

Jurgen
author: **6** Cabell (James Branch)
trade: **10** pawnbroker

juridical
5 legal **8** juristic

jurisdiction
3 law, see **4** sway **5** might, power, range, reach, scope, venue **6** county, domain, parish, sphere **7** command, compass, control, diocese, mastery **8** dominion, province **9** authority, bailiwick, territory **10** domination
suffix: **3** dom

jurisprudence
3 law

jury
5 panel **9** committee
decision: **7** verdict

just
3 all, apt, due, fit **4** even, fair, good, meet, only, true **5** equal, happy, legal, quite, right, sharp **6** as well, barely, cogent, hardly, honest, in toto, merely, proper, scarce, simply, square, wholly **7** condign, exactly, fitting, merited, totally, upright, utterly **8** all in all, deserved, faithful, rightful, scarcely, squarely, suitable, unbiased **9** befitting, equitable, expressly, honorable, impartial, justified, objective, precisely, requisite, uncolored, veracious, veridical **10** accurately, altogether, completely, felicitous, legitimate, scrupulous **11** appropriate, undistorted, well-founded **12** unprejudiced, well-grounded **13** conscientious, dispassionate, rhadamanthine

justice
3 law **5** court, judge **6** equity **7** honesty **8** evenness, fairness **10** magistrate **12** impartiality

justification
6 excuse, reason **7** account, apology, defense **8** apologia **9** rationale **10** apologetic **11** explanation

justify
5 argue, claim **6** assert, defend, excuse, uphold, verify **7** account, bear out, confirm, contend, explain, support, warrant **8** maintain, validate **9** vindicate **11** corroborate, explain away, rationalize **12** authenticate, substantiate

justly
4 well **5** fitly **6** nicely **7** rightly **8** decently, properly **9** correctly, fittingly **10** decorously **11** befittingly

jut
4 hang, poke, pout **5** bulge, jetty, pouch **6** beetle **7** project **8** bend over, lean over, overhang, protrude, stand out, stick out **9** outthrust **10** projection, protrusion **12** protuberance

jute
5 gunny **6** burlap **7** sacking
Indian: **4** desi

Juvenal's forte
6 satire

juvenile
3 kid **5** child, green, young, youth **6** callow, infant, moppet, unripe **8** immature, young one, youthful **9** unfledged, youngling, youngster **11** undeveloped

juvenility
5 youth **7** puberty **9** greenness, youthhood **10** pubescence, springtide, springtime **11** adolescence **12** youthfulness

juxtaposed
8 abutting, adjacent, touching **9** adjoining, bordering **10** approximal, contiguous **12** conterminous

Kk

kabob
7 shaslik 8 shashlik 9 shashlick

kaddish
6 cantor, prayer

kady
3 hat 5 derby

Kafka, Franz
character: 4 Olga 5 Samsa (Gregor)
6 Joseph (K.)
novel: 7 Amerika 8 The Trial 9 The
Castle

kaiser
5 ruler 7 emperor, monarch
9 sovereign

kaka
6 parrot

kakariki
6 lizard 8 parakeet

kakatoe
6 parrot 8 cockatoo

kale
4 cole 7 cabbage, collard 8 bore-
cole, colewort

kaleidoscopic
7 diverse, various 8 colorful
10 variegated

Kali
aspect: 5 Durga 7 Parvati
husband: 4 Siva 5 Shiva

kalium
9 potassium

kalong
3 bat 8 fruit bat

Kama
god of: 4 love
mount: 6 parrot 7 sparrow
wife: 4 Rati

kambal
5 shawl 7 blanket

kamik
4 boot

kamikaze
7 suicide 8 airplane, suicidal

kampong
6 hamlet 7 village

Kampuchea
see **Cambodia**

kangaroo
4 euro 6 leaper 7 bettong, wallaby
8 boongary, wallaroo 9 marsupial
10 macropodid
herd: 3 mob
male: 6 boomer
young: 4 joey

kangaroo bear
5 koala

kangaroo rat
7 potoroo

kans
5 grass 6 glagah

Kansas
capital: 6 Topeka
college: 5 Tabor
fort: 5 Riley
largest city: 7 Wichita
nickname: 14 Jayhawker State,
Sunflower State
prison: 11 Leavenworth

kaolin
4 clay

kapelle
5 choir 9 orchestra

kaput
6 ruined 7 done for 8 defeated,
finished 9 destroyed

karakul
5 sheep

karakurt
6 spider 9 black wolf

Kareah's son
7 Johanan 8 Jonathan

karma
4 aura 5 force, power 6 spirit

kaross
3 rug 7 garment

kasha
4 mush 5 grain

katabasis
7 retreat 9 troparion

Katharina
father: 8 Baptista
suitor: 9 Petruchio

Katrina's suitor
9 Brom Bones 12 Ichabod Crane

katydid
6 insect 11 grasshopper

katzenjammer
6 clamor, nausea 8 hangover,
headache

kava
3 awa 5 shrub 6 pepper

kayak
4 boat 5 canoe

kayo
8 knockout

Kazantzakis hero
5 Zorba

kea
6 parrot

Keats poem
5 Lamia 8 Endymion, Hyperion, Isabella, To Autumn 11 Ode to
Psyche

kedge
6 anchor

keel
4 boat, drop, fall, ship 5 barge,
pitch, ridge, slump, upset 6 carina,
go down, plunge, topple, tumble
7 capsize 8 overturn 11 center-
board

keelbird
3 ani

keen
4 agog, avid, wail, yowl 5 acute, alert, eager, honed, nutty, sharp, smart 6 ardent, bewail, clever, fervid, gung ho, lively, shrewd 7 animate, anxious, athirst, fervent, thirsty, whetted, zealous 8 animated, appetent, spirited 9 impatient, pervervid, sensitive, sprightly, unblunted, vivacious 10 breathless, perceptive, razor-sharp 11 penetrating, penetrative, quick-witted, sharp-witted 12 enthusiastic, quick-sighted, sharp-sighted

keenness
3 wit 4 edge 6 acumen 9 sharpness 10 astuteness, shrewdness 11 discernment, penetration, percipience 12 incisiveness, perspicacity

keep
3 own, pen 4 curb, fend, have, hold, jail, mind, obey, save 5 carry, check, stock 6 bridle, comply, detain, direct, follow, hold in, living, lockup, manage, ordain, prison, retain 7 abstain, alimony, carry on, conduct, conform, control, forbear, inhibit, observe, operate, possess, refrain, reserve, support 8 conserve, hold back, hold down, maintain, preserve, restrain, withhold 9 celebrate, constrain, solemnize 10 livelihood, sustenance 11 commemorate, maintenance, subsistence

keep back
3 dam 4 deny, hold, save 6 detain, refuse, retain, retard 7 reserve 8 disallow, withhold

keeper
5 guard 6 custos, pastor, warden 7 curator 8 cerberus, claviger, guardian, watchdog 9 constable, custodian

keeping
4 care, ward 5 trust 6 charge, saving 7 custody 9 salvation 10 caretaking 12 conservation, guardianship

keep on
7 persist 8 continue 9 persevere

keep out
3 bar 4 hold 5 debar 6 detain, retain 7 reserve 8 hold back, withhold

keepsake
5 relic, token 6 trophy 7 memento 8 giftbook, memorial, reminder, souvenir 11 remembrance 12 remembrancer

keep up
7 sustain 8 continue, maintain, preserve

keeve
3 tub, vat 4 kier 5 basin

kef
4 hemp 7 languor, tobacco 10 dreaminess 12 tranquillity

keg
3 tun 4 butt, cask, pipe 6 barrel 7 barrico 8 hogshead

kegler
6 bowler

keister, keester
7 satchel 8 buttocks, suitcase

keitloa
5 rhino

keloid
4 scar

kelp
3 ash 4 agar, alga 5 varec 7 seaweed

Kemuel
father: 5 Nahor
mother: 6 Milcah
son: 9 Hashabiah

ken
4 view 5 grasp, range, reach, scope, sight 7 horizon, purview 10 perception

kenaf
4 hemp, jute 6 ambari 8 hibiscus

kench
3 bin 9 enclosure

Kenilworth author
5 Scott (Walter)

kennel
3 den 4 pack 5 drain, house, sewer 6 gutter 7 confine, shelter 9 enclosure

keno
4 game
similar to: 5 beano, bingo, lotto

Kentucky
capital: 9 Frankfort
largest city: 10 Louisville
nickname: 14 Bluegrass State
state bird: 8 cardinal
state flower: 9 goldenrod

Kentucky bluegrass
3 poa

Kenya
capital: 7 Nairobi
monetary unit: 8 shilling

kepi
3 cap

kerchief
6 hankie 8 babushka, bandanna, headrail, kaffiyeh
Scottish: 5 curch

kerf
3 cut 4 slit 5 notch 6 groove

kermis
4 fair 8 carnival, festival

kernel
3 nub, nut 4 core, crux, gist, meat, pith, seed 5 grain 6 matter, nubbin, upshot 7 nucleus 9 substance
combining form: 4 cary, kary 5 caryo, karyo

Kerouac novel
6 Big Sur 9 On the Road

kestrel
4 bird, hawk 6 falcon, fanner 9 windhover

ketch
4 boat 8 sailboat

ketone
5 irone 7 acetone, camphor, muscone 8 acridone, butanone, civetone

kettle
3 pot, vat 6 vessel 7 caldron, marmite, pothole 8 cauldron, flambeau

kettledrum
5 naker, party 6 timbal, tymbal
Arabian: 6 atabal

Keturah's husband
7 Abraham

kevel
5 cleat, staff 6 cudgel, hammer, timber 7 bollard

key
3 cay 4 isle, reef, tone 5 islet, pitch, vital 6 clavis, cotter, island, legend, opener, samara, spline, ticket 7 central, digital 8 critical, passport, password, solution, tonality 9 important 10 open sesame
combining form: 5 clavi, clavo, cleid 6 cleido
notch: 4 ward

keyboard
6 manual 7 clavier 8 pedalier 10 claviature

key fruit
6 samara

key man
9 locksmith

keynote
4 tone 5 theme, tonic 7 feature

keynoter
6 orator 7 speaker

Keystone State
12 Pennsylvania

Keziah's father
3 Job

khaki
5 cloth, color 7 uniform

khamsin
4 wind

khan
5 chief, ruler 9 chieftain, sovereign

khedive
5 ruler 7 viceroy

Khomeini, e.g.
4 imam

Ki
brother, consort: 2 An
mother: 5 Nammu
son: 5 Enlil

kiang
3 ass

kibble
4 meal 5 grain, grind

kibbutz
4 farm 7 commune 10 collective, settlement

kibe
4 chap 5 crack 9 chilblain

kibitzer
5 prier, pryer, snoop 6 butt-in
7 meddler 8 busybody, observer, quidnunc 9 spectator 10 pragmatist, rubberneck

kick
4 bang, boot, fuss, punt, wail
5 whine 6 except, murmur, object, repine, thrill, wallop 7 grumble, protest 8 complain 11 expostulate, remonstrate

kicker
4 crab 5 crank 6 griper, grouch, punter 7 growler 8 grumbler, sorehead, sourpuss 10 complainer

kick off
4 open 5 begin, start 6 launch
8 commence, embark on, initiate
10 embark upon, inaugurate

kick out
2 ax 4 drop, fire, sack 5 chase, chuck, eject, evict 6 bounce 7 boot out, cashier, dismiss, extrude
8 throw out 9 discharge

kickshaw
3 toy 5 goody, treat 6 bauble, dainty, morsel, tidbit, titbit, trifle
8 delicacy

kid
3 bud, fun, guy, rag, rib 4 dupe, fool, gull, hoax, jest, joke, josh, razz 5 child, jolly, trick, youth
6 banter, befool, moppet 8 flimflam, hoodwink, juvenile, young one 9 bamboozle, youngling, youngster

kidnap
6 abduct, waylay 8 shanghai
10 spirit away

kidney
5 gland, organ
combining form: 4 reni, reno 5 nephr
6 nephro 7 nephron, nephros
Scottish: 4 neer

kidney-shaped
8 reniform

kielbasa
7 sausage

kier
3 vat

kilderkin
3 keg 4 cask 6 barrel

kilim
3 mat, rug 6 carpet

kill
3 zap 4 bane, down, hang, slay, veto 5 croak, scrag, shoot 6 cut off, finish, lay low, murder, poison, stifle 7 butcher, destroy, execute, garrote, put away, take off 8 carry off, dispatch, immolate, massacre, negative, strangle 9 non-placet, sacrifice, slaughter 10 annihilate
11 assassinate, exterminate

killer
6 gunman, hit man, slayer 7 torpedo 8 assassin, homicide, murderer
combining form: 4 cide 6 ctonus

killer whale
4 orca 7 grampus

killing
5 blood 6 murder 8 foul play, homicide 9 slaughter 12 manslaughter
combining form: 5 cidal
of a race: 8 genocide
of bacteria: 11 bactericide
of brother: 10 fratricide
of father: 9 parricide, patricide
of king: 8 regicide
of mother: 9 matricide

of self: 7 suicide
of sister: 10 sororicide

Kilmer poem
5 Trees

kiln
4 bake, burn, fire, oast, oven
7 furnace

kilt
5 skirt 7 filabeg, filibeg 8 fillebeg
fabric: 5 plaid 6 tartan

kilter
4 trim 5 order, shape 6 fettle, repair 7 fitness 9 condition

kimono
4 gown, robe
sash: 3 obi

kin
3 sib 4 clan, folk, race, sept
5 stock, tribe 6 family 7 kindred, lineage, related 8 kinsfolk, relation, relative 9 cousinage

kind
3 ilk, way 4 good, mild, sort, type, warm 5 breed, class, genre, genus, order 6 benign, gender, genial, gentle, humane, kidney, nature, stripe, tender 7 affable, amiable, clement, cordial, feather, lenient, species, variety 8 merciful, obliging, tolerant 9 benignant, character
10 altruistic, benevolent, charitable, forbearing, propitious, responsive
11 complaisant, considerate, description, good-hearted, good-humored, good-natured, openhearted, sympathetic, warmhearted
12 eleemosynary, good-tempered, humanitarian 13 compassionate, philanthropic

kindle
4 fire, move, stir, wake, whet
5 light, rally, rouse, waken
6 arouse, awaken, bestir, excite, foment, ignite, incite 7 inflame, provoke 9 challenge, instigate, stimulate

kindliness
5 amity 6 comity 8 goodwill
10 friendship 11 benevolence
12 friendliness

kindly
4 well 6 benign 7 benefic
8 friendly, gracious 9 attentive, benignant, heedfully 10 generously, neighborly 11 considerate, goodhearted 12 thoughtfully
13 considerately

kindness
5 favor 7 service 8 clemency, courtesy, goodwill, sympathy 10 indul-

gence **11** benevolence
12 dispensation

kindred
  3 sib **4** akin, clan, folk, race, sept **5** house, stock, tribe **6** agnate, allied, family **7** cognate, connate, lineage, related **8** incident **10** affiliated, connatural **11** consanguine

king
  3 rex **4** czar, tsar **5** baron, mogul, ruler **6** tycoon **7** magnate, monarch **9** sovereign
  Albanian: **3** Zog **7** William
  Assyrian: **6** Sargon **11** Sennacherib, Shalmaneser
  Babylonian: **6** Sargon **9** Hammurabi **10** Belshazzar
  Belgian: **6** Albert **7** Leopold **8** Baudouin
  Bohemian: **9** Wenceslas **10** Wenceslaus
  Damascus: **8** Benhadad
  Danish: **4** Abel, Eric, Gorm, Hans, John, Olaf **5** Sweyn **6** Canute, Harold, Magnus **8** Nicholas, Waldemar **9** Christian, Frederick **11** Christopher
  Dutch: **7** William
  Egyptian: **3** Tut **4** Pepi, Seti **5** Khufu, Menes, Necho **6** Cheops, Ramses **7** Harmhab, Osorkon, Psamtik, Ptolemy **8** Ikhnaton, Thothmes, Thutmose **9** Amenhotep, Sesostris **11** Tutankhamen
  English: **4** John **5** Henry, James **6** Alfred, Canute, Edmund, Edward, Egbert, George, Harold **7** Charles, Richard, Stephen, William **8** Ethelred **9** Athelstan, Ethelbald, Ethelbert
  French: **3** Odo, roi **4** John **5** Henry, Louis, Pepin, Raoul **6** Philip, Robert, Rudolf **7** Charles, Francis, Lothair **9** Hugh Capet **11** Charlemagne
  German: **4** Karl **5** Louis **6** Lothar, Ludwig **7** Charles, Lothair
  Greek (modern): **4** Paul **6** George **9** Alexander **11** Constantine
  Hawaiian: **10** Kamehameha
  Hungarian: **6** Attila
  Indian: **4** raja **5** rajah
  Irish: **9** Brain Boru
  Italian: **7** Humbert
  Jordanian: **5** Talal **7** Hussein **8** Abdullah
  Judah: (see at **Judah**)
  Judean: **5** Herod
  Lydian: **5** Gyges **7** Croesus **8** Alyattes
  Norwegian: **4** Eric, Erik, Inge, Olaf **5** Sweyn **6** Haakon, Harald, Harold, Magnus, Sigurd, Sverre

  Ostrogothic: **9** Theodoric
  Persian: **5** Cyrus **6** Darius, Xerxes
  Portuguese: **4** John **5** Henry, Louis, Peter **6** Carlos, Edward, Manuel, Sancho **7** Alfonso **9** Ferdinand, Sebastian
  Prussian: **7** Wilhelm, William **9** Frederick, Friedrich
  relating to: **5** regal, royal
  Saudi Arabian: **4** Saud **6** Faisal **9** Abdul-Aziz
  Scottish: **4** John **5** David, Edgar, James **6** Duncan **7** Macbeth, Malcolm, William **9** Alexander, Donalbane **10** David Bruce **11** Robert Bruce
  Spanish: **3** rey **5** Louis **6** Philip **7** Alfonso, Amadeus, Charles **9** Ferdinand **10** Juan Carlos
  Spartan: **8** Leonidas
  Swedish: **4** Eric, John **5** Oscar **6** Birger, Gustav, Haakon, Magnus **7** Charles **8** Gustavus, Waldemar **9** Frederick, Sigismund, Sten Sture
  Visigothic: **6** Alaric

King Arthur
  birthplace: **8** Tintagel
  chronicler: **8** Geoffrey
  court site: **7** Camelot **8** Caerleon
  deathplace: **6** Camlan
  father: **5** Uther
  father-in-law: **9** Laodogant, Leodegran **11** Leodegrance
  foster father: **5** Ector
  jester: **7** Dagonet
  knight: **3** Kay **4** Bors **5** Balan, Balin **6** Gareth, Gawain, Modred **7** Galahad, Geraint, Lamerok, Mordred, Tristan **8** Bedivere, Lancelot, Parsifal, Percival, Tristram **9** Percivale
  lance: **3** Ron
  last abode: **6** Avalon
  last name: **9** Pendragon
  magician: **6** Merlin
  mother: **6** Ygerne **7** Igraine
  nephew: **6** Gareth, Modred **7** Mordred
  queen: **9** Guinevere
  shield: **7** Pridwin
  sister: **7** Morgain **11** Morgan le Fay
  slayer: **6** Modred **7** Mordred
  son: **6** Modred **7** Mordred
  steward: **3** Kay
  sword: **9** Excalibur
  victim: **6** Modred **7** Mordred
  wife: **9** Guinevere

king crab
  7 limulus

kingdom
  5 realm **6** domain, empire **7** demesne

kingfish
  4 cero **7** croaker, whiting **8** mulloway

kingfisher
  4 bird **6** alcedo, dacelo **7** halcyon **10** kookaburra

kingly
  5 regal, royal **6** lordly, regnal **8** imperial, majestic, powerful, puissant **9** imperious, masterful, monarchal, sovereign **10** monarchial **11** monarchical

King Philip
  9 Metacomet

Kingsley play
  7 Dead End **10** Men in White

Kingu
  consort: **6** Tiamat
  slayer: **6** Marduk

kink
  4 bend, curl, turn, whim **5** cramp, crick, quirk, snarl, twist **6** buckle, tangle **12** imperfection

kinky
  3 odd **5** outré, ultra, weird **6** farout **7** bizarre, crooked, deviant, strange, twisted **10** outlandish

kiosk
  5 booth **8** pavilion **9** newsstand **11** summerhouse

kip
  3 bed **4** hide, pelt, skin **5** sleep

Kipling, Rudyard
  trio: **3** rag **4** bone **10** hank of hair
  work: **3** Kim, **6** L'Envoi **8** Gunga Din, Mandalay **10** Fuzzy Wuzzy **11** Recessional **13** Soldiers Three, The Jungle Book

kirsch
  6 brandy

kirtle
  4 coat, gown **5** dress, tunic

Kish
  father: **3** Ner **4** Abdi **5** Abiel, Jeiel **6** Jehiel
  son: **4** Saul

kismet
  3 lot **4** doom, fate **5** moira, weird **7** destiny, portion **12** circumstance

kiss
  4 buss, peck, skim **5** brush, graze, shave, smack **6** glance, smooch **8** osculate

kisser
  4 face **5** mouth

Kiss sculptor
5 Rodin (Auguste)

kit
3 bag, box, set 6 outfit 7 package
9 container 10 collection

kitchen
6 galley 7 cuisine 8 scullery
appliance: (see at **appliance**)
boss: 4 chef; (see also **cooking**)

kite
4 bird, hawk, sail 5 scram 6 begone, decamp, get out 7 skiddoo, take off 8 clear out, hightail
9 skedaddle

kith
7 friends, kindred 9 neighbors

kittenish
3 coy 6 elvish, frisky, impish 7 coltish, larkish, playful, roguish 8 prankish 10 frolicsome 11 mischievous

kitty
3 cat, pot 4 pool 6 feline, stakes
7 jackpot

kiwi
4 bird 5 fruit 7 apteryx

kleptomaniac
5 thief 10 shoplifter

klutz
3 oaf 4 gawk, lout, lump 5 looby
6 lubber, lummox 7 lobster, palooka 9 schlemiel

knack
3 set 4 bent, gift, hang, head, nose, turn 5 skill, swing, trick 6 genius, talent 7 ability, aptness, command, know-how, mastery 8 facility
9 dexterity, expertise, expertism
10 expertness, mastership

knapsack
3 bag 4 case, pack 8 backpack, packsack, rucksack 9 haversack

knave
4 heel, jack 5 rogue, scamp 6 rascal, varlet 7 lowlife, villain 8 coistrel 9 miscreant, scoundrel
10 blackguard

knavery
5 fraud 8 mischief, trickery, villainy
9 rascality

knavish
5 lying 6 shifty 7 roguish 8 unhonest 9 deceitful, dishonest 10 mendacious, untruthful

knee
4 genu 5 joint
armor: 6 poleyn

bend: 5 kneel 9 genuflect
bone: 7 patella

kneeler
5 stool 7 cushion 8 prie-dieu

knell
4 bong, peal, ring, toll 5 chime
6 summon 7 warning

knickknack
3 toy 4 dido 5 curio, virtu 6 bauble, gadget, gewgaw, trifle 7 biblelot, novelty, trinket, whatnot 8 gimcrack, souvenir 9 bric-a-brac, objet d'art 11 rattletraps

knife
3 cut, ulu 4 bolo, shiv, stab
5 blade, bowie, corer, gouge, panga, slice, sword 6 barong, colter, coutel, cutter, dagger, kuttar, parang, sickle 7 cleaver, couteau, machete, whittle 8 yataghan
case: 6 sheath
maker: 6 cutler 7 grinder
surgical: 6 catlin 7 catling, scalpel
8 bistoury

knifelike
5 acute, sharp 8 piercing, shooting, stabbing

knight
3 dub, sir 5 eques 6 ritter 8 cavalier, chessman, horseman 9 caballero, chevalier
code: 8 chivalry
competition: 7 listing, tilting 8 jousting 10 tournament
flag: 6 pennon 8 gonfalon, gonfanon
legendary: 8 douzeper
servant: 4 page 5 valet 6 squire
title: 3 sir
wife: 4 lady

knighthood
8 chivalry

knightly
5 brave, noble 7 gallant
10 chivalrous

Knight of the Round Table
see **King Arthur**

Knight of the Rueful Countenance
10 Don Quixote

knit
4 bind, heal, join, mend, purl
5 plait, unite, weave 6 cement, stitch 7 conjoin, crochet, wrinkle
8 contract 10 intertwine

knitting
9 handiwork

material: 4 yarn
stitch: 3 rib 4 purl 6 garter
11 stockinette
tool: 6 needle

knob
3 bun, bur, nub 4 bump, burr, dial, hill, lump, node, peak, umbo
5 bulge, gnarl, knoll, mound 6 button, finial, handle, nubble, pommel
7 hillock 12 protuberance
combining form: 3 tyl 4 tylo 6 condyl
7 condylo

knobkerrie
3 bat 4 club, mace 5 billy
6 cudgel 7 war club 8 bludgeon
9 billy club, truncheon

knock
3 bob, hit, rap, tap 4 blow, bump, lick, skin, swat, tunk, wipe
5 blame, clout, pound, swipe, thump 7 censure, condemn 8 denounce 9 criticize, reprehend, reprobate 10 denunciate

knock down
3 get, win 4 drop, earn, fell, gain, make 5 floor, level
6 ground, lay low 7 acquire, bring in, flatten 8 bowl over

knocker
5 momus 6 carper, critic, Zoilus
7 caviler 9 aristarch 10 criticizer
11 fault-finder

knock off
4 do in, halt, quit, stop, take
5 cease 6 deduct, desist, finish, murder 7 execute, put away, take off, take out 8 discount, draw back, give over, leave off, subtract, surcease, take away 9 liquidate, substract 11 assassinate, discontinue

knockout
2 K.O. 4 kayo 5 dandy, peach
6 beauty, eyeful, looker, lovely
7 stunner 8 jim-dandy 9 humdinger
11 crackerjack

knock over
3 rob 4 down, drop, fell, loot
5 floor, rifle, upset, whelm
6 ground, lay low, topple 7 flatten, overset, plunder, ransack, stick up, tip over 8 bowl down, overcome, overturn 9 bring down, overpower, overthrow, overwhelm, prostrate

knoll
4 hill, knob 5 mound 7 hillock

knot
3 bow, tie, web 4 bond, bump, burr, link, loop, lump, maze, mesh, node, snag, yoke 5 bunch, gnarl, hitch, nexus, skein, snarl 6 jungle, morass, tangle 7 mizmaze 8 ligament, ligature, vinculum 9 labyrinth
in fiber: 3 nep
kind: 4 bend, loop, slip 5 hitch, honda 6 granny, splice, square 7 bowline

knotty
4 hard 5 rough, tough 6 daedal, rugged, sticky, uphill 7 complex, gordian, twisted 8 involved, terrible 9 Byzantine, difficult, effortful, elaborate, intricate 10 formidable 11 complicated 12 labyrinthine

knout
4 flog, lash, whip

know
3 see, wot 4 feel 5 grasp, savor, sever, taste 6 fathom, intuit, suffer 7 cognize, discern, realize, sustain, undergo 8 separate 9 apprehend, extricate, recognize 10 apperceive, appreciate, comprehend, difference, discrepate, experience, severalize, understand
Scottish: 3 ken

knowable
5 lucid 8 luminous 9 graspable 10 cognizable, fathomable 11 cognoscible 12 intelligible 13 apprehensible

know-how
3 art 5 craft, knack, skill 7 ability, command, cunning, mastery 9 dexterity, expertise, expertism 10 adroitness, expertness, mastership

knowing
3 hep, hip 4 gash, sage, wise 5 alive, awake, aware, blasé, canny, quick, sharp, slick, smart 6 brainy, bright, clever, sophic 7 gnostic, witting, worldly 8 mondaine, sensible, sentient 9 brilliant, cognizant, conscious, insighted, observant, sagacious, world-wise 10 conversant, discerning, insightful, perceptive 11 intelligent, quick-witted, ready-witted, sharp-witted, worldly-wise 12 apprehensive, disenchanted, disentranced, nimble-witted, sophisticate 13 disillusioned, sophisticated
combining form: 7 gnostic 9 gnostical

know-it-all
6 smarty 7 wise guy 8 wiseacre, wisehead 10 smart aleck 11 smarty-pants, wisecracker, wisenheimer

knowledge
3 ken 4 data, lore, news 5 facts 6 wisdom 7 science 8 evidence, learning 9 cognition, education, erudition 10 cognizance 11 information, scholarship 12 intelligence 13 enlightenment
combining form: 5 gnosy, sophy 6 gnosia, gnosis
from meditation: 5 jnana
lack of: 9 ignorance
mystical: 6 gnosis
suffix: 3 ics
systematized: 7 science
universal: 8 pansophy 9 pantology

knowledgeable
4 sage, wise 5 sharp, smart 6 brainy, bright, clever, sophic 7 gnostic, knowing 9 brilliant, insighted, sagacious 10 discerning, insightful, perceptive 11 intelligent, quick-witted, ready-witted

know-nothing
4 dolt, dope, rude 5 dummy, dunce, idiot 6 dimwit 7 lackwit, pinhead, wantwit 8 ignorant, untaught 9 benighted, ignoramus, untutored 10 illiterate, uneducated, unlettered 11 empty-headed

knuckle
5 joint
combining form: 6 condyl 7 condylo

knucklehead
5 dunce 8 clodpate, numskull 10 thickskull

knuckle under
3 bow 4 cave 5 defer, yield 6 submit 7 succumb 10 capitulate

knurl
4 bead, knob, knot 5 ridge

K.O.
4 kayo 8 knockout

koan
7 paradox

kobold
5 gnome 6 goblin, spirit, sprite

Kohath
father: 4 Levi
sister: 8 Jochebed
son: 5 Izhar

Kohinoor
7 diamond

kohlrabi
6 turnip 7 cabbage

kokoon
3 gnu

kola
3 nut 7 extract

Kolaiah's son
4 Ahab

komatik
4 sled 6 sledge

kook
3 nut 5 crank 6 cuckoo 7 lunatic 8 crackpot 9 ding-a-ling, harebrain, screwball 10 crackbrain

kopeck
4 coin
one hundred: 5 ruble

Korah
father: 4 Esau 7 Eliphaz
mother: 10 Oholibamah

Koran
chapter: 4 sura
revealer of: 7 Gabriel
scholar: 5 ulama, ulema

Korea
see **North Korea; South Korea**

Korean
dynasty: 2 Yi
national dish: 6 kimchi

kosher
3 fit 4 pure 5 clean 6 proper 7 genuine 10 legitimate

Koussevitzky
5 Serge 6 Sergei 9 conductor

kowtow
4 fawn 5 cower, toady 6 cringe, grovel 7 honey up, truckle 8 bootlick 11 apple-polish

kraal
3 hut, pen 6 corral 8 manyatta 9 enclosure

krater
6 vessel
ovoid: 6 kelebe

Kriemhild
brother: 7 Gunther
husband: 5 Etzel 6 Attila 9 Siegfried
slayer: 10 Hildebrand
victim: 5 Hagen

kris
6 dagger

Krishna
avatar of: 6 Vishnu
brother: 8 Balarama
father: 8 Vasudeva

mother: 6 Devaki
uncle: 5 Kansa
victim: 5 Kansa

Krupp works site
5 Essen

krypton
symbol: 2 Kr

kudize
4 hail 6 praise 7 acclaim, applaud, commend 9 recommend 10 compliment

kudo
7 bouquet, orchids 10 compliment

kudos
4 bays 5 award, badge, glory, honor 6 praise, renown 7 laurels 8 accolade, eminence, prestige 10 decoration, prominence, prominency 11 distinction

kudu
8 antelope

kukri
5 sword

kumquat
5 fruit
kin: 6 orange

kusu
5 mouse

kuttar
6 dagger

kvass
4 beer

kylin
7 unicorn

kylix
3 cup 7 chalice

kyphosis
8 humpback 9 hunchback

Laadah
father: 6 Shelah
grandfather: 5 Judah

laager
4 camp, tent 6 encamp 7 bivouac

Laban
daughter: 4 Leah 6 Rachel
father: 7 Bethuel
grandfather: 5 Nahor
sister: 7 Rebekah

label
3 tag 4 band, mark 6 marker, ticket 8 classify
adhesive: 7 sticker

labium
3 lip

labor
3 tug 4 moil, task, toil, work 5 drive, grind 6 strain, strive 7 slavery, travail 8 bullwork, drudgery, endeavor, slogging, struggle 10 birth pangs, childbirth, donkeywork 12 childbearing
group: 3 AFL, CIO 5 ILGWU, union
leader: 5 Hoffa (Jimmy), Lewis (John L.), Meany (George) 6 Chavez (Cesar) 7 Gompers (Samuel), Reuther (Walter) 8 Randolph (Asa Philip)

laboratory
device: 4 etna 5 flask 6 beaker, mortar, pestle, retort 7 pipette 8 crucible, test tube 12 Bunsen burner

laborer
3 man 4 hand, peon 5 hunky, navvy 6 bohunk, toiler, worker 7 workman 8 workhand 9 operative 10 roustabout, workingman
Mexican: 7 bracero
Oriental: 5 cooly 6 coolie

laborious
4 hard 5 heavy 6 uphill 7 arduous, labored, onerous, operose 8 toilsome 9 difficult, effortful, strenuous 10 burdensome

La Brea
4 pits 7 tar pits
fossil: 10 sabertooth

labyrinth
3 web 4 knot, maze, mesh 5 skein, snarl 6 jungle, morass, tangle 7 mizmaze
builder: 8 Daedalus
monster: 8 Minotaur

labyrinthine
6 daedal, knotty 7 complex, gordian 8 involved, tortuous 9 Byzantine, elaborate, intricate 11 complicated

lace
3 net, tat, tie 4 beat, cord, lash, trim 5 adorn, braid, frill, liven, plait, twine 6 defeat, fabric, fasten, ribbon, string, thrash, thread 7 entwine, tatting 8 decorate, openwork 9 embroider 10 embroidery, intertwine, shoestring 11 needlepoint
edge: 5 picot
ground: 6 réseau
into: 5 abuse 6 attack 7 condemn
kind: 6 bobbin 7 Alençon, guipure, Maltese, Mechlin 8 Argentan, Brussels, Venetian 9 Chantilly 10 colberteen, colbertine 11 needlepoint 12 Valenciennes
make: 3 tat
pattern: 5 toilé

Lacedaemon
6 Sparta

lacerate
3 cut, rip 4 rend, tear 5 wound 6 mangle, pierce

lachrymose
3 sad 5 teary, weepy 7 tearful, weeping 8 mournful

lack
4 need, want 6 dearth, defect 7 absence, default, deficit, failure, require 8 shortage, underage 9 privation 10 deficiency, inadequacy, scantiness

lackadaisical
4 idle, lazy, limp 7 die-away, languid, passive 8 fainéant, indolent, listless, romantic, slothful 9 enervated, incurious 10 languorous, spiritless

lacking
3 shy 4 away, gone, sans 5 minus, short 6 absent, devoid 7 missing, omitted, wanting, without 8 awanting 9 defective, deficient 10 inadequate, incomplete, uncomplete 12 insufficient

lackluster
3 dim, mat 4 dead, drab, dull, flat 5 blind, muted, prosy, rusty 6 leaden 7 prosaic 8 lifeless 9 colorless, tarnished

Laconian
7 Spartan
king: 5 Lelex, Myles

laconic
4 curt 5 brief, pithy, short, terse 7 brusque, concise 8 succinct 11 compendiary, compendious 12 breviloquent

lacquer
5 gloss 6 finish 7 shellac, varnish

lacquered metalware
4 tole

lacrosse
team: 3 ten

lactate
4 salt 5 ester 7 secrete

lacteal
5 milky

lacuna
3 gap 5 break 6 breach, hiatus 7 interim 8 interval 12 interruption

lad
3 boy, son, tad 5 youth 6 shaver 9 shaveling, stripling
Scottish: 6 callan 7 callant

ladder
3 run 5 scale 6 series
adjunct: 4 rung 6 rundle

ladderlike
6 scalar 11 scalariform

lade
3 dip, tax 4 bail, clog, load, pack,
ship, stow 5 ladle, scoop, weigh
6 burden, charge, cumber, saddle,
weight 8 encumber

lading
4 haul, load 5 cargo 6 burden
7 freight, payload

ladle
3 dip 4 bail, lade 5 scoop, spoon
6 dipper

Ladon
6 dragon
father: 7 Phorcus, Phorcys
mother: 4 Ceto
slayer: 8 Heracles, Hercules

lady
French: 4 dame
Italian: 5 donna 7 signora
Muslim: 5 begum
Spanish: 4 doña 6 senora

lady ___
4 crab, fern, luck, palm 5 chair, tulip 6 beetle, friend, killer 7 cracker
9 bountiful

ladybird
6 beetle 7 pintail

ladybug
6 beetle
Australian: 7 vedalia

Lady Chatterley's Lover
author: 8 Lawrence (David Herbert)
character: 6 Connie 7 Mellors
9 Constance

Lady of the Lake, The
5 Ellen, Nimue 6 Vivien
author: 5 Scott (Walter)

Lady Windermere's Fan
author: 5 Wilde (Oscar)

Laertes
father: 8 Acrisius, Polonius
sister: 7 Ophelia
son: 7 Ulysses 8 Odysseus
wife: 8 Anticlea

La Fontaine's forte
5 fable

lag
4 drag, last, poke, slow, stay, tire
5 dally, delay, final, tarry, trail
6 dawdle, deport, latest, latter, loiter, put off, retard 7 closing,

slacken 8 eventual, hindmost, terminal, ultimate 10 concluding

lager
4 beer

laggard
4 slow 6 loafer, remiss 7 dawdler,
unhasty 8 comatose, dawdling,
delaying, dilatory, lingerer, loiterer,
slowpoke, sluggish 9 apathetic, impassive, lazybones, leisurely, lethargic, loitering, slow coach, straggler, unhurried 10 deliberate,
phlegmatic

La Gioconda
composer: 10 Ponchielli (Amilcare)
painter: 7 da Vinci (Leonardo)

lagniappe
3 tip 4 perk 7 cumshaw, largess,
palm oil 8 gratuity 9 pourboire
10 perquisite

lagomorph
4 hare, pika 6 rabbit

lagoon
4 pond, pool 5 liman, sound
7 channel

___ La Guardia
8 Fiorello

Lahmi
brother: 7 Goliath
slayer: 7 Elhanan

laic
6 layman

lair
3 den 4 cave 5 couch, haunt,
lodge 6 burrow 7 hideout, retreat
8 hideaway

Laius
father: 8 Labdacus
slayer, son: 7 Oedipus
wife: 7 Jocasta

lake
3 sea 4 loch, mere, pond, pool
5 lough 6 lagoon
Adriatic: 6 Varano
Alberta: 6 Louise
Algeria: 5 Hodna
Alps: 6 Annecy
Arizona-Nevada: 4 Mead
Armenia: 5 Sevan 6 Gokcha,
Sevang 9 Lychnitis
Aswan's: 6 Nasser
Australia: 4 Eyre 5 Carey, Cowan,
Frome, Wells 6 Barlee 7 Amadeus,
Everard, Torrens 8 Gairdner
Austria: 5 Atter, Traun 6 Kammer
8 Attersee 9 Kammersee
Bolivia: 5 Poopo
Botswana: 5 Ngami
British Columbia: 4 Pitt 5 Atlin

California: 4 Mono, Tule 5 Clear,
Eagle, Honey
Cambodia: 8 Tonle Sap
Canada: 4 Dyke 8 Manitoba
central Africa: 4 Kivu 5 Mweru
6 Albert
Central America: 5 Guija
central Europe: 5 Leman 6 Geneva,
Lugano 7 Ceresio 8 Bodensee
9 Constance
central North America: 5 Rainy
Chile: 4 Laja 5 Ranco
China: 6 Poyang 8 Dongting
Colorado: 5 Grand
combining form: 4 limn 5 limni,
limno 6 limnia (plural) 7 limnion
Connecticut: 6 Bantam 7 Gardner
8 Highland 10 Candlewood,
Pocotopaug
Denmark: 5 Esrum
east Africa: 6 Rudolf 7 Turkana
east Asia: 6 Khanka 7 Xingkai
8 Hsingkai
east central Africa: 8 Victoria
10 Tanganyika
east China: 3 Tai 5 Dalai, Hulun
Ethiopia: 4 Tana, Zwai 5 Abaya,
Shala, Shamo, Tsana 8 Stefanie
9 Chew Bahir
Finland: 5 Inari
Florida: 5 Worth 10 Okeechobee
Germany: 5 Ammer, Chiem 8 Am-
mersee, Chiemsee
Ghana: 5 Volta
Great: 4 Erie 5 Huron 7 Ontario
8 Michigan, Superior
Greece: 5 Bolbe, Volvi
Guatemala: 7 Atitlan
Honduras: 5 Yojoa
Honshu: 3 Omi 4 Biwa, Suwa, Yodo
Hungary: 7 Balaton 10 Plattensee
Idaho: 4 Waha 5 Grays 6 Priest
11 Coeur d'Alene, Pend Oreille
India: 3 Dal 5 Wular 6 Chilka
Indonesia: 4 Poso, Toba 5 Ranau
Iowa: 5 Storm
Iran: 5 Niriz, Shahi, Urmia 8 Mati-
anus, Urumiyeh 9 Bakhtigan
Ireland: 3 Gur, Ree 4 Conn, Derg,
Mask 5 Allen, Arrow, Leane
Israel: 12 Bahr Tabariya, Sea of
Galilee
Israel-Jordan: 7 Dead Sea
Italy: 4 Como, Iseo, Nemi 5 Garda
6 Albano 7 Bolsena, Perugia
8 Maggiore 9 Trasimene
Japan: 4 Imba 8 Imbanuma
Kazakhstan: 7 Balqash 8 Balkhash
largest inland: 10 Caspian Sea
Louisiana: 4 Soda 5 Black, White
9 Catahoula 13 Pontchartrain
Maine: 3 Big 6 Sebago 9 Moose-
head

Mali: **4** Debo
Manitoba: **4** Gods **5** Cedar, Moose
8 Winnipeg
Mexico: **7** Chapala
Michigan: **4** Burt
Minnesota: **3** Red **4** Cass, Gull,
Swan **5** Leech **6** Itasca **9** Mille
Lacs **10** Minnetonka, of the Woods
11 Lac qui Parle
Minnesota-Wisconsin: **5** Pepin
Mongolian: **3** Har **5** Har Us, Khara
8 Khara Usu
Montana: **8** Medicine
mountain: **4** tarn
Myanmar: **4** Inle
Nevada: **4** Ruby **7** Pyramid
New Hampshire: **4** Echo **5** Squam
7 Sunapee **13** Winnipesaukee
New Jersey: **5** Union
New York: **4** Long **5** Chazy, Keuka
6 Cayuga, George, Oneida, Ot-
sego, Owasco, Placid, Seneca
7 Crooked, Saranac **8** Onondaga,
Saratoga **10** Chautauqua **11** Can-
andaigua, Skaneateles
New Zealand: **4** Ohau **5** Hawea,
Taupo **6** Pukaki, Wanaka
8 Wakatipu
Nicaragua: **7** Managua
North Africa: **4** Chad
North America: **9** Champlain
Northern Ireland: **5** Neagh
Northwest Territories: **4** Gras
5 Baker, Garry, Pelly **9** Great Bear
10 Great Slave
Norway: **5** Mjosa
Nova Scotia: **7** Bras d'Or
Ontario: **4** Rice, Seul **5** Trout
Oregon: **5** Abert **6** Crater **7** Mal-
heur, Wallowa
Paraguay: **4** Ypoa
Peru: **5** Junin **13** Chinchaycocha
Philippines: **4** Bato, Taal **5** Lanao
6 Bombon
Poland: **5** Mamry, Mauer
Quebec: **5** Minto, Payne
Russia: **3** Seg **5** Chany, Ilmen, La-
cha, Onega **6** Ladoga **7** Rybinsk
10 Eltonskoye **11** Ladozhskoye
saline: **5** chott, shott
Saskatchewan: **4** Cree **5** Ronge
Scotland: **3** Ard, Awe **4** Doon, Earn,
Ness, Oich, Shin, Sloy **5** Leven, Lo-
chy, Maree, Morar, Shiel
6 Lomond
Siberia: **6** Baikal, Baykal
South Africa: **4** Kosi
South America: **5** Merin, Mirim
8 Titicaca
South Carolina: **11** Wateree Pond
South Dakota: **5** Andes
southeast Africa: **5** Nyasa **6** Nyassa
southern United States: **5** Caddo

southwest Europe: **5** Ohrid
7 Okhrida
Sudan: **2** No
Sweden: **5** Asnen, Roxen **6** Siljan,
Vetter **7** Malaren, Vattern
Switzerland: **3** Zug **4** Biel, Joux
5 Zuger **6** Bieler, Bienne, Brienz,
Sarnen, Sarner, Zurich **7** Lucerne,
Lungern **8** Brienzer, Zuricher
9 Neuchatel, Zurichsee
Tadzhikistan: **7** Karakul
Tanzania: **5** Rukwa
Tibet: **4** Na-mu **6** Nam Tso, Tengri
Turkey: **2** Ak **3** Tuz, Van **4** Bafa,
Nice **5** Iznik, Sugla **6** Nicaea
Uganda: **5** Kyoga
Utah: **6** Powell, Sevier **9** Great Salt
volcanic: **8** Ilopango
Wales: **4** Bala
Washington: **4** Omak **5** Moses
6 Chelan **9** Wenatchee
western China: **4** Ai-pi **6** Ebinur
western United States: **4** Bear
5 Tahoe
Wisconsin: **5** Green **9** Winnebago
Yellowstone National Park: **5** Heart,
Lewis **8** Shoshone
Zaire: **5** Tumba
Zambia: **9** Bangweolo, Bangweulu

lake duck
7 mallard

lake herring
5 cisco

Lake poet
7 Southey (Robert) **9** Coleridge
(Samuel Taylor) **10** Wordsworth
(William)

lakes
central North America: **5** Great
Connecticut: **4** Twin
Egypt: **5** Balah
Maine: **8** Rangeley
New Hampshire: **11** Connecticut
New York: **6** Finger
Saskatchewan: **5** Quill
Twin: **8** Washinee **9** Washining
Wisconsin: **4** Four

Lakmé
aria: **8** Bell Song
composer: **7** Delibes (Leo)

Lakshmi
husband: **6** Vishnu
son: **4** Kama

lalapalooza
5 beaut

lam
3 hit **4** beat, drub, pelt, slip
5 paste, pound **6** batter, escape,
flight, hammer, pummel, thrash,

wallop **7** getaway **8** breakout, escaping **10** escapement

La Mancha's knight
10 Don Quixote

lamb
4 cade, dupe, yean **5** sheep **6** cosset **8** yeanling
leg of: **5** gigot

lambaste
3 pan **4** beat, drub, flay, lick, pelt,
slam, slap, trim, whip **5** paste,
pound, roast, scold, score, slash,
smear **6** assail, attack, berate,
hammer, pummel, scathe, scorch,
thrash, wallop **7** blister, censure,
clobber, reprove, scarify, scourge,
shellac, smother **8** denounce, harangue, lash into, squabash **9** castigate, criticize, excoriate **10** tongue-
lash

lambent
6 bright, lucent **7** beaming, glowing, radiant **8** luminous, lustrous
9 brilliant, effulgent, refulgent
12 incandescent

lamblike
4 meek **5** ovine **6** gentle

lamb of God
8 Agnus Dei

Lamb's pseudonym
4 Elia

lame
3 ill **4** halt, limp, sick, weak **6** feeble, sickly **7** cripple, halting, hip-
shot, limping **8** crippled, disabled
13 incapacitated

lamebrain
3 oaf **4** dope **5** dunce, noddy,
stupe **6** noodle **7** schnook **8** dumbhead **10** dunderhead

Lamech
daughter: **6** Naamah
father: **9** Methusael **10** Methuselah
son: **4** Noah **5** Jabal, Jubal
9 Tubalcain
wife: **4** Adah **6** Zillah

lament
3 cry, rue **4** keen, moan, pine, pity,
sigh, wail, weep **5** dirge, elegy,
mourn **6** bemoan, bewail, grieve,
plaint, regret, repent, repine **7** deplore, despair, elegize **8** jeremiad
9 complaint

lamentable
3 sad **4** dire **6** rueful, woeful
7 doleful, pitiful **8** dolesome, dolorous, grievous, mournful **9** plaintive,
sorrowful **10** afflictive, calamitous,
deplorable, lugubrious, melancholy

11 distressing, regrettable, unfortunate **13** heartbreaking

Lamerok
father: **9** Pellinore
lover: **8** Margawse
slayer: **6** Gawain

lamia
3 hag, hex **5** bruja, witch **9** sorceress **10** witchwoman **11** enchantress

Lamia
country: **5** Libya
form: **7** serpent
lover: **4** Zeus

lamina
5 blade, flake, layer, plate

lamp
3 arc, eye, orb **4** bulb, davy **5** klieg, light, torch **6** ocular, oculus, peeper, winker **7** lantern **10** candelabra **11** candelabrum
floor: **8** torchère
hanging: **10** chandelier

lampblack
4 soot **6** carbon

Lampetia
father: **6** Apollo, Helios
husband: **9** Asclepius
mother: **6** Neaera
sister: **9** Phaethusa

lampoon
4 mock **5** squib **6** satire **7** pasquil **8** ridicule, satirize **10** pasquinade

lamprey
3 eel

lanai
5 porch **7** terrace, veranda

lanate
5 hairy **6** woolly

lance
3 cut **4** spit **5** blade, spear, spike **6** impale, pierce, skewer, skiver, weapon **7** javelin **8** transfix **11** transpierce

Lancelot, Launcelot
father: **3** Ban
lover: **6** Elaine **9** Guinevere
son: **7** Galahad
victim: **6** Gawain

lancer
Prussian: **4** ulan **5** uhlan

land
3 get, win **4** dirt, gain, have, home, soil **5** acres, annex, catch, earth, light, manor, perch, roost, shore, terra, tract **6** alight, debark, estate, ground, obtain, pick up, quinta, secure, settle **7** acquire,

acreage, country, procure, set down, sit down **8** plottage **9** disembark, touch down **10** terra firma **13** mother country
alluvial: **5** delta
along a river: **5** carse **7** bottoms
area: **7** terrain, terrene
barren: **5** waste **6** desert
combining form: **3** geo **4** chor, gaea **5** choro
cultivated: **4** farm **5** tilth **7** tillage
for grazing: **3** lea, ley **5** range **6** meadow **7** pasture
high: **4** hill, mesa **7** plateau **8** mountain
level: **4** mesa **5** plain **7** plateau
low: **4** vale **6** valley **9** intervale
measure: **3** rod **4** acre **7** centare **8** centiare
open: **5** field, plain
piece: **3** lot **6** estate, parcel
reclaimed: **6** polder
relating to: **8** agrarian
sloping: **6** cuesta
strip: **7** isthmus
wet: **3** bog, fen **4** moor **5** marsh, swamp **6** marish **7** maremma

land east of Eden
3 Nod

landing place of the Ark
6 Ararat

landlord
6 lessor

landmark
5 bound, cairn **9** milestone

Land of Cakes
8 Scotland

Land of Enchantment
9 New Mexico

Land of Lakes
8 Michigan

Land of Lincoln
8 Illinois

Land of Milk and Honey
6 Israel

land of Nod
5 sleep

Land of Opportunity
8 Arkansas

Land of Plenty
6 Goshen

Land of the Midnight Sun
6 Norway

Land of the Rising Sun
5 Japan

landowner
6 squire, yeoman
Anglo-Saxon: **5** thane, thegn

Dutch: **7** patroon
Scottish: **5** laird

landscape
5 scene **7** picture, scenery **8** painting
gardener: **9** topiarist

lane
3 way **4** path, road **5** aisle, alley, byway, track **6** street **7** loaning, pathway **8** footpath **10** passageway

Langobard
see **Lombard**

lang syne
4 past, yore **8** foretime **9** yesterday **10** yesteryear

language
4 cant **5** argot, idiom, lingo, prose, slang **6** jargon, patois, speech, tongue **7** dialect, lexicon, palaver **10** dictionary, vernacular, vocabulary **11** terminology
ambiguous: **6** jargon **8** newspeak **10** double-talk
ancient: **5** Greek, Latin **6** Hebrew **8** Sanskrit
artificial: **2** Ro **3** Ido **7** Volapük **9** Esperanto
classical: **5** Greek, Latin
combining form: **5** gloss, glott **6** glosso, glotto
expert: **8** linguist
informal: **5** lingo, slang
meaningless: **9** gibberish
mixed: **6** pidgin
pretentious: **6** hot air **7** bombast **8** claptrap
regional: **7** dialect
relating to: **10** linguistic
Romance: **6** French **7** Catalan, Italian, Spanish **8** Romanian, Rumanian **10** Portuguese
secret: **4** cant, code **5** argot
structure: **6** syntax **7** grammar
suffix: **3** ese
written: **5** prose

languid
4 limp, slow, weak **5** inert **6** supine, torpid **7** die-away **8** comatose, inactive, listless, slothful, sluggish **9** apathetic, enervated, impassive, lethargic **10** languorous, phlegmatic, spiritless **11** languishing **13** lackadaisical

languishing
4 limp **6** pining **7** die-away, languid, longing **8** fainéant, indolent, listless, weakened, yearning **9** enervated, enfeebled **10** languorous, spiritless **11** debilitated **13** lackadaisical

languor

3 kef, kif 4 coma 5 blues, dumps, ennui, sleep 6 stupor, tedium, torpor 7 fatigue, slumber 8 doldrums, dullness, hebetude, lethargy 9 lassitude, torpidity, weariness 10 depression, exhaustion

languorous

3 lax 4 limp, slow 5 loose, slack 7 die-away, laggard, languid, passive, relaxed 8 dilatory, fainéant, indolent, indulged, listless, pampered, slothful 9 enervated, leisurely 10 spiritless 11 languishing 13 lackadaisical

lank

4 bony, lean 5 gaunt, lanky, spare 6 gangly, skinny 7 angular, scraggy, scrawny 8 gangling, rawboned 10 attenuated, extenuated

lanyard

4 cord, line, rope

Laocoon

city: 4 Troy
killer: 7 serpent

Laodamia

father: 7 Acastus
husband: 11 Protesilaus

Laomedon

daughter: 7 Hesione
father: 4 Ilus
kingdom: 4 Troy
mother: 8 Eurydice
slayer: 8 Heracles, Hercules
son: 5 Priam 8 Tithonus

Laos

capital: 9 Vientiane
monetary unit: 3 kip

lap

3 lip, sip 4 lave, ride, wash 5 bathe, slosh, swash 6 bubble, burble, gurgle 7 overlie, shingle 8 override 9 imbricate

lapidary

6 cutter 7 jeweler 8 engraver, polisher

lapideous

5 stony

lapillus

4 lava 6 cinder

lapin

6 rabbit

Lapiths

foes: 8 centaurs
king: 5 Ixion

lappet

4 flap, fold, moth 5 lapel 6 infula

Lappidoth's wife

7 Deborah

Lapsang

3 tea

lapse

3 err, sin 4 bull, slip, trip, vice 5 boner, crime, error, fluff, slide 6 breach, bungle, foible, recede, return, revert 7 blooper, blunder, decline, descend, failing, frailty, mistake, offense, subside 8 trespass 9 backslide, decadence, recession, violation 10 apostatize, declension, degenerate, devolution, recidivate, regression, retrograde 11 backsliding, deteriorate 12 degeneration 13 deterioration, retrogression, transgression

Laputan

6 absurd 9 visionary

lar

3 god 6 gibbon, spirit

larboard

4 left, port

larcenist

4 prig 5 thief 6 nimmer, robber 7 burglar, filcher, stealer 8 pilferer 9 purloiner

larceny

4 lift 5 pinch, steal, theft 7 looting, robbery 8 burglary, stealage, stealing, thievery, thieving 10 purloining
kind: 5 grand, petty

lard

3 fat 6 fatten, grease 10 shortening

larder

6 pantry

large

3 big, fat 4 bull, huge, vast 5 ample, bulky, grand, great, hefty, husky, jumbo, major 6 goodly 7 extreme, immense, mammoth, massive, outsize, sizable 8 colossal, enormous, gigantic, oversize 9 excessive, extensive, monstrous 10 exorbitant, immoderate, inordinate, large-scale, monumental, prodigious, stupendous, tremendous, voluminous 11 extravagant
combining form: 3 meg 4 macr, mega 5 macro, megal 6 megalo

largess

3 tip 4 boon, gift, perk 5 favor 7 cumshaw, present 8 gratuity 9 lagniappe, pourboire 10 perquisite 11 benevolence

lariat

4 rope 5 lasso, noose, reata, riata
part: 5 honda, hondo
user: 6 cowboy, drover 10 cowpuncher

lark

4 bird, dido 5 antic, caper, prank, shine, trick 6 frolic 7 rollick 8 carousal, escapade 10 shenanigan, tomfoolery 11 monkeyshine

larrup

4 beat, drub, dust, flog, hide, lash, lick, whip 5 mop up, whale 6 lather, stripe, thrash 7 clobber, scourge, shellac 8 lambaste 9 overwhelm 10 flagellate

larva

3 bot 4 grub, worm 5 eruca 6 dobson, maggot 7 atrocha 8 cercaria, hornworm, mealworm 10 case bearer, helgramite 11 caterpillar 12 hellgrammite
amphibian: 7 tadpole
crustacean: 4 zoea
flatworm: 5 redia
free-swimming: 7 planula
mollusk: 7 veliger
moth: 8 leafworm
tapeworm: 6 measle

larynx

8 voice box

lasagna

5 pasta 7 noodles

lascivious

3 hot 4 fast, lewd 5 gross 6 coarse, wanton 7 goatish, lustful, obscene, satyric 8 prurient 9 lecherous, libertine, lickerish, salacious 10 libidinous, licentious, passionate 11 incontinent 12 concupiscent

lash

3 jaw, wag 4 beat, bind, boil, bolt, dash, flay, flog, hide, pour, race, rush, tear, teem, wave, whip 5 baste, chase, fling, scold, shoot, slash, whale 6 charge, drench, lather, scathe, scorch, stripe, switch, thrash, waggle, woggle 7 bawl out, blister, chew out, scarify, scourge, tell off, upbraid 8 lambaste 9 castigate, excoriate 10 flagellate

lassitude

5 blues, dumps, ennui, sleep 6 apathy, stupor, tedium, torpor 7 fatigue, languor, slumber 8 doldrums, dullness, hebetude, lethargy 9 disregard, impotence, tiredness, torpidity, unconcern, weariness 10 depression, exhaustion, torpid-

ness **11** disinterest, insouciance **12** heedlessness, indifference, listlessness

lasso
   see **lariat**

last
   3 end, lag **5** abide, final **6** endure, latest, latter, utmost **7** closing, dernier, extreme, perdure, persist **8** continue, eventual, furthest, hindmost, rearmost, remotest, terminal, ultimate **9** outermost, umpteenth, uttermost **10** bottommost, concluding **11** terminating
   next to: **6** penult **11** penultimate

last extremity
   9 bitter end

lasting
   3 old **6** stable **7** abiding, durable, endless, eternal **8** enduring, lifelong **9** continual, diuturnal, incessant, indelible, perduring, perennial, permanent, unceasing **10** continuing, continuous, perdurable, persisting

Last of the Goths
   8 Roderick

Last of the Mohicans, The
   5 Uncas
   author: **6** Cooper (James Fenimore)
   character: **4** Cora **5** Alice, Magua, Uncas **11** Natty Bumppo **12** Chingachgook

Last of the Saxons
   6 Harold

Last Supper, The
   painter: **7** da Vinci (Leonardo)

Las Vegas district
   5 Strip

latch
   4 bolt **5** catch **6** fasten **8** fastener
   British: **5** sneck

latchet
   4 lace **5** strap, thong

late
   3 new, old **4** cold, dead, once, past **5** tardy **6** asleep, bygone, former, modern, recent, whilom **7** belated, defunct, extinct, onetime, overdue, quondam **8** deceased, departed, lifeless, sometime

Late George Apley, The
   author: **8** Marquand (John P.)

latent
   4 idle **5** inert **6** hidden, unripe **7** abeyant, dormant, lurking **8** immature, inactive **9** concealed, po-

tential, prepatent, quiescent, unmatured
   combining form: **5** crypt, krypt **6** crypto, krypto

later
   4 anon, next, soon **5** after, infra **6** behind **7** by and by, ensuing **8** latterly, tomorrow **9** afterward, posterior **10** afterwhile, subsequent **12** postliminary, subsequently **13** subsequential

lateral
   4 pass, side **8** sideways

laterally
   8 crabwise, sideling, sidelong, sideward, sideways, sidewise

latest
   3 lag **4** last **5** final **6** latter, newest **7** closing **8** eventual, hindmost, rearmost, terminal, ultimate **10** concluding

latex
   5 paint **8** emulsion
   product: **6** balata, chicle, rubber

lath
   4 slat **5** stave, stick, strip **8** forepole

lather
   4 flap, flog, foam, hide, lash, moil, soap, stew, suds, whip **5** froth, spume, storm, yeast **6** bustle, clamor, dither, hassle, hubbub, pother, stripe, thrash, tumult **7** scourge, turmoil, whoopla **8** rowdydow **9** agitation, commotion, confusion

Latin
   5 Roman **7** Italian **8** Hispanic
   after: **4** post
   always: **6** semper
   and: **2** et
   before: **4** ante, prae
   book: **5** liber
   boy: **4** puer
   bronze: **3** aes
   brother: **6** frater
   but: **3** sed
   day: **4** dies
   dog: **5** canis
   foot: **3** pes
   force: **3** vis
   friend: **6** amicus
   god: **4** deus
   goddess: **3** dea
   grammarian: **7** Donatus
   hand: **5** manus
   is: **3** est
   law: **3** ius, jus, lex
   light: **3** lux
   peace: **3** pax

   pronoun: **2** tu **3** ego, nos, vos
   road: **3** via **4** iter
   see: **4** vide
   that is: **5** id est
   thing: **3** res
   this: **3** hic, hoc **4** haec
   thus: **3** sic
   war: **6** bellum
   wife: **4** uxor
   woman: **6** femina
   year: **5** annus

Latin-American
   country: **4** Cuba, Peru **5** Chile **6** Belize, Brazil, Guyana, Mexico, Panama **7** Bolivia, Ecuador, Uruguay **8** Colombia, Honduras, Paraguay **9** Argentina, Costa Rica, Guatemala, Nicaragua **10** El Salvador
   revolutionary: **6** Castro (Fidel) **7** Bolivar (Simon), Guevara (Ché)

Latinus
   daughter: **7** Lavinia
   father: **6** Faunus **8** Odysseus
   son-in-law: **6** Aeneas
   wife: **5** Amata

latitude
   4 play, room **5** scope, space **6** leeway, margin **7** freedom **9** elbowroom

latke
   7 pancake **11** griddle cake

Latona
   4 Leto
   daughter: **5** Diana **7** Artemis
   father: **5** Coeus
   mother: **6** Phoebe
   son: **6** Apollo

Latter-day Saint
   6 Mormon

lattice
   4 grid **5** grate **7** grating, trellis

Latvia
   capital: **4** Riga

Latvian
   4 Lett
   coin: **7** santims
   measure: **4** stof **5** faden, kanne, stoff, stoof, vedro **6** kulmet, sagene, versta **8** krouchka

laud
   4 hymn **5** adore, bless, cry up, extol **6** admire, praise, revere **7** flatter, glorify, magnify, worship **8** eulogize, venerate **9** celebrate, reverence **10** panegyrize

laudable
   6 worthy **9** admirable, deserving, estimable, meritable, praisable

11 commendable, meritorious, thankworthy **12** praiseworthy

laugh
 3 yuk **4** beam, crow, grin, ha-ha, roar **5** smile, smirk, snort, tehee, whoop **6** cackle, giggle, guffaw, hee-haw, simper, titter **7** chortle, chuckle, snicker, sniggle **10** cachinnate

laughable
 4 rich **5** comic, droll, funny, witty **6** jocose **7** amusing, comical, jocular, mocking, risible **8** derisive, derisory, farcical, gelastic, humorous **9** diverting, facetious, ludicrous **10** ridiculous **12** entertaining

laughing
 5 riant **8** derisive

laughingstock
 4 butt, fool, jest, joke, mark, mock **5** sport **6** jestee, target **7** mockery **8** derision **9** pilgarlic

launch
 4 cast, fire, hurl, open, toss **5** begin, fling, heave, pitch, set up, sling, start, throw **6** get off **7** jump off, kick off, usher in **8** commence, embark on, initiate **9** institute, introduce, originate **10** inaugurate

launching
 7 lift-off, takeoff **8** blast-off

launder
 4 wash **5** clean **7** cleanse

Laura's lover
 8 Petrarch

laurels
 4 bays **5** award, badge, honor, kudos **8** accolade **10** decoration **11** distinction

laurel tree nymph
 6 Daphne

lava
 2 aa **4** rock, slag **5** magma **6** latite, scoria **8** andesite, trachyte
 cooled: **8** pahoehoe
 fragment: **8** lapillus
 stream: **4** flow **6** coulee

lavalava
 5 cloth, skirt

lavaliere
 7 pendant **8** necklace

lavatory
 2 WC **3** loo **4** head, john **5** basin, privy **6** johnny, toilet **7** latrine **8** bathroom, washroom **11** convenience, water closet

lave
 3 lap, lip **4** pour, wash **5** bathe

Lavinia
 father: **7** Latinus
 husband: **7** Aeneas
 mother: **5** Amata

Lavinium's founder
 6 Aeneas

lavish
 4 free, lush **5** grand, spend, waste **7** opulent, profuse, riotous **8** gorgeous, prodigal, splendid, squander **9** exuberant, luxuriant, luxurious, profusive, sumptuous

law
 3 act, lex **4** bill, code, doom, rule **5** axiom, canon, edict, nomos, Torah **6** assize, custom, decree, equity **7** command, dictate, justice, mandate, precept, statute, theorem **8** decretum, exigency **9** enactment, institute, necessity, ordinance, prescript, principle **10** principium, regulation **11** commandment, fundamental **12** constitution, prescription
 body of: **4** code **7** pandect **12** constitution
 combining form: **4** nomy
 degree: **3** LLB, LLD
 expert: **5** judge **6** jurist **7** justice
 practitioner: **6** lawyer **7** counsel **8** attorney
 relating to: **5** jural, legal **7** canonic **8** forensic, juristic **9** judiciary
 violation of: **3** sin **4** tort **5** crime, malum **6** felony

lawbreaker
 5 felon **6** sinner **8** criminal, offender, scofflaw, violator **10** malefactor

lawcourt
 3 bar **8** tribunal

lawful
 3 due **5** legal, licit **7** condign **8** bona fide, innocent, rightful **9** allowable **10** legitimate

lawgiver
 5 Moses, solon **10** legislator

lawlessness
 4 riot **5** chaos **6** strife **7** anarchy, discord **8** conflict, variance **9** mobocracy **10** ochlocracy

lawman
 7 marshal, officer, sheriff **9** policeman

Law of Moses
 5 Torah **10** Pentateuch

Lawrence novel
 8 Kangaroo **9** Aaron's Rod **10** The Rainbow **11** Women in Love **13** Sons and Lovers

Lawrence of ___
 6 Arabia

lawrencium
 symbol: **2** Lr

lawsuit
 4 case **5** cause **6** action **10** litigation

lawyer
 6 jurist, legist **7** counsel, pleader **8** advocate, attorney **9** barrister, counselor, solicitor **10** mouthpiece **12** jurisconsult, jurisprudent **13** attorney-at-law
 dishonest: **7** shyster **11** pettifogger
 fictional: **10** Perry Mason
 French: **6** avocat
 Indian: **5** vakil **6** vakeel

lawyers' patron saint
 4 Ives

lax
 4 ease, easy, open **5** loose, slack **6** loosen, remiss **7** ease off, lenient, slacken **8** careless, derelict **9** forgetful, negligent, oblivious, unmindful, untighten **10** behindhand, delinquent, neglectful, regardless **12** disregardful

lay
 3 aim, air, bet, fix, put, set **4** aria, cast, cite, even, game, hymn, lied, play, song, tune, turn **5** ditty, flush, level, offer, place, plane, point, put on, refer, stake, stick, train, wager **6** adduce, allege, assign, ballad, charge, credit, direct, expose, gamble, impute, melody, settle, smooth, spread, strain, warble, zero in **7** address, advance, ascribe, descant, flatten, incline, measure, melisma, melodia, present, profane, secular, subject, uncover **8** accredit, diapason, smoothen, temporal, unsacred **9** attribute, establish

lay aside
 4 cast, save, shed **5** chuck, ditch, put by, scrap **6** reject, slough **7** discard, neglect **8** jettison, salt away **9** throw away

lay by
 4 save **5** amass, hoard, store **7** deposit **8** salt away

lay down
 3 set **4** cede **5** leave, waive, yield **6** assign, decree, define, give up, impose, ordain, resign **7** abandon,

dictate **8** hand over **9** establish, prescribe, surrender **10** relinquish

lay eggs
5 spawn **8** oviposit

layer
3 hen, ply **4** coat, film, seam, tier **5** paver, sheet **6** folium, lamina, veneer **7** coating, provine, stratum **8** laminate, membrane, sandwich, stratify
combining form: **5** cline, lamin, ptych **6** lamell, lamino, ptycho, strati **7** lamelli
inner: **6** lining
of odds: **6** bookie **9** bookmaker
of skin: **6** dermis **9** epidermis
outer: **4** skin **6** veneer

lay for
6 ambush, waylay **8** surprise

lay in
see **lay by**

lay low
4 down, fell, hide, kill, slay **5** floor, level, scrag **6** cut off, finish, ground **7** destroy, flatten, mow down, put away, take off **8** bowl down, bowl over, dispatch **9** knock down, knock over, throw down

layman
4 laic **7** secular

lay off
4 halt, quit, stop **5** avoid, cease **7** dismiss, measure **9** disemploy **11** discontinue

lay open
4 bare, show **6** expose, reveal **7** uncover

lay out
3 pay **4** give, plan **5** spend **6** design, expend, map out, outlay, set out **7** arrange, fork out **8** disburse, shell out

lay waste
4 ruin **6** ravage **7** destroy **8** desolate **9** devastate

lazar
5 leper

Lazarus' sister
4 Mary **6** Martha

laze
3 bum **4** idle, lazy, loaf, loll **5** sloth **6** dawdle, loiter, lounge, slouch **7** goof off **8** idleness, laziness, malinger **9** goldbrick, indolence

laziness
5 sloth **6** slouch **8** idleness **9** indolence

lazy
3 bum, lax **4** idle, loaf, loll **5** drony, inert, slack **6** dawdle, loiter, lounge, remiss, supine, torpid **7** goof off, languid, passive, workshy **8** comatose, fainéant, inactive, indolent, listless, slothful, sluggish, trifling **9** easygoing, goldbrick, lethargic, negligent, shiftless, slowgoing

Lazy Susan
4 tray **9** turntable

lea
6 fallow, meadow **7** pasture **8** unplowed **9** grassland

leach
4 suck **7** draw out **9** lixiviate, percolate **11** bloodsucker

lead
3 get, see **4** dean, head, move, show, star **5** bring, doyen, guide, metal, pilot, route, steer, usher **6** bullet, ceruse, direct, escort, induce, leader **7** captain, conduct, convert, plumbum, precede, preface, prevail **8** graphite, persuade, shepherd **9** introduce **10** bellwether
combining form: **5** plumb **6** molybd, plumbo **7** molybdo
ore: **6** galena **8** galenite **9** anglesite, cerrusite
oxide: **6** sinter
sounding: **7** plummet
symbol: **2** Pb

lead astray
4 undo **6** delude, entice, seduce **7** corrupt, deceive, degrade, pervert

leaden
3 dun **4** drab, dull, flat, gray **5** heavy, inert **8** dragging, lifeless, sluggish **9** plumbeous

leader
4 boss, cock, dean, duce, head, lead, lion, lord **5** chief, doyen, guide, pilot **6** bigwig, herald, honcho, master, rector **7** captain, foreman, general, headman, manager, notable **8** big-timer, big wheel, chairman, director, eminence, hierarch, luminary, superior **9** chieftain, commander, conductor, dignitary, dominator, harbinger, pacemaker, precursor, president, principal, straw boss **10** bellwether, chairwoman, forerunner, notability, pacesetter **11** chairperson
authoritarian: **10** Big Brother

combining form: **4** arch
Cossack: **6** ataman, hetman
German: **6** führer **7** fuehrer
Japanese: **6** shogun
military: **7** admiral, general, warlord **9** commander **12** field marshal
Muslim: **4** caid **5** calif **6** caliph, mollah, mullah
national: **7** premier **9** president **12** chief of state
religious: **4** pope **5** rabbi **6** bishop, priest **7** prelate **8** hierarch

leading
4 arch, head, main **5** chief, first, noted **6** famous **7** initial, popular, premier **8** champion, foremost, headmost **9** inaugural, notorious, principal, prominent, well-known

lead on
3 toy **4** bait, fool, lure, toll **5** dally, decoy, flirt, tempt **6** allure, coquet, entice, entrap, seduce, trifle, wanton **8** inveigle **11** string along

leaf
4 foil, olla, page, scan **5** blade, bract, folio, frond, petal, scale, sepal **6** browse, spathe **7** dip into, run over **8** glance at **10** glance over, run through **11** flip through, riff through, skim through **12** thumb through **13** riffle through
aperture: **5** stoma
axis: **6** rachis
combining form: **5** phyll **6** phylla (plural), phyllo **7** phyllum
edge: **9** crenation
lily: **3** pad
part: **4** lobe, vein **5** blade, costa, stoma **7** petiole, stipule, tendril
pine: **6** needle
scale: **8** ramentum
vein: **5** costa

leafage
7 foliage, umbrage, verdure

leaflet
5 pinna, sheet, tract **6** folder **8** circular, pamphlet

leafy
4 lush **5** green **7** foliate, foliose, folious **8** foliated, laminate

league
4 band, bond, club, loop, tier **5** class, grade, group, guild, order, union, unite, wheel **6** concur **7** circuit, combine, conjoin, society **8** alliance, category, coadjute, division, grouping, sodality **9** anschluss, coalition, cooperate **10** conference, federation, fellowship, fraternity, pigeonhole **11** association, brother-

hood, confederacy **13** confederation

Leah
daughter: **5** Dinah
father: **5** Laban
husband: **5** Jacob
sister: **6** Rachel
son: **4** Levi **5** Judah **6** Reuben, Simeon **7** Zebulun **8** Issachar

leak
3 out **4** drip, ooze, seep **5** bilge, break, crack **6** escape, get out **7** come out

leaky
6 porose, porous

lean
3 jut, tip **4** bend, bony, cant, hang, heel, lank, list, look, slim, tend, thin, tilt, turn, worn **5** curve, gaunt, grade, lanky, sheer, slant, slope, spare **6** beetle, divert, meager, skinny, slight, wasted **7** angular, deflect, haggard, incline, pinched, recline, scraggy, scrawny, slender, stringy, wizened **8** bend over, gradient, overhang, rawboned, spare-set **10** cadaverous

Leander's beloved
4 Hero

Leandre
beloved: **7** Lucinde
father: **7** Geronte

Leaning Tower site
4 Pisa

lean-to
3 hut **5** shack **7** shelter

leap
3 hop, lop **4** buck, jump, loup, over, rise, soar **5** arise, bound, caper, clear, mount, vault **6** ascend, bounce, gambol, hurdle, spring **7** saltate **8** capriole, surmount
ballet: **4** jeté **9** entrechat
by a horse: **7** gambade, gambado **9** ballotade

leaping light
3 arc

Lear
daughter: **5** Regan **7** Goneril **8** Cordelia
servant: **4** Kent

learn
3 con, get, see **4** find, hear **5** study **6** master, peruse, pick up, tumble **7** catch on, find out, realize, unearth **8** discover, memorize **9** ascertain, determine

learned
4 sage, wise **6** astute **7** bookish, erudite **8** abstruse, academic, cultured, educated, esoteric, pedantic, polymath **9** recondite, scholarly **10** cultivated, scholastic

learner
5 pupil **7** scholar, student, trainee **10** apprentice

learning
4 lore **6** wisdom **7** science **8** booklore, pedantry **9** education, erudition, knowledge **11** scholarship
man of: **7** egghead, scholar, teacher **9** professor **12** intellectual

lease
3 let **4** hire, rent **7** charter **8** contract

leash
3 tie **4** bind, clog, cord, curb, rope **5** strap **6** fetter, hamper, hobble, hog-tie, tether **7** shackle, trammel **9** entrammel
hawk's: **4** lune

leather
3 tan **4** hide, skin, whip **6** thrash
kind: **3** kid, kip, oak **4** alum, bock, buff, calf, napa, ooze, roan **5** aluta, basil, crown, grain, japan, mocha, strap, suede, whang **6** castor, comber, latigo, levant, oxhide, patent, roller, saddle, skiver **7** buffalo, canepin, carding, chamois, hemlock, morocco, ostrich, peccary, rutland, saffian **8** capeskin, cheverel, cordovan, cordwain, shagreen
maker: **5** tawer **6** tanner **7** tannery
piece: **4** rand, welt **5** strap, thong, trank
prepare: **3** sam, tan, taw **4** mull **5** curry, sammy
soft: **5** aluta, mocha, suede **8** cabretta

Leatherneck
6 marine

Leatherstocking Tales, The
author: **6** Cooper (James Fenimore)
title: **10** The Prairie **11** The Pioneers **13** The Deerslayer, The Pathfinder

leave
2 go **3** let **4** cede, drop, exit, have, quit, will **5** allot, allow, scram, waive, yield **6** assent, assign, commit, decamp, depart, desert, devise, escape, get off, give up, legate, maroon, permit, resign, retire, strand, suffer, vacate **7** abandon, confide, consent, consign, entrust, forsake, get away, holiday, pull out

8 bequeath, emigrate, hand over, sanction, vacation, withdraw **9** allowance, apportion, surrender, terminate **10** permission, relinquish, sufferance **13** authorization

leaved
7 foliate, foliose, folious **8** foliated

leaven
5 imbue, steep, yeast **6** infuse, invest, temper, vivify **7** enliven, ingrain, qualify, quicken, suffuse **8** moderate **9** inoculate

leavening agent
5 yeast **12** baking powder

leave of absence
5 exeat **8** furlough

leave off
4 halt, quit, stop **5** cease **6** desist **8** give over, knock off, surcease **11** discontinue

leave out
4 omit, skip **5** elide **7** exclude

Leaves of Grass author
7 Whitman (Walt)

leavings
4 heel, junk, lees, orts, rest **5** dregs, scrap **7** balance, remains, remanet, remnant, residue, rubbish **8** discards, portions, residual, residuum **9** fragments, remainder

Lebanon
capital: **6** Beirut
monetary unit: **5** pound

lecher
4 rake, roué **9** debauchee, libertine

lecherous
4 fast, lewd **7** goatish, lustful, satyric **9** libertine, salacious **10** lascivious, libidinous, licentious **11** incontinent

lectern
4 desk **5** stand

lecture
4 talk **5** scold, speak **6** preach, sermon, speech **7** address, oration, prelect **8** briefing **9** discourse **10** allocution

lecturer
6 docent, orator, reader **7** speaker, teacher **9** professor **10** praelector

Leda
daughter: **5** Helen **12** Clytemnestra
father: **8** Thestius
husband: **9** Tyndareus
lover: **4** swan, Zeus
son: **6** Castor, Pollux

ledge
4 berm, lode, sill 5 berme, ridge, shelf

ledger
4 book 6 record 8 monument
9 footstone, headstone, tombstone
10 gravestone 11 grave marker

lee
5 haven 6 harbor 7 shelter

leech
4 worm 6 sponge, sucker
7 sponger 8 barnacle, hanger-on, parasite 10 freeloader 11 bloodsucker 12 lounge lizard

Leeds' river
4 Aire

leer
4 look, ogle 5 empty, fleer, smirk, sneer 6 glance 7 grimace

leery
4 wary 8 doubtful 10 suspicious
11 distrustful

lees
5 draff, dregs 6 dunder, refuse
7 deposit, grounds, vinasse 8 leavings, sediment 9 settlings
11 precipitate

leeward
8 downwind

leeway
4 play, room 5 scope, space
6 margin 8 latitude 9 elbowroom

left
4 port 8 larboard

left-handed
8 southpaw

left-hand page
5 verso

leftovers
see **leavings**

leftward
4 levo 5 aport, laevo 8 levogyre
10 levogyrate
go: 3 haw

leg
3 gam, run 4 gamb, limb, walk
5 gambe, shank 6 gammon 7 support 8 cabriole 9 appendage, drumstick
bone: 4 shin 5 femur, tibia 6 fibula
7 patella
part: 4 calf, crus, foot, knee, shin
5 ankle, thigh 6 cnemis

legacy
4 gift 6 devise 7 bequest 8 heritage 9 heritance, patrimony
10 birthright 11 inheritance

legal
5 licit 6 lawful 7 juridic 8 innocent
9 juridical 10 legitimate
matter: 3 res 4 case, suit
order: 4 writ 7 summons
8 subpoena
party: 6 suitor 8 litigant 9 defendant, plaintiff
restraint: 8 estoppel

legal aid group
4 ACLU

legal tender
4 cash 5 money 6 dollar
8 currency

legate
4 will 5 envoy, leave 6 deputy, devise 8 bequeath, delegate, emissary, governor 10 ambassador

legatee
4 heir 9 inheritor

legend
4 lore, myth, saga 5 fable, story
6 mythos, mythus 7 caption, fiction
8 folklore 9 mythology, tradition

legendary
6 fabled, mythic 7 fabular 8 fabulous, mythical 12 mythological

legerdemain
5 magic 8 trickery 9 conjuring

legging
5 chaps 6 puttee 7 gambade, gambado 11 spatterdash
12 antigropelos

leghorn
4 fowl 5 straw 7 chicken

legible
5 clear 8 distinct, readable

legion
4 army, host, many, rout 5 cloud, crowd, flock 6 scores, sundry
7 various 8 numerous, populous
9 multitude

legislate
5 enact

legislation
3 act, law 4 bill 7 statute

legislator
3 rep 5 solon 6 deputy 7 senator
8 lawgiver, lawmaker 9 statesman
10 politician 11 congressman

legislature
4 diet 5 house, junta 6 senate
7 council 8 assembly, congress
10 parliament
Communist: 6 soviet 9 politburo, presidium
czarist Russian: 4 duma

Danish: 9 Folketing
Finnish: 9 Eduskunta
German: 9 Bundesrat, Bundestag
Iceland: 7 Althing
Israel: 7 Knesset
Norway: 8 Storting
one-house: 10 unicameral
Poland: 4 Sejm
Spain: 6 Cortes
Sweden: 7 Riksdag
two-house: 9 bicameral

legitimate
4 fair, just, true 5 legal, licit, sound, usual, valid 6 cogent, lawful, normal 7 natural, regular, typical
8 innocent, rightful 9 customary
10 recognized

leg of lamb
5 gigot

Legree type
6 tyrant

legume
3 pea, pod, soy 4 bean, guar, seed, soya 5 pulse 6 lentil 7 soybean 9 bird's-foot, vegetable

leg up
5 boost

lei
6 wreath 7 garland 8 necklace

Leibnitz's invention
8 calculus

Leif Ericson
discovery: 7 Vinland
father: 4 Eric

leisure
4 ease, rest, time 6 casual, repose
10 relaxation 12 requiescence

leisurely
3 lax 4 easy, slow 5 slack 7 delayed, laggard, relaxed, restful, unhasty 8 dilatory 9 slackened, unhurried

leitmotiv
5 theme 6 motive

lemma
5 bract, theme 7 premise, theorem

lemon
3 dud 4 bomb, bust, flop 5 fruit, loser 7 failure

lemur
4 maki, vari 5 indri, locis, potto
6 aye-aye, colugo, macaco 7 half-ape, tarsier 9 babacoote

lend
4 give, loan 5 allow, grant
6 oblige 7 advance, furnish 11 accommodate

length
4 term 5 orbit, range, reach, realm, scope 6 radius 7 compass, purview, stretch, yardage 8 distance, panorama

lengthen
4 draw 6 expand, extend 7 draw out, prolong, spin out, stretch 8 elongate, increase, protract 10 prolongate
Scottish: 3 eke

lengthy
4 long 8 dragging, drawn-out, elongate, extended, longsome, overlong 9 elongated, prolonged 10 protracted

leniency
5 mercy 8 clemency 9 tolerance 10 indulgence, toleration 11 forbearance

lenient
3 lax 4 easy, kind, mild, soft 5 balmy, bland, faint 6 benign, gentle, kindly, smooth, tender 7 amiable, clement 8 excusing, humoring, merciful, obliging, spoiling, tolerant 9 benignant, condoning, forgiving, indulgent, indulging, pampering, pardoning 10 charitable, forbearing

lenity
5 grace, mercy 7 caritas, charity 8 clemency 10 humaneness, tenderness

lens
5 glass 6 lentil 8 meniscus
kind: 5 toric 6 convex 7 bifocal, concave 8 trifocal

lentigo
5 nevus 7 freckle

lentil
4 lens, seed 6 legume

Leofric's wife
6 Godiva

Leoncavallo opera
9 Pagliacci

leonine
8 lionlike

Leonora
alias: 7 Fidelio
husband: 9 Florestan

leopard
3 cat 7 panther
relating to: 7 pardine

Leo star
7 Regulus

leper
6 pariah 7 Ishmael, outcast 8 castaway, derelict 10 Ishmaelite 11 untouchable

Leper King
7 Baldwin

Leper Priest
6 Damien

lepers' hospital
9 lazaretto

lepers' island
7 Molokai

lepidopter
4 moth 6 insect 9 butterfly

Leporello's master
11 Don Giovanni

leprechaun
3 elf 5 fairy 6 sprite
trade: 8 cobbling

Lesage hero
7 Gil Blas

Lesbos poet
6 Sappho 7 Alcaeus

lesion
3 cut 4 flaw, sore 5 ulcer, wound 6 injury 10 impairment

Lesotho
capital: 6 Maseru
monetary unit: 4 loti

lessen
4 clip, crop, ease, thin, wane 5 abate, close, drain, lower, taper 6 dilute, minify, reduce, shrink, weaken 7 abridge, assuage, curtail, dwindle, lighten, relieve 8 amputate, decrease, diminish, minimize, mitigate, taper off, truncate 9 attenuate

lessening
5 letup 8 decrease, slowdown 9 abatement

lesser
3 low 5 dinky, lower, minor, small, under 6 nether 8 inferior, small-fry 9 secondary, small-time, subjacent 11 minor-league 13 insignificant

lesson
4 text 5 chide, moral, study 6 monish, rebuke 7 lecture, reading, reprove, tick off 8 admonish, call down, exercise, reproach 9 reprimand 11 instruction

lessor
6 bailor 8 landlady, landlord

let
4 have, hire, rent 5 allow, grant, lease, leave 6 permit, suffer 7 approve, certify, charter, concede, endorse, license 8 accredit, sanction 9 authorize

letdown
5 slump 7 decline 10 depression

let go
4 emit, fire, free 6 unhand 7 dismiss, release 9 discharge

lethal
5 fatal 6 deadly, mortal, poison 7 deathly 9 pestilent, poisonous

lethargic
4 dull, idle, slow 5 dopey, heavy, inert 6 stolid, stupid, supine, torpid 7 dormant, laggard, languid, passive 8 comatose, dilatory, inactive, listless, sluggish 9 apathetic, impassive 10 languorous, phlegmatic, slumberous, spiritless 12 hebetudinous 13 lackadaisical

lethargy
4 coma 5 sleep, sloth 6 apathy, phlegm, stupor, torpor 7 inertia, languor, slumber 8 dullness, hebetude, idleness, laziness 9 disregard, inanition, indolence, inertness, lassitude, torpidity, unconcern 10 inactivity, supineness, torpidness 11 disinterest, impassivity, insouciance, passiveness

lethe
8 oblivion 13 forgetfulness

let in
5 admit

Leto
see **Latona**

let off
5 spare 6 excuse, exempt 7 absolve, relieve 8 dispense 9 discharge

let on
3 own 4 avow, tell 5 admit, allow, grant, own up, spill 6 betray, fess up, reveal, unveil 7 concede, confess, divulge, uncover 8 disclose, give away

letter
2 ar, ef, el, em, en, ex 3 bee, cee, cue, dee, ess, gee, jay, kay, pee, tee, vee, wye, zed, zee 4 line, mail, memo, note, rune 5 aitch, print, vowel 6 report, screed, symbol 7 epistle, message, missive 8 dispatch, inscribe 9 consonant
airmail: 8 aerogram
Anglo-Saxon: (see **Anglo-Saxon**)
Arabic: (see **alphabet**)
Greek: (see **alphabet**)
Hebrew: (see **alphabet**)

kind: **5** chain, roman **6** italic, uncial **8** Dear John

large: **7** capital **9** majuscule, upper case

small: **9** lower case, miniscule

lettuce
3 cos **4** Bibb, head **6** Boston **7** iceberg, romaine, Simpson **10** butterweed

let up
3 ebb **4** fall, wane **5** abate **6** relent **7** die away, die down, ease off, slacken

letup
5 break **7** respite **9** reduction

Levant, Levantine
7 eastern

levee
4 dike, dock, pier, quay, slip **5** berth, jetty, wharf **10** embankment

level
3 aim, lay, par **4** akin, cast, down, drop, even, fell, flat, like, raze, same, tier, true, turn **5** alike, equal, floor, flush, plane, point, train **6** direct, ground, smooth, zero in **7** address, aligned, flatten, incline, mow down, planate, regular, similar, uniform **8** parallel, smoothen **9** bring down

lever
3 bar, lam, pry **4** jack **5** helve, jimmy, peavy, prize **6** peavey, tappet **7** crowbar

leverage
5 power **9** influence

leveret
4 hare

Levi
father: **5** Jacob
mother: **4** Leah
son: **6** Kohath, Merari **7** Gershon

leviathan
4 huge **5** giant, titan, whale **7** immense, mammoth, monster **8** behemoth, enormous, gigantic **9** cyclopean **10** gargantuan **11** elephantine

Leviathan author
6 Hobbes (Thomas)

levitate
4 lift, rise **5** float **7** suspend

levity
5 folly, humor **8** buoyancy **9** absurdity, flippancy, frivolity, lightness, silliness

levy
3 set, tax **4** duty **5** exact, lay on, place, put on, wrest, wring **6** assess, charge, impose, impost, tariff **10** assessment

lewd
4 base, fast **5** bawdy, gross **6** coarse **7** lustful, obscene, satyric, whorish **8** improper, indecent **9** lecherous, libertine, salacious **10** indelicate, lascivious, libidinous, licentious **11** incontinent

Lewis and Clark interpreter
9 Sacagawea, Sacajawea

Lewis novel
7 Babbitt **9** Dodsworth **10** Arrowsmith, Main Street **11** Elmer Gantry

lexicographer
8 compiler

American: **6** Porter (Noah) **7** Webster (Noah) **9** Worcester (Joseph)

English: **4** Wyld (Henry) **6** Fowler (Francis, Henry), Murray (James), Onions (Charles) **7** Craigie (William), Johnson (Samuel)

French: **6** Littré (Paul-Emile) **8** Larousse (Pierre)

lexicon
4 cant **6** jargon **7** palaver **8** language, wordbook **9** word-hoard, word-stock **10** dictionary, vocabulary **11** onomasticon, terminology

liable
3 apt **4** open, tied **5** bound, given, prone **6** likely **7** exposed, subject **8** amenable, beatable, inclined, vincible **9** obnoxious, sensitive **10** answerable, assailable, attackable, chargeable, penetrable, vulnerable **11** accountable, conquerable, responsible, susceptible

liaison
4 bond **5** amour **6** affair **7** affaire **8** intrigue **12** relationship

liar
6 fibber **7** Ananias, fibster **8** fabulist, perjurer **9** falsifier **12** prevaricator

female: **8** Sapphira

libation
5 drink **6** liquid **7** potable **8** beverage, potation

libel
6 defame, malign, vilify **7** asperse, calumny, slander, traduce **8** tear down, travesty **9** burlesque, denigrate **10** calumniate, caricature, scandalize

libelous
8 debasing **9** invidious, maligning, traducing, vilifying **10** backbiting, calumnious, defamatory, derogative, detracting, detractive, detractory, malevolent, pejorative, scandalous, slanderous

liberal
4 free, open, wide **5** ample, broad **6** lavish, plenty **7** copious, lenient, profuse, radical **8** abundant, advanced, generous, handsome, prodigal, tolerant **9** bounteous, bountiful, exuberant, indulgent, plenteous, plentiful, unsparing **10** benevolent, bighearted, charitable, forbearing, freehanded, munificent, openhanded

liberate
4 free **5** loose, remit **6** detach, loosen, unbind, unhook **7** manumit, release, unchain **8** untangle **9** discharge, unshackle **10** emancipate **12** disembarrass

liberator
7 messiah
of Argentina: **9** San Martin (Jose de)
of Chile: **8** O'Higgins (Bernardo)
of Ecuador: **5** Sucre (Antonio Jose de)
of Scotland: **5** Bruce (Robert the)
of South America: **7** Bolivar (Simon)

Liberia
capital: **8** Monrovia
monetary unit: **6** dollar

Liberian
language: **3** Kwa
native: **3** Kru, Vai **4** Gola, Toma **5** Bassa, Grebo **6** Kruman

libertine
4 fast, lewd, rake, roué **7** lustful, satyric **9** debauchee, lecherous, salacious **10** lascivious, libidinous, licentious

liberty
5 leave **7** freedom, license **8** autonomy, delivery **10** liberation **12** emancipation, independence

libidinous
3 hot **4** fast, lewd **5** gross **6** coarse **7** goatish, lustful, obscene, satyric **8** prurient **9** lecherous, libertine, lickerish, salacious **10** lascivious, licentious, passionate **11** incontinent **12** concupiscent

Libni
father: **5** Mahli **7** Gershon
grandfather: **4** Levi

librarian
5 Dewey (Melvil)

library
7 archive 9 athenaeum 11 bibliotheca, reading room
desk: 6 carrel

Libya
capital: 7 Tripoli
chief export: 3 oil
largest city: 7 Tripoli
monetary unit: 5 dinar
father: 7 Epaphus
son: 5 Belus 6 Agenor

license
3 let 5 allow, leave 6 enable, laxity, permit, suffer 7 certify, empower, freedom, liberty 8 accredit, passport, sanction, variance 9 authorize, looseness, slackness

licentious
3 lax 4 fast, lewd 5 loose, randy 6 amoral, animal, carnal 7 corrupt, fleshly, immoral, lustful, relaxed, satyric, sensual, unmoral 8 depraved, scabrous 9 abandoned, debauched, dissolute, lecherous, libertine, oversexed, reprobate, salacious 10 lascivious, libidinous, profligate 11 incontinent 12 unprincipled

lichen
4 moss 6 archil, litmus 7 oakmoss
genus: 5 Usnea

licit
5 legal 6 lawful 8 approved, innocent, licensed 10 authorized, legitimate, sanctioned

lick
3 hit, lap, rap 4 beat, cast, dash, down, drub, flog, hint, swat, whip, wipe 5 knock, smack, smear, swipe, taste, throw, tinge, touch, trace, whiff 6 hurdle, master, thrash, tongue 7 clobber, conquer, shellac, smother 8 lambaste, overcome, surmount 9 overwhelm

lickerish
see **libidinous**

lickety-split
4 fast 5 apace 7 flat out, hastily, quickly, rapidly, swiftly 8 speedily 9 posthaste 13 expeditiously

licorice
4 root 5 candy
pill: 6 cachou

lid
3 cap, top 5 cover 8 covering
moss: 9 operculum

lie
3 fib 4 flam, myth, rest, tale 5 dwell, exist, fable, libel, story 6 canard, delude, inhere, palter, repose, reside 7 beguile, consist, deceive, distort, falsify, falsity, forgery, lie down, mislead, perjure, perjury, recline, untruth 8 misguide, misstate, nontruth, untruism 9 falsehood, fish story, mendacity, misinform 10 dishonesty, distortion, equivocate, exaggerate, inaccuracy, inveracity, stretch out, taradiddle 11 fraudulence, misinstruct, prevaricate 12 misstatement, song and dance

Liebestraum composer
5 Liszt (Franz)

lied
4 aria, hymn, song 5 ditty 7 descant

lie down
4 rest 6 repose 7 recline 10 stretch out

lief
4 fain 6 freely, gladly 9 willingly

liege
4 true 5 loyal 6 ardent, vassal 7 staunch 8 constant, faithful, resolute 9 steadfast

lien
5 claim 6 charge 8 interest, mortgage

lieu
5 place, stead

lieutenant
3 aid 4 aide, zany 7 officer 9 assistant, coadjutor 10 aide-de-camp, coadjutant

life
3 bio, man, vim 4 body, brio, dash, élan, soul, zing 5 being, blood, oomph, verve 6 energy, esprit, memoir, mortal, person, spirit 8 creature, vitality 9 animation, biography, existence, personage 13 autobiography
animal: 5 fauna
animal and plant: 5 biota
combining form: 2 bi 3 bia, bio 4 bium, bius 5 biont 6 bioses (plural), biosis, biotic
plant: 5 flora
relating to: 5 vital 8 biologic 10 biological
science: 7 biology

life jacket
7 Mae West

lifeless
4 cold, dead, drab, dull, flat, late 5 amort, inert, prosy 6 asleep, torpid 7 defunct, extinct, prosaic 8 deceased, departed 9 colorless, exanimate, inanimate 10 lackluster, lusterless

lifelike
6 verist 8 accurate, veristic 9 realistic

life of ___
5 Riley 8 the party

Life with Father author
3 Day (Clarence)

lift
2 up 3 aid, nip 4 doff, hand, heft, help, hook, jack, rear, rise, soar 5 arise, exalt, filch, heave, hoist, mount, pinch, raise, shrug, steal, surge, swipe, theft, tower 6 ascend, aspire, assist, pick up, pilfer, recall, relief, repeal, revoke, rocket, snitch, succor, take up, uphold, uprear 7 comfort, elevate, larceny, magnify, purloin, rescind, reverse, secours, support, upraise 8 levitate, stealage, stealing, thievery

lift-off
6 launch 7 takeoff 9 launching

ligament
3 tie 4 band, bond, knot, link, yoke 5 nexus 8 ligature, vinculum

ligature
see **ligament**

Ligeia author
3 Poe (Edgar Allan)

light
3 gay, hit 4 airy, bump, dawn, deft, easy, fair, fast, fire, lamp, land, luck, meet, morn, neon, soft 5 blond, dizzy, flash, giddy, loose, minor, perch, petty, roost, royal, small, sunny, torch 6 aurora, beacon, bright, candle, casual, chance, facile, flimsy, fluffy, happen, ignite, illume, kindle, little, meager, settle, simple, slight, smooth, strobe, swimmy, tumble, wanton 7 downing, flighty, inflame, lantern, lighten, morning, set down, sit down, slender, stumble, sunrise, trivial, unheavy, whorish 8 cheerful, cockcrow, daybreak, daylight, enkindle, illumine, luminous, skittish, swimming, trifling, unchaste 9 frivolous, small-beer, touch down 10 bird-witted, chandelier, effortless, illuminate
combining form: 4 luci, phos, phot 5 lumin, photo 6 lumini, lumino

measure: 3 lux 4 phot 5 lumen
6 candle 7 candela
refractor: 5 prism
relating to: 6 photic
ring: 4 halo 6 corona 7 aureola,
aureole
science: 6 optics 7 photics
source: 3 sun 4 lamp

light-emitting
suffix: 6 escent

lighten
4 dawn, ease, fade, thin 5 allay
6 bleach, dilute, illume 7 assuage,
mollify, relieve 8 brighten, illumine,
mitigate 9 alleviate, attenuate, extenuate 10 illuminate

light-headed
5 dizzy, giddy 6 swimmy 7 flighty
8 swimming 9 frivolous 10 bird-
witted 11 vertiginous

lighthearted
3 gay 4 glad 5 happy, jolly, merry
6 blithe, jocund, jovial, joyful, joyous, lively 7 buoyant, festive, gleeful 8 carefree, cheerful, mirthful,
spirited, volatile 9 expansive, resilient, sprightly, vivacious 10 blithesome, free-minded, insouciant
12 effervescent, happy-go-lucky,
high-spirited

lighthouse
5 guide, phare 6 beacon, pharos
7 warning 8 guidance 9 direction

lightless
3 dim 4 dark, dusk 5 dusky, murky
6 gloomy 7 obscure 9 tenebrous
10 caliginous 11 unillumined

lightness
6 gaiety, levity 8 buoyancy, vivacity 9 flippancy, frivolity 10 elasticity, liveliness, resiliency, volatility
11 flightiness 12 cheerfulness
13 effervescence, expansiveness

lightning bug
7 firefly

lignite
4 coal 9 brown coal

likable
6 genial 8 friendly, pleasant, pleasing 10 attractive

like
2 as 3 dig 4 akin, same, such, will,
wish 5 close, elect, enjoy, equal,
match 6 admire, agnate, allied,
choose, esteem, please, prefer, regard, relish, select 7 approve, cognate, endorse, kindred, related, respect, similar, uniform 8 parallel,
selfsame, suchlike 9 analogous,

consonant, identical 10 appreciate,
comparable, comprehend, equivalent, resembling
combining form: 3 sym, syn 4 home
5 homeo, homoe, homoi
6 homoeo, homoio
suffix: 2 ar, ic, ly 3 ine, ish, oid
4 eous, ical 5 oidal

likelihood
6 chance 11 probability

likely
3 apt 4 rosy 5 given, prone 6 liable, mortal 7 earthly, hopeful, roseate 8 inclined, possible, probable,
probably 9 assumably, doubtless,
promising 10 presumably,
promiseful

liken
5 match 6 equate 7 compare, paragon 8 parallel 10 assimilate

likeness
4 copy, twin 5 image 6 effigy, simile 7 analogy, picture, replica 8 affinity, equality, identity, sameness
9 agreement, facsimile, semblance
10 comparison, conformity, photograph, similarity, similitude, uniformity 11 equivalence, parallelism,
resemblance

likewise
2 so 3 and, too 4 also, more
5 along 6 as well, withal 7 besides
8 moreover 9 similarly 11 furthermore

liking
4 lust, mind, will 5 fancy, gusto,
taste 8 affinity, appetite, fondness,
penchant, pleasure, soft spot, velleity, weakness 11 inclination
12 predilection
combining form: 4 phil 5 phile
6 philic 7 philous

Lilith
husband: 4 Adam
successor: 3 Eve

lilliputian
3 wee 4 runt, tiny 5 dwarf, midge,
pygmy, teeny, weeny 6 midget, minute, peewee, teensy, teenty 7 manikin 8 Tom Thumb 10 diminutive,
homunculus, teeny-weeny
12 teensy-weensy

lilt
3 air 4 sing, song, tune 5 swing

lily
3 pad 4 aloe, ixia, sego 5 calla, tiger, white, yucca 6 flower 7 leopard 8 mariposa
combining form: 6 crinus

Lily ___
4 Pons

lily of France
10 fleur-de-lis

lily-livered
6 coward, craven 7 chicken, gutless, unmanly 8 cowardly
9 spunkless 11 poltroonish
12 poor-spirited 13 pusillanimous

lily-white
4 good, pure 8 innocent, virtuous
9 blameless, exemplary, guiltless,
righteous 10 inculpable

lima
4 bean, seed 7 mollusk

liman
3 bay 6 lagoon 7 estuary

limb
3 arm, fin, leg 4 twig, wing
5 bough, devil, rogue, scamp,
shoot, spray, sprig 6 branch, member, rascal, switch 7 villain 8 mischief, scalawag 9 appendage

limber
5 agile, lithe, loose 6 pliant, supple
7 elastic, lissome, plastic, pliable,
springy 8 flexible 9 lithesome,
resilient

limbo
5 dance 6 prison 8 oblivion

lime
5 color, fruit, green 6 citrus

limen
9 threshold

limerick
4 poem 5 verse 8 fishhook
writer: 4 Lear (Edward)

limestone
4 malm, tufa 5 chalk 6 marble, oo-
lite, oolith 7 coquina

lime tree
4 teil 6 linden

limit
3 bar, end, fix, rim, set 4 brim,
curb, edge, term 5 brink, check,
pinch, quota, verge 6 assign, border, curfew, define, hinder, lessen,
margin, narrow 7 appoint, extreme, mark out, measure 8 contract, deadline, restrain, restrict
9 constrict, demarcate, determine,
extremity, prescribe

limitless
4 vast 8 infinite, termless 9 unbounded 10 indefinite, unmeasured
11 innumerable, undrainable

12 immeasurable, incalculable, unfathomable 13 inexhaustible

limn
4 draw 5 image 6 depict, render,
sketch 7 picture, portray 8 describe 9 delineate, interpret,
represent

Limoges product
9 porcelain

limp
3 lax 4 halt, lame, wilt 5 hitch,
loose, slack 6 falter, flabby, floppy,
hobble, muddle, sleazy, supple,
toddle, totter, waddle, wobble
7 die-away, flaccid, languid, relaxed, shuffle, stagger, stumble
9 enervated 10 languorous,
spiritless

limpid
4 pure 5 clear, lucid 10 see-
through 11 translucent, transparent

limping
4 halt, lame 5 gimpy 8 lameness
12 claudication

Lincoln
assassin: 5 Booth (John Wilkes)
biographer: 7 Masters (Edgar Lee)
8 Sandburg (Carl)
debater: 7 Douglas (Stephen)
law partner: 7 Herndon (William)
mother: 5 Nancy (Hanks)
nickname: 9 Honest Abe
12 Railsplitter
photographer: 5 Brady (Mathew)
secretary of state: 6 Seward
(William)
secretary of war: 7 Stanton (Edwin)
wife: 8 Mary Todd

line
3 job, pad, ray, row, way 4 abut,
file, join, path, rank, road, rope,
tier, work 5 align, array, goods,
march, order, queue, range, route,
touch, train, verge, wares 6 adjoin,
border, butt on, column, course,
policy, polity, series, string 7 arrange, calling, contour, echelon,
marshal, passage, profile, program, pursuit 8 business, neighbor,
ordinate, sequence 9 procedure,
vendibles 10 employment, figuration, occupation, silhouette,
succession
curved: 3 arc
mathematical: 6 vector
metrical: 5 verse 6 verset 8 versicle
weather map: 6 isobar

lineage
4 clan, folk, race 5 birth, blood,
house, stock, tribe 6 family, origin,

stirps 7 descent, kindred 8 ancestry, pedigree

lineal
6 direct 10 hereditary

lineament
7 contour, feature, outline, profile
10 figuration, silhouette

lineation
see **lineament**

lined
5 ruled 7 lineate, striate, striped
8 lineated, streaked, wrinkled

linen
4 lawn 5 cloth, toile 6 byssus, damask, dowlas, fabric, forfar, napery,
sheets 7 batiste, bedding, cambric,
Holland, taffeta 8 cretonne,
lingerie
fiber: 3 tow 4 line
source: 4 flax

liner
4 ship 6 insert, vessel

Linet, Lynette
brother: 6 Liones
husband: 6 Gareth

linger
3 lag 4 bide, drag, mope, poke,
stay, wait 5 abide, amble, dally,
delay, drift, mosey, tarry 6 bummel, dawdle, loiter, put off, remain,
stroll 11 stick around

lingerie
6 undies 9 underwear

lingo
4 cant 5 argot, slang 6 jargon, patois, patter 7 dialect 10 vernacular

linguist
8 polyglot 11 philologist

linguistics
9 philology

liniment
3 oil 6 lotion 8 ablution, ointment

lining
6 facing, insert 8 wainscot
combining form: 6 pleura

link
3 tie 4 bond, join, knot, yoke
5 nexus, unite 6 couple, relate
7 combine, conjoin, connect 8 catenate, vinculum 9 associate,
conjugate

linksman
6 golfer

linnet
5 finch

lint
3 fur 4 down, flue, fuzz, pile
5 floss, fluff 7 charpie 9 ravelings

lion
3 cat, VIP 4 king, puma 5 chief
6 big boy, cougar, leader 7 notable 8 bigtimer, eminence, luminary
9 carnivore
group: 5 pride
young: 3 cub

lioness headed goddess
3 Mut 6 Sekhet

lionhearted
4 bold 5 brave 7 valiant 8 fearless, intrepid, unafraid, valorous
9 dauntless 10 courageous

lionlike
7 leonine

lion monkey
7 tamarin 8 leoncito, marmoset

Lion of Judah
13 Haile Selassie

lip
3 rim 4 brim, buss, edge, kiss,
lave, peck, wash 5 bathe, smack
6 labium, labrum, margin, smooch
8 osculate
relating to: 6 labial

lipid
3 fat, wax

lipped
7 labiate 9 bilabiate

lip server
8 pharisee, Tartuffe 9 hypocrite

liquefy
3 run 4 flux, fuse, melt, thaw, thin
6 soften 8 dissolve

liqueur
4 ouzo, raki 5 crème, noyau
6 kummel 7 cordial, curaçao, rata-
fia, rosolio, sloe gin 8 absinthe, an-
isette, prunelle 10 chartreuse,
pousse-café

liquid
5 drink, fluid, sauce, water
6 golden, lotion, mellow, watery
7 honeyed 8 beverage, emulsion,
Hyblaean 11 mellifluent, mellifluous
aromatic: 7 eugenol 8 terpinol
container: 3 cup, jug, mug 4 vial
5 glass 6 bottle, goblet 7 pitcher,
tumbler
corrosive: 5 oleum
flammable: 3 gas, oil 5 ether, furan
6 butane, toluol 7 alcohol, dioxine,
ligroin, toluene 8 furfuran, gasoline, ligroine, propenol, pyridine
measure: 2 cc, ml, oz, pt, qt 3 cup,

gal **4** pint **5** liter, ounce, quart **6** gallon
medicinal: **8** liniment, ointment
oily: **5** fusel **6** octane
resinous: **6** tallol
scented: **7** cologne, perfume
thick: **5** sirup, syrup **8** molasses
volatile: **6** hexane **7** naphtha, pentane **8** isoprene, phenetol

liquidate
3 pay **4** cool, do in, quit **5** clear, pay up, purge **6** murder, remove, settle, square **7** satisfy **8** amortize, clear off

liquor
4 grog **5** booze, drink **7** alcohol, potable, spirits **8** beverage, potation **9** aqua vitae, drinkable, firewater, inebriant, moonshine **10** intoxicant
add: **4** lace **5** spike
homemade: **9** moonshine **10** bathtub gin
inferior: **5** hooch, smoke **6** rotgut
kind: **3** gin, rum, rye **5** vodka **6** brandy, geneva, scotch **7** bourbon, whiskey **8** vermouth
malt: **3** ale **4** beer **5** stout
measure: **4** dram
Mexican: **5** sotol **6** mescal **7** tequila
Oriental: **4** sake, saki **6** arrack, samshu

liquor cabinet
10 cellarette

lissome
5 agile, lithe **6** limber, supple **8** flexible

list
3 tip **4** book, cant, file, heel, lean, menu, note, post, roll, tilt **5** count, index, slant, slope **6** agenda, detail, enroll, record, roster **7** catalog, incline, itemize, recline, specify, tick off **8** glossary, inscribe, numerate, register, roll call, schedule, tabulate **9** chronicle, enumerate, inventory **10** specialize **13** particularize

listen
4 hark, hear, heed, note **6** attend, harken **8** overhear **9** eavesdrop

listeners
8 audience

listless
4 dull, limp **6** drowsy, sleepy **7** dieaway, languid **9** apathetic, enervated **10** languorous **11** languishing **13** lackadaisical

listlessness
6 apathy **8** doldrums, lethargy **9** disregard, lassitude, unconcern **11** disinterest, insouciance **12** indifference

litany
4 list **5** chant **6** ektene, prayer **7** synapte **8** rogation

literal
5 exact **7** precise **8** verbatim **11** word-for-word

literally
6 direct **8** verbatim **11** word for word

literary
7 bookish, erudite, learned **8** lettered, well-read

literary style
suffix: **3** ese

literary work
4 book, opus, play, poem **5** cento, drama, essay, novel **10** short story

literature
4 kind **5** prose **6** poetry **7** fiction **10** nonfiction

lithe
4 lean, slim, thin **5** agile, spare **6** lissom, slight, supple, svelte **7** lissome, slender **8** graceful

lithium
symbol: **2** Li

lithographer
4 Ives (James Merritt) **7** Currier (Nathaniel)
French: **5** Redon (Odilon)

Lithuanian
4 Balt **6** Baltic
capital: **7** Vilnius
coin: **6** centas

litigant
4 suer **6** suitor

litigation
4 case, suit **6** action **7** lawsuit

litter
3 bed **4** hash, junk **5** offal, trash, waste, young **6** basket, debris, jumble, jungle, muddle, refuse, tumble **7** garbage, rubbish, rummage, shuffle **8** mishmash, scramble **9** offspring, stretcher

little
3 set, wee **4** mean, puny, tiny **5** borne, light, minor, petty, short, small **6** bantam, casual, minute, monkey, narrow, paltry, petite, rarely, seldom **7** bigoted, limited,

niggard, selfish, trivial, unoften **8** smallish **9** hidebound, illiberal, niggardly, secondary, small-beer **10** collateral, diminutive, fortuitous, hardly ever, incidental, provincial, shoestring, subsidiary **11** unimportant

Little Bighorn victor
11 Sitting Bull

little by little
8 inchmeal **9** gradually, piecemeal

Little Corporal
8 Napoleon

Little Dipper
constellation: **9** Ursa Minor
star: **5** North **7** Polaris

little finger or toe
7 minimus

Little Minister
author: **6** Barrie (James)
character: **5** Gavin **6** Babbie **7** Dishart

little one
suffix: **2** el, et, ey **2** ia (plural), ie **3** cle, ium, kin, ock, ula, ule, uli (plural) **4** ella, ette, illa, ling, ulae (plural), ulum, ulus **5** ellae (plural), illae (plural)

Little Women
author: **6** Alcott (Louisa May)
character: **2** Jo **3** Amy, Meg **4** Beth
surname: **5** March

liturgy
4 form, rite **7** service **8** ceremony **9** formality **10** ceremonial, observance

livable
4 cosy, snug **5** homey **6** viable **8** bearable, homelike **9** endurable

live
2 be, is **3** are **4** fare **5** abide, dwell, exist, green, vital **6** reside **7** breathe, dynamic, hang out, running, subsist, working

livelihood
3 art, fee, job, pay **4** keep, wage **5** bread, craft, trade **6** living, salary **7** alimony, stipend, support **9** emolument **10** handicraft, profession, sustenance **11** maintenance, subsistence

liveliness
4 brio, élan **5** verve **6** spirit **8** vibrance, vibrancy, vitality, vivacity

lively
3 gay **4** busy, fast, keen, pert, spry, yare **5** agile, alert, brisk, catty,

fussy, jazzy, jolly, merry, peppy, zippy **6** active, blithe, bright, brisky, chirpy, frisky, jocund, nimble **7** animate, buoyant, chipper, dashing, driving, elastic, gleeful, hopping, humming, popping, rousing **8** animated, bustling, cheerful, chirping, chirrupy, hustling, mirthful, spirited, volatile **9** cock-a-hoop, energetic, expansive, hilarious, resilient, sprightly, vivacious

liven
5 cheer **6** vivify **7** animate, quicken

live oak
6 encina

liver
4 foie **5** hepar **7** denizen **8** habitant, occupant, resident **9** indweller **10** inhabitant
combining form: **5** hepat **6** hepato
disease: **9** cirrhosis, hepatitis
lobster's: **8** tomalley

liverwort
8 hepatica **9** bryophyte

livestock
6 cattle **7** animals

live wire
6 dynamo, peeler **7** hustler, rustler **8** go-getter **11** self-starter

livid
3 wan **4** ashy, pale **5** ashen, dusky, lurid, murky, waxen **6** doughy, gloomy, grisly, pallid, sultry **8** blanched **9** colorless

living
4 keep, salt **5** bread, vital **6** active, around, extant, zoetic **7** alimony, animate, dynamic, support **8** animated, existent **9** operative **10** livelihood, sustenance
combining form: **3** ont **4** onto, vivi

living being
8 creature
combining form: **2** zo **3** ont, zoa (plural), zoo **4** onto, zoon

living room
6 parlor **7** parlour **10** lebensraum

lizard
3 dab, eft, uma **4** adda, gila, newt, seps, uran **5** agama, anole, gecko, skink, teiid, tokay, varan, waral **6** dragon, goanna, iguana, moloch, worral, worrel **7** cheecha, monitor, reptile **8** basilisk, lacertid, slowworm, whiptail **9** alligator, blindworm, chameleon, crocodile **10** chuckwalla, salamander

combining form: **4** saur **5** saura, sauro **6** sauria (plural)
genus: **3** Uta **5** Agama **6** Ameiva, Anolis **7** Lacerta

llama
6 alpaca **7** guanaco
country: **4** Peru
habitat: **5** Andes

Lloyd's business
9 insurance

lo
4 hark, look

load
3 tax **4** bale, bear, care, cram, drag, duty, fill, glut, haul, lade, onus, pack, pile, task **5** cargo, carry, choke, drain, flood, gorge, laden, swamp, weigh **6** burden, charge, convey, cumber, debase, doctor, dope up, lading, parcel, saddle, weight **7** freight, surfeit **8** encumber, pressure, shipment **9** liability, millstone, transport

loaded
4 full **7** brimful **8** brimming **9** chock-full

loaf
3 bum **4** idle, laze, lazy **6** dawdle **9** goldbrick

loafer
3 bum **4** shoe, slug **5** idler **6** slouch **8** deadbeat, dolittle, fainéant, slugabed, sluggard **9** do-nothing, lazybones

loam
4 dirt, sand, silt, soil **7** topsoil
deposit: **5** loess

loan
4 lend **5** prest **7** advance, imprest

loan shark
6 lender, usurer **7** Shylock **11** moneylender

loath
6 afraid, averse **7** uneager **8** hesitant **9** reluctant, unwilling **10** indisposed

loathe
4 hate **5** abhor, spurn **6** detest, refuse, reject **7** decline, despise **8** execrate **9** abominate, repudiate

loathsome
4 foul, ugly, vile **5** nasty **7** hateful, hideous **8** horrible **9** invidious, obnoxious, offensive, repellent, repugnant, repulsive, revolting **10** disgusting

lob
3 hit **4** shot, step, toss, vein **5** stair, throw

lobby
4 hall **5** foyer **8** anteroom **9** vestibule

lobe
4 flap **7** lobulus

lobo
4 wolf **10** timber wolf

lobster
10 crustacean
African: **12** Cape crawfish
claw: **5** chela **6** pincer
female: **3** hen
male: **4** cock
trap: **3** pot **5** creel

local
6 native **7** endemic, insular, topical
combining form: **3** top **4** topo

locale
4 area, site **5** place, scene, venue **6** region **8** district, vicinage, vicinity **11** mise-en-scène **12** neighborhood

locality
4 area, belt, home, seat, site, zone **5** field, haunt, range, tract **6** domain, region, sector, sphere **7** habitat, section **8** district, province, vicinage **9** bailiwick, territory **12** neighborhood

localize
8 pinpoint

locate
3 spy **4** espy, find, site, spot **5** place, trace **6** settle **7** situate, station, uncover **8** discover, pinpoint, position **9** establish

locating device
5 lidar, radar, sonar

location
4 area, site, spot **5** locus, place, point, scene, where **7** habitat

loch
3 bay **4** lake

lock
3 fix **4** bolt, curl, hank, tuft **5** click, latch, tress **6** bundle, fasten, secure **7** ringlet **8** fastener **9** fastening

Locke's tabula ____
4 rasa

lockjaw
7 tetanus, trismus

Locksley Hall author
8 Tennyson (Alfred)

lockup
3 jug, pen 4 coop, jail 6 cooler, prison

loco
3 mad 5 crazy 6 insane

locomotive
5 cheer, dolly, train 6 engine 7 movable 8 moveable 9 camelback
small: 5 dinky 6 dinkey
type: 5 steam 6 diesel 8 electric

Locrine
daughter: 7 Sabrina
father: 4 Brut 6 Brutus
lover: 9 Estrildis
wife: 9 Gwendolen

locum tenens
3 sub 6 fill-in 7 stand-in 9 alternate, surrogate 10 substitute 11 pinch hitter, replacement, succedaneum

locust
5 carob 6 cicada, insect 11 grasshopper

locust bird
5 stork 7 grackle

locution
4 word 6 phrase 10 expression

lode
4 lead, vein 7 deposit

lodestar
5 guide 6 leader

lodestone
6 magnet 9 magnetite

lodge
3 cot, den, fix, hut, inn 4 camp, club, hold, lair, root, take 5 admit, board, cabin, couch, embed, hotel, house, infix, motel, put up, shack 6 accept, bestow, billet, burrow, harbor, hostel, shanty, tavern 7 auberge, contain, cottage, hospice, ingrain, quarter, receive 8 domicile, entrench, hostelry 9 entertain, roadhouse 11 accommodate, caravansary, public house

lodger
5 guest 6 renter, roomer, tenant

loess
4 loam 7 deposit

loft
3 bin 5 attic, raise 6 garret

loftiness
5 pride 6 height, morgue 7 disdain, hauteur, stature 9 arrogance, superbity

lofty
3 big 4 airy, epic, high, tall 5 grand, noble, proud 6 aerial, august, raised, superb 7 exalted, haughty, soaring, spiring, stately, sublime, topless, utopian 8 arrogant, cavalier, elevated, eloquent, generous, imposing, insolent, majestic, superior, towering 9 ambitious, grandiose, magnified, visionary 10 benevolent, chivalrous, disdainful 11 aggrandized, considerate, magnanimous, overbearing, pretentious, skyscraping 12 greathearted, supercilious

log
4 book, note, wood 5 diary, stick 6 record, timber 7 journal
mover: 7 cantdog

logarithm inventor
6 Napier (John)

loge
3 box 5 booth, stall 9 enclosure

logger
9 lumberman 10 lumberjack, woodcutter
legendary: 10 Paul Bunyan

loggerhead
6 shrike, turtle

loggia
6 arcade 7 balcony, gallery

logic
6 reason 9 reasoning
specious: 7 sophism 9 sophistry

logical
4 sane 5 clear, lucid, sound, valid 6 cogent, subtle 7 telling 8 analytic, sensible 10 compelling, convincing, reasonable

logjam
7 impasse 8 blockage, deadlock, stoppage

logo
4 mark 5 brand 9 trademark

logograph
6 puzzle 7 anagram

logroll
4 birl

logrolling contest
5 roleo

logy
4 dull, slow 5 dopey, heavy 6 drowsy, groggy, torpid 8 listless, sluggish

Lohengrin
composer: 6 Wagner (Richard)
father: 8 Parsifal, Parzival
wife: 4 Elsa

loincloth
African: 5 pagne
Hindu: 5 dhoti, dhuti 6 dhooti
Indian: 5 lungi 6 lungyi

Loire, city on the
5 Blois, Tours 6 Nantes 7 Orléans

Lois
daughter: 6 Eunice
grandson: 7 Timothy

loiter
3 bum, lag 4 drag, idle, laze, lazy, loaf, poke 5 dally, delay, tarry, trail 6 dawdle, diddle, lounge, put off

Loki
father: 8 Farbauti
mother: 3 Nal 6 Laufey
offspring: 3 Hel 4 Hela 6 Fenris 7 Midgard
slayer: 8 Heimdall
victim: 6 Balder
wife: 5 Sigyn 9 Angurboda

Lolita author
7 Nabokov (Vladimir)

loll
3 bum 4 idle, laze, lazy 5 droop, slump, tarry 6 dawdle, diddle, slouch

Lollards' leader
8 Wycliffe (John)

lombard
6 cannon

Lombard king
5 Cleph 6 Alboin, Audoin 7 Aistulf, Aripert, Authari 9 Liudprand

London
borough: 5 Brent 6 Barnet, Bexley, Ealing, Harrow, Sutton 7 Barking, Bromley, Chelsea, Croydon, Enfield, Hackney, Lambeth 8 Haringey, Havering, Hounslow, Lewisham 9 Greenwich, Islington, Redbridge 10 Kensington 11 Westminster
cathedral: 7 St. Paul's
clock: 6 Big Ben
district: 4 Soho 5 Acton 7 Chelsea, Mayfair
gallery: 4 Tate
policeman: 5 bobby
prison: 7 Newgate
river: 6 Thames
square: 9 Leicester, Trafalgar
street: 4 Bond 5 Fleet 6 Strand

7 Downing **9** Whitehall **10** Piccadilly
subway: **4** tube

London novel
9 White Fang **10** Martin Eden, The Sea Wolf **11** The Iron Heel **16** The Call of the Wild

lone
4 only, sole, solo **5** alone **6** single, unique **8** deserted, forsaken, isolated, secluded, separate, singular, solitary

lonely
4 lorn **5** alone **7** forlorn **8** deserted, homesick, lonesome, solitary

loneness
8 solitude **9** isolation

loner
6 hermit **7** outcast, recluse **8** outsider, solitary

Lone Ranger, The
creator: **7** Striker (Fran)
companion: **5** Tonto
horse: **6** Silver
trademark: **4** mask **12** silver bullet

lonesome
see **lonely**

Lone Star State
5 Texas

long
3 age, aim, yen **4** ache, aeon, itch, lust, miss, pine, sigh, want **5** crave, dream, wordy, yearn **6** aspire, hanker, hunger, prolix, thirst **7** diffuse, dog's age, lengthy, suspire, verbose **8** blue moon, coon's age, dragging, drawn-out, eternity, extended **9** diffusive, extensive **10** protracted

long dozen
8 thirteen

long-drawn-out
7 lengthy **8** dragging **10** protracted

Longfellow poem
8 Christus, Hiawatha, Hyperion, Kavanagh **10** Evangeline **11** My Lost Youth **12** A Psalm of Life

long for
4 ache, pine, want **5** covet, crave, yearn

longing
3 yen **4** wish **6** desire, thirst **7** craving **8** appetite

Long, Long Ago composer
5 Bayly (Thomas)

longshoreman
9 stevedore

long-suffering
7 patient **8** humility, meekness, patience **9** lowliness **11** forbearance, patientness, resignation, subduedness

long suit
5 forte **6** medium, métier, oyster **8** eminency, strength **9** specialty **10** specialism

long-winded
5 wordy **6** prolix **7** diffuse, lasting, lengthy, verbose **9** redundant **10** palaverous

loo
6 toilet

look
3 air, mug, see **4** cast, face, gape, gawk, heed, hope, lean, leer, mien, mind, note, ogle, peek, peep, peer, seem, show, spot, tend, view **5** await, front, glare, gloat, sight, slant, sound, stare, watch **6** appear, aspect, attend, beware, divine, expect, eyeful, glance, glower, goggle, notice, regard, squint, survey, visage **7** count on, display, exhibit, express, glimpse, incline, observe, seeming **8** forecast, foretell, indicate, manifest **9** count upon **10** appearance, expression, rubberneck **11** countenance, physiognomy

look after
4 tend **6** attend **7** care for

look at
3 eye, see **4** ogle, view **6** behold **7** examine

look back
6 recall, review **7** reflect **8** remember **9** reminisce

look down
5 abhor, scorn, scout **7** contemn, despise, disdain, overtop **8** dominate, outstare **9** tower over **10** tower above

looker
6 beauty, eyeful, lovely **8** knockout

looker-on
6 viewer **7** watcher, witness **8** beholder, by-sitter, observer **9** bystander, spectator **10** eyewitness

look for
4 seek **5** await

looking glass
6 mirror

look into
5 study **7** examine, inspect **11** investigate

look out
4 mind **6** beware

lookout
4 ward **5** guard, scape, vigil, vista, watch **6** affair, cupola, picket, sentry **7** concern, palaver **8** business, prospect, sentinel, watchman **9** crow's nest, firetower, occasions, vigilance **10** observance, watchtower **9** widow's walk **11** observation, observatory, perspective **12** surveillance

loom
4 brew, bulk, hulk, near, rear, show **5** tower **6** appear, come on, emerge, gather, impend, make up, weaver **8** approach, stand out, threaten **9** forthcome
part: **3** lam **4** caam **5** easer **6** heddle **7** harness, shuttle, treadle, trundle

loon
3 nut **4** bird **5** grebe

loony
3 nut **5** batty, crazy, silly, wacky **6** absurd, dement, insane, madman, maniac **7** foolish, lunatic, madling **9** bedlamite, non compos **10** Tom o' Bedlam **11** harebrained **12** preposterous

loony bin
6 asylum **8** madhouse, nuthouse **9** funny farm **10** booby hatch, crazy house

loop
3 arc, eye **4** ansa, arch, bend, coil, curl, gird, knot, ring **5** beset, curve, noose, picot, wheel **6** begird, circle, girdle, league, staple, wreath **7** circlet, circuit, compass **8** encircle, surround **9** encompass **13** circumference

looped
5 drunk **11** intoxicated

loophole
3 out **6** outlet **7** opening

loose
3 lax **4** bate, ease, easy, fast, fire, free, limp, undo, vent **5** abate, clear, let up, light, relax, shoot, slack, unbar, unfix, unpin, untie **6** flabby, remiss, unbind, unbolt, undone, unglue, unhook, unlace, unlash, unlock, unsnap, wanton **7** ease off, flaccid, manumit, re-

laxed, release, slacken, unchain, unclasp, unhitch, unlatch, unleash, unscrew, unstick, unstrap, whorish **8** detached, liberate, mitigate, reckless, separate, unbuckle, unbutton, unchaste, unfasten **9** alleviate, desultory, discharge, disengage, negligent, take out on, unbandage, untighten **10** capricious, disjointed, emancipate, incoherent, inconstant, unattached, unconfined, unfastened **11** disenthrall, extravagant, nonadhesive, unconnected **12** disconnected, unrestrained

loose end
6 detail **8** fragment

loose-fitting
5 baggy **6** droopy

loose-lipped
see **loquacious**

loosen
3 lax **4** ease, free **5** relax, slack, untie **6** unbind **7** ease off, manumit, release, slacken, unchain **8** liberate, unbuckle, unfasten **9** discharge **10** emancipate

loosen up
5 relax **6** unbend, unwind **7** ease off

loot
3 rob **4** sack, swag **5** booty, dough, lucre, money, prize, rifle, spoil **6** boodle **7** pillage, plunder, ransack, relieve, seizure, stick up **9** knock over **10** plunderage **11** filthy lucre

looter
5 thief **6** reaver, riever **8** marauder, pillager, ravisher

lop
3 cut **4** chop, clip, jump, leap, trim **5** bound, droop, slump, vault **6** bounce, hurdle, slouch, spring **7** pendent, saltate **8** truncate

lope
3 jog, run **4** gait, romp, skip, trip **6** spring, sprint **7** skitter

lopsided
6 uneven **7** crooked, difform, unequal **8** top-heavy, unsteady **9** irregular **10** asymmetric, off-balance, unbalanced **13** unsymmetrical

loquacious
5 gabby, talky, wordy **6** chatty, prolix **7** verbose **9** jabbering, talkative **10** babblative **11** looselipped **12** loose-tongued, multiloquent **13** overtalkative

lord
2 Mr. **3** man, sir **4** boss, cock, earl, peer **5** noble, put on, swank, swell **6** affect, master, mister **7** husband, overawe, peacock, pretend, swagger **8** governor, nobleman, overbear **9** tyrannize
feudal: **5** liege **8** seigneur, suzerain
Muslim: **6** sayyid

Lord High Executioner
4 Koko

Lord Jim author
6 Conrad (Joseph)

lordly
5 grand, noble, proud **6** august, puffed, uppity **7** haughty, swollen **8** affected, arrogant, cavalier, imposing, insolent, magnific, majestic, princely, snobbish, superior **9** egotistic, grandiose **10** disdainful **11** dictatorial, magisterial, magnificent, overbearing **12** supercilious **13** authoritarian, high-and-mighty

Lord of the Flies author
7 Golding (William)

Lord's Prayer
9 Our Father **11** Paternoster

lore
4 myth, saga, tale **5** fable **6** custom, legend, mythos, wisdom **7** folkway, science **9** knowledge, mythology, tradition **11** information **12** old wives' tale, superstition

Lorelei
5 siren **9** temptress **10** seductress **11** femme fatale
poet: **5** Heine (Heinrich)
river: **5** Rhine
victim: **6** sailor **7** mariner

Lorenzo's beloved
7 Jessica

lorgnette
8 eyeglass **10** opera glass

Lorna Doone
author: **9** Blackmore (Richard)
hero: **4** Ridd (John)

___-Lorraine
6 Alsace

lose
3 rid, rob **4** drop, fail, fall, miss, oust, slip, tine, tyne **5** clear, shake, yield **6** divest, give up, mislay **7** bereave, decline, deprive, forfeit, regress, succumb **8** misplace, shake off, throw off, unburden **9** sacrifice, surrender

lose feathers
4 molt

loser
3 dud **4** bomb, bust, flop **5** lemon **7** also-ran, convict, failure **8** jailbird

loss
4 leak, ruin **5** havoc, waste **6** damage, defeat, injury **7** failure, forfeit **8** decrease **9** confusion, mislaying, privation, ruination, sacrifice **10** divestment, forfeiture, misplacing **11** bereavement, deprivation, deprivement, destruction

lost
4 dead, gone **6** absent, astray, bygone, damned, doomed, hidden, musing, passed, ruined **7** bemused, defunct, extinct, faraway, lacking, mislaid, missing **8** absorbed, departed, distrait, vanished **9** condemned, daydreamy, graceless **10** abstracted **11** inconscient, irrevocable, preoccupied, unconscious, unconverted **12** absentminded, incorrigible, irredeemable, irreformable, unregenerate

Lost Horizon
author: **6** Hilton (James)
land: **9** Shangri-La

lot
3 cut, ilk, set **4** bite, body, doom, fate, give, heap, kind, lump, mass, much, part, peck, plat, push, sort, type, yard **5** allow, array, batch, block, breed, bunch, clump, crowd, field, group, moira, patch, quota, share, slice, tract, weird **6** assign, barrel, bundle, circle, clutch, decree, kidney, kismet, parcel, stripe **7** cluster, destiny, feather, fortune, mete out, partage, portion, species **8** allocate, clearing, frontage **9** admeasure, aggregate, allowance, apportion, character, great deal

Lot
father: **5** Haran
sister: **5** Iscah **6** Milcah
son: **4** Moab **5** Ammon
uncle: **7** Abraham

Lotan's father
4 Seir

lothario
5 Romeo **7** amorist, Don Juan, gallant **8** Casanova, paramour

Loti, Pierre
5 Viaud (Louis-Marie-Julien)

lotion
3 oil **4** balm **8** ablution, liniment, ointment

lottery
6 raffle 7 drawing 11 sweepstakes

lotus-eater
7 dreamer

loud
5 gaudy, harsh, noisy, showy
6 brassy, brazen, flashy, garish, hoarse, tawdry, tinsel, vulgar
7 blaring, blatant, booming, chintzy, glaring, pealing, raucous, ringing, roaring 8 piercing, resonant, sonorous, strident 9 deafening, obnoxious, obtrusive, offensive
10 bigmouthed, resounding, stentorian, stertorous, thunderous 11 ear-piercing, full-mouthed, fulminating, stentorious 12 ear-splitting

loudmouth
7 stentor 8 blowhard, braggart

loudspeaker
6 woofer 7 tweeter

Louise composer
11 Charpentier (Gustave)

Louisiana
capital: 10 Baton Rouge
county: 6 parish
largest city: 10 New Orleans
nickname: 11 Creole State 12 Pelican State
state flower: 8 magnolia
university: 3 LSU
6 Tulane 9 Grambling

lounge
3 bar, bum, lie, pub, tap 4 idle, laze, lazy, loaf, loll, sofa 5 dally, drift, slack 6 dawdle, loiter, saloon
7 barroom, buvette, lie down, recline, taproom

lounge lizard
3 fop 4 buck, dude 5 blood, dandy, leech 6 sponge, sucker
7 coxcomb, sponger 8 barnacle, hanger-on, macaroni, parasite
9 exquisite 10 freeloader 11 Beau Brummel, bloodsucker, petit-maître

Lourdes saint
10 Bernadette

louse
3 cur, dog, rat 4 snot, toad
5 aphid, skunk, snake 6 cootie, psylla, slater, wretch 7 stinker
egg: 3 nit

louse up
4 mess, ruin 5 botch 6 bobble, bollix, bungle, mucker

lout
3 oaf 4 boor, dolt, gawk, hick, lump, mock, quiz, razz, rube, twit
5 churl, klutz, looby, rally, scout, taunt, yokel 6 deride, galoot, lubber, lummox, rustic 7 bumpkin, hayseed, lobster, palooka, peasant
8 ridicule, stinkard 10 clodhopper

Louvre masterpiece
8 Mona Lisa 11 Venus de Milo

lovable
4 dear 6 genial 7 winning, winsome 8 adorable, alluring, charming, engaging, fetching, pleasing
9 appealing, endearing, ravishing, seductive 10 attractive, bewitching, enchanting, entrancing 11 captivating, enthralling

love
3 pet 4 dear, like, lust, zeal
5 adore, amour, ardor, crush, Cupid, deify, exalt, fancy, honey, piety, prize, sweet, value 6 admire, affair, caress, cosset, cuddle, dandle, desire, enamor, fealty, fervor, fondle, liking, regard, revere 7 ardency, cherish, darling, emotion, idolize, loyalty, passion, romance, worship 8 devotion, fidelity, fondness, idolatry, treasure, venerate, yearning 9 adoration, affection, delight in, sentiment, sweetling
10 allegiance, appreciate, attachment, enthusiasm, honeybunch, sweetheart 11 amorousness, infatuation
combining form: 5 phily 6 philia
French: 5 amour
Italian: 5 amore

love apple
6 tomato

lovebird
6 budgie, parrot 10 budgerigar

love feast
5 agape

love god
4 Amor, Eros, Kama 5 Bhaga, Cupid

love goddess
5 Athor, Freya, Venus 6 Hathor, Inanna, Ishtar 7 Astarte 9 Aphrodite, Ashtoreth

love letter
8 mash note 9 valentine 10 billet-doux

lovely
4 fair, rare 5 sweet 6 beauty, dainty, eyeful, looker, pretty 7 stunner 8 alluring, charming, delicate, engaging, graceful, handsome, knockout 9 beauteous, beautiful, exquisite 10 attractive, bewitching, delectable, delightful, enchanting, entrancing 11 captivating, good-looking

love-potion
7 philter, philtre 11 aphrodisiac

lover
3 fan, man 4 beau, buff 5 flame, hound, leman, Romeo 6 addict, master, steady, votary 7 amorist, devotee, Don Juan, gallant, habitué
8 fancy man, lothario, mistress, paramour 9 boyfriend, inamorata, inamorato 10 aficionado, girl friend
of beauty: 7 esthete 8 aesthete
of books: 11 bibliophile

love song
5 canso 6 ballad, serena
8 serenade

love story
7 romance

love token
4 ring 6 amoret

loving
4 dear, fond, kind 6 ardent, erotic, tender 7 amatory, amorous, bound up, cordial, devoted, fervent 8 attached, enamored, faithful 9 attentive 10 benevolent, infatuated, passionate, solicitous 11 considerate, impassioned, warmhearted
12 affectionate
combining form: 4 phil 5 phile, philo
6 philic 7 philous

low
3 bad, cut, moo, raw 4 base, blue, deep, down, flat, mean, neap, poor, rude, vile, weak 5 brief, broke, cheap, crass, crude, dizzy, faint, gross, needy, rough, short, under 6 abject, ailing, coarse, fallen, humble, lesser, nether, offish, poorly, scurvy, sickly, sordid, undear, unwell, vulgar, woeful 7 cut-rate, ignoble, nominal, popular, reduced, scrubby, scruffy, servile, slashed, uncouth, underly 8 atypical, baseborn, beggared, cast down, dejected, dirt poor, downcast, feverish, indigent, inferior, mediocre, moderate, off-color, plebeian, uncostly, unwashed, wretched 9 declining, depressed, destitute, inelegant, miserable, penurious, subjacent, subnormal, woebegone
10 despicable, economical, indisposed, marked down, reasonable, spiritless, subaverage, unennobled
11 crestfallen, downhearted

lowbred
7 boorish, loutish **8** churlish, cloddish, lubberly **9** unrefined **10** unpolished **11** uncivilized

low-cost
5 cheap **6** undear **7** popular **10** affordable, reasonable **11** inexpensive

low-down
4 base, mean, ugly, vile **6** scurvy **7** ignoble, servile **8** wretched **10** despicable

lowdown
4 dope **5** facts **11** information

lower
3 cut **4** clip, drop, fall, pare, peer, rail, sink **5** abase, abate, couch, decry, demit, droop, frown, gloom, scowl, shave, slash, stare, under **6** bemean, debase, demean, demote, humble, lesser, menace, nether, reduce **7** cut back, cut down, deflate, degrade, demerit, depress, descend, detrude, devalue, let down **8** cast down, inferior, mark down, overcast, submerge, threaten, write off **9** devaluate, downgrade, humiliate, subjacent
combining form: **4** bath, cato **5** batho
prefix: **5** infra

Lower Depths author
5 Gorki, Gorky (Maksim)

lowest
5 least **6** bottom **7** deepest **9** undermost **10** bottommost, nethermost, rock-bottom

lowest point
5 nadir **6** trough
on earth: **7** Dead Sea

low-grade
4 hack, mean, poor **6** common **8** declassé, inferior **10** second-rate **11** second-class **12** second-drawer

low-key
4 soft **5** sober **7** subdued **8** softened **9** toned down

lowland
4 flat, vale **6** valley **7** bottoms
Scottish: **6** lallan **7** lalland

Lowlander
4 Scot **8** Scotsman

lowlife
4 heel, worm **5** knave, rogue **6** mucker, no-good, rascal, wretch **7** villain **8** wormling **9** miscreant, scoundrel **10** blackguard

lowly
4 base, mean, meek **6** humble, modest **7** ignoble, mundane, prosaic, servile, workday **8** baseborn, everyday, obeisant, plebeian, retiring, unwashed, workaday

low-pitched
4 bass

low-pressure
6 casual, degagé **7** relaxed, unfussy **8** informal **9** easygoing **10** unreserved **13** unconstrained

low-priced
5 cheap **6** undear **7** popular **8** uncostly **10** reasonable **11** inexpensive

low-spirited
4 blue, down **8** dejected, downcast **9** depressed, heartsore, woebegone

low tide
3 ebb **4** neap

loyal
4 firm, true **5** liege **6** ardent, trusty **7** devoted, staunch **8** constant, faithful, resolute **9** allegiant, steadfast

loyalist
4 Tory **7** patriot

loyalty
5 ardor, truth **6** fealty **8** adhesion, devotion, fidelity, trueness **9** adherence, constancy **10** allegiance, attachment **12** faithfulness

lozenge
4 pill **5** candy **6** tablet, troche **7** diamond, rhombus, tabella **8** pastille

LSD
4 acid
user: **8** acidhead

lubricate
3 oil **6** grease **7** moisten

lubricious
4 lewd **5** slick **6** fickle, greasy, slippy, wanton **8** slippery, slithery, ticklish, unstable, variable, volatile **9** lecherous, salacious, uncertain **10** changeable, inconstant **13** temperamental

lucent
5 clear **6** bright **7** beaming, crystal, radiant, shining **8** clear-cut, luminous, pellucid **9** brilliant, unblurred **11** unambiguous

Lucia di Lammermoor
composer: **9** Donizetti (Gaetano)

lucid
4 sane **5** clear, right **6** bright, normal **7** beaming, crystal, lambent, radiant **8** all there, clear-cut, knowable **9** brilliant, effulgent, graspable, refulgent, unblurred **10** fathomable **11** transparent, unambiguous **12** compos mentis, incandescent, intelligible, transpicuous **13** apprehensible

lucidity
3 wit **4** mind **6** reason, sanity, senses **7** clarity **8** saneness **9** clearness, plainness, soundness **12** distinctness, explicitness

Lucifer
5 devil, fiend, Satan **6** diablo **7** Old Nick, serpent **8** Apollyon **9** Beelzebub **10** Old Scratch **13** Old Gooseberry

Lucinde
beloved: **7** Leandre **9** Clitandre
father: **7** Geronte **10** Sganarelle

luck
3 hap, hit, lot **4** bump, juju, meet, weal, zemi **5** break, charm, fluke, light **6** amulet, chance, fetish, happen, hazard, kismet, mascot, tumble **7** fortune, godsend, periapt, stumble **8** accident, fortuity, occasion, talisman, windfall **9** advantage **10** phylactery **11** opportunity **13** fortunateness
token: **5** charm **6** amulet, clover, mascot **8** talisman **9** horseshoe

luckless
7 hapless, unhappy **8** ill-fated, untoward, wretched **9** miserable **10** ill-starred **11** star-crossed, unfortunate **12** misfortunate

lucky
4 well **5** happy **6** benign **9** favorable, fortunate **10** auspicious, beneficial, felicitous, profitable, propitious **12** advantageous, providential
Scottish: **5** canny

lucrative
4 good **6** paying **7** gainful **10** productive, profitable, well-paying, worthwhile **11** moneymaking **12** advantageous

Lucrezia _____
6 Borgia

ludicrous
5 antic, awful, comic, droll, funny, silly **6** absurd **7** bizarre, comical, foolish, risible **8** farcical, gelastic **9** fantastic, grotesque, laughable

Lud's town
6 London

lug
3 box, tow 4 bear, buck, drag, draw, haul, jerk, pack, pull, snap, tote, worm, yank 5 carry, ferry, shlep 6 convey, schlep, twitch 9 transport, vellicate

luggage
4 bags 7 baggage 9 suitcases

lugubrious
3 sad 4 dour, glum 5 black, bleak 6 dismal, dreary, gloomy, morose, rueful, somber, sullen, woeful 7 doleful, joyless 8 dolesome, mournful 9 cheerless, plaintive, saturnine, sorrowful 10 depressant, depressing, lamentable, melancholy, oppressing, oppressive 11 dispiriting

lukewarm
4 cool 5 tepid 8 hesitant 9 uncertain, undecided 10 indecisive, irresolute, irresolved, unresolved, wishy-washy 11 halfhearted, uncommitted

lull
3 ebb 4 balm, calm, hush, wane 5 abate, allay, comma, let up, pause, quiet, still 6 becalm, settle, soothe, temper 7 compose, die away, die down, ease off, qualify, slacken, subside 8 abeyance, interval, moderate 9 pausation 10 quiescence 11 tranquilize

lullaby
4 song 8 berceuse 10 cradlesong
Scottish: 5 baloo, balow

lumber
3 tax 4 clog, lade, load, logs, plod, slog, wood 5 barge, clump, stump, weigh 6 burden, charge, saddle, timber, trudge

lumberjack
see **logger**

Lumber State
5 Maine

luminance
10 brightness

luminary
3 big, sun, VIP 4 lion, name, star 5 light, nabob 6 leader 7 big name, notable 8 big-timer, eminence, somebody 9 celebrity 10 notability 12 leading light

luminous
5 clear, lucid 6 bright, lucent 7 beaming, crystal, fulgent, lam-

bent, radiant, shining 8 clear-cut, knowable, pellucid 9 brilliant, effulgent, graspable, refulgent, unblurred 10 fathomable 11 translucent, transparent 12 incandescent

lummox
3 oaf 4 boor, gawk, lout 5 klutz, looby 7 lobster, palooka

lump
3 bit, gob, lot, oaf, wad 4 bear, blob, bulk, chip, clod, clot, gawk, heap, hunk, knot, lout, mass, much, peck, pile, welt 5 abide, batch, block, brook, bulge, bunch, chunk, crumb, hunch, klutz, looby, piece, scrap, stand, wedge 6 barrel, digest, endure, lubber, morsel, nugget 7 lobster, palooka, portion, stomach, swallow 8 swelling 12 protuberance

lumpy
3 raw 4 rude 5 crude, rough 8 clumpish, unformed 9 rough-hewn, undressed

lunacy
5 folly, mania 7 fatuity, foolery, inanity, madness 8 delirium, insanity 9 absurdity, asininity, craziness, silliness, stupidity, unbalance 10 aberration, alienation, ineptitude, insaneness 11 derangement, distraction, foolishness, psychopathy, witlessness 13 senselessness

lunar
dark area: 4 mare 5 maria (plural)
valley: 4 rill 5 rille

lunatic
3 mad, nut 4 kook, loon 5 crank, crazy, loony, raver, wacky 6 absurd, crazed, cuckoo, dement, insane, madman, maniac, psycho 7 cracked, foolish, madling, unsound 8 crackpot, demented, demoniac, deranged, paranoid 9 bedlamite, ding-a-ling, energumen, fantastic, harebrain, neuropath, non compos, screwball 10 crackbrain, Tom o' Bedlam

lunch
4 meal, nosh 5 snack 6 tiffin

luncheonette, lunchroom
4 café 6 eatery 7 beanery 8 snack bar 9 cafeteria 10 coffee shop 11 eating house 12 sandwich shop

lune
5 leash

lung
5 organ 8 breather
combining form: 5 pneum, pulmo

6 pneumo, pulmon 7 pulmoni, pulmono
disease: 9 emphysema, pneumonia 12 tuberculosis

lunge
4 dive, stab 5 burst, drive, pitch 6 thrust

lunkhead
3 oaf 4 boob, dolt, goof 5 booby, chump, dunce

lupine
6 fierce 7 wolfish 10 bluebonnet

lurch
3 bob, yaw 4 bent, jerk, reel, rock, roll, snap, swag, sway, tilt, toss, wave, yank 5 swing, waver, weave, whirl 6 bumble, careen, falter, plunge, seesaw, swerve, teeter, tilter, topple, totter, twitch, wallow, wobble 7 blunder, leaning, stagger, stumble 8 flounder, penchant, tendency

lure
3 bag 4 bait, call, draw, fake, pull, rope, toll, trap, wile 5 blind, catch, charm, decoy, tempt, train, trick 6 ambush, appeal, cajole, come-on, draw in, draw on, entice, entrap, invite, lead on, seduce, suck-in 7 attract, beguile, bewitch, capture, con game, enchant, ensnare, gimmick, wheedle 8 blandish, delusion, illusion, inveigle 9 captivate, fascinate, incentive, seduction, siren song 10 attraction, camouflage, enticement, inducement, seducement, temptation
fishing: 3 fly 4 herl, worm 5 spoon 6 minnow 8 bucktail

lurid
3 wan 4 ashy, grim, pale 5 ashen, livid, waxen 6 doughy, malign, sultry 7 baleful, ghastly, hideous, macabre, malefic, tabloid 8 blanched, gruesome, horrible, sinister, terrible 9 colorless 10 horrifying, maleficent, terrifying 11 sensational

lurk
4 hide, slip 5 creep, skulk, slide, slink, sneak, steal 7 gumshoe 9 pussyfoot

luscious
4 rare, rich 5 sapid, tasty, yummy 6 Capuan, choice, deluxe, florid, ornate, rococo, savory 7 baroque, darling, opulent, piquant, sensual 8 adorable, heavenly, palatial, sensuous 9 ambrosial, epicurean, exquisite, palatable 10 appetizing, delectable, delightful, flamboyant,

flavorsome **11** distinctive, scrumptious, upholstered

lush
  3 sot **4** rich **5** drunk, yummy **6** bibber, boozer, Capuan, deluxe **7** opulent, profuse, riotous, sensual, tippler **8** adorable, drunkard, heavenly, palatial, prodigal, sensuous **9** ambrosial, delicious, epicurean, exuberant, inebriate, luxuriant, luxurious, profusive, sumptuous **10** boozehound, delectable, delightful, voluptuous

Lusitania
  4 ship **5** liner **8** Portugal

lust
  3 rut, yen **4** ache, heat, itch, long, pine, urge, wish **5** crave, letch, yearn **6** desire, fervor, hanker, hunger, libido, thirst **7** craving, lechery, passion **8** appetite, coveting, cupidity, priapism, salacity, satyrism, yearning **9** carnality, eroticism, lubricity, prurience, pruriency **10** aphrodisia, appetition, excitement, satyriasis **11** nymphomania **13** concupiscence, lecherousness

luster
  4 glow **5** glaze, gleam, glint, gloss, sheen, shine **6** polish **8** radiance **9** afterglow **10** brightness, brilliance, brilliancy, effulgence, luminosity, refulgence **11** candescence, iridescence, opalescence

lusterless
  3 dim, mat, wan **4** dead, drab, dull, flat **5** blind, faded, muted, prosy **7** prosaic

lustful
  3 hot **4** fast, lewd **5** rutty **7** burning, goatish, itching, ruttish, satyric **8** prurient **9** lecherous, libertine, lickerish, salacious **10** hot-blooded, lascivious, libidinous, licentious, passionate **11** incontinent **12** concupiscent

lustrate
  5 purge **6** purify **7** cleanse

lustration
  9 catharsis, cleansing

lustrous
  5 nitid, shiny **6** bright, gleamy, glossy, sheeny **7** fulgent, lambent, radiant, shining **8** gleaming, glinting, polished, splendid **9** brilliant,

burnished, effulgent, refulgent, sparkling **10** glimmering, glistening **11** resplendent **12** incandescent

lusty
  4 hale, huge, vast **5** hardy, vital **6** mighty, potent, robust, strong **7** dynamic, healthy, immense, massive **8** enormous, vigorous, whacking, whopping **9** energetic, strenuous **10** full-bodied, prodigious, red-blooded, tremendous

lusus
  5 freak **7** monster **8** abortion **11** miscreation, monstrosity

lute
  4 clay, ring, seal **6** cement **7** bandora, bandore **10** chitarrone, instrument
  Arabic: **3** oud
  Greco-Roman: **7** pandura **8** pandoura
  Oriental: **3** tar
  Russian: **7** bandura
  Spanish: **8** banduria
  two-necked: **7** theorbo

lutenist
  4 Mace (Denis, Thomas) **5** Bream (Julian) **6** Gallot (Antoine, Jacques, Henry Francois), Mouton (Charles), Radolt (Wenzel Ludwig von) **7** Bakfark (Balint), Dowland (John, Robert), Gautier (Jacques, Pierre), Perrine **8** Capirola (Vincenzo), Gaultier (Denis, Ennemond)

Lutetia
  5 Paris

luxuriant
  4 lush, posh, rank, rich **5** plush **6** Capuan, fecund, lavish **7** fertile, opulent, profuse, riotous **8** fruitful, luscious, palatial, prodigal, prolific **9** exuberant, sumptuous

luxuriate
  4 bask, love, riot, roll **5** eat up, enjoy, feast, revel **6** overdo, wallow, welter **7** indulge, rollick **11** overindulge

luxurious
  4 lush, posh, rich **5** awful, fancy, grand, plush, showy **6** Capuan, costly, deluxe, lavish, palace, plushy **7** opulent, sensual, stately **8** imposing, majestic, palatial, splendid **9** elaborate, epicurean, expensive, grandiose

10 impressive **11** extravagant, languishing, magnificent
  situation: **7** fat city **10** bed of roses, easy street

luxury
  5 frill **6** dainty **7** amenity, comfort **8** delicacy **10** redundancy **11** superfluity **12** extravagance **13** embellishment

Lycaon
  daughter: **8** Callisto
  father: **8** Pelasgus
  mother: **8** Meliboea

Lycidas author
  6 Milton (John)

Lycomedes
  daughter: **8** Deidamia
  victim: **7** Theseus

Lycus
  brother: **7** Nycteus
  father: **7** Pandion
  slayer: **6** Zethus **7** Amphion
  wife: **5** Dirce

Lydian
  king: **5** Gyges **7** Croesus **8** Alyattes
  queen: **7** Omphale

lye
  7 caustic **8** lixivium

Lynceus
  brother: **4** Idas
  father: **8** Aphareus

lynch
  4 hang **6** murder

Lynette
  see **Line**

lynx
  3 cat **6** bobcat **7** caracal **9** catamount

Lyra star
  4 Vega

lyre
  4 harp **6** kissar **10** instrument

lyric
  3 ode **4** odic, poem **5** melic **6** poetic **7** melodic, musical

lyric drama
  5 opera

Lysander's beloved
  6 Hermia

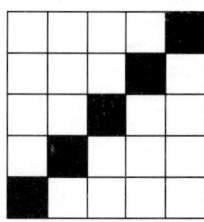

Maacah

father: 5 Nahor 6 Talmai
7 Absalom
husband: 5 David 6 Jehiel, Machir
8 Rehoboam
son: 5 Hanan 6 Abijam, Achish
7 Absalom 10 Shephatiah

Maaseiah

father: 6 Jotham 7 Shallum
son: 7 Azariah 8 Zedekiah
9 Zephaniah

macabre

4 grim 5 lurid 6 deadly, grisly, horrid 7 deathly, ghastly, ghostly, hideous 8 gruesome, horrible, terrible
9 deathlike, ghostlike 10 horrifying, unpleasant

macaque

6 monkey, rhesus

macaroni

3 fop 4 buck, dude 5 dandy
7 coxcomb

Macbeth

character: 4 Ross 5 Angus 6 Hecate,
Lennox 7 Fleance
slayer: 7 Macduff
successor: 7 Malcolm
title: 5 thane
victim: 6 Banquo, Duncan

mace

3 bat, rod 4 beat, bilk, club 5 baton, billy, staff 6 cudgel, strike
8 bludgeon 9 billy club 10 knob-kerrie, nightstick

Macedonia

capital: 5 Pella 6 Skopje
king: 6 Philip 9 Alexander
last king: 7 Perseus

machete

4 bolo 5 knife 6 guitar

Machiavelli work

9 The Prince 11 The Mandrake

machinate

4 plot 6 devise, scheme, wangle
7 collude, connive, finagle 8 cogitate, conspire, contrive, engineer,
intrigue, maneuver 9 scheme out

machine

3 car 4 auto 5 buggy, golem, motor, robot 6 device 7 autocar, fashion, vehicle 8 motorcar 9 automaton 10 automobile, conveyance
11 standardize
component: 3 cam 4 belt, gear, seal
5 brake, chain, screw, shaft
6 clutch, spring 7 linkage
8 coupling
excavating: 7 backhoe
humanlike: 5 robot
laboratory: 10 centrifuge

machine-gun

6 strafe

machine gun inventor

7 Gatling (Richard)

machinery

4 gear, tool 5 agent, means, organ, works 6 agency, device, gadget, medium, outfit, tackle 7 channel, utensil, vehicle 8 matériel,
tackling 9 apparatus, appliance,
equipment, implement 10 instrument 11 contraption, contrivance

Machir's father

6 Ammiel 8 Manasseh

Macher Picchu resident

4 Inca

mackle

4 blur

macrocosm

5 world 6 cosmos, nature 8 creation, universe

McTeague author

6 Norris (Frank)

mad

3 ire 4 daft, fury, rage, rash, sore,
waxy, wild 5 anger, angry, crazy,
irate, irked, loony, rabid, wacky,
wrath, wroth 6 absurd, enrage,
heated, insane, ireful 7 cracked,
enraged, foolish, frantic, furious, incense, invalid, lunatic, steam up,
umbrage 8 choleric, demented,
deranged, frenetic, frenzied, of-
fended, outraged, worked up,
wrathful 9 affronted, delirious, fantastic, hilarious, illogical, indignant,
infuriate, senseless, sophistic
10 corybantic, exasperate, fallacious, irrational, reasonless, unbalanced

Madagascar

capital: 10 Tananarive 12 Anta-
nanarivo
export: 5 sugar 6 cloves, coffee
7 vanilla
monetary unit: 5 franc

Madame Bovary

4 Emma
author: 8 Flaubert (Gustave)

Madame Butterfly

character: 9 Cho-Cho-San, Cio-Cio-
San, Pinkerton, Sharpless
composer: 7 Puccini (Giacomo)

madcap

4 rash 5 brash, hasty 8 reckless
9 hotheaded 10 ill-advised, incautious 11 thoughtless 13 inconsiderate

Mad Cavalier

6 Rupert (Prince)

madden

3 ire 5 anger, craze 6 enrage,
frenzy 7 derange, incense, possess, shatter, steam up, umbrage,
unhinge 8 distract 9 infuriate,
unbalance

Madeira

capital: 7 Funchal
export: 4 wine 5 sugar 7 bananas

made-to-order

6 custom 10 customized 11 custom-built

madhouse

5 chaos 6 asylum, bedlam 8 loony
bin 9 funny farm 10 booby hatch

madman
3 ass, nut 4 bawd, fool, jerk, loon 5 idiot, loony, ninny 6 dement, donkey, maniac, psycho 7 jackass, lunatic 8 imbecile 9 bedlamite, non compos 10 nincompoop, Tom o' Bedlam

madness
4 rage 6 lunacy, rabies 7 ecstasy 8 insanity 9 unbalance 10 aberration, alienation, enthusiasm 11 derangement, distraction, psychopathy

Madonna initials
3 BVM

Madras
9 Tamil Nadu
founder: 3 Day (Francis)

Madrid museum
5 Prado

madrigal
4 glee, poem, song 8 part-song

madrigalist
Dutch: 8 Arcadelt (Jacques)
English: 4 Byrd (William) 6 Morley (Thomas), Wilbye (John) 7 Tomkins (Thomas), Weelkes (Thomas)
Flemish: 8 Willaert (Adriaan)
Italian: 5 Festa (Costanzo) 7 Landini (Francesco) 8 Marenzio (Luca) 10 Monteverdi (Claudio)

maelstrom
4 eddy, fury 5 storm, whirl 6 vortex 7 turmoil 9 commotion, confusion, whirlpool

maestro
see **conductor**

magazine
4 dump, Life, Time 5 cache, daily, depot, organ, store 6 annual, armory, digest, review, weekly 7 arsenal, gazette, journal, McCall's, monthly, Playboy, Redbook, TV Guide 8 biweekly 9 bimonthly, newspaper, quarterly, warehouse, Woman's Day 10 depository, lumber room, periodical, repository, semiweekly, storehouse 11 publication 12 Family Circle 13 Reader's Digest

maggot
4 grub, whim 5 fancy, freak, humor, larva 6 notion, vagary 7 boutade, caprice, conceit

Magi
6 Gaspar 8 Melchior 9 Balthazar
gift: 4 gold 5 myrrh 12 frankincense

magian
6 mystic, witchy, wizard

7 charmer, warlock 8 conjurer, sorcerer, wizardly 9 enchanter, sorcerous 11 necromancer, necromantic 12 thaumaturgic

magic
5 charm, wicca 6 augury, mystic, witchy 7 alchemy, bewitch, conjury, devilry, gramary, sorcery 8 deviltry, divining, exorcism, gramarye, satanism, witchery, witching, wizardly, wizardry 9 conjuring, diablerie, diabolism, marvelous, occultism, sorcerous, sortilege, voodooism 10 mumbo jumbo, necromancy, prodigious, remarkable, stupendous, witchcraft 11 abracadabra, bewitchment, enchantment, incantation, legerdemain, necromantic, soothsaying, thaumaturgy 12 thaumaturgic, unbelievable

magical
6 mystic, witchy 8 wizardly 9 sorcerous 10 bewitching 11 necromantic 12 thaumaturgic

Magic Flute composer
6 Mozart (Wolfgang Amadeus)

magician
4 seer 5 brujo, witch 6 medium, shaman, voodoo, wizard 7 augurer, charmer, diviner, Houdini, prophet, warlock 8 conjurer, exorcist, satanist, sorcerer 9 archimage, diabolist, enchanter, exorciser, invocator, trickster, voodooist 10 soothsayer 11 illusionist, medicine man, necromancer, thaumaturge
Arthurian: 6 Merlin

magicking
7 sorcery 8 witchery, wizardry 9 conjuring 10 necromancy, witchcraft 11 bewitchment, enchantment, thaumaturgy

Magic Mountain, The
author: 4 Mann (Thomas)
character: 7 Castorp

magisterial
5 bossy, puffy, wiggy 6 lordly, stuffy 7 bloated, pompous 8 arrogant, dogmatic, insolent 9 dictative, imperious, important, masterful 10 disdainful, high-handed, imperative, peremptory, pontifical 11 doctrinaire, domineering, overbearing 12 supercilious 13 authoritarian, authoritative, self-important

Magister Ludi author
5 Hesse (Hermann)

magistrate
5 court, judge 7 bencher, justice 8 official

ancient Greek: 5 ephor 6 archon
ancient Roman: 5 edile 6 aedile, pretor 7 duumvir, praetor, questor 8 quaestor
Italian: 7 podesta
Scottish: 6 bailie
Venice (former): 4 doge

Magna Carta
king: 4 John
place signed: 9 Runnymede

magnanimous
3 big 5 great, lofty, noble 7 liberal 8 generous, knightly, princely 9 forgiving, unselfish 10 altruistic, benevolent, chivalrous, highminded 11 noble-minded

magnate
4 czar, king, lion, name, peer 5 baron, mogul, nabob 6 biggie, big gun, fat cat, figure, prince, tycoon 8 big-timer, nobleman 9 personage, plutocrat

magnesium
symbol: 2 Mg

magnet
8 terrella 9 lodestone

magnetic
7 drawing 8 alluring 9 appealing, arresting, seductive 10 attracting, attractive, bewitching, enchanting 11 captivating, charismatic, fascinating 12 irresistible
substance: 4 iron 7 ferrite

magnetism
5 charm 6 allure, appeal, glamor 7 glamour 8 charisma, witchery 10 witchcraft 11 fascination

magnetize
4 draw, lure, take, wile 5 charm 6 allure 7 attract, bewitch, enchant 9 captivate, fascinate

magnification unit
8 diameter

magnificence
8 grandeur, splendor 13 sumptuousness

magnificent
5 grand, noble, proud 6 august, lordly, superb 7 opulent, stately, sublime 8 glorious, gorgeous, imposing, majestic, splendid, standout 9 brilliant, grandiose, inspiring, luxurious, sumptuous 11 extravagant, outstanding, resplendent, splendorous, superlative 13 splendiferous

magnifier
4 lens
jeweler's: 5 loupe

magnify

3 pad 4 hymn, laud, rise 5 add to, bless, boost, color, cry up, erect, exalt, extol, fudge, honor, mount, rouse, swell 6 beef up, deepen, dilate, expand, extend, praise, uprear 7 amplify, augment, distend, enhance, enlarge, ennoble, glorify, inflate, sublime 8 eulogize, heighten, increase, maximize, multiply, overdraw, overplay, redouble 9 aggravate, celebrate, embellish, embroider, intensate, intensify, overpaint, overstate 10 aggrandize, exaggerate, overcharge, overstress, panegyrize 13 overemphasize

magnifying

combining form: 4 micr 5 micro

magniloquent

7 aureate, flowery, swollen 8 sonorous 9 bombastic, overblown 10 euphuistic, rhetorical 11 declamatory

magnitude

4 pith, size, tune 5 order, range 6 extent, import, matter, moment, number, volume, weight 7 bigness, caliber, measure, quality 8 enormity, hugeness, loudness, quantity, vastness, vicinity 9 greatness, immensity, largeness 10 dimensions, importance, proportion 11 consequence, sizableness, weightiness

Magnolia State

11 Mississippi

magnum opus

7 classic 10 masterwork 11 chef d'oeuvre, masterpiece, tour de force

Magog's king

3 Gog

magpie

4 bird, crow 6 gabber, prater 7 blabber 8 jabberer, prattler 9 bandar-log, blabmouth, chatterer 10 chatterbox, piping crow 12 blabbermouth 13 miscellaneous

maguey

5 agave, fiber 7 cantala
relative: 4 aloe

magus

6 wizard 7 charmer, warlock 8 conjurer, sorcerer 9 enchanter 11 necromancer

Magyar

9 Hungarian

Mahalath

father: 7 Ishmael 8 Jerimoth
husband: 4 Esau 8 Rehoboam

mah-jongg piece

4 tile

Mahli, Mahali

brother: 5 Mushi
father: 6 Merari

Mahlon

father: 9 Elimelech
mother: 5 Naomi
wife: 4 Ruth

Mahol's son

5 Darda, Heman 6 Calcol

Maia

father: 5 Atlas
mother: 7 Pleione
sisters: 8 Pleiades
son: 6 Hermes 7 Mercury

maid

3 gal 4 girl, lass, miss 5 biddy, bonne, missy, wench 6 damsel, lassie, virgin 7 servant 8 charlady, domestic, factotum 9 charwoman, hired girl 10 au pair girl, handmaiden
lady's: 7 abigail

maiden

3 gal 4 burd, girl, lass, miss 5 first, fresh, missy, prime, wench 6 burdie, damsel, intact, lassie, unused, virgin 7 damosel, damozel, initial, pioneer, primary, untaken, untried 8 earliest, original, virginal 10 old-maidish, spinsterly 11 husbandless, spinsterish 12 undeflowered
combining form: 7 parthen 8 partheno
Muslim: 5 houri
Norse mythological: 6 valkyr 8 valkyrie, walkyrie

maidenhair tree

6 gingko, ginkgo

maidenhead

5 hymen 6 purity 9 freshness, virginity

maidenhood

9 virginity

maiden lady

7 old maid 8 spinster 10 spinstress

Maid of Astolat

6 Elaine

Maid of Orleans, The

4 Joan 7 Pucelle
author: 8 Schiller (Friedrich von)

___ mail

3 air 5 chain

maim

4 maul 5 break 6 batter, bung up, mangle, mayhem 7 cripple, disable, dislimb 8 massacre, mutilate,

paralyze 9 disfigure, dismember, hamstring

main

3 big, sea 4 blue, deep, head, line, star, very 5 brine, chief, drink, great, major, ocean, sheer, vital 7 capital, high sea, leading, stellar 8 cardinal, foremost 9 essential, paramount, principal 10 preeminent, prevailing 11 controlling, fundamental, outstanding, predominant

Maine

capital: 7 Augusta
college: 5 Bates, Colby 7 Bowdoin
highest point: 10 Mt. Katahdin
largest town: 8 Portland
motto: 6 dirigo 7 I direct
nickname: 11 Lumber State 13 Pine Tree State

mainstay

3 key 4 prop 5 brace, staff 6 crutch, pillar, sinews 7 standby, support 8 backbone, buttress, upholder 9 supporter, sustainer

Main Street author

5 Lewis (Sinclair)

maintain

4 aver, avow, save 5 argue, claim, guard, right 6 affirm, assert, avouch, back up, defend, insist, keep up, manage, stress, uphold 7 care for, carry on, contend, correct, declare, husband, justify, persist, profess, protect, protest, rectify, support, warrant 8 continue, preserve 9 cultivate, emphasize, vindicate 10 provide for

maintenance

4 care, keep, salt 5 bread 6 living, upkeep 7 alimony, support 10 livelihood 11 subsistence 12 alimentation
worker: 7 janitor 9 custodian

maize

4 milo 10 Indian corn

majestic

5 grand, noble, regal, royal 6 august, kingly, lordly 7 courtly, stately 8 elevated, imperial, imposing, kinglike, magnific, princely 9 dignified, grandiose, monarchal, sovereign 10 monarchial 11 ceremonious, magnificent, monarchical

major

3 big 4 fell, main, star, ugly 5 chief, grave, hefty, large 6 better, higher, larger 7 capital, greater, serious, sizable, stellar 8 grievous, superior 9 dangerous, extensive, principal 10 large-scale, preemi-

nent **11** outstanding, predominant **12** considerable

Major Barbara author
4 Shaw (George Bernard)

majority
4 edge **6** margin

make
3 act, eat, fit, fix, get, lay, net, run, set, tap, win **4** bear, brew, draw, earn, form, gain, head, mold, name, reap, sire **5** begin, build, catch, cause, clear, draft, enact, equal, erect, force, forge, frame, hatch, infer, judge, reach, ready, shape, spawn, start, write **6** attain, behave, coerce, compel, create, deduce, deduct, derive, draw on, draw up, effect, extend, father, finger, gather, intend, oblige, ordain, output, parent, secure, seduce, set out **7** achieve, acquire, appoint, bring in, clean up, collect, compose, concuss, count as, destine, fashion, harvest, perform, prepare, proceed, produce, serve as, shotgun, stretch, take off **8** assemble, break for, comprise, conclude, drag down, draw down, generate, initiate, light out, nominate, traverse **9** constrain, construct, designate, establish, fabricate, formulate, knock down, originate, procreate, strike out **10** bring about, constitute **11** manufacture, put together
amends: **5** atone
a metallic sound: **5** chink, clang
a mistake: **3** err **4** goof
ashen: **6** blanch
a statement: **7** expound
a witty remark: **4** jest
bare: **5** strip **6** denude
believe: **7** pretend
certain: **6** assure **8** convince
cheerful: **6** solace
coins: **4** mint
different: **6** change
fast: **3** fix **4** gird **6** secure
hair curly: **5** crimp **6** buckle
happy: **5** bless **6** please **7** satisfy
holy: **6** hallow
inoperative: **5** annul
into a law: **5** enact
known: **3** air **6** expose, reveal, spread **7** declare, divulge, uncover **8** announce, disclose, proclaim
less severe: **6** weaken **8** mitigate **9** attenuate
manifest: **7** explain
melodious: **6** attune
merry: **5** cheer
numb: **4** daze, stun
presentable: **5** groom

quiet: **4** calm **5** allay, quell **6** pacify **7** appease
ready beforehand: **7** prepare
red: **5** flush
rigid: **5** brace **7** stiffen
sacred: **8** sanctify
slick: **3** oil **9** lubricate
small: **8** belittle
smaller: **8** compress
strong: **7** fortify
suffix: **2** en, fy **3** ify
suitable: **5** adapt
supremely happy: **7** beatify
unclean: **4** soil
understandable: **7** clarify
useful: **7** utilize
use of: **6** employ
vigorous: **8** energize

make-believe
7 charade, feigned, fiction, pageant **8** disguise, pretense **9** insincere, pretender **10** pretension

make off
2 go **3** fly, run **4** bolt, flee, quit, skip **5** leave, scoot, skirr **6** decamp, depart, escape, retire **7** abscond, run away, scamper **8** withdraw **9** skedaddle

make out
2 go **3** dig, see **4** draw, show **5** catch, grasp, infer, judge, prove, score **6** accept, arrive, deduce, deduct, derive, follow, gather, take in, thrive **7** collect, compass, discern, prosper, succeed **8** conclude, flourish, get along **9** apprehend, determine, establish, interpret **10** comprehend, understand **11** demonstrate

make over
4 cede, deed **5** alien **6** assign, convey, reform, remise **7** remodel **8** alienate, renovate, transfer **10** abalienate

makeshift
6 refuge, resort **7** stopgap **8** recourse, resource **9** expedient, temporary **10** expediency, substitute **11** provisional **13** rough-and-ready

make similar to
suffix: **2** fy **3** ify

make up
3 fit, fix, get, mix, pay, sue, woo **4** fuse, meld, rise **5** atone, blend, court, frame, merge, ready, spark **6** decide, derise, gather, invent, mingle, offset, pursue, redeem, set off, settle **7** address, advance, arrange, balance, compile, compose, concoct, prepare, replace, reprint

8 approach, atone for, compound, comprise, contrive, intermix, outweigh **9** formulate, improvise, interfuse **10** compensate

makeup
3 lie **4** cast, face, form, mold, plan, vein **5** fiber, grain, humor, paint, setup, shape, stamp, style **6** design, nature, powder, stripe, temper **7** fiction **8** ordering, war paint **9** blackface, character, formation **10** complexion, maquillage **11** arrangement, composition, disposition, grease paint, personality, replacement, temperament **12** architecture, compensation, constitution, construction, organization
eye: **4** kohl **7** mascara
facial: **5** rouge **6** powder

maladroit
5 brash, inept **6** clumsy, gauche **7** awkward, halting, unhandy **8** bumbling, bungling, tactless **9** ham-handed, impolitic, lumbering, stumbling, unpolitic, unskilled, untactful **10** blundering, left-handed, ungraceful **11** floundering, heavy-handed **12** undiplomatic

malady
3 ill **7** ailment, disease, illness **8** disorder, sickness, syndrome **9** affection, complaint, condition, infirmity **10** affliction
suffix: **4** itis

malaise
7 disease **8** debility **9** infirmity **10** feebleness, infirmness, sickliness **11** decrepitude **13** unhealthiness

Malaprop creator
8 Sheridan (Richard Brinsley)

malapropos
5 inapt, undue **8** ill-timed, improper, mistimed, unseemly, untimely **10** unsuitable **11** ill-seasoned, inopportune, unbefitting **12** unseasonable, unseasonably **13** inappropriate, inopportunely

malaria
6 miasma **8** paludism
transmitter: **8** mosquito

malarkey
4 guff **5** hooey **6** bunkum, bushwa **7** hogwash, twaddle **8** nonsense **9** poppycock **10** balderdash **12** blatherskite

Malawi
capital: **8** Lilongwe
export: **3** tea **7** tobacco
largest city: **8** Blantyre
monetary unit: **6** kwacha

Malaysia
capital: **11** Kuala Lumpur
export: **3** tin **6** rubber, timber **7** palm oil

Malchiel
father: **6** Beriah
grandfather: **5** Asher

Malchijah, Malchiah
father: **5** Harim **6** Parosh, Rechab

Malchishua's father
4 Saul

malcontent
5 crank, rebel **6** anarch, griper, grouch, kicker, unruly **7** growler **8** factious, frondeur, grumbler, mutineer, mutinous, restless, revolter, sorehead **9** alienated, anarchist, estranged, insurgent, seditious **10** bellyacher, complainer, rebellious **11** disaffected, disgruntled, disobedient, faultfinder, ungratified **12** contumacious, dissatisfied, ungovernable

mal de ___
3 mer

Maldives capital
4 Male

maldonite
9 black gold

male
3 tom **5** fella, manly **6** manful, virile **7** manlike **9** masculine, staminate
combining form: **4** andr **5** andro
dark-haired: **6** brunet

malediction
5 curse **7** malison **8** anathema

malefactor
5 felon, knave, rogue **6** rascal, sinner **8** criminal, evildoer, offender **9** miscreant, scoundrel, wrongdoer **10** blackguard, lawbreaker

malefic
see **malicious**

malevolence
5 spite **6** grudge, malice, spleen **7** despite, ill will **9** hostility, malignity **10** abhorrence, antagonism **11** abomination, detestation **12** spitefulness **13** maliciousness

malevolent
4 evil **6** bitchy, malign, wicked **7** baleful, hateful, hurtful, vicious **8** sinister, spiteful **9** injurious, malicious, malignant **10** despiteful

malfunction
6 glitch

Mali
capital: **6** Bamako
monetary unit: **5** franc
product: **4** fish **6** cotton **7** peanuts

malice
4 bane, bile, hate **5** spite, venom **6** animus, enmity, grudge, hatred, poison, spleen **7** despite, ill will, umbrage **8** meanness **9** animosity, antipathy **10** bitterness, resentment **11** hatefulness, malevolence **12** spitefulness **13** invidiousness

malicious
4 evil, mean **5** catty, green, nasty, petty **6** bitchy, wicked, witchy **7** baneful, hateful, heinous, jealous, spitish **8** spiteful, venomous, virulent **9** green-eyed, poisonous, poison-pen, rancorous **10** despiteful, malevolent

maliciousness
see **malevolence**

malign
4 evil, slur, soil **5** decry, libel, smear, stain, sully, taint **6** befoul, defame, defile, revile, smirch, vilify, wicked **7** asperse, baleful, baneful, blacken, detract, hateful, hostile, noxious, pollute, slander, spatter, tarnish, traduce, vicious **8** backbite, besmirch, derogate, inimical, sinister, spiteful, tear down, virulent **9** bespatter, denigrate, disparage, injurious, rancorous **10** calumniate, depreciate, despiteful, maleficent, malevolent, pernicious, scandalize, villainize, vituperate **11** deleterious, detrimental, opprobriate **12** antagonistic, antipathetic

malignant
4 evil **6** wicked **7** baleful, hateful, vicious **8** devilish, fiendish, spiteful **9** injurious, rancorous **10** despiteful, diabolical, malevolent

malison
5 curse **8** anathema **11** commination, imprecation, malediction

mall
4 lane **5** alley **6** mallet **9** concourse, esplanade, promenade **10** passageway **11** median strip

malleable
6 pliant, supple **7** ductile, plastic

malleate
4 beat **5** pound **6** hammer

mallet
6 hammer, strike

Mallothi's father
5 Heman

Malluch's father
4 Bani **5** Harim

malodorous
4 foul, gamy, high, olid, rank, vile **5** fetid, fuggy, funky, fusty, musty, nasty, reeky, rough, stale **6** frowsy, putrid, rancid, rotten, smelly, stinky, strong, whiffy **7** decayed, noisome, noxious, reeking, spoiled, stenchy, tainted, ungodly **8** improper, indecent, mephitic, polluted, stinking, unseemly, untoward **9** offensive, poisonous, stenchful **10** decomposed, indelicate, nauseating, unbecoming **11** ill-smelling **12** pestilential

Malta
capital: **8** Valletta
monetary unit: **4** lira **5** pound
product: **8** textiles

Maltese Falcon, The
author: **7** Hammett (Dashiell)
detective: **5** Spade (Sam)

maltreat
5 abuse **6** ill-use, misuse **7** outrage **8** disserve

mammal
3 ass **5** camel, daman, hippo, hyrax **6** alpaca, colugo, dassie **7** bearcat, primate **8** elephant **12** hippopotamus
African: **5** okapi, zebra, zoril **7** zorilla, zorille, zorillo **8** aardvark, aardwolf
aquatic: **5** yapok **6** desman, dugong, narwal, yapock **7** cowfish, manatee, narwhal, platypi (plural) **8** cetacean, narwhale, platypus, porpoise, sirenian **10** platypuses (plural)
arboreal: **5** lemur **6** cuscus **7** opossum **8** kinkajou, lemuroid
Australian: **5** coala, koala **8** kangaroo
burrowing: **8** moldwarp, starnose, suricate
carnivorous: **3** cat, dog, fox **4** bear, lion, mink, seal, wolf **5** genet, hyena, otter, panda, pekan, ratel, sable, tiger **6** badger, grison, marten, racoon, teledu, walrus **7** dasyure, genette, linsang, polecat, raccoon **8** carcajou, mongoose, mungoose
catlike: **5** civet
doglike: **6** jackal
extinct: **6** quagga **8** mastodon, stegodon
feline: **4** lion **5** tiger, tigon **6** tiglon **7** leopard, lioness, tigress
flying: **3** bat
gnawing: **3** rat **6** beaver, rodent **7** leporid **8** squirrel

goatlike: **4** tahr **5** takin

harelike: **5** hyrax **7** hyraces (plural), hyraxes (plural) **8** hyracoid

hoofed: **2** ox **3** cow, pig **4** deer, goat, owse, oxen (plural) **5** camel, owsen (plural), sheep, tapir **6** alpaca, ovibos **7** peccary **8** ruminant, ungulate **12** hippopotamus

horned: **4** goat

insect-eating: **4** mole **5** shrew **6** tanrec, tenrec **8** hedgehog

long-necked: **7** giraffe

marine: **3** orc **4** orca **6** walrus **7** dolphin, grampus

marsupial: **9** bandicoot

nocturnal: **6** wombat

raccoon-like: **8** cacomixl

ruminant: **4** deer **5** llama, moose, sheep **6** vicuña **7** vicugna

small: **4** pika **8** hedgehog, hedgepig

South American: **7** guanaco

toothless: **5** sloth **8** edentate, pangolin **9** armadillo

tropical: **5** coati

unweaned: **8** suckling

with flippers: **8** pinniped

wolflike: **5** hyena **6** hyaena

mammoth
4 huge **5** giant, whale **7** monster **8** colossal, enormous, gigantic **9** leviathan, monstrous **10** behemothic, gargantuan, mastodonic **11** elephantine

Mamre's brother
4 Aner **6** Eshcol

man
2 he, Mr. **3** boy, guy **4** body, buck, chap, cuss, gent, lord, soul **5** being, brace, flesh, lover, skate **6** fellow, galoot, mister, mortal, person, police, vassal **7** bruiser, fortify, husband, John Law, officer **8** bluecoat, creature, humanity, paramour **9** boyfriend, humankind, mortality, personage **10** individual **11** Homo sapiens

brass: **5** Talos, Talus

castrated: **6** eunuch

combining form: **4** andr **5** andro, homin **6** homini

eccentric: **6** codger, geezer

French: **5** homme

Italian: **4** uomo

Latin: **3** vir **4** homo

Spanish: **6** hombre

Yiddish: **6** mensch

young: **3** boy, lad **8** springal **9** springald, stripling

manage
2 do **3** run **4** fare, keep **5** get by, get on, guide, shift **6** afford, direct,

effect, govern, handle, ordain **7** achieve, carry on, conduct, control, execute, husband, operate, steward, succeed **8** carry out, contrive, dominate, engineer, get along, work upon **9** cultivate, stagger on, supervise **10** accomplish, administer, adulterate, bring about **11** superintend **12** riding school, stagger along **13** muddle through

management
4 care **6** charge **7** conduct, running **8** handling, intrigue **9** oversight **10** conducting, intendance **11** supervising, supervision

manager
4 exec **6** gerent **7** handler, officer **8** director, official, producer **9** conductor, executive **10** impresario, supervisor **13** administrator

museum: **7** curator

suffix: **3** eer

Manahath's father
6 Shobal

Man and Superman author
4 Shaw (George Bernard)

Manassas battle
7 Bull Run

Manasseh, Manasses
brother: **7** Ephraim
father: **6** Hashum, Joseph **8** Hezekiah **10** Pahathmoab
grandfather: **5** Jacob
grandson: **6** Gilead
mother: **7** Asenath
son: **6** Machir

man-at-arms
2 GI **7** fighter, soldier, warrior **10** serviceman **11** fighting man

mancipium
5 slave **7** bondman, chattel **8** bondsman **9** bondslave

Mandalay author
7 Kipling (Rudyard)

mandarin
4 duck, tree **5** elder **6** orange **8** official **9** tangerine **10** bureaucrat

mandate
4 fiat, word **5** edict, order, ukase **6** behest, charge, decree **7** bidding, command, dictate **9** authority **10** imperative, injunction **13** authorization

mandatory
6 forced **7** binding, needful **8** required **9** de rigueur, essential, imperious, necessary, requisite **10** commanding, compelling, compulsory, imperative **11** involuntary **12** irremissible **13** indispensable

mandible
3 jaw

Manette's daughter
5 Lucie

maneuver
3 jig, ply **4** move, plan, play, plot, ploy, step **5** feint, swing, trick, wield **6** design, device, gambit, handle, jockey, scheme, tactic, wangle **7** beguile, exploit, finagle, finesse, gimmick, measure **8** artifice, demarche, dispense, engineer, exercise, intrigue, movement, navigate **9** machinate, procedure, stratagem **10** manipulate, proceeding, subterfuge **11** contrivance, machination **12** manipulation

maneuvering room
8 latitude

Man for All Seasons, A
author: **4** Bolt (Robert)
subject: **4** More (Thomas)

manful
see **manly**

manganese
ore: **10** pyrolusite
symbol: **2** Mn

manger
4 rack **6** cratch, trough

mangle
3 mar **4** hack, iron, maul **5** press **6** batter, damage, deface, deform, impair, injure, padder **7** butcher, contort, distort **9** disfigure

mangy
5 seedy **6** shabby, sleazy, tagrag **7** scruffy, squalid **8** decrepit, tattered **9** moth-eaten **10** down-atheel

manhandle
4 maul **5** abuse **6** batter **7** rough up **8** maltreat, mistreat **10** knock about, roughhouse, slap around

Manhattan
purchaser: **6** Minuit (Peter)
school: **9** Juilliard
university: **8** Columbia

mania
4 rage **5** craze, fancy, thing **6** fetish, hangup **7** madness, passion **8** fixation, idée fixe, insanity **9** cacoëthes, fixed idea, obsession **10** compulsion, enthusiasm **11** fascination, infatuation

maniac
3 bug, mad, nut **4** loon, wild **5** bigot, crazy, fiend, freak, loony, rabid **6** crazed, dement, insane, madman, raging, zealot **7** berserk,

cracked, fanatic, frantic, furious, lunatic, madling, ranting, unsound, violent 8 demented, deranged, frenetic, frenzied 9 bedlamite, delirious, non compos 10 enthusiast

manifest
4 mark, show, told, vent 5 clear, overt, plain, shown, utter, voice 6 appear, embody, evince, expose, ostend, patent 7 display, evident, evinced, exhibit, express, obvious 8 apparent, distinct, divulged, evidence, palpable, proclaim, revealed 9 disclosed, evidenced, incarnate, objectify, personify, personize, prominent 10 illustrate, indication, noticeable 11 demonstrate, exteriorize, externalize, materialize, personalize, unambiguous

manifestation
4 show 7 display 8 epiphany 10 revelation
combining form: 5 phany

manifold
5 boost 6 beef up, expand 7 augment, diverse, enlarge, magnify 8 compound, increase, multiply, numerous 9 aggregate, multiform, multiplex 10 aggrandize, multiphase 11 diversiform, polymorphic 12 multifarious, multivarious

manikin
4 puny, runt 5 dwarf, midge, pygmy 6 midget, peewee 8 Tom Thumb 10 diminutive, homunculus

Manila
founder: 7 Legazpi (Miguel Lopez de)
victor: 5 Dewey (George)

manipulate
3 ply, rig, use 4 play 5 swing, wield 6 direct, doctor, handle, jockey, juggle, manage 7 beguile, conduct, control, exploit, finesse 8 dispense, engineer, maneuver 9 machinate 10 tamper with

Manitoba
capital: 8 Winnipeg
university: 7 Brandon 13 Saint Boniface

mankind
5 flesh, human 6 humans, people 8 humanity 9 mortality 11 homo sapiens

manlike
4 male 6 virile 8 hominoid, humanoid 9 masculine 10 anthropoid

manly
4 bold, male 5 brave 6 virile 7 gal-

lant, valiant 8 fearless, intrepid, unafraid, valorous 9 dauntless, masculine, undaunted 10 courageous

man-made
9 synthetic 10 artificial, factitious
object: 8 artefact, artifact

Mann character
7 Castorp 10 Felix Krull

manner
3 use, way 4 form, kind, mien, mode, sort, tone, turn, vein, wise, wont 5 habit, modus, mores, style, trick, usage 6 custom, method, system 7 bearing, fashion, p's and q's quomodo 8 behavior, decorums, demeanor, habitude, practice, protocol 9 amenities, etiquette, technique 10 civilities, consuetude, deportment, elegancies 11 affectation, formalities, peculiarity, proprieties 12 affectedness, idiosyncrasy
combining form: 4 wise
suffix: 2 ic, ly 4 ical

mannered
6 cutesy 8 affected 9 conscious 13 self-conscious

mannerism
4 airs, lugs, pose 7 oddness 9 prettyism, queerness 10 preciosity 11 affectation, peculiarity, singularity 12 eccentricity, idiosyncrasy 13 artificiality

mannerless
4 rude 7 ill-bred, uncivil 8 impolite 11 disgracious 12 discourteous 13 disrespectful

mannerly
5 civil 6 polite 7 civilly, genteel 8 politely 9 courteous 10 respectful 12 respectfully

Manoah's son
6 Samson

Manon composer
8 Massenet (Jules)

Manon Lescaut
author: 7 Prevost (Abbé)
composer: 7 Puccini (Giacomo)

manor
4 land 5 acres, villa 6 castle, estate, quinta 7 château 12 landed estate

manservant
5 valet 6 butler

mansion
4 hall 5 house, villa 6 castle, estate 7 château

manslaughter
5 blood 6 murder 7 bump-off, killing 8 foul play, homicide

manslayer
6 killer 8 homicide, murderer

mantic
7 fatidic 8 Delphian, oracular 9 sibylline, vaticinal 11 prophetical

mantle
4 glow, pink, robe, rose 5 blush, cloak, color, cover, flush, rouge 6 pinken, redden 7 crimson
combining form: 7 chlamyd 8 chlamydo

Manto
father: 8 Tiresias
husband: 7 Rhacius
son: 6 Mopsus

man-to-man
4 open 5 frank 6 candid 10 unreserved 11 openhearted, unconcealed, undisguised, unvarnished 12 undissembled

mantra
2 om 4 hymn 5 chant 6 prayer 11 incantation

manual
4 text 5 guide 6 primer 7 primary 8 Baedeker, handbook, hornbook, textbook 9 guidebook, vade mecum 10 compendium 11 abecedarium, enchiridion
religious: 9 catechism
worker: 7 laborer

manufactory
4 mill 5 plant, works

manufacture
4 form, make, mold 5 forge, frame, shape 6 create, invent 7 fashion, produce 8 creation 9 fabricate 10 production 11 put together

manumit
4 free 5 loose 6 loosen, unbind 7 release, set free, unchain 8 liberate 9 discharge, unshackle 10 emancipate

manure
4 dung 6 ordure 7 excreta 9 excrement 10 fertilizer

manuscript
4 hand
ancient: 5 codex 7 codices (plural)
red part: 6 rubric

Man Without a Country, The
author: 4 Hale (Edward Everett)
character: 5 Nolan

many
4 much 5 monie 6 divers, legion, myriad, sundry 7 copious, diverse, several, various 8 abundant, manifold, multiple, numerous, populous 9 abounding, bounteous, bountiful,

countless, multitude, plentiful
10 multiplied, voluminous **12** multifarious, multiplicate, multitudinal
13 multitudinous
combining form: **4** poly **5** multi, pluri

Maon's father
7 Shammai

Mao's successor
3 Hua (Kuo-feng)

map
4 plan, plat **5** chart, draft, graph
6 design, lay out, set out, sketch, survey **7** arrange, diagram, drawing, explore, outline, picture, tracing **9** cartogram, delineate
collection: **5** atlas
line: **6** isohel **7** contour, isobath, isogone, isogram, isogriv, isohyet, isotach **8** isarithm, isocheim, isochime, isogloss, isogonal, isogonic, isograph, isopleth, isotherm
maker: **12** cartographer
making: **11** cartography, chorography

map projection
5 Bonne, conic **6** Albers **8** gnomonic, Mercator **9** Mollweide, polyconic **10** sinusoidal **12** orthographic **13** stereographic

maquillage
4 face **5** paint **6** makeup **8** war paint

mar
4 flaw, harm, hurt, ruin, scar, warp
5 spoil, wreck **6** bruise, damage, deface, deform, impair, injure, injury **7** blemish, scratch, tarnish, vitiate **9** prejudice
the countryside: **6** litter

marabou
4 silk **5** stork **12** adjutant bird

Marat
colleague: **6** Danton (Georges)
slayer: **6** Corday (Charlotte)

maraud
4 raid **5** foray, harry **6** harass

marauder
6 bandit, bummer, looter, pirate, raider, sacker **7** brigand, cateran, forager, ravager, spoiler, wrecker
8 pillager, ravisher **9** buccaneer, desperado, despoiler, plunderer, spoliator **10** depredator, freebooter

marble
3 mib, mig **4** immy, migg **5** aggie, rance **6** blotch, miggle, mottle, streak **7** cipolin, glassie, steelie

Marble Faun, The
author: **9** Hawthorne (Nathaniel)
character: **5** Hilda **6** Kenyon, Miriam **9** Donatello
setting: **4** Rome

marblehearted
5 stony **7** callous **8** hardened, obdurate **9** heartless, unfeeling
10 hard-boiled **11** cold-blooded
13 unsympathetic

marcelled hair
4 wavy

march
2 go **3** hem, rim **4** abut, jibe, join, line, move **5** agree, check, fit in, get on, skirt, sling, stalk, tally, touch **6** accord, adjoin, border, butt on, course, extend, fringe, parade, square, stride, travel **7** advance, headway, ongoing, proceed **8** anabasis, boundary, dovetail, frontier, get along, neighbor, outlands, parallel, progress, traverse **9** periphery, provinces, territory **10** borderland, correspond
11 advancement

March
date: **4** ides
sisters: **2** Jo **3** Amy, Meg **4** Beth

March Hare creator
7 Carroll (Lewis)

March King
5 Sousa (John Philip)

Mardi Gras
8 carnival **10** Fat Tuesday
city: **10** New Orleans

Marduk, Merodach
city: **7** Babylon
consort: **8** Zarpanit **9** Sarpanitu
father: **2** Ea
victim: **5** Kingu

mare
3 sea **5** horse **6** equine

Mareshah's son
6 Hebron

mare's nest
3 din **4** hoax, sell **5** babel, cheat, fraud, put on, spoof **6** clamor, hubbub, humbug, racket, uproar
7 swindle **8** flimflam **9** imposture
10 hullabaloo

margarine
4 oleo

margin
3 hem, rim **4** abut, brim, edge, join, line, play, room, side
5 bound, brink, frame, scope, shore, skirt, touch, verge **6** border,

fringe, leeway **7** connect, minimum, outline, selvage **8** latitude, neighbor, surround, trimming **9** elbowroom, perimeter, periphery
of shortcoming: **6** leeway
tiny: **4** hair

Marguerite's lover
5 Faust

Maria ___
5 Elena **7** Stuarda

Marianas
discoverer: **8** Magellan (Ferdinand)
island: **4** Rota **5** Pagan **6** Guguan, Saipan, Tinian **7** Agrihan, Aguijan

marijuana
3 boo, pot **4** hash, hemp, weed
5 grass, joint **6** moocah, reefer
7 hashish **8** cannabis

marina
4 dock **5** basin **8** boatyard **9** esplanade, promenade

marine
5 naval **6** dipsey, dipsie, gyrene
7 abyssal, aquatic, bathyal, benthic, deep-sea, fluvial, neritic, oceanic, pelagic **8** bathybic, nautical, seagoing, seamanly **9** bathysmal, seafaring, thalassic **10** fluviatile, lacustrine, oceangoing, seamanlike
12 hydrographic, navigational
13 oceanographic
crustacean: **8** barnacle
deposit: **5** coral
plant: **4** alga, kelp **7** seaweed

mariner
3 gob, tar **4** jack, salt **6** rating, sailor, sea dog, seaman **7** jack-tar, old salt, swabbie **8** seafarer **9** sailorman, shellback, tarpaulin
10 bluejacket

marionette
6 puppet **10** bufflehead

marital
6 wedded **7** married, nuptial, spousal **8** conjugal, hymeneal
9 connubial

maritime
7 oceanic **8** nautical **9** thalassic
12 navigational

mark
3 aim, jot, map, sap, say, see, use
4 butt, cull, dupe, duty, fish, fool, goal, gull, heed, logo, look, note, pick, read, show, sign, type, view
5 bound, brand, chart, chump, elect, grade, index, label, limit, stamp, token, trait **6** assign, attend, behold, choose, denote, emblem, evince, lay off, lay out, notice, ob-

ject, optate, opt for, ostend, pigeon, prefer, rating, record, regard, select, sucker, symbol, target, victim, virtue **7** bespeak, betoken, delimit, destine, discern, exhibit, fall guy, feature, gudgeon, indicia, initial, measure, observe, pick out, purpose, qualify, quality, scratch, signify, symptom **8** ambition, evidence, function, indicate, logotype, manifest, perceive, proclaim, property, register **9** affection, attention, attribute, character, demarcate, designate, determine, objective, quaesitum, signalize, single out **10** importance, indication **11** differentia, distinction, distinguish **12** characterize
a tree: **5** blaze
by cutting: **4** nick **5** notch **6** scribe
distinctive: **7** indicia **8** indicium
identifying: **6** signet
low-water: **5** datum
musical notation: **6** corona **7** fermata
of insertion: **5** caret
of omission: **8** ellipsis **10** apostrophe
over a vowel: **5** breve **6** accent, macron
over n: **5** tilde
punctuation: **4** dash **5** colon, comma **6** hyphen, period **9** semicolon
skate: **4** cusp
time: **5** count
under a letter: **7** cedilla
with welts: **4** wale

Mark
cousin: **8** Barnabas
mother: **4** Mary

mark down
3 cut **4** clip, pare **5** decry, lower, shave, slash **6** reduce **7** cut back, devalue **8** write off **9** devaluate **10** depreciate, underprize, undervalue

marked
5 noted **6** signal **7** pointed, salient **8** striking **9** arresting, prominent **10** noticeable, remarkable **11** conspicuous, outstanding **12** considerable **13** distinguished
man: **4** Cain

market
4 give, sell, shop, vend **5** cheap, store **6** outlet, retail, tryste **8** showroom **9** traffic in, wholesale **11** merchandise
kind: **4** flea **5** money, stock

marketable
3 fit **4** good **5** sound **7** selling **8** vendible **9** wholesome **10** commercial

marketplace
4 souk **5** agora, bazar **6** bazaar, rialto

marksman
4 shot **7** deadeye, shooter

marl
4 clay **5** earth **9** fertilize

marlin
9 spearfish

Marlowe play
8 Edward II **9** Dr. Faustus **11** Tamburlaine **13** The Jew of Malta

marmalade fruit
6 orange, quince

marmot
10 prairie dog

Marpessa
abductor: **4** Idas
father: **6** Evenus

Marquand character
4 Gray, Moto **5** Apley, Wayde **6** Pulham **7** Goodwin

Marquis
cat: **9** Mehitabel
cockroach: **5** Archy

marriage
5 match, union **6** bridal **7** nuptial, spousal, wedding, wedlock **8** espousal, monogamy, nuptials, polygamy, polygany **9** espousals, matrimony **11** conjugality **12** connubiality
combining form: **4** gamy **6** gamous
notice: **5** banns
outside a group: **7** exogamy
second: **6** bigamy, digamy
within a group: **8** endogamy

marriageable
6 nubile

marriage broker
9 go-between **10** matchmaker
Jewish: **8** shadchan

marriage portion
3 dot **5** dower, dowry

marrow
4 core, meat, pith, soul **5** heart, stuff **6** bottom, kernel **7** essence **9** substance **10** virtuality **12** essentiality, quintessence

marry
3 tie, wed **4** join, link, mate, wive, yoke **5** catch, hitch **6** couple, relate, splice, spouse **7** combine, conjoin, espouse, husband **9** associate, conjugate

Mars
6 planet
combining form: **4** areo
moon: **6** Deimos, Phobos
relating to: **7** martian; (see also **Ares**)

Marseillaise composer
13 Rouget de Lisle (Claude-Joseph)

marsh
3 bog, fen **4** mire, ooze, quag **5** bayou, glade, swail, swale, swamp **6** maskeg, morass, muskeg, slough **7** baygall, wetland **8** moorland, quagmire **9** swampland
combining form: **4** helo **6** paludi

marshal
5 array, guide, order, rally, space, usher **6** direct, escort, muster **7** arrange, dispose, officer **8** mobilize, organize, shepherd **9** methodize **10** distribute

marshland
see **marsh**

marshlight
7 spunkie **11** ignis fatuus

Martha
brother: **7** Lazarus
sister: **4** Mary

martial
7 warlike **8** militant, military, spirited **9** bellicose, combative **10** aggressive, mettlesome, pugnacious **11** belligerent

Martial's forte
7 epigram

Martin Chuzzlewit author
7 Dickens (Charles)

Martinique
capital: **12** Fort-de-France
discoverer: **8** Columbus (Christopher)

martyr
4 Paul, rack **5** Agnes, Alban, James, Peter, saint, wring **6** George, harrow, Justin **7** afflict, agonize, crucify, Cyprian, Stephen, torment, torture **8** Ignatius, Lawrence, Polycarp, sufferer **9** Joan of Arc, Sebastian **10** excruciate
Protestant: **6** Ridley (Nicholas) **7** Cranmer (Thomas), Latimer (Hugh)

marvel
6 wonder **7** miracle, portent, prodigy, stunner **9** horehound, sensation **10** phenomenon **12** astonishment

marvelous
5 awing, nifty, super, swell **6** divine, dreamy, groovy, peachy

7 amazing, awesome, ripping
8 glorious, pleasant, striking, stunning, superior, terrific, wondrous
9 agreeable, enjoyable, excellent, hunky-dory, rewarding, wonderful
10 astounding, incredible, phenomenal, prodigious, satisfying, staggering, stupendous, surprising
11 astonishing, bewildering, confounding, exceptional, pleasurable, sensational, spectacular **12** awe-inspiring, supernatural, unimaginable
13 extraordinary, inconceivable

Marx, Karl
book: **10** Das Kapital
collaborator: **6** Engels (Friedrich)

Marx brother
5 Chico, Harpo, Zeppo **7** Groucho

Mary
husband: **6** Clopas, Joseph
8 Alphaeus
kinswoman: **9** Elisabeth
son: **4** Mark **5** James, Jesus, Joses

Maryland
academy, university: **7** U.S. Naval
11 Towson State **12** Johns Hopkins
capital: **9** Annapolis
largest city: **9** Baltimore
nickname: **12** Cockade State, Old Line State

mascot
4 juju, luck, zemi **5** charm **6** amulet, bat boy, fetish **7** periapt **8** talisman **10** phylactery

masculine
4 male **5** manly **6** manful, robust, virile **7** manlike **9** unwomanly
combining form: **4** andr **5** andro

masculinity
8 machismo, virility **9** manliness

mash
4 mess, pulp **6** accost, bruise, jumble, jungle, litter, muddle, suitor, tumble **7** clutter, rummage **8** scramble **10** sweetheart **12** hugger-mugger

masher
4 wolf **5** flirt **6** chaser **7** Don Juan **8** Casanova **9** ladies' man, philander, womanizer **10** lady-killer
11 philanderer

mash note
10 billet-doux, love letter

mask
4 blur, face, pose, sham, show, veil **5** block, cloak, color, cover, front, guard, guise, put-on, visor **6** aspect, defend, domino, facade, fak-

ery, flavor, screen, shield, veneer, visard, vizard **7** dress up, frisket, muffler, posture, pretext, protect, secrete, seeming, veiling **8** coloring, disguise, pretense **9** dissemble, doughface, false face, safeguard, semblance **10** appearance, camouflage, false front, simulation
11 affectation, dissembling, dissimulate **12** disguisement **13** dissimulation

masonry
9 brickwork, stonework
in a frame: **7** nogging

masquerade
4 face, pose, show, veil **5** cloak, color, cover, front **6** facade, pass as **7** pass for, pass off, posture
8 disguise **10** camouflage
12 attitudinize

mass
3 lot, sum, wad **4** bank, body, bulk, clot, core, glob, heap, hill, lump, much, pack, peck, pile
5 clump, group, mound, shock, stack, total, whole **6** corpus, nugget, object, staple, volume **7** expanse, globule, pyramid, wadding
8 assemble, mountain **9** aggregate, great deal, magnitude, stockpile, substance **10** generality **11** aggregation, proletariat **12** conglomerate
combining form: **4** onco **5** oncho
confused: **7** clutter **9** imbroglio
for departed: **7** requiem
ice: **4** calf, floe
indefinite: **3** gob
jumbled: **8** pell-mell, scramble
metal: **5** ingot
muddy: **6** sludge
of hair: **3** mop
of individuals: **5** crowd, horde, swarm **13** agglomeration
part: **6** proper **8** ordinary
rock: **4** dome
rounded: **4** knob
suffix: **3** ium, ome
swollen: **4** cere
tight: **4** knot

Massachusetts
capital: **6** Boston
college, university: **3** MIT **5** Clark, Curry, Smith, Tufts **6** Babson, Boston **7** Amherst, Harvard **8** Brandeis, Williams **9** Hampshire, Holy Cross, Merrimack, Radcliffe, Wellesley **11** Springfield **12** Mount Holyoke, Northeastern
highest point: **10** Mt. Greylock

nickname: **8** Bay State **9** Old Colony
state bird: **9** chickadee

massacre
4 kill **6** mangle, murder, pogrom
8 butchery, decimate, genocide, mangling, mutilate **9** bloodbath, bloodshed, slaughter **10** annihilate, blood purge, decimation **11** exterminate, internecion

massage
3 rub **5** knead **7** rubdown

Massa's father
7 Ishmael

Massenet opera
5 Le Cid, Manon, Sapho, Thais
7 Werther

massive
4 huge, vast **5** bulky, giant, grand, heavy, hefty, hulky, jumbo, large, solid **6** mighty, mortal **7** compact, hulking, immense, mammoth, notable, weighty **8** colossal, cracking, cumbrous, enormous, gigantic, towering **9** fantastic, monstrous, ponderous **10** cumbersome, monumental, prodigious, stupendous, tremendous **11** elephantine, mountainous

master
3 get **4** best, boss, cock, down, guru, head, lick, rule, tame, whiz
5 adept, bwana, chief, crack, learn, lover, marse, ruler, sahib, swami, throw, tutor **6** artist, direct, domine, expert, genius, govern, honcho, hurdle, leader, pick up, ruling, savant, subdue, victor, wizard **7** artiste, captain, conquer, headman, maestro, overman, padrone, prevail, rabboni, regnant, skilled, subduer, triumph **8** defeater, dominant, dominate, employer, fancy man, governor, hierarch, overcome, overlord, overseer, paramour, regulate, skillful, superior, surmount, virtuoso **9** ascendant, authority, boyfriend, chieftain, conqueror, dominator, paramount, prevalent, principal, sovereign
10 proficient, subjugator, vanquisher **11** controlling, crackerjack, domesticate, domesticize, domiciliate, overbearing, predominant, predominate
combining form: **4** arch

masterdom
8 dominion **9** ascendant, dominance, supremacy **10** ascendancy, domination, prepotence, prepotency **11** preeminence, sovereignty

masterful

4 deft 5 adept, bossy, crack
6 adroit, expert 7 skilled, supreme
8 absolute, despotic, dogmatic, imperial, skillful, vigorous 9 arbitrary, dexterous, dictative, energetic, imperious 10 autocratic, high-handed, imperative, peremptory, preeminent, proficient, self-willed, tyrannical 11 crackerjack, dictatorial, doctrinaire, domineering, magisterial, overbearing, superlative
12 transcendent 13 authoritarian, authoritative, high-and-mighty

masterly

5 adept, crack 6 expert 7 skilled, supreme 8 skillful 10 preeminent, proficient 11 crackerjack, superlative 12 transcendent

Master of Ballantrae

6 Durrie
author: 9 Stevenson (Robert Louis)

masterpiece

7 classic 9 objet d'art 10 magnum opus 11 chef d'oeuvre, tour de force

mastery

4 sway 5 knack, might, power, skill
7 ability, command, control, know-how 8 dominion 9 authority, expertise, expertism 10 ascendancy, domination, expertness 11 superiority 12 jurisdiction

masticate

4 chew, pulp 5 champ, chomp, chump, crush, munch, smash
6 bruise, crunch, squash 7 chumble, pulpify, scrunch 8 macerate, ruminate 9 break down

mastodonic

see **mammoth**

mast support

4 bibb

mat

3 dim, rug 4 dead, dull, felt, flat, shag 5 blind, doily, muted 6 carpet 10 lackluster, lusterless

matador

6 torero 8 toreador 11 bullfighter
adjunct: 6 muleta
move: 4 pase 5 faena 8 veronica

Mata Hari

3 spy

match

3 con, pit, tie, vie 4 anti, bout, game, like, meet, suit, twin
5 adapt, array, equal, event, liken, rival, touch 6 amount, double, equate, fellow, oppose 7 compare, compeer, counter, opposer, paragon, play off, stack up 8 analogue, approach, opponent, parallel 9 adversary, companion, correlate, duplicate, encounter, measure up, oppugnant, partake of 10 antagonist, assimilate, complement, coordinate, engagement, equivalent, reciprocal, supplement 11 counterpart, countertype 12 correspond to
13 correspondent, harmonize with
a bet: 3 see
friction: 5 fusee, fuzee 7 lucifer
8 locofoco

matchless

4 only 5 alone 6 unique 9 unequaled, unrivaled 10 inimitable
11 unparagoned 12 incomparable, unparalleled

matchmaker

see **marriage broker**

mate

3 pal, tie, wed 4 chum, pair, peer, twin 5 amigo, breed, buddy, equal, hitch, marry, parti, sosie
6 cohort, couple, double, fellow, friend, helper, splice, spouse 7 compeer, consort, partner 8 alter ego, confrere, familiar 9 associate, companion, confidant, copartner, duplicate, procreate 10 complement, crossbreed, equivalent, reciprocal
11 cater-cousin, concomitant
12 acquaintance 13 accompaniment

maté

3 tea 5 holly 8 beverage

material

3 big 4 real, true 5 ad rem, being, cloth, gross, stuff, tapis, thing, vital
6 actual, animal, bodily, carnal, entity, fabric, matter, object 7 apropos, earthly, element, fleshly, germane, sensual, weighty, worldly
8 apposite, cardinal, palpable, physical, pointful, relevant, sensible, tangible 9 apparatus, component, corporeal, equipment, essential, important, machinery, momentous, objective, pertinent, substance 10 applicable, individual, ingredient, meaningful, phenomenal 11 applicative, applicatory, appreciable, constituent, fundamental, perceptible, significant, substantial 12 considerable
13 consequential
building: 5 adobe, brick 7 plywood, shingle 8 concrete

cementing: 7 plaster
combining form: 3 hyl 4 hylo
combustible: 8 kindling
cushioning: 4 foam
glutinous: 7 gelatin
hard: 7 carbide
hard covering: 6 stucco
indecent: 4 smut
insulating: 7 lagging 10 fiberglass
leftover: 5 waste 7 rubbish
petrified: 8 gemstone

materialistic

6 carnal, earthy 7 earthly, mundane, profane, secular, sensual, worldly

materialize

4 loom, rise, show 5 issue, reify
6 appear, embody, emerge, entify, show up, spring, typify 8 manifest
9 incarnate, objectify, personify, personize, take shape 10 pragmatize 11 exteriorize, hypostatize
12 substantiate

matériel

4 gear 6 outfit, tackle 8 tackling
9 apparatus, equipment, machinery
11 habiliments 13 accouterments, accoutrements, paraphernalia

maternal

6 mother 8 motherly

maternally related

5 enate

mathematician

American: 5 Wiles (Andrew)
6 Peirce (Charles S.), Veblen (Oswald), Wiener (Norbert)
British: 6 Stokes (George)
Dutch: 7 Huygens (Christiaan)
English: 6 Newton (Isaac), Taylor (Brook), Turing (Alan), Wallis (John)
7 Pearson (Karl), Russell (Bertrand)
9 Whitehead (Alfred North, Henry)
French: 5 Borel (Emile), Comte (Auguste), Viète (François) 6 Galois (Evariste), Pascal (Blaise), Picard (Charles-Emile) 7 Fourier (Jean-Baptiste), Laplace (Marquis de), Vernier (Pierre) 8 Painlevé (Paul), Poincaré (Jules-Henri) 9 Descartes (René)
German: 5 Gauss (Carl), Wolff (Freiherr von) 6 Staudt (Karl von)
7 Riemann (Georg) 11 Weierstrass (Karl)
Greek: 6 Euclid 10 Archimedes, Pythagoras
Italian: 8 Volterra (Vito) 10 Torricelli (Evangelista)
Norwegian: 7 Stormer (Fredrik)
Russian: 11 Lobachevsky (Nikolay)

Scottish: **4** Tait (Peter) **6** Napier (John) **8** Stirling (James)

Swiss: **5** Sturm (Jacques) **7** Steiner (Jakob)

mathematics
branch: **7** algebra **8** calculus, geometry **10** arithmetic **12** trigonometry
proven statement in: **7** theorem

___ Mather
6 Cotton **7** Richard **8** Increase

Matred
daughter: **9** Mehetabel
father: **7** Mezahab
son-in-law: **5** Hadar

matriarch
4 dame **6** mother **7** dowager **10** grande dame **13** materfamilias

matrimonial
6 bridal, wedded **7** marital, married, nuptial, spousal **8** conjugal, hymeneal **9** connubial **11** epithalamic

matrimony
7 wedlock **8** marriage **11** conjugality **12** connubiality

matrix
3 die **6** cradle, gangue, strike **10** groundmass, truth table

matron
4 dame **7** dowager **10** grande dame, parlormaid

Mattaniah
father: **4** Bani, Elam, Mica **5** Asaph, Heman, Zattu **6** Josiah **10** Pahathmoab
grandson: **5** Hanan
son: **6** Zaccur **8** Shemaiah

Mattatha
father: **6** Nathan
grandfather: **5** David

Mattathias
father: **5** Simon **6** Ananos **7** Absalom, Boethus **10** Theophilus
son: **8** Josephus

matter
3 pus **4** body, core, gist, head, mail, mean, meat, pith, text, to-do, tune **5** being, cause, count, motif, order, point, range, sense, stuff, theme, thing, topic, value, weigh, worry **6** affair, amount, burden, entity, extent, import, motive, object, source, upshot **7** concern, signify, subject **8** argument, business, material, vicinity **9** grievance, magnitude, substance, suppurate **10** individual **11** constituent, predicament **12** circumstance

added to book: **8** addendum, appendix
coloring: **3** dye **6** indigo **7** pigment **8** tinction **10** indigo blue
combining form: **3** hyl **4** hylo
decayed organic: **4** duff
diffused: **5** vapor
in dispute: **5** issue
inferior: **5** trash
waste: **5** dross **6** sewage **7** excreta
white: **4** alba
worthless: **4** slag **7** garbage

matter-of-fact
3 dry **4** cold **5** prose, prosy, sober, sound, stoic **6** earthy, stolid **7** prosaic, prosing **9** apathetic, impassive, objective, practical, pragmatic, realistic **10** hard-boiled, hardheaded, impersonal, phlegmatic, unaffected **11** cold-blooded, commonplace, down-to-earth, emotionless **12** unidealistic **13** unimpassioned, unsentimental

Matthew's father
8 Alphaeus

Mattithiah's father
4 Nebo **7** Shallum **8** Jeduthun

mattress
3 pad **4** sack
case: **4** tick
fabric: **7** ticking
straw: **6** pallet

mature
3 age, due **4** grow, ripe, wane **5** adult, grown, olden, owing, ready, ripen, round **6** flower, grow up, mellow, season, unpaid **7** advance, blossom, decline, develop, grown-up, outgrow, overdue, payable, ripened **8** progress **9** developed, full-blown, full-grown
combining form: **3** tel **4** tele, telo

maudlin
5 mushy, silly **6** addled, slushy, sticky **7** fuddled, mawkish, muddled **8** bathetic, confused, romantic **9** befuddled **11** sentimental, tear-jerking

Maugham character
4 Kear, Liza **5** Carey, Rosie, Sadie **7** Mildred **8** Craddock **10** Strickland

maul
3 paw, row **4** bang, bash, club, fray, lash, mace, whip **5** abuse, brawl, broil, flail, melee, pound, set-to **6** batter, beetle, buffet, fracas, hammer, injure, molest, sledge

7 rough up, ruction **8** dogfight, maltreat **9** manhandle **10** donnybrook

Mauna ___
3 Loa

maunder
3 bat, gad **5** drift, mooch, range **6** ramble **9** gallivant

Mauritania
capital: **10** Nouakchott
monetary unit: **7** ouguiya

Mauritius
capital: **9** Port Louis
export: **5** sugar
monetary unit: **5** rupee

Maurois biographee
4 Hugo (Victor), Sand (George) **5** Byron (Lord), Dumas (Alexandre) **6** Proust (Marcel) **7** Shelley (Percy Bysshe) **8** Disraeli (Benjamin)

mauve
6 purple, violet

maven, mavin
5 adept **6** expert, master **8** virtuoso **9** authority **10** past master, proficient **12** professional

maverick
5 stray **8** bohemian, unmarked **9** unbranded **13** nonconformist

maw
4 crop **7** stomach **9** poppy seed

mawkish
4 flat **5** banal, mushy **6** slushy, sticky **7** cloying, maudlin **8** bathetic, romantic **9** sickening **10** lovey-dovey, nauseating **11** sentimental, tear-jerking

maxilla
3 jaw **4** bone

maxim
3 law **4** rule **5** axiom, gnome, large, moral, motto **6** dictum, saying, truism **7** brocard, precept, proverb, theorem **8** aphorism, apothegm **9** platitude, prescript **11** commonplace

maximal
3 top **6** utmost **7** highest, topmost **8** greatest

maximize
7 magnify **8** overplay **10** overstress **13** overemphasize

maximum
3 top **6** utmost **7** highest, largest, supreme, topmost **8** extremum, greatest

may
5 shrub 6 spirea 8 hawthorn

maybe
7 perhaps 8 possible, possibly
9 perchance 10 indecision
11 uncertainty

Mayflower
document: 7 Compact
passengers: 8 pilgrims

mayhem
4 maim 7 cripple, dislimb 8 mutilate 9 dismember

mayor
11 burgomaster
Chicago (former): 5 Daley (Richard)
New York (former): 9 La Guardia (Fiorello)
Spanish: 7 alcalde

Mayor of Casterbridge, The
author: 5 Hardy (Thomas)
character: 8 Henchard

maze
3 web 4 knot, mesh 5 skein, snarl
6 jungle, morass, tangle 7 confuse
8 bewilder, mishmash 9 labyrinth
10 hodgepodge, miscellany
11 gordian knot

MD
3 doc 6 doctor, medico 7 medical
8 sawbones 9 mediciner, physician

meadow
3 lea, ley 9 grassland
low-lying: 5 haugh

meadow beauty
9 deer grass

meadow bird
8 bobolink

meadow chicken
8 sora rail

meadow hen
4 coot, rail 7 bittern

meadowlark
4 bird 5 acorn

meadow mushroom
6 agaric

meadow sorrel
4 dock

meager
4 bare, bony, lank, lean, mere, poor, thin 5 gaunt, lanky, scant, short, skimp, spare 6 lenten, scanty, scrimp, shabby, skimpy, skinny, slight, sparse 7 angular, minimum, scraggy, scrawny, scrimpy 8 exiguous, inferior, raw-boned, scrimpit 9 deficient, miserable 10 inadequate 12 insufficient

meal
3 eat 4 chow, fare, feed, grub, take 5 board, feast, lunch, salep, snack, table 6 brunch, devour, dinner, farina, feed on, ingest, picnic, repast, spread, supper 7 consume, nooning 8 victuals 9 breakfast, collation, partake of, refection
army: 4 mess

mealy
6 spotty, uneven 8 farinose 9 pollinose 11 farinaceous

mean
3 aim, low, mid, par, set, way
4 base, fair, hack, hint, mode, name, norm, pile, plan, poor, sick, so-so, ugly, want, wish 5 agent, borne, cheap, count, cruel, imply, lousy, lowly, mingy, organ, pesky, purse, rough, small, spell, tatty, tight, tough, weigh 6 agency, ailing, attest, center, common, denote, design, desire, donsie, estate, humble, import, intend, little, manner, matter, medial, medium, method, middle, narrow, offish, ornery, paltry, pocket, poorly, rugged, scrimy, scummy, scurvy, shabby, shoddy, sickly, sleazy, stingy, system, trashy, unwell, wealth, wicked 7 add up to, ashamed, average, betoken, capital, central, channel, connote, express, fairish, fashion, fortune, ignoble, limited, lowborn, miserly, nest egg, niggard, pitiful, propose, purpose, savings, scrimpy, signify, suggest, underly, vehicle 8 baseborn, beggarly, count for, déclassé, indicate, inferior, intimate, kindless, low-grade, mediocre, middling, ministry, moderate, off-color, ordinary, pitiable, plebeian, rubbishy, unwashed 9 apparatus, bastardly, designate, difficult, equipment, low-minded, machinery, niggardly, penurious, troublous, vexatious 10 despicable, despisable, formidable, indisposed, instrument, second-rate, unennobled 11 closefisted, contemplate, indifferent, ineffectual, second-class, tight-fisted, troublesome 12 contemptible, intermediary, intermediate, narrow-fisted, second-drawer

meander
4 roam, rove, turn, wind 5 drift, range, snake, stray, twist 6 ramble 7 traipse 8 vagabond 9 gallivant, labyrinth

meandering
5 snaky 7 sinuous, winding 8 flexuous, tortuous 10 convoluted, serpentine 11 anfractuous

meandrous
see **meandering**

meaning
3 aim 4 hint, plan 5 drift, force, point, sense, tenor, value 6 animus, design, effect, import, intent, object, syntax 7 essence, message, purport, purpose 9 intention, substance 10 definition, denotation, intendment, intimation, suggestion 11 acceptation, connotation, implication, significant 12 significance, significancy 13 signification, understanding

meaningful
4 rich 6 facund 7 weighty 8 eloquent, material, pregnant 9 important, momentous 10 expressive 11 sententious, significant, substantial 12 considerable 13 consequential

meaningless
5 blank, empty 6 vacant 7 fustian 10 unpurposed 13 insignificant

meanings
diverse: 8 polysemy
study of: 9 semantics

means
5 funds, money 6 agency, assets 7 quomodo 8 finances 9 apparatus, equipment, resources 10 instrument 11 wherewithal

meantime
8 interval

measly
4 poor, puny 5 petty 6 paltry 7 trivial 8 blighted, inferior, niggling, picayune, piddling, trifling 10 picayunish 12 pettifogging

measure
4 beat, bill, deal, meed, move, part, size, step, test, tune 5 bound, dance, gauge, index, limit, meter, metre, quota, rhyme, scale, share, shift, swing, weigh 6 amount, bounds, degree, effort, extent, figure, govern, melody, ration, reckon, resort, rhythm, size up, strain, survey 7 cadence, cadency, caliper, compute, delimit, mark out, melodia, portion, project, quantum, stopgap 8 calliper, estimate, indicate, maneuver, proposal, regulate, resource, rhythmus, standard 9 al-

lotment, allowance, benchmark, calculate, calibrate, criterion, demarcate, determine, expedient, magnitude, makeshift, procedure, yardstick **10** delimitate, dimensions, indication, moderation, proceeding, proportion, temperance, touchstone **11** denominator, proposition **13** apportionment
area: **4** acre **7** hectare **9** square rod **10** square foot, square inch, square mile, square yard **11** square meter
arrow weight: **8** shilling
butter: **4** span
capacity: **4** gill, peck, pint **5** liter, minim, quart **6** bushel, gallon **8** fluidram **10** cubic meter, fluidounce, milliliter
cloth: **3** ell
combining form: **6** metric **8** metrical
depth: **5** plumb, sound
electrical: **7** coulomb
Hebrew: (see at **Hebrew**)
horse height: **4** hand
interstellar space: **6** parsec
length: **3** rod **4** foot, inch, mile, yard **5** cubit (ancient), meter **9** kilometer **10** centimeter
liquid: **4** pint **5** pipet, quart **6** gallon **7** pipette
metrical foot: **8** monopody
mixed drinks: **6** jigger
of advantage: **4** lead
of comparison: **8** standard
out: **5** batch
paper: **4** ream
printer's: **2** em, en **4** pica **5** point
radioactive decay: **8** halflife
rotation: **5** angle
silk size: **8** drammage
Spanish dry: **5** fanga **6** fanega
strength of solution: **7** titrate
surface: **3** are
thermodynamic: **7** entropy **8** enthalpy
volume: **9** cubic foot, cubic inch, cubic yard **10** cubic meter

Measure for Measure
character: **6** Angelo, Juliet **7** Claudio, Mariana **8** Isabella **9** Vincentio
setting: **6** Vienna

measurement
4 area **6** degree **8** capacity, quantity **9** dimension **11** mensuration
rain: **8** udometry
weight: **6** metage

measure up
3 tie **4** meet **5** equal, match, rival, touch

measuring
combining form: **5** metry
device for liquid: **7** venturi
rod: **8** dipstick
stick: **8** yardwand
tube: **5** buret **7** burette

meat
4 core, food, gist, pith, pork, veal **5** flesh, jerky, sense, short, steak **6** burden, matter, thrust, upshot **7** charqui, edibles, nurture **8** victuals **9** foodstuff, provender, substance **10** provisions **11** comestibles
broiled: **8** barbecue, grillade
broth: **8** bouillon
cake: **6** burger
cured: **7** biltong
cut: **3** rib **4** loin, rump **5** chuck, flank, plate, round, shank **7** brisket, sirloin **8** rib roast **9** club steak, rump roast, short loin, short ribs **10** blade roast, flank steak, round steak, T-bone steak **11** arm pot roast **12** boneless neck, pinbone steak, sirloin steak **13** blade rib roast, crosscut shank
dealer: **7** butcher
deer: **7** venison
dried: **5** jerky
fastening pin: **6** skewer
holding rod: **4** spit
juices: **5** gravy
minced: **7** rissole
packer: **5** Swift **6** Armour
raw: **6** gobbet
roasting shop: **10** rotisserie
rounded mass of: **9** croquette
seasoned: **7** sausage **8** pastrami, pastromi
sheep: **6** mutton
side: **8** sowbelly
skewered: **5** kabab, kabob, kebob
slice: **6** cutlet, rasher
small portion: **6** collop
tough part: **7** gristle

meat-eating
11 carnivorous

meathead
3 oaf **4** gawk, lout, lump **5** klutz, looby **6** lubber **7** palooka

Mebd
husband: **6** Ailill
victim: **10** Cuchulainn

Mecca
country: **11** Saudi Arabia
pilgrimage: **4** hadj, hajj
port: **5** Jidda
shrine: **5** Caaba, Kaaba

mechanic
7 artisan **9** automatic, machinist **10** uninspired

mechanism
4 gear **5** ratch, slide, steer **6** cutoff, infeed, rachet **7** ratchet **8** rackwork, signaler **9** apparatus
bookbinder's: **7** gripper
card game: **7** holdout
clutch: **8** throwout
dam: **7** tripper
fastening: **5** catch
firearm: **7** ejector, gunlock
guiding: **5** apron
part: **7** trippet
printing: **8** elevator
raising: **4** lift
timepiece: **7** setting

meddle
3 pry **4** fool, nose **5** snoop **6** butt in, dabble, horn in, invade, kibitz, monkey, putter, tamper, tinker **7** intrude, obtrude **8** busybody, trespass **9** interfere, interlope, intervene **10** mess around, monkey with, tamper with

meddlesome
4 busy **9** intrusive, obtrusive, officious **11** impertinent **13** polypragmatic

Medea
brother: **8** Absyrtus
father: **6** Aeëtes
husband: **5** Jason **6** Aegeus
son: **6** Medeus
victim: **6** Creusa, Glauce, Glauke

medial
3 mid **4** fair, mean **6** center, middle **7** average, central, fairish, halfway, midmost **8** middling, moderate **10** centermost, middlemost **11** equidistant, indifferent **12** intermediary, intermediate

median
see **medial**

mediate
6 convey, liaise, step in **9** intercede, interfere, interpose, intervene

mediator
5 judge **6** broker **7** arbiter **9** go-between, middleman **10** interagent, interceder, peacemaker **11** intercessor

medical
3 doc **6** doctor **9** physician
instrument: **11** cardiograph, stethoscope

medical treatment
combining form: 5 iatry 6 iatric
7 iatrics 8 iatrical

medicament
4 cure 6 physic, remedy
9 pharmacon
inert: 7 placebo

medication
see **medicament**

medicinal
4 drug 8 biologic, salutary, sanative 12 pharmaceutic
extract: 10 belladonna

medicine
4 cure 5 bromo 6 physic, remedy
7 anodyne, nostrum 8 busulfan,
poultice 9 pharmacon 11 antipyretic, magical rite 12 magical
power
ball: 4 pill
bottle: 4 vial
branch: 7 surgery 8 posology 9 pathology 10 bariatrics, geriatrics,
gynecology, obstetrics, pediatrics
cathartic: 8 evacuant 9 purgative
combining form: 5 iatro 8 pharmaco
quantity of: 4 dose 6 dosage
shell: 7 capsule
soothing: 7 nervine 8 lenitive,
sedative

medicine man
6 doctor, kahuna, shaman

medieval
guild: 5 Hanse
military unit: 5 lance
study: 5 logic 6 trivia (plural)
7 grammar, trivium 8 rhetoric

mediocre
3 bad 4 fair, hack, mean, poor, soso 6 common 7 average, fairish
8 inferior, middling, moderate, ordinary, passable 10 bush-league
11 commonplace

meditate
4 muse, roll 6 intend, ponder
7 purpose, revolve 8 consider, mull
over, ruminate, turn over 9 reflect
on 10 deliberate 11 contemplate

meditator
4 yogi 5 yogin

Mediterranean
11 Mare Nostrum 12 Mare
Internum
coastal region: 7 Riviera
eastern shores: 6 Levant
island: (see at **island**)
vessel: 5 setee 6 settee
wind: 6 solano 7 mistral, sirocco

medium
3 par 4 fair, mean, so-so 5 agent,
forte, organ, radio 6 agency, métier, milieu, normal, oyster, vulgar
7 ambient, average, channel, climate, fairish, neutral, popular, vehicle 8 ambience, eminency, long
suit, middling, ministry, moderate,
passable, standard 9 go-between,
run-of-mine, tolerable 10 atmosphere, compromise, instrument,
middle-rate, strong suit, television
11 clairvoyant, environment
nutrient: 7 culture
of exchange: 5 money
of radio transmission: 3 air
7 airwave

medley
4 brew, olio 6 jumble 7 mélange
8 pastiche 9 pasticcio, patchwork,
potpourri 10 assortment, hodgepodge, miscellany 11 gallimaufry

Medusa
6 Gorgon
father: 7 Phorcus, Phorcys
mother: 4 Ceto
offspring: 7 Pegasus 8 Chrysaor
sister: 6 Stheno 7 Euryale
slayer: 7 Perseus

meed
3 due 4 part, plum 5 merit, prize,
quota, share 6 amount, carrot, desert, ration, reward 7 guerdon,
measure, portion, premium, quantum 8 dividend 9 allotment, allowance 12 recompensing, satisfaction
13 apportionment

meek
4 mild, tame, weak 5 lowly 6 gentle, humble, modest 7 lenient, patient 8 moderate, tolerant 10 forbearing, submissive, unassuming
13 long-suffering

meerschaum
4 pipe 6 gravel 9 sepiolite

meet
3 apt, fit, hit, sit, tie 4 bump, espy,
face, fair, fill, find, good, join, just,
luck, open, spot 5 brave, catch,
clash, close, cross, equal, event, focus, front, greet, happy, hit on,
light, match, right, rival, touch,
unite 6 accost, answer, chance, descry, detect, engage, happen, oppose, proper, salute, settle, suffer,
take on, tumble, turn up, tussle, useful 7 affront, collide, contest, convene, fitting, fulfill, grapple, hit
upon, satisfy, stumble, sustain, un-

dergo, wrestle 8 approach, assemble, come upon, concours, conflict,
confront, converge, cope with, suitable 9 concenter, conformed, encounter, equitable, impinge on,
measure up, rencontre 10 applicable, congregate, convenient, experience, felicitous, provide for, reconciled 11 appropriate, competition
a bet: 3 see
a need: 7 suffice
athletic: 8 gymkhana
by appointment: 10 rendezvous

meeting
4 moot, talk 5 tryst 6 parley, powwow 7 contest, session 8 assembly, conclave, concours, conflict,
congress, junction 9 concourse, encounter, gathering, rencontre
10 concursion, conference, confluence 11 competition 12 intersection
Anglo-Saxon: 5 gemot 6 gemote
place: 5 forum
spiritual: 6 séance

Mefistofele composer
5 Boito (Arrigo)

Megaera
see **Erinyes**

megaphone
7 address 8 bullhorn
10 mouthpiece

Megara
father: 5 Creon
husband: 8 Heracles, Hercules
king: 5 Nisus

megillah
5 story 6 scroll 7 account

megrim
4 urge, whim 5 fancy, freak, humor, whiff 6 whimsy 7 boutade,
caprice, conceit, impulse, vertigo
8 crotchet, migraine 9 dizziness

Mehetabel
husband: 5 Hadar
mother: 6 Matred
son: 7 Delaiah

Mehitabel
3 cat
creator: 7 Marquis (Don)
friend: 5 Archy

Mein Kampf author
6 Hitler (Adolf)

meiosis
7 litotes 12 cell division

Meistersinger
4 Folz (Hans) 5 Sachs (Hans)

melancholic
3 sad 6 triste 7 joyless 8 mournful
9 depressed, saddening
10 depressing

melancholy
3 sad 5 blues, dumps, ennui,
gloom, sorry 6 dismal, dreary,
gloomy, misery, rueful, somber, tedium, triste, woeful 7 boredom, despair, dismals, doleful, joyless,
moanful, pensive, sadness, sighful,
unhappy, wailful 8 dejected, dolesome, dolorous, funereal, mournful,
saddened, sombrous 9 dejection,
plaintive, saddening, sorrowful
10 afflicting, depressing, depression, disturbing, lachrymose, lamentable, lugubrious, perturbing, reflective, thoughtful 11 desperation,
disquieting, unhappiness 12 dis-
composing, heavyhearted, mournfulness, wretchedness 13 misera-
bleness

mélange
see **medley**

Melanippe's son
6 Aeolus

Melanippus
father: 7 Theseus
slayer: 10 Amphiaraus
victim: 6 Tydeus

Melchior
companion: 6 Gaspar 9 Balthazar
gift: 4 gold

Melchizedek's kingdom
5 Salem

meld
3 mix 4 fuse 5 blend, merge 6 mingle 8 compound 9 interfuse
10 amalgamate, interblend 11 intermingle

Meleager
beloved: 8 Atalanta
father: 6 Oeneus
mother: 7 Althaea
victim: 4 boar

Melech's father
5 Micah

melee
3 row 4 fray, hash, riot, stew
5 brawl, broil, brush, clash, fight
6 affray, fracas, jumble, ruckus
7 ruction, scuffle 8 dogfight, mishmash, pastiche, skirmish 9 potpourri, scrimmage 10 donnybrook,
free-for-all, hodgepodge, miscellany

Melicertes
father: 7 Athamas
mother: 3 Ino

meliorate
4 help 5 amend 6 better, soften
7 improve

Mélisande's lover
7 Pelleas

melisma
3 air, lay 4 song, tune 6 strain,
warble 7 cadenza, descant, measure 8 diapason

mellifluous
5 sweet 6 dulcet, golden, liquid,
smooth 7 honeyed, silvery 8 euphonic, Hyblaean, resonant 9 accordant 13 golden-tongued, silver-
tongued

mellisonant
5 sweet 6 dulcet 7 tuneful 8 euphonic 10 euphonious

mellow
3 age 4 aged 5 ripen 6 genial,
golden, grow up, liquid, mature
7 develop, honeyed, matured,
ripened

melodic
5 sweet, tuned 6 dulcet 7 musical,
songful, tuneful 8 canorous
10 euphonious

melodious
5 lyric, sweet, tuned 6 dulcet 7 musical, songful, tuneful 8 euphonic,
soundful 9 cantabile

melody
3 air, lay 4 sing, song, tune
5 canto 6 lyrics, strain, warble
7 descant, measure 8 bel canto,
diapason, vocalize 11 tunefulness

melon
4 pepo 5 gourd, mango 6 casaba,
papaya 7 cassaba 8 honeydew
10 cantaloupe

Melpomene
see **Muse**

melt
3 rin, run 4 bake, burn, cook, flux,
fuse, thaw, warm 5 blend, broil,
roast, sweat 6 scorch, soften,
spleen 7 liquefy, liquify, swelter
8 dissolve, liquesce, perspire, un-
freeze 9 disappear 10 deliquesce
down: 6 render
together: 4 fuse

Melville
character: 3 Pip 4 Ahab, Toby
5 Bembo, Chase 6 Cereno, Jermin,
Pierre 7 Fayaway, Ishmael 8 Bar-
tleby, Queequeg, Starbuck
novel: 4 Omoo 5 Mardi, Typee

6 Pierre 7 Redburn 8 Moby Dick
11 White Jacket

member
3 cut 4 part 5 penis, piece
6 clause, moiety, parcel 7 portion,
section, segment 8 division
architectural: 3 fan 7 cornice
armed forces: 5 cadet 6 airman,
Marine, sailor 7 soldier
chivalry order: 6 knight
combining form: 3 mer 4 crat, mere
5 ocrat
gang: 7 mobster 8 henchman
10 hatchet man
Girl Scout: 7 brownie, Cadette
household: 8 familiar
legislative: 7 senator
mendicant order: 5 friar 9 Dominican
middle class: 7 burgher
monastic order: 4 monk 5 friar
6 hermit
Parliament: 2 MP
political party: 4 Tory, Whig 7 Liberal 8 Democrat, Laborite 9 Communist, Socialist 10 Republican
12 Conservative
secret society: 7 DeMolay, tongman
8 Klansman, Ku Kluxer
senior male: 5 doyen
service club: 4 Lion 8 Kiwanian,
Rotarian
structural: 4 arch
suffix: 2 ad, id
triangular: 5 gable

membrane
6 pleura 7 pleurae (plural)
bodily: 6 serosa 7 serosae (plural)
brain: 3 pia
combining form: 3 vel 5 chori, hymen 6 chorio, hymeno, mening,
myring 7 meningi, meningo,
myringo
diffusion through: 7 osmosis
dividing: 5 septa (plural) 6 septum
ear: 8 tympanum
enclosing: 8 indusium
thin: 6 lamina 7 lamella, laminae
(plural) 8 lamellae (plural)
wing: 8 patagium

memento
5 relic, token, trace 6 shadow, trophy 7 vestige 8 keepsake, reminder, souvenir 11 remembrance
12 remembrancer

Memnon
father: 8 Tithonus
mother: 3 Eos 6 Aurora
slayer: 8 Achilles

memoir
3 bio 4 life 6 record, report, thesis

8 anecdote, tractate, treatise
9 biography, discourse, monograph
10 monography 11 confessions, remembrance 12 disquisition, dissertation, recollection, reminiscence
13 autobiography

memoirist
7 Boswell 10 biographer

memorable
6 rubric 9 deathless, momentous, red-letter 10 impressive, noteworthy, remembered 11 significant
13 distinguished

memorandum
4 chit, note 5 diary 6 letter, minute, notice 7 epistle, message, missive, tickler 8 dispatch, notation, reminder 9 directive 12 announcement

memorial
4 note 5 relic, token, trace 6 record, trophy 7 relique 8 keepsake, monument, reminder, souvenir
10 dedicatory, enshrining 11 celebrative, remembrance 12 consecrative, remembrancer 13 commemoration, commemorative, commemoratory
mound: 4 carn 5 cairn

memorial park
8 cemetery, God's acre 9 graveyard 10 necropolis 11 polyandrium 12 burial ground, potter's field 13 burying ground

memorize
3 con, get 5 learn, study
8 remember

memory
4 mind 6 recall 8 mind's eye, souvenir 9 anamnesis, awareness, retention 10 cognizance, reflection
11 remembrance 12 recollection, reminiscence 13 concentration, consciousness, retentiveness, retrospection
assisting: 8 mnemonic
combining form: 4 mnem 5 mnemo 6 mnesia
loss: 7 amnesia

menace
4 loom, risk 5 alarm, lower, peril, scare 6 danger, hazard, threat
7 imperil, jeopard, torment 8 endanger, frighten, jeopardy, threaten 10 jeopardize

ménage
5 folks, house 6 family 8 quarters
9 household 12 housekeeping

Menahem
father: 4 Gadi
son: 8 Pekahiah
victim: 7 Shallum

mend
3 fix, sew 4 cure, darn, do up, gain, heal, vamp 5 patch, ready, renew 6 bushel, cobble, doctor, look up, perk up, reform, remedy, repair, revamp 7 correct, improve, patch up, rebuild, rectify, redress, restore, service 8 overhaul, renovate 9 condition, refurbish 10 ameliorate, convalesce, recuperate, rejuvenate 11 recondition, reconstruct

mendacious
5 false, lying, wrong 6 shifty 7 fibbing, knavish, roguish 8 unhonest 9 deceitful, dishonest, paltering
10 untruthful 12 equivocating
13 prevaricating

mendacity
7 dodging, fibbery, hedging 8 boggling, caviling, shifting 9 falsehood, quibbling 12 equivocation, sidestepping 13 truthlessness

mendelevium
symbol: 2 Md

mendicancy
7 beggary, bumming, cadging
8 mooching, sponging 11 panhandling

mendicant
5 friar 6 beggar 7 begging

Mending Wall author
5 Frost (Robert)

Menelaus
brother: 9 Agamemnon
father: 6 Atreus
kingdom: 6 Sparta
mother: 6 Aerope
wife: 5 Helen

menial
5 lowly 6 humble 7 servile, slavish
8 obeisant 10 obsequious
11 subservient

Men in White author
8 Kingsley (Sidney)

Menlo Park inventor
6 Edison (Thomas Alva)

menopause
11 climacteric 12 change of life

Menotti, Gian Carlo
character: 5 Amahl
opera: 9 The Consul, The Medium
12 The Telephone

men's store
12 haberdashery

mental
5 inner 6 genial 7 psychic 8 thinking 9 reasoning, spiritual 10 immaterial, telepathic 11 ideological, intelligent 12 intellective, intellectual
13 psychological
faculty: 6 memory

mentality
3 wit 5 sense 6 brains 7 outlook
9 mother wit 10 brainpower
12 intelligence

mention
4 cite, name, note 5 quote, refer 6 advert, allude, detail 7 refer to, specify 8 instance 9 designate, reference 10 denominate

mentor
5 coach 7 teacher

Mentor's pupil
10 Telemachus

menu
4 card, diet 5 carte 7 regimen
10 bill of fare 11 carte du jour
item: 4 soup 5 salad 6 entrée
7 dessert 9 appetizer

Mephibosheth
father: 4 Saul 8 Jonathan
mother: 6 Rizpah

Mephistophelian
7 satanic 8 devilish, diabolic

mephitic
4 olid 5 fetid, funky, musty 6 poison, smelly 7 noisome, noxious, reeking, stenchy 8 stinking, toxicant, venomous, virulent 9 poisonous 10 malodorous

Merab
father: 4 Saul
husband: 6 Adriel

Meraioth
father: 6 Ahitub 8 Zerahiah
son: 5 Zadok

Merari
brother: 6 Kohath 7 Gershon
daughter: 6 Judith
father: 4 Levi
son: 5 Mahli, Mushi

mercenary
4 grub, hack 5 venal 6 drudge, slavey 7 corrupt, grubber, soldier
8 hireling

merchandise
4 line, sell 5 cargo, goods, stock, trade, wares 6 deal in, job lot, market, retail 7 effects, staples, traffic

9 publicize, vendibles
11 commodities

merchandiser
9 tradesman 11 businessman

merchant
5 buyer 6 dealer, jobber, seller,
trader, vender, vendor 7 peddler
8 purveyor, retailer 9 tradesman
10 specialist, trafficker, wholesaler
11 businessman, storekeeper
guild: 5 hansa, hanse
Hindu: 6 banian, banyan
League: 9 Hanseatic
ship: 5 oiler 6 argosy, coaler, gal-
iot, packet, tanker, trader 7 collier,
galliot, steamer 8 Indiaman
9 freighter
wine: 7 vintner

Merchant of Venice
7 Antonio
character: 6 Portia 7 Jessica, Lorenzo, Nerissa, Shylock 8 Bassanio

merciful
4 easy, kind 6 benign, humane,
kindly 7 clement, lenient, sparing
8 tolerant 9 condoning, forgiving,
indulgent, pardoning 10 charitable, forbearing 11 softhearted
13 compassionate

merciless
4 grim 5 cruel, harsh 6 mortal, savage, wanton 9 cutthroat, ferocious,
unpitying 10 gratuitous, implacable, ironfisted, unyielding 11 uncalled-for, unflinching, unrelenting
12 unappeasable

mercurial
6 adroit, clever, fickle, mobile
7 buoyant, cunning, elastic, movable 8 ticklish, unstable, variable,
volatile 9 expansive, ingenious, resilient, sprightly 10 capricious,
changeable, inconstant, lubricious
12 effervescent 13 temperamental

mercury
5 azoth 9 poison ivy 11 quicksilver
ore: 8 cinnabar
symbol: 2 Hg

Mercury
6 planet; (see also **Hermes**)

Mercutio
friend: 5 Romeo
slayer: 6 Tybalt

mercy
4 pity, ruth 5 grace 6 lenity 7 caritas, charity 8 clemency, goodwill,
kindness, leniency 9 benignity, tolerance 10 compassion, generosity,

kindliness 11 benevolence, forbearance 13 commiseration
petition for: 5 kyrie 8 miserere

mere
3 fen 4 bare, lake, pool, pure, very
5 marsh 9 undiluted

Mered's father
5 Ezrah

merely
3 but 4 just, only 5 quite 6 simply,
wholly

Meremoth's father
4 Bani 5 Uriah

meretricious
4 loud 5 gaudy 6 brazen, flashy,
garish, tawdry, tinsel 7 blatant,
chintzy, glaring 8 delusive, delusory 9 deceptive, insincere
10 misleading

merganser
4 duck, smew

merge
3 mix 4 fuse, join 5 blend, unify,
unite 6 mingle 7 combine 8 coalesce, compound 9 commingle, interfuse 10 amalgamate, interblend
11 consolidate, intermingle

mergence
see **merging**

merger
5 union 9 coalition 11 coadunation, combination, unification
12 amalgamation 13 consolidation

merging
5 union 9 coalition 11 coadunation, combination, unification
13 consolidation

meridian
4 acme, apex, peak 6 apogee, climax, comble, summit, zenith
8 pinnacle

merit
3 due 4 earn, rate 5 arete, award,
lumps, repay, value, worth 6 reward, rights, virtue 7 caliber, deserts, deserve, entitle, justify, quality, requite, stature, warrant
9 deserving 10 excellence, excellency, perfection, recompense

meritable
see **meritorious**

merited
3 due 4 just 5 right 7 condign
8 deserved, rightful, suitable 9 requisite 11 appropriate 13 rhadamanthine

meritorious
6 worthy 8 laudable 9 admirable,
deserving, estimable, honorable,
praisable 11 commendable, thankworthy 12 praiseworthy

merlin
6 falcon 10 pigeon hawk

mermaid
7 manatee 8 sirenian
11 sirenomelus

Merodach
see **Marduk**

Merope
father: 5 Atlas 8 Oenopion
husband: 7 Polybus 8 Sisyphus
11 Cresphontes
lover: 5 Orion
mother: 7 Pleione
sisters: 8 Pleiades
son: 7 Aepytus, Glaucus

merriment
4 glee 5 mirth, revel 6 gaiety 7 jollity, revelry, whoopee 8 hilarity,
reveling 9 festivity, jocundity, joviality 10 jocularity, jubilation
13 entertainment

merry
3 gay, mad 4 boon, gean, glad,
high, wild 5 happy, jolly, riant,
sharp 6 blithe, jocund, jovial, joyful, joyous, lively 7 festive, gleeful,
intense 8 animated, cheerful, glee-
some, laughing, mirthful 9 hilarious, sprightly, vivacious 10 blithesome 12 lighthearted 13 unconstrained

merry-andrew
4 zany 5 clown 7 buffoon 9 harlequin 10 mountebank

merrymaking
5 party, revel 6 gaiety 7 jollity, revelry, whoopee 8 pleasure 9 enjoyment, festivity, revelment 10 indulgence 12 conviviality

Merry Widow composer
5 Lehar (Franz)

Merry Wives of Windsor, The
character: 3 Nym 4 Ford, Page
5 Caius 6 Fenton, Pistol 7 Slender
8 Falstaff

mesa
5 bench 7 plateau 9 cartouche,
tableland

mescal
5 agave 6 cactus, liquor, maguey

mesh
3 net, web 4 knot, maze, nett

5 skein, snarl **6** accord, engage, jungle, morass, tangle **7** mizmaze, netting, network **8** entangle **9** harmonize, interlock, labyrinth **10** coordinate

Mesha
father: **9** Shaharaim
kingdom: **4** Moab
mother: **6** Hodesh

Meshech's father
7 Japheth

meshuggaas
4 guff **6** drivel **7** twaddle **8** claptrap, nonsense **9** poppycock **10** balderdash

Meshullam
father: **4** Bani **5** Zadok **9** Berechiah, Besodeiah **10** Shephatiah, Zerubbabel **12** Meshillemith
son: **5** Sallu **7** Hilkiah

Meshullemeth
husband: **8** Manasseh
son: **4** Amon

mesmeric
5 siren **7** drawing **8** alluring, charming **9** glamorous **10** attractive, bewitching, enchanting **11** captivating

mesmerize
4 grip, hold **7** catch up **8** enthrall, entrance **9** fascinate, hypnotize, spellbind

Mesopotamia
civilization: **7** Assyria **9** Babylonia
river: **6** Tigris **9** Euphrates

mess
4 hash, mull, play **5** botch, catch, gum up, mix up, snafu, wreck **6** bobble, bollix, bungle, dabble, doodle, fiddle, fright, goof up, jumble, muddle, potter, puddle, putter, tinker, trifle **7** bitch up, confuse, desight, eyesore, louse up **8** botchery, disarray, dishevel, disorder, shambles, wreckage **9** confusion **10** disarrange, hodgepodge, miscellany **11** monstrosity
up: **5** touse **6** tousle, touzle, untidy

message
4 note, word **5** sense **6** import, letter, report **7** epistle, evangel, meaning, mission, purport **8** dispatch, telegram **9** directive, telegraph **10** communiqué, intendment, memorandum **11** acceptation **12** significance **13** communication, signification

Messalina's husband
8 Claudius

mess around
4 fool, idle, wolf **5** flirt **6** butt in, dabble, dawdle, doodle, fiddle, horn in, meddle, potter, puddle, putter, tinker **7** intrude **8** busybody, womanize **9** associate, interfere, interlope, manhandle, philander **10** monkey with, tamper with

messenger
4 post **5** envoy **6** herald **7** apostle, courier **8** emissary **9** character, go-between **11** internuncio **12** intermediary
God's: **5** angel
of the gods: **6** Hermes **7** Mercury
Turkish: **6** chiaus, chouse

Messiah composer
6 Handel (George Frideric)

messy
5 dirty, grimy **6** botchy, sloppy, unneat, untidy **7** raunchy, unkempt **8** careless, ill-kempt, slapdash, slipshod, slovenly **10** disheveled, unthorough **12** unfastidious
abode: **3** sty

Mestor
father: **7** Perseus
mother: **9** Andromeda

metal
4 gold **5** steel, sword **6** bronze
alloy: (see **alloy**)
casting mold: **5** ingot
corrosion: **4** rust
design: **7** chasing
dross: **4** slag
drum: **8** canister
fittings: **5** brass
in mass: **7** bullion
layer: **7** plating
lump: **6** nugget
magnetic: **4** iron
piece: **4** slug
refuse: **6** scoria
sheath: **5** armor
substance: **5** alloy
surface scum: **5** dross
thin: **4** foil, leaf **5** plate
type: **7** quadrat
unite: **6** solder
worker: **5** smith **10** blacksmith

metallic element
3 tin **4** gold, iron, lead, zinc **6** barium, cobalt, copper, nickel, radium, silver, sodium **7** arsenic, bismuth, lithium, mercury, uranium **8** aluminum, platinum, tungsten, vanadium **9** magnesium, manganese, potassium, strontium **10** molybdenum

metamere
6 somite **7** segment

metamorphic
rock: **5** slate **6** gneiss, marble, schist **9** quartzite, soapstone

metamorphose
3 age **5** ripen **6** change, mature **7** commute, convert, develop **9** transform, translate, transmute **11** transfigure **12** transmogrify

metamorphosis
6 change **8** changing
combining form: **3** ody

Metamorphosis author
5 Kafka (Franz)

metanoia
7 rebirth **10** conversion

metaphor
5 trope **6** simile **7** analogy **8** allegory **10** comparison, similitude

metaphorical compound
7 kenning

metaphysical
8 bodiless, numinous, superior **9** unearthly, unfleshly **10** discarnate, immaterial, superhuman, suprahuman **12** supermundane, supernatural, supramundane, supranatural, transcendent **13** preternatural
poet: **5** Donne (John) **7** Crashaw (Richard), Herbert (George), Marvell (Andrew)

mete
4 deal, dole, give **5** allot **6** parcel **7** portion **8** allocate, dispense **9** apportion

meteor
8 fireball **12** shooting star
exploding: **5** bolis **6** bolide
shower: **5** Lyrid **6** Leonid, Taurid **7** Aquarid, Geminid, Orionid, Perseid **10** Quadrantid
suffix: **2** id

meteorite
8 aerolite, aerolith **10** siderolite

meter
4 beat, scan **5** rhyme, swing **6** rhythm **7** cadence, cadency, measure, versify

metheglin
4 mead **8** beverage
ingredient: **5** honey

method
3 way **4** form, line, mode, modi (plural), plan, wise **5** means, modus, order, style, track **6** course, design, manner, schema, scheme,

system **7** fashion, formula, pattern, process, routine, technic, wrinkle **8** practice **9** procedure, technique **11** orderliness **13** modus operandi
careful: **8** strategy
of employing troops: **6** tactic
of procedure: **2** MO **4** game

methodical
5 exact **7** careful, orderly, precise, regular **9** organized **10** scrupulous, systematic **12** systematized

Methuselah
father: **5** Enoch
grandson: **4** Noah
son: **6** Lamech

Methushael
father: **8** Mehujael
son: **6** Lamech

meticulous
4 neat **5** exact, fussy, picky **6** strict **7** careful, finicky, heedful **8** punctual, thorough **10** pernickety **11** microscopic, painstaking **12** conscionable

métier
3 art **4** mode **5** craft, forte, trade **7** calling **8** business, eminency, long suit, vocation **10** handicraft, profession, strong suit

metrical foot
4 iamb **5** iambi (plural), ionic, paeon **6** cretic, dactyl, iambic, iambus **7** anapest, pyrrhic, spondee, triseme, trochee **8** bacchius, choriamb, spondaic, tribrach, trochaic

metric unit
area: **7** centare, deciare, hectare
capacity: **5** liter **9** decaliter, deciliter, kiloliter **10** centiliter, hectoliter, milliliter
length: **5** meter **9** decameter, decimeter, kilometer **10** centimeter, hectometer, millimeter, myriameter
mass and weight: **4** gram **7** quintal **8** decagram, decigram, kilogram **9** centigram, hectogram, metric ton, milligram
volume: **5** stere **9** decastere, decistere

metropolis
4 city **7** capital **13** mother country

metropolitan
5 urban **6** urbane **10** archbishop

mettle
4 guts **5** heart, pluck, spunk **6** spirit, temper **7** cojones, courage **10** resolution **12** spiritedness **13** dauntlessness

mettlesome
4 edgy **5** beany, fiery **6** spunky **7** gingery, peppery **8** skittish, spirited **9** excitable, startlish **10** high-strung **11** high-hearted **12** high-spirited

mew
3 hem, pen **4** cage, coop, gull, molt, mure **5** fence **6** corral, immure, shut in **7** enclose **8** hideaway

mewl
4 meow **5** whine **7** whimper

Mexico
aborigine: **4** Maya **5** Aztec
coin: **7** centavo
conqueror: **6** Cortes, Cortez (Hernan, Hernando)
crop: **5** sisal
emperor: **10** Maximilian
estate: **8** hacienda
ethnic group: **6** Indian **7** Mestizo
export: **6** coffee, cotton, sulfur **9** petroleum
food: **4** masa, taco **5** chili, salsa **6** tamale **7** burrito, panocha, penuche, tostada **8** frijoles, tortilla **9** enchilada, guacamole **10** quesadilla **11** chimichanga
house: **5** jacal
language: **7** Spanish
liquor: **7** tequila
monetary unit: **4** peso
oil enterprise: **5** PEMEX
reformer: **6** Juarez (Benito)
revolutionist: **5** Villa (Pancho) **6** Zapata (Emiliano) **8** Carranza (Venustiano)
stimulant: **6** mescal

mezzanine
5 story **7** balcony **8** entresol

mezzo-soprano
American: **5** Elias (Rosalind), Horne (Marilyn), Jones (Sissieretta) **6** Bumbry (Grace) **7** Verrett (Shirley) **8** Troyanos (Tatiana), von Stade (Frederica)
Austrian: **6** Ludwig (Christa)
English: **5** Baker (Janet)
Italian: **8** Cossotto (Fiorenza)

Miami
bowl: **6** Orange
chief: **12** Little Turtle
county: **4** Dade
stadium: **9** Joe Robbie
team: **4** Heat **7** Marlins **8** Dolphins, Panthers

miasma
4 smog

mib
5 agate **6** marble

mica
4 talc **7** biotite **8** silicate

Mica
father: **6** Zichri **12** Mephibosheth
grandfather: **8** Jonathan

Micah
father: **9** Meribbaal
son: **5** Abdon

Micaiah
father: **5** Imlah, Uriel **8** Gemariah
grandfather: **7** Absalom
husband: **8** Rehoboam
mother: **5** Tamar
son: **6** Abijah, Achbor

Michelangelo
painting: **10** Holy Family **12** Last Judgment
statue: **5** David, Moses, Pietà **7** Bacchus

Michener novel
5 Space, Texas **6** Hawaii, Poland **8** Caravans, Sayonara **9** The Source **10** Centennial, Chesapeake **11** The Covenant, The Drifters **16** The Fires of Spring **18** The Bridges of Toko-ri

Michigan
capital: **7** Lansing
college: **4** Alma
highest point: **9** Mt. Curwood
largest city: **7** Detroit
nickname: **9** Lake State **14** Wolverine State
state bird: **5** robin
state flower: **12** apple blossom

microfilm sheet
5 fiche

Micronesia
political division: **4** Guam **5** Nauru **6** Tuvalu **8** Kiribati

microorganism
4 germ **5** virus **6** aerobe **7** bacilli (plural), microbe **8** bacillus, bacteria (plural), pathogen, protozoa (plural) **9** bacterium, protozoan

microphone
3 bug **4** mike
shield: **4** gobo

microscope
7 magnify **9** magnifier **10** instrument
part: **5** stage **6** mirror **8** eyepiece **9** objective

microscopic
4 tiny **5** small **6** minute

midday
4 noon, sext 8 noontide, noontime

middle
4 core, mean 5 mesne, waist
6 center, medial, median 7 central,
halfway 8 interior 10 centermost
11 equidistant, intervening 12 intermediary, intermediate
combining form: 3 mes 4 medi, meso
5 medio, mesio

Middle America country
4 Cuba 5 Haiti 6 Mexico, Panama
8 Honduras 9 Costa Rica, Guatemala, Nicaragua 10 El Salvador

Middle Atlantic State
7 New York 9 New Jersey
12 Pennsylvania

middlebrow
4 boob 7 Babbitt 10 philistine

middle class
11 bourgeoisie

middle-class
9 bourgeois

middle ear
bone: 5 incus 6 stapes 7 malleus
membrane: 7 eardrum 8 tympanum

Middle East country
4 Iran, Iraq, Oman 5 Egypt, Qatar,
Sudan, Syria, Yemen 6 Cyprus, Israel, Jordan, Kuwait, Turkey 7 Bahrain, Lebanon 11 Saudi Arabia

Middle Kingdom
5 China

middleman
6 broker 7 bailiff 8 mediator 9 go-
between 10 interagent, interceder
11 intercessor 12 entrepreneur,
intermediary, intermediate 13 intermediator

Middlemarch author
5 Eliot (George)

middle-of-the-road
8 moderate 9 soft-shell

middling
4 fair, mean, poor, so-so 6 fairly,
flitch, medium, rather 7 average,
fairish 8 inferior, mediocre, moderate 10 moderately, second-rate
11 indifferent 12 intermediate

midge
3 fly 4 runt 5 dwarf, pygmy 6 peewee 7 manikin 8 mannikin, Tom
Thumb 10 homunculus 11 lilliptu-
tian
larva: 9 bloodworm

midget
3 wee 4 runt, tiny 5 dwarf, pygmy,

teeny 6 peewee, punkie, teensy
7 manikin 8 dwarfish, mannikin,
Tom Thumb 9 miniature 10 diminutive, homunculus 11 hop-o'-my-
thumb, lilliputian

Midian
father: 7 Abraham
mother: 7 Keturah

mid-Victorian
4 fogy, prig 5 prude 6 fogram, fossil, square 7 puritan 8 bluenose,
mossback 9 Mrs. Grundy 10 antiquated, fuddy-duddy, goody-goody
12 old-fashioned 13 stick-in-the-mud

midwife
10 accoucheur
Scottish: 5 howdy 6 howdie

mien
3 air, set 4 look, port 6 aspect,
manner 7 address, bearing, seeming 8 demeanor, presence 9 mannerism 10 appearance, deportment, expression 11 comportment

miff
3 fit 4 beef, spat 5 pique, run-in
7 dispute, dudgeon, offense, quarrel, rhubarb, umbrage 8 squabble
10 conniption, falling-out, resentment 11 altercation

mig
6 marble

might
3 arm 4 beef, sway, thew
5 brawn, force, means, power,
sinew 6 energy, muscle 7 ability,
command, control, mastery, potency, strings 8 capacity, strength
9 authority, lustiness, resources,
strong arm 10 capability, competence, domination 12 forcefulness,
jurisdiction, powerfulness, vigorous-
ness 13 energeticness

mighty
4 high, huge, very 5 grand, great
6 august, heroic, hugely, moving,
potent, strong, wieldy 7 eminent,
immense, massive, notable, violent
8 enormous, forceful, forcible, gigantic, imposing, powerful, puissant, rattling, renowned, whacking,
whopping 9 efficient, extremely,
strenuous 10 impressive, monumental, prodigious, tremendous 11 efficacious, exceedingly, illustrious
12 surpassingly 13 extraordinary
combining form: 3 din 4 dein, dino
5 deino

Mignon composer
6 Thomas (Ambroise)

mignonette
4 herb 6 reseda

migrant
5 mover, nomad 6 mobile 7 drifter
8 traveler, wanderer

migrate
4 move, roam, rove, trek 5 drift,
range, shift 6 wander 8 nomadize,
transfer

migration
6 moving 8 diaspora, movement
of professionals: 10 brain drain

migratory
5 nomad 6 errant, mobile, moving,
roving 7 nomadic, ranging
9 wandering

Milan
family: 6 Sforza 8 Visconti
opera house: 7 La Scala

Milcah
brother: 3 Lot
father: 5 Haran 10 Zelophehad
husband: 5 Nahor
son: 7 Bethuel

mild
4 calm, easy, meek, soft, tame
5 balmy, bland, faint 6 benign,
choice, dainty, docile, gentle,
smooth 7 amiable, clement, lenient,
subdued 8 delicate, moderate,
obeisant, obliging 9 benignant,
exquisite, temperate 10 forbearing,
submissive

mildew
4 mold 6 fungus, growth

___ mile
7 statute 8 nautical

mileage recorder
8 odometer

milepost
5 event 6 marker 8 occasion

milestone
5 event 8 landmark, occasion

milieu
6 medium 7 ambient, climate, setting 8 ambience 10 atmosphere
11 environment, mise-en-scéne
12 surroundings

militant
5 pushy 7 fighter, martial, pushful,
pushing, scrappy, warlike 8 fighting 9 assertive, assertory, bellicose,
combative, truculent 10 aggressive,
pugnacious 11 belligerent, contentious, quarrelsome 12 gladiatorial
13 self-assertive

military
5 troop 6 forces 7 martial, warlike
9 soldierly 10 jingoistic, servicemen
11 armed forces, soldierlike
12 chauvinistic, warmongering
alliance: 4 NATO
base: 4 camp, fort, post 5 depot,
field 6 billet 8 barracks, garrison,
quarters 10 encampment
officer: 5 major 7 captain, colonel,
general 9 brigadier 10 lieutenant
prisoner: 3 POW
school: 3 OCS, OTS 4 ROTC,
USMA 9 West Point
sector: 10 combat zone 11 battle-
front
store: 2 BX, PX 10 commissary
storehouse: 5 depot, étape 6 armory
7 arsenal
supplies: 8 matériel, ordnance
unit: 5 corps, squad, troop 7 company, platoon 8 division, regiment
9 battalion 11 battle group
vehicle: 4 jeep, tank 9 half-track

militate
4 tell 5 count, weigh

milk
4 draw, pump, rook, suck 5 bleed,
drain, educe, empty, evoke, exact,
mulct, nurse, stick, sweat, wring
6 elicit, evince, extort, fleece, suckle
7 exhaust, exploit, extract
coagulated: 4 curd
combining form: 4 lact 5 lacti, lacto
6 galact 7 galacto
curdled: 5 leben 7 clabber
fermented: 5 kefir, kumys 6 kumiss,
kumyss, yogurt 7 koumiss, mat-
zoon, yoghurt
liquid part: 4 whey
store: 5 dairy
sugar: 7 lactose

milk shake
6 frappe 7 frosted

milksop
4 baby 5 sissy 6 coward 7 doormat 8 weakling 9 jellyfish 10 effeminate, namby-pamby, pantywaist 11 Milquetoast, mollycoddle

milky
4 meek, mild, tame 5 white
6 chalky, gentle 7 lacteal, lactean
8 timorous

Milky Way
combining form: 6 galact 7 galacto

mill
4 beat, slug 5 dress, fight, plant,
quern, shape, works 6 finish,
thrash 7 factory, machine 11 manufactory

Miller, Arthur
film: 10 The Misfits
play: 9 All My Sons 11 The Crucible
12 After the Fall 16 Death of a
Salesman 18 A View From the
Bridge
salesman: 5 Loman (Willy)

mill fever
10 byssinosis

million
combining form: 3 meg 4 mega

millionth
combining form: 4 micr 5 micro

Mill on the Floss author
5 Eliot (George)

millstone
3 tax 4 duty, load, onus, task
6 burden, charge, weight 9 buhrstone 10 affliction, deadweight

Milne bear
4 Pooh

Milquetoast, Caspar
creator: 7 Webster (Harold Tucker);
(see also **milksop**)

Miltiades' victory
8 Marathon

Milton work
5 Comus 7 Lycidas 8 L'Allegro
12 Areopagitica, Paradise Lost

mime
3 act 5 actor 6 act out, player
7 trouper 8 thespian 9 performer,
playactor, represent
12 impersonator
famous: 7 Marceau (Marcel)

mimic
2 do 3 act, ape 4 copy, mock,
play 5 actor, enact 6 hit off, mummer, parody, parrot, player 7 copycat, imitate, perform, take off,
trouper 8 simulate, thespian, travesty 9 burlesque, imitation, pantomime, performer, personate, playactor 11 impersonate 12 impersonator

mimicry
4 echo, mock 5 apery 6 parody
9 imitation 10 caricature

mince
3 cut 4 chop, hash 5 cut up, strut
6 finick, sashay 7 finnick 8 moderate, restrain 9 euphemize

mincing
4 nice 5 fussy 6 dainty, la-di-da,
too-too 7 finical, finicky, genteel,
stilted 8 affected, delicate 9 squeamish 10 fastidious, particular, pernickety 11 persnickety

mind
3 eye, see, wit 4 care, espy, keep,
look, mood, nous, obey, soul, tend,
tone, vein, view, will, wits 5 brain,
fancy, humor, power, study, watch,
weigh, worry 6 at-
tend, behold, belief, beware,
brains, comply, descry, desire, follow, govern, liking, memory, notice, ponder, psyche, reason, sanity, senses, spirit, strain, temper
7 care for, conform, discern, dislike, faculty, feeling, look out, observe, opinion, oversee, perpend,
purpose 8 consider, function, lucidity, perceive, pleasure, remember,
saneness, think out, villeity, watch
out 9 intellect, intention, mentality,
sentiment, soundness, supervise,
think over 10 brainpower, conviction, discipline, excogitate, gray
matter, persuasion 11 disposition,
inclination, superintend, temperament 12 intelligence, recollection
13 consciousness
combining form: 3 noo 5 menti,
phren, psych 6 phreni, phreno,
psycho

mindful
5 alert, alive, awake, aware
7 knowing 8 sensible, vigilant
9 attentive, au courant, cognizant,
conscious, observant, observing,
regardful 10 conversant 12 apprehensive 13 conscientious

mindless
3 mad 4 nuts 5 nutsy, silly 6 insane, maniac, simple, stupid 7 asinine, foolish, lunatic 9 nitwitted
10 unthinking 11 sheepheaded
13 unintelligent

mine
3 dig, pit, sap 4 lode, vein, well,
work 5 delve, drill, scoop 6 burrow, quarry, spring 7 bonanza, extract 8 eldorado, excavate, Golconda, treasury 10 excavation,
wellspring 13 treasure-house, treasure trove
coal: 8 colliery
French: 4 à moi 6 le mien

mine gas
9 blackdamp, chokedamp

miner
6 digger, pitman 7 collier

mineral
5 beryl, topaz, trona 6 augite, bar-
ite, garnet, iolite, pinite, rutile,
sphene, spinel, sulfur, zircon 7 ap-
atite, azurite, bornite, calcite, ci-

trine, coesite, cyanite, jadeite, kernite, kunzite, olivine, zeolite 8 boracite, cinnabar, dolomite, epsomite, fayalite, feldspar, fluorite, hematite, lazulite, lazurite, siderite, sodalite, stibnite, triplite, wellsite 9 aragonite, celestite, cerussite, danburite, fosterite, kaolinite, lawsonite, magnetite, malachite, muscovite, phenakite, scapolite, tridymite, turquoise, wulfenite 10 chalcedony, orthoclase, pyrrhotite, tourmaline 11 alexandrite, chrysoberyl, melanterite 12 brazilianite, chalcopyrite, tincalconite 13 rhodochrosite

combining form: 3 ine, ite 4 lite, lith, lyte, xene 5 oryct 6 orycto
flaky: 4 mica
greasy: 4 talc 10 serpentine
hard: 6 spinel 7 diamond 8 corundum
iridescent: 4 opal
nonmetallic: 5 boron 6 gypsum, halite 8 asbestos, graphite
shiny: 4 gold 6 galena, pyrite, silver
soft: 4 talc 6 gypsum 8 graphite
transparent: 6 quartz

mineral water
7 seltzer

Minerva
see **Athena**

mingle
3 mix 4 meld 5 merge 6 commix, make up 7 combine, concoct 8 intermix 9 socialize

mingy
4 mean 5 tight 6 stingy 7 scrimpy 8 ungiving 9 niggardly, penurious 11 closefisted

miniature
3 wee 4 copy, tiny 5 model, small, teeny, weeny 6 little, minute, teensy 8 portrait 9 itty-bitty 10 diminutive, small-scale, teeny-weeny 11 lilliputian 12 illumination

minify
5 dwarf 6 lessen, shrink 7 abridge, curtail 8 diminish

minim
3 jot 4 atom, iota 5 grain, speck 6 minute, smitch 7 modicum, smidgen 8 particle
music: 8 half note, half rest

minimal
5 basic 6 lowest 8 littlest, smallest 9 slightest

minimize
5 decry, dwarf 6 reduce 7 run down 8 belittle, derogate, discount

9 disparage, dispraise 10 depreciate 11 detract from

minimum
3 dab, jot 4 hair, iota, whit 5 least, speck 6 lowest, margin 7 smidgen 8 particle, pittance, smallest

minion
4 idol, toad 6 yes-man 7 darling, spaniel 8 creature, favorite, truckler 9 sycophant, toadeater, underling 10 bootlicker 11 lickspittle, subordinate

minister
4 tend 5 agent, clerk, serve 6 cleric, curate, divine, parson 8 clerical, preacher, reverend 9 churchman, clergyman 10 ambassador 12 ecclesiastic
of state: 10 chancellor

minister plenipotentiary
5 envoy

ministry
4 mean 5 agent, organ 6 agency, clergy, medium 7 channel, vehicle 10 instrument

Minnehaha's husband
8 Hiawatha

Minnesota
capital: 6 St. Paul
nickname: 11 Gopher State 14 North Star State
state bird: 10 common loon

minor
4 fair 5 dinky, light, lower, petty, small, youth 6 casual, infant, lesser, little, medium, slight 7 average, trivial 8 inferior, mediocre, piddling, small-fry, trifling 9 dependent, secondary, small-beer, small-time 10 bush-league, second-rate, shoestring 11 indifferent, unimportant 12 unnoticeable 13 insignificant

minority
6 nonage 7 infancy 10 immaturity

minor-league
5 dinky, small 6 lesser 8 small-fry 9 secondary, small-time 11 unimportant

Minos
daughter: 7 Ariadne, Phaedra
father: 4 Zeus 7 Jupiter
kingdom: 5 Crete
monster: 8 Minotaur
mother: 6 Europa
son: 9 Androgeos
wife: 8 Pasiphaë

Minotaur
father: 4 bull
home: 9 labyrinth
mother: 8 Pasiphaë
slayer: 7 Theseus

minstrel
4 bard, wait 6 harper, singer 7 gleeman 8 jongleur 9 balladist 10 troubadour
end man: 7 Mr. Bones, Mr. Tambo
instrument: 4 lute 10 tambourine

mint
3 pot, wad 4 coin, pile 6 boodle, bundle, intact, packet, unused 7 fire-new, fortune, perfect, spannew 8 brand-new, lavender, original, spang-new, unmarred 9 blue curls, bugleweed, spearmint 10 peppermint 11 spanking-new 12 spick-and-span

Minuit's purchase
9 Manhattan

minus
4 less, sans 7 lacking, wanting, without 8 awanting, subtract 10 deficiency

minute
3 jot, wee 4 full, tiny 5 crack, flash, jiffy, light, petty, shake, small, teeny, weeny 6 little, moment, second, teensy, tittle 7 careful, instant, precise, trivial 8 detailed, itemized, thorough, trifling 9 breathing, clocklike, itty-bitty, small-beer 10 blow-by-blow, meticulous, particular, scrupulous, teeny-weeny 11 lilliputian, punctilious, split second, unimportant 13 infinitesimal, insignificant

minutes
6 record 7 summary

minutiae
5 ropes 6 trivia 7 details 9 small beer 10 ins and outs, triviality 11 particulars, small change 13 small potatoes

miracle
4 feat 6 marvel, wonder 7 portent, prodigy, stunner 9 sensation 10 phenomenon

miraculous
7 amazing, strange 8 superior 9 marvelous, unearthly, wonderful 10 astounding, prodigious, staggering, superhuman, suprahuman 11 astonishing, spectacular 12 supermundane, supernatural, supramundane, supranatural 13 preternatural

mirage
8 delusion, illusion, phantasm
11 fata morgana, ignis fatuus
13 hallucination

Miranda
father: **8** Prospero
lover: **9** Ferdinand

mire
3 bog, fen, mud **4** muck, ooze, quag, sink, soil, trap **5** cling, delay, embog, marsh, slush, stick, swamp **6** cleave, detain, enmesh, entrap, hang up, morass, retard, slow up, tangle **7** baygall, bog down, embroil, ensnare, involve, set back, slacken **8** entangle, slow down **9** implicate

Miriam's brother
5 Aaron, Moses

mirror
5 glass, ideal, image, model **6** embody, typify **7** example, pattern, reflect **8** ensample, exemplar, paradigm, speculum, standard **9** archetype, beau ideal, body forth, epitomize, exemplify, personify, pier glass, reflector, represent, symbolize **10** illustrate **11** cheval glass, emblematize **12** looking glass
sight: **5** image
signaling: **5** helio **10** heliograph, heliotrope

mirth
3 fun, joy **4** glee **5** cheer **6** gaiety, levity **7** jollity **8** gladness, hilarity **9** frivolity, happiness, jocundity, joviality, merriment, rejoicing **10** jocularity, joyfulness **12** cheerfulness

mirthful
3 gay **5** jolly, merry, riant **6** blithe, jocund, jovial **7** festive **10** blithesome **12** lighthearted

miry
4 oozy **5** boggy, muddy

misadventure
4 bull, slip, woes **5** boner, error, lapse **6** howler, mishap **7** blunder, faux pas, tragedy **8** accident, calamity, casualty, disaster **9** cataclysm **11** catastrophe

misanthropic
7 cynical **8** reserved, solitary **9** reclusive **10** antisocial **11** standoffish

misappropriate
5 steal **8** embezzle

misbegotten
7 bastard, natural **8** baseborn, deformed, spurious **10** fatherless, un-

fathered **12** contemptible, illegitimate

misbehaving
3 bad **7** naughty

misbehavior
8 rudeness **10** misconduct, wrongdoing

miscalculate
3 err **8** discount, miscount, misgauge, overlook **9** disregard, overprize, overvalue **10** underprize, undervalue

miscarry
4 fail, flop **5** abort

miscellaneous
3 odd **4** many **5** mixed **6** divers, motley, sundry, varied **7** diverse, jumbled, mingled **8** assorted, chowchow, unsorted **9** different, disparate, divergent, scrambled **10** commingled, unassorted **12** conglomerate **13** heterogeneous

miscellany
3 ana **4** brew, hash, olio, posy, stew **5** album, melee, salad **6** jumble, medley, motley, muddle **7** garland, mélange, mixture, omnibus **8** analects, chowchow, mixed bag, pastiche, porridge **9** anthology, colluvies, congeries, pasticcio, patchwork, potpourri **10** assortment, cumulation, hodgepodge, hotchpotch, salmagundi **11** aggregation, combination, florilegium, gallimaufry, odds and ends, olla podrida, smorgasbord

mischance
6 mishap **7** tragedy **8** accident, casualty **9** adversity **10** misfortune **11** contretemps

mischief
3 ill **4** evil, harm, hurt, limb, ruin **5** devil, prank, rogue, scamp **6** damage, injury, rascal, strife **7** devilry, discord, dissent, outrage, roguery, trouble, villain, waggery **8** conflict, deviltry, division, hardship, scalawag, variance **9** devilment, diablerie, disaccord, skeezicks **10** contention, difference, difficulty, dissension **11** rapscallion, roguishness, waggishness **12** sportiveness

mischief-maker
3 imp **4** puck **5** devil, knave, rogue, scamp **6** rascal **7** villain **8** scalawag **9** prankster, trickster **11** rapscallion

mischievous
3 bad, ill, paw, sly **4** evil, foxy **5** antic, risky **6** artful, impish, irking, tricky, vexing, wicked **7** harmful, hurtful, irksome, larkish, naughty, playful, puckish, roguish, tricksy, waggish **8** annoying, damaging, prankish, sportive **9** bothering, injurious **10** bothersome, frolicsome, ill-behaved

mischievousness
4 evil, harm, hurt **6** injury **7** devilry, roguery, teasing, waggery **8** annoying, deviltry **9** devilment, diablerie, pestering

miscolor
4 warp **5** belie, twist **6** garble **7** distort, falsify, pervert **12** misrepresent

misconduct
10 wrongdoing **11** impropriety, malfeasance, misbehavior **12** malversation

miscreant
4 heel **5** knave, rogue **6** rascal, wretch **7** corrupt, heretic, infidel, lowlife, vicious, villain **8** depraved, infamous, perverse **9** heretical, nefarious, scoundrel, unhealthy **10** blackguard, degenerate, flagitious, unbeliever, villainous

miscue
4 miss, slip, trip **5** error, fluff, lapse **6** slipup **7** blooper, blunder, mistake

misdeed
3 sin **5** crime, wrong **7** offense **13** transgression

misdoubt
4 fear **5** dread **7** suspect **8** distrust **9** apprehend, suspicion

mise-en-scène
3 set **4** site **6** locale, medium, milieu **7** ambient, climate, setting **8** ambience, stage set **10** atmosphere **11** environment **12** stage setting, surroundings

miser
3 hog, pig **4** skin **5** chuff, hunks, nabal, piker, stiff **7** glutton, niggard, scrooge **8** muckworm, tightwad **9** skinflint **10** cheapskate

miserable
6 dolent, rueful, woeful **7** doleful, forlorn, piteous, pitiful, ruthful **8** dolorous, hopeless, shameful, wretched **9** afflicted, sorrowful, worthless **10** despairing, despon-

dent, melancholy 12 contemptible 13 discreditable

Miserables, Les
author: 4 Hugo (Victor)
character: 6 Javert 7 Cosette, Fantine, Valjean

miserly
4 mean 5 close, tight 6 abject, greedy, sordid, stingy 7 ignoble 8 covetous, grasping, stingily 9 penurious, scrimping 10 avaricious 11 closefisted, tightfisted 12 cheeseparing, parsimonious 13 penny-pinching

misery
3 woe 5 agony, dolor, grief 6 sorrow 7 anguish, passion, sadness, squalor 8 calamity, distress 9 adversity, dejection, privation, suffering 10 affliction, depression, desolation, melancholy 11 despondency, unhappiness 12 wretchedness

misfortune
3 woe 4 harm 5 cross, trial 7 tragedy, trouble 8 accident, calamity, casualty, disaster 9 adversity, cataclysm 10 affliction, visitation 11 catastrophe, contretemps, tribulation
Scottish: 6 dirdum

misgiving
4 fear 5 doubt, qualm 7 anxiety, presage 8 distrust 9 prenotion, suspicion 11 premonition 12 apprehension, presentiment

misguided
5 wrong 9 erroneous 10 ill-advised

Mishael
brother: 8 Elzaphan
cousin: 5 Aaron
father: 6 Uzziel

Misham's father
6 Elpaal

mishandle
5 abuse 7 pervert, rough up 10 knock about, prostitute, roughhouse, slap around

mishap
7 tragedy 8 accident, casualty 9 adversity 11 contretemps

mishmash
6 jumble, jungle, litter, medley, muddle, tumble 7 clutter, mélange, mixture, rummage 8 pastiche, scramble 9 pasticcio, patchwork, potpourri 10 hodgepodge, hotchpotch

misidentify
7 confuse 8 confound

misinterpret
3 err 7 misread

mislay
4 lose

mislead
3 lie 4 dupe, fool, lure 5 bluff, cheat, tempt 6 betray, delude, entice, illude, juggle, seduce, take in 7 beguile, deceive 8 hoodwink, inveigle 11 double-cross

misleading
5 false, wrong 8 delusive, delusory, specious 9 deceitful, deceiving, deceptive 10 fallacious, inaccurate 11 casuistical, sophistical

mismatch
3 jar 5 clash 6 jangle 7 discord 8 conflict 9 disaccord 12 disharmonize

misplace
4 lose

misrepresent
3 lie 4 gild, mask, warp 5 belie, cloak, color, dress, feign, gloss, twist, wrest 6 garble, palter, weasel, wrench 7 confuse, deceive, distort, falsify, pervert, varnish 8 disguise, simulate 9 dissemble, embellish, embroider 10 camouflage, equivocate 11 counterfeit, prevaricate

misrepresentation
3 fib, lie 4 tale 5 story 6 canard 7 falsity, untruth 8 untruism 9 falsehood

miss
3 err, gal 4 fail, girl, maid, omit 5 avoid, wench 6 damsel, escape, forget, ignore, lassie, maiden, slight 7 failure, neglect 8 discount, overlook 9 disregard

Missa Solemnis composer
9 Beethoven (Ludwig van)

misshape
4 warp, wind 6 deform 7 contort, distort, torture 9 deformity 10 distortion 12 malformation

missile
4 bolt, dart 5 arrow, shell, spear 6 bullet, rocket 10 cannonball, projectile
underwater: 7 torpedo; (see also **guided missile**)

mission
4 goal, task 5 trade 6 errand 7 calling, embassy, purpose 8 busi-

ness, legation, lifework, ministry, vocation

missionary
5 agent 7 apostle 8 emissary, promoter 10 colporteur, evangelist, revivalist 12 propagandist

Mississippi
capital: 7 Jackson
highest point: 9 Woodall Mt.
motto: 14 By Valor and Arms
nickname: 10 Bayou State 13 Magnolia State
state flower: 8 magnolia
university: 12 Jackson State

missive
4 memo, note 6 letter 7 epistle

Miss Julie author
10 Strindberg (August)

Miss Lonelyhearts author
4 West (Nathanael)

Miss-Nancyish
5 sissy 6 prissy 7 epicene, unmanly 9 pansified, sissified 10 effeminate

Missouri
capital: 13 Jefferson City
college: 5 Avila, Drury
nickname: 11 Show Me State 12 Bullion State
state flower: 9 hawthorne

misstate
4 warp 5 belie, color, twist 6 garble 7 distort, falsify, pervert

misstatement
3 fib, lie 4 tale 7 falsity, untruth 8 untruism 9 falsehood 10 taradiddle 13 prevarication

misstep
4 bull, slip 5 boner, error, fluff, lapse 6 slipup 7 blooper, blunder, faux pas

mist
3 dim, fog 4 blur, film, haze, murk 5 befog, brume, cloud, smaze 7 becloud, obscure 9 overcloud

mistake
3 err 4 bull, slip, trip 5 addle, boner, error, fluff, folly, lapse 6 boo-boo, bungle, jumble, lapsus, muddle, slight, slipup, tumble 7 blooper, blunder, confuse, neglect 8 confound, omission, omitting 9 confusion, slighting 10 inaccuracy, neglecting

mister
3 man, sir 4 lord 7 husband
French: 8 monsieur
German: 4 herr

Italian: **6** signor
Spanish: **5** senor

Mister Roberts author
6 Heggen (Thomas)

mistreat
5 abuse **6** ill-use **7** outrage

mistress
4 amie **5** lover, woman **6** harlot
7 bedmate, hetaira **8** dulcinea,
ladylove, paramour **9** concubine,
courtesan, inamorata, kept woman
10 chatelaine, girl friend
of Charies II: **4** Gwyn (Nell) **8** Villiers (Barbara)
of Edward III: **7** Perrers (Alice)
of Henry II (England): **8** Clifford
(Rosamund)
of Henry II (France): **9** de Poiters
(Diane)
of Louis XV: **9** Pompadour (Madame de)

mistrust
5 alarm, doubt, scare **6** appall, dismay, wonder **7** concern, dispute,
dubiety, foresee, surmise, suspect
8 frighten, question **9** apprehend,
challenge, dubiosity, suspicion
10 anticipate, foreboding, skepticism **11** incertitude, uncertainty,
uncertitude **12** apprehension,
presentiment

mistrustful
7 jealous **10** suspicious

misty
3 dim **4** hazy **5** foggy, mushy,
vague **6** cloudy, vapory **7** obscure,
unclear **8** confused, vaporous
10 indistinct

misunderstanding
7 quarrel **9** imbroglio
12 disagreement

misuse
5 abuse **7** outrage, pervert **8** illtreat, maltreat **10** prostitute
of a word: **8** malaprop

mite
3 bit, jot **4** atom, iota **5** grain,
minim, ounce, speck **6** acarid, minute, tittle **7** chigger, modicum, smidgen **8** molecule, particle, smidgeon
combining form: **4** acar **5** acari,
acaro
family: **8** oribatid

mitigate
4 ease **5** abate, allay, relax, slake
6 lessen, soften, temper **7** assuage,
lighten, mollify, relieve **8** palliate
9 alleviate, meliorate

mitigation
4 ease **6** relief **8** easement
10 moderation, palliation
11 alleviation

mitosis
12 cell division, karyokinesis
stage: **8** anaphase, prophase
9 metaphase, telophase

mix
4 fuse, join, link, lump, meld, stir
5 blend, braid, merge, unite
6 blunge, fusion, jumble, make up,
mingle, tangle, work in **7** amalgam, combine, concoct, confuse,
conjoin **8** coalesce, comingle, compound, confound, immingle **9** associate, commingle, interflow, interfuse **10** amalgamate, crossbreed,
inosculate, interblend **11** interfusion, intermingle, misidentify
12 amalgamation

mixable
8 miscible

mixed
6 impure, motley, varied **8** chowchow **9** irregular **11** promiscuous
12 conglomerate, multifarious
13 heterogeneous, miscellaneous

mixed bag
4 olio **5** salad **6** jumble, medley
8 pastiche **10** assortment, hodgepodge, miscellany **11** gallimaufry

mixed-blooded person
7 mestizo, mulatto **8** octoroon
9 half-breed

mixologist
6 barman **7** tapster **9** barkeeper,
bartender

mixture
4 brew, hash, olio **5** alloy, blend
6 fusion, medley **7** amalgam, compost, farrago, mélange **8** compound, mishmash, solution **9** composite, potpourri **10** concoction,
confection **11** interfusion
12 amalgamation

mix up
5 addle, dizzy **6** fuddle, jumble,
muddle, tumble **7** confuse, derange, disrupt, fluster, misdeem,
mistake **8** befuddle, bewilder, confound, disarray, disjoint, disorder,
distract **9** distemper **10** disarrange,
discompose **11** disorganize,
misidentify

mix-up
4 hash, mess, mull, muss **5** blend,
botch, melee **6** fusion, muddle,
tangle **8** botchery, compound,

shambles **9** composite, confusion
11 interfusion

mizmaze
3 web **4** knot, mesh **5** skein, snarl
6 jungle, morass, tangle **9** confusion, labyrinth **12** bewilderment

mks unit
3 lux, ohm **4** mole, volt, watt
5 farad, henry, hertz, joule, lumen,
meter, metre, tesla, weber **6** ampere, kelvin, newton, pascal, second **7** candela, coulomb, siemens
8 kilogram

Mnemosyne
6 Memory
daughters: **5** Muses
father: **6** Uranus
lover: **4** Zeus
mother: **2** Ge **4** Gaea

Moabite
city: **3** Kir
god: **7** Chemosh
king: **5** Eglon, Mesha

Moab's father
3 Lot

moan
4 weep **5** groan **6** bewail, grieve,
lament **7** deplore **8** complain

mob
3 set **4** camp, clan, gang, herd,
push, ring, riot, rout, scum **5** cabal,
crowd, crush, dregs, horde, posse,
press, swarm, trash **6** circle, clique,
masses, rabble, throng **7** coterie,
ingroup **8** canaille, riffraff, unwashed **9** camarilla **11** proletariat

mobile
5 fluid **6** liquid, moving **7** migrant,
movable, protean **8** moveable, unstable, unsteady, variable, weathery **9** all-around, changeful, manysided, mercurial, migrative,
migratory, unsettled **10** capricious,
changeable, inconstant **11** migratorial

mobile phone area
4 cell

mobilize
5 drive, impel, rally **6** muster, propel, set off **7** actuate, marshal
8 activate, assemble, organize
9 circulate

Moby Dick
5 whale
author: **8** Melville (Herman)
character: **3** Pip **6** Daggoo, Parsee
7 Ishmael **8** Queequeg, Starbuck,
Tashtego
pursuer: **4** Ahab

ship: 6 Pequod

moccasin
3 pac 6 loafer 7 slipper 8 larrigan

mock
3 ape 4 butt, copy, defy, fake, gibe, jape, jeer, jest, joke, lout, quiz, razz, sham, twit 5 bogus, dummy, false, farce, feign, mimic, phony, quasi, rally, scout, sneer, sport, taunt 6 affect, assume, betray, delude, deride, ersatz, humbug, illude, jester, juggle, parody, pseudo 7 beguile, buffoon, deceive, imitate, mislead, sell out, take off 8 derision, ridicule, simulate, so-called, spurious, travesty 9 burlesque, disregard, imitation, pilgarlic, simulated 10 artificial, caricature, fictitious, substitute 11 counterfeit, double-cross 13 laughingstock

mockery
4 butt, jest, joke, sham 5 farce, sport 6 japery, jester, parody, satire 7 take-off 8 derision, ridicule, travesty 9 burlesque, imitation, pilgarlic 10 caricature 13 laughingstock

mocking
8 derisive, sardonic

mode
3 cry, fad, way 4 chic, rage, vein, wise 5 craze, state, style, vogue 6 custom, furore, manner, method, status, system 7 fashion, posture 9 condition, situation, technique 10 convention, dernier cri

model
4 copy, type, very 5 dummy, frame, gauge, ideal, shape 6 design, effigy, emblem, mirror, mockup, symbol 7 classic, epitome, example, fashion, imitate, manikin, paragon, pattern, perfect, replica, typical 8 ensample, exemplar, flawless, mannikin, nonesuch, paradigm, standard 9 archetype, beau ideal, blueprint, classical, criterion, exemplary, miniature, nonpareil 10 apotheosis, embodiment, prototypal, touchstone 11 commendable 12 indefectible, paradigmatic, prototypical, quintessence, reproduction
combining form: 3 typ 4 typo
preliminary: 8 maquette

moderate
3 ebb 4 calm, cool, even, fair, fall, mean, mild, slow, soft, so-so, wane 5 abate, bland, let up, small, sober 6 gentle, lessen, medium, paltry, reduce, relent, slight, soften, steady, subdue, temper 7 average, chasten, control, cushion, die away, die down, ease off, equable, fairish, lighten, qualify, relieve, slacken, subside, trivial 8 attemper, constant, decrease, diminish, discreet, mediocre, middling, piddling, restrain, trifling 9 alleviate, constrain, soft-shell, temperate, unextreme 10 abstemious, controlled, middle-road, reasonable, restrained 11 indifferent, unexcessive 12 conservative 13 unimpassioned

moderation
7 control, measure 9 restraint 10 abstinence, limitation, temperance 13 temperateness

moderator
5 judge 7 arbiter 8 chairman, examiner, governor, mediator 10 peacemaker 11 chairperson

modern
3 new 4 late 5 fresh, novel 6 latter, recent 7 current 8 neoteric, up-to-date 9 new-sprung, prevalent 10 coincident, concurrent, newfangled, present-day, prevailing 11 concomitant 12 contemporary, new-fashioned
combining form: 2 ne 3 neo

modernize
5 renew 6 update 7 refresh, restore 8 renovate 9 refurbish 10 rejuvenate

modest
3 coy, dry, shy 4 meek, nice, prim, pure 5 clean, lowly, plain, timid 6 chaste, decent, demure, humble, prissy, proper, seemly, silent, simple, stuffy 7 bashful, prudish 8 decorous, discreet, moderate, priggish, reserved, reticent, retiring, spotless 9 diffident, stainless, temperate, unassured, undefiled, unsullied 10 immaculate, reasonable, unassuming, unboastful 11 inelaborate, puritanical, straitlaced, unassertive, unblemished, unelaborate, unpresuming, withdrawing 12 self-effacing, unornamented, unpretending 13 unembellished, unembroidered, unpretentious

Modest Proposal author
5 Swift (Jonathan)

modesty
7 decency, pudency, reserve 8 chastity, humility, pudicity, timidity 10 diffidence

modicum
3 bit, jot 4 atom, iota, whit 5 grain, minim, ounce, scrap 7 soupçon 8 particle

modify
4 turn, vary 5 alter, amend 6 change, mutate, temper 7 qualify 8 mitigate, moderate, restrain 9 refashion

modish
4 chic 5 smart, swank 6 with-it 7 dashing 9 exclusive 11 fashionable

Modred, Mordred
father: 6 Arthur
mother: 8 Margawse
slayer, victim: 6 Arthur

modulate
4 sing 6 intone, temper 8 restrain

modus
3 way 4 wise 5 means 6 manner, method, system 7 fashion 9 technique

modus ___
7 vivendi 8 operandi

mogul
4 czar, king, lord 5 baron, nabob, ruler 6 prince, tycoon 7 magnate

Mohammed
see **Muhammad**

Mohawk chief
5 Brant (Joseph) 8 Hiawatha

Mohican chief
5 Uncas

moiety
3 cut 4 half, part 5 piece 6 member, parcel 7 element, portion, section, segment 8 division 9 component

moil
3 tug 4 grub, to-do, work 5 churn, drive, grind, labor, swirl 6 bustle, clamor, drudge, hubbub, lather, strain, strive, uproar 7 chaffer, ruction, slavery, travail, trouble, wrangle 8 drudgery, plugging, rowdydow, slogging 9 commotion, confusion 10 hurly-burly, turbulence

moira
3 lot 4 doom, fate 5 weird 6 kismet 7 destiny, portion 12 circumstance

moist
3 wet 4 damp, dank, dewy 5 gooey, humid, mushy, sappy, soggy, soupy 6 drippy, slushy, steamy, sticky, watery 7 dampish, maudlin, tearful, wettish

moisten
3 wet **6** dampen **8** humidify, saturate

moisture
5 vapor **11** tearfulness **13** precipitation
combining form: **4** hygr **5** hygro

moistureless
3 dry **4** arid, sere **7** bone-dry, parched, thirsty **8** droughty **9** unwatered **10** desiccated

molar
5 tooth **7** grinder
combining form: **3** myl **4** mylo

molasses
7 treacle **8** theriaca **10** blackstrap

mold
3 die, hug, lot **4** cast, form, kind, make, soil, sort, type **5** adapt, build, class, erect, forge, frame, knead, shape, stamp **6** design, fungus, growth, nature **7** fashion, pattern **8** template **9** character, construct **11** description, put together
combining form: **5** plasm, plast, plasy **6** plases (plural), plasia, plasis, plasma

moldable
6 pliant, supple **7** ductile, fictile, plastic, pliable **9** adaptable, malleable

molder
3 rot **4** turn **5** decay, spoil, taint, waste **7** crumble, putrefy **9** break down, decompose **11** deteriorate **12** disintegrate

molding
4 bead, cove, gula, list, reed, tore **5** angle, congé, ogive, talon, thumb **6** baston, nebulé, reglet **7** annulet, beading, cornice, reeding **8** cincture **9** baseboard
compound: **4** beak, ogie **8** cymatium **9** cyma recta **10** serpentine **11** cyma reversa
edge: **5** arris
flat: **4** band, face **5** bevel, splay **6** fascia, fillet, listel, regula **7** chamfer
simple curve: **4** roll **5** flute, ovolo, torus **6** scotia **8** astragal

moldy
5 dated, fusty, musty, passé **6** bygone, old hat, rococo **7** ancient, archaic **8** mildewed, outdated **9** crumbling, moth-eaten **10** antiquated **12** old-fashioned

mole
4 pier, quay **5** jetty, nevus **6** bur-row, tunnel **9** birthmark **10** breakwater
combining form: **5** talpi

molecule
3 bit, jot **4** atom, iota **5** minim, ounce, speck **7** modicum **8** fraction, fragment, particle

molest
3 vex **4** bait, raid **5** annoy, harry, tease **6** bother, harass, heckle, pester **7** disturb, torment, trouble **9** persecute

Moll Flanders author
5 Defoe (Daniel)

mollify
4 calm, ease **5** allay, relax **6** pacify, soften, soothe, temper **7** appease, assuage, lighten, placate, relieve, sweeten **8** mitigate **9** alleviate **10** ameliorate, conciliate, propitiate

mollusk
6 chiton
bivalve: **4** clam **6** bankia, cockle, mussel, oyster, teredo **7** geoduck, scallop **8** shipworm
cephalopod: **5** squid **7** octopus **8** argonaut, nautilus **10** cuttlefish
part: **6** mantle, radula, siphon
tooth shell: **9** dentalium
univalve: **4** slug **5** conch, cowry, murex, snail, whelk **6** cowrie, limpet, triton **7** abalone **10** nudibranch, periwinkle

mollusk-like
8 limacine

Molly ___
7 Maguire, Pitcher

mollycoddle
4 baby **5** humor, sissy, spoil **6** cocker, cosset, pamper **7** cater to, doormat, indulge, milksop, protect **8** weakling **9** jellyfish **10** goody-goody, pantywaist **11** Milquetoast **12** invertebrate

molt
4 cast, shed, slip **6** change, slough **7** discard, ecdysis **8** exuviate

molted covering
7 exuviae

molten
6 heated, melted **7** glowing

molten rock
4 lava **5** magma

molybdenum
symbol: **2** Mo

moment
4 pith, time **5** crack, flash, jiffy, point, shake, while **6** import, minute, second, weight **7** instant **8** juncture, occasion **9** breathing, magnitude **10** importance **11** consequence, split second, weightiness **12** significance **13** consideration

momentary
5 brief, quick, short **8** fleeting, fugitive, volatile **9** ephemeral, fugacious, transient **10** evanescent, short-lived, transitory **11** impermanent

momentous
3 big **5** grave **7** epochal, fateful, serious, weighty **8** eventful, material **9** important **10** meaningful **11** significant, substantial **12** considerable **13** consequential

momentousness
4 pith **6** import, weight **9** magnitude **10** importance **11** consequence, weightiness **12** significance

momus
6 carper, critic, Zoilus **7** caviler, knocker **9** aristarch **10** criticizer **11** faultfinder, smellfungus

Monaco
casino: **10** Monte Carlo
prince: **6** Ranier
princess (former): **5** Grace

monad
3 one **4** atom, unit **8** zoospore

Mona Lisa
10 La Gioconda
painter: **7** da Vinci (Leonardo)

monarch
4 czar, king, raja, tsar, tzar **5** queen, rajah, ruler **6** kaiser, prince **7** emperor **9** potentate, sovereign

monarchical
5 regal, royal **6** kingly **8** imperial, kinglike, majestic **9** sovereign

monarch's daughter
8 princess
Portuguese, Spanish: **7** infanta

monarch's son
6 prince
French: **7** dauphin
Portuguese, Spanish: **7** infante

monastery
5 abbey **6** friary, priory **7** convent, nunnery
Buddhist: **8** lamasery
Eastern Orthodox: **5** laura
head: **5** abbot, prior **7** hegumen

___ **Mondrian**
4 Piet

monetary
6 fiscal, pocket 9 financial, pecuniary 10 numismatic

monetary rate
7 millage

monetary unit
see at individual countries

money
4 bill, cash, coin, gelt, loot, pelf, swag 5 bread, chips, dough, funds, lucre, moola, rhino, rocks 6 boodle, change, dinero, mammon, mazuma, moolah, riches, specie, wampum, wealth 7 cabbage, capital, coinage, lettuce, needful, scratch, stipend 8 bankroll, currency, finances, treasure 9 resources 10 greenbacks 11 filthy lucre, legal tender

moneyed
4 rich 7 opulent, wealthy 8 affluent 10 well-heeled

moneygrubber
4 skin 5 chuff, miser, nabal, stiff 7 niggard, scrooge 8 muckworm 9 skinflint 10 cheapskate

moneymaking
6 paying 7 gainful 9 lucrative 10 profitable, well-paying, worthwhile 12 advantageous, remunerative

monger
4 hawk, rend 6 dealer, hawker, peddle, spread, trader, vendor 7 higgler, packman, peddler 8 huckster, outcrier

Mongol conqueror
9 Tamerlane 10 Kublai Khan 11 Genghis Khan, Tamburlaine

mongrel
3 cur 4 mule, mutt 5 cross 6 hybrid 7 bastard 9 crossbred, half blood, half-breed 10 crossbreed

monish
5 chide 6 rebuke 7 reprove, tick off 8 call down, reproach 9 reprimand

monition
6 caveat 7 caution, warning 11 forewarning

monitor
4 test 5 check, watch 7 adviser, observe 8 reminder 9 counselor
lizard: 7 varanid

Monitor
designer: 8 Ericsson (John)
opponent: 8 Virginia 9 Merrimack

monitory
7 warning 8 advisory 10 cautionary, cautioning, counseling 11 admonishing

monk
5 friar 7 brother 8 monastic 9 anchorite
Buddhist: 4 lama 5 bonze
Eastern Orthodox: 7 caloyer
Hindu: 8 sannyasi
Roman Catholic: 9 Dominican 10 Cistercian, Franciscan
room: 4 cell
shaven crown: 7 tonsure
title: 3 dom, fra 5 padre

monkey
3 imp, sap 4 dupe, fool, gull, mark 5 cebid, gamin, small 6 bantam, butt in, ceboid, horn in, little, meddle, petite, simian, sucker, tamper, urchin, victim 7 fall guy 8 busybody, easy mark, smallish 9 interfere, interlope 10 tamper with 11 intermeddle
combining form: 6 pithec 7 pitheco
New World: 4 saki, titi 5 sajou 6 howler, spider, uakari, woolly 7 sapajou, tamarin 8 capuchin, marmoset, squirrel 11 douroucouli
Old World: 4 douc, mona 5 Diana, drill, patas 6 grivet, guenon, langur, rhesus, vervet 7 colobus, hanuman, macaque 8 entellus, mandrill, mangabey, talapoin, wanderoo 9 proboscis 10 Barbary ape

monkeyshine
4 dido, lark 5 antic, caper, prank, trick 6 frolic 10 shenanigan, tomfoolery

monocratic
8 absolute, despotic 9 arbitrary, autarchic, tyrannous 10 autocratic, tyrannical

monogram
6 cipher, sketch 7 outline 8 initials

monograph
5 study 6 memoir, thesis 8 tractate, treatise 9 discourse 12 disquisition, dissertation

monopolize
3 hog 5 sew up 6 absorb, corner, manage 7 consume, control, engross

monopoly
5 trust 6 cartel, corner 7 control 9 ownership, syndicate 10 consortium 11 exclusivity

monotonous
4 blah, dull, poky, same 6 dreary, stodgy 7 humdrum, uniform 8 bansic, unvaried 10 pedestrian 11 repetitious

monotony
6 tedium 7 humdrum 8 flatness, sameness 10 uniformity

monster
4 huge, ogre 5 demon, devil, fiend, freak, giant, lusus, teras, whale 6 ogress 7 mammoth, titanic 8 abortion, behemoth, colossal, enormous, giantess, gigantic 9 hellhound, leviathan, manticore 10 behemothic, gargantuan 11 elephantine, miscreation
biblical: 5 Rehab 8 Behemoth 9 Leviathan
combining form: 4 pagi (plural) 5 pagus, terat 6 terato
female: 6 Gorgon, Medusa, Scylla
fire-breathing: 6 dragon, Typhon 7 Chimera 8 Chimaera
fowl-dragon: 10 cockatrice
French: 8 Tarasque
horse-fish: 11 hippocampus
hundred-armed: 9 Enceladus
hundred-eyed: 5 Argus
hundred-handed: 8 Briareus
lion-eagle: 7 griffin
serpent-headed: 6 gorgon
study of: 10 teratology
three-bodied: 6 Geryon
three-headed dog: 8 Cerberus
two-headed dog: 6 Orthos
water: 6 kraken, nicker
winged dragon: 6 wivern, wyvern
woman-bird: 5 Harpy
woman-lion: 6 Sphinx
woman-serpent: 7 Echidna; (see also dragon)

___ **monster**
4 Gila

monstrosity
4 mess 5 freak, lusus, sight 6 fright 7 desight, eyesore 8 abortion 11 miscreation

monstrous
3 big 4 huge, rank, vast 5 awful, large 6 crying, mighty, mortal 7 glaring, heinous, hideous, immense, mammoth, massive, titanic 8 colossal, cracking, deformed, dreadful, enormous, gigantic, horrible, infamous, shocking, towering 9 atrocious, desperate, fantastic, malformed, unnatural 10 flagitious, gargantuan, impressive, monumental, outrageous, prodigious, scandalous, stupendous, tremendous 11 elephantine, magnificent

Montagues'enemies
8 Capulets

Montaigne's forte
5 essay

Montana
capital: 6 Helena
highest point: 11 Granite Peak
largest town: 8 Billings
nickname: 13 Mountain State, Treasure State
state flower: 10 bitterroot

Monteverdi opera
5 Orfeo 7 Arianna

Montezuma
conqueror: 6 Cortes, Cortez (Hernan, Hernando)
people: 6 Aztecs
revenge: 8 diarrhea

month
combining form: 4 meno
current: 7 instant
following: 7 proximo
Hindu: 3 Pus 4 Asin, Jeth, Magh 5 Aghan, Chait, Sawan 6 Asargh, Bhadon, Kartik, Phagun 7 Baisakh
Jewish: 2 Ab 4 Adar, Elul, Iyar 5 Nisan, Sivan, Tebet 6 Kislev, Shebat, Tammuz, Tishri 7 Heshvan
Muslim: 4 Rabi 5 Rajab, Safar 6 Jumada, Sha 'ban 7 Ramadan, Shawwal 8 Muharram 9 Dhu'l-Hijja, Dhu'l-Qa'dah
preceding: 6 ultimo

Montmartre church
10 Sacré Coeur

monument
5 relic, stela, stupa 6 ledger, record 7 chaitya, example, memento, tribute 8 archives, cenotaph, document, memorial 9 footstone, headstone, tombstone 10 gravestone 11 commemorate, grave marker, memorialize, testimonial
prehistoric: 6 dolmen, menhir 8 cromlech, megalith

monumental
4 huge, vast 6 mighty, mortal 7 immense, mammoth, massive 8 cracking, enormous, gigantic, towering 9 fantastic, monstrous 10 prodigious, stupendous, tremendous 11 inestimable, mountainous 12 overwhelming

moocah
3 pot 5 grass 8 cannabis 9 marijuana

mooch
3 bat, beg 4 roam, rove 5 amble, cadge, drift, range, slink, sneak, steal, stray 6 ramble, sponge, wander 7 meander, saunter 8 straggle

mooching
7 beggary, bumming, cadging 9 mendicity 10 mendicancy 11 panhandling

mood
3 air 4 aura, feel, mind, tone, vein, whim 5 humor 6 aspect, spirit, strain, temper, timbre 7 caprice, emotion, feeling 8 ambiance, ambience 9 character, semblance 10 atmosphere 11 disposition, personality, temperament

moody
3 sad 4 glum 5 sulky 6 fickle, gloomy, grumpy 7 pensive 8 unstable 9 humorsome, mercurial, whimsical 10 capricious, inconstant 13 temperamental

moon
4 gape 5 dream 6 dawdle 9 satellite
combining form: 5 selen 6 seleni, seleno
dark area: 4 mare 5 maria (plural)
god: 3 Sin 5 Nanna 6 Meztli
goddess: 4 Luna 5 Diana, Tanit 6 Hecate, Hekate, Selena, Selene, Tanith 7 Artemis, Astarte; (see also satellite)

Moon and Sixpence author
7 Maugham (W. Somerset)

mooncalf
4 dolt, fool 5 idiot, ninny 6 doodle, madman 7 jackass, tomfool 8 imbecile

Moon River composer
7 Mancini (Henry)

moonshine
4 bosh, jake 5 hokum 6 bunkum, humbug 7 bootleg, eyewash 8 homebrew, malarkey, nonsense 10 balderdash, bathtub gin, flapdoodle 11 mountain dew 12 blatherskite

Moonstone, The
author: 7 Collins (Wilkie)
detective: 4 Cuff

moor
3 bog, fen 4 fell 5 berth, catch 6 anchor, Berber, fasten, Muslim, secure 8 Moroccan
fictional: 7 Othello

moose
6 cervid
female: 3 cow
male: 4 bull
relative: 3 elk 4 deer

moot
5 argue, plead 6 broach, debate 7 agitate, bring up, canvass, discept, discuss, dispute, dubious, suggest, suspect 8 arguable, disputed, doubtful 9 debatable, introduce, thrash out, uncertain, unsettled, ventilate 10 disputable, toss around 11 problematic 12 questionable 13 controversial

mooting
6 debate 8 forensic 9 dialectic 11 disputation 13 argumentation

mop
3 mug 4 swab, wipe 5 mouth 7 grimace, shellac, trounce

mope
4 ache, pout, sulk 5 ample, brood, drift, grump, mosey 6 bummel, dawdle, grieve, linger, stroll 7 despond, saunter

mopes
5 blues, dumps 7 dismals, sadness 8 dolefuls 10 depression, melancholy 11 unhappiness 12 mournfulness

mopey
3 low 4 blue, down 6 droopy 8 cast down, dejected, downcast 9 depressed 10 dispirited, spiritless

moppet
3 bud, kid, tot 4 chit, tyke 5 chick, child, youth 8 juvenile, young one 9 youngster

mop up
4 beat, drub, dust, lick, whip 6 absorb, garner 7 shellac, trounce 8 lambaste 9 overwhelm

moral
4 good, just, pure, rule 5 axiom, gnome, maxim, noble, right 6 chaste, decent, dictum, honest, proper, teachy, truism 7 brocard, ethical, preachy, upright 8 aphorism, apothegm, didactic, elevated, sermonic, virtuous 9 honorable, righteous 10 high-minded, principled, scrupulous 11 right-minded, sermonizing 13 conscientious

morale
4 mood 5 vigor 6 esprit, spirit 9 assurance 10 confidence 13 esprit de corps

moralistic
5 noble 7 ethical 8 didactic, virtuous 9 righteous 10 principled 11 right-minded

morality
5 ethic, mores 6 virtue 7 probity 8 goodness 9 rectitude, rightness 11 saintliness, uprightness 13 righteousness

moralize
6 preach 7 lecture 9 preachify, sermonize 11 pontificate

morals
5 mores 6 ethics 9 standards

morass
3 bog, fen, web 4 knot, maze, mesh, mire, quag 5 marsh, skein, snarl, swamp 6 jungle, tangle 7 mizmaze 8 quagmire

moratorium
3 ban 5 delay 8 suspense 10 suspension

moray
3 eel

morbid
4 dark, sick 5 moody 6 gloomy, grisly, morose, sickly, sullen 7 unsound 8 diseased, gruesome 9 saturnine, unhealthy 11 melancholic, unwholesome 12 pathological

mordacious
see **mordant**

mordancy
7 acidity 8 acerbity, acridity, acrimony, asperity, pungency 10 causticity, trenchancy

mordant
4 keen 5 salty, sharp 6 biting 7 burning, caustic, pungent 8 incisive, scathing 9 sarcastic, trenchant

Mordecai
cousin: 6 Esther
father: 4 Jair
mother: 6 Esther

more
3 new, too 4 also, else, plus 5 added, again, along, extra, fresh, older, other 6 as well, better, nearer, withal 7 another, besides, farther, further, greater 8 likewise, moreover 10 additional
combining form: 4 pleo, plio 5 pleio

More book
6 Utopia

moreover
3 and, too, yet 4 also, then 6 as well, withal 7 besides, further 8 likewise 11 furthermore 12 additionally

morepork
3 owl 9 frogmouth

mores
6 ethics, habits 7 customs, manners 8 decorums, folkways, morality 9 amenities, etiquette 10 civilities 11 proprieties

Morgana's brother
6 Arthur

morgue
5 pride 7 disdain, hauteur 8 mortuary 9 arrogance, loftiness, superbity 11 haughtiness

moribund
5 dying, going 6 fading 7 dormant 8 decaying, expiring 10 regressing 13 deteriorating

Mormon Church
administrative unit: 4 ward 5 stake
founder: 5 Smith (Joseph)
leader: 5 Young (Brigham)
priest: 5 elder

Mormon State
4 Utah

morn
see **morning**

morne
4 cold 5 black, bleak 6 dismal, gloomy 8 desolate 9 cheerless 10 depressant, depressing, depressive

morning
4 dawn 5 light, sunup 6 aurora 7 dawning, sunrise 8 cockcrow, daybreak, daylight, forenoon
moisture: 3 dew 8 dewdrops
song: 6 aubade

Morocco
capital: 5 Rabat
largest city: 10 Casablanca
monetary unit: 6 dirham

moron
4 fool, zany 5 ament, dummy, dunce, idiot 6 cretin, stupid 7 dullard, half-wit 8 dullhead, dumbbell, imbecile 9 ignoramus, simpleton

moronic
4 dull 6 simple, stupid 7 brutish 8 backward, imbecile, retarded 9 dim-witted 10 half-witted, slow-witted 12 feebleminded, simpleminded

morose
4 dour, glum, sick, sour, ugly 5 gruff, sulky, surly, testy 6 cranky, crusty, gloomy, morbid, sickly, sullen 7 crabbed, unhappy 8 choleric 9 irascible, saturnine, splenetic 10 ill-humored

Morpheus
father: 6 Hypnos
god of: 5 sleep

Morse code
dash: 3 dah
dot: 3 dit

morsel
3 bit 4 bite, tapa 5 crumb, goody, mug-up, piece, scrap, snack, taste, treat 6 dainty, tidbit, titbit 8 delicacy, fragment, kickshaw, mouthful 11 bonne bouche

mortal
3 man 4 body, grim, weak 5 awful, being, fatal, frail, human, party 6 deadly, finite, lethal, person 7 deathly, earthly, extreme, fleshly, massive, tedious 8 creature, hominine, possible, probable, ruthless, temporal, towering 9 fantastic, merciless, monstrous, personage, pestilent 10 implacable, individual, ironfisted, monumental, prodigious, relentless, stupendous, tremendous, unyielding 11 conceivable, mortiferous, unflinching, unrelenting 12 overpowering, pestilential, unappeasable

mortality
5 flesh 7 mankind 8 fatality, humanity 9 humankind, lethality 10 deadliness

mortally
4 very 7 awfully, fatally, vitally 8 terribly 9 extremely, intensely 10 dreadfully, grievously 11 exceedingly

Morte d'Arthur author
6 Malory (Thomas)

mortgage
4 hock, pawn 6 pledge 10 obligation

mortician
8 embalmer 10 undertaker

mortiferous
5 fatal 6 deadly, lethal, mortal 7 deathly 9 pestilent 12 pestilential

mortified
5 stern 6 severe, shamed 7 ascetic, ashamed, austere 9 chagrined

mortuary
8 tumulary 10 sepulchral 11 funeral home

mosaic
5 inlay 7 chimera 8 terrazzo 9 composite, patchwork 12 tessellation
piece: 6 smalto 7 tessera 8 tesserae (plural)

Moscow
citadel: 7 Kremlin
resident: 9 Muscovite

Moses
brother: 5 Aaron
brother-in-law: 5 Hobab

deathplace: **4** Nebo
father-in-law: **6** Jethro
sister: **6** Miriam
son: **7** Eliezer, Gershom
spy: **5** Caleb
successor: **6** Joshua
wife: **8** Zipporah

mosey
4 mope **5** amble, drift **6** bummel, linger, ramble, stroll, wander **7** saunter

Moslem
see **Muslim**

mosque
6 masjid
niche: **6** mihrab
prayer caller: **7** muezzin
pulpit: **6** mimbar
turret: **7** minaret

mosquito
5 culex **7** culicid **8** culicine
genus: **5** Aëdes, Culex **9** Anopheles

moss
9 bryophyte
kind: **4** peat **8** sphagnum
part: **4** seta **7** capsule, rhizoid
study of: **8** bryology

mossback
4 fogy, hick **5** yokel **6** fogram, fossil, rustic, square **7** bumpkin, hayseed **9** hillbilly **10** clodhopper, fuddy-duddy, provincial **12** antediluvian, backwoodsman, mid-Victorian **13** stick-in-the-mud

most
3 too **4** best, much, nigh, very **5** about, chief, super **6** all but, better, nearly, utmost **7** greater, highest, largest, maximum **8** greatest, majority, mightily, mortally, well-nigh **9** eminently, extremely, principal **10** remarkably **11** exceedingly, practically **12** surpassingly **13** approximately

mostly
6 mainly **7** chiefly, largely, overall, usually **9** generally, primarily **11** principally **13** predominantly

mote
3 dot **4** hill **5** point, speck **6** barrow, height **7** tumulus **8** flyspeck, particle

moth
6 tineid **7** tineoid **8** bombycid
immature: **5** larva **6** larvae (plural) **11** caterpillar
kind: **4** luna **7** codling, tussock **8** Cecropia, silkworm **9** browntail
order: **11** Lepidoptera

moth-eaten
4 worn **5** dated, dingy, faded, moldy, passé, seedy **6** bygone, old hat, patchy, rococo, shabby, tag-rag **7** archaic, raggedy, run-down, unkempt **8** decrepit, outdated, outmoded, tattered **10** antiquated, down-at-heel, threadbare **11** dilapidated

mother
2 ma **3** dam, mom **4** mama, root **5** fount, mamma, mammy, mater, momma, mommy, mummy, nurse, serve **6** mammie, origin, source, wait on **7** care for, nurture, produce, rootage **9** prototype, rootstock **10** minister to, provenance, wellspring
combining form: **4** matr **5** matri, matro

mother country
4 home, land, soil **8** homeland **10** fatherland

Mother Courage author
6 Brecht (Bertolt)

mother-of-pearl
5 nacre

Mother of Presidents
8 Virginia

Mother of the Gods
3 Ops **4** Rhea

motif
4 head, text **5** point, theme, topic **6** design, device, figure, matter **7** pattern, subject **8** argument **13** subject matter

motion
4 flag, move, sign, stir, sway **5** swing **6** signal **7** gesture **8** carriage, movement, proposal, stirring, wavering **9** agitation, signalize **10** suggestion **11** application, fluctuation, oscillation
combining form: **3** cin, kin **4** cino, kine, kino, moto **5** cinet, kinet, phoro **6** cineto, kineto, praxia, praxis **7** cinesia, kinesia

motionless
5 fixed, inert, rigid, still **6** static **8** becalmed, immobile, immotile, immotive, stagnant, unmoving **9** immovable, sedentary, steadfast, unmovable **10** stationary, stock-still, stone-still

motion picture
see **movie**

motivate
4 move **5** impel, pique, rouse **6** excite, incite, induce **7** innerve, inspire, provoke, quicken **9** galvanize, influence, innervate, stimulate

motivation
4 spur **5** drive **7** impetus, impulse **8** catalyst, stimulus **9** incentive, stimulant **10** incitation, incitement **11** instigation

motive
3 aim, end **4** good, head, spur, text **5** cause, point, theme, topic **6** design, device, figure, intent, matter, object, reason, spring **7** impulse, pattern, purpose, subject **8** argument, stimulus **9** incentive, intention **10** incitement, inducement

motley
4 fool **5** idiot, mixed, salad **6** jester, jumble, medley, varied **7** dappled, diverse, mottled, piebald **8** assorted, chowchow, discolor, pastiche **9** colluvies, multihued **10** assortment, hodgepodge, miscellany, multicolor, variegated, versicolor **11** gallimaufry, promiscuous, varicolored **12** conglomerate, multicolored, multifarious, parti-colored, versicolored **13** heterogeneous, miscellaneous
combining form: **5** parti, party

motor
3 car **4** auto, ride, tool **5** buggy, drive, pilot, wheel **6** engine **7** autocar, machine **10** automobile

motorbike
5 moped

motorboat
7 cruiser, inboard **8** outboard, runabout **12** cabin cruiser

motorcar
4 auto **5** buggy **10** automobile

motorcycle
7 chopper **8** minibike **9** trail bike
adjunct: **7** sidecar

motorist
6 driver **7** autoist **8** operator **12** automobilist

Motown
7 Detroit

mottle
4 spot **6** blotch, marble **7** splotch

motto
3 cry **5** adage, axiom, maxim **6** byword, saying, slogan, war cry **7** precept **8** aphorism **9** battle cry, catchword, watchword **10** shibboleth **11** catchphrase, rallying cry

moue
3 mow, mug **4** face, pout **5** mouth **7** grimace **8** mouthing

mound

4 bank, cock, heap, hill, hump, mass, pile **5** cairn, drift, shock, stack **6** barrow, tumuli (plural) **7** bulwark, hillock, rampart, tumulus **8** mountain **9** elevation **10** embankment

Buddhist: **5** stupa
burial, Eastern Europe: **6** kurgan
burial, Peruvian: **5** huaca
of detritus: **4** kame
of sand: **4** dune
of stones: **5** cairn
Polynesian: **3** ahu
prehistoric: **4** terp
Scottish: **5** toman

mound-like

7 tumular

mount

2 up **3** alp, wax **4** back, hill, lift, peak, pony, rise, show, soar, upgo **5** arise, build, climb, frame, horse, put on, rouse, scale, stage, steed, stuff **6** ascend, aspire, deepen, expand, uprear **7** advance, augment, enhance, enlarge, magnify, produce, support, upclimb, upsurge **8** bestride, escalade, escalate, heighten, increase, multiply, redouble **9** aggravate, intensate, intensify **10** promontory

mountain

3 alp, lot **4** bank, dome, heap, hill, hulk, lump, mass, mesa, much, peak, peck, pile, slew **5** bluff, butte, drift, mound, shock, stack **6** hurdle, sierra **8** obstacle **10** impediment **11** obstruction

Alaska: **4** Bona **6** Denali **7** Foraker, Sanford **8** Wrangell
Alberta: **6** Castle **10** Eisenhower
Alps' highest: **5** Blanc
Angola's highest: **4** Moco
Antarctica: **4** Mohl **7** Gardner **9** Elizabeth **12** Vinson Massif
Appalachians: **10** Kittatinny
Argentina: **9** Aconcagua
Australia: **4** Ziel **5** Bruce **6** Cradle **9** Kosciusko
beyond the: **10** tramontane **11** transalpine
biblical: **5** Horeb, Tabor **6** Hermon **8** Har Tavor
Black Hills: **10** Harney Peak
Bolivia: **6** Sorata **8** Illimani
Borneo: **8** Kinabalu, Kinabulu
California: **5** Guyot **7** Palomar, Whitney **8** Tuolumne **10** Buena Vista, Sonora Peak, Stanislaus
China: **4** Emei, Song
Colorado: **9** Pikes Peak **13** Purgatory Peak
combining form: **3** ore, oro **4** oreo

Connecticut's highest: **8** Frissell
Costa Rica: **6** Blanco **14** Chirripó Grande
Cyprus' highest: **7** Olympus, Troodos
depression: **3** col
Dominican Republic: **6** Duarte **8** Trujillo
Egypt: **4** Musa **5** Sinai
Fiji: **8** Victoria **9** Tomaniivi
foot: **8** piedmont
Gabon: **8** Iboundji
Georgia: **8** Springer **10** Oglethorpe
Germany: **7** Zollern **11** Fichtelberg
Greece: **3** Ida **5** Athos, Levka **7** Helicon **9** Parnassus, Psiloriti **10** Pendelikon, Pentelicus
Greenland: **9** Gunnbjørn
Himalayas: **10** Kula Kangri
India: **5** Japvo
Indonesia: **4** Lawu **5** Kwoka, Lawoe, Raung **6** Raoeng
Israel: **5** Meron **6** Carmel
Ivory Coast: **5** Nimba
Japan: **4** Fuji **5** Iwate **7** Fujisan **8** Fujiyama **9** Iwate-yama **10** Fujino-Yama
Java: **5** Liman
Jordan: **3** Hor **5** Hārūn
Malaysia: **5** Ophir, Tahan **6** Ledang
Mediterranean entrance: **5** Calpe **15** Rock of Gibraltar
New York: **4** Bear
North America's highest: **6** Denali **8** McKinley
Oman: **4** Sham
Pakistan: **9** Tirich Mir
Papua New Guinea: **7** Wilhelm
Pennine Alps: **4** Rosa
Philippines: **3** Apo, Iba **4** Labo **5** Silay
ridge: **4** spur **5** arête, crest **7** sawbuck
Romania: **11** Moldoveanul
South America: **7** Roraima
South Dakota: **10** Custer Peak
Syria: **4** Druz **5** Druze, Duruz
Tanzania: **11** Kilimanjaro
Tasmania's highest: **4** Ossa
Tennessee: **7** Jumpoff, Lookout **11** Chimney Tops **13** Clingmans Dome
Togo: **4** Agou
Vermont: **11** Glastenbury
Vietnam: **8** Ngoo Linh
West Africa: **8** Cameroon
western hemisphere's highest: **9** Aconcagua
world's highest: **7** Everest; (see also peak)

mountain chain

Asia: **8** Tien Shan
Greece: **4** Oeta
Turkey: **6** Taurus

mountain climbing

equipment: **2** ax **3** axe, nut **5** piton **7** crampon **9** carabiner
maneuver: **6** rappel **10** rappelling

mountain dew

see moonshine

mountain formation

7 orogeny **9** orogenesy **10** orogenesis

mountain group

Germany: **4** Harz
Idaho: **10** Clearwater
New York: **8** Catskill **10** Adirondack
Sinai: **9** Gebel Musa
Slovakia: **5** Tatra, Tatry **9** High Tatra
South Dakota-Wyoming: **10** Black Hills
Utah: **5** La Sal
Washington: **7** Olympic
Zimbabwe: **11** Matopo Hills **12** Matoppo Hills

mountainous

4 huge, vast **6** mighty **7** immense, mammoth, massive **8** enormous, gigantic **10** monumental, prodigious

mountain pass

Afghanistan-Pakistan: **6** Khyber
Alps: **5** Gries
California: **4** Muir **6** Sonora
China-Myanmar: **5** Namni
Colorado: **3** Ute **5** Mosca, Muddy, Music, Raton
Europe: **8** Moravian
Greece: **5** Rupel
Hindu Kush Mts.: **5** Dorah, Durah
Pakistan: **5** Bolan, Gomal, Gumal
Sierra Nevada: **4** Mono
Switzerland: **5** Furka, Gemmi **7** Grimsel **8** Lötschen
Tunisia: **5** Faïd
Ukrainian: **5** Uzhok
Wyoming: **5** Union

mountain range

Alaska: **6** Brooks **7** Chugach **8** Wrangell
Alaska-Canada: **10** Saint Elias
Algeria: **3** Zab
Alps: **8** Bavarian
ancient Edom: **4** Seir
Antarctica: **9** Ellsworth
Appalachian: **4** Bald, Blue **5** Green **6** Unicoi **10** Great Smoky **12** Great Smokies
Arizona: **8** Maricopa **10** Chiricahua
Australia: **7** Darling **10** Macpherson
Brazil: **5** Organ
California: **4** Inyo **6** Nevada **7** Klamath **10** San Gabriel **13** San Bernardino
Canada: **10** Laurentian
central Asia: **9** Hindu Kush **11** Paropamisus

China: **5** Helan
Colorado: **7** San Juan
Czech Republic-Slovakia: **11** West Beskids
England: **12** Pennine Chain
Ethiopia: **4** Gugu
Eurasia: **8** Caucasus
Europe: **4** Jura **8** Pyrenees
France: **6** Vosges **8** Cévennes
Germany: **4** Rhön **13** Thüringer Wald
Greece: **6** Othris, Othrys, Pindus **7** Olympus **8** Taygetus
Hawaii: **7** Waianae
Himalayas: **8** Anapurna **9** Annapurna
Idaho: **5** Lemhi **7** Wasatch
India: **7** Vindhya **12** Eastern Ghats, Western Ghats
Indonesia: **5** Maoke
Iran: **6** Elburz
Iran-Turkmenistan: **8** Kopet Dag
Ireland: **7** Wicklow
Italy: **9** Apennines
Kazakhstan-Russia: **4** Ural
Kyrgyzstan: **4** Alai
McKinley's: **6** Alaska
Massachusetts: **6** Hoosac
Mexico: **11** Sierra Madre
Minnesota: **6** Mesabi
New Hampshire: **12** Presidential
New Jersey: **6** Ramapo
New Zealand: **12** Southern Alps
North Carolina: **5** Black
Northern Ireland: **6** Mourne
Pakistan: **8** Sulaiman
Papua New Guinea: **6** Albert **11** Owen Stanley
Philippines: **11** Sierra Madre
Rockies: **11** Medicine Bow
Russia: **8** Barguzin, Stanovoi
Scandinavia: **5** Kölen **6** Kjølen
Slovakia-Poland: **11** East Beskids
South Africa: **9** Nieuwveld **10** Kwathlamba, Quathlamba **11** Drakensberg
South Asia: **5** Ladak **6** Ladakh
Spain: **6** Morena, Toledo **8** Maladeta **10** Cantabrian
United States: **7** Cascade **8** Gallatin, Ouachita
Utah: **5** Uinta
Venezuela: **6** Mérida
Wales: **8** Cambrian
Washington: **6** Chelan
Wyoming: **5** Teton **11** Sierra Madre
Yosemite National Park: **9** Cathedral

mountains
Algeria: **6** Hoggar **7** Ahaggar
England: **8** Cumbrian
Idaho: **10** Clearwater
New Hampshire: **5** White

New York: **8** Catskill **10** Adirondack
Pennsylvania: **6** Pocono
Slovakia: **5** Tatra, Tatry **9** High Tatra
study of: **7** orology
Sudan: **4** Nuba
Utah: **5** La Sal
Washington: **7** Olympic
western North America: **11** Coast Ranges

mountain sickness
4 veta **7** soroche

Mountain State
7 Montana **12** West Virginia

mountain system
Asia: **5** Altai **8** Himalaya **9** Himalayas
Europe: **4** Alps **10** Carpathian
Iran: **6** Zagros
North Africa: **5** Atlas
North America: **5** Rocky **7** Rockies **11** Appalachian **12** Appalachians
Scotland: **9** Grampians **13** Grampian Hills
South America: **5** Andes

mountebank
3 gyp **5** cheat, quack **6** con man **7** diddler, sharper **8** swindler **9** charlatan, defrauder, pretender, quackster **11** flimflammer, quacksalver **12** double-dealer, saltimbanque **13** confidence man

Mount St. Helens
7 volcano

mourn
3 rue **6** bemoan, bewail, grieve, lament, sorrow **7** protest

mournful
3 sad **4** dire **5** sorry **6** dismal, rueful, somber, triste, woeful **7** doleful, joyless, unhappy **8** dolesome, dolorous, funereal, grievous, saddened **9** plaintive, saddening, sorrowful **10** afflictive, calamitous, deplorable, depressing, dispirited, lamentable, lugubrious, melancholy **11** distressing, melancholic, regrettable, unfortunate **12** heavyhearted

mournfulness
5 blues, dumps, gloom **7** sadness **9** dejection **10** depression, melancholy, the dismals **11** unhappiness

Mourning Becomes Electra
author: **6** O'Neill (Eugene)

mourning period
Jewish: **5** shiva **6** shibah, shivah

mourning symbol
7 armband

mouse
3 pry **4** hunt, nose, poke, slip **5** creep, glide, slide, snoop, steal **6** shiner **7** explore, saunter **8** black eye, busybody
combining form: **2** my **3** myo, mys

mouth
3 eat, gab, gob, mop, mow, yap **4** blow, brag, crow, face, guff, moue, puff, rail, rant, rave, sass, talk, tell, trap **5** boast, orate, prate, sauce, speak, spill, vaunt, voice **6** betray, mumble, palate, recite, reveal, tongue **7** blab out, declaim, divulge, grimace, soapbox, speaker, unclose **8** back talk, bloviate, disclose, discover, entrance, give away, harangue, perorate **9** gasconade, impudence, pronounce, spokesman **10** embouchure, volubility **11** rodomontade, spokeswoman **12** embouchement, spokesperson
combining form: **3** ori, oro **4** stom **5** stoma, stome, stomi, stomo, stomy **6** stomat, stomia, stomum **7** stomata, stomate, stomato, stomous **9** stomatous

mouthing
3 mow, mug **4** face **7** grimace

mouthlike opening
5 stoma **7** stomata (plural)

mouthpiece
7 speaker **9** spokesman **11** spokeswoman **12** spokesperson

mouthward
4 orad

mouth-watering
5 sapid, tasty **6** savory, toothy **8** tasteful **9** aperitive, delicious, palatable, relishing **10** appetizing **11** good-tasting

mouthy
5 talky **9** bombastic, garrulous, talkative

movable
5 loose **6** mobile, motile, moving, roving **8** unstable, unsteady **10** changeable **11** unsteadfast

movables
5 goods **7** effects **8** chattels **10** belongings

move
2 go **3** act, hum **4** bear, blow, exit, goad, go on, lead, live, spur, step, stir, sway, turn, void **5** bring, budge, carry, drive, exist, get on, impel, leave, march, pique, rouse, shift, start, touch **6** acquit, affect,

behave, convey, demean, depart, deport, excite, get off, incite, induce, kindle, motion, prompt, propel **7** actuate, advance, agitate, animate, breathe, comport, conduct, convert, disturb, get away, impress, innerve, inspire, measure, migrate, proceed, propose, provoke, pull out, replace, request, suggest, take off **8** activate, dislodge, displace, evacuate, get along, maneuver, mobilize, motivate, persuade, progress, relocate, resettle, stirring, supplant, transfer, transmit, withdraw **9** dislocate, galvanize, influence, innervate, instigate, stimulate, supersede, transport **10** proceeding

movement
3 act **4** deed, stir, time **5** tempo, trend **6** action, motion, rhythm **8** activity, dynamism, liveness, maneuver, stirring, tendency
away: **6** exodus
combining form: **3** cin, kin **4** cino, kine, kino **5** cinet, kinet **6** cineto, kineto **7** cinesia, kinesia
music: **4** moto
reflex: **5** taxis
stimulated: **7** kinesis

movie
4 cine, film, show **5** flick **6** cinema **7** picture **9** photoplay **11** picture show **13** motion picture, moving picture
combining form: **4** cine
cowboy: **5** oater **7** western
short: **4** clip **8** newsreel

movie director
American: **2** Oz (Frank) **3** Lee (Spike), Ray (Nicholas) **4** Coen (Joel), Ford (John), Wise (Robert) **5** Allen (Woody), Capra (Frank), Cukor (George), Demme (Jonathan), Hawks (Howard), Kazan (Elia), Lucas (George), Roach (Hal), Stone (Oliver), Vidor (King), Wyler (William), Zwick (Ed) **6** Altman (Robert), Beatty (Warren), Burton (Tim), Curtiz (Michael), Gibson (Mel), Howard (Ron), Huston (John), Welles (Orson), Wilder (Billy) **7** Cameron (James), Coppola (Francis Ford), Costner (Kevin), De Mille (Cecil B.), Fleming (Victor), Kubrick (Stanley), Nichols (Mike), Pollack (Sidney), Redford (Robert), Stevens (George), Sturges (Preston) **8** Eastwood (Clint), Flaherty (Robert), Griffith (David Wark), Levinson (Barry), Lubitsch (Ernst), Marshall (Penny), Minnelli (Vincente), Scorsese (Mar-

tin), Zemeckis (Robert) **9** Hitchcock (Alfred), Preminger (Otto), Spielberg (Steven), Sternberg (Josef von), Streisand (Barbra), Tarantino (Quentin), Zinnemann (Fred) **10** Heckerling (Amy)
Australian: **4** Weir (Peter) **6** Noonan (Chris) **9** Armstrong (Gillian), Beresford (Bruce)
Austrian: **4** Lang (Fritz) **8** Stroheim (Erich von)
British: **4** Lean (David) **5** Ivory (James), Scott (Ridley) **6** Figgis (Mike), Frears (Stephen), Jordan (Neil), Newell (Mike), Parker (Alan), Powell (Michael) **7** Branagh (Kenneth), Forsyth (Bill), Gilliam (Terry) **10** Richardson (Tony) **11** Schlesinger (John)
Chinese: **3** Lee (Ang) **5** Zhang (Yimou)
French: **4** Tati (Jacques) **5** Malle (Louis) **6** Godard (Jean-Luc), Renoir (Jean), Rohmer (Eric) **8** Truffaut (François)
German: **6** Herzog (Werner) **10** Fassbinder (Rainer) **11** Riefenstahl (Leni)
Italian: **5** Leone (Sergio) **6** De Sica (Vittorio) **7** Fellini (Federico) **8** Pasolini (Pier Paolo), Visconti (Luchino) **9** Antonioni (Michelangelo) **10** Bertolucci (Bernardo), Rossellini (Roberto), Wertmuller (Lina), Zeffirelli (Franco)
Japanese: **8** Kurosawa (Akira)
New Zealand: **7** Campion (Jane)
Polish **7** Holland (Agnieszka)
Russian: **10** Eisenstein (Sergei)
Spanish: **6** Buñuel (Luis) **9** Almodovar (Pedro)
Swedish: **7** Bergman (Ingmar) **10** Zetterling (Mai)

movie producer
American: **5** Mayer (Louis B.), Roach (Hal) **6** Kramer (Stanley), Warner (Jack L.), Welles (Orson), Zanuck (Darryl, Richard) **7** De Mille (Cecil B.), Goldwyn (Samuel), Sennett (Mack) **8** Griffith (David Wark), Selznick (David O.)
Austrian: **9** Reinhardt (Max)
French: **6** Renoir (Jean)

moving
5 astir **6** mobile **7** emotive, rousing **8** arousing, exciting, gripping, pathetic, poignant, rallying, stirring, touching, unstable, unsteady **9** actuating, affecting, affective, awakening, emotional, provoking, transient **10** ambulatory, impressive **11** stimulating, unsteadfast

moving picture
see **movie**

moving stairs
9 escalator

mow
3 cut, mop, mug **4** bank, clip, cock, crop, down, drop, face, fell, heap, hill, kill, moue, pile, rick, rout **5** drift, floor, level, mouth, shock, smash, stack **6** ground **7** grimace **8** bowl down, bowl over, mouthing **9** bring down, knock down, throw down

moxie
2 go **3** pep **4** birr, grit, guts, tuck **5** heart, nerve, pluck, spunk, vigor **6** energy, mettle, spirit **7** cojones, courage, potency **8** backbone **9** fortitude, hardihood **10** resolution **13** dauntlessness

Mozart
birthplace: **8** Salzburg
cataloger: **6** Köchel (Ludwig)
deathplace: **6** Vienna
opera: **8** Idomeneo **10** Magic Flute **11** Don Giovanni **12** Cosi fan Tutte

MP's prey
4 AWOL **8** deserter

Mr. Moto star
5 Lorre (Peter)

Mrs. Grundy
4 prig **5** prude **7** puritan **8** bluenose, comstock **9** nice Nelly **10** goody-goody

much
3 lot, oft **4** good, heap, long, lots, lump, many, mass, most, nigh, pack, peck, pile, scad, very **5** about, often **6** all but, almost, highly, hugely, nearly, plenty **7** greatly, notably **8** abundant, lashings, ofttimes, well-nigh **9** eminently, extremely, great deal, multitude **10** frequently, oftentimes, repeatedly
combining form: **4** poly **5** multi

Much Ado About Nothing
character: **4** Hero **7** Claudio, Don John **8** Beatrice, Benedick

much as
4 when **5** while **6** albeit, though **7** howbeit, whereas **8** although

muck
3 goo **4** crap, dirt, dung, gook, goop, grub, gunk, junk, mess, mire, murk, plod, slog, slum, soil, toil **5** dirty, filth, grime, grind, gumbo, muddy, offal, slave, slime, swill, trash, waste **6** debris, drudge, lit-

ter, manure, refuse, sludge, smirch, smooch, smudge, smutch **7** garbage, rubbish

muckamuck
3 VIP **5** nabob **6** bigwig **7** big shot, notable **8** somebody **9** dignitary **10** notability

mucker
3 cad, oaf **4** boor, punk, worm **5** botch, chuff, churl, clown, gum up, rough, rowdy, tough, yahoo **6** bobble, bollix, bungle, no-good, wretch **7** bitch up, blunder, grobian, louse up, lowlife, ruffian, toughie **8** bullyboy, wormling **9** roughneck **10** clodhopper

mucky
4 foul **5** black, dirty, dungy, humid, messy, muddy, muggy, murky, nasty, soggy **6** cloudy, filthy, grubby, sordid, sticky, sultry **7** clouded, squalid, unclean

mucous
5 slimy **6** viscid

mucronate
5 acute, piked, sharp **6** peaked **7** pointed **8** acicular **9** aciculate, acuminate, acuminous, cuspidate

mucus
9 secretion

mud
4 dirt, mire, ooze, rile, roil **5** dregs, slime **6** depths, sludge
combining form: **3** pel **4** pelo

muddle
3 mix **4** blow, daze, hash, limp, mess, muck, mull, muss, rile, roil **5** addle, botch, mix up, muddy, ravel, snarl, waste **6** ataxia, drivel, foul up, fuddle, fumble, huddle, jumble, jungle, litter, mess up, mumble, murmur, muss up, mutter, tangle, tumble **7** clutter, confuse, fluster, fritter, perplex, rummage, shuffle, snarl up, stumble, stupefy, swallow **8** befuddle, bewilder, botchery, cast away, confound, disarray, disorder, distract, entangle, mishmash, scramble, shambles, squander, throw off, unsettle **9** confusion, throw away **10** complicate, disarrange, discompose, frivol away, trifle away **11** blunder away, disorganize

muddled
5 drunk, tight, tipsy, vague **6** cloudy **7** mixed-up **8** inchoate **9** disguised, pixilated **10** disjointed, disordered, incoherent, incohesive, inebriated **11** intoxi-

cated, unconnected, unorganized **12** disconnected, uncontinuous **13** discontinuous

muddlehead
4 dolt **5** dunce, idiot, moron **6** dimwit **7** fathead **8** dumbbell **9** blockhead, simpleton **11** chowderhead

muddle through
2 do **4** fare **5** get by, get on, shift **6** manage **8** get along **9** stagger on **12** stagger along

muddy
3 dim, fog **4** base, blur, drab, dull, fade, foul, miry, oozy, pale, rile, roil, soil **5** befog, black, cloud, dirty, dungy, grime, murky, riley, roily, soily **6** cloudy, gloomy, sordid, turbid **7** becloud, begrime, bemired, confuse, squalid, subfusc, tarnish, unclean, unclear **8** confused **9** uncleanly

mudfish
6 bowfin

mud hen
4 coot, rail

muezzin's faith
5 Islam

muff
4 blow, flub **5** botch, error, fluff **6** bobble, bollix, bungle, fumble, goof up **7** louse up

muffle
4 dull, mute, veil **5** shush **6** dampen, deaden, lessen, shroud, soften, stifle, subdue, wrap up **7** envelop, repress, silence, smother, squelch **8** bundle up, strangle, suppress, tone down **10** overspread

muffler
4 mask, veil **5** cloak, cover, guise, scarf **6** facade, veneer **8** disguise **10** masquerade **12** disguisement

muffler mangler
3 rut **7** pothole **9** chuckhole

mug
3 cup, mop, mow **4** boob, dolt, dope, face, fool, moue, phiz, punk, puss, thug, toby **5** dunce, grail, idiot, mouth, rough, rowdy, stein, stoup, tough **6** dimwit, mucker, seidel, visage **7** assault, chalice, grimace, ruffian, tankard **8** bullyboy, dumbbell, features, mouthing, numskull, plug-ugly, schooner **9** blockhead, ignoramus, roughneck **11** countenance

mugger
4 thug **9** assailant, assaulter

muggy
4 damp **5** humid, moist, mucky, soggy **6** moisty, sticky, sultry **7** dampish, wettish

Muhammad, Mohammed
adopted son: **3** Ali
birthplace: **5** Mecca
camel: **5** Kaswa
daughter: **6** Fatima
deathplace: **6** Medina
deity: **5** Allah
father: **8** Abdallah, Abdullah
father-in-law: **7** Abu Bakr
flight: **6** hegira, hejira
follower: **6** Moslem, Muslim
horse: **5** Buraq **7** Alborak
religion: **5** Islam
son: **7** Ibrahim
son-in-law: **3** Ali
successor: **5** calif **6** caliph **7** Abu Bakr
tribe: **7** Koreish
uncle: **8** Abu Talib
wife: **5** Aisha **6** Ayesha **7** Khadija

mulct
4 fine, milk, rook **5** bleed, cheat, stick, sweat **6** amerce, fleece **7** deceive, defraud, forfeit, penalty, swindle **8** penalize **10** amercement

mule
5 cross **6** hybrid **7** bastard, mongrel **9** crossbred, half blood, halfbreed **10** crossbreed

muleheaded
see **mulish**

mulish
5 balky **6** unruly **8** perverse, stubborn **9** obstinate, pigheaded **10** bullheaded, headstrong, inflexible, refractory, self-willed, unyielding **11** stiff-necked, wrongheaded

mull
4 hash, mess, muse, muss, numb, poke, roll, stir **5** addle, blunt, botch, dally, delay, mix-up, tarry, think **6** ball up, bemuse, benumb, dawdle, deaden, fuddle, linger, loiter, mess-up, muddle, ponder, put off **7** confuse, crumble **8** befuddle, bewilder, botchery, cogitate, consider, distract, meditate, ruminate, shambles, throw off, turn over **9** pulverize **10** deliberate, dillydally **11** desensitize **13** procrastinate

mulligrubs
4 sulk **5** blues, dumps, gloom, mumps, pouts **6** grumps **7** sullens

9 dejection 10 depression, melancholy

multicolored
4 pied 6 motley 7 dappled 8 discolor 10 variegated, versicolor

multifarious
4 many 5 mixed 6 legion, motley, sundry, varied 7 diverse, various 8 assorted, chowchow, manifold, numerous, populous 10 voluminous 11 diversiform, promiscuous 12 conglomerate 13 heterogeneous, miscellaneous

multiform
7 diverse 8 manifold 11 diversiform 12 multifarious, multivarious

multiformity
7 variety 8 multeity 9 diversity 11 diverseness, variousness 12 multiplicity

multihued
see **multicolored**

multilateral
9 many-sided

multiloquent
5 gabby, talky 6 chatty 9 garrulous, talkative 10 babblative, loquacious 11 loose-lipped 12 loose-tongued

multiplex
see **multiform**

multiplicity
3 lot 4 mass, much, peck 6 barrel 7 variety 8 multeity 9 diversity, great deal 11 diverseness, variousness

multiply
3 wax 4 bear, rise 5 beget, boost, breed, build, mount 6 beef up, expand, extend, spread 7 amplify, augment, enlarge, magnify, produce, upsurge 8 generate, heighten, increase 9 procreate, propagate, reproduce 10 aggrandize

multitude
3 mob 4 army, host, many, rout 5 cloud, crowd, crush, drove, flock, horde, press, swarm 6 legion, oodles, public, scores, squash, throng 7 numbers

multitudinal
see **multitudinous**

multitudinous
4 many 6 legion, myriad, sundry 7 various 8 manifold, numerous, populous 9 countless 10 innumerous, numberless, voluminous 11 innumerable 12 multifarious

multivocal
7 blatant 8 strident 9 clamorous, equivocal 10 boisterous, vociferant, vociferous 11 loudmouthed, openmouthed 12 obstreperous

mum
4 dumb, mute 5 still 6 silent 7 silence 8 wordless 10 speechless

mumble
4 chew 5 mouth, rumor 6 muddle, murmur, mutter 7 maunder, swallow, whisper 9 undertone 11 susurration

mumbo jumbo
7 mummery 9 gibberish 10 hocus pocus 11 abracadabra

mummer
4 mime 5 actor, mimic 6 player 7 trouper 8 thespian 9 performer, playactor 12 impersonator

mummery
6 acting 9 gibberish, hypocrisy 10 hocus pocus, mumbo jumbo 11 abracadabra

mummify
4 wilt 5 dry up, wizen 6 welter, wither 7 shrivel

mumpish
4 dour, ugly 5 sulky, surly 6 morose, sullen 9 saturnine

munch
3 eat 4 bite, chew 5 champ, chomp, chump 6 crunch 7 chumble, scrunch 8 ruminate 9 masticate

mundane
5 lowly 6 cosmic, earthy 7 earthly, prosaic, sensual, terrene, workday, worldly 8 banausic, everyday, telluric, workaday 9 sublunary, tellurian 11 commonplace, terrestrial, uncelestial 13 materialistic

municipal
4 city, home 5 urban 6 native 7 burghal 8 domestic, internal, national 9 intestine

munificent
4 free 6 lavish 7 liberal 8 generous, handsome 9 bounteous, bountiful, unsparing 10 freehanded, openhanded

munitions maker
5 Krupp

muralist
4 Sert (José María) 6 Benton (Thomas Hart), Giotto, Orozco (José Clemente), Rivera (Diego) 7 La Farge (John) 9 Siqueiras (David) 12 Michelangelo 16 Puvis de Chavannes (Pierre-Cecile); (See also **painter**)

murder
4 cool, do in, hang, kill, slay 5 abate, blood, lynch, scrag 6 finish, mangle, rub out 7 abolish, blot out, destroy, execute, garrote, killing, put away, root out, smother 8 foul play, homicide, knock off, strangle, uncreate 9 eradicate, liquidate, slaughter 10 annihilate, asphyxiate, decapitate, extinguish, guillotine 11 assassinate, electrocute, exterminate 12 manslaughter
brother: 10 fratricide
father: 9 patricide
king: 8 regicide
mother: 9 matricide
parent: 9 parricide
sister: 10 sororicide

murderer
6 killer, slayer 7 butcher 8 assassin, homicide 9 manslayer 11 slaughterer

Murder in the Cathedral
author: 5 Eliot (Thomas Stearns)
character: 5 Henry 7 Beckett

murderous
6 brutal 9 ferocious 11 devastating 12 bloodthirsty

mure
3 pen 4 cage, wall 5 fence, hedge 6 shut in, thrust 7 close in, enclose, envelop, squeeze

murk
3 dim, fog 4 foul, haze, mist, soil 5 bedim, cloud, dirty, gloom, grime, muddy 6 besoil, darken, smirch, smudge 7 becloud, begrime, obscure, tarnish 8 darkness 9 obfuscate

murky
3 dim, dun 4 dark, drab, dull, dusk, foul 5 black, dirty, dusky, foggy, misty, muddy, nasty, roily 6 cloudy, filthy, gloomy, grubby, opaque, somber, sordid, turbid 7 obscure, squalid, subfusc, unclean 8 nubilous 9 ambiguous, equivocal, sibylline, tenebrous 10 caliginous

murmur
3 cry, hum 4 buzz, fuss, kick, purr, talk, wail 5 croak, drone, rumor, scold, whine 6 fumble, gossip, grouch, grouse, muddle, mumble, mutter, repine, report, rumble

7 grumble, hearsay, swallow, whisper **8** complain **9** grapevine, grumbling, undertone **11** scuttlebutt, susurration

muscle
4 beef, thew **5** brawn, force, might, power, sinew **6** energy **7** potency **8** strength **9** necessity, strong arm
arm: **6** biceps **7** triceps
back: **9** trapezius
calf: **6** soleus
chest: **10** pectoralis
combining form: **2** ei (plural) **3** eus, mya **6** muscul, myaria (plural) **7** musculo
jaw: **8** masseter
kind: **6** flexor, tensor **7** dilator, evertor, levator, rotator **8** abductor, adductor, extensor
loin: **5** psoas
neck: **8** platysma
shoulder: **7** deltoid **10** deltoideus
study of: **7** myology
thigh: **8** gracilis **9** sartorius

muscle-bound
5 rigid, stiff **6** wooden **7** buckram, stilted **9** cardboard

muscular
4 ropy, wiry **5** beefy, burly, husky, stout **6** brawny, mighty, robust, sinewy, strong, sturdy, supple **7** fibrous, stringy, well-set **8** athletic, forceful, powerful, stalwart, vigorous, well-knit **9** Herculean, well-built

muse
4 bard, poet **5** study, think **6** ponder, trance **7** reflect, reverie **8** cogitate, meditate, mull over, ruminate, turn over **10** deliberate, excogitate **11** contemplate

Muse
father: **4** Zeus **7** Jupiter
mother: **9** Mnemosyne
of astronomy: **6** Urania
of choral song: **11** Terpsichore
of comedy: **6** Thalia
of dancing: **11** Terpsichore
of epic poetry: **8** Calliope
of history: **4** Clio
of love poetry: **5** Erato
of lyric poetry: **5** Erato
of music: **7** Euterpe
of pastoral poetry: **6** Thalia
of sacred poetry: **8** Polymnia **10** Polyhymnia
of tragedy: **9** Melpomene

museum
5 salon **7** exhibit, gallery **8** atheneum **10** collection, repository **11** pinacotheka

Mushi's father
6 Merari

mushroom
4 grow **5** burst, go off **6** blow up, expand, spread **7** explode **8** detonate
combining form: **3** myc **4** myco **5** mycet **6** myceto
edible: **5** morel **10** champignon **11** chanterelle
kind: **6** agaric, bolete **7** inky cap, russula
part: **3** cap **4** gill, ring **5** stipe, volva **6** pileus **7** annulus **8** mycelium
poisonous: **7** amanita **8** death cup **9** toadstool

mushy
4 hazy, soft, weak **5** foggy, misty, pappy, pulpy, vague **6** cloudy, quaggy, spongy, sticky, vapory **7** blurred, maudlin, mawkish, pulpous, squashy, squishy, squushy **8** bathetic, effusive, romantic, sluggish, squelchy, vaporous **10** lovey-dovey **11** sentimental, tear-jerking

music
abbreviation: **2** ff, mf, mp, pp, sf **3** sfz
bass staff lines: **5** GBDFA
bass staff spaces: **4** ACEG
characteristic phrase: **9** leitmotif, leitmotiv
chord: **5** tonic **8** dominant **9** augmented **10** diminished
embellishment: **3** run **4** turn **5** trill **7** cadenza, mordent, roulade **8** arpeggio, flourish **9** grace note
for eight: **5** octet
for five: **7** quintet
for four: **7** quartet
for nine: **5** nonet
for one: **4** solo
for seven: **6** septet
for six: **6** sextet
for three: **4** trio
for two: **3** duo **4** duet
god: **6** Apollo
hall: **7** cabaret, theater
instrumental form: **3** jig **4** jazz, reel **5** étude, fugue, gigue, march, polka, rondo, suite, swing, waltz **6** minuet, pavane, sonata **7** bourrée, gavotte, mazurka, prelude, ragtime, toccata **8** chaconne, concerto, courante, fantasia, galliard, nocturne, overture, rhapsody, ricercar, saraband, serenade, symphony, tone poem **9** allemande, polonaise **11** rock and roll
medley: **4** olio
morning: **6** aubade
Muse: **7** Euterpe
night: **8** nocturne, serenade
note: **4** half **5** breve, minim, neume, whole **6** eighth **7** quarter **9** sixteenth
patron saint: **7** Cecilia
period: **6** Modern, Rococo **7** Baroque **8** Medieval, Romantic **9** Classical
reformer: **5** Guido (of Arezzo)
symbol: **3** bar, key **4** clef, flat, note, rest, slur, turn **5** sharp, staff **7** fermata, mordent **9** alla breve **10** accidental
treble staff lines: **5** EGBDF
treble staff spaces: **4** FACE
vocal form: **3** air **4** aria, hymn, lied, mass, song **5** canon, chant, motet, opera, round **6** anthem, ballad **7** cantata, chanson, chorale **8** cavatina, madrigal, operetta, oratorio, serenade **9** cabaletta

musical
4 show **5** revue **6** turned **7** chiming, lyrical, melodic, songful, tuneful **8** blending, harmonic **9** consonant, melodious, symphonic **10** harmonious **11** symphonious

musical composition
4 aria, hymn, opus, solo **5** étude, fugue, motet, opera, psalm, rondo, suite **6** anthem, ballad, sonata, verset **7** cantata, chanson, chorale, prelude, requiem, toccata **8** concerto, madrigal, nocturne, operetta, oratorio, postlude, serenade, sonatina, symphony **9** bagatelle, cabaletta, interlude, toccatina **10** intermezzo

musical direction
accented: **7** marcato **8** sforzato **9** sforzando
airy: **7** sfogato
all: **5** tutti
as written: **3** sta
bold: **6** audace
brisk: **4** vivo **6** vivace **7** allegro, animato
connected: **6** legato
detached: **8** spiccato, staccato
dignified: **8** maestoso
disconnected: **8** staccato
dying away: **7** calando
emotional: **12** appassionato
emphatic: **7** marcato
evenly: **10** egualmente
excited: **7** agitato **9** spiritoso

fast: 4 vite, vivo 5 tosto 6 presto, veloce, vivace 7 allegro 10 tostamente

faster: 7 stretto 11 accelerando

fluctuating tempo: 6 rubato

forcefully: 7 furioso

freely: 9 ad libitum

gay: 7 giocoso

gentle: 5 dolce 7 amabile, amoroso 9 affettuso

graceful: 6 adagio 8 grazioso

half: 5 mezzo

heavy: 7 pesante

held firmly: 6 tenuto

hurried: 7 agitato

joyous: 7 giocoso

less: 4 meno

little: 4 poco

little by little: 9 poco a poco

lively: 4 vite 6 vivace 7 allegro, animato, giocoso 9 capriccio

loud: 5 forte

louder: 9 crescendo

lovingly: 7 amabile, amoroso

majestic: 8 maestoso

moderate: 7 andante 8 moderato

moderately loud: 2 mf 10 mezzo forte

moderately soft: 2 mp 10 mezzo piano

muted: 5 sorda, sordo

passionless: 6 freddo

plaintive: 7 dolente 8 doloroso

playful: 7 giocoso 10 scherzando

plucked: 9 pizzicato

quick: 4 vite, vivo 5 tosto 6 presto, veloce, vivace 7 allegro 10 tostamente

quickening: 11 affrettando

repeat: 2 DC 3 bis 6 da capo

sad: 7 dolente 8 doloroso

separate: 6 divisi

showily: 10 brilliante

silent: 5 tacet

singing: 9 cantabile

sliding: 9 glissando

slow: 5 grave, largo, tardo 6 adagio 7 andante 9 larghetto

slowing: 3 rit 6 ritard 10 ritardando 11 rallentando

smooth: 5 dolce 6 legato 8 grazioso

soft: 5 dolce, piano

softening: 10 diminuendo 11 decrescendo

solemn: 5 grave

sorrowful: 7 dolente 8 doloroso

spirited: 4 vivo 6 audace, vivace 7 animato 9 spiritoso

stately: 7 pomposo 8 maestoso

strong: 5 forte

sustained: 6 tenuto 9 sostenuto

sweet: 5 dolce

tender: 7 amabile, amoroso 10 affettuoso

together: 4 a due

tranquil: 7 calmato

very fast: 11 prestissimo

very loud: 2 ff 10 fortissimo

very soft: 2 pp 10 pianissimo

musical drama
5 opera 8 operetta 9 singspiel

musical group
4 band, trio 5 choir, combo 6 chorus 7 quartet 8 ensemble, glee club, symphony 9 orchestra

musical instrument
African: 5 mbira, sansa, zanza 7 kalimba, marimba

ancient: 4 lyre, rote 5 crwth, rotte, shawm 6 cither, syrinx, trigon 7 cithara, mandola, pandura, panpipe, serpent, sistrum, theorbo

Arabic: 3 oud 6 atabal

bagpipe: 7 musette, pibroch

biblical: 4 asor, harp, horn, pipe 5 flute 6 cymbal, sabeca, tabret 7 timbrel, trumpet 8 psaltery

brass: 4 horn, tuba 5 bugle 6 cornet 7 althorn, clarion, helicon, saxhorn, trumpet 8 trombone 10 French horn

Chinese: 3 kin

Indian: 4 vina 5 sarod, sitar, veena

Japanese: 4 biwa, koto 7 samisen

keyboard: 5 organ, piano 6 spinet 7 celesta, cembalo, clavier 8 calliope, melodeon, virginal 9 accordion 10 clavichord, concertina, pianoforte 11 harpsichord

medieval: 4 lute 5 naker, rebab, rebec, shawm, tabor 6 citole 7 cow horn, gittern, mandola, panpipe 8 cornetto, doucaine, dulcimer, gemshorn, hornpipe, Jew's harp, oliphant, recorder 9 monochord, rommelpot 10 clavichord, hurdygurdy

percussion: 4 bell, drum 5 guiro, piano 6 cymbal, maraca 7 marimba, timbrel, tympani 8 bass drum, castanet, triangle 9 snare drum, xylophone 10 kettledrum, tambourine, vibraphone

Persian: 6 santir

pipe: 6 syrinx 7 bagpipe, musette, panpipe 9 cornemuse

reed: 4 oboe 7 bassoon 8 clarinet 9 harmonica, saxophone 11 English horn

Renaissance: 4 viol 5 regal, shawm 6 curtal, lirone, spinet 7 bagpipe, bandora, cittern, rackett, sackbut, serpent, theorbo, vihuela, violone 8 crumhorn, penorcon, recorder, virginal 9 angelique, cornamuse, orpharion, pandurina 10 bassanello, chitarrone, colascione 11 harpsichord

Russian: 9 balalaika

stringed: 3 oud 4 asor, harp, lute, lyre, vina, viol 5 banjo, cello, piano, rebec, sitar, viola 6 fiddle, guitar, violin, zither 7 bandora, cittern, gittern, kantele, pandura, ukulele 8 autoharp, dulcimer, mandolin 10 contrabass, double bass 11 harpsichord, violoncello

suffix: 3 ina, ine

toy: 5 kazoo 7 ocarina

two-necked: 7 theorbo

woodwind: 4 oboe 5 flute 7 bassoon, piccolo 9 flageolet, saxophone 11 English horn

musical interval
5 fifth, major, minor, sixth, third 6 ditone, fourth, octave, second 7 perfect, seventh, tritone

musical syllable
2 do, fa, la, mi, re, si, ti, ut 3 Ela, sol

Guido's: 2 ut 3 Ela

musician
4 bard 5 piper 6 player 7 jazzman 8 minstrel, virtuoso 9 performer

muskeg
3 bog, fen 4 mire, quag 5 marsh, swamp 6 slough 7 baygall

musket
5 fusil 6 dragon 7 dragoon 9 flintlock, matchlock 12 muzzleloader

medieval: 8 culverin

Musketeer
5 Athos 6 Aramis 7 Porthos

author: 5 Dumas (Alexandre)

friend: 9 d'Artagnan

muskmelon
10 cantaloupe

Muslim, Moslem
ascetic: 4 Sufi 5 fakir 7 dervish 8 marabout

Bible: 5 Koran

body of scholars: 5 ulema

branch: 4 Shia 5 Sunni

caller to prayer: 7 muezzin

call to prayer: 4 adan, azan

cap: 3 taj

creed: 6 Kelima 7 Kalimah

devil: 5 Eblis

festival: 3 Eed 6 Bairam

garment: 4 izar 5 ihram 6 chador
god: 5 Allah
holy city: 5 Mecca 6 Medina
holy war: 5 jahad, jehad, jihad
judge: 4 cadi
lawyer: 5 mufti
marriage: 4 mota, muta
mendicant: 5 fakir
monastery: 5 ribat 7 khankah
month: (see at **month**)
month of fasting: 7 Ramadan
mosque: 6 masjid
mystic: 4 Sufi
nonbeliever: 5 Kafir 6 Kaffir
nymph: 5 houri
pilgrim: 4 haji 5 hadji, hajji
pilgrimage: 3 haj 4 hadj, hajj
priest: 4 imam
prophet: 8 Mohammed, Muhammad
religion: 5 Islam
saint: 3 pir 6 santon
saint's tomb: 3 pir
shrine: 5 Caaba, Kaaba 6 Kaabeh
student: 5 softa
teacher: 4 alim 5 mulla 6 mullah
temple: 6 mosque
title: 3 aga 4 agha, emir, said 5 calif, emeer, sayid 6 caliph
tradition: 5 sunna 6 sunnah; (see also **mosque; Muhammad**)

muss
4 mess 5 botch, mix-up, upset
6 jumble, mess-up, muddle, rumple
7 disrupt, rummage, wrinkle
8 botchery, disarray, dishevel, disorder, shambles 10 disarrange
11 disorganize

mussel
5 naiad
genus: 4 Unio 7 Mytilus 8 Anodonta
larva: 9 blackhead

Mussolini, Benito
7 Fascist 8 dictator
title: 4 Duce (Il)

mussy
5 messy 6 sloppy, sloven, unneat, untidy 7 unkempt 8 ill-kempt, slobbery, slovenly 10 disheveled

must
4 duty, have, need, want 5 ought
6 charge, devoir, should 9 committal, condition, essential, necessity, requisite 10 commitment, obligation, sine qua non 11 requirement
12 precondition, prerequisite

muster
4 call, roll 5 breed, cause, crowd, enter, get up, group, hatch, raise, rally 6 enlist, enroll, gather, induce,

invoke, join up, number, roster, sample, sign on, sign up, summon, work up 7 collect, company, convene, develop, include, marshal, produce 8 assemble, assembly, comprise, congress, engender, generate, mobilize, occasion, organize
9 congeries, forgather, gathering, inventory 10 accumulate, assemblage, collection, congregate, rendezvous 11 aggregation, examination 12 accumulation, congregation

muster out
8 separate 9 discharge
10 demobilize

musty
4 dull, rank, sour 5 dirty, fetid, funky, moldy, stale, tired, trite
6 frowsy, old hat, smelly, whiffy
7 noisome, spoiled, squalid 8 shopworn, timeworn 10 antiquated, malodorous, threadbare

Mut
husband: 4 Amen, Amon
son: 5 Chons 6 Chonsu, Khonsu

mutable
5 fluid 6 fickle, mobile, shifty
7 protean 8 slippery, unstable, unsteady, variable, wavering, weathery 9 changeful, mercurial, uncertain, unsettled 10 capricious, changeable, inconstant 11 fluctuating, vacillating 12 inconsistent

mutate
4 turn, vary 5 alter 6 change, modify 7 commute 9 refashion, transform, transmute, transpose
11 transfigure 12 metamorphize, metamorphose, transmogrify

mutation
4 turn 6 change 7 novelty 9 variation 10 alteration, innovation 11 vicissitude 12 modification

mute
3 mum 4 dumb 6 dampen, deaden, muffle, reduce, silent, soften, stifle 8 silencer, wordless
9 voiceless 10 speechless 12 inarticulate, unarticulate

muted
3 dim, mat 4 dead, dull, flat
5 blind 6 silent 10 lackluster, lusterless, speechless

mutedly
6 weakly 7 faintly 9 sotto voce

mutilate
3 mar 4 geld, hurt, maim 5 alter, spoil, unsex 6 change, damage,

deface, injure, mangle, mayhem, neuter 7 cripple, dislimb 8 castrate
9 disfigure, dismember, sterilize
11 desexualize

mutineer
5 rebel 6 anarch 8 frondeur, revolter 9 anarchist, insurgent
10 malcontent

mutinous
6 unruly 8 factious 9 insurgent, seditious, turbulent 10 rebellious
12 contumacious 13 insubordinate

mutiny
5 rebel 6 revolt 9 insurrect, rebellion 11 rise against 12 insurrection

mutt
3 cur, dog 4 boob, dolt, dope
5 dunce, idiot 6 dimwit 7 mongrel
8 dumbbell, numskull 9 blockhead, ignoramus

Mutt and ___
4 Jeff

mutter
5 croak, growl, rumor, scold 6 fumble, grouch, grouse, muddle, mumble, murmur 7 grumble, swallow, whisper 9 undertone 11 susurration

muttonchops
9 burnsides, sideburns 10 sideboards 11 dundrearies 12 sidewhiskers

muttonhead
3 oaf 5 dunce, idiot 8 clodpate, numskull 9 blockhead 10 thickskull

mutual
5 joint 6 common, public, shared, united 7 related 8 communal, conjoint, conjunct 9 connected 10 associated, reciprocal, respective
prefix: 2 co 5 inter

muzzle
3 gag, mug 4 face, nose, phiz
5 snout 6 nuzzle, visage 8 features, restrain 11 countenance

My Antonia author
6 Cather (Willa)

My Last Duchess author
8 Browning (Robert)

My Lost Youth author
10 Longfellow (Henry Wadsworth)

myrmecology subject
3 ant

myrmidon
8 follower, hireling, retainer 9 attendant, underling 11 subordinate

Myron's statue
10 Discobolus

Myrrha's son
6 Adonis

mysterious
6 arcane, mystic, occult, secret
7 cryptic, obscure, strange 8 abstruse, esoteric, numinous 9 ambiguous, enigmatic, equivocal, recondite, unguessed 10 cabalistic, unknowable 11 enigmatical, inscrutable, ungraspable 12 impenetrable, incognizable, inexplicable, unexaminable, unfathomable
13 unaccountable

mystery
5 poser 6 enigma, puzzle, riddle, secret 7 arcanum, problem, stumper 9 conundrum 10 closed book, perplexity, puzzlement
13 Chinese puzzle, mystification
story: 8 whodunit

mystic
4 seer 5 magic, vague 6 arcane,

magian, occult, secret, witchy
7 magical, obscure 8 anagogic, esoteric, numinous, quixotic, telestic, wizardly 9 enigmatic, mysterial, sorcerous, unguessed 10 cabalistic, mysterious, unknowable 11 inscrutable, necromantic 12 impenetrable, thaumaturgic 13 unaccountable

mystical
4 deep, holy 6 covert, divine, orphic, sacred, secret 7 cryptic, furtive, sub-rosa 8 anagogic, hush-hush, orphical, profound, stealthy, telestic 9 spiritual 10 miraculous, symbolical 11 clandestine 12 hugger-mugger, supernatural, supranatural 13 hole-and-corner

mysticism
8 cabalism, quietism

mystify
6 puzzle 7 confuse, perplex 8 befuddle, bewilder 9 obfuscate

mystifying
4 dark 7 cryptic 8 Delphian
9 enigmatic

myth
4 lore, saga, tale 5 fable, story
6 legend 7 fiction, figment, parable 8 allegory, apologue, creation, folklore 9 invention, tradition 11 fabrication

mythical
6 unreal 7 created, fictive 8 fabulous, fanciful, invented 9 fantastic, fictional, imaginary, legendary, visionary 10 fictitious 12 mythological

mythological
see **mythical**

mythologist
5 Tylor (Edward) 6 Frazer (James)
5 Müller (Friedrich Max) 9 Euhemerus 10 Malinowski (Bronislaw)

mythology
see **myth**

Nn

Naamah
brother: 9 Tubalcain
father: 6 Lamech
husband: 7 Solomon
mother: 6 Zillah
son: 8 Rehoboam

Naaman
disease: 7 leprosy
father: 4 Bela
grandfather: 8 Benjamin
healer: 6 Elisha

Naam's father
5 Caleb

Naarah's husband
6 Ashhur

nab
3 nip 4 hook, nail, take 5 catch, pinch, run in, seize, steal 6 arrest, clutch, collar, detain, pickup, pull in, snatch 7 capture, grapple 9 apprehend

nabal
5 chuff, hunks, miser, stiff 7 niggard, scrooge 8 muckworm, tightwad 9 skinflint 12 moneygrubber

Nabal's wife
7 Abigail

nabob
6 biggie, bigwig, fat cat 7 notable 8 big chief, eminence 9 dignitary 10 notability

Nabokov novel
3 Ada 4 Pnin 6 Lolita, The Eye 7 Despair, The Gift 8 Mashenka, Pale Fire, The Event 10 The Defense, The Exploit

nacre
13 mother-of-pearl

nada
7 nullity, vacuity 8 nihility 11 nothingness 12 nonexistence

Nadab
brother: 4 Kish 5 Abihu

father: 5 Aaron, Jeiel 6 Gibeon 8 Jeroboam
mother: 6 Maacah 8 Elisheba
slayer: 6 Baasha

nadir
4 base, foot 6 bottom
opposite: 6 zenith

nag
3 egg, irk, vex 4 bait, carp, fuss, goad, jade, prod, ride, urge 5 annoy, chivy, harry, hound, tease, worry 6 badger, bother, carp at, harass, heckle, hector, needle, peck at, pester, plague 7 henpeck, torment 8 harangue, irritate

Nahash's daughter
7 Abigail, Zeruiah

Nahath
father: 5 Reuel
grandfather: 7 Elkanah

Nahor
brother: 5 Haran 7 Abraham
concubine: 6 Reumah
father: 5 Serug, Terah
grandson: 7 Abraham
son: 5 Terah 7 Bethuel
wife: 6 Milcah

Nahshon
brother-in-law: 5 Aaron
father: 9 Amminadab
grandson: 4 Boaz
sister: 8 Elisheba
son: 6 Salmon

naiad
5 nymph

naif
7 ingenue

nail
3 bag, get 4 brad, spad, stud, tack, trap 5 catch, clone, spike, sprig 6 collar, secure, tacket, unguis, ungula 7 capture, prehend, ungulae (plural) 8 sparable
combining form: 4 helo, onyx 5 on-

ych, ungui 6 onycho 7 onychia 8 onychium

naive
4 easy 5 fresh 6 simple 7 artless, natural 8 gullible, innocent, original, unartful 9 ingenuous, unstudied 10 fleeceable, unaffected, unschooled 11 susceptible

naked
3 raw 4 bald, bare, mere, nude, open, pure 5 clear, sheer 6 meager, peeled, scanty, simple, unclad 7 denuded, evident, exposed, obvious, unarmed 8 buffbare, garbless, manifest, palpable, revealed, stripped 9 au naturel, colorless, destitute, disclosed, unclothed, uncolored, uncovered, undressed 10 discovered
combining form: 4 gymn, nudi 5 gymno

Naked and the Dead author
6 Mailer (Norman)

namby-pamby
3 sop 4 baby, flat 5 banal, bland, inane, sissy 6 jejune 7 doormat, insipid, milksop, sapless 8 weakling 9 driveling, innocuous, jellyfish 10 pantywaist, wishy-washy 11 Milquetoast, mollycoddle 12 milk-and-water 13 characterless

name
3 dub, nom, tab, tag, tap 4 call, cite, clan, make, race, term 5 alias, label, nomen, quote, state, style, title 6 byword, family, finger, handle, report, repute, rubric, ticket 7 appoint, baptize, declare, entitle, epithet, mention, moniker, notable, publish, specify 8 announce, christen, cognomen, identify, instance, luminary, monicker, nominate, somebody 9 advertise, celebrity, character, designate, incognito, pseudonym, recognize, sobriquet, stipulate 10 denominate, hypoco-

rism, nom de plume, notability, reputation **11** appellation, appellative, designation
ancient Rome: **7** agnomen **8** prenomen
assumed: **5** alias **9** sobriquet
combining form: **4** onym **7** onomato
family: **8** cognomen
fictitious: **9** pseudonym
giver: **6** eponym

namely
5 to wit **8** scilicet **9** expressly, specially, videlicet **10** especially **12** particularly, specifically
abbreviation: **3** viz

nana
5 nurse **9** nursemaid **11** nurserymaid

Nana
author: **4** Zola (Emile)
mother: **8** Gervaise

Nanna
brother: **6** Nergal, Ninazu
father: **5** Enlil
husband: **6** Balder
mother: **6** Ninlil
son: **3** Utu
wife: **6** Ningal

nanny
see nana

Naomi
4 Mara
daughter-in-law: **4** Ruth **5** Orpah
husband: **9** Elimelech
meaning: **8** pleasant
son: **6** Mahlon **7** Chilion

nap
3 nod **4** doze, rest, shag **5** break, cover, let up, pause, relax, sleep, unlax **6** drowse, siesta, snooze **7** respite **10** forty winks

nape
6 scruff

Naphish's father
7 Ishmael

Naphtali
brother: **3** Dan
father: **5** Jacob
mother: **6** Bilhah
son: **4** Guni **5** Jezer **7** Jahzeel, Jahziel, Shallum

naphtha
7 solvent **9** petroleum

napkin
5 cloth, doily, towel **9** handcloth

napoleon
4 boot **6** pastry **8** card game **9** solitaire
bid: **7** blucher **10** wellington

Napoleon
adversary: **6** Nelson (Horatio) **7** Kutuzov (Mikhail) **10** Wellington (Duke of)
birthplace: **7** Ajaccio (Corsica)
brother: **5** Louis **6** Jerome, Joseph, Lucien
brother-in-law: **5** Murat (Joachim)
deathplace: **8** St. Helena
defeat: **7** Leipzig **8** Waterloo **9** Trafalgar
father: **5** Carlo
island of exile: **4** Elba **8** St. Helena
marshal: **3** Ney (Michel) **5** Murat (Joachim), Soult (Nicolas-Jean) **6** Suchet
nickname: **14** Little Corporal
sister: **5** Maria **8** Carlotta, Carolina
victory: **3** Ulm **4** Jena, Lodi **5** Ligny **6** Abukir, Arcole, Wagram **7** Bautzen, Dresden, Marengo **8** Borodino **10** Austerlitz
wife: **9** Josephine **11** Marie Louise

narcissism
6 vanity **7** conceit **8** self-love, vainness **9** vainglory **10** self-esteem **11** amour propre, self-conceit **13** conceitedness

narcissistic
4 vain **7** stuck-up **8** conceity **9** conceited **12** vainglorious **13** self-conceited

Narcissus
father: **9** Cephissus
mother: **7** Liriope
rejected admirer: **4** Echo

narcotic
3 hop **4** dope, drug, junk **5** opium **6** heroin, opiate **7** anodyne, cocaine, hashish **8** hasheesh, hypnotic, morphine, nepenthe, somnific **9** somnolent, soporific **10** somnorific **11** somniferous, soporifical
peddler: **6** dealer, pusher

nark
3 rat **4** fink **5** peach, stool **6** canary, inform, snitch, squeak, squeal **7** tipster **8** betrayer, informer, squeaker, squealer **10** talebearer **11** stool pigeon

narrate
4 tell, yarn **5** state, story **6** detail, dilate, recite, relate, report **7** descant, recount **8** describe, rehearse **9** discourse

narrative
4 epic, myth, saga, tale, yarn **5** fable, story **6** legend, report **7** account, history, recital, version **8** anecdote **9** chronicle

medieval French: **5** roman **7** romance
prose: **5** novel **7** novella

narrow
3 set **4** mean **5** close, fixed, limit, small, taper, tense **6** lessen, little, meager, paltry, strait **7** bigoted, limited, precise **8** contract, decrease, definite, obdurate, straiten **9** confining, constrict, hidebound, illiberal **10** brassbound, constringe, inexorable, inflexible, intolerant, restricted

narrowly
6 barely **8** scarcely

narrow-minded
5 petty **7** bigoted, shallow **9** hidebound, illiberal **10** brassbound, intolerant, provincial, unenlarged

nasal
6 rhinal, twangy **9** nosepiece
combining form: **4** rhin **5** rhino

nascency
5 birth **6** origin

nascent
7 initial **9** beginning, inceptive, incipient **10** initiative, initiatory **12** introductory

Naseby victor
7 Fairfax (Thomas) **8** Cromwell (Oliver)

nasicorn
10 rhinoceros

nasty
4 evil, foul, icky, mean, vile **5** black, cheap, dirty, gross, snide, soily **6** coarse, filthy, grubby, horrid, impure, malign, oafish, ribald, smutty, tawdry, vulgar, wicked **7** hateful, ill-bred, obscene, raunchy, spitish, squalid, unclean, vicious **8** improper, indecent, spiteful, unseemly **9** loathsome, malicious, malignant, offensive, repugnant, repulsive, uncleanly, vexatious **10** disgusting, disturbing, indecorous, indelicate, malevolent

natant
8 swimming

Nathan
father: **4** Bani **5** Attai, David
son: **5** Zabad

national
4 home **5** civic, civil **6** public **7** citizen, subject **8** domestic, internal **9** intestine, municipal

National Basketball Association
Atlanta: 5 Hawks
Boston: 7 Celtics
Charlotte: 7 Hornets
Chicago: 5 Bulls
Cleveland: 9 Cavaliers
Dallas: 9 Mavericks
Denver: 7 Nuggets
Detroit: 7 Pistons
Golden State: 8 Warriors
Houston: 7 Rockets
Indiana: 6 Pacers
Los Angeles: 6 Lakers 8 Clippers
Miami: 4 Heat
Milwaukee: 5 Bucks
Minnesota: 12 Timberwolves
New Jersey: 4 Nets
New York: 6 Knicks
Orlando: 5 Magic
Phoenix: 4 Suns
Portland: 12 Trail Blazers
Sacramento: 5 Kings
San Antonio: 5 Spurs
Seattle: 11 SuperSonics
Toronto: 7 Raptors
Utah: 4 Jazz
Vancouver: 9 Grizzlies
Washington: 7 Bullets

National Football League
Arizona: 9 Cardinals
Atlanta: 7 Falcons
Buffalo: 5 Bills
Carolina: 8 Panthers
Chicago: 5 Bears
Cincinnati: 7 Bengals
Cleveland: 6 Browns
Dallas: 7 Cowboys
Denver: 7 Broncos
Detroit: 5 Lions
Green Bay: 7 Packers
Houston: 6 Oilers
Indianapolis: 5 Colts
Jacksonville: 7 Jaguars
Kansas City: 6 Chiefs
Los Angeles: 7 Raiders
Miami: 8 Dolphins
Minnesota: 7 Vikings
New England: 8 Patriots
New Orleans: 6 Saints
New York: 4 Jets 6 Giants
Philadelphia: 6 Eagles
Phoenix: 9 Cardinals
Pittsburgh: 8 Steelers
St. Louis: 4 Rams
San Diego: 8 Chargers
Seattle: 8 Seahawks
Tampa Bay: 4 Bucs
Washington: 8 Redskins

national historical park
Alaska: 5 Sitka
Idaho: 8 Nez Percé
Kentucky-Tennessee: 13 Cumberland Gap
Maryland-West Virginia: 12 Harpers Ferry
Massachusetts: 9 Minute Man
New York: 8 Saratoga

National Hockey League
Anaheim: 11 Mighty Ducks
Boston: 6 Bruins
Buffalo: 6 Sabres
Calgary: 6 Flames
Chicago: 10 Black Hawks
Colorado: 9 Avalanche
Dallas: 5 Stars
Detroit: 8 Red Wings
Edmonton: 6 Oilers
Florida: 8 Panthers
Hartford: 7 Whalers
Los Angeles: 5 Kings
Montreal: 9 Canadiens
New Jersey: 6 Devils
New York: 7 Rangers 9 Islanders
Ottawa: 8 Senators
Philadelphia: 6 Flyers
Pittsburgh: 8 Penguins
St. Louis: 5 Blues
San Jose: 6 Sharks
Tampa Bay: 9 Lightning
Toronto: 10 Maple Leafs
Vancouver: 7 Canucks
Washington: 8 Capitals
Winnipeg: 4 Jets

nationalism
10 patriotism
excessive: 8 jingoism 10 chauvinism

National League
Atlanta: 6 Braves
Chicago: 4 Cubs
Cincinnati: 4 Reds
Colorado: 7 Rockies
Florida: 7 Marlins
Houston: 6 Astros
Los Angeles: 7 Dodgers
Montreal: 5 Expos
New York: 4 Mets
Philadelphia: 8 Phillies
Pittsburgh: 7 Pirates
St. Louis: 9 Cardinals
San Diego: 6 Padres
San Francisco: 6 Giants

national military park
Alabama: 13 Horseshoe Bend
Arkansas: 8 Pea Ridge
Mississippi: 9 Vicksburg
Pennsylvania: 10 Gettysburg
South Carolina: 13 Kings Mountain
Tennessee: 6 Shiloh

national monument
Alabama: 11 Russell Cave
Alaska: 9 Aniakchak
Arizona: 5 Tonto 6 Navajo 7 Saguaro, Wupatki 8 Tuzigoot
10 Chiricahua, Pipe Spring, Tumacacori 11 Hohokam Pima 12 Sunset Crater, Walnut Canyon
California: 8 Cabrillo, Lava Beds 9 Muir Woods, Pinnacles 10 Joshua Tree 11 Death Valley
Colorado: 10 Yucca House
Colorado-Utah: 8 Dinosaur 9 Hovenweep
Florida: 12 Fort Matanzas 13 Fort Jefferson
Georgia: 8 Ocmulgee 11 Fort Pulaski 13 Fort Frederica
Iowa: 12 Effigy Mounds
Louisiana: 12 Poverty Point
Maryland: 11 Fort McHenry
Minnesota: 9 Pipestone 12 Grand Portage
Nebraska: 9 Homestead 11 Scotts Bluff
New Mexico: 5 Pecos 7 El Morro 9 Bandelier, El Malpais, Fort Union 10 Aztec Ruins, White Sands
New York: 11 Fort Stanwix 13 Castle Clinton
South Carolina: 10 Fort Sumter 13 Congaree Swamp
South Dakota: 9 Jewel Cave
Utah: 11 Cedar Breaks 13 Rainbow Bridge
Wyoming: 11 Devils Tower, Fossil Butte

national park
Alaska: 6 Denali, Katmai 9 Lake Clark 10 Glacier Bay 11 Kenai Fjords, Kobuk Valley
Angola: 4 Iona, Mupa
Arizona: 11 Grand Canyon
Arkansas: 10 Hot Springs
Botswana: 5 Chobe
California: 7 Redwood, Sequoia 8 Yosemite 11 King's Canyon
Chad: 5 Manda
Colombia: 5 Uraba
Colorado: 9 Mesa Verde 13 Rocky Mountain
eastern Africa: 10 Mount Kenya
Florida: 8 Biscayne 10 Everglades
Hawaii: 9 Haleakala
India: 5 Kanha
Japan: 5 Nikko
Kentucky: 11 Mammoth Cave
Kenya: 4 Meru 5 Tsavo 10 Royal Tsavo
Lake Superior: 10 Isle Royale
Maine: 6 Acadia
Malaysia: 8 Kinabalu
Minnesota: 9 Voyageurs
Montana: 7 Glacier
Nevada: 10 Great Basin
Oregon: 10 Crater Lake
Poland: 5 Ojcow, Tatra
South Africa: 6 Kruger

South Dakota: 8 Badlands, Wind Cave
Sri Lanka: 4 Yala
Sweden: 5 Sarek
Tanzania: 5 Ruaha 9 Serengeti
Texas: 7 Big Bend
Utah: 4 Zion 6 Arches 11 Bryce Canyon, Canyonlands, Capitol Reef
Virginia: 10 Shenandoah
Washington: 7 Olympic 12 Mount Rainier 13 North Cascades
Wyoming: 10 Grand Teton
Wyoming-Idaho-Montana: 11 Yellowstone
Zambia: 5 Kafue
Zimbabwe: 13 Rhodes Inyanga, Victoria Falls

native
3 raw 4 home, wild 5 crude, local 6 impure, inborn, innate, normal, simple 7 connate, endemic, indigen, natural 8 agrarian, agrestal, domestic, indigene, inherent, internal, national, ungraded, unsorted 9 inherited, intestine, municipal 10 aboriginal, congenital, connatural, indigenous, unacquired, unaffected
Acadian Louisiana: 5 Cajun
China: 3 Han 9 Celestial
India: 5 sepoy
Japan: 9 Nipponese
London: 7 Cockney
New England: 4 Yank 6 Yankee
New York: 13 Knickerbocker
suffix: 2 er 3 ese, ier, ite, ote, yer

Native Son author
6 Wright (Richard)

Nativity
4 noel, Xmas, yule 5 birth 8 yuletide 9 Christmas

natty
4 jimp 5 doggy, jimpy, sassy, smart 6 dapper, spiffy, spruce, sprucy 7 bandbox, doggish 11 well-groomed

natural
4 easy, feeb, fool, open, wild, zany 5 ament, frank, idiot, moron, naive, plain, typic, usual, white 6 candid, common, cretin, folksy, inborn, innate, native, normal, rustic, simple 7 artless, bastard, connate, general, genuine, half-wit, regular, sincere, typical 8 agrarian, agrestal, baseborn, homespun, ignorant, imbecile, inherent, innocent, spurious, unartful 9 blackjack, childlike, guileless, impulsive, ingenuous, ingrained, inherited, prevalent, primitive, simpleton, unfeigned, unla-

bored, unstudied, untutored, unworldly 10 congenital, fatherless, indigenous, legitimate, provincial, unacquired, unaffected, unfathered, unschooled 11 commonplace, instinctive, misbegotten, spontaneous, undesigning

naturalist
American: 4 Muir (John) 5 Hyatt (Alpheus) 7 Audubon (John James), Verrill (Addison, Alpheus)
English: 3 Ray (John) 5 White (Gilbert) 6 Darwin (Charles) 7 Wallace (Alfred) 10 Williamson (William)
French: 5 Fabre (Jean-Henri) 7 Lamarck (Chevalier de), Réaumur (René-Antoine)
Scottish: 6 Wilson (Alexander) 10 Richardson (John)

nature
3 ilk, way 4 kind, sort, type 5 being, humor, shape, world 6 cosmos, figure, kidney, kosmos, makeup, stripe, temper 7 anatomy, essence, texture, variety 8 creation, essentia, megacosm, universe 9 character, framework, macrocosm, normality 10 complexion 11 description, disposition, macrocosmos, personality, temperament 12 essentiality

naught
3 nil 4 zero 5 zilch 6 cipher, ruined 7 nothing 8 goose egg 11 nonexistent, nothingness 12 nonexistence

naughty
3 bad, paw 4 evil 5 rowdy 6 unruly, wicked 7 froward, wayward, willful 8 contrary, perverse 9 ruffianly 10 disorderly, headstrong, ill-behaved, indecorous, refractory 11 disobedient, intractable, misbehaving, mischievous 12 obstreperous, recalcitrant, ungovernable

nauseate
5 abhor, repel 6 loathe, reluct, revolt, sicken 7 disgust, repulse

nauseated
4 sick 6 queasy, queazy 7 carsick 9 squeamish

nauseating
4 foul, icky 5 nasty 7 noisome 9 loathsome, offensive, repugnant, repulsive, sickening

nauseous
see **nauseated**

Nausicaa
father: 8 Alcinous
mother: 5 Arete

nautical
5 naval 6 marine 7 oceanic 8 maritime 12 navigational
instrument: 3 aba 7 compass, pelorus, sextant

Navajo
dwelling: 5 hogan

naval hero
5 Jones (John Paul), Perry (Matthew, Oliver Hazard) 8 Farragut (David, George), Lawrence (James)

nave
3 hub

navel
6 middle 7 nombril 9 umbilicus 11 belly button
combining form: 6 omphal 7 omphalo

navigate
4 move, sail, walk 5 pilot, steer

navigation
6 voyage 7 passage 8 piloting, seacraft, shipping

navigational system
5 loran 6 shoran 7 teleran

navigator
5 flyer, pilot 6 airman 7 copilot
Danish: 6 Bering (Vitus)
Dutch: 6 Tasman (Abel) 7 Barents (Willem)
English: 4 Cook (Captain James) 5 Cabot (John, Sebastian), Drake (Francis) 6 Hudson (Henry) 7 Gilbert (Humphrey), Raleigh (Walter) 9 Vancouver (George)
French: 7 Cartier (Jacques) 9 La Perouse (Comte de)
Italian: 6 Caboto (Giovanni) 8 Columbus (Christopher), Vespucci (Amerigo) 9 Verrazano (Giovanni)
Norwegian: 4 Eric (the Red) 8 Ericsson 12 Leif Eriksson
Portuguese: 4 Dias (Bartolomeu, Dinis) 6 Cabral (Pedro Alvars), da Gama (Vasco) 8 Magellan (Ferdinand)
Spanish: 9 Fernandez (Juan)

navy
5 fleet

Nazi
9 Hitlerite 10 brownshirt
admiral: 6 Dönitz (Karl), Raeder (Erich) 7 Doenitz (Karl)
air force: 9 Luftwaffe
armed forces: 9 Wehrmacht
collaborator: 5 Laval (Pierre) 8 Quisling (Vidkun)
concentration camp: 6 Belsen, Dachau 9 Auschwitz 10 Buchenwald, Nordhausen

field marshal: 5 Model (Walter)
6 Keitel (Wilhelm), Paulus (Friedrich), Rommel (Erwin) 9 Rundstedt (Karl von) 10 Kesselring (Albert)
greeting: 4 Heil
leader: 3 Ley (Robert) 4 Hess (Rudolf), Röhm (Ernst) 5 Roehm (Ernst) 6 Führer, Göring (Hermann), Hitler (Adolph) 7 Fuehrer, Goering (Hermann), Himmler (Heinrich) 8 Goebbels (Joseph), Heydrich (Reinhard) 9 Rosenberg (Alfred)
police: 2 SS 7 Gestapo
propagandist: 8 Goebbels (Joseph)
submarine: 5 U-boat
surrender signer: 4 Jodl (Alfred) 6 Keitel (Wilhelm)
symbol: 6 fylfot 8 swastika
tactic: 10 blitzkrieg
tank: 6 panzer

NCO
3 cpl, sgt 8 corporal, sergeant

neap
4 tide

near
2 by 4 nigh 5 about, circa, close, round 6 almost, around, beside, narrow, stingy 7 close by, closely, close on 8 adjacent, approach, stingily 9 immediate, proximate, thriftily 10 intimately 11 approximate, at close hand, closefisted
combining form: 5 juxta
prefix: 2 ad, ep 3 eph, epi 4 peri, pros 5 plesi 6 plesio

nearby
4 nigh 5 about, aside, circa, close, handy, round 6 around, beside 7 closeby, close on, vicinal 8 adjacent 9 immediate, proximate 10 contiguous, convenient 11 neighboring

nearest
4 next 8 proximal

nearsighted
6 myopic

neat
3 net 4 deft, nice, prim, pure, snug, tidy, trig, trim 5 clean, clear, exact, kempt, plain 6 adroit, clever, dainty, dapper, spruce, sprucy 7 chipper, correct, finicky, orderly, precise, primsie, regular, unmixed 8 accurate, spotless, straight 9 ingenious, shipshape, undiluted 10 fastidious, gratifying, immaculate, methodical, systematic 11 uncluttered, well-groomed 12 spickand-span 13 unadulterated

neb
3 ear, nib, tip 4 beak, bill, nose 6 pecker

Nebaioth
brother: 5 Kedar
father: 7 Ishmael

Nebraska
capital: 7 Lincoln
college, university: 4 Dana 5 Doane 9 Creighton
Indian: 4 Otoe
largest city: 5 Omaha
state flower: 9 goldenrod

nebula
6 galaxy

nebulous
4 hazy 6 turbid 7 clouded 10 indistinct

necessary
5 vital 6 needed 7 certain 8 cardinal, inerrant, integral, unerring 9 essential, important, inerrable, mandatory, momentous, requisite 10 compelling, compulsory, imperative, ineludible, inevasible, inevitable, obligatory, unevadable 11 fundamental, ineluctable, inescapable, significant, unavoidable, unescapable 12 constraining, prerequisite 13 indispensable

necessitate
3 ask 4 take 5 crave 6 compel, demand 7 call for, require 9 constrain, force into

necessitous
see **needy**

necessity
4 call, must, need 5 cause 6 duress 7 poverty 8 coercion, exigency, occasion 9 condition, essential, requisite 10 compulsion, constraint, obligation, sine qua non 11 needfulness, requirement 12 precondition, prerequisite 13 requisiteness

neck
3 pet 4 kiss 5 beard 6 behead, cervix, collet, fondle, smooch, strait 7 embrace 8 gorgerin 9 decollate 10 decapitate, guillotine
back of: 4 nape 5 nucha 6 scruff
ornament: 6 gorget, torque

necklace
4 band 5 chain 6 locket 7 rivière 8 carcanet

neckpiece
3 boa 5 scarf

necktie
5 ascot 6 cravat 10 four-in-hand

adjunct: 6 tiepin 8 tie clasp

necrology
4 obit 8 obituary

necromancy
5 magic 7 sorcery 8 witchery, wizardry 9 conjuring, magicking 10 witchcraft 11 bewitchment, enchantment, thaumaturgy

necropolis
8 boneyard, boot hill, cemetery, God's acre 9 graveyard 12 burial ground

necropsy
7 autopsy 10 postmortem

need
3 use 4 call, duty, have, lack, long, must, pine, want, wish 5 claim, covet, crave, drive, exact, ought, yearn 6 charge, demand, desire, devoir, hanker, hunger, penury, thirst 7 deficit, poverty, require 8 exaction, exigency, occasion, poorness, shortage 9 committal, indigence, necessity, privation, requisite 10 commitment, compulsion, deficiency, dependence, obligation 11 destitution, requirement

neediness
4 want 6 penury 7 poverty 9 indigence, privation 11 destitution

needle
3 dun 5 annoy, tease, worry 6 harass, pester, plague 7 bedevil, hagride, obelisk, pricker, syringe
blunt: 6 bodkin
case: 4 etui
combining form: 3 acu
hole: 3 eye

needlefish
3 gar

needlelike
7 styloid 8 belonoid
part: 7 acicula

needlepoint lace
7 alençon

needle-shaped
6 acuate 7 acerose, acerous, aciform

needlework
6 sewing 7 crochet, sampler, seaming, tatting 8 knitting 10 crocheting, embroidery

needy
4 poor 6 hard up 8 dirt poor, indigent, strapped 9 destitute, penniless, penurious 11 impecunious, necessitous 12 impoverished, unprosperous

ne'er-do-well
6 bad lot, no-good, waster
7 rounder, wastrel 9 shiftless
10 profligate, scapegrace
11 incompetent

nefarious
4 rank 5 gross 6 putrid, rotten
7 corrupt, glaring, heinous 8 flagrant, infamous, perverse 9 miscreant, monstrous 10 degenerate, detestable, outrageous, villainous

negate
4 deny, undo, void 5 abate, annul, cross, quash 6 impugn 7 abolish, gainsay, nullify, redress, vitiate
8 negative, traverse 9 cancel out, disaffirm, frustrate 10 annihilate, contradict, contravene, counteract, invalidate, neutralize
12 countercheck

negative
2 no 3 nix 4 deny, kill, veto 5 annul, cross, minus 6 impugn 7 adverse, gainsay, nullify, redress, refusal 8 abrogate, disprove, traverse 9 cancel out, disaffirm, frustrate, non-placet 10 contradict, contravene, counteract, invalidate, neutralize 11 detrimental, unfavorable
battery terminal: 5 anode
ion: 5 anion
Scottish: 3 nae
sign: 5 minus

neglect
4 fail, miss, omit, pass 5 elide, scant, scorn, shirk 6 forget, ignore, pass by, reject, slight 7 blink at, default, disdain, dismiss, failure
8 brush off, discount, omission, overleap, overlook, overpass, pass over, shrug off, slur over 9 blink away, disregard, oversight, pretermit, shrug away 10 brush aside, slough over

neglectful
see **negligent**

negligee
4 gown 8 camisole 9 nightgown

negligent
3 lax 5 slack 6 remiss 7 offhand
8 careless, derelict, discinct, heedless, slipshod, slovenly 9 incurious, unheedful, unstudied 10 behindhand, delinquent, regardless, unthinking 11 inadvertent, inattentive, indifferent, thoughtless, unconcerned 12 disregardful 13 inconsiderate

negligible
4 slim 5 small 6 remote, slight
7 outside, slender 8 trifling

negotiate
4 leap, over 5 agree, clear, vault
6 adjust, handle, hurdle, manage, settle 7 arrange, bargain, compose, concert, conduct 8 complete, contract, covenant, overleap, surmount, transact 10 accomplish

Nehemiah's father
5 Azbuk 9 Hachaliah

Nehushta
father: 8 Elnathan
husband: 9 Jehoiakim
son: 10 Jehoiachin

neigh
6 nicker, whinny 7 snicker, snigger

neighbor
4 abut, join, line 5 march, touch, verge 6 adjoin, border, butt on, corner 8 border on

neighborhood
4 area, tune 5 order, range 6 extent, matter 8 district, locality, vicinage, vicinity 9 magnitude, proximity

neighborly
6 social 7 cordial 8 amicable, friendly, gracious, sociable 10 gregarious, hospitable 11 cooperative

nematode
4 worm 7 eelworm 9 roundworm

Nemean predator
4 lion

neon
3 gas
symbol: 2 Ne

neonate
see **newborn**

neophyte
see **newcomer**

Neoptolemus
7 Pyrrhus
father: 8 Achilles
slayer: 7 Orestes
victim: 5 Priam
wife: 8 Hermione

Nepal
capital: 8 Katmandu 9 Kathmandu
forest land: 5 Terai
monetary unit: 5 rupee

nepenthe
6 opiate 7 anodyne 8 narcotic

Nepheg
brother: 5 Korah 6 Zichri
father: 5 David, Izhar

Nephele
daughter: 5 Helle
husband: 7 Athamas
son: 7 Phrixos, Phrixus

Nephthys
brother, husband: 3 Set 4 Seth

Neptune
6 planet
satellite: 6 Nereid, Triton; (see also Poseidon)

Ner
father: 5 Abiel, Jeiel
son: 5 Abner

Nereides
6 Thetis 7 Galatea 10 Amphitrite
father: 6 Nereus
mother: 5 Doris

Nereus
daughters: 8 Nereides
emblem: 7 trident
father: 6 Pontus
mother: 2 Ge 4 Gaea
wife: 5 Doris

Nergal
brother: 5 Nanna 6 Ninazu
father: 5 Enlil
mother: 6 Ninlil

Neriah
father: 8 Maaseiah
son: 6 Baruch 7 Seraiah

Nerissa's husband
8 Gratiano

Nero
birthplace: 4 Rome
mother: 9 Agrippina
successor: 5 Galba
tutor: 6 Seneca
victim: 5 Lucan 6 Seneca 7 Octavia, Poppaea 9 Agrippina
wife: 7 Octavia, Poppaea

Nero Wolfe creator
5 Stout (Rex)

nerve
4 face, gall, grit, guts, sand, vein
5 brass, cheek, cheer, crust, heart, moxie, spunk, steel 6 daring 7 animate, chirk up, hearten, sciatic, stamina 8 audacity, backbone, boldness, embolden, inspirit, strength, temerity 9 assurance, brashness, encourage, enhearten, fortitude, hardihood, hardiness
10 confidence, effrontery, strengthen 11 presumption
cell: 6 neuron
cell group: 7 ganglia (plural)
8 ganglion
combining form: 4 neur 5 neura, neuro

cranial: **4** vagi (plural) **5** optic, vagus **8** abducens
ending: **8** receptor
lesion: **8** neuritis

nerve center
3 hub **4** seat **5** focus, heart **8** polestar **10** focal point

nervous
4 edgy **5** jerky, jumpy, timid **6** feisty, goosey, spooky **7** fidgety, fretful, jittery, uptight, waspish **8** aflutter, agitated, critical, forcible, skittery, skittish, snappish, spirited, twittery, unsteady, volatile **9** difficult, excitable, irritable, querulous, unrestful **10** high-strung **12** apprehensive

nervy
4 bold, edgy, pert, wise **5** brash, fresh, jerky, jumpy, sassy, smart, tense **6** cheeky, goosey, spooky, uneasy **7** fidgety, forward, jittery, restive, twitchy, uptight **8** impudent, intrepid, twittery **9** excitable, unrestful **10** high-strung **11** smart-alecky

ness
4 cape **8** headland **10** promontory

Nessus' victim
8 Heracles, Hercules

nest
3 den **4** aery, home, lair, nidi (plural) **5** aerie, eyrie, nidus **6** nidify **7** hangout, shelter **8** smuggery **11** aggregation
eagle's: **4** aery **5** aerie, eyrie
wasp's: **8** vespiary

nest egg
5 hoard, stock, store **7** backlog, reserve **9** inventory, reservoir, stockpile

nestle
4 snug **5** house **6** burrow, cuddle, nuzzle **7** shelter, snuggle

Nestor
father: **6** Neleus
kingdom: **5** Pylos

net
4 gain, gist, make, mesh, pure **5** basic, catch, clear, seine, tulle, yield **6** maline **7** clean up, essence, malines
combining form: **5** dicty **6** dictyo
conical: **5** trawl
fishing: **5** seine
hair: **5** snood

Nethanel
brother: **5** David

father: **5** Jesse **7** Pashhur **8** Obededom
son: **8** Shemaiah

Nethaniah's father
5 Asaph **6** Jehudi **7** Ishmael

nether
3 low **5** lower, under **6** lesser **8** inferior **9** subjacent

Netherlands
capital: **9** Amsterdam
de facto capital: **8** The Hague
monetary unit: **6** florin, gulden **7** guilder
patron saint: **10** Willibrord
piano city: **3** Ede

netherworld
3 pit **4** hell **5** abyss, hades, Sheol **6** blazes **7** inferno **9** perdition **11** Pandemonium

netlike
9 reticular **10** reticulate

nettle
3 get, vex **4** huff, rile, roil **5** peeve, pique, upset **6** incite, put out, stir up **7** agitate, disturb, perturb, provoke **8** irritate **10** discompose, exasperate

nettle rash
5 hives **9** urticaria

nettlesome
5 spiny **6** thorny **7** prickly **9** irritable **10** irritating

network
3 web **4** mesh **8** gridiron **9** reticulum
anatomical: **4** rete **5** retia (plural)

neurotic
6 phobic **7** nervous **8** unstable **9** obsessive **10** compulsive

neuter
3 fix **4** geld **5** alter, unsex **6** change, worker **7** sexless **8** castrate, mutilate **9** sterilize **11** desexualize **12** intransitive

neutral
4 calm, cool, easy **5** aloof **6** normal **7** hueless, relaxed **8** abstract, clinical, composed, detached, middling, unbiased **9** collected, colorless, impartial **10** achromatic, impersonal, nonchalant, pokerfaced **11** indifferent, unpassioned **13** disinterested, dispassionate

neutralize
5 annul **6** defeat, negate, offset, subdue **7** balance, conquer, nullify, redress **8** abrogate, negative, overcome, override, overrule **9** cancel

out, frustrate **10** compensate, counteract, invalidate **11** countervail **12** countercheck, counterpoise

Nevada
capital: **10** Carson City
largest city: **8** Las Vegas
nickname: **11** Silver State **14** Sagebrush State
state flower: **9** sagebrush

névé
4 firn, snow

never-ending
7 endless, eternal **8** immortal **9** ceaseless **11** amaranthine, everlasting

never-failing
4 firm, sure **6** steady **7** abiding **8** enduring **9** steadfast **11** unfaltering, unqualified **12** wholehearted **13** unquestioning

nevertheless
3 but, yet **5** still **6** though, withal **7** howbeit, however **8** after all **11** still and all

nevus
4 mole **9** birthmark

new
5 fresh, novel **6** afresh, lately, modern, of late, recent **7** another, revived, strange **8** neoteric, pristine **9** first-hand, recreated, refreshed, renovated **10** additional, unfamiliar **11** modernistic, regenerated **12** unaccustomed **13** reinvigorated
combining form: **2** ne **3** cen, neo, nov **4** caen, ceno, novo **5** caeno
word: **7** coinage, neology **9** neologism

newcomer
4 colt, tyro **6** novice, rookie **8** beginner, chechako, freshman, neophyte **9** immigrant, novitiate **10** apprentice, tenderfoot

New Deal agency
3 CCC, NRA, TVA, WPA

Newfoundland
capital: **10** Saint Johns
discoverer: **5** Cabot (John)
part: **8** Labrador

new gas
4 neon

New Hampshire
capital: **7** Concord
college: **9** Dartmouth **10** Keene State **12** Saint Anselms
highest point: **12** Mt. Washington
largest city: **10** Manchester
motto: **13** Live Free or Die
nickname: **12** Granite State

state bird: 11 purple finch
state flower: 11 purple lilac

New Jersey
capital: 7 Trenton
college, university: 4 Drew 6 Upsala
7 Rutgers 9 Princeton, Seton Hall
10 Bloomfield 11 Saint Peters
largest city: 6 Newark
nickname: 11 Garden State
state bird: 9 goldfinch
state flower: 6 violet

New Mexico
capital: 7 Santa Fe
largest city: 11 Albuquerque
state bird: 10 roadrunner
state flower: 5 yucca

news
4 dope, poop, word 5 rumor 6 advice, gossip, report, tattle 7 lowdown, tidings 9 knowledge, speerings 11 information, scuttlebutt
12 announcement, intelligence
agency: 2 AP 3 UPI 4 Tass
7 Reuters

newspaper
5 daily, organ 6 review 7 journal, tabloid 8 magazine 10 periodical
publisher: 6 Hearst (William Randolph)

newt
3 eft 6 triton
green: 5 ebbet

New Testament
see at **Bible**

New York
academy, college, (university): 3 RPI
4 Iona, Pace, SUNY 5 Keuka, Kings, Nyack, Pratt, Siena, Utica
6 CW Post, Elmira, Hunter, Ithaca, Marist, Queens, Vassar 7 Adelphi, Colgate, Cornell, Fordham, Hofstra, Niagara, St. Johns, Yeshiva
8 Brooklyn, Canisius, Columbia, Hamilton, Hartwick, Skidmore, Syracuse 9 Juilliard, Manhattan, St. Francis, St. Josephs, West Point
10 Long Island 13 Sarah Lawrence, St. Bonaventure
capital: 6 Albany
motto: 9 Excelsior 10 Ever Upward
nickname: 11 Empire State
state flower: 4 rose

New York City
6 Gotham
borough: 5 Bronx 6 Queens
8 Brooklyn, Richmond 9 Manhattan

New Zealand
capital: 10 Wellington
discoverer: 6 Tasman (Abel)

monetary unit: 6 dollar
parrot: 3 kea

next
4 then 5 after, below, infra, later, since 6 behind, coming, second
7 by and by, closest, ensuing 8 latterly 9 afterward, following, proximate 10 afterwhile, contiguous, succeeding

nexus
3 tie 4 bond, knot, link, yoke 8 ligament, ligature, vinculum
10 connection

Nez Percé chief
6 Joseph

niagara
5 flood, spate 6 deluge 7 torrent
8 cataract, flooding, overflow
9 cataclysm 10 inundation

nib
4 beak, bill 5 tooth 6 pecker
8 pen point

nibble
4 bite, gnaw, peck, pick

Nicanor's father
9 Patroclus

Nicaragua
capital: 7 Managua
monetary unit: 7 cordoba
neighbor: 8 Honduras 9 Costa Rica

nice
4 fine, good, mild, neat, rare, sage, wise 5 exact, fussy, picky, right, rigid 6 benign, chaste, choosy, comely, dainty, decent, proper, queasy, seemly, strict, subtle 7 affable, careful, clement, correct, finical, finicky, fitting, precise, refined, welcome 8 accurate, becoming, clerkish, decorous, delicate, finespun, hairline, picksome, pleasant, pleasing, precieux, precious, rigorous, suitable, virtuous 9 agreeable, befitting, congenial, enjoyable, exquisite, favorable, finicking, judicious 10 attractive, conforming, delightful, discerning, fastidious, gratifying, meticulous, old-maidish, particular, pernickety, personable, scrupulous

niche
4 nook 5 place 6 cranny, crater, nestle, recess 7 byplace, secrete

Nicholas Nickleby author
7 Dickens (Charles)

nick
4 deny, hack 5 cut in, notch, score, snipe 6 charge, record 9 indenture
11 indentation

nickname
3 tag 5 label, style 6 byword, handle 7 epithet, miscall, moniker
8 cognomen 9 sobriquet
10 hypocorism

Nicomede
conquest: 10 Cappodocia
dramatist: 9 Corneille (Pierre)
half-brother: 6 Attale
stepmother: 7 Arsinoë

nictate
3 bat 4 wink 5 blink 7 twinkle

nictitate
see **nictate**

nifty
4 cool, keen, neat 5 adept, dandy, dilly, handy, peach, smart, super, swell 6 clever, corker, groovy, peachy 7 stylish 8 jim-dandy, knockout, splendid, terrific

Niger
capital: 6 Niamey
export: 7 uranium
monetary unit: 5 franc

Nigeria
capital: 5 Lagos
monetary unit: 5 naira
people: 3 Ibo 4 Igbo
product: 3 tin 4 coal 5 cocoa
6 rubber

niggard
5 miser

niggardly
5 close, tight 6 scanty, stingy 7 miserly 9 penurious 11 closefisted, tightfisted 12 cheeseparing, parsimonious 13 penny-pinching

niggling
5 petty 6 measly, paltry, peanut
8 picayune, piddling, trifling
10 picayunish

nigh
2 by 4 near 5 about, circa, close, round 6 all but, almost, around, beside, nearby, nearly 7 close on
8 approach 9 immediate, proximate 10 near-at-hand 11 approximate, at close hand, practically

night blindness
10 nyctalopia

nightfall
3 eve 4 dusk, even 6 sunset 7 evening, sundown 8 eventide, gloaming, owl-light, twilight

nighthawk
6 petrel 7 bullbat 10 goatsucker
Australian: 8 morepork

nightingale
6 thrush

nightjar
5 potoo 10 goatsucker

nightly
9 nocturnal

nightmare
5 dream, fancy, worry 6 vision
7 fantasy, incubus 8 daydream,
phantasm, phantasy, succubus
12 apprehension

nightshade
7 henbane 10 belladonna
weedy: 11 bittersweet

nightstick
3 bat 4 club, mace 5 baton, billy
6 cudgel 8 bludgeon 9 billy club,
truncheon

Nike
father: 6 Pallas
mother: 4 Styx

nil
4 zero 6 naught, nought 7 nothing
11 nonexistent

Nile
6 Al-Bahr
dam: 6 Makwar 9 Aswan High
10 Gebel Aulia
explorer: 5 Baker (Sir Samuel), Bruce
(James), Grant (James Augustus),
Speke (John Hanning)
queen: 4 Cleo 9 Cleopatra
section: 4 Abai, Abay 5 Abbai

nilgai
8 antelope, blue bull

nimble
3 yar 4 deft, spry, yare 5 agile,
alert, brisk, catty, fleet, handy,
light, quick, zippy 6 active, adroit,
brisky, clever, limber, lively 8 vigilant, watchful 9 dexterous, lightsome, sprightly, wide-awake

nimble-witted
3 hep 4 wise 5 canny, quick,
sharp, slick, smart 7 knowing

Nimrod
6 hunter
father: 4 Cush

Ninazu
brother: 5 Nanna 6 Nergal
father: 5 Enlil
mother: 6 Ninlil

nincompoop
3 ass 4 fool, jerk 5 idiot, ninny
6 donkey 7 jackass, tomfool
8 imbecile 9 simpleton

nine
12 baseball team

combining form: 3 non 4 nona
5 ennea
goddesses: 5 Muses
group: 6 ennead
inches: 4 span
instruments: 5 nonet

nine day devotion
6 novena

Nine Worlds
3 Hel 6 Asgard 7 Alfheim, Midgard 8 Niflheim, Vanaheim
10 Jotunnheim 12 Muspellsheim
13 Svartalfaheim

ninny
see **nincompoop**

Ninsun's son
9 Gilgamesh

ninth
combining form: 3 non 4 nona

Nintu
consort: 4 Enki
son: 6 Ninsar

Ninurta
father: 5 Enlil
victim: 3 Kur

Ninus
father: 5 Belus
wife: 9 Semiramis

Niobe
brother: 6 Pelops
father: 8 Tantalus
husband: 7 Amphion
sister-in-law: 5 Aedon

nip
3 bit, dig, hop, nab 4 balk, dart,
dash, dram, drop, hook, jolt, jump,
lift, nail, peck, shot, slug, soak,
swig 5 blast, booze, check, chill,
clamp, drink, hurry, pinch, sever,
snort, steal, swill 6 arrest, blight,
guzzle, imbibe, snatch, tank up,
thwart, tipple 7 cabbage, snifter,
swizzle 8 compress, cutpurse, liquor up, piquancy, toothful 9 frustrate 10 pickpocket

nipper
3 bud, kid 4 rack 5 chick, child
6 cunner, moppet 8 brakeman, juvenile, young one 9 youngling,
youngster

nipping
3 icy 4 cold, cool 5 chill, sharp
6 arctic, chilly, frosty 7 caustic, glacial, shivery 8 freezing

nipple
3 pap 4 teat 8 mammilla
combining form: 4 mast 5 masto
6 papill 7 papillo

nipple-shaped
9 mammiform

Nippon
5 Japan

nippy
see **nipping**

nirvana
4 Zion 5 bliss, dream 6 Canaan,
heaven 7 elysium 8 empyrean,
oblivion, paradise 10 Civitas Dei
12 New Jerusalem

nisse
3 elf, fay 5 fairy, pixie 6 kobold,
sprite 7 brownie

Nisus
betrayer, daughter: 6 Scylla
father: 7 Pandion

nitid
6 bright, glossy 8 lustrous

nitrogen
5 azote
combining form: 2 az 3 azo

nitwit
4 dope, simp 5 cluck, dunce 7 pinhead 9 dumb bunny, dumb cluck,
simpleton

nix
2 no 3 nay 4 kill, nope, veto
6 naught, nought 7 nothing
8 negative

Njord, Njorth
daughter: 5 Freya
son: 4 Frey
wife: 6 Skadhi, Skathi

no
3 nae, nay, nix 6 denial
combining form: 5 nulli

no-account
see **no-good**

Noachian
3 old 4 aged 5 hoary 6 age-old
7 ancient, antique 8 timeworn
9 venerable 12 antediluvian

Noah
father: 6 Lamech 10 Zelophehad
grandson: 4 Aram 6 Canaan
great grandson: 3 Hul
landing place: 6 Ararat
son: 3 Ham 4 Shem 6 Canaan
7 Japheth

Nobel Prize Winner
chemistry:
1901: 8 van't Hoff (Jacobus)
1902: 7 Fischer (Emil)
1903: 9 Arrhenius (Svante)
1904: 6 Ramsay (William)
1905: 9 von Baeyer (Adolph)
1906: 7 Moissan (Henri)

1907: 7 Buchner (Eduard)
1908: 10 Rutherford (Ernest)
1909: 7 Ostwald (Wilhelm)
1910: 7 Wallach (Otto)
1911: 5 Curie (Marie)
1912: 8 Grignard (François), Sabatier (Paul)
1913: 6 Werner (Alfred)
1914: 8 Richards (Theodore)
1915: 11 Willstatter (Richard)
1918: 5 Haber (Fritz)
1920: 7 Nernst (Walther)
1921: 5 Soddy (Frederick)
1922: 5 Aston (Francis)
1923: 5 Pregl (Fritz)
1925: 9 Zsigmondy (Richard)
1926: 8 Svedberg (Theodor)
1927: 7 Wieland (Heinrich)
1928: 7 Windaus (Adolf)
1929: 6 Harden (Athur) 12 Euler-Chelpin (Hans)
1930: 7 Fischer (Hans)
1931: 5 Bosch (Carl) 7 Bergius (Friedrich)
1932: 8 Langmuir (Irving)
1934: 4 Urey (Harold)
1935: 11 Joliot-Curie (Frederic, Irene)
1936: 5 Debye (Peter)
1937: 6 Karrer (Paul) 7 Haworth (Walter)
1938: 5 Kuhn (Richard)
1939: 7 Ruzicka (Leopold) 9 Butenandt (Adolph)
1943: 6 Hevesy (Georg von)
1944: 4 Hahn (Otto)
1945: 8 Virtanen (Artturi)
1946: 6 Sumner (James) 7 Stanley (Wendell) 8 Northrup (John)
1947: 8 Robinson (Robert)
1948: 8 Tiselius (Arne)
1949: 7 Giauque (William)
1950: 5 Alder (Kurt), Diels (Otto)
1951: 7 Seaborg (Glenn) 8 McMillan (Edwin)
1952: 5 Synge (Richard) 6 Martin (Archer)
1953: 10 Staudinger (Hermann)
1954: 7 Pauling (Linus)
1955: 10 du Vigneaud (Vincent)
1956: 7 Semenov (Nikolay) 11 Hinshelwood (Cyril)
1957: 4 Todd (Alexander)
1958: 6 Sanger (Frederick)
1959: 9 Heyrovsky (Jaroslav)
1960: 5 Libby (Willard)
1961: 6 Calvin (Melvin)
1962: 6 Perutz (Max) 7 Kendrew (John)
1963: 5 Natta (Giulio) 7 Ziegler (Karl)
1964: 7 Hodgkin (Dorothy) 8 Woodward (Robert)
1966: 8 Mulliken (Robert)

1967: 5 Eigen (Manfred) 6 Porter (George) 7 Norrish (Ronald)
1968: 7 Onsager (Lars)
1969: 6 Barton (Derek), Hassel (Odd)
1970: 6 Leloir (Luis)
1971: 8 Herzberg (Gerhard)
1972: 5 Moore (Stanford), Stein (William) 8 Anfinsen (Christian)
1973: 7 Fischer (Ernst) 9 Wilkinson (Geoffrey)
1974: 5 Flory (Paul)
1975: 6 Prelog (Vladimir) 9 Cornforth (John)
1976: 8 Lipscomb (William)
1977: 9 Prigogine (Ilya)
1978: 8 Mitchell (Peter)
1979: 5 Brown (Herbert) 6 Wittig (Georg)
1980: 4 Berg (Paul) 6 Sanger (Frederick) 7 Gilbert (Walter)
1981: 5 Fukui (Kenichi) 8 Hoffmann (Roald)
1982: 4 Klug (Aaron)
1983: 5 Taube (Henry)
1984: 10 Merrifield (R. Bruce)
1985: 5 Karle (Jerome) 8 Hauptman (Herbert)
1986: 3 Lee (Yuan) 7 Polanyi (John) 10 Herschbach (Dudley)
1987: 4 Cram (Donald), Lehn (Jean-Marie) 8 Pedersen (Charles)
1988: 5 Huber (Robert) 6 Michel (Hartmut) 11 Deisenhofer (Johann)
1989: 4 Cech (Thomas) 6 Altman (Sidney)
1990: 5 Corey (Elias)
1991: 5 Ernst (Richard)
1992: 5 Marcus (Rudolph)
1993: 5 Smith (Michael) 6 Mullis (Kary)
1994: 4 Olah (George)
1995: 6 Molina (Mario) 7 Crutzen (Paul), Rowland (F. Sherwood)

economics:
1969: 6 Frisch (Ragnar) 9 Tinbergen (Jan)
1970: 9 Samuelson (Paul)
1971: 7 Kuznets (Simon)
1972: 5 Arrow (Kenneth), Hicks (John)
1973: 8 Leontief (Wassily)
1974: 5 Hayek (Friedrich von) 6 Myrdal (Gunnar)
1975: 8 Koopmans (Tjalling) 11 Kantorovich (Leonid)
1976: 8 Friedman (Milton)
1977: 5 Meade (James), Ohlin (Bertil)
1978: 5 Simon (Herbert)
1979: 5 Lewis (Arthur) 7 Schultz (Theodore)
1980: 5 Klein (Lawrence)
1981: 5 Tobin (James)

1982: 7 Stigler (George)
1983: 6 Debreu (Gerard)
1984: 5 Stone (Richard)
1985: 10 Modigliani (Franco)
1986: 8 Buchanan (James)
1987: 5 Solow (Robert)
1988: 6 Allais (Maurice)
1989: 8 Haavelmo (Trygve)
1990: 6 Miller (Merton), Sharpe (William) 9 Markowitz (Harry)
1991: 5 Coase (Ronald)
1992: 6 Becker (Gary)
1993: 5 Fogel (Robert), North (Douglass)
1994: 4 Nash (John) 6 Selten (Reinhard) 8 Harsanyi (John)
1995: 5 Lucas (Robert)

literature:
1901: 9 Prudhomme (Sully)
1902: 7 Mommsen (Theodor)
1903: 8 Bjornson (Bjornstjerne)
1904: 7 Mistral (Frederic) 9 Echegaray (Jose)
1905: 11 Sienkiewicz (Henryk)
1906: 8 Carducci (Giosue)
1907: 7 Kipling (Rudyard)
1908: 6 Eucken (Rudolf)
1909: 8 Lagerlof (Selma)
1910: 8 von Heyse (Paul)
1911: 11 Maeterlinck (Maurice)
1912: 9 Hauptmann (Gerhart)
1913: 6 Tagore (Rabindranath)
1915: 7 Rolland (Romain)
1916: 13 von Heidenstam (Verner)
1917: 9 Gjellerup (Karl) 11 Pontoppidan (Henrik)
1919: 9 Spitteler (Carl)
1920: 6 Hamsun (Knut)
1921: 6 France (Anatole)
1922: 9 Benavente (Jacinto)
1923: 5 Yeats (William Butler)
1924: 7 Reymont (Wladyslaw)
1925: 4 Shaw (George Bernard)
1926: 7 Deledda (Grazia)
1927: 7 Bergson (Henri)
1928: 6 Undset (Sigrid)
1929: 4 Mann (Thomas)
1930: 5 Lewis (Sinclair)
1931: 9 Karlfeldt (Erik Axel)
1932: 10 Galsworthy (John)
1933: 5 Bunin (Ivan)
1934: 12 Pirandello (Luigi)
1936: 6 O'Neill (Eugene)
1937: 12 Martin du Gard (Roger)
1938: 4 Buck (Pearl)
1939: 9 Sillanpaa (Frans Eemil)
1944: 6 Jensen (Johannes)
1945: 7 Mistral (Gabriela)
1946: 5 Hesse (Hermann)
1947: 4 Gide (Andre)
1948: 5 Eliot (Thomas Stearns)
1949: 8 Faulkner (William)
1950: 7 Russell (Bertrand)
1951: 10 Lagerkvist (Par Fabian)

1952: **7** Mauriac (Francois)
1953: **9** Churchill (Winston)
1954: **9** Hemingway (Ernest)
1955: **7** Laxness (Halldor)
1956: **7** Jimenez (Juan Ramon)
1957: **5** Camus (Albert)
1958: **9** Pasternak (Boris)
1959: **9** Quasimodo (Salvatore)
1960: **5** Perse (Saint-John)
1961: **6** Andric (Ivo)
1962: **9** Steinbeck (John)
1963: **7** Seferis (George)
1964: **6** Sartre (Jean-Paul)
1965: **9** Sholokhov (Mikhail)
1966: **5** Agnon (Shmuel Yosef), Sachs (Nelly)
1967: **8** Asturias (Miguel Angel)
1968: **8** Kawabata (Yasunari)
1969: **7** Beckett (Samuel)
1970: **12** Solzhenitsyn (Alexander)
1971: **6** Neruda (Pablo)
1972: **4** Böll (Heinrich)
1973: **5** White (Patrick)
1974: **7** Johnson (Eyvind) **9** Martinson (Edmund)
1975: **7** Montale (Eugenio)
1976: **6** Bellow (Saul)
1977: **10** Aleixandre (Vicente)
1978: **6** Singer (Isaac Bashevis)
1979: **6** Elytis (Odysseus)
1980: **6** Milosz (Czeslaw)
1981: **7** Canetti (Elias)
1982: **13** Garcia Marquez (Gabriel)
1983: **7** Golding (William)
1984: **7** Siefert (Jaroslav)
1985: **5** Simon (Claude)
1986: **7** Soyinka (Wole)
1987: **7** Brodsky (Joseph)
1988: **7** Mahfouz (Naguib)
1989: **4** Cela (Camilo Jose)
1990: **3** Paz (Octavio)
1991: **8** Gordimer (Nadine)
1992: **7** Walcott (Derek)
1993: **8** Morrison (Toni)
1994: **2** Oe (Kenzaburo)
1995: **6** Heaney (Seamus)

peace:
1901: **5** Passy (Frederic) **6** Dunant (Jean-Henri)
1902: **5** Gobat (Charles Albert) **8** Ducommun (Elie)
1903: **6** Cremer (William)
1905: **10** von Suttner (Bertha)
1906: **9** Roosevelt (Theodore)
1907: **6** Moneta (Ernesto) **7** Renault (Louis)
1908: **5** Bajer (Fredrik) **9** Arnoldson (Klas Pontus)
1909: **9** Beernaert (Auguste) **13** d'Estournelles (Paul)
1911: **5** Asser (Tobias), Fried (Alfred)

1912: **4** Root (Elihu)
1913: **10** La Fontaine (Henri)
1919: **6** Wilson (Woodrow)
1920: **9** Bourgeois (Leon)
1921: **5** Lange (Christian Louis) **8** Branting (Karl Hjalmar)
1922: **6** Nansen (Fridtjof)
1925: **5** Dawes (Charles) **11** Chamberlain (Austen)
1926: **6** Briand (Aristide) **10** Stresemann (Gustav)
1927: **6** Quidde (Ludwig) **7** Buisson (Ferdinand)
1929: **7** Kellogg (Frank)
1930: **9** Soderblom (Nathan)
1931: **6** Addams (Jane), Butler (Nicholas)
1933: **6** Angell (Norman)
1934: **9** Henderson (Arthur)
1935: **9** Ossietzky (Carl von)
1936: **13** Saavedra Lamas (Carlos)
1937: **5** Cecil (Robert)
1945: **4** Hull (Cordell)
1946: **4** Mott (John) **5** Balch (Emily Greene)
1949: **3** Orr (John Boyd)
1950: **6** Bunche (Ralph)
1951: **7** Jouhaux (Leon)
1952: **10** Schweitzer (Albert)
1953: **8** Marshall (George)
1957: **7** Pearson (Lester)
1958: **4** Pire (Dominique Georges)
1959: **9** Noel-Baker (Philip)
1960: **7** Luthuli (Albert John)
1961: **12** Hammarskjold (Dag)
1962: **7** Pauling (Linus)
1964: **4** King (Martin Luther)
1968: **6** Cassin (Rene)
1970: **7** Borlaug (Norman)
1971: **6** Brandt (Willy)
1973: **8** Le Duc Tho **9** Kissinger (Henry)
1974: **4** Sato (Eisaku) **8** MacBride (Sean)
1975: **8** Sakharov (Andrey)
1976: **8** Corrigan (Mairead), Williams (Betty)
1978: **5** Begin (Menachem), Sadat (Anwar el-)
1979: **12** Mother Teresa
1980: **8** Esquivel (Adolfo Perez)
1982: **6** Myrdal (Alva) **12** Garcia Robles (Alfonso)
1983: **6** Walesa (Lech)
1984: **4** Tutu (Desmond)
1986: **6** Wiesel (Elie)
1987: **12** Arias Sanchez (Oscar)
1989: **9** Dalai Lama
1990: **9** Gorbachev (Mikhail)
1991: **13** Aung San Suu Kyi
1992: **6** Menchu (Rigoberta)
1993: **7** de Klerk (Frederik), Mandela (Nelson)

1994: **5** Peres (Shimon), Rabin (Yitzhak) **6** Arafat (Yasir)
1995: **7** Rotblat (Joseph)

physics:
1901: **8** Roentgen (Wilhelm)
1902: **6** Zeeman (Pieter) **7** Lorentz (Hendrik Antoon)
1903: **5** Curie (Marie, Pierre) **9** Becquerel (Antoine-Henri)
1904: **8** Rayleigh (Lord)
1905: **6** Lenard (Philipp)
1906: **7** Thomson (Joseph John)
1907: **9** Michelson (Albert)
1908: **8** Lippmann (Gabriel)
1909: **5** Braun (Karl) **7** Marconi (Guglielmo)
1910: **11** van der Waals (Johannes)
1911: **4** Wien (Wilhelm)
1912: **5** Dalen (Nils)
1914: **7** von Laue (Max)
1915: **5** Bragg (Wilham)
1917: **6** Barkla (Charles)
1918: **6** Planck (Max)
1919: **6** Stark (Johannes)
1920: **9** Guillaume (Charles)
1921: **8** Einstein (Albert)
1922: **4** Bohr (Niels)
1923: **8** Millikan (Robert)
1924: **8** Siegbahn (Karl)
1925: **5** Hertz (Gustav) **6** Franck (James)
1926: **6** Perrin (Jean-Baptiste)
1927: **6** Wilson (Charles) **7** Compton (Arthur)
1928: **10** Richardson (Owen)
1929: **7** Broglie (Louis-Victor de)
1930: **5** Raman (Chandrasekhara)
1932: **10** Heisenberg (Werner)
1933: **5** Dirac (Paul) **11** Schrodinger (Erwin)
1935: **8** Chadwick (James)
1936: **4** Hess (Victor) **8** Anderson (Carl)
1937: **7** Thomson (George) **8** Davisson (Clinton)
1938: **5** Fermi (Enrico)
1939: **8** Lawrence (Ernest)
1943: **5** Stern (Otto)
1944: **4** Rabi (Isidor Isaac)
1945: **5** Pauli (Wolfgang)
1946: **8** Bridgman (Percy)
1947: **8** Appleton (Edward)
1948: **8** Blackett (Patrick)
1949: **6** Yukawa (Hideki)
1950: **6** Powell (Cecil)
1951: **6** Walton (Ernest) **9** Cockcroft (John)
1952: **5** Bloch (Felix) **7** Purcell (Edward)
1953: **7** Zernike (Frits)
1954: **4** Born (Max) **5** Bothe (Walther)

1955: **4** Lamb (Willis) **5** Kusch (Polykarp)
1956: **7** Bardeen (John) **8** Brattain (Walter), Shockley (William)
1957: **3** Lee (Tsung Dao) **4** Yang (Chen Ning)
1958: **4** Tamm (Igor) **5** Frank (Ilya) **9** Cherenkov (Pavel)
1959: **5** Segre (Emilio) **11** Chamberlain (Owen)
1960: **6** Glaser (Donald)
1961: **9** Mossbauer (Rudolf) **10** Hofstadter (Robert)
1962: **6** Landau (Lev)
1963: **5** Mayer (Maria) **6** Jensen (J. Hans), Wigner (Eugene)
1964: **5** Basov (Nikolay) **6** Townes (Charles) **9** Prochorov (Alexander)
1965: **7** Feynman (Richard) **8** Tomonaga (Sin-itiro) **9** Schwinger (Julian)
1966: **7** Kastler (Alfred)
1967: **5** Bethe (Hans)
1968: **7** Alvarez (Luis)
1969: **8** Gell-Mann (Murray)
1970: **4** Néel (Louis) **6** Alfven (Hannes)
1971: **5** Gabor (Dennis)
1972: **6** Cooper (Leon) **7** Bardeen (John) **10** Schrieffer (John)
1973: **5** Esaki (Leo) **7** Giaever (Ivar) **9** Josephson (Brian)
1974: **4** Ryle (Martin) **6** Hewish (Antony)
1975: **4** Bohr (Aage) **9** Mottelson (Ben), Rainwater (L. James)
1976: **4** Ting (Samuel) **7** Richter (Burton)
1977: **4** Mott (Nevill) **8** Anderson (Philip), Van Vleck (John)
1978: **6** Wilson (Robert) **7** Kapitsa (Pyotr), Penzias (Arno)
1979: **5** Salam (Abdus) **7** Glashow (Sheldon) **8** Weinberg (Steven)
1980: **5** Fitch (Val) **6** Cronin (James)
1981: **8** Schawlow (Arthur), Siegbahn (Kai) **11** Bloembergen (Nicholaas)
1982: **6** Wilson (Kenneth)
1983: **6** Fowler (William) **13** Chandrasekhar (Subrahmanyan)
1984: **6** Rubbia (Carlo) **11** van der Meere (Simon)
1985: **8** Klitzing (Klaus von)
1986: **5** Ruska (Ernst) **6** Binnig (Gerd), Rohrer (Heinrich)
1987: **6** Müller (K. Alex) **7** Bednorz (J. Georg)
1988: **8** Lederman (Leon), Schwartz (Melvin) **11** Steinberger (Jack)
1989: **4** Paul (Wolfgang) **6** Ramsey (Norman) **7** Dehmelt (Hans)

1990: **6** Taylor (Richard) **7** Kendall (Henry) **8** Friedman (Jerome)
1991: **8** De Gennes (Pierre-Gilles)
1992: **7** Charpak (Georges)
1993: **5** Hulse (Russell) **6** Taylor (Joseph)
1994: **5** Shull (Clifford) **10** Brockhouse (Bertram)
1995: **4** Perl (Martin) **6** Reines (Frederick)

physiology or medicine:
1901: **10** von Behring (Emil)
1902: **4** Ross (Ronald)
1903: **6** Finsen (Niels)
1904: **6** Pavlov (Ivan)
1905: **4** Koch (Robert)
1906: **5** Golgi (Camillo) **11** Ramon y Cajal (Santiago)
1907: **7** Laveran (Charles)
1908: **7** Ehrlich (Paul) **11** Metchnikoff (Elie)
1909: **6** Kocher (Emil)
1910: **6** Kossel (Albrecht)
1911: **10** Gullstrand (Allvar)
1912: **6** Carrel (Alexis)
1913: **6** Richet (Charles)
1914: **6** Barany (Robert)
1919: **6** Bordet (Jules)
1920: **5** Krogh (August)
1922: **4** Hill (Archibald) **8** Meyerhof (Otto)
1923: **7** Banting (Frederick), Macleod (John)
1924: **9** Einthoven (Willem)
1926: **7** Fibiger (Johannes)
1927: **13** Wagner-Jauregg (Julius)
1928: **7** Nicolle (Charles)
1929: **7** Eijkman (Christiaan), Hopkins (Frederick)
1930: **11** Landsteiner (Karl)
1931: **7** Warburg (Otto)
1932: **6** Adrian (Edgar) **11** Sherrington (Charles)
1933: **6** Morgan (Thomas)
1934: **5** Minot (George) **6** Murphy (William) **7** Whipple (George)
1935: **7** Spemann (Hans)
1936: **4** Dale (Henry) **5** Loewi (Otto)
1937: **12** Szent-Gyorgyi (Albert)
1938: **7** Heymans (Corneille)
1939: **6** Domagk (Gerhard)
1943: **3** Dam (Henrik) **5** Doisy (Edward)
1944: **6** Gasser (Herbert) **8** Erlanger (Joseph)
1945: **5** Chain (Ernst) **6** Florey (Howard) **7** Fleming (Alexander)
1946: **6** Muller (Hermann)
1947: **4** Cori (Carl, Gerty) **7** Houssay (Bernardo)
1948: **7** Mueller (Paul)

1949: **4** Hess (Walter) **5** Moniz (Antonio)
1950: **5** Hench (Philip) **7** Kendall (Edward) **10** Reichstein (Tadeus)
1951: **7** Theiler (Max)
1952: **7** Waksman (Selman)
1953: **5** Krebs (Hans) **7** Lipmann (Fritz)
1954: **6** Enders (John), Weller (Thomas) **7** Robbins (Frederick)
1955: **8** Theorell (Hugo)
1956: **7** Cournand (Andre), Richards (Dickinson) **9** Forssmann (Werner)
1957: **5** Bovet (Daniel)
1958: **5** Tatum (Edward) **6** Beadle (George) **9** Lederberg (Joshua)
1959: **5** Ochoa (Severo) **8** Kornberg (Arthur)
1960: **6** Burnet (Macfarlane) **7** Medawar (Peter)
1961: **6** Bekesy (Georg von)
1962: **5** Crick (Francis) **6** Watson (James) **7** Wilkins (Maurice)
1963: **6** Eccles (John), Huxley (Andrew) **7** Hodgkin (Alan)
1964: **5** Bloch (Konrad), Lynen (Feodor)
1965: **5** Jacob (Francois), Monod (Jacques) **5** Lwoff (Andre)
1966: **4** Rous (Francis) **7** Huggins (Charles)
1967: **4** Wald (George) **6** Granit (Ragnar) **8** Hartline (H. Keffer)
1968: **6** Holley (Robert) **7** Khorana (H. Gobind) **9** Nirenberg (Marshall)
1969: **5** Luria (Salvador) **7** Hershey (Alfred) **8** Delbruck (Max)
1970: **4** Katz (Bernard) **7** Axelrod (Julius) **8** Von Euler (Ulf)
1971: **10** Sutherland (Earl)
1972: **6** Porter (Rodney) **7** Edelman (Gerald)
1973: **6** Frisch (Karl von), Lorenz (Konrad) **9** Tinbergen (Nikolaas)
1974: **4** Duve (Christian) **6** Claude (Albert), Palade (George)
1975: **5** Temin (Howard) **8** Dulbecco (Renato) **9** Baltimore (David)
1976: **8** Blumberg (Baruch), Gajdusek (D. Carleton)
1977: **5** Yalow (Rosalyn) **7** Schally (Andrew) **9** Guillemin (Roger)
1978: **5** Arber (Werner), Smith (Hamilton) **7** Nathans (Daniel)
1979: **7** Cormack (Allan) **10** Hounsfield (Godfrey)
1980: **5** Snell (George) **7** Dausset (Jean) **10** Benacerraf (Baruj)
1981: **5** Hubel (David) **6** Sperry (Roger), Wiesel (Torsten)

1982: **4** Vane (John) **9** Bergstrom (Sune) **10** Samuelsson (Bengt)
1983: **10** McClintock (Barbara)
1984: **5** Jerne (Niels) **7** Koehler (Georges) **8** Milstein (Cesar)
1985: **5** Brown (Michael) **9** Goldstein (Joseph)
1986: **5** Cohen (Stanley) **14** Levi-Montalcini (Rita)
1987: **8** Tonegawa (Susumu)
1988: **5** Black (James), Elion (Gertrude) **9** Hitchings (George)
1989: **6** Bishop (J. Michael), Varmus (Harold)
1990: **6** Murray (Joseph), Thomas (E. Donnall)
1991: **5** Neher (Erwin) **7** Sakmann (Bert)
1992: **5** Krebs (Edwin) **7** Fischer (Edmond)
1993: **5** Sharp (Phillip) **7** Roberts (Richard)
1994: **6** Gilman (Alfred) **7** Rodbell (Martin)
1995: **5** Lewis (Edward) **9** Wieschaus (Eric) **15** Nüsslein-Volhard (Christiane)

Nobel's invention
8 dynamite

nobility
7 peerage, royalty **8** eminence, noblesse **11** aristocracy, superiority

noble
4 peer **5** grand, lofty, moral **6** august, lordly, worthy **7** eminent, ethical, stately **8** baronial, elevated, heroical, highborn, highbred, imposing, magnific, majestic, princely, sterling, virtuous, wellborn **9** estimable, excellent, grandiose, honorable, righteous **10** highminded, impressive, moralistic, principled **11** illustrious, magnificent, outstanding, right-minded **12** aristocratic

nobleman
4 duke, peer **5** baron **6** prince **7** baronet **8** principe
British: **4** earl **8** viscount
European: **7** marquis **8** marquess
French: **5** comte **7** vicomte
German: **4** Graf **5** burgrave, margrave **9** landgrave
Indian: **6** sardar, sirdar **8** maharaja
Italian: **8** marchese
Japanese (former): **6** daimio, daimyo
Scandinavian: **4** jarl
Spanish: **7** hidalgo

noblewoman
4 lady **7** baronne, duchess, peeress **8** baroness, countess, princess

European: **8** marquise
Italian: **8** marchesa

nobody
4 none, zero **5** no man, no one, zilch **6** cipher **7** nothing, nullity, whiffet **8** whipster **9** nonentity

nocturnal
5 night **7** nightly **10** night piece

nocuous
3 bad, ill **6** nocent **7** harmful, hurtful **8** damaging **9** injurious **11** deleterious, detrimental, mischievous

nodding
4 dozy **6** drowsy, sleepy, snoozy **8** slumbery **9** pendulous, somnolent, soporific **10** slumberous

noddle
4 bean, head, poll **6** noggin **9** headpiece

noddy
4 dope, fool, jack, tern **5** dunce, stupe **6** fulmar, noodle **7** schnook **8** dumbhead **9** lamebrain, razorbill, simpleton

node
4 knob **5** point **11** predicament **12** entanglement, protuberance

nog
3 ale, peg, pin **5** block

Nogah's father
5 David

noggin
4 bean, head, pate, poll **6** noddle, noodle

no-good
4 worm **6** bad lot, draffy, drossy, mucker, waster, wretch **7** inutile, lowlife, nothing, rounder, wastrel **8** unworthy, wormling **9** no-account, valueless, worthless **10** ne'er-do-well, profligate, scapegrace

Nohah's father
8 Benjamin

noise
3 din **4** blab, talk **5** babel, rumor, sound **6** clamor, gossip, hubbub, racket, ruckus, rumpus, tattle, uproar **7** ruction, sonance, stridor **8** resonant **11** pandemonium
explosive: **6** report

noiseless
4 hush **5** quiet, still, whist **6** silent, stilly

noisemaker
4 horn **6** rattle **7** clapper

noisette
5 hazel

noisome
4 foul, rank, vile **5** dirty, fetid, funky, fusty, musty, nasty **6** filthy, horrid, putrid, rancid, sickly **7** harmful, noxious, squalid **8** nidorous, stinking **9** offensive, repulsive, revolting, sickening, unhealthy **10** disgusting, insalutary, malodorous, nauseating, unsalutary **11** destructive, distasteful, unhealthful **12** insalubrious

noisy
4 loud **7** blatant, clamant, rackety, squeaky **8** clattery, overloud, sonorous, strident **9** clamorous, turbulent **10** boisterous, clangorous, strepitous, tumultuous, uproarious, vociferous **12** obstreperous

nomad
6 roving
Arabic: **6** beduin **7** bedouin

nomadic
6 roving **7** vagrant **8** vagabond **9** itinerant, itinerate, wandering, wayfaring **11** perambulant, peripatetic **13** perambulatory

nom de plume
see **pen name**

nomen
4 name, noun **5** style, title **7** moniker **11** appellation, appellative, designation

nomenclature
4 list, name **7** catalog **9** designate **11** appellation, designation, terminology

nominal
5 rated **6** formal **7** alleged, seeming, titular **8** apparent, so-called, trifling **9** pretended, professed **10** ostensible **11** approximate **12** substantival **13** insignificant

nominate
3 tap **4** call, name **5** offer **6** tender **7** appoint, name off, present, proffer, propose, purpose

nonage
7 infancy **8** minority **10** immaturity

nonchalant
4 cool, easy, glad **5** light **6** casual, smooth **8** careless, cheerful, composed **9** collected, unruffled **10** effortless **11** unflappable **12** lighthearted **13** imperturbable

noncleric
4 laic **6** layman

nonclerical
3 lay

nonclerics
5 laity

noncommittal
7 neutral 8 reserved 10 restrained

nonconformist
5 rebel 6 hippie 7 beatnik, heretic, sectary 8 bohemian, maverick 9 dissenter, dissident, heretical, heterodox, sectarian 10 schismatic, separatist, unorthodox 11 misbeliever, schismatist

nonconformity
6 heresy, schism 7 dissent 9 misbelief 10 dissidence, heterodoxy 11 unorthodoxy 13 individualism

nonentity
4 zero 5 aught, zilch 6 cipher, nobody 7 nothing, nullity, sad sack, whiffet 8 small fry, unperson, whipster 9 obscurity, rushlight, small beer

nonesuch
5 ideal, jewel 7 paragon 9 matchless, nonpareil, unequaled, unrivaled

nonetheless
3 yet 5 still 6 though, withal 7 howbeit, however 8 after all 11 still and all

nonexistence
4 nada 7 nullity, vacuity 8 nihility 11 nothingness

nonflammable
7 apyrous 13 incombustible

nonfunctional
7 useless 8 unusable 10 unworkable 11 impractical 13 impracticable, unserviceable

non-Hawaiian
5 haole

non-Jew
3 goy 5 goyim (plural) 7 gentile

nonmilitary
8 civilian

non-Muslim
6 giaour

no-nonsense
5 grave, sober, staid 6 sedate, solemn, somber 7 earnest, serious, weighty 10 sobersided

nonpareil
see **nonesuch**

nonpartisan
4 fair, just 9 equitable, impartial, objective, uncolored 11 indifferent 12 unprejudiced 13 undistinctive

nonplus
4 balk, beat, faze 5 stick, stump, throw 6 baffle, boggle, flurry, muddle, puzzle, rattle, stymie, thwart 7 buffalo, confuse, dilemma, fluster, mystify, perplex, stagger 8 confound, overcome, paralyze, quandary 9 dumbfound, frustrate

nonprofessional
3 lay 4 laic, tyro 7 amateur, dabbler 9 smatterer 10 dilettante 11 abecedarian

nonrational
3 mad 7 invalid 9 illogical, sophistic 10 fallacious, reasonless, unreasoned 12 unreasonable

nonreactive
5 inert

nonreligious
3 lay 7 godless, profane, secular 8 temporal

nonresistant
7 passive 8 resigned, yielding 10 submissive 11 acquiescent

nonsense
3 rot 4 blah, bosh, bull, bunk, crap, gook, guff, jazz, punk, tosh 5 bilge, drool, folly, fudge, Greek, hokum, hooey, trash 6 babble, blague, bunkum, bushwa, drivel, hot air, humbug, jabber, piffle 7 baloney, blather, eyewash, flubdub, foolery, fooling, hogwash, inanity, rubbish, trifles, twaddle 8 buncombe, claptrap, falderal, falderol, flimflam, malarkey, pishposh, slipslop, tommyrot, trumpery 9 gibberish, moonshine, poppycock 10 applesauce, balderdash, double-talk, flapdoodle, meshuggaas, tomfoolery 11 jabberwocky, whangdoodle, windbaggery 12 blatherskite, fiddle-faddle, fiddlesticks, flummadiddle 13 horsefeathers
British: 10 codswallop

nonsensical
5 inane 6 absurd 7 foolish 9 unmeaning 12 preposterous

nonsuccess
6 defeat 7 failure

nonviolent
6 irenic 7 pacific 8 pacifist, peaceful 9 peaceable 12 pacificatory

noodle
4 bean, dope, head, poll 5 chump, dunce, ninny, noddy, stupe 6 noggin 7 schnook 8 dumbhead 9 blockhead, lamebrain, simpleton 10 dunderhead

nook
4 cove, hole 5 niche 6 alcove, corner, cranny, recess 7 byplace 9 cubbyhole

Noon Wine author
6 Porter (Katherine Anne)

noose
3 tie 4 bond, hang 5 lasso, scrag, snare 6 entrap, gibbet, secure 7 turn off 8 string up

Nordhoff's partner
4 Hall (James)

norm
3 par 4 mean, type 5 maxim, model 6 median 7 average, pattern

Norma
composer: 7 Bellini (Vincenzo)
librettist: 6 Romani (Felice)

normal
4 mean, sane 5 lucid, right, typic, usual 6 common 7 average, general, natural, regular, typical 8 all there, ordinary, standard 9 customary, prevalent 11 commonplace 12 compos mentis

Normandy's capital
5 Rouen

Norns
5 fates, Skuld, Urdur 9 Verthandi

Norris novel
4 Blix 6 The Pit 8 McTeague 10 The Octopus

Norse
abode of the dead: 8 Niflheim
alphabet: 5 Runic
archer: 4 Egil
bard: 5 scald, skald
chieftain: 4 jarl, Rolf 5 Rollo
demon: 4 Mara, Surt 5 Surtr
dragon: 6 Fafnir 8 Nithhogg
epic: 4 Edda
explorer: 4 Erik 8 Ericsson, Eriksson
first man: 3 Ask 4 Askr
first woman: 5 Embla
giant: 4 Egil, Wade, Wate, Ymer, Ymir 5 Aegir, Egill, Hymir, Jotun, Mimir 6 Fafnir, Jotunn
giantess: 4 Egia, Norn, Nott
god: 2 As, Ve 3 Asa, Ass 4 Surt, Vali, Vili 5 Aesir (plural), Surtr, Vanir (plural) 6 Hoenir, Vithar 7 Vitharr
blind: 4 Hoth 5 Hoder, Hodur, Hothr
chief: 4 Odin 5 Othin, Wodan, Woden, Wotan

guardian: 7 Heimdal 8 Heimdall 9 Heimdallr
messenger: 6 Hermod 7 Hermodr
of beauty: 5 Baldr 6 Balder, Baldur
of evil: 4 Loke, Loki
of fertility: 4 Frey 5 Freyr
of justice: 7 Forsete, Forseti
of light: 3 Dag
of peace: 5 Baldr 6 Balder, Baldur
of poetry: 5 Brage, Bragi
of the hunt: 3 Ull 4 Ullr
of the seas: 5 Njord 6 Njoerd, Njorth 4 Hler 5 Aegir, Gymir
of the sky: 4 Odin 5 Othin
of thunder: 4 Thor 5 Donar
of war: 3 Tiu, Tiw, Tyr, Zio, Ziu
wolf: 6 Fenrir
goddess: 3 dis 4 Saga 5 disir (plural) 7 Asynjur
of fate: 3 Urd 4 Norn, Urth, Wyrd 5 Skuld 9 Verthandi
of healing: 3 Eir
of love: 5 Freya
of marriage: 5 Frigg 6 Frigga
of night: 4 Natt, Nott
of storms: 3 Ran
of the earth: 5 Joerd, Jorth
of the moon: 5 Nanna
of the sea: 3 Ran
of the sky: 5 Frigg 6 Frigga
of the underworld: 3 Hel 4 Hela
of youth: 4 Idun 5 Ithun 6 Ithunn
gods' abode: 6 Asgard
hall of heroes: 8 Valhalla
king: 4 Atli, Olaf
nobleman: 4 jarl
patron saint: 4 Olaf
poem: 4 rune
poet: 5 scald, skald
rainbow bridge: 7 Bifrost
sea serpent: 4 Wade, Wate 6 kraken 7 Midgard
smith: 6 Völund
tale: 4 saga
toast: 5 skoal
watchdog: 4 Garm 5 Garmr
world's destruction: 8 Ragnarok
world tree: 8 Ygdrasil 10 Yggdrasill

north
combining form: 4 arct 5 arcto

North African
country: 5 Egypt, Libya 7 Algeria, Morocco, Tunisia
fruit: 3 fig 4 date
garment: 4 haik
grass: 4 alfa 7 esparto
jackal: 4 dieb
language: 6 Arabic, Berber
Muslim sect: 6 Sanusi 7 Senussi
people: 6 Berber, Hamite 7 bedouin
seaport: 4 Oran, Sfax 6 Annaba 7 Tangier 10 Casablanca

North America
country: 4 Cuba 5 Haiti 6 Canada, Mexico, Panama 7 Bahamas, Grenada, Jamaica 8 Dominica, Honduras 9 Costa Rica, Guatemala, Nicaragua 10 El Salvador, Saint Lucia 12 United States
ethnic group: 5 Negro 6 Indian 7 Mestizo, Spanish
language: 6 Creole, French 7 English, Nahuatl, Spanish

North Carolina
capital: 7 Raleigh
college, university: 4 Duke, Elon 8 Davidson 10 Wake Forest
largest city: 9 Charlotte
nickname: 12 Tar Heel State
state bird: 8 cardinal
state flower: 7 dogwood

North Dakota
capital: 8 Bismarck
largest town: 5 Fargo
nickname: 10 Sioux State

northern
4 pike 6 boreal 11 hyperborean

northern limit of the world
5 Thule

North Korea
capital: 9 Pyongyang
monetary unit: 3 won

North Star State
9 Minnesota

Northwest Passage author
7 Roberts (Kenneth)

Northwest Territories
capital: 11 Yellowknife
district: 8 Franklin, Keewatin 9 Mackenzie

north wind
see at **wind**

Norway
capital: 4 Oslo
inlet: 5 fiord, fjord
monetary unit: 5 krone
patron saint: 4 Olaf
plateau region: 5 fjeld

Norwegian
goblin: 5 nisse
language: 5 Norse 6 Bokmal 7 Bokmaal, Nynorsk, Riksmal 8 Landsmal, Riksmaal 9 Landsmaal

nose
3 pry 4 beak, bent, bump, gift, head, poke 5 aroma, flair, knack, prier, pryer, scent, smell, sniff, snift, snoop, snoot, snout, snuff 6 butt-in, genius, muzzle, nuzzle, pecker, talent 7 aptness, faculty, meddler, Paul Pry, smeller, sneezer 8 busybody, kibitzer, quidnunc, smell out 9 olfaction, proboscis, schnozzle
combining form: 3 nas 4 nasi, naso 5 rhina, rhine 6 rhinus, rrhine 7 rhina, rhine, rrhine
kind: 3 pug 5 Roman 8 aquiline
lengthener: 3 lie
opening: 7 nostril

nosebleed
6 yarrow 9 epistaxis

nose-dive
3 dip 4 drop, fall, skid 6 plunge, tumble 7 plummet

nosegay
4 posy 7 bouquet

nosey
see **nosy**

nosh
5 snack

Nostradamus
5 augur 6 auspex 7 prophet 8 foreseer, haruspex 9 predictor 10 forecaster, foreteller, prophesier

Nostromo author
6 Conrad (Joseph)

nostrum
6 elixir 7 cure-all, panacea

nosy
5 peery 6 prying, snoopy 7 curious 9 intrusive 11 inquisitive, inquisitory

not
prefix: 2 an, il, im, in, ir, un 3 ant, dis, non 4 anth, anti

notability
3 VIP 4 lion, name 5 celeb, chief 6 leader 7 big name, big shot 8 bigtimer, eminence, luminary, somebody 9 celebrity, dignitary

notable
3 big, VIP 4 czar, king, lion, name, star 5 baron, celeb, chief, famed, great, light, mogul, nabob, nawob, power 6 big boy, biggie, big gun, bigwig, famous, fat cat, figure, leader, prince, rubric 7 big name, big shot, eminent, magnate, mugwump, pooh-bah 8 big chief, big noise, bigtimer, big wheel, eminence, great gun, luminary, renowned, somebody, striking 9 big cheese, celebrity, character, dignitary, important, muckamuck, personage, prominent, red-letter 10 celebrated, celebrious, noteworthy 11 conspicuous, heavyweight, illustrious, personality 13 distinguished, high-muck-a-muck

notarize
7 certify 8 validate

notch
3 cut, gap, peg 4 gash, mark, nick, nock, rung, step 5 cleft, grade, score, stage 6 degree, indent, record 7 scratch 8 incision, undercut 9 indenture 10 depression 11 indentation

note
3 cry, jot, see 4 call, chit, heed, mark, memo, mood, odor, show, song, tone, view 5 motif, smell, sound, tenor 6 descry, letter, regard, remark 7 comment, discern, element, epistle, jotting, missive, observe 8 annotate, eminence, indicate, perceive, reminder 9 attention, knowledge 10 cognizance, commentary, memorandum, observance, reputation 11 distinction, distinguish, information, observation 12 obiter dictum

notebook
3 log 5 diary 6 cahier 7 journal

noted
6 famous 7 eminent, leading, popular 9 prominent, well-known

noteworthy
6 patent, rubric 7 evident, notable 8 manifest, nameable 9 memorable, prominent, red-letter 10 noticeable, observable, remarkable 11 conspicuous, exceptional, outstanding 12 considerable 13 extraordinary

nothing
3 nil, nix 4 zero 5 aught, nihil, ought, zilch 6 cipher, draffy, drossy, naught, nobody, no-good, nought, trifle 7 inutile, nullity, whiffet 8 goose egg, unworthy, whipster 9 bagatelle, no-account, nonentity, valueless, worthless
French: 4 rien
German: 6 nichts
Latin: 5 nihil
Spanish: 4 nada

nothingness
4 nada, void 5 death 6 vacuum 7 nullity, vacuity 8 nihility 9 emptiness 12 nonexistence

notice
2 ad 3 see 4 care, espy, heed, mark, memo 5 favor, grasp, greet, refer, sense, sight 6 advert, descry, regard, remark, review 7 comment, concern, discern, observe, respect, thought 8 civility, critique, perceive, reviewal 9 attention, criticism, directive, recognize 10 book review, cognizance, evaluation, memorandum, observance 11 acknowledge, distinguish, information, observation 12 announcement

noticeable
6 marked, patent, signal 7 evident, obvious, pointed, salient 8 manifest, striking 9 arresting, arrestive, prominent 10 noteworthy 11 conspicuous, eye-catching, outstanding, sensational, significant, spectacular

notify
4 clew, clue, post, tell, warn 6 advise, fill in, inform, reveal, signal, wise up 7 apprise, declare, divulge, publish 8 acquaint, announce, disclose, discover, proclaim 9 broadcast 10 promulgate

notion
4 clue, hint, idea, term, whim 5 fancy, freak, humor, image 6 maggot, phrase 7 boutade, caprice, conceit, concept, inkling, thought 8 crotchet, telltale 9 knowledge 10 impression, knickknack 12 apprehension 13 understanding

notional
5 ideal 6 unreal 7 fancied, shadowy 8 fanciful, imagined 9 crotchety, imaginary, visionary, whimsical 10 conceptual 11 theoretical

notorious
5 noted 6 famous 7 leading, popular 8 ill-famed, infamous 9 prominent, well-known

Nott's horse
8 Hrimfaxi

Notus
6 Auster
brother: 5 Eurus 6 Boreas 8 Zephyrus
father: 6 Aeolus 8 Astraeus
mother: 3 Eos

noun
4 name 7 nominal 11 substantive
inflectional form: 4 case
suffix: 2 et, ia, ic 3 ent, ery, ier, ing, ion, ist 4 ence
verbal: 6 gerund

nourish
4 rear 5 nurse, raise 6 foster, nursle, suckle 7 bring up, build up, nurture, support 8 maintain 9 cultivate 10 breastfeed, provide for, strengthen

nourishment
3 pap 4 food, keep 6 living 7 aliment, pabulum, support 8 nutrient 10 sustenance 11 maintenance

___nous
5 entre

nouveau riche
7 parvenu, upstart 8 roturier 9 arriviste

Nova Scotia
capital: 7 Halifax
original name: 6 Acadia, Acadie

novel
3 new, odd 5 fresh 6 modern, recent, unique 7 special, strange, unusual 8 neoteric, original, peculiar, singular, uncommon 9 different, new-sprung 10 newfangled, unfamiliar 11 modernistic 12 new-fashioned

novelty
5 curio, sport 6 bauble, change, gewgaw, trifle 7 bibelot, newness, trinket, whatnot 8 gimcrack, mutation 9 objet d'art 10 innovation, knickknack

novice
3 cub 4 boot, colt, punk, tyro 6 greeny, rookie 7 amateur, learner, recruit, student, trainee 8 beginner, freshman, inexpert, neophyte, newcomer, prentice 9 fledgling, greenhorn, novitiate, postulant 10 apprentice, tenderfoot

Novum Organum author
5 Bacon (Francis)

now
2 as 3 for 4 away 5 since, today 6 at once, hereat, seeing 7 anymore, because, present, whereas 8 as long as, directly, existing, first off, up-to-date 9 forthwith, instanter, instantly, presently, right away, sometimes 10 inasmuch as 11 considering, immediately, straightway

now and again
7 at times, betimes 9 sometimes

now and then
see **now and again**

Nox, Nyx
brother: 6 Erebus
daughter: 3 Day 4 Eris 5 Light
father: 5 Chaos
husband: 6 Erebus
son: 6 Charon, Hypnos 8 Thanatos

noxious
5 fetid 6 deadly, putrid, sickly 7 baneful, noisome 8 stinking

9 pestilent, unhealthy **10** insalutary, unsalutary **11** distasteful, pestiferous, unhealthful, unwholesome

nozzle
5 eject, spray **9** nose about

nuance
4 dash **5** shade, tinge, touch **6** nicety **7** soupçon **8** subtlety **9** gradation, suspicion **10** refinement, suggestion

nub
4 core, crux, gist, knob, lump, meat, pith **5** point, short **6** kernel, upshot **9** substance **12** protuberance

Nubian
8 Cushitic

nucha
4 nape

nuclear agency
3 AEC, NRC

nuclear particle
5 meson **6** proton **7** neutron

nucleus
3 bud **4** core, germ, head, kern, ring, seed **5** focus, spark **6** embryo
material: **8** karyotin

Nudd's son
6 Edeyrn

nude
3 raw **4** bald, bare **5** naked, stark **6** peeled, unclad **7** unrobed **8** buffbare, stripped **9** au naturel, unattired, unclothed, uncovered, undressed **10** dishabille, stark-naked **11** garmentless

nudge
3 dig, jab, jog, toe **4** near, poke, prod **5** punch **9** ease along

nugatory
4 idle, vain **5** empty **6** hollow, otiose **7** invalid **9** worthless

nugget
3 gob, wad **4** clod, hunk, lump **5** chunk, clump, hunch

nuisance
4 harm, pest **6** bother, injury, pester, plague **7** nudnick **8** irritant, pesterer **9** besetment **10** botherment **11** botheration **12** exasperation

null
3 bad, nil **4** knur, void, zero **5** annul, empty, knurl **7** destroy, expunge, invalid, useless **9** worthless **10** obliterate **11** ineffective, ineffectual, nonexistent **13** inefficacious, insignificant

nullify
4 undo **5** abate, annul, limit, quash **6** efface, negate, offset **7** abolish, confine, vitiate **8** abrogate, restrict **10** annihilate, compensate, counteract, invalidate, neutralize **11** countervail

nullity
4 nada, zero **5** zilch **6** cipher, nobody **7** nothing, vacuity, whiffet **8** whipster **9** annulment, nonentity **11** nothingness **12** nonexistence

numb
4 dead, dull, mull **5** aloof, blunt, chill, frost **6** asleep, casual, deaden, freeze, remote **8** comatose, deadened, detached **9** incurious, insensate, senseless, stupefied, uncurious, unfeeling **10** insensible, insentient **11** desensitize, indifferent, insensitive, unconcerned, unconscious **12** anesthetized, desensitized, uninterested

number
5 add up, count, digit, run to, sum to, tally, total **6** amount, cipher, come to, figure **7** chiffer, include, integer, numeral, numeric, ordinal, run into, several, sum into **8** cardinal, numerate, paginate **9** aggregate, enumerate
added to another: **6** augend
combining form: **7** arithmo
large indeterminate: **7** zillion
resulting from division: **8** quotient
resulting from multiplication: **7** product
resulting from subtraction: **10** difference
science: **11** mathematics
whole: **7** integer

number one
4 main **5** chief, major **6** Grade A **7** capital, stellar **8** dominant, fivestar, foremost, superior **9** excellent, first-rate, front-rank, numero uno, top-drawer **10** blue-ribbon, firstclass, preeminent **11** first-string, outstanding, predominant

numbness
6 stupor
combining form: **4** narc **5** narco

numeral
5 digit **6** cipher, figure, number **7** chiffer, integer **11** whole number

numerate
4 list, tale, tell **5** count, tally **6** number **7** tick off

numerous
3 big **4** many **5** great, large **6** legion, sundry **7** several, umpteen, various **8** populous **9** plentiful **10** voluminous **12** multifarious, multitudinal **13** multitudinous

Numitor
brother: **7** Amulius
daughter: **9** Rea Silvia **10** Rhea Silvia
grandson: **5** Remus **7** Romulus

numskull
4 dolt **5** dunce **8** bonehead, clodpate **9** blockhead, thickhead

numskulled
5 dense, thick **6** stupid **9** fatheaded **10** beefheaded **11** blockheaded, thickheaded, thick-witted

nunnery
7 convent **10** sisterhood
head: **8** superior

Nun's son
6 Joshua

nuptial
6 bridal, wedded **7** marital, married, spousal, wedding **8** conjugal, hymeneal **9** connubial, espousals **11** matrimonial

nurse
4 feed, nana, rear, suck **5** humor, nanny, serve **6** attend, foster, mother, pamper, suckle, wait on **7** advance, care for, cherish, educate, forward, further, indulge, nourish, nurture, promote **9** cultivate **10** minister to
children's: **5** nanny **6** nannie
English: **11** Nightingale (Florence)
Indian: **4** ayah
Oriental: **3** ama **4** amah

nursemaid
4 nana **5** nanny **6** minder, nannie, sitter **9** governess **10** babysitter
Indian: **4** ayah
Oriental: **3** ama **4** amah

nursery
6 crèche **7** brooder

nurture
4 feed, food, grub, rear **5** nurse, raise, train **6** cradle, foster, nursle, school, uphold, viands **7** bolster, bring up, cherish, edibles, educate, nourish, support, sustain **8** tutelage, victuals **9** cultivate, provender **10** discipline, provisions, upbringing **11** comestibles

nut
2 en **3** bug **4** kook, loon **5** acorn,

bigot, crank, fiend, freak, issue, loony, pecan, tryma **6** almond, cashew, cuckoo, dement, madman, maniac, zealot **7** fanatic, filbert, hickory, lunatic, madling, problem, trymata (plural) **8** crackpot, question **9** bedlamite, ding-a-ling, harebrain, macadamia, non compos, pistachio, screwball **10** crackbrain, enthusiast, Tom o' Bedlam
combining form: **4** cary, kary **5** caryo, karyo
European shrub: **7** filbert
of a violin bow: **4** frog, heel

Nut
consort: **3** Geb, Keb
daughter: **4** Isis **8** Nephthys
son: **2** Ra **6** Osiris

nuthouse
6 asylum **8** loony bin **9** funny farm **10** booby hatch

Nutmeg State
11 Connecticut

nutria
5 coypu

nutriment
3 pap **4** food, keep **5** bread **6** living **7** pabulum, support **10** livelihood, sustenance **11** maintenance, subsistence

nutrition
study of: **8** sitology

nutritious
9 healthful, wholesome **10** nourishing

nuts
3 mad **4** daft, wild **5** batty, crazy, wacky **6** insane, screwy **7** cracked **8** demented **10** unbalanced

nutshell
3 sum **5** sum up **6** digest **7** summate **8** condense **9** epitomize, inventory, summarize, synopsize

nutty
see **nuts**

nuzzle
4 push, root, snug **5** nudge **6** burrow, cuddle, nestle, snudge, thrust **7** snoozle, snuggle

Nycteus
brother: **5** Lycus
daughter: **7** Antiope

nymph
5 deity, larva **6** maiden
changed into a bear: **8** Callisto
changed into a laurel: **6** Daphne
changed into a rock: **4** Echo
mountain: **5** oread
of Muslim paradise: **5** houri
sea: **6** Nereid **7** Calypso
water: **5** naiad **6** undine
wood: **5** dryad

Nym's crony
8 Falstaff

Nyx
see **Nox**

Oo

oaf
2 ox **3** dub **4** boob, bull, clod, dolt, gawk, goof, goon, hulk, lout, lump, slob **5** beast, booby, brute, chump, clown, dunce, klutz, looby **6** bohunk, galoot, lubber, lummox, slouch **7** bruiser, fathead, gorilla, lobster, lumpkin, palooka **8** bonehead, dolthead, lunkhead, meathead **9** blockhead, blunderer, lamebrain, simpleton

oak
4 tree, wood **9** broadleaf
African: **7** turtosa
family: **8** Fagaceae
fruit: **5** acorn
genus: **7** Quercus
kind: **3** bur, pin, red **4** bear, cork, holm, ilex, live **5** black, holly, roble, white **6** barren, cerris, encina **7** durmast, English, moss-cup, valonia **9** blackjack
Mexican: **8** chaparro
young: **7** oakling **8** flittern

oar
3 row **4** pole, pull **5** rower, scull **6** paddle **7** paddler
part: **4** loom, palm **5** blade, shaft **6** button, collar
pin: **5** thole

oarsman
3 bow **5** rower **6** stroke **7** sculler
director: **3** cox **8** coxswain

oasis
3 spa **4** wadi, wady **6** refuge, relief
ancient: **4** Merv
Egypt: **4** Siwa **5** Gafsa **6** Dakhla **7** Farafra **8** Ammonium
Libya: **5** Mizda, Sebha **6** Sabhah **7** Gadames **8** Ghudamis
Niger: **5** Bilma
Saudi Arabia: **5** Hofuf, Taima **7** Al-Hufuf

oat
5 grain, grass **6** cereal

genus: **5** Avena
Scottish: **3** ait

oater
7 western **10** horse opera

oath
3 vow **4** cuss **5** curse, swear **6** pledge **8** cussword **9** expletive, profanity, swearword **11** affirmation
mild: **3** gee **4** darn, drat, gosh **5** by gor, golly

oatmeal
6 burgoo **8** porridge
Scottish: **8** drammock

Obadiah
father: **4** Azel **6** Jehiel **8** Izrahiah, Shemaiah
son: **8** Ishmaiah

obdurate
4 firm, hard **5** harsh, rigid, rough **6** dogged, mulish, rugged **7** adamant, callous **8** stubborn **9** heartless, immovable, unbending, unfeeling **10** brassbound, hard-boiled, inexorable, inflexible, relentless, unyielding **11** coldhearted, hardhearted, stiff-necked, unemotional **12** stonyhearted **13** unsympathetic

obeah
5 charm, magic

Obed
father: **4** Boaz **6** Ephlal **8** Shemaiah
mother: **4** Ruth
son: **5** Jesse **7** Azariah

Obededom's father
8 Jeduthun

obedient
5 loyal **6** docile **7** duteous, dutiful, slavish **8** amenable, biddable, obeisant, yielding **9** compliant, sheeplike, tractable **10** law-abiding, submissive **11** acquiescent, subservient

obeisance
3 bow **5** congé, honor, kotow

6 curtsy, fealty, homage, kowtow, salaam **7** gesture, loyalty **9** deference, reverence **10** allegiance

Oberon
messenger: **4** Puck
wife: **7** Titania

Oberto composer
5 Verdi (Giuseppe)

obese
3 fat **5** gross, heavy, plump, pudgy, stout **6** fleshy, portly **7** porcine **9** corpulent **10** overweight **11** upholstered

obey
3 bow **4** heed, keep, mind **5** agree, defer, yield **6** accede, assent, comply, follow, regard, submit **7** conform, fulfill, observe, satisfy **8** carry out **9** acquiesce

obfuscate
3 dim **4** murk **5** befog, cloud, gloom **6** darken, shadow **7** becloud, confuse, obscure **8** overcast **9** adumbrate

obi
4 sash

obiter dictum
4 note **6** remark **7** comment **10** commentary **11** observation

obituary
9 necrology

object
3 aim, end, jib, use **4** balk, body, bulk, duty, goal, item, kick, mark, mass, rail, rant, rave, view **5** being, demur, frown, spurn, storm, stuff, thing **6** boggle, doodad, entity, except, gadget, matter, target, volume **7** article, dissent, protest, purpose, stickle **8** complain, disfavor, function, material **9** challenge, criticize, deprecate, disesteem, objective, substance **10** disapprove, discommend, individual

objection
5 demur **7** protest **8** demurral, de-

murrer, question **9** challenge, exception **10** difficulty **12** remonstrance **13** remonstration

objectionable
4 vile **5** unfit **8** unwanted **9** abhorrent, invidious, loathsome, obnoxious, offensive, repellent, repugnant, repulsive, revolting, unwelcome **10** censurable, ill-favored, unpleasant, unsuitable **11** distasteful, undesirable **12** disagreeable

objective
3 aim, end, use **4** duty, fair, goal, mark **5** gross, outer **6** object, target **7** outside, outward, purpose **8** ambition, external, function, material, physical, sensible, tangible, unbiased **9** corporeal, equitable, impartial, quaesitum, uncolored **10** impersonal, phenomenal **11** substantial **12** unprejudiced **13** dispassionate

objet d'art
5 curio, vertu (plural), virtu (plural) **6** bauble, gewgaw, trifle **7** bibelot, novelty, trinket, whatnot **8** gimcrack **10** knickknack

objurgate
4 damn **5** curse, decry **7** censure, reprove **8** execrate **9** castigate **12** anathematize

oblate
4 monk **5** offer

oblation
6 corban, korban **8** offering **9** sacrifice **12** presentation

obligated
5 bound **8** beholden, indebted

obligation
3 vow **4** call, debt, duty, must, need, oath, part **5** cause, ought, place **6** burden, charge, devoir, pledge **7** promise **8** business, contract, occasion **9** arrearage, committal, liability, necessity, restraint **10** commitment, compulsion, constraint **11** requirement **12** indebtedness

obligatory
7 binding **8** required **9** imperious, mandatory **10** compulsory, imperative

oblige
3 aid **4** help, make **5** avail, favor, force **6** assist, coerce, compel, please, profit **7** benefit, concuss, gratify, shotgun **9** constrain **10** contribute **11** accommodate

obliged
5 bound **8** beholden, grateful, indebted, thankful

obliging
4 easy, kind, mild **5** civil **7** amiable, lenient **11** complaisant, good-humored, good-natured **12** good-tempered

oblique
6 sloped, tilted, tipped **7** leaning, pitched, sloping, tilting **8** circular, inclined, indirect, pitching **9** inclining

obliterate
4 raze, x out **5** erase **6** cancel, delete, efface **7** blot out, expunge, wipe out **8** black out, cross out **10** annihilate

oblivion
5 lethe, limbo **6** pardon **7** amnesty, nirvana **13** forgetfulness, obliviousness

oblivious
7 unaware **8** absorbed, ignorant **9** forgetful, unknowing, unmindful, unwitting **10** unfamiliar, uninformed **11** incognizant, unconscious

oblong
4 oval **7** ellipse **9** elongated, rectangle **11** rectangular

obloquy
4 slam, slur **5** abuse, odium, shame **6** infamy **7** calumny, censure **8** disgrace, dishonor, ignominy **9** aspersion, contumely, discredit, disesteem, disrepute, invective, stricture **10** opprobrium, reflection, scurrility **12** billingsgate, vituperation

obnoxious
4 open, vile **5** prone **6** liable, odious **7** exposed, hateful, subject **9** abhorrent, invidious, offensive, repellent, repugnant, revulsive, sickening **10** disgusting

oboe
4 reed **7** hautboy **8** hautbois, woodwind

oriental: **6** surnai, surnay

obscene
4 foul, lewd, rank, vile **5** bawdy, crude, dirty, gross, lurid, nasty **6** coarse, crusty, earthy, filthy, impure, ribald, risqué, smutty, sultry, vulgar **7** hideous, noisome, profane, raunchy **8** barnyard, horrible, indecent, scabrous **9** offensive, repellent, repugnant, salacious, sickening **10** disgusting, fescennine, lascivious, nauseating, scurrilous

11 foulmouthed, unprintable **12** pornographic, scatological

obscure
3 dim, far, fog, odd **4** blur, dark, dusk, fuzz, haze, hide, mask, mist, murk, veil **5** bedim, befog, belie, blear, blind, cloak, close, cloud, cover, dusky, faint, gloom, lowly, minor, murky, shade, shady, vague **6** bemask, bleary, cloudy, darken, dim out, far-off, gloomy, hidden, humble, mystic, opaque, remote, screen, secret, shadow, shroud **7** becloud, clouded, conceal, cryptic, devious, dislimn, distant, eclipse, falsify, removed, retired, shadowy, unclear, unfamed, unknown, unnoted **8** abstruse, Delphian, disguise, esoteric, lonesome, mystical, nameless, nubilous, overcast, puzzling, secluded, solitary **9** adumbrate, ambiguous, difficult, enigmatic, equivocal, illegible, lightless, obfuscate, overcloud, sibylline, tenebrous, uncertain, undefined, unheard-of **10** caliginous, camouflage, fuliginous, ill-defined, indecisive, indefinite, indistinct, mysterious, overshadow, umbrageous, unemphatic, unexplicit, unrenowned **11** double-edged, double-faced, inscrutable, out-of-the-way, sequestered, unimportant **12** inaccessible, inconclusive, inexplicable, misrepresent, uncelebrated, unfathomable, unnoticeable **13** inconspicuous, unilluminated

obsequies
5 rites **7** funeral

obsequious
6 menial **7** dutiful, fawning, servile, slavish **8** obedient, obeisant, toadying **9** parasitic **10** submissive **11** deferential, subservient, sycophantic

observance
4 heed, mark, note, rite **6** notice, regard, remark, ritual **7** liturgy, service **8** ceremony **9** attention, formality **10** ceremonial, cognizance **11** observation

observant
5 alert, awake, aware **6** arrect **7** heedful, mindful **8** watchful **9** advertent, attentive, regardful **10** thoughtful

observation
4 heed, mark, note **6** notice, regard, remark **7** comment **9** attention **10** cognizance, commentary **12** obiter dictum

observatory

5 tower **7** lookout, outlook
8 overlook
famous: **4** Lick **6** Wilson, Yerkes
7 Palomar
instrument: **9** telescope

observe

3 see **4** espy, keep, look, mark,
mind, note, obey, twig, view
5 sight, study, watch **6** behold,
comply, follow, notice, remark, revere **7** comment, conform, discern
8 perceive, venerate **9** celebrate,
reverence, solemnize **10** animadvert, commentate **11** commemorate

obsessed

4 held **5** beset, queer **6** dogged,
hipped **7** gripped, haunted,
plagued **8** harassed, overcome,
troubled **9** bedeviled, bewitched,
dominated, hagridden, possessed
12 prepossessed

obsession

5 craze, mania, thing **6** fetish,
hang-up **8** fixation
13 preoccupation

obsolete

3 old **4** dead **5** passé **6** démodé,
old hat **7** worn-out **8** old-timey, outmoded, time-worn **10** superseded
12 old-fashioned

obstacle

3 bar, dam, rub **4** bump, clog,
snag, wall **5** block, catch, crimp,
hitch **6** hamper, hurdle **7** barrier
8 handicap, hardship, mountain,
traverse **9** hindrance **10** difficulty,
impediment **11** Chinese wall, encumbrance, obstruction, vicissitude

obstinate

4 deaf **5** balky, muley, stiff, tough
6 dogged, mulish, unruly **7** crabbed, staunch, willful **8** contrary, obdurate, perverse, renitent, resolute,
stubborn, unpliant **9** pigheaded, resistant, steadfast, unbudging, unpliable **10** bullheaded, hardheaded,
headstrong, inexorable, inflexible,
muleheaded, refractory, self-willed,
unyielding **11** incompliant, intractable, opinionated, stiff-necked,
wrongheaded **12** closed-minded,
intransigent, pertinacious, pervica-
cious, recalcitrant

obstreperous

4 loud **5** noisy **6** unruly **7** blatant
8 strident **9** clamorous **10** boisterous, multivocal, vociferant, vociferous **11** disobedient, loudmouthed, openmouthed

obstruct

3 bar, dam, gag **4** clog, fill, plug,
stop **5** block, brake, choke, close
6 hinder, impede, screen, shroud
7 congest, occlude, shut off, shut
out, stopper, trammel **8** block out
10 bottleneck, overslaugh

obstruction

3 bar, dam, rub **4** snag **5** hitch
6 hamper, hurdle **8** mountain, obstacle **9** hindrance **10** impediment

obtain

3 buy, eke, get, win **4** earn, gain,
have, reap **5** annex, reach **6** pick
up, secure **7** acquire, chalk up,
procure **8** purchase

obtrude

5 cut in **6** butt in, horn in, impose
7 presume **8** chisel in, infringe

obtrusive

4 busy **5** pushy **7** forward **9** bumptious, officious **10** meddlesome
11 impertinent

obtuse

4 dull, mild **5** blunt, dense, thick
6 stupid

obverse

4 face, side **5** front **10** complement

obviate

4 ward **5** avert, deter **7** forfend,
prevent, rule out **8** preclude, stave
off **9** forestall, interfere, interpose,
intervene

obvious

5 clear, overt, plain **6** patent **7** blatant, evident, glaring **8** apparent,
distinct, manifest, palpable
10 plain as day **11** conspicuous,
unambiguous, unequivocal

oca

5 tuber **6** sorrel

___O'Casey, dramatist

4 Sean

occasion

3 use **4** call, need, shot, show, time
5 basis, break, breed, cause, event,
hatch, right, thing, while **6** chance,
demand, excuse, ground, induce,
look-in, moment, reason, squeak,
work up **7** episode, instant, opening, produce, provoke, warrant
8 engender, generate, incident,
milepost, muster up **9** happening,
milestone, necessity **10** antecedent,
foundation, obligation, occurrence
11 determinant, opportunity **12** circumstance **13** justification

occasional

3 few, odd **4** rare **6** casual, random, scarce, seldom **8** sporadic,
uncommon **10** incidental, infrequent, unfrequent

Occidental

7 Western **9** Westerner

occlude

4 clog, fill, plug, stop **5** block,
choke, close **7** congest, stopper
8 obstruct

occult

4 bury, deep, hide **5** cache, eerie,
heavy, magic, stash, weird **6** arcane, orphic, screen, secret, voodoo **7** conceal, secrete **8** abstruse,
ensconce, esoteric, hermetic, mystical, profound **9** recondite, unearthly **10** acroamatic, cabalistic,
mysterious **12** supernatural
ability: **3** ESP
combining form: **5** crypt, krypt
6 crypto, krypto

occupant

5 liver **6** inmate, tenant **7** denizen,
dweller, resider **8** habitant, resident **9** indweller **10** inhabitant
suffix: **3** ite

occupation

3 job **4** line, work **5** trade **6** career, métier **7** calling, pursuit **8** business **9** occupancy, residence
10 employment, habitation,
settlement

occupy

3 use **4** busy, fill, hold **5** seize
6 engage, people, tenant **7** engross, immerse, inhabit **8** populate

occur

3 hap **4** pass **6** befall, betide,
chance, happen, strike **7** come off,
develop, fall out **9** transpire

occurrence

2 go **3** hap **4** pass **5** event, state,
thing **7** episode **8** exigency, incident, juncture, occasion **9** adventure, condition, emergency, happening, situation
extraordinary: **7** miracle
unexpected: **8** surprise **9** bombshell

ocean

3 sea **4** blue, deep, main **5** brine,
drink **6** Arctic, Indian **7** Pacific
8 Atlantic **9** Antarctic
movement: **4** tide, wave

Oceania

country: **4** Fiji **8** Kiribati **9** Australia
10 New Zealand **12** Western Sa-
moa

ethnic group: 6 Fijian, Indian, Papuan, Samoan 7 British 10 Melanesian, Polynesian 11 Micronesian
language: 5 Hindi, Maori 6 Fijian, Papuan, Pidgin, Samoan 7 English 10 Melanesian

oceanic
6 marine 7 pelagic 8 maritime 9 thalassic

Ocean State
11 Rhode Island

Oceanus
daughter: 5 Doris 7 Oceanid 8 Eurynome
father: 6 Uranus
mother: 2 Ge 4 Gaea
sister: 6 Tethys
son: 6 Peneus 7 Alpheus
wife: 6 Tethys

ocellus
3 eye 7 eyespot

ocelot
3 cat 7 wildcat

octave
4 cask, note 5 eight, scale 6 eighth

Octavia
brother: 8 Augustus
grandson: 8 Caligula
husband: 4 Nero 6 Antony

octopus
7 mollusk 9 devilfish 10 cephalopod
arm: 8 tentacle
genus: 7 Polypus
kin: 5 squid 10 cuttlefish

ocular
3 eye, orb 4 lamp 5 optic 6 oculus, peeper, visual, winker 7 optical, seeable, visible 8 viewable, visional

"Odalisque" painter
6 Ingres (Jean-Auguste-Dominique) 7 Matisse (Henri)

odd
4 lone, only, rare 5 extra, fluky, queer, rummy, weird 6 casual, chance, single, uneven 7 curious, erratic, oddball, strange, unusual 8 peculiar, singular, unpaired 9 eccentric, unmatched 13 idiosyncratic
combining form: 5 azygo

oddball
4 case, quiz 5 queer, weird 6 oddity, weirdo, zombie 7 bizarre, curious, strange 8 original, peculiar 9 character, eccentric 10 outlandish 13 idiosyncratic

oddity
4 case, quiz 5 quirk 8 original 9 character, curiosity, eccentric 12 idiosyncrasy

odd job
5 chore

odds and ends
4 olio 5 melee 6 jumble, medley, motley, scraps 7 mélange, mixture 8 oddments, sundries 9 etceteras, leftovers, potpourri 10 assortment, hodgepodge, miscellany

ode
4 hymn, poem 5 lyric, psalm, verse
part: 5 epode 7 strophe 11 antistrophe

Oded's son
7 Azariah

Odets play
9 Golden Boy 10 Night Music 12 Awake and Sing, Paradise Lost 14 The Country Girl 15 Waiting for Lefty

odeum
4 hall 7 theater

Odin
brother: 2 Ve 4 Vili
daughter-in-law: 5 Nanna
father: 3 Bor
hall: 8 Valhalla
horse: 8 Sleipnir
maiden: 8 Valkyrie
mansion: 9 Gladsheim
mother: 6 Bestla
raven: 5 Hugin, Munin
ring: 8 Draupnir
ship: 7 Naglfar 11 Skidbladnir
son: 3 Tyr 4 Thor, Vali 6 Balder
spear: 7 Gungnir
sword: 4 Gram
throne: 10 Hlidskjalf 11 Hlithskjalf
wife: 4 Fria, Rind 5 Frigg 6 Frigga
wolf: 4 Geri 5 Freki

odious
4 foul, vile 6 horrid 7 hateful 8 hateable 9 abhorrent, invidious 10 abominable, despicable, detestable

odium
4 blot, blur, hate, onus, slur, spot 5 brand, shame, stain 6 hatred, infamy, stigma 7 obloquy 8 black eye, disgrace, dishonor, ignominy 9 discredit, disesteem, disrepute 10 opprobrium 11 bar sinister

odontalgia
9 toothache

odor
4 funk 5 aroma, scent, smell
combining form: 3 osm 4 osma, osmo
offensive: 5 stink 6 stench

odorous
5 heady, sweet 6 smelly, strong 7 pungent, reeking, scented 8 aromatic, fragrant, redolent, smelling

Odysseus
7 Ulysses
dog: 5 Argos
enchantress: 5 Circe
father: 7 Laertes
friend: 6 Mentor
harasser: 8 Poseidon
herb: 4 moly
kingdom: 6 Ithaca
mother: 8 Anticlea
son: 9 Telegonus 10 Telemachus
swineherd: 7 Eumaeus
voyage: 7 odyssey
wife: 8 Penelope

Odyssey author
5 Homer

Oedipus
brother-in-law: 5 Creon
daughter: 6 Ismene 8 Antigone
father: 5 Laius
foster father: 7 Polybus
foster mother: 8 Periboea
kingdom: 6 Thebes
mother: 7 Jocasta
son: 8 Eteocles 9 Polynices 10 Polyneices
victim: 5 Laius
wife: 7 Jocasta

Oeneus
kingdom: 7 Calydon
son: 8 Meleager
wife: 7 Althaea

oenochoe
3 jug 7 pitcher
relative: 4 olpe

Oenomaus
charioteer: 8 Myrtilus
daughter: 10 Hippodamia
kingdom: 4 Pisa
slayer: 6 Pelops

Oenone
husband: 5 Paris
rival: 5 Helen

oeuvre
4 work 6 corpus, output

of
French: 2 de
German: 3 aus, von

offal

4 junk **5** trash, waste **6** debris, litter, refuse, spilth **7** carrion, garbage, rubbish **9** sweepings
fish: **5** gurry

off-balance

6 uneven **7** unequal **8** lopsided **9** irregular **10** asymmetric **13** unsymmetrical

off-center

9 eccentric

off-color

3 low **4** blue, mean, racy **5** broad, salty, shady, spicy **6** ailing, poorly, purple, risqué, sickly, unwell, wicked **7** underly **10** indisposed, suggestive

offend

3 sin, vex **4** gall, hurt, miff **5** break, pique, shock, sting, upset, wound **6** appall, breach, excite, insult, nettle **7** affront, disturb, horrify, infract, mortify, outrage, provoke, violate **8** aggrieve, distress, infringe, irritate, trespass **9** disoblige, displease

offender

5 felon **6** sinner **8** criminal, violator **10** lawbreaker, malefactor

offense

3 fit, pet, sin **4** huff, miff, tort **5** anger, crime, onset, pique, scene, tizzy **6** attack, catfit, delict, felony, insult, onfall **7** affront, assault, dudgeon, flare-up, misdeed, tantrum, umbrage **8** delictum, outburst **9** explosion, indignity, offensive, onslaught **10** aggression, assailment, conniption, resentment **11** displeasure, indignation, misdemeanor

offensive

3 bad **4** evil, foul, grim, icky, rank, vile **5** awful, lurid, nasty, onset **6** attack, grisly, horrid, odious, onfall **7** assault, beastly, fulsome, ghastly, hideous, noisome, obscene **8** dreadful, gruesome, horrible, shocking, terrible, unsavory **9** abhorrent, appalling, atrocious, frightful, loathsome, onslaught, repellent, repugnant, repulsive, revolting, sickening **10** abominable, aggression, assailment, detestable, disgusting, nauseating, ungrateful, unpleasant **11** uncongenial, unpalatable, unwholesome **12** disagreeable, unappetizing **13** objectionable

offer

3 bid, lay, try **4** cite, give, pose, seek, show **5** assay, essay **6** adduce, allege, extend, strive, tender **7** advance, attempt, display, exhibit, hold out, present, proffer, propose **8** endeavor, proposal, struggle

offering

4 alms, gift **6** corban, korban, victim **7** charity, present **8** donation, oblation **9** sacrifice **11** benefaction, beneficence **12** contribution

offhand

6 casual **8** informal **9** extempore, impromptu, unstudied **10** improvised **11** extemporary, unrehearsed

office

3 job **4** duty, post, role, spot **5** berth, place **6** billet **7** station **8** business, function, position, province **9** situation **10** connection **11** appointment
head: **4** boss **7** manager
machine: **6** copier **9** stenotype **10** calculator, typewriter
seeker: **9** candidate **10** politician
suffix: **2** cy **3** ate, dom, ure **4** ship
worker: **5** clerk, steno **6** typist **9** secretary **10** bookkeeper **12** stenographer

officer

3 cop **4** exec **6** noncom, police **7** John Law, manager **8** official **9** executive
abbreviation: **2** Lt. **3** Adm., Col., Ens., Gen., Maj. **4** Capt., Cmdr. **5** Comdr., Lieut.
army: **5** major **7** captain, colonel, general **10** lieutenant
British: **9** brigadier
court: **7** bailiff
king's: **11** chamberlain
law-enforcement: **3** cop **6** deputy, police **7** marshal, sheriff **9** constable, patrolman, policeman
naval: **4** mate **6** ensign **7** admiral, captain **9** commander, commodore **10** lieutenant
noncommissioned: **5** sarge **8** corporal, sergeant
petty: **5** bosun, chief **6** yeoman **7** teleman **9** boatswain
prison: **5** guard **6** warden

official

4 exec **7** cleared, manager, officer **8** approved, endorsed **9** canonical, cathedral, certified, executive, ex officio **10** authorized, ex cathedra, sanctioned **13** administrator, authoritative
city or town: **5** mayor **8** alderman **9** selectman **10** councilman
diplomatic: **5** envoy **6** consul **7** attaché **10** ambassador
governmental: **6** syndic

parish: **6** beadle
sports: **3** ref, ump **6** umpire **7** referee **8** linesman
university: **4** dean **6** bursar **7** provost **9** registrar **10** chancellor

officious

4 busy **9** intrusive, obtrusive **10** meddlesome **11** impertinent **13** polypragmatic

offing

6 future **7** by-and-by **9** aftertime, afterward, hereafter **10** background

offscouring

5 filth, leper **6** pariah, refuse **7** Ishmael, outcast **8** castaway, derelict **10** Ishmaelite **11** untouchable

offset

4 stop **5** check **6** contra, make up, redeem, set off **7** balance **8** atone for, outweigh **10** compensate **11** countervail

offshoot

5 scion **6** branch **7** spin-off **9** byproduct, outgrowth **10** derivative, descendant

offspring

3 kid, son **4** seed **5** brood, hatch, issue, scion, spawn, swarm, young **7** produce, product, progeny **8** children **9** posterity **10** descendant **11** progeniture
combining form: **3** gen, ped **4** geno, paed, paid, pedo **5** paedo, paido, proli

Of Human Bondage

author: **7** Maugham (W. Somerset)

Of Mice and Men

author: **9** Steinbeck (John)
character: **6** George, Lennie

ogee

3 ess **4** arch **5** curve **7** molding

Ogier the ___

4 Dane

ogive

4 arch

ogle

3 eye **4** gape, gaze, leer, look **5** stare **6** goggle **10** rubberneck

ogre

5 beast, bogey, demon, giant **6** booger **7** bugbear, monster **8** bogeyman **9** boogeyman
Algonquian: **7** windigo

ogress

5 harpy, scold, shrew, vixen **6** amazon, virago **8** fishwife **9** termagant, Xanthippe

Ohio

capital: 8 Columbus
college, university: 5 Akron, Hiram, Miami 6 Dayton 7 Antioch, Denison, Oberlin 8 Defiance, Ursuline 9 Kent State
largest city: 9 Cleveland
nickname: 12 Buckeye State
state bird: 8 cardinal

Oholibamah

father: 4 Anah
husband: 4 Esau

oil

3 fat, gas 4 balm, fuel, lube, oleo 5 oleum 6 anoint, grease 7 blarney, incense, lanolin 8 flattery, soft soap 9 adulation, lubricant, lubricate, petroleum
combining form: 3 ole 4 eleo, olei, oleo 5 elaeo, elaio
consecrated: 6 chrism
fragrant: 5 attar 6 neroli
fuel: 3 gas 8 gasoline, kerosene, kerosine
relating to: 5 oleic
ship: 6 tanker
source: 5 olive, shale
well: 6 gusher

Oil! author

8 Sinclair (Upton)

oilbird

8 guacharo

oily

5 fatty, slick, soapy, suave 6 greasy, smarmy, smooth 7 fulsome 8 unctious, unctuous 10 oleaginous

ointment

4 balm, nard 5 cream, salve 6 cerate, chrism, lotion 7 unction, unguent 8 calamine, dressing, liniment 9 demulcent, emollient 11 embrocation

OK, okay

3 aye, yea, yes 5 favor 6 agreed 7 approve, certify, endorse 8 accredit, all right, approval, blessing, sanction

Okinawa capital

4 Naha

Oklahoma

city: 3 Ada 4 Enid 5 Tulsa
nickname: 11 Sooner State
state flower: 9 mistletoe
university: 11 Oral Roberts

okra

4 soup 5 bendy, gumbo 8 hibiscus

old

4 aged, late, once, past 5 dated, hoary, passé, solid, stale 6 by-gone, démodé, former, steady, versed, whilom 7 ancient, antique, archaic, elderly, lasting, onetime, overage, quondam, skilled, staying, veteran 8 enduring, lifelong, Noachian, outmoded, seasoned, sometime, timeworn 9 erstwhile, long-lived, perennial, perpetual, practical, practiced, primitive, venerable 10 antiquated, continuing, inveterate
Scottish: 4 auld

old age

10 feebleness, senescence 11 decrepitude, elderliness, senectitude
combining form: 6 geront, presby 7 geronto, presbyo
relating to: 6 senile 8 gerontal, gerontic 9 geriatric

Old Bailey

5 court

Old Colony State

13 Massachusetts

Old Curiosity Shop author

7 Dickens (Charles)

Old Dominion State

8 Virginia

Old English letter

see **Anglo-Saxon**, ++letter

Old Faithful

6 geyser

old-fashioned

4 aged 5 dated, dowdy, drink, fusty, moldy, mossy, passé 6 bygone, crusty, démodé, old hat, quaint, rococo, stodgy 7 ancient, antique, archaic, belated, demoded, disused, fogyish, outworn, vintage 8 cocktail, obsolete, outdated, outmoded, unmodern 9 discarded, moss-grown, moth-eaten, out-of-date, Victorian 10 antiquated, fuddy-duddy, moss-backed

old hand

3 vet 7 veteran 9 longtimer

old hat

5 dated, stale, tired, trite 6 cliché, démodé 7 antique, archaic, clichéd, old-time, vintage 8 shopworn, timeworn, well-worn 9 hackneyed, out-of-date 10 antiquated, oldfangled, threadbare

Old Ironsides

12 Constitution
poet: 6 Holmes (Oliver Wendell)

old liner

4 tory 5 right 7 diehard 8 rightist, standpat 11 bitter-ender, right-winger, standpatter 12 conservative

Old Line State

8 Maryland

old maid

7 fusspot 8 spinster

Old North State

13 North Carolina

Old Rough and Ready

6 Taylor (Zachary)

Olds' car

3 Reo

Old Scratch

5 devil, fiend, Satan 7 Lucifer, Old Nick, serpent 8 Apollyon 9 Beelzebub

old-time

5 dated 6 bygone, old hat, versed 7 antique, archaic, skilled, veteran, vintage 8 seasoned 9 practical, practiced 10 antiquated 11 experienced

old-timer

3 vet 5 elder 6 senior 7 ancient, old hand, oldster, veteran 10 golden-ager

old womanish

5 anile

Old World

6 Europe

oleaginous

see **oily**

oleaster

5 olive 9 olive tree

olecranon

9 funny bone

oleo

9 margarine

oleoresin

10 turpentine

oleum

3 oil

olfaction

5 sense, smell 7 osmesis 8 smelling

olid

4 rank 5 fetid, funky 6 putrid, rancid, smelly 7 stenchy 8 mephitic, stinking 10 malodorous

olio

4 brew, hash, stew 6 medley 7 mélange, mixture 8 mishmash 9 potpourri 10 assortment, hodgepodge, miscellany 11 olla podrida

olive

genus: 4 Olea
stuffing: 7 pimento 8 pimiento

Oliver Twist

author: 7 Dickens (Charles)
character: 5 Bates, Fagin, Nancy,

Sikes **6** Bumble **7** Dawkins **12** Artful Dodger

olia podrida
see olio

Ollie's pal
4 Stan

Olympian
3 god **5** lofty **7** athlete, exalted **8** majestic **10** competitor

Olympics
5 games **6** sports **9** athletics
place of origin: **6** Athens
symbol: **5** flame, torch

Oman
capital: **6** Masqat, Muscat
monetary unit: **4** rial

Omar
4 poet **7** Khayyém
country: **6** Persia
father: **7** Eliphaz
poem: **8** Rubáiyát

omega
3 end **6** ending, letter
kin: **3** zee

omelet
4 eggs
kind: **7** foo yong, Spanish, western

omen
4 bode, sign **5** augur, token **6** augury, boding **7** auspice, betoken, portend, portent, presage, promise, warning **8** bodement, forebode, foreshow **9** foretoken **10** foreshadow, prognostic

ominous
4 dire, dour, evil, grim **6** dismal, malign **7** baleful, baneful, direful, doomful, fateful, hostile, malefic, unlucky **8** lowering, menacing, sinister **9** ill-boding, ill-omened **10** forbidding, maleficent, portentous, unfriendly **11** apocalyptic, threatening **12** inauspicious, inhospitable, unpropitious

omission
3 cut, gap **4** skip, slip **5** blank, break, chasm, error, lapse **6** hiatus, lacuna **8** eclipsis, ellipsis, overlook **9** exclusion
mark: **5** caret **8** ellipsis **10** apostrophe

omit
3 cut **4** dele, drop, fail, skip **5** elide **6** cancel, delete, except, forget, ignore, slight **7** blink at, neglect **8** discount, leave out, overlook, overpass

Omni and Cobo
6 arenas

omnibus
3 ana **4** posy **5** album **7** garland, vehicle **8** analects **9** anthology **10** miscellany **11** florilegium
horse-drawn: **10** shillibeer

omnipotent
3 god **5** deity **6** divine **7** godlike **8** almighty **9** unlimited **11** all-powerful

omnipresent
7 allover, endless **8** infinite, unending **9** boundless, limitless, universal **10** ubiquitous **12** immeasurable

omniscient
4 wise **7** learned **10** all-knowing

omnium-gatherum
see olio

Omphale
domain: **5** Lydia
slave: **8** Heracles, Hercules

omphalos
5 navel **9** umbilicus **10** focal point

Omri's father
4 Imri **6** Becher **7** Michael

on
4 atop, over, upon, with **5** about, above, along, forth **7** forward

onager
5 kiang **8** catapult

Onan's father
5 Judah

once
3 odd **4** ever, late, past **5** at all **6** anyway, before, bygone, former, whilom **7** already, anywise, earlier, onetime, quondam **8** formerly, sometime
Scottish: **4** anes **5** yince

once-over
6 glance, survey **10** inspection **11** examination

one
3 wed **4** join, link, lone, only, sole, unit **5** monad, unite **6** number, relate, single, unique, united **7** connect, numeral **8** coagment, coalesce, separate, singular, solitary **9** associate, coadunate, undivided **10** individual, particular
combining form: **3** mon **4** heno, mono
French: **2** un **3** une
German: **3** ein **4** eine
prefix: **3** uni
Scottish: **2** ae **3** ane, yae
Spanish: **2** un **3** uno

one and a half
combining form: **6** sesqui

one-eyed giant
7 Cyclops **10** Polyphemus

one-handed god
3 Tiu, Tyr

one-horse town
4 burg **6** Podunk **7** mudhole **11** whistle-stop

one hundred
6 centum
years: **7** century

O'Neill, Eugene
heroine: **4** Anna, Nina
play: **3** Ile **4** Gold **11** The Hairy Ape **12** Ah Wilderness, Anna Christie, Emperor Jones **13** Marco Millions **15** The Iceman Cometh **16** Strange Interlude, The Great God Brown

oneiric
6 dreamy **8** anagogic

oneness
5 unity **7** allness, unicity **8** entirety, identity, sameness, totality, uniquity **9** wholeness **10** entireness, singleness, uniqueness **11** singularity **12** completeness, selfsameness, singularness **13** identicalness, individuality

onerous
4 hard **5** heavy, hefty, tough **6** taxing, trying, unruly **7** arduous, driving, exigent, weighty **8** exacting, grievous, toilsome, unwieldy **9** demanding, difficult, laborious, ponderous **10** burdensome, cumbersome, oppressive **11** heavy-headed

oneself
combining form: **3** aut **4** auto

one-sided
6 biased, unfair, unjust, warped **7** bigoted, colored, partial **8** lopsided, partisan, weighted **9** jaundiced **10** prejudiced

onetime
4 late, once, past **6** bygone, former, whilom **7** quondam **8** formerly **9** erstwhile

on hand
4 here **7** present

Onias' son
5 Simon

onion
4 bulb **5** cibol **7** shallot **8** eschalot
bulb: **3** set
genus: **6** Allium
kin: **4** leek **6** garlic

kind: 3 red 5 green 7 Bermuda, Danvers, Spanish
roll: 5 bialy
young: 8 scallion

only
3 but, one, yet 4 just, lone, mere, save, sole, solo 5 alone 6 except, merely, simply, single, solely, unique 7 however 8 entirely, peerless, separate, singular, solitary 9 matchless, unequaled, unmatched

onomasticon
7 lexicon 8 wordbook

onomatopoeic
5 mimic 6 echoic 7 mimetic, mimical 9 emulative, imitative 10 simulative

onomatopoetic
see **onomatopoeic**

onrush
see **onslaught**

onset
4 dawn 5 birth, start 6 attack, onfall, origin, outset, setout 7 assault, dawning, offense, opening 8 outstart 9 beginning, offensive, onslaught 10 aggression, assailment 12 commencement

onslaught
5 onset 6 attack, onfall, onrush 7 assault, offense 9 offensive 10 aggression, assailment

Ontario
capital: 7 Toronto
university: 4 York 5 Brock, Trent 8 McMaster

on the other hand
3 but 7 however

on the whole
7 en masse 8 all in all 9 generally 10 altogether, by and large

onto
4 atop

onus
3 tax 4 blot, blur, duty, load, slur, spot, task 5 blame, brand, fault, guilt, odium, stain 6 burden, charge, stigma, weight 8 black eye 9 millstone 10 deadweight

onward
4 alee, away 5 ahead, along, forth 7 forward

onyx
3 jet 4 inky 5 black, ebony, jetty, raven, sable 9 pitch-dark 10 chalcedony, pitchblack 11 atramentous

oodles
4 gobs, heap, slew, tons 5 loads, scads 7 jillion 10 quantities

ooid
4 oval 5 ovate, ovoid 7 oviform

oolong
3 tea

oomph
3 vim 4 brio, dash, élan, gimp, life, push 5 drive, verve, vigor 6 esprit, pizazz, spirit 7 pizzazz 8 strength, vitality 9 animation

ooze
3 mud 4 leak, seep, weep 5 bleed, exude, marsh, slime, sweat 6 strain 7 secrete 8 transude

opah
4 fish 5 cravo

opal
3 gem 5 glass, jewel, stone 7 girasol, hyalite 8 girasole 9 cacholong

opaque
4 dark, dull 5 dense, vague 6 cloudy, stupid 7 obscure, unclear 8 nubilous

OPEC nation
4 Iran, Iraq 5 Gabon, Libya, Qatar 6 Kuwait 7 Algeria, Ecuador, Nigeria 9 Indonesia, Venezuela 11 Saudi Arabia

open
3 cut, tap 4 ajar, bare, free, gash, hole, meet, undo, wide 5 agape, begin, break, clear, cover, frank, naked, overt, plain, prone, slash, start, swell, untie 6 billow, breach, broach, candid, dilate, expand, expose, extend, fan out, gaping, get off, launch, liable, mantle, patent, peeled, pierce, public, reveal, spread, unbolt, unfold, unlock, unseal, unshut, unstop, unveil, unwrap, usable 7 convene, denuded, jump off, kick off, outdoor, outside, release, ringent, rupture, subject, unblock, unclose, uncover, unlatch, without, yawning 8 commence, disclose, doubtful, embark on, initiate, outdoors, patulous, stripped, unbarred, unbolted, unclench, unclosed, unclothe, unlocked, unsealed 9 agreeable, ambiguous, available, dehiscent, dubitable, equivocal, obnoxious, operative, outspread, perforate, reachable, securable, sensitive, uncertain, uncovered, undecided, unimpeded, unsettled 10 accessible, attainable, embark upon, employable, inaugu-

rate, indecisive, obtainable, out-of-doors, outstretch, overspread, unfastened 11 practicable, problematic, susceptible, unconcealed, undisguised, unvarnished 12 undissembled, unobstructed, unrestricted
poetic: 3 ope
slightly: 4 ajar

open-air
7 outdoor, outside 8 alfresco 9 out-of-door 10 hypaethral

open-and-shut
5 clear, plain 6 patent 7 evident, obvious 8 apparent, distinct, manifest

openhanded
4 free 5 clear, plain 6 patent 7 evident, liberal, obvious 8 apparent, distinct, generous 9 bounteous, bountiful, unsparing 10 bighearted, munificent

openhearted
4 kind, warm 5 frank, plain 6 candid

opening
2 os 3 gap, ora (plural) 4 dawn, door, gate, hole, pass, pore, rift, rima, shot, show, slit, slot, time, vent 5 birth, break, chasm, chink, cleft, crack, debut, mouth, onset, start, stoma 6 breach, chance, eyelet, lacuna, look-in, outlet, outset, setout, squeak 7 crevice, dawning, fissure, orifice, pinhole, ventage 8 aperture, crevasse, débouché, occasion, outstart, overture 9 beginning 11 opportunity
bodily: 4 pore 5 hilum, hilus 7 foramen, orifice, ostiole 8 fenestra
combining form: 4 pora, pore, pyle 5 stoma, stome, stomi, stomy, trema 6 stomia, stomum 7 stomata (plural), stomate, tremata (plural)
ship's: 5 hatch 8 hatchway, porthole

openmouthed
5 agape 6 amazed, gaping 7 blatant 8 strident 9 clamorous 10 boisterous, multivocal, vociferant, vociferous

open sesame
3 key 6 ticket 8 passport, password

opera
7 musical
comic: 5 buffa 6 bouffe
glasses: 9 lorgnette
kind: 4 soap 5 comic, grand, horse, space
part: 3 act 4 aria 5 scena

solo: 4 aria
star: 4 diva 10 prima donna
text: 8 libretto (see also individual titles and composers)

operate
2 go 3 act, cut, ply, run, use
4 keep, play, take, work 5 drive,
pilot, react, steer, wield 6 behave,
direct, handle, manage, open up,
ordain 7 carry on, conduct, control, perform 8 function, maneuver
10 manipulate

operation
3 use 4 play 6 action 7 surgery
8 exercise, exertion, function
9 appliance, procedure 10 employment, exercising

operative
4 hand, live, open 5 agent, alive
6 active, usable, worker 7 dynamic, laborer, running, working,
workman 8 mechanic, workhand
9 Pinkerton

operator
5 agent 6 doctor, driver 7 autoist,
surgeon 8 motorist 9 conductor
suffix: 3 ist 4 ster

operculum
3 lid 4 flap

operetta composer
5 Lehar (Franz), Suppe (Franz von)
6 Straus (Oscar) 7 Herbert (Victor),
Romberg (Sigmund), Strauss (Johann) 8 Sullivan (Arthur) 9 Offenbach (Jacques)

operose
4 busy, hard 5 tough 6 severe
7 arduous 8 diligent, sedulous, toilsome 9 assiduous, difficult, effortful, laborious

Ophelia
beloved: 6 Hamlet
brother: 7 Laertes
father: 8 Polonius

ophidian
5 snake 9 snakelike

Ophir's father
6 Joktan

opiate
4 dope, drug 6 deaden, sleepy
7 anodyne 8 hypnotic, narcotic,
nepenthe, somnific 9 soporific
10 somnorific

opine
4 deem, hold, view 5 judge, think
6 accept, regard 7 believe, suppose

opinion
3 eye 4 idea, mind, view 5 tenet,
think 6 belief, notion, theory 7 feeling, thought 8 attitude, estimate,
judgment, reaction 9 sentiment
10 assumption, conclusion, conjecture, conviction, estimation, impression, persuasion 11 speculation,
supposition
express an: 4 vote 5 judge
9 criticize

opium
4 dope, drug 8 narcotic
derivative: 6 heroin 7 codeine, meconin, narcein 8 laudanum, morphine, narceine 9 narcotine,
paregoric
prepared: 6 chandu
source: 5 poppy

opossum
9 marsupial
kin: 8 kangaroo

oppidan
8 townsman

opponent
3 con, foe 4 anti 5 enemy, match,
rival 7 nemesis, opposer 9 adversary, assailant, combatant, oppugnant 10 antagonist, competitor
12 counteragent

opportune
3 fit 5 happy 6 timely 7 timeous
9 favorable, well-timed 10 auspicious, felicitous, propitious, prosperous 11 appropriate

opportunity
4 hope, pass, room, shot, show,
time, turn 5 break, space, spell
6 chance, look-in, prayer, relief,
squeak 7 opening 8 juncture,
occasion

oppose
3 pit, vie 4 buck, duel, face 5 array, beard, fight, match, repel
6 combat, differ, object, refute, repugn, resist 7 contest, counter, dispute, play off 8 confront, contrast,
traverse 9 withstand 10 contradict

opposite
2 to 4 foil 5 polar 6 contra, facing, unlike 7 antonym, counter, inverse, obverse, opposed, reverse,
unalike 8 antipode, antipole, contrary, contrast, converse, separate
9 antipodal, diametric, different,
divergent, unrelated, unsimilar
10 antipodean, antithesis, antonymous, dissimilar 11 contrasting,
counterpole, independent, uncon-
nected 12 antagonistic, antithetical, counterpoint 13 contradictory
combining form: 7 enantio
French: 8 en face de
prefix: 2 ob 3 dis 5 retro 6 contra
7 counter

opposition
3 con 8 defiance 9 animosity, hostility 10 antagonism, antithesis,
resistance 11 contrariety

oppress
5 harry, wrong 6 burden, harass,
sadden, subdue 7 afflict, conquer,
depress, outrage, torment, torture,
trouble 8 aggrieve, distress, overcome 9 overthrow, persecute,
subjugate

oppressive
4 hard 5 black, bleak, harsh,
heavy, tough 6 dismal, gloomy, severe, somber, taxing 7 exigent,
onerous, weighty 8 exacting, grievous 9 demanding 10 burdensome,
depressing 11 dispiriting 12 discouraging 13 disheartening

oppressive force
4 onus, yoke 6 burden, weight
10 juggernaut

oppressor
6 despot, tyrant 8 dictator 9 strong
man

opprobrious
7 abusive 8 ill-famed, infamous,
scurrile 9 invective, notorious, truculent 10 scurrilous, vituperous
12 contumelious, vituperative,
vituperatory

opprobrium
5 abuse, odium, scorn, shame 6 infamy 7 obloquy 8 disgrace, dishonor, ignominy 9 discredit, disesteem, disrepute 10 scurrility
12 vituperation

oppugn
3 tug, war 5 fight 6 battle
7 contend

Ops
4 Rhea
consort: 6 Cronus, Saturn
daughter: 5 Ceres 7 Demeter

opt
4 cull, mark, pick, take 5 elect
6 choose, decide, prefer, select
9 single out

optical
6 ocular, visual 8 visional
instrument: 4 lens 5 glass, scope
7 transit 9 magnifier, optometer,

periscope, telescope
10 microscope

optimist
   5 hoper **7** dreamer **8** idealist, micawber **9** Pollyanna **10** positivist

optimistic
   4 fond, rosy **5** merry, sunny
6 bright, hoping, upbeat **7** assured, hopeful **8** cheerful, sanguine
9 confident **12** Pollyannaish

option
   5 right **6** choice **8** election **9** privilege, selection **10** preference
11 alternative, prerogative

optional
   4 free **8** elective **9** voluntary
11 alternative, facultative
13 discretionary
   item: **5** add-on

opulence
   6 plenty, riches, wealth **9** affluence

opulent
   4 lush, rich **5** plush, showy, swank
6 Capuan, deluxe, lavish **7** elegant, moneyed, profuse, wealthy
8 affluent, luscious, palatial, prodigal **9** exuberant, luxuriant, luxurious, profusive, sumptuous

opuntia
   6 cactus

or
   4 else, gold **6** golden, yellow
9 otherwise

oracle
   4 sage, seer **6** medium, vision
8 prophecy **10** apocalypse, revelation
   site: **6** Claros, Delphi, Didyma, Dodona **9** Epidaurus

oracular
   5 vatic **6** mantic **7** fatidic **8** Delphian **9** prophetic, sibylline, vaticinal

oral
   4 told **5** vocal **6** sonant, spoken, verbal, voiced **7** related, uttered
8 narrated, viva voce **9** recounted, unwritten

orange
   5 color, fruit **6** citrus **8** jacinthe
   brownish: **6** Titian
   deep: **11** bittersweet
   genus: **6** Citrus
   kin: **9** tangerine **10** grapefruit
   kind: **4** sour **5** blood, chino, navel, Osage, sweet **7** Seville **8** bergamot, mandarin, Valencia
   seed: **3** pip
   skin: **4** rind

orangutan
   3 ape **4** mias **5** pongo

orate
   4 rant, rave **5** mouth, speak, spiel
7 bombast, declaim, elocute, soapbox **8** blah-blah, bloviate, harangue, perorate **9** sermonize, speechify **11** rodomontade

oration
   6 sermon, speech **7** address
9 discourse
   funeral: **6** eulogy

orator
   7 demagog, speaker **9** demagogue
   American: **4** Clay (Henry) **5** Bryan (William Jennings), Henry (Patrick)
7 Calhoun (John C.), Douglas (Stephen), Webster (Daniel)
   British: **5** Burke (Edmund) **8** Disraeli (Benjamin) **9** Churchill (Winston), Gladstone (William)
   French: **8** Mirabeau (Comte de)
   Greek: **5** Corax **8** Pericles
11 Demosthenes
   Roman: **6** Cicero

oratory
   6 chapel **8** rhetoric **9** elocution, eloquence **11** speechcraft

orb
   3 eye **4** ball, lamp **5** globe, round
6 circle, ocular, oculus, peeper, sphere, winker

orbit
   4 path **5** ambit, range, reach, scope, sweep, track **6** extent, radius
   farthest point: **5** apsis **6** apogee
8 aphelion
   nearest point: **5** apsis **7** perigee
10 pericenter, perihelion

orchard
   5 copse **6** garden **8** arbustum
10 plantation

orchestra
   4 band **5** combo, group **7** gamelan **8** ensemble, symphony
12 philharmonic
   leader: **9** conductor
   section: **5** brass **6** string **8** woodwind **10** percussion

orchestrate
   5 blend, score, unify **7** arrange
9 harmonize, integrate **10** symphonize, synthesize

orchid
   6 flower
   kind: **5** faham, vanda **7** calypso, pogonia **8** cattleya, oncidium **9** cymbidium **11** cypripedium

   petal: **3** lip **8** labellum
   product: **5** faham, salep
   tuber: **5** salep

Orcus
   see **Hades**

ordain
   4 keep **5** order **6** decree, direct, impose, manage **7** carry on, command, conduct, dictate, lay down, operate **9** prescribe

ordeal
   5 cross, trial **7** calvary **8** crucible
10 affliction, visitation
11 tribulation

order
   3 bid, fix, ilk, row, set **4** case, club, fiat, gear, kind, line, plan, rank, rule, sort, tell, trim, tune, type, warn, word **5** align, array, breed, chain, edict, genus, grace, grade, guild, range, right, shape, train, union **6** adjust, behest, branch, charge, codify, decree, direct, enjoin, estate, extent, fettle, kidney, kilter, league, line up, matter, method, nature, police, repair, sequel, series, settle, status, stripe, system **7** aptness, arrange, arrayal, bidding, bracket, command, decorum, dictate, dispose, feather, fitness, mandate, marshal, pattern, probity, routine, society **8** approach, organize, regiment, regulate, sequence, sodality, tidiness, vicinity **9** allotment, amendment, arrayment, closeness, condition, following, integrity, magnitude, methodize, propriety, proration, proximity, rectitude, rightness, routinize **10** adjustment, allocation, correction, expediency, fellowship, fraternity, injunction, permission, pigeonhole, procession, properness, seemliness, streamline, succession, timeliness **11** alternation, arrangement, association, brotherhood, collocation, consecution, correctness, description, disposition, hierarchize, orderliness, progression, suitability, systematize
   good: **6** eutaxy
   lack of: **5** chaos **6** ataxia **7** anarchy, clutter **9** confusion
11 pandemonium
   of business: **6** agenda, docket
   of preference: **8** priority

orderly
   4 aide, neat, snug, tidy, trig, trim
5 alike, exact **6** batman, formal
7 chipper, correct, precise, regular,

uniform **8** accurate, methodic, picked up **9** shipshape **10** methodical, systematic **11** uncluttered, well-groomed **12** businesslike

ordinal
4 book **6** number
suffix: **2** nd, st, th **3** eth

ordinance
3 law **4** fiat, rule **5** canon, edict **6** decree **7** precept, statute **8** decretum **9** prescript **10** capitulary, regulation

ordinary
4 so-so **5** banal, plain, trite, usual **6** common, normal **7** mundane, natural, prosaic, regular, routine **8** everyday, familiar, frequent, workaday **9** customary, plain Jane, quotidian **10** uneventful **11** commonplace **12** unnoteworthy

ordnance
4 guns **6** cannon **7** weapons **8** supplies **9** artillery **10** ammunition

ordure
9 excrement
combining form: **4** copr, scat **5** copro, scato

ore
4 gold, rock **5** metal **6** copper, silver **7** mineral **8** platinum
analysis: **5** assay
deposit: **4** lode, vein
excavation: **5** stope
iron: **5** ocher **8** goethite, hematite, limonite
lead: **6** galena
process: **8** leaching, smelting
refuse: **4** slag **5** dross, matte **6** scoria
smelted: **6** speiss **7** regulus

oread
5 nymph

Oreb's slayer
6 Gideon

Oregon
capital: **5** Salem
largest city: **8** Portland
nickname: **11** Beaver State, Sunset State **12** Webfoot State

Orel's river
3 Oka

Orestes
father: **9** Agamemnon
friend: **7** Pylades
mother: **12** Clytemnestra
sister: **7** Electra **9** Iphigenia

victim: **9** Aegisthus **12** Clytemnestra
wife: **8** Hermione

organ
5 agent, means **6** agency, medium, review **7** channel, journal, vehicle **8** magazine, ministry **9** newspaper **10** instrument, periodical
ancient: **6** syrinx **9** hydraulus
barrel: **10** hurdy-gurdy
bodily: **3** ear, eye **4** lung, nose **5** gland, heart, liver **6** kidney, larynx, spleen, tongue, tonsil, viscus **9** intestine
combining form: **6** viscer **7** visceri, viscero
mouth: **9** harmonica
part: **4** pipe, reed, stop **5** pedal, valve **6** blower **7** console, tremolo **8** keyboard, pedalier **9** wind chest
reed: **8** melodeon **9** harmonium
stop: **4** oboe, sext **5** gamba, quint, viola **6** dolcan, dulcet **7** bassoon, celesta, melodia, subbass, tertian **8** carillon, dulciana, gemshorn
tactile: **6** feeler **8** tentacle

organ cactus
7 saguaro

organism
4 unit **5** being, biont, plant **6** animal
disease-producing: **4** germ **5** virus **7** microbe **8** pathogen **9** bacterium
single-celled: **5** monad **6** amoeba **9** protozoan
suffix: **5** acean

organist
American: **3** Fox (Virgil) **5** Biggs (E. Power) **6** Newman (Anthony)
Danish: **9** Buxtehude (Dietrich)
Dutch: **9** Sweelinck (Jan)
English: **6** Wesley (Samuel) **7** Gibbons (Christopher, Edward, Ellis, Orlando)
French: **5** Widor (Charles) **6** Franck (Cesar) **8** Messiaen (Olivier) **10** Schweitzer (Albert)
German: **4** Bach (Carl Philipp, Johann Christian, Johann Christoph, Johann Sebastian, Wilhelm Friedemann, Wilhelm Friedrech) **6** Walcha (Helmut) **7** Richter (Anton, Ernst, Ferdinand, Johann, Karl)
Italian: **7** Germani (Fernando) **8** Gabrieli (Andrea, Giovanni)

organization
4 body, club, unit **5** group, guild, setup **6** agency **11** arrangement, association
college: **4** frat **8** sorority **10** fraternity
criminal: **4** gang **5** Mafia

fraternal: (see **fraternal society**)
government: (see **government agency**)
lack of: **5** chaos
political: **4** bloc **5** party **7** apparat, machine

organize
4 form **5** array, found, order, rally, set up, start **6** create, muster **7** arrange, dispose, marshal **8** mobilize **9** construct, establish, institute, integrate, methodize, systemize **10** constitute, coordinate **11** put together

orgy
3 bat **4** romp, soak, tear **5** binge, fling, party, revel, spree **6** ran-tan **7** blowoff, carouse, debauch, rampage, splurge, wassail **8** carousal **9** bacchanal **10** saturnalia **11** bacchanalia

oriel
3 bay **6** window

orient
5 adapt, pearl, sheen **6** adjust, luster **8** acquaint **11** accommodate

Orient
4 Asia, East **7** Far East

Oriental
5 Asian **7** Asiatic, Chinese, Eastern **8** Japanese
chieftain: **4** khan
coin: **3** sen, yen
dish: **5** pilaf
drink: **3** tea **4** sake, tuba **6** arrack
inn: **4** khan **5** serai **11** caravansary **12** caravanserai
litter: **4** kago **5** dooly **6** doolie **9** palanquin
market: **3** suq **4** souk **6** bazaar
nana: **4** amah
prince: **4** raja
ruler: **4** khan, raja, shah **5** calif, nawab, rajah **6** caliph, sultan
storm: **7** monsoon
taxi: **7** ricksha **8** rickshaw **10** jinrikisha
title: **4** raja **5** rajah
weight: **4** tael **5** catty, liang
worker: **6** coolie

orifice
see **opening**

oriflamme
4 flag **5** color **6** banner, pennon **7** pendant, pennant **8** bannerol, gonfalon, standard, streamer

origin
4 root, seed, well **5** birth, blood, start **6** source, whence **7** descent, genesis, lineage **8** ancestry, foun-

tain, nascence, nascency, pedigree
9 beginning, inception, maternity,
parentage, paternity **10** derivation,
extraction, provenance, wellspring
combining form: **4** geny
of a word: **9** etymology

original
3 new **4** case, quiz **5** first, model,
novel, prime **6** maiden, mother, native, oddity, unique, zombie **7** initial, oddball, pattern, pioneer, primary **8** creative, earliest, inventor
9 archetype, character, demiurgic,
deviceful, eccentric, ingenious, innovator, inventive, precedent, precursor, primitive, prototype, underived **10** archetypal, forerunner,
innovative, innovatory, introducer
prefix: **4** arch **5** arche, archi

originate
4 coin, flow, make, open, rise, sire,
stem **5** arise, begin, birth, breed,
hatch, issue, set up, spawn, start
6 create, father, launch, parent,
spring **7** emanate, proceed, produce, usher in **8** come from, commence, generate, hail from, initiate,
stem from **9** institute, introduce,
procreate **10** derive from, inaugurate, spring from

originator
4 sire **5** maker **6** author, father
7 creator, founder **8** inventor **9** architect, generator, innovator, patriarch **10** introducer

oriole
4 bird **8** troupial
European: **6** loriot
genus: **7** Icterus
golden: **5** pirol **6** loriot
kind: **6** golden **7** orchard **8** Bullock's **9** Baltimore

Orion
6 hunter **13** constellation
beloved: **3** Eos
belt: **7** Ellwand
father: **7** Hyrieus **8** Poseidon
slayer: **5** Diana **7** Artemis
star: **5** Rigel **9** Bellatrix
10 Betelgeuse

orison
4 plea, suit **6** appeal, prayer **8** entreaty, petition **11** application,
imploration, imprecation
12 supplication

Orithyia
lover: **6** Boreas
son: **5** Zetes **6** Calais

Orlando author
5 Woolf (Virginia)

Orlando Furioso author
7 Ariosto (Ludovico)

Orleans heroine
9 Joan of Arc

orlop
4 deck

ornament
3 gem **4** bead, deck, trim **5** adorn,
jewel, prank **6** bedeck, enrich, finial, tassel **7** dress up, garnish, jewelry, pendant, whatnot **8** beautify,
decorate, filigree **9** embellish, embroider, lavaliere **10** lavalliere
architectural: **7** crocket **10** ball-
flower
Christmas tree: **4** bulb **5** angel
6 tinsel
lip: **6** labret
shoulder: **7** epaulet

ornate
4 lush, rich **5** fancy, showy
6 florid, frilly, gilded, rococo **7** aureate, baroque, labored, opulent
8 luscious, overdone **9** elaborate,
luxuriant, luxurious, sumptuous
10 flamboyant, overworked

ornery
4 mean **5** balky, nasty, waspy
6 cranky **7** bearish, froward, restive, waspish, wayward **8** cankered, contrary, perverse, stubborn,
vinegary **9** crotchety **10** vinegarish
11 wrongheaded **12** cantankerous,
cross-grained

ornithic
5 avian

ornithologist
American: **4** Bond (James) **7** Audu-
bon (John James), Bartram
(William)
English: **5** Gould (John)
Scottish: **6** Wilson (Alexander)

ornithon
6 aviary

orotund
4 full, loud **5** round **7** aureate,
flowery, ringing, vibrant **8** plangent, resonant, sonorant, sonorous
9 bombastic, consonant **10** euphuistic, oratorical, resounding, rhetorical, stentorian **11** declamatory
12 magniloquent **13** grandiloquent

Orpah
husband: **7** Chilion
sister-in-law: **4** Ruth

orphan
4 lost, waif **5** alone, Annie **6** bereft
7 cast-off, ignored **8** forsaken,
slighted, solitary **9** abandoned,

foundling, neglected **10** parentless,
unparented

Orpheus
father: **6** Apollo **7** Oeagrus
home: **6** Thrace
instrument: **4** lyre
mother: **8** Calliope
wife: **8** Euridice

ort
3 bit **5** scrap **6** morsel **7** leaving,
remnant **8** leftover

orthodox
4 good, tory **5** right, sound
6 proper, square **7** correct, diehard, fogyish, oldline **8** accepted,
admitted, approved, official, received, standard, straight **9** canonical, customary **10** button-down,
recognized, sanctioned **11** reactionary, traditional **12** acknowledged, conservative, conventional
13 authoritative

orthography
8 spelling

ortolan
4 sora **7** bunting **8** bobolink

Orwell novel
10 Animal Farm

oryx
7 gemsbok **8** antelope

os
4 bone **5** esker, mouth **7** orifice

oscillate
4 sway, vary **5** squeg, swing, waver **7** vibrate **9** fluctuate, pendulate

osculate
3 lip **4** buss, kiss, peck **5** smack

osier
3 rod **6** willow **7** dogwood

Osiris
brother: **3** Set **4** Seth
crown: **4** atef
father: **3** Geb, Keb, Seb
mother: **3** Nut
scribe: **5** Thoth
sister: **4** Isis
slayer: **3** Set **4** Seth
son: **5** Horus **6** Anubis
wife: **4** Isis

osmium
symbol: **2** Os

osmosis
4 flow **9** diffusion **10** absorption
12 assimilation

osprey
4 hawk **8** fish hawk

Ossa and ___
6 Pelion

osseous
4 bony

ossicle
4 bone 5 incus 6 stapes 7 malleus

ossify
3 set 6 harden

ossuary
3 urn 4 tomb 5 vault

ostensible
7 alleged, seeming 8 apparent, illusive, illusory, semblant, so-called, supposed 9 pretended, professed, purported

ostentation
4 show 7 display 9 showiness

ostentatious
4 loud 5 gaudy, showy, swank 6 chichi 7 splashy 8 peacocky 10 flamboyant, peacockish 11 pretentious

ostiole
4 pore 5 mouth 7 orifice 8 aperture

ostracism
5 exile 9 expulsion 10 banishment, relegation 11 deportation 12 displacement

ostracize
3 cut 4 oust, snob, snub 5 exile, expel 6 banish, deport 7 cast out, expulse 8 displace, throw out 9 blackball 10 expatriate 12 cold-shoulder

ostrich
female: 3 hen
genus: 8 Struthio
male: 4 cock

Ostrogoth king
9 Theodoric

otalgia
7 earache

Otello composer
5 Verdi (Giuseppe) 7 Rossini (Gioacchino)

o tempora! o ___!
5 mores

Othello
ensign: 4 Iago
lieutenant: 6 Cassio
victim, wife: 9 Desdemona

other
combining form: 3 all 4 allo 5 heter 6 hetero

others
4 rest 9 remainder
and: 4 et al 6 et alii

Othniel
brother: 5 Caleb
father: 5 Kenaz
wife: 6 Achsah

Othni's father
8 Shemaiah

otic
5 aural 8 auditory 9 auricular

otiose
4 idle, lazy, vain 5 empty 6 futile, hollow 7 surplus, useless 8 nugatory 11 inexcusable, purposeless, superfluous 13 supernumerary

Otis
7 bustard

Ottawa chief
7 Pontiac

otter
genus: 5 Lutra 7 Enhydra

ottoman
4 seat 5 couch 9 footstool

Ottoman
4 Turk 7 Turkish
ruler: 5 Osman 8 Suleyman

Otus
5 giant
brother: 9 Ephialtes
father: 6 Aloeus 8 Poseidon
mother: 9 Iphimedia
slayer: 6 Apollo

ouch
2 ow 3 cry 5 bezel, jewel 6 brooch, buckle 7 setting 8 bracelet, necklace 11 exclamation

ounce
3 cat 4 atom, doit, dram, drop 5 crumb, grain, minim, shred 6 weight 7 leopard, measure, smidgen 8 particle

ouph
3 elf

our
French: 5 notre
German: 5 unser
Italian: 6 nostra

Our Town author
6 Wilder (Thornton)

oust
3 bar, rob 4 lose 5 eject, evict, expel 6 banish, deport, remove 7 bereave, cast out, deprive, expulse, kick out 8 displace, relegate 9 ostracize, transport 10 disinherit, dispossess

out
4 away, free, leak, show 5 break, chase, chuck, douse, eject, evict, forth, loose 6 absent, quench 7 dismiss, extrude, showing 9 transpire 10 extinguish
of control: 4 wild 7 chaotic
of gas: 5 tired 9 exhausted
of line: 4 awry, rude 5 askew, fresh
of place: 13 inappropriate
of sorts: 5 cross 7 grouchy, peevish 9 irritable
of the ordinary: 3 odd 7 strange, unusual

outage
7 failure 8 blackout 12 interruption

out-and-out
5 gross, sheer, utter 7 perfect 8 absolute, complete, positive 10 consummate 13 thoroughgoing

outback
4 bush 10 wilderness

outboard
5 motor

outbreak
4 dawn, rash 5 burst, flare, onset 6 plague, revolt 8 epidemic, eruption 9 beginning 12 commencement

outbreathe
6 exhale, expire

outburst
4 gale, gust, tiff 5 flare, sally, scene, storm 6 access, fantod, frenzy, tirade 7 flare-up, rapture, tantrum, torrent 8 eruption 9 explosion

outcast
4 hobo 5 exile, leper, tramp 6 pariah 7 Ishmael, vagrant 8 castaway, derelict, vagabond 9 reprobate 10 expatriate, Ishmaelite 11 offscouring, untouchable
Japanese: 3 eta

outclass
4 best 5 excel 7 surpass

outcome
4 fate 5 event, issue 6 effect, result, sequel, upshot 8 causatum 9 aftermath 11 aftereffect, consequence

outcrop
4 rock 5 ledge 6 basset

outcry
4 yell 5 shout 6 clamor, tumult, upturn 7 ferment 8 upheaval 9 commotion

outdare
4 defy, face 5 beard, brave, front
7 venture 9 challenge

outdated
see **out-of-date**

outdo
3 top 4 beat, best, down 5 excel,
trump, worst 6 better, defeat, exceed 7 surpass, upstage
9 transcend

outdoor
7 open-air 8 alfresco
10 hypaethral

outer
5 ectad, ectal 6 remote 7 surface
8 exterior, external 9 extrinsic
10 extraneous 11 superficial

outermost
4 last 5 final 7 extreme 8 farthest,
furthest, remotest

outfit
3 arm, kit, rig 4 band, firm, gear
5 corps, dress, equip, getup, guise,
house, party, troop 6 tackle, troupe
7 appoint, company, concern, costume, furnish 8 accouter, accoutre,
business, ensemble, materiel, tackling 9 apparatus, equipment, machinery 10 enterprise 11 habiliments 12 organization
13 accouterments, accoutrements,
establishment, paraphernalia

outflow
4 flux 6 efflux 8 drainage, effluent

outfox
see **outwit**

outgrowth
4 tuft 5 child, issue, shoot
6 branch, effect, member, result
7 process, product, spin-off 8 offshoot, swelling 9 by-product, offspring, processus 10 derivative,
descendant 11 aftereffect, consequence, enlargement, excrescence,
excrescency

outhouse
5 jakes, privy 7 latrine

outing
4 trip 5 jaunt, sally 6 junket, picnic
9 excursion 10 roundabout

outland
5 rural 6 rustic 7 bucolic, country
8 agrestic, pastoral 10 campestral,
provincial 11 countrified

outlandish
3 odd 4 back, wild 5 alien, kinky,
queer, ultra, weird 6 remote, vulgar 7 bizarre, curious, extreme,
foreign, strange, uncouth, unusual

8 barbaric, frontier, peculiar, singular 9 barbarian, barbarous, graceless, monstrous, tasteless, unsettled
10 unorthodox 11 extravagant

outlaw
3 ban 5 taboo 6 badman, bandit,
enjoin, forbid, gunman 7 inhibit
8 criminal, prohibit, renegade
9 desperado, interdict

outlay
4 cost, give 5 spend 6 expend
7 expense 8 disburse 11 expenditure 12 disbursement

outlet
4 exit, hole, shop, vent 5 store
6 egress, escape 7 opening, orifice, release 8 aperture, showroom

outline
3 hem, map, rim 4 edge, form,
limn, plan 5 bound, chart, draft,
shape, skirt, trace 6 border, figure,
fringe, margin, projet, sketch
7 contour, profile 8 skeleton, surround, syllabus 9 adumbrate
10 figuration, silhouette
11 skeletonize

outlive
7 survive

outlook
4 side, view 5 angle, scape, scene,
sight, slant, vista 8 prospect 9 direction, viewpoint 10 standpoint
11 observatory, perspective, point
of view

outlying
3 far 6 far-off, remote 7 distant, faraway, removed 8 far-flung

outmoded
see **out-of-date**

out-of-date
3 old 5 dowdy, passé, tacky 6 démodé, frumpy, stodgy 7 antique,
archaic, oldtime, vintage 8 frumpish 9 unstylish 10 antiquated
12 old-fashioned

out-of-the-way
5 aside 6 remote, secret 7 devious,
obscure, removed, retired
8 lonesome

outpouring
4 flow, gush 8 effusion, outburst

output
4 crop, gain, take 5 yield 6 profit
7 harvest, produce, product
10 production

outrage
4 harm, hurt, rape, ruin 5 abuse,
anger, force, spoil, wrong 6 defile,

ill-use, injury, insult, misuse, offend,
ravish 7 affront, oppress, violate
8 aggrieve, deflower, ill-treat, maltreat, mischief, mistreat

outrageous
5 awful, gross 6 crying, horrid, unholy, wicked 7 beastly, ghastly, obscene, ungodly 8 dreadful, flagrant, horrible, shocking, terrible
9 desperate 10 abominable, impossible 11 intolerable, unchristian, uncivilized 12 unreasonable

outré
5 kinky, ultra 7 bizarre, strange

outrigger
4 prao, prau, proa 5 canoe, prahu

outright
3 all 5 gross, total, utter, whole
6 entire 7 perfect 8 absolute, complete, positive 10 consummate
11 unmitigated 13 thoroughgoing

outrun
4 beat 6 exceed 7 surpass

outset
4 dawn 5 birth, start 7 dawning,
opening 9 beginning
12 commencement

outshine
see **outdo**

outside
3 bar, but, off, top 4 open, over,
past, save, slim 5 after, alien, small
6 beyond, except, remove, saving,
slight, utmost 7 foreign, maximal,
maximum, open-air, slender, topmost 8 alfresco, exterior, external
9 apart from, excluding 10 hypaethral, negligible 11 exclusive of
prefix: 2 ec, ex 3 ect, exo 5 extra,
extro

outsider
5 alien 7 inconnu 8 stranger
9 foreigner

outsmart
see **outwit**

outspoken
4 free, open 5 bluff, blunt, frank,
plain, round, vocal 6 candid, direct
8 explicit, strident 10 forthright,
pointblank

outspread
4 open 6 expand, extend, unfold

outstanding
3 due 4 main, star 5 chief, major,
noted 6 marked, mature, signal, superb, unpaid 7 capital, notable,
overdue, payable, salient, stellar
8 dominant 9 arrestive, principal,

prominent, unsettled **10** noticeable, preeminent, remarkable **11** conspicuous, magnificent, predominant, superlative

outstart
4 dawn **5** birth, onset **7** dawning, opening **9** beginning **12** commencement

outstrip
3 top **4** beat, best, lose, pass **5** excel **6** better, exceed **7** surpass **8** distance

outsweepings
4 junk **5** trash, waste **6** debris, litter, refuse **7** garbage, rubbish

outward
4 over **5** ectad, ectal, overt **7** visible **8** apparent, exterior, external **10** ostensible **11** superficial

outweigh
6 make up, offset, redeem, set off **7** balance **8** atone for, overbear **10** compensate **11** countervail, overbalance

outwit
3 fox **4** dupe, foil, gull, have, hoax, undo **5** trick **6** befool **8** hoodwink **9** bamboozle, frustrate, overreach

outworn
see **out-of-date**

ouzel
4 bird **6** thrush **9** blackbird

oval
4 ooid **5** track **7** ellipse **8** elliptic **9** egg-shaped **11** ellipsoidal

ovation
6 homage, praise **8** applause

oven
4 kiln, lehr, oast **5** range, stove **6** calcar

over
2 by, on **3** mid, off, too **4** amid, anew, atop, away, done, leap, past, upon, with **5** about, above, again, aloft, clear, cross, due to, ended, extra, midst, round, vault **6** across, afresh, around, beyond, de novo, during, higher, hurdle, unduly **7** athwart, greater, outside, outward, owing to, through **8** exterior, external, finished, once more, superior, surmount **9** because of, extremely, immensely, negotiate **10** throughout **11** excessively, superjacent **12** inordinately, transversely
French: **3** sur
German: **4** über

prefix: **2** ep **3** eph, epi, sur **5** extra, hyper, super, supra
Spanish: **5** sobre

overabundance
6 excess **7** surfeit, surplus **8** plethora **10** surplusage **11** superfluity

overact
3 ham, mug **4** rant **5** emote, spout

overage
see **overabundance**

overall
6 global, mainly, mostly **7** chiefly, general, largely **8** sweeping **9** generally, inclusive, primarily **10** high and low, tar and wide **11** principally **13** comprehensive, predominantly

overalls
5 pants **8** trousers

over and above
6 beside, beyond **7** besides **8** as well as

over and over
3 oft **4** much **5** often **8** ofttimes **10** frequently, oftentimes, repeatedly

overbearing
5 bossy, proud **6** lordly, master **7** haughty, pompous, regnant **8** absolute, arrogant, cavalier, despotic, dominant, imperial, insolent, superior **9** ascendant, imperious, masterful, paramount, prevalent, sovereign **10** autocratic, disdainful, highhanded, imperative, peremptory, tyrannical **11** magisterial, predominant, predominate **12** preponderant, supercilious **13** high-and-mighty

overblown
3 big, fat **4** arty **5** gross, heavy, obese, stout, tumid, windy **6** fleshy, portly, turgid **7** aureate, flowery, porcine **8** dropsied, imposing, inflated, sonorous **9** bombastic, corpulent, dropsical, flatulent, tumescent **10** arty-crafty, euphuistic, oratorical, rhetorical **11** declamatory, exaggerated, pretentious **12** high-sounding, magniloquent **13** grandiloquent

overbold
6 arrant, brassy, brazen **7** blatant **8** impudent **9** barefaced, shameless, unabashed **10** unblushing **11** brazenfaced

overcast
3 cap, dim **4** dull, gray, hazy **5** cloud, cover, crown, dirty, heavy

6 cloudy, darken, shadow, sullen **7** becloud, blanket, louring, obscure **8** brooding, lowering, nubilous **9** adumbrate **10** oppressive

overcharge
3 gyp, pad **4** clip, skin, soak **5** gauge, stick **6** fleece **7** magnify **9** embellish

overcoat
6 capote, raglan, ulster **7** paletot, surtout **9** balmacaan, inverness **12** chesterfield

overcome
3 win **4** beat, best, down, lick **5** drown, throw, whelm **6** defeat, hurdle, master **7** conquer, outlive, prevail, triumph **8** surmount **9** prostrate
by grief: **8** dejected, downcast **10** dispirited **12** disconsolate **13** broken-hearted

overconfident
5 brash, cocky **6** uppity **7** pushful **9** presuming **10** brassbound **12** presumptuous

overdo
7 exhaust, fatigue **10** exaggerate

overdue
4 late **5** lated, owing, tardy **6** mature, unpaid **7** belated, payable **9** unsettled **10** behindhand, unpunctual **11** outstanding

overemphasize
7 magnify **10** exaggerate

overflow
4 brim, pour, slop, teem **5** drown, flood, slosh, spate, spill, swamp, whelm **6** deluge, engulf, excess **7** cascade, niagara, surfeit, surplus, torrent **8** cataract, flooding, inundate, plethora, spillage, submerge **9** cataclysm **10** inundation, surplusage **11** superfluity

overflowing
4 rife **5** alive, awash **7** replete, teeming **8** thronged **13** superabundant

overgrown
4 lush, rank **5** braky, copsy, dense, thick **6** brushy, jungly **7** brambly **8** thickety **9** thicketed

overhang
3 jut **4** poke, pout **5** bulge, jetty, pouch **6** beetle **7** project **8** protrude

overhaul
3 fix **4** do up, mend, take **5** catch, patch **6** doctor, repair, revamp

7 rebuild 8 renovate 11 recondition, reconstruct

overhead
5 above, aloft 7 expense

overindulgence
6 excess 8 gluttony 12 immoderation, intemperance

overindulgent
9 excessive 10 immoderate, inordinate, untempered 11 intemperate 12 unrestrained

overkill
6 excess 7 surfeit, surplus 8 plethora 10 surplusage 11 superfluity

overlap
7 shingle 9 imbricate

overlay
3 cap 4 coat 5 cover, crown 6 veneer 7 blanket 8 covering

overload
4 glut 6 excess 7 surfeit

overlook
4 boss, fail, omit, skip 5 blank, chasm 6 forget, ignore, slight, survey 7 blink at, condone, neglect 8 chaperon, discount, dominate, omission 9 blink away, chaperone, disregard, supervise 10 tower above

overlord
5 chief, ruler 8 suzerain 9 chieftain

overpass
4 fail, omit 6 bridge, forget, ignore 7 blink at, neglect 8 discount 9 blink away, disregard

overplay
6 accent 7 magnify, point up, stretch 8 maximize 9 dramatize 10 accentuate, exaggerate 11 hyperbolize

overpower
4 rout 5 crush, drown, whelm 6 defeat, master, reduce, subdue 7 conquer 8 bear down, vanquish 9 prostrate, subjugate

overreach
3 gyp 4 beat, bilk, undo 5 cheat, cozen 6 chouse, diddle, outfox, outwit 7 defraud 8 flimflam, outslick, outsmart 11 outmaneuver

override
3 lap 4 veto 7 nullify, shingle 9 imbricate

overriding
7 central, pivotal, primary 8 cardinal 9 principal

overrule
4 sway, veto 5 reign 6 govern

overrun
4 beat, drub, lick, raid, trim, whip 5 beset, foray, smear, spill, swarm 6 exceed, infest, inroad, invade, thrash 7 outstep, surpass 8 lambaste

overseas
5 alien 6 abroad, exotic 7 foreign, strange 11 transmarine, ultramarine

oversee
3 run 4 boss 5 watch 6 survey 8 chaperon 9 chaperone, supervise 11 quarterback, superintend

overseer
4 boss, head 5 chief 7 foreman, manager 8 chaperon 9 chaperone 10 supervisor

overshadow
3 dim 4 haze 5 cloud, cover 6 darken 7 becloud, obscure 9 adumbrate

overshoe
4 boot 6 arctic, galosh, patten, rubber

oversight
4 care, skip 5 aegis, blank, chasm, check, error, guard 6 charge 7 conduct, control, custody, default, failure, keeping, mistake, neglect, running 8 handling, omission, tutelage 10 ciceronage, intendance, management 11 chaperonage

overslaugh
3 bar, dam 5 block, brake 6 hinder, impede 8 obstruct

oversoon
5 early 7 betimes 8 previous, untimely 9 premature 11 prematurely

overspread
3 cap 5 beset, cover, crown 6 infest 7 blanket

overstate
3 pad 5 color, fudge 7 magnify 9 embellish, embroider 10 exaggerate

overstep
6 exceed 7 surpass 8 infringe, trespass 10 transgress

overstock
6 excess 7 surplus 9 remainder 10 surplusage

overstress
7 magnify 8 maximize 10 exaggerate

overswarm
4 raid 5 beset, foray 6 infest, inroad, invade

overt
4 open 6 patent 7 obvious, outward, visible 8 apparent, manifest

overtake
4 pass

over there
3 yon 6 yonder

overthrow
4 down, fell, oust, rout, ruin 5 purge, upset 6 defeat, depose, remove, topple, tumble, unseat 7 beating, conquer, debacle, destroy, licking, unhorse 8 dethrone, downcast, drubbing 9 liquidate, trouncing 10 defeasance 11 shellacking 12 vanquishment

overtone
4 hint 8 harmonic 10 suggestion 11 association, connotation, implication

overture
3 bid 5 proem 6 tender 7 advance, preface, prelude 8 approach, exordium, foreword, preamble, prologue, proposal 9 prelusion 11 proposition 12 introduction, prolegomenon

overturn
3 tip 4 coup, down 5 upend, upset 6 keel up, topple, tumble 7 capsize, shake-up, unhorse 9 prostrate 10 revolution

overweening
5 brash 6 uppish, uppity 7 forward, pushful 8 arrogant 10 immoderate 12 presumptuous 13 self-assertive

overweight
3 fat 5 gross, heavy, obese, stout 6 fleshy, portly 9 corpulent

overwhelm
4 beat, bury, drub, lick, ruin, sink, trim, whip 5 crush, drown, flood, floor, lower, smear, swamp, upset, wreck 6 deluge, engulf, thrash 7 destroy, disturb, shatter, shellac, smother 8 inundate, submerge 9 devastate, downgrade, dumbfound, prostrate 10 demoralize 11 subordinate

overwhelmed
5 agape 6 aghast 7 stunned 13 thunderstruck

overword
6 burden 7 refrain

Ovid work
5 Fasti **7** Tristia **8** Heroides
13 Metamorphoses

oviform
4 ooid, oval **5** ovate **6** ooidal
9 egg-shaped

ovine
5 sheep **9** sheeplike

ovoid
  see **oviform**

ovule
3 egg
fertilized: **4** seed

ovum
3 egg **6** gamete **7** egg cell

owing
3 due **6** mature, unpaid **7** overdue,
payable **9** unsettled

owing to
4 over **7** through **9** because of

owl
Australian: **7** boobook **8** morepork
cry: **4** hoot
genus: **4** Otus
kind: **3** elf **4** barn, gray, lulu **5** eagle, gnome, madge, pygmy, snowy
6 barred, horned **7** saw-whet
screech **9** long-eared **10** short-
eared **11** great horned
resembling: **8** strigine
snowy: **7** harfang

Owl and Pussycat author
4 Lear (Edward)

own
4 avow, have, hold **5** admit, allow,
enjoy, grant, let on **6** fess up, retain **7** concede, confess, possess
11 acknowledge

owner
4 lord **8** landlady, landlord **9** possessor **10** proprietor

ownership
4 hand **5** title **8** dominion, property
10 possession **11** proprietary
perpetual: **8** mortmain

ox
3 yak **4** anoa, buff, gaur, musk,
zebu **5** bison, gayal, steer **6** bovine, ovibos **7** banteng, bantery,
brahman, buffalo
Asian: **4** zebu
attachment: **4** yoke
combining form: **4** bovi
extinct: **4** urus **7** aurochs
family: **7** Bovidae
relating to: **6** bovine
Scottish: **4** nowt, owse
wild: **4** anoa, gaur **7** banteng
8 saladang, seladang

oxeye
5 daisy **6** flower

oxford
4 shoe **5** cloth, sheep

oxide
calcium: **4** lime **9** quicklime
ferric: **4** rust
sodium: **4** soda

oxidize
4 rust

oxygen
3 air, gas **5** ozone **7** element
discoverer: **9** Lavoisier
form: **5** ozone
liquid: **3** lox

oyster
5 forte **6** medium **7** bivalve,
mollusk
bed: **4** park **6** claire, cultch
combining form: **5** ostre **6** ostrei,
ostreo
eggs: **5** spawn
genus: **6** Ostrea **11** Crassostrea
Long island: **9** bluepoint
product: **5** pearl
shell: **4** test **5** shuck
young: **4** spat

oysterbird
5 tirma **10** sanderling

oysterfish
6 tautog

oyster grass
4 kelp **10** sea lettuce

Oz
creator: **4** Baum (Frank)
inhabitant: **8** Munchkin

Ozark State
8 Missouri

Ozem
brother: **5** David
father: **5** Jesse **9** Jerahmeel

Ozni's father
3 Gad

Ozymandias author
7 Shelley (Percy Bysshe)

P p

pabulum
4 food 7 aliment 8 nutrient 9 nutriment 10 sustenance 11 nourishment

pace
3 rut 4 gait, hoof, rate, step, time, walk 5 grind, speed, tempo, tread, troop 6 timing 7 example, fluency, forerun, precede, proceed, routine, traipse 8 ambulate, antecede, celerity, rapidity, regulate, velocity 9 quickness, rapidness, swiftness, treadmill

pachyderm
8 elephant

pacific
4 calm, meek, mild 6 gentle, irenic, placid, serene 8 dovelike, peaceful, tranquil 9 appeasing, peaceable

Pacificator, Great
4 Clay (Henry)

Pacific Ocean discoverer
6 Balboa (Vasco Nunez de)

pacifist
4 dove 6 irenic 8 appeaser, peaceful 9 peaceable 10 nonviolent, satyagrahi 11 peacemonger

pacify
4 calm, ease, lull 5 allay, quiet, still 6 settle, soften, soothe, subdue, temper 7 appease, assuage, mollify, placate

pack
3 jam, lot, lug, mob, ram, wad 4 bear, cram, fill, heap, load, lump, mass, much, pile, stow, tamp, tote 5 carry, choke, crowd, ferry, group, store, stuff, troop 6 barrel, bestow, bundle, charge, convey, depart 7 compact 8 compress 9 container

pack animal
3 ass 4 mule 5 burro, camel, horse, llama 6 donkey 7 jackass, sumpter 13 beast of burden

packed
4 full 5 awash 7 brimful, crowded, stuffed 8 brimming 9 chock-full

packet
3 pot, wad 4 boat, mint, pile 6 boodle, bundle, parcel 7 fortune

pact
4 bond 6 treaty 7 bargain, concord 8 alliance, covenant 9 agreement

pad
3 mat, wad 5 fudge, guard, quilt, stuff 6 muffle, shield, tablet, trudge 7 bolster, cushion, magnify, stretch 8 overdraw 9 embellish, embroider, overpaint, overstate 10 exaggerate, overcharge

paddle
3 fin, oar, row 4 pull 5 spank 6 dabble, thrash 7 flipper

pagan
7 gentile, heathen, infidel, profane 8 idolator 9 infidelic 10 unbeliever
god: 4 idol

page
4 book, call, leaf 5 folio, sheet 6 locate, summon 7 writing
left-hand: 5 verso
reverse: 5 verso
right-hand: 5 recto

pageant
4 sham, show 7 charade 8 disguise, pretense 9 spectacle 10 exhibition

Pagiel's father
5 Ocran 6 Ochran

Pagliacci
character: 5 Canio, Nedda, Tonio 6 Silvio
composer: 11 Leoncavallo (Ruggero)

pagoda
2 ta 3 taa 6 alcove, gazebo, temple 9 belvedere 11 garden house, summerhouse

pail
6 bucket, piggin

pain
3 ail, irk, try 4 ache, care, hurt, pang 5 agony, cramp, grief, throe, upset, wound 6 effort, grieve, harass, harrow, injure, stitch, stress, twinge 7 afflict, agonize, anguish, crucify, provoke, torment, torture, travail, trouble 8 aggrieve, convulse, distress, lacerate 9 suffering 10 affliction, discomfort, excruciate
abdominal: 5 colic
back: 7 lumbago
combining form: 3 alg 4 agra, algo, noci 5 agrae (plural), algia, algic 6 odynia, odynic
ear: 6 otalgy 7 otalgia
intensity unit: 3 dol
muscular: 7 myalgia

painful
3 raw 4 sore 5 acute, sharp 6 aching, bitter 7 algetic, galling, hurting, irksome, racking 8 annoying, grievous, piercing, shooting, stabbing, stinging, unsavory 9 agonizing, harrowing, torturous, upsetting, vexatious 10 afflictive, tormenting

painkiller
6 opiate 7 anodyne 8 morphine, narcotic 9 analgesic 10 anesthetic

painstaking
5 exact, fussy 7 careful, heedful 8 diligent, exacting, punctual 9 laborious 10 meticulous, scrupulous 11 punctilious

paint
4 coat, daub, face, limn 5 color, japan, stain 6 depict, fresco, makeup 7 portray 9 delineate, represent 10 maquillage

painter

6 artist

American: **4** Haas (Richard), West (Benjamin), Wood (Grant) **5** Abbey (Edwin Austin), Henri (Robert), Hicks (Edward), Homer (Winslow), Johns (Jasper), Kroll (Leon), Marin (John), Moses (Grandma), Peale (Anna, Charles Willson, James, Raphaelle, Rembrant, Sarah, Titian), Ryder (Albert), Shahn (Ben), Sloan (Eric, John), Weber (Max), Wyeth (Andrew, Jamie, Newell Convers) **6** Benton (Thomas Hart), Catlin (George), Copley (John Singleton), Eakins (Thomas), Hassam (Childe), Hopper (Edward), Inness (George), Leutze (Emanuel), Martin (Agnes, Homer), Rivers (Larry), Rothko (Mark), Stella (Frank), Stuart (Gilbert), Tanguy (Yves), Thorpe (Thomas), Warhol (Andy) **7** Allston (Washington), Bellows (George), Cassatt (Mary), La Farge (John), O'Keeffe (Georgia), Parrish (Maxfield), Pollock (Jackson), Sargent (John Singer), Sheeler (Charles), Tiffany (Louis Comfort), Tworkov (Jack), Wiggins (Carleton) **8** Melchers (Gari), Rockwell (Norman), Sullivan (Patrick), Trumbull (John), Whistler (James Abbott McNeil) **9** Feininger (Lyonel), Remington (Frederic), Twachtman (John Henry), Vanderlyn (John) **10** Motherwell (Robert), Whittredge (Thomas) **12** Lichtenstein (Roy)

Austrian: **9** Kokoschka (Oskar)

Belgian: **6** Campin (Robert) **8** Magritte (Rene)

Canadian: **4** Kane (Paul) **6** Harris (Lawren), Watson (Homer) **7** Jackson (Alexander Young), Thomson (Tom) **9** MacDonald (James Edward Hervey)

Chinese: **4** Wu Li **6** Ma Yüan **7** Wang Wei **8** Yen Li-pen

Dutch: **4** Hals (Franz), Lely (Peter), Maas (Nicolas) **5** Bosch (Hieronymus), Steen (Jan) **6** Potter (Paul) **7** de Hooch (Pieter), de Witte (Emanuel de), Hobbema (Meindert), van Gogh (Vincent), Vermeer (Jan) **8** Mondrian (Piet), Ruisdael (Jacob van), Ruysdael (Salomon), Terborch (Gerard) **9** Rembrandt, Wouwerman (Philips) **11** Terbrugghen (Hendrik)

English: **4** John (Augustus), Lear (Edward) **5** Bacon (Francis), Blake (William), Brown (Ford Madox), Lewis (Wyndham), Watts (George)

6 Romney (George), Turner (Joseph Mallord William), Wilson (Richard) **7** Hogarth (William), Kneller (Godfrey), Millais (John), Raeburn (Henry) **8** Lawrence (Thomas), Reynolds (Joshua), Rossetti (Dante Gabriel) **9** Constable (John), Nicholson (Ben, William) **12** Gainsborough (Thomas)

Flemish: **4** Goes (Hugo van der) **6** Rubens (Peter Paul), Weyden (Rogier van der) **7** Memling (Hams), Teniers (David), Van Dyck (Anthony), Van Eyck (Hubert, Jan) **8** Breughel, Brueghel (Abraham, Ambrose, Jan, Pieter)

French: **4** Doré (Gustave), Dufy (Raoul) **5** Corot (Camille), David (Jacques-Louis), Degas (Edgar), Leger (Fernand), Manet (Edouard), Monet (Claude), Puvis (Pierre), Redon (Odilon), Vouet (Simon) **6** Braque (Georges), Breton (Andre), Claude (of Lorrain), Clouet (François, Jean) Gerome (Jean-Leon), Greuze (Jean-Baptiste), Ingres (Jean-Auguste-Dominique), Le Brun (Charles), Le Nain (Antoine, Louis, Mathieu), Millet (Jean-Francois), Renoir (Pierre-Auguste), Seurat (Georges), Sisley (Alfred), Tanguy (Yves), Vernet (Carle, Horace, Joseph) **7** Bonheur (Rosa), Bonnard (Pierre), Cézanne (Paul), Chardin (Jean-Baptiste), Courbet (Gustave), Daumier (Honore), Duchamp (Gaston, Marcel), Gauguin (Paul), Matisse (Henri), Morisot (Berthe), Poussin (Nicolas), Rouault (Georges), Utrillo (Maurice), Watteau (Antoine) **8** Dubuffet (Jean), Pissarro (Camille), Rousseau (Henri, Theodore), Vlaminck (Maurice de), Vuillard (Edouard) **9** Delacroix (Eugene), Fragonard (Jean-Honore), Gericault (Theodore), Laurencin (Marie) **10** Meissonier (Jean-Louis) **11** Le Corbusier

German: **5** Dürer (Albrecht), Ernst (Max), Grosz (George), Nolde (Emil) **6** Muller (Friedrich "Maler'') **7** Cranach (Lucas), Holbein (Hans), Lochner (Stefan), Schwind (Moritz von), Zoffany (Johann) **8** Kirchner (Ernst), Kollwitz (Käthe) **9** Grünewald (Matthias), Kandinsky (Wassily) **10** Schongauer (Martin), Wohlgemuth (Michael)

Greek: **6** Zeuxis **7** Apelles **10** Polygnotus

Irish: **5** Yeats (Jack, John Butler)

Italian: **4** Reni (Guido), Rosa (Salvator), Tura (Cosme) **5** Campi (Anto-

nio, Bernardino, Giulio, Vincenzo), Lippi (Fra Filippo, Filippino, Lorenzo), Piero (della Francesca, di Cosimo), Sarto (Andrea del) **6** Cosimo (Agnolo di, Piero di), Giotto, Romano (Giulio), Sodoma (IL), Titian, Vasari (Giorgio) **7** Bellini (Gentile, Giovanni, Jacopo), Chirico (Giorgio De), Cimabue, da Vinci (Leonardo), Fiesole (Giovanni da), Martini (Simone), Orcagna, Peruzzi (Baldassare), Raphael, Tiepolo (Giovanni), Uccello (Paolo), Zuccari (Taddeo) **8** Del Sarto (Andrea), Fabriano (Gentile da), Giordano (Luca), Mantegna (Andrea), Masaccio, Montagna (Bartolommeo), Perugino, Pontorno (Jacopo da), Severini (Gino), Veronese (Paolo), Vivarini (Alvise, Antonio, Bartolomeo) **9** Carpaccio (Vittore), Correggio, Francesca (Piero della) **10** Caravaggio, Modigliani (Amedeo), Signorelli (Luca), Tintoretto, Verrocchio (Andrea del), Zuccarelli (Francesco) **11** Ghirlandajo (Domenico) **12** Michelangelo, Parmigianino

Japanese: **5** Korin **6** Sesshu

Lithuanian: **7** Soutine (Chaim)

Mexican: **6** Orozco (Jose), Rivera (Diego), Tamayo (Rufino) **9** Siqueiros (David)

Norwegian: **5** Munch (Edvard)

Russian: **7** Chagall (Marc), Roerich (Nikolay) **9** Kandinsky (Wassily)

Scottish: **6** Ramsay (Allan) **7** Nasmyth (Alexander), Raeburn (Henry)

Spanish: **4** Dali (Salvador), Goya (Francisco), Gris (Juan), Miro (Joan), Sert (Jose Maria) **6** Ribera (Jose), Rincon (Antonio del), Tapies (Antonio) **7** El Greco, Herrera (Francisco de), Murillo (Bartolomé Esteban), Picasso (Pablo), Zuloaga (Ignacio) **8** Zurbaran (Francisco de) **9** Velazquez (Diego)

Swedish: **4** Zorn (Anders) **6** Roslin (Alexander)

Swiss: **4** Klee (Paul), Witz (Konrad)

painting

3 oil **7** acrylic, picture **10** watercolor

circular: **5** tondo

combining form: **6** chromy

one-color: **8** monotint **10** monochrome

plaster: **5** secco **6** fresco

style: **6** cubism, Gothic, pop art, rococo **7** baroque, Bauhaus, dadaism, fauvism, realism **8** Barbizon, futurism **9** Byzantine, geometric, mannerism **10** avant-garde, classi-

cism, surrealism **11** romanticism **13** expressionism, impressionism
technique: **3** oil **6** fresco, gouche, pastel **7** polymer, tempera **9** encaustic **10** watercolor
tool: **5** brush, easel, knife, paint **6** canvas **7** palette
wall: **5** mural

pair
3 duo, two **4** dyad, join, mate, span, team, yoke **5** brace, match, unite **6** couple **7** doublet, twosome **8** geminate

Pakistan
capital: **9** Islamabad
largest city: **7** Karachi
monetary unit: **5** rupee
province: **4** Sind **6** Punjab **11** Baluchistan

pal
4 chum, mate **5** buddy, crony **6** comate, friend **7** comrade, partner **9** associate, companion **11** confederate

paladin
see **douzeper**

Palal's father
4 Uzai

Palamedes
brother: **6** Sforza **8** Achilles
father: **8** Nauplius
slayer: **7** Corinda, Ulysses **8** Odysseus

palatable
5 sapid, tasty, yummy **6** savory, toothy **8** luscious, pleasing, saporous, savorous, tasteful, tempting **9** aperitive, delicious, relishing, saporific, savorsome, toothsome **10** appetizing, delightful, flavorsome

palate
4 zest **5** gusto, heart, taste **6** relish

palatial
4 lush, rich **5** large, noble, plush **6** Capuan, deluxe, ornate **7** opulent, stately **8** luscious, splendid **9** luxuriant, luxurious, sumptuous **10** impressive **11** magnificent, upholstered

palaver
3 gas, yak **4** blab, cant, chat, guff, tack **5** clack **6** affair, babble, hot air, jargon, parley **7** chatter, concern, lexicon, lookout, prattle, seminar **8** business, colloquy, dialogue **10** colloquium, conference, discussion, rap session **12** conversation

palaverous
5 windy, wordy **6** prolix **7** diffuse, verbose **9** redundant **10** longwinded

pale
3 dim, wan **4** ashy, dull, fade, gray, sick, weak **5** ashen, faint, fence, inane, livid, lurid, muddy, pasty, stake, waxen, white **6** anemic, blanch, chalky, doughy, feeble, jejune, pallid, picket, sallow, sickly, watery, whiten **7** ghastly, insipid, tarnish, waxlike **8** blanched, encircle, waterish, whitened **9** bloodless, colorless, deathlike

paleness
6 pallor

palinode
5 unsay **6** abjure, recall, recant **7** retract **8** forswear, take back, withdraw **10** retraction **11** recantation

pall
4 bore, cloy, glut, jade, sate, tire **5** cloak, drape, ennui, gorge, weary **6** canopy, clothe, mantle, stodge **7** disgust, satiate, surfeit **8** covering **11** counterpane

palladium
symbol: **2** Pd

Pallas
brother: **6** Aegeus
father: **7** Pandion
slayer: **7** Theseus
wife: **4** Styx; (see also **Athena**)

palliate
4 ease, hide, mask **5** cloak, cover, glass, gloze, salve **6** excuse, lessen, soften, temper, veneer, whiten **7** conceal, condone, cover up, lighten, qualify, varnish **8** disguise, mitigate, moderate, prettify **9** alleviate, dissemble, extenuate, glass over, gloze over, sugarcoat, whitewash

pallid
3 wan **4** ashy, dull **5** ashen, waxen **6** anemic, doughy, watery **8** blanched, waterish **9** bloodless, colorless

Pallu
father: **6** Reuben
son: **5** Eliab

pally
4 cozy **6** chummy **8** intimate

palm
3 tip **4** hide **5** bribe, merus, prize **6** thenar **7** conceal
beverage: **4** nipa **5** assai

fiber: **4** bass, bast **6** gomuti **7** bassine **8** piassava
fruit: **4** date **7** coconut **11** coquilla nut
kind: **3** fan, wax **4** coco, date, doom, hemp, nipa, sago **5** areca, assai, betel, datil, ivory, royal, tucum **6** gomuti, grigri, grugru, jupati, raffia, rattan **7** cabbage, feather, palmyra, talipot **8** carnauba, palmetto, piassava **12** Washingtonia
leaf: **4** olla **5** frond
starch: **4** sago
vine: **6** rattan

palmer
7 pilgrim

Palmetto State
13 South Carolina

palm lily
2 ti

palm off
5 foist **7** deceive

Palmyra's queen
7 Zenobia

palooka
3 oaf **4** gawk, lout, lump **5** klutz **6** lubber, lummox

palpable
4 sure **5** clear, plain **6** patent **7** certain, evident, obvious, seeming, tactile **8** apparent, distinct, manifest, positive, striking, tangible **9** arresting **10** noticeable **11** perceptible, unequivocal

palpate
4 feel **5** touch **6** finger, handle

palpitate
4 beat **5** pulse, throb **6** quiver **7** flutter, pulsate **12** pitter-patter

palter
3 fib, lie **5** evade, fence **6** haggle, parley **7** bargain, chaffer, falsify **10** equivocate **11** prevaricate

Palti
father: **5** Laish, Raphu
wife: **6** Michal

Paltiel's father
5 Azzan

paltry
3 low, set **4** base, mean, poor, puny, vile **5** borne, cheap, petty, small, tatty, trash **6** common, little, measly, narrow, shabby, shoddy, sleazy, slight, trashy **7** limited, lowdown, pitiful, rubbish, trivial **8** beggarly, inferior, picayune, piddling, rubbishy, trifling **9** worthless **10** de-

spicable, picayunish **11** ineffectual, Mickey Mouse, unimportant **13** insignificant

paludous place
5 marsh

Pamela author
10 Richardson (Samuel)

pamper
3 pet **4** baby **5** humor, spoil **6** caress, cocker, coddle, cosset, cuddle, dandle, fondle, regale, tickle **7** cater to, cherish, gratify, indulge **11** mollycoddle
Irish: **6** cosher

pamphlet
5 tract **6** folder **7** booklet, leaflet **8** brochure **10** broadsheet

pan
3 rap **5** basin, blame, cut up, knock, trash **6** attack **7** censure, condemn **8** denounce, ridicule **9** criticize, reprehend

Pan
5 Inuus **6** Faunus
father: **6** Hermes
invention: **6** syrinx
lower part: **4** goat
mother: **8** Penelope
pipe: **6** syrinx
seat of worship: **7** Arcadia
son: **7** Silenus

panacea
4 cure **6** elixir, relief, remedy **7** cure-all, nostrum **10** catholicon

Panacea's father
9 Asclepius **11** Aesculapius

pancake
8 flapjack, slapjack
French: **5** crepe
Jewish: **5** latke **6** blintz **7** blintze
Russian: **5** blini

Pandarus
6 archer **8** procuror
father: **6** Lycaon
slayer: **8** Diomedes

pandect
4 code **6** aperçu, digest, précis, sketch, survey **8** syllabus **10** compendium

pandemoniac
7 avernal, hellish, riotous, stygian **8** infernal, plutonic **9** cimmerian, plutonian

pandemonium
3 din **4** hell, sink **5** babel, Sodom **6** clamor, hubbub, jangle, racket, tumult, uproar **7** cesspit **8** cess-

pool, disorder **9** confusion **10** hullabaloo, tintamarre

pander
4 pimp **5** bully, cadet, cater **8** fancy man, procurer **9** procuress

Pandion
daughter: **6** Procne **9** Philomela
son: **6** Pallas

Pandora
creator: **10** Hephaestus
husband: **10** Epimetheus

pandurina
4 lute

panegyric
6 eulogy, praise **7** tribute **8** citation, encomium **9** laudation **10** salutation

panegyrical
9 laudative, laudatory, praiseful **10** eulogistic **11** encomiastic

panegyrize
4 hymn, laud **5** bless, cry up, extol **6** praise **7** glorify, magnify **8** eulogize **9** celebrate

panel
4 gore, jury **5** board, label **6** hurdle

pan-fry
5 sauté

pang
4 ache, pain, stab **5** agony, prick, spasm, throe **6** stitch, twinge **7** anguish, torment

Pangloss' pupil
7 Candide

panhandler
6 beggar

panic
4 fear, wild **5** alarm, dread, scare **6** dismay, frenzy, fright, horror, terror **8** cold feet, frighten, hysteria, stampede **11** trepidation **13** consternation

panoply
4 pomp, show **5** armor, array, shine **6** parade **7** display, fanfare

panorama
4 view **5** orbit, range, reach, scene, scope, sweep, vista **6** extent, radius **7** compass, purview **9** cyclorama

pan out
5 click **6** go over **7** come off, succeed

pant
3 aim **4** blow, gasp, gulp, huff, long, puff, wind, wish **5** chuff,

heave, throb, yearn **6** aspire, desire, hunger, thirst, wheeze **7** pulsate **9** palpitate

Pantagruel
5 giant
companion: **7** Panurge
father: **9** Gargantua
mother: **7** Badebec

Pantaloon's daughter
9 Columbine

Panthea's husband
9 Abradatus

pantomime
6 ballet, dancer **7** charade **12** harlequinade

pantry
6 closet, larder **7** buttery

pants
5 jeans **6** slacks **7** drawers **8** britches, knickers, trousers

pantywaist
5 sissy **7** doormat, milksop

Panurge's companion
10 Pantagruel

Paolo's lover
9 Francesca

pap
4 food, mash, pulp, slop **5** paste, trash **7** aliment, garbage, rubbish **9** nutriment **10** sustenance **11** nourishment

papal
8 pontific **9** apostolic **10** pontifical
cape: **5** fanon, orale
court: **5** Curia
decree: **8** decretal
envoy: **6** nuncio **8** ablegate
letter: **4** bull **10** encyclical

paper
4 card **5** essay, sheet, theme **6** letter, report **7** article, nominal **8** clerical, document **9** monograph, newspaper, wallpaper **10** memorandum **11** composition, publication **12** dissertation
arrangement: **3** pad **6** tablet
coarse: **9** newsprint
collection: **4** file **7** dossier
combining form: **6** papyro
copying: **6** carbon
currency: **5** scrip
measure: **4** page, ream **5** quire, sheet
roll: **6** scroll
scrap: **4** chad
size: **3** cap **4** demi, demy **5** atlas, crown, folio, legal, royal, sexto, sixmo **6** octavo, quarto **7** emperor

8 elephant, foolscap, imperial
10 typewriter
stiff: 9 cardboard, wallboard
12 Bristol board
strong: 5 kraft 6 manila
thin: 4 bank 6 pelure, tissue
9 onionskin
transparent: 8 glassine
writing: 3 rag 6 vellum 9 parchment

paper folding
Japanese: 7 origami

paphian
6 erotic, wanton

pappy
3 dad 4 soft 5 mushy 6 father,
spongy 7 pulpous, squashy,
squishy, squushy 8 squelchy, yielding 9 succulent

par
4 mean, norm 5 equal 6 median
7 average 8 equality, sameness,
standard

parable
4 myth, tale 5 fable, story
8 allegory

parachute
7 bailout, skydive 8 paradrop
part: 5 riser 6 canopy 7 harness,
ripcord

paraclete
6 helper 8 advocate, consoler
9 comforter 10 Holy Spirit
11 intercessor

parade
4 brag, pomp, show 5 array,
boast, flash, march, shine, strut
6 expose, flaunt, reveal 7 declare,
display, disport, divulge, exhibit,
fanfare, listing, marshal, panoply,
publish, recital, show off, trot out
8 brandish, disclose, movement,
proclaim 9 advertise, cavalcade,
formation, pageantry, promenade
10 exhibition, masquerade

paradigm
5 ideal, model 6 mirror 7 example,
pattern 8 ensample, exemplar, standard 9 archetype, beau ideal,
prototype

paradise
4 Eden, Zion 5 bliss 6 Canaan,
heaven, utopia 7 arcadia, elysium,
nirvana 8 empyrean 9 Cockaigne,
fairyland, Shangri-la 10 Civitas
Dei, lubberland, wonderland
12 New Jerusalem, promised land

Paradise Lost author
6 Milton (John)

paragon
3 gem 4 love, pick, tops 5 champ,
cream, ideal, jewel, liken, match,
model, peach, trump 6 beauty,
equate, lovely 7 compare, epitome, pattern, phoenix 8 champion,
exemplar, last word, nonesuch, parallel, ultimate 9 archetype, beau
ideal, nonpareil 10 apotheosis,
assimilate

Paraguay
capital: 8 Asuncion
monetary unit: 7 guarani

parallel
4 akin, even, like 5 align, alike,
along, equal, liken, match 6 agnate, double, equate, line up
7 compare, similar, uniform 8 analogue 9 analogous, collimate, collo-
cate, consonant, correlate, duplicate 10 assimilate, comparable,
comparison, correspond, equivalent, similarity 11 counterpart,
countertype, duplication, resemblance 13 correspondent,
corresponding

parallelogram
5 rhomb 6 oblong, square 7 rhombus 8 rhomboid 9 rectangle

paralysis
5 palsy 9 impotence
combining form: 5 lyses, lysis, plegy
6 plegia

paralyze
4 daze, maim, stun 5 close, daunt
6 appall, bemuse, benumb,
deaden, disarm, dismay, weaken
7 astound, cripple, destroy, disable,
horrify, nonplus, petrify, prevent,
stupefy, unnerve 8 demolish, enfeeble, knock out, shut down 9 prostrate 11 flabbergast
12 incapacitate

paramount
5 above, chief 6 master 7 capital,
regnant, supreme 8 cardinal,
crowning, dominant, headmost, superior 9 sovereign, uppermost
10 commanding, preeminent

paramour
5 lover, Romeo 6 master 7 amorist,
Don Juan, gallant 8 Casanova,
fancy man, lothario, mistress 9 boyfriend, inamorata, inamorato
10 girl friend

parapet
4 wall 7 bastion, bulwark, rampart
10 battlement, breastwork
part: 6 merlon

paraphernalia
4 gear 6 outfit, tackle 8 materiel,
tackling 9 apparatus, equipment,
machinery, materials, trappings
11 furnishings, habiliments 13 accouterments, accoutrements,
appurtenances

paraphrase
6 reword 7 restate, version 9 rendering, summarize, translate
10 transcribe 11 restatement,
translation

parasite
4 laze 5 idler, leech, toady 6 infest, sponge, sucker 7 sponger
8 barnacle, deadbeat, ectozoan,
entozoan, hanger-on 9 dependent,
sycophant 10 freeloader, smell-
feast 11 bloodsucker

parasitic
7 fawning 8 cowering, cringing,
sponging, toadying, toadyish
9 groveling, kowtowing, leechlike,
truckling 11 bootlicking, freeload-
ing, sycophantic

___ paratus
6 semper

paravane
5 otter

parboil
4 stew 5 sweat 6 seethe, simmer

Parcae
5 Fates
name: 4 Nona 5 Morta 6 Decuma

parcel
3 box, cut, lot 4 body, clot, deal,
mete, pack, part, plot, wrap 5 allot, array, batch, bunch, clump,
group, piece, quota, share, tract
6 assign, bundle, clutch, divide,
member, moiety, packet, ration
7 cluster, package, portion, prorate, section, segment 8 allocate,
disburse, disperse, division, fragment 9 apportion 10 distribute

parch
3 dry 4 burn, sear 5 roast, toast
6 scorch 7 shrivel 9 dehydrate,
desiccate, exsiccate

parchment
5 paper 6 vellum 8 document

pardon
4 free 5 remit, spare 6 accept, excuse 7 absolve, amnesty, condone,
forgive, justify, release 8 liberate,
reprieve, tolerate 9 acquittal, exculpate, indemnity, remission 10 absolution, indulgence 11 exculpation,

exoneration, forgiveness, vindication

pardonable
6 venial 9 excusable

pare
3 cut 4 clip, crop, flay, peel, skin, trim 5 lower, prune, scalp, shave, shear, skive, slash, strip 6 reduce, remove 7 curtail, cut back, cut down, whittle 8 diminish

parent
4 make, sire 5 cause, hatch, spawn 6 author, create, father, mother, origin 7 forbear, produce 8 ancestor, begetter, forebear, generate 9 originate, procreate 10 forefather, progenitor

parenthetically
6 obiter 8 by the bye, by the way 9 in passing

parentless
6 orphan 8 orphaned

par excellence
4 fine 5 prime 6 famous 7 classic 8 champion, superior 9 classical, number one 10 first-class 12 preeminently

pariah
5 leper 7 Ishmael, outcast 8 castaway, déclassé, derelict 10 Ishmaelite 11 offscouring, untouchable
Japanese: 3 eta

Paris
beloved: 5 Helen
betrothed: 6 Juliet
father: 5 Priam
mother: 6 Hecuba
slayer: 11 Philoctetes
wife: 6 Oenone

Paris
ancient name: 7 Lutetia
avenue: 13 Champs-Elysées
basilica: 10 Sacré Coeur
cathedral: 9 Notre Dame
city hall: 12 Hôtel de Ville
college: 8 Sorbonne
garden: 9 Tuileries 10 Luxembourg
island: 11 Île de la Cité
museum: 4 Army 5 Cluny 6 Louvre
palace: 6 Louvre 7 Bourbon
patron saint: 9 Geneviève
racecourse: 7 Auteuil
river: 5 Seine
section: 8 Left Bank 9 Right Bank 10 Montmartre 12 Latin Quarter
stock exchange: 6 Bourse
subway: 5 Metro
tower: 6 Eiffel

Parisina
author: 5 Byron (Lord)
husband: 3 Azo
lover: 4 Hugo
slayer: 3 Azo

parity
7 analogy 8 equality, likeness, nearness, sameness 9 closeness 10 adequation, similarity, similitude 11 equivalence

parka
6 anorak, jacket 8 pullover

park designer
4 Vaux (Calvert) 6 Paxton (Joseph) 7 Alphand (Jean), Olmsted (Frederick Law)

parlance
4 talk 5 idiom 6 phrase, speech 7 diction, wordage, wording 8 phrasing, verbiage 9 verbalism 11 phraseology

parley
3 bet, use 4 chat, talk 5 speak, treat 6 advise, confab, confer, huddle, powwow 7 consult, discuss, meeting, utilize 8 collogue, colloquy, converse, dialogue 9 discourse 10 conference, converse in, discussion, rap session 11 confabulate 12 conversation 13 confabulation

parliament
see **legislature**

parlor
5 salon

parlous
4 very 5 hairy, risky 6 chancy, damned, mighty, wicked 7 greatly 8 critical 9 dangerous, extremely, hazardous 11 exceedingly, excessively

Parnassian
4 poet

parochial
5 petty 6 narrow 7 bigoted, insular 9 sectarian, small-town 10 provincial

parody
3 ape, rib 4 mock 5 mimic, spoof 6 satire, send-up 7 imitate, takeoff 8 ridicule, spoofery, travesty 9 burlesque, imitation 10 caricature

paronomasia
3 pun 9 calembour

parous
6 gravid 8 childing, enceinte, pregnant 9 expectant, expecting

parrot
4 copy, echo 5 mimic, polly 6 repeat 7 chatter, imitate
kind: 3 ara, kea 4 jako, kaka, lory 5 macaw 6 Amazon, budgie, kakapo 8 cockatoo, lorikeet, lovebird, parakeet 9 cockatiel, parrakeet 10 budgerigar

parrot fever
11 psittacosis

parrot fish
4 loro 5 lauia 6 scarid

parry
4 duck, fend, ward 5 avert, avoid, block, dodge, evade, fence, shirk 7 deflect, prevent 8 preclude, sidestep 9 forestall

Parsifal
composer: 6 Wagner (Richard)
magician: 8 Klingsor
quest: 5 grail
son: 9 Lohengrin
temptress: 6 Kundry

parsimonious
4 mean 5 cheap, close, tight 6 frugal, stingy 7 miserly 9 niggardly, penurious 11 closefisted, tightfisted 12 cheese-paring 13 pennypinching

parson
5 clerk 6 cleric, divine, rector 8 clerical, minister, preacher, reverend 9 churchman, clergyman 12 ecclesiastic

parsonage
5 manse

parson bird
3 poe, tui 4 koko

part
3 bit, cut, lot 4 bite, chip, duty, meed, role, side, some, spot, unit 5 allot, chunk, organ, piece, place, quota, scrap, sever, share, slice 6 behalf, cleave, detach, detail, divide, member, moiety, office, ration, region, sector, sunder 7 break up, disjoin, dissect, element, measure, portion, quality, quantum, quarter, section, segment 8 dissever, district, disunite, division, fraction, fragment, function, separate 9 allotment, allowance, component
combining form: 3 mer 4 mere, mero, mery, toma, tome, tomy 5 meric, meris, parti 6 merous

partake
5 share 6 accept 7 receive 11 participate

Parthenon
  sculptor: **7** Phidias
  site: **9** Acropolis

partial
  6 biased, unfair, warped **7** colored, half-way **8** one-sided **9** jaundiced **10** fractional, incomplete, prejudiced **11** fragmentary, predilected, predisposed
  prefix: **4** demi, semi

partiality
  4 bent, bias **7** leaning **8** penchant, tendency **9** inclining, prejudice **10** chauvinism **11** inclination **12** one-sidedness, predilection

participant
  4 aide **5** actor **6** fellow, helper, sharer **7** sharing **8** confrere **9** colleague

participate
  5 share **7** partake

particle
  3 ace, bit, dot, jot, ray **4** atom, damn, doit, dram, drop, hoot, iota, mite, mote, snap, spot, whit **5** atomy, crumb, fleck, grain, minim, ounce, scrap, shred, speck, whoop **6** morsel, smidge, smitch, tittle **7** dribbet, granule, modicum, smidgen **8** fragment **9** scintilla
  atomic: **3** ion **5** anion **6** cation
  combining form: **5** plast
  elementary: **3** psi, tau **4** kaon, muon, pion **5** boson, meson **6** baryon, hadron, lambda, lepton, photon, proton **7** fermion, hyperon, neutron, nucleon, upsilon **8** electron, mesotron, neutrino, positron
  hypothetical: **5** gluon, quark **6** parton **8** graviton
  suffix: **2** id
  virus: **6** virion
  with negative charge: **8** electron
  with positive charge: **6** proton **8** positron

motley
  7 piebald **8** skewbald **9** multihued **10** variegated

particular
  3 one **4** full, item, lone, nice, only, sole **5** fussy, picky, point, thing **6** dainty, detail, minute, single, unique **7** careful, correct, element, finical, finicky, precise, several, special, unusual **8** accurate, detailed, distinct, especial, exacting, itemized, separate, solitary, specific, thorough **9** clocklike, finicking **10** blow-by-blow, fastidious, individual, meticulous, pernickety, respec-

tive, scrupulous, speciality **11** appropriate, persnickety, punctilious

particularize
  4 list **6** detail **7** itemize, specify **8** separate **9** enumerate, inventory, stipulate **11** specificate **13** individualize

parting
  4 last **5** adieu, congé, final **7** good-bye **8** farewell **10** divergence, separation **11** leave-taking, valedictory

partisan
  5 blind **6** backer, biased, cohort, warped **7** colored, devoted, devotee, die-hard, fanatic, patriot, sectary **8** adherent, advocate, champion, disciple, follower, henchman, one-sided, sectator, stalwart, upholder **9** factional, guerrilla, irregular, jaundiced, satellite, sectarian, supporter
  combining form: **4** crat **5** ocrat

partition
  4 deal, wall **6** divide, lot out, screen **7** divorce, dole out, portion, rupture, section, split-up **8** disburse, dispense, disperse, division **9** severance **10** detachment, distribute, measure out, separation

partner
  4 ally, chum, mate, wife **5** buddy, crony **6** cohort, fellow **7** comrade, husband **8** confrere, sidekick **9** assistant, associate, bedfellow, colleague, companion **10** accomplice, consociate **11** confederate
  prefix: **2** co

partnership
  4 firm **5** tie-up **6** hookup **7** cahoots, company **8** alliance **11** association, combination, conjunction **12** consociation, togetherness **13** participation

parturient
  6 gravid, parous **8** childing, enceinte, pregnant **9** expecting

parturition
  5 birth **7** bearing **8** delivery **10** childbirth **12** childbearing
  combining form: **4** toky

party
  4 ball, band, bevy, bloc, body, crew, fete, orgy, ring, side **5** actor, being, bunch, cabal, corps, covey, group, human, revel, troop, union **6** fiesta, mortal, outfit, person, sharer, social, soiree **7** carouse, cluster, combine, company, debauch, faction, shindig **8** alli-

ance, assembly, carousal, creature, litigant, wingding **9** bacchanal, coalition, gathering, personage **10** detachment, individual, saturnalia **11** bacchanalia, celebration, combination, participant
  food: **4** cake **6** canapé **8** crudités, ice cream **11** hors d'oeuvre

parvenu
  7 upstart **8** roturier **9** arriviste **12** nouveau riche

Pasha or Baba
  3 Ali

Pashhur
  father: **5** Immer **8** Malchiah
  son: **8** Gedaliah

Pasiphaë
  daughter: **7** Ariadne, Phaedra
  husband: **5** Minos
  son: **8** Minotaur

pass
  2 go **3** die, end, hap, hie, jog, top **4** beat, buck, fare, give, hand, omit, pose, wend **5** cease, lapse, occur, outdo, reach, relay, spend, while **6** crisis, demise, depart, elapse, exceed, expire, forget, hand on, happen, ignore, perish, permit, push on, repair, roll on, slight, slip by, strait, travel **7** approve, blink at, come off, decease, develop, devolve, journey, neglect, proceed, succumb **8** bequeath, exigency, fade away, fork over, hand down, juncture, outmatch, outshine, outstrip, overlook, peter out, transmit **9** blink away, disregard, emergency, terminate, transcend, transpire, while away
  Afghanistan: **5** Murgh
  Afghanistan-Pakistan: **6** Khyber
  Alaska: **5** White
  Alps: **3** col **5** Cenis, Loibl **7** Brenner, Ljubelj, Simplon **9** St. Bernard
  California: **5** Cajon
  China-India: **9** Karakoram
  Colorado: **3** Ute
  into law: **5** enact
  Pakistan: **5** Kilik
  Russian: **12** Caspian Gates
  Tennessee: **10** Cumberland
  Turkey: **13** Cilician Gates
  Wyoming: **5** South

passable
  4 open **9** navigable, reachable, tolerable, unblocked **10** accessible, attainable, negotiable, travelable

passably
  4 so-so **6** enough, fairly, rather **9** averagely, tolerably **10** moderately

passage
3 way **4** exit, fare, hall, line, path, road, text **5** route, shift **6** access, arcade, avenue, course, egress, strait, trajet, travel, tunnel, voyage **7** areaway, channel, couloir, excerpt, hallway, journey, traject, transit **8** corridor, transfer, traverse **9** enactment, quotation **10** transition, traversing **11** transmittal **12** transference, transmission **13** transmittance
air: **7** windway
arched: **6** arcade
Atlantic-Pacific: **9** Northwest
combining form: **4** meat, pora **5** meato
money: **4** fare
roofed: **6** arcade **9** breezeway
to water's edge: **4** ghat

Passage to India author
7 Forster (Edward Morgan)

pass away
2 go **3** die **4** drop **6** cash in, demise, depart, elapse, expire, perish **7** decease, succumb

pass by
4 fail, omit **6** forget, ignore **7** neglect **8** overlook **9** disregard

passé
4 dead **5** dated **6** démodé, old hat **7** belated, demoded, disused, extinct, outworn **8** obsolete, outdated, outmoded **9** out-of-date **10** antiquated, superseded **12** old-fashioned **13** superannuated

passed master
5 maven, mavin **6** artist, expert, wizard **7** artiste **8** virtuoso **9** authority

passel
4 body, clot **5** array, batch, bunch, clump, group **6** bundle **7** battery, cluster

passenger
4 fare **8** traveler, wayfarer
hidden: **8** stowaway
vessel: **5** liner **7** steamer

passerine bird
see **bird**, *songbird*

passing
5 death, sleep **6** demise **7** cursory, decease, elusory **8** fleeting, illusive, illusory **9** ephemeral, fugacious, momentary, transient **10** evanescent, short-lived, transitory

passion
3 ire **4** fire, fury, heat, itch, love, lust, rage, urge, zeal **5** agony, amour, anger, ardor, crush, dolor **6** béguin, desire, fervor, hurrah, misery, temper **7** craving, ecstasy, emotion, feeling, panting, rapture **8** appetite, devotion, distress, lyricism, outbreak, outburst **9** affection, calenture, eagerness, eroticism, prurience, pruriency, sentiment, suffering, transport **10** aphrodisia, appetition, dedication, enthusiasm, heartthrob, sensuality **11** affectivity, amorousness, infatuation, lustfulness **12** sensuousness **13** concupiscence, lickerishness

passionate
3 hot **5** fiery, testy **6** ardent, fervid, steamy, sultry **7** amorous, blazing, burning, excited, fervent, flaming, glowing, goatish, lustful, peppery, satyric **8** headlong, prurient, vehement **9** impetuous, irascible, lickerish, quickened, steamed up **10** hotblooded, lascivious, libidinous, stimulated **11** high-powered, hot-tempered, precipitate **12** concupiscent, high-pressure, unrestrained **13** quick-tempered

passive
4 idle **5** inert, quiet, stoic **6** asleep, docile, latent, sleepy, stolid **7** bearing, patient **8** enduring, inactive, resigned, yielding **9** apathetic, compliant, lethargic, quiescent, tractable **10** nonviolent, phlegmatic, submissive **11** acquiescent, unresistant

pass on
3 die **6** convey, depart, expire, impart **7** decease **8** transmit **11** communicate

pass out
5 faint, swoon

pass over
4 fail, omit, pass **6** forget, ignore **7** neglect **8** overlook **9** disregard

Passover
5 Pasch
bread: **4** azym **5** azyme, matzo **6** matzoh
meal: **5** seder

past
2 by **3** ago, old **4** gone, late, once, yore **5** above, after, prior **6** beyond, bygone, former, goneby, whilom **7** onetime, outside, present, quondam, without **8** anterior, foretime, lang syne, previous, sometime **9** antiquity, erstwhile, foregoing, precedent, preceding, yesterday **10** antecedent, yesteryear

combining form: **6** preter **7** praeter
prefix: **5** retro

pasta
5 dough, paste
kind: **4** ziti **7** gnocchi, lasagna, pastina, ravioli **8** alfabeto, linguine, linguini, macaroni, rigatoni, tortelli **9** canneloni, quadrucci, spaghetti **10** malfattini, tagliolini, tortellini, vermicelli **11** cappelletti, stricchetti **12** paglia e fieno

paste
4 beat, drub, glue **5** dough, pound, stick, stuff **6** attach, batter, buffet, cement, pummel, spread, thrash, wallop **7** belabor **8** adhesive, lambaste, material

Pasternak hero
7 Zhivago

pasticcio
see **pastiche**

pastiche
6 medley **7** mélange **8** mishmash **9** potpourri **10** assortment, hodgepodge, hotchpotch, miscellany **11** gallimaufry

pastime
4 game **5** hobby, sport **9** amusement, diversion **10** recreation **13** entertainment

past master
see **passed master**

pastoral
5 rural **6** rustic **7** bucolic, country, idyllic, outland **8** agrarian, agrestic, innocent **10** campestral, outcountry, provincial

pastor's assistant
6 curate

pastry
3 bun, pie **4** baba, cake, flan, tart **5** torte **6** cornet, Danish, éclair, gâteau, kolach, pirogi, strata, torten (plural) **7** baklava, beignet, bouchée, dariole, fritter, gâteaux (plural), kolacky, palmier, savarin, strudel, tartlet **8** napoleon, papillon, piroshki, turnover, vacherin **9** barquette, cream puff, gugelhupf, kugelhupf, madeleine, petit four, vol-au-vent **10** cheesecake **11** profiterole **12** millefeuille
kind: **4** filo, puff **5** choux, flaky **6** phyllo
shell: **7** timbale **8** meringue

pasty
5 gluey **6** chalky, pallid, sickly

patch
3 bit, fix **4** do up, mend **5** cover,

scrap **6** doctor, emblem, repair, revamp

patchwork
4 hash, olio, stew **5** salad **6** jumble **8** mishmash **10** hodgepodge, hotchpotch, miscellany, salmagundi

patchy
6 spotty, uneven **9** irregular

pate
4 head, poll **5** brain, crown **6** noddle, noggin, noodle

pâté de ___
8 foie gras

patella
7 kneecap, kneepan

patent
4 open, rank **5** clear, gross, plain **7** evident, glaring, license, obvious **8** apparent, distinct, flagrant, manifest, palpable, unclosed **9** privilege, prominent

paternal
8 fatherly

path
3 way **4** fare, lane, line, road, walk **5** byway, route, track, trail **6** artery, avenue, course, street **7** highway, passage **9** boulevard **12** thoroughfare

pathetic
3 sad **4** poor **6** moving, rueful **7** piteous, pitiful **8** pitiable **9** affecting

Pathfinder
author: **6** Cooper (James Fenimore)
hero: **6** Bumppo (Natty)

pathogen
4 germ **5** virus **6** fungus **9** bacterium

pathological condition
suffix: **2** ia

pathos
4 pity **9** poignance, poignancy

pathway
5 track, trail **6** course

patience
4 cool **9** composure, endurance, passivity, suffering, tolerance **10** equanimity, submission, sufferance, toleration **11** forbearance, longanimity, passiveness, resignation, self-control **13** long-suffering

patient
4 case, meek **6** patron **8** enduring **9** admitting, undaunted **11** susceptible **13** long-suffering
man: **3** Job

patina
4 film **6** finish **7** surface **10** coloration

patio
5 court **7** terrace **9** courtyard

patois
4 cant **5** argot, lingo, slang **6** jargon **7** dialect **10** colloquial, vernacular

patriarch
4 sire **5** maker **6** author, father, gaffer **7** creator, founder **8** inventor **9** architect, generator, graybeard **10** originator
biblical: **5** David, Isaac, Jacob **7** Abraham

patrician
6 aristo **9** blue blood, gentleman **10** aristocrat

patriciate
5 elite **6** flower, gentry **7** aristoi, quality **8** optimacy **9** blue blood, gentility **10** upper crust **11** aristocracy

patrimony
6 legacy **8** heritage **9** heritance **10** birthright **11** inheritance

patriot
8 loyalist, partisan **9** flag-waver, guerrilla, irregular **11** nationalist
overzealous: **5** jingo **8** jingoist **10** chauvinist

Patroclus
friend: **8** Achilles
slayer: **6** Hector

patrol
5 scout, watch **7** protect

patrolman
3 cop **6** police **7** John Law, officer

patrol wagon
10 Black Maria

patron
5 angel **6** avowry, backer, client, surety **7** sponsor **8** backer-up, customer

patronage
5 aegis, trade **6** custom **7** backing, subsidy, traffic **8** auspices, business, cronyism **9** clientage, clientele **10** protection **11** benefaction, sponsorship **12** guardianship **13** pork-barreling

patronize
3 use **5** deign, favor **7** protect, support **8** frequent **10** condescend

patron saint
of beggars, cripples: **5** Giles
of children: **8** Nicholas

of England: **6** George
of fishermen: **5** Peter
of France: **5** Denis
of Ireland: **7** Patrick
of lawyers: **4** Ives
of musicians: **7** Cecilia
of Norway: **4** Olaf
of physicians: **4** Luke
of sailors: **4** Elmo **8** Nicholas
of Scotland: **6** Andrew
of shoemakers: **7** Crispin
of Spain: **5** James **8** Santiago
of Wales: **5** David
of winegrowers: **7** Vincent
of workers: **6** Joseph

patsy
3 sap **4** dupe, fool, goat, gull, mark **5** chump **6** pigeon, sucker, victim **7** fall guy **9** scapegoat **11** whipping boy

patter
3 jaw, yak **4** cant, chat **5** argot, clack, lingo, prate, slang **6** babble, gabble, jargon, patois **7** chatter, dialect, prattle **9** yakety-yak **10** vernacular

pattern
4 plan **5** ideal, model, motif, order **6** design, device, figure, method, mirror, motive, system **7** example **8** ensample, exemplar, original, paradigm, standard, template **11** arrangement, orderliness

paucity
4 lack **6** dearth **7** fewness, poverty **8** scarcity **10** scarceness **13** insufficiency

Paulina's husband
7 Camillo **9** Antigonus

___ Paulo
3 São

Paul the Apostle
birthplace: **6** Tarsus
companion: **5** Silas, Titus **7** Artemas, Timothy **8** Barnabas
original name: **4** Saul
place of conversion: **8** Damascus
prosecutor: **9** Tertullus
teacher: **8** Gamaliel
tribe: **8** Benjamin

paunch
3 pod **4** draw **5** belly, bowel, tummy **6** venter **7** abdomen, embowel, stomach **8** potbelly **9** bay window

pauper
4 bust, ruin **5** break **6** beggar **7** almsman, have-not, lazarus **8** bankrupt, indigent **10** down-and-out, impoverish

pauperism
4 need, want 6 penury 7 beggary, poverty 9 indigence, neediness 11 destitution

pause
3 gap 4 halt, hush, lull, stop, wait 5 break, comma, lapse, letup 6 hiatus, recess 7 caesura, respite 8 interval 9 cessation, interlude 10 hesitation, suspension 12 intermission, interruption

pave
3 lay, tar 5 cover, floor 7 overlie, surface 8 blacktop

pavement
6 tarmac 7 macadam 8 concrete, flagging, sidewalk

paw
4 feel, foot, hand 5 touch 6 finger, handle 7 palpate

pawn
4 hock, tool 5 token 6 pledge, puppet, stooge 7 earnest, warrant 8 impledge

Pax
see **Irene**

Pax
3 Dei 6 Romana 10 Brittanica

pay
3 fee 4 give, hire, quit, wage 5 clear, remit, spend, yield 6 defray, expend, lay out, outlay, pony up, render, return, salary, settle, square, tender 7 bring in, cough up, fork out, guerdon, requite, satisfy, stipend 8 clear off, disburse, pungle up, shell out 9 discharge, emolument, indemnify, liquidate, plunk down, reimburse 10 compensate, recompense, remunerate

payable
3 due 5 owing 6 mature, unpaid 7 overdue 9 unsettled 11 outstanding

payload
4 haul 5 cargo 6 burden, lading 7 freight

payment
3 fee, tax 4 duty 6 return 7 premium 12 compensation

payoff
3 fix 5 bribe 6 climax, profit, reward 8 decisive 11 retribution

PDQ
6 at once 8 directly, right off 9 forthwith, instanter, instantly, right away 11 immediately, straightway

pea
6 legume

peace
3 pax 4 calm, ease, rest 5 amity, order, quiet 6 repose 7 concord, harmony 8 serenity 11 tranquility 12 tranquillity

peaceable
6 irenic 7 amiable, pacific 8 amicable, friendly, pacifist 10 neighborly, nonviolent 11 complaisant 12 pacificatory

peaceful
4 cool 6 irenic, placid, steady 7 equable, pacific 8 composed, constant, pacifist 9 collected, unruffled 10 nonviolent

pause:
5 truce

peacemaker
8 appeaser, mediator, placater 10 arbitrator, negotiator 11 pacificator

peace officer
3 cop 6 police 7 John Law, officer 9 patrolman, policeman

peach
3 rat 4 blab 5 dandy, nifty 6 betray, inform, snitch, squeak, squeal 8 jim-dandy 9 freestone, humdinger, nectarine 10 clingstone 11 crackerjack

Peach State
7 Georgia

peachy
4 fine, nice 6 divine 8 glorious 9 excellent, hunky-dory, marvelous

peacockish
5 showy, swank 6 chichi 7 splashy 10 flamboyant 11 pretentious

peacock-like
8 pavonine

peak
3 alp, top 4 acme, apex, bill, roof 5 abate, crest, crown, mount, visor 6 apogee, lessen, rebate, recede, summit, vertex, zenith 7 dwindle 8 capsheaf, capstone, decrease, diminish, meridian, mountain, pinnacle, taper off
Adirondack: 9 Whiteface
Africa's highest: 4 Kibo
Alaska-Canada: 12 Mt. Saint Elias
Andes: 4 Ruiz 5 Torrá
Apennines: 5 Amaro
Argentina: 4 Azul 5 Negra, Payún
Bavaria: 5 Arber
Berkshires: 10 Mt. Greylock

Black Hills: 10 Mt. Rushmore
Bolivia: 5 Cuzco, Tahua, Ubina 6 Sajama
Borneo: 4 Raja
California: 6 Sonora 7 Palomar 8 Half Dome, Mt. Shasta 9 Excelsior
California's highest: 9 Mt. Whitney
Canada: 5 Keele
Canaries: 5 Teide 8 Tenerife
Carpathian: 4 Rysy
Catskill: 5 Mt. Vly 8 Mt. Pisgah
Caucasus: 5 Ushba 6 Elbrus
Chile: 4 Mayo, Pili 5 Paine, Pular
Colombia: 4 Tama 5 Neiva
Colorado: 3 Ute 5 Pikes 9 Purgatory
combining form: 3 acr, akr 4 acro, akro
Cuba: 8 Turquino
Ecuador: 10 Chimborazo
England: 11 Scafell Pike
Ethiopia: 4 Guna 5 Holla
France: 5 Pilat
French Guiana: 5 Amana
Georgia: 16 Springer Mountain
Glacier National Park: 8 Kootenai
Greece: 6 Mt. Ossa 6 Pelion
Himalayas: 3 Api 5 Kamet 7 Lhotse I 8 Lhotse II 10 Gasherbrum
Honshū: 4 Yari 10 Yarigatake
Idaho: 13 Mt. Pend Oreille
Iran: 8 Damavand
Japan: 4 Sobo 5 Oyama 7 Sobozan
Java: 6 Slamet
Jordan: 8 Mt. Gilead
Karakoram Range: 10 Masherbrum
Karakoram Range's highest: 7 Dapsang 12 Godwin Austen
Maine: 10 Mt. Katahdin 10 Saddleback
Montana: 8 Gallatin
Nevada: 5 Mt. Ely
Newfoundland: 9 Gros Morne
New Hampshire: 11 Mt. Monadnock
New Zealand: 5 Mt. Una 6 Mt. Cook 7 Aorangi 10 Mt. Aspiring
Oahu: 5 Kaala
Oregon: 6 Mt. Hood
Papua New Guinea: 10 Mt. Victoria
Pennine Alps: 10 Matterhorn, Mont Cervin
Philippines: 4 High
Pyrenees: 11 de Vignemale
Russia's highest: 6 Elbrus
Scotland: 8 Ben Nevis
Spain: 5 Yelmo 8 Mulhacén
Switzerland: 3 Dom 4 Dôle, Tödi 5 Eiger, Mönch 6 La Dôle, Rusein 7 Pilatus 8 Jungfrau
U.S.S.R.'s highest: 9 Communism
Utah: 5 Kings
Venezuela: 7 Mt. Icutú

Vermont: 8 Haystack, Stratton
10 Mt. Ascutney 11 Mt. Mansfield
Washington: 9 Mt. Olympus, Mt.
Rainier 13 Mt. Saint Helens
White Mts.: 12 Mt. Washington
Wyoming: 10 Grand Teton 11 Elk
Mountain
Yukon: 4 King 7 Mt. Logan

peaked
3 wan 4 pale, sick 5 acute, drawn,
piked, sharp 6 sickly 7 pointed
8 acicular 9 aciculate, acuminate,
acuminous, cuspidate

peal
4 bell, bong, ring, toll 5 chime,
knell

peanut
4 mani, puny 5 petty, small 6 goober, measly, paltry 8 earthnut,
picayune

pear
4 Bosc 5 Anjou, Hardy 6 Comice,
Garber, Seckel 7 Kieffer, LeConte
8 Bartlett
cider: 5 perry

Pearl Mosque site
4 Agra

Pearl of the Pacific
4 Guam

pearly
8 nacreous

pear-shaped
8 pyriform

peasant
4 boor, carl, hick, kern, peon, serf
5 churl, knave, yokel 6 rustic
7 bumpkin, hayseed, redneck, villein 9 hillbilly
Arab: 6 fellah
Latin-American: 9 campesino
Russian: 5 mujik 6 moujik, muzhik,
muzjik

peccary
7 tayassu 8 javelina

peck
3 lip, lot, nag 4 beak, buss, fuss,
kiss, much 5 smack 6 carp at,
smooch 7 henpeck 8 osculate
9 great deal

pecker
3 neb, nib 4 beak, bill, nose
5 snoot, snout 9 proboscis

peculate
8 embezzle

peculiar
3 odd 5 queer, weird 6 proper,
unique 7 bizarre, curious, oddball,
strange, unusual 8 singular 9 dia-

critic, eccentric 10 diagnostic, individual 11 distinctive

peculiarity
4 mark 5 savor, trait 7 feature,
quality 8 property 9 affection,
attribute, character

pecuniary
6 fiscal 8 monetary 9 financial

pedagogue
5 tutor 7 teacher 12 schoolmaster

Pedaiah
brother: 9 Shealtiel
father: 6 Parosh 7 Kolaiah
grandson: 9 Jehoiakim
son: 4 Joed, Joel

pedal digit
3 toe

pedantic
3 dry 4 arid, dull 5 booky 7 bookish, donnish, erudite, inkhorn,
learned 8 academic, didactic
9 dryasdust, schoolish 10 scholastic
11 book-learned

peddle
4 hawk, push, sell, vend 5 shove
6 monger 8 huckster

peddler
6 hawker, monger, pusher, vendor
7 chapman, higgler, packman,
roadman 8 huckster, mongerer,
outcrier 9 cheap-jack, cheap-john,
piepoudre 10 colporteur
12 costermonger

pedestal part
4 base, dado 6 plinth 7 surbase

pedestrian
4 blah, dull 5 banal, heavy, inane
6 dreary, jejune, stodgy 7 humdrum, prosaic 8 banausic, monotone, plodding, truistic 10 monotonous, wishy-washy
11 commonplace 13 unimaginative

pedigree
5 blood 6 origin, stemma 7 descent, lineage 8 ancestry, purebred
9 genealogy, pureblood 10 extraction, family tree

peduncle
4 stem

peek
6 glance 7 glimpse

peel
4 bark, pare, skin 5 flake, scale,
strip 8 flake off 9 exfoliate 10 desquamate 11 decorticate, excorticate

peeled
4 bare, open 5 naked 7 denuded,
exposed 8 stripped 9 uncovered

peep
3 pip, spy 4 chip, look, ogle, peer
5 cheep, chirp, stare, tweet
6 glance, peek in, squeak 7 chipper, chirrup, chitter, glimpse, look-
see, peek out, tweedle, twitter
8 look-over, oeillade

peeping tom
5 snoop 6 peeper, voyeur
7 prowler, snooper

peer
3 eye, pry 4 bore, gape, gawk,
gaze, lord 5 equal, glare, gloat,
noble, snoop, stare 6 goggle,
squint 9 associate
British: 4 duke, earl 5 baron 7 marquis 8 viscount
highest: 4 duke
lowest: 5 baron

Peer Gynt
author: 5 Ibsen (Henrik)
beloved: 7 Solveig
composer: 5 Grieg (Edvard)
mother: 3 Ase

peerless
4 only 5 alone 6 unique 8 dominant 9 matchless, nonpareil, paramount, sovereign, unequaled, unmatched, unrivaled 11 unparagoned 12 unparalleled

peeve
3 get, irk 4 miff, rile, roil 5 pique
6 nettle, put out 7 disturb, provoke
8 irritate 9 aggravate
10 exasperate

peevish
5 huffy, waspy 7 carping, fretful,
pettish, waspish 8 captious, caviling, critical, petulant, snappish
9 fractious, irritable

peewee
4 runt, tiny 5 dwarf, midge, pygmy
6 midget 7 manikin, minikin
8 dwarfish, Tom Thumb 9 miniature
10 diminutive, homunculus
11 lilliputian

Peewee or Della
5 Reese

peg
3 pin 4 plod, plug 5 dowel, prong,
stake, throw 6 attach 8 identify

Pegasus
5 horse, steed
rider: 11 Bellerophon

Pekah
father: 8 Remaliah
slayer: 6 Hoshea
victim: 8 Pekahiah

Pekahiah
father: 7 Menahem
slayer: 5 Pekah

Pelatiah's father
4 Ishi 7 Benaiah 8 Hananiah

Peleg
father: 4 Eber
son: 3 Reu

Peleus
brother: 7 Telamon
father: 6 Aeacus
half brother: 6 Phocus
son: 8 Achilles
victim: 8 Eurytion
wife: 6 Thetis

pelf
5 money, rhino, stuff 7 needful

Pelias
country: 6 Iolcus
father: 8 Poseidon
half brother: 5 Aeson
son: 7 Acastus

Pelican State
9 Louisiana

Pelion and ___
4 Ossa

Pelleas
beloved: 9 Mélisande
brother, slayer: 6 Golaud

Pelles
daughter: 6 Elaine
grandson: 7 Galahad

pellet
3 wad 4 ball, dung, shot 5 bolus
6 bullet

Pellinore
slayer: 6 Gawain
son: 5 Torre 6 Dornar 7 Lamerok
8 Percival 9 Agglovale

pell-mell
5 chaos, snarl 6 ataxia, huddle,
muddle, rashly 7 clutter, hotfoot
8 disarray, disorder, headlong,
stampede 9 confusion, hurriedly
10 carelessly, heedlessly 11 hurry-
scurry, impetuously 12 indiscreetly
13 helter-skelter, incontinently

pellucid
5 clear, sheer 6 limpid, lucent
7 crystal 8 clear-cut, luminous 9 unblurred 10 see-through 11 crystalline, translucent

Pelops
father: 8 Tantalus
son: 6 Atreus 8 Pittheus, Thyestes
wife: 10 Hippodamia

pelota
see **jai alai**

pelt
3 fly, fur 4 beat, drub, fell, hide,
rush, skin, whop 5 fleet, haste,
hurry, pound, scoot 6 batter, hammer, jacket, pummel, thrash, wallop
7 beeline, belabor, hotfoot

pen
3 hem, mew 4 cage, coop, crib,
jail, yard 5 fence, hedge 6 cooler,
corral, kennel, prison, shut in, stylus
7 close in, enclose

penalize
4 fine 5 judge, mulct 6 amerce,
punish 7 chasten, condemn, correct
8 chastise 9 castigate 10 discipline

penalty
4 fine, loss 5 mulct 7 forfeit
10 amercement

penance
3 rue 4 ruth 7 remorse 9 atonement, attrition, penitence, penitency
10 contrition, repentance
11 compunction

penchant
4 bent 7 leaning 8 tendency 9 inclining 10 proclivity, propensity
11 disposition, inclination
12 predilection

pendant
4 flag, jack 5 color 6 banner, ensign, pennon 7 pennant 8 bannerol, standard, streamer 9 correlate 10 complement

pendent
7 hanging, pensile 9 pendulant,
pendulous, suspended, undecided,
unsettled 12 undetermined

pending
6 during 9 undecided, unsettled
12 undetermined

___ Pendragon
5 Uther

pendulous
6 wobbly 7 hanging, pendent, pensile 8 wavering 9 faltering, suspended, tentative 10 hesitating
11 vacillating

Penelope
father: 7 Icarius
father-in-law: 7 Laertes
husband: 7 Ulysses 8 Odysseus
mother: 8 Periboea

son: 10 Telemachus
suitor: 7 Agelaus

penetrable
6 porose, porous 8 pervious
9 permeable

penetrate
3 jab 4 bore, go in, stab 5 break,
drill, drive, enter, knife, prick
6 charge, come in, insert, invade,
pierce 7 ingress, pervade 8 encroach, permeate, puncture, saturate, trespass 9 insinuate, introduce, percolate, perforate,
transfuse 10 impregnate

penetrating
4 keen 5 acute, crisp, sharp 6 astute, biting, shrewd 7 cutting, ingoing 8 clear-cut, incisive 9 trenchant
11 quick-witted, sharp-witted
12 quick-sighted, sharp-sighted

Peneus
daughter: 6 Daphne
father: 7 Oceanus
mother: 6 Tethys

Peninnah's husband
7 Elkanah

peninsula
4 neck 10 chersonese
Alaska: 5 Kenai 6 Seward
Australia: 6 Tasman
Barents Sea: 5 Kanin
British colony: 9 Gibraltar
Canada: 8 Labrador
Cape Cod: 9 Race Point 12 Mono-
moy Point
Chile: 5 Swett
Costa Rica: 3 Osa
Denmark: 7 Jutland
eastern United States: 8 Delmarva
Estonia: 5 Sorve
Florida: 8 Pinellas 9 Canaveral
France: 5 Giens
Greece: 4 Acte 10 Chalcidice
11 Peloponnese 12 Peloponnesus
Guam: 5 Orote
Hong Kong: 7 Kowloon
Honshū: 3 Izu 5 Miura
Massachusetts: 7 Cape Ann, Cape
Cod
Mexico: 7 Yucatan 14 Baja
California
Michigan: 8 Keweenaw
Middle East: 5 Sinai
New Guinea: 4 Huon
New Jersey: 9 Sandy Hook
New Zealand: 5 Banks, Mahia
Northern Territory: 4 Gove
Northwest Territories: 4 Hall 7 Boo-
thia 8 Melville
Ontario: 5 Bruce

Persian Gulf: **9** Ras Tanura **13** Ras at Tannurah
Quebec: **5** Gaspé
Russia: **4** Kola **5** Taman, Yamal **6** Kolski, Taimyr **9** Kamchatka
Scotland: **7** Cantyre, Kintyre
South Australia: **4** Eyre **5** Yorke **6** Yorkes
southeast Asia: **5** Malay **9** Indochina **12** Farther India
southeastern Europe: **6** Balkan
southwestern Asia: **6** Arabia **7** Arabian
southwestern Europe: **7** Iberian
Texas: **9** Matagorda
Tierra del Fuego: **5** Mitre
Turkey: **8** Anatolia **9** Asia Minor
Ukraine: **5** Kerch
Wales: **5** Gower, Lleyn
Washington: **7** Olympic
west Africa: **11** Sierra Leone
Wisconsin: **4** Door

Peninsular State
7 Florida

penis
7 phallus

penitence
3 rue **4** ruth **5** grief, qualm **6** regret, sorrow **7** anguish, penance, remorse, sadness, scruple **8** distress, humbling **10** contrition, debasement, repentance **11** compunction, degradation, humiliation, self-reproof **12** contriteness, self-reproach

penitent
5 sorry **8** contrite **9** regretful, repentant **10** apologetic, remorseful

penitentiary
see **prison**

penman
5 clerk **6** author, scribe, writer **12** calligrapher **13** calligraphist

penmanship
4 hand **6** ductus, script **7** writing **11** calligraphy, chirography, handwriting

pen name
6 anonym **9** pseudonym **10** nom de plume
Addison (Joseph): **4** Clio
Arouet (François-Marie): **8** Voltaire
Beyle (Marie-Henri): **8** Stendhal
Blair (Eric): **12** George Orwell
Brontë (Anne): **9** Acton Bell
Brontë (Charlotte): **10** Currer Bell
Brontë (Emily): **9** Ellis Bell
Clemens (Samuel): **9** Mark Twain
Dickens (Charles): **3** Boz

Dodgson (Charles Lutwidge): **12** Lewis Carroll
Dupin (Amandine-Aurore): **10** George Sand
Evans (Mary Ann): **11** George Eliot
Faust (Frederick): **8** Max Brand
Franklin (Benjamin): **11** Poor Richard
Geisel (Theodore): **7** Dr. Seuss
Glidden (Frederick): **9** Luke Short
Lamb (Charles): **4** Elia
Munro (Hector Hugh): **4** Saki
Poquelin (Jean-Baptiste): **7** Molière
Porter (William Sidney): **6** O. Henry
Ramé (Maria Louise): **5** Ouida
Russell (George): **2** AE
Thibault (Jacques-Anatole-François): **13** Anatole France
Viaud (Louis-Marie-Julien): **10** Pierre Loti

pennant
4 flag, jack **5** color **6** banner, ensign, pennon **7** pendant **8** standard, streamer **9** banderole

penniless
4 poor **5** broke **8** bankrupt **11** impecunious

pennilessness
see **penury**

pennon
4 flag, jack **5** color **6** banner, ensign **8** bannerol, gonfalon, gonfanon **9** banderole, oriflamme

Pennsylvania
battlefield: **10** Gettysburg
capital: **10** Harrisburg
college, university: **5** Gratz, Thiel **6** Drexel, Lehigh, Temple **7** La Salle **8** Alliance, Bryn Mawr, Bucknell **9** Dickinson, Lafayette, St. Joseph's, Villanova **10** Pittsburgh, Swarthmore
nickname: **13** Keystone State
state bird: **12** ruffed grouse
state flower: **14** mountain laurel

penny pincher
5 miser, piker, stiff **7** niggard **8** tightwad **9** skinflint **10** cheapskate **11** cheeseparer **12** moneygrubber

penny-pinching
5 close, tight **6** stingy **7** miserly **9** niggardly, penurious **11** closefisted, tightfisted **12** cheeseparing, parsimonious

pensile
7 hanging, pendent **9** pendulant, pendulous, suspended

pensioner
7 retiree **8** retirant

pensive
3 sad **4** blue **6** musing **7** wistful **8** absorbed, saddened, thinking **9** pondering, withdrawn **10** abstracted, cogitative, meditative, melancholy, reflecting, reflective, ruminating, ruminative, thoughtful **11** preoccupied, speculative **13** contemplative

Pentateuch
5 Torah **6** Exodus **7** Genesis, Numbers **9** Leviticus **11** Deuteronomy

Penthesilea
queen of: **7** Amazons
slayer: **8** Achilles

Pentheus
grandfather: **6** Cadmus
king of: **6** Thebes
mother: **5** Agave

Penuel
father: **3** Hur **7** Shashak
grandfather: **5** Judah

penumbra
5 shade **6** shadow **7** umbrage

penurious
4 poor **5** close, needy, tight **6** stingy **7** miserly **8** beggared, dirt poor, indigent **9** destitute, niggardly **10** avaricious **11** closefisted, impecunious, necessitous, tightfisted **12** cheeseparing, impoverished, parsimonious **13** penny-pinching

penury
4 need, want **7** poverty **8** poorness **9** indigence, neediness, privation **11** destitution

peon
4 serf **5** slave **6** drudge, slavey, toiler **7** laborer, peasant **9** dray horse, workhorse **11** galley slave
Anglo-Saxon: **4** esne

peonage
4 yoke **6** thrall **7** bondage, helotry, serfdom, slavery **9** servitude, thralldom, villenage **11** enslavement

people
3 kin, men **4** folk **5** plebs **6** occupy, plebes, public, tenant **7** inhabit, society **8** populace, populate **9** commonage, commoners, common men, community, plebeians **10** commonalty **11** inhabitants, rank and file, third estate
combining form: **4** demo, ethn **5** ethno

pep
2 go **3** vim **4** dash, push **5** getup, punch, verve, vigor **6** energy,

starch **7** potency **8** vitality **9** animation, hardihood **10** get-up-and-go, liveliness

pepo
5 gourd, melon **6** squash **7** pumpkin **8** cucumber

pepper
3 dot **5** chili, speck **7** cayenne, freckle, paprika, pimento, speckle, stipple **8** capsicum, pimiento, sprinkle **9** bespeckle

peppery
4 keen, racy **5** alert, cross, fiery, spicy, zesty **6** cranky, lively, snappy, spunky **7** gingery, piquant, pungent **8** choleric, poignant, spirited **9** irascible, temperish **10** mettlesome, passionate **11** high-hearted, hot-tempered **12** high-spirited **13** quick-tempered

peppy
4 keen **5** alert **6** bright, lively **7** animate **8** animated, spirited **9** sprightly, vivacious

Pepys' journal
5 Diary

Pequod
cabin boy: **3** Pip
captain: **4** Ahab
harpooner: **6** Daggoo **8** Queequeg, Tashtego
mate: **8** Starbuck

Pequot sachem
5 Uncas

per
2 by **3** via **4** with **7** by way of, through **8** by dint of **9** by means of

perambulate
4 walk **6** stroll **8** traverse **9** promenade

per capita
3 all **4** each **5** aside **6** apiece

perceive
3 see **4** espy, feel, know, mark, mind, note, take **5** grasp, seize, sense **6** behold, descry, detect, divine, notice **7** discern, observe, realize **8** identify **9** apprehend, recognize **10** comprehend, understand

perceptible
5 clear, lucid **6** signal **8** palpable, sensible, tangible **10** cognizable, detectable, noticeable, observable **11** appreciable, conspicuous, discernible, perspicuous **12** recognizable

perception
4 idea **5** image **6** acumen, notion **7** conceit, concept, insight, thought **9** cognition **10** impression

perceptive
4 keen, sage, wise **5** acute, aware, sharp **6** sophic **7** gnostic, knowing **9** insighted, sagacious, sensitive **10** discerning, insightful, prehensile, prehensive, responsive

perch
3 bar, set **4** land **5** light, roost **6** alight, settle **7** set down, sit down, station

perchance
5 maybe **7** perhaps **8** possibly

percipience
3 wit **6** acumen **8** keenness **10** astuteness, shrewdness **11** discernment, penetration **12** perspicacity

percolate
4 ooze, seep, sift **5** exude **6** charge, filter, strain **7** pervade **8** permeate, saturate, transude **9** penetrate, transfuse **10** impregnate **11** impenetrate

percussion
3 jar **4** bump, jolt **5** clash, crash, shock **6** impact **9** collision **10** concussion
instrument: (see at **musical instrument**)

Perdita
father: **7** Leontes
mother: **8** Hermione

perdition
3 pit **4** hell **5** abyss, hades **7** Gehenna, inferno **9** barathrum, damnation **10** underworld **11** netherworld, Pandemonium

Père Goriot author
6 Balzac (Honoré)

peregrination
4 trek, trip **7** journey, travels **10** expedition

peremptory
5 bossy, fixed **7** certain, decided **8** absolute, decisive, imperial, positive **9** imperious, masterful, obstinate **10** high-handed, imperative **11** domineering, magisterial, overbearing

perennial
3 old **7** durable **8** enduring, lifelong **9** continual, long-lived, permanent, perpetual, unceasing **10** continuing, inveterate, perdurable **11** long-lasting

Perez
brother: **5** Zerah
father: **5** Judah
mother: **5** Tamar

perfect
3 fit **4** full, pure, rank, very **5** exact, gross, ideal, model, right, round, sheer, sleek, slick, sound, utter, whole **6** choate, entire, expert, intact, needed, polish, proper, refine, simple, smooth **7** express, precise, unmixed **8** absolute, complete, finished, flawless, integral, masterly, outright, positive, required, suitable, unbroken, unflawed **9** downright, excellent, fleckless, masterful, requisite, unalloyed, undamaged, undiluted, uninjured **10** consummate, impeccable, unimpaired

perfection
5 arête, ideal, merit **6** virtue **7** paragon, quality **9** integrity, wholeness **10** entireness, excellence, excellency **12** completeness

perfidious
5 false, venal **6** untrue **7** unloyal **8** disloyal, recreant **9** alienated, deceitful, dishonest, estranged, faithless, mercenary **10** traitorous, unfaithful **11** treacherous

perfidiousness
see **perfidy**

perfidy
6 deceit **7** falsity, sellout, treason **8** betrayal, foul play **9** falseness, treachery **10** disloyalty, infidelity **13** faithlessness

perforate
3 pit **4** bore **5** drill, drive, prick, probe, punch **6** pierce **8** puncture **9** penetrate

perform
2 do **3** act, end **4** play, take, work **5** enact, react **6** behave, effect, finish, wind up **7** achieve, execute, fulfill, operate, playact **8** bring off, complete, function **9** discourse, implement, personate **10** accomplish, perpetrate

peformance
3 act **4** deed, feat, show, work **5** stunt **6** acting, action **7** concert, exploit, matinee **8** behavior, efficacy **9** discharge, execution **10** efficiency **11** fulfillment **12** presentation

performer
4 doer, mime 5 actor, mimic
6 mummer, player, worker 7 actress, artiste, trouper 8 thespian
9 playactor 12 impersonator
suffix: 3 ant, ent

perfume
4 balm 5 aroma, cense, scent,
smell, spice 6 sachet 7 bouquet, incense, odorize 9 aromatize, fragrance, redolence
source: 4 musk 5 attar, myrrh, orris
6 chypre 8 bergamot

perfumer
6 Chanel (Coco)

perfunctory
4 cool 5 stock, usual 6 wooden
7 cursory, routine, unaware 8 careless, standard 9 automatic
10 impersonal, mechanical 11 indifferent, involuntary, superficial,
unconcerned 12 uninterested

pergola
5 arbor, bower

perhaps
5 maybe 6 theory 7 suppose
8 feasibly, possibly 9 perchance
10 conjecture, imaginably 11 conceivably, speculation

periapt
4 juju, luck, zemi 5 charm 6 amulet, fetish, mascot 8 talisman
10 phylactery

Pericles
father: 10 Xanthippus
mistress: 7 Aspasia
mother: 8 Agariste

peril
4 risk 6 danger, hazard, menace
7 jeopard 8 endanger, exposure,
jeopardy, openness 9 liability
10 compromise, jeopardize, subjection 12 endangerment

perilous
5 hairy, risky, shaky 6 chancy,
touchy, wicked 7 tottery, unsound
8 delicate, dreadful, ticklish, unstable, unsteady 9 dangerous, desperate, hazardous, unhealthy 10 jeopardous 11 treacherous

___ Perilous
5 Siege

perimeter
3 hem, rim 4 brim, edge 5 ambit,
brink, skirt, verge 6 border, fringe,
margin 7 circuit, compass
8 boundary 9 periphery 13 circumference

period
3 age, end, era 4 days, span, stop,
term, time 5 close, epoch 6 ending, season 7 closing, closure
8 duration 9 cessation 10 conclusion, generation 11 termination

periodical
5 organ 6 review 7 journal 8 magazine 9 alternate, newspaper,
recurrent, recurring 10 isochronal
11 isochronous 12 intermittent

Peri opera
5 Dafne 8 Euridice

peripatetic
6 roving 7 nomadic, vagrant 8 ambulant, vagabond 9 itinerant, itinerate, wandering, wayfaring
11 perambulant

periphery
see **perimeter**

periphrasis
see **pleonasm**

perish
3 die, end 4 pass 5 cease 6 demise, depart, expire, vanish 7 decease, decline, go under, succumb
8 collapse, pass away 9 disappear

perjure
3 lie 5 trick 6 delude 7 deceive,
mislead 8 forswear 10 equivocate
11 prevaricate

perk
4 gain, mend 6 look up 7 freshen,
improve, smarten 9 percolate
10 ameliorate, convalesce, perquisite, recuperate

permanent
5 fixed 6 stable 7 abiding, durable, lasting 8 constant, enduring
9 continual, diuturnal, perduring,
perennial 10 invariable, perdurable 12 imperishable

permeable
6 porose, porous 8 passable, pervious 10 penetrable

permeate
4 fill, soak 5 imbue, steep
6 charge, drench, imbrue, infuse,
invade 7 diffuse, ingrain, pervade,
suffuse 8 saturate 9 interfuse, penetrate, percolate, transfuse 10 impregnate, infiltrate 11 impenetrate

permissible
7 allowed 8 approved, bearable,
endorsed 9 allowable, permitted,
tolerable, tolerated 10 acceptable,
admissible, authorized, sanctioned
11 unforbidden 12 unprohibited

permission
5 leave 6 permit 7 consent, license
8 approval, sanction 9 allowance
10 acceptance, sufferance 11 approbation, endorsement 12 acquiescence 13 authorization

permit
3 let 4 have 5 admit, allow, grant,
leave 6 suffer 7 consent 8 sanction, tolerate 9 allowance, authorize 10 permission, sufferance
13 authorization

permitted
5 licit

permutation
5 sport 6 change 7 novelty 10 alteration, innovation 11 vicissitude
12 modification

pernicious
3 bad 4 evil 5 fatal, swart, toxic
6 deadly, lethal, malign, mortal,
wicked 7 baleful, baneful, harmful,
hurtful, killing, malefic, miasmic,
noxious, ruinous 8 damaging, sinister, venomous, virulent 9 malignant, miasmatic, pestilent, poisonous 10 maleficent 11 deleterious,
destructive, detrimental, devastating

Pernod flavor
5 anise 8 licorice

perorate
4 rant, rave 5 mouth 7 declaim,
soapbox 8 bloviate, harangue

perpend
4 mind 5 study, weigh 6 ponder
8 consider, think out 9 think over
10 excogitate 11 contemplate

perpendicular
5 plumb 7 stand-up, upright
8 straight, vertical 10 straight-up

perpetrate
2 do 4 pull 5 wreak 6 commit, effect 7 inflict, execute, perform

perpetual
7 endless, eternal 8 constant,
unending 9 ceaseless, continual, incessant, perennial, unceasing
10 continuous 11 everlasting, unremitting 12 interminable

perpetuate
4 keep 6 secure 7 bolster, support,
sustain 8 conserve, eternize, maintain, preserve 10 eternalize
11 immortalize

perplex
4 balk, pose 5 amaze, befog,
ravel, snarl 6 baffle, bemuse, muddle, puzzle, tangle, thwart

7 astound, confuse, ensnarl, mystify, nonplus, perturb, stumble **8** astonish, bewilder, confound, entangle, surprise **10** complicate, discompose **11** intertangle

perquisite
3 tip **5** right **6** income **7** cumshaw, largess **8** appanage, gratuity **9** lagniappe, pourboire, privilege **10** birthright **11** prerogative

per se
5 alone **6** as such, solely **8** in itself

persecute
4 bait, rack, ride **5** harry, hound, worry, wrong **6** harass, heckle, molest **7** afflict, dragoon, oppress, outrage, torment, torture **8** aggrieve

Persephone
4 Kore **10** Proserpina
father: **4** Zeus **7** Jupiter
husband: **5** Hades, Pluto
mother: **5** Ceres **7** Demeter

Perseus
father: **4** Zeus **7** Jupiter
grandfather: **8** Acrisius
mother: **5** Danaë
victim: **6** Medusa **8** Acrisius
wife: **9** Andromeda

perseverance
8 tenacity **9** diligence, endurance **11** persistence **13** steadfastness

persevere
see **persist**

persevering
see **persistent**

Persian
fairy: **4** peri
fire worshiper: **5** Parsi **6** Parsee
governor: **6** satrap
mystic: **4** sufi
poet: **5** Hafez **8** Firdausi, Firdawsī **11** Omar Khayyam
prophet: **9** Zoroaster
robe: **6** caftan
sacred books: **6** Avesta
sun-god: **7** Mithras
title: **4** shah
writing: **9** cuneiform

persiflage
6 banter **8** backchat, badinage, raillery, repartee, snip-snap

persist
4 go on, last **5** abide **6** endure, hang on, linger, obtain **7** carry on, perdure, prevail **8** continue **9** persevere **12** carry through

persistence
3 run **6** course **8** duration **9** endurance **10** continuity **11** continuance **12** continuation
combining form: **6** stasia, stasis

persistent
6 dogged **7** archaic **8** enduring **9** insistent, primitive, steadfast, tenacious, unevolved **10** determined, relentless, unshakable **11** perseverant, persevering, undeveloped, unremitting **13** perseverative

persnickety
4 nice **5** fussy, picky **6** choosy **7** finicky **8** clerkish **10** fastidious

person
3 guy, man, one **4** body, chap, coot, life, self, soul **5** being, human, stick **6** entity, fellow, galoot, mortal **8** creature, specimen **10** individual
admirable: **6** mensch
ambitious: **8** go-getter **10** up-and-comer
betrothed: **6** fiancé **7** fiancée
clumsy: **5** klutz **6** kludge
combining form: **6** prosop **7** prosopo
contemptible: **3** cad **4** heel **5** knave **6** varlet
distinguished: **3** VIP **5** great
dressy: **12** clotheshorse
eighty-year-old: **12** octogenarian
energetic: **10** ball of fire
guilty: **7** culprit
meek: **7** nebbish
ninety-year-old: **12** nonagenarian
non-Jewish: **3** goy **7** gentile
of mixed ancestry: **5** métis **7** mestizo, mulatto **8** octoroon
one-hundred-year-old: **11** centenarian
rude: **4** boor
rural: **4** hick
sixty-year-old: **12** sexagenarian
virtuous: **6** zaddik **7** tzaddik
wealthy: **3** nob **5** nabob

personable
6 comely **7** shapely **8** charming, handsome **10** attractive **11** good-looking

personage
3 VIP **4** body, life, soul **5** being, chief, human, nabob **6** bigwig, mortal **7** big shot, notable **8** creature, eminence, somebody **9** dignitary **10** individual, notability **11** personality

personal
3 own **5** privy **7** private, special **8** peculiar **10** individual, particular
combining form: **4** idio

personal effects
5 goods, stuff, traps **6** things, tricks **10** belongings **11** possessions

personality
3 ego, VIP **5** chief, humor, nabob, seity **6** makeup, nature, temper **7** big shot, ipseity, notable, selfdom **8** eminence, identity, selfhood, selfness, somebody **9** character, dignitary, personage **10** complexion, notability **11** disposition, singularity, temperament **13** individualism, individuality

personate
2 do **3** act **4** play **5** enact **6** embody, mirror, typify **7** perform, play-act **9** discourse, epitomize, exemplify, personify, represent **10** illustrate **11** emblematize

personify
6 embody, mirror, typify **8** manifest **9** body forth, epitomize, exemplify, incarnate, objectify, represent, symbolize **10** illustrate **11** emblematize, exteriorize, externalize, materialize, personalize, reincarnate **12** substantiate

perspective
5 scape, vista **7** lookout, outlook **8** prospect **9** viewpoint

perspicacious
4 keen **5** cagey, heady **6** argute, astute, shrewd **9** astucious, sagacious **10** perceptive **11** penetrating, sharp-witted **12** quick-sighted, sharp-sighted

perspicacity
3 wit **6** acumen **8** astucity, keenness **10** astuteness, shrewdness **11** discernment, penetration, percipience

perspicuity
7 clarity **8** lucidity **9** clearness, limpidity, plainness **12** explicitness

perspicuous
5 clear, lucid **6** lucent **7** crystal **8** clear-cut, luculent, luminous, pellucid **9** unblurred **11** unambiguous

perspiration
4 work **5** sweat **9** exudation
abnormal: **8** hidrosis

perspire
5 sweat **7** swelter

persuadable
8 amenable, exorable, suasible, swayable **9** acceptant, acceptive, receptive

persuade

3 win 4 coax, draw, lead, move, sway 5 bring, touch 6 affect, assure, entice, induce, impress, satisfy, win over 8 convince, talk into 9 argue into, prevail on 11 bring around, prevail upon

persuasible

see **persuadable**

persuasion

3 ilk, lot 4 bias, cast, cult, mind, mold, sect, sort, type, view 5 class, creed, faith, order 6 belief, church, nature 7 feeling, opinion 8 religion 9 character, communion, prejudice, sentiment 10 cajolement, connection, conviction, partiality 11 affiliation, description 12 denomination

Persuasion author

6 Austen (Jane)

pert

4 arch, bold, keen, rude, wise 5 alert, fresh, nervy, sassy, saucy, smart 6 bantam, brazen, bright, cheeky, daring, lively 7 animate, forward 8 animated, impudent, spirited 9 audacious, sprightly, vivacious 11 smart-alecky 13 disrespectful

pertain

4 join, vest 5 apply 6 bear on, belong, relate 7 combine, concern, connect 8 bear upon 9 associate

pertaining to

suffix: 2 al, an, ar, ic 3 ean, ese, ial, ile, ine, ist, ory 4 ical 5 ative, istic 6 itious 7 istical

pertinacious

6 dogged, mulish 7 willful 8 perverse, stubborn 9 obstinate, tenacious 10 bullheaded, headstrong, inflexible, refractory, self-willed, unshakable, unyielding

pertinent

3 apt, fit 5 ad rem 7 apropos, germane 8 apposite, material, pointful, relevant 10 applicable, pertaining 11 applicative, applicatory, appropriate

perturb

5 upset, worry 6 bother, dismay, flurry 7 agitate, disturb, fluster, trouble 8 disquiet, unsettle 10 discompose, disconcert

Peru

capital: 4 Lima

conqueror: 7 Pizarro (Francisco)
monetary unit: 3 sol

peruse

4 read, scan 5 study 6 survey 7 examine

pervade

4 fill 5 bathe, imbue 6 charge 8 permeate, saturate 9 penetrate, percolate, transfuse 10 impregnate 11 impenetrate

perverse

5 balky 6 cranky, mulish, ornery, putrid, rotten 7 corrupt, froward, restive, vicious, wayward 8 contrary, depraved, stubborn 9 irritable, miscreant, nefarious, obstinate, unhealthy 10 degenerate, headstrong, refractory, self-willed, unyielding, villainous 11 stiff-necked, wrongheaded 12 cross-grained, pertinacious, unreasonable

pervert

4 ruin, skew, warp 5 abuse, belie, color, twist 6 debase, garble, misuse 7 corrupt, debauch, deprave, distort, falsify, outrage 8 ill-treat, maltreat, misapply, miscolor, misstate, mistreat 9 animalize, brutalize, misemploy, mishandle 10 bastardize, bestialize, demoralize, misimprove, prostitute 12 misrepresent

pervious

6 porose, porous 9 permeable 10 penetrable

pesky

4 mean, ugly 8 annoying 9 troublous, vexatious 10 bothersome 11 troublesome

pessimist

5 cynic 7 killjoy 9 Cassandra, defeatist, doomsayer, worrywart 10 fussbudget 11 crepehanger, misanthrope

pessimistic

6 gloomy 7 cynical 10 despairing

pest

4 bane 5 worry 6 bother, pester, plague, vermin 7 heckler, nudnick, trouble 8 badgerer, irritant, nuisance, vexation 9 annoyance, besetment, tormentor

pester

4 ride 5 annoy, devil, harry, tease, worry 6 badger, bother, harass, plague 7 bedevil, hagride, torment 8 irritant, nuisance 9 annoyance, beleaguer, besetment, tantalize 10 botherment 11 botheration

pesticide

3 DDT 7 biocide 9 fungicide, germicide, vermicide 11 bactericide, insecticide, microbicide, rodenticide

pestiferous

6 deadly 7 baneful, noxious 9 pestilent 10 pernicious 12 pestilential

pestilence

5 curse 6 plague 7 scourge

pestilential

5 fatal 6 deadly, lethal, mortal, vexing 7 baneful, deathly, noxious 9 pestilent 10 irritating, pernicious 11 mortiferous

pestle

4 mano 5 pilum 6 muller
vessel: 6 mortar

pet

3 hug 4 dear, love, pout, sulk 5 grump, loved 6 caress, cosset, cuddle, dandle, fondle, stroke 7 beloved, cherish, darling, embrace, indulge 8 blue-eyed, favorite

petcock

3 tap 4 gate 5 valve 6 faucet, spigot 7 hydrant 8 stopcock

peter

4 fade, fail 5 abate, cease 6 lessen, rebate, recede 7 dwindle 8 decrease, diminish, taper off 9 drain away

Peter Pan

author: 6 Barrie (James)
character: 4 John 5 Wendy 7 Michael 9 Tiger Lily 10 Tinker Bell
dog: 4 Nana
pirate: 4 Hook, Smee

Peter the Apostle

brother: 6 Andrew
father: 5 Jonah
original name: 5 Simon

Peter the Great

father: 6 Alexis
wife: 7 Eudoxia 9 Catherine

Pethuel's son

4 Joel

petite

3 wee 5 dwarf, small 6 bantam, little, monkey 8 smallish 9 miniature 10 diminutive 11 lilliputian

petition

3 ask, beg, sue 4 plea, pray, suit 5 plead, sue to 6 appeal, orison, prayer, sue for 7 beseech, entreat, implore, request 8 entreaty 10 sup-

plicate **11** application, imploration, imprecation **12** supplication

Petrarch's beloved
5 Laura

Petrified Forest author
8 Sherwood (Robert)

petrify
4 daze, numb, stun **5** alarm **6** appall, bedaze, bemuse, benumb, dismay **7** horrify, startle, stupefy, terrify **8** frighten, paralyze

Petruchio's wife
9 Katharina, Katharine

pettifogger
6 lawyer **7** shyster **10** bush lawyer **13** jackleg lawyer

pettish
see **petulant**

petty
4 base, mean, puny **5** light, minor, small **6** casual, little, measly, paltry, peanut **7** pimping, trivial, unvital **8** childish, niggling, peddling, picayune, piddling, piffling, trifling **9** frivolous, hair-drawn, small-beer **10** irrelevant, negligible, picayunish, shoestring, ungenerous **11** impertinent, Mickey Mouse, unimportant

petty officer
6 noncom, yeoman

petulant
5 cross, huffy, sulky, testy, waspy **7** fretful, grouchy, peevish, pettish, waspish **8** snappish **9** fractious, irascible, irritable, querulous

peyote
6 cactus, mescal
drug: **9** mescaline

Phaedra
father: **5** Minos
husband: **7** Theseus
mother: **8** Pasiphaë
sister: **7** Ariadne
stepson: **10** Hippolytus

Phaëthon's father
6 Helios **7** Phoebus

phantasm
5 dream, fancy, ghost, shade **6** mirage, shadow, spirit, vision **7** eidolon, fantasy, fiction, specter **8** daydream, delusion, illusion, revenant, spectrum **9** invention, nightmare **10** apparition **11** fabrication, ignis fatuus **13** hallucination

phantom
5 ghost, shade **6** eidola (plural), shadow, spirit **7** eidolon, specter **8** phantasm, revenant, spectrum **10** apparition

Phanuel's daughter
4 Anna

pharaoh
3 Tut **4** Seti **6** Ahmose, Ramses **7** Harmhab **8** Ikhnaton, Thutmose **9** Amenhotep, Merneptah **11** Tutankhamen

pharisaism
4 cant **9** hypocrisy **10** sanctimony, Tartuffery, Tartuffism **12** pecksniffery

pharisee
8 Tartuffe **9** hypocrite, lip server **10** dissembler **12** dissimulator

pharmacist
8 druggist **10** apothecary
British: **7** chemist

pharos
6 beacon **10** lighthouse

Pharsalus, battle of
vanquished: **6** Pompey
victor: **6** Caesar (Julius)

phase
4 hand, look, side, view **5** angle, color, facet, state **6** aspect **7** posture **8** position **9** condition, semblance, situation, viewpoint **10** appearance, complexion

PhD exam
5 orals

pheasant
5 argus, monal **8** tragopan

Phebe's husband
7 Silvius

Phèdre author
6 Racine (Jean)

phenomenal
4 rare **5** gross **6** unique **7** unusual **8** material, physical, sensible, singular, tangible, unwonted **9** corporeal, objective **10** remarkable **11** exceptional, substantial, unthinkable **13** extraordinary

phenomenon
4 fact **5** event **6** marvel, wonder **7** anomaly, miracle, paradox, portent, prodigy, reality, stunner **9** actuality, sensation **10** experience, uniqueness **11** peculiarity, singularity, unusualness

philander
4 wolf **5** chase, dally, flirt **6** chaser, masher, pursue, trifle **7** Don Juan **8** Casanova, womanize **9** ladies' man, womanizer **10** fool around, lady-killer, mess around, play around **11** philanderer

philanthropic
4 good **6** giving, humane **8** donating **10** altruistic, benevolent, bighearted, charitable, freehanded **11** civic-minded, freehearted, kindhearted, magnanimous, openhearted **12** contributing, eleemosynary, greathearted, humanitarian

philanthropist
American: **6** Girard (Stephen) **7** Cornell (Ezra) **8** Carnegie (Andrew) **9** Rosenwald (Julius) **11** Rockefeller (John Davison)
English: **11** Wilberforce (William)
Swedish: **5** Nobel (Alfred)

Philemon's wife
6 Baucis

philharmonic
4 band **8** symphony **9** orchestra

Philip of Macedonia
father: **7** Amyntas
son: **9** Alexander

philippic
6 tirade **8** diatribe, harangue, jeremiad

Philippics author
6 Cicero

Philippines
capital: **6** Manila
discoverer: **8** Magellan (Ferdinand)
hero: **5** Rizal (Jose)
language: **7** Spanish, Tagalog, Visayan **8** Filipino
liberator: **9** MacArthur (Douglas)
monetary unit: **4** peso
president: **6** Marcos (Ferdinand), Aquino (Corazon)

Philippi victor
6 Antony (Marc) **8** Octavian

Philip the Tetrarch
father: **5** Herod
mother: **9** Cleopatra

philistine
4 boob, boor, lout **5** clown **7** Babbitt **8** boeotian **9** barbarian, bourgeois, vulgarian **10** capitalist, middlebrow **11** materialist

Philistine
champion: 7 Goliath
city: 4 Gath, Gaza 5 Ekron 6 Ashdod 8 Ashkelon
foe: 5 David 6 Samson
god: 5 Dagon

Philoctetes
father: 5 Poeas
victim: 5 Paris

Philomela
11 nightingale
father: 7 Pandion
ravisher: 6 Tereus
sister: 6 Procne

philosopher
American: 5 Adler (Mortimer), James (Henry, William), Quine (Willard), Royce (Josiah) 6 Langer (Susanne) 7 Marcuse (Herbert) 9 Santayana (George)
Arab: 8 Avicenna
British: 7 Russell (Bertrand) 12 Wittgenstein (Ludwig)
Chinese: 6 Lao-tsu 7 Mencius, Tai Chen 9 Confucius
Danish: 11 Kierkegaard (Soren)
Dutch: 7 Spinoza (Baruch)
English: 4 Mill (John Stuart), More (Henry, Thomas) 5 Bacon (Francis), Locke (John), Moore (George), Occam (William) 6 Hobbes (Thomas), Ockham (William) 7 Bentham (Jeremy), Russell (Bertrand), Spencer (Herbert), Whewell (William) 9 Whitehead (Alfred North)
Finnish: 11 Westermarck (Edward)
French: 5 Comte (Auguste), Taine (Hippolyte) 6 Pascal (Blaise), Sartre (Jean-Paul), Valery (Paul) 7 Abelard (Peter) 8 Maritain (Jacques), Rousseau (Jean-Jacques), Teilhard (Pierre) 9 Descartes (Rene) 10 Saint-Simon (Comte de), Schweitzer (Albert)
German: 4 Kant (Immanuel), Marx (Karl) 5 Hegel (Georg Wilhelm Friedrich), Wolff (Christian von) 6 Fichte (Immanuel, Johann), Herder (Johann von) 7 Jaspers (Karl), Leibniz (Gottfried) 8 Spengler (Oswald) 9 Heidegger (Martin), Nietzsche (Friedrich), Schelling (Friedrich von) 12 Schopenhauer (Arthur) 14 Albertus Magnus
Greek: 4 Zeno 5 Plato, Timon 6 Thales 7 Gorgias, Proclus 8 Diogenes, Epicurus, Longinus, Socrates 9 Aristotle 10 Anaxagoras, Democritus, Empedocles, Heraclitus, Parmenides, Protagoras, Pytha-gorus, Xenocrates, Xenophanes 11 Anaximander 12 Theophrastus
Indian: 13 Gautama Buddha
Irish: 8 Berkeley (George)
Italian: 6 Ficino (Marsilio)
Jewish: 5 Buber (Martin), Philo 12 Philo Judaeus
Roman: 6 Seneca (Lucias Annaeus) 8 Boethius (Anicius), Plotinus 9 Lucretius
Scottish: 4 Hume (David), Mill (James), Reid (Thomas) 7 Stewart (Dugald)
Spanish: 6 Suarez (Francisco) 13 Ortega y Gasset (Jose)
Swedish: 10 Swedenborg (Emanuel)

philosophers' stone
6 elixir

philosophical
4 calm 8 composed, rational 9 temperate

philosophy
3 tao 4 yoga 5 deism 7 dualism, inquiry, wholism 8 stoicism 10 empiricism, pragmatism 12 Cartesianism

Phineas
beloved: 9 Andromeda
tormentors: 7 Harpies
wife: 9 Cleopatra

Phinehas
father: 3 Eli 7 Eleazar
grandfather: 5 Aaron

phlegm
6 apathy 7 ataraxy 8 calmness, coolness, stoicism 9 composure, sangfroid, stolidity, unconcern 10 equanimity 11 impassivity, nonchalance

phlegmatic
3 dry 4 calm, dull 5 aloof, stoic 6 stolid 8 sluggish 9 apathetic, impassive, incurious, lethargic 11 indifferent, unconcerned

Phlegyas
daughter: 7 Coronis
father: 4 Ares, Mars
son: 5 Ixion

phobia
see **fear**

Phobos
4 moon 9 satellite
brother: 6 Deimos
father: 4 Ares, Mars

Phocus
father: 6 Aeacus 8 Ornytion
half brother: 6 Peleus 7 Telamon
mother: 8 Psamathe

slayer: 6 Peleus 7 Telamon
wife: 7 Antiope

Phoebe
5 Diana 7 Artemis
daughter: 4 Leto
father: 9 Leucippus
mother: 2 Ge 4 Gaea

phoebus
3 sun 7 daystar

Phoebus
see **Apollo**

Phoenician
city: 4 Acre, Tyre 5 Sidon
colony: 8 Carthage
god: 4 Baal 6 Eshmun
goddess: 6 Baltis 7 Astarte

Phoenix
4 bird
brother: 5 Cilix
pupil: 8 Achilles
sister: 6 Europa
team: 4 Suns

phony
4 fake, hoax, sham 5 bogus, cheat, faker, false, fraud, put-on, snide, spoof 6 humbug, pseudo 7 swindle 8 impostor, spurious 9 brummagen, charlatan, imposture, pinchbeck, pretender 11 counterfeit

photograph
3 mug, pic 4 film, snap 5 kodak, shoot 6 glossy 7 filmize, picture, tintype 8 cinemize, likeness, snapshot 9 snapshoot
three dimensional: 8 hologram

photographer
8 camerist, photoist 9 cameraman 10 shutterbug 11 snapshooter
famous: 3 Ray (Man) 4 Capa (Robert), Haas (Ernst), Hine (Lewis), Riis (Jacob) 5 Adams (Ansel), Arbus (Diane), Atget (Eugene), Brady (Mathew), Evans (Frederick, Walker), Horst (Horst Peter), Karsh (Yousuf), Lange (Dorothea), Model (Lisette), Parks (Gordon), Smith (W. Eugene), Weber (Bruce), White (Clarence, Minor) 6 Abbott (Berenice), Avedon (Richard), Beaton (Cecil), Brandt (Bill), Coburn (Alvin), Curtis (Edward S.), Newton (Helmut), Porter (Eliot), Rowell (Galen), Siegel (Eliot), Strand (Paul), Talbot (William Henry Fox), Weegee, Weston (Brett, Edward) 7 Brassaï, Cameron (Julia Margaret), Emerson (Peter), Jackson (William Henry), Kertész (Andre), Salomon (Erich), Siskind (Aaron), Snowdon (Earl of), Thom-

son (John), Watkins (Carleton) **8** Callahan (Harry), Cosindas (Marie), Daguerre (Louis-Jacques-Mande), Kasebier (Gertrude), Scavullo (Francesco), Steichen (Edward), Steinert (Otto) **9** Caponigro (Paul), Feininger (Andreas, T. Lux), Leibovitz (Annie), Meyrowitz (Joel), O'Sullivan (Timothy), Rejlander (Oscar), Rothstein (Arthur), Stieglitz (Alfred), Winogrand (Garry) **10** Cunningham (Imogen), Heartfield (John), Moholy-Nagy (Laszlo) **11** Bourke-White (Margaret), Eisenstaedt (Alfred) **12** Mapplethorpe (Robert) **14** Cartier-Bresson (Henri)

photographic
5 exact, vivid **7** graphic **8** accurate, detailed **9** pictorial **11** picturesque
solution: **4** hypo **5** fixer, toner **7** reducer **9** developer

phrase
3 put **4** term, word **5** couch, idiom **6** byword, slogan **7** diction, express, styling, wordage, wording **8** locution, parlance, verbiage **9** catchword, formulate, verbalism, watchword **10** expression, shibboleth

Phrixus
father: **7** Athamus
mother: **7** Nephele
sister: **5** Helle
wife: **9** Chalciope

Phrontis
brother: **5** Argus, Melas **9** Cytisorus
father: **7** Phrixus
mother: **9** Chalciope

Phrygian
god: **3** Men **4** Atys **5** Attis
goddess: **6** Cybele
king: **5** Midas **7** Gordius

phthisis
2 TB **11** consumption, white plague **12** tuberculosis

phylactery
4 juju, luck, zemi **5** charm **6** amulet, fetish, mascot **7** periapt **8** talisman

physic
4 cure, heal **5** purge **6** remedy **7** relieve **8** medicant, medicine **9** cathartic, purgative **10** medicament, medication

physical
5 brute, gross, lusty **6** bodily, car-

nal **7** fleshly, natural, somatic **8** corporal, material, sensible, tangible, visceral **9** corporeal, elemental, objective **10** elementary, phenomenal **11** substantial

physician
2 MD **3** doc **5** medic **6** doctor, medico **7** medical, surgeon **9** mediciner **10** specialist **12** practitioner
American: **4** Rush (Benjamin), Salk (Jonas) **5** Minot (George), Spock (Benjamin), Still (Andrew) **6** Jarvik (Robert), Murphy (John), Weller (Thomas) **7** Huggins (Charles), Robbins (Frederick), Theiler (Max) **8** Richards (Dickinson) **9** Sternberg (George Miller)
Arab: **8** Avicenna
Austrian: **6** Mesmer (Anton)
Canadian: **5** Osler (William)
combining form: **5** iatro **7** iatrist
English: **4** Ross (Ronald) **6** Harvey (William), Jenner (Edward, William), Willis (Thomas) **8** Sydenham (Thomas)
French: **5** Widal (Fernand) **7** Laveran (Charles) **10** Schweitzer (Albert)
German: **7** Sylvius (Franciscus)
Greek: **6** Galen **11** Hippocrates
Italian: **7** Galvani (Luigi)
slang: **8** sawbones
South African: **7** Barnard (Christiaan)
Swiss: **10** Paracelsus; (see also **Nobel Prize Winner**, *physiology or medicine;* **surgeon**)

physicist
American: **4** Rabi (Isidor Isaac), Ting (Samuel) **5** Fermi (Enrico), Gibbs (J. Willard), Kusch (Polykarp), Mayer (Maria-Goeppert), Pauli (Wolfgang), Pupin (Michael), Segre (Emilio), Smyth (Henry Dewolf), Stern (Otto) **6** Teller (Edward), Townes (Charles), Wigner (Eugene) **7** Goddard (James), Purcell (Edward) **8** Einstein (Albert), Gell-Mann (Murray), McMillan (Edwin), Millikan (Clark, Robert), Mulliken (Robert), Shockley (William), Van Allen (James) **9** Michelson (Albert), Schwinger (Julian) **11** Oppenheimer (J. Robert)
Austrian: **4** Mach (Ernst) **7** Doppler (Christian) **11** Schrodinger (Erwin)
British: **6** Stokes (George) **7** Tyndall (John) **8** Thompson (Benjamin, Silvanus)
Chinese: **4** Yang (Chen Ning)
Danish: **4** Bohr (Aage, Niels)
Dutch: **6** Zeeman (Pieter) **7** Huygens (Christian), Lorentz (Hendrik), Zer-

nike (Frits) **11** Van der Waals (Johannes)
English: **4** Snow (Charles Percy) **5** Jeans (James), Joule (James) **6** Dalton (John), Kelvin (Baron), Newton (Isaac), Powell (Cecil) **7** Faraday (Michael), Hodgkin (Dorothy), Thomson (George, Joseph, William) **8** Rayleigh (Lord), Robinson (Robert) **9** Wollaston (William) **10** Richardson (Owen), Rutherford (Ernest), Wheatstone (Charles)
French: **4** Néel (Louis) **5** Arago (François) **6** Ampere (Andre-Marie), Perrin (Jean-Baptiste) **7** Coulomb (Charles-Augustin de), Kastler (Alfred), Reaumur (Rene-Antoine de) **8** Lippmann (Gabriel)
German: **3** Ohm (Georg) **4** Laue (Max von), Wien (Wilhelm) **5** Hertz (Gustav, Heinrich), Stark (Johannes) **6** Jensen (Hans), Lenard (Philipp), Nernst (Walther), Planck (Max) **7** Meitner (Lise) **8** Roentgen (Wilhelm) **9** Helmholtz (Hermann von), Kirchhoff (Gustav), Mossbauer (Rudolf) **10** Fahrenheit (Daniel), Hofstadter (Robert)
Indian: **5** Raman (Chandrasekhara)
Irish: **6** Walton (Ernest)
Italian: **5** Rossi (Bruno), Volta (Alessandro) **7** Galileo, Galvani (Luigi) **10** Torricelli (Evangelista)
Japanese: **6** Yukawa (Hideki) **8** Tomonaga (Shin'ichirō)
Mexican: **8** Vallarta (Manuel)
Russian: **4** Tamm (Igor) **6** Landau (Lev) **9** Prokhorov (Aleksandr)
Scottish: **4** Tait (Peter) **6** Wilson (Charles) **7** Maxwell (James Clerk)
Swedish: **7** Rydberg (Johannes) **8** Angstrom (Anders), Siegbahn (Kai, Karl)
Swiss: **6** Zwicky (Fritz) **7** Piccard (Auguste); (see also **Nobel Prize Winner**, *physics*)

physiologist
English: **8** Starling (Ernest)
German: **5** Weber (Ernst), Wundt (Wilhelm) **7** Schwann (Theodor) **9** Helmholtz (Hermann von)
Italian: **11** Spallanzani (Lazzaro); (see also **Nobel Prize Winner**, *physiology or medicine*)

physique
4 body, form **5** build, frame, habit, shape **6** figure **7** anatomy, habitus **9** structure **12** constitution **13** configuration

pianist
American: **4** Nero (Peter), Wild (Earl) **5** Arrau (Claudio), Davis (Anthony),

Janis (Byron), Tatum (Art), Watts (Andre) **6** Duchin (Peter), Joplin (Scott), Serkin (Peter, Rudolf), Waller (Fats) **7** Cliburn (Van), Istomin (Eugene), Ohlsson (Garrick), Perahia (Murray), Winston (George) **8** Graffman (Gary), Grainger (Percy), Horowitz (Vladimir), Pennario (Leonard) **10** Johannesen (Grant), Rubinstein (Arthur)
Austrian: **6** Czerny (Karl) **8** Schnabel (Artur) **9** Rosenthal (Moriz)
Bulgarian: **11** Weissenberg (Alexis)
Cuban: **5** Bolet (Jorge)
English: **4** Hess (Myra) **5** Katin (Peter), Ogdon (John) **6** Curzon (Clifford)
Finnish: **8** Palmgren (Selim)
French: **6** Cortot (Alfred-Denis) **7** Cziffra (Gyorgy) **9** Entremont (Philippe) **11** Saint-Saens (Camille)
German: **5** Bülow (Hans von) **6** Kempff (Wilhelm) **8** Schumann (Clara, Robert) **9** Gieseking (Walter)
Hungarian: **5** Liszt (Franz) **6** Vasary (Tamas)
Italian: **6** Busoni (Ferruccio) **8** Clementi (Muzio)
Polish: **6** Chopin (Frederic) **7** Hofmann (Josef) **9** Landowska (Wanda) **10** Paderewski (Ignacy)
Russian: **6** Berman (Lazar), Gilels (Emil) **7** Richter (Sviatoslav) **8** Pachmann (Vladimir von) **9** Ashkenazy (Vladimir), Prokofiev (Sergey) **10** Rubinstein (Anton) **12** Rachmaninoff (Sergey)
Spanish: **6** Iturbi (Jose) **8** Granados (Enrique) **10** de Larrocha (Alicia)
Swiss: **4** Anda (Geza)

piano
5 grand **6** softly, spinet **7** quietly, upright
builder: **5** Knabe (William), Stein (Johann), Zumpe (Johann) **7** Baldwin (Dwight) **8** Steinway (Henry) **9** Bechstein (Friedrich) **10** Chickering (Jonas), Cristofori (Bartolomeo), Silbermann (Johann)
inventor: **10** Cristofori (Bartolomeo)
key: **7** digital
pedal: **6** damper **7** celeste

Piazza Tales author
8 Melville (Herman)

picaroon
5 rogue, rover, thief **6** pirate, sea dog **7** brigand, corsair, sea wolf **8** sea rover **9** buccaneer, sea robber **10** freebooter

picayune
see **piddling**

Piccini's rival
5 Gluck (Christoph)

pick
3 top **4** beak, best, cull, gaff, mark, take **5** elect, elite, pluck, pride, prime, prize **6** choice, choose, chosen, optate, opt for, prefer, select **8** plectrum, selected **9** exclusive, single out

picket
3 peg **4** pale, post, ward **5** guard, stake, watch **6** sentry, tether **7** lookout **8** palisade, sentinel, watchman

pick handle
5 helve

pickle
3 fix, jam **4** dill, spot **5** brine, souse **6** capers, corner, plight, scrape **7** dilemma, gherkin, trouble **8** marinate **11** predicament

pickpocket
5 thief **8** cutpurse **11** purse cutter
slang: **3** dip

pick up
3 get **4** cull, gain, land, lift, rear **5** annex, glean, hoist, learn, pinch, raise, renew, run in **6** arrest, detain, garner, gather, master, obtain, pull in, reopen, resume, uphold, uplift, uprear **7** acquire, compass, elevate, extract, procure, restart, upraise **8** continue **9** apprehend **10** recommence

pickup
5 truck **6** arrest **9** detention **10** arrestment, hitchhiker **11** arrestation, improvement **12** acceleration, apprehension

picky
4 nice **5** fussy **6** choosy, dainty **7** finical, finicky **9** finicking **10** fastidious, particular **11** persnickety

picnic
4 snap **5** cinch **6** breeze, outing
beach: **8** clambake

picture
4 cine, copy, draw, film, idea, limn, show **5** flick, image, movie, photo, pinup, print **6** depict, render **7** drawing, portray, tableau **8** describe, painting, portrait **9** delineate, depiction, interpret, photoplay, portrayal, represent **10** simulacrum **11** delineation, description, portraiture, presentment **13** spitting image
stand: **5** easel

picture show
4 cine, film **5** flick, movie **9** photoplay

piddling
4 puny **5** petty **6** measly, paltry **7** trivial **8** niggling, trifling **11** Mickey Mouse

pie
4 flan, tart **5** pasty **6** affair, pastry **7** cobbler **8** business, crustade, turnover

piece
3 cut **4** part **6** member, moiety, parcel **7** portion, section, segment **8** division, fraction, fragment

pièce de résistance
8 main dish **9** showpiece **11** centerpiece, chef d'oeuvre, masterpiece

piecemeal
7 gradual **8** bit by bit **9** gradually **10** step-by-step

pie chart
5 graph **11** circle graph

pier
4 dock, quay, slip **5** berth, jetty, levee, wharf **6** column, pillar **8** pilaster
architectural: **4** anta

pierce
3 cut **4** bore, gash, gore, slit, stab **5** slash, slice, spear **6** incise, riddle, skewer **8** transfix **9** penetrate, perforate **10** run through

piercing
4 high, keen, loud, thin **5** acute, sharp **6** argute, piping, shrill, treble **7** blaring, roaring **8** shooting, stabbing **9** knifelike **10** stentorian **12** earsplitting
tool: **3** awl

piety
5 ardor **6** fealty, fervor **7** loyalty **8** devotion, fidelity, holiness, sanctity **9** godliness, reverence **10** allegiance, devoutness **12** faithfulness

piffle
4 bosh **5** hooey **6** bunkum **7** twaddle **8** malarkey, nonsense, pishposh **10** balderdash, flapdoodle **12** blatherskite

pig
3 hog **5** swine **6** farrow, porker **7** casting, glutton
breed: **5** Duroc **8** Tamworth **9** Berkshire, Hampshire, Yorkshire
combining form: **3** hyo **7** choerus
female: **3** sow **4** gilt

feral: **9** razorback
litter: **6** farrow
male: **4** boar **6** barrow
meat: **3** ham **4** pork **5** bacon **7** sausage **8** chitlins **9** chitlings **12** chitterlings
wild: **7** peccary, warthog **8** babirusa **9** babirussa
young: **4** gilt **5** shoat **6** farrow, piglet

pigeon
3 sap **4** dupe, fool, gull, hoax, mark **5** chump, decoy **6** culver, sucker **7** fall guy, gudgeon **8** flimflam, hoodwink **9** bamboozle, victimize **11** hornswoggle
genus: **7** Columba
house: **4** cote, loft
kind: **4** barb, rock **5** homer **6** pouter, roller **7** carrier, crowned, dragoon, fantail, jacobin, tumbler **8** carneaux
relative: **4** dove
young: **5** squab

pigeonhole
4 slot, sort, tier **5** class, cubby, grade, group, niche **6** assort, league **7** catalog, cubicle **8** category, classify, grouping **9** cubbyhole **10** categorize

pigeon pea
3 dal **4** dhal, herb

piggish
6 greedy **7** selfish, swinish **10** gluttonous

pigheaded
6 mulish **7** willful **8** perverse, stubborn **9** obstinate **10** headstrong, self-willed, unyielding **11** intractable, stiff-necked

pigment
3 dye **5** color, paint, stain **8** colorant, dyestuff, tincture
black: **9** lampblack
blue: **4** cyan **5** azure, smalt **6** indigo **7** cyanine **8** cerulean **9** verdigris **11** ultramarine
brown: **5** sepia
umber: **6** bister, sienna
combining form: **5** chrom **6** chromo
dark: **7** melanin
green: **7** celadon **8** viridian **10** biliverdin
orange: **7** realgar **8** carotene
red: **4** lake
minium: **7** carmine, crimson, pimento, scarlet, sinopia **8** lycopene **9** bilirubin, vermilion **10** vermillion
toxic: **8** gossypol
yellow: **5** ocher, ochre **6** flavin, lu-

tein **7** flavine, xanthin **8** luteolin, massicot

pigpen
3 sty **4** dump, mess

pigsty
see **pigpen**

piker
3 bum, vag **5** miser, stiff **7** drifter, floater, niggard, vagrant **8** roadster, tightwad, vagabond **9** skinflint **10** cheapskate **11** cheeseparer **12** moneygrubber, penny pincher

pilaster
4 anta, pier **6** column, pillar

Pildash
father: **5** Nahor
mother: **6** Milcah

pile
3 fur, lot, mow, nap, pot, wad **4** bank, cock, down, fill, flue, fuzz, heap, hill, lint, load, lump, mass, mint, much, pack, peck, pyre, rick **5** choke, drift, floss, fluff, hoard, mound, shock, stack **6** barrel, barrow, boodle, bundle, charge, jumble, packet **7** edifice, fortune, haycock, hayrick, pyramid, tumulus, windrow **8** erection, haystack, mountain **9** aggregate, amassment, great deal, structure **10** assemblage, collection **11** aggregation, glomeration **12** accumulation

pileous
5 hairy **6** fleecy, pilose, woolly **7** hirsute **9** whiskered

pileup
5 crash, smash **7** crack-up, smashup **8** accident **9** collision

pilfer
3 rob **4** lift **5** filch, pinch, steal, swipe **6** finger, snitch, thieve **7** purloin **11** appropriate

pilferer
4 prig **5** thief **6** nimmer **7** filcher, stealer **8** larcener **9** larcenist

pilgarlic
4 butt **5** sport **6** jestee **8** baldhead **13** laughingstock

pilgrim
5 hadji, hajji **6** palmer **8** traveler, wanderer, wayfarer
famous: **5** Alden (John) **6** Carver (John) **8** Bradford (William), Brewster (William)

pilgrimage
4 hadj, hajj, trip **7** journey

Pilgrims' interpreter
7 Squanto

Pilgrim's Progress
8 allegory
author: **6** Bunyan (John)
hero: **9** Christian

pill
4 ball **5** bolus **6** pellet, pilule **7** capsule

pillage
3 nab **4** lift, loot, sack **5** filch, pinch, steal, swipe, usurp, waste **6** devour, maraud, pilfer, ravage, thieve **7** despoil, plunder, purloin **8** arrogate, desolate, spoliate **9** depredate, desecrate, devastate **10** confiscate **11** appropriate

pillager
6 looter, raider, sacker **7** forager, ravager, spoiler **8** marauder, ravisher **9** plunderer **10** freebooter

pillar
4 pier, post, prop **5** pylon, shaft, stela, stele **6** column, stelae (plural) **7** obelisk **8** backbone, mainstay, pedestal, pilaster
combining form: **4** cion, styl **5** ciono, style, stylo **6** stelic, stylar

Pillar of Hercules
5 Abila, Abyla, Calpe

pillow
3 pad **7** bolster, cushion

pilose
see **pileous**

pilot
3 ace **4** auto, dean, lead, show, tool **5** doyen, drive, flier, guide, motor, route, steer, wheel **6** airman, direct, escort, flyboy, leader **7** aviator, birdman, conduct **8** aviatrix, helmsman, shepherd

pimp
6 pander **8** fancy man, procurer

pimple
3 dot, zit **4** boil, spot, stud **6** papule **7** abscess, pustule, speckle **8** furuncle, sprinkle **9** carbuncle

pin
3 fid, peg **4** clip **5** affix, dowel, stake, thole **6** broach, brooch, cotter, fasten, secure

pinch
3 nab, nip **4** lift **5** exact, filch, gouge, run in, screw, skimp, spare, steal, stint, swipe, theft, tweak, wrest, wring **7** larceny, squeeze **8** exigency, juncture, stealing, thievery, thieving, zero hour **9** appre-

hend, detention, emergency, shake down 10 arrestment, crossroads, purloining

pinchbeck
4 fake, sham 5 bogus, false, phony, snide 6 pseudo 8 spurious 9 brummagen 11 counterfeit

pinch hitter
3 sub 6 fill-in 7 stand-in 9 alternate, surrogate 10 substitute 11 locum tenens, replacement, succedaneum

Pindar
home: 6 Thebes
poems: 4 odes

pine
4 ache, fret, long, mope, sigh 5 brood, crave, dream, yearn 6 grieve, hanker, hunger, lament, repine, thirst 7 agonize

Pine Tree State
5 Maine

pinguid
3 fat

pinhead
4 fool, simp 5 dense, dunce 6 dimwit, nitwit, stupid 7 doltish, lackwit, wantwit

Pinkerton
6 shamus 9 detective, operative 10 private eye

pinnacle
3 top 4 acme, apex, peak 5 crest, crown 6 apogee, climax, summit, zenith 8 capsheaf, meridian 11 culmination
of a glacier: 5 serac

pinniped
4 seal 6 walrus

Pinocchio author
7 Collodi (Carlo) 9 Lorenzini (Carlo)

pinochle
card: 3 ace, ten 4 jack, king, nine 5 queen
term: 4 meld 5 widow 7 auction
two-handed: 7 goulash

pinpoint
4 spot 5 exact, place 6 finger 7 precise 8 diagnose, identify 9 recognize 11 determinate, distinguish 13 diagnosticate

pinto
4 pied 5 overo, paint 7 painted, piebald, tobiano 8 skewbald

pint-size
3 wee 4 tiny 5 teeny, weeny

6 midget, pocket, teensy 9 miniature 10 diminutive, pocket-size

pioneer
5 first, prime 6 maiden 7 initial, primary, settler 8 colonist, earliest, original
famous: 5 Boone (Daniel), Bowie (Jim), Clark (William), Lewis (Meriwether) 6 Carson (Kit), Colter (John) 7 Bridger (Jim), Chapman (John), Fremont (John C.), Whitman (Marcus) 8 Crockett (Davy)

pious
4 holy 5 godly 6 devout 8 priestly 9 pietistic, prayerful, religious

pip
3 dot 4 blip, peep, root, seed, spot 5 image, speck

pipe
3 keg, tun 4 butt, cask 5 carry 6 barrel, convey, funnel, siphon 7 channel, conduct, conduit, traject 8 hogshead
ceremonial: 7 calumet
combining form: 3 aul 4 aulo 5 solen 6 siphon, soleno 7 siphono
part: 4 bowl, stem

pipe down
5 dry up, quiet 6 dumb up, shut up

pipe dream
6 bubble 7 chimera, fantasy, rainbow 8 illusion, phantasy

pipeline
7 channel, conduit 8 supplier 10 connection

piquant
4 racy, tart 5 spicy, zesty 6 biting, snappy 7 peppery, pungent 8 poignant 9 sparkling 10 appetizing

pique
3 irk 4 huff, miff, move, rile, roil 5 annoy, peeve, plume, preen, pride, rouse, snuff 6 excite, irking, nettle, put out 7 dudgeon, innerve, offense, provoke, quicken, umbrage 8 irritate, motivate, vexation 9 aggravate, annoyance, galvanize, innervate, stimulate 10 exasperate, irritation, resentment

piranha
6 caribe

pirate
5 rover 6 looter, raider, robber, sea dog 7 brigand, corsair, sea wolf 8 marauder, picaroon, pillager, sea rover 9 buccaneer, plunderer, privateer, sea robber 10 freebooter
Celtic: 5 Fomor 8 Fomorian

flag: 10 Jolly Roger
French: 7 Laffite (Jean), Lafitte (Jean)
Scottish: 4 Kidd (William)

Pirithous' wife
10 Hippodamia

pirogue
5 canoe

pirouette
4 gyre, spin 5 twirl, whirl 6 gyrate 9 whirligig

piscator
6 angler 9 fisherman

pismire
3 ant

pistol
7 handgun 8 revolver 9 derringer
case: 7 holster

pit
3 vie 4 hell, hole 5 abyss, chasm, hades, match 6 cavity, oppose 7 counter, Gehenna, inferno, play off 9 barathrum, perdition 10 underworld 11 netherworld, Pandemonium

Pit and the Pendulum author
3 Poe (Edgar Allan)

pitch
3 dip, yaw 4 cant, cast, dive, drop, fall, fire, hurl, rock, roll, swag, tilt, tone, toss 5 burst, drive, fling, heave, lunge, lurch, sling, slump, spiel, throw 6 go down, launch, plunge, seesaw, tilter, topple, tumble, unseat 7 buck off, unhorse 8 keel over 12 song and dance

pitch-black
see **pitch-dark**

pitch-dark
3 jet 4 ebon, inky 5 black, ebony, jetty, raven, sable 11 atramentous

pitched
6 sloped, tilted, tipped 7 leaning, oblique, sloping, tilting 8 inclined 9 inclining

pitcher
4 ewer, olla, toby 5 cruse 7 creamer
area: 5 mound
handle: 3 ear 4 ansa

pitch in
5 begin, set to, start 6 chip in, fall to, jump in, kick in 8 commence, jump into, start off 9 subscribe 10 buckle down, contribute 11 come through

piteous
4 poor 6 rueful, ruined 7 pitiful

8 pathetic, pitiable
12 commiserable

pitfall
4 lure, risk, trap 5 peril, snare
6 danger, hazard 7 springe
8 deadfall, trapfall 9 booby trap,
mousetrap 12 entanglement

pith
3 nub 4 core, gist, meat, pulp,
root, soul 5 focus, heart 6 center,
import, kernel, marrow, matter, upshot, weight 7 essence, nucleus
9 magnitude, substance 10 importance 11 consequence, weightiness
12 essentiality, significance

Pithon's father
5 Micah

pithy
4 curt 5 brief, crisp, meaty, short,
terse 7 compact, concise, marrowy
8 succinct 12 epigrammatic
13 short and sweet

pitiable
see **pitiful**

pitiful
3 sad 4 poor 5 cheap, sorry 6 rueful, scummy, scurvy, shabby, woeful
7 forlorn, piteous 8 beggarly, pathetic, pitiable, wretched 9 miserable, sorrowful 10 despicable, despisable 12 commiserable,
contemptible, heartrending

pitiless
5 cruel, stony 6 brutal, savage
8 inhumane, ruthless 9 barbarous,
cutthroat, heartless, merciless, unfeeling, unpitying 10 relentless, unmerciful 11 coldhearted, hardhearted, ironhearted
12 stonyhearted 13 marblehearted

pittance
3 bit 4 mite 5 scrap, trace 6 trifle
7 dribble, driblet, smidgen

pity
3 rue 4 ache, ruth 5 mercy 7 feel
for 8 clemency, sympathy 10 compassion 11 commiserate
13 commiseration

pivot
4 turn, veer, whip 5 avert, sheer,
swing, wheel, whirl 6 divert, swivel
7 deflect

pivotal
3 key 5 vital 6 ruling 7 central,
crucial 8 cardinal 9 essential
10 overriding

pixie
3 elf, fay 5 antic, devil, fairy, nisse,
rogue, scamp 6 elvish, impish, ras-

cal, sprite 7 brownie, coltish, playful, puckish 8 prankish, scalawag,
slyboots 9 skeezicks

pixieish
5 antic 6 elvish, frisky, impish
7 playful, puckish 9 kittenish, pixilated 11 mischievous

pixilated
5 drunk 6 elvish, pranky, stoned
7 larkish, muddled, playful, puckish, roguish, waggish 9 disguised
10 frolicsome, inebriated
11 intoxicated

Pizarro
city founded: 4 Lima
conquest: 4 Peru
victims: 5 Incas

placard
4 bill, post 6 poster 7 affiche
8 handbill

placate
4 calm 6 pacify, soothe 7 appease, assuage, comfort, mollify,
sweeten 10 conciliate, propitiate
11 tranquilize

place
3 fix, job, lay, put, set 4 area, call,
lieu, loci (plural), post, rank, site,
spot, zone 5 berth, judge, locus,
point, posit, state, stick, tract, where
6 billet, finger, office, reckon, region, settle, status 7 deposit, footing, install, situate, station 8 capacity, diagnose, district, estimate,
identify, locality, location, pinpoint,
position, standing, vicinity 9 character, establish, recognize
combining form: 3 top 4 chor, loco,
topo, topy 5 choro
of ease: 10 bed of roses
of sin: 5 Sodom
suffix: 3 ary, ery, ory 4 aria (plural),
oria (plural) 5 arium, orium

place-name
7 toponym

placid
4 calm, easy, mild 5 quiet, still
6 hushed, irenic, poised, serene,
stilly 7 halcyon 8 composed,
peaceful, tranquil 9 collected, easygoing, unruffled 10 unagitated, untroubled 12 self-composed
13 imperturbable, self-possessed

plague
3 vex 4 bane, fret, gnaw, pest,
rash 5 annoy, beset, curse, harry,
hound, tease, worry 6 bother, harass, hassle, hector, pester 7 afflict,
bedevil, disease, hagride, scourge,
torment, trouble 8 epidemic, inva-

sion, irritant, nuisance, outbreak
9 annoyance, beleaguer, besetment
10 affliction, black death, botherment, pestilence 11 botheration,
infestation

plain
3 dry, lea 4 bald, bare, moor,
neat, open, pure 5 campo, clear,
frank, heath, llano, stark, usual,
veldt 6 candid, homely, modest,
pampas, patent, severe, simple,
steppe, tundra 7 austere, evident,
obvious, prairie, routine, savanna,
Spartan, unmixed 8 apparent, discreet, distinct, everyday, homespun,
manifest, ordinary, palpable, savannah, straight, uncomely, unpretty, workaday 9 inelegant, quotidian, unadorned, undiluted
10 unaffected, unalluring,
unhandsome

plainclothesman
4 dick 6 sleuth 7 gumshoe 8 hawkshaw, Sherlock 9 detective
12 investigator

plain Jane
5 usual 7 routine 8 everyday, ordinary, workaday 9 quotidian
12 unremarkable

plainness
7 clarity 8 lucidity 9 clearness,
limpidity

plainsong
5 chant 12 cantus firmus

plainspoken
4 open 6 candid, direct 10 forthright 11 undisguised, unvarnished

plaintive
3 sad 6 rueful, woeful 7 doleful, el-
egiac, piteous, pitiful 8 dolesome,
dolorous, mournful 9 sorrowful
10 lamentable, lugubrious,
melancholy

plait
4 fold 5 braid, weave 7 pigtail
10 intertwine

plan
3 aim, map, way 4 cast, mean,
plot 5 chart, draft, frame, order
6 animus, budget, design, devise,
intend, intent, lay out, map out,
method, policy, projet, scheme, set
out, sketch, system 7 arrange, concert, meaning, outline, pattern, program, project, propose, purpose,
regimen, work out 8 conspire, contrive, engineer, organize, platform,
schedule, strategy, think out 9 blueprint, calculate, figure out, formulate, intention 10 intendment

plane

3 jet, lay 4 even, flat 5 flush, level
6 smooth 7 flatten 8 aircraft, air-
liner, smoothen

plane surface

4 area

planet

4 Mars 5 Earth, Pluto, Venus 6 Saturn, Uranus 7 Jupiter, Mercury,
Neptune
brightest: 5 Venus
closest to sun: 7 Mercury
farthest from sun: 5 Pluto
largest: 7 Jupiter
path: 5 orbit
red: 4 Mars
ringed: 6 Saturn
satellite: 4 moon
shadow: 5 umbra
small: 8 asteroid
smallest: 7 Mercury

planetary

6 global 7 immense 8 colossal,
enormous 9 universal, worldwide

plangent

5 round 6 rotund 7 orotund, ringing, vibrant 8 resonant, sonorant,
sonorous 9 consonant
10 resounding

plank

4 slab 5 board 6 lumber, timber
7 deposit, support

plant

3 fix, pot, set, sow 4 bury, grow,
hide, mill, root, seed, tomb
5 cache, cover, imbed, inter, place,
put in, stash, works 6 entomb, inhume, occult, screen 7 conceal,
factory, lay away, put away, secrete 8 colonize, populate
9 cultivate
African: 4 aloe 6 acacia 8 stapelia
angiosperm: 5 dicot 7 monocot
aquatic: 4 reed 5 lotus, sedge
7 awlwort, cattail, fanwort, papyrus
8 duckweed, eelgrass, hornwort,
pondweed 9 water lily 10 watercress 11 bladderwort
12 pickerelweed
Australian: 6 mallee 7 banksia
8 blackboy 10 eucalyptus
body: 4 stem 7 thallus
bract: 5 glume 8 phyllary
bulbous: 4 lily 5 camas, onion, tulip
7 jonquil 8 hyacinth 9 narcissus
cactus: 5 nopal 6 cereus, mescal
7 opuntia, saguaro 11 prickly pear
carnivorous: 6 sundew 10 butterwort
12 pitcher plant 13 Venus's-flytrap
cell layer: 5 suber 7 phellem

climbing: 3 ivy 4 vine 5 betel, liana,
vetch 6 bryony, derris, smilax
7 creeper, jasmine 8 bignonia, fumi-
tory, moonseed, scammony, wisteria 12 morning glory
coloring agent: 8 carotene 11 chlorophyll, xanthophyll
combining form: 4 phyt 5 chore,
cocci (plural), oecia (plural), phyta
(plural), phyte, phyto
cone-bearing: 3 fir, yew 4 pine 5 cedar, cycad 6 gingko, ginkgo,
spruce 7 conifer, cypress, redwood
10 arborvitae, gymnosperm
desert: 4 aloe 5 agave 6 cactus,
cholla 8 mesquite, ocotillo 9 palo-
verde 11 brittlebush, Welwitschia
disease: 3 rot 4 gall, mold, rust,
scab, smut, wilt 5 ergot 6 blight,
mildew, mosaic 7 blister 8 clubroot
9 black spot 10 black heart
epiphyte: 6 orchid 8 air plant 9 bro-
meliad 11 Spanish moss
evergreen: 3 fir 4 pine 6 spruce
7 lycopod 8 boxberry, clubmoss
9 bearberry 11 wintergreen
12 partridge pea
extinct: 8 calamite
fern: 5 royal 6 Boston 7 bracken
8 polypody, staghorn 10 cliffbrake,
maidenhair
flowerless: 4 alga, fern, kelp, moss
5 algae (plural), fungi (plural) 6 fungus, lichen 7 seaweed 8 clubmoss
9 bryophyte, equisetum, horsetail,
liverwort
fluid: 3 gum, sap 4 milk 5 latex,
resin
garden: 4 iris, ixia, lily, pink, rose
5 aster, calla, canna, daisy, oxlip,
pansy, peony, phlox, stock, tulip
6 betony, cosmos, crocus, dahlia,
lupine, malope, oxalis, salvia, violet, zinnia 7 anemone, begonia,
bluecap, cowslip, fuchsia, gentian,
jonquil, lobelia, petunia, statice,
verbena 8 bluebell, cyclamen, daffodil, foxglove, gardenia, geranium, hyacinth, larkspur, marigold,
primrose, sweet pea 9 amaryllis,
campanula, carnation, cineraria,
gladiolus, hollyhock, ligularia, narcissus, pimpernel, portulaca, saxifrage, sunflower 10 delphinium,
marguerite, mignonette, nasturtium,
snapdragon 11 forget-me-not
12 rhododendron, sweet william
13 bleeding heart, chrysanthemum
gland: 7 nectary
grain: 3 oat, rye 4 corn, rice
5 maize, wheat 6 barley, millet
9 buckwheat

hallucinogenic: 4 hemp 6 mescal
8 cannabis 9 marihuana,
marijuana
herb: 4 balm, mint, sage 5 basil,
calla, tansy, thyme 6 catnip, cicely,
fennel 7 bitters, boneset, caraway,
figwort, ginseng, parsley, saffron,
vanilla 8 geranium, lavender, marjoram, rosemary, valerian 9 calendula, celandine, cineraria, corian-
der, horehound, portulaca,
spearmint, spikenard 10 elecam-
pane, pennyroyal
largest: 7 sequoia
life: 5 flora
marine: 4 kelp 5 fucus 7 seaweed
10 sea lettuce
marsh: 4 reed 5 carex, sedge
7 bogbean, bulrush, calamus, cattail 8 red maple, sphagnum
11 loosestrife
medicinal: 4 aloe, sage 5 poppy,
senna, tansy 6 catnip, fennel, garlic, ipecac, nettle 7 aconite, boneset, camphor, hemlock, henbane,
juniper, lobelia, mustard, parsley
8 camomile, cinchona, licorice,
pilewort, wormwood 9 asafetida,
chamomile, dandelion, monkshood
10 peppermint 11 assafoetida
microscopic: 4 mold 6 diatom 7 eu-
glena 8 bacteria (plural)
9 bacterium
mushroom: 5 morel 7 amanita
10 champignon 11 chanterelle
oldest: 11 bristlecone
onion-like: 4 leek 5 chive 7 shallot
8 scallion
opening: 5 stoma 7 stomata (plural)
parasitic: 6 dodder, fungus 9 mistletoe 10 beechdrops
part: 3 bud, nut, sap 4 bark, bulb,
cell, cone, corm, leaf, pome, root,
seed, stem, wood 5 drupe, fruit,
grain, spore, thorn, tuber, xylem
6 catkin, flower, nectar, phloem, raceme 7 rhizome 8 lenticel 9 cellulose, cotyledon 11 chlorophyll,
chloroplast 13 inflorescence
pest: 5 aphid, scale 6 chafer, thrips,
weevil 7 cutworm 8 fruit fly, wireworm 9 gypsy moth 10 can-
kerworm, leafhopper, phylloxera
11 codling moth
poisonous: 4 poke, upas 5 sumac
6 castor, croton, datura 7 amantia,
cassava, cowbane, henbane, lobelia, tobacco 8 foxglove, larkspur,
locoweed, mayapple, oleander,
pokeweed 9 baneberry, monkshood 10 belladonna, jimsonweed,
manchineel, nightshade

product: 3 dye, tar 4 cork, drug, food, rope 5 fiber, paper, resin, rosin 6 lumber, rubber 7 alcohol, perfume, tobacco 10 turpentine
saprophytic: 5 fungi (plural) 6 fungus 10 Indian pipe
shrub: 3 box 5 broom, furze, lilac, sumac 6 azalea, datura, hyssop, privet, spirea 7 begonia, dogwood, spiraea 8 hawthorn, magnolia, oleander, plumbago, viburnum 9 forsythia
succulent: 5 agave 6 cactus 10 bitterroot
suffix: 2 ad 4 ales (plural) 5 aceae (plural), ineae (plural)
support: 7 trellis
thorny: 4 rose 5 briar 6 cactus, nettle, teasel, teazel, teazle 7 caltrop, thistle 8 cockspur 9 cocklebur
tissue: 5 xylem 6 phloem 7 cambium, medulla 8 meristem
unit of structure: 6 telome
wild flower: 4 ramp 5 bluet, calla, daisy 6 adonis, lupine 7 arbutus, cowslip, gentian 8 fireweed, hepatica, toadflax, trillium 9 bloodroot, buttercup, campanula, columbine, dandelion, goldenrod
young: 5 scion, shoot 6 sprout 7 cutting 8 seedling

plantlike
7 phytoid

plant louse
5 aphid

plaster
3 dab 4 coat, daub, sham 5 cover, gesso, salve, smear 6 bedaub, mortar, remedy, smudge, soothe, stucco

plastic
4 soft 5 vinyl 6 pliant, supple 7 ductile, organic, pliable 8 creative, flexible, moldable 9 adaptable, formative, malleable 10 sculptural

plat
3 lot, map 4 plan 5 chart, floor, tract 6 parcel 7 surface 8 platform

plate
4 base, coat, disc, dish, disk, tile 5 layer, paten, scute, slice 6 fascia, lamina, plaque 7 lamella, overlay
kind: 4 blue, home

plateau
4 mesa 5 table 6 upland 9 altiplano, tableland
arid: 4 puna
barren: 5 field 6 paramo
dry: 5 karoo 6 karroo

platform
3 map 4 bank, base, dais, deck, plan 5 forum, ledge, shelf, stage 6 design, podium, pulpit, scheme 7 balcony, pattern, rostrum 9 banquette 11 declaration
temporary: 7 staging 8 scaffold
wooden: 9 boardwalk

platinum
symbol: 2 Pt

platitude
6 cliché, truism 7 bromide 8 banality, prosaism 10 prosaicism, shibboleth

Plato
father: 7 Ariston
literary form: 6 dialog 8 dialogue
original name: 10 Aristocles
school: 7 Academy
work: 3 Ion 4 Meno 5 Crito, Lysis 6 Laches, Phaedo 7 Apology, Gorgias 8 Phaedrus, Republic 9 Charmides, Symposium

platoon
3 lot, set 4 team, unit 5 array, batch, bunch, clump, group, squad 6 parcel 7 battery, cluster 8 division 9 formation

platter
6 salver 8 trencher

platypus
8 duckbill

plaudits
5 kudos 6 praise 7 acclaim 8 applause, encomium 11 acclamation, approbation

plausible
8 credible 10 believable, creditable

play
3 act, bet, fun, use 4 game, jest, joke, ploy, romp, room, take, wile 5 dally, drama, enact, feint, flirt, scope, serve, sport, stake, treat, trick, wager 6 cavort, comedy, device, fiddle, fidget, frolic, gambit, gamble, gambol, handle, jockey, leeway, margin, trifle 7 beguile, delight, disport, exploit, finesse, gimmick, perform, roister, rollick, twiddle 8 artifice, latitude, maneuver, pleasure, recreate 9 amusement, dalliance, discourse, diversion, elbowroom, enjoyment, pantomime, personate, stratagem 10 manipulate, recreation
kind: 5 farce, opera 6 comedy 7 musical, tragedy 8 one-acter, operetta 9 melodrama, pantomime

part: 3 act 5 exode, scene 8 epilogue, prologue

playact
2 do 7 perform 9 discourse, personate 11 impersonate

playboy
4 roué

play down
4 mute 6 soften 9 soft-pedal 11 deemphasize

player
4 mime 5 actor, mimic 6 mummer 7 actress, trouper 8 thespian 9 performer 11 participant 12 impersonator

playful
3 gay 5 antic, jolly, merry, pixie 6 blithe, elvish, frisky, impish, jocund, joking, jovial, lively, pranky, wicked 7 coltish, dashing, gleeful, jocular, larking, larkish, puckish, roguish, waggish 8 gamesome, humorous, mirthful, pixieish, playsome, prankful, prankish, sportive 9 kittenish, pixilated, sprightly, whimsical 10 frolicsome, rollicking 11 mischievous 12 lighthearted

play off
3 pit, vie 5 match 6 oppose 7 counter

play on words
3 pun

play up
6 stress 7 feature 9 emphasize, italicize, underline 10 underscore

playwright
6 author, writer 9 dramatist 10 dramatizer, dramaturge

plaza
5 green 6 common, square 9 carrefour 11 marketplace

plea
4 suit 5 alibi 6 appeal, excuse, orison, prayer 7 apology, pretext, request 8 entreaty, overture, petition 11 application, imploration, imprecation 12 supplication
defendant's: 4 nolo 6 guilty 9 not guilty

plead
3 beg, sue 4 pray 5 brace, crave 6 appeal 7 beseech, entreat, implore 9 importune 10 supplicate

pleasant
4 fair, fine, glad, good, nice 5 clear, sunny, sweet, tasty 6 cheery, genial, joyful, joyous, pretty 7 amiable, clarion, likable,

welcome 8 amicable, charming, cheerful, cheering, engaging, gracious, grateful, likeable, pleasing, sunshine, sunshiny, tasteful 9 agreeable, appealing, cloudless, congenial, convivial, enjoyable, favorable, unclouded 10 delightful, gratifying, undarkened
and unpleasant: 11 bittersweet

pleasantry
3 fun 4 jest, joke 6 banter 10 jocularity

please
4 like, suit, will, wish 5 agree, amuse, elate, elect, enjoy 6 arride, choose, tickle 7 content, delight, gladden, gratify, happify, indulge, satisfy 9 delectate, titillate

pleasing
4 good, nice 5 nifty 6 comely, pretty, seemly 7 welcome, winning 8 charming, grateful, suitable 9 agreeable, congenial, favorable, palatable 10 attractive, delectable, delightful, enchanting, gratifying 11 pleasurable 12 satisfactory

pleasingly plump
6 zaftig, zoftig

pleasurable
see **pleasing**

pleasure
3 fun, joy 4 will 5 bliss, fancy, mirth 6 arride, liking, relish 7 delight, gladden, gratify, happify, joyance 8 felicity, fruition, gladness, hedonism, velleity 9 amusement, delectate, diversion, enjoyment, happiness, merriment

pleasuremonger
8 hedonist, sybarite

pleat
4 fold 5 crimp 6 crease 7 flounce

pleated
7 plicate

plebeian
3 low 4 base, mean 5 lowly 6 coarse, common, homely, humble, vulgar 7 ignoble, ill-bred, low-born 8 baseborn, everyday, ordinary, unwashed

plebeians
see **populace**

plectrum
4 pick

pledge
3 row 4 bail, bond, gage, hock,

oath, pass, pawn, seal, word 5 drink, swear, toast, token 6 engage, plight, surety 7 earnest, hostage, promise, warrant 8 contract, covenant, guaranty, mortgage, security, warranty 9 assurance, certainty, guarantee, undertake 11 impignorate

pledget
3 wad 8 compress

Pleiades
4 Maia 6 Merope 7 Alcyone, Celaeno, Electra, Sterope, Taygeta 8 Asterope
brightest star: 7 Alcyone

plenteous
see **plentiful**

plentiful
4 full, rich 5 ample 6 bumper, galore, plenty 7 copious, fertile, fulsome, liberal, opulent, profuse, teeming 8 abundant, affluent, bursting, fruitful, generous, prolific, swarming, swimming 9 abounding, bounteous, bountiful, plenteous, unstinted

plenty
3 lot 4 heap, much, pack, peck, pile 5 ample 7 copious, liberal 8 abundant, generous, mountain, opulence 9 abundance, bounteous, bountiful, great deal, plenteous, plentiful 10 cornucopia

pleonasm
8 verbiage 9 tautology, verbality 10 periphrase, redundancy, roundabout 11 periphrasis 13 circumambages

plethora
4 glut 5 flood 6 deluge, excess 7 surfeit, surplus 8 fullness, overflow, overkill, overmuch, overplus 9 repletion 10 surplusage 11 superfluity 13 overabundance

plexus
4 rete 7 network

pliable
see **pliant**

pliant
4 limp, soft 5 lithe 6 limber, supple 7 ductile, plastic, tensile, willowy 8 flexible, moldable, workable, yielding 9 adaptable, compliant, malleable, tractable 11 manipulable 13 manipulatable

plica
4 fold, ruck 5 ridge, rivel 6 crease,

furrow, rimple 7 crinkle, wrinkle 11 corrugation

plight
3 box, fix, jam, vow 4 hole, spot, word 5 swear, engage, pickle, pledge 6 scrape 7 betroth, dilemma, promise 8 covenant, quandary 9 betrothal 10 difficulty, engagement 11 predicament

plighted
7 engaged 8 intended 9 affianced, betrothed 10 contracted

plod
4 grub, slog, slop, toil 5 grind, slave, tramp, tromp 6 drudge, stodge, trudge 7 trample 8 footslog, plunther

plot
4 plan 5 cabal, covin, tract 6 design, devise, parcel, scheme 7 collude, compact, connive, diagram, outline 8 cogitate, conspire, contrive, engineer, intrigue, practice, scenario 9 collusion, conniving, machinate, scheme out 10 complicity, connivance, conspiracy 11 machination

plover
4 bird 5 pewit, stilt 7 lapwing 8 dotterel, killdeer
relative: 9 sandpiper, turnstone

plow
3 dig 4 till, turn 5 break 6 furrow, trench 8 turn over 9 cultivate
part: 4 beam, frog 5 share 8 landside 9 moldboard

ploy
4 ruse, scam, wile 5 feint, trick 6 device, gambit 7 gimmick 8 artifice, maneuver 9 stratagem

pluck
3 tug 4 grit, guts, pick, pull 5 cheek, heart, nerve, spunk 6 daring, mettle, snatch, spirit, tweeze 7 bravery, cojones, courage 8 gameness 10 resolution

plucky
4 bold, game 5 brave 6 feisty, spunky 7 doughty 8 fearless 9 dauntless, unfearing 10 courageous 11 undauntable

plug
3 tap 4 bung, clog, cork, fill, pack, puff, push, stop, tout 5 block, blurb, boost, choke, close, spile 7 congest, occlude, promote, puffing, stopper, stopple, tampion, tompion, write-up 8 obstruct 9 advertise

plug-ugly
3 mug 4 thug 5 rowdy, tough, yahoo 6 mucker 7 ruffian 8 bullyboy
9 roughneck

plum
5 prize 6 reward 7 guerdon, premium 8 dividend
dried: 5 prune
kind: 4 Agen 6 Damson, Duarte
7 bullace 8 Hortulan, Salicina
9 Green Gage, myrobalan
spiny: 10 blackthorn

plumage
8 feathers
early: 4 down

plumb
5 delve, probe, sound 6 fathom
7 explore, plummet 8 absolute, vertical 10 straight-up
13 perpendicular

plume
5 pique, preen, pride 7 feather
8 aigrette

plummet
3 dip 4 drop, fall, sink, skid
5 crash 6 plunge, tumble 7 decline, descend 8 collapse, decrease, nose-dive 11 precipitate

plump
3 fat 5 buxom, podgy, pudgy,
round, stout, tubby 6 chubby,
fleshy, portly, rotund 8 roly-poly
10 roundabout

plunder
3 rob 4 loot, swag 5 booty, prize,
rifle, spoil 6 boodle 7 despoil, pillage, ransack, relieve, stick up
9 knock over

plunderage
4 loot, swag 5 booty, prize, spoil
6 boodle

plunderer
6 looter, raider, sacker 7 forager,
ravager 8 marauder, pillager, ravisher 9 despoiler 10 freebooter

plunge
3 dig, dip, ram, run 4 dive, drop,
fall, rush, sink, skid, stab 5 burst,
douse, drive, lunge, pitch, slump,
stick 6 charge, go down, thrust,
topple, tumble 7 immerse, plummet
8 keel over, nose-dive, submerge

plus
4 more, over 5 asset, boost, build
6 beef up, excess, expand 7 augment, enlarge, magnify, overage,
surplus 8 compound, increase
9 overstock 10 oversupply

plush
4 posh 6 Capuan, deluxe 7 opulent 8 luscious, palatial 9 luxuriant,
luxurious, sumptuous
11 upholstered

Pluto
3 Dis 5 Hades
brother: 4 Zeus 7 Jupiter, Neptune
8 Poseidon
father: 6 Cronus, Saturn
mother: 3 Ops 4 Rhea
wife: 10 Persephone, Proserpina

plutonic
6 Hadean 7 avernal, hellish, stygian 8 chthonic, infernal 9 chthonian, cimmerian, Tartarean 10 sulphurous 11 pandemoniac

plutonium
symbol: 2 Pu

Plutus
father: 6 Iasion
god of: 6 riches, wealth
mother: 5 Ceres 7 Demeter

ply
4 bend, fold 5 exert, layer, swing,
throw, wield 6 handle, put out
7 belabor 8 dispense, exercise,
maneuver 9 importune
10 manipulate

pneuma
4 soul 5 anima 6 animus, psyche,
spirit 9 élan vital 10 vital force

pneumatic
4 airy 6 aerial 11 atmospheric

Pocahontas
father: 8 Powhatan
husband: 5 Rolfe (John)

pock
3 pit 4 hole, spot 6 pimple
7 pustule

pocket
3 bag, nab, wee 4 hook, lift, sack,
tiny 5 filch, pinch, pouch, purse,
steal, swipe, weeny 6 accept, cavity 7 capsule, conceal, dead end,
impasse, swallow 8 abstract, bear
with, cul-de-sac, dwarfish, monetary, pint-size, tolerate, tough out
9 condensed, financial, itsy-bitsy,
miniature, pecuniary 10 blind
alley, diminutive
billiards: 4 pool

pocket money
6 change 9 petty cash 11 small
change

pocket-size
4 tiny 6 midget, minute, peewee

8 dwarfish, pint-size 9 itsy-bitsy,
miniature 10 diminutive

pod
3 bag, gam, sac 4 boll, case, hull,
husk, skin 5 shell, shuck 6 cocoon,
paunch, school 7 capsule, silique
8 potbelly, seedcase 9 bay window 11 corporation
combining form: 7 siliqui
plant: 3 pea 4 bean, okra 5 chili,
gumbo 6 cassia, cowpea, legume,
lentil, peanut, pepper 8 capsicum,
mesquite, milkweed 9 lespedeza

pod-bearing tree
5 carob 6 locust 7 catalpa

podiatry
9 chiropody

Poe, Edgar Allan
detective: 5 Dupin
poem: 6 Lenore 7 Israfel, To Helen,
Ulalume 8 Eldorado, For Annie,
The Raven 10 Annabel Lee
tale: 6 Ligeia, Shadow 7 Morella,
Silence 10 The Gold Bug

poem
3 ode 4 epic, epos, idyl, rime,
rune, song 5 ditty, elegy, epode,
idyll, lyric, rhyme, verse 6 ballad,
epopee, jingle, rondel, sonnet
7 rondeau 8 limerick, madrigal
closing: 5 envoi, envoy
combining form: 5 stich
division: 4 foot, line 5 canto, epode,
stich, verse 6 stanza 7 refrain
8 epilogue, prologue
Japanese: 5 haiku, tanka
of eight lines: 6 octave 7 triolet
of four lines: 8 quatrain
of fourteen lines: 6 sonnet
of three lines: 7 triplet
pastoral: 7 eclogue, georgic
short: 5 ditty 7 epigram

poet
4 bard, muse, scop 5 odist, skald
6 lyrist 7 elegist 8 idyllist, lyricist,
satirist 9 balladist, sonneteer, sonnetist 10 Parnassian
American: 3 Poe (Edgar Allan)
4 Dove (Rita), Hass (Robert), Nash
(Ogden), Read (Thomas), Tabb
(John Banister), Tate (Allen) 5 Auden (Wystan Hugh), Benèt (Stephen
Vincent), Crane (Hart), Field (Eugene), Frost (Robert), Guest (Edgar),
Moore (Marianne), Plath (Sylvia),
Pound (Ezra), Riley (James Whitcomb), Wylie (Elinor) 6 Barlow
(Joel), Bryant (William Cullen),
Ciardi (John), Dunbar (Paul), Kilmer
(Joyce), Lanier (Sidney), Lowell

(Amy, James Russell, Robert), Millay (Edna St. Vincent), Ransom (John Crowe), Seeger (Alan), Strand (Mark), Taylor (Edward), Warren (Robert Penn), Wilbur (Richard) **7** Emerson (Ralph Waldo), Jeffers (Robinson), Lindsay (Vachel), Markham (Edwin), Merrill (James), Nemerov (Howard), Roethke (Theodore), Shapiro (Karl), Stevens (Wallace), Whitman (Walt) **8** Cummings (Edward Estlin), Ginsberg (Allen), MacLeish (Archibald), Robinson (Edwin Arlington), Teasdale (Sara), Whittier (John Greenleaf), Williams (Charles Kenneth, William Carlos) **9** Dickinson (Emily), Santayana (George) **10** Bradstreet (Anne), Longfellow (Henry Wadswworth) **12** Wigglesworth (Michael)
Anglo-Saxon: **7** Caedmon, Cynwulf **8** Cynewulf
Arab: **5** Jarir
Australian: **8** Paterson (Andrew Barton)
Belgian: **11** Maeterlinck (Maurice)
Canadian: **5** Pratt (Edwin John) **7** Roberts (Charles G. D.)
Chinese: **4** Li Po, Tu Fu
Danish: **5** Ewald (Johannes)
English: **3** Gay (John) **4** Gray (Thomas), Owen (Wilfred), Pope (Alexander), Rowe (Nicholas), Tate (Nahum), Wyat (Thomas) **5** Blake (William), Byron (Lord), Donne (John), Eliot (Thomas Stearns), Noyes (Alfred), Wilde (Oscar), Wyatt (Thomas), Young (Edward) **6** Arnold (Matthew), Brooke (Rupert), Cowper (William), Dryden (John), Graves (Robert), Milton (John), Savage (Richard), Sidney (Philip), Surrey (Earl of), Symons (Arthur), Waller (Edmund), Warton (Thomas), Watson (William), Wotton (Henry) **7** Chaucer (Geoffrey), Herrick (Robert), Hopkins (Gerard Manley), Housman (Alfred Edward), Layamon, Patmore (Coventry), Quarles (Francis), Shelley (Percy Bysshe), Skelton (John), Southey (Robert), Spender (Stephen), Spenser (Edmund) **8** Betjeman (John), Browning (Elizabeth, Robert), Langland (William), Lovelace (Richard), Meredith (George), Rossetti (Christina, Dante Gabriel), Suckling (John), Tennyson (Alfred Lord), Thompson (Francis) **9** Coleridge (Samuel Taylor), Swinburne (Algernon) **10** Wordsworth (William) **11** Shakespeare (William)

Finnish: **8** Runeberg (Johan Ludvig)
French: **5** Marot (Clement) **6** Musset (Alfred de), Valery (Paul), Villon (François) **7** Bourget (Paul), Chenier (Andre de, Marie-Joseph), Gautier (Theophile), Rimbaud (Arthur), Ronsard (Pierre de) **8** Malherbe (François de), Mallarmé (Stephane), Verlaine (Paul) **9** Lamartine (Alphonse de) **10** Baudelaire (Charles) **11** Apollinaire (Guillaume)
German: **5** Heine (Heinrich), Rilke (Rainer Maria), Storm (Theodor Woldsen) **6** Goethe (Johann Wolfgang von), Uhland (Ludwig) **7** Walther, Wolfram **8** Schiller (Friedrich von) **9** Klopstock (Friedrich Gottlieb)
Greek: **5** Arion, Homer **6** Erinna, Hesiod, Pindar, Sappho **7** Agathon, Thespis **8** Anacreon **9** Simonides **10** Apollonius, Theocritus
Hindu: **5** Naidu (Sarojini) **6** Tagore (Rabindranath) **8** Kalidasa
Hungarian: **6** Zrinyi (Miklos)
Irish: **5** Moore (Thomas), Synge (John Millington), Wolfe (Charles), Yeats (William Butler) **8** Stephens (James)
Italian: **4** Rosa (Salvator), Vida (Marco) **5** Dante, Tasso (Torquato) **7** Ariosto (Ludovico), Manzoni (Alessandro), Montale (Eugenio) **8** Leopardi (Giacomo), Petrarch **9** D'Annunzio (Gabriele), Marinetti (Filippo Tommaso), Ungaretti (Giuseppe)
medieval: **8** minstrel, trouvère, trouveur **10** troubadour
nonsense: **4** Lear (Edward)
Norwegian: **8** Björnson (Bjornstjerne), Welhaven (Johan) **9** Wergeland (Henrik)
Persian: **4** Sadi **5** Attar, Hafiz **11** Omar Khayyam
Roman: **4** Ovid **6** Horace, Vergil, Virgil **7** Juvenal, Statius **8** Catullus, Tibullus **9** Lucretius
Russian: **7** Pushkin (Aleksandr), Yesenin (Sergey) **9** Kheraskov (Mikhail), Pasternak (Boris)
Scottish: **4** Hogg (James), Muir (Edwin) **5** Burns (Robert), Scott (Alexander, Walter) **6** Ramsay (Allan) **7** Thomson (James)
Spanish: **7** Jimenez (Juan Ramon) **11** Garcia Lorca (Federico)
Swedish: **5** Sachs (Nelly) **6** Tegner (Esaias) **8** Snoilsky (Carl Johan) **9** Karlfeldt (Erik Axel)
Swiss: **5** Amiel (Henri Frederic) **9** Spitteler (Carl)

Welsh: **6** Thomas (Dylan) **7** Aneurin, Watkins (Vernon)

poetaster
6 rhymer, verser **7** bardlet **8** bardling, verseman **9** rhymester, versifier

poetic
5 lyric **6** bardic, dreamy **8** romantic

poetic contraction
see at **contraction**

poet laureate
3 Pye (Henry) **4** Rowe (Nicholas), Tate (Nahum) **6** Austin (Alfred), Cibber (Colley), Dryden (John), Hughes (Ted), Jonson (Ben) **7** Bridges (Robert), Southey (Robert) **8** Betjeman (John), Davenant (William), Day-Lewis (Cecil), Shadwell (Thomas), Tennyson (Alfred Lord) **9** Masefield (John), Whitehead (William) **10** Wordsworth (William)

Pogo creator
9 Walt Kelly

poignancy
6 pathos

poignant
4 keen, racy **5** acute, sharp, spicy, zesty **6** moving, snappy, urgent **7** cutting, peppery, piquant, pungent **8** incisive, piercing, touching **9** affecting **10** impressive

point
3 aim, awn, bit, dot, jag, nib, tip **4** apex, barb, beak, bill, cape, cast, cusp, edge, head, hint, item, mite, mote, naze, site, snag, spot, tine, turn **5** brink, force, imply, level, locus, motif, place, prong, punch, refer, speck, spike, steer, theme, topic, trace, verge **6** allude, detail, direct, matter, moment, motive, tip-off, zero in **7** address, article, cogency, element, feature, instant, station, subject, suggest **8** argument, flyspeck, foreland, headland, indicate, juncture, location, particle, position, validity **9** birthmark, character, punctuate, situation, threshold, validness **10** particular, promontory **12** significance

Point Counter Point author
6 Huxley (Aldous)

pointed
5 acute, peaky, piked, sharp **6** marked, peaked, signal **7** salient **8** acicular, striking **9** aciculate, acu-

minate, acuminous, arresting, cuspidate, mucronate, prominent

pointer
3 dog, tip 4 dial, hint 5 arrow, steer 6 tip-off 9 indicator

pointillist
6 Seurat (Georges)

point of view
5 angle 7 outlook 11 perspective

point out
8 indicate

poise
4 hang, tact 5 float, grace, hover 6 aplomb, stasis, steady 7 address, balance, ballast, dignity 8 calmness, elegance, serenity 9 assurance, diplomacy, equipoise, stabilify, stabilize 10 confidence 11 delicatesse, equilibrium, savoir faire, stabilitate, tactfulness, tranquility

poised
4 calm, easy 6 placid, serene 8 composed, tranquil 9 collected, easygoing, possessed 13 self-possessed

poison
4 bane, harm, loco, warp 5 stain, taint, toxic, toxin, venom, virus 6 debase, infect, toxine, toxoid 7 botulin, cacodyl, corrupt, debauch, deprave, destroy, envenom, pervert, vitiate 8 mephitic, toxicant, venenate, venomous, virulent 9 contagion 10 corruption, demoralize 13 contamination
arrow: 4 inée 5 urare, urari 6 antiar, curara, curure 7 ouabain, woorali, woorari 8 antiarin
combining form: 3 tox 4 toxi, toxo 5 toxic 6 toxico

poisoning
food: 8 botulism
lead: 8 plumbism

poisonous
5 fatal, toxic 6 deadly, lethal, mortal 7 baneful, miasmal, miasmic, nocuous, noxious, toxical 8 mephitic, toxicant, venenous, venomous, virulent 9 miasmatic, pestilent 10 nauseating, pernicious
alkaloid: 8 nicotine 10 strychnine
element: 7 arsenic

poke
3 box, dig, hit, jab, jog, jut, lag, pry 4 chop, cuff, dolt, dope, drag, nose, pout, prod, push, sock, stab, stir 5 bulge, chump, clout, dally, delay, dunce, idiot, moron, mouse,

nudge, punch, rouse, shove, smack, snoop, spank, tarry, trail 6 arouse, awaken, beetle, buffet, cowboy, dawdle, dimwit, loiter, pierce, put off, putter, thrust 7 project 8 busybody

poker
bet total: 3 pot
form: 4 stud 8 baseball
hand: 4 pair 5 flush 8 straight 9 full house 10 royal flush 13 straight flush
stake: 4 ante
term: 3 see 4 call, draw, open 5 raise
token: 4 chip

poker-faced
5 grave, sober, staid 6 sedate, solemn, somber 7 earnest, neutral, serious

poky
4 blah, dull 6 dreary, stodgy 7 humdrum 8 banausic, monotone 10 monotonous

Poland
capital: 6 Warsaw
labor leader: 6 Walesa (Lech)
monetary unit: 5 zloty

polar
8 opposite

pole
4 punt, spar 5 shaft, stick, stilt
Indian: 5 totem
Scottish: 5 caber

polecat
5 fitch, skunk 7 fitchet

polestar
3 hub 4 seat 5 focus, guide, heart 6 center 10 focal point 11 nerve center

policeman
3 cop 4 fuzz, heat 5 bobby 6 copper, peeler 7 gumshoe, John Law, officer, trooper 8 bluecoat, Dogberry, flatfoot, gendarme 9 constable, patrolman 12 peace officer
Italian: 11 carabiniere
Parisian: 4 flic 8 gendarme
Spanish: 10 carabinero
Turkish: 6 kavass 7 zaptiah, zaptieh

policy
3 wit 4 line 6 course, govern, wisdom 7 program 8 sagacity 9 procedure

polio vaccine developer
4 Salk (Jonas) 5 Sabin (Albert)

polish
3 rub, wax 4 buff 5 glaze, glint, gloss, round, sheen, shine, sleek,

slick 6 glance, luster, pumice, refine, smooth 7 brush up, burnish, culture, perfect, touch up 8 breeding, brighten 10 refinement

Polish
dumpling: 7 pierogi
patriot: 9 Kosciusko (Thaddeus)
pope: 8 John Paul
sausage: 8 kielbasa
soldier: 7 Pulaski (Casimir)

polish off
5 eat up, shift, swill 6 devour, punish 7 consume, put away 8 dispatch

polite
5 civil 7 courtly, genteel 8 mannerly 9 attentive, courteous 10 thoughtful 11 considerate 12 well-mannered

politeness
8 chivalry, civility, courtesy

politic
4 wise 7 cunning, prudent, tactful 8 delicate, tactical 9 advisable, expedient, judicious 10 diplomatic 11 worldly-wise

political
association: 4 bund
meeting: 6 caucus
party: 3 GOP 9 Communist, Socialist 10 Democratic, Republican
system: 7 fascism 9 communism, democracy, socialism

politics
conservative: 8 rightism
liberal: 7 leftism

poll
4 clip, crop, head, nape 5 shear 6 noddle, noggin, noodle, survey 7 canvass

pollack, pollock
6 saithe 8 bluefish, coalfish

pollard
3 top 4 crop 8 truncate 10 detruncate

pollen-producing organ
6 stamen

pollex
5 thumb

polliwog
7 tadpole

polltaker
6 Gallup

pollute
4 foul, soil 5 dirty, taint 6 befoul, defile 7 corrupt, profane 11 contaminate

pollution
4 smog 8 impurity 10 defilement

Pollux
10 Polydeuces
brother: 6 Castor
father: 4 Zeus
mother: 4 Leda
sister: 5 Helen 12 Clytemnestra

Pollyanna
8 optimist 10 daydreamer
author: 6 Porter (Eleanor)

Pollyannaish
8 cheerful, sanguine 10 optimistic

Polonius
daughter: 7 Ophelia
slayer: 6 Hamlet
son: 7 Laertes

poltergeist
5 ghost 6 spirit

poltroon
4 funk 6 coward, craven, funker
7 dastard, gutless, quitter, unmanly
8 cowardly 9 spunkless 11 lily-livered, yellowbelly

Polyclitus statue
4 Hera

Polydorus
father: 5 Priam 6 Cadmus
mother: 6 Hecuba 8 Harmonia
slayer: 8 Achilles 10 Polymestor
11 Polymnestor

polygon
eight-sided: 7 octagon
five-sided: 8 pentagon
four-sided: 8 tetragon
nine-sided: 7 nonagon
seven-sided: 8 heptagon
six-sided: 7 hexagon
ten-sided: 7 decagon
three-sided: 8 triangle
twelve-sided: 9 dodecagon

Polyhymnia
4 Muse
invention: 4 lyre

Polynesian
5 Maori 6 Samoan, Tongan 8 Hawaiian, Tahitian 9 Marquesan

Polynices
brother: 8 Eteocles
father: 7 Oedipus
mother: 7 Jocasta
wife: 5 Argia 6 Argeia

polyp
5 zooid 7 hydroid
freshwater: 5 hydra

Polyphemus
7 cyclops
beloved: 7 Galatea

father: 8 Poseidon
victim: 4 Acis

pome
4 pear 5 apple 6 quince
8 hawthorn

pommel
4 knob 6 finial

pomp
4 form, show 5 array, shine 6 parade, ritual 7 display, fanfare, liturgy, panoply 8 ceremony, splendor 9 formality

pompano
4 fish 6 permit 8 carangid
10 butterfish

Pompeii's volcano
8 Vesuvius

pom-pom
4 ball, tuft

pompous
4 vain 5 proud, puffy, wiggy
6 stuffy 7 aureate, bloated, flowery, stilted, stuck-up 8 arrogant, sonorous 9 bombastic, important,
overblown 10 egocentric, euphuistic, hoity-toity, pontifical, rhetorical
11 declamatory, highfalutin, magisterial, pretentious

pond
4 mere 5 stank 6 lagoon, salina
combining form: 4 limn 5 limni,
limno

ponder
4 mind, mull, muse 5 brood, study,
think, weigh 6 reason 7 perpend,
reflect, revolve 8 appraise, cogitate, consider, evaluate, meditate,
mull over, muse over, ruminate,
think out, turn over 9 speculate,
think over 10 deliberate, excogitate
11 contemplate

ponderous
4 dull 5 heavy, hefty, stiff, vapid
6 dreary, stodgy, stuffy, wooden
7 buckram, humdrum, massive, onerous, stilted, weighty 8 plodding,
unwieldy 10 burdensome, cumbersome, oppressive

poniard
6 dagger

Ponocrates' pupil
9 Gargantua

Ponte Vecchio
city: 8 Florence
river: 4 Arno

Pontiac's tribe
6 Ottawa

pontiff
4 pope 6 bishop

pontifical
5 puffy, wiggy 6 stuffy 7 bloated,
pompous 8 arrogant, dogmatic
9 episcopal, important
11 magisterial

pony
4 crib, trot 5 horse 6 cayuse
breed: 6 Exmoor 8 Shetland

Pooh creator
5 Milne (Alan Alexander)

pooh-pooh
3 boo 4 bird, hiss, hoot, razz
5 bazoo 7 catcall, dismiss, kiss off
9 raspberry

pool
3 pot, pul 4 mere 5 chain, group,
kitty, trust 6 cartel, lagoon, laguna,
puddle 7 combine, jackpot
9 syndicate
player: 7 Mosconi (Willie) 13 Minnesota Fats

poor
3 bad, low 4 base, flat, hack,
mean, punk 5 amiss, broke, cheap,
needy, scant, skimp, spare, stony,
tatty, wrong 6 common, crummy,
humble, meager, paltry, rotten, rueful, scanty, scrimp, shoddy, skimpy,
sleazy, sparse, trashy 7 piteous,
pitiful, scrawny, scrimpy, squalid,
trivial 8 bankrupt, beggared, beggarly, déclassé, exiguous, indigent,
inferior, low-grade, pathetic, pitiable, rubbishy, strapped 9 deficient,
destitute, insolvent, moneyless,
penceless, penniless, penurious, un-
moneyed 10 bankrupted, down-
and-out, pauperized, second-rate,
stone-broke 11 fortuneless,
impecunious, indifferent, necessitous, second-class, unfavorable
combining form: 3 mal

poorly
3 low 4 mean 6 ailing, offish,
sickly, unwell 8 off-color 10 indisposed 11 undesirably
13 ineffectively

pop
3 dad, dot, gun, hit, try 4 dada,
dart, ding, jump, papa, shot, slap,
slog, sock, soda, stab, swat
5 break, catch, crack, daddy,
drink, fling, shoot, smite, whack,
whirl 6 attack, effort, father, strike
7 assault, attempt, explode, instant
8 backfire
in: 3 see 4 call 5 visit 6 by, look
up, stop by 8 come over

pop artist
5 Blake (Peter) **6** Warhol (Andy)
7 Hockney (David), Indiana (Robert)
9 Oldenburg (Claes), Wesselman
(Tom) **12** Lichtenstein (Roy)

pope
3 Leo **4** John, Mark, Paul, Pius
5 Caius, Conon, Donus, Felix, Gaius, Lando, Linus, Peter, Soter, Urban **6** Adrian, Agatho, Fabian, Julius, Lucius, Martin, Sixtus, Victor
7 Anterus, Clement, Damasus, Gregory, Hadrian, Hyginus, Marinus, Paschal, Pontian, Romanus, Sergius, Stephen, Zosimus **8** Agapetus, Anicetus, Benedict, Boniface, Calixtus, Eugenius, Eusebius, Formosis, Gelasius, Hilarius, Honorius, Innocent, John Paul, Liberius, Nicholas, Pelagius, Siricius, Theodore, Vigilius, Vitalian **9** Adeodatus, Alexander, Anacletus, Callistus, Celestine, Cornelius, Densdedit, Dionysius, Eutychian, Evaristus, Hormisdas, Marcellus, Miltiades, Severinus, Silverius, Silvester, Sisinnius, Sylvester, Symmachus, Valentine, Zacharias **10** Anastasius, Melchiades, Sabinianus, Simplicius, Zephyrinus **11** Christopher, Constantine, Eleutherius, Eutychianus, Marcellinus, Telesphorus

Pope poem
10 The Dunciad **12** An Essay on
Man **16** The Rape of the Lock

Popeye
accessory: **4** pipe
baby: **8** Sweet Pea
energizer: **7** spinach
friend: **5** Wimpy **8** Olive Oyl
occupation: **6** sailor
rival: **5** Bluto

poplar
5 abele, alamo, aspen **9** tulip tree
10 cottonwood **12** balm of Gilead
North American: **6** balsam

Poppaea's husband
4 Nero

poppycock
3 rot **4** bosh, guff **5** bilge, hokum
6 bunkum **8** malarkey, nonsense
10 balderdash **12** blatherskite, fiddle-faddle

populace
5 plebs **6** masses, people, plebes
9 commonage, commoners, common men, plebeians **10** commonalty **11** rank and file, third estate
combining form: **3** dem **4** demo

popular
4 rife **5** cheap, noted **6** famous, public, ruling, vulgar **7** current, favored, general, leading, rampant, regnant **8** approved, favorite **9** notorious, preferred, prevalent, prominent, well-known, well-liked
10 democratic, prevailing, widespread

populate
6 occupy, people, tenant **7** inhabit

populous
7 crowded **8** numerous

Poratha's father
5 Haman

porcelain
Chinese: **9** Lowestoft
English: **3** Bow **5** Derby, Spode
6 Minton **7** Bristol, Chelsea
8 Caughley, Wedgwood
French: **6** Sèvres **7** Limoges
German: **7** Dresden, Meissen
ingredient: **6** kaolin **8** petuntse
Italian: **6** Doccia
Japanese: **5** Imari

porch
5 lanai **7** galilee, passage, veranda **8** verandah

porcine
see **portly**

porcupine
5 porky, prick **7** echidna
8 hedgehog

porgy
4 scup **6** sparid **7** margate, pinfish
8 menhaden

Porgy and Bess composer
8 Gershwin (George)

Porgy author
7 Heyward (Dubose)

Po River
cities: **5** Milan, Padua, Turin **6** Verona **7** Brescia

pork
3 ham, pig **5** bacon, swine
8 sowbelly
cut: **3** ham **4** jowl, loin, side **7** fatback **8** forefoot, hind foot, spare rib **9** picnic ham **10** Boston butt

pork-barreling
9 patronage

pornographic
7 obscene

porous
5 leaky **6** leachy **8** pervious **9** permeable **10** cancellate, cancellous, penetrable **13** insubstantial

porridge
4 stew **5** brose, salad **6** crowdy, sowans, sowens **7** crowdie

port
3 air, set **4** goal, mien **5** cover, haven **6** asylum, covert, harbor, refuge, riding **7** address, bearing, retreat, shelter **8** demeanor, larboard, presence **9** anchorage, harborage, roadstead, sanctuary
10 deportment **11** comportment, destination; (see also **seaport**)

portable
5 handy **6** mobile, wieldy

portal
4 door, gate **5** entry **7** doorway
8 entrance, entryway
11 entranceway

portcullis
3 bar **4** shut **7** grating, lattice

portend
4 bode, omen **5** augur **7** betoken, predict, presage, promise, signify
8 forebode, forecast, foreshow, foretell, indicate, prophesy **9** adumbrate, foretoken **10** foreshadow, vaticinate

portent
4 omen, sign **6** augury, boding, marvel, wonder **7** miracle, presage, prodigy, stunner **8** bodement
9 foretoken, sensation

portentous
7 pompous, weighty **8** inflated
9 marvelous **10** prodigious

porter
5 carry, hamal **6** bearer, hamaul, hammal, redcap **7** carrier, drogher
9 transport **10** doorkeeper
airport: **6** skycap

Portia
husband: **6** Brutus **8** Bassanio
maid: **7** Nerissa

portion
3 cut, lot **4** bite, doom, fate, meed, part **5** dower, endow, moira, piece, quota, share, slice, weird **6** divide, kismet, member, moiety, parcel **7** deal out, destiny, dole out, measure, mete out, partage, prorate, quantum, segment **8** dispense, division
largest: **10** lion's share
unused: **8** leftover

portly
3 fat **5** heavy, obese, stout **6** fleshy
7 weighty **8** imposing **9** corpulent, overblown **10** overweight

portmanteau
9 gladstone 12 traveling bag

portrait
4 bust 5 image 6 double, ringer, statue 7 picture 10 similitude, simulacrum

portray
4 limn 5 cameo, enact, image 6 depict, render 7 picture 8 describe 9 delineate, interpret, represent

portrayal
7 picture 9 depiction 11 delineation, description, presentment

Portugal
9 Lusitania
capital: 6 Lisbon
coin: 7 centavo
export: 4 cork, wine 8 textiles
monetary unit: 6 escudo
premier: 7 Salazar (Antonio de)

pose
3 ask, dog, put, sit 4 airs, fake, give, lugs, sham 5 befog, feign, offer, query, strut 6 baffle, extend, pass as, prefer, puzzle, stance, tender 7 confuse, hold out, pass for, pass off, peacock, perplex, present, pretend, profess, proffer, propone, purport, show off, stumble, suggest 8 attitude, bewilder, carriage, confound, pretense, propound, question 9 mannerism 10 grandstand, masquerade, pretension 11 affectation, proposition 12 attitudinize

Poseidon
7 Neptune
brother: 4 Zeus 5 Hades, Pluto 7 Jupiter
consort: 4 Tyro 6 Medusa 7 Demeter
father: 6 Cronus
mother: 4 Rhea
offspring: 7 Pegasus
son: 5 Orion 6 Neleus, Pelias 7 Antaeus 10 Polyphemus
weapon: 7 trident
wife: 10 Amphitrite

posh
4 chic, tony 5 smart, swank 7 à la mode 9 exclusive 11 fashionable

posit
6 assume, thesis 7 premise, presume 9 apriorism 10 assumption, presuppose 11 presumption

position
3 job 4 rank, side, site, spot, view 5 angle, berth, color, locus, place, point, situs, slant, stand, state, where 6 belief, billet, cachet, locate, office, stance, status 7 dignity, emplace, footing, stature 8 attitude, capacity, judgment, prestige, standing 9 character, viewpoint 10 standpoint
troops: 6 deploy

positive
4 firm, hard, rank, sure 5 clear, gross, sound, utter 6 actual 7 assured, certain, decided, express, factual, genuine, perfect 8 absolute, cocksure, complete, definite, emphatic, explicit, forceful, forcible, outright, specific 9 clockwise, confident, doubtless, downright, energetic, practical 10 consummate, inarguable, reasonable, sure-enough, undeniable 11 categorical, indubitable, irrefutable, right-handed, unambiguous, undoubtable, unequivocal, unmitigated 12 indisputable, irrebuttable, undisputable, unmistakable

possess
3 own 4 bear, have, hold, keep 5 carry, enjoy 6 retain

possessed
4 calm, easy 6 placid, serene 8 tranquil

possession
8 property 9 ownership 11 proprietary

possessive
7 jealous

possessive pronoun
see at **pronoun**

possibility
2 if 9 potential 11 contingency

possible
6 latent, likely, mortal, viable 7 dormant, earthly 9 expedient, potential

possibly
5 maybe 7 perhaps 9 perchance

post
3 job, set 4 clew, clue, mail, spot, tell, warn 5 berth, place 6 advise, billet, fill in, inform, notify, office, wise up 7 apprise, placard, station 8 acquaint

poster
4 bill, sign 6 banner, notice 7 affiche, placard 8 handbill 9 billboard, broadside, signboard 12 announcement 13 advertisement

posterior
4 back, hind, rear, rump, seat, tail 5 after, later 6 behind, hinder, retral 7 ensuing, rear end, tail end 8 backside, buttocks, hindmost, rearward 10 subsequent 13 subsequential

posterity
4 seed 5 brood, issue 6 scions 7 progeny 8 children 9 offspring 11 descendants, progeniture

posthaste
4 fast 5 fleet, quick, rapid, swift 6 speedy 7 flat-out, fleetly, quickly, rapidly, swiftly 8 full tilt, speedily 9 breakneck 10 harefooted 11 expeditious 12 lickety-split

postimpressionist painter
6 Seurat (Georges) 7 Cezanne (Paul), Gauguin (Paul), Van Gogh (Vincent)

postmortem
7 autopsy 8 necropsy

postpone
5 defer, delay 6 hold up, put off, shelve 7 hold off, lay over, suspend 8 hold over, prorogue, reprieve 9 carry over

postulate
4 aver, call 5 claim, exact 6 affirm, assert, assume, demand, thesis 7 premise, presume, require, solicit 9 apriorism, challenge 10 assumption, presuppose 11 presumption, requisition, supposition

posture
3 sit 4 mien, mode 5 state 6 manner, stance, status 7 bearing, pass for, pass off 8 attitude, carriage 9 condition, situation 10 deportment, masquerade 12 attitudinize

posy
3 ana 5 album, bloom 6 flower 7 blossom, bouquet, corsage, garland, nosegay, omnibus 8 analects 9 anthology 10 miscellany 11 florilegium

pot
3 bet, wad 4 ante, mint, olla, pile, weed 5 grass, kitty, stake, wager 6 boodle, bundle 7 fortune 8 cannabis 9 marihuana, marijuana, sideswipe
small: 6 pipkin

potable
4 pure 5 clean, drink, fresh 6 liquor 8 beverage 9 drinkable

potassium
6 kalium
ore: 6 sylvin 7 sylvine, sylvite

potato
3 yam 4 spud 5 praty, tater 6 murphy

bud: **3** eye
cooked strips of: **11** French fries

potbelly
5 stove **6** paunch **9** bay window

potency
3 pep **4** birr, tuck **5** force, might, power, sinew, vigor **6** energy, muscle, virtue **8** strength **9** hardihood, puissance **10** capability **13** effectiveness

potent
5 lusty **6** mighty, robust, strong, virile **8** forceful, forcible, powerful

potential
6 latent, likely **7** abeyant, dormant, lurking **8** possible, probable **9** plausible, prepatent, quiescent **10** imaginable **11** conceivable, possibility

pother
3 ado **4** cark, flap, fret, fuss, stew, stir, to-do **5** furor, whirl, worry **6** bustle, clamor, flurry, furore, hassle, hubbub, tumult, uproar **7** turmoil **9** agitation, annoyance, commotion, confusion, whirlpool, whirlwind **10** hurly-burly, turbulence

potion
7 philter, philtre

Potiphar's slave
6 Joseph

Potiphera
daughter: **7** Asenath
son-in-law: **6** Joseph

potpourri
4 hash, olio **6** medley **7** mélange **8** mishmash, pastiche **9** patchwork **10** assortment, hodgepodge, miscellany, salmagundi

potshot
3 cut, dig **4** gibe, jeer **5** crack **6** insult **9** aspersion, criticism, sideswipe

potter
4 mess **6** doodle, fiddle, puddle **10** mess around
English: **8** Wedgwood (Josiah)

Potter, Beatrix
creation: **11** Peter Rabbit

potter's field
8 cemetery, God's acre **9** graveyard

pottery, glazed
5 delft

pouch
3 bag, jut, sac **4** sack **5** bulge, burse **6** beetle, pocket **7** project, saccule **8** overhang, protrude, sacculus, stand out
bodily: **5** bursa

pouf
5 quilt **9** comforter

poultice
7 plaster **8** compress, dressing **9** cataplasm

poultry
4 fowl
type: **4** duck, swan **5** goose, quail **6** grouse, pigeon, turkey **7** chicken, ostrich, peacock **8** pheasant **9** partridge

pounce
5 swoop, talon **6** emboss, powder

pound
3 bat **4** bang, bash, beat, belt, biff, blow, drub, pelt, slam, sock **5** crack, drive, grave, smack, stamp **6** batter, buffet, hammer, pummel, thrash, wallop **7** belabor, impress **8** malleate

pound and sponge
5 cakes

pour
3 run **4** beat, emit, flow, gush, lash, rain, rill, roll, rush, teem, void **5** flood, issue, skink, spate, surge, swarm **6** decant, deluge, drench, sluice, spring, stream **7** cascade, give off, niagara, proceed, torrent **8** cataract, flooding, inundate, overflow
forth: **6** effuse

pourboire
3 tip **7** cumshaw, largess **8** gratuity **9** lagniappe **10** perquisite

pout
3 pet **4** moue, sulk **5** bulge, grump **7** project **8** overhang, protrude

poverty
4 need, want **6** penury **7** beggary, borasca **8** poorness, scarcity **9** indigence, indigency, necessity, neediness, pauperism, privation, suffering **10** mendicancy, scarceness **11** destitution **13** destituteness, insufficiency, insufficiency, pennilessness
combining form: **5** penia

poverty-stricken
see **penurious**

POW camp
German: **6** stalag

powder
4 bray, buck, dust, talc **5** crush **6** talcum **8** sprinkle **9** comminute, pulverize, triturate **10** besprinkle **12** contriturate
medicinal: **7** lupulin

power
3 arm, vis **4** dint, sway **5** force, might, right, sinew, steam, vigor, vires (plural) **6** energy, muscle, talent, virtue, weight **7** ability, command, control, dynamis, faculty, mastery, potence, potency, voltage **8** aptitude, capacity, dominion, dynamism, function, imperium, prestige, strength **9** authority, direction, dominance, endowment, influence, masterdom, privilege, puissance, strong arm, supremacy **10** ascendancy, birthright, capability, competence, domination, management **11** prerogative, sovereignty, superiority **12** jurisdiction, potentiality **13** effectiveness
combining form: **5** dynam **6** dynamo
in Hindu philosophy: **4** maya
reduction: **8** brownout
sacred: **4** kami
unit of: **4** watt

powerful
4 able **5** great **6** mighty, potent, strong, wieldy **7** capable, dynamic, weighty **8** almighty, dominant, forcible, puissant, vigorous **9** competent, effective, effectual, efficient, energetic, strenuous **10** convincing, invincible **11** efficacious, influential **13** authoritative

powerless
4 weak **5** inert, unfit **6** feeble, infirm, supine **7** passive **8** decrepit, impotent, inactive, nugatory **9** incapable **11** incompetent, ineffective

powwow
4 chat, talk **5** treat **6** advise, confab, confer, huddle, parley **7** consult, meeting **8** collogue **10** conference **11** confabulate

poyou
6 peludo **9** armadillo

practicable
4 open **5** handy, utile **6** useful **9** operative **10** functional

practical
5 handy, sober, utile **6** usable, useful, versed **7** old-time, skilled, veteran **8** banausic, implicit, sea-

soned, sensible **9** pragmatic, realistic **10** functional, hard-boiled, hardheaded **11** down-to-earth, experienced, serviceable **12** businesslike

practically
4 most, much, nigh **5** about **6** all but, almost, nearly **8** as good as, as much as, well-nigh **9** in essence

practice
3 use, way **4** form, mode, plot, wont **5** cabal, covin, drill, habit, trick, usage **6** custom, follow, manner, method, pursue, repeat, scheme, system, usance **7** execute, fulfill, iterate, perform, process, utility **8** drilling, exercise, habitude, intrigue, rehearse **9** procedure **10** conspiracy, convenance, convention, proceeding
suffix: **2** cy **3** ery, ics, ism

practitioner
combining form: **4** path
suffix: **5** ician

pragmatic
9 practical, realistic **10** hard-boiled, hardheaded, unromantic **11** down-to-earth

pragmatist
7 realist

prairie antelope
9 pronghorn

prairie apple
9 breadroot

prairie berry
9 trompillo

prairie chicken
6 grouse

prairie hen
11 clapper rail

prairie potato
9 breadroot

prairie wolf
6 coyote

praise
4 hail, hymn, laud **5** bless, cry up, erect, exalt, extol, honor, psalm, roose **6** anthem, belaud, extoll, kudize, uprear **7** acclaim, adulate, applaud, commend, dignify, enhance, ennoble, flatter, glorify, hosanna, magnify, plaudit, puffery, resound, sublime **8** eulogize, heighten, proclaim, psalmody **9** celebrate, intensify, recommend **10** aggrandize, compliment, panegyrize

expression of: **8** accolade **9** encomium

praiseworthy
7 palmary **8** laudable **9** admirable, deserving, estimable, meritable **11** commendable, meritorious

prance
4 step **5** strut, tread **6** curvet, foot it, hoof it, jaunce, sashay **8** cakewalk

prank
4 deck, lark, play, trim, whim **5** adorn, antic, caper, fancy, fix up, freak, spiff, sport, trick **6** bedeck, didoes, doll up, frolic, gambol, levity, shines, vagary, wheeze, whimsy **7** caprice, conceit, deck out, doll out, dress up, fooling, garnish, gussy up, rollick **8** beautify, decorate, escapade, ornament, spruce up **9** capriccio, embellish, frivolity, high jinks, horseplay, lightness, rowdiness, smarten up **10** roughhouse, shenanigan, skylarking, tomfoolery **11** monkeyshine
Scottish: **6** shavie

prate
3 gab, jaw, yak **4** blab, blow, brag, chat, crow, puff, yack **5** boast, clack, drool, mouth, vaunt **6** babble, drivel, gabble, jabber, waffle, yabber **7** blabber, blather, chatter, palaver, twaddle, twattle **9** gasconade, yakety-yak **11** rodomontade

prater
6 magpie **9** bandar-log, blabmouth **10** chatterbox **12** blabbermouth

prattle
see **prate**

prattler
see **prater**

prawn
6 shrimp **8** crevette **13** Norway lobster

praxis
3 use **4** wont **5** habit, trick, usage **6** custom, manner **8** habitude **10** consuetude

Praxiteles statue
6 Hermes **8** The Satyr

pray
3 beg **5** brace, crave, daven, doven, plead **6** appeal **7** beseech, entreat, implore **8** meditate **10** supplicate

prayer
4 plea, suit **6** appeal, beggar, litany, orison, suitor **7** angelus, begging, complin, worship **8** blessing, compline, entreaty, petition, pleading **9** adoration, imploring, suppliant **10** beseeching, supplicant **11** application, imploration, imprecation, supplicator **12** supplication
beads: **6** rosary
ending: **4** amen
for the dead: **7** requiem
Jewish: **7** kaddish, kiddush **9** kaddishim (plural)
period: **6** novena **7** triduum
shawl: **6** tallis, tallit **7** tallith

prayer book
6 missal **8** breviary
Jewish: **6** mahzor, siddur **7** machzor

prayerful
4 holy **5** godly, pious **6** devout

praying figure
5 orant

preach
7 address, lecture **8** advocate, homilize, moralize **9** sermonize **10** evangelize

preacher
6 cleric, divine, parson **7** evangel **8** clerical, homilist, minister, reverend **9** churchman, clergyman **10** evangelist **12** ecclesiastic

preacher bird
5 vireo

preaching friar
9 Dominican

preamble
5 proem **8** exordium, foreword, overture, prologue **12** introduction, prolegomenon

precarious
4 iffy **5** risky **6** touchy, tricky **7** dubious **8** delicate, doubtful, insecure, ticklish, unstable **9** sensitive, uncertain

precaution
8 prudence **9** foresight, safeguard **10** providence **11** forethought

precede
4 lead, pace, rank **5** forgo, usher **6** forego, herald **7** forerun, outrank **8** announce, antedate **9** introduce

precedence
8 priority

precedent
4 past **5** prior **6** former **7** example **8** anterior **9** foregoing

preceding

4 past 5 prior 6 before, former
7 ahead of, prior to 8 anterior, hitherto 9 erstwhile 10 heretofore
11 in advance of
prefix: 4 ante

precept

3 law 4 rule 5 axiom, canon,
dogma, edict, tenet 6 behest, decree 7 bidding, statute 8 decretum,
doctrine 9 ordinance, principle
10 injunction, regulation
11 fundamental

preceptive

8 didactic 9 mandatory

preceptor

5 tutor 7 teacher 9 principal
10 headmaster

precinct

6 domain, region, sector, sphere
7 quarter, section 8 district, dominion, province 9 bailiwick, territory

precious

3 pet 4 dear, nice, rare, rich
5 fussy, loved, picky, showy 6 artful, chichi, choice, choosy, costly,
la-di-da 7 beloved, darling, finicky,
genteel, studied 8 affected, blue-
eyed, favorite, overnice, prizable,
valuable 9 exquisite, priceless,
prizeable, recherché 10 fair-
haired, fastidious, invaluable,
particular

precipitancy

4 rush 5 haste 9 hastiness 10 sud-
denness 11 hurriedness

precipitant

5 hasty 6 abrupt, sudden 7 hurried, rushing 8 headlong
9 impetuous

precipitate

4 lees 5 dregs, event, hasty, issue,
sheer, steep 6 abrupt, effect, madcap, result, sequel, sudden, upshot
7 arduous, deposit, grounds, hurried, rushing 8 headlong, sediment
9 aftermath, breakneck, hotheaded,
impatient, impetuous, impulsive, ov-
erhasty, settlings 10 headstrong, refractory, unexpected, unforeseen
11 aftereffect, consequence,
subitaneous

precipitation

4 hail, lees, rain, rush, snow
5 dregs, haste, sleet 7 deposit,
grounds 8 sediment 9 hastiness,
settlings 11 hurriedness

precipitous

5 hasty, sheer, steep 6 abrupt, sudden 7 hurried, rushing 8 headlong

précis

6 aperçu, digest, sketch, survey
7 pandect, sylloge 8 syllabus
10 compendium

precise

4 nice, prim, very 5 exact, fixed,
right, rigid 6 narrow, prissy,
proper, stuffy 7 correct, genteel,
limited, missish, prudish 8 accurate, definite, priggish, rigorous,
specific 9 clocklike, stringent
10 particular

preciseness

see **precision**

precision

4 care, heed 6 timing 8 accuracy
9 exactness 10 definitude, exactitude 11 carefulness, correctness

preclude

4 quit, stop, ward 5 avert, cease,
deter 7 forfend, obviate, rule out
8 stave off 9 forestall
11 discontinue

precondition

4 must 9 essential, necessity, requisite 10 sine qua non
11 requirement

precursor

6 herald 8 foregoer 9 harbinger,
prototype 10 antecedent,
forerunner

predate

7 forerun 8 antecede

predatory

9 rapacious, raptorial, vulturine,
vulturous

predecessor

7 forbear 8 ancestor, forebear,
foregoer 9 prototype 10 antecedent, forerunner

predestine

see **preordain**

predetermine

see **preordain**

predeterminism

8 fatalism

predicament

3 box, fix, jam 4 hole, pass, soup,
spot 5 Dutch, pinch, rigor, state
6 corner, pickle, plight, scrape,
strait 7 dilemma, impasse, posture,
trouble 8 asperity, exigency, hardness, hardship, hot water, juncture,

quagmire 9 condition, deep water,
emergency, situation 10 difficulty

predicate

4 aver, avow, base, rest, stay
5 found 6 affirm, assert, avouch,
depose, ground 7 declare, profess,
protest 9 establish

predict

5 augur, guess, infer, judge 7 for-
bode, foresee, portend, suppose,
surmise 8 conclude, forebode, forecast, forefeel, foreshow, foretell,
prophesy, soothsay 9 adumbrate
10 conjecture, vaticinate
13 prognosticate

predictor

4 seer 5 augur, weird 6 auspex
7 prophet 8 foreseer, haruspex
10 forecaster, foreteller, prophesier,
soothsayer 11 Nostradamus

predilection

4 bent 7 leaning 8 penchant, tendency 9 inclining 10 proclivity,
propensity

predispose

4 bend, bias, sway 6 strike
7 incline

predisposed

4 fain 5 prone, ready 7 willing
8 inclined

predisposition

4 bent 7 leaning 8 penchant, tendency 9 inclining 10 proclivity,
propensity

predominant

4 main 5 chief, major 6 master
7 capital, general, primary 9 number one, paramount, principal, sovereign 11 outstanding, overbearing

predominate

4 rule 5 reign 6 master 7 regnant
9 ascendant, paramount, prevalent,
sovereign 11 overbearing

preeminence

6 renown 7 primacy 8 dominion
9 masterdom, supremacy 10 ascendancy, domination 11 distinction,
superiority

preeminent

4 main 5 chief, major 7 capital,
stellar, supreme 8 dominant, towering, ultimate 9 number one, principal 10 surpassing 11 outstanding,
unequalable, unmatchable 12 incomparable, transcendent
prefix: 4 arch

preempt
4 take 5 annex, seize, usurp 6 assume 8 accroach, arrogate 9 sequester 10 commandeer, confiscate 11 appropriate, expropriate

preen
5 plume, pride, primp

preface
4 lead 5 proem, usher 6 prolog 8 exordium, foreword, overture, preamble, prologue 9 introduce 12 introduction

prefatory
8 proemial 9 inductive, preludial 12 introductory

prefer
3 put 4 cull, mark, pick, pose, take 5 elect 6 choose, optate, opt for, select

preference
6 choice, option 8 druthers, election 9 elevation, prelation, promotion, selection, upgrading 10 partiality

prefigure
4 hint 9 adumbrate 10 foreshadow

pregnancy
6 cyesis 9 fertility, gestation, gravidity

pregnant
4 rich 5 heavy 6 facund, gravid, parous 7 weighty 8 childing, eloquent, enceinte 9 expecting, momentous 10 expressive, meaningful, parturient 11 sententious

prehend
3 bag, get 4 nail, take 5 catch 6 collar, secure 7 capture

prehensile
6 grabby, greedy 8 covetous, desirous, grasping 11 acquisitive

preindicate
6 herald 7 forerun, presage 8 announce, foreshow 9 harbinger

prejudice
3 mar 4 bend, bias, harm, hurt, skew 5 angle, slant, spoil 6 damage, impair, injure, racism, sexism 7 bigotry, blemish, dispose, incline, leaning, tarnish, vitiate 9 influence 10 partiality 12 one-sidedness, partisanship

prejudicial
3 bad 4 evil 7 harmful, nocuous 8 damaging 9 injurious 11 deleterious, detrimental, mischievous

preknow
3 see 6 divine 7 foresee 8 forefeel 9 apprehend, visualize 10 anticipate

preliminary
5 basic 7 fitting 8 proemial, readying 9 elemental, inductive 11 fundamental 12 introductory

preliterate
9 primitive

prelude
5 proem 8 exordium, foreword, overture, prologue 12 introduction, prolegomenon

premature
5 early 8 oversoon, untimely 9 overearly

premeditated
7 advised, studied 8 designed, studious 10 considered, deliberate, thought-out

premier
4 arch, head 5 chief, first 7 leading 8 champion, foremost 9 principal

premise
5 posit 6 assume, thesis 9 apriorism, postulate 10 assumption 11 postulation, supposition

premium
4 agio, meed, plum 5 prize 6 carrot, reward 7 guerdon 8 buckshee, dividend, superior 11 exceptional

premonition
9 misgiving 10 foreboding 12 apprehension

preoccupied
4 deep, lost, rapt 6 absent, intent 7 bemused, engaged, faraway, wrapped 8 distrait, immersed 9 engrossed, forgetful, wrapped up 10 abstracted 11 inconscient 12 absentminded

preordain
4 fate 6 doom to 7 destine 9 determine 10 predestine 11 foredestine

preparation
7 fitness 8 training 9 readiness 11 compounding

preparatory
9 preludial, prelusive 11 prefatorial, preliminary

prepare
3 fit, fix, get 4 busk, gird, make 5 brace, dower, draft, endow, endue, equip, frame, prime, ready, steel, train 6 draw up, make up,

outfit, supply 7 confect, dispose, fortify, furnish, provide 9 formulate 10 strengthen
for publication: 4 edit 6 redact
leather: 5 curry

prepared
3 set 5 ready

preponderance
8 dominion 9 ascendant, masterdom, supremacy 10 ascendancy, domination

preponderant
8 dominant, superior 9 paramount, sovereign 11 overbearing

preponderate
4 rule 5 reign 8 domineer

preposition
2 at, by, in, of, on, to, up 3 but, cum, ere, for, off, out, per, via 4 amid, down, from, into, like, onto, over, save, thru, till, unto, upon, with 5 about, above, after, along, among, anent, below, circa, since, tween, twixt, under, until 6 aboard, across, amidst, around, before, behind, beside, beyond, contra, except, gainst, inside, mongst, toward, versus, within 7 against, amongst, athwart, beneath, besides, between, betwixt, despite, outside, through, towards, without 10 throughout, underneath

prepossess
4 bias 5 imbue 6 absorb, engage, occupy 7 engross, immerse, involve 9 influence, prejudice, preoccupy

prepossessing
10 attractive

preposterous
4 wild 5 crazy, loony, silly, wacky 6 absurd, insane 7 foolish 9 fantastic 10 irrational 11 extravagant, harebrained 12 unreasonable

preposterousness
5 folly 8 insanity 9 absurdity

prerequisite
4 must 9 condition, essential, necessary, necessity 10 imperative, sine qua non 11 necessitous, requirement

prerogative
5 right 8 appanage, immunity 9 exemption, privilege 10 birthright, perquisite

presage
4 bode, omen 5 augur 6 augury, boding, herald 7 bespeak, betoken, forerun, portend, portent, pre-

dict, promise **8** announce, bodement, forebode, forecast, foreshow, foretell, indicate, prophesy, soothsay **9** adumbrate, foretoken, harbinger, misgiving, prenotion **10** foreboding, foreshadow, prognostic, vaticinate **12** apprehensive **13** prognosticate

presbyter
5 elder **6** priest

prescience
9 foresight

prescribe
3 fix, set **6** assign, choose, decide, decree, define, impose, ordain, select, settle **7** dictate, lay down, pick out **9** determine

prescript
3 law **4** rule **5** edict **6** decree **8** decretum **9** institute, ordinance **10** regulation

prescription
3 law **4** rule **5** edict **6** decree **8** decretum **9** institute, ordinance

presence
3 air **4** look, mien, port **6** aspect **7** address, bearing, seeming **8** demeanor

present
3 aim, lay, now **4** boon, cast, cite, gift, give, head, past, pose, show **5** favor, level, offer, point, today, train **6** adduce, allege, bestow, devote, direct, donate, extant, extend, modern, tender **7** address, advance, hand out, hold out, instant, largess, proffer **8** acquaint, nowadays, todayish, up-to-date **9** introduce **12** contemporary, newfashioned

presentable
3 fit **6** decent, proper **9** befitting **11** appropriate

presentiment
see **premonition**

presently
3 now **4** anon, soon **5** today **7** by and by **8** nowadays

preservation
4 care, ward **5** guard **6** saving, shield **7** defense, keeping **9** safeguard **10** husbanding **11** conservancy, safekeeping

preserve
3 can, jam **4** save **6** keep up, pickle **7** sustain **8** maintain **9** confiture

preside
3 run **4** head, keep **5** chair **6** direct, handle, manage, ordain **7** carry on, conduct, control, operate, oversee

president
United States: **4** Bush (George), Ford (Gerald R.), Polk (James K.), Taft (William H.) **5** Adams (John, John Quincy), Grant (Ulysses S.), Hayes (Rutherford B.), Nixon (Richard M.), Tyler (John) **6** Arthur (Chester A.), Carter (Jimmy), Hoover (Herbert), Monroe (James), Pierce (Franklin), Reagan (Ronald), Taylor (Zachary), Truman (Harry S.), Wilson (Woodrow) **7** Clinton (Bill), Harding (Warren), Jackson (Andrew), Johnson (Andrew, Lyndon) Kennedy (John F.), Lincoln (Abraham), Madison (James) **8** Buchanan (James), Coolidge (Calvin), Fillmore (Millard), Garfield (James), Harrison (Benjamin, William H.), McKinley (William), Van Buren (Martin) **9** Cleveland (Grover), Jefferson (Thomas), Roosevelt (Franklin D., Theodore) **10** Eisenhower (Dwight D.), Washington (George)

press
3 hug, jam, ram **4** bear, cram, iron, mass, move, pack, pile, push, rice, tamp **5** clasp, crowd, crush, drive, drove, elbow, force, horde, impel, shove, stuff **6** enfold, gather, goffer, hustle, jostle, propel, sadden, sinter, squash, squish, squush, throng, thrust **7** collect, embrace, gauffer, imprint, squeeze, squelch, squoosh **8** assemble, bulldoze, shoulder **9** constrain, multitude, weigh down **10** congregate

pressing
4 dire **5** acute **6** direct, urgent **7** clamant, crucial, exigent, instant **8** critical **9** clamorous, immediate, insistent **10** imperative **11** importunate

pressure
4 push, rush **5** drive, impel **6** strain, stress **7** tension **9** overpress
combining form: **4** tono **5** piezo
instrument: **9** barometer
unit: **3** bar **5** barye

prestige
4 rank, sway **5** power, state **6** cachet, credit, renown, status, weight **7** dignity, stature **8** eminence, position, standing **9** authority, influence **10** prominence, prominency **11** consequence, distinction

prestigious
5 famed, great **7** eminent, notable **8** renowned **9** prominent **10** celebrated **13** distinguished

presto
4 fast **7** flat-out, hastily, quickly, rapidly **8** chop-chop, full tilt **9** posthaste **12** lickety-split **13** expeditiously

presumably
6 likely **9** doubtless

presume
5 guess, opine, posit, think **6** impose, reason **7** intrude, obtrude, suppose, surmise **8** infringe **9** postulate **10** conjecture

presuming
see **presumptuous**

presumption
4 face, gall **5** brass, cheek, nerve, posit **6** thesis **9** apriorism, brashness, postulate **10** confidence, effrontery

presumptuous
4 smug **5** brash, lofty **6** uppish, uppity **7** forward, pushful, pushing **9** confident **10** brassbound, complacent **11** inexcusable, overweening, self-assured

presuppose
5 guess, infer, judge, posit, think **6** assume, deduce, expect, gather, reckon **7** believe, imagine, surmise, suspect **9** postulate

presupposition
5 guess, posit **6** belief, thesis **7** surmise **8** judgment **9** apriorism, inference, judgement, postulate **10** conjecture

pretend
3 act **4** fake, sham **5** bluff, feign, guess, put on, think **6** affect, assume, delude **7** beguile, deceive, mislead, profess, purport, suppose, surmise **8** simulate

pretender
4 fake **5** faker, fraud, phony **6** humbug **8** impostor

pretense
3 air **4** face, fake, mask, sham **5** claim, cloak, color, cover, fraud, guise, title **6** deceit, facade, humbug **7** charade, pageant **8** coloring, disguise **9** deception, imposture, mannerism **10** false front, masquerade **11** affectation, make-believe

pretension
5 claim, title 7 charade, pageant
8 disguise 11 make-believe
13 ambitiousness

pretentious
3 big 4 arty 5 lofty, put-on, showy,
swank, tumid 6 chichi, la-di-da, too-
too, turgid 7 aureate, feigned,
flowery, genteel, mincing, pompier,
splashy, stilted, utopian 8 affected,
imposing, inflated, peacocky
9 bombastic, grandiose, overblown, visionary 10 arty-crafty, euphuistic, flamboyant, peacockish,
rhetorical 12 high-sounding,
magniloquent
speech: 7 bombast

preternatural
7 deviant 8 aberrant, abnormal,
atypical, numinous, superior
9 anomalous, deviative, unearthly,
untypical 10 miraculous, superhuman, suprahuman 11 heteroclite
12 supermundane, supramundane

pretext
4 mask 5 alibi, cloak, cover, front,
guise 6 excuse 8 pretense

pretty
4 cute, fair, good, some 5 bonny,
ducky 6 adroit, bonnie, clever,
comely, fairly, incony, kind of,
lovely, rather, seemly, sort of,
wicked 7 cunning, darling, dollish
8 handsome, skillful, somewhat
9 beauteous, beautiful 10 attractive, moderately, more or less
11 good-looking

prevail
4 beat, rule 5 reign 6 affect, master 7 conquer, impress, triumph
8 dominate, domineer, overcome,
override

prevailing
see **prevalent**

prevalent
4 rife 5 usual 6 common, master,
normal, ruling, wonted 7 general,
natural, popular, rampant, regnant,
regular, typical 8 dominant 9 ascendant, customary, paramount,
sovereign 10 accustomed, widespread 11 commonplace

prevaricate
3 fib, lie 6 palter 7 falsify
12 misrepresent

prevarication
3 fib, lie 4 tale 5 lying, story 6 canard 7 falsity 9 falsehood

prevaricator
4 liar 6 fibber 7 Ananias, fibster
8 perjurer 9 falsifier 11 storyteller

prevent
3 bar, dam 4 balk, foil, ward
5 avert, block, check, debar, deter
6 arrest, baffle, forbid, hinder, impede, thwart 7 forfend, inhibit, obviate, rule out, shut out 8 obstruct,
prohibit, stave off 9 forestall, frustrate, interdict, interrupt
10 anticipate
access: 9 barricade

previous
4 fore, past 5 prior 6 before, former 7 earlier, forward 8 anterior,
oversoon 9 foregoing, in advance,
overearly 10 antecedent,
beforehand

previously
4 once 6 before 7 already, earlier,
priorly 8 formerly 9 erstwhile
10 heretofore

prey
4 game 5 chase 6 quarry, victim
8 casualty, underdog 9 bottom dog

Priam
daughter: 6 Creusa 8 Polyxena
9 Cassandra
father: 8 Laomedon
grandfather: 4 Ilus
kingdom: 4 Troy
slayer: 7 Pyrrhus 11 Neoptolemus
son: 5 Paris 6 Hector, Lycaon 7 Helenus, Troilus 9 Deiphobus,
Polydorus
wife: 6 Arisbe, Hecuba

Priapus
father: 7 Bacchus 8 Dionysus
mother: 5 Venus 9 Aphrodite

price
3 tab 4 cost, rate, toll 6 charge, tariff 7 expense

priceless
6 costly, valued 8 precious, valuable 9 cherished, treasured
10 invaluable

prick
3 cut, jab, sic 4 bore, goad, hole,
prod, slit, spur, stab, urge 5 drill,
egg on, enter, pique, punch, rowel,
slash, sting, thorn 6 excite, exhort,
prompt, propel 8 puncture 9 perforate, stimulate

prickly
5 burry, spiny 6 nettly, thorny, tingly, twitty 7 brambly, fretful, peevish, pettish, waspish 8 annoying,

petulant, snappish 9 fractious, irritable 10 bothersome, nettlesome

pride
3 fat, top 4 best, brag, crow, face,
pick 5 boast, cream, elite, pique,
plume, preen, scorn, vaunt
6 choice, egoism, flower, morgue
7 bighead, conceit, dignity, disdain, egotism, hauteur 8 contempt,
smugness, vainness 9 arrogance,
cockiness, gasconade, insolence,
loftiness, self-glory, self-trust, superbity, vainglory 10 felicitate, self-esteem, self-regard 11 amour propre,
haughtiness, self-opinion, self-respect 12 congratulate, snobbish-
ness 13 condescension, self-
assurance

Pride and Prejudice author
6 Austen (Jane)

prier
5 snoop 6 butt-in 7 meddler, Paul
Pry 8 busybody, quidnunc
10 rubberneck

priest
9 clergyman 10 chancellor
11 chamberlain
ancient Roman: 6 fecial, fetial, flamen 8 pontifex
Buddhist: 4 lama
Celtic: 5 druid
French: 4 abbé, curé
Indian: 6 shaman
military: 5 padre 8 chaplain
Muslim: 4 imam
of Bacchus: 6 maenad 9 bacchante

priestly
8 hieratic 10 sacerdotal
12 sacerdotical

prig
5 prude, thief 6 Grundy, nimmer,
stuffy, wowser 7 filcher, genteel,
prudish, puritan, stealer 8 bluenose, comstock, larcener, pilferer
9 larcenist, Mrs. Grundy, nice
Nelly, purloiner, Victorian
10 goody-goody, tight-laced 11 puritanical, straitlaced

priggish
4 smug 6 stuffy 7 genteel, prudish
9 Victorian 10 complacent, self-loving, tight-laced 11 puritanical, self-
pleased, straitlaced 13 self-contented, self-esteeming,
self-righteous, self-satisfied

prim
4 neat, nice, snug, tidy 5 rigid, stiff
6 formal, proper, stuffy, wooden
7 chipper, correct, genteel, missish,
orderly, precise, prudish 8 deco-

rous, straight **9** bluenosed, shipshape, Victorian **10** ceremonial,
tight-laced **11** ceremonious,
puritanical, straitlaced, uncluttered,
well-groomed **12** conventional

prima facie
11 self-evident

primary
4 main **5** basal, basic, chief, first
6 bottom, direct **7** initial, pioneer,
radical **8** earliest, original **9** first-
hand, immediate, underived **10** underlying **11** fundamental **12** foundational, underivative
combining form: **4** prot **5** proto
prefix: **4** arch **5** archi

primate
3 ape, man **5** human **6** monkey
7 gorilla **10** anthropoid, chimpanzee, human being **11** Homo
sapiens
nocturnal: **7** tarsier
small: **6** galago

prime
3 top **4** best, fine, morn, move, pick
5 cream, elite, first, sunup, youth
6 aurora, choice, excite, famous,
spring **7** capital, initial, morning,
provoke, quicken **8** cock-
crow, daybreak, earliest, motivate,
original, superior **9** dayspring, excellent, first-rate, galvanize, stimulate, underived **10** first-class, juvenility, springtide **11** adolescence

primer
4 book **6** reader **8** hornbook

primeval
10 aboriginal; (see also **primordial**)

primitive
5 basic, early **7** archaic **8** original
9 barbarian, elemental, essential,
underived, unevolved **10** elementary, persistent, substratal, underlying **11** fundamental, nonliterate,
preliterate, uncivilized, undeveloped **12** uncultivated
combining form: **4** pale **5** palae, paleo **6** archae, archeo, palaeo, palaio **7** archaeo
prefix: **4** arch **5** arche, archi

primogenitor
7 forbear **8** ancestor, forebear
9 ascendant **10** forefather

primordial
5 early, first **8** earliest, original
10 elementary **11** fundamental, undeveloped

primordium
6 anlage, origin **9** beginning

primp
5 fix up, preen, slick, spiff **6** doll up
7 deck out, doll out, dress up, gussy
up

prince
Anglo-Saxon: **8** atheling
Arab: **4** emir **5** emeer
Austrian: **8** archduke
Ethiopian: **3** ras
Indian: **4** raja **5** rajah
Muslim: **4** amir **5** ameer
of demons: **9** Beelzebub
of Monaco: **7** Rainier
of the church: **8** cardinal
of Wales: **7** Charles

Prince and the Pauper author
5 Twain (Mark)

Prince Edward Island
capital: **13** Charlottetown
discoverer: **7** Cartier (Jacques)

Prince Igor composer
7 Borodin (Aleksandr)

princely
5 grand, noble, royal **6** august,
lordly **8** baronial, imposing **9** grandiose **11** magnificent

princess
mythical: **3** Ino
of Monaco: **5** Grace

principal
4 arch, head, main, star **5** chief,
first, major **7** capital, leading, premier, primary, stellar **8** champion,
dominant, foremost **10** preeminent
11 outstanding, predominant
combining form: **4** prot **5** proto
prefix: **4** arch **5** archi

principium
3 law **5** axiom, basis **7** element,
theorem **10** foundation
11 fundamental

principle
3 law **4** form, rule **5** axiom, basis,
canon, tenet, usage **6** ground **7** precept, theorem **8** polestar **10** convention, foundation **11** fundamental

principled
5 moral, noble **7** ethical **8** virtuous
9 righteous **10** moralistic

print
4 type **5** litho, stamp, write **7** engrave, impress, publish, typeset
10 impression
style: **5** roman **6** italic **7** cursive

printer
English: **6** Caxton (William)
Italian: **6** Bodoni (Giambattista)
8 Manutius (Aldus)

printers' mark
see **proofreaders' mark**

printer's receptacle
7 hellbox

printing
7 edition, reissue **10** impression
measure: **2** em, en **4** pica **5** agate
6 cicero
plate: **6** stereo **7** linecut
process: **4** roto **7** gravure
style: **6** gothic

prior
see **previous**

priority
5 order **8** ordering **9** supremacy
10 ascendancy, precedence

prison
3 pen **4** jail, keep **6** cooler, lockup
7 bastile, dungeon, slammer **8** bastille, stockade **11** reformatory
12 penitentiary
California: **10** San Quentin
former: **8** Alcatraz, Sing-Sing
New York: **6** Attica **12** Rikers Island
Northern Ireland: **4** Maze
resident: **6** inmate **7** convict
8 jailbird

prissy
6 stuffy **7** epicene, finicky, genteel,
missish, prudish, unmanly **9** pansified, sissified, squeamish, Victorian
10 effeminate, fastidious, tight-laced
11 puritanical, straitlaced **12** Miss-
Nancyish

pristine
4 pure **8** earliest, original

privacy
7 secrecy **9** seclusion

private
6 closet, hidden, hushed, inside, secret **7** soldier **8** discreet, personal
9 concealed **10** closed-door
12 confidential

private detective
see **detective**

privately
7 sub rosa **8** covertly, in camera,
secretly **9** by stealth **10** stealthily

privation
4 lack, loss, need, want **6** dearth,
defect, losing, misery, penury **7** absence, default, poverty **8** distress,

poorness **9** indigence, mislaying, neediness, suffering **10** misplacing **11** deprivement, divestiture

privilege
4 boon **5** favor, right **8** appanage **9** allowance **10** birthright, concession, perquisite **11** prerogative
pope-granted: **6** indult

privy
2 WC **4** head, john **5** jakes **6** buried, covert, hidden, johnny, toilet **7** latrine **8** lavatory, obscured, outhouse, personal, shrouded, stealthy, ulterior **9** backhouse, concealed **11** convenience, water closet

prize
3 pry, top **4** best, loot, meed, pick, plum, swag **5** award, booty, cream, elite, jimmy, lever, spoil, value **6** boodle, carrot, choice, esteem, reward, trophy **7** cherish, guerdon, jackpot, plunder, premium **8** dividend, treasure **10** appreciate, plunderage **11** outstanding

prizefighting
8 pugilism **10** fisticuffs

pro
3 for, vet, wiz **4** whiz, with **5** adept, doyen **6** expert, master **9** authority, in favor of **10** masterhand

probable
6 likely **7** seeming **8** apparent, rational **10** reasonable

probe
3 ask **4** quiz, sift **5** query, quest, scout **6** go into **7** delving, dig into, examine, explore, feel out, inquest, inquire, inquiry **8** look into, research, sound out **9** catechize, delve into **11** inquire into, inquisition, interrogate, investigate, reconnoiter **13** investigation

probity
6 virtue **7** honesty **8** goodness **9** integrity, rectitude, rightness **11** uprightness

problem
3 nut **5** issue **6** enigma, puzzle **7** bugaboo, bugbear, dilemma, example, mystery

problematic
4 moot, open **7** dubious, suspect **8** arguable, doubtful, mootable **9** ambiguous, debatable, dubitable,

uncertain, unsettled **10** disputable, indecisive, precarious **12** questionable

proboscis
4 beak, nose **5** snoot, snout **7** smeller

procedure
4 line, move, step **6** course, method, policy, polity **7** measure, program **8** demarche, maneuver

proceed
2 go **3** hie **4** fare, flow, head, move, pass, rise, stem, wend **5** arise, get on, issue, march, segue **6** push on, repair, spring, travel **7** advance, emanate, journey **8** get along, progress **9** originate **10** derive from

proceedings
8 goings-on
recorded: **4** acta

proceeds
4 gain **5** lucre **6** profit, return **8** earnings

process
3 way **4** mode, wise **5** modus **6** manner, method, system **7** fashion, recycle, routine **9** operation, outgrowth, technique
combining form: **4** typy
suffix: **2** al, th **3** ing, ism, sis **4** ance, ence, esis, osis **7** ization

procession
5 order **6** parade, series **8** sequence **9** cavalcade **11** consecution
combining form: **4** cade

proclaim
4 mark, show, vent **5** bruit, utter, voice **6** blazon, evince, herald, ostend **7** clarion, declare, exhibit, publish **8** announce, evidence, manifest, promulge **9** advertise, broadcast, ventilate **10** annunciate, bruit about, illustrate, promulgate **11** blaze abroad, demonstrate

proclivity
see **penchant**

Procne
father: **7** Pandion
husband: **6** Tereus
sister: **9** Philomela
son: **4** Itys

procrastinate
3 lag **4** drag, poke, stay **5** dally, defer, delay, tarry **6** dawdle, lin-

ger, loiter, put off **7** prolong, suspend **8** postpone

procreate
4 bear, make, sire **5** beget, breed, hatch, spawn **6** father, mother, parent **7** produce **8** engender, generate, multiply **9** originate, propagate, reproduce

Procris' husband and slayer
8 Cephalus

Procrustean ___
3 bed

proctor
9 supervise **10** supervisor

procure
3 get **4** draw, gain, have, land **5** annex **6** draw in, draw on, induce, obtain, pick up **7** acquire, compass, win over

prod
3 dig, jab, jog, sic **4** goad, poke, spur, urge **5** egg on, nudge, pique, prick, punch **6** excite, exhort **9** stimulate

prodigal
4 lush **6** lavish, waster **7** opulent, profuse, riotous, spender, wastrel **8** unthrift **9** exuberant, luxuriant, profusive **10** high roller, profligate, squanderer **11** scattergood, spendthrift, wastethrift

prodigious
4 huge, vast **6** mighty, mortal **7** amazing, immense, mammoth, massive **8** colossal, cracking, enormous, gigantic, towering **9** fantastic, marvelous, monstrous, wonderful **10** astounding, miraculous, monumental, staggering, stupendous, surprising

produce
4 bear, form, give, grow, make, show, sire **5** beget, breed, build, cause, erect, frame, get up, hatch, mount, put on, raise, spawn, stage, yield **6** create, draw on, effect, father, output, parent, secure, work up **7** deliver, fashion, outturn, turn out **8** engender, generate, multiply, muster up **9** construct, cultivate, fabricate, originate, procreate, propagate **10** bring about **11** manufacture, put together
combining form: **3** fer, gen **4** gene **5** genic **6** genous **7** genetic

product
5 fruit, yield **6** effect, output, result **7** harvest, outcome, outturn, turnout

8 multiple, offshoot 9 handiwork, outgrowth 11 consequence
combining form: 3 ade, ine, ite

production
5 fruit, yield 6 output 7 outturn, turnout
combining form: 4 geny, gony 7 genesia, poiesis 8 fication

productive
4 rich 6 fecund 7 fertile 8 childing, fruitful, prolific, spawning 11 proliferant

proem
see **prologue**

profane
3 lay 4 foul 5 dirty, nasty, pagan 6 coarse, ethnic, filthy, smutty, unholy, vulgar 7 earthly, gentile, heathen, impious, infidel, mundane, obscene, raunchy, secular, ungodly, worldly 8 indecent, temporal, unsacred 9 infidelic 10 irreverent, unhallowed 11 blasphemous, terrestrial 12 sacrilegious 13 irreverential

profanity
4 oath 5 curse 7 cursing, cussing 8 swearing 9 blasphemy 10 execration 11 imprecation

profess
4 aver, avow 6 affirm, assert, avouch, depose 7 declare, protest, purport 8 constate 9 predicate

profession
3 art, job 5 craft, trade 6 career, métier 7 calling 8 vocation 10 handicraft
suffix: 4 ship

professional
3 pro 4 paid, whiz 5 adept 6 artist, expert, master 7 artiste 8 virtuoso 9 authority 10 past master, proficient

professor
3 don 7 teacher

proffer
4 give, pose 5 offer 6 extend, tender 7 hold out, present 8 proposal 10 invitation, suggestion 11 proposition

proficiency
5 march, skill 7 advance, headway, ongoing 8 anabasis, progress 9 adeptness

proficient
4 able, whiz 5 adept, crack 6 artist, expert, master 7 artiste, capable, drilled, skilled 8 finished, masterly, skillful, virtuoso 9 authority, competent, effective, effectual, effi-

cient, exercised, masterful, practiced, qualified 10 checked-out, consummate, past master 11 crackerjack, experienced 12 accomplished, professional

profile
4 line 7 contour, outline 9 lineament, lineation 10 figuration, silhouette

profit
3 net 4 gain, take 5 avail, lucre, serve, yield 6 output, return 7 benefit, cleanup, killing, outturn, product, receipt, turnout, work for 8 cleaning, earnings, proceeds

profitable
6 paying 7 gainful 9 lucrative 10 well-paying, worthwhile 11 moneymaking 12 advantageous, remunerative

profligate
6 bad lot, no-good, waster 7 rounder, spender, wastrel 8 prodigal, unthrift, wasteful 9 abandoned, dissolute, reprobate 10 high roller, licentious, ne'er-do-well, scapegrace, squanderer 11 scattergood, spendthrift, wastethrift

profound
3 low 4 deep, hard, wise 5 heavy 6 occult, orphic, secret 7 abysmal, intense 8 abstruse, esoteric, hermetic 9 intensive

profoundness
5 abyss, depth 8 deepness 10 profundity

profundity
see **profoundness**

profuse
4 lush 6 lavish 7 copious, liberal, opulent, riotous, teeming 8 abundant, generous, prodigal, swarming 9 abounding, bounteous, bountiful, excessive, exuberant, luxuriant 10 immoderate, munificent

profusive
see **profuse**

progenitor
4 sire 8 ancestor, forebear 9 ascendant 10 forefather

progeny
see **posterity**

prognosis
4 cast 5 weird 8 forecast, prophecy 9 prevision 10 prediction 11 foretelling

prognostic
4 omen, sign 6 augury, boding

7 portent, presage 8 bodement 9 foretoken

prognosticate
see **predict**

program
4 bill, card, line, plan, sked 5 slate 6 agenda, course, docket, policy, polity 8 calendar, schedule 9 procedure, timetable 10 bill of fare
theater: 8 playbill

progress
2 go 4 fare, grow, move 5 get on, march 6 course, growth 7 advance, headway, ongoing, passage, proceed, promote 8 anabasis, get along, upgrowth 9 evolution, flowering, unfolding 10 evolvement 11 advancement, development, proficiency
planned: 7 telesis

progressing
5 afoot 8 under way

progression
3 row 5 chain, order, train 6 course, growth, sequel, series 7 advance 8 sequence, upgrowth 9 evolution, flowering, unfolding 10 evolvement, succession 11 alternation, consecution, development

progressive
4 wide 5 broad 7 liberal, radical 8 advanced, stepwise, tolerant

prohibit
3 ban, bar 5 taboo 6 enjoin, forbid, outlaw 7 inhibit 9 interdict

prohibited
5 taboo 6 banned 7 illegal, illicit 8 verboten 9 forbidden

project
3 jut, see 4 cast, feat, gest, plan, poke, pout 5 bulge, chart, image, pouch, thing, think 6 affair, beetle, design, devise, extend, intend, matter, scheme, vision 7 arrange, concern, diagram, dope out, emprise, exploit, feature, imagine, prolong, propose, purpose, venture 8 business, conceive, envisage, envision, game plan, lengthen, overhang, protrude, stand out, stick out, strategy 9 adventure, blueprint, delineate, visualize 10 enterprise 11 proposition, undertaking
trivial: 10 boondoggle

projecting
7 salient

projection
3 jut 4 bump, hook, knob, spur 5 bulge, bunch, ledge, point, spine

8 eminence, forecast, salience, swelling 9 extension, outthrust 10 prominence, protrusion

projet
4 plan 5 draft

proletariat
3 mob 4 mass 6 rabble 7 workers 8 canaille, laborers

prolific
4 rich 6 fecund 7 fertile 8 breeding, childing, fruitful, spawning, swarming 9 abounding 10 generating, productive 11 propagating, reproducing 12 reproductive

prolix
5 windy, wordy 7 diffuse, irksome, tedious, verbose 8 tiresome 9 prolonged, redundant, wearisome 10 long-winded, palaverous, protracted

prolixity
9 verbalism, verbosity, windiness, wordiness 11 verboseness

prologue
5 proem 7 preface, prelude 8 exordium, foreword, overture, preamble 9 prelusion 12 introduction, prolegomenon

prolong
4 draw, last 6 endure, extend 7 draw out, persist, spin out, stretch 8 continue, elongate, lengthen, protract

prolonged
4 long 7 lengthy 8 dragging, drawn-out, longsome, overlong 10 protracted

promenade
4 deck, walk 5 dance 6 parade, stroll 7 balcony, gallery 9 boardwalk

Prometheus
brother: 5 Atlas 9 Menoetius 10 Epimetheus
creation: 3 man
father: 7 Iapetus
gift to man: 4 fire
mother: 7 Clymene
rescuer: 8 Heracles, Hercules

prominence
6 renown 8 eminence, prestige, salience 10 importance, projection 11 distinction
combining form: 8 tubercul 9 tuberculo

prominent
5 famed, great, noted 6 famous, marked, signal 7 eminent, leading,

notable, popular, salient 8 renowned, striking 9 arresting, arrestive, notorious, well-known 10 celebrated, celebrious, noticeable, remarkable 11 conspicuous, illustrious, outstanding 13 distinguished
person: 3 VIP 6 bigwig 7 grandee

promiscuous
5 mixed 6 motley, random, varied 7 aimless 8 assorted, chowchow 9 desultory, haphazard, hit-or-miss, irregular, unplanned 10 designless 11 purposeless

promise
3 vow 4 bode, oath, omen, pass, pawn, word 5 agree, augur, swear, token 6 accede, assent, assure, engage, ensure, insure, pledge, plight 7 bargain, betoken, compact, consent, earnest, portend, presage, warrant 8 contract, covenant, forebode, foreshow, security 9 assurance, foretoken, guarantee, undertake

promised land
4 Zion 6 Canaan, heaven, utopia 7 arcadia 8 paradise 9 cockaigne, fairyland, shangri-la 10 lubberland, wonderland

promising
4 rosy 6 likely 7 hopeful, roseate 11 encouraging, rose-colored

promissory note
3 IOU

promontory
4 beak, bill, cape, head, naze, peak 5 point 8 foreland, headland

promote
3 aid, cry 4 help, plug, puff, push 5 boost, serve 6 foster, impart, prefer 7 advance, build up, elevate, forward, further, upgrade 8 ballyhoo 9 advertise, encourage, publicize 10 press-agent

promoter
5 agent

promotion
7 advance, buildup, puffery 9 elevation, prelation, publicity, upgrading 10 preference, preferment 11 advancement, advertising 13 advertisement

prompt
3 apt, cue, get, sic 4 draw, fast, goad, prod, spur, urge 5 alert, egg on, prick, quick, rapid, ready, swift 6 exhort, induce, propel, speedy, timely 7 win over 8 convince, persuade, punctual, talk into

promulgate
4 toot 5 sound 7 declare, publish 8 announce, proclaim 9 advertise, broadcast 10 annunciate 11 disseminate

prone
3 apt 4 fain, flat, open 5 given, level, ready 6 liable, likely, minded, supine 7 exposed, subject, willing 8 disposed, inclined, resupine 9 decumbent, obnoxious, prostrate, reclining, recumbent, sensitive 11 predisposed, susceptible

prong
3 nib 4 fang, fork, stab, tine 5 point

pronghorn
6 cabree 8 antelope

pronoun
archaic: 2 ye 3 thy 4 thou 5 thine
demonstrative: 4 that, this 5 these, those
indefinite: 3 all, any, few, one 4 both, each, none, some 5 no one, other 6 anyone, either, nobody 7 another, anybody, neither, nothing, someone 8 anything, somebody 9 everybody, something 10 everything
personal: 2 he, it, my, we 3 her, him, his, its, our, she, you 4 hers, mine, ours, them, they, your 5 their, yours 6 theirs
possessive: 2 my 3 her, his, its, our 4 hers, mine, ours, your 5 their, yours 6 theirs
reflexive: 6 itself, myself 7 herself, himself, oneself, ourself 8 yourself 9 ourselves 10 themselves, yourselves
relative: 3 who 4 that, what, whom 5 which, whose, whoso 6 whomso 7 whoever 8 whatever, whomever 9 whichever, whosoever 10 whatsoever, whomsoever 11 whichsoever

pronounce
3 say 5 speak, utter 6 recite 7 declare, phonate 9 enunciate 10 articulate

pronounced
7 assured, decided 8 clear-cut, definite

pronouncement
9 statement 11 declaration, publication 12 proclamation, promulgation

pronto
4 fast 6 at once 7 quickly

8 promptly **9** posthaste
11 immediately

pronunciation
6 speech **9** utterance
distinctive: **4** burr **5** drawl, twang
6 accent
study: **8** orthoepy **9** phonetics

proof
4 test **6** galley **8** argument, evidence **9** testament, testimony
10 impression **11** attestation
12 confirmation

proofreaders' mark
3 cap, rom **4** dele, ital, stet **5** caret

prop
3 leg **4** stay **5** brace, carry, shore
6 bear up, buoy up, column, upbear, uphold **7** bolster, shore up, support, sustain **8** buttress
12 underpinning

propaganda
4 hype **8** agitprop **9** publicity

propagandist
7 apostle **9** missioner **10** colporteur, evangelist, missionary

propagate
4 bear, grow **5** beget, breed, raise, strew **6** spread **7** diffuse, produce, radiate **8** disperse, generate, multiply **9** circulate, cultivate, procreate, reproduce **10** distribute
11 disseminate

propel
4 goad, move, prod, push, spur, urge **5** drive, egg on, impel, power, prick, shove **6** exhort, prompt, thrust **7** actuate

propellant
4 fuel, spur **7** impetus, impulse
8 catalyst, stimulus **9** incentive, stimulant **10** incitation, motivation
11 provocative

propeller
3 fan, oar **5** screw **6** paddle

propensity
see **penchant**

proper
3 apt, due, fit **4** able, good, just, meet, nice, prig, prim, true **5** exact, happy, right **6** au fait, comely, decent, prissy, stuffy, useful **7** capable, correct, desired, fitting, genteel, missish, precise, prudish
8 accurate, becoming, decorous, peculiar, priggish, rightful, rigorous, suitable **9** befitting, competent, diacritic, qualified **10** applicable, conforming, convenient, diagnostic,

felicitous, individual **11** appropriate, comme il faut, distinctive, puritanical, straitlaced
combining form: **4** orth **5** ortho

property
4 land, mark **5** trait, worth **6** estate, realty, riches, virtue, wealth
7 feature, fortune, quality **8** dominion **9** affection, attribute, character, ownership, resources, substance
10 possession, real estate
conveyor: **7** alienor
private: **8** peculium
recipient: **7** alienee
seller: **7** Realtor
transfer: **8** alienate

prophecy
4 cast **5** weird **6** oracle, vision
8 forecast **9** prevision, prognosis
10 apocalypse, prediction, revelation **11** foretelling

prophesier
4 seer **5** augur **6** auspex
7 prophet **8** foreseer, haruspex
9 predictor **10** forecaster, foreteller
11 Nostradamus

prophesy
5 augur **7** portend, predict, presage **8** forecast, foretell, soothsay
9 adumbrate **10** vaticinate
13 prognosticate

prophet
4 seer **5** augur **6** auspex, oracle
7 seeress **8** foreseer, haruspex
9 predictor **10** forecaster, foreteller, prophesier, soothsayer
11 Nostradamus
Arthurian: **6** Merlin
Major: **6** Daniel, Isaiah **7** Ezekiel
8 Jeremiah
Minor: **4** Amos, Joel **5** Hosea, Jonah, Micah, Nahum **6** Haggai
7 Malachi, Obadiah **8** Habakkuk
9 Zechariah, Zephaniah

prophetess
4 Anna **5** Sibyl **6** Huldah, Miriam
7 Deborah, Noadiah **9** Cassandra

prophetic
5 vatic **6** mantic, mystic **7** fatidic, strange, vatical **8** Delphian, oracular **9** sibylline, vaticinal **10** mysterious, revelatory **11** apocalyptic, prophetical

propinquity
7 kinship **8** nearness **9** closeness, immediacy, proximity **10** contiguity

propitiate
5 adapt, atone **6** adjust, pacify
7 appease, assuage, conform, con-

tent, mediate, mollify, placate, satisfy, sweeten **9** intercede, reconcile
10 conciliate

propitiatory
7 lustral **9** expiative, expiatory, purgative

propitious
4 good, rosy **5** brave, white **6** benign, bright, dexter, timely, toward, useful **7** benefic, helpful, timeous
8 favoring **9** favorable, fortunate, opportune, well-timed **10** auspicious, beneficial, prosperous, seasonable **12** advantageous

proponent
6 backer **8** advocate, champion
9 expounder, supporter

proportion
4 rate, size, tune **5** ratio, scale
6 attune, degree, extent **7** balance, conform, harmony, measure, prorate **8** symmetry

proportional
5 equal **7** in scale **8** relative
9 dependent **10** contingent, reciprocal **11** correlative, symmetrical
12 commensurate **13** commensurable, corresponding

proposal
3 bid **4** idea, plan **6** motion, scheme **7** outline, proffer, project
10 invitation, suggestion
11 proposition
final: **9** ultimatum

propose
3 aim, ask, put **4** mean, plan, pose
5 offer **6** design, intend, prefer, submit, tender **7** move for, present, purpose, request, solicit, suggest
8 nominate, propound, theorize
11 contemplate

proposition
3 put **4** pose **5** lemma, offer **6** prefer, thesis **7** premise, proffer, propose, suggest, theorem **8** proposal, propound **10** invitation, suggestion

propound
3 put **4** pose **6** prefer **7** propone, propose, suggest **11** proposition

proprietor
5 owner **6** holder **9** possessor

propriety
5 order **6** manner **7** aptness, decency, decorum, dignity, fitness
8 meetness **9** etiquette, rightness
10 expediency, properness, seemliness **11** correctness, orderliness, suitability **12** appositeness, cor-

rectitude, decorousness, suitableness

propulsion
4 fuel, push 5 drive, power

prorate
5 allot, divvy, quota, share 6 divide, parcel, ration 7 portion
9 apportion

prorogate
see **prorogue**

prorogue
4 rise, stay 5 defer, delay, remit
6 hold up, put off, recess, shelve
7 adjourn, hold off 8 dissolve, hold over, postpone 9 prorogate, terminate

prosaic
4 drab, dull, flat 5 lowly, prose, prosy 6 actual, boring, common
7 factual, irksome, literal, mundane, tedious, workday 8 everyday, lifeless, ordinary, workaday 9 colorless, practical 10 lackluster, lusterless, uneventful 11 commonplace

proscenium
5 stage 9 forestage 10 foreground

proscribe
3 ban 4 damn, doom 7 condemn
8 prohibit, sentence

proscription
3 ban 5 taboo 11 forbiddance, prohibition 12 interdiction

prosecute
3 sue 5 press 6 charge, indict

prosecutor
2 DA 6 lawyer 7 accuser
public: 6 fiscal

proselyte
7 convert, recruit 8 neophyte

____ prosequi
5 nolle

prospect
4 mine, sift 5 probe, scape, vista
6 go into 7 dig into, explore, lookout, outlook 8 look into
9 candidate

prosper
3 dow 4 boom 5 score, yield 6 arrive, thrive 7 augment, make out, produce, succeed, turn out 8 flourish, increase

prosperity
4 boom, ease 6 growth, riches, wealth 7 arrival, benefit, success, welfare 8 interest, thriving 9 abundance, advantage, affluence, ex-

pansion, inflation, well-being
10 easy street 12 flying colors

Prospero
daughter: 7 Miranda
servant: 5 Ariel
slave: 7 Caliban

prosperous
4 easy, rich, well 5 happy, lucky, lusty, palmy 6 robust, strong, timely
7 booming, halcyon, opulent, roaring, thrifty, timeous, wealthy, well-off 8 affluent, thriving, well-to-do
9 desirable, favorable, fortunate, opportune, well-fixed, well-timed
10 auspicious, convenient, felicitous, propitious, seasonable, successful, well-heeled 11 appropriate, comfortable, flourishing, substantial

prostitute
4 bawd, doxy, drab, moll 5 abuse, madam, poule, quean, whore
6 callet, debase, harlot, hooker, misuse, pickup, tomato, wanton
7 cocotte, corrupt, cruiser, Cyprian, debauch, deprave, hustler, joy girl, Paphian, vitiate 8 call girl, meretrix, misapply, strumpet 9 cocodette, misemploy, mishandle, party girl 10 misimprove, street girl
11 fille de joie, nightwalker
12 camp follower, streetwalker
reformed: 8 Magdalen

prostitution
8 harlotry, whoredom 10 social evil
13 streetwalking
house of: 7 brothel 8 bordello

prostrate
4 down, drop, fell, flat, poop
5 floor, level, prone, whelm 6 disarm, ground, lay low, tucker 7 cripple, disable, exhaust, frazzle, outtire, outwear, wear out 8 knock out, overcome, paralyze 9 decumbent, knock over, overpower, overwhelm, reclining, recumbent, throw down

protagonist
4 hero, star 5 actor 6 leader 8 advocate, champion 9 spokesman

protean
5 fluid 6 mobile 7 mutable 8 unstable, unsteady, variable, weathery
9 changeful, unsettled
10 changeable

protect
4 fend, save 5 cover, guard 6 defend, harbor, screen, secure, shield

7 bulwark, shelter 8 conserve, preserve 9 safeguard

protected
4 safe 6 immune

protection
3 pad 4 ward 5 aegis, armor, bribe, graft, guard 6 safety, shield
7 defense, squeeze 8 armament, security 9 extortion, safeguard, shakedown

protector
5 armor, guard 6 patron, shield
7 tutelar 8 guardian

protégé
4 ward 5 pupil 7 student

protein
4 zein 5 actin, opsin 6 avidin, enzyme, fibrin, globin 7 albumin, elastin, fibroin, histone, keratin, legumin, sericin 8 creatine, globulin, glutelin, prolamin, protamin, proteose, vitellin
complex: 6 mucoid
derivative: 7 peptone
poisonous: 5 abrin, ricin
source: 4 eggs, fish, meat, milk
6 cheese

pro tem
6 acting, supply 7 interim 9 ad interim, temporary 10 pro tempore

protest
4 aver, avow, kick 5 demur, fight
6 affirm, assert, avouch, combat, depose, except, object, oppose, picket, resist 7 declare, profess
8 constate, demurral, demurrer
9 challenge, objection

Protestant
5 Amish 6 Mormon, Quaker, Shaker 7 Baptist, Lollard, Pilgrim, Puritan 8 Anglican, Lutheran, Moravian 9 Adventist, Mennonite, Methodist, Unitarian 12 Episcopalian, Presbyterian
Bohemian: 7 Hussite
dissenter: 7 sectary
French: 8 Huguenot
martyr: (see at **martyr**)

prototypal
see **prototypical**

prototype
5 model 8 ancestor, foregoer, original 9 archetype, precursor
10 antecedent, antecessor, forerunner, protoplast 11 predecessor

prototypical
5 ideal, model 7 classic 9 classical, exemplary 10 archetypal

protozoan

4 cell 5 ameba 6 amoeba 7 arcella, ciliate, stentor 10 flagellate, paramecium

protract

see **prolong**

protrude

3 jut 4 poke, pout 5 bulge, pouch 6 beetle 7 project 8 overhang, stand out, stick out

protrusion

3 jut, nub 4 bump, hump 5 bulge 8 eminence, swelling 9 outthrust 10 projection 12 protuberance

protuberance

see **protrusion**

protuberate

see **protrude**

proud

4 vain 5 huffy, lofty, noble, wiggy 6 lordly, stuffy, superb 7 bloated, haughty, pompous, stuck-up, sublime 8 arrogant, cavalier, glorious, gorgeous, insolent, misproud, orgulous, scornful, splendid, superior, toplofty 9 conceited, hubristic, imperious, important, masterful 10 disdainful, dismissive, high-handed 11 domineering, magnificent, overbearing, pretentious, resplendent, splendorous, toploftical 12 contemptuous, narcissistic, ostentatious, proudhearted, supercilious

prove

3 try 4 show, test 5 argue, check 6 attest, verify 7 bespeak, betoken, confirm, examine, make out 8 document, indicate 9 determine, establish 11 corroborate, demonstrate 12 substantiate

provenance

4 root, well 6 origin, source, whence 8 fountain 9 inception 10 derivation, wellspring 11 provenience

provender

see **provisions**

provenience

see **provenance**

proverb

3 saw 4 word 5 adage, axiom, maxim 6 byword, saying

provide

4 feed, give, hand 5 cater, endow, equip 6 afford, supply 7 deliver, furnish, support 8 dispense, hand over, maintain

provided

2 if 6 if only 8 equipped

providence

6 thrift 7 caution, economy 8 prudence 9 canniness, foresight, frugality, husbandry 10 discretion, precaution 11 forethought, thriftiness 12 discreetness

provident

5 canny, chary 6 frugal, saving, Scotch 7 sparing, thrifty 9 stewardly 10 economical, unwasteful

providential

4 kind, well 5 happy, lucky 6 kindly 9 benignant, fortunate

province

4 area, duty, role, walk, work 5 field 6 domain, office, sphere 7 calling, demesne, pursuit, terrain 8 business, district, dominion, function 9 bailiwick, champaign, territory 10 department
Greek: 4 nome 8 nomarchy

provincial

4 hick, jake, rube 5 clown, local, rural 6 rustic 7 bigoted, bucolic, bumpkin, country, hayseed, insular, outland, peasant 8 agrestic, pastoral 9 hidebound, parochial, sectarian, small-town 10 campestral, out-country 11 countrified

provision

4 term 6 clause 7 proviso, strings 9 condition 11 reservation, stipulation

provisional

4 iffy 7 stopgap 9 dependent, makeshift, provisory, temporary, tentative 10 contingent 11 conditional 13 rough-and-ready

provisions

4 feed, food, grub 6 viands 7 edibles, nurture 8 supplies, victuals 9 provender 11 comestibles
dealer: 8 chandler

proviso

see **provision**

provocation

6 irking, vexing 8 vexation 9 annoyance, bothering, provoking 10 harassment

provocative

4 goad, push, spur 7 impetus, impulse 8 stimulus 9 incentive 10 incitation, incitement, motivation 11 challenging

provoke

3 bug, get, irk, vex 4 abet, fire, fret, gall, move, rile, roil, stir, wake, whet 5 anger, annoy, breed, cause, chafe, exalt, get up, grate, hatch, pique, prime, raise, rally, rouse, set on, upset, waken 6 abrade, arouse, awaken, bestir, bother, excite, foment, harass, incite, induce, inform, insult, kindle, madden, put out, ruffle, stir up, thrill, whip up 7 animate, build up, enthuse, incense, inflame, innerve, inspire, outrage, perturb, produce, quicken 8 engender, exercise, generate, irritate, motivate, muster up, occasion, titivate 9 aggravate, challenge, electrify, galvanize, innervate, instigate, stimulate, titillate

provost

4 head 6 keeper 7 marshal 8 director 13 administrator

prow

3 bow 4 beak, stem 5 front

prowess

5 skill, valor 7 address, heroism, sleight 8 deftness, valiance, valiancy 9 dexterity, gallantry, readiness 10 adroitness 12 valorousness 13 dexterousness

prowl

4 hunt, pace, roam 5 creep 6 wander

proximate

4 near, next, nigh, rude 5 close, rough 6 nearby 8 imminent 9 immediate, impending 10 near-at-hand

proximity

8 nearness, vicinity 9 adjacency, closeness, immediacy 10 contiguity 11 propinquity 12 togetherness

proxy

5 agent, power 6 deputy, factor 8 assignee, attorney 9 authority

prude

4 prig 6 Grundy 7 old fogy, old maid, Puritan 8 bluenose, comstock 9 Mrs. Grundy, nice Nelly 10 fuddy-duddy, fuss-budget, goody-goody, spoilsport, wet blanket 12 stuffed shirt

prudence

3 wit 6 acumen, thrift, wisdom 7 caution, economy, insight 8 astucity, keenness, sagacity, sageness, sapience 9 canniness, chariness, foresight, frugality, husbandry

10 astuteness, discretion, expediency, precaution, providence, shrewdness 11 calculation, forethought, penetration, percipience, thriftiness 12 discreetness, perspicacity

prudent

4 sage, sane, wary, wise 5 canny, chary 7 politic, sapient 8 cautious, sensible, tactical 9 advisable, expedient, judicious

prudish

4 prim 5 stern 6 prissy, proper, severe, strict, stuffy 7 austere, genteel 8 priggish 9 Victorian 11 puritanical, straitlaced

prune

3 cut, lop 4 clip, crop, dolt, dope, pare, plum, thin, trim 5 brash, chump, dunce, fruit, idiot, moron, shave, shear, skive

prurience

4 itch, lust 6 desire 7 passion 9 eroticism 11 lustfulness 13 concupiscence

prurient

3 hot 4 lewd 5 bawdy 6 erotic 7 goatish, lustful, satyric, sensual 9 lickerish 10 lascivious, libidinous, passionate 12 concupiscent

pruritic

5 itchy

Prussian

aristocrat: 6 Junker 12 Hohenzollern
prime minister: 8 Bismarck (Otto von)
ruler: 7 Wilhelm 9 Frederick

pry

4 lift, nose, open, peek, poke, rear, turn 5 hoist, jimmy, lever, mouse, prize, raise, snoop, twist 6 divide, pick up, take up, uphold, uplift, uprear 7 crowbar, disjoin, elevate, upraise 8 busybody, separate

psalm

3 ode 4 hymn, laud, poem, song 5 cry up, extol 6 praise 7 glorify, magnify 8 eulogize 9 celebrate
book: 7 psalter
selection: 6 hallel
word: 5 selah

psalmist

4 poet 5 Asaph, David 6 cantor

pseudo

4 fake, mock, sham 5 bogus, false, phony, snide, wrong 8 spurious 9 brummagem, pinchbeck 11 counterfeit

pseudonym

5 alias 6 ananym, anonym 7 pen name 9 incognito, stage name 10 nom de plume 11 nom de guerre; (see also **pen name**)

psyche

4 mind, soul 5 anima 6 animus, pneuma, spirit 9 élan vital 10 vital force
part: 2 id 3 ego 8 superego

Psyche's beloved

4 Eros 5 Cupid

psychiatrist

6 shrink
American: 9 Menninger (Karl)
Austrian: 5 Adler (Alfred)
Swiss: 4 Jung (Carl) 9 Rorschach (Hermann)

psychic

6 mental 7 sensile 8 cerebral, sensible, sentient 9 sensitive, spiritual 10 responsive, susceptive, telepathic 11 impressible, susceptible 12 intellective, intellectual, supersensory 13 psychological
American: 5 Cayce (Edgar)
power: 3 ESP

psychoanalyst

5 Freud (Sigmund), Fromm (Erich) 6 Horney (Karen)

psychological

6 mental 7 psychic 8 cerebral 9 psychical 12 intellective, intellectual

psychologist

6 shrink
American: 3 May (Rollo) 5 James (William) 6 Rogers (Carl), Terman (Lewis), Watson (John), Yerkes (Robert) 7 Skinner (Burrhus Frederic) 8 Brothers (Joyce) 9 Thorndike (Edward Lee)
English: 4 Ward (James) 8 Spearman (Charles), Tichener (Edward)
German: 5 Wundt (Wilhelm) 6 Muller (Georg), Stumpf (Carl) 10 Wertheimer (Max)
Swiss: 4 Jung (Carl) 6 Piaget (Jean)

psychopathy

6 lunacy 7 madness 8 insanity 9 unbalance 10 aberration, alienation, insaneness 11 derangement, distraction

psychotic

3 mad 5 crazy 6 insane 8 schizoid

ptarmigan

6 grouse

ptomaine

6 poison

pub

3 bar, inn 6 tavern 7 barroom, rummery, taproom 8 drinkery, groggery, grogshop

puberty

5 youth 6 spring 9 greenness, youthhood 10 juvenility, pubescence, springtide, springtime 11 adolescence
combining form: 4 hebe

public

4 open 5 civic, civil, joint, state, suite, urban 6 common, mutual, people, shared, vulgar 7 general, popular, society 8 audience, communal, conjoint, conjunct, national, open-door 9 clientage, clientele, community, following, hangers-on, municipal, prevalent, universal 10 accessible, government, widespread 11 intermutual

publican

8 boniface, taverner 9 barkeeper, collector, innholder, innkeeper, saloonist 12 saloonkeeper, tax collector

publication

4 book 5 paper 7 journal 8 magazine, pamphlet 9 broadcast, newspaper 10 periodical 11 declaration
list: 12 bibliography

public house

3 inn 5 hotel, lodge 6 hostel, tavern 7 auberge, hospice 8 hostelry 9 road-house 11 caravansary

publicity

4 hype, plug, puff 5 blurb 6 hoopla 7 buildup, puffery, réclame, write-up 8 ballyhoo, hard sell 9 promotion 11 advertising 12 announcement

publicize

3 cry 4 hype, plug, puff, push, tout 5 boost, bruit, extol 7 advance, build up, promote, trumpet 8 announce, headline, skywrite 9 advertise, broadcast 10 press-agent, promulgate 11 circularize 12 propagandize

publish

3 air 4 toot, vent 5 issue, print, utter 6 broach, get out, market, put out 7 declare, express, produce 8 announce, bring out, proclaim 9 advertise, broadcast, ventilate 10 annunciate, distribute, promulgate 11 blaze abroad, disseminate

publisher
6 editor 7 printer 10 journalist

Puccini, Giacomo
heroine: 4 Mimi
opera: 5 Edgar, Tosca 7 Le Villi
8 La Bohème, Turandot 12 Manon
Lescaut, Suor Angelica

puck
3 elf, imp 4 disk 5 fairy 6 spirit,
sprite 9 hobgoblin, prankster

pucker
4 fold 5 purse 6 cockle 7 wrinkle
8 contract

puckish
5 antic 6 impish, wicked 7 larkish,
playful, roguish, waggish 8 prankish, sportive 11 mischievous

Puck's master
6 Oberon

pudding
4 duff 6 burgoo 7 custard, dessert,
tapioca
baked: 10 brown Betty

pudgy
5 plump, round, squab, tubby
6 chubby, plumpy, rotund, squdgy,
stumpy 8 plumpish, roly-poly
10 roundabout

pueblo
4 town 7 village 8 dwelling
ceremonial room: 4 kiva

puerile
6 boyish 7 babyish 8 childish,
immature

Puerto Rico
capital: 7 San Juan
discoverer: 8 Columbus (Christopher)

puff
3 cry 4 blow, brag, crow, drag,
draw, gasp, huff, pant, plug, pouf,
pull, push 5 blurb, boast, boost,
heave, mouth, prate, quilt, vaunt
6 praise 7 build up, puffing, write-
up 8 inhaling 9 advertise, comforter, gasconade, laudation,
publicize

puffer
8 blowfish 9 globefish

puffery
7 buildup 9 promotion, publicity
11 advertising 12 press-agentry

puffin
4 bird 9 sea parrot 10 shearwater

puff up
5 bloat, swell 7 inflate

puffy
5 wiggy 6 stuffy 7 bloated, pompous 8 arrogant 9 important

10 pontifical 11 magisterial 13 self-
important

pug
3 bun, dog 4 nose 5 boxer, track
9 footprint

pugilism
4 ring 6 boxing 10 fisticuffs
13 prizefighting

pugilist
5 boxer 7 fighter

pugnacious
5 pushy 7 defiant, pushing,
scrappy, warlike 8 brawling, militant 9 bellicose, combative, truculent 10 rebellious 11 belligerent,
contentious, quarrelsome

pugnacity
5 fight 6 attack 10 aggression
12 belligerence 13 combativeness

puisne
5 judge, later 6 junior 9 associate

puissance
4 sway 5 clout, force, might,
power, sinew, vigor 6 energy, muscle, virtue 7 potency 8 strength
9 influence

puissant
6 mighty, potent, ruling, strong
8 forceful, forcible, powerful
10 commanding

pukka
4 real, true 5 right 7 genuine
8 bona fide 9 authentic, simon-pure

pule
3 cry 5 whine 7 whimper

Pulitzer Prize winner, fiction
1918: 5 Poole (Ernest)
1919: 10 Tarkington (Booth)
1921: 7 Wharton (Edith)
1922: 10 Tarkington (Booth)
1923: 6 Cather (Willa)
1924: 6 Wilson (Margaret)
1925: 6 Ferber (Edna)
1926: 5 Lewis (Sinclair)
1927: 9 Bromfield (Louis)
1928: 6 Wilder (Thornton)
1929: 8 Peterkin (Julia)
1930: 7 La Farge (Oliver)
1931: 6 Barnes (Margaret)
1932: 4 Buck (Pearl)
1933: 9 Stribling (Thomas
Sigismund)
1934: 6 Miller (Caroline)
1935: 7 Johnson (Josephine)
1936: 5 Davis (Harold)
1937: 8 Mitchell (Margaret)
1938: 8 Marquand (John)
1939: 8 Rawlings (Marjorie Kinnan)
1940: 9 Steinbeck (John)
1942: 7 Glasgow (Ellen)

1943: 8 Sinclair (Upton)
1944: 6 Flavin (Martin)
1945: 6 Hersey (John)
1947: 6 Warren (Robert Penn)
1948: 8 Michener (James)
1949: 7 Cozzens (James Gould)
1950: 7 Guthrie (Alfred Bertram)
1951: 7 Richter (Conrad)
1952: 4 Wouk (Herman)
1953: 9 Hemingway (Ernest)
1955: 8 Faulkner (William)
1956: 6 Kantor (MacKinlay)
1958: 4 Agee (James)
1959: 6 Taylor (Robert Lewis)
1960: 5 Drury (Allen)
1961: 3 Lee (Harper)
1962: 7 O'Connor (Edwin)
1963: 8 Faulkner (William)
1965: 4 Grau (Shirley Ann)
1966: 6 Porter (Katherine Anne)
1967: 7 Malamud (Bernard)
1968: 6 Styron (William)
1969: 7 Momaday (N. Scott)
1970: 8 Stafford (Jean)
1972: 7 Stegner (Wallace)
1973: 5 Welty (Eudora)
1975: 6 Shaara (Michael)
1976: 6 Bellow (Saul)
1978: 9 McPherson (James Alan)
1979: 7 Cheever (John)
1980: 6 Mailer (Norman)
1981: 5 Toole (John Kennedy)
1982: 6 Updike (John)
1983: 6 Walker (Alice)
1984: 7 Kennedy (William)
1985: 5 Lurie (Alison)
1986: 8 McMurtry (Larry)
1987: 6 Taylor (Peter)
1988: 8 Morrison (Toni)
1989: 5 Tyler (Anne)
1990: 8 Hijuelos (Oscar)
1991: 6 Updike (John)
1992: 6 Smiley (Jane)
1993: 6 Butler (Robert Olen)
1994: 6 Proulx (E. Annie)
1995: 7 Shields (Carol)

pull
3 don, get, lug, oar, row, tow, tug,
win 4 drag, draw, gain, haul,
have, jerk, land, lure, puff, push,
tear, yank 5 clout, drive, heave, impel, put on, shove 6 appeal, assume, commit, evulse, obtain, paddle, pick up, secure, strain, strike,
take on, wrench 7 chalk up, extract, procure 9 influence, seduction 10 allurement, attraction, perpetrate, persuasion 12 drawing
power

pull down
4 raze, ruin 5 wreck 7 destroy
8 decimate, demolish, destruct, tear
down 9 dismantle 10 annihilate

pullet
3 hen

pulley
5 wheel 6 sheave
watch's: 5 fusee, fuzee

pull in
3 bit, nab 4 curb 5 check, pinch, run in 6 arrest, bridle, detain, hold in, pick up 7 inhibit 8 hold back, hold down, restrain

pulling
8 traction
cable for: 7 towline

Pullman
3 car 7 sleeper

pull out
4 exit, quit 5 leave, pluck 6 depart, get off, retire 7 retreat, take off 8 shove off, withdraw

pull through
7 recover, ride out, survive

pullulate
4 flow, teem 5 crawl, swarm 6 abound

pull up
4 halt, stop 6 draw up, haul up

pulp
4 mash, pith 5 crush 6 bruise, squash 7 bagasse, becrush

pulpit
4 ambo 7 lectern 8 ministry, platform
Muslim: 6 minbar

pulsate
4 beat, drum, pump, roar 5 pound, throb, thrum 7 vibrate 9 fluctuate, oscillate, palpitate

pulse
4 beat 5 throb 6 rhythm
combining form: 6 crotic 7 sphygmo
relating to: 8 sphygmic

pulverize
4 beat, bray, buck, mill, mull, ruin 5 crush, flour, grate, grind, smash, wreck 6 abrade, crunch, powder, rub out 7 atomize, break up, crumble, destroy, shatter, smatter 8 decimate, demolish, destruct, dynamite, fragment, levigate, splinter, tear down 9 comminute, micronize, triturate 11 fragmentize 12 contriturate

puma
3 cat 6 cougar

pumice
5 glass, stone

pummel
4 beat, drub, pelt 5 pound 6 batter, buffet, hammer, thrash, wallop 7 belabor

pump
3 tap 4 draw, shoe 5 draft, drain 6 siphon 7 draw off, syringe

pumpernickel
3 rye 5 bread

pumpkin
4 pepo 5 fruit 6 cushaw, squash 12 jack-o'-lantern

pun
4 joke 9 calembour, equivoque 11 paronomasia

punch
3 box, dig, hit, jab, jog, pep 4 bang, bore, cuff, poke, prod, push, slap, snap, sock, stab 5 clout, drill, drive, force, getup, nudge, paste, point, prick, smack, vigor 6 buffet, starch, strike 7 cogency 8 puncture, uppercut, validity, vitality 9 perforate, validness 13 effectiveness

punch bowl
8 monteith

puncheon
4 tool 5 stamp

puncher
5 boxer 6 cowboy

Punch's wife
4 Judy

punctilious
4 nice 5 exact, fussy 6 formal 7 careful, heedful 8 punctual 9 observant 10 meticulous, scrupulous 11 painstaking

punctual
5 exact, fussy, quick, ready 6 prompt, timely 7 careful, heedful 10 meticulous

punctuate
4 mark 5 point 6 divide 8 separate

punctuation mark
4 dash 5 brace, colon, comma 6 hyphen, parens, period 7 bracket, virgule 8 diagonal, ellipsis 9 semicolon 10 apostrophe 11 parenthesis

puncture
3 jab 4 bore, hole, stab 5 drill, prick, punch, shoot 6 blow up, riddle 7 explode 8 disprove 9 discredit, perforate 11 perforation
surgical: 8 centesis

pundit
4 sage 5 swami 6 critic 7 teacher

pungency
4 tang, zest 8 piquancy

pungent
3 hot 4 keen, racy, rich, salt 5 acute, salty, sharp, spicy, tangy, zesty 6 biting, bitter, snappy 7 cutting, peppery, piquant 8 exciting, incisive, poignant 9 trenchant 11 provocative, stimulating

punish
3 fix 4 fine, whip 5 mulct, shift, swill 6 amerce, avenge 7 chasten, consume, correct, put away, put down, reprove, revenge, scourge, torture 8 chastise, lambaste, penalize 9 castigate, criticize, polish off 10 discipline

punishment
3 rod 4 fine 5 mulct 7 penalty, reproof, revenge 8 punition 9 criticism 10 amercement, avengement, correction, discipline 11 castigation 12 chastisement
Scottish: 6 dirdum

punitive
5 penal 8 punitory 9 punishing 11 castigating 12 correctional, disciplinary

punk
4 bosh, colt, hood, thug 5 rough, rowdy, tough, yahoo 6 bunkum, hot air, mucker, novice, rookie 7 baloney, hogwash, hoodlum, ruffian, toughie 8 beginner, bullyboy, claptrap, neophyte, newcomer, nonsense 9 fledgling, novitiate, roughneck 10 apprentice, balderdash

punt
4 boat, kick

puny
4 weak 5 frail, petty 6 feeble, infirm, measly, paltry, sickly, weakly 7 fragile, trivial, unsound 8 decrepit, niggling, picayune, piddling, trifling 10 picayunish

pupa
9 chrysalid, chrysalis

pupil
5 cadet, tutee 7 learner, scholar, student 8 disciple
French: 5 élève

puppet
4 doll, dupe, pawn, tool 5 slave 6 stooge 7 cat's-paw

puppy
3 dog 5 whelp

Purcell opera
13 Dido and Aeneas

purchase
3 buy 4 take 6 obtain 7 acquire
11 acquisition

purchaser
4 user 5 buyer 6 client, emptor, patron, vendee 7 shopper 8 consumer, customer

pure
4 good, neat 5 clean, fresh, gross, plain, sheer, total, utter 6 chaste, decent, modest, simple 7 blasted, blessed, classic, genuine, perfect, plenary, sinless, unmixed 8 absolute, complete, infernal, innocent, spotless, straight, virtuous 9 authentic, blameless, exemplary, guiltless, inviolate, out-and-out, righteous, stainless, unalloyed, undefiled, undiluted, unsullied 10 confounded, immaculate, inculpable, unblamable, unblighted, unprofaned 11 unblemished, unmitigated, unqualified 13 unadulterated

purebred
8 pedigree 9 pedigreed 10 registered 11 full-blooded
12 thoroughbred

puree
4 soup 5 paste

purely
3 all 4 just 5 quite 6 in toto, wholly 7 exactly, totally, utterly 8 all in all 10 altogether

purfle
4 trim 6 border 8 decorate, ornament

purgation
9 catharsis, cleansing 10 lustration

purgative
5 jalap 7 lustral 9 cathartic, expiatory

purge
3 rid 4 oust 5 clear, debar, eject, erase, expel 6 purify, remove 7 absolve, cleanse, dismiss, exclude, expunge, shut out, wipe out 8 disabuse, lustrate, undelude 9 eliminate, expurgate, liquidate, undeceive 11 exterminate

purification
5 grace 7 rebirth 9 atonement, catharsis, cleansing, expiation, purgation, salvation 10 absolution, lustration, redemption 11 expurgation, forgiveness 12 regeneration
sacrament: 7 baptism

purify
5 atone, clean, purge, remit 6 filter, refine 7 absolve, baptize, clarify, cleanse, expiate 8 depurate, lustrate 9 elutriate, expurgate

Purim
11 Feast of Lots

purist
7 diehard, Puritan 8 Atticist 9 precisian 10 classicist 11 bitter-ender 12 conservative, precisionist

puritan
4 prig 5 prude 6 Grundy 8 bluenose, comstock 9 Mrs. Grundy, nice Nelly

puritanical
4 prim 6 narrow, prissy, strict, stuffy 7 bigoted, genteel, prudish 8 priggish, rigorous 9 blue-nosed, hidebound, illiberal, victorian 10 intolerant, tight-laced 11 strait-laced 12 narrow-minded

purity
8 chastity 9 innocence

purl
4 eddy, knit 5 gurge, swirl, whirl, whorl 6 stitch, swoosh 9 whirlpool

purlieu
5 haunt 6 resort 7 hangout

purlieus
6 bounds, limits 7 compass, suburbs 8 boundary, confines, environs 9 outskirts, precincts

purloin
5 filch, pinch, steal, swipe 6 pilfer, rip off, snitch, thieve 7 cabbage 11 appropriate

purloiner
4 prig 5 thief 6 nimmer 7 filcher, stealer 8 larcener, pilferer 9 larcenist

purple
4 blue, plum, racy 5 broad, grape, lilac, mauve, regal, salty, shady, spicy 6 florid, maroon, murrey, orchid, risqué, turgid, violet, wicked 7 flowery, pompous, stilted 8 lavender, off-color 9 bombastic, high-flown, overblown 10 oratorical, rhetorical, suggestive

Purple Heart
5 award, medal

purport
4 core, gist, meat, pith 5 drift, sense, tenor 6 burden, matter, thrust, upshot 7 meaning, message 9 substance 10 intendment 11 acceptation, connotation, implication 12 significance, significancy

purported
7 alleged, reputed, rumored 8 academic, so-called, supposed 9 pretended, professed, suspected 10 ostensible, postulated 11 presupposed, speculative

purpose
3 aim, use 4 duty, goal, mark, mean, plan 5 point 6 animus, decide, design, intend, intent, object, ponder, target 7 meaning, mission, resolve 8 ambition, conclude, consider, function, meditate, proposal 9 determine, direction, intention, objective 10 aspiration, intendment

purposeless
6 random 7 aimless, fustian, unaimed, useless 8 feckless 9 desultory, haphazard, hit-or-miss, irregular, senseless, unhelpful, unplanned, worthless 10 designless, unpurposed 11 meaningless, nonsensical, purportless 12 unprofitable

purposely
9 expressly 10 designedly, explicitly, prepensely 12 deliberately 13 intentionally

purr
3 hum 6 murmur

purse
3 bag, sum 4 knit 5 money, pouch, prize 6 pucker, wallet 7 handbag 9 clutch bag 10 pocketbook, prize money
Scottish: 7 sporran

pursual
5 chase, quest 6 search 7 pursuit

pursue
3 woo 4 hunt, seek 5 chase, chivy, court, hound, spark, stalk, track, trail 6 badger, follow 7 address, oppress, persist 8 make up to 9 persecute, persevere

pursuit
3 job 4 hunt, line, work 5 chase, quest 6 racket, search 7 calling, seeking 8 business, reaching 9 following, obtaining 10 employment, occupation

pursy
see **portly**

purvey
6 obtain, supply 7 provide

purview
3 ken 5 ambit, orbit, range,

reach, scope, sweep **6** extent, radius **7** compass

pus
6 fester
combining form: **2** py **3** pyo

push
3 dig, jam, lot, pep, ram, set
4 bang, bear, bump, butt, goad, move, plug, prod, snap, spur
5 boost, build, bunch, crowd, crush, drive, drove, elbow, force, getup, group, horde, hunch, impel, nudge, press, punch, shove, vigor
6 beef up, circle, expand, hustle, jostle, launch, peddle, propel, squash, squish, squush, starch, throng, thrust **8** ambition, bulldoze, compound, increase, oversell, pressure, shoulder, stimulus, vitality
9 advertise, incentive **10** aggrandize, enterprise, get-up-and-go, incitation, incitement, initiative

push around
4 bait, ride **5** bully, chivy, hound **6** badger, heckle, hector **8** bullyrag

pushful
5 brash **6** uppish, uppity **7** assured, forward, pushing **8** imposing, militant **9** assertive, assertory, confident, intrusive, obtruding, obtrusive, officious, presuming **10** aggressive **11** overweening **12** presumptuous **13** self-asserting, self-assertive

Pushkin
novel: **12** Eugene Onegin
play: **12** Boris Godunov

push off
2 go **4** exit, quit **5** leave **6** depart, get off **7** get away, pull out **8** withdraw

push on
2 go **3** hie **4** fare, pass, wend **6** repair, travel **7** journey, proceed

pushover
3 pie **4** snap **5** cinch, setup **6** breeze, picnic **8** duck soup, kid stuff **10** child's play

pushy
see **pushful**

pusillanimous
6 coward, craven **7** chicken, gutless, unmanly **8** cowardly, poltroon **9** spunkless **11** lily-livered, poltroonish

puss
3 cat, kid, mug **4** face **5** child **6** kisser, kitten, moppet, nipper, visage **8** juvenile

pussyfoot
4 lurk, slip **5** creep, dodge, evade, glide, hedge, skulk, slide, slink, sneak, steal **6** weasel **7** gumshoe, shuffle **8** sidestep **10** equivocate, tergiverse **12** tergiversate

pustule
4 boil, wart **5** whelk **6** pimple **7** abscess **8** furuncle **9** carbuncle

put
3 air, fix, lay, set **4** call, give, levy, pose, turn, vent, word **5** couch, exact, focus, judge, place, rivet, state, stick **6** assess, fasten, fixate, impose, phrase, prefer, reckon, render, return, settle **7** express, propose, replace, restore, suggest **8** estimate, give back, propound **9** concenter

putative
7 reputed **8** supposed **11** conjectural, suppositive, suppository **12** hypothetical

put away
4 bury, do in, kill, slay, stow **5** inter, plant, scrag, swill **6** cut off, entomb, finish, inhume, lay low, murder, punish **7** bump off, consume, destroy, dismiss, divorce, execute, reposit, take off, unmarry **8** carry off, dispatch, knock off **9** liquidate

put back
6 demote, return **7** replace, restore **8** give back **9** reinstate

put by
4 save **5** lay in, lay up **7** lay away **8** lay aside, salt away

put down
4 bump, bust **5** break, crush, quash, quell, shift, swill **6** demote, humble, punish, quench, squash, subdue **7** consume, declass, degrade, demerit, disrate, put away **8** disgrade, suppress **9** downgrade

put in
3 sow **4** seed **5** plant **6** insert

put off
5 delay, elude, repel **7** suspend **8** dissuade, postpone **9** frustrate **10** disconcert

put on
3 act, don, kid **4** fake, hire, pose, sham, show **5** bluff, feign, get on, mount, stage **6** affect, assume, draw on, employ, engage, slip on, strike, take on **7** mislead

put-on
3 act **4** face, fake, mask, sell, sham, show **5** cheat, cloak, cover,

faked, guise, phony, posed, spoof **6** deceit, facade, parody **7** assumed, disguise, mannered, spurious **9** deception, imposture **10** artificial, false front, masquerade

put on the block
4 sell

put out
3 ply, vex **4** gall, rile, roil **5** annoy, douse, exert, grate, issue, throw, wield **6** burn up, quench **7** inflame, publish, trouble **8** exercise, irritate **9** aggravate, disoblige, displease, incommode **10** discommode, dissatisfy, exasperate, extinguish **13** inconvenience

putrefy
3 rot **4** turn **5** decay, spoil, taint **6** molder **7** crumble **9** break down, decompose **12** disintegrate

putrid
3 bad **4** foul, high, olid **5** fetid **6** rancid, rotten, smelly, whiffy **7** corrupt, decayed, noisome, reeking, spoiled, vicious **8** depraved, nidorous, perverse **9** nefarious **10** malodorous
combining form: **4** sapr **5** sapro

putter
4 club, mess **6** dawdle, doodle, fiddle, golfer, puddle, tinker **10** boondoggle

putting area
5 green

put together
4 form, join, make **5** build, erect, frame, shape, unite **7** fashion, produce **9** construct, fabricate

putty
3 mud **4** clay **6** cement

put up
3 can, hut **4** bunk, hike, jump, make, rear **5** board, boost, build, erect, forge, house, lodge, raise, set up, shape **6** bestow, billet, harbor, jack up, uprear **7** elevate, quarter **8** domicile, escalate, increase **9** construct
with: **4** bear **5** stand **6** endure

puzzle
3 why **4** foil, pose **5** addle, amaze, befog, poser, rebus, upset **6** baffle, enigma, fuddle, muddle, riddle **7** anagram, confuse, disturb, mystery, mystify, nonplus, perplex, problem, stumble **8** acrostic, befuddle, bewilder, confound, distract

9 conundrum, crossword, dumb-found, frustrate **10** closed book, disconcert, puzzlement **11** brainteaser
Chinese: **7** tangram

puzzle out
5 break, solve **6** cipher, unfold **7** clear up, dope out, unravel **8** decipher, unriddle **9** figure out

Pygmalion
father: **5** Belus
playwright: **4** Shaw (George Bernard)
sister: **4** Dido
statue, beloved: **7** Galatea
victim: **8** Sichaeus

pygmy
4 runt, tiny **5** dwarf, midge **6** midget, peewee **7** manikin, minikin **8** dwarfish, Tom Thumb **10** diminutive, homunculus, pocket-size **11** lilliputian

Pylades
companion: **7** Orestes
father: **9** Strophius
wife: **7** Electra

pylon
4 post **5** tower **7** gateway

Pym's creator
3 Poe (Edgar Allan)

Pynchon novel
15 Gravity's Rainbow

pyramid
4 bank, heap, hill, mass, pile, tomb **5** drift, mound, stack **7** windrow
builder: **5** Khufu **6** Cheops

Pyramus' beloved
6 Thisbe

pyre
4 heap, pile

pyromaniac
8 arsonist

pyrosis
9 heartburn

pyrotechnics
9 fireworks

Pyrrha's husband
9 Deucalion

Pyrrhonian
7 doubter, skeptic, zetetic **10** unbeliever

Pyrrhus
kingdom: **6** Epirus
victory: **7** Asculum; (see also Neoptolemus)

Pythias' friend
5 Damon

python
3 boa **5** snake

pyx
3 box **4** case **5** chest **6** coffer, vessel

Qq

Qatar's capital
4 Doha

Q.E.D. word
4 erat, quod

q.t., on the
8 in secret, secretly

qua
2 as 4 bird 5 heron

quack
3 cry 4 honk, sham 7 shammer
9 charlatan, pretender, quackster,
simulator 10 mountebank
12 saltimbanque
combining form: 5 pseud 6 pseudo

quad
see **quadrangle**

quadra
5 frame 6 border, fillet, listel, plinth

quadragenarian
8 fortyish

quadrangle
4 yard 5 court 6 figure, square
9 courtyard, curtilage, enclosure

quadrant
6 fourth 10 instrument

quadratic
6 square 10 foursquare

quadriga
7 chariot

quadrille
5 dance, ombre 8 card game

quadrillion
combining form: 4 peta

quadrillionth
combining form: 5 femto

quadrivium subject
5 music 8 geometry 9 astronomy
10 arithmetic

quaestor
5 judge 8 official 9 paymaster,
treasurer 10 prosecutor

quaff
3 sip 4 toss 5 drink, sup up 6 imbibe, sup off 7 swallow

quagga
3 ass

quaggy
4 soft 5 boggy, mushy, pappy,
pulpy 6 spongy 7 squashy,
squishy, squushy 8 squelchy,
yielding

quagmire
3 bog, box, fen, fix, jam 4 hole,
mire 5 marsh, swamp 6 corner,
morass, pickle, plight, scrape,
slough 7 dilemma 9 marshland
11 predicament

quahog
4 clam 11 cherrystone

quail
4 bird 5 colin, cower, wince
6 blanch, blench, cringe, flinch,
recoil, shrink 7 massena, shudder,
squinch, tremble 8 bobwhite
flock of: 4 bevy
young: 7 cheeper 8 squealer

quaint
3 odd 5 droll, funny, queer 7 antique, archaic, curious, oddball,
strange, unusual 8 peculiar, singular 9 eccentric, laughable, whimsical 10 antiquated

quake
3 jar 5 shake, shock, waver
6 dither, quaver, quiver, shiver,
tremor 7 shudder, temblor, tremble,
twitter, vibrate 8 trembler, tremblor
9 fluctuate

Quaker
6 Friend 9 broadbrim
city: 12 Philadelphia
colonizer: 4 Penn (William)
founder: 3 Fox (George)
gray: 5 acier

poet: 6 Barton (Bernard) 8 Whittier
(John Greenleaf)
state: 12 Pennsylvania

qualification
5 might 7 ability 8 adequacy, aptitude, capacity 10 capability,
competence

qualified
3 fit 4 able, good 5 fixed, tried
6 au fait, proper, proved, tested
7 capable, limited, partial,
quizzed, trained 8 definite, eligible, examined, modified, reserved
9 competent 10 catechized, determined, instructed, restricted 11 conditional, disciplined

qualify
4 mark 6 assign, impute, soften
7 ascribe, certify, entitle, license,
prepare 8 moderate 9 attribute,
authorize

quality
4 fine, mark, rank 5 arete, class,
elite, grade, merit, place, prime, savor, state, trait, value, worth 6 factor, flower, gentry, Grade A, status,
virtue 7 aristoi, caliber, element,
feature, footing, society, station, stature 8 capacity, five-star, position,
property, standing, superior 9 affection, attribute, blue blood, character, excellent, first-rate, gentility,
parameter, situation 10 blue-ribbon, excellence, first-class, patriciate, perfection, superbness
essential: 8 suchness
suffix: 2 cy, ty 3 ice, ity 4 ance,
ancy, ence, ency, hood, ness, ship

qualm
5 demur, doubt 6 squeam, unease
7 scruple 8 mistrust 9 agitation,
misgiving, objection, suspicion
10 conscience, foreboding, impa-
tience, insecurity, reluctance, uneasiness 11 compunction, nervousness,
uncertainty 12 apprehension, per-

turbation, presentiment, remonstrance **13** unwillingness

qualmish
5 queer **6** queasy **9** nauseated

quandary
3 fix, jam **6** pickle, plight, scrape **7** dilemma **11** predicament

quantity
4 body, bulk, dose, unit **5** total **6** amount, budget, degree **9** aggregate
fixed: **8** constant
small: **3** bit, jot, ray **4** atom, dram, drop, iota, mite, whit **5** grain, scrap, shred, speck **7** modicum, smidgen

Quantrill's ___
7 raiders

quantum
3 sum **4** body, bulk, meed, part **5** quota, share, total **6** amount, budget, ration **7** measure, portion **9** aggregate, allotment, allowance **13** apportionment
of radiant energy: **6** photon
of vibrational energy: **6** phonon
theory originator: **6** Planck (Max)

quarantine
6 cut off **7** isolate **9** interdict, isolation

quarrel
3 row, war **4** beef, bolt, bump, dust, feud, fray, fuss, miff, spat, tiff, tile, vary **5** argue, arrow, brawl, broil, clash, fight, melee, run-in, scrap, set-to, words **6** affray, battle, bicker, chisel, differ, divide, dustup, fracas, hassle, ruckus, rumpus, squall, strife, thwart **7** bobbery, brabble, cast out, collide, contend, diamond, discord, dispute, dissent, fall out, rhubarb, ruction, scuffle, wrangle **8** catfight, conflict, squabble, to-and-fro, variance **9** altercate, bickering, brannigan, caterwaul, disaccord, imbroglio, scrimmage **10** contention, difference, difficulty, dissension, donnybrook, falling-out, free-for-all **11** altercation, battle royal, controversy, embroilment **12** disagreement

quarrelsome
6 brawly **7** adverse, counter, crabbed, hostile, scrappy, warlike **8** brawling, cankered, inimical, militant, ructious **9** bellicose, brawlsome, combative, irascible, irritable, rancorous, truculent **10** battlesome, pugnacious **11** bel-

ligerent, contentious **12** disputatious **13** argumentative

quarry
3 pit **4** game, mine, prey **5** chase, delve, pluck **6** victim **7** lozenge

quart
6 fourth
four: **6** gallon
metric: **5** liter, litre

quarter
3 hut **4** area, bunk, part **5** board, house, lodge, put up **6** barrio, billet, canton, fourth, harbor, sector **7** barrack, section **8** district, division, domicile, locality, precinct, quadrant **9** entertain **11** domiciliate
circle: **8** quadrant
note: **8** crotchet
pint: **4** gill
ship's: **6** fo'c'sle **10** forecastle
year, Scottish: **5** raith

quarterback
4 boss **6** survey **7** oversee **9** supervise **10** footballer

quartet
4 four **6** tetrad **7** quatuor **8** foursome **10** quadruplet, quaternion

quartz
4 onyx, sard **5** agate, smoky **6** jasper, rubace **7** citrine, rubasse, sardius **8** amethyst, sardonyx, sunstone **9** cairngorm, carnelian **10** chalcedony

quash
4 undo, void **5** abate, annul, crush, quell **6** negate, quench, stifle, vacate **7** abolish, nullify, put down, repress, smother, squelch, vitiate **8** abrogate, dissolve, strangle, suppress **9** discharge

quasi
6 almost **7** seeming, virtual

Quasimodo
9 hunchback
creator: **4** Hugo (Victor)
occupation: **10** bell ringer
residence: **9** Notre Dame

quat
3 sty **4** beat, boil **6** squash **7** upstart

quaver
5 quake, shake, waver **6** dither, falter, shiver, tremor **7** shudder, tremble, twitter **8** hesitate **9** vacillate

quawk
5 heron **10** night heron

quay
4 dock, pier, slip **5** berth, jetty, levee, wharf

quean
4 bawd **5** wench, whore **6** harlot **7** hustler **8** meretrix **10** prostitute

queasy
4 open **5** fishy, queer, shady **6** qualmy **7** dubious **8** doubtful, qualmish **9** ambiguous, doubtable, nauseated, squeamish

Quebec
college, university: **5** Laval, Lévis **6** McGill **9** Concordia
largest city: **8** Montreal
peninsula: **5** Gaspé
vehicle: **7** caleche

queen
4 card **6** regina **7** goddess, monarch **8** chessman **9** sovereign
Austria-Hungary: **12** Maria Theresa
Belgian: **6** Astrid
Danish: **8** Margaret, Margrete
Egyptian: **9** Cleopatra **10** Hatshepsut
English: **4** Anne, Mary **8** Victoria **9** Elizabeth
French and English: **7** Eleanor
Netherlands: **7** Beatrix, Juliana **10** Wilhelmina
of heaven: **4** Mary, moon **7** Astarte
of Isles: **6** Albion
of Ithaca: **8** Penelope
of Navarre: **8** Margaret
of Scots: **4** Mary
of Sheba: **6** Balkis
of the Adriatic: **6** Venice
of the Antilles: **4** Cuba
of the East: **7** Zenobia
of the fairies: **3** Mab **7** Titania
of the gods: **4** Hera, Juno, Sati
of the Nile: **9** Cleopatra
of the North: **9** Edinburgh
of the underworld: **3** Hel **4** Hela **10** Persephone, Proserpina
Spanish: **8** Isabella
Swedish: **9** Christina

Queen Anne's Lace
6 carrot

Queen of Spades
author: **7** Pushkin (Aleksandr)
composer: **11** Tchaikovsky (Pyotr)

Queensland
capital: **8** Brisbane
explorer: **4** Cook (Captain James)

Queeg's command
5 Caine

queer
5 droll, funny, weird **6** qualmy,

queasy 7 bizarre, curious, dubious, oddball, strange, unusual 8 doubtful, obsessed, peculiar, qualmish, singular 9 eccentric, laughable, squeamish 10 outlandish

quell
5 crush, quash 6 quench, squash 7 conquer, put down 8 overcome, suppress, vanquish 9 subjugate 10 extinguish

Quemoy's neighbor
4 Amoy

quench
3 end, out 4 raze, ruin, sate 5 allay, crush, douse, quash, quell, slake, wreck 6 lessen, put out, reduce, squash 7 appease, assuage, content, destroy, gratify, lighten, put down, relieve, satiate, satisfy, shatter 8 decimate, decrease, demolish, destruct, diminish, mitigate, suppress 9 alleviate, terminate 10 extinguish

quenelle
8 meatball 9 forcemeat

quern
4 mill

querulous
5 huffy, waspy 6 crying 7 fretful, peevish, pettish, wailing, waspish, weeping 8 petulant, snappish 9 bemoaning, deploring, fractious, irritable, lamenting 10 blubbering, whimpering

query
3 ask 4 quiz 7 concern, dubiety, examine, inquire, inquiry 8 mistrust, question 9 catechize, dubiosity, dubitancy, suspicion 10 skepticism 11 interrogate, questioning, uncertainty, uncertitude 13 interrogation, interrogatory

quest
3 bay 4 howl, hunt, seek, wail 5 probe 6 search 7 delving, inquiry, probing, pursual, pursuit, seeking, ululate 8 pursuing, research 9 cast about, ferret out, pursuance, search for, search out 11 inquisition

question
3 ask, nut 4 poll, quiz 5 demur, doubt, issue, query 7 debrief, dispute, examine, inquire, inquiry, problem, protest, suspect 8 demurral, demurrer, mistrust 9 catechize, challenge, objection 10 difficulty, puzzle over 11 interrogate, wonder about 12 hesitate over, remonstrance 13 interrogation, interrogatory

questionable
4 moot 5 vague 6 unsure 7 dubious, obscure 8 arguable, doubtful, mootable, unlikely, untrusty 9 debatable, equivocal, refutable, trustless, uncertain 10 disputable, fly-by-night, improbable, unreliable 11 problematic 12 undependable

questioning
5 query 6 show-me 7 curious, inquiry 8 aporetic 9 inquiring, quizzical, skeptical 11 incredulous, inquisitive, unbelieving 12 disbelieving, disquisitive 13 interrogation, interrogatory, investigative

quetzal
4 bird, coin 6 trogon

queue
3 row 4 file, line, rank, tier 5 braid

quibble
4 carp 5 argue, cavil 6 argufy, bicker, hassle 7 chicane, dispute, wrangle 8 pettifog, squabble 9 criticize

quick
3 apt 4 able, core, deft, fast, keen, pith, root, wise 5 acute, agile, apace, brisk, canny, fleet, hasty, heart, rapid, ready, sharp, slick, smart, swift 6 abrupt, adroit, center, clever, nimble, prompt, speedy, sudden 7 capable, flat-out, hastily, knowing, rapidly, swiftly 8 speedily 9 breakneck, competent, dexterous, effective, effectual, impetuous, posthaste 10 expeditive, harefooted 11 expeditious, intelligent, quick-witted, sharp-witted 12 lickety-split, nimble-witted 13 expeditiously
combining form: 3 oxy 5 tachy

quick bread
6 muffin 7 biscuit

quicken
4 goad, move, spur, stir, wake 5 hurry, liven, pique, rouse, speed 6 arouse, awaken, excite, hasten, induce, step up, vivify 7 actuate, animate, enliven, innerve, provoke, shake up, swiften 8 activate, energize, motivate, vitalize 9 galvanize, innervate, stimulate 10 accelerate, exhilarate, invigorate, vivificate

quickness
4 gait, pace 5 speed 8 celerity, legerity, rapidity, velocity 9 rapidness, swiftness

quicksand
3 bog 4 mire, syrt 6 syrtis

quicksilver
7 mercury 9 mercurial

quick-tempered
5 cross, ratty 6 cranky 7 peppery 8 choleric 9 irascible 10 passionate

quick-witted
3 apt, hep 4 keen, wise 5 acute, alert, canny, ready, sharp, slick, smart, witty 6 brainy, bright, clever, prompt 7 knowing 8 humorous 9 brilliant, facetious 11 intelligent, penetrating, penetrative

quid
3 cut, wad 4 chew 5 pound 9 sovereign

quiddity
6 trifle 7 essence, quibble

quidnunc
see **rumormonger**

quiescent
4 calm 5 quiet, still 6 hushed, latent, placid, stilly 7 abeyant, dormant, halcyon, lurking 10 untroubled

quiet
4 calm, hush, idle, lull, stop 5 abate, allay, inert, plain, shush, still, tasty, whist 6 asleep, becalm, homely, hushed, lessen, placid, settle, shut up, silent, simple, sleepy, soothe, stilly, subdue 7 compose, halcyon, hushful, passive, silence, subdued 8 choke off, decrease, inactive, tasteful 9 cessation, noiseless, soundless, stillness 10 restrained, untroubled 11 inobtrusive, termination, tranquilize, unobtrusive

quietus
5 death, sleep 6 demise 7 decease, passing, silence 8 curtains 10 inactivity

quill
3 pen 5 spine, spool 6 bobbin 7 feather 8 plectrum

quill pig
9 porcupine

quilt
4 pouf, puff 8 bedcover 9 bedspread, comforter, eiderdown 11 counterpane
design: 8 trapunto

quink
5 brant, goose

quintessence
4 meat, pith, soul 5 stuff 6 bottom, marrow 7 epitome 8 last word, ultimate 9 substance 12 essentiality

quintessential
4 pith, soul 5 ideal, model, stuff 6 bottom, marrow 7 classic, essence, typical 9 classical, exemplary, substance 10 archetypal, prototypal 12 prototypical

quintillion
combining form: 3 exa

quintillionth
combining form: 4 atto

quintuple
8 fivefold

quintuplets
famous: 6 Dionne

quip
3 gag 4 gibe, gird, jape, jeer, jest, joke 5 crack, fleer, flout, sally, scoff, sneer 8 drollery 9 wisecrack, witticism

quipster
3 wag, wit 5 comic, droll, joker 6 jester 8 comedian, funnyman, humorist, jokester

quirk
4 bend, quip 5 crook 6 groove, retort 7 channel 9 mannerism 11 peculiarity

quirt
4 whip

quisling
7 traitor 8 turncoat

quit
3 act, pay 4 bear, drop, exit, halt, stop 5 carry, cease, chuck, clear, leave, pay up 6 behave, demean, depart, deport, desert, desist, get off, resign, retire, secede, settle, square 7 abandon, comport, conduct, forsake, get away, satisfy, take off 8 clear off, give over, knock off, leave off, renounce, surcease, withdraw 9 discharge, liquidate, surrender, terminate, throw over 10 relinquish 11 discontinue

quite
3 all, far 4 just, well 5 fully, in all 6 in toto, purely, rather, wholly 7 all told, exactly, totally, utterly 8 all in all, cleverly, entirely, somewhat 9 perfectly 10 altogether, completely, thoroughly

quittance
6 amends 7 redress 8 reprisal 9 indemnity 10 recompense, reparation 11 restitution 12 compensation

quitter
4 funk 6 coward, craven, funker 7 chicken 8 poltroon 11 yellowbelly

quiver
4 beat 5 flash, gleam, glint, pulse, quake, shake, throb 6 dither, glance, shiver, tremor 7 glimmer, glisten, glitter, pulsate, shimmer, shudder, sparkle, tremble, twinkle, twitter 9 palpitate

quiverleaf
5 aspen

quiver tree
4 aloe

Quixote
see **Don Quixote**

quixotic
8 fanciful, illusory, romantic 9 fantastic, visionary 10 chimerical, idealistic 11 impractical

quiz
3 ask 4 lout, mock, razz, twit 5 query, rally, scout, taunt 6 deride, oddity, zombie 7 examine, inquire, oddball 8 original, question, ridicule 9 catechize, character, eccentric 11 interrogate

quizzical
6 show-me 7 curious, probing 8 aporetic 9 searching, skeptical 11 incredulous, inquisitive, questioning, unbelieving 12 disbelieving

quizzing glass
7 monocle

quodlibet
6 debate, medley 8 fantasia, question

quoin
5 angle, facet, wedge 6 corner 7 lozenge 8 keystone, voussoir

quoit
4 ring, rope 5 cover 6 circle

quoits
4 game
peg: 3 hob

quondam
3 old 4 late, once, past 6 bygone, former, whilom 7 onetime 8 sometime 9 erstwhile

quorum
7 council 8 majority

quota
3 cut, lot 4 bite, meed, part 5 share, slice 6 divide, parcel, ration 7 measure, partage, portion, prorate, quantum 9 allotment, allowance, apportion

quotation
3 bid 5 offer, price 7 excerpt, passage

quotation mark
French: 9 guillemet

quote
4 cite, list, mark 5 refer 6 adduce, notice, set off 7 excerpt

quotidian
5 daily, plain, usual 7 diurnal, routine 8 everyday, ordinary, workaday 9 circadian 12 unremarkable

Quo Vadis
author: 11 Sienkiewicz (Henryk)
character: 4 Nero 5 Lygia, Peter 8 Vinicius 9 Petronius

Rr

Ra
son: 6 Khonsu
wife: 3 Mut

Raamah
father: 4 Cush
son: 5 Dedan, Sheba

Rabbi Ben Ezra author
8 Browning (Robert)

rabbit
4 cony 5 bunny, coney, lapin
castrated: 5 lapin
female: 3 doe
fictional: 5 Fiver, Hazel, Mopsy, Peter 6 Flopsy, Harvey 7 Thumper 8 Crusader, Ricochet 9 Bugs Bunny 10 Cottontail 11 Easter Bunny
food: 5 salad 6 carrot 7 lettuce

rabbitlike
8 leporine

rabble
3 mob 4 many, raff, rout, scum 5 dregs, scurf, trash 6 masses, people, polloi, public, ragtag 7 doggery 8 canaille, populace, riffraff, unwashed, varletry 9 hoi polloi, other half, tag and rag 10 commonalty, roughscuff 11 bourgeoisie, proletariat, rank and file

rabble-rouser
9 demagogue

Rabelais character
9 Gargantua 10 Pantagruel

rabid
3 mad 4 keen, wild 5 crazy, ultra 6 crazed, insane 7 extreme, fanatic, frantic, furious, radical, zealous 8 demented, deranged, frenetic, frenzied, obsessed, ultraist 9 delirious, extremist 10 corybantic 12 enthusiastic

rabies
5 lyssa 11 hydrophobia

raccoon
5 panda 10 cacomistle
relative: 5 coati 10 coatimundi

race
4 boil, bolt, clan, dash, drag, folk, gill, lash, rush, tear, type 5 breed, brook, chase, creek, fling, house, shoot, speed, stock, tribe 6 career, charge, course, endure, family, nation, people, runnel, stream 7 culture, kindred, lineage, Negroid, rivulet, running, variety 8 marathon 9 Caucasian, Mongoloid
auto: 5 rally 6 rallye 9 grand prix
combining form: 3 gen 4 geno, phyl 5 ethno, phylo

racecourse
4 oval, turf 5 track
combining form: 4 drom 5 drome, dromo

racehorse
champion: 5 Kelso 6 Forego 7 Man O' War 8 Affirmed, Citation 9 Riva Ridge 10 War Admiral 11 Forward Pass, Seattle Slew, Secretariat 12 Native Dancer

Rachel
father: 5 Laban
husband: 5 Jacob
servant: 6 Bilhah
sister: 4 Leah
son: 6 Joseph 8 Benjamin

rachis
4 back 5 spine 8 backbone 9 vertebrae

rachitic
5 shaky 6 wobbly 7 rackety, rickety 10 rattletrap

rachitis
7 rickets

___ Rachmaninoff
6 Sergei

racing enthusiast
8 railbird

rack
3 try 4 pain 5 frame, wring 6 harrow, martyr 7 afflict, agonize, crucify, oppress, sawbuck, torment, torture 8 distress, sawhorse 9 persecute 10 excruciate

racket
3 din 5 babel 6 clamor, hubbub, jangle, tumult, uproar 8 brouhaha 10 hullabaloo 11 pandemonium

rack up
3 win 4 gain 5 reach, score 6 attain 7 achieve, realize 10 accomplish

raconteur
11 storyteller

racy
4 blue 5 broad, fiery, salty, shady, spicy, zesty 6 purple, risqué, snappy, wicked 7 gingery, peppery, piquant, pungent 8 off-color, spirited 10 suggestive

Radames' beloved
4 Aïda

radar image
4 blip

Raddai
brother: 5 David
father: 5 Jesse

radiance
5 glory 8 splendor

radiant
4 glad 6 bright, cheery, lucent 7 beaming, fulgent, lambent 8 cheerful, luminous 9 brilliant, effulgent, refulgent 12 incandescent

radiate
4 beam, burn 5 gleam, shine, strew 6 spread 7 diffuse, diverge 8 disperse 9 circulate, eradicate, propagate

radiation unit
3 rem, rep 8 roentgen

radiator
6 cooler, heater 11 transmitter

radical
4 acyl, root 5 basal, basic, pinko, rabid, rebel, ultra, vital 6 bottom

7 extreme, fanatic, primary **8** advanced, agitator, cardinal, inherent, nihilist, reformer, tolerant, ultraist **9** anarchist, essential, extremist, insurgent, intrinsic **10** separatist, subversive, underlying **11** broadminded, fundamental, out-and-outer, progressive, reactionary **12** foundational, revolutional, secessionist **13** revolutionary
combining form: **2** yl **3** oyl **5** ylene
mathematical: **4** surd

radicle
4 root **5** radix **9** hypocotyl

radio
8 wireless
frequency range: **8** waveband

radioactive debris
7 fallout

radium
symbol: **2** Ra

radius
5 ambit, orbit, range, reach, scope, sweep **6** extent **7** compass, purview **9** extension

radix
4 base, root **6** etymon, source

radon
5 niton **6** thoron **7** actinon
symbol: **2** Rn

raffish
4 fast, wild **6** sporty **8** rakehell **12** devil-may-care

raffle
4 game **6** refuse **7** lottery, rubbish, serrate **8** riffraff

raft
3 lot, rnat **4** slew **5** balsa, float

rafter
4 beam, bird **10** flycatcher

rag
3 fun, jaw, kid, rib **4** fool, jive, joke, josh, rail, rant, razz **5** baste, jolly, scold, tease **9** newspaper

ragamuffin
3 bum **4** hobo, waif **5** tramp **6** loafer, orphan **7** ragshag, vagrant, wastrel **8** vagabond **9** scarecrow

rage
3 cry, fad, ire, mad **4** boil, burn, chic, fume, fury, mode, rant, whim **5** anger, craze, fancy, freak, mania, style, upset, vogue, wrath **6** blow up, frenzy, furore, seethe, vagary **7** bristle, caprice, conceit, fashion, flare up **8** acerbity, acrimony, asperity, boil over, crotchet,

hysteria **9** agitation **10** dernier cri **11** indignation

ragged
4 rent, torn **5** dingy, faded, seedy **6** frayed, shabby **7** patched, shreddy, worn-out **8** battered, frazzled, tattered **10** threadbare **11** dilapidated

raging
4 wild **5** dirty, rough **6** stormy **7** furious **8** blustery **9** turbulent **10** blustering **11** tempestuous

rags
5 dress **6** attire, shreds, things **7** apparel, clothes, raiment, ribbons, tatters **8** clothing **10** attirement **11** habiliments, odds and ends

ragtag
see **rabble**

ragwort
7 senecio **10** butterweed

Rahab
husband: **6** Salmon
son: **4** Boaz

raid
3 rob **4** loot, sack **5** foray, harry, onset, rifle, waste **6** harass, inroad, invade, maraud, pirate, ravage **7** assault, despoil, overrun, plunder **8** invasion, picaroon, spoliate **9** devastate, incursion, irruption, onslaught, overswarm

raider
6 looter, pirate, sacker **7** forager, ravager, spoiler **8** marauder, picaroon, pillager, ravisher **9** plunderer **10** freebooter **11** bushwhacker

rail
3 jaw **4** rate **5** scold **6** berate, revile **7** bawl out, upbraid **8** banister **10** balustrade, tongue-lash, vituperate

rail bird
4 sora

railing
8 banister **10** balustrade
part: **8** baluster

raillery
6 satire **10** lampoonery **13** satiricalness

railroad
5 frame **9** iron horse
car: **5** coach, diner, stock **6** hopper **7** caboose, gondola, Pullman
engine: **10** locomotive
station: **5** depot
underground: **6** subway
worker: **6** porter **7** fireman **8** brake-

man, engineer **9** conductor **10** dispatcher **11** gandy dancer

raiment
4 clad, duds, garb, togs **5** array, dress **6** attire, clothe, things **7** apparel, clothes, garment **8** clothing, enclothe **10** attirement **11** habiliments

rain
6 mizzle, shower **7** drizzle **8** downpour
combining form: **4** hyet **5** hyeto, ombro, pluvi **6** pluvia, pluvio
fine: **6** serein

rainbow
3 arc **4** iris **5** gamut **7** fantasy **8** illusion, phantasy **9** pipe dream
bridge: **7** Bifrost
chaser: **9** visionary
combining form: **4** irid **5** irido
goddess: **4** Iris

rainbow fish
5 guppy, trout **6** wrasse

raincoat
3 mac **4** mack **6** poncho **7** slicker **10** mackintosh

rain gauge
8 udometer

rain leader
9 downspout

rain tree
9 monkeypod

raise
2 up **4** abet, ante, grow, hike, jack, jump, lift, pump, rear **5** boost, breed, build, erect, exalt, hoist, put up **6** foment, gather, incite, jack up, muster, pick up, stir up, take up, upbear, uphold, uplift, uprear, whip up **7** bring up, collect, elevate, enhance, inflate, produce, provoke **8** addition, assemble, congress, heighten, increase **9** accession, accretion, construct, cultivate, forgather, increment, instigate, propagate, resurrect **10** congregate, rendezvous **12** augmentation
nap: **5** tease
spirits: **5** elate

raisin
7 sultana

raison d' ____
4 être

raja
4 king **5** chief, ruler **6** prince **9** dignitary

rake
3 cad **4** beat, comb, grub, roué, tool **5** angle, scour, slope **6** for-

age, rascal, search **7** coxcomb, playboy, ransack, rummage **8** fine-comb **9** implement, libertine **10** profligate **11** inclination

rakehell
4 fast, wild **6** rascal, sporty **7** raffish **8** rascally **9** dissolute, libertine **10** licentious, profligate **12** devil-may-care

rake's look
4 ogle

Rake's Progress engraver
7 Hogarth (William)

rakish
see **rakehell**

rally
4 fire, lout, mock, quiz, race, razz, stir, twit, wake, whet **5** harry, renew, rouse, scout, taunt, tease, waken, worry **6** arouse, awaken, bestir, deride, harass, kindle, muster, perk up, pick up **7** brace up, enliven, marshal, recover, refresh, restore **8** mobilize, organize, ridicule **9** challenge, come round, tantalize **10** invigorate

rallying cry
5 motto **6** slogan

ram
5 Aries, crash, drive, sheep, stick, stuff **6** plunge, strike, thrust **7** jampack, warship

Rama's wife
4 Sita

ramble
3 gad **4** roam, rove, turn, walk **5** drift, range, stray **6** depart, sprawl, stroll, wander **7** digress, diverge, excurse, meander, saunter, traipse **8** divagate, straggle **9** gallivant

rambunctious
5 rowdy **6** unruly **7** raucous **8** rowdyish **9** termagant, turbulent **10** boisterous, rowdydowdy, tumultuous

ramification
6 branch **8** offshoot **9** branching, outgrowth **11** consequence

Ramona author
7 Jackson (Helen Hunt)

ramose
8 branched

ramp
5 apron, climb, storm **6** easing

rampage
4 orgy **5** binge, fling, spree **6** uproar **7** splurge, turmoil

rampageous
4 wild **6** unruly **7** riotous

rampant
4 rank, rife **6** ruling **7** current, popular, regnant **9** excessive, prevalent **10** immoderate, inordinate, widespread

rampart
7 bastion, bulwark, parapet **10** breastwork

ramshackle
7 rickety **10** dissipated **11** dilapidated

ram's mate
3 ewe

ranch
8 estancia, hacienda
worker: **6** cowboy, gaucho **7** cowgirl, cowhand, cowpoke **10** cowpuncher

rancid
4 high, olid **5** fetid **6** putrid, smelly, whiffy **7** noisome, reeking **8** nidorous **10** malodorous

rancor
6 animus, enmity **9** animosity, antipathy, hostility, virulence **10** antagonism, bitterness

rancorous
4 evil **6** bitter, malign, wicked **7** hateful, hostile, vicious **8** spiteful, virulent **9** malicious, malignant, vitriolic **10** despiteful, malevolent **12** antagonistic

Rand, Ayn
novel: **6** Anthem **12** Fountainhead **13** Atlas Shrugged

random
4 spot **7** aimless, anywise, unaimed **8** slapdash **9** desultory, haphazard, hit-or-miss, irregular, unplanned **10** accidental, contingent, designless, fortuitous, incidental, objectless **11** any which way, haphazardly, promiscuous, purposeless

randy
4 lewd **7** lustful, satyric **9** lecherous, libertine **10** lascivious, libidinous, licentious **11** incontinent

range
3 ken, row, run **4** area, bias, home, line, roam, rove, site, sort, span, tune, vary **5** align, ambit, drift, field, gamut, haunt, orbit, order, reach, realm, scope, space, stray, sweep, width **6** assort, circle, differ, domain, extend, extent, length, line up, matter, radius, ram-ble, sphere, spread, wander **7** compass, dispose, earshot, expanse, eyeshot, habitat, horizon, meander, purview, stretch **8** confines, locality, panorama, province, straggle, vicinity **9** fluctuate, gallivant, magnitude, territory

range finder
9 telemeter **10** tachymeter

rangy
5 lanky **6** gangly **7** spindly **8** gangling

rani's mate
4 raja **5** rajah

rank
3 row **4** file, foul, line, lush, olid, rate, sort, tier **5** class, dirty, fetid, funky, grade, gross, grown, humid, order, place, queue, state, utter **6** assort, cachet, coarse, estate, filthy, lavish, putrid, rancid, smelly, smutty, status, string, vulgar **7** arrange, capital, dignity, echelon, footing, glaring, noisome, obscene, peerage, perfect, precede, profuse, rampant, raunchy, reeking, station, stature **8** absolute, capacity, classify, complete, evaluate, flagrant, gentrice, indecent, outright, position, positive, prestige, standing, stinking **9** character, downright, egregious, exuberant, loathsome, luxuriant, overgrown, repulsive, situation **10** consummate, malodorous, noticeable **11** consequence, conspicuous, outstanding, unmitigated
honorary: **8** brevetcy
suffix: **2** cy

rank and file
5 plebs **6** people, plebes **8** populace **9** commonage, commoners, common men, plebeians **10** commonalty **11** third estate

rankle
3 irk, vex **5** annoy **6** bother, fester, harass, obsess, plague **7** torment **8** irritate **9** aggravate **10** exasperate

ransack
3 rob **4** beat, comb, grub, loot, rake **5** rifle, scour **6** forage, search **7** plunder, relieve, rummage, stick up **8** finecomb

Ran's husband
5 Aegir

ransom
3 buy **4** free **6** redeem, regain **7** recover, release **8** liberate, retrieve

rant
3 jaw, rag **4** huff, rage, rail, rate, rave **5** mouth, orate, scold **6** berate **7** bawl out, bluster, bombast, declaim, fustian, soapbox **8** bloviate, harangue, perorate, rhetoric **10** vituperate **11** rodomontade

ranula
4 cyst

rap
3 bob, hit, wig **4** chat, chin, lick, skin, swat, talk, tunk, wipe, yarn **5** blame, knock, prose, swipe **6** rebuke **7** censure, chiding, condemn, reproof **8** causerie, denounce, reproach **9** criticize, reprehend, reprimand, reprobate **10** admonition, conference, denunciate, discussion

rapacious
6 fierce **8** ravening, ravenous **9** predative, predatory, raptorial, vulturine, vulturish, vulturous **10** gluttonous **11** predatorial

rapacity
5 greed **6** demand **7** avarice, avidity **8** cupidity, exaction, voracity

rape
4 cole, ruin **5** spoil **6** defile, ravage, ravish **7** debauch, despoil, outrage, plunder, seizure, violate **9** violation **10** spoliation

Rape of the Lock
author: **4** Pope (Alexander)
heroine: **7** Belinda

Raphael
birthplace: **6** Urbino (Italy)
subject: **7** Madonna
teacher: **8** Perugino

rapid
4 fast **5** agile, brisk, fleet, hasty, quick, swift **6** nimble, speedy **7** hurried **9** breakneck, quickened **10** expeditive **11** expeditious

rapidity
4 gait, pace **5** speed **8** celerity, velocity **9** quickness, swiftness

rapids
6 dalles **10** whitewater

rapine
7 pillage, plunder **10** spoliation

Rappaccini's Daughter
8 Beatrice
author: **9** Hawthorne (Nathaniel)

rapport
5 unity **7** concord, harmony

rapscallion
see **rascal**

rap session
6 confab, parley **7** palaver **8** colloquy **10** colloquium, conference, discussion

rapt
4 deep **6** intent **7** engaged **8** absorbed, immersed **9** engrossed, wrapped up **11** preoccupied

raptorial
see **rapacious**

rapture
6 heaven **7** ecstasy **8** rhapsody **9** transport **13** seventh heaven

rara ___
4 avis

rare
3 few **4** fine, thin **6** choice, dainty, scarce, seldom, select, subtle, unique **7** elegant, subtile, tenuous, unusual **8** delicate, singular, sporadic, superior, uncommon, unwonted **9** attenuate, exquisite, recherché **10** attenuated, infrequent, occasional, unfrequent, unordinary **11** exceptional **13** extraordinary

rarefied
4 thin **6** subtle **7** subtile, tenuous **9** attenuate **10** attenuated

rarefy
4 thin **9** attenuate

rarely
5 extra **6** little, seldom **7** unoften **9** extremely, unusually **10** hardly ever

raring
4 agog, avid, keen **5** eager **6** ardent **7** anxious, athirst, thirsty **9** impatient **10** breathless

rarity
6 oddity **7** fewness **8** scarcity

rascal
5 devil, knave, rogue, scamp **7** lowlife, skellum, villain **8** mischief, scalawag **9** miscreant, scoundrel, skeezicks **10** blackguard **11** rapscallion
Irish: **8** spalpeen

rash
5 hasty, silly **6** abrupt, daring, madcap, plague, sudden, unwary, unwise **7** foolish **8** careless, epidemic, headlong, heedless, outbreak, reckless **9** audacious, daredevil, foolhardy, hotheaded, impetuous, imprudent, impulsive, unadvised, venturous **10** ill-advised, incautious, incogitant, indiscreet, mad-brained, unthinking **11** adventurous, injudicious, precipitate, precipitous, temerarious, thoughtless, venturesome **12** unconsidered **13** adventuresome, inconsiderate

rasp
4 file **5** grate **6** scrape, wheeze **7** scratch

raspberry
3 boo **4** bird, hiss, hoot, pooh, razz **5** bazoo **7** catcall **8** pooh-pooh

raspy
3 dry **5** harsh, rough **6** hoarse, snappy **7** grating, jarring, peevish, pettish, raucous **8** petulant, prickish, snappish **9** irritable

rat
3 pad **4** fink, heel, scab **5** louse **6** defect, desert, inform, rodent, snitch, squeak, squeal **7** caitiff, stoolie **8** apostate, defector, informer, recreant, renegade, renounce, runagate, squealer, turncoat **9** bandicoot, repudiate, turnabout **10** apostatize, tergiverse **11** stool pigeon
female: **3** doe

rate
3 tab **4** cost, earn, rail, rank **5** assay, class, grade, merit, price, scale, scold, set at, value **6** assess, berate, charge, degree, revile, survey, tariff **7** apprize, bawl out, chew out, deserve, upbraid, valuate **8** appraise, classify, estimate, evaluate, price tag **10** proportion, tongue-lash

rather
5 quite **6** enough, fairly, in lieu, kind of, pretty, sort of **7** instead **8** passably, somewhat **9** averagely, tolerably **10** moderately, more or less **11** alternately **12** considerably **13** alternatively

ratify
5 enact **7** approve, confirm, endorse, license **8** accredit, sanction, validate

rating
4 mark, rank **5** grade **6** rebuke **8** standing

ratio
5 scale **7** percent **8** quotient **10** proportion

ratiocination
8 judgment, sequitur **9** inference, reasoning **10** conclusion

ration

4 dole, meed, part 5 allot, quota, share 6 assign, divide, parcel 7 measure, mete out, prorate, quantum 8 allocate, division 9 allotment, allowance 10 assignment 13 apportionment

rational

4 calm, cool, sane 5 lucid, sober, sound 6 normal, stable 7 logical, prudent 8 sensible 9 judicious 10 consequent, reasonable 11 circumspect, intelligent, level-headed

rationale

6 reason 11 explanation 13 justification

rationalize

7 explain, justify 10 account for

rattail

4 file, fish, mule 5 spoon 6 cactus, fescue 8 tapering 9 grenadier

rattan

4 cane, palm, stem

rattle

3 gab, jaw, yak 4 chat, faze 5 abash, addle, clack, run on, upset 6 babble, gabble 7 chatter, clatter, confuse, disturb, perplex 8 bewilder, confound, distract 9 discomfit, embarrass

rattlebrained

5 dizzy, giddy, silly 7 flighty 8 skittish 9 frivolous 11 empty-headed

rattling

4 very 6 damned, mighty 7 parlous 8 snapping, spanking, whacking, whopping 9 extremely 11 exceedingly

ratty

5 cross, testy 6 cranky, shabby, tetchy, touchy 7 peppery, unkempt 8 choleric 9 irascible, temperish

raucous

3 dry 5 gruff, harsh, rough, rowdy 6 hoarse, unruly 7 brusque, grating, jarring, squawky 8 rowdyish, strident 9 termagant, turbulent 10 boisterous, disorderly, rowdy-dowdy, stridulent, stridulous, tumultuous 11 rumbustious

raunchy

4 foul 5 dirty, messy, nasty 6 coarse, filthy, sloppy, smutty, unneat, untidy, vulgar 7 obscene, unkempt 8 ill-kempt, indecent, slipshod, slovenly 10 disheveled

ravage

3 rob 4 loot, raze, ruin, sack

5 crush, harry, havoc, spoil, strip, waste, wreck 6 devast, devour, invade 7 despoil, destroy, overrun, pillage, plunder, ransack, scourge 8 deflower, demolish, desolate, encroach, spoliate, trespass 9 depredate, desecrate, devastate, overpower, overthrow, overwhelm

rave

4 rant 5 drool, mouth, orate 7 declaim, enthuse, soapbox 8 bloviate, harangue, perorate, rhapsody 10 rhapsodize

ravel

5 snarl 6 muddle, tangle 7 perplex 8 entangle 10 complicate

ravelings

4 lint

Ravel work

6 Bolero

raven

3 jet 4 bird, ebon, inky, prey 5 black, ebony, jetty, sable 7 despoil, plunder 9 pitch-dark 10 pitch-black
combining form: 5 corax
relating to: 7 corvine

Raven, The

author: 3 Poe (Edgar Allan)
refrain: 9 Nevermore

ravenous

6 hungry 7 starved 8 edacious, famished, starving 9 rapacious, voracious

ravine

3 cut, gap 4 gulf, pass 5 abyss, chasm, cleft, clove, gorge, gulch, gully, notch 6 arroyo, canyon, clough, coulee, defile, gutter, nullah 7 crevice, fissure 8 barranca, barranco, crevasse
Mt. Washington's: 9 Tuckerman

ravish

3 rob 4 rape 5 spoil 6 defile 7 despoil, outrage, pillage, violate 8 deflower, entrance, overcome 9 deflorate, enrapture, transport

raw

4 nude, rude 5 crass, crude, fresh, green, gross, naked, rough, young 6 callow, coarse, impure, native, unclad, unhewn, unripe, vulgar 7 uncouth, untried 8 buff-bare, stripped, uncooked, unformed, ungraded, unsorted, untaught, unversed 9 au naturel, inelegant, roughhewn, run-of-mine, unclothed, undressed, unmatured, unrefined,

untutored 10 stark-naked, unfinished, unpolished, unseasoned 11 unfashioned, unpracticed 13 inexperienced

rawboned

4 bony, lank, lean 5 gaunt, lanky, spare 6 skinny 7 angular, scraggy, scrawny

ray

4 beam, beta 5 alpha, gamma, gleam, light, manta, shaft, shine, shoot, skate, trace 6 radius, streak 7 radiate, sawfish, torpedo 8 particle 9 irradiate, radiation

raze

4 ruin, undo 5 wrack, wreck 6 unmake 7 destroy, unbuild, unframe 8 decimate, demolish

razor

3 cut 5 shave

razz

3 kid, rag, rib 4 fool, jest, joke, josh, lout, mock, quiz, twit 5 jolly, rally, scout, taunt 6 banter, deride, heckle, ridicule; (see also **raspberry**)

RBI

11 run batted in

re

4 as to 5 as for 7 apropos 9 as regards, regarding 10 as respects, concerning, respecting 13 with respect to

reach

2 go 3 get, ken, run, win 4 buck, come, gain, hand, make, move, pass, show, sway 5 ambit, get at, get in, orbit, range, scope, score, sweep, touch 6 affect, arrive, attain, extend, extent, rack up, radius, show up, turn up 7 achieve, compass, contact, horizon, purview, realize, stretch 8 approach 9 extension, influence 10 accomplish

react

6 behave 7 respond

___ reaction

5 chain 7 nuclear 8 chemical

reactionary

4 fogy, tory 5 blimp, right 7 diehard, fogyish, old-line, radical 8 mossback, orthodox, rightist, royalist 11 bitter-ender, right-winger, standpatter 12 conservative

reactionist

see **reactionary**

reactivate
5 renew 6 revive 8 rekindle, renovate, retrieve, revivify 9 resurrect 10 revitalize 11 resuscitate

read
3 say 4 mark, scan, show 5 proof 6 peruse, record 7 dictate 8 indicate, register
inability to: 8 dyslexia

readable
7 legible

reader
6 lector, primer 8 bookworm 9 anthology

readily
4 well 6 easily, freely 7 lightly 12 effortlessly

readiness
4 ease 5 skill 7 address, fluency, prowess, sleight 8 alacrity, dispatch, facility, goodwill 9 dexterity, eloquence 10 expedition, volubility 11 promptitude

reading
7 version 9 rendition

readjust
6 modify 7 reorder 8 reorient 9 rearrange, reshuffle 10 reorganize 11 reconstruct, reorientate

ready
3 apt, fit, fix, get, set 4 fain, gird, live, make, prep, ripe 5 adept, brace, prime, prone, psych, quick, steel 6 active, expert, make up, minded, primed, prompt 7 dynamic, fortify, prepare, skilled, willing 8 adjusted, disposed, imminent, inclined, masterly, prepared, skillful 9 qualified 10 proficient, strengthen 11 predisposed

real
4 true 5 being, pucka, pukka, sound, valid 6 actual, honest 7 certain, genuine, sincere 8 bona fide, existing 9 authentic, necessary, undoubted, unfeigned, veridical 10 undeniable 12 indisputable

realism
6 verism 7 verismo

realistic
4 hard, sane 5 sober, sound 6 astute, earthy, shrewd 8 lifelike, rational, sensible, veristic 9 practical, pragmatic 10 hard-boiled, hard-headed, reasonable, unromantic 11 down-to-earth, nonacademic, pragmatical, utilitarian 12 matter-of-fact 13 unsentimental

reality
4 fact 5 truth

realize
3 win 4 gain 5 fancy, image, reach, score, think 6 attain, rack up, vision 7 achieve, feature, imagine 8 conceive, envisage, envision 10 accomplish

realm
5 orbit, range, scope, sweep 6 empire, extent, radius 7 compass, purview
suffix: 3 dom

reanimation
7 rebirth, revival 10 renascence, resurgence 11 renaissance 12 risorgimento

reap
5 glean 6 garner, gather, thresh 7 harvest 8 ingather

rear
4 back, hind, lift, ramp, rump, seat, tail 5 after, breed, build, erect, fanny, hoist, nurse, put up, raise, set up 6 behind, bottom, foster, hinder, pick up, retral, take up, uphold, uplift 7 bring up, elevate, hind end, nurture, upraise 8 backside, buttocks, hindmost 9 construct, posterior

rear end
4 rump, seat, tail 5 fanny 6 behind, bottom 8 backside, buttocks, derriere

rearmost
4 last 5 final 6 latest, latter 7 closing 8 eventual, terminal, ultimate 10 concluding

rearrange
see **readjust**

rearward
4 back 9 posterior

Rea Silvia, Rhea Silvia
father: 7 Numitor
son: 5 Remus 7 Romulus

reason
3 why, wit 4 mind, nous 5 cause, infer, proof, think 6 ground, motive, sanity, senses, spring, whyfor 7 account, reflect 8 argument, cogitate, logicize, lucidity, occasion, persuade, saneness 9 cerebrate, inference, intellect, rationale, soundness, speculate, wherefore 10 antecedent, deliberate 11 determinant, explanation 13 consideration, justification, ratiocination, understanding

reasonable
3 low 5 cheap, sound 6 modest, undear 7 logical, low-cost, popular 8 discreet, moderate, rational, sensible, uncostly 9 low-priced, temperate, unextreme 10 affordable, consequent, controlled, restrained 11 inexpensive, intelligent

reasoning
5 logic

reasonless
3 mad 4 daft 5 crazy 6 crazed, insane 7 cracked, invalid, lunatic 8 demented, deranged 9 bedlamite, illogical, sophistic 10 fallacious, irrational 11 nonrational

rebate
5 taper 6 lessen, reduce, refund 7 dwindle 8 decrease, diminish, discount, taper off 9 abatement, deduction, drain away, reduction 11 subtraction

Rebecca
beloved: 7 Ivanhoe
father: 5 Isaac

Rebekah
brother: 5 Laban
father: 7 Bethuel
husband: 5 Isaac
nurse: 7 Deborah
son: 4 Esau 5 Jacob

rebel
6 anarch, mutiny, revolt, rise up 7 radical 8 attacker, debunker, frondeur, mutineer, opponent, revolter, ultraist 9 adversary, anarchist, assailant, extremist, insurgent, insurrect 10 antagonist, iconoclast, malcontent 11 rise against 13 revolutionary, revolutionist

rebellion
6 mutiny, revolt 8 sedition 10 revolution 12 insurrection

rebellious
8 mutinous 9 alienated, estranged, insurgent 11 disaffected 13 insubordinate

rebirth
7 revival 8 metanoia 10 conversion, renascence, resurgence 11 reanimation, renaissance 12 resurrection, risorgimento

rebound
7 recover 8 ricochet, snap back

rebuff
5 repel 6 reject 7 fend off, hold off, keep off, repulse, ward off 8 stave off

rebuke
3 rap, wig 5 chide, scold, scorn
6 earful, lesson, monish 7 chiding,
lecture, reproof, reprove, tick off
8 admonish, call down, reproach,
scolding 9 reprimand, talking-to
10 admonition 12 admonishment,
dressing down 13 tongue-lashing

rebut
5 break, evert, repel 6 refute 7 confute, fend off, hold off, keep off, repulse, ward off 8 confound, disprove, stave off 10 controvert,
disconfirm

recalcitrant
4 wild 6 unruly 8 opposing, stubborn, untoward 9 fractious, obstinate, resisting 11 indomitable,
intractable

recall
4 cite, lift, stir 5 educe, evoke, renew, rouse, unsay, waken 6 abjure, arouse, awaken, elicit, memory, remind, repeal, retain, revive,
revoke 7 bethink, extract, rescind,
restore, retract, reverse 8 forswear,
palinode, remember, take back,
withdraw 9 anamnesis, dismantle,
recollect, reinstate, reminisce
10 retrospect 12 recollection,
reminiscence

recant
5 unsay 6 abjure 7 retract 8 forswear, palinode, take back,
withdraw

recap
4 tire 7 retread

recapitulate
5 sum up, unite 9 summarize

recapitulation
3 sum 5 sum-up 6 précis, resumé
7 epitome, summary 9 summing-up

recede
3 ebb 4 back 5 abate, close, taper
6 depart, lessen, reduce, retire
7 dwindle, regress, retract, retreat
8 decrease, diminish, fall back,
withdraw 9 drain away 10 retrograde, retrogress

receipts
6 income 7 revenue

receive
4 take 5 admit 6 take in

received
5 sound 8 accepted, orthodox
9 canonical 10 sanctioned 13 authoritative

receiver
5 donee, fence 9 treasurer

recent
3 new 4 late 5 fresh, novel 6 latest, modern 8 neoteric 9 new-
sprung 10 newfangled 11 modernistic 12 new-fashioned
combining form: 2 ne 3 cen, neo
4 caen, cene, ceno 5 caeno

receptacle
5 torus 6 cupule 8 placenta 9 container 10 repository
laundry: 6 hamper
narrow: 6 trough

receptive
4 open 8 amenable, friendly, suasible, swayable 9 acceptant
10 accessible, open-minded, responsive 11 persuadable, persuasible, suggestible, sympathetic

recess
4 nook 5 niche 6 alcove 7 adjourn
8 dissolve, prorogue 9 prorogate,
terminate

Recessional author
7 Kipling (Rudyard)

recessive
8 retiring 9 withdrawn

recherché
3 new 4 rare 5 fresh, novel
6 choice, dainty, exotic, select 7 elegant, unusual 8 delicate, original,
superior, uncommon

recidivate
5 lapse 7 relapse 9 backslide

recipe
7 formula 12 prescription

reciprocal
4 mate, twin 5 match 6 double, fellow 9 companion, duplicate
10 coordinate
combining form: 6 allelo
prefix: 5 inter

reciprocate
5 repay 6 retort, return 7 requite
8 exchange, serve out 9 retaliate
10 compensate, recompense
11 interchange

recital
5 story 9 discourse, narration, recountal 10 recounting
11 description
combining form: 3 log 5 logue

recite
4 tell 5 chant, count, state 6 number, relate, report 7 narrate, recount 8 describe, rehearse 9 enumerate

reckless
4 rash, wild 5 brash, hasty 6 daring, madcap 8 carefree 9 audacious, daredevil, desperate, foolhardy, hotheaded, uncareful,
venturous 10 ill-advised, incautious,
mad-brained 11 adventurous,
temerarious, venturesome 13 adventuresome, inconsiderate,
irresponsible

reckon
3 add, put, sum 4 call, cast, deem,
foot, view 5 count, guess, judge,
lot on, place, total 6 bank on, cipher, figure, number, regard, rely
on 7 account, build on, compute,
count on, lot upon, surmise, trust in,
trust to 8 bank upon, consider, depend on, estimate, rely upon 9 calculate, enumerate 10 conjecture,
depend upon 11 approximate, calculate on

reckoning
3 tab 4 bill 5 score 7 account, invoice 8 figuring 9 ciphering, statement 10 arithmetic, estimation
11 calculation, computation

reclaim
7 recover, restore 9 restitute 10 rejuvenate 11 recondition, reconstruct 12 rehabilitate

recline
3 lie, tip 4 cant, heel, lean, list,
rest, tilt 5 slant, slope 6 lounge, repose 7 lie down 10 stretch out

reclining
4 flat 5 prone 9 decumbent, prostrate, recumbent 10 procumbent

recluse
6 hermit 7 eremite 8 cenobite, hermetic, secluded, solitary 9 anchorite, seclusive 10 cloistered
11 sequestered
female: 7 ancress 9 anchoress

reclusive
8 eremitic, reserved, solitary 10 antisocial 11 standoffish 12 misanthropic

recognition
6 credit 9 awareness 10 cognizance
combining form: 5 gnosy 6 gnosia,
gnosis

recognize
4 know, note, spot 5 admit, agree,
place 6 finger, notice, recall, remark 7 observe 8 diagnose, identify, pinpoint, remember 11 acknowledge, determinate, distinguish

recoil

3 shy 4 balk, duck 5 dodge, quail, quake, shake, start, stick, waver, wince 6 blanch, blench, falter, flinch, shrink, swerve 7 shudder, squinch, stickle, tremble 8 hesitate, reel back

recollect

4 cite, stir 5 rally, rouse, waken 6 arouse, awaken, recall, remind, retain, revive 7 bethink 8 remember 9 reminisce 10 retrospect

recollection

6 memory, recall 9 anamnesis 11 remembrance 12 reminiscence

recommence

5 renew 6 pick up, reopen, resume, take up 7 restart 8 continue

recommend

4 hail, tout 6 advise, commit, kudize, praise 7 acclaim, applaud, consign, counsel, entrust 8 advocate 10 compliment

recommendation

6 advice 8 approval 9 character, reference 11 credentials, endorsement, testimonial

recompense

3 pay 5 award, grant, repay 6 accord, amends, offset, return, reward 7 balance, redress, requite 8 reprisal 9 indemnify, indemnity, quittance, reimburse, retaliate, vouchsafe 10 compensate, remunerate, reparation 11 reciprocate, restitution

reconcile

3 fit 4 suit, tune 5 adapt 6 adjust, attune, square, tailor 7 conform 8 quadrate 9 harmonize, integrate 10 coordinate, proportion 11 accommodate

recondite

4 dark, deep, hard 5 heavy, runic 6 mystic, occult, orphic, secret 7 cryptic, learned, obscure 8 abstruse, academic, anagogic, esoteric, hermetic, mystical, pedantic, profound 9 difficult, enigmatic, scholarly, sibylline 10 cabalistic

recondition

3 fix 4 do up, mend 5 patch 6 doctor, repair, revamp 7 rebuild, reclaim, restore 8 overhaul 9 restitute 10 rejuvenate 12 rehabilitate

reconnoiter

5 probe, scout

reconsider

5 amend 6 review, revise 7 correct, draw off, rethink, re-treat, reweigh, sleep on 9 reexamine, think over 10 reevaluate

reconstruct

3 fix 4 do up, mend 5 patch 6 doctor, repair, retool, revamp 7 rebuild, reclaim, reorder, restore 8 overhaul, readjust, reorient 9 rearrange, reshuffle, restitute 10 rejuvenate, reorganize 12 rehabilitate

record

3 say 4 date, disc, mark; read, show 5 enrol 6 annals, enroll 7 archive, journal 8 archives, document, register 9 chronicle
combining form: 4 gram 5 graph
of a meeting: 7 minutes
of past events: 7 history
of proceedings: 4 acta
ship's: 3 log 7 logbook

recorder

5 flute

record player

5 phono 9 turntable 10 phonograph

recount

4 tell 5 state 6 recite, relate, report 7 narrate 8 describe, rehearse

recoup

6 regain 7 get back, recruit 8 retrieve 9 repossess

recourse

5 shift 6 refuge, resort 7 stopgap 9 expedient, makeshift 10 expediency

recover

4 heal, mend 5 rally, renew, rewin 6 offset, perk up, redeem, regain, resume, retake, revive 7 balance, get back, improve, rebound, reclaim, recruit, refresh, restore 8 reoccupy, retrieve, snap back 9 come round, reacquire, recapture, repossess, restitute 10 bounce back, compensate, convalesce, recuperate, rejuvenate 12 rehabilitate

recreant

3 rat 5 false 6 coward, untrue 7 unloyal 8 apostate, defector, disloyal, renegade, turncoat 9 faithless, turnabout 10 perfidious, traitorous, unfaithful

recreate

4 play 5 amuse, renew, sport 6 divert 7 disport, refresh, restore 9 entertain

recreation

3 fun 4 ease, play 5 mirth, sport 6 frolic, repose 7 disport, leisure, rollick 9 amusement, diversion 13 entertainment

recrudesce

5 react, recur, renew 6 return, revert, revive 7 reoccur

recruit

4 hire, mend 5 raise, renew 6 enlist, muster, novice, recoup, regain, repair, rookie 7 draftee, get back, rebuild, recover, refresh, restore 8 beginner, enlistee, freshman, neophyte, newcomer, renovate, retrieve 9 fledgling, novitiate, repossess 10 apprentice, tenderfoot

rectifier

4 tube 5 diode 8 detector

rectify

4 mend 5 amend, emend, right 6 repair 7 correct, rebuild

rectitude

6 virtue 7 honesty, probity 8 goodness, justness, morality 9 rightness 11 uprightness 13 righteousness

rector

6 pastor 9 clergyman 10 headmaster

rectory

5 manse 9 parsonage

recumbent

4 flat 5 prone 9 prostrate, reclining

recuperate

4 gain, mend 6 look up, perk up 7 improve 10 convalesce

recur

6 repair, repeat, resort, return, revert 7 iterate 8 turn back 9 reiterate 10 recrudesce

recurrent

see **recurring**

recurring

8 periodic 9 alternate 10 isochronal, periodical 11 isochronous 12 intermittent
combining form: 6 ennial

red

4 laky, puce, ruby 5 gules, ocher, rouge, ruddy 6 bloody, cerise, florid, wanton 7 carmine, flushed, glowing, oxblood, radical, rubious, scarlet, stammel, vermeil 8 flagrant, sanguine 9 carnation
combining form: 4 rhod 5 pyrrh,

pyrro, rhodo **6** erythr, pyrrho
7 erythro

Red
6 commie **9** Bolshevik, Communist

redact
4 edit **5** frame **6** revise **7** compose

Red and the Black author
8 Stendhal

red ape
9 orangutan

red arsenic
7 realgar

red-backed parrot
7 grassie

red-backed sandpiper
6 dunlin **10** blackheart

Red Badge of Courage
author: **5** Crane (Stephen)
hero: **7** Fleming (Henry)

red-bellied snipe
9 dowitcher

red benjamin
9 birthroot

redbird
8 cardinal **13** summer tanager

redbird cactus
7 jewbush

red blindness
10 protanopia

red blood cell
11 erythrocyte

red-blooded
5 lusty, vital **7** dynamic **8** vigorous
9 energetic, strenuous

redbreast
4 knot **5** robin

red-breasted snipe
9 dowitcher

redbuck
6 impala

Redburn author
8 Melville (Herman)

red carp
8 goldfish

red chalk
4 bole **6** ruddle

red cobalt
9 erythrite

red copper ore
7 cuprite

Red Cross
founder: **6** Barton (Clara)
Knight: **6** George

red currant
4 goya

redden
3 rud **4** glow, pink, rose, ruby
5 blush, color, flush, rouge, ruddy
6 mantle, pinken, rubify, rubric, ruddle **7** crimson **11** incarnadine

red dog
5 dhole, flour **8** card game

redecorate
9 refurbish

redeem
3 buy **4** free **5** loose **6** make up,
offset, ransom, set off, unbind
7 balance, manumit, release, unchain **8** atone for, liberate, outweigh **10** compensate

redeemer
6 savior **7** messiah, saviour

redemption
6 ransom **7** release **9** atonement,
expiation, salvation **11** deliverance

redeye
4 rudd **7** whiskey **8** rock bass, warmouth **10** copperhead

redfish
4 drum **6** salmon **11** channel bass

red grouper
5 negre

red grouse
8 moorbird, moorfowl, moor game

red hickory
6 pignut **9** mockernut

red hind
7 graysby **8** cabrilla

red-hot
2 up **5** fiery **6** ardent, fervid
7 abreast, blazing, boiling, burning, flaming, glowing **8** scalding,
sizzling, up-to-date **9** au courant,
scorching **10** blistering, passionate,
sweltering **11** impassioned

red hot cattail
8 chenille

red Indian paint
9 bloodroot

red ink
7 deficit

red inkberry
8 pokeweed

red ironbark
5 mugga **8** eucalypt

red iron ore
8 hematite

red lauan
8 tanguile

red lead
6 minium

red lead ore
8 crocoite

red-legged crow
6 chough

red-legged plover
9 turnstone

red-letter
6 rubric **7** notable **8** nameable
9 memorable **10** noteworthy,
observable

red-light district
5 levee, stews **10** tenderloin

red mite
7 chigger

red-neck
4 hick, rube **5** yokel **6** rustic
7 bumpkin, hayseed, peasant **9** hillbilly **10** provincial **12** backwoodsman

red-necked gazelle
5 addra

redo
5 renew **6** revamp **7** remodel, restyle **8** refinish, renovate **9** reproduce, restyling **10** redecorate,
repetition

red ocher
4 bole

redolence
4 balm **5** aroma, scent, spice
7 bouquet, incense, perfume
9 fragrance

redolent
5 balmy, spicy, sweet **6** aromal, savory **7** perfumy **8** aromatic, fragrant, perfumed **9** ambrosial, re-
mindful **11** reminiscent

redouble
4 rise **5** mount, rouse **6** deepen
7 enhance, magnify **8** heighten
9 intensify

redoubt
4 fort **7** citadel **8** fastness, fortress
10 stronghold

redoubtable
5 awful, famed, great **6** famous
7 eminent, fearful **8** dreadful, horrible, horrific, renowned, shocking,
terrible **9** appalling, frightful, prominent **10** celebrated **11** illustrious
13 distinguished

redound
6 accrue 7 conduce 10 contribute

red pine
4 rimu 10 Douglas fir

Red Planet
4 Mars

redpoll
6 linnet

redraft
6 revamp, review, revise, rework 7 restyle, revisal, rewrite 8 rescript, revision, work over 9 recension

redrawer
6 winder

redress
5 annul, venge 6 amends, avenge, negate 7 revenge 8 negative, reprisal 9 balancing, cancel out, frustrate, indemnity, quittance, vengeance, vindicate 10 counteract, neutralize, offsetting, recompense, reparation 11 restitution, retaliation 12 compensation, countercheck

red roe
5 coral

redroot
7 alkanet, pigweed

red sable
8 kolinsky

red silk cotton
5 simal

red silver ore
9 proustite 11 pyrargyrite

red snapper
6 rasher

red sorrel
7 roselle

red squirrel
9 chickaree

red-stalk aster
6 cocash

reduce
3 cut 4 bate, clip, diet, pare, slow 5 abate, break, crush, lower, shave, slash, taper 6 debase, defeat, demote, humble, lessen, rebate, recede, subdue, weaken 7 conquer, cripple, curtail, cut back, cut down, declass, deflate, degrade, demerit, disable, disrate, dwindle 8 bear down, beat down, decrease, diminish, discount, disgrade, enfeeble, mark down, roll back, slim down, step down, taper off, unweight, vanquish 9 downgrade, drain away, humiliate, overpower, scale down, subjugate,

undermine 10 depreciate, slenderize

reductio ad ___
8 absurdum

reduction
6 rebate 7 cutback, cutdown 8 discount, markdown 9 abatement 11 downgrading
combining form: 5 lyses (plural), lysis

redundancy
8 pleonasm, tumidity, verbiage 9 inflation, prolixity, tautology, turgidity 10 flatulence, periphrase, roundabout 11 periphrasis, superfluity

redundant
5 extra, spare, windy, wordy 6 prolix 7 diffuse, surplus, verbose 9 iterating 10 long-winded, palaverous 11 reiterating, repetitious, superfluous 13 supernumerary

red vitriol
9 bieberite, colcothar

redware
7 boccaro

red whelk
6 buckie

redwing
7 gadwall

redwing blackbird
6 maizer

redwood
5 rohun 7 amboyna, sequoia 8 mahogany 10 Scotch pine

reed
4 pipe 5 arrow
weaver's: 4 slay, sley 6 sleigh

reedy
4 slim, thin 6 slight, stalky, twiggy 7 slender, squinny, tenuous 9 attenuate

reef
4 lode, vein 7 bioherm

reek
4 funk 5 smell, stink 6 stench

reeking
4 rank 5 fetid, funky, fusty 6 putrid, rancid, smelly 7 noisome 10 malodorous

reel
3 bob 4 spin, sway, swim, turn 5 lurch, swing, waver, weave, whirl 6 careen, falter, teeter, topple, totter, wobble 7 stagger, stumble 8 titubate

reestablish
5 renew 6 recall, revive 7 restore 9 reinstate 11 reintroduce

reevaluate
6 review 7 rethink, re-treat, reweigh 9 think over 10 reconsider

reeve
4 ruff 6 thread 8 official 10 magistrate

reexamine
see **reevaluate**

refashion
4 turn, vary 5 alter 6 change, modify

refection
4 feed, meal 6 repast

refectory
10 dining hall

refer
4 cite, name 5 apply, quote 6 advert, advise, allude, assign, charge, credit, hand in, impute, insert, submit 7 ascribe, bring up, mention, specify 8 accredit, instance, point out 9 attribute

referee
3 ump 5 judge 6 umpire 7 adjudge, arbiter 9 arbitrate 10 adjudicate, arbitrator

reference book
5 atlas 6 manual 7 almanac 10 dictionary 12 encyclopedia

reference guide
5 index

referendum
4 poll

refine
6 polish, smooth 7 improve, perfect

refined
4 nice 6 subtle, urbane 7 genteel 8 cultured, debonair, delicate, finespun, polished, précieux, well-bred 9 distingué 10 cultivated

refinement
5 couth, grace 6 finish, polish 7 culture, dignity, suavity 8 breeding, civility, courtesy, elegance, urbanity 10 politeness 11 cultivation

reflect
4 echo 5 glass, image, study, think, weigh 6 mirror, ponder, reason 7 sparkle 8 cogitate 9 cerebrate 10 deliberate

reflecting
7 pensive 8 lustrous 10 cogitative, meditative, ruminative, thoughtful
light: 8 relucent
suffix: 6 escent

reflective
7 pensive 8 thinking 9 pondering 10 cogitative, meditative, ruminative, thoughtful

reflux
6 ebbing 9 condenser, returning

reform
5 amend, emend 7 correct, improve

Reformation leader
4 Knox (John) 6 Calvin (John), Luther (Martin) 7 Zwingli (Huldrych)

reformatory
3 pen 4 jail 6 cooler, lockup, prison 7 borstal 8 stockade 12 penitentiary

refractory
6 mulish 8 perverse, stubborn 9 obstinate 10 bullheaded, headstrong, self-willed, unyielding 11 intractable, stiff-necked

refrain
4 curb, deny, halt, keep, stop 5 check 6 arrest, chorus 7 forbear, inhibit 8 hold back, withhold 9 interrupt

refresh
4 rest 5 amuse, renew 6 divert, update, vivify 7 animate, enliven, quicken, restore 8 recreate, renovate 9 modernize, stimulate 10 rejuvenate

refresher
5 drink, tonic 6 bracer 9 stimulant

refrigerant
3 ice 5 freon 7 ammonia, cooling 13 carbon dioxide

refrigerator
6 fridge, icebox 9 condenser

refuge
4 port 5 cover, haven, shift 6 asylum, covert, harbor, resort, shield 7 hideout, retreat, shelter, stopgap 8 hideaway, immunity, recourse, resource 9 expedient, harborage, makeshift, sanctuary

refugee
2 DP 5 exile 6 emigré 7 evacuee 8 emigrant, fugitive 10 expatriate

refulgent
6 bright 7 beaming, radiant 8 luminous 9 brilliant

refund
5 repay 6 rebate 9 reimburse, repayment

refurbish
5 renew 6 update 7 restore, retouch 8 renovate 9 modernize 10 rejuvenate

refuse
3 jib 4 deny, dump, junk, nill 5 dreck, offal, spurn, swill, trash, waste 6 debris, kelter, litter, lumber, reject, scraps, spilth 7 decline, dismiss, garbage, rubbish 8 disallow, dustheap, keep back, riffraff, turn down, withhold 9 reprobate, repudiate, sweepings 10 disapprove

refutation
8 disproof, elenchus

refute
5 break, evert, rebut 8 confound, disprove 10 controvert, disconfirm

regain
6 recoup 7 get back, recover, recruit 8 reassume, reoccupy, retrieve 9 repossess
possession: 7 replevy 8 replevin

regal
6 august, kingly 7 queenly, stately, sublime 8 glorious, imposing, kinglike, majestic, princely, splendid 9 monarchal, sovereign 10 monarchial 11 magnificent, monarchical, resplendent

regale
5 feast 6 dinner, spread 7 banquet

regalia
5 cigar 6 finery 8 frippery 9 full dress

Regan
father: 4 Lear
husband: 8 Cornwall
sister: 7 Goneril 8 Cordelia

regard
4 care, deem, heed, mark, note, rate, view 5 assay, favor, honor, value 6 admire, assess, esteem, homage, notice, reckon, remark 7 account, concern, prizing, respect, valuing 8 approval, consider, estimate, interest 9 attention, curiosity, deference 10 admiration, cherishing, cognizance, estimation, observance, solicitude 11 approbation, carefulness, heedfulness, observation 12 appreciation, satisfaction 13 consciousness, consideration
as perfect: 8 idealize

regardful
6 arrect 7 duteous 9 advertent, attentive, intentive, observant, observing

regarding
4 as to, in re 5 about, anent 6 anenst 7 apropos 10 as respects 13 with respect to

regatta
4 race 6 fabric 7 liberty

regenerate
6 reform, revive 9 reproduce

regent
5 ruler 8 governor 9 professor

regicide's victim
4 king

regimen
4 rule 9 governing 10 government

region
4 area, belt, part, walk, zone 5 field, tract 6 domain, sector, sphere 7 demesne, terrain 8 province, vicinity 9 bailiwick, territory 12 neighborhood
elevated: 8 highland

regional
5 areal, local 9 localized 10 provincial

register
3 say 4 list, mark, read, roll, show 6 enroll, record 7 catalog 8 indicate

regnant
4 rife 6 master, ruling 7 current, popular 9 paramount, prevalent, sovereign 10 prevailing, widespread

regress
6 revert 9 throw back

regret
3 rue, woe 4 care 5 demur, grief, mourn, qualm 6 bemoan, bewail, grieve, lament, repent, sorrow 7 anguish, apology, deplore, scruple 9 deprecate, heartache, penitence 10 affliction, contrition, disapprove, heartbreak 11 compunction

regretful
5 sorry 8 contrite, penitent 9 repentant 10 apologetic 11 attritional, penitential

regrettable
4 dire 6 woeful 8 grievous 10 afflictive, calamitous 11 distressing, unfortunate 13 heartbreaking

regular
3 set 4 even 5 fixed, gross, typic, usual, utter 6 common, normal, steady 7 equable, general, natural, orderly, perfect, settled, typical, uni-

form **8** absolute, complete, constant, methodic, ordinary, outright, positive **9** clocklike, customary, downright, prevalent **10** consummate, methodical, systematic **11** commonplace, unmitigated **12** run-of-the-mill

regulate
3 fix **5** order **6** adjust, temper, tune up **7** arrange **8** organize **9** methodize **11** systematize

regulation
3 law **4** rule **5** canon, edict **6** curfew, decree **7** precept, statute **8** decretum **9** ordinance, prescript

regulator
8 governor

Rehabiah
father: **7** Eliezer
grandfather: **5** Moses

rehabilitate
7 reclaim, recover, restore **11** recondition

rehearse
5 drill, state **6** recite, relate, report **7** iterate, narrate, recount **8** describe, exercise, practice **10** run through

Rehoboam
father: **7** Solomon
kingdom: **5** Judah **6** Israel
mother: **6** Naamah

reign
4 king, rule, sway **6** govern **7** prevail **8** dominate, domineer, overrule **11** predominate **12** preponderate

reimburse
3 pay **5** repay **7** balance, requite **9** indemnify **10** compensate, remunerate

rein
4 cool **7** collect, compose, control, repress, smother **8** restrain, suppress

reinforce
4 prop **5** super **6** pillar **7** augment, bolster, enlarge, fortify, sustain **8** buttress, energize, increase, multiply **10** invigorate, strengthen

reinstate
5 renew **6** recall, return, revive **7** put back, replace, restore **8** give back **11** reestablish

reintroduce
5 renew **6** recall, revive **7** restore **11** reestablish

reinvestment
8 plowback

reiterate
5 renew, resay **6** repeat **7** reprise

reject
4 cast, jilt, junk, shed **5** debar, scrap, spurn **6** rebuff, refuse, slough **7** cashier, decline, discard, dismiss, exclude, shut out **8** jettison, throw out, turn down **9** eliminate, reprobate, repudiate, throw away **10** disapprove

rejoice
3 joy **5** exult, glory **7** gladden

rejoin
5 reply **6** answer, come in, retort **7** respond

rejoinder
5 reply **6** answer, retort, return **7** respond **8** antiphon, response

rejuvenate
5 renew **7** reclaim, recover, refresh, restore **9** modernize, refurbish **11** recondition, reconstruct

Rekem's father
6 Hebron

rekindle
5 renew **6** revive **8** renovate, retrieve, revivify **9** resurrect **10** reactivate, revitalize **11** resuscitate

relate
4 join, link, tell, yoke **5** apply, unite **6** assign, bear on, couple, credit, depict, detail, impute, render, report **7** connect, divulge, express, itemize, pertain, recount **8** bear upon, describe, disclose **9** appertain, pronounce

related
4 akin **5** alike **6** agnate, allied **7** cognate, connate, germane, kindred **8** incident **9** analogous, identical, pertinent **10** connatural **11** consanguine
by marriage: **7** affined

relating to
suffix: **2** al, an, ar, ic **3** ean, ese, ial, ile, ine, ist, ory **4** ical **5** ative, istic **6** itious **7** istical

relation
3 kin **7** kinsman **9** kinswoman
on father's side: **6** agnate
on mother's side: **5** enate

relative
2 ma, pa **3** kin, mom, sib, sis, son **4** aunt, mama, nana, papa, sibb **5** madre, mamma, mammy, momma, niece, pappy, pater, poppa, uncle **6** agnate, cousin, father, mother, nephew, parent, sister **7** brother, cognate, kinsman, sibling **8** daughter, cognate **9** dependent, kinswoman **10** contingent, grandchild **11** approximate, conditional, grandfather, grandmother, grandparent **13** granddaughter

relatives
7 kinfolk **8** kinfolks

relax
4 ease, loll, rest **5** loose, slack **6** lollop, loosen, lounge, rest up, unbend, unwind **7** ease off, slacken **8** loosen up **9** untighten

relaxation
4 ease, rest **6** repose **7** leisure **9** amusement **11** assuagement **12** requiescence

relaxed
4 mild, soft **5** loose, slack **6** breezy, casual, dégagé, gentle **7** lenient, sinuous, unfussy **8** flexuous, informal **9** easygoing **10** unreserved **11** low-pressure

release
4 emit, free, vent **5** issue, loose, unfix, yield **6** acquit, loosen, pardon, ransom, resign, unbind, uncage, uncoil **7** give off, give out, manumit, unchain, unleash **8** liberate, throw off, unfetter, untether **9** discharge, exculpate, exonerate, surrender, take out on, unshackle **10** emancipate
conditional: **6** parole

relegate
5 exile, expel, refer **6** banish, charge, commit, credit, deport **7** commend, confide, consign, entrust, expulse **8** accredit, displace, hand over, turn over

relent
3 ebb **4** fall, wane **5** abate, let up **7** die away, die down, ease off, slacken, subside **8** moderate

relentless
4 grim **5** cruel, rigid **6** dogged, fierce, mortal, strict **7** adamant, inhuman **8** obdurate, rigorous **9** ferocious, stringent, unbending **10** implacable, inexorable, inflexible, ironfisted, unyielding **11** unflinching **12** unappeasable

relevant
3 apt, fit **5** ad rem **6** allied, proper **7** apropos, cognate, fitting, germane, weighty **8** apposite, material, pointful, suitable **9** allowable, important, pertinent **10** admissible, applicable **11** applicative, applicatory, appropriate

reliable
4 safe **5** sound, tried, valid **6** cogent, proven, secure, trusty **7** certain, telling **8** accurate, apposite, attested, inerrant, unerring, verified **9** authentic, confirmed, validated **10** dependable **11** trustworthy **12** tried and true

reliance
4 hope **5** faith, stock, trust

relic
5 token, trace **6** shadow, trophy **7** memento, vestige **8** keepsake, memorial, reminder, souvenir **11** remembrance

relict
5 widow **8** residual

relief
3 aid **4** ease, hand, help, lift **6** assist, succor **7** comfort, secours, support **8** easement **9** allayment, softening **10** assistance, lightening, mitigation **11** alleviation, appeasement, assuagement

relieve
3 aid, rob, sub **4** ease, help, loot **5** allay, quiet, rifle, spare, spell **6** excuse, exempt, fill in, lessen, let off, reduce, soften, solace, soothe, subdue, supply, temper **7** absolve, appease, assuage, benefit, comfort, console, lighten, mollify, plunder, qualify, ransack, stick up, subvene **8** decrease, diminish, dispense, mitigate, moderate, palliate, take over **9** alleviate, discharge

religion
4 cult, sect **5** creed, faith **6** belief, church

religious
3 nun **4** holy, just, monk, true **5** godly, moral, noble, pious **6** devout, priest, sister, votary **7** ethical, staunch, upright, votress **8** faithful, monastic, votaress, votarist **9** pietistic, prayerful, steadfast
foot-washing ceremony: **6** maundy
offering: **8** oblation
order member: **5** friar **8** cenobite

relinquish
4 cast, cede, quit, shed **5** forgo, leave, waive, yield **6** desert, forego, give up, resign **7** abandon, discard, forbear, forsake, lay down, throw up **8** abdicate, abnegate, hand over, lay aside, renounce **9** sacrifice, surrender

relish
4 like, tang, zest **5** enjoy, flair, gusto, heart, sapor, savor, smack, taste **6** admire, flavor, liking, loving, palate **7** leaning **8** enjoying, penchant, pleasure, sapidity **9** delight in, diversion, enjoyment, prejudice **10** appreciate, propensity **11** delectation

relucent
7 radiant, shining **10** reflecting

reluctant
3 shy **4** wary **5** chary, loath **6** afraid, averse **7** uneager **8** backward, cautious **9** unwilling **10** indisposed
prophet: **5** Jonah

rely on
5 trust **7** count on **8** depend on

remain
4 bide, stay, wait **5** abide, tarry **6** linger **7** survive **11** stick around

remainder
6 excess **7** balance, residue, surplus **8** leavings, leftover, residual, residuum

remains
4 body, mort **5** stiff **6** corpse, debris, fossil **7** balance, cadaver, carcass, residue **8** leavings, residual, residuum

remark
3 see **4** heed, note **5** glass **6** notice, postil, saying **7** comment, discern, mention, observe **8** exegesis, perceive, scholium **9** assertion, attention, statement, utterance **10** animadvert, annotation, cognizance, commentary, commentate, exposition **11** observation
in a play: **5** aside
witty: **7** epigram

remarkable
4 rare **6** signal, unique **7** salient, strange, unusual, weighty **8** peculiar, singular, striking, uncommon, unwonted **9** arresting, arrestive, important, momentous, prominent **10** unordinary **11** conspicuous, exceptional, outstanding, significant, uncustomary **13** extraordinary

___ Remarque
5 Erich (Maria)

remedial
6 curing **7** healing **8** curative, sanative, sanatory **9** vulnerary **11** restorative

remedy
4 cure, drug, heal **6** elixir, physic **7** cure-all, nostrum, panacea **8** antidote, biologic, medicant, medicine, specific **9** medicinal, pharmacon **10** corrective, medicament, medication **11** counterstep

remember
4 cite **5** educe, evoke **6** elicit, recall, relive, retain **9** recollect **10** retrospect

remembrance
4 gift **5** favor, relic, token **6** memory, recall, trophy **7** memento, present **8** keepsake, memorial, souvenir **9** anamnesis **12** recollection

remind
3 jog **4** warn **5** alert **6** advise, prompt **8** admonish

reminder
4 hint, memo, note, sign **5** relic, token **6** notice, trophy **7** gesture, memento, warning **8** keepsake, memorial, souvenir **10** admonition, expression, indication, intimation, memorandum, suggestion

reminisce
see **remember**

reminiscence
6 memory, recall **9** anamnesis **12** recollection

remise
4 cede, deed **5** alien **6** assign, convey **8** alienate, make over, sign over, transfer

remiss
3 lax **4** lazy **5** slack **8** careless, derelict, fainéant, indolent, slothful **9** negligent **10** behindhand, delinquent, neglectful, regardless **12** disregardful

remit
4 send, ship, stay **5** defer, delay, route **6** excuse, hold up, pardon, put off, shelve **7** address, condone, consign, forgive, forward, hold off **8** dispatch, postpone

remnant
4 heel, rest **7** balance, oddment, residue **8** leavings, residual, residuum

remodel
6 revamp **11** reconstruct

remonstrance
5 demur **7** protest **8** demurral, demurrer, question **9** challenge, objection

remonstrate
4 kick **5** fight **6** combat, except, object, oppose, resist **7** protest **9** withstand

remonstration
see **remonstrance**

remora
4 clog, drag 11 shark sucker, sucking fish

remorse
3 rue 6 regret 7 penance 9 attrition, penitence, penitency 10 contrition, repentance 11 compunction 12 contriteness

remorseful
see **regretful**

remorsefulness
see **remorse**

remote
3 far, off 4 back, slim 5 aloof, small 6 casual, far-off, secret, slight 7 devious, distant, faraway, obscure, outside, retired, slender 8 detached, far-flung, frontier, lonesome, off-lying, outlying, ulterior 9 incurious, uncurious, unsettled, withdrawn 10 negligible, outlandish 11 indifferent, out-of-the-way, unconcerned 12 uninterested
combining form: 3 tel 4 dist, pale, tele 5 disto, palea, paleo 6 palaeo, palaio

remotest
6 utmost 7 extreme, outmost 9 outermost, uttermost 11 furthermost

remove
4 doff, ship, skim 5 douse, erase, purge, shift 6 efface, put off, unseat 7 blot out, cast off, disturb, expunge, extract, take off, take out 8 dislodge, displace, displant, evacuate, take away, throw off, transfer, withdraw 9 clear away, dislocate, eliminate, eradicate, extirpate, liquidate 10 obliterate 11 exterminate
from office: 6 depose
hair: 8 depilate
prefix: 2 de
surgically: 6 resect

removed
3 far 5 alone, aloof, apart 6 far-off, secret 7 devious, distant, faraway, isolate, obscure 8 detached, far-flung, isolated, lonesome, off-lying, outlying

remunerate
3 pay 5 award, grant, repay 6 accord 7 guerdon, requite 9 indemnify, reimburse, vouchsafe 10 recompense

remunerative
6 paying 7 gainful 9 lucrative 10 profitable, well-paying, worthwhile 11 moneymaking 12 advantageous

Remus
brother: 7 Romulus
father: 4 Mars
mother: 10 Rhea Silvia
slayer: 7 Romulus

renaissance
see **rebirth**

renal
7 nephric

rend
3 rip 4 rive, tear 5 split 6 cleave, divide

render
3 put 4 limn, turn 5 image 6 depict, govern, return 7 execute, picture, portray 8 carry out, describe 9 delineate, interpret, represent, translate, transpose 10 administer 12 administrate
suffix: 2 en

rendering
7 version 10 paraphrase 11 restatement, translation

rendezvous
4 date 5 haunt, raise, tryst 6 gather, muster, resort 7 collect, hangout, purlieu 8 assemble, congress 9 forgather 10 congregate, engagement 11 appointment, assignation

rendition
7 reading, version 11 translation

renegade
3 rat 5 rebel 7 heretic 8 apostate, defector, deserter, forsaker, recreant, turncoat 9 abandoner, insurgent, turnabout 10 iconoclast, schismatic 13 tergiversator

renege
5 welsh 6 cry off, resile 7 back off, back out 8 back down 9 backpedal

renew
4 mend 5 fresh, resay 6 pick up, recall, reform, reopen, repair, repeat, resume, revise, revive, take up, update 7 correct, freshen, iterate, rebuild, rectify, refresh, remodel, reprise, restart, restore 8 continue, make over, rekindle, retrieve, revivify 9 modernize, refurbish, reinstate, reiterate, resurrect 10 ingeminate, reactivate, recommence, rejuvenate, revitalize 11 reestablish, reintroduce

rennet
8 abomasum

renounce
3 rat 4 quit, turn 5 chuck, demit

6 defect, desert, resign 7 abandon, forsake 8 abdicate, disclaim 9 repudiate, throw over 10 apostatize, tergiverse

renovate
5 clean 6 revive 7 cleanse, refresh, restore 8 rekindle, retrieve, revivify 9 modernize, refurbish, resurrect 10 revitalize

renown
4 fame 5 éclat, kudos 6 repute 8 eminence, prestige 9 celebrity, notoriety 10 prominence, prominency, reputation 11 distinction, preeminence

renowned
5 famed, great 6 famous, lauded, signal 7 eminent, notable, praised 8 extolled 9 acclaimed, prominent 10 celebrated, celebrious 11 illustrious, outstanding 13 distinguished

rent
3 let 4 hire, rift, torn 5 break, lease, split 6 breach, schism, sublet 7 charter, fissure, mangled, rupture 8 fracture, sublease

rental
4 flat 5 rooms, suite 8 lodgings, tenement 9 apartment

renter
6 lessee

renunciation
6 denial 8 forgoing, yielding 9 eschewing, sacrifice, surrender 10 abjurement, forbearing, self-denial 11 forswearing

reopen
5 renew 6 pick up, resume, take up 7 restart 8 continue 10 recommence

reorder
6 retool 7 permute 8 readjust 9 rearrange, reshuffle 11 reconstruct 12 reconstitute

reorganization
7 shake-up 8 overturn, turnover

reorganize
6 retool 7 rebuild, refound 8 readjust, renovate, resettle 9 rearrange, reshuffle 10 regenerate 11 reconstruct, reestablish 12 reconstitute

reorient
6 retool 8 readjust 9 rearrange, reshuffle

repair
3 fix, hie, run 4 case, do up, fare, mend, pass, trim, turn, wend 5 apply, order, patch, recur, refer, shape 6 doctor, estate, fettle, kilter,

push on, resort, revamp, travel **7** fitness, journey, proceed, rebuild, service **8** overhaul **11** recondition

reparation
6 amends, reward **7** redress **8** requital **9** atonement, indemnity, quittance **10** adjustment, recompense, settlement

repartee
3 wit **5** humor, irony **6** banter, retort, satire **7** riposte, sarcasm **8** backchat, badinage, comeback, response, snip-snap **9** rejoinder **10** back answer, persiflage

repast
4 feed, meal **9** refection

repay
5 award **6** accord, offset **7** balance, requite **9** indemnify, reimburse **10** compensate, recompense, remunerate

repeal
4 lift, void **6** recall, revoke **7** rescind, reverse **9** dismantle

repeat
4 copy, echo, harp, ring **5** chime, ditto, quote, recap, recur, renew, rerun, resay **6** parrot, recite, rehash, relate, retell, return **7** imitate, iterate, recount, restate **8** hash over, rehearse **9** duplicate, reiterate **12** recapitulate

repeater
7 firearm **10** recidivist

repeating
7 iterant

repel
4 buck **5** fight, rebut **6** combat, oppose, rebuff, reluct, resist, revolt, sicken **7** contest, disgust, dispute, fend off, hold off, keep off, ward off **8** nauseate, stave off

repellent
4 foul, vile **5** nasty **7** noisome **8** aversive, kindless, ungenial **9** invidious, loathsome, obnoxious, offensive, revolting, revulsive **10** disgusting **11** uncongenial

repent
3 rue **6** regret **7** deplore

repentance
3 rue **4** ruth **7** remorse **9** penitency **10** contrition **11** compunction **12** contriteness

repentant
see **regretful**

repetition
4 copy **7** recital **8** iterance **9** rehearsal

rephrase
6 reword **7** restate

repine
4 fret, fuss, kick, wail **6** murmur **8** complain **10** discontent

replace
5 renew, shift **6** change, recoup, regain, return **7** put back, recover, restore **8** give back, retrieve, supplant, take back **9** reinstate, restitute, supersede

replacement
3 sub **6** fill-in **7** stand-in **9** alternate, surrogate **10** substitute **11** locum tenens, pinch hitter, succedaneum

replenish
5 refit, renew, stock **7** restore

replete
4 full, rife **5** alive, awash **6** jammed, loaded **7** brimful, crammed, crowded, stuffed, teeming **8** brimming, swarming, thronged **9** abounding, chock-full **11** overflowing

replica
4 copy **5** ditto **6** carbon **9** duplicate, facsimile **10** carbon copy

replicate
4 copy

reply
6 answer, come in, rejoin, retort, return **7** respond **8** response **9** rejoinder

report
3 cry **4** buzz, chat, dirt, fame, name, news, talk, word **5** brief, ondit, rumor, state, story **6** advice, canard, gossip, impart, murmur, notice, recite, relate, review, rumble, speech, tattle **7** account, chatter, comment, hearsay, history, narrate, prating, recount, scandal, tidings, version **8** advisory, bulletin, chitchat, describe, rehearse **9** character, chronicle, grapevine, narrative, small talk, statement

reporter
7 newsman **10** journalist
inexperienced: **3** cub

repose
3 lie **4** rest **7** leisure, lie down, recline, renewal **10** relaxation, stretch out **11** refreshment, restoration **12** requiescence

repository
5 depot, store **7** arsenal **8** magazine **10** storehouse

repossess
see **regain**

reprehend
3 rap **4** rate, skin **5** blame, chide, knock, scold **6** berate, rebuke **7** censure, condemn, upbraid **8** admonish, denounce **9** criticize **10** denunciate

reprehensible
5 amiss **6** guilty, sinful, unholy **8** blameful **11** blameworthy **13** demeritorious

represent
4 body, copy, limn, mean, show **5** draft, image **6** denote, depict, embody, mirror, relate, render, sketch, typify **7** display, exhibit, express, imitate, narrate, outline, picture, portray, realize, signify, suggest **8** describe **9** body forth, delineate, epitomize, exemplify, interpret, personate, personify, symbolize **10** illustrate, substitute **11** emblematize, impersonate, personalize

representation
6 symbol **7** picture **8** likeness **9** portrayal **11** portraiture

representative
4 case **5** agent, envoy, ideal, model, typal, typic **6** deputy, sample **7** classic, example, typical **8** delegate, emissary, instance, monotype, sampling, specimen **9** catchpole, classical, exemplary **10** archetypal, prototypal **11** case history **12** illustrative, prototypical

repress
4 cool **5** shush **6** muffle **7** collect, compose, control, smother, squelch **8** restrain

repression
4 curb **5** check **7** choking, control, subdual **8** crushing, quashing, quelling, stifling **9** clampdown, crackdown, quenching, restraint, squashing **10** smothering

reprieve
7 respite

reprimand
3 rap, wig **5** chide **6** lesson, monish, rebuke **7** chiding, tick off **8** admonish, call down **10** admonition **12** admonishment

reprisal
6 amends **7** redress, revenge **8** avenging, revanche **9** indemnity, quittance, vengeance **10** avengement, recompense **11** counterblow, retaliation, retribution

reprise
5 renew, resay 7 iterate 9 reiterate

reproach
3 rap, wig 5 blame, chide, taunt
6 lesson, monish, rebuke 7 censure, chiding, upbraid 8 admonish,
call down 9 discredit 10 admonition 12 admonishment

reprobate
3 bad, rap 4 evil, heel, skin
5 blame, knock, spurn, wrong 6 refuse, reject, sinful, wicked 7 censure, condemn, decline, dismiss, immoral, lowlife, vicious, villain
8 denounce, roperipe, turn down
9 abandoned, criticize, dissolute,
miscreant, scoundrel 10 blackguard, disapprove, iniquitous, licentious 12 unprincipled

reproduce
4 bear, copy 5 beget, breed 7 imitate 8 generate, multiply 9 duplicate, procreate, propagate
11 reduplicate

reproduction
see **replica**

reproductive cell
3 egg 4 ovum 5 sperm, spore
6 gamete 7 agamete

reproof
3 rap, wig 6 rebuke 7 chiding
8 scolding 10 admonition
12 admonishment

reprove
4 warn 5 blame, chide, scold
6 lesson, monish, punish, rebuke
7 censure, chasten, correct, counsel, tick off 8 admonish, call down,
lambaste 9 criticize

reptile
5 snake 6 caiman, cayman, gavial,
lizard, turtle 7 tuatara 8 hatteria,
tortoise 9 crocodile, sphenodon
combining form: 6 herpet 7 herpeto
extinct: 8 dinosaur

republic
5 state 6 nation
Africa: 4 Chad, Mali, Togo 5 Benin,
Congo, Egypt, Gabon, Ghana, Kenya, Niger, Sudan, Zaire 6 Angola, Gambia, Guinea, Malawi,
Rwanda, Uganda, Zambia 7 Algeria, Burundi, Comoros, Liberia, Namibia, Senegal, Somalia, Tunisia
8 Botswana, Cameroon, Djibouti,
Tanzania 9 Cape Verde 10 Ivory
Coast, Madagascar, Mauritania,

Mozambique 11 Sierra Leone
12 Guinea-Bissau
Asia: 4 Iran, Iraq, Laos 5 China, India, Syria, Yemen 6 Turkey
7 Vietnam 8 Maldives, Mongolia,
Pakistan, Sri Lanka 9 Indonesia,
Singapore 10 Bangladesh, North
Korea, South Korea 11 Philippines
Central America: 4 Cuba 5 Haiti
6 Panama 7 Ecuador 8 Honduras
9 Costa Rica, Guatemala,
Nicaragua
Europe: 5 Italy 6 France, Greece,
Poland 7 Albania, Austria, Finland,
Germany, Hungary, Iceland, Ireland, Romania, Rumania 8 Bulgaria, Portugal 9 San Marino
Pacific: 5 Nauru 8 Kiribati
South America: 4 Peru 5 Chile 6 Brazil, Guyana 7 Bolivia, Uruguay
8 Colombia, Paraguay 9 Argentina, Venezuela

Republican Party
3 GOP
mascot: 8 elephant

Republic author
5 Plato

repudiate
4 deny 5 spurn 6 defect, desert,
disown, refuse, reject 7 abandon,
decline, disavow, discard, dismiss,
forsake 8 disallow, disclaim, renounce, turn down 10 apostatize,
disapprove, tergiverse

repugnance
4 hate 6 hatred, horror 8 aversion,
loathing 11 abomination,
detestation

repugnant
4 foul, vile 5 alien, nasty 6 creepy,
horrid 7 foreign, noisome 8 aversive, gruesome 9 abhorrent, extrinsic, invidious, loathsome, obnoxious, offensive, repulsive, revolting,
revulsive 10 disgusting

repulse
5 rebut 6 rebuff, reluct, revolt,
sicken 7 disgust, fend off, hold off,
keep off, ward off 8 nauseate,
stave off

repulsion
see **repugnance**

repulsive
see **repugnant**

reputation
4 fame, name 5 éclat 6 credit, renown, weight 8 prestige 9 authority, celebrity, character, influence,
notoriety

reputed
8 putative, supposed 9 estimable
10 creditable 11 conjectural,
respectable, suppositive 12 hypothetical, supposititious

request
3 ask, sue 4 pray 5 apply 6 appeal, desire, invite 7 solicit 8 entreaty, petition

Requiem for a Nun author
8 Faulkner (William)

requin
5 shark 8 cub shark, man-eater

require
3 ask 4 call, lack, need, take, want
5 claim, crave, exact 6 demand
7 call for, solicit 11 necessitate

required
6 needed 9 mandatory 10 compulsory, obligatory 12 compulsatory

requirement
4 must, need, want 6 demand
9 condition, essential, necessity
10 sine qua non

requisite
3 due 4 just, must 5 right
6 needed 7 condign, merited,
needful 8 deserved, rightful, suitable 9 condition, essential, necessity 10 sine qua non 11 appropriate 12 precondition

requisition
4 call 5 claim, exact 6 demand
7 solicit 9 challenge, postulate

requital
7 revenge 8 avenging, revanche
9 vengeance 10 avengement
11 counterblow, retaliation,
retribution

requite
3 pay 5 repay 6 return 7 content,
revenge, satisfy 9 indemnify, reimburse 10 compensate
11 reciprocate

reredos
6 screen 7 brazier 9 partition

rescind
4 lift 6 recall, repeal, revoke
7 reverse

rescue
4 free, save 6 ransom, redeem, regain 7 deliver, manumit, recover,
release 8 conserve, liberate, preserve, retrieve 9 extricate
10 emancipate 11 disentangle
12 disembarrass

research
   5 probe, quest 7 delving, inquest, inquiry, probing 11 inquisition 13 investigation

resect
   6 cut out, excise 9 extirpate

resemblance
   6 simile 7 analogy 8 affinity, likeness, parallel 9 alikeness 10 comparison, similarity, similitude

resemble
   5 favor 8 look like, simulate

resembling
   combining form: 4 form 5 iform
   suffix: 2 ar 3 ful 4 eous, itic

resentful
   4 sore 6 bitter, piqued, sullen 7 envious, jealous 9 grudgeful

resentment
   4 huff, miff 5 pique, spite 6 animus, malice, rancor 7 dudgeon, ill will, offense, umbrage 9 animosity, antipathy, malignity 10 antagonism, malignancy

reservation
   5 terms 7 proviso, strings

reserve
   4 book, fund, hold, keep 5 hoard, stock, store 6 detain, engage, retain, supply 7 backlog, bespeak, keep out, nest egg 8 contract, hold back, keep back, withhold 9 inventory, preengage, stockpile

reserved
   3 shy 5 aloof, close 6 formal, modest, offish, silent 7 bashful, distant, limited 8 eremitic, modified, reticent, solitary, taciturn 9 diffident, qualified, reclusive, withdrawn 10 antisocial, unsociable 11 ceremonious, close-lipped, constrained, standoffish, tight-lipped 12 closemouthed

reservoir
   5 hoard, stock, store 7 backlog, nest egg 9 inventory, stockpile

reside
   3 lie 4 live 5 dwell, exist 6 endure, inhere, occupy, people, tenant 7 consist, hang out, inhabit 8 continue, domicile

residence
   4 home 5 abode, house 8 domicile, dwelling 9 occupancy 10 commorancy, habitation, occupation, settlement 11 inhabitancy 12 inhabitation

resident
   5 liver 7 denizen, dweller 8 habitant, occupant 9 indweller 10 inhabitant

residential area
   5 exurb 6 suburb 7 exurbia 8 suburbia

resident of
   suffix: 2 er 3 ese, ier, ite, yer

residual
   4 heel 7 balance, remains, remanet, remnant 8 leavings 9 remainder

residue
   3 ash 4 heel 7 balance, remains, remanet, remnant 8 bone char, leavings 9 bone black, remainder 11 animal black
   from honey: 7 slumgum
   metallic: 4 slag
   mineral: 4 calx

resign
   4 cede, drop, quit 5 demit, leave, waive, yield 6 give up, submit 7 abandon 8 abdicate, hand over, renounce 9 surrender, terminate 10 relinquish

resignation
   7 modesty 8 meekness, patience 9 lowliness 10 compliance, conformity, humbleness 11 forbearance, longanimity, patientness 12 acquiescence

resigned
   7 passive 8 yielding 10 submissive 11 acquiescent, unresistant, unresisting

resile
   6 recede, recoil 7 rebound, retract, retreat

resilient
   4 airy 6 bouncy, supple, whippy 7 buoyant, elastic, springy, stretch 8 flexible, stretchy, volatile 9 expansive

resin
   4 balm 5 copal, damar, roset 6 dammar 7 acrylic, copaiba
   aromatic: 6 balsam, mastic 8 sandarac
   fossil: 8 retinite
   fragrant: 4 tolu 5 elemi 6 storax, styrax 7 ladanum 8 labdanum, olibanum
   gum: 4 kino 5 myrrh 7 benzoin 8 bdellium
   medicinal: 6 guaiac 8 guaiacum
   of an insect: 3 lac

synthetic: 8 phenolic
used by bees: 8 propolis

resist
   4 balk, buck, defy, duel, foil, stem 5 check, fight, repel 6 assail, attack, baffle, combat, hinder, impugn, oppose, thwart 7 assault, contest, counter, dispute, gainsay 8 obstruct, traverse 9 frustrate, withstand 10 contradict, contravene

resistance unit
   3 ohm

resistor
   8 rheostat

resolute
   3 set 4 bent, fast, true 5 loyal 6 ardent, intent, steady 7 decided, settled, staunch 8 constant, decisive, faithful, stubborn 9 allegiant, obstinate, steadfast 10 determined 12 pertinacious

resolution
   4 guts 5 heart, pluck, spunk 6 mettle, spirit 7 courage 8 analysis, decision, firmness 11 decidedness 13 dauntlessness, determination, purposiveness

resolve
   3 fix, rid 4 rule, work 5 break, clear, purge 6 decide, dispel, figure, settle, unfold 7 analyze, clear up, dissect, unravel, work out 8 conclude, decipher, decision, disabuse, disperse, firmness, unriddle 9 anatomize, breakdown, decompose, determine, dissipate, puzzle out 11 decidedness 13 determination, purposiveness

resonant
   3 fat 4 deep, full, loud, rich 5 noisy, round 6 mellow, rotund 7 beating, booming, orotund, pulsing, ringing 8 enhanced, plangent, powerful, profound, sonorous, sounding, strident 9 pulsating, thrilling, throbbing 10 clangorous, heightened, stentorian, thundering, thunderous 11 intensified 13 reverberating

resort
   2 go 3 den, inn, spa, use 4 nest, turn 5 apply, haunt, haven, hotel, lodge, recur, refer, shift 6 affect, devote, direct, employ, harbor, refuge 7 address, hang out, purlieu, retreat, riviera, stopgap, utilize 8 frequent, recourse 9 expedient, makeshift 10 substitute
   beach: 4 lido

resound

4 echo, hymn, laud **5** bless, cry up, extol **6** praise **7** glorify, magnify **9** celebrate

resounding

5 round **6** rotund **7** orotund, reboant, vibrant **8** emphatic, forceful, plangent, sonorant, sonorous **9** assertive, consonant

resource

3 way **4** hope, mode, step **5** dodge, means, shift **6** device, lash-up, manner, method, refuge, relief, string, system **7** fashion, measure, stopgap **8** artifice, creation **9** expedient, invention, makeshift, stratagem, surrogate

resources

5 means, worth **6** assets, riches, wealth **7** capital, fortune **8** property **9** substance

respect

3 awe **4** fear **5** favor, honor **6** admire, devoir, esteem, regard, revere **7** account, worship **8** consider, venerate **9** adoration, reverence **10** admiration, estimation, veneration **13** consideration

respectable

4 done, good, nice **5** right **6** comely, decent, proper, worthy **7** correct, reputed **8** adequate, all right, becoming, decorous **9** befitting **11** conforming, sufficient **11** appropriate **12** satisfactory **13** well-thought-of

respectful

5 civil **6** polite **7** duteous **8** gracious, obeisant, reverent **9** attentive, courteous **10** venerating **11** deferential, reverential

respecting

4 as to, in re **5** about **7** apropos **9** as regards

respire

7 breathe

respite

3 ten **4** blow, ease, lull **5** break, pause, spell **6** breath, recess **7** leisure **8** breather, reprieve **12** intermission

resplendent

5 proud **6** superb **7** blazing, flaming, glowing, sublime **8** glorious, gorgeous

respond

3 act **5** react, reply **6** answer, behave, come in, rejoin, retort, return **8** antiphon

response

5 reply **6** answer, retort, return **8** antiphon **9** rejoinder

involuntary: **6** reflex **7** tropism

responsibility

4 duty, onus **6** burden, charge

responsible

6 liable **10** answerable, dependable **11** accountable

responsive

4 warm **6** tender **7** sensile **8** replying, sensible, sentient, suasible, swayable **9** acceptant, answering **11** impressible, kindhearted, persuadable, persuasible, softhearted, susceptible, sympathetic

rest

3 bed, lie, nap, nod, sit **4** base, calm, doze, ease, hang, heel, loaf, loll, lull, seat, stay **5** basis, count, found, hinge, let up, lie by, pause, peace, quiet, relax, sleep, spell, unlax **6** bottom, depend, ease up, excess, ground, lay off, lounge, repose, snooze, unbend **7** balance, breathe, ease off, footing, leisure, let down, lie down, recline, remains, remanet, remnant, seating, silence, slacken, slumber, surplus **8** interval, leavings, overplus, serenity, slack off, vacation **9** deferring, establish, placidity, predicate, remainder, stillness

restate

6 reword **8** rephrase **9** translate **10** paraphrase

restatement

7 version **9** rendering **10** paraphrase **11** translation

restaurant

4 café **5** diner **6** eatery **7** beanery, tearoom, teashop **8** teahouse **9** brasserie, cafeteria **10** coffee shop **11** coffeehouse

price: **8** a la carte, prix fixe **10** table d'hôte

worker: **4** chef, cook **6** busboy, waiter **7** maître d' **8** waitress **10** dishwasher, headwaiter **12** maître d'hôtel

____ Restaurant

6 Alice's

restful

6 placid **7** easeful, relaxed **8** tranquil

restitute

6 return **7** reclaim, recover, replace **8** take back **10** rejuvenate **11** recondition, reconstruct **12** rehabilitate

restitution

6 amends **7** redress **8** reprisal **9** indemnity, quittance **10** recompense

restive

4 edgy **5** balky, nervy, tense **6** ornery, uneasy **7** fidgety, froward, uptight, wayward **8** contrary, perverse

restiveness

7 ferment, turmoil **8** disquiet **10** inquietude **11** disquietude

restless

5 itchy, jumpy **6** fitful, fretty, uneasy **7** fidgety, fretful, jittery, nervous, unquiet **8** agitated, fretsome, troubled **9** disturbed, perturbed, spasmodic, unsettled

restlessness

see **restiveness**

restorative

5 tonic **6** curing **7** healing **8** remedial, roborant, sanatory **9** remedying, vulnerary, wholesome **10** astringent

restore

4 cure, heal, save, stir **5** amend, rally, renew, right, rouse **6** arouse, better, recall, recoup, redeem, reform, regain, remedy, repair, return, revise, revive, update **7** correct, get back, improve, put back, reclaim, recover, recruit, rectify, refresh, replace **8** give back, renovate, retrieve, revivify, take back **9** modernize, refurbish, reinstate **10** rejuvenate **11** recondition, reconstruct, reestablish, reintroduce **12** rehabilitate

restrain

3 bit, gag **4** cool, curb, keep, rein, stop **5** block, check, cramp, crimp, leash **6** arrest, bridle, coarct, halter, hamper, hinder, hold in, impede, muzzle, pull in, temper **7** collect, compose, control, forbear, harness, inhibit, prevent, repress, smother **8** hold back, hold down, moderate, modulate, obstruct, suppress, underact, withhold

trade: **7** embargo

restrained

5 quiet, tasty **7** aseptic, subdued **8** discreet, moderate, retiring, tasteful **9** shrinking, temperate, unaffable, unextreme, withdrawn **10** controlled, reasonable

restraint

5 cramp **7** durance, embargo **8** pullback **11** confinement

legal: **5** estop

restrict

3 bar, tie 4 bind 5 limit 6 shrink
7 confine, delimit 8 prelimit 10 delimitate 12 circumscribe
a will: 6 entail

restriction

4 curb 5 brake, check, cramp,
limit, stint 7 control 10 constraint
11 confinement

restyle

6 redraw, revamp, revise, rework
7 redraft, rewrite 8 work over

result

3 end 5 close, ensue, issue 6 answer, effect, finish, sequel, upshot
7 outcome, product 8 sequence, solution 9 aftermath 10 conclusion,
production 11 aftereffect, consequence, eventuality, termination
incidental: 7 spinoff
suffix: 7 ization

resume

4 go on 5 renew 6 keep up, pick
up, recoup, regain, reopen, retake,
take up 7 carry on, reclaim, recover 8 continue, reoccupy, retrieve 10 recommence

resumé

5 sum-up 7 epitome, summary
9 summation, summing-up

resurgence

7 rebirth, revival 11 reanimation
12 risorgimento

resurrect

5 raise, renew 6 revive 8 rekindle,
renovate, retrieve, revivify 10 reactivate, revitalize

resurrection

7 rebirth, revival 10 renascence
11 renaissance 12 reviviscence,
risorgimento

resuscitate

see **resurrect**

retail

4 sell 6 market 11 merchandise

retain

3 own 4 have, hold, keep 7 possess, reserve 8 continue, hold
back, keep back, preserve, remember, withhold

retainer

3 fee 6 lackey, minion 7 servant
8 employee, follower 9 dependent

retaliate

5 repay 6 avenge, punish 7 requite, revenge 10 recompense
11 reciprocate

retaliation

see **reprisal**

retaliatory

prefix: 7 counter

retard

4 balk, clog, mire 5 delay, embog,
stunt 6 baffle, detain, fetter, hamper, hang up, hinder, impede,
lessen, reduce, slow up 7 bog
down, inhibit, set back, slacken
8 decrease, restrain, slow down
10 decelerate

retarded

3 dim 4 dull, dumb, slow
6 opaque, simple, stupid 7 moronic
8 backward, imbecile 9 dim-witted
10 half-witted, slow-witted
11 exceptional

retch

3 gag 4 keck 5 heave, vomit

retention

6 memory 7 holding, keeping,
storage

reticent

see **reserved**

reticulate

6 meshed, netted 10 cancellate

retinue

4 band 5 suite, train 7 company,
cortege 9 entourage, following

retire

2 go 3 bed 4 drop, exit, quit
5 leave, yield 6 depart, get off, recede, resign, turn in, vacate
7 abandon, dismiss, get away, pension, retreat, take off 8 fall back,
give back, run along, withdraw
9 discharge, surrender, terminate
10 pension off, relinquish
12 superannuate

retired person

7 emerita 8 emeritus

retirement allowance

7 pension

retiring

3 shy 5 timid 6 demure, modest
7 aseptic, bashful, rabbity 8 backward, reserved 9 diffident, unaffable, unassured, withdrawn 10 restrained 11 unassertive

retool

7 reequip, reorder 8 readjust, reorient 9 rearrange, reshuffle
10 reorganize

retort

3 gag, mot 4 jape, jest, joke, quip,
snap 5 crack, repay, reply, sally
6 answer, come in, rejoin, return
7 respond, revenge, riposte 8 anti-

phon, comeback, repartee, reprisal, response 9 rejoinder

retract

4 back 5 unsay 6 abjure, disown,
recall, recant, recede, revoke 7 exclude, rescind, rule out, suspend,
unswear 8 fall back, forswear, palinode, take back, withdraw

retral

4 back, hind, rear 5 after 6 hinder
8 backward, hindmost 9 posterior
10 retrograde

retread

4 tire 5 recap

retreat

2 go 3 den, fly 4 back, flee, port,
quit 5 cover, haven, leave, quail
6 asylum, bow out, covert, decamp,
depart, escape, harbor, recede, recoil, refuge, shrink, vacate 7 abandon, back out, pull out, shelter
8 back down, crawfish, evacuate,
fall back, give back, hightail, withdraw 9 climb down, harborage,
sanctuary
religious: 5 asram 6 ashram

retrench

3 cut 4 omit 5 slash 6 delete, excise, lessen, reduce 7 abridge, curtail, cut back, shorten 9 economize

retribution

3 pay 6 return 7 revenge 8 avenging, reprisal, requital, revanche
9 vengeance 10 avengement, punishment, recompense 11 counterblow
goddess of: 3 Ate 4 Fury 7 Nemesis

retrieve

5 renew 6 recall, recoup, regain,
rescue, revive 7 get back, recover,
recruit, salvage 8 rekindle, renovate, revivify 9 repossess, resurrect
10 reactivate, revitalize

retrograde

4 back, sink 5 lapse 6 invert, recede, retral, revert, worsen 7 decline, descend, inverse, relapse, retreat, reverse 8 backward,
decadent, fall back, inverted, rearward 9 backslide 10 degenerate,
disimprove 11 deteriorate 12 disintegrate, recapitulate

retrogress

see **revert**

retrospect

4 cite 6 recall, remind, review, revive 7 bethink 8 remember, revision 9 reminisce 10 afterlight
13 reexamination

retrospective
6 review **8** backward **10** exhibition

return
3 lob, pay **4** gain, give **5** lucre, react, recur, renew, repay, reply, yield **6** advert, answer, bestow, come in, profit, rebate, regain, rejoin, render, retort, revert, rotate **7** bring in, put back, rebound, recover, reentry, reflect, replace, reprise, requite, respond, restore, revenue, reverse, revolve **8** antiphon, comeback, earnings, feedback, give back, proceeds, response, take back, turn back **9** reinstate, rejoinder, repayment, repercuss, restitute, retaliate, reversion **10** recompense, recrudesce, recurrence **11** reciprocate **12** reappearance, reoccurrence

Return of the Native
author: **5** Hardy (Thomas)
character: **4** Clym **8** Eustacia

Reuben
brother: **6** Joseph
father: **5** Jacob
mother: **4** Leah
son: **5** Carmi **6** Hanoch, Hezron, Phallu

Reuel
father: **4** Esau **7** Ibnijah
mother: **8** Basemath
son: **5** Zerah **6** Mizzah, Nahath **7** Shammah **8** Eliasaph
son-in-law: **5** Moses

revamp
5 patch, renew **6** redraw, repair, rework **7** rebuild, redraft, restyle, rewrite **8** make over, overhaul, renovate **11** recondition, reconstruct

reveal
3 bid, rat **4** avow, bare, blab, leak, open, show, talk, tell, vent **5** admit, break, let on, mouth, peach, spill **6** betray, expose, impart, squeak, unmask, unveil **7** bespeak, blab out, breathe, confess, declare, display, divulge, exhibit, give out, publish, unbosom, unclose, uncover, whisper **8** announce, decipher, disclose, discover, give away, unclothe **9** broadcast, uncertain **11** acknowledge, communicate

revel
4 bask, hell, orgy, riot, roll **5** feast, gloat, spree **6** frolic, gaiety, wallow, welter **7** carouse, delight, indulge, jollity, roister, rollick, royster, wassail, whoopee, whoopla, whoop-up **8** carnival, festival **9** cel-

ebrate, festivity, high jinks, luxuriate, merriment, whoop-de-do **10** skylarking **11** merrymaking

revelation
4 tora **5** torah **6** oracle **8** epiphany, prophecy **9** discovery **10** apocalypse, disclosure **13** manifestation

reveler
8 bacchant, carouser **10** merrymaker

revelry
6 gaiety **7** jollity, wassail, whoopee, whoopla, whoop-up **8** carousal **9** festivity, high jinks, merriment, whoop-de-do **10** skylarking **11** merrymaking

revenant
5 ghost, shade **6** shadow, spirit, wraith **7** phantom, specter **8** phantasm **9** recurring **10** apparition

revenge
6 defend **7** justify, redress **8** reprisal, requital **9** vindicate **11** counterblow, retaliation, retribution

revenue
2 in **4** rent **5** gains, wages, yield **6** income, profit, return, salary **7** comings **8** earnings, interest, proceeds, receipts

reverberant
6 hollow **7** reboant **8** resonant

reverberate
4 echo, ring **5** repel **7** rebound, reflect, resound

revere
4 love **5** adore, enjoy, exalt, honor, prize, value **6** admire, esteem, hallow, regard **7** cherish, magnify, respect, worship **8** treasure, venerate **10** appreciate

revered
9 venerable

reverence
3 awe **4** fear **5** adore, dread, honor, piety **6** fealty, homage **7** loyalty, worship **8** devotion, venerate **9** deference, obeisance, solemnity
gesture of: **3** bow **8** kneeling **11** genuflexion **12** genuflection

reverend
3 sri **4** holy **5** abbot, clerk **6** clergy, cleric, divine, parson, sacred **8** clerical, minister, preacher **9** churchman, clergyman, monsignor, venerable **11** patriarchal **12** ecclesiastic

reverent
6 devout **7** dutiful **10** respectful

reverie
4 muse **5** dream, study **6** musing, trance, vision **7** fantasy, thought **8** daydream, dreaming **10** absorption, brown study, meditation **11** abstraction, daydreaming

reversal
4 turn **5** check **6** change, switch **7** backset, setback, turning **8** backfire **9** about-face, inversion, turnabout, volte-face

reverse
4 lift, turn **5** annul, check, polar, shift, verso **6** change, contra, defeat, invert, recall, repeal, revoke **7** backset, capsize, counter, rescind, set back, subvert **8** antipode, antipole, backward, contrary, converse, disaster, exchange, opposite, overrule, overturn, transfer **9** about-face, antipodal, backwards, diametric, dismantle, overthrow, transpose, turnabout, volte-face **10** antipodean, antithesis, misfortune, right-about, transplace
prefix: **2** de, ob **3** dis, dys

reversion
4 turn **5** lapse **6** return **7** atavism, escheat, relapse **9** about-face, throwback, turnabout, volte-face **10** right-about **11** backsliding, changeabout

revert
4 turn **5** lapse, react, recur **6** change, return **7** decline, escheat, inverse, regress, relapse **8** turn back **9** backslide, throw back, transpose **10** degenerate, recrudesce, retrograde, retrogress, transplace

revetment
7 sodwork **9** barricade **10** embankment

review
4 edit, scan **5** audit, organ, recap, study **6** notice, parade, revise, survey **7** account, brushup, checkup, comment, journal, recense, redraft, rethink, re-treat, revisal, reweigh **8** analysis, critique, magazine, rescript, revision, scrutiny **9** checkover, criticism, criticize, recension, reexamine, think over **10** afterlight, inspection, periodical, reconsider, reevaluate, reflection, retrospect **11** examination **13** reexamination, retrospection, second thought

revile
4 hate, rail, rate 5 abuse, libel, scold 6 berate, defame, malign, vilify 7 asperse, bawl out, chew out, slander, traduce, upbraid 8 backbite, disgrace, execrate, reproach 9 blaspheme 10 calumniate, tongue-lash, vituperate

revise
4 edit 5 alter, amend, emend 6 change, polish, redact, redraw, reform, revamp, review, rework, update 7 correct, improve, perfect, recense, redraft, restyle, rewrite, upgrade 8 overhaul, rescript, work over 9 recension 10 blue-pencil, reorganize

revitalize
see **revive**

revival
7 rebirth, renewal 8 wakening 10 renascence, resurgence 11 reanimation, renaissance, restoration 12 regeneration, rejuvenation, reproduction, resurrection, reviviscence, risorgimento 13 recrudescence, resuscitation

revive
4 wake 5 rally, renew, rouse 6 arouse, exhume, recall 7 bethink, enliven, freshen, quicken, refresh, respire, restore 8 activate, energize, reawaken, rekindle, remember, renovate, retrieve, revivify, vitalize 9 galvanize, reanimate, recollect, refreshen, reinstate, resurrect, stimulate 10 reactivate, recuperate, regenerate, rejuvenate, revitalize 11 reestablish, reintroduce, resuscitate 12 reinvigorate

revivify
see **revive**

revoke
4 lift, void 5 adeem, annul, erase 6 abjure, cancel, recall, recant, remind, renege, repeal 7 abolish, expunge, nullify, rescind, retract, reverse 8 abrogate, forswear 10 invalidate 11 countermand

revolt
4 defy, riot 5 rebel, repel 6 mutiny, offend, oppose, reluct, resist, sicken, uprise, uproar 7 boycott, disgust, repulse 8 mutineer, nauseate, overturn, renounce, sedition, uprising 9 insurrect, overthrow, rebellion 11 rise against, turn against 12 insurrection

revolter
5 rebel 6 anarch 8 frondeur, muti-neer 9 anarchist, insurgent 10 malcontent

revolting
4 foul, ugly, vile 5 nasty 6 horrid 7 hideous, noisome 8 shocking 9 loathsome, offensive, repellent, repugnant, repulsive 10 disgusting, nauseating

revolution
4 gyre, reel, riot, roll, spin, turn 5 cycle, round, twirl, wheel, whirl 6 change 7 circuit, shake-up 8 disorder, gyration, overturn, rotation, sedition, turnover, uprising 9 overthrow, pirouette, rebellion

revolutionary
5 rabid, rebel, ultra 7 extreme, fanatic, radical 8 mutineer, rotating, ultraist 9 extremist, insurgent 10 malcontent
American: 4 Reed (John) 5 Shays (Daniel)
French: 5 Marat (Jean-Paul) 8 Mirabeau (Comte de) 11 Robespierre (Maximilien)
Irish: 4 Tone (Wolfe)
Mexican: 5 Villa (Pancho) 6 Zapata (Emiliano)
Russian: 5 Kirov (Sergey) 7 Trotsky (Leon) 8 Kerensky (Aleksandr) 9 Kropotkin (Pyotr)

revolutionist
see **revolutionary**

revolutionize
5 alter 6 change, modify, recast, redraw, reform, revamp, revise 7 remodel, restyle 8 overturn 9 overthrow, refashion, transform 11 transfigure 12 metamorphose

revolve
4 birl, chaw, gyre, muse, roll, spin, turn 5 orbit, round, wheel, whirl 6 circle, gyrate, ponder, rotate 7 agitate, circuit 8 consider, gyration, meditate, mull over, rotation, ruminate, turn over

revolver
3 gat, gun, rod 6 pistol 7 firearm, handgun

revulsion
4 hate 6 hatred, horror 8 aversion, loathing 9 repulsion 10 abhorrence, repugnance 11 abomination, detestation

reward
4 meed, plum 5 bonus, booty, crown, medal, prize 6 bounty, carrot, trophy 7 guerdon, premium 8 dividend, requital 10 compensate, honorarium, recompense, re-munerate 12 compensation, remuneration

reword
see **restate**

rework
6 redraw, revamp, revise 7 redraft, restyle, rewrite

rewrite
see **revise**

Reynard the ____
3 Fox

Rezon's father
6 Eliada

rhadamanthine
3 due 4 just 5 right 7 condign, merited 8 deserved, rightful, suitable 9 requisite 11 appropriate

Rhadamanthus
5 judge
brother: 5 Minos
father: 4 Zeus 7 Jupiter
mother: 6 Europa

rhapsodic
8 ecstatic, effusive 9 emotional

Rhea
3 Ops
daughter: 4 Hera, Juno 5 Ceres, Vesta 6 Hestia 7 Demeter
father: 6 Uranus
husband: 6 Cronus, Saturn
mother: 2 Ge 4 Gaea
son: 4 Zeus 5 Hades, Pluto 7 Jupiter, Neptune 8 Poseidon

Rheingold, Das
character: 4 Loki 5 Freya, Wotan 6 Fafner, Fasolt 8 Alberich
composer: 6 Wagner (Richard)

rheostat
6 dimmer 8 resistor

rhesus
6 monkey 7 macaque

rhetoric
4 rant 6 speech 7 bombast, fustian, oratory 8 rhapsody 9 discourse, elocution, eloquence, verbosity 11 highfalutin, rodomontade, speechcraft 13 lexiphanicism
term: 6 aporia, ecbole, simile 7 epandos, litotes 8 metaphor 10 apostrophe, digression 12 alliteration, onomatopoeia

rhetorical
4 glib 5 gassy, grand, showy, tumid, vocal, windy 6 florid, fluent, mouthy, ornate, purple, turgid 7 aureate, flowery, orotund, pompous, stilted, swollen 8 eloquent, forensic, imposing, inflated, over-

done, sonorous, swelling
9 bombastic, grandiose, high-flown, overblown, tumescent **10** articulate, euphuistic, figurative, flamboyant, oratorical **11** declamatory, embellished, exaggerated, highfalutin, overwrought, pretentious **12** high-sounding, magniloquent, orchidaceous, ostentatious **13** grandiloquent

rhetorician
6 orator, writer **7** speaker
Roman: **11** Quintillian

Rhine River
city: **4** Bonn, Köln **5** Mainz **7** Cologne **8** Mannheim **9** Weisbaden **10** Dusseldorf
golden ring: **9** Rheingold, Rhinegold
nymph: **7** Lorelei
tributary: **3** Aar, Ill, Lek **4** Aare, Lahn, Main, Ruhr, Waal

rhinoceros
5 badak **6** borele **7** keitloa, upeygan **8** nasicorn
feature: **4** horn
relative of: **5** tapir

rhizome
4 root, stem **5** shoot **6** branch

Rhode Island
capital: **10** Providence
college, university: **5** Brown **6** Bryant **10** Providence **11** Salve Regina
founder: **8** Williams (Roger)
nickname: **10** Ocean State **11** Little Rhody
state flower: **6** violet

Rhodesia
see **Zimbabwe**

rhombus
7 diamond, lozenge **13** parallelogram

rhonchus
5 snore

Rhone River
lake: **6** Geneva
mountain: **4** Jura
town: **4** Lyon **5** Arles **6** Geneva
tributary: **5** Isère, Saône

rhubarb
3 row **4** beef **5** plant, run-in, set-to **7** dispute, quarrel, yawweed **8** pieplant **9** bickering **11** altercation, controversy

rhyme
4 beat, poem, rune, song **5** agree, check, meter, poesy, swing, verse **6** accord, cohere, poetry, rhythm

7 cadence, cadency, comport, conform, consist, consort, measure **8** dovetail, rhythmus **10** correspond

rhymer
4 bard, poet **5** rimer **7** bardlet **8** bardling, poetling, rimester, verseman **9** poetaster, poeticule, versifier **11** versemonger

rhymester
see **rhymer**

rhythm
4 beat, lilt, time **5** meter, pulse, swing, tempo **6** accent **7** cadence, cadency, measure **8** movement, sequence

rhythmic
6 poetic **7** pulsing, regular **8** cadenced, measured, metrical **9** cadential, pulsating

rialto
4 mart **6** market **8** district, exchange

riant
3 gay **4** boon **5** jolly, merry **6** blithe, bright, jocund, jovial **7** festive, gleeful, smiling **8** cheerful, laughing, mirthful

riata
4 rope **5** lasso **6** lariat

rib
3 fun, kid, rag **4** band, bone, dike, fool, jest, joke, josh, purl, razz, stay, wale **5** chaff, costa, ridge, tease **6** banter, costae (plural), lierne
combining form: **4** cost **5** costi, costo, pleur **6** pleuri, pleuro
relating to: **6** costal **7** costate

ribald
5 devil, rogue, scamp **6** coarse, rascal, risqué, vulgar **7** obscene **8** indecent, mischief, scalawag, slyboots **9** skeezicks **10** irreverent **11** rapscallion

ribbon
3 bow **4** band, tape **5** braid, reins, shred, strip **6** cordon, fillet, stripe, tatter **7** bandeau, banding, binding **8** fragment, tressure **9** banderole
combining form: **4** taen **5** taeni **6** taenio

rice
4 boro, paga, twig **5** arroz, bigas, canin, macan **6** branch **7** risotto
boiled with meat: **5** pilaf, pilau
combining form: **4** oryz **5** oryzi, oryzo

cooked with meat: **7** risotto **9** jambalaya
drink: **4** saki **7** pangasi
field: **3** cut **4** padi **5** paddy, sawah
husk: **5** lemma, shood, shude
long-stemmed: **4** aman
mountain: **5** smilo
short-stemmed: **3** aus

rich
3 fat **4** dear, easy, high, lush, oofy, warm **5** ample, flush, heavy, meaty, plump, round, sweet, vivid **6** absurd, costly, creamy, daedal, facund, fecund, florid, fruity, hearty, mellow, monied, ornate, potent, rococo, sating, superb **7** amusing, baroque, cloying, copious, fertile, filling, moneyed, opulent, orotund, pinguid, wealthy, well-off **8** abundant, affluent, childing, eloquent, fruitful, well-to-do **9** abounding, bountiful, elaborate, laughable, luxuriant, oversweet, plentiful, satiating, sumptuous, well-fixed **10** expressive, flamboyant, meaningful, productive, prosperous, well-heeled **11** comfortable
person: **5** Midas, nabob **7** Croesus **9** plutocrat

Richardson work
6 Pamela **8** Clarissa **15** Clarissa Harlowe

Richelieu's successor
7 Mazarin

riches
4 gold, pelf, weal **5** booty, lucre, worth **6** mammon, wealth **7** fortune **8** opulence, property, treasure **9** resources
demon of: **6** Mammon

rick
3 mow **4** bank, cock, heap, hill, pile, ruck **5** drift, shock, stack

rickety
4 weak **5** shaky **6** feeble, senile, wobbly **7** unsound **8** rachitic, unstable, unsteady **10** ramshackle, rattletrap

ricochet
3 dap **4** skim, skip **5** bound, carom, graze **6** bounce, glance, recoil **7** rebound

rid
4 free, lose, quit, shed **5** clear, empty **6** remove, uproot **7** abolish, deliver, release, relieve **8** liberate, shake off, throw off, unburden **11** disencumber

riddle

3 pan, why **4** crux, sift **5** griph, rebus **6** enigma, pierce, puzzle, screen **7** griphus, mystery, perplex, problem **8** permeate, separate **9** conundrum, penetrate, perforate **10** puzzlement

ride

2 go **3** rib **4** auto, bait, last, lift, sail, spin, tour, trip, turn **5** chivy, coast, drift, drive, float, glide, hound, motor, tease **6** badger, banter, canter, gallop, harass, heckle, hector **7** journey, oppress, overlap, overlie, shingle, survive, torment, torture **8** bullyrag, carousel, ridicule **9** carrousel, excursion, imbricate, persecute

ride out

7 outlast, weather

rider

6 clause, cowboy, jockey, knight **7** codicil **8** addendum, addition, appendix, horseman, reinsman **9** amendment **10** equestrian, supplement

ridge

3 rib, top **4** bank, brow, fold, hill, keel, reef, roll, ruck, seam, spur, wave **5** arris, chine, costa, crest, knurl, ledge, plica, quill, rivel, spine **6** crease, divide, furrow, rideau, rimple, saddle, summit **7** annulet, breaker, costula, crinkle, hogback, hummock, wrinkle **8** headland, shoulder **9** razorback **11** corrugation
gravelly: **5** esker
on the skin: **4** welt
sharp: **7** hogback

ridicule

3 guy, pan **4** gibe, haze, jape, jeer, lout, mock, quiz, razz, ride, twit **5** chaff, flout, mimic, rally, roast, scoff, scout, sneer, squib, taunt **6** deride, satire **7** lampoon, mockery, pillory, sarcasm **8** derision, raillery, satirize, travesty **9** burlesque **10** caricature
god of: **5** Momus
object of: **4** butt **13** laughingstock

ridiculous

5 antic, comic, dotty, droll, funny, rough, silly **6** absurd, insane **7** amusing, bizarre, comical, foolish, mocking, risible, ungodly **8** derisive, derisory, farcical, gelastic, improper, indecent, unseemly **9** cockamamy, fantastic, grotesque, laughable, ludicrous **10** indeco-

rous, irrational, outrageous, unbecoming **12** preposterous

riding

academy: **6** manège
costume: **5** habit
pants: **8** jodhpurs
whip: **4** crop **5** quirt

Rienzi composer

6 Wagner (Richard)

rife

4 full, rank **5** alive, ariot **6** active, filled, strong **7** current, popular, rampant, regnant, replete, teeming **8** abundant, manifest, numerous, swarming, thronged **9** abounding, plentiful, prevalent **10** prevailing, widespread **11** overflowing

riff

4 scan, skim **6** browse

riffle

4 fret, scan, skim, wave **5** rapid, shoal **6** browse, cockle, dimple, ripple **7** dip into, run over, shuffle **8** glance at **10** glance over, run through **11** flip through, leaf through, skim through **12** thumb through

riffraff

3 mob **4** junk, mass, scum **5** dregs, offal, trash, waste **6** debris, kelter, litter, rabble, refuse, tagrag **7** garbage, rubbish **8** canaille, unwashed **11** proletariat

rifle

3 arm, gun, rob **4** loot **5** piece, steal, yager **6** furrow, groove, jaeger, weapon **7** carbine, despoil, firearm, pillage, plunder, ransack, relieve **9** chassepot
accessory: **6** ramrod
kind: **6** Garand, Mauser **7** Enfield **8** Browning **9** Remington **10** Winchester **11** Springfield
pin: **4** tige

rift

3 gap **4** flaw, rent, rima, rime, rive **5** break, chasm, chink, cleft, crack, split **6** breach, cleave, divide, hiatus, schism **7** blemish, fissure, opening, rupture **8** crevasse, division, fracture, interval, rimation

rig

3 arm, fit, fix **4** gear, hoax, wind **5** dress, equip, getup, guise, trick **6** fit out, outfit, setout, tackle **7** appoint, arrange, costume, derrick, furnish, turn out **8** accouter, accoutre, carriage, equipage **9** apparatus, equipment

rigadoon

5 dance

rigamarole

see **rigmarole**

rigging

3 net **4** duds, gear, togs **5** dress, lines, ropes **6** attire, chains, tackle, things **7** apparel, clothes, raiment **8** clothing

right

3 apt, due, fit, ius, jus, now **4** away, bang, dead, done, fair, good, hale, jura (plural), just, nice, real, sane, tory, true, very, well **5** amend, amply, claim, clear, droit, emend, exact, fully, happy, legal, lucid, quite, sharp, sound, spang, title, whole **6** at once, comely, common, decent, dexter, direct, equity, highly, honest, lawful, normal, patent, proper, square, strict **7** condign, correct, diehard, exactly, fitting, fogyish, freedom, genuine, healthy, liberty, license, merited, notably, old-line, parlous, precise, rectify, redress, utterly **8** accurate, adequate, all there, appanage, becoming, bona fide, decorous, deserved, directly, easement, entirely, faithful, first off, interest, old liner, orthodox, properly, rigorous, smack-dab, squarely, standpat, straight, suffrage, suitable, suitably, usufruct **9** authentic, authority, befitting, equitable, extremely, fittingly, forthwith, franchise, honorable, instanter, perfectly, precisely, privilege, propriety, requisite, simon-pure, tolerable, undoubted, veracious, veridical, veritable, wholesome **10** acceptable, acceptably, accurately, adequately, altogether, applicable, becomingly, completely, concession, felicitous, perquisite, properness, remarkably, scrupulous, straightly, sufficient, sure-enough, well-liking **11** appropriate, bitter-ender, comme il faut, correctness, exceedingly, immediately, indubitable, prerogative, reactionary, standpatter, undistorted **12** compos mentis, conservative
combining form: **4** orth, rect **5** dextr, ortho, recti **6** dextro
feudal: **4** soke
legal: **5** droit **8** usufruct
royal: **6** regale **7** regalia (plural)

right away

3 now **6** at once **8** directly, first off, straight **9** forthwith, instanter, instantly **11** immediately, straightway

righteous
4 good, holy, just, pure 5 godly, moral, noble, pious 6 devout, worthy 7 ethical, sinless, upright 8 innocent, virtuous 9 blameless, equitable, exemplary, guiltless 10 inculpable, moralistic, principled

righteousness
6 equity, virtue 7 justice, probity 8 goodness, holiness, justness, morality 9 rectitude 11 uprightness

rightful
3 apt, due, fit 4 fair, just, true 5 legal 6 honest, lawful, proper 7 condign, fitting, merited 8 deserved, suitable 9 befitting, equitable, impartial, requisite 10 applicable, legitimate 11 appropriate

right-handed
7 dextral 8 dextrous 9 clockwise, dexterous

right-hand page
5 recto

rightist
4 tory 7 diehard 8 old liner, standpat 11 bitter-ender, reactionary, right-winger, standpatter 12 conservative

right-minded
5 moral, noble 7 ethical 8 virtuous 10 moralistic, principled

Rights of Man author
5 Paine (Thomas)

rigid
3 set 4 firm, hard, taut 5 fixed, solid, stein, stiff, tough 6 formal, severe, strait, strict 7 adamant, austere, buckram, hard-set 8 hard-line, ironclad, obdurate, rigorist, rigorous 9 draconian, immovable, impliable, inelastic, stringent, unbending 10 adamantine, inexorable, inflexible, ironhanded, motionless, relentless, unflexible, unyielding 11 immalleable

rigidity
5 frost 6 turgor 7 buckram 8 hardness, turgency 9 stiffness
muscular: 8 myotonia

rigmarole
6 ramble 8 nonsense 9 procedure 10 balderdash

Rigoletto
composer: 5 Verdi (Giuseppe)
daughter: 5 Gilda

rigor
5 trial 7 cruelty 8 asperity, hardness, hardship, severity 9 austerity, harshness, roughness, sharpness, sternness 10 affliction, difficulty, exactitude, strictness, visitation 11 tribulation, vicissitude 13 inflexibility

rigorous
4 hard, nice 5 exact, harsh, right, rigid, rough, stern, stiff 6 bitter, brutal, proper, rugged, severe, strait, strict 7 ascetic, correct, drastic, onerous, precise 8 accurate, exacting 9 draconian, inclement, stringent 10 burdensome, inexorable, inflexible, ironhanded, oppressive

rile
3 mud, vex 4 roil 5 anger, annoy, grate, muddy, peeve, pique, upset 6 muddle, nettle, put out 7 agitate, disturb, inflame, provoke 8 irritate 9 aggravate

rim
3 hem, lip 4 bank, boss, brim, edge, ring 5 bezel, bezil, bound, brink, skirt, verge 6 border, flange, fringe, margin, shield 7 annulus, horizon, outline 8 boundary, surround 9 perimeter, periphery
of a basket: 4 hoop
of a cask: 5 chime, chine
of an insect's wing: 6 termen
of a spoked wheel: 5 felly 6 felloe
of a volcanic crater: 5 somma

rima
4 rift 5 chink, cleft, crack, split 7 fissure 8 aperture

rime
3 ice 4 cake, rift 5 chink, cleft, crack, crust, frost, split 7 encrust, fissure, incrust 10 incrustate 12 incrustation

Rimmon's son
6 Baanah, Rechab

rimple
4 fold, ruck 5 crimp, plica, ridge, rivel, screw 6 crease, furrow, ruck up, rumple 7 crimple, crinkle, crumple, scrunch, wrinkle 11 corrugation

Rinaldo
beloved: 8 Angelica
cousin: 7 Orlando
father: 5 Aymon
horse: 6 Bayard
mother: 3 Aya
sister: 10 Bradamante
uncle: 11 Charlemagne

rind
4 bark, husk, peel, skin 5 crust
of roast pork: 9 crackling

ring
3 bee, eye, hem, mob, rim 4 bail, band, bell, bloc, bong, camp, clan, cric, ding, dirl, echo, gird, gyre, hoop, loop, peal, toll 5 anlet, arena, bague, bezel, cabal, chime, clang, cycle, group, knell, knoll, party, rigol, round, sound 6 begird, boxing, circle, clique, collar, collet, dindle, famble, girdle, staple 7 annulus, clangor, combine, compass, coterie, faction, ferrule, grommet, ingroup, resound, vibrate 8 bracelet, cincture, encircle, pugilism, surround 9 camarilla, coalition, encompass 11 combination, reverberate
around sun or moon: 5 broch 6 corona
combining form: 3 gyr 4 cycl, gyro 5 cyclo
curtain: 3 eye
for a compass: 6 gimbal
for a lampshade: 4 harp 7 gallery
harness: 3 dee 6 button, larigo, terret, territ
heraldic: 7 annulet
in a hinge: 7 gudgeon
of chain: 4 link 7 belcher
of color: 8 stocking
of dots around a coin: 8 graining
of leaves or flowers: 6 wreath 7 garland
of light: 4 halo 5 glory 6 corona, nimbus 7 aureole 8 halation
of Odin: 8 draupnir
of rope or metal: 4 hank 6 becket 7 garland, grommet, snotter, thimble
of two hoops: 5 gemel 6 gemmel, gimmal
on a key, pocket watch or scissors handle: 3 bow
on an archery target: 4 sous 5 souse
relating to: 7 annular
rubber, for a fruit jar: 4 lute
used as a valve or diaphragm: 5 wafer
used for securing a bird: 6 vervel
used to enclose deer: 7 tinchel
wedding: 4 band

Ring and the Book author
8 Browning (Robert)

ringed
8 annulate, circular 9 encircled 10 surrounded

ringer
4 fake, spit 5 image 6 double 7 picture 8 impostor, portrait 9 direct hit 10 simulacrum 13 spitting image

ringing

5 round **6** bright, fervid, jangle, rotund **7** clangor, orotund, vibrant **8** decisive, plangent, resonant, sonorant, sonorous **9** consonant **10** resounding

ringleader

4 boss **5** chief **6** honcho **10** instigator, mastermind

ringlet

4 curl, lock **5** tress **7** tendril

rinse

4 lave, wash **5** douse, swill **6** douche, sluice **7** cleanse
the mouth: **6** gargle

riot

4 hell, howl **5** brawl, melee, revel, smash, spree **6** attack, bedlam, clamor, émeute, excess, frolic, jumble, scream, tumult, uproar **7** anarchy, carouse, debauch, dispute, misrule, quarrel, revelry, roister, wassail **8** carousal, disorder, uprising **9** anarchism, commotion, distemper, sensation **10** donnybrook **11** disturbance

riotous

4 loud, lush, wild **5** noisy **6** lavish, stormy, wanton **7** bacchic, opulent, profuse **8** bacchian, prodigal, roaring **9** exuberant, luxuriant, profusive **10** boisterous **11** saturnalian **12** unrestrained

rip

3 cut **4** rend, rent, rive, spit, tear **5** shred, slash, split **6** attack, cleave, sunder **7** sputter **8** lacerate, splutter

ripe

3 fit **4** aged, late **5** adult, grown, ready **6** mature, mellow, timely **7** grown-up, matured, overdue **8** complete, finished **9** developed, full-blown, full-grown, perfected, virtuosic, well-timed **10** consummate, seasonable **11** full-fledged

ripen

3 age **4** grow **6** better, grow up, mature, mellow, season **7** develop, enhance, improve, perfect **8** heighten, maturate **9** intensify

ripening early

4 rath **5** rathe **8** rareripe

riposte

5 reply **6** retort, return, thrust **8** comeback, repartee **10** back answer **13** counterattack

ripping

4 fine **5** grand, nifty, super, swell

6 divine, peachy **7** capital **8** glorious, splendid, terrific **9** admirable, excellent, marvelous, wonderful **10** remarkable **11** sensational

ripple

3 cut, lap **4** curl, fret, riff, wave **5** acker **6** cockle, dimple, lipper, popple, riffle, rimple **7** crinkle, wrinkle

rip-roaring

5 noisy **6** lively **8** exciting **9** hilarious **10** boisterous, uproarious

ripsnorter

5 dandy **8** jim-dandy **9** humdinger **11** crackerjack

riptide

8 undertow

Rip Van Winkle

author: **6** Irving (Washington)
dog: **4** Wolf

rise

2 up **3** wax **4** come, flow, grow, head, hike, lift, rear, soar, stem, well **5** awake, begin, boost, build, climb, get up, issue, mount, occur, raise, rebel, rouse, scale, sit up, stand, start, surge, swell, tower **6** ascend, ascent, aspire, awaken, befall, betide, chance, deepen, emerge, expand, growth, happen, recess, revolt, spring, thrive, uprear **7** adjourn, advance, augment, bristle, develop, elevate, emanate, enhance, enlarge, fall out, magnify, pile out, proceed, prosper, roll out, stand up, succeed, surface, turn out, upgrade, upstand, upsurge **8** addition, dissolve, eminence, heighten, increase, levitate, multiply, prorogue, redouble, upspring **9** accession, accretion, aggravate, ascension, increment, intensate, intensify, originate, prorogate, terminate, transpire **10** derive from
above: **8** surmount
abruptly: **9** skyrocket
again: **7** resurge **9** resurrect
against: **5** rebel **6** mutiny, revolt **9** insurrect
and fall: **4** tide **5** heave **6** welter
and shine: **5** get up **7** pile out, roll out, turn out
gradually: **4** loom
swiftly: **4** boil, boom **6** spring
up: **4** fume, rear, well **5** rebel, swell, tower **6** ascend, revolt **9** insurrect

Rise of Silas Lapham author

7 Howells (William Dean)

riser

4 step

risible

5 comic, droll, funny **7** comical **8** farcical, gelastic **9** laughable, ludicrous **10** ridiculous

risk

4 dare, defy, face, luck, meet **5** beard, brave, peril, stake, wager **6** chance, danger, gamble, hazard, menace **7** fortune, imperil, jeopard, venture **8** accident, confront, endanger, exposure, jeopardy, openness **9** adventure, encounter, liability **10** compromise, jeopardize

risky

4 bold **5** hairy **6** chancy, daring, touchy, wicked **7** parlous, unsound **8** delicate, perilous, ticklish **9** dangerous, hazardous, sensitive, unhealthy **10** jeopardous, precarious **11** speculative, treacherous

risqué

3 raw **4** blue, foul, lewd, racy, sexy **5** broad, crude, dirty, gross, salty, shady, spicy **6** coarse, daring, earthy, purple, ribald, vulgar, wicked **7** naughty, obscene, raunchy **8** indecent, off-color, scabrous **9** audacious, inelegant, salacious, unrefined **10** indecorous, indelicate, suggestive

rite

4 cult, form **6** fetish, honors, office **7** liturgy, mystery, service **8** ceremony, hierurgy, occasion **9** formality, ordinance, procedure, sacrament, solemnity **10** ceremonial, initiation, observance **11** celebration, sacramental
aborigine: **4** bora
American Indian: **8** huskanaw **11** huskanawing
Buddhist: **6** pansil
funeral: **6** exequy **7** obsequy **8** exequies
Hindu: **4** puja **5** pooja, sradh **6** poojah, sradha **7** sraddha
Jewish: **4** bris **5** berit, briss, brith **6** berith **7** tashlik **8** tashlich **12** circumcision
Mayan: **3** kex
of initiation or purification: **7** baptism
of knighthood: **8** accolade
of prophecy: **6** augury
of recognition of merit: **8** accolade; (see also **sacrament**)

ritual

see **rite**

ritzy

6 modish **7** elegant, haughty **8** snobbish **9** expensive, luxurious **11** fashionable **12** ostentatious

rival

3 tie, try, vie **4** even, meet, peer, side **5** equal, fight, match, touch **6** amount, strive **7** attempt, compete, contend, contest, emulate, entrant, feuding **8** approach, emulator, opponent, rivalize, struggle **9** adversary, competing, contender, measure up, partake of **10** antagonist, competitor, contending, contestant **11** comparative, competition
prefix: **3** ant **4** anth, anti

rivalry

6 strife **7** contest, warfare **8** conflict, jealousy, striving, tug-of-war **9** emulation **11** competition

rive

3 hew, rip **4** chop, plow, rend, tear **5** burst, sever, smash, split **6** cleave, divide, pierce, shiver, sunder, thrust **7** shatter **8** fracture, fragment, lacerate, separate, splinter, splitter **11** splinterize

river

Africa: **4** Bomu **5** Congo, Mbomu, Zaire **6** Atbara **7** Aruwimi, Atbarah, Zambesi, Zambeze, Zambezi **9** Astaboras
Alabama: **5** Coosa **6** Mobile **7** Conecuh, Perdido **9** Tombigbee **10** Tallapoosa
Alaska: **5** Kobuk **6** Copper, Noatak, Tanana **7** Koyukuk, Susitna **9** Kuskokwim
Albania: **4** Drin **5** Drini
Argentina: **5** Negro **6** Parané **7** Matanza
arm: **6** branch **9** tributary
Asia: **3** Ili **4** Amur, Oxus **5** Indus **6** Jayhun, Sutlej **7** Oedanes **8** Amu Darya **9** Dyardanes **11** Brahmaputra
Australia: **4** Daly **5** Roper, Yarra **6** Barwon, Culgoa, Dawson, DeGrey, Murray **7** Darling, Fitzroy, Lachlan **8** Victoria **10** Yarra Yarra
Austria: **4** Enns
bank: **5** levee
Belgium: **5** Rupel, Senne, Weser **6** Dender, Dindar, Ourthe **8** Visurgis
Bolivia: **4** Beni **5** Abuná **6** Mamoré
Borneo: **5** Kajan
bottom: **3** bed
Brazil: **3** Ica **4** Pará, Paru **5** Negro, Xingu **6** Paraná **7** Madeira, Tapajós, Tapajoz
British Columbia: **6** Skeena **10** Bella Coola
California: **3** Eel, Pit **4** Kern, Yuba **6** Merced **7** Feather, Salinas, Trin-

ity **8** Tuolumne **9** Mokelumne **10** Sacramento, Stanislaus
Cambodia: **8** Tonle Sap
Canada: **3** Bow **4** Back **5** Moose, Peace **6** Beaver, Fraser, Nelson, Ottawa **8** Gatineau, Saguenay **9** Athabasca, Great Fish, Mackenzie, Richelieu **11** Assiniboine
Carolinas: **7** Catawba
central Africa: **6** Ubangi
central Asia: **5** Orhon **6** Gandak, Orkhon **8** Syr Darya
central Canada: **5** Slave
central Europe: **4** Eger, Elbe, Labe, Ohře **5** Albis **6** Danube
central United States: **3** Fox **5** Grand **6** Neosho, Platte, Wabash **8** Keya Paha, Missouri, Niobrara **9** Tennessee, Verdigris **10** Republican, Saint Croix **11** Mississippi
channel: **6** alveus
Chile: **3** Loa **5** Itata, Maule **6** Bío-Bío **8** Valdivia
China: **2** Si, Xi, Zi **3** Bei, Hun, Wei **4** Dong **5** Baihe, Huang, Hwang, Tarim **6** Yellow **7** Kashgar, Yangtze
China-North Korea: **4** Yalu
Colombia: **4** Tomo **6** Atrato **9** Magdalena
Colorado: **5** Yampa **8** Gunnison
combining form: **5** fluvi, potam **6** fluvio, potamo
Connecticut: **6** Thames **7** Niantic, Shepaug **9** Naugatuck **10** Farmington, Housatonic, Quinnipiac **11** Willimantic
crossing: **4** ford
current: **4** eddy **6** rapids
Czech Republic: **4** Iser **6** Jizera, Moldau, Vltava
dam: **4** weir
Denmark: **4** Stor
dried bed: **4** wadi **5** waddy
drowned: **7** estuary
East Africa: **4** Juba **5** Tsavo **6** Songwe
East Asia: **4** Yalu **5** Amnok **7** Oryokko
eastern United States: **7** Potomac
Ecuador: **4** Napo **10** Esmeraldas
England: **3** Esk, Exe, Nen, Ure **4** Aire, Avon, Eden, Nene, Ouse, Tees, Tyne, Wear, Yare **5** Swale, Trent **6** Mersey, Ribble, Thames
Ethiopia: **3** Omo **4** Baro, Dawa
Europe: **4** Oder **5** Saale **6** Danube, Ticino
Florida: **6** Indian **9** Kissimmee **10** Saint Johns **12** Apalachicola
France: **3** Ain, Lot, Var **4** Aire, Aude, Cher, Eure, Gers, Loir, Oise, Orne, Saar, Tarn, Yser **5** Adour,

Aisne, Drôme, Indre, Isère, Loire, Marne, Saare, Sâone, Seine, Somme, Yonne **6** Allier, Ariège, Scarpe, Vienne **7** Durance, Garonne, La Riège **8** Charente, Dordogne
Georgia: **6** Etowah, Oconee **8** Altamaha, Ocmulgee **13** Chattahoochee
Germany: **3** Ems, Rur **4** Eder, Eger, Elbe, Isar, Main, Rems, Ruhr **5** Hunte, Lippe, Rhine, Spree, Werra, Weser **6** Neckar
Germany-Poland: **4** Oder
Ghana: **5** Volta
god: **7** Alpheus, Inachus **8** Achelous
Greece: **3** Iri **4** Arta **5** Lerna, Lerne **7** Alpheus, Eurotas **8** Achelous **9** Arakhthos
hazard: **4** snag **6** rapids **7** Lorelei
Honduras: **4** Ulúa **5** Aguán **6** Patuca
Iberian: **5** Douro, Duero
Idaho: **5** Lemhi
Illinois: **8** Mackinaw
India: **4** Sind **5** Sindh, Tapti **6** Chenab, Jhelum, Kaveri, Kistna **7** Cauvery, Krishna **8** Acesines, Godavari
Indian subcontinent: **5** Ganga **6** Ganges
inlet: **5** bayou **6** slough
Iran: **3** Kor **4** Mand, Mund **5** Kārūn **8** Safīd Rud, Sefīd Rud
Ireland: **3** Lee **4** Deel, Erne, Suir **5** Boyne, Clare, Foyle **6** Barrow, Liffey **7** Shannon
Italy: **2** Po **4** Adda, Arno, Liri, Nera **5** Adige, Arnus, Etsch, Liris, Oglio, Padus, Piave, Tiber **6** Ollius, Rapido, Tevere, Trebia **7** Athesis, Rubicon, Secchia, Tiberis, Trebbia **8** Rubicone, Volturno
Kansas: **6** Pawnee
Kazakhstan-Russia: **4** Ural **5** Tobol **6** Irtysh
Kenya: **4** Athi, Tana
Kubla Khan's: **4** Alph
land: **4** holm **5** carse, flats **7** bottoms
Latvia: **2** Aa **5** Gauja
Latvia-Lithuania: **7** Lielupe
Lebanon: **6** Litani
Little Rock's: **8** Arkansas
living in: **9** rheophile
living on the bank of: **8** riparian
longest: **4** Nile
Louisiana: **11** Atchafalaya
Maine: **8** Kennebec **9** Aroostook, Penobscot
Malaysia: **9** Trengganu **10** Terengganu
Maryland: **8** Monocacy, Patapsco, Patuxent **9** Nanticoke

Massachusetts: 7 Charles, Taunton 9 Westfield 10 Housatonic
Mexico: 6 Pánuco, Sonora 7 Tabasco 8 Grijalva
Michigan: 4 Cass 5 Flint, Huron 7 Detroit, Saginaw 8 Manistee, Muskegon 9 Cheboygan, Kalamazoo 10 Michigamme, Shiawassee
Mississippi: 5 Pearl, Yazoo 10 Pascagoula
Moldova-Ukraine: 8 Dneister
Missouri: 5 Osage
Montgomery's: 7 Alabama
mouth: 4 lade 5 delta
Myanmar (Burma): 4 Pegu 8 Chindwin, Irrawady
Nebraska: 4 Loup 6 Nemaha, Platte 7 Elkhorn
Netherlands: 4 Waal 5 Issel, Yssel 6 Ijssel 7 Vahalis
New England: 4 Saco 6 Nashua 9 Merrimack 10 Blackstone 11 Connecticut 12 Androscoggin
New Jersey: 6 Rahway 7 Passaic, Raritan 8 Tuckahoe
New York: 4 East 5 Tioga 6 Hudson, Mohawk, Oneida, Oswego, Seneca 7 Chemung, Niagara 8 Chenango, Cohocton 9 Conhocton
New Zealand: 7 Waikato
Nicaragua: 4 Coco 7 Segovia
Nigeria: 5 Benin
North Carolina: 3 Haw, Tar 5 Neuse 6 Chowan 8 Alamance
northeast North America: 13 Saint Lawrence
northeast United States: 4 Ohio 6 Hoosic 7 Genesee, Hocking 8 Delaware, Mahoning 9 Allegheny 11 Monongahela, Susquehanna
Northern ireland: 4 Bann 6 Mourne
North Korea: 5 Daido 7 Taedong
northwest North America: 5 Yukon
northwest United States: 5 Snake 7 Klamath 8 Columbia 11 Pend Oreille
Norway: 4 Tana, Teno
nymph: 4 nais 5 naiad
obstruction: 4 snag
of fire: 9 Phlegeton
of forgetfulness: 5 Lethe
of ice: 7 glacier
of woe: 7 Acheron
Ohio: 5 Miami 8 Cuyahoga, Sandusky 9 Muskingum 10 Tuscarawas
Oklahoma: 8 Cimarron
Oregon: 5 Rogue 6 Owyhee 7 Malheur 8 McKenzie 9 Clackamas, Deschutes 10 Willamette
Panama: 5 Tuira 7 Chagres

Papua New Guinea: 3 Fly 5 Sepik
Paraguay: 3 Apa 9 Pilcomayo
Pennsylvania: 6 Lehigh 10 Schuylkill
Peru: 5 Rímac, Santa 7 Marañón 8 Apurímac, Huallaga, Urubamba
Philippines: 4 Abra, Agno 5 Pasig 7 Cagayan 8 Cotabato, Mindanao, Pampanga
Poland: 3 San 7 Vistula
Portugal: 4 Sado 7 Mondego
relating to: 7 fluvial, potamic 9 fluminose, fluminous
Rhode Island: 7 Seekonk 8 Sakonnet 10 Providence
Romania: 5 Arges
Russia: 2 Ob, Om 3 Don, Oka, Ufa, Usa 4 Kama, Kara, Lena, Msta, Neva, Sura, Svir 5 Onega, Terek, Volga 6 Anadyr, Angara, Belaya, Kolima, Kolyma, Ussuri, Vyatka 7 Dnieper, Pechora, Yenisei, Yenisey 8 Barguzin, Kostroma, Voronezh, Vychegda
Russia-Ukraine: 6 Donets
sacred: 5 Ganga 6 Ganges
São Paulo's: 5 Tietê
Scotland: 3 Dee, Don, Esk, Tay 4 Doon, Nith, Spey, Tyne 5 Afton, Annan, Clyde, Forth, Tweed 6 Teviot 7 Deveron 8 Findhorn
Shanghai's: 7 Huang-p'u, Hwang Pu
Sicily: 5 Salso 6 Simeto
siren: 7 Lorelei
Slovakia: 3 Vag, Vah 4 Gran, Hron, Waag 5 Garam, Nitra 6 Neutra, Nyitra
South Africa: 4 Vaal 6 Orange
South America: 3 Apa 6 Amazon 8 Amazonas, Orellana, Paraguay 9 Pilcomayo
South Carolina: 6 Saluda, Santee 7 Wateree 8 Congaree
South Dakota: 3 Bad
southeast Africa: 7 Limpopo 9 Crocodile
southeast Asia: 6 Dza-chu, Mekong 7 Salween 8 Lan-ts'ang
southeast United States: 6 Pee Dee 7 Noxubee, Washita 8 Escambia, Ouachita, Suwannee 10 Okanoxubee
southern United States: 6 Sabine
South Korea: 3 Kŭm
southwest Asia: 5 Dijla 6 Jordan, Tigris 8 Hiddekel 9 Euphrates
southwest United States: 4 Gila, Zuni 5 Pecos 6 Colorado
Spain: 4 Ebro 6 Aragon 12 Guadalquivir
Sweden: 4 Göta 5 Kalix
Switzerland: 3 Aar 4 Aare 5 Reuss
Syria: 6 Khabur 7 Orontes

Tasmania: 4 Huon
Tbilisi's: 4 Kura
Texas: 5 Llano 6 Brazos, Nueces 7 San Saba, Trinity 9 Guadalupe
Texas-Mexico: 8 Rio Bravo 9 Rio Grande
tidal: 7 estuary
Tokyo's: 6 Sumida
Turkey: 4 Aras 5 Araks 6 Seihun, Seyhan
Ukrainian: 3 Bug 4 Alma
underworld: 4 Styx 5 Lethe 7 Acheron, Cocytus 10 Phlegethon
Uruguay: 5 Negro
Utah: 5 Uinta, Weber 6 Jordan, Sevier
valley: 6 strath
Venezuela: 5 Apure, Caura 6 Caroní 7 Orinoco
Vermont: 3 Mad 5 Onion, White 8 Winooski
Virginia: 3 Dan 5 James 7 Rapidan 9 Nansemond 10 Appomattox, Shenandoah 12 Chickahominy, Rappahannock
wailing: 7 Cocytus
Wales: 4 Dyfi 5 Clwyd, Dovey, Teifi
Washington: 6 Skagit, Yakima 9 Klickitat, Snohomish, Wenatchee
West Africa: 5 Niger 6 Gambia 7 Senegal
western North America: 8 Columbia, Flathead
western United States: 7 Laramie 11 Yellowstone
West Virginia: 7 Kanawha
Wisconsin: 8 Kickapoo 9 Menominee
Wyoming: 8 Shoshone 10 Gros Ventre 11 Medicine Bow

___ Rivera, Painter
5 Diego

river duck
4 teal 6 wigeon 7 mallard, widgeon 9 greenwing

river horse
5 hippo 12 hippopotamus

riverine
7 potamic

rivet
3 fix 4 bolt, brad, stud 5 affix 6 attach, fasten 8 fastener

rivulet
3 run 4 burn, gill, race, rill 5 bache, bayou, bourn, brook, creek 6 runlet, runnel, stream 7 channel 9 streamlet

Rizpah
father: 4 Aiah

lover: 4 Saul
son: 6 Armoni 12 Mephibosheth

roach
4 fish, rock, spot 6 braise

road
3 way 4 fare, lane, line, path
5 drive, going, route, track 6 artery, avenue, career, causey, course, street 7 highway, journey, passage 8 causeway, chaussée, crossway, highroad, pavement, speedway, turnpike 9 boulevard 12 thoroughfare
along a cliff: 8 corniche
around a city: 6 bypass 7 beltway
bend: 7 hairpin
edge: 4 berm 8 shoulder
French: 6 chemin
in or to a mine: 4 bord 5 board
  8 footrill
Irish: 6 boreen 8 beallach
machine: 4 harl 5 paver 6 grader
  9 bulldozer
narrow (in England): 4 loke 5 drang, drong 8 driftway
of stones: 7 telford
raised: 5 agger
Roman: 3 via 4 iter
Scottish: 4 brae 8 beallach
side: 5 biway 6 branch 8 shunpike
Spanish: 6 camino
surface: 3 tar 6 bricks, gravel, stones 7 macadam 8 concrete, pavement
temporary: 7 shoofly
zigzag: 10 switchback

roadblock
7 barrier 8 blockade 9 barricade

road book
3 map 5 atlas 9 gazetteer, itinerary

roadhouse
3 inn 5 hotel, lodge 6 hostel, tavern 7 auberge, hospice 8 hostelry 11 caravansary

roadman
6 hawker, monger, vendor 7 drummer, higgler, packman, peddler 8 huckster, mongerer, salesman 9 canvasser

roadrunner
6 cuckoo 7 paisano

road rut
7 pothole 9 chuckhole

roam
3 bat, gad, run 4 rove, walk
5 drift, prowl, range, stray 6 ramble, stroll, travel, wander 7 mean-der 8 gadabout, straggle, vagabond 9 gallivant

roamer
5 gipsy, gypsy, nomad, rover
6 gadder, walker 7 drifter, rambler 8 gadabout, stroller, traveler, vagabond, wanderer 9 meanderer 12 peregrinator, rolling stone

roar
3 cry, din 4 bawl, bell, boom, bray, howl, rout, yell 5 laugh, shout 6 bellow, clamor, outcry, scream, shriek 7 bluster, rebound, ululate 9 repercuss 10 vociferate 11 reverberate
bullring: 3 ole
low: 5 brool
of a boar: 5 fream
of the surf: 3 rut 4 rote

roast
4 bake, cook, flay, melt, razz, roti 5 broil, parch, score, slash 6 scathe, scorch 7 blister, lambast, swelter, torrefy, torrify 8 lambaste, lash into, ridicule 9 castigate, excoriate

rob
3 cop, mug 4 fake, flap, lift, loot, lose, nick, oust, pelf, roll, sack, take 5 bribe, cheat, filch, harry, heist, pinch, pluck, reave, rifle, spoil, steal, touch 6 burgle, divest, hijack, hold up, hustle, pilfer, pirate, ravage, ravish, snatch, snitch, thieve 7 bereave, defraud, deprive, despoil, pillage, plunder, purloin, ransack, relieve, stick up, swindle 8 jackroll 9 knock over, strong-arm 10 burglarize

robber
4 yegg 5 crook, thief 6 bandit, catman, pirate, rifler 7 brigand, footpad, heister, ladrone, raffles, reifier 8 hightoby, hijacker, swindler 9 holdup man 10 cat burglar, highwayman, sandbagger, stickup man 12 housebreaker
grave: 5 ghoul
Irish: 8 woodkern
murderous (in India and Burma): 6 dacoit
of pedestrians: 3 pad 7 footpad
on high seas: 6 pirate

robbery
3 job 5 heist, theft 6 holdup, piracy 7 larceny, stickup 8 banditry
Scottish: 4 reif

robe
3 aba 4 mant, wrap 5 cloak, cover, habit 6 caftan, clothe, mantle, revest 7 becloak, costume, garment, manteau 8 clothing, covering, dalmatic, vestment
ancient Greek tragedian's: 5 syrma
baptismal: 7 chrisom
bishop's: 6 chimer 7 chimere
coronation: 8 colobium
Eastern Orthodox: 10 sticharion
Indian: 4 jama 6 khalat, khilat
Jewish: 6 kittel
knight's: 6 cyclas
Latin: 5 stola
loose: 5 camis, camus 6 kimona
Mexican: 5 manga
monarch's: 7 pluvial
of Roman emperors: 6 purple
of tartan: 7 arisaid
Turkish: 6 dolman
woman's: 5 cymar, simar, symar

Robinson Crusoe author
5 Defoe (Daniel)

robot
5 golem 7 android, machine 8 automata (plural) 9 automaton

Rob Roy author
5 Scott (Walter)

robust
4 hale, hard, iron, rude 5 hardy, lusty, sound, stout, wally 6 browny, hearty, potent, rugged, sinewy, strong 7 booming, healthy, roaring, thrifty, valiant 8 athletic, muscular, thriving, vigorous 9 strapping 10 boisterous, full-bodied, prospering, prosperous 11 flourishing 12 concentrated

robustious
6 rugged 7 boorish, ill-bred, loutish, lumpish 8 churlish, clownish, lubberly 9 unrefined 10 unpolished

rock
3 fly, zip 4 bill, crag, oner, reel, roll, rush, slip, sway, toss 5 boner, error, fluff, geode, heave, hurry, pitch, quake, shake, speed, swing 6 barrel, bullet, bungle, dollar, gangue, hustle, miscue, rocket, slipup, totter 7 agitate, blooper, blunder, boulder, breccia, concuss, hotfoot, misstep, tremble 8 astonish, convulse, undulate 9 oscillate
basaltic: 5 wacke
cavity: 3 vug 4 vugg, vugh
combining form: 4 lite, lith, lyte, petr, saxi 5 clast, petri, petro, phyre
decomposed: 6 gossan
fissile: 5 shale
foliated: 8 phyllite

formation: **4** sial **5** nappe **6** pluton **7** rimrock, terrane **8** isocline, syncline
fragment: **8** xenolith
fragmental: **8** psephite
granular: **6** norite
igneous: **4** lava, sial, sima **6** basalt, dunite, gabbro, ophite, pumice **7** diabase, diorite, felsite, granite, greisen, picrite, sienite, syenite **8** eruptive, felstone, obsidian, porphyry, trachyte, traprock **9** tachylyte **10** travertine
layer: **8** regolith **10** mantlerock
mass: **5** scree **9** batholith
metamorphic: **5** slate **6** gneiss, marble, schist **8** eclogite, ganister, mylonite **9** quartzite, soapstone
molten: **4** lava
protruding: **5** scaur
sedimentary: **4** clay, coal **5** chalk, chert, coral, flint, shale **6** pelite **8** mudstone, psammite **9** limestone, sandstone, siltstone
silicate: **8** hornfels
siliceous: **9** buhrstone
soft: **7** tripoli
suffix: **3** ite
volcanic: **4** tuff **5** trass **6** basalt, taxite, terras **8** pumicate, rhyolite, tephrite

rock badger
4 cony **5** coney, hyrax

rock bass
6 redeye **8** cabrilla

rock bottom
4 pith, root, soul **5** stuff **6** lowest, marrow **7** essence **8** cheapest **9** lowermost, substance, undermost **10** nethermost

rockbound
5 rigid **7** adamant **8** obdurate **9** unbending **10** inexorable, inflexible, unyielding **12** single-minded

rocker
6 cradle **7** shoofly

rocket
3 fly, zip **4** soar, whiz **5** arise, haste, hurry, mount, smoke, surge, tower, whish **6** ascend, bullet **7** missile, shoot up **8** firework, starship
engineer: **8** Von Braun (Wernher)
landing: **7** reentry **10** splashdown
launcher: **7** bazooka
launching: **7** liftoff **8** blastoff

rocketry
father of: **7** Goddard (Robert)

rockfish
5 reina, viuva **6** gopher, rasher, tambor **7** corsair, garrupa, grouper **8** bocaccio

___ Rockne
5 Knute

rock-ribbed
see **rockbound**

rockweed
4 tang **5** fucus **7** seatang, seaweed

rocky
4 dull, hard, weak **5** dizzy, reefy, shaky, stony **6** stoney, tricky, wobbly **7** petrean **8** bouldery, obdurate, ticklish, unstable, unsteady **9** bloodless, difficult, insensate, rockbound, steadfast **11** insensitive

rocky hill
3 tor

rococo
4 arty **6** florid, ornate **7** baroque **8** luscious **9** fantastic **10** flamboyant

rod
3 bar, gad, guy **4** bolt, came, cane, good, pole, scob, slab, ward **5** ingot, lytta, osier, perch, power, spoke, staff, stick, strip **6** billet, broach, carbon, etalon, pistol, raddle, skewer, switch, toggle **7** baculus, crowbar, scepter, spindle **8** punition, revolver **9** authority **10** correction, discipline, oppression, punishment **11** castigation **12** chastisement
bundle of: **6** fasces
combining form: **5** rhabd **6** rhabdo
glassmaking: **5** punty

rodent
3 rat **4** cavy, cony, degu, hard, mole, paca, pika, utia, vole **5** cavie, coney, coypu, gundi, hutia, jutia, lerot, mouse, zokor **6** agouti, agouty, beaver, biting, cururo, gerbil, gopher, jerboa, marmot, murine, nutria, rabbit **7** chincha, hamster, lemming, leveret, muskrat **8** abrocome, capibara, capybara, chipmunk, cricetid, dormouse, gerbille, leporide, pacarana, sewellel, squirrel, tuco tuco, viscacha, vizcacha, water rat **9** guinea pig, porcupine **10** chinchilla, field mouse, prairie dog, springhare **11** kangaroo rat, meadow mouse, pocket mouse **12** pocket gopher
aquatic: **5** coypu **6** beaver, coypou, nutria **7** muskrat **8** musquash

burrowing: **6** gerbil, gopher **7** hamster **8** gerbille, viscacha, vizcacha
Eurasian: **6** suslik
family: **5** murid **6** murine **7** Muridae, sciurid **9** Sciuridae **10** Cricetidae **12** Octodontidae
furry: **10** chinchilla
genus: **3** Mus **5** Lepus
relating to: **8** rosorial
South American: **4** mara

rodeo
7 contest, roundup **9** enclosure **10** exhibition **11** competition
animal: **5** horse, steer **10** Brahma bull
event: **10** calf roping **11** bulldogging **12** bronco riding
performer: **5** clown **6** cowboy

___ Rodin
7 Auguste

rodomontade
4 blow, brag, crow, puff, rant **5** boast, mouth, prate, pride, vaunt **6** blower, braggy, vanity **7** bluster, boaster, bombast, bragger, fustian, vaunter **8** blowhard, boastful, boasting, braggart, bragging, puckfist, rhapsody, rhetoric, vaunting **9** gasconade, vainglory **11** braggadocio

Rodomonte
beloved: **8** Doralice
slayer: **8** Ruggiero

Rodrigo Diaz de Bivar
5 el Cid

rod-shaped
7 virgate **8** bacillar, rhabdoid **9** bacillary, virgulate

roe
2 ra **3** ova, pea **4** deer, eggs, hart, hind **5** coral, spawn **6** caviar **7** caviare

Roentgen's discovery
4 X ray

rogation
3 law **6** decree, litany, prayer **7** inquiry **8** petition, proposal **12** supplication

___ Rogers
3 Roy **4** Will

rogue
3 boy, guy, gyp, imp **4** heel, kite **5** cheat, crank, devil, gipsy, gypsy, hempy, knave, scamp **6** beggar, canter, chiaus, coquin, harlot, rascal **7** cheater, culprit, erratic, lowlife, sharper, villain **8** mischief, pic-

aroon, scalawag, swindler
9 defrauder, miscreant, scoundrel, skeezicks, trickster **10** blackguard, delinquent, mountebank
11 rapscallion
relating to: **10** picaresque

roguery

5 fraud **7** devilry, waggery **8** deviltry, mischief, trickery **9** devilment, diablerie **11** waggishness
12 sportiveness

roguish

3 coy, sly **4** arch **5** antic, lying
6 impish, pranky, shifty, wicked
7 knavish, larkish, playful **8** espiègle, prankful, prankish
11 mischievous

roil

3 mud, vex **4** foul, rile **5** annoy, dirty, grate, muddy, peeve **6** befoul, burn up, muddle, nettle
7 blunder, disturb, inflame, pollute, provoke, turmoil **8** irritate **9** aggravate **10** exasperate **11** contaminate

roily

5 muddy, riley **6** turbid

roister

4 hell, riot **5** revel, spree **6** frolic
7 carouse, wassail

Roland

7 Orlando
beloved: **4** Aude
betrayer: **4** Gano **7** Ganelon
friend: **6** Oliver **7** Olivier
horn: **7** Olivant
sword: **8** Durandal, Durendal
uncle: **11** Charlemagne

role

3 bit **4** duty, face, look, part, show
5 guise **6** aspect, office **7** seeming
8 business, clothing, function, province **9** character, semblance
10 appearance

roll

3 bun, gad, rob **4** bask, bolt, bunn, clew, coil, file, flow, furl, gush, gyre, list, muse, pour, roam, rock, rota, rove, toss, turn, wind, wrap
5 drape, drift, growl, heave, pitch, range, revel, stray, surge, troll
6 bundle, circle, enwrap, goggle, grovel, gyrate, muster, ponder, ramble, roster, rotate, rumble, scroll, stream, swathe, wallow, wander, welter, whelve, wintle, wrap up **7** biscuit, brioche, catalog, envelop, grumble, indulge, revolve, rissole, rollick, swaddle, trundle **8** enswathe, involute, meditate,

mull over, register, ruminate, schedule, turn over
of coins: **7** rouleau
sweet: **8** schnecke

roll about

6 wallow, welter

roll back

5 lower **6** reduce **7** repulse

roll call

4 list **6** roster **7** catalog **8** register, schedule

rolled

8 obvolute
backward: **8** revolute
together: **9** convolute

roller

4 wave **5** finer, inker, winch
6 caster, fascia, rowlet **7** breaker, carrier **8** cylinder

roller derby round

3 jam

rollick

4 bask, lark, play, roll, romp **5** caper, frisk, revel, sport **6** cavort, frolic, gambol, wallow, welter **7** indulge **8** escapade

rollicking

3 gay **4** glad, wild **5** antic, happy, merry **6** jovial, joyful, joyous, lively
7 playful **8** cheerful **9** hilarious, sprightly **10** frolicsome
12 lighthearted

rolling stock

4 cars **6** trucks **7** coaches, engines
8 cabooses, Pullmans, sleepers, trailers **11** locomotives

rolling stone

5 rover **6** roamer **7** drifter, rambler
8 wanderer **9** meanderer

roll up

4 furl **10** accumulate

roly-poly

see **rotund**

Roman

5 brave, Latin, papal **7** Italian
amphitheater: **9** Colosseum
assembly: **5** forum **6** senate
7 comitia
building: **5** Forum **6** Circus **8** basilica, Pantheon
clan: **4** gens
comedy writer: **7** Plautus (Titus), Terence
conspirator: **6** Brutus (Marcus Junius)
7 Cassius (Gaius) **8** Catiline
date: **4** Ides **7** calends, kalends
emperors: **4** Nero, Otho **5** Galba
(Servius Sulpicius), Nerva (Marcus

Cocceius), Titus, Verus (Lucius Aurelius) **6** Julian, Trajan **7** Hadrian, Maximus (Magnus Clemens, Marcus Clodius, Petronius), Severus (Lucius Septimius) **8** Augustus, Caligula, Claudius, Commodus (Lucius Aelius), Domitian, Tiberius, Valerian
9 Caracalla, Vespasian **10** Diocletian, Theodosius **11** Constantine, Valentinian
entrance hall: **5** atria (plural)
6 atrium
epic: **6** Aeneid
epigrammatist: **7** Martial
family: **7** Gracchi
Fates: **4** Nona **5** Morta **6** Decuma, Parcae
founder: **5** Remus **7** Romulus
fountain: **5** Trevi
garment: **4** toga **5** palla, sagum, stola, stole, tunic
general: **5** Sulla (Lucius Cornelius), Titus **6** Antony (Marc), Marius (Gaius), Scipio (Publius Cornelius)
8 Agricola (Gnaeus Julius)
god: **4** deus
blind: **6** Plutus
chief: **4** Jove **7** Jupiter
messenger: **7** Mercury
of agriculture: **6** Saturn
of animals: **6** Faunus
of death: **4** Mors
of dreams: **8** Morpheus
of fire: **6** Vulcan
of gates and doors: **5** Janus
of healing: **11** Aesculapius
of heaven: **6** Uranus
of households: **5** Lares **7** Penates
of love: **4** Amor **5** Cupid
of medicine: **11** Aesculapius
of mirth: **5** Comus
of regeneration: **7** Priapus
of sleep: **6** Somnus
of the sea: **6** Pontus **7** Neptune, Proteus
of the sun: **3** Sol **6** Apollo
of the underworld: **3** Dis **5** Orcus, Pluto **8** Dispater
of the wind: **5** Eurus, Notus **6** Aeolus, Aquilo, Auster, Boreas **8** Favonius, Zephyrus
of war: **4** Mars **8** Quirinus
of wealth: **6** Plutus
of wine: **7** Bacchus
of woods: **6** Faunus
two-faced: **5** Janus
goddess: **3** dea
of agriculture: **5** Ceres
of beauty: **5** Venus
of dawn: **6** Aurora
of flowers: **5** Flora
of handicrafts: **7** Minerva
of harvests: **3** Ops

of health: 7 Minerva
of hope: 4 Spes
of hunting: 5 Diana
of justice: 7 Astraea
of love: 5 Venus
of marriage: 4 Juno
of night: 3 Nox
of peace: 3 Pax
of springs: 7 Juturna
of strife: 9 Discordia
of the earth: 6 Tellus
of the hearth: 5 Vesta
of the moon: 4 Luna
of the sea: 10 Amphitrite
of the underworld: 10 Proserpina
of victory: 6 Vacuna
of war: 7 Bellona
of wisdom: 7 Minerva
of womanhood: 4 Juno
greeting: 3 ave
helmet: 5 galea 6 cassis
hero: 6 Caesar (Julius) 11 Cincinnatus (Lucius Quinctius)
hill: 7 Caelian, Viminal 8 Aventine, Palatine, Quirinal 9 Esquiline 10 Capitoline
historian: 4 Livy 5 Nepos (Cornelius)
king: 7 Romulus, Servius, Tullius 12 Ancus Martius 13 Numa Pompilius
military formation: 3 ala 6 alares (plural) 7 phalanx
miltary unit: 6 cohort, legion 7 maniple
officer: 9 centurion
official: 5 augur, edile 6 aedile, censor, consul, lictor 7 praetor, prefect, tribune 8 irenarch, quaestor
people: 5 Laeti 6 populi (plural) 7 populus, Sabines 8 plebians 9 plebeians 10 patricians
philosopher: 4 Cato (Marcus Porcius) 6 Seneca (Lucius Annaeus)
physician: 11 Aesculapius
port: 5 Ostia
procurator: 6 Pilate (Pontius)
racecourse: 6 circus
road: 4 iter
slave: 9 Spartacus
statesman: 4 Cato (Marcus Porcius) 5 Pliny 6 Caesar (Julius), Cicero (Marcus Tullius), Seneca (Lucius Annaeus) 7 Agrippa (Marcus Vipsanius) 8 Augustus, Maecenas (Gaius)
symbol of authority: 6 fasces

roman à ___
4 clef

romance
3 woo 4 gest, love, tale 5 amour, court, fable, fancy, feign, geste, novel, story 6 affair 7 fantasy, fiction 8 stardust 10 love affair

Romance language
6 French 7 Catalan, Italian, Spanish 8 Romanian, Rumanian 9 Provençal 10 Portuguese

Romania
capital: 9 Bucharest
monetary unit: 3 leu

romantic
4 wild 5 ideal, mushy 6 ardent, dreamy, exotic, gothic, poetic, slushy, sticky, unreal 7 maudlin, mawkish, strange 8 bathetic, fabulous, fanciful, invented, quixotic 9 fantastic, imaginary, visionary 10 idealistic, lovey-dovey 11 extravagant, sentimental

Romany
5 gipsy, gypsy

Romeo
7 amorist, Don Juan, gallant 8 Casanova, lothario, paramour
beloved: 6 Juliet
enemy: 6 Tybalt
father: 8 Montague
friend: 8 Mercutio

Rommel, Erwin
nickname: 9 Desert Fox

romp
4 play, roil, rout 5 caper, frisk 6 cavort, frolic, gambol, hoyden 7 courant, gammock, rollick, runaway, skylark

Romulus
brother: 5 Remus
father: 4 Mars
mother: 10 Rhea Silvia
victim: 5 Remus

rondure
3 orb 4 ball 5 globe, round 6 circle, sphere

rood
5 cross 8 crucifix

roof
3 hip, top 4 apex, deck, dome, flat, peak 5 cover, crest, crown, haven, house 6 cupola, harbor, palate, shield, summit, vertex 7 chamber, mansard 8 covering, housetop 9 fastigium
automobile: 8 fastback
false: 7 cricket
material: 3 tar, tin 4 tile 5 paper, slate, straw, terne 6 copper, gravel, thatch 8 shingles
of a cavern: 4 dome
of the mouth: 6 palate
part: 3 hip 4 eave 7 cricket
peak: 3 hip
structure: 9 penthouse

type: 5 gable 6 cupola 7 gambrel, mansard 9 butterfly 10 jerkinhead
vaulted: 4 dome

roofer
5 tiler

rook
4 bird, crow, milk 5 bleed, cheat, mulct, raven, steal, stick, sweat 6 castle, fleece 7 defraud, swindle

rookery
5 roost 8 building

rookie
4 colt, tyro 6 novice 7 recruit, trainee 8 beginner, freshman, neophyte, newcomer 9 novitiate 10 apprentice, tenderfoot

room
3 den, hut 4 aula, cell, hall, play, rein, seat, sway 5 board, divan, house, lodge, place, put up, range, roost, salon, scope, space, study 6 billet, camera, harbor, leeway, margin, reside, studio 7 boudoir, cabinet, chamber, cubicle, expanse, gallery, lodging 8 domicile, latitude 9 apartment, clearance
ancient Roman: 5 atria (plural), oecus 6 atrium 7 fumaria 8 aedicule
eating: 4 nook 7 cenacle, kitchen 9 refectory
food storage: 6 larder, pantry
for paintings: 7 gallery
for small meetings: 7 seminar
in a monastery: 4 cell 6 lavabo 8 locutory 9 refectory 11 calefactory
in a prison: 4 cell 7 dungeon
in a tower: 6 belfry
next to dining room: 7 servery
on a ship: 5 cabin 6 galley
public: 7 theater
round: 7 rotunda

room and board
7 lodging 8 lodgment

roomer
5 guest 6 lodger, tenant 7 boarder

roomy
4 wide 5 ample, broad, large, spacy 7 spacial 8 spacious 9 capacious 10 commodious

Roosevelt, F.D.
birthplace: 8 Hyde Park
dog: 4 Fala
message: 12 fireside chat
mother: 4 Sara
predecessor: 6 Hoover (Herbert)
program: 7 New Deal
successor: 6 Truman (Harry)
wife: 7 Eleanor

roost
3 hut, sit 4 land, nest, room
5 board, house, light, lodge, perch, put up 6 alight, billet, garret, harbor, settle 7 dovecot, lodging, quarter, set down, sit down 8 domicile, dovecote 9 touch down

rooster
4 cock 5 capon, gallo 8 gamecock
11 chanticleer

root
3 dig, fix 4 base, bulb, core, grub, moot, pith, soul, stem, well 5 basis, cheer, embed, grout, heart, infix, lodge, plant, quick, radix, shout, stuff, tuber 6 bottom, center, etymon, ground, marrow, origin, rise to, settle, source 7 applaud, bedrock, essence, footing, ingrain, radical, support 8 entrench, fountain, radicate, wellhead 9 beginning, establish, inception, substance
10 derivation, foundation
aromatic: 7 ginseng
combining form: 4 rhiz 5 rhiza, rhizo 6 rhizae (plural), rrhiza 7 rrhizae (plural)
edible: 3 oca, oka, roi, yam 4 beet, eddo 6 carrot, ginger, radish, turnip 7 parsnip 8 rutabaga, tuckahoe
fragrant: 4 khus 5 orris 6 cuscus, kuskus 7 vetiver 8 khuskhus
main: 7 taproot
medicinal: 5 jalap 7 ginseng, zedoary
relating to: 7 radical
starch: 4 arum
tropical: 4 taro
word: 6 etymon
yielding red dye: 4 chay, choy 5 chaya, choya 6 madder

rootlet
7 radicel, radicle, rhizoid

root out
4 grub, stub 6 evulse 7 abolish, blot out, destroy, wipe out 8 demolish 9 eradicate, extirpate 10 annihilate, deracinate, extinguish
11 exterminate

Roots author
5 Haley (Alex)

rope
3 gad, guy, tie, toe 4 bind, cord, hemp, line, stay 5 belay, bight, brace, cable, chord, hoose, lasso, longe, riata, sheet, widdy 6 becket, binder, fasten, halter, hawser, lariat, shroud, strand, string, tether 7 aweband, binding, bobstay, hal-

yard, lashing, marline, outhaul, painter, towline 8 backstay, buntline, downhaul, inveigle, jackstay, lifeline, prolonge
loop: 7 cringle
maker: 8 strander
mooring: 6 hawser
of flowers: 3 lei
saving: 8 lifeline
ship's: 4 vang 6 parral, parrel, ratlin 7 laniard, lanyard, marline, marling, ratline, swifter 8 rattling

ropedancer
7 acrobat 11 funambulist

rope off
6 cordon

ropes
8 minutiae 10 ins and outs, procedures, techniques

ropy
4 wiry 6 sinewy 7 fibrous, stringy 8 muscular

roque
7 croquet

rorqual
5 whale 7 finback

Rosalind's beloved
7 Orlando

rosary
5 beads 7 chaplet, garland 8 beadroll

rose
4 glow, pink 5 blush, color, flush, rouge 6 mantle, pinken, redden 7 crimson 10 erysipelas
Chinese: 8 Cherokee
combining form: 4 rhod 5 rhodo, roseo
cotton: 7 cudweed
feature: 5 thorn
kind: 4 moss 5 Peace, Vogue 6 Circus, damask 7 Fashion, Granada, Iceberg, New Dawn, Pascali, Tiffany 8 Rubaiyat 9 Floradora, Montezuma, polyantha, Tropicana 10 Floribunda 11 grandiflora, Mount Shasta 12 Crimson Glory, Paul's Scarlet, Red Pinocchio 13 Golden Showers 14 Queen Elizabeth
wild: 8 eglatere

roseate
3 red 4 pink 6 blushy, bright, florid, likely 7 auroral, flushed, healthy, hopeful 8 aurorean, blooming, blushful, blushing, cheerful, rubicand 9 favorable, promising 10 optimistic, promiseful

rose-colored
see **roseate**

rosemary
4 mint 8 costmary 9 rosmarine

Rosenkavalier composer
7 Strauss (Richard)

rose of ____
6 Sharon

rose oil
5 attar

Rose Tattoo author
8 Williams (Tennessee)

rosette
7 cockade 8 ornament

Rosh's father
8 Benjamin

Rosinante's master
7 Quixote (Don)

Rosmersholm author
5 Ibsen (Henrik)

____ Rossetti
5 Dante 9 Christina 12 Dante Gabriel
work: 8 Sing-Song 11 Annus Domini, Seek and Find, Sister Helen 12 Beata Beatrix 14 The House of Life

Rossini opera
6 Otello 8 Tancredi 11 William Tell

Rostand hero
6 Cyrano

roster
4 list, roll, rota 5 slate 6 muster, scroll 7 catalog 8 beadroll, register, roll call, schedule 10 muster roll

rostrum
4 beak, dais 5 snout 6 pulpit 7 lectern, tribune 8 platform 9 proboscis

rosy
see **roseate**

rot
3 ret 4 bosh, bull, crap, sink, turn, warp 5 bilge, chaff, decay, hooey, spoil, stain, taint, trash 6 banter, debase, fester, molder, worsen 7 corrode, corrupt, crumble, debauch, decline, deprave, descend, hogwash, pervert, putrefy, rubbish, vitiate 8 nonsense 9 animalize, break down, decompose, poppycock 10 bestialize, degenerate, demoralize, disimprove, retrograde 11 deteriorate 12 disintegrate 13 decomposition

rotary
6 circle 8 gyratory, spinning

rotate
4 gyre, pass, roll, spin, turn
5 pivot, twirl, wheel 6 circle, follow, gyrate 7 precess, relieve, revolve, succeed, trundle 8 exchange, rotiform, windmill
9 alternate 10 circumduct
11 interchange
a log: 4 birl

rotation
4 gyre, turn 5 round, wheel, whirl
7 circuit, turning 8 gyration
10 revolution

rote
4 list, pace 5 grind, learn
6 course, custom, groove, memory, repeat, system 7 routine 8 practice
9 automatic, treadmill 10 memorizing, repetition 12 memorization

rotten
2 up 3 bad, bum 4 foul, poor, punk, sour 5 amiss, fetid, nasty, wrong 6 crappy, putrid 7 carrion, corrupt, decayed, spoiled, tainted, touched, unhappy, unsound, vicious
8 chiselly, depraved, perverse, unstable 9 nefarious, offensive, putrified, unhealthy 10 abominable, decomposed, degenerate, flagitious, putrescent, undermined, unpleasant, villainous 11 displeasing
12 disagreeable 13 disintegrated
combining form: 4 sapr 5 sapro

rotter
3 cad, cur 7 bounder, shirker, slacker 9 yellow dog
10 blackguard

rotund
3 fat 5 beefy, buxom, dumpy, obese, plump, podgy, pudgy, round, squat, stout, thick, tubby
6 chubby, chunky, plumpy, spuddy, stocky, stubby 7 paunchy, ringing, vibrant 8 heavyset, plangent, plumpish, resonant, roly-poly, sonorant, sonorous, thickset 9 consonant, spherical 10 potbellied, resounding, roundabout

rouge
3 red 4 glow, pink, rose 5 blush, color, flush 6 mantle, pinken, redden 7 crimson

rough
3 bad, dry, raw 4 curt, firm, hard, punk, rude, wild 5 bluff, blunt, brief, brute, bumpy, crass, crude, draft, gross, gruff, hairy, harsh, heavy, raspy, rowdy, short, solid, tight, tough, uncut, yahoo 6 abrupt, broken, brushy, burred, choppy, coarse, craggy, crusty, hispid, hoarse, jagged, knotty, mucker, raging, rugged, severe, sketch, stormy, trying, uneven, unhewn, vulgar 7 arduous, boorish, brusque, cragged, furious, grating, jarring, operose, outline, rasping, raucous, ruffian, scraggy, toughie, tricksy, uncivil, uncouth, ungodly, unlevel, violent 8 asperous, block out, blustery, bullyboy, chalk out, churlish, impolite, improper, indecent, scabrous, skeleton, stormful, unformed, unseemly, unsmooth 9 adumbrate, difficult, imperfect, inclement, inelegant, ironbound, laborious, manhandle, mishandle, proximate, strenuous, turbulent, undressed, unrefined 10 blustering, boisterous, formidable, indecorous, indelicate, knock about, malodorous, ridiculous, slap around, stridulent, stridulous, tumultuous, unbecoming, undecorous, unfinished, ungracious, unpolished 11 approximate, shortspoken, skeletonize, tempestuous, unfashioned 12 characterize, discourteous
combining form: 6 trachy

roughhewn
4 rude 5 crude, plain, rough 8 unformed, unworked 9 undressed
10 unfinished, unpolished 11 unfashioned 12 uncultivated

roughhouse
7 fooling, rough up 9 high jinks, horseplay, manhandle, mishandle, rowdiness 10 knock about, skylarking, slap around

roughneck
see **ruffian**

roughness
7 crudity 8 acrimony, asperity
10 inequality, unevenness
12 irregularity

rough out
5 draft 6 sketch 7 outline 8 block out, chalk out, skeleton 9 adumbrate 11 skeletonize
12 characterize

rough up
9 manhandle, mishandle 10 knock about, roughhouse, slap around

round
2 by 3 arc, bow, hem, orb 4 arch, back, ball, bend, bent, bold, fast, free, full, gird, gyre, most, near, nigh, over, rich, ring, tour, turn 5 about, again, ample, arced, bowed, brisk, crook, curve, cycle, globe, harsh, large, orbed, plain, plump, podgy, pudgy, sleek, slick, tubby, vocal, wheel, whirl 6 all but, almost, arched, around, begird, beside, chubby, circle, curved, girdle, mellow, nearby, nearly, plumpy, polish, refine, rotund, smooth, sphere 7 annular, arrondi, bulbous, circuit, compass, orotund, perfect, ringing, rondure, spheric, through, vibrant 8 arciform, as good as, backward, circular, complete, conglobe, encircle, ensphere, finished, globular, gyration, plangent, plumpish, resonant, roly-poly, rotation, sonorant, sonorous, surround, vigorous, well-nigh 9 consonant, curvation, curvature, encompass, in reverse, just about, orbicular, outspoken, spherical 10 conglobate, free-spoken, resounding, revolution, throughout 11 circulation, curvilinear, cylindrical
combining form: 5 globo, troch, ventr 6 trocho, ventri, ventro
prefix: 4 peri

roundabout
4 tour 5 jaunt, plump, tubby
6 chubby, detour, junket, outing, plumpy, rotary, rotund 7 circuit, curving, oblique, winding 8 circular, indirect, pleonasm, plumpish, roly-poly, verbiage 9 excursion, runaround, tautology, verbality
10 circuitous, collateral, meandering, periphrase 11 periphrasis

rounded
4 bent 5 arced, bowed, curvy, round 6 arched, convex, curved, mellow 7 arrondi, gibbous 8 arciform, complete, sonorous 9 curvesome, Junoesque, perfected 10 curvaceous 11 approximate, curvilinear 13 well-developed

rounder
4 rake, roué 6 bad lot, no-good, waster 7 wastrel 10 ne'er-do-well, profligate, scapegrace

roundly
4 most, well 5 about, à fond, fully, quite 6 all but, almost, nearly, wholly 7 bluntly, sharply, smartly, utterly 8 as good as, bitterly, candidly, entirely, promptly, well-nigh 9 just about, perfectly 10 altogether, completely, scathingly

round off
3 cap 5 crown 6 climax, top off
9 culminate, finish off

round robin
6 letter, series 7 protest 8 petition, sequence 10 tournament

round trip
4 tour 7 circuit 9 excursion

round up
5 group 6 gather 7 cluster, collect 8 assemble

rouse
4 call, move, rise, stir, wake, whet 5 alarm, awake, mount, pique, rally, waken 6 awaken, bestir, deepen, excite, foment, incite, kindle, revive, vivify 7 agitate, animate, disturb, enhance, enliven, innerve, magnify, provoke, quicken 8 heighten, motivate, redouble 9 aggravate, challenge, galvanize, innervate, instigate, intensate, intensify, stimulate

rousing
3 gay 4 keen 5 alert, brisk, peppy 6 bright, lively 7 animate, dashing 8 animated, exciting, spirited, stirring 9 inspiring, sprightly 10 exhilarant, eye-popping 11 stimulating, superlative 12 exhilarating, exhilarative, intoxicating

Rousseau work
5 Emile

roust
4 move, stir 5 pique, rouse 6 excite 7 innerve, provoke, quicken 8 motivate 9 galvanize, stimulate

roustabout
4 hand 6 worker 7 laborer, workman 8 deckhand, floorman, workhand 9 operative 10 workingman

rout
3 mob 4 army, bawl, beat, drub, dust, fuss, herd, host, lick, mass, roar, romp, root, whip 5 chase, cloud, crowd, dregs, drive, eject, expel, flock, trash 6 bellow, clamor, defeat, dig out, dispel, flight, hunt up, legion, number, rabble, scores, soiree, throng, wallop 7 beating, bluster, clobber, conquer, debacle, hunt out, licking, rummage, runaway, shellac, warming 8 cakewalk, drubbing, hunt down, lambaste, riffraff, stampede, walkaway, walkover 9 clean up on, hoi polloi, multitude, other half, overthrow, reception 10 defeasance, demoralize 11 proletariat

route
3 way 4 lead, line, path, road, send, ship, show 5 guide, pilot, remit, steer, track, trail 6 course, direct, divert, escort 7 address, channel, circuit, conduct, consign, forward, highway, journey, passage 8 dispatch, shepherd, transmit 9 direction, itinerary

routine
3 act, bit, rut 4 pace, rote 5 drill, grind, habit, plain, usual 6 course, groove, wonted 7 chronic, regular 8 accepted, everyday, habitual, ordinary, standard, workaday 9 customary, plain Jane, quotidian, treadmill 10 accustomed 11 commonplace 12 unremarkable

rove
3 gad 4 move, roam 5 drift, prowl, range, stray 6 ramble, wander 7 meander, traipse 8 vagabond 9 gallivant

rover
3 gad 5 stray 6 gadder, pirate, roamer, sea dog 7 corsair, drifter, floater, rambler, sea wolf 8 gadabout, picaroon, runabout, traveler, wanderer 9 buccaneer, itinerant, meanderer, sea robber 10 freebooter 11 peripatetic 12 rolling stone

roving
6 errant, mobile 7 nomadic, roaming, vagrant 8 rambling, vagabond 9 itinerant, itinerate, wandering, wayfaring 10 discursive 11 perambulant, peripatetic

row
3 oar 4 beef, file, fray, fuss, line, list, pull, punt, rank, sail, scud, spat, tier, tiff 5 align, brawl, broil, chain, fight, melee, mouth, order, queue, run-in, scrap, scull, set-to, swath, train 6 affray, bicker, clamor, fracas, paddle, propel, sequel, series, string 7 brabble, dispute, echelon, quarrel, rhubarb, wrangle 8 argument, sequence, squabble 9 bickering, caterwaul, commotion 10 falling-out, succession 11 altercation, consecution, disturbance, progression

rowdy
4 punk, rude 5 rough, tough, yahoo 6 mucker, unruly, vulgar 7 hoodlum, raffish, raucous, ruffian, toughie 8 bullyboy, stubborn 9 roughneck, turbulent 10 boisterous, disorderly, tumultuous 11 rumbustious

Rowena
father: 7 Hengist
guardian: 6 Cedric
husband: 7 Ivanhoe 9 Vortigern

Roxana
husband: 9 Alexander
rival: 7 Statira

royal
3 top 4 easy 5 grand, light, noble, prime, regal 6 august, facile, kingly, lordly, simple, smooth, superb 7 stately 8 baronial, champion, five-star, glorious, imperial, imposing, kinglike, majestic, princely, splendid, superior 9 classical, excellent, front-rank, grandiose, monarchal, number one, sovereign 10 effortless, monarchial 11 magnificent, monarchical

royalist
4 Tory 5 blimp, white 7 Bourbon, diehard 8 Cavalier 11 reactionary

rub
3 bar, irk, vex 4 buff, fret, gall, rasp, rile, snag, wear, wipe 5 annoy, chafe, crimp, erode, glaze, gloss, grate, graze, grind, peeve, scour, scrub, shine 6 abrade, bother, glance, hamper, hurdle, nettle, polish, ruffle, scrape, smooth, stroke 7 burnish, corrade, furbish, massage, provoke 8 irritate, obstacle, traverse 9 aggravate, excoriate, hindrance 10 difficulty, exasperate, impediment 11 obstruction

Rubaiyat author
11 Omar Khayyam

rubber
4 nose 5 snoop 6 butt-in, eraser 7 Paul Pry, trouble 8 busybody, quidnunc 9 whetstone 10 caoutchouc, misfortune 11 nosey Parker 12 intermeddler
basis: 5 latex
hard: 7 ebonite
synthetic: 8 neoprene
tree: 5 Hevea 7 manihot

Rubber City
5 Akron (Ohio)

rubberneck
3 eye 4 gape, gaze, look, ogle 5 prier, pryer, snoop, stare 6 butt-in, goggle 7 meddler, tourist, tripper 8 busybody, kibitzer, quidnunc, sight-see 9 buttinsky, sightseer 10 pragmatist

12 intermeddler

rubbish

3 pap, rot **4** bosh, crap, junk, slop **5** bilge, dreck, dross, hooey, offal, trash, waste, wrack **6** debris, kelter, litter, pablum, refuse, rubble **7** garbage, hogwash **8** nonsense, tommyrot **9** poppycock, sweepings **11** foolishness

rubbishy

4 base, mean, poor **5** cheap, tatty **6** common, paltry, shoddy, sleazy, trashy **9** worthless

rube

4 boor, hick **5** yahoo **6** rustic **7** bucolic, bumpkin, hayseed, redneck **9** hillbilly **10** clodhopper, provincial **12** backwoodsman

rubicund

3 red **5** flush, ruddy **6** florid **7** flushed, glowing **8** sanguine **11** full-blooded

rubidium

symbol: **2** Rb

rub out

4 do in, kill, raze, ruin **5** smash, wreck **6** finish, murder **7** bump off, destroy, put away, shatter **8** decimate, demolish, destruct, knock off **9** liquidate **10** annihilate, extinguish, obliterate **11** assassinate

rubric

3 rud **4** name, ruby **5** canon, class, nomen, ruddy, style, title **6** redden, rubify, ruddle **7** concept, notable **8** category, cognomen, nameable **9** memorable, red-letter **10** noteworthy, observable **11** appellation, appellative, designation, incarnadine **12** compellation, denomination

ruck

3 mob **4** fold, heap, mass, pile **5** crimp, crowd, group, plica, ridge, rivel, screw **6** crease, furrow, jumble, muster, pucker, rimple, rumple **7** company, crimple, crinkle, crumple, scrunch, wrinkle **9** congeries, gathering, multitude **10** assemblage, collection, generality **11** aggregation, corrugation

rucksack

4 pack **8** backpack

ruckus

3 row **4** coil, fuss, to-do **5** brawl, broil, melee, scrap **6** fracas, furore, hassle, rumpus, shindy, uproar **7** dispute, quarrel, shindig, wrangle **8** squabble **9** bickering, commotion, confusion **10** falling-out **11** altercation, controversy, disturbance

ruction

see **ruckus**

ruddle

see **redden**

ruddy

3 red **4** rosy, ruby **5** flush, vivid **6** blowsy, florid, lively, redden, rubify, rubric **7** bronzed, flushed, glowing **8** blooming, rubicund, sanguine **11** full-blooded, incarnadine

rude

3 ill, raw **4** curt, wild **5** bluff, crass, crude, fresh, green, gross, gruff, harsh, lumpy, rough, surly **6** abrupt, bitter, callow, clumsy, coarse, crusty, Gothic, ribald, rugged, savage, simple, stormy, unhewn, vulgar **7** angular, boorish, brusque, crabbed, Hunnish, ill-bred, incivil, inexact, loutish, natural, uncivil, uncouth **8** arrogant, barbaric, churlish, clownish, ignorant, impolite, impudent, inexpert, insolent, inurbane, tactless, unformed, unlicked, unsubtle, untaught, unversed, unworked **9** barbarian, barbarous, benighted, dissonant, elemental, imperfect, imprecise, incondite, inelegant, intrusive, makeshift, primitive, proximate, rough-hewn, truculent, turbulent, undressed, unfleshed, unrefined, unwrought **10** cacophonic, discordant, illiterate, immoderate, mannerless, meddlesome, uncultured, uneducated, unfinished, ungracious, unhandsome, unlettered, unmannered, unmannerly, unpolished, unschooled **11** approximate, cacophonous, disgracious, disharmonic, empty-headed, ill-mannered, impertinent, know-nothing, rudimentary, uncalled-for, uncivilized, uncourteous, unfashioned, unmitigated, unpracticed, unprocessed **12** discourteous, inharmonious, unconversant, uncultivated, unharmonious, uninstructed **13** disrespectful

rudiment

5 basic **6** anlage **7** element, vestige **9** beginning, essential **11** fundamental

rudimentary

5 basal, basic **7** initial **8** simplest **9** beginning, elemental, vestigial **10** elementary **11** fundamental, undeveloped

prefix: **3** pro

rue

3 woe **4** care, pity, ruth **5** dolor, grief, mourn **6** bewail, grieve, lament, regret, repent, sorrow **7** anguish, deplore, penance, remorse **8** sympathy **9** heartache, penitence, penitency **10** affliction, compassion, contrition, heartbreak, repentance **11** compunction **12** contriteness

rueful

3 sad **4** poor **5** sorry **6** dolent, woeful **7** doleful, piteous, pitiful, ruthful **8** contrite, dolesome, dolorous, hopeless, mournful, pathetic, penitent, pitiable, wretched **9** afflicted, depressed, miserable, oppressed, plaintive, sorrowful **10** despairing, despondent, lamentable, lugubrious, melancholy **11** weighed down

ruff

5 frill, perch **6** collar, fringe, pigeon, ruffle **9** sandpiper **11** pumpkinseed

female: **5** reeve

ruffian

4 hood, punk, thug **5** bully, rough, rowdy, tough, yahoo **6** brutal, coarse, mucker **7** gorilla, hoodlum, toughie **8** bullyboy, hooligan **9** roughneck, strong arm

ruffle

3 bug, fan, irk, rub, vex **4** blow, fret, gall, wear, wind **5** annoy, chafe, erode, frill, graze, jabot, pleat, ruche **6** abrade, bother, gather, nettle, ripple, winnow **7** agitate, corrade, dispute, disturb, provoke, stiffen, trouble, wrinkle **8** dishevel, disorder, distract, drumbeat, exercise, furbelow, irritate, skirmish **10** disarrange, discompose

Rufus' father

5 Simon

rug

3 mat **4** wrap **5** cover **6** carpet, runner **7** blanket, laprobe **8** covering

kind: **3** rag, rya **6** dhurry, hooked **7** braided, flokati, Persian **8** Aubusson, Oriental **10** Savonnerie

rugby

formation: **5** scrum **9** scrummage

goal: **7** dropped, penalty

period: **4** half

player: 6 center, hooker, winger
8 standoff 9 scrum half
scoring: 3 try 4 goal 10 conversion
team: 7 fifteen
term: 4 heel 5 match 7 convert,
dribble, hand off, knock on 9 fair
catch
time-out: 8 stoppage
version: 5 union 6 league

rugged

3 dry 4 hard, rude, wild 5 burly,
hardy, harsh, heavy, husky, rough,
stern, tough 6 bitter, brawny, brutal, coarse, craggy, hoarse, jagged, knotty, robust, severe, strong,
sturdy, uneven 7 arduous, austere,
boorish, grating, ill-bred, jarring,
loutish, lumpish, operose, rasping,
raucous, scraggy, unlevel 8 asperous, churlish, clownish, lubberly,
muscular, rigorous, scabrous, stalwart, unsmooth, vigorous 9 difficult, inclement, laborious, strenuous, unrefined, weathered
10 formidable, robustious, stridulent, stridulous, unpolished
11 intemperate

Ruggiero

guardian: 7 Atlante
sister: 7 Marfisa
slayer: 11 Tisaphernes
wife: 10 Bradamante

ruin

4 balk, bane, beat, bilk, bust, dash,
do in, doom, draw, fall, foil, harm,
hurt, loss, maim, raze, sack, undo
5 break, decay, drain, havoc,
spoil, use up, waste, wrack, wreck
6 baffle, beggar, blight, damage,
debase, deface, devour, fold up,
impair, injury, mangle, pauper, ravage, reduce, thwart, unmake 7 atrophy, break up, corrupt, decline,
deplete, despoil, destroy, exhaust,
outrage, pillage, unbuild, undoing,
unframe, vitiate, wipe out, wrecker
8 bankrupt, calamity, clean out, collapse, decimate, demolish, desolate, dishonor, downfall, draw
down, mischief, mutilate, spoliate
9 confusion, crumbling, decadence,
depredate, desecrate, destroyer,
devastate, disfigure, disrepair,
downgrade, frustrate, overthrow,
pauperize 10 circumvent, declension, degeneracy, degenerate, devolution, dilapidate, disappoint, impoverish 11 destruction,
devastation, dissolution 12 degeneration 13 deterioration

ruination

4 bane, loss 5 havoc 7 undoing
8 downfall 9 confusion, destroyer
11 destruction, devastation

ruinous

5 fatal 7 fateful 8 wrackful, wreckful 10 calamitous, disastrous, pernicious, shattering 11 cataclysmic,
destructive 12 annihilative,
catastrophic

rule

3 law 4 lead, sway 5 axiom, by-
law, canon, edict, gnome, guide,
habit, infer, judge, maxim, moral,
order, reign 6 assize, course, custom, decide, decree, deduce, dictum, direct, figure, gather, govern,
manage, method, regime, settle,
truism 7 brocard, command, control, decorum, precept, preside,
prevail, regency, regimen, resolve,
statute 8 aphorism, apothegm, conclude, decretum, doctrine, dominate, domineer, dominion, overrule
9 authority, determine, etiquette, influence, ordinance, principle, procedure, propriety 10 regulation
11 fundamental
absolute: 8 autarchy
by a god: 8 thearchy, theonomy
combining form: 4 nomy 5 archy

Rule Britannia composer

4 Arne (Thomas)

rule out

3 bar 4 bate, ward 5 avert, debar,
deter 6 except, forbid, refuse 7 exclude, forfend, obviate, prevent,
scratch, suspend 8 count out, preclude, prohibit, stave off 9 eliminate, forestall

ruler

4 king, lord 5 queen 6 archon, dy-
nast, ferule, gerent, prince, regent,
satrap, sultan 7 emperor, monarch,
viceroy 8 governor, hierarch, oli-
garch, pentarch, princess, theocrat
9 dominator, imperator, matriarch,
patriarch, potentate, sovereign
12 straightedge
absolute: 6 despot, tyrant 8 autocrat, dictator, omniarch, overlord
Arab: 4 amir, emir 5 emeer, sheik
6 sharif, sheikh, sherif, sultan
Asian: 4 khan
Byzantine Empire: 6 exarch
combining form: 4 arch
Egyptian: 7 pharaoh
family: 7 dynasty
Iranian: 4 shah
one of four: 8 tetrarch
one of seven: 8 heptarch

one of three: 7 triarch 8 triumvir
Persian: 6 satrap
Russian: 4 czar, tsar, tzar
Turkish: 3 bey, dey

ruling

3 law 4 rife 5 chief, edict, ukase
6 decree 7 central, current, pivotal,
popular, rampant, regnant, statute
8 cardinal, decision 9 directive,
prevalent 10 overriding, prevailing,
widespread 11 predominant

Rumania

see **Romania**

rumble

3 cry 4 boom, buzz, clap, peal,
roar, roll, talk 5 blast, burst, crack,
crash, growl, ondit, rumor 6 gossip, murmur, report, uproar 7 hearsay, quarrel, resound, thunder
9 complaint, grapevine 11 disturbance, scuttlebutt

ruminant

3 cow, yak 4 deer, goat, tahr 5 bison, camel, goral, llama, okapi, serow, sheep, takin 6 alpaca, cattle,
musk ox, vicuña 7 buffalo, chamois, chewing, giraffe, guanaco
8 antelope
stomach: 5 rumen 6 omasum 8 abomasum 9 reticulum

ruminate

4 chew, mull, muse, roll 5 champ,
chomp, chump, munch, think,
weigh 6 crunch, ponder 7 chumble,
reflect, revolve, scrunch 8 cogitate, consider, meditate, mull over,
turn over 9 masticate 10 deliberate, excogitate 11 contemplate

ruminative

7 pensive 8 thinking 9 pondering
10 cogitative, meditative, reflecting,
reflective, thoughtful 11 speculative
13 contemplative

rummage

4 beat, comb, fish, grub, hash,
mash, poke, rake, rout, seek 5 mix
up, scour 6 dig out, forage, hunt
up, jumble, jungle, litter, mess up,
muddle, search, spy out, tumble
7 clutter, disrupt, disturb, examine,
hunt out, ransack 8 disarray, disorder, finecomb, hunt down, mishmash, scramble 9 ferret out, patchwork, potpourri, search out
10 collection, disarrange, discompose, hotchpotch, miscellany, scrutinize 11 disorganize

rummy

3 odd 4 lush 5 drunk, queer
6 boozer, lusher 7 bizarre, curious,

guzzler, oddball, strange, swiller, tippler **8** drunkard, peculiar, singular **9** eccentric, inebriate **10** boozehound

rumor
4 blab, buzz, talk, word **5** on-dit, story **6** gossip, mumble, murmur, mutter, report, rumble, tattle **7** hearsay, tidings, whisper **9** grapevine, undertone **11** scuttlebutt, susurration

rumormonger
5 tabby **6** gossip **8** gossiper, quidnunc, telltale **9** carrytale **10** talebearer

rump
4 beam, hind, rear **5** fanny **6** behind, bottom **7** rear end **8** backside, buttocks, derriere, haunches **9** posterior
combining form: **3** pyg **4** pyga, pygo **5** pygal, pygia

rumple
4 fold, muss **5** crimp, screw **6** tousle **7** crimple, crinkle, scrunch, wrinkle

rumpus
see **ruckus**

run
2 go **3** act, dig, fly, get, ram, set, use, wax **4** bolt, come, dart, dash, flee, flit, flow, flux, fuse, gill, grow, hare, herd, hunt, keep, line, make, melt, move, pour, race, rush, shin, sink, skip, stab, tear, thaw, trip, turn, vary, work **5** apply, blend, brook, chase, creek, drift, drive, fleet, haste, hurry, range, reach, recur, refer, scoot, skirr, speed, stick, swing, tenor, trend **6** become, bustle, career, course, direct, escape, extend, gallop, govern, handle, hustle, manage, ordain, plunge, repair, resort, runnel, scorch, scurry, sprint, stream, thrust **7** bearing, bootleg, carry on, conduct, current, hotfoot, liquefy, make off, operate, proceed, retreat, rivulet, scamper, scuttle, smuggle, stretch **8** dissolve, duration, function, highball, liquesce, tendency, traverse **9** direction, endurance, skedaddle **10** continuity, contraband, deliquesce **11** continuance, persistence **12** continuation, prolongation

run across
4 meet **8** discover **9** encounter

runagate
3 rat, vag **4** hobo **5** tramp **7** drifter, floater, vagrant **8** apos-

tate, defector, fugitive, recreant, renegade, roadster, turncoat, vagabond, wanderer **9** turnabout

run along
2 go **4** exit, quit **5** leave **6** depart, get off **7** pull out, take off **8** shove off

runaround
6 detour, escape **7** come off, elusion, evasion **8** escaping, eschewal, shunning **9** avoidance **10** roundabout

run away
4 bolt, flee **5** elope **6** desert, escape **7** abscond **8** stampede

runaway
8 decisive, deserter, fugitive

run down
3 hit **4** stop **5** decry, trace **6** pursue **7** downcry **8** belittle, derogate, diminish **9** disparage, dispraise **10** depreciate **11** detract from, opprobriate

run-down
5 dingy, seedy, tacky, tired **6** shabby, tagrag **8** decrepit, tattered, untended **9** exhausted, neglected **10** broken-down, down-at-heel, uncared-for **11** dilapidated

rune
4 poem, song **5** charm, ogham, poesy, rhyme, spell, verse **6** poetry **11** conjuration, incantation

rung
4 step **5** grade, notch, spoke, stage, stair, tread **6** degree, handle **10** crosspiece

run in
3 nab **4** bust **5** pinch, visit **6** arrest, come by, detain, drop by, look up, pick up, stop by **9** apprehend

run-in
3 row **4** tiff **5** brush, fight, set-to **6** hassle **7** dispute, quarrel, rhubarb **8** skirmish **9** bickering, encounter **10** falling-out, velitation **11** altercation

run into
4 meet **6** become **9** encounter

runnel
see **rivulet**

runner
3 rug **5** agent, blade, miler, racer **6** carpet, stolon **8** operator, sprinter **9** messenger

running
4 care, easy, live, race **5** alive **6** active, charge, fluent, linear,

smooth **7** conduct, cursive, dynamic, flowing, working **8** handling, roadwork, together **9** operative, oversight **10** continuous, effortless, intendance, management **11** continually, functioning, night and day, supervision **12** continuously, successively **13** consecutively
combining form: **4** drom **5** dromo **7** dromous

running mate
3 pal **4** chum **5** buddy, crony **7** comrade **9** associate, companion

run-of-the-mill
4 fair, mean **5** typic, usual **6** common, medium, normal **7** average, general, natural, regular, typical **8** mediocre, middling, moderate, ordinary, uncommon **9** prevalent **11** commonplace, indifferent **12** intermediate **13** unexceptional

run on
3 gab, jaw, yak **4** chat, talk **5** clack **6** babble, gabble, rattle **7** chatter, prattle **8** continue

run out
4 fail, flow, oust **5** exile, expel **6** banish, deport, elapse, expire **7** cast out, give out **8** complete, displace **9** ostracize, transport

run over
5 spill **6** exceed, repeat **7** examine **8** overbrim, overfill, overflow, rehearse

runt
5 dwarf, midge, pygmy **6** midget, peewee **7** manikin **8** Tom Thumb **10** homunculus **11** hop-o'-my-thumb, lilliputian

run through
2 go **4** scan **5** spend, use up **6** browse, expend, finish, pierce **7** consume, dip into, examine, exhaust **8** glance at, rehearse, transfix **10** glance over

runty
4 puny **5** small **7** stunted **8** dwarfish **10** diminutive, undersized **12** contemptible

run up
3 wax **4** rise **5** build, erect, mount **6** expand **7** augment, enlarge **8** increase, multiply, snowball **9** construct **10** accumulate

runway
4 path **5** strip, track, trail **6** bridge **7** channel **8** airstrip, platform

rupture
4 hole, open, part, rend, rent, rift,

rive **5** break, burst, sever, split **6** breach, cleave, divide, hernia, schism, sunder **7** blowout, break up, disjoin, disrupt, dissect, divorce, fissure, parting, split-up **8** disunion, disunite, division, fracture, separate **9** partition **10** detachment, separation **11** dissolution, divorcement

combining form: **7** rrhexes (plural), rrhexis

R.U.R.
author: **5** Čapek (Karel)
character: **5** robot

rural
6 rustic, simple **7** bucolic, country, idyllic, natural, outland **8** agrestic, arcadian, pastoral, villatic **10** campestral, out-country, provincial **11** countrified

ruse
3 jig **4** hoax, ploy, wile **5** dodge, feint, fraud, trick **6** deceit, gambit **7** gimmick **8** artifice, maneuver, trickery **9** stratagem **10** subterfuge

rush
3 fly, run **4** boil, bolt, dart, dash, flit, flow, flux, lash, race, scud, tear, tide, whiz **5** break, chase, drift, fleet, fling, flood, haste, hurry, onset, sally, scoot, shoot, spate, speed, surge **6** attack, barrel, bustle, career, charge, course, hasten, hurtle, irrupt, plunge, stream **7** assault, cattail, current **8** stampede, vanquish **9** hastiness, overpower **11** hurriedness **12** precipitance, precipitancy **13** precipitation

rushing
5 hasty **6** abrupt, sudden **7** hurried

8 headlong **9** impetuous **11** precipitant, precipitate, precipitous, subitaneous

Russian
family: **7** Romanov **9** Stroganov
monk: **8** Rasputin
peasant: **5** kulak, mujik **6** moujik, muzhik, muzjik
ruler: (see **czar**)
saint: **15** Alexander Nevsky
villa: **5** dacha

rustic
3 jay, yap **4** hick, jake, rube, rude **5** churl, clown, plain, rough, rural, swain, yokel **6** farmer, joskin, simple, sturdy, sylvan, woodsy **7** artless, bucolic, bumpkin, country, granger, hayseed, hillman, hoosier, outland, peasant, plowboy, plowman, redneck, uncouth **8** agrestic, mossback, pastoral **9** chawbacon, greenhorn, hillbilly **10** campestral, clodhopper, countryman, exurbanite, husbandman, out-country, provincial **11** countrified, country jake, mountaineer **12** backwoodsman

rustle
5 haste, hurry, speed, steal, swish **6** forage, hustle, swoosh **7** crinkle **8** celerity, dispatch, susurrus **9** swiftness **10** expedition, speediness

rustler
5 thief **6** dynamo, peeler **7** hustler **8** go-getter, live wire **11** self-starter

Rustum's son and victim
6 Sohrab

rusty
3 dry **4** slow **5** harsh, hoary, inept, rough **6** hoarse, rugged **7** grating,

jarring, rasping, raucous, restive **8** outmoded, strident **10** discolored

rut
4 heat, pace, rote **5** grind, track **6** estrus, furrow, groove **7** channel, routine **9** treadmill

rutabaga
5 swede **6** turnip

ruth
3 rue **4** pity **5** grief, mercy **6** regret, sorrow **7** penance, remorse, sadness **8** distress, sympathy **9** attrition, penitence, penitency **10** compassion, contrition, repentance **11** compunction

Ruth
husband: **4** Boaz **6** Mahlon
mother-in-law: **5** Naomi
son: **4** Obed

ruthenium
symbol: **2** Ru

ruthful
6 dolent, rueful, tender, woeful **7** doleful, pitiful **8** dolorous, wretched **9** afflicted, miserable, sorrowful

ruthless
4 grim **5** cruel **6** mortal, savage **8** pitiless **9** ferocious, merciless, unsparing **10** implacable, ironfisted, relentless, unyielding **11** unflinching, unrelenting **12** unappeasable

ruttish
3 hot **5** rutty **7** goatish, lustful, satyric **9** lickerish, salacious **10** lascivious, libidinous **12** concupiscent

Rwanda
capital: **6** Kigali
monetary unit: **5** franc

Ss

Sabatini novel
11 Scaramouche 12 Captain Blood

sabbatical
4 rest 5 leave

saber
5 sword

sabertooth
3 cat 5 tiger

sable
3 jet 4 dark, ebon, inky 5 black, dusky, ebony, jetty, murky, raven 6 gloomy, mammal, somber 9 pitch-dark 10 pitch-black

sabot
4 clog, shoe

sabotage
5 block, wreck 6 damage, hamper, hinder, injury 7 break up, destroy, subvert 8 obstruct, wreckage, wrecking 9 frustrate, undermine 10 impairment, subversion 11 undermining 12 subversivism

Sabra
father: 7 Ptolemy
husband, rescuer: 8 St. George
son: 3 Guy 5 David 9 Alexander

Sabrina
father: 7 Locrine
mother: 9 Estrildis

sac
4 cyst 5 pouch

Sacar
father: 8 Obededom
son: 5 Ahiam

saccharine
5 sweet 6 sugary, syrupy 7 candied, cloying, honeyed, sugared 9 disarming, oversweet 11 deferential, sugar-coated 12 ingratiating

sacerdotal
8 priestly 9 religious 10 priestlike 11 ministerial

sachem
4 boss 5 chief 6 leader

sachet
3 bag 6 powder 7 perfume

sack
2 ax 3 bag, bed 4 base, drop, fire, raid, ship, wine 5 expel, pouch, strip, waste 6 bounce, devour, forage, pocket, ravage 7 boot out, cashier, despoil, dismiss, kick out, pillage 8 desolate, spoliate 9 container, depredate, desecrate, devastate, terminate

sackbut
8 trombone

sacque
6 jacket

sacrament
4 rite, sign 6 symbol 7 baptism, penance 8 ceremony 9 eucharist, matrimony 10 holy orders 12 confirmation

sacrarium
6 chapel, shrine 7 oratory, piscina 8 sacristy 9 sanctuary

sacred
4 holy 5 godly 6 immune 7 angelic, blessed, guarded, saintly 8 defended, hallowed, numinous 9 cherished, inviolate, spiritual, unprofane 10 inviolable, sacrosanct, sanctified 11 consecrated, sacramental
combining form: 4 hagi, hier, sacr 5 hagio, hiero, sacro
monkey: 6 baboon, rhesus 7 hanuman
place: 7 sanctum
weed: 7 vervain

sacrifice
4 cede, drop, give, lose 5 forgo, yield 6 devote, donate, eschew, martyr, victim 7 forbear, forfeit, offer up 8 dedicate, hecatomb, immolate, oblation, offering

sacrilege
7 impiety, offense 9 blasphemy, violation 11 desecration, irreverence, profanation

sacrilegious
7 impious, profane, ungodly 10 irreverent 11 blasphemous, irreligious

sacristan
6 sexton

sacristy
6 vestry

sacrosanct
6 sacred 8 esteemed, regarded 9 inviolate, respected 10 inviolable

sad
4 blue, down 5 drear, dumpy, sorry 6 dismal, dreary, gloomy, morose, triste, woeful 7 doleful, dumpish, joyless, piteous, pitiful, unhappy 8 dejected, desolate, dolorous, downbeat, downcast, grieving, mournful, pathetic, pitiable, saddened, tristful 9 depressed, mirthless, sorrowful, woebegone 10 afflicting, depressing, dispirited, lamentable, melancholy 11 melancholic 12 heavyhearted

sadden
7 depress, oppress 9 weigh down

saddle
3 tax 4 lade, load, task 5 weigh 6 burden, charge, cumber, hamper, impede, impose, weight 7 aparejo, inflict 8 encumber, restrict
adjunct: 7 stirrup
covering: 7 mochila
part: 6 cantle, pommel 8 tapadera, tapadero
strap: 5 cinch, girth 6 latigo 7 harness

sadness
3 woe 4 funk 5 blues, dinge, downs, dumps, gloom, grief, mopes 6 misery, sorrow 7 anguish, dis-

mals, megrims **8** doldrums, dolefuls, glumness, mourning **9** dejection, dysphoria, moodiness **10** blue devils, depression, desolation, melancholy **11** despondency, forlornness, melancholia, unhappiness **12** downcastness, hopelessness, listlessness, mournfulness **13** sorrowfulness

safari
4 hunt, trek, trip **7** caravan **10** expedition

safe
4 wary **5** chary **6** intact, secure, unhurt **7** careful, guarded, healthy **8** cautious, defended, discreet, gingerly, guarding, harmless, innocent, riskless, shielded, unharmed **9** innocuous, protected, sheltered, shielding, uninjured, unscathed, wholesome **10** inviolable, protecting, scatheless, sheltering **11** calculating, circumspect, considerate, impregnable, inoffensive, uninjurious **12** invulnerable, safeguarding, unassailable, unthreatened

safety
5 cover **7** defense, shelter **8** security **9** assurance **10** protection **13** inviolability
org.: **4** OSHA

sag
3 dip **4** bend, drop, flag, flap, flop, sink, slip, swag, wilt **5** basin, droop, slide, slump **6** dangle, hollow, slouch **7** decline, drop off, falloff, sinkage, sinking **8** downturn, fall away, settling, sinkhole **9** concavity, downslide, downswing, downtrend **10** depression

saga
4 edda, epic, tale **5** story **6** legend **9** narrative

sagacious
4 sage, wise **5** cagey, heady, smart **6** argute, astute, clever, shrewd **7** gnostic, knowing, prudent, sapient **8** critical **9** astucious, far-seeing, insighted, judicious **10** discerning, insightful, perceptive **11** intelligent **13** knowledgeable, perspicacious

sagacity
5 grasp **6** wisdom **7** insight **8** prudence, sageness, sapience, wiseness **10** perception **11** discernment, penetration, sensitivity **13** comprehension, judiciousness, understanding

sagamore
5 chief **6** sachem

sage
4 mint, sane, wise **5** acute **6** expert, master, nestor, savant, sophic **7** gnostic, knowing, learned, probing, prudent, sapient, scholar, wise man **8** polymath, profound, sensible **9** insighted, judgmatic, judicious, sagacious **10** discerning, insightful, perceptive **11** penetrating, philosophic **13** knowledgeable
Hindu: **5** rishi **6** pandit **7** mahatma

Sagebrush State
6 Nevada

sage cock
6 grouse

Sage of ___
Chelsea: **7** Carlyle (Thomas)
Concord: **7** Emerson (Ralph Waldo)
Emporia: **5** White (William Allen)
Ferney: **8** Voltaire
Monticello: **9** Jefferson (Thomas)
Pylos: **6** Nestor

sagging
8 swayback

Sagittarius
6 archer **7** centaur **13** constellation

saguaro
6 cactus

saharan
3 dry **4** arid, sere **6** barren **8** deserted

sail
3 fly **4** boat, dart, flit, scud, skim, wing **5** fleet, float, mizen, shoot, skirr, sweep, yacht **6** cruise, mizzen **7** spencer **9** spinnaker
triangular: **3** jib **5** genoa

sailboat
4 bark, yawl **5** ketch, skiff, sloop **8** skipjack

sailing vessel
4 brig, saic **5** xebec **6** barque **7** frigate, galleon **8** schooner **10** barkentine, brigantine

sailor
3 tar **4** jack, salt **5** jacky **6** seaman, swabby **7** jack-tar, mariner, swabbie, yachter **8** seafarer, shipmate **9** tarpaulin, yachtsman **10** bluejacket
British: **5** limey
fictional: **6** Sinbad
patron saint: **4** Elmo

song:
6 chanty **7** chantey **9** barcarole

saint
biography: **11** hagiography
list: **9** hagiology; (see also **patron saint**)

Saint, the
12 Simon Templar
creator: **9** Charteris (Leslie)

Saint Anthony's cross
3 tau

Saint Elmo's Fire
9 corposant

Saint Joan author
4 Shaw (George Bernard)

Saint John's bread
5 carob

saintly
4 holy **5** godly, pious **6** devout, seraph, worthy **7** angelic, upright **8** seraphic, virtuous **9** righteous

Saint Paul's Church (London)
designer: **4** Wren (Christopher)

Saint Peter's Basilica
architect: **7** Bernini (Gian Lorenzo) **12** Michelangelo
sculpture: **5** Pietà

Saint Vitus' dance
6 chorea

sake
3 end **4** good **5** drink **7** purpose

salaam
3 bow **8** greeting

salacious
4 fast, lewd **7** lustful, satyric **9** lecherous, libertine **10** lascivious, libidinous, licentious **11** incontinent

salad
4 brew, hash, stew, toss **5** chef's **6** Caesar **7** mélange
item: **3** egg **4** bean, cuke, herb **5** cress, fruit, olive, onion **6** carrot, celery, cheese, endive, pepper, potato, radish, tomato **7** anchovy, cabbage, crouton, lettuce, parsley, spinach **8** chick-pea, coleslaw, cucumber, garbanzo, mushroom, scallion **10** watercress **11** cauliflower

salamander
3 eft **4** newt **8** mudpuppy, waterdog
Mexican: **7** axolotl

salient
6 marked, moving, signal **7** obvious, weighty **8** striking **9** arresting, arrestive, important, intrusive, obtru-

sive, pertinent, prominent **10** impressive, noticeable, pronounced, remarkable **11** conspicuous, outstanding, significant

saline
4 salt **5** briny, salty **8** brackish **10** saliferous

saliva
4 spit **5** water **6** slaver, sputum **7** spittle

salivate
5 drool **6** drivel, slaver **7** dribble, slabber, slobber

___ Salk
5 Jonas

sallow
3 wan **4** pale **6** willow, yellow

sally
3 gag **4** gust, jape, jest, joke, quip **5** burst, crack, jaunt **6** junket, outing **7** flare-up **8** drollery, eruption, outburst **9** excursion, explosion, wisecrack, witticism

salmagundi
see **hodgepodge**

salmon
4 parr, pink **5** smolt **6** grilse **7** essling, geelbec, sockeye **9** brandling
female: **4** raun
male: **6** kipper
smoked: **3** lox

Salmon
father: **3** Hur **7** Nahshon
grandfather: **5** Caleb
son: **4** Boaz

Salmoneus
brother: **7** Athamas **8** Sisyphus
daughter: **4** Tyro
father: **6** Aeolus
mother: **7** Enarete

Salome
composer: **7** Strauss (Richard)
father: **5** Herod
husband: **6** Philip **7** Zebedee **11** Aristobulus
mother: **8** Herodias
son: **4** John **5** James

salon
4 hall, shop **5** suite **6** parlor **9** apartment, reception

saloon
3 bar **4** hall **6** tavern **7** barroom, cantina, gallery, taproom **8** drinkery

salt
3 tar **4** jack, keep, NaCl **5** brine, salty **6** sailor, saline, seaman **7** jack-tar, mariner **8** salinize **9** sailorman, tarpaulin **10** saliferous

salt away
4 save **5** lay by, lay in, lay up, put by **8** lay aside

saltpeter
5 niter, nitre

saltworks
6 salina **7** saltern

salty
4 blue, racy **5** briny, broad, shady, spicy **6** purple, risqué, saline, wicked **7** caustic, mordant **8** brackish, off-color, scathing **9** trenchant **10** mordacious, saliferous, suggestive

salubrious
4 good **7** bracing, healthy **8** hygienic, salutary **9** healthful, wholesome **11** stimulating **12** invigorating

Salus
see **Hygeia**

Salu's son
5 Zimri

salutation
2 hi **4** hail **5** hello **7** Dear Sir **8** greeting
Arab: **6** salaam
French: **5** salut
German: **4** heil
Hawaiian: **5** aloha
Italian: **4** ciao
Latin: **3** ave
Spanish: **4** hola

salute
4 hail, heil **5** greet **6** accost, call to **7** address **8** greeting

salvage
4 save **6** ransom, redeem, regain, rescue **7** deliver, reclaim, recover **8** retrieve

salvation
6 saving **7** keeping **9** preserval **11** conservancy, safekeeping **12** conservation, preservation, sustentation

Salvation Army founder
5 Booth (General William)

salve
3 aid **4** balm **5** cream **6** cerate, chrism, remedy **7** unction, unguent **8** ointment **9** emollient, lubricant

salver
4 tray

salvo
4 hail **5** burst, spray, storm **6** shower, volley **7** barrage, tribute **9** broadside, cannonade, discharge, fusillade **11** bombardment, testimonial **12** appreciation

samaritan
6 helper **8** welldoer **10** benefactor

same
4 idem, like, very **5** equal, exact **7** coequal, identic, similar **8** constant **9** duplicate, identical, unfailing, unvarying **10** comparable, consistent, equivalent, invariable, tantamount, unchanging

Samoa's capital
4 Apia **8** Pago Pago

samovar
3 urn

sampan
4 boat **5** skiff

sample
4 case, part, sign, unit **5** piece, taste **7** element, example, portion, segment **8** fragment, instance, sampling, specimen **10** indication, individual **11** case history, constituent **12** illustration

Samson
betrayer: **7** Delilah
birthplace: **5** Zorah
deathplace: **4** Gaza
father: **6** Manoah
tribe: **3** Dan

Samson Agonistes author
6 Milton (John)

Samuel
father: **7** Elkanah
grandson: **5** Heman
mother: **6** Hannah

samurai
7 soldier, warrior
code: **7** bushido

San Antonio
team: **5** Spurs
landmark: **5** Alamo

sanctify
5 bless **6** hallow **10** consecrate

sanctimonious
5 false **7** canting **9** deceiving, pharisaic **11** pharisaical **12** hypocritical, pecksniffian **13** self-righteous

sanction
2 OK 4 fiat, okay 5 leave 6 permit, ratify 7 approve, certify, consent, endorse, license, support 8 accredit, approval 9 allowance, authorize 10 commission, permission, sufferance 11 approbation, endorsement 12 confirmation, ratification 13 authorization, encouragement

sanctity
8 holiness 9 godliness 11 saintliness, uprightness 13 righteousness

sanctuary
4 port 5 bamah, cover, haven, oasis 6 asylum, covert, harbor, refuge, shrine 7 retreat, sanctum, shelter 9 harborage, holy place

sanctum
6 shrine 9 holy place, sanctuary

sandal
4 zori 8 huarache, huaracho
winged: 7 talaria (plural)

sandbar
4 reef, spit 7 tombolo

sand hill
4 dune

sandpiper
4 knot, ruff, stib 5 reeve, terek 6 dunlin, teeter

sandstone deposit
6 flysch

sandwich
3 BLT, sub 4 club 5 hoagy 6 hoagie 7 grinder 9 submarine
combining form: 6 burger
shop: 4 deli

sandy
6 beachy, gritty 7 arenose, arenous 8 sabulose, sabulous

sane
3 fit 4 good, hale, sage, well, wise 5 lucid, right, sober, sound 6 cogent, normal 7 healthy, logical, prudent, sapient 8 all there, balanced, oriented, rational, sensible 9 judgmatic, judicious, wholesome 10 compelling, convincing, reasonable, well-liking 11 levelheaded 12 compos mentis

San Francisco
hill: 3 Nob 7 Russian
tower: 4 Coit

sangfroid
6 phlegm 7 ataraxy 9 aloofness, composure, unconcern 10 equanimity 11 self-control 12 indifference

sanguinary
4 gory 6 bloody 7 imbrued 9 homicidal, murdering, murderous 12 bloodstained, bloodthirsty

sanguine
4 gory 5 flush, ruddy 6 bloody, florid, secure, upbeat 7 assured, flushed, glowing, hopeful, imbrued 8 rubicund 9 confident, expectant, homicidal, murdering, murderous 10 optimistic, undoubtful 11 full-blooded, self-assured 12 bloodstained, bloodthirsty, Pollyannaish, undespairing 13 self-confident

sanitary
5 clean 8 hygienic 9 healthful

sanity
3 wit 4 mind 6 reason, senses 8 lucidity, saneness 9 soundness 12 intelligence 13 comprehension

Sanskrit
5 Indic 8 language
dialect: 4 Pali
epic: 8 Ramayana
school: 3 tol
Scripture: 4 Veda

Santa Lucia composer
5 Denza (Luigi)

sap
4 dupe, fool, gull, mark, ruin 5 blunt, chump, drain, wreck 6 pigeon, sucker, weaken 7 cripple, deplete, destroy, disable, exhaust, fall guy, saphead, unbrace 8 enervate, enfeeble, knock out 9 attenuate, schlemiel, undermine 10 debilitate

Saph's slayer
8 Sibbecai

sapid
5 tasty 6 savory 8 saporous 9 aperitive, palatable, relishing, toothsome 10 appetizing, flavorsome

sapience
see **sagacity**

sapient
see **sagacious**

sapling
4 tree 5 youth

Sapphira
coconspirator, husband: 7 Ananias

Sappho
forte: 6 poetry
island: 6 Lesbos

sappy
5 crazy, loony, mushy, silly, soupy 6 absurd, drippy, insane, slushy,

sticky 7 foolish, maudlin, mawkish 8 bathetic 11 harebrained, sentimental

Saracen
4 Arab 6 Muslim
hero: 9 Rodomonte

Sarah
husband: 7 Abraham
maid: 5 Hagar
son: 5 Isaac

sarcasm
3 wit 4 gibe, jest 5 humor, irony, scorn 6 rancor, satire 7 mockery 8 acerbity, acrimony, mordancy, raillery, repartee, ridicule, sneering 9 invective, sharpness 10 causticity, lampooning 13 corrosiveness
writer: 7 ironist

sarcastic
3 dry 4 tart 5 acerb, sharp 6 biting, ironic 7 acerbic, caustic, cutting, cynical, jeering, mocking, mordant, pungent, satiric 8 incisive, sardonic, scathing, scornful, stinging 9 corrosive, trenchant

sarcophagus
4 tomb 6 coffin

sardine
4 sild 7 herring 8 pilchard

Sardinia's capital
8 Cagliari

sardonic
3 wry 6 ironic 7 caustic, cynical, jeering, mocking, satiric 8 derisive, scornful, sneering 9 corrosive, sarcastic, saturnine 10 disdainful 12 contemptuous

sarong
5 skirt 7 garment

Sarpedon
brother: 5 Minos 12 Rhadamanthus
father: 4 Zeus 7 Jupiter
mother: 6 Europa 8 Laodamia

Sartor ____
8 Resartus

Sartre work
4 Kean 6 Nausea 7 The Wall 8 The Flies 10 Baudelaire, Saint Genet

sash
4 belt 6 girdle 8 ceinture, cincture 9 waistband

sashay
4 perk 5 mince, strut 6 prance 7 flounce, swagger

Saskatchewan's capital
6 Regina

sass
4 guff 5 cheek, mouth, sauce
8 back talk, saucebox 9 insolence,
sassiness 12 impertinence

sassafras
3 tea 6 saloop

sassy
4 bold, pert, wise 5 doggy, fresh,
lippy, natty, nervy, smart 6 brazen,
cheeky, dapper, spiffy, spruce,
sprucy 7 bandbox, doggish, forward 8 impudent, malapert, sparkish 9 audacious, unabashed
11 smart-alecky, well-groomed

Satan
5 beast, demon, deuce, devil,
fiend, viper 6 diablo 7 Lucifer, Old
Nick, serpent, villain 8 Apollyon,
devil-god, renegade, succubus
9 archfiend, Beelzebub 10 Old
Scratch 13 Old Gooseberry

satanic
4 evil 6 wicked 7 demonic 8 demoniac, demonian, devilish, diabolic, fiendish 9 saturnine
10 serpentine, unhallowed
11 diabolonian

satanism
9 diabolism

satchel
3 bag 4 case 5 pouch 6 valise

sate
4 cloy, fill, glut, jade, pall 5 gorge,
stuff 6 stodge 7 overeat, satiate,
surfeit 8 overfill 9 overstuff

satellite
4 moon 6 cohort, minion 7 sectary,
sputnik 8 adherent, disciple, favorite, follower, henchman, incident,
partisan, sector 9 ancillary, attendant, attending, supporter
of Jupiter: 2 Io 6 Europa 8 Callisto,
Ganymede
of Mars: 6 Deimos, Phobos
of Neptune: 6 Nereid, Triton
of Saturn: 4 Rhea 5 Dione, Janus,
Mimas, Titan 6 Phoebe, Tethys
7 Iapetus 8 Hyperion 9 Enceladus
of Uranus: 5 Ariel 6 Oberon 7 Miranda, Titania, Umbriel

satiate
see **sate**

satire
5 irony, spoof, squib 6 banter, parody 7 mockery, pasquil, takeoff
8 chaffing, raillery, ridicule, spoofery, travesty 10 causticity, lampoonery, pasquinade, persiflage

satiric
6 ironic 7 caustic, mocking 8 chaffing, farcical, ironical, spoofing
9 bantering, parodying 10 lampooning, ridiculing

satirist
English: 5 Swift (Jonathan)
7 Marston (John)
French: 8 Rabelais (François),
Voltaire
Greek: 8 Menippus
Roman: 6 Horace 7 Juvenal, Persius
9 Petronius

satirize
4 mock 5 spoof 6 parody 7 cartoon, censure, lampoon 8 ridicule

satisfaction
6 amends 8 pleasure 9 atonement
10 attainment 11 contentment, fulfillment, restitution 13 gratification

satisfactory
2 OK 4 fair, good, okay 5 solid,
sound, valid 6 cogent, decent,
enough 8 adequate, all right, passable 9 competent, sufficing, tolerable 10 acceptable, convincing,
sufficient 11 comfortable
13 unexceptional

satisfy
3 pay 4 fill, meet, quit, sate, suit
5 clear, humor, pay up, serve 6 answer, assure, induce, pacify,
please, settle, square 7 appease,
content, fulfill, gladden, gratify, indulge, placate, satiate, suffice, win
over 8 clear off, convince, inveigle,
persuade, pleasure 9 conform to
10 comply with

satrap
5 ruler 7 viceroy 8 governor,
henchman 11 subordinate

saturate
3 sop, wet 4 soak, wash 5 bathe,
imbue, madid, probe, souse, steep
6 douche, drench, infuse,
pierce, soaked, sodden, soused
7 instill, pervade, soaking, sopping,
suffuse 8 drenched, dripping, permeate, waterlog 9 inoculate, penetrate, percolate, transfuse

Saturn
see **Cronus**

saturnalia
4 orgy 5 party 7 debauch 9 bacchanal 11 bacchanalia

saturnine
4 dark, dour, glum, ugly 5 grave,
staid, sulky, surly 6 gloomy, mop-
ing, morose, silent, solemn, somber,

sullen 7 crabbed, serious 8 funereal, reserved, taciturn

satyric
4 lewd 5 horny, randy 7 goatish,
lustful 8 prurient 9 lecherous, libertine, lickerish, salacious 10 lascivious, libidinous, licentious, passionate 12 concupiscent

sauce
4 guff, sass 5 mouth 6 relish 7 topping 8 back talk, pertness 9 condiment, impudence
kind: 3 soy 4 hard, lear, mole
5 bercy, chili, curry, dashi, gravy,
melba, pesto, salsa 6 catsup,
chivry, Mornay, panada, Robert,
tartar, tomato 7 catchup, chutnee,
chutney, ketchup, marengo, New-
burg, piquant, soubise, supreme,
tartare, velouté 8 béchamel, dux-
elles, marinara, matelote, noisette,
normande, normandy, poivrade,
poulette, ravigote, remolade
9 bearnaise, lyonnaise, mariniere,
remoulade 10 bordelaise, Proven-
çale 11 hollandaise, vinaigrette

saucy
see **sassy**

Saudi Arabia
capital: 6 Riyadh
monetary unit: 5 riyal

Saul
concubine: 6 Rizpah
cousin: 5 Abner
daughter: 5 Merab 6 Michal
father: 4 Kish
son: 8 Jonathan
successor: 5 David
uncle: 3 Ner
wife: 7 Ahinoam

saunter
4 mope, roam, rove, walk 5 amble,
drift, mosey, tarry 6 bummel, linger, loiter, ramble, stroll, wander
7 meander 8 ambulate

sausage
5 wurst 6 banger, kishka, kishke,
salami, Vienna, wiener 7 baloney,
bologna, boloney, chorizo, saveloy
8 cervelat, chaurice, drisheen, kielbasa, pemmican 9 bratwurst, frankfort, frankfurt, pepperoni, Thuringer
10 knackwurst, knockwurst, liver-
wurst, mortadella 11 frankforter,
frankfurter

sausage-shaped
10 botuliform

savage
4 fell, grim, rude, wild 5 brute,
cruel, feral, harsh, rabid, rough

6 bloody, brutal, fierce, Gothic, Hunnic, rugged 7 bestial, brutish, Hunnish, inhuman, untamed, vicious, wolfish 8 barbaric, inhumane, primeval, ravenous, unbroken 9 barbarian, barbarous, butcherly, ferocious, heartless, murderous, primitive, rapacious, truculent, unsubdued, voracious 10 implacable, relentless 11 coldhearted, uncivilized, unharnessed, unrelenting 12 bloodthirsty, uncontrolled, uncultivated, unsocialized

savanna
5 plain 9 grassland

savant
4 sage 7 scholar, wise man

save
3 bar, but, yet 4 bank, keep, only, Stow 5 cache, guard, hoard, lay by, lay in, lay up, put by, set by, skimp, spare 6 bating, defend, except, keep up, manage, rescue, saving, scrimp, shield, unless 7 barring, besides, collect, deliver, deposit, however, husband, lay away, protect, reclaim, reserve, salvage, store up, sustain, unchain 8 conserve, lay aside, maintain, preserve, salt away, squirrel 9 aside from, economize, excluding, safeguard, stash away, stockpile, unshackle 10 accumulate 11 exclusive of

saving
3 but 6 beside, except 7 barring, besides, sparing, thrifty 9 aside from, except for, excluding, preserval, provident, salvation, stewardly 10 economical, husbanding, unwasteful 11 conservancy, safekeeping 12 conservation, preservation, sustentation

savoir faire
4 tact 5 grace, poise, taste 6 aplomb 7 address, dignity, manners 8 elegance 9 blaséness, diplomacy 10 confidence, experience, refinement 11 delicatesse, tactfulness 13 self-assurance

savor
4 feel, know, mark, tong 5 sapor, scent, smack, smell, taste, tinge, trait 6 flavor, relish, virtue 7 feature, quality 8 property, sapidity 9 affection, attribute, character 10 experience

savory
5 balmy, sapid, spicy, sweet, tasty 6 aromal 7 flavory, gustful, perfumy

8 aromatic, fragrant, perfumed, pleasing, redolent, tempting 9 ambrosial, aperitive, palatable, relishing, toothsome 10 appetizing, flaversome

saw
3 hew 4 word 5 adage 6 byword, saying 7 proverb

___ saw
3 bow, jig, pit, rip 4 band, buck, buzz, fret, hack, whip 5 chain, crown, saber 6 coping, scroll 7 compass, keyhole 8 circular, crosscut

sawbuck
5 horse 6 tenner 7 trestle 9 workhorse

sawhorse
see **sawbuck**

saw-toothed
7 serrate, serried 8 serrated 11 denticulate

Saxon
serf: 4 esne
warrior: 5 thane

say
4 aver, avow, cite, give, mark, most, much, nigh, read, show, talk, tell 5 about, mouth, quote, speak, state, utter, voice 6 affirm, almost, assert, nearly, recite, record, remark, repeat 7 breathe, chime in, comment, declare, deliver, express, phonate, protest 8 announce, bring out, decision, indicate, proclaim, register, throw out 9 authority, enunciate, just about, pronounce 10 animadvert, articulate

saying
3 mot 4 word 5 adage, axiom, maxim 6 byword, dictum, truism 7 proverb

scab
5 crust 6 eschar 13 strikebreaker

scabbard
6 sheath

scabby
4 mean 5 scaly 7 blotchy 10 scurrilous

scabrous
5 downy, harsh, rough, scaly 6 craggy, jagged, knobby, knotty, rugged, scabby, scurfy, thorny, uneven 7 bristly, prickly, scraggy, unlevel 8 asperous, unsmooth

scads
3 lot 4 gobs, heap, much, slew, wads 5 loads, reams 6 oodles

7 jillion, million, umpteen, zillion 8 slathers, thousand, trillion 9 great deal, multitude 10 quantities

scaffold
5 stage 7 staging 8 platform

Scala, La
city: 5 Milan
production: 5 opera

scalawag
see **scamp**

scald
4 bard, boil, burn, poet 6 scorch

scale
4 peel, rate, skin, upgo 5 climb, flake, gauge, mount, ratio, scute, strip 6 ascend, degree, scutum, squama 7 chip off, measure 8 escalade, escalate, flake off, spall off 9 exfoliate 10 desquamate, proportion 11 decorticate, excorticate
auxiliary: 7 vernier
earthquake: 7 Richter
temperature: 6 Kelvin 7 Celsius 10 centigrade, Fahrenheit

scallion
4 leek 5 onion 7 shallot

scalp
4 skin 5 cheat 6 trophy

scalpel
5 knife 7 dissect

scamp
5 devil, joker, pixie, rogue 6 rascal, ribald 7 villain 8 mischief, scalawag, slyboots 9 prankster, skeezicks 11 rapscallion

scamper
3 fly, run 4 bolt, dash, flee, scud, shin, skip 5 scoot, shoot, skirr 6 scurry, sprint 7 dash off, make off, rush off, scuddle, scuttle, tear off, whip off, whiz off 8 hurry off, light out 9 hasten off, hurry away, skedaddle, speed away

scan
3 eye 4 view 5 audit 6 browse, review, survey 7 perusal, run over 8 analysis, glance at, scrutiny 9 check-over 10 glance over, inspection, run through 11 examination, flip through, leaf through, observation, riff through, skim through 12 thumb through

scandal
4 tale 7 calumny 8 reproach 9 aspersion, discredit, disrepute 10 backbiting, defamation, detraction

scandalize
4 slur **5** libel, shock, smear **6** defame, malign **7** asperse, slander **9** denigrate **10** calumniate

scandalmonger
5 tabby **6** gossip **8** gossiper, quidnunc, telltale **9** backbiter, carrytale, muckraker **10** talebearer

scandalous
7 heinous **8** libelous, shocking **9** atrocious, desperate, maligning, monstrous, traducing, vilifying **10** backbiting, calumnious, defamatory, detracting, detractive, outrageous, slanderous

Scandinavia
6 Norway, Sweden **7** Denmark, Finland, Iceland

Scandinavian
see **Norse**

scant
4 poor **5** chary, close, short, skimp, spare, stint, tight **6** meager, meagre, scarce, scrimp, skimpy, sparse **7** scrimpy, wanting **8** exiguous **9** deficient **10** inadequate **12** insufficient

scantiness
4 lack **6** dearth **7** deficit, failure, paucity, poverty **8** scarcity, shortage, sparsity, underage **10** deficiency, inadequacy, scarceness, sparseness **11** defalcation **13** insufficience, insufficiency

scanty
see **scant**

scapegoat
4 mark **5** patsy **6** target, victim **7** fall guy **11** whipping boy

Scapin
5 rogue, valet
author: **7** Molière
employer: **7** Léandre

scar
3 cut, mar **4** flaw, scab **5** score **6** damage, deface, defect, keloid **7** blemish, blister, scratch **8** cicatrix, pockmark **9** cicatrize, disfigure **13** disfigurement
on a seed: **5** hilum

scarab
6 beetle

scaramouch
see **scamp**

scarce
3 few, shy **4** just, rare **5** scant, short **6** barely, hardly, scanty, seldom **7** failing, wanting **8** sporadic,

uncommon **9** curtailed, deficient, shortened, truncated **10** inadequate, infrequent, occasional **12** insufficient

scarceness
see **scantiness**

scarcity
see **scantiness**

scare
3 awe **5** alarm, panic, spook **6** freeze, fright **7** horrify, petrify, shake up, startle, terrify **8** affright, frighten, paralyze **9** terrorize

scarf
3 boa **5** ascot, fichu, nubia, plaid, shawl, stole **8** babushka, liripipe
Latin-American: **6** tapalo
long: **6** rebozo

Scarlet Letter, The
author: **9** Hawthorne (Nathaniel) *character:* **5** Pearl, Roger **6** Arthur, Hester

Scarlet Pimpernel author
5 Orczy (Baroness Emmuska)

Scarlett's home
4 Tara

scary
6 afraid, aghast, spooky **7** anxious, fearful **8** spookish **9** terrified **10** frightened

scat
4 flee, jazz **5** scoot, scram **7** singing

scathe
4 flay **5** slash **6** scorch **7** blister, scarify, scourge **8** lambaste, lash into **9** castigate, excoriate

scathing
5 salty **6** brutal **7** burning, caustic, mordant, searing **9** scorching, trenchant **10** mordacious, sulphurous

scatological
4 foul **5** dirty, nasty **6** coarse, filthy, smutty, vulgar **7** obscene, raunchy **8** indecent

scatter
3 sow **4** cast, part, shed **5** sever, straw, strew **6** dispel, divide, splash **7** bestrew, break up, disband, discard, disject, diverge, spatter **8** dispense, disperse, separate, splatter, sprinkle **9** broadcast, dissipate **10** besprinkle, distribute **11** disseminate

scatterbrained
5 dizzy, giddy, silly **7** flighty, foolish **9** frivolous

scavenge
5 clean **7** cleanse, collect, extract, salvage

scavenger
5 hyena **7** vulture

scenario
4 plot **6** script **7** outline **10** screenplay

scene
3 set **4** site, spot, view **5** arena, field, place, sight, vista **6** locale, milieu, sphere **7** compass, culture, outlook, setting, tableau **8** backdrop, hangings, locality, location, stage set **10** background **11** environment, mise-en-scène **12** stage setting

scenery
3 set **5** decor, props **7** setting **8** stage set **9** furniture **10** properties **11** furnishings, mise-en-scène **12** stage setting

scent
4 balm, nose, odor **5** aroma, smell, sniff, snuff, spice, whiff **7** bouquet, essence, incense, odorize, perfume **9** aromatize, fragrance, redolence

scepter
4 mace **5** baton, staff **11** sovereignty

schedule
4 list, roll, sked, time **5** chart, slate, table **6** agenda, docket, record, roster **7** catalog, program **8** calendar, register, roll call **9** catalogue, timetable

scheme
4 plan, plot **5** cabal, order **6** design, device, devise **7** collude, connive, project **8** cogitate, conspire, contrive, game plan, intrigue, ordering, practice, proposal, strategy **9** blueprint, expedient, machinate **10** conspiracy **11** arrangement, contrivance, machination

schism
4 rent, rift **5** break, chasm, cleft, split **6** breach, heresy **7** dissent, fissure, rupture **8** cleavage, division, fracture **10** dissidence, divergence, heterodoxy, separation **11** unorthodoxy **12** estrangement

schizoid
5 split

schlemiel
4 fool **7** bungler **10** ne'er-do-well

schlepp
3 lug **4** drag, haul, jerk

schmaltzy
5 showy 6 florid 11 sentimental

schnoz
4 beak, nose

scholar
4 sage 5 pupil 6 savant 7 bookman, student, wise man 8 literati (plural), polymath 10 classicist
Hindu: 6 pundit
Muslim: 5 ulama, ulema

scholarly
7 erudite, learned, trained 8 educated, studious 10 scholastic 12 intellectual

scholarship
7 science 8 learning 9 education, erudition, knowledge 11 eruditeness, learnedness

scholastic
5 booky 6 versed 7 bookish, erudite, learned 8 academic, lettered, literary, pedantic 9 scholarly 10 conversant 11 book-learned, quodlibetic
life: 8 academia

school
3 gam, pad 4 lead, show 5 guide, shoal, teach, train 6 direct, inform, manage 7 academy, advance, college, control, educate 8 instruct 9 cultivate 10 discipline
French: 5 école, lycée
grounds: 6 campus
Jewish: 5 heder 7 yeshiva 8 yeshivah
judo: 4 dojo
organization: 3 PTA, PTO
religious: 8 seminary
term: 7 quarter 8 semester

schoolbook
4 text 6 primer, reader 7 speller

School for Scandal author
8 Sheridan (Richard Brinsley)

schooner
4 ship 5 stein, stoup 6 goblet, seidel 7 tumbler

science
4 lore 6 wisdom 8 learning 9 education, erudition, knowledge 11 information, scholarship
combining form: 4 logy 5 logia, sophy
of agriculture: 8 agronomy
of animals: 7 zoology
of armorial bearings: 8 heraldry
of criminal punishment: 8 penology
of environment: 7 ecology
of fermentation: 8 zymology
of government: 8 politics
of health: 7 hygiene 9 hygienics
of heredity: 8 genetics
of human behavior: 10 psychology
of lawmaking: 8 nomology
of measuring time: 8 horology 10 chronology 11 chronometry
of motion: 8 kinetics
of mountains: 7 orology
of nutrition: 8 sitology
of plants: 6 botany
of projectiles: 10 ballistics
of soils: 8 agrology
of the earth: 7 geology
of time: 10 chronology 11 chronometry
of tumors: 8 oncology
suffix: 3 ics

scientific classification
8 taxonomy

sci-fi writer
3 Lem (Stanislaw) 4 Pohl (Frederick) 5 Clark (Arthur), Niven (Larry), Verne (Jules), Wells (Herbert George) 6 Aldiss (Brian), Asimov (Isaac), Bishop (Michael), Butler (Octavia), Delany (Samuel), Le Guin (Ursula), Miller (Walter) 7 Ballard (James Graham), Ellison (Harlan), Herbert (Frank), Van Vogt (Alfred Elton), Zelazny (Roger) 8 Anderson (Poul), Bradbury (Ray), Heinlein (Robert), Sturgeon (Theodore) 10 Silverberg (Robert)

scimitar
5 saber, sword

scintilla
3 jot 4 iota 5 trace 8 particle

scintillate
5 flash, gleam, glint 6 glance 7 glimmer, glisten, glitter, shimmer, sparkle, twinkle 9 coruscate

scoff
3 boo 4 gibe, jeer, jest, mock, twit 5 fleer, flout, rally, scorn, sneer, taunt 6 deride, quip at 7 contemn, despise, disdain, scout at 8 poohpooh, ridicule

scold
3 jaw, rag, wig 4 chew, lash, rail, rant, rate 5 baste, blame, brace, chide, croak, grill, grunt, harpy, hound, shrew, vixen 6 amazon, berate, grouch, grouse, harass, murmur, mutter, ogress, rebuke, revile, tongue, virago 7 bawl out, blister, censure, chew out, grumble, reprove, tell off, upbraid 8 admonish, denounce, execrate, fishwife, lambaste, objurate, reproach 9 criticize, dress down, excoriate, reprehend, reprimand, reprobate, termagant, Xanthippe 10 tonguelash, vituperate

sconce
4 head, poll 5 cover 6 noggin, noodle, screen 7 shelter 11 candlestick

scoop
3 dig, dip 4 bail, beat, grub, lade, lift 5 gouge, ladle, spade 6 dig out, gather, pick up, shovel 8 excavate 9 exclusive

scoot
3 fly, run, zip 4 bolt, dash, flee, rush, shin, skip 5 fleet, hurry, scram, skirr 6 barrel, bustle, hasten, hustle, scurry, sprint 7 beeline, make off, scamper 8 highball 9 skedaddle

scope
4 area, play, room 5 ambit, orbit, range, reach, sweep 6 extent, leeway, margin, radius 7 breadth, compass, purview 8 fullness, latitude, wideness 9 amplitude, elbowroom, extension

Scopes trial lawyer
5 Bryan (William Jennings) 6 Darrow (Clarence)

scorch
4 bake, burn, cook, flay, melt, sear 5 broil, roast, slash 6 scathe, seethe, simmer 7 blister, scarify, scourge, swelter 8 lambaste, lash into 9 castigate, excoriate

score
3 cut, tab, win 4 bill, flay, gain, gash, goal, line, mark, nick, slit 5 cleft, notch, reach, slash, tally, total 6 arrive, attain, furrow, groove, grudge, rack up, record, scorch, scotch, thrive 7 account, achieve, invoice, make out, prosper, realize, ream out, scarify, scourge, scratch, succeed 8 flourish, lambaste, lash into 9 castigate, excoriate, reckoning, serration, statement 10 accomplish

scorn
4 gibe, jeer, mock, pooh 5 abhor, flout, scoff, scout, taunt 6 gibing 7 contemn, despise, despite, disdain, jeering, mockery 8 contempt, derision, despisal, flouting, look down, ridicule, scoffing, taunting 11 despisement 13 disparagement

Scorpius star
7 Antares

Scotch cocktail
6 Rob Roy

Scotch fiddle
4 itch, scab

scoter
7 sea coot, sea duck

Scotland's capital
9 Edinburgh

Scott, Sir Walter
novel: 6 Rob Roy 7 Ivanhoe, Waverly 8 The Abbot 9 Woodstock 10 Kenilworth 11 Redgauntlet, The Talisman
poem: 7 Marmion

___ Scott case
4 Dred

Scottish
cap: 11 tam-o'-shanter
child: 5 bairn
hero: 5 Bruce (Robert) 7 Wallace (William)
hill: 4 brae
landowner: 5 laird
outlaw: 6 Rob Roy
patron saint: 6 Andrew
plaid: 6 tartan
pudding: 6 haggis
spirit: 5 kelpy 6 kelpie
trousers: 5 trews

scoundrel
see **scamp**

scour
3 eat, fan, fly 4 beat, bite, comb, find, flit, flux, gnaw, grub, rake, rout, seek 5 erode, fleet, hurry, range, rifle, scrub, smoke, speed 6 bullet, forage, rocket, search 7 beeline, corrode, eat away, look for, ransack, rummage 8 finecomb, highball, wear away 9 ferret out 13 fine-tooth comb

scourge
3 hit 4 flay, flog, hide, lash, sack, whip, whop 5 curse, flail, knout, slash, waste, whale 6 lather, plague, ravage, scathe, scorch, stripe, thrash 7 blister, despoil, pillage, scarify 8 desolate, lambaste, lash into, spoliate 9 castigate, depredate, desecrate, devastate, excoriate 10 flagellate, pestilence

Scourge of God
6 Attila

scouting group
3 BSA, GSA

scow
3 hoy 5 barge 6 garvey 7 lighter

scowl
5 frown, glare, gloom, lower 6 glower

scrabble
6 scrawl 7 clamber, scratch 8 scramble, scribble, squiggle

scraggy
4 bony, lank, lean 5 gaunt, harsh, lanky, rough, spare 6 jagged, rugged, skinny, uneven 7 angular, dwarfed, scrawny, scrubby, spindly, stunted, unlevel 8 asperous, gangling, rawboned, scabrous, skeletal 9 spindling, undersize

scram
4 kite 6 begone, decamp, get out 7 skiddoo, take off 8 clear out, hightail 9 skedaddle

scramble
4 hash 6 jumble, jungle, litter, muddle, ramble, scurry, sprawl, tumble 7 clamber, clutter, rummage, scuttle, shuffle 8 mishmash, scrabble, straggle

scrap
3 bit, end, jot, ort, row 4 cast, chip, dump, fray, junk, shed, spat, tiff, whit 5 brawl, broil, crumb, fight, set-to, shred, speck, waste, whoop 6 affray, bicker, fracas, reject, slough, smitch, tittle 7 bobbery, brabble, cashier, cutting, discard, fall out, quarrel, scuffle, wrangle 8 fragment, jettison, leftover, particle, squabble, throw out 9 caterwaul, scrappage, throw away

scrape
3 fix, jam, rub 4 hole, rasp, spot 5 chafe, get by, grate, graze, grind, pinch, screw, scuff, shave, skimp, spare, stint 6 abrade, corner, pickle, plight, scrimp 7 dilemma, scratch, trouble 8 get along, struggle 11 predicament

scrappy
6 brawly 7 warlike 8 brawling, militant 9 bellicose, brawlsome, combative, truculent 10 battlesome, pugnacious 11 belligerent, contentious, quarrelsome

scratch
4 claw, rake, rasp 5 grate, score 6 scotch, scrape, scrawl 8 scrabble, scribble, squiggle

scrawl
6 doodle 7 scratch 8 inscribe, scrabble, scribble, squiggle

scrawny
4 bony, lank, lean 5 gaunt, lanky, spare 6 skinny 7 angular, scraggy 8 rawboned

scream
3 cry, yip 4 howl, riot, roar, wail, yell, yowl 5 blare, shout 6 bellow, screak, shriek, shrill, squeak, squeal 7 grumble, protest, screech 8 complain 9 caterwaul

screech
4 hoot 6 pierce, screak, scream, shriek, shrill, squeal

screen
4 blip, bury, fend, hide, sift, sort 5 cache, cloak, close, cover, guard, shade, sieve, stash 6 censor, choose, defend, embosk, riddle, secure, select, shadow, shield, shroud 7 bulwark, conceal, cover up, extract, pick out, protect, seclude, secrete, shut off, shut out, sort out, umbrage, wall off 8 blindage, block out, disguise, ensconce, obstruct, separate 9 expurgate, filter out, inumbrate, safeguard, winnow out 10 bowdlerize, camouflage
Japanese: 5 shoji

screw
5 crimp, exact, gouge, pinch, skimp, spare, stint, wrest, wring 6 extort, rimple, ruck up, rumple, scrape, scrimp, skinch, wrench 7 crimple, crinkle, crumple, scrunch, squeeze, wrinkle 8 thumbkin 9 shake down

screwy
3 mad 4 daft, nuts 5 wacky 6 insane 7 cracked, lunatic, unsound 10 unbalanced

scribble
5 write 6 scrawl, scribe 7 jot down, scratch 8 scrabble, squiggle

scribe
5 clerk, write 6 author, writer 7 copyist 9 secretary

scrimmage
4 fray 5 brawl, broil, brush, clash, fight, melee, set-to 6 affray, fracas, mellay 7 scuffle 8 skirmish 10 donnybrook, free-for-all

scrimp
4 save 5 stint 6 save up, scrape 9 economize

script
4 hand, text 10 penmanship 11 calligraphy, chirography, handwriting

scrivener
6 notary, scribe, writer 7 copyist

scrooge
5 miser 7 niggard 8 muckworm, tightwad 9 skinflint 10 cheapskate 12 moneygrubber

scrub
3 rub 4 buff, drop, wash 5 brush, scour 6 cancel, mallee, maquis, polish 7 call off, cleanse 8 inferior 9 chaparral, secondary, subaltern, underling 11 subordinate

scruff
4 nape, neck

scruffy
5 seedy, tacky 6 shabby, tagrag 7 run-down, scrubby 8 tattered 10 down-at-heel, threadbare

scrumptious
5 yummy 8 adorable, heavenly, luscious 9 ambrosial, delicious 10 delectable, delightful

scruple
3 bit, jot 4 atom, balk, fret, iota 5 demur, grain, qualm, scrap, shred, worry 7 modicum 8 particle, question 9 faltering, hesitancy 11 compunction

scrupulous
4 just, true 5 exact, fussy, right 6 honest, strict 7 careful, heedful, upright 8 critical, punctual 9 honorable 10 fair-minded, fastidious, meticulous, upstanding 11 painstaking, punctilious 12 conscionable 13 conscientious

scrutinize
3 eye 4 comb, scan 5 audit, probe, study, watch 6 peruse, survey 7 analyze, canvass, check up, dig into, dissect, examine, eyeball, inspect 8 consider, look over, pore over 9 check over 11 contemplate, perlustrate

scrutiny
3 eye 4 scan 5 audit, watch 6 look-in, review, survey 7 look-see 8 analysis, eagle eye, lookover 9 check-over 10 inspection 11 examination 12 surveillance 13 perlustration

scuba diver
7 frogman 8 aquanaut

scuff
6 scrape 7 scratch, shamble, shuffle

scuffle
3 row 4 cuff, fray 5 brawl, broil, fight, scrap, set-to 6 affray, fracas, shovel, tussle 7 bobbery, grapple, shamble, shuffle, wrestle

scull
3 oar, row 4 boat 6 propel

sculpt
5 carve 6 chisel

sculptor
American: 4 Gabo (Naum), Taft (Lorado) 5 Andre (Carl), Pratt (Bela), Segal (George), Smith (David), Story (William) 6 Aitkin (Robert), Calder (Alexander), French (Daniel Chester), Powers (Hiram), Zorach (William) 7 Borglum (Gutzon), Noguchi (Isamu) 8 Lachaise (Gaston), Lipchitz (Jacques), Nadelman (Elie), Nevelson (Louise) 9 Bourgeois (Louise), Mestrovic (Ivan), Remington (Frederic) 12 Saint-Gaudens (Augustus)
Czech: 6 Stursa (Jan)
Danish: 6 Thorvaldsen (Bertel), Thorwaldsen (Bertel)
Dutch: 6 Sluter (Claus)
English: 5 Moore (Henry), Watts (George) 7 Epstein (Jacob), Flaxman (John) 8 Hepworth (Barbara)
French: 3 Arp (Hans, Jean) 4 Bloc (Andre) 5 Rodin (Auguste) 6 Dubois (Paul), Houdon (Jean-Antoine) 7 Maillol (Aristide), Pevsner (Antoine) 9 Bartholdi (Frederic-Auguste), Roubillac (Louis-François)
Greek: 5 Myron 7 Phidias 10 Polyclitus, Praxiteles 11 Polycleitus
Italian: 5 Leoni (Leone), Salvi (Niccolò, Nicola) 6 Canova (Antonio), Pisano (Andrea, Nino), Robbia (Andrea, Giovanni, Girolamo, Luca della) 7 Bernini (Gian Lorenzo), Cellini (Benvenuto), da Vinci (Leonardo), Orcagna, Quercia (Jacopo della) 8 Ghiberti (Lorenzo), Vittoria (Alessandro) 9 Donatello, Sansovino (Jacopo) 10 Verrocchio (Andrea del) 12 Michelangelo
Rhodian: 9 Polydorus
Romanian: 8 Brancusi (Constantin)
Russian: 7 Zadkine (Ossip)
Swedish: 6 Milles (Carl)
Swiss: 10 Giacometti (Alberto)

scum
3 cur, mob 5 dregs, dross, skunk, snake, trash 6 masses, rabble,

refuse 7 stinker 8 canaille, riffraff, unwashed

scummy
3 low 4 base, mean, vile 5 cheap, sorry 6 scurvy, shabby 8 beggarly, pitiable 10 despicable, despisable 12 contemptible

scurrilous
4 foul 5 dirty, gross, nasty 6 coarse, filthy, smutty, vulgar 7 abusive, obscene, raunchy 8 indecent 9 insulting, invective, offending, offensive, outraging, truculent 10 outrageous, vituperous 11 opprobrious 12 blackguardly, contumelious, vituperative, vituperatory

scurry
3 fly, run 4 dart, dash, shin, tear 5 scoot, shoot 6 sprint 7 scamper, scuffle, scutter, scuttle, skelter

scurvy
see **scummy**

scut
4 tail

scuttlebutt
4 buzz, talk 5 on-dit, rumor 6 gossip, report, rumble 7 hearsay 9 grapevine

Scylla
4 rock
father: 5 Nisus
lover: 5 Minos; (see also **Charybdis**)

scythe handle
5 snath 6 snathe

sea
4 blue, deep, main 5 brine, briny, drink, ocean
Antarctica: 4 Ross 5 Davis 7 Weddell 8 Amundsen
Arctic: 4 Kara 7 Chukchi 8 Beaufort, Karskoye 9 Chuckchee, Norwegian 11 Chukotskoye 12 East Siberian
Asia-Europe: 5 Black
Asia Minor: 7 Icarian
Atlantic: 5 North 7 Weddell 9 Caribbean
Australia-Indonesia: 7 Arafura
Balkan Peninsula-Italy: 8 Adriatic
Bay of Bengal: 7 Andaman
China-Korea: 5 Huang, Hwang 6 Yellow
combining form: 3 mer 4 mari 5 pelag 6 pelago 7 thalass 8 thalasso
Corsica-Italy: 10 Tyrrhenian
Denmark-Norway: 8 Skagerak 9 Skagerrak
Denmark-Sweden: 8 Kattegat
England-Ireland: 5 Irish

Fiji: **4** Koro
France-Italy: **8** Ligurian
Greece: **5** Crete
Greece-Italy: **6** Ionian
Greece-Turkey: **6** Aegean **8** Thracian
Honshu: **6** Sagami
Indian Ocean: **4** Savu, Sawu **5** Timor **7** Arabian
Indonesia: **4** Bali **6** Flores
inland: **3** Red **4** Aral **7** Caspian
Japan: **3** Iyo, Suo **6** Inland
largest island: **7** Caspian
Malay Archipelago: **5** Banda
Mexico: **6** Cortes
Netherlands: **6** Wadden
North Atlantic: **8** Sargasso
Northern Europe: **6** Baltic, Ostsee **8** Suevicum **10** Baltiskoye
North Pacific: **6** Bering
Novaya Zemlya-Svalbard: **7** Barents
off Scotland: **8** Hebrides
off Sweden: **5** Aland
Pacific: **4** Java **5** China, Coral **6** Maluku **7** Celebes, Eastern, Molucca, Solomon **9** East China, Moluksche **10** South China
Philippine: **4** Sulu
Russia: **5** White **7** Okhotsk
Russia-Ukraine: **4** Azov **9** Azovskoye
South Pacific: **4** Ross **6** Tasman **8** Amundsen
Turkey: **7** Marmara **9** Propontis
West Pacific: **5** Ceram, Japan **8** Bismarck **10** Philippine

sea anemone
  7 actinia

seabird
  see **bird**, **++aquatic**

sea channel
  6 strait **7** euripus

sea coot
  6 scoter **9** guillemot

sea cucumber
  7 trepang **11** holothurian

sea dog
  see **sailor**

sea duck
  5 eider, scaup **6** scoter **9** merganser

sea eagle
  3 ern **4** erne **6** osprey

seafood dish
  4 clam, crab, tuna **5** scrod **6** oyster, shrimp **7** lobster, scallop

seagoing
  8 maritime, nautical

seal
  5 sigil, stamp **6** cachet, signet **7** sticker

bearded: **6** makluk
eared: **5** otary
female: **3** cow **5** matka
herd: **3** pod **5** patch
male: **8** seecatch
young: **3** pup

sealant
  4 lute **6** luting

sea lily
  7 crinoid

seallike
  7 phocine

seam
  4 bond **5** joint, union **7** joining **8** coupling, junction, juncture **10** connection

seaman
  see **sailor**

sea monster
  3 Orc
legendary: **6** kraken

seamount
flat-topped: **5** guyot

seamy
  5 dirty, rough, seedy **6** sordid **12** disreputable

séance
  7 meeting, session, sitting
holder: **6** medium

seaport
Adriatic: **5** Split **6** Spljet
Aegean: **5** Vathy
Alaska: **9** Anchorage
Albania: **5** Vlona, Vlorë
Algeria: **4** Bona, Oran **5** Arzew **6** Annaba **9** Arsenaria, Cherchell, Shershell
Angola: **6** Lobito **7** Cabinda **8** Benguela **9** Mocamedes
Argentina: **7** La Plata
Australia: **4** Eden **6** Bowen **8** Brisbane, Wallaroo **10** Wollongong
Azores: **5** Horta
Balearic: **5** Ibiza
Baltic: **5** Visby
Belgium: **6** Ostend
Benin: **6** Kotonu **7** Cotonou
Black Sea: **5** Odessa
Bosnia and Herzegovina: **4** Omis
Brazil: **3** Rio **4** Para **5** Bahia, Belem, Natal **6** Recife, Santos **8** Salvador **10** Pernambuco **11** Pôrto Alegre, São Salvador **12** Rio de Janeiro
Bulgaria: **5** Varna
Cameroon: **5** Campo, Duala, Kampo, Kribi
Canaries: **8** Arrecife
Celebes: **7** Makasar **8** Macassar, Makassar

Chile: **4** Lebu, Lota **5** Ancud, Arica **8** Coquimbo **10** Valparaiso
China: **4** Amoy **6** Lushun, Xiamen
Colombia: **6** Lorica **9** Cartagena
Corsica: **5** Calvi
Costa Rica: **10** Puntarenas
Crimean: **10** Sevastopol
Croatia: **4** Senj **5** Zadar **9** Dubrovnik
Cuba: **5** Banes
Cyprus: **7** Limasol **8** Limassol **9** Famagusta
Delaware: **5** Lewes
Denmark: **5** Arhus, Ronne, Vejle **6** Aarhus, Alborg **7** Aalborg **8** Elsinore
Djibouti: **4** Obok **5** Obock **6** Tajura **8** Tadjoura
Ecuador: **5** Manta **9** Guayaquil
Egypt: **4** Said **8** Al Qusayr, Al Quseir, El Qoseir **10** Alexandria
England: **10** Portsmouth
Equatorial Guinea: **4** Bata
Eritrea: **4** Aseb
Estonia: **5** Parnu **6** Pyarnu **7** Tallinn
Ethiopia: **4** Zula
Finland: **3** Abo **4** Kemi, Oulu, Pori, Vasa **5** Hango, Kotka, Rauma, Turku, Vaasa **8** Uleaborg **10** Bjorneborg
Florida: **5** Miami, Tampa **9** Pensacola **12** Apalachicola, Jacksonville
France: **4** Meze, Nice **5** Havre, Nizza **6** Calais, Cannes, Toulon **7** Dunkirk, Le Havre, Lorient **8** Bordeaux, Boulogne **9** Cherbourg, Dunkerque, Marseille **10** Marseilles
French Polynesia: **7** Papeete
Georgia: **9** Brunswick
Georgia, Republic of: **4** Poti
Germany: **4** Kiel **5** Bremen, Emden, Husum **6** Wismar **8** Cuxhaven **11** Bremerhaven **13** Wilhelmshaven
Ghana: **4** Keta **6** Kwitta
Greece: **4** Kimi, Kyme **5** Pylos, Syros, Volos **7** Piraeus **8** Peiraeus
Guatemala: **7** San José **10** Livingston
Gulf of Aden: **5** Alula
Haiti: **5** Cayes **8** Aux Cayes
Honduras: **8** Trujillo
India: **3** Goa **4** Puri **5** Marud **6** Old Goa **9** Jagannath **10** Juggernaut
Ionian: **5** Corfu
Iran: **4** Jask **7** Bushehr, Bushire
Iraq: **5** Basra
Ireland: **4** Cork **5** Sligo **6** Dingle, Tralee **10** Balbriggan
Israel: **4** Acre, Akko, Elat, Yafa **5** Accho, Eilat, Elath, Haifa, Jaffa, Joppa **9** Ptolemais, Sycaminum
Italy: **4** Bari **5** Anzio, Gaeta, Genoa, Pizzo, Trani **6** Naples, Pe-

saro, Venice **7** Leghorn, Rapallo, Salerno, Taranto, Trieste, Venedig **8** Sorrento **10** Senigallia
Ivory Coast: **4** Tabu **5** Tabou
Jamaica: **10** Montego Bay
Japan: **5** Kochi, Rumoi, Ujina, Uraga **6** Sasebo **7** Fukuoka **8** Nagasaki, Yokohama
Java: **5** Tegal, Tuban **8** Samarang, Semarang, Surabaja, Tjirebon
Jordan: **5** Akaba, Aqaba, Elath **6** Aelana
Latvia: **4** Riga **9** Ventspils
Lebanon: **5** Saida **7** Tripoli
Libya: **4** Homs **5** Khoms **6** Tobruk
Lithuania: **5** Memel **8** Klaipeda
Madagascar: **8** Tamatave
Maine: **7** Belfast **8** Portland
Malaysia: **4** Miri, Weld **5** Pekan **6** Melaka, Pinang **7** Malacca **10** George Town
Massachusetts: **9** Fall River
Mauritius: **5** Louis
Mediterranean: **4** Gaza, Oran, Said **5** Genoa, Haifa, Jaffa **6** Bayrut, Beirut **7** Algiers, Bizerte, Catania, Tripoli **8** Benghazi **9** Barcelona **10** Alexandria, Marseilles
Mexico: **8** Acapulco, Veracruz
Minorca: **5** Mahon
Moluccas: **5** Ambon
Montenegro: **5** Kotov
Morocco: **3** Sla **4** Safi, Sale **5** Ceuta, Saffi **6** Agadir **7** Larache, Tangier **10** Casablanca
Mozambique: **5** Beira, Pemba **6** Amelia, Xai Xai **11** Porto Amelia
New Hampshire: **10** Portsmouth
New Zealand: **8** Auckland
Nicaragua: **5** Brito
Nigeria: **8** Harcourt
Niger mouth: **5** Bonny
North Korea: **4** Yuki **5** Unggi
Norway: **4** Bodo, Moss **5** Vadso **6** Tromso **9** Stavanger, Trondheim, Trondhjem **11** Fredrikstad
Oman: **3** Sur **5** Sohar **6** Matrah
Pakistan: **5** Pasni
Panay: **6** Iloilo
Papua New Guinea: **3** Lea
Peru: **3** Ilo **4** Eten **5** Paita, Pisco
Philippines: **4** Cebu **5** Davao, Laoag **6** Aparri, Cavite, Iloilo, Manila **7** Legaspi **8** Tacloban **9** Zamboanga
Poland: **6** Gdynia **7** Gdingen, Stettin **8** Szczecin
Portugal: **4** Faro **5** Lagos **6** Oporto **7** Funchal **9** Lacobriga
Puerto Rico: **5** Ponce
Russia: **3** Kem **5** Anapa, Sochi **6** Vyborg **11** Kaliningrad, Vladivostok

Ryukyu: **4** Naha, Nawa
Sakhalin Island: **8** Korsakov
Saudi Arabia: **4** Wejh **5** Jidda, Qatif, Yanbu, Yenbo **6** Juddah **7** Djeddah
Scotland: **3** Ayr **4** Oban **5** Alloa, Largs, Leven **6** Dundee
Sicily: **5** Avola **7** Messina, Palermo **8** Syracuse
Slovenia: **5** Kopar, Koper, Piran
Somalia: **7** Berbera, Kismayu **9** Chisimaio
South Africa: **6** Durban **8** Cape Town, Kaapstad
South Carolina: **10** Charleston
South Korea: **5** Mason, Mokpo **6** Inch'on, Jinsen **7** Masampo **8** Chemulpo
Spain: **4** Adra, Noya, Vigo **5** Cadiz, Gadir, Gijon, Marin **6** Abdera **8** Alicante **9** Cartagena, Las Palmas
Sri Lanka: **10** Batticaloa
Sumatra: **6** Padang
Sweden: **4** Umea **5** Gavle, Lulea, Malmo, Pitea, Ystad **8** Göteborg **10** Gothenburg
Tanzania: **5** Lindi, Tanga
Thailand: **4** Trat **8** Bang Phra
Tunisia: **4** Sfax **5** Gabes **7** Bizerte, Safaqis
Turkey: **4** Rize **5** Coruh, Sinop **6** Coroch
Ukraine: **7** Kherson
U.S. Virgin Islands: **8** St. Thomas
Vanuatu: **4** Vila
Vietnam: **6** Da Nang **7** Tourane **8** Haiphong, Nha Trang
Virginia: **10** Portsmouth
Yemen: **5** Mocha, Mokha **7** Hodeida; (see also **seaport capital**)

seaport capital
4 Aden, Apia, Lomé, Suva **5** Accra, Adana, Alger, Dakar, Lagos **6** Banjul, Belize, Bissão, Bissau, Boston, Dublin, Eblana, Havana, Juneau, Kuwait, Lisbon, Maputo, Masqat, Muscat, Roseau **7** Algiers, Batavia, Colombo, Icosium, Jakarta, Moresby, San Juan **8** Al-Jazā'ir, Al-Kuwait, Bathurst, Castries, Djakarta, Freetown, Hamilton, Helsinki, Honolulu, Kingston, La Habana, Monrovia, Valletta **9** Annapolis, Mogadishu, Nukualofa, Porto-Novo, Reykjavík, Singapore **10** Bridgetown, Daressalem, Libreville, Mogadiscio, Paramaribo **11** Dar es Salaam, Port of Spain **12** Port-au-Prince

sear
3 dry **5** parch **6** burn up, scorch,

sizzle **7** shrivel **9** cauterize, dehydrate, desiccate, exsiccate

search
4 beat, comb, grub, hunt, peer, rake, scan, seek **5** check, delve, frisk, quest, rifle, scour, study **6** ferret, forage, pry out **7** examine, hunting, inspect, manhunt, pursual, pursuit, ransack, rummage, run down, seeking **8** finecomb, look over, pursuing, scavenge, scout out, skirmish **9** cast about, ferret out, pursuance, scrimmage, shake down **10** scrutinize **11** scout around **13** fine-tooth comb
for gold: **7** fossick

sea robber
5 rover **6** pirate **7** corsair **8** picaroon **9** buccaneer **10** freebooter

sea rover
see **sea robber**

seasickness
8 mal de mer **9** naupathia

season
3 fit **4** fall, salt, term, time **5** spice, steel, train **6** autumn, harden, pepper, period, school, spring, summer, winter **7** prepare, toughen **8** marinade, marinate **9** acclimate, climatize **10** case harden, discipline **11** acclimatize

seasonable
3 apt **6** timely **7** apropos, timeous **8** relevant **9** favorable, opportune, pertinent, well-timed **10** auspicious, convenient, propitious, prosperous **11** appropriate

seasoning
4 herb, sage, salt **5** spice **6** fennel, garlic, pepper **7** cayenne, mustard, paprika **9** condiment

seat
3 bed, hub, put, sit **4** base, beam, rest **5** basis, focus, heart, place, usher **6** behind, bottom, center, settee **7** footing, fulcrum **8** backside, basement, buttocks, derriere, polestar **9** establish, fundament, posterior **10** focal point, foundation, groundwork **11** nerve center
church: **3** pew
on a camel or elephant: **6** howdah
upholstered: **9** banquette

sea urchin
7 echinus **8** echinoid

seaweed
4 agar, alga, kelp **5** dulse **6** murlin **7** henware **9** carrageen **11** badderlocks

brown: 6 fucoid 8 gulfweed, rockweed, sargasso
edible: 4 ulva 7 redware
purple: 9 carrageen, Irish moss

Sea Wolf, The
author: 6 London (Jack)
captain: 10 Wolf Larsen
ship: 5 Ghost

Sebastian
brother: 6 Alonso
sister: 5 Viola

secede
4 quit 5 leave 8 withdraw

seclude
4 hide 6 closet, immure, retire,
screen 7 confine, enclose, isolate,
shut off 8 cloister, separate, withdraw 9 sequester

seclusion
7 privacy 8 solitude 9 aloneness,
isolation 10 detachment, retirement, separation, withdrawal
11 privateness 12 separateness

second
3 aid 4 abet, back, wink 5 flash,
jiffy, trice 6 assist, minute, moment
7 endorse, instant, support
9 twinkling
combining form: 4 deut 5 deuto
6 deuter 7 deutero

secondary
3 sub 5 dinky, minor, scrub, small,
under 6 lesser 7 derived, subject
8 borrowed, derivate, inferior,
small-fry 9 accessory, dependent,
resultant, small-time, subaltern, tributary, underling 10 collateral, consequent, derivative, secondhand,
subsequent 11 minor-league, subordinate, subservient
prefix: 3 sub

second-class
4 hack, mean, poor 6 common
8 déclassé, inferior, low-grade

secondhand
4 used, worn 7 derived
8 borrowed

second-rate
see **second-class**

second-string
3 sub 10 substitute

secrecy
4 hush 7 silence, stealth 8 hush-
hush 10 censorship, covertness,
subterfuge 11 concealment, furtiveness

secret
4 deep 5 heavy, sneak 6 covert,
hidden, occult, orphic, remote
7 devious, furtive, obscure, removed, retired, sub-rosa 8 abstruse, esoteric, hermetic, hush-
hush, lonesome, mystical, profound,
screened, stealthy, unavowed
9 concealed, recondite 10 acroamatic, classified, restricted, undeclared, undercover 11 clandestine,
out-of-the-way, underhanded
12 confidential, hugger-mugger
13 surreptitious, under-the-table
combining form: 5 crypt, krypt
6 crypto, krypto

secret agent
3 spy 8 emissary

secretaire
4 desk 10 escritoire

secretary
4 desk 5 clerk 6 scribe 10 amanu-
ensis, escritoire
king's: 10 chancellor

secrete
4 bury, hide 5 cache, cover, exude, plant, stash 6 screen 7 conceal, deposit 8 ensconce, withhold

secretly
7 sub rosa 8 covertly 9 furtively
10 stealthily

secret society
3 KKK 4 Poro, tong 5 Mafia 7 ca-
morra 10 Ku Klux Klan

sect
4 cult 5 creed, faith 6 church 8 religion 9 communion 10 connection,
persuasion 12 denomination

sectarian
5 local 7 insular 8 splinter 9 dissident, heretical, heterodox, parochial, small-town 10 provincial,
schismatic, unorthodox
13 nonconformist

sectary
5 bigot, rebel 6 cohort, hippie
7 beatnik, heretic, liberal, radical
8 adherent, bohemian, disciple, follower, henchman, maverick, partisan, sectator 9 dissenter, dissident,
satellite, supporter, Young Turk
10 schismatic, separatist 11 misbeliever, schismatist 13 nonconformist, revolutionary

section
3 cut 4 area, belt, part, zone
5 field, piece, slice, split, tract 6 divide, member, moiety, parcel, region, sector, sphere 7 break up,
portion, quarter, segment 8 district,
division, locality, precinct, separate, vicinity 9 territory
11 subdivision
combining form: 4 tome, tomy

sector
7 quarter, section 8 district,
precinct

secular
3 lay 7 profane 8 temporal, unsacred 11 nonclerical
12 nonreligious

secure
3 bag, fix, get, set 4 bind, fast,
fend, firm, gain, have, iron, land,
lock, make, moor, nail, safe, sure,
take 5 annex, catch, cause, chock,
cinch, clamp, cover, fixed, guard,
rivet, solid, sound, tight, tried 6 anchor, assure, cement, clinch, collar,
defend, draw on, effect, ensure,
fasten, insure, obtain, pick up, pinion, pledge, screen, shield, stable,
strong, trusty 7 acquire, assured,
bulwark, capture, chalk up, prehend, procure, produce, protect, settled, staunch, tie down 8 balanced,
reliable, riskless, sanguine 9 confident, safeguard, tenacious 10 batten down, bring about, dependable, underwrite, undoubtful
11 established, self-assured, trustworthy 12 tried and true 13 self-
confident

security
4 bail, bond, pawn, ward 5 aegis,
armor, guard, token 6 pledge,
safety, shield, surety 7 defense,
earnest, warrant 8 armament, firmness, guaranty, safeness, strength,
warranty 9 assurance, guarantee,
safeguard, soundness, stability
10 protection, stableness, steadiness 13 certification

sedan
3 car 4 auto, limo 10 automobile

sedate
4 calm 5 grave, sober, staid
6 placid, proper, seemly, serene,
solemn, somber 7 earnest, serious,
weighty 8 composed, decorous,
tranquil 9 collected, dignified, unruffled 10 no-nonsense, sobersided
13 dispassionate, imperturbable

sedative
4 balm 7 calmant 8 barbital, hyo-
scine, pacifier, quietive 9 calmative
10 depressant 11 barbiturate
12 sleeping pill, tranquilizer

sedentary
4 lazy 7 settled 8 inactive
10 stationary

sediment
4 lees, silt, slag 5 draff, dregs,
dross 6 scoria 7 bottoms, deposit,
grounds, heeltap 9 recrement,
settlings 11 precipitate
13 precipitation
layer: 5 varve

sedition
4 coup 6 action, mutiny, putsch, revolt, strike 7 protest, treason 8 uprising 9 coup d'etat, rebellion
10 alienation, revolution 12 disaffection, estrangement, insurrection

seditious
7 lawless, violent 8 disloyal, factious, mutinous 9 alienated, dissident, faithless, insurgent 10 perfidious, rebellious, traitorous
11 disaffected, treacherous

seduce
4 bait, coax, lure, rape, ruin, undo
5 decoy, tease, tempt, train 6 allure, betray, delude, entice, entrap,
lead on, ravish 7 corrupt, debauch,
deceive, degrade, enslave, mislead, pervert, violate 8 deflower,
entrance, inveigle 9 overpower,
overwhelm

seducer
7 Don Juan 8 lothario

seduction
4 call, draw, lure, pull, rape, ruin
6 appeal 9 siren song, violation
10 allurement, attraction, corruption, perversion, ravishment,
seducement, temptation
11 deflowering

seductive
5 siren 7 drawing, vampish 8 alluring, magnetic 9 desirable
10 attracting, attractive, bewitching, enchanting 11 captivating, fascinating, provocative

seductress
5 siren 7 Lorelei 9 temptress
11 femme fatale

sedulous
4 busy 6 active 7 operose 8 diligent, hustling 9 assiduous
10 persistent 11 industrious, persevering, unremitting

see
4 call, date, espy, gape, gaze,
have, hear, know, lead, look,
mark, mind, note, peek, peep,
peer, scan, show, take, twig, vide,

view 5 catch, fancy, glare, grasp,
guide, learn, pilot, pop in, probe,
route, sight, stare, steer, study,
think, visit, watch, weigh 6 accept,
attend, behold, come by, descry,
direct, divine, drop by, drop in, escort, follow, go with, look in, look
up, notice, pierce, ponder, remark,
step in, stop by, stop in, suffer, take
in, tumble, vision 7 catch on, conduct, discern, examine, feature,
find out, foresee, glimpse, imagine,
inspect, look out, make out, observe, preknow, previse, realize,
sustain, take out, undergo, unearth
8 appraise, come over, conceive,
consider, discover, envisage, envision, forefeel, foreknow, perceive,
shepherd, watch out 9 accompany,
apprehend, ascertain, determine,
penetrate, prevision, recognize, visualize 10 anticipate, comprehend,
experience, scrutinize, understand
11 distinguish 12 discriminate

seed
3 bud, sow 4 core, germ 5 brood,
image, issue, ovule, plant, put in,
spark 6 embryo, kernel, notion, scions 7 conceit, concept, nucleus,
progeny 8 children, rudiment 9 offspring, posterity 10 conception, impression 11 descendants,
progeniture
aromatic: 6 fennel
coating: 5 testa 6 testae (plural)
combining form: 3 gon 4 cocc,
gono, spor 5 cocci, cocco, sperm,
spori, sporo 6 sperma, spermi,
spermo 7 spermae (plural), spermat
8 spermato
covering: 4 aril
medicinal: 7 ignatia
of a bean: 7 haricot
of an herb: 3 pea, soy 4 soya
7 soybean
of a vine: 6 peanut
palm tree: 6 jarina
poisonous: 10 castor bean
prickly: 6 bonduc
vessel: 3 pod 5 fruit, pyxis 7 pyxi-
des, pyxidia (plural), silicle, siliqua
8 pyxidium, sillique

seedcase
3 pod

seedy
5 dingy, faded, messy, tired
6 droopy, shabby, untidy, wilted
7 run-down, sagging, unkempt, wilt-
ing 8 decrepit, drooping, flagging,
slovenly, tattered 9 neglected, overgrown 10 bedraggled, down-at-
heel, threadbare

seek
3 dig, try 4 fish, hunt, nose, root
5 assay, delve, essay, mouse, offer,
quest, sniff 6 strive 7 attempt, bird-
dog 8 endeavor, smell out, struggle
9 cast about, ferret out, search for,
search out, undertake

seem
4 hint, look 5 imply, sound 6 appear 7 suggest 8 intimate, resemble 9 insinuate

seeming
combining form: 5 quasi

seemly
4 nice 5 right 6 decent, proper
7 correct 8 becoming, decorous,
pleasing 9 befitting, congenial,
congruous, consonant 10 compatible, conforming, consistent
11 comme il faut

seep
4 drip, flow, leak, ooze, weep
5 bleed, exude, sweat 6 strain
8 transude

seer
5 augur 6 auspex 7 prophet 8 foreseer, haruspex 9 predictor 10 forecaster, foreteller 11 Nostradamus

seesaw
3 yaw 4 cant, lean, list, rock, roll,
swag, sway, tilt, toss 5 lurch, pitch
6 teeter, tilter 7 bascule, incline

seethe
3 sop 4 boil, burn, fret, fume, rage,
soak, stew, stir, teem 5 anger,
churn, erupt, souse, steam, steep,
swarm 6 abound, blow up, bubble,
drench, simmer, sizzle, sodden
7 bristle, ferment, flare up, parboil
8 boil over, overflow, saturate, waterlog 10 bubble over, impregnate

see-through
5 clear 6 limpid 8 pellucid
11 translucent, transparent

segment
3 cut 4 part 5 piece 6 divide,
member, moiety, parcel, set off
7 isolate, portion, seclude, section
8 division, separate 10 categorize

sego
4 lily

segregate
6 choose, cut off, enisle, island, select, single 7 isolate 8 close off, insulate, separate 9 sequester
10 disconnect

segregation
9 apartheid, isolation, seclusion

10 jim crowism, separation, separatism **12** separateness
13 ghettoization

Segub's father
4 Hiel **6** Hezron

seidel
3 cup, mug **5** stein, stoup

seine
3 net **5** trawl

seismologist
7 Richter (Charles)

seize
3 nab **4** grab, take **5** annex, catch, grasp, usurp **6** abduct, arrest, clutch, kidnap, occupy, secure, snap at, snatch, strike **7** afflict, capture, grapple, impound, preempt **8** accroach, arrogate, carry off, overtake, take over **9** apprehend, latch onto, sequester, spirit off **10** commandeer, confiscate, fasten onto, spirit away **11** appropriate, expropriate

seizure
3 fit **4** turn **5** spell, throe **6** access, attack, taking **9** breakdown **10** convulsion

seldom
3 few **4** rare **6** hardly, little, rarely, scarce **7** unoften **8** scarcely, sporadic, uncommon **10** hardly ever, infrequent, occasional **11** irregularly **12** infrequently, occasionally, sporadically

select
3 top **4** best, cull, fine, mark, pick, rare, take **5** elect, elite **6** choice, choose, chosen, culled, dainty, optate, opt for, picked, prefer, single **7** elegant, favored **8** blue-chip, delicate, eclectic, screened, superior **9** exclusive, exquisite, preferred, recherché, single out, weeded out **11** winnowed out

selection
5 draft **6** acumen, choice, option **7** culling, excerpt, insight, picking **8** choosing, drafting, election **10** preference **11** alternative, discernment

selective
5 fussy, picky **6** choosy **7** choosey, finicky **8** eclectic **10** particular, scrupulous

Seled's father
5 Nadab

Selene
4 Luna **6** Hecate **7** Artemis
beloved: **8** Endymion

brother: **6** Helios
father: **8** Hyperion
mother: **4** Thea

selenium
symbol: **2** Se

self
3 ego
combining form: **3** aut **4** auto

self-acting
9 automatic

self-assertive
4 bold, sure **6** uppish, uppity **7** forward, pushful, pushing **8** cocksure, militant **9** audacious, intrusive, obtrusive, officious, presuming **10** aggressive, meddlesome **11** impertinent, overweening **12** presumptuous

self-assurance
6 aplomb **8** coolness **9** composure, sangfroid, self-trust **10** confidence, equanimity **13** collectedness

self-assured
4 smug **6** secure **8** sanguine **9** confident **10** undoubtful

self-complacent
4 smug **8** priggish

self-composed
4 calm, easy **6** placid, poised, serene **8** tranquil **9** collected, possessed

self-confidence
6 aplomb, hutzpa **7** chutzpa, hutzpah **8** chutzpah, sureness **9** assurance, cockiness, self-trust **12** sanguineness **13** self-assurance

self-confident
5 cocky, janty **6** jaunty, secure **7** assured, cockish **8** sanguine **10** undoubtful

self-conscious
4 prim **5** stiff **6** formal, uneasy **7** anxious, flaunty, stilted **8** affected, mannered **9** ill at ease **10** artificial **12** ostentatious

self-control
4 will **7** balance, dignity, reserve **9** stability, willpower **10** constraint, discipline

self-defense
4 judo **6** aikido, karate **7** jujitsu, jujutsu

self-destruction
7 suicide **8** felo-de-se, hara-kiri

self-discipline
4 will **9** willpower

self-effacing
3 shy **5** timid **6** modest **7** bashful, rabbity **8** backward, retiring **9** diffident, unassured **11** unassertive

self-esteem
5 pride **6** vanity **7** conceit **10** narcissism **11** amour propre

self-evident
5 clear, plain **7** obvious **8** manifest **10** prima facie **12** unmistakable

self-explanatory
5 clear, plain **7** evident, obvious **8** manifest

self-governing
7 popular **10** autonomous, democratic

self-importance
5 pride **6** egoism **7** conceit, egotism **9** arrogance, pomposity, vainglory

self-important
5 puffy, wiggy **6** stuffy **7** bloated, pompous **8** arrogant **10** pontifical **11** magisterial

self-indulgent
9 sybaritic **10** hedonistic, sybaritish **11** sybaritical

self-interest
6 egoism

selfish
6 stingy **7** hoggish, hoglike **8** egoistic **9** egotistic **10** egocentric **11** egomaniacal

self-love
6 vanity **7** conceit, narcism **8** vainness **9** vainglory **10** narcissism **11** amour propre **13** conceitedness

self-possessed
4 calm, easy **5** aloof **6** placid, poised, serene **8** composed, reserved, tranquil **9** collected, easygoing

self-proclaimed
9 soi-disant **10** self-styled

Self-Reliance author
7 Emerson (Ralph Waldo)

self-respect
5 pride **11** amour propre

self-righteous
7 canting **9** pharisaic **11** pharisaical **12** hypocritical, pecksniffian **13** sanctimonious

self-sacrificing
6 kindly **8** generous, selfless **9** unselfish **10** charitable **13** philanthropic

self-satisfied
4 smug 8 priggish 10 complacent

self-seeking
7 selfish 8 egoistic, selfhood 9 egotistic 10 egocentric 11 egomaniacal

self-service
  combining form: 5 teria

self-serving
  see **self-seeking**

self-starter
6 dynamo, peeler 7 hustler, rustler 8 go-getter, live wire

self-styled
5 quasi 7 would be 8 so-called 9 self-given, soi-disant

self-taught
12 autodidactic

sell
3 net 4 draw, hawk, mart, sale, vend 5 bring, fetch, trade, yield 6 barter, betray, deal in, market, peddle, retail, return 7 auction, bring in, command, realize, traffic 8 exchange

sell out
4 dump, move 5 cross 6 betray, delude, humbug, take in, unload 7 beguile, deceive, mislead 8 close out 9 four-flush, sacrifice 11 double-cross

selvage
4 edge

semblance
3 air 4 aura, face, feel, look, mask, mood, pose, show, veil 5 front, guise 6 aspect, facade, simile, veneer 7 analogy, feeling, seeming, showing 8 affinity, disguise, likeness 9 alikeness 10 appearance, atmosphere, comparison, false front, masquerade, similarity, similitude, simulacrum 11 resemblance

Semele
  father: 6 Cadmus
  mother: 8 Harmonia
  sister: 3 Ino 5 Agave 7 Autonoe
  son: 7 Bacchus 8 Dionysus

semi
4 demi, half, hemi 6 partly 7 partial

seminar
8 colloquy 10 colloquium, conference

Seminole chief
7 Osceola

Semiramis
  husband: 5 Ninus
  kingdom: 7 Babylon

Semite
3 Jew 4 Arab 6 Hebrew 7 Maobite 8 Assyrian 9 Canaanite 10 Babylonian, Phoenician

Senapo
  daughter: 8 Clorinda
  kingdom: 8 Ethiopia

senate
7 council 8 assembly 11 legislature

senator
5 solon 8 lawmaker 10 legislator

send
4 mail, post, rush, ship 5 relay, remit, route 6 assign, commit, export, launch, thrill 7 address, advance, airmail, consign, enthuse, forward, mission, traject 8 allocate, delegate, dispatch, expedite, transmit 9 electrify
  back: 6 remand
  forth: 4 emit 7 emanate

senectitude
  see **senescence**

Senegal
  capital: 5 Dakar
  monetary unit: 5 franc

senescence
6 old age 8 caducity 11 elderliness, senectitude

senile
3 old 4 aged, weak 5 aging 6 doting, feeble 7 ancient, doddery 8 decrepit, doddered 9 doddering, enfeebled, senescent, shattered

senility
6 dotage 7 decline 8 caducity 10 senescence

senior
5 doyen, elder, older 6 better 7 ancient, doyenne, oldster 8 brass hat, higher-up, old-timer, superior 10 golden-ager

Sennacherib
  domain: 7 Assyria
  father: 6 Sargon
  kingdom: 7 Assyria
  slayer, son: 8 Sharezer 11 Adrammelech

sensation
4 bomb 5 sense 6 marvel, wonder 7 feeling, miracle, portent, prodigy, stunner 8 response 9 bombshell 10 impression, perception, phenomenon 11 sensibility, sensitivity 13 consciousness, sensitiveness

combining form: 8 esthesio 9 aesthesio

sensational
3 hot 5 boffo, juicy, livid, lurid, smash 6 coarse, divine, groovy, marked, signal, sultry, vulgar 7 colored, piquant, pointed, pungent, rousing, salient, sensory, sensual, tabloid 8 crashing, glorious, slambang, smashing, stunning 9 arresting, hunky-dory, marvelous, prominent, sensatory, sensitive, sensorial, superfine 10 impressive, noticeable, remarkable 11 conspicuous, extravagant, outstanding

sense
3 wit 4 core, deem, feel, gist, hold, know, meat, pith 5 focus, short, smell, think 7 believe, feeling, meaning, message, nucleus, purport, realize 8 consider, gumption, judgment, perceive, prudence 9 awareness, foresight, mentality, mother wit, substance 10 anticipate, brainpower, cognizance, discretion, intendment 11 acceptation, discernment, penetration, recognition 12 appreciation, intelligence, significance, significancy 13 comprehension, consciousness, signification, understanding
  sixth: 3 ESP

Sense and Sensibility author
6 Austen (Jane)

senseless
4 cold, dead, numb, surd 5 silly 6 asleep, numbed, simple, wooden 7 foolish, trivial, unaware, unwitty, witless 8 benumbed, comatose, deadened, mindless 9 brainless

senselessness
5 folly 7 inanity 8 insanity 9 absurdity, craziness, dottiness, silliness, stupidity 11 foolishness, witlessness 12 illogicality

sense organ
3 ear, eye 4 nose, skin 6 tongue

sensibility
5 heart, sense 7 emotion, feeling, insight 8 keenness 9 affection, sensation 11 discernment, penetration, sensitivity

sensible
4 good, sage, sane, wise 5 alive, awake, aware, gross, smart, solid, sound 6 noting, patent, seeing 7 evident, knowing, logical, obvious, prudent, sapient, sizable, witting 8 concrete, imaginal, manifest,

material, palpable, physical, rational, sentient, tangible **9** au courant, cognizant, conscious, corporeal, judgmatic, judicious, objective, observing, remarking, sensitive, weighable **10** consequent, conversant, detectable, observable, perceiving, perceptual, phenomenal, reasonable, responsive

sensitive
4 keen, open, sore **5** acute, aware, prone, sharp, tense **6** liable, seeing, touchy, tricky **7** exposed, feeling, knowing, nervous, psychic, sensile, sensory, sensual, subject **8** affected, delicate, disposed, inclined, sensible, sentient, ticklish, unstable **9** cognizant, conscious, emotional, impressed, irritable, obnoxious, sensatory, sensorial **10** high-strung, influenced, insultable, perceiving, perceptive, precarious, responsive, susceptive, umbrageous **11** emotionable, impressible, predisposed, sensational, susceptible **13** understanding

sensitive plant
6 minosa
family: **3** pea

sensual
4 lush **6** animal, carnal, earthy **7** fleshly, mundane, sensory, worldly **8** banausic, luscious, sensuous, temporal **9** epicurean, luxurious, sensatory, sensitive, sensorial **10** voluptuous **11** irreligious, sensational, unspiritual **13** materialistic

sensuous
4 lush **6** carnal, fleshy **7** bacchic, fleshly, sensual **8** luscious **9** dionysiac, Dionysian, epicurean, luxurious, sybaritic **10** hedonistic, voluptuous **12** sensualistic **13** self-indulgent

sentence
4 damn, doom, rule **5** blame, judge **6** devote, ordain, punish **7** adjudge, condemn **8** denounce, penalize **9** proscribe **10** adjudicate

sententious
4 rich **5** crisp, pithy, terse **6** facund **7** concise, piquant **8** eloquent, pregnant **10** aphoristic, expressive, meaningful **11** significant

sentiment
3 eye **4** bias, mind, view **6** belief **7** emotion, feeling, leaning, opinion, passion, posture **8** penchant,

position, tendency **9** affection, inclining, sensation **10** conception, conviction, partiality, persuasion, propensity **11** affectivity, disposition, inclination **12** emotionalism

sentimental
4 soft **5** gooey, gushy, inane, moist, mushy, sappy, sobby, soupy, sweet, vapid **6** dreamy, drippy, jejune, loving, slushy, sobful, sticky, sugary, syrupy, tender **7** gushing, insipid, maudlin, mawkish **8** bathetic, effusive, romantic, schmalzy **9** misty-eyed, nostalgic, rosewater **10** lovey-dovey, moonstruck, namby-pamby, passionate, saccharine, soft-boiled, sugar-candy **11** tear-jerking **12** affectionate **13** demonstrative

sentimentalist
5 softy **6** softie

sentimentality
4 mush **7** schmalz **8** schmaltz

sentinel
see **sentry**

sentry
4 ward **5** guard, watch **6** picket **7** lookout, outpost **8** sentinel, watchman

separate
3 one **4** comb, free, know, lone, only, part, sift, sole, sort **5** apart, halve, ravel, sever, split **6** cut off, detach, dispel, divide, enisle, island, single, sunder, unglue, unique, unjoin, unknit, unlink, winnow **7** break up, discern, disjoin, dislink, dispart, dissect, diverse, divorce, isolate, quarter, rupture, scatter, several, split up, unravel, various **8** alienate, autarkic, close off, detached, diffract, discrete, disjoint, disperse, dissever, dissolve, distinct, disunify, disunite, estrange, insulate, peculiar, solitary, splinter, uncouple, unmingle, unsolder **9** autarchic, different, discharge, disengage, disrelate, extricate, muster out, segregate, sequester, sovereign, uncombine **10** autonomous, demobilize, difference, discrepate, disengaged, disgregate, dissociate, particular, severalize **11** compartment, dichotomize, disassemble, discontinue, distinctive, distinguish, independent **12** disaggregate, disconnected, discriminate **13** differentiate
flax: **7** hatchel
into filaments: **6** sleave

separation
6 schism **7** breakup, divorce, parting, rupture, split-up **8** disunion, disunity, division, shedding **9** apartheid, dichotomy, dispersal, partition **10** detachment, diffluence, diremption, dissection, separatism, trichotomy **11** disjointure, disjunction, disrelation, dissolution, divorcement, segregation **12** dissociation **13** disconnection, sequestration

separatism
9 apartheid **11** segregation

separatist
7 heretic, sectary **9** dissenter, dissident **10** schismatic **11** misbeliever, schismatist **13** nonconformist

sepia
3 ink **4** gray **5** brown

sepulcher
4 bury, tomb **5** grave, inter, plant **6** burial, entomb, inhume **7** lay away, put away

sequel
3 end, row **5** chain, close, issue, order, train **6** effect, ending, finish, result, series, upshot **7** closing, outcome **8** causatum, epilogue, sequence **9** aftermath, finishing **10** succession **11** aftereffect, alternation, consecution, consequence, development, eventuality, progression, termination **12** continuation

sequence
3 row **5** chain, issue, order, train **6** effect, result, sequel, series, upshot **7** outcome **8** disposal, grouping, ordering **9** aftermath, cavalcade, placement **10** procession, succession **11** aftereffect, alternation, arrangement, consecution, disposition, eventuality, progression **12** distribution

sequential
6 serial **9** succedent **10** succeeding, successive **11** consecutive **12** successional

sequester
4 hide, take **5** annex, seize **6** attach, cut off, enisle, island **7** impound, isolate, preempt, seclude, secrete **8** accroach, arrogate, cloister, close off, insulate, separate **9** segregate **10** commandeer, confiscate, dispossess **11** appropriate, expropriate

seraglio
5 harem 6 bagnio 7 brothel, lupanar 8 bordello

Serah's father
5 Asher

Seraiah
brother: 6 Baruch 7 Othniel
father: 5 Asiel, Kenaz 7 Hilkiah
9 Tanhumeth
grandson: 4 Jehu 6 Jeshua
son: 4 Joab 7 Jozadak 9 Joshibiah

seraphic
4 pure 7 angelic, sublime

sere
3 dry 4 arid 5 parch 7 bone-dry,
thirsty 8 droughty 9 unwatered,
waterless 12 moistureless

Sered's father
7 Zebulun

serene
4 calm, easy 5 quiet, still 6 placid,
poised 7 resting 8 composed,
tranquil

serf
4 esne, peon 5 churl, helot, slave
6 thrall 7 villein
freeborn: 7 colonus

series
3 row, run, set 4 tier 5 chain,
group, scale, train 6 catena, column, parade, sequel, string 8 category, sequence 9 cavalcade, gradation 10 procession, succession
11 alternation, consecution, continuance, progression 12 continuation

serious
4 fell, grim, hard, ugly 5 grave,
heavy, major, sober, staid, stern,
tough 6 intent, sedate, severe, solemn, somber, steady 7 arduous,
austere, earnest, intense, operose,
pensive, unfunny, weighty 8 grievous, menacing, resolute, sobering
9 dangerous, difficult, humorless,
important, laborious, strenuous,
unamusing 10 determined, formidable, meditative, no-nonsense,
poker-faced, purposeful, reflective,
sobersided, thoughtful, unhumorous
11 significant, steady-going,
threatening 12 businesslike
13 contemplative

sermon
6 homily, preach, tirade 7 lecture
8 harangue 9 preaching
10 preachment 11 exhortation

sermonize
6 preach 7 descant, discuss, dissert
8 dilate on, homilize, moralize

9 discourse, expatiate, preachify
10 dilate upon, dissertate,
evangelize

serpent
5 devil, fiend, Satan, snake
6 dipsas
combining form: 4 ophi 5 ophio,
ophis
fabled: 8 basilisk
mythical: 10 cockatrice
sound: 4 hiss

serpentine
5 snaky 7 crooked, demonic, devious, satanic, sinuous, winding
8 demoniac, demonian, devilish, diabolic, fiendish, flexuous, tortuous
9 meandrous, snakelike 10 convoluted, meandering

serrated
6 scored 7 notched, serried,
toothed 8 indented, saw-edged,
sawtooth 10 saw-toothed
11 denticulate

Serug
father: 3 Reu
son: 5 Nahor

servant
4 maid 5 valet 6 butler, menial
7 famulus, footman 8 domestic,
handmaid, houseboy, houseman,
servitor 9 attendant 11 chamberlain, chambermaid
India: 4 syce
kitchen: 8 scullion
Wodehouse: 6 Jeeves

serve
3 act, fit, use 4 make, play, suit,
take, work 5 avail, nurse, put in,
spend, treat 6 foster, handle,
mother, profit, wait on 7 advance,
benefit, care for, forward, further,
promote, satisfy, service, suffice, undergo, work for 8 deal with, function, minister 9 advantage, encourage, officiate 10 minister to

service
3 use 4 duty, rite 5 avail, cater, favor 6 action, combat, ritual 7 account, fitness, liturgy 8 ceremony,
courtesy, fighting, kindness 9 advantage, formality, relevance
10 active duty, ceremonial, indulgence, observance, usefulness
12 dispensation 13 applicability

servile
3 low 4 base, mean, ugly, vile
6 abject, menial, scurvy, sordid
7 ignoble, passive, slavish, toadish
8 obedient, obeisant 9 groveling
10 despicable, obsequious, submis-

sive 11 bootlicking, subservient,
unresisting

servility
4 yoke 7 bondage, helotry, peonage, serfage, serfdom, slavery
9 servitude, thralldom
11 enslavement

serving
6 dollop 7 portion

sesame
3 til
grass: 4 gama
seed: 8 gingelly

session
6 assize 7 meeting, sitting
combining form: 4 fest

set
3 aim, dry, fit, fix, gel, kit, lay, lot,
put 4 firm, jell, park, sink 5 affix,
array, batch, brood, bunch, crowd,
fixed, group, place, put on, ready,
rigid, scene, sited, stick 6 anchor,
belong, circle, clique, gelate, go
down, harden, impose, placed,
rooted, secure, stated 7 arrange,
certain, cluster, congeal, decided,
deposit, descend, dictate, emplace,
express, faction, install, jellify, lay
down, limited, located, prepare,
scenery, situate, specify, station,
valuate 8 appraise, ensconce, estimate, evaluate, fastened, grouping,
prepared, resolute, resolved, situated, solidify, specific 9 confirmed,
designate, establish, prescribe,
specified, stipulate, tenacious, unbending 10 assortment, determined, entrenched, gelatinize,
inflexible, positioned, prescribed,
stipulated, unyielding 11 established, mise-en-scène
a gem: 6 collet
right: 7 redress

set apart
7 isolate, seclude 8 dedicate

set aside
4 void 5 annul 8 overrule

set back
4 mire 5 delay, embog 6 detain,
hang up, retard, slow up

setback
5 check 6 defeat, rebuff 7 reverse
8 comedown, obstacle, reversal
9 hindrance 10 impediment,
regression

set down
4 land 5 light, perch, roost
6 alight, record 9 establish, touch
down

set fire to
4 burn 6 ignite 7 emblaze, inflame

set free
7 manumit, unloose 8 liberate, unloosen, untangle 10 emancipate

Seth
brother: 4 Abel, Cain
father: 4 Adam
mother: 3 Eve
son: 4 Enos

set off
5 start 7 actuate, balance 8 activate, atone for, outweigh 9 circulate 10 compensate 11 countervail 12 counterpoise

set out
4 head, plan 5 start, state 6 design, intend 7 arrange, present, take off 9 undertake

Set's victim
6 Osiris

setting
5 scene 7 scenery 11 mise-en-scène
for a stone: 4 ouch

settle
3 fix, lay, pay, put 4 calm, land, lull 5 allay, clear, light, pay up, perch, place, quiet, roost, stick, still 6 alight, becalm, clinch, decide, soothe, square, wind up 7 arrange, clean up, compose, concert, install, resolve, satisfy, set down, sit down 8 clear off, colonize, conclude, ensconce 9 determine, discharge, establish, negotiate, reconcile, touch down 11 tranquilize

settlement
7 quietus, village 8 decision 9 agreement 10 conclusion, habitation, resolution 13 determination
Israeli: 6 moshav

settler
7 pioneer 8 colonist 9 colonizer

set-to
3 row 4 fray 5 brawl, broil, brush, fight, run-in, scrap 6 affray, fracas, hassle 7 bobbery, dispute, quarrel, rhubarb, scuffle 8 skirmish 9 bickering, encounter 10 falling-out, velitation 11 altercation

set up
4 blow, open, rear 5 elate, erect, found, put up, raise, stand, start, treat 6 create, excite, launch 7 build up, commove, inspire, start up, usher in 8 generate, initiate, organize, spirit up 9 construct, estab-

lish, hammer out, institute, introduce, originate

seven
combining form: 4 hept, sept 5 hepta, septi
group of: 6 heptad 8 hebdomad

seventeenth century
8 seicento

sever
3 cut 4 chop, part 5 carve, slice, split 6 cleave, divide, sunder 7 break up, dissect, divorce 8 disjoint, separate

severe
3 raw 4 dear, dour, grim, hard, sore 5 acute, bleak, grave, harsh, heavy, rigid, sharp, smart, sober, stern, tough 6 bitter, brutal, crimpy, rugged, savage, stormy, strict, wintry 7 arduous, ascetic, austere, drastic, extreme, hostile, intense, onerous, painful, serious, weighty 8 blustery, exacting, rigorous, toilsome 9 difficult, effortful, inclement, laborious, mortified, strenuous, stringent 10 astringent, blistering, blustering, forbidding, inflexible, iron-willed, oppressive, unpleasant, unyielding 11 disciplined, heavy-handed, intemperate, restrictive 12 disagreeable, inhospitable

sew
4 darn, mend, seam 5 baste 6 needle, stitch, suture

sewing
aid: 7 thimble
case: 4 etui
kit: 5 hussy 9 housewife

sewing-machine inventor
4 Howe (Elias)

sexless
6 neuter 7 epicene

sex manual
9 Kama-sutra

sexton
9 custodian, sacristan

sexual
combining form: 3 gam, gon 4 gamo, gono

sexual desire
4 eros

sexy
4 blue, racy 5 broad, salty, shady, spicy 6 erotic, purple, risqué 8 off-color 10 suggestive

Sganarelle
brother: 6 Ariste
daughter: 7 Lucinde

ward: 7 Leonore 8 Isabelle
wife: 7 Martine

Shaaph
father: 5 Caleb 6 Jahdai
mother: 6 Maacah

shabby
4 bare, mean, poor 5 cheap, dingy, dowdy, faded, mangy, ratty, seedy, shady, sorry, tacky, tired 6 ruined, scummy, scurvy, shoddy, sleazy, sordid, tagrag 7 outworn, rickety, ruinous, run-down, scrubby, scruffy, squalid, worn-out, wrecked 8 beggarly, decaying, decrepit, desolate, dog-eared, pitiable, shameful, slipshod, tattered 9 abandoned, miserable, moth-eaten, neglected, worm-eaten 10 bedraggled, broken-down, despicable, despisable, disfigured, down-at-heel, inglorious, ramshackle, threadbare 11 dilapidated, disgraceful, ignominious 12 contemptible, deteriorated, dishonorable, disreputable 13 deteriorating, discreditable, unrespectable

shack
3 cot, hut 4 camp 5 cabin, hovel, lodge 6 shanty 7 cottage

shackle
3 tie 4 clog, curb, gyve, lash, rope 5 bilbo, bonds, chain, gyves, irons, leash, strap 6 anklet, chains, collar, fetter, hamper, hobble, hog-tie, pinion, secure 7 enchain, fetters, garrote, leg-iron, manacle, trammel 8 bracelet, handcuff 9 entrammel

shad
4 fish 7 clupeid, herring

shade
3 hue 4 cast, hint, tint, tone, veil 5 bogey, color, cover, ghost, spice, tinge, trace, umbra 6 awning, nuance, screen, shadow, spirit, streak 7 dimness, phantom, shelter, soupçon, specter, umbrage 8 darkness, penumbra, phantasm, tincture 9 blackness, gradation, intensity, inumbrate, obscurity, suspicion, variation 10 apparition, difference, saturation, suggestion 11 adumbration, distinction, obscuration

shadow
3 dim, dog, tag 4 haze, hint, tail 5 bedim, bedog, cloud, relic, shade, shady, smack, tinge, touch, trace, trail, umbra 6 breath, screen, shaded, spirit, wraith 7 becloud, eidolon, memento, obscure,

phantom, predict, specter, suggest, umbrage, umbrous, vestige 8 forecast, foretell, overcast, penumbra, phantasm, revenant, shadowed, tincture 9 adumbrate, inumbrate, overcloud, prefigure, suspicion 10 apparition, intimation, suggestion, umbrageous 11 adumbration, prefigurate
combining form: 3 sci 4 scia, scio, skia

shadowbox
4 spar

shadowy
3 dim 4 dark 5 faint, vague 7 ghostly 8 adumbral 10 indistinct

shady
4 blue, dark, racy 5 bosky, broad, dusky, fishy, salty, spicy 6 purple, risqué, shabby, shoddy, wicked 7 clouded, shadowy, suspect, umbrous 8 doubtful, off-color, screened, shadowed, shameful 9 equivocal, sheltered, uncertain, undecided 10 impugnable, indecisive, inglorious, suggestive, suspicious, umbrageous 11 disgraceful, ignominious 12 dishonorable, disreputable 13 discreditable
spot: 4 glen

shaft
3 cut, jab, ray, rod 4 axle, barb, beam, dart, pole, stem 5 arrow, lance, shoot, spear 6 thrust 7 chimney, potshot 8 short end
of a vehicle: 5 thill

shag
3 mat, nap, rug 5 chase, fetch 7 thicket 9 cormorant

shaggy
5 bushy, rough 7 thrummy, unkempt

shake
3 jar, jog, rid 4 deal, flit, jerk, jolt, lose, rock, roil, slip, whip 5 avoid, churn, clear, crack, daunt, elude, flash, jiffy, quail, quake, shock, trill, upset, waver, worry 6 appall, bother, bounce, dismay, dither, escape, jiggle, joggle, jostle, jounce, minute, moment, outwit, quaver, quiver, rattle, ruffle, second, shimmy, shiver, stir up, tremor, wiggle 7 agitate, chatter, commove, concuss, disturb, flicker, flitter, flutter, horrify, instant, perturb, shudder, stagger, temblor, tremble, twitter, unnerve, vibrate 8 convulse, disorder, disquiet, throw off, tremblor, unburden, unsettle, unstring 9 breathing, fluctuate, oscillate, pal-

pitate 10 discompose, earthquake 11 consternate, split second

shake down
5 frisk, gouge, pinch, screw, wrest, wring 6 extort, search, wrench 7 squeeze

Shakespeare, William
mother: 9 Mary Arden
play: 6 Hamlet, Henry V 7 Henry IV, Henry VI, Macbeth, Othello 8 King John, King Lear, Pericles 9 Cymbeline, Henry VIII, Richard II 10 Coriolanus, Richard III, The Tempest 11 As You Like It 12 Julius Caesar, Twelfth Night
theater: 5 Globe
wife: 12 Anne Hathaway

Shakespearean actor
4 Kean (Edmund) 5 Evans (Maurice) 7 Branagh (Kenneth), Garrick (David), Gielgud (John), Olivier (Laurence) 8 Ashcroft (Peggy), Macready (William), Redgrave (Michael), Scofield (Paul) 10 Richardson (Ralph)

shaky
4 weak 6 aquake, ashake, dickey, infirm, unsure, wobbly 7 aquiver, dubious, quaking, quivery, rackety, rickety, suspect, tottery, trembly, unclear, unsound 8 doubtful, insecure, rachitic, rootless, unstable, unsteady, wavering 9 fluctuant, quivering, tottering, trembling, tremorous, tremulous, uncertain, unsettled 10 indecisive, precarious, rattletrap 11 problematic, vacillating

shale
4 rock 5 slate

shallot
4 herb, tube 5 onion 8 eschalot

shallow
4 idle, vain 5 empty, petty, shoal 6 hollow, paltry 7 cursory, flighty, sketchy, surface, trivial 8 trifling 9 depthless 10 bird-witted, shallowish, uncritical 11 superficial

shallows
6 lagoon

Shallum
father: 5 Shaul, Zadok 6 Jabesh, Josiah, Sismai, Tikvah 8 Colhozeh, Naphtali 9 Hallohesh
mother: 6 Bilhah
nephew: 8 Jeremiah
slayer: 7 Menahem
son: 6 Mibsam 7 Hilkiah 8 Maaseiah
victim: 9 Zechariah

shalom
5 peace 8 farewell, greeting

sham
3 act, ape, lie 4 cant, copy, fake, hoax, mock, sell 5 bluff, bogus, cheat, dummy, false, farce, feign, phony, put on, snide, spoof 6 affect, assume, create, deceit, ersatz, facade, fakery, invent, pseudo 7 assumed, feigned, imitate, mislead, mockery, plaster, pretend 8 affected, flimflam, simulate, so-called, spurious, travesty 9 brummagem, burlesque, deception, hypocrisy, imitation, imposture, pinchbeck, simulated, synthetic 10 artificial, caricature, false front, fictitious, pharisaism, sanctimony, substitute, Tartuffery, Tartuffism 11 adulterated, counterfeit, make believe 12 pecksniffery
combining form: 5 pseud 6 pseudo

Shamariah
see **Shemariah**

Shama's father
6 Hotham

Shamash
6 sun-god
father: 3 Sin
sister: 6 Ishtar
wife: 2 Ai 3 Aya

shamble
see **shuffle**

shambles
4 mess 5 botch, mix-up 6 mess-up, muddle 8 botchery, wreckage 9 confusion

shame
5 abash, guilt, odium 6 infamy 7 chagrin, obloquy 8 disgrace, dishonor, ignominy 9 discredit, disesteem, disrepute 10 opprobrium 11 self-reproof 12 self-reproach 13 embarrassment, mortification

shameless
4 bold, lewd 6 arrant, brassy, brazen, cheeky 7 blatant 8 immodest, impudent, overbold 9 abandoned, audacious, bald-faced, barefaced, dissolute, unabashed 10 highhanded, outrageous, profligate, unblushing 11 brazenfaced, disgraceful 12 presumptuous

Shamgar's father
5 Anath

Shamir's father
5 Micah

Shammah
brother: 5 David
father: 4 Agee 5 Jesse, Reuel

grandfather: **4** Esau **7** Ishmael
son: **7** Jonadab **8** Jonathan

Shammai's father
4 Onam **5** Ezrah, Rekem

Shammua
father: **5** David, Galal **6** Bilgah, Zaccur
mother: **9** Bathsheba
son: **4** Abda

Shamsherai's father
7 Jeroham

shanghai
6 abduct, kidnap

Shangri-la
4 Zion **6** heaven, utopia **7** arcadia
8 paradise **9** Cockaigne, fairyland
10 lubberland, wonderland
12 promised land

shank
3 leg **4** shin, stem **5** stalk, tibia

shanty
3 cot, hut **4** camp **5** cabin, hovel, lodge, shack **7** cottage

shape
3 fit **4** case, cast, form, look, make, mold, plan, trim **5** build, forge, frame, order, state, whack **6** aspect, devise, estate, fettle, figure, kilter, repair, tailor, work up **7** fashion, fitness **8** assemble **9** condition, construct, fabricate, semblance **10** appearance **12** conformation **13** configuration
combining form: **5** morph **6** morpho

shapeable
4 soft **6** pliant **7** ductile

shapeless
8 formless, inchoate, unformed **9** amorphous, unshapely

shapely
4 trim **5** buxom **6** comely **7** regular, rounded **8** balanced, clean-cut **9** Junoesque **10** curvaceous, statuesque, well-turned **11** clean-limbed, full-figured, symmetrical **12** proportioned

Shaphan
grandson: **8** Gedaliah
son: **6** Ahikam **8** Gemariah **9** Jaazaniah

Shaphat
father: **4** Hori **5** Adlai **8** Shemaiah
son: **6** Elisha

Sharai's father
4 Bani

share
3 cut, lot **4** bite, meed, part **5** claim, quota, slice, stake **6** assign, divide, parcel, quotum, ration

7 deal out, dole out, give out, measure, mete out, partage, partake, portion, prorate, quantum, rake-off **8** dispense, interest, quotient **9** allotment, allowance, apportion **10** commission, experience, percentage, proportion **11** participate **13** apportionment

shared
5 joint **6** common, mutual, public **8** communal, conjoint, conjunct
prefix: **2** co

Sharezer
father, victim: **11** Sennacherib

shark
5 cheat **8** swindler
kind: **4** blue, gata, haye, mako, sand, tope **5** nurse, tiger, whale, white **7** basking, dogfish, leopard **8** mackerel, maneater, thresher **9** porbeagle **10** great white, hammerhead
skin: **8** shagreen

sharp
3 hep, sly **4** acid, cute, fast, high, keen, sour, thin, tony, trig, wise **5** acrid, acute, alert, blunt, canny, harsh, honed, peaky, piked, quick, short, slick, smart, swank, swish **6** adroit, argute, biting, bitter, brainy, bright, clever, nimble, peaked, piping, severe, shrewd, shrill, snappy, tonish, treble **7** austere, caustic, dashing, exactly, intense, knowing, odorous, pointed, prickly, stylish, whetted **8** acicular, drilling, incisive, original, piercing, shooting, stabbing, stinging, virulent **9** aciculate, acuminate, acuminous, agonizing, amaroidal, brilliant, cuspidate, ingenious, knifelike, precisely, sensitive, unblunted, unethical, vitriolic **10** accurately, astringent, paralyzing, perceptive, ungracious **11** acrimonious, double-edged, intelligent, penetrating, penetrative, quick-witted, ready-witted, resourceful, suffocating, thoughtless **12** excruciating, nimble-witted, quick-sighted **13** inconsiderate, strong-scented, unceremonious
combining form: **3** oxy **5** acuto

sharp-edged
8 cultrate

sharpen
4 edge, file, hone, whet **5** dress, grind, strop **6** stroke

sharper
3 gyp **5** cheat **6** con man **7** diddler **8** swindler **9** defrauder, trick-

ster **10** mountebank **12** double-dealer

sharpie
see **sharper**

sharpness
4 edge **6** acumen **8** acrimony, keenness **12** incisiveness

sharpshooter
8 marksman

sharp-sighted
4 keen **5** acute **7** lyncean **8** hawk-eyed, lynx-eyed **9** eagle-eyed **11** penetrating, penetrative, quick-witted

sharp-witted
3 hep **4** keen, wise **5** acute, canny, quick, slick, smart **6** shrewd **7** knowing **10** discerning **11** intelligent

Shashai's father
4 Bani

Shashak's father
6 Elpaal

shatter
4 dash, raze, rend, rive, ruin, snap **5** break, burst, clack, crack, crash, crush, shoot, smash, split, wrack, wreck **6** bicker, crunch, rattle, shiver **7** clatter, clitter, destroy **8** decimate, demolish, destruct, fragment, splinter, splitter **9** pulverize **10** annihilate **11** fragmentize, splinterize **12** disintegrate

shatterable
5 frail **7** fragile **8** delicate, shattery **9** breakable, frangible **11** fracturable

Shaul's father
6 Simeon

shave
3 cut **4** clip, crop, kiss, pare, skim, trim **5** brush, graze, lower, prune, shear, shred, skive, slash **6** glance, reduce, scrape, sliver **7** cut back, cut down, shingle, tonsure, whittle **8** mark down

shaveling
3 boy, lad, son, tad **6** laddie **9** stripling

shaver
3 boy, lad **5** child, razor **6** barber **9** youngster

shawl
4 maud, wrap **5** cloak, manta **6** chadar, chador, sarape, serape **7** blanket, tallith

shawm's descendant
4 oboe

Shawnee chief
8 Tecumseh 9 Cornstalk

Shaw play
6 Geneva 7 Candida 9 Pygmalion, Saint Joan 11 Misalliance
12 Major Barbara

sheaf
6 bundle 7 cluster

Sheal's father
4 Bani

Shealtiel
father: 4 Neri 8 Jeconiah
son: 10 Zerubbabel

shear
3 cut, mow 4 barb, clip, crop,
pare, snip, trim 5 prune, shave,
skive 6 barber 8 manicure

Shearjashub's father
6 Isaiah

shears
8 scissors

shearwater
4 bird 6 hagdon, haglet 7 skimmer

sheath
4 case, skin 5 cover 8 scabbard
combining form: 4 cole 5 coleo,
theca

sheathe
4 case, clad, face, side, skin, wrap
5 cover, panel 6 encase, jacket
7 envelop 8 surround

Sheba
father: 6 Bichri
queen: 6 Balkis

shebang
3 hut 6 affair 8 business

Sheber
father: 5 Caleb
mother: 6 Maacah

Shebuel
father: 5 Heman 7 Gershom
grandfather: 5 Moses

Shecaniah
father: 6 Jehiel 8 Jehaziel
son: 7 Hattush 8 Shemaiah
son-in-law: 6 Tobiah

Shechem's father
5 Hamor 6 Gilead 8 Shemidah

shed
3 hut 4 abri, cast, doff, drop, junk,
molt, slip 5 scrap 6 divest, lean-to,
reject, slough 7 cashier, cast off,
discard, ecdysis, take off 8 exuviate, jettison, throw out 9 throw
away

Shedeur's son
6 Elizur

sheen
5 glaze, glint, gloss, shine 6 finish,
luster, polish 9 shininess

sheeny
see *shiny*

sheep
5 dumba, ovine
Australian: 7 jumbuck
breed: 5 Tunis 6 Dorper, Dorset,
Merino, Navajo, No-Tail, Oxford,
Panama, Romney 7 Cheviot, Col-
bred, Karakul, Lincoln, Ryeland,
Suffolk 8 Columbia, Cotswold, Pol-
warth 9 Hampshire, Leicester, Mon-
tadale, Southdown 10 Corriedale,
Debouillet 11 Rambouillet
coat: 4 wool 6 fleece
disease: 3 gid 5 braxy 6 sturdy
female: 3 ewe
male: 3 ram 6 wether
meat: 6 mutton
relating to: 5 ovine
Scottish: 9 blackface
skin: 4 slat
sound: 5 bleat
tender of: 8 shepherd
wild: 3 sha 5 urial 6 aoudad, ar-
gali, bharal, nahoor, oorial 7 big-
horn, mouflon 8 moufflon
young: 3 teg 4 hogg, lamb

sheepish
4 meek 5 timid 7 abashed, bashful
9 diffident 11 embarrassed

sheepskin
4 roan 5 basil 6 mouton
7 diploma 9 parchment
prepare: 3 taw

sheer
3 dip 4 airy, pure, skew, slue, thin,
turn, veer, whip 5 avert, filmy,
gauzy, pivot, steep, utter, wheel,
whirl 6 abrupt, arrant, divert,
flimsy, simple, swerve 7 chiffon, deflect, perfect, unmixed 8 absolute,
complete, gossamer, outright 9 out-
and-out, unalloyed, undiluted 10 diaphanous, see through 11 precipitate, precipitous, transparent,
unmitigated

sheet
4 leaf, page, sail 5 cover, linen,
paper 9 newspaper
combining form: 6 pallio

sheet ___
3 ice 4 film 5 glass, metal, music
6 anchor

Shehariah's father
7 Jeroham

Shelah
father: 5 Judah 8 Arphaxad
son: 4 Eber

Shelemiah
father: 5 Cushi 6 Abdeel, Binnui
8 Hananiah
son: 5 Jucal 6 Irijah 8 Hananiah

Sheleph's father
6 Joktan

Shelesh's father
5 Helem

shelf
4 bank, edge, reef, sill 5 ledge,
shoal 6 gradin, mantel 7 gradine
8 sandbank

shell
3 pod 4 boat, bomb, case, hull,
husk, rake, skin 5 blitz, conch,
shuck 6 pepper 7 bombard, capsule, grenade, mollusk 9 cannonade, cartridge
combining form: 5 conch 6 concho,
ostrac 7 ostraca, ostraco
defective: 3 dud
explosive: 4 bomb
layer: 5 nacre
ornamental: 5 cowry 6 cowrie
study: 10 conchology

shellac
4 beat, drub, lick, rout, trim, whip
5 resin, smear 6 defeat, thrash
7 smother, trounce 8 lambaste,
vanquish

Shelley
elegy: 7 Adonais
poem: 7 Alastor 8 Queen Mab,
The Cloud 10 Ozymandias, To a
Skylark

shellfish
4 clam, crab 5 conch, cowry,
prawn 6 cockle, limpet, mussel,
oyster, triton 7 abalone, lobster,
mollusk, scallop 8 barnacle
10 crustacean

shell out
3 pay 4 give 5 spend 6 expend,
outlay 8 disburse

shell-shaped
6 spiral 9 cochleate

Shelomi's son
6 Ahihud

Shelomith
father: 5 Dibri, Izhar 8 Rehoboam
9 Josiphiah 10 Zerubbabel
mother: 6 Maacah

shelter
3 den, hut, lee 4 abri, cote, fold,
hide, port, roof, shed, tent 5 arbor,
benab, bower, cloak, cover, haven,
house, shack, tower 6 asylum, burrow, covert, defend, harbor, ref-

uge, shield **7** chamber, defense, foxhole, hideout, hospice, housing, lodging, pergola, pillbox, protect, retreat **8** hideaway, security **9** dwellings, harborage, hermitage, hidey-hole, sanctuary **10** quarterage, retirement
for a car: **6** garage
for aircraft: **6** hangar
for cows: **4** barn, byre
toward: **4** alee

shelve
4 dish, drop, stay, tilt **5** defer, delay, stock, waive **6** give up, hold up, put off **7** hold off **8** hold over, postpone, prorogue

Shem
brother: **3** Ham **7** Japheth
father: **4** Noah

Shemaiah
father: **4** Joel **7** Delaiah **8** Adonikam, Nethanel, Obededom **9** Elizaphan, Shecaniah
son: **5** Uriah **6** Urijah **7** Delaiah, Obadiah

Shemariah's father
4 Bani **5** Harim **8** Rehoboam

Shema's father
4 Joel **6** Hebron

Shemer's father
5 Mahli

Shemida's father
6 Gilead

Shemuel's father
4 Tola **7** Ammihud

shenanigan
4 game, lark, play, ploy, ruse, wile **5** antic, caper, prank, stunt, trick **6** device, didoes, frolic, shines **7** fast one, gimmick, whizzer **8** goings-on, maneuver **9** stratagem **10** tomfoolery **11** legerdemain, monkeyshine

Shenazzar's father
8 Jeconiah **10** Jehoiachin

Sheol
see **hades**

Shephatiah
father: **5** David **6** Maacah, Mattan **11** Jehoshaphat
mother: **6** Abital

shepherd
3 see **4** lead, show, tend **5** guide, pilot, route, steer, watch **6** direct, escort, leader **7** conduct **8** guardian
dog: **6** Collie
stick: **4** kent **5** crook, staff

Shephi, Shepho
father: **6** Shobal

Sheridan play
7 Pizarro **9** The Critic, The Rivals

sheriff
6 lawman **7** marshal, officer
aide: **6** deputy

Sherlock Holmes
6 sleuth **7** gumshoe **8** hawkshaw **9** detective **12** investigator
creator: **5** Doyle (Arthur Conan)
sidekick: **6** Watson

sherry
4 fino, wine **7** oloroso **11** amontillado

Sherwood play
13 Idiot's Delight, The Road to Rome **14** The Petrified Forest, Waterloo Bridge

Sheshai's father
4 Anak

Sheshan's servant
5 Jarha

shibboleth
3 tag **6** byword, clich'e, phrase, slogan, truism **7** bromide **8** banality, password, prosaism **9** catchword, platitude, watchword **10** prosaicism **11** catchphrase

shield
4 fend, roof, ward **5** aegis, armor, cover, guard, haven, house **6** defend, harbor, screen, secure **7** buckler, bulwark, protect, shelter **8** defilade **9** safeguard **10** escutcheon
band: **4** fess
bullfighter's: **9** burladero
combining form: **4** scut **5** aspid, scuti **6** aspido
large: **5** pavis **6** pavise
light: **5** targe
part: **4** boss, umbo **7** bordure
Roman: **6** scutum **7** clipeus, testudo

shield-like
7 peltate, scutate **9** scutiform

shift
3 yaw **4** bend, bout, move, stir, tack, time, tour, turn, vary **5** alter, budge, get by, get on, spell, stint, trick **6** change, make do, manage, remove, swerve **7** disturb, replace, shuffle **8** get along, relocate, transfer **9** deviation, dislocate **10** alteration, changeover, conversion, deflection, transition

shiftless
4 lazy

shifty
5 cagey, lying, shady **6** crafty, sneaky, tricky **7** cunning, devious, dodging, elusive, evasive, furtive, knavish, mutable, roguish **8** guileful, indirect, slippery, sneaking, unhonest, unstable, unsteady, variable **9** collusive, conniving, deceitful, dishonest, insidious, shuffling, uncertain, underhand **10** changeable, fraudulent, inconstant, mendacious, untruthful **11** duplicitous, treacherous, underhanded **12** equivocating **13** prevaricate, prevaricatory

Shilem's father
8 Naphtali

Shilhi
daughter: **6** Azubah
grandson: **11** Jehoshaphat

shill
5 blind, decoy, stick **6** capper

shilling
3 bob

shilly-shally
4 halt **5** waver **6** dither, falter, wobbly **7** halting, stagger, whiffle **8** hesitate, to-and-fro, wavering **9** faltering, hesitancy, vacillate, whiffling **10** hesitating, hesitation, indecision **11** vacillating, vacillation, vacillatory **12** irresolution

Shilshah's father
6 Zophah

Shimea
brother: **5** David
father: **5** David, Jesse
son: **7** Jonadab **8** Jonathan

Shimeam's father
7 Mikloth

Shimei
brother: **8** Conaniah, Cononiah **10** Zerubbabel
father: **4** Bani, Gera, Kish **6** Hashum, Jahath **7** Gershon **8** Jeduthun
grandfather: **4** Levi

Shimeon's father
5 Harim

shimmer
5 flash, gleam, glint, spark **7** glimmer, glisten, glitter, spangle, sparkle, twinkle **8** blinking, sparking **9** coruscate **11** coruscation, scintillate **13** scintillation

shimmy
5 dance, shake **7** chemise, vibrate

Shimrath's father
6 Shimei

Shimri's father
5 Hosah 8 Shemaiah 9 Elizaphan

Shimrith's son
9 Jehozabad

Shimron's father
8 Issachar

shin
3 run 4 dash 5 scoot, tibia
6 scurry, sprint 7 scamper

shindig
4 ball, bash, coil, fête, gala, to-do
5 dance, party 6 affair, furore,
ruckus, rumpus, shindy, uproar
7 shebang 8 foofaraw
9 commotion

shine
3 ray, rub 4 beam, buff, burn,
glow, pomp, show 5 array, flare,
flash, glare, glaze, gleam, glint,
gloss, sheen 6 finish, glance, luster,
parade, polish 7 burnish, display,
fanfare, furbish, glimmer, glisten,
panoply, radiate, sparkle, twinkle
9 luminesce 10 incandesce

shiner
4 fish 8 black eye, cyprinid

Shinto gods
4 kami

shiny
6 glossy, sheeny 7 fulgent 8 gleaming, lustrous, polished 9 burnished
10 glistening

ship
4 boat, move, send 5 remit, route,
shift 6 direct, export, remove 7 address, consign, disturb, forward,
freight 8 dispatch, transfer, transmit
ancient: 5 knorr 6 galley 7 galleon,
trireme
attendant: 7 steward
beam: 7 carling, keelson
berth: 4 dock, slip
boat: 6 dinghy
body: 4 hull
cabin: 9 stateroom
commercial: 5 liner, oiler 6 argosy,
tanker, trader 9 freighter
crew member: 4 hand, mate 5 bosun
6 purser, sailor
deck: 4 boat, main, poop 5 orlop
6 bridge 10 forecastle
fishing: 6 lugger 7 trawler
fleet: 6 armada
floor: 4 deck
front: 3 bow 4 prow, stem
8 cutwater
hoister: 4 boom 5 davit 7 capstan
kitchen: 6 galley
left side: 4 port 8 larboard

merchant: (see **commercial**)
military: 6 cutter, PT boat 7 carrier,
cruiser 9 destroyer, submarine
officer: 4 mate 5 bosun 6 purser
7 captain, steward
of the desert: 5 camel
part: 3 bow 4 beam, deck, helm,
hold, hull, keel, mast, stem 5 bilge,
hatch, stern 6 bridge, rudder
7 scupper
partition: 7 bulwark 8 bulkhead
personnel: 4 crew
platform: 9 crow's nest, gangboard,
gangplank
post: 4 mast 7 bollard
prison: 4 brig
projection: 7 sponson
rear: 5 stern
record: 3 log
right side: 9 starboard
room: 4 brig 5 cabin 6 galley
rope: 4 line 7 halyard
sailing: 4 brig, dhow, prao, prau,
proa, yawl 5 ketch, prahu, sloop,
xebec 6 chebec, lugger 7 caravel,
galleon 8 bilander, schooner
spar: 6 bumkin
steerer: 4 helm 6 tiller
storage area: 4 hold
submersible: 9 submarine
11 bathyscaphe
to the rear of: 3 aft 5 abaft 6 astern
valve: 7 seacock
window: 4 port 8 porthole

Shiphi's father
5 Allon

Shiphtan's son
6 Kemuel

shipment
5 cargo 8 delivery

Ship of Fools author
6 Porter (Katherine Anne)

ships
group of: 4 navy 5 fleet, flota 6 armada 8 flotilla

shipshape
4 neat, snug, tidy, trig, trim 7 chipper, orderly 11 spic-and-span,
uncluttered, well-groomed 12 spick-
and-span

shire
5 horse 6 county 8 district

shirk
4 duck, lurk, shun, slip 5 creep,
dodge, fence, parry, skulk, slink,
sneak, steal 6 bypass, eschew
8 sidestep

shirker
see **slacker**

shirt
4 sark 6 camisa, camise, jersey
7 garment 8 guernsey, pullover
armored: 6 byrnie
hair: 6 cilice
kind: 3 tee 4 polo 5 dress, sport
Scottish: 4 jupe

shirty
3 mad 4 waxy 5 angry, irate,
wroth 6 heated, ireful, wrathy
8 choleric, wrathful

Shiva, Siva
consort: 3 Uma 4 Devi, Kali
5 Durga, Gauri 6 Ambika, Chandi
7 Parvati 9 Haimavati
son: 6 Ganesa, Skanda 7 Ganesha
10 Karttikeya

shiver
4 rive 5 burst, quake, shake, smash
6 dither, quaver, quiver, tremor
7 shatter, shudder, tremble, twitter
8 fragment, splinter, splitter
11 splinterize

Shiza's son
5 Adina

shoal
3 bar 4 bank, hook, reef, spit 7 barrier, sandbar, shallow, tombolo
8 sandbank, sand reef, seamount
9 coral reef 11 barrier reef,
superficial

Shobab
father: 5 Caleb, David
mother: 6 Azubah 9 Bathsheba

Shobal's father
3 Hur 4 Seir

Shobi's father
6 Nahash

shock
3 jar 4 bank, bump, cock, hill, jolt,
pile, rick 5 clash, crash, floor,
mound, quake, shake, smash, stack
6 appall, impact, insult, offend,
sicken, trauma, tremor 7 astound,
disgust, horrify, outrage, pyramid,
shake up, startle, temblor 8 astonish, knock out, nauseate, surprise,
tremblor 9 collision, electrify, stockpile 10 concussion, earthquake,
percussion, scandalize, traumatism
11 prostration 12 stupefaction

shock absorber
6 spring 7 dashpot, snubber

shocking
5 awful, lurid 6 crying, horrid
7 burning, direful, fearful, glaring,
heinous 8 dreadful, horrible, hor-

rific, shameful, terrible **9** appalling, atrocious, desperate, frightful, monstrous **10** formidable, outrageous, scandalous **11** disgraceful, unspeakable

shoddy
4 base, mean, poor **5** cheap, dingy, seedy, shady, tacky, tatty **6** common, paltry, shabby, sleazy, trashy **7** run-down, scruffy **8** rubbishy, shameful **9** makeshift, scambling **10** broken-down, down-at-heel, inglorious **11** dilapidated, disgraceful, ignominious **12** dishonorable, disreputable **13** discreditable

shoe
3 bal, pac **4** boot, clog, geta, mule, pump **5** gilly, plate, sabot, tegua, wedge **6** brogan, brogue, buskin, crakow, gaiter, galosh, gillie, loafer, oxford, patten, sandal **7** chopine, ghillie, slipper, sneaker **8** balmoral, moccasin, platform, plimsoll **9** brodequin, pampootie, spectator **10** clodhopper, espadrille
accessory: **4** horn, tree **6** polish
armored: **8** solleret
athlete's: **7** sneaker
form: **4** last, tree
kind: **8** elevator, open-toed **10** high-heeled
part: **3** tip, toe **4** arch, heel, lace, lift, sole, vamp **5** shank, upper **6** box toe, collar, foxing, insole, lining, throat, tongue **7** counter, outsole **8** backstay
protective: **6** galosh, rubber
Roman: **6** caliga, sandal
shiner: **6** polish **9** bootblack
wooden: **5** sabot **7** chopine

shoelace tip
5 aglet **6** aiglet

shoeless
6 unshod **8** barefoot

shoemaker
5 soler **7** cobbler, crispin
patron saint: **7** Crispin
Scottish: **6** souter

Shogun author
7 Clavell (James)

Shoham's father
7 Jaaziah

Shomer
father: **5** Heber
son: **9** Jehozabad

shoo-in
9 sure thing

shoot
3 bud, fly, gun, ray **4** beam, bolt, dart, dash, fire, lash, race, raze, ruin, rush, sail, scud, skim, spew, tear **5** blast, chase, fling, float, loose, photo, shaft, skirr, snipe, spurt, wrack, wreck **6** branch, charge **7** destroy, explode, project, shatter **8** decimate, demolish, destruct, disprove, puncture **9** discharge, discredit **10** annihilate, photograph
combining form: **5** blast, thall **6** blasto, thalli, thallo

shooting
5 acute, sharp **7** gunplay **8** piercing, stabbing **9** knifelike

shooting star
6 meteor **8** fireball

shoot up
4 soar **6** rocket **9** skyrocket

shop
4 hunt **5** store **6** market, outlet **8** boutique, emporium, showroom

shoplift
3 bag, cop **4** palm **5** pinch, steal, swipe **6** pilfer, rip off, snitch

shop owner
3 cit **8** merchant, retailer **10** proprietor

shopworn
5 stale, tired, trite **6** cliché **7** clichéd **8** overused **9** hackneyed **10** overworked **13** stereotypical

shore
4 bank, prop, stay **5** beach, brace, brink, carry, coast **6** bear up, column, rivage, strand, upbear, uphold **7** bolster, support, sustain **8** buttress, littoral, seacoast **9** coastland, coastline, riverbank, riverside, waterside **10** embankment, waterfront **11** underpinner **12** underpinning

shorebird
see at **bird**

short
3 shy **4** core, curt, gist, meat, pith **5** aback, bluff, blunt, brief, crisp, dumpy, gruff, scant, sharp, skimp, spare, squat, stint, terse, thick **6** abrupt, amount, burden, chunky, crusty, low-set, meager, scanty, scarce, skimpy, snippy, sparse, stubby, sudden, thrust, upshot **7** asudden, brittle, brusque, compact, concise, crumbly, crunchy, curtate, failing, fragile, friable, lacking, laconic, needing, pointed, pur-

port, scrimpy, slender, squatty, summary, unaware, wanting **8** abridged, abruptly, delicate, exiguous, lessened, snippety, succinct, suddenly, thickset, unawares **9** curtailed, decreased, decurtate, deficient, forthwith, irascible **10** diminished, inadequate, ungracious **11** abbreviated, compendiary, compendious **12** breviloquent, insufficient, unexpectedly, unsufficient **13** inconsiderate, unceremonious
combining form: **5** brevi **6** brachy

shortage
4 lack **5** pinch **6** dearth **7** deficit, failure **8** underage **10** deficiency, inadequacy, scantiness
in container: **6** ullage

shortcoming
3 sin **5** fault **7** demerit **10** deficiency **12** imperfection

shortcut
6 bypass, cutoff

shorten
3 bob, cut **4** clip, dock **5** elide, slash **6** lessen, reduce, shrink **7** abridge, bobtail, curtail, cut back, excerpt **8** compress, condense, contract, decrease, diminish, minimize, retrench, truncate **10** abbreviate

shorthand
11 stenography
method: **5** Gregg **6** Pitman

shorthanded
7 wanting **11** undermanned **12** understaffed

shortly
4 anon, soon **6** pronto **7** briefly, by and by, in brief, quickly, tersely **8** directly **9** concisely, presently **10** succinctly **11** laconically

shortness
7 brevity

shortsighted
6 myopic

short-spoken
4 curt **5** bluff, blunt, brief, gruff **6** abrupt, crusty, snippy **7** brusque **8** snippety

short-tempered
5 testy **6** touchy **9** irascible

Shoshoni chief
8 Washakie **9** Pocatello

shot
2 go **3** nip, pop, try **4** dram, drop, jolt, show, slug, stab, time **5** break, carom, crack, fling, snort, whack,

whirl **6** chance **7** snifter **8** occasion, toothful **11** opportunity

shoulder

4 edge, push, side **5** elbow, press, shove **6** axilla, hustle, jostle **8** bulldoze
bone: **7** scapula **8** clavicle
combining form: **2** om **3** omo
covering: **6** tippet **8** scapular
muscle: **7** deltoid
relating to: **7** humeral **8** scapular

shoulder blade

7 scapula

shout

3 cry **4** bark, bawl, bray, call, howl, roar, yell **5** blare, whoop **6** bellow, clamor, holler, scream, shriek **7** exclaim **10** vociferate

shove

3 dig, jab, jam **4** cram, poke, prod, push **5** drive, elbow, press **6** hustle, jostle, peddle, propel, thrust **8** bulldoze, shoulder

shovel

3 dig **4** grub **5** scoop, scuff, spade **6** dig out **7** scuffle, shamble, shuffle **8** excavate

shoveler

4 duck **9** broadbill

shovelhead

7 catfish

shove off

2 go **4** exit, quit **5** leave **6** depart, get off **7** pull out, take off **8** run along

show

3 air, get, say, see **4** cine, come, fair, film, lead, look, loom, mark, pomp, read **5** array, flash, flick, front, get in, guide, mount, movie, offer, pilot, prove, revue, sport, stage, steer, vaunt **6** appear, arrive, blazon, chance, direct, emerge, escort, evince, expose, flaunt, lay out, look-in, ostend, parade, record, reveal, set out, submit, turn up, unveil **7** conduct, display, disport, divulge, exhibit, fanfare, make out, panoply, picture, present, produce, proffer, project, seeming, trot out **8** brandish, disclose, evidence, flourish, indicate, manifest, occasion, proclaim, register, shepherd **9** determine, establish, photoplay, represent, semblance, spectacle **10** appearance, exhibition, exposition, illustrate, simulacrum **11** demonstrate, materialize, opportunity, performance

13 demonstration, motion picture, moving picture

Show Boat

author: **6** Ferber (Edna)
composer: **4** Kern (Jerome)

showcase

7 exhibit, vitrine

shower

3 tub **4** hail, rain, wash **5** bathe, burst, party, salvo, spray, storm **7** barrage, shatter, spatter **8** downpour, rainfall **9** broadside, cannonade, fusillade **10** cloudburst **11** bombardment

showman

8 producer
famous: **4** Cody (William Frederick) **6** Barnum (Phineas Taylor)

Show Me State

8 Missouri

show off

4 brag **5** boast, flash **6** expose, flaunt, parade **7** display, disport, exhibit, swagger, trot out **8** brandish

showoff

3 ham **6** hotdog **7** hotshot **13** exhibitionist

showpiece

3 gem **5** jewel, prize **11** chef d'oeuvre, masterpiece

show up

3 get **4** come **5** get in, reach **6** arrive, debunk, expose, turn up, unmask **7** uncloak, undress **8** discover, unshroud **9** discredit **10** invalidate

showy

3 gay **4** arty, loud **5** gaudy, jazzy, swank **6** chichi, flashy, garish, ornate, sporty, tawdry **7** opulent, splashy **8** gorgeous, overdone, peacocky **9** luxurious, sumptuous **10** flamboyant, peacockish **11** overwrought, pretentious, resplendent, sensational **12** meretricious, orchidaceous, ostentatious

shrapnel

8 fragment **10** projectile

shred

3 bit, dag, rag **4** iota **5** crumb, grate, ounce, scrap, shave, speck **6** sliver **7** modicum, smidgen **8** fragment, particle

shrew

5 harpy, scold, vixen, witch **6** amazon, ogress, rodent, virago **8** fish-

wife, she-devil, spitfire **9** termagant, Xanthippe

shrewd

3 sly **4** cagy, foxy, keen, tidy, wise **5** acute, cagey, canny, heady, sharp, slick, smart **6** argute, astute, clever, crafty, polite, smooth **7** knowing, probing, prudent **8** piercing, sensible **9** astucious, ingenious, judicious, sagacious **10** farsighted **11** foresighted, intelligent, penetrating, quick-witted **13** perspicacious

shriek

3 cry **4** yell **5** blare, shout **6** screak, scream, shrill, squawk, squeal **7** screech

shrill

4 high, keen, thin **5** acute, sharp **6** argute, piping, scream, shriek, squeal, treble **7** screech **8** piercing, strident

shrimp

4 runt **5** prawn **6** peanut **10** crustacean
combining form: **5** caris

shrine

3 box **4** tomb **5** altar **6** temple **7** sanctum **9** holy place, reliquary, sanctuary **10** sanctorium
Buddhist: **5** stupa **6** dagoba

shrink

3 shy **4** fail, funk, wane **5** cower, demur, quail, slink, start, wince **6** blanch, blench, boggle, cringe, crouch, flinch, huddle, recede, recoil, retire, weaken, wither **7** dwindle, retreat, scruple, squinch **8** compress, condense, contract, draw back, withdraw **9** constrict, fall short, shrivel up, waste away **11** concentrate

shrinking

3 shy **5** timid **7** aseptic **8** retiring **9** unaffable, withdrawn **10** restrained **11** unexpansive

shrive

4 free **5** purge **6** pardon **7** confess

shrivel

4 wilt **5** dry up, parch, wizen **6** welter, wither

Shropshire Lad author

8 Houseman (Alfred Edward)

shroud

3 lop **4** hide, veil, wrap **5** cloak, close, cover, shade **6** enfold, enwrap, invest, screen **7** enclose, envelop, shut off, shut out **8** block out, cerement, obstruct **9** cerecloth

shrouded
5 privy **6** buried, covert, hidden
7 guarded **8** obscured, ulterior
9 concealed

shrub
3 lop **4** bush **5** elder, erica, hazel, plant, prune **6** cercis, muskit, privet **7** arboret, dyeweed, guayule **8** barberry, bluewood, boxthorn, inkberry, ironweed, rosebush **9** bearberry **10** bladdernut
Asian: **4** bago **5** ramee, ramie **6** kerria **8** caragana, japonica **10** beauty bush
climbing: **7** jasmine
combining form: **5** thamn **6** thamno
desert: **5** retem **6** alhagi **7** ephedra
dwarf: **6** bonsai
East Indian: **3** aal **4** sunn
European: **4** cade **8** woodbind, woodbine
evergreen: **3** box, kat, yew **4** ilex, khat, titi **5** furze, heath, holly, pyxie, savin, taxus, thuja, thuya, toyon, yapon **6** kalmia, laurel, myrtle, nandin, protea, sabine, savine, yaupon **7** boxwood, heather, jasmine, juniper, rosebay **8** lambkill, oleander, rosemary, tamarisk
flowering: **5** lilac, ribes, tiara, wahoo **6** azalea, daphne, laurel, myrtle, spirea, wicopy **7** chamise, chamiso, fuchsia, mahonia, maybush, rhodora, spiraea, weigela **8** magnolia, mezereon, mezereum, nineback, oleander, oleaster, shadblow, shadbush, snowball, snowbell, snowbush, tornillo, viburnum, wistaria, wisteria
fragrant: **4** mint, sage **5** thyme **8** rosemary **10** basil thyme
genus: **4** Inga, Itea **7** Solanum **8** Euonymus
hardwood: **6** cornel
Mexican: **8** ocotillo
ornamental: **6** privet **7** deutzia, jetbead, syringa, woodwax **9** bluebeard
pasture: **8** cowberry
prickly: **4** whin **5** briar, chico, furze, gorse **7** bramble, rhamnus **8** hawthorn, mesquite **9** buckthorn
South American: **4** coca **7** rhatany
thicket: **6** maquis **7** macchia **9** chaparral
tropical: **4** kava **5** guava, henna **7** camelia, lantana **8** buddleia, camellia, gardenia **10** frangipani
West Indian: **4** anil **7** acerola

shrug
6 jacket **7** gesture
off: **5** evade **8** minimize

Shua
father: **5** Heber
son-in-law: **5** Judah

Shuah
father: **7** Abraham
mother: **7** Keturah

Shual's father
6 Zophah

shuck
3 pod **4** case, cast, hull, husk, junk, peel, shed, skin **5** chuck, ditch, scrap, shell, strip **6** reject, slough **7** discard **8** jettison **11** decorticate

shudder
5 quake, shake **6** dither, gyrate, quaver, quiver, shimmy, shiver, tremor **7** frisson, tremble, twitter

shuffle
4 hash, limp, mash **5** dodge, evade, hedge, scuff **6** jumble, jungle, litter, mess up, muddle, shovel, tumble, weasel **7** clutter, disrupt, disturb, rummage, shamble, stumble **8** disarray, disorder, mishmash, sidestep **9** dislocate, pussyfoot **10** disarrange, discompose, equivocate, tergiverse **11** disorganize **12** tergiversate

Shuham's father
3 Dan

shun
3 shy **4** duck, snub **5** avoid, elude, evade **6** double, escape, eschew, refuse, reject **7** decline, disdain

Shuni's father
3 Gad

shunt
4 move, turn **5** avert, shift **6** change, divert, switch **7** deflect, head off, shuttle **8** transfer **9** sidetrack

shush
4 hush **5** quiet, still **6** muffle, shut up **7** repress, silence, squelch **8** choke off, strangle, suppress

shut
4 lock, seal **5** close **6** fasten **7** confine **10** batten down
loudly: **4** slam

Shute, Nevil
novel: **7** Marazan **9** Pied Piper **10** On the Beach **11** So Disdained

Shuthelah's father
7 Ephraim

shut in
3 hem, pen **4** cage, coop, mure, wall **5** fence **6** immure **7** close in, confine, enclose, envelop **8** imprison

shut-in
7 invalid **12** convalescent

shut out
3 bar **5** close **6** screen, shroud **7** exclude **8** obstruct

shutter
5 blind **6** screen

shuttle
5 shunt **6** bobbin **9** alternate

shuttlecock
4 bird **6** birdie

shut up
3 gag **4** hush **5** dry up, quiet, shush, still **6** dumb up **7** dummy up, silence **8** choke off, pipe down **9** quiet down

shy
3 coy, gag, jib, pot **4** balk, bilk, duck, meek, shun, wary **5** avoid, chary, demur, elude, evade, loath, quail, scant, short, timid **6** afraid, averse, blench, boggle, demure, double, escape, eschew, modest, recoil, scanty, scarce, shrink **7** bashful, failing, fearful, lacking, nervous, potshot, rabbity, scruple, stickle, stumble, uneager, wanting **8** backward, cautious, hesitant, inturned, reserved, retiring, sheepish, skittish, timorous **9** conscious, deficient, diffident, introvert, reluctant, sideswipe, unassured, unwilling **10** backhanded, inadequate, indisposed, shamefaced, suspicious **11** circumspect, disinclined, introverted, unassertive **12** apprehensive, insufficient, introversive, self-effacing, unsufficient **13** self-conscious

Shylock
6 usurer **9** loan shark
daughter: **7** Jessica

shyster
11 pettifogger

Siam
see **Thailand**

Siamese coin
see **coin,** *Thailand*

sib
3 kin **4** akin **6** sister **7** brother, kindred, related **8** relative

Sibbecai's victim
4 Saph

Sibelius composition
9 Finlandia

Siberian
antelope: 5 saiga
dog: 5 husky
gulf: 2 Ob
native: 5 Tatar, Yakut 6 Tartar
9 Mongolian
plain: 6 steppe
storm: 5 buran
tent: 4 yurt

sibilate
4 buzz, fizz, hiss, whiz 5 swish,
whisk 6 fizzle, sizzle, wheeze
7 whisper

sibling
6 sister 7 brother

sibyl
4 seer 7 prophet 10 prophetess
13 fortune-teller

sic
2 so 4 abet, goad, prod, spur,
thus, urge 5 egg on, favor, prick
6 exhort, prompt, propel 7 agitate
8 catalyze, inspirit 9 instigate

Sicilian
secret organization: 5 Mafia
volcano: 4 Etna

Sicily's capital
7 Palermo

sick
3 ill 4 down, mean, weak 5 amiss,
fed up, funny, lousy, peaky, rocky,
tired, weary 6 ailing, faulty,
flawed, laid up, morbid, morose,
peaked, rotten, unwell, wobbly
7 fevered 8 confined, diseased
9 defective, disgusted, imperfect,
tottering, unhealthy 10 disordered,
indisposed 11 debilitated

sicken
5 repel, upset 6 reluct, revolt 7 derange, disgust, repulse, unhinge
8 disorder, nauseate, unsettle

sickle
5 blade, mower 8 crescent

sickly
3 ill, low 4 down, mean, puny,
weak 5 pecky 6 ailing, morbid,
morose, offish, peaked, poorly, unwell 7 noisome, noxious, underly
8 diseased, off-color 9 unhealthy
10 indisposed, insalutary, unsalutary 11 unhealthful, unwholesome
12 insalubrious

sickness
3 ill 6 malady 7 ailment, disease,
illness 8 disorder, syndrome, unhealth 9 affection, complaint, condition, infirmity 10 affliction, un-

wellness 12 diseasedness
13 indisposition, unhealthiness

sic transit gloria ___
5 mundi

side
4 clad, face, hand, part, skin 5 angle, facet, flank, phase, slant, stand
6 aspect, sector, stance 7 outlook,
posture, sheathe 8 attitude, position
9 direction, viewpoint 10 standpoint 11 disposition
combining form: 5 later, pleur 6 la-
teri, latero, pleuri, pleuro
sheltered: 3 lee

sideboard
5 table 6 buffet 8 credence
for wine: 8 cellaret 10 cellarette

sideboards
see **sideburns**

sideburns
9 burnsides 10 sideboards 11 dundrearies, muttonchops

side by side
8 together
combining form: 3 par 4 para

sidekick
3 pal 7 partner 9 assistant,
companion

sidereal
6 astral, starry 7 stellar

side road
5 byway 8 bystreet, shunpike

sidestep
4 duck 5 avoid, burke, dodge,
evade, fence, hedge, parry, shirk,
skirt 6 bypass, weasel 9 pussyfoot
10 circumvent, equivocate
12 tergiversate

sidetrack
5 shunt 6 divert, switch

sidewalk
6 paving 7 walkway 8 pavement
9 banquette

sidewhiskers
see **sideburns**

side with
4 back 6 uphold 7 support 8 advocate, backstop, champion

sidle
4 ease, edge, slip 7 saunter

siege
4 bout 5 spell 6 attack 7 seizure
9 onslaught

Siegfried
mother: 9 Sieglinde
slayer: 5 Hagen
sword: 7 Balmung

vulnerable spot: 4 back 8 shoulder
wife: 9 Kriemhild

Sienkiewicz novel
8 Quo Vadis

sierra
4 fish 5 range

Sierra ___
5 Ancha, Leone, Madre 6 Blanca,
Nevada

siesta
3 nap 5 sleep 6 catnap, dog nap,
snooze 10 forty winks

sieve
4 sift 5 clack, tabby 6 gossip,
screen 8 colander, gossiper, quidnunc, strainer 10 talebearer

Sif's husband
4 Thor

sift
4 bolt, comb, cull, sort 5 probe,
sieve 6 filter, go into, screen, winnow 7 dig into, explore 8 filtrate,
look into, prospect, separate
9 delve into 11 inquire into,
investigate

sigh
3 sob 4 ache, blow, gasp, howl,
long, lust, moan, pant, pine, roar
5 crave, dream, groan, sough,
whine 6 exhale, hanker, hunger,
murmur, thirst, wheeze 7 breathe,
respire, suspire, whisper, whistle

sight
3 aim, eye, spy 4 espy, look, mess,
view 5 scene 6 fright, seeing, vision 7 eyesore, outlook
11 monstrosity
combining form: 4 opsy 5 opsia,
opsis
relating to: 5 optic 6 ocular, visual
7 optical

sightseer
7 tourist 10 rubberneck

sign
3 cue, ink 4 flag, hint, mark, omen,
show 5 index, proof, token, trace
6 motion, signal, symbol 7 earmark, endorse, exhibit, gesture, indicia, initial, symptom, vestige,
warning 8 evidence, exponent, reminder 9 autograph, character, indicator, subscribe 10 expression,
indication, suggestion 11 attestation 13 gesticulation, symbolization
commercial: 4 neon
directional: 5 arrow
of the zodiac: (see **zodiac sign**)

signal

3 cue 4 flag 5 alarm, alert, siren
6 beckon, famous, marked, motion,
tocsin, wigwag 7 eminent, gesture,
salient 8 high sign, movement, peculiar, renowned, striking 9 arresting, arrestive, prominent 10 individual, noticeable, remarkable
11 conspicuous, distinctive, illustrious, outstanding
distress: 3 SOS 6 Mayday

signature

3 ink 4 name, sign 9 autograph,
subscribe 11 John Hancock
flourish: 6 paraph

signet

4 ring, seal 5 stamp

significance

4 pith 5 merit, sense 6 credit,
import, moment, virtue, weight
7 meaning, message, purport
8 prestige 9 authority, influence,
magnitude 10 excellence, importance, intendment, perfection
11 acceptation, consequence,
weightiness

significant

3 big 4 rich 5 sound, valid 6 cogent, facund 7 telling, weighty
8 eloquent, forceful, material, powerful 9 important, momentous
10 compelling, convincing, expressive, meaningful 11 sententious,
substantial 12 considerable
13 consequential

signification

4 gist 5 sense 6 import 7 essence,
meaning, message, purport 8 im-
plying 9 substance 10 intendment
11 acceptation, implication
12 construction 13 understanding

signify

4 bear, mean, show 5 carry, count,
spell, weigh 6 convey, denote, import, intend, matter 7 add up to,
bespeak, connote, express, purport

sign over

4 cede, deed 5 alien 6 assign, remise 8 alienate, make over, transfer 10 abalienate

sign up

4 join 5 enrol, enter 6 enlist, enroll,
join up, muster

Sigurd

horse: 5 Grani
slayer: 5 Hogni
victim: 6 Fafnir
wife: 6 Gudrun

Sigyn's husband

4 Loki

silage

6 fodder

silence

3 gag 4 calm, dumb, hush, lull,
mute 5 death, quash, quell, quiet,
shush, sleep, still 6 dampen,
deaden, demise, muffle, muzzle,
shut up, squash 7 decease, passing, quietus, secrecy, squelch
8 choke off, curtains, hush-hush,
quietude, suppress 9 quietness,
stillness

silent

3 mum 4 dumb, hush, mute
5 close, muted, quiet, still, tacit,
whist 6 curbed, stilly 7 checked,
hushful 8 reserved, reticent, taciturn, unspoken, unvoiced, wordless
9 inhibited, noiseless, secretive,
soundless, unuttered, voiceless
10 incoherent, restrained, speechless, tongue-tied, unsociable
11 close-lipped, shut-mouthed, tight-
lipped, unexpressed 12 closemouthed, close-tongued, inarticulate, tight-mouthed

silhouette

4 line 6 shadow 7 contour, outline,
profile 9 lineament, lineation 10 figuration 11 delineation

silicon

symbol: 2 Si

silk

5 fiber, honan 7 foulard 8 sarcenet, sarsenet
fabric: 4 gros 5 caffa, ninon, Pekin,
satin, surah, tulle 6 cendal, mantua, pongee, samite, sendal, tussah
7 taffeta, tussore
factory: 8 filature
hat: 6 topper
maker: 4 worm 7 thrower
raw: 5 grège 6 greige
source: 6 cocoon
waste: 4 noil 5 floss
wild: 6 tussah 7 tussore
yarn: 4 tram

silkworm

3 eri 6 bombyx, tussah 7 tussore
8 bombycid

sill

5 bench, ledge, shelf 9 threshold

silliness

5 folly 7 inanity 8 insanity 9 absurdity, craziness, dottiness
11 foolishness, witlessness 12 illogicality 13 senselessness

silly

3 off 4 daft 5 crazy, daffy, dizzy,
empty, funny, giddy, loony, sappy,
wacky 6 absurd, insane, simple,
unwise 7 asinine, fatuous, flighty,
foolish, unwitty, vacuous, witless
8 ignorant 9 fantastic, nitwitted,
senseless 10 bird-witted, irrational,
weak-headed, weak-minded
11 empty-headed, harebrained,
light-headed, sheep-headed
12 preposterous, unreasonable
13 rattlebrained, unintelligent

silt

4 scum, soil 5 dregs 7 deposit, residue 8 sediment

silver

4 coin 5 money, shiny 6 argent, dulcet 7 bullion, element 8 argentum,
flatware, lustrous, sterling 9 argentine, tableware
relating to: 5 lunar 8 argentic 9 argentine, argentous
symbol: 2 Ag

silverfish

6 insect, tarpon

silver fox

5 caama

silversmith

6 Revere (Paul)

silver-tongued

4 glib 7 voluble 8 eloquent

silvery

6 argent 7 frosted, shining 9 ar-
gentate, argentine, argentous, brilliant 10 glittering, shimmering

Silvia's beloved

9 Valentine

Simeon

father: 5 Jacob
mother: 4 Leah
son: 4 Ohad 6 Nemuel

simian

3 ape 6 monkey 10 anthropoid

similar

4 akin, like 5 alike 6 agnate 7 uniform 8 parallel, suchlike 9 analogous, consonant 10 comparable,
reciprocal 11 correlative 13 complementary, corresponding
combining form: 3 hol, hom 4 holo,
home, homo 5 homeo, homoe,
homoi 6 homoeo, homoio

similarity

6 simile 7 analogy 8 affinity, likeness, parallel 9 alikeness, closeness, collation, semblance 10 comparison, similitude, synonymity

11 association, coincidence, correlation, resemblance

similarly
2 so 4 also 8 likewise

simile
7 analogy 8 affinity, likeness, metaphor 9 alikeness, semblance 10 comparison, similarity, similitude 11 resemblance
word: 2 as 4 like

similitude
4 copy 6 double, simile 7 analogy, replica 8 affinity, likeness, metaphor 9 alikeness, semblance 10 comparison, similarity 11 resemblance

simmer
4 boil, stew, stir 5 churn 6 bubble, seethe 7 ferment, parboil, smolder

simmer down
4 cool 7 collect, compose, control, repress, smother, subside 8 restrain, suppress 9 quiet down, re-collect

Simon
brother: 5 Jesus 6 Andrew
father: 5 Jonah
new name: 5 Peter
son: 5 Judas, Rufus 9 Alexander

Simon ___
5 Magus 6 Legree 8 of Cyrene 9 the Zealot

Simon Maccabeus
father: 10 Mattathias
nickname: 6 Thassi
slayer: 7 Ptolemy

simp
5 dunce 6 dimwit, nitwit 7 lackwit, pinhead, wantwit 13 featherweight

simper
5 smirk

simple
4 dull, dumb, dupe, easy, mere, pure, slow, soft 5 crass, dense, dopey, light, naive, plain, royal, sheer, silly, stark 6 doting, facile, modest, smooth, spoony, stupid 7 artless, asinine, fatuous, foolish, idiotic, moronic, natural, perfect, unmixed, unwitty, witless 8 absolute, backward, childish, discreet, gullible, ignorant, imbecile, mindless, retarded, trusting, unartful, untaught 9 brainless, childlike, credulous, dim-witted, ingenuous, nitwitted, senseless, unalloyed, unstudied 10 effortless, half-witted, illiterate, slow-witted, unaffected, uneducated, unschooled, weak-headed, weakminded 11 fundamental, inelaborate, sheepheaded, undecorated, unelaborate, unmitigated, unqualified 12 feebleminded, unartificial, unbeautified, uncompounded, unornamented 13 inexperienced, unadulterated, unintelligent, unpretentious, untroublesome
combining form: 3 apl 4 aplo, hapl 5 haplo

simpleminded
4 dull, slow 6 stupid 7 moronic 8 imbecile, retarded 9 dim-witted 10 half-witted, slow-witted

simpleton
4 dolt, fool, zany 5 ament, dummy, dunce, idiot, moron 6 cretin, stupid 7 bungler, dullard, half-wit, natural 8 dullhead, dumbbell, imbecile 9 ignoramus

simplify
6 reduce 7 abridge, clarify, clean up, cut down, shorten 8 boil down 10 disinvolve, streamline, unscramble 11 disentangle 13 straighten out

simply
3 but 4 just, only 6 merely

simulacrum
4 copy, face, show, spit 5 guise, image 6 double, ersatz, ringer 7 picture, seeming, showing 8 portrait 9 imitation, semblance 10 appearance 13 spitting image

simulate
3 act, ape 4 copy, fake, pose, sham 5 bluff, favor, feign, mimic, put on 6 affect, assume 7 imitate, play-act, pretend 8 resemble 11 counterfeit

simulated
4 fake, mock, sham 5 dummy, false, phony 6 ersatz 8 spurious 9 imitation 10 artificial, fictitious, substitute

simultaneous
6 coeval 8 agreeing 10 coetaneous, coexistent, coexisting, coinciding, concurrent, concurring, synchronal, synchronic 11 synchronous 12 contemporary

simultaneously
6 at once 8 together 12 coincidently, concurrently

sin
3 err 4 debt, evil, tort 5 crime, fault, wrong 6 offend 7 demerit 8 hamartia, iniquity, trespass 9 diablerie 10 deficiency, transgress, wickedness, wrongdoing 11 shortcoming 12 imperfection
deadly: 4 envy, lust 5 anger, pride, sloth 8 gluttony 12 covetousness

Sin
7 moon-god
daughter: 6 Ishtar
son: 7 Shamash
wife: 6 Ningal

since
2 as 3 for 4 next 5 after, below 6 behind, seeing 7 because, whereas 8 as long as 9 following 10 inasmuch as 11 considering 12 subsequent to
Scottish: 4 syne

sincere
4 dear, open, real, true 5 frank, meant, plain 6 actual, candid, devout, hearty, honest 7 genuine, serious 8 bona fide, faithful, heartful, truthful 9 authentic, heartfelt, unfeigned 10 aboveboard, forthright, heart-whole, unaffected 11 undesigning, whole-souled 12 frankhearted, undissembled, wholehearted 13 unpretentious

sincerity
6 candor 8 goodwill 9 bona fides, good faith 11 earnestness

sinecure
4 snap 5 cinch

sine qua non
4 must 9 condition, essential, necessity, requisite 11 requirement 12 precondition, prerequisite

sinew
5 force, might, power 6 energy, muscle, tendon 7 potency 8 strength

sinewy
4 ropy, wiry 5 tough 6 brawny, strong, sturdy 7 fibrous, stringy 8 athletic, muscular 9 tenacious

sinful
3 bad, low 4 base, evil, vile 5 amiss, wrong 6 guilty, unholy, wicked 7 immoral, peccant, vicious 8 blamable, blameful, culpable, damnable, shameful 9 reprobate 10 censurable, iniquitous 11 blameworthy, disgraceful 13 demeritorious, reprehensible

sing
3 hum 4 hymn, lilt, lull, tune 5 carol, chant, croon, yodel 6 intone, warble 7 confess, descant,

lullaby **8** serenade, vocalize
10 cantillate

singe
4 burn, char **6** scorch

singer
4 alto, bass **5** tenor **6** cantor
7 crooner, soloist, songman, soprano **8** baritone, choirboy, songster, vocalist **9** balladeer, balla-
dier, chorister
cabaret: **11** chansonnier
female: **9** chanteuse, chantress
10 cantatrice
opera: **4** diva **5** buffa, buffo
religious: **6** cantor

singing
exercise: **7** solfège
group: **4** duet, trio **5** choir **6** chorus
7 quartet
voice: **4** alto, bass **5** tenor **7** soprano **8** baritone **9** contralto
12 mezzo-soprano

single
3 hit, one **4** free, lone, only, open,
sole **5** frank, plain, unwed **6** candid, maiden, screen, unique, virgin
7 base hit, special **8** celibate, distinct, especial, separate, singular,
solitary, specific, unshared **9** exclusive, unmarried **10** individual,
particular, spouseless, unattached,
unfettered
combining form: **3** apl, mon **4** aplo,
hapl, mono **5** haplo
prefix: **3** uni

single-minded
4 open **5** frank, plain, rigid **6** candid **7** adamant, bigoted, diehard
8 obdurate **9** unbending **10** brassbound, inexorable, inflexible, relentless, unyielding

single out
4 cull, mark, pick, take **5** elect
6 choose, optate, opt for, prefer,
select

singular
3 odd **4** lone, only, rare, sole, solo
5 alone, queer, weird **6** unique
7 bizarre, certain, curious, oddball,
strange, unusual **8** definite, discrete, peculiar, solitary, uncommon,
unwonted **9** exclusive **10** individual, outlandish, particular, respective, unexampled, unordinary
11 exceptional **13** extraordinary

singularity
5 seity, unity **7** ipseity, oneness,
selfdom **8** identity, selfhood, selfness **10** singleness **11** personality

13 individualism, individuality,
particularity

singularize
4 mark **7** qualify **9** signalize
11 distinguish, individuate **12** characterize **13** individualize

sinister
4 dark, dire, evil **6** malign **7** baleful, doomful, fateful, malefic, ominous **8** lowering, menacing **9** ill-
boding, ill-omened, malicious
10 maleficent, portentous **11** apocalyptic, threatening **12** inauspicious, unpropitious

sink
3 dip, pit, ram, rot, run, sag, set,
sty **4** dive, pool, stab **5** abase, basin, demit, drive, droop, lower,
slump, Sodom, stoop **6** bemean,
debase, demean, go down, hollow,
humble, plunge, thrust, worsen
7 cesspit, decline, degrade, depress, descend, founder, go under,
let down, subside, torpedo **8** cast
down, cesspool, hellhole, submerge, submerse **9** concavity, humiliate **10** degenerate, depression,
disimprove, retrograde **11** deteriorate, pandemonium **12** Augean stable, disintegrate

sinker
4 drop **5** pitch **6** weight

sinkhole
3 dip, sag **5** basin **6** hollow
8 cesspool **9** concavity
10 depression

sinless
4 pure **8** innocent

Sinn ___
4 Fein

sinuous
4 wavy **5** shaky **7** twisted, winding
8 flexuous, tortuous **9** meandrous
10 convoluted, meandering, serpentine **11** anfractuous, snake-shaped

sinus
6 cavity, hollow, recess

Sioux
6 Dakota
chief: **8** Red Cloud **10** Crazy Horse
11 Sitting Bull
people: **3** Ofo **4** Crow **6** Biloxi, Tu-
telo **7** Catawba, Hidatsa
9 Winnebago

sip
4 toss **5** drink, quaff, sup up, taste
6 imbibe, sup off **7** swallow

siphon
3 tap **4** draw, pipe, pump **5** carry,
draft, drain **6** convoy, funnel
7 channel, conduct, draw off, traject **8** transmit

sir
4 lord **5** title **6** knight, mister
9 gentleman

sire
4 lord **5** beget, breed, hatch,
maker, spawn **6** author, create, father, parent **7** creator, founder,
produce **8** generate, inventor **9** architect, generator, originate, patriarch, procreate **10** originator
11 progenerate

siren
4 vamp **7** charmer, drawing, enticer, Lorelei **8** alluring, magnetic
9 seductive, temptress **10** attracting, attractive, bewitching, enchanting, seductress **11** captivating, fascinating, femme fatale
of silent screen: **4** Bara (Theda)

Siren
5 Ligea **8** Leucosia **10** Parthenope
German: **7** Lorelei

sirenian
6 dugong, sea cow **7** manatee

siren song
4 bait, lure, trap **5** decoy, snare
6 come-on **10** allurement, enticement, seducement, temptation

sissy
4 baby **6** prissy **7** doormat, epicene, milksop, unmanly **8** weakling
9 jellyfish **10** effeminate, pantywaist **11** Milquetoast, mollycoddle

sister
3 nun **4** girl **7** sibling **8** relative

Sister Carrie author
7 Dreiser (Theodore)

sisterly
7 sororal

Sisyphus
brother: **7** Athamas **9** Salmoneus
father: **6** Aeolus
mother: **7** Enarete
son: **7** Glaucus

sit
4 meet, open, pose, rest, seat
5 brood, cover, perch, squat **6** settle **7** convene, install, posture
8 ensconce

Sita
abductor: **6** Ravana
husband, rescuer: **4** Rama

sitarist
7 Shankar (Ravi)

sit down
4 land 5 light, perch, roost
6 alight, settle 9 touch down

site
3 dig 4 home, spot 5 haunt, locus,
place, point, range, scene, where
6 locale 7 habitat, station 8 locality, location, position

sit-in
7 protest

sitting
6 séance 7 session
prolonged: 8 sederunt

Sitting Bull's tribe
5 Sioux

sitting duck
4 butt, mark 6 target

situate
3 put, set 4 site 5 place 6 locate
8 position

situation
3 job 4 mode, post, rank, site, spot
5 berth, locus, place, point, state,
where 6 billet, office, status 7 bargain, footing, posture, station 8 location, position, standing
9 condition

situs
5 place

Siva
see **Shiva**

six
combining form: 3 hex, sex 4 hexa,
sexi 5 sexti
group of: 5 hexad 6 hexade, sestet,
sextet 7 sestole, sextole 8 sestolet,
sextette 9 sextuplet
on a die: 4 sice
relating to: 6 senary

sixfold
9 sextuplex

six-shooter
3 gun 6 pistol 8 revolver

sixth sense
3 ESP

sizable
3 big 4 good 5 hefty, large, major
8 sensible 9 extensive 10 giant-
sized, large-scale 11 respectable
12 considerable

size
4 area, body, bulk, mass 5 width
6 extent, height, length, spread, volume 7 bigness, breadth, expanse,

measure, stretch 9 amplitude, dimension, extension, greatness,
largeness, magnitude 10 dimensions, proportion 11 measurement

sizzle
3 fry 4 buzz, fizz, hiss, sear, whiz
5 swish, whish 6 wheeze, whoosh
8 sibilate

sizzling
3 hot 5 fiery 6 baking, red-hot, torrid 7 burning 8 broiling, scalding,
white-hot 9 scorching

skald
4 bard, poet

Skanda
6 war-god
brother: 6 Ganesa 7 Ganesha
father: 4 Siva 5 Shiva

skate
4 fish, skid 5 glide, slide 6 fellow
blade: 6 runner
kind: 6 figure, hockey

skating site
3 ice 4 rink

skedaddle
3 fly, run 4 bolt, flee, kite, skip
5 scoot, scram, screw, skirr, split
6 begone, cut out, decamp, get out
7 make off, scamper, skiddoo, take
off, vamoose 8 clear out, hightail

skeleton
5 bones, draft, frame 6 sketch 7 diagram, outline 9 framework
marine: 5 coral, shell

skeptic
5 cynic 7 doubter, scoffer, zetetic
8 agnostic 10 headshaker, Pyrrhonian, Pyrrhonist, questioner, unbeliever 11 disbeliever

skeptical
6 show-me 7 cynical 8 aporetic,
doubtful, doubting 9 quizzical
10 dissenting, suspicious 11 incredulous, mistrustful, questioning, unbelieving 12 disbelieving, freethinking

skepticism
5 doubt, qualm 6 wonder 7 concern, dubiety 8 mistrust 9 dubiosity, suspicion 11 incertitude,
uncertainty

skerry
4 isle, reef

sketch
4 draw, line, plot 5 draft, trace
7 aperçu 6 depict, design, detail,
lay out, map out, précis, survey
7 develop, diagram, outline, pan-

dect, sylloge 8 block out, chalk
out, rough out, skeleton, syllabus
9 adumbrate, blueprint, delineate
10 compendium 11 skeletonize
12 characterize 13 diagrammatize

sketchy
5 rough 7 cursory, shallow 8 skeletal 9 depthless 11 superficial

skew
3 dip 4 bias, skid, slip, slue, veer
5 angle, sheer, slant, slide
6 swerve 8 train off

skewer
3 rod 4 spit 5 lance, spear, spike
6 impale, skiver 8 transfix 9 brochette 11 transpierce

ski
5 glide, slide
lift: 4 J-bar, T-bar 5 chair 7 gondola

skid
3 dip 4 drop, fall, skew, slue, veer
5 sheer, slide 6 plunge, tumble
7 plummet, spinout 8 nose-dive

skid row
4 slum 6 bowery

skier
American: 3 Moe (Tommy) 4 Kidd
(Billy) 5 Mahre (Phil) 7 Johnson
(Bill)
Austrian: 6 Proell (Annemarie)
7 Klammer (Franz), Schranz (Karl)
expert: 6 kanone
French: 5 Killy (Jean-Claude)
Italian: 5 Tomba (Alberto) 6 Theoni
(Gustavo)
Swedish: 8 Stenmark (Ingemar)

skiff
4 boat 7 rowboat

skiing
area: 3 run 5 slope
cross-country: 7 touring
event: 6 schuss, slalom 8 downhill
11 giant slalom
horse-drawn: 9 skijoring
kind: 6 Alpine, Nordic
position: 7 vorlage
technique: 6 wedeln 8 snowplow,
traverse
turn: 7 christy 8 christie

skill
3 art 5 craft, knack 7 ability, address, command, cunning, know-
how, mastery, prowess, sleight
8 deftness 9 dexterity, expertise,
expertism, readiness 10 adroitness,
expertness, mastership 13 dexterousness

combining form: 6 techno, techny
suffix: 3 ics 4 ship

skillet
3 pan 6 frypan, spider 9 frying pan

skillful
4 deft, good 5 adept, crack 6 adroit, clever, daedal, expert, master, pretty, wicked 7 learned, skilled, versant 8 masterly 9 masterful, workmanly 10 proficient, well-versed 11 crackerjack, workmanlike

skim
3 dap, fly 4 dart, kiss, sail, scud, skip 5 brush, carom, float, graze, shave, shoot, skirr 6 glance 8 ricochet

skimpy
3 shy 4 poor 5 scant, short, spare 6 meager, scanty, scarce, scrimp, sparse 7 failing, scrimpy, wanting 8 exiguous 9 deficient 10 inadequate 12 insufficient

skim through
4 scan 6 browse 8 glance at 10 glance over

skin
3 fur, gyp, pod, rap 4 clad, clip, face, fell, hide, pare, peel, pelt, rind, side, soak 5 blame, cheat, cover, fleet, haste, hurry, knock, miser, nabal, scale, stick, stiff, strip 6 barrel, bucket, bullet, con man, fleece, hasten, hustle, sheath, slough 7 beeline, censure, condemn, diddler, grifter, niggard, scrooge, sharper, sheathe 8 denounce, highball, swindler, tightwad 9 criticize, defrauder, dermatous, excoriate, reprehend, reprobate, sheathing 10 cheapskate, denunciate, overcharge 11 cheeseparer, decorticate, excorticate, flimflammer
animal: 4 coat, hide, pelt 6 hackle, peltry
bird: 7 pteryla
combining form: 3 cut 4 cuti, derm, scyt 5 derma, dermo, dermy, scyto 6 dermat, dermia, dermis 7 cutaneo, dermata (plural), dermato, epiderm 8 epidermo
depression: 6 dimple
disease: 4 acne 5 hives, mange 6 eczema 10 dermatitis
dry: 5 scurf
fold: 5 plica
layer: 5 derma 6 corium, dermis 7 corneum, cuticle 9 epidermis

opening: 4 pore
protuberance: 4 mole, wart 6 pimple
rabbit: 5 coney
retating to: 6 dermal 9 cuticular, epidermal
seal: 5 sculp
spot: 7 freckle
tumor: 3 wen

skinflint
5 chuff, miser, nabal 7 niggard 8 muckworm, tightwad 10 cheapskate 11 cheeseparer

skink
4 soup 6 lizard

skinny
4 bony, lank, lean 5 gaunt, lanky, spare, weedy 6 twiggy 7 angular, scraggy, scrawny 8 rawboned, skeletal 9 emaciated

Skin of Our Teeth author
6 Wilder (Thornton)

skip
3 dap, fly, hop, run 4 bolt, flee, jump, leap, lope, skim, trip 5 blank, bound, caper, carom, chasm, frisk, graze, scoot, skirr 6 bounce, cavort, curvet, gambol, glance, spring 7 make off, scamper, skitter 8 omission, overlook, ricochet 9 oversight, skedaddle 10 hippety-hop

skipjack
3 fop 4 fish 6 beetle 8 sailboat

skipper
6 leader 7 captain 9 commander

skirl
6 scream, shriek

skirmish
4 fray 5 brush, clash, melee, run-in, set-to 6 affray, ambush, attack, mellay 7 assault 9 encounter, scrimmage 10 velitation

skirr
3 fly, run 4 bolt, dart, flee, sail, scud, skim, skip 5 float, scoot, shoot 7 make off, scamper 9 skedaddle

skirt
3 hem, rim 4 brim, duck, edge, skip 5 avoid, bound, brink, burke, dodge, elude, evade, hedge, verge 6 border, bypass, define, detour, escape, fringe, ignore, margin 7 garment 8 sidestep, surround 9 perimeter, periphery 10 circumvent, equivocate
ballet: 4 tutu
feature: 3 hem 4 slit

long: 4 maxi
Scottish: 4 kilt
short: 4 mini
style: 5 A-line

skit
3 act 4 jibe 5 caper, taunt 6 parody, shtick, sketch 7 schtick 9 burlesque

skitter
3 hop 4 lope, skip, trip 6 spring

skittery
see **skitterish**

skittish
4 edgy 5 dizzy, giddy 7 flighty, nervous, restive 8 agitable, unstable, volatile 9 alarmable, excitable, frivolous, startlish 10 capricious, unreliable

skivvies
9 underwear

skoal
5 drink, toast

skua
4 bird 6 jaeger

skulduggery
8 foul play, trickery

skulk
4 lurk, slip 5 creep, shirk, slink, sneak, steal 7 gumshoe 9 pussyfoot

skull
4 bone, head, mind 5 brain 7 cranium 8 brainpan 9 braincase
back of: 7 occiput
bone: 5 vomer 6 zygoma 7 ethmoid, frontal 8 parietal, sphenoid, temporal
jawless: 9 calvarium
joint: 6 suture
part: 3 jaw 5 inion 6 basion

skullcap
5 calot 6 beanie, pileus 7 calotte 8 yarmulke 9 calvarium, zucchetto

skunk
3 cur, dog 4 beat, drub, lick, scum, snot, toad, whip 5 snake 6 thrash 7 polecat, shellac 8 conepate, lambaste 9 overwhelm
genus: 8 Mephitis

sky
5 azure 6 heaven, welkin 7 heavens 8 empyrean 9 firmament
combining form: 4 uran 5 urano
sky-blue: 5 azure 8 cerulean 9 caerulean

sky chief
5 pilot

skylarking

5 revel 7 fooling, revelry, wassail, whoopee, whoopla, whoop-up 9 high jinks, horseplay, revelment, rowdiness, whoop-de-do 10 roughhouse 12 roughhousing

skylight

6 window

skyline

7 horizon

sky pilot

5 padre 6 cleric, divine, parson 8 chaplain, clerical, minister, preacher 9 churchman, clergyman 12 ecclesiastic

skyrocket

4 rise, soar 5 climb 7 shoot up 8 upspring

sky sighting

3 UFO

slab

3 bar, rod 4 tile 5 ingot, slice, stick, strip 6 billet

slabber

5 drool 6 drivel, slaver 7 dribble 8 salivate

slack

3 lax, off 4 down, ease, lazy, slow, soft, weak 5 inert, loose, relax 6 feeble, infirm, loosen, remiss, slow-up 7 ease off, laggard, passive, relaxed 8 careless, derelict, dilatory, fainéant, inactive, indolent, slothful, slowdown, sluggish, stagnant, unsteady 9 leisurely, lethargic, negligent, untighten

slacken

3 ebb, lax 4 ease, fall, mire, wane 5 abate, delay, embog, let up, loose, relax 6 detain, hang up, loosen, relent, retard, slow up 7 bog down, die away, die down, ease off, set back, subside 8 moderate, slow down 9 untighten 10 decelerate

slacker

5 idler 6 loafer 7 shirker, slinker 8 slugabed, sluggard 9 goldbrick

slag

4 lava 5 dross 6 cinder, debris, scoria

slake

5 allay 6 deaden, quench 7 crumble, hydrate, satisfy

slam

3 bat, dig, hit, jab, rap 4 bang, bash, beat, belt, blow, boom, clap, ding, drub, flay, mace, slug, slur, swat, wham 5 blast, burst, crack, crash, fling, knock, pound, slash, slate, smack, smash, swipe, whack 6 batter, cudgel, hammer, scathe, strike, thwack, wallop 7 clobber, obloquy, potshot, scourge 8 lambaste, lash into 9 aspersion, bastinado, castigate, stricture

slammer

3 jug, pen 4 jail 6 cooler, prison

slander

4 hurt, slur, tale 5 belie, libel, smear 6 assail, attack, damage, defame, injure, malign 7 asperse, calumny, scandal, traduce 8 muckrake, roorback, strumpet, tear down 9 black wash, denigrate 10 backbiting, calumniate, defamation, detraction, muckraking 11 mud-slinging 12 back-stabbing, belittlement, depreciation 13 disparagement

slang

4 cant 5 argot, lingo 6 jargon, patois, patter 7 dialect 10 vernacular

slant

3 aim, tip 4 bank, bend, bias, cant, heel, lean, list, side, skew, tilt, veer, warp 5 angle, aside, bevel, color, focus, grade, point, slope, splay, train, twist 6 aslope, direct, orient, swerve 7 decline, descend, deviate, distort, diverge, incline, leaning, outlook, recline 8 gradient, sideways, sidewise 9 direction, influence, obliquely, prejudice, viewpoint 10 standpoint 11 concentrate, inclination 12 predilection
combining form: 4 clin 5 clino

slap

3 box, hit, pop, try 4 bash, blip, chop, cuff, drub, flay, poke, shot, slam, stab, swat, wham 5 clout, crack, fling, punch, score, slash, smack, spank, whack, whirl 6 buffet, insult, scathe, strike 7 affront, despite, scourge 8 haymaker, lambaste, lash into 9 castigate, contumely, indignity

slapdash

5 messy 6 botchy, random, sloppy, untidy 7 aimless 8 careless, slipshod, slovenly 9 desultory, haphazard, hit-or-miss, irregular 10 designless, unthorough

slaphappy

7 foolish 8 carefree, reckless 10 punch-drunk

slash

3 cut 4 clip, flay, gash, hack, pare, slit 5 lower, shave, slice 6 hackle, haggle, incise, pierce, reduce, scathe, scorch 7 abridge, blister, curtail, cut back, cut down, scarify, scourge, shorten 8 lambaste, lash into, mark down, retrench 9 castigate, excoriate 10 abbreviate

slasher

5 knife, razor, sword 9 swordsman 12 swashbuckler

slat

4 lath 5 board, stave, strip 6 louver 7 airfoil 9 sheepskin

slate

4 gray, list, rock, tile 6 record, tablet, ticket 7 shingle 8 schedule 9 designate

slaughter

4 kill, maim, slay 6 mangle, murder 7 butcher, carnage, torture, wipe out 8 butchery, decimate, hecatomb, massacre, mutilate 9 bloodbath, bloodshed 10 annihilate 11 destruction, exterminate 12 annihilation

slaughterhouse

8 abattoir

Slav

4 Pole, Serb, Sorb, Wend 5 Croat, Czech 6 Bulgar, Slovak 7 Russian, Serbian, Slovene 8 Bohemian, Croatian, Moravian 9 Bulgarian, Ruthenian, Ukrainian

slave

4 grub, help, peon, plod, serf, slog, toil 5 grind, helot 6 drudge, menial, thrall, toiler, vassal 7 bondman, chattel, servant 8 bondsman 9 dray horse, mancipium, workhorse
feudal: 4 serf
harem: 9 odalisque
liberated: 8 freedman
Muslim: 8 Mameluke
Spartan: 5 helot

slave driver

6 tyrant 8 martinet, rawhider 10 taskmaster 11 Simon Legree

slaver

4 fawn, spit 5 cower, drool, toady, water 6 cringe, drivel, grovel, kowtow, saliva 7 dribble, honey up, slabber, slobber, spittle, truckle 8 bootlick, salivate

slavery

4 moil, toil, work, yoke 5 grind, labor 6 drudge, thrall 7 bondage, helotry, peonage, serfdom 8 bull-

work, drudgery, plugging **9** servitude, thralldom, villenage **10** donkeywork

Slavic apostle
5 Cyril **9** Methodius

slavish
3 low **4** hard, tame **5** apish, heavy, rough **6** knotty, menial, rugged **7** operose, servile, subdued **8** obeisant, wretched **9** difficult, emulative, imitative, laborious, miserable, spineless, strenuous **10** formidable, obsequious, uninspired, unoriginal **11** subservient

slay
4 do in, down, kill **6** cut off, finish, lay low, murder **7** butcher, destroy, execute, put away **8** dispatch, knock off **9** liquidate, slaughter **11** assassinate

slayer
4 bane **6** killer **8** homicide, murderer

sleazy
3 low **4** mean, thin **5** cheap, dingy, seedy, tacky, tatty **6** cheesy, common, flabby, flimsy, floppy, paltry, shabby, shoddy, slight, trashy **7** flaccid, run-down, tenuous **9** gossamery **10** broken-down, down-at-heel **11** dilapidated **12** disreputable

sled
4 luge, pung **6** sleigh **7** coaster, travois **8** toboggan
Russian: **6** troika

sled dog
5 husky **8** malamute

sledge
6 hammer, sleigh
Eskimo: **7** komatik

sleek
4 oily **5** round, slick **6** glassy, glossy, polish, refine, smarmy, smooth **7** perfect **8** lustrous, polished **10** glistening

sleep
3 nap **4** coma, doze, rest **5** death, relax, sopor **6** demise, repose, siesta, snooze, torpor **7** decease, languor, passing, quietus, shut-eye, silence, slumber **8** dullness, hebetude, lethargy **9** lassitude, torpidity **10** defunction, torpidness **11** dissolution, slumberland
bringer: **7** sandman
combining form: **4** hypn, narc **5** hypno, narco, somni
god: **6** Hypnos, Hypnus, Somnus

sleeper
4 beam **7** Pullman, support **8** dormeuse, long shot

sleeping
4 abed **7** dormant **8** comatose
disease: **10** narcolepsy

sleeplessness
8 insomnia

sleepwalker
12 somnambulist

sleepy
4 dozy **5** dazed, dopey, inert, quiet **6** drowsy, opiate, snoozy, torpid **7** nodding, passive, poppied, yawning **8** comatose, hypnotic, inactive, listless, narcotic, oscitant, sleeping, sluggish, slumbery, somnific **9** heavy-eyed, lethargic, somnolent, soporific **10** nepenthean, slumbering, slumberous, somnorific **11** somniferous

sleigh
4 pung, sled **6** sledge

sleight
4 play, ploy, ruse, wile **5** skill, trick **6** device **7** address, gimmick, prowess **8** artifice, deftness, maneuver **9** dexterity, readiness, stratagem **10** adroitness **13** dexterousness

sleight of hand
5 magic, trick **9** dexterity **11** legerdemain

slender
4 lean, slim, thin, trim **5** lithe, reedy, scant, short, small **6** remote, scanty, scarce, skinny, slight, stalky, svelte, twiggy **7** outside, spindly, squinny, tenuous, wanting **8** slimmish **9** attenuate, deficient **10** inadequate, negligible **12** insufficient

sleuth
3 tec **4** dick **7** gumshoe **8** hawkshaw, Sherlock **9** detective **10** private eye **12** investigator

slice
3 cut, lot **4** bite, gash, part, slit **5** carve, quota, sever, share, slash, split **6** cleave, incise, pierce, sunder **7** dissect, partage, portion, segment **8** dissever **9** allotment, allowance

slick
4 oily, slip, wise **5** canny, fix up, glide, quick, round, sharp, sleek, slide, smart, soapy, spiff **6** doll up, glossy, greasy, polish, refine, slippy, smarmy, smooth **7** deck out,

doll out, dress up, fulsome, gussy up, knowing, perfect, slither **8** glissade, slippery, slithery, spruce up, unctious, unctuous **10** lubricious, oleaginous **11** quick-witted, sharp-witted

slicker
4 dude **6** gypper **7** cheater, diddler, oilskin, sharper **8** raincoat, swindler **9** defrauder, trickster **11** flimflammer

slide
3 dip, sag **4** drop, fall, flow, lurk, move, skid, slip **5** chute, coast, crawl, creep, drift, glide, shift, shirk, skate, skulk, slick, slink, slump, sneak, spill, steal **6** stream, tumble **7** decline, drop off, fall off, slither **8** downturn, fall away, glissade **9** downswing, downtrend

slight
4 fail, omit, skip, slim, thin **5** flout, reedy, scoff, small **6** flimsy, forget, ignore, remote, sleazy, stalky, subtle, twiggy **7** blink at, contemn, despise, neglect, outside, slender, squinny, tenuous **8** delicate, discount, overlook, overpass, smallish **9** attenuate, blink away, disregard, gossamery, pint-sized **10** negligible

slim
4 thin **5** canny, lithe, reedy, small **6** adroit, clever, narrow, remote, skinny, slight, stalky, svelte, twiggy **7** cunning, lissome, outside, slender, squinny, tenuous **9** attenuate, dexterous, ingenious, lithesome **10** negligible

slim down
4 diet **6** reduce **10** slenderize

slime
3 mud **4** muck, ooze, scum, slum **6** sludge
combining form: **3** myx **4** myxa, myxo

slimy
4 oozy, vile **7** viscous

sling
4 cast, fire, hang, hurl, sock, toss **5** fling, heave, march, pitch, stalk, throw **6** dangle, depend, launch, stride **7** suspend **8** catapult

slink
4 lurk **5** creep, shirk, skulk, slide, sneak, steal **6** weasel **7** gumshoe, sneaker **8** sneaksby **9** pussyfoot

slip
3 dip, lam, sag **4** bull, dock, drop, fall, lose, lurk, molt, pier, quay,

shed, sink, skid, trip **5** berth, boner, crash, creep, erode, error, fluff, glide, jetty, lapse, levee, mouse, shake, shirk, skulk, slick, slide, slink, slump, sneak, steal, wharf **6** bungle, escape, flight, go down, slough, soften, topple **7** blooper, blunder, decline, drop off, fall off, faux pas, getaway, gumshoe, mistake, plummet, slither **8** breakout, downturn, escaping, exuviate, fall away, glissade, nosedive, prolapse, throw off **9** downslide, downswing, downtrend, pussyfoot

slipper
4 mule, shoe **5** brake, romeo, scuff **6** juliet, sandal **8** babouche, pantofle

slippery
3 icy **4** eely, oily **5** slick **6** greasy, lubric, shifty **7** mutable **8** slithery, unstable, unsteady, variable **9** uncertain **10** changeable, inconstant, lubricious

slipshod
5 messy, tacky **6** botchy, faulty, shabby, shoddy, sloppy, tagrag, unneat, untidy **7** inexact, raunchy, scrubby, scruffy, unkempt **8** careless, fouled-up, ill-kempt, messed-up, slapdash, slovenly, tattered **9** botched-up, haphazard, imperfect, neglected, negligent, slaphappy **10** bedraggled, disheveled, down-at-heel, inaccurate

slipup
5 boner, error, fluff, lapse **6** bungle, miscue **7** blooper, blunder, mistake **9** oversight

slit
3 cut **4** gash, rent, tear **5** slash, slice **6** incise, pierce **7** opening **8** roulette

slither
4 lurk, slip **5** creep, glide, prowl, sidle, slick, slide, slink, snake, sneak, steal **8** glissade, undulate

slithery
5 slick **6** greasy, slippy **8** slippery **10** lubricious

sliver
5 carve, shave, shred, slice **6** haggle **8** splinter

slob
4 boor, clod **6** sloven

slobber
4 gush **5** drool **6** drivel, slaver **7** dribble, slabber **8** salivate

sloe
4 plum **10** blackthorn

slog
3 hit **4** ding, grub, plod, slop, sock, toil **5** catch, clout, grind, slave, smite, whack **6** drudge, stodge, strike, trudge **8** plunther

slogan
4 word **5** idiom, motto **6** byword, phrase **8** locution **9** catchword, watchword **10** expression, shibboleth **11** catchphrase

sloop
4 boat, dray **8** longboat, sailboat

slop
3 mud, pap **4** bolt, cram, food, gulp, plod, slog, toil, wolf **5** douse, plash, slosh, spill, squab, swash **6** englut, gobble, guzzle, pablum, splash, splosh, stodge, trudge **7** rubbish, spatter, splurge, spurtle **8** footslog, plunther, splatter **11** ingurgitate

slope
3 tip **4** bend, cant, heel, lean, list, rise, skew, swag, sway, tilt **5** grade, pitch, scarp, slant **6** ascent, escarp, glacis **7** descent, incline, leaning, recline, versant **8** gradient **9** acclivity, declivity, deviation, obliquity **10** deflection **11** inclination, obliqueness
combining form: **5** cline **6** clinal

sloppy
4 poor, soft **5** drunk, gushy, messy **6** botchy, clumsy, unneat, untidy **7** awkward, gushing, muddled, unkempt **8** careless, effusive, ill-kempt, mediocre, slapdash, slipshod, slobbery, slovenly **9** disguised, pixilated **10** amateurish, disheveled, inebriated, slobbering, unthorough **11** intoxicated

slosh
3 bat, lap **4** bang, bash, belt, blow, bolt, cram, dash, gulp, gush, roar, rush, slam, slop, wash, wolf **5** churn, crack, douse, plash, pound, smack, swash, whirl **6** babble, bubble, burble, englut, gobble, gurgle, guzzle, ripple, splash, wallop **7** spatter, splurge, spurtle **8** splatter **9** bespatter **11** ingurgitate

slot
5 niche, notch, track, trail **6** groove, keyway **7** keyhole, opening, passage **10** pigeonhole

sloth
4 laze **6** acedia, apathy, idling, lazing, slouch **7** languor, loafing **8** idleness, laziness, lethargy **9** faineancy, heaviness, indolence, lassitude, torpidity **10** ergophobia **11** inattention, languidness **12** heedlessness, listlessness, slothfulness, sluggishness **13** shiftlessness
three-toed: **2** ai
two-toed: **4** unav

slothful
4 idle, lazy **5** drony **7** work-shy **8** fainéant, indolent **9** easygoing, slowgoing

slouch
3 bum, hat, lop, oaf, sag **4** bend, gawk, laze, lean, loaf, loll, lout, lump, slug, wilt **5** droop, idler, klutz, looby, sloth, slump, stoop **6** loafer, lounge, lubber **7** saunter, shamble, shuffle, trollop **8** dolittle, fainéant, idleness, laziness, meathead, slugabed, sluggard **9** do-nothing, indolence, lazybones **12** slothfulness, sluggishness

slough
3 arm, bay, bog, fen, mud **4** cast, cove, gulf, junk, mire, molt, shed, slip, sump **5** bayou, firth, inlet, marsh, scrap, swamp **6** harbor, morass, reject **7** cashier, discard **8** exuviate, jettison, quagmire, throw out **9** marshland, swampland, throw away

sloven
5 messy **6** sloppy, untidy **7** unkempt **8** careless, ill-kempt, slipshod, uncombed **10** disheveled

slow
3 low, off **4** down, dull, late, poky **5** brake, rusty, slack, tardy **6** leaden, retard, simple, steady, stupid **7** halting, laggard, lagging, limited, reduced, unhasty **8** backward, crawling, dawdling, delaying, dilatory, dragging, flagging, measured, plodding, retarded, sluggish, stagnant **9** dim-witted, leisurely, snaillike, unhasting, unhurried **10** deliberate, half-witted, snail-paced, straggling, unhurrying

slowpoke
5 snail **6** lagger **7** dawdler, laggard **8** lingerer, loiterer **9** slowcoach, straggler

sludge
3 mud **4** mire, muck, ooze, slob **5** slime **8** sediment

slue
3 dip 4 skew, turn, veer 5 sheer
6 swerve 8 train off

sluff
7 discard

slug
3 bum, hit, nip, tot 4 belt, dram,
drop, jolt, shot, slam 5 blast, idler,
larva, smash, snail, snort 6 loafer,
slouch, sloven, wallop 7 clobber,
slacker, snifter 8 dolittle, fainéant,
toothful 9 do-nothing, lazybones
genus: 5 Limax

sluggard
3 bum 5 idler 6 loafer, slouch
7 dawdler, laggard, lie-abed,
shirker 8 dolittle, fainéant, slowpoke, slugabed 9 do-nothing, goldbrick, lazybones, slow coach
10 sleepyhead

slugger
5 boxer 6 batter, hitter

sluggish
3 off 4 down, lazy, logy, slow
5 dopey, heavy, slack, stiff 6 bovine, draggy, leaden, stupid, torpid
7 costive, lumpish 8 comatose,
dragging, slothful 9 apathetic, lethargic, stupified 10 slumberous
12 hebetudinous

sluice
4 flow, gush, pour, roll, soak, wash
5 douse, flush, surge 6 drench,
stream

slum
4 dump 6 ghetto 7 skid row

slumber
4 coma, doze 5 sleep 6 drowse,
stupor, torpor 7 lanquor 8 dullness,
hebetude, lethargy 9 lassitude,
torpidity

slumberous
see **sleepy**

slump
3 dip, lop, sag 4 drop, fall, flag,
loll, slip 5 droop, pitch, slide
6 cave in, go down, plunge, slouch,
topple, tumble 7 decline, drop off,
falloff, trollop 8 collapse, downturn, fall away, keel over 9 downslide, downswing, downtrend, recession 10 depression, stagnation

slur
4 blot, blur, lisp, onus, slam, spot
5 brand, odium, smear, stain 6 befoul, defame, insult, malign, slight,
stigma 7 blacken, obloquy, traduce

8 black eye, tear down 9 aspersion, bespatter, denigrate, stricture
10 calumniate

slurp
4 suck 5 lap up, slosh, smack, swill
6 guzzle 8 wolf down

slush
3 mud 4 mire, muck, snow 5 grout
6 drivel

sly
4 deep, foxy, lurk, slim, wily 5 cagey, canny, creep, shady, skulk,
slick, slide, slink, smart, sneak, steal
6 adroit, artful, astute, clever, covert, crafty, shifty, smooth, sneaky,
subtle, tricky 7 crooked, cunning,
devious, furtive, gumshoe, slanter,
unfrank, vulpine 8 guileful, scheming, slippery, stealthy 9 designing,
dexterous, dishonest, ingenious,
insidious, masterful, predatory, sub-
dolous, underhand 11 calculating,
clandestine, underhanded 12 disingenuous, unscrupulous
13 Machiavellian

slyboots
see **scamp**

slyness
3 art 5 craft 7 cunning 8 artifice,
foxiness, wiliness 9 cageyness,
canniness 10 artfulness, craftiness

smack
3 bat, bop, box, lip 4 bash, belt,
biff, blip, blow, buss, chop, cuff,
dash, hint, kiss, lick, peck, reek,
slap, sock, tang 5 clout, crack,
punch, sapor, savor, smash, smell,
spank, stink, taste, tinge, trace 6 buffet, flavor, relish, smooch 7 soupçon, suggest 8 osculate, resemble,
sapidity, tincture 9 suspicion
10 sprinkling

small
3 off, set, wee 4 mean, mini, puny,
slim, tiny 5 borne, dinky, light, micro, minor, petty, short 6 bantam,
lesser, little, minute, monkey, narrow, paltry, petite, remote, slight
7 cramped, limited, outside, slender, trivial 8 picayune, piddling,
pint-size, trifling 9 miniature, minuscule, secondary, two-by-four
10 diminutive, negligible, picayunish, undersized 11 ineffectual,
minor-league, unimportant 12 inconsequent 13 insignificant
amount: see **particle**
combining form: 4 lept, micr, mini,
olig, parv 5 lepto, oligo, parvi,
parvo

small fry
4 kids 8 children

small-minded
4 mean 6 narrow 7 bigoted
9 hidebound, illiberal 10 brassbound, intolerant, unenlarged

smallness
abnormal: 6 nanism 8 dwarfism

small one
suffix: 2 el, et, ey, ia (plural), ie
3 cle, ium, kin, ock, ula, ule, uli
(plural) 4 ella, ette, illa, ling, ulae
(plural), ulum, ulus 5 ellae (plural),
illae (plural)

smallpox
7 variola

small talk
6 babblo, banter 7 chatter, prattle
8 babbling, badinage, chitchat,
repartee, trifling 9 bavardage,
prattling

smalt
4 blue 5 glass

smarmy
4 oily 5 sleek, slick, soapy
6 glassy, glossy, sleeky 7 fulsome
8 polished, unctious, unctuous
10 oleaginous

smart
3 hep 4 ache, bite, bold, burn,
chic, hurt, pain, pert, trig, wise
5 alert, canny, fresh, nervy, prick,
quick, sassy, saucy, sharp, slick,
sting, swank, swish 6 brainy,
bright, cheeky, clever, dapper,
modish, shrewd, spruce, suffer, tingle, with-it 7 dashing, knowing,
stylish 8 impudent 9 brilliant, exclusive, sprightly 11 fashionable, intelligent, quick-witted, ready-witted,
sharp-witted

smart aleck
7 show-off, wise guy 8 wiseacre
9 know-it-all 11 wisecracker, wisenheimer 12 grandstander
13 exhibitionist

smart-alecky
4 wise 5 fresh, nervy, sassy
6 cheeky 8 impudent 9 bold-faced
10 procacious

smarten
5 fix up, primp, slick, spiff 6 doll
up, spruce 7 deck out, doll out,
dress up, gussy up 8 spruce up

smart set
3 ton 5 elite 6 bon ton 7 aristoi,
society, who's who 10 blue bloods,

upper crust **11** aristocracy, Four
Hundred

smash
3 hit, jar, wow **4** bang, bash, belt,
blow, boom, bump, clap, jolt, raze,
rive, ruin, slam, slug, sock, wham,
whop **5** blast, burst, clash, crack,
crash, shock, whack, wreck **6** impact, pileup, shiver, wallop **7** clobber, crack-up, debacle, destroy,
shatter, smashup **8** collapse, decimate, demolish, destruct, fragment,
knockout, splinter, splitter, tear
down **9** bastinado, breakdown,
collision, sensation, succès fou
10 annihilate, bell ringer, percussion **11** splinterize

smashup
5 crash, wreck **6** pileup **7** crack-
up, debacle **8** collapse
9 breakdown

smattering
3 few **7** handful **10** sprinkling

smear
3 dab, rub, tar **4** beat, coat, daub,
drub, foil, lick, slur, soil, trim, whip
5 cover, smarm, stain, sully, taint
6 bedaub, befoul, defame, defile,
malign, smirch, smudge, spread,
thrash **7** asperse, blacken, overlay,
plaster, repulse, shellac, slander,
smother, tarnish **8** besmirch, discolor, lambaste **9** bespatter, denigrate, frustrate **10** calumniate,
overspread

smell
4 funk, hint, nose, odor, reek
5 aroma, scent, sense, smack, sniff,
snuff, stink, trace, whiff **6** detect,
stench **7** soupçon **8** tincture **9** fragrance, redolence, suspicion **10** intimation, suggestion
combining form: **3** osm **4** osma,
osmo

smell, sense of
9 olfaction, osphresis

smelly
4 olid, rank **5** fetid, funky, reeky
6 foetid, putrid, rancid, stinky
7 noisome, reeking, stenchy **8** stinking **10** malodorous

smelt
4 flux, slag **6** reduce, refine,
speise, speiss, tomcod **7** scorify
8 sparling **9** sand borer, sand
lance, whitebait, sand lance

smidgen
see **particle**

smile
4 beam, grin **6** simper

smirch
see **smudge**

smirk
4 grin, leer **5** fleer, sneer **6** simper

smitch
see **particle**

smite
3 bat, hit, try **4** belt, dash, ding,
slog, sock **5** catch, clout, whack
6 harrow, martyr, strike **7** afflict,
agonize, clobber, crucify, torment,
torture **10** excruciate

smithereens
6 pieces **9** fragments, particles

smitten
6 mashed, soft on **8** enamored,
spoony on **10** spoony over

smoke
4 cure, floc, fume **8** fumigate
9 cigarette

smoking material
3 pot **4** hash **5** cigar, joint **6** reefer
7 hashish, tobacco **9** cigarette, cig-
arillo, marihuana, marijuana

smolder
4 boil, stir **5** burst, churn, erupt
6 bubble, seethe, simmer **7** explode, ferment **9** fulminate

smooch
3 lip **4** buss, foul, kiss, peck, soil
5 dirty, grime, smack **6** besoil,
smirch, smudge, smutch **7** begrime,
tarnish **8** osculate

smooth
3 lay **4** bald, easy, even, fair, flat,
mild, soft **5** balmy, bland, faint,
flush, level, light, plane, preen,
round, royal, sleek, slick, suave
6 evenly, facile, flatly, fluent, gentle, glossy, polish, polite, refine,
simple, sleeky, trowel, urbane, ve-
lure **7** courtly, cursive, flatten, flowing, jagless, lenient, perfect, planate, running **8** glabrate, glabrous,
hairless, soothing, unbroken, wave-
less **9** agreeable, civilized, courteous, uniformly **10** effortless, ripple-
less, unwrinkled
combining form: **3** lio **4** leio, liss
5 lisso

smoothen
3 lay **4** even **5** flush, level, plane
7 flatten

smooth-spoken
5 vocal **6** fluent **8** eloquent **10** articulate

smorgasbord
4 hash **6** jumble, medley **7** mélange **8** mishmash, pastiche **9** potpourri **10** hodgepodge, miscellany
11 gallimaufry

smother
4 beat, cool, cork, drub, lick, rein,
trim, whip **5** choke, quash, quell,
smear **6** hush up, muffle, quench,
stifle, thrash **7** clobber, collect,
compose, control, quackle, repress,
shellac, squelch **8** lambaste, restrain, suppress **9** suffocate
10 asphyxiate

smudge
3 dab **4** daub, foul, soil **5** dirty,
grime, smear, stain, sully, taint
6 bedaub, besoil, blotch, defile,
smirch **7** begrime, besmear, plaster, splotch, tarnish **8** besmirch

smug
4 tidy **5** slick **6** spruce **8** priggish
10 complacent **11** self-pleased
13 self-contented, self-satisfied

smuggle
3 run **7** bootleg **10** contraband

smut
4 blot, soil **5** dirty, smear, stain,
taint **6** defile **7** bestain **8** besmirch,
discolor

smutty
4 foul **5** dirty, nasty **6** coarse,
filthy, vulgar **7** obscene, raunchy
8 indecent **12** scatological

Smyrna
5 Izmir

snack
3 tea **4** bite, nosh, tapa **5** mug-up
6 morsel **9** collation **11** refreshment

snaffle
3 bit

snag
3 bar, rub **4** clog, curb, drag
5 brake, crimp **6** hamper, hold-up,
hurdle **8** obstacle, traverse **10** impediment **11** obstruction

snail
8 escargot, ramshorn, slowpoke
9 band shell

snake
3 boa, cur, dog **4** scum, snot, toad
5 crawl, creep, prick, skunk, slide
6 python **7** serpent, slither **8** anaconda, ophidian, undulate
combining form: **4** ophi **5** ophio,
ophis
poisonous: **3** asp **4** habu **5** adder,
cobra, coral, krait, mamba, viper

6 elapid, taipan 7 rattler 8 cerastes, pit viper, ringhals 10 bushmaster, copperhead, fer-de-lance 11 cottonmouth 13 water moccasin
South African: 5 aboma

snakebird
6 darter 7 anhinga

snake crane
7 cariama

snake-eater
7 markhor 8 mongoose 13 secretary bird

snakelike
7 anguine 8 ophidian

snakeroot
7 bugbane 10 wild ginger 11 blazing star

snakeweed
7 bistort 13 poison hemlock

snakewood
9 nux vomica 10 frangipani

snaky
7 sinuous, winding 8 flexuous, tortuous 9 meandrous 10 convoluted, meandering, serpentine 11 anfractuous

snap
3 bit, jot, lug, pep, pie 4 bang, bark, dram, drop, hoot, iota, jerk, push, yank 5 cinch, drive, getup, grain, lurch, punch, setup, vigor 6 breeze, picnic, starch, twitch 7 crackle, modicum 8 duck soup, fragment, kid stuff, particle, pushover, sinecure, vitality 9 soft touch, vellicate 10 child's play

snap back
7 rebound, recover

snape
5 taper

snappy
4 fast, racy, tony, trig 5 fleet, hasty, huffy, quick, rapid, raspy, ready, sharp, smart, spicy, swank, swift, swish, zesty 6 lively, prompt, speedy, twitty 7 dashing, peppery, piquant, pungent, raspish, stylish 8 animated, petulant, poignant, prickish 9 breakneck, fractious, irritable, vivacious 10 harefooted 11 expeditious

snare
4 bait, lure, trap 5 catch, decoy, tempt 6 come-on, enmesh, entrap, seduce, tangle 7 catch up, chicane, ensnarl, involve, springe, trammel 8 entangle 9 chicanery, deception, embrangle 10 allurement, enticement, entrapment, seducement, temptation 12 inveiglement

snarl
3 jam, web 4 bark, gnar, knot, maze, mesh, muck 5 chaos, gnarr, ravel, skein, swarm 6 ataxia, huddle, jungle, morass, muddle, tangle 7 clutter, mizmaze, perplex 8 disarray, disorder, entangle, mishmash 9 confusion, intricacy, labyrinth 10 complexity, complicate 11 intertangle 12 complication, entanglement 13 intricateness

snatch
3 nab 4 grab, jerk, nail, take, yank 5 catch, cotch, nip up, seize 6 clutch, whip up, wrench 7 grapple

sneak
3 cur, sly 4 heel, lurk, slip, toad, worm 5 crawl, creep, glide, knave, louse, prowl, shirk, skulk, skunk, slide, slink, steal 6 covert, secret, tiptoe, weasel 7 furtive, gumshoe, hangdog, reptile, slither, smuggle, sub-rosa 8 hush-hush, slyboots, stealthy 9 pussyfoot, scoundrel 10 blackguard, undercover 11 clandestine

sneaky
6 shifty 7 devious 8 guileful, indirect 9 underhand 11 duplicitous, underhanded

sneer
4 gibe, gird, grin, jest, pish 5 fleer, flout, scoff, smile, smirk 6 quip at 7 detract, scout at 8 belittle 9 disparage, underrate

snicker
5 laugh, tehee 6 giggle, guffaw, hee-haw, titter 7 chortle, chuckle

snide
4 fake, sham 5 bogus, false, phony 6 pseudo 7 corrupt, crooked 8 spurious 9 brummagem, dishonest, pinchbeck 11 counterfeit

sniff
4 nose 5 scent, smell

snifter
3 nip, tot 4 dram, drop, jolt, shot, slug 5 snort 8 toothful

snippety
see **snippy**

snippy
4 curt 5 bluff, blunt, brief, gruff, short 6 abrupt, crusty 7 brusque

snit
3 fit 4 flap, fume, huff, stew 5 panic, pique, sweat, tizzy 6 dither, frenzy, swivet, taking 7 seizure 10 conniption

snitch
3 cop, nip, rat 4 beak, hook, lift, tell 5 filch, peach, pinch, steal, swipe 6 inform, squeal, tattle 7 purloin, tattler, tipster 8 betrayer, informer, squealer 11 stool pigeon

snob
5 toady 6 poseur 7 high-hat, parvenu, sneerer, tinhorn, upstart 8 popinjay 9 sycophant

snobbish
5 aloof, potty, ritzy 6 remote, snooty, snotty, uppish, uppity 7 haughty, high-hat, pompous 9 high-flown 10 hoity-toity 11 patronizing, pretentious 12 supercilious 13 condescending

snook
5 cobia 6 robalo 12 sergeant fish

snoop
3 pry, spy 4 mess, nose, peek, peep, peer, poke 5 mouse, prier, pryer, stare 6 butt-in, meddle 7 intrude, meddler, Paul Pry 8 busybody, quidnunc 9 detective, inspector, interfere 10 rubberneck

snooper
3 spy 7 meddler 9 detective, inspector 12 investigator

snoopy
4 nosy 5 peery 6 prying 7 curious 11 inquisitive, inquisitory 13 inquisitorial

snoot
see **snout**

snooty
see **snobbish**

snooze
3 nap 5 dover 6 catnap, dog nap, siesta 10 forty winks

snore
8 rhonchus

snort
3 nip, tot 4 dram, drop, jolt, shot, slug 7 snifter 8 toothful

snot
3 cur, dog, pig, rat, sod 4 puke, scum, toad 5 knave, louse, rogue, skunk, snake 6 wretch 7 high-hat, lowlife, reptile, stinker, villain 8 stinkard 9 scoundrel, stinkaroo

snout
4 beak, nose 6 pecker 7 smeller
combining form: 6 rhynch 7 rhyncho 8 rhynchus

snow
combining form: 4 chio 5 chion 6 chiono
glacial: 4 firn, névé
melted: 5 slush
pellet: 7 graupel
ridge: 8 sastruga, zastruga

snow apple
8 mushroom

snowball
3 wax 4 rise 5 build, mount, run up 6 expand 7 augment, upsurge 8 increase, multiply

snowberry
6 blolly

snowbird
9 fieldfare, ivory gull

Snow-Bound author
8 Whittier (John Greenleaf)

snow eater
7 chinook

snow finch
9 brambling

snow goose
4 wavy 5 wavey

snow grouse
9 ptarmigan

snowlike
7 niveous

snowstorm
8 blizzard

snub
3 cut 5 spite, swank 6 slight 7 high-hat, put down 9 ostracize 12 cold-shoulder

snuff
4 kill, nose, odor 5 aroma, pinch, scent, smell, sniff 6 rappee 8 maccaboy

snug
4 cosy, cozy, easy, neat, soft, tidy, trig, trim 5 comfy, cushy 6 burrow, cuddle, nestle, nuzzle 7 chipper, croodle, easeful, orderly 9 shipshape 11 comfortable

snuggle
5 spoon 6 burrow, cuddle, curl up, huddle, nestle, nuzzle

so
3 sae 4 also, ergo, much, then, thus, very 5 hence 6 thusly 7 awfully, parlous 8 likewise 9 extremely, similarly, therefore, thereupon 11 accordingly, exceedingly 12 consequently

soak
3 wet 4 clip, lush, skin, swig 5 douse, drink, imbue, souse, steep 6 boozer, drench, fleece, infuse, seethe 7 guzzler, immerse, insteep, overwet 8 bedrench, drunkard, permeate, saturate, submerge 9 penetrate 10 impregnate, overcharge
flax: 3 ret

soap
4 suds 7 flatter
hard: 7 castile
ingredient: 3 lye

soapbox
4 rant, rave 5 mouth, orate 7 declaim 8 bloviate, harangue, perorate

soaproot
8 sand lily

soapstone
8 steatite

soapwood
8 wild pear

soapwort
7 cowherd 11 bouncing Bet

soar
2 up 3 fly 4 lift, rise 5 arise, climb, mount, shoot 6 ascend, aspire, rocket, uprear 7 shoot up 9 skyrocket

sob
3 cry 4 blub, wail, weep 6 boohoo 7 blubber

sober
4 calm, cool, hard, soft 5 grave, staid 6 low-key, placid, proper, sedate, serene, solemn 7 earnest, serious, subdued, weighty 8 composed, decorous, forgoing, low-keyed, moderate, rational, reserved, softened, tranquil 9 abstinent, collected, continent, eschewing, inhibited, practical, pragmatic, realistic, temperate, toned down 10 abnegating, abstaining, abstemious, controlled, forbearing, hardboiled, hardheaded, no-nonsense, reasonable, refraining, restrained 11 abstentious, constrained, disciplined, down-to-earth 12 matter-of-fact, unidealistic 13 imperturbable, self-possessed, unimpassioned

sobriety
7 gravity 9 soberness 10 abstinence, continence, sedateness, temperance 11 seriousness

sobriquet
6 byname, byword 8 nickname 10 hypocorism

so-called
6 formal 7 alleged, nominal, titular 8 supposed 9 pretended, professed, purported 10 ostensible

soccer
cup: 5 World
official: 7 referee 8 linesman
player: 6 booter, goalie, kicker, winger 7 forward, link man, striker, sweeper 8 defender, fullback, halfback 10 goalkeeper
player of renown: 4 Pele
term: 3 net 4 boot, chip, kick, trap 6 corner, header, tackle, volley 7 dribble, kickoff, throw-in 8 backheel, free kick, goal kick, goal line 9 touchline 10 center spot, corner flag, corner kick 11 dropped ball, halfway line, penalty kick, penalty spot

sociable
5 close 6 genial 7 cordial 8 familiar, gracious, intimate 9 congenial, convivial 10 gregarious 11 goodnatured

social
6 genial 7 amusing, cordial 8 friendly, gracious, pleasant 9 convivial 10 gregarious, hospitable 11 pleasurable 12 entertaining 13 companionable
class: 5 caste

Social Contract author
8 Rousseau (Jean-Jacques)

socialist
American: 4 Debs (Eugene) 6 Ripley (George), Thomas (Norman)
English: 4 Webb (Sidney) 6 Morris (William)
French: 7 Viviani (René)
German: 4 Marx (Karl) 6 Engels (Friedrich) 9 Luxemburg (Rosa) 10 Liebknecht (Wilhelm)

socialize
3 mix 5 party 6 mingle 9 associate

social worker
4 Riis (Jacob), Wald (Lillian D.) 6 Addams (Jane) 7 Alinsky (Saul D.), Lathrop (Julia C.)

society
4 club 5 elite, guild, order, union 6 flower, gentry, league, masses, people, public 7 aristoi, company, quality, who's who 8 populace, sodality 9 community 10 fellowship, fraternity, patriciate, upper class,

upper crust 11 aristocracy, association, brotherhood 13 companionship
girl: 3 deb 9 debutante
high: 9 beau monde, haut monde

Society Islands
capital: 7 Papeete
discoverer: 7 Queirós (Pedro Fernandes de)

sociologist
American: 4 Ward (Lester Frank) 5 Balch (Emily Green), Whyte (William H.) 6 Du Bois (William Edward Burghardt), Sumner (William Graham) 7 Johnson (Charles Spurgeon), Riesman (David)
English: 7 Spencer (Herbert)
French: 8 Durkheim (Emile)
German: 5 Weber (Max)
Italian: 6 Pareto (Vilfredo)
Swedish: 6 Myrdal (Alva, Gunnar)

sock
3 bop, box, hit 4 bash, belt, blow, chop, cuff, ding, slap, slog 5 clout, punch, smack, smash, whack 6 argyle, buffet, strike, thwack 8 stocking

socks
4 hose 7 hosiery

Socrates
birthplace: 6 Athens
poison: 7 hemlock
pupil: 5 Plato
wife: 8 Xantippe

sodality
4 club 5 guild, order, union 6 league 7 society 10 fellowship, fraternity 11 association, brotherhood

sodden
3 wet 4 soak 5 soppy, souse, steep 6 drench, seethe, soaked, soused 7 soaking, sopping 8 drenched, dripping, saturate, waterlog 9 saturated 11 wringing-wet

Sodi's son
7 Gaddiel

sodium
7 natrium
symbol: 2 Na

Sodom and ____
8 Gomorrah

sofa
5 couch, divan 7 ottoman 9 banquette

Sofia native
6 Bulgar 9 Bulgarian

soft
4 cozy, easy, mild, snug 5 balmy, bland, comfy, cushy, downy, faint, mushy, pappy, pulpy, silky, silly, sleek, sober, wooly 6 doughy, flabby, fleshy, gentle, low-key, pliant, quaggy, satiny, silken, simple, smooth, spongy, spoony, tender, woolly 7 cottony, easeful, fatuous, foolish, lenient, pillowy, pliable, pulpous, squashy, squishy, subdued, velvety, witless 8 cushiony, formless, low-keyed, moderate, squelchy, woollike, workable, yielding 9 malleable, temperate, toned down 10 weak-headed, weak-minded 11 comfortable 12 compressible

soft-cover
9 paperback

soft hail
7 graupel

softhearted
4 warm 6 tender 10 responsive 11 sympathetic 13 compassionate

soft palate
5 velum

soft-pedal
6 dampen, hush up, muffle, subdue 7 conceal, cushion, silence 8 disguise, play down, suppress, tone down, tune down 11 de-emphasize

soft-soap
3 con 4 coax 6 cajole 7 blarney, flatter, wheedle 8 blandish 9 sweet-talk

Sohrab and Rustum author
6 Arnold (Matthew)

soil
3 mud, tar 4 daub, dirt, foul, home, land, loam, mess, muck, murk 5 crock, dirty, earth, glebe, grime, muddy, smear, stain, sully, taint 6 bedaub, defile, ground, smirch, smooch, smudge, smutch 7 begrime, besmear, country, drabble, draggle, dry land, pedocal, pollute, regosol, tarnish 8 bedabble, besmirch, discolor, homeland, laterite, lithosol, pedalfer, planosol, rendzina, sierozem, solonets, solonetz 10 fatherland, motherland, terra firma 11 contaminate
aggregate: 3 ped
clay: 5 gault
combining form: 2 ge 3 geo, ped 4 agro, pedo
dark: 9 chernozem
deposit: 5 loess 7 eluvium
infertile: 6 podsol, podzol

layer: 4 gley, sola (plural) 5 solum
prairie: 8 brunizem
rich: 6 hotbed
soft: 4 mool
tropical: 7 latosol

sojourn
4 stay, stop 5 abide, tarry, visit 6 linger 7 layover 8 stopover 9 tarriance

Sol
3 sun 7 daystar, phoebus
horse: 4 Eous 5 Ethon 9 Erythreos; (see also **Helios**)

solace
5 cheer 6 buck up 7 comfort, console, upraise

solar disk
4 Aten

solarium
7 sunroom

solder
4 weld 5 braze

soldier
2 GI 4 swad 5 perdu 6 perdue 7 dogface, fighter, pandoor, pandour, pikeman, private, trooper, warrior 8 doughboy, fusileer, fusilier, partisan, rifleman 9 free lance, guerrilla, man-at-arms, mercenary 10 carabineer, serviceman 11 condottiere, fighting man, infantryman
ancient Greece: 7 hoplite, peltast
British: 5 Tommy 7 redcoat
cavalry: 6 hussar 8 chasseur
Celtic: 4 kern 5 kerne
Confederate: 3 reb
French: 5 poilu 6 Zouave
German: 5 jerry
Greek: 6 evzone 7 palikar
India: 5 jawan, sowar 7 jemadar, jemidar
irregular: 8 guerilla 9 guerrilla
Prussian: 4 ulan 5 uhlan
Turkish: 8 janizary 9 janissary

sole
3 one 4 lone, only 5 alone, unwed 6 bottom, single, unique 8 separate, singular, unshared 9 exclusive

solecism
5 boner, break, gaffe 7 blooper, faux pas 8 slangism 9 indecorum, vulgarism 11 impropriety

solemn
4 full 5 grand, grave, sober, staid 6 august, formal, sedate, somber 7 earnest, plenary, serious, stately, weighty 8 majestic 10 ceremonial, impressive, no-nonsense, sobersided 11 ceremonious, magnificent

solemnize
4 keep 5 honor 7 dignify, observe
8 venerate 9 celebrate
11 commemorate

solicit
3 ask, beg 4 call, drum, tout, turn
5 apply, claim, exact, refer 6 demand, desire, drum up, resort 7 beseech, bespeak, canvass, implore, request, require 9 challenge, postulate 11 requisition

solicitous
4 avid, keen 5 eager 6 ardent, raring 7 anxious, athirst, thirsty
8 appetent 9 impatient

solicitude
4 care, heed 5 qualm, worry 6 regard, unease 7 anxiety, concern, scruple 8 disquiet 9 attention
10 uneasiness 11 compunction, concernment 12 presentiment, watchfulness 13 consideration

solid
4 firm, hard 5 sound 6 cogent, firmly, hardly, secure, square, stable 7 telling 9 compacted, unanimous 10 convincing

solidarity
5 union, unity 6 esprit, fixity 7 oneness 8 cohesion, firmness 9 integrity 10 singleness 12 cohesiveness, togetherness 13 esprit de corps, undividedness

solidify
3 dry, set 4 cake 6 harden 7 congeal 8 compress, concrete, contract, indurate

solitary
3 one 4 lone, lorn, only 5 alone, aloof 6 hermit, lonely, offish, single, unique 7 distant, recluse, uncouth 8 derelict, deserted, desolate, eremitic, forsaken, lonesome, reserved, separate, singular 9 abandoned, reclusive, withdrawn 10 antisocial, insociable, particular, unattended, unexampled, unsociable
11 standoffish 12 misanthropic, unrepeatable 13 companionless, unaccompanied

solitude
8 loneness 9 aloneness, isolation, seclusion 10 detachment, loneliness, quarantine, retirement, withdrawal 11 confinement 12 lonesomeness, separateness

solo
4 lone 5 alone

Solomon
brother: 8 Adonijah
daughter: 7 Taphath 8 Basemath
father: 5 David
kingdom: 6 Israel
mother: 9 Bathsheba
son, successor: 8 Rehoboam
victim: 4 Joab 8 Adonijah

Solomon Islands' capital
7 Honiara

solution
6 answer, result
salt: 6 saline

solve
3 fix 4 work 5 break 6 decide, settle, unfold 7 clear up, dope out, explain, unravel, work out 8 construe, decipher, unpuzzle, unriddle 9 determine, elucidate, enlighten, figure out, interpret, puzzle out

Somalia
capital: 9 Mogadishu
monetary unit: 8 shilling

somatic
6 bodily, carnal 7 fleshly 8 corporal, physical 9 corporeal

somber
3 dim 4 dark, dusk 5 black, bleak, dusky, grave, murky, staid 6 dismal, dreary, gloomy, sedate, solemn 7 earnest, obscure, serious, weighty 8 funereal 9 lightless, tenebrous 10 caliginous, depressing, depressive, no-nonsense, sobersided, tenebrific 11 dispiriting

sommelier's offering
4 wine

somniferous
see sleepy

somnolent
see sleepy

Somnus
brother: 4 Mors
god of: 5 sleep
mother: 3 Nox

song
3 air, cry, lay 4 aria, call, glee, hymn, lied, note 5 ditty, lyric, paean, piece, poesy, rhyme, verse 6 ballad, melody, poetry 7 calypso, chanson, descant 8 alleluia, cavatina
biblical: 8 canticle
boat: 9 barcarole 10 barcarolle
combining form: 4 melo
French: 7 chanson
funeral: 5 dirge
German: 4 lied 6 lieder (plural)
lamentation: 8 threnode, threnody

medieval: 8 sirvente
morning: 6 aubade
of joy: 5 paean
operatic: 4 aria 8 cavatina
9 cabaletta
Portuguese: 4 fado
sacred: 5 psalm
sailor's: 6 chanty 7 chantey, shantey
short: 8 canzonet
wedding: 8 hymeneal

song and dance
5 pitch, spiel

songbird
see at bird

Song of Myself author
7 Whitman (Walt)

Song of Solomon
9 Canticles

songwriter
8 composer, lyricist

Sonja ____
5 Henie

Sonnambula composer
7 Bellini (Vincenzo)

sonnet
developer: 8 Petrarch
part: 5 octet 6 octave, sestet

Son of the Middle Border author
7 Garland (Hamlin)

sonorous
5 noisy, round 6 rotund 7 aureate, flowery, orotund, rackety, ringing, vibrant 8 clattery, noiseful, plangent, resonant, voiceful 9 bombastic, consonant, overblown 10 euphuistic, oratorical, resounding, rhetorical, uproarious 11 declamatory 12 magniloquent
13 grandiloquent

soon
6 any day

Sooner State
8 Oklahoma

soothe
3 pat 4 balm, calm, hush, lull 5 allay, salve, still 6 becalm, pacify, settle, subdue 7 comfort, compose, console, massage, mollify, placate
11 tranquilize

soothsay
5 augur 7 portend, predict, presage 8 forecast, foretell, prophesy 9 abumbrate 13 prognosticate

soothsayer
5 augur 6 auspex 7 prophet

8 foreseer, haruspex 9 predictor
10 forecaster, foreteller, prophesier
ancient Roman: 6 auspex
8 haruspex
blind: 8 Tiresias; (see also **prophet**)

sop

3 buy, fix, wet 4 have, soak
5 bribe, douse, drown, sissy, souse,
steep 6 buy off, deluge, drench,
seethe, sodden, square 7 doormat,
douceur 8 gratuity, saturate, waterlog, weakling 10 namby-pamby,
pantywaist, tamper with 11 Milquetoast, mollycoddle

Sopater's father

7 Pyrrhus

sophic

4 sage, wise 7 gnostic, knowing
9 insighted, sagacious 10 discerning, insightful, perceptive
13 knowledgeable

sophism

see **sophistry**

sophisticate

6 debase 10 adulterate
11 disillusion

sophisticated

5 adult, blasé, bored, couth, jaded,
salty, suave 6 daedal, knotty, mature, smooth, svelte, urbane 7 complex, cynical, gordian, knowing,
worldly 8 involved, mondaine,
schooled, seasoned, well-bred
9 Byzantine, elaborate, intricate,
practiced, skeptical, world-wise
10 world-weary 11 experienced,
worldly wise 12 cosmopolitan, disenchanted, disentranced, labyrinthine 13 disillusioned

sophistry

7 fallacy 8 delusion 9 ambiguity,
casuistry, deception 12 equivocation, speciousness, spuriousness
13 deceptiveness

Sophocles play

4 Ajax 7 Electra 8 Antigone
10 Oedipus Rex

Sophonisba

brother: 8 Hannibal
father: 9 Hasdrubal
husband: 6 Syphax

soporiferous

6 opiate 8 hypnotic, narcotic, somnific 9 somnolent 10 somnorific
12 somnifacient

soporific

4 dozy 6 drowsy, opiate, sleepy,
snoozy 7 calming, nodding, numbing 8 hypnotic, narcotic, sedative,

slumbery 9 deadening, somnolent
10 anesthetic, quietening, slumberous 11 somniferous 12 somnifacient 13 tranquilizing

soprano

American: 4 Pons (Lily) 5 Costa
(Mary), Gluck (Alma), Moffo
(Anna), Moore (Grace), Price (Leon-
tyne), Sills (Beverly) 6 Arroyo (Mar-
tina), Battle (Kathleen), Callas (Ma-
ria), Curtin (Phyllis), Donath (Helen),
Farrar (Geraldine), Garden (Mary),
Munsel (Patrice), Norman (Jessye),
Peters (Roberta), Piazza (Margue-
rite), Resnik (Regina) 7 Farrell (Ei-
leen), Kirsten (Dorothy), Stevens
(Rise), Traubel (Helen) 8 Ponselle
(Rosa)
Australian: 5 Melba (Nellie) 10 Suth-
erland (Joan)
Austrian: 7 Rysanek (Leonie) 8 Sem-
brich (Marcella)
Canadian: 7 Stratas (Teresa)
French: 7 Crespin (Regine)
German: 6 Leider (Frida) 7 Lehmann
(Lilli, Lotte) 11 Schwarzkopf
(Elisabeth)
Italian: 5 Freni (Mirella), Grisi (Giu-
ditta, Giulia), Patti (Adelina)
6 Scotto (Renata) 7 Tebaldi (Re-
nata) 10 Tetrazzini (Luisa)
11 Ricciarelli (Katia)
Mexican: 8 Cruz-Romo (Gilda)
Norwegian: 8 Flagstad (Kirsten)
Romanian: 8 Cotrubas (Ileana)
Spanish: 7 Caballe (Montserrat)
8 Berganza (Teresa) 12 de los An-
geles (Victoria)
Swedish: 4 Lind (Jenny) 7 Nilsson
(Birgit); (see also **mezzo-soprano**)

sorcerer

4 mage 5 magus 6 wizard
7 charmer, warlock 8 conjurer,
conjuror, magician 9 enchanter,
voodooist 11 necromancer

sorceress

3 hag, hex 5 bruja, Circe, lamia,
witch 10 witchwoman

sorcery

5 magic 8 diablery, witchery,
witching, wizardry 9 conjuring
10 necromancy, witchcraft 11 bewitchment, enchantment, incantation, thaumaturgy
African: 3 obe, obi 4 obia 5 obeah

sordid

3 low 4 base, foul, mean, vile
5 black, dirty, dowdy, nasty, seamy
6 blowsy, filthy, frowsy, grubby, impure, scurvy, sodden 7 ignoble,
low-down, servile, squalid, unclean

8 slattern, wretched 9 uncleanly
10 despicable, slatternly

sore

5 angry, vexed 6 aching, bitter
7 algetic, chancre, hurtful, hurting,
painful 9 rancorous, resentful
10 afflictive

sorehead

4 crab 6 griper, grouch 7 grouser,
growler 8 grumbler, sourpuss
10 complainer, malcontent

sorrel

4 dock 7 roselle

sorrow

3 rue, sob, woe 4 care, moan
5 agony, dolor, grief, groan, mourn
6 grieve, misery, regret 7 anguish,
remorse, sadness 8 distress, grieving, mourning 9 dejection, heartache, suffering 10 affliction, depression, heartbreak, melancholy
11 lamentation, unhappiness
12 mournfulness, wretchedness

sorrowful

6 dolent, rueful, tragic, triste, woeful
7 doleful, ruthful 8 dolesome, dolorous, mournful, tragical, tristful,
wretched 9 afflicted, miserable,
plaintive 10 lamentable, lugubrious, melancholy

sorry

3 bad, sad 4 mean, poor 5 cheap
6 cheesy, paltry, scummy, scurvy,
shabby, shoddy 7 scruffy, unhappy
8 beggarly, contrite, mournful, penitent, pitiable, saddened, trifling,
wretched 9 miserable, regretful, repentant 10 apologetic, despicable,
despisable, inadequate, melancholy, remorseful 11 attritional, disgraceful, penitential 12 compunctious, contemptible, heavyhearted

sort

3 ilk, lot, set 4 body, comb, cull,
kind, pick, sift, type 5 array, batch,
class, group, order, suite 6 choose,
clutch, parcel, riddle, screen, select,
stripe, winnow 7 battery, catalog,
species, unravel, variety 8 classify,
separate 9 catalogue, character
10 categorize, pigeonhole

sortie

5 sally

sortilege

7 sorcery 8 witchery 10 divination

so-so

4 fair 6 enough, fairly, medium,
rather, subpar 7 average, fairish
8 mediocre, middling, moderate,

passable, passably, somewhat
9 averagely, tolerably **10** moderately **11** indifferent **12** run-of-the-
mill

sot

4 lush **5** drunk **6** bibber, boozer
7 guzzler, tippler **8** drunkard **9** inebriate **10** boozehound

sotto voce

3 low **5** aside **6** softly, weakly
7 faintly, mutedly, quietly **9** muffledly, privately **11** mutteringly

souchong

3 tea

sough

4 sigh **7** suspire

soul

4 life, pith **5** anima, being, bosom,
heart, human, stuff, wight **6** animus, bottom, breast, marrow, mortal, person, pneuma, psyche, spirit
7 essence **8** creature, noumenon,
vitality **9** élan vital, personage, substance **10** conscience, individual,
virtuality, vital force **11** personality
12 essentiality, quintessence
combining form: **4** thym **5** psych,
thymo **6** psycho

soul singer

5 Baker (Anita), Brown (James),
Flack (Roberta) **6** Sledge (Percy)
7 Charles (Ray), Pickett (Wilson),
Redding (Otis) **8** Franklin (Aretha)

sound

3 fit **4** firm, hale, look, ping, sane,
seem, well **5** audio, exact, music,
noise, plumb, probe, right, sober,
solid, valid, whole **6** appear, cogent, fathom, intact, secure, stable,
unhurt **7** correct, declare, earshot,
feel out, healthy, hearing, logical,
perfect, precise, publish, sonance,
sonancy, telling **8** accepted, accurate, announce, flawless, orthodox,
proclaim, rational, received, sensible, unbroken, unmarred **9** advertise, broadcast, canonical, errorless, faultless, resonance,
undamaged, uninjured, vibration,
wholesome **10** annunciate, consequent, convincing, impeccable,
promulgate, reasonable, sanctioned, satisfying, unimpaired
11 disseminate, intelligent, rightminded, sober-minded, unblemished, well-founded **12** satisfactory,
well-grounded **13** authoritative,
reverberation
combining form: **3** son **4** phon, soni,
sono **5** audio, audit, phone, phony
6 audito, phonia

high-pitched: **4** ping, ting
of a horn: **7** tantara
of disapproval: **7** catcall
pleasant: **7** euphony
quality: **6** timbre
repeating: **7** ratatat **8** rataplan
resounding: **8** resonant
ringing in ears: **8** tinnitus
rustling: **8** froufrou
science: **6** sonics **7** phonics
throaty: **8** guttural

Sound

Alaska: **5** Cross
Antarctica: **7** McMurdo
Australia: **4** King **5** Broad
Bahamas: **5** Exuma
Canada: **4** Howe **6** Nansen
Connecticut-New York: **10** Long Island
English Channel: **8** Plymouth
Georgia: **8** Altamaha
Greenland: **5** Smith
Gulf of Mexico: **8** Suwannee
11 Mississippi
Massachusetts: **8** Vineyard
9 Nantucket
New England: **11** Block Island
North Carolina: **4** Core **5** Bogue
7 Pamlico, Roanoke **9** Albemarle,
Currituck
Northwest Territories: **4** Peel **8** Melville **9** Lancaster **12** Prince Albert
Norwegian Sea: **8** Scoresby
Ontario: **4** Owen
Scotland: **3** Hoy **4** Jura, Mull **5** Inner
Spitsbergen: **4** Bell
Washington: **5** Puget

Sound and the Fury, The

author: **8** Faulkner (William)
character: **5** Benjy, Caddy, Jason
7 Quentin
family: **7** Compson

soundness

3 wit **4** mind **6** health, reason, sanity, senses **8** lucidity, security,
strength **9** stability

sound off

7 speak up **8** speak out

soup

beet: **6** borsch **7** borscht
bowl: **6** tureen
clear: **5** broth **8** bouillon, consommé, julienne
cold: **8** gazpacho **11** vichyssoise
curry: **12** mulligatawny
okra: **5** gumbo
seafood: **7** chowder
thick: **5** gumbo, puree **6** bisque,
burgoo
vegetable: **10** minestrone

soupçon

see **particle**

soupy

5 mushy, sobby **6** drippy, slushy,
sticky **7** maudlin, mawkish **11** sentimental, tear-jerking

sour

3 bad, dry **4** acid, keen, tart
5 acerb, acrid, sharp, tangy
6 acidic, bitter, rotten, turned **7** acerbic, acetose, unhappy **8** acescent, vinegary **9** acidulous,
fermented

source

4 dawn, rise, root, well **5** cause,
fount, onset, start **6** mother, origin,
parent, rising, spring, whence
7 dawning, opening, rootage
8 fountain, starting, wellhead **9** beginning, inception, paternity, rootstock **10** antecedent, authorship,
birthplace, derivation, provenance,
wellspring **11** determinant, origination, provenience **12** fountainhead

sourness

7 acidity **8** acerbity **10** discontent

sourpuss

4 crab **5** crank **6** griper, grouch,
kicker **7** grouser, killjoy **8** sorehead **10** complainer

south

combining form: **3** not **4** noto **5** austr
6 austro
French: **3** sud

South Africa

capital: **8** Cape Town, Pretoria
12 Bloemfontein
colonizer: **9** Pretorius (Andries,
Marthinus)
enclave: **7** Lesotho
grassland: **4** veld
largest city: **12** Johannesburg
monetary unit: **4** rand
settlers: **5** Boers

South America

country: **4** Peru **5** Chile **6** Brazil,
Guyana **7** Bolivia, Ecuador, Surinam, Uruguay **8** Colombia, Paraguay, Suriname **9** Argentina,
Venezuela
ethnic group: **5** Negro **6** Aymara,
Creole, Indian **7** Mestizo, Mulatto,
Quechua, Spanish **10** Amerindian,
Portuguese
language: **6** Aymara **7** Guarani,
Quechua, Spanish **10** Portuguese

South Carolina

capital: **8** Columbia
college, university: **5** Coker **6** Furman
7 Clemson

nickname: **13** Palmetto State
state flower: **13** yellow jasmine

South Dakota
capital: **6** Pierre
largest town: **10** Sioux Falls
nickname: **11** Coyote State **13** Sunshine State

southerly
7 austral

South Korea
capital: **5** Seoul
monetary unit: **3** won

South-West Africa
7 Namibia
capital: **8** Windhoek

south wind
see at wind

souvenir
5 relic, token **6** trophy **7** memento **8** keepsake, memorial, reminder **11** remembrance **12** remembrancer

sovereign
4 fine, free **5** regal, royal **6** kingly, master, regent **7** capital, guiding, highest, padshah, regnant **8** autarkic, champion, dominant, five-star, kinglike, loftiest, majestic, padishah, separate **9** ascendant, autarchic, classical, directing, excellent, monarchal, number one, paramount, prevalent **10** autonomous, blue-ribbon, commanding, first-class, monarchial **11** independent, monarchical, overbearing, predominant, predominate **12** preponderant, self-governed

soviet
7 council **9** committee

sow
4 seed, toss **5** drill, fling, plant, put in, straw, strew **7** bestrew, disject, scatter **9** broadcast **11** disseminate
combining form: **3** hyo **7** choerus

spa
5 baths, hydro, wells **6** resort, waters **7** springs **13** watering place
Czech: **6** Bilina **8** Karlsbad
English: **4** Bath **6** Buxton **9** Harrogate
French: **3** Dax **5** Évian
German: **3** Ems **5** Baden **6** Bad Ems **9** Kissingen

space
4 area, room **6** cavity, spread **7** breadth, expanse, stretch **8** distance, interval, universe **9** amplitude, expansion

spaced-out
4 high **5** doped **6** stoned, zonked **7** drugged **8** hopped-up, turned on

spacious
3 big **4** vast, wide **5** ample, great, large, roomy **7** immense **8** enormous, extended **9** boundless, expansive, extensive

spade
3 dig **4** grub **5** scoop **6** dig out, shovel **8** excavate

Spade, Sam
9 detective
creator: **7** Hammett (Dashiell)

Spain
ancient name: **8** Hispania
capital: **6** Madrid
former leader: **6** Franco (Francisco)
monetary unit: **6** peseta

spall
4 chip **5** flake **8** fragment

span
4 term, time **8** duration, interval

spangle
4 trim **5** adorn, flash, gleam **7** glimmer, glisten, glitter, shimmer, sparkle, twinkle **8** decorate, ornament **9** coruscate **11** scintillate

Spaniard
9 Castilian

Spanish
combining form: **7** Hispano
folksong: **6** tonada
hero: **5** El Cid **8** Palmerin
penal settlement: **8** presidio
saint: **7** Dominic **8** Ignatius
title: **5** señor **6** señora **8** señorita
wine: **4** sack

Spanish fly
9 cantharis

spank
3 box **4** blip, cuff, slap, sock **5** clout, punch, smack **6** buffet

spar
3 box **5** stall **7** dispute, wrangle **8** longeron
ship's: **4** yard **6** bumkin, sprite **7** boomkin, jibboom, spright, yardarm **8** bowsprit

spare
4 bony, lank, lean, poor, save **5** extra, gaunt, lanky, lay by, lay in, lay up, pinch, put by, scant, screw, short, skimp, stint **6** de trop, excess, excuse, exempt, let off, meager, scanty, scrape, scrimp, skimpy, skinny **7** absolve, angular, lay away, relieve, scraggy, scrawny,

scrimpy, surplus **8** dispense, exiguous, lay aside, rawboned, salt away **9** discharge **11** superfluent, superfluous

sparing
4 wary **5** canny, chary, tight **6** frugal, saving, Scotch, stingy **7** thrifty **8** ungiving **9** provident, stewardly **10** economical, unwasteful **11** tightfisted **12** parsimonious

spark
3 bud, woo **4** beau, germ, seed **5** court, lover, swain, wooer **6** embryo, incite, suitor **7** gallant **8** activate

sparker
5 swain, wooer **6** suitor

sparkle
5 flash, gleam, glint **6** glance **7** glimmer, glisten, glitter, shimmer, twinkle **9** coruscate **11** coruscation, scintillate **13** scintillation

sparkling
6 lively **8** animated **9** brilliant **12** effervescent

sparling
5 smelt

sparse
4 poor, rare **5** scant, skimp **6** meager, scanty, scarce, scrimp, skimpy **7** scrimpy **8** exiguous, sporadic, uncommon **9** dispersed, scattered **10** infrequent, occasional

Sparta
10 Lacedaemon
country: **7** Laconia
hero, king: **8** Leonidas
opponent: **6** Athens

Spartacus
author: **4** Fast (Howard)
slayer: **7** Crassus

spasm
3 fit, tic **4** pang **5** burst, crick, throe
muscular: **6** clonus

spasmodic
6 catchy, fitful, spotty **8** sporadic, spurtive **9** desultory

spat
3 row **4** beef, miff, tiff **5** fight, scrap **6** bicker, hassle **7** brabble, dispute, fall out, quarrel, wrangle **8** squabble **9** bickering, brannigan, caterwaul **10** falling-out **11** altercation

spate
4 flow, flux, pour, rain, rush, tide **5** drift, flood, river, spurt **6** deluge,

series, stream **7** current, torrent **8** cataract, flooding, overflow **9** cataclysm **10** inundation

spatter
3 few **4** slop, slur, spit, spot **5** douse, plash, slosh, smear, swash **6** befoul, bespot, defame, malign, smatch, sparge, splash, splosh **7** asperse, blacken, handful, splurge, spurtle, traduce **9** denigrate **10** scattering, smattering, sprinkling

spawn
4 make, sire **5** hatch **6** create, father, parent **7** produce **8** generate **9** originate, procreate

speak
4 talk, tell **5** blurt, drawl, mouth, orate, shout, spout, utter, voice **6** assert, convey, intone, mumble, murmur, mutter, parley **7** address, declaim, declare, descant, lecture, phonate, prelect, whisper **8** converse, dilate on, intonate, perorate, splutter, vocalize **9** discourse, expatiate, verbalize
confusedly: **8** splutter
for: **7** testify
hesitantly: **7** stammer

speaker
9 spokesman **10** mouthpiece

spear
4 bore, pike, ream, spit **5** drill, gouge, lance, spike, stick **6** impale, pierce, skewer, skiver **7** fishgig, harpoon, leister, trident **8** transfix **9** penetrate **11** transpierce

special
4 rare **6** unique **7** express **8** peculiar, uncommon **9** earmarked **10** designated, particular **11** distinctive, exceptional

specialist
suffix: **5** ician

specialize
4 list **7** itemize **9** enumerate, inventory **13** particularize

species
4 kind, sort, type **5** breed, class, order

specific
3 set **6** strict **7** express, limited **8** clean-cut, clear-cut, definite, especial, explicit, reserved **10** individual, particular **11** categorical, unambiguous

specify
3 fix, set **4** cite, list, name **5** limit **6** detail, settle **7** itemize, mention,

pin down, precise **8** instance **9** condition, determine, enumerate, establish, inventory, stipulate **13** particularize

specimen
4 case, sort, type **6** sample **7** example, neotype, variety **8** instance, sampling **12** illustration
animal or plant: **8** holotype
typical: **8** topotype

specious
4 idle, vain **5** empty, false, wrong **6** hollow, untrue **7** seeming, unsound **8** apparent, nugatory **9** beguiling, colorable, erroneous, illogical, incorrect, plausible **10** inaccurate

speciousness
7 fallacy, sophism **8** delusion **9** casuistry, deception, sophistry **12** equivocation

speck
3 bit, dot, jot **4** atom, iota, mite, mote, tick **5** crumb, grain, point **6** pepper, smitch **7** freckle, stipple **8** molecule, particle, pinpoint, sprinkle

speckle
3 dot **4** spot, stud **5** flake, fleck **6** dapple, pepper, pimple **7** stipple **8** sprinkle

spectacle
4 show **7** display, pageant **10** exhibition **13** demonstration
combining form: **4** cade

spectacular
5 stagy **7** amazing **8** dramatic, striking, wondrous **9** marvelous, thrilling, wonderful **10** astounding, eye-popping, histrionic, miraculous, prodigious, staggering, stupendous, theatrical **11** astonishing, sensational

spectator
4 seer **5** gazer **6** viewer **7** watcher, witness **8** beholder, observer, onlooker **9** bystander, perceiver **10** eyewitness

Spectator, The
author: **6** Steele (Richard) **7** Addison (Joseph)

specter
5 ghost, shade, umbra **6** shadow, spirit **7** eidolon, phantom **8** phantasm, revenant **10** apparition

spectral
6 ghosty, spooky **7** ghastly, ghostly, phantom, shadowy **9** deathlike, ghostlike, unearthly

10 cadaverous, corpselike, shadowlike **11** disembodied, phantomlike

spectrum
5 bogey, ghost, shade **6** spirit **7** eidolon **8** phantasm, revenant **10** apparition

speculate
5 study, think, weigh **6** reason, review **7** reflect **8** cogitate, theorize **9** cerebrate **10** deliberate, excogitate

speculation
6 review, theory **7** perhaps, suppose, thought **8** studying, weighing **9** brainwork **10** conjecture

speculative
5 pensy **6** closet, musing **7** curious, pensive **8** academic, thinking **9** inquiring **10** reflecting, ruminating, thoughtful **11** questioning, theoretical

Spedding biographee
5 Bacon (Francis)

speech
4 talk **5** idiom, voice **6** debate, parley, tongue **7** address, dialect, lecture, monolog, oration, voicing **8** harangue, language, parlance, speaking, uttering **9** discourse, monologue, utterance **10** allocution, expressing, expression, vernacular, vocalizing **11** declamation **12** articulation, vocalization **13** verbalization
defect: **4** lisp **7** stutter

speechcraft
7 oratory **8** rhetoric **9** elocution

speechless
3 mum **4** dumb, mute **6** silent **7** aphonic

speed
3 aid, fly, rev, run, zip **4** clip, ease, gait, pace, race, rush, tear, whiz **5** chase, haste, hurry, tempo, woosh **6** barrel, bucket, burn up, career, course, good on, hasten, hustle, rustle, smooth, spur on, step up, whoosh **7** quicken, swiften **8** alacrity, celerity, dispatch, expedite, fastness, highball, legerity, rapidity, velocity **9** fleetness, quickness, rapidness, swiftness **10** accelerate, cannonball, expedition, facilitate

speedy
4 fast **5** agile, brisk, fleet, hasty, quick, rapid, ready, swift **6** nimble, prompt, raking **8** hasteful **9** breakneck **10** harefooted **11** expeditious

spell
2 go 3 bit, fix, hex 4 bout, time, tour, turn 5 charm, shift, stint, throe, trick, while 6 access, attack, period, streak, voodoo 7 bewitch, enchant, relieve, seizure, stretch 9 ensorcell 11 conjuration, incantation

spellbind
4 grip, hold 5 charm 7 catch up 8 enthrall 9 fascinate, mesmerize

spelling
11 orthography
bad: 10 cacography

spell out
7 explain, expound 8 construe 9 explicate, interpret

spend
3 pay 4 blow, drop, give, pass 5 use up, waste 6 lay out, outlay 7 consume, exhaust, fork out, hand out, splurge 8 disburse, shell out, squander 9 dissipate, throw away, while away 10 contribute, run through
wisely: 7 husband

spender
6 waster 7 wastrel 8 prodigal, unthrift 10 high roller, profligate, squanderer 11 scattergood, wastethrift

spendthrift
see **spender**

spent
5 all in 6 bleary, effete, used up 7 drained, far-gone, worn-out 8 depleted 9 exhausted, washed-out

spew
4 gush 5 belch, eject, eruct, erupt, expel, flood, vomit 6 irrupt, spit up 7 bring up, throw up, upchuck 8 disgorge

sphagnum
4 moss

sphere
3 orb 4 ball, walk 5 field, globe, realm, round 6 circle, domain 7 demesne, rondure, terrain 8 conglobe, dominion, province 9 bailiwick, champaign, territory 10 conglobate 12 jurisdiction

spherical
5 round 6 global 7 globate, globose, globous 8 globated, globular 9 orbicular
combining form: 5 globo

Sphinx
builder: 6 Khafre
father: 6 Typhon

head: 3 man, ram 4 hawk 5 woman
mother: 7 Echidna
query: 6 riddle
site: 4 Giza 6 Thebes

spice
4 balm, cast, dash, hint, lick 5 aroma, clove, scent, smack, smell, taste, tinge, touch, trace 6 ginger, nutmeg 7 bouquet, incense, perfume 8 cinnamon 9 fragrance, redolence

Spice Islands
8 Moluccas

spick-and-span
3 new 4 mint, neat, snug, tidy, trig, trim 5 clean, fresh 6 spruce 7 chipper, orderly 8 brand-new 9 shipshape 11 uncluttered, well-groomed

spicy
4 blue, racy 5 broad, fiery, salty, shady, sweet, zesty 6 aromal, purple, risqué, savory, snappy, wicked 7 gingery, peppery, perfumy, piquant, pungent, scented, zestful 8 aromatic, fragrant, off-color, perfumed, poignant, redolent, spirited 9 ambrosial 10 suggestive 12 high spirited 13 sophisticated

spider
6 frypan 7 araneid, skillet 8 arachnid 9 frying pan 10 black widow
combining form: 6 arachn 7 arachno

spider monkey
7 sapajou

spiel
4 line 5 pitch 12 song and dance

spieler
6 gypper 7 cheater, diddler, grifter, sharper, slicker 8 swindler 9 defrauder 11 flimflammer 12 double-dealer

spigot
3 tap 4 cock, gate 5 valve 6 faucet 7 hydrant, petcock 8 stopcock

spike
5 lance, piton, spear 6 impale, skewer, skiver 8 transfix 11 transpierce

spile
4 bung 5 spout 8 forepole

spill
4 drip, drop, slop, tell 5 mouth, spray, squab 6 betray, reveal, splash 7 blab out, divulge, dribble, overrun, run over, spatter 8 disclose, discover, give away, overfill, overflow, well over

Spillane detective
10 Mike Hammer

spin
4 gyre, reel, ride, swim, turn 5 dizzy, drive, giddy, mix up, swirl, twirl, wheel, whirl 6 gyrate, muddle, rotate 7 fluster, revolve, vibrate 9 oscillate, pendulate, pirouette, whirligig
a log: 4 birl
out: 4 draw 6 extend 7 prolong, stretch 8 elongate, lengthen, protract 10 prolongate

spinal column
6 rachis
curvature: 7 lordoma 8 lordosis
part: 8 vertebra; (see also **spine**)

spindle
3 pin, rod 5 newel 6 rachis

spindly
5 lanky, rangy 6 gangly

spine
4 back 6 rachis 8 backbone 9 vertebrae

spineless
4 weak 8 impotent 9 weak-kneed 10 emasculate, inadequate, weak-willed 11 ineffective, ineffectual 12 invertebrate

spin-off
8 offshoot 9 by-product, outgrowth 10 derivative, descendant

_____ Spinoza
6 Baruch

spinster
7 old maid 10 maiden lady

spiny
6 thorny 7 prickly 8 echinate 10 nettlesome

spiral
4 coil, curl, wind 5 helix, twine, twist 7 entwine, helical, helices (plural), wreathe 8 gyroidal, volution 9 cochleate, corkscrew
combining form: 3 gyr 4 gyro 5 helic 6 helico

spire
4 coil, curl 5 twist, whorl 6 sprout 7 steeple 8 pinnacle 9 germinate

spirit
3 pep, vim, zip 4 brio, dash, élan, gimp, grog, guts, life, mood, snap, soul, tone, zeal, zing 5 anima, ardor, drive, force, heart, might, moxie, oomph, pluck, power, shade, spunk, umbra, verve, vigor 6 animus, daimon, energy, esprit, fervor, ginger, mettle, morale,

pneuma, psyche, shadow, starch, temper, timbre, wraith **7** cojones, courage, eidolon, passion, phantom, specter, spectre **8** phantasm, revenant, strength, vitality **9** animation, briskness, character, élan vital, substance **10** apparition, enthusiasm, get-up-and-go, liveliness, resolution, vital force **13** dauntlessness
away: **6** abduct, kidnap, snatch
combining form: **4** thym **5** psych, thymo **6** psycho, thymia **7** pneumat **8** pneumato
evil: **5** afrit, demon **6** afreet **7** erlking, shaitan, sheitan
female: **5** nymph **7** banshee, banshie, nymphet
good: **7** eudemon **8** eudaemon
Hopi: **7** kachina, katcina
Persian: **4** peri

spirited
3 hot **4** avid, bold, game, keen **5** alert, beany, brave, eager, fiery, nervy, peppy, sharp **6** ardent, bright, gritty, lively, plucky, spunky **7** animate, chipper, fervent, gingery, peppery, valiant, zealous **8** animated, cheerful, fearless, intrepid, resolute **9** audacious, dauntless, sprightly, vivacious **10** courageous, mettlesome, passionate **11** high-hearted **12** enthusiastic

spirits
5 booze, drink **6** liquor, tipple **9** aqua vitae, firewater
low: **5** blues **8** doldrums **10** blue devils, melancholy

spiritual
4 high **5** lofty **6** church, mental, sacred **7** saintly **8** bodiless, cerebral, churchly, elevated, mystical, numinous, platonic **9** unfleshly **10** discarnate, high-minded, immaterial, unphysical **11** disembodied, incorporeal, nonmaterial, nonphysical **12** metaphysical, supernatural, supramundane

spiritualist
6 mystic

spit
5 lance, spear **6** impale, saliva, skewer, skiver, slaver, sputum **7** spatter, sputter **8** splutter, transfix **9** brochette **11** expectorate

spite
6 grudge, malice, rancor, spleen **7** ill will, revenge **9** vengeance **10** malignancy **11** malevolence **12** vengefulness **13** maliciousness

spiteful
4 evil **5** catty **6** malign, wicked **7** cattish, hostile, vicious **9** malicious, malignant, rancorous **10** malevolent, vindictive **12** antagonistic

Spitta biographee
4 Bach (Johann Sebastian)

spitting image
4 twin **6** double, ringer **7** picture **8** portrait **10** simulacrum

spittoon
8 cuspidor

splash
3 sop, wet **4** slop, soak **5** douse, drown, slosh, spray, swash, throw **6** dabble, drench, squirt **7** spatter, splurge, spurtle **8** sprinkle

splatter
4 slop **5** douse, plash, slosh, swash **6** splosh **7** splurge, spurtle

spleen
see **spite**

splendor
4 pomp **5** adorn, glory, value, worth **6** beauty **8** grandeur **10** brilliancy, excellence **12** magnificence

splice
3 tie **4** join, mate **5** unite

splinter
4 rive **5** burst, smash, spail, spale **6** shiver **7** shatter **8** fragment

split
3 cut, rip **4** part, rend, rent, rift, rima, rime, rive, tear **5** break, carve, chasm, chink, cleft, crack, sever, slice **6** breach, cleave, cloven, divide, schism, sunder **7** break up, disjoin, dissect, divorce, fissate, fission, fissure, rupture **8** cleavage, dissever, fracture, rimation, separate **10** alienating, estranging **11** dichotomize
combining form: **5** schiz **6** schizo **7** schisto

splotch
4 blob, blot, spot **5** fleck, stain **6** bespot, dapple, marble, motley, mottle **9** harlequin, variegate

splurge
4 orgy, slop **5** binge, douse, fling, plash, slosh, spree, swash **6** splash, splosh **7** rampage, spatter, spurtle **8** splatter **12** extravagance

spoil
3 mar, rot **4** baby, grab, harm, haul, hurt, loot, rape, ruin, sack, swag, take, turn **5** booty, decay,

favor, force, humor, louse, prize, queer, snafu, taint, waste, wreck **6** boodle, cocker, coddle, cosset, damage, defile, impair, injure, molder, oblige, pamper, ravage, ravish **7** blemish, cater to, crumble, destroy, indulge, outrage, pillage, plunder, putrefy, tarnish, violate, vitiate **8** deflower, demolish, desolate, pickings, spoliate **9** break down, decompose, deflorate, depredate, desecrate, devastate **10** plunderage, spoliation **11** acquisition, mollycoddle

spoilsport
7 killjoy

spoke
3 bar, rod **5** chock, stake **8** baluster **11** obstruction

sponge
5 leech, mooch **7** moocher **8** parasite **10** freeloader
material: **8** mesoglea
opening: **6** oscula (plural), oscule **7** osculum, ostiole

sponger
5 leech **7** moocher **8** parasite **10** freeloader

spongy
4 soft **5** mushy, pappy, pulpy **6** quaggy **7** pulpous, squashy, squishy **8** squelchy, yielding

sponsor
5 angel **6** backer, patron, surety **8** advocate, backer-up, champion, Maecenas, mainstay, promoter, upholder **9** guarantor, preferrer, supporter **10** benefactor

sponsorship
4 egis **5** aegis **7** backing **8** auspices **9** patronage

spontaneous
7 natural, offhand **8** unforced **9** automatic, extempore, impromptu, impulsive, unstudied **10** improvised, unprompted **11** instinctive, unmeditated **13** unconstrained

spontoon
3 bat **4** club, mace **5** baton, billy **6** cudgel **8** bludgeon **9** billy club, truncheon **10** nightstick

spoof
4 dupe, fake, fool, hoax, sell, sham **5** cheat, farce, phony, put-on, trick **6** befool, deceit, parody, send-up **7** chicane, takeoff **8** flimflam, hoodwink **9** bamboozle, deception, imposture **11** hornswoggle

spook
3 spy 5 agent, alarm, ghost, scare
6 fright 7 specter, startle, terrify
8 affright, frighten 9 terrorize
10 ghostwrite 13 undercover man

spooky
5 eerie, jumpy, nervy, weird
6 goosey 7 fidgety, jittery, nervous,
ominous, uncanny 8 twittery 9 unearthly, unrestful 10 high-strung

spool
4 wind 6 bobbin, holder

spoon
3 pet, woo 4 neck 5 court, ladle,
scoop 7 scraper

spoonbill
8 shoveler 9 ruddy duck
10 paddlefish

Spoon River Poet
7 Masters (Edgar Lee)

spoony
5 silly 6 simple 7 fatuous, foolish,
unwitty, witless 10 weak-headed,
weak-minded 11 sheepheaded
over/on: 6 mashed 7 smitten
8 enamored

spoor
4 step 5 track, tract 7 vestige
8 footstep 9 footprint

sporadic
3 few 4 rare 6 catchy, fitful,
scarce, seldom, single, spotty
8 separate, uncommon 9 desultory,
irregular, spasmodic 10 infrequent,
occasional, unfrequent

sport
3 fun 4 game, jest, joke, mock,
play 6 frolic, racing, trifle 7 mockery, show off 9 diversion, high
jinks, horseplay, pilgarlic
10 recreation
indoor: 6 boxing, hockey, squash
7 bowling 8 handball 9 wrestling
10 acrobatics, basketball, gymnastics 11 racquetball, table tennis
Olympic: 4 judo 6 boxing, diving,
hockey, rowing 7 archery, cycling,
fencing, shot put 8 canoeing, football, high jump, long jump, marathon, shooting, swimming, yachting
9 decathlon, pole vault, water polo,
wrestling 10 basketball, gymnastics, pentathlon, triple jump, volleyball 11 discus throw, hammer
throw 12 javelin throw, steeplechase 13 weightlifting
water: 6 diving, rowing 7 sailing,
surfing 8 canoeing, swimming,
yachting

winter: 6 hockey, skiing 7 curling,
lugeing, skating 8 biathlon, sled-
ding 10 ski jumping 11 bobsled-
ding, tobogganing

sporting house
6 bagnio 7 brothel 8 bordello,
seraglio

sportive
5 antic 6 frisky, impish 7 larkish,
playful, roguish, waggish 8 gamesome 10 frolicsome
11 mischievous

sportiveness
7 devilry, roguery, waggery 8 deviltry, mischief 9 devilment

spot
3 fix, jam, job, nip, see 4 drop,
espy, find, iota, mite, onus, post,
site, slug, whit 5 brand, catch,
fleck, hit on, locus, place, point,
speck 6 blotch, corner, dapple, descry, detect, dollop, finger, macula,
mottle, office, pickle, pimple, plight,
random, scrape, stigma, turn up
7 aimless, dilemma, freckle, hit
upon, smidgen, spatter, speckle,
splotch, station, unaimed 8 diagnose, flyspeck, identify, location,
maculate, meet with, particle, pinpoint, position 9 bespatter, encounter, haphazard, hit-or-miss, irregular, recognize, situation, unplanned
10 connection, designless 11 determinate, distinguish, predicament
combining form: 5 macul 6 maculi,
maculo

spotless
4 pure 5 clean 6 chaste, decent,
modest 7 cleanly 8 hygienic, sanitary, unsoiled 9 undefiled, unsullied
10 immaculate 11 unblemished

spotted eagle ray
6 obispo

spouse
4 mate, wife 5 hubby 7 consort,
husband

spout
5 chute, falls, sault 6 nozzle 7 cascade 8 cataract 9 waterfall

sprain
4 pull, tear, turn 5 break, throw,
twist 6 wrench 7 stretch 8 fracture
9 dislocate

sprawl
4 loll 5 drape, slump 6 extend,
lounge, ramble, slouch, spread
7 stretch 8 scramble, straddle,
straggle 11 spread-eagle

spray
3 fog 4 hose 7 aerosol 8 atomizer,
fumigate, nebulize

spread
3 jam, lay, set, sow 4 deal, oleo,
open, pâté, push 5 feast, jelly,
noise, space, splay, strew, sweep
6 butter, dinner, expand, extend,
fan out, pass on, peddle, regale,
retail, unfold 7 banquet, breadth,
diffuse, expanse, overrun, perfuse,
pervade, radiate, scatter, slather,
stretch, suffuse 8 bedcover, coverlet, dispense, disperse, distance,
mushroom, permeate, transmit
9 amplitude, broadcast, circulate,
diffusion, dissipate, expansion, extension, profusion, propagate
10 distribute, outstretch 11 communicate, counterpane, disseminate,
enlargement
on: 5 apply

spree
3 bat, jag 4 bust, hell, orgy, riot,
tear 5 binge, fling, revel 6 bender,
frolic, rantan 7 carouse, rampage,
roister, splurge, wassail 8 carousal

sprig
4 brad, heir 5 dowel, scion 6 figure 7 pintail 9 ruddy duck

sprightly
3 gay 4 keen, yare 5 agile, alert,
antic, brisk, perky, sharp, smart,
zippy 6 active, breezy, brisky,
clever, frisky, lively, nimble, volant
7 animate, coltish, playful, pungent
8 animated, spirited, sportive 9 vivacious 10 frolicsome, keen-witted,
rollicking, unpedantic 11 quick-
witted 13 scintillating

spring
3 hop, lop 4 bolt, come, flow,
head, jump, leap, loom, lope, rise,
root, skip, stem, trip, well 5 arise,
begin, birth, bound, cause, fount,
hatch, issue, start, vault, youth
6 appear, arrive, bounce, emerge,
geyser, hurdle, motive, origin, reason, source, tittup, uncoil, updive,
vernal 7 budtime, come out, emanate, impetus, proceed, puberty, rebound, saltate, skitter, startle
8 come from, commence, excitant,
fountain, stimulus, wellhead
9 greenness, originate, stimulant,
youthhood 10 derive from, incitement, juvenility 12 fountainhead,
youthfulness
back: 6 resile
combining form: 4 cren 5 creno

springe
5 noose, snare 7 pitfall 8 deadfall, trapfall 9 booby trap, mousetrap

springlike
6 vernal

springy
6 supple, whippy 7 elastic, stretch 8 flexible, stretchy 9 recoiling, resilient 10 rebounding

sprinkle
3 dot 4 dust, spot 5 shake, speck, strew 6 pepper, powder, sparge 7 asperse, drizzle, freckle, scatter, speckle, stipple 9 bespeckle

sprint
3 run 4 dash, shin 5 scoot 6 scurry 7 scamper

sprite
3 elf, fay 5 fairy, nisse, pixie 7 brownie
water: 5 kelpy 6 kelpie

spritz
3 jet 5 spurt 6 squirt

sprout
3 bud 4 grow 5 scion, shoot 6 ratoon, sucker 8 offshoot 9 germinate
combining form: 4 clad 5 blast, clado 6 blasto, blasty 7 blastic

spruce
4 trim 5 natty, sassy 6 dapper, spiffy 11 well-groomed
up: 5 slick, spiff 6 doll up 7 deck out, gussy up

spry
4 yare 5 agile, brisk, quick, ready, sound, zippy 6 active, brisky, lively, nimble, prompt, robust, volant 7 healthy 8 vigorous 9 energetic

spud
6 potato 8 spade lug

___ spumante
4 asti

spume
4 foam, suds 5 froth, yeast 6 lather

spunk
4 grit, guts, sand 5 heart, moxie, nerve, pluck 6 mettle, spirit 7 cojones, courage 8 backbone 9 fortitude 10 doggedness, resolution 13 dauntlessness

spunky
4 bold 5 beany, brave, fiery, gutsy 6 plucky 7 doughty, gingery, peppery 8 fearless, spirited 9 dauntless, unfearing 10 courageous,

mettlesome 11 high-hearted, undauntable 12 high-spirited

spur
3 sic 4 goad, prod, stir, urge 5 egg on, favor, prick, rally, rouse, rowel 6 arouse, awaken, exhort, prompt, propel 7 impetus, impulse 8 catalyst, excitant, stimulus 9 actuation, incentive, instigate, stimulant 10 activation, incitation, incitement, motivation 11 countenance

spurious
4 fake, mock, sham 5 bogus, dummy, false, phony, put-on, snide 6 ersatz, pseudo, unreal 7 assumed, bastard, feigned, pretend 8 affected, baseborn 9 brummagem, imitation, pinchbeck, pretended, simulated, ungenuine 10 apocryphal, artificial, substitute 11 counterfeit, make-believe, misbegotten, unauthentic 12 illegitimate
combining form: 4 noth 5 notho, pseud 6 pseudo

spurn
5 flout, scoff, scorn, scout, sneer 6 refuse, reject 7 conspue, contemn, decline, despise, disdain, dismiss 8 turn down 9 reprobate, repudiate 10 disapprove

spurt
3 jet 5 spout, surge 6 spritz, sprout, squirt

sputter
3 pop 4 fizz, hiss, rage, rant, rave, spit 6 gibber, jabber 7 bluster, crackle

spy
5 agent, scout, snoop, spook 6 beagle, sleuth 7 gumshoe 8 informer, saboteur 9 detective 12 investigator 13 undercover man
name: 4 Boyd (Belle), Hari (Mata) 5 André (John)

Spy, The
author: 6 Cooper (James Fenimore)

spying
9 espionage

Spyri's heroine
5 Heidi

squab
5 couch 6 pigeon 7 cushion

squabble
see **spat**

squalid
3 low 4 base, foul, mean, ugly, vile 5 black, dingy, dirty, nasty, seedy, soily 6 filthy, frowzy, grubby, impure, scurvy, shabby, shoddy, sleazy, sloppy 7 ignoble, low-

down, run-down, scrubby, unclean, unkempt 8 slipshod, slovenly, wretched 10 broken-down, despicable, disheveled, slatternly 11 dilapidated 12 disreputable

squall
3 caw, yap, yip 4 bark, bawl, beef, feud, howl, roar, wail, yaup, yawp, yell, yelp, yowl 5 brawl, croak, fight, shout 6 bellow, hassle, shriek, squeal 7 dispute, quarrel, screech 9 bickering 10 falling-out 11 altercation

squander
4 blow 5 waste 7 consume, fritter 8 fool away, unthrift 9 dissipate, overdoing, throw away 10 frivol away, lavishness, trifle away 11 prodigality, prodigalize 12 extravagance, extravagancy, wastefulness

squanderer
see **spender**

square
3 fit, fix, pay, sop 4 bang, boxy, even, fair, fogy, have, jibe, just, quit, suit 5 adapt, agree, bribe, clear, equal, exact, fit in, green, pay up, plaza, right, sharp, spang 6 accord, adjust, buy off, common, fogram, fossil, settle, tailor 7 balance, boxlike, conform, exactly, satisfy 8 check out, clear off, coincide, dovetail, mossback, orthodox, quadrate, smack-dab, straight, unbiased 9 discharge, equitable, harmonize, impartial, liquidate, objective, precisely, quadratic, reconcile 10 accurately, button-down, correspond, fuddy-duddy 12 conventional 13 stick-in-the-mud

squash
3 jam 4 cram, mash, pepo, pulp 5 crush, gourd, press, quell 7 put down, squeeze, squelch, squidge 8 suppress 10 annihilate, extinguish
variety: 5 acorn 6 cushaw, cymlin, Sibley, turban 7 cymling, dunkard, Hubbard, scallop 8 cymbling, pattypan, zucchini 9 butternut, cocozelle, crookneck 10 Marblehead

squat
5 dumpy, hunch, stoop, thick 6 chunky, crouch, hunker, stocky, stubby 8 heavyset, thickset 10 hunker down 11 thick-bodied

squawfish
4 chub 8 cyprinid

squawk
3 caw, yap, yip 4 beef, crab, fuss,

yaup, yawp **5** bitch, bleat, gripe
6 yammer **7** protest **8** complain

squeak
3 rat **4** pipe, shot, show, talk, time
5 grate, peach **6** change, inform,
look-in, scream, snitch **7** opening,
screech **8** occasion **11** opportunity

squeal
3 rat, yip **4** howl, rasp, talk, yell,
yowl **5** bitch, bleat, creak, grate,
gripe, peach **6** inform, screak,
scream, shriek, shrill, snitch,
squawk **7** screech **8** complain

squealer
4 fink **6** canary, snitch **7** ratfink,
tipster **8** betrayer, informer **10** talebearer **11** stool pigeon

squeamish
5 dizzy, fussy, queer, shaky, upset
6 dainty, qualmy, queasy **7** finical,
finicky **8** nauseous **9** finicking, nauseated, unsettled **10** fastidious, particular, pernickety **11** persnickety,
vertiginous

squeamishness
6 nausea

squeeze
3 hug, jam **4** bear, cram, push
5 clasp, crowd, crush, exact,
gouge, juice, pinch, press, screw,
wrest, wring **6** eke out, enfold, extort, squash, squish, squush, wrench
7 embrace, extract, scratch **8** compress, contract **9** shake down

squelch
5 shush **6** muffle, squash, squish,
stifle **7** repress, squidge **8** strangle,
suppress

squib
4 fire **6** filler **7** lampoon **8** scribble,
shoot off **9** detonator

squid
7 calamar, mollusk **8** calamary
10 cephalopod
kin: **7** octopus **10** cuttlefish

squiggle
4 worm **6** scrawl, writhe **7** scratch
8 scrabble, scribble

squinch
5 quail, start, wince **6** blanch,
blench, recoil, shrink

squint
4 bent **5** trend **10** hagioscope,
strabismus

squire
5 judge, lover **6** escort, lawyer
7 gallant **9** accompany

squirm
4 toss, worm **6** wiggle, writhe
7 agonize, wriggle

squirrel
5 hoard, stash
African: **5** xerus
red: **9** chickaree

squirrel-like
8 sciuroid

squirt
3 jet, pup **4** pour **5** puppy, sprat,
spray, sprit, spurt, surge, twerp
6 splurt, spritz, stream **7** spatter

squish
3 jam **4** bear, push **5** crush, press
7 squeeze, squelch

squishy
4 soft **5** pulpy **6** quaggy, spongy
7 pulpous **8** squelchy

Sri Lanka
capital: **7** Colombo
export: **3** tea **6** rubber
former name: **6** Ceylon
monetary unit: **5** rupee

SRO
7 sellout

SS chief
7 Himmler (Heinrich)

S-shaped
7 sigmoid **9** sigmoidal

stab
2 go **3** dig, pop, ram, run, try
4 dirk, poke, shot, sink, slap
5 crack, drive, fling, prick, prong,
punch, spear, stick, whack, whirl
6 dagger, pierce, plunge, thrust
7 bayonet, poniard **8** puncture,
stiletto

Stabat ____
5 Mater

stabile
6 steady **9** sculpture **10** stationary

stabilize
3 fix, set **4** prop **5** poise **6** fixate,
secure, settle, steady **7** balance, ballast, support, sustain

stable
3 set **4** even, fast, firm, safe, sure
5 fixed, solid, sound **6** poised, secure, steady, strong, sturdy **7** lasting, staunch, uniform **8** balanced,
constant, enduring, resolute **9** diuturnal, perduring, permanent, steadfast, unvarying **10** perdurable, unchanging, unshakable

stack
4 bank, cock, heap, hill, load,
mass, pile **5** drift, mound **7** pyramid

stadium
4 bowl **5** arena **6** garden **8** coliseum **9** gymnasium

staff
3 rod **4** club, prop, rung, wand
6 cudgel **7** support
bishop's: **7** crosier, crozier
medical: **8** caduceus

stage
4 give, open, play, rung, show,
step **5** grade, level, mount, notch,
phase, put on **6** degree, period
7 execute, perform, present,
produce
direction: **4** exit **5** enter **6** exeunt
scenery: **8** backdrop
show: **4** play **5** drama, revue **7** musical **9** burlesque **10** vaudeville
signal: **3** cue
whisper: **5** aside

stage set
5 scene **7** scenery, setting **11** mise-
en-scène

stagger
4 halt, reel, sway **5** amaze, floor,
lurch, shift, stump, swing, waver,
weave, wheel **6** boggle, careen,
dither, falter, puzzle, teeter, topple,
totter, wobble **7** astound, nonplus,
perplex, shatter, stumble, whiffle
8 astonish, bowl over, hesitate, paralyze, titubate **9** devastate, dumbfound, knock over, overpower,
overwhelm, vacillate

stagnant
5 stale **6** static **8** immobile, unmoving **10** motionless, stationary

stagnate
6 stifle **7** trammel **8** stultify,
vegetate

staid
4 cool, smug **5** grave, sober **6** formal, sedate, solemn, somber, stuffy
7 earnest, serious, starchy, weighty
8 composed, decorous, priggish

stain
3 dye, tar **4** blot, blur, daub, flaw,
onus, slur, smut, soil, spot **5** brand,
color, crock, odium, smear, sully,
taint, tinge **6** bedaub, blotch, debase, defect, defile, embrue, imbrue, smirch, smudge, smutch,
stigma **7** besmear, blemish, corrupt, debauch, deprave, pervert,
pigment, tarnish **8** besmirch, black
eye, colorant, discolor, dyestuff,
tincture
combining form: **5** macul **6** maculi,
maculo

staircase
handrail: 8 banister
outdoor: 6 perron
post: 5 newel 8 baluster

stake
3 bet, lay, pot, set 4 ante, back, game, play 5 claim, put on, share, wager 6 gamble 7 finance 8 bankroll, interest 10 capitalize

stale
4 rank 5 dusty, fetid, fusty, moldy, musty, tired, trite 6 cliché, smelly 7 clichéd, noisome, reeking, stenchy 8 shopworn, timeworn 9 hackneyed 10 malodorous 11 commonplace, stereotyped

stalemate
3 tie 4 draw 7 dogfall 8 deadlock, standoff

stalk
4 hunt, prey 5 chase, drive, march, sling, track 6 ambush, follow, pursue, stride, walk up 8 flush out
flower: 8 peduncle
leaf: 7 petiole
short: 5 stipe

stall
4 halt 5 booth, brake, check, kiosk, stand 6 arrest, put off 7 hold off 11 compartment

stalwart
4 bold 5 brave, husky, stout, tough 6 brawny, sinewy, strong, sturdy 7 valiant 8 athletic, fearless, intrepid, muscular, unafraid, valorous 9 dauntless, tenacious, undaunted 10 courageous

stamen
combining form: 4 andr 5 andro 9 stemonous
part: 6 anther 8 filament

stamina
9 endurance, tolerance 10 toleration

stammer
6 gibber, jabber 7 sputter, stutter 8 hesitate, splutter

stamp
3 ilk, lot 4 cast, etch, kind, mint, mold, seal, sort, type 5 clomp, clump, drive, grave, infix, pound, print, tromp 6 hammer, incuse, stripe 7 impress, imprint, sticker, trample 8 hallmark, inscribe 9 character 10 impression

stampede
4 bolt, dash, rout, rush, tear 5 chase, fling, shoot 6 charge 8 pell-mell

stamps
7 postage

stance
4 pose 5 color 7 posture 8 attitude, carriage, position, positure

stanch
4 stem, stop

stanchion
4 prop 5 brace 7 support

stand
4 bear, take 5 abide, booth, brook, kiosk, treat 6 endure, suffer 7 stomach, swallow 8 attitude, position, tolerate
artist's: 5 easel
having three legs: 6 tripod, trivet
ornamental: 7 étagère
stiffly: 7 bristle

standard
3 law, par 4 flag, jack, mean, norm, rule 5 axiom, color, gauge, ideal, model 6 assize, banner, belief, ensign, median, mirror, pennon 7 average, example, measure, pattern, pennant 8 bannerol, ensample, exemplar, paradigm, streamer 9 archetype, banderole, beau ideal, benchmark, criterion, principle, yardstick 10 touchstone 11 fundamental

stand-in
3 sub 6 second 9 alternate, assistant, surrogate 10 substitute 11 locum tenens, pinch hitter, replacement, succedaneum

standing
4 rank, term 5 place 6 cachet, status 7 dignity, footing, station, stature 8 capacity, position, prestige 9 character, situation 11 consequence

standoff
see **stalemate**

standoffish
5 aloof 7 distant 8 eremitic, reserved, solitary 9 reclusive, withdrawn 10 antisocial, insociable, unsociable 12 misanthropic

stand out
3 jut 4 bulk, loom, poke, pout 5 bulge, pouch 6 beetle 7 project 8 overhang, protrude

standpatter
4 tory 7 diehard 8 old liner, rightist 11 bitter-ender, right-winger 12 conservative

standpoint
4 side 5 angle, slant 7 outlook 9 direction

standstill
4 halt, stop 5 check, pause 6 arrest 8 deadlock 9 cessation

Stanford site
8 Palo Alto

Stanley Kowalski's wife
6 Stella

Stanley's car
7 steamer

Stan's pal
5 Ollie

stanza
7 strophe
combining form: 5 stich
of eight lines: 6 octave 8 octonary
of four lines: 6 ballad 8 quatrain
of six lines: 6 sestet, sextet 7 sextain
of three lines: 6 tercet 7 triplet 8 tristich
Persian: 8 rubaiyat

star
4 main, nova 5 actor, chief, major, novae (plural) 6 étoile 7 actress, capital 8 asterisk, dominant 9 principal 10 preeminent 11 outstanding, predominant
bright: 4 Vega 5 Deneb, Rigel, Spica 6 Altair, Pollux, Sirius 7 Antares, Canopus, Capella, Procyon 8 Arcturus 9 Aldebaran, Archernar, Fomalhaut 10 Beta Crucis, Betelgeuse 11 Alpha Crucis 12 Beta Centauri 13 Alpha Centauri
combining form: 4 astr 5 aster, astro 6 astero, sidero
five-pointed: 8 pentacle
giant: 10 Betelgeuse
six-pointed: 8 hexagram
suffix: 2 id

starch
2 go 3 pep 4 bang, push, snap 5 drive, getup, punch, vigor 6 amylum 7 stiffen 8 vitality
combining form: 4 amyl 5 amylo

star-crossed
6 doomed 7 hapless, unhappy, unlucky 8 ill-fated, luckless, untoward 10 ill-starred 11 unfortunate 12 misfortunate

Stardust composer
10 Carmichael (Hoagy)

stare
3 eye 4 bore, gape, gawk, gaze, look, ogle, peer 5 gloat 6 goggle 7 fisheye 10 rubberneck

stark
3 raw 4 bare, firm, nude, pure 5 bleak, clear, empty, naked, quite, rigid, sheer, stout, utter 6 barren,

robust, strict, unclad, vacant, wholly **8** absolute, complete, desolate, stripped **9** au naturel, out-and-out **10** absolutely

starry
6 astral **7** stellar **8** sidereal **9** stellular

Star-Spangled Banner writer
3 Key (Francis Scott)

start
4 bolt, dawn, draw, edge, jump, leap, odds, open **5** alpha, arise, begin, bound, bulge, crank, enter, found, intro, onset, quail, set up, wince **6** blanch, blench, bounce, create, embark, flinch, get off, launch, outset, recoil, setout, shrink, spring, take up, tee off **7** actuate, dawning, genesis, infancy, kickoff, opening, pioneer, proceed, squinch, trigger, vantage **8** activate, commence, drawback, embark on, handicap, initiate, organize **9** advantage, allowance, beginning, establish, institute, originate **10** inaugurate **12** commencement

startle
3 awe **4** bolt, jolt, jump **5** alarm, scare, shock, spook **8** affright, astonish, frighten, surprise

starved
6 hungry **8** famished, ravenous, underfed

stash
4 bury, hide **5** cache, hoard, plant **7** conceal, secrete **8** ensconce, squirrel

stasis
5 poise **7** balance **9** equipoise **11** equilibrium

state
3 air, put, say **4** aver, mode, rank, tell, vent **5** opine, place, utter **6** affirm, assert, cachet, define, recite, relate, report **7** declare, deliver, dignity, enounce, explain, expound, express, footing, narrate, posture, recount **8** attitude, bring out, capacity, describe, position, prestige, set forth, standing **9** character, condition, elucidate, enunciate, interpret, situation, ventilate **11** body politic
subdivison: **6** county
suffix: **2** cy, th **3** ate, dom, ery, ion, ism, ity **4** ance, ancy, ence, ency, hood, ment, ness, oses (plural), osis, ship **5** ation **7** isation, ization

state
easternmost: **5** Maine
largest: **6** Alaska
smallest: **11** Rhode Island
southernmost: **6** Hawaii

State abbreviation
Alabama: **2** AL **3** Ala.
Alaska: **2** AK **4** Alas.
Arizona: **2** AZ **4** Ariz.
Arkansas: **2** AR **3** Ark.
California: **2** CA **3** Cal. **5** Calif.
Colorado: **2** CO **3** Col. **4** Colo
Connecticut: **2** CT **4** Conn.
Delaware: **2** DE **3** Del.
Florida: **2** FL **3** Fla.
Georgia: **2** GA
Hawaii: **2** Hi
Idaho: **2** ID **3** Ida.
Illinois: **2** IL **3** Ill.
Indiana: **2** IN **3** Ind.
Iowa: **2** IA, Io.
Kansas: **2** KS **3** Kan., Kas. **4** Kans.
Kentucky: **2** KY **3** Ken.
Louisiana: **2** LA
Maine: **2** ME
Maryland: **2** MD
Massachusetts: **2** MA **4** Mass.
Michigan: **2** MI **4** Mich.
Minnesota: **2** MN **4** Minn.
Mississippi: **2** MS **4** Miss.
Missouri: **2** MO
Montana: **2** MT **4** Mont.
Nebraska: **2** NE **3** Neb. **4** Nebr.
Nevada: **2** NV **3** Nev.
New Hampshire: **2** NH
New Jersey: **2** NJ
New Mexico: **2** NM **4** N. Mex.
New York: **2** NY
North Carolina: **2** NC **4** N. Car.
North Dakota: **2** ND **4** N. Dak.
Ohio: **2** OH
Oklahoma: **2** OK **4** Okla.
Oregon: **2** OR **3** Ore. **4** Oreg.
Pennsylvania: **2** PA **4** Penn. **5** Penna.
Rhode island: **2** RI
South Carolina: **2** SC **4** S. Car.
South Dakota: **2** SD **4** S. Dak.
Tennessee: **2** TN **4** Tenn.
Texas: **2** TX **3** Tex.
Utah: **2** UT
Vermont: **2** VT **4** Verm.
Virginia: **2** VA **4** Virg.
Washington: **2** WA **4** Wash.
West Virginia: **2** WV **3** W. Va.
Wisconsin: **2** WI **3** Wis. **4** Wisc.
Wyoming: **2** WY **3** Wyo.

stately
5 grand, noble, preux, regal, royal **6** august, formal, kingly, lordly, solemn **7** courtly, gallant **8** gracious, imperial, imposing, magnific, ma-

jestic, princely **9** dignified, grandiose **10** ceremonial **11** ceremonious, magnificent

statement
3 tab **4** bill, vent, word **5** score, voice **6** dictum **7** account, invoice, recital **9** narrative, reckoning, testimony, utterance **10** deposition, expression **11** description **12** vocalization **13** verbalization
introductory: **7** preface **8** foreword, prologue

stateroom
5 cabin

statesman
10 politician
American: **3** Hay (John Milton) **4** Clay (Henry), Hull (Cordell), Otis (James), Root (Elihu) **5** Henry (Patrick), Lodge (Henry Cabot), Vance (Cyrus) **6** Bunche (Ralph), Bunker (Ellsworth), Dulles (John Foster), Kennan (George F.), Morris (Gouverneur), Sumner (Charles) **7** Acheson (Dean), Hancock (John), Kellogg (Frank B.), Lansing (Robert), Sherman (John, Roger), Stimson (Henry L.), Webster (Daniel) **8** Franklin (Benjamin), Hamilton (Alexander), Harriman (Averell), Pinckney (Charles, Thomas), Randolph (Edmund Jennings, John, Payton), Rutledge (John), Stevenson (Adlai), Trumbull (Jonathan, Joseph) **9** Kissinger (Henry) **10** Stettinius (Edward Reilly)
Australian: **9** Wentworth (William Charles)
Austrian: **6** Renner (Karl) **7** Kaunitz (Wenzel von) **8** Dollfuss (Engelbert) **10** Metternich (Klemens von) **13** Schwarzenberg (Felix zu)
Canadian: **4** King (William Lyon Mackenzie) **7** Laurier (Wilfrid) **8** Thompson (John Sparrow) **9** Macdonald (John Alexander, John Sandfield), Mackenzie (Alexander, William Lyon)
Chinese: **3** Yen (Hsishan) **4** Kung (Hsiang-hsi), Wang (Anshih, Chingwei), Yuan (Shih-kai) **9** Sun Yat-Sen
Dutch: **6** de Witt (Johan de) **7** Grotius (Hugo), Stikker (Dirk)
East German: **8** Ulbricht (Walter)
English: **3** Fox (Charles, Henry) **4** Eden (Anthony, George, William), More (Thomas), Peel (Arthur, Robert, William), Pitt (William), Vane (Henry) **5** Cecil (Robert, William), North (Francis, Frederick, Roger) **6** Morley (John), Sidney (Algernon, Henry, Philip, Robert),

Temple (Henry, William), Wolsey (Thomas) **7** Halifax (Earl of), Reading (Marquis of), Russell (John, William), Stanley (Edward George, Edward Henry), Stewart (Robert), Warwick (Earl of) **8** Cromwell (Oliver, Thomas), Disraeli (Benjamin), Robinson (George Frederick Samuel), Villiers (George) **9** Cavendish (Spencer, William), Churchill (Randolph, Winston), Gladstone (William), Salisbury (Earl, Marquis of), Strafford (Earl of), Wellesley (Arthur, Richard Colley) **10** Palmerston (Lord), Rockingham (Marquis of), Sunderland (Earl of), Walsingham (Francis), Wellington (Duke of) **11** Chamberlain (Austen, Joseph, Neville), Shaftesbury (Earl of) **12** Chesterfield (Earl of)

Finnish: **9** Stahlberg (Kaarlo Juho)
French: **5** Sully (Duc de) **6** Guizot (Francois-Pierre-Guillaume), Thiers (Louis-Adolphe), Turgot (Anne-Robert-Jacques) **7** Herriot (Edouard), Mazarin (Jules), Schuman (Robert), Viviani (Rene) **8** Hanotaux (Gabriel) **9** Lafayette (Marquis de), Millerand (Alexandre), Richelieu (Duc de) **10** Clemenceau (Georges) **11** Tocqueville (Alexis de)
German: **5** Wirth (Joseph) **10** Stresemann (Gustav)
German-Danish: **9** Struensee (Johann Friedrich)
Greek: **6** Zaimis (Alexandros) **8** Pericles **9** Aristides **11** Cleisthenes, Demosthenes **12** Themistocles
Israeli: **5** Begin (Menachem), Dayan (Moshe)
Italian: **6** Cavour (Conte di), Crispi (Francesco) **7** Orlando (Vittorio Emanuele) **11** Machiavelli (Niccolo)
Japanese: **5** genro, Kanoe **6** Kanoye
Norwegian: **6** Nansen (Fridtjof)
Polish: **7** Zaleski (August) **9** Pilsudski (Jozef) **10** Paderewski (Ignacy)
Prussian: **5** Stein (Karl)
Roman: **4** Cato (Marcus Porcius) **6** Cicero (Marcus Tullius), Pompey, Seneca (Lucius Annaeus) **7** Agrippa (Marcus Vipsanius) **8** Gracchus (Gaius, Tiberius), Maecenas (Gaius) **9** Symmachus (Quintus Aurelius)
Russian: **5** Witte (Sergey) **7** Molotov (Vyacheslav) **8** Potemkin (Grigory) **9** Vyshinsky (Andrey)
Scottish: **4** Knox (John)
South American: **9** San Martin (Jose de)
Swiss: **4** Ador (Gustave) **5** Welti (Emil)

static
5 fixed, inert, rigid, stuck **6** stable, steady, sticky **7** stabile, stalled, stopped **8** constant, immobile, inactive, stagnant, unmoving **9** immovable **10** unchanging **13** unfluctuating

station
3 set **4** post, rank, site, spot **5** depot, locus, place, point, state, where **6** assign **7** appoint. footing **8** capacity, standing **9** character

stationary
5 fixed **6** static **8** immobile, stagnant, unmoving **9** immovable **10** motionless, stock-still

statue
base: **6** plinth **8** pedestal
gigantic: **8** Colossus
Greek: **5** atlas **7** telamon **8** caryatid
religious: **5** Pietà
small: **8** figurine

statuesque
4 tall, trim **7** shapely **10** well-turned **11** clean-limbed

stature
see **status**

status
4 rank **5** merit, place, worth **6** cachet, rating, renown **7** caliber, dignity, footing, posture, quality **8** capacity, eminence, position, prestige, standing **9** character, condition, situation **10** prominence **11** consequence, distinction

statute
3 act, law **4** rule **5** canon, edict **6** assize, decree **7** precept **8** decretum **9** enactment, ordinance **10** regulation

staunch
4 fast, firm, sure, true **5** liege, loyal **6** ardent, secure, stable, strong **8** constant, faithful, resolute **9** allegiant, steadfast

stave off
4 ward **5** avert, block, deter, parry, rebut, repel **6** rebuff **7** forfend, obviate, prevent, repulse, rule out, ward off **8** preclude **9** forestall

stay
3 lag **4** base, bide, halt, live, prop, rest, stop, wait **5** abide, brace, check, dally, defer, delay, dwell, found, remit, shore, tarry, visit **6** arrest, bottom, column, ground, linger, loiter, put off, remain, shelve **7** adjourn, sojourn, support, suspend **8** buttress, hold over, intermit, postpone, prorogue, stop over

9 establish, interrupt, predicate **10** dillydally, hang around **11** stick around

steadfast
4 firm, sure, true **5** fixed, liege, loyal, rigid **6** ardent **7** abiding, adamant, patient, staunch **8** constant, enduring, faithful, immobile, immotile, immotive, obdurate, resolute, stubborn **9** allegiant, immovable, unbending, unmovable **10** inexorable, inflexible, relentless, unwavering, unyielding **11** irremovable, unfaltering, unflinching, unqualified **12** never-failing, single-minded, wholehearted **13** unquestioning

steady
3 set **4** beau, even, fast, sure **5** fixed, flame, liege, lover, loyal, poise **6** ardent, stable, static **7** abiding, ballast, beloved, certain, durable, equable, stabile, staunch, uniform **8** constant, enduring, faithful, ladylove, reliable, resolute, truelove, unshaken **9** allegiant, boyfriend, inamorata, inamorato, stabilify, stabilize, unvarying **10** changeless, girl friend, sweetheart, unchanging, unswerving, unwavering **11** unfaltering **12** unchangeable, unflickering, wholehearted **13** unfluctuating

steak
4 club, cube **5** chuck, flank, round, T-bone **6** rib eye **7** sirloin **9** Delmonico, hamburger, Salisbury **10** tenderloin **11** porterhouse **13** chateaubriand

steal
3 cop, nab, nim, nip, rob **4** glom, grab, hook, kite, lift, loot, lurk, slip, take **5** annex, creep, filch, glide, grasp, heist, mooch, mouse, pinch, poach, prowl, rifle, seize, shirk, sidle, skulk, slide, slink, sneak, swipe, theft **6** burgle, collar, fleece, hijack, pilfer, pocket, rustle, smouch, snatch, snitch, thieve, tiptoe **7** bargain, gumshoe, larceny, pillage, plunder, purloin **8** shanghai, shoplift, thievery, thieving **9** pussyfoot **10** burglarize **11** appropriate
a vehicle: **6** hijack **8** highjack

stealing
7 larceny
combining form: **5** klept **6** klepto

stealthy
3 sly **4** wily **5** catty, quiet, sneak **6** covert, crafty, feline, secret, shifty, silent, slinky, sneaky **7** catlike, cunning, furtive, sub-rosa **8** hush-hush,

skulking, slinking, sneaking
9 noiseless **10** pantherine, pan-
therish, undercover **11** clandestine
12 hugger-mugger **13** surreptitious

steam
5 force, might, power, sinew **6** energy, muscle **7** potency **8** strength
9 puissance
combining form: **5** atmid **6** atmido

steam bath
5 sauna

steamboat structure
5 texas

steamer
4 boat, clam, ship

steam organ
8 calliope

steamship abbreviation
2 SS

steed
5 horse **7** charger

steel
4 gird **5** brace, cheer, nerve, rally,
ready **6** buck up **7** animate, chirk
up, fortify, hearten, prepare **8** embolden, inspirit **9** encourage, enhearten, reinforce **10** strengthen

steep
3 sop **4** high, soak **5** dizzy, imbue,
lofty, sheer **6** abrupt, drench, infuse
7 arduous, extreme, suffuse **8** elevated, saturate **9** excessive **10** exorbitant, immoderate, impregnate,
inordinate **11** precipitate,
precipitous

steeple
5 spire **6** flèche

steer
3 see, tip **4** lead, show **5** guide, pilot, point, route **6** direct, escort, tip-
off **7** channel, conduct **8** shepherd
a racing rowboat: **3** cox **8** coxswain
a ship: **4** conn, helm, luff **7** boxhaul

stein
3 cup, mug **5** stoup **6** goblet, seidel **7** tankard

Steinbeck novel
10 Cannery Row, East of Eden
12 Of Mice and Men, Tortilla Flat
13 Grapes of Wrath

Steinway product
5 piano

stellar
4 main **5** chief, major **6** astral,
starry **7** capital, shining **8** dominant, gleaming, luminous, lustrous,
sidereal, starlike **9** principal
10 preeminent **11** outstanding, predominant

stem
4 flow, head, rise, stop **5** arise,
check, issue **6** arrest, spring, stanch
7 control, emanate, proceed **8** peduncle **9** originate **10** derive from
covering: **5** ocrea
plant: **4** halm **5** haulm
suffix: **3** ome
underground: **5** tuber **7** rhizoma,
rhizome

stench
4 funk, reek **5** smell, stink

stenchful
see **smelly**

stentorian
4 loud **5** rough **7** blaring, orotund,
roaring **8** gravelly, piercing
9 clamorous **10** loud-voiced, vociferous **11** fullmouthed, loudmouthed
12 earsplitting **13** clarion-voiced

step
3 act **4** hoof, move, pace, rung,
walk **5** dance, grade, notch, spoor,
stage, stair, track, tract, tread,
troop **6** action, degree, prance
7 measure, traipse **8** ambulate
9 footprint, procedure
10 proceeding
dance: **3** pas
one of a series: **6** gradin **7** gradine

step-by-step
7 gradual **9** piecemeal

stepmotherly
8 novercal

steppe
5 plain
Kazakhstan: **6** Kirgiz **10** Betpak-Dala

Steppenwolf author
5 Hesse (Hermann)

stereotypical
4 hack **5** stale, trite **6** cliché, common **7** clichéd **8** bathetic, shopworn, timeworn **9** hackneyed
11 commonplace

sterile
3 dry **4** arid, bare, dead, flat
5 stale, vapid **6** barren, effete, fallow, jejune **7** insipid, worn-out
8 desolate, impotent, infecund
9 fruitless, infertile **10** uncreative,
unfruitful, uninspired, unoriginal, un-
prolific **12** unproductive

sterilize
3 fix **4** geld, spay **5** alter, unsex
6 change, neuter **8** caponize, castrate, mutilate, sanitate, sanitize
10 emasculate, poulardize

sterilized
7 aseptic

sterling
4 pure, true **5** noble **6** worthy
9 estimable, honorable

stern
4 grim **5** sober, stony **6** flinty, severe, strict **7** ascetic, austere
9 mortified **10** astringent, implacable, inexorable, inflexible
11 unrelenting

sternward
3 aft

Sterope
father: **5** Atlas
mother: **7** Pleione
sisters: **8** Pleiades

Stevenson novel
9 Kidnapped

stew
4 boil, brew, cark, flap, fret, fume,
fuss, hash, olio, olla, slum, snit
5 civet, daube, salmi, sweat, tizzy,
worry **6** burgoo, dither, jumble,
lather, medley, paella, pother, ra-
gout, salmis, scouse, seethe, simmer, swivet, tumult **7** goulash, mélange, parboil, puchero, turmoil
8 mishmash, mulligan, pot-au-feu
9 agitation, Brunswick, cassoulet,
commotion, confusion, pasticcio,
potpourri **10** capilotade, hodgepodge, hotchpotch, miscellany, turbulence **11** olla podrida, rata-
touille, slumgullion **13** bouillabaisse

steward
6 manage **7** manager

Stheno
see **Gorgon**

stick
3 bar, dig, fix, gag, get, jib, lay,
nod, put, ram, rod, run, set, shy
4 balk, beat, clip, glue, milk, pole,
rook, sink, skin, slab, soak, stab
5 affix, baton, bleed, blind, cling,
decoy, demur, drive, ingot, mulct,
paste, place, shill, strip, stump,
sweat **6** adhere, attach, billet, boggle, capper, cement, cleave, cohere, fasten, fleece, plunge, settle,
strain, thrust **7** buffalo, nonplus,
scruple, stumble **9** establish, shillaber **10** overcharge
combining form: **5** rhabd **6** rhabdo

stick around
4 bide, stay, wait **5** abide, tarry
6 linger, remain

sticker
4 seal **5** stamp

stick-in-the-mud
4 fogy **6** fogram, fossil, square
8 mossback **10** fuddy-duddy

stick out

3 jut 4 bear, poke, pout, push, take
5 abide, brook, bulge, pouch,
stand 6 beetle, endure, strike
7 project, protend, stomach, support 8 overhang, protrude, tolerate
9 outthrust 10 outstretch

stick up

3 rob 4 loot 5 rifle 7 plunder, ransack, relieve 9 knock over

sticky

4 hard 5 gluey, gooey, gummy,
heavy, humid, muggy, mushy,
rough, soggy, tacky 6 cloggy,
knotty, resiny, rugged, slushy,
stodgy, sultry, viscid 7 maudlin,
mawkish, operose, viscous 8 adhesive, bathetic, resinous, romantic
9 difficult, laborious, strenuous
10 formidable 11 sentimental, tearjerking

stiff

3 dry, set 4 arid, body, dull, hard,
lush, mort, skin 5 drunk, miser, nabal, rigid, stark, steep, stock, tense,
undue 6 boozer, corpse, mulish,
wooden 7 buckram, cadaver, carcass, extreme, guzzler, muddled,
niggard, scrooge, stilted, studied,
swiller 8 drunkard, hardened, tightwad, towering 9 cardboard, disguised, excessive, impliable, inebriate, inelastic, obstinate, petrified,
pixilated, resistant, skinflint, unbending 10 boozehound, bullheaded, cheapskate, exorbitant,
hardheaded, immoderate, inebriated, inflexible, inordinate, mechanical, self-willed, unflexible,
unyielding 11 extravagant,
immalleable, incompliant, intoxicated, intractable 12 closedminded, pertinacious

stiffen

6 harden, tauten 7 bolster, buckram, support, thicken 8 rigidify, solidify 9 constrict, formalize, stabilize 10 immobilize

stifle

4 mute 5 burke, choke 6 dampen,
deaden, hush up, muffle 7 smother,
trammel 8 stagnate, stultify, suppress 9 suffocate 10 asphyxiate

stigma

4 blot, blur, onus, slur, spot
5 brand, odium, shame, stain, taint
6 smudge, smutch 8 black eye, disgrace, dishonor, tainting 11 bar
sinister 12 besmirchment

stigmatize

7 censure 8 denounce, identify
9 designate

still

3 too, yet 4 also, balm, calm, even,
hush, lull, more 5 allay, along,
quiet, shush, whist 6 as well, becalm, hushed, placid, serene, settle,
shut up, silent, though, withal 7 besides, compose, deathly, halcyon,
howbeit, however, hushful, silence
8 after all, choke off, likewise,
moreover, peaceful, quietude, stagnant, tranquil 9 deathlike, noiseless, quietness, soundless 10 motionless, untroubled 11 furthermore,
nonetheless, tranquilize, unperturbed 12 additionally,
nevertheless

stilt

4 bird, pole 8 longlegs

stilted

4 prim 6 formal, la-di-da, too-too,
wooden 7 aureate, buckram, flowery, genteel 8 affected, decorous,
sonorous 9 bombastic, cardboard
10 euphuistic

stilt-like bird

6 avocet

stimulant

4 goad, spur 7 caffein, impetus, impulse 8 caffeine, catalyst, excitant
9 incentive 10 incitation, incitement, motivation

stimulate

4 move, whet 5 pique, rouse, set
up 6 arouse, excite, vivify 7 commove, enliven, innerve, inspire, provoke, quicken 8 activate, dynamize, energize, motivate, spirit up,
vitalize 9 galvanize, innervate
10 exhilarate

stimulus

4 goad, push, spur 5 boost, cause
6 motive, urging 7 impetus, impulse, piquing 8 catalyst, stressor
9 incentive 10 excitement, incitation, incitement, inducement, invitation, motivation, propellant 11 instigation, provocation, provocative
13 encouragement

sting

4 bite, burn 5 smart

stinging

8 aculeate

stingy

4 mean 5 close, scant, tight 6 frugal, narrow, scrimy 7 chinchy, costive, miserly, niggard, save-all,

scrimpy, sparing, thrifty 8 pinching,
ungiving 9 niggardly, penny-wise,
penurious 10 economical, hardfisted, hardhanded, ironfisted,
pinchpenny, ungenerous 11 closefisted, tightfisted 12 cheeseparing,
parsimonious 13 narrowhearted,
penny-pinching

stink

4 funk, reek 5 smell 6 stench 7 malodor 8 malaroma

stinker

3 cur, dog 4 scum, snot 5 skunk,
snake

stinking

see **smelly**

stinky

see **smelly**

stint

2 go 3 job 4 bout, duty, task, time,
tour, turn 5 chare, chore, cramp,
pinch, scant, screw, share, shift,
short, skimp, spare, spell, trick
6 amount, devoir, scrape, scrimp,
skinch 8 quantity 9 allotment, stricture 10 assignment, limitation
11 restriction

stipend

3 fee, pay 4 hire, wage 5 award
6 salary 7 payment 9 emolument
13 consideration

stipple

3 dot 5 speck 6 pepper, streak
7 freckle, speckle 8 sprinkle
9 bespeckle

stipulate

5 state 6 detail 7 provide, specify
9 designate 13 particularize

stipulation

5 limit, terms 7 proviso, strings
9 provision

stir

3 ado, can, din, jug, mix, pen, set
4 abet, boil, fuss, jail, keep, moil,
move, rout, wake, whet 5 awake,
churn, drive, impel, raise, rally,
rouse, roust, set on, waken, whirl
6 arouse, awaken, bubble, bustle,
excite, flurry, foment, furore, hubbub, incite, kindle, motion, pother,
seethe, simmer, tumult, whip up
7 actuate, agitate, ferment, inspire,
provoke, quicken 8 activate, energize, movement, vitalize 9 agitation, challenge, commotion, galvanize, instigate, stimulate
11 disturbance, pandemonium

stirrup
6 stapes

stithy
5 anvil

stock
4 clan, folk, fund, have, hope, keep, race 5 carry, faith, hoard, house, tribe, trust 6 family, supply 7 backlog, furnish, kindred, lineage, nest egg, reserve 8 estimate, judgment, reliance 9 appraisal, inventory, reservoir 10 assessment, confidence, dependence, estimation, evaluation

stockade
3 can, jug 4 coop, jail 6 cooler, lockup, prison 8 hoosegow 9 calaboose, guardroom

stock exchange
6 bourse

stockings
4 hose 7 hosiery

stockpile
4 bank, heap, hill, hive, mass 5 amass, drift, hoard, lay up, mound, stack, store, uplay 6 garner, roll up 7 backlog, nest egg, pyramid, reserve, store up 8 cumulate, mountain 9 inventory, reservoir 10 accumulate

stocky
3 fat 5 bunty, cobby, dumpy, lumpy, plump, pudgy, short, squab, squat, thick 6 chuffy, chumpy, chunky, low-set, squdgy, stubby, stuggy, stumpy 7 lumpish 8 heavyset, thickset 9 corpulent 11 thickbodied

stodge
4 cloy, fill, flut, jade, pall, plod, sate, slog, slop, toil 5 gorge 6 trudge 7 filling, satiate, surfeit 8 footslog, plunther

stodgy
4 blah, dull 5 dowdy, dumpy, gluey, gooey, gummy, heavy, tacky 6 boring, claggy, clarty, cloggy, dreary, frumpy, sticky 7 humdrum, weighty 8 banausic, frumpish, outmoded, pedantic, plodding 9 hidebound, out-of-date, ponderous, unstylish 10 monotonous, pedestrian, unexciting

stoic
3 dry 5 aloof 7 patient, Spartan 8 detached, resigned 9 apathetic, impassive 10 phlegmatic 11 indifferent, indomitable, unconcerned

stoicism
4 grit, guts, sand 5 pluck 6 apathy 8 backbone 9 fortitude, stolidity 11 impassivity 13 insensibility
founder: 4 Zeno

stoke
4 feed, poke, stir, tend 6 supply

Stoker, Bram
novel: 7 Dracula

stolid
3 dry 4 dull, dumb, slow 5 blunt, dense, inert 6 bovine, obtuse, supine 7 passive 8 inactive, rocklike 9 apathetic, impassive 10 phlegmatic

stomach
3 gut 4 bear, craw, take 5 abide, belly, brook, stand, taste, tummy 6 digest, endure, paunch, venter 7 abdomen, swallow 8 appetite, tolerate 9 appetence
combining form: 5 gastr 6 gaster, gastro, ventri, ventro 7 gastero, gastria
enzyme: 6 pepsin, rennin
muscle: 7 pylorus
ruminant: 5 rumen 6 omasum 8 abomasum 9 reticulum
Scottish: 4 kyte

stomachache
5 colic, gripe 6 misery 8 distress 12 collywobbles

stomp
5 tramp 7 trample

stone
3 gem 4 buhr, rock 5 lapis, logan, stane 6 pebble, testis 7 boulder, lapides (plural), surface 8 calculus
base: 6 plinth
block of: 8 monolith
chip: 5 spall 6 gallet
combining form: 4 lite, lith, lyte
cosmic: 6 meteor 9 chondrite, meteorite
for grinding grains: 6 metate
fruit: 5 drupe
memorial: 7 obelisk
monument: 8 megalith
of a fruit: 3 pit 6 pyrene
precious: 6 ligure

＿＿＿ Stone
7 Blarney, Rosetta

stonecrop
5 sedum

stoned
4 high 5 boozy, doped, drunk 6 canned, lushed, zonked 7 drugged, muddled 8 hopped-up, turned on, wiped out 9 disguised, pixilated, plastered, spaced-out 10 inebriated, tripped out 11 intoxicated

stonelike
7 lithoid

Stooge
3 Moe (Howard) 5 Curly (Howard), Larry (Fine)

stool pigeon
3 rat 4 fink, nark, pimp, sing 5 peach 6 canary, inform, snitch, squeak, squeal 7 tipster

stoop
3 dip 4 duck, sink, thaw 5 deign, favor, kneel, porch, relax 6 accord, crouch, oblige, unbend 7 concede, descend, portico 10 condescend 11 accommodate

stop
3 bar, can, dam, end, see 4 balk, call, clog, fill, halt, plug, quit, stay, stem, wall 5 block, brake, cease, check, choke, close, stall, tarry 6 arrest, cut off, desist, draw up, ending, haul up, hinder, kibosh, lay off, pull up, stanch 7 barrier, break up, bring up, closing, congest, disrupt, occlude, prevent, shut off, sojourn, suspend, turn off 8 blockade, knock off, leave off, obstruct, surcease 9 barricade, cessation, interrupt, roadblock, terminate 10 conclusion, desistance, standstill 11 discontinue, refrain from, termination
blood: 6 stanch
up: 4 cork, plug 7 occlude 8 obturate

stopgap
5 shift 6 refuge, resort 8 recourse, resource 9 expedient, makeshift 10 expediency, substitute 11 provisional

stopover
5 visit 7 sojourn 9 tarriance
for troops: 5 étape

stoppage
6 strike
combining form: 5 stasi 6 stases (plural), stasia, stasis
work: 6 hartal, strike

stopper
4 clog, fill, plug 5 block, choke, close 7 congest, occlude 8 obstruct

store
3 bin 4 fund, hive, pack, shop, tank 5 amass, cache, depot, hoard, lay up, stash 6 bestow, bought, garner, market, outlet, roll

up, shoppe, supply **7** arsenal, backlog, deposit, nest egg, reserve **8** cumulate, emporium, magazine, mothball, showroom, squirrel **9** inventory, reservoir, stockpile, warehouse **10** accumulate, depository, repository
candle: **9** chandlery
in a silo: **6** ensile **8** ensilage
shoe: **7** bootery

storehouse
5 depot **7** arsenal, granary **8** magazine **10** depository, repository

storekeeper
8 merchant

storeroom
6 larder, pantry **7** buttery

storm
4 hail, to-do **5** beset, buran, burst, salvo **6** assail, attack, bustle, clamor, easter, fall on, hassle, hubbub, pother, strike, volley **7** aggress, assault, barrage, clatter, ruction, typhoon **8** drumfire, fall upon **9** broadside, cannonade, commotion, fusillade **10** hurly-burly **11** bombardment

storm trooper
10 brownshirt

stormy
4 foul, wild **5** dirty, dusty, murky, rough **6** raging **7** furious, howling, roaring **8** blustery **9** turbulent **10** blustering, rip-roaring **11** tempestuous, threatening

story
3 fib, lie **4** tale, yarn **5** conte, fable **6** canard, legend, report **7** account, falsity, fiction, märchen, untruth, version **8** allegory, anecdote, folktale **9** chronicle, fairy tale, falsehood, narration, narrative **11** description, fabrication **13** prevarication
involved: **8** megillah
moral: **7** parable
short: **5** conte **8** anecdote

storyteller
4 liar **6** fibber **8** fabulist **9** raconteur

stoup
4 font **5** basin **6** flagon **7** tankard

stout
3 ale, fat **4** bold, brew, hard **5** brave, heavy, obese, tough **6** fleshy, heroic, portly, strong, sturdy **7** porcine, valiant, weighty **8** fearless, intrepid, resolute, stal-

wart, valorous **9** corpulent, steadfast, tenacious **10** courageous, invincible, overweight **11** indomitable, thick-bodied

Stout detective
5 Wolfe (Nero)

stouthearted
4 bold **5** brave **7** doughty, valiant **8** fearless, intrepid, unafraid **9** dauntless, undaunted **10** courageous

stove
4 kiln **5** range **8** potbelly

stow
4 pack **6** steeve **9** warehouse

stower
9 stevedore

Stowe work
4 Dred

strabismus
6 squint

straddle
6 ramble, sprawl, stride **8** bestride, scramble, sprangle **11** spreadeagle

straggle
4 roam, rove **5** drift, range, stray **6** ramble, wander **7** maunder, meander

straight
4 fair, good, neat, pure **5** plain, right **6** at once, direct, honest, linear, square **7** unmixed **8** directly, first off, orthodox **9** forthwith, instanter, right away, undiluted **10** aboveboard, button-down, forthright, unmodified **11** immediately **12** concentrated, conventional, plain dealing **13** unadulterated, undeviatingly, uninterrupted
combining form: **4** orth, rect **5** ortho, recti

straightaway
3 now **6** at once **8** directly, first off **9** forthwith, instanter **11** immediately

straightedge
5 razor

straighten
4 true **5** align **6** unbend, uncurl
up: **4** tidy

straightforward
5 frank **6** candid, direct, honest **7** precise **8** clearcut **9** outspoken **11** undeviating

strain
3 air, irk, lay, tax, try, tug **4** hint, mind, moil, mood, ooze, pull, seep, toil, tone, tune, vein, work **5** drive, labor, shade, sweat, tinge, touch, trace **6** harass, melody, streak, stress, strive, warble **7** descant, measure, melisma, soupçon, tension, trouble **8** diapason, distress, pressure, transude **9** suspicion **10** suggestion

strait
4 bind, pass **5** pinch **6** crisis **7** squeeze **8** exigency, hardship, juncture **9** crossroad, emergency **10** difficulty, perplexity **11** contingency
Adriatic Sea-Ionian Sea: **7** Otranto
Africa-Madagascar: **10** Mozambique
Alaska: **3** Icy
Alaska-Russia: **6** Bering
Albania-Greece: **5** Corfu
Asia-Europe: **11** Dardanelles
Atlantic-Baffin Island: **5** Davis
Atlantic-Gulf of Mexico: **7** Florida
Atlantic-Mediterranean: **9** Gibraltar
Atlantic-Nantucket Sound: **8** Muskeget
Atlantic-North Sea: **7** English
Atlantic-Pacific: **5** Drake **8** Magellan
Atlantic-Saint Lawrence: **5** Cabot
Baffin Island-Quebec: **6** Hudson
Bering Sea-Sea of Okhotsk: **5** Kuril **6** Kurile
Bismarck Sea-Solomon Sea: **6** Vitiaz
Canada: **3** Rae **5** Dease
East China Sea: **5** Korea **8** Tsushima
East China-South China: **6** Taiwan **7** Formosa
England-France: **5** Dover
Flores Sea-Indian Ocean: **4** Sape
Flores Sea-Savu Sea: **4** Alor
Indian Ocean-Java Sea: **5** Sunda
India-Sri Lanka: **4** Palk
Indonesia: **4** Alas, Alor, Bali **5** Tioro **6** Lombok **7** Dampier, Makasar **8** Makassar, Surabaja
Inner Hebrides: **5** Tiree
Iran-Oman: **6** Hormuz
Italy: **7** Messina
Japan: **4** Yura **5** Bungo, Kitan **7** Hayasui
Japan-Sakhalin Island: **4** Sōya
Lake Huron: **10** Mississagi
Lake Huron-Lake Michigan: **8** Mackinac
Malay Archipelago: **5** Wetar
Malaysia-Singapore: **6** Johore
Malay-Sumatra: **7** Malacca
New Jersey-Staten Island: **7** van Kull
New South Wales-Tasmania: **4** Bass
New Zealand: **4** Cook

Northwest Territories: **6** Barrow
8 Franklin, Victoria **13** Prince of
Wales
Nova Scotia: **5** Canso
Pacific-San Francisco Bay: **10** Golden
Gate
Pacific-South China Sea: **5** Luzon
Philippines: **5** Bohol, Tanon **6** Iloilo
7 Basilan
Russia: **4** Kara
Suvu Sea-Timor Sea: **4** Roti
Sea of Azov-Black Sea: **5** Kerch
7 Enikale
Sea of Japan: **5** Tatar
Solomon Islands: **12** Bougainville
South China Sea: **7** Mindoro
9 Singapore
Turkey: **8** Bosporus **9** Karadeniz
Vancouver-Washington: **10** Juan de
Fuca
Wales: **5** Menai
Washington Sound: **4** Haro

straitlaced
4 prig, prim **6** narrow, prissy, strict,
stuffy **7** genteel, prudish **8** priggish, rigorous **9** hidebound, Victorian **10** intolerant **11** puritanical
12 narrow-minded

strand
4 bank **5** beach, coast, shore,
wreck **6** pile up **8** cast away
9 shipwreck

strange
3 new, odd **5** alien, crazy, fishy,
funny, kinky, kooky, nutty, outré,
queer, weird **6** exotic, far-out,
freaky, quaint **7** amazing, bizarre,
curious, erratic, oddball, offbeat,
uncanny, uncouth, unknown, unusual **8** aberrant, abnormal, atypical, peculiar, romantic, singular,
wondrous **9** eccentric, fantastic,
grotesque, marvelous, wonderful
10 astounding, miraculous, mysterious, off-the-wall, outlandish, stupendous, surprising, unfamiliar
11 astonishing, exceptional, spectacular **12** unaccustomed
13 idiosyncratic
combining form: **3** xen **4** xeno

Strange Interlude author
6 O'Neill (Eugene)

stranger
4 unco **5** alien **7** inconnu, visitor
8 outcomer, outsider, wanderer
9 auslander, foreigner, immigrant,
transient

strangle
5 burke, choke, shush **6** garote,

muffle, quelch **7** garotte, garrote
8 suppress, throttle

strapping
6 robust

stratagem
4 play, plot, ploy, ruse, wile
5 feint, trick **6** device, gambit **8** artifice, intrigue, maneuver **10** conspiracy **11** machination

strategy
4 plan **6** design, scheme **7** project
8 game plan **9** blueprint

stratum
3 bed **5** layer

Strauss
opera: **6** Salome **7** Elektra
13 Rosenkavalier
tone poem: **7** Don Juan **10** Don
Quixote

straw
3 sow **5** blond **6** flaxen, golden,
thatch
braided: **6** sennit
bundle: **8** windling
Japanese: **4** toyo
mat: **6** tatami
plaited: **7** leghorn

strawberry nettle
6 urtica

stray
3 err, gad **4** roam, rove **5** range
6 depart, errant, ramble, random,
wander **7** deviate, devious, digress, diverge, erratic, excurse, meander, runaway, traipse **8** divagate, sporadic **9** gallivant,
wandering

streak
4 hint, spot, vein **5** fleck, shade,
tinge, touch, trace **6** dapple, marble, mottle, strain, strake, stripe
7 striate **8** tincture **9** suspicion, variegate **10** intimation, suggestion
of color: **5** vitta

streaked
8 brindled, grizzled

stream
3 run **4** burn, flow, flux, gill, gush,
pour, race, roll, rush, tide **5** bourn,
brook, creek, drift, flood, spate,
surge **6** bourne, branch, rindle,
runlet, runnel, sluice **7** current, rivulet **8** affluent
combining form: **5** fluvi **6** fluvio
rapid: **7** torrent
small: **4** sike, syke
verbal: **10** blue streak

streamer
4 flag, jack **5** color **6** banner, ensign, pennon **7** pendant, pennant
8 banderol, bannerol, standard

streamline
8 simplify

street
3 way **4** drag, path, road **5** drive,
track **6** artery, avenue, ruelle
7 highway, roadway **9** boulevard
12 thoroughfare
border: **7** curbing
material: **6** cobble **7** asphalt
11 cobblestone
narrow: **4** wynd
show: **5** raree

streetcar
4 tram **7** trolley

Streetcar Named Desire, A
author: **8** Williams (Tennessee)
character: **6** Stella **7** Blanche,
Stanley

Street Scene author
4 Rice (Elmer)

strength
5 brawn, force, might, power,
sense, sinew **6** burden, energy,
muscle **7** potency, purport **8** firmness, security **9** soundness, stability, substance, toughness **10** stableness, steadiness, sturdiness

strengthen
4 beef, gird **5** brace, ready, sinew,
steel **6** anneal, tone up **7** animate,
chirk up, ensteel, fortify, hearten,
prepare, support, toughen **8** embolden, energize, fortress, inspirit
9 encourage, enhearten, reinforce,
undergird **10** invigorate

strenuous
4 hard, mean **5** lusty, tough, vital
6 uphill, wicked **7** dynamic, operose, toilful **8** toilsome, vigorous
9 difficult, effortful, energetic, Herculean, laborious

Strephon
8 shepherd
beloved: **5** Chloe **6** Urania

stress
3 irk, try **4** pain **5** pinch **6** accent,
burden, harass, import, play up,
strain, weight **7** feature, tension,
trouble **8** emphasis, pressure **9** emphasize, italicize, underline
10 importance, underscore
12 accentuation
in poetry: **5** ictus

stretch

3 run **4** area, draw, time **5** fudge, range, reach, scope, space, spell, sweep, tract, while **6** extend, extent, length, limber, region, spread, supple, whippy **7** breadth, compass, draw out, elastic, expanse, magnify, prolong, purview, spin out, springy, tighten **8** distance, elongate, flexible, lengthen, protract **9** amplitude, dimension, embellish, embroider, expansion, overstate, resilient **10** exaggerate

on a frame: **6** tenter

out: **3** lie **4** rest **6** repose, sprawl

stretchable

7 elastic, tensile **8** tensible

stretched

4 taut

stretcher

5 dooly **6** dhooly, gurney, leader, litter **7** tail fly **8** tall tale

strew

3 sow **4** dust **5** cover **6** pepper, spread **7** diffuse, disject, radiate, scatter **8** disperse, sprinkle **9** broadcast, circulate, dissipate, propagate **10** distribute **11** disseminate

strict

4 dour, grim, just, true **5** harsh, right, rigid, tough **8** exacting, faithful, rigorous **9** draconian, unsparing, veracious, veridical **10** forbidding, hard-boiled, ironhanded, oppressive **11** undistorted **12** unpermissive

stricture

4 slam, slur **5** cramp, stint **7** obloquy **9** aspersion **10** limitation, reflection **11** restriction **12** ball and chain **13** animadversion

stride

5 march, sling, stalk **8** straddle

strident

4 loud **5** harsh **6** hoarse **7** blatant, dinsome, grating, jarring, rasping, raucous, squawky **9** clamorous **10** boisterous, stentorian, stertorous, vociferant, vociferous **11** loudmouthed **12** obstreperous

strife

4 fray **5** brawl, broil, fight **6** affray, combat, fracas **7** contest, discord, dispute, dissent, quarrel, rivalry, warfare, wrangle **8** argument, conflict, disunity, squabble, tug-of-war, variance **9** disaccord, emulation **10** contention, difference, dissension, dissidence **11** altercation, competition, controversy

strike

3 hit, pop, rap **4** bang, bash, beat, dash, deal, ding, give, kick, knap, mace, poke, rack, slam, slap, slog, slug, sock, swat, whap, whop **5** beset, carry, clout, crash, flick, knack, knock, occur, punch, smack, smite, storm, swipe, thump, whack **6** affect, assail, attack, cudgel, fall on, fillip, hammer, harrow, pummel, thrash **7** afflict, aggress, assault, deliver, impress, inflict, inspire, percuss, torment, torture **8** fall upon **9** detection, discovery, influence

striking

5 showy, vivid **6** cogent, marked, signal **7** salient, telling **8** forceful, powerful **9** arresting, arrestive, prominent **10** compelling, noticeable, remarkable **11** conspicuous, outstanding

Strindberg play

6 Easter **8** Comrades **9** Miss Julie, The Father **10** Master Olaf **12** Dance of Death, Gustavus Vasa, The Creditors

string

3 row **4** file, line, rank, tier **5** chain, order, queue, shift, train **6** refuge, resort, sequel, series **7** echelon, stopgap **8** recourse, resource, sequence **9** expedient, makeshift **10** substitute, succession

up: **4** hang **5** noose, scrag **6** gibbet

string along

3 toy **4** fool **5** dally, flirt **6** coquet, lead on, trifle, wanton

stringent

see **strict**

stringy

4 ropy, wiry **6** sinewy **7** fibrous **8** muscular

strip

3 bar, rod **4** band, bare, doff, flay, husk, peel, sack, skin, slab **5** ingot, scale, stick, waste **6** billet, denude, devest, divest, expose, fillet, flitch, ravage, ribbon **7** bandeau, banding, deprive, disrobe, pillage, take off, uncover, undress **8** bankrupt, denudate, desolate, spoliate, unclothe **9** depredate, desecrate, devastate, dismantle **11** decorticate, excorticate

leather: **5** thong

of wood: **4** lath, slat

skin: **6** flench, flense

stripe

3 ilk **4** band, flog, hide, kind, lash, sort, type, whip **5** breed, order, whale **6** fillet, kidney, lather, ribbon, strake, streak, striate, thrash **7** bandeau, banding, feather, scourge, species, variety **10** flagellate

stripling

3 boy, lad

stripper

6 peeler, teaser **9** ecdysiast

stripteaser

see **stripper**

strive

3 try, tug, vie **4** cope, moil, seek, toil, work **5** assay, essay, labor, offer **6** resist, strain **7** attempt, travail **8** endeavor, struggle **9** undertake

stroke

3 hit, pet **4** hone, whet **6** caress, soothe **8** apoplexy **9** heartbeat

stroll

4 mope, muck, turn, walk **5** amble, drift, mosey, paseo **6** bummel, linger, ramble **7** saunter

stroller

4 pram **5** tramp **6** go-cart **7** vagrant

strong

4 fast, firm, hard, rich, sure **5** hardy, large, lusty, stout, tough **6** ardent, brawny, heroic, mighty, potent, robust, rugged, secure, sinewy, stable, sturdy, wieldy **7** durable, staunch, unmixed **8** enduring, forceful, muscular, powerful, stalwart, straight, vigorous **9** strapping, tenacious, undiluted **10** ablebodied, full-bodied, spirituous **12** concentrated

strong-arm

5 bully **6** bounce, hector **7** dragoon **8** bludgeon, browbeat, bulldoze, bullyrag **9** terrorize **10** intimidate

strongbox

6 coffer

stronghold

4 fort **7** citadel, redoubt **8** fastness, fortress

strong point

5 forte

strong suit

5 forte **6** medium, métier, oyster **8** eminency

strontium
  symbol: **2** Sr

strophe
  6 stanza

structure
  4 form, pile **5** build, frame **6** fabric, format, makeup, system **7** anatomy, complex, edifice, network **8** building, erection, skeleton **9** framework **10** morphology **11** arrangement, composition **12** construction
  combining form: **5** morph **6** morpho

struggle
  3 try, vie **4** agon **5** assay, essay, offer, trial **6** hassle, strive, tussle **7** attempt, compete, grapple, scuffle **8** endeavor, flounder, striving **9** undertake **11** undertaking

strumpet
  4 jade, slut **5** hussy, tramp, trull, wench **6** harlot, wanton **7** jezebel, trollop **8** slattern

strut
  6 flaunt, parade, prance, sashay **7** flounce, peacock, swagger

stub
  4 snag **5** fence, guard **6** strike **9** pulverize

stubborn
  5 balky, rigid, stunt **6** dogged, mulish, ornery, wilful **7** adamant, bullish, wayward, willful **8** obdurate **9** obstinate, pigheaded, steadfast, unbending **10** bullheaded, headstrong, inexorable, inflexible, rebellious, refractory, relentless, unyielding **11** intractable **12** cantankerous, contumacious, single-minded

stubby
  5 dumpy, puggy, squat **6** chumpy, chunky, squdgy, stocky, stuggy, stumpy **7** puggish **8** heavyset **11** thick-bodied

stuck-up
  4 vain **8** conceity **9** conceited **12** narcissistic, vainglorious

stud
  3 dot **4** male, nail, post, spot **5** cleat **6** button, pillar, pimple **7** speckle, upright **8** sprinkle

student
  5 pupil **6** premed **7** protégé
  college: **13** undergraduate
  combining form: **3** log **5** logue
  female: **4** coed
  first-year: **8** freshman
  fourth-year: **6** senior

French: **5** élève **8** étudiant
military: **5** cadet
Muslim: **5** softa
naval officer: **5** middy **10** midshipman
of a guru: **5** chela
placement: **8** tracking
second-year: **9** sophomore
third-year: **6** junior
wandering: **7** goliard

studio
  4 shop **7** atelier, bottega **8** workroom, workshop

Studs Lonigan creator
  7 Farrell (James T.)

study
  3 con, den, vet **4** heed, mind, muse, view **5** learn, weigh **6** debate, lesson, musing, ponder, survey, trance **7** analyze, canvass, check up, examine, inspect, reverie **8** consider, exercise, memorize, think out, weighing **9** attention, check over, pondering, think over **10** excogitate, meditation, rumination, scrutinize **11** abstraction, application, contemplate **12** deliberation **13** concentration, consideration, contemplation
  combining form: **5** sophy
  group: **7** seminar
  hard: **4** cram
  suffix: **3** ics

stuff
  3 jam, ram **4** cram, pith, soul, tamp **5** being, crowd, gorge **6** entity, marrow, matter, object, things **7** essence, jam-pack **8** material, overcram, overfill **9** substance **10** individual, virtuality **12** essentiality, quintessence

stuffed shirt
  4 prig, smug **5** Blimp, prude **7** diehard **10** fuddy-duddy **12** Colonel Blimp

stuffing
  3 gut, tar **6** tripes **7** innards, insides, inwards, pudding, viscera **8** dressing, entrails **9** internals

stuffy
  4 dull, prim **5** close, fuggy, heavy, humid, stivy, thick, wiggy **6** narrow, prissy, proper, shut-up, stodgy, sultry **7** airless, bloated, genteel, humdrum, pompous, prudish **8** arrogant, priggish, stagnant, stifling **9** hidebound, illiberal, important, Victorian **10** breathless, oppressive, pontifical, tight-laced **11** magisterial, puritanical, straitlaced,

suffocating **12** narrow-minded **13** self-important

stultify
  4 dull **5** check **6** deaden, impair, stifle, weaken **7** inhibit, nullify, repress, smother, trammel **8** enfeeble, restrain, stagnate, suppress **9** suffocate **10** constipate, discourage, invalidate

stumble
  3 err, sin **4** slip, trip **5** demur, error **6** falter **7** blunder, scruple, stagger, stammer **8** hesitate

stump
  3 get **4** beat, dare, defi, defy **5** barge, stick **6** cartel, lumber **7** buffalo, galumph, nonplus **8** defiance **9** challenge

stun
  4 daze **5** amaze **6** bedaze, bemuse, benumb, dazzle **7** astound, nonplus, petrify, stupefy **8** bewilder, knock out, paralyze **11** flabbergast

stunt
  4 curb, feat **5** check, dwarf, runty, trick **6** impair, runted **7** runtish, scrunty **8** hold back, suppress

stupefy
  4 daze, dull, faze **5** addle, blunt **6** bedaze, bemuse, benumb, rattle **7** nonplus, petrify **8** hebetate, paralyze

stupendous
  7 amazing, massive **8** cracking, towering, wondrous **9** fantastic, marvelous, monstrous, wonderful **10** astounding, miraculous, monumental, prodigious, staggering **11** astonishing, spectacular

stupid
  4 dull, dumb, slow **5** brute, crass, dense, dopey, dummy, dunce, heavy, idiot, moron, silly, thick **6** dummel, goosey, oafish, simple, torpid **7** asinine, brutish, doltish, dullard, fatuous, foolish, idiotic, lumpish, pinhead **8** backward, blockish, comatose, dullhead, dumbbell, dummkopf, duncical, ignorant, retarded, sluggish **9** blear-eyed, fatheaded, half-assed, ignoramus, imbecilic, lethargic, lumbering, pinheaded, simpleton **10** beefheaded, beef-witted, half-witted, numskulled, slow-witted, slumberous **11** blockheaded, thickheaded, thick-witted **12** beetleheaded, hammerheaded, hebetudinous **13** chuckleheaded

stupor
4 coma 5 sleep 6 torpor 7 languor, slumber 8 dullness, hebetude, lethargy, narcosis 9 lassitude, torpidity 10 anesthesia
13 insensibility
combining form: 4 narc 5 narco

sturdy
5 sound, stout, tough 6 strong
7 healthy 8 stalwart 9 tenacious
11 substantial

sturgeon
6 beluga
roe: 6 caviar 7 caviare

Sturm und Drang
6 unrest 7 ailment, ferment, turmoil
8 disquiet 10 inquietude 11 disquietude, restiveness 12 restlessness

St. Vitus' ___
5 dance

sty
3 den, pen 4 dump, sink 5 Sodom
6 pigpen 7 cesspit, piggery
8 cesspool

stygian
7 avernal, hellish 8 infernal, plutonic 9 cimmerian, plutonian
11 pandemoniac

style
3 fad, way 4 chic, mode, rage, tone, vein 5 craze, decor, thing, vogue 6 manner 7 fashion, wording 9 designate 10 dernier cri
11 appellation, appellative
hair: 4 coif 8 coiffure
suffix: 5 esque

stylish
2 in 3 mod, new 4 chic, posh, tony, trig 5 doggy, natty, nifty, ritzy, sassy, sharp, showy, sleek, slick, smart, swank, swell 6 chichi, classy, dapper, dressy, modern, modish, new-day, rakish, snappy, snazzy, spiffy, tonish, trendy, with-it
7 à la mode, dashing, doggish, swagger 8 spiffing, up-to-date
9 exclusive 10 newfangled 11 fashionable, modernistic, pretentious
12 new-fashioned, ostentatious

Stymphalides' slayer
8 Heracles, Hercules

styx
5 nymph, river 7 hateful
father: 7 Oceanus
ferryman: 6 Charon
location: 5 Hades
mother: 6 Tethys

Suah's father
6 Zophah

suave
5 bland, slick 6 genial, polite, smooth, urbane 7 affable, cordial, courtly, fulsome, politic, refined, tactful, worldly 8 cultured, gracious, polished, sociable, unctuous, well-bred 9 courteous, distingué
10 cultivated, diplomatic, soft-spoken 12 ingratiating
13 sophisticated

sub
5 under 6 fill-in 7 stand-in 9 alternate, dependent, secondary 10 collateral 11 locum tenens, pinch hitter, replacement

subaltern
8 inferior 9 secondary, underling

subdue
5 crush, quash, quell 6 defeat, master, quench, reduce 7 conquer, put down, squelch 8 bear down, beat down, suppress, vanquish 9 overpower, subjugate

subdued
4 soft, tame 5 quiet, sober 6 low-key, mellow 7 neutral, serious
8 low-keyed, softened, tasteful, tempered 9 moderated, toned down
10 controlled, restrained, submissive 11 inobtrusive, unobtrusive

subjacent
3 low 5 lower, under 6 lesser, nether 8 inferior

subject
3 apt 4 core, head, meat, open, text 5 motif, point, prone, theme, topic, under 6 expose, liable, likely, matter, motive 7 citizen, exposed, lay open, problem, servile, slavish, uncover 8 argument, material, notional, question 9 dependent, leitmotif, leitmotiv, obnoxious, secondary, sensitive, substance, tributary 10 collateral 11 subordinato, subservient, susceptible

subjective
6 biased 10 prejudiced

subjugate
see **subdue**

sublime
4 holy 5 erect, exalt, grand, honor, ideal, lofty, noble, proud 6 august, divine, sacred, superb 7 dignify, ennoble, exalted, glorify, magnify, stately 8 elevated, glorious, gorgeous, majestic, splendid 9 spiri-

tual 10 aggrandize 11 distinguish, magnificent, resplendent, splendorous 12 transcendent
13 splendiferous

submarine
detector: 5 sonar

submerge
3 dip 4 duck, dunk, sink, soak
5 douse, drown, flood, souse, swamp, whelm 6 deluge, drench, engulf, go down 7 founder, go under, immerse 8 inundate, overflow, saturate

submerse
see **submerge**

submissive
4 tame 6 menial 7 obeying, servile, slavish, subdued, unerect
8 resigned, uxorious, yielding
9 complying 10 bowing down
11 acquiescent, conformable, subservient, unresistant, unresisting
12 nonresistant, nonresisting

submit
3 bow 4 cave, fall 5 bring, defer, offer, refer, yield 6 go down, hand in, send in, tender 7 deliver, go under, knuckle, present, proffer, provide, succumb, suggest 8 theorize
9 surrender 10 capitulate
11 buckle under 12 knuckle under

subordinate
5 minor, scrub, under 7 adjunct, subject 8 adjuvant, inferior, parergal 9 accessory, auxiliary, dependent, satellite, secondary, subaltern, tributary, underling
10 collateral, subsidiary

suborn
6 incite, induce 9 instigate

sub rosa
8 covertly, in camera, secretly 9 by stealth, furtively, privately 10 stealthily 12 hugger-mugger 13 clandestinely

subscribe
3 ink, yes 4 sign 5 agree, favor
6 accede, adhere, assent 7 approve, consent, endorse 8 sanction
9 acquiesce, autograph, signature
10 contribute

subsequent
4 next 5 after, later 6 serial 7 ensuing 9 following, posterior, resultant, resulting, succedent 10 sequential, succeeding, successive
11 consecutive
prefix: 4 post

subservient

4 mean 6 abject, menial 7 fawning, ignoble, servile, slavish 8 adjuvant, cowering, cringing, obeisant, resigned 9 accessory, ancillary, auxiliary, compliant, truckling 10 collateral, obsequious, submissive 11 acquiescent

subside

3 ebb 4 fall, lull, wane 5 abate, let up 7 die away, die down, ease off, slacken 8 moderate

subsidiary

5 minor 6 back-up 8 adjuvant 9 accessory, ancillary, tributary 10 collateral

subsidize

4 back, fund, help 5 endow 7 finance, promote

subsidy

4 gift 5 grant 6 reward 10 subvention 13 appropriation

subsist

2 be 4 live, move 7 breathe

subsistence

4 keep, salt 5 bread 6 living 7 alimony, support 10 sustenance 11 maintenance 12 alimentation

substance

3 nub 4 body, bulk, core, crux, gist, mass, meat, pith, soul 5 being, drift, focus, heart, point, sense, short, stuff, tenor, thing, worth 6 amount, bottom, burden, center, corpus, entity, import, kernel, marrow, matter, nubbin, object, riches, staple, thrust, upshot, wealth 7 essence, fortune, meaning, nucleus, purport 8 additive, material, property, strength, sum total 9 resources 10 individual, virtuality 12 essentiality, quintessence
combining form: 3 hyl 4 hylo 5 phane, state
transparent: 6 hyalin 7 hyaline

substantial

3 big 4 easy, snug, well 5 gross, solid 6 strong 7 weighty, well-off 8 material, physical, sensible, tangible, well-to-do 9 corporeal, important, momentous, objective, well-fixed 10 meaningful, phenomenal, prosperous, well-heeled 11 comfortable, significant 12 considerable

substantiate

3 try 4 test 5 prove 6 embody, verify 7 bear out, confirm, justify

8 manifest, validate 9 incarnate, objectify, personify, personize 11 corroborate, demonstrate, exteriorize, externalize, materialize, personalize 12 authenticate

substantive

4 firm, noun, real 5 solid 8 definite 9 essential

substitute

4 mock, sham, swap 5 dummy, false, locum, other, proxy, trade 6 back-up, change, deputy, double, ersatz, fill-in, refuge, resort, second, switch 7 another, replace, reserve, standby, stand-in, stopgap 8 exchange, recourse, resource, spurious, supplant 9 alternate, expedient, imitation, makeshift, simulated, surrogate 10 additional, artificial, expediency, suppletory, understudy 11 alternative, locum tenens, pinch hitter, replacement, succedaneum
combining form: 5 pseud 6 pseudo
suffix: 4 ette

substratum

4 base, core, meat, root, seat 5 basis, stuff 6 bottom, ground 7 bedrock, footing 10 foundation, groundwork 12 underpinning

substructure

4 base, seat 5 basis 6 bottom 10 foundation, groundwork

subsume

4 have 6 embody, take in 7 contain, embrace, include, involve 9 encompass 10 comprehend

subterfuge

5 cheat, fraud 6 dupery 7 chicane 8 trickery 9 chicanery, deception 10 dishonesty 11 highbinding 13 double-dealing

subterranean

4 cave 6 cavern, grotto 9 underfoot 10 underearth 11 underground

subtile

4 rare, thin 7 elusive, tenuous 8 rarefied

subtle

3 sly 4 deep, fine, foxy, nice, wily 6 artful, astute, crafty 7 cunning, logical, refined 8 analytic, delicate, finespun, guileful, hairline, skillful 9 dexterous, insidious 10 analytical

subtract

4 take 6 deduct 7 take off, take out 8 discount, draw back, knock off, take away

subtraction

6 rebate 8 discount 9 abatement
word: 7 minuend 9 remainder

suburbs

7 fringes 8 environs, outskirt, purlieus

subversion

8 sabotage, wreckage, wrecking 10 destroying 11 demolishing, destruction, undermining

subvert

4 ruin 5 upset, wreck 6 debase 7 corrupt, deprave, destroy 8 demolish, overturn, sabotage 9 overthrow, undermine

subway

British: 4 tube 11 underground
French: 5 métro

succeed

2 go 4 boom 5 click, ensue, score 6 arrive, follow, go over, pan out, thrive, win out 7 catch on, come off, make out, prevail, prosper, triumph 8 flourish, get ahead, prove out 9 supervene 10 accomplish

success

3 hit 7 arrival, killing, triumph, victory 10 attainment, prosperity 11 achievement

successful

5 smash 7 notable 8 smashing, thriving 10 noteworthy, prosperous 11 flourishing

succession

3 row 5 chain, cycle, order, round, suite, train 6 course, sequel, series, string 8 sequence 11 consecution

succinct

4 curt 5 blunt, brief, short, terse 7 brusque, concise, laconic, summary 11 compendiary, compendious 12 breviloquent

succor

3 aid 4 hand, help, lift 6 assist, relief 7 comfort, secours, support 8 ministry 10 assistance, sustenance 11 maintenance, nourishment 12 ministration

succubus

5 demon, devil, fiend, Satan 9 archfiend

succulent

5 juicy, sappy

succumb

3 bow, die 4 cave, drop, fall, pass, wilt 5 defer, yield 6 cash in, cave in, demise, depart, expire, go

down, peg out, perish, resign, submit **7** decease, give out, go under, knuckle **8** collapse, pass away **9** break down, surrender **10** capitulate **11** buckle under **12** knuckle under

such
4 akin, like, said, that **5** alike **7** similar **8** parallel **9** aforesaid, analogous **10** comparable, equivalent **13** corresponding

suck
3 lap, sip **4** draw **5** nurse **6** absorb, imbibe, inhale

sucker
3 gyp, sap **4** beat, bilk, dupe, fool, gull, mark **5** cheat, chump, cozen, leech **6** diddle, pigeon, sponge **7** defraud, fall guy, saphead, sponger **8** barnacle, hanger-on, parasite **9** schlemiel **10** freeloader

suckle
5 nurse **7** nourish **10** breast-feed

Sudan
capital: **8** Khartoum
monetary unit: **5** pound

sudden
4 fast **5** fleet, hasty, rapid, swift **6** abrupt **7** hurried, rushing **8** headlong **9** forthwith, impetuous, quickened **11** precipitant, precipitate, precipitous, subitaneous

suds
4 beer, foam, soap **5** froth, spume **6** lather

sue
3 woo **5** court, spark **6** appeal **7** address, implead **8** litigate, make up to, petition

suer
8 litigant

suet
3 fat **6** tallow
combining form: **5** steat **6** steato

Suez Canal
builder: **9** de Lesseps (Ferdinand-Marie)
city: **8** Ismailia, Port Said

suffer
3 bow, let, see **4** bear, have, know, lump, take **5** abide, admit, allow, brook, leave, stand, yield **6** accept, endure, permit, submit **7** agonize, anguish, receive, stomach, sustain, swallow, undergo **8** tolerate **9** acquiesce **10** experience **11** countenance

sufferance
5 leave **6** permit **7** consent **8** sanction **10** permission **13** authorization

sufferer
6 victim
combining form: **4** path

suffering
5 agony, dolor **6** misery **7** passion **8** distress **9** adversity **10** misfortune
combining form: **5** pathy **6** pathic

suffice
2 do **5** serve **6** enough

sufficient
3 due **5** ample **6** common, decent, enough, plenty **8** adequacy, adequate, all right, pleasing **9** agreeable, competent, plenteous, plentiful, tolerable **10** acceptable, competence **11** comfortable **12** commensurate, satisfactory **13** commensurable, proportionate, unexceptional
poetic: **4** enow

suffix
adjective: **2** al, an, ar, er, ic, ly **3** ant, ary, ean, ent, ese, est, eth, fic, ful, ial, ian, ile, ine, ish, ist, oid, ory, ose, ous **4** able, eous, ible, ical, ious, less **5** ative, istic, oidal, ulent **6** escent, itious **7** istical
noun: **2** ad, al, cy, ee, er, et, il, on, or, th, ty **3** ade, ana, ant, ard, ata, ate, dom, een, eer, ery, ese, ice, ics, ier, ile, ine, ing, ion, ism, ist, ite, ity, ium, ive, ode, oma, ome, one, ote, sis **4** ance, ancy, ence, ency, esis, ette, etum, iana, itis, ling, ment, ness, osis, ship, ster, trix, tron **5** arian, arium, aster, ation, iasis, ician, onium, orium, tress **7** escence, isation, ization
verb: **2** ed, en, fy, le **3** ate, ify, ing, ise, ize **4** lyse, lyze

suffocate
5 burke, choke, stive **6** stifle **7** quackle, smother **8** strangle **10** asphyxiate

suffrage
4 vote **5** voice **6** ballot **9** franchise

suffragist
4 Catt (Carrie Chapman), Howe (Julia), Paul (Alice) **5** Stone (Lucy) **7** Anthony (Susan B.), Stanton (Elizabeth Cady) **8** Woodhull (Victoria Claflin) **9** Pankhurst (Emmeline)

suffuse
5 imbue, steep **6** invest, leaven

7 ingrain **9** inoculate, interject, interpose, introduce

sugar
6 aldose, fucose, xylose **7** glucose, lactose, maltose, mannose, pentose, sorbose, sucrose, sweeten **8** fructose, furanose, levulose **10** saccharose
combining form: **3** lyx **4** gluc, glyc, lyxo, sucr, thre **5** gluco, glyco, sucro, threo **7** sacchar **8** sacchari, saccharo
from palm sap: **7** jaggery
Mexican: **7** panocha, panoche
source: **4** beet, cane, corn **5** maple
suffix: **3** ose **5** ulose

sugarcane refuse
7 bagasse

sugarcoat
5 candy, honey, white **6** veneer, whiten **7** sweeten, varnish **8** palliate **9** extenuate, gloss over, gloze over, whitewash **10** blanch over, edulcorate

suggest
3 put **4** hint, pose **5** imply, point **6** prefer, submit **7** connote, propose **8** indicate, intimate, propound, theorize **9** adumbrate, insinuate

suggestion
3 cue **4** clue, hint, vein, wind **5** shade, smack, tinge, trace **6** advice, strain **7** inkling, proffer **8** allusion, innuendo, overtone, proposal, reminder, telltale **9** suspicion, undertone

suggestive
4 blue, racy, sexy **5** broad, salty, shady, spicy **6** erotic, purple, risqué, wicked **8** off-color **9** evocative

suicidal pilot
8 kamikaze

suicide
8 felo-de-se, hara-kiri **10** self-murder **13** self-slaughter
Japanese: **7** seppuku

suit
2 do, go **3** fit **4** case, jibe, plea **5** adapt, agree, befit, cause, check, serve, tally **6** accord, action, adjust, appeal, asking, become, go with, orison, please, prayer, square, tailor **7** conform, enhance, flatter, lawsuit, request, satisfy, suffice **8** check out, entreaty, petition, quadrate **9** agree with, reconcile **10** go together, requesting, soliciting, tailor-make **11** accommodate,

application, imploration, imprecation 12 solicitation, supplication 13 harmonize with

type: 4 zoot 6 monkey, vested 9 paternity 10 pin-striped 11 class action

suitable

3 apt, due, fit 4 good, just, meet, nice 5 happy, right 6 proper, seemly, useful 7 condign, fitting, merited 8 deserved, eligible, rightful 9 requisite 10 convenient, felicitous 11 appropriate

suitcase

3 bag 4 grip 6 valise

suite

3 lot, row, set 4 body, flat, sort 5 array, batch, chain, group, rooms, train 6 clutch, parcel, rental, sequel, series, string 7 battery, lodging, retinue 8 chambers, sequence, tenement 9 apartment, entourage, following

suitor

4 beau 5 asker, lover, spark, swain, wooer 7 gallant, sparker 8 cavalier, paramour 9 boyfriend 10 petitioner

sulfur

9 brimstone
combining form: 3 thi 4 thio

sulk

4 mope, pout 5 brood, frown, gloom, grump, scowl 6 glower

sulky

4 cart, dour, glum 5 huffy, moody, surly, testy 6 cranky, gloomy, morose, touchy 7 crabbed 9 irritable, querulous, saturnine 12 cantankerous

sullen

4 dour, glum, mean, sour, ugly 5 black, cross, moody, pouty, surly 6 crabby, gloomy, grumpy, morose 7 crabbed, cynical, fretful, hostile, mumpish, peevish, pouting 8 frowning, lowering, petulant, scowling 9 glowering, saturnine, tenebrose, tenebrous 10 ill-humored, malevolent, sourpussed, tenebrific 11 pessimistic

Sullivan's partner

7 Gilbert (William Schwenck)

sully

3 tar 4 soil 5 shame, smear, stain, taint 6 defile 7 besmear, pollute, tarnish 8 besmirch, discolor, disgrace

Sultan of Swat

8 Babe Ruth

sultry

3 hot 5 close, humid, livid, lurid, mucky, muggy, soggy, stivy 6 baking, red-hot, sticky, stuffy, torrid 7 airless, burning, tabloid 8 broiling, sizzling, smothery, stifling 9 scorching 10 breathless, sweltering 11 sensational

sum

3 add, all, tot 4 bulk, mass, tote 5 gross, total, whole 6 amount, digest, entity, figure, resumé, system 7 epitome 8 condense, entirety, integral, nutshell, totality, totalize 9 aggregate, epitomize, integrate, inventory, synopsize
small: 7 peanuts 8 pittance

Sumatra

country: 9 Indonesia
highest peak: 8 Kerintji
largest city: 5 Medan
shrew: 4 tana

Sumerian

city: 2 Ur 4 Umma
dragon: 3 Kur
god: 2 An 3 Abu, Kur, Utu 4 Enki 5 Enlil, Lahar, Nanna, Nintu 6 Dumuzi, Nergal, Ninazu 7 Enkimdu
goddess: 2 Ki 6 Ningal, Ninlil

summarize

5 brief, recap 6 digest, resumé 8 condense, nutshell 9 epitomize, inventory, synopsize 10 retrograde 12 recapitulate

summary

4 curt 5 brief, short, terse 6 aperçu, précis, resumé 7 compact, compend, concise, epitome, laconic, outline, roundup, rundown 8 drumhead, overview, scenario, succinct, synopses (plural), synopsis 9 compacted, inventory 11 compendiary, compendious 12 breviloquent

summerhouse

6 alcove, gazebo, pagoda 9 belvedere

summery

7 estival 8 aestival

summit

3 top 4 acme, apex, peak, roof 5 crest, crown 6 apogee, climax, vertex, zenith 8 capsheaf, capstone, meridian, pinnacle 9 fastigium 11 culmination

combining form: 3 ace, acr, akr 4 acro, akro, apic 5 apici, apico

summon

3 bid 4 beck, call, cite 5 order 6 beckon, call in, enjoin, muster 7 command, conjure, convene, convoke, subpena 8 assemble, subpoena

sump

3 bog, fen 4 mire, quag 5 marsh, swamp 6 morass, slough 8 quagmire 9 swampland

sumptuous

4 lush, rich 5 grand, plush 6 Capuan, deluxe, lavish, superb 7 opulent 8 gorgeous, imposing, luscious, palatial, splendid 9 grandiose, luxuriant, luxurious 10 impressive 11 resplendent 12 awe-inspiring

sun

3 orb, Sol 4 bask, star 7 daystar, phoebus 8 daylight, insolate, luminary, radiance 9 radiation 13 celestial body
combining form: 4 heli 5 helio
disk: 4 Aten
god: 2 Ra 3 Lug, Sol, Tem, Utu 4 Amen, Atmu, Atum, Inti, Lleu, Llew, Lugh, Utug 5 Horus, Sunna, Surya 6 Apollo, Babbar, Helios, Marduk 7 Khepera, Ninurta, Phoebus, Shamash 8 Hyperion, Merodach

Sun Also Rises, The

author: 9 Hemingway (Ernest)
character: 6 Ashley (Brett), Barnes (Jake)

sunder

3 cut, rip 4 rend, rive 5 break, carve, sever, slice, split 6 cleave, divide 7 break up, disjoin, disrupt, dissect, divorce 8 disjoint, dissever, disunite, separate 11 dichotomize

sundew

7 drosera

sundial part

6 gnomon

sundries

7 notions 8 oddments 9 etceteras 11 odds and ends

sundry

4 many, some 6 divers, legion 7 diverse, several, various 8 manifold, numerous, populous 9 different 10 voluminous 12 multifarious, multitudinal 13 miscellaneous, multitudinous

sunfish
4 opah 8 bluegill

Sunflower State
6 Kansas

sun-god
see at **sun**

Sun King
8 Louis XIV

sunny
4 fair, fine, warm 5 clear, happy
6 blithe, bright, cheery, chirpy,
golden 7 clarion 8 cheerful, chirrupy, pleasant, rainless 9 brilliant,
cloudless, lightsome, unclouded
10 undarkened

sunrise
4 dawn, morn 5 light 6 aurora
7 dawning, morning 8 cockcrow,
daybreak, daylight
goddess: 3 Eos 6 Aurora

sun-room
8 solarium

sunset
3 eve 4 dusk 7 evening 8 twilight

Sunset State
6 Oregon

Sunshine State
7 Florida 11 South Dakota

sunspot portion
5 umbra 8 penumbra

sunup
see **sunrise**

sup
3 eat 4 dine 5 drink, quaff 6 imbibe 7 swallow 8 mouthful

superannuate
6 retire 7 outdate, outmode 8 obsolete 9 antiquate, obsolesce
10 pension off

superb
4 best, fine, rich 5 grand, lofty, noble, prime, proud, super 7 elegant,
exalted, optimal, optimum, opulent,
rousing, stately, sublime, supreme
8 crashing, elevated, glorious, gorgeous, imposing, majestic, slambang, splendid, standout 9 excellent, marvelous, wonderful
11 magnificent, outstanding, resplendent, sensational, splendorous, superlative 13 splendiferous

supercilious
5 proud 6 lordly, sniffy, snifty,
snippy, snuffy 7 haughty 8 arrogant, cavalier, insolent, sneering,
sniffish, snobbish, superior 10 dis-

dainful 11 overbearing 13 high-
and-mighty

superficial
5 hasty, shoal 6 casual, slight
7 cursory, general, shallow,
sketchy, surface 8 skin-deep, smat-
tery 9 depthless 10 uncritical

superfluity
5 frill, luxus 6 excess, luxury
7 amenity, surfeit, surplus, teeming
8 overflow, overkill, overmuch,
overplus, plethora, swarming
10 surplusage 11 overflowing,
prodigality 12 extravagance
13 overabundance

superfluous
4 over 5 extra, spare 6 de trop, excess 7 surplus, unasked, useless
8 needless, unneeded, unwanted
9 excessive, redundant 10 gratuitous 11 dispensable, uncalled-for,
unnecessary 12 nonessential

superhuman
6 divine 7 demigod, uncanny 8 numinous 9 unearthly, unnatural
10 miraculous 13 extraordinary,
preternatural

superintend
4 boss 5 guide 6 direct, manage,
survey 7 control, oversee 8 chaperon, overlook 10 administer
11 quarterback

superintendence
4 care 6 charge 7 conduct, running 8 handling 9 authority, direction, oversight 10 management,
presidence

superior
4 fine, head, lord, over, rare
5 above, dandy, elder, lofty, major,
prime, proud, upper 6 better,
choice, dainty, famous, higher, select, senior 7 capital, elegant,
greater, haughty, premium, primary, unusual 8 arrogant, brass
hat, cavalier, delicate, dominant,
five-star, higher-up, insolent, numinous 9 excellent, exquisite, first-
rate, marvelous, overlying,
recherché, unearthly 10 disdainful,
first-class, miraculous, noteworthy,
preeminent, preferable, remarkable, suprahuman 11 exceptional,
first-string, heavyweight, overbearing, predominant 13 high-and-
mighty, preternatural

superiority
6 better 7 victory 8 whip hand
9 advantage, dominance, seniority,

supremacy, upper hand
10 ascendancy

superjacent
4 over 6 higher 7 greater
9 overlying

superlative
4 best 8 finished, peerless, standout
10 consummate 11 magnificent,
outstanding 12 accomplished

superlative degree
suffix: 3 est

Superman
9 Clark Kent
cartoonist: 7 Shuster (Joe)
girl friend: 8 Lois Lane

supernatural
5 magic 6 divine 7 uncanny, unusual 8 heavenly, numinous
9 celestial, spiritual, unearthly
10 miraculous, paranormal, phenomenal 12 metaphysical
13 extraordinary

supernatural being
3 elf, god 5 angel, deity, demon,
fairy, gnome, nymph, troll 6 seraph, spirit 7 banshee, goddess
10 leprechaun
Muslim: 4 jinn
Persian: 4 peri

supernumerary
5 extra, spare 6 de trop, excess
7 surplus

supersede
7 replace, succeed 8 displace, outplace, set aside, supplant

supervene
5 ensue 6 follow 7 succeed

supervise
3 run 4 boss 5 guide, steer 6 direct, govern, manage, survey 7 conduct, control, monitor, oversee,
proctor, referee 8 chaperon, overlook 10 administer 11 quarterback

supervision
4 care 6 charge 7 conduct, running 8 handling 9 oversight
10 intendance, management

supervisor
7 foreman

supine
5 inert, prone, slack 6 abject
7 passive 8 inactive, indolent
11 indifferent

supper club
4 café 6 nitery 7 cabaret, hot spot
8 nightery 9 night spot

supplant

4 oust **5** eject, expel, usurp
6 bounce, cut out **7** cast out, replace **8** crowd out, displace, force
out, outplace **9** overthrow,
supersede

supple

4 wiry **5** agile, lithe, withy **6** limber, nimble, pliant, whippy **7** ductile, elastic, lissome, plastic, pliable,
springy, stretch, willowy **8** flexible,
graceful, moldable, stretchy
9 adaptable, lithesome, malleable,
resilient

supplement

3 add, eke **5** rider **6** append **7** adjunct, codicil **8** addendum, addi-
tion, appendix **9** accessory
10 complement

suppliant

5 asker **6** beggar, prayer, suitor
9 solicitor **10** petitioner

supplicant

see **suppliant**

supplicate

3 beg, sue **4** pray **5** crave, plead
6 appeal, invoke **7** beseech, entreat, implore, solicit **8** petition
9 importune

supplication

4 plea, suit **6** appeal, orison,
prayer **8** entreaty, petition **11** application, imploration, imprecation

supplies

8 matériel **9** materials

supply

3 fit, man **4** feed, find, fund, give,
hand, help **5** cache, equip, hoard,
stock, store **6** outfit, purvey, succor
7 deliver, fulfill, furnish, provide, reserve, surplus **8** dispense, hand
over, transfer, turn over **9** inventory, provision, reservoir, stockpile

support

3 aid **4** back, base, bear, hand,
help, keep, lift, prop, root, side,
stay, take **5** abide, adopt, boost,
brace, bread, brook, carry, favor,
shore, strut, truss **6** anchor, assist,
bear up, behalf, buoy up, column,
crutch, defend, endure, girder, living, pillar, relief, second, succor,
suffer, upbear, uphold, verify **7** alimony, applaud, approve, backing,
bolster, bracing, comfort, confirm,
embrace, endorse, espouse, footing, fortify, fulcrum, nourish, nurture, pull for, secours, shore up,
stiffen, sustain, toehold **8** advocate,

backstop, buttress, champion, foothold, mainstay, maintain, sanction,
side with, underpin **9** encourage,
reinforce, underprop **10** assistance,
foundation, livelihood, provide for,
strengthen, sustenance **11** corroborate, maintenance, subsistence,
underpinning **12** alimentation, sustentation, underpinning
of a bridge: **8** abutment

supporter

4 ally **6** cohort, patron **7** booster,
sectary **8** adherent, advocate,
champion, disciple, exponent, follower, henchman, partisan, sector
9 expounder, proponent, satellite
combining form: 4 crat **5** ocrat
suffix: 3 ite

suppose

4 deem, take **5** allow, guess, infer,
judge, opine, think **6** assume, expect, gather, reckon, repute, theory
7 believe, imagine, perhaps, presume, pretend, surmise, suspect
8 conclude, consider **10** conjecture, understand **11** speculation

supposition

5 posit **6** theory, thesis **7** premise,
surmise **9** apriorism, postulate
10 assumption, conjecture, estimation, hypothesis **11** postulation, presumption, speculation

supposititious

6 unreal **7** dubious, fictive, reputed
8 doubtful, fanciful, illusory, putative, spurious **9** fantastic, fictional,
imaginary, pretended, simulated
10 chimerical, fictitious, fraudulent
11 conjectural **12** hypothetical,
questionable

suppress

4 cool, curb, hide, kill, rein, stop
5 burke, check, choke, crush,
drown, dwarf, quash, quell, shush,
spike, stunt **6** arrest, censor, cut off,
hush up, muffle, quench, retard,
squash, stifle, subdue **7** abolish, collect, compose, conceal, control, destroy, prevent, put down, silence,
smother, squelch, swallow **8** prohibit, restrain, slap down, strangle,
withhold **9** overpower, overthrow
10 annihilate, extinguish

suppurate

6 fester

supra

5 above

supremacy

4 sway **5** power **7** control, mastery
8 dominion **9** ascendant, authority,

dominance, masterdom **10** ascendancy, domination, mastership, prepotence, prepotency **11** preeminence, sovereignty, superiority
12 predominance, principality
13 preponderance, preponderancy,
transcendence

supreme

4 last **5** alone, chief, final **6** master, superb, utmost **7** highest, maximum, perfect **8** absolute, crowning,
foremost, peerless, towering, ultimate **9** excellent, marvelous, paramount, sovereign, unequaled, unmatched, unrivaled **10** preeminent,
surpassing **11** unequalable, unmatchable, unsurpassed **12** incomparable, transcendent, unparalleled
13 unsurpassable

Supreme Being

3 God **5** Allah **7** creator, Jehovah
11 the Almighty

surcease

3 end **4** halt, quit, rest, stop **6** desist **7** refrain, suspend **8** give over,
knock off, leave off, postpone
9 cessation **11** discontinue

sure

3 set **4** fast, firm, safe **5** cocky,
fixed **6** indeed, secure, stable,
steady, strong **7** abiding, certain,
staunch **8** absolute, arrogant, cocksure, definite, enduring, inerrant,
positive, reliable, surefire, unerring,
unshaken **9** confident, convinced,
inerrable, steadfast **10** convincing,
dependable, infallible, undeniable,
unshakable, unwavering **11** indubitable, trustworthy, unequivocal, unfaltering, unqualified **12** indisputable, never-failing, wholehearted
13 incontestable, uncontestable,
unquestioning

sure thing

6 shoo-in, winner **9** certainty

surety

4 bail, bond **5** angel **6** backer, patron, pledge **7** sponsor **8** backer-
up, guaranty, security, warranty
9 certainty, certitude, guarantee,
guarantor **10** confidence,
conviction

surface

3 top **4** face, pave, rise, skin
5 cover, facet **6** come up, facing,
finish, patina, veneer **7** outside
8 covering, exterior **11** superficial

surfeit

4 cloy, fill, glut, jade, pall, sate
5 gorge, stall **6** excess, stodge

7 replete, satiate, satisfy, surplus
8 overfill, overflow, overkill, overmuch, overplus, plethora **10** surplusage **11** overindulge, superfluity **13** overabundance

surge
4 flow, gush, pour, rise, roll, rush, wave **5** swell **6** billow, sluice, stream **7** upswell

surgeon
8 sawbones
American: **4** Mayo (Charles, William), Reed (Walter) **6** Thorek (Max) **7** Cushing (Harvey), DeBakey (Michael) **8** McDowell (Ephraim)
British: **6** Hunter (John)
English: **5** Paget (James) **6** Lister (Joseph)
French: **4** Paré (Ambroise) **5** Broca (Paul)
heart: **7** Barnard (Christiaan)
South African: **7** Barnard (Christiaan)
Swiss: **6** Kocher (Emil Theodor)
type: **4** oral **5** brain, heart **7** plastic **8** thoracic

surgery
9 operation
instrument: **5** clamp, curet, lance, probe **6** gorget, lancet, splint, stylet, trocar **7** forceps, scalpel

surgical removal
8 ablation
combining form: **6** ectomy

surly
4 dour, glum, rude, ugly **5** cross, gruff, sulky **6** crusty, grumpy, morose, sullen **7** bearish, boorish, crabbed, haughty, waspish **8** churlish, snappish **9** fractious, irritable, saturnine **10** ungracious **11** ill-mannered **12** discourteous

surmise
see **suppose**

surmount
3 cap, top **4** best, down, leap, lick, over **5** clear, crest, crown, excel, outdo, throw, vault **6** better, finish, hurdle, master, outtop **7** conquer, surpass **8** outstrip, outtower, overcome, overleap **9** negotiate, terminate, transcend

surpass
3 cap, cob, top **4** beat, best, pass, rank **5** excel, outdo, outgo, trump **6** better, exceed, outrun, outvie **7** eclipse, outpace, outrank, outstep **8** distance, outclass, outmatch, outpoint, outrange, outrival, outshine, outstrip, outweigh, overstep **9** tran-

scend **10** outperform, overshadow **11** outdistance

surplice
5 cotta, ephod **8** vestment

surplus
5 extra, spare **6** de trop, excess **7** overage, reserve, surfeit **8** overflow, overkill, overmuch, plethora **9** overstock, remainder **10** oversupply **11** superfluent, superfluity, superfluous **13** overabundance, supernumerary

surprise
4 faze, grab, stun **5** amaze, catch, floor, grasp, seize **6** ambush, dismay, lay for, rattle, waylay, wonder **7** astound, capture, nonplus, stagger, startle, stupefy **8** astonish, bewilder, bowl over, confound, drygulch, overcome **9** amazement, bushwhack, discomfit, dumbfound, overpower **10** disconcert **11** flabbergast **12** astonishment

surrender
4 cede, fall **5** leave, waive, yield **6** commit, give in, give up, go down, resign, submit **7** abandon, concede, consign, go under, succumb **8** dedition, hand over, yielding **9** relenting **10** capitulate, relinquish, submission, succumbing **11** appeasement **12** capitulation
sign: **9** white flag

surreptitious
see **stealthy**

surrogate
3 sub **6** deputy, fill-in, refuge, resort **7** stand-in, stopgap **8** recourse, resource **9** alternate, expedient, makeshift **10** expediency, substitute **11** alternative, locum tenens, pinch hitter, replacement, succedaneum

surround
3 hem, rim **4** edge, gird, loop, ring **5** beset, bound, limit, round, skirt, verge **6** begird, border, circle, engulf, fringe, girdle, margin **7** compass, confine, embosom, enclave, enclose, envelop, environ, outline **8** encircle **9** encompass **10** circumvent **12** circumscribe

surrounding
5 about **12** circumjacent
prefix: **4** peri **6** circum

surroundings
6 medium, milieu **7** ambient, climate **8** ambience **10** atmosphere **11** environment, mise-en-scène

surveillance
3 eye, tab **4** tout **5** vigil, watch **7** lookout **8** eagle eye, scrutiny, stakeout **9** vigilance

survey
3 con, vet **4** boss, rate, scan, view **5** assay, audit, set at, study, value **6** aperçu, assess, digest, précis, review, search, sketch **7** canvass, check up, examine, inspect, oversee, pandect, preview, sylloge, valuate **8** analysis, appraise, chaperon, estimate, evaluate, overlook, scrutiny, syllabus **9** check over, supervise **10** compendium, inspection, scrutinize **11** examination, quarterback, superintend **13** perlustration

survive
4 last **6** endure, revive **7** carry on, outlast, outlive, outwear, persist, recover, ride out **8** continue, live down **11** come through, pull through

Surya
6 sun-god
son: **4** Manu, Yama **5** Karna **6** Asvins **7** Sugriva
temple site: **7** Konarak

susceptible
4 easy, open **5** naive, prone **6** liable **7** exposed, sensile, subject **8** disposed, gullible, inclined, sensible, sentient **9** obnoxious, receptive, sensitive **10** fleeceable, responsive, vulnerable **11** impressible, predisposed **12** nonresistant

Susi's son
5 Gaddi

suspect
4 open **5** doubt, guess, shaky, think **6** assume, expect, gather, unsure **7** believe, dubious, imagine, suppose, unclear **8** conceive, distrust, doubtful, misdoubt, mistrust **9** doubtable, uncertain **10** disbelieve, understand **11** problematic

suspend
3 bar **4** bate, hang, stay, stop **5** debar, defer, delay, hover, sling **6** dangle, depend, except, hold up, put off, shelve **7** adjourn, exclude, hold off, rule out **8** count out, intermit, postpone, prorogue **9** eliminate **11** discontinue

suspended
7 hanging, pendant, pensile **8** dangling, swinging **9** pendulant, pendulous

suspenders
6 braces 8 galluses

suspense
5 worry 6 unease 7 anxiety, concern, mystery 11 uncertainty 12 apprehension

suspension
4 stop 5 delay 7 latency 8 abeyance, abeyancy, doldrums, dormancy, stoppage 9 remission 10 moratorium, quiescence, quiescency 11 cold storage, withholding 12 intermission, interruption

suspicion
4 cast, hint 5 doubt, shade, smell, tinge, touch, trace, whiff 6 wonder 7 concern, dubiety 8 distrust, mistrust 9 dubiosity, misgiving 10 foreboding, intimation, skepticism, suggestion 11 incertitude, uncertainty, uncertitude

suspicious
4 wary 5 chary, leery, queer, shaky 6 unsure 7 careful, dubious, jealous, suspect 8 cautious, doubtful, watchful 9 doubtable, skeptical, uncertain 10 borderline 11 distrustful, mistrustful, problematic, unbelieving 12 questionable

suspire
4 sigh

sustain
4 bear, feed, prop, save 5 abide, brace, brook, carry, stand 6 bear up, buoy up, endure, foster, hold up, keep up, succor, suffer, upbear, uphold 7 bolster, confirm, nourish, nurture, prolong, receive, shore up, stomach, support, undergo 8 buttress, continue, preserve, tolerate 9 underprop, withstand 10 experience, strengthen

sustenance
3 pap 4 food, keep, meat, salt 5 bread 6 living, viands 7 aliment, alimony, pabulum, support 9 nutriment 10 livelihood 11 maintenance, nourishment, subsistence 12 alimentation

susurration
6 mumble, murmur, mutter, rustle 7 whisper 9 undertone

suture
4 line, seam 6 stitch

swab
3 mop 5 clean

swaddle
4 roll, wrap 5 drape 6 enwrap,

swathe, wrap up 7 bandage, envelop 8 enswathe

swag
3 yaw 4 flag, loot, tilt, wilt 5 booty, droop, lurch, money, pitch, prize, spoil 6 boodle, seesaw, tilter 7 plunder 10 plunderage

swagger
4 brag, cock, lord 5 boast, strut, swank, swash, swell 7 bluster, peacock 8 flourish 11 pontificate, swashbuckle

swain
4 beau 5 lover, spark, wooer 6 suitor 7 admirer, sparker 9 boyfriend

swallow
3 sip 4 bear, bolt, down, gulp, take 5 abide, brook, drink, quaff, stand 6 absorb, accept, digest, endure, imbibe, ingest 7 believe, consume, stomach 8 bear with, tolerate 11 ingurgitate

swamp
3 bog, fen 4 mire, moss, muck, quag 5 drown, flood, glade, marsh, whelm 6 deluge, engulf, morass, muskeg, slough 7 baygall, bottoms 8 inundate, overcome, overflow, quagmire, submerge 9 marshland, overwhelm
Everglades: 10 Big Cypress
Georgia: 10 Okefenokee
North Carolina-Virginia: 6 Dismal 11 Great Dismal

Swamp Fox
6 Marion (Francis)

swan
female: 3 pen
male: 3 cob 4 cobb
young: 6 cygnet

Swanhild
father: 6 Sigurd
mother: 6 Gudrun

swank
4 cock, lord, tony, trig 5 sharp, showy, swell, swish 6 chichi, classy, lively, snappy, tonish, trendy, with-it 7 peacock, splashy, stylish, swagger 8 peacocky 10 flamboyant, peacockish 11 pontificate, pretentious 12 orchidaceous, ostentatious

swap
5 trade, truck 6 barter, change, switch 7 bargain, traffic 8 exchange 10 substitute

swarm
4 flow, host, teem 5 crawl, crowd, flock, group, horde 6 abound, throng 7 overrun 9 multitude, pullulate 10 congregate

swarthy
4 dark 5 dusky 8 bistered 11 black-a-vised, dark-skinned

swash
3 lap 4 dash, slop 5 douse, plash, slosh 6 bubble, burble, gurgle, splash, splosh 7 bluster, spatter, splurge, spurtle, swagger 8 splatter

swat
3 bat, box, hit, rap 4 belt, blow, cuff, lick, slog, slug, sock 5 clout, knock, smack, smash, smite, swipe, whack 6 buffet, strike, wallop 7 clobber

swathe
see **swaddle**

sway
3 get 4 bend, bias, move, rock, rule 5 carry, lurch, might, power, range, reach, reign, scope, sweep, swing, touch, waver, weave 6 affect, careen, direct, govern, manage, spread, strike, totter, waddle, wobble 7 command, dispose, expanse, impress, incline, inspire, mastery, stagger, stretch, strings 8 overrule 9 amplitude, authority, dominance, influence, oscillate, pendulate, vacillate 10 domination, predispose 11 fluctuation 12 jurisdiction

swear
3 vow 4 bind, cuss, damn, oath, rail, rant 5 abuse, curse 6 adjure, affirm, assert, attest, bedamn, depone, depose, pledge, plight, revile, vilify 7 declare, promise, testify 8 covenant, cussword, execrate 9 blaspheme, expletive, imprecate 10 asseverate, vituperate

swearword
4 cuss, oath 5 curse 9 expletive, obscenity 10 scurrility

sweat
4 emit, fume, milk, moil, ooze, rook, seep, snit, stew, toil, weep, work 5 bleed, exude, grind, labor, mulct, stick, tizzy 6 fleece, strain, swivet 7 excrete, slavery, travail 8 bullwork, drudgery, perspire, transude 10 donkeywork
combining form: 4 hidr 5 hidro

sweater
8 cardigan, pullover, slipover

sweat out
2 go 4 bear, lump, take, wait
5 abide, brook, stand 6 endure
7 stomach 8 tolerate

sweaty
3 wet 6 clammy, sticky 7 labored
8 perspiry 10 perspiring

Sweden
capital: 9 Stockholm
monetary unit: 5 krona

Swedish Nightingale
4 Lind (Jenny)

sweep
3 fly 4 flit, sail, wing 5 ambit,
broom, clean, clear, drive, fleet,
orbit, range, reach, scope, surge
6 extent, radius 7 compass, purview 9 extension

sweeping
6 all-out 7 blanket, general, overall
8 whole-hog 9 all-around, extensive, inclusive, out-and-out, wholesale 12 all-embracing 13 comprehensive, thoroughgoing

sweepings
4 dust, junk 5 trash, waste 6 debris, litter, refuse 7 garbage,
rubbish

sweet
5 candy, honey, spicy 6 aromal,
dulcet, lovely, savory, sugary, syrupy 7 angelic, dessert, melodic,
odorous, perfumy, scented, winning, winsome 8 aromatic, engaging, euphonic, fragrant, heavenly,
loveling, luscious, perfumed, pleasant, pleasing, redolent 9 agreeable, ambrosial, beautiful, delicious
10 delectable, delightful
combining form: 4 glyc 5 glyco

Sweet ___, song
7 Adeline

sweeten
5 candy, honey, sugar 6 pacify,
refine, soften, solace 7 appease,
assuage, lighten, mollify, placate,
relieve 9 sugarcoat, sugar over
10 conciliate, propitiate

sweet potato
3 yam

sweet-talk
3 con 4 coax 6 banter, cajole
7 blarney, wheedle 8 blandish,
soft-soap

swell
4 cock, grow, keen, lord, neat,
pout, puff 5 bloat, bulge, dandy,
nifty, pouch, super, surge, swank

6 billow, blow up, dilate, expand,
groovy, tumefy 7 amplify, augment,
balloon, distend, inflate, peacock,
swagger, upsurge 8 increase, over-
blow, terrific 9 marvelous,
wonderful
British: 3 nob 4 toff

swelled head
5 pride 6 egoism 7 conceit, egotism 9 arrogance, vainglory
10 narcissism 11 amour propre
13 conceitedness

swelling
3 sty 4 bubo, gall, node 5 edema,
tumid, tumor 6 bunion, growth
7 aureate, flowery, gibbous 8 tu-
bercle 9 bombastic, carbuncle,
chilblain, tumescent 10 euphuistic,
rhetorical 12 inflammation, magniloquent 13 grandiloquent

sweltering
3 hot 5 fiery 6 baking, sultry, torrid
7 burning 8 broiling, sizzling
9 scorching

swerve
3 dip, err 4 skew, slue, turn, veer
5 sheer, shift, stray, waver 6 depart, totter, wander 7 deflect, deviate, digress, diverge 8 train off

swift
4 fast 5 fleet, hasty, quick, rapid,
ready 6 prompt, raking, snappy,
speedy, sudden 7 flat-out, fleetly,
quickly, rapidly 8 full tilt, headlong,
promptly, speedily 9 breakneck
10 harefooted

___ Swift
3 Tom 8 Jonathan
character: 8 Gulliver

swiftness
4 gait, pace 5 haste, hurry, speed
6 hustle, rustle 8 celerity, dispatch,
rapidity, velocity 9 quickness, rapidness 10 expedition, speediness

swig
4 drag, pull 5 booze, draft, drink,
swill 6 guzzle, imbibe, tipple
7 swizzle

swill
4 slop, swig, tope 5 booze, draft,
drink, offal, rinse, slops, trash,
waste 6 debris, guzzle, refuse,
spilth, tank up, tipple 7 consume,
garbage, hogwash, put away, put
down, rubbish, swizzle 9 polish off

swim
4 reel, spin, turn 5 float, swoon,
whirl 9 dizziness

swimmer
7 natator

swimming stroke
5 crawl 7 dolphin, trudgen 9 butterfly, dogpaddle

swindle
3 con, gyp 4 beat, bilk, dupe,
fake, hoax, rook, scam, sell, sham,
skin 5 bunco, cheat, cozen, fraud,
phony, rogue 6 chouse, diddle,
humbug 7 defraud 8 flimflam 9 imposture, victimize

swine
see **hog**

swing
3 ply, wag 4 beat, hang, rock, roll,
sway, turn, veer, wave, whip
5 avert, flail, knack, lurch, meter,
pivot, rhyme, sheer, trick, weave,
wheel, whirl, wield 6 careen, divert, handle, jiggle, rhythm, rotate,
stroke, switch, waggle, wiggle,
wigwag, wobble 7 cadence, cadency, deflect, measure, revolve,
stagger, vibrate 8 brandish, dispense, maneuver, undulate 9 fluctuate, oscillate, pendulate
10 manipulate

swinish
5 brute, feral, gross 6 animal,
brutal, coarse, ferine, greedy
7 beastly, bestial, boarish, brutish,
porcine, sensual

swipe
3 cop, hit, nab, rap 4 blow, conk,
hook, lick, lift, swat, wipe 5 draft,
heist, knock, pinch, steal 6 pilfer,
snatch, snitch, strike

swirl
4 eddy, purl, roil 5 curve, gurge,
twist, whirl, whorl 6 swoosh, vortex
9 whirlpool 11 convolution

swish
2 in 4 buzz, fizz, flog, hiss, tony,
whiz 5 smart, swank, whisk
6 classy, fizzle, sizzle, tonish,
trendy, wheeze, whoosh, with-it
7 stylish 8 sibilate 9 exclusive

Swiss Family Robinson author
4 Wyss (Johann David)

switch
3 rod, wag 4 beat, flog, lash,
swap, wand, wave, whip 5 shift,
shunt, trade, whisk 6 change,
strike, waggle, woggle 7 scourge
8 exchange 9 sidetrack
10 substitute

Switzerland
capital: 4 Bern

largest city: 6 Zurich
monetary unit: 5 franc

swivel
4 turn 5 swing

swivet
see **snit**

swizzle
see **swig**

swollen
5 bulgy, tumid 6 turgid 7 aureate, bulbous, bulging, flowery, pompous 8 enlarged, inflated, varicose 9 bombastic, distended, tumescent 10 euphuistic, rhetorical 12 magniloquent 13 grandiloquent
combining form: 4 phys 5 physo

swoon
4 coma, daze, fade 5 drown, faint 6 torpor 7 die away, pass out, rapture, syncope 8 black out

swoosh
4 eddy, gush, purl 5 gurge, swirl, whirl, whorl

sword
4 épée, foil, kris, pata 5 estoc, saber 6 barong, bilboa, creese, rapier, toledo 7 cutlass 8 claymore, falchion, scimitar, yataghan

sword of ___
8 Damocles

sword-shaped
6 ensate 8 ensiform

sworn
6 avowed 7 devoted, settled 8 affirmed 9 confirmed, hard-shell 10 deep-rooted, deep-seated, entrenched, inveterate

sybarite
7 epicure 8 hedonist 10 voluptuary

sybaritic
6 carnal 7 sensual 8 sensuous 9 epicurean, luxurious 10 apolaustic, hedonistic, voluptuous 13 self-indulgent

sycophancy
7 calumny, scandal, slander 8 toadying 10 backbiting, defamation, detraction 12 backstabbing, belittlement, depreciation 13 disparagement

sycophant
5 toady 6 flunky, lackey, minion, stooge, yes-man 7 defamer, fawning 8 bootlick, cowering, cringing, groveler, lickspit, parasite, toadying, toadyish 9 easy rider, flatterer, groveling, kowtowing, parasitic,

slanderer 10 bootlicker, self-seeker 11 bootlicking, lickspittle 13 apple-polisher

sycophantic
7 fawning, servile, slavish 8 cowering, cringing, toadying, toadyish 9 groveling, kowtowing, parasitic, truckling 10 defamatory, obsequious, slanderous 11 bootlicking

Sycorax's son
7 Caliban

syllable
3 bit, jot 4 atom, iota, whit 5 crumb, ounce, shred 7 modicum 8 particle
deletion: 7 apocope
last: 8 ultima
lengthening of: 7 ectasis
next to last: 6 penult
shortening: 7 elision, systole
stressed: 5 arsis

syllabus
6 aperçu, digest, précis, sketch, survey 7 epitome, outline, pandect, summary 8 abstract, headnote, synopsis 10 compendium

sylvan
5 bosky, woody 6 rustic, wooded
deity: 3 Pan 4 Faun 5 dryad, satyr 6 Faunus 7 Silenus 8 Arethusa, Silvanus, Sylvanus

symbol
4 logo, mark, note, sign, type 5 badge, motif, stamp, token 6 design, device, emblem, figure, mascot 7 pattern 9 attribute, character 10 indication
chemical: see individual element
Egyptian: 4 ankh
musical: 4 clef, flat, hold, note, rest, turn 5 presa, shake, sharp, trill 7 fermata, mordent, natural 8 arpeggio 9 crescendo 10 diminuendo 11 decrescendo

symbolic
10 emblematic 11 allegorical

symbolist poet
7 Rimbaud (Arthur) 8 Mallarmé (Stéphane), Verlaine (Paul)

symbolize
6 embody, mirror, typify 7 express, signify 9 body forth, epitomize, exemplify, personify, represent 10 illustrate 11 emblematize

symmetrical
5 equal 7 regular 8 balanced 12 commensurate, proportional 13 commensurable

symmetry
5 order 7 balance, harmony 8 equality, evenness 9 agreement, congruity 10 conformity, proportion, regularity 11 arrangement

sympathetic
4 kind, warm 6 benign, humane, kindly, tender 8 amenable, favoring, friendly 9 agreeable, approving, benignant, congenial, congruous, consonant, favorable, receptive 10 compatible, consistent, responsive 11 kindhearted, softhearted, warmhearted 12 appreciating, well-disposed 13 compassionate, comprehending, understanding

sympathize
4 ache, pity 7 condole, feel for 10 appreciate, comprehend, understand 11 commiserate 13 compassionate

sympathy
3 rue 4 pity, ruth 5 heart 6 accord, warmth 7 empathy, harmony 8 affinity, kindness 9 agreement 10 benignancy, benignness, compassion, condolence, kindliness, tenderness 11 sensitivity 13 commiseration

symphonic
7 chiming, musical 8 blending, harmonic 9 consonant 10 harmonious

symphony
4 band 7 concord, harmony 9 orchestra 10 consonance 11 concert band 12 philharmonic

symptom
4 mark, note, sign 5 index, token 7 indicia 8 evidence 10 indication 11 significant

symptoms
8 syndrome

synagogue
8 assembly, building 9 community 12 congregation

synchronize
5 agree 6 concur 8 coincide

synchronous
6 coeval 8 existing 10 coetaneous, coexistent, coexisting, concurrent 11 concomitant 12 contemporary, simultaneous

syncope
4 coma 5 faint, swoon 8 blackout

syndicate
4 pool 5 chain, group, trust, union 6 cartel 7 combine 11 association,

partnership **12** conglomerate, organization

syndrome
3 ill **6** malady **7** ailment, disease **8** disorder, sickness **9** affection, complaint, condition, infirmity **11** concurrence

synergic
8 coacting, coactive, conjoint

synod
4 body **7** council, meeting **8** assembly **10** convention, judicatory **11** convocation

synopsis
5 brief **7** epitome, summary **8** abstract, boildown, breviary, breviate **10** abridgment, conspectus **12** condensation

synopsize
3 sum **5** sum up **6** digest **7** summate **8** condense, nutshell **9** epitomize, inventory, summarize

synthesis
5 blend, union **11** combination **13** incorporation

synthesize
5 blend, unify **7** combine **9** harmonize, integrate

synthetic
7 man-made **10** artificial, fabricated

Syria
capital: **8** Damascus
monetary unit: **5** pound

Syrinx
5 nymph **7** panpipe
pursuer: **3** Pan

syrup
4 corn **5** maple **7** sorghum **8** molasses
almond-flavored: **6** orgeat

syrupy
5 gooey, moist, mushy, sappy, sobby, sweet **6** drippy, dulcet, slushy, sticky **7** maudlin **11** sentimental

system
3 sum, way **4** code, mode, plan, wise **5** modus, order, setup, whole **6** entity, manner, method, scheme **7** complex, fashion, network, pattern, process, regimen **9** technique **10** regularity **11** arrangement, disposition, orderliness

systematic
7 logical, ordered, orderly, regular **8** arranged, methodic **9** organized **10** analytical, methodical **12** businesslike

systematize
5 array, order **6** adjust, codify **7** arrange, catalog, dispose, marshal **8** classify, organize, regiment **9** methodize

system of weights
4 troy **11** avoirdupois

Tt

tab
3 eye, tag 4 bill, cost, rate
5 check, price, score, watch
6 charge, tariff 7 account, invoice
8 eagle eye, price tag, scrutiny
9 reckoning, statement
12 surveillance

tabard
4 cape, coat 5 tunic 7 pendant

tabby
3 cat 6 feline, gossip 7 rumorer
8 gossiper, quidnunc, telltale
9 carrytale 10 newsmonger, talebearer 12 gossipmonger
13 scandalmonger

tabellion
6 scribe

tabernacle
6 church, temple 10 house of God
13 house of prayer

tabes
7 atrophy, wasting

Tabitha's Greek name
6 Dorcas

table
4 fare, list 5 bench, board, chart,
stand 6 buffet, record, teapoy, upland 7 counter, plateau 8 mahogany 9 sideboard
ornament: 7 epergne 11 centerpiece
spread: 4 oleo 6 butter
wheeled: 4 cart
writing: 4 desk 9 secretary
10 escritoire

table d' ___
4 hôte

table game
see at **game**

tableland
4 mesa 6 upland 7 plateau
Alabama-West Virginia:
10 Cumberland
Arizona: 5 Kanab 6 Kaibob

England: 8 Dartmoor
India: 5 Malwa; (see also **plateau**)

tablet
3 bar, pad 4 cake, disk, pill, slab
5 panel, slate 6 troche 7 lozenge
combining form: 4 plac 5 pinac,
pinak, placo 6 pinaco
ornamental: 9 cartouche
stone: 5 stela, stele
writing: 3 pad 7 fanfold 8 triptych

Table Talk author
6 Selden (John)

table talk expert
13 deipnosophist

tableware
4 cups 5 bowls, forks 6 dishes,
knives, plates, silver, spoons
7 glasses, saucers

tabloid
5 livid, lurid, short 9 newspaper
11 sensational

taboo
3 ban 4 don't 6 enjoin, forbid, outlaw 7 inhibit 8 prohibit, sanction
9 interdict, restraint 10 inhibition,
limitation, regulation 11 forbiddance, prohibition, reservation,
restriction 12 interdiction,
proscription

tabor
4 drum

taboret
5 stand, stool 7 cabinet

Tabrimmon
father: 6 Hezion
son: 8 Benhadad

tabula ___
4 rasa

tabulation
5 chart, tally

tache
5 clasp 6 buckle

tacit
6 silent, unsaid 7 assumed, implied

8 hinted at, implicit, inferred, unspoken, unvoiced 9 alluded to, intimated, suggested, unuttered 10 undeclared, understood
11 unexpressed 12 inarticulate

taciturn
5 close 6 silent 7 laconic 8 reserved, reticent, wordless 10 silen-
tious 11 close-lipped, tight-lipped
12 closemouthed

Tacitus work
7 Annales 8 Germania 9 Historiae

tack
3 pin, yaw 4 bend, brad, link, nail,
turn 5 shift 6 double, swerve, zigzag 7 tangent 9 deviation 10 alteration, deflection, digression

tackle
3 rig 4 gear 5 throw 6 attack, burton, outfit, take on 7 lineman, rigging 8 matériel, set about 9 apparatus, equipment, machinery,
undertake 10 footballer, plunge
into 11 clothesline, habiliments
13 accouterments, paraphernalia

tacky
5 cheap, crude, dingy, dowdy,
faded, gaudy, messy, seedy
6 blowsy, frowsy, frumpy, shabby,
sloppy, sticky, stodgy, tagrag, untidy 7 run-down, unkempt 8 frumpish, outmoded, slovenly 9 incorrect,
inelegant, out-of-date, tasteless, unstylish 10 broken-down, down-at-
heel, threadbare, unbecoming, unsuitable 11 dilapidated

tact
5 poise, skill 6 acumen 7 finesse,
suavity 8 civility, courtesy, deftness,
urbanity 9 diplomacy, gallantry
10 adroitness, perception, politeness, smoothness 11 delicatesse,
savoir faire, sensitivity

tactful
4 deft 5 suave 6 adroit, urbane

7 politic, skilled 8 delicate, discreet, polished, skillful 9 sensitive 10 diplomatic, perceptive

tactical
4 wise 7 politic, prudent 8 delicate 9 advisable, expedient 10 diplomatic, short-range

tactics
4 plan 6 method, system 9 maneuvers

tactile
8 palpable, tangible 9 touchable

taction
5 touch 7 contact 9 palpation

tad
3 bit, boy, lad, son 5 child 6 laddie 9 shaveling, stripling

tadpole
8 polliwog, pollywog

taffy
5 candy 8 flattery

tag
3 dog, end 4 flap, game, tail 5 bedog, label, trail 6 cliché, follow, shadow, ticket, truism 7 bromide 8 banality, prosaism 9 platitude 10 prosaicism, shibboleth

tagrag
5 dingy, faded, seedy, tacky 6 shabby 7 run-down 10 bedraggled, down-at-heel, threadbare 11 dilapidated

Tahan's father
7 Ephraim

Tahash's father
5 Nahor

Tahath's father
5 Bered 7 Eleadah

Tahiti
capital: 7 Papeete
painter: 7 Gauguin (Paul)

tail
3 dog, end, eye, tag 4 butt, rear 5 bedog, cauda, hound, trail 6 follow, pursue, shadow 7 hind end, rear end 8 backside, buttocks 9 posterior
relating to: 6 caudal
short: 4 scut

tailed
7 caudate

tailless
7 acaudal, anurous 8 ecaudate

tailor
3 fit, sew 4 suit 5 adapt, alter, style 6 adjust, sartor, square 7 conform, shape up 8 clothier, dovetail,

quadrate, seamster 9 reconcile 11 accommodate
Hindu: 5 darzi 6 durzee

taint
3 hue, rot, tar 4 blur, foul, harm, hurt, smut, soil, turn 5 brand, cloud, color, decay, dirty, smear, spoil, stain, sully 6 befoul, damage, defile, molder, smudge, smutch 7 besmear, blacken, crumble, pollute, putrefy, tarnish 8 besmirch, discolor 9 break down, decompose, discredit 10 stigmatize 11 contaminate

taipan
5 snake 8 merchant

Taiwan
7 Formosa
capital: 6 Taipei

taj
3 cap

Taj Mahal
9 mausoleum
builder: 9 Shah Jahan
site: 4 Agra

take
3 bag, buy, cut, eat, get, gyp, nab, use, win 4 bear, beat, bilk, cull, down, draw, grab, grip, haul, pick 5 abide, admit, annex, brook, catch, charm, cheat, clasp, cozen, grasp, seize, share, stand, think, treat 6 accept, allure, assume, choose, clutch, collar, deduct, devour, endure, follow, gather, income, ingest, obtain, opt for, prefer, secure, select, snatch, strike, suffer 7 attract, believe, call for, capture, consume, defraud, enchant, grapple, imagine, receive, require, stomach, suppose, swallow 8 arrogate, contract, deal with, discount, flimflam, knock off, proceeds, purchase, receipts, subtract, tolerate 9 apprehend, captivate, fascinate, partake of, single out, substract 10 commandeer, comprehend, confiscate, sicken with, understand 11 appropriate 12 come down with
account of: 6 notice
advantage of: 5 abuse 7 exploit
after: 6 follow 8 resemble
apart: 7 analyze, dissect 9 dismantle
care: 6 beware
care of: 3 fix 4 tend 5 nurse 6 attend
exception: 6 object
five: 4 rest
from: 7 deprive, detract 8 subtract
it easy: 5 relax

on the: 7 corrupt
part: 4 join 5 share 11 participate
place: 5 occur 6 happen
the cake: 3 win
to: 4 like
to task: 5 scold 7 reprove
turns: 9 alternate
unawares: 8 surprise

take away
5 decry, wrest 6 deduct, remove 7 deprive, detract 8 belittle, derogate, diminish, discount, draw back, knock off, minimize, subtract, withdraw, write off 9 disparage, substract 10 depreciate 11 detract from

take back
5 unsay 6 abjure, recall, recant, return 7 replace, restore, retract 8 forswear, palinode, withdraw 9 repossess, restitute

take down
5 lower 6 reduce, tackle 8 dismount 9 dismantle, dismember 11 disassemble

take in
3 see 4 fool, have 5 admit, bluff, catch, grasp, trick 6 absorb, accept, betray, delude, embody, follow, illude 7 beguile, compass, contain, deceive, embrace, include, involve, receive, subsume 8 flimflam 9 apprehend, encompass, four-flush 10 assimilate, comprehend, understand 11 double cross

take off
2 go 3 ape 4 doff, down, exit, head, kill, kite, mock, quit, slay 5 douse, leave, mimic, scram 6 begone, decamp, deduct, depart, finish, get out, lay low, parody, remove, set out 7 destroy, get away, imitate, pull out, skiddoo, vamoose 8 clear out, discount, dispatch, draw back, hightail, light out, subtract, withdraw 9 burlesque, skedaddle, strike out, substract

takeoff
4 jato, rato 6 launch, parody, send-up 7 lift-off 8 blast-off, travesty 9 burlesque 10 caricature
area: 3 pad 6 runway

take on
3 add, don 4 face, hire, meet, pull 5 adopt, annex 6 append, assume, employ, engage, strike 7 embrace, espouse, subjoin 9 encounter

take out
4 date, vent 5 loose 6 deduct, remove 7 release, unleash 8 dis-

count, draw back, knock off, subtract, withdraw **9** clear away, eliminate, substract

take over
    5 seize, spell, usurp **7** relieve

take up
    3 use **4** lift, open, rear **5** adopt, begin, enter, hoist, raise, renew, set to, start **6** assume, resume, tackle, uphold, uplift, uprear **7** elevate, embrace, espouse, kick off, restart, upraise **8** commence, continue, initiate **10** recommence

talc
    4 mica **6** powder **7** agalite **8** steatite **9** soapstone

tale
    3 fib, lie, sum **4** myth, saga, tote, yarn **5** fable, story, total, whole **6** canard, legend **7** calumny, falsity, fiction, scandal, slander, untruth **8** anecdote, entirety, sum total, totality, untruism **9** aggregate, falsehood, narration, narrative **10** backbiting, defamation, detraction **12** backstabbing, belittlement, depreciation **13** disparagement, prevarication
    epic: **4** saga
    woeful: **8** jeremiad

talebearer
    4 fink **5** tabby **6** canary, gossip, snitch **7** rumorer, tattler, tipster **8** gossiper, informer, quidnunc, squealer **10** newsmonger **11** rumormonger, stool pigeon **13** scandalmonger

talent
    4 bent, gift, nose **5** craft, flair, forte, money, skill **6** genius **7** aptness, faculty **9** endowment, expertise

Tale of Two Cities, A
    author: **7** Dickens (Charles)
    character: **6** Carton (Sidney), Darnay (Charles) **7** Defarge, Manette (Alexander), Manette (Lucie)

Tales of a Traveller author
    6 Irving (Washington)

Tales of a Wayside Inn author
    10 Longfellow (Henry Wadsworth)

Tales of Hoffman composer
    9 Offenbach (Jacques)

talipot
    4 palm

talisman
    4 juju, luck, zemi **5** charm, saffi **6** amulet, fetish, mascot, saphie **7** periapt **10** phylactery

Talisman, The
    author: **5** Scott (Walter)

talk
    3 gab, rap, yak **4** blab, buzz, chat, chin, sing, yarn **5** on-dit, prate, rumor, run on, speak, utter, voice **6** babble, dialog, gabble, gossip, parley, patter, powwow, report, speech, squeal, tattle **7** address, chatter, declaim, gabfest, hearsay, lecture, prattle **8** causerie, colloque, colloquy, converse, dialogue, harangue, perorate, vocalize **9** discourse, grapevine, hold forth, speechify, utterance, verbalize **10** allocution, discussion **11** scuttlebutt **12** conversation, deliberation **13** confabulation, verbalization
    about: **7** discuss
    back: **4** sass
    combining form: **3** log **4** logy **5** logia, logue
    foolish: **4** bunk **6** babble **7** chatter, palaver
    indistinctly: **6** mumble, mutter
    over: **7** discuss
    slowly: **5** drawl
    small: **8** chitchat
    wildly: **4** rant, rave

talkative
    4 glib **5** gabby, vocal **6** chatty, fluent, mouthy **7** gossipy, voluble **9** garrulous **10** babblative, loquacious **11** loose-lipped **12** loosetongued, multiloquent **13** multiloquious

tall
    4 high **5** lanky, lofty, rangy **8** towering **11** skyscraping **12** altitudinous

tallow
    3 fat **4** suet **6** grease
    combining form: **4** sebi, sebo **5** stear, steat **6** stearo, steato

tally
    4 jibe **5** agree, count, fit in, match, score **6** accord, number, square **7** balance, catalog, conform, itemize **8** numerate **9** catalogue, enumerate, harmonize, inventory **10** correspond

Talmai
    daughter: **6** Maacah
    father: **4** Anak
    grandson: **7** Absalom

talon
    4 claw

talus
    5 ankle, scree, slope

tam
    3 cap

Tamar
    brother: **7** Absalom
    father: **5** David **7** Absalom
    father-in-law: **5** Judah
    half brother: **5** Amnon
    husband: **2** Er
    seducer: **5** Amnon
    son: **5** Perez, Zerah

tamarisk
    4 atle **5** athel, atlee

tambour
    3 cup **4** bell, drum, wall **7** drummer

tambourine
    4 dove, drum **7** timbrel

Tamburlaine the Great author
    7 Marlowe (Christopher)

tame
    4 meek, mild **6** docile, gentle, master, pliant **7** pliable, subdued, trained **8** amenable, biddable, broken in, domestic, obedient **9** tractable **10** submissive **11** domesticate, domesticize, domiciliate, housebroken **12** domesticated

Taming of the Shrew, The
    character: **6** Bianca **8** Baptista **9** Katharina, Petruchio

Tammany boss
    5 Tweed (William)

Tammuz' lover
    6 Ishtar

tam-o'-shanter
    3 cap

tamp
    3 jam, mat, ram **4** cram, pack **5** pound, stuff

tampion
    4 plug

tan
    3 sun, taw **4** beat, ecru, flog, whip **5** beige, brown, toast **6** bronze, darken, thrash

tanager
    4 bird, yeni

Tancred, Tancredi
    beloved: **8** Clorinda
    father: **3** Odo
    mother: **4** Emma
    victim: **8** Clorinda

tandem
    4 pair **8** carriage

tang
    3 nip **4** bite, odor, zest **5** aroma, sapor, savor, smack, taste **6** flavor,

relish **8** piquancy, pungency, sapidity **9** spiciness

tangible
7 tactile **8** embodied, material, palpable, physical, sensible **9** corporeal, touchable **10** detectable, observable, phenomenal **11** appreciable, discernible, perceptible, substantial

tangle
3 mat, web **4** knot, maze, mesh, muck, trap **5** benet, catch, mix up, ravel, skein, snare, snarl **6** entrap, foul up, jungle, morass, muddle **7** catch up, embroil, ensnare, ensnarl, involve, mizmaze, perplex **9** implicate, labyrinth **10** complicate

Tanglewood Tales author
9 Hawthorne (Nathaniel)

tango
5 dance

tank
3 vat **5** basin **7** cistern, pachuca, vehicle **8** aquarium **9** container, reservoir
American: **7** Sherman
German: **6** panzer
part: **6** turret

tankard
3 mug **5** stoup **6** flagon **9** blackjack

tanker
4 ship **5** oiler

Tannhäuser composer
6 Wagner (Richard)

tantalize
4 bait, gnaw **5** annoy, harry, taunt, tease, worry **6** harass, pester, plague **7** bedevil, hagride, torment **9** beleaguer, frustrate

Tantalus
daughter: **5** Niobe
father: **4** Zeus
son: **6** Pelops

tantamount
4 same **5** alike, equal **8** selfsame **9** duplicate, identical **10** equivalent

tantara
5 blare **7** fanfare

tantivy
4 rush **6** gallop **8** headlong

tantrum
3 fit

Tanzania
capital: **11** Dar es Salaam
monetary unit: **8** shilling

Taoism founder
6 Lao Tzu

tap
3 bar, bob, hit, pub, rap **4** cock, draw, name, pump, tunk **5** draft, drain, knock, nudge, thump, valve **6** faucet, finger, siphon, spigot, strike **7** appoint, barroom, draw off, hydrant, petcock **8** nominate, stopcock **9** designate

tape
4 band, belt, bind **5** strip **6** fillet, record, ribbon **7** bandage, measure
kind: **5** inkle **6** ferret **7** masking **8** adhesive **9** measuring
machine: **8** recorder

taper
4 wick **5** abate, close, spire **6** lessen, reduce **7** dwindle **8** decrease, diminish **9** drain away

tapering
5 conic, spiry **6** terete **7** conical, pointed **8** fusiform, subulate **9** acuminate

tapestry
5 arras, kilim **6** dossal **7** curtain, Gobelin, hanging
pattern: **7** cartoon
tool: **6** broché

tapeworm
6 taenia **8** parasite
body: **8** strobila
combining form: **4** taen **5** taeni **6** taenio
head: **6** scolex

Taphath's father
7 Solomon

tapioca
7 cassava, pudding

Tappuah's father
6 Hebron

taproom
3 bar, pub **6** saloon, tavern

tapster
6 barman **7** barmaid **9** barkeeper, bartender **10** mixologist

tar
4 jack, pave, salt, soil **5** pitch, smear, stain, sully, taint **6** defile, sailor, seaman **7** asphalt, besmear, mariner **8** besmirch **9** sailorman

taradiddle
3 fib, lie **5** story **6** canard **7** falsity **9** falsehood **13** prevarication

tarantella
5 dance

tarantula
6 spider

Taras Bulba author
5 Gogol (Nikolay)

tarboosh
3 fez, hat

tardy
3 lax **4** late, slow **7** belated, delayed, laggard, overdue **8** detained, dilatory **10** behindhand, delinquent, unpunctual

tare
4 seed **5** vetch **6** weight

target
3 aim **4** butt, goal, mark **6** object, victim **9** objective, quaesitum **11** sitting duck
center: **8** bull's-eye
shooter's: **10** clay pigeon

Tar Heel State
13 North Carolina

tariff
3 tab, tax **4** cost, duty, levy, rate **5** price **6** charge, impost **8** price tag **10** assessment

Tarkington, Booth
character: **6** Penrod

tarn
4 lake, pool

tarnish
3 dim, mar, tar **4** dull, fade, foul, harm, hurt, pale, soil **5** dirty, grime, muddy, smear, spoil, sully, taint **6** besoil, damage, impair, injure, smirch, smudge, smutch **7** begrime, besmear, blemish **8** besmirch, discolor

taro
4 dalo, eddo, gabe, gabi **5** aroid, tania **6** yautia **7** dasheen, malanga
product: **3** poi

tarpaulin
4 jack, salt **5** cover **6** sailor, seaman **7** mariner **9** sailorman

tarpon
4 fish **5** oxeye

tarry
3 lag **4** bide, drag, poke, stay, wait **5** abide, dally, delay, trail, visit **6** linger, loiter, put off, remain **8** stop over **11** stick around **13** procrastinate

Tarshish's father
6 Bilhan

tarsus
5 ankle

tart
3 dry, pie 4 acid, sour 5 acerb, sharp 6 pastry 7 acerbic, acetose, piquant, pungent 9 acidulous

Tartar
6 Mongol 7 Turkish 8 Mongolic 9 Mongolian

Tartuffe author
7 Molière

Tarzan
creator: 9 Burroughs (Edgar Rice)
mate: 4 Jane

task
3 job 4 duty, lade, load, toil, work 5 chare, chore, labor, stint, weigh 6 burden, charge, devoir, errand, lumber, saddle, weight 7 mission, project 8 encumber 10 assignment 11 undertaking

Tasmanian
4 wolf 5 devil
pine: 4 Huon

Tasmania's capital
6 Hobart

tassel
4 tuft 5 adorn 6 fringe 7 pendant 8 ornament

Tasso
patron: 4 Este (Alfonso II d')
work: 6 Aminta 7 Rinaldo 18 Jerusalem Delivered

taste
3 eat, sip, try 4 dash, feel, hint, tang, zest 5 grace, gusto, heart, sapor, savor, smack, tinge, touch, whiff 6 degust, flavor, liking, palate, polish, relish, trifle 7 finesse, stomach 8 appetite, elegance, fondness, sapidity, soft spot, tincture, weakness 9 appetence 10 experience, partiality, refinement, sprinkling 11 inclination
combining form: 6 geusia
kind: 4 salt, sour 5 sweet 6 bitter
lacking: (see tasteless)
organ: 3 bud

tasteless
4 dull, flat, wild 5 bland, vapid 6 vulgar 7 insipid 8 barbaric, unsavory 9 barbarian, barbarous, graceless, inelegant, savorless, unrefined 10 flavorless, outlandish, unflavored, unpolished 11 ill-flavored, unpalatable 12 unappetizing 13 uninteresting

tasty
5 sapid 6 savory, toothy 9 palatable, relishing, toothsome 10 appetizing, flavorsome

Tate
7 Gallery

tatou
9 armadillo

tatter
3 rag, rip 4 tear 5 shred

tattered
5 dingy, seedy, tacky 6 frayed, ragged, shabby, tagrag 7 run-down, shreddy 8 frazzled 10 bedraggled, broken-down, threadbare 11 dilapidated

tattle
4 blab, buzz, talk 5 rumor 6 gossip, report 7 hearsay 9 grapevine 11 scuttlebutt

tattler
see talebearer

tattletale
see talebearer

tatty
4 base, mean, poor 5 cheap 6 common, paltry, shoddy, sleazy, trashy 8 rubbishy

taunt
4 gibe, lout, mock, razz, twit 5 scout, tease 6 deride 7 provoke 8 reproach, ridicule

taurine
6 bovine

Taurus
4 bull
star: 9 Aldebaran

taut
5 close, tense, tight

tautology
8 pleonasm, verbiage 9 verbality 10 periphrase, redundancy, roundabout 11 periphrasis 13 circumambages

tavern
3 bar, inn, pub 5 hotel, lodge 6 bistro, hostel, saloon 7 auberge, barroom, hospice, taproom 8 alehouse, drinkery, hostelry 9 roadhouse 11 caravansary, public house 12 watering hole

taverner
8 boniface, publican 9 barkeeper, innholder, innkeeper, saloonist 12 saloonkeeper

taw
5 stake 6 marble

tawdry
4 loud 5 gaudy 6 brazen, flashy, garish, tinsel 7 blatant, chintzy, glaring 12 meretricious

tawny
3 tan 4 dark 5 brown 6 tanned
combining form: 5 fusco, pyrrh, pyrro 6 pyrrho

tax
4 duty, lade, levy, load, onus, scot, toll 5 abuse, tithe 6 assess, burden, cumber, impost, saddle, strain, tariff, weight 7 tollage, tribute 8 encumber 10 assessment, deadweight
agency: 3 IRS
feudal: 7 scutage, tallage
kind: 4 geld 5 sales, tithe 6 excise, income 7 chevage, prisage 8 property 9 surcharge
on salt: 7 gabelle
rate: 10 assessment

taxi
3 cab, car 4 hack

taxing
5 tough 6 trying 7 exigent, onerous, weighty 8 exacting, grievous 9 demanding 10 burdensome, oppressive

Taygeta
father: 5 Atlas
mother: 7 Pleione
sisters: 8 Pleiades

tazza
3 cup 4 vase

Tchaikovsky, Peter
ballet: 8 Swan Lake 10 Nutcracker
opera: 12 Eugene Onegin 13 Queen of Spades

tea
5 drink, party 6 repast 8 beverage 9 marijuana, reception
black: 5 bohea, oopak, pekoe 8 souchong
cake: 6 cookie
genus: 4 Thea
ingredient: 8 caffeine
kind: 4 herb, Java 5 Assam, black, bohea, green, hyson, ledum, pekoe 6 Ceylon, congou, oolong 7 cambric 8 souchong 9 sassafras
of India: 10 Darjeeling

teach
5 coach, train, tutor 6 impart, school 7 educate, instill 8 instruct 9 enlighten, inculcate 12 indoctrinate

teacher
4 guru, prof **5** coach, guide, tutor
6 docent, master, mentor, pedant
7 edifier, maestro, trainer **8** educator, magister **9** pedagogue, preceptor, professor **10** instructor
12 schoolmaster
Hindu: **5** swami
Jewish: **5** rabbi **7** rabboni
Muslim: **3** pir **5** mulla **6** mollah, mullah
organization: **3** NEA
religious: **8** mystagog **9** catechist

Tea for Two composer
7 Youmans (Vincent)

team
4 club, crew, gang, join, pair, side, yoke **5** group, squad, wagon
8 carriage
baseball: **4** nine
basketball: **4** five **7** quintet
football: **6** eleven
kind: **2** JV **6** jayvee **7** varsity
supporter: **3** fan

tear
3 cut, rip, run **4** bolt, dash, gash, lash, race, rend, rift, rive, rush, slit
5 chase, fling, sever, shoot, shred, slash, speed, split **6** career, charge, cleave, course, incise, sunder, tatter **8** lacerate

tear away
6 avulse

tear down
4 raze, ruin, slur **5** smear, wrack, wreck **6** defame, malign **7** asperse, destroy, shatter, slander
8 demolish, destruct **9** denigrate
10 annihilate, calumniate, scandalize

tearful
3 sad **5** weepy **6** crying **7** bawling, sobbing, weeping **8** mourning
9 lamenting, sniveling **10** blubbering, lachrymose

tear-jerking
5 mushy **6** slushy, sticky **7** maudlin, mawkish **8** bathetic, romantic
11 sentimental

teary
see **tearful**

teary-eyed
5 blear

tease
3 kid, rip **4** gnaw, josh, twit **5** annoy, chaff, harry, taunt, worry
6 harass, pester, plague **7** bedevil
8 ridicule **9** beleaguer

teaser
television: **5** promo

Tebah
father: **5** Nahor
mother: **6** Reumah

teched
4 daft **5** batty, crazy **6** crazed, insane **7** cracked, lunatic **8** demented, deranged **9** bedlamite

technicality
6 detail **8** loophole

technique
3 way **4** mode, wise **5** modus
6 manner, method, system
7 fashion
combining form: **4** urgy

tectonic
10 structural

ted
5 strew **6** spread **7** scatter

tedious
3 dry **4** arid, dull **5** dusty **6** boring, tiring **7** insipid, irksome **8** boresome, bromidic, drudging, weariful
9 dryasdust, wearisome
13 uninteresting

tedium
4 yawn **5** ennui **7** boredom **8** doldrums, dullness, monotony

teem
4 flow **5** crawl, swarm **6** abound
9 pullulate

teeming
4 lush, rife **5** alive **6** aswarm **7** replete **8** swarming, thronged
9 abounding **11** overflowing

teen
5 youth **8** juvenile **9** youngster
10 adolescent

tee off
4 open **5** begin, drive, enter, start
6 take up **8** commence, initiate

teeter
5 lurch **6** falter, seesaw, topple, totter, wobble **7** stagger, stumble

teeth
false: **8** dentures
grinding: **7** bruxism
having: **7** dentate
problem: **5** decay **6** caries
8 overbite
relating to: **6** dental; (see also **tooth**)

teg
3 doe **4** deer **5** sheep

tegua
8 moccasin

teju
6 lizard

telamon
5 atlas
counterpart: **8** caryatid

Telamon
brother: **6** Peleus
father: **6** Aeacus
half-brother: **6** Phocus
son: **4** Ajax **6** Teucer

Telegonus
father: **7** Ulysses **8** Odysseus
mother: **5** Circe

telegraph
4 wire **5** cable **6** signal
code: **5** Morse

Telemachus
father: **7** Ulysses **8** Odysseus
mother: **8** Penelope

telephone
4 buzz, call, dial, ring **5** phone
6 ring up
inventor: **4** Bell (Alexander Graham)

Telephus
father: **8** Heracles, Hercules
mother: **4** Auge

telescope
5 glass **8** compress, condense, spyglass

television
2 TV **4** tube **5** video **8** boob tube
antenna: **10** rabbit ears
award: **4** Emmy
British: **5** telly
children's: **6** kidvid
frequency: **3** UHF, VHF
interference: **4** snow
network: **3** ABC, BBC, CBS, Fox, NBC, NET, PBS
pioneer: **5** Baird (John Logie)
8 Zworykin (Vladimir)
program: **4** news, show **5** rerun
6 series, sitcom **7** western **8** game show, talk show **9** broadcast, docudrama, soap opera **11** infomercial
12 infotainment
tube: **4** kine **9** kinescope

tell
3 bid, say **4** clew, clue, post, tale, warn **5** mouth, order, spill, state, tally, utter **6** advise, betray, charge, direct, enjoin, fill in, inform, notify, number, relate, reveal, wise up **7** blab out, command, de-

clare, divulge, narrate **8** bring out, disclose, discover, give away, instruct, numerate

teller
5 clerk **7** cashier, counter **8** informer, narrator

telling
5 solid, sound, valid **6** cogent **10** convincing, satisfying **12** satisfactory

tell off
3 jaw **4** rail **5** scold **6** berate, revile **7** bawl out, chew out, upbraid **8** call down **10** tongue-lash, vituperate

tell on
6 snitch, tattle

telltale
3 cue **4** clue, hint, wind **5** clack, tabby **6** gossip, notion **7** inkling **8** gossiper, quidnunc **9** carrytale **10** indication, intimation, newsmonger, suggestion, talebearer **12** gossipmonger **13** scandalmonger

tellurian
6 earthy **7** earthly, mundane, terrene, worldly **9** sublunary **11** terrestrial, uncelestial

tellurium
symbol: **2** Te

Tema's father
7 Ishmael

temblor
5 quake, shake, shock **6** quaker, tremor **10** earthquake

temerarious
4 rash **6** daring **8** heedless, reckless **9** audacious, daredevil, foolhardy, imprudent, venturous **10** incautious **11** adventurous, injudicious, venturesome **13** adventuresome

temerity
4 gall **5** nerve **6** daring **8** audacity, rashness **9** assurance, brashness, hardihood, hardiness **11** impetuosity **12** heedlessness, impertinence, recklessness **13** foolhardiness

temper
4 curb, mind, mood, tone, vein **5** humor **6** dilute, makeup, season, soften, spirit, strain, timbre **7** passion **8** moderate, modulate, restrain, tone down **10** complexion

11 personality **13** individualism, individuality

temperament
4 mood **5** humor **6** makeup, nature **9** character **10** complexion **11** disposition, personality

temperamental
5 moody **6** fickle **8** ticklish, unstable, variable, volatile **9** humorsome, mercurial, uncertain **10** capricious, changeable, inconstant

temperance
7 control, measure **8** sobriety **9** austerity **10** abstinence, continence, moderation **11** refrainment, self-control **12** moderateness
advocate of: **6** Nation (Carry) **7** Willard (Frances)

temperate
4 calm, even **5** sober **6** modest, steady **8** discreet, moderate **9** abstinent, continent, regulated, unextreme **10** abstemious, controlled, reasonable, restrained **11** abstentious, unexcessive **12** conservative **13** unimpassioned

temperature
4 heat **5** fever **6** warmth **9** intensity

tempest
4 gale, rage, wind **5** storm **6** tumult, uproar **9** commotion, hurricane

Tempest, The
character: **5** Ariel **7** Caliban, Miranda **8** Prospero **9** Ferdinand

tempestuous
4 wild **5** rough **6** raging, stormy **7** furious, violent **8** blustery **9** turbulent, unbridled **10** blustering, tumultuous

temple
4 fane **6** church **10** house of God, tabernacle **13** house of prayer
ancient: **4** naos **5** speos **8** pantheon
Aztec: **6** teopan **8** teocalli
Buddhist: **2** ta **3** taa, wat
Eastern: **6** pagoda
Greek: **6** hieron **9** Parthenon
sanctuary: **5** cella **6** adytum **10** penetralia

tempo
4 pace, rate, time **5** speed **6** rhythm
fast: **6** presto **7** allegro
moderate: **7** andante
slow: **5** grave, lento **6** adagio

temporal
3 lay **6** earthy **7** mundane, pro-

fane, secular, sensual, worldly **8** banausic, unsacred **13** materialistic

temporary
6 acting, pro tem, supply **7** interim **9** ad interim, transient **10** pro tempore

tempt
3 woo **4** bait, lure, risk, vamp **5** decoy, train **6** allure, entice, entrap, invite, lead on, seduce **7** solicit **8** inveigle **9** tantalize

temptation
4 bait, lure, trap **5** decoy, snare **6** come-on **10** allurement, enticement, seducement **12** inveiglement

temptress
4 vamp **5** siren **7** Delilah, Lorelei **10** seductress **11** femme fatale

ten
cents: **4** dime
combining form: **3** dec, dek **4** deca, deka **5** decem
dollars: **7** sawbuck
mills: **4** cent
thousand: **6** myriad
years: **6** decade

tenacious
3 set **4** fast, firm, true **5** fixed, stout, tight, tough **6** dogged, secure, strong, sturdy, viscid **7** viscose, viscous **8** resolute, stalwart, stubborn **9** obstinate, steadfast **10** bulldogged, persisting **11** bulldoggish, persevering **12** pertinacious

tenacity
8 firmness **10** resolution

tenant
6 holder, lessee, occupy, people, renter **7** boarder, dweller, inhabit **8** occupant, populate **9** collibert
feudal: **4** leud **6** bordar, vassal **7** socager, sokeman
Indian: **7** chakdar
Irish: **7** cottier

tenantable
7 livable **9** habitable, lodgeable **10** occupiable **11** inhabitable

Ten Commandments
9 Decalogue

tend
4 care, lean, look, mind, till, work **5** dress, labor, nurse, serve, watch **7** care for, conduce, incline, redound **8** minister **10** contribute

tendency

3 run **4** bent, bias **5** drift, tenor, trend **7** current, leaning **8** penchant **9** inclining **10** proclivity, propensity **11** disposition, inclination **12** predilection
combining form: **5** phily **6** philia
suffix: **4** itis

tendentious

6 biased **7** colored, partial **8** one-sided, partisan **10** prejudiced

tender

4 fond, give, mild, pose, soft, sore, warm **5** offer **6** extend, gentle, humane, loving, submit **7** hold out, lenient, present, proffer, propose **8** yielding **9** forgiving **10** benevolent, charitable, responsive **11** considerate, kindhearted, softhearted, sympathetic, warmhearted **12** affectionate **13** commiserative, compassionate

tenderfoot

4 colt, tyro **6** novice, rookie **8** beginner, freshman, neophyte, newcomer **9** novitiate **10** apprentice

Tender Is the Night author

10 Fitzgerald (F. Scott)

tendon

4 band, cord **5** sinew

tendril

4 curl **6** cirrus **7** ringlet

tenebrific

5 black, bleak **6** dismal, dreary, gloomy, somber **8** funereal **10** oppressive **11** dispiriting **13** disheartening

tenebrous

3 dim **4** dark, dusk **5** dusky, murky, vague **6** gloomy **7** obscure, unclear **9** ambiguous, equivocal, lightless, sibylline, uncertain **10** caliginous, unexplicit **13** unilluminated

tenement

4 flat **5** rooms, suite **6** rental **7** lodging **8** building **9** apartment

tenet

3 ism **5** canon, dogma **8** doctrine

tenfold

6 denary

Tennessee

capital: **9** Nashville
college, university: **5** Bryan **10** Vanderbilt
largest city: **7** Memphis
nickname: **14** Volunteer State
state flower: **4** iris

tennis

award: **8** Davis Cup
item: **3** net **4** ball **6** racket **7** racquet
kind: **5** table **7** doubles, singles **8** platform
score: **4** love **5** deuce
serve: **3** ace
shoe: **7** sneaker
stroke: **3** cut, lob **4** chop, drop **5** serve, slice **6** volley **8** backhand, forehand
term: **3** let, set **5** court, fault **7** service **9** advantage, backcourt

tennis champ

4 Ashe (Arthur), Borg (Bjorn), Cash (Pat), Graf (Steffi), King (Billie Jean), Noah (Yannick), Wade (Virginia) **5** Budge (Don), Chang (Michael), Court (Margaret Smith), Evert (Chris), Gomez (Andres), Laver (Rod), Lendl (Ivan), Perry (Fred), Seles (Monica), Stich (Michael), Vilas (Guillermo), Wills (Helen) **6** Agassi (André), Austin (Tracy), Becker (Boris), Edberg (Stephan), Fraser (Neale), Gibson (Althea), Kramer (Jack), Muster (Thomas), Pierce (Mary), Stolle (Fred), Tilden (Bill) **7** Connors (Jimmy), Courier (Jim), Emerson (Roy), Lacoste (Rene), McEnroe (John), Nastase (Ilie), Sampras (Pete) **8** Bruguera (Sergi), Connolly (Maureen), Gonzalez (Pancho), Martinez (Conchita), Newcombe (John), Rosewall (Ken), Sabatini (Gabriela), Wilander (Mats) **10** Mandlikova (Hana) **11** Navratilova (Martina) **14** Sanchez Vicario (Arantxa)

Tennyson poem

4 Maud **5** Ulysses **8** Tiresias **10** Enoch Arden, In Memoriam **12** Locksley Hall

tenor

3 run **4** body, mood, tone **5** drift, voice **6** singer **7** current, meaning, purport **8** tendency **9** substance
American: **5** Lanza (Mario) **6** Hadley (Jerry), Peerce (Jan), Tucker (Richard) **8** Melchior (Lauritz) **9** McCormack (John), McCracken (James)
Canadian: **7** Vickers (Jon)
Czech: **6** Slezak (Leo)
German: **10** Wunderlich (Fritz)
Italian: **5** Gigli (Beniamino) **6** Caruso (Enrico) **7** Corelli (Franco) **8** Bergonzi (Carlo) **9** del Monaco (Mario), di Stefano (Giuseppe), Pavarotti (Luciano)
Spanish: **7** Domingo (Placido) **8** Carreras (Jose)

Swedish: **5** Gedda (Nicolai) **8** Björling (Jussi) **9** Bjoerling (Jussi)

tenpins

7 bowling

tense

4 edgy, taut **5** nervy, tight **6** uneasy **7** anxious, jittery, restive, uptight **8** strained
grammatical: **4** past **6** future **7** perfect, present **8** preterit **9** preterite **10** pluperfect **11** progressive

tension

6 nerves, strain, stress, unease **7** anxiety **8** pressure, tautness **9** agitation **10** discomfort, uneasiness **11** nervousness, uptightness

tent

4 camp **5** bivvy, cover, lodge **6** canopy, encamp, laager, maroon **7** bivouac, shelter
Eskimo: **5** tupik
kind: **3** pup **4** bell, pawl, yort **5** Baker, tepee **6** teepee, wigwam **7** kibitka, marquee, wickiup **8** pavilion, umbrella
maker: **4** Omar
material: **6** canvas
part: **3** fly, guy, peg **4** pole

tentacle

3 arm **6** feeler

tentative

4 test **5** trial **6** wobbly **7** halting **8** hesitant **9** faltering, makeshift, provisory, uncertain **10** irresolute **11** conditional, provisional, vacillating, vacillatory **12** provisionary

tenth

5 tithe
combining form: **4** deci

tenuous

4 rare, slim, thin, weak **5** reedy **6** feeble, flimsy, slight, stalky, subtle, twiggy **7** slender, squinny, subtile **8** ethereal, rarefied **9** attenuate **10** attenuated **11** implausible **13** insubstantial, unsubstantial

tenure

4 grip, hold, term **5** clamp, clasp, grasp, gripe **6** clench, clinch, clutch, estate **7** grapple
feudal: **7** burgage

tepid

4 mild, warm **7** warmish **8** lukewarm, milk-warm **9** temperate **11** halfhearted, indifferent

tequila source

6 mescal

Terah's son
5 Abram, Haran, Nahor
7 Abraham

teras
7 monster

terbium
symbol: 2 Tb

Terentia's husband
6 Cicero

Tereus
son: 4 Itys
wife: 6 Procne

tergiversate
3 rat 4 turn 5 dodge, evade, hedge 6 defect, desert, weasel 7 shuffle 8 renounce, sidestep 9 pussyfoot, repudiate 10 apostatize, equivocate

term
3 dub 4 call, name, span, time, word 5 bound, hitch, spell 6 detail, period, tenure 7 article, baptize, stretch 8 christen, duration 9 designate 10 denominate, limitation, particular

termagant
5 harpy, rowdy, scold, shrew, vixen 6 amazon, ogress, unruly, virago 7 raucous 8 fishwife 9 rowdy 9 turbulent, Xanthippe 10 boisterous, disorderly, rowdydowdy, tumultuous 11 rumbustious

terminable
6 finite 7 endable, limited 9 limitable

terminal
3 end, lag 4 last 5 depot, final 6 latest, latter 7 closing, station 8 eventual, hindmost, ultimate 10 concluding
negative: 7 cathode
positive: 5 anode

terminate
2 ax 3 end 4 drop, fire, halt, quit, rise, sack, stop 5 close, leave 6 bounce, finish, recess, resign, wind up, wrap up 7 abolish, adjourn, boot out, cashier, dismiss, kick out 8 complete, conclude, dissolve, prorogue, ultimate 9 determine, discharge, prorogate 10 extinguish 11 discontinue

terminology
4 cant 6 jargon 7 lexicon, palaver 8 language 10 dictionary, vocabulary

termite
3 ant

tern
4 trio 5 scray 8 schooner
genus: 6 Sterna

ternary
6 triple 9 threefold

terpsichore
see **Muse**

terrace
4 bank, dais, deck, roof, step 5 bench, porch 7 balcony, portico 8 platform

terra-cotta
4 clay 7 pottery

terra firma
4 dirt, land, soil 5 earth 6 ground 7 dry land

terrain
4 turf, walk 5 field 6 domain, sphere 7 demesne 8 dominion, province 9 bailiwick, champaign, territory 10 topography

terrapin
6 turtle

terrestrial
6 earthy 7 earthly, mundane, profane, prosaic, secular, terrene, worldly 8 telluric 9 earthlike, sublunary, tellurian 10 earthbound

terrible
3 bad 4 grim, hard 5 awful, heavy, tough 6 fierce, grisly, horrid, severe 7 arduous, fearful, furious, ghastly, hideous, intense, macabre, vicious, violent 8 dreadful, gruesome, horrible, horrific, shocking, toilsome, vehement 9 appalling, desperate, difficult, exquisite, frightful, laborious, strenuous 10 formidable, horrifying
combining form: 3 din 4 dein, dino 5 deino

terrier
3 dog
kind: 3 fox 4 blue, bull, Skye 5 cairn, Irish, Welsh 6 Boston 8 Airedale, Lakeland 9 Yorkshire

terrific
5 super, swell 6 superb 7 fearful 8 dreadful, glorious, horrible, horrific, shocking 9 appalling, frightful, marvelous, upsetting, wonderful 10 formidable 11 magnificent, sensational, terrorizing

terrify
3 awe 4 stun 5 alarm, scare 7 startle 8 affright, frighten 9 terrorize

terrifying
4 grim 6 grisly, horrid 7 ghastly, hideous, macabre 8 gruesome, horrible, terrible 10 horrifying

territory
4 area, belt, land, turf, walk, zone 5 field, tract 6 domain, region, sphere 7 demesne, terrain 8 dominion, province 9 bailiwick, champaign

terror
4 fear 5 alarm, dread, panic 6 dismay, fright, horror 9 trepidity 11 fearfulness, trepidation 13 consternation

terrorist
4 thug 6 bomber 7 Jacobin 8 alarmist

terrorize
3 cow 5 alarm, bully, scare 6 fright, hector 7 dragoon 8 affright, bludgeon, browbeat, bulldoze, bullyrag, frighten 9 strongarm 10 intimidate

terry
4 loop 6 fabric 8 toweling

terse
4 curt, taut 5 brief, crisp, pithy, short 7 compact, concise, laconic, summary 8 succinct 11 compendiary, compendious 12 breviloquent

tertiary
5 third

tessera
3 die 4 tile 6 tablet, ticket

test
3 try 4 exam, quiz 5 assay, check, essay, final, prove, trial, try on 6 sample, trying, try out, verify 7 confirm, examine, mid-term, proving 8 sounding, trial run 10 experiment 11 demonstrate, examination 12 experimental

testa
4 coat 5 shell 8 episperm 10 integument

testament
4 will 5 proof 7 witness 8 evidence 9 scripture, testimony 11 attestation, testimonial 12 confirmation

tester
5 frame 6 canopy, prover 7 assayer

testifier
7 witness 8 deponent 9 proselyte

testify
5 argue, swear 6 attest, depone, depose 7 bespeak, betoken, point to, witness 8 announce, indicate

testimonial
5 proof, salvo, token 6 salute 7 tribute, witness 8 evidence, memorial, monument 9 character, reference, testament 10 indication 11 attestation, credentials 12 appreciation, confirmation

testimony
5 proof 7 witness 8 evidence 10 indication 11 affirmation, attestation 12 confirmation 13 documentation

testy
5 cross, ratty 6 cranky, tetchy, touchy 7 grouchy 8 choleric 9 irascible, irritable, temperish 10 ill-humored 12 cantankerous 13 quick-tempered

tetanus
7 lockjaw, trismus

tetchy
see **testy**

tête-à-tête
4 chat, coze, talk 7 vis-à-vis 8 causerie 10 discussion 12 conversation

tether
3 tie 4 bind, rope 5 cable, chain, scope 6 fasten

Tethys
daughters: 9 Oceanides
father: 6 Uranus
husband: 7 Oceanus
mother: 2 Ge 4 Gaea 5 Terra

tetrad
4 four 7 quartet, quatuor 8 foursome 9 quartetto 10 quaternion

Teucer
father: 7 Telamon 9 Scamander
stepbrother: 4 Ajax

Teutonic
6 German 8 Germanic
language: 5 Dutch 6 Danish, German, Gothic 7 English, Flemish, Frisian, Swedish 9 Afrikaans, Norwegian

Texas
capital: 6 Austin
college, university: 3 SMU 4 Rice 5 Lamar, Wiley 6 Baylor
largest city: 7 Houston
nickname: 13 Lone Star State
state flower: 10 bluebonnet

text
4 head 5 motif, point, theme, topic 6 matter, motive 7 subject 8 argument 13 subject matter

textbook
6 manual, primer

textile
6 fabric
dealer: 6 mercer
machine: 8 calender
shop: 7 mercery
treat: 9 mercerize

texture
3 web 5 being, fiber 6 fabric, nature 7 essence

Thackeray novel
9 Pendennis 10 Vanity Fair 11 Henry Esmond

Thailand
4 Siam
capital: 7 Bangkok
language: 3 Lao
monetary unit: 4 baht 5 tical
temple: 3 wat

Thaïs
7 hetaera 9 courtesan
author: 6 France (Anatole)
composer: 8 Massenet (Jules)

thalassic
6 marine 7 oceanic 8 maritime

Thalia
see **Graces; Muse**

thallium
symbol: 2 Tl

Thanatopsis author
6 Bryant (William Cullen)

Thanatos
5 death
brother: 6 Hypnos
mother: 3 Nyx

thankful
7 obliged 8 grateful 12 appreciative

thanks
2 ta 5 grace 8 blessing 9 gratitude 11 benediction 12 appreciation, thanksgiving

Thanksgiving
5 feast 7 holiday
first celebrant: 6 Indian 7 Pilgrim
food: 6 turkey

thatch
4 roof 5 cover

that is
2 i.e.
Latin: 5 id est

Thaumas
daughter: 4 Iris 5 Aello, Harpy 7 Celaeno, Ocypete
daughters: 7 Harpies
father: 6 Pontus
mother: 2 Ge 4 Gaea
wife: 7 Electra

thaumaturgic
5 magic 6 magian, mystic, witchy 7 magical 8 wizardly 9 sorcerous 11 necromantic

thaumaturgy
5 magic 7 sorcery 8 witchery, wizardry 9 conjuring 10 necromancy, witchcraft 11 bewitchment, enchantment, incantation

thaw
3 run 4 flux, fuse, melt 7 liquefy 8 dissolve, liquesce 10 deliquesce

the
7 article
French: 2 la, le 3 les
German: 3 das, der, die
Italian: 2 il, la
Spanish: 2 el, la 3 las, los

Thea
daughter: 6 Selene
father: 6 Uranus
husband: 8 Hyperion
mother: 2 Ge 4 Gaea

theater
4 hall 5 drama, house, odeum, stage 6 boards 9 playhouse 10 footlights
award: 4 Tony
entrance: 5 foyer, lobby
Greek: 5 odeum
movie: 6 cinema
outdoor: 7 drive-in
part: 3 box, pit 4 loge 5 skene, stage, wings 7 balcony, parodos, parquet 10 proscenium

theatrical
5 stagy 6 staged 8 affected, dramatic, mannered, thespian 10 artificial, histrionic 11 dramaturgic, exaggerated 12 melodramatic
agent: 6 Morris (William)
device: 4 prop
group: 6 troupe

Theban Eagle
6 Pindar

Thebes
founder: 6 Cadmus
king: 5 Laius 7 Oedipus
queen: 7 Jocasta

theft
4 lift 5 pinch, steal 6 piracy 7 lar-

ceny, robbery, robbing, swiping
8 burglary, filching, stealage, stealing, thievery, thieving **9** pilferage,
pilfering **10** purloining
combining form: **5** klept **6** klepto

The Golden
3 Ass **4** Bowl **5** Bough **6** Fleece,
Legend

theme
4 head, text **5** essay, motif, paper,
point, topic **6** matter, motive, thesis
7 article, subject **8** argument
11 composition **13** subject matter

Themis
father: **6** Uranus
goddess of: **3** law **7** justice
husband: **4** Zeus **7** Jupiter
mother: **2** Ge **4** Gaea

then
2 so **4** also, anon, ergo, thus, when
5 again, hence **7** besides, further
9 therefore, thereupon **10** in addition **11** accordingly **12** additionally, consequently

thence
4 away **7** thereof **9** therefrom

theologian
American: **7** Edwards (Jonathan),
Niebuhr (Reinhold), Tillich (Paul),
Walther (Carl)
Dutch: **6** Jansen (Cornelis)
English: **4** Bede (Venerable) **5** Pusey
(Edward), Watts (Isaac) **6** Alcuin,
Wesley (John) **7** Langton (Stephen)
8 Pelagius, Wycliffe (John)
French: **6** Calvin (John) **7** William (of
Auvergne, of Auxerre) **8** Sabatier
(Auguste)
German: **6** Rahner (Karl) **7** Eckhart
(Meister) **9** Niemoller (Martin)
14 Albertus Magnus
Greek: **9** Zygomalas (Theodore)
Italian: **7** Aquinas (Thomas), Socinus
(Fausto, Laelius)
Scottish: **10** Duns Scotus (John)
Spanish: **6** Suarez (Francisco) **7** Vito-
ria (Francisco de) **8** Servetus
(Michael)
Swedish: **9** Soderblom (Nathan)
Swiss: **5** Barth (Karl), Vinet
(Alexandre-Rodolphe)

Theologica
5 Summa

theological
school: **8** seminary
virtue: **4** hope **5** faith **7** charity

theorbo
4 lute **8** archlute

theorem
3 law **4** rule **5** axiom **9** principle
10 principium **11** fundamental

theoretical
5 ideal **8** abstract, academic, notional, unproved **11** conjectural,
speculative **12** hypothetical, transcendent **13** problematical,
suppositional

theorize
6 submit **7** suggest **9** postulate

theory
7 perhaps, premise, suppose, surmise **8** supposal **10** conjecture,
hypothesis **11** speculation,
supposition
astronomical: **7** big bang
combining form: **4** logy **5** logia,
ology
suffix: **3** ism

therapy
9 treatment
combining form: **5** pathy **6** pathic

therefore
2 so **4** ergo, then, thus **5** hence
11 accordingly **12** consequently

therefrom
6 thence

thereupon
4 then **6** at once

therm
7 calorie

thermal
3 hot **4** warm
unit: **3** Btu **6** degree **7** calorie

thermometer
9 indicator
kind: **7** Celsius, Reaumur **10** centigrade, Fahrenheit

Thersander's father
9 Polynices

Thersites' slayer
8 Achilles

The Saint
12 Simon Templar

the same
4 idem **5** ditto **8** likewise
9 identical

thesaurus
7 lexicon **10** dictionary
editor: **5** Roget (Peter Mark)

Theseus
father: **6** Aegeus
mother: **6** Aethra
slayer: **9** Lycomedes
son: **10** Hippolytus

victim: **6** Sciron **8** Minotaur
10 Procrustes
wife: **7** Phaedra

thesis
5 essay, point, posit **6** belief, memoir **7** premise **8** tractate, treatise
9 apriorism, discourse, monograph,
postulate **10** contention, exposition,
monography **11** postulation, proposition, supposition **12** disquisition,
dissertation

thespian
4 mime **5** actor, mimic **6** mummer,
player **7** trouper **8** dramatic, theatral, theatric **9** performer, playactor
10 histrionic, theatrical **11** dramaturgic **12** impersonator

Thespis' forte
5 drama **7** tragedy

Thessalian hero
5 Jason **8** Achilles

___ the Terrible
4 Ivan

"The Thinker" sculptor
5 Rodin (Auguste)

Thetis
6 Nereid
father: **6** Nereus
husband: **6** Peleus
mother: **5** Doris
son: **8** Achilles

theurgist
8 magician

thew
4 beef **5** brawn, might, power,
sinew **6** muscle **8** strength

thick
3 fat **4** dull, dumb, wide **5** broad,
bulky, burly, close, dense, dumpy,
husky, obese, squat **6** chummy,
chunky, flimsy, obtuse, stocky, stupid **7** compact, crammed,
crowded, doltish, massive, viscous
8 blockish, duncical, familiar, heavyset, intimate **10** numskulled
combining form: **4** dasy, hadr
5 hadro, pachy

thicket
4 bosk, bush, wood **5** clump,
copse, grove **6** bosket, tangle
7 boscage, coppice, spinney
9 brushwood, chaparral
Scottish: **4** rone

thickness
5 layer **7** density **9** callosity

thief
3 dip, nip **4** prig **5** ganef **6** bandit,

lifter, looter, nimmer, pirate, robber
7 booster, burglar, filcher, stealer
8 hijacker, larcener, pilferer **9** larcenist, purloiner **10** cat burglar,
pickpocket, shoplifter
12 housebreaker

thieve
3 nip **4** hook, lift **5** filch, pinch,
steal, swipe **6** pilfer, snitch
7 purloin

thievery
see **theft**

thievish
9 larcenous

thigh
3 ham **5** flank **6** gammon
bone: 5 femur
combining form: 3 mer **4** mero
5 cruro, merus **6** femoro
relating to: 6 crural

thimble
3 cup **5** cover

thin
3 cut **4** fine, high, lank, lean, puny,
rare, slim, weak **5** acute, gaunt,
lanky, reedy, sharp, spare, wispy
6 argute, dilute, flimsy, meager,
piping, rarefy, shrill, skinny, slight,
sparse, stalky, treble, twiggy, watery, weaken **7** scrawny, slender,
squinny, subtile, tenuous **8** piercing, rarefied, rawboned, skeletal,
twiglike, wiredraw **9** attenuate, extenuate **10** attenuated **11** implausible, watered-down **12** unconvincing **13** unsubstantial
combining form: 4 lept **5** lepto

thing
2 go **3** act, cry, fad **4** deed, item,
mode, rage **5** being, craze, doing,
event, mania, point, stuff, style,
vogue **6** action, affair, detail, entity, fetish, furore, matter, object
7 article, concern, element, episode, fashion **8** business, existent,
fixation, incident, material, occasion **9** existence, happening, obsession, substance **10** dernier
cri, individual, occurrence,
phenomenon
additional: 5 bonus
in law: 3 res
insignificant: 6 trifle
rare: 4 oner
single: 4 unit
suffix: 2 ia (plural) **3** ant, ory **4** oria
(plural) **5** orium
to do: 3 job **5** chore
unusual: 5 freak **6** oddity
worthless: 4 junk **5** waste

thingamajig
5 gizmo **6** dingus, doodad, gadget, jigger **7** dofunny **9** doohickey
10 thingumbob

things
4 duds, togs **5** dress, goods, stuff,
traps **6** attire, tricks **7** apparel,
clothes, effects, plunder, raiment
8 chattels, clothing, movables
10 attirement, belongings, habiliment, possession
for sale: 11 merchandise

think
4 deem, feel, mull, muse **5** brood,
fancy, guess, opine, study, weigh
6 assume, expect, gather, ideate,
ponder, reason **7** believe, imagine,
perpend, presume, realize, reflect,
suppose, surmise, suspect **8** cogitate, conceive, consider, envisage,
envision, logicize, meditate, ruminate **9** cerebrate, speculate, visualize **10** conjecture, deliberate,
excogitate, logicalize **11** contemplate, rationalize
out: 4 plan
piece: 7 article

third
8 tertiary
combining form: 4 trit **5** trito
power: 4 cube

third degree
5 grill **8** grilling **13** interrogation

third estate
5 plebs **6** people, plebes **8** populace **9** commonage, commoners,
plebeians **10** commonalty **11** rank
and file

Third Man, The
author: 6 Greene (Graham)

thirst
3 yen **4** ache, itch, long, lust, pine
5 crave, yearn **6** hanker, hunger

thirsty
3 dry **4** agog, arid, avid, keen,
sere **5** eager **6** ardent **7** anxious,
athirst, bone-dry, parched **8** appetent, droughty **9** impatient, unwatered, waterless **12** moistureless

this and that
8 oddments, sundries **9** etceteras
11 odds and ends

Thisbe's lover
7 Pyramus

This Side of Paradise author
10 Fitzgerald (F. Scott)

thistle
4 weed **7** caltrop
Russian: 10 tumbleweed

thistlebird
9 goldfinch

thither
3 yon **5** there **6** yonder

thole
3 peg, pin

___ Thomas, Welsh author
5 Dylan

Thomas à ___
6 Becket, Kempis

Thomas' Greek name
7 Didymus

Thomas opera
6 Mignon

Thompson
5 Sadie **7** Dorothy, Francis, J. Walter **8** Benjamin

thong
4 lace, lash, rein **5** romal, strap,
strip **7** amentum, babiche, latchet
8 whiplash

Thor
5 Donar
father: 4 Odin
god of: 7 thunder
hammer: 8 Mjollnir
mother: 5 Jordh, Jorth

thorax
5 chest

Thoreau, Henry David
friend: 7 Emerson (Ralph Waldo)
work: 6 Walden

thorium
symbol: 2 Th

thorn
5 briar, brier, spine **7** acantha, spinule **9** annoyance **10** irritation
combining form: 4 spin **5** spini, spino
6 acanth **7** acantho, spinoso
8 acanthus

thorny
5 sharp, spiny **6** tricky **7** prickly,
spinate **9** difficult, vexatious
10 nettlesome **11** troublesome

thorough
4 full **6** minute **8** complete, detailed, itemized, whole-hog **9** clocklike **10** blow-by-blow, exhaustive

thoroughbred
5 horse **8** pedigree, purebred
9 pedigreed, pureblood **11** fullblooded

thoroughfare
3 way **4** drag, path, road **5** track
6 artery, avenue, street **7** highway
9 boulevard

thoroughgoing
4 rank 5 gross, utter 8 absolute, complete, outright, whole-hog 9 out-and-out 10 consummate, exhaustive 11 straight-out, unmitigated

though
3 yet 5 still, while 6 albeit 7 however, whereas 8 after all 11 nonetheless 12 nevertheless

thought
4 idea, mind 5 image 6 musing, notion 7 concept, opinion 9 brainwork, pondering 10 cogitation, conception, meditation, reflection, rumination 11 cerebration, speculation 12 deliberation, intellection 13 contemplation
combining form: 3 log 4 logo

thoughtful
6 polite 7 careful, gallant, heedful, logical, mindful, pensive, serious 8 gracious, rational, studious, thinking 9 attentive, courteous, pondering, regardful 10 cogitative, meditative, reflecting, reflective, ruminative, solicitous 11 considerate 12 intellectual 13 contemplative

thoughtless
4 rash, rude 5 brash, hasty 6 madcap 7 selfish 8 careless, feckless, heedless, impolite, reckless, uncaring 9 hotheaded, unheeding, unrecking 10 ill-advised, incautious, mad-brained, ungracious, unthinking 11 inadvertent 12 discourteous, irreflective, unreflective 13 inconsiderate

thousand
combining form: 4 kilo
dollars: 5 grand
years: 10 millennium

thousandth
10 millesimal
combining form: 5 milli

thrall
4 yoke 7 bondage, helotry, peonage, serfdom, slavery 9 servitude, villenage 11 enslavement

thrash
4 beat, drub, flog, hide, lash, lick, maul, pelt, whip 5 paste, pound, smear, whale 6 batter, buffet, larrup, pummel, stripe, wallop 7 belabor, scourge, shellac 8 lambaste 10 flagellate

thrash out
4 moot 5 argue 6 debate 7 agi-
tate, canvass, discept, discuss, dispute 10 kick around, toss around

thread
4 line, vein, yard 5 fiber, reeve, weave 6 strand, stream, string 8 filament
ball of: 4 clew, clue
combining form: 3 mit, nem 4 fili, mito, nema, neme, nemo 5 nemat 6 nemata (plural), nemato
dental: 5 floss
holder: 6 bobbin
kind: 4 silk, yarn 5 floss, lisle, watap 6 cotton, lingel 8 surgical
loose: 8 raveling 9 ravelling
surgical: 5 seton 6 catgut, suture

threadbare
4 hack, worn 5 dingy, faded, seedy, stale, tacky, tired, trite 6 cliché, frayed, ragged, shabby, tagrag 7 clichéd, run-down, worn-out 8 bathetic, shopworn, tattered, timeworn, well-worn 10 down-at-heel 11 commonplace, dilapidated

threadlike
6 filose

threads
8 clothing

threat
6 duress, menace 7 warning

threaten
3 cow 4 warn 5 augur 6 menace 7 caution, portend, presage 8 browbeat, bulldoze, forebode, forewarn 10 intimidate

three
4 trey 5 crowd
combining form: 3 ter, tri
group of: (see threesome)

threefold
5 trine 6 thrice, triple

Three Musketeers
5 Athos 6 Aramis 7 Porthos
author: 5 Dumas (Alexandre)

Threepenny Opera, The
author: 6 Brecht (Bertolt)
music: 5 Weill (Kurt)

threescore
5 sixty

Three Sisters, The
4 Olga 5 Irina, Masha
author: 7 Chekhov (Anton)

Three Soldiers author
9 Dos Passos (John)

threesome
4 trio 5 triad, trine 6 triple, triune, troika 7 trinity 11 triumvirate

three-wheeler
8 tricycle

threnody
5 dirge, elegy

thresh
4 beat, flog, whip 5 flail 6 strike

threshold
3 eve 4 edge, gate 5 brink, limen, point, verge

thrice
9 threefold
a day: 3 t.i.d. 8 ter in die

thrift
7 economy 8 prudence 9 frugality, husbandry 11 economizing

thriftiness
see **thrift**

thrifty
5 canny, chary 6 frugal, robust, saving 7 booming, roaring, sparing 8 thriving 9 provident, stewardly 10 conserving, economical, preserving, prospering, prosperous, unwasteful 11 flourishing

thrill
4 bang, boot, kick, send 6 excite, wallop 7 enthuse 9 electrify, galvanize 10 excitement 11 titillation

thriller
6 gothic 7 chiller, mystery, shocker 9 dime novel 13 penny dreadful

thrive
2 go 4 boom, grow 5 score 6 arrive 7 develop, make out, prosper, succeed 8 flourish

throat
3 maw 4 gula, tube 6 groove, gullet 7 channel, weasand, weazand
combining form: 3 der 4 dero 6 bronch 7 broncho
inflammation: 5 croup 6 angina, quinsy 10 laryngitis
relating to: 8 guttural
upper: 4 gula
warmer: 5 scarf

throb
4 ache, beat 5 pulse 7 pulsate 9 palpitate

throe
3 fit 4 ache, pain, pang 5 spell 6 access, attack, stitch, twinge 7 seizure 10 convulsion

thrombus
4 clot

throne
4 apse, seat 5 chair, gaddi, power 8 cathedra 11 sovereignty

throng

4 host, pack, push **5** bunch, crowd, crush, drove, flock, group, horde, press **6** squash **9** multitude

throttle

5 choke **7** garrote **8** strangle **11** accelerator

through

2 by **3** per, via **4** done, over, past, with **5** about, due to, ended, round **6** around, direct **7** by way of, done for, owing to **8** by dint of, complete, finished, straight, washed-up **9** because of, by means of, completed, concluded **10** by virtue of, terminated, throughout **13** uninterrupted

prefix: **2** di **3** dia, per

throughout

3 mid **4** amid, over **5** about, midst, round **6** around, during **7** all over, overall **10** everyplace, everywhere, far and near, far and wide, high and low

combining form: **3** hol **4** holo

Through the Looking Glass

author: **7** Carroll (Lewis)

character: **5** Alice

throw

3 peg, put **4** cast, fire, hurl, toss **5** fling, heave, pitch, sling **6** launch, propel, unseat **7** buck off, project, unhorse

in the towel: **4** quit **6** give up

throw away

4 blow, cast, junk, shed **5** scrap, waste **6** reject, slough **7** cashier, consume, discard, fritter **8** jettison, squander

throw back

6 reject, revert **7** regress **10** retrogress

throwback

7 atavism **9** reversion

throw down

4 fell **5** level **6** lay low **8** bowl over **9** knock over, overthrow, prostrate

the gauntlet: **4** defy **9** challenge

throw off

3 rid **4** emit, lose, shed, slip, vent **5** addle, eject, expel, issue, mix up, shake **6** ball up **7** confuse, fluster, give out, release **8** befuddle, bewilder, distract, unburden

the track: **6** derail **7** confuse, mislead

throw out

4 cast, junk, shed **5** addle, chuck, eject, evict, mix up, scrap **6** ball

up, reject, slough **7** cashier, confuse, discard, dismiss, extrude, fluster **8** befuddle, bewilder, distract, jettison

throw up

4 barf **5** heave, vomit **7** upchuck **8** disgorge **10** jerry-build

thrush

4 bird **5** robin, veery **8** bluebird

European: **5** mavis, ousel, ouzel **6** mistle **9** blackbird, mistletoe **11** nightingale

thrust

3 dig, jab, ram, run **4** core, gist, meat, pith, push, sink, stab **5** drive, sense, short, shove, stick **6** burden, plunge, propel, upshot **7** intrude, purport, riposte **9** substance

thug

3 mug **4** goon, hood, punk **5** bully, rough, rowdy, tough, yahoo **6** gunman, mucker **7** hoodlum, mobster, ruffian **8** gangster, hooligan, plugugly **9** cutthroat, roughneck, strong arm **10** hatchet man

thulium

symbol: **2** Tm

thumb

5 digit, hitch **6** pollex **8** pollices (plural) **9** hitchhike

thumb through

4 scan **6** browse **7** dip into, run over **8** glance at **10** glance over

thunder

4 bang, roar **6** rumble **8** rumbling **11** fulmination

combining form: **5** bront **6** bronto, ceraun **7** cerauno, kerauno

thunderbolt

9 lightning

thunderclap

see **thunder**

thunder lizard

10 brontosaur

thunderstruck

5 agape **7** aghast, shocked, stunned **8** dismayed **9** staggered **10** bewildered, confounded **11** dumbfounded, overwhelmed

Thurber character

11 Walter Mitty

thurify

5 cense

thus

2 so **3** sic **4** ergo, then **5** hence **9** therefore, thereupon, thus and so **11** accordingly **12** consequently

French: **5** ainsi

Thus Spoke Zarathustra

author: **9** Nietzsche (Friedrich)

thwack

3 bop **4** biff, blow, sock, whop **5** crack, pound, smack, whack

thwart

4 balk, beat, bilk, curb, dash, foil, ruin **6** arrest, baffle, scotch, stymie **8** traverse **9** checkmate, crosswise, frustrate **10** circumvent, disappoint, transverse **11** transversal

Thyestes

brother: **6** Atreus

daughter: **7** Pelopia

father: **6** Pelops

mother: **10** Hippodamia

son: **9** Aegisthus

Tiamat

husband: **4** Apsu

slayer: **6** Marduk

tiara

5 crown **6** diadem **9** headdress

Tibetan

animal: **3** yak **5** manul

coin: **5** tanga

gazelle: **3** goa

monk: **4** lama

people: **6** Bhotia, Sherpa

Tibet's capital

5 Lhasa

tibia

8 shinbone

Tibni's father

6 Ginath

tic

5 spasm **6** twitch **9** twitching

tick

6 credit, insect **8** arachnid, parasite **11** bloodsucker

combining form: **4** acar **5** acari, acaro

ticker

4 bomb **5** clock, heart, watch

ticket

3 key, tag **4** vote **5** label, slate **6** ballot **8** passport, password **10** open sesame **12** carte d'entrée

seller: **7** cashier, scalper

tickle

4 stir **5** amuse, tease, touch **6** arouse, excite, please, tingle **7** delight, gratify, provoke **9** stimulate, titillate

ticklish

5 risky, rocky **6** fickle, touchy, tricky **8** delicate, unstable, variable, volatile **9** mercurial, sensitive, uncertain **10** capricious, changeable, inconstant, precarious

tick off
3 irk **4** list **5** chide **6** monish, rebuke **7** reprove **8** admonish, call down, numerate, reproach **9** enumerate, reprimand

tidal flood
4 bore **5** eagre

tidbit
5 goody, treat **6** dainty, morsel **8** delicacy, kickshaw **11** bonne bouche

tide
4 flow, flux, rush **5** drift, flood, spate, surge **6** stream **7** current, holiday
lowest: **4** neap
type: **3** ebb, low **4** high, neap **5** flood **6** spring

tidings
4 news, word **6** advice **7** message **9** speerings **11** information **12** intelligence

tidy
4 neat, snug, trig, trim **7** chipper, orderly **9** shipshape **11** uncluttered, well-groomed **12** spick-and-span

tie
3 rod, wed **4** band, bind, bond, cord, draw, gird, join, knot, lash, link, mate, moor, rope, yoke **5** ascot, cinch, equal, jabot, leash, marry, match, nexus **6** attach, cravat, fasten, fetter, hamper, hobble, secure, splice **7** connect, dogfall, shackle, trammel, truss up **8** deadlock, fastener, ligament, ligature, standoff, vinculum **9** entrammel, fastening, stalemate **10** attachment, four-in-hand

tier
3 row **4** file, line, rank **5** class, grade, group, queue, story **6** league, string **7** echelon **8** category, grouping

tiff
3 row **4** spat **5** run-in, scrap **6** bicker **7** brabble, dispute, fall out, quarrel, rhubarb, wrangle **8** squabble **9** bickering, caterwaul **10** falling-out **11** altercation

tiffany
5 gauze **11** cheesecloth

tiger
3 cat **6** feline **9** carnivore
young: **3** cub

tight
3 set **4** fast, firm, hard, snug, taut, trim **5** cheap, close, dense, drunk, fixed, tense, thick **6** firmly, secure, stingy **7** compact, crowded, drunken, fixedly, miserly, solidly **9** niggardly, penurious, tenacious **10** contracted, inebriated **11** closefisted, constricted, intoxicated, steadfastly **12** cheeseparing, parsimonious **13** pennypinching

tightfisted
see **stingy**

tight-lipped
5 close **6** silent **8** reserved, reticent, taciturn **12** closemouthed, close-tongued

tightwad
4 skin **5** miser, nabal, stiff **7** niggard, scrooge **9** skinflint **10** cheapskate **11** cheeseparer

Tikvah's son
7 Shallum **8** Jahaziah

tile
3 hat **5** brick, guard, plate, slate **6** domino, tegula **7** abacula, tessera
roofing: **7** pantile

till
2 to **3** sow **4** plow, tend, turn, up to, work **5** until **6** before, harrow **7** prior to **9** cultivate **11** in advance of

tillable
6 arable **10** cultivable **12** cultivatable

tillage
4 farm, land **5** crops **11** cultivation

tiller
4 helm **6** farmer, rudder **7** steerer

Tilon's father
6 Shimon

tilt
3 tip, yaw **4** cant, cock, heel, lean, list, swag **5** grade, lurch, pitch, slant, slope **6** seesaw **7** incline, leaning, recline **8** gradient **11** inclination

timbal
4 drum **10** kettledrum

timber
3 log **4** balk, beam, tree, wood **5** board, joist, plank, trees, weald, woods **6** forest, girder, lumber, rafter **8** woodland
decay: **4** dote, doze
joint: **4** coak
mine: **5** stull

Philippine: **5** lauan
ship's: **3** rib **4** bibb, keel, mast, skeg **7** stemson **8** sternson
supporting: **4** stud **6** purlin, putlog, rafter **8** puncheon
uncut: **8** stumpage
wolf: **4** lobo

timbre
4 mood, tone **6** spirit, temper

timbrel
4 drum **10** tambourine

time
2 go **3** age, bit, day, era **4** book, bout, date, hour, pace, plan, shot, show, span, term, tour, turn **5** break, clock, epoch, set up, shift, space, spell, stint, tempo, trick, while **6** chance, look-in, moment, period, season, squeak **7** instant, opening, program, stretch **8** duration, occasion, schedule **11** opportunity
ahead of: **5** early
combining form: **5** chron, semic **6** chrono **8** chronous
gone by: **4** past **9** yesterday
long: **3** age, eon, era **4** aeon
of day: **4** dawn, dusk, noon **5** night **6** sunset **7** evening, morning, sunrise **8** daybreak, twilight **9** afternoon
olden: **4** yore **10** yesteryear
period: **3** age, day, eon, era **4** aeon, hour, week, year **5** epoch, month **6** decade, minute, moment, second **7** century, instant **9** fortnight **10** millennium
present: **3** now
relating to: **8** temporal
short: **5** jiffy **6** moment, second **7** instant
suffix: **2** ad
to come: **6** future **8** tomorrow
waste: **4** loaf **5** dally **6** loiter

time and again
3 oft **5** often **8** ofttimes **10** frequently, oftentimes, repeatedly **11** over and over

timeless
7 ageless, endless, eternal **8** dateless, unending **9** ceaseless, continual, perpetual, unceasing **10** intemporal **11** everlasting, unremitting **12** interminable

timely
3 fit **4** meet, soon **5** early **6** likely, prompt, proper **7** betimes, fitting, timeous **8** punctual, suitable **9** favorable, opportune, promising, well-timed **10** auspicious, propi-

tious, prosperous, seasonable, seasonably **11** appropriate

Time Machine, The
author: **5** Wells (Herbert George)

Time magazine founder
4 Luce (Henry Robinson)
6 Hadden (Briton)

Time of Your Life, The
author: **7** Saroyan (William)

timepiece
5 clock, watch **7** horloge, sundial **8** horologe **9** clepsydra **11** chronograph, chronometer, chronoscope

timetable
4 card, plan, sked **6** agenda, docket **7** program **8** calendar, schedule

timeworn
3 old **4** aged, hack **5** hoary, stale, trite **6** age-old **8** Noachian **9** hackneyed, venerable **12** antediluvian

time zone, U.S.
7 central, eastern, Pacific **8** mountain

timid
3 coy, shy **4** mild, wary **5** chary, mousy, pavid **6** afraid, demure, gentle, modest, yellow **7** bashful, chicken, fearful, halting, nervous, panicky, rabbity **9** diffident, faltering, milk-toast, mouselike, shrinking, tentative, unassured, uncertain **10** irresolute **11** unassertive, vacillating, vacillatory **12** apprehensive, fainthearted

Timna
brother: **5** Lotan
father: **4** Seir
son: **6** Amalek

Timon's servant
7 Flavius

timorous
5 timid **7** fearful **8** quailing, undaring **9** quivering, recoiling, shivering, shrinking, trembling **10** shuddering

Timothy's associate
4 Paul

tin
3 box, can **5** metal **7** element, stannum **9** container
combining form: **5** stann **6** stanni, stanno
mining region: **8** stannary
relating to: **7** stannic **8** stannous
sheet: **6** latten
symbol: **2** Sn

tincture
3 dye **4** cast, hint, tint **5** color, shade, stain, tinge, touch, trace **6** streak **8** colorant, dyestuff **10** complexion, intimation, suggestion

tinder
4 punk **8** kindling

tine
5 point, prong, spike **6** branch

tinge
3 dye, hue **4** cast, hint, tint, tone **5** color, shade, tinct, touch, trace **6** strain **8** tincture **10** complexion, intimation, sprinkling, suggestion

tinker
3 fix **4** mend, mess **6** doodle, fiddle, mender, potter, puddle, putter, repair **9** repairman **10** mess around

tinkle
3 gab, gas, jaw, yak **4** chat, ting **5** chink, clack, clink, plink **6** babble, jangle, jingle, rattle, tingle **7** chatter, prattle

tinny
4 thin **5** cheap, harsh **8** metallic

Tin Pan Alley acronym
5 ASCAP

tinsel
4 loud **5** gaudy **6** brazen, flashy, garish, tawdry **7** blatant, chintzy, glaring **8** ornament **9** clinquant **12** meretricious

tint
3 dye, hue **4** cast, tone, wash **5** color, shade, tinge, touch **7** touch up **8** tincture **10** coloration, complexion **12** pigmentation

tiny
3 wee **5** bitsy, dwarf, minim, pygmy, small, teeny, weeny **6** midget, minute, peewee, pocket, teensy, teenty, weensy **7** minikin **8** dwarfish, pint-size **9** itsy-bitsy, itty-bitty, miniature, minuscule **10** diminutive, minuscular, pocketsize, teeny-weeny **11** lilliputian, microscopic **12** teensy-weensy **13** infinitesimal

tip
3 cap, cue, top **4** apex, cant, clue, cusp, heel, hint, lean, list, peak, perk, tilt **5** point, slant, slope, steer, upset **6** advice, topple **7** cumshaw, incline, largess, overset, pointer, recline **8** forecast, gratuity, overturn, turn over **9** baksheesh, knock over, logniappe, overthrow, pourboire

10 perquisite, prediction **11** information
combining form: **3** acr, akr **4** acro, akro, apic **5** apici, apico

tip-off
4 hint **5** point, steer **7** pointer, warning **8** giveaway, jump ball **10** indication

Tippecanoe and ___ too
5 Tyler

tippet
4 band, barb, cape **5** scarf

tipple
3 bib, sip **4** grog, soak, swig **5** booze, drink, swill **6** guzzle, imbibe, liquor, spirit, tank up **7** swizzle **8** liquor up **9** aqua vitae, firewater

tippler
3 sot **4** lush, soak **5** drunk, toper **6** bibber, boozer **7** tosspot **8** drunkard **9** inebriate

tipstaff
7 bailiff

tipster
4 fink, nark **6** canary, snitch **7** tattler **8** betrayer, informer, squealer **10** talebearer **11** stool pigeon

tipsy
5 drunk, tight **7** drunken **8** unsteady **10** inebriated **11** intoxicated

tiptoe
5 creep, steal **7** gumshoe **9** pussyfoot

tirade
4 rant **5** abuse **6** screed **7** censure **8** berating, diatribe, harangue, jeremiad **9** invective, philippic **10** revilement **11** rodomontade **12** condemnation, denunciation, vituperation **13** tongue-lashing

tire
3 sap **4** bore, hoop, jade, pall, poop, wear **5** drain, ennui, weary, wheel **6** tucker, weaken **7** exhaust, fatigue, wear out **8** enervate, enfeeble, wear down **10** debilitate
airless: **4** flat **7** blowout
kind: **4** bias, snow **6** radial **7** retread **9** whitewall

tiredness
7 fatigue **8** collapse **9** lassitude, weariness **10** exhaustion **11** prostration

tireless
4 busy **6** active **8** untiring **9** weariless **10** unflagging, unwearying

11 unweariable **12** enthusiastic
13 indefatigable, inexhaustible

Tiresias
4 seer **10** soothsayer

tiresome
4 dull, hard **6** boring, jading, tiring
7 irksome, onerous, tedious **8** boresome, drudging **9** difficult, wearisome **10** burdensome, oppressive

Tirhanah
father: **5** Caleb
mother: **6** Maacah
uncle: **9** Jerahmeel

Tiriac of tennis
3 Ion

tiring
see *tiresome*

Tirol, Tyrol
capital: **9** Innsbruck
country: **7** Austria
mountains: **4** Alps

Tirzah's father
10 Zelophehad

Tisiphone
see *Erinyes*

tissue
3 web **4** mesh **5** fiber, gauze,
paper **6** fabric
anatomical: **4** tela **5** fiber **6** diploe
8 ganglion **10** epithelium
combining form: **4** hist **5** histi, histo,
hypho **6** histio
connective: **6** stroma, tendon
9 cartilage
kind: **3** fat **5** nerve **6** muscle **7** nervous **8** muscular **10** connective,
epithelial
layer: **6** dermis **7** stratum
plant: **4** bast, wood **5** xylem
6 phloem

Titan
father: **6** Uranus
female: **4** Rhea **6** Tethys, Themis
male: **6** Cronus **7** Iapetus, Oceanus
mother: **2** Ge **4** Gaea

Titan, The
author: **7** Dreiser (Theodore)

Titania's husband
6 Oberon

titanic
4 huge **5** great **6** mighty **8** colossal, enormous, gigantic **9** cyclopean, Herculean, monstrous
10 gargantuan, tremendous

titanium
symbol: **2** Ti

tithe
3 tax **5** tenth

Tithonus
beloved by: **3** Eos
father: **8** Laomedon

Titian painting
5 Danaë **8** Ecce Homo **10** Holy
Family **12** Rape of Europa **13** Maltese Knight, Medea and Venus, Venus and Cupid **14** Worship of
Venus

title
3 dub, due **4** call, deed, dibs,
name, term **5** claim, merit, nomen
7 baptize, caption, heading
8 christen, cognomen, pretense
9 designate **10** denominate, pretension **11** appellation, appellative,
designation **12** championship,
compellation, denomination
Dutch: **7** mynheer
ecclesiastic: **8** reverend
feminine: **2** Ms. **3** Mrs. **4** dame,
lady, ma'am, miss **5** madam **6** milady, missus **8** mistress
French: **6** madame **8** monsieur
12 mademoiselle
German: **4** Frau, Herr **8** Fraulein
holder: **5** noble **8** champion
Indian: **3** sri **4** raja, shri **5** sahib
7 bahadur
Islamic: **6** sayyid **9** ayatollah
Italian: **5** donna **6** signor **7** signora
9 signorina
monk's: **3** fra **7** brother
of nobility: **3** sir **4** Duke, Earl, King,
Lord, sire **5** Baron, Count, Queen
6 Prince **7** Baronet, Marquis
8 Archduke, Princess, Viscount
Oriental: **4** khan
Persian: **5** mirza

titmouse
4 bird **6** tomtit, verdin **7** bushtit
9 chickadee

Tito
4 Broz (Josip)

titter
5 laugh, tehee **6** giggle, guffaw,
hee-haw **7** chortle, chuckle, snicker

tittle
3 bit, jot **4** atom, iota, mite
5 minim, speck **6** smitch **7** smidgen
8 particle

titular
6 formal **7** nominal **8** so-called

Tityus
father: **4** Zeus
slayer: **6** Apollo

Tiu
see *Tyr*

tizzy
4 fume, snit, stew **5** sweat **6** dither,
swivet

T-man
5 agent **8** revenuer

TNT
8 dynamite **9** explosive

to
2 at **3** ere, for **4** ante, till **5** until
6 before, toward, up till **7** against,
ahead of, prior to **8** opposite,
touching **9** preceding **11** in advance of
be sure: **6** indeed **9** certainly
prefix: **2** ac, ad, af, ag, al, ap, as,
at
Scottish: **3** tae
wit: **3** viz **6** namely **8** scilicet

toad
4 agua, hyla, scum **6** anuran,
peeper **7** crapaud, stinker **8** lickspit, truckler **9** amphibian, sycophant **10** batrachian, bootlicker,
footlicker **11** lickspittle
combining form: **7** batrach **8** batracho **9** batrachus
genus: **4** Bufo

toady
4 fawn **5** cower, kotow **6** cringe,
flunky, grovel, kowtow **7** honey up,
truckle **8** bootlick, lickspit, truckler
9 brownnose, sycophant **10** bootlicker, footlicker **11** apple-polish,
lickspittle

To Althea from ___
6 Prison
author: **8** Lovelace (Richard)

toast
5 bread, brown, drink, skoal
6 cheers, pledge, prosit, salute
7 wassail
Jewish: **7** lehayim **8** lechayim
kind: **5** melba **6** French **8** zwieback

toastmaster
2 MC **5** emcee

To a Waterfowl author
6 Bryant (William Cullen)

tobacco
4 leaf, weed
cask: **8** hogshead
chewing: **4** chaw, quid
Cuban: **4** capa
ingredient: **3** tar **8** nicotine
juice: **6** ambeer
kind: **4** shag **5** bogie, snuff **6** bright,
burley **7** caporal, perique, Turkish
9 broadleaf, mundungus

pipe: 4 heel 6 dottle
rolled: 5 cigar
Turkish:
  7 latakia

Tobacco Road author
  8 Caldwell (Erskine)

to be
  Latin: 4 esse

Tobias
  father: 5 Tobit
  son: 8 Hyrcanus

toboggan
  4 sled 7 coaster

toby
  3 cup, mug 5 cigar

tocsin
  3 SOS 4 sign 5 alarm, alert 6 alarum, signal

today
  3 now 7 present 8 nowadays
  9 presently

toddle
  4 walk 6 stroll 7 saunter

toddy
  3 sap 5 drink

to-do
  4 coil, fuss 5 whirl 6 clamor, furore, hassle, hubbub, hurrah, pother, ruckus, rumpus, shindy, tumult, uproar 7 turmoil 9 commotion
  10 hurly-burly

toe
  3 tip 5 digit, touch
  big: 6 hallux
  combining form: 6 dactyl, digiti
  7 dactylo, dactyly 8 dactylia
  9 dactylism, dactylous
  little: 7 minimus

toehold
  7 footing

toffee
  5 candy

toga
  4 gown, rope, wrap 5 tunic

together
  6 at once, joined, united 7 jointly
  8 mutually 10 conjointly 11 concertedly 12 coincidently, collectively, concurrently
  prefix: 2 co 3 col, com, con, cor, sym, syn

togetherness
  5 union 7 cahoots 8 alliance, cohesion 10 connection, solidarity
  11 affiliation, association, combination, conjunction, partnership

Togo
  capital: 4 Lome
  monetary unit: 5 franc

tog out
  5 fix up, slick, spiff 6 doll up
  7 dress up, gussy up 8 spruce up
  9 smarten up

togs
  4 duds 5 dress 6 attire, things
  7 apparel, clothes, raiment 8 clothing 10 attirement, habiliment

To Have and to Hold author
  8 Johnston (Mary)

To His Coy Mistress author
  7 Marvell (Andrew)

toil
  3 net, tug 4 grub, plod, slog, slop, work 5 drive, grind, labor, slave, sweat 6 drudge, stodge, strain, strive, trudge 7 travail 8 bullwork, drudgery, footslog, plunther, slogging

toiler
  4 peon 5 slave 6 drudge, slavey
  9 dray horse, workhorse 11 galley slave

toilet
  4 head, john 5 dress, privy
  6 johnny 7 latrine 8 bathroom, lavatory 11 convenience, water closet
  British: 3 loo

toilsome
  4 hard 6 uphill 7 arduous, labored, operose 9 difficult, effortful, laborious, strenuous

Toi's son
  5 Joram 7 Hadoram, Jehoram

Tokay
  4 wine

token
  4 mark, pawn, sign 5 index, relic
  6 pledge, trophy 7 earnest, gesture, indicia, memento, minimal, symptom, warrant 8 evidence, keepsake, memorial, reminder, security, souvenir 9 indicator 10 expression, indication 11 remembrance 12 remembrancer

Tokyo
  formerly: 3 Edo
  island: 6 Honshu

Tola's father
  4 Puah 8 Issachar

tolerable
  2 OK 4 fair 6 common, decent
  7 livable 8 adequate, all right, bearable 9 endurable 10 acceptable, sufferable, sufficient 11 presentable, respectable, supportable, sustainable 12 satisfactory

tolerably
  4 so-so 6 enough, fairly, pretty, rather 8 passably 9 averagely
  10 moderately

tolerance
  7 stamina 8 clemency, lenience, leniency, patience 9 endurance
  10 indulgence, resistance, steadiness, sufferance 11 forbearance
  13 steadfastness

tolerant
  4 easy 5 broad 7 clement, lenient, liberal 9 condoning, forgiving, indulgent 10 charitable, forbearing, open-minded, permissive
  11 broad-minded, progressive, sympathetic 13 understanding

tolerate
  4 bear, take 5 abide, allow, brook, stand 6 accept, endure, permit, suffer 7 condone, stomach, swallow
  8 bear with, tough out
  11 countenance

Tolkien creature
  3 Ent 6 Hobbit

toll
  3 tax 4 bait, bell, bong, cost, lure, peal, ring 5 chime, decoy, knell, price, tempt 6 allure, charge, entice, entrap, lead on, seduce 7 expense, lockage 8 inveigle

tollbooth
  11 customhouse

Tolstoy novel
  11 War and Peace 12 Anna Karenina

tomato
  5 fruit 9 love apple

tomb
  4 bury 5 grave, inter, plant 6 burial, inhume 7 lay away, put away
  8 mausolea (plural) 9 mausoleum, sepulcher, sepulture
  11 ensepulcher
  ancient Egyptian: 7 mastaba
  8 mastabah
  circular: 6 tholoi (plural), tholos
  empty: 8 cenotaph

tomboy
  6 gamine, hoyden

Tom Brown's School Days
  author: 6 Hughes (Thomas)

tombstone
  6 ledger 8 memorial, monument
  11 grave marker
  inscription: 3 RIP 8 hic jacet

tome
4 book 6 volume

tomfool
3 ass 4 fool, jerk 5 crazy, idiot,
loony, ninny, silly 6 absurd, donkey, insane 7 foolish, jackass 8 imbecile 9 fantastic 10 nincompoop
11 harebrained 12 preposterous

tomfoolery
4 dido, lark 5 antic, caper, prank,
shine, trick 6 frolic 7 hogwash, rubbish, twaddle 8 claptrap, malarkey, nonsense 9 poppycock
10 balderdash, shenanigan
11 monkeyshine 12 blatherskite

Tom Jones author
8 Fielding (Henry)

tommyrot
4 bash, bull, crap 5 bilge, hooey,
trash 7 hogwash, rubbish
8 nonsense

Tom o'Bedlam
3 nut 4 loon 5 loony 6 dement,
madman, maniac 7 lunatic, madling 9 bedlamite, non compos

tomorrow
6 future, mañana

Tom Sawyer
author: 5 Twain (Mark)
character: 5 Becky 8 Huck Finn, In-
jun Joe 9 Aunt Polly 10 Muff Potter

Tom Thumb
4 runt 5 dwarf, midge, pygmy
6 midget, peewee 7 manikin
10 homunculus 11 lilliputian

ton
3 fad 4 chic, rage 5 craze, style,
vogue 6 furore 7 fashion

tone
3 hue 4 cast, mode, mood, tint,
vein 5 color, humor, pitch, shade,
style, tinge 6 accent, manner,
spirit, strain, temper, timbre 7 fashion 10 inflection
combining form: 4 phon 5 phono

toned down
4 mute, soft 5 sober 6 low-key,
mellow 7 subdued 8 low-keyed,
softened

tongue
4 lick 6 glossa, lingua, speech
7 dialect 8 language
10 vernacular
click of: 3 tch
combining form: 4 glot 5 gloss, lingu
6 glossa, glosso, lingua, lingui, lin-
guo 7 glossia

tongue-lash
3 wig 4 lash, rail 5 scold 6 berate
7 bawl out, chew out, tell off,
upbraid

tonguelike part
7 languet

tonic
5 sharp 7 bracing 8 renewing,
roborant 9 animating 10 astringent, quickening, refreshing, vitalizing 11 restorative, stimulating,
stimulative 12 exhilarating,
exhilarative, invigorating
13 strengthening
extract: 4 cola 9 berberine

tonsorialist
6 barber

tony
2 in 4 chic 5 swank, swish 6 modish 7 a la mode, stylish 9 exclusive
11 fashionable

too
4 also, ever, more, over, very
5 along 6 as well, highly, overly,
unduly, withal 7 awfully, besides,
greatly, notably 8 likewise, moreover, overfull, overmuch 9 extremely, immensely 10 remarkably,
strikingly 11 exceedingly, excessively, furthermore 12 additionally,
exorbitantly, immoderately, inordinately, unmeasurably
13 exceptionally

tool
3 awl, zax 4 pawn 5 drive 6 puppet, rimmer, stooge 7 cat's-paw,
hayfork, machine, rounder, utensil
8 picklock 9 implement, mechanism
10 instrument
axlike: 3 adz
barrel making: 5 croze 6 crozer
boring: 5 auger, drill
carving: 6 veiner
cleaving: 4 froe
cobbler's: 3 awl
cutting: 2 ax 3 adz, axe, saw
4 adze 5 knife 6 shears 8 billhook
digging: 4 pick 7 mattock
engraving: 5 burin 7 scauper
farm: 6 seeder
filing: 4 rasp 7 riffler
garden: 3 hoe 4 rake 5 spade
6 trowel, weeder
grasping: 6 pincer 7 tweezer
8 tweezers
mining: 6 trepan
prehistoric: 5 flint 6 eolith
pruning: 6 shears 8 secateur
rubbing: 9 burnisher
scooping: 6 router

toothed: 3 saw 7 rippler
woodworking: 3 saw 5 bevel, plane
6 chisel, hammer

toot
3 bat, jag 4 bust, tear 5 binge,
drunk, sound, spree 6 bender
7 blowoff, carouse

tooth
5 molar 7 incisor 8 bicuspid,
premolar
combining form: 4 dent, odon, odus
5 denti, dento, odont 6 odonta,
odonto, odonty 7 dentate, odontes,
odontia
cuspid: 6 canine 8 dogtooth,
eyetooth
cutting: 10 carnassial
decay: 6 caries
doctor: 7 dentist
pointed: 4 fang 6 canine, cuspid
small: 8 denticle
surface: 5 mensa

toothless
8 edentate

toothsome
5 sapid, tasty 6 savory 8 pleasant,
pleasing, tasteful 9 agreeable, delicious, palatable, relishing 10 appetizing, attractive 11 good-tasting

top
3 cap, tip 4 acme, apex, beat,
best, clip, crop, cusp, dock, face,
fine, head, peak, pick, roof
5 cream, crest, crown, elite, excel,
outdo, point, pride, prime, prize
6 apical, better, choice, climax, exceed, height, summit, utmost, vertex
7 capital, highest, maximal, maximum, outside, pollard, surface, surpass 8 five-star, loftiest, outshine,
outstrip, pinnacle, superior, surmount 9 excellent, fastigium, first-
rate, transcend, uppermost 10 first-
class 11 culmination, first-string
combining form: 3 acr, akr 4 acro,
akro

tope
3 nip 4 soak 5 booze, drink, shark
6 guzzle, imbibe, tank up, tipple
7 swizzle 8 liquor up

toper
3 sot 4 lush, soak 5 drunk 6 bibber, boozer 7 tippler, tosspot
8 drunkard 9 inebriate

Tophet
4 hell 5 hades, Sheol 6 blazes
7 Gehenna, inferno 9 barathrum,
perdition 10 underworld 11 Pandemonium

topic
4 head, text 5 issue, motif, point, theme 6 matter, motive 7 subject 8 argument 11 proposition 13 subject matter

top-notch
4 fine 5 prime 7 capital 8 five-star, superior 9 excellent, first-rate 10 first-class 11 first-string

top off
3 cap 5 crown 6 climax 8 round off 9 culminate, finish off

topography
7 terrain

topple
4 drop, fall 5 lurch, pitch, slump, upset 6 falter, go down, plunge, teeter, totter, tumble, wobble 7 overset, stagger, stumble, tip over, unhorse 8 keel over, overturn, turn over 9 knock over, overthrow

topsy-turvy
8 cockeyed, inverted, unhinged 10 disjointed, disordered, downside-up, upside-down 11 disarranged

toque
3 cap, hat

tor
4 hill, peak 5 mound 8 pinnacle

torch
7 firebug 8 arsonist, flambeau 10 incendiary

toreador
6 torero 7 matador 11 bullfighter

torment
3 try 4 bait, hurt, pain, rack 5 smite, wring 6 harass, harrow, heckle, molest, plague 7 afflict, agonize, crucify, torture, trouble 8 distress 9 persecute 10 excruciate

torn
4 rent 7 mangled 9 lacerated

tornado
7 cyclone, twister 9 whirlwind

toro
4 bull

torpedo
3 gun 4 mine 6 gunman, hit man 8 assassin 9 cutthroat, explosive 10 gunslinger, hatchet man, projectile, triggerman

torpid
5 dopey 8 comatose, sluggish 9 lethargic 10 slumberous 12 hebetudinous

torpor
4 coma 5 sleep 6 stupor 7 languor 8 dullness, hebetude, lethargy 9 lassitude, passivity, stolidity 10 stagnation 12 listlessness

torque
5 chain, twist 6 collar

torrent
5 flood, spate 6 deluge 7 niagara 8 cataract, flooding, overflow 9 cataclysm 10 inundation, outpouring

torrid
3 hot 5 fiery 6 ardent, fervid, heated, red-hot, sultry 7 blazing, burning, flaming 8 broiling, scalding, sizzling, white-hot 9 scorching 10 hot-blooded, passionate, sweltering 11 impassioned

tort
3 sin 4 evil 5 crime, wrong 8 iniquity 9 diablerie 10 wrongdoing

tortilla
4 cake, taco

Tortilla Flat author
9 Steinbeck (John)

tortoise
6 turtle 8 terrapin 9 chelonian
freshwater: 4 emyd
shell: 8 carapace

tortuous
5 snaky 7 sinuous, winding 8 flexuous, involute, involved 9 meandrous 10 convoluted, meandering, serpentine 11 anfractuous, vermiculate

torture
3 try 4 hurt, maim, rack, warp 5 smite, wring 6 deform, harrow, mangle 7 afflict, agonize, contort, crucify, distort, oppress, torment 8 misshape, mutilate 10 excruciate

tory
5 right 7 diehard, fogyish, old-line 8 loyalist, old liner, orthodox, rightist, standpat 11 bitter-ender, reactionary, right-winger, standpatter 12 conservative

Tosca
character: 5 Mario 7 Scarpia
composer: 7 Puccini (Giacomo)

___ Toscanini
6 Arturo

tosh
5 bilge, hooey 6 bunkum 7 eyewash 8 malarkey, nonsense, pishposh

toss
4 cast, fire, flip, hurl, rock, roll 5 bandy, drink, fling, heave, pitch, quaff, sling, throw 6 imbibe, launch, seesaw, squirm, writhe 7 agonize

tosspot
see **tippler**

tot
3 add, nip, sum 4 cast, dram, drop, foot, jolt, shot, slug 5 child, snort, total 6 figure 7 snifter, summate, toddler

totable
8 portable

total
3 add, all, sum 4 body, bulk, cast, come, foot, full, tale 5 add up, equal, gross, run to, smash, sum to, utter, whole, wreck, yield 6 all-out, amount, budget, entire, figure, number 7 crack up, destroy, full-out, overall, perfect, plenary, quantum, run into, stack up, sum into, summate 8 absolute, complete, comprise, demolish, entirety, outright, positive, quantity, result in 9 aggregate, consist of, full-blown, full-scale, inclusive, out-and-out, unlimited 10 consummate, unreserved 11 unmitigated 13 comprehensive, thoroughgoing
combining form: 3 hol 4 holo

totalitarian
6 all-out 7 full-out 8 absolute 9 full-blown, full-scale, unlimited 11 dictatorial 13 authoritarian

totality
3 all, sum 4 tale 5 gross, whole 6 entity, system 7 allness, oneness 8 entirety, integral 9 aggregate, integrate, wholeness 10 entireness 12 completeness

totalize
3 add, sum, tot 6 figure 7 summate

tote
3 add, lug 4 bear, buck, cart, haul, pack 5 carry, ferry 6 convey, figure 7 summate 9 transport

totem
4 clan, pole 6 emblem
pole: 3 xat

To the Lighthouse author
5 Woolf (Virginia)

totter
4 reel 5 lurch, wheel 6 falter, topple, wobble 7 stagger, stammer 8 titubate

touch

3 dab, pat, paw, rub 4 abut, dash, feel, hand, hint, join, line, meet, move, palm, stir, sway 5 brush, carry, graze, march, probe, shade, smack, thumb, tinge, verge 6 adjoin, affect, amount, arouse, border, butt on, caress, excite, finger, fondle, handle, streak, strike, stroke 7 contact, feeling, impress, inspire, palpate, quicken, taction, toy with, verge on 9 influence, palpation, stimulate, tactility

combining form: 6 thigmo

touchable

7 tactile 8 palpable, tangible

touch down

4 land 5 light, perch, roost 6 alight, settle 9 six points

touching

2 to 4 as to, in re 5 about, anent, as for 6 moving, tender 7 against, apropos, meeting, piteous, pitiful, tangent 8 abutting, adjacent, pitiable, poignant, stirring 9 adjoining, affecting, as regards, bordering, impinging 10 approximal, as respects, concerning, contiguous, impressive, juxtaposed, responsive 11 overlapping, sympathetic, tearjerking 12 conterminous 13 compassionate

touchstone

4 test 5 check, gauge, proof, scale, trial 7 measure 8 standard 9 barometer, benchmark, criterion, yardstick 13 demonstration

touch up

4 do up 5 fix up 6 polish 7 brush up, improve, perfect

touchy

5 cross, dicey, miffy, ratty, risky, testy 6 cranky, tetchy, tricky, unsafe 7 harmful 8 choleric, delicate, ticklish, volatile 9 hazardous, irascible, sensitive, temperish 10 precarious 11 thin-skinned 13 oversensitive, quick-tempered, temperamental, unpredictable

tough

3 bad, fit, mug 4 goon, hard, hood, punk, taut, thug 5 bully, fixed, hardy, harsh, lusty, rigid, rough, rowdy, stiff, stout, teuch, teugh, yahoo 6 accept, anneal, flinty, ghetto, mucker, mulish, narrow, robust, rugged, severe, strict, strong, sturdy, taxing, trying, unsafe, uphill, viscid 7 arduous, drastic, exigent, healthy, hoodlum, labored, onerous, ruffian, steeled, toilful, viscose, viscous, weighty 8 bullyboy, exacting, grievous, hardcase, hardened, hard-line, hooligan, obdurate, plug-ugly, rigorous, seasoned, stalwart, stubborn, toilsome, vigorous 9 arbitrary, confirmed, dangerous, demanding, difficult, effortful, hardshell, immutable, inner city, laborious, obstinate, pigheaded, resistant, roughneck, strenuous, tenacious 10 bullheaded, burdensome, disorderly, hard-bitten, hardboiled, hardfisted, hardhanded, hardheaded, headstrong, inflexible, oppressive, refractory, self-willed, unyielding 11 conditioned, intractable, procrustean, unalterable, unbreakable 12 pertinacious, withstanding

toughen

6 anneal, harden, season 7 develop 9 acclimate, climatize 10 strengthen 11 acclimatize

toughie

4 punk 5 heavy, rough, rowdy, yahoo 6 mucker 7 ruffian 8 bullyboy 9 roughneck

toupee

3 wig 6 peruke, wiglet 7 periwig, wiggery

tour

4 bout, time, trip, turn 5 round, shift, spell, stint, trick 6 travel, troupe 7 circuit 9 round trip 10 roundabout

tour de force

4 deed, feat 7 classic, exploit 10 magnum opus, masterwork 11 achievement, chef d'oeuvre, masterpiece

tour guide

8 cicerone

tourist

7 tripper, visitor 8 traveler 9 sightseer, traveller 10 day-tripper, rubberneck 12 excursionist

tournament

4 tilt 5 joust 7 tourney

tousle

4 mess, muss 6 rumple 8 dishevel, disorder

tout

4 laud, plug 5 vigil, watch 6 herald, praise 7 acclaim, lookout, promote, trumpet 8 ballyhoo, proclaim 9 publicize, vigilance

tow

3 lug, tug 4 drag, draw, haul, pull

toward

6 contra, facing 7 against, apropos, benefic, helpful, vis-à-vis 8 favoring, fronting 9 favorable, regarding 10 beneficial, propitious

prefix: 2 ac, ad, af, ag, al, ap, as, at, il, im, in, ir 4 pros

suffix: 2 ad

towel word

3 his 4 hers

tower

5 spire 7 overtop 8 dominate, look down, overlook

Babylonian: 8 ziggurat

on a mosque: 7 minaret

small: 6 turret

towering

4 airy, high, tall 5 dizzy, lofty, undue 6 aerial 7 extreme, massive, soaring, spiring, supreme 8 ultimate 10 exorbitant, immoderate, inordinate, monumental, preeminent, prodigious, stupendous, surpassing, tremendous 11 extravagant, skyscraping 12 altitudinous, overpowering, overwhelming, transcendent

towhee

5 finch

to wit

3 viz 6 namely 8 scilicet 9 videlicetis

town

4 burg 6 podunk 7 borough, village

medieval: 5 bourg

town and ___

4 gown 7 country

townsman

3 cit 6 townee 7 burgher, citizen, oppidan

town square

Italian: 6 piazza

toxic

6 poison 8 mephitic, venomous, virulent 9 poisonous

toxin

5 venin, venom 6 poison

toy

3 pet 4 fool, play 5 curio, dally, flirt, sport, tease 6 bauble, caress, coquet, cosset, cuddle, dandle, frolic, gewgaw, lead on, popgun, trifle, wanton 7 bibelot, disport, dreidel, novelty, trinket, whatnot 8 gimcrack, pinwheel 9 plaything

10 fiddle with, knickknack 11 string along

trace
4 hint, mark 5 relic, shade, smell, tinge, track, trail, tread, whiff 6 nuance, shadow, strain, streak 7 memento, soupçon, vestige 9 suspicion 10 intimation

trachea
8 windpipe

track
3 dog, way 4 drag, find, mark, path, road, sign, step, tail, walk 5 chase, cover, print, spoor, trace, trail, tread 6 artery, avenue, follow, pursue, shadow, street, travel 7 footway, highway, imprint, monitor, pathway, vestige 8 footpath, footstep, hunt down, pass over, smell out, traverse 9 footprint
combining form: 4 ichn 5 ichno

track-and-field event
4 dash, race 7 shot put 8 footrace, high jump, long jump 9 broad jump, decathlon, pole vault, relay race 10 heptathlon, pentathlon, triple jump 11 discus throw 12 steeplechase

tract
3 lot 4 area, belt, plat, plot, zone 6 parcel, region 7 portion, terrain 9 territory

tractable
6 docile, pliant 7 pliable, subdued 8 amenable, biddable, flexible, obedient 10 manageable

tractate
6 memoir, thesis 8 treatise 9 discourse, monograph 10 monography 12 disquisition, dissertation

tractor
maker: 5 Deere (John)

trade
3 art 4 deal, sell, swap, work 5 craft, truck 6 barter, change, custom, market, métier, peddle, switch 7 bargain, calling, pursuit, traffic 8 business, commerce, exchange, industry, merchant, vocation 9 patronage 10 employment, handicraft, occupation, profession, substitute 11 merchandise
illicit: 11 black market
suffix: 3 ery

trademark
4 logo 5 brand 8 logotype

trade route
7 sea-lane

tradition
4 lore, myth 6 custom, legacy, legend, mythos 8 folklore, heritage 9 mythology 10 convention

traditional
3 old 4 oral 5 fixed, usual 6 common, spoken, verbal 7 popular 8 habitual, orthodox 9 ancestral, customary, unwritten 10 immemorial 11 established, word-of-mouth 12 acknowledged, conventional, tralatitious

traditionalist
6 purist 9 precisian 12 precisionist

traditionalistic
4 tory 5 right 7 die-hard, fogyish, old-line 8 orthodox 11 reactionary 12 conservative

traduce
5 libel 6 betray, defame, malign, vilify 7 asperse, slander, violate 8 disgrace 9 denigrate 10 calumniate, scandalize

Trafalgar commander
6 Nelson (Horatio)

traffic
4 push, swap 5 fence, trade, truck 6 barter, custom, deal in, travel 7 bargain, bootleg 8 business, commerce, dealings, exchange, industry 9 communion, patronage 11 black-market, intercourse

trafficker
6 dealer, trader

tragedy
3 lot 4 blow, woes 5 curse, shock 6 mishap 8 calamity, disaster 9 adversity, cataclysm, mischance 10 misfortune 11 catastrophe, contretemps 12 misadventure

trail
3 dog, lag, tag 4 drag, flag, halt, path, plod, poke, tail 5 bedog, chase, chivy, dally, delay, tarry, trace, track 6 dawdle, falter, follow, linger, loiter, pursue, shadow, trudge 7 draggle, footway, gumshoe, pathway, traipse 8 footpath, footwalk 10 bridle path
emigrant: 6 Oregon
Florida: 7 Tamiami
Georgia-Maine: 11 Appalachian
Indian: 5 Great

trailer truck
4 semi

train
3 aim, lay, row, run 4 bait, cast, head, line, lure, tier, toll, turn 5 chain, coach, decoy, level, order, point, scale, shape, suite, teach, tempt 6 allure, course, direct, entice, harden, lead on, school, season, seduce, sequel, series, thread, zero in 7 develop, educate, incline, retinue 8 accustom, instruct, inveigle, sequence 9 cultivate, entourage, following, gradation, habituate 10 discipline, succession 11 alternation, consecution, progression

training
7 tuition 8 teaching, tutelage 9 education, schooling 11 instruction
horses: 6 manege

train off
3 dip 4 skew, slue, veer 5 sheer 6 swerve

traipse
3 gad 4 dowd, drab, drag, hoof, pace, roam, rove, slut, step, walk 5 dowdy, drift, mooch, range, trail, tread, troop 6 foot it, ramble, wander 7 draggle, meander 8 ambulate, slattern 9 gallivant 11 draggle-tail

trait
4 mark 5 point, savor 6 virtue 7 feature, quality 8 property 9 affection, attribute, birthmark, character 11 denominator

traitor
5 Judas 6 Arnold 8 betrayer, quisling, renegade, renegado, traditor, turncoat

traitorous
5 false 6 untrue 7 unloyal 8 apostate, disloyal, mutinous, recreant, renegade 9 alienated, estranged, faithless, seditious 10 perfidious, rebellious, unfaithful 11 disaffected, treacherous, unpatriotic

traject
4 pipe 5 carry 6 convey, funnel, siphon 7 channel, conduct 8 transmit

tram
3 car 7 trolley 9 streetcar

trammel
3 tie 4 bind, clog, curb 5 leash, limit 6 enmesh, fetter, hamper, hobble, hog-tie, stifle 7 confine, enchain, ensnarl, manacle, shackle 8 entangle, handcuff, stagnate, stultify 9 embrangle, entrammel 12 circumscribe

tramontane
7 foreign 10 outlandish 11 transalpine

tramp

3 vag **4** hike, hobo, jade, plod, thud, walk **5** march, stamp, stomp **6** ramble, stodge, stroll, trudge **7** drifter, floater, saunter, traipse, vagrant **8** derelict, footslog, vagabond **9** walkabout **10** street arab

trample

5 pound, stamp, stomp, tromp **7** tread on **8** override

trance

4 muse **5** study **6** ravish **7** reverie **8** enravish, hypnosis **9** enrapture, transport **10** brown study

tranquil

4 calm, easy **5** quiet, still **6** irenic, placid, poised, serene, stable, steady **7** pacific, restful **8** composed, peaceful **9** collected, easygoing **13** self-possessed

tranquilize

4 balm, calm, hush, lull **5** quiet, still **6** becalm, sedate, settle, soothe, subdue **7** compose

tranquilizer

6 downer, opiate **8** diazepam, pacifier, sedative **10** depressant

transaction

4 bond, pact **7** bargain, compact, dealing **8** contract, covenant **9** agreement **10** convention

transcend

3 top **4** beat, best **5** excel, outdo **6** better, exceed **7** surpass **8** outshine, outstrip

transcendent

5 ideal **7** perfect, supreme **8** abstract, towering **10** consummate, preeminent, surpassing **11** theoretical, unequalable, unmatchable **12** hypothetical, incomparable **13** unsurpassable

Transcendentalist

7 Emerson (Ralph Waldo), Thoreau (Henry David)

transcribe

4 copy **5** write **6** record **9** translate **13** transliterate

transfer

4 cede, deed, feed, find, give, hand, move, ship **5** alien, carry, shift **6** assign, change, convey, remise, remove, supply **7** convert, deliver, devolve, disturb, provide **8** alienate, dispense, hand over, make over, relocate, sign over, turn over **9** carry over, dislocate **10** abalienate

transfix

4 spit **5** lance, spear, spike **6** impale, skewer, skiver

transform

5 alter **6** change, mutate **7** commute, convert **8** denature **12** metamorphize, metamorphose

transformation

5 shift **10** alteration, changeover, conversion

transfuse

6 charge **7** pervade **8** permeate, saturate **9** penetrate, percolate **10** impregnate **11** impenetrate

transgress

3 sin **5** break **6** breach, offend **7** infract, violate **8** infringe, overstep, trespass **10** contravene

transient

7 passing **8** fleeting, flitting, fugitive, temporal, unstable, volatile **9** ephemeral, fugacious, momentary, temporary **10** evanescent, short-lived, transitory **11** impermanent **12** momentaneous **13** insubstantial

transit

5 shift **6** travel **7** passage **8** carriage, carrying **9** transport **10** alteration, conveyance **12** transporting

transition

5 shift **6** change, growth **7** passage **8** progress **9** evolution **10** alteration, conversion **11** development **13** metamorphosis
musical: **5** segue

transitory

see **transient**

translate

3 put **4** turn **6** change, render, reword **7** commute, convert, restate **8** rephrase **9** interpret **10** paraphrase **12** metamorphose

translation

7 version **9** rendering **10** paraphrase **11** restatement

translucent

5 clear, lucid **6** limpid **7** crystal, obvious **8** apparent, clear-cut, luminous, pellucid **9** unblurred **10** seethrough
combining form: **4** hyal **5** hyalo

transmarine

7 oversea **8** overseas

transmission

7 gearbox

combining form: **8** phoreses (plural), phoresis

transmit

4 pipe, send, ship **5** break, carry, radio, route **6** convey, funnel, hand on, impart, pass on, siphon **7** address, channel, conduct, consign, forward, instill, traject **8** bequeath, dispatch, hand down

transmogrify

see **transform**

transmute

see **transform**

transoceanic message

9 cablegram

transparent

5 clear, filmy, gauzy, lucid, plain, sheer **6** flimsy, limpid, lucent **7** crystal, tiffany **8** clear-cut, gossamer, luminous, pellucid **9** tralucent, unblurred **10** diaphanous, seethrough, translucid **11** crystalline, translucent
combining form: **4** hyal **5** hyalo **7** diaphan **8** diaphano

transpire

3 hap, out **4** leak **5** occur **6** befall, betide, chance, happen **7** develop

transport

3 lug, wow **4** bear, buck, move, oust, pack, send, slay, tote **5** ardor, carry, exile, expel, ferry, truck **6** banish, convey, deport, excite, fervor, heaven, ravish, stir up, thrill, trance, uplift **7** agitate, cast out, delight, ecstasy, elevate, expulse, inflame, passion, provoke, quicken, rapture, transit, vehicle **8** carriage, carrying, displace, enravish, entrance, relegate, rhapsody **9** carry away, enrapture, happiness, stimulate **10** conveyance, enthusiasm, imparadise

transportation

6 moving **7** hauling, transit, vehicle **8** carriage, carrying **10** conveyance

transpose

4 turn **6** change, invert, render, revert **7** commute, convert, inverse, reverse **12** metamorphose

transubstantiate

see **transform**

transude

4 ooze, seep, weep **5** bleed, sweat **6** strain

Transvaal

capital: **8** Pretoria
natives: **7** Bushmen **10** Hottentots
resource: **4** gold

transversal
4 bent **6** thwart **8** crossing **9** crosswise **12** intersecting

transverse
5 cross **6** across, thwart **7** crossed, oblique **8** crossing, diagonal **9** crosswise

trap
3 net **4** bait, lure, plot, ploy, ruse, snag, tree, wile **5** benet, catch, decoy, feint, snare **6** ambush, come-on, gambit, tangle **7** catch up, ensnare **8** artifice, birdlime, entangle, intrigue, maneuver **9** ambuscade, stratagem **10** allurement, conspiracy, enticement, seducement, temptation **11** machination **12** inveiglement
an animal: **8** deadfall

trappings
4 gear **5** dress **10** decoration **13** embellishment

Trappist
4 monk
writer: **6** Merton (Thomas)

trash
3 mob, rot **4** bosh, crap, junk, plod, scum, slog, slop, toil **5** bilge, dregs, hokum, offal, waste, wreck **6** bunkum, debris, kelter, litter, masses, rabble, refuse, shlock, stodge, trudge **7** garbage, rubbish **8** canaille, claptrap, doggerel, dustheap, footslog, leavings, malarkey, nonsense, plunther, riffraff, unwashed **9** sweepings, vandalize **11** proletariat

trash can
7 dustbin

trashy
4 base, mean, poor **5** cheap, tatty **6** common, cruddy, paltry, shoddy, sleazy **8** rubbishy **9** third-rate

trauma
4 blow **5** shock, upset **6** stress **8** collapse **11** disturbance

travail
4 moil, task, toil, work **5** grind, labor, pains **6** drudge **7** slavery **8** bullwork, drudgery, plugging, struggle **10** birth pangs, childbirth **11** parturition **12** childbearing, contractions

travel
2 go **3** hie **4** fare, pass, roam, tour, trek, wend **5** cover, cross, jaunt, track **6** move on, push on, repair, voyage **7** explore, journey, passage, proceed, process, traffic, transit **8** pass over

travelable
8 passable **9** navigable **10** negotiable

traveling library
10 bookmobile

traverse
3 bar, rub **4** buck, deny, duel, snag, walk **5** cover, cross, fight, repel **6** combat, hamper, hurdle, impugn, negate, oppose, patrol, resist, thwart, travel **7** contest, dispute, gainsay **8** crossing, negative, obstacle, pass over **9** crosswise, disaffirm, withstand **10** contradict, contravene, crisscross, impediment **11** obstruction, perambulate

travesty
3 ape **4** mock, sham **5** farce, mimic **6** parody **7** imitate, mimicry, mockery, take off **8** ridicule **9** burlesque **10** caricature, distortion **12** exaggeration
satanic: **9** Black Mass

Traviata, La
character: **7** Alfredo, Germont **8** Violetta
composer: **5** Verdi (Giuseppe)

trawl
3 net **4** fish **5** troll **7** setline

tray
6 salver, server **7** platter **8** teaboard
revolving: **9** lazy Susan

treacherous
5 false, hairy, Punic, risky **6** chancy, tricky, untrue, wicked **7** unloyal, unsound **8** disloyal, perilous, recreant, ticklish **9** betraying, dangerous, deceptive, faithless, hazardous, unhealthy **10** jeopardous, misleading, perfidious, precarious, traitorous, unfaithful **12** falsehearted

treachery
7 perfidy, sellout, treason **9** falseness **10** disloyalty, infidelity **11** double cross **13** double dealing, faithlessness

treacle
5 syrup **6** remedy **8** molasses

tread
4 hoof, pace, step, walk **5** dance, march, stamp, stomp, trace, track, tramp, tromp, troop **6** foot it, hoof it, prance, stride **7** traipse, trample **8** ambulate

treadle
5 lever, pedal

treadmill
3 rut **4** pace, rote **5** grind **6** groove **7** routine

treason
6 deceit **7** perfidy **8** betrayal, sedition **9** duplicity, treachery **10** disloyalty, misprision **13** deceitfulness, faithlessness, seditiousness

treasure
4 find, plum, save **5** catch, guard, pearl, prize, trove, value **6** esteem, revere **7** apprize, cherish, idolize, worship **8** conserve, preserve, venerate **9** reverence **10** appreciate

Treasure Island
author: **9** Stevenson (Robert Louis)
narrator: **10** Jim Hawkins

treasurer
6 bursar, purser **11** chamberlain

Treasure State
7 Montana

treasure trove
4 find, mine **7** bonanza **8** eldorado, Golconda, gold mine

treasury
4 mine **5** chest **6** coffer, museum **7** bonanza, gallery **8** archives, eldorado, Golconda, gold mine, war chest **9** exchequer **10** depositary, depository, repository, storehouse
state: **4** fisc

treat
3 use **5** goody, nurse, serve **6** advise, confab, confer, dainty, doctor, do with, handle, huddle, manage, morsel, parley, physic, powwow, regard, tidbit, titbit **7** care for, consult **8** collogue, deal with, delicacy, kickshaw, medicate, medicine **10** minister to **11** bonne bouche, confabulate
animals: **3** vet
leather: **3** tan, taw **6** shammy, shamoy **7** chamois, tanning

treatise
4 book **6** memoir, thesis **7** writing **8** argument, tractate **9** discourse, monograph **10** discussion, exposition, monography **12** disquisition, dissertation
combining form: **3** log **4** logy **5** logia, logue
suffix: **3** ics

treatment
4 care **7** therapy
combining form: **6** praxes (plural), praxis

treaty

4 pact 6 accord 7 charter, compact, concord 8 contract, covenant 9 agreement, concordat 10 convention

treble

4 high, thin 5 acute, sharp 6 argute, piping, shrill 8 piercing

tree

African: 4 akee, cola, shea 5 limba, sassy 6 baobab 7 avodire, bubinga 8 sasswood 9 berberine

Asian: 4 dhak, upas 6 banyan, kamala

Australian: 7 blue gum 8 lacewood, quandong 9 casuarina

branch: 5 bough

Brazilian: 3 apa, ule 7 arariba, seringa, wallaba

Chinese: 4 tung 5 yulan 6 gingko, ginkgo, litchi 7 kumquat

citrus: 4 lime 5 lemon 6 orange 8 bergamot 10 calamondin

combining form: 3 dry 4 dryo 5 dendr 6 dendra (plural), dendro 7 dendron

coniferous: 3 fir, yew 4 pine 5 alder, cedar, larch 6 spruce 7 cypress, hemlock, juniper, redwood, sequoia

dwarf: 8 arbuscle 10 chinquapin

East Indian: 4 neem, poon, teak, toon 6 banyan, deodar, durian, durion 7 amboina, amboyna, cajaput, cajeput, cajuput, champac, champak, deodara 11 chaulmoogra

elm: 4 wych

Ethiopian: 5 cusso, kusso 6 kousso

Eurasian: 5 abele, rowan 6 medlar

European: 5 osier 8 bourtree, caprifig

European oak: 7 murmast

evergreen: 3 fir, yew 4 atle, pine, titi 5 athel, bunya, carob, cedar, piñon, taxus, thuja, thuya 6 arbute, cullay, dahoon, jarrah, loquat, mallee, pinyon, sapota 7 arbutus, camphor, conifer, inkwood, juniper, lentisk, madrona, madrone, madrono, peebeen, quillai, redwood, sequoia 8 eucalypt, loblolly, longleaf, tamarisk 9 balsam fir 12 balm of Gilead

evergreen oak: 6 encina

fig: 5 pipal 6 peepul

flowering: 5 sumac 6 acacia, sumach 7 dogwood 8 sourwood

hardwood: 3 oak 5 beech, birch, ebony, maple 6 cherry, copalm, cornel, walnut 7 bilsted, hickory,

shittah 8 chestnut, mahogany 9 primavera

Japanese: 4 kaki 7 zelkova

linden: 8 basswood

mulberry: 8 sycamine

North African: 5 babul 7 babbool

nut-bearing: 4 cola, kola 5 hazel, pecan, piñon 6 almond, cashew 7 buckeye, filbert, hickory 9 pistachio

oak: 5 roble 8 bluejack

oil-yielding: 3 ebo 4 eboe, tung 7 cajaput, cajeput, cajuput

ornamental: 3 box 5 holly 6 gingko, ginkgo, mimosa, myrtle, redbud 8 laburnum, magnolia 9 poinciana 12 rhododendron

palm: 4 coco, nipa 5 ratan 6 cohune, gomuti, grugru, pinang, raffia, raphia, rattan 7 babassu, coquito, talipot 8 carnauba, ladypalm

Peruvian: 8 cinchona

Philippine: 4 dita, pili 6 bataan, molave 7 tindalo 10 calamondin

resinous: 10 candlewood

rubber: 3 ule

shade: 3 elm, oak 5 maple 6 linden 8 sycamore 10 chinaberry

softwood: 5 alamo 6 tupelo 8 black gum, corkwood; (see also **coniferous**)

South American: 3 apa 4 ombu 7 wallaba 8 oiticica 9 Brazil nut

swamp: 11 bald cypress

tropical: 4 akee, ohia, sago, teak 5 areca, assai, balsa, cacao, ceiba, genip, lehua, mahoe, mamey, mamie 6 acajou, balata, baobab, bustic, citrus, degame, degami, fustic, kabiki, mammee, mammey, padauk, padouk, santol, souari 7 arnotto, bebeeri, genipap, logwood, majagua, mameyes, palmyra, quassia, soursop 8 allspice, barbasco, cocobola, cocobolo, jelutong, mahogany, mangrove, milkwood, palmetto, porkwood, rosewood, simaruba, soapbark, sweetsop, tamarind 9 candlenut, cherimoya, jacaranda 10 breadfruit, manchineel 11 candleberry, coconut palm

trunk: 4 bole

willow: 5 osier, sauch, saugh 6 poplar

young: 7 sapling

tree frog

genus: 4 Hyla

trefoil

4 leaf 6 clover

part: 3 arc

trek

4 trip 7 journey, travels 10 expedition

trellis

6 screen 7 lattice

tremble

3 jar 5 quake, shake 6 dither, quaver, quiver, shiver, tremor 7 shudder, twitter, vibrate

Scottish: 4 dirl

tremblor

see **temblor**

tremendous

4 huge, vast 5 awful 6 mighty, mortal 7 fearful, immense, massive, titanic 8 colossal, cracking, dreadful, enormous, gigantic, horrible, shocking, terrible, terrific, towering 9 appalling, fantastic, frightful, monstrous 10 formidable, monumental, prodigious, stupendous

tremolo

7 vibrato

tremor

3 jar 5 quake, shake, shock 6 dither, quaver, quiver, shiver 7 shudder, temblor, tremble, twitter, vibrate 8 tremblor 10 earthquake

muscular: 8 dystaxia

Scottish: 6 dindle

tremulous

5 aspen, quaky, shaky 6 aguish, aquake, ashake 7 aquiver, ashiver, quaking, quivery, shaking, shivery 9 quivering, shivering, trembling, tremorous, tremulant, vibrating 11 palpitating

trench

4 sink 5 ditch, drain, drill, fosse, gully, verge 6 border, furrow, trough 8 approach

Caribbean: 6 Cayman

combining form: 5 bothr 6 bothro

trenchant

5 acrid, crisp, salty 6 biting 7 caustic, cutting, ingoing, mordant, probing, satiric 8 clear-cut, incisive, piercing, sardonic, scathing 9 sarcastic 10 mordacious, razor-sharp 11 penetrating

trencher

4 tray 7 platter

trend

3 fad, run 4 flow, mode, rage, wind 5 craze, drift, style, swing, tenor, vogue 6 furore 7 current, fashion 8 movement, tendency 9 direction 10 dernier cri

trendy
2 in 3 hep, hip 4 tony 5 faddy
6 modish, tonish, with-it 7 a la
mode, faddish, stylish 11 fashionable, ultramodern

Trent's Last Case author
7 Bentley (Edmund Clerihew)

trepidation
4 fear 5 alarm, dread, panic
6 dismay, fright, horror, terror
13 consternation

trepidity
4 fear 5 alarm, dread, panic
6 dismay, fright, horror, terror
13 consternation

trespass
3 err, sin 5 lapse, poach 6 breach,
invade, offend 7 intrude 8 encroach, entrench, infringe, invasion
9 interlope, intrusion, obtrusion, violation 10 infraction, transgress
11 intermeddle 12 encroachment,
infringement 13 contravention,
transgression

tress
4 curl, hair, lock 5 braid, plait

trestle
4 buck 5 horse 7 sawbuck 8 sawhorse 9 workhorse

tret
9 allowance

triad
4 trio 5 trine 6 triple, triune, troika
7 trinity 9 threesome 11 triumvirate

trial
3 try, woe 4 care, test 5 agony,
cross, essay, grief, rigor, worry
6 hassle, misery, ordeal, sorrow
7 anguish, attempt, calvary, trouble
8 crucible, distress, endeavor, hardship, striving, struggle 9 adversity,
suffering 10 affliction, difficulty, experiment, heartbreak, misfortune,
visitation 11 tribulation
12 experimental

trial balloon
6 feeler

trial run
4 test 10 experiment

triangle type
5 right 6 obtuse 7 scalene 9 isos-
celes 11 equilateral

triangular
6 cuneal 7 cuneate, hastate
combining form: 6 trigon 7 trigono

tribal unit
7 phratry

tribe
4 clan, folk, race 5 house, stock
6 family 7 kindred, lineage
combining form: 4 phyl 5 phylo

tribulation
5 cross, trial 6 ordeal 7 calvary
8 crucible, wronging 10 affliction, oppression, visitation
11 persecution

tribunal
3 bar 5 court 8 lawcourt

tributary
3 sub 5 minor, under 7 subject
8 influent 9 dependent, satellite,
secondary 10 collateral
11 subordinate

tribute
5 salvo 6 eulogy 8 citation, encomium 9 panegyric 10 salutation
11 recognition, testimonial
12 appreciation
feudal: 6 heriot

trice
4 wink 5 shake 6 moment, second
7 instant 9 twinkling 11 split
second

trick
3 jig 4 bout, dupe, feat, fool, gull,
hang, hoax, lark, play, ploy, ruse,
sham, tour, turn, wile 5 antic,
blind, bluff, caper, craft, cully,
curve, dodge, feint, fraud, knack,
prank, shaky, shift, slick, spell, stall,
stint, stunt 6 chouse, device, didoes, frolic, gambit, outwit, praxis,
scheme, shines, touchy 7 boutade,
chicane, dodgery, finagle, gimmick, sleight 8 artifice, escapade,
flimflam, hoodwink, maneuver, outtrump, skin game, unstable 9 bamboozle, deception, defective,
diversion, stratagem, victimize
10 expediency, red herring, shenanigan, tomfoolery, unreliable
11 contrivance, hornswoggle, monkeyshine 12 undependable
13 practical joke, untrustworthy
Scottish: 6 shavie

trickery
5 cheat, fraud 7 chicane, knavery
8 hokypoky 9 chicanery, deception, fourberie 10 hanky-panky
11 double-cross, highbinding
13 double-dealing, sharp practice

trickle
4 drib, drip, drop, weep 5 trill 7 distill, dribble

trickster
5 cheat 6 con man 7 cheater, did-

dler, grifter, sharper 8 conjurer,
magician, swindler 9 defrauder
11 flimflammer, illusionist
12 double-dealer

tricksy
5 rough, tight 6 trying 7 arduous
8 prankish

tricky
3 sly 4 foxy, wily 5 rocky 6 artful,
astute, crafty, quirky, shifty, touchy
7 cunning 8 delicate, delusive, delusory, gimmicky, guileful, ticklish,
unstable 9 deceitful, deceptive, difficult, dishonest, insidious, sensitive
10 misleading, precarious
12 undependable

trident
5 spear 7 scepter

tried
6 proved, secure, tested, trusty
7 staunch 8 approved, faithful, reliable 9 certified, steadfast 10 dependable 11 trustworthy

tried and true
6 secure, trusty 8 reliable 10 dependable 11 trustworthy

trifle
3 toy 4 fico, fool, mash, muck, play
5 curio, dally, flirt, use up, waste
6 bauble, burn up, coquet, fiddle,
fidget, gewgaw, lead on, misuse,
mucker, wanton 7 bibelot, consume, fribble, fritter, novelty, trinket,
twiddle, whatnot 8 fool away, gimcrack, kickshaw, play with, squander 9 dissipate, objet d'art, philander, throw away 10 frivol away,
knickknack, mess around, potter
away 11 prodigalize, string along

trifolium
6 clover 8 shamrock

trig
4 chic, neat, prim, snug, tidy, trim
5 sharp, smart, swank 6 classy,
modish, snappy 7 chipper, dashing, orderly, stylish 9 shipshape
11 fashionable, spic-and-span, uncluttered, well-groomed 12 spick-
and-span

triggerman
3 gun 5 bravo 6 gunman, hit man
7 torpedo 8 assassin 9 cutthroat
10 gunslinger, hatchet man

trigonometric function
see at **function**

trill
4 drib, drip, drop, weep 5 shake
7 distill, dribble, trickle

trillion
combining form: **4** tera, treg **5** trega

trillionth
combining form: **4** pico

trim
3 cut, fit **4** beat, clip, crop, deck, drub, lick, neat, pare, snug, tidy, trig, whip **5** adorn, order, prank, prune, shape, shave, shear, skive **6** barber, bedeck, dapper, fettle, kilter, repair, ricrac, spruce, sprucy, thrash **7** chipper, dress up, fitness, garnish, orderly, shapely, shellac **8** beautify, clean-cut, decorate, lambaste, manicure, ornament, rickrack, shapeful **9** condition, embellish, shipshape **10** statuesque, well-turned **11** clean-limbed, spic-and-span, streamlined, uncluttered, well-groomed **12** spick-and-span
a tree: **5** prune **7** pollard

trine
see **triad**

Trinidad and Tobago
capital: **11** Port of Spain
monetary unit: **6** dollar

trinity
see **triad**

trinket
5 curio **6** bauble, gewgaw, tinsel, trifle **7** bibelot, novelty, whatnot **8** frippery, gimcrack, kickshaw, nicknack **9** plaything **10** knickknack

trinkets
10 bijouterie

trio
of goddesses: **5** Fates **6** Furies, Graces; (see also **triad**)

trip
3 hop, run **4** bull, lope, skip, slip, tour, trek **5** boner, error, fluff, lapse **6** bungle, spring **7** blooper, blunder, journey, mistake, skitter, stumble, travels **10** expedition

tripes
4 guts **7** innards, insides, inwards, viscera **8** entrails, stuffing **9** internals

triple
4 trio **5** triad, trine **6** treble, triune, troika **7** trinity **9** threesome **11** triumvirate

Triple Crown winner
1919: **9** Sir Barton
1930: **10** Gallant Fox
1935: **5** Omaha
1937: **10** War Admiral

1941: **9** Whirlaway
1943: **10** Count Fleet
1946: **7** Assault
1948: **8** Citation
1973: **11** Secretariat
1977: **11** Seattle Slew
1978: **8** Affirmed

tripped out
4 high **5** doped **6** stoned, zonked **7** drugged **8** hopped-up, turned on, wiped out **9** spaced-out

Triptolemus
father: **6** Celeus
gift to man: **5** grain
mother: **9** Metaneira

Tristan, Tristam
beloved: **6** Iseult, Isolde

triste
3 sad **7** joyless **8** mournful **9** saddening **10** depressing, melancholy **11** melancholic

Tristram Shandy author
6 Sterne (Laurence)

trite
3 set **4** dull, flat, hack **5** banal, chain, corny, musty, stale, stock, tired, vapid **6** cliché, common, jejune, old hat, used-up **7** clichéd, drained, prosaic, worn-out **8** bathetic, bromidic, mildewed, ordinary, shopworn, timeworn, well-worn **9** hackneyed **10** threadbare **11** commonplace, stereotyped **13** platitudinous, stereotypical

triton
3 eft **4** newt **10** salamander

Triton
6 merman
attribute: **5** conch
father: **7** Neptune **8** Poseidon
mother: **10** Amphitrite

triturate
4 bray, buck **5** crush, grind **6** powder **9** comminute, pulverize

triumph
3 joy, win **4** beat, best, gain **5** exult, glory **6** master **7** conquer, delight, prevail, prosper, succeed, victory **8** conquest, jubilate, overcome, reveling, surmount **9** exultance, festivity, jubilance **10** ascendancy, exultation, jubilation **11** surmounting, vanquishing **12** vanquishment

triumphal
see **triumphant**

triumphant
8 exultant, exulting, jubilant **9** rejoicing

triumvirate
see **triad**

Triumvirate, First
member: **6** Caesar (Julius), Pompey (the Great) **7** Crassus (Marcus Licinius)

Triumvirate, Second
member: **6** Antony (Marc) **7** Lepidus (Marcus Aemilius) **8** Octavius (Gaius)

triune
see **triad**

trivet
4 rack **5** stand **6** tripod

trivia
8 minutiae **9** small beer **11** small change **13** small potatoes

trivial
4 puny **5** light, minor, petty **6** casual, little, measly, paltry, slight **7** shallow **8** captious, picayune, trifling **9** fribbling, frivolous, small-beer **10** negligible, picayunish, shoestring **11** Mickey Mouse, superficial, unimportant **13** insignificant

troche
6 tablet **7** lozenge **8** pastille

troglodyte
7 caveman **11** cave dweller

troika
8 carriage; (see also **triad**)

Troilus
beloved: **8** Cressida
father: **5** Priam
mother: **6** Hecuba
slayer: **8** Achilles

Troilus and ___
8 Cressida, Criseyde

Trojan
horse builder: **5** Epeus
king: **5** Priam
priest: **7** Laocoon
soothsayer: **7** Helenus **9** Cassandra
warrior: **5** Paris **6** Aeneas, Agenor, Hector **9** Euphorbus

Trojan Horse builder
5 Epeus **6** Epeius

troll
4 fish, lure, roll, sing **5** angle, dwarf, giant

trolley
3 car **4** cart, tram **8** carriage **9** streetcar

Trollope, Anthony
novel: **11** Ayala's Angel, Phineas

Finn **12** Phineas Redux **13** The
Claverings

trombone
4 wind **5** brass **7** sackbut

tromp
4 beat, drub, hike, pelt, slog
5 pound, stamp, stomp, tramp
6 batter, buffet, pummel, thrash,
trudge **7** belabor, trample
8 lambaste

troop
4 army, band, hoof, host, pace,
step, walk **5** corps, tread **6** foot it,
forces, legion, outfit **7** company,
traipse **8** ambulate, assembly, military, soldiers **9** gathering, multitude
10 collection, combatants, servicemen **11** armed forces

trope
5 irony **6** simile **8** metaphor, metonymy **10** synecdoche

Trophonius
brother: **8** Agamedes
temple site: **6** Delphi

trophy
5 relic, token **7** memento **8** keepsake, memorial, reminder, souvenir
11 remembrance **12** remembrancer

tropical
3 hot **4** warm **6** jungly, sultry, torrid **10** equatorial

tropical cyclone
see typhoon

tropical storm
see typhoon

Tropic of Cancer author
6 Miller (Henry)

Tros' son
4 Ilus **8** Ganymede

trot
3 jog **4** crib, gait, lope, pony
11 translation

troth
8 espousal **10** engagement

trot out
4 show **5** flash **6** expose, flaunt,
parade **7** display, disport, exhibit,
show off **8** brandish

Trotsky, Leon
associate: **5** Lenin (Vladimir)

troubadour
4 bard, poet **6** rhymer **8** jongleur,
minstrel, musician **9** balladist,
rhymester

trouble
3 ado, ail, irk, try, vex **4** care,
cark, fret, fuss, pain **5** annoy,
Dutch, harry, haunt, pains, rowel,
trial, upset, while, worry **6** bother,
bustle, effort, flurry, harass, kiaugh,
pester, plague, pother, put out,
strain, stress **7** afflict, agitate, disturb, intrude, perturb, torment **8** disquiet, distress, exertion, hardship,
hot water, impose on, irritate, mischief, put about, vexation **9** disoblige, incommode **10** difficulty, discommode, discompose, disconcert,
impose upon **11** bedevilment, elbow grease, predicament
13 inconvenience

troublemaker
6 heller **7** hellion, inciter **8** agitator, inflamer **10** instigator

troublesome
4 mean, ugly **5** pesky **6** vexing,
wicked **7** painful **8** alarming, annoying **9** upsetting, vexatious
10 bothersome, disturbing
11 disquieting

troublous
4 mean, ugly **5** pesky **6** stormy,
wicked **9** turbulent, vexatious

trough
3 hod **4** bowl, tank **5** basin, drain
6 manger, vessel **7** channel
9 container
combining form: **5** bothr **6** bothro

trounce
4 beat, drub, rout, trim, whip
5 whomp **6** thrash, wallop **7** clobber, shellac **9** overwhelm

troupe
4 band **5** corps, party **6** outfit
7 company

trouper
4 mime **5** actor, mimic **6** mummer,
player **7** artiste **8** thespian **9** performer, playactor **11** entertainer
12 impersonator

trousers
5 pants **6** slacks **8** britches
tartan: **5** trews

trout
kind: **3** sea **4** char, lake **5** brook,
brown, river **7** rainbow **8** speckled
9 steelhead

Trovatore, Il
character: **7** Azucena, Leonora, Man-
rico **11** Count di Luna
composer: **5** Verdi (Giuseppe)

trove
5 hoard **9** amassment, colluvies
10 collection, cumulation **11** aggregation **12** accumulation
13 agglomeration

Troy
5 Ilium
epic of: **5** Iliad
excavator: **10** Schliemann (Heinrich)
founder: **4** Ilus
modern site: **9** Hissarlik; (see also
Trojan)

truant
4 idle **7** shirker **8** shirking
13 irresponsible

truce
4 lull **5** letup, pause, peace **6** accord **7** respite **9** armistice, cease-
fire

truck
3 van **4** swap **5** lorry, trade **6** barter, handle, peddle, retail **7** bargain, traffic **8** commerce, dealings,
exchange
military: **6** camion

truckers' communicators
3 CBs

truckle
3 tag **4** fawn, tail **5** cower, toady,
trail **6** cringe, follow, grovel, kowtow **7** honey up, succumb **8** bootlick **11** apple-polish

truckler
4 toad **5** toady **7** spaniel **8** lickspit
9 sycophant, toadeater **10** bootlicker, footlicker **11** lickspittle

truculent
4 fell, grim **5** cruel, harsh, rough,
sharp **6** cowing, fierce, savage, severe **7** abusive, inhuman, scrappy,
warlike, wolfish **8** bullying, inhumane, militant, scathing, scurrile
9 barbarous, bellicose, combative,
ferocious, invective, trenchant, vitriolic **10** pugnacious, scurrilous, terrifying, vituperous **11** belligerent,
browbeating, contentious, frightening, opprobrious, quarrelsome, terrorizing **12** contumelious, gladiatorial, intimidating, vituperative,
vituperatory

trudge
4 plod, slog, slop, toil, trek
6 stodge **8** footslog, plunther

true
4 just, real, very **5** liege, loyal,
right, sooth, valid **6** actual, ardent,
honest, kosher, strict, trusty **7** fac-

tual, genuine, precise, staunch, un-
faked, upright **8** accurate, bona
fide, constant, faithful, resolute, rightful, unfabled **9** allegiant, authentic,
honorable, steadfast, trustable, undoubted, unfeigned, veracious, veridical, veritable **10** creditable, dependable, legitimate, sure-enough,
undeniable **11** appropriate, indubitable, trustworthy, undesigning,
undistorted **12** indisputable, undissembled **13** authoritative
  combining form: **2** eu **4** orth **5** ortho

true-blue
  5 loyal **8** faithful **10** unswerving

truism
  4 rule **5** axiom, gnome, maxim,
moral **6** cliché, dictum, gospel, verity **7** brocard, bromide **8** aphorism, apothegm, veracity **9** platitude **10** shibboleth
11 commonplace

Truk Island
  3 Tol **4** Moen, Udot, Uman **5** Fefan
6 Dublon

truly
  3 yea **4** even, very, well **6** easily,
indeed, really, surely, verily **7** de
facto **8** actually **9** genuinely, veritably **10** absolutely, positively
11 confidently, doubtlessly,
undoubtedly

Truman, Harry S
  birthplace: **5** Lamar (Missouri)
  predecessor: **3** FDR
  successor: **3** DDE

trump
  3 cap, top **4** beat, best, pass, ruff
5 excel, outdo **6** better **7** manille,
surpass **8** clincher, outstrip,
spadille

trumpery
  4 base, mean, poor **5** bilge,
cheap, hokum **6** bunkum, bushwa,
cheesy, common, paltry, shoddy,
trashy **7** twaddle **8** claptrap, flimflam, malarkey, nonsense, rubbishy
10 double-talk

trumpet
  4 horn, tout **6** herald **8** ballyhoo
  call: **6** sennet
  ram's horn: **6** shofar

trumpeter
  4 Hirt (Al) **5** André (Maurice),
Baker (Chet), Davis (Miles), James
(Harry) **6** Alpert (Herb), Voisin (Roger) **7** Schwarz (Gerard) **8** Eld-
ridge (Roy) **9** Armstrong (Louis),

Gillespie (Dizzy) **10** McPartland
(Jimmy)

truncate
  3 lop, top **4** crop **5** shear **6** cut off
7 abridge, pollard **10** abbreviate

truncheon
  3 bat **4** club, mace **5** billy
6 cudgel **8** bludgeon **9** billy club
10 knobkerrie, nightstick

trundle
  3 bed, tub **4** bowl, cart, haul, push,
roll **5** churn, wheel **6** lumber

trunk
  3 box **4** body, case, stem **5** chest,
torso **7** channel, circuit, luggage
  elephant: **9** proboscis
  tree: **4** bole

truss
  3 tie **4** bind, pack **5** brace **7** support **9** supporter **10** strengthen

trust
  4 care, hope, pool, rely, ward
5 chain, faith, group, lot on, stock
6 assume, bank on, belief, cartel,
charge, commit, credit, rely on
7 build on, combine, confide, consign, count on, custody, keeping,
presume **8** bank upon, credence,
depend on, reckon on, reliance,
rely upon, sureness **9** assurance,
certainty, certitude, syndicate
10 confidence, conviction, dependence, depend upon **11** calculate
on, safekeeping **12** conglomerate,
guardianship, positiveness
  Scottish: **6** lippen

trustworthy
  4 true **5** exact, tried, valid **6** honest, secure **7** upright **8** accurate,
credible, faithful, reliable **9** authentic, realistic, veracious **10** convincing, dependable, scrupulous
12 tried and true **13** authoritative

trusty
  4 firm **5** sound, tried **6** secure, stable **7** convict, turnkey **8** credible,
faithful, reliable **9** authentic
10 convincing, dependable **11** pre-
dictable, responsible **12** tried and
true

truth
  5 axiom, maxim, sooth **6** candor,
gospel, verity **7** lowdown, reality,
veritas **8** veracity **9** precision, rightness **11** genuineness **12** authenticity, veridicality **13** veraciousness,
veritableness
  goddess: **4** Maat
  serum: **11** scopolamine

truthful
  4 real **5** frank **6** candid, honest
7 factual, sincere, veridic **8** accurate **9** realistic, veracious, veridical

truthfulness
  5 truth **6** verity **8** veracity **12** veridicality **13** veraciousness

try
  2 go **3** aim, irk, pop, vex **4** pain,
rack, seek, shot, slap, stab, test
5 annoy, assay, check, crack, essay, exert, fling, offer, prove, trial,
whack, whirl, wring **6** aspire,
bother, harass, harrow, hassle,
martyr, strain, stress, strive **7** afflict,
agonize, attempt, crucify, test out,
torment, torture, trouble **8** distress,
endeavor, striving, struggle **9** undertake **10** excruciate, experiment

trying
  5 rough, tight, tough **6** sticky, taxing, tricky, vexing **7** arduous, exigent, irksome, onerous, tricksy,
weighty **8** annoying, exacting
9 demanding, strenuous **10** bothersome, burdensome, irritating, oppressive **11** troublesome

try out
  8 audition

tryst
  4 date **7** meeting **10** engagement,
rendezvous **11** appointment,
assignation

tsetse fly
  8 glossina

tsunami
  9 tidal wave

'' ___ tu''(aria)
  3 Eri

tub
  3 vat **4** bath, wash **5** keeve
6 shower **8** dumpling **10** butterball

tuba
  7 helicon

Tubalcain
  father: **6** Lamech
  mother: **6** Zillah

Tubal's father
  7 Japheth

tubby
  5 plump, podgy, pudgy **6** chubby,
plumpy, rotund **8** plumpish, roly-
poly **10** roundabout

tube
  2 TV **4** duct, hose, pipe **5** buret, pipet **6** siphon, subway, tunnel, ves-

sel **7** burette, conduit, cuvette, pipette, syringe **8** pipe-line
anatomical: **3** vas **4** duct, vasa (plural) **7** salpinx **9** salpinges (plural)
combining form: **5** solen **6** siphon, soleno, syring **7** siphoni, siphono, syringo

tuber
4 bulb, corm, stem **6** potato **7** rhizome

tuberculosis
2 TB **8** phthisis **11** consumption, white plague

tuck
2 go **3** pep **4** birr, chow, eats, feed, food, grub, meat **5** bread, moxie, scoff, vigor **6** energy, viands **7** potency **9** hardihood, provender

tucker
4 poop, wilt **5** gruel **7** exhaust, frazzle, tire out, wear out **8** knock out **9** prostrate

tuft
5 clump, mound **7** cluster
combining form: **4** loph **5** lophi, lopho **6** lophio
of feathers: **7** panache
of hair: **4** tate
ornamental: **6** pompon
vascular: **6** glomus

tufted
8 floccose

tug
3 lug, tow, war **4** drag, draw, haul, moil, pull, toil, work **5** drive, fight, labor **6** battle, oppugn, strain, strive **7** contend

tug-of-war
6 strife **7** contest, rivalry, warfare **8** conflict, striving **9** emulation **11** competition

tuition
8 teaching, training, tutelage **9** education, schooling **11** instruction

tumble
3 dip, hit **4** bump, down, drop, fall, fell, hash, hear, luck, mash, meet, skid, trip **5** floor, learn, level, light, mix up, pitch, snafu, upset **6** chance, foul up, go down, happen, jumble, litter, mess up, muddle, muss up, plunge, topple **7** catch on, clutter, confuse, descend, disturb, find out, flatten, overset, plummet, rummage, shuffle, snarl up, unearth, unhorse **8** bowl down, bowl over, come down, disarray, discover, disorder, keel over, mishmash, nose-dive, overturn, scramble, unsettle **9** ascertain, bring down, determine, knock down, knock over, overthrow **10** disarrange, discompose

tumbledown
7 rickety **10** ramshackle

tumbler
5 glass **11** cartwheeler

tumbrel
4 cart **5** wagon **7** vehicle **8** dumpcart

tumescent
6 turgid **7** aureate, bloated, bulging, flowery, swollen **8** dropsied, inflated, swelling **9** bombastic, dropsical, flatulent, overblown **10** euphuistic, rhetorical **12** magniloquent **13** grandiloquent

tumid
see **tumescent**

tummy
3 gut **5** belly **6** paunch, venter **7** abdomen, stomach

tumor
3 wen **4** cyst **5** myoma **6** emerod, glioma, lipoma, myxoma **7** desmoid, emeroid, myeloma, neuroma, osteoma, sarcoma **8** blastoma, hepatoma, lymphoma, neoplasm, teratoma **9** carcinoma
benign: **7** fibroid, fibroma
combining form: **3** oma **4** cele, myom, onco **5** myomo, omato (plural), oncho **6** gangli **7** ganglio
hard: **8** scirrhus
soft: **5** gumma

tumult
3 din **4** flap, stew, to-do **5** babel, noise, whirl **6** clamor, dither, hassle, hubbub, jangle, lather, outcry, pother, racket, uproar, upturn **7** ferment, turmoil **8** disorder, paroxysm, seething, upheaval **9** agitation, commotion, confusion, maelstrom **10** convulsion, hullabaloo, hurly burly, turbulence **11** disturbance, pandemonium **12** unsettlement

tumultuous
5 rowdy **6** unruly **7** raucous **8** rowdyish **9** termagant, turbulent **10** boisterous, disorderly, rowdydowdy **11** rumbustious

tumulus
4 hill **5** mound **6** barrow **7** hillock

tun
3 keg, vat **4** butt, cask, pipe **6** barrel **8** hogshead

tuna
6 bonito **7** bluefin **8** albacore, dogtooth, skipjack **9** yellowfin

tune
3 air, fix, lay **4** dial, sing, sync **5** carol, chant, chime, order, range, synch **6** accord, adjust, chorus, extent, matter, melody, strain, warble **7** concert, concord, conform, descant, harmony, measure, melisma, melodia **8** diapason, regulate, vicinity, vocalize **9** agreement, harmonize, integrate, magnitude, reconcile **10** consonance, coordinate, proportion **11** accommodate, composition, concordance **12** neighborhood, reconciliate

tuneful
5 sweet, tuned **6** dulcet **7** lyrical, melodic, musical, songful **8** euphonic **9** melodious **10** euphonious **11** mellisonant

tungsten
7 wolfram

tunic
5 gipon, jupon **6** caftan, kaftan, kirtle
Greek: **6** chiton

tunicate
4 salp **5** salpa **6** salpid **8** ascidian, doliolid **9** sea squirt

Tunisia
monetary unit: **5** dinar
ruins: **8** Carthage

tunnel
4 tube **6** burrow **7** conduit **8** crawlway
Alps: **7** Simplon
France: **4** Rove
Hudson river: **7** Holland, Lincoln
Nevada: **5** Sutro
railroad: **6** Hoosac **7** Cascade

tunny
4 tuna **7** bluefin

Turandot
character: **3** Liu **5** Calaf
composer: **7** Puccini (Giacomo)
suitor: **5** Calaf

turban
6 pugree **7** pugaree, puggree **8** bandanna, puggaree **9** headdress

turbid
4 dark **5** dense, mucky, muddy, murky, riley, roily, smoky, thick **6** cloudy, opaque **7** clouded, obscure

turbulence
3 din **4** flap, stew **5** babel, fight **6** dither, fracas, lather, pother, tumult, uproar **7** turmoil **9** agitation, commotion, confusion **10** unruliness **11** pandemonium

turbulent
4 fast, wild **5** roily, rough, rowdy **6** raging, stormy, unruly **7** boiling, furious, howling, moiling, raucous, riotous, roaring, ruffled **8** agitated, blustery, brawling, mutinous, rowdyish, stormful, swirling **9** clamorous, convulsed, stirred up, termagant **10** blustering, boisterous, disorderly, rip-roaring, roisterous, roughhouse, rowdy-dowdy, tumultuous **11** rumbustious, tempestuous, uninhibited **12** rambunctious **13** tempest-tossed

turf
3 sod **4** area **5** divot, track **6** region, sphere, swarth **7** terrain **9** racetrack, territory

turgid
see **tumescent**

turkey
disease: 9 blackhead
female: 3 hen
head growth: 5 snood **7** dewbill
male: 3 tom **7** gobbler
throat pouch: 6 wattle
young: 5 poult

Turkey
capital: 6 Ankara
largest city: 8 Istanbul
monetary unit: 4 lira **5** pound

turkey buzzard
4 aura

Turkey in the ___
5 Straw

Turkish
empire: 7 Ottoman
governor: 4 vali
inn: 6 imaret
music: 9 janissary
palace: 5 serai
province: 7 vilayet
soldier: 5 nizam **8** janizary **9** janissary
sultan: 5 Ahmed, Selim **7** Bajazet, Bayezid, Ilderim
sword: 8 yataghan
title: 3 aga, bey **4** agha **5** pasha **6** vizier

turmeric
4 herb **5** spice **8** curcumin **9** bloodroot

turmoil
4 flap, moil, riot, stew, to-do **5** whirl **6** clamor, dither, hassle, hubbub, lather, pother, strife, tumult, unease, unrest, uproar **7** anxiety, ferment, garboil **8** disorder, disquiet, distress, upheaval **9** agitation, commotion, confusion **10** disruption, hurly burly, inquietude, turbulence, uneasiness **11** anxiousness, disquietude, jitteriness, nervousness, restiveness **12** restlessness **13** Sturm und Drang

turn
3 aim, yaw, zag, zig **4** bend, bias, bout, cast, eddy, grow, gyre, plow, reel, roll, sour, spin, swim, tack, tour, vary, veer, whip, wind **5** alter, angle, avert, curve, orbit, pivot, point, refer, round, sheer, shunt, spell, stint, swing, swirl, train, twirl, twist, upset, weave, whirl **6** become, change, circle, defect, desert, detour, direct, divert, gyrate, hang on, invert, modify, mutate, obvert, plow up, render, repair, resort, revert, rotate, sicken, sprain, switch, swivel, wrench, zero in, zigzag **7** circuit, convert, deflect, derange, deviate, digress, diverge, flexure, hinge on, inverse, passade, reflect, reverse, revolve **8** disorder, flection, gyration, mutation, renounce, reversal, rotation, unsettle **9** about-face, deviation, oscillate, pirouette, rechannel, refashion, repudiate, reversion, sidetrack, translate, transpose, variation, volte-face **10** alteration, apostatize, change into, circumduct, deflection, double back, revolution, right-about, tergiverse, transplace **11** changeabout, reversement **12** modification, tergiversate
combining form: 4 trop **5** trope, tropy **6** tropic **7** trophic, tropism, tropous
to stone: 8 lapidify

turnabout
3 rat **6** coward **7** quitter, reverse **8** apostate, defector, recreant, renegade, reversal, runagate **9** about-face, reversion, volte-face **10** backslider, right-about **11** changeabout, reversement **13** tergiversator

turn aside or away
4 skew, veer, ward **5** avert, shunt **6** divert **7** deflect, shuttle

turn back
5 react, recur, repel **6** return, revert **10** recrudesce

turncoat
3 rat, spy **7** quisler, traitor **8** apostate, betrayer, defector, deserter, quisling, recreant, renegade, runagate **9** straggler, turnabout **13** tergiversator

turn down
4 veto **5** spurn **6** refuse, reject **7** decline, dismiss **9** reprobate, repudiate **10** disapprove

turned on
4 high **5** doped **6** stoned, zonked **7** drugged **8** hopped-up **9** spaced-out **10** tripped out

turn in
3 bed **5** rat on **6** betray, retire **7** deliver, produce **8** hand over, inform on

turning point
4 crux **5** pivot **6** climax, crisis **8** landmark

turnip
5 swede **8** rutabaga
Scottish: 4 neep

turnip-shaped
8 napiform

turn left
3 haw

Turn of the Screw, The
author: 5 James (Henry)
character: 5 Flora, Miles **10** Peter Quint
composer: 7 Britten (Benjamin)

turn over
4 feed, find, give, hand, muse, plow, roll **5** break, upset **6** assign, commit, give up, plow up, ponder, supply, topple **7** commend, confide, consign, deliver, entrust, furnish, overset, provide, revolve **8** delegate, meditate, ruminate, transfer **9** overthrow **10** deliberate, relinquish

turnpike
4 road **7** highway, tollway **8** toll road

turn right
3 gee

turn up
3 get **4** come, espy, find, show, spot **5** catch, get in, hit on, pop in, reach **6** appear, arrive, descry, detect, louden, roll in, show up **7** hit upon, uncover, unearth **8** meet with **9** encounter, track down **11** materialize

Turnus
beloved: **7** Lavinia
slayer: **6** Aeneas

turpentine
7 galipot, solvent, thinner
ingredient: **6** pinene
tree: **4** pine **9** terebinth

turret
5 tower **8** bartizan

turtle
8 terrapin, tortoise **9** chelonian
edible part: **7** calipee **8** calipash
sea: **6** ridley **8** hawkbill
shell: **8** carapace
shell part: **8** plastron

Tuscany
city: **4** Pisa **8** Florence
river: **4** Arno
tower: **4** Pisa
wine: **7** chianti

tusk
4 fang **5** ivory, tooth

tussle
4 spar **5** scrap **6** hassle **7** grapple,
scuffle, wrestle **8** skirmish

tutelage
see **tuition**

tutor
5 coach, teach **6** docent, mentor
7 teacher **9** pedagogue
10 instructor

Tut's tomb discoverer
6 Carter (Howard)

TV
see **television**

twaddle
3 jaw, yak **4** bosh, chat **5** clack,
drool, prate, run on **6** babble,
dither, drivel, gabble, hot air
7 blabber, blather, chatter, prattle
8 claptrap, malarkey, nonsense,
tommyrot, wish-wash **9** poppycock
10 balderdash

Twain biographer
5 Paine (Albert)

tweak
3 jog **4** jerk, pull **5** pinch **6** snatch,
twitch

Twelfth Night character
5 Maria, Viola **6** Olivia **8** Malvolio
9 Sebastian, Toby Belch

twelve
combining form: **5** dodec **6** dodeca

twenty
combining form: **4** icos **5** icosa, icosi

twerp
4 brat, fool, jerk **5** sprat **6** squirt
7 upstart

twibil
2 ax **3** axe **8** battle-ax **9** battle-axe

twice
3 bis **7** twofold
combining form: **2** di **3** bis
prefix: **2** bi **3** dis

twice a day
3 b.i.d. **8** bis in die

twice a year
8 biannual

Twice-Told Tales author
9 Hawthorne (Nathaniel)

twig
5 shoot, sprig **6** branch
bundle of: **5** fagot **6** faggot

twiggy
4 slim, thin **5** reedy **6** slight, stalky
7 slender, squinny, tenuous
9 attenuate

twilight
3 end, eve **4** dusk **5** gloom **6** sunset **8** gloaming, glooming, owl light
9 attenuate, nightfall

Twilight of the Gods
8 Ragnarok

twill
5 cloth, serge, weave **6** fabric
9 gabardine **11** herringbone

twin
4 dual, like, mate **5** match **6** bifold, binary, double, fellow, paired
7 matched, similar, twofold
8 matching **9** companion, duplicate, identical **10** coordinate,
reciprocal
combining form: **5** didym **6** didymo

Twin Cities
6 St. Paul **11** Minneapolis

twine
4 coil, curl, wind **5** twist **6** enmesh,
spiral, tangle **7** entwine, wreathe
8 entangle **9** corkscrew
10 interweave

twinge
4 ache, pain, pang **5** throe
6 stitch

twinkle
3 bat **4** wink **5** blink, flash, gleam,
glint, light, shake, shine, trice
6 minute, moment, second **7** flicker,
glimmer, glisten, glitter, instant,
light up, nictate, shimmer, sparkle
9 coruscate, nictitate, twinkling

10 illuminate **11** coruscation, scintillate, split second **13** scintillation

twin stars
6 Castor, Pollux

twirl
4 gyre, spin **5** whirl **6** gyrate
9 pirouette, whirligig

twist
3 wry **4** coil, curl, kink, slub, turn,
warp, wind, wisp **5** belie, color,
gnarl, pivot, quirk, thraw, twine,
wring **6** garble, intort, spiral,
sprain, squirm, torque, widdle,
wrench, writhe **7** contort, distort,
entwine, falsify, intwine, pervert,
wreathe, wriggle **8** miscolor, misstate, squiggle **9** corkscrew
12 misrepresent
combining form: **4** spir **5** spiri, spiro

twisted
3 wry **4** awry **5** askew **6** knurly,
thrawn, warped **7** tortile

twister
7 cyclone, tornado **9** whirlwind

twit
4 jive, josh, lout, mock, quiz, razz
5 blame, chide, rally, scout, taunt,
tease **6** deride **7** censure, reprove
8 reproach, ridicule **9** reprehend

twitch
3 lug, nip, tic **4** jerk, snap, yank
5 grasp, lurch, pinch, pluck, tweak
6 clutch, snatch **9** vellicate

twitter
3 gab, jaw **4** chat, chip, peep
5 cheep, chirp, quake, run on,
shake, tweet **6** babble, cackle,
dither, quaver, quiver, rattle, shiver,
tremor **7** chatter, chipper, chirrup,
chitter, prattle, shudder, tremble,
tweedle

twittery
5 jumpy, nervy **6** goosey, spooky
7 fidgety, jittery, nervous **9** flustered **10** high-strung

two
3 duo **4** duet, pair **5** twain
6 couple
combining form: **2** dy **3** bis, duo,
dyo
divide into: **4** fork **6** bisect
9 bifurcate
prefix: **2** bi **3** twi

twofold
4 dual, twin **5** binal, duple **6** binary, double, duplex, dyadic,
paired **9** dualistic
combining form: **2** di **4** dipl **5** diphy,
diplo **6** diphyo

Two Gentlemen of Verona
character: 5 Julia 6 Silvia, Thurio
7 Proteus 9 Valentine

two-horned
10 bicornuate

twosome
3 duo 4 dyad, pair 5 brace 6 couple 7 doublet

two-time
5 bluff 6 delude, humbug, illude, juggle, take in 7 beguile, deceive, mislead 11 double-cross

two-wheeler
4 bike 5 cycle 7 bicycle, scooter
10 velocipede

two-winged
9 dipterous

Two Years Before the Mast
author
4 Dana (Richard Henry)

Tybalt
cousin: 6 Juliet
family: 7 Capulet
slayer: 5 Romeo
victim: 8 Mercutio

Tyche
goddess of: 7 fortune

tycoon
4 czar, king 5 baron, mogul, nabob 6 prince 7 magnate

tyke
3 dog 5 child, hound 6 canine
7 mongrel

tympanum
7 eardrum 9 middle ear

Tyndareus
kingdom: 6 Sparta
wife: 4 Leda

type
3 cut, ilk, lot, way 4 cast, form, kind, mold, sort 5 breed, class, genre, order, print, serif, stamp

6 kidney, nature, stripe 7 feather, species, variety 8 category 9 character 10 persuasion 11 description
bar: 4 slug
combining form: 5 morph 6 morpho
jumbled: 2 pi 3 pie
measure: 2 em, en 4 pica 5 point
set: 7 compose
setter: 10 compositor
size: 4 pica 5 agate, pearl
stroke: 5 serif
style: 5 roman 6 Gothic, italic
7 Fraktur 8 boldface, sanserif
9 lightface, sans serif
tray: 6 galley

Typee
author: 8 Melville (Herman)
character: 4 Toby

typewriter
part: 3 key 6 platen, spacer
type size: 4 pica 5 elite

Typhon
3 Set 7 monster 8 Typhoeus
offspring: 6 Sphinx 7 Chimera
8 Cerberus, Chimaera
wife: 7 Echidna

typhoon
9 hurricane 13 tropical storm

typical
5 ideal, model, usual 6 common, normal, old hat 7 classic, general, natural, regular 9 classical, exemplary, prevalent 11 commonplace

typical of
suffix: 2 ic, ly 3 ish, ist 4 ical 5 istic
7 istical

typify
6 embody, mirror 9 body forth, epitomize, exemplify, personify, represent, symbolize 10 illustrate
11 emblematize

typo
5 error 8 misprint

typographer
7 printer 10 compositor

Tyr
3 Tiu
brother: 4 Thor
father: 4 Odin
god of: 3 war
mother: 5 Jordh, Jorth

tyrannical
5 harsh 6 brutal 8 absolute, despotic 9 arbitrary, autarchic, roughshod 10 autocratic, monocratic, oppressive

tyrannize
5 crush 7 dictate, oppress, shackle, trample 8 dominate, domineer, overlord 9 despotize, terrorize

tyrannous
6 lordly 8 absolute, despotic 9 arbitrary, autarchic, fascistic 10 autocratic, monocratic 12 totalitarian

tyranny
7 fascism 8 totality 9 autocracy, despotism, terrorism 10 absolutism, domination, oppression
12 dictatorship

tyrant
4 duce 6 despot 8 autocrat, dictator 9 oppressor, strong man
12 totalitarian

Tyrian ___
6 purple

tyro
4 colt 6 novice, rookie 7 amateur, dabbler 8 beginner, freshman, neophyte, newcomer 9 novitiate, smatterer 10 apprentice, dilettante, tenderfoot, uninitiate 11 abecedarian

Tyrol
see **Tirol**

Tzar
see **czar**

Uu

übermensch
7 overman 8 superman

ubiquitous
7 allover 9 universal 10 everywhere 11 omnipresent

Uel's father
4 Bani

Uganda
capital: 7 Kampala
monetary unit: 8 shilling

ugly
3 bad, low 4 base, dour, fell, foul, glum, mean, ugly, vile 5 awful, cross, grave, major, pesky, plain, sulky, surly, toady 6 cranky, gloomy, homely, morose, sordid, sullen, wicked 7 bizarre, crabbed, hideous, ignoble, low-down, serious, servile, vicious 8 grievous, gruesome, uncomely, unlovely, wretched 9 dangerous, grotesque, repelling, repugnant, repulsive, saturnine, troublous, unsightly, vexatious 10 despicable, ill-favored, ill-looking, uninviting, unpleasing 11 ill-tempered, threatening, troublesome, unbeautiful 12 unattractive

Ugly Duckling author
8 Andersen (Hans Christian)

ugni blanc
4 wine 9 Trebbiano

ukase
5 edict, order 6 decree, ruling 7 command 9 directive 12 proclamation

Ukraine
capital: 4 Kiev
folk dance: 5 gopak
soldier: 7 cossack

Ulalume author
3 Poe (Edgar Allan)

Ulam's father
5 Eshek

ulcer
4 sore
kind: 6 peptic 8 duodenal
mouth: 10 canker sore

uliginous
3 wet 4 damp, oozy 5 moist, muddy 6 swampy

ulna
5 cubit 7 cubitus, forearm

Ulrica
5 sibyl, sybil, witch

Ulster hero
4 Emer, Medb 5 Cu Roi, Etain, Noisi 6 Ailill, Fergus 7 Cathbad, Conaire, Da Derga, Deirdre 8 MacDatho 9 Conchobar, Cuchullin, Finnabair 10 Cuchulainn

ulterior
4 dark 5 later, privy 6 buried, covert, future, hidden, latent 7 cryptic, further, guarded, obscure, remoter, thither 8 obscured, shrouded 9 ambiguous, concealed, enigmatic, equivocal 10 subsequent, succeeding 11 undisclosed

ultimate
3 end, lag 4 dire, last 5 basic, close, final, grand, lofty 6 finish, latest, latter, utmost, wind up, wrap up 7 closing, epitome, exalted, extreme, maximum, sublime, supreme 8 absolute, complete, conclude, earliest, empyreal, empyrean, eventual, farthest, hindmost, last word, original, terminal, towering 9 determine, elemental, terminate 10 apotheosis, concluding, consummate, preeminent, surpassing 11 categorical, fundamental, unequalable, unmatchable 12 incomparable, quintessence, transcendent 13 unsurpassable

ultimatum
5 order 6 demand, threat

ultra
5 kinky, outré, rabid 6 beyond, far-out 7 extreme, fanatic, forward, radical 9 excessive, extremist, fanatical 10 outlandish 11 extravagant

ultraconservative
4 tory 5 blimp, white 7 Bourbon, diehard 8 royalist 9 right-wing 11 reactionary, reactionist 13 reactionarist

ultraist
5 rabid 7 extreme, fanatic, radical 9 extremist

ultramarine
7 new blue, oversea 8 overseas 10 French blue 11 lapis lazuli, transmarine

ululate
3 bay 4 hoot, howl, wail, yelp 5 quest 6 bewail, lament 7 screech

Ulysses
author: 5 Joyce (James)
character: 5 Bloom, Molly 6 Boylan 7 Dedalus (Stephen); (see also **Odysseus**)

umber
5 brown, shade 6 darken, shadow 8 grayling 9 hammerkop

umbilicus
4 core 5 heart, hilum, navel
combining form: 6 omphal 7 omphalo

umbra
4 fish 5 ghost, shade 6 shadow 7 eidolon, phantom 8 darkness, phantasm, revenant 10 apparition

umbrage
3 ire 4 fury, huff, miff, rage 5 anger, doubt, pique, shade, trace, umbra, wrath 6 enrage, irking,

madden, offend, screen, shadow
7 dudgeon, foliage, incense, leafage, offense, pretext, steam up, verdure **8** nettling, vexation **9** annoyance, infuriate, provoking, semblance, suspicion **10** irritation, resentment **11** displeasure **12** exasperation

umbrageous
5 shady **6** shaded, shadow
7 shadowy **8** shadowed **9** resentful
11 belligerent

umbrella
5 guard, shade **6** brolly, pileus,
screen **7** parasol, shelter **10** protection **11** bumbershoot
large: **4** gamp

umbrous
5 shady **6** shaded, shadow
7 shadowy **8** shadowed

umph
see **oomph**

umpire
5 judge **7** adjudge, arbiter, referee
9 arbitrate **10** adjudicate,
arbitrator
call: **3** out **4** balk, ball, safe **6** strike

unabashed
6 arrant, brassy, brazen **7** blatant
8 impudent, overbold **9** barefaced,
shameless **10** unblushing
11 brazenfaced

unabbreviated
see **unabridged**

unable
8 helpless, impotent **9** incapable
11 incompetent, inefficient, unqualified **13** incapacitated

unabridged
5 uncut, whole **6** entire, intact
8 complete, undocked **11** uncondensed, whole-length **13** unabbreviated

unacceptable
4 poor **7** boorish **8** below par, unwanted **9** unwelcome **10** ill-favored, unpleasing, unsuitable
11 undesirable **12** inadmissible
13 below standard, exceptionable,
objectionable

unaccompanied
4 bare, sole **5** alone, apart **6** single **7** isolate, removed **8** detached,
isolated

unaccomplished
7 jackleg **8** dabbling, ungifted
9 unskilled **10** amateurish, dilet-

tante, incomplete, unfinished
12 dilettantish, dilettantist

unaccountable
6 arcane, mystic **7** strange **8** numinous **9** mysterial, unguessed
10 cabalistic, mysterious, unknowable **11** inscrutable **12** impenetrable, inexplicable, unfathomable
13 inexplainable, irresponsible,
unexplainable

unaccustomed
3 new **6** unused **7** strange **8** uncommon **10** unfamiliar

unacquainted
7 strange, unaware, unusual **8** ignorant **9** oblivious, unknowing, unwitting **10** unfamiliar, uninformed
11 incognizant **12** inconversant,
uninstructed **13** inexperienced

unacquired
6 inborn, innate, native **7** connate,
natural **9** inherited **10** congenital,
connatural, indigenous

unadorned
3 dry **4** bald, bare **5** naked, plain,
stark **6** rustic, simple **7** austere
11 undecorated, unelaborate, ungarnished **12** unbeautified, unornamented **13** unembellished, unembroidered, unpretentious

unadulterated
4 neat, pure **5** plain, sheer **6** honest, simple **7** genuine, perfect, sincere, unmixed **8** absolute, straight
9 unalloyed, undiluted **11** unmitigated, unqualified

unadvisable
see **inadvisable**

unaffable
7 aseptic **8** retiring **9** shrinking,
withdrawn **10** restrained
11 unexpansive

unaffected
4 easy, real **5** naive, plain **6** rustic,
simple **7** artless, natural, sincere
9 ingenuous, unstudied, untouched,
untutored **10** unschooled **12** unartificial, uninfluenced

unafraid
4 bold, cool, sure **5** brave **7** assured, defiant, valiant **8** composed,
fearless, intrepid, valorous **9** audacious, confident, dauntless, undaunted **10** courageous
13 imperturbable

unaimed
6 random **7** aimless **9** desultory,
haphazard, hit-or-miss, unplanned

10 designless **11** purposeless
12 unconsidered

unalike
7 distant, diverse, unequal, various
9 different, disparate, divergent,
unsimilar **10** dissimilar

unalloyed
4 deep, pure **5** sheer, solid **6** simple, virgin **7** genuine, perfect, unmixed **8** absolute **9** undiluted
11 unmitigated, unqualified
13 unadulterated

unalluring
5 plain **6** homely **8** uncomely, unpretty **10** unhandsome **11** unbeauteous, unbeautiful **12** unattractive

unalterable
see **inalterable**

unambiguous
5 clear, lucid, plain **6** patent
7 crystal, evident, express, obvious
8 apparent, clean-cut, clear-cut, definite, distinct, explicit, luminous,
manifest, palpable, pellucid, specific **9** unblurred **10** definitive
11 categorical, translucent, transparent **12** transpicuous

unanimated
4 cold, dead, dull, flat **5** vapid
6 asleep **7** insipid

unanimous
5 solid **6** agreed, united **8** agreeing, univocal **10** concordant,
concurrent, harmonious **11** consentient **13** consentaneous

unanimously
5 as one

unappeasable
4 grim **6** mortal **8** ruthless **9** insatiate, merciless, unsatiate **10** implacable, insatiable, ironfisted, quenchless, relentless, unyielding **11** unflinching, unrelenting **12** unquenchable **13** unsatisfiable

unappetizing
4 flat **7** insipid **8** unsavory **9** savorless, tasteless **10** flavorless **11** distasteful, ill-flavored, unpalatable
12 unattractive **13** uninteresting

unappreciative
9 thankless **10** ungrateful,
unthankful

unapproachable
5 aloof **6** offish **7** distant, stately
8 reserved **9** unbending, withdrawn **10** insociable, unsociable
11 standoffish, ungetatable, un-

reachable **12** inaccessible, unattainable

unarm
see **disarm**

unarmed
4 bare **5** inerm **8** unbarbed **11** defenseless
combining form: **5** anopl **6** anoplo

unartful
5 naive **6** simple **7** artless, natural **9** ingenuous, unstudied **10** unaffected, unschooled **12** unartificial

unarticulate
see **inarticulate**

unasked
5 unbid **6** wanton **8** arrogant, impudent, unbidden, unsought, unwanted **9** uninvited, unwelcome, voluntary **10** gratuitous **11** overbearing, spontaneous, uncalled-for, unrequested **12** presumptuous, supererogant, unacceptable

unassailable
5 stout, tough **6** secure, strong, sturdy **8** stalwart **9** tenacious **10** invincible, unbeatable **11** impregnable, indomitable **12** inexpugnable, invulnerable, undefeatable **13** inconquerable, unconquerable

unassertive
3 shy **4** meek **5** timid **6** modest **7** bashful, rabbity **8** backward, retiring **9** diffident, unassured **12** self-effacing

unassuming
3 shy **4** meek **5** lowly **6** humble, modest, simple **7** natural **8** retiring

unassured
3 shy **5** timid **6** modest, unsafe, unsure **7** bashful, rabbity **8** backward, insecure, retiring **9** diffident **10** unreliable **11** unassertive, unconfident **12** self-effacing, undependable **13** untrustworthy

unattached
4 free **5** loose **6** single **9** unmarried

unattractive
4 rude, ugly **5** plain **6** homely **8** frumpish, uncomely, unpretty **9** unlikable **10** unalluring, ungracious, unhandsome, unlikeable **11** unbeauteous, unbeautiful

unauthentic
7 bastard **8** spurious **9** ungenuine **10** apocryphal

unavailing
4 vain **6** futile **7** useless **8** abortive, bootless, gainless **9** fruitless **11** ineffective, ineffectual **12** unproductive

unavoidable
7 certain **9** necessary **10** ineludible, inevasible, inevitable, returnless, unevadable **11** ineluctable, inescapable, unescapable

unavoidably
8 perforce **10** helplessly, inevitably, willy-nilly **11** inescapably, whether or no

unaware
5 aback, short **6** sudden **7** unready **8** ignorant, suddenly **9** oblivious, unknowing, unwitting **10** unfamiliar, uninformed, unprepared **11** incognizant, inconversant, unacquainted, unexpectedly, uninstructed

unawares
5 aback, short **8** suddenly **12** unexpectedly

unbalance
5 craze **6** frenzy, lunacy, madden **7** derange, madness, unhinge **8** distract, insanity **10** aberration, alienation, insaneness **11** derangement, distraction, instability, psychopathy

unbalanced
3 mad **4** daft **5** batty, wacky **6** crazed, insane, uneven **7** unequal, unsound **8** demented, deranged, lopsided **9** irregular **10** asymmetric **13** unsymmetrical

unbeautiful
4 ugly **5** plain **6** homely **7** hideous **8** uncomely, unpretty **9** unsightly **10** ill-favored, ill-looking, unalluring, unhandsome **12** unattractive

unbecoming
4 rude **5** inapt, inept, rough, undue **6** clumsy, gauche, indign, unmeet **7** awkward, beneath, ungodly **8** improper, indecent, uncomely, unseemly, untimely, untoward, unworthy **9** incorrect, inelegant, maladroit **10** indecorous, indelicate, malapropos, malodorous, undecorous, unsuitable **11** disgraceful, unbefitting **12** unattractive, unseasonable **13** inappropriate

unbefitting
see **unbecoming**

unbelievable
4 thin, weak **5** thick **6** flimsy **8** fabulous **9** fantastic **10** improbable, incredible **11** implausible, incogitable, unthinkable **12** insupposable, unconvincing, unimaginable **13** inconceivable, unsubstantial

unbeliever
5 pagan **6** giaour **7** atheist, doubter, heretic, infidel, scoffer, skeptic, zetetic **8** agnostic **10** headshaker, Pyrrhonian, Pyrrhonist **11** free-thinker

unbelieving
6 show-me **8** aporetic, doubting **9** quizzical, skeptical **11** distrusting, incredulous, questioning **12** disbelieving

unbending
5 aloof, rigid, stern, stiff **6** offish **7** distant **8** obdurate, reserved, resolute **9** impliable, inelastic, withdrawn **10** brassbound, inexorable, inflexible, insociable, relentless, unflexible, unsociable, unswayable, unyielding **11** immalleable, incompliant, standoffish **12** single-minded

unbiased
4 fair, just **5** aloof, equal **8** detached, tolerant **9** equitable, impartial, objective, uncolored **12** uninterested, unprejudiced **13** dispassionate

unbidden
7 unasked **8** unsought **9** uninvited **11** unrequested

unbind
4 free, undo **5** loose, unfix, untie **6** detach, loosen, ungird **7** absolve, deliver, manumit, release, unchain, unloose **8** dissolve, liberate, unfasten, unloosen, unswathe **9** discharge, disengage, unshackle **10** emancipate

unblamable
4 good, pure **8** innocent, virtuous **9** exemplary, guiltless, righteous **10** inculpable

unblemished
4 pure **5** clean, sound, whole **6** chaste, decent, intact, modest, unhurt **7** perfect **8** flawless, spotless, unmarred **9** stainless, undamaged, undefiled, uninjured, unsullied **10** immaculate, unimpaired

unblock
3 ope **4** open, undo **6** unshut, unstop **7** unclose

unblunted
4 keen **5** honed, sharp **7** whetted **10** razor-sharp

unblurred
5 clear, lucid 7 crystal 8 clear-cut, luminous, pellucid 11 translucent, transparent, unambiguous 12 transpicuous

unbolt
4 open 5 unbar, unpin 6 loosen, unlock 8 unfasten

unbosom
4 open, tell 6 betray, reveal, unveil 7 divulge, unclose, uncover 8 disclose, discover 9 uncurtain

unbound
4 free 5 loose 10 unconfined, unfastened

unbounded
4 huge, open 7 endless 8 infinite 9 boundless, limitless, unchecked, unlimited 10 indefinite, unmeasured 11 measureless 12 immeasurable, uncontrolled, unrestrained

unbridled
4 free 5 loose 7 violent 9 dissolute, unchecked 10 licentious, ungoverned 11 uninhibited 12 uncontrolled, unrestrained

unbroken
3 one 5 solid, sound, whole 6 entire, intact, single, unhurt 7 perfect, untamed 8 straight, unmarred, unplowed 9 continual, undamaged, undivided, uninjured, unsubdued 10 continuous, unimpaired 13 uninterrupted

unburden
3 rid 4 ease, lose 5 clear, empty 6 unload 7 relieve 8 shake off, throw off 9 discharge 11 disencumber

uncalled-for
4 rude 5 silly 6 absurd, wanton 7 foolish, incivil, unasked, uncivil 8 baseless, impolite, needless, unneeded 9 intrusive, officious, unfounded, unneedful 10 bottomless, gratuitous, groundless, ungracious, ungrounded, unrequired 11 disgracious, ill-mannered, impertinent, inessential, unessential, unnecessary, unwarranted 12 discourteous, preposterous, supererogant 13 disrespectful

uncanny
4 eery 5 eerie, scary, weird 6 creepy, spooky 7 ghostly, strange 9 unearthly, unnatural 10 mysterious, superhuman 11 supernormal, supranormal 12 supernatural 13 superordinary

uncared-for
7 run-down 8 untended 9 neglected

uncareful
4 wild 8 feckless, reckless 10 incautious 13 irresponsible

uncaring
8 feckless, heedless 9 oblivious, unheeding, unrecking 10 unthinking 11 inadvertent, thoughtless 12 irreflective, unreflective

unceasing
7 endless, eternal 8 constant, unending 9 ceaseless, continual, incessant, perpetual 10 continuous 11 everlasting, unremitting 12 interminable 13 uninterrupted

unceremonious
4 curt 5 bluff, blunt, sharp, short 6 abrupt 8 familiar, informal 9 irregular 10 ungracious, unofficial 11 thoughtless 13 inconsiderate

uncertain
4 asea, dark, hazy, iffy, moot, open 5 fluky, vague 6 chancy, fickle, fitful, queasy, shifty, unsure, wobbly 7 dubious, erratic, halting, mutable, obscure, protean, suspect, unclear 8 aleatory, arguable, doubtful, flickery, hesitant, insecure, mootable, slippery, ticklish, unstable, unsteady, variable, volatile 9 ambiguous, debatable, equivocal, faltering, fluctuant, mercurial, sibylline, tenebrous, tentative, undecided, unsettled, whimsical 10 borderline, capricious, changeable, disputable, inconstant, indecisive, indefinite, irresolute, lubricious, precarious, unexplicit 11 problematic, vacillating, vacillatory 12 incalculable, questionable, undependable, unexpectable, wiggle-waggle 13 indeterminate, problematical, temperamental, unforeseeable, unpredictable, untrustworthy

uncertainty
5 doubt, maybe, query, worry 6 bother, gamble, wonder 7 anxiety, concern, dubiety, reserve, trouble 8 disfaith, disquiet, distress, distrust, mistrust, suspense 9 agitation, dubiosity, dubitancy, suspicion 10 hesitation, skepticism, uneasiness 12 doubtfulness, perturbation

unchain
4 free 5 loose 6 loosen, unbind 7 manumit, release 8 liberate 9 discharge, unshackle 10 emancipate

unchangeable
4 fast 5 fixed 7 eternal 8 constant 9 immovable, immutable, unmovable 10 inflexible, invariable 11 inalterable, unalterable 12 unmodifiable

unchanging
4 even, same 6 stable, static, steady 7 equable, eternal, forever, settled, stabile, uniform 8 constant 9 immutable, steadfast, unfailing, unvarying 10 consistent, invariable, stationary 13 unfluctuating

unchaste
4 easy, fast, lewd 5 bawdy, dirty, light, loose 6 coarse, impure, wanton 7 haggard, immoral, obscene, scarlet, unclean 9 uncleanly

unchecked
4 free 5 loose 7 rampant 9 unbounded, unbridled 11 uninhibited

uncivil
4 rude, wild 5 crass, crude, rough 6 brutal, coarse, crusty, Gothic, rugged, savage 7 Hunnish, ill-bred, incivil 8 barbaric, clownish, impolite 9 barbarian, barbarous 10 indecorous, ungracious, unsuitable 11 disgracious, ill-mannered, impertinent, uncivilized, uncourteous 12 discourteous, uncultivated 13 disrespectful

uncivilized
4 rude, wild 6 brutal, Gothic, Hunnic, rugged, savage, unholy, wicked 7 boorish, Hunnish, ill-bred, loutish, lowbred, ungodly 8 barbaric, churlish, cloddish 9 barbarian, barbarous, unrefined 10 outrageous, uncultured, unmannerly, unpolished 12 uncultivated 13 unenlightened

unclad
see unclothed

uncle
Dutch: 3 oom
Scottish: 3 eme
Spanish: 3 tio

unclean
4 foul, tref, vile 5 black, dirty, nasty, soily 6 common, filthy, grubby, impure 7 defiled, immoral, obscene, squalid 8 polluted, profaned, unchaste 10 desecrated 11 unwholesome

unclear
3 dim 4 hazy, open 6 bleary, blurry, opaque, unsure 7 dubious, obscure, shadowy, suspect

8 doubtful, nebulose, nebulous
9 ambiguous, equivocal, tenebrous, uncertain, undefined, unsettled
10 ill-defined, indistinct, unexplicit
11 problematic

Uncle Remus creator
6 Harris (Joel Chandler)

Uncle Tom's Cabin
author: 5 Stowe (Harriet Beecher)
character: 5 Eliza, Topsy 6 Legree (Simon) 9 Little Eva

Uncle Vanya author
7 Chekhov (Anton)

uncloak
6 debunk, expose, show up, unmask 7 undress 8 discover, unshroud

unclothe
5 strip 6 denude, devest, divest, expose, reveal, unveil 7 display, disrobe, uncloak, uncover, undress
8 disclose 10 dishabille

unclothed
3 raw 4 nude 5 naked 6 unclad
8 buff-bare, stripped 9 au naturel, undressed 10 stark-naked

unclouded
4 fair, fine, open 5 clear, sunny
7 clarion 8 pleasant, rainless, sunshiny 10 undarkened

uncluttered
4 neat, snug, tidy, trig, trim 7 chipper, orderly 9 shipshape 11 spic-and-span, well-groomed 12 spick-and-span

uncolored
4 fair, just 5 equal 8 unbiased
9 equitable, impartial, objective
12 unprejudiced 13 dispassionate

uncombed
5 messy 6 sloppy, unneat, untidy
7 unkempt 8 ill-kempt, slipshod, slovenly 10 disheveled
12 unfastidious

uncombine
4 free, part 5 loose, sever 6 divide, sunder 7 disjoin 8 disjoint, dissever, disunite, separate
11 dichotomize

uncomely
4 ugly 5 inapt, inept, plain, undue
6 homely 7 hideous 8 improper, indecent, unpretty, untimely 9 unsightly 10 ill-favored, ill-looking, malapropos, unalluring, unbecoming, unhandsome, unsuitable
11 unbeauteous, unbeautiful, unbefitting 12 unattractive 13 inappropriate

uncomfortable
4 sick 5 harsh 6 queasy, uneasy
7 prickly 8 easeless, scratchy
11 distressing 13 disconcerting

uncommon
3 few, odd 4 rare 5 novel
6 choice, scarce, seldom, unique
7 special, strange, unusual 8 esoteric, especial, singular, sporadic, unwonted 10 infrequent, occasional, remarkable, unfrequent, unordinary 11 exceptional, unthinkable 12 unaccustomed, unimaginable 13 extraordinary

uncommunicative
4 dumb 5 aloof, close 6 offish, silent 7 distant, private 8 reserved, reticent, taciturn 9 unbending, withdrawn 10 insociable, unsociable
11 close-lipped, standoffish, tight-lipped 12 closemouthed, close-tongued, tight-mouthed

uncompassionate
5 stony 7 callous 8 obdurate
9 heartless, unfeeling 10 hard-boiled 11 coldhearted, hardhearted, unemotional 12 stony-hearted 13 unsympathetic

uncompliant
5 rigid 8 obdurate 9 untending
10 brassbound, inexorable, inflexible, unswayable, unyielding 12 single-minded

uncomplicated
5 basic, plain 6 honest, simple
10 elementary

uncomplimentary
9 slighting 10 derogatory, detracting, pejorative 11 disparaging, dyslogistic 12 depreciative, depreciatory

uncomprehensible
see **incomprehensible**

uncompromising
4 firm 5 rigid, stern, tough 6 strict
7 extreme 8 hard-line, obdurate
9 unbending 10 brassbound, determined, inexorable, inflexible, relentless, unyielding 11 uncompliant
12 intransigent, single-minded

unconcealed
4 bare, open 5 frank, overt, plain
6 candid 8 apparent 11 openhearted, undisguised, unvarnished
12 undissembled 13 undissembling

unconcern
4 cool 6 apathy 8 coolness, lethargy 9 disregard, lassitude
11 disinterest, insouciance, noncha-

lance 12 heedlessness, indifference, listlessness 13 unmindfulness

unconcerned
4 cool 5 aloof 6 casual, remote
8 composed, detached 9 apathetic, collected, incurious, lethargic, uncurious, unmindful, withdrawn
10 nonchalant 11 indifferent 12 uninterested 13 disinterested

unconditional
4 free 5 frank, utter 6 simple 8 absolute, explicit, termless
10 unreserved

unconfined
3 lax 4 free 5 loose 9 boundless, limitless, unlimited 12 unrestrained

uncongenial
8 aversive, kindless 9 repellent, repugnant, unlikable 10 discordant, unpleasing 11 displeasing, inconsonant 12 antipathetic, inharmonious, unattractive, unharmonious
13 unsympathetic

unconnected
5 gappy 7 muddled 8 detached, inchoate, rambling, separate
10 disjointed, disordered, incoherent, incohesive 11 unorganized
12 uncontinuous 13 discontinuous

unconquerable
6 secure 9 resistant 10 impassable, invincible, unbeatable 11 impregnable, indomitable, insuperable
12 inexpugnable, invulnerable, unassailable, undefeatable

unconscionable
5 undue 6 unholy, wicked 7 extreme, ungodly 8 towering 9 barbarous, excessive 10 exorbitant, immoderate, inordinate, outrageous
11 extravagant, unchristian, uncivilized, unwarranted 12 unmeasurable, unprincipled, unreasonable, unscrupulous 13 unjustifiable, unwarrantable

unconscious
3 out 4 cold 5 brute 6 asleep, blotto, torpid 7 out cold, stunned, unaware 8 comatose, ignorant, mindless 10 insensible

unconsciousness
4 coma 5 faint 6 torpor, trance

unconsidered
4 puny, rash 5 brash, hasty, petty, small 6 paltry, random 7 aimless, trivial 8 picayune, reckless, trifling
9 desultory, haphazard, hit-or-miss, hotheaded, unadvised, unplanned
10 designless, ill-advised, incau-

tious, objectless **11** promiscuous, thoughtless **12** inconsequent

unconsolable
see **inconsolable**

unconstrained
4 easy, free **6** casual, dégagé, simple **7** natural, relaxed, unfussy **8** familiar, informal, outgoing **9** easygoing, expansive **10** unreserved **11** low-pressure **13** demonstrative

unconstraint
4 ease **7** abandon, freedom, naiveté **10** simplicity **11** naturalness, spontaneity **13** impulsiveness, ingenuousness

uncontrollable
4 wild **6** unruly **8** indocile **9** fractious **11** indomitable, intractable **12** recalcitrant, unmanageable **13** insuppressive, irrepressible, uncontainable, undisciplined

uncontrolled
4 free, wild **5** loose **9** irregular, unbounded, unmanaged **10** hysterical, licentious, ungoverned **11** unregulated **12** unrestrained

unconventional
3 odd **5** loose, outré, queer **6** casual **7** devious, offbeat, strange, unusual **8** Bohemian, informal **10** unorthodox **13** unceremonious

unconversant
3 raw **5** green, young **6** callow **7** untried **8** unversed **9** unfleshed **10** unseasoned **11** unpracticed **13** inexperienced

unconvincing
4 thin, weak **5** fishy, thick **6** flimsy **10** improbable, incredible **11** implausible **12** unbelievable **13** inconceivable, unsubstantial

uncooked
3 raw

uncork
6 unplug **7** release

uncorrectable
8 cureless, hopeless **9** incurable, insanable, uncurable **10** impossible **11** immedicable, irreparable **12** irremediable **13** unrecoverable

uncorrupted
4 pure **5** naive **6** virgin **8** innocent, pristine **9** unspoiled

uncouple
3 cut **5** loose, unfix **6** detach **8** abstract, unfasten **9** disengage **10** disconnect, dissociate **12** disassociate

uncourteous
4 rude **7** uncivil **8** impolite **10** ungracious **11** disgracious, ill-mannered, impertinent, uncalled-for **13** disrespectful

uncouth
3 odd, raw **4** lorn, rude **5** crass, crude, gross, queer, rough, rummy **6** coarse, quaint, vulgar **7** awkward, bizarre, boorish, curious, erratic, ill-bred, loutish, oddball, strange, uncivil **8** backwood, derelict, deserted, desolate, forsaken, impolite, solitary, ungainly **9** abandoned, eccentric, inelegant, unrefined **10** uncultured, unpolished **11** disgracious, ill-mannered, impertinent, uncalled-for **12** discourteous, uncultivated **13** disrespectful
person: **3** oaf **4** boor, lout **5** yokel **6** bumkin, rustic **7** bumpkin

uncover
4 bare, open, tell **5** strip **6** betray, denude, detect, divest, expose, remove, reveal, unmask, unveil **7** display, divulge, lay open, subject, unbosom, unclose, undrape, unearth **8** disclose, unclothe **9** uncurtain

uncovered
4 bare, open **5** naked **6** peeled **7** denuded, exposed **8** stripped, unmasked

uncritical
6 casual **7** cursory, inexact, offhand, shallow, sketchy **8** careless, slipshod **9** depthless, imprecise **10** inaccurate **11** perfunctory, superficial

uncrown
6 depose, unmake **8** dethrone, discrown, displace **9** disthrone **11** disenthrone

unction
3 oil **4** balm **5** cream, salve **6** cerate, chrism **7** suavity **8** ointment

unctuous
3 fat **4** oily **5** fatty, slick, soapy, suave **6** greasy, smarmy **7** fulsome **10** oleaginous

uncultivated
3 raw **4** arid, rude, wild **5** crass, crude, feral, gross, rough **6** coarse, desert, fallow, Gothic, incult, native, savage, sloven **7** deserty, Hunnish, natural, uncivil **8** agrarian, agrestal, barbaric **9** barbarian, barbarous, inelegant **11** uncivilized

uncultured
3 raw **4** rude **5** crass, crude, gross,

uncurbed
9 audacious **10** ungoverned, unhampered **11** uninhibited, untrammeled **12** uncontrolled, unrestrained

uncustomary
4 rare **6** unique **7** unusual **8** singular, uncommon, unwonted **10** unordinary **11** exceptional, unthinkable **13** extraordinary

uncut
5 whole **6** entire **8** complete, undocked **10** full-length, unabridged **11** uncondensed, whole-length **13** unabbreviated

undamaged
5 sound, whole **6** intact, unhurt **8** flawless, unbroken, unmarred **9** uninjured **10** unimpaired **11** unblemished

undaring
5 timid **8** timorous

undarkened
4 fair, fine **5** clear, sunny **7** clarion **8** pleasant, rainless, sunshiny **9** cloudless, unclouded

undaunted
4 bold **5** brave **7** Spartan, valiant **8** fearless, intrepid, valorous **9** audacious, confident **10** courageous **11** unconquered

undeceive
5 purge **8** disabuse, undelude **11** disillusion

undecided
4 moot, open **6** unsure **7** dubious, pendent, pending, unclear **8** doubtful, wavering **9** equivocal, uncertain, unsettled **10** borderline, indecisive **12** undetermined

undecipherable
9 illegible **10** unreadable

undecisive
see **indecisive**

undeclared
5 tacit **6** secret, unsaid **7** implied **8** implicit, inferred, unspoken, wordless **9** unuttered **10** understood **11** unexpressed

undecorated
5 plain **6** homely, simple **9** unadorned **11** inelaborate, ungarnished **12** unbeautified, unorna-

mented **13** unembellished, unembroidered

undefiled
4 pure **5** clean **6** chaste, decent, intact, modest, virgin **8** innocent, spotless, virtuous **9** stainless, unsullied **10** immaculate **11** unblemished

undefined
3 dim **5** faint, vague **6** bleary **7** obscure, shadowy, unclear **10** indistinct **12** undetermined

undemonstrated
7 untried **8** unproved, untested **11** unpracticed

undemonstrative
3 icy **4** calm, cold, cool **5** aloof, chill **6** frigid **7** aseptic, distant, glacial, laconic **8** reserved, retiring **9** shrinking, unaffable, withdrawn **10** restrained, unsociable **11** emotionless, indifferent, standoffish, unemotional, unexpansive **12** uninterested

undeniable
4 real, true **6** actual **7** certain **8** positive, unfabled **9** veridical **10** inarguable **11** indubitable, unequivocal **12** indisputable, undisputable **13** incontestable, uncontestable

undependable
5 trick **6** casual, tricky, unsafe, unsure **7** dubious, erratic **8** untrusty **9** trustless, unassured **10** fly-by-night, unreliable **12** questionable **13** irresponsible, untrustworthy

under
3 low, sub **5** below, lower, neath **6** lesser, nether **7** beneath, subject **8** inferior **9** dependent, secondary, subjacent, tributary **10** collateral, underneath **11** subordinate
prefix: **3** hyp, sub **4** hypo

underage
4 lack **7** deficit, failure **8** shortage **10** deficiency, inadequacy, scantiness **11** defalcation **13** insufficience, insufficiency

undercarriage
5 frame **6** struts **8** supports **9** framework **11** landing gear

undercover
6 covert, secret **7** furtive, sub rosa **8** hush-hush **11** clandestine **12** hugger-mugger **13** hole-and-corner, surreptitious, under-the-table
person: **3** spy **4** mole **5** agent, spook **9** detective **10** counterspy **12** counteragent

undercroft
5 crypt, vault **7** chamber **8** catacomb

underdeveloped
7 dwarfed, stunted **8** backward **10** behindhand **13** unprogressive

underdog
4 prey **5** loser **6** victim **8** casualty **9** dark horse

underdone
4 rare

underestimate
8 disprize, minimize **9** underrate **10** undervalue

undergarment
3 bra **4** slip **5** teddy **6** bodice, briefs, cilise, corset, girdle, shorts, skivvy, undies **7** chemise, dessous, drawers, panties, step-ins **8** flimsies, knickers, lingerie, pretties, skivvies **9** brassiere, petticoat, underwear **10** foundation

undergo
3 bow, see **4** bear, have, know, pass **5** abide, carry, defer, serve, yield **6** endure, submit, suffer **7** sustain **8** tolerate **10** experience

undergoer
suffix: **2** ee

undergraduate
4 coed **6** junior, senior **7** student **8** freshman **9** sophomore

underground
5 train **6** hidden, secret, subway **7** beneath, illegal, off-beat **8** hypogeal, hypogean **9** underfoot **10** undercover, underearth **11** disapproved **12** subterranean **13** surreptitious **14** counterculture

underhand
3 sly **4** mean, wily **5** shady **6** crafty, secret, shifty, sneaky, tricky, unfair **7** crooked, cunning, devious, furtive, hangdog, oblique, stealth **8** guileful, indirect, sinister, sneaking **9** deceitful, dishonest, insidious **10** circuitous, fraudulent **11** duplicitous

underhanded
3 sly **4** mean **5** shady **6** secret, shifty, sneaky, unfair **7** devious **8** guileful, indirect, sneaking, unfairly **9** deceitful **10** circuitous, fraudulent **11** clandestine, duplicitous, shorthanded, undermanned **12** understaffed

underived
5 prime **7** primary **8** original **9** primitive

underlease
6 sublet **8** sublease, underlet

underlet
6 sublet **8** sublease **10** underlease

underlie
4 bear **7** subtend, support

underline
4 mark **6** legend, play up, stress **7** caption, feature **9** emphasize, italicize **10** underscore

underling
5 scrub **6** menial, minion **8** inferior **9** secondary, subaltern **11** subordinate **12** poor relation

underlying
5 basal, basic, vital **6** bottom, covert **7** crucial, needful, obscure, primary, radical **8** cardinal, critical, implicit **9** elemental, essential, necessary, primitive **10** elementary, substratal **11** fundamental **12** foundational **13** indispensable

Under Milk Wood author
6 Thomas (Dylan)

undermine
3 sap **4** cave, foil, ruin **5** blunt, drain, erode, wreck **6** impair, thwart, weaken **7** cripple, disable, founder, subvert, unbrace **8** enfeeble, sabotage, supplant **9** attenuate, frustrate **10** debilitate, demoralize **12** unstrengthen

undermost
6 bottom, lowest **9** lowermost **10** bottommost, nethermost, rock-bottom

underneath
4 sole **5** below **6** bottom, secret **9** underside **10** undercover **12** undersurface **13** surreptitious
prefix: **5** intra

underpin
4 base, prop, root, seat, stay **5** brace, shore **7** justify, support **8** buttress, maintain **12** substantiate

underpinning
4 base, prop, root, seat, stay **5** basis, brace, shore **6** column, ground **7** bedrock, footing, seating, support **8** buttress **10** foundation, groundwork, substratum **12** substruction, substructure **13** underpropping

underpowered
4 slow, weak **6** anemic **8** sluggish

underprivileged
4 poor **5** needy **7** hapless, unlucky **8** deprived, ill-fated **9** depressed **10** ill-starred **11** handicapped, un-

fortunate **12** impoverished **13** disadvantaged

underprize
5 decry, lower **7** devalue **9** devaluate, write down **10** depreciate, devalorize, undervalue

underprop
4 stay **5** brace, shore **6** buoy up, uphold **7** bolster, support, sustain **8** buttress

underpropping
4 prop, stay **5** brace, shore **6** column **7** support **8** buttress

underrate
5 decry, lower **7** devalue **8** discount, mark down, write off **9** devaluate, write down **10** depreciate, devalorize, undervalue **13** underestimate

underscore
6 play up, stress **7** feature **9** emphasize, italicize, underline

undersexed
4 cold **6** frigid **9** inhibited **11** passionless **12** unresponsive

underside
4 sole **6** bottom **10** underneath **12** undersurface
combining form: **6** infero

undersized
4 puny **5** dwarf, runty, scrub, small **6** little **7** scrubby, stunted

understand
3 con, dig, get, ken, see **4** have, know, sabe, take, twig **5** catch, fancy, grasp, guess, infer, savvy, seize, sense, think **6** accept, assume, deduce, expect, fathom, figure, follow, gather, reason, take in **7** believe, cognize, discern, imagine, presume, realize, suppose, surmise, suspect **8** conceive, conclude, consider, perceive **9** apprehend, interpret, penetrate **10** appreciate, comprehend, conjecture

understandable
3 lay **5** clear, lucid, plain **6** simple **7** popular **8** clear-cut, exoteric, knowable, luminous **9** graspable, unblurred **10** fathomable **11** unambiguous **12** intelligible **13** apprehensible

understanding
3 ken, wit **4** deal, idea **5** grasp, sense **6** accord, humane, import, kindly, notion, reason, treaty **7** compact, concept, empathy, entente, insight, knowing, meaning, message, purport **8** attitude, con-

tract, daylight, judgment, sympathy **9** agreement, awareness, diagnosis, intellect, intuition, knowledge, tolerance **10** acceptance, intendment **11** acceptation, discernment, intelligent, penetration, sympathetic **12** apprehension, intelligence, significance, significancy **13** comprehension, signification

understatement
7 litotes

understood
5 clear, lucid, tacit **6** unsaid **7** implied **8** implicit, inferred, unspoken, wordless **9** unuttered **10** undeclared **11** unexpressed

understudy
6 double **7** stand-in **10** substitute **11** replacement

undertake
2 do, go **3** try **4** dare, pass, seek **5** assay, begin, essay, offer, start **6** accept, assume, engage, incept, pledge, strive, take on, take up **7** attempt, certify, emprise, execute, perform, promise, warrant **8** commence, contract, covenant, endeavor, struggle

undertaker
8 embalmer **9** mortician **12** entrepreneur

undertaking
3 job, try **4** task **5** essay, trial **6** cautio, charge, effort, hassle, scheme, voyage **7** attempt, calling, emprise, emprize, project, venture **8** covenant, endeavor, striving, struggle **9** adventure **10** enterprise **11** proposition

under-the-table
6 covert, secret **7** furtive, sub-rosa **8** stealthy **10** undercover **11** clandestine **13** surreptitious

undertone
4 hint **5** aside, rumor **6** mumble, murmur, mutter **7** inkling, subtone, whisper **8** overtone **10** suggestion **11** association, connotation, implication, susurration

undertow
4 eddy **6** vortex **7** current, riptide, sea puss **8** seapoose, sea purse

undervalue
see **underrate**

underwater
9 submarine **10** subaquatic, subaqueous
breathing apparatus: **5** scuba
captain: **4** Nemo
chamber: **7** caisson

device: **8** paravane
missile: **7** torpedo
sound detector: **5** sonar

underwear
see **undergarment**

underwood
5 frith **7** boscage, coppice **10** underbrush **11** undergrowth

underworld
4 hell **5** abyss, hades, Orcus, Sheol **6** Erebus, Tophet **7** Gehenna, inferno, xibalba **8** gangland **9** barathrum **11** netherworld, Pandemonium
boatman: **6** Charon
deity: **3** Dis **4** Bran **5** Pluto **6** Osiris **8** Dispater
goddess: **6** Hecate **10** Persephone
organization: **5** Mafia
relating to: **8** chthonic
watchdog: **8** Cerberus

underwrite
4 back, sign **6** assure, insure, pay for **7** endorse, finance, sponsor, support **9** subscribe

undesigning
4 real, true **6** honest, simple **7** artless, genuine, sincere **9** unfeigned **10** heart-whole **12** undissembled

undesirable
8 unwanted **9** unwelcome **10** ill-favored **12** inadmissible, unacceptable **13** exceptionable, objectionable

undesired
8 unsought, unwanted, unwished **9** unwelcome **10** quenchless

undestroyable
see **indestructible**

undetermined
3 dim **5** faint, unset, vague **6** bleary **7** dubious, obscure, pendent, pending, shadowy, unclear **8** aoristic, doubtful **9** equivocal, undecided, undefined, unsettled **10** ill-defined, indistinct

undeveloped
5 crude **6** latent **7** archaic **8** backward, immature, juvenile **9** primitive, unevolved **10** behindhand, persistent **13** unprogressive

undiluted
4 mere, neat, pure **5** plain, sheer **6** simple **7** perfect, unmixed **8** absolute, straight **9** unalloyed **11** unmitigated, unqualified **13** unadulterated

undiplomatic
5 brash **8** tactless **9** impolitic, maladroit, unpolitic, untactful

undisciplined
4 wild 6 unruly, wanton 8 untoward 9 fractious, untrained 11 intractable 12 recalcitrant, ungovernable, unmanageable

undisclosed
6 hidden, sealed, secret 8 ulterior 12 confidential

undisguised
4 bald, open 5 frank, overt, plain 6 candid 9 barefaced 11 openhearted, unconcealed, unvarnished 12 undissembled 13 undissembling

undissembled
4 open, real, true 5 frank, plain 6 candid, honest 7 genuine, sincere 9 unfeigned 10 heart-whole 11 openhearted, unconcealed, undesigning, undisguised, unvarnished

undistinguished
5 gross 6 common 8 mediocre, noteless 9 unnotable 12 unnoteworthy

undistorted
4 just, true 5 clear, right 6 strict 8 faithful 9 veracious, veridical

undivided
3 one 5 fixed, total, whole 6 entire, intact 8 complete, unbroken 10 continuous, unswerving 12 concentrated, undistracted

undo
3 ope 4 have, open, raze, ruin 5 abate, annul, loose, quash, unfix, untie, wrack, wreck 6 defeat, diddle, negate, outfox, outwit, seduce, unbind, unmake, unshut, unsnap, unstop 7 abolish, debauch, destroy, nullify, unblock, unbuild, unclose, unframe, unloose, unravel, vitiate 8 abrogate, decimate, demolish, outreach, outslick, outsmart, unfasten, unloosen 9 disengage, outjockey, overreach 10 annihilate, invalidate, outgeneral 11 outmaneuver

undoing
4 bane, ruin 8 downfall 9 destroyer, overthrow, ruination 11 destruction

undoubtedly
4 well 5 truly 6 easily, indeed, really, surely 7 frankly 11 doubtlessly, indubitably

undoubtful
6 secure 7 assured 8 sanguine 9 confident 11 self-assured 13 self-confident

undress
see **unclothe**

undressed
3 raw 4 nude, rude 5 crude, naked, rough 6 unclad, unhewn 8 buff-bare, stripped, unformed, unworked 9 au naturel, roughhewn, unclothed 10 stark-naked, unfinished, unpolished 11 unfashioned

undue
5 dizzy, inapt, inept, unapt 7 extreme 8 ill-timed, improper, towering, untimely 9 excessive, unfitting 10 exorbitant, immoderate, inordinate, unsuitable 11 extravagant, unwarranted 12 unreasonable, unseasonable 13 inappropriate, unjustifiable, unwarrantable

undulant fever
11 brucellosis

undulate
4 roll, swag, sway, wave 5 snake, swing 6 ripple 7 slidder, slither 9 fluctuate

unduly
3 too 4 ever, over 6 overly 8 overfull, overmuch 9 extremely, immensely 11 excessively 12 inordinately

undutiful
7 impious

undying
7 ageless, endless, eternal 8 immortal, unending 9 continual, deathless, unceasing 10 continuing, persistent 12 imperishable, interminable, unquenchable

uneager
3 shy 5 loath 6 afraid, averse 8 backward, hesitant 9 reluctant, unwilling 10 indisposed 11 disinclined

unearth
3 dig, see 4 hear, show 5 delve, learn 6 exhume, expose, reveal, tumble 7 catch on, exhibit, find out, uncover 8 disclose, discover 9 ascertain, determine

unearthly
4 eery 5 balmy, crazy, eerie, loony, silly, wacky, weird 6 absurd, insane, spooky 7 awesome, foolish, uncanny, ungodly 8 numinous, superior, terrific 9 appalling, fantastic 10 miraculous, mysterious, outlandish, superhuman, suprahuman 12 preposterous, supermundane, supernatural, supranatural 13 preternatural

unease
4 care 5 worry 6 unrest 7 anxiety, concern, tension, trouble 8 disquiet 9 abashment, confusion 10 discomfort, discontent, solicitude 11 concernment, displeasure, disquietude, uptightness 12 apprehension, discomfiture, discomposure 13 disconcertion, embarrassment

uneasiness
see **unease**

uneasy
4 edgy 5 nervy, shaky, tense 6 unsure 7 anxious, awkward, careful, fidgety, restive, suspect, unquiet, uptight, worried 8 agitated, doubtful, restless 9 ambiguous, concerned, difficult, disturbed, doubtable, perturbed, uncertain, unrestful, unsettled 10 borderline, disquieted, precarious, solicitous, unpeaceful, untranquil 13 uncomfortable

uneducated
4 rude 6 simple 8 ignorant, untaught 9 benighted, untutored 10 illiterate, unlettered, unschooled 11 empty-headed, know-nothing 12 uninstructed

unembellished
3 dry 5 plain 6 simple 7 austere, prosaic 9 unadorned 11 undecorated, unelaborate, ungarnished 12 unbeautied, unornamented 13 unembroidered, unpretentious

unembroidered
see **unembellished**

unemotional
3 dry, icy 4 cold, cool 5 chill, stoic, stony 6 frigid 7 callous, glacial, stoical 8 obdurate 9 heartless, impassive, unfeeling 10 hardboiled, phlegmatic 11 coldhearted, hardhearted, indifferent 12 stonyhearted 13 dispassionate, unsympathetic

unemployed
4 free, idle 5 fired 6 otiose, unused 7 jobless, laid off 8 inactive, workless 9 unengaged 10 unoccupied

unending
7 eternal, undying 8 constant, immortal, timeless 9 ceaseless, continual, perpetual 10 continuous 11 amaranthine, everlasting, unremitting 12 interminable 13 uninterrupted

unenlightened
7 heathen 8 backward, ignorant 9 benighted 13 unprogressive

unenthusiastic
4 cold, cool 8 lukewarm 9 apathetic, unexcited 10 spiritless 11 perfunctory 12 uninterested

unequal
5 impar 6 uneven, unfair, unjust, unlike 7 distant, diverse, unalike, various 8 inferior, lopsided, variable 9 different, disparate, divergent, irregular, unsimilar 10 asymmetric, dissimilar, off-balance 11 fluctuating 12 overbalanced 13 unsymmetrical
combining form: 4 anis 5 aniso

unequalable
7 supreme 8 towering, ultimate 10 preeminent, surpassing 11 unmatchable 12 incomparable, transcendant 13 unsurpassable

unequaled
4 only 5 alone 6 unique 7 supreme 8 nonesuch, peerless 9 matchless, unmatched, unrivaled 10 surpassing 11 unparagoned 12 unparalleled 13 unprecedented

unequipped
5 unfit 8 unfitted 9 incapable 10 ineligible, unprepared 11 incompetent, unqualified 12 disqualified

unequivocal
5 clear, plain 6 direct, patent 7 certain, decided, evident, obvious 8 apparent, definite, distinct, explicit, manifest, palpable, positive 10 undeniable 11 categorical, indubitable 12 indisputable, undisputable 13 incontestable, uncontestable

unerasable
see **inerasable**

unerring
4 dead, sure, true 5 exact 7 certain, correct, precise 8 accurate, reliable 9 unfailing 10 dependable, infallible 11 trustworthy

unescapable
see **inevitable**

unessential
8 needless, unneeded 9 extrinsic, unneedful 10 unrequired 11 dispensable, uncalled-for, unimportant, unnecessary 13 insubstantial

unethical
5 venal, wrong 6 amoral 7 corrupt, immoral 9 mercenary 10 praetorian 12 unprincipled, unscrupulous

unevadable
see **inevitable**

uneven
3 odd 4 wavy 5 bumpy, erose, harsh, jaggy, rough 6 craggy, jagged, patchy, rugged, spotty, unfair, unjust, unlike 7 scraggy, streaky, unequal, unlevel, varying 8 asperous, lopsided, scabrous, scraggly, scratchy, unsmooth 9 anomalous, differing, disparate, irregular 10 asymmetric, discrepant, ill-matched, off-balance, unbalanced 11 fluctuating 12 inconsistent, overbalanced 13 unsymmetrical

unevenness
4 bump, wave 7 anomaly 8 asperity, imparity 9 disparity, roughness 10 inequality 12 irregularity 13 disproportion

uneventful
6 common 7 prosaic 8 ordinary 11 commonplace 12 unnoteworthy 13 unexceptional

unexampled
4 lone, only, sole, solo 5 alone 6 unique 8 singular, solitary 12 unrepeatable

unexceptional
5 usual 6 common, decent 7 prosaic, regular 8 adequate, all right, ordinary 9 tolerable 10 acceptable, sufficient, uneventful 11 commonplace 12 satisfactory, unnoteworthy 13 unimpeachable

unexcited
4 calm 5 level, stoic 7 stoical 8 tranquil

unexciting
4 dead, dull, tame 6 boring 7 prosaic 13 uninteresting

unexpectedly
5 aback, short 6 sudden 7 unaware 8 abruptly, suddenly, unawares 10 unawaredly 12 accidentally

unexpended
6 saving 7 reserve, surplus 8 left over 9 remaining

unexperienced
see **inexperienced**

unexpired
5 alive, valid 8 left over 9 operative, remaining

unexplicit
4 hazy 5 vague 7 obscure, unclear 8 nebulous, nubilous 9 ambiguous, equivocal, tenebrous, uncertain 10 indistinct

unexpressed
5 tacit 6 silent, unsaid 7 implied 8 implicit, inferred, unspoken, wordless 9 unuttered, voiceless 10 undeclared, understood

unfadable
4 fast 7 sunfast 9 colorfast

unfaded
5 fresh 6 bright

unfailing
4 same, sure 6 deadly 7 certain 8 constant, reliable, surefire, unerring 9 unvarying 10 consistent, infallible, invariable, unchanging, unflagging 13 inexhaustible

unfair
4 foul, hard 5 wrong 6 biased, shabby, uneven, unjust 7 devious, unequal 8 wrongful 9 dishonest, inequable, unethical 11 inequitable, underhanded, unequitable, unrighteous 12 dishonorable

unfairness
5 wrong 8 inequity 9 injustice 10 unjustness

unfaithful
5 false 6 untrue 7 infidel, traitor, unloyal 8 disloyal, recreant, turncoat 9 faithless 10 adulterous, inaccurate, perfidious, traitorous 11 treacherous 13 untrustworthy

unfaltering
4 firm, sure, true 5 brave 6 steady 7 abiding 8 enduring, unerring 9 steadfast 11 unqualified 12 never-failing, wholehearted 13 unquestioning

unfamiliar
3 new 6 exotic 7 curious, foreign, strange, unaware, unknown 8 ignorant, peculiar 9 oblivious, unknowing, unwitting 10 remarkable, uninformed 11 incognizant 12 inconversant, unaccustomed, unacquainted, uninstructed

unfamiliarity
9 ignorance, innocence, inscience, nescience 11 unawareness 13 unknowingness

unfashionable
5 dated, passé 6 démodé 8 outmoded 9 out-of-date

unfasten
4 free, open, undo 5 loose, unbar, unfix, unpin, untie 6 detach,

loosen, unbind, unlace, unlock, unsnap **7** unhitch, unloose **8** unanchor, unloosen, untether **9** disengage

unfathomable
7 abysmal **8** profound **9** plumbless, soundless **10** bottomless, fathomless, mysterious, unknowable **11** inscrutable, ungraspable **12** impenetrable, incognizable

unfavorable
3 bad, ill **4** evil, foul, poor **6** averse, unfair, unkind **7** adverse, awkward, froward, hostile, unhappy **8** backward, contrary, inimical, negative, sinister, unkindly **11** detrimental
prefix: **3** dys

unfavorably
4 awry **5** amiss, badly, wrong **6** afield, astray

unfearful
4 bold **5** brave **7** valiant **8** fearless, intrepid, valorous **9** audacious, dauntless, undaunted **10** courageous

unfeasible
10 impossible, infeasible, unworkable **11** impractical **12** irrealizable, unattainable, unrealizable **13** impracticable

unfeeling
4 cold, dead, dull, hard, numb **5** crass, cruel, harsh, stern, stony, surly, tough **6** asleep, brutal, leaden, marble, numbed, severe, stolid, unkind **7** callous **8** benumbed, churlish, deadened, exacting, hardened, obdurate, pitiless, ruthless **9** apathetic, bloodless, crotchety, heartless, inanimate, indurated, insensate, merciless, senseless, unamiable, uncordial **10** hardboiled, insensible, insentient **11** cold-blooded, coldhearted, hardhearted, insensitive, ironhearted, unemotional **12** anesthetized, cantankerous, curmudgeonly, roughhearted, stonyhearted **13** marblehearted, unsusceptible, unsympathetic

unfeigned
4 open, real, true **6** hearty, honest **7** genuine, natural, sincere **9** heartfelt **11** undesigning **12** undissembled, wholehearted

unfertile
see **infertile**

unfinished
3 raw **4** rude **5** crude, rough **6** unhewn **7** jackleg, sketchy **8** dabbling, unformed, ungifted, unworked **9** imperfect, roughhewn, undressed, unskilled **10** amateurish, dilettante, incomplete, unpolished **11** unfashioned **12** dilettantish, dilettantist

Unfinished Symphony composer
8 Schubert (Franz)

unfit
3 bad **4** sick **5** inapt, inept, wrong **6** faulty, unmeet **7** awkward, unhandy **8** bungling, disabled, improper, inexpert, unsuited **9** illsuited, incapable, maladroit **10** blundering, discordant, illadapted, ineligible, unbecoming, unequipped, unskillful, unsuitable **11** handicapped, heavyhanded, incompetent, incongruous, inefficient, maladjusted, uncongenial, unqualified **12** disqualified, incompatible, infelicitous, inharmonious, unproficient **13** inappropriate, incapacitated
Jewish law: **4** tref **6** trefah **7** terefah

unfitting
5 inapt, inept, unapt **8** improper, unseemly **10** malapropos, unbecoming, unsuitable **13** inappropriate

unfix
4 undo **5** loose **6** detach, loosen, unbind **7** unloose **8** abstract, dissolve, uncouple, unfasten, unloosen, unsettle **9** disengage **10** disconnect, dissociate **12** disassociate

unflagging
6 steady **8** constant, tireless, untiring **9** weariless **10** unwearying **11** unweariable **13** indefatigable, inexhaustible

unflappable
4 cool, easy **7** relaxed **8** composed **9** collected, unruffled **10** nonchalant **13** imperturbable

unflawed
7 perfect **8** absolute, flawless **9** fleckless **10** impeccable **11** noteperfect **12** indefectible

unfledged
5 green, young **6** callow, infant, unripe **8** immature, juvenile, youthful **11** undeveloped, unfeathered

unflexible
see **inflexible**

unflinching
4 firm, grim **5** level **6** mortal **7** staunch **8** resolute, ruthless **9** merciless, steadfast **10** implacable, ironfisted, relentless, unwavering, unyielding **11** unrelenting **12** unappeasable

unfluctuating
4 even **6** stable, steady **7** equable, stabile, uniform **8** constant **9** unvarying **10** unchanging

unfold
4 open, show **5** break, burst, solve **6** deploy, evince, evolve, expand, expose, extend, fan out, flower, reveal, spread, unfurl, unroll, untuck, unwrap **7** blossom, clear up, develop, display, divulge, dope out, exhibit, explain, release, resolve, unravel **8** decipher, disclose, dissolve, evidence, manifest, unriddle **9** elaborate, explicate, figure out, outspread, puzzle out **10** outstretch **11** demonstrate

unforbearing
9 impatient **10** intolerant **11** unindulgent

unforced
4 easy **7** natural, willful, willing, witting **9** voluntary **10** deliberate **11** intentional **12** unprescribed

unforeseen
6 sudden **10** accidental, unexpected

unforgivable
9 untenable **10** inexpiable **11** inexcusable **12** indefensible, unpardonable **13** unjustifiable

unformed
4 rude **5** crude, rough **6** callow, unhewn **8** formless, inchoate, unshaped, unworked **9** amorphous, roughhewn, shapeless, uncreated, undressed **10** unfinished, unpolished **11** undeveloped, unfashioned

unfortunate
3 bad, ill, sad **4** dire, poor **5** inept **6** woeful, wretch **7** awkward, hapless, malefic, unhappy, unlucky **8** grievous, ill-fated, luckless, untoward, wretched **9** graceless, ill-chosen, miserable **10** afflictive, calamitous, deplorable, ill-starred, lamentable **11** distressing, regrettable, star-crossed **12** inauspicious,

infelicitous, misfortunate, unsuccessful **13** heartbreaking

unfounded
    4 idle, vain **8** baseless **9** deceptive, dishonest **10** bottomless, chimerical, gratuitous, groundless, mendacious, misleading, ungrounded, untruthful **11** uncalledfor, unwarranted

unfrequented
    5 empty **6** lonely **8** isolated, solitary

unfriendly
    3 ill **4** cold, cool, foul **5** chill **6** bitter, chilly, fierce, frosty, remote **7** hostile **8** inimical, unsocial **10** inimicable

unfruitful
    6 barren, effete, wasted **7** sterile, useless **8** impotent, infecund **9** infertile **12** unproductive, unprofitable

unfurl
    4 open **6** spread, unfold, unroll, unwind **7** develop

unfurnished
    4 bare **6** vacant

unfussy
    6 casual, common, dégagé **7** relaxed **8** informal **9** easygoing **10** unreserved **11** low-pressure **13** unconstrained

ungainly
    5 gawky, lanky, splay **6** clumsy **7** awkward, boorish, lumpish, uncouth **8** clownish, lubberly, unlicked, unwieldy **9** lumbering, maladroit **10** blundering **11** elephantine, splathering

ungarnished
    3 dry **5** plain **6** modest, simple **9** unadorned **11** inelaborate, unelaborate **12** unornamented **13** unembellished, unembroidered

ungenerous
    4 mean, puny **5** close, harsh, nasty, petty, small, tight **6** paltry, peanut, shabby, stingy **7** miserly **8** grudging, picayune, trifling, ungiving **9** niggardly, penurious **12** inconsequent, parsimonious **13** pennypinching

ungenuine
    7 bastard **8** spurious **10** apocryphal **11** unauthentic

ungiving
    4 mean **5** close, tight **6** stingy

7 miserly, save-all **9** niggardly, penurious **11** tightfisted **12** parsimonious

ungodly
    see **unholy**

ungovernable
    4 wild **6** unruly **7** froward **8** untoward **9** fractious, unbridled **10** disorderly, headstrong, rebellious **11** intractable **12** recalcitrant, unmanageable **13** irrepressible, undisciplined

ungoverned
    8 uncurbed **9** audacious **10** unhampered **11** uninhibited, untrammeled **12** unrestrained

ungraceful
    5 lanky **6** clumsy **7** angular, awkward, halting **8** untoward **9** inelegant

ungracious
    4 hard, rude **5** gruff, sharp, short **7** uncivil **8** churlish, impolite, snappish **9** offensive **10** unmannerly, unpleasant **11** disgracious, ill-mannered, impertinent, thoughtless, uncalled-for, uncourteous **12** discourteous, unattractive **13** disrespectful, inconsiderate, unceremonious

ungraded
    3 raw **5** crude **6** impure, native **8** unsorted **9** run-of-mine, unrefined

ungraspable
    10 unknowable **12** impenetrable, incognizable, unfathomable

ungrateful
    4 foul **6** unkind **7** hideous **8** horrible **9** loathsome, offensive, repellent, repugnant, repulsive, revolting, thankless **10** disgusting, unthankful **13** unappreciated

ungratified
    9 uncontent **10** discontent, malcontent **11** disgruntled, uncontented, unsatisfied **12** discontented, dissatisfied, malcontented

ungrounded
    8 baseless **9** unfounded **10** bottomless, gratuitous, groundless, uninformed **11** uncalled-for, unwarranted **12** uninstructed

unguarded
    6 unwary **7** unalert **8** careless **9** imprudent **10** incautious, unvigilant, unwatchful **11** defenseless, thoughtless, unprotected

unguent
    4 balm **5** cream, salve **6** cerate, ceroma, chrism **7** unction **8** ointment **9** lubricant

ungulate
    3 hog, pig **4** deer **5** horse, tapir **6** hoofed **8** amblypod, elephant **10** rhinoceros

unhallowed
    6 impure, unholy **7** demonic, impious, profane, satanic, ungodly **8** demoniac, demonian, devilish, diabolic, fiendish **10** desecrated, irreverent, serpentine **11** diabolonian **13** irreverential

unhampered
    4 free **5** loose **6** direct **8** uncurbed **9** audacious, expedited **10** ungoverned **11** expeditious, uninhibited, untrammeled **12** unrestrained

unhandsome
    4 mean, rude **5** plain **6** homely **7** ill-bred, uncivil **8** impolite, uncomely, unpretty **10** unalluring, unbecoming, ungracious **11** disgracious, ill-mannered, impertinent, unbeauteous, unbeautiful **12** discourteous, unattractive **13** disrespectful

unhandy
    5 inapt, inept, unapt **6** clumsy, gauche, wooden **7** awkward, halting, inadept, unhappy **8** bumbling, cumbrous, inexpert, unfacile, unwieldy **9** ham-handed, maladroit, ponderous **10** cumbersome, unskillful **11** undexterous **12** inconvenient, unproficient

unhappiness
    3 woe **5** blues, dolor, dumps, gloom, grief, worry **6** misery, mishap, sorrow, unrest **7** dismals, illluck, sadness **9** dejection **10** depression, melancholy **12** mournfulness, wretchedness

unhappy
    3 bad, sad **4** evil, sour **5** black, bleak, inept, sorry **6** clumsy, dismal, dreary, gauche, gloomy, rotten, wooden **7** awkward, halting, joyless, unhandy, unlucky **8** bumbling, chisely, dejected, ill-fated, luckless, mournful, saddened, untoward, wretched **9** cheerless, graceless, ill-chosen, maladroit, woebegone **10** depressant, ill-starred, melancholy, oppressive, unpleasant **11** dispiriting, displeasing, heavyhanded, melancholic, star-crossed, unfortunate **12** disagreeable,

heavyhearted, inauspicious, infelicitous, misfortunate

unharmed
4 safe **6** unhurt **9** unscathed **10** scatheless

unharness
6 disarm, divest, ungear **7** outspan, unhitch, unhorse, unstrap **8** untackle

unhealthiness
7 disease, illness, malaise **8** debility, disorder, sickness **9** infirmity **10** affliction, feebleness, infirmness, sickliness **11** decrepitude **12** diseasedness **13** indisposition

unhealthy
3 bad, ill **4** sick **5** hairy, risky **6** chancy, infirm, putrid, queasy, rotten, sickly, unhale, wicked **7** corrupt, noisome, noxious, unsound, vicious **8** depraved, diseased, perilous, perverse **9** dangerous, hazardous, nefarious **10** degenerate, flagitious, insalutary, jeopardous, unsalutary, villainous **11** treacherous, unwholesome **12** insalubrious

unheard-of
3 new **7** obscure, strange, unfamed, unknown, unnoted **8** nameless **10** unrenowned **12** uncelebrated **13** extraordinary, unprecedented

unheeding
4 deaf **8** careless, feckless, heedless, ignoring, uncaring **9** unrecking **10** unnoticing, unthinking, unwatchful **11** inadvertent, inattentive, inobservant, insensitive, thoughtless, unobservant, unobserving **12** disregarding, irreflective, unperceiving, unreflective

unhesitating
4 free **5** ready **8** haltless **9** immediate **10** forthright **12** wholehearted

unhinge
4 turn **5** craze, upset **6** bother, flurry, frenzy, madden, sicken, untune **7** agitate, derange, disturb, fluster, perturb **8** disorder, disquiet, distract, unsettle **9** unbalance **10** discompose

unholy
5 amiss, rough **6** guilty, impure, sinful, wicked **7** corrupt, impious, profane, raucous, ungodly **8** blamable, blameful, culpable, dreadful, fiendish, god-awful, improper, indecent, shocking, unseemly, untoward **9** atheistic, atrocious, barbarous,

frightful, malicious, unearthly **10** censurable, indecorous, indelicate, irreverent, malodorous, outrageous, scandalous, unbecoming, undecorous, unhallowed **11** blameworthy, unbelieving, unchristian, uncivilized **13** demeritorious, irreverential, reprehensible

unhorse
5 pitch, throw **6** topple, tumble, unseat **7** buck off, overset **8** dislodge, dismount, overturn, unsaddle **9** overthrow

unhurried
4 easy, slow **7** laggard, unhasty **8** dilatory **9** leisurely **10** deliberate

unhurt
4 safe **5** sound, whole **6** entire, intact **7** perfect **8** unbroken, unharmed, unmarred **9** undamaged, uninjured **10** unimpaired

unicity
7 oneness **8** uniquity **10** singleness, uniqueness

unicorn
antelope: **5** takin
Chinese: **5** kilin, kylin **6** chi-lin
fish: **7** narwhal

unidealistic
4 hard **5** sober **9** practical, pragmatic, realistic **10** hard-boiled, hardheaded **11** down-to-earth, unfantastic **12** matter-of-fact

unification
5 union **6** hookup, merger **7** joining, linkage, melding, merging **8** alliance, coupling, mergence **9** coalition **10** connection **11** affiliation, coadunation, combination **12** interlocking **13** consolidation

uniform
4 akin, even, like, suit **5** alike, blues, dress, equal, khaki, level **6** agnate, livery, outfit, stable, steady, whites **7** equable, ordered, orderly, regular, similar, stabile **8** constant, parallel **9** analogous, consonant, unvarying **10** comparable, compatible, consistent, invariable, monotonous, unchanging **11** homogeneous **13** corresponding, unfluctuating
combining form: **2** is **3** iso

uniformity
7 oneness **8** equality, evenness, monotony, sameness

uniformly
6 always, evenly, flatly, smooth **8** smoothly

unify
3 tie **4** bind **5** blend, merge, order, unite **6** cement **7** arrange, compact **8** coalesce, organize **9** harmonize, integrate **10** articulate, centralize, symphonize, synthesize **11** concatenate, concentrate, consolidate, orchestrate, systematize

unilluminated
3 dim **4** dark, dusk **5** dusky, murky **6** gloomy **7** obscure **9** lightless, tenebrous **10** caliginous

unimaginable
4 rare **6** unique **7** unusual **8** singular, uncommon, unwonted **10** incredible, unknowable, unordinary **11** exceptional, incogitable, unthinkable **12** insupposable, unbelievable **13** extraordinary, inconceivable

unimaginative
4 dull **7** limited, literal, prosaic **10** pedestrian

unimpaired
4 free **5** fresh, sound, whole **6** entire, intact, unhurt **7** perfect **8** unbroken, unmarred **9** undamaged, uninjured

unimpassioned
4 calm, cold **5** sober, stoic **6** placid, steady, stolid **8** moderate, tranquil **9** impassive, temperate **10** impersonal, phlegmatic **11** cold-blooded, emotionless **12** matter-of-fact

unimpeachable
6 common, decent **8** adequate, all right **9** blameless, faultless, tolerable **10** acceptable, sufficient **12** satisfactory **13** unexceptional

unimportant
5 light, minor, petty, small **6** casual, little, paltry **7** trivial **9** small-beer **10** negligible, shoestring **13** insignificant

unindifferent
6 biased **7** colored, partial **8** one-sided, partisan **9** jaundiced, unneutral **10** prejudiced **11** tendentious **12** prepossessed

uninformed
7 unaware **8** ignorant **9** oblivious, unknowing, unwitting **10** unfamiliar **11** incognizant **12** inconversant, unacquainted, uninstructed

uninhabited
4 wild **5** empty **6** desert, vacant **8** deserted, desolate

uninhibited

3 lax **4** free, open **5** loose **8** uncurbed **9** audacious **10** boisterous, ungoverned, unhampered **11** untrammeled **12** unrestrained

uninitiate

4 tyro **7** amateur, dabbler **9** smatterer **10** dilettante **11** abecedarian

uninjured

5 sound, whole **6** entire, intact, unhurt **7** perfect **8** unbroken, unmarred **9** undamaged **10** unimpaired

uninspired

4 dull **6** stodgy **7** sterile **9** ponderous **10** uncreative, unoriginal **11** elephantine, heavy-footed, heavy-handed, noncreative, uninventive **13** unoriginative

uninstructed

4 rude **7** unaware **8** ignorant, untaught **9** benighted, oblivious, unknowing, untutored, unwitting **10** illiterate, uneducated, unfamiliar, uninformed, unlettered **11** empty-headed, incognizant, know-nothing **12** inconversant, unacquainted

unintelligent

4 dumb **5** brute **6** obtuse, simple, stupid, unwise **7** asinine, fatuous, foolish, vacuous, witless **8** ignorant, mindless **9** brainless, insensate, senseless **10** irrational, weakheaded, weak-minded

unintended

see **unintentional**

unintentional

6 chance, random **9** causeless, haphazard, undevised, unplanned, unthought, unwitting **10** accidental, undesigned, unexpected, unforeseen, unpurposed, unthinking **11** inadvertent, purposeless, unlooked-for **13** unanticipated

uninterested

5 aloof **6** casual, remote **8** detached **9** incurious, uncurious, withdrawn **11** indifferent, unconcerned

uninteresting

3 dry **4** arid, drab, dull, flat **5** dusty, stale **6** boring, jejune, prolix, stupid **7** humdrum, insipid, tedious **8** bromidic, tiresome, weariful **9** colorless, dryasdust, wearisome **10** unexciting

uninterrupted

6 direct **7** endless, eternal, through **8** constant, straight, unending **9** ceaseless, continual, incessant, perpetual, unceasing **10** continuous **11** everlasting, unremitting **12** interminable

uninvited

7 unasked **8** unbidden, unsought **11** unrequested

union

4 bloc, club, seam **5** alloy, group, guild, hansa, hanse, joint, order **6** enosis, fusion, league, merger **7** amalgam, joining, melding, merging, society **8** alliance, congress, coupling, junction, juncture, marriage, mergence, sodality, together **9** anschluss, coalition **10** connection, federation, fellowship **11** association, brotherhood, coadunation, coalescence, combination, confederacy, unification **13** confederation, consolidation

combining form: 3 zyg **4** gamy, zygo **6** gamous

labor: 3 AFL, CIO, UAW **5** ILGWU

of two gametes: 7 zygoses (plural), zygosis

Union Of Soviet Socialist Republics

see **U.S.S.R.**

unique

3 odd, one **4** lone, only, rare, sole, solo **5** alone, queer **6** single **7** special, strange, unusual **8** peculiar, peerless, separate, singular, solitary, uncommon, unwonted **9** matchless, unequaled, unmatched, unrivaled **10** particular, unexampled, unordinary **11** exceptional, unparagoned **12** unparalleled, unrepeatable **13** extraordinary

uniqueness

4 mark, note **6** import, moment, oddity **7** oneness, unicity **10** notability, quaintness, singleness **11** curiousness, peculiarity, singularity, strangeness, unusualness **12** memorability, significance

_____-Unis

5 Etats

unit

3 one **4** item **5** digit, group, monad, whole **6** entity **7** element, measure **10** individual

administrative: 6 agency, bureau **8** district

boy scout: 5 troop

educational: 6 course

military: (see at military)

of acceleration: 3 gal

of action: 7 episode

of advertising space: 4 line **6** column **7** milline

of a fire department: 9 battalion

of an element: 4 atom **8** molecule

of angular measure: 6 radian **7** centrad

of area: 4 acre **6** morgen **7** hectare

of astronomical distance: 6 parsec **9** light-year

of brightness: 5 stilb **7** lambert

of capacity: 2 cc, ml **4** gill, peck, pint **5** liter, litre, minim, ounce, quart **6** bushel, firkin, gallon **8** fluidram

of computer information: 3 bit

of conductance: 3 mho **7** siemens

of distance: 4 mile **5** meter **7** furlong

of electricity: 3 amp **4** volt, watt **6** ampere **7** coulomb

of electromotive force: 4 volt

of energy: 3 erg **5** joule **7** quantum **8** watt-hour

of explosive force: 7 megaton

of fineness: 5 carat, karat

of fluidity: 3 rhe

of force: 4 dyne **6** newton **7** poundal

of frequency: 5 hertz **7** fresnel

of grain: 5 sheaf **6** thrave

of heat: 3 BTU **5** therm **7** calorie

of illumination: 3 lux **4** phot

of inductance: 5 gauss, henry

of length: 3 mil **4** foot, inch, yard **5** fermi, meter **6** micron

of loudness: 4 phon, sone **7** decibel

of lumber: 9 board foot

of magnetic flux: 5 weber **7** maxwell

of magnetic induction: 5 tesla

of magnetic intensity: 5 gamma **7** oersted

of magnetomotive force: 7 gilbert

of pressure: 3 bar **4** torr **5** barye **10** atmosphere

of radiation: 3 rad **8** roentgen

of radioactivity: 5 curie

of resistance: 3 ohm

of solar radiation: 7 langley

of sound absorption: 5 sabin

of speech: 4 word **6** toneme **7** phoneme **8** morpheme, syllable

of speed: 3 CPS, MPH, RPM **4** knot

of temperature: 6 degree, kelvin

of time: 3 day **4** beat, bell, hour, week **5** month **6** minute, season, second **8** svedberg

of viscosity: 5 poise

of weight: 3 ton **4** dram, gram, tael **5** carat, grain, ounce, pound, stein, tonne **6** drachm, kantar, gigaton, kiloton, millier, quintal, scruple

ancient Roman: 5 libra

Asian: 5 Picul, tical 6 cattie, miskal
British: 3 tod
Chinese: 5 liang
Hebrew: 5 gerah
Indian: 3 ser 4 tola
Muslim: 4 rotl
Russian: 4 pood
Turkish: 3 oka, oke
of work: 3 erg 5 ergon, joule
social: 4 clan 5 tribe 6 family
7 chapter

unite
3 add, mix, sew, tie, wed 4 ally,
band, bind, bond, fuse, join, knit,
link, weld 5 blend, graft, marry,
merge, unify 6 adhere, adjoin, attach, cement, concur, couple,
gather, league, mingle, relate, solder, splice 7 combine, conjoin,
connect 8 assemble, coadjute, coalesce, compound, copulate, federate 9 affiliate, aggregate, associate, commingle, cooperate
10 amalgamate, federalize 11 concentrate, confederate, incorporate
12 conglutinate

United Arab Emirates
5 Ajman, Dubai 7 Sharjah 8 Abu
Dhabi, Fujairah

United Kingdom
capital: 6 London
monetary unit: 5 pound
part: 5 Wales 7 England
8 Scotland

United Nations
secretary-general: 3 Lie (Trygve)
5 Thant (U) 8 Waldheim (Kurt)
12 Boutros-Ghali (Boutros), Hammarskjold (Dag) 14 Perez de Cuel-
lar (Javier)

unities, dramatic
4 time 5 place 6 action

unity
5 union 7 concord, harmony, oneness, rapport 8 identity, sodality,
soleness, uniquity 9 agreement,
communion, congruity 10 singleness, solidarity, uniformity, uniqueness 11 conformance, conjunction,
singularity 12 selfsameness, singularness 13 individuality

universal
3 all 5 broad, total, whole 6 common, cosmic, entire, global 7 allover, general, generic 8 catholic,
ecumenic, sweeping 9 extensive,
planetary, unlimited, worldwide
10 ecumenical, ubiquitous 11 omnipresent 12 all-embracing, all-inclusive, all-pervading, cosmopolitan
combining form: 3 omn 4 omni

universe
3 all 5 world 6 cosmos, nature,
system 8 creation, megacosm
9 macrocosm 11 macrocosmos
combining form: 4 cosm 5 cosmo

unjust
4 hard 5 cruel, wrong 6 unfair,
wicked 7 unequal 8 improper,
wrongful 9 dishonest, inequable
10 iniquitous 11 inequitable, unequitable, unrighteous

unjustifiable
5 undue 7 invalid 9 untenable
10 inexpiable 11 inexcusable,
unwarranted

unkempt
5 messy 6 frowsy, frowzy, shaggy,
sloppy, unneat, untidy 7 ruffled,
tousled 8 draggled, ill-kempt,
scraggly, slipshod, slovenly, strub-
bly, uncombed 10 disarrayed, disheveled 12 unfastidious

unkind
3 bad, ill 4 mean, vile 5 cruel,
harsh, rough, stern 6 severe 8 ungenial 9 inclement 10 ungenerous,
ungracious 11 unfavorable

unknit
4 undo 5 ravel, relax, untie
7 unravel

unknowable
6 arcane, mystic 8 mystical, numinous 9 enigmatic, mysterial, unguessed 10 cabalistic, mysterious
11 inscrutable, ungraspable
12 impenetrable, incognizable,
unexaminable, unfathomable, unimaginable 13 inconceivable

unknowing
7 unaware 8 ignorant 9 oblivious,
unwitting 10 unfamiliar, uninformed 11 incognizant 12 inconversant, unacquainted, uninstructed

unknown
6 nobody, secret 7 obscure,
strange, unfamed, unnoted 8 nameless 9 anonymous, incognito, unheard-of 10 unfamiliar, unrenowned 12 uncelebrated
Scottish: 6 unkent

unlawful
7 bootleg, illegal, illicit, lawless
8 criminal, improper, wrongful
9 irregular, nefarious 10 contraband, flagitious, iniquitous
11 black-market, intolerable
12 illegitimate 13 exceptionable,
objectionable

unlearned
7 natural 8 ignorant, untaught
9 inerudite, unbookish, untutored
10 illiterate, uneducated, unstudious
11 instinctive, unscholarly

unleash
4 free, vent 5 loose 7 release

unless
3 but 4 save 6 except, saving
7 without 9 excepting

unlettered
see **uneducated**

unlike
7 distant, diverse, unequal, various
9 different, disparate, divergent, unsimilar 10 dissimilar

unlikely
5 unfit 7 dubious 8 doubtful 10 improbable, unsuitable 11 unpromising 12 questionable, unattractive

unlikeness
8 alterity, contrast 9 otherness
10 difference, divergence, divergency 11 discrepancy, distinction
12 disagreement, dissemblance
13 dissimilarity, dissimilitude,
inconsistence

unlimited
4 vast 5 total 6 all-out 7 endless,
full-out 8 infinite 9 boundless, full-
blown, full-scale, unbounded, undefined, universal 10 indefinite,
unconfined, unmeasured 11 measureless, untrammeled 12 immeasurable, totalitarian, unrestricted
13 indeterminate

unload
4 drop, dump, land 5 empty, un-
box 6 debark, remove, unlade, un-
pack, unship, unstow 7 deliver,
lighten, off-load, relieve, uncrate
8 jettison 9 disburden, discharge,
disembark, liquidate, stevedore
11 disencumber

unloose, unloosen
4 undo 5 unfix 6 unbind 7 unrivet
8 unfasten 9 disengage

unloyal
see **disloyal**

unlucky
3 bad, ill 4 dire 7 baleful, baneful,
direful, doomful, fateful, hapless,
ominous, unhappy 8 ill-fated, tragical, untoward 9 ill-boding, ill-
omened 10 calamitous, disastrous,
ill-starred 11 apocalyptic,

cataclysmic, star-crossed, unfortunate **12** catastrophic, misfortunate

unman
4 undo **5** abase, crush, drain, unfit **7** degrade, deplete, exhaust, unnerve **8** castrate, enervate, paralyze, unstring **9** prostrate **10** disqualify, emasculate, impoverish

unmanageable
4 wild **6** unruly **7** restive **8** indocile **9** fractious **10** disorderly **11** indomitable, intractable **12** recalcitrant, ungovernable **13** undisciplined

unmanly
5 sissy **6** coward, craven, prissy **7** chicken, epicene, gutless **8** childish, cowardly, poltroon **9** pansified, sissified, spunkless **10** effeminate **11** lily-livered **12** Miss-Nancyish, poor-spirited **13** pusillanimous

unmannered
4 open, rude **5** frank, plain **6** candid **7** boorish, ill-bred, uncivil **8** impolite, man-to-man **10** ungracious, unmannerly **11** disgracious, openhearted, undisguised, unvarnished **12** discourteous, undissembled **13** disrespectful

unmarred
5 sound, whole **6** entire, intact, unhurt **7** perfect **8** pristine, unbroken

unmarried
4 lone, sole **5** unwed **6** single **10** spouseless

unmask
6 debunk, expose, reveal, show up, unveil **7** uncloak, undress **8** disclose, discover, unshroud

unmatchable
7 supreme **8** towering, ultimate **10** preeminent, surpassing **11** unequalable **12** incomparable, transcendent **13** unsurpassable

unmatched
3 odd **4** only **5** alone **6** unique **8** peerless, unpaired **9** matchless, unequaled, unrivaled **11** unparagoned **12** unparalleled

unmerciful
5 cruel **8** pitiless, ruthless **9** merciless, unpitying **10** relentless

unmethodical
7 cursory, erratic **9** desultory

unmindful
7 unaware **8** careless, heedless **9** forgetful, negligent, oblivious, unwitting **10** neglectful **11** inattentive

unmistakable
4 flat, open **5** clear, frank, plain **6** patent **7** evident, express **8** apparent, distinct, manifest, palpable, univocal

unmitigated
4 mere, pure, rank **5** gross, sheer, utter **6** arrant, damned, simple **7** perfect, unmixed **8** absolute, clearcut, complete, outright **9** out-and-out, unalloyed, undiluted **10** unmodified **11** straight-out, unqualified **13** thoroughgoing, unadulterated

unmixed
4 deep, mere, neat, pure **5** plain, sheer, utter **6** simple **7** perfect, sincere **8** absolute, straight **9** unalloyed, undiluted **11** unmitigated, unqualified **13** unadulterated

unmodern
3 old **5** dated, passé **7** antique, archaic, old-time, vintage **9** out-of-date **10** antiquated, oldfangled **12** old-fashioned

unmodifiable
5 fixed **8** constant, straight **9** immovable, immutable, unmovable **10** inflexible, invariable **11** inalterable, unalterable **12** unchangeable

unmovable
see **immovable**

unmoved
4 calm, cool, firm **5** stony **6** serene **7** adamant **8** obdurate, stubborn, unshaken **9** apathetic, impassive

unmoving
5 inert **6** static **8** immobile, stagnant **10** stationary

unnamed
8 nameless **9** anonymous **10** innominate **12** undesignated

unnatural
6 off-key **7** deviant, uncanny **8** abnormal **9** anomalous, divergent, irregular, unregular **10** superhuman **11** supernormal, supranormal **13** superordinary

unneat
5 messy **6** sloppy, untidy **7** unkempt **8** careless, ill-kempt, slipshod, slovenly, uncombed **12** unfastidious

unnecessary
6 excess, lavish **7** profuse, surplus **8** needless, prodigal **9** redundant **10** gratuitous, unrequired **11** inessential, superfluous, uncalled-for, unessential

unneeded
see **unnecessary**

unnerve
3 sap **5** unman, upset **6** weaken **7** agitate, perturb **8** bewilder, castrate, confound, distract, enervate, enfeeble, unstring **9** undermine **10** emasculate

unneutral
6 biased, warped **7** colored, partial **8** one-sided, partisan **9** jaundiced **10** prejudiced **11** tendentious **12** prepossessed

unnoted
7 obscure, unfamed, unknown **8** nameless **9** unheard-of **10** unobserved, unremarked, unrenowned **12** uncelebrated, unconsidered

unobservant
9 unheeding **10** unnoticing, unwatchful **11** inattentive **12** unperceiving

unobserving
see **unobservant**

unobstructed
4 open **5** clear **8** unclosed

unobtrusive
5 quiet, tasty **7** subdued **8** tasteful **10** restrained

unoccupied
4 free, idle **5** empty **10** unemployed

unofficial
8 informal **9** irregular **13** unceremonious

unorganized
7 muddled **8** inchoate **10** disjointed, disordered, incoherent, incohesive **11** unconnected **12** disconnected, uncontinuous **13** discontinuous

unoriginal
3 dry **4** arid, dull **5** staid **6** barren, stodgy, stuffy **7** prosaic, sterile, unfired **10** uncreative, uninspired **11** noncreative, uninventive

unornamented
3 dry **5** plain **6** simple **9** unadorned **11** inelaborate, unelaborate, ungarnished **12** unbeautified **13** unembellished, unembroidered

unorthodox
9 dissident, heretical, sectarian **10** schismatic **13** nonconformist

unorthodoxy
6 heresy, schism **7** dissent **9** disbelief **10** dissidence **13** nonconformism, nonconformity

unpaid
3 due **5** owing **6** mature **7** overdue, payable **8** freewill, wageless **9** unsettled, voluntary, volunteer **10** gratuitous **11** outstanding **13** uncompensated, unrecompensed, unremunerated

unpalatable
4 flat, thin, weak **5** washy **6** bitter, watery **7** galling, insipid, painful **8** grievous, nauseous, unsavory **9** loathsome, savorless, sickening, tasteless **10** afflictive, flavorless **11** distasteful, ill-flavored **12** unappetizing

unparalleled
5 alone **6** unique **8** peerless **9** matchless, unequaled, unmatched, unrivaled

unperceiving
see **unobservant**

unpermissive
5 rigid **6** strict **8** rigorist, rigorous **9** draconian, stringent **10** ironhanded

unphysical
8 bodiless **9** asomatous **10** discarnate, immaterial, unembodied **11** disembodied, incorporeal, nonmaterial

unpierceable
10 impervious **11** impregnable **12** impenetrable

unpitying
9 merciless **10** unmerciful

unplanned
6 random **7** aimless, unaimed **9** desultory, haphazard, hit-or-miss, undevised, unthought **10** designless, undesigned, unintended, unpurposed **11** inadvertent, purposeless **12** unconsidered **13** unintentional

unpleasant
3 bad **4** sour **5** seamy **6** rotten **7** unhappy **11** displeasing, distasteful **12** disagreeable
combining form: 3 cac **4** caco

unpliable
6 mulish **8** perverse, stubborn **9** obstinate, pigheaded **10** bullheaded, headstrong, self-willed **12** pertinacious

unplug
3 ope **4** open **6** uncork **7** unblock **10** disconnect

unpolished
4 rude **5** crude, rough **6** unhewn **7** boorish, ill-bred, incivil, loutish, lowbred, uncivil **8** churlish, cloddish, impolite, unformed, unworked **9** roughhewn, undressed, unrefined **10** uncultured, unfinished, ungracious **11** clodhopping, disgracious, ill-mannered, uncivilized, unfashioned **12** discourteous **13** disrespectful

unpracticed
3 raw **5** fresh, green **6** callow **7** untried **8** untested, unversed **13** inexperienced

unpredictable
4 iffy **6** chancy **7** erratic **9** fluctuant, uncertain, whimsical **10** capricious

unprejudiced
4 fair, just **5** equal **8** unbiased **9** equitable, impartial, objective, uncolored **13** dispassionate

unpressed
7 wrinkly

unpretentious
5 plain **6** modest, simple **10** unaffected **11** inelaborate, unelaborate, ungarnished **12** unbeautified **13** unembellished

unpretty
5 plain **6** homely **8** uncomely **10** unalluring, unhandsome **11** unbeauteous, unbeautiful **12** unattractive

unprincipled
5 venal **7** corrupt, crooked **9** abandoned, dishonest, dissolute, mercenary, reprobate, unethical **10** licentious, praetorian, profligate **12** unscrupulous

unproductive
4 vain **6** barren, futile **7** useless **8** impotent, infecund **9** fruitless, infertile, unbearing, unfertile **10** unavailing **11** ineffectual, unavailable **12** hardscrabble

unprofitable
4 idle, vain **7** useless

unprogressive
8 backward, ignorant **9** benighted **10** behindhand **11** undeveloped **13** unenlightened

unpropitious
4 dire **7** adverse, baleful, baneful, counter, fateful, ominous, unlucky **9** ill-boding, ill-omened **11** threatening **12** antagonistic

unprosperous
3 low **4** poor **5** broke, needy **8** indigent **9** destitute, penurious **11** fortuneless, impecunious **12** impoverished

unprotected
6 unsafe **8** helpless, insecure **9** unguarded **10** undefended, unshielded **11** defenseless, unsheltered

unproved
7 untried **8** untested

unpunctual
4 late **5** lated, tardy **7** belated, overdue **10** behindhand

unqualified
4 firm, pure, rank, sure **5** clear, gross, sheer, unfit, utter **6** entire, simple, steady **7** abiding, blasted, blessed, express, perfect, unmixed **8** absolute, complete, enduring, explicit, infernal, unfitted **9** incapable, out-and-out, steadfast, unalloyed, undiluted, unlimited, unskilled **10** confounded, ineligible, unequipped, unreserved, unsuitable **11** incompetent, unfaltering, unmitigated **12** never-failing, wholehearted **13** unadulterated, unconditional

unquenchable
9 insatiate, unsatiate **10** insatiable

unquestionable
4 flat, real, true, very **7** certain, genuine **8** bona fide, positive **9** authentic, downright, undoubted, up-and-down **10** sure-enough **11** established, well-founded **12** well-grounded

unquestioning
4 firm, sure **5** fixed **6** steady **7** abiding **8** enduring, unshaken **9** steadfast **10** unshakable **12** never-failing

unravel
5 break, solve **6** unfold, unknit **7** dope out, resolve, unsnarl **8** decipher, dissolve, unriddle, untangle **9** extricate, figure out, puzzle out **11** disentangle

unreadable
9 illegible

unreal
7 fictive **8** chimeric, fanciful, illusory **9** fantastic, fictional, imaginary **10** chimerical, fictitious **12** suppositious
combining form: 5 pseud **6** pseudo

unrealistic
8 fanciful **10** ivory-tower **11** impractical, unpractical **12** ivory-towered **13** ivory-towerish

unreasonable
3 mad **5** loose, undue **7** invalid **8** improper, overmuch, unlawful,

wrongful **9** arbitrary, excessive, illogical, sophistic **10** fallacious, immoderate, inordinate, irrational, peremptory, reasonless, unrightful **11** incongruous, nonrational, unwarranted

unreasoned
3 mad **7** invalid **9** illogical, sophistic **10** fallacious, irrational, reasonless **11** nonrational

unrecompensed
6 unpaid **13** uncompensated

unrefined
3 raw **4** rude **5** crass, crude, gross, rough **6** coarse, impure, native, vulgar **7** boorish, ill-bred, loutish, lowbred, natural, uncouth **8** churlish, cloddish, ungraded, unsorted **9** inelegant, roughcast, roughhewn, run-of-mine, undressed **10** uncultured, unpolished **11** clodhopping, uncivilized, unprocessed

unreflective
8 careless, feckless, heedless, uncaring **9** unheeding **10** unthinking **11** inadvertent, thoughtless

unrehearsed
7 offhand **9** extempore, impromptu, unstudied **10** improvised **11** extemporary

unrelated
8 discrete, separate **9** disjoined

unrelenting
4 grim **6** mortal **8** ruthless **9** merciless **10** implacable, ironfisted, unyielding **11** unflinching **12** unappeasable

unreliable
5 false, slick **6** fickle, shifty, tricky, unsafe, unsure, untrue **7** dubious, inexact **8** slippery, untrusty **9** faithless, trustless, unassured **10** fly-by-night, inaccurate, inconstant, perfidious, unfaithful **11** vacillating **12** falsehearted **13** untrustworthy

unreligious
7 godless

unremarkable
5 plain, usual **7** routine **8** everyday, ordinary, workaday **9** plain Jane, quotidian

unremitting
7 endless **8** constant, unending **9** ceaseless, continual, perpetual, unceasing **12** interminable **13** uninterrupted

unremorseful
7 unsorry **10** impenitent, regretless, uncontrite

unremunerated
6 unpaid

unrenowned
7 obscure, unfamed, unknown, unnoted **8** nameless **9** unheard-of **12** uncelebrated

unrepentant
7 unsorry **10** impenitent, regretless, uncontrite **11** remorseless

unrepresentative
7 deviant **8** aberrant, abnormal, atypical **9** anomalous, untypical **11** heteroclite

unrequested
7 unasked **8** unbidden, unsought **9** uninvited

unrequired
8 needless, unneeded **9** omissible, unneedful **11** dispensable, inessential, uncalled-for, unessential, unnecessary **12** nonessential

unreserved
4 open **5** frank, plain **6** breezy, candid, casual, dégagé **7** relaxed, unfussy **8** informal, outgoing, outright **9** easygoing, expansive **11** low-pressure, openhearted, unconcealed, undisguised, unvarnished **12** undissembled **13** demonstrative, unconstrained

unresolved
8 hesitant, wavering **9** faltering, uncertain **10** hesitating, indecisive, irresolute, undecisive **11** vacillating **12** shilly-shally

unrespectable
5 shady **6** shabby, shoddy **8** shameful, inglorious **11** disgraceful, ignominious

unresponsive
4 cold **6** frigid **9** inhibited **10** insentient, undersexed **11** insensitive, passionless **13** insusceptible, unimpressible, unsusceptible

unresponsiveness
6 apathy, phlegm **8** stoicism **9** stolidity **11** impassivity **13** insensibility

unrest
5 chaos **6** tumult **7** ailment, anarchy, ferment, turmoil, unquiet **8** disorder, disquiet, upheaval **9** agitation, commotion, confusion **10** convulsion, inquietude, turbulence **11** disquietude, restiveness **13** Sturm und Drang

unrestrained
4 free, open **5** bluff, blunt, frank, loose **6** candid **7** brusque, rampant **8** outgoing, reinless, uncurbed

9 audacious, excessive, expansive **10** forthright, immoderate, inordinate, ungoverned, unhampered, untempered **11** intemperate, plainspoken, uninhibited, untrammeled **13** demonstrative, overindulgent

unrestraint
4 ease **7** abandon **11** naturalness, spontaneity **13** impulsiveness

unrestricted
4 free, open **6** public **10** accessible

unrighteous
6 unfair, unjust **9** inequable **11** inequitable, unequitable

unripe
5 green, young **6** callow, infant **8** immature, juvenile, youthful **9** unfledged

unrivaled
4 only **5** alone **6** unique **8** peerless **9** matchless, unmatched **11** unparagoned **12** unparalleled

unrobe
see **unclothe**

unroll
6 extend, uncoil, unfurl, unwind **7** open out

unromantic
4 cool, hard **5** sober **9** practical, pragmatic, realistic **10** hard-boiled, hardheaded **11** down-to-earth **12** matter-of-fact **13** unsentimental

unruffled
4 calm, cool **6** serene **8** composed, tranquil **9** collected **10** nonchalant **11** unflappable **13** imperturbable

unruly
4 hard, wild **5** rowdy, tough **7** froward, naughty, raffish, raucous, wayward **8** contrary, indocile, perverse, rowdyish, untoward **9** fractious, obstinate, ruffianly, termagant, turbulent **10** boisterous, disorderly, rampageous, rebellious, rowdy-dowdy, tumultuous **11** disobedient, indomitable, intractable, rumbustious **12** contumacious, incorrigible, obstreperous, rambunctious, recalcitrant, ungovernable, unmanageable **13** insubordinate, undisciplined

unsacred
3 lay **7** profane, secular **8** temporal

unsafe
5 risky, shaky **6** chancy **7** erratic, tottery, unsound **8** insecure, perilous, unstable **9** dangerous, hazard-

ous, unassured, uncertain **10** jeopardous, unreliable **12** undependable **13** untrustworthy

unsaid
5 tacit **7** implied **8** implicit, inferred, nonvocal, unspoken, wordless **9** unuttered **10** undeclared, understood **11** unexpressed

unsalutary
7 noisome, noxious **9** unhealthy
11 unhealthful, unwholesome
12 insalubrious

unsatisfactory
3 bad, bum **4** poor, punk **5** amiss,
wrong **6** rotten

unsatisfiable
9 insatiate **10** quenchless

unsavory
4 flat **7** insipid **9** tasteless **10** flavorless **11** distasteful, ill-flavored,
unpalatable **12** unappetizing

unsay
6 abjure, recall, recant **7** retract
8 forswear, palinode, take back,
withdraw

unscathed
4 safe **8** unharmed

unscented
8 odorless

unschooled
5 naive **6** simple **7** artless, natural
8 ignorant, untaught **9** benighted,
ingenuous, unstudied, untutored
10 illiterate, unaffected, uneducated, unlettered **11** emptyheaded,
know-nothing **12** unartificial,
uninstructed

unscramble
5 untie **7** untwine **8** untangle **9** extricate **10** disembroil, disentwine,
unentangle **11** disencumber, disentangle **12** disembarrass

unscrupulous
5 shady, venal **6** crafty **7** corrupt,
crooked **8** improper, scheming, sinister, unseemly, wrongful **9** deceitful, dishonest, mercenary, underhand, unethical **10** praetorian
12 questionable, unprincipled

unseasonable
5 inapt, inept, unapt, undue **8** ill-
timed, improper, mistimed, untimely
10 malapropos, unbecoming **11** inopportune, unfortunate **12** inauspicious, inconvenient, infelicitous
13 inappropriate

unseasoned
3 raw **5** fresh, green, young **6** callow **7** untried **8** unversed **9** un-

fleshed **11** unpracticed
13 inexperienced

unseat
5 pitch, throw **6** depose, remove
7 buck off, unhorse **8** dethrone

unseemliness
9 indecorum **10** inelegance
11 impropriety

unseemly
5 crude, inapt, inept, rough, rowdy,
unapt **6** coarse **7** raffish, ungodly
8 ill-timed, improper, indecent, untoward **9** inelegant, ruffianly, unrefined **10** indecorous, indelicate,
malapropos, malodorous, unbecoming, undecorous, unsuitable
11 unbefitting **13** inappropriate

unseen
9 invisible

unsentimental
see **unromantic**

unserviceable
7 useless **11** impractical **12** unfunctional **13** nonfunctional

unsettle
4 turn **5** upset **6** bother, flurry, jumble, sicken **7** agitate, derange, disturb, fluster, perturb, rummage,
trouble, unhinge **8** disarray, disorder, disquiet **9** incommode **10** disarrange, discommode, discompose
11 disorganize

unsettled
3 due **4** back, open **5** fluid **6** mature, mobile, queasy, remote, un-
easy, unpaid **7** clouded, dubious,
mutable, overdue, payable, pendent, pending, protean, unclear,
unquiet **8** doubtful, frontier, restless,
unstable, unsteady, variable, weathery **9** changeful, dubitable, uncertain, undecided, unrestful
10 changeable, indecisive, unpeaceful, untranquil **11** outstanding, problematic **12** undetermined

unsex
3 fix **4** geld **5** alter **6** change, neuter **8** castrate, mutilate **9** sterilize
11 desexualize

unshackle
4 free **5** loose **6** loosen, unbind
7 manumit, release, unchain **8** liberate **9** discharge **10** emancipate

unshakable
4 firm, sure **5** fixed **6** steady
7 abiding **9** steadfast **10** unwavering **11** unfaltering **12** never-failing **13** unquestioning

unshaped
8 formless, inchoate, unformed
9 amorphous

unshared
4 sole **6** single **9** exclusive

unship
6 unlade, unload, unstow **7** off-load
9 disburden, discharge

unshod
8 barefoot, shoeless **10** unsandaled

unshroud
6 debunk, expose, show up, unmask **7** uncloak, undress
8 discover

unshut
3 ope **4** open, undo **6** unstop
7 unblock, unclose

unsightly
4 drab, dull, ugly **7** hideous **8** uncomely **9** ill-shaped, unshapely
10 ill-favored, ill-looking, lackluster,
unesthetic **11** unbeautiful

unsimilar
6 unlike **7** distant, diverse, unalike,
unequal, various **9** different, disparate, divergent

unskilled
5 green, inept **7** amateur, jackleg
10 amateurish **12** dilettantish,
dilettantist **13** unworkmanlike

unskillful
5 inapt, inept, unapt **6** clumsy,
gauche **7** awkward, inadept, unhandy, unready **8** inexpert, unexpert, unfacile, unfitted **9** butcherly,
incapable **11** incompetent, inefficient, undexterous, unqualified
12 unproficient **13** unworkmanlike

unsleeping
5 alert **7** wakeful **8** open-eyed, vigilant, watchful **9** wide-awake

unsmooth
5 harsh, rough **6** craggy, jagged,
ruffly, rugged, uneven **7** scraggy,
unlevel **8** asperous, scabrous

unsnarl
see **untangle**

unsociable
3 shy **4** cool **5** aloof, timid **6** offish, remote, shut-in **7** distant,
prickly **8** brooding, reserved, solitary, standoff **9** diffident, exclusive,
secretive, sensitive, unbending,
withdrawn **11** indifferent, standoffish **12** inaccessible

unsoiled
5 clean **7** cleanly **8** spotless
9 taintless, unsullied **10** immaculate

unsophisticated

5 crude, green, naive 6 callow, simple 7 artless, genuine, natural, uncouth 9 ingenuous, untutored, unworldly 10 unaffected, unschooled 12 unartificial

unsorted

3 raw 5 crude, mixed 6 impure, motley, native, varied 8 ungraded 9 unrefined 11 promiscuous 12 multifarious 13 heterogeneous, miscellaneous

unsought

7 unasked 8 unbidden, unwanted, unwished 9 undesired, uninvited, unwelcome 11 unrequested

unsound

3 mad 4 daft, weak 5 batty, false, frail, hairy, risky, wrong 6 chancy, crazed, faulty, flawed, flimsy, infirm, insane, untrue, weakly, wicked 7 cracked, damaged, fragile, lunatic 8 decrepit, demented, deranged, perilous, specious 9 dangerous, erroneous, hazardous, imperfect, incorrect, unhealthy 10 inaccurate, jeopardous, unbalanced 11 treacherous 13 insubstantial, unsubstantial
mentally: 6 insane

unsparing

4 free 6 severe 7 liberal 8 generous, handsome 9 bounteous, bountiful 10 freehanded, munificent, openhanded

unspeakable

6 odious 7 hateful 9 atrocious, loathsome, obnoxious, offensive, repellent, repugnant, repulsive, revolting 10 disgusting, outrageous 11 distasteful 13 inexpressible, unexpressible

unspoiled

6 intact, virgin 8 pristine, untapped, virginal 9 undefiled, untouched

unspoken

4 mute 5 tacit 6 hinted, silent, unsaid 7 implied 8 implicit, inferred, unstated, unvoiced, wordless 9 intimated, suggested, unuttered 10 undeclared, understood 11 unexpressed

unstable

4 weak 5 fluid, rocky, shaky 6 dickey, fickle, mobile, moving, shifty, tricky, unsure, wobbly 7 buoyant, dubious, elastic, protean, suspect 8 doubtful, freakish, insecure, rootless, slippery, ticklish, volatile, wavering, weathery 9 am-biguous, changeful, fluctuant, mercurial, resilient, uncertain, unsettled 10 borderline, capricious, inconstant, lubricious, precarious 11 vacillating 12 effervescent 13 temperamental

unsteady

5 fluid, rocky, tippy 6 jiggly, mobile, moving, shifty, wobbly 7 movable, mutable, protean, rickety, tottery 8 slippery, staggery, tittuppy, variable, weathery 9 changeful, uncertain, unsettled 10 changeable, inconstant
British: 5 wonky

unsteel

5 unarm 6 disarm 7 win over

unstop

3 ope 4 open, undo 6 uncork, unplug, unshut 7 unblock, unclose

unstow

6 unlade, unload, unship 7 off-load 9 disburden, discharge

unstrengthen

3 sap 5 blunt 6 weaken 7 cripple, disable, unbrace 8 enfeeble 9 attenuate, undermine 10 debilitate

unstudied

5 naive 6 simple 7 artless, natural, offhand 8 unversed 9 extempore, impromptu, ingenuous, unlearned, untutored 10 improvised, unaffected, unschooled 11 extemporary, spontaneous, unrehearsed 12 unartificial

unstylish

5 dowdy, tacky 6 démodé, frumpy, stodgy 8 frumpish, outmoded 9 out-of-date

unsubstantial

4 thin, weak 5 frail, shaky 6 feeble, flimsy, infirm, weakly 7 fragile, tenuous, unsound 8 bodiless, decrepit, insecure 9 spiritual 10 immaterial, improbable, incredible, unembodied, unphysical 11 implausible, incorporeal, nonmaterial, nonphysical 12 metaphysical, unbelievable, unconvincing, undependable 13 inconceivable

unsuccess

4 bomb, flop 6 defeat 7 failure, reverse, setback

unsuitable

5 inapt, inept, undue, unfit 6 unmeet 7 unhappy 8 ill-timed, improper, unfitted, untimely 9 ill-suited 10 ill-adapted, unbecoming 11 unbefitting 13 inappropriate

unsuited

5 inapt, unfit 6 unmeet 8 unfitted 10 ill-adapted, inadequate 12 inadmissible, unacceptable 13 disappointing, inappropriate, objectionable

unsullied

4 pure 5 clean 6 chaste, decent, modest 7 cleanly 8 spotless, unsoiled 9 stainless, taintless, undefiled 10 immaculate 11 unblemished

unsure

4 open, weak 5 shaky 6 dickey, wobbly 7 dubious, unclear 8 doubtful, insecure, rootless, unstable, untrusty, wavering 9 fluctuant, trustless, unassured, uncertain, undecided 10 borderline, indecisive, suspicious, unreliable 11 problematic, unconfident, vacillating 12 questionable, undependable 13 untrustworthy

unsurpassable

7 supreme 8 towering, ultimate 10 preeminent 12 transcendent

unsusceptible

9 impassive 10 insentient 11 insensitive 12 unresponsive

unsuspecting

6 unwary 9 credulous

unsuspicious

see **unsuspecting**

unswayable

5 rigid 8 obdurate 10 inflexible, relentless, unyielding 11 uncompliant 12 single-minded

unswerving

see **unfaltering**

unsymmetrical

6 uneven 7 unequal 8 lopsided 9 irregular 10 off-balance 12 overbalanced

unsympathetic

4 cold, cool 6 frigid 7 callous 8 aversive, kindless, lukewarm, obdurate, ungenial 9 heartless, repellent, repugnant, unfeeling, unlikable 10 dislikable, hard-boiled, unpleasant, unpleasing 11 coldhearted, displeasing, halfhearted, hardhearted, indifferent, uncongenial, unemotional 12 stonyhearted 13 disinterested

untactful

5 brash 9 impolitic, maladroit, unpolitic 12 undiplomatic

untamed

4 wild 5 feral 9 unsubdued

untangle
7 unsnarl, untwine, untwist 9 discumber, extricate 10 disembroil, disentwine, unscramble 11 disencumber 12 disembarrass

untapped
6 virgin 8 virginal 9 unspoiled, untouched

untaught
8 ignorant 9 benighted, untutored 10 illiterate, uneducated, unlettered, unschooled 11 empty-headed, know-nothing 12 uninstructed

untempered
9 excessive 10 immoderate, inordinate 12 unrestrained 13 overindulgent

untended
7 run-down 9 neglected 10 uncared-for

Unter den ___
6 Linden

untested
7 untried 8 unproved 11 unpracticed

unthankful
9 thankless 10 ungrateful

unthinkable
4 rare 6 unique 7 unusual 8 singular, uncommon, unwonted 10 incredible, unordinary 11 exceptional 13 extraordinary

unthinking
8 careless, feckless, heedless, uncaring 9 unheeding 11 inadvertent, thoughtless 12 irreflective, unreflective

unthorough
5 messy 6 botchy, sloppy, untidy 8 careless, slapdash, slipshod, slovenly

unthought
9 undevised, unplanned 10 undesigned, unintended, unpurposed 11 inadvertent 13 unintentional

unthrift
5 waste 6 lavish, waster 7 spender, wastrel 8 prodigal, squander 9 overdoing 10 high roller, lavishness, profligate, squanderer 11 improvident, prodigality, scattergood 12 extravagance, extravagancy, wastefulness

unthrifty
6 lavish 8 prodigal, wasteful 10 thriftless 11 extravagant, improvident

untidy
5 messy 6 botchy, sloppy, unneat 7 unkempt 8 careless, ill-kempt, slapdash, slipshod, slovenly, uncombed 10 disheveled, unthorough 12 unfastidious

untie
6 loosen, unknot, unlace, unlash 8 unstring 9 extricate 10 disembroil, disentwine, unentangle, unscramble 11 disencumber, disentangle 12 disembarrass

untighten
3 lax 4 ease 5 loose, relax, slack 6 loosen 7 ease off, slacken

until
2 to 4 till, up to 5 since 6 before 7 prior to 11 in advance of

untimely
4 soon 5 early, inapt, unapt, undue 8 ill-timed, improper, mistimed, oversoon, previous 9 overearly, premature 10 malapropos, unsuitable 11 ill-seasoned, inopportune 12 intempestive, unseasonable 13 inappropriate

untiring
8 tireless 9 weariless 10 unflagging, unwearying 11 unweariable 13 indefatigable, inexhaustible

untold
4 huge, vast 6 mighty 7 immense, mammoth, titanic 8 enormous, gigantic 9 countless, monstrous, uncounted, unrelated 10 innumerous, numberless, prodigious, unnumbered 11 innumerable, uncountable 12 unnumberable

untouchable
5 leper 6 pariah 7 Ishmael, outcast 8 castaway, déclassé, derelict, outcaste, outsider 10 Ishmaelite 11 offscouring

untouched
4 pure 5 sound, whole 6 entire, intact, virgin 7 perfect 8 flawless, pristine, unmarred, untapped, virginal 9 undamaged, unspoiled 11 unblemished

untoward
4 wild 5 rough 6 unruly 7 hapless, ungodly, unhappy, unlucky 8 ill-fated, improper, indecent, indocile, luckless, unseemly 9 fractious 10 ill-starred, indecorous, indelicate, unbecoming, undecorous 11 intractable, star-crossed, unfortunate 12 misfortunate, recalcitrant, ungovernable, unmanageable 13 undisciplined

untrained
see **unskilled**

untrammeled
8 uncurbed 9 audacious 10 ungoverned, unhampered 11 uninhibited 12 unrestrained

untried
3 raw 5 fresh, green 6 callow, unripe 8 immature, unproved, untested, unversed 9 half-baked 10 unseasoned 11 unpracticed 12 unconversant 13 inexperienced

untroubled
4 calm 5 quiet, still 6 hushed, placid, stilly 7 halcyon

untroublesome
4 easy 5 light, royal 6 facile, simple, smooth 10 effortless

untrue
5 false, wrong 7 inexact, unloyal, unsound 8 disloyal, forsworn, perjured, recreant, specious 9 erroneous, faithless, imprecise, incorrect, unprecise 10 inaccurate, perfidious, traitorous, unfaithful 11 treacherous
combining form: 5 pseud 6 pseudo

untruism
3 fib, lie 4 tale 5 story 6 canard 7 bouncer 9 falsehood 13 prevarication

untrustworthy
6 unsafe, unsure 7 dubious 9 unassured 10 fly-by-night, unreliable 12 questionable, undependable

untruth
3 fib, lie 4 tale 5 error, story 6 canard 7 fallacy, falsity 9 falsehood, falseness 13 erroneousness, prevarication

untruthful
5 false, lying, wrong 6 shifty 7 knavish, roguish 8 delusive, delusory, unhonest 9 deceitful, deceptive, dishonest, incorrect 10 inaccurate, mendacious, misleading

untruthfulness
7 fibbery 9 falsehood, mendacity 10 unveracity

untune
5 upset 6 bother, flurry 7 agitate, disturb, fluster, perturb, unhinge 8 disquiet 10 discompose

untutored
see **unschooled**

untwine
see **untangle**

untwist
see **untangle**

untypical
see **unusual**

unusable
7 useless 11 impractical 12 unfunctional 13 nonfunctional

unused
4 idle 6 vacant

unusual
3 odd 4 rare 6 freaky, quaint, unique 7 bizarre, curious, deviant, oddball, strange 8 aberrant, abnormal, freakish, peculiar, singular, uncommon, unwonted 9 anomalous, eccentric, untypical 10 outlandish, unordinary 11 exceptional, unthinkable 12 unimaginable 13 extraordinary
combining form: 4 anom 5 anomo

unusually
5 extra 6 rarely 8 uncommon 9 extremely 10 uncommonly

unutterable
5 awful 7 awesome 8 wondrous 9 marvelous, wonderful 10 incredible, prodigious 13 inexpressible, unexpressible

unuttered
see **unspoken**

unvaried
5 alike 7 uniform 10 monotonous

unvarnished
see **undisguised**

unvarying
see **unchanging**

unveil
see **uncover**

unversed
3 raw 5 fresh, green 6 callow 7 untried 9 unfleshed 10 unseasoned 11 unpracticed 12 unconversant 13 inexperienced

unvigilant
6 unwary 7 unalert 9 unguarded 10 incautious, unwatchful

unvital
5 petty 6 paltry, peanut 7 trivial 8 piddling, trifling 12 inconsequent

unvoiced
see **unspoken**

unwanted
see **unwelcome**

unwarranted
5 undue 8 baseless 9 unfounded 10 bottomless, gratuitous, groundless, ungrounded 11 uncalled-for 12 unreasonable 13 unjustifiable

unwary
4 rash 5 brash, hasty 7 unalert 8 reckless 9 credulous, hotheaded, unadvised, unguarded 10 ill-advised, incautious, unvigilant 11 thoughtless 12 unsuspecting, unsuspicious 13 inconsiderate

unwashed
3 low, mob 4 base, mean, scum 5 dregs, lowly, trash 6 humble, masses, rabble 7 ignoble, lowborn 8 baseborn, canaille, plebeian, riffraff 10 unennobled 11 proletariat

unwasteful
5 canny, chary 6 frugal, saving 7 sparing, thrifty 9 provident, stewardly 10 economical

unwatchful
7 unalert 9 unguarded, unheeding 10 incautious, unnoticing, unvigilant 11 inattentive, inobservant, unobservant, unobserving 12 unperceiving

unwatered
3 dry 4 arid, sere 7 bone-dry, thirsty 8 droughty 9 waterless 12 moistureless

unwavering
see **unfaltering**

unwearying
6 steady 8 constant, tireless, untiring 9 unceasing, weariless 10 unflagging 12 interminable 13 indefatigable, inexhaustible

unwed
see **unmarried**

unwelcome
7 unasked 8 unsought, unwanted, unwished 9 obnoxious, repellent, undesired 10 ill-favored, unpleasant, unpleasing 11 distasteful, undesirable 12 inadmissible, unacceptable 13 exceptionable, objectionable

unwell
3 ill, low 4 mean, sick 5 frail, rocky, shaky 6 ailing, feeble, infirm, offish, poorly, queasy, sickly, weakly, wobbly 7 underly 8 offcolor, qualmish 9 squeamish 10 indisposed

unwholesome
4 foul 6 sickly 7 baneful, harmful, hideous, hurtful, noxious, obscene 8 horrible 9 injurious, offensive, re-

pellent, repulsive, unhealthy 10 disgusting, insalutary, pernicious, unsalutary 11 deleterious, detrimental, unhealthful 12 insalubrious

unwieldy
5 bulky, heavy 6 clumsy 7 awkward, massive, onerous, unhandy 8 cumbrous 9 lumbering, ponderous 10 burdensome, cumbersome 11 encumbering 12 inconvenient, unmanageable

unwilling
4 loth 5 loath 6 afraid, averse 7 uneager 8 backward, hesitant 9 reluctant 10 indisposed 11 disinclined

unwind
5 relax, unlax 6 unbend, unreel, unroll 7 ease off 8 loosen up

unwise
5 inane, inept, naive 7 fatuous, foolish, unsound, witless 8 childish, immature 9 ill-judged, impolitic, imprudent, misguided, senseless 10 ill-advised, indiscreet 11 impractical, injudicious, thoughtless, undesirable, unfortunate 13 inappropriate, unintelligent

unwished
see **unwelcome**

unwishful
4 loth 5 loath 6 afraid, averse 7 uneager 8 backward, hesitant 9 reluctant 10 indisposed 11 disinclined

unwitting
7 unaware 8 ignorant 9 forgetful, oblivious, unknowing, unmindful 10 unfamiliar, uninformed 11 incognizant 12 inconversant, unacquainted, uninstructed

unwitty
5 silly 6 simple 7 asinine, fatuous, foolish, witless 8 mindless 9 brainless 10 weak-headed, weak-minded

unwonted
4 rare 6 unique 7 unusual 8 singular, uncommon 10 unordinary 11 exceptional, unthinkable 12 unimaginable 13 extraordinary

unworkable
7 useless 10 impossible, infeasible, unfeasible 11 impractical 12 unfunctional 13 nonfunctional

unworked
4 rude 5 crude, rough 6 unhewn 8 unformed 9 roughhewn, un-

dressed **10** unfinished, unpolished **11** unfashioned

unworkmanlike
5 inept **8** inexpert, unexpert **9** incapable, unskilled **10** unskillful **11** incompetent, inefficient

unworldly
5 naive **6** astral, dreamy, simple **7** artless, natural **9** daydreamy, ingenuous, unstudied, untutored, visionary **10** unaffected, unschooled **11** daydreaming **12** unartificial

unworthy
6 drossy, no-good **7** inutile, nothing **9** no-account, valueless, worthless

unwrap
see **uncover**

unwrinkled
6 smooth

unwritten
4 oral **6** spoken, verbal **11** traditional, word-of-mouth

unwrought
see **unworked**

unyielding
4 firm, grim, hard **5** fixed, rigid, stern, stiff, tough **6** mortal, mulish **8** hardcore, hard-line, obdurate, ruthless, stubborn **9** impliable, inelastic, merciless, obstinate, pigheaded **10** bullheaded, headstrong, implacable, inexorable, inflexible, ironfisted, refractory, relentless, self-willed, unflexible, unswayable **11** immalleable, incompliant, intractable, uncompliant, unflinching, unrelenting **12** pertinacious, single-minded, unappeasable

unyoke
5 untie **6** unbind, unlink **7** disjoin, outspan, unhitch

up
4 hike, jump, lift, rise, soar **5** arise, boost, mount, raise **6** ascend, aspire, au fait, red-hot, uprear, versed **7** abreast, versant **8** familiar, increase, informed **9** au courant **10** acquainted, conversant, down-to-date **12** contemporary
prefix: **2** an **3** ana, sur

up-and-coming
4 keen **5** alert, eager, ready **7** go-ahead **9** gumptious **12** enterprising

upbear
4 prop **5** brace, carry **7** bolster, shore up, support, sustain **8** buttress

upbeat
4 fond **8** sanguine **10** optimistic **12** Pollyannaish

upbraid
4 lash, rate **5** scold **6** berate, revile **7** bawl out, chew out **8** bless out **10** tongue-lash, vituperate

upchuck
4 barf, spew **5** vomit **6** spit up **7** bring up, throw up **8** disgorge

upcoming
7 nearing **8** foreseen **11** approaching, prospective

up-country
4 bush **6** sticks **8** backland, backwash, frontier **9** backwater, backwoods, boondocks **10** hinterland

update
5 renew **7** refresh, restore **8** renovate **9** modernize, refurbish **10** rejuvenate

Updike novel
10 Rabbit, Run, The Centaur, Bech is Back **11** Rabbit Redux **12** Rabbit at Rest, Rabbit is Rich

upend
4 beat, drub, lick, trim, whip **6** wallop **7** clobber, shellac, trounce **9** overwhelm

upgrade
3 wax **4** hike, rise **5** boost **6** prefer **7** advance, elevate, promote **8** increase **12** breakthrough

upgrowth
8 progress **9** evolution, flowering, unfolding **10** evolvement **11** development, progression

upheaval
6 change, clamor, outcry, tumult, upturn **7** ferment, heaving **8** churning, disaster, stirring **9** cataclysm, commotion **10** alteration, convulsion **11** catastrophe

uphill
4 hard **6** rugged **7** arduous, labored, operose **8** toilsome **9** difficult, effortful, laborious, strenuous

uphold
3 aid **4** back, help, lift, prop, rear **5** brace, carry, hoist, raise **6** assist, bear up, buoy up, defend, pick up, take up, upbear, uplift, uprear **7** bolster, elevate, justify, shore up, support, sustain, upraise **8** advocate, backstop, buttress, champion, maintain, side with **9** underprop, vindicate

upland
5 table **7** plateau

uplift
4 rear **5** edify, hoist, raise **6** illume, pick up, take up, uphold, uprear **7** elevate, improve, upraise **8** illumine **9** enlighten, irradiate **10** illuminate

upon
4 atop
prefix: **2** ep **3** eph, epi

upper class
5 elite **6** flower, gentry **7** quality, society, who's who **9** blue blood, gentility **11** aristocracy

upper crust
see **upper class**

upper hand
6 better **7** victory **9** advantage **11** superiority

uppermost
3 top **6** apical **7** highest **8** loftiest

uppity
5 brash **7** forward, pushful, pushing **9** presuming **11** overweening **12** presumptuous **13** self-asserting, self-assertive

upraise
4 lift, rear **5** cheer, hoist **6** buck up, pick up, solace, take up, uphold, uplift, uprear **7** comfort, console, elevate

uprear
4 lift, rise, soar **5** arise, build, erect, exalt, hoist, honor, mount, put up, raise **6** ascend, aspire, pick up, take up, uphold, uplift **7** dignify, elevate, ennoble, glorify, magnify, sublime, upraise **9** construct **10** aggrandize **11** distinguish

upright
4 fair, good, just, pure, true **5** erect, moral, noble **6** arrect, honest, raised **7** ethical, stand-up **8** elevated, virtuous **9** blameless, equitable, exemplary, honorable, impartial, righteous **10** highminded, principled, scrupulous, straight-up, upstanding **13** conscientious
combining form: **4** orth **5** ortho

uprightness
6 virtue **7** honesty, probity **8** morality, nobility **9** integrity, rectitude **12** reputability

uprising
6 revolt **9** rebellion **10** revolution **12** insurrection

uproar

3 din 4 coil, to-do 5 babel, brawl, broil, chaos, furor, melee, whirl 6 clamor, fracas, furore, hassle, hubbub, jangle, pother, racket, ruckus, rumpus, shindy, tumult 7 shindig, turmoil 8 brouhaha, disorder, foofaraw 9 commotion, confusion 10 hullabaloo, hurly-burly, tintamarre, turbulence 11 pandemonium

uproarious

5 noisy 7 rackety 8 clattery, noiseful, sonorous 10 clangorous

uproot

4 grub, move 5 abate, shift 6 uptear 7 abolish, blot out, destroy, replace, subvert, wipe out 8 demolish, displace, overturn, supplant, uncreate 9 eradicate, extirpate, overthrow, supersede 10 annihilate, transplant 11 exterminate

upset

3 ail 4 bend, cark, turn 5 curve, lay up, mix up, unman, worry 6 bother, flurry, invert, jumble, muddle, sicken, suffer, topple, tumble 7 afflict, agitate, derange, disturb, fluster, invalid, perturb, reverse, rummage, tip over, trouble, unhinge, unnerve 8 bewilder, confound, disarray, disorder, disquiet, distract, distress, overturn, turn over, unsettle 9 indispose, knock over, overthrow 10 debilitate, disarrange, discompose 12 incapacitate

upshot

4 core, gist, meat, pith 5 event, issue, sense, short 6 burden, climax, effect, ending, finish, result, sequel, thrust 7 outcome, purport 9 aftermath, substance 10 completion, conclusion 11 aftereffect, consequence, culmination, eventuality, termination

upside-down

5 snafu 7 chaotic, haywire, jumbled, mixed-up 8 confused, fouled-up, inverted, reversed 10 downside-up, topsy-turvy 13 helter-skelter

upspring

4 flow, head, rise 5 arise, get up, issue 6 uprise 7 emanate, proceed, stand up 9 originate 10 derive from

upstanding

see **upright**

upstart

3 cad 4 boor, lout, slob 5 comer, rowdy 6 mucker 7 bounder, parvenu 8 outsider, roturier 9 arriviste, roughneck, vulgarian 11 guttersnipe 12 nouveau riche 13 social climber

upsurge

3 wax 4 rise 5 build, mount 6 expand 7 augment, enlarge 8 heighten, increase, multiply

uptight

4 edgy 5 nervy, tense 6 uneasy 7 restive

uptightness

6 unease 7 tension

up till

2 to 5 until 6 before 7 prior to 11 in advance of

up to

4 till 5 until 6 before 11 in advance of

up-to-date

6 modern, modish, red-hot, timely 7 abreast, a la mode, dashing, fitting, stylish 8 advanced, suitable 9 au courant, expedient, opportune 10 convenient 12 contemporary

Urania

see **Muse**

Uranus

mother, wife: 2 Ge 4 Gaea
offspring: 6 Titans 8 Cyclopes
overthrower, son: 6 Cronus

urban

4 city, town 5 civic 6 public 7 burghal, oppidan, popular, village 9 inner city, municipal 12 metropolitan

urbane

5 bland, civil, suave 6 poised, smooth 7 affable, genteel, refined 8 balanced, cultured, gracious, obliging, polished, well-bred 9 civilized, courteous, distingué 10 cultivated 12 cosmopolitan, metropolitan

urbanize

6 citify

urchin

3 imp 4 brat 5 child, gamin, scamp, whelp 7 dickens, mudlark 8 bratling 10 ragamuffin, street arab 11 guttersnipe, hobbledehoy
combining form: 6 echino

Urdur, Urth

see **Norn**

urge

3 egg, sic 4 coax, goad, itch, lust, prod, push, rush, sick, spur 5 drive, egg on, hurry, impel, press, prick, set on, shove, tar on, tarre 6 cajole, compel, desire, exhort, hustle, incite, motive, needle, prompt, propel, spring 7 craving, impulse, passion, provoke, solicit, wheedle 8 appetite, blandish, pressure 9 constrain, encourage, incentive 10 appetition 12 high-pressure

urgency

8 entreaty, exigence, instancy, pressure 10 insistence 11 importunity

urgent

6 crying 7 burning, clamant, driving, instant 8 pressing 9 clamorous, demanding, impelling, insistent 10 imperative 11 importunate

Uriah, Urijah

father: 8 Shemaiah
slayer: 9 Jehoiakim
son: 8 Meremoth
wife: 9 Bathsheba

Uriel

9 archangel
father: 6 Kohath
grandson: 6 Abijah

Uris, Leon

novel: 5 QBVII 6 Exodus, The Haj, Trinity 9 Battle Cry 13 The Angry Hills

Uri's son

5 Geber 7 Bezalel

urn

4 vase 7 samovar
Greek: 7 amphora

Ursa Major

9 Great Bear

Ursa Minor

10 Little Bear
star: 7 Polaris

Ur's son

7 Eliphal

Uruguay

capital: 10 Montevideo
monetary unit: 4 peso

usable

4 open 9 operative 10 accessible, functional

usage

3 way 4 form, lead, wont 5 habit, trick 6 choice, custom, manner, praxis 7 guiding, process 8 ceremony, guidance, habitude, practice 9 formality, procedure 10 conve-

nance, convention, preference, proceeding
combining form: 4 nomo

use

3 ply, run, way 4 duty, goal, mark, need, play, take, talk, wont, work 5 apply, avail, habit, inure, serve, speak, treat, trick, value, wield, worth 6 bestow, custom, demand, employ, govern, handle, manage, manner, object, parley, praxis, profit, target 7 account, benefit, control, exploit, fitness, operate, purpose, service, utility, utilize 8 accustom, ceremony, deal with, efficacy, exercise, exertion, function, habitude, impose on, occasion, practice, regulate 9 advantage, appliance, formality, habituate, objective, operation, relevance 10 converse in, employment, exercising, impose upon, manipulate 11 application, familiarize 12 adaptability, availability 13 applicability

used

8 shopworn 10 secondhand

used up

5 all in, spent 6 bleary, effete 7 drained, far-gone, worn-out 8 depleted 9 exhausted, washed-out

useful

3 fit 4 good, meet 5 brave, handy, utile 6 proper, toward 7 benefic, helpful 8 favoring, suitable 9 favorable, practical 10 beneficial, convenient, functional, propitious 11 appropriate, practicable, serviceable 12 advantageous

usefulness

7 account, service, utility 9 advantage, relevance 13 applicability

useless

4 vain 6 futile 7 fustian, inutile 8 abortive, unusable 10 unavailing, unpurposed, unworkable 11 impractical, ineffective, ineffectual, unavailable 12 unfunctional, unproductive 13 impracticable, nonfunctional, unserviceable

user

6 addict 7 pothead 8 utilizer
suffix: 4 ster

use up

3 eat 4 draw 5 drain, spend 6 devour, expend, finish 7 consume, deplete, exhaust 8 bankrupt, draw down 10 impoverish, run through

usher

4 lead 7 precede, preface 9 introduce

usher in

5 set up 6 launch 8 initiate 9 institute, introduce, originate 10 inaugurate

U.S.S.R, former

capital: 6 Moscow
leader: 5 Beria (Lavrenty), Lenin (Vladimir) 6 Stalin (Joseph) 7 Gromyko (Andrey), Kosygin (Aleksey), Molotov (Vyacheslav) 8 Andropov (Yury), Brezhnev (Leonid), Bukharin (Nikolay), Podgorny (Nikolay), Zinovyev (Grigory) 9 Chernenko (Konstantin), Gorbachev (Mikhail) 10 Khrushchev (Nikita)
monetary unit: 5 ruble
republic: 5 Tajik, Uzbek 6 Kazakh, Kirgiz, Latvia, Russia 7 Armenia, Estonia, Georgia, Tadzhik, Turkmen, Ukraine 8 Moldavia 9 Kirgiziya, Lithuania 10 Azerbaijan, Belorussia, Kazakhstan, Tajikistan, Uzbekistan 12 Turkmenistan

usual

4 rife 5 plain, typic 6 common, normal, wonted 7 chronic, current, general, natural, regular, routine, typical 8 accepted, everyday, familiar, ordinary, workaday 9 customary, plain Jane, prevalent, quotidian 10 accustomed, prevailing 11 commonplace 12 unremarkable

usually

7 as a rule 8 commonly, wontedly 9 sometimes 10 by ordinary, frequently, now and then, ordinarily 11 customarily, now and again 12 consistently, once and again

usurer

7 Shylock 9 loan shark

usurp

6 assume, cutout 7 preempt 8 accroach, arrogate, displace, supplant 10 commandeer 11 appropriate

Utah

capital: 12 Salt Lake City
college, university: 10 Weber State 12 Brigham Young
neighbor: 5 Idaho 6 Nevada 7 Arizona, Wyoming 8 Colorado
nickname: 11 Mormon State 12 Beehive State
state flower: 8 sego lily

utensil

4 fork, tool 5 knife, spoon 8 coquille, teaspoon 9 implement 10 instrument
cooking: (see at **kitchen**)

uterus

4 womb

Uther Pendragon

son: 6 Arthur
wife: 6 Ygerne 7 Igraine

utile

5 handy 6 useful 9 practical 10 functional 11 practicable, serviceable

utilitarian

4 hard 7 practic 9 practical, pragmatic, realistic 10 unromantic 11 down-to-earth, pragmatical 12 matter-of-fact
philosopher: 4 Mill (John Stuart) 7 Bentham (Jeremy)

utility

3 use 7 account, fitness, service 9 advantage, relevance 10 usefulness

utilize

3 use 5 apply 6 bestow, employ, handle 7 advance, exploit, forward, further, promote 8 exercise

utmost

3 top 7 extreme, maximal, maximum, outside 8 damndest, darndest, farthest, furthest, remotest 9 damnedest, darnedest

utopia

4 Zion 6 heaven 7 arcadia 8 paradise 9 Cockaigne, dreamland, fairyland, Shangri-la 10 dreamworld, lubberland, never-never, wonderland 12 promised land

Utopia author

4 More (Thomas)

utopian

5 ideal, lofty 6 edenic 7 dreamer 8 abstract, arcadian, idealist 9 ambitious, grandiose, ideologue, visionary 10 idealistic, impossible, millennial, unfeasible 11 pretentious 12 otherworldly 13 castle-builder, impracticable

Uttar Pradesh

capital: 7 Lucknow
country: 5 India

utter

3 say 4 blue, dang, darn, durn, pure, rank, talk, tell 5 black, blank,

gross, sheer, speak, stark, state, total, voice **6** arrant, blamed, dashed, deuced **7** blasted, blessed, chime in, declare, deliver, dog-gone, flat-out, goldarn, perfect, regular **8** absolute, all-fired, blighted, blinding, bring out, complete, crashing, infernal, outright, positive, throw-out, vocalize **9** dad-blamed, dad-burned, downright, out-and-out, verbalize **10** blithering, confounded, consummate, dad-blasted, double-dyed **11** come out with, straight-out, unmitigated, unqualified **13** blankety-blank, thoroughgoing

utterance
4 talk, vent, word **5** parol, voice **6** speech **8** speaking, vocalism **9** discourse, statement **10** expression **12** articulation, vocalization **13** verbalization

utterly
3 all **4** just, well **5** à fond, fully, plumb, quite **6** in toto, purely, wholly **7** exactly, totally **8** all in all, entirely **9** perfectly **10** altogether, completely, thoroughly

uttermost
7 extreme **8** farthest, furthest, remotest

Utu
6 sun-god
father: **5** Nanna
mother: **6** Ningal

Uzai's son
5 Palal

Uzal's father
6 Joktan

Uzbek capital
8 Tashkent

Uzzah
father: **6** Shimei **8** Abinadab
son: **6** Shimea

Uzzi
father: **4** Bani **5** Bukki **6** Michri
son: **4** Elah **8** Zerahiah

Uzziah
father: **5** Harim, Shaul **7** Amaziah
son: **6** Jotham **8** Jonathan

Uzziel
brother: **5** Amram, Izhar
father: **6** Kohath **8** Harhaiah, Jeduthun
grandfather: **4** Levi
son: **6** Sithri **7** Mishael **8** Elzaphan

vacancy
4 void 6 vacuum 7 vacuity 8 voidness 9 blankness, emptiness 11 vacuousness 12 desertedness

vacant
4 bare, idle, void 5 blank, clear, empty, inane, stark, unlet 6 unused 7 deadpan, untaken, vacuous, witless 8 unfilled 10 tenantless, unoccupied 11 emptyheaded, thoughtless 12 inexpressive, unexpressive

vacate
4 quit, void 5 annul, clear, empty, leave, quash 6 give up, repeal, revoke 7 abandon, rescind, retract, reverse 8 abrogate, dissolve, part from, part with 9 discharge 10 relinquish

vacation
4 rest, trip 5 break, leave 6 recess 7 holiday, respite, time off 8 furlough 12 intermission
resort: 3 spa

vacationer
7 tourist, tripper

vaccination
4 shot 7 booster 9 injection 11 inoculation

vaccine
4 shot 5 serum
inventor: 6 Jenner (Edward)

vacillate
3 wag 4 halt, swag, sway 5 dally, waver 6 dawdle, dither, falter, seesaw, teeter, waggle, wigwag, wobble 7 stagger, swither, whiffle 8 hesitate 9 alternate 12 fiddle-faddle, shilly-shally, teeter-totter, wiggle-waggle

vacillating
4 weak 5 shaky, timid 6 dickey, fickle, unsure, wobbly 7 erratic, halting, unfixed 8 dallying, dawdling, doubtful, doubting, hesitant, insecure, rootless, shifting, stalling, unstable, unsteady, volatile, wavering 9 demurring, eccentric, faltering, fluctuant, mercurial, pendulous, tentative, uncertain, unsettled, weak-kneed, whiffling 10 changeable, hesitating, inconstant, indecisive, irresolute, undecisive, unresolved 11 fluctuating, oscillating 12 double-minded, shilly-shally, wiggle-waggle 13 dillydallying

vacillation
5 doubt 8 dallying, demurral, stalling, to-and-fro, wavering 9 hesitancy 10 hesitation, indecision 12 irresolution, shilly-shally 13 dillydallying

vacuity
4 hole, nada, void 6 cavity, hollow 7 inanity, nullity, vacancy 8 bareness, dullness, nihility, voidness 9 blankness, bleakness, emptiness, inaneness, stupidity 10 barrenness, hollowness 11 nothingness, vacuousness 12 desolateness, nonexistence

vacuous
4 bare, dull, void 5 blank, clear, empty, inane, silly, stark 6 stupid, vacant 7 foolish, shallow 11 empty-headed, superficial

vacuousness
7 vacancy, vacuity 8 voidness 9 blankness, emptiness

vacuum
4 void 5 space 9 emptiness

vacuum tube
5 diode 6 triode 7 pentode, tetrode
casing: 4 bulb
suffix: 4 tron

vade mecum
5 guide 6 manual 8 Baedeker, handbook 9 guidebook 10 compendium 11 enchiridion

vadimonium
4 bond 6 pledge 8 contract, security

___ Vadis
3 Quo

vagabond
3 bum 4 hobo, roam, rove 5 drift, gypsy, piker, range, rogue, rover, stiff, stray, tramp 6 beggar, boomer, canter, picaro, ramble, roamer, roving, wander 7 drifter, floater, gangrel, meander, migrant, nomadic, swagger, swagman, traipse, tramper, vagrant 8 bohemian, clochard, derelict, picaroon, roadster, runabout, runagate, straggle, traveler, wanderer 9 itinerant, itinerate, straggler, transient, wandering, wayfaring 10 street arab 11 perambulant, peripatetic, Weary Willie 13 parambulatory

vagarious
5 kinky 7 erratic 8 freakish, whimsied 9 arbitrary, whimsical 10 capricious 12 unreasonable

vagary
3 bee 4 kink, whim 5 dream, fancy, freak, humor, quirk 6 megrim 7 boutade, caprice, conceit, fantasy 8 crotchet, day-dream

vagrancy
6 roving 7 hoboism, roaming 8 nomadism, rambling 9 itineracy, wandering 10 itinerancy

vagrant
see **vagabond**

vague
3 dim 4 hazy 5 blear, faint, foggy, misty, muddy, mushy 6 bleary, blurry, cloudy, dreamy, opaque, vapory 7 bleared, obscure, shadowy, unclear, unplain 8 nebulous, vaporous 9 ambiguous, dreamlike, equivocal, tenebrous, uncertain

10 ill-defined, indefinite, indistinct, unexplicit **12** undetermined **13** indeterminate, unsubstantial

vain
4 idle, puny, void **5** empty, pensy, petty, proud **6** futile, hollow, otiose, paltry **7** foppish, haughty, stuck-up, trivial, useless **8** abortive, arrogant, boastful, bootless, conceity, dandyish, delusive, delusory, egoistic, nugatory, trifling **9** conceited, fruitless, valueless, worthless **10** egocentric, misleading, profitless, unavailing **11** coxcombical, ineffective, ineffectual, unavailable **12** narcissistic, self-exalting, unproductive, unprofitable, vainglorious **13** inefficacious, self-conceited, self-important, swollen-headed

vainglorious
7 stuck-up **8** insolent, vaunting **9** conceited **10** disdainful **12** narcissistic, supercilious **13** self-conceited

vainglory
5 pride **6** egoism **7** bombast, conceit, egotism **8** parading **9** arrogance, flaunting, self-glory, self-pride **10** exhibition **11** haughtiness, self-opinion **12** boastfulness

vainness
see **vanity**

valance
5 drape **7** curtain, drapery

vale
4 dale, glen **5** combe **6** valley **8** farewell

valediction
7 good-bye **8** farewell

valedictory
7 good-bye, parting **8** farewell **9** departing

valentine
4 card **7** beloved **10** sweetheart

Valentine
beloved: **6** Silvia
sister: **8** Margaret
slayer: **5** Faust
twin brother: **5** Orson
wife: **9** Clerimond

valet
3 man **4** goad **7** servant **10** manservant

Vali
father: **4** Odin
guardian of: **7** justice

mother: **4** Rind **5** Rindr
victim: **5** Hoder

valiance
see **valor**

valiant
see **valorous**

valid
4 just, true **5** legal, licit, solid, sound **6** cogent, lawful, potent, strong **7** telling **8** attested, decisive, verified **9** confirmed, effective, effectual **10** acceptable, conclusive, convincing, definitive, determined, persuasive, satisfying **11** established **12** corroborated, demonstrated, satisfactory **13** determinative, substantiated

validate
5 prove **6** ratify, verify **7** approve, bear out, confirm, endorse, justify, probate **8** legalize, sanction **11** corroborate, rubber-stamp **12** authenticate, substantiate

validity
5 force, point, punch **7** cogency, gravity, potency **8** efficacy **9** soundness **13** effectiveness

validness
see **validity**

valise
3 bag **4** grip **7** luggage **8** gripsack, suitcase

Valjean's pursuer
6 Javert

Valkyrie
6 maiden **8** Brynhild

valley
4 dale, dell, glen, vale **5** basin, combe, gorge, gully, swale **6** canyon, dingle, hollow, ravine, rincon **10** depression
Africa-Asia: **4** Rift **9** Great Rift
Alps: **11** Grindelwald
ancient Greece: **5** Nemea
arid: **6** bolson
California: **4** Napa **5** Death, Squaw **8** Imperial, Yosemite **11** San Fernando
Dead Sea area: **6** Arabah
Dominican Republic: **5** Cibao
Egypt: **6** Kharga
England: **5** Doone
Germany: **4** Ruhr
Greece: **5** Tembi, Tempe
India: **4** Kulu
Ireland: **5** Avoca, Ovoca
Israel: **4** Elah
Lebanon: **4** Bika

moon: **5** rille
New York: **6** Sleepy **12** Sleepy Hollow
Pennsylvania: **7** Nittany
Scotland: **7** Glen Roy
steep: **6** ravine
Switzerland: **5** Hasli
Virginia: **10** Shenandoah
volcanic: **5** atrio
Washington: **11** Grand Coulee

vallum
4 wall **7** rampart

Valmiki's epic
8 Ramayana

valor
4 guts, sand **6** mettle, spirit **7** bravery, courage, heroism, prowess **8** backbone, tenacity, valiance, valiancy **9** fortitude, gallantry **10** resolution

valorous
4 bold **5** brave **7** doughty, valiant **8** fearless, intrepid **9** audacious, dauntless, undaunted **10** courageous

valuable
4 dear **6** costly, prized, worthy **7** admired **8** esteemed, precious, property **9** expensive, priceless, respected, treasured **11** appreciated

valuate
4 rate **5** assay, set at **6** assess, survey **8** appraise, estimate

valuation
4 cost **5** price, worth **6** charge, rating **7** account, opinion **8** estimate, judgment **9** appraisal **10** assessment, estimation **12** appraisement

value
4 cost, rate **5** assay, gauge, merit, price, prize, set at, worth **6** assess, charge, esteem, figure, reckon, revere, survey, virtue **7** account, apprize, caliber, care for, cherish, compute, expense, quality, stature **8** appraise, estimate, treasure, venerate **9** appraisal, reverence **10** appreciate, assessment
Scottish: **4** feck

valueless
6 draffy, drossy, no-good **7** inutile, nothing **8** unworthy **9** worthless

valve
3 tap **4** cock, gate **6** faucet, poppet, spigot **7** hydrant, petcock, shutoff **8** stopcock
cardiac: **6** mitral **8** bicuspid

vamoose
  3 git 4 kite, scat 5 scram 6 begone, decamp, get out 7 skiddoo, take off 8 clear out, hightail 9 skedaddle

vamp
  3 fix 4 do up, mend 5 fix up, flirt, frame, patch, siren 6 cook up, devise, invent, make up, repair 7 brush up, charmer, concoct, dream up, enticer, furbish, hatch up, rebuild, touch up 8 contrive, coquette, overhaul 9 formulate, inveigler, refurbish, temptress 10 gold digger, seductress 11 enchantress, femme fatale, recondition, reconstruct

vampire
  3 bat 7 Dracula 9 Nosferatu 11 bloodsucker

van
  3 car 4 head, lead 5 truck, wagon 6 leader 7 vehicle

vandal
  4 lout 6 looter, ruiner 7 defacer, hoodlum, ravager, ruffian, spoiler, wrecker 8 hooligan, pillager, ruinator 9 despoiler, destroyer, plunderer, spoliator 10 devastator, iconoclast

vandalize
  3 mar 5 trash, wreck 6 deface, rip off, tear up 7 destroy

Vandal king
  8 Genseric

Vandyke
  5 beard

vane
  3 arm 9 indicator 11 weathercock

vanguard
  9 forefront

Vaniah's father
  4 Bani

vanilla
  7 extract

vanish
  3 die 4 fade, melt 5 clear 8 dissolve, evanesce, melt away 9 disappear, evaporate 13 dematerialize

vanity
  6 egoism 7 conceit 8 self-love 9 vainglory

Vanity Fair author
  9 Thackeray (William Makepeace)

vanquish
  4 beat 5 crush 6 defeat, humble, reduce, subdue 7 conquer, subvert, trample 8 bear down, beat down, overturn, surmount 9 overpower, subjugate

vanquisher
  5 champ 6 master, victor, winner 7 subduer 8 champion, defeater 9 conqueror 10 subjugator

vanquishment
  4 rout 6 defeat 7 beating, debacle, licking, mastery, subdual 8 drubbing 9 overthrow, trouncing 10 defeasance 11 shellacking, subjugation

vantage
  4 draw, edge, odds 5 bulge, start 8 deadwood, handicap 9 allowance, head start

vapid
  4 dull, flat, weak 5 inane 6 jejune 7 insipid, sapless 9 driveling, innocuous, milk-toast, tasteless 10 flavorless, namby-pamby, wishywashy 13 unimaginative, uninteresting

vapor
  3 fog, gas 4 haze, mist, smog 5 brume, cloud, smoke, steam 6 breath, nimbus
  combining form: 3 atm 4 atmo, mano 5 atmid 6 atmido 7 pneumat 8 pneumato
  condensed: 3 dew
  frozen: 4 rime 5 frost
  noxious: 6 miasma

vaporize
  4 boil 9 evaporate

vaporous
  4 airy, hazy 5 foggy, gassy, misty, mushy, vague, wispy 6 aerial, cloudy, unreal 7 gaseous 8 ethereal, illusory 13 unsubstantial

vaquero
  6 cowboy 8 herdsman

varia
  10 miscellany

variable
  5 fluid 6 fickle, fitful, mobile, shifty 7 mutable, protean, unequal 8 slippery, ticklish, unstable, unsteady, volatile, weathery 9 changeful, irregular, mercurial, spasmodic, uncertain, unequable, unsettled, ununiform 10 capricious, changeable, inconstant 13 temperamental

variance
  6 change, strife 7 discord, dissent 8 conflict, disunity, division, severing 9 deviation, disaccord, sundering, variation 10 contention, difference, dissension, dissidence, separation 11 fluctuation

variation
  4 turn 5 shift 6 change 8 mutation, variance 9 disparity 10 alteration, deflection, difference, divergence 11 discrepancy 12 modification 13 dissimilarity

varicolored
  see **variegated**

varicose
  7 cirsoid, dilated, swollen

varied
  5 mixed 6 motley 8 assorted, chowchow 11 promiscuous 12 conglomerate, multifarious 13 heterogeneous, miscellaneous

variegated
  4 pied 5 pinto 6 calico, motley, mottle 7 checked, dappled, flecked, freaked, marbled, mottled, piebald, spotted 8 discolor, skewbald, speckled, stippled, streaked 9 checkered, multihued, spattered 10 multicolor, parti-color, polychrome, versicolor 11 varicolored 12 multicolored, parti-colored, versicolored 13 polychromatic

variety
  3 ilk 4 kind, rank, sort, type 5 grade 6 medley, nature, stripe 7 species 8 multeity 9 character, diversity, variation 10 assortment, miscellany 11 description, diverseness, variousness 12 multiformity, multiplicity 13 heterogeneity

various
  4 many, some 6 divers, legion, sundry, unlike, varied 7 certain, distant, diverse, several, unalike, unequal, variant, varying 8 assorted, changing, discrete, distinct, numerous, peculiar, populous, separate 9 different, disparate, divergent, unsimilar 10 dissimilar, individual, omnigenous, voluminous 11 distinctive 12 multifarious, multitudinal 13 heterogeneous, miscellaneous, multitudinous

varlet
  5 knave 6 rascal 9 scoundrel

varmint
  6 animal, rascal 7 critter

varnish
  4 coat 5 glaze, japan, white 6 veneer, whiten 7 shellac 8 palliate 9 extenuate, gloss over, gloze over,

sugarcoat, whitewash **10** blanch over
component: **5** resin

vary
3 run **4** part, turn **5** alter, range **6** change, depart, differ, divide, extend, modify, mutate **7** deviate, digress, discord, dissent, diverge, qualify **8** disagree, modulate, separate **9** disaccord, refashion

vase
3 jar, urn **4** ewer **6** crater, krater, vessel **7** amphora, potiche **8** boughpot

Vashni's father
6 Samuel

Vashti's husband
6 Xerxes **9** Ahasuerus

vassal
4 esne, leud, serf **5** helot, liege, slave **6** tenant, varlet **7** bondman, feodary, homager, peasant, servant, subject **8** liegeman **9** dependent, underling **11** beneficiary, subordinate
high-ranking: **7** vavasor **8** vavasour
office: **5** feoff

vast
3 big **4** huge, wide **5** ample, broad, giant, large **6** cosmic **7** immense, titanic **8** colossal, enormous, far-flung, gigantic, spacious, whopping **9** capacious, expansive **10** monumental, tremendous, widespread **12** astronomical

vastness
8 enormity, hugeness **9** immensity, magnitude **12** enormousness

vat
3 tub, tun **4** back, beck, cask, kier, tank **5** keeve, kieve **6** barrel, vessel **7** cistern **8** cauldron
cheese: **7** chessel

vatic
6 mantic **7** fatidic **8** Delphian, oracular **9** prophetic, sibylline **11** apocalyptic, prophetical

Vatican
chapel: **7** Sistine
church: **11** Saint Peter's
ruler: **4** Pope
site: **4** Rome

vaticinal
see **vatic**

vaticinate
4 call **5** augur **7** portend, predict, presage **8** forecast, foretell, prophesy **9** adumbrate **13** prognosticate

vaudeville
4 song **5** revue **7** variety **9** burlesque **13** entertainment

vaudevillian
5 actor, comic **6** dancer, singer **7** acrobat **9** performer **11** entertainer

vault
3 hop, lop, pit **4** arch, cave, dome, jump, leap, over, rise, room, soar, tomb **5** bound, clear, crypt, mount **6** ascend, bounce, cavern, cellar, hurdle, spring, upleap **7** saltate **8** catacomb, overjump, overleap, surmount, upspring **9** negotiate **10** undercroft

vaulting
7 emulous **8** aspiring **9** ambitious **12** enthusiastic **13** opportunistic

vaunt
4 blow, brag, crow, puff **5** boast, mouth, prate **6** expose, flaunt, parade **7** display, exhibit, show off **8** brandish **9** gasconade **11** rodomontade

Ve
brother: **4** Odin, Vili
victim: **4** Ymir

veal
4 calf
cutlet: **9** schnitzel
roasted: **10** fricandeau
shank: **8** osso buco

vector
7 carrier

Vedic
god: **4** Agni, Soma, Vayu, Yama **5** Aditi, Bhaga, Dyaus, Indra, Mitra, Rudra **6** Aditya, Varuna **7** Savitar
goddess: **4** Usas **5** Ushas
hymn: **6** mantra
language: **8** Sanskrit
treatise: **9** Upanishad
writing: **7** Samhita

veer
3 dip, yaw **4** skew, slue, turn, whip **5** avert, pivot, sheer, shift, twist, wheel, whirl **6** depart, divert, swerve **7** bear off, deflect, deviate, digress, diverge **8** angle off, train off **9** volte-face

vega
5 plain **6** meadow

vegetable
3 pea, soy, yam **4** bean, beet, corn, kale, leek, okra, soya, taro, wort **5** chive, cress, green, onion, plant **6** carrot, celery, cowpea, endive, garlic, lentil, peanut, pepper, potato, radish, sorrel, squash, tomato, turnip **7** cabbage, chayote, dullard, lettuce, mustard, parsley, parsnip, pumpkin, rhubarb, salsify, shallot, soybean, spinach **8** broccoli, collards, cucumber, eggplant, kohlrabi, lima bean, rutabaga, scallion **9** artichoke, asparagus, muskmelon **10** watermelon **11** cauliflower, horseradish, sweet potato
dish: **5** salad
mold: **5** humus
oyster: **7** salsify
pear: **7** chayote
seller: **6** grocer **7** grocery **12** costermonger
sponge: **5** luffa
spread: **4** oleo **9** margarine

vegetarian
9 herbivore

vegetate
4 idle, laze **8** languish, stagnate **9** hibernate

vegetation
5 flora **6** growth, plants **7** verdure **8** greenery
floating: **4** sudd **8** pleuston

vehement
3 hot **4** wild **5** rabid **6** ardent, fervid, fierce, hearty, heated, lively, potent **7** fervent, frantic, furious, intense, vicious, violent, zealous **8** emphatic, forceful, powerful, terrible **9** delirious, desperate, energetic, exquisite, perfervid **10** passionate, pronounced **11** impassioned **12** concentrated

vehicle
3 bus, car, van **4** auto, tool **5** agent, buggy, means, organ, sedan, wagon **6** agency, medium, vector **7** carrier, channel **8** ministry **9** implement, transport **10** automobile, conveyance, instrument
baby's: **4** pram **8** carriage, stroller
child's: **4** bike **5** trike **7** bicycle, scooter **8** tricycle
combining form: **6** mobile
farm: **4** wain **7** tractor
horse-drawn: **4** cart, dray **5** buggy, lorry, sulky, wagon **6** hansom, landau **8** carriage
military: **4** jeep, tank
one-wheeled: **8** unicycle
passenger: **3** bus, cab, car **4** auto, taxi **7** ricksha
public: **3** bus **4** tram **5** train **6** subway **7** omnibus, trolley
Roman: **7** chariot
winter: **4** sled **6** sleigh **8** snowplow

veil
4 hide, mask, wrap 5 cloak, color, cover, front, guise 6 enfold, enwrap, facade, invest, mantle, screen, shroud 7 blanket, conceal, cover up, curtain, enclose, envelop, secrete 8 calyptra, coloring, disguise, enshroud 10 camouflage, false front, overspread, spread over
Muslim: 7 yashmak
netting: 6 maline 7 malines

vein
3 way 4 hint, line, lode, mind, mode, mood, seam, tone, tube, vena 5 humor, shade, style, tenor, tinge, touch, trace 6 fettle, manner, nature, spirit, strain, streak, temper, vessel 7 channel, fashion 8 tincture 9 character, suspicion 10 complexion, suggestion 11 disposition, temperament
combining form: 3 ven 4 veni, veno 5 phleb 6 phlebo
deposit: 3 ore
fluid: 5 blood
leaf: 3 rib
leg: 7 saphena
neck: 7 jugular
small: 6 venule
varicose: 5 varix

velar
7 palatal

veldt
5 plain 6 meadow 9 grassland

velitation
5 brush, run-in, set-to 8 skirmish 9 encounter

velleity
4 mind, will, wish 5 fancy 6 liking 8 pleasure, volition 11 inclination

vellicate
3 jig, lug, nip 4 jerk, snap, yank 5 lurch, pinch 6 fidget, jiggle, twitch

velocipede
4 bike 5 cycle 7 bicycle 10 two-wheeler

velocity
3 bat 4 gait, pace 5 haste, hurry, speed 7 headway, impetus 8 celerity, dispatch, momentum, rapidity 9 quickness, rapidness, swiftness 10 expedition

velum
4 veil 8 membrane

velvet
5 cloth 6 fabric, profit 8 winnings
on: 4 rich, safe 7 wealthy

velvety
4 soft 5 plush, silky, sleek, slick 6 glossy, plushy, satiny, silken, smooth 7 cottony 10 velutinous

venal
4 hack, paid 6 sordid 7 buyable, corrupt, crooked, ignoble, vicious 8 bribable, hireling, infamous 9 mercenary, nefarious, unethical 10 flagitious, iniquitous, praetorian 11 corruptible, purchasable 12 unprincipled, unscrupulous

vend
4 give, hawk, sell, toot 5 sound 6 blazon, market, monger, peddle 7 declare, publish 8 announce, huckster, proclaim 9 advertise, broadcast 10 promulgate

vendee
5 buyer 6 emptor 9 purchaser

vendetta
4 feud 9 blood feud

vendible
7 salable 8 sellable 10 marketable

vendibles
5 goods, wares 11 commodities, merchandise

vendor
6 duffer, hawker, seller 7 higgler, packman, peddler, roadman 8 huckster, merchant, outcrier, salesman 9 cheap-jack, cheap-john

vendue
4 sale 7 auction

veneer
4 face, mask, show, veil 5 cover, front, gloss, white 6 facade, whiten 7 coating, varnish 8 disguise, palliate 9 extenuate, gloss over, gloze over, sugarcoat, whitewash 10 blanch over, false front

venerable
3 old 4 aged 5 hoary 6 age-old, sacred 7 ancient, antique, elderly, honored, revered, stately 8 imposing, Noachian, reverend, timeworn 9 admirable, dignified, estimable, honorable 10 reverenced, worshipful 11 patriarchal, reverential 12 antediluvian

venerate
5 adore, honor 6 revere 7 idolize, worship 9 reverence

veneration
3 awe 5 dulia, honor 6 esteem, homage 7 respect, worship 9 reverence

venery
4 game 5 chase 7 hunting

venesection
10 phlebotomy 12 bloodletting

Venetian
boat: 7 gondola
boatman: 9 gondolier
canal: 3 rii (plural), rio
ruler: 4 doge
street: 5 canal

Venezuela
capital: 7 Caracas
monetary unit: 7 bolivar

Venezuelan
herdsman: 7 llanero
liberator: 7 Bolívar (Simón)
people: 5 Carib 6 Timote

venge
7 redress 9 vindicate

vengeance
6 return 7 revenge 8 avenging, reprisal, requital, revanche 9 repayment 10 avengement 11 counterblow, retaliation, retribution

vengeful
7 hostile 8 inimical, wreakful 9 rancorous 10 vindictive 12 antagonistic

venial
5 minor 7 trivial 8 harmless, trifling 9 allowable, excusable, tolerable 10 forgivable, pardonable, remittable 13 insignificant

Venice of the East
7 Bangkok

Venice of the North
9 Stockholm

Veni, Creator ___
8 Spiritus

venireman
5 juror

venison
4 deer

veni, vidi, ___
4 vici

venom
4 bane 5 virus 6 poison, rancor 7 ill will, vitriol 9 contagion, malignity, virulence

venomous
5 toxic 6 deadly, malign, poison 7 baleful, malefic 8 mephitic, toxicant, viperish, viperous, virulent 9 malignant, poisonous, viperlike 10 maleficent, malevolent

vent

3 air, put 4 emit, give, hole, slit, slot 5 issue, loose, state, utter, voice 6 assert, outlet 7 cast out, declare, exhaust, express, give off, give out, opening, orifice, release, unleash 8 aperture, throw off 9 discharge, statement, take out on, utterance 10 expression 12 articulation, vocalization 13 verbalization

venter

3 gut 5 belly 6 paunch 7 abdomen, stomach

ventilate

3 air, put 4 give, moot 5 state 6 broach, debate, go into, take up, talk of 7 bring up, discuss, express, publish 8 rap about, talk over 9 advertise, broadcast, introduce, thresh out 10 deliberate

ventral area

7 abdomen
combining form: 5 gastr 6 gaster, gastri, gastro 7 gastero

ventricle

7 chamber
combining form: 4 cele, coel 5 coele

ventriloquist

companion: 5 dummy
famous: 6 Bergen (Edgar)

venture

3 bet, try 4 dare, defy, face, feat, gest, risk 5 beard, brave, crack, fling, front, peril, stake, wager 6 banter, chance, expose, gamble, hazard 7 attempt, emprise, exploit, imperil, jeopard, lay open, operate, outdare, outface, play for 8 endanger, jeopardy 9 adventure, challenge, speculate 10 enterprise, jeopardize 11 speculation, undertaking

venturesome

4 bold, rash 5 brave, stout 6 daring, sturdy 8 overbold, reckless, stalwart 9 audacious, daredevil, foolhardy 11 adventurous, temerarious

venturous

see **venturesome**

venue

4 side, site 5 place 6 ground, locale

Venus

6 planet, Vesper 8 Hesperus; (see also **Aphrodite**)

Venus de ___

4 Milo

___ vera

4 aloe

veracious

4 just, true 5 right, valid 6 direct, strict 8 accurate, faithful, truthful 9 veridical 11 true-tongued, undeceitful, undeceptive, undistorted, unvarnished 12 truth-telling 13 truth-speaking

veracity

4 fact 5 truth 6 gospel, truism, verity 7 honesty 8 accuracy 9 actuality, exactness, frankness 11 correctness, factualness 12 truthfulness, veridicality

veranda

5 lanai, porch 6 piazza 7 balcony, gallery, portico

verb

auxiliary: 2 am, be, do, is 3 are, can, did, had, has, may, was 4 have, must, were, will 5 could, might, shall, would 6 should
form: 6 active, gerund 7 passive 10 infinitive, participle
kind: 10 transitive 12 intransitive
linking: 6 copula
mood: 8 optative 10 imperative, indicative 11 subjunctive
suffix: (see at **suffix**)
tense: 4 past 6 aorist, future 7 perfect, present 9 predicate 10 pluperfect

verbal

4 oral 6 spoken 7 literal 8 verbatim 9 unwritten 11 traditional, word-for-word, word-of-mouth

verbalism

6 phrase 7 diction, styling, wordage, wording 8 parlance, phrasing, verbiage 9 prolixity, verbosity, windiness, wordiness 10 prolixness 11 phraseology, verboseness

verbalization

4 talk 6 speech 8 speaking 9 discourse, utterance

verbalize

3 air, say 4 give, talk, vent, word 5 speak, state, utter, voice 7 express 8 vocalize 9 ventilate

verbatim

5 close, exact 6 direct, strict, verbal 7 exactly, literal, precise 8 directly, faithful 9 literally, literatim, precisely 10 accurately 11 word-for-word

verbiage

6 phrase 7 diction, wordage, wording 8 parlance, phrasing, pleo-

nasm 9 floridity, tautology, verbalism, verbality, verbosity 10 floridness, periphrase, redundancy, roundabout 11 periphrasis, phraseology

verbose

5 windy, wordy 6 prolix 7 diffuse, flowery 9 redundant 10 long-winded, palaverous, pleonastic 11 tautologous 12 magniloquent, periphrastic 13 grandiloquent

verboseness

see **verbosity**

verbosity

7 bombast 8 verbiage 9 prolixity, verbalism, windiness, wordiness 10 prolixness, redundancy 11 verboseness

verboten

5 taboo 6 banned 8 outlawed 9 forbidden 10 disallowed, prohibited, unlicensed 11 disapproved 12 unauthorized, unsanctioned

verdant

3 raw 5 green 6 grassy

verdict

6 ruling 7 finding, opinion 8 decision, judgment

Verdi opera

4 Aida 6 Ernani, Oberto, Otello 7 Nabucco 8 Don Carlo, Falstaff 9 Rigoletto 10 La Traviata 11 Il Trovatore

verdure

5 green 7 foliage, leafage, umbrage 8 greenery 10 vegetation

verge

3 hem, lip, rim 4 abut, brim, edge, join, lean, line 5 bound, brink, march, point, skirt, touch 6 adjoin, border, butt on, fringe, margin, tend to, trench 7 incline, outline, selvage, touch on 8 approach, neighbor, surround 9 threshold, touch upon 10 border line, tend toward 11 butt against, communicate

Vergil

epic: 6 Aeneid
poems: 8 Bucolics, Georgics

veridical

see **veracious**

verification

5 proof 12 confirmation

verify

3 try 4 test 5 prove 6 settle 7 bear out, confirm, justify 8 document, validate 9 establish 11 corrobo-

rate, demonstrate **12** authenticate, substantiate

verily
3 yea **4** even **5** truly **6** indeed

verisimility
5 color **12** plausibility

veritable
4 real, true, very **6** actual **7** factual, genuine **8** bona fide, undenied **9** authentic, undoubted, unrefuted **10** sure-enough **11** indubitable

verity
5 truth **6** gospel, truism **8** veracity **12** truthfulness, veridicality **13** veraciousness

vermeil
4 ruby

vermiform
8 wormlike

vermilion
3 red

vermin
4 lice, mice, rats **5** fleas **7** bedbugs

verminous
6 filthy **7** noxious **9** offensive

Vermont
capital: **10** Montpelier
college, university: **7** Norwich **10** Middlebury, St. Michael's
state bird: **12** hermit thrush
state flower: **9** red clover

vernacular
4 cant **5** argot, idiom, lingo, slang **6** jargon, patois, patter, speech, tongue, vulgar **7** dialect, vulgate **8** language **10** colloquial **12** mother tongue

vernacularism
8 slangism, solecism **9** barbarism, vulgarism **10** corruption **11** impropriety

vernal
6 spring **10** springlike

Verne, Jules
character: **4** Fogg (Phileas), Nemo **12** Passepartout
submarine: **8** Nautilus

versant
2 up **6** au fait **7** abreast **8** familiar, informed **9** au courant **10** acquainted

versatile
4 able **5** handy **6** adroit, facile, gifted, mobile **7** elastic, plastic, pliable, skilled **8** flexible, skillful, talented **9** adaptable, all-around, dex-

terous, many-sided **10** conversant **11** well-rounded

verse
3 lay, ode **4** epic, poem, rune, song **5** lyric, poesy, rhyme, stich **6** ballad, jingle, poetry, sonnet, stanza **11** familiarize
analysis: **8** scansion
four-line: **8** quatrain
six-line: **6** sestet
three-line: **6** tercet
two-line: **7** couplet
writer: **4** poet; (see also **poem**)

versed
2 up **3** old, vet **5** adept **6** au fait **7** abreast, old-time, skilled, versant, veteran **8** familiar, informed, seasoned **9** au courant, competent, practical, practiced **10** acquainted, conversant **11** experienced

verseman
4 bard, poet **6** rhymer **9** poetaster, rhymester, versifier **12** balladmonger

versicolor
see **variegated**

versifier
see **verseman**

version
4 tale **5** story **6** report **7** account, history, reading **9** chronicle, narrative, rendering, rendition, rewording **10** paraphrase **11** restatement, translation **12** condensation **13** clarification, restipulation

versus
3 con **6** contra **7** against, vis-à-vis **11** over against

vertebra
4 bone
combining form: **7** spondyl **8** spondyli (plural), spondylo **9** spondylus
kind: **6** dorsal, lumbar, sacral **8** cervical, thoracic

vertebrae
4 back **5** spine **6** rachis **8** backbone **12** spinal column

vertebrate
6 animal
characteristic: **5** spine **7** cranium
kind: **4** bird, fish, frog **5** shark **6** mammal **7** lamprey, reptile

vertex
3 cap, top **4** apex, peak, roof **5** crest, crown **6** apogee, summit, tip-top, zenith **9** fastigium

Verthandi
see **Norn**

vertical
5 erect, plumb, sheer, steep **7** upright **9** up-and-down **10** straight-up **13** perpendicular
combining form: **4** orth **5** ortho

vertiginous
5 dizzy, giddy, light **6** rotary, swimmy **8** swimming **11** lightheaded

vertigo
6 megrim **9** dizziness

verve
3 pep, vim, zip **4** brio, dash, élan, fire, life, zest, zing **5** gusto, oomph **6** bounce, esprit, spirit, spring **8** buoyancy, vivacity **9** animation **10** elasticity, liveliness, resiliency

very
2 so **3** too **4** bare, mere, most, much, real, same, true **5** ideal, model, pesky, quite, super, truly **6** damned, highly, hugely, mighty, really **7** awfully, de facto, genuine, greatly, notably, parlous, precise, vitally **8** actually, bona fide, mightily, mortally, rattling, selfsame, snapping, spanking, terribly, whacking, whopping **9** authentic, eminently, extremely, genuinely, identical, tellingly, undoubted, veritable, veritably **10** dreadfully, insatiably, remarkably, strikingly, sureenough, thoroughly **11** exceedingly, indubitable **12** surpassingly **13** exceptionally
French: **4** très
German: **4** sehr
Scottish: **3** gey

vesicle
3 sac **4** cyst **6** cavity **7** bladder, blister

Vesper
5 Venus **8** Hesperus **11** evening star

vespers
6 prayer **7** service **8** evensong

⸺ Vespucci
7 Amerigo

vessel
3 ama, can, cup, jar, pan, pot, pyx, tub, urn **4** boat, bowl, drum, ewer, pail, ship, tank, tube, vase, vein **5** canal, craft, cruse, laver **6** artery, barrel, bottle, bucket, firkin, flagon, kettle, krater, pottle, situla **7** cresset, pitcher **8** crucible **10** receptacle
combining form: **3** vas **4** ange, angi, vasi, vaso **5** angia (plural), angio

6 angium, arteri, vascul 7 arterio, vasculo

drinking: 3 cup, mug 4 toby 5 cylix, flask, glass, gourd, kylix, stein, stoup 6 goblet, seidel 7 tankard, tumbler

Indian: 4 lota 5 lotah

sailing: (see at **ship**)

Scottish: 3 cog 6 cootie, quaich, quaigh 7 yetling

vest
4 coat 6 belong, invest, jacket, weskit 7 empower, pertain 9 appertain, authorize, waistcoat

Vesta
see **Hestia**

vestal
3 nun 4 pure 6 chaste, virgin 8 virginal

vestibule
4 hall 5 entry, foyer, lobby 6 portal 7 narthex, portico 8 anteroom, entryway 11 antechamber 12 entrance hall

vestige
3 rag, tag 4 path, step 5 relic, scrap, spoor, trace, track, tract, trail 6 shadow 7 memento, remains, remnant 8 footstep 9 footprint, remainder

vestment
3 alb 4 cope, garb, gown, pall, robe 5 amice, cotta, dress, fanon, orale, stole, tunic 6 rochet, sakkos 7 cassock, garment, maniple, pallium, tunicle 8 chasuble, cincture, dalmatic, parament, surplice 9 phelonion

ancient Hebrew: 5 ephod

vestry
4 room 6 closet 8 sacristy

vesture
5 cover 6 clothe 7 apparel, costume, envelop, garment 8 clothing

Vesuvius
7 volcano

vetch
4 tare
bitter: 3 ers 5 ervil

veteran
4 wise 6 expert, master, versed 7 old hand, old-time, skilled, worldly 8 old-timer, seasoned 9 longtimer, practical, practiced 10 past master 11 experienced 13 sophisticated

veto
3 nix 4 deny, kill 6 defeat, forbid, refuse, reject 7 decline 8 disallow,

negative, prohibit 9 blackball, nonplacet

vex
3 bug, ire, irk 4 chaw, fret, gall 5 anger, annoy, chafe, tease 6 abrade, bother, plague 7 provoke, torment 8 exercise 9 embarrass, infuriate

vexation
6 irking 9 annoyance, bothering, provoking 10 harassment, irritation 11 aggravation, bedevilment, provocation

vexatious
4 mean, ugly 5 pesky 6 wicked 9 troublous 11 troublesome

via
2 by 3 per 4 over, road, with 5 along 7 by way of, passage, through 8 by dint of 9 by means of 10 by virtue of

viable
6 doable 8 feasible, possible, workable 11 practicable

viaduct
6 bridge

vial
5 ampul, flask, glass, phial 6 ampule, beaker, bottle, vessel 7 ampoule 8 test tube

viands
4 eats, fare, feed, food, grub 7 edibles, nurture 8 victuals 9 provender 10 provisions 11 comestibles

viator
8 traveler, wayfarer

vibrant
5 alive, round, vital 6 rotund 7 orotund, ringing 8 plangent, resonant, sonorant, sonorous 9 consonant 10 resounding

vibrate
3 jar 4 rock 5 quake, shake, trill, twang 6 shiver, tremor 7 shudder, tremble

vibration
4 vibe 5 quake, shake, trill 6 quaver, quiver, tremor 7 flutter, shaking 8 fremitus 9 trembling 11 oscillation
Scottish: 6 dindle

vicar
6 priest 8 minister 9 clergyman

Vicar of Wakefield
author: 9 Goldsmith (Oliver)
character: 8 Primrose

vice
3 ill, sin 4 evil, flaw 5 fault, wrong 6 defect, foible 7 blemish, failing, frailty 9 depravity, indecency 10 corruption, debasement, debauchery, immorality, perversion, unchastity, wickedness 11 shortcoming

vice-president
4 veep 9 executive
American: 4 Burr (Aaron), Bush (George), Ford (Gerald), Gore (Albert), King (William) 5 Adams (John), Agnew (Spiro), Dawes (Charles), Gerry (Elbridge), Nixon (Richard Milhous), Tyler (John) 6 Arthur (Chester), Colfax (Schuyler), Curtis (Charles), Dallas (George), Garner (John Nance), Hamlin (Hannibal), Hobart (Garret), Morton (Levi), Quayle (Dan), Truman (Harry), Wilson (Woodrow) 7 Barkley (Alben), Calhoun (John Caldwell), Clinton (George), Johnson (Andrew, Lyndon Baines, Richard Mentor), Mondale (Walter), Sherman (James Schoolcraft), Wallace (Henry), Wheeler (William) 8 Coolidge (Calvin), Fillmore (Millard), Humphrey (Hubert Horatio), Marshall (Thomas), Tompkins (Daniel), Van Buren (Martin) 9 Fairbanks (Charles), Hendricks (Thomas), Jefferson (Thomas), Roosevelt (Theodore), Stevenson (Adlai) 11 Rockefeller (Nelson) 12 Breckinridge (John)

viceroy
5 nabob, ruler 6 exarch, satrap 7 khedive 8 governor 9 butterfly

vice versa
10 contrawise, conversely 12 contrariwise

vicinage
4 area 8 district, locality, vicinity 12 neighborhood

vicinity
4 area 5 range 6 extent, matter, region 8 district, locality, nearness, vicinage 9 magnitude, proximity 12 neighborhood

vicious
4 evil, mean, wild 5 feral, wrong 6 fierce, malign, putrid, rotten, savage, sinful, wicked 7 brutish, corrupt, furious, hateful, immoral, intense, violent 8 depraved, infamous, perverse, spiteful, terrible, vehement 9 desperate, malicious, malignant, miscreant, nefari-

ous, rancorous, reprobate
10 degenerate, despiteful, flagitious, iniquitous, malevolent, villainous **12** blood-thirsty

vicissitude
5 rigor, trial **6** change **7** novelty, variety **8** asperity, hardness, hardship, mutation, reversal **9** adversity, diversity, mischance **10** affliction, difficulty, innovation, misfortune **11** permutation, progression, tribulation, ups and downs

victim
4 butt, dupe, fool, gull, mark, prey **5** chump **6** pigeon, quarry, sucker **7** fall guy, gudgeon **8** casualty, offering, underdog **9** bottom dog, sacrifice

victimize
4 dupe, fool, gull, hoax **5** trick **6** pigeon **8** flimflam, hoodwink, immolate **9** bamboozle, sacrifice **11** hornswoggle

victor
3 top **5** champ, first **6** master, winner **7** subduer **8** champion, defeater **9** conquerer **10** subjugator, vanquisher

Victoria, Queen
family: **7** Hanover
father: **6** Edward
husband: **6** Albert
son: **6** Edward

Victorian
4 prig, prim **6** prissy, stuffy **10** old-maidish, tight-laced **11** puritanical, straitlaced **12** old-fashioned

victory
3 win **6** better **7** command, control, mastery, success, triumph **8** conquest, dominion, walkaway, walkover, whip hand **9** advantage, supremacy, upper hand **11** subjugation, superiority
costly: **7** Pyrrhic
easy: **8** cakewalk, walkaway
monument: **4** arch **13** Arc de Triomphe
reward: **6** spoils
sign: **3** vee
symbol: **4** flag **6** laurel, wreath

Victory author
6 Conrad (Joseph)

victuals
4 chow, eats, feed, food, grub **6** viands **7** edibles **9** provender **10** provisions **11** comestibles

___ Vidal
4 Gore

videlicet
3 viz **5** to wit **6** namely **8** scilicet

vie
3 pit **5** match, rival **6** oppose, outvie **7** compete, contend, contest, counter, play off **9** challenge

Viennese
city hall: **7** Rathaus
family: **8** Hapsburg
palace: **7** Hofburg
park: **6** Prater

Vientiane's land
4 Laos

Vietnam
capital: **5** Hanoi
monetary unit: **4** dong

Vietnamese New Year
3 Tet

view
3 aim, con, eye, see, vet **4** deem, espy, goal, look, mark, mind, plan, scan **5** audit, scene, sight, study, vista **6** behold, belief, descry, design, look at, notice, notion, object, regard, review, survey **7** canvass, check up, discern, examine, feeling, inspect, observe, opinion, outlook, picture, scenery **8** analysis, consider, gaze upon, look upon, panorama, perceive, prospect, scrutiny **9** check over, objective, sentiment **10** conviction, inspection, persuasion, scrutinize **11** contemplate, distinguish, examination, perlustrate **13** perlustration

viewable
6 ocular, visual **7** seeable, visible

viewer
7 watcher, witness **8** beholder, bysitter, looker-on, observer, onlooker **9** bystander, spectator **10** eyewitness

viewing instrument
5 glass, scope **7** glasses **9** telescope **10** binoculars, microscope
combining form: **5** scope

viewpoint
3 eye **4** side **5** angle, slant, stand **7** outlook, posture **8** attitude, position **9** direction **10** estimation, standpoint **11** perspective

vigil
4 tout **5** watch **7** lookout **12** surveillance, watch and ward

vigilance
see **vigil**

vigilant
4 agog, avid, keen **5** acute, alert, awake, aware, eager, sharp **7** anxious, wakeful **8** open-eyed, watchful **9** attentive, sharp-eyed, wide-awake **10** unsleeping

vignette
5 scene **6** sketch **7** picture **8** ornament

vigor
3 pep, vim, zip **4** bang, beef, birr, dash, fire, push, snap, tuck, zing **5** drive, force, getup, might, moxie, oomph, power, punch, steam **6** bounce, energy, muscle, spirit, starch **7** ability, potency **8** dynamism, strength, virility, vitality **9** hardihood, lustiness, manliness, puissance, soundness **10** capability, enterprise, get-up-and-go **11** healthiness

vigorous
5 brisk, hardy, husky, lusty, proud, stout, tough, vital **6** hearty, lively, potent, robust, sinewy, strong, sturdy **7** dashing, driving, dynamic, healthy, zealous **8** athletic, bouncing, muscular, powerful, slashing, spirited **9** energetic, exuberant, masterful, strenuous **10** mettlesome, red-blooded, survigorous **11** hard-driving, hard-hitting **13** rough-and-ready

Viking
see **Norse**

vile
3 low **4** base, evil, foul, mean, ugly **5** gross, nasty **6** coarse, horrid, sordid, vulgar **7** debased, ignoble, low-down, noisome, obscene, servile, squalid **8** depraved, wretched **9** abhorrent, corrupted, debauched, loathsome, offensive, perverted, repugnant, repulsive, revolting **10** despicable, disgusting **12** contemptible

Vili
brother: **2** Ve **4** Odin
victim: **4** Ymir

vilify
5 abuse, libel **6** assail, attack, berate, defame, malign, misuse **7** asperse, outrage, slander, traduce **8** denounce, mistreat, tear down **9** denigrate **10** calumniate, villainize

villa
5 manor 6 castle, estate 7 chateau, mansion

village
4 burg, town 5 bourg, thorp 6 hamlet 7 townlet
African: 4 dorp, stad 5 kraal
Indian: 6 bustee, pueblo
Japanese: 4 mura
Jewish: 6 shtetl
Malay: 7 campong, kampong
Russian: 3 mir

Village Blacksmith author
10 Longfellow (Henry Wadsworth)

villain
4 heel 5 devil, heavy, knave, rogue, scamp 6 meanie, rascal, sinner 7 lowlife 8 criminal, evildoer, mischief, offender, roperipe, scalawag 9 miscreant, reprobate, scoundrel, skeezicks 10 blackguard, malefactor 11 rapscallion
classic: 4 Iago

villainous
6 putrid, rotten 7 corrupt, debased, heinous, vicious 8 contrary, infamous, perverse 9 abandoned, atrocious, dissolute, miscreant, nefarious, offensive, perverted 10 degenerate, detestable, flagitious, outrageous, profligate 13 objectionable

villainy
5 crime 9 depravity

villein
7 peasant 8 villager

villenage
4 yoke 6 thrall 7 bondage, helotry, peonage, serfdom, slavery 9 servitude, thralldom 11 enslavement

vim
4 brio, dash, élan, kick, life, push, zing 5 oomph, verve 6 esprit, pepper, spirit 9 animation

vinaigrette
3 box 4 cart 5 sauce, wagon 6 bottle

vinculum
3 tie 4 bond, knot, link, yoke 5 nexus 8 ligament, ligature

vindicable
6 venial 7 tenable 9 excusable 10 condonable, defensible 11 inoffensive, justifiable, warrantable

vindicate
4 free 5 argue, claim, clear, guard,

prove, venge 6 acquit, assert, avenge, defend, refute, second, shield, uphold 7 absolve, bear out, confute, contend, justify, protect, redress, revenge, support, warrant 8 advocate, disprove, maintain, plead for 9 exculpate, exonerate 10 disculpate 11 rationalize

vindictive
5 nasty 6 malign 8 punitive, spiteful, vengeful, wreakful 9 malicious, malignant, merciless 10 implacable, relentless, revengeful 11 unrelenting

vine
3 hop, ivy, pea 4 gogo, soma 5 betel, buaze, guaco, kudzu, liana, liane, luffa, maile 6 cowage, cowpea, loofah, maypop 7 chayote, climber, copihue, creeper, cupseed 8 catbrier, clematis 10 chilebells 11 bittersweet
combining form: 4 viti
East Indian: 6 pikake

vinegar
3 vim 6 acetum 8 sourness
combining form: 4 acet 5 aceto
relating to: 6 acetic
steep in: 6 pickle

vinegarish
4 sour 5 waspy 6 bitter, cranky, ornery 7 bearish, waspish 8 cankered 9 crotchety, irascible 12 cantankerous, cross-grained

Vinegar Joe
8 Stilwell (Joseph)

vinegary
4 sour 6 acetic 7 acetose, acetous

vineyard
7 grapery
French: 3 cru

Vinland discoverer
8 Ericsson, Eriksson (Leif)

vintage
3 old 4 crop, wine 5 dated, passé 6 démodé 7 antique, archaic, classic, harvest 8 outdated, outmoded 9 classical 10 antiquated 12 old-fashioned

Viola
brother: 9 Sebastian
husband: 6 Orsino

Viola da ____
5 gamba

violate
3 err, sin 4 rape 5 break, force, spoil 6 breach, defile, offend, ravish 7 infract, outrage 8 deflower,

infringe, overpass, trespass 9 deflorate, disregard, trample on 10 contravene, transgress 11 trample upon

violation
5 break, crime, wrong 6 breach 7 offense 8 defacing, trespass 9 blasphemy, sacrilege 10 defacement, illegality, infraction 11 desecration, misdemeanor, profanation 12 encroachment, infringement 13 contravention, transgression

violence
4 fury, riot 5 clash, force 6 attack, duress, frenzy, tumult, uproar 7 assault, rampage 8 coercion, foul play, savagery, struggle 9 onslaught 10 compulsion, constraint

violent
5 acute, harsh, rough 6 fierce, mighty, potent, strong 7 cutting, extreme, furious, intense, vicious 8 forceful, forcible, piercing, powerful, terrible, vehement 9 desperate, exquisite, splitting 10 immoderate, inordinate 11 destructive 12 concentrated

violently
4 hard 5 madly 6 wildly 8 fiercely, stormily 9 furiously, ruinously 10 frenziedly 11 combatively, frantically, turbulently 12 tumultuously 13 destructively

violet
5 mauve 6 flower, purple

violin
6 fiddle 10 instrument
kind: 4 bass 5 Amati, cello, Strad 7 quinton 10 double bass, Guarnerius, Stradivari 12 Stradivarius
part: 3 bow, nut, peg, rib 4 neck 5 belly 6 bridge, corner, pegbox, saddle, scroll, string 8 chin rest, purfling 11 fingerboard
precursor: 5 gigue, rabab, rebec 6 vielle

violinist
American: 5 Elman (Mischa), Fodor (Eugene), Rabin (Michael), Ricci (Ruggiero), Stern (Isaac) 6 Midori, Powell (Maud), Rosand (Aaron) 7 Heifetz (Jascha), Menuhin (Yehudi), Szigeti (Joseph) 8 Kreisler (Fritz), Milstein (Nathan), Spalding (Albert), Zukofsky (Paul) 9 Zimbalist (Efrem)
Belgian: 5 Ysaye (Eugene-Auguste) 8 Grumiaux (Arthur)
Canadian: 6 Staryk (Steven)

Chinese: 4 Chen (Chong)
Czech: 3 Suk (Josef)
French: 12 Francescatti (Zino)
German: 6 Mutter (Anne-Sophie) 9 Hindemith (Paul)
Hungarian: 6 Tatrai (Vilmos) 7 Joachim (Joseph)
Israeli: 7 Perlman (Itzhak) 8 Zukerman (Pinchas)
Italian: 6 Viotti (Giovanne Battista) 7 Corelli (Arcangelo), Vivaldi (Antonio) 8 Paganini (Niccolo) 9 Geminiani (Francesco)
Romanian: 6 Enescu (George)
Russian: 8 Oistrakh (David), Spivakov (Vladimir)

violin maker
4 Salo (Gasparo da) 5 Amati (Andrea, Antonio, Girolamo, Nicolo) 7 Maggini (Giovanni) 8 Guarneri (Andrea, Giuseppe, Pietro) 10 Stradivari (Antonio, Francesco, Omobono)

VIP
4 lion 6 biggie, bigwig, fat cat, leader 7 big shot, notable, someone 8 big wheel, luminary, somebody 9 big cheese

viper
3 asp 5 adder, snake 10 bushmaster, copperhead, fer-de-lance 11 rattlesnake

virago
5 harpy, scold, shrew, vixen 6 amazon, ogress 8 fishwife 9 termagant, Xanthippe

Virgil
see **Vergil**

virgin
3 new 4 pure 5 fresh, unwed 6 intact, maiden, single, vestal 8 celibate, innocent, primeval, pristine, unmarred, untapped 9 abstinent, unmarried, unspoiled, unsullied, untouched 10 spouseless 12 undeflowered
combining form: 7 parthen 8 partheno

virginal
4 pure 6 intact, maiden 8 untapped 9 unspoiled, untouched 12 undeflowered

Virgin Goddess
5 Diana 7 Artemis

Virginia
capital: 8 Richmond
college, institute, university: 7 Hampton 8 Richmond 11 Old Dominion 13 Randolph Macon 14 William and Mary
nickname: 11 Old Dominion
state bird: 8 cardinal

Virginian, The
author: 6 Wister (Owen)
character: 7 Trampas

Virginia willow
4 itea

Virgin Islands of the U.S.
6 St. John 7 St. Croix 8 St. Thomas

virginity
6 purity 8 chastity 10 chasteness, maidenhead, maidenhood

Virgin Queen
10 Elizabeth I

Virgo star
5 Spica

viridity
5 youth 9 freshness, greenness, innocence

virile
4 male 5 manly 6 manful, potent, robust 7 driving, manlike, mannish 8 decisive, forceful 9 energetic, masculine

virose
5 fetid 6 poison 9 poisonous

virtual
5 basic 8 implicit 9 essential, practical 11 fundamental 12 constructive

virtuality
4 pith, soul 5 stuff 6 bottom, marrow 7 essence 9 substance 12 essentiality, quintessence

virtually
6 almost, nearly 7 morally 8 actually 9 basically, in essence 10 absolutely 11 essentially, practically 13 fundamentally

virtue
4 dint, mark 5 arête, merit, piety, trait, value, vigor, worth 7 caliber, feature, potency, probity, quality, stature 8 efficacy, goodness, morality, property 9 affection, attribute, character, puissance, rectitude, rightness 10 excellence, excellency, perfection 11 uprightness 13 effectiveness, effectualness, righteousness
cardinal: 4 hope 5 faith 7 charity, justice 8 prudence 9 fortitude 10 temperance

virtuosic
4 ripe 6 expert 8 finished 9 masterful, perfected 10 consummate 12 accomplished

virtuoso
4 whiz 6 artist, expert, master, musico, wizard 7 artiste, dabster 8 musician 9 authority 10 past master 12 professional

virtuous
4 good, pure 5 moral, noble 6 worthy 7 ethical, sinless 8 innocent, spotless 9 blameless, effective, effectual, efficient, exemplary, faultless, guiltless, righteous, unsullied, untainted 10 inculpable, moralistic, principled, unblamable 11 efficacious, right-minded, untarnished

virulent
5 sharp, toxic 6 biting, bitter, malign, poison 7 cutting, hateful, hostile 8 mephitic, scathing, spiteful, stabbing, toxicant, venomous 9 malignant, poisonous, rancorous, vitriolic 10 unfriendly 12 antagonistic

virus
4 bane, germ 5 venom 6 poison 9 contagion, infection

vis
5 force, might, power

visage
3 mug 4 cast, face, look, phiz 6 kisser 8 features 10 expression 11 countenance

vis-à-vis
6 contra, facing, toward, versus 7 against 8 fronting, opposite 9 tête-à-tête 10 coordinate 11 counterpart, over against

viscera
4 guts 7 innards, insides, inwards 8 entrails, stuffing 9 internals
combining form: 9 splanchno

visceral
3 gut 5 inner 8 interior, internal, intimate 9 intuitive 11 instinctive, instinctual

viscid
see **viscous**

viscount
4 peer 7 sheriff 8 nobleman

viscous
4 ropy, sizy 5 gummy, slimy, stiff, thick, tough 6 sticky 9 glutinous, semifluid, tenacious

vise
4 grip, tool 5 clamp

Vishnu
4 Hare, Hari
avatar: 4 Rama 5 Kurma 6 Buddha,

Matsya, Vamena, Varaha
7 Krishna **9** Narasinha
consort: **3** Sri **4** Shri **7** Lakshmi
home: **4** Meru

visible
4 seen **6** ocular, visual **7** seeable
8 apparent, viewable

Visigoth
conquest: **4** Rome
king: **6** Alaric

vision
3 eye **4** muse **5** dream, fancy,
image, sight, think **6** beauty, oracle, seeing **7** fantasy, feature,
imagine, realize **8** conceive, daydream, envisage, eyesight, phantasm, phantasy, presence, prophecy **9** nightmare, visualize
10 apocalypse, apparition, phenomenon, revelation
combining form: **4** opsy, opto **5** opsia, opsis **6** optico
deceptive: **6** mirage
defect: (see at eye)
in bright light: **8** photopia
in dim light: **8** scotopia
relating to: **5** optic **6** visual **7** optical
without: **5** blind

visionary
5 ideal, lofty, noble **6** astral,
dreamy, musing **7** dreamer, exalted, radical, utopian **8** idealist
9 ambitious, daydreamy, grandiose, ideologue, unworldly **10** abstracted, idealistic **11** daydreaming, impractical, pretentious
12 otherworldly **13** castle-builder,
introspective

visionless
4 dark **5** blind **7** eyeless **9** sightless **10** stone-blind

Vision of Sir Launfal, The
author
6 Lowell (James Russell)

visit
3 gam, see **4** call, chat, chin, pain,
stay, talk, yarn **5** pop in, run in,
tarry, wreak, wreck **6** avenge,
bother, come by, drop by, drop in,
impose, look in, look up, punish, reside, step in, stop by, stop in **7** afflict, force on, inflict, sojourn, trouble **8** colloque, come over,
converse, frequent, stopover
9 force upon, tarriance
often: **8** frequent

visitation
4 call **5** cross, trial **6** ordeal **7** calvary **8** calamity, crucible, disaster

9 mischance **10** affliction **11** catastrophe, tribulation

visitor
5 guest **6** caller **7** company, invitee

vison
4 mink

visor
4 bill, mask, peak **6** domino, vizard **8** eyeshade **9** doughface, false
face

vista
4 view **5** range, scape, scene,
scope, sight **6** survey **7** lookout,
outlook **8** panorama, prospect
11 perspective

visual
5 optic **6** ocular **7** optical, seeable,
visible **8** viewable, visional **11** discernible, perceivable, perceptible

visualize
3 see **4** view **5** fancy, image, think
6 call up, divine **7** feature, foresee,
imagine, picture, preknow, previse,
realize **8** conceive, envisage, envision, forefeel, foreknow **9** apprehend, conjure up, objectify, prevision **10** anticipate

vital
5 alive, lusty **6** living, needed,
zoetic **7** animate, dynamic, needful
8 animated, cardinal, integral, required, vigorous **9** breathing, energetic, essential, requisite, strenuous
10 red-blooded **11** fundamental
12 constitutive, prerequisite
13 indispensable

vital force
4 soul **5** anima **6** animus, pneuma,
psyche, spirit **9** élan vital

vitality
see **vigor**

vitalize
5 liven, pep up **6** actify, excite, vivify **7** animate, enliven, provoke,
quicken **8** activate, activize, dynamize, energize **9** galvanize,
stimulate **10** invigorate, strengthen

vitally
4 very **6** hugely **7** notably, parlous
9 extremely **10** remarkably, strikingly **11** exceedingly **12** surpassingly **13** exceptionally

vitals
see **viscera**

vitamin
6 biotin, niacin **7** choline, folacin
8 carotene, inositol, thiamine **9** co-
balamin, folic acid, pyridoxal

10 calciferol, pyridoxine, riboflavin,
tocopherol **12** ascorbic acid, bio-
flavonoid, meso-inositol

Vito Nuova, La
author: **5** Dante

vitellus
4 yolk

vitiate
3 mar **4** harm, hurt, soil, undo
5 abate, annul, quash, spoil, sully,
taint **6** damage, debase, defile, impair, injure, negate **7** abolish,
blemish, corrupt, debased, debauch, deprave, nullify, pervert, tarnish **8** abrogate, depraved **9** brutalize, corrupted, debauched,
perverted, prejudice **10** annihilate,
bastardize, bestialize, demoralize,
invalidate

vitreous
6 glassy

vitriol
7 sulfate **9** virulence

vitriolic
6 bitter **7** hostile **8** virulent **9** rancorous **12** antagonistic

vituperate
4 lash, rail, rate **5** abuse, curse,
scold **6** bark at, berate, malign, revile, yell at **7** asperse, bawl out,
chew out, condemn, growl at, upbraid **8** lambaste **10** tongue-lash

vituperation
5 abuse, blame **7** censure, obloquy
8 scolding **9** contumely, invective
10 revilement, scurrility **12** billingsgate **13** tongue-lashing

vituperative
6 severe **7** abusive, railing **8** critical, scolding, scurrile **9** invective,
truculent **10** censorious, scurrilous
11 opprobrious **12** contumelious

vivacious
3 gay **4** cant, keen **5** alert, brash,
canty, zesty **6** breezy, lively **7** animate, playful, vibrant **8** animated,
spirited, sportive **9** ebullient, exuberant, sprightly **10** frolicsome
12 effervescent, high-spirited

vivacity
see **verve**

Vivaldi, Antonio
epithet: **12** il prete rosso, the red
priest

___ vivant
3 bon

vivarium

3 zoo

vivid

3 gay 4 keen, rich 5 acute, alive, brave, sharp 6 bright, colory, lively, living 7 graphic, intense 8 animated, colorful, dramatic, eloquent, spirited, vigorous 9 pictorial 10 expressive, meaningful, theatrical 11 dramaturgic, picturesque 12 photographic

vivify

5 liven, renew 6 excite, revive 7 animate, enliven, quicken, refresh, restore 9 galvanize

vixen

3 fox, nag 5 harpy, scold, shrew 6 amazon, ogress, virago 8 fishwife 9 termagant, Xanthippe

viz

5 to wit 6 namely 8 scilicet 9 videlicet

vizard

4 mask 5 visor 6 domino 9 doughface, false face

vocabulary

4 cant 5 words 6 jargon 7 lexicon, palaver 8 language 9 word-hoard, word-stock 10 dictionary 11 phraseology, terminology

vocal

4 oral 6 fluent, sonant, spoken, voiced 7 uttered, voicing 8 eloquent 9 expressed, intonated, outspoken 10 articulate, expressing, expressive, free-spoken

vocalic

5 vowel 6 vowely 9 vowellike

vocalist

6 singer 8 songster 9 performer 11 entertainer

vocalization

5 mouth, voice 6 speech 7 diction, voicing 8 mouthing, sounding, speaking, uttering 9 utterance 11 enunciation 12 articulation 13 verbalization

vocalize

4 sing, talk, tune 5 chant, speak, utter, voice 6 convey, impart, let out 7 express 9 enunciate, pronounce, verbalize 11 communicate

vocal organ

6 larynx
bird: 6 syrinx

vocation

3 art, job 4 work 5 craft, trade 6 métier 7 calling, mission 8 lifework 10 handicraft, occupation, profession

vocative

4 case 6 fluent 7 voluble 9 garrulous

vociferate

3 cry 4 call, yell 5 hallo, hollo, shout 6 holler

vociferous

4 loud 5 noisy 6 shrill 7 blatant, dinsome 8 strident 9 clamorous 10 boisterous, multivocal 11 distracting, loudmouthed, openmouthed 12 obstreperous

vogue

3 cry, fad 4 chic, mode, rage 5 craze, style, trend 6 bon ton, furore 7 fashion 10 dernier cri 11 stylishness

voice

3 put, say 4 talk, tell, vent 5 sayso, sound, speak, utter 6 phrase, speech 7 present, recount 8 vocalize 9 enunciate, formulate, pronounce, statement, utterance, verbalize 10 articulate, expression
combining form: 4 phon 5 phone, phono, phony 6 phonia
female: 4 alto 5 mezzo 7 soprano 9 contralto
high: 5 tenor 7 soprano 8 falsetto
in grammar: 6 active 7 passive
Latin: 3 vox
male: 4 bass 5 tenor 8 baritone
quality: 5 pitch 6 timbre
quiet: 7 whisper
relating to: 5 vocal 8 phonetic
without: 4 dumb, mute

voice box

6 larynx

voiced

4 oral 5 vocal 6 sonant, spoken 10 articulate

voiceless

3 mum 4 dumb, mute 6 silent 10 speechless 12 inarticulate, unarticulate

void

3 bad, gap 4 bare, emit, flow, hole, null, pour 5 abyss, annul, clear, drain, eject, empty, quash, scant, short 6 bereft, cavity, devoid, hollow, remove, vacant, vacate, vacuum 7 denuded, deplete, give off, invalid, negated, vacuity, vacuous 8 abrogate, deprived, dissolve, evacuate, innocent, throw out 9 destitute, discharge, eliminate 10 disembogue

voiture

3 car 8 carriage

volage

5 dizzy, giddy 7 flighty 9 frivolous 10 bird-witted 11 empty-headed, hare-brained 13 rattlebrained

volant

4 spry, yare 5 agile, brisk, catty, zippy 6 active, lively, nimble 9 sprightly

volary

6 aviary 8 birdcage

volatile

4 airy, edgy 6 bouncy, fickle, lively 7 buoyant, elastic, flighty, protean 8 agitable, fleeting, flippant, fugitive, skittery, skittish, ticklish, unstable, variable 9 alarmable, ephemeral, excitable, expansive, explosive, frivolous, fugacious, mercurial, momentary, resilient, startlish, transient 10 capricious, changeable, evanescent, inconstant, lubricious, short-lived, transitory 11 impermanent, light-minded 12 effervescent 13 temperamental

volatility

6 levity 9 animation, flippancy, frivolity, lightness 11 flightiness, inconstancy, instability, variability 13 changeability, mercurialness, sprightliness

volcanic

crater: 4 maar
explosion: 8 eruption
glass: 8 obsidian
matter: 3 ash 4 lava, tufa, tuff 5 magma, trass 6 scoria
mound: 4 cone 7 hornito
passage: 6 throat 7 conduit
vent: 8 fumarole 9 solfatara

volcano

8 mountain
Alaska: 11 Mount Katmai
Andes: 5 Omate 12 Huaina Putina
Antarctica: 11 Mount Erebus
Azores: 4 Alto
California: 10 Lassen Peak
Canaries: 5 Teide 8 Tenerife
Colombia: 5 Huila, Pasto 6 Purace 7 Galeras
Costa Rica: 4 Poás 5 Barba, Irazú
Ecuador: 8 Cotopaxi
extinct: 5 Iriga 8 Mauna Kea 9 Mount Popa 10 Mount Kenya
Guatemala: 4 Agua 5 Fuego 7 Atitlán
Hawaii: 8 Mauna Loa

Honshu: **4** Nasu **5** Asama, Azuma **6** Bandai **8** Nasudake **9** Asama-yama
Iceland: **5** Askja, Hekla
Indonesia: **7** Tambora **9** Gunung Awu **10** Peak of Bali **11** Gunung Agung
island: **8** Krakatau, Krakatoa
Italy: **8** Vesuvius **9** Stromboli
Japan: **3** Aso **5** Unzen **6** Asosan
Java: **4** Gede **5** Bromo, Gedeh, Kelud, Salak
Madeira: **5** Ruivo
Martinique: **10** Mount Pelee
Mexico: **6** Colima **7** Orizaba **9** Paricutin **12** Popocatepetl
New Zealand: **7** Ruapehu **9** Ngauruhoe
Philippines: **4** Taal **10** Mount Mayon **13** Mount Pinatubo
Saint Vincent: **9** Soufrière
Sicily: **4** Etna **5** Aetna
Solomons: **5** Balbi
South America: **5** Lanín, Maipo
Sumatra: **5** Dempo
Washington: **16** Mount Saint Helens

___ volente
3 Deo

volition
4 will **6** choice, desire, option **8** election **9** selection **10** preference

volley
4 hail, shot **5** burst, round, salvo, storm **6** shower **7** barrage **8** drumfire

volplane
5 glide

Volpone
3 fox
author: **6** Jonson (Ben)
servant: **5** Mosca

Volsung
grandson: **6** Sigurd **9** Siegfried
great-grandfather: **4** Odin
son: **7** Sigmund

Voltaire
drama: **5** Zaïre **6** Alzire, Brutus, Mèrope, Oedipe **7** Mahomet **8** Tancrède
novel: **5** Zadig **7** Candide
real name: **6** Arouet (François Marie)

volte-face
4 turn, veer, whip **5** avert, pivot, sheer, wheel, whirl **6** divert **7** deflect, reverse **8** reversal **9** about-face, face about, reversion, turnabout **10** right-about **11** changeabout, reversement

voluble
4 glib **6** fickle, fluent **8** vocative **9** talkative **13** silver-tongued

volume
4 body, book, bulk, mass, size, tome **6** amount, object **7** content **8** capacity, loudness, quantity

voluminous
4 full, many **6** legion, sundry **7** several, various **8** numerous **12** multifarious, multitudinal **13** multitudinous

Volumnia's son
10 Coriolanus

Völund
5 smith **7** Wayland
brother: **4** Egil **5** Egill

voluntary
4 free **5** opted **6** chosen **7** elected, willful, willing, witting **8** elective, optional, unforced **10** autonomous, deliberate, volitional **11** independent, intentional **12** unprescribed

volunteer
5 offer **6** enlist
hospital: **12** candy striper

Volunteer State
9 Tennessee

voluptuous
4 lush **6** wanton **7** sensual **8** luscious, sensuous **9** abandoned, dissolute, epicurean, excessive, indulgent, luxurious **10** dissipated **12** sensualistic

volute
6 scroll, spiral

volution
5 twist, whorl

vomit
3 gag **4** barf, spew **5** eject, expel, retch **6** spit up **7** bring up, throw up, upchuck **8** disgorge **11** regurgitate

vomiting
6 emesis

Von Flotow opera
6 Martha

Vonnegut, Kurt
work: **10** Cat's Cradle **11** Player Piano **16** The Sirens of Titan **18** Slaughterhouse Five **20** Breakfast of Champions **22** Happy Birthday Wanda June

Von Stroheim film
5 Greed **10** Queen Kelly **12** Foolish Wives **13** Blind Husbands, Grand Illusion, The Merry Widow **15** Sunset Boulevard

voodoo
3 hex **4** jinx, mage **5** charm, magus, obeah, spell, witch **6** whammy, wizard **7** bewitch, enchant, warlock **8** conjurer, magician, sorcerer **9** enchanter, ensorcell **10** Indian sign **11** necromancer

voodooist
4 mage **5** magus **6** wizard **7** charmer, warlock **8** conjurer, magician, sorcerer **9** enchanter **11** necromancer

Vophsi's son
5 Nahbi

voracious
4 avid **6** greedy, hungry, sating **7** gorging **8** covetous, edacious, grasping, ravening, ravenous **9** devouring, rapacious, satiating **10** gluttonous, insatiable, surfeiting **11** acquisitive

vorago
5 abyss, chasm

vortex
4 eddy, gyre **5** spout, whirl **6** spiral **9** maelstrom, whirlpool

votary
3 fan **4** buff **5** freak, hound, lover **6** addict, zealot **7** admirer, amateur, devotee, fancier, habitué **8** disciple **10** aficionado

vote
4 poll **5** elect **6** ballot, choice, choose, decide, ratify, ticket **7** opinion **8** election, suffrage **9** franchise
affirmative: **3** aye, nod, yea, yes **6** placet
kind: **5** proxy, straw, voice **6** secret **7** write-in **10** plebiscite, referendum
negative: **2** no **3** nay
right to: **8** suffrage **9** franchise

voter
7 chooser, elector
kind: **8** absentee

vouch
5 prove **6** assure, attest, uphold, verify **7** certify, confirm, support, witness **9** guarantee **11** corroborate **12** substantiate

voucher
4 chit **5** proof **7** receipt **9** affidavit **10** credential **11** certificate

vouchsafe
4 give **5** award, deign, favor, grant, stoop **6** accord, oblige **7** concede **10** condescend **11** accommodate

vow
4 oath, swan **5** swear **6** assert, pledge, plight, prayer **7** declare, promise **8** covenant

vowel
5 vocal **6** letter
kind: **4** long **5** glide, schwa, short **9** diphthong
omission: **7** aphesis **11** contraction
variation: **6** ablaut, umlaut

vowely
5 vocal **7** vocalic

voyage
4 tour, trip **6** cruise, travel **7** journey **9** excursion **10** expedition, pilgrimage

voyeur
6 peeper **10** peeping Tom

Vronski's lover
12 Anna Karenina

Vulcan
see **Hephaestus**

vulgar
3 low, raw **4** base, rude, vile, wild **5** crass, crude, dirty, gross, nasty, rough **6** coarse, public, ribald, smutty, spoken **7** general, obscene, popular, profane, uncouth **8** barbaric, barnyard, improper, indecent, unseemly **9** barbarian, barbarous, graceless, idiomatic, incorrect, inelegant, loathsome, offensive, repulsive, revolting, tasteless, unrefined **10** colloquial, indecorous, indelicate, outlandish, ungraceful, unpolished, vernacular **12** scatological

vulgarism
8 slangism, solecism **9** barbarism **10** corruption **11** impropriety **13** vernacularism, vernacularity

vulgate
6 patois **10** colloquial, vernacular

Vulgate translator
6 Jerome

vulnerability
8 exposure, openness, weakness **9** liability **11** vincibility

vulnerable
4 open, weak **6** liable **7** exposed

vulnerary
6 curing **7** healing **8** curative, remedial, sanative, sanatory **9** remedying, wholesome **11** restorative

vulpine
3 sly **4** foxy, wily **6** artful, astute, crafty, tricky **7** cunning **8** guileful **9** insidious

vulture
4 hook, lift **5** filch, pinch, steal, swipe **6** condor, snitch **7** buzzard **8** aasvogel **11** lammergeier
food: **7** carrion

vulturine
9 predative, predatory, rapacious, raptorial **10** predacious

Ww

wacky
3 mad 4 nuts 5 crazy, loony, silly
6 absurd, crazed, insane
7 cracked, foolish, lunatic 8 demented, deranged 11 harebrained
12 preposterous

wad
3 gob, pot 4 bomb, clod, hunk,
lump, mint, pile 5 chunk, clump,
hunch 6 boodle, bundle, nugget,
packet 7 fortune

waddy
3 peg 4 club 5 stick 6 cowboy
7 rustler

wade
4 ford, plod
into: 6 attack

wadi
3 bed 4 wash 5 gully 6 ravine

wafer
4 cake, disk 7 cracker

waft
4 gust, puff, wave 5 drift, float,
whiff

wag
3 wit 4 beat, card, lash, wave,
zany 5 clown, comic, cutup, droll,
joker, shake 6 jester, kidder, madcap, switch, twitch, waggle, wiggle, wigwag, woggle 7 farceur,
show-off 8 comedian, funnyman,
humorist, jokester, quipster 9 oscillate, prankster 11 wisecracker

wage
3 fee, pay 4 hire, take 6 income,
return, reward, salary 7 stipend
8 earnings, receipts 9 emolument
10 recompense 12 compensation,
remuneration

wager
3 bet, lay, pot, set 4 ante, game,
play, risk 5 put on, stake
6 chance, gamble, hazard, impone
7 venture 9 adventure

waggery
3 gag 4 jape, jest, joke, quip
5 crack 7 devilry, roguery 8 deviltry, drollery, mischief 9 devilment,
wisecrack, witticism 10 impishness
11 roguishness, waggishness
12 sportiveness

waggish
4 arch, pert 5 antic, comic, droll,
funny, saucy, witty 6 impish, jocose
7 comical, jocular, playful, puckish,
roguish 8 humorous, prankish,
sportive 9 facetious, laughable, ludicrous 10 frolicsome
11 mischievous

waggle
4 beat, lash, sway, wave 6 switch,
waddle, wobble

Wagner, Richard
birthplace: 7 Leipzig
deathplace: 6 Venice
father-in-law: 5 Liszt (Franz)
heroine: 5 Senta
opera: 6 Rienzi 8 Parsifal 9 Lohengrin, Siegfried 10 Die Walküre,
Tannhäuser 12 Das Rheingold
recurring theme: 9 leitmotif, leitmotiv
wife: 5 Minna 6 Cosima

wagon
3 car, van 4 cart, dray, wain
5 gilly 6 telega 7 fourgon, vehicle

wah
5 panda

wahoo
4 fish 5 shrub 8 basswood, mackerel 11 burning bush

waif
5 stray 7 vagrant 8 wanderer
9 foundling

wail
3 bay, cry, sob 4 bawl, blub, fuss,
howl, keen, kick, weep, yowl
5 quest, whine 6 boohoo, murmur,
repine, squall 7 blubber, ululate
8 complain

wailful
6 rueful, woeful 7 doleful 8 dolesome, mournful 9 plaintive, sorrowful 10 lamentable, lugubrious,
melancholy

wain
5 wagon

waistband
4 belt, sash 6 girdle 8 ceinture,
cincture

waistcoat
4 vest 6 jerkin

wait
4 bide, stay 5 abide, nurse, serve,
tarry 6 expect, linger, mother, remain 7 care for, foresee 10 anticipate, minister to 11 stick around

waiter
6 garçon 7 servant 9 attendant

Waiting for ___
5 Godot, Lefty

waive
4 cede, stay 5 allow, defer, delay,
grant, leave, yield 6 give up, hold
up, put off, resign, shelve 7 abandon, concede, hold off, suspend
8 hand over, hold over, postpone
9 surrender 10 relinquish

wake
4 stir, whet 5 arise, get up, rally,
renew, rouse 6 arouse, bestir, kindle 7 freshen, roll out 9 challenge
mower's: 5 swath

wakeful
5 alert 8 restless, vigilant, watchful
9 sleepless

waken
see **wake**

Walden author
7 Thoreau (Henry David)

wale
3 rib 4 weal, welt 5 ridge, wheal,
whelk

Wales
5 Cymru
capital: **7** Cardiff
language: **6** Cymric
Latin name: **7** Cambria
patron saint: **5** David

walk
3 leg, run **4** foot, hike, hoof, pace, plod, race, reel, slog, step, turn **5** amble, field, march, mince, strut, stump, tramp, tread, troop **6** airing, domain, foot it, lumber, parade, ramble, sashay, sphere, stride, stroll, strunt, toddle, trudge **7** alameda, demesne, saunter, stretch, terrain, traipse **8** ambulate, dominion, province, traverse **9** bailiwick, champaign, promenade, territory **11** base on balls, perambulate **12** deambulation

walkaway
4 romp, rout

walking shorts
8 Bermudas

walking stick
4 cane **5** staff **6** kebbie **8** ashplant

walk out
5 leave **6** strike

walkway
4 path **7** catwalk **9** promenade
ancient Greek: **4** stoa

wall
3 bar, hem **4** cage, coop, stop **5** block, fence, hedge **6** corral, immure **7** barrier, close in, enclose, envelop **8** blockade **9** barricade, roadblock
hanging: **8** tapestry
painting: **5** mural
protective: **7** parapet
top of: **6** coping

wallaba tree
3 apa

wallaby
8 kangaroo

wallet
8 billfold **10** pocketbook
items: **5** bills

wallop
3 bat, bop, jar **4** bang, bash, beat, belt, blow, boot, bump, drub, jolt, kick, lick, pelt, slam, slug, trim, whip, whop **5** baste, blast, clash, crash, paste, pound, shock, smack, smash **6** buffet, impact, pummel, thrash, thrill, thwack **7** belabor, shellac, trounce **8** lambaste **9** collision **10** percussion

walloping
4 huge **5** giant **7** immense, mammoth, monster **8** colossal, enormous, gigantic **10** gargantuan, prodigious

wallow
4 bask, roll **5** enjoy, lurch, revel **6** welter **7** blunder, indulge, rollick, stumble **8** flounder **9** delight in, luxuriate

___ Walpole, writer
6 Horace

walrus
6 mammal
relative: **4** seal
tooth: **4** tusk

___ Walton, writer
5 Izaak

waltz
3 zip **6** breeze

Waltz King
7 Strauss (Johann)

Wampanoag chief
9 Massasoit, Metacomet **10** King Philip

wampum
5 beads, money, sewan **6** shells

wan
4 ashy, pale, weak, worn **5** ashen, livid, waxen **6** anemic, doughy, pallid, sickly **7** haggard **8** blanched, bleached, boneless, impotent **9** bloodless, colorless, forceless, spineless, washed-out **10** cadaverous, emasculate **11** ineffective, ineffectual, slack-spined **12** invertebrate

wand
3 rod **4** pole, tube **5** baton, staff
combining form: **5** rhabd **6** rhabdo

wander
3 bat, bum, err, gad **4** roam, roll, rove **5** amble, drift, gypsy, mooch, range, stray, tramp **6** depart, gander, ramble, stroll **7** deviate, digress, diverge, excurse, maunder, meander, saunter, traipse **8** divagate, straggle, vagabond **9** gallivant

wanderer
5 nomad, rover **6** errant, roamer **7** drifter, pilgrim, rambler, tzigane, vagrant **9** meanderer **12** rolling stone

wane
3 ebb **4** fail, fall **5** abate, let up **6** relent, shrink, weaken **7** decline,

die away, die down, dwindle, ease off, slacken, subside **8** moderate **9** fall short, waste away

wangle
7 finagle **8** engineer, maneuver, outflank **9** machinate, overreach **10** outgeneral **11** outmaneuver

want
4 lack, must, need, wish **5** covet, crave, ought **6** dearth, defect, demand, desire, penury, should **7** absence, default, poverty, require **8** exigency, poorness **9** indigence, necessity, neediness, privation **10** desiderate, inadequacy, meagerness, scantiness, skimpiness **11** destitution, requirement **12** exiguousness **13** insufficiency

wanting
3 shy **4** away, gone, sans **5** minus, scant, short **6** absent, scanty, scarce **7** failing, lacking, missing, omitted, without **9** defective, deficient **10** inadequate, incomplete, uncomplete **12** insufficient, unsufficient

wanton
3 lax, toy **4** doxy, easy, fast, fool, jade, slut **5** cruel, dally, flirt, hussy, light, loose, slack, tramp, trifle, wench **6** coquet, harlot, lead on, trifle **7** baggage, cyprian, jezebel, trollop, unasked, wayward, whorish **8** contrary, perverse, slattern, spiteful, strumpet, unchaste **9** malicious **10** gratuitous, malevolent, prostitute **11** string along, uncalled-for **12** supererogant

wapiti
3 elk **4** deer, stag

war
3 tug **4** feud **5** fight **6** battle, combat, oppugn, strife **7** contend, crusade **8** struggle
German: **5** krieg **10** blitzkrieg
god: **3** Tyr **4** Ares, Mars, Odin **5** Wodan, Woden
goddess: **4** Enyo **5** Anath **6** Inanna, Ishtar **7** Bellona
Latin: **6** bellum
Muslim: **5** jehad, jihad
relating to: **7** martial

War and Peace
author: **7** Tolstoy (Leo)
composer: **9** Prokofiev (Sergey)

warble
3 air, lay **4** sing, tune **6** melody, strain **7** descant, measure, melisma, melodia **8** diapason

warbler
7 kinglet 8 songster 9 blackpoll
11 gnatcatcher
European: 10 chiffchaff

war club
3 bat 4 mace 5 baton 6 cudgel
8 bludgeon 9 truncheon
10 knobkerrie

war cry
5 motto 6 slogan
Greek: 5 alala

ward
4 balk, care, fend, foil, halt, stay,
turn 5 aegis, armor, avert, block,
check, deter, guard, parry, rebut,
repel, trust, watch 6 divert, picket,
rebuff, sentry, shield, stymie, thwart
7 custody, defense, deflect, fend
off, forfend, hold off, keeping, keep
off, lookout, obviate, prevent, repulse, rule out 8 armament, preclude, security, sentinel, stave off,
watchman 9 forestall, frustrate, interrupt, safeguard 10 protection
11 safekeeping 12 guardianship

warden
6 custos, jailer, keeper, ranger
8 cerberus, claviger, guardian,
watchdog 9 custodian

wardrobe
4 room 5 trunk 6 closet 7 armoire
12 clothespress

ware
4 shun 5 avoid, awake, aware,
cloth, goods 7 fabrics, knowing,
pottery 8 sensible 9 cognizant,
conscious

warehouse
4 pack, stow 5 étape, guard, store
6 bestow 7 protect, shelter, storage
8 entrepôt 11 accommodate
oriental: 6 godown

wares
4 line 5 goods 9 vendibles
11 commodities, merchandise

warfare
6 strife 7 contest, rivalry 8 conflict,
striving 9 emulation 11 competition
combining form: 5 machy

warhorse
7 charger, courser

warlike
7 hawkish, martial, warring 8 battling, fighting, militant, military, ructious 9 bellicose, combative, truculent 10 contending, pugnacious
11 belligerent, contentious, quarrelsome 12 gladiatorial

warlock
4 mage 5 magus 6 wizard
7 charmer 8 conjurer, magician,
sorcerer 9 enchanter, voodooist
11 necromancer

warm
4 heat 5 tepid 6 ardent 7 affable,
cordial, fervent, sincere, zealous
8 gracious 9 heartfelt 10 passionate, responsive 11 kindhearted,
softhearted, sympathetic 12 enthusiastic, wholehearted
13 compassionate
air: 7 thermal

warmed-over
5 stale, tired, trite 6 old hat 7 clichéd 8 shopworn, timeworn, well-
worn 9 hackneyed, twice-told

warmhearted
4 kind, warm 6 benign, kindly, tender 8 outgoing 9 benignant 10 responsive 11 sympathetic
13 compassionate

warn
3 bid, tip 4 clew, clue, post, tell
5 alert, guide, order 6 advise, beacon, charge, direct, enjoin, fill in,
inform, monish, notify, wise up
7 apprise, caution, command, counsel 8 acquaint, instruct

warning
3 tip 4 hint 6 advice, caveat
7 caution, counsel, sematic 8 guidance, monition, monitory 10 admonition, admonitory, cautionary, cautioning, monitorial, suggestion
11 admonishing, commonition
legal: 6 caveat

War of the Worlds author
5 Wells (Herbert George)

warp
4 bend, kink, wind 5 color, twist,
wrest 6 debase, deform, garble,
wrench 7 confuse, contort, corrupt,
debauch, deprave, distort, pervert,
torture, vitiate 8 miscolor, misshape
9 brutalize 10 bastardize, bestialize, demoralize 12 misrepresent

warrant
4 back, pawn, word 5 argue, basis, claim, state, token 6 affirm, assert, assure, defend, ensure, insure,
pledge, secure 7 call for, certify,
contend, earnest, justify, require,
sponsor 8 guaranty, maintain, mittimus, security 9 assurance, guarantee, stipulate, vindicate 10 foundation

warranty
4 bail, bond 6 surety 8 guaranty,
security 9 guarantee

warrior
2 GI 4 hero, swad 7 fighter, soldier 9 man-at-arms 10 serviceman
11 fighting man
female: 6 Amazon
Japanese: 7 samurai

Warsaw
castle: 5 Zamek
river: 7 Vistula

warship
see **ship,** *military*

wart
6 lesion 7 verruca

wary
4 safe 5 canny, chary, leery 6 frugal, saving, scotch 7 careful,
guarded, sceptic, skeptic, sparing,
thrifty 8 cautious, discreet, doubting, gingerly, vigilant, watchful
9 provident, stewardly 10 suspicious, unwasteful 11 calculating,
circumspect, considerate, distrustful

wash
3 lap, lip, tub 4 lave, ride, suds
5 bathe, clean, drift, float, slosh,
swash 6 bubble, burble, gurgle,
shower, sluice 7 launder, shampoo

washed-out
5 all in, spent 6 bleary, effete, used
up 7 drained, far-gone, worn-out
8 depleted 9 exhausted

washed-up
4 done 7 done for, through
8 finished

washing
4 bath 6 lavage 8 ablution
ceremonial: 6 lavabo

Washington
capital: 7 Olympia
largest city: 7 Seattle
nickname: 12 Chinook State 14 Evergreen State
state bird: 9 goldfinch
state flower: 12 rhododendron

Washington, D.C. designer
7 L'Enfant

Washington's home
11 Mount Vernon

Washington Square author
5 James

wash out
4 cast, fail, flop, junk, shed 5 elute,
scrap 6 reject, slough 7 cashier,

discard, flummox **8** jettison **9** throw away

wasp
6 hornet, vespid

waspish
5 huffy, sharp **6** cranky, ornery **7** bearish, crabbed, fretful, peevish, pettish **8** cankered, contrary, perverse, petulant, snappish, spiteful **9** crotchety, fractious, impatient, irritable, malicious, querulous **10** vinegarish **12** cantankerous, crossgrained

waspy
see **waspish**

wassail
3 bat **4** bust, hell, riot, soak, tear **5** binge, revel, spree **6** bender, frolic, ran-tan **7** carouse, revelry, roister, whoopee, whoopla, whoop-up **8** carousal **9** high jinks, revelment **10** skylarking

waste
4 blow, fail, junk, sack, wane, wild **5** offal, trash **6** barren, debris, desert, devour, drivel, kelter, litter, ravage, refuse, sewage, shrink, trifle, weaken **7** badland, consume, despoil, dwindle, fritter, garbage, pillage, rubbish, sullage **8** cast away, desolate, emaciate, fool away, misspend, riot away, spoilage, spoliate, squander, unthrift, wild land, wildness **9** deprecate, desecrate, devastate, dissipate, fall short, overdoing, sweepings, throw away **10** frivol away, lavishness, muddle away, potter away, trifle away, wilderness **11** blunder away, dribble away, prodigality, prodigalize **12** extravagance, extravagancy
allowance: **4** tret
from a mine: **7** mullock
maker: **5** haste
time: **5** dally **6** dawdle, footle, piddle

waste away
4 fail, wane **5** dwine **7** atrophy, decline

wasted
4 worn **5** gaunt **6** meager **7** wizened **8** skeletal, withered **9** emaciated, shriveled **10** cadaverous

wasteful
6 lavish **8** prodigal **10** thriftless **11** extravagant, improvident

wastefulness
8 squander, unthrift **9** overdoing

10 lavishness **11** prodigality **12** extravagance, extravagancy

wasteland
4 wild **6** barren, desert **8** wildness **10** wilderness

Waste Land author
5 Eliot (Thomas Stearns)

waster
5 idler **6** loafer, no-good **7** lounger, rounder, spender, wastrel **8** prodigal, unthrift **9** fritterer **10** dissipater, high roller, ne'er-do-well, profligate, scapegrace, squanderer **11** scattergood, spendthrift

wastrel
3 rip **4** rake, roué **5** idler, knave, rogue, scamp **6** lecher, loafer, no-good, rascal **7** lounger, rounder, spender **8** prodigal, scalawag, unthrift **9** fritterer, libertine, scoundrel **10** blackguard, black sheep, dissipater, high roller, ne'er-do-well, profligate, scapegrace, squanderer **11** rapscallion, scattergood, spendthrift

watch
3 eye, see, spy, tab **4** look, mind, scan, tend, tout, ward **5** guard, vigil **6** attend, follow, picket, sentry **7** care for, examine, eyeball, inspect, lookout, monitor, surveil **8** eagle eye, scrutiny, sentinel, watchman **9** timepiece, vigilance **10** scrutinize **11** chronograph, chronometer **12** surveillance
chain: **3** fob
maker: **10** horologist

watchdog
6 custos, keeper, warden **8** cerberus, claviger, guardian **9** custodian

watcher
6 viewer **7** guarder, lookout, witness **8** beholder, by-sitter, guardian, looker-on, observer, onlooker **9** bystander, spectator **10** eyewitness
combining form: **6** scopus

watchfire
6 beacon

watchful
4 wary **5** alert, chary, quick, ready **6** prompt **7** wakeful **8** cautious, open-eyed, vigilant **9** wide-awake **10** unsleeping **11** circumspect
Scottish: **5** tenty **6** tentie

watchman
4 ward **5** guard **6** picket, sentry **7** lookout **8** sentinel

watch out
4 mind **6** beware **7** look out

watchtower
7 lookout **10** lighthouse

watchword
6 slogan **10** shibboleth **11** catchphrase, countersign

water
5 fluid **6** dilute, liquid **7** moisten **8** irrigate, moisture, snowmelt
body: **3** bay, sea **4** gulf, lake, pool **5** ocean **6** lagoon, strait **9** reservoir
combining form: **4** aqua, aqui, aquo, hydr **5** hydat, hydro **6** hydato, limnia (plural) **7** limnion
French: **3** eau
goddess: **4** Nina **7** Anahita, Anaitis
Latin: **4** aqua
Spanish: **4** agua

water buffalo
4 arna **7** carabao
female: **5** arnee

water clock
9 clepsydra

water closet
2 WC **4** head, john **5** privy **6** johnny, toilet **7** latrine **8** lavatory **11** convenience
British: **3** loo

watercourse
4 duct **5** canal **6** course **7** channel, conduit **8** aqueduct, headrace, tailrace

water cow
7 manatee

water eagle
6 osprey

watered-down
4 thin, weak **5** washy **6** dilute, watery **7** diluted **8** waterish

water elephant
12 hippopotamus

waterfall
4 eddy **5** chute, falls, sault, shoot, spout, surge **6** rapids, riffle, vortex **7** cascade **8** cataract **9** whirlpool
California: **8** Yosemite
Canada: **5** Grand
Canada-U.S.: **7** Niagara
former Nile: **5** Ripon
Kentucky: **5** Great **10** Cumberland
Niagara: **8** American, Canadian **9** Horseshoe
Oregon: **9** Multnomah
Snake river: **4** Twin **8** Shoshone
Washington: **10** Snoqualmie
world's highest: **5** Angel

Yellowstone: **5** Tower
Zambezi: **8** Victoria

waterfinder
6 dowser

water hole
desert: **5** oasis

water horse
6 kelpie **11** hippocampus

watering hole
3 bar, pub **4** café **5** haunt, oasis
6 lounge, nitery, resort, saloon, tavern **7** barroom, cabaret, hangout,
hot spot, purlieu **8** drinkery,
nightery **9** nightclub, nightspot
10 rendezvous, supper club
11 discotheque

water jar
4 ewer, lota, olla **5** banga, lotah
6 hydria, kalpis

waterless
3 dry **4** arid, sere **7** bone-dry,
thirsty **8** droughty **9** unwatered
12 moistureless
combining form: **6** anhydr **7** anhydro

waterlog
3 sap **4** soak **5** souse, steep
6 drench, sodden **7** insteep
8 saturate

water nymph
4 lily **5** naiad **6** Nereid **7** Oceanid
9 dragonfly
female: **5** nixie

water oscillation
6 seiche

water pipe
5 hooka **6** hookah **8** narghile,
nargileh

water plant
7 aquatic **10** hydrophyte

water rat
4 vole **6** rodent **7** muskrat

water spirit
6 undine

waterspout
6 funnel **10** cloudburst

water sprite
see **water nymph**

water tank
7 cistern

waterwheel
5 noria **6** sakieh

watery
4 pale, thin, weak **5** banal, bland,
vapid, washy **6** anemic, dilute, jejune, pallid, sluicy **7** diluted, insipid, sapless **9** bloodless
10 namby-pamby, wishy-washy

wattle
3 rod **4** pole **10** interweave

wattle and ____
4 daub

wave
3 wag **4** beat, flap, lash **6** marcel,
ripple, switch, waggle, woggle
7 flutter, ripplet **8** brandish,
undulate
combining form: **3** cym, kym **4** cymo,
kymo
large: **7** tsunami

waver
4 halt, trim **5** hedge, shift **6** dither,
falter, palter, seesaw, teeter
7 flicker, stagger, whiffle **8** hesitate
9 vacillate **12** shilly-shally, wiggle-
waggle

wavering
4 weak **5** shaky **6** dickey, unsure,
wobbly **7** halting **8** insecure, rootless, to-and-fro, unstable **9** faltering, fluctuant, hesitancy, vacillant,
whiffling **10** hesitating, hesitation,
indecision **11** vacillating, vacillation, vacillatory **12** irresolution,
shilly-shally, wiggle-waggle

Waverly author
5 Scott (Walter)

wavy pattern
5 moiré

wax
3 get, run **4** come, grow, hike, rise,
turn **5** boost, build, lipid, mount
6 become, expand **7** augment, enlarge, upgrade, upsurge
8 heighten, increase, multiply, paraffin, simonize
combining form: **3** cer **4** cero

waxen
3 wan **4** ashy, pale **5** ashen, livid
6 doughy, pallid **8** blanched
9 colorless

waxlike
9 ceraceous

way
3 ilk **4** adit, door, kind, lane,
mode, path, road, sort, type, wise,
wont **5** alley, breed, class, entry,
habit, modus, order, route, style,
track, trick, usage **6** access, artery,
avenue, course, custom, entrée,
manner, method, praxis, street, system **7** fashion, ingress, species, variety **8** distance, entrance, habitude, practice **9** admission,
boulevard, technique **10** admittance, consuetude **12** thoroughfare
combining form: **3** ode

wayfaring
6 roving **7** nomadic, vagrant
8 vagabond **9** itinerate, itinerate,
wandering **11** perambulant, peripatetic **13** perambulatory

waylay
6 ambush **8** surprise

Way of All Flesh author
6 Butler (Samuel)

Way of the World author
8 Congreve (William)

way or sea ____
5 farer

wayward
5 balky **6** fickle, ornery **7** erratic,
froward, restive **8** contrary, freakish, perverse, unstable, variable,
whimsied **9** arbitrary, vagarious,
whimsical **10** capricious, inconstant
11 wrongheaded **12** cross-grained

we
French: **4** nous
German: **3** wir
Italian: **3** noi
Spanish: **8** nosotros

weak
3 wan **4** puny, thin **5** faint, frail,
shaky, washy **6** dickey, dilute, feeble, flimsy, infirm, sickly, unsure,
watery, wobbly **7** diluted, fragile,
rickety, sapless, spindly, unsound
8 boneless, decrepit, impotent, insecure, rootless, thewless, unstable,
wavering **9** enfeebled, fluctuant,
forceless, powerless, spineless, uncertain **10** emasculate, improbable,
impuissant, inadequate, incredible,
irresolute, unreliable **11** debilitated, implausible, ineffective, ineffectual, slack-spined, vacillating,
watered-down **12** invertebrate,
unbelievable, unconvincing, undependable **13** insubstantial,
unsubstantial
combining form: **4** lept **5** lepto **6** asthen **7** astheno

weaken
3 cut, sap **4** fade, fail, flag, thin,
wane **5** blunt, unman **6** damage,
dilute, impair, infirm, injure, lessen,
reduce, shrink, soften **7** cripple, decline, disable, dwindle, unbrace,
unnerve **8** enervate, enfeeble, languish, minimize, paralyze **9** attenuate, fall short, undermine, waste
away **10** debilitate, emasculate
11 deteriorate **12** incapacitate,
unstrengthen

weak-kneed
5 timid **6** wobbly **8** wavering **9** fal-

tering, uncertain, whiffling **10** irresolute **11** vacillating
12 double-minded, wiggle-waggle

weakling
3 sop **4** baby, butt, drip, mark
5 sissy **6** misfit, sucker **7** doormat, milksop, sad sack **8** mama's boy, pushover **9** jellyfish **10** mother's boy, namby-pamby, pantywaist, sissy-pants **11** Milquetoast, mollycoddle **12** invertebrate **13** sissy-britches

weakness
5 taste **6** foible, liking **7** frailty
8 adynamia, appetite, fondness, soft spot **12** Achilles' heel

weal
4 wale, welt **5** ridge, wheal, whelk
6 stripe **7** welfare **9** well-being

weald
5 woods **6** forest, timber **8** woodland **10** timberland

wealth
4 mean, pelf **5** goods, worth **6** assets, estate, mammon, riches **7** capital, fortune **8** golconda, holdings, nabobism, opulence, property **9** resources, substance **11** possessions
combining form: **4** plut **5** pluto

Wealth of Nations author
5 Smith (Adam)

wealthy
4 rich **7** moneyed, opulent
8 affluent

wean
5 alien, spean **8** alienate, disunify, disunite, estrange **9** disaffect

weapon
3 gun **4** bola, bolo, club, dart, dirk, épée, foil, mace, nuke, pike **5** arrow, knife, lance, rifle, saber, sabre, sling, spear, sword **6** dagger, magnum, musket, pistol, poleax, rapier **7** bazooka, carbine, firearm, halberd, halbert, javelin, machete, missile, poleaxe, shotgun, trident **8** battle-ax, catapult, crossbow, petronel, revolver, spontoon, tomahawk **9** battle-axe, blackjack, boomerang, derringer **11** blunderbuss **13** brass knuckles

weapons
7 arsenal

wear
3 rub **4** fray, gall, jade, tire
5 chafe, drain, erode, graze, grind, weary **6** abrade, ruffle, tatter
7 corrode, fatigue, frazzle

wear away
3 eat **4** bite, gnaw **5** erode, scour
6 abrade **7** corrode

wear down
4 jade, tire **5** drain, weary
6 weaken **7** exhaust, fatigue

weariness
5 ennui **7** fatigue **9** lassitude, tiredness **10** exhaustion

wearisome
see **tiresome**

wear out
3 fag **4** poop **6** tucker **7** exhaust, frazzle, outtire **8** knock out, overstay, overtoil **9** prostrate

weary
4 bore, jade, pall, sick, tire, worn
5 drain, fed up, jaded, tired
6 tucker, weaken **7** fatigue **8** enfeeble, fatigued, footsore, footworn, overtire, overwork, wear down, worn down **9** disgusted
10 debilitate

weasand
6 gullet, throat **8** windpipe

weasel
5 dodge, evade, hedge, slink, sneak, stoat **6** ermine, ferret **7** shuffle, sneaker **8** sidestep, sneaksby
9 pussyfoot **10** equivocate, tergiverse **12** tergiversate
Scottish: **8** whittret

weather
5 clime **7** climate
combining form: **6** meteor **7** meteoro

weathercock
4 vane

weave
4 reed, spin, sway **5** braid, lurch, swing, twill **6** careen, damask, pleach, raddle, tissue, wattle, wobble **7** stagger, texture

weaverbird
4 taha **6** whidah, whydah
8 avadavat

Weaver of Raveloe
6 Marner (Silas)

weaver's reed
4 slay, sley

web
3 net **4** knot, maze, mesh **5** fiber, skein, snare, snarl, toils **6** cobweb, fabric, jungle, meshes, morass, tangle **7** ensnare, mizmaze, network, texture **8** entangle **9** labyrinth **10** enmeshment, entrapment

11 embroilment, ensnarement, involvement **12** entanglement
combining form: **5** hypho
of a feather: **5** vexil **8** vexillum

Weber opera
6 Oberon **9** Euryanthe **13** Der Freischütz

_____ Webster
4 Noah **6** Daniel

wed
3 tie **4** join, link, mate, yoke
5 catch, marry, unite **6** marrow, relate, splice **7** combine, conjoin, connect, espouse **9** associate

wedded
7 marital, married, nuptial, spousal
8 conjugal, hymeneal **9** connubial
11 matrimonial

wedding
6 bridal **7** spousal **8** espousal, marriage, nuptials

wedding anniversary
fifteenth: **7** crystal
fifth: **6** wooden
fiftieth: **6** golden
first: **5** paper
seventy-fifth: **7** diamond
tenth: **3** tin
twentieth: **5** china
twenty-fifth: **6** silver

wedge-shaped
7 cuneate, sphenic

wedlock
8 marriage **9** matrimony **11** conjugality **12** connubiality

wee
4 tiny **5** teeny **6** minute, teensy, weensy **7** teentsy **9** miniature
10 diminutive, teeny-weeny **11** lilliputian **12** teensy-weensy

weed
4 dock, tare **5** chess **6** darnel, dodder, lupine, nettle, sorrel, teasel
7 burdock, burseed, hemlock, mullein, solanum, thistle, tobacco
8 amaranth, charlock, gromwell, purslane, toadflax **9** cocklebur, dandelion, glasswort, goldenrod, horsetail, knotgrass, marijuana, poison ivy, poison oak, stickseed
10 cinquefoil
European: **6** spurry **7** spurrey
8 pingrass
killer: **8** paraquat **9** herbicide
Western: **4** loco

week
8 hebdomad
two weeks: **9** fortnight

weep

3 cry, sob 4 blub, drib, drip, drop, moan, ooze, seep, wail 5 bleed, exude, greet, sweat, trill 6 bemoan, bewail, boohoo, grieve, lament, strain 7 blubber, deplore, distill, dribble, trickle 8 transude

weepy

5 teary 7 maudlin, tearful 10 lachrymose

weevil

4 boll 7 billbug 8 curculio
tropical: 7 zyzzyva

weft

3 web 4 pick, woof, yarn 6 fabric, thread

weigh

3 tax 4 lade, load, mind, rate, tare 5 count, study 6 burden, charge, cumber, lumber, ponder, saddle, weight 7 balance, perpend 8 appraise, consider, encumber, evaluate, militate, think out 9 think over 10 excogitate 11 contemplate

weigh down

5 press 6 sadden 7 depress, oppress

weight

3 tax 4 duty, lade, load, onus, pith, task 6 burden, charge, credit, cumber, debase, import, lumber, moment, saddle 7 potency 8 efficacy, encumber, prestige 9 authority, influence, magnitude, millstone 10 adulterate, importance 11 consequence 12 forcefulness, forcibleness, powerfulness, significance
allowance: 4 tare, tret 7 scalage
apothecary: 4 dram 5 grain, pound 7 scruple
Asian: 6 cattie
combining form: 3 bar 4 baro
gem: 5 carat
measure of: 3 ton 4 dram, gram 5 grain, ounce, pound 7 long ton, scruple 8 kilogram, short ton 9 metric ton
system: 3 net 4 troy 6 metric 10 apothecary 11 avoirdupois

weightiness

4 pith 6 import, moment, weight 9 magnitude 10 importance 11 consequence 12 significance

weight lift

5 press 6 snatch 12 clean and jerk

weighty

3 big, fat 5 grave, gross, heavy, hefty, obese, sober, staid, stout, tough 6 fleshy, portly, sedate, se-

vere, solemn, somber, taxing 7 earnest, exigent, massive, onerous, porcine, serious 8 cumbrous, exacting, grievous, material 9 corpulent, demanding, important, momentous, ponderous 10 burdensome, cumbersome, meaningful, no-nonsense, oppressive, overweight, sobersided 11 significant, substantial 12 considerable 13 consequential

weir

3 dam 9 fishgarth

weird

3 lot, odd 4 cast, doom, eery, fate 5 awful, eerie, moira, queer 6 creepy, kismet, spooky 7 bizarre, curious, destiny, eldrich, fearful, oddball, portion, strange, uncanny, uncouth 8 dreadful, eldritch, forecast, haunting, horrific, peculiar, prophecy, singular, supernal 9 eccentric, prevision, prognosis, unearthly, unnatural 10 mysterious, outlandish, prediction 11 foretelling, inscrutable 12 awe-inspiring, circumstance, supernatural 13 preternatural

welcome

4 hail 5 greet 6 genial 7 cordial 8 pleasant, pleasing 9 agreeable, congenial, favorable 10 contenting, gratifying, satisfying 11 pleasurable, pleasureful, sympathetic

weld

5 unite 6 solder 11 consolidate

welfare

4 good 7 benefit, fortune, success 8 interest 9 advantage, happiness, well-being 10 prosperity

welkin

3 sky 7 heavens 9 firmament

well

3 far, fit 4 easy, hale, sane 5 amply, clear, fitly, fully, happy, lucky, quite, right, sound, truly 6 aright, freely, indeed, justly, kindly, likely, nicely, origin, rather, really, source, wholly 7 happily, healthy, lightly, perhaps, readily, rightly, roundly, utterly 8 decently, entirely, facilely, fountain, possibly, probably, properly, smoothly, somewhat, suitably 9 correctly, favorably, fittingly, fortunate, inception, perfectly, tolerably, wholesome 10 acceptably, adequately, altogether, becomingly, completely, decorously, generously, pleasantly, prosperous, provenance, swimmingly, thoroughly 11 approvingly, befittingly,

comfortable, doubtlessly, fortunately, provenience, substantial 12 considerably, effortlessly, fountainhead, prosperously, providential, satisfyingly, successfully 13 appropriately, significantly
combining form: 2 eu

well-being

4 ease, good 7 benefit, welfare 8 euphoria, interest, thriving 9 abundance, advantage 10 easy street, prosperity

well-bred

6 urbane 7 genteel, refined 8 cultured, polished 9 distingué 10 cultivated

well-built

5 hunky, solid

well-developed

5 curvy 7 rounded 9 curvesome, Junoesque 10 curvaceous 11 curvilinear

well-disposed

8 friendly 9 receptive 11 sympathetic

Welles movie

7 Macbeth, Othello 8 The Trial 11 Citizen Kane, The Third Man, Touch of Evil 16 Chimes at Midnight

well-favored

4 fair 6 comely, lovely, pretty 8 handsome 9 beauteous, beautiful 10 attractive 11 good-looking

well-fixed

see **well-to-do**

well-founded

4 good, just 5 meaty, pithy, sound, valid 6 cogent 7 telling 8 rational, reasoned 9 justified 10 reasonable 11 fundamental, substantial

well-groomed

4 neat, snug, tidy, trig, trim 5 doggy, natty, sassy 6 dapper, spiffy, spruce, sprucy 7 chipper, doggish, orderly 8 sparkish 9 shipshape 11 spic-and-span, uncluttered 12 spick-and-span

wellhead

see **wellspring**

well-heeled

see **well-to-do**

Wellington

horse: 10 Copenhagen
victory: 7 Vitoria 8 Talavera, Waterloo 9 Salamanca

well-known
5 noted **6** famous **7** leading, popular **9** important, notorious, prominent **11** conspicuous, outstanding

well-liked
7 favored, popular **8** favorite **9** preferred

well-mannered
5 civil **6** polite **7** genteel **9** courteous

well-nigh
4 most, much, nigh **5** about **6** all but, almost, nearly **8** as good as, as much as **11** essentially, practically

well-off
see **well-to-do**

well-paying
7 gainful **9** lucrative **10** profitable, worthwhile **11** moneymaking **12** advantageous, remunerative

well-proportioned
see **well-turned**

wellspring
4 root **6** origin, source **8** fountain **9** inception **10** provenance **11** provenience **12** fountainhead

well-thought-of
7 reputed **9** estimable, reputable **10** creditable **11** respectable

well-timed
7 timeous **9** favorable, opportune **10** auspicious, propitious, prosperous, seasonable

well-to-do
4 easy, rich **7** wealthy **8** affluent **10** prosperous **11** comfortable, substantial

well-turned
4 trim **7** shapely **8** shapeful **10** statuesque **11** clean-limbed

well-worn
5 stale, tired, trite **9** hackneyed **10** threadbare **11** commonplace, stereotyped

welsh
6 cry off, renege, resile **7** back off, back out **8** back down **9** backpedal, backwater **10** declare off **11** crawfish out

Welsh
see **Cymric**

welt
4 wale, weal **5** ridge, wheal, whelk

welter
4 bask, roll, wilt **5** dry up, mummy, revel, wizen **6** wallow, wither **7** in-dulge, mummify, rollick, shrivel **9** luxuriate

____ Welty, writer
6 Eudora

wen
4 cyst **6** growth **11** excrescence

wench
3 gal **4** girl, jade, lass, maid, miss **5** hussy, missy, tramp, trull **6** damsel, lassie, maiden, wanton **7** jezebel, servant, trollop **8** slattern, strumpet

wend
2 go **3** hie **4** fare, pass **6** push on, repair, travel **7** journey, proceed

werewolf
11 lycanthrope

Werther's beloved
5 Lotte

Wesleyan
9 Methodist

West
8 Occident

West African
baboon: **5** drill **8** mandrill
city: **5** Accra, Dakar, Lagos
country: **4** Togo **5** Benin, Gabon, Ghana **6** Gambia, Guinea **7** Liberia, Nigeria, Senegal **8** Cameroon **10** Ivory Coast **11** Sierra Leone
fetish: **4** juju
native: **3** Ibo **5** Hausa **7** Ashanti

western
5 oater **9** shoot-em-up **10** horse opera

Western novelist
4 Grey (Zane) **5** Short (Luke) **6** Judson (Edward Zane Carroll), L'Amour (Louis), Wister (Owen) **7** Guthrie (Alfred Bertram) **8** McMurtry (Larry)

Western organization
3 OAS **4** NATO

Western Samoa
capital: **4** Apia
monetary unit: **4** tala

West Indies
boat: **7** drogher
country: **4** Cuba **5** Haiti **7** Grenada, Jamaica **8** Dominica **10** Saint Lucia **13** Bahama Islands
language: **6** Creole, French **7** English, Spanish

West Point
father of: **6** Thayer (Sylvanus)
freshman: **5** plebe
student: **5** cadet

West Side Story
composer: **9** Bernstein (Leonard)
heroine: **5** Maria
lyricist: **8** Sondheim (Stephen)

West Virginia
capital: **10** Charleston
nickname: **13** Mountain State
state bird: **8** cardinal
state flower: **12** rhododendron

west wind
see at **wind**

wet
3 dew, sop **4** damp, dank, lave, soak, wash **5** bedew, douse, drown, drunk, madid, moist, rainy, rinse, soggy, soppy, souse, water **6** dampen, deluge, drench, drippy, soaked, sodden, soused, sweaty, vapory **7** moisten, slopped, soaking, sopping **8** drenched, dripping, humidify, irrigate, saturate **9** saturated **10** inebriated **11** intoxicated
combining form: **4** hygr **5** hygro

wet blanket
7 killjoy **10** spoilsport

wether
4 goat **5** sheep

wetland
3 bog, fen **5** marsh, swamp

whack
2 go **3** bat, hit, pop, try **4** bash, blow, ding, shot, slap, slog, sock, stab, whop **5** catch, crack, fling, smack, smash, whirl **6** strike, thwack, wallop **7** stagger

whale
4 flog, hide, lash, whip **5** giant **6** stripe, thrash **7** mammoth, monster, scourge **8** behemoth **9** leviathan **10** flagellate
arctic: **7** bowhead
combining form: **3** cet **4** ceto
group: **3** pod
killer: **4** orca
kind: **3** sei **4** blue **5** right, sperm **6** baleen, beluga, killer **7** narwhal, rorqual **8** cachalot
tale: **8** Moby Dick
toothed: **9** blackfish
young: **4** calf

whalebone
6 baleen

wham
4 bang, boom, clap, slam **5** blast, burst, crack, crash, smash

whammy
3 hex **4** jinx **6** hoodoo, voodoo **10** Indian sign

wharf
4 dock, pier, quay, slip 5 berth, jetty, levee

Wharton novel
10 Ethan Frome 12 House of Mirth 13 The Buccaneers 16 Age of Innocence

whatnot
5 curio 6 bauble, gewgaw, trifle 7 bibelot, novelty, trinket 8 gimcrack 9 objet d'art 10 knickknack

wheal
4 wale, welt 5 whelk 6 strake, streak, stripe

wheat
5 durum, emmer, spelt, trigo 6 speltz 7 einkorn
beard: 3 awn
beat: 6 thresh
chaff: 4 bran
crushed: 6 bulgur
disease: 4 rust, smut

wheedle
3 con 4 coax 6 cajole 7 blarney 8 blandish, soft-soap 9 sweet-talk

wheel
4 auto, gyre, loop, reel, tire, tool, turn, veer, whip 5 avert, cycle, dolly, drive, motor, pilot, pivot, round, sheer, whirl 6 circle, divert, league, totter 7 circuit, deflect, stagger 8 gyration, rotation, titubate 9 volte-face 10 charioteer, conference, revolution 11 association, circulation
combining form: 5 troch 6 trocho
part: 3 hub, rim 5 spoke
rim: 5 felly 6 felloe
spoke: 6 radius
toothed: 3 cog 4 gear

wheel-like
8 rotiform

wheelman
6 driver 7 cyclist 8 helmsman

wheel-shaped
5 round 7 trochal 8 circular

wheeze
4 buzz, fizz, hiss, lark 5 antic, caper, prank, swish, trick 6 didoes, fizzle, frolic, shines, sizzle, whoosh 7 whisper 8 sibilate 10 shenanigan 11 monkeyshine

whelk
4 wale, weal, welt 5 wheal

whelm
5 drown, flood, swamp 6 deluge, engulf 8 inundate, overcome, over-flow, submerge 9 knock over, overpower, overwhelm, prostrate

whelp
3 boy, cub, pup 4 girl 5 child, puppy

when
4 anon 5 again, while 6 albeit, much as, though 7 howbeit, whereas 8 although

where
4 site, spot 5 locus, place, point 7 station, whither 8 location, position 9 situation

whereas
2 as 3 for, now 4 when 5 since, while 6 albeit, much as, seeing, though 7 because, howbeit 8 although, as long as 10 inasmuch as 11 considering

wherefore
3 why 5 proof 6 ground, reason, whyfor 8 argument

wherewithal
5 means, money 9 resources

wherry
4 boat 5 barge 7 rowboat

whet
4 edge, hone, stir, wake 5 rally, rouse, waken 6 arouse, awaken, bestir, kindle 7 sharpen, zakuska 9 antipasto, appetizer, challenge 11 hors d'oeuvre

whiff
4 dash, hint 5 shade, smack, tinge, trace 6 breath, trifle 7 soupçon 8 tincture

whiffet
4 zero 5 zilch 6 cipher, nobody 7 nothing, nullity 8 whipster 9 nonentity

whiffle
4 halt 5 waver 6 dither, falter 7 stagger 8 hesitate 9 vacillate 12 shilly-shally, wiggle-waggle

while
2 as 3 bit 4 pass, time, when 5 fleet, pains, space, spell, spend 6 albeit, effort, moment, much as, though 7 beguile, howbeit, instant, stretch, trouble, whereas 8 although, exertion, occasion

whim
3 bee 4 idea 5 dream, fancy, freak, humor 6 megrim, vagary, vision 7 boutade, caprice, conceit, fantasy, thought 8 crotchet 11 disposition, inclination

whimper
3 cry 4 mewl, pule 5 whine

whimsical
4 iffy 6 chancy 7 erratic, wayward 8 freakish, whimsied 9 arbitrary, fluctuant, uncertain, vagarious 10 capricious 12 incalculable 13 unpredictable

whimsy
4 idea 5 dream, fancy, freak, humor 6 megrim, vagary, vision 7 boutade, caprice, conceit, fantasy, thought 8 crotchet 9 capriccio 11 disposition, inclination

whine
4 fuss, kick, pule, wail 6 murmur, repine, snivel, yammer 7 whimper 8 complain

whinny
5 neigh 6 nicker 7 whicker

whiny
5 raspy, waspy 6 snappy, twitty 7 peevish, raspish, waspish 8 snappish 9 irritable, querulous

whip
3 set 4 abet, beat, cane, drub, dust, flog, hide, lash, lick, rout, trim, turn, veer 5 avert, blast, curry, mop up, pivot, quirt, raise, set on, sheer, upend, whale, wheel, whirl, whisk, whomp 6 cudgel, defeat, divert, foment, incite, lather, stir up, stripe, subdue, switch, thrash, wallop 7 curbash, deflect, kurbash, overrun, provoke, rawhide, scourge, shellac, trounce 8 bludgeon, courbash, kourbash, lambaste, overcome, vanquish 9 bastinado, instigate, overwhelm 10 flagellate 13 cat-o'-nine-tails
braided: 10 blacksnake
combining form: 6 mastig, mastix 7 mastigo
riding: 4 crop

whippersnapper
see **whiffet**

whipping boy
4 goat 5 patsy 7 fall guy 9 scapegoat

whippy
6 supple 7 elastic, springy, stretch 8 flexible, stretchy 9 resilient

whir
3 fly 4 buzz 5 chirr 6 chirre 7 revolve, vibrate

whirl
2 go 3 ado, pop, try 4 eddy, flit, fuss, gyre, moil, reel, shot, slap, spin, stab, stir, swim, turn, veer,

whip, whiz **5** avert, crack, fleet, fling, gurge, hurry, pivot, round, sheer, speed, stave, storm, twirl, whack, wheel, whish, whisk **6** barrel, bullet, bustle, divert, flurry, furore, gyrate, hassle, hubbub, pother, swoosh, vortex **7** circuit, clatter, deflect, ruction, stagger, whoopla **8** gyration, rotation, rowdydow **9** commotion, maelstrom, pirouette **10** hurly-burly, revolution **11** circulation

whirligig
4 gyre, spin **6** beetle, gyrate **8** carousel **9** carrousel, pirouette **12** merry-go-round

whirlpool
3 ado **4** eddy, fuss, purl, stir **5** gurge, whorl **6** bustle, flurry, furore, pother, swoosh, vortex **8** vortices (plural) **9** maelstrom, whirlwind
combining form: **4** dino

whirlwind
2 oe **3** ado **4** fuss, stir **6** bustle, flurry, furore, pother, whirly **7** tornado **9** dust devil, hurricane, rainspout, sand spout **10** sand column, waterspout

whish
3 fly **4** buzz, fizz, flit, hiss, whiz **5** fleet, hurry, speed, stave, whirl **6** bullet, fizzle, sizzle, wheeze **7** whisper **8** sibilate

whisk
3 fly, zip **4** beat, flit, whip, whiz **5** hurry, speed **6** barrel, bullet

whisker
3 ace **4** hair **11** hairbreadth

whiskered
5 hairy **6** fleecy, pilose, woolly **7** barbate, bearded, hirsute, pileous

whiskers
5 beard **6** beaver

whiskey
3 rye **5** hooch, usque **6** hootch, Scotch **7** bourbon **8** usquabae, usquebae
with beer chaser: **11** boilermaker

whisper
4 buzz, dash, fizz, hint, hiss, whiz **5** rumor, shade, swish, tinge, touch, trace, whiff **6** breath, fizzle, mumble, murmur, mutter, rustle, sizzle, wheeze, whoosh **7** breathe, confide **8** sibilate **9** suspicion, undertone **11** susurration

whist
4 game, hush **5** quiet, still **6** silent, stilly **7** hushful **9** noiseless, soundless
card hand: **10** Yarborough

whistle
4 pipe **5** flute **6** signal

whit
3 bit, jot **4** atom, damn, hoot, iota **5** shred, whoop **7** modicum **8** particle

white
5 hoary, milky **6** albino, benign, blanch, bleach, blench, bright, dexter **7** decolor **8** palliate **9** canescent, extenuate, favorable, fortunate, gloss over, gloze over, sugarcoat **10** auspicious, blanch over, decolorize, propitious
combining form: **3** alb **4** albo, cali, calo, leuc, leuk **5** callo, leuco, leuko
egg's: **5** glair **6** glaire **7** albumen

white cliffs of ___
5 Dover

White Fang author
6 London (Jack)

White House
designer: **5** Hoban (James)
first occupant: **5** Adams (Abigail, John)

white lightning
7 bootleg **9** moonshine **10** bathtub gin **11** mountain dew

whiten
3 dim **4** dull, fade, pale **5** frost **6** blanch, bleach, blench, silver, veneer **7** decolor, grizzle, lighten, varnish **8** etiolate, palliate **9** extenuate, gloss over, gloze over, sugarcoat **10** blanch over, decolorize

white plague
2 TB **8** phthisis **11** consumption **12** tuberculosis

whitewash
6 veneer **7** varnish **8** palliate **9** extenuate, gloss over, gloze over, sugarcoat **10** blanch over

whither
5 where **7** whereto **9** whereunto **11** whereabouts

whiting
4 fish, hake

Whitsunday
9 Pentecost

Whittier poem
7 Ichabod, Laus Deo **9** Snow-Bound **10** Maud Muller **11** Barefoot Boy **14** Telling the Bees **16** Barbara Frietchie

whittle
3 cut **4** pare **5** carve, shape

whiz
3 fly, zip **4** buzz, fizz, flit, hiss, zoom **5** adept, hurry, speed, swish, whirl, whish, whisk **6** bullet, expert, fizzle, master, sizzle, wheeze, whoosh, wizard **7** whisper **8** sibilate, virtuoso **10** past master **12** professional

whole
3 all, fit, sum **4** full, hale, sane **5** fixed, gross, right, sound, total **6** choate, entire, entity, intact, system, unhurt, unrent **7** gestalt, perfect, plenary **8** complete, entirety, flawless, integral, outright, sum total, totality, unbroken, unmarred **9** aggregate, exclusive, integrate, undamaged, undivided, uninjured, untouched **10** unimpaired, unswerving **11** unblemished **12** concentrated, undistracted
combining form: **3** hol, pan **4** holo, pano, toti **7** integri

wholehearted
4 sure **6** ardent, hearty, steady **7** abiding, earnest, fervent, genuine, serious, sincere **8** bona fide, enduring **9** authentic, heartfelt, steadfast, unfeigned **10** passionate, unwavering **11** impassioned, unfaltering, unqualified **13** unquestioning

whole-hog
8 complete, thorough **9** full-dress **10** exhaustive **13** thoroughgoing

wholeness
5 vigor **6** health **7** allness, oneness **8** entirety, haleness, totality **9** integrity, soundness **10** entireness, heartiness, perfection, robustness **11** healthiness **12** completeness

whole note
9 semibreve

whole number
5 digit **6** cipher, figure **7** chiffer, integer, numeral

wholesome
3 fit **4** good, hale, safe, sane, well **5** right, sound **6** curing **7** healing, healthy **8** curative, hygienic, remedial, salutary, sanative, sanatory **9** healthful, remedying, vulnerary **10** salubrious, well-liking **11** restorative

wholly
3 all **4** just, well **5** fully, quite **6** in toto, purely **7** exactly, roundly, to-

tally, utterly **8** all in all, entirely
9 perfectly **10** altogether, completely, thoroughly
combining form: 4 toti

whomp
4 beat, drub, whip **5** smear
6 thrash, wallop **7** shellac, trounce
8 lambaste

whoopee
3 fun **5** revel **6** gaiety **7** jollity, revelry, wassail **8** reveling **9** festivity,
high jinks, merriment, revelment
10 skylarking **11** merrymaking

whoopla
4 to-do **5** revel, whirl **6** clamor,
hassle, pother, tumult, uproar **7** revelry, turmoil, wassail **9** commotion,
high jinks, revelment **10** hurly-burly,
skylarking

whop
3 bat, bop **4** bash, beat, biff, blow,
drub, sock **5** baste, pound, smack,
whack **6** batter, buffet, hammer,
pummel, thwack, wallop **7** belabor
8 lambaste

whopping
4 huge, much, very **6** damned,
highly, hugely, mighty **7** awfully,
immense **8** colossal, enormous, gigantic **10** gargantuan, prodigious
11 exceedingly

whorl
4 eddy, purl **5** gurge, swirl
6 swoosh **9** whirlpool
combining form: 7 spondyl
8 spondylo

why
5 proof **6** enigma, ground, puzzle,
reason, riddle **7** mystery **8** argument **9** conundrum, wherefore
10 puzzlement **13** Chinese puzzle,
mystification

wicked
3 bad **4** blue, evil, mean, racy,
ugly **5** antic, broad, hairy, pesky,
risky, salty, shady, spicy, wrong
6 adroit, au fait, chancy, clever,
cursed, impish, malign, pranky,
purple, risqué, sinful, unholy **7** hateful, heinous, immoral, larkish, playful, roguish, ungodly, unsound, vicious **8** fiendish, off-color, perilous,
prankful, prankish, spiteful **9** barbarous, dangerous, hazardous, malicious, malignant, rancorous, reprobate, troublous, unhealthy,
vexatious **10** despiteful, iniquitous,
jeopardous, malevolent, outrageous, suggestive **11** mischie-

vous, treacherous, troublesome, unchristian, uncivilized

wickedness
3 sin **4** debt, evil, vice **5** wrong
9 depravity **10** corruption,
immorality

wicker
3 rod **4** twig **5** osier, withe

wicket
4 arch, door, gate, hoop **6** window

wickiup
3 hut **5** lodge, tepee **7** shelter

wide
5 ample, broad, roomy **6** scopic,
sweepy **7** liberal, radical **8** advanced, extended, scopious, spacious, tolerant **9** capacious, expansive, extensive **10** commodious
11 broad-minded, progressive
combining form: 4 eury, lati

widen
4 ream **6** dilate **7** broaden
9 breadthen

wideness
5 scope **7** breadth **8** fullness
9 amplitude

widespread
4 rife **6** ruling **7** current, popular,
rampant, regnant **9** prevalent
10 prevailing

widget
5 gizmo **6** gadget, jigger
7 gimmick

width
5 ambit, orbit, range, scope **6** circle, length, radius **7** breadth, compass **8** panorama **9** extension

wield
3 ply **5** exert, swing, throw **6** handle, put out **7** conduct, control
8 dispense, exercise, maneuver
10 manipulate
the gavel: 7 preside

wieldy
6 mighty, strong **8** powerful

wiener
3 dog **5** frank **6** hot dog **11** frankfurter, wienerwurst

wife
3 Mrs. **4** mate **5** bride **6** matron,
missis, missus, spouse **7** consort,
dowager **8** helpmate, helpmeet
9 other half
Latin: 4 uxor
of a rajah: 4 rani **5** ranee

wifely
7 uxorial

wig
3 jaw, rap **4** rail, rate **5** scold
6 berate, peruke, rebuke, revile,
toupee **7** bawl out, chiding, reproof, upbraid **8** reproach **9** reprimand **10** admonition, tongue-lash
12 admonishment

wiggle
4 worm **6** squirm, writhe
8 squiggle
Scottish: 5 hotch

wight
5 being, human **6** mortal, person
8 creature **9** personage **10** human
being, individual

wigwam
3 hut **5** lodge, tepee

wild
3 mad **4** fast **5** crazy, dirty, feral,
rabid, rough, waste **6** barren, brutal, desert, ferine, Gothic, raging,
rakish, savage, stormy, unruly, vulgar **7** badland, frantic, furious,
Hunnish, natural, raffish, uncivil, untamed, vicious **8** agrarian, agrestal, barbaric, blustery, carefree,
feckless, frenetic, frenzied, rakehell,
reckless, stormful, untoward **9** barbarian, barbarous, delirious, fantastic, fractious, graceless, tasteless,
turbulent, uncareful, unsubdued,
wasteland **10** blustering, corybantic, incautious, outlandish, wilderness **11** extravagant, intractable,
tempestuous, uncivilized **12** devil-
may-care, preposterous, recalcitrant, uncultivated, ungovernable,
unmanageable **13** irresponsible,
undisciplined
combining form: 5 agrio

wild ass
5 kiang **6** onager

Wild Duck author
5 Ibsen (Henrik)

wildebeest
3 gnu

wilderness
5 waste **6** barren, desert **7** badland **9** backlands, wasteland
10 hinterland **11** backcountry

Wilder play
7 Our Town **13** The Matchmaker
17 The Skin of Our Teeth

wild-eyed
6 raving **7** radical **9** visionary

wild ox
4 anoa

wile
4 draw, ploy, ruse 5 charm, feint, guile, trick 6 allure, deceit, device, gambit 7 attract, beguile, bewitch, chicane, cunning, enchant, gimmick 8 artifice, maneuver, trickery 9 captivate, chicanery, fascinate, magnetize, stratagem 13 dissimulation

wiliness
3 art 5 craft 7 cunning, slyness 8 artifice, foxiness 9 cageyness, canniness 10 artfulness, craftiness

will
4 like, mind, wish 5 elect, fancy, leave 6 choose, devise, legate, liking, please 8 bequeath, pleasure, velleity, volition 9 testament 10 discipline 11 inclination, self-command, self-control, self-mastery 13 determination, self-restraint
addition: 7 codicil
maker: 8 testator 9 testatrix
without: 9 intestate

willful
6 dogged, mulish, unruly 7 decided 8 factious, perverse, resolved, stubborn, unforced 9 obstinate, pigheaded, purposive, voluntary 10 deliberate, determined, headstrong 11 intentional, intractable, stiff-necked, wrongheaded 12 contumacious, pertinacious, unprescribed

Williams play
10 Camino Real 13 The Rose Tattoo 16 Cat on a Hot Tin Roof, Sweet Bird of Youth 17 The Glass Menagerie 18 Suddenly Last Summer

William Tell composer
7 Rossini (Gioacchino)

willies
5 jumps 6 creeps, dither, shakes 7 jitters, shivers 9 whim-whams 13 heebie-jeebies

willing
3 apt 4 fair, game, open 5 prone, ready 6 minded, prompt 7 forward, witting 8 disposed, inclined, unforced 9 agreeable, compliant, favorable, voluntary 10 deliberate 11 intentional, predisposed 12 unprescribed

willow
5 osier, salix 6 sallow
flower cluster: 6 catkin
kind: 5 crack, pussy, white 6 basket 7 weeping

willowy
4 tall 5 lithe 6 pliant 7 slender

8 graceful

wilt
3 sag 4 drop, flag, swag 5 droop, dry up, mummy, wizen 6 cave in, peg out, welter, wither 7 give out, mummify, shrivel, succumb 8 collapse 9 break down

wily
3 sly 4 deep, foxy 6 artful, astute, clever, crafty, shrewd, tricky 7 cunning, knowing 8 guileful 9 insidious, sagacious

wimble
4 bore 5 auger, brace, scoop 6 gimlet

Wimbledon's game
6 tennis

wimple
4 veil, wrap 6 ripple
wearer: 3 nun

win
3 get 4 beat, earn, gain, have, make, take 5 annex, reach, score, yield 6 attain, defeat, obtain, pick up, rack up, secure 7 achieve, acquire, bring in, chalk up, conquer, procure, produce, realize, triumph, victory 8 conquest, drag down, draw down, overcome 9 knock down 10 accomplish
over: 6 disarm, induce 8 convince, persuade, talk into 9 prevail on

wince
5 cower, quail, start 6 blanch, blench, cringe, flinch, recoil, shrink 7 squinch

wind
3 fan, nil 4 bend, blow, clue, coil, curl, gale, gird, gust, hint, reel, warp, wrap 5 curve, spool, twine, twist, weave 6 breath, breeze, circle, deform, enlace, girdle, naught, notion, nought, ruffle, spiral, winnow, zephyr 7 contort, distort, enclose, entwine, envelop, inkling, meander, monsoon, nothing, torture, wreathe 8 easterly, encircle, misshape, surround, westerly 9 corkscrew 10 indication, intimation, suggestion
California: 8 Santa Ana
cold: 4 bise, bora 6 sansar, sarsar 7 mistral, pampero, wulliwa 8 williwaw, willywaw
combining form: 4 anem 5 anemo, venti, vento
east: 5 Eurus
gentle: 6 breeze, zephyr 7 cat's-paw
hot: 6 ghibli, samiel, shamal, simoom, solano 7 sirocco

instrument: 3 sax 4 horn, oboe, tuba, vane 5 flute 7 bassoon, trumpet 8 trombone 10 anemometer 11 weather vane
into: 8 aweather
measure of speed: 4 knot
Mediterranean: 7 etesian 8 levanter
north: 6 Boreas
scale: 8 Beaufort
south: 5 Notus 6 Auster
southwest: 8 libeccio
stormy: 4 gale 7 cyclone, tornado, twister 9 hurricane 11 northeaster
warm: 4 föhn 5 foehn 7 chinook
west: 6 zephyr 8 Favonius, Zephyrus

winding
5 snaky 6 spiral 7 bending, coiling, crooked, curving, devious, sinuous 8 flexuous, indirect, tortuous, twisting 9 meandrous 10 circuitous, convoluted, meandering, roundabout, serpentine 11 anfractuous

windmill
fighter: 9 Don Quixote
sail: 3 awe

window
3 bay, eye 4 pane 5 oriel 6 dormer 7 fenster, lucarne, luthern, opening 8 aperture, casement, jalousie
cover: 5 blind 7 curtain, shutter
French: 7 fenêtre
over a door: 7 transom 8 fanlight
part: 4 came, pane, sash, sill 5 frame
projecting: 3 bay 5 oriel
relating to: 9 fenestral
roof's: 6 dormer 8 skylight
Scottish: 7 winnock
ship's: 4 port 8 porthole
ticket: 7 guichet

windpipe
6 throat 7 trachea
combining form: 6 bronch, trache 7 bronchi, broncho, tracheo 8 bronchio

windrow
4 bank, heap, hill, mass, pile 5 drift, mound, stack 6 furrow 7 pyramid 8 mountain

wind up
3 end 4 halt 5 close 6 finish, settle, wrap up 7 clean up 8 complete, conclude 9 determine, terminate

windup
3 end 5 close 6 ending, finale, finish 10 conclusion

windy
4 airy 5 blowy, brisk, fresh, gusty,

tumid, wordy **6** breezy, drafty, prolix, turgid **7** diffuse, verbose **8** blustery, dropsied, inflated **9** dropsical, flatulent, overblown, redundant **10** palaverous

wine
4 vino **5** drink, juice **8** beverage
aromatized: **8** vermouth **9** hippocras, Quinquina
beverage: **5** clary, mulse, negus, punch **6** bishop **8** sangaree **9** hippocras
bottle: **6** fiasco, magnum **8** decanter, jeroboam, rehoboam **9** balthazar **10** methuselah, salmanazar **14** nebuchadnezzar
cabinet: **8** cellaret
cask: **3** tun, vat **4** butt, pipe **8** puncheon
cellar: **6** bodega
combining form: **2** en **3** eno, oen **4** oeno
discoverer: **4** Noah
disorder: **5** casse
distillate: **6** brandy, cognac
dry: **3** sec **4** brut
film: **8** beeswing
flavor: **4** mull
fortified: **4** port **6** Malaga, sherry **7** Madeira, marsala
fragrance: **4** nose **7** bouquet
golden: **4** Bual **7** Amoroso, Madeira, Moscato, Oloroso, Sercial **8** Bucellas, Moscatel, muscatel
lover: **9** oenophile **11** oenophilist
maker: **7** vintner **8** vigneron **13** viticulturist
merchant: **7** vintner
pitcher: **4** olpe **5** olpae (plural) **8** oenochoe
red: **4** port, tent **5** Gamay, Macon, Marco, Medoc, Rioja **6** Aleyor, Barolo, Beaune, claret, Shiraz, Volnay **7** Almissa, Barbera, Chianti, Falerno, Inferno, Margaux **8** Aleatico, Alicante, Ambonnay, Bordeaux, Burgundy, cabernet, Gragnano, Julienas, Nebbiolo, Sassella **9** Adlesberg, Hermitage, Lambrusco, Pinot Noir, St. Emilion, zinfandel **10** Barbaresco, Beaujolais, Roussillon, Sangiovese, Valtellina, Verdicchio **11** Affenthaler, Mavrodaphne, Petite Sirah **12** Valpolicella
relating to: **5** vinic **6** vinous
residue: **4** marc
rice: **4** sake
richness: **4** body
sediment: **4** lees **5** dregs
shop: **6** bistro, bodega
sparkling: **4** sekt **8** cold duck, mous-

seux, sparkler, Spumante **9** champagne, Lambrusco
specialist: **9** enologist **10** oenologist
spiced: **9** hippocras
steward: **9** sommelier
study of: **7** enology **8** oenology
sweet: **4** Bual, port, tent **5** Almus, Tokay **6** Albana, canary, d'Yquem, Malaga, muscat **7** Almissa, bastard, Catawba, Madeira, malmsey, marsala, Moscato, Oloroso, Orvieto, Vouvray **8** Aleatico, Alicante, Malvasia, Moscatel, muscadel, muscatel, sauterne **9** Sauternes **11** Mavrodaphne, scuppernong
sweeten: **4** mull
unfermented: **4** must
vessel: **3** ama **5** amula **7** chalice
white: **4** hock, sock **5** Almus, Rhine, Soave **6** Alella, Barsac, Gentil, Graves, Saumur, Valmur **7** Banyuls, Catawba, Chablis, Chacoli, Conthey, Dezaley, Falerno, Moselle, Orvieto, Vouvray **8** Aiglerie, Amarante, Bordeaux, Frascati, Riesling, Semillon, Sylvaner, Traminer, Vaudesir, vermouth **9** champagne, Hermitage, Meursault, Neuchatel, Sansevero, Teneriffe, Zeltinger **10** chardonnay, Hochheimer, Montrachet **11** Chenin Blanc, Niersteiner, Rudesheimer, scuppernong **12** Geisenheimer **13** liebfraumilch **14** sauvignon blanc
year: **7** vintage

wing
3 ala, arm, ell, fly **4** flit, limb, sail **5** annex, block, bulge, fleet, pinna, sweep **9** expansion, extension **10** projection, protrusion **12** prolongation, protuberance
combining form: **3** ali **4** pter **5** ptera, ptero **6** pterus, pteryg **7** pterous, pterygo
relating to: **4** alar **5** alary **6** pteric

winged
5 alate **7** pennate
deity: **4** Amor, Eros, Nike **5** Cupid **6** Hermes **7** Mercury
horse: **7** Pegasus
monster: **5** harpy

wingless
7 apteral **8** apterous

winglike
4 alar **7** aliform
part: **3** ala **4** alae (plural)

wink
3 bat **5** blink, shake, trice **6** minute, moment, second **7** instant, nictate, twinkle **9** nictitate, twinkling **11** split second

winner
6 victor **8** champion **9** conqueror

Winnie-the-Pooh
author: **5** Milne (Alan Alexander)
character: **3** Roo **5** Kanga **6** Piglet, Tigger

winning
5 sweet **6** dulcet, profit **8** conquest, engaging

winnow
3 fan **4** blow, comb, sift, sort, wind **6** delete, remove, ruffle **8** separate

winsome
5 sweet **6** dulcet **7** lovable, winning **8** adorable, cheerful, engaging, lovesome

winter
6 season
French: **5** hiver
Spanish: **8** invierno

Winter's Tale character
7 Camillo, Leontes, Perdita **8** Florizel, Hermione **9** Polixenes

wintry
3 icy **4** cold **5** hoary, snowy **6** frigid, hiemal, stormy **8** hibernal, storming

wipe
3 mop **4** x out **5** abate, annul, erase, towel **6** cancel, delete, efface **7** abolish, blot out, expunge **8** black out, decimate, massacre **9** eradicate, extirpate, slaughter **10** annihilate, extinguish, obliterate **11** exterminate

wire
3 rod **4** cord, line **5** cable **6** thread **7** message **8** telegram **9** telegraph
measure: **3** mil **5** gauge

wireless
5 radio

wiry
4 lean, ropy **6** sinewy **7** fibrous, stringy **8** muscular

Wisconsin
capital: **7** Madison
college, university: **5** Ripon **9** Marquette
largest city: **9** Milwaukee
nickname: **11** Badger State
state bird: **5** robin
state flower: **6** violet

wisdom
4 lore **5** sense **7** insight, science **8** gumption, judgment, sagacity, sageness, saneness, sapience **9** good sense, knowledge **10** horse sense, shrewdness **11** common

wise

sense, information **12** perspicacity **13** judiciousness, sagaciousness
combining form: **5** sophy

wise

3 hep, hip, way **4** bold, clew, clue, flip, keen, mode, pert, post, sage, sane, tell, warn, wily **5** acute, alert, aware, brash, cagey, canny, cocky, fresh, lippy, modus, nervy, quick, sassy, saucy, sharp, slick, smart **6** advise, artful, astute, bright, cheeky, crafty, fill in, inform, manner, method, notify, shrewd, smooth, sophic, system, tricky **7** apprise, cunning, fashion, forward, gnostic, knowing, politic, prudent, sapient **8** acquaint, arrogant, discreet, flippant, impudent, insolent, sensible, slippery, tactical **9** advisable, bold-faced, expedient, insighted, intuitive, judgmatic, judicious, provident, sagacious **10** cogitative, discerning, insightful, perceptive, procacious, reflective, thoughtful **11** foresighted, impertinent, intelligent, quick-witted, sharp-witted, smart-alecky **12** nimble-witted **13** contemplative, knowledgeable, perspicacious
old man: **6** Nestor
person: **4** sage **6** savant **7** scholar

wiseacre

see **wise guy**

wisecrack

3 gag **4** jape, jest, joke, quip **5** sally **7** waggery **9** witticism

wise guy

6 smarty **9** know-it-all **10** smart aleck **11** smarty-pants

Wise Men

see **Magi**

wish

4 hope, like, long, want, will **5** covet, crave, elect, fancy, foist, yearn **6** desire, expect, impose, please **7** longing **10** desiderate

wishbone

7 furcula **8** furculum

wishful

5 eager **7** longing **8** desirous

wishy-washy

4 weak **5** banal, bland, vapid **6** jejune, watery **7** insipid, languid, sapless **8** listless, waterish **9** enervated, savorless **10** flavorless, namby-pamby, pantywaist, spiritless **13** characterless

wisp

5 strip **6** streak **7** handful

8 fragment

wispy

5 frail **8** nebulous

wisteria

4 fuji, vine

Wister novel

12 The Virginian

wistful

3 sad **7** pensive **10** meditative, melancholy

wit

3 ESP, wag **4** head, mind **5** brain, comic, droll, grasp, humor, joker, sense **6** acumen, brains, esprit, jester, reason, sanity, satire, senses, wisdom **7** balance, insight, punster, sensing **8** astucity, comedian, funnyman, humorist, jokester, keenness, lucidity, prudence, quipster, repartee, sagacity, sageness, saneness, sapience, wordplay **9** alertness, awareness, mentality, smartness, soundness **10** astuteness, brainpower, brilliance, cleverness, divination, gray matter, perception, shrewdness **11** discernment, penetration, percipience, rationality **12** apprehension, clairvoyance, intelligence, perspicacity **13** comprehension, sagaciousness, understanding

witch

3 hag, hex **4** drab, trot **5** biddy, bruja, charm, crone, lamia, spell **6** beldam, voodoo **7** enchant **8** magician, sorcerer **9** ensorcell, sorceress **11** enchantress
companion: **3** cat
group: **5** coven
male: **6** wizard **7** warlock
meeting: **6** sabbat
Scottish: **6** cummer
town: **5** Endor
vehicle: **5** broom

witchcraft

5 charm, magic **6** allure, appeal, voodoo **7** glamour, hexerei, sorcery **8** charisma, witchery, wizardry **9** conjuring, magnetism **10** black magic, necromancy **11** enchantment, fascination, incantation, thaumaturgy

witch hazel

8 hornbeam **11** tobaccowood, winterbloom
lotion: **9** hamamelin

witchy

5 magic **6** magian, mystic **7** magical **8** wizardly **9** sorcerous **11** necromantic **12** thaumaturgic

with

2 by, on **3** for, per, pro, via **4** over, upon **5** about **7** by way of, through **8** by dint of **9** by means of, in favor of **10** by virtue of
French: **4** avec
German: **3** mit
Italian: **3** con
Latin: **3** cum
prefix: **2** co **3** col, com, con, cor, sym, syn

withal

3 too, yea, yet **4** also, more **5** still **6** as well, though **7** besides, howbeit, however **8** after all, moreover **9** per contra **11** furthermore, nonetheless **12** additionally, nevertheless

withdraw

2 go **4** exit, quit **5** leave, quail, unsay **6** abjure, depart, get off, recall, recant, recede, recoil, remove, retire, secede, shrink **7** get away, retract, retreat, take off, take out **8** fall back, forswear, give back, palinode, run along, take away, take back

withdrawal

4 exit **6** egress, exodus **7** exiting, pullout, retreat **8** offgoing **9** departure, egression **10** setting-out
from reality: **6** autism

withdrawn

4 cool **5** aloof **6** casual, offish, remote **7** aseptic, distant **8** detached, reserved, retiring, solitary **9** incurious, shrinking, unaffable, uncurious **10** restrained, unsociable **11** indifferent, standoffish, unconcerned, unexpansive **12** uninterested
from reality: **8** autistic

wither

3 age, dry **4** wane, wilt **5** dry up, mummy, wizen **6** shrink, welter **7** decline, mummify, shrivel

withered

4 sere **8** shrunken

withhold

3 bit **4** curb, deny, keep **5** check **6** bridle, detain, refuse, retain **7** abstain, forbear, inhibit, keep out, refrain, reserve **8** disallow, keep back, restrain **9** constrain

within

4 into **5** among **6** inside **7** indoors, inwards **8** interior
combining form: **3** end, ent **4** endo, ento

prefix: 2 il, im, in, ir 5 infra, inter, intra, intro

with-it
2 in 4 tony 5 swank, swish 6 modish, tonish, trendy 7 à la mode, stylish 11 fashionable

without
4 open, past, sans 5 after, minus 6 beyond 7 lacking, open air, outside, wanting 8 awanting, outdoors 10 out-of-doors
combining form: 4 lipo
Latin: 4 sine
suffix: 4 less

with respect to
2 re 4 as to 5 as for 7 apropos 8 touching 9 as regards, regarding 10 concerning

withstand
4 bear, buck, duel 5 abide, fight, repel 6 combat, endure, oppose, resist, suffer 7 contest, dispute 8 tolerate, traverse

withy
4 twig 5 osier 6 branch, willow

witless
4 daft 5 crazy, silly 6 crazed, insane, simple, stupid 7 asinine, cracked, unwitty 8 demented, deranged, mindless 9 bedlamite, brainless, nitwitted, senseless 10 reasonless, weak-headed, weak-minded

witlessness
5 folly 7 inanity 8 insanity 9 absurdity, craziness, dottiness, silliness 11 foolishness 13 senselessness

witness
3 see 4 view 5 argue, proof, vouch 6 attest, viewer 7 bespeak, betoken, certify, testify, watcher 8 announce, beholder, by-sitter, evidence, indicate, looker-on, observer, onlooker 9 bystander, spectator, testament, testimony 11 attestation, testimonial 12 confirmation

witticism
3 gag, mot, pun 4 jape, jest, joke, quip 5 crack 6 bon mot 7 waggery 8 drollery 9 wisecrack

wittiness
5 humor 6 comedy 8 drollery 9 drollness, funniness

witting
4 ware 5 alive, awake, aware 7 knowing, willful, willing 8 sensible, sentient, untorced 9 cognizant,

conscious, voluntary 10 deliberate 11 intentional

witty
5 funny 6 clever, jocose 7 amusing, jocular, probing, risible 8 humorous, piercing 9 diverting, facetious, sparkling 10 ridiculous 11 penetrating 12 entertaining 13 scintillating

witty saying
3 mot 4 quip 7 epigram 8 facetiae (plural)

wiz
6 artist, expert, master 8 virtuoso 9 authority 10 past master

wizard
4 mage, sage, whiz 5 magus 6 artist, expert, master 7 warlock 8 conjurer, magician, sorcerer, virtuoso 9 archimage, authority, enchanter 10 past master, proficient 11 necromancer

wizardly
5 magic 6 magian, mystic, witchy 7 magical 9 sorcerous 11 necromantic 12 thaumaturgic

Wizard of Menlo Park
6 Edison (Thomas Alva)

Wizard of Oz
author: 4 Baum (Lyman Frank)
character: 7 Dorothy 9 Scarecrow 10 Tin Woodman 12 Cowardly Lion
dog: 4 Toto

wizardry
5 magic 7 sorcery 8 witchery 9 conjuring, magicking 10 necromancy, witchcraft 11 bewitchment, enchantment, incantation

wizen
3 dry 4 wilt 5 dry up, mummy 6 welter, wither 7 mummify, shrivel

wobble
4 sway 5 lurch, quake, shake, swing, waver, weave 6 careen, dither, falter, quaver, quiver, shimmy, shiver, teeter, topple, totter 7 shudder, stagger, stumble

wobbly
4 weak 5 shaky 6 dickey, unsure 7 halting, rackety, rickety, shaking 8 hesitant, insecure, rachitic, rootless, unstable, unsteady, wavering 9 faltering, fluctuant, tentative, uncertain 10 irresolute, rattletrap 11 vacillating, vacillatory 12 wiggle-waggle

Wodehouse character
6 Jeeves, Psmith 7 Wooster 8 Mulliner

Woden
see **Odin**

woe
3 rue 4 care 5 grief 6 misery, regret, sorrow 7 anguish, sadness, trouble 9 bemoaning, bewailing, deploring, heartache 10 affliction, heartbreak 11 lamentation, unhappiness 12 wretchedness

woebegone
3 low 4 blue, down, worn 5 black, bleak 6 dismal, dreary, gloomy, shabby 8 dejected, downcast, funereal 9 depressed 10 depressing, dispirited, lugubrious, melancholy, oppressive, tenebrific 11 crestfallen, dilapidated, dispiriting, downhearted 12 disconsolate

woeful
3 sad 4 dire 5 grave, wrung 6 dismal, dolent, paltry, racked, rueful 7 crushed 8 dejected, dolesome, dolorous, downcast, grievous, harrowed, mournful, overcome, stricken, tortured, wretched 9 afflicted, depressed, heartsick, miserable, plaintive, sorrowful 10 afflictive, calamitous, deplorable, dispirited, lamentable, lugubrious, melancholy 11 distressing, downhearted, low-spirited, regrettable, unfortunate 12 disconsolate, inconsolable 13 heartbreaking, unprecedented

wold
5 plain

wolf
4 bolt, cram, grub, gulp, lobo, roué, slop 6 canine, chaser, coyote, englut, gobble, guzzle, lecher, masher 7 amorist, Don Juan, rounder 8 Casanova, lothario, womanize 9 ladies' man, libertine, philander, womanizer 10 fool around, lady-killer, mess around, play around, profligate 11 ingurgitate, philanderer
combining form: 3 lyc 4 lyco
genus: 5 Canis
group: 4 pack
young: 5 whelp

wolfish
4 fell, grim 5 cruel 6 fierce, lupine, savage 7 inhuman 8 inhumane 9 barbarous, ferocious, truculent

wolverine
8 carcajou

European: 7 glutton
genus: 4 Gulo

Wolverine State
8 Michigan

woman
4 dame, lady 5 madam 6 female, matron 8 mistress
attractive: 4 peri 5 belle 6 beauty, eyeful, looker 7 stunner 8 knockout
Australian: 4 bint
combining form: 3 gyn 4 gyne, gyno, gyny 5 gynec, gyneo 6 gynaec, gynaeco, gyneco, gynous 7 gynaeco
courageous: 7 heroine
dignified: 6 matron 7 dowager 10 grande dame
dowdy: 5 frump
Dutch: 4 vrow 5 vrouw
English: 6 milady
first, biblical: 3 Eve
first, mythological: 7 Pandora
French: 5 femme
German: 4 frau 8 fräulein
Hawaiian: 6 wahine
Indian: 5 squaw
intellectual: 12 bluestocking
Italian: 3 donna 7 signora
lewd: 5 hussy 6 harlot, wanton 7 trollop
little: 3 Mrs. 4 wife
old: 3 hag 4 dame 5 crone 6 beldam, carlin, gammer, granny
pregnant: 7 gravida
resembling: 8 gynecoid
royal: 5 queen 8 princess
sailor: 4 Wave
scheming: 7 jezebel
servant: 4 maid
slovenly: 8 slattern
soldier: 3 Wac
Spanish: 4 doña 6 senora
strong: 6 amazon, virago
unmarried: 4 miss 6 maiden 8 spinster
young: 4 girl, lass 6 lassie, maiden

womanize
4 wolf 9 philander 10 fool around, mess around, play around

womanizer
4 wolf 6 chaser, masher 7 Don Juan 8 Casanova 9 ladies' man, philander 10 lady-killer 11 philanderer

womb
6 uterus
combining form: 4 metr, uter 5 metra, metro, utero 6 hyster, metria (plural) 7 hystero, metrium

wombat
9 marsupial

women
hatred of: 8 misogyny
organization of: 3 DAR, NOW 7 sorosis 8 sorority

Women in Love author
8 Lawrence (David Herbert)

wonder
3 awe 5 amaze, doubt 6 marvel 7 concern, dubiety, miracle, portent, prodigy, stunner 8 mistrust 9 amazement, dubiosity, marveling, sensation, suspicion 10 admiration, phenomenon, skepticism 11 incertitude, uncertainty, uncertitude 12 astonishment, bewilderment

wonderful
5 great, super, swell 6 divine, groovy, peachy 7 amazing, strange 8 glorious, terrific, wondrous 9 marvelous 10 astounding, miraculous, staggering, stupendous, surprising 11 astonishing, sensational

wondrous
7 amazing, strange 9 marvelous, wonderful 10 astounding, miraculous, stupendous, surprising 11 astonishing, spectacular

wont
3 apt, use, way 5 habit, inure, trick, usage 6 custom, manner 8 accustom, habitude, practice 9 habituate 10 consuetude 11 familiarize

wonted
5 usual 7 chronic, routine 8 accepted, habitual 9 customary 10 accustomed

woo
3 sue 5 court, spark 6 pursue 7 address 8 make up to 10 sweetheart

wood
5 weald 6 forest, lumber, timber 10 timberland
combining form: 3 hyl, xyl 4 hylo, lign, xylo 5 ligni, ligno, xylon, xylum
decayed: 4 punk
eater: 7 termite
for burning: 5 fagot 6 tinder 8 kindling
golf: 5 spoon 6 driver 7 brassie
hard: 3 elm, eng, oak 4 ebon, poon, rata, teak 5 beech, birch, ebony, maple 6 cherry, walnut 8 chestnut, mahogany, sycamore
imperfection: 4 knot 5 gnarl

kind: 5 xylem 6 phloem
light: 5 balsa
made of: 5 treen
pattern in: 5 grain 6 figure
product: 3 tar 5 paper 10 turpentine
soft: 4 pine

wood alcohol
6 methyl 8 methanol

woodchuck
6 marmot 9 groundhog

wood coal
7 lignite

wooded
5 bosky 6 sylvan 8 sylvatic

wooden
4 dull 5 inept, stiff, treen 6 clumsy, gauche 7 buckram, halting, stilted, unhandy 8 bumbling 9 cardboard, ham-handed, maladroit 11 heavy-handed, muscle-bound

woodland
5 weald, woods 6 forest, timber

wood nymph
5 dryad

woodpecker
7 flicker, piculet, wryneck 9 sapsucker
genus: 5 Picus
kind: 5 downy, green, hairy 8 imperial, pileated 9 redheaded 11 ivory-billed
relating to: 6 picine 8 piciform

woodsman
6 logger, ranger 7 bushman 8 forester 11 bushwhacker

wood sorrel
3 oca 6 oxalis 7 begonia 8 shamrock

woodsy
6 rustic, sylvan

woodwind
4 oboe 5 flute 7 bassoon 8 clarinet 9 saxophone 10 instrument

woodworker
9 carpenter 12 cabinetmaker

woody
6 xyloid 8 ligneous
(see also **wooded**)

Woody Allen film
5 Alice, Zelig 7 Bananas, Sleeper 9 Annie Hall, Interiors, Manhattan, Radio Days, September 12 Love and Death 16 Husbands and Wives

wooer
   4 beau 5 spark, swain 6 suitor
   7 sparker

woof
   4 weft, yarn 5 weave 6 fabric,
   thread 7 texture

wool
   3 fur 4 coat, hair 6 fleece
   coarse: 3 abb
   combining form: 3 lan 4 erio, lani,
   lano
   cut: 5 shear
   fabric: 4 felt 5 baize, crepe, serge,
   tweed 6 covert, kersey, mohair,
   poplin, shoddy, velour 7 duvetyn,
   flannel, worsted 8 cashmere, chenille 9 gabardine 10 broadcloth
   fat: 7 lanolin
   kind: 4 hogg 6 angora, hogget,
   virgin
   low-quality: 5 mungo 6 shoddy
   matted: 7 daglock, taglock
   musk-ox: 6 qiviut
   process: 7 carding 8 skirting
   source: 4 goat, lamb 5 camel,
   llama, sheep

woolly
   5 hairy 6 fleecy, lanate, lanose, pilose 7 hirsute, lanated, pileous
   9 whiskered

woozy
   4 sick, weak 5 dizzy 6 blurry
   8 nauseous

word
   3 cry, put, say, vow 4 buzz, news,
   oath, talk, tell, term 5 order, rumor,
   state 6 advice, behest, charge,
   convey, gossip, pledge, plight, report, rumble, saying 7 bidding,
   command, dictate, express, hearsay, mandate, message, promise,
   tidings, vocable, warrant 8 locution
   9 assurance, directive, formulate,
   guarantee, speerings, statement, utterance 10 commitment, expression, injunction 11 countersign, declaration, information, scuttlebutt
   12 announcement, intelligence
   13 communication, pronouncement
   combining form: 3 log 4 logo, onym
   7 onomato
   connective: 11 conjunction
   group: 6 clause, phrase 8 sentence
   misused: 8 malaprop
   11 malapropism
   naming: 4 noun
   new: 7 coinage 9 neologism
   of action: 4 verb
   of honor: 4 oath 7 promise
   origin: 9 etymology
   part: 8 syllable

root: 6 etymon
scrambled: 7 anagram
shortened: 11 contraction
   12 abbreviation
square: 10 palindrome
with opposite meaning: 7 antonym
with same meaning: 7 synonym
with some pronunciation: 7 homonym
   9 homophone
with some spelling: 7 homonym
   9 homograph

wordbook
   7 lexicon 8 libretto 9 thesaurus
   10 dictionary

word for word
   8 verbatim

wordiness
   8 verbiage 9 prolixity, verbalism,
   verbosity, windiness 10 prolixness
   11 verboseness

word-of-mouth
   4 oral 6 spoken, verbal 9 unwritten

wordy
   4 glib 5 tumid, windy 6 prolix, turgid 7 diffuse, verbose, voluble
   8 inflated 9 bombastic, flatulent,
   garrulous, redundant, talkative
   10 long-winded, loquacious, palaverous, rhetorical

work
   2 go 3 act, fix, job, run, tug, use
   4 duty, line, moil, opus, take, tend,
   till, toil 5 chore, craft, dress, drive,
   grind, labor, react, solve, sweat,
   trade 6 behave, drudge, effort,
   handle, métier, racket, strain, strive
   7 calling, operate, perform, pursuit,
   resolve, slavery, travail, trouble
   8 bullwork, business, drudgery, exertion, function, plugging, slogging,
   striving, vocation 9 cultivate
   10 employment, handicraft, occupation, profession
   combining form: 3 erg 4 ergo
   together: 9 cooperate
   11 collaborate
   unit: 3 erg 5 joule

workaday
   4 dull 5 lowly, plain, usual 7 mundane, prosaic, routine 8 everyday,
   ordinary 9 quotidian
   11 commonplace

worker
   4 doer, hand 6 toiler, wallah 7 artisan, laborer 8 employee, mechanic, operator 9 craftsman, operative 10 roustabout
   combining form: 5 ergat 6 ergato
   fellow: 7 comrade, partner

   9 colleague
   group: 4 crew, gang 5 shift, staff,
   union
   hard: 5 slave 6 beaver, drudge
   itinerant: 6 boomer 7 migrant
   slow: 7 plodder
   unskilled: 4 peon 7 jackleg, laborer

working
   4 busy, live 5 alive 6 active 7 dynamic, engaged, running 8 employed, occupied 9 operative
   11 functioning
   not: 5 kaput 6 broken

workless
   4 idle 7 jobless 10 unemployed

workman
   see **worker**

work out
   3 fix 5 solve, train 7 resolve
   8 exercise

workout
   8 exercise, practice

work over
   4 redo 6 beat up, redraw, rehash,
   revamp, revise, rework 7 redraft,
   restyle, rewrite 9 manhandle

workroom
   3 lab 4 shop 6 studio 7 atelier
   10 laboratory

works
   4 mill 5 plant 7 factory

Works and Days author
   6 Hesiod

world
   5 earth, globe 6 cosmos, kosmos,
   nature, planet 8 creation, megacosm, universe 9 macrocosm
   11 macrocosmos
   combining form: 4 cosm 5 cosmo

worldly
   5 blasé 6 earthy 7 earthly, knowing, mundane, sensual, terrene
   8 banausic, mondaine, telluric, temporal 9 sublunary, tellurian 11 terrestrial 12 disenchanted, sophisticate 13 disillusioned, materialistic,
   sophisticated

World War I
   battle: 5 Marne, Somme, Ypres
   6 Verdun 7 Jutland, Lemberg
   10 Tannenberg
   battle line: 9 Siegfried
   hero: 4 York (Alvin) 8 Pershing (John
   J.) 12 Rickenbacker (Eddie)
   treaty: 10 Versailles

World War II
   admiral: 6 Halsey (William "Bull"),
   Nimitz (Chester)
   alliance: 4 Axis 6 Allies

battle: 5 Anzio, Bulge 6 Bataan, Midway, Tarawa, Warsaw 7 Iwo Jima, Okinawa 8 Normandy 10 Stalingrad
general: 6 Patton (George), Rommel (Erwin) 7 Bradley (Omar) 10 Eisenhower (Dwight David), Montgomery (Bernard)
hero: 6 Murphy (Audie)
journalist: 4 Pyle (Ernie)
vehicle: 4 jeep
weapon: 5 A-bomb 6 rocket

worldwide
6 cosmic, global 8 catholic 9 planetary, universal 10 ecumenical 12 cosmopolitan
combining form: 5 globo

worm
3 eel, loa, lug 4 grub, nema 5 borer, fluke, leech 6 edge in, maggot, mucker, no-good, squirm, wiggle, work in, wretch, writhe 7 carbora, distome, lowlife, serpent, triclad, wriggle 8 helminth, nematode, squiggle 9 insinuate, planarium, trematode 10 infiltrate
combining form: 5 nemat, vermi 6 nemato, scolec, scolex 7 scoleco 8 helminth 9 helmintho
marine: 3 lug 4 naid 6 nereis, palolo 7 annelid, tubifex 11 chaetognath
parasitic: 5 fluke, leech 7 ascarid, ascaris, cestode, filaria 8 strongyl, trichina
relating to: 7 vermian
resembling: 11 helminthoid

worm-eaten
6 pitted 7 decayed, worn-out 10 antiquated

worn
5 drawn, erose, jaded, tired, weary 6 eroded 7 haggard, pinched, wearied 8 careworn, fatigued

worn-out
4 sere 5 all in, spent, stale, tired, trite 6 bleary, effete, used up 7 cliché d, drained, far-gone 8 depleted 9 exhausted, hackneyed, washed out 10 threadbare 11 stereotyped

worried
8 distrait, harassed, troubled 9 tormented 10 distracted, distraught, distressed

worry
3 ail, dun, nag, tew, try, vex 4 care, cark, fret, fuss, gnaw, stew, test 5 annoy, beset, harry, tease, trial, upset 6 bother, harass, needle, pester, plague, pother, unease 7 afflict, anguish, anxiety, bedevil, disturb, hagride, oppress, torment, torture, trouble 8 aggrieve, distress 9 beleaguer, tantalize 10 solicitude, uneasiness 11 concernment, disquietude
without: 8 carefree

worrywart
7 fusspot 9 Cassandra, pessimist 11 crepehanger

worse
4 less 6 poorer 8 inferior

worsen
3 rot 4 sink 6 debase 7 decline, degrade, descend 10 degenerate, retrograde 11 deteriorate

worship
4 love 5 adore 6 dote on, revere 7 idolize, lionize, liturgy 8 dote upon, idolatry, venerate 9 adoration, affection, reverence 10 veneration 11 idolization
combining form: 5 latry
object of: 3 god 4 icon, idol
place of: 5 altar 6 church, mosque, shrine, temple 9 cathedral, synagogue

worshiper
6 votary 7 devotee 8 disciple
combining form: 5 later

worst
4 beat, best, down 5 least, outdo 6 defeat, lowest

worsted
4 yarn 5 serge 6 fabric, poplin 9 gabardine

wort
4 herb 5 plant

worth
4 mark, note 5 merit, price, value 6 moment, riches, wealth 7 account, caliber, fortune, quality, stature 8 property 9 resources, substance, valuation

worthless
4 mean 5 junky, sorry 6 draffy, drossy, no-good, trashy 7 fustian, inutile, nothing, useless 8 feckless, unworthy 9 cheapjack, incapable, valueless 11 incompetent, meaningless, purposeless, unqualified 12 contemptible

worthwhile
4 good 6 paying 7 gainful 9 lucrative 10 profitable, well-paying 11 moneymaking 12 advantageous, remunerative

worthy
4 good 5 noble 6 divine 8 laudable, pleasing, precious, sterling 9 admirable, deserving, desirable, estimable, honorable, meritable, praisable, priceless 10 invaluable, satisfying 11 commendable, meritorious

Wotan
see **Odin**

Wouk
novel 13 The Winds of War 14 The Caine Mutiny

wound
3 cut 4 blow, harm, hurt 6 damage, injure, injury, lesion, trauma 8 lacerate 10 laceration
combining form: 7 traumat 8 traumato
discharge: 3 pus
sign: 4 scab, scar 5 blood 7 blister

wow
3 hit 4 bang 5 smash 7 success 9 succès fou 10 bell ringer 11 exclamation

Wozzeck composer
4 Berg (Alban)

wrack
4 kelp, raze, ruin, undo 5 wreck 6 unmake 7 destroy, seaweed, unbuild, unframe 8 decimate, demolish

wraith
5 ghost, shade, spook 6 shadow, spirit 7 phantom, specter 8 phantasm 10 apparition

wrangle
3 row 4 spat, tiff 5 argue, fight, scrap 6 argufy, bicker, fracas, hassle 7 brabble, dispute, fall out, quarrel, quibble 8 squabble 9 bickering, caterwaul 11 altercation

wrangler
6 cowboy 9 disputant

wrap
4 foil, mask, roll, veil 5 cloak, drape, paper, shawl 6 enfold, invest, muffle, shroud, swathe 7 blanket, enclose, envelop, muffler, swaddle 8 bundle up, enshroud, enswathe, wax paper 10 camouflage

wrapped up
4 deep, rapt 6 intent 7 engaged 8 absorbed, immersed 9 engrossed 11 preoccupied

wrapper

4 gown 5 cover, shawl 6 jacket

wrap up

see **wind up**

wrath

3 ire 4 fury, rage 5 anger 8 acerbity, acrimony, asperity 10 resentment 11 indignation

wrathful

3 mad 4 waxy 5 angry, irate, wroth 6 heated, ireful, wrothy

wreak

5 exact, visit, wreck 6 impose 7 force on, inflict 9 force upon

wreath

3 lei 4 bays 5 crown, torse 6 anadem, laurel 7 chaplet, coronal, coronet, garland

wreathe

4 coil, curl, wind 5 twine, twist 6 spiral 7 contort, entwine 9 corkscrew

wreck

3 dog 4 do in, heap, hulk, raze, ruin, undo 5 beach, crash, crate, smash, total, visit, wrack, wreak 6 damage, impose, jalopy, junker, pileup, ravage, strand, unmake 7 clunker, crack-up, debacle, despoil, destroy, disable, force on, inflict, plunder, smashup, subvert, unbuild, unframe 8 bankrupt, cast away, collapse, decimate, demolish, sabotage 9 breakdown, force upon, undermine, vandalize

wreckage

6 jetsam 7 flotsam 8 sabotage 9 driftwood 10 subversion 11 undermining

wrench

3 wry 4 pull, tool, turn, warp 5 exact, force, gouge, pinch, screw, twist, wrest, wring 6 coerce, compel, extort, garble, sprain 7 distort, pervert, squeeze 9 constrain, shake down 12 misrepresent

kind: 6 monkey 7 ratchet

wrest

3 wry 4 warp 5 exact, gouge, pinch, screw, twist, wring 6 extort, garble, wrench 7 confuse, distort, extract, pervert, squeeze 9 shake down 12 misrepresent

wrestle

4 moil, toil 5 essay, exert, fight, labor 6 strain, strive, tussle 7 contend, grapple, scuffle, stretch, travail 8 endeavor, struggle

wrestling

hold: 4 lock 6 nelson 8 headlock, scissors

kind: 4 sumo

term: 3 pin 4 fall 5 throw 8 takedown

wretch

3 cur, dog 4 scum, snot, toad, worm 5 devil, knave, rogue, skunk, snake 6 mucker, no-good, rascal, rotter 7 caitiff, lowlife, stinker, villain 8 scalawag, stinkard, wormling 9 scoundrel, stinkaroo 10 blackguard, ne'er-do-well 11 rapscallion

wretched

3 low 4 base, mean, vile 6 abject, dismal, dolent, paltry, rueful, scurvy, sordid, woeful 7 doleful, forlorn, ignoble, piteous, pitiful, ruthful, servile 8 dolorous, hopeless, pitiable 9 afflicted, miserable, sorrowful 10 despairing, despicable, despondent, melancholy

wretchedness

3 woe 6 misery 11 unhappiness

wriggle

4 worm 6 squirm, writhe 8 squiggle

wring

3 wry 4 rack 5 exact, gouge, pinch, screw, wrest 6 extort, harrow, martyr, wrench 7 afflict, agonize, torment, torture 10 excruciate

the neck: 5 scrag

wringing-wet

5 soppy 6 soaked, sodden, soused 7 soaking, sopping 8 drenched, dripping 9 saturated

wrinkle

4 fold, line, ruck, ruga, seam 5 crimp, plica, ridge, rivel, screw 6 crease, furrow, method, rimple, ruck up, rumple 7 crimple, crinkle, crumple, novelty, scrunch, shrivel 9 crow's foot 10 innovation 11 corrugation

wrinkled

5 lined 6 rugate, rugose, rugous, rumply 8 rugulose

wrist

5 joint 6 carpus

bone: 6 carpal, hamate, lunate 8 capitate, pisiform 9 navicular 10 triangular 11 multangular

combining form: 4 carp 5 carpo

writ

5 breve, brief, order, tales 6 capias, elegit, venire 7 mandate, precipe, summons, warrant 8 document, mandamus, mittimus, praecipe, replevin, subpoena 10 certiorari, distringas, injunction 12 habeas corpus

write

3 ink, jot, pen 4 draw, note, sign 5 chalk, draft 6 author, indite, pencil, scrawl, scribe 7 compose, dot down, engross, scratch 8 inscribe, scribble 10 correspond

write down

4 note 6 record

write off

5 decry, lower 6 cancel 7 devalue, downcry, run down 8 belittle, derogate, discount, mark down, minimize 9 devaluate, disparage, downgrade, underrate 10 depreciate, undervalue 11 detract from

writer

4 poet 6 penman, scribe 7 penster 8 composer, novelist

bad: 4 hack

combining form: 7 grapher; (see also **author**)

writhe

4 bend, curl, toss, worm 5 twist 6 squirm, wiggle 7 agonize, contort, distort, wriggle 8 squiggle

writing

4 book, hand 5 essay, paper, print, prose, words 6 letter, script 7 epistle 8 document, longhand 9 allograph, signature 10 literature, manuscript, penmanship 11 calligraphy, composition, inscription, publication

character: 6 letter 9 cuneiform 10 hieroglyph

combining form: 4 gram 6 grapho, graphy 7 graphia

for the blind: 7 braille

instrument: 3 pen 5 chalk, quill 6 pencil, stylus

kind: 5 prose, verse 6 poetry

sacred: 5 Bible, Koran 6 Talmud, Tantra 9 scripture

secret: 4 code

surface: 5 board, paper, slate 6 scroll 9 parchment

wrong

3 bad, ill, off, sin 4 awry, debt, evil, harm, hurt, poor, tort 5 abuse, amiss, badly, crime, false, inapt, unfit 6 afield, astray, injure, injury, offend, rotten, sinful, untrue, wicked 7 immoral, oppress, outrage, vicious 8 aggrieve, ill-treat, improper, inequity, iniquity, maltreat,

mistaken, mistreat **9** diablerie, erroneous, grievance, incorrect, injustice, misguided, persecute, reprobate, unfitting **10** inaccurate, iniquitous, unfairness, unjustness, unsuitable, wickedness **11** unfavorably **12** infelicitous **13** inappropriate

prefix: **3** mis

wrongdoer

5 felon **6** sinner **8** criminal, offender **9** miscreant **10** malefactor

wrongdoing

3 sin **4** evil, tort **5** crime **7** misdeed, offense **8** iniquity **9** diablerie, violation **10** misconduct **11** malefaction, misbehavior

wrongful

7 illegal, illicit, lawless **8** criminal, unlawful **12** illegitimate

wrongheaded

5 balky **6** mulish, ornery **7** froward, restive, wayward **8** contrary, perverse, stubborn **9** obstinate **10** self-willed **11** stiff-necked **12** cross-grained, pertinacious

wrought

4 made **6** formed, shaped, worked **7** created **8** finished, hammered **9** fashioned, processed **10** ornamented **12** manufactured

up: **7** excited, stirred

wry

4 bent **5** twist, wrest, wring **6** ironic, wrench **7** cynical, twisted **8** sardonic

wryneck

10 woodpecker

Wuthering Heights

author: **6** Brontë (Emily)
character: **7** Hindley **9** Catherine **10** Heathcliff

Wycliffite

7 Lollard

Wyoming

capital: **8** Cheyenne
city: **6** Casper **7** Laramie
nickname: **13** Equality State
state bird: **10** meadowlark

Xx

x
3 chi, ten **4** kiss, mark **5** annul, cross, erase, error, times, wrong **6** cancel, delete, efface **7** blot out, expunge, mistake, wipe out **8** abscissa, black out **9** signature **10** obliterate

Xanadu
country: **5** China
river: **4** Alph

xanthic
6 yellow **9** yellowish

Xanthippe
3 nag **5** harpy, scold, shrew, vixen **6** nagger, ogress, virago **8** fishwife **9** termagant
husband: **8** Socrates

xanthous
6 yellow

xebec
4 boat, ship **6** vessel **10** pirate ship

xenium
4 gift **7** present

xenon
symbol: **2** Xe

Xenophon work
8 Anabasis **9** Cyropedia, Hellenica

Xeres
4 wine **5** Jerez **6** sherry

xerophyte
6 cactus

xerosis
7 dryness

Xerxes
defeat: **7** Salamis
father: **6** Darius
kingdom: **6** Persia

mother: **6** Atossa
wife: **6** Esther

Xmas
4 Noel, yule **8** Nativity, yuletide **9** Christmas

X ray
discoverer: **8** Roentgen (Wilhelm)
science: **9** radiology **13** roentgenology

xurel
4 scad **6** saurel

xyloid
5 woody **8** ligneous

xylophone
5 saron, vibes **7** gambang, gamelan, marimba **8** gamelang, gigelira, sticcado **10** vibraphone

xystus
4 stoa, walk **5** porch **7** portico, terrace

Yy

yacht
4 boat, race, sail, ship 5 craft
6 cruise, sonder 8 keelboat

yahoo
4 lout, punk 5 brute, clown, rough,
rowdy, tough 6 mucker, savage
7 bumpkin, ruffian, toughie 8 bullyboy 9 roughneck

Yahweh
3 God 6 Jahvah 7 Jehovah

yak
2 ox 3 gab, jaw 4 blab, chat
5 clack, laugh, prate 6 babble,
gabble, jabber, sarlak, sarlyk, yammer 7 blabber, buffalo, chatter, palaver, prattle

yakety-yak
3 gab, jaw 4 blab, chat 5 clack,
prate 6 babble, gabble, jabber
7 blabber, chatter, palaver, prattle

Yale
3 Eli 4 lock 10 university

Yalta participant
6 Stalin (Joseph) 9 Churchill (Winston), Roosevelt (Franklin Delano)

yam
3 ube, ubi 5 tugui 6 igname, potato 7 boniata 11 sweet potato

yammer
3 cry, gab, jaw, yak 4 chat, crab,
fuss, yaup, yawp, yell 5 bleat,
clack, gripe, whine, yearn 6 babble, clamor, gabble, squawk
7 chatter, grumble, prattle 8 complain 9 bellyache, yakety-yak

yank
3 lug, tug 4 grab, jerk, pull, snap,
tear 5 hoick, lurch 6 clutch, evulse,
snatch, twitch 7 extract 9 vellicate

yap
4 bark, hick, jake, yelp 5 clown,
mouth, scold 6 bowwow, rustic
7 bumpkin, chatter, hayseed 9 hill-

billy 10 clodhopper, provincial
12 backwoodsman

yard
4 lawn, quad, spar 5 court, garth,
patio, stick 9 curtilage, enclosure
10 playground, quadrangle
enclosed: 5 garth, patio
five and one-half: 3 rod
part of: 4 foot, nail
shelter: 6 gazebo
sixteenth of: 4 nail
two hundred and twenty: 7 furlong

yardstick
5 gauge 7 measure 8 standard
9 benchmark, criterion
10 touchstone

yare
4 spry 5 agile, brisk, catty, ready
6 active, brisky, lively, nimble, volant 9 sprightly

yarn
3 rap 4 chat, chin, garn, tale, talk
5 fiber, floss, grain, prose, story,
visit 6 caddis, cotton, crewel,
strand, thread 7 caddice, gen-
appe, schappe 8 anecdote, causerie, colloque, converse 9 narration,
narrative
ball of: 4 clew, clue
coil: 5 skein 6 skeane
cotton: 10 candlewick
for fastening a sail: 6 roband, robbin
woolen: 6 crewel, worset 7 worsted
8 shetland

yate
8 eucalypt

yaw
4 bend, gape, swag, tack, tilt, turn,
veer, yawn 5 lurch, pitch, shift
6 double, seesaw, swerve, tilter
7 deviate 9 deviation 10 deflection

yawn
4 gape 5 ennui 6 tedium 7 boredom 8 doldrums

yawning
5 agape, bored 6 gaping 7 chasmal 8 oscitant 9 cavernous

yawp
3 bay, caw, cry 4 bawl, crab, fuss,
gape 5 bleat, gripe 6 squall,
squark, squawk, yammer
8 complain

yaws
4 pian 9 frambesia

yea
2 ay, OK 3 aye, nay, too, yes, yet
4 also, even, more, okay 5 along,
truly 6 agreed, assent, as well,
indeed, really, verily 7 besides 8 all
right, likewise, moreover, positive
11 affirmative 12 additionally

yeanling
3 kid 4 lamb 7 newborn

year
academic: 7 session
combining form: 6 ennial
division: 5 month 6 season
9 trimester
kind: 4 leap 5 lunar, solar 6 fiscal
8 calendar, sidereal, tropical
12 astronomical
Latin: 5 annus
Scottish: 7 towmond, towmont

yearbook
5 annal 6 annual 7 almanac,
annuary

yearling
4 colt

Yearling
author: 8 Rawlings (Marjorie Kinnan)
character: 4 Jody

yearly
6 annual 8 annually

yearn
3 yen 4 ache, burn, long, lust,
pant, pine, sigh, wish 5 covet,

crave, dream **6** desire, grieve, hanker, hunger, thirst, yammer

yearning
4 wish **5** eager **6** desire, hanker **7** craving, wistful **8** homesick, lovesick

years
eight: **9** octennial
five: **7** lustrum **12** quinquennial, quinquennium
four: **11** quadrennial, quadrennium
one hundred: **7** century **9** centenary **10** centennial
one thousand: **10** millennium
ten: **6** decade **9** decennary, decenniad, decennial, decennium
three: **9** triennial, triennium

yeast
3 bee **4** barm, foam, suds **5** froth, spume **6** lather, leaven **7** ferment

yeasty
5 dizzy, giddy, light **6** frothy **7** flighty **8** restless **9** exuberant, fribbling, frivolous **11** light-headed

Yeats
beloved: **9** Maud Gonne
birthplace: **6** Dublin
play: **7** Deirdre **9** Purgatory **12** The Herne's Egg
poem: **9** Byzantium **11** Lapis Lazuli

yegg
5 thief **6** robber **7** burglar **8** criminal **11** safecracker

yell
3 cry, yip **4** call, howl, roar, wail, weep, yowl **5** cheer, hallo, hollo, shout, whoop **6** bellow, bemoan, bewail, clamor, holler, lament, outcry, scream, shriek, squall, squeal, yammer **7** deplore, roaring **10** vociferate

yellow
4 mean **5** amber, blake, favel, lemon, ochre **6** coward, craven, flavid, flaxen, golden, sallow **7** gutless, mustard, saffron, unmanly, xanthic **8** cowardly, xanthous **9** jaundiced, spunkless **11** lily-livered **12** dishonorable **13** pusillanimous
brownish: **3** dun **5** aloma, amber, straw **6** manila
combining form: **4** flav **5** chrys, flavo, luteo, xanth **6** chryso, xantho
dye: **5** morin **6** orlean **7** annatto **9** morindone
grayish: **4** ecru
greenish: **5** olive **6** acacia **10** chartreuse

yellowbelly
3 rat **4** funk **6** coward, craven, funker **7** chicken, dastard, quitter **8** poltroon

yellow dog
3 cad, cur **6** rotter **7** bounder

yellowhammer
5 ammer, finch, skite **6** gladdy **7** bunting, flicker, yeldrin **8** yoldring

yellowish brown
4 gold **7** mustard **9** butternut **12** butterscotch

Yellowstone attraction
4 bear **6** geyser **11** Old Faithful

yelp
3 cry, yap, yip **4** bark **5** boast, shout **6** outcry, squeal **8** complain

Yemen
capital: **4** San'a
monetary unit: **4** rial **5** dinar, riyal

yen
4 ache, long, lust, pine, sigh, urge **5** crave, yearn **6** desire, hanker, hunger, thirst **7** craving, longing

yeoman
5 churl, clerk **6** farmer **7** freeman **8** retainer **9** assistant, attendant, beefeater, landowner **10** freeholder **11** subordinate

yeomanly
5 brave, loyal **6** sturdy **8** faithful **9** laborious **11** hardworking

yes
2 OK **3** aye, yea, yeh, yep, yup **4** okay, yeah **5** agree **6** accede, agreed, assent, gladly **7** consent, exactly **8** all right **9** acquiesce, assuredly, certainly, precisely, subscribe, willingly **11** affirmation, affirmative, undoubtedly
French: **3** oui
German: **2** ja
Italian: **2** si
Russian: **2** da
Spanish: **2** si

yes-man
5 dummy, toady **6** minion, stooge **7** spaniel **8** bootlick, groveler, truckler **9** sycophant **10** bootlicker

yesterday
4 past, yore **8** foretime
French: **4** hier

yesteryear
4 past, yore **8** foretime

yet
3 but, too **4** also, even, more, only, save **5** along, so far, still **6** as well, except, though, withal **7** besides, earlier, finally, further, howbeit, however, someday, thus far **8** after all, hitherto, likewise, moreover, sometime, somewhen **10** eventually, ultimately **11** furthermore, nonetheless, still and all **12** additionally, nevertheless

Yevtushenko poem
7 Babi Yar

Ygerne
see **Igraine**

yield
3 bow, net, pay **4** bear, bend, cave, cede, cess, crop, emit, fail, fold, give, obey, quit, vent **5** admit, agree, allow, award, break, bring, defer, eject, grant, leave, offer, repay, waive **6** accede, accord, afford, bounty, buckle, comply, fold up, give up, impart, output, profit, relent, render, resign, return, reward, soften, submit, supply, tender **7** abandon, bring in, concede, consent, crumple, deliver, furnish, harvest, hold out, indulge, knuckle, outturn, produce, product, proffer, provide, revenue, succumb, truckle, turnout **8** collapse, hand over **9** acquiesce, discharge, surrender **10** capitulate, production, recompense, relinquish **11** buckle under **12** knuckle under

yielding
4 meek, soft, waxy **5** mushy, pappy, pulpy **6** feeble, flabby, limber, pliant, quaggy, spongy, supple **7** bearing, flaccid, flexile, passive, squashy, squishy, squushy **8** flexible, resigned, squelchy **9** tractable **10** manageable, submissive **11** acquiescent, unresistant, unresisting **12** nonresistant, nonresisting
combining form: **6** ferous

yin and ___
4 yang

yip
4 howl, yell, yelp, yowl **6** scream, squeal

yoga
posture: **5** asana

yoke
3 tie, wed **4** bail, bond, join, knot, link, pair, span, team **5** bangy, hitch, marry, nexus, unite **6** banghy, couple, inspan, tackle **7** bond-

age, combine, conjoin, connect, harness, helotry, oppress, peonage, serfage, serfdom, slavery **8** ligament, ligature, vinculum **9** associate, conjugate, servility, servitude, thralldom **10** oppression **11** enslavement

combining form: **3** zyg **4** zygo

part: **5** oxbow

yokel

3 oaf **4** boor, clod, hick, jake, rube **6** rustic **7** bucolic, bumpkin, hayseed **8** Abderite **9** chawbacon, hillbilly **10** clodhopper **12** backwoodsman

yolk

6 center, yellow **7** essence

combining form: **6** lecith, vitell **7** lecitho, vitello

egg: **8** vitellus

yon

see **yonder**

yonder

5 there **7** farther, further, thither

yore

4 past **8** foretime **10** yesteryear

you

2 ye **3** one **4** thee, thou

French: **2** te, tu **4** vous

German: **2** du **3** sie

young

3 fry, new, raw **4** baby, rude, tyro, weak **5** brood, fresh, green **6** callow, infant, junior, litter, unripe **7** untried **8** childish, immature, juvenile, unformed, unversed, youthful **9** unfledged, unfleshed **10** unfinished, unseasoned **11** unpracticed **13** inexperienced

animal: **3** cub, fry, pup **4** calf, colt, fawn, foal, joey, lamb **5** puppy

bird: **5** chick

hare: **7** leveret

sheep, goat: **6** yeelin **8** yeanling

younger

6 junior

youngling

see **youngster**

Young Lions author

4 Shaw (Irwin)

youngster

3 boy, cub, kid, lad, tad, tot **4** girl, lass, tike **5** chick, child **6** moppet, shaver, urchin **8** juvenile

suffix: **4** ling

youth

5 prime **6** spring **7** puberty **8** juvenile, teenager **9** fledgling, stripling **10** adolescent, callowness, immaturity, juvenility, pubescence, springtide, springtime **11** adolescence **12** inexperience

ancient Greek: **7** ephebos, ephebus

goddess of: **4** Hebe

mythological: **6** Adonis, Apollo, Icarus **8** Ganymede

time of: **9** salad days; (see also **youngster**)

youthful

5 fresh, green, young **6** boyish, callow, infant, junior, maiden, unripe, virgin **7** puerile **8** immature, juvenile, virginal **9** beardless, unfledged

yowl

3 cry, yip **4** bawl, howl, wail, yell, yelp **6** scream, squall, squeal

yucca

5 palma **9** bear grass

Yugoslavia

capital: **8** Belgrade

monetary unit: **5** dinar

president: **4** Broz (Josip), Tito (Marshal)

former republic: **7** Croatia **8** Slovenia **9** Macedonia **17** Bosnia-Herzegovina

republic: **6** Kosovo, Serbia **9** Vojvodina **10** Montenegro

Yukon

capital: **10** Whitehorse

region: **8** Klondike

town: **6** Dawson

yule

4 Noel, Xmas **8** Nativity, yuletide **9** Christmas **13** Christmastide

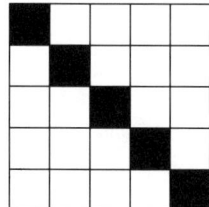

Zz

Zabbai
father: 5 Bebai
son: 6 Baruch

Zabud's father
6 Nathan

Zaccur
father: 4 Imri 5 Asaph 7 Jaaziah
9 Mattaniah
son: 5 Hanan

Zacharias
father: 9 Barachias
son: 4 John 6 Joseph
wife: 9 Elisabeth

Zadoke
daughter: 7 Jerusha
father: 5 Baana, Immer 6 Ahitub
8 Meraioth
grandson: 6 Jotham
son: 7 Ahimaaz, Shallum

Zaire
capital: 8 Kinshasa
former name: 5 Congo 12 Belgian
Congo

zakuska
4 whet 9 antipasto, appetizer
11 hors d'oeuvre

Zalmunna's slayer
6 Gideon

Zambia
capital: 6 Lusaka
monetary unit: 6 kwacha

zampogna
7 bagpipe, panpipe

zany
3 wag 4 card, fool 5 ament,
clown, comic, crazy, cutup, dotty,
idiot, joker, moron, nutty 6 cretin
7 buffoon, farceur, half-wit, pranker
8 clowning, clownish, comedian,
funnyman, humorist, imbecile,
jokester 9 harlequin, prankster, simpleton, trickster

Zauberflöte composer
6 Mozart (Wolfgang Amadeus)

zeal
4 fire, zest 5 ardor, gusto 6 desire,
energy, fervor, hurrah, spirit
7 avidity, passion, urgency 8 devotion, keenness 9 calenture, eagerness, intensity, readiness, sincerity,
vehemence 10 enthusiasm, fanati-
cism, fierceness 11 earnestness,
seriousness

zealot
3 bug, nut 5 bigot, fiend, freak
6 maniac, votary 7 devotee, fanatic, sectary 8 adherent, disciple,
follower, partisan 10 enthusiast

zealous
4 avid, keen, warm 5 afire, eager,
fired, nutty, rabid 6 ardent, fervid,
gung ho, hearty 7 devoted, earnest, fanatic, fervent 8 frenetic, obsessed, wild-eyed 9 dedicated,
possessed 12 enthusiastic

Zebadiah
father: 6 Asahel 7 Jeroham
11 Meshelemiah
uncle: 4 Joab

Zebah's slayer
6 Gideon

Zebedee
son: 4 John 5 James
wife: 6 Salome

zebra
4 duaw
extinct: 6 quagga
resembling: 7 zebrine, zebroid

Zebulun
brother: 4 Levi 5 Judah 6 Simeon
father: 5 Jacob
mother: 4 Leah
son: 4 Elon 5 Sered 7 Jahleel

zecchino
6 sequin

Zechariah
daughter: 3 Abi 6 Abijah
father: 4 Elam, Iddo 5 Bebai, Hosah
7 Isshiah 8 Jehoiada, Jeroboam,
Jonathan 9 Berechiah 11 Jebere-
chiah, Jehoshaphat, Meshelemiah
grandson: 8 Hezekiah
slayer: 7 Jehoram, Shallum
son: 4 Iddo 8 Jahaziel

Zedekiah
brother: 8 Jehoahaz
father: 6 Josiah 8 Hananiah, Jeconiah, Maaseiah 9 Chenaanah
mother: 7 Hamutal

Zeeb's slayer
6 Gideon

zenana
5 harem, harim 8 seraglio

zenith
4 acme, apex, peak 6 apogee, climax, height, summit, vertex 8 capstone, meridian, pinnacle
11 culmination
opposite: 5 nadir

Zenobia
husband: 9 Odenathus
kingdom: 7 Palmyra

Zeno follower
5 stoic

Zephaniah
father: 8 Maaseiah
son: 6 Josiah

Zephi, Zepho
father: 7 Eliphaz
grandfather: 4 Esau

Zephon's father
3 Gad

Zephyrus
4 wind 6 breeze 8 west wind
father: 6 Aeolus 8 Astraeus
mother: 3 Eos 6 Aurora
wife: 4 Iris

zeppelin
5 blimp 7 airship 9 dirigible

Zerah
brother: 5 Perez
father: 5 Judah, Reuel 6 Simeon
grandfather: 4 Esau
mother: 5 Tamar

Zerbino
beloved: 8 Isabella
friend: 7 Orlando
sister: 7 Ginevra
slayer: 11 Mandricardo

Zeresh's husband
5 Haman

zero
2 oh 3 aim, lay, nil, nul 4 cast, head, nowt, null, turn, void 5 aught, blank, empty, level, ought, point, train, zilch 6 cipher, direct, naught, nobody, nought 7 address, nothing, nullity, scratch, whiffet 8 goose egg, whipster 9 nonentity

Zeruah
husband: 5 Nebat
son: 8 Jeroboam

Zerubbabel
daughter: 9 Shelomith
father: 7 Pedaiah
grandfather: 10 Jehoiachin
son: 4 Ohel

Zeruiah
brother: 5 David
sister: 7 Abigail
son: 4 Joab 6 Asahel 7 Abishai

zest
4 edge, élan, tang, zeal 5 ardor, gusto, heart, taste 6 fervor, flavor, palate, relish 7 delight, ecstasy, elation, passion 8 piquancy, pleasure 9 eagerness, enjoyment 10 enthusiasm 11 delectation 12 satisfaction

zesty
4 racy 5 spicy 6 breezy, hearty, snappy 7 peppery, piquant, pungent 8 poignant

Zetes
brother: 6 Calais
father: 6 Boreas
mother: 8 Orithyia
slayer: 8 Heracles, Hercules

zetetic
6 seeker 7 doubter, skeptic 10 headshaker, pyrrhonian, pyrrhonist, unbeliever

Zethus
brother: 7 Amphion

father: 4 Zeus 7 Jupiter
mother: 7 Antiope

Zeus
7 Jupiter
brother: 5 Hades 8 Poseidon
daughter: 3 Ate 4 Hebe, Kore 5 Helen, Irene 6 Athena 7 Artemis, Astraea 9 Aphrodite 10 Persephone, Proserpina 12 Clytemnestra
father: 6 Cronus
lover: 2 Io 4 Leda, Leto, Maia 5 Danae, Dione, Metis 6 Aegina, Europa, Latona, Semele, Themis 7 Alcmene, Antiope, Demeter 8 Callisto, Eurynome
messenger: 4 Iris
mother: 4 Rhea
nurse: 8 Cynosura
oracle: 6 Dodona
shield: 5 aegis
sister: 4 Hera, Juno 6 Hestia
son: 4 Ares 5 Arcas, Argus, Minos 6 Aeacus, Apollo, Hermes, Zethus 7 Amphion, Perseus 8 Dionysus, Heracles, Hercules, Sarpedon, Tantalus
tree: 3 oak
wife: 4 Hera, Juno 5 Metis 6 Themis

Zibiah
husband: 7 Ahaziah
son: 7 Jehoash

Zichri
father: 5 Asaph 6 Shimei 7 Jeroham, Shashak
son: 4 Joel 7 Amasiah, Eliezer 10 Elishaphat
victim: 8 Maaseiah

zigzag
4 tack, turn 5 angle, crank, weave 7 chevron 8 flexuose, flexuous

zilch
4 zero 5 aught, ought 6 cipher, naught, nobody, nought 7 nothing, nullity, whiffet 8 goose egg, whipster 9 nonentity

Zillah
husband: 6 Lamech
son: 9 Tubalcain

Zilpah's son
3 Gad 5 Asher

zimarra
5 cloak 7 cassock, soutane

Zimbabwe
capital: 6 Harare
former name: 8 Rhodesia

Zimran
father: 7 Abraham
mother: 7 Keturah

Zimri
father: 5 Zerah
grandfather: 5 Judah
victim: 4 Elah

zinc
impure oxide: 5 tutty
ingot: 7 spelter
ore: 6 blende 10 sphalerite
symbol: 2 Zn

zing
3 pep, vim, zip 4 brio, dash, élan, life, snap 5 ardor, force, oomph, verve, vigor 6 energy, esprit, spirit 9 animation, eagerness 10 enthusiasm

zingel
5 perch

Zion
5 bliss 6 canaan, heaven, Israel, utopia 7 arcadia, elysium, nirvana 8 empyrean, paradise 9 cockaigne, fairyland, Shangri-la 10 Civitas Dei, wonderland 12 New Jerusalem, promised land 13 Abraham's bosom

Zionist
American: 5 Szold (Henrietta)
English: 8 Zangwill (Israel)
German: 6 Nordau (Max Simon)
Hungarian: 5 Herzl (Theodor)
Israeli: 5 Buber (Martin) 8 Weizmann (Chaim)

zip
3 fly, pep, vim 4 dash, rush, snap, whiz, zing 5 force, hurry, speed, waltz, whisk 6 breeze, bustle, energy, hasten, hustle

zipper
8 fastener

Zipporah
father: 5 Reuel 6 Jethro
husband: 5 Moses
son: 7 Eliezer, Gershom

Zippor's son
5 Balak

zippy
4 keen, spry, yare 5 agile, alert, brisk, catty, ready 6 active, brisky, lively, nimble, snappy 7 dynamic, intense 8 forceful 9 sprightly

zircon
6 jargon 7 jargoon
variety: 7 jacinth 8 hyacinth, starlite

zirconium
symbol: 2 Zr

zither
Chinese: 3 kin
Japanese: 4 koto

Ziza
  father: 8 Rehoboam
  mother: 6 Maacah

zodiac sign
  3 Leo (the Lion) 5 Aries (the Ram),
  Libra (the Balance), Virgo (the Virgin) 6 Cancer (the Crab), Gemini
  (the Twins), Pisces (the Fishes), Taurus (the Bull) 7 Scorpio (the Scorpion) 8 Aquarius (the Water
  Bearer) 9 Capricorn (the Goat)
  11 Sagittarius (the Archer)

zoetic
  5 alive, vital 6 living 7 animate
  8 animated

Zohar
  father: 6 Simeon
  son: 6 Ephron

Zoheth's father
  4 Ishi

Zoilus
  5 momus 6 carper, critic 7 caviler,
  knocker 9 aristarch, belittler
  10 criticizer 11 faultfinder,
  smellfungus

Zola, Emile
  work: 4 Nana 6 Verité 7 J'accuse

8 Germinal 9 La Débâcle 10 L'As-
sommoir 13 Thérèse Raquin

zombie
  5 drink, snake 6 python 8 cocktail

zone
  4 area, band, belt 5 tract 6 region,
  sector 7 section, segment
  9 territory
  ecological: 7 ecotone

zonked
  4 high 5 doped, drunk, tight
  6 stoned 7 drugged, drunken
  8 hopped-up, turned on 9 spaced-
  out 10 inebriated, tripped out
  11 intoxicated

zoologist
  American: 5 Clark (Eugenie), Hyatt
  (Alpheus) 6 Carson (Rachel), Fos-
  sey (Dian), Kinsey (Alfred), Osborn
  (Henry Fairfield), Yerkes (Robert)
  7 Ditmars (Raymond), Merriam
  (Clinton)
  British: 6 Darwin (Charles), Huxley
  (Julian, Thomas) 7 Goodall (Jane),
  Medawar (Peter) 9 Lankester
  (Edwin)
  Dutch: 10 Swammerdam (Jan)
  French: 6 Cuvier (Georges)

German: 7 Haeckel (Ernst), Spemann
  (Hans)
  Norwegian: 6 Nansen (Fridtjof)
  South African: 5 Broom (Robert)
  Swedish: 8 Linnaeus (Carolus)

zoophyte
  5 coral 6 sponge 7 hydroid 8 bryozoan 9 gorgonian 10 sea anemone 12 invertebrate

Zoroastrian
  demon: 4 deva
  god: 10 Ahura Mazda
  sacred writings: 6 Avesta

zucchetto
  7 calotte 8 skullcap

Zur
  brother: 4 Kish
  daughter: 5 Cozbi
  father: 5 Jeiel

Zuriel's father
  7 Abihail

zweiback
  5 bread, toast 7 biscuit

zygomatic bone
  5 malar 9 cheekbone

zygote
  6 oocyst 7 oosperm